Western Europe

Susie **Ashworth**
Davi**d** Atkinson
Chris Baty
Andr**ew** Bender
Geert Cole
Dunca**n** Garwood
Susie **G**rimshaw
Kat**h**ryn Hanks

Sarah Johnstone
Alex Landragin
Matt Lane
Cathy Lanigan
Leanne Logan
Craig MacKenzie
Lisa Mitchell
Sally O'Brien

Josephine
  Quintero
Kalya Ryan
Andrew Stone
Rachel Suddart
Dani Valent
Vivek Wagle
David Willett

LONELY PLANET PUBLICATIONS
Melbourne • Oakland • London • Paris

WESTERN EUROPE

Western Europe
6th edition – January 2003
First published – January 1993

Published by
Lonely Planet Publications Pty Ltd ABN 36 005 607 983
90 Maribyrnong St, Footscray, Victoria 3011, Australia

Lonely Planet Offices
Australia Locked Bag 1, Footscray, Victoria 3011
USA 150 Linden St, Oakland, CA 94607
UK 10a Spring Place, London NW5 3BH
France 1 rue du Dahomey, 75011 Paris

Photographs
Many of the images in this guide are available for licensing from
Lonely Planet Images.
w www.lonelyplanetimages.com

Front cover photograph
Broken layer of cloud above Eiffel Tower, Paris, France
(Vince Streano, Getty Images)

ISBN 1 74059 313 8

text & maps © Lonely Planet Publications Pty Ltd 2003
photos © photographers as indicated 2003

GR and PR are trademarks of the FRRP (Fédération Française de la
Randonée Pédestre).

Printed by The Bookmaker International Ltd
Printed in China

Contents – Text

GERMANY

GREECE

IRELAND

ITALY

SWITZERLAND 1067

Contents – Maps

7

The Authors

Susie Ashworth
Susie updated the Switzerland and Liechtenstein chapters. Years spent in the sleepy Blue Mountains in her teens inspired her to hit the road as soon as possible.

She caught her first glimpse of the stunning Swiss Alps during her obligatory year-long backpacking trip in the late 1980s, where she gained an addiction to Lindt chocolate that remains a problem to this day. Since then, she's done odd jobs in London, written headlines and corrected spelling for magazines in Sydney, and travelled rural Oz with her life packed into a camper trailer. These days, she works as an editor at Lonely Planet and lives in Melbourne with her partner and two cats.

David Atkinson
David updated parts of the France chapter. He is a London-based freelance writer, specialising in travel, and has previously both lived and worked in Vietnam and Japan. During this time, he was mistaken for a gun runner, ate freshly killed snake and learned to do a mean karaoke Elvis medley. His stories have been published in the *Guardian*, the *Weekend FT*, the *South China Morning Post* and *Time Magazine Asia*. He is a member of the British Guild of Travel Writers.

Chris Baty
Chris updated parts of the Germany chapter – his first authoring assignment for Lonely Planet. His deep admiration for the German people began in 1992, when a study abroad program took him deep into the maw of a Northern European winter. Heeding the example of the savvy natives, Chris soon discovered that beer and chocolate, in sufficient quantities, can sate the body's need for actual sunlight. He hasn't been the same since. Chris lives in Oakland, California, where he supplements his vast travel writing fortune with other equally questionable part-time occupations: music journalism and novel writing.

Andrew Bender
Andrew updated parts of the Germany chapter. Yet another LP author with an MBA, Andy worked with companies in Japan and the US but leapt to write full time after selling his first travel article. His writing has since appeared in *Travel & Leisure*, *Fortune*, *In Style* and the *Los Angeles Times*. He also reviews restaurants (hence no photo, but trust us, he's cute) and edits the *Kyoto Diary*, a journal of Japanese culture. His other LP titles include *Germany* (2002) and *Norway* (2002).

At home in Los Angeles, he's an inline skater at the beach, eats Asian food and schemes over ways to spoil his nephews, Ethan and Matthew.

Duncan Garwood

Duncan updated parts of the Italy chapter. His writing career has so far taken him from the vaporous depths of London's largest sewage farm to the more traditional attractions of northern and central Italy.

His first taste of travelling came with a four-month trip to India prior to a history degree at York University and a spell in corporate journalism.

However, he gave up leafy Berkshire for life in the Italian sun, and currently lives in the wine-rich hills overlooking Rome. He divides his time between writing, dreaming and teaching English to, among others, Italian Miss World contenders.

Susie Grimshaw

Susie updated the Portugal chapter. Born in Cheshire, she was itching to travel from an early age and read American Studies at university in the hopes of securing an exchange placement on the other side of the pond.

The economic climate at the time did not permit such frivolous behaviour, so she went off her own bat and has never looked back, chalking up the miles in the US, Asia and Europe. Susie was delighted to return to Portugal so she could resume her comparative study of custard tarts. Previously, she nobly volunteered to review restaurants for *Out to Eat London*.

Kathryn Hanks

Kathryn updated parts of the Britain chapter. She graduated with a degree in English and before taking up predictable career route number one (journalism) she followed the English graduate's second predictable career path (teaching), this time in the altogether more exciting realms of Tanzania. Hence she gleefully seized the opportunity to cram her passport full of stamps from various East African countries.

She had to be dragged back to her native UK to spend two years editing a business magazine; however, she was fortunate enough to be rescued by Lonely Planet and to have the chance to show readers what Britain's really like.

Sarah Johnstone

Sarah updated the Austria chapter. She's not really keen on author biographies, but the publishers insist. A freelance journalist raised in Queensland but based in London, she has previously worked for Reuters, Virgin Atlantic's in-flight magazine *Hot Air*, and *Business Traveller*, among others.

Her writing has also appeared in the *Times*, the *Independent on Sunday* and the *Face*. A great big coward, somehow Sarah still occasionally finds herself in places like Soweto or Libya (before the UN embargo was lifted – oops). A serial hugger of central heating systems the world over, she managed to find the Austrian outdoors a bit chilly, too.

Alex Landragin

Alex updated the Andorra chapter and parts of the France chapter. He was born in France's Champagne region before his father landed an antipodean winemaking job and the family moved to Australia. After university studies in English and a couple of unremarkable careers, he worked as a staff writer and Web editor at Lonely Planet's Melbourne HQ before opting for a life on the road.

During the sunny, tumultuous weeks of a presidential election campaign, Alex and his father drove the backroads of western France and Andorra at breakneck speed, racing from one restaurant to the next with bottomless appetites, with updating work slotted in between meals.

Alex has also updated sections of Lonely Planet's *Australia* and *Victoria* guides and between assignments writes fiction in wine country near Melbourne.

Matt Lane

Matt updated parts of the Germany chapter. Born in England, he grew up in country Australia where he started what was to be a checkered noncareer in journalism.

Three newspaper jobs, a stint in television, some freelancing and travel, and one-third of a graphic design degree later, he wound up at Lonely Planet.

This is Matt's third LP job. He has also worked on *Australia* and *Queensland*. He lives in northeast Victoria, Australia, with his wife.

Cathy Lanigan

Cathy updated the Netherlands chapter. She worked as a journalist, turkey egg collector, newspaper editor, and politician between stints travelling in Europe, Asia, the Middle East and North Africa. She now works for Lonely Planet recruiting authors and occasionally being one.

When not traipsing around the world with her partner and two-year-old in tow, she hangs out in country Victoria, Australia. Cathy has contributed to Lonely Planet's *Middle East* guide and updated *Travel with Children*.

Leanne Logan & Geert Cole

Leanne and Geert updated the Belgium and Luxembourg chapters and parts of the Britain chapter. Leanne, a journalist from Australia, and Geert, a stained-glass artist from Belgium, met over a decade ago and have been writing and updating Lonely Planet guides ever since. This time round they were aided, and occasionally distracted, by their six-month-old daughter, Eleonor. Good at finding dead cockroaches under hotel beds and testing the breaking point of restaurant staff, Eleonor made life on the road more fun than ever. When not travelling, the trio can be found tending vegies, planting trees and watching wallabies at their rural retreat in northern New South Wales, Australia.

Craig MacKenzie

Craig updated the Introduction and the Facts for the Visitor chapter. Born in Kinlochleven in the Scottish West Highlands, he was told he was on a two-week holiday back in 1963 when he arrived in Melbourne, Australia, as an unwitting nine-year-old migrant. He's still in Melbourne having spent over 15 years with the Fairfax media group as a sports journalist and subeditor with freelance stints on SBS radio and TV. Seeking a haven for industrial misfits he joined Lonely Planet as a book editor in June, 1996. He's still seeking that haven. He's balding, overweight, smokes long panatellas and drinks pints of Guinness.

Lisa Mitchell

Lisa updated parts of the Greece chapter. She discovered the world was big on a spree across Europe, the UK, Southeast Asia and Australia in the '80s. She returned to earn her byline deciphering 'techno goss' in the computer press, spat the CPU, and became a writer and editor of lifestyle sections on a city newspaper. She sashayed momentarily into TV drama, later joining a women's magazine in dot com land. As deadlines and pocket money allow, Lisa pants up small mountains in high places.

Her playgrounds include Alaska, Colorado, British Columbia, Patagonia and New Zealand. She works as a freelance writer in Melbourne.

Sally O'Brien

Sally updated parts of the Italy chapter. Born in Melbourne, and raised in Seoul and Sydney, Sally edited various Lonely Planet titles before deciding to try her luck as an author. She's written for *Sydney*, *Australia* and *Sicily*, and covered Rome and Southern Italy for this book, where she amused one and all with her imaginative Italian and her version of driving on the right-hand side of the road. She's happy to keep getting sent there, despite predictably strange occurrences at train, bus and ferry stations and the aforementioned driving fiascos. When not authoring, she likes tea drinking and procrastinating.

Josephine Quintero

Josephine updated parts of the Spain chapter. Born in England, she started travelling with a backpack and guitar in the late '60s (didn't everyone?), stopping off in Israel on a kibbutz for a year. This led her, in a roundabout romantic sort of way, to move to California. After graduating from UC Berkeley, Josephine worked as a journalist for local newspapers and glossy magazines. Further travels took her to Kuwait where she edited the *Kuwaiti Digest*, and made several side trips, including to Yemen and India. She was briefly held hostage during the Iraqi invasion of Kuwait, and moved to the more relaxed shores of Andalucía shortly thereafter. She has worked as a ghostwriter on several books, including a spy thriller and several biographies. She has also contributed to more than 15 guidebooks, with an emphasis on the Iberian peninsula, and writes regularly for in-flight magazines, including *Highlife* (British Airways) and *Red Hot* (Virgin Airways).

Kalya Ryan

Kalya updated the Getting There & Away chapter and parts of the Britain chapter. She grew up in Sydney and northern New South Wales then spent some time educating herself in Canberra.

She was shacked up in Edinburgh for a year, but now calls Melbourne home (mainly because Lonely Planet agrees to pay her to edit guidebooks there). She likes pina coladas and getting caught in the rain...no, that's a lie, she prefers beer and avoids rain whenever she can.

Andrew Stone

Andrew updated the Ireland chapter. He began travelling early, living in Africa and Iran before he was nine. Aged 10 he moved to Burgess Hill, an English town that can, and sometimes does, claim to be the place where greyhound racing legend Ballyregan Bob chose to retire.

A journalistic career followed (for Andrew, not the dog) in the giddy world of business periodicals, on a distribution industry weekly.

Sadly, the excitement of supply chain logistics soon put too much of a strain on his heart, and doctors' advice then forced his resignation.

Deciding to travel in Asia awhile, he based himself in Hong Kong where he got up late, played too much Tetris and watched Korean sitcoms, while his family thought he was writing city guidebooks. After a lengthy stint doing nothing in particular in Australia and New Zealand he returned to the UK and took on this, his first assignment with Lonely Planet.

Rachel Suddart

Rachel updated the Getting Around chapter. Originally from the Lake District, and a graduate of Manchester University, she spent several years trying to work out how to combine her love for writing with her incurable wanderlust.

In 2000 she had her first taste of authorship when she took part in a BBC documentary.

After getting her foot stuck firmly in the door she took on a full-time role in Lonely Planet's London office which is where you'll find her now (probably singing along to some dodgy rock music). She has contributed to several LP titles.

Dani Valent

Dani updated parts of the France chapter. In eight years of travel writing for Lonely Planet, she has worked on over a dozen guides to destinations on four continents.

She still loves coming home to Melbourne, Australia, where she dreams about making the perfect *crème brûlée* and playing Aussie Rules football for Carlton (editor's note: she'd get a game at the moment).

Vivek Wagle

Vivek updated parts of the Spain chapter. Dragging him kicking and screaming from his native land of India was probably the best way to introduce him to a life of itinerancy. After years of bouncing around the globe from Jakarta, Indonesia, to Washington, DC, with family and friends, he settled down long enough to earn an unbelievably practical degree in philosophy at Harvard University. But the experiential world soon won out over noumenal quandaries, propelling Vivek to enter the travel-writing business. After a stint as an editor in Lonely Planet's Oakland office, he hit the road once again as an author. To this day, he's not quite sure what time zone he's in at any given moment.

David Willett

David updated parts of the Greece chapter. He is a freelance journalist based near Bellingen on the mid-north coast of New South Wales, Australia. He grew up in Hampshire, England, and wound up in Australia in 1980 after stints working on newspapers in Iran (1975–78) and Bahrain. He spent two years working as a sub-editor on the Melbourne *Sun* before trading a steady job for a warmer climate. Between jobs, David has travelled extensively in Europe, the Middle East and Asia. He is a regular visitor to Athens as coordinator of Lonely Planet's *Greece* and co-author of the *Athens* city guide. He is also the author of Lonely Planet's *Tunisia*, and has contributed to various other guides, including *Africa*, *Australia*, *Indonesia*, *South-East Asia*, *Mediterranean Europe* and *Western Europe*.

This Book

Many people have helped to create this 6th edition. Among the major contributors to past editions were Mark Armstrong, Janet Austin, Mark Balla, Carolyn Bain, Neal Bedford, Lou Callan, Stefano Cavedoni, Fionn Davenport, Paul Dawson, Rob van Driesum, Richard Everist, Steve Fallon, Susan Forsyth, Helen Gillman, Jeremy Gray, Rosemary Hall, Anthony Haywood, Paul Hellander, Mark Honan, John King, Clem Lindenmayer, Frances Linzee Gordon, Sarah Mathers, Scott McNeely, John Noble, Tim Nollen, Oda O'Carol, David Peevers, Nick Ray, Daniel Robinson, Miles Roddis, Andrea Schulte-Peevers, Sean Sheehan, Corinne Simcock, Damien Simonis, Tom Smallman, David Stanley, Robert Strauss, Dorinda Talbot, Bryn Thomas, Rebecca Turner, Ryan Ver Berkmoes, Greg Videon, Gary Walsh, Tony Wheeler, Julia Wilkinson, Nicola Williams, Neil Wilson and Pat Yale.

Western Europe is part of Lonely Planet's Europe series, which includes *Eastern Europe*, *Mediterranean Europe*, *Central Europe*, *Scandinavian Europe* and *Europe on a shoestring*. Lonely Planet also publishes phrasebooks to these regions.

FROM THE PUBLISHER

This was bigger than *Ben Hur*. The coordinating editor was Craig MacKenzie and the coordinating designer was Jacqui Saunders. They were assisted by Susie Ashworth, Gus Poó y Balbontin, Yvonne Bischofberger, Csanad Csutoros, Hunor Csutoros, Pete Cruttenden, Piotr Czajkowski, James Ellis, Simone Egger, Susannah Farfor, Justin Flynn, Karen Fry, Cris Gibcus, Nancy Ianni, Evan Jones, Joelene Kowalski, Valentina Kremenchutskaya, Kusnander, Sally Morgan, Jarrad Needham, Jacqueline Nguyen, Darren O'Connell, Leanne Peake, Adrian Persoglia, Cherry Prior, Nina Rousseau, Anastasia Safioleas, John Shippick, Sarah Sloane, Nick Stebbing, Linda Suttie, Nick Tapp, Simon Tillema, Gina Tsarouhas, Celia Wood and Helen Yeates. Also helping out were Gerilyn Attebery, Kerryn Burgess, David Burnett, Tony Davidson, Bruce Evans, Liz Filluel, Huw Fowles, Quentin Frayne, Mark Germanchis, Mark Griffiths, Kieran Grogan, James Hardy, Errol Hunt, Rachel Imeson, David Kemp, Emma Koch, Chris Lee Ack, Adriana Mammarella, Mary Neighbour, Daniel New, Robert Reid, Diana Saad, Jane Thompson, Ray Thomson, Sam Trafford, Andrew Tudor, Vivek Wagle, Chris Wyness and Isabelle Young. Thanks also to Lonely Planet Images.

ACKNOWLEDGMENTS

Grateful acknowledgment is made for reproduction permission: Penguin Books Ltd: Excerpt from *The Italians*, Luigi Barzini (1964).

Thanks also to Mountain High Maps ® Copyright © 1993 Digital Wisdom, Inc.

THANKS
Many thanks to the travellers who used the last edition and wrote to us with helpful hints, advice and interesting anecdotes. Your names appear in the back of this book.

Foreword

ABOUT LONELY PLANET GUIDEBOOKS

The story begins with a classic travel adventure: Tony and Maureen Wheeler's 1972 journey across Europe and Asia to Australia. There was no useful information about the overland trail then, so Tony and Maureen published the first Lonely Planet guidebook to meet a growing need.

From a kitchen table, Lonely Planet has grown to become the largest independent travel publisher in the world, with offices in Melbourne (Australia), Oakland (USA), London (UK) and Paris (France).

Today Lonely Planet guidebooks cover the globe. There is an ever-growing list of books and information in a variety of media. Some things haven't changed. The main aim is still to make it possible for adventurous travellers to get out there – to explore and better understand the world.

At Lonely Planet we believe travellers can make a positive contribution to the countries they visit – if they respect their host communities and spend their money wisely. Since 1986 a percentage of the income from each book has been donated to aid projects and human rights campaigns, and, more recently, to wildlife conservation.

> Although inclusion in a guidebook usually implies a recommendation we cannot list every good place. Exclusion does not necessarily imply criticism. In fact there are a number of reasons why we might exclude a place – sometimes it is simply inappropriate to encourage an influx of travellers.

UPDATES & READER FEEDBACK

Things change – prices go up, schedules change, good places go bad and bad places go bankrupt. Nothing stays the same. So, if you find things better or worse, recently opened or long-since closed, please tell us and help make the next edition even more accurate and useful.

Lonely Planet thoroughly updates each guidebook as often as possible – usually every two years, although for some destinations the gap can be longer. Between editions, up-to-date information is available in our free, quarterly *Planet Talk* newsletter and monthly email bulletin *Comet*. The *Scoop* section of our website covers news and current affairs relevant to travellers. Lastly, the *Thorn Tree* bulletin board and *Postcards* section carry unverified, but fascinating, reports from travellers.

Tell us about it! We genuinely value your feedback. A well-travelled team at Lonely Planet reads and acknowledges every email and letter we receive and ensures that every morsel of information finds its way to the relevant authors, editors and cartographers.

Everyone who writes to us will find their name listed in the next edition of the appropriate guidebook, and will receive the latest issue of *Comet* or *Planet Talk*. The very best contributions will be rewarded with a free guidebook.

We may edit, reproduce and incorporate your comments in Lonely Planet products such as guidebooks, websites and digital products, so let us know if you don't want your comments reproduced or your name acknowledged.

How to contact Lonely Planet:
Online: e talk2us@lonelyplanet.com.au, w www.lonelyplanet.com
Australia: Locked Bag 1, Footscray, Victoria 3011
UK: 10a Spring Place, London NW5 3BH
USA: 150 Linden St, Oakland, CA 94607

Introduction

Western Europe means many things to many people. Some marvel at its diversity of cultures and languages crammed into such a small area, the wealth of its museums, theatre and architecture, and the seemingly endless shopping opportunities, restaurants and nightlife on offer in many of its bustling cities. Others are attracted to Western Europe's varied scenery, from sun-drenched beaches and dense forests to mountain lakes and snow-capped peaks. Many citizens of the Americas and Australasia see Western Europe as their ancestral homeland and birthplace of much of their culture and civilisation. Almost all visitors are delighted by the minimal amount of bureaucracy, the well-developed tourist facilities and efficient transport that make it possible to explore this fascinating region with a minimum of fuss.

Western Europe is often looked upon as the hub of the developed world – at least historically. Though its growth rate is not what it was in the heady days of the 1950s and '60s, Western Europe remains an economic powerhouse and a leader in art, literature and music. For the visitor to the region, the biggest problem is simply choosing where to go, and what to see and do. There are magnificent museums and galleries such as the British Museum in London, the Louvre in Paris and the Prado in Madrid. There are architectural treasures like the Parthenon in Athens, Gaudí's fantastic church in Barcelona and Germany's fairy-tale castles. And there are superb natural features: the soaring Swiss Alps, the magnificent stretches of rugged coastline in western Ireland and the tranquil, sunny islands of Greece. For the energetic, there are walking trails ranging from the high-altitude circuit of Mont Blanc in France to the West Highland Way in Scotland, ski runs from Andorra to Zermatt in Switzerland and there's sailing, windsurfing and swimming all along the Atlantic, Baltic and Mediterranean coasts. And there are places where it's simply just fun to be, whether it's clubbing in Berlin, pub-crawling through Dublin or watching the world go by from a sidewalk café in Paris or Rome.

Western Europe provides an insight into the history, people and culture of this diverse collection of countries and offers practical information to help you make the most of your time and money.

There's information on how to get to Western Europe and how to get around once you're there. There are extensive details on what to see, where to see it and how much it costs. The thousands of recommendations about places to stay range from French camping grounds and German hostels to Spanish *pensions* and Irish B&Bs. Cafés, restaurants and bars are covered in equally exhaustive detail, with suggestions which cover every budget – from the cheapest of cheap eats to the ideal place for that big splurge. There are even recommendations on what to buy and where to buy it.

Western Europe is a wonderful region to visit and there is a whole lot out there waiting to be enjoyed. This newly updated edition of *Western Europe* will guide you, so don't procrastinate any longer about that trip of a lifetime – go now!

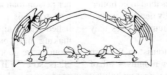

Facts for the Visitor

HIGHLIGHTS
The Top 10
There is so much to see in Western Europe that compiling a Top 10 is next to impossible. Nevertheless, we've compiled this list. You may agree with some entries, while some omissions may raise your hackles – it's OK, we've got broad shoulders:

1. Paris
2. London
3. Rome
4. Berlin
5. Amsterdam
6. The Alps
7. Venice
8. Scotland's Highlands and Islands
9. Florence and Tuscany
10. Greek island-hopping

Other possibilities include Barcelona, Munich, the Algarve, western Ireland, Hamburg, the North Frisian Islands, Umbria, Provence, Corsica, the Pyrenees, the wine cellars of Oporto, Bruges, Edinburgh, Languedoc-Roussillon and the Yorkshire Dales.

PLANNING
A bit of prior knowledge and careful planning can make your travel budget stretch further. You'll also want to make sure that the things you plan to see and do will be possible when you'll be travelling.

Lonely Planet's *Read This First – Europe* is an excellent source of important preliminary information.

When to Go
Any time can be the best time to visit Western Europe, depending on what you want to see and do. Summer lasts roughly from June to September and offers the best weather for outdoor pursuits in the northern half of Europe. In the southern half (Mediterranean coast, Iberian Peninsula, southern Italy and Greece), where the summers tend to be hotter, you can extend that period by one or even two months either way, when temperatures may also be more agreeable.

You won't be the only tourist in Western Europe during the summer months – all of France and Italy, for instance, goes on holiday in August. Prices can be high, accommodation fully booked and the sights packed. You'll find much better deals – and far fewer crowds – in the shoulder seasons on either side of summer; in April and May, for instance, flowers are in bloom and the weather can be surprisingly mild, and Indian summers are common in September and October.

On the other hand, if you're keen on winter sports, resorts in the Alps and the Pyrenees begin operating in late November and move into full swing after the New Year, closing down when the snows begin to melt in March or even April.

The Climate and When to Go sections in individual country chapters explain what to expect and when to expect it, and the climate charts in country chapters will help you compare the weather in different destinations. As a rule, spring and autumn tend to be wetter and windier than summer and winter. The temperate maritime climate along the Atlantic is relatively wet all year, with moderate extremes in temperature. The Mediterranean coast is hotter and drier, with most rainfall occurring during the mild winter. The continental climate in eastern Germany and the Alps tends to have much stronger extremes in weather between summer and winter.

When summer and winter are mentioned throughout this book we generally mean high and low tourist seasons, ie, for summer read roughly May to September and for winter read October to April.

What Kind of Trip
Travelling Companions If you decide to travel with others, keep in mind that travel can put relationships to the test like few other experiences. Make sure you agree on itineraries and routines beforehand, and try to remain flexible about everything – even in the heat of an August afternoon in Paris or Berlin. Travelling with someone else does have financial benefits as single rooms are more expensive per person than a double in most countries.

If travel is a good way of testing established friendships, it's also a great way of making new ones. Hostels and camping grounds are good places to meet fellow travellers, so even if you're travelling alone you need never be lonely.

The Getting Around chapter has information on organised tours.

Maps

Good maps are easy to come by once you're in Europe, but you might want to buy a few beforehand to plan and track your route. The maps in this book will help you get an idea of where you might want to go and will be a useful first reference when you arrive in a city. Proper road maps are essential if you're driving or cycling.

For some European cities (eg, Amsterdam, Berlin, London, Paris, Rome and Brussels) Lonely Planet has detailed maps. Michelin maps are also good and, because of their soft covers, they fold up easily so you can stick them in your pocket.

Some people prefer the maps meticulously produced by Freytag & Berndt, Kümmerly + Frey and Hallwag. As a rule, maps published by European automobile associations (the AA in Britain, the ADAC and AvD in Germany etc) are excellent and sometimes free if membership of your local association gives you reciprocal rights. Some of the best city maps are produced by Falk; RV Verlag's EuroCity series is another good bet. Tourist offices are often another good source for (usually free and fairly basic) maps.

What to Bring

It's very easy to find almost anything you need in Western Europe and, since you'll probably buy things as you go along, it's better to start with too little rather than too much.

A backpack is still the most popular method of carrying gear as it is convenient, especially for walking.

Travelpacks – a combination backpack/ shoulder bag – are very popular. The backpack straps zip away inside the pack when they are not needed, so you almost have the best of both worlds. Backpacks or travelpacks are always much easier to carry than a bag, and can be made reasonably theft-proof with small padlocks.

Another alternative is a large, soft zip bag with a wide shoulder strap so it can be carried with relative ease. Forget suitcases unless you're travelling in style, but if you do take one, make sure it has wheels to allow you to drag it along behind you.

As for clothing, the climate will have a bearing on what you take along, but always be prepared for rain at any time of year. Remember that insulation works on the principle of trapped air, so several layers of thin clothing are warmer than a single thick one (and will be easier to dry). You'll also be much more flexible if the weather suddenly turns warm. Bearing in mind that you can buy virtually anything on the spot, a minimum packing list could include:

- underwear, socks and swimming gear
- a pair of jeans and maybe a pair of shorts or a skirt
- a few T-shirts and shirts
- a warm sweater
- a solid pair of walking shoes
- sandals or thongs for showers
- a coat or jacket
- a raincoat, waterproof jacket or umbrella
- a medical kit and sewing kit
- a padlock
- a Swiss Army knife
- soap and a towel
- toothpaste, toothbrush and other toiletries

RESPONSIBLE TOURISM

As a visitor, you have a responsibility to the local people and to the environment. For guidelines on how to avoid offending locals you meet, read the following Appearances & Conduct section. When it comes to the environment, the key rules are to preserve natural resources and to leave the countryside as you find it. Those Alpine flowers look much better on the mountainside than squashed in your pocket (and many species are protected anyway).

Wherever you are, littering is irresponsible and offensive. Mountain areas have fragile ecosystems, so stick to prepared paths whenever possible, and always carry your rubbish away with you.

Do not use detergents or toothpaste (even if they are listed as biodegradable) in or close to any watercourses.

If you just gotta go when you're out in the wilderness somewhere, bury human waste in holes at least 15cm deep and at least 100m from any watercourse.

Recycling is an important issue, especially in Austria, Germany and Switzerland, and you will be encouraged to follow suit. Traffic congestion on the roads is a major problem, and visitors will do themselves and residents a favour if they forgo driving and use public transport.

Western Europe World Heritage List

AUSTRIA
Graz's historic centre
Hallstatt-Dachstein (Salzkammergut) cultural landscape
Palaces and gardens of Schönbrunn near Vienna
Semmering railway
Salzburg's historic city centre
Vienna's historic centre
Wachau's cultural landscape (between Melk and Krems)

BELGIUM
Belfries of Flanders and Wallonia
Bruges' historic centre
Canal du Centre's Four Lifts and their environs, La Louviere and Le Roeulx, Hainault Province
Flemish Béguinages throughout Flanders
Grand Place, Brussels
Major town houses of architect Victor Horta, Brussels
Neolithic flint mines at Spiennes, Mons
Notre Dame Cathedral in Tournai

FRANCE
Abbey of St Rémi and Tau Palace at Reims
Amiens Cathedral
Arc-et-Senans' Royal Saltworks
Arles' Roman and Romanesque monuments
Avignon's historic centre
Bourges Cathedral
Carcassonne
Canal du Midi
Chartres Cathedral
Chateau of Versailles and gardens
Church of Saint Savin sur Gartempe
Corsica's Cape Girolata, Cape Porto, Les Calanche and Scandola Natural Reserve
Fontainebleau Palace and Park
Fontenay's Cistercian abbey
Grande Île section of Strasbourg
Lascaux and other caves in the Vézére Valley

Loire Valley between Sully-sur-Loire and Chalonnes
Lyon's historic centre
Mont Saint Michel and its bay
Notre Dame and the banks of the Seine in Paris
Pilgrimage routes to Santiago de Compostela
Place Stanislas, Place de la Carriére and Place d'Alliance in Nancy
Pont du Gard Roman aqueduct near Nîmes
Provins, town of medieval fairs
Pyrenees – Mont Perdu
Roman theatre and triumphal arch at Orange
St Émilion
Vézelay's Basilica

GERMANY
Aachen Cathedral
Abbey and Altenmünster of Lorsch
Lübeck
Augustusburg and Falkenlust Castles at Brühl
Bamberg
Bauhaus sites in Weimar and Dessau
Berlin's Museuminsel (Museum Island)
Cologne Cathedral
Classical Weimar
Garden kingdom of Dessau-Wörlitz
Goslar and mines of Rammelsberg Hildesheim's Cathedral and St Michael's Church
Luther memorials in Eisleben and Wittenberg
Maulbronn Monastery complex
Messel fossil site
Monastic island of Reichenau
Palaces and parks of Potsdam and Berlin
Quedlinburg's Collegiate Church, castle and old town
Speyer Cathedral
Trier's Roman monuments, cathedral and Liebfrauen Church

Völklingen ironworks
Wartburg Castle
Wies' pilgrimage church
Würzburg's Residence and Court Gardens
Zollverein coal mine in Essen

GREECE
Acropolis in Athens
Bassae's Temple of Apollo Epicurius
Delos
Delphi archaeological site
Epidaurus archaeological site
Hora, the Monastery of Saint John and the Cave of the Apocalypse on Patmos
Medieval city of Rhodes
Meteora
Monasteries of Daphni, Hossios Luckas and Nea Moni at Chios
Mount Athos
Mycenae and Tyrins' archaeological sites
Mystras
Olympia's archaeological site
Pythagorio, Hereon at Samos
Thessaloniki's Early Christian and Byzantine monuments
Vergina's archaeological site

IRELAND
Boyne Valley archaeological sites
Skellig Michael

ITALY
Aeolian Islands
Agrigento's archaeological area
Alberobello's trulli
Aquileia archaeological area and the patriarchal Basilica
Archaeological areas of Pompei, Herculaneum and Torre Annunziata
Assisi, St Francis' Basilica and other Franciscan sites
Caserta's Royal Palace with the park, aqueduct of Vanvitelli and the San Leucio complex
Castel del Monte
Cilento and Vallo di Diano National Park with archaeological sites of Paestum and Velia, and Certosa di Padula

Western Europe World Heritage List

Cinque Terre, Port Venere
and islands
Costiera Amalfitana
Crespi d'Adda
Ferrara, the Renaissance city
Florence's historic centre
Matera's sassi (traditional
stone houses)
Milan's Church of Santa
Maria delle Grazie and
convent including *The Last
Supper* by Leonardo da Vinci
Modena's cathedral, Torre
Civica and Piazza Grande
Naples' historic centre
Padua's botanical garden
Pienza's historic centre
Pisa's Piazza del Duomo
Ravenna's Early Christian
monuments and mosaics
Rome's historic centre
San Gimignano's historic centre
Savoy's royal house residences
Siena's historic centre
Su Nuraxi fortress at Barumini
Urbino's historic centre
Valle Camonica's rock carvings
Vatican City
Venice and its lagoon
Verona
Villa Adriana and Villa d'Este,
Tivoli
Villa Romana del Casale
Vincenza and its Palladian villas
LUXEMBOURG
Old quarter and fortifications
of Luxembourg City
NETHERLANDS
Amsterdam's Defence Line
DF Wouda steam pumping
station
Droogmakerij de Beemster
(Beemster Polder)
Kinderdijk-Elshout's mill
network
Reitveld Schröder House
Schokland and surrounds
Willemstad's historic area
PORTUGAL
Alcobaça's Monastery
Alto Douro wine region
Angra do Heroismo, Azores

Batalha Monastery
Côa Valley's prehistoric rock-art
Convent of Christ in Tomar
Évora's historic centre
Guimarães historic centre
Lisbon's Monastery of the
Hieronymites and Tower
of Belém
Madeira's Laurisilva
Oporto's historic centre
Sintra's cultural landscape
SPAIN
Albaicín Moorish quarter of
Granada
Alcalá de Henares university
and historic area
Altamira Cave
Aragon's Mudejar architecture
Aranjuez cultural landscape
Archaeological site of Atapuerca
Ávila's old town section
Barcelona's Güell park and
palace, Casa Mila, Palace of
the Música Catalana and Sant
Pau hospital
Burgos Cathedral
Cáceres' old town section
Catalan Romanesque churches
of the Vall de Boí
Córdoba's historic centre
Cuenca's walled city
Doñana National Park
El Escorial near Madrid
Garajonay National Park
Ibiza's biodiversity and culture
La Alhambra, El Generalife
summer palace and Iberian
Peninsula's rock art
Las Médulas
Lugo's Roman walls
Monuments of Oviedo and
the kingdom of Asturias
Mérida's archaeological
ensemble
Palmeral of Elche
Poblet Monastery
Pyrenees – Mont Perdu
Royal Monastery of Santa
María de Guadeloupe
Salamanca's old town
San Millán de Cogolla's Yuso
and Suso Monasteries

San Cristóbal de la Laguna
Santiago de Compostela's old
town and route
Segovia's old town and
aqueduct
Sevilla's cathedral, Alcázar
Archivo de Indias
Tárraco's archaeological
ensemble
Toledo's historic centre
Valencia's La Lonja de
la Seda (silk exchange)
SWITZERLAND
Bellinzona's three castles,
defensive wall and ramparts
Bern's old city section
Jungrau-Aletsch-Bietschhorn
Müstair's Convent of St John
St Gall Convent
UK
Bath
Blaenavon industrial landscape
Blenheim Palace
Bermuda's historic St George
and related fortifications
Canterbury Cathedral, St
Augustine's Abbey and St
Martin's Church
Derwent Valley mills
Dorset and east Devon coast
Durham Castle and Cathedral
Edinburgh (old and new towns)
Giant's Causeway and the
Causeway Coast
Gough Island Wildlife Reserve
Greenwich
Gwynedd's castles and town
walls
Hadrian's Wall
Henderson Island
Ironbridge Gorge
Neolithic Orkney
New Lanark
Saltaire
St Kilda
Stonehenge and Avebury
Studley Royal Park and ruins
of Fountains Abbey
Tower of London
Westminster Abbey, West-
minster Palace and St
Margaret's Church

Appearances & Conduct

Although dress standards are fairly informal in northern Europe, your clothes may well have some bearing on how you're treated in southern Europe.

Dress casually, but keep your clothes clean, and ensure sufficient body cover (eg, trousers or a knee-length dress) if your sightseeing includes churches, monasteries, synagogues or mosques.

Wearing shorts away from the beach or camping ground is not very common among men in Europe.

Some nightclubs and fancy restaurants may refuse entry to people wearing jeans, a tracksuit or sneakers (trainers); men might consider packing a tie as well, just in case.

While nude bathing is usually restricted to certain beaches, topless bathing is very common in many parts of Europe.

Nevertheless, women should be wary of taking their tops off as a matter of course. The basic rule is that if nobody else seems to be doing it, then you shouldn't either – and stick to this rule.

You'll soon notice that Europeans are heavily into shaking hands and even kissing when they greet one another. Don't worry about the latter with those you don't know well, but get into the habit of shaking hands with virtually everyone you meet. In many parts of Europe, it's also customary to greet the proprietor when entering a shop, café or a quiet bar, and to also say goodbye when you leave.

VISAS & DOCUMENTS
Passport

Your most important travel document is your passport, which should remain valid until well after you return home. If it's just about to expire, renew it before you go. This may not be easy to do overseas, and some countries insist that your passport remains valid for a specified period (usually three months beyond the date of your departure from that country).

Applying for or renewing a passport can take anywhere from just an hour to several months, so don't leave it till the last minute. Bureaucratic wheels usually turn much faster if you do everything in person instead of relying on the post or agents, but check first what you need to take with you: photos of a certain size, your birth certificate, population register extract, signed statements, exact payment in cash etc.

Australian citizens can apply at a post office or the passport office in their state capital; Britons can pick up application forms from major post offices, and the passport is issued by the regional passport office; Canadians can apply at regional passport offices; New Zealanders can apply at any district office of the Department of Internal Affairs; US citizens must apply in person (but may usually renew by mail) at a US Passport Agency office or at some courthouses and post offices.

Once you start travelling, carry your passport at all times and guard it carefully (see Copies later in this section for advice about carrying copies of your passport and other important documents). Camping grounds and hotels sometimes insist that you hand over your passport for the duration of your stay, which is very inconvenient, but a driving licence or Camping Card International usually solves the problem.

Citizens of the European Union (EU) and those from certain other European countries (eg, Switzerland) don't need a valid passport to travel to another EU country or even some non-EU countries; a national identity card is sufficient. If you want to exercise this option, check with your travel agent or the embassies of the countries you plan to visit.

Visas

A visa is a stamp in your passport or on a separate piece of paper permitting you to enter the country in question and stay for a specified period of time.

Often you can get the visa at the border or at the airport on arrival, but not always – check first with the embassies or consulates of the countries you plan to visit – and seldom on trains.

There's a wide variety of visas, including tourist, transit and business ones. Transit visas are usually cheaper than tourist or business visas, but they only allow a very short stay (one or two days) and usually are difficult to extend.

Most readers of this book, however, will have very little to do with visas. With a valid passport they'll be able to visit most European countries for up to three (sometimes even six) months, provided they have some sort of onward or return ticket and/or 'sufficient means of support' (money).

In line with the Schengen Agreement there are no passport controls at the borders between Austria, Belgium, Denmark, Finland, France, Germany, Greece, Iceland, Italy, Luxembourg, the Netherlands, Norway, Portugal, Spain and Sweden; an identity card should suffice, but it's always safest to carry your passport. Britain, Ireland, Liechtenstein and Switzerland are still not full members of Schengen.

Border procedures between EU and non-EU countries can still be fairly thorough, though citizens of Australia, Canada, Israel, Japan, New Zealand and the USA do not need visas for tourist visits to any Schengen country.

All non-EU citizens visiting a Schengen country and intending to stay there for longer than three days or to visit another Schengen country are supposed to obtain an official entry stamp in their passport either at the point of entry or from the local police within 72 hours.

This is very loosely enforced, however, and in general registering at a hotel will be sufficient.

For those who do require visas, it's important to remember that these will have a 'use-by' date, and you'll be refused entry after that period has elapsed. It may not be checked when entering these countries overland, but major problems can arise if it is requested during your stay or on departure and you can't produce it.

Visa requirements can change, and you should always check with the individual embassies or a reputable travel agent before travelling.

It's generally easier to get your visas as you go along, rather than arranging them all beforehand.

Carry spare passport photos (you may need from one to four every time that you apply for a visa).

Travel Insurance

A travel insurance policy to cover theft, loss and medical problems is a good idea. The policies handled by STA Travel and other student travel organisations are usually good value.

Some policies offer lower and higher medical expense options; the higher ones are chiefly for travellers from countries such as the USA that have extremely high medical costs. There is a wide variety of policies available so check the small print.

Some policies specifically exclude 'dangerous activities', which can include scuba diving, motorcycling and even trekking. A locally acquired motorcycle licence is not valid under some policies.

You may prefer a policy that pays doctors or hospitals directly rather than you having to pay on the spot and claim later. If you have to claim later, make sure that you keep all your documentation.

Some policies ask you to call back (reverse charges) to a centre in your home country where an immediate assessment of your problem is made. Check that the policy covers ambulances or an emergency flight home.

EU nationals can obtain free emergency treatment on presentation of an E111 form, validated in their home country. Note, however, that this form does not provide health cover in Switzerland or Andorra.

Driving Licence & Permits

Many non-European driving licences are valid in Europe, but it's still a good idea to bring along an International Driving Permit (IDP), which can make life much simpler, especially when hiring cars and motorcycles.

Basically a multilingual translation of the vehicle class and personal details which are noted on your local driving licence, an IDP is not valid unless it is accompanied by your original licence. An IDP can be obtained for a fairly small fee from your local automobile association – take a passport photo and a valid licence.

Camping Card International

The Camping Card International (CCI) is a camping ground ID that can be used instead of a passport when checking into a camping ground and includes third party insurance. As a result, many camping grounds offer a small discount (usually 5% to 10%) if you sign in with one.

CCIs are issued by automobile associations, camping federations or, sometimes, on the spot at camping grounds. In the UK, the AA and RAC issue them to their members for UK£6.50.

Hostel Cards

A hostelling card is useful – if not always mandatory – for those staying at hostels.

Some hostels in Western Europe don't require that you be a hostelling association member, but they often charge less if you are and have a card.

Many hostels will issue one on the spot or after a few stays, though this might cost a bit more than getting it in your home country. See Hostels under Accommodation later in this chapter.

Student & Youth Cards

The most useful of these is the International Student Identity Card (ISIC), a plastic ID-style card with your photograph, which provides discounts on various forms of transport (which includes the airlines and local public transport), cheap or free admission to a variety of museums and sights, and inexpensive meals in some student cafeterias and some restaurants.

If you're aged under 26 but not a student, you can apply for an International Youth Travel Card (IYTC, formerly GO25) issued by the Federation of International Youth Travel Organisations (FIYTO) or the Euro<26 card.

Both go under different names in different countries and give much the same discounts and benefits as an ISIC.

All these cards are issued by student unions, hostelling organisations or youth-oriented travel agencies.

Seniors Cards

Museums and other sights, public swimming pools and spas, and transport companies frequently offer discounts to retired people/old-age pensioners/those over 60 (slightly younger for women).

Make sure you bring proof of age; that suave *signore* in Italy or that polite Parisian *mademoiselle* is not going to believe you're a day over 39.

European nationals aged 60 and over can get a Railplus Card. For more information see Cheap Tickets under Train in the Getting Around chapter.

International Health Certificate

You'll require this yellow booklet only if you are travelling to Western Europe from certain regions of Asia, Africa and South America, where diseases such as yellow fever are prevalent. See Immunisations under Health later in this chapter for more detailed information on jabs.

Copies

All important documents (passport data page and visa page, credit cards, travel insurance policy, air/bus/train tickets, driving licence etc) should be photocopied before you leave home. Leave one copy with someone at home and keep another with you.

While you're on the road add the serial numbers of your travellers cheques (cross them off as you cash them) to these photocopies and remember to keep all this emergency material separate from your passport, cheques and cash.

You should add some emergency money (eg, US$50 to US$100 in cash) to this separate stash as well.

If you do lose your passport, notify the police immediately to get a statement, and contact your nearest consulate.

It's also a good idea to store details of your vital travel documents in Lonely Planet's free online Travel Vault in case you lose photocopies or can't be bothered with them. Your password-protected Travel Vault is accessible online anywhere in the world – create it at [w] www.ekno.lonelyplanet.com.

EMBASSIES & CONSULATES

See individual country chapters for the addresses of embassies and consulates.

Getting Help from Your Embassy

As a tourist, it's vitally important to realise what your own embassy – the embassy of the country of which you are a citizen – can and cannot do.

Generally speaking, it won't be much help in emergencies if the trouble you're in is remotely your fault.

Remember that you are bound by the laws of the country that you are in. Your embassy will show little sympathy towards you if you end up in jail after committing a crime locally, even if such actions are legal in your own country.

In genuine emergencies you might get some assistance, but only if other channels have been exhausted. For example, if you need to get home urgently, a free ticket home is exceedingly unlikely as the embassy would expect you to have insurance. If you have all your money and documents stolen, it might assist with getting a new passport, but a loan for onward travel is almost always out of the question.

The Euro

The European Central Bank's much anticipated roll-out of new euro coins and bank-
notes took place on 1 January 2002 in all 12
participating euro zone countries – Austria,
Belgium, Finland, France, Germany, Greece,
Ireland, Italy, Luxembourg, the Netherlands,
Portugal and Spain.

The euro has the same value in all EU member countries.

There are seven euro notes (five, 10, 20, 50,
100, 200 and 500 euros) and eight euro coins
(one and two euros, then one, two, five, 10,
20 and 50 cents).

One side is standard for all euro coins and
the other side bears a national emblem of participating countries.

So, if you stumble across some Deutsch-
marks or francs on your travels, you're staring
at museum pieces, albeit that old currencies
can still be exchanged at central banks in the
euro zone countries.

Treat the euro as you would any major
world currency.

Just as you'd exchange, say, US dollars for
euros in the euro zone, you'll find yourself exchanging euros for a local currency outside the
euro zone (although in the UK, for example,
some big stores and some tourist attractions
accept euros).

And think of its portability and usability
throughout Western Europe.

country	unit		euro
Australia	A$1	=	€0.59
Canada	C$1	=	€0.72
Japan	¥100	=	€0.86
New Zealand	NZ$1	=	€0.48
South Africa	R1	=	€0.10
UK	UK£1	=	€1.64
USA	US$1	=	€1.15

MONEY
Exchanging Money

Most EU countries now have a single currency
called the euro (see the boxed text 'The Euro'
on this page).

US dollars, pounds sterling and Swiss
francs are easily exchanged in Europe. You
lose out through commissions and customer
exchange rates every time you change money,
so if you only visit Portugal, for example, you
are better off buying euros straight away from
your bank at home.

All Western European currencies (well, the
few that remain) are fully convertible, but get
rid of any Scottish and Northern Irish pounds
before leaving the UK as they can (eg, in
Canada) attract a lower rate of exchange than
English pounds. Yes, they are all legal tender,
all pounds sterling and although it doesn't
make much sense your protestations at, say, a
Thomas Cook office in Toronto, could fall on
deaf ears. Ours did.

Most airports, central train stations, large
hotels and many border posts have banking
facilities outside normal office hours, sometimes on a 24-hour basis. You'll often find
automatic exchange machines outside banks
or tourist offices that accept the currencies of
up to two dozen countries. Post offices in
Europe often perform banking tasks and outnumber banks in remote places; they also
tend to be open longer hours. Be aware,
though, that while they always exchange
cash, they might balk at handling travellers
cheques unless they're denominated in the
local currency.

The best exchange rates are usually at
banks. *Bureaux de change* usually – but not
always by any means – offer worse rates or
charge higher commissions. Hotels are almost always the worst places for exchanging
money.

Both American Express and Thomas Cook
offices usually do not charge commission for
changing their own cheques, however, they
may offer a less favourable exchange rate than
the banks.

Cash Nothing beats cash for convenience, or
risk. If you lose it, it's gone forever and very
few travel insurers will come to your rescue.
Those that will, limit the amount to somewhere around US$300.

For tips on carrying your money safely,
see Theft under Dangers & Annoyances later
in this chapter.

It's still a good idea, though, to bring some
local currency in cash, if only to tide you over
until you get to an exchange facility or find an
automatic teller machine (ATM). The equivalent of, say, US$50 or US$100 should usually
be enough. Some extra cash in an easily exchanged currency (eg, US dollars) is also a
good idea.

Travellers Cheques & Eurocheques

The main idea of carrying travellers cheques rather than cash is the protection they offer from theft, though they are losing their popularity as more travellers – including those on tight budgets – deposit their money in their bank at home and withdraw it through ATMs as they go along.

American Express, Visa and Thomas Cook travellers cheques are widely accepted and have efficient replacement policies. If you're going to remote places, it's worth sticking to American Express as small local banks may not always accept other brands.

When you change cheques, don't look at just the exchange rate; ask about fees and commissions as well. There may be a service fee per cheque, a flat transaction fee or a percentage of the total amount irrespective of the number of cheques. Some banks charge fees (often exorbitant) to change cheques but not cash; others do the reverse.

Guaranteed personal cheques are another way of carrying money or obtaining cash. Eurocheques, which are available if you have a European bank account, are guaranteed up to a certain limit. When you cash them (eg, at post offices), you will be asked to show your Eurocheque card bearing your signature and registration number, and perhaps a passport or ID card. Your Eurocheque card should be kept separately from the cheques. Many hotels and merchants refuse to accept Eurocheques because of the relatively large commissions applied.

ATMs & Credit Cards

If you're not familiar with the options, ask your bank to explain the workings and the relative merits of credit, credit/debit, debit, charge and cash cards.

A major advantage of credit cards is that they allow you to pay for expensive items (eg, airline tickets) without having to carry great wads of cash around. They also allow you to withdraw cash at selected banks or from the many ATMs that are linked up internationally. However, if an ATM in Europe swallows a card that was issued outside Europe, it can be a major headache. Also, some credit cards aren't linked to ATM networks unless you ask your bank to do this.

Cash cards, which you use at home to withdraw money directly from your bank account or savings account, can be used throughout Europe at ATMs linked to international networks like Cirrus and Maestro.

Credit and credit/debit cards like Visa and MasterCard are widely accepted. MasterCard is linked to Europe's extensive Eurocard system, and Visa (sometimes called Carte Bleue) is particularly strong in France and Spain. However, these cards often have a credit limit that is too low to cover major expenses like long-term car rental or airline tickets and can be difficult to replace if lost abroad. Also, when you get a cash advance against your Visa or MasterCard credit card account, your issuer charges a transaction fee and/or finance charge. With some issuers, the fees can reach as high as US$10 *plus* interest per transaction so it's best to check with your card issuer before leaving home and compare rates.

Charge cards like American Express and Diners Club have offices in the major cities of most countries that will replace a lost card within 24 hours. However, charge cards are not widely accepted off the beaten track.

Another option is Visa TravelMoney, a prepaid travel card that gives 24-hour access to your funds in local currency via Visa ATMs. The card is PIN-protected and its value is stored on the system, not on the card. So if you lose the card, your money's safe. Visa TravelMoney can be purchased in any amount from both Citicorp and Thomas Cook/ Interpayment.

If you want to rely heavily on bits of plastic, go for two different cards – an American Express or Diners Club, for instance, along with a Visa or MasterCard. Better still is a combination of credit or cash card and travellers cheques so you have something to fall back on if an ATM swallows your card or the banks in the area are closed.

A word of warning – fraudulent shopkeepers have been known to quickly make several charge slip imprints with your credit card when you're not looking, and then simply copy your signature from the one that you authorise. Try not to let your card out of sight, and always check your statements upon your return.

International Transfers

Telegraphic transfers are not very expensive but, despite their name, can be quite slow. Be sure to specify the name of the bank and the name and address of the branch where you'd like to pick it up.

It's quicker and easier to have money wired via an American Express office (US$60 for US$1000). Western Union's Money Transfer system (available at post offices in some countries) and Thomas Cook's MoneyGram service are also popular.

Costs

This book provides a range of prices to suit every budget. See the Facts for the Visitor sections in the individual country chapters for specific information regarding travelling expenses.

Tipping & Bargaining

In many European countries it's common (and the law in France) for a service charge to be added to restaurant bills, in which case no tipping is necessary. In others, simply rounding up the bill is sufficient. See the individual country chapters for more details.

Some bargaining goes on in the markets, but the best you should hope for is a 20% reduction on the initial asking price.

Taxes & Refunds

A kind of sales tax called value-added tax (VAT) applies to most goods and services throughout Western Europe; it's 20% in Ireland, 19.6% in France, 18% in Greece, 17.5% in the UK, 16% in Germany and 7.5% in Switzerland. In most countries, visitors can claim back the VAT on purchases that are being taken out of the country. Those actually *residing* in one EU country are not entitled to a refund on VAT paid on goods bought in another EU country. Thus an American citizen living in London is not entitled to a VAT rebate on items bought in Paris, while an EU passport holder residing in New York is.

The procedure for making the claim is fairly straightforward, though it may vary somewhat from country to country and there also are minimum-purchase amounts imposed. First of all make sure the shop offers duty-free sales (often identified with a sign reading 'Tax-Free for Tourists'). When making your purchase, ask the shop attendant for a VAT refund voucher (sometimes called a Tax-Free Shopping Cheque) filled in with the correct amount and the date. This can either be refunded directly at international airports on departure or stamped at ferry ports or border crossings and mailed back for refund.

CUSTOMS

Duty-free goods are no longer sold to those travelling from one EU country to another. For goods purchased at airports or on ferries *outside* the EU, the usual allowances apply for tobacco (200 cigarettes, 50 cigars or 250g of loose tobacco), alcohol (1L of spirits or 2L of liquor with less than 22% alcohol by volume; 2L of wine) and perfume (50g of perfume and 0.25L of *eau de toilette*).

Do not confuse these with *duty-paid* items (including alcohol and tobacco) bought at normal shops and supermarkets in another EU country, where certain goods might be more expensive. (Cigarettes in France, for example, are half the price they are in the UK.) Then the allowances are more generous: 800 cigarettes, 200 cigars or 1kg of loose tobacco; 10L of spirits (more than 22% alcohol by volume), 20L of fortified wine or aperitif, 90L of wine or 110L of beer; and unlimited quantities of perfume.

POST & COMMUNICATIONS
Post

From major European centres, airmail typically takes about five days to North America and a week to Australasian destinations, though mail from the UK can be much faster and from Greece much slower. Postage costs vary from country to country, as does post office efficiency – the Italian post office is notoriously unreliable.

You can collect mail from poste restante sections at major post offices. Ask people writing to you to print your name clearly and underline your surname. When collecting mail, your passport may be required for identification and you may have to pay a small fee. If an expected letter is not awaiting you, ask to check under your given name; letters commonly get misfiled. Post offices usually hold mail for about a month, but sometimes less (in Germany, for instance, they only keep mail for two weeks). Unless the sender specifies otherwise, mail will always be sent to the city's main post office (or GPO in the UK and Ireland).

You can also have mail (but not parcels) sent to you at American Express offices so long as you have an American Express card or are carrying American Express travellers cheques. When you buy the cheques, ask for a booklet listing all the American Express offices worldwide.

Telephone

You can ring abroad from almost any phone box in Europe. Public telephones accepting stored-value phonecards (available from post offices, telephone centres, newsstands and retail outlets) are virtually the norm now; in some countries (eg, France) coin-operated phones are almost impossible to find.

There's a wide range of local and international phonecards. Lonely Planet's ekno global communication service provides low-cost international calls, a range of innovative messaging services, an online travel vault where you can securely store all your important documents, free email and travel information, all in one easy service. You can join online at **W** www.ekno.lonelyplanet.com, where you can also find the best local access numbers to connect to the 24-hour customer service centre to join or find out more. Once you have joined, always check the ekno website for the latest access numbers for each country and updates on new features.

For local calls you're usually better off with a local phonecard.

Without a phonecard, you can ring from a booth inside a post office or telephone centre and settle your bill at the counter. Reverse-charge (collect) calls are often possible, but not always. From many countries, however, the Country Direct system lets you phone home by billing the long-distance carrier you use at home. The numbers can often be dialled from public phones without even inserting a phonecard.

Area codes for individual cities are provided in the country chapters. For country codes, see Appendix – Telephones at the back of this book.

Toll-free numbers throughout Western Europe generally have an 0800 prefix (also 0500 in Britain). You'll find toll-free emergency numbers (ambulance, fire brigade, police) under Dangers & Annoyances in the Facts for the Visitor sections of the country chapters.

Fax

You can send faxes and telexes from most main post offices in Western Europe.

Email & Internet Access

The major Internet service providers (ISPs) such as **AOL** (**W** www.aol.com), **CompuServe** (**W** www.compuserve.com) and the **AT&T** (**W** www.att.com) organisation, have dial-in nodes throughout Europe; it's best to download a list of the dial-in numbers before you leave home. If you access your Internet email account at home through a smaller ISP or your office or school network, your best option is either to open an account with a global ISP, like those mentioned above, or to rely on Internet cafés and other public access points to collect your mail.

If you do intend to rely on Internet cafés, you'll need to carry three pieces of information with you so you can access your Internet email account: your incoming (POP or IMAP) mail server name, your account name, and your password. Your ISP or network supervisor will give you these. Armed with this information, you should be able to access your Internet email account from Internet-connected machines throughout the world, provided they run some kind of email software (remember that Netscape and Internet Explorer both have mail modules). Most ISPs also enable you to receive your emails through their website, which only requires you to remember your account name and password. It pays to become familiar with the process for doing this before you leave home.

You'll find Internet cafés throughout Europe; check the country chapters in this book, and see **W** www.netcafeguide.com for an up-to-date list. You may also find public Internet access in post offices, libraries, hostels, hotels, universities and so on.

DIGITAL RESOURCES

The Internet is a rich resource for travellers. You can research your trip, hunt down bargain air fares, book hotels, check weather conditions or chat with locals and other travellers about the best places to visit.

Airline Information What airlines fly where, when and for how much.
W www.travelocity.com

Airline Tickets Name the price you're willing to pay for an airline seat and if an airline has an empty seat for which it would rather get something than nothing, US-based Priceline lets you know.
W www.priceline.com

Currency Conversions Exchange rates of hundreds of currencies worldwide.
W www.xe.net/ucc

Lonely Planet There's no better place to start your Web explorations than the Lonely Planet website. Here you'll find succinct summaries on travelling to most places on earth, postcards from other travellers and the Thorn Tree bulletin board, where you can ask questions before you go or dispense advice when you get back. You can also find travel news and updates to many of our most popular guidebooks, and the subWWWay section links you to the most useful travel resources elsewhere on the Web.

W www.lonelyplanet.com

Tourist Offices Lists tourist offices at home and around the world for most countries.

W www.towd.com

Train Information Train fares and schedules on the most popular routes in Europe, including information on rail and youth passes.

W www.raileurope.com

NEWSPAPERS & MAGAZINES

Keeping up with the news in English is obviously no problem in the UK or Ireland. In larger towns in the rest of Western Europe you can buy the excellent *International Herald Tribune* on the day of publication, as well as the colourful but superficial *USA Today*. Among other English-language newspapers widely available are the *Guardian,* the *Financial Times* and the *Times*. Also readily available are *Newsweek, Time* and the *Economist*.

RADIO & TV

Close to the Channel, you can pick up British radio stations, particularly BBC's Radio 4. There are also numerous English-language broadcasts – or even BBC World Service and Voice of America (VOA) rebroadcasts on local AM and FM radio stations. Otherwise, you can pick up a mixture of the BBC World Service and BBC for Europe on medium wave at 648kHz AM and on short wave at 1296kHz, 6195kHz, 9410kHz, 12095kHz (a good daytime frequency), 15485kHz and 17640kHz, depending on the time of day. BBC Radio 4 broadcasts on long wave at 198kHz. VOA can usually be found at various times of the day on 7170kHz, 9530kHz, 9690kHz, 9760kHz, 11825kHz, 15165kHz, 15205kHz, 15335kHz and 15580kHz.

Cable and satellite TV have spread across Europe with much more gusto than radio. Sky TV and Eurosport can be found in many upmarket hotels throughout Western Europe, as can CNN, BBC Prime and other networks. You can also pick up many cross-border TV stations, including British stations close to the Channel.

VIDEO SYSTEMS

If you want to record or buy video tapes to play back home, you won't get a picture if the image registration systems are different. Europe generally uses PAL (Secam in France), which is incompatible with the North American and Japanese NTSC system. Australia also uses PAL.

PHOTOGRAPHY & VIDEO

Both your destination and the weather will dictate what film to take or buy locally. In places like Ireland and Britain, where the sky is often overcast, photographers should bring higher-speed film (eg, 200 ISO). For southern Europe (or northern Europe under a blanket of snow and sunny skies) slower film (100 ISO or lower) is the answer.

Lonely Planet's *Travel Photography* by Richard I'Anson will help you capture pictures you've always wanted.

Film and camera equipment are available everywhere in Western Europe, but obviously shops in larger cities and towns have a wider selection.

Avoid buying film at tourist sites in Europe (eg, at kiosks below the Eiffel Tower in Paris or at the Tower of London). It may have been stored badly or reached its sell-by date. It will certainly be expensive.

Properly used, a video camera can give a fascinating record of your holiday. Unlike still photography, video 'flows' so, for example, you can shoot scenes of countryside rolling past the train window. Make sure you keep the batteries charged and have the necessary charger, plugs and transformer for the country you are visiting. In most countries, it is possible to obtain video cartridges easily in large towns and cities, but make sure you buy the correct format. It is usually worth buying at least a few cartridges duty-free at the start of your trip.

TIME

Most of the countries covered in this book are on Central European Time (GMT/UTC plus one hour), the same time used from Spain to Poland. Britain and Ireland are on GMT/UTC and Greece is on East European Time (GMT plus two hours).

Clocks are advanced one hour for daylight-saving time on the last Sunday in March, and set back on the last Sunday in October. During daylight-saving time Britain and Ireland are GMT/UTC plus one hour, Central European Time is GMT/UTC plus two hours and Greece is GMT/UTC plus three hours.

ELECTRICITY
Voltages & Cycles

Most of Europe runs on 220V, 50Hz AC. The exceptions are the UK, which has 240V, and Spain, which usually has 220V but sometimes still the old 110V or 125V, depending on the network (some houses can have both). Some old buildings and hotels in Italy (including Rome) might also have 125V. All EU countries were supposed to have been standardised at 230V by now, but like many things in the EU, this is taking longer than anticipated.

Check the voltage and cycle (usually 50Hz) used in your home country. Most appliances that are set up for 220V will handle 240V without modifications (and vice versa); the same goes for 110V and 125V combinations. It's always preferable to adjust your appliance to the exact voltage if you can (some modern battery chargers and radios will do this automatically). Just don't mix 110/125V with 220/240V without a transformer (which will be built into an adjustable appliance).

Several countries outside Europe (such as the USA and Canada) have 60Hz AC, which will affect the speed of electric motors even after the voltage has been adjusted to European values. CD and tape players (where motor speed is all-important) will be useless, but things like electric razors, hair dryers, irons and radios will be fine.

Plugs & Sockets

The UK and Ireland use a design with three flat pins – two for current and one for earth/grounding. Most of Continental Europe uses the 'europlug' with two round pins. Many europlugs and some sockets don't have provision for earth since most local home appliances are double-insulated; when provided, earth usually consists of two contact points along the edge, although Italy, Greece and Switzerland use a third round pin in such a way that the standard two-pin plug still fits the sockets (not always in Italy and Switzerland).

If your plugs are of a different design, you'll need an adaptor. Get one before you leave, since the adaptors available in Europe usually go the other way. If you find yourself without one, however, a specialist electrical-supply shop should be able to help.

WEIGHTS & MEASURES

The metric system is in use throughout Western Europe. However, in Britain nonmetric equivalents are used by much of the population (distances continue to be given in miles and milk and beer are sold in pints, not litres). In Germany, cheese and other food items are often sold per *Pfund*, which means 500g.

Continental Europe shows decimals with commas and thousands with full stops (for numbers with four or more digits the French use full stops or spaces).

There's a metric conversion chart on the inside cover of this book.

HEALTH

Travel health depends on your predeparture preparations, your daily health care while travelling and how you handle any medical problem that does develop.

Predeparture Planning

Immunisations Jabs aren't usually necessary for travel in Western Europe, but find out from your doctor, a travel health centre or an organisation such as the US-based **Centers for Disease Control and Prevention** (**W** www
.cdc.gov) what the current recommendations are for travel to your destination(s). It's a good idea to make sure your tetanus, diphtheria and polio vaccinations are up to date before travelling. Other vaccinations that may be recommended include typhoid, hepatitis A, hepatitis B, rabies and tick-borne encephalitis.

Although there is no risk of yellow fever in Europe, if you are arriving from a yellow-fever infected area (most of sub-Saharan Africa and parts of South America) you'll need proof of yellow fever vaccination before you will be allowed to enter Greece or Portugal (if arriving in or coming from the Azores or Madeira).

Remember to leave enough time for any vaccinations – say, six weeks before travel – and record them on an International Health Certificate (see that section under Visas & Documents earlier in this chapter).

Health Insurance Make sure that you have adequate health insurance. See Travel Insurance under Visas & Documents earlier in this chapter for details.

Travel Health Guides *Travel with Children* from Lonely Planet includes advice on travel health for younger children.

Travellers Thrombosis

Sitting inactive for long periods of time on any form of transport (bus, train or plane), especially if in cramped conditions, can give you swollen feet and ankles, and may increase the possibility of deep vein thrombosis (DVT).

DVT is when a clot forms in the deep veins of your legs. DVT may be symptomless or you may get an uncomfortable ache and swelling of your calf. What makes DVT a concern is that in a minority of people, a small piece of the clot can break off and travel to the lungs to cause a pulmonary embolism, a very serious medical condition.

To help prevent DVT during long-haul travel, you should move around as much as possible and while you are sitting you should flex your calf muscles and wriggle your toes every half-hour. It's also a good idea to drink plenty of water or juices during the journey to prevent dehydration, and, for the same reason, avoid drinking lots of alcohol or caffeinated drinks. In addition, you may want to consider wearing support stockings if you have had leg swelling in the past or you are over 40 years.

If you are prone to blood clotting or you are pregnant, you will need to discuss preventive measures with your doctor before you leave.

There are also a number of excellent travel health sites on the Internet. The World Health Organization at w www.who.int and the US Centers for Disease Control and Prevention at w www.cdc.gov have good sites, while the Lonely Planet website at w www.lonelyplanet .com/weblinks/wlheal.htm has a number of excellent links.

Other Preparations Make sure you're healthy before you start travelling. If you are going on a long trip make sure your teeth are OK. If you wear glasses take a spare pair and your prescription.

If you require a particular medication take an adequate supply, as it may not be available locally. Take part of the packaging showing the generic name, rather than the brand, which will make getting replacements easier. To avoid any problems, it's a good idea to have a legible prescription or letter from your doctor to show that you legally use the medication.

Basic Rules

Food Salads and fruit should be safe throughout Europe. Ice cream is usually OK, but beware if it has melted and been refrozen. Take great care with fish or shellfish (cooked mussels that haven't opened properly can be dangerous, for instance), and avoid under-cooked meat.

If a place looks clean and well run, and if the vendor also looks clean and healthy, then the food is probably safe. In general, places that are packed with travellers or locals will be fine. Be careful with food that has been cooked and left to go cold.

Picking mushrooms is a favourite pastime in some parts of Europe as autumn approaches, but make sure you don't eat any that haven't been positively identified as safe. Many cities and towns set up inspection tables at markets or at entrances to national parks to separate the good from the deadly.

Water Tap water is almost always safe to drink in Europe, but the quality can vary in Greece and southern Italy. Be wary of natural water unless you can be sure that there are no people or cattle upstream; run-off from fertilised fields is also a concern. If you are planning extended hikes where you have to rely on natural water, it may be useful to know about water purification.

The simplest way of purifying water is to boil it thoroughly. Vigorous boiling should be satisfactory; however, at high altitude water boils at a lower temperature, so germs are less likely to be killed. Boil it for longer in these environments.

Consider purchasing a water filter for a long trip. Alternatively, iodine is effective in purifying water and is available in tablet form. Follow the directions carefully and remember that too much iodine can be harmful. Chlorine tablets will kill many pathogens, but not some parasites such as giardia and amoebic cysts.

Medical Problems & Treatment

Local pharmacies or neighbouring medical centres are good places to visit if you have a small medical problem and can explain what the problem is. Hospital casualty wards will help if it's more serious. Major hospitals and emergency numbers are mentioned in the various country chapters of this book and sometimes indicated on the maps. Tourist offices and hotels can put you on to a doctor or dentist, and your embassy or consulate will probably know one who speaks your language.

Environmental Hazards

Altitude Sickness This can occur above 3000m, however, very few treks or ski runs in the Austrian, French, Italian or Swiss Alps reach heights of 3000m or more – Mont Blanc is one exception – so altitude sickness is unlikely. Headache, vomiting, dizziness, extreme faintness, and difficulty in breathing and sleeping are all signs to heed. Treat mild symptoms with rest and simple painkillers. If mild symptoms persist or get worse, descend to a lower altitude and seek medical advice.

Heat Exhaustion & Prickly Heat Dehydration and salt deficiency can cause heat exhaustion and can lead to severe heatstroke (see the following section). Take time to acclimatise to high temperatures, drink sufficient liquids and do not do anything too physically demanding.

Salt deficiency is characterised by fatigue, lethargy, headaches, giddiness and muscle cramps; salt tablets may help, but adding extra salt to your food is better.

Prickly heat is an itchy rash caused by excessive perspiration trapped under the skin. It usually strikes people who have just arrived in a hot climate. Keeping cool, bathing often, drying the skin and using a mild talcum or prickly heat powder, wearing loose clothing or resorting to air-conditioning may help.

Sunburn You can get sunburn surprisingly quickly, even through cloud, and particularly at high altitude. Use a sunscreen, a hat, and a barrier cream for your nose and lips. Calamine lotion or a commercial after-sun preparation are good for mild sunburn. Protect your eyes with good quality sunglasses, particularly if you will be near water, sand or snow.

Heatstroke This serious and occasionally fatal condition can occur if the body's heat-regulating mechanism breaks down and the body temperature rises to dangerous levels. Long, continuous periods of exposure to high temperatures and insufficient fluids can leave you vulnerable to heatstroke.

The symptoms are: feeling unwell, not sweating very much (or at all) and a high body temperature (39° to 41°C or 102° to 106°F). Where sweating has ceased, the skin becomes flushed and red. Severe, throbbing headaches and lack of coordination will also occur, and the sufferer may be confused or aggressive. Eventually the victim will become delirious or convulse. Hospitalisation is essential, but in the interim get victims out of the sun, remove their clothing, cover them with a wet sheet or towel and then fan continually. Give fluids if they are conscious.

Hypothermia The weather in Europe's mountains can be extremely changeable at any time of the year. Skiers and hikers should always be prepared for very cold and wet weather.

Hypothermia occurs when the body loses heat faster than it can produce it and the core temperature of the body falls. It is surprisingly easy to progress from very cold to dangerously cold due to a combination of wind, wet clothing, fatigue and hunger, even if the air temperature is above freezing.

It is best to dress in layers; silk, wool and some of the new artificial fibres are all good insulating materials. A hat is important, as a lot of heat is lost through the head. A strong, waterproof outer layer and a 'space' blanket for emergencies are essential. Carry basic supplies, including food containing simple sugars to generate heat quickly and fluid to drink.

Symptoms of hypothermia are exhaustion, numb skin (particularly toes and fingers), shivering, slurred speech, irrational or violent behaviour, lethargy, stumbling, dizzy spells, muscle cramps and violent bursts of energy. Irrationality may take the form of sufferers claiming they are warm and trying to take off their clothes.

To treat mild hypothermia, first get the person out of the wind and/or rain, remove their clothing if it's wet and replace it with dry, warm clothing. Give them hot liquids – not alcohol – and some high-kilojoule, easily digestible food. Do not rub victims; instead, allow them to slowly warm themselves. This should be enough to treat the early stages of hypothermia. The early recognition and treatment of mild hypothermia is the only way to prevent severe hypothermia, which is a critical condition.

Infectious Diseases

Diarrhoea Simple things like a change of water, food or climate can all cause a mild bout of diarrhoea, but a few rushed toilet trips with no other symptoms is not indicative of a major problem.

Dehydration is the main danger with any diarrhoea, particularly in children or the elderly as dehydration can occur quite quickly. Under all circumstances, fluid replacement (at least equal to the volume being lost) is the most important thing to remember. Weak black tea with a little sugar, soda water, or soft drinks allowed to go flat and diluted 50% with clean water are all good. With severe diarrhoea a rehydrating solution is preferable to replace minerals and salts lost. Commercially available oral rehydration salts (ORS) are very useful; add them to boiled or bottled water. In an emergency you can make up a solution of six teaspoons of sugar and half a teaspoon of salt to a litre of boiled or bottled water. Keep drinking small amounts often. Stick to a bland diet as you recover.

Over-the-counter diarrhoea remedies such as loperamide or diphenoxylate (sold under many different brand names) can be used to bring relief from the symptoms, although they do not actually cure the problem. Only use these drugs if you do not have access to toilets, eg, if you *must* travel. Note that these drugs are not recommended for children under 12 years.

In certain situations antibiotics may be required: severe diarrhoea, diarrhoea with blood or mucus (dysentery), any diarrhoea accompanied by fever, profuse watery diarrhoea, persistent diarrhoea that does not improve after 48 hours. These suggest a more serious cause of diarrhoea and in these situations over-the-counter diarrhoea remedies should be avoided and you should consult a doctor.

Fungal Infections These infections occur more commonly in hot weather and are usually found on the scalp, between the toes (athlete's foot) or fingers, in the groin and on the body (ringworm). You get ringworm (which is a fungal infection, not a worm) from infected animals or other people. Moisture encourages these infections.

To prevent fungal infections wear loose, comfortable clothes, avoid artificial fibres, wash frequently and dry yourself carefully. If you do get an infection, wash the infected area at least daily with a disinfectant or medicated soap and water, and rinse and dry well. Apply an antifungal cream or powder like tolnaftate. Try to expose the infected area to air or sunlight as much as possible and wash all towels and underwear in hot water – change them often and let them dry in the sun.

Hepatitis This is a general term for inflammation of the liver. The symptoms are similar in all forms of the illness, and include fever, chills, headache, fatigue, feelings of weakness and aches and pains, followed by loss of appetite, nausea, vomiting, abdominal pain, dark urine, light-coloured faeces, jaundiced (yellow) skin and yellowing of the whites of the eyes. People who have had hepatitis should avoid alcohol for some time after the illness, as the liver needs time to recover.

Hepatitis A is transmitted by contaminated food and drinking water. You should seek medical advice, but there is not much you can do apart from resting, drinking lots of fluids, eating lightly and avoiding fatty foods. Hepatitis E is transmitted in the same fashion as hepatitis A – it can be particularly serious in pregnant women.

Hepatitis B is spread through contact with infected blood, blood products or body fluids, for example through sexual contact, unsterilised needles and blood transfusions, or contact with blood via small breaks in the skin. Other risk situations include having a shave, tattoo or body piercing with contaminated equipment. The symptoms of hepatitis B may be more severe than type A and the disease can lead to long-term problems such as chronic liver damage, liver cancer or a long term carrier state. Hepatitis C and D are spread in the same way as hepatitis B and can also lead to long-term complications.

HIV & AIDS Infection with the human immunodeficiency virus (HIV) may lead to acquired immune deficiency syndrome (AIDS), which is a fatal disease. Any exposure to blood, blood products or body fluids may put the individual at risk. The disease is often transmitted through sexual contact or dirty needles – vaccinations, acupuncture, tattooing and body piercing can be potentially as dangerous as intravenous drug use. HIV/AIDS can also be spread through infected blood transfusions; blood used in European hospitals is screened for HIV and should be safe.

HIV testing is required in Germany for any foreigner staying more than 180 days in Bavaria. Foreign test results are not accepted. Anyone seeking residence, work and student permits in Spain must submit to a medical exam, which may include an AIDS test.

Sexually Transmitted Diseases

HIV/AIDS and hepatitis B can be transmitted through sexual contact – see the relevant sections earlier for more details. Other STIs include gonorrhoea, herpes and syphilis; sores, blisters or rashes around the genitals and discharges or pain when urinating are common symptoms. In some STIs, such as wart virus or chlamydia, symptoms may be less marked or not observed at all, especially in women. Chlamydia infection can cause infertility in men and women before any symptoms have been noticed. Syphilis symptoms eventually disappear completely but the disease continues and can cause severe problems in later years. While abstinence from sexual contact is the only 100% effective prevention, using condoms is also effective.

Cuts, Bites & Stings

Bedbugs & Lice Bedbugs live in various places, but particularly in dirty mattresses and bedding, evidenced by spots of blood on bedclothes or on the wall. Bedbugs leave itchy bites in neat rows. Calamine lotion or a sting relief spray may help.

All lice cause itching and discomfort. They make themselves at home in your hair (head lice), your clothing (body lice) or in your pubic hair (crabs). You catch lice through direct contact with infected people or by sharing combs, clothing and the like. Powder or shampoo treatment will kill the lice and infected clothing should then be washed in very hot, soapy water and left in the sun to dry.

Ticks You should always check all over your body if you have been walking through a potentially tick-infested area, as ticks can cause skin infections and other more serious diseases. If a tick is found attached, press down around the tick's head with tweezers, grab the head and gently pull upwards. Avoid pulling the rear of the body as this may squeeze the tick's gut contents through the attached mouth parts into the skin, increasing the risk of infection and disease. Smearing chemicals on the tick will not make it let go and is not recommended.

Lyme disease is a tick-transmitted infection that may be acquired in parts of Europe. The illness usually begins with a spreading rash at the site of the tick bite and is accompanied by fever, headache, extreme fatigue, aching joints and muscles, and mild neck stiffness. If untreated, these symptoms usually resolve over several weeks but over subsequent weeks or months disorders of the nervous system, heart and joints may develop. Treatment works best early in the illness. Medical help should be sought.

Ticks can carry encephalitis, a virus-borne cerebral inflammation. Tick-borne encephalitis can occur in forest and rural areas of Western Europe including Austria and Germany. You might consider getting an FSME (meningo-encephalitis) vaccination if you plan to do extensive hiking and camping between May and September. The symptoms include blotches around the bite, which is sometimes pale in the middle. Headache, stiffness and other flu-like symptoms, as well as extreme tiredness, appearing a week or two after the bite, can progress to more serious problems. Medical help must be sought.

Rabies The only Western European countries that are rabies-free are Britain, Greece, Ireland, Italy, Portugal and Switzerland. Many animals can be infected (such as dogs, cats, bats and monkeys) and it is their saliva that is infectious. Any bite, scratch or even lick from an animal should be cleaned immediately and thoroughly. Scrub with soap and running water, and then apply alcohol or iodine solution. Local medical advice should be sought immediately as to the possibility of rabies in the region. A course of injections may then be required in order to prevent the onset of symptoms and death.

Snakes To minimise your chances of being bitten always wear boots, socks and long trousers when walking through undergrowth where snakes may be present. Don't put your hands into holes and crevices, and be careful when collecting firewood.

Snake bites do not cause instantaneous death, and antivenins are usually available. If bitten by a snake that could be venomous, immediately wrap the bitten limb tightly, as you would for a sprained ankle, and then attach a splint to immobilise it. Keep the victim still and seek medical help, if possible with the dead snake for identification. Don't attempt to catch the snake if there is a possibility of being bitten again. Tourniquets and sucking out the poison are comprehensively discredited.

Women's Health

Antibiotic use, synthetic underwear, sweating and contraceptive pills can lead to fungal vaginal infections, especially when travelling in hot climates. Fungal infections are characterised by a rash, itch and discharge. The usual treatment is with antifungal pessaries or cream but if you can't get hold of these, they can also be treated with a highly diluted vinegar or lemon-juice douche, or with yogurt. Maintaining good personal hygiene and wearing loose-fitting clothes and cotton underwear may help prevent these infections.

Sexually transmitted infections are a major cause of vaginal problems. Symptoms include a smelly discharge, painful intercourse and sometimes a burning sensation when urinating. Medical attention should be sought and male sexual partners must also be treated. For more details see Sexually Transmitted Infections earlier in this Health section. Besides abstinence, the best thing is to practise safer sex using condoms.

WOMEN TRAVELLERS

Frustrating though it may be, women travellers continue to face more challenging situations when travelling than men do. If you are a woman traveller, especially a solo woman, you may find it helpful to understand the status of local women to better understand the responses you illicit from locals. Hopes of travelling inconspicuously, spending time alone and absorbing the surroundings are often thwarted by men who assume a lone woman desires company, or who seemingly find it impossible to avert their penetrating gaze. Bear in mind that most of this behaviour, which can come across as threatening, is more often than not harmless. Don't let it deter you! The more women that travel, alone or in pairs or groups, the less attention women will attract and, in time, the more freedom women will feel to gallivant across the globe, *sans* beau in tow.

Despite feminism's grip on many European countries, women remain underrepresented in positions of power, in both governmental and corporate spheres. In spite of the exciting progress to elevate the status of women in recent years, women's leadership at the upper echelons of institutions still leaves a lot to be desired, and in many areas, you may notice the glut of women in low-paid, menial jobs. As is the case worldwide, women remain overrepresented among the illiterate and unemployed.

Women travellers will find Western Europe relatively enlightened, and shouldn't often have to invent husbands that will be joining them soon or muscle-bound boyfriends that will be back any minute. If you do find yourself in an uncomfortable situation or area, jump in a taxi if you possibly can (and worry about the cost later), or pipe up and make a racket. Parts of Portugal, Spain, Italy and Greece remain very conservative, so you may decide to dress demurely in the hope that you'll blend in a little better.

GAY & LESBIAN TRAVELLERS

This book lists contact addresses and gay and lesbian venues in the individual country chapters; look in the Facts for the Visitor and Entertainment sections.

The *Spartacus International Gay Guide* (Bruno Gmünder, US$39.95) is a good male-only international directory of gay entertainment venues in Europe and elsewhere. It's best when used in conjunction with listings in local gay papers, usually distributed for free at gay bars and clubs. For lesbians, *Women's Travel in Your Pocket* (Ferrari Publications, US$15.95) is a good international guide.

DISABLED TRAVELLERS

If you have a physical disability, get in touch with your national support organisation (preferably the 'travel officer' if there is one) and ask about the countries you plan to visit. They often have complete libraries devoted to travel, and they can put you in touch with travel agents who specialise in tours for the disabled.

The British-based **Royal Association for Disability & Rehabilitation** (RADAR: ☎ 020-7250 3222, fax 7250 0212; W www.radar.org.uk; 12 City Forum, 250 City Rd, London EC1V 8AF) publishes a useful guide entitled *Holidays & Travel Abroad: A Guide for Disabled People* (UK£8) that includes planning, transport and accommodation information.

SENIOR TRAVELLERS

Senior citizens are entitled to many discounts in Europe on things like public transport, museum admission fees etc, provided they show proof of their age. In some cases they might need a special pass. The minimum qualifying age is generally 60 or 65 for men and slightly younger for women.

In your home country, a lower age may already entitle you to all sorts of interesting travel packages and discounts (on car hire, for instance) through organisations and travel agents that cater for senior travellers. Start hunting at your local senior citizens advice bureau. European residents over 60 are eligible for the Railplus Card; see Cheap Tickets under Train in the Getting Around chapter for details.

TRAVEL WITH CHILDREN

Successful travel with young children requires planning and effort. Don't try to overdo things; even for adults, packing too much into the time available can cause problems. And make sure the activities include the kids as well – balance that day at the Louvre with a day at Disneyland Paris. Include children in the trip planning; if they've helped to work out where you will be going, they will be much more interested when they get there. Europe is the home of Little Red Riding Hood, Cinderella, King Arthur and Tintin and is a great place to travel with kids. Lonely Planet's *Travel with Children* by Cathy Lanigan (with a foreword by Maureen Wheeler) is an excellent source of information.

Most car-rental firms in Europe have children's safety seats for hire at a nominal cost, but it's essential that you book them in advance. The same goes for highchairs and cots (cribs); they're standard in most restaurants and hotels, but numbers are limited. The choice of baby food, formulas, soy and cow's milk, disposable nappies (diapers) and the like is as great in the supermarkets of most Western European countries as it is at home, but the opening hours might be different. Run out of nappies on Saturday afternoon and you're in for a messy weekend.

DANGERS & ANNOYANCES

On the whole, you should experience few problems travelling in Western Europe – even alone – as the region is well developed and relatively safe. But do exercise common sense. The Basque separatist movement remains active as does soccer hooliganism. Whatever you do, don't leave friends and relatives back home worrying about how to get in touch with you in case of an emergency. Work out a list

of places where they can contact you or, best of all, phone home now and then or email.

Theft

Theft is definitely a problem in Europe, and nowadays you also have to be wary of other travellers. The most important things to guard are your passport, papers, tickets and money – in that order. It's always best to carry these next to your skin or in a sturdy leather pouch on your belt. Train station lockers or luggage storage counters are useful places to store your bags (but *never* valuables) while you get your bearings in a new town. Be very suspicious about people who offer to help you operate your locker. Carry your own padlock for hostel lockers.

You can lessen the risks further by being careful of snatch thieves. Cameras or shoulder bags are an open invitation for these people, who sometimes operate from motorcycles or scooters and expertly slash the strap before you have a chance to react. A small daypack is better, but watch your rear. Be very careful at cafés and bars; loop the strap around your leg while seated.

Pickpockets are most active in dense crowds, especially in busy train stations and on public transport during peak hours. A common ploy is for one person to distract you while another zips through your pockets. Beware of gangs of kids – dishevelled-looking *and* well dressed – waving newspapers and demanding attention. In the blink of an eye, a wallet or camera can go missing.

Be careful even in hotels; don't leave valuables lying around in your room.

Parked cars containing luggage and other bags are prime targets for petty criminals in most cities, particularly cars with foreign number plates and/or rental-agency stickers. While driving in cities, beware of snatch thieves when you pull up at the lights – keep doors locked and windows rolled up high.

In case of theft or loss, always report the incident to the police and ask for a statement. Otherwise your travel-insurance company won't pay up.

Drugs

Always treat drugs with a great deal of caution. There are a lot of drugs available in Western Europe, sometimes quite openly (eg, in the Netherlands), but that doesn't mean they're legal. Even a little harmless hashish can cause a great deal of trouble in some places.

Don't even think about bringing drugs home with you either. With what they may consider 'suspect' stamps in your passport (eg, Amsterdam's Schiphol airport), energetic customs officials could well decide to take a closer look.

ACTIVITIES

Europe offers countless opportunities to indulge in more active pursuits than sightseeing. The varied geography and climate supports the full range of outdoor pursuits: windsurfing, skiing, fishing, trekking, cycling and mountaineering. For more local information, see the individual country chapters.

Cycling

Along with hiking, cycling is the best way to really get close to the scenery and the people, keeping yourself fit in the process. It's also a good way to get around many cities and towns.

Much of Western Europe is ideally suited to cycling. In the northwest, the flat terrain ensures that bicycles are a popular form of everyday transport, though rampant headwinds often spoil the fun. In the rest of the region, hills and mountains can make for heavy going, but this is offset by the dense concentration of things to see. Cycling is a great way to explore many of the Mediterranean islands, though the heat can get to you after a while (make sure you drink enough fluids).

Some popular cycling areas among holidaymakers include the Belgian Ardennes, the west of Ireland, the upper reaches of the Danube in southern Germany, the coasts of Sardinia and Apulia, anywhere in the Alps (for those fit enough) and the south of France.

If you are arriving from outside Europe, you can often bring your own bicycle along on the plane (see Bicycle in the Getting Around chapter). Alternatively, this book lists many places where you can hire one (make sure it has plenty of gears if you plan anything serious), though apart from in Ireland hire places might take a dim view of rentals lasting more than a week.

See the introductory Getting Around chapter for more information on bicycle touring, and the Getting Around sections in individual country chapters for rental agencies and tips on places to go to.

Skiing

In winter, Europeans flock to the hundreds of resorts located in the Alps and Pyrenees for downhill skiing and snowboarding, though cross-country is very popular in some areas.

A skiing holiday can be an expensive one due to the costs of ski lifts, accommodation and the inevitable après-ski drinking sessions. Equipment hire (or even purchase), on the other hand, can be relatively cheap if you follow the tips in this book, and the hassle of bringing your own skis may not be worth it. As a rule, a skiing holiday in Europe will work out twice as expensive as a summer holiday of the same length. Cross-country skiing costs less than downhill since you don't rely as much on ski lifts.

The skiing season generally lasts from early December to late March, though at higher altitudes it may extend an extra month either way. Snow conditions can vary greatly from one year to the next and from region to region, but January and February tend to be the best (and busiest) months.

Ski resorts in the French and Swiss Alps offer great skiing and facilities, but are also the most expensive. Expect high prices, too, in the German Alps, though Germany has cheaper (but far less spectacular) options in the Black Forest and Harz Mountains. Austria is generally slightly cheaper than France and Switzerland (especially in Carinthia). Prices in the Italian Alps are similar to Austria (with some upmarket exceptions like Cortina d'Ampezzo), and can be relatively cheap, given the right package.

Possibly the cheapest skiing in Western Europe is to be found in the Pyrenees in Spain and Andorra, and in the Sierra Nevada range in the south of Spain. Both Greece and Scotland also boast growing ski industries – especially good value in Greece. See the individual country chapters for more detailed information.

Hiking

Keen hikers can spend a lifetime exploring Europe's many exciting trails. Probably the most spectacular are to be found in the Alps and Italian Dolomites, which are crisscrossed with well-marked trails; food and accommodation are available along the way in season. The equally sensational Pyrenees are less developed, which can add to the experience as you often rely on remote mountain villages for rest and sustenance. Hiking areas that are less well known but nothing short of stunning are Corsica, Sardinia and northern Portugal. The Picos de Europa range in Spain is also rewarding and Scotland's West Highland Way has gained world renown.

The **Ramblers' Association** (☎ 020-7339 8500; **w** www.ramblers.org.uk) is a charity that promotes long-distance walking in the UK and can help with maps and information. The British-based **Ramblers Holidays** (☎ 01707-331133; **w** www.ramblersholidays.co.uk) in Hertfordshire offers hiking-oriented trips in Europe and elsewhere.

Every country in Europe has national parks and other interesting areas that may qualify as a trekker's paradise, depending on your preferences. Guided treks are often available for those who aren't sure about their physical abilities or who simply don't know what to look for. Read the Hiking information in the individual country chapters in this book and take your pick.

Windsurfing & Surfing

After swimming and fishing, windsurfing could well be the most popular of the many water sports on offer in Europe. It's easy to rent sailboards in many tourist centres, and courses are usually available for beginners.

Believe it or not, you can also go surfing in Europe. Forget the shallow North Sea and Mediterranean, and the calm Baltic, but there can be excellent surf, and an accompanying surfer scene, in southwest England and west Scotland (wetsuit advisable!), along Ireland's west coast, the Atlantic coast of France and Portugal, and along the north and southwest coasts of Spain.

Boating

Europe's many lakes, rivers and diverse coastlines offer a variety of boating options unmatched anywhere in the world. You can canoe in Finland, raft down rapids in Slovenia, charter a yacht in the Aegean, hire a catamaran in the Netherlands, row on a peaceful Alpine lake, join a Danube River cruise from Amsterdam to Vienna (see the introductory Getting Around chapter), rent a sailing boat on the Côte d'Azur or dream away on a canal boat along Britain's (or Ireland's or France's) extraordinary canal network – the possibilities are endless. The country chapters have more details.

COURSES

If your interests are more cerebral, you can enrol in courses in Western Europe on anything from language to alternative medicine. Language courses are available to foreigners through universities or private schools, and are justifiably popular since the best way to learn a language is in the country where it's spoken. But you can also take courses in art, literature, architecture, drama, music, cooking, alternative energy, photography and organic farming, among other subjects.

The individual country chapters in this book give pointers on where to start looking. In general, the best sources of detailed information are the cultural institutes maintained by many European countries around the world; failing that, try their national tourist offices or embassies. Student exchange organisations, student travel agencies and organisations such as the YMCA/YWCA and Hostelling International (HI) can also put you on the right track. Ask about special holiday packages that include a course.

WORK

European countries aren't keen on handing out jobs to foreigners when unemployment rates are what they are in some areas. Officially, an EU citizen is allowed to work in any other EU country, but the paperwork isn't always straightforward for long-term employment and after three months they will probably need to apply for a residency permit. Other country/nationality combinations require special work permits that can be almost impossible to arrange, especially for temporary work. That doesn't prevent enterprising travellers from topping up their funds occasionally by working in the hotel or restaurant trades at beach or ski resorts or teaching a little English, and they don't always have to do this illegally either.

The UK, for example, issues special 'working holiday' visas to Commonwealth citizens aged between 17 and 27, valid for two years. In France you can get a visa for work as an au pair if you are going to follow a recognised course of study (eg, a French-language course) and complete all the paperwork before leaving your country. Your national student exchange organisation may be able to arrange temporary work permits to several countries through special programmes. For more details on working as a foreigner, see Work in the Facts for the

Visitor sections of the individual country chapters.

If you have a parent or grandparent who was born in an EU country, you may have certain rights you never knew about. Get in touch with that country's embassy and ask about dual citizenship and work permits – if you go for citizenship, also ask about any obligations, such as military service and residency. Ireland is particularly easy-going about granting citizenship to people with an Irish parent or grandparent, and with an Irish passport, the EU is your oyster. Be aware that your home country may not recognise dual citizenship.

If you do find a temporary job, the pay may be less than that offered to local people. The one big exception is teaching English, but these jobs are hard to come by – at least officially. Other typical tourist jobs (picking grapes in France, washing dishes in Alpine resorts) often come with board and lodging, and the pay is little more than pocket money, but you'll have a good time partying with other travellers.

If you play an instrument or have other artistic talents, you could try working the streets. As every Peruvian pipe player (and his fifth cousin) knows, busking is fairly common in major Western European cities like Amsterdam and Paris, but is illegal in some parts of Switzerland and Austria. In Belgium and Germany it has been more or less tolerated in the past but crackdowns are not unknown. Most other countries require municipal permits that can be hard to obtain. Talk to other street artists before you start.

Selling goods on the street is generally frowned upon and can be tantamount to vagrancy, apart from at flea markets. It's also a hard way to make money if you're not selling something special. Most countries require permits for this sort of thing. It's fairly common, though officially illegal, in the UK, Germany and Spain.

There are several references and websites that publicise specific positions in Western Europe. **Transitions Abroad** (w *www.trans abroad.com*) publishes *Work Abroad: The Complete Guide to Finding a Job Overseas* and the *Alternative Travel Directory: The Complete Guide to Work, Study and Travel Overseas* as well as a colour magazine, *Transitions Abroad*. Its website lists paid positions and volunteer and service programmes. **Action Without Borders** (w *www.idealist.org*) and

GoAbroad.com (w *www.goabroad.com*) list hundreds of jobs and volunteer opportunities.

Work Your Way Around the World by Susan Griffith gives good, practical advice on a wide range of issues. Its publisher, **Vacation Work** (w *www.vacationwork.co.uk*), has many other useful titles, including *Summer Jobs Abroad*, edited by David Woodworth. *Working Holidays*, published by the Central Bureau for Educational Visits & Exchanges in London, is another good source.

Volunteer Work

Organising a volunteer work placement is a great way to gain a deeper insight into local culture. If you're staying with a family, or working alongside local colleagues, you'll probably learn much more about life there than you would if you were travelling through the country.

In some instances volunteers are paid a living allowance, sometimes they work for their keep and other programmes require the volunteer to pay.

There are several Internet sites that can help you search for volunteer work opportunities in Western Europe. As well as websites mentioned earlier, **WorkingAbroad** (w *www .workingabroad.com*) has an excellent website for researching possibilities and applying for positions.

The **International Willing Workers On Organic Farms** (WWOOF; w *www.wwoof .org*) association has organisations all over Western Europe. If you join a WWOOF organisation, you can arrange to live and work on a host's organic farm.

ACCOMMODATION

The cheapest places to stay in Europe are camping grounds, followed by hostels and accommodation in student dormitories. Cheap hotels are virtually unknown in the northern half of Europe, but guesthouses, *pensions*, private rooms and B&Bs often offer good value. Self-catering flats and cottages are worth considering with a group, especially if you plan to stay somewhere for a while.

See the Facts for the Visitor sections in individual country chapters for an overview of the local accommodation options. During peak holiday periods accommodation can be hard to find, and unless you're camping it's advisable to book ahead. Even camping grounds can fill up, especially in or around big cities.

Reservations

Cheap hotels in popular destinations (eg, Paris, London, Rome) – especially the well-run ones smack in the middle of desirable or central neighbourhoods – fill up quickly. It's a good idea to make reservations as many weeks ahead as possible, at least for the first night or two. A three-minute international phone call to reserve a room (followed, if necessary, by written confirmation and/or deposit) is a lot cheaper and less frustrating than wasting your first day in a city looking for a place to stay. Increasingly, places offering accommodation in Western Europe can be contacted via email and often have a listing on accommodation websites.

If you arrive in a country by air and without a reservation, there is often an airport accommodation booking desk, although it rarely covers the lower strata of hotels. Tourist offices often have extensive accommodation lists, and the more helpful ones will go out of their way to find you something suitable. In most countries the fee for this service is very low and, if accommodation is tight, it can save you a lot of running around. This is also an easy way to get around any language problems. Agencies offering private rooms can be good value. Staying with a local family doesn't always mean that you'll lack privacy, but you'll probably have less freedom than in a hotel.

Sometimes people will come up to you on the street offering a private room or a hostel bed. This can be good or bad, there's no hard-and-fast rule – just make sure it's not way out in a dingy suburb somewhere and that you negotiate a clear price. As always, be careful when someone offers to carry your luggage; they might relieve you of more than the load off your back.

Camping

Camping is immensely popular in Western Europe (especially among Germans and the Dutch) and provides the cheapest accommodation. There's usually a charge per tent or site, per person and per vehicle. The national tourist offices should provide booklets or brochures listing camping grounds all over their country. See Visas & Documents earlier in this chapter for information on the Camping Card International.

In large cities, most camping grounds will be some distance from the centre. For this reason, camping is most popular with people who have their own transport. If you're on foot, the money you save by camping can quickly be eaten up by the cost of commuting to/from a town centre. You may also need a tent, sleeping bag and cooking equipment, though not always. Many camping grounds hire bungalows or cottages accommodating from two to eight people.

Camping other than at designated camping grounds is difficult because the population density of Western Europe makes it hard to find a suitable spot to pitch a tent away from prying eyes. It is also illegal without permission from the local authorities (the police or local council office) or from the owner of the land (don't be shy about asking – you may be pleasantly surprised by the response).

In some countries, such as Austria, the UK, France and Germany, free camping is illegal on all but private land, and in Greece it's illegal altogether. This doesn't prevent hikers from occasionally pitching their tent for the night, and they'll usually get away with it if they have only a small tent, are discreet, stay only one or two nights, take the tent down during the day and do not light a campfire or leave rubbish. At worst, they'll be woken up by the police and asked to move on.

Hostels

Hostels offer the cheapest (secure) roof over your head in Europe, and you don't have to be a youngster to use them. Most hostels are part of the national youth hostel association (YHA), which is affiliated with what was formerly called the IYHF (International Youth Hostel Federation) and has been renamed Hostelling International (HI) in order to attract a wider clientele and move away from the emphasis on 'youth'. The situation remains slightly confused, however. Some countries, such as the USA and Canada, immediately adopted the new name, but many European countries will take a few years to change their logos. In practice it makes no difference; IYHF and HI are the same thing and the domestic YHA almost always belongs to the parent group.

There are also some privately run hostels, although it's mainly in Britain, Ireland and Germany that private backpacker hostels have really taken off.

Technically, you're supposed to be a YHA or HI member to use affiliated hostels, but you can often stay by paying an extra charge and this will usually be set against future membership. Stay enough nights as a non-member and you're automatically a member.

In Bavaria, in Germany, the strict maximum age for anyone, except group leaders or parents accompanying a child, is 26, although most countries don't adhere to an age limit.

To join the HI, you can ask at any hostel or contact your local or national hostelling office. There's a very useful website at **w** www .iyhf.org with links to most HI sites. The offices for English-speaking countries appear below. Otherwise, check the individual country chapters for addresses.

Australia
Australian Youth Hostels Association (☎ 02-9261 1111, fax 9261 1969, **e** yha@yhansw.org.au), 422 Kent St, Sydney, NSW 2000

Canada
Hostelling International Canada (☎ 613-237 7884, fax 237 7868, **e** info@hihostels.ca), 205 Catherine St, Suite 400, Ottawa, Ont K2P 1C3

England & Wales
Youth Hostels Association (☎ 01629-592600, fax 592702, **e** customerservices@yha.org .uk), Trevelyan House, Dimple Rd, Matlock, Derbyshire DE4 3YH

Ireland
An Óige (Irish Youth Hostel Association; ☎ 01-830 4555, fax 830 5808, **e** mailbox@anoige .ie), 61 Mountjoy St, Dublin 7

New Zealand
Youth Hostels Association of New Zealand (☎ 03-379 9970, fax 365 4476, **e** info@yha.org.nz), PO Box 436, Level 3, 193 Cashel St, Christchurch

Northern Ireland
Hostelling International Northern Ireland (☎ 028-9031 5435, fax 9043 9699, **e** info@hini.org .uk), 22–32 Donegall Rd, Belfast BT12 5JN

Scotland
Scottish Youth Hostels Association (☎ 01786-891400, fax 891333, **e** info@syha.org.uk), 7 Glebe Crescent, Stirling FK8 2JA

South Africa
Hostelling International South Africa (☎ 021-424 2511, fax 424 4119, **e** info@hisa.org.za), PO Box 4402, St George's House, 73 St George's Mall, Cape Town 8001

USA
Hostelling International/American Youth Hostels (☎ 202-783-6161, fax 783-6171, **e** hiayhserv@hiayh.org), 733 15th St NW, Suite 840, Washington DC 20005

At a hostel, you get a bed for the night plus use of communal facilities, which often include a kitchen where you can prepare your own meals. You are usually required to have a sleeping sheet and simply using your sleeping bag is not permitted. If you don't have your own approved sleeping sheet, you can usually hire or buy one. Hostels vary widely in character, but the growing number of travellers and the increased competition from other forms of accommodation, particularly private 'backpacker hostels', have prompted many hostels to improve their facilities and cut back on rules and regulations. Increasingly, hostels are open all day, curfews are disappearing and 'wardens' with sergeant-major mentalities are an endangered species. In some places you'll even find hostels with single and double rooms. Everywhere the trend has been towards smaller dormitories with just four to six beds.

There are many hostel guides with listings available, including HI's *Europe* (UK£8.50) and the England & Wales YHA's *YHA Accommodation Guide* (UK£2.99, free to members), as well as a couple of cooperatively produced guides to the Irish backpacker hostels. Many hostels accept reservations by phone or fax, but usually not during peak periods; they'll often book the next hostel you're heading to for a small fee. You can also book hostels through national hostel offices. Popular hostels can be heavily booked in summer and limits may even be placed on how many nights you can stay.

University Accommodation
Some university towns rent out student accommodation during holiday periods. This is very popular in France and the UK (see those chapters for more details) as universities become more accountable financially.

Accommodation will sometimes be in single rooms (more commonly in doubles or triples) and may have cooking facilities. Inquire at the college or university, at student information services or at local tourist offices.

B&Bs, Guesthouses & Hotels
There's a huge range of accommodation above the hostel level. In the UK and Ireland myriad B&Bs are the real bargains in this field, where you get a room (a bed) and breakfast in a private home. In some areas every other house will have a B&B sign out the front. In other countries similar private

accommodation – though often without breakfast – may go under the name of pension, guesthouse, *Gasthaus*, *Zimmer frei*, *chambre d'hôte* and so on. Although the majority of guesthouses are simple affairs, there are more expensive ones where you'll find en suite bathrooms and other luxuries.

Above this level are hotels, which at the bottom of the bracket may be no more expensive than B&Bs or guesthouses, while at the other extreme extend to luxury five-star properties with price tags to match. Although categorisation depends on the country, the hotels recommended in this book will generally range from no stars to one or two stars. You'll often find inexpensive hotels clustered around the bus and train station areas, which are always good places to start hunting.

Check your hotel room and the bathroom before you agree to take it, and make sure you know what it's going to cost – discounts are often available for groups or for longer stays. Ask about breakfast; sometimes it's included, but other times it may be obligatory and you'll have to pay extra for it. If the sheets don't look clean, ask to have them changed right away. Check where the fire exits are.

If you think a hotel room is too expensive, ask if there's anything cheaper; often, hotel owners may have tried to steer you into more expensive rooms. In southern Europe in particular, hotel owners may be open to a little bargaining if times are slack. In France and the UK it is common practice for business hotels (usually more than two stars) to slash their rates by up to 40% on Friday and Saturday nights when business is dead. Save your big hotel splurge for the weekend.

FOOD

Few regions in the world offer such a variety of cuisines in such a small area as Western Europe. The Facts for the Visitor sections in the individual country chapters contain details of local cuisines, and the Places to Eat sections list many suggestions.

Restaurant prices vary enormously. The cheapest places for a decent meal are often the self-service restaurants in department stores. University restaurants are dirt cheap, but the food tends to be bland and you may not be allowed in if you're not a local student. Kiosks often sell cheap snacks that can be as much a part of the national cuisine as the fancy dishes.

Self-catering – buying ingredients at a shop or market and preparing them yourself – can be a cheap and wholesome way of eating. Even if you don't cook, a lunch on a park bench with half a loaf of fresh bread, some local cheese, salami and a tomato or two, washed down with a bottle of local wine, can be one of the recurring highlights of your trip. It also makes a nice change from restaurant food.

If you have dietary restrictions – you're a vegetarian or you keep kosher, for example – tourist organisations may be able to advise you or provide lists of suitable restaurants. We list some vegetarian and kosher restaurants in this book.

In general, vegetarians needn't worry about going hungry in Western Europe; many restaurants have one or two vegetarian options, and southern European menus in particular tend to contain many vegetable dishes and salads.

DRINKS

So much to drink, so little time. Western Europe is a wine and beer connoisseur's haven. What else would you expect of the home of Grolsch, Guinness, ouzo, port and whisky, not to mention the most famous wines in the history of viniculture? Can you feel the champagne bubbles tickling your nostrils?

Afterthought – nonalcoholic options, coffee and tea are readily available. See Drinks in the Facts for the Visitor sections of the country chapters for specific information.

Getting There & Away

Step one of your trip is actually getting to Western Europe, and in these days of severe competition among airlines there are plenty of opportunities to find cheap tickets to a variety of gateway cities.

You can almost rule out shipping as a means of arriving in Western Europe via the Atlantic – only a handful of ships still carry passengers on this route; they don't sail often and are very expensive, even compared with full-fare air tickets. It's a slightly different story if you are travelling from Scandinavia or North Africa, for example, as there are a reasonable number of shipping companies plying these routes. Some travellers still arrive or leave overland – the options being Africa, the Middle East and Asia via Russia on the Trans-Siberian Railway from China.

AIR

Always remember to reconfirm your onward or return bookings by the specified time – at least 72 hours before departure on international flights. Otherwise there's a real risk that you'll turn up at the airport only to find that you've missed your flight because it was rescheduled, or that you've been reclassified as a 'no show' and 'bumped'.

Buying Tickets

An air ticket alone can gouge a great slice out of anyone's budget, but you can reduce the cost by digging for discounted fares. Stiff competition has resulted in widespread discounting which is good news for travellers! The only people likely to be paying full fare these days are travellers flying in 1st or business class. Passengers that fly in economy can usually manage some sort of discount.

Be sure to buy carefully and flexibly, as it's still possible to end up paying exorbitant amounts for a journey.

For long-term travel there are plenty of discount tickets that are valid for 12 months, allowing multiple stopovers with open dates. For short-term travel cheaper fares are available by travelling midweek, staying away at least one Saturday night or taking advantage of short-lived promotional offers.

When you're looking for bargain air fares, go to a travel agent rather than directly to the airline. From time to time, airlines do have

promotional fares and special offers, but generally they only sell fares at the official listed price. One exception to this rule is the expanding number of 'no-frills' carriers operating in the USA and northwest Europe, which mostly sell direct to travellers. Unlike the 'full-service' airlines, no-frills carriers often make one-way tickets available at around half the return fare, meaning that it is easy to put together a return ticket when you fly to one place but leave from another.

The other exception is booking on the Internet. Many airlines, full-service and no-frills, offer some excellent fares to Web surfers. They may sell seats by auction or simply cut prices to reflect the reduced cost of electronic selling. Many travel agents around the world have websites, which can make the Internet a quick and easy way to compare prices, a good start for when you're ready to begin negotiating with your favourite travel agency. Online ticket sales work well if you are doing a simple one-way or return trip on specified dates. However, online super-fast fare generators are no substitute for a travel agent who knows all about special deals, has strategies for avoiding inconvenient stopovers and can offer advice on everything from which airline has the best vegetarian food to the best travel insurance to bundle with your ticket.

The days when some travel agents would routinely fleece travellers by running off with their money are, happily, almost over. Paying by credit card generally offers protection, as most card issuers provide refunds if you can prove you didn't get what you paid for. Similar protection can be obtained by buying a ticket from a bonded agent, such as one covered by the Air Transport Operators Licence (ATOL) scheme in the UK. Agents who only accept cash should hand over the tickets straight away and not tell you to 'come back tomorrow'. After you've made a booking or paid your deposit, call the airline and confirm that the booking was made. It's generally not advisable to send money (even cheques) through the post unless the agent is very well established – some travellers have reported being ripped off by fly-by-night mail-order ticket agents.

You may decide to pay more than the rock-bottom fare by opting for the safety of a better known travel agent. Companies such as STA Travel, which has offices worldwide, or Council Travel in the USA, are not going to disappear overnight and they offer good prices to most destinations.

If you purchase a ticket and later want to make changes to your route or get a refund, you need to contact the original travel agent. Airlines only issue refunds to the purchaser of a ticket – usually the travel agent who bought the ticket on your behalf. Many travellers change their routes halfway through their trips, so think carefully before you buy a ticket that is not easily refunded.

Student & Youth Fares Full-time students and people under 26 have access to better deals than other travellers. The better deals may not always be cheaper fares but can include more flexibility to change flights and/or routes. You have to show a document proving your date of birth, a valid International Student Identity Card (ISIC) or an International Youth Travel Card (IYTC) when buying your ticket and boarding the plane. See ⓦ www.istc.org for more information.

Frequent Flyers Most of the airlines offer frequent-flyer deals that can earn you a free air ticket or other goodies. To qualify, you have to accumulate sufficient mileage with the same airline or airline alliance. Many airlines have 'blackout periods', or times when you cannot fly for free on your frequent-flyer points (Christmas and Chinese New Year, for example). The worst thing about frequent flyer programmes is that they tend to lock you into one airline, and that airline may not always have the cheapest fares or most convenient flight schedule.

Courier Flights These flights are a great bargain if you're lucky enough to find one. Air-freight companies expedite delivery of urgent items by sending them with you as your baggage allowance. You are permitted to bring along a carry-on bag, but that's often all. In return, you get a steeply discounted ticket.

There are other restrictions: courier tickets are sold for a fixed date and schedule changes can be difficult to make. If you buy a return ticket, your schedule will be even more rigid. You need to clarify before you fly what restrictions apply to your ticket, and don't expect a refund once you've paid.

Booking a courier ticket takes some effort. They are not readily available and arrangements have to be made a month or more in advance. You won't find courier flights on all routes either – just on the major air routes.

Courier flights are occasionally advertised in the newspapers, or you could contact air-freight companies listed in the phone book. You may even have to go to the air-freight company to get an answer – the companies aren't always keen to give out information over the phone. **Travel Unlimited** *(PO Box 1058, Allston, MA 02134, USA)* is a monthly travel newsletter based in the USA that publishes many courier-flight deals from destinations worldwide. A 12-month subscription to the newsletter costs US$25, or US$35 for readers outside the USA. Another possibility (at least for US residents) is to join the International Association of Air Travel Couriers (IAATC). The membership fee of US$45 gets members a bimonthly update of air-courier offerings, access to a fax-on-demand service with daily updates of last-minute specials and the bimonthly newsletter *Travel Guide International*. For more information, contact **IAATC** *(☎ 352-475-1584; ⓦ www .courier.org)*. However, be aware that joining this organisation does not guarantee that you'll get a courier flight.

Second-Hand Tickets You'll occasionally see advertisements on youth-hostel bulletin boards and newspapers for 'second-hand tickets'. That is, somebody purchased a return ticket or a ticket with multiple stopovers and now wants to sell the unused portion of the ticket. Unfortunately, these tickets, if used for international travel, are usually worthless, as the name on the ticket must match the name on the passport of the person checking in. Some people reason that the seller of the ticket can check you in with his or her passport, and then give you the boarding pass – wrong again! Usually the immigration people want to see your boarding pass, and if it doesn't match the name in your passport, then you won't be able to board your flight.

Travellers with Special Needs

Most international airlines can cater to people with special needs – travellers with disabilities, people with young children and even children travelling alone.

Travellers with special dietary preferences (vegetarian, kosher etc) can request the appropriate meals with advance notice. If you are travelling in a wheelchair, most of the international airports can provide an escort from the check-in desk to the plane where needed, and ramps, lifts, toilets and phones are generally available.

Airlines usually allow babies up to two years of age to fly for 10% of the adult fare, although a few may allow them to fly free of charge. Reputable international airlines usually provide nappies (diapers), tissues, talcum and all the other paraphernalia needed to keep babies clean, dry and half-happy. For children between the ages of two and 12, the fare on international flights is usually 50% of the regular fare or 67% of a discounted fare.

The USA

Discount travel agents in the USA are known as consolidators. San Francisco is the ticket consolidator capital of America, although some cheap deals can be found in Los Angeles, New York and other big cities. Consolidators can be found through the Yellow Pages or the major daily newspapers.

The *New York Times*, *LA Times*, *Chicago Tribune* and *San Francisco Chronicle* all have weekly travel sections in which you'll find any number of travel agents' ads. **Council Travel** (W *www.counciltravel.com*), America's largest student travel organisation, has around 70 offices in the USA; its **head office** (☎ 212-822-2700; 205 E 42 St, New York, NY 10017) is in New York. **STA Travel** (☎ 800-781-4040; W *www.statravel.com*) has offices in major cities. Call for office locations.

You should be able to fly from New York to London or Paris and back for US$400 to US$500 in the low season and US$500 to US$850 in the high season. Equivalent fares from the west coast are US$100 to US$300 higher.

On a stand-by basis, one-way fares can work out to be remarkably cheap. New York-based **Airhitch** (W *www.airhitch.org*) can get you to/from Europe for US$194/228/262/206 each way from the east coast/midwest/west coast/southeast.

Another option is a courier flight. A New York–London return ticket can be had for as little as US$210 in the low season. See Courier Flights under Buying Tickets earlier in this chapter.

Canada

Canadian discount air-ticket sellers are also known as consolidators and their air fares tend to be about 10% higher than those sold in the USA. The *Globe & Mail*, *Toronto Star*, *Montreal Gazette* and *Vancouver Sun* carry travel agents' ads and are a good place to look for cheap fares.

Travel CUTS (☎ 1-866-246-9762; W *www.travelcuts.com*) is Canada's national student travel agency and has offices in all major cities.

Airhitch (see The USA earlier in this chapter) has stand-by fares to major European cities from Toronto, Montreal and Vancouver.

Australia

Cheap flights from Australia to Europe generally go via Southeast Asian capitals, involving stopovers at Kuala Lumpur, Bangkok or Singapore. If a long stopover between connections is necessary, transit accommodation is sometimes included in the price of the ticket. If it's at your own expense, it may be worth considering a more expensive ticket.

Quite a few travel offices specialise in discount air tickets. Some travel agents, particularly smaller ones, advertise cheap air fares in the travel sections of weekend newspapers, such as the *Age* in Melbourne and the *Sydney Morning Herald*.

Two well-known agents for cheap fares are STA Travel and Flight Centre. **STA Travel** (☎ 03-8417 6911; W www.statravel.com.au; 260 Hoddle St, Abbotsford, VIC 3067) has offices in all major cities and on many university campuses. Call ☎ 1300 733 035 Australia-wide for the location of your nearest branch. **Flight Centre** (☎ 133 133 Australia-wide; W www.flightcentre.com.au) has a **central office** (82 Elizabeth St, Sydney, NSW 2000), and there are over one hundred offices throughout Australia.

Thai, Malaysia, Qantas and Singapore airlines cost from about A$1300 (low season) up to A$2500. All have frequent promotional fares so it pays to check newspapers daily. Flights to/from Perth are a couple of hundred dollars cheaper.

Another option for travellers wanting to go to Britain between November and February is to hook up with a charter flight returning to Britain. These low-season, one-way fares do have restrictions, but may work out to be considerably cheaper. Ask your travel agent.

New Zealand
As in Australia, **STA Travel** (☎ 0508 782 872; W www.statravel.com.au) and **Flight Centre** (☎ 0800 24 35 44; W www.flightcentre.co.nz) are popular travel agents in New Zealand. The cheapest fares to Europe are routed through Asia. A discounted return flight to London from Auckland costs around NZ$2000.

Africa
Nairobi and Johannesburg are probably the best places in Africa to buy tickets to Europe, thanks to the many bucket shops and the lively competition between them. **STA Travel** (☎ 27 11 482 4666; W www.statravel.co.za) in Johannesburg and the **Africa Travel Centre** (☎ 021-423 555) in Cape Town are worth trying for cheap tickets. You're looking at paying approximately R6700 for a flight from Johannesburg to London.

Several West African countries such as Senegal and The Gambia offer cheap charter flights to France and London. Charter fares from the UK to Morocco and Tunisia can be quite cheap if you're lucky enough to find a seat.

Asia
Singapore and Bangkok are the discount airfare capitals of Asia. Shop around and ask the advice of other travellers before handing over any money. STA Travel operates branches in Tokyo, Osaka, Singapore, Bangkok, and Kuala Lumpur.

In India, tickets may be slightly cheaper from the bucket shops around Delhi's Connaught Place. Check with other travellers about their current trustworthiness.

LAND
Train
It's possible to travel to most Western European destinations from many other parts of Europe, as well as from both Morocco and Turkey, via the **Inter-Rail network** (W www .raileurope.co.uk).

It *is* possible to get to Western Europe by rail from Central and eastern Asia, though count on spending at least eight days doing it. Four different routes wind their way to Moscow: the Trans-Siberian (9297km from Vladivostok), the Trans-Mongolian (7860km from Beijing) and the Trans-Manchurian (9001km from Beijing), which all use the same tracks across Siberia but have different routes east of Lake Baikal; the Trans-Kazakhstan runs between Moscow and Urumqi in northwestern China. Prices vary enormously, depending on where you buy the ticket and what is included – advertised 2nd-class fares cost around US$345 from Beijing to Moscow. Websites worth consulting for trans-Siberian packages include:

W www.finnsov.fi
W www.monkeyshrine.com
W www.regent-holidays.co.uk
W www.trans-siberian.co.uk

There are countless travel options between Moscow and Western Europe. Most people will opt for the train, usually to/from Berlin, Munich or Vienna. Lonely Planet's *Trans-Siberian Railway* is a comprehensive guide to the route with details of costs, travel agencies that specialise in the trip and highlights.

Overland Trails
In the early 1980s, the overland trail to/from Asia lost much of its popularity as the Islamic regime in Iran made life difficult for most independent travellers.

Despite the fact that in recent years Iran appears to be rediscovering the merits of tourism, the war in Afghanistan and unsettled conditions in southern Pakistan and northwest

India will prevent the trickle of travellers turning into a flood for the time being.

Discounting the complicated Middle East route via Egypt, Jordan, Syria, Turkey and Eastern Europe, going to/from Africa involves a Mediterranean ferry crossing (see Sea later in this chapter). Due to unrest in Africa, the most feasible overland routes through that continent have all but closed down.

Travelling by private transport beyond Western Europe requires plenty of paperwork and other preparations. A detailed description is beyond the scope of this book, but the following Getting Around chapter tells you what's required within Western Europe.

SEA
Mediterranean Ferries

There are many ferries across the Mediterranean between Africa and Western Europe. The ferry you take will depend on your travels in Africa, but the options include: Spain–Morocco, Italy–Tunisia, and France–Morocco and France–Tunisia. There are also ferries between Greece and Israel via Cyprus.

Ferries are often filled to capacity in summer, especially to/from Tunisia, so it's advisable to book well in advance if you're taking a vehicle across. See the relevant country chapters.

Passenger Ships & Freighters

Regular, long-distance passenger ships disappeared with the advent of cheap air travel and were replaced by a small number of luxury cruise ships. Cunard's *Queen Elizabeth 2* sails between New York and Southampton 20 times a year; the trip takes six nights each way and costs around US$4000 for the return trip in a standard double cabin, though there are also one-way and 'fly one-way' deals.

A more adventurous alternative is as a paying passenger on a freighter.

Freighters are far more numerous than cruise ships and there are many more routes from which to choose. *Travel by Cargo Ship* (Cadogan) is a useful resource. Passenger freighters typically carry six to 12 passengers (more than 12 would require a doctor on board) and, though less luxurious than dedicated cruise ships, give you a real taste of life at sea.

Schedules tend to be flexible and costs vary, but seem to hover around US$100 a day; vehicles can often be included for an additional fee.

DEPARTURE TAX

Some countries charge you a fee for the privilege of leaving from their airports. Some also charge port fees when departing by ship. Such fees are *usually* included in the price of your ticket, but it pays to check this when purchasing it.

If not, you'll have to have the fee ready when leaving. Details of departure taxes are given at the end of the Getting There & Away sections of individual country chapters.

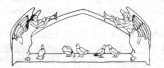

Getting Around

Travel within most of the EU, whether by air, rail or car, has been made easier following the Schengen Agreement. This abolished border controls between signed-up states. Britain and Ireland are the only EU countries currently outside the agreement.

AIR

Air travel is best viewed as a means to get you to the starting point of your itinerary rather than as your main means of travel. It lacks the flexibility of ground transport and generally can be expensive for short trips.

Since 1997 air travel within the EU has been deregulated. This 'open skies' policy allows greater flexibility in routing, wider competition and lower prices. Air travel is still dominated by the large state-run and private carriers, but these have been joined by several no-frills small airlines that sell budget tickets directly to the customer. They operate routes from the UK to most countries in continental Europe, though note they sometimes use smaller, less convenient airports.

Refer to the Air Travel Glossary in the previous Getting There & Away chapter for information on types of air tickets. London is a good centre for picking up cheap, restricted-validity tickets. Amsterdam and Athens are other good places for discount tickets in Western Europe. For more information, see the individual country chapters. Some airlines, such as the UK-based **easyJet** (W *www.easyJet .com)*, give discounts for tickets purchased via the Internet.

So-called open-jaw returns, by which you can travel into one city and exit from another, are worth considering, though they sometimes work out to be more expensive than simple returns. In the UK, **Trailfinders** (☎ *020-7937 1234)* and **STA Travel** (☎ *020-7361 6161;* W *www.statravel.co.uk)* can give you tailor-made versions of these tickets. Your chosen cities don't necessarily have to be in the same country.

STA Travel sells tickets to all travellers but caters especially to young people and students. Other travel agencies include **Bridge the World** (☎ *0870 444 7474; 4 Regent Place, London W1R 5FB)* and **Flightbookers** (☎ *020-7757 2000; 177-178 Tottenham Court Rd, London W1P 9LF)*.

If you are travelling alone, courier flights are a possibility. You get cheap passage in return for accompanying packages or documents through customs and delivering them to a representative at the destination airport. EU integration and electronic communications mean there's increasingly less call for couriers, but you might find something. British Airways, for example, offers courier flights through the **Travel Shop** (☎ *0870 606 1133)*.

Across Europe many travel agencies have ties with STA Travel, where cheap tickets can be purchased and STA Travel-issued tickets can be altered (usually for a US$25 fee). Outlets in major cities include **Voyages Wasteels** *(France* ☎ *08 03 88 70 04; 11 rue Dupuytren, 75006 Paris)* and **STA Travel** (☎ *030-311 0950; Goethestrasse 73, 10625 Berlin)*. See the individual country chapters for more information on travel agencies and getting to and from countries in Western Europe.

Getting between airports and city centres is rarely a problem in Western Europe thanks to effective public transport networks, though it can be rather time-consuming in large cities like Paris.

BUS
International Buses

International bus travel tends to take second place to going by train.

The bus has the edge in terms of cost, sometimes quite substantially, but is generally slower and less comfortable. Europe's biggest network of international buses is provided by a group of bus companies which operates under the name of **Eurolines** (W *www.euro lines.com)*.

Eurolines' representatives (which may also be able to advise you on other bus companies and deals) include:

Deutsche-Touring (☎ 069-79 03 50) Am Römerhof 17, Frankfurt

Eurolines Austria (☎ 01-712 04 53), Autobusbahnhof Wien-Mitte, Landstrasse Hauptstrasse, 1030 Vienna

Eurolines France (☎ 08-36 69 52 52) Gare Routière Internationale, 28 Ave du Général de Gaulle, 75020 Paris

Eurolines Italy (☎ 064 40 40 09) Ciconvallazione Nonentana 574, Lato Stazione Tiburtina, Rome

Eurolines Nederland (☎ 020-560 87 88) Rokin 10, 1012 KR Amsterdam
Eurolines UK (☎ 0870 514 3219) 52 Grosvenor Gardens, London SW1

Eurolines UK has six circular explorer routes, always starting and ending in London (no youth/senior reductions). The very popular London–Amsterdam–Brussels–Paris route is UK£62; London–Dublin–Galway–Killarney–Cork–London costs UK£59.

Eurolines also offers passes. Compared to rail passes, they're cheaper but not as extensive or as flexible. They cover 46 cities as far afield as Dublin, Bucharest, Rome and Madrid in Western Europe. Most trips must be international; a few internal journeys are possible between major cities in France, Germany, Spain and Italy. The cost is UK£229 for 30 days (UK£186 for youths and senior citizens) or UK£267 for 60 days (UK£205). The passes are cheaper off season.

On ordinary return trips, youths aged under 26 and seniors over 60 pay less. For example, a London–Munich return ticket costs UK£83 for adults or UK£75 for youths/seniors. Return tickets are valid for six months.

Busabout (☎ 020-7950 1661; w www.busabout.com; 258 Vauxhall Bridge Rd, Victoria, London SW1, England), operates buses that complete set circuits round Europe, stopping at major cities. You get unlimited travel per sector, and can 'hop-on, hop-off' at any scheduled stop, then resume with a later bus. Buses are often oversubscribed, so prebook each sector to avoid being stranded.

Departures are every two days from April to October, or May to September for Spain and Portugal. The circuits cover all countries in continental Western Europe, and you can pay to 'add on' Greece, Scandinavia and/or a London-Paris link.

Busabout's Consecutive Pass allows unlimited travel within the given time period. For a one-month pass the cost is UK£329 for adults or UK£289 for students and those under 26. Passes are also available for 14/21 days, two or three months, or for the whole season. The Flexipass allows you to select travel days within the given time period. Six days in one month costs UK£169/149 adult/youth while 25 days in four months will set you back UK£549/499.

See the individual country chapters for more information about long-distance buses.

National Buses

Domestic buses provide a viable alternative to the rail network in most countries. Again, compared to trains they are usually slightly cheaper and somewhat slower. Buses tend to be best for shorter hops such as getting around cities and reaching remote villages. They are often the only option in mountainous regions. Advance reservations are rarely necessary. On many city buses you usually buy your ticket in advance from a kiosk or machine and validate it on entering.

See the individual country chapters and city sections for more details on local buses.

TRAIN

Trains are a popular way of getting around: they are comfortable, frequent, and generally on time. The Channel Tunnel makes it possible to get from Britain to continental Europe using the **Eurostar** (w www.eurostar.com). See the France and Britain Getting There & Away sections later in this book.

In some countries, such as Spain, Portugal and (to some extent) Italy, fares are reasonably low; in others, European rail passes make travel more affordable. Supplements and reservation costs are not covered by passes, and pass holders must always carry their passport for identification purposes.

If you plan to travel extensively by train, it might be worth getting hold of the *Thomas Cook European Timetable*, which gives a complete listing of train schedules and indicates where supplements apply or where reservations are necessary. It is updated monthly and is available from **Thomas Cook** (w www.thomascook.com) outlets and bookshops in the UK, and in the USA from **Forsyth Travel Library** (☎ 800-367 7984; w www.forsyth.com). In Australia, bookshops can usually order-in copies if none are in stock.

If you intend to do a lot of train travel in one or a handful of countries – Benelux, say – it might be worthwhile getting hold of the national timetables that are published by the state railroads. The *European Planning & Rail Guide* is an informative annual **magazine** (USA ☎ 877-441 2387; w www.budgeteuropetravel.com) primarily geared towards North American travellers. It's free within the USA; send US$3 if you want it posted anywhere else.

Paris, Amsterdam, Munich, Milan and Vienna are important hubs for international rail connections. See the relevant city sections for details and budget ticket agents.

Note that European trains sometimes split en route in order to service two destinations, so even if you know you're on the right train, make sure you're in the correct carriage too.

Express Trains

Fast trains or those that make few stops are identified by the symbols EC (EuroCity) or IC (InterCity). The French TGV, Spanish AVE and German ICE trains are even faster. Supplements can apply on fast trains, and it is a good idea (sometimes obligatory) to make seat reservations at peak times and on certain lines.

Overnight Trains

These trains will usually offer a choice of couchette or sleeper if you don't fancy sleeping in your seat with somebody else's elbow in your ear. Again, reservations are advisable as sleeping options are allocated on a first-come, first-served basis.

Couchette bunks are comfortable enough, if lacking a bit in privacy. There are four per compartment in 1st class or six in 2nd class. A bunk costs around UK£10 for most international trains, irrespective of the length of the journey.

Sleepers are the most comfortable option, offering beds for one or two passengers in 1st class, and two or three passengers in 2nd class. Charges vary depending upon the journey, but they are significantly more expensive than couchettes. Most long-distance trains have a dining (buffet) car or an attendant who wheels a snack trolley through carriages. If possible buy your food before travelling as onboard prices tend to be high.

Security

You should be quite safe travelling on most trains in Western Europe but it pays to be security conscious nonetheless. Keep an eye on your luggage at all times (especially when stopping at stations) and lock compartment doors at night.

Rail Passes

Shop around, as pass prices can vary between different outlets. Once purchased, take care of your pass, as it cannot be replaced or refunded if lost or stolen. European passes get reductions on Eurostar through the Channel Tunnel and on ferries on certain routes (eg, between France and Ireland). In the USA, **Rail Europe** (☎ 800-438 7245; w www.raileurope.com) sells all sorts of rail passes.

Eurail These passes can only be bought by residents of non-European countries, and are supposed to be purchased before arriving in Europe. However, Eurail passes *can* be purchased within Europe, so long as your passport proves you've been there for less than six months, but the outlets where you can do this are limited, and the passes will be more expensive than getting them outside Europe. The London office for **Rail Europe** (☎ 0870 584 8848; w www.raileurope.co.uk; 179 Piccadilly, London) is one such outlet; another is **Drifters Travel Centre** (☎ 020-7402 9171; 22 Craven Terrace, London). Passes cannot be booked over the telephone with Rail Europe. You must make a personal call to the travel centre. If you've lived in Europe for more than six months, you are eligible for an Inter-Rail pass, which is a better buy.

Eurail passes are valid for unlimited travel on national railways and some private lines in the Western European countries of Austria, Belgium, France (including Monaco), Germany, Greece, Ireland, Italy, Luxembourg, the Netherlands, Portugal, Spain and Switzerland (including Liechtenstein).

Eurail is also valid on some ferries between Italy and Greece. Reductions are given on some other ferry routes and on river/lake steamer services in various countries.

Eurail passes offer reasonable value to those aged under 26. A Youthpass gives unlimited 2nd-class travel within a choice of five validity periods: 15/21 days (UK£325/415) or one/two/three months (UK£525/740/925). The Youth Flexipass, also for 2nd class, is valid for freely chosen days within a two-month period: 10 days for UK£390 or 15 days for UK£510. Overnight journeys commencing after 7pm count as the following day's travel. The traveller must fill out in ink the relevant box in the calendar before starting a day's travel.

For those aged over 26, the equivalent passes provide 1st-class travel. The standard Eurail pass for 15/21 days costs UK£470/605 or for one/two/three months UK£750/1065/1320. The Flexipass costs UK£545/730 for 10/15 days within two months. Two to five people travelling together can get a 'saver' version of either pass, saving about 15%. Eurail passes for children are also available.

Europass Also for non-Europeans, Europass gives unlimited travel on freely chosen days within a two-month period. Youth (aged under 26) and adult (solo, or two to five sharing) versions are available, and purchasing requirements and sales outlets are as for Eurail passes. They are cheaper than Eurail passes as they cover only France, Germany, Italy, Spain and Switzerland. The youth/adult price is UK£190/295 for a minimum five travel days, or UK£430/615 for a maximum 15 days. 'Associate countries' can be added on to the basic pass – prices vary. These associate countries are Austria, Hungary, Belgium, Luxembourg, the Netherlands, Greece (including ferries from Italy) and Portugal.

Inter-Rail These passes are available to European residents of more than six months standing (passport identification is required). Terms and conditions vary slightly from country to country, but in the country of origin there is only a discount of around 50% on the normal fares.

The Inter-Rail pass is split into zones. In Western Europe, Zone A is Ireland and Britain (though if you buy your Zone A pass in Britain, you get only 34% off, or no discount at all with the 26+ version); C is Denmark, Germany, Switzerland and Austria; E is France, Belgium, the Netherlands and Luxembourg; F is Spain and Portugal; G is Italy, Greece and Italy–Greece ferries. The other zones cover Scandinavia and parts of Eastern Europe.

The normal Inter-Rail pass is for people aged under 26, though travellers over 26 can get the Inter-Rail 26+ version. The price for any one zone is UK£139 (UK£209 for 26+) for 22 days. Multizone passes are valid for one month: two zones cost UK£189 (UK£265), three zones UK£209 (UK£299) and the all-zone global pass is UK£249 (UK£355).

Euro Domino There is a Euro Domino pass for each of the countries covered in the Inter-Rail pass, and it's worth considering if you're homing in on a particular region. They're sold in Europe to European residents. Adults (travelling 1st or 2nd class) and youths under 26 can opt for three to eight days valid travel within one month. Examples of adult/youth prices for eight days in 2nd class are UK£77/£59 for the Netherlands and UK£167/£125 for Germany.

National Rail Passes If you're intending to travel extensively within one country, check which national rail passes are available. These can sometimes save you a lot of money; details can be found in the Getting Around sections in the individual country chapters. You need to plan ahead if you intend to take this option, as some passes can only be purchased prior to arrival in the country concerned. Some national flexi passes, near-equivalents to the Domino passes mentioned above, are only available to non-Europeans.

Cheap Tickets
European rail passes are only worth buying if you plan to do a reasonable amount of inter-country travelling within a short space of time. Plan your itinerary carefully. Don't overdo the overnight travelling. Although it can work out to be a great way of saving time and money you don't want to be too tired to enjoy the next day of sightseeing.

When weighing up options, consider the cost of other cheap ticket deals, including advance purchase reductions, one-off promotions or special circular-route tickets. Normal international tickets are valid for two months, and you can make as many stops as you like en route; make your intentions known when purchasing, and inform the train conductor how far you're going before they punch your ticket.

For a small fee, European residents can buy a Railplus Card, entitling the holder to a 25% discount on international train journeys. In most countries (eg, in the UK) it is sold only to people aged over 60 who hold a valid British Senior Card. The Railplus card costs UK£12 and lasts for one year. However, some national rail networks may make the Railplus Card available also to young people or other travellers.

CAR & MOTORCYCLE
Travelling with your own vehicle allows increased flexibility and the option to get off the beaten track. Unfortunately, cars can be inconvenient in city centres when you have to negotiate one-way streets or find somewhere to park amid a confusing concrete jungle. Various car-carrying trains (motorail) can help you avoid long, tiring drives. Eurotunnel through the Channel Tunnel transports cars; see Getting There & Away in the Britain and France chapters later in this book.

Paperwork & Preparations

Proof of ownership of a private vehicle should always be carried (Vehicle Registration Document for British-registered cars) when touring Europe. An EU driving licence is acceptable for driving throughout Europe. However, old-style green UK licences are no good for Spain or Italy and should be backed up by a German translation in Austria.

If you have any other type of licence it is advisable or necessary to obtain an International Driving Permit (IDP) from your motoring organisation (see Visas & Documents in the earlier Facts for the Visitor chapter). Always check what type of licence is required in your chosen destination prior to departure.

Third party motor insurance is compulsory in Europe. Most UK motor insurance policies automatically provide this for EU countries. Get your insurer to issue a Green Card (which may cost extra), an internationally recognised proof of insurance, and check that it lists all the countries you intend to visit. You'll need this in the event of an accident outside the country where the vehicle is insured. Also ask your insurer for a European Accident Statement form, which can simplify things if the worst happens. Never sign statements you can't read or understand – insist on a translation and sign that only if it's acceptable. For non-EU countries make sure you check the requirements with your insurer. For further advice and more detailed information contact **Association of British Insurers** (☎ 020-600 3333, W www.abi.org.uk).

Taking out a European motoring assistance policy is a good investment, such as the AA Five Star Service or the RAC European Motoring Assistance. Expect to pay about UK£50 for 14 days cover with a 10% discount for association members. Non-Europeans might find it cheaper to arrange international coverage with their national motoring organisation before leaving home. Ask your motoring organisation for details about free services offered by affiliated organisations around Western Europe.

Every vehicle travelling across an international border should display a sticker showing its country of registration. A warning triangle, to be used in the event of breakdown, is compulsory almost everywhere. Some recommended accessories are a first-aid kit (which is compulsory in Greece), a spare bulb kit (compulsory in Spain) and a fire extinguisher (compulsory in Greece). Bail bonds are not required for Spain. In the UK, contact **RAC** (☎ 0800 550055; W www.rac.co.uk) or **AA** (☎ 0870 550 0600) for more information.

Road Rules

Motoring organisations can supply members with country-by-country information about motoring regulations, or they may produce motoring guidebooks for general sale. The RAC (see Paperwork & Preparations earlier in this chapter) provides comprehensive and destination-specific notes offering a summary of national road rules and regulations.

With the exception of Britain and Ireland, driving is on the right. Vehicles brought over from either of these countries should have their headlights adjusted to avoid blinding oncoming traffic at night (a simple solution on older headlight lenses is to cover up a triangular section of the lens with tape). Priority is usually given to traffic approaching from the right in countries that drive on the right-hand side.

Take care with speed limits, as they vary from country to country. You may be surprised at the apparent disregard of traffic regulations in some places (particularly in Italy and Greece), but as a visitor it is always best to be cautious. In many countries, driving infringements are subject to an on-the-spot fine. Always ask for a receipt.

European drink-driving laws are particularly strict. The blood-alcohol concentration (BAC) limit when driving is between 0.05% and 0.08%, but in certain areas it can be *zero* per cent. See the introductory Getting Around sections in the country chapters for more details on traffic laws.

Roads

Conditions and types of roads vary across Western Europe, but it is possible to make some generalisations. The fastest routes are four- or six-lane dual carriageways/highways, ie, two or three lanes either side (motorway, autobahn, autoroute, autostrada etc). These roads are great in terms of speed and comfort but driving can be dull with little or no interesting scenery. Some of these roads incur tolls (eg, in Italy, France and Spain) or have a general tax for usage (Switzerland and Austria), but there will usually be an alternative route you can take. Motorways and other primary routes are almost always in good condition.

Road surfaces on minor routes are not perfect in some countries (eg, Greece), although normally they will be more than adequate. These roads are narrower and progress is generally much slower. To compensate, you can expect much better scenery and plenty of interesting villages along the way.

Rental

The big international firms will give you reliable service and a good standard of vehicle. Usually you will have the option of returning the car to a different outlet at the end of the rental period. Prebook for the lowest rates – if you walk into an office and ask for a car on the spot, you will pay over the odds, even allowing for special weekend deals. Fly-drive combinations and other programmes are worth looking into. You should be able to make advance reservations online at the websites of the following companies:

Avis (W www.avis.com)
Budget (W www.budget.com)
Europcar (W www.europcar.com)
Hertz (W www.hertz.com)

Brokers can cut hire costs. **Holiday Autos** (UK ☎ 0870 400 4477; W www.holidayautos .com) has low rates and offices or representatives in over 20 countries. In the USA call **Kemwel Holiday Autos** (☎ 877-820 0668). In the UK, a competitor with even lower prices is **Autos Abroad** (☎ 020-7287 6000; W www .autosabroad.co.uk).

If you want to rent a car and haven't prebooked, look for national or local firms, which can often undercut the big companies. Nevertheless, you need to be wary of dodgy deals where they take your money and point you towards some clapped-out wreck.

No matter where you rent it is imperative to understand exactly what is included in your rental agreement (collision waiver, unlimited mileage etc). Make sure you are covered with an adequate insurance policy. Ask in advance if you are allowed to drive a rented car across borders, such as from Germany (where hire prices are low) to Austria (where they're high).

The minimum rental age is usually 21 or even 23, and you'll probably need a credit card. Note that prices at airport rental offices are usually higher than at branches in the city centre.

Motorcycle and moped rental is common in some countries, such as Italy, Spain, Greece and the south of France. Sadly, it's also common to see inexperienced riders leap on rented bikes and very quickly fall off them again, leaving a layer or two of skin on the road in the process.

Purchase

Britain is probably the best place to buy as second-hand prices are good and, whether buying privately or from a dealer, the absence of language difficulties will help you establish exactly what you are getting and what guarantees you can expect in the event of a breakdown. See the Britain Getting Around section later in this book for information on purchase paperwork and European insurance.

Bear in mind that you will be getting a car with the steering wheel on the right in Britain. If you want left-hand drive and can afford to buy new, prices are usually reasonable in Greece, France, Germany, Belgium, Luxembourg and the Netherlands. Paperwork can be tricky wherever you buy, and many countries have compulsory roadworthiness checks on older vehicles.

Leasing

Leasing a vehicle has none of the hassles of purchasing and can work out considerably cheaper than hiring over longer periods. The Renault Eurodrive scheme provides new cars for non-EU residents for a period of between 17 and 170 days. Under this arrangement, a Renault Clio 1.2 for 24 days, for example, would cost UK£340 (if picked up/dropped off in France), including insurance and roadside assistance. Check out the options before leaving home. In the USA, Kemwel Holiday Autos (see Rental earlier in this chapter) arranges European leasing deals.

Camper Van

A popular way to tour Europe is for three or four people to band together to buy or rent a camper van. London is the usual embarkation point. Look at the advertisements in London's free magazine TNT if you wish to form or join a group. TNT is also a good source for purchasing a van, as is the Loot newspaper.

Some second-hand dealers offer a 'buyback' scheme for when you return from the Continent, but we've received warnings that some dealers don't fully honour their refund commitments. Anyway, buying and reselling privately should be more advantageous if you have the time. A reader recommended **Down Under Insurance** (☎ 020-7402 9211; w www .downunderinsurance.co.uk) for European cover.

Camper vans usually feature a fixed high-top or elevating roof and two to five bunk beds. Apart from the essential camping gas cooker, professional conversions may include a sink, fridge and built-in cupboards. Prices and facilities vary considerably and it's certainly worth getting advice from a mechanic to see if you are being offered a fair price. Getting a mechanical check (from UK£35) is also a good idea. Once on the road you should be able to keep budgets lower than backpackers using trains, but don't forget to set some money aside for emergency repairs.

The main advantage of going by camper van is flexibility. Transport, accommodation and storage are all taken care of. Unfortunately the self-contained factor can also prove to be one of the downsides. Conditions can get very cramped, tempers can become frayed and your romantic hippy-style trail may dissolve into the camper-van trip from hell. Other disadvantages include having to leave your gear inside when you are exploring. Invest in good locks and try to keep the inside tidy with your belongings stored away at all times.

Motorcycle Touring

Western Europe is made for motorcycle touring, with good-quality winding roads, stunning scenery and an active motorcycling scene. The weather is not always reliable though so make sure your wet-weather gear is up to scratch. The wearing of helmets for rider and passenger is compulsory everywhere in Western Europe. Austria, Belgium, France, Germany, Luxembourg, Portugal and Spain also require that motorcyclists use headlights during the day; in other countries it is recommended.

On ferries, motorcyclists can sometimes be squeezed in without a reservation although booking ahead is certainly advisable during peak travelling periods. Take note of local custom about parking motorcycles on footpaths (sidewalks). Though this is illegal in some countries, the police usually turn a blind eye so long as the vehicle doesn't obstruct pedestrians. Don't try this in Britain. Your feeble excuses to traffic wardens will fall on deaf ears.

If you are thinking of touring Europe on a motorcycle try contacting the **British Motorcyclists Federation** (☎ 0116-254 8818) for help and advice. An excellent source of information for travellers interested in more adventurous biking activities can be found at w www.horizonsunlimited.com.

Fuel

Fuel prices can vary enormously from country to country (though it's always more expensive than in North America or Australia) and may bear little relation to the general cost of living. Motoring organisations such as the **RAC** (UK ☎ 0906-470 1740) can supply more details.

Unleaded petrol is widely available throughout Western Europe. Diesel is usually significantly cheaper, though the difference is only marginal in Britain, Ireland and Switzerland.

TAXI

Taxis in Western Europe are metered and rates are high. There might also be supplements (depending on the country) for things like luggage, the time of day, the location from which you boarded and for extra passengers. Good bus, rail and underground (subway/metro) railway networks make the taking of taxis all but unnecessary, but if you need one in a hurry they can usually be found idling near train stations or outside big hotels.

Lower fares make taxis more viable in some countries, such as Spain, Greece and Portugal. Don't underestimate the local knowledge that can be gleaned from taxi drivers. They can often tell you about the liveliest places in town and know all about events happening during your stay.

BICYCLE

A tour of Western Europe by bike may seem like a daunting prospect but help is at hand. The **Cyclists' Touring Club** (CTC; ☎ 0870 873 0060; w www.ctc.org.uk; Cotterell House, 69 Meadrow, Godalming, Surrey GU7 3HS) is based in the UK and offers its members an information service on all matters associated with cycling (including cycling conditions, detailed routes, itineraries and maps). If they are not able to answer your questions the chances are they will know someone who can. Membership costs UK£27 for adults, UK£10 for those aged under 25 and UK£16.50 for those over 65.

The key to a successful trip is to travel light. What you carry should be largely determined by your destination and type of trip. Even for the shortest and most basic trip it's worth carrying the tools necessary for repairing a puncture. Other things you might want to consider packing are spare brake and gear cables, spanners, allen keys, spare spokes of the correct length and strong adhesive tape.

Before you set off ensure that you are competent at carrying out basic repairs. There's no point in weighing yourself down with equipment that you haven't got a clue how to use. Always check over your bike thoroughly each morning and again at night when the day's touring is over. Take a good lock and always use it when you leave your bike unattended.

The wearing of helmets is not compulsory but is certainly advised. A seasoned cyclist can average about 80km a day but this depends on the terrain and how much weight you are carrying. Don't overdo it – there's no point in burning yourself out during the initial stages.

For more information on cycling, see Activities in the earlier Facts for the Visitor chapter and in the individual country chapters.

Rental

It is easy to rent bicycles in Western Europe and you can often negotiate good deals. Rental periods vary. Local tourist offices will carry information on rental outlets. Occasionally you can drop the bicycle off at a different location so you don't have to double back on your route. See individual country chapters for more details.

Purchase

For major cycling tours, it's best to have a bike you're familiar with, so consider bringing your own (see the following Transporting a Bicycle section) rather than buying on arrival. If you can't be bothered with the hassle then there are plenty of places to buy in Western Europe (shops sell new and second-hand bicycles or you can check local papers for private vendors). Note that you will require a specialist bicycle shop for a machine capable of withstanding touring. CTC can provide members with a leaflet about purchasing bicycles. Cycling is very popular in the Netherlands and Germany, and they are good places to pick up a well-equipped touring bicycle. European prices are quite high (certainly higher than in North America), but non-Europeans should be able to claim back VAT on the purchase.

Transporting a Bicycle

If you want to bring your bicycle to Western Europe, you should be able to take it with you on the plane relatively easily. You can either take it apart and pack everything in a bike bag or box, or simply wheel it to the check-in desk, where it should be treated as a piece of luggage. You may have to remove the pedals and turn the handlebars sideways so that it takes up less space in the aircraft's hold; check with the airline well in advance, ie, before you pay for your ticket. If your bicycle and other luggage exceed your weight allowance, ask about alternatives or you may suddenly find yourself being charged a fortune for excess baggage.

Within Western Europe, bikes can usually be transported as luggage on slower trains, subject to a small supplementary fee.

Fast trains can rarely accommodate bikes: they might need to be sent as registered luggage and may end up on a different train from the one you take. This is often the case in France and Spain. Eurostar charges UK£20 to send a bike as registered luggage on its routes. You can transport your bicycle with you on Eurotunnel through the Channel Tunnel.

The European **Bike Express** (UK ☎ 01642-251 440; w www.bike-express.co.uk) is a coach service where cyclists can travel with their bicycles. It runs in the summer from northeast England to France, Italy and Spain, with pick-up/drop-off points en route. The maximum return fare is UK£179 (£10 off for CTC members).

HITCHING

Hitching is never entirely safe in any country in the world, and we don't recommend it. Travellers who decide to hitch should understand that they are taking a small but potentially serious risk. People who do choose to hitch will be safer if they travel in pairs and let someone know where they plan to go.

Hitching can be the most rewarding and frustrating way of getting around. Rewarding, because you get to meet and interact with local people and are forced into unplanned detours that may yield unexpected highlights off the beaten track. Frustrating, because you may get stuck on the side of the road to nowhere with nowhere (or nowhere cheap) to stay. Then it begins to rain...

That said, hitchers can end up making good time, but obviously your plans need to be flexible in case a trick of the light makes you appear invisible to passing motorists. A man and woman travelling together is probably the best combination. Two or more men must expect some delays; two women together will make good time and should be relatively safe. A woman hitching on her own is taking a big risk, particularly in parts of southern Europe.

Don't try to hitch from city centres; take public transport to suburban exit routes. Hitching is usually illegal on motorways (freeways) – stand on the slip roads, or approach drivers at petrol stations and truck stops. Look presentable and cheerful, and make a cardboard sign indicating your intended destination in the local language. Never hitch where drivers can't stop in good time or without causing an obstruction. At dusk, give up and think about finding somewhere to stay. If your itinerary includes a ferry crossing (for instance, across the Channel), it might be worth trying to score a ride before the ferry rather than after, since vehicle tickets sometimes include all passengers free of charge. This also applies to Eurotunnel via the Channel Tunnel.

It is sometimes possible to arrange a lift in advance: scan student notice boards in colleges, or contact car-sharing agencies. Such agencies are particularly popular in France (Allostop Provoya, Auto-Partage) and Germany (Mitfahrzentralen); see the relevant country chapters.

For general facts, destination-based information and ride-share options, w www.bugeurope.com may be helpful. The useful w www.hitchhikers.org connects hitchhikers and drivers worldwide.

BOAT
Ferry
Several ferry companies compete on all the main ferry routes, and the resulting service is comprehensive but complicated. The same ferry company can have a host of different prices for the same route, depending upon the time of day or year, the validity of the ticket or the length of your vehicle. It is worth planning (and booking) ahead where possible as there may be special reductions on off-peak crossings and advance-purchase tickets. Most ferry companies adjust prices according to the level of demand (so-called 'fluid' or 'dynamic' pricing) so it may pay to offer alternative travel

dates. Vehicle tickets usually include the driver and a full complement of passengers.

P&O Stena Line is one of the largest ferry companies in the world. It serves British, Irish and some Scandinavian routes. P&O Portsmouth and Brittany Ferries sail direct between England and northern Spain, taking 24 to 35 hours. The shortest cross-Channel route is Dover to Calais (also the busiest), though there is now great competition from the Channel Tunnel. You can book ferry tickets online (often at a discount) on the following websites:

w www.Brittany-ferries.com
w www.poportsmouth.com
w www.posl.com
w www.seafrance.com

Hoverspeed (☎ 0870 240 8070; w www .hoverspeed.co.uk) is quicker – Dover to Calais takes only 50 minutes – yet is competitively priced.

Italy (Brindisi or Bari) to Greece (Corfu, Igoumenitsa and Patras) is also a popular route. The Greek islands are connected to the mainland and each other by a spider's web of routings; Lonely Planet's *Greek Islands* gives details.

Rail-pass holders are entitled to discounts or free travel on some lines (see the earlier Train section). Food on ferries is often expensive (and lousy), so it is worth bringing your own when possible. It is also worth knowing that if you take your vehicle on board, you are usually denied access to it during the voyage.

Steamer
Europe's main lakes and rivers are served by steamers, and as you'd expect, schedules are more extensive in the summer months. Rail-pass holders are entitled to some discounts (see the earlier Train section). Extended boat trips should be considered as relaxing and scenic excursions; viewed merely as a functional means of transport, they can be very expensive.

Long cruises are possible in the Mediterranean and along Europe's rivers, however, you'll need a boatload of cash. Since the early 1990s the Danube has been connected to the Rhine by the Main-Danube canal in Germany. The *Viking Europe* does 13-day cruises along this route, from Vienna to Amsterdam, between May and September. In Britain, you may make bookings through

Noble Caledonia *(☎ 020-752 0000;* W *www .noble-caledonia.co.uk)*. In the USA, you can book through **Uniworld** *(☎ 800-360 9550;* W *www.cruiseuniworld.com)*.

ORGANISED TOURS

Package tours, whether tailor-made or bog standard, cater for all tastes, interests and ages. See your travel agent or look in the small ads in newspaper travel pages. The Internet is also an excellent resource to find unusual tours that might not receive media or trade attention.

Specialists include **Ramblers Holidays** *(☎ 01707-331133;* W *www.ramblersholi days.co.uk)* in Britain for hiking trips and **CBT Tours** *(☎ 800-736-2453;* W *www.cbt tours.com)* in the USA for bicycle trips.

Young revellers can party on Europe-wide bus tours. Contiki and Top Deck offer camping or hotel-based bus tours for the 18 to 35 age group. The duration of Contiki's tours are five to 46 days. **Contiki** *(☎ 020-8290 6777;* W *www.contiki.com)* and **Top Deck** *(☎ 020-7370 4555;* W *www.topdecktravel.co.uk)* have London offices, as well as offices or representatives in Europe, North America, Australasia and South Africa.

For people aged over 50, **Saga Holidays** *(*W *www.sagaholidays.com)* offers holidays ranging from cheap coach tours to luxury cruises and it has cheap travel insurance. There's a **UK office** *(☎ 0800 300500; Saga Building, Middelburg Square, Folkestone, Kent CT20 1AZ, England)* and a **US office** *(☎ 617-262-2262; 222 Berkeley St, Boston, MA 02116)*.

National tourist offices in most countries offer organised trips to points of interest. These may range from one-hour city tours to several-day circular excursions. They often work out more expensive than going it alone, but are sometimes worth it if you are pressed for time.

A short city tour will give you a quick overview of the place and can be a good way to begin your visit.

Andorra

The principality of Andorra, nestled in the Pyrenees mountains between France and Spain, covers an area of just 464 sq km. Although tiny, this political anomaly is at the heart of some of Europe's most dramatic scenery. It's also a budget skiing venue and duty-free shopping haven. These activities, together with great summer walking, attract over eight million visitors a year and bring not only wealth but some unsightly development around the capital of Andorra la Vella.

From the Middle Ages until as recently as 1993, Andorra's sovereignty was invested in two 'princes': the Catholic bishop of the Spanish town of La Seu d'Urgell and the French president (who inherited the job from France's pre-Revolutionary kings). Nowadays, democratic Andorra is a 'parliamentary co-princedom', the bishop and president remaining joint but largely nominal heads of state. Andorra is a member of the United Nations and the Council of Europe, but not a full member of the EU.

Andorrans form only about a quarter of the total population of 66,000, and are outnumbered by Spaniards. The official language is Catalan, which is related to both Spanish and French. Most people speak a couple of these languages and sometimes all three, while younger people, especially in the capital and ski resorts, manage more than a smattering of English also.

Facts for the Visitor

VISAS & DOCUMENTS
Visas aren't necessary; the authorities figure that if Spain or France let you in, that's good enough for them – but bring your passport or national ID card with you.

EMBASSIES & CONSULATES
Andorra has embassies in France and Spain, both of whom have reciprocal diplomatic missions in Andorra.

MONEY
Although it's not a full member of the EU, Andorra (which previously used the Spanish

At a Glance

- **Andorra la Vella** – quaint Casa de la Vall, parliament of one of the world's smallest nations
- **La Massana** – gateway to the ski centres of Arinsal and Pal

Capital	Andorra la Vella
Population	66,000
Official Language	Catalan
Currency	euro
Time	GMT/UTC+0100
Country Phone Code	☎ 376

Andorra la Vella pp62-3

peseta) has chosen to make life simpler for itself by opting for the euro. There are many ATMs and banks throughout the country, especially in Andorra la Vella.

POST & COMMUNICATIONS
Post
Andorra has no postal system of its own; France and Spain each operate separate systems with their own Andorran stamps, which are needed only for international mail (letters within the country are delivered free). Regular French and Spanish stamps cannot be used in Andorra.

It's usually swifter to route international mail (except letters to Spain) through the French postal system.

ANDORRA

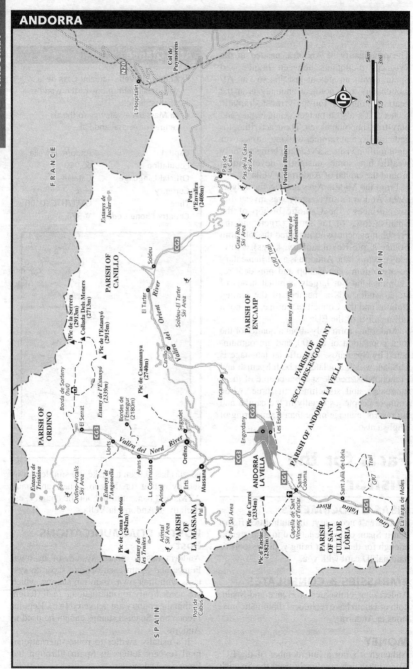

ANDORRA

N20

L'Hospitalet

Col de
Puymorens

FRANCE

Estanys de
Juclar

Pas de
la Casa

Pas de la Casa
Ski Area

Port
d'Envalira
(2408m)

Portella Blanca

Pic de la Serrera
(2913m)

Collada Dels Meners
(2713m)

Pic de l'Estanyó
(2915m)

Grau Roig
Ski Area

Estany de
Montmalús

GR7 Trail

PARISH OF
CANILLO

Soldeu

Borda de Sorteny
(hut)

Estany de l'Estanyó
(2339m)

El Tarter

Soldeu-El Tarter
Ski Area

El Serrat

Pic de Casamanya
(2740m)

Orient

River

Bordes de
l'Ensegur
(2180m)

PARISH OF
ORDINO

Canillo

Valira del

SPAIN

PARISH OF
ENCAMP

Estany de l'Illa

Llorts

Valira del Nord River

Segudet

Encamp

Estanys de
Tristaina

Ordino-Arcalís
Ski Area

Estany de
l'Angonella

Arans

Ordino

CG3

CG2

Les Escaldes

PARISH OF
ESCALDES-ENGORDANY

La Cortinada

PARISH OF ANDORRA LA VELLA

Pic de Coma Pedrosa
(2942m)

Arinsal

Erts

La
Massana

Engordany

Estany de
les Truites

PARISH
OF
LA MASSANA

Pal

Pic de Carroi
(2334m)

ANDORRA
LA VELLA

CG3

CG2

Santa
Coloma

CG1

Sant Julià de Lòria

Arinsal
Ski Area

Pal Ski Area

Capella de Sant
Vicenç d'Enclar

CG1

GR7
Trail

SPAIN

Pic d'Enclar
(2382m)

Valira

River

Sant Vincenç d'Enclar

GR7 Trail

PARISH
OF SANT
JULIÀ DE
LÒRIA

Port de
Cabús

Gran

La Farga de Moles

0   2.5   5km
0   1.5   3mi

Telephone

Andorra's country code is ☎ 376. The cheapest way to make an international call is to buy a *teletarja* (phonecard, sold for €3 at tourist offices and kiosks) and ring off-peak (9pm to 7am plus all day Sunday). At these times a three-minute call to Europe or the US costs €1.62 (€2.31 to Australia). You can't make a reverse-charge (collect) call from Andorra.

Email & Internet Access

There are a couple of Internet café options in Andorra la Vella (see Information under Andorra la Vella later in this chapter) and Hostal Pobladó in Arinsal, 10km northwest of Andorra la Vella (see Places to Stay under Arinsal later in this chapter).

TIME

Andorra is one hour ahead of GMT/UTC in winter (two hours ahead from the last Sunday in March to the last Sunday in September).

BUSINESS HOURS

Shops in Andorra la Vella are generally open 9.30am to 1pm and 3.30pm to 8pm daily, except (usually) Sunday afternoon.

ACTIVITIES

Above the main valleys, you'll find attractive lake-dotted mountain country, good for skiing in winter and walking in summer. The largest and best ski resorts are Soldeu-El Tarter and Pas de la Casa/Grau Roig. Others – Ordino-Arcalís, Arinsal and Pal – are a bit cheaper but often colder and windier. Ski passes cost €19 to €30 a day, depending on location and season; downhill ski-gear is €8 to €10 a day, and snowboards are €15 to €18 a day.

Tourist offices provide a useful English-language booklet, *Sport Activities*, describing numerous hiking and mountain-bike routes. In summer, mountain bikes can be rented in some resorts for around €18 a day.

ACCOMMODATION

Tourist offices stock a comprehensive free brochure, *Hotels, Restaurants, Apartaments i Cámpings*. Be warned, however, that prices it quotes are merely indicative.

There are no youth hostels and, outside Andorra la Vella, few budget options for independent travellers. In compensation, there are plenty of camping grounds, many beautifully situated. In high season (December to March

Emergency Services

The Europe-wide telephone number ☎ 112 can be used for the police, fire brigade and ambulance.

and July/August), some hotels put prices up substantially and others don't take in independent travellers.

For walkers, Andorra has 26 off-the-beaten-track *refugis* (mountain refuges); all except one are unstaffed and free. If you're trekking, ask at tourist offices for the free *Mapa de Refugis i Grans Recorreguts*, which pinpoints and describes them all.

Getting There & Away

The only way to reach Andorra, unless you trek across the mountains, is by road.

FRANCE

Autocars Nadal (☎ 821 138) operates two buses a day (€20, four hours) on Monday, Wednesday, Friday and Sunday, linking Toulouse's Gare Routière (bus station) and Andorra la Vella.

By rail, take a train from Toulouse to either L'Hospitalet (2¼ to 2¾ hours, four daily) or Latour-de-Carol (2½ to 3¼ hours). Two daily connecting buses link Andorra la Vella with both L'Hospitalet (€6.80) and Latour-de-Carol (€8.20). On Saturday, up to five buses run from L'Hospitalet to Pas de la Casa, just inside Andorra.

SPAIN

Alsina Graells (☎ 827 379) runs up to seven buses daily between Barcelona's Estació del Nord and Andorra la Vella's bus station (€18, four hours).

Eurolines (☎ 860 010) has four services daily (€17.88) between Andorra (departing from the car park of Hotel Diplomátic) and Barcelona's Sants bus station.

Samar/Andor-Inter (☎ 826 289) operates three times weekly between Andorra and Madrid (€27, nine hours) via Zaragoza (€13).

La Hispano Andorrana (☎ 821 372) operates five to eight buses daily between La Seu d'Urgell, just across the border, and Carrer

Doctor Nequi in Andorra la Vella (€2.05, hourly until 9pm).

Getting Around

BUS
Ask at a tourist office for a timetable of the eight bus routes, run by **Cooperativa Interurbana** (☎ 820 412), which follow Andorra's three main highways.

Destinations from the Avinguda Príncep Benlloch stop in Andorra la Vella include Ordino (€0.84, every half-hour), Arinsal (€1.38, four daily), Soldeu (€2.16, hourly) and Pas de la Casa (€4.36, up to four daily).

CAR & MOTORCYCLE
The speed limit is 40km/h in populated areas and 90km/h elsewhere. Two problems are the recklessness of local drivers on the tight, winding roads and Andorra la Vella's horrendous traffic jams. Bypass the worst of the latter by taking the ring road around the south side of town.

Petrol in Andorra is about 25% cheaper than in Spain or France.

Andorra la Vella

pop 23,300
The town of Andorra la Vella (elevation 1029m) is squeezed into the Riu Gran Valira Valley and is mainly engaged in retailing electronic and luxury goods. With the constant din of jackhammers and shopping-mall architecture, you might be in Hong Kong – but for the snowcapped peaks and an absence of noodle shops!

Orientation
Andorra la Vella is strung out along the main drag, whose name changes from Avinguda del Príncep Benlloch to Avinguda de Meritxell to Avinguda de Carlemany. The tiny historic quarter is split by this heavily trafficked artery. The town merges with the once-separate villages of Escaldes and Engordany to the east and Santa Coloma to the southwest.

Information
Tourist Offices The helpful **municipal tourist office** (☎ 827 117; Plaça de la Rotonda; open 9am-1pm & 4pm-8pm Mon-Sat,

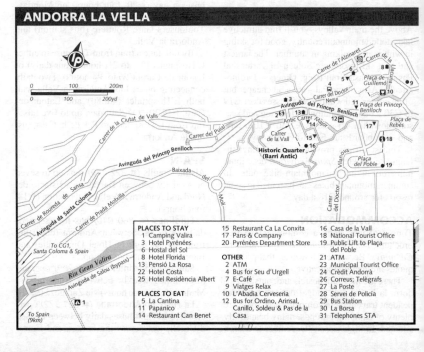

ANDORRA LA VELLA

PLACES TO STAY
1 Camping Valira
3 Hotel Pyrénées
6 Hostal del Sol
8 Hotel Florida
13 Pensió La Rosa
22 Hotel Costa
25 Hotel Residència Albert

PLACES TO EAT
5 La Cantina
11 Papanico
14 Restaurant Can Benet

15 Restaurant Ca La Conxita
17 Pans & Company
20 Pyrénées Department Store

OTHER
2 ATM
4 Bus for Seu d'Urgell
7 E-Café
9 Viatges Relax
10 L'Abadia Cerveseria
12 Bus for Ordino, Arinsal, Canillo, Soldeu & Pas de la Casa

16 Casa de la Vall
18 National Tourist Office
19 Public Lift to Plaça del Poble
21 ATM
23 Municipal Tourist Office
24 Crèdit Andorrà
26 Correus; Telègrafs
27 La Poste
28 Servei de Policia
29 Bus Station
30 La Borsa
31 Telephones STA

9am-7pm Sun, 9am-9pm daily July & Aug) sells stamps and telephone cards.

The **national tourist office** (☎ 820 214; open 10am-1.30pm Mon-Sun, 3pm-7pm Mon-Sat Oct-June, 9am-1pm Mon-Sun, 3pm-7pm Mon-Sat July-Sept) is just off Plaça de Rebés.

Money There are ATMs sprinkled liberally throughout this mercantile city. **Crèdit Andorrà** (Avinguda de Meritxell 80) has a 24-hour banknote exchange machine that accepts 15 currencies. Banks abound, and are open 9am to 1pm and 3pm to 5pm weekdays and to noon Saturday.

American Express is represented by **Viatges Relax** (☎ 822 044; Carrer de Mossèn Tremosa 2).

Post & Communications The French post office is **La Poste** (Carrer de Pere d'Urg 1) while **Correus i Telègrafs** (Carrer de Joan Maragall 10) is the Spanish one. Both are open 8.30am to 2.30pm weekdays and 9am to noon Saturday.

You can make international calls from pay phones or from the **Servei de Telecomunica-**cions d'Andorra (STA; Avinguda de Meritxell 112; open 9am-9pm daily), which also has a fax service.

E-Café (☎ 865 677; Alzinaret 5; open 10am-9pm Mon-Fri & 4pm-8pm Sat Aug & Sep), just off Plaça de Guillemó, charges €3.60 an hour for Net access and is a cheerful place to log on. **Future@point** (☎ 828 202; Carrer de la Sardana 6; open 10am-11pm daily) charges €3.05 per hour.

Things to See & Do

The small **Barri Antic** (Historic Quarter) was the heart of Andorra la Vella when the principality's capital was little more than a village. The narrow cobblestone streets around the **Casa de la Vall** are flanked by attractive stone houses.

Built in 1580 as a private home, the Casa de la Vall has served as Andorra's parliament building since 1702. Downstairs is **El Tribunal de Corts** (☎ 829 129), the country's only courtroom. Free guided tours (available in English) are given 9.30am to 1pm and 3pm to 7pm Monday to Saturday (daily in August, at other times 10am to 2pm Sunday). In summer, book at least a week ahead to ensure a

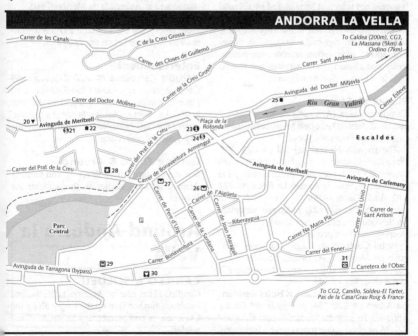

ANDORRA LA VELLA

ANDORRA

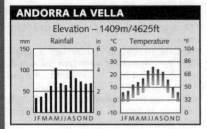

ANDORRA LA VELLA
Elevation – 1409m/4625ft

place – though individuals can often be squeezed in at the last minute.

The **Plaça del Poble**, a large public square just south of Plaça de Rebés, occupies the roof of a modern government office building. Giving excellent views, it's a very popular local gathering place, especially during the evening.

The free public lift in the southeast corner will whisk you away to the car park below.

Pamper yourself at **Caldea** (☎ 800 995; 3hr tickets €22.80; open 10am-11pm daily) in Escaldes, a 10-minute walk upstream from Plaça de la Rotonda.

Enclosed in what looks like a futuristic cathedral is Europe's largest spa complex of lagoons, hot tubs and saunas, fed by thermal springs.

If you've enough left in the kitty for some **shopping**, you can make savings on things like sports gear, photographic equipment, shoes and clothing, where prices are around 25% less than in Spain or France.

Places to Stay
Camping Valira (Avinguda de Salou; sites 2 people & tent €12; open year-round) has a small indoor swimming pool.

The friendly **Hostal del Sol** (☎ 823 701; Plaça de Guillemó; singles/doubles with shower €12/24) provides spruce rooms. Also in the Barri Antic is **Pensió La Rosa** (☎ 821 810; Antic Carrer Major 18; dorm beds €13, singles/doubles €19/22) which provides plain singles/doubles, plus triples, quads and a room sleeping up to six people.

Hotel Costa (☎ 821 439; 3rd floor, Avinguda de Meritxell 44; singles/doubles €11/20) has clean, no-frills rooms – the entrance is in the shopping arcade.

Also very basic but clean is **Hotel Residèn-cia Albert** (☎ 820 156; Avinguda del Doctor Mitjavila 16; singles/doubles/triples €20/35/42). Most good-value rooms have a bathroom.

More upmarket, the delightful **Hotel Florida** (☎ 820 105, fax 861 925; e hotelflorida@andorra.ad; Carrer La Lacuna 15; singles/doubles low season €28/36, high season €40/67.30), one block from Plaça de Guillemó, provides well-equipped rooms (rates include breakfast).

Although the rooms are good value at **Hotel Pyrénées** (☎ 860 006, fax 820 265; e ph@mypic.ad; singles/doubles €33/52.30), you must take half-board in peak periods.

Places to Eat
Pans & Company (Plaça de Rebés 2) is good for baguettes with a range of fillings (€2.50-3.30). **La Cantina** (Plaça de Guillemó; salads €4.50-6.60, 3-course set menu €7.20) is a friendly family-run place offering good salads and pizzas.

In the Barri Antic, **Papanico** (Avinguda del Príncep Benlloch; tapas €1.75-5) is fun for morning coffee to late-night snacks. **Restaurant Ca La Conxita** (Placeta de Monjó 3; meal €16-20) is a bustling family place. Around the corner there is the **Restaurant Can Benet** (Antic Carrer Major 9; mains €8.50-15), which is equally delightful.

There are fast-food outlets opposite the bus station and at Avinguda de Meritxell 105.

For self-caterers, the **Pyrénées department store** (Avinguda de Meritxell 21) has a well-stocked supermarket on the 2nd floor.

Entertainment
L'Abadia Cerveseria (☎ 820 825; Cap del Carrer 2; open 6pm-3am Mon-Sat) is a great place to sample an amber liquid in the wee hours. **La Borsa** (Avinguda de Tarragona; open Thur-Sat) is an old favourite among the city's several nightclubs.

Getting There & Around
See the Getting There & Away and Getting Around sections earlier in this chapter for options.

Around Andorra la Vella

CANILLO & SOLDEU
Canillo, 11km east of Andorra la Vella, and Soldeu, a further 7km up the valley along the CG2, are as complementary as summer and winter.

In summer, Canillo offers canyon clambering, a *vía ferrata* climbing gully and climbing wall, the year-round Palau de Gel with ice rink and swimming pool, guided walks and endless possibilities for hiking (including an easy, signposted nature walk which follows the valley downstream from Soldeu). The helpful tourist office (☎ 851 002) is on the main road at the east end of the village.

In winter, Soldeu and its smaller neighbour El Tarter come into their own as 23 lifts (including a cabin lift up from Canillo) connect 86km of runs with a vertical drop of 850m. The slopes, wooded in their lower reaches, are often warmer than Andorra's other more exposed ski areas and offer the Pyrenees' finest skiing and snowboarding. Lift passes for one/ three days cost €24.50/63 (low season) and €27.50/70.50 (high season).

Places to Stay
Year-round, accommodation in Canillo is markedly less expensive than in Andorra La Vella. Of its five camping grounds, Camping Santa Creu (☎ 851 462; person/tent/car €2.85/2.85/2.85) is the greenest and quietest. Hostal Aina (☎ 851 434, fax 851 747; beds €10.22, with breakfast €12.63) offers dormitory accommodation – ring ahead in winter as it is often full.

Hotel Canigó (☎ 851 024, fax 851 824; rooms €18.25 per person, with breakfast €21.85) provides comfortable and value-for-money lodging.

Places to Eat
On Soldeu's main drag, the cheerful restaurant situated at the Hotel Bruxelles (sandwiches €2.70-3.50, menu €8) does well-filled sandwiches, whopping burgers and a tasty *menu*.

Entertainment
The music pounds on winter nights in Soldeu. Pussy Cat and its neighbour, Fat Albert, both one block from the main drag, rock until far too late for impressive skiing next day.

Getting There & Around
Buses run from Andorra la Vella to El Tarter and Soldeu (€2.16, 40 minutes, hourly) between 9am to 8pm. In winter there are free shuttle buses (just flash your ski pass) between Canillo and the two upper villages. These run approximately hourly (with a break from noon to 3pm) until 11pm.

All three villages are also on the bus route between Andorra la Vella and the French railheads of Latour-de-Carol and L'Hospitalet (see the main Getting There & Away section earlier in this chapter).

ORDINO & AROUND
Despite recent development, Ordino (population 1000), on highway CG3 8km north of Andorra la Vella, retains its Andorran character, with most buildings still in local stone. At 1000m it's a good starting point for summer activity holidays. The tourist office (☎ 737 080; open 9am-1pm Mon-Sun, 3pm-7pm Mon-Sat) is beside the CG3.

Things to See & Do
Museu d'Areny i Plandolit (☎ 836 908) is a 17th-century manor house with a richly furnished interior.

Within the same grounds is the far from nerdy Museo Postal de Andorra. It has an interesting 15-minute audiovisual program (available in English) and stamps by the thousand, issued by France and Spain specifically for Andorra (see Post & Communications earlier in this chapter). Admission to each museum costs €2.40. Both are open 9.30am to 1.30pm and 3pm to 6.30pm Tuesday to Saturday, plus Sunday morning.

There are some excellent walking trails around Ordino.

From the hamlet of Segudet, 500m east of Ordino, a path goes up through fir woods to the Coll d'Ordino (1980m), reached in about 1½ hours. Pic de Casamanya (2740m), with knock-me-down views, is some two hours north of the col.

Other trails lead off from the tiny settlements beside the CG3 north of Ordino. A track (three hours one way) heads west from Llorts (1413m) up the Riu de l'Angonella Valley to a group of lakes, the Estanys de l'Angonella, at about 2300m.

Just north of El Serrat (1600m), a secondary road leads 4km east to the Borda de Sorteny mountain refuge (1969m), from where trails lead into the high mountain area.

From Arans (1385m), a trail goes northeastwards to Bordes de l'Ensegur (2180m), where there's an old shepherd's hut.

Places to Stay & Eat
The cheapest option you'll find in Ordino is the cavernous Hotel Casamanya (☎ 835 011;

ANDORRA

singles/doubles €28/32). **Bar Restaurant Quim** (Plaça Major; menu €8.50) has a basic menu. Next door, the **Restaurant Armengol** (menu €10) has a good range of meat dishes. Up the valley and some 200m north of Llorts is **Camping Mitxéu** (☎ 850 022; 2 people & tent €7.20; open mid-June–mid-Sept), one of Andorra's most beautiful camp sites. Bring your own provisions. **Hotel Vilaró** (☎ 850 225; singles/doubles €15/27.65) is 200m south of Ordino.

Getting There & Away

Buses between Andorra la Vella and Ordino (€0.84) run about every half-hour from 7am to 9pm daily. Buses to El Serrat (€1.45) – via Ordino – leave Andorra la Vella at both 1pm and 8.30pm. The valley is also served by four buses daily (10 in the ski season) linking Ordino and Arcalís.

ARINSAL

During winter, Arinsal, 10km northwest of Andorra la Vella, has good skiing and snowboarding and a lively après-ski scene. There are 13 lifts (including a smart cabin lift to hurtle you up from the village), 28km of pistes and a vertical drop of 1010m. In summer, Arinsal is a good departure point for medium mountain walks. From Aparthotel Crest at Arinsal's northern extremity, a trail leads northwest, then west to **Estany de les Truites** (2260m), a natural lake. The steepish walk up takes around 1½ hours. From here, it's another 1½ to two hours to bag **Pic de la Coma Pedrosa** (2964m), Andorra's highest point.

Places to Stay

Just above Estany de les Truites is **Refugi de Coma Pedrosa** (☎ 327 955; €7; open June-late Sept). It does snacks and meals (dinner

€11). The large, well-equipped **Camping Xixerella** (☎ 836 613; sites per adult/tent/car €4.50/4.50/4.50; open year-round), between Arinsal and Pal, has an outdoor swimming pool. In Arinsal, **Hostal Poblado** (☎ 835 122, fax 836 879; e hospoblado@andornet.ad; basic singles/doubles €15/29, with shower €20/39, with bathroom €27.50/42; open July–mid-June), beside the cabin lift, is friendliness itself. It has a lively bar (which offers Internet access on the side), and breakfast is an extra €3.

Places to Eat

As a change from the plentiful snack and sandwich joints, try **Refugi de la Fondue**, which does cheese or meat fondue dishes. **Restaurant el Moli** (pasta & pizza €5.50-7.50) bills itself as Italian – and indeed offers the usual staple pastas and pizzas – but also has more exotic fare. **Rocky Mountain** has a gringo menu with dishes such as T-bone steak and 'New York style cheesecake'. All three options are situated on the main road.

Entertainment

In winter, Arinsal fairly throbs after sunset. In summer, it can be almost mournful. When the snow's around, call by **Surf** (meat dishes €7.50-13.50) near the base of the cabin lift. A pub, dance venue and restaurant, it specialises in juicy Argentinian meat dishes. **Quo Vadis** occasionally has live music.

Getting There & Away

Buses leave Andorra la Vella for Arinsal (€1.38) via La Massana at 9.30am, 1pm and 6.15pm. There are also more than 10 buses daily between La Massana and Arinsal. In winter, Skibus (€2) runs five times daily between La Massana and Arinsal.

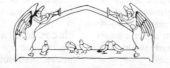

Austria

What a difference a century makes, huh? Under the rule of the mighty Habsburgs, Austria (Österreich) began the 1900s as the dominant political force in central Europe. Today that era of empire, or *Kaiserzeit*, is but a memory; after one of the biggest downsizings in history, the modern state has long reconciled itself to being a minor player in European affairs.

In the world of tourism, however, Austria remains a superpower, hanging out the *'Zimmer frei'* (rooms vacant) sign year-round. Its Schwarzenegger-sized Alps invite sports fans up for a spot of skiing, snowboarding or hiking. Its baroque architecture and Art Deco paintings woo culture vultures. And its homegrown strains of Mozart and Strauss serenade visitors, to gently win them over.

Facts about Austria

HISTORY

In its early years, the land that became Austria was invaded by successive tribes and armies using the Danube Valley as a conduit to new lands – Celts, Romans, Vandals, Visigoths, Huns, Avars and Slavs all came and went. In 803, Charlemagne established a territory in the Danube basin known as the Ostmark, and the area became Christianised and predominantly Germanic. The Ostmark was undermined by invading Magyars but was re-established by Otto I in 955. In 962, Pope John XII crowned Otto as Holy Roman Emperor of the German princes.

A period of growth and prosperity followed under the reign of the Babenbergs, and the territory became a duchy in 1156. Influence in what is now Lower Austria expanded and Styria also came under central control in 1192. The last Babenberg died in 1246 without an heir. The duchy's future was uncertain until, in 1278, it fell into the hands of the Habsburgs, who ruled Austria until WWI.

The Habsburg Dynasty

Austrian territory gradually expanded under the Habsburgs. Carinthia (Kärnten) and Carniola were annexed in 1335, followed by Tirol in 1363. However, the family preferred to extend its territory without force. Much of Vorarlberg, for example, was purchased from

bankrupt lords, while significant gains were achieved through marriage. Intermarriage was extremely effective, although it did have a genetic side-effect; a distended lower jaw became an increasingly visible family trait, albeit discreetly ignored in official portraits.

In 1477, Emperor Maximilian 1 gained control of Burgundy and the Netherlands by marrying Maria of Burgundy. His eldest son, Philip, was wed to the Infanta of Spain in 1496. In 1516, Philip's son became Charles I of Spain, a title granting control of vast overseas territories. Three years later, he also became Charles V of the Holy Roman Empire.

These acquisitions were too diverse for one person to rule effectively, so Charles handed over the Austrian territories to his younger brother Ferdinand in 1521. Ferdinand, the first Habsburg to live in Vienna, also ruled Hungary and Bohemia. In 1556, Charles abdicated as emperor and Ferdinand I was crowned in his place. Charles' remaining territory was inherited by his son, Philip II, thereby splitting the Habsburg dynasty into two distinct lines – the Spanish and Austrian.

In 1571, when the emperor granted religious freedom, most Austrians turned to Protestantism. Five years later, new emperor Rudolf II embraced the Counter-Reformation and many people reverted to Catholicism – not always without coercion. The attempt to impose Catholicism on Protestant areas of Europe led to the devastating Thirty Years' War. Peace was finally achieved in 1648 with the Treaty of Westphalia, signalling the end of the push for Catholic control over Europe. But there were other threats. In 1683, as they had once before in 1529, Turkish troops advanced as west as Vienna. Their siege of the city lasted two months before it was repelled.

In 1740, Maria Theresa ascended the throne, despite being ineligible to do so as a woman. Her rule lasted 40 years, and is generally acknowledged as the era in which Austria developed as a modern state. She centralised control, established a civil service, reformed the army and the economy, and introduced a public education system. Progress was halted when Napoleon defeated Austria at Austerlitz in 1805 and forced the abolition of the title of Holy Roman Emperor.

European conflict dragged on until the settlement at the Congress of Vienna in 1814–15, which was dominated by the Austrian foreign minister, Metternich. Austria was left with control of the German Confederation, however, it suffered internal upheaval during the 1848 revolutions and eventual defeat in the 1866 Austro-Prussian War.

Defeat led to exclusion from Bismarck's new German empire and the formation of the dual monarchy of Austria-Hungary in 1867 under Emperor Franz Josef. The dual monarchy established a common defence, foreign and economic policy, but retained two separate parliaments.

Another period of prosperity followed and Vienna, in particular, flourished. The situation changed in 1914 when the emperor's nephew, Archduke Franz Ferdinand, was assassinated in Sarajevo on 28 June. A month later, Austria-Hungary declared war on Serbia and WWI began.

Post-Habsburgs

Franz Josef died in 1916, in the middle of the war. His successor abdicated at its conclusion in 1918 and the Republic of Austria was created on 12 November. In 1919, the new, reduced state was forced to recognise the independent states of Czechoslovakia, Poland, Hungary and Yugoslavia, which, along with Transylvania (now in Romania), had previously been under Habsburg control. Losing so much land caused severe economic difficulties and political and social unrest.

More problems ensued during the rise of National Socialism in Germany during the 1930s. The Nazis tried to start a civil war in Austria and succeeded in killing Chancellor Dolfuss in 1934. Hitler manipulated the new chancellor to increase the power of the National Socialists in Austria, and was so successful that German troops met little resistance when they invaded Austria in 1938 and brought it into the German Reich. A national referendum that April supported the *Anschluss* (annexation).

Austria was bombed heavily in WWII, and in 1945 the victorious Allies restored it to its 1937 frontiers. Allied troops from the USA, UK, Soviet Union and France remained in the country and divided it into four zones. Vienna, in the Soviet zone, was also divided into four zones. Fortunately, free movement between zones allowed Vienna to escape the fate that eventually befell Berlin, though the period of occupation was generally a tough time. The ratification of the Austrian State Treaty and the withdrawal of the occupying powers were not completed until 1955, when Austria proclaimed its neutrality.

Since WWII, Austria has worked hard to overcome economic difficulties. It established a free-trade treaty with the EU (then known as the EC) in 1972, and applied for membership

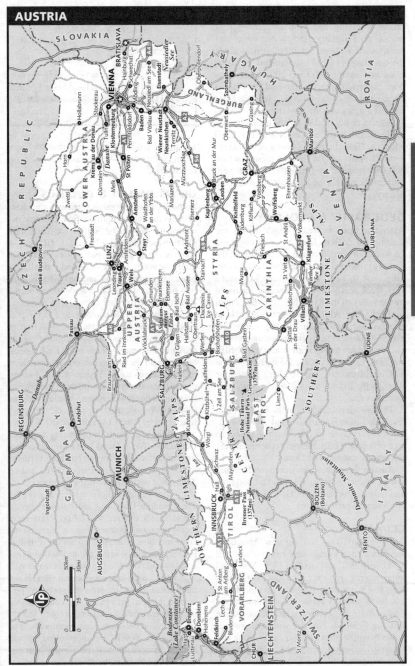

AUSTRIA

in 1989. In a 1994 referendum, 66.4% voted in favour of joining, and Austria became part of the EU on 1 January 1995. Since then, most Austrians have been rather ambivalent about the advantages of EU membership. EU relations worsened in 1999 and 2000 when sanctions were temporarily imposed on Austria after members of the far-right Freedom Party entered a new coalition government.

After such political woes, the country again made world headlines in November 2000 when the Gletscherbahn railway in the ski resort of Kaprun caught fire in a mountain tunnel. One hundred and fifty-five people were killed, making this the worst alpine disaster in history.

GEOGRAPHY & ECOLOGY
Austria occupies an area of 83,855 sq km, extending for 560km from west to east, and 280km from north to south. Two-thirds of the country is mountainous, with three chains running west to east. The Northern Limestone Alps reach nearly 3000m. These are separated by the valley of the River Inn from the Central (or High) Alps, which have the tallest peaks in Austria. Most mountains in this region are above 3000m and many ridges are topped with glaciers, which makes north-south travel difficult. The Grossglockner is the highest peak at 3797m. Elsewhere, the Southern Limestone Alps partly form a natural border with Italy and Slovenia.

The most fertile land is in the Danube Valley. Cultivation is intensive and 90% of Austria's food is home-grown. North of Linz is an area of forested hills; the only other relatively flat area is southeast of Graz.

Austria is highly environmentally conscious. Recycling is legally enforced, and flora and fauna are protected in Hohe Tauern, Europe's largest national park.

CLIMATE
Average rainfall is 71cm per year. Maximum temperatures in Vienna are January 1°C, April 15°C, July 25°C and October 14°C. Minimum temperatures are lower by about 10°C (summer) to 4°C (winter). Salzburg and Innsbruck can be as hot as Vienna, but a couple of degrees colder on winter nights. Some people find the *Föhn* – a hot, dry wind that sweeps down from the mountains in early spring and autumn – rather uncomfortable. That's not all. Folk wisdom holds the *Föhn* responsible for

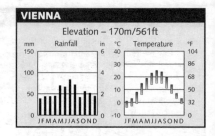

anything from restless farm animals and poor exam performances to increased car accidents or suicides.

GOVERNMENT & POLITICS
As head of the federal government, the chancellor is the central political figure – a role occupied by Wolfgang Schüssel at least until elections scheduled for late 2003. The head of state is the president, who is elected separately by voters for six years and formally appoints the chancellor. Thomas Klestil, well into his second term as president, has been a particularly active and high-profile player.

Austria is divided into nine federal provinces *(Bundesländer)*, each one with its own head of government *(Landeshauptmann)* and provincial assembly *(Landtag)*. Each assembly has a degree of local autonomy and elects representatives to the Federal Council *(Bundesrat)*, the upper house of the national parliament. The lower house is the National Council *(Nationalrat)*, which is elected every four years by voters over the age of 18.

In 1999, after decades in power, the Social Democrats (SPÖ) failed to win a viable electoral majority. Their former coalition partners, the right-wing People's Party (ÖVP), led by Schüssel, eventually formed a government instead with the far-right Freedom Party (FPÖ). The Freedom Party was led by Jörg Haider, notorious for making several pro-Nazi statements during his political career. International condemnation prompted Haider to resign as FPÖ leader, but he remained its dominant personality and continued to court controversy.

Austria's love-hate relationship with Haider hints that at least some pro-Nazi sentiment persists in Austria. Previously, the country faced international embarrassment over the 1986 appointment of President Kurt Waldheim, who served in a WWII unit implicated in war crimes. Waldheim was the United Nations' General Secretary in the 1970s.

ECONOMY

Austria's economy is reasonably strong (unemployment under 6%, inflation under 8%), despite few natural resources. Deposits of oil and natural gas are supplemented by hydroelectric power and imported coal. Agriculture and forestry employ 5% of the population.

The economy is bolstered by a large contingent of foreign workers, particularly from Eastern Europe. Austria generally has a trade deficit, which is usually offset by income from tourism. Its main exports are machinery, metallurgical products and textiles.

The country's wide-ranging welfare services, including free education and health care (for locals), generous pensions and housing, are being threatened by proposed Government cutbacks. Privatisation has bitten into Austria's nationalised industries.

POPULATION & PEOPLE

Austria has a population of about 8.1 million. Vienna is the most populous city with 1.6 million people, followed by Graz (245,000), Linz (208,000), Salzburg (145,000), and Innsbruck (111,000). On average, there are 96 inhabitants per sq km. Native Austrians are mostly of Germanic origin.

ARTS

Austria is renowned for its musical heritage. European composers were drawn to the country by the Habsburgs' generous patronage during the 18th and 19th centuries. The various classical music forms – symphony, concerto, sonata, opera and operetta – were developed and explored in Austria by the era's most eminent exponents. Haydn, Mozart, Beethoven, Brahms and Schubert all made Vienna their home during this period. The waltz also originated in the city in the 19th century and the genre was perfected by Johann Strauss senior and junior.

Musical innovation continued in the 20th century with Arnold Schönberg. Today, Austrian orchestras have a global reputation, and important music festivals are held annually in Vienna, Salzburg and Graz.

Architecture is another important tradition. The Gothic style was popular, before architect Fischer von Erlach developed a distinct Austrian baroque style from the Italian model in the 17th century. (The Church of St Charles in Vienna is one example.) In the late 19th century, the Austrian Secessionist movement embraced Art Nouveau (*Jugendstil*). But architects Otto Wagner, creator of the Post Office Savings Bank, and Adolf Loos moved progressively away from ornamentation to functionalism.

Secessionist painter Gustav Klimt and the expressionists Egon Schiele and Oskar Kokoschka also emerged in the early 20th century. By that time, elaborate Art Nouveau household objects from the Vienna Workshops (Wiener Werkstätte) had overtaken the more traditional Biedermeier style of furniture design of 100 years before.

SOCIETY & CONDUCT

Traditional costumes are still worn in rural areas of Tirol, but you're more likely to see them during celebrations. Traditional attire for men is shorts with wide braces, and jackets without collars or lapels. The best-known form of dress for women is the Dirndl: pleated skirt, apron, and a white, pleated corsage with full sleeves.

Many festivals act out ancient traditions, such as welcoming the spring with painted masks and bells.

The departure of herders and cattle to high alpine pastures in early summer and their return in autumn are the cause of much jollity in village life.

It is customary to greet people, even shop assistants, with the salute '*Grüss Gott*', and to say '*Auf Wiedersehen*' before leaving. Upon being introduced to someone, shake hands.

RELIGION

Roman Catholicism is embraced by 80% of the population; many of the remainder are Protestants, concentrated in both Burgenland and Carinthia, or nondenominational. Religion plays an important part in many Austrians' lives.

LANGUAGE

About 98% of Austrians speak German, although there are Croatian- and Slovenian-speaking pockets in the southeastern provinces of Burgenland and Carinthia respectively.

English is widely understood in cities. In smaller towns, hotel and railway staff usually know some English, but don't bank on it.

Knowledge of some German is appreciated. See the Language chapter at the back of the book for pronunciation guidelines and useful words and phrases.

AUSTRIA

Facts for the Visitor

HIGHLIGHTS

With its rich history, musical heritage and architectural jewels housing myriad art treasures, Vienna is usually the top of most travellers' list. Picture-book Salzburg, with its mementos of Mozart and stunning skyline, usually comes next. Innsbruck and particularly Graz, a new European Culture Capital, are vibrant provincial capitals with plenty to explore. To ski or snowboard, head to one of the many resorts concentrated in Tirol, such as Kitzbühel or St Anton am Arlberg.

SUGGESTED ITINERARIES

Depending on the length of your stay, you might want to see and do the following:

Two days
Vienna – see the central sights, visit the opera and sample a few *Heurigen* (wine taverns).

One week
Spend four days in Vienna, including a Danube cruise; two days in Salzburg; and one day visiting the Salzkammergut lakes.

Two weeks
Spend five days in Vienna, three days in Salzburg (with a day trip to the Werfen ice caves), two days at the Salzkammergut lakes, two days in Innsbruck and two days in Graz.

One month
Visit the same places as the two-week scenario at a more leisurely pace and adding an alpine resort. If the time of year permits, travel south through the Hohe Tauern National Park and over the Grossglockner, stopping in Lienz en route to Graz and Klagenfurt.

PLANNING
When to Go

Summer sightseeing and winter sports make Austria a year-round destination, though alpine resorts are pretty dead between seasons, ie, May, June and November. The summer high season is July and August. Christmas to late February is the winter high season in the ski resorts, though Christmas and New Year are also peak times elsewhere.

Maps

Freytag & Berndt of Vienna publishes good maps in varying scales. Its 1:100,000 series and 1:50,000 blue series are popular with hikers. Extremely detailed maps are produced by

---

Flood Damage

At the time of writing Austria was facing an estimated clean-up bill of around €2 billion following the floods that hit the northern part of the country in the summer of 2002, although the consequences of the flood damage for travellers do not appear to be as serious as in the neighbouring Czech Republic and Germany.

---

the Austrian Alpine Club. Bikeline maps are good for cyclists.

What to Bring

Pack warm clothing for nights at high altitude. A series of thinner layers is better than bulky, thick woollens.

TOURIST OFFICES
Local Tourist Offices

Local tourist offices (usually called *Kurverein*, *Verkehrsamt* or *Tourismusverband*) are efficient and helpful, and can be found in all towns and villages of touristic interest. Beware that local tourist office hours change from one year to the next, so the hours that we list may have changed by the time you arrive. Most offices have a room-finding service, often without commission. Maps are always available and usually free. Each region has a provincial tourist board.

Tourist Offices Abroad

Austrian National Tourist Office (ANTO) branches abroad include:

Australia (☎ 02-9299 3621, fax 9299 3808, e info@antosyd.org.au) 1st floor, 36 Carrington St, Sydney, NSW 2000

UK (☎ 020-7629 0461, fax 7499 6038, e info@anto.co.uk) 14 Cork St, London W1S 3NS

USA (☎ 212-944 6880, fax 730 4568, e info@oewnyc.com) PO Box 1142, New York, NY 10108-1142

Some offices aren't open to personal callers, so phone first. There are also tourist offices located in Budapest, Dublin, Milan, Munich, Paris, Tokyo, and Zürich. New Zealanders can get information from the Austrian consulate in Wellington (see Embassies & Consulates later in this section).

VISAS & DOCUMENTS

Visas are not required for EU, US, Canadian, Australian or New Zealand citizens. Visitors may stay a maximum of three months (six months for Japanese). There are no time limits for EU and Swiss nationals, but they should register with the police before taking up residency. Most African and Arab nationals require a visa.

EMBASSIES & CONSULATES
Austrian Embassies & Consulates

Diplomatic representation abroad includes:

Australia (☎ 02-6295 1533, fax 6239 6751, ⓦ www.austriaemb.org.au) 12 Talbot St, Forrest, Canberra, ACT 2603
Canada (☎ 613-789 1444, fax 789 3431, ⓔ embassy@austro.org) 445 Wilbrod St, Ottawa, ON K1N 6M7
New Zealand (☎ 04-499 6393, fax 499 6392) Austrian Consulate, Level 2, Willbank House, 587 Willis St, Wellington – does not issue visas or passports; contact the Australian office for these services
UK (☎ 020-7235 3731, fax 7235 8025, ⓦ www.austria.org.uk) 18 Belgrave Mews West, London SW1X 8HU
USA (☎ 202-895 6700, fax 895 6750, ⓔ obwascon@sysnet.net) 3524 International Court NW, Washington, DC 20008

Embassies & Consulates in Austria

The following foreign embassies are in Vienna. All these countries have a consulate in Vienna too, but not necessarily at the same address. Check the telephone book for more detailed listings of embassies *(Botschaften)* or consulates *(Konsulate)*.

Australia (☎ 01-506 74 04), Mattiellistrasse 2–4
Canada (☎ 01-531 38-3000) 01, Laurenzerberg 2
Czech Republic (☎ 01-894 37 41) 14, Penzingerstrasse 11–13
Germany (☎ 01-711 54-0) 03, Metternichgasse 3
Hungary (☎ 01-537 80-300) 01, Bankgasse 4–6
Italy (☎ 01-712 51 21-0) 03, Rennweg 27
New Zealand The embassy (☎ 030 20 62 10) is in Berlin, Germany; Vienna has only an honorary consul (☎ 01-318 85 05)
Slovakia (☎ 01-318 90 55) 19, Armbrustergasse 24
Switzerland (☎ 01-795 05-0) 03, Prinz Eugen Strasse 7
UK (☎ 01-716 13-0) 03, Jaurèsgasse 12
USA (☎ 01-313 39-0) 09, Boltzmanngasse 16

Foreign consulates in other cities include:

Germany (☎ 0662-84 15 91-0) Bürgerspitalplatz 1-II, Salzburg
Italy (☎ 0512-58 13 33) Conradstrasse 9, Innsbruck; (☎ 0662-87 83 01) Bergstrasse 22, Salzburg
Switzerland (☎ 0662-62 25 30), Alpenstrasse 85, Salzburg
UK (☎ 0662-84 81 33) Alter Markt 4, Salzburg; (☎ 0512-58 83 20) Kaiserjägerstrasse 1/1, Innsbruck
USA (☎ 0662-84 87 76), Alter Markt 1, Salzburg

CUSTOMS

Duty-free shopping has been abolished within the EU, so there are no set limits on goods purchased within the EU for personal use. People aged 17 or over can bring in 200 cigarettes (or 50 cigars or 250g of tobacco), 2L of wine and 1L of spirits from non-EU countries.

MONEY

In 2002, Austria switched from the Austrian Schilling to the euro, with a minimum of fuss. See the boxed text 'The Euro' in the introductory Facts for the Visitor chapter.

Both Visa and MasterCard credit cards are more widely accepted than American Express (AmEx) and Diners Club, though some places accept no cards at all.

If you're coming from outside the euro zone, beware that exchange rates and commission charges can vary between banks, and it pays to shop around. Changing cash usually attracts lower commission rates, but always check first. Some private exchange offices charge as much as 10% commission on transactions. But AmEx offices don't have the best rates, but their commission charges are low (for Austria) – from about €1.85 for cash and €3.65 for travellers cheques; no commission applies on AmEx's own travellers cheques. The post office charges 1% (€2.20 minimum) for cash but doesn't change cheques. Train stations charge about €3 for cash and €4.70 minimum for cheques. Banks typically charge €7 to €8. Avoid changing a lot of low-value cheques because commission costs will be higher.

The most efficient way to manage your money in Austria is with the ATM withdrawal/debit card you use at home to access your bank account. If it has a Cirrus or Plus sign on it – and most today have – the card will work in many of the Bankomat machines (ATMs) around Austria. The small fee for making overseas transactions is much lower than the interest you'd be charged for a cash advance on your credit card.

Sending funds electronically is quick and efficient using Western Union or AmEx – and there's no fee at the receiving end.

Costs

Expenses are average for Western Europe, and prices are highest in big cities and ski resorts. Budget travellers can get by on €40 a day, after rail-card costs; double this if you want to avoid self-catering or staying in hostels. The *minimum* you can expect to pay per person is €10/22 for a hostel/hotel and €3.50/5.80 for a lunch/dinner, excluding drinks.

Tipping & Bargaining

In restaurants, it is customary to round off the bill so that it includes an approximate 10% tip and pay it directly to the server. (Sadly, Austrian waiters are not particularly renowned for friendly or speedy service.) Taxi drivers will expect tips of 10%. Prices are fixed, so bargaining for goods is not generally an option.

Taxes & Refunds

Value-added tax, or VAT (*Mehrwertsteuer* or *MwSt*), is charged at 10% (eg, travel, food and museum entry) and 20% (drinks and luxury goods). Prices are always displayed inclusive of all taxes.

For purchases over €75, non-EU residents can reclaim the MwSt (though one-third will be absorbed in charges), either upon leaving the EU or afterwards. Ensure the shop has the forms that need to be filled out at the time of purchase. Present the documentation to customs on departure for checking and stamping. The airports at Vienna, Salzburg, Innsbruck, Linz and Graz have counters for instant refunds, as do some land crossings, but you can only claim your refunds here if you're not going to another EU country. You can also reclaim by post.

POST & COMMUNICATIONS
Post

Post office hours vary: typical hours in smaller towns are 8am to noon and 2pm to 6pm Monday to Friday (money exchange to 5pm), and 8am to 11am Saturday, but a few main post offices in big cities are open daily till late, or even 24 hours. Stamps are also available in tobacco (*Tabak*) shops.

Postcards and standard letters (up to 20g) cost €0.51 both within Austria and to Europe. Standard letters to other destinations cost €1.09.

Poste restante is *Postlagernde Sendungen* in German. Mail can be sent care of any post office and is held for a month (address it to 'Postamt', followed by the postcode); a passport must be shown to collect mail. AmEx will also hold mail for 30 days for customers who have its charge card.

Telephone & Fax

Call charges dropped after telecommunications liberalisation in 1998, and it now costs €0.12 a minute to call anywhere in Austria, be it next door or across the country.

The minimum tariff in phone boxes is €0.20, but as some now take only phonecards (*Telefon-Wertkarte*) it's often more convenient to buy one of those. In 2002, these were streamlined into just two denominations – €3.63 and €7.27 – but this seems likely to change in subsequent years.

International direct dialling is nearly always possible. To call collect, you have to dial a freephone number; ask directory assistance on ☎ 118200. Calls to Germany, Switzerland and Italy are €0.50 per minute, to the rest of Europe and the USA €0.67. The national and international cheap rate applies from 6pm to 8am, and on weekends; rates drop greatly for national calls, but only marginally for international calls.

Of course, telephones in hotels cost much more than public pay phones. Cut-price telephone call centres in cities offer the best rates.

Email & Internet Access

There is public Internet access in most towns; see the individual city sections. Terminals in coffee houses and bars tend to be more expensive than in dedicated Internet cafés, and it's always worth keeping an eye out for cheaper online facilities in public libraries. The **Bignet** chain (**w** *www.bignet.at; see individual city sections)* has reliable well-equipped outlets in Vienna, Salzburg and Linz. Many post offices now also offer Internet access, although you need to buy a prepaid card before using these 'surf points'. The same card works at Bignet outlets.

Phone Quirks

Don't worry if a telephone number you're given has only four digits, as many as nine or somewhere in between. The Austrian system often adds direct-dial (DW) extensions to the main number – after a hyphen. Thus, say ☎ 12 345 is a main number, ☎ 12 345-67 will be an extension, which could be a phone or fax. Mostly, a -0 gives you the switchboard operator. In this chapter, where an organisation's phone and fax numbers are based on the same main number the fax is only marked by a hyphen and extension number. In these cases, you send a fax by dialling the main number, dropping the phone extension (if there is one, ie, any digits following a hyphen) and adding the fax extension.

DIGITAL RESOURCES

Most Austrian businesses have email addresses and websites. The **Austrian National Tourist Office website** (**w** *www.austria-tourism.at*) is an excellent starting point; the **Austrian Press & Information Service** (**w** *www.austria.org*) offers weekly news and visa details. Another useful website for travellers is the **Austrian Railways** (*Österreiche Bundesbahnen or ÖBB;* **w** *www.oebb.at*) home pages, which have details of train times and fares. Budget travellers might also find quite useful the listing of university canteens, or *mensas,* at **w** www.mensen.at.

BOOKS

Lonely Planet has guides to both *Austria* and *Vienna,* and Western/Central Europe phrasebooks. *The Xenophobe's Guide to the Austrians* by Louis James is both informative and amusing, while Graham Greene's evocative spy story *The Third Man,* John Irving's *Setting Free the Bears* and Arthur Schnitzler's *Dream Story* are all set in Austria. The last is a lot easier to fathom than its Stanley Kubrick movie adaptation *Eyes Wide Shut.*

NEWSPAPERS & MAGAZINES

English-language newspapers and magazines (*The Times, International Herald Tribune, Newsweek)* are available for €2.20 to €3.80.

RADIO & TV

FM4 is a news and music station, mostly in English, with hourly news until 7pm. It's on 103.8FM in Vienna. Austria has only two (terrestrial) national TV channels (ORF 1 and 2), and a national cable channel (ATV). Many hotels have multilingual cable TV.

PHOTOGRAPHY & VIDEO

The Niedermeyer chain is one of the cheapest stores for buying film; a roll of Kodak Farbwelt 100 print film with 36 exposures costs €3.69, Elite Chrome slide film €4.99 (without mounting and processing). Austria uses the PAL video system.

TIME

Austrian time is GMT/UTC plus one hour. Clocks go forward one hour on the last Saturday night in March and back again on the last Saturday night in October.

LAUNDRY

Look out for *Wäscherei* for self-service or service washes. Expect to pay around €7 to wash and dry a load. Many hostels have cheaper laundry facilities.

TOILETS

There is no shortage of public toilets, however, some cubicles may have a charge of €0.35 to €0.50.

WOMEN TRAVELLERS

Women should experience no special problems. Physical violations and verbal harassment are less common than in many other countries. Vienna has a **Rape Crisis Hotline** (☎ *01-717 19*).

GAY & LESBIAN TRAVELLERS

Public attitudes to homosexuality are less tolerant than in most other Western European countries, except perhaps in Vienna. A good information centre in Vienna is **Rosa Lila** (☎ *01-586 8150; 06, Linke Wienziele 102*). The age of consent for gay men is 18; for everyone else it's 14. Vienna has a Pride march, the Rainbow Parade, on the last Saturday in June.

SENIOR TRAVELLERS

With proof of age, senior travellers are entitled to many public transport and sightseeing discounts. The official qualifying age in Austria is 65 for men and 60 for women, however, some attractions do offer discounts for those aged 62 and over. Vienna-based

Seniorenbüro der Stadt Wien (☎ 01-4000-8580; 08, Schlesingerplatz 2; open 8am-3.30pm Mon-Fri) can give advice.

DISABLED TRAVELLERS

Many sights and venues have wheelchair ramps.

Local tourist offices usually have good information on facilities for the disabled; the Vienna office, for example, has a free 90-page booklet.

Car drivers have free, unlimited parking in blue zones with the international disabled sticker.

DANGERS & ANNOYANCES

You always need to beware of theft, even in a relatively orderly country like Austria. Pickpockets particularly work in Vienna's two main train stations and pedestrian centre, and there has been some trouble with unlicensed people offering rooms at the Westbahnhof in Vienna.

Some anti-foreigner feeling exists. It tends to be directed at East European, Turkish and African immigrants, but if you're a tourist who comes from one of those places, or look like you do, you could be in for some unnecessary questioning by police.

Take care in the mountains; helicopter rescue is expensive unless you are covered by insurance (assuming they find you in the first place).

BUSINESS HOURS

Shops are usually open at 8am (except Sunday), and close between 6pm and 7.30pm on weekdays, and 1pm to 5pm on Saturday. They sometimes close for up to two hours at noon, except in big cities.

Some shops in train stations have extended hours. Banking hours can vary but are commonly 9am to 12.30pm and 1.30pm to 3pm Monday to Friday, with late (5.30pm) closing on Thursday.

Emergency Services

The emergency number for the police is ☎ 133, for an ambulance ☎ 144, for a doctor (after hours) ☎ 141, in the case of fire ☎ 122, and if you require an alpine rescue ☎ 140. For emergency vehicle breakdown assistance phone ☎ 120 or ☎ 123.

PUBLIC HOLIDAYS & SPECIAL EVENTS

Public holidays are 1 and 6 January, Easter Monday, 1 May, Ascension Day, Whit Monday, Corpus Christi, 15 August, 26 October, 1 November, and 8, 25 and 26 December.

Numerous local events take place throughout the year, so it's worth checking with the tourist office. ANTO compiles an updated list of annual and one-off events. Vienna and Salzburg have almost continuous music festivals (see their Special Events headings). Linz has the Bruckner Festival in September.

There are trade fairs in Vienna, Innsbruck and Graz in September. Religious holidays provide an opportunity to stage colourful processions. Look out for Fasching (Shrovetide carnival) in early February, maypoles on 1 May, midsummer night's celebrations on 21 June, the autumn cattle roundup at the end of October, much flag-waving on national day on 26 October and St Nicholas Day parades on 5 and 6 December.

ACTIVITIES
Skiing & Snowboarding

Austria has world-renowned skiing and snowboarding areas, particularly in the Vorarlberg and Tirol regions. There are plenty of winter sports in Salzburg province, Upper Austria and Carinthia, where prices can be lower. Equipment can always be hired at resorts.

Generally, you need a complete or partial day pass to ride on ski lifts, although coupons for individual rides are sometimes available. For one day, count on spending €20 to €38 for a ski pass. Rental generally starts at €15 for downhill equipment and €11 for cross-country rental; rates drop for multiple days. The skiing season starts in December and lasts well into April at higher altitude resorts. Year-round skiing is possible at the Stubai Glacier near Innsbruck.

Hiking & Mountaineering

Walking and climbing are popular with visitors and Austrians alike. Mountain paths are marked with direction indicators, and most tourist offices have maps of hiking routes. There are 10 long-distance national hiking routes, and three European routes pass through Austria. Options include the northern alpine route from Lake Constance to Vienna, via Dachstein, or the central route from Feldkirch to Hainburger Pforte, via Hohe Tauern.

Mountaineering should not be undertaken without proper equipment or experience. Tirol province has many mountain guides and mountaineering schools; these are listed in the *Walking Guide Tirol*, free from the ANTO and the Tirol regional tourist office (see Information under Innsbruck later in this chapter). The **Austrian Alpine Club** *(Österreichischer Alpenverein, ÖAV;* ☎ *0512-58 78 28, fax 58 88 42;* **w** *www.alpenverein-ibk.at; Wilhelm Greil Strasse 15, A-6010 Innsbruck)* has touring programmes, and also maintains a list of alpine huts. These are situated between 900m and 2700m in hill-walking regions; they're inexpensive and often have meals or cooking facilities. Members of the club take priority but anyone can stay. It's a good idea to book huts. The Austrian Alpine Club can give you the phone numbers to book specific huts, and some are also listed on its website.

Spa Resorts

There are spa resorts throughout the country, identifiable by the prefix *Bad* (Bath), eg, Bad Ischl. While perfect for the self-indulgent pampering which stressed-out city-dwellers nowadays so often crave, they also promise more traditional healing cures for respiratory, circulatory and other ailments.

WORK

EU nationals can work in Austria without a permit. Everyone else must obtain a work permit and (except for seasonal work) a residency permit in advance.

In ski resorts, there are often jobs going with unsociable hours – clearing snow, cleaning chalets or working in restaurants and ski-equipment shops. Employers face big fines if they're caught employing workers illegally.

ACCOMMODATION

Reservations are recommended in July and August and at the peak times of Christmas and Easter. Reservations are binding on either side and compensation may be claimed if you do not take a reserved room or if a reserved room is unavailable.

A cheap and widely available option is to take a room in a private house (€12 to €22 per person). Look out for the ubiquitous *Zimmer frei* (rooms vacant) signs. See Hiking & Mountaineering under Activities earlier in this chapter for information on alpine huts. Tourist offices can supply lists of all types of accommodation, and often make reservations. Accommodation sometimes costs more for a single night's stay. Prices are lower out of season. Assume breakfast is included in prices listed in this chapter, unless otherwise stated.

In many resorts (rarely in towns) a guest card is issued to people who stay overnight, which offers useful discounts. Check with the tourist office if you're not offered one at your resort accommodation.

Guest cards are funded by a resort tax of around €1 to €1.50 per night, which is added to the accommodation tariff. Prices quoted for accommodation in this book generally include this tax.

Camping

There are more than 400 camping grounds, but most close in the winter. They charge around €2.60 to €5.80 per person, plus about €3 for a tent and €3 for a car.

Free camping in camper vans is OK (in tents it's illegal), except in urban and protected rural areas. Just don't set up equipment outside the van. Contact the **Austrian Camping Club** *(Österreichischer Camping Club;* ☎ *01-711 99-1272; Schubertring 1-3, A-1010 Vienna).*

Hostels

In Austria there is an excellent network of HI-affiliated hostels *(Jugendherbergen)*. Membership cards are always required, except in a few private hostels. Nonmembers pay a surcharge of about €3 per night for a guest card; after six nights, the guest card counts as a full membership card. Some hostels will accept reservations by telephone, and some are part of the worldwide computer reservations system. Hostel prices are around €10 to €18. Austria has two hostel associations: **Österreichischer Jugendherbergsverband** *(*☎ *01-533 53 53, fax 535 08 61;* **e** *backpacker-austria@or.at;* **w** *www.oejhv.or.at; 01, Schottenring 28, A-1010 Vienna)* and **Österreichischer Jugendherbergswerk** *(*☎ *01-533 18 33, fax -85;* **w** *www.oejhw.or.at; 01, Helferstorferstrasse 4, Vienna).*

Hotels & Pensions

With very few exceptions, rooms are clean and adequately appointed. Expect to pay from €25/45 for a single/double. In low-budget accommodation, a room with a private shower may mean a room with a shower cubicle

AUSTRIA

rather than a proper en suite bathroom. Prices in the major cities (particularly in Vienna) are significantly higher than in the untouristed rural areas. A small country inn *(Gasthaus* or *Gasthof)* or a guesthouse *(Pension)* tends to be much more intimate than a hotel. Self-catering chalets or apartments are common in ski resorts.

FOOD

The main meal is at midday. Most restaurants have a set meal of the day *(Tagesteller* or *Tagesmenu)*, which provides the best value for money. The cheapest deal is in university restaurants *(mensas)*; these are only listed if they are open to all. Wine taverns are fairly cheap eateries, and Asian restaurants and pizzerias are plentiful. For a stand-up snack, head for a sausage *(Wurst)* stall or *Würstel Stand*.

Hearty soups often include dumplings *(Knödel)* or pasta. *Wiener Schnitzel*, a veal or pork cutlet coated in breadcrumbs, is Austria's best-known dish, but *Chicken Huhn* is also popular. Paprika is used to flavour several dishes, including *Gulasch* (beef stew). Look out for regional dishes such as *Tiroler Bauernschmaus*, a selection of meats served with sauerkraut, potatoes and dumplings. Austrians eat lots of meat, although it's increasingly easier for vegetarians to find things to eat.

Famous desserts include *Strudel* (baked dough filled with a variety of fruits) and *Salzburger Nockerl* (an egg, flour and sugar pudding). Pancakes are also popular.

DRINKS

Eastern Austria specialises in producing white wines. Heuriger wine is the year's new vintage. It's avidly consumed, even in autumn while still semi-fermented (called *Sturm)*. Austria is famous for its lager beer; some well-known brands include Gösser, Schwechater, Stiegl and Zipfer. Also try *Weizenbier* (wheat beer). Beer is usually served by the 0.5L or 0.3L; in eastern Austria, these are respectively called a *Krügerl* and a *Seidel*.

Leading historian Simon Schama has wryly observed that when it was under attack in 1683, Austria managed to 'resist the Turkish siege but (was) defenceless against the coffee bean'. There are competing stories as to exactly how Austrians developed a taste for their

enemy's beverage – from spies infiltrating the Turkish army to sacks of beans abandoned outside Vienna's gates. But the fact is even today locals love to linger over a cup in coffee houses *(Kaffeehäuse* or *Café Konditoreien)*. Drinks come in more than a dozen variations, but the *Grosser Brauner* and, in Vienna, the milky, foamy *Melange* are probably the most popular.

ENTERTAINMENT

Late-night bars, clubs and music venues proliferate in Vienna, Graz, Innsbruck and Salzburg and there is plenty of convivial (and sometimes rowdy) après ski in many winter resorts.

In cinemas (cheaper on Monday) some films are dubbed, but look for OF, meaning *Original Fassung* (original-language production), or OmU, meaning *Original mit Untertiteln* (original language with subtitles).

The main season for opera, theatre and concerts is September to June. Cheap, standing-room tickets are often available shortly before performances begin.

SHOPPING

Confectionery and local crafts such as textiles, pottery, painted glassware, woodcarving and wrought-iron work make popular souvenirs.

Getting There & Away

AIR

The airports at Vienna, Linz, Graz, Salzburg, Innsbruck and Klagenfurt all receive international flights. Vienna is the busiest airport, with several daily, nonstop flights to major transport hubs such as Amsterdam, Berlin, Frankfurt, London, Paris and Zürich.

LAND
Bus

Buses depart from London's Victoria Station five days a week (daily in summer), arriving in Vienna 22 hours later (adult and student UK£65/99 one way/return, senior UK£59/89). See the Vienna Getting There & Away section later in this chapter for services to Eastern Europe. The website for Eurolines in Austria is **w** www.eurolines.at.

Train

Austria has excellent rail connections. Vienna is its main hub (see its Getting There & Away section for details); Salzburg has at least hourly trains to Munich with onward connections north. Express services to Italy go via Innsbruck or Villach; trains to Slovenia are routed through Graz.

Reserving 2nd-class train seats in Austria costs €3.60; in 1st class it's free. Supplements sometimes apply on international trains.

Car & Motorcycle

There are many entry points from the Czech Republic, Hungary, Slovakia, Slovenia, and Switzerland; main border crossings are open 24 hours. There are no border controls to/from Germany and Italy.

Austria levies fees for its entire motorway network and tourists not only need to choose between a 10-day pass (€7.60/4.30 for cars/motorcycles), a two-month pass (€21.80/10.90) or a yearly pass (€72.60/29), they must also clearly display the toll label *(Vignette)* on their vehicle. Passes are available at borders, on freeways or from service stations. Without one, you will face an on-the-spot fine of up to €220 or, if you don't pay up immediately, an enormous €2180 fine. For details, see **w** www.vignette.at.

RIVER

Steamers and hydrofoils operate along the Danube in the summer. See the Vienna and The Danube Valley sections later in this chapter for details.

DEPARTURE TAX

There is no departure tax to pay at the airport, as all taxes are included in the ticket price.

Getting Around

AIR

There are several flights a day from Vienna to Graz, Klagenfurt, Innsbruck, Salzburg and Linz. The main national carrier is Austrian Airlines; its subsidiary, Tyrolean Airlines, has nonstop flights between most domestic airports. Schedules change half-yearly.

BUS

Yellow or orange/red buses are operated by the post office or Austrian Railways; either way, they're called *Bundesbus*. Sometimes, buses duplicate rail routes, but generally they operate in the more inaccessible mountainous regions. They are clean, efficient and run on time. Advance reservations are possible, but sometimes you can only buy tickets from the drivers. The fares are comparable to the train fares. For national information call **Bundesbus** (☎ *01-711 01*).

TRAIN

Trains are efficient and frequent. The state network covers the whole country, and is supplemented by a few private lines. Eurail and Inter-Rail passes are valid on the former; inquire about the latter. Despite what it says on your pass, Austrian Railways does not charge a supplement for national travel on faster EC (Eurocity) and IC (Intercity) trains. 'We're not in Germany here, you know,' one conductor reassured us. Many stations have information centres where staff speak English. Tickets can be purchased on the train, but they cost about €3 extra. In this chapter, fares quoted are for 2nd class.

Trains are relatively expensive and Austria has withdrawn most of its rail passes. You could consider buying a Euro Domino Pass (see the introductory Getting Around chapter earlier in this book) – the Austrian version costs UK£68/108 for three/eight days. The Vorteilscard (under 26/over 26/senior €18.17/93.75/25.44; valid one year) reduces fares by 50%. If you're not under 26 or a senior, it's only worth buying if you stay a while. For

---

Bahn-storming

Austria is embarking on a major renovation of its train stations in 2003–04. It shouldn't cause any disruption to services, but be aware that facilities in and around stations, such as bus stops, banks and tourist information desks, might be shifted. Twenty stations will be affected. Work will be under way in 2003 on stations in: Baden, Feldkirch, Graz, Klagenfurt, Krems an der Donau, Leoben, Linz, Wels, Wien Mitte and Wiener Neustadt. In 2004, renovation begins in Attnang Puchheim, Bruck an der Mur, St Pölten and Salzburg. Wien Nord (Praterstern), Wien Südbahnhof, Wien Westbahnhof, Wien Heiligenstadt and Wien Hütteldorf will also receive a makeover then.

under-26s and seniors, however, if offers great savings even for short stays. Even without a VORTEILScard, reduced fares are sometimes available for those aged under 26; wave your passport and ask.

Stations are called *Bahnhof* (train station) or *Hauptbahnhof* (main train station). Single/return tickets for journeys over 100km are valid for three days/one month and you can break your journey, however, tell the conductor first.

Some provinces have zonal day passes, (valid for trains and buses), which may save money compared with buying ordinary tickets. Nationwide train information can be obtained by dialling ☎ 05-1717 (local rate).

CAR & MOTORCYCLE

Visitors require an international driver's licence. Traffic drives on the right. Roads are generally good, but care is needed on difficult mountain routes. In addition to the absolutely vital motorway tax (see Car & Motorcycle in the Getting There & Away section earlier in this chapter), there are hefty toll charges for some mountain tunnels. The tourist office has details of the few roads and passes closed in winter.

Give way to vehicles from the right. On mountain roads, Bundesbuses always have priority; otherwise, priority lies with uphill traffic.

Drive in low gear on steep downhill stretches. There's a steep on-the-spot fine for drink-driving (over 0.05% blood alcohol content) and your licence may be confiscated. The usual speed limits are 50km/h in towns, 130km/h on motorways and 100km/h on other roads. Snow chains are highly recommended in winter.

Many city streets have restricted parking (called blue zones), normally limiting parking during shopping hours. Parking is unrestricted on unmarked streets.

Cars can be transported by train; Vienna is linked by a daily motorail service to Feldkirch, Innsbruck, Salzburg and Villach.

Motorcyclists must have their headlights on during the day and crash helmets are compulsory for both them and their passengers.

Contact the **Austrian Automobile Club** (*Österreichischer Automobil, Motorrad und Touring Club, ÖAMTC*; ☎ *01-711 99-0; Schubertring 1-3, A-1010 Vienna*).

For emergency vehicle breakdown assistance phone ☎ 120 or ☎ 123.

Rental

Hertz, Avis, Budget and Europcar have offices in major cities. With all the usual caveats about it being cheaper to book ahead and on weekends, you should expect to pay between €30 and €60 a day to rent from a multinational. Local rental agencies may be cheaper; tourist offices should have details. The minimum age for renting small cars is 19, or 25 for larger 'prestige' cars. Many contracts forbid customers to take cars outside Austria.

BICYCLE

Bicycles can no longer be hired from train stations, and at the time of writing private operators were only beginning to step into the breach. Some hostels rent bikes, but if you get stuck ask the tourist office. You can expect to pay anything from €6 a day in smaller cities to a hefty €30 in Vienna. Cycling is popular even though sometimes strenuous on steep minor roads. You can always take your bike on slow trains (€2.95/6.55/19.65 for a daily/weekly/monthly ticket); on fast trains you might have to send your bike as registered luggage (€10.20).

HITCHING

Lonely Planet doesn't recommend hitching, as it is never entirely safe. Additionally, in Austria, it's illegal for minors under 16 to hitch in Burgenland, Upper Austria, Styria and Vorarlberg, or for anyone to hitch on motorways. Otherwise, trucks are usually your best bet, particularly when stopped at border posts or truck parking stops *(Autohof)*. Show your destination on a sign and stay clear of the route from Salzburg to Munich; it's been named one of Europe's most difficult spots to get a lift. Austria has only one *Mitfahrzentrale* hitching agency – see Hitching under Getting There & Away in the Vienna section later for details.

BOAT

The only services along the Danube are scenic pleasure cruises, but these can be a good way of getting from A to B if you have the time, money and inclination. The larger Salzkammergut lakes have ferry services.

LOCAL TRANSPORT

Buses, trams and underground railways are efficient and reliable. Most towns have an integrated system and offer good-value daily or

24-hour tickets (€2.90 to €4.30), which are available in advance from dispensers or Tabak shops. Even single tickets can sometimes only be purchased prior to boarding buses/trams. On-the-spot fines apply to those caught travelling without tickets, though some locals are prepared to take the risk.

Taxis are metered. If you need one, look around train stations and large hotels.

For a rundown on mountain transport, see the introductory Getting Around section in the Switzerland chapter later in this book.

ORGANISED TOURS

These vary from two-hour walks in city centres to all-inclusive packages at ski resorts. Inquire at tourist offices.

Vienna

☎ 01 • pop 1.6 million

Vienna, the capital of Austria, is so like an eccentric grandmother that it's hard not to feel affection for her. Her home is full of the treasures of a full and colourful life, from Habsburg riches to the outpourings of Art Nouveau artists such as Gustav Klimt. She has nostalgic memories of famous old companions, including Johann Strauss, who created the waltz, and Sigmund Freud, the father of psychoanalysis – all of which make her a great storyteller. And even if her grumpy manners, and her continual smoking and wearing fur, make you want to shout at her occasionally, Vienna (Wien) has made progress in the last decade in shaking off a deeply ingrained conservatism. Since Austria's central European neighbours were released from communism in the early 1990s, this frontline Cold War city has opened up a bit to the world.

Orientation

Many historic sights are in the old city, the *Innere Stadt*. This is encircled by the Danube Canal (Donaukanal) to the northeast and a series of broad boulevards called the Ring or Ringstrasse. Most attractions in the centre are within walking distance of each other. St Stephen's Cathedral, right in the heart of the city, is the principal landmark.

When reading addresses, remember the number of a building within a street *follows* the street name. Any number *before* the street name denotes the district, of which there are

23. District 1 (the Innere Stadt) is the central region, mostly within the Ring. Generally, the higher the district number, the further it is from the city centre. The middle two digits of postcodes refer to the district, hence places with a postcode 1010 are in district 1, and 1230 means district 23.

The main train stations are Franz Josefs Bahnhof to the north, Westbahnhof to the west and Südbahnhof to the south; transferring between them is easy. Most hotels and pensions are in the centre and to the west.

Information

Tourist Offices The main tourist office (☎ 24 555, fax -666; e info@info.wien.at; w www.info.wien.at; 01, Am Albertinaplatz; open 9am-7pm daily) can provide information, including an excellent city map, and same-day hotel bookings (€2.90). Postal inquiries should be simply addressed to the Vienna Tourist Board, A-1025 Wien.

Information and room reservations (€3.50 to €4 commission) are also available in Westbahnhof and Südbahnhof (6.30am or 7am until 9pm or 10pm daily). There is also an **information and hotel reservation counter** (open 8am-11pm Mon-Fri, 9am-7pm Sat & Sun) in the arrival hall of the airport.

The **Austria Information Office** (☎ 587 20 00; fax 588 66-20; e oeinfo@oewwien.via.at; 04, Margaretenstrasse 1; open 10am-5pm Mon-Wed & Fri, 10am-6pm Thur) also has information. **Jugend-Info Wien** (☎ 17 99; 01, Babenbergerstrasse 1; open noon-7pm Mon-Sat), a youth information centre, can get tickets for varied events at reduced rates for those aged between 14 and 26. Its phone number is not accessible from outside Austria. Information on municipal facilities is available in the **Rathaus** (Town Hall; ☎ 525 50).

For sports, however, contact the **Sportamt** (☎ 4000-84111; Ernst-Happel-Stadion, 02, Meiereistrasse 7).

Tourist offices and hotels sell the Vienna Card (€15.25), providing admission discounts and a free 72-hour travel pass.

Money Banks are open from 8am or 9am to 3pm Monday to Wednesday and Friday, and to 5.30pm on Thursday; smaller branches close from 12.30pm to 1.30pm. Numerous Bankomat ATMs allow cash withdrawals. Train stations have extended hours for exchanging money.

AUSTRIA

AUSTRIA

VIENNA

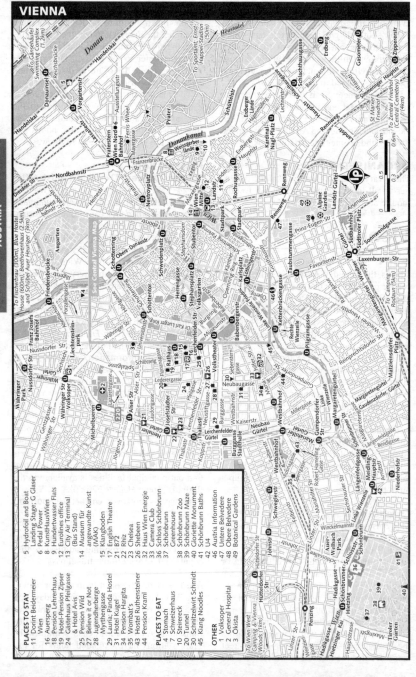

PLACES TO STAY
11 Dorint Beidermeier Wien
16 Auersperg
18 Pension Lehrerhaus
19 Hotel-Pension Zipser
24 Gästehaus Pfeilgasse
8 Hotel Avis
25 Pension Wild
27 Believe it or Not
28 Jugendherberge Myrthengasse
29 Hunta, Landa Hostel
31 Hotel Kugel
34 Pension Hargita
35 Wombat's
43 Hostel Ruthensteiner
44 Pension Kraml

PLACES TO EAT
4 Stomach
7 Schweizerhaus
10 Steirereck
20 Tunnel
30 Schnitzelwirt Schmidt
45 Kiang Noodles

OTHER
1 Volksoper
2 General Hospital
3 Okita
5 Hydrofoil and Boat Landing Stage; G Glaser
6 Pedal Power
8 KunstHausWien
12 Hundertwasser Flats
13 Euroline's office
City Akr Terminal (Bus Stand)
14 Museum für angewandte Kunst (MAK)
15 Klangboden
17 English Theatre
21 Rhiz
23 Chelsea
26 Shebeen
32 Haus Wien Energie
36 Camera Club
37 Schönbrunn
38 Greenhouse
39 Schönbrunn Zoo
40 Schönbrunn Maze
41 Gloriette Monument
42 Schönbrunn Baths
46 U4
47 Austria Information
47 Untere Belvedere
48 Obere Belvedere
49 Botanical Gardens

Post & Communications The main post office *(Hauptpost 1010; 01, Fleischmarkt 19; open 24hr)* is close to the Danube Canal. There are also post offices open long hours daily at Südbahnhof, Franz Josefs Bahnhof and Westbahnhof.

Email & Internet Access For a listing of public Internet centres, go to Jugend-Info Wien (see under Tourist Offices earlier in this section). Some places are free, like **Haus Wien Energie** *(☎ 58 20 00; 06, Mariahilfer Strasse 63; open shop hours)*. The most central Internet cafés are a branch of **Bignet** *(Kärntner Strasse 61; open daily)*, which charges €1.45 for 10 minutes' Net access and **Surfland Internetcafe** *(Krugerstrasse 10; open daily)*, where the initial charge is €1.40 then it's €0.08 a minute afterwards. Most hostels have Internet access.

Travel Agencies Handily located in the middle of Kärntnerstrasse is **American Express** *(☎ 515 40, fax -777; 01, Kärntner Strasse 21-23; open 9am-5.30pm Mon-Fri, 9am-noon Sat)*. The **Österreichisches Komitee für Internationalen Studienaustausch** *(ÖKISTA; ☎ 401 48-0, fax -2290; e info@ oekista.co.at; 09, Garnisongasse 7; open 9am-5.30pm Mon-Fri)* is a specialist in student and budget fares, linked to STA Travel. Around town you'll find other **branches** *(☎ 401 48-0; 09, Türkenstrasse 6 • ☎ 502 43-0; 04, Karlsgasse 3)*.

Bookshops The **British Bookshop** *(☎ 512 19 45; 01, Weihburggasse 24-6)* has the most English-language titles. **Shakespeare & Co Booksellers** *(☎ 535 50 53; 01, Sterngasse 2)* has new and second-hand books. **Freytag & Berndt** *(☎ 533 85 85; 01, Kohlmarkt 9)* stocks a vast selection of maps. **Reisebuchladen** *(☎ 317 33 84; 09, Kolingasse 6)* has many Lonely Planet guides.

Medical & Emergency Services For medical attention, try the **Allgemeines Krankenhaus** *(general hospital; ☎ 404 00; 09, Währinger Gürtel 18-20)*. For out-of-hours dental treatment call ☎ 512 20 78.

Things to See & Do

Walking is the best way to see the centre. Architectural riches confront you at nearly every corner, testimony to the power and wealth of the Habsburg dynasty. Ostentatious public buildings and statues line both sides of the Ring, so doing a circuit of this boulevard by tram (or foot or bicycle) is strongly recommended. The stand-out buildings include the neo-Gothic Rathaus, the Greek Revival-style Parlament (in particular the Athena statue), the 19th-century Burgtheater and the baroque Karlskirche (St Charles' Church). Carefully tended gardens and parks intersperse the stonework.

Walk north up the pedestrian-only Kärntner Strasse, a thoroughfare of plush shops, trees, café tables and street entertainers. It leads directly to Stephansplatz and the prime landmark of **Stephansdom** (St Stephen's Cathedral).

The latticework spire of this 13th-century Gothic masterpiece rises high above the city. Take the lift up the **north tower** *(admission €3.50)* or the stairs up the higher **south tower** *(admission €2.50)* for a view that's only slightly impeded by building work on the cathedral.

Some of the internal organs of the Habsburgs reside in the **Katakomben** *(catacombs; admission €3; open daily)*, which are also in Stephansdom. Others are located in the **Augustinerkirche** *(01, Augustinerstrasse 3)*. You will find the flower-strewn coffin of the celebrated Empress Elisabeth ('Sissi'), alongside that of her husband, the penultimate emperor, Franz Josef, in the morbid but compelling **Kaisergruft** *(01, Neuer Markt/Tegetthofstrasse; admission €3.60)*.

From Stephansplatz, turn west down Graben, which is dominated by the knobbly outline of the **Plague Column**. If you turn right into Tuchlaubenstrasse and left into Schulterstrasse, you'll come to the concrete **Jewish memorial** for Holocaust victims. If you turn left from Graben into Kohlmarkt and walk down, you'll reach the St Michael's Gateway of the **Hofburg** (Imperial Palace).

The Hofburg has been periodically enlarged since the 13th century, resulting in a mix of architectural styles. The Spanish Riding School office is to the left within the entrance dome (see Entertainment later in this chapter). Opposite are the **Kaiserappartements** *(adult/senior & student under 26 €6.90/5.40; open daily)*. Walk into the large courtyard, and take a left into the small Swiss Courtyard. Here you'll find the **Burgkapelle** (Royal Chapel; see Vienna Boys' Choir under Entertainment,

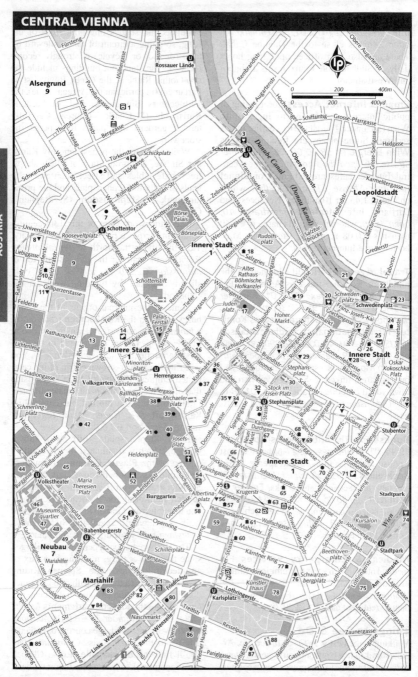

CENTRAL VIENNA

CENTRAL VIENNA

PLACES TO STAY
10   Pension Residenz
18   Schweizer Pension Solderer
24   Pension Dr Geissler
26   Hotel Post
36   Pension Nossek
57   Hotel Sacher & Café
60   Hotel Bristol;
      Korso Restaurant
61   Hotel-Pension Suzanne
63   Hotel zur Wiener Staatsoper
65   Music Academy & Mensa
68   Hotel Kaiserin Elisabeth
77   Hotel Imperial
85   Kolping-Gästehaus
89   Hotel im Palais
      chwarzenberg

PLACES TO EAT
6   Café Stein
8   University Mensa & Café
11   Café Einstein
15   Café Central
16   Esterházykeller
27   Griechenbeisl
28   Restaurant Bauer
29   Pizza Bizi
31   Wrenkh
32   DO & CO
34   Trzesniewski
35   Café Hawelka
56   Café Mozart
69   Immervoll
72   Gulaschmuseum
73   Café Prückl

83   Ra'mien
84   Café Sperl
86   Technical University Mensa

OTHER
1   International Theatre
2   Sigmund Freud Museum
3   Flex
4   Billy's Bones
5   Ökista
7   Reisebuchladen
      (Bookshop & Tourguide)
9   University
12   Rathaus (City Hall)
13   Burgtheater (National
      Theatre)
14   Hungarian Embassy
17   Jewish Memorial
19   Shakespeare & Co
      Booksellers
20   Krah Krah
21   Marienbrücke
22   Schwedenbrücke
23   Danube Canal
      Tour Landing Stage
25   Main Post Office
30   Stephansdom
      (St Stephen's Cathedral)
33   Österreichische Werkstätten
37   Freytag & Berndt
38   Kaiserappartements
39   Spanish Riding School
40   Schatzkammer
41   Burgkapelle
42   Volksgarten

43   Parlament
44   Volkstheater
45   Naturhistoriches Museum
46   Museum of Modern Art
      (MUMOK, Stiftung
      Ludwig Wien)
47   Kunsthalle
48   Leopold Museum
49   ZOOM Children's
      Museum
50   Musuem of Fine Arts
51   Jugend-Info Wien
52   Hofburg
53   Augustinerkirche
54   Albertina
55   Main Tourist Office
58   State Ticket Office
59   Staatsoper (State Opera)
62   Surfland Internetcafe
64   Haus der Musik
66   Kaisergruft
67   American Express
70   British Bookshop
71   US Consulate
74   Meierei im Stadtpark
75   Konzerthaus;
      Akademietheater
76   Austrian Airlines
78   Musikverein
79   Bignet
80   DDSG Blue Danube
81   Secession Building
82   Wiener Festwochen
87   ÖKISTA
88   Karlskirche

later in this section), and the **Schatzkammer** *(Imperial Treasury; adult/senior & student under 27 €7/5; open Wed-Mon)*. The latter contains treasures and relics spanning 1000 years, including the crown jewels. Allow an hour or more to get round.

Schloss Schönbrunn The Habsburgs' summer palace was the sumptuous 1440-room **Schloss Schönbrunn** *(☎ 811 13-0; 13, Schönbrunner Schlossstrasse 47; U-Bahn No 4; self-guided 22-/40-room tour €7.50/9.80, students €6.90/7.99; open 8.30am-5pm daily Apr-Oct, 8.30am-4.30pm Nov-Mar)*. Today, it's a world-renowned tourist attraction; so much so, that sometimes in summer it's too crowded to fully appreciate. Inside the palace of this mini-Versailles, you'll traipse through progressively more luxurious apartments, the most impressive being the **Audience Rooms**. It's worth noting that these are only included in the 40-room grand tour.

Other points of interest within the grounds include the formal gardens and fountains, the **maze** *(adult/concession €2.10/1.45)*, the **Palmenhaus** *(greenhouse; adult/concession €3.30/2.20)* and the **Gloriette Monument** *(adult/concession €2.10/1.45)*, whose roof offers a wonderful view over the palace grounds and beyond. There is even a **Tiergarten** *(zoo; adult/concession €9/6)*.

Two combined tickets in the summer (€14/17.20) provide good value if you're interested in several features. And the Schönbrunn public swimming baths have now been reopened after extensive renovation (see Watersports under Activities later in this section).

Schloss Belvedere This palace *(combined admission adult/student €7.50/5; open 10am-6pm Tues-Sun)* consists of two main buildings housing the **Österreichische Galerie** *(Austrian Gallery; ☎ 795 57-261)*. One building is the **Obere Belvedere** *(Upper Belvedere;*

03, *Prinz Eugen Strasse 27*), where you'll find instantly recognisable works, such as Gustav Klimt's *The Kiss*, accompanied by other late-19th-/early-20th-century Austrian works. The other is **Untere (Lower) Belvedere** *(03, Rennweg 6A)* which contains a baroque museum. The buildings sit at opposite ends of a manicured garden.

Kunsthistorisches Museum A huge range of the art amassed by the Habsburgs is showcased at the **Museum of Fine Arts** *(☎ 525 24-0; ☒ www.khm.at; 01, Maria Theresien-Platz; adult/concession €8.70/6.50; open 10am-6pm Tues-Sun, 10am-10pm Thur)*. The collection includes works by Rubens, van Dyck, Holbein and Caravaggio. Paintings by Peter Brueghel the Elder, including *Hunters in the Snow*, also feature. There is an entire wing full of ornaments, clocks and glassware, in which you'll see Cellini's stunning salt-cellar. If you can stay the distance, a collection of Greek, Roman and Egyptian antiquities also awaits.

Secession Building This extremely popular Art Nouveau 'temple of art' *(☎ 587 53 07; Friedrichstrasse 12; adult/student €5.09/2.91; open 10am-6pm Tues-Sun, to 10pm Thur)* was built in 1898 and bears an intricate golden dome that the Viennese say looks like a 'golden cabbage'. And it does. Inside, the highlight is the 34m-long *Beethoven Frieze* by Klimt.

KunstHausWien Hey, where did the floor go? This fairytale gallery *(☎ 712 04 91-0; 03, Untere Weissgerberstrasse 13; adult/concession €8/6 for entry to Hundertwasser collection, or €14/11 with temporary exhibitions, half-price Mon; open 10am-7pm daily)* certainly sweeps you off your feet with its uneven surfaces, irregular corners and coloured ceramics. Designed by Friedensreich Hundertwasser in order to house his art, it's vaguely reminiscent of Anton Gaudi's buildings in Barcelona and a leading example of organic architecture well before the Guggenheim Museum in Bilbao, Spain, came along. Down the road there's a block of residential flats by Hundertwasser, on the corner of Löwengasse and Kegelgasse.

Museums Quarter The **Leopold Museum** *(☎ 525 70-0; 07, Museumsplatz 1; adult/concession €9/5.50; open 11am-7pm Wed-*

Mon, to 9pm Fri)* is the highest-profile spot in Vienna's new Museumsquartier, containing as it does the world's largest collection of Egon Schiele paintings. However, the complex also includes the new main home of the **Museum of Modern Art** *(MUMOK, Stiftung Ludwig Wien; ☎ 525 00; adult/concession €6.50/5; open 9am-6pm Tues-Sun, to 9pm Thur)*, the **City Art Gallery** *(Kunsthalle; ☎ 521 89-33; adult/concession €8/6.50; open 10am-7pm daily, to 10pm Thur)* and the **Zoom Children's museum** *(☎ 522 67 48; adult/child €4.50/3.50; open 9am-4pm Mon-Fri, 11am-5pm Sat & Sun)*. A combined ticket to all (€25) can be bought from the ticket office in the complex.

Other Museums It doesn't begin to do justice to the **Haus der Musik** *(House of Music; ☎ 516 48-51; ☒ www.haus-der-musik.at; Seilerstätte 30; adult/student & senior €8.50/6.50; open 10am-10pm daily)* to list its myriad features.

Its interactive electronic displays allow you to create 'brain operas' through your movement and touch, to virtually conduct the Vienna Philharmonic Orchestra, to make your own CD and listen to snatches of sound from Broadway to the moon. Blah, blah, blah. More simply put, after a deceptively slow start, this amazing museum tickles your eardrums and blows your mind.

With your neurons still buzzing, a good next stop is the **Sigmund Freud Museum** *(☎ 319 1596; 09, Bergasse 19; admission €4.36; open 9am-6pm July-Sept, otherwise to 5pm)*. It's more a memorial to Freud himself than an explication of his psychoanalytical theories, though.

The **Albertina** *(☎ 534 83; ☒ www.albertina.at)* is reopening in mid-March 2003 after a lengthy refurbishment, which means Albrecht Dürer's *Hare*, among others, will be on display again. The **Museum für angewandte Kunst** *(MAK; ☎ 711 36-0; 01, Stubenring 5; adult/concession €2.20/1.10 permanent exhibition, €6.60/3.30 temporary exhibitions, free Sat; open Tues-Sun)* displays Art Deco objects from the Wiener Werkstatte and 20th-century architectural models.

Some former homes of the great composers, including one of Mozart's, are also open to the public; ask at the tourist office.

Cemeteries Beethoven, Schubert, Brahms and Schönberg have memorial tombs in the

Zentralfriedhof (Central Cemetery; 11, Simmeringer Hauptstrasse 232-244), about 4km south of the centre. Mozart also has a monument here, but he is actually buried in the **St Marxer Friedhof** (Cemetery of St Mark; 03, Leberstrasse 6-8). Initially unmarked, his grave now has a poignant memorial.

Naschmarkt This **market** (06, Linke Wienzeile; open 6am-6pm Mon-Sat) consists primarily of fruit, vegetable and meat stalls, but there are a few stalls selling clothing and curios as well. There is also an atmospheric **flea market** (open Sat). Snack bars provide cheap, hot food, especially kebabs.

Prater If you're a fan of the film The Third Man, you might look forward to riding the **Riesenrad** (giant wheel; €4.36) in this amusement park as a great way to relive a classic cinema moment. Truth be told, you'll be too busy jostling for space to recall the immortal speech actor Orson Welles made in one of the gondolas. So, give in – just enjoy the view as the Ferris wheel languidly takes you 65m aloft. More hardened adrenalin junkies will prefer the Prater's faster-spinning rides.

Activities
Hiking To the west of the city, the rolling hills and marked trails of the Vienna Woods are perfect for walkers; the Wander bares Wien leaflet, available from the Sportamt, outlines hiking routes and how to reach them. The Lower Austria Information office has a free map of routes further from the city.

Watersports You can swim, sail, boat and windsurf in the stretches of water known as the Old Danube, northeast of the Donaustadt island and the New Donau, which runs parallel to and just north of the Donaukanal (Danube Canal). There are stretches of river bank with unrestricted access. Alternatively, go to much-loved **Schönbrunn baths** (full day/afternoon including locker €9.50/6.50; open May-Sept). Or try the swimming complex **Gänsehäufel** (full day/afternoon including locker €8.50/6.50; open May-Sept).

Organised Tours
Several companies offer tours of the city and surrounding areas, either by coach, foot (try the Third Man Tour, which visits spots featured in the famous film, including the underground sewers) or bicycle; contact **Pedal Power** (☎ 729 72 34; 02, Ausstellungsstrasse 3). **Reisebuchladen** (☎ 317 33 84; 09, Kolingasse 6) gives an interesting tour of 'alternative' Vienna (€24). Boat operators conduct tours of the Danube Canal; the tourist office has details. See also The Danube Valley section later in this chapter.

Special Events
The Vienna Festival, from mid-May to mid-June, has a wide-ranging programme of the arts. Contact the **Wiener Festwochen** (☎ 589 22-22, fax -49; w www.festwochen.or.at; Lehárgasse 11, A-1060 Vienna; open Jan–mid-June) for details.

Vienna's Summer of Music runs from mid-July to mid-September; contact **KlangBoden** (☎ 4000-8410; 01, Stadiongasse 9). Reduced student tickets go on sale at the venue 10 minutes before the performance.

At the end of June, look out for free rock, jazz and folk concerts in the Donauinselfest. The free open-air Opera Film Festival on Rathausplatz runs throughout July and August.

Vienna's traditional Christmas market (Christkindlmarkt) takes place in front of the city hall between mid-November and 24 December. Other seasonal events include New Year concerts and gala balls (January and February), the Vienna Spring Marathon (April/May) and the Schubert Festival (November). The tourist office does not sell tickets, but has details.

Places to Stay – Budget
Vienna can be a budget traveller's nightmare. Cheaper places are often full, especially in summer. Reserve beforehand, or at least phone before turning up.

Tourist offices (see under Information earlier this section) list private rooms and offer a useful Camping pamphlet. They will also book rooms.

Camping To get to the **Wien West** (☎ 914 23 14; 14, Hütteldorfstrasse 80; site per adult/tent/car €5/3/2; open all year), take U4 or the S-Bahn to Hütteldorf, then bus No 148 or 152. **Camping Rodaun** (☎ 888 41 54; 23, An der Au 2; site per adult/tent/car €5.45/4.36/1.09; open late Mar–mid-Nov) is another option. Take S1 or S2 to Liesing then bus No 60A.

AUSTRIA

Hostels Undoubtedly, the Viennese des-res (most desirable residence) of the savvy backpacker is **Wombat's** (☎ 897 23 36, fax 897 25 77; e wombats@chello.at; 15, Grangasse 6; dorm beds/doubles €14/18). This hostel's clean, modern dorms and doubles have won it favourable word-of-mouth from all quarters, and it's been adding extra rooms.

Nearby is **Hostel Ruthensteiner** (☎ 893 42 02, fax 893 27 96; e info@hostel.ruthen steiner.com; 15, Robert Hamerling Gasse 24; beds in large/small dorms €11.50/13, triples/ doubles €19/20, key deposit €10). It's an older building, but it has a nice garden and is still very lively. There are small extra charges for sheets, credit card payments and breakfast.

Moving towards the centre, in an area of cheap restaurants and second-hand clothes shops, you'll find **Jugendherberge Myrthengasse** (☎ 523 63 16, fax 523 58 49; e hos tel@chello.at; 07, Myrthengasse 7; beds in 4–6-bed dorms/doubles €15/17 including breakfast & sheets). It's based in two buildings, with reception in the main one. Although the desk is staffed 24 hours a day, check-in is limited to between 11am and 4pm.

The dorms can feel a bit claustrophobic in both **Believe It or Not** (☎ 526 46 58; 07, Apartment 14, Myrthengasse 10; dorm beds €12.50) and **Panda Hostel** (☎ 522 53 53; 07, 3rd floor, Kaiserstrasse 77; dorm beds €12). However, both of these private hostels offer kitchen facilities, if no breakfast, and are friendly places. Panda is linked to **Lauria** (see Hotels & Pensions later in this section).

There are also two large HI hostels out in the suburbs: to get to **Brigittenau** (☎ 332 82 94, fax 330 83 79; e jgh1200wien@chello.at; 20, Friedrich Engels Platz 24; beds in dorms without/with shower €15/16) take the U6 to Handelskai and then bus 11A one stop to Friedrich Engels Platz; and for **Hütteldorf-Hacking** (☎ 877 02 63, fax -2; e jgh@wigast .com; 13, Schlossberggasse 8; dorm beds from €13.90) take the U4 to Hütteldorf and leave the station by the Habikgasse exit.

Student Residences These are available to tourists from 1 July to 30 September while students are on holiday. The cheapest, and one of the nicest, is the **Blue Hostel House** (☎ 369 55 85-0, fax -12; 19, Peter Jordan Strasse 29; singles/doubles with shared facilities €16/ 26.20). It's not that near to the centre, though. Other *Studentenheime* to consider include:

Gästehaus Pfeilgasse & Hotel Avis (☎ 401 74, fax 401 76-20; 08, Pfeilgasse 4-6; singles/ doubles/triples with shared facilities €21/38/ 51, with bathroom €46/62/81) and **Music Academy** (☎ 514 84-7700, fax -7799; e jag ersberger@mdw.ac.at; 01, Johannesgasse 8; singles/doubles with shared facilities €33/58, with private bathroom €36/70). If you want to book a room contact this last one by fax or email, rather than phone.

Auersperg (☎ 406 25 40, fax 406 25 49-13; 09, Auerspergstrasse 9; singles/doubles with shared facilities €28/46, with private bathroom €38/64) is one of several establishments that can be booked through **Albertina Hotels** (☎ 512 74 93, fax 512 1968; w www.albertina-hotels.at).

Hotels & Pensions A great place for young couples or small groups of travellers is **Lauria** (☎ 522 25 55; e lauria.apartments@chello.at; 07, 3rd floor, Kaiserstrasse 77; twins/doubles €35/40, with shower €60, triples €45-60, with shower €70, quads without/with shower €70/80, 4-person apartments €105, first night supplement €5). Its rooms are comfortable and personable, there's a kitchen and you get your own key.

Pension Lehrerhaus (☎ 404 23 58-100, fax -69; 08, Lange Gasse 20; singles/doubles without shower & toilet €27/49, with facilities €34/57, surcharge for single-night stays €1.50) was designed to accommodate visiting teachers, but now offers excellent value to all travellers with its basic but clean rooms. Breakfast is not included in the tariff.

Kolping-Gästehaus (☎ 587 56 31, fax 586 36 3; e reservierung@wien-zentral.kolping .at; 06, Gumpendorfer Strasse 39; singles without shower & toilet €22; singles/doubles with facilities from €52/65) is a student residence, rather than one for teachers, so there's an institutional feel to its rooms, but they're comfortable and conveniently located all the same.

Pension Hargita (☎ 526 19 28, fax 526 04 92; e pension@hargita.at; 07, Andreasgasse 1; singles/doubles without bathroom 31/45, with bathroom €35/65) surely must be the cleanest and most charming in Vienna for the price. The owner's warm manner, pastel-coloured rooms and spruced-up entrance hall will make you forgive the absence of a lift. If you can get a room, that is. Book ahead; breakfast is available on request.

Family-run and traditionally decorated **Pension Kraml** (☎ 587 85 88, fax 586 75 73; e pension.kraml@chello.at; 06, Brauergasse 5; singles/doubles without bathroom €26/48, with bathroom €43/65) is another sound choice. The breakfast here is generous.

Friendly **Hotel Kugel** (☎ 523 33 55, fax -5; 07, Siebensterngasse 43; singles/doubles without shower & toilet €33/45, with facilities from €42/64; no credit cards) is near tram tracks, but you don't hear much noise inside. The four-poster beds in some of its more upmarket rooms make it popular with American tourists, but it offers good bargains as well.

Proud to call itself 'gay-friendly, everyone-friendly', **Pension Wild** (☎ 406 51 74, fax 402 21 68; 08, Langegasse 10; singles €37-65, doubles €45-90) has been doing some renovation of late. So it now has luxury rooms, as well as its traditionally cheaper accommodation, with showers and toilets outside the rooms. By the way, 'Wild' is the family name, not a description.

Places to Stay – Mid-Range
Schweizer Pension Solderer (☎ 533 81 56, fax 535 64 69; e schweizer.pension@chello.at; 01, Heinrichsgasse 2; singles/doubles from €36/56, with shower & toilet €60/80) is a cosy hotel in the northern part of the city centre. **Hotel Post** (☎ 515 83-0, fax -808; 01, Fleischmarkt 24; singles/doubles without bathroom €42/68, with bathroom €72/111) is right in the heart of things. With its parquet flooring in the rooms, long carpeted hallways and decorative cast-iron lift, it feels like a grand old 19th-century boarding house. The rooms without bathrooms are a fantastic bargain.

Don't be deterred by the slow lift to nearby **Pension Dr Geissler** (☎ 533 28 03, fax 533 26 35; 01 Postgasse 14; singles/doubles without private facilities from €39/50, with private facilities from €65/88). Inside, it's been renovated in a pleasantly baroque style.

Baroque is also the style favoured by **Hotel-Pension Suzanne** (☎ 513 25-07, fax -00; e info@pension-suzanne.at; 01, Walfischgasse 4; singles/twins/doubles €69/87/99) and **Pension Nossek** (☎ 533 70 41-0, fax 535 36 46; 01, Graben 17; singles €43-65, doubles €98-120; no credit cards). Both are right in the centre, close to the madding crowds.

A little further out, close to the university, you'll find **Pension Residenz** (☎ 406 47 86-0, fax -50; e vienna@pension-residenz.co.at; 01, Ebendorferstrasse 10; singles/doubles €58/87). Also traditionally decorated, with white, light-coloured fittings, it's a pleasant place to stay.

Hotel-Pension Zipser (☎ 404 54-0, fax 408 52 66-13; e zipser@netway.at; 08, Lange Gasse 49; singles/doubles from €67/101) has elegant contemporary furnishings and some rooms have balconies facing a garden.

Hotel zur Wiener Staatsoper (☎ 513 12 74, fax -15; e office@zurwienerstaatsoper.at; 01, Krugerstrasse 11; singles/doubles from €76/109) is famous for its appealing facade. Its rooms are small, but its prices great for such a central location.

Places to Stay – Top End
If anything, Vienna has a glut of four- and five-star hotels. Every major chain is here, from Best Western, Hilton and InterContinental to Marriott and Radisson SAS.

Even the city's most recognisable names now belong to groups, including the **Hotel Sacher** (☎ 514 56-0, fax -810; 01, Philharmoniker Strasse 4; singles/doubles from €200/298), **Hotel Bristol** (☎ 515 16-0, fax -550; 01, Kärntner Ring 1; singles/doubles both from €335) and **Hotel Imperial** (☎ 501 10-0; fax -410; 01, Kärntner Ring 16; singles/doubles from €406/486).

Slightly kinder on the wallet is the pleasant and central **Kaiserin Elisabeth** (☎ 515 26, fax -7; e info@kaiserinelisabeth.at; 01, Weihburggasse 13; singles €73-113, doubles €193). Delightful **Dorint Biedermeier Wien** (☎ 71 671-0, fax -716; 03, Landstrasser Hauptstrasse 28; singles/doubles from €129/159) is memorably located in a mews with shops and restaurants.

One of Vienna's most exclusive addresses is **Hotel im Palais Schwarzenberg** (☎ 798 4515, fax 798 4714; 03, Schwarzenbergplatz 9; singles/doubles from €233/262).

Places to Eat
You can buy groceries outside normal shopping hours at the train stations; prices are considerably higher except in a **Billa supermarket** (Franz Josefs Bahnhof; open 7am-7.30pm daily). Westbahnhof has a large shop in the main hall, which is open 5.30am to 11pm daily; and Südbahnhof has a few tiny kiosks open daily till late. There is another **Billa supermarket** (open 7.30am-10pm daily) in the airport.

Würstel stands are scattered around the city and provide a quick snack of sausage and bread for around €2.50.

Vienna's best known dish, the Wiener Schnitzel, is available everywhere; goulash is also common. Vienna is renowned for its excellent pastries and desserts, which are very effective at transferring the bulk from your moneybelt to your waistline.

Places to Eat – Budget The best deal is in the various student cafeterias (mensas). They're usually only open for weekday lunches between 11am and 2pm. Meals are €3.20 to €4.80, often with a reduction for students. **University Mensa** (01, Universitätsstrasse 7) has an adjoining **café** (open 8am-6pm Mon-Fri). **Technical University Mensa** (04, Resselgasse 7-9) is also convenient. **Music Academy Mensa** (01, Johannesgasse 8) is the only one inside the Ring.

Tunnel (08, Florianigasse 39; breakfast €2.50, lunch specials €4, pizzas €5-7, other mains €4-10; open daily) is also a student haunt. The food is satisfying, although you might have to wait a while for it to arrive.

There are several cheap places in the centre to fuel up. **Trzesniewski** (01, Dorotheergasse 1; open sandwiches €0.73 each; open Mon-Sat) is the most traditional, albeit not for those with a phobia about egg, onions or fish, one of which is on every tiny open sandwich for sale. While you eat standing up and wash your food down with a beer, you can make believe that you're one of the Austrian Emperor's minions on the way home from a hard day at the factory.

Pizza Bizi (01, Rotenturmstrasse 4; pizzas €5.70; open daily) is rather less quaint – a fact that hardly registers with the multilingual crowd who flock here for the prices and convenience. The restaurant is self-service.

Gulaschmuseum (01, Schulerstrasse 20; vegie & meat dishes from €6, lunch menu €6.18; open daily) serves every type of goulash you can imagine, and quite a few you can't – including the actually rather celebrated chocolate goulash for dessert.

Visiting **Café Einstein** (01, Rathausplatz 4; schnitzels from €4.20, other meat & vegie mains from €5.50; open daily) is a smart move. By the university, it has some of the cheapest Wiener Schnitzels in town. For a more authentic Viennese atmosphere, venture into **Schnitzelwirt Schmidt** (07, Neubaugasse

52; schnitzels from €5.10; open Mon-Sat). Perhaps it's having to carry such huge portions to the tables that makes the waiters here so temperamental.

The Rabelaisian adventures continue in the Prater park, where **Schweizerhaus** (02, Strasse des Ersten Mai 116; open daily Mar-Oct) serves Hintere Schweinsstelze (roasted pork hocks). Mustard or horseradish are recommended accompaniments to these massive chunks of meat on the bone.

Relaxed Asian noodle bar **Ra'mien** (06, Gumperndorferstrasse 9; mains from €6.80; open Tues-Sun) provides a change with refreshing, if not particularly spicy soups, noodles and other, meat and vegetarian, dishes. Those who arrive alone may be seated at one of the long communal benches. **Kiang Noodles** (06 Joanelligasse 3) is another, more upmarket noodle bar. It's a chain, but this is one of the most conveniently located.

Places to Eat – Mid-Range & Top-End Its name means 'always full' and **Immervoll** (☎ 513 522 88; 01 Weihburggasse 17; mains from €6.90; open daily) pretty well is. Customers can't resist its pleasant environment and dishes including gnocchi and Wiener Schnitzel.

Wrenkh (☎ 533 15 26; 01, Bauernmarkt 10; lunch menus €11.04; open daily) is a classy vegetarian restaurant, featuring some lip-smacking Mediterranean, Austrian and Asian dishes – from risotto to tofu.

Once a real insider's tip, **Stomach** (☎ 310 20 99; 9 Seegasse 26; mains from €10, open Wed-Sat) is now such a favourite that it pays to book ahead. Delicious Styrian and Italian cuisine is served in its rustic room and pleasant garden. Fantastic.

Much more touristy is **Griechenbeisl** (01, Fleischmarkt 11; mains from €12; open daily). However, this interlocking collection of rooms is atmospheric and full of history.

The busy **DO & CO** (☎ 535 39 69; 01, Haas Haus, Stephansplatz 12; mains from €13; open daily) has great food and views. One half serves Asian dishes, the other international cuisine. Book ahead.

The long-standing gourmet temple **Steirereck** (☎ 713 31 68; 08, Rasumofskygasse 2; mains around €24; open Mon-Fri) has had some competition in recent years. When Viennese go out for a grand meal, they might just as easily choose **Restaurant Bauer** (☎ 512 98

71; 01, Sonnenfelsgasse 17; mains from €18; open Mon-Fri) or **Korso** *(☎ 515 16-546; 01, Mahlerstrasse 2; mains from €28.50; open Sun-Fri)* at Hotel Bristol.

Coffee Houses 'Vienna's coffee houses are full of people who want to be alone...without feeling lonely,' wrote the local 19th-century author Alfred Polgar. Sometimes today it's hard to get that sense of personal space when the city's most famous cafés are brimming over with other curious visitors.

A good Viennese café provides somewhere to relax, people-watch and catch up on international newspapers. Sadly, you don't really find that in the hectic **Hotel Sacher Café** *(01, Philharmonikerstrasse 4)* or **Café Mozart** *(01 Albertinaplatz 2)*.

Russian revolutionary Leon Trotsky might also spin in his grave to see how commercial his former chess haunt now feels. But the high moulded ceilings and palms in **Café Central** *(01, Herrengasse 14; open Mon-Sat)* go a long way to offsetting the touristy aura.

Inside the slightly worn, 1950s-style **Café Prückl** *(01, Stubenring 24; open daily)*, you get the feeling that you're surrounded by more locals – whether they be trendy students or refined old ladies.

One of the most charmingly unspoilt of Vienna's coffee houses is the **Café Sperl** *(06, Gumpendorfer Strasse 11; open daily, except Sun in July & Aug)*. Original architectural features, a dishevelled pile of papers, billiards tables and a cast of interesting characters can make you reluctant to finish your coffee.

Café Hawelka *(01, Dorotheergasse 6; open Wed-Mon)* is smoky, crowded, noisy, with nicotine-stained walls – which is precisely why its many regulars love it.

It's not strictly a coffee house and other Internet cafés have overtaken its Web facilities, but **Café Stein** *(09, Währinger Strasse 6; open Mon-Sat)* is still a regular fixture on the Vienna scene – for trendy students and arty types.

Across the city, full-sized coffees cost roughly €2.80 to €3.50 – but then the custom is to take one's time.

Entertainment

From the sweet strains of Mozart, to the smoky dub lounge of celebrity DJ duos Kruder & Dorfmeister or Pulsinger & Tunakan, Vienna prefers to take its entertainment sitting down. (It's no coincidence this city has spawned a band called the Sofa Surfers.) There are still plenty of chances to drink and dance the night away, though, as you'll find by flipping through listings magazines *City* (€1) and *Falter* (€2.05). The tourist office has copies of *Vienna Scene* and produces monthly events listings.

The state ticket office, **Bundestheaterverkassen** *(☎ 514 44-7880; 01, Goethegasse 1)*, sells tickets without commission for the Staatsoper, Volksoper, Burgtheater and Akademietheater. For other places, try **Wien Ticket** *(☎ 588 85)* in the hut by the Oper; it charges little or no commission for cash sales.

Cheap standing-room *(Stehplatz)* tickets are often the best deal (see the following sections for details). By contrast, concert tickets touted on the streets by numerous be-wigged Mozart wannabes are truly overpriced.

Cinema & Theatre Check local papers for listings. All cinema seats are cheaper (€5.40 rather than €8.30) on Monday. There are performances in English at the **English Theatre** *(☎ 402 82 84; w www.englishtheatre.at; 08, Josefsgasse 12)* and the **International Theatre** *(☎ 319 62 72; 09, Porzellangasse 8)*. If you understand German, try either the **Burgtheater** *(☎ 514 44-4145; 01, Dr Karl Lueger Ring 2)* or the **Akademietheater** *(☎ 514 44; 01 Lisztstrasse 1)*.

Classical Music In a city that Beethoven, Brahms, Haydn, Mozart and Schubert once called home and where even today buskers often have classical training, it's a pity not to visit the opera or orchestra.

Performances at the **Staatsoper** *(State Opera; ☎ 514 44-2960; 01, Opernring 2; seats €5.10-179, standing room €3.65)*, are lavish, formal affairs, where people dress up. The **Volksoper** *(People's Opera; ☎ 514 44-3670; 09 Währinger Strasse 78; tickets €3.65-72, standing room €1.50-20.64)* puts on more modern or niche performances and is a little more relaxed in atmosphere. At both these venues, standing-room tickets go on sale an hour before each performance, and you may need to queue three hours before that for major productions. An hour before the curtain goes up, unsold tickets also go on sale at cheap prices (from €3.65) to students under 27 (home university ID plus ISIC card necessary).

The **Musikverein** *(☎ 505 18 90; 01, Bösendorferstrasse 12; seats from €15-110,* *standing room* (€5-7) is the opulent and acoustically perfect (unofficial) home of the world-class Vienna Philharmonic Orchestra. Here, standing tickets can be bought three weeks in advance at the box office.

There are no performances in July and August. Ask the tourist office for details of free concerts at the Rathaus or in churches.

Vienna Boys' Choir Never mind Johnny-come-lately global chart-toppers like NSync or Boyzone, the Vienna Boys' Choir *(Wiener Sängerknaben)* is *the* original boy band. The choir performs at the **Burgkapelle** *(music chapel;* ☎ *533 99 27;* e *hofmusikkapelle@ asn-wien.ac.at; inside the Hofburg; seats €5.10-27.65, standing room free, tickets available Fri & 8.15am Sun; performances 9.15am Sun, except July–mid-Sept).* Formed in 1498, the choir has been around longer than ex-Take That singer Robbie Williams, had more hit records than the short-lived Bros and looks more angelic than golden-haired Hanson. True, the individual members are a trifle younger than most teen stars, but their concerts are routinely sold out and there's often a crush of fans to meet them afterwards. These classical singers have even recently recorded a cover version of a Metallica song. Whatever next? Perhaps a guest performance by Ozzy Osbourne.

The choir also performs regularly in the **Konzerthaus** *(03, Lotheringerstrasse 20; 3.30pm Fri in May, June, Sept & Oct).*

Spanish Riding School The famous Lipizzaner stallions strut their stuff in the Spanish Riding School *(fax 535 01 86;* e *tickets@ srs.at; seats €33-145, standing room €22-25)* behind the Hofburg. Performances are sold out months in advance, so write to the Spanische Reitschule, Michaelerplatz 1, A-1010 Wien, or ask in the office about cancellations (unclaimed tickets are sold 45 minutes before performances); there's no phone. Deal directly with the school to avoid the hefty 20% to 30% commission charged by travel agents.

You need to be pretty keen on horses to pay the prices asked, although a few of the tricks, such as a stallion bounding along on its hind legs like a demented kangaroo, do stick in the mind. Tickets to watch the horses train can be bought the same day (€14.50). Training is from 10am to noon, Tuesday to Saturday, from mid-February to mid-December except

in July and August when the stallions go on holiday. These sessions are only intermittently interesting, and if you try around 11am you can usually get in fairly quickly. Watching the weekly final rehearsal (€20; Friday or Saturday) is also an option.

Nightclubs & Bars The area around Ruprechtsplatz, Seitenstettengasse and Rabensteig in the Innere Stadt has been dubbed the 'Bermuda Triangle' for the way drinkers disappear into its numerous pubs and clubs, but you'd have to seriously overindulge to become lost in the small *Bermudadreieck*. Venues here are lively and inexpensive, but not particularly atmospheric.

Krah Krah *(01, Rabensteig 8)* has 50 different brands of beer and is open 11am until late.

Other good places for a beer are the shady garden at **Fischerbräu** *(Billrothstrasse 17)* or smoky Irish pub **Billy's Bones** *(Schickplatz 4)*. **Shebeen** *(Lerchenfelderstrasse 45-47)* is a popular evening spot for travellers and expats alike.

If you head for the U-Bahn arches near the Gürtel you'll find a good choice of bars. **Chelsea** *(08, Lechenfelder Gürtel 29-31)* has DJs, occasional indie bands, and English football via satellite. **Rhiz** *(No 37-38)* is a comfy hang-out, favouring modern electronic music, while **B72** *(No 72)*, is slightly more posey. It features varied bands and DJs.

Laidback **Camera Club** *(07, Neubaugasse 2)*, still aspires to being an Amsterdam coffee shop rather than a Viennese disco, but it's not quite as popular as it once was.

More serious clubbing goes on in the young and lively **Flex** *(near Schottenring U-bahn & Donaukanal)* by the water, and in **Volksgarten** *(01, Burgring 1)*, which is three linked venues: a café with DJs and a garden, a disco with theme evenings, and a more formal 'Walzer Dancing' place. **Meierei im Stadtpark** *(Heumarkt 3)* is another favourite for catching up on Vienna's DJ scene. When the weekend crush there gets too much, you can always cool off in the surrounding park.

U4 *(12, Schönbrunner Strasse 222)* is one of Vienna's longest-standing discos. Each night has a different theme. Sunday is 1960s and '70s music; Thursday is gay night.

Heurigen Wine taverns or *Heurigen* sell 'new' wine produced on the premises, a concession first granted by Emperor Joseph II;

traditionally they can be identified by a green wreath or branch hanging over the door. Outside tables are common and there's a selection from inexpensive hot and cold buffet counters.

Heurigen usually have a relaxed atmosphere, which becomes increasingly lively as the evening progresses. The more touristy taverns feature traditional live music; native Viennese, however, tend to prefer a music-free environment. Opening times are approximately 4pm to 11pm, and wine costs around €2.50 a *Viertel* (0.25L).

Heurigen are concentrated in the wine-growing suburbs to the north, south and west of the city. Taverns are so close together that it is best to pick a region and just explore.

The Heurigen areas of Nussdorf and Heiligenstadt are near each other at the terminus of tram D. In 1817, Beethoven lived in the **Beethovenhaus** *(19, Pfarrplatz 3, Heiligenstadt)*. Down the road (bus No 38A from Heiligenstadt or tram 38 from the Ring) is Grinzing, an area favoured by tour groups (count the tour buses lined up outside in the evening). There are several Heurigen in a row where Cobenzlgasse and Sandgasse meet. Alternatively, catch bus 38A east to Ambrüstergasse and follow Kahlenberger Strasse to **Schübel Auer** *(19 Kahlenberger Strasse; open Mon-Sat)*, which has a great food buffet and atmosphere.

Stammersdorf (tram No 31) and Strebersdorf (tram No 32) are cheaper, quieter regions. At **Esterházykeller** *(01, Haarhof 1; open from 11am daily, closed Sat & Sun evenings)* you can get an approximate taste of the Heurigen experience without leaving the centre.

Shopping
Waltzing along the shopaholic's mecca of Kärntner Strasse, a good place to stop is the **Österreiche Werkstätten** *(Kärntner Strasse 6)*, for Art Deco-type jewellery and household objects in the Viennese tradition. Other local specialities include lamps, handmade dolls, wrought-iron and leather goods. Some prices include VAT, which can be claimed back (see Taxes & Refunds under Money in the Facts for the Visitor section earlier in this chapter).

Getting There & Away
Air Regular scheduled flights link Vienna to Linz, Salzburg, Innsbruck, Klagenfurt and Graz. There are daily nonstop flights to all major European destinations. Check with

Austrian Airlines *(☎ 1789; city office: 01, Kärntner Ring 18)*.

Bus Since the central bus station at Wien Mitte was closed in 2000, departures are split between different locations. Buses to Budapest (€28, 3½ hours) leave opposite the offices of **Eurolines** *(☎ 7102 0453; w www.eurolines.at; 03, Invalidenstrasse 5-7; open daily)*. Eurolines buses to Prague depart twice daily from 01, Rathausplatz 5 (€23.30, five hours). Meanwhile, the ÖBB services to Bratislava (€10.90, 1½ hours) leave from Südtirolerplatz near Südbahnhof. Call ☎ 93000-34305 for details of these.

Train Schedules are subject to change, and not all destinations are exclusively serviced by one station, so check with train information centres in stations or call ☎ 05-1717.

International trains leave from either Westbahnhof or Südbahnhof. Westbahnhof has trains to Western and northern Europe and western Austria. Services head to Salzburg roughly every hour; some continue to Munich and terminate in Paris (14½ hours total). To Zürich, there are two day trains (€77.80, nine hours) and one night train (same fare, plus charge for fold-down seat/couchette). Eight trains a day go to Budapest (€32.80, 3½ hours).

Südbahnhof has trains to Italy (eg, Rome, via Venice and Florence), Slovakia, the Czech Republic, Hungary and Poland, and southern Austria. Five trains a day go to Bratislava (€13.80, 1½ hours) and four to Prague (€36, five hours), with two of those continuing to Berlin (10 hours in total).

Wien-Mitte Bahnhof handles local trains only and Franz Josefs Bahnhof has local and regional trains.

Car & Motorcycle The Gürtel is an outer ring road which joins up with the A22 on the north bank of the Danube and the A23 southeast of town. All the main road routes intersect with this system, including the A1 from Linz and Salzburg, and the A2 from Graz.

Hitching Hitchhikers and drivers are linked through **Rot-Weiss-Rot Mitfahrzentrale** *(☎ 408 22 10; e office@mfz.at)*. There's no physical office, however, you can phone 24 hours a day, seven days a week. Some examples of the fares for hitchers are Salzburg

€18.20, Innsbruck €25.45, Frankfurt €36.35 and Munich €25.45.

Boat Fast hydrofoils travel eastwards in the summer to Bratislava and Budapest, once per day. To Bratislava (Wednesday to Sunday, 1½ hours) costs €19/29 one way/return. To Budapest (at least daily, 5½ hours) costs €65/89. Bookings can be made through **DDSG Blue Danube** (☎ 588 80-0, fax -440; **w** www .ddsg-blue-danube.at; 01, Friedrichstrasse 7) or **G Glaser** (☎/fax 726 08 20; **w** www.mem bers.aon.at/danube; 02, Handelskai 265).

Heading west, a series of boats ply the Danube between Krems and Passau (in Germany), though services originating in Vienna are very infrequent. More operators are listed in The Danube Valley section later in this chapter.

Getting Around

To/From the Airport
Some 19km from the city centre is **Wien Schwechat airport** (☎ 7007-2233). There are buses every 20 or 30 minutes, 24 hours a day, between the airport and the city air terminal at the Hotel Hilton (€5.80). Buses also run every 30 or 60 minutes from Westbahnhof and Südbahnhof between 3.30am and midnight. By 2003, the reconstructed S-Bahn (S7 line) to the airport might be running again from Wien Mitte, instead of Sudbahnhof. However, it's best to check before setting out for the station (☎ 93000-2300). Taxis should cost €25 to €30. **C&K Airport Service** (☎ 1731) does the trip for a €21 fixed fare.

Public Transport
Vienna has a comprehensive and unified public transport network. Flat-fare tickets are valid for trains, trams, buses, the underground (U-Bahn) and suburban (S-Bahn) trains.

All advance-purchase tickets must be validated in the machines before use. Routes are outlined in the free tourist office map. Single tickets cost €1.60 via machines on buses/trams. Otherwise they cost €1.30 each from ticket machines in U-Bahn stations; it's the same rate in multiples of four/five from ticket offices, machines or Tabak shops. You may change lines on the same trip.

Children under six always travel free; those under 16 go free on Sunday, public holidays and during Vienna school holidays (photo ID necessary).

Daily passes (Stunden-Netzkarte) cost €4.30 (valid 24 hours from first use) or €10.90 (valid 72 hours). Validate the ticket in the machine at the beginning of your first journey. An eight-day multiple-user pass (8-Tage-Karte) costs €21.80; validate the ticket once per day per person. Weekly tickets, valid Monday to Sunday, cost €11.20.

Ticket inspections are not very frequent, but fare dodgers who are caught pay an on-the-spot fine of €40.70, plus the fare. Austrian and European rail passes are valid on the S-Bahn only. Public transport finishes around midnight, but there's also a comprehensive night bus service. They run every 30 minutes nightly, around the Ring and to the suburbs, and tickets are €1 (day tickets/passes not valid).

Car & Motorcycle
Parking is a problem in the city centre and the Viennese are impatient drivers. Using public transport is therefore preferable while sightseeing. Blue parking zones allow a maximum stop of 1½ or two hours from 9am to 8pm (to 7pm in the Innere Stadt) on weekdays.

Parking vouchers (€0.40 per 30 minutes) for these times can be purchased in Tabak shops and banks. The cheapest parking garage in the centre is situated at Museumsplatz and the cost is €2 per hour, €12 for 24 hours).

Taxi
They are metered for city journeys: €2 or €2.10 flag fall, plus €1.09 or €1.38 per kilometre – the higher rate is on Sunday and at night. There is a €2 surcharge (€2.10 at night) for phoning a radio taxi.

Bicycle
With bikes no longer available from train stations, the best thing is to ask your hostel or hotel for small local operators. **Pedal Power** (☎ 729 72 34; 02, Ausstellungsstrasse 3; 1st-day/half-day rental €27/17) is the city's dominant operator, although its prices are rather steep. Tips für Radfahrer is available from the tourist office and shows circular bike tours.

Fiacres
Before hiring one of these horse-drawn carriages (Fiakers) by the Stephansdom, it's worth asking yourself whether these are pony traps or tourist traps.

Sure, they're kind of cute, but at €65 for a 40-minute ride... well, you do the maths.

The Danube Valley

The strategic importance of the Danube (Donau) Valley as an east-west corridor meant that control of the area was hotly contested throughout history. As a result, there are hundreds of castles and fortified abbeys throughout the region.

The 36km Wachau section of the Danube, between Krems and Melk, is the river's most picturesque stretch, with wine-growing villages, forested slopes and vineyards at every bend.

Several companies operate boats along the Danube, generally from early April to late October. **DDSG Blue Danube** (☎ 01-588 80-0, fax -440; w www.ddsg-blue-danube.at; 01, Friedrichstrasse 7, Vienna) has three departures daily (one daily in April and October) passing through the Wachau. From Melk to Krems (1¾ hours, downstream) or from Krems to Melk (three hours, upstream) costs €15.50/20.50 one way/return; shorter journeys between Melk and Spitz cost €9/12 one way/return. **Brandner** (☎ 07433-25 90-21; e schiffahrt@brander.at) offers the same trips at the same prices.

Ardagger (☎ 07479-64 64-0; e dsa@pgv .at) connects Linz and Krems three times a week in each direction during the summer. **Donauschiffahrt Wurm & Köck** (☎ 0732-78 36 07; w www.donauschiffahrt.com; Untere Donaulände 1, Linz) has twice daily services between Linz and Passau in Germany (six hours), which stop in the Wachau.

G Glaser (☎/fax 01-726 08 20; w www .members.aon.at/danube; 02, Handelskai 265, Vienna) sails between Passau and Budapest, stopping at Krems and Melk en route. Most operators carry bicycles free of charge.

The route by road is also scenic. Hwy 3 links Vienna and Linz and stays close to the north bank of the Danube much of the way. There is a cycle track along the south bank from Vienna to Krems, and along both sides of the river from Krems to Linz.

St Pölten is the state capital of Lower Austria, but contact the Lower Austria Information Office mentioned in the Vienna section earlier for region-wide information.

If you stay in the Wachau, be sure to get the guest card. The benefits include free entry to Melk's open-air swimming pool during the summer.

KREMS AN DER DONAU
☎ 02732 • pop 23,000

The historic town of Krems sits on the Danube's north bank, surrounded by terraced vineyards. It consists of three linked areas: Krems, the smaller town of Stein, and the connecting suburb of Und. That's why locals joke that *'Krems und Stein sind drei Städte'* (Krems and Stein are three towns). To best appreciate the surroundings, stroll in and around the cobbled, pedestrian-only main thoroughfare of Landstrasse, noting the baroque houses and adjoining courtyards, gothic churches and ancient city walls.

You'll find the **tourist office** (☎ 826 76; e austropa.krems@netway.at; Undstrasse 6) in the **Kloster Und**, where there are also wine tastings. **Net-Café** (Untere Landstrasse 35) offers Internet access, while bike rental is available from **Hentschl** (☎ 822 83; Wiener-strasse 129).

One of the highlights is the **Weinstadt Museum** (☎ 80 15 67; Körnermarkt 14; adult/concession €3.60/2.50; open 10am-6pm Tues-Sun Mar-Nov). In a former medieval Dominican monastery, it houses some captivatingly ancient animal sculptures.

Places to Stay & Eat

Budget options include **ÖAMTC Camping Krems** (☎ 844 55; Wiedengasse 7; €3.65/2.20-4.36/3.65 per person/tent/car), near the boat station, as well as the HI **Jugendherberge** (☎ 834 52; Ringstrasse 77; dorm beds from €12.20). Both are open April to October.

Gästehaus Einzinger (☎ 823 16, fax -6; Steiner Landstrasse 82, Krems-Stein; singles/doubles €36/48) has atmospheric, individually designed rooms around a leafy courtyard. The stairs are rather precarious, but the decoration is sweet.

Gästehaus Weingut Hutter (☎ 820 06; e hutter-krems@yline.com; Weinzierlbergstrasse 10, Krems; singles/doubles from €31/56) is one of the nicest 'Winzers', where you stay with a wine-growing family in the hills above the town.

You'll find places to eat and a supermarket along Obere and Untere Landstrasse. The tourist office has the opening times of local Heurigen.

Getting There & Away

The boat station *(Schiffsstation)* is a 20-minute walk west from the train station along

Donaulände. Between three and five buses leave daily from outside the train station to Melk (€5.80, 65 minutes). Trains to Vienna (€10.40, one hour) arrive at Franz Josefs Bahnhof.

DÜRNSTEIN
☎ 02711 • pop 1000

Dürnstein, west by road or rail from Krems, is where English king Richard I (the Lionheart) was imprisoned in 1192. His unscheduled stopover on the way home from the Crusades came courtesy of Austrian Archduke Leopold V, whom he had insulted. A trip today to the ruins of the **Künringerburg** castle hints that the kidnapped English monarch, at least potentially, had wonderful views of the Danube.

For more about Dürnstein, contact the **Rathaus** (☎ 219, fax 442; e duernstein@net way.at; Hauptstrasse) or the makeshift **tourist office** (☎ 200; in the train station car park; open Apr-Oct).

MELK
☎ 02752 • pop 6500

Featured in both the epic medieval German poem *Nibelungenlied* and Umberto Eco's bestselling novel *The Name of the Rose*, Melk's impressive Benedictine monastery endures as a major Wachau landmark.

Orientation & Information

The train station is some 300m from the town centre. Walking straight ahead from the train station exit, along Bahnhofstrasse you immediately come to the **post office** (Postamt 3390; open 8am-noon, 2pm-6pm Mon-Fri & 8am-10am Sat), where money exchange is available. Turn right here into Abt Karl Strasse if you're going to the HI hostel. Otherwise, carry straight on. The quickest way to the central Rathausplatz is through the small Bahngasse path (right of the cow's head mural at the bottom of the hill), rather than veering left into Hauptplatz.

Turn right from Bahngasse into Rathausplatz, and right again at the end, following the signs to the **tourist office** (☎ 523 07-410, fax -490; e melk@smaragd.at; Babenbergerstrasse 1; open 9am-noon & 2pm-6pm Mon-Fri & 10am-2pm Sat Apr-Oct; 9am-7pm Mon-Sat & 10am-2pm Sun July & Aug; closed Nov-Mar). Internet access is available at **Teletechnik Wepper** (Wienerstrasse 3).

Things to See & Do

On a hill overlooking the town is the ornate golden abbey **Stift Melk** (☎ 555-232; w www .stiftmelk.at; adult/senior/student under 27 from €5.09/4.72/2.54, guided tours €1.45 extra; open 9am-5pm daily Apr-Nov, to 6pm May-Sept, open for guided tours only Nov-Mar). Once a noble abode, then home to monks since the 11th century, the current building was erected in the 18th century after a devastating fire. Consequently, it's an elaborate example of baroque architecture, most often lauded for its imposing marble hall and beautiful library, but just as unforgettable for the curved terrace connecting these two rooms. You can easily imagine past abbots pausing to take in the views of the Danube and feeling like lord of all they surveyed. (The film *The Name of the Rose* was shot elsewhere.)

Explanatory booklets are available in various languages for €3.50, or phone ahead if you want a tour in English, which works out cheaper.

Places to Stay & Eat

Camping Melk (sites per adult/tent/car €2.60/2.60/1.90; open Mar-Oct) is on the west bank of the canal that joins the Danube. Reception is in restaurant **Melker Fährhaus** (☎ 532 91; Kolomaniau 3; dishes from €5.75; open daily Mar-Oct).

The HI **Jugendherberge** (☎ 526 81, fax 542 57; Abt Karl Strasse 42; dorm beds €11.90, under-19s €9.90; open Apr-Nov, reception closed 10am-5pm) levies a €0.80 surcharge for single-night stays. During the day you can reserve a bed and leave your bags.

Gasthof Weisses Lamm (☎ 540 85; Linzer Strasse 7; from €20 per person) has basic, but reasonably pleasant rooms. On the premises is **Pizzeria Venezia** (open daily), with many tasty pizzas starting at €5.80. **Gasthof Goldener Stern** (☎ 522 14, fax -4; Sterngasse 17; singles/doubles €25/42 without shower & toilet, from €32/54 with private facilities) has been recently renovated, but has retained some cheaper rooms. Even when the adjoining restaurant is shut on Tuesday and Wednesday, the hotel desk is open.

Restaurant **Pasta e Pizza** (Jakob Prandtauerstrasse 4; pizzas from €6) is tucked away from the main tourist trail.

There is a **Spar supermarket** (Rathausplatz 9) for self-caterers.

Street café in-crowd, Innsbruck, Austria

Interior, Museum of Fine Arts, Vienna, Austria

Life on the edge, Andorra la Vella, Andorra

As an in-line skater defies gravity, Vienna's Burgtheater is a captive audience

LEANNE LOGAN

Guildhalls, Grote Markt, Antwerp, Belgium

BRYN THOMAS

Prime real estate in Weymouth, England

PAUL JOHN DOYLE

Party girls, Notting Hill Carnival, London, England

NEIL SETCHFIELD

Party guys, London, England

DOUG McKINLAY

At the third stroke, it will be... Big Ben, London

Getting There & Away

Boats leave from the canal by Pionierstrasse, 400m behind the monastery. Trains to Vienna Westbahnhof (€12, 60 to 70 minutes) are direct or via St Pölten.

LINZ

☎ 0732 • pop 208,000

Poor Linz. Essentially industrial by nature, it discovered years ago that its small old-town centre couldn't compete with Vienna or Salzburg. Its biggest claims to 'fame' were having been Adolf Hitler's favourite town and having a type of cake – Linzer Torte – named after it. So the city decided to carve out a niche for itself in contemporary culture and technology.

Orientation & Information

Most of the town is on the south bank of the Danube. The **tourist office** (☎ 7070-1777, fax 700 11; Hauptplatz 1; open 8am-7pm Mon-Fri, 10am-7pm Sat & Sun, to 6pm Nov-Apr) has a free room-finding service and sells the Linz Museums Card (10 museums for €7.27) and the Linz Card (10 museums, sightseeing tour, restaurant voucher, multiple discounts for €20). It's on the main square, which is reached from the train station via tram No 3 outside.

If you prefer to walk, turn right (northeast) out of the station, then left (north-north-west) at the far side of the park and continue along Landstrasse for 10 minutes.

The large **post office** (Postamt 4020; open 7am-10pm Mon-Fri, 9am-6pm Sat, 9am-1pm Sun) is to the left of the train station exit.

The **provincial tourist office** (☎ 77 12 64, fax 60 02 20; e info@upperaustria.or.at; Schillerstrasse 50; open 9am-noon & 1pm-4.30pm Mon-Thur, 9am-noon Fri) has information on Salzkammergut.

You can surf the Internet at **Bignet** (Promenade 3), while the **Lilo** suburban train station (☎ 65 43 76; Coulinstrasse 30) has bike rental. A **Creditanstalt** bank on Hauptplatz changes money.

Things to See & Do

Suspended from the ceiling of the **Ars Electronica Center** (☎ 72 72-0; Hauptstrasse 2; adult/student €6/3; open 10am-6pm Wed-Sun), and wearing a virtual reality headset, you get an idea of what it's like to fly, as well as having a glimpse of the future. This art and technology centre on the Danube's north bank offers several simulated experiences, including the world's only public 'Cave', a virtual environment where you can travel through space and time. More prosaically, free Internet access is included.

The **Neue Galerie** (☎ 7070 3600; Blütenstrasse 15; adult/student from €5/3; open 10am-6pm Mon-Fri, to 10pm Thur, 10am-1pm Sat) continues the shock-of-the-new theme, with temporary exhibitions ranging from Keith Haring to modern local artists.

The remarkable stained-glass windows depicting the history of the town in the neo-Gothic **Neuer Dom** (New Cathedral; entrances on Hafnerstrasse & Herrenstrasse) have been supplemented by modern designs, too.

For more traditional sightseeing, stroll around the large, baroque **Hauptplatz** or head to the **Schlossmuseum** (castle museum; ☎ 77 44 19; Tummelplatz 10; adult/concession €4/2.20; open Tues-Sun).

Looking like something out of a Western movie, the **Pöstlingbergbahn** (funicular railway; €3.20 return) wends its way to the ornate church and children's grotto railway atop the Pöstlingberg hill.

Tickets for classic music performances during autumn's **Bruckner Festival** (☎ 77 52 30; Brucknerhaus Kasse, Untere Donaulände, A-4010 Linz) should be booked early. The *Pflasterspektakel* performing arts street festival is in summer.

Places to Stay

Camping is southeast of town at **Pichlinger See** (☎ 30 53 14; Wiener Bundesstrasse 937; adult/tent & car €4/9.08; open Apr-Oct).

There are three HI hostels in Linz. The pick of them really is the **Jugendgästehaus** (☎ 66 44 34, fax -75; Stanglhofweg 3; dorm beds €14.39, singles/doubles €19.48/26.74) on bus routes 17, 19 and 27. Dorms are rather cramped in the **Jugendherberge** (☎ 78 27 20, fax 78 17 894; e zentral@jutel.at; Kapuzinerstrasse 14; dorm beds for over/under 19 €12/15; closed around Nov-Mar). The **Landesjugendherberge** (☎ 73 70 78, fax -15; Blütenstrasse 19-23; dorm beds for over/under 19 €9.08/10.90, plus small heating charge Nov-April) caters primarily for school groups and entry is, peculiarly, through a multistorey car park. Each hostel closes its reception at intermittent times, so phone ahead.

AUSTRIA

Recently renovated **Wilder Mann** (☎/fax 65 60 78; e wilder-mann@aon.at; Goethestrasse 14; singles/doubles without shower & toilet €26.20/46.60, with bathroom €31.30/53.80) offers good value in a city that's otherwise pretty short of budget accommodation options.

The mid-priced rooms at **Goldener Anker** (☎/fax 77 10 88; Hofgasse 5; singles/doubles from €42/70) are also quite comfortable and convenient.

Hotel Wolfinger (☎ 77 32 91-0, fax -55; Hauptplatz 19; singles/doubles without shower €40/60, with bathroom €79/110) is a wonderful former cloister renovated in a baroque style. Sadly, it has a very limited number of cheaper rooms.

Places to Eat

There's a **Billa supermarket** (Landstrasse 44), heading towards town from the train station, as well as many Würstel stands.

Mangolds (Hauptplatz 3; salads from €1.13 per 100g; open Mon-Sat) offers self-serve vegie food. The **Josef Stadtbräu** (Landstrasse 49; weekday lunches €6.90) is a popular evening haunt for its beer and beer garden, but it also attracts midday diners. Chinese food is found at **Lotos** (Landstrasse 11; lunch €5.01), and Mexican at **Los Caballeros** (Landstrasse 32; lunch €6.40).

Etagen Bieserl (Domgasse 8; mains from €6.70) is a lively, friendly place to partake of homy Austrian lunches and dinners. Just try not to spoil your appetite beforehand by sampling too much Linzer Torte, a heavy nuttytasting sponge filled with strawberry jam, at **Café Glockenspiel** (Hauptplatz 18)!

Stiegelbräu zum Klosterhof (Landstrasse 30; most mains from €11; open daily) has a huge beer garden, but also a fine gastronomical reputation and seems popular for business lunches and tourist outings alike.

Getting There & Around

Linz is approximately halfway between Salzburg and Vienna on the main road and rail routes. Trains to Salzburg (€16.50) and Vienna (€21.80) both take between 1¼ and two hours.

Trains leave approximately every hour. City transport tickets are bought before you board: €0.70 per journey or €2.90 for a day card. Some of the bus services stop early in the evening.

The South

The two main southern states, Styria (Steiermark) and Carinthia (Kärnten) retain elements of Italian, Slovenian and Hungarian culture, with which they have historical connections.

GRAZ
☎ 0316 • pop 245,000

Graz hopes its reign as European City of Culture in 2003 will bring it the same lasting success as previous incumbents such as Helsinki, Reykjavík and, er, Bergen in Norway. A new art gallery resembling a mutant human organ in design should at least focus some attention on the much-underrated Styrian capital.

Orientation

Austria's second largest city is dominated by its Schlossberg, or castle hill, which looms over the medieval town centre. The River Mur cuts a north-south path west of the hill, dividing the old centre from the main train station. Tram Nos 3, 6 and 14 run from the station to the central Hauptplatz. Several streets radiate from this square, including café-lined Sporgasse and the main pedestrian thoroughfare, Herrengasse, which leads to Jakominiplatz, a major transport hub.

Information

At the train station, there is a basic **tourist information desk** (open 8.30am-5.30pm Mon-Fri). More detailed information is available from the **main tourist office** (☎ 80 75-0, fax -15; e info@graztourismus.at; Herrengasse 16; open 9am-6pm Mon-Fri, 9am-3pm Sat, 10am-3pm Sun Oct-May, 1-2hr later in Jun-Sept). Send mail at the **main post office** (Hauptpostamt 8010; Neutorgasse 46; open 7.30am-8pm Mon-Fri, 8am-noon Sat).

Bicycle (☎ 82 13 57-0; Kaiser-Franz-Josef Kai 56) can rent you a set of two wheels. **Café Zentral** (Andreas Hofer Platz) has Internet access.

Things to See & Do

The tourist office organises guided walks of the city (from €7.50), daily in summer and on Saturday in winter. However, most visitors head straight for the **Schlossberg** to enjoy the views and see the remnants of the city's fortress. These include a **bell tower**, **bastion** and **garrison museum** and the charming

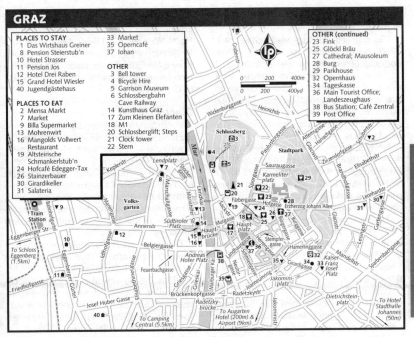

GRAZ

PLACES TO STAY		OTHER (continued)
1 Das Wirtshaus Greiner	33 Market	23 Fink
8 Pension Steierstub'n	35 Operncafé	25 Glöckl Bräu
10 Hotel Strasser	37 Iohan	27 Cathedral; Mausoleum
11 Pension Jos		28 Burg
12 Hotel Drei Raben	**OTHER**	29 Parkhouse
15 Grand Hotel Wiesler	3 Bell tower	32 Opernhaus
40 Jugendgästehaus	4 Bicycle Hire	34 Tageskasse
	5 Garrison Museum	36 Main Tourist Office;
PLACES TO EAT	6 Schlossbergbahn	Landeszeughaus
2 Mensa Markt	Cave Railway	38 Bus Station; Café Zentral
7 Market	14 Kunsthaus Graz	39 Post Office
9 Billa Supermarket	17 Zum Kleinen Elefanten	
13 Mohrenwirt	18 M1	
16 Mangolds Vollwert	20 Schlossberglift; Steps	
Restaurant	21 Clock tower	
19 Altsteirische	22 Stern	
Schmankerlstub'n		
24 Hofcafé Edegger-Tax		
26 Stainzerbauer		
30 Girardikeller		
31 Salateria		

AUSTRIA

clock tower – with its minute and hour hands reversed – which is the emblem of Graz. There are three main ways to ascend: the glass **Schlossberglift** hewn through the hill, the **Schlossbergbahn** funicular railway, and the 260 steps near the lift. Gates are sometimes locked at the top of other paths.

The old town below the hill is a Unesco World Heritage Site. Among its highlights are the **cathedral** (cnr Hofgasse & Bürgergasse) and the **Burg** complex of the Styrian parliament across from it on Hofgasse. Left of the door marked 'Stiege III', there's a **double-winding staircase** as good as any perspective-defying drawing by MC Escher.

The **Mausoleum** of Ferdinand II, behind the cathedral, will be closed for restoration until mid-2003. After that, the tourist office will have admission details.

The **Landeszeughaus** (Armoury; ☎ 82 87 96; Herrengasse 16; adult/student €4.30/60; open 9am-5pm Tues-Sun Mar-Oct, 10am-3pm Tues-Sun Nov & Dec) is lined with row upon deadly row of armour and weapons and explains Graz's history in resisting invasions by Ottoman Turks. Undeniably, these 32,000 pieces represent an important social legacy,

but being in their company is a rather chilling experience.

Schloss Eggenberg (☎ 58 32 64-0; Eggenberger Allee 90; tram No 1; adult/senior or student €5.45/4.30; open Tues-Sun Apr-Oct), an opulent residence 4km west of the centre, harks back to the city's 17th-century past while the bizarre, bubble-shaped **Kunsthaus Graz** (Südtiroler Platz) is shaping up to be part of its future. The opening is scheduled for September 2003, but some local politicians may try to enforce a more conventional design until the last moment possible.

Graz already has many funky street sculptures. Several temporary installations, including an artificial island in the River Mur, will join them for the cultural capital celebrations. Contact **Graz 2003** (☎ 2003; W www.graz03 .at) for information.

Places to Stay

Graz is the nearest city to the Austrian Grand Prix circuit at Spielberg, so some hotels will inevitably fill up when that event is on (in May).

Camping Central (☎ 378 51 02, fax 69 78 24; Martinhofstrasse 3; bus No 32 from Jakominiplatz; single tent site with 1/2 people

€13/20; open Apr-Nov) is 5.5km southwest of the centre.

Closer in is the HI **Jugendgästehaus** (☎ 71 48 76, fax -88; Idlhofgasse 74; beds in 4-bed dorms/doubles with shower & toilet €17/ 21.50, cheaper dorms without private facilities €14 on request, €2.50 surcharge for single-night stays; reception open 7am-10pm Mon-Fri, 7am-10am & 5pm-10pm Sat, Sun & holidays). Right from the cartoon motifs on its facade, it sets a friendly tone.

Hotel Strasser (☎ 71 39 77, fax 71 68 56; e hotel@clicking.at; Eggenberger Gürtel 11; singles/doubles without shower €25.50/42, with shower €32/53) has spacious, well-kept rooms that make it a pleasant surprise for a cheap hotel close to the train station.

The same applies for nearby **Pension Jos** (☎ 71 05 05, fax 71 04 06; Friedhofgasse 14; singles/doubles from €29/51). Rooms come with their own, admittedly small, bathrooms. There's a bell by the driveway to attract attention on arrival.

Pension Steierstub'n (☎/fax 71 68 55; Lendplatz 8; singles/doubles €35/62) seems luxurious for the price, and the pumpkin seeds, rather than chocolates, on the pillow are a nice local touch. But avoid being home around 5pm, when the oompah musicians next door crank it up for an hour or so.

Das Wirtshaus Greiner (☎ 68 50 90, fax -4; e das.wirtshaus.greiner@eunet.at; Grabenstrasse 64; singles/doubles from €40/72) emits a refined air with its white walls and polished floorboards. The restaurant/reception closes at weekends, so phone ahead at those times.

Hotel Stadthalle Johannes (☎/fax 83 77 66; Münzgrabenstrasse 48; singles/doubles from €43/64) has older Italianate decor, but it's been well looked after. A convenient location, a tram stop outside and a nearby sister hotel to accommodate extra guests, add to its appeal.

At **Hotel Drei Raben** (☎ 71 26 86, fax 71 59 59-6; e dreiraben@vivat.at; Annenstrasse 43; singles/doubles from €59/93) you also get value for money. This friendly, modern hotel has satellite TV in all rooms.

The inside of **Augarten** (☎ 208 00-0, fax -80; Schönaugasse 53; singles/doubles from €110/150) aims for a *Wallpaper** magazine style. Expensive modern furnishings in clean lines, with artwork to match, make this a sought-after address.

However, the accolade of being Graz's grande dame of hotels goes to the **Grand Hotel Wiesler** (☎ 70 66-0, fax -76; e wiesler@weitzer.com; Grieskai 4; singles/doubles from €159/209). Its sumptuous Art Deco features include a tiled mural created by a student of Gustav Klimt.

Places to Eat

The Annenpassage shopping centre opposite the train station has a **Billa supermarket**, but if you're self-catering don't miss the **farmers markets** (Kaiser-Franz-Josef Platz; open Mon-Sat • Lendplatz; open Sat). Lendplatz market is reported to operate on weekdays also, but this didn't happen during our visit. It specialises in local produce, including many varieties of apples, fresh fruit juices and schnapps.

Cheap eats are available all around the university, especially at the **Mensa Markt** (Schubertstrasse 2-4; menus for €3.56, €3.85 & €4.29) as well as the cellar bar **Girardikeller** (Leonhardstrasse 28; pizzas, lasagnes, Spätzle all €4; open 5pm-2am Tues-Fri, 6pm-2am Sat, plus 4am-9am 'breakfast club' Fri, Sat & Sun).

Vegetarian lunches are served at **Salateria** (Leonhardstrasse 18; mains from €3.30; open 11am-2pm Mon-Fri), and at other times at **Mangolds Vollwert Restaurant** (Griesgasse 11; salad from €1.05 per 100g; open 11am-8pm Mon-Fri, 11am-4pm Sat).

Thanks to its salads in pumpkinseed oil, fish specialities and *Pfand'l* grilled pan dishes, Styrian cuisine feels healthier than other regional Austrian cooking. Good places to sample it include the low-key inn **Mohrenwirt** (Mariahilfer Strasse 16; mains from €5; open Sat-Wed), the rustic **Altsteirische Schmankerlstub'n** (Sackstrasse 10; mains from €9; open daily) and the high-quality **Stainzerbauer** (Bürgergasse 4; mains from €12; closed Sun).

Iohan (☎ 82 13 12; Landhausgasse 1; mains from €13; open Tues-Sat for dinner) is the city's classiest restaurant. It's located in the former cold storage room of the city hall.

When looking for a typical Austrian coffee house, **Hofcafé Edegger-Tax** (Hofgasse 8; open Mon-Fri, Sat morning) might tempt with its stunning sculptured wood facade, but **Operncafé** (Opernring 22; open daily) is more atmospheric inside.

Entertainment

Many favourite nightspots double as restaurants, among them **Stern** *(Sporgasse 38)*, which draws a wide crowd, and the more exclusive **Fink** *(Freheitsplatz 2)*. **Zum Kleinen Elefanten** *(Neu Weltgasse 3)* is a relaxed café that also hosts a wide range of live bands.

Graz, like Vienna, has an area of bars known as the Bermudadreieck. This one is located between Sporgasse, Färbergasse and Stempfergasse, where you'll find venues ranging from the humble **Glöckl Bräu** *(Glockenspielplatz 2-3)* to the third-floor **M1** *(Färbergasse 1)*, favoured by the beautiful people. M1 is more relaxed by day, when it's pleasant just to have a drink on its rooftop terrace.

If the weather's warm, you also want to head for **Parkhouse** *(Stadtpark 2)*. This island of bonhomie in the city park is a great place to meet locals, and at night, with music pumping out at the trees, there's a special vibe.

Graz hosts classical and other musical events throughout the year. The **Tageskasse** *(☎ 8000; Kaiser Josef Platz 10)* sells tickets without commission for the **Opernhaus** (opera). Cheap student deals, last-minute returns as well as standing-room tickets are all available.

Getting There & Away

Low-cost Ryanair flies from London Stansted daily; check **w** www.ryanair.com for prices. Direct IC trains to Vienna's Südbahnhof depart every two hours (€24.70, 2¾ hours). Trains depart every two hours to Salzburg (€33.40, 4¼ hours), either direct or changing at Bischofshofen. Two daily direct trains depart for Ljubljana (€32.70, four hours), and every hour or two to Budapest via Szentgotthard and Szombathely (€41, 6½ hours). Trains to Klagenfurt (€26.10, three hours) go via Bruck an der Mur. The bus station is at Andreas Hofer Platz. The A2 autobahn from Vienna to Klagenfurt passes a few kilometres south of the city.

Getting Around

Public transport tickets cover the Schlossbergbahn (castle-hill railway) that runs from Sackstrasse up the Schlossberg and bus No 631 to/from the airport. Tickets cost €1.45 each (€11.63 for a strip of 10). The 24-hour/weekly passes cost €3.05/7.27. If you're driving, blue parking zones allow a three-hour stop (€0.50 for 30 minutes) during specified times.

AROUND GRAZ

The stud farm that produces the Lipizzaner stallions which perform in Vienna is about 40km west of Graz at **Piber** *(adult/senior/ student €10/8/5; open Easter-end Oct)*. Get basic details from the Graz tourist office. It's also possible to make a day trip from Graz to **Bärnbach**, where there's a remarkable parish church created by Hundertwasser and other artists.

KLAGENFURT

☎ 0463 • pop 87,000

The capital of Carinthia (Kärnten), Klagenfurt seems rather unassuming to be the seat of power of Austria's most controversial politician in recent years. Jörg Haider was first elected provincial governor here in 1989, but the tourist industry revolves around the nearby lake and theme park of tiny famous buildings instead.

Orientation & Information

The heart of the city is Neuer Platz (New Square), which is 1km north of the main train station; walk straight down Bahnhofstrasse and turn left into Paradiesergasse to get there. Across the square, in the Rathaus, you'll find the **tourist office** *(☎ 53 72 23, fax 53 72 95;* **e** *tourismus@klagenfurt.at; open 8am-8pm Mon-Fri, 10am-5pm Sat, 10am & holidays May-Sept, 8am-6.30pm Mon-Fri, 10am-3pm Sat & Sun otherwise)*. The **main post office** *(Postamt 9010; Dr Hermann Gasse)* is one block west of Neuer Platz. Bikes can be hired from **Verein Zweirad Impulse** *(☎ 51 63 10)*, which has several rental points around town. Internet access is available at **Gates Cafebar** *(Waagplatz 7)*.

Things to See & Do

The **Neuer Platz** (New Square) is dominated by the town emblem, the Dragon Fountain. At the west end of the pedestrianised **Alter Platz** (Old Square) is the 16th-century **Landhaus**, with a striking **Hall of Arms** *(Wappensaal; adult/student €2/1; open Sat & Sun Apr-Sept)*. Paintings of 655 coats of arms cover the walls, while the trompe l'oeil ceiling creates the illusion of a balcony above them.

The **Wörther See**, 4km west of the centre, is one of the region's warmer lakes, thanks to subterranean thermal springs. You can swim or go boating in summer. Steamers also embark on circular tours; get details from **STW**

AUSTRIA

(☎ 211 55; e schifffahrt@stw.at). Neighbouring Europa Park has various attractions, including the touristy **Minimundus** (☎ 211 94-0; Villacher Strasse 241; adult/senior & student/child €10/8.50/4.50; open daily Apr-Oct), which displays more than 150 models of famous international buildings on a 1:25 scale.

Places to Stay
Choose **Camping Strandbad** (☎ 211 69, fax -93) in Europa Park and you'll be close to many major attractions in summer.

The modern HI **Jugendherberge** (☎ 23 00 20, fax -20; Neckheimgasse 6; beds in 4-bed dorms €16.30, doubles €19.93; reception open 7am-11am, 5pm-10pm) is also near the university and Europa Park and offers Internet access. Bus 12 is the closest stop.

Back in town, **Pension Klepp** (☎ 322 78; Platzgasse 4; singles/doubles €22/36.50 without breakfast) is a good, cheap option.

Hotel Liebetegger (☎ 569 35, fax -6; Völkermarkter Strasse 8; singles/doubles €32/51 without breakfast) is classier and more recently renovated.

Places to Eat
The **University Mensa** (Universitätsstrasse 90; mains from €4.10; open 11am-2.30pm Mon-Fri) is by Europa Park, while back in the centre, the stalls in the **Benediktinerplatz market** serve hot meals for only about €4.

Gasthaus Pirker (cnr Adlergasse & Lidmanskygasse; mains from €5.80) has cheap Austrian food, while **Zum Augustin** (Pfarrhofgasse 2; mains from €7.20) impresses just as much with its tasty regional food as it does with its range of beers. Hip **Pankraz** (8 de Mai Strasse 16; sandwiches €3.50) is mainly a café, but does sell snacks. It attracts a wide range of people from students and Goths to yuppies.

Getting There & Around
Ryanair flies from London daily. Trains to Graz depart every one to two hours (€33.40, three hours). Trains to western Austria, Italy and Germany go via Villach, 40 minutes away.

Bus drivers sell single tickets (€1.60), while a strip of 10 costs €12 from ticket machines. Passes for 24 hours cost €3.30, for a week €13. For the Europa Park vicinity, take bus No 10, 11, 12, 20, 21 or 22 from Heiligengeistplatz in the centre. To the airport, take bus No 42 or a taxi (about €15).

Salzburg

☎ 0662 • pop 145,000

Salzburg certainly has chocolate-box appeal (literally, in fact, when it comes to the rows of Mozartkugeln confectionery named after its most famous son). From its quaint old town nestled below the medieval Hohensalzburg Fortress to its baroque palace and manicured gardens, the city presents one picture-postcard vista after another.

If that and Mozart weren't enough to explain why it's Austria's second biggest tourist destination after Vienna, there's also the Von Trapp family story, which was partly filmed here. Yup, them thar' hills are alive to The Sound of Music.

Orientation
The city centre is split by the River Salzach. The old part of town (mostly pedestrianised) is on the left (south) bank, with the Hohensalzburg Fortress on the hill above. Most attractions are this side of the river, as is the fashionable shopping street of Getreidegasse. On the right (north) bank is the new town and business centre, where you'll find most of the cheaper hotels.

Information
Tourist Offices The **main tourist office** (☎ 889 87-330, hotel reservations ☎ 889 87-314, fax -32; Mozartplatz 5; open 9am-6pm daily May-Oct, to 7pm in Dec, July & Aug, 9am-6pm Mon-Sat otherwise) will book rooms, at €2.20 commission for up to two people or €4 for three people or more. There is a **provincial information section** (☎ 66 88 0; open 9am-6pm Mon-Fri, 9am-3.30pm Sat) in the same building as the main tourist office.

The information office at the train station on platform 2a is also open throughout the year; the Mitte (central) office at Münchner Bundesstrasse 1 and that in the south at Park & Ride Parkplatz, Alpensiedlung Süd, Alpenstrasse, are open from Easter to November; the office in the north, at Autobahnstation Kasern, is open from June to September.

Tourist offices and hotels sell the Salzburg Card, which provides free museum entry and public transport, and gives various reductions. The price is €18/26/32 for 24/48/72 hours (students get a 10% discount).

SALZBURG

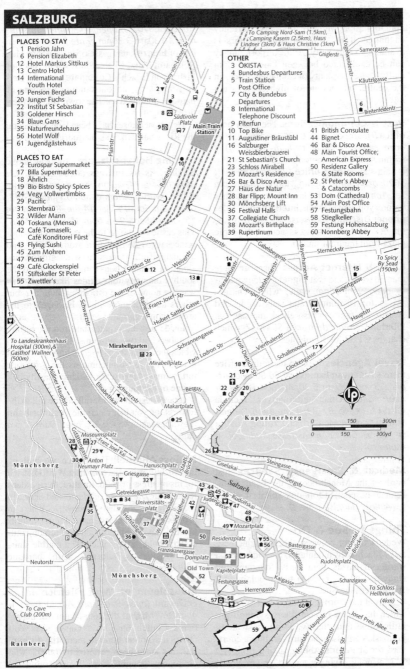

PLACES TO STAY
1. Pension Jahn
6. Pension Elizabeth
12. Hotel Markus Sittikus
13. Centro Hotel
14. International Youth Hotel
15. Pension Bergland
20. Junger Fuchs
22. Institut St Sebastian
23. Goldener Hirsch
34. Blaue Gans
56. Naturfreundehaus
56. Hotel Wolf
61. Jugendgästehaus

PLACES TO EAT
2. Eurospar Supermarket
5. Billa Supermarket
18. Ährlich
19. Bio Bistro Spicy Spices
24. Vegy Vollwertimbiss
29. Pacific
31. Sternbräu
32. Wilder Mann
40. Toskana (Mensa)
42. Café Tomaselli; Café Konditorei Fürst
43. Flying Sushi
45. Zum Mohren
47. Picnic
49. Café Glockenspiel
51. Stiftskeller St Peter
55. Zwettler's

OTHER
3. ÖKISTA
4. Bundesbus Departures
5. Train Station Post Office
7. City & Bundesbus Departures
8. International Telephone Discount
9. Piterfun
10. Top Bike
11. Augustiner Bräustübl
16. Salzburger Weissbierbrauerei
21. St Sebastian's Church
23. Schloss Mirabell
25. Mozart's Residence
26. Bar & Disco Area
27. Haus der Natur
28. Bar Flipp; Mount Inn
30. Mönchsberg Lift
36. Festival Halls
37. Collegiate Church
38. Mozart's Birthplace
39. Rupertinum
41. British Consulate
44. Bignet
46. Bar & Disco Area
48. Main Tourist Office; American Express
50. Residenz Gallery & State Rooms
52. St Peter's Abbey & Catacombs
53. Dom (Cathedral)
54. Main Post Office
57. Festungsbahn
58. Stieglkeller
59. Festung Hohensalzburg
60. Nonnberg Abbey

AUSTRIA

Money Banks are open 8am to noon and 2pm to 4.30pm Monday to Friday. Currency exchange at the train station counters is available to 8pm daily. At the airport, money can be exchanged between 8am and 8pm daily. There are plenty of exchange offices in the centre, but beware of high commission rates.

Post & Communications The **main post office** (*Hauptpostamt 5010; Residenzplatz 9; open 7am-7pm Mon-Fri, 8am-10am Sat*) is within sight of the tourist office. There's also a train station **post office** (*Bahnhofspostamt 5020; open 7am-8.30pm Mon-Fri, 8am-2pm Sat, 1pm-6pm Sun*) for last-minute dispatches before you leave town. **International Telephone Discount** (*Kaiserschützenstrasse 8; open 9am-11pm daily*) is across the large plaza from the train station.

Email & Internet Access There are more than 30 workstations at **Bignet** (*Judengasse 5-7; open 9am-10pm daily*) which charges €1.45 for 10 minutes and sells drinks and sweets, but you can also check messages at **Piterfun** (*Ferdinand-Porsche-Strasse 7*) which charges €1.80 for 10 minutes.

Travel Agencies Next to the tourist office there's **American Express** (*☎ 80 80; Mozartplatz 5; open 9am-5.30pm Mon-Fri, 9am-noon Sat*). Other alternatives include **ÖKISTA** (*☎ 45 87 33; Fanny-von-Lehnert Strasse 1; open Mon-Fri*) and **Young Austria** (*☎ 62 57 58-0; Alpenstrasse 108a; open Mon-Fri*).

Medical & Emergency Services Just north of the Mönchsberg is the Landeskrankenhaus hospital, **St Johanns-Spital** (*☎ 44 82-0; Müllner Hauptstrasse 48*).

Things to See & Do

Wedged tightly between the Kapuzinerberg and Mönchsberg mountains, the old city is a warren of plazas, courtyards, fountains and churches, which Unesco has proclaimed a World Heritage Site.

Start at the **Dom** (cathedral) on Domplatz, which has three bronze doors symbolising faith, hope and charity. Head west along Franziskanergasse, and turn left into a courtyard for **St Peter's Abbey**, dating from AD 847. Among lovingly tended graves you'll find the entrance to the **catacombs** (*adult/ student €1/0.70; open 10.30am-5pm summer, 10.30am-3.30pm winter*). The western end of Franziskanergasse opens out into Max Reinhardt Platz, where you'll see the back of Fisher von Erlach's **Collegiate Church** (*Universitätsplatz*), an outstanding example of baroque architecture. The town is at its prettiest at night.

New boat cruises have been launched along the River Salzach. Ask the tourist office.

Festung Hohensalzburg Towering above Salzburg is its **fortress** (*☎ 84 24 30-11; Mönchsberg 34; admission to grounds only €3.56, with interiors & audio guide €7.12; open 9am-6pm 15 Mar-14 Jun, 8.30am-7pm 15 Jun-14 Sept, 9am-5pm 15 Sept-14 Mar*). This castle was home to the many archbishopprinces who ruled Salzburg from AD 798, and the magnificent views from its grounds include an isolated house in a big field to the south. Some city tour guides like to say this was the home of the official executioner, but others admit it more likely belonged to the archbishop's groundskeeper.

Inside are the ornate state rooms, torture chambers and two museums. The opulence in which the archbishops lived is impressive, but perhaps not as compelling as the grotesque torture masks and scary-looking chastity belt in one of the museums.

It takes 15 minutes to walk up the hill to the fortress, or you can catch the **Festungsbahn** (*Festungsgasse 4; €2.80; open 9am-10pm daily*).

Schloss Mirabell This palace was built by the worldly prince-archbishop Wolf Dietrich for his mistress in 1606. Its attractive gardens featured in *The Sound of Music*, and brides in white dresses and their grooms flock here in droves in summer to have their pictures taken. 'Musical Spring' concerts (among others) are held in the palace. The marble staircase inside is adorned with baroque sculptures.

Mausoleum of Wolf Dietrich In the graveyard (*open 9am-7pm Apr-Oct, 9am-4pm Nov-Mar*) of the 16th-century St Sebastian's Church on Linzer Gasse sits Wolf Dietrich's not-so-humble memorial to himself. It's since been restored by others, who obviously thought it worth preserving the amusingly bombastic epitaphs here. Both Mozart's father and widow are buried in the graveyard.

Museums It's supremely ironic that although Mozart found Salzburg stifling and couldn't wait to leave, his life here is one of the city's major tourist drawcards. People flock to Mozart's **Geburtshaus** (Birthplace; ☎ 84 43 13; Getreidegasse 9; adults/students & seniors €5.50/4.50; open 9am-6pm daily, to 7pm July & Aug) and his **Wohnhaus** (Residence; ☎ 87 42 27-40; Makartplatz 8; admission & hours as for Geburtshaus) to see musical instruments, sheet music, letters, family paintings and other memorabilia of the composer's early years. A combined ticket to both houses is €9 (students and seniors €7). The Wohnhaus is more extensive, and houses the **Mozart Sound and Film Museum** (admission free).

In the **Residenz** (☎ 80 42-2690; Residenzplatz 1; €7.25/5.50 adult/student), you can visit the archbishops' baroque state rooms and a gallery housing good 16th- and 17th-century Dutch and Flemish paintings. The **Rupertinum** (☎ 80 42 23 36; Wiener Philharmoniker Gasse 9; adult/student €7/4.36; open 10am-5pm Tues-Sun) contains contemporary art.

The **Haus der Natur** (Museum of Natural History; ☎ 84 26 53 Museumsplatz 5; adult/senior/student under 27 €4.50/4/2.50; open 9am-5pm daily) is a surprise hit in a city normally preoccupied with music and the baroque. Schoolchildren and adults flock to see rooms full of crystals, watch the moon diorama, watch sharks being fed and generally learn about the animal world.

Organised Tours

One-hour walking tours (€8) of the old city leave from the main tourist office. Other tours of Salzburg mostly leave from Mirabellplatz, including regular *Sound of Music* tours.

This tour is enduringly popular with the English-speaking visitors, even if there's a certain tackiness about it.

It lasts three to four hours, costs around €29 and takes in sights in the city, including a passing wave at the **Nonnberg Abbey** that featured in the movie, as well as some neighbouring Salzkammergut.

Some visitors find the proceedings quite dull. Yet, if you go with a group with the right tongue-in-cheek enthusiasm, it can be brilliant fun. Consider yourself blessed if you find

yourself among manic Julie Andrews impersonators flouncing in the fields, screeching 'the hills are alive', or with loutish youths who skip about chanting 'I am 16 going on 17'. Unfortunately, there's no longer access to the summer house where this last song was performed, as, according to one reader:

The gazebo is now locked. No tourists can leap from bench to bench as a result of an 85-year-old fan imitating Liesel and falling – breaking a hip.
J Smethurst

Special Events

The **Salzburg International Festival** (w www .salzburgfestival.at) takes place from late July to the end of August, and includes music ranging from Mozart (of course!) to contemporary. Several events take place each day in different locations. Prices range from €12 to €340. The cheapest tickets are for standing-room, which can usually be booked beforehand. Most things sell out months in advance. Write for information as early as October to: **Kartenbüro der Salzburger Festspiele** (Postfach 140, A-5010 Salzburg). Try checking closer to the event for cancellations – inquire at the **ticket office** (☎ 80 45, fax -401; Herbert von Karajan Platz 11; open 9.30am-7pm, until the last daily performance during the festival), behind the horse fountain. Other important music festivals are at Easter and Whit Sunday.

Places to Stay

Ask for the tourist office's hotel brochure, which gives prices for hotels, pensions, hostels and camping grounds. Accommodation is at a premium during festivals.

Camping Just north of the A1 Nord exit is **Camping Kasern** (☎/fax 45 05 76; e camp ingkasern@aon.at; Carl Zuckmayer Strasse 4; sites per adult/car/tent €4.50/3/3; open Apr-Oct). **Camping Nord-Sam** (☎/fax 66 04 94; Samstrasse 22a; sites per adult/car & tent €5.50/8; open Easter & May-Sept) is slightly closer to town.

Private Rooms The tourist office's list of private rooms and apartments doesn't include the Kasern area, as this is just north of the city limits. But this area, up the hill from the Salzburg-Maria Plain mainline train station (warning – not the Maria-Plain station on the local train network), has the best bargains.

AUSTRIA

Haus Lindner (☎ 45 66 81; e info@haus-lindner.at; Panoramaweg 5; €15 per person in double & triple rooms) is one of the most popular. Its comfortable rooms and its homy atmosphere make it feel like you're staying with friends. Although breakfast is provided, there are kitchen facilities, too.

Another good option among the forest of 'Zimmer frei' (rooms vacant) signs is neighbouring **Haus Christine** (☎ 45 67 73; Panoramaweg 3; €14-15 per person).

Hostels If you're travelling to party, head for the sociable **International Youth Hotel** (YoHo; ☎ 87 96 49, fax 87 88 10; e office@yoho.at; w www.yoho.at; Paracelsusstrasse 9; 8-bed dorms/4-bed dorms/doubles €14/16/19, including 1 free shower a day; open all day). There's a bar with loud music and cheap beer, the staff are mostly young, native English-speakers, outings are organised and The Sound of Music is screened daily. This place accepts phone reservations no earlier than one day in advance, although you can book ahead on the Internet. There are separate charges for extra showers (€1), lockers (€0.50 to €1) and breakfast (€3).

The large HI **Jugendgästehaus** (☎ 84 26 70-0, fax 84 11 01; e jgh.salzburg@jgh.at; Josef Preis Allee 18; 8-bed dorms/4-bed dorms/doubles from €13.34/17.44/21.80, surcharge for single-night stays €2.50; check-in from 11am, although reception closed intermittently during the day) is probably the most comfortable hostel. It has free lockers, a bar and a small kitchen. Daily Sound of Music tours are the cheapest in town at €25.45 for anybody who shows up by 8.45am or 1.30pm. The film is also shown daily.

To reach **Institut St Sebastian** (☎ 87 13 86, fax -85; e office@st-sebastian-salzburg.at; Linzer Gasse 41; dorm beds without/with sheets €14.50/16.70, singles/doubles without shower & toilet €26/38.50, with facilities €30.50/52.30), you turn through the gate marked 'Feuerwache Bruderhof'. This hostel has a roof terrace and kitchens, but the sound of church bells is loud in some rooms.

The **Naturfreundehaus** (☎/fax 84 17 29; Mönchsberg 19; dorm beds €12.50-13.50, showers €0.80; 1am curfew, open mid-April to mid-Oct) compensates for its fairly ordinary dorm rooms with priceless views over the city. High on the Mönchsberg hill, this hostel is reached via the Mönchsberg lift

(€2.40 return) from A Neumayr Platz or by climbing the stairs from Toscanini Hof, behind the Festival Halls. There's also a café. Sometimes, its too cold to open the unheated rooms, so phone ahead.

Hotels & Pensions – Budget Centrally located **Junger Fuchs** (☎ 87 54 96; Linzer Gasse 54; singles/doubles/triples €25.50/33.50/44 without breakfast) remains a solid, if unremarkable, budget choice. Its cramped stairwell opens out into reasonably sized rooms with wooden floorboards.

Rooms at **Pension Jahn** (☎ 87 14 05, fax 87 55 35; Elisabethenstrasse 31; singles/doubles from €31/43, doubles with private shower €64) are also fairly spartan, but clean. And the pension is handy for the train station.

Gasthof Wallner (☎ 84 50 23, fax -3; Aiglhofstrasse 15; singles/doubles €26/42, singles/doubles/quads with private bathroom €40/60/85) hardly seems like it's in Salzburg, as it lies on the opposite side of the Mönchsberg from the old town. However, it's only a 10-minute ride from the centre on bus No 29 from Hanuschplatz. The reception faces a main road, but the pleasant, airy rooms are in a separate building set back from the street.

Pension Elisabeth (☎/fax 87 16 64; Vogelweiderstrasse 52; singles/doubles €33/39, singles/doubles with bathroom €42/64) has been nicely renovated in recent years, making it Salzburg's top budget choice. It's near the Breitenfelderstrasse stop of bus No 15, which heads for town every 15 minutes.

Hotels & Pensions – Mid-Range & Top End For an option that really does possess the personal atmosphere it boasts of, try **Pension Bergland** (☎ 87 23 18, fax -8; e pkuhn@berglandhotel.at; Rupertgasse 15; singles/doubles €50/80). Small, family-run, with individual touches in each folksy room, it's a 15-minute walk from the old town.

The friendly staff at **Centro Hotel** (☎ 88 22 21, fax -55; e centro-hotel@Salzburg.co.at; Auerspergstrasse 24; singles/doubles €66/104) are happy to show you to the lift or free overnight parking. This is a fairly new hotel and its modern rooms are spotless, if a trifle bland. The hotel caters for many youth groups.

Hotel Markus Sittikus (☎ 87 11 21-0, fax -58; Markus Sittikus Strasse 20; singles/doubles €73/110) is more formal, possibly due to its location near the Salzburg Congress Centre.

With all mod cons, however, it's a very pleasant place to stay.

Being housed in medieval buildings, many hotels in the historic city centre have rather musty and gloomy interiors. **Hotel Wolf** (☎ 84 34 53-0, fax 84 24 23-4; e office@hotelwolf .com; Kaigasse 7; singles/doubles from €68/ 98) manages to avoid that, while retaining the essential character of its 500-year-old abode. It's an ideal mix of quaint bedrooms and tasteful bathrooms.

Blaue Gans (☎ 84 24 91, fax -9; e office@ blauegans.at; Getreidegasse 41-43; singles/ doubles from €115/119) also offers modern luxury (just think blond-wood furniture and frosted-glass bathroom doors) in a historic setting.

If you prefer baroque decor, **Goldener Hirsch** (☎ 80 84-0, fax 84 33 49; Getreidegasse 37; singles/doubles from €129/165) is one of the best places in town.

Places to Eat

There's a **fruit and vegetable market** at Mirabellplatz on Thursday morning. On Universitätsplatz and Kapitelplatz there are **market stalls** and **fast-food stands**. There's a **Billa supermarket** (Schallmooser Hauptstrasse) and a **Eurospar supermarket** (open 8am-7pm Mon-Fri, 7.30am-5pm Sat) situated by the train station.

Places to Eat – Budget The most convenient university mensa is **Toskana** (Sigmund Haffner Gasse 11), where lunches are served from 11.30am to 2pm on weekdays, and cost from €2.50 for students, €3.50 for others.

Sushi and salads are available from **Flying Sushi** (Rudolfskai 8; boxes to eat-in or takeaway from €5.80).

For vegetarian nourishment on weekdays, try **Vegy Vollwertimbiss** (Schwarzstrasse 21; salads from €3, lunch menu €7.20; open 11am-5pm), or the holistic **Bio Bistro Spicy Spices** (☎ 87 07 12; Wolf-Dietrich-Strasse 1; mains €5, salads €3). At weekends, you can walk 15 minutes to the latter's sister restaurant **Spicy by Sead** (Schallmooser Hauptstrasse 48), which offers much the same deal.

Picnic (Judengasse 15; sandwiches from €4.72, pasta from €5.67; open daily May-Sept, otherwise closed on Tues) seems an enduringly popular joint. It serves cheap snacks, including 'big sandwiches' so big you can't get your mouth around them.

Wilder Mann (in the passageway off Getreidegasse 20; mains €5-7.90; open Mon-Fri), serves traditional Austrian food in a friendly, bustling environment. Tables, both inside and out, are often so packed it's almost impossible not to get chatting with fellow diners.

Stadtalm (Mönchsberg 19c; mains from €6.80; open daily mid-Apr–mid-Oct) is a great place to tuck into a well-priced meal while you admire the view.

For coffee houses, try **Café Tomaselli**, **Café Konditorei Fürst** (both on Alter Markt) or **Café Glockenspiel** (Mozartplatz 2).

Places to Eat – Mid-Range & Top End

Just off Mozartplatz, **Zwettler's** (Kaigasse 3; mains €6.50-10.50; open Mon-Sat for dinner) serves up Italo-Austrian cuisine, from Wiener Schnitzel, Styrian chicken breast and beef goulash to spinach gnocchi. Its Salzburger Nockerl (soufflé) is renowned.

Ährlich (Wolf Dietrich Strasse 7; mains €9.50-16.30; open Mon-Sat) has given local cuisine a healthy twist, and serves vegetarian as well as meat-based mains.

However, for a complete antidote to feeling weighed down by stodgy fare, sample the sharp, fresh tastes of Thai restaurant **Pacific** (☎ 84 22 88; Franz Josef Kai 13; noodle dishes from €7, curries from €11; open Mon-Sat evenings).

Two huge dining complexes, with a series of different rooms, hark back to a different era, although both are a bit touristy. **Sternbräu** (between Getreidegasse 36 & Griesgasse 23; mains from €5.60; open daily) serves Austrian food, such as Tafelspitz, and fish when in season. The adjoining courtyard features a self-service summer buffet and a pizzeria. **Stiftskeller St Peter** (☎ 84 12 68-34; St Peter Bezirk I/4; mains from €10; open daily) is more upmarket. It offers healthy options like asparagus or cottage cheese, smoked salmon and wasabi, but determinedly old-fashioned dishes are also on the menu. Even if you don't eat in the complex's baroque main salon, have a quick look inside.

Cellar restaurant **Zum Mohren** (☎ 484 23 87; Judengasse 9; mains from €12; open Mon-Sat) offers traditional food in a reasonably formal environment.

Entertainment

When you enter **Augustiner Bräustübl** (Augustinergasse 4-6; open 3pm-11pm Mon-Fri,

AUSTRIA

2.30pm-11pm Sat & Sun) you hear the contented hum of the crowd well before you descend the steps into the beer halls or garden. The brew produced by local monks – served in litre (€5) or half-litre (€2.50) ceramic mugs – is doing a good job as a social lubricant. Other convivial beer halls include **Stieglkeller** *(Festungsgasse 10; open 10am-10pm daily Apr-Oct)*, which has a garden overlooking the town, and **Salzburger Weissbierbrauerei** *(cnr Rupertgasse & Virgilgasse)*.

There's a lively stretch of bars, clubs and discos near the Hotel Altstadt on Rudolfskai, including **Irish pubs** with live music. Directly across the river, there's also a little scene along Steingasse. However, things in both these strips generally quieten down soon after midnight. Real night owls need to head to **Bar Flip** *(Gstättengasse 17)*, or **Mount Inn** *(Gstättengasse 21)*, establishments which both keep humming until 4am.

The legendary **Cave Club** *(☎ 84 00 26; w www.cave-club.at; Leopoldskronstrasse 26)* is still pumping out hard-core techno. Phone ahead or check the website to see what's on.

Shopping

The obvious souvenir is confectionery, particularly *Mozartkugeln*. These chocolate-coated combinations of nougat and marzipan cost around €0.45 per piece (cheaper in supermarkets), available individually or in presentation packs.

Getting There & Away

Air The airport *(☎ 85 80)* handles regular scheduled flights to Amsterdam, Brussels, Frankfurt, London, Paris and Zürich. Contact **Austrian Airlines** *(☎ 85 45 11-0)* there or go online to no-frills **Ryanair** *(w www.ryanair.com)*, which has two flights a day (three on Saturday) from London.

Bus Bundesbuses to Kitzbühel (€12 one way, 2¼ hours, at least three times daily) and other ski resorts depart from Südtiroler Platz across from the train station post office. Those to the Salzkammergut region now leave from just to the left of the main station exit. Destinations include Bad Ischl (€7.40, 1¾ hours), Mondsee (€4.50, 50 minutes), St Gilgen (€4.50, 50 minutes) and St Wolfgang (€6.70, 1½ hours). There are timetable boards at each departure point and a bus information office

in the train station. Alternatively, call ☎ 4660-333 for information.

Train Fast trains leave for Vienna (€33.40, 3¼ hours) via Linz every hour. The express service to Klagenfurt (€26.10, three hours) goes via Villach. The quickest way to Innsbruck (two hours) is by the 'corridor' train through Germany via Kufstein; trains depart at least every two hours and the fare is €27.60. There are trains every 30 to 60 minutes to Munich (€21.60, two hours).

Car & Motorcycle Three autobahns converge on Salzburg and form a loop round the city: the A1 from Linz, Vienna and the east; the A8/E52 from Munich and the west; and the A10/E55 from Villach and the south. Heading south to Carinthia on the A10, there are two tunnels through the mountains; the combined toll is €10 (€7 for motorcycles).

Getting Around

To/From the Airport Salzburg airport is 4km directly west of the city centre. Bus No 77 goes there from the main train station. A taxi costs about €12.

Bus Bus drivers sell single bus tickets for €1.60. Other tickets must be bought from the automatic machines at major stops, Tabak shops or tourist offices. Day passes are €2.90 and weeklies cost €9. Prices are 50% less for children aged six to 15 years; those under six travel free.

Car & Motorcycle Don't drive in the city centre. Parking places are scarce and much of the old town is pedestrianised. The largest central park is the Altstadt Garage under the Mönchsberg. Attended car parks cost €1.40 to €2.40 an hour. On streets with automatic ticket machines (blue zones), a three-hour maximum applies (€3, or €0.50 for 30 minutes) during specified times – usually shopping hours.

Other Transport Flag fall in a taxi is €2.40 (€3.20 at night), plus about €1.10 per kilometre inside the city or €1.60 per kilometre outside the city. To book a taxi, call ☎ 87 44 00. **Top Bike** *(☎ 0676 476 72 59)* rents bikes from the Intertreff Café just outside the train station and from the main city bridge. A pony-and-trap *(fiaker)* ride for up to four passengers costs €30.50 for 25 minutes.

AROUND SALZBURG
Hellbrunn

Four kilometres south of Salzburg's old-town centre is the popular **Schloss Hellbrunn** *(☎ 82 03 72-0; Fürstenweg 37; adult/student €7.50/5.50; open 9am-4.30pm, April & Oct, to 5.30pm in May, June & Sept, to 10pm in July & Aug)*. Built in the 17th century by bishop Markus Sittikus, Wolf Dietrich's nephew, this castle is mainly known for its ingenious trick fountains and water-powered figures. When the tour guides set them off, expect to get wet! Admission includes a tour of the **baroque palace**. Other parts of the garden (without fountains) are open year-round and free to visit.

The **Hellbrunn Zoo** *(adult/student €6.50/4.70; open 8.30am-6.60pm daily in summer, 8.30am-4.30pm daily in winter)* is as naturalistic and open-plan as possible.

Getting There & Away City bus No 55 runs to the palace every half-hour from Salzburg Hauptbahnhof, via Rudolfskai in the old town (Salzburg tickets are valid).

Hallein
☎ 06245 • pop 20,000

Hallein's prime attraction is the **salt mine** *(Salzbergwerk; ☎ 825 85 15; open 9am-5pm daily Apr-Oct, 11am-3pm Nov-Mar)* at Bad Dürrnberg, situated on the hill above. Much of Salzburg's past prosperity was dependent upon salt mines, and this one is the easiest to visit from the city. Some people rave about the experience, while others find the one-hour tour disappointing and overpriced (adults/student €15.50/9.30). Careering down the wooden slides in the caves is fun, and you get a brief raft trip on the salt lake, but there's little else to see. Overalls are supplied. The salt-mine tours in the Salzkammergut are cheaper – see the Salzkammergut section later in this chapter.

The Hallein **tourist office** *(☎ 853 94; e info-tg@eunet.at; Mauttorpromenade; open 9am-6pm Mon-Thur, 9am-8pm Fri-Sat, 10am-3pm Sun July–mid-Sept, otherwise 10am-6pm Mon-Thur, 10am-8pm Fri)* is on the narrow island adjoining the Stadtbrücke.

Getting There & Away Hallein is 30 minutes or less from Salzburg by bus or train (€3). Since the cable-car service was discontinued, the only way to reach Bad Dürrnberg is with a car or by taking the bus (€1.60) from outside the station. You could also hike to the mine, though it's a steep 40-minute climb – at the church with the bare concrete tower, turn left along Ferchl Strasse, and follow the sign pointing to the right after the yellow Volksschule building.

Werfen
☎ 06468 • pop 3000

Werfen is a rewarding day trip from Salzburg. The **Hohenwerfen Fortress** *(adult/student €9/7.50; open daily Apr-Nov)* stands on the hill above the village. Originally built in 1077, the present building dates from the 16th century. Admission includes an exhibition, a guided tour of the interior and a dramatic falconry show, where birds of prey swoop low over the heads of the crowd. The walk up from the village takes 20 minutes.

The **Eisriesenwelt Höhle** *(Giant Ice Caves; ☎ 5646; adult/student & senior €7.20/6.50 without cable car; open 1 May-26 Oct)* in the mountains are the largest accessible ice caves in the world. The vast, natural ice formations inside are elaborate and beautiful. Take warm clothes because it gets cold inside and the tour lasts 75 minutes. Some elderly visitors find the going too arduous. The cable-car fare is often included in the quoted price.

Both attractions can be visited in one day if you start early (tour the caves first, and be at the castle by 3pm for the falconry show). The **tourist office** *(☎ 5388; e info@werfen.at; Markt 24; open 9am-5pm Mon-Fri mid-Aug–mid-July, 9am-7pm Mon-Fri & 5pm-7pm Sat mid-July–mid-Aug)* is in the village main street.

Getting There & Around Werfen (and Hallein) can be reached from Salzburg by Hwy 10. By train (€6) it takes 50 minutes. The village is a five-minute walk from Werfen station. Getting to the caves is more complicated, though scenic. A minibus service (€5.50 return) from the station operates along the steep, 6km road to the car park, which is as far as cars can go. A 15-minute walk then brings you to the cable car (€8.80/8 return adult/concession) from which it is a further 15-minute walk to the caves. Allow four hours return from the station, or three hours from the car park (peak-season queues may add an hour). The whole route can be hiked, but it's a very hard four-hour ascent, rising 1100m above the village.

Salzkammergut

Salzkammergut, named after its salt mines, is a picturesque holiday region of mountains and lakes east of Salzburg. The main season is summer, when hiking and water sports – or simply relaxing – are popular pursuits. In winter, some hiking paths stay open and there's downhill or cross-country skiing. The Salzkammergut Lammertal ski region includes 80 cable cars and lifts, serving 145km of ski runs; the general ski pass costs €51 for a minimum two days. You can also get one-day passes for individual resorts.

Orientation & Information

Bad Ischl is the geographical centre of Salzkammergut. The largest lake is Attersee, situated to the north. Most of the lakes south of Bad Ischl are much smaller, the largest there being Hallstätter See. West of Bad Ischl is the Wolfgangsee.

Because the area straddles several of Austria's federal provinces, various details are available from provincial tourist offices in Salzburg and Linz (see individual city sections). Once within the region, a central point of information is **Salzkammergut Touristik** (☎ 06132-240 00-0; **e** office@salzkammergut.co.at; Götzstrasse 12, Bad Ischl; open 9am-8pm daily). Staff are helpful, but because it's a private agency they might try to sell you holiday packages.

The area is dotted with hostels and affordable hotels. Rooms in private homes often come with a surcharge for single-night stays (€3 to €4), but are still usually the best deals. Tourist offices can supply accommodation lists and generally make free bookings. Some lodgings close in winter. Resorts have a holiday/guest card (Gästekarte) offering discounts in the whole region; ask for this if it is not offered. Your hotel, hostel or camping ground must stamp the card for it to be valid.

If you plan to stay a while, buy the Salzkammergut Card for €4.90. It's valid between May and October for the duration of your visit and provides a 25% discount on sights, ferries, cable cars and some Bundesbuses.

Getting Around

The major rail routes bypass the heart of Salzkammergut, but regional trains cross the area in a north-south direction. You get on this route from Attnang Puchheim on the Salzburg-Linz line. The track from here connects Gmunden, Traunkirchen, Ebensee, Bad Ischl, Hallstatt and Obertraun. When you're travelling from a small unstaffed station (unbesetzter Bahnhof), you buy your ticket on the train; no surcharge applies. After Obertraun, the railway continues east via Bad Aussee before connecting with the main Bischofshofen-Graz line at Stainach Irdning. Attersee can also be reached via Vöcklamarkt, the next stop on the Salzburg–Linz line before Attnang Puchheim.

Regular Bundesbuses connect the region's towns and villages, though less frequently on weekends. Timetables are displayed at stops, and tickets can be bought from the driver.

Passenger boats ply the waters of the Attersee, Traunsee, Mondsee, Hallstätter See and Wolfgangsee.

To reach Salzkammergut from Salzburg by car or motorcycle, take the A1 or Hwy 158.

BAD ISCHL

☎ 06132 • pop 13,000

WWI – or what became WWI – was declared in Bad Ischl. It's an unlikely birthplace for such brutality, given that it's a spa resort devoted to rather more relaxing and healthier pursuits (and now a genteel retirees' paradise to boot). However, in the 19th and early 20th centuries, it was fashionable for Austria's power-brokers to 'take the cure' in the town's salty waters. Emperor Franz Josef was enjoying his annual summer holiday here in 1914 when difficulties with Serbia demanded his urgent attention.

Orientation & Information

The town centre rests within a bend of the River Traun. If you turn left into the main road as you come out of the train station, you will see the **tourist office** (Kurdirektion; ☎ 277 57-0, fax -77; **e** office@badischl.at; Bahnhofstrasse 6; open 8am-6pm Mon-Fri, 9am-3pm Sat, 10am-1pm Sun July-Sept, 8am-5pm Mon-Fri, 8am-noon Sat Oct-June) almost immediately. A telephone lobby in its doorway can be used to make free hotel bookings after hours. The **post office** (Postamt 4820), along the road at Aübockplatz, changes money (cash only). Salzkammergut Touristik (see the introductory Salzkammergut Orientation & Information section earlier) offers bike rentals and Internet access.

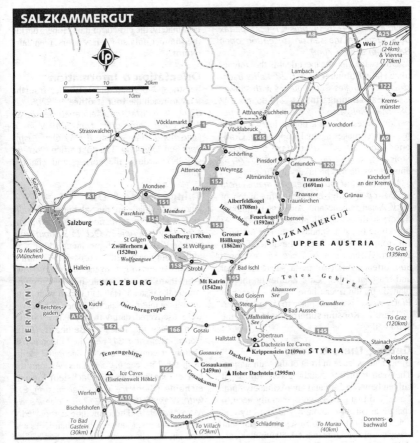

SALZKAMMERGUT

AUSTRIA

Things to See & Do

The **Kaiservilla** (☎ 232 41; Kaiserpark; tours €9.50; open daily May–mid-Oct) was Franz Josef's summer residence and shows he loved little better than huntin', shootin' and fishin'; it's decorated with an obscene number of animal trophies. The villa can be visited only by guided tour (in German but with written English translations), during which you'll pick up little gems like the fact that Franz Josef was conceived in Bad Ischl after his mother, Princess Sophie, took a treatment to cure her infertility in 1828. There are several 40-minute tours daily during the main season, but one is also offered every Wednesday from January to April.

The teahouse of Franz Josef's wife, Elisabeth, is now a **photo museum** (entry €1.50).

Free *Kurkonzerte* (spa concerts) are held regularly during summer; the tourist office has venues and times. An operetta festival takes place in July and August; for details and advance reservations, call ☎ 238 39.

Bad Ischl has downhill skiing from **Mt Katrin** (a winter day-pass costs €18) and various cross-country skiing routes. In summer, the Mt Katrin cable car costs €12 return. The **salt mine** (Salzbergwerk) is south of town; tours cost €10.90, are conducted daily from May to late September and receive mixed reviews.

The tourist office has information on health treatments in the resort.

Places to Stay & Eat

In the town centre behind Kreuzplatz is the HI **Jugendgästehaus** (☎ 265 77, fax -75; Am

Rechensteg 5; dorm beds €12.50, singles/ doubles €25.44/36.34, plus €1-1.50 spa tax depending on the season; reception open 8am-1pm & 5pm-7pm).

Otherwise, the cheapest deal is the immaculate **Haus Rothauer** *(☎ 236 28; Kaltenbachstrasse 12; singles €20, doubles with shower €48)*. **Haus Baumgartner** *(☎ 241 66, fax 222 08; Maxquellgasse 26; rooms €20-27 per person)* is less modern, but its leafy location by the river makes it equally appealing. **Goldener Ochs** *(☎ 235 29-0, fax -50; Grazer Strasse 4; singles/doubles from €41/74)* is amazing value for the luxury it offers.

Umeko *(Rettenbachweg 1; mains from €6.50; open daily)* is a delightful fusion of tasty Asian cuisine and Austrian farmhouse decor, high on a hill above the river. At lunchtime (except Sunday) you can eat your fill from the €5.80 buffet. Laidback **Blauen Enzian** *(Wirerstrasse 2; dishes €8-14; closed Sun)* offers a variety of pasta, salads, regional and seasonal dishes. **Café Zauner** on the Esplanade by the river (there's also a branch at Pfarrgasse 2) is a great place to sit in summer.

There's a **Konsum supermarket** behind the Trinkhalle.

Getting There & Away

Bundesbuses leave in front of the train station. They run hourly to Salzburg (€7.40) via St Gilgen between 5am and approximately 8pm. To St Wolfgang (€3), you generally need to change at Strobl (although you can buy one ticket straight through). Buses go to Hallstatt every couple of hours (€3.60, 50 minutes), arriving in the village itself. Some services continue to Obertraun.

Trains depart roughly hourly. It costs €2.80 to Hallstatt station, to which you must add the €1.80 cost of the boat to the village (see the Hallstatt Getting There & Away section later). The train fare to Salzburg (two hours), via Attnang Puchheim, is €15.50.

HALLSTATT
☎ 06134 • pop 1150

There's evidence of human settlement at Hallstatt as long as 4500 years ago – and who wouldn't want to move into such a breathtaking location as early as possible? The village, now a designated Unesco World Heritage Site, perches on a steep mountainside, beside a placid lake. Mining salt in the peak above was the main activity for thousands of years.

Today, tourism is the major money-spinner. Fortunately, the crowds of day-trippers during the summer only stay a few hours, then calm returns.

Orientation & Information

Seestrasse is the main street. Turn left from the ferry to reach the **tourist office** *(☎ 8208, fax 8352;* e *hallstatt-info@eunet.at; Seestrasse 169; open 9am-noon, 1pm-5pm Mon-Fri year-round, 10am-5pm Sat May-Oct, 10am-2pm Sun July-Aug)*. The **post office** *(Postamt 4830)* is around the corner, and changes money.

Things to See & Do

Above the village are the **Salzbergwerk** *(saltworks; ☎ 8400; admission €14; open 9am-4pm daily late Apr–26 Oct, to 3.30pm from mid-Sept)*. Riding the funicular up adds €5.50 to the salt mine ticket, or costs €7.50 return if you just want to get up the mountain. However, there are two scenic hiking trails you could take instead. Hallstatt is rich with archaeological interest. Near the mine, 2000 graves were discovered, dating from 1000 to 500 BC. Don't miss the macabre **Beinhaus** *(Bone House; admission €1)* near the village parish church; it contains rows of decorated skulls from the 15th century and later. Around the lake at Obertraun are the **Dachstein Rieseneishöhle** *(Giant Ice Caves; admission €8, with Mammoth Cave €12.30; open early May–mid-Oct)*. These include a reportedly spectacular giant stone (rather than ice) cave with sheer walls meeting in an arched ceiling called the Mammoth Cave. A cable car provides easy access.

Places to Stay & Eat

Some private rooms are only available during the busiest months of July and August; others require a minimum three-night stay. Ask at the tourist office, which will telephone around without charge.

For camping there's **Campingplatz Höll** *(☎ 8322; Lahn 201; sites per adult/tent/car €5.80/3.70/2.90; open Apr-Oct)*. Tax is extra. There are two hostels: the HI **Jugendherberge** *(☎ 8212; Salzbergstrasse 50; dorm beds without/with sheets €9.30/12.60; open around May-Oct, check-in 5pm-6pm)*, which is usually full with groups in July and August, and the **TVN Naturfreunde Herberge** *(☎/fax 8318; Kirchenweg 36; dorm beds without/*

with sheets €10/12.50). At both the hostels breakfast is available for €2.50.

Friendly and charming **Tauchergasthof Hallberg** (☎ 8709, fax 828 65; Seestrasse 113; per person €35-60) is near the tourist office, and the hub of the lake's scuba diving community.

Hallstatt's steep pavements certainly help you work up an appetite. Good restaurants include **Bräu Gasthof** (Seestrasse 120; dishes from €7.40; open daily 1 May-26 Oct) for typical Austrian food in an old-fashioned atmosphere, **Gasthof Weisses Lamm** (Mortonweg 166; mains from €7.50) which has some healthier options, and **Grüner Anger** (Lahn 10; mains from €7) near the HI hostel.

Nearby, **Obertraun** is another possible base: there's a **youth hostel** (☎ 06131-360; Winkl 26) and restaurants with affordable rooms. Ask the local **tourist office** (☎ 06131-351; e tourismus@obertraun.or.at).

Getting There & Away
There are some six buses a day to/from Obertraun and Bad Ischl. Until the 'Parkterrasse' stop downtown reopens, you can only alight in one place in Hallstatt – at 'Lahn', just south of the road tunnel. Beware, as services finish very early and the last guaranteed departure from Bad Ischl is 4.10pm. There are at least nine train services a day from Bad Ischl (€2.80, 50 minutes). The station is across the lake from the village, but the ferry captain waits for trains to arrive before making the short crossing (€1.80). Though trains run later, the last ferry departs the train station at 6.44pm (leaving Hallstatt at 6.10pm). Parking in the village is free if you have a guest card, though car access is restricted in the summer.

WOLFGANGSEE
You can swim or go boating on this lake, climb the mountain above it or just sit on the shore, gazing at the scenery. However, its proximity to Salzburg means the Wolfgangsee can become crowded in summer.

Orientation & Information
The lake is dominated by the Schafberg on the northern shore. Next to it is the resort of St Wolfgang. On the main street by the entrance to the road tunnel you'll find the **tourist office** (☎ 06138-2239-0; e info@stwolfgang .at; open 9am-noon Mon-Sat & 2pm-5pm Mon, Tues, Thur & Fri Sept-June, 8am-8pm

Mon-Sat, noon-6pm Sun July & Aug). St Gilgen, on the western shore, provides easy access to Salzburg, 29km away. Its **tourist office** (☎ 06227-2348; e info@stgilgen .co.at; Mozartplatz 1; open 9am-noon Mon-Fri & 2pm-5pm Mon, Tues, Thur & Fri Sept-June, 8.30am-7pm Mon-Sat, 9am-noon Sun July & Aug) is in the Rathaus.

Things to See & Do
St Wolfgang's 14th-century **Pilgrimage Church** (open 9am-6pm daily), still attracts pilgrims. Today they're mainly interested in seeing the winged high altar, created by Michael Pacher between 1471 and 1481. Its eight large painted panels depict scenes from the life of Christ, and while the four outermost paintings once remained folded inwards much of the time, they now seem to be always open. For those churchgoers who find that one altar is not enough, there's an additional baroque double altar in the middle of the nave.

Another major attraction is the **Schafberg** (1783m). Some people like to climb mountains because they're there; others of us prefer the less strenuous train ride to the top. The first group will love the four-hour hike to the peak. The rest need to get there between early May and the end of October, when the Schafberg cog-wheel railway operates. It runs approximately hourly during the day and costs €12.70 to the top and €20.90 return. There is also a stop halfway up.

Hot-air ballooning and paragliding are also popular (ask at the tourist office) and **St Gilgen** offers good views and some pleasant swimming spots.

Places to Stay & Eat
Camping Appesbach (☎ 06138-2206; Au 99; sites per adult €5, tent & car €6; open Easter-Oct) is on the lakefront, 1km from St Wolfgang heading towards Strobl.

St Gilgen has a good HI **Jugendgästehaus** (☎ 06227-2365; Mondseestrasse 7; dorm beds/twin rooms/doubles €12.35/14.53/ 18.16; check-in 5pm-7pm), where some of the rooms have a lake view.

Both St Wolfgang and St Gilgen have numerous pensions, private rooms and holiday apartments. Most start at about €18 per person, although a few cheaper deals are available. The tourist offices have listings or will phone around for you without charge.

In St Wolfgang, the chalet-style **Gästehaus Raudaschl** (☎ 06138-2329; Pilgerstrasse 4; singles/doubles from €30/56) is lively and friendly.

Rooms in smaller **Pension Ellmauer** (☎/fax 06138-2388; Markt 183; singles/doubles €33/54) are of a much higher standard and have lake views.

In St Gilgen, you could try **Pension Pichler** (☎ 06227-7113; Helenenstrasse 8; rooms per person €21-28) across the highway from the centre of town, for a welcoming, cheap option.

Alternatively, you could try **Haus Schernthaner** (☎ 06227-2402, fax -2; e garni-scherntaner@aon.at; Schwarzenbrunnerstrasse 4; singles/doubles €36.50/64) which is both pleasant and central.

There are many places to eat in both towns, from cheap snack joints to quaint touristy restaurants. Just follow your nose.

Getting There & Away
A ferry operates from Strobl to St Gilgen, stopping at various points en route, including St Wolfgang. Services are from late April to 26 October, but are more frequent from early July to early September. The journey from St Wolfgang to St Gilgen takes 45 to 50 minutes (€4.30), with boats sailing during the high season approximately twice an hour between 8am and 8pm.

Buses from St Wolfgang to St Gilgen and Salzburg go via Strobl on the east side of the lake. St Gilgen is 50 minutes from Salzburg by bus, with hourly departures till at least 8.30pm. The fare is €4.50.

NORTHERN SALZKAMMERGUT
West of Attersee is **Mondsee**, a lake whose warm water makes it a favourite swimming spot. Mondsee village has an attractive church that was used in the wedding scenes of *The Sound of Music*.

East of Attersee is Traunsee and its three main resorts: Gmunden, Traunkirchen and Ebensee. Gmunden is famous for its twin castles linked by a causeway on the lake, and the manufacture of ceramics.

Buses go east from Gmunden to Grünau (or take the train from Wels). This out-of-the-way destination has a good backpacker hostel, **The Tree House** (☎ 07616-8499; e treehousehotel@hotmail.com; Schindlbachstrasse 525; dorm beds/doubles €13.80/16.44).

Tirol

Hooray for Tirolliwood! Its wonderful mountain scenery makes Tirol (sometimes spelled Tyrol) an ideal playground for hikers and mountaineers and its glitzy ski resorts add glamour. The province is divided in two: East Tirol has been isolated from the main part of the state ever since prosperous South Tirol was ceded to Italy at the end of WWI.

Train and bus journeys within Tirol are cheaper using VVT tickets, which can only be bought within Tirol (from train stations etc). These tickets can be combined with city passes. The system is quite complicated; the **IVB Kundenbüro** (☎ 0512-53 07-103; Stainerstrasse 2, Innsbruck) can give information.

INNSBRUCK
☎ 0512 • pop 111,000
As a two-time host to the winter Olympics – in 1964 and 1976 – Innsbruck could be easily mistaken for a sports-mad destination with little else to offer than skiing, snowboarding and a landmark ski-jump. How wrong that would be. An important trading post since the 12th century, the city also boasts the cultural legacy of being home to one branch of the Habsburgs. Emperor Maximilian erected the golden roof in the old town.

Orientation
Innsbruck lies in the valley of the River Inn, scenically squeezed between the northern chain of the Alps and the Tuxer mountain range to the south. The town centre is very compact, with the Hauptbahnhof only a 10-minute walk from the pedestrian-only, old town centre (Altstadt). The main street in the Altstadt is Herzog Friedrich Strasse.

Information
Tourist Offices The main tourist office (☎ 53 56-36, fax -41; e info@innsbruck .tvb.co.at; Burggraben 3; open 9am-6pm Mon-Sun) books hotel rooms (€3 commission) and sells ski passes and public transport tickets. Ask for the free tear-off map sheet, rather than buying one.

There are hotel reservation centres (open 9am-8pm daily, to 9.15pm in July, Aug & around Christmas) located in the main train station and at motorway exits near the city. The **youth waiting room** (Jugendwarteraum;

INNSBRUCK

PLACES TO STAY
1 Jugendherberge St Nikolaus
4 Romantik Hotel Schwarzer Adler
17 Weinhaus Happ
19 Gasthof Innbrücke
20 Gasthof Weisses Lamm
25 Weisses Kreuz
44 Pension Stoi

PLACES TO EAT
2 Restaurant Rama
5 SOWI lounge
7 Novembar
9 Dengg
12 Gasthaus Goldenes Dachl
13 Café Galerie
18 Elferhaus
21 Markthalle
23 Weisses Rössl
24 Sweet Basil
27 Feinkost Hörtnagl
34 Café Central
37 University Mensa
39 Restaurant Philippine

OTHER
3 Café am Hofgarten
6 Landestheater
8 Hofkirche; Volkskunst Museum
10 Hofburg
11 Stadtturm; Panini
14 Cathedral
15 Dom
16 Goldenes Dachl; Maximilian Museum
22 IVB Kundenbüro
26 Main Tourist Office
28 Treibhaus
29 Tiroler Landesmuseum Ferdinandeum
30 Cinematograph
31 Post Office
32 International Telephone Discount
33 Bubble Point Wasch Salon
35 St Anne's Column
36 Couch Club
38 University Clinic
40 Main Post Office
41 Triumphal Arch
42 Tirol Information Office
43 ÖKISTA
45 Neuner Sport
46 German Consulate
47 Bundesbus Station

AUSTRIA

open mid-Sept–mid-July) in the train station also offers useful information.

The **Tirol Information office** (☎ 72 72, fax -7; e tirol.info@tirolwerbung.at; Maria Theresien Strasse 55; open 8am-6pm Mon-Fri) also has information.

Ask your hotel for the complementary 'Club Innsbruck' membership card. It provides various discounts and benefits, such as free guided mountain hikes between June and September. The Innsbruck Card, available at the main tourist office, gives free entry to museums and free use of public transport. It costs €18.89/23.98/29.07 for 24/48/72 hours.

Money There are various exchange bureaus around town (compare rates and commission) as well as Bankomats. The tourist office also exchanges money, however, it charges a hefty commission.

Post & Communications The **main post office** (Hauptpostamt 6010; Maximilianstrasse 2; open 7am-11pm Mon-Fri, 7am-9pm Sat, 8am-9pm Sun) is yet another place for changing cash. There's also a **train station post office** (Brunecker Strasse 1-3; open 7am-7pm Mon-Fri).

Email & Internet Access Owned by someone who's obviously seen the film *My Beautiful Laundrette* a few times, the fabulous, neon-coloured **Bubble Point Wasch Salon** (Brixner Strasse 1) allows you to read your email cheaply while doing your laundry. Internet access costs €1 for 10 minutes.

Travel Agencies Agencies include ÖKISTA
(☎ 58 89 97; Wilhelm Greil Strasse 17; open
9am-5.30pm Mon-Fri).

Medical Services The University Clinic
(☎ 504-0; Anichstrasse 35) is also called the
Landeskrankenhaus.

Things to See & Do
For an overview of the city, climb the 14th-
century **Stadtturm** (City Tower; ☎ 56 15 00;
Herzog Friedrich Strasse; adult/student & senior €2.50/2.00; open 10am-5pm daily, to
8pm in summer). Across the square is the famous **Goldenes Dachl** (Golden Roof) comprising 2657 gilded copper tiles dating from
the 16th century. Emperor Maximilian used to
observe street performers from the balcony beneath. Inside the building, there's a Maximilian **museum** (☎ 58 11 11; Herzog Friedrich
Strasse 15; adult/student/senior €3.63/2.91/
1.45). A minute or so north of the Golden
Roof is the baroque cathedral. After visiting
the cathedral, turn back southwards and note
the elegant 15th- and 16th-century buildings as
you stroll down Maria Theresien Strasse to the
1767 **Triumphal Arch**.

Hofburg The Imperial Palace (☎ 58 71 86;
Rennweg 1; adult/senior/student €5.45/4/
3.63; open 9am-4.30pm daily) dates from
1397, but has been rebuilt and restyled several
times since, particularly by Empress Maria
Theresa. It's impressive, but can't compete
with Schönbrunn in Vienna. The baroque
Giant's Hall is a highlight. There are three
guided tours daily in German (€2.18). Alternatively, for a do-it-yourself tour, buy the explanatory booklet in English (€1.81).

Hofkirche Diagonally across Universitätsstrasse from the palace is the Imperial Church
(☎ 58 43 02; Universitätsstrasse 2; adult/
student under 27 €2.20/1.45, admission free
Sun & holidays; visits 9am-5pm Mon-Sat, before 8am, noon-3pm & after 5pm Sun). Major
restoration means the empty sarcophagus of
Maximilian I will be under wraps until autumn 2003 or later. Although you're now forbidden to touch the 28 giant statues of
Habsburgs lining either side of the cask, these
thankfully aren't being refurbished; it would
be a shame to erase the traces of numerous in-
quisitive hands, which have polished parts of
the dull bronze, including Kaiser Rudolf's

codpiece! Combined tickets (adult/student
€5.45/4.00) are available for the church and
adjoining **Volkskunst Museum** (Folk Art Museum; 9am-5pm Mon-Sat, 9am-noon Sun).

Schloss Ambras Located in a spacious park
on a hill east of the centre, this medieval
castle (☎ 34 84 46; Schlossstrasse 20; adult/
concession €7.50/5.50 Apr-Oct, otherwise
€4.30/2.90; open 10am-5pm daily Apr-Oct,
otherwise 2pm-5pm Wed-Mon) was greatly
extended by Archduke Ferdinand II in the 16th
century. It features a Renaissance Spanish
Hall, an armoury and various portraits including one of Vlad IV Tzespech Dracul – the
model for Dracula. You can reach the castle on
tram No 3 or 6, or bus K. From April to October, there's also an hourly shuttle bus from
Maria Theresien Strasse, just north of Anichstrasse on the opposite side of the road.

Alpine Zoo The zoo (☎ 29 23 23; Weiherburggasse 37; adult/child €5.80/2.90; open
9am-6pm daily, to 5pm in winter) is north of
the River Inn and houses a comprehensive collection of alpine animals, including amorous
bears and combative ibexes. Walk up the hill
to get there or take the Hungerburgbahn (funicular railway), which is free if you buy your
zoo ticket at the Hungerburgbahn station.

Tiroler Landesmuseum Ferdinandeum
This major museum (☎ 594 89; Museumstrasse 15) is due to reopen in summer 2003
after a lengthy renovation and rearrangement
of its collection, including Gothic statues and
altarpieces. Phone for details, or ask at the
tourist office.

Swarovski Kristallwelten The Crystal
Worlds (☎ 05224 51080; e scs.visitors-cen
tre@swarovski.com; Kristallweltenstrasse 1;
admission €5.45; open 9am-6pm daily) is a
series of caverns featuring the famous Swarovski crystals. Greats like Salvador Dali, Andy
Warhol and Keith Haring designed some of
the displays, which are all very sparkly. The
centre in Wattens is best reached by Bundesbus (€6.20 return, 30 minutes), which leaves
from the train station.

Skiing
The ski region around Innsbruck has been totally refurbished, with the long-awaited reopening of the Mutters area, and new chair

lifts and cable cars connecting previously separate runs. A one-day ski pass is €20 to €26,
depending on the area, and there are several
versions of multiday tickets available. Downhill equipment rental starts at €15. With 'Club
Innsbruck', ski buses are free.

You can ski or snowboard all year at the
popular **Stubai Glacier**. A one-day pass costs
€35. Catch the white IVB Stubaltalbahn bus,
departing roughly hourly from the bus station,
or ask the tourist office about the free ski bus
in winter. The journey there takes 80 minutes
and the last bus back is usually at 5.30pm.
Several places offer complete packages to the
glacier, which compare favourably with going
it alone. The tourist office package for €46.51
includes transport, passes and equipment
rental. In winter, if you take the free ski bus,
there's a cheaper €41.42 package.

Places to Stay
Camping West of the town centre, **Camping
Innsbruck Kranebitten** (*☎/fax 28 41 80;
Kranebitter Allee 214; sites per adult/tent/car
€5.55/3/3; open year-round*) has a restaurant
on site.

Private Rooms The tourist office has lists of
private rooms in Innsbruck and Igls ranging
from €15 per person. Igls is south of town; get
there by tram No 6 or bus J. Further afield is
Haus Wolf (*☎ 54 86 73; Dorfstrasse 48, Mutters; dorm beds €14*). Rooms have one to three
beds, and rates include a big breakfast. Take
the Stubaitalbahn tram from in front of the train
station to Birchfeld (€1.82, 30 minutes).
Trams depart every 50 minutes till 10.30pm.

Hostels None of Innsbruck's hostels is particularly convenient, but **Jugendherberge St
Nikolaus** (*☎ 28 65 15, fax -14; e innsbruck@
hostelnikolaus.at; Innstrasse 95; dorm beds
from €13, plus €0.80 surcharge for first night,
doubles €18.20; check-in 5pm-10pm*) is
probably the best located. It has a bar and
restaurant and is a sociable place. There's
more privacy, but, more of a draught too, in
the hostel's sister **Glockenhaus pension**
(*Weiherburggasse 3; singles/doubles €29/
43.60*) up the hill.

The **Jugendherberge Innsbruck** (*☎ 34 61
79, fax -12; Reichenauerstrasse 147; dorm
beds 1st night/additional nights €12.05/
9.50; curfew 11pm, closed 10am-3pm summer, 10am-5pm rest of year*) is a huge, Soviet-

style concrete monstrosity that's more pleasant inside than out. Rates are €0.50 less if
you're aged under 18. It has a kitchen and
washing machines and is reached by bus O
from Museumstrasse.

Two extra hostels to try in summer are **St
Paulus Hostel** (*☎ 34 42 91; Reichenauerstrasse 72; open mid-June–early Sept*) and
Jugendwohnheim Fritz Prior (*☎ 58 58 14,
fax -4; Rennweg 17b; open July, Aug & New
Year*). Both have similar prices to the above
hostels, with check-in from 5pm.

Hotels & Pensions A pleasant choice is
Pension Paula (*☎ 29 22 62, fax 29 30 17;
e office@pensionpaula.at; Weiherburggasse
15; singles/doubles without shower & toilet
€26/44, with facilities €33/53*) which has
been made even more pleasant as it has been
renovating its bathrooms. Guests aren't deterred by the uphill walk (with great views), so
book ahead.

Two other cheapish options are situated on
the northern bank of the River Inn: **Gasthof
Innbrücke** (*☎ 28 19 34, fax 27 84 10; e inn
bruecke@magnet.at; Innstrasse 1; singles/
doubles without shower & toilet €25.50/
43.60, with facilities €32.70/58.20*) and the
Gasthof Weisses Lamm (*☎ 831 56; Maria-
hilfstrasse 12; singles/doubles €33/55*).

If you stay at **Pension Stoi** (*☎ 58 54 34, fax
872 82; Salurner Strasse 7; singles/doubles
without shower & toilet €29/47, with facilities €34/54*) you'll need to breakfast elsewhere but that's a small price to pay for such
decent, centrally located rooms. Coming from
the train station, turn left after the Neuner
Sport shop.

Binders (*☎ 334 36-0, fax 334 39-99; Dr
Glatz Strasse 20; singles without shower &
toilet €36/49, with facilities from €43/64*) is
for those whose taste for modern comfort and
style exceeds their budget. Even those rooms
without shower and toilet feel luxurious and
the breakfast room and other public spaces are
just nice to be in, too.

Two hotels in the old town stand out.
Weisses Kreuz (*☎ 594 79, fax -90; e hotel
.weisses.kreuz@eunet.at; Herzog Friedrich
Strasse 31; singles from €35, singles/doubles
with shower & toilet from €59/89*), once
played host to Mozart and resonates with history. Across the street, **Weinhaus Happ** (*☎ 58
29 80, fax -11; e office@weinhaus-happ.at;
Herzog Friedrich Strasse 14; singles/doubles

AUSTRIA

from €51/88) has some rooms with views of the Golden Roof.

Innsbruck's most opulent accommodation is the **Romantik Hotel Schwarzer Adler** *(☎ 58 71 09, fax 56 16 97; e romantikhotel-innsbruck@netway.at; Kaiserjägerstrasse 2; singles/ doubles from €98/140)*. Its rooms are individually styled and its over-the-top suites include one fitted by Versace and another with Swarovski crystals.

Places to Eat

A group of international restaurants has diffused Innsbruck's focus on Tirolean cuisine. Whether you think that's a good thing or not depends on how much you crave a break from calorific regional specialities.

For groceries and fresh produce, there is the supermarket **Feinkost Hörtnagl** *(Burggraben)* or a large indoor food market by the river in **Markthalle** *(Herzog Siegmund Ufer; open Mon-Fri & Sat morning)*.

You enjoy great views of the Alps lunching at **University Mensa** *(Herzog Siegmund Ufer 15; mains from €4.60; open 11am-1.30pm Mon-Thur, 11am-2pm Fri & Sat)*. Another mensa option is the **SOWI lounge** *(Universitätsstrasse 15; mains from €3; open 8am-5pm Mon-Thur, 10am-3pm Fri)*.

The first floor of self-service restaurant **Panini** *(cnr of Hofgasse & Herzog Friedrich Strasse; meals from €3.60)*, next door to the Stadtturm, overlooks the Golden Roof, so it's a great viewpoint if you can get into it in summer.

Nearby **Elferhaus** *(Herzog Friedrich Strasse 11; daily menus €6.35 & €8.70)* has sausages, burgers and other fare to accompany its vast range of beers.

Nonmeat eaters will find solace at vegie **Restaurant Philippine** *(☎ 58 91 57; Müllerstrasse 9; daily menus €6.80 & €7.80; open 11.30am-2pm, 6.30pm-8pm Mon-Sat)*.

The ever-popular **Restaurant Rama** *(Innstrasse 81; Indian meals around €8; open Tues-Sun)*, also known as Shashi's, provides vegetarian options, as well as meat, curries and pizzas.

Italian-influenced **Sweet Basil** *(Herzog Friedrich Strasse 31; mains from €9.80)* is one of a new breed of trendy restaurants. Another is **Dengg** *(Riesengasse 11-13; light dishes €4.50, mains from €13)*, serving everything from Italian focaccia, Thai coconut curry soup and international fish and meat dishes.

Novembar *(Universitätstrasse 1; small meals from €6.60, mains from €12.40)* is one of Innsbruck's 'in' haunts. Overlooking the square in front of the Hofburg, it attracts a wide range of customers, from students to suits.

Of course, old-school Austrian eateries survive. **Gasthaus Goldenes Dachl** *(Hofgasse 1; open daily)* offers Tirolean specialities such as *Bauerngröstl*, a pork, bacon, potato and egg concoction which is served with salad (€9.65). **Weisses Rössl** *(Kiebachgasse 8; daily menu €6.90; open Mon-Sat)* is another favourite for regional food.

The traditional **Café Central** *(Gilmstrasse 5; specials from €7.30; open daily)* is a great place to hang out, snacking and reading the English newspapers. The actual coffee can be dire, though. For a delicious café latte, make tracks instead for **Café Galerie** *(Pfarrgasse 6)* near the cathedral.

Entertainment

The tourist office sells tickets for 'Tirolean evenings' (€30 for alpine music, folk dancing, yodelling and one drink), classical concerts, and performances in the **Landestheater** *(Rennweg 2)*. Commission is usually charged.

If these don't appeal, 'eyebk' as local hipsters call it, has a pretty good bar and club scene. Firstly, Elferhaus, Sweet Basil, Novembar, Café Galerie (see Places to Eat earlier) all double as very popular bars. **Dom** *(Pfarrgasse 3)* is another. Hopefully, **Café im Hofgarten** *(Rennweg 6A)* will still be running its student nights on Tuesday. With a student card that shows you're over 20, they've been letting you have six drinks for €10 after 8pm. Although the official address is Rennweg it is actually some distance away in the Hofgarten.

Additionally, under the railway arches along Ingenieur Etzel Strasse, there is a row of late-night bars (mostly opening after midnight). Walk along and take your pick. Then, there's the hip **Couch Club** *(Anichstrasse 7; open Thur-Sat)* and the arty, community-minded **Treibhaus** *(☎ 58 68 74; Angerzellgasse 8)*, which hosts live music, short-film festivals and the like and has a play area for kids. On Sunday, there's a 'jazz breakfast' from 10.30am and 'five o'clock tea'.

Cinematograph *(☎ 57 85 00; Museumstrasse 31)* is a good place to catch independent films in their original language.

Getting There & Away

Air Tyrolean Airways flies daily to Amsterdam, Frankfurt, Paris, Vienna and Zürich.

Bus Bundesbuses leave from the south end of the main train station, which has been undergoing refurbishment. Meanwhile, bus tickets and information have been available from, you guessed it, the north end of the station.

Train Fast trains depart seven times a day for Bregenz (2¾ hours) and every two hours to Salzburg (two hours). Regular express trains head north to Munich (via Kufstein; two hours) and south to Verona (3½ hours). Connections are hourly to Kitzbühel (€13.30 1¼ hours). On many trains to Lienz, people travelling on Austrian passes must pay a surcharge for travelling through Italy. On the 6.56am, 1.56pm and 5.53pm 'corridor' services, this is not the case, but otherwise the situation can vary, so it's best to ask before boarding. Alternatively, call ☎ 05-1717, available 24 hours.

Car & Motorcycle The A12 and the parallel Hwy 171 are the main roads to the west and east. Hwy 177, to the west of Innsbruck, heads north to Germany and Munich. The A13 motorway is a toll road (€7.99) southwards through the Brenner Pass to Italy; it includes the impressive Europabrücke (Europe Bridge) several kilometres south of the city. Toll-free Hwy 182 follows the same route, passing under the bridge.

Getting Around

The airport is 4km west of the centre. To get there, take bus F, which leaves from opposite the main train station half-hourly (hourly on Saturday afternoon and Sunday) and passes through Maria Theresien Strasse.

Single tickets, including to the airport, cost €1.60. A 24-hour pass is €3.20 and a weekly €10.10.

Private transport is a real hassle in the city centre. Most central streets are blue zones with maximum parking of 1½ hours; the charge is €0.50 per 30 minutes (tickets from pavement dispensers). Parking garages (eg, under the Altstadt) are €10 and upwards per day.

Taxis cost €3.80 for the first 1.3km, then €1.31 per kilometre. A taxi to the airport costs around €10. Bike rental is available from **Neuner Sport** (☎ 56 15 01; *Salurner Strasse 5*).

KITZBÜHEL
☎ 05356 • **pop 8200**
Kitzbühel is a fashionable and prosperous winter resort, offering excellent skiing.

Orientation & Information

From the main train station to the town centre is 1km. You emerge from the train station onto Bahnhofstrasse and walk straight ahead, then turn left onto Josef Pirchl Strasse; take the right fork (no entry for cars), which is still Josef Pirchl Strasse, and continue past the post office (Postamt 6370).

The **tourist office** (☎ 62155-0, fax 62307; e *info@kitzbuehel.com; Hinterstadt 18; open daily high season, Mon-Fri & Sat morning low season)* is in the centre.

The staff are not always that helpful, but ask about the guest card, which offers various discounts. There is Internet access at **Kitz Video** (*Schlossergasse 10*).

Activities

Skiing In winter, there is good intermediate skiing on Kitzbüheler Horn to the north and Hahnenkamm to the south. A one-day general ski pass costs €32, though some pensions/hotels can offer 'Ski Hit' reductions before mid-December or after mid-March. The cost of a day's ski rental is around €11/9 for downhill/cross-country. The professional Hahnenkamm downhill ski race takes place in mid to late January.

Hiking Dozens of summer hiking trails surround the town; the tourist office gives free maps and free guided hikes. Get a head start to the heights with the three-day cable-car pass for €32.70.

There is an alpine flower garden (free) on the slopes of the Kitzbüheler Horn (toll-road for drivers). The scenic Schwarzsee lake is a fine location for summer swimming.

Places to Stay & Eat

Rates often rise by €2 to €4 for stays of one or two nights. Prices are higher at Christmas and Easter, in July and August (the summer high season), but they peak during the winter high season, which are the prices quoted here. Quite a few private rooms and apartments are available.

Alternatively, you can pitch your tent at **Campingplatz Schwarzsee** (☎ 628 06; *Reither Strasse 24; open year-round)* by the lake.

Now that Jugendhotel Kaiser no longer takes backpackers or other individual travellers, the closest place to stay to the train station is **Pension Hörl** *(☎/fax 631 44; Josef Pirchl Strasse 60; singles/doubles without shower €18/36, with shower €20/40)*. It's cheap, friendly and a lot more comfortable than its jumble-sale decor first suggests.

Renovated **Pension Schmidinger** *(☎/fax 631 34; Ehrenbachgasse 3; €32 per person)* offers bright, comfortable rooms. So does conveniently located **Pension Mühlberger-hof** *(☎ 62835, fax 644 88; Schwarzseestrasse 6; from €33 per person per night)*. The owners here serve breakfast with produce from their farm.

On Bichlstrasse there's a **Billa supermarket** *(open daily high season)*, while grocery store **Asia Markt** *(Josef Pirchl Strasse 16; meals from €4.50; open Mon-Sat)* serves light, weekday lunches and early evening meals.

A trip to Kitzbühel isn't complete without visiting **Huberbräu Stüberl** *(Vorderstadt 18; mains from €6.45; open daily)*, where diners and drinkers congregate around the Austrian food and beers. The Tex-Mex place **La Fonda** *(Hinterstadt 13; mains around €6-7; open evenings)* is similarly popular. The Anglophile **Hölzl** *(Jochbergerstrasse 4; open daily)* is mainly a bar, but also lays on pork sandwiches *(€4)*. It's particularly busy with tour groups on Saturday in winter.

Pricier **Zinnkrug** *(Untere Gänsbachgasse 12)* is known for its pork spare ribs *(€15.60)*.

Getting There & Away

Direct trains to Innsbruck *(€3.30, one to two hours, depending on the service)* only leave Kitzbühel every two hours or so, but there are hourly services to Wörgl, where you can change for Innsbruck. Trains to Salzburg *(€19.60, two hours)* leave roughly hourly. Slower trains stop at Kitzbühel-Hahnenkamm, which is closer to the centre than the main Kitzbühel stop.

Getting to Lienz by public transport is awkward. The train is slow and the bus is infrequent *(€9.96, two hours)*. There are four bus departures Monday to Friday and two each on Saturday and Sunday.

Heading south to Lienz, you pass through some marvellous scenery. Hwy 108 (the Felber Tauern Tunnel) and Hwy 107 (the Grossglockner mountain road, closed in winter) both have toll sections.

KUFSTEIN
☎ 05372 • pop 15,000

A 13th-century **fortress** *(☎ 602 350; admission €8/4.50 July & Aug; €7/4 Easter-July & Sept-mid-Nov)* dominates Kufstein town centre. Inside is a wide-ranging but not over-large **Heimat Museum**, and a massive 'Heroes Organ' (recital at noon, and at 5pm in summer, which is audible all over town). There is a lift to the fortress, which is included in the entry price.

A free city bus goes to the nearby **Hechtsee** lake in summer.

Information

The **tourist office** *(☎ 62207; ⓔ kufstein@netway.at; Unterer Stadtplatz 8; open Mon-Fri year-round, Sat morning in summer)* is in the centre of town, across the River Inn and three minutes' walk from the train station. It makes room reservations without charge.

Places to Stay & Eat

Should you decide to stay overnight, ask for the guest card. There is a **camping ground** *(☎ 622 29-55; Salurner Strasse 36)* by the river. A few blocks southeast of the castle is **Pension Striede** *(☎ 623 16, fax -33; Mitterndorfer Strasse 20; rooms per person €23/46)*, with hospital-like rooms with shower and toilet. There are several affordable places to eat on Stadtplatz, and a **supermarket**.

Getting There & Away

Kufstein is on the main Innsbruck-Salzburg 'corridor' train route. To reach Kitzbühel *(€6.90, one hour)*, change at Wörgl; the easiest road route is also via Wörgl.

LIENZ
☎ 04852 • pop 13,000

Many travellers view the capital of East Tirol principally as a handy stopover on the way to Italy, but it's also a good base for skiing or hiking. That's thanks to the jagged Dolomite mountain range, which crowds the southern skyline.

Orientation & Information

The town centre is within the junction of the Rivers Isel and Drau. To reach pivotal Hauptplatz from the train station, cross the road (or take the 'Zur Stadt' exit) and follow the street past the post office (Postamt 9900). Staff at the **tourist office** *(☎ 652 65, fax -2;*

[e] lienz@netway.at; Europaplatz 1; open 8am-6pm Mon-Fri, 9am-noon Sat, also Sun summer & winter high seasons) will find rooms free of charge, or you can use the hotel board (free telephone) outside. **Probike** (☎ 735 76; Amlacherstrasse 1a) rents bicycles; to get on the Internet visit **Net-Planet/ Odin's** (Schweizergasse 3).

Things to See & Do
Schloss Bruck (adult/senior/student €7/5/4; open 10am-6pm daily May-Nov) displays the powerful, if sometimes dour, paintings of local artist Albin Egger (1868–1926), as well as some folk art.

There is downhill skiing on the nearby **Zettersfeld** and **Hochstein** peaks; a one-day ski pass covering both is €26. However, the area around Lienz is more renowned for its cross-country skiing; the town fills up for the annual **Dolomitenlauf** cross-country skiing race in mid-January.

In summer, hiking is good in the mountains. The cable cars are closed during the off-season (April, May, October and November).

Places to Stay
Just south of the town, **Camping Falken** (☎ 640 22; Eichholz 7; open mid-Dec–Oct) is the best place in Austria to wash your clothes. At least, that's according to the quirky newspaper article on its laundrette wall, which praises the view while you wait.

Most of the private rooms around the town don't have quite the same close-up of the Dolomite range but are great value nonetheless. Some allow a single night's stay, like the **Haus Egger** (☎ 720 98; Alleestrasse 33; rooms per person €14) or the **Gästehaus Masnata** (☎ 655 36; Drahtzuggasse 4; apartments around €19-20 per person).

Gästehaus Gretl (☎ 621 06; Schweizergasse 32; singles/doubles €23/46) has been recently renovated, adding TVs to the rooms. There is courtyard parking, but the guesthouse is closed between seasons.

The atmospheric, spacious **Altstadthotel Eck** (☎ 647 85, fax -3; [e] altstadthotel.eck@ utanet.at; Hauptplatz 20; singles/doubles from €55/110) provides all the comfort you'd expect from one of the town's leading hotels.

Places to Eat
There are **ADEG supermarkets** on Hauptplatz and Tiroler Platz. **Imbissstube** (Albin Egger Strasse 5) offers mouth-watering rotisserie chicken sprinkled with spices. A Hendl (half-chicken) with a roll is just €3.

Pick Nick Ossi (Europaplatz 2; snacks from €2.91) has a range of salads, pizzas and other fast food. **Vinothek** (Zwergergasse 4; mains from €6.80) is a popular place, with many Italian-style dishes.

There are lots of places to try regional dishes, such as **Adlerstüberl** (Andrä Kranz Gasse 5; meals from €7.80), which has daily specials. **Goldener Fisch** (Kärntner Strasse 9; menus for €8.10 & €10.80) is also good.

Getting There & Away
Except for the 'corridor' route to Innsbruck (see the Innsbruck Getting There & Away section earlier in this chapter), trains to the rest of Austria connect via Spittal Millstättersee to the east. Trains to Salzburg (€24.70) take at least three hours. Villach, between Spittal and Klagenfurt, is a main junction for rail routes to the south. To head south by car, you must first divert west or east along Hwy 100.

Hohe Tauern National Park

Flora and fauna are protected in this 1786 sq km hiking paradise that straddles Tirol, Salzburg and Carinthia.

It contains **Grossglockner** (3797m), Austria's highest mountain, which towers over the 10km-long Pasterze Glacier. The best viewing point is **Franz Josefs Höhe**, reached from Lienz by Bundesbus. The bus runs from mid-June to late September and the return fare is covered by a zonal day pass for Carinthia (available in Lienz; €10.20), plus a €2.67 toll for the park. For longer stays, you should ask about the seven-day Bundesbus pass for the park (€22.60).

The route north (Hwy 107, the Grossglockner Hochalpenstrasse) is breathtakingly scenic. Along the way you pass Heiligenblut (buses year-round from Lienz), where there's a HI **Jugendherberge** (☎ 04824-2259; Hof 36; open mid-Dec–mid-Oct). By car, you can reach Franz Josefs Höhe from May to November, but the daily toll for using the road is €25.44 for cars and €16.71 for motorcycles. An eight-day pass is €33.43 and €22.53 respectively. There are places to stay overnight.

AUSTRIA

Cyclists and hikers pay nothing to enter the park.

Farther west, Felbertaurenstrasse also goes north-south through the park. For the tunnel section, there's a toll of €10 for cars and €8 for motorcycles. At the northern end of the park, turn west along Hwy 165 to reach **Krimml Falls**. These triple-level falls make a great spectacle. It takes 1½ hours to walk to the top, where there's an equally good view looking back down the valley.

Vorarlberg

The small state of Vorarlberg trickles down from the Alps to the shores of Lake Constance (Bodensee) and provides a convenient gateway to Germany, Liechtenstein and Switzerland. To travel the province you can buy VVV tickets, similar to VVT tickets (see the Tirol introduction earlier in this chapter).

BREGENZ
☎ 05574 • pop 27,500
With its face to the waters of Lake Constance and its disproportionate number of expensive clothes stores, Bregenz feels more like a posh seaside village than the provincial capital it is. The town is busiest during its annual music festival.

Orientation & Information
Bregenz is on Lake Constance's eastern shore. Turn left at the main train station exit and take Bahnhofstrasse to the centre (five minutes). Among the first things you'll see is the **tourist office** (☎ 4959-0, fax -59; e tourismus@bregenz.at; Bahnhofstrasse 14; open 9am-noon Mon-Sat & 1pm-5pm Mon-Fri, to 7pm daily during the Bregenz Festival).

The **post office** (Postamt 6900; Seestrasse; open 8am-7pm Mon-Fri, to 2pm Sat) is a few minutes further on. The tourist office provides free Internet access, while after-hours Web surfers should head for **S'Logo** (Kirchstrasse 47; open 5pm-midnight daily). Bundesbuses leave from outside the train station.

Things to See & Do
The **Bregenz Festival** runs for four weeks in July and August, when operas and classical works are performed from a floating stage on the lake's edge. If you want tickets contact the **Kartenbüro** (☎ 407-6, fax -400; w www

.bregenzerfestspiele.com; Postfach 311, A-6901) about nine months beforehand.

Even when the last diva has trilled the festival's closing note, there's spectacular sightseeing from the **Pfänder** mountain. A **cable car** (adults/seniors return €9.50/8.60; 9am-7pm daily; closed 2 weeks in Nov) carries you up and back.

Bregenz has several landmark buildings in wildly different styles, from the baroque **St Martin's Tower** in the old town to its – love it or loathe it – shimmering modern block of an art gallery, the **Kunsthaus**.

Places to Stay & Eat
The least expensive site is **Camping Lamm** (☎ 717 01; Mehrerauerstrasse 51; adult/tent/car €3.27/3.27/2.54; open May–mid-Oct), 1.5km west of the station. The HI **Jugendgästehaus Bregenz** (☎ 42867, fax -88; e jgh.bregenz@jgh.at; Mehrerauerstrasse 5; dorm beds from €15-17, doubles or singles available off-peak for €5-7 extra; open year-round) is near the skateboard park. To get to this hostel from the train station, get on the walkway above the platforms, then head for the 'Zum See' exit, not the 'Kassenhalle' (ticket office) exit, and continue past the casino.

Private singles/doubles start at €18/22; ask at the tourist office, which has a room-booking service (€3).

Two budget options in the centre are **Pension Gunz** (☎/fax 436 57; Anton Schneider Strasse 38; singles/doubles without shower €29/46, with shower from €31/52; reception open Wed-Mon) and **Pension Sonne** (☎ 425 72, fax -4; e office@bbn.at; Kaiserstrasse 8; singles/doubles without shower & toilet €35/66, with facilities €40/78; closed winter). For a once-in-a-lifetime experience, stay at **Gästehaus am Tannenbauch** (☎ 441 74; Im Gehren 1; €22-37 per person; open May-Oct). The ornate breakfast room, decorated with family memorabilia, is fit for a Habsburg – which you wouldn't realise from the house's reasonably humble exterior.

Trek through the first-floor clothes department in the GWL centre on Römerstrasse into **Leutbühel** (Römerstrasse 2; lunches from €6.30; open Mon-Sat) for salads and sausage dishes. Or tuck into Greek food at **Poseidon** (Kornmarktstrasse 2; most lunch dishes from €8.30; open daily).

Gösserbräu (Anton Schneider Strasse 1; dishes €6-9; open Tues-Sun) serves up local cuisine that's hearty rather than stodgy; its vegetarian mushroom goulash with dumplings is delicious. **Goldener Hirschen** *(Kirchstrasse 8; dishes €6.40-17.80; open Wed-Mon)* is another popular choice for Austrian food.

Getting There & Away

Trains to Munich (€44.60, 2½ hours) go via Lindau. There are also regular departures to St Gallen and Zürich. Trains to Innsbruck (€23.20, 2¾ hours) depart every two hours. Feldkirch is on the same route (€11.80, 30 minutes).

Boat services operate from late May to late October, with a reduced schedule from early March. For information, call ☎ 428 68. Bregenz to Constance by boat (via Friedrichshafen) takes about 3½ hours and there are about seven departures a day. Special boat passes offer discounts.

FELDKIRCH

☎ 05522 • pop 29,000

Granted its town charter in 1218, Feldkirch retains many medieval buildings, including the **Schattenburg** castle and **museum** *(adult/student €2/1; open Tues-Sun Dec-Oct)*. The musical **Feldkirch Festival** *(☎ 05576-720 91, fax 754 50; w www.feldkirchfestival.at)* takes place in May to June. The town rests in the Liechtenstein border region, not an immediately obvious location for a **Tibetan monastery**, but one exists. Ask at the tourist office for information about hikes to the monks' **Peace Stupa** monument.

Information

Feldkirch tourist office *(☎ 734 67, fax 798 67; e tourismus@feldkirch.at; Herrengasse 12; open 9am-6pm Mon-Fri, 9am-noon Sat; closed lunchtime in winter)* reserves rooms free of charge.

Places to Stay & Eat

The HI **Jugendherberge** *(☎ 731 81, fax 793 99; Reichsstrasse 111; beds in dorms/doubles from €10.80/14.50, €2 heating charge in winter; reception open 8am-10pm; hostel closed 2 weeks early Dec)* truly is one of Austria's most memorable, situated in a refurbished medieval infirmary with exposed timber and historic features.

Private rooms and budget pensions are scarce, but you can try **Haus Greiner** *(☎ 811*

48; Rundblick 8; €20 per person per night) or **Gasthof Engel** *(☎/fax 720 56; Liechtensteiner Strasse, Tisis; singles/doubles with hall shower €28/46)*. Both are on the bus route to Liechtenstein, but Gasthof Engel's reception is closed Monday and Tuesday. In the centre, **Gasthof Lingg** *(☎ 720 62, fax -6; Kreuzgasse 10; singles/doubles €60/65)* is good value for those travelling in pairs.

For meat eaters, the best daytime deal is at delicatessen **Metzgerei Spieler** *(Johanitergasse 6; menu €4.72)*; for an Austrian dinner, you could try **Johanniterhof** *(Marktgasse 1; menus €8.30)*.

Some vegie options are available at **Dogana** *(Neustadt 20; sandwiches from €3.40, menus €8.40)*, which is a trendy but relaxed place to hang out.

Getting There & Away

Two buses an hour (one per hour on weekends) depart for Liechtenstein from outside the train station. Travelling to Liechtenstein's capital, Vaduz (€3.60, 40 minutes), often requires a change in Schaans.

From Schaans, you can catch a train to Buchs and onward to major Swiss destinations, including Zürich.

ARLBERG REGION

The Arlberg region, shared by Vorarlberg and neighbouring Tirol, has some of the best skiing in Austria. Summer is less busy, when many bars are closed.

St Anton am Arlberg is the largest resort, where you're as likely to hear a cheery antipodean 'G'day' or Scandinavian *'God dag'* as you are to hear an Austrian *'Grüss Di'*. There are good medium-to-advanced runs here, as well as nursery slopes on Gampen and Kapall. The **tourist office** *(☎ 05446-226 90; e st.anton@netway.at)* on the main street, has details. Head diagonally left from the train station to find it.

Lech, a more upmarket resort, is a favourite with royalty and film stars. Runs are predominantly medium to advanced. For details, contact the **Lech tourist office** *(☎ 05583-2161-0; e lech-info@lech.at)*.

A ski pass valid for 83 ski lifts in Lech, Zürs, Stuben, St Anton and St Christoph costs €37 for one day and €171 for six (reductions for children and seniors). Rental starts at €15 for both downhill and cross-country skis and poles.

Places to Stay & Eat

Accommodation is mainly in a bewildering number of small B&Bs. The tourist office has brochures. Alternatively, try the accommodation board with free telephones outside its office. Many budget places (prices from €26 per person in winter high season) are booked months or even years in advance.

Central **Haus Wannali** (☎ 05446-2350; Arlberg Strasse 509; per person €37) has a friendly atmosphere and entertaining regulars, but the views are also worth the ski-bus ride and walk to the new **Pension Strolz Christian** (☎ 05446-301 19, fax -4; Ing Gomperz Strasse 606; per person €38). When the hunger pangs hit, there is a **Spar supermarket** on the main street and good pizzas at **Pomodoro**. At night, there is certainly a whiff of testosterone in the St Anton air. By about 6pm, people are often bawling rock standards from the door of **Piccadilly**, while it takes slightly longer for things to get going in **Kandahar**, which also serves Indian food. **Krazy Kanguruh** is a popular bar on the slopes.

Getting There & Away

St Anton is on the main railway route between Bregenz and Innsbruck, less than 1½ hours from both. St Anton is close to the eastern entrance of the Arlberg Tunnel, the toll road connecting Vorarlberg and Tirol. The tunnel toll is €9.45/7.25 for cars/motorcycles. You can avoid the toll by taking the B197, but no vehicles with trailers are allowed on this winding road. There is a choice of about 3/12 buses a day in summer/winter to Lech (€3.42, 40 minutes) from St Anton.

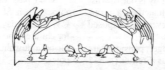

Belgium

Think of Belgium (België in Flemish, Belgique in French) and it's 'Bruges, beer and chocolate' that generally spring to mind. While Brits might add 'boring' to that list and businesspeople would arrive at the 'European Union', few other word associations are likely to pop up. Belgium, you see, has an identity problem. A little country surrounded by Europe's big guys, it's been fought over by bossy neighbours for most of its history. Nationhood only came about less than 200 years ago, and since then rivalry between the two main language communities – the Flemish and the Walloon – has kept nationalism at bay.

Belgium has plenty to fascinate the visitor. This much-embattled country spawned Western Europe's first great towns and it was here that medieval artists are credited with inventing oil painting. To these historically-rich art towns add fab restaurants, thousands of bars and cafés, great beer and chocolate, avant-garde fashion, rich Art Nouveau architecture and some lovely rural corners in the hilly Ardennes. Belgium's not boring, it just hasn't learnt to boast.

Facts about Belgium

HISTORY

Belgium's position between France, Germany, the Netherlands and, across the North Sea, England has long made it one of Europe's main battlegrounds.

Prosperous throughout the 13th and 14th centuries, the Flemish towns of Ypres, Bruges and Ghent were the first major cities, booming on the manufacturing and trading of cloth. Their craftspeople established powerful guilds (organisations to stringently control arts and crafts) whose elaborate guildhalls you'll see in many cities. However, the Flemish weavers were ruined by competition from England and, due largely to Bruges' refusal to handle the foreign cloth as well as the silting of its river, the towns faded. Trade moved eastward to Antwerp, which soon became the greatest port in Europe.

When Protestantism swept Europe in the 16th century, the Low Countries (present-day

Belgium, the Netherlands and Luxembourg, often referred to as the Benelux) embraced it, much to the chagrin of their ruler, the fanatically Catholic Philip II of Spain. He sent the cruel Inquisition to enforce Catholicism, thus inflaming the smouldering religious tensions. The eruption came with the Iconoclastic Fury, in which Protestants ran riot, ransacking the churches. Philip retaliated with a force of 10,000 soldiers, and thousands of citizens

BELGIUM

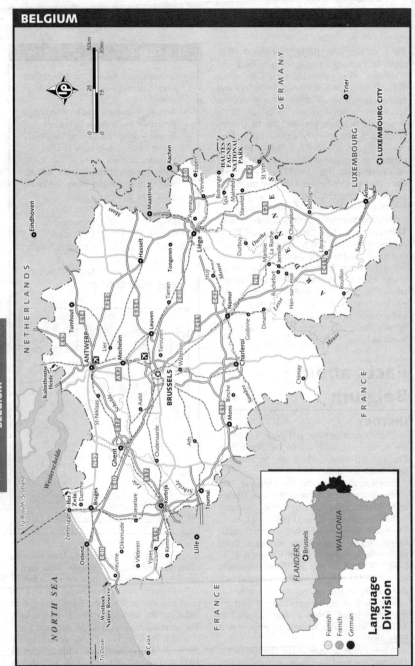

BELGIUM

Language
Division

Flemish
French
German

were imprisoned or executed before war broke out in 1568. The Revolt of the Netherlands lasted 80 years, and in the end roughly laid the region's present-day borders. Holland and its allied provinces victoriously expelled the Spaniards while Belgium and Luxembourg stayed under their rule.

For the next 200 years Belgium remained a battlefield for successive foreign powers. After the Spaniards, the Austrians came and in turn the French. The largely unpopular French occupation ended in 1814 with the creation of the United Kingdom of the Netherlands, which incorporated Belgium and Luxembourg. Napoleon was finally trounced the following year at the Battle of Waterloo near Brussels. In 1830 the Catholic Belgians revolted, winning independence from the Netherlands and forming their own kingdom.

The ensuing years saw the start of Flemish nationalism, with tension growing between Flemish (Dutch) and French speakers which would eventually lead to a language partition that divided the country (see Population & People later in this chapter).

In 1885 the then king, Léopold II, personally acquired the Congo in Africa. He was later disgraced over the continuing slave trade there. In the early 1900s the Congo was made a Belgian colony; much-disputed independence was granted in 1960.

Despite Belgium's neutral policy, the Germans invaded in 1914. Used as a bloody battleground throughout WWI, the town of Ypres was wiped off the map. During WWII the whole country was taken over within three weeks of a surprise German attack in May 1940. Controversy over the questionable early capitulation by the then king, Léopold III, led to his abdication in 1950 in favour of his son, King Baudouin, whose popular reign ended with his death (at age 62) in 1993.

Childless, Baudouin was succeeded by his brother, the present King Albert II. Thanks to a relatively recent change of law allowing women to rule, Albert's granddaughter, Elizabeth, born in 2001, is the first female heir to the Belgian throne.

Postwar Belgium was characterised by an economic boom, later accentuated by Brussels' appointment as headquarters of the EU and North Atlantic Treaty Organization (NATO).

During the 1990s, political and judicial scandals have left Belgium with the nickname

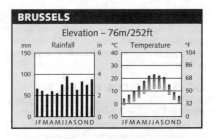

BRUSSELS

Elevation – 76m/252ft

of the 'Italy of the north'. The most famous incident, the Dutroux affair, involved suspected murderer and paedophile, Marc Dutroux, and resulted in 300,000 Belgians taking to the streets of Brussels in 1996 to protest the nation's malfunctioning police and judicial systems. Reform has been slow and that, combined with the continuing friction between the Flemish and Walloon communities, has left many Belgians questioning the future of their country.

GEOGRAPHY
Occupying 30,520 sq km, Belgium is one of Europe's smallest nations, sandwiched between the Netherlands, Germany, Luxembourg and France. The north is flat, the south dominated by the hilly, forested Ardennes, and the 66km North Sea coastline monopolised by resorts, save for a few patches of windswept dunes.

CLIMATE
The country has a generally mild, maritime climate. July and August are the warmest months. They are also the wettest, although precipitation is spread pretty evenly over the year. The Ardennes is often a few degrees colder than the rest of the country, with occasional snow from November to March.

ECOLOGY & ENVIRONMENT
Water and noise pollution, urbanisation and waste management are the most pressing environmental issues. Public concern over these issues has led to growing support for the Green parties, which are a part of the present coalition government.

Belgium's largest nature reserve is Hautes Fagnes National Park, a region of swampy heath and woods in the Ardennes. Other important reserves include the Kalmthoutse Heide (heather and dunes) north of Antwerp, as well as Het Zwin (polders and mudflats)

BELGIUM

and the Westhoek (dunes), which sit at either end of Belgium's coastal strip. By anyone's standards these reserves are small, and the country's flora and fauna are under enormous pressure to survive.

GOVERNMENT & POLITICS

Belgium is a constitutional hereditary monarchy, led by King Albert II and a parliament. In 1993 the government was decentralised by creating three regional governments representing the Flemish and Walloon communities (Flanders and Wallonia respectively) as well as the Brussels-Capital region.

The overall political scene has long been dominated by the (Catholic) Christian Democrats, Socialists and Liberals, though support for the Green parties as well as the ultra-right-wing Vlaams Blok (Flemish Block) is on the increase. The latter is particularly strong in Antwerp, where it gained a third of the vote in the 2000 municipal election.

The Liberals emerged from the last national election in 1999 as the leading political force and formed a coalition government with the Socialists and Greens. The Prime Minister, Guy Verhofstadt, is Belgium's first Liberal leader in more than half a century.

ECONOMY

Over the centuries, Belgium's economic prosperity has swung between one language community and the other, starting with Flanders' medieval textile wealth, which was later supplanted by Wallonia's mining and steel industries. The latter's decline means Flanders is again the country's industrial backbone. The economy as a whole, however, is struggling with a huge public debt and relatively high unemployment (8.4%). In 2001, the GDP was US$259 billion. The main industries are chemicals, car manufacturing, textiles, iron and steel. Agriculture (cereals), horticulture and stock breeding are also important.

POPULATION & PEOPLE

While spread over 10 provinces, Belgium's population is basically split in two: the Flemish and the Walloons. Indeed, many people call themselves Flemish or Walloon first, and Belgian second. Language is the dividing factor, made official in 1962 when an invisible line – or Linguistic Divide as it's called – was drawn across the country, cutting it almost equally in half. To the north lies Flanders (Vlaanderen), whose Flemish speakers make up 60% of Belgium's population of 10.2 million. To the south is Wallonia (La Wallonie), where French-speaking Walloons make up most of the remainder. To complicate matters, Brussels is officially bilingual but predominantly French speaking. It lies within the Flemish region but is governed separately. There's also a tiny German-speaking enclave in the east of Wallonia.

The roots of the language issue can be traced back to Roman times, however, it was formalised with the establishment of the Belgian constitution. The ruling elite made French the official language and banned Flemish. Over the years this divisive issue has caused many political and social conflicts.

ARTS

Belgium has produced many influential painters of world renown. The master of early Flemish painting is undoubtedly Jan van Eyck (c. 1390–1441), who perfected the technique of oil painting and founded the Flemish school. He worked in both Bruges, and The Hague in the Netherlands. The 16th-century painter and draughtsman Pieter Brueghel the Elder (1525–69) regained fame in the 20th century for landscapes and religious paintings.

Pieter Paul Rubens (1577–1640) dominated Flemish painting during the 17th century. He founded a studio and consolidated his reputation as the most important exponent of baroque painting in Europe. In 2002, one of Rubens' works, *Massacre of the Innocent*, was sold in London for £135 million – a record for a painting auctioned in Britain. The famous portrait painter Anthony (Antoon) van Dyck (1599–1641) and his contemporary Jacob Jordaens (1593–1678) were natives of Antwerp and graduated from the Rubens studio.

The start of the 20th century saw the beginnings of sinuous Art Nouveau architecture in Brussels. The movement was led by Henri van de Velde and Victor Horta. The latter was famed for interiors that displayed few straight lines – ceilings simply became curved continuations of walls. Stained glass and wrought iron fashioned in stylised natural forms were also used. The painter René Magritte (1898–1967) lived most of his life in Brussels, but his disturbing surreal images have earned him an enduring international reputation.

Belgians who became famous in the music world include Adolphe Sax (1814–94), who

Foreboding and formidable – the Cuillin Hills on the Isle of Skye, Scotland

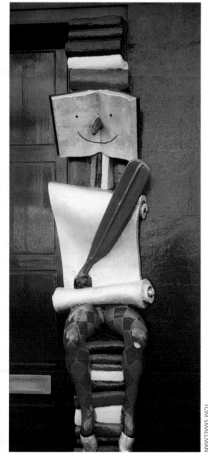

All puffed out, Scotland

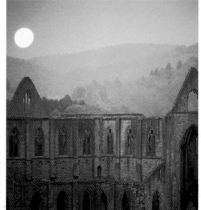

Fringe festival office entrance, Edinburgh, Scotland

Ghostly Tintern Abbey, Wales

RICHARD I'ANSON

Napoleon-era architecture, Paris

MARTIN MOOS

Fast-food sculpture on the Champs-Élysées, Paris, France

JOHN HAY

Mona Lisa has the classiest address in town – the Louvre, Paris, France

JON DAVISON

Nice tans, nice weather, Nice, Côte d'Azur, France

invented the saxophone; Jean 'Toots' Thiele-mans (1922–), whose harmonica playing earnt him fame in the jazz scene; and the raspy-voiced Jacques Brel, who rose to star-dom in Paris in the 1950s for his songs about Belgium that are still popular today.

The country's most prestigious classical music event is the Concours Musical International Reine Élisabeth de Belgique (Queen Elisabeth International Musical Competition), which attracts young talent from around the world.

Very little local literature has been translated into English. One book you may want to get hold of is *The Sorrow of Belgium* by Hugo Claus, which describes wartime Belgium through the eyes of a Flemish adolescent. Marguerite Yourcenar is arguably the country's most famous female poet and writer. Liège detective novelist Georges Simenon is famed for his detective character, Inspector Maigret.

Comic strips are a Belgian forte. Hergé, the creator of Tintin, is one of the country's best known cartoonists.

SOCIETY & CONDUCT

With their history of foreign domination, Belgians are used to visitors and their different habits, and there are few social taboos that travellers are likely to break. It is customary to greet shopkeepers and café/pub owners when entering their premises. The possession of cannabis for personal use was decriminalised in Belgium in 2001.

RELIGION

Long a Catholic stronghold, Belgium has experienced a decrease in church attendances but religious traditions continue, influencing many aspects of daily life, including politics and education.

LANGUAGE

See the History and Population & People sections earlier in this chapter for information on language. For a rundown of Flemish (Dutch), French and German languages, see the Language chapter at the back of this book. English is widely spoken – less so in Wallonia.

For travellers, the Linguistic Divide will cause few problems. The most confusing part will be on the road, when the sign you're following to Bergen (as it's known in Flemish) disappears and the town of Mons (the French name) appears.

Facts for the Visitor

HIGHLIGHTS

Here are some of Belgium's highlights:

Beers
Duvel, Westmalle Triple, Cantillon Gueuze, Hoegaarden, Rochefort 10, Oerbier, Delirium Tremens
Cycling
Anywhere in Flanders for flat terrain; Wallonia for mountain biking
Hiking
La Roche, Rochefort or the Hautes Fagnes areas of the Ardennes
Museums & Sights
Grand Place, Musée Horta, Old England Building and Musées Royaux des Beaux-Arts in Brussels; Belfry, Begijnhof and canal cruise in Bruges; Onze Lieve Vrouwkathedraal and Rubenshuis in Antwerp; Flanders Fields Museum in Ypres
Pubs
Falstaff and Le Greenwich in Brussels; 't Brugs Beertje in Bruges; Oud Arsenaal in Antwerp

SUGGESTED ITINERARIES

Depending on the length of your stay, you might want to see and do the following:

Two days
One day each in Brussels and Bruges.
One week
Two days each in Brussels and the Ardennes, and one day each in Antwerp, Bruges and Ypres.
Two weeks
Three days in and around Brussels, two days each in Antwerp and the Ardennes, two days in Bruges and Ypres, two days in coastal resorts, and one day each in Ghent, Namur and Liège.
One month
This should give you plenty of time to explore the previously-mentioned places and discover a few new places of your own.

PLANNING
When to Go

Spring is the best time to go, as there's less chance of rain, many flowers (including daffodils and tulips) are in bloom and tourist crowds are minimal.

Maps

The best road maps of Belgium are those produced by Michelin – map No 909 (scale:

BELGIUM

1:350,000) covers Belgium and Luxembourg. The Institut Géographique National (IGN) publishes topographical maps (on a scale of 1:25,000). Lonely Planet's comprehensive foldout Brussels City Map contains five maps at a scale of 1:15,000.

TOURIST OFFICES
Local Tourist Offices

The Flemish and Walloon tourist authorities (Toerisme Vlaanderen and Office de Promotion du Tourisme, respectively) have a joint office (☎ 02-504 03 90, fax 02-504 02 70; e info@toerismevlaanderen.be; e info@ opt.be) at Rue du Marché aux Herbes 63, B-1000 Brussels. Much of the tourist literature is free.

Tourist Offices Abroad

Belgian tourist offices abroad include:

Canada
(☎ 514-484 3594, fax 489 8965) PO Box 760, Succursale NDG, Montreal, Que H4A 3S2
France
(☎ 01 47 42 41 18, fax 01 47 42 71 83) blvd des Capucines 21, 75002 Paris
Germany
(☎ 0221-27 75 90, fax 27 75 91) Cäcilienstrasse 46, 50667 Cologne
The Netherlands
Flanders: Toerisme Vlaanderen-Brussel (☎ 070-416 81 10, e verkeersbureau@ toerisme-vlaanderen.nl) Koninginnegracht 86, NL-2514 AJ The Hague
Wallonia: Belgisch Verkeersbureau voor de Ardennen en Brussel (☎ 023-534 44 34, e belgisch.verkeersbureau@wxs.nl) PO 2324 NL-2002 CH Haarlem
UK
Flanders: Tourism Flanders-Brussels (☎ 020-7458 0044, 0800-954 5245, fax 7458 0045, e info@flanders-tourism.org) 31 Pepper St, London E14 9RW
Wallonia: Belgian Tourist Office Brussels-Ardennes (☎ 0800-954 5245, fax 7531 0393, e info@belgiumtheplaceto.be) 217 Marsh Wall, London E14 9FJ
USA
(☎ 212-758 8130, fax 355 7675, e info@ visitbelgium.com) 780 Third Ave, Suite 1501, New York, NY 10017

VISAS & DOCUMENTS

Visitors from many countries need only a valid passport for three-month visits. Regulations are basically the same as for entering the Netherlands (for more details, see the

Facts for the Visitor section in the Netherlands chapter).

EMBASSIES & CONSULATES
Belgian Embassies & Consulates

Belgian representation abroad includes:

Australia (☎ 02-6273 2501, fax 6273 3392) 19 Arkana St, Yarralumla, Canberra, ACT 2600
Canada (☎ 613-236 7267/69, fax 236 7882) 4th floor, 80 Elgin St, Ottawa, Ont K1P 1B7
New Zealand (Honorary Consulate, ☎ 09-379 6690, fax 309 9570) 18 Waterloo Quadrant, Auckland
UK (☎ 020-7470 3700, fax 7259 6213) 103-105 Eaton Square, London SW1 9AB
USA (☎ 202-333 6900, fax 333 3079) 3330 Garfield St NW, Washington DC 20008

Embassies & Consulates in Belgium

All the following embassies and consulates are in Brussels:

Australia (☎ 02-231 05 00, fax 02-230 68 02) Rue Guimard 6, B-1040
Canada (☎ 02-741 06 11, fax 02-741 06 43) Ave de Tervueren 2, B-1040
France (☎ 02-548 87 11, fax 02-513 68 71) Rue Ducale 65, B-1000
Germany (☎ 02-774 19 11, fax 02-772 36 92) Ave de Tervueren 190, B-1150
Ireland (☎ 02-230 53 37, fax 02-230 53 12) Rue Froissart 89, B-1040
Luxembourg (☎ 02-737 57 00, fax 02-737 57 10) Ave de Cortenbergh 75, B-1000
The Netherlands (☎ 02-679 17 11, fax 02-679 17 75) Ave Herrmann-Debroux 48, B-1160
New Zealand (☎ 02-512 10 40, fax 02-513 48 56) Square de Meeus 1, 7th floor, B-1000
UK (☎ 02-287 62 11, fax 02-287 63 55) Rue d'Arlon 85, B-1040
USA (☎ 02-508 21 11, fax 02-511 27 25) Blvd du Régent 27, B-1000

MONEY

Belgium's currency is the euro (see the boxed text 'The Euro' in the introductory Facts for the Visitor chapter for details).

Exchanging Money

Banks are the best place to change money, charging no commission on cash, and €2.48 on travellers cheques. Out of hours there are exchange bureaus which generally offer lower rates. All major credit cards are widely accepted. You'll find ATMs in major cities and at Zaventem (Brussels) airport.

Costs

If you stay at hostels and eat very cheaply you can get by on between €35 and €40 per day. Because of the country's size, getting around is not a major cost. Most museums offer concessions for students and seniors.

Tipping & Bargaining

Tipping is not obligatory and bargaining not customary.

Taxes & Refunds

Value-added tax, or VAT (BTW in Flemish, TVA in French), is calculated at 6% for food, hotels and camping grounds, and either 17% or the more common 21% for everything else. To get a rebate, your purchase invoice has to be stamped by customs as you leave. You send it back to the shop and it'll forward the refund. Alternatively, buy from shops affiliated with the Tax Cheque Refund Service (see Money in the Netherlands chapter for details).

POST & COMMUNICATIONS
Post

Post offices are generally open 8am or 9am to 5pm or 6pm weekdays and on Saturday mornings. Letters (under 20g) cost €0.42 within Belgium, €0.52 in the EU, €0.74 in the rest of Europe or €0.84 elsewhere. They average seven to nine days to reach places outside Europe and two to three days inside. Poste restante can attract a €0.35 fee (often waived).

Telephone

Belgium's international country code is ☎ 32. To telephone abroad, the international access code is ☎ 00 (see the Telephones appendix).

In 2000, Belgium introduced a single telephone zone for the entire country. This means it costs the same to make a telephone call within Brussels as to call, for example, Bruges from Brussels. At the same time, area codes were incorporated into phone numbers. So if you're anywhere in Belgium (including in Brussels) and are phoning, for example, Brussels, the number you dial must include the '02' area code.

Phone calls are metered and cost a minimum of €0.30. Telephone numbers prefixed with 0900 or 070 are pay-per-minute numbers (from €0.20 to €0.45 per minute). Numbers prefixed with 0800 are free calls.

Call boxes take €0.10, €0.20, €0.50, €1 and €2 coins as well as €5 and €10 Telecards

(Belgacom phonecards), available from post offices and newsagents. International calls can be made using XL-Call phonecards (€5, €10 or €20), also available from post offices. A three-minute phone call to the USA from a phone box costs €3.

For travellers with mobile phones, Belgium uses GSM 900/1800, which is compatible with the rest of Europe and Australia but not with the North American GSM 1900 or the system used in Japan.

Fax

Faxes can be sent and received from Belgacom shops (known as *teleboetieks* or *téléboutiques*) and cost €1.61 for the first page to many destinations including the UK, USA and Australia, plus €0.62 for each additional page. Receiving a fax costs €0.25 per page.

Email & Internet Access

Internet cafés are plentiful; expect to pay €3 to €4.50 per hour.

DIGITAL RESOURCES

Excellent websites offering heaps of information on transport, accommodation and tourism, plus links to other Some Belgium-related sites are W www.visitbelgium.com and W www.trabel.com. For an overview of Brussels go to W www.bruxelles.irisnet.be.

BOOKS

Lonely Planet's *Belgium & Luxembourg* guide has comprehensive coverage of both these countries. For an affectionate look at Belgium's many idiosyncrasies, pick up *A Tall Man in a Low Land*, written by Englishman Harry Pearson.

Brussels and Antwerp have stores specialising in English-language books; alternatively, head to a chain store like FNAC or Standaard Boekhandel.

FILMS

Dominique Deruddere's comedy *Everybody Famous* was nominated for an Academy Award in the best foreign-language category in 2001. Another recently acclaimed Belgian film is *Rosetta* by the Dardenne brothers – it won the Palme d'Or at Cannes in 1999. Other noted films include *The Eighth Day* and *Toto le Héros*, both by Jaco Van Dormael; *The Sexual Life of the Belgians* by Jan Bucquoy and *Daens* by Stijn Coninckx.

BELGIUM

NEWSPAPERS & MAGAZINES

American and English newspapers and magazines are widely available. *Le Soir* (French) and *De Standaard* (Flemish) are the best national daily newspapers.

The English-language *Bulletin* magazine (€2.50) comes out on Thursday and has national news and a good entertainment guide.

RADIO & TV

The BBC's World Service can be picked up on 648kHz AM. Two popular Belgian radio stations are Radio 1 (Flemish) and Radio 21 (French). The main Belgian TV channels are TV1, VTM and Kanaal 2 (Flemish), and RTBF1 and ARTE (French). Most homes have cable TV and can access a myriad of international stations, which includes the BBC and CNN.

TIME

Belgium runs on Central European Time. At noon in Belgium it's 11am in London, 6am in New York, 3am in San Francisco, 6am in Toronto, 9pm in Sydney and 11pm in Auckland. Daylight-saving time comes into effect at 2am on the last Sunday in March, when clocks are moved an hour forward; they're moved an hour back again at 2am on the last Sunday in October. The 24-hour clock is commonly used.

LAUNDRY

Self-service laundries *(wassalon/laverie)* on average charge €2.50 for a 5kg wash and €0.20 per dryer cycle.

TOILETS

Public toilets (€0.30 fee) are few and far between so duck into a pub or café.

WOMEN TRAVELLERS

Women should encounter few problems travelling around Belgium. However, in the event of rape or attack, contact **SOS Viol** (☎ 02-534 36 36) or **Helpline** (☎ 02-648 40 14).

GAY & LESBIAN TRAVELLERS

Attitudes to homosexuality are becoming less conservative and same-sex marriages are now legal. The age of consent is 16.

Flanders' biggest gay/lesbian organisation is **Federatie Werkgroepen Homoseksualiteit** *(FWH;* ⓦ *www.fwh.be; Kammerstraat 22)* in Ghent. It has a café and also operates an information and help hotline which is called **Holebifoon** (☎ *09-238 26 26; open 6pm-10pm daily).*

The main French-speaking gay/lesbian group is **Tels Quels** (☎ *02-512 45 87, fax 02-511 31 48; Rue du Marché au Charbon 81)* in Brussels. This bar-cum-information centre is one of the few meeting places in Brussels frequented by both sexes. It also runs a helpline, **Télégal** (☎ *02-502 79 38; open 8pm-midnight daily).*

La Loba (☎ *02-512 03 47; Galerie Bortier, Rue St Jean, Brussels)* is a women's bookshop and lesbian information centre.

The Belgian Pride parade is held on the first weekend of May.

DISABLED TRAVELLERS

Belgium is not terribly user-friendly for travellers with a mobility problem. Some government buildings, museums, hotels and restaurants have lifts and/or ramps, but not the majority. Wheelchair users will be up against rough, uneven pavements, and will need to give an hour's notice when travelling by train.

For more information, contact **Mobility International** (☎ *03-236 51 19, fax 03-272 27 93; Koorstraat 1, B-3510 Kermt).*

SENIOR TRAVELLERS

Most museums and other attractions offer reductions to seniors over 65. Travellers aged over 65 pay only €2.50 for a return day trip by train (2nd class) to anywhere in Belgium.

On the whole, getting around should pose few major problems, although at some train stations, platforms are low-set, making it difficult to climb into carriages.

TRAVEL WITH CHILDREN

Belgians love kids and there is plenty to keep the youngsters occupied. Children usually enjoy canal rides in Bruges, the Atomium in Brussels, the caves at Han-sur-Lesse in the Ardennes and a bike ride in the countryside. Indulging in waffles, chocolates and *frites* (chips) is sure to be a winner.

DANGERS & ANNOYANCES

Belgium is, in general, very safe. The only danger you're likely to encounter is a big night out on Belgian beer.

As in some other parts of Western Europe, racism has increased during the past decade.

Emergency Services

The national emergency numbers are police ☎ 101 and fire/ambulance ☎ 100. The ☎ 112 emergency number used for much of Europe can also be used. For 24-hour roadside assistance in the event of breakdown, the Touring Club de Belgique offers Touring Secours (☎ 070-34 47 77).

Hostility here is primarily directed at the nation's immigrant populations, particularly Turks and Moroccans.

LEGAL MATTERS

Police usually treat tourists with respect. Under Belgian law, you must carry either a passport or national identity card at all times. Should you be arrested, you have the right to ask for your consul to be immediately notified.

BUSINESS HOURS

In general, shops are open 8.30am or 9am to noon and 2pm to 6pm Monday to Saturday. Shops in some cities also open on Sunday. Banks are open 9am to noon or 1pm, and 2pm to 4pm or 5pm weekdays, and Saturday mornings. In large cities, shops and banks often don't close for lunch.

PUBLIC HOLIDAYS & SPECIAL EVENTS

Public holidays include New Year's Day, Easter Monday, Labour Day (1 May), Ascension Day, Whit Monday, Festival of the Flemish Community (11 July, Flanders only), Belgium National Day (21 July), Assumption (15 August), Festival of the Walloon Community (27 September, Wallonia only), All Saints' Day (1 November), Armistice Day (11 November) and Christmas Day.

The religious festival of Carnival is celebrated throughout Belgium, but is at its most colourful in the villages of Binche and Stavelot. There's a swarm of local and national, artistic or religious festivals – pick up the tourist office's free brochure.

ACTIVITIES

The Ardennes is Belgium's outdoor playground. The hilly, forested terrain favours kayaking, hiking or mountain biking on a *vélo tout terrain* (VTT – a mountain bike) and, in winter, cross-country skiing. Cycling is also a hit in flat Flanders – for more details see Bicycle in the Getting Around section.

WORK

Nationals from EU countries do not require a work permit to work in Belgium. Non-EU nationals cannot seek employment here without having a work permit issued before they arrive. Given Belgium's high unemployment, chances of finding work as a non-EU national are slim.

ACCOMMODATION

In summer all forms of accommodation are heavily booked. The national tourist office will reserve accommodation for free and has camping and hotel brochures, as well as booklets on B&Bs and rural houses available for weekly rental. Once you're in Belgium, local tourist offices offer free accommodation booking services (you pay a deposit that is deducted from your room rate).

Camping rates vary widely, but on average you'll be looking at between €6.50 and €13 for two adults, a tent and vehicle.

There are private hostels in some cities. Otherwise, Belgium has two HI hostelling groups. The **Vlaamse Jeugdherbergcentrale** (☎ 03-232 72 18, fax 03-231 81 26; e info@ vjh.be; Van Stralenstraat 40, B-2060 Antwerp) runs hostels in Flanders. Its Walloon counterpart is **Les Auberges de Jeunesse** (☎ 02-219 56 76, fax 02-219 14 51; e info@ laj.be; Rue de la Sablonnière 28, B-1000 Brussels). The rates for members range from €12.50 to €14.50 per night in a dorm. Some hostels have single/double rooms for €22.50/ 17.50 per person. Nonmembers pay €2.50 extra for the first six nights. Prices include breakfast and sheets.

B&Bs/guesthouses (*gastenkamers* in Flemish; *chambres d'hôtes* in French) are rapidly gaining ground in Belgium – prices range from €30 to €60 for singles and €45 to €80 for doubles. Unfortunately many B&Bs will not accept stays of one night; those that do generally levy a surcharge.

Budget hotels charge €35 to €50 for a single room and from €50 to €70 for doubles. Breakfast is usually included; the cheaper rooms have communal bathroom facilities. The starting price for mid-range single/double hotel rooms is about €70/80. Top-end establishments start at around €110/130, or in Brussels €180/220. Some of the mid-range

BELGIUM

and top-end hotels in Brussels (and also in other cities such as Antwerp and Liège) drop their rates dramatically on Friday and Saturday nights, when all the businesspeople have gone home. Great deals can be had.

FOOD

Belgian cuisine is highly regarded throughout Europe – some say it's second only to French, while in others' eyes it's equal. Combining French style with German portions, you'll rarely have reason to complain.

Meat and seafood are abundantly consumed, and then of course there are frites – chips or fries – which the Belgians swear they invented and which, judging by availability, is a claim few would contest.

Snacks

The popularity of frites cannot be understated. Every village has at least one *frituur/friture* where frites are served in a paper cone or dish, smothered until almost unrecognisable with large blobs of thick mayonnaise and eaten with a small fork in a mostly futile attempt to keep your fingers clean. Another favourite snack is a *belegd broodje/sandwich garni* – half a baguette filled with an array of garnishes.

On the sweet side, *wafels/gaufres* (waffles) are eaten piping hot from market stalls. Then there are Belgium's famous filled chocolates, better known as *pralines* (see Shopping later in this chapter for details).

Main Dishes

Meat, poultry and hearty vegetable soups figure prominently on menus, but it's *mosselen/moules* (mussels) cooked in white wine and served with a mountain of frites that's regarded as the national dish. Cultivated mainly in the Delta region in the Netherlands, the rule of thumb for mussels is: eat them during the months that include an 'r', and don't touch the ones that haven't opened properly when cooked.

Game, including pheasant and boar, is an autumn speciality from the Ardennes (also famed for its hams). Horse, rabbit and guinea fowl are typical offerings. In spring, asparagus from Mechelen is a firm favourite. When dining out, the *dagschotel/plat du jour* (dish of the day) is often the cheapest option. Even better value is the *dagmenu/menu du jour* (menu of the day), which comprises anything from three

to six courses. Many cafés and brasseries cater for vegetarians (but not vegans).

DRINKS

Beer rules – and deservedly so. The quality is excellent and the variety incomparable – somewhere upwards of 400 types, from standard lagers to specialist brews. The most noted are the abbey-brewed Trappist beers, dark in colour, grainy in taste and dangerously strong (from 6% to 12% alcohol by volume). *Lambiek/lambic* is a spontaneously fermented beer which is available sweet or sour depending on what's added during fermentation – *gueuze*, a sour variety, is the most famous. Beer prices match quality, with a 250mL lager costing €1.50 to €2.30, and a 330mL Trappist €2.80 to €4.20. For beer recommendations, see Highlights at the start of the Facts for the Visitor section.

ENTERTAINMENT

Nightlife centres around the ubiquitous bars and cafés but there are plenty of other options including opera, theatre, dance, music festivals and puppet theatres. Cinemas in Flanders usually screen films in their original language with Flemish subtitles, while those in Wallonia tend to dub them into French. Screenings are sometimes cheaper on Monday.

SHOPPING

Lace, chocolate and beer are the specialities, but the first two don't come cheap. A lace handkerchief will set you back between €5 and €25.

Pralines cost €17 to €36 per kilo depending on quality and where you buy them. They're sold everywhere – from the local bakery or supermarket deli, to specialist chain stores like Leonidas and Godiva or, at the top end, independent establishments such as Wittamer in Brussels and Del Rey in Antwerp.

Getting There & Away

AIR

Belgium's national airline, Sabena, went down the gurgler in 2001. In its place rose **SN Brussels Airlines** (☎ 070-35 11 11), which flies to many European destinations as well as to some countries in sub-Saharan Africa.

The country's main international airport is Zaventem (also known as Brussels National), 14km northeast of Brussels. Much smaller airports servicing a tiny number of international flights include Deurne, close to Antwerp, and Brussels South (55km south of Brussels) at Charleroi.

Airline passengers departing from Zaventem pay a €17.50 departure tax; from Deurne it's €8 and from Brussels South it's €7 (this tax is commonly included in airline tickets).

LAND
Bus
Eurolines operates international bus services to and from Belgium. Tickets can be bought from its offices in Antwerp, Brussels or Liège, or from travel agencies. Reduced fares for people aged under 26 or over 60 are offered. In July and August, some fares – such as those to London – are subject to a peak season supplement.

Eurolines has regular buses to many Western, Eastern, Mediterranean and Central European destinations, as well as Scandinavia and North Africa. Depending on the destination and the time of year, its buses stop in Brussels, Antwerp, Bruges, Ghent and Liège. To most major destinations there's just one price, irrespective of where in Belgium you depart from. Given Belgium's small size, there's also not much difference in journey times – for example, Brussels–Paris takes 3¾ hours, and from Antwerp it takes 4¾ hours.

Services from Brussels include Amsterdam (€15, four hours, seven daily), Cologne (€19, four hours, one daily), London (€46, 8½ hours, four daily) and Paris (€17, 3¾ hours, eight daily).

Train
Belgium built continental Europe's first railway line (Brussels–Mechelen) in the 1830s. The national network is run by the Belgische Spoorwegen/Société National des Chemins de Fer Belges, whose logo is a 'B' in an oval. Major train stations have information offices open until 7pm (until 9pm in Brussels). For all international inquiries – including Eurostar and Thalys trains – call ☎ 02-528 28 28.

Brussels is the international hub and has three main train stations – Gare du Nord, Gare Centrale and Gare du Midi. Gare du Midi is the main one for international connections: Eurostar and Thalys fast trains stop here only.

Eurostar (ⓦ www.eurostar.com) trains between Brussels and London (2¾ hours, nine trains daily) operate through the Channel Tunnel. Standard 2nd-class fares are €223/352 one way/return, however, cheaper weekend and mid-week fares are available (conditions apply).

Thalys (ⓦ www.thalys.com) fast trains connect Brussels with Paris (€61.20, 1½ hours, hourly), Cologne (€33.90, 2½ hours, seven trains daily) and Amsterdam (€36.90, 2½ hours, 10 daily). Cheaper Thalys fares are available on weekends and for trips booked well in advance. Those aged under 26 receive a 50% discount.

Examples of one-way, 2nd-class adult fares and journey times with ordinary trains from Brussels to some neighbouring countries include Amsterdam (€30, 2½ hours, hourly), Cologne (€29.50, three hours, every two hours), and Luxembourg City (€23.80, 2¾ hours, hourly). On weekends, all return fares are reduced by 40%.

Car & Motorcycle
The main motorways into Belgium are the E19 from the Netherlands, the E40 from Germany, the E411 from Luxembourg and the E17 and E19 from France. For details on car ferries between Belgium and the UK, see the following section.

SEA
Hoverspeed (ⓦ www.hoverspeed.com) sails a high-speed Seacat from Ostend to Dover (England) in two hours (twice daily). The one-way fare for a car and one adult is around €225; passengers are charged €37.

Superfast Ferries (ⓦ www.superfast.com) is a new service operating between Zeebrugge and Rosyth near Edinburgh in Scotland. The overnight voyage takes 17½ hours. One-way fares for cars range from €92 to €228, depending on the season; passenger fares start at €70 in a nine-bed cabin.

There's no departure tax when leaving Belgium by sea.

Getting Around

BUS
Buses connect towns and villages in more remote areas, particularly throughout the Ardennes. Local tourist offices will generally

have details, or contact the regional bus information office in Namur (see the Namur Getting There & Away section later in this chapter for details).

TRAIN

Belgium's public transport system is dominated by its efficient rail network. There are four levels of service: InterCity (IC) trains (which are the fastest), InterRegional (IR), local (L) and peak-hour (P) commuter trains. Depending on the line, there will be an IC and an IR train every half-hour or hour. Most train stations have either luggage lockers (€1.50/2.80/3.30 for small/medium/large lockers for 24 hours) or luggage rooms, which are generally open from 6am to 9pm and charge €2.23 per article per day. For all national train information, call ☎ 02-555 25 55.

Costs

First-class fares are 50% more than 2nd class. On weekends, return tickets within Belgium are reduced by 40% for a single passenger or the first in a group (to a maximum of six people), and 60% for the rest of the group.

Another option to consider if you're travelling in a small group (three to five people) is a Multi Pass. It costs €35/40/44 for three/four/five people (one person must be over 26 years) and is valid for one journey anywhere in the country.

Discount excursion tickets, known as B-Excursions, to a huge number of destinations around the country are also well worth inquiring about.

Many rail passes are available. The Benelux Tourrail, which gives five days travel in one month in Belgium, the Netherlands and Luxembourg, costs €174/116 in 1st/2nd class for those aged 26 and over, and €87 (2nd class only) for under 26s.

The B-Tourrail pass gives five days travel in one month within Belgium for €90/58 in 1st/2nd class. The Rail Pass costs €90/58, gives 10 one-way trips anywhere in Belgium and is valid for one year. For those under 26, the equivalent of the Rail Pass is the Go Pass (€39; valid in 2nd class for six months).

CAR & MOTORCYCLE

Drive on the right and give way to the right. The speed limit is 50km/h in towns, 90km/h outside towns and 120km/h on motorways. The blood alcohol limit is 0.05%. Fuel prices

per litre are €1.10 for super, €1 for lead-free and €0.75 for diesel. More motoring information can be obtained from the **Touring Club de Belgique** (☎ 02-233 22 11; Rue de la Loi 44, B-1040 Brussels).

Car rental (including insurance, VAT and unlimited kilometres) ranges from around €45 to €70 a day or €180 to €240 a week. Rental firms include **Avis** (☎ 02-537 12 80; Rue Américaine 145); **Budget** (☎ 02-646 51 30; Ave Louise 327b); **Hertz** (☎ 02-513 28 86; Blvd Maurice Lemonnier 8); and **National/Alamo** (☎ 02-753 20 60; Zaventem airport).

BICYCLE

Getting around by bike is feasible in Flanders where many roads have separate cycle lanes. Bikes can be hired from private operators in some cities (see Getting Around in the appropriate city). A more expensive option is to hire one from a train station – prices are €6.50/8.90 per half/full day (plus a €12.50 deposit) and the bike must be returned to the same station. Bikes can be taken on trains (only from stations in cities and major towns) for €4.10.

HITCHING

It's illegal on motorways and you'll find few Belgians hitching these days.

TaxiStop agencies (see Travel Agencies under Information in the Brussels section) match drivers with travellers on the road for a reasonable fee.

LOCAL TRANSPORT

Buses and trams (and small metro systems in Brussels and Antwerp) are efficient and reliable. Single tickets cost €1 or you can buy a multistrip ticket – 10 strips for €7.50 – or a one-day card for €2.90. Services generally run until about 11pm or midnight.

Taxis are metered and expensive (€1.60 per kilometre). You'll find them outside train stations.

ORGANISED TOURS

From Brussels, it's possible to take day trips by bus to Waterloo (€22.50, 4½ hours), Ghent and Bruges (€31, 9½ hours) or Antwerp (€23.50, 5½ hours), or even to the Ardennes and Luxembourg City (€37, 12 hours) or Paris (€50, 14 hours). The main operator is **De Boeck** (☎ 02-513 77 44; Rue de la Colline 8, B-1000 Brussels).

Brussels

pop 970,500

Brussels (Brussel in Flemish, Bruxelles in French) is an unpretentious mix of grand edifices and modern skyscrapers. Its character largely follows that of the nation it governs: modest, confident, but rarely striving to overtly impress.

From a 6th-century marshy village on the banks of the Senne (filled in long ago for sanitary reasons), this bilingual city is now headquarters of the EU and NATO, and home to Europe's most impressive central square.

Orientation

The Grand Place, Brussels' imposing 15th-century market square, sits dead centre in the Petit Ring, a pentagon of boulevards enclosing central Brussels. Many of the main sights are within the ring, but there's also plenty to see outside. Gare Centrale, Brussels' most central train station, is about five minutes' walk from the Grand Place; Gare du Midi, where most international trains arrive, is 2.5km from the famous square.

Almost everything in Brussels – from the names of streets to train stations – is written in both Flemish and French. We have used the French versions in this book.

Information

Tourist Offices There are two offices: one for Brussels, another for national information.

Tourist Information Brussels (TIB; ☎ 02-513 89 40, fax 02-513 83 20; e info@brus selstourism.be; open 9am-6pm Mon-Sat Jan-Easter; 9am-6pm daily Easter-Sept; 9am-6pm Mon-Sat, 10am-2pm Sun Oct-Dec) is in the city hall on the Grand Place. It sells two discount passes – the Most of Brussels (€15.60), which gives access to most of the top attractions, and the Brussels Passport (€7.50), a booklet containing discounts to museums/restaurants and two public transport one-day cards.

The **national tourist office** (☎ 02-504 03 90, fax 02-504 02 70; Rue du Marché aux Herbes 63; open 9am-6pm daily May-Oct; 9am-6pm Mon-Sat, 9am-1pm Sun Nov-Apr) is another source of information.

Money Outside banking hours, there are exchange bureaus at the airport (open until 10pm), at Gare Centrale and Gare du Nord (both open to 8.30pm) and another at Gare du Midi (open to 10pm). ATMs are at the airport and on the Grand Place. A good central exchange agency is **Baslé** (Rue au Beurre 23). You can also try **Thomas Cook** (☎ 02-513 28 45; Grand Place 4).

Post & Communications The **main post office** (1st floor, Centre Monnaie, Blvd Anspach; open 8am-6pm Mon-Fri, 9.30am-3pm Sat) is near Place de Brouckère.

Faxes can be sent and collected from the **Belgacom Téléboutique** (fax 02-223 32 01; Centre Monnaie, Blvd Anspach; open 9am-6pm Mon-Sat) which is in the same building as the post office.

Email & Internet Access To get online there's **easyEverything** (☎ 02-211 08 20; Place de Brouckère 9; open 8am-11.30pm). It charges €1 for 30 to 60 minutes, depending on the time of day.

Travel Agencies A good general travel agency is **Usit/Connections** (☎ 02-550 01 00; Rue du Midi 19). **AirStop/TaxiStop** (AirStop: ☎ 070-23 31 88, TaxiStop: ☎ 070-22 22 92; Rue du Fossé aux Loups 28) offer cheap charter flights and paid rides (€3.30 per 100km) in cars going to other European cities.

Bookshops Two specialist English-language bookshops are **Waterstones** (☎ 02-219 27 08; Blvd Adolphe Max 71) and **Sterling Books** (☎ 02-223 62 23; Rue du Fossé aux Loups 38).

Laundry Self-service laundries include **Primus Wash** (Rue Haute), and **Wash Club** (Place St Géry 25).

Medical & Emergency Services For 24-hour medical emergencies including ambulance services, simply dial ☎ 100. **Helpline** (☎ 02-648 40 14) is a Brussels-based, 24-hour English-speaking crisis line and information service.

Things to See & Do

Grand Place is the obvious place to start when exploring within the Petit Ring.

It once was home to the craft guilds, whose rich guildhalls – topped by golden figures glistening by day and illuminated by night – line the square.

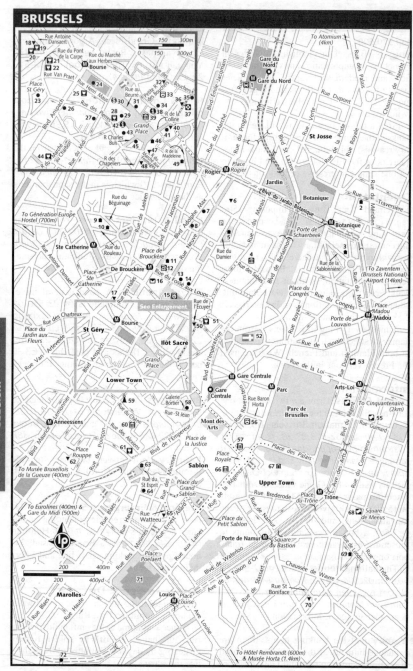

BRUSSELS

BELGIUM

BRUSSELS

PLACES TO STAY
2   Centre Vincent van Gogh
3   Jacques Brel Hostel/Les
    Auberges de Jeunesse
5   Sleep Well Hostel
9   Hôtel Noga
10 Résidence Les Écrins
11 Hôtel Métropole
46 Hôtel Saint Michel
49 Hôtel Le Dixseptiéme
63 Bruegel Hostel
69 B&B Guilmin

PLACES TO EAT
6   Super GB Supermarket (City
    2 Shopping Centre)
17 Super GB Supermarket
18 Le Pain Quotidien
32 Aux Armes de Bruxelles
36 Taverne du Passage
40 Panos
47 Frites/Pitta-Bread Places
48 Brasserie de la Roue d'Or
50 Hémisphères
62 Comme Chez Soi
65 Le Perroquet
70 L'Ultime Atome

BARS
19 L'Archiduc

20 Le Greenwich
21 Bizon
22 Roi des Belges
25 Falstaff
28 The Music Village
44 Tels Quels
51 À la Mort Subite
61 La Fleur en Papier Doré

OTHER
1   Eurolines Bus Station/Main
    Office
4   Centre Belge de la Bande
    Dessinée
7   Waterstones (Bookshop)
8   ARAU
12 easyEverything
13 AirStop/TaxiStop
14 Sterling Books
15 Théâtre Royal de la Monnaie
16 Main Post Office/Belgacom
    Téléboutique
23 Wash Club
24 Bourse (Stock Exchange)
26 Ancienne Belgique
27 Usit/Connections
29 Thomas Cook
30 Baslé
31 Galler
33 Théâtre Royal de Toone

34 De Biertempel
35 Neuhaus
37 Galeries St Hubert
38 National Tourist Office
39 Musée de la Ville de
    Bruxelles
41 De Boeck
42 Tourist Information Brussels
    (TIB)
43 Hôtel de Ville (City Hall)
45 Art-Nouveau Plaque/Everard
    't Serclaes Statue
52 Saints Michel & Gudule
    Cathedral
53 French Embassy
54 US Embassy
55 Australian Embassy
56 Palais des Beaux-Arts
58 La Loba Bookshop
59 Manneken Pis
60 House of Manneken Pis
64 Primus Wash
66 Musées Royaux des
    Beaux-Arts
67 Old England Building/Musée
    des Instruments de Musique
67 Palais Royal
68 NZ Embassy
71 Palais de Justice
72 Porte de hal

BELGIUM

Off the Grand Place to the south on Rue Charles Buls is an example of the city's once-famous Art Nouveau cult – an 1899 **gilded plaque** dedicated to the city by its appreciative artists. It's beside a reclining **statue of Everard 't Serclaes**, a 14th-century hero – rub his gleaming torso for good luck.

Manneken Pis, the statue of a small boy peeing, is a couple of blocks to the southwest on the corner of Rue du Chêne and Rue de l'Étuve. So famous is this little fellow that he has his own museum, the **House of Manneken Pis** (*Rue du Chêne 19; open 9am-5pm Mon-Fri*).

One block northeast of the Grand Place is the **Galeries St Hubert**, Europe's oldest glass-covered shopping arcade (and home to Neuhaus, one of the oldest chocolate shops) and, farther north, the impressive **Centre Belge de la Bande Dessinée** (see Museums). Alternatively, head east up the hill past the Gare Centrale to Rue Royale and the refinement of the upper town. Here you'll find the **Palais Royal**, Paul Saintenoy's Art Nouveau showpiece; the **Old England Building** (home to a superb museum of musical instruments)

and the **Musées Royaux des Beaux-Arts** (see Museums for details). From here it's a short walk to the **Sablon**, an exclusive area known for its many antique shops.

Museums The Grand Place is home to several museums including the **Musée de la Ville de Bruxelles** (*adult/concession €2.50/2; open 10am-5pm Tues-Fri, 10am-1pm Sat & Sun*) which gives a historical rundown on the city.

The **Musées Royaux des Beaux-Arts** (W *www.fine-arts-museum.be; Rue de la Régence 3; adult/concession €5/3.50; open 10am-5pm Tues-Sun*) houses Belgium's premier collections of ancient and modern art. Flemish Primitives, Brueghel and Rubens are well represented.

The **Musée des Instruments de Musique** (W *www.mim.fgov.be; Rue Montagne de la Cour 2; adult/concession €3.75/2.50; open 9.30am-5pm Mon-Fri, 10am-5pm Sat & Sun*) boasts the world's biggest collection of musical instruments. It's housed in the stunning Old England building, a must-see Art Nouveau example.

Tintin fans should not miss the **Centre Belge de la Bande Dessinée** *(Rue des Sables 20; admission €6.20; open 10am-6pm Tues-Sun)*. It has the nation's best ensemble of comic-strip art and occupies an airy Art Nouveau building designed by Victor Horta.

Several museums draw you out of the Petit Ring. **Musée Horta** *(Rue Américaine 25; tram No 92; adult/concession €4.95/3.70; open 2pm-5.30pm Tues-Sun)* in St Gilles was Victor Horta's house and is an excellent introduction to the Art Nouveau movement.

To the east, **Cinquantenaire** *(metro Mérode)* is a large museum conglomerate – art, history, military and motor vehicles sit together in a huge complex.

About 500m northwest of Gare du Midi is **Musée Bruxellois de la Gueuze** *(Rue Gheude 56; admission €3; open 9am-5pm Mon-Fri, 10am-5pm Sat)* in Anderlecht, a working brewery using traditional methods. You can sample Brussels' unique gueuze beer.

Musée Magritte *(Rue Esseghem 135; metro Belgica then tram No 18; admission €6; open 10am-6pm Wed-Sun)* in Jette opens up the world of surrealist artist René Magritte.

Other Attractions The **Atomium** *(Blvd du Centenaire; metro Heysel, tram No 81 to Heysel; adult/concession €5.45/4.50; open 9am-7.30pm daily Apr-Sept, 10am-5.30pm daily Oct-Mar)*, in the northern suburb of Laeken, is a space-age leftover from the 1958 World Fair. It represents an iron molecule enlarged 165 billion times.

The biggest **market** is Sunday morning's food and general goods market around Gare du Midi.

Organised Tours

De Boeck *(☎ 02-513 77 44; Rue de la Colline 8)* runs a 2¾-hour bus tour of major sights costing €20 (students/children €18/10).

It also has the Visit Brussels Line, a hop-on hop-off bus that stops at 12 places around the city. Tickets cost €12.50 (students/children €11.50/8).

From mid-June to mid-September **Chatterbus** *(☎ 02-673 18 35)* has a 2½-hour walking tour (€7.50) of the old centre led by Brusselians; phone for details.

For specialised tours such as Horta and Art Nouveau, or Brussels in the Art Deco era, contact the **ARAU** *(☎ 02-219 33 45; W www.arau.org; Blvd Adolphe Max 55)* or the TIB.

Special Events

The most prestigious annual event is the Ommegang, a 16th-century-style procession staged within the illuminated Grand Place in early July. Just as popular is the biennial flower carpet that colours the square in mid-August every second year (even-numbered years). Immerse yourself in music at the annual Brussels Jazz Marathon (last weekend in May). The Grand Place, together with the Sablon and Place Ste Catherine, also hosts free open-air concerts throughout summer.

Places to Stay

Camping Head 10km south to the small camping ground, **Beersel** *(☎ 02-331 05 61, fax 02-378 19 77; Steenweg op Ukkel 75; site per adult/child €3/2, per tent/car €2/1.35; open year-round)*. Tram No 55 (direction: Uccle) stops 3km away, from where you take bus UB to Beersel.

Hostels Three HI-affiliated hostels are dotted around Brussels, all with the same prices – dorm beds cost from €12.50 to €14.50 and singles/doubles cost €22.50/17.50 per person. The most central is **Bruegel** *(☎ 02-511 04 36, fax 02-512 07 11; e brussel@vjh.be; Rue du St Esprit 2)*.

About 15 minutes' walk from the centre is **Jacques Brel** *(☎ 02-218 01 87, fax 02-217 20 05; e brussels.brel@laj.be; Rue de la Sablonnière 30)*. **Génération Europe** *(☎ 02-410 38 58, fax 02-410 39 05; e brussels.europe@laj.be; Rue de l'Éléphant 4)*, is a 20-minute walk northwest of the Grand Place.

Central, modern and popular is **Sleep Well** *(☎ 02-218 50 50, fax 02-218 13 13; e info@sleepwell.be; Rue du Damier 23; beds in 6-bed/8-bed dorm €14.55/12.80, singles/doubles per person €24.45/18.75, triple/quad per person €18.75/16.15)*.

The newly renovated **Centre Vincent van Gogh** *(☎ 02-217 01 58, fax 02-219 79 95; e chab@ping.be; Rue Traversière 8; beds in 6-bed/10-bed dorm €11.50/9, singles/doubles €21/15.50)* is hip, but is has an age limit of 35 years. It's 1.25km uphill north of Gare Centrale or take the metro to Botanique.

Guesthouses For B&B accommodation, contact **Bed & Brussels** *(☎ 02-646 07 37, fax 02-644 01 14; W www.bnb-brussels.be)*.

Don't be put off by the lacklustre facade of **B&B Guilmin** *(☎ 02-512 92 90, fax 02-502*

41 01; e ph.guilmin@belgacom.net; Rue de Londres 19; metro Trône; singles/doubles €57/77; one-night supplement €13). The four rooms here are gorgeous.

Hotels In the appealing Ste Catherine quarter, 10 minutes' walk northwest of the Grand Place, you will find the **Résidence Les Écrins** (☎ 02-219 36 57, fax 02-223 57 40; e les .ecrins@skynet.be; Rue du Rouleau 15; rooms without/with bath €50/70). Just off Ave Louise is the homy **Hôtel Rembrandt** (☎ 02-512 71 39, fax 02-511 71 36; e rembrandt@ brutele.be; Rue de la Concorde 42; singles/ doubles without private bathroom €37/54, with bathroom €60/75).

One of the best mid-range choices is **Hôtel Noga** (☎ 02-218 67 63, fax 02-218 16 03; e info@nogahotel.com; Rue du Béguinage 38; singles/doubles Fri & Sat €60/75, Sun-Thur from €75/95). It's well positioned in the Ste Catherine quarter. If you'd prefer to be dead centre then the **Hôtel Saint Michel** (☎ 02-511 09 56, fax 02-511 46 00; e hotel saintmichel@hotmail.com; Grand Place 11; singles/doubles €63/90, with a view €110/ 130) is the place. Predictably, it's overpriced, but that's to be expected with such a unique location.

Top-end hotels are abundant. The most charming is **Hôtel Le Dixseptième** (☎ 02-502 57 44, fax 02-502 64 24; e ledixsep tieme@net7.be; Rue de la Madeleine 25; singles/doubles Fri & Sat €130/155, Sun-Thur from €180/205). For belle époque luxury, head to **Hôtel Métropole** (☎ 02-217 23 00, fax 02-218 02 20; e info@metropole hotel.be; Place de Brouckère 31; rooms Fri & Sat €115, singles/doubles Sun-Thur from €275/325).

Places to Eat
Restaurants Brussels' dining heart is Rue des Bouchers (Butcher's Street), near the Grand Place. Here you'll find lobster, crab, mussels and fish awaiting conspicuous consumption in one terrace restaurant after another. Most are tourist traps – **Aux Armes de Bruxelles** (☎ 02-511 55 98; Rue des Bouchers 13; mains around €20; open Tues-Sun) is a notable exception. Expect efficient service and Belgian classics.

Taverne du Passage (☎ 02-512 37 31; Galerie de la Reine 30; dishes €12-21; open noon-midnight daily), in Galeries St Hubert, has been serving no-nonsense Belgian cuisine since 1928, dished up by the friendliest waiters you'll find.

Brasserie de la Roue d'Or (☎ 02-514 25 54; Rue des Chapeliers 26; lunch €9.80, dinner mains €13-22) does traditional food in surrealist surroundings.

Ask any Bruxellois to name the city's finest restaurant and the answer is always **Comme Chez Soi** (☎ 02-512 29 21; Place Rouppe 23; mains from €45, menus €62-139; open Tues-Sat), which serves French cuisine. Reservations are essential.

Cafés For some wholesome savoury pies and filled sandwiches in a nonsmoking environment there's **Le Pain Quotidien** (☎ 02-502 23 61; Rue Antoine Dansaert 16), a country-style bakery-cum-tearoom.

Hémisphères (☎ 02-513 93 70; Rue de l'Écuyer 65; mains €8-10) does Middle Eastern food in silky surroundings.

In the Sablon, **Le Perroquet** (☎ 02-512 99 22; Rue Watteeu 31) is an Art Nouveau café with salads (€7.50-9.30), stuffed pitta bread (from €5) and vegetarian fare.

L'Ultime Atome (☎ 02-513 48 84; Rue St Boniface 14; mains €7-15; kitchen open until midnight) is off the beaten track but the ambience is invigorating, the food eclectic and there's a huge range of beers.

Fast Food & Self-Catering The Rue du Marché aux Fromages near the Grand Place is stacked with **frites/pitta-bread places**. For a half-baguette sandwich (€2.50), head to **Panos** (Rue du Marché aux Herbes 85).

There are two handy **Super GB supermarkets** (City 2 shopping centre, Rue Neuve • Rue des Halles; open 9am-8pm Mon-Sat).

Entertainment
The Bulletin magazine's 'What's On' guide lists live contemporary and classical music, opera, dance and what's screening in the cinema scene. Otherwise, there are enough bars and cafés for a very long pub crawl.

Le Greenwich (Rue des Chartreux 7), **À la Mort Subite** (Rue Mont aux Herbes Potagères 7), **La Fleur en Papier Doré** (Rue des Alexiens 53), and **Falstaff** (Rue Henri Maus 17) are all wonderful old cafés each with a unique ambience.

Roi des Belges (Rue Van Praet 35) is where the young and trendy flock, while nearby

BELGIUM

Bizon (*Rue du Pont de la Carpe 7*) is a happening grunge bar with occasional live bands.

Those who love Art Deco and live jazz shouldn't go past the **L'Archiduc** (*Rue Antoine Dansaert 6*).

For more jazz there's **The Music Village** (*Rue des Pierres 50*).

Fuse (*Rue Blaes 208; metro Port de Hal; open from 10pm Thur-Sat*) is the city's biggest club.

For information on gay and lesbian venues, ask at the bar of **Tels Quels** (☎ *02-512 45 87, fax 02-511 31 48; Rue du Marché au Charbon 81*).

Local and international bands play at **Ancienne Belgique** (☎ *02-548 24 24; Blvd Anspach 110*).

Main performing arts venues are **Palais des Beaux-Arts** (☎ *02-507 82 00; Rue Ravenstein 23*) and **Théâtre Royal de la Monnaie** (☎ *02-229 12 11; Place de la Monnaie*).

For something different there's the **Théâtre Royal de Toone** (☎ *02-511 71 37; Petite Rue des Bouchers 21*), a marionette theatre where the cast speaks the local Brussels dialect.

Shopping

Head to the Sablon area for antiques. **Neuhaus** (*Galeries St Hubert*), and **Galler** (*Rue au Beurre 44*) are just two of the many exclusive chocolate shops.

De Biertempel (*Rue du Marché aux Herbes 56*) stocks hundreds of varieties of Belgian beers. Rue Antoine Dansaert is good for avant-garde fashion, and Ave Louise is the stamping ground for designer boutiques.

Getting There & Away

For details on international services, see Getting There & Away earlier in this chapter.

Bus The main office of **Eurolines** (☎ *02-274 13 50; Rue du Progrès 80*) is next to Gare du Nord, and most of its buses depart from here. There's a smaller **office** (☎ *02-538 20 49; Ave Fonsny 9*), near Gare du Midi.

Train There are **train information offices** (*open 6.30am-9pm*) at Gare du Nord, Gare Centrale and Gard du Midi; the latter is the main station for international trains. For all national inquiries call ☎ 02-555 25 55.

For prices and journey times from Brussels to other Belgian cities and towns, check individual Getting There & Away sections.

Getting Around

Public transport maps are available at the tourist offices or metro information kiosks.

To/From the Airport The international airport, Zaventem, is connected to all three central stations (€2.35, 30 minutes, four trains hourly). Taxis generally charge approximately €25 to €30.

Public Transport Brussels' bus, tram and metro network is operated by the Société des Transports Intercommunaux de Bruxelles (MIVB in Flemish, STIB in French). Single-journey tickets cost €1.40, five-/10-journey cards are €6/9 and a one-day card (valid for two people on Saturday or Sunday) is €3.60. Valid on all public transport, tickets can be bought from metro stations or bus drivers; the one-day card is also available from the TIB. Public transport runs until about midnight.

Car See the introductory Getting Around section for details on travelling by car and car rental.

Taxi There are plenty of ranks around the city, or phone **Taxis Bleus** (☎ *02-268 00 00*) or **Taxis Verts** (☎ *02-349 49 49*).

AROUND BRUSSELS

Waterloo, the battleground where Napoleon was defeated and European history changed course in 1815, is 18km south of Brussels. Unless you're a war or history buff, it's staid. What's more, the most important sites are spread over several kilometres, making it tedious to get around with public transport (bus W from Porte de Hal in Brussels). Consider a day trip (see Organised Tours in the introductory Getting Around section).

To the southeast of Brussels is the **Forêt de Soignes**, an ideal spot for walking among beech and oak trees.

The **Musée Royal de l'Afrique Centrale** (☎ *02 769 52 11; Leuvensesteenweg 13; metro Montgomery then tram No 44; adult/concession €4/1.50; open Tues-Sun*) at Tervuren is 14km east of Brussels. It has artefacts from the Democratic Republic of Congo, collected during the reign of Léopold II.

About 25km east of Brussels, **Leuven** (Louvain in French) is a lively student town which is home to Belgium's oldest university (dating from 1425). The main sight is the flamboyant 15th-century town hall. From Brussels, there are two trains per hour (€3.80, 30 minutes).

Antwerp

pop 456,706

Worldly, seedy, historic, hedonistic – that's Antwerp (Antwerpen in Flemish, Anvers in French). Second in size to Brussels and more likable, Antwerp produced one of the 17th century's best-known artists, Pieter Paul Rubens, and is Belgium's most underrated drawcard.

With a prime spot on the Schelde River, Antwerp came to the fore as Western Europe's greatest economic centre in the early 16th century. But the times of prosperity were short-lived. When Protestants smashed the city's cathedral in 1566 as part of the Iconoclastic Fury, the Spanish ruler Philip II sent troops to take control. Ten years later the unpaid garrison mutinied, ransacking the city – in three nights they massacred 8000 people in the Spanish Fury. The final blow came in 1648 when the Dutch closed the Schelde to all non-Dutch ships, blocking Antwerp's vital link to the sea. It wasn't until Napoleon arrived and the French rebuilt the docks that Antwerp got back on its feet.

Today compact Antwerp brims with self-confidence. As a world port, its air is international, although at times down-at-heel. The world's largest diamond-cutting industry is run from behind the discreet facades of the Jewish quarter, while in the small fashion district, avant-garde designers set next season's styles. Cosmopolitan, full of contrasts, fun... Antwerp in a nutshell.

Orientation

Antwerp's old centre, where many of its sights are concentrated, is based around the Grote Markt, a 20-minute walk from the main train station, Centraal Station. Other sights are spread around Het Zuid, the city's trendiest area (about 1.25km south of the Grote Markt).

Information

Tourist Offices The **tourist office** (☎ 03-232 01 03, fax 03-231 19 37; **e** visit@ antwerpen.be; Grote Markt 13; open 9am-5.45pm Mon-Sat, 9am-4.45pm Sun) dispenses information.

Money Competitive exchange rates (for cash or US$ travellers cheques only) are offered by **Leo Stevens exchange bureau** (☎ 03-232 18 43; De Keyserlei 64; open 9am-5pm Mon-Fri). **Travelex** (☎ 03-226 29 53; Koningin Astridplein 33; open 8.30am-9pm Mon-Fri, 9am-9pm Sat, 10am-7pm Sun) is another handy option. There's a **KBC Bank** (☎ 03-206 82 10; Eiermarkt 20) in the base of the Torengebouw (Europe's first skyscraper).

Post & Communications The **main post office** (Groenplaats 43) is in the old centre; handy branch offices are opposite Centraal Station and on Jezusstraat. The **Belgacom Teleboetiek** (Jezusstraat 1) sells phonecards and handles faxes.

Email & Internet Access For ambient surroundings try **2Zones** (☎ 03-232 24 00; Wolstraat 15; open 11am-midnight daily) which has Internet access for €4.50 per hour. If pricing dictates there's the no-frills **Internet Café** (☎ 03-234 38 13; Korte Koepoortstraat 9) charging €1.50/3 for 30/60 minutes.

Bookshops An excellent range of second-hand English novels is available at either **De Slegte** (☎ 03-231 66 27; Wapper 5) or cosy **Jenny Hannivers** (☎ 0486-28 97 75; Jezuietenrui 11). For travel guides and maps try **Atlas & Zanzibar** (☎ 03-227 27 23; Wolstraat 7). **Mekanik Strip** (☎ 03-234 23 47; St Jacobsmarkt 73) is cartoon kingdom.

Laundry Head to the **Wassalon** (Nationalestraat 18) for washing.

Things to See & Do

Start exploring at the **Grote Markt**, with its impressive **Stadhuis** (City Hall), imposing guildhalls and voluptuous Brabo Fountain.

The city's skyline is best viewed from the raised **promenades** (known as wandelterrassen), leading off from Steenplein, or from the river's west bank, accessible by the **St Annatunnel**, a pedestrian tunnel under the Schelde at St Jansvliet.

Museums The major museums mostly charge €5 (concession €2.50), or you can buy a three-museum discount ticket for €7.50. Many museums are free on Friday. All those described here, unless stated otherwise, are open 10am to 4.45pm Tuesday to Sunday.

BELGIUM

ANTWERP

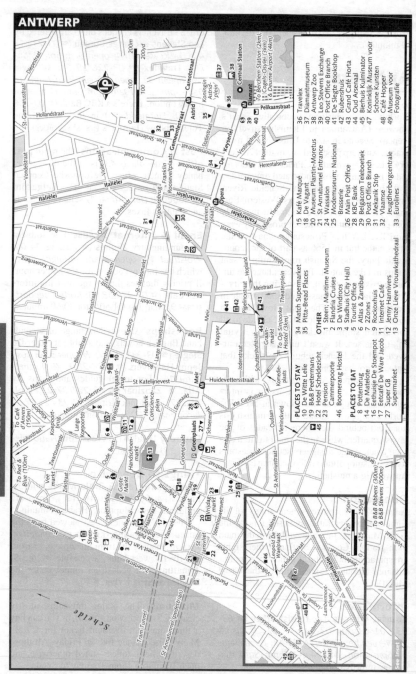

PLACES TO STAY
10 De Witte Lelie
19 B&B Peetermans
22 Hotel Scheldezicht
23 Pension
   Cammerpoorte
46 Boomerang Hostel

PLACES TO EAT
8 Pottenbrug
14 De Matelote
16 Eethuisje De Stoempot
17 Eetcafé De Ware Jacob
27 Café GB
   Supermarket
34 Match Supermarket
35 Pitta-Bread Places

OTHER
1 Steen; Maritime Museum
2 Flandria Cruises
3 De Windroos
4 Stadhuis (City Hall)
5 Tourist Office
6 Atlas & Zanzibar
7 2Zones
9 Rockoxhuis
11 Internet Café
12 Jenny Hannivers
13 Onze Lieve Vrouwkathedraal

15 Kafé Marqué
18 De Vagant
20 Museum Plantin-Moretus
21 St Annatunnel Entrance
24 Wassalon
25 Modemuseum; National
   Brasserie
26 Main Post Office
28 KBin Bank
29 Belgacom Teleboetiek
30 Post Office Branch
31 Mekanik Strip
32 Vlaaikens
33 Jeugdherbergcentrale
   Eurolines

36 Travelex
37 Diamantmuseum
38 Antwerp Zoo
39 Leo Stevens Exchange
40 Post Office Branch
41 De Slegte Bookshop
42 Rubenshuis
43 Grand Café Horta
44 Oud Arsenaal
45 Bierhuis Kulminator
47 Koninklijk Museum voor
   Schone Kunsten
48 Café Hopper
49 Museum voor
   Fotografie

The **Rubenshuis** (*Rubens' House; Wapper 9; adult/concession €5/2.50*) tops most visitors' lists although his best-known works are in Onze Lieve Vrouwkathedraal. Another fine 17th-century home is **Rockoxhuis**, (*Keizerstraat 12; adult/concession €2.50/1.25*). For more Rubens, as well as Flemish Primitives and contemporary works, there's **Koninklijk Museum voor Schone Kunsten** (*Royal Museum of Fine Arts; Leopold de Waelplaats 1-9; adult/concession €5/4*) in Het Zuid.

The 16th-century home and workshop of a prosperous printing family, **Museum Plantin-Moretus** (*Vrijdagmarkt 22; adult/concession €4/2*) displays antique presses and splendid old globes.

The **Steen**, the city's medieval riverside castle at Steenplein, houses a **maritime museum** (*adult/concession €4/2*).

The city's excellent **Museum voor Fotografie** (*Photography Museum; Waalsekaai 47; admission €2.50/1.25*) is closed until spring 2003.

The long-awaited **Modemuseum** (*MOMU; Fashion Museum; Nationalestraat 28; adult/concession €5/3*) opened late in 2002.

The new **Diamantmuseum** (*Koningin Astridplein 19; adult/concession €5/3; open 10am-6pm daily May-Oct, 10am-5pm Nov-Apr, closed Jan*) uses interactive displays to trace aspects of the city's diamond industry. To get a glimpse of the amount of diamonds and gold being traded in Antwerp, wander along Pelikaanstraat or Vestingstraat near Centraal Station any time during the day (except Saturday when Shabbat, the Jewish holy day, closes everything down).

Onze Lieve Vrouwkathedraal With its 120m spire, the splendid **Cathedral of Our Lady** (*entry from Handschoenmarkt; adult/concession €2/1.50; open 10am-5pm Mon-Fri, 10am-3pm Sat, 1pm-4pm Sun*) is Belgium's largest Gothic cathedral and home to four paintings by Rubens, including the *Descent from the Cross*.

Antwerp Zoo The Antwerp Zoo (*Koningin Astridplein 26; admission €13/8.50; open 9am-4.30pm or 6pm daily*) is one of the world's oldest. In parts it's state-of-the art but there are also some horrible old cages.

Cogels-Osylei This is a street of radical *fin-de-siècle* houses built in eclectic styles

ranging from Art Nouveau to the classical or neo-Renaissance. It's a little way from the centre but well worth a wander – tram No 11 (direction: Deurne Eksterlaar) runs along it.

Markets The Vrijdagmarkt offers second-hand goods on Friday morning. Vogelmarkt, held on Theaterplein, is a lively food market on Saturday and has general stuff on Sunday. Hoogstraat and Kloosterstraat are good hunting grounds for bric-a-brac.

Boat Trips Cruises run by **Flandria** (*☎ 03-231 31 00; Steenplein*) include Schelde trips (€6.50, 50 minutes) or port excursions (€8.50, 1½ hours).

Places to Stay

Camping On the west bank of the Schelde there's **De Molen** (*☎ 03-219 81 79; St Annastrand; bus No 81 or 82; open Apr-Sept; tent site €2.10, per adult €1.60*).

Hostels The HI-affiliated hostel, **Op Sinjoorke** (*☎ 03-238 02 73, fax 03-248 19 32; e antwerpen@vjh.be; Eric Sasselaan 2*) is 10 minutes from Centraal Station by tram No 2 (direction: Hoboken) or bus No 27 (direction: Zuid) – get off at Bouwcentrum and follow the signs.

Boomerang (*☎ 03-238 47 82; Volkstraat 49; bus No 23 direction: Zuid from Centraal Station; dorm beds €12, sheets €2.50*) is ultra laid-back. Give it a miss if you like things homy.

Guesthouses For a warm welcome and comfy rooms there's **B&B Stevens** (*☎ 03-259 15 90; e greta.stevens@pandora.be; Molenstraat 35; bus No 290; singles/doubles Mon-Fri from €36/47, Sat-Sun €60*).

B&B Ribbens (*☎ 03-248 15 39; e marleen.engelen@yucon.be; Justitiestraat 43; bus No 290; singles/doubles from €35/60*) is decadently spacious with 5m-high ceilings and old-style furnishings.

Handily placed is **B&B Peetermans** (*☎/fax 03-231 37 92; e enich.anders@antwerpen .be; Leeuwenstraat 12; singles/doubles €45/50, triples/quads €65/80*), home of a stone sculptor.

Hotels The **Hotel Scheldezicht** (*☎ 03-231 66 02, fax 03-231 90 02; e hotelschelde zicht@pi.be; St Jansvliet 12; singles/doubles/*

triples €35/50/60, with bath €38/55/65) is
well located on a leafy square near the river
and has spacious rooms.

A dependable mid-range choice is **Pension
Cammerpoorte** *(☎/fax 03-231 28 36; Steen-
houwersvest 55; singles/doubles €50/60)*.
Its 16 rooms are brightly coloured and some
have kitchenettes at no extra charge.

De Witte Lelie *(☎ 03-226 19 66, fax 03-
234 00 19;* e *hotel@dewittelelie.be; Keizerstraat 16; singles/doubles from €169/223)*
sports 10 luxurious rooms furnished in a winning mix of modern and antique.

Places to Eat

Craving mashed potatoes? Go no further than
Eethuisje De Stoempot *(☎ 03-231 36 86;
Vlasmarkt 12; mains €8; open Fri-Tues)*.
This down-to-earth eatery offers traditional
homestyle meals at prices to match.

Eetcafé De Ware Jacob *(☎ 03-213 37 89;
Vlasmarkt 19; meals €7-12; open Tues-Sun)* is
a brown café which is known for its convivial
atmosphere.

Pottenbrug *(☎ 03-231 51 47; Minder-
broedersrui 38; dishes €10.50-17)* is a tasteful
old bistro that's appealed to locals for years.

Movers and groovers mingle at the new
National Brasserie *(☎ 03-227 56 56; Nationalestraat 32; dishes €14-20; open 8am-
11.30pm)* which is near the Modemuseum.

For fine seafood there's one port of call –
De Matelote *(☎ 03-231 32 07; Haarstraat 9;
mains from €24; open Tues-Sat)*.

Pitta-bread places reign in the streets near
Centraal Station. Self-caterers will find a
Super GB supermarket in the Grand Bazaar
shopping centre at Groenplaats, and a **Match
supermarket** in the Keyser Centre on De
Keyserlei.

Entertainment

With some 4000 bars and cafés, Antwerp is a
party city.

For **terrace cafés**, head to Groenplaats or
to the more intimate Handschoenmarkt. The
Oud Arsenaal *(Pijpelincxstraat 4)* is a quirky
local haunt (and the beers are among the
cheapest in town). **De Vagant** *(Reyndersstraat
21)* deals out 200 *jenevers* (Belgian gins).
Bierhuis Kulminator *(Vleminckveld 32)* is *the*
place to sink a host of Belgian brews – there's
more than 600 on the menu. Go glamorous at
Grand Café Horta *(Hopland 2)*.

For live jazz, head to the **Café Hopper**
(Leopold De Waelstraat 2) in Het Zuid.

Kafé Marqué *(Grote Pieter Potstraat 3;
open from 11pm Fri & Sat)* is a central club
doing rock and Britpop. A hipper-than-thou
club crowd heads to **Café d'Anvers** *(Ververs-
rui 15; open Fri-Sun)* in the sailor's quarter.
Red & Blue *(Lange Schipperskapelstraat 11)*
bills itself as the country's biggest gay disco.

Getting There & Away

Bus For bus information, see Getting There
& Away at the start of this chapter. Buses de-
part from the **Eurolines** *(☎ 03-233 86 62;
Van Stralenstraat 8)* office.

Train Antwerp has two main train stations –
Centraal Station, about 1.5km from the old
city centre, and Berchem station, 2km southeast of Centraal Station. The magnificent
Centraal Station is undergoing extensive underground expansion, expected to be finished
in 2005 (until then you may find train services into Centraal Station disrupted).

National connections from Antwerp include IC trains to Brussels (€5.30, 35 minutes), Bruges (€10.80, 70 minutes) and Ghent
(€6.80, 45 minutes). There are also frequent
trains to Amsterdam (€25-31, two hours).

Getting Around

A good network of buses, trams and a
premetro (a tram that runs underground for
part of its journey) is run by De Lijn. Public
transport information kiosks are at premetro
stations Diamant (in front of Centraal Station) and Groenplaats.

The main bus hubs are Koningin Astridplein next to Centraal Station and Franklin
Rooseveltplaats a few blocks west. Hire bikes
from **De Windroos** *(☎ 03-480 93 88, Steenplein 1a)* for €2.50/12.50 per hour/day.

Ghent

pop 230,000
Medieval Europe's largest city outside Paris
is Ghent (known as Gent in Flemish, Gand in
French). Its glory lies in its industrious and
rebellious past. Sitting on the junction of the
Leie and Schelde Rivers, by the mid-14th
century it had become Europe's biggest cloth
producer, importing wool from England and
employing thousands of people. Townsfolk

were well known for their armed battles for civil liberties and against the heavy taxes imposed upon them. It's not picturesque like Bruges is today, but as it's home to many students it's ultimately more realistic.

Orientation

Unlike many Belgian cities, Ghent does not have one central square. Instead, the medieval core is a row of open areas separated by two imposing churches and a belfry. The Korenmarkt is the westernmost square, and is technically the city's centre – it's a 25-minute walk from the main train station, St Pietersstation, or there's a regular connection (tram Nos 1, 10 and 11). Halfway between the two there's the university quarter, based along St Pietersnieuwstraat.

Information

The **tourist office** (☎ 09-266 52 32, fax 09-225 62 88; e toerisme@gent.be; Botermarkt 17a; open 9am-6.30pm daily Easter-early Nov, 9.30am-4.30pm mid-Nov–Easter) can help with inquiries.

The **Europabank** (St Pietersstation) and the **Goffin Change** (Mageleinstraat 36) are both

open daily. There's a **post office** (Lange Kruisstraat 55) and a **laundrette** (Oudburg 25).

Things to See & Do

Ghent's most noteworthy sight is the Van Eyck brothers' *Adoration of the Mystic Lamb*, which is housed in the **crypt** (admission €2.50; open 9.30am-4.45pm Mon-Sat, 1pm-4.30pm Sun Easter-Nov; 10.30am-3.45pm Mon-Sat, 1pm-3.30pm Sun Nov-Easter) of **St Baafskathedraal** (entry on St Baafsplein; admission free; open 8.30am-6pm daily). This 15th-century painting is a lavish representation of medieval religious thinking and one of the earliest known oil paintings.

Rising from the old Cloth Hall, the 14th-century **belfort** (belfry; Botermarkt; adult/concession €3/1.75; open 10am-1pm & 2pm-6pm daily) affords spectacular views of the city.

With moat, turrets and arrow slits, the fearsome 12th-century **Gravensteen** (St Veerleplein 11; adult/concession €6.20/1.20; open 9am-6pm daily, 9am-5pm Nov-Mar) is the quintessential castle. It was built to protect the townsfolk as well as to intimidate them into law-abiding submission.

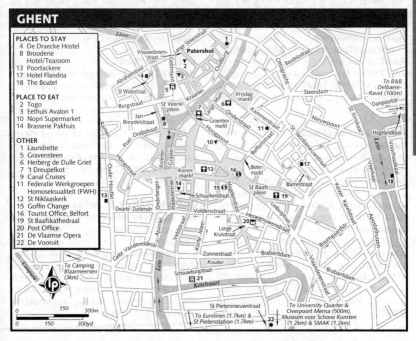

The **Museum voor Schone Kunsten** (*Citadelpark*) is home to some Flemish Primitives and a couple of typically nightmarish works by Hieronymus Bosch. Across the road is **SMAK**, the city's contemporary art museum. Both museums are open 10am to 6pm Tuesday to Saturday; admission to each is €2.50/1.20.

City **canal cruises** (€4.50/9 for 40/90 minutes) depart from the Graslei and Korenlei.

Places to Stay

Camping A long way west of the city there's **Camping Blaarmeersen** (☎ 09-221 53 99; *Zuiderlaan 12; adult/child €4/2, site per tent/car €4/2.25; open Apr-Sept*). Catch bus No 9 from the station then bus No 38.

Hostels Ghent's attractive hostel is the **De Draecke** (☎ 09-233 70 50, fax 09-233 80 01; e gent@vjh.be; *St Widostraat 11; beds in 6-bed dorm with bath €14.50, doubles €35*) which occupies a renovated warehouse in the heart of town. Take tram No 1, 10 or 11 from the train station to St Veerleplein.

Guesthouses The **Gilde der Gentse Gastenkamers** (*GGG;* ☎ 09-233 30 99; w www.bedandbreakfast.gent-be; *Tentoonstelling slaan 69, 9000 Ghent*) organises the city's B&B accommodation.

One excellent option is **B&B Delbaere-Ravet** (☎/fax 09-233 43 52; e s.deravet@worldonline.be; *Hagelandkaai 38; singles/doubles €35/50*). Take bus No 70 or 71 from St Pietersstation to the Dampoortstation bus stop.

Hotels The **Hotel Flandria** (☎ 09-223 06 26, fax 09-233 77 89; e gent@flandria-centrum.be, Barrestraat 3; *singles/doubles €33/38*) is a warren of cheap but decent rooms. More atmospheric is **Brooderie** (☎ 09-225 06 23; *Jan Breydelstraat 8; singles/doubles with shared bath from €38/58*), a bakery-cum-tearoom which has four lovely rooms upstairs.

The **Boatel** (☎ 09-267 10 30, fax 09-267 10 39; e info@theboatel.com; *Voorhoutkaai 29a; singles/doubles from €72/95*) is a renovated canal boat with nice rooms.

Poortackere (☎ 09-269 22 10, fax 09-269 22 30; e info@monasterium.be; *Oude Houtlei 50-58; hotel rooms €70/120, guestrooms €45/95*) is a converted convent with a luxu-

rious, ground-floor hotel and a first-floor *gastenverblijf* with smaller and sober guestrooms.

Places to Eat

The student ghetto around Pietersnieuwstraat, about 10 minutes' walk southeast of the Korenmarkt, is the best area for cheap eats. Here you'll find the **Overpoort mensa** (☎ 09-264 71 10; *Overpoortstraat 49; open lunch & dinner Mon-Fri; meals from €5*), a self-service student cafeteria.

Eethuis Avalon 1 (☎ 09-224 37 24; *Geldmunt 32; mains €8-10; open lunch only Mon-Sat*) is a quaint vegetarian restaurant. Another wholesome place is the **Brooderie** (☎ 09-225 06 23; *Jan Breydelstraat 8*), a rustic, nonsmoking tearoom (see Places to Stay earlier).

Restaurants are dotted around the Patershol quarter, a thicket of cobbled lanes with an old-world ambience. **Togo** (☎ 09-223 65 51; *Vrouwebroersstraat 21; mains from €13*) has been around for years and is consistently good. It specialises in African cuisine.

Brasserie Pakhuis (☎ 09-223 55 55; *Schuurkenstraat 4; mains €15-25, 3-course lunchtime menu €10.50*) occupies a restored textile warehouse and draws young and old alike.

Self-caterers should try the **Nopri supermarket** (*Hoogpoort 42*).

Entertainment

Herberg De Dulle Griet (*Vrijdagmarkt 50*) is one of the city's best-known beer pubs, while tiny **'t Dreupelkot** (*Groentenmarkt 12*) specialises in jenevers and has a pleasant waterfront terrace.

De Vooruit (☎ 09-267 28 28; *St Pietersnieuwstraat 23*) is the venue for dance and theatre. Opera is most commonly performed at **De Vlaamse Opera** (☎ 09-225 24 25; *Schouwburgstraat 3*).

Getting There & Away

The **Eurolines office** (☎ 09-220 90 24; *Koningin Elisabethlaan 73*) is 100m from the train station; buses leave from here.

For help with rail queries, go to the **train station information office** (☎ 09-222 44 44; *open 7am-9pm daily*). There are IC trains to Antwerp (€6.80, 45 minutes), Bruges (€4.70, 20 minutes), Brussels (€6.40, 45 minutes) and Ypres (€8.30, one hour).

Getting Around
The public transport information kiosk outside the station sells tickets and has free tram/bus maps.

Bruges

pop 120,000
Bruges (Brugge in Flemish) could be described as the 'perfect' tourist attraction.

Suspended in time centuries ago when its lifeline – the Zwin estuary – silted up, it is now one of Europe's best-preserved medieval cities and Belgium's most visited town. In 2000 Bruges' historic centre was added to Unesco's World Heritage List.

Bruges was a prosperous cloth manufacturing town and the centre of Flemish Primitive art between the 12th and 15th centuries. When the Zwin silted Bruges died, its wealthy merchants abandoning it for Antwerp, leaving unoccupied homes and deserted canals.

More than two million tourists inundate this little city each year and, at the height of summer, it seethes.

Stay around late on a midsummer evening, or time your visit for spring when daffodils carpet tranquil Begijnhof, and Bruges will reveal its age-old beauty.

Orientation
Central Bruges fits neatly into an oval-shaped series of canals. It's great for amblers, with sights sprinkled within leisurely walking distance of its compact centre. There are two central squares, the Markt and the Burg. The train station is about 1.5km south of the Markt and buses shuttle regularly between the two.

Information
Tourist Offices The main **tourist office** (☎ 050-44 86 86, fax 050-44 86 00; e to erisme@brugge.be; Burg 11; open 9.30am-6.30pm Mon-Fri, 10am-noon & 2pm-6.30pm Sat & Sun Apr-Sept; 9.30am-5pm Mon-Fri, 9.30am-1pm & 2pm-5.30pm Sat Oct-Mar) handles inquiries and has a handful of luggage lockers in the foyer.

Inside the train station there's an **information booth** (open 10am-6pm Mon-Sat).

Money Good rates are offered at **Weghsteen & Driege Exchange** (☎ 050-33 33 61; Oude Burg 6; open 9am-noon & 2pm-4.30pm Mon-Fri); it handles cash only. The **BBL Bank** (Markt 19) is central. Alternatively, there's the tourist office's **exchange bureau** (open daily).

Post & Communications Send mail at the **post office** (Markt 5). Faxes can be sent and received at **Copy House** (☎ 050-33 59 43, fax 050-34 61 92; Oude Burg 22a).

Email & Internet Access Get online cheaply at **Happyrom** (Ezelstraat 8) for €3 per hour; there's no staff nor atmosphere. For conversation and conviviality try **The Coffee Link** (☎ 050-34 99 73; w www.thecoffeelink.com; Mariastraat 38) where terminals cost €5 per hour.

Laundry The **Ipsomat** (Langestraat 151), and the **Belfort Wassalon** (Ezelstraat 51) are self-service laundries.

Things to See & Do
Being so small, Bruges is the sort of place you get to know quickly. It has plenty of sights and things to do, from climbing the belfry to cruising the canals.

You can also start a walking tour at the **Markt**, the city's medieval core, from which rises the mighty **belfort** (see later in this section). The nearby **Burg**, connected to the Markt by an alley lined with lace shops, features Belgium's oldest **Stadhuis** (town hall), as well as the **Heiligbloed-Basiliek** (Basilica of the Holy Blood), where a few coagulated drops of Christ's blood are said to be kept. From the Burg, go through the archway marking Blinde Ezelstraat (Blind Donkey St) to the **Vismarkt** (fish market). From here, Steenhouwersdijk leads into **Groenerei**, a short but delightful promenade along a pretty part of the canal.

Immediately west of Vismarkt is **Huidenvettersplein**, a dinky little square lined with popular restaurants. This is the start of the **Dijver**, along which you'll find departure points for **canal cruises**, as well as the town's premier museums. Nearby is the **Onze Lieve Vrouwekerk**, which houses Michelangelo's *Madonna and Child*, a delicate statue and his only sculpture to leave Italy in his lifetime. Across from the church, in the old St Jans-hospitaal complex on Mariastraat, is the newly opened **Memlingmuseum**. Farther south along Mariastraat, signs lead to the

BELGIUM

BRUGES

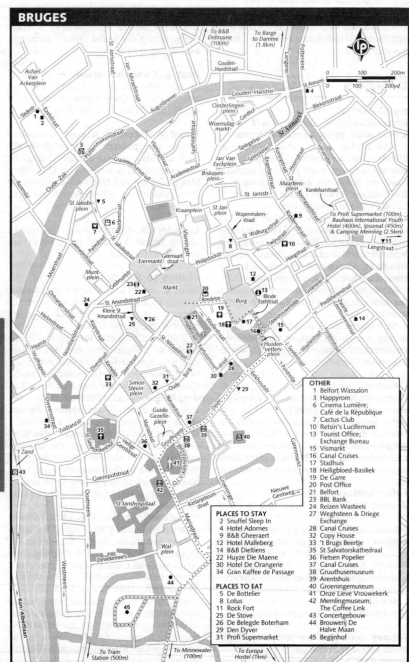

To B&B Debruyne (100m)
To Barge to Damme (1.8km)

To Profi Supermarket (100m), Bauhaus International Youth Hotel (400m), Ipsomat (450m) & Camping Memling (2.5km)

To B&B Debruyne (100m)

To Train Station (500m)
To Minnewater (100m)
To Europa Hostel (1km)

OTHER
1 Belfort Wassalon
3 Happyrom
6 Cinema Lumière;
  Café de la Rêpublique
7 Cactus Club
10 Retsin's Lucifernum
13 Tourist Office;
   Exchange Bureau
15 Vismarkt
16 Canal Cruises
17 Stadhuis
18 Heiligbloed-Basiliek
19 De Garre
20 Post Office
21 Belfort
23 BBL Bank
24 Reizen Wasteels
27 Weghsteen & Driege
   Exchange
28 Canal Cruises
32 Copy House
33 't Brugs Beertje
35 St Salvatorskathedraal
36 Fietsen Popelier
37 Canal Cruises
38 Gruuthusemuseum
39 Arentshuis
40 Groeningemuseum
41 Onze Lieve Vrouwekerk
42 Memlingmuseum;
   The Coffee Link
43 Concertgebouw
44 Brouwerij De
   Halve Maan
45 Begijnhof

PLACES TO STAY
2 Snuffel Sleep In
4 Hotel Adornes
9 B&B Gheeraert
12 Hotel Malleberg
14 B&B Dieltiens
22 Huyze Die Maene
30 Hotel De Orangerie
34 Gran Kaffee de Passage

PLACES TO EAT
5 De Bottelier
8 Lotus
11 Rock Fort
25 De Stove
26 De Belegde Boterham
29 Den Dyver
31 Profi Supermarket

Begijnhof (see later in this section), from where you can easily cross to the **Minnewater**, once an inner-city port. The waterway is edged by a tranquil park.

Museums A discount ticket (€15), valid for five museums of your choice, is a worthwhile option if you plan to visit the following museums (all open 9.30am to 5pm Tuesday to Sunday).

The **Groeningemuseum** *(Dijver 12; admission €7)* is home to the city's prized collection of art from the 14th to 20th centuries. Most notable is the impressive section on Flemish Primitives. The **Arentshuis** *(Dijver 16; admission €2.50)* contains two collections: lace, and the artwork of Frank Brangwyn, a Bruges-born artist of British parentage. An excellent collection of both applied and decorative arts is displayed in the recently reorganised **Gruuthusemuseum** *(Dijver 17; admission €5)*. The prestigious **Memlingmuseum** *(Mariastraat 38; admission €7)* occupies the recently restored, 12th-century St Janshospitaal complex (a former hospital) and houses works by Hans Memling, one of the early Flemish Primitives.

Belfort Climb 366 steps to reach the top of this 83m-high belfry *(adult/concession €5/3; open 9.30am-5pm daily)*. The view rewards the sweat and effort.

Begijnhof The Begijnhof was home to a 13th-century religious community of unmarried or widowed women who were known as *begijnen* (Beguines). It's lined with modest, whitewashed houses which these days are inhabited by single women of all ages. The large convent at the rear of the square is home to Benedictine nuns.

The Begijnhof is about a 10-minute walk south of the Markt.

Brouwerij De Halve Maan Half Moon Brewery *(Walplein 26)* shows the workings of one of Belgium's many little breweries. Tours (€3.70) run hourly from 11am to 4pm daily (less frequent in winter).

Canal Cruises Boats depart from jetties south of the Burg every 20 minutes between 10am and 6pm daily early March to mid-November (weekends only for the rest of the year). Tours (adult/concession €5.20/2.60) last 30 minutes and queues are often horrendous.

Horse-drawn Carriages Five people can tuck under a blanket and see Bruges in this time-honoured fashion. Board at the Markt and expect to pay €27.50 for 30 minutes.

Organised Tours
Bruges by bike, bus, foot – name it and you can tour by it. The tourist office has details.

One highly recommended company is **Quasimodo** *(☎ 050-37 04 70, freecall 0800 97525; e info@quasimodo.be)*. It offers two bike trips (€16/14 for those aged over/under 26): a three-hour (8km) tour of Bruges; or a four-hour (25km) cycle to the Dutch border. Alternatively there are two minibus tours (€40/38 including lunch) – on one you'll indulge in waffles, beer and chocolates; the other takes in Ypres and its WWI memorials.

Places to Stay
Camping The nicest camping ground is **Memling** *(☎ 050-35 58 45; Veltemweg 109; sites per adult/tent/car €2.80/2.50/3.30; open year-round)*. Take bus No 11 from the train station.

Hostels Several hostels compete for Bruges' backpacker market.

The newly renovated **Snuffel Sleep In** *(☎ 050-33 31 33, fax 050-33 32 50; e info@snuffel.be; Ezelstraat 47-49; dorm beds €11-13, double rooms €15)* has funky rooms, friendly staff and a kitchen for guests. Breakfast costs €2. Catch bus No 3 or 13 from the train station.

Gran Kaffee de Passage *(☎ 050-34 02 32, fax 050-34 01 40; Dweersstraat 26-28; bus 'Centrum' from the train station; dorm beds €12.50, doubles with breakfast from €35)* has modern dorms as well as a hotel section next door. Breakfast costs €2 and the **restaurant** here is enticing.

The **Bauhaus International Youth Hotel** *(☎ 050-34 10 93, fax 050-33 41 80; e bauhaus@bauhaus.be, Langestraat 135; bus No 6 or 16 from the train station; dorm beds €11, singles/doubles €15.50/29, with private shower €24/36)* is big and constantly expanding. It has a bar, restaurant and Internet café, but it's all a bit soulless.

The HI-affiliated hostel, **Europa** *(☎ 050-35 26 79, fax 050-35 37 32; e brugge@vjh.be; Baron Ruzettelaan 143; dorm beds €12.50, beds in 4-bed room €14.50)*, is 500m south of the city walls but lacks atmosphere.

BELGIUM

Guesthouses There's a swarm of B&Bs and many represent excellent value.

The three lofty rooms at the **B&B Gheeraert** (☎ 050-33 56 27, fax 050-34 52 01; e paul.gheeraert@skynet.be, Riddersstraat 9; singles/doubles/triples €45/50/70) are simply gorgeous.

B&B Dieltiens (☎ 050-33 42 94, fax 050-33 52 30; e koen.dieltiens@skynet.be; Waalsestraat 40; singles/doubles €45/50, triples/quads €70/90, one-night supplement €7.50) has been welcoming visitors for years and the hospitality still shines.

Those adverse to stairs should head to the **B&B Debruyne** (☎ 050-34 76 07, fax 050-34 02 85; e marie.debruyne@advalvas.be; Lange Raamstraat 18; singles/doubles €45/50, triples/quads €70/90), a highly original home.

Hotels The **Hotel Malleberg** (☎ 050-34 41 11, fax 050-34 67 69; Hoogstraat 7; singles/doubles €60/72, triples/quads €100/117) is an immaculate two-star hotel with eight lovely rooms.

In the often overlooked St Anna quarter is charming **Hotel Adornes** (☎ 050-34 13 36, fax 050-34 20 85; e hotel.adornes@proximedia.be; St Annarei 26; singles/doubles from €75/80). It occupies three old gabled houses.

For a room with a view of the Markt there's **Huyze Die Maene** (☎ 050-33 39 59, fax 050-33 44 60; e huyzediemaene@padora.be; Markt 17; singles/doubles from €107/116, one-night supplement per person €5). This place is predominantly a brasserie but it has three fabulous rooms upstairs.

One of Bruges' most opulent but discreet choices is **Hotel De Orangerie** (☎ 050-34 16 49, fax 050-33 30 16; e info@orangerie.com; Kartuizerinnenstraat 10; singles/doubles from €173/198; breakfast €19). It's on a quiet backstreet overlooking the Dijver Canal.

Places to Eat

For a sandwich, try the rustic little **De Belegde Boterham** (☎ 050-34 91 31; Kleine St Amandsstraat).

The pleasant **Lotus** (☎ 050-33 10 78; Wapenmakerstraat 5; small/large meals €7.90/8.45; open lunch only Mon-Sat) is a stylish vegetarian restaurant.

Forget time at **De Bottelier** (☎ 050-33 18 60; St Jakobsstraat 50; mains €10-14); the

menu here will suit most. **Rock Fort** (☎ 050-33 41 13; Langstraat 15; dishes €13-19) does fusion cuisine in intimate surroundings.

The cavernous **Den Dyver** (☎ 050-33 60 69; Dijver 5; 3-course menu including drinks €42) uses the nation's many beers to spice up traditional cuisine.

De Stove (☎ 050-33 78 35; Kleine St Amandsstraat 4; mains €16-20) specialises in seafood and is refined and charming.

Self-caterers should head to **Profi supermarkets** (Oude Burg 22 • Langestraat 55).

Entertainment

If you're fanging for a beer, or better still, 300 different types of them, just go directly to **'t Brugs Beertje** (Kemelstraat 5). Another great bar is **De Garre** (Garre 1).

Retsin's Lucifernum (Twijnstraat 8; open from 9pm Fri & Sat) is one of Belgium's weirdest places to drink – a huge mansion strewn with moody paintings.

Live contemporary and world music generally happens at the **Cactus Club** (☎ 050-33 20 14; St Jakobsstraat 33). The **Cinema Lumière** (☎ 050-34 34 65; St Jakobsstraat 36a) screens foreign and mainstream films. Next door at **Café de la République** (St Jakobsstraat 36) you can find out what's happening around town. For performing arts there's the new **Concertgebouw** ('t Zand).

Getting There & Away

Bus From mid-May through mid-September, there's a daily Eurolines bus from Bruges to London (€46, six hours). **Reizen Wasteels** (☎ 050-33 65 31; Geldmuntstraat 30a) sells tickets.

Train The **station information office** (☎ 050-38 23 82; open 7am-8.30pm daily) can help with rail queries. IC trains go to Brussels (€10.30, one hour), Antwerp (€10.80, 70 minutes), Ghent (€4.70, 20 minutes) and Kortrijk (€5.60, 40 minutes), from where hourly connections go to Ypres (€8.45, 1½ hours).

Getting Around

There's a small network of buses, most leaving from the Markt, and many pass by the train station. For route and timetable information ring ☎ 059-56 53 53.

Rent bikes from **Fietsen Popelier** (☎ 050-34 32 62; Mariastraat 26) for €6/9 per half/full day.

BELGIUM

AROUND BRUGES

The famous, poppy-filled **battlefields of Flanders** draw many people south for a day or longer (see the Ypres section). In the opposite direction, the former fishing village of **Damme** is just 5km away, connected by the Napoleon Canal, and popular as a day-trip destination for the canal barge *Lamme Goedzak* (€5/6.50 one way/return).

Ypres

pop 35,000

Stories have long been told about the WWI battlefields of Flanders. There were the tall red poppies that rose over the flat, flat fields; the soldiers who disappeared forever in the quagmire of battle; and the little town of Ypres (Ieper in Flemish), which was wiped off the map.

Sitting in the country's southwest corner, Ypres and its surrounding land were the last bastion of Belgian territory unoccupied by the Germans in WWI. As such, the Ypres Salient was a barrier to a German advance towards the French coastal ports around Calais. More than 300,000 Allied soldiers were killed here during four years of fighting that left the medieval town flattened. Convincingly rebuilt, its outlying farmlands are today dotted with cemeteries and memorials, and in early summer, the poppies still flower.

Orientation & Information

The town's hub is the Grote Markt. It's a 10-minute walk from the train station – head straight up Stationsstraat and, at the end, turn left onto Tempelstraat and then right onto Boterstraat. Three blocks on is Renaissance-style Lakenhalle (cloth hall) with its 70m-high belfry.

The **visitors centre** (☎ 057-22 85 84, fax 057-22 85 89; Grote Markt; open 9am-6pm daily Apr-Sept, 9am-5pm Oct-Mar) is in the Lakenhalle.

Things to See

Ypres ranked alongside Bruges and Ghent as an important cloth town in medieval times, and its postwar reconstruction holds true to its former prosperity.

The excellent **In Flanders Fields Museum** (Grote Markt 34; W www.inflandersfields.be; adults/children €7.50/3.50; open 10am-5pm or 6pm daily Apr-Sept, 10am-5pm or 6pm Tues-Sun Oct-Mar) is a moving testament to the wartime horrors experienced by ordinary people.

One of the saddest reminders of the Great War is Ypres' **Meensepoort** (Menin Gate), inscribed with the names of 55,000 British and Commonwealth troops who were lost in the trenches and who have no graves.

A bugler sounds the last post here at 8pm every evening. It's about 300m from the tourist office.

Around Ypres, in outlying fields and hamlets, are 170 **cemeteries** and many **memorials** to those who died on the Ypres Salient. These wartime reminders are scattered over a large area – if you have limited time it's best to go with an organised tour (see the following section).

Organised Tours

Several companies offer tours of the cemeteries and the important battle sites. **Salient Tours** (☎ 057-91 02 23) has been around for years and runs 2½ hour/four hour tours for €15/22. **Flanders Battlefield Tours** (☎ 057-36 04 60) is a newcomer and it charges €10/14. Alternatively, join **Quasimodo's** tour (see Organised Tours under Bruges for details). Book ahead for all tours.

Places to Stay & Eat

For camping, there's **Jeugdstadion** (☎ 057-21 72 82; e info@jeugdstadion.be; Leopold III laan 16; tent site €1.50, per person €3), 900m southeast of the town centre. The closest private hostel is **De Iep** (☎/fax 057-20 88 11; Poperingseweg 34; dorm beds €14.10), 2km west of town.

The new **B&B Hortensia** (☎ 057-21 24 06; Rijselsestraat 196; singles/doubles/triples €42/54/69) is modern, spacious and a treat.

An affordable central hotel is the old fashioned **Old Tom** (☎ 057-20 15 41, fax 057-21 91 20; e oldtom@pandora.be; singles/doubles €49/58).

Hotel Regina (☎ 057-21 88 88, fax 057-21 90 20; e info@hotelregina.be; Grote Markt 45) has two types of rooms – old and very ordinary 'classics' for €75, or new and beautifully rustic 'executive' rooms for €100.

Cafés and restaurants line Grote Markt – a good choice is **In het Klein Stadhuis** (☎ 057-21 55 42; mains €10.60-15.50), a simple brasserie right next to the town hall.

BELGIUM

Eethuis De Ecurie (☎ 057-21 73 78; Rijselsestraat 49; dishes €13-17) offers innovative cuisine and an enticing atmosphere (despite once being a horse stable).

For picnic supplies, there's the **Super GB supermarket** (Vandepeereboomplein 15).

Getting There & Around

Direct hourly trains go to Kortrijk (€3.20, 30 minutes) and Ghent (€8.30, one hour).

For Brussels (€12.70, 1½ hours), Antwerp (€14.20, two hours), Bruges (€8.45, 1½ hours) and Tournai (€6.80, one hour), change trains in Kortrijk.

Regional buses leave from outside the train station.

Rent bicycles from the Jeugdstadion (see Places to Stay earlier) for €5 per day.

Tournai

pop 68,365

The Walloon town of Tournai (Doornik in Flemish), together with Tongeren in Flanders, is classed as the oldest city in Belgium. Just 10km from the French border and some 80km southwest of Brussels, it was once a Roman trading settlement called Tornacum, though there are few reminders of these times. The town's focal point, the five-towered cathedral, is one of the country's finest (however, it's expected to be closed until about 2009).

Orientation & Information

The train station is a 10-minute walk from the centre of town – head straight up Rue Royale until you reach the cathedral. To the left up the hill is the **tourist office** (☎ 069-22 20 45, fax 069-21 62 21; e tourisme@tournai.be; Vieux Marché aux Poteries 14; open 9am-6pm or 7pm Mon-Fri, 10am-1pm & 3pm-6pm Sat, 10am-noon & 2pm-6pm Sun), near the base of the belfry.

Things to See & Do

Tournai's austere 12th-century **cathedral** is undergoing extensive repairs after tornado damage in 1999. It'll probably be closed for a decade. The treasury (entry via Rue des Chapeliers) has remained open (check with the tourist office for opening hours).

After a decade-long face-lift, the 13th-century **belfry** (Vieux Marché aux Poteries;

admission €2) has reopened. Climb the 257 steps for a great view.

The town's most prestigious museum is the **Musée des Beaux-Arts** (Enclos St Martin; admission €3), in a building designed by Victor Horta. The **Musée de la Tapisserie et des Arts du Tissu** (Museum of Tapestry and Cloth Arts; Place Reine Astrid; admission €2.50) is testament to the revival of the city's historically important tapestry industry. Both museums are open 10am to noon and 2pm to 5.30pm Wednesday to Monday.

Places to Stay & Eat

The **Camping de l'Orient** (☎ 069-22 26 35; Vieux Chemin de Mons; bus W from station; tent site €2.50, per person €2.50) is 4km southeast of town.

The pleasant, HI-affiliated **Auberge de Jeunesse** (☎ 069-21 61 36, fax 069-21 61 40; Rue St Martin 64; dorm beds €12.50, singles/doubles €22.50/35) is a 20-minute walk from the station.

Hôtel d'Alcantara (☎ 069-21 26 48, fax 069-21 28 24; Rue des Bouchers St Jacques 2; singles/doubles from €73/83) is a charmingly discreet hotel with modern rooms.

Two good restaurant options include: **L'Écurie d'Ennetières** (☎ 069-21 56 89; Ruelle d'Ennetières; mains €7.50-12.50), a lovely mid-range French restaurant, or consider the excellent **Le Pressior** (☎ 069-22 35 13; Vieux Marché aux Poteries 2; mains €17-19).

Pita Pyramide (☎ 069-84 35 83; Rue Tête d'Or 7) has stuffed pitta breads for €3.80. Picnic supplies can be had from the **Super GB supermarket** across the road.

Getting There & Away

There are regular trains to Kortrijk (€3.80, 40 minutes), Brussels (€9.30, one hour) and Ypres via Kortrijk (€6.80, one hour).

Liège

pop 189,903

Liège (Luik in Flemish) is one of those cities people tend to love or loathe. Sprawled along the Meuse River in the eastern part of Wallonia, it's busy and gritty and is the sort of place that takes time to know. If you're passing en route to the Ardennes, stop off to see its evocative museums.

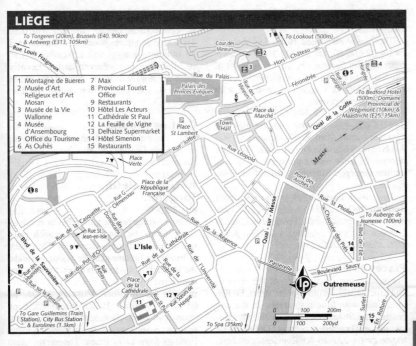

LIÈGE

To Tongeren (20km), Brussels (E40, 90km)
& Antwerp (E313, 105km)

Rue Louis Fraigneux

1 Montagne de Bueren
2 Musée d'Art
   Religieux et d'Art
   Mosan
3 Musée de la Vie
   Wallonne
4 Musée
   d'Ansembourg
5 Office du Tourisme
6 As Ouhès
7 Max
8 Provincial Tourist
   Office
9 Restaurants
10 Hôtel Les Acteurs
11 Cathédrale St Paul
12 La Feuille de Vigne
13 Delhaize Supermarket
14 Hôtel Simenon
15 Restaurants

To Lookout (500km)
Cour des Mineurs
Château
Hors Château
Rue du Palais
Palais des Princes Evêques
Place du Marché
Town Hall
Rue Joffre
Place St Lambert
Rue Léopold
Quai de la Goffe
Meuse
Rue Hongrée
Rue St Georges
To Bedford Hotel
(500m), Domaine
Provincial de
Wégimont (10km) &
Maastricht (E25, 35km)
Pont des Arches
Rue St Pholien
To Auberge de
Jeunesse (100m)
Chaussée des Prés
Blvd de l'Est
Place Verte
Place de la République Française
Rue G Clémenceau
Rue de la Casquette
Rue des Dominicains
Rue Jean-en-Isle
L'Isle
Blvd de la Sauvenière
Rue des Urbanistes
Rue du Pont d'Or
Rue d'Amay
Rue sur la Fontaine
Rue de la Cathédrale
Rue de la Régence
Rue de l'Université
Quai sur Meuse
Passerelle
Boulevard Saucy
Outremeuse
Rue Surlet
Rue En Roture
Place de la Cathédrale
Rue de la Sirène
Rue Sœurs de Hasque
Rue St Paul
To Gare Guillemins (Train
Station), City Bus Station
& Eurolines (1.3km)
To Spa (35km)

0   100   200m
0   100   200yd

Orientation

The central district is strewn along the western bank of the Meuse River, which splits in two creating the island of Outremeuse. The main train station, Gare Guillemins, is 2km south of Place St Lambert, the city's heart.

Information

The main **Office du Tourisme** (☎ 04-221 92 21, fax 04-221 92 22; e office.tourisme@ liege.be; Féronstrée 92; open 9am-5pm or 6pm Mon-Fri, 10am-4pm Sat, 10am-2pm Sun) can help with information.

For regional information, head to the **provincial tourist office** (Fédération du Tourisme de la Province de Liège; ☎ 04-232 65 10; Blvd de la Sauvenière 77).

At Gare Guillemins there's a small bureau dispensing city and provincial information.

Things to See & Do

Excellent views of the city can be enjoyed from the top of **Montagne de Bueren** – an impressive flight of 373 stairs which lead up from Hors Château. On Sunday morning there's **La Batte**, which is a street market stretching along 1.5km of riverfront quays.

The area around the tourist office is old and quite picturesque and home to the city's best museums. The **Musée d'Art Religieux et d'Art Mosan** (Museum of Religious Art and Art from the Meuse Valley; Rue Mère Dieu; admission €2.50; open 11am-6pm Tues-Sat, 11am-4pm Sun) is stuffed with relics and paintings from the region. The nearby **Musée de la Vie Wallonne** (Walloon Life Museum; Cour des Mineurs; admission €2; open 10am-5pm Tues-Sat, 10am-4pm Sun) presents local customs from days gone by. Life as it was for some in the 18th century is depicted in the **Musée d'Ansembourg** (Féronstrée 114; admission €1.50; open 1pm-6pm Tues-Sun), a Regency-style mansion. Don't miss the six-faced clock.

Places to Stay

One of the closest camping grounds is **Domaine Provincial de Wégimont** (☎ 04-377 99 02; Chaussée de Wégimont 76; open Feb-Dec) in Ayeneux, 10km east of Liège.

The big HI-affiliated **Auberge de Jeunesse** (☎ 04-344 56 89, fax 04-344 56 87; e liege@laj.be; Rue Georges Simenon 2; bus No 4 from Gare Guillemins; dorm beds

€12.80, singles/doubles €20.50/30) is in Outremeuse.

The newly renovated **Hôtel Les Acteurs** (☎ 04-223 00 80, fax 04-221 19 48; e lesac teurs@skynet.be; Rue des Urbanistes 10; bus No 1 or 4 from the station; singles/doubles from €50/60) is a breath of fresh air, with modern, comfy rooms.

Hôtel Simenon (☎ 04-342 86 90, fax 04-344 26 69; e simenon@swing.be; Blvd de l'Est 16; rooms from €62) occupies a 1908 Art Nouveau house in Outremeuse. The gaily decorated rooms reflect the writings of local author Georges Simenon. Breakfast costs €6.20.

The city's finest hotel is the riverfront **Bedford** (☎ 04-228 81 11, fax 04-227 45 75; e hotelbedford@pophost.eunet.be; Quai St Léonard 36; singles/doubles Sat-Sun €91/101, Mon-Fri €209/234).

Places to Eat

For serene surroundings, cross the river to Outremeuse with an old cobbled street, En Roture, lined with little restaurants. In the city centre, Rue St-Jean-en-Isle is filled with restaurants and brasseries. Nearby, **La Feuille de Vigne** (☎ 04-222 20 10; Rue Sœurs de Hasque 12; meals €7.50-9; open noon-3pm Mon-Sat) is a health-food-shop-cum-vegetarian eatery. One of the best brasseries is **As Ouhès** (☎ 04-223 32 25; Place du Marché 21; dishes €10-17), specialising in rich Walloon cuisine (servings are extra generous and prices reasonable). For superb seafood, the answer is **Max** (☎ 04-222 08 59; Place Verte 2; mains €21-33, 4-course menu €50).

Self-caterers should try **Delhaize supermarket** (Place de la Cathédrale).

Getting There & Away

Bus The office of **Eurolines** (☎ 04-222 36 18; Rue des Guillemins 94) is near the main train station. Buses depart from 50m away on the corner of Rue des Guillemins and Rue d'Artois.

Train The principal station, Gare Guillemins, is 2km from Place St Lambert and is connected by bus No 1 or 4. There's a **train information office** (☎ 04-224 26 10; open 7am-9.30pm daily).

The Thalys fast train connects Liège with Cologne (€23.30, 1¼ hours, seven trains daily) but there are also cheaper, normal trains

(€18.80, 1½ hours, eight daily). Other regular connections include Brussels (€10.80, 1¼ hours, two trains hourly), Maastricht (€7, 30 minutes, hourly) and Luxembourg City (€24.30, 2½ hours, seven daily). Locally, there are hourly trains to Namur (€6.40, 50 minutes), Spa (€3.20, 50 minutes) and Tongeren (€3.30, 30 minutes).

Getting Around

Inner-city buses leave from the right as you leave Gare Guillemins. Bus No 1 or 4 plies between here and the centre.

AROUND LIÈGE
Tongeren
pop 30,000

Flemish Tongeren is about 20km north of Liège. It has the honour (together with Tournai) of being Belgium's oldest city. The original locals put up considerable resistance under the leadership of Ambiorix when the area was conquered by Roman troops in 15 BC. The impressive **Gallo-Roman Museum** (☎ 012-67 03 30; Kielenstraat 15; admission €5; open noon-5pm Mon, 9am-5pm Tues-Fri, 10am-6pm Sat & Sun) in the heart of town has many findings from early times. Tongeren is also well known for its Sunday **antique market**.

For more information, visit the **tourist office** (☎ 012-39 02 55, fax 012-39 11 43; Stadhuisplein 9; open 8.30am-noon & 1pm-4.30pm Mon-Fri, 10am-4pm Sat & Sun).

Overnighters will find a pleasant HI hostel, **Begijnhof** (☎ 012-39 13 70, fax 012-39 13 48; e tongeren@vjh.be; St Ursulastraat 1; dorm beds €12.50) or the mid-range **Hotel Lido** (☎ 012-23 19 48, fax 012-39 27 27; Grote Markt 19; singles/doubles €60/70).

Spa
pop 11,000

Spa was for centuries the luxurious retreat of royalty and the wealthy who drank, bathed and cured themselves in mineral-rich waters. Now a run-down reminder of the past, it's pleasant enough for a day or overnight.

The town is about 35km southeast of Liège, connected by regular trains (see the Liège Getting There & Away section). The local **Office du Tourisme** (☎ 087-79 53 53, fax 087-79 53 54; e officetourismespa@skynet .be; Place Royale 41; open 9am-6pm Mon-Fri, 10am-6pm Sat & Sun) can assist you regarding any inquiries.

Hautes Fagnes National Park

Bordering the Eifel Hills in Germany, with which it forms one geographical entity, the Hautes Fagnes park is a region of swampy heath and woods. Within the park is the **Botrange Nature Centre** (☎ 080-44 03 00, fax 080-44 44 29; e botrange.centrenature@ skynet.be; Route de Botrange 131; admission adult/concession €3/1.50; open 10am-6pm daily) close to the highest point in Belgium – the Signal de Botrange (694m). This area is a popular base for hikers, cyclists and cross-country skiers.

For those wanting just a short walk (1½ hours) through this bleak but interesting landscape, head to the boardwalk at the Fagne de Polleur, nearby at Mt Rigi.

The Botrange Nature Centre is about 50km east of Liège.

It takes at least 1¼ hours to get to on public transport from Liège – take the train to Verviers and then bus No 390 in the direction of Elsenborn.

The Ardennes

Home to deep river valleys and high forests, Belgium's southeastern corner is often overlooked by travellers hopping between the old art towns and the capital. But here, in the provinces of Namur, Liège and Luxembourg, you'll find tranquil villages nestled into the grooves of the Meuse, Lesse and Ourthe Valleys or sitting atop the verdant hills. Historically, this is where the Battle of the Bulge once raged.

The town of Namur is the best base for exploration. It's well positioned on the train line to Luxembourg and has rail and bus connections to some of the region's less accessible spots. Without your own transport, getting around this region can take time.

NAMUR
pop 105,000

Just 50km southeast of Brussels, Namur (Namen in Flemish) is the capital of Wallonia. The town is relatively small and picturesque, and is dominated by its 15th-century citadel.

The **tourist office** (☎ 081-24 64 49; Square Léopold; open 9.30am-6pm daily) is 200m to the left of the station, as you leave. There's also a small tourist kiosk at Place du Grognon at the base of the citadel.

Things to See & Do

Perched dramatically above the town, the **citadel** (☎ 081-22 68 29; admission free) can be reached either on foot, by car along the Route Merveilleuse, or by a shuttle bus (€1) which departs half-hourly from the tourist office. Guided visits cost €6/3 for adults/children.

Of the handful of museums, the two most intriguing are the **Félicien Rops** (☎ 081-22 01 10; Rue Fumal 12; admission €2.50/1.25), which has works by the 19th-century Namurborn artist who fondly illustrated erotic lifestyles, and the tiny **Trésor du Prieuré d'Oignies** (☎ 081-23 03 42; Rue Julie Billiart 17; admission €1.25/0.50), a one-roomed hoard of exquisite Gothic treasures in a modern convent.

Places to Stay & Eat

Campers can head to **Camping Les Tilleuls** (☎ 082-61 12 31; Rue de la Plage; bus No 433 from the bus station) at Godinne, about 15km south of Namur, en route to Dinant.

About 3km from the train station there's the riverfront **Auberge de Jeunesse** (☎ 081-22 36 88, fax 081-22 44 12; e namur@ laj.be; Ave F Rops 8; bus No 3 or 4 from the station; dorm beds €14.50).

At the **Grand Hôtel de Flandre** (☎ 081-23 18 68, fax 081-22 80 60; Place de la Station 14; singles/doubles from €56/73) there are no-nonsense rooms.

For considerably more charm try **Hôtel Les Tanneurs** (☎ 081-24 00 24, fax 081-24 00 25; e info@tanneurs.com; Rue des Tanneries 13; singles €31-193, doubles €49-215). Every room in this unique establishment is different and the prices reflect standards of luxury.

Tea Time Café (☎ 0496-52 44 22; Rue St Jean 35) serves excellent filled baguettes (€3.25) as well as crepes and waffles.

Snacks plus French-style meals are served at **Brasserie Henry** (☎ 081-22 02 04; Place St Aubain 3; mains €8.50-15, 3-course menu €21.50; open noon-midnight).

Getting There & Away

From Namur's **train station** (☎ 081-25 22 22) there are trains to Brussels (€6.40, one hour, half-hourly), Luxembourg City (€21.50, 1¾ hours, hourly) and Liège (€6.40, 50 minutes, hourly). For information on regional trains, see Getting There & Away sections for

BELGIUM

Dinant, Han-sur-Lesse, Rochefort, La Roche-en-Ardenne and Bastogne.

Local and regional buses are operated by TEC (☎ 081-25 35 55; office open 7am-7pm daily) which has an office opposite the train station. Regional buses leave from the bus station near the C&A department store (to the left of the train station as you leave).

DINANT
pop 12,500

This distinctive town, 28km south of Namur, is one of the Ardennes' touristy hot spots. Its bulbous cathedral competes for attention with the cliff-front citadel, while below, a hive of boat operators compete for the Meuse River day-trippers or the Lesse Valley kayakers. The tourist office (☎ 082-22 28 70; e info@dinant-tourisme.be; Ave Cadoux 8; open 8.30am-6pm Mon-Fri, 10am-4.30pm Sat & Sun) can assist visitors.

Things to See & Do

The citadel is open all year and accessible by cable car – a combined ticket costs €5/3.75 for adults/children.

Several companies have kayaking trips leaving from Houyet 21km upriver, and ending at Anseremme next to Dinant five hours later. Try Kayaks Ansiaux (☎ 082-22 23 25; Rue du Vélodrome 15) in Anseremme.

More sedate are the boat cruises that go down the Meuse. Companies include Bateaux Bayard (☎ 082-22 30 42; Quai No 10, Blvd Churchill), which offers a 45-minute return trip to Anseremme (adults/children €4.80/3.50) and a 3½-hour return cruise to Hastière (€11/9).

Places to Stay

Hotels are not plentiful and there's no hostel (the nearest is in Namur). The Hôtel de la Couronne (☎ 082-22 24 41; e info@hotellacouronne.com; Rue Sax 1; singles/doubles from €50/62) is pleasant and central. The new riverfront Hôtel Ibis (☎ 082-21 15 00; e hotelibis.dinant@belgacom.net; Rempart d'Albeau 16; singles/doubles from €75/84) is architecturally bland, however, it boosts the meagre accommodation scene.

Getting There & Away

There are hourly trains from Namur to Dinant (€3.40, 30 minutes). Bus No 34 (50 minutes, one every two hours) connects the two.

HAN-SUR-LESSE & ROCHEFORT
pop 23,500

The millennia-old limestone grottoes are the drawcard of these two villages, which sit just 8km apart on the Lesse and the Lomme Rivers respectively.

The impressive Han caves (adults/children €10.30/5.90; open 10am-noon & 1.30pm-4.30pm Apr-Oct, tours at 11.30am, 1pm, 2.30pm and 4pm Nov, Dec, Feb & Mar) are a little way out of town – a tram will take you to the entrance and a boat will bring you back. Rochefort's cave, known as the Grotte de Lorette (adults/children €5.95/3.95; open Easter–early-Nov), is much smaller and less impressive.

Local information offices include the Han tourist office (☎ 084-37 75 96; e han.tourisme@euronet.be; Place Théo Lannoy) as well as the Rochefort tourist office (☎ 084-34 51 72; e valdelesse@tiscalinet.be; Rue de Behogne 5).

Places to Stay

Camping La Lesse (☎ 084-37 72 90; Rue du Grand Hy; open Mar-Nov) is in Han. In Rochefort there's Camping Communal (☎ 084-21 19 00; open Easter-31 Oct).

Both villages have private hostels which have dormitory-style accommodation costing €12.50 for people 26 years and over, or €10 for under 26s.

Contact Han Gîte d'Étape hostel (☎ 084-37 74 41; e g.han@skynet.be; Rue du Gîte d'Étape 10; open year-round) or try the Rochefort Gîte d'Étape hostel (☎ 084-21 46 04; e giterochefort@skynet.be; Rue du Hableau 25).

In Han, the grey stone Hôtel des Ardennes (☎ 084-37 72 20, fax 084-37 80 62; Rue des Grottes 2; singles/doubles from €48/60) has local charm and a good restaurant. Rochefort has a better range of hotel options including the bright Hotel La Fayette (☎ 084-21 42 73; e hotel.lafayette@swing.be; Rue Jacquet 87; singles/doubles from €37/42) or atmospheric Le Vieux Logis (☎ 084-21 10 24, fax 084-22 12 30; Rue Jacquet 71; singles/doubles €48/58).

Getting There & Away

Take the Namur-Luxembourg train to Jemelle (40 minutes, hourly) and transfer to the hourly bus No 29 (seven minutes to Rochefort, 14 minutes to Han).

LA ROCHE-EN-ARDENNE
pop 4100

Hugging a bend in the Ourthe River, La Roche is a vibrant little town, hidden in a deep valley, crowned by a ruined **castle** and surrounded by verdant hills much enjoyed by hikers. If you want to get into kayaking or mountain biking, this is your playground. The **tourist office** (☎ 084-36 77 36; e in lolr@skynet.be; Place du Marché 15) dispenses information. At **Ardenne Adventures** (☎ 084-41 19 00; Rue du Hadja 1) you can hire mountain bikes and kayaks, and it also organises white-water rafting (October to March only).

Places to Stay
Camping Le Vieux Moulin (☎ 084-41 13 80; Petite Strument 62; sites per adult/tent €2.50/7.50; open Easter-Oct) is beautifully positioned.

Villa Les Olivettes (☎ 084-41 16 52, fax 084-41 21 69; e info@lesolivettes; Chemin de Soeret 12; dorm beds €15, singles/doubles from €54/74) is popular with horse-riding enthusiasts. In addition to hotel rooms, it has a separate auberge with dormitory-style accommodation (four to eight beds); breakfast is not included.

For a quaint B&B, head to **Le Vieux La Roche** (☎ 084-41 25 86; e levieuxlaroche@online.be; Rue du Chalet 45; rooms €38), with five homy rooms.

The captivating **Moulin de la Strument** (☎ 084-41 15 07, fax 084-41 10 80; e strument@skynet.be; Petite Strument 62; singles/doubles €60/66) is a hotel/restaurant with eight rooms beside a babbling stream.

Places to Eat
Succulent crepes are the house speciality of **Le Clos René** (☎ 084-41 26 17; Rue Châmont 30; crepes €4-5). It's in the heart of town and prices are reasonable. Note the glass floor.

For both classic French cuisine and ultra-attentive service, you should head to **La Clairefontaine** (☎ 084-41 24 70; Route de Hotton 64; 3-course/6-course menu €19/52), an old-fashioned hotel/restaurant 1.5km from town.

The **Spar supermarket** (Quai du Gravier 1) has picnic supplies.

Getting There & Away
From Namur, take a Luxembourg-bound train to Marloie, then bus No 15 to La Roche (35 minutes, eight daily).

BASTOGNE
pop 12,500

It was here, north of Arlon and close to the Luxembourg border, that thousands of soldiers and civilians died during the Battle of the Bulge in the winter of 1944–45. Testament to these events is a huge, star-shaped **American memorial**, known also as Mardasson, on a hill 2km from Bastogne. The neighbouring **Bastogne Historical Centre**, (☎ 061-21 14 13; open 10am-4.30pm daily Feb-June & Sept-Dec, 9.30am-6pm daily July-Aug; admission €7.50/5) is an unimpressive glorification of war.

The new **tourist office** (☎ 061-21 27 11; Place McAuliffe) is in the heart of town.

Places to Stay
Camping de Renval (☎ 061-21 29 85; Route de Marche 148; open 16 Jan-Dec) is 1km from the tourist office. **Hôtel du Sud** (☎ 061-21 11 14; e info@hotel-du-sud.be; Rue de Marche 39; singles/doubles from €45/54) has passable rooms. More upmarket is **Hôtel Collin** (☎ 061-21 43 58; e infos@hotel-collin.com; Place McAuliffe 8; singles/doubles from €67/80).

Getting There & Away
From Namur, take a Luxembourg-bound train to the rail junction of Libramont, from where bus No 163b departs every two hours for Bastogne's defunct train station (35 minutes).

BELGIUM

LA ROCHE-EN-ARDENNE
pop 4100

BASTOGNE
pop 12,500

Britain

The first stop on many people's European tour, Britain can easily occupy a trip of its own. London is booming and has a definite buzz and vibrancy. At one stage of its history this small island ruled half the world's population and had a major impact on many of the rest. For those whose countries once lay in the shadow of its great empire a visit may almost be a cliche, but it's also essential – a peculiar mixture of homecoming and confrontation.

To the surprise of many, Britain remains one of the most beautiful islands in the world. All the words, paintings and pictures that have been produced are not just romantic, patriotic exaggerations.

In terms of area, Britain is small, but the more that you explore the bigger it seems to become. Visitors from the New World are often fooled by this magical expansion and try to do too much too quickly. JB Priestley observed of England: 'She is just pretending to be small'. Covering it all in one trip is impossible – and that's before you start thinking of Scotland and Wales.

The United Kingdom comprises Britain (England, Scotland and Wales) as well as Northern Ireland. Its full name is the United Kingdom of Great Britain and Northern Ireland. This chapter confines itself only to the island of Britain, the largest of the British Isles, the Channel Islands and Scotland's outlying islands – the Inner and Outer Hebrides in the west and Orkney and Shetland in the northeast. For reasons of geographical and practical coherence, Northern Ireland is dealt with alongside the Irish Republic in the Ireland chapter.

Sometimes in summer it can feel as if the whole world has come to Britain, but it's certainly possible to avoid the rush. Don't spend all your time in the big, tourist-ridden towns; rather, pick a small area and spend at least a week or so wandering around country lanes and villages.

Facts about Britain

HISTORY
See the England, Scotland and Wales individual sections later in this chapter for information about their history.

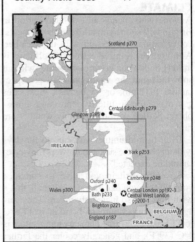

GEOGRAPHY & ECOLOGY
Britain has an area of 240,000 sq km, about the same size as New Zealand or half the size of France. It is less than 600mi from south to north and under 300mi at its widest point.

There are no great mountains in terms of height, but this does not prevent a number of ranges from being spectacular. The mountains

BRITAIN

161

of Snowdonia in northwest Wales, the Cumbrian mountains in northwest England, and the Glenkens in southwest Scotland all reach around 1000m. The Grampians form the mountainous barrier between the Scottish Lowlands and Highlands, and include Ben Nevis, at 1343m the highest mountain on the island.

The seas surrounding the British Isles are shallow, and relatively warm because of the influence of the warm North Atlantic Current, also known as the Gulf Stream. This creates a temperate, changeable, maritime climate with few extremes of temperature but few cloudless sunny days!

With almost 57 million people living on a relatively small island, environmental issues, especially in relation to pollution from the ever-growing number of cars, are forcing their way on to the agenda. Britain has several high-profile environmental pressure groups. For more information try **Greenpeace** (☎ 020-7865 8100; e info@uk .greenpeace.org; Cannonbury Villas, London N1 2PN).

CLIMATE

Anyone who spends an extended period in Britain will soon sympathise with the locals' conversational obsession with the weather. Although in relative terms the climate is mild (London can go through winter without snowfall) and the annual rainfall not spectacular (912mm, or 35 inches), grey skies can make for an utterly depressing atmosphere. Settled periods of sunny weather are rare.

Even in midsummer you can go for days without seeing the sun, and showers (or worse) should be expected.

To enjoy Britain you have to convince yourself that you *like* the rain – after all, that's what makes it so incredibly green! The average July temperature in London is 17.6°C (64°F), and the average January temperature is 4°C (39°F), and generally cooler the farther north you go.

GOVERNMENT & POLITICS

As yet the United Kingdom doesn't have a written constitution. Instead it operates under a mixture of parliamentary statutes, common law (a body of legal principles based on precedents that go back to Anglo-Saxon customs) and convention.

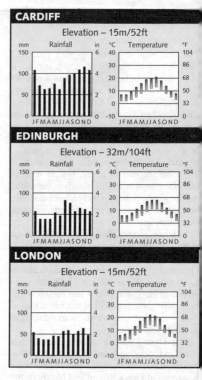

The monarch is the head of state, but real power has been whittled away to the point where the current Queen Elizabeth II is a figurehead who acts almost entirely on the advice of 'her' ministers and Parliament.

Parliament has three separate elements: the Queen, the House of Commons and the House of Lords. In practice, the supreme body is the House of Commons, which is directly elected every five years. Voting is not compulsory, and candidates are elected if they win a simple majority in their constituencies. There are 659 constituencies (seats) – 529 for England, 40 for Wales, 72 for Scotland and 18 for Northern Ireland.

The House of Lords consists of the Lords Spiritual (26 senior bishops of the Church of England), the Lords Temporal (all hereditary and life peers), and the Lords of Appeal (or 'law lords').

None are elected by the general population, and the Labour government has pledged to remove the hereditary peers within the next few years.

BRITAIN

To Shetland Islands (see inset)

ORKNEY ISLANDS
Mainland
Stromness
Hoy
Pentland Firth
Thurso
Wick

SHETLAND ISLANDS
Foula
Lerwick

OUTER HEBRIDES
Lewis
St Kilda
North Uist
Harris
South Uist
The Minch

North West Highlands
Ullapool
Moray Firth
Elgin
Peterhead
Inverness
Kyle of Lochalsh
Aviemore
Skye
Loch Ness
Spey
Dee
Aberdeen

Rhum
Fort William
Ben Nevis (1343m)
SCOTLAND
Grampians
Braemar

INNER HEBRIDES
Coll
Tiree
Mull
Oban
Loch Awe
Montrose
Dundee
Arbroath
Perth
St Andrews

ATLANTIC OCEAN

Colonsay
Jura
Loch Lomond
Stirling
Kirkaldy
Firth of Forth
Dunbar
Islay
GLASGOW
Motherwell
EDINBURGH

NORTH SEA

Arran
Kilmarnock
Galashiels
Berwick-upon-Tweed
Ayr
Sanquhar
Tweed
Jedburgh
Galloway
Nith
Ashington
Derry
Dumfries
NEWCASTLE-UPON-TYNE
Tyne
Stranraer
Larne
Carlisle
Sunderland
NORTHERN IRELAND
North Channel
Solway Firth
Workington
Durham
BELFAST
Lake District
Cambrian Mtns
Darlington
Middlesbrough
Douglas
Windermere
North York Moors
Scarborough
Isle of Man
Lancaster
Yorkshire Dales
Ure
Ouse
Bridlington

IRISH SEA

Blackpool
Blackburn
York
DUBLIN
Dun Laoghaire
Southport
LEEDS
Humber
KINGSTON-UPON-HULL
Holyhead
LIVERPOOL
MANCHESTER
Grimsby
Anglesey
Colwyn Bay
Bangor
Rhyl
Chester
Peak
SHEFFIELD
Lincoln
NORTH SEA
Wrexham
Stoke-on-Trent
Snowdonia
Derby
Boston
The Wash
Cardigan Bay
Shrewsbury
Nottingham
King's Lynn
Aberystwyth
Cambrian Mtns
BIRMINGHAM
Leicester
Norwich
ENGLAND
Coventry
Peterborough
The Fens
Wexford
Worcester
Ely
Bury St Edmunds
Rosslare
WALES
Hereford
Northampton
Cambridge
Ipswich
St George's Channel
Llandovery
Stratford-upon-Avon
Fishguard
St David's
Wye
Cheltenham
Gloucester
Luton
Colchester
Harwich
CELTIC SEA
Brecon Beacons
Merthyr Tydfil
The Cotswolds
Oxford
Pembrokeshire Coast
Pembroke
Llanelli
Swansea
Newport
Swindon
The Chilterns
Windsor
Thames
Southend-on-Sea
CARDIFF
Reading
LONDON
Bristol Channel
Bristol
Bath
Guildford
North Downs
Canterbury
Ramsgate
Dover
Channel Tunnel

CHANNEL ISLANDS
Alderney
Cherbourg
St Peter Port
FRANCE
Guernsey
Sark
Jersey
St Helier

Exmoor
Barnstaple
Taunton
Salisbury
Winchester
South Downs
Hastings
Eastbourne
Boulogne
Calais
Bude
Exeter
Exe
Southampton
Bournemouth
Brighton
Portsmouth
Newquay
Tamar
Dartmoor
Torquay
Weymouth
Isle of Wight
THE CHANNEL
Penzance
Truro
Plymouth
Land's End
Isles of Scilly

See Channel Islands inset
Cherbourg
Alderney

Dieppe
FRANCE

0   50   100km
0   30   60mi

BRITAIN

If the Lords refuses to pass a bill, but it is passed twice by the Commons, it is sent to the Queen for her automatic assent.

The Queen appoints the leader of the majority party in the House of Commons as prime minister; all other ministers are appointed on the recommendation of the prime minister, most from the House of Commons. Ministers are responsible for government departments. The senior ministers make up the Cabinet, which, although answerable to Parliament, meets confidentially and in effect manages the government and its policies.

For the last 150 years a predominantly two-party system has operated. Since 1945 either the Conservative Party or the Labour Party has held power, the Conservatives largely drawing their support from suburbia and the country-side, and Labour from urban industrialised areas.

Put crudely, the Conservatives are right wing, free-enterprise supporters, and Labour is left wing in the social-democratic tradition. In recent years, however, the Labour Party has shed most of its socialist credo, and the Conservatives have softened their hard-right approach. In both the 1997 and 2001 elections, Tony Blair led the Labour Party to landslide victories. In the last few years Scotland and Wales have been given their own elected parliaments and London has voted for its first elected mayor, the mercurial Ken Livingstone. However, promises to replace the first-past-the-post electoral system that has exaggerated the seesaw politics of the past half-century, with an alternative vote or proportional representation system, have not materialised. Still, the Labour Party looks set for a few more years in power, so time is likely on its side. The next election is due by 2006.

ECONOMY

Until the 18th century the economy was based on agriculture and the manufacture of woollen cloth. In the late 18th century the empire and the Industrial Revolution allowed Britain to become the first industrialised trading nation, and the population of South Wales, the Midlands, Yorkshire and the Scottish Lowlands expanded rapidly. Conditions for workers were appalling, but 19th-century Britain dominated world trade.

In the 20th century, a considerable proportion of industry was nationalised (railways, utilities, coal mines, steel, shipbuilding, even the motor industry), a process that was reversed under Margaret Thatcher.

Today free enterprise rules the roost, and although manufacturing continues to play an important role (particularly in the Midlands), service industries like banking and finance have grown rapidly (particularly in London and the southeast). Most of the traditional mining, engineering and cotton industries (especially in the Midlands and north) have disappeared.

The last 20 years have seen a battle against inflation (2.5% in 2001) and unemployment. By the start of the 21st century, the economy had emerged from the doldrums, although unemployment is still high in areas like Liverpool.

POPULATION & PEOPLE

Britain has a population of almost 57 million people, an average 236 inhabitants per square kilometre, making the island one of the most crowded on the planet. The majority are concentrated in and around London, Birmingham, Manchester, Liverpool, Sheffield and Nottingham.

Since WWII there has been significant immigration from the ex-colonies, especially the West Indies, Bangladesh, Pakistan and India. The 1990s also saw an influx of refugees from troubled areas of the world like Somalia and eastern Turkey. Outside London and big northern cities, however, the population is overwhelmingly white.

ARTS

The greatest artistic contributions from the British have been in theatre, literature and architecture. Although there are notable individual exceptions, there is not an equivalent tradition of great painters, sculptors or composers.

Literature

For anyone who has studied 'English' literature, travelling in the footsteps of the great English, Scottish and Welsh writers, and their fictional characters, can be one of the highlights of a British visit. Hundreds of famous books capture specific moments in time, favourite landscapes or particular groups of people. This guide can only suggest where to start.

In the beginning was Chaucer and his *Canterbury Tales*. This book may be responsible for more boring lectures than any other, but in its natural environment it comes to life, providing a vivid insight into medieval society, in particular into the lives of pilgrims on their way to Canterbury. Neville Coghill has written a good modern translation.

The next great figure to blight schoolchildren's lives was Shakespeare. Despite this, many will be tempted to visit Stratford-upon-Avon, where he lived, and the new Globe Theatre in London, built close to the site where he acted, and where many of his plays were originally staged.

The most vivid insight into 17th-century London life comes courtesy of Samuel Pepys' *Diary*. In particular, he gives the most complete account of the Plague and the Great Fire of London.

The popular English novel, as we know it, only really appeared in the 18th century. If you plan to spend time in the Midlands, read Elizabeth Gaskell's *Mary Barton*, which paints a sympathetic picture of the plight of workers during the Industrial Revolution. This was also the milieu about which Charles Dickens wrote most powerfully. *Hard Times*, set in fictional Coketown, paints a brutal picture of the capitalists who prospered in it.

Jane Austen wrote about a very different, prosperous, provincial middle class. The intrigues and passions boiling away under the stilted constraints of 'propriety' are beautifully portrayed in *Emma* and *Pride and Prejudice*.

If you visit the Lake District you'll find countless references to William Wordsworth, the romantic poet who lived there for the first half of the 19th century. Modern readers may find him difficult, but at his best he has an exhilarating appreciation of the natural world.

More than most writers, Thomas Hardy was dependent on a sense of place and on the relationship between place and people. This makes his best work an evocative picture of Wessex, the region of England centred on Dorchester (Dorset) where he lived. *Tess of the D'Urbervilles* is one of his greatest novels.

Moving into the 20th century, DH Lawrence chronicled life in coal-mining Nottinghamshire in the brilliant *Sons and Lovers*. Written in the Depression of the 1930s, George Orwell's *Down and Out in Paris and London* describes his grim existence as a temporary vagrant. About the same time, Graham Greene wrote of the seedy side of Brighton in *Brighton Rock*.

One of the funniest and most vicious portrayals of late-20th-century Britain is Martin Amis' *London Fields*, while Hanif Kureishi writes of growing up in London's Pakistani community in *The Buddha of Suburbia* and Caryl Phillips writes of the Caribbean immigrants' experience in *The Final Passage*. Irvine Welsh's *Trainspotting*, which explores the world of Scottish heroin addiction, was made into a successful film.

Of the straightforward modern travelogues, the most successful has been Bill Bryson's highly entertaining and perceptive *Notes from a Small Island*.

The Kingdom by the Sea by Paul Theroux, and Jonathan Raban's *Coasting* are both a little bit dated, but nonetheless readable. Nick Danziger's *Danziger's Britain* strips the gloss and the jokes aside to reveal the darker side of 'Cool Britannia'.

Architecture

Wherever you travel in Britain you'll not be far from a beautiful medieval church or cathedral. Perhaps the most distinctive architectural phenomenon in the country, however, is the huge number of extraordinary country houses that dot the landscape.

The 18th- and 19th-century aristocrats knew quality when they saw it and surrounded themselves with treasures in the most beautiful houses and gardens of Europe.

Although their successors have often inherited the arrogance of their ancestors, it is fortunate that inheritance taxes have forced many of them to open their houses and priceless art collections to the public. Even on a short visit you should try and visit Hatfield House, Blenheim Palace, Castle Howard or one of the other great stately homes.

Much of Britain's modern architecture is, however, regarded as a failure. Exceptions are works by Richard Rogers and Norman Foster, whose multifarious buildings dot the capital. Foster designed Stansted airport, while Rogers was responsible for the Lloyd's Building. He's also the brains behind the controversial Millennium Dome in Greenwich, which cost the public £1 billion and attracted less than half the 11 million visitors anticipated by the government.

Some of the most interesting architectural developments of recent years have not been new buildings so much as adaptations of existing buildings for new uses.

BRITAIN

Fine examples are London's Oxo Tower, which has been converted into a mixture of flats and eateries, and the Bankside power station, which now is the awesome Tate Modern gallery.

SOCIETY & CONDUCT

It is difficult to generalise about the British, but there's no doubt they are a creative, energetic and aggressive people whose impact on the world has been disproportionate to their numbers. They're also a diverse bunch, as one would expect given the variety of peoples who have made this island their home – from the original inhabitants, to the Celts, Romans, Angles, Jutes, Saxons, Vikings, Normans, Huguenots and Jews, and to the relatively recent arrivals from Asia, Africa and the Middle East.

Many people have strong preconceptions about the British but, if you're one of them, you'd be wise to abandon them. The most common stereotype is of a reserved, anally retentive politeness and conservatism. Remember, however, that this is one of the planet's most crowded islands and some of these characteristics have developed as a method of coping with the constant crush of people. Regional and class differences may have shrunk, but accents and behaviour still vary widely depending on where you are and with which class you are mingling.

The extraordinary scenes following the death of Diana, Princess of Wales, probably laid to rest the cliches about the British 'stiff upper lip'. And the words 'cold' and 'inhibited' don't generally leap to mind when you're mixing with the working classes, the northern English, the Welsh, or the Scots.

Visit a nightclub in one of the big cities, a football match, a local pub, or a country B&B and you might more readily describe the Brits as uninhibited, exhibitionist, passionate, aggressive, humorous, sentimental and entirely hospitable.

It's certainly true that no other country in the world has more obsessive hobbyists – train *and* bus spotters, twitchers (bird-watchers), sports supporters, fashion victims, royalists, model-makers and collectors of every description, heritage preservationists, ramblers, pet owners, gardeners...

Britain is a country of sceptical individualists who resent any intrusion on their privacy or freedom, so it's hardly surprising that their flirtation with socialism was brief. Change happens slowly, and only after proceeding through endless consultations, committees, departments and layers of government. As a result, most things (including the cities) have developed organically and chaotically. This is a country where streets are rarely straight and trains rarely run on time.

Despite the cynics who proclaim that Britain is in a state of terminal decline, the major cities remain cultural powerhouses. You can only wonder what will appear next. A new tribe on the cutting edge of popular culture like the mods, hippies, new romantics, punks or goths? Or a new political or economic movement like industrialisation, imperialist capitalism, parliamentary democracy, socialism or Thatcherism?

RELIGION

The Church of England (C of E), a Christian church that became independent from Rome in the 16th century, is the largest, wealthiest and most influential in Britain. Along with the Church of Scotland, it's an 'established' church, meaning that it's the official national church, with a close relationship to the state; the Queen appoints archbishops and bishops on the advice of the prime minister. The traditionally conservative C of E has shown some signs of recognising the need for change. In 1994, after many years of debate, the first women were ordained as priests. The debate has now moved on to the acceptability of gay clergy.

Although in a similar position as a national church, the Church of Scotland is quite different from the C of E – it is not subject to any outside authority and is much more a child of the Reformation.

Other significant Protestant churches, or 'free' churches with no connection to the state, include Methodist, Baptist and United Reformed churches and the Salvation Army. Women have been priests in all these churches for some years.

Since the 16th century, Roman Catholics have experienced several periods of terrible persecution; one modern legacy is the ongoing problem of Northern Ireland. They did not gain political rights until 1829 or a formal structure until 1850, but today about one in 10 Britons considers themselves Catholic.

Recent estimates suggest there are now over one million Muslims and significant numbers of Sikhs and Hindus in Britain. But although attendances at Sunday church services continue to fall, the majority of the British population probably still regard themselves as Christian.

LANGUAGE

English may be one of the world's most widely spoken languages, but the language as it's spoken in some parts of Britain is sometimes incomprehensible to overseas visitors – even to those who think they've spoken it all their lives.

For more about the languages that are spoken in Britain, see the Facts about Scotland and the Facts about Wales sections later in this chapter.

Facts for the Visitor

HIGHLIGHTS

Of Britain's many attractions, the most outstanding are listed here:

Castles Tower of London, Windsor, Dover, Leeds (near Canterbury), Conwy, Alnwick, Edinburgh
Cathedrals Canterbury, Salisbury, Winchester, Wells, York, Durham
Coastline Beachy Head (East Sussex), Land's End to St Ives (Cornwall), Tintagel (Cornwall), Ilfracombe to Lynton/Lynmouth (Devon), St David's to Cardigan (Wales), Scarborough to Saltburn (North Yorkshire), the Scottish coastline (particularly the west coast)
Historic Towns Salisbury, Winchester, Bath, Oxford, Cambridge, Shrewsbury, St David's, York, Whitby, Durham, Edinburgh, St Andrews
Houses Hampton Court Palace, Hatfield House (London), Knole House (Kent), Blenheim Palace (Oxfordshire), Chatsworth (Derbyshire), Castle Howard (North Yorkshire)
Islands Orkney, Skye, Lewis and Harris (Scotland)
Museums & Galleries British Museum, Victoria & Albert Museum, Science Museum, Natural History Museum, National Gallery, Tate Galleries (London), HMS Victory (Portsmouth), Ironbridge Gorge (near Shrewsbury), Castle Museum (York), Burrell Collection (Glasgow)
National Parks & Nature Regions Exmoor National Park, the Cotswolds, Brecon Beacons National Park, Pembrokeshire Coast National Park, Peak District National Park, Lake District National Park, Scottish Highlands (especially the west coast)
Other Highlights Avebury prehistoric complex, Hadrian's Wall

SUGGESTED ITINERARIES

Depending on the length of your stay, you might want to see and do the following:

Two days Visit London.
One week Visit London, Oxford, the Cotswolds, Bath and Bristol.
Two weeks Visit London, Salisbury, Avebury, Bath, Bristol, Wells, Oxford, York and Edinburgh.
One month Visit London, Cambridge, York, Edinburgh, Inverness, Isle of Skye, Fort William, Oban, Glasgow, the Lake District, Snowdonia (North Wales), Shrewsbury, the Cotswolds, Wells, Bath, Avebury and Oxford, before returning to London.
Two months As for one month, but stay in one or two places for a week, and do a week-long walk.

PLANNING
When to Go

July and August are the busiest months, and should be avoided if possible. The crowds in London and popular cities like Oxford, York and Edinburgh have to be seen to be believed. You are just as likely to get good weather in spring and autumn, so May to June and September to October are the best times to visit, although October is getting too late for the Scottish Highlands.

Maps

The best introductory map to Britain is published by the British Tourist Authority (BTA), and is widely available.

Drivers will find there is a range of excellent road atlases. If you plan to go off the beaten track you will need a 3mi to the inch scale or better.

The Ordnance Survey caters to walkers, with a wide variety of maps at different scales. Its Landranger maps, at 1:50,000 or about 1¼ inches to the mile, are ideal. Look out for Harveys hiking maps, which can sometimes be more user-friendly and up to date than Ordnance Survey maps.

What to Bring

Since anything you think of can be bought in major towns and cities (including Vegemite), pack light and pick up extras as you go along.

TOURIST OFFICES

The British Tourist Authority (BTA) has a remarkably extensive collection of information, quite a lot of it free and relevant to budget

BRITAIN

travellers. Make sure you contact the BTA before you leave home, because some of the material and discounts are only available outside Britain. Overseas, it represents the regional tourist boards.

Tourist Information Centres (TICs) can be found even in small towns. They can give invaluable advice on accommodation and cheap ways of seeing the area, often including excellent guided walking tours.

Tourist Offices Abroad

There are more than 40 BTA offices worldwide. The addresses of some overseas offices are as follows:

Australia (☎ 02-9377 4400, fax 9377 4499) Level 16, The Gateway, 1 Macquarie Place, Circular Quay, Sydney, NSW 2000
Canada (☎ 905-405 1720, fax 405 1835) Suite 120, 5915 Airport Rd, Mississauga, Ont L4V 1T1
New Zealand (☎ 09-303 1446, fax 776 965) Level 17, NZI House, 151 Queen St, Auckland 1
South Africa (☎ 011-325 0343) Lancaster Gate, Hyde Lane, Hyde Park, Sandton 2196
USA *Chicago:* (in-person visits only) 625 N Michigan Avenue, Suite 1001, Chicago IL 60611
New York: (☎ 1 800 GO 2 BRITAIN) 7th floor, 551 Fifth Avenue, Suite 701, New York, NY 10176-0799

VISAS & DOCUMENTS
Visas

Visa regulations are always subject to change, so it's essential to check with your local embassy, high commission or consulate before leaving home.

Currently, you don't need a visa if you are a citizen of Australia, Canada, New Zealand, South Africa or the USA. Tourists are generally permitted to stay for up to six months, but are prohibited from working. Citizens of the EU can live and work in Britain free of immigration control – they don't need a visa to enter the country.

The immigration authorities have always been tough, and this is unlikely to change; dress neatly when entering the country, and carry some evidence that you have sufficient funds to support yourself. A credit card and/or an onward ticket will help. People have been refused entry because they happened to be carrying documents (perhaps

work references) that suggested they intended to work.

Work Permits

EU nationals don't need a work permit, but all other nationalities must have one to work legally. If the *main* purpose of your visit is to work, you basically have to be sponsored by a British company.

However, if you're a citizen of a Commonwealth country, and aged between 17 and 26 inclusive, you may apply for a Working Holiday Entry Certificate that allows you to spend up to two years in the UK, and to take work that is 'incidental to a holiday'.

You must apply to your nearest UK mission overseas, prior to your arrival. It is not possible to switch from being a visitor to a working holiday–maker, nor is it possible to claim back any time spent out of the UK during the two-year period.

If you're a Commonwealth citizen and have a parent born in the UK, you may be eligible for a Certificate of Entitlement to the Right of Abode, which means you can live and work in Britain free of immigration control.

If you are a Commonwealth citizen and have a grandparent born in the UK, or if the grandparent was born before 31 March 1922 in what is now the Republic of Ireland, you may qualify for a UK Ancestry-Employment Certificate, which means you can work full-time for up to four years in the UK.

Visiting students from the USA can get a work permit allowing them to work for six months; you have to be at least 18 years old and a full-time student at a college or university. The permit is available through the **Council on International Educational Exchange** (☎ 212-822 2600; **W** *www.ciee.org; 633 3rd Ave, 20th floor, New York, NY 10017*). Contact the council for current details and fees.

If you have queries once you are in the UK, contact the **Home Office, Immigration & Nationality Department** (☎ 0870 606 7766; **W** *www.ind.homeoffice.gov.uk; Lunar House, Wellesley Rd, Croydon CR9 2BY; East Croydon train station*).

Driving Licence

Your normal driving licence is legal for 12 months from the date you last entered the country; for stays longer than a year you should apply for a British licence at a post office.

See the introductory Facts for the Visitor chapter for information on international student identity and discount cards.

EMBASSIES & CONSULATES
UK Embassies

UK embassies in Western Europe are listed in the relevant country chapters in this book. Other UK embassies abroad include:

Australia – British High Commission (☎ 02-6270 6666) Commonwealth Ave, Yarralumla, Canberra, ACT 2600

Canada – British High Commission (☎ 613-237 1530) 80 Elgin St, Ottawa, Ont K1P 5K7

Japan – British Embassy (☎ 03-3265 5511) 1 Ichiban-cho, Chiyoda-ku, Tokyo 102

New Zealand – British High Commission (☎ 04-472 6049) 44 Hill St, Wellington 1

South Africa – British High Commission (☎ 21-461 7220) 91 Parliament St, Cape Town 8001

USA – British Embassy (☎ 202-462 1340) 3100 Massachusetts Ave NW, Washington DC 20008

Embassies & Consulates in the UK

Countries with diplomatic representation in the UK include the following:

Australian High Commission (☎ 020-7379 4334) Australia House, The Strand, London WC2; tube Temple

Canadian High Commission (☎ 020-7258 6600) 1 Grosvenor Square, London W1X; tube Bond St

French Consulate (☎ 020-7838 2000) 21 Cromwell Rd, London SW7; tube South Kensington

German Embassy (☎ 020-7824 1300) 23 Belgrave Square, London SW1; tube Hyde Park Corner

Irish Embassy (☎ 020-7235 2171) 17 Grosvenor Place, London SW1; tube Hyde Park Corner

Japanese Embassy (☎ 020-7465 6500) 101–104 Piccadilly, London W1V; tube Green Park

Netherlands Embassy (☎ 020-7590 3200) 38 Hyde Park Gate, London SW7; tube Gloucester Rd

New Zealand High Commission (☎ 020-7930 8422) New Zealand House, 80 Haymarket, London SW1; tube Piccadilly Circus

South African High Commission (☎ 020-7451 7299) South Africa House, Trafalgar Square, London WC2; tube Trafalgar Square

Spanish Consulate (☎ 020-7589 8989) 20 Draycott Place, London SW3; tube Sloane Square

US Embassy (☎ 020-7499 9000) 24 Grosvenor Square, London W1A; tube Bond St

CUSTOMS

For imported goods there's a two-tier system: the first for goods bought duty-free, the second for goods bought in an EU country where tax and duty have been paid. Duty-free purchases within the EU have been phased out.

The second tier is relevant because a number of products (eg, alcohol and tobacco) are much cheaper on the Continent. Under single-market rules, as long as tax and duty have been paid somewhere in the EU, there is no prohibition on importing them within the EU, so long as they are for individual consumption. A thriving business has developed with Britons making day trips to France to load their cars up with cheap beer, wine and cigarettes – the savings can more than pay for the trip.

For more details on duty-free and duty-paid goods, see Customs in the introductory Facts for the Visitor chapter.

MONEY
Currency

No euros here...yet! And it's unlikely that there will be any in the next couple of years. The currency is the pound sterling (£), and there are 100 pence (p) in a pound. One and 2p coins are copper; 5p, 10p, 20p and 50p coins are silver; the bulky £1 coin is gold-coloured; and the £2 coin is coloured gold and silver. The word pence is rarely used in common language; like its written counterpart it is abbreviated and pronounced *pee*.

Notes (bills) come in £5, £10, £20 and £50 denominations and vary in colour and size. You may also come across notes issued by several Scottish banks, including a £1 note; they are legal tender on both sides of the border, though shopkeepers in England and Wales may be reluctant to accept them in which case ask a bank to swap them for you.

Exchange Rates

country	unit		pound sterling
Australia	A$1	=	£0.35
Canada	C$1	=	£0.41
euro zone	€1	=	£0.65
Japan	¥100	=	£0.48
New Zealand	NZ$1	=	£0.29
USA	US$1	=	£0.65

Exchanging Money

Bureaux de Change & Banks Be careful using *bureaux de change*; they may offer good

BRITAIN

exchange rates, but they frequently levy outrageous commissions and fees. Make sure you establish the rate, the percentage commission and any fees in advance.

The bureaus at international airports are exceptions to the rule. They charge less than most high-street banks (ie, major or city-centre banks) and cash sterling travellers cheques for free.

Bank hours vary, but you'll be safe if you visit between 9.30am and 3.30pm, Monday to Friday. Some banks are open on Saturday, generally from 9.30am till noon. Once again, the total cost of foreign exchange can vary quite widely; in particular, watch for the minimum charge.

It's difficult to open a bank account, although if you're planning to work, it may be essential. Building societies tend to be more welcoming and often have better interest rates. Look for a bank or building society current account that pays interest, gives you a cheque book and guarantee card, and has access to ATMs (called cashpoints in Britain). You'll need a (semi-) permanent address, and you'll smooth the way considerably if you have a reference or introductory letter from your bank manager at home, *plus* bank statements for the previous year. Owning credit/charge cards also helps. If your bank at home is affiliated with a UK bank you may be able to set up a UK account before you even leave home, but you'll need to allow at least four weeks to organise it.

Travellers Cheques & Credit Cards
Travellers cheques are rarely accepted outside banks or used for everyday transactions so you need to cash them in advance.

Your cheques should ideally be in pounds. Use American Express or Thomas Cook – they are widely recognised, well represented and don't charge for cashing their own cheques.

Thomas Cook has an office in all of the decent-sized towns, and American Express has representation in most cities.

Visa, MasterCard, Access, American Express and Diners Club cards are widely used, although most B&Bs require cash. If your bank has an agreement with an international money system such as Cirrus, Maestro or Plus, you can often withdraw money direct from your home account using ATMs in Britain.

Costs
Britain is extremely expensive and London is horrendous. While you are in London you will need to budget around £30 to £35 a day just for bare survival. Any sightseeing, restaurant meals or nightlife will be on top of that. There's not much point visiting if you can't participate in some of the city's life, so if possible add another £15 to £20. Costs will obviously be even higher if you choose to stay in a central hotel and eat restaurant meals.

Once you start moving around the country, particularly if you have a transport pass of some description, or you're walking or hitching, the costs can drop. Fresh food is roughly the same price as in Australia and the US. However, without including long-distance transport, and assuming you stay in hostels, you'll still need £20 to £25 per day.

If you hire a car or use a transport pass, stay in B&Bs, eat one sit-down meal a day, and don't stint on entry fees, you'll need £50 to £65 per day (not including long-distance transport costs). Most modest B&Bs charge £20 to £25 per person and dinner will cost between £8 and £15; add £5 for lunch and snacks, and around £8 to £10 for admission fees and miscellaneous supplies. If you're travelling by car you'll probably average a further £10 a day on petrol and parking; if you travel by some sort of pass you will probably need to average a couple of pounds a day on local transport or for hiring a bike.

Throughout this chapter admission costs are often given as adult/concession (concession referring to students and seniors). Admission fees for children are usually around half of those of adults. Kids under five often get in free.

Tipping & Bargaining
Taxi drivers and waiters all expect 10% tips. Some restaurants include a service charge (tip) of 10% to 15% on the bill, but this should be clearly advertised. Prices are almost always fixed. Bargaining is only really expected if you're buying second-hand gear, especially vehicles. Always check whether there are discounts for students, youth/seniors or YHA hostel members.

Taxes & Refunds
Value-added tax (VAT) is a 17.5% sales tax levied on virtually all goods and services, but not on food and books. Restaurant menu prices must by law include VAT.

In some cases it's possible to claim a refund of VAT paid on goods – a considerable saving. If you have spent fewer than 365 days living in Britain out of the two years prior to making the purchase, and if you are leaving the EU within three months of making the purchase, you are eligible.

There are a number of companies that offer a centralised refunding service to shops. Participating shops carry a sign in their window. You can avoid bank charges usually encountered when cashing pound travellers cheques by using a credit card for purchases and requesting that your VAT refund be credited to your card account. In some cases, cash refunds are now available at the major airports.

POST & COMMUNICATIONS
Post
Post office hours can vary, but most are open 9am to 5pm Monday to Friday, and to noon on Saturday. Within the UK, 1st-class mail is quicker and more expensive (27p per letter) than 2nd-class mail (19p).

Airmail letters to Europe are 37p, to the Americas and Australasia 45p (up to 10g) and 65p (up to 20g). An airmail letter to the USA or Canada will generally take less than a week; to Australia or New Zealand, around a week.

Telephone
Since British Telecom (BT) was privatised, several companies have started competing for its business. However, most public phone booths are still operated by BT.

The famous red phone booth survives in conservation areas. More usually you'll see glass cubicles of two types: one takes cash, while the other uses prepaid, plastic debit cards and, increasingly, credit cards.

All phones come with reasonably clear instructions. If you're likely to make some calls (especially international) and don't want to be caught out, make sure you buy a phonecard. There are numerous cheap phonecards around that massively undercut BT rates on international calls. Take note however that some of these phonecards can only be used from a private phone – if you intend using a public phone make sure you buy a suitable phonecard.

Most BT services are expensive; even directory assistance calls (☎ 192) from a public telephone cost 20p.

Local & National Calls Dial ☎ 100 for a BT operator. Local calls are charged by time, and national calls (including Scotland, Wales and Northern Ireland) are charged by time and distance. Standard rates apply 8am to 6pm Monday to Friday; the cheap rate is 6pm to 8am, Monday to Friday; and the weekend rate is midnight Friday to midnight Sunday.

Note that any number that begins with the code 0870 is charged at the national rate; a number that begins with the code 0845 is charged at the (cheaper) local rate.

International Calls You should dial ☎ 155 to get the international operator. Direct dialling is cheaper, but some budget travellers prefer operator-connected reverse-charge (collect) calls. To get an international line (for international direct dialling) dial ☎ 00, then the country code, area code (drop the first zero if there is one) and number.

Purchase the discount phonecards advertised on newsagent windows in major towns and cities or look for the independently operated telecom centres. International rates offered at these places are generally the lowest available.

For more on international calls see the Telephone Appendix at the end of this book.

Fax
Most hotels have fax machines. Some shops also offer fax services, advertised by a sign in the window.

Email & Internet Access
To collect your email visit one of the growing number of Internet cafés. Some hostels and pubs also offer Internet services. Expect to pay around £2 or £3 per hour. Alternatively many public libraries offer free Internet access but you often need to book in advance.

DIGITAL RESOURCES
Britain is second only to the USA in its number of websites, and there are many that are of interest to travellers. Towns, tourist boards, attractions, hostels, B&Bs, hotels and transportation companies all have websites. You'll find some listed throughout this chapter. The Lonely Planet site (**w** www.lonelyplanet.com .au) offers a speedy link to numerous sites for travellers. Also see the UK Travel Guide (**w** www.uktravel.com).

BRITAIN

BOOKS

There are countless guidebooks covering every nook and cranny of the British Isles. When you arrive, one of your first stops should be at bookshop or map shop – see the London Bookshops section later.

Lonely Planet

For greater detail, look for Lonely Planet's *Britain*, *England*, *Scotland* or *Wales* guidebooks as well as the *London* and *Edinburgh* city guides. *London Condensed* provides essential information in a handy format. Hikers and cyclists should check Lonely Planet's *Walking in Britain* and *Cycling Britain* guides.

Guidebooks & Travel

For information on history, art and architecture, the *Blue Guide* series is excellent. The separate guides to *England* (£15.99), *Scotland* (£16.99), and *Wales* (£12.99) have scholarly information on all the important sites.

Numerous books list B&Bs, restaurants, hotels, country houses, camping and caravan parks, self-catering cottages etc. The objectivity of many of these books is questionable as the places they cover have to pay for the privilege of being included; however, they can still be useful. Those published by the tourist authorities are reliable (although not comprehensive) and are widely available in information centres, usually for around £5.

Individual long-distance walking trails are all covered by the *National Trail Guides* series published by Aurum Press, usually costing around £10.99. For shorter walks (two to 4½ hours), the *Pathfinder Guide* series (£10.95) is recommended, with good maps and descriptions.

NEWSPAPERS & MAGAZINES

There are few countries in the world where you can wake up to such a range of newspapers. The quality daily papers are the *Independent*, the *Guardian*, the *Telegraph* and the *Times*. At the other extreme, outrageous tabloids like the *Sun*, and on Sunday the *News of the World*, continue to plumb new depths. Curiously, media magnate Rupert Murdoch owns both the *Times* and the *Sun*. There's an equally diverse range of magazines.

RADIO & TV

There are five regular TV channels – BBC1, ITV and Channel 5 are quite mainstream, while BBC2 and Channel 4 are rather more serious – plus Murdoch's satellite Sky TV and numerous cable channels. Radio also has a mix of BBC and commercial stations. Try BBC Radio 4 for news and drama; Five Live for sport; Galaxy, Heart, Virgin Radio or Capital Radio (London) for pop/rock/dance; Jazz FM for jazz; and Classic FM for classical music.

TIME

Wherever you are in the world, the time on your watch is measured in relation to the time in London's Greenwich Mean Time (GMT).

Daylight-saving time (also known as British summer time) confuses the issue, but to give you an idea, New York is five hours behind GMT, San Francisco is eight hours behind, and Sydney is 10 hours ahead of GMT. Phone the international operator on ☎ 155 to find out the exact difference.

ELECTRICITY

The standard voltage throughout Britain is 240V AC, 50Hz. Plugs have three square pins and adapters are widely available. For more information see Electricity in the Facts for the Visitor chapter at the start of this book.

WEIGHTS & MEASURES

Under an EU directive in 2000, Britain moved from imperial to metric weights and measures, although nonmetric equivalents are still widely used. The EU granted a permanent exemption for speed and distance measurements, thus road signs and car odometers continue to be given in miles. Pubs are also permitted to continue pulling pints of beer, and milkmen may go on leaving a pint of milk on the doorstep. Most other liquids are sold in litres. For conversion tables, see the inside back cover of this book.

LAUNDRY

You'll find a laundrette on every high street. A single load (wash and dry) costs between £2.50 and £3.50.

TOILETS

Public toilets are well signposted. There may be a charge of 10p to 20p for their use.

WOMEN TRAVELLERS

Women will find Britain a reasonably enlightened country. Lone travellers should have no problems, although common-sense caution should be observed in big cities, especially when walking alone at night. Hitchhiking, while possible, is extremely risky. Some pubs still retain a heavy masculine atmosphere but on the whole they're becoming increasingly family-friendly.

The **Council Rape & Crisis Support Group** (☎ 020-8572 0100) gives confidential advice and support to women who have been sexually assaulted.

GAY & LESBIAN TRAVELLERS

London, Manchester and Brighton are Britain's main gay and lesbian centres. You'll also find gay and lesbian information centres in most other cities and large towns. Check the listings in *Gay Times*, available from newsagents, for details of major events such as London Pride (end of June or early July). The age of consent is 16.

DISABLED TRAVELLERS

The **Royal Association for Disability and Rehabilitation** (RADAR; ☎ 020-7250 3222; 12 City Forum, 250 City Rd, London EC1V 8AF) publishes a useful guide, *Holidays and Travel Abroad: A Guide for Disabled People*, which gives a good overview of facilities available. For disabled travellers in the capital, it also stocks *Access in London* (£8).

SENIOR TRAVELLERS

All senior citizens (over 60s) are entitled to discounts on public transport, museum admission fees etc, provided they show proof of their age. Sometimes a pass must be purchased to qualify for discounts. Rail companies offer a Senior Citizens' Railcard (£18 for one year) giving a third off fares. Coach companies have similar cards. National Express, for example, has a senior's coach card (£9) that gives various discounts over one year.

USEFUL ORGANISATIONS

Membership of the Youth Hostels Association (YHA) is a must. There are more than 300 hostels in Britain and members are also eligible for an impressive list of discounts. For more information and contact details see Accommodation later in this chapter. For information on the various ISIC and FIYTO cards see this book's introductory Facts for the Visitor chapter.

Membership of English Heritage and the National Trust is worth considering, especially if you are going to be in Britain for an extended period and are interested in fine historical buildings. Both are nonprofit organisations dedicated to environmental preservation and care for many spectacular sites.

Australasian Club Drifters Travel (☎ 020-7402 9171) 22A Craven Terrace W2, offers back-up services like mail holding, local information, discounts on film processing, freight forwarding and equipment purchase, and cheap tours. It's mainly aimed at Aussies and Kiwis, but anyone is welcome. Membership is £10.

English Heritage (EH) Most EH (☎ 020-7973 3000) properties cost nonmembers around £2.50 to enter. A year's adult membership costs £31.50 and gives free entry to all EH properties, half-price entry to Historic Scotland and Cadw (Welsh) properties, and an excellent guidebook and map. You can join at most major sites. Alternatively you can buy a seven-/14-day pass for £13.50/17.50.

Great British Heritage Pass This pass gives you access to National Trust and English Heritage properties and some of the expensive private properties. A seven-/15-/30-day pass costs £30/45/60. It's available overseas (ask your travel agent or contact the nearest Thomas Cook office) or at the British Travel Centre in London.

National Trust (NT) Most NT (☎ 020-7222 9251) properties cost nonmembers from £1 to £6 to enter. Adult membership is £32, under 26 is £15. It gives free entry to all British properties, and an excellent guidebook and map. You can join at most major sites. There are reciprocal arrangements with the National Trust organisations in Scotland, Australia, New Zealand, Canada and the USA (the Royal Oak Foundation), all of which are cheaper to join.

DANGERS & ANNOYANCES

Britain is remarkably safe considering its size and the disparities in wealth. City crime is certainly not unknown, so caution, especially at night, is necessary. Pickpockets and bag snatchers operate in crowded public places.

When travelling by tube at night in London, choose a carriage with other people and avoid some of the deserted tube stations in the suburbs; a bus can be a better choice. Avoid large groups of young lads after the pubs shut down (11pm), as violence is worryingly commonplace in town centres across Britain.

Drugs of every description are widely available, especially in the clubs where ecstasy (not all of it pure) is at the heart of the rave scene. Nonetheless, all the usual dangers associated with black-market drugs apply.

BRITAIN

Cannabis is still illegal, although possession of small quantities usually warrants only a caution.

Hotel/hostel touts descend on backpackers at London Underground stations like Earl's Court, Liverpool St and Victoria. Treat their claims with scepticism and don't accept offers of free lifts (you could end up miles away). Be careful of unauthorised taxi drivers approaching you at these same stations; play safe and stick with the regulated black cabs.

The big cities have many beggars; if you must give don't wave a full wallet around and carry some change in a separate pocket. It is preferable, however, to donate to a recognised charity. **Shelter** (☎ 020-7505 2000; e info@shelter.org.uk; 88 Old St, London EC1) is a voluntary organisation that helps the homeless; or consider buying the Big Issue (£1.20), an interesting weekly magazine available from street vendors who benefit directly from sales.

Britain is not without racial problems, particularly in some of the deprived suburbs of big cities, but in general tolerance prevails. Few visitors have problems associated with their skin colour.

BUSINESS HOURS

Offices are open 9am to 5pm Monday to Friday. Shops may be open for longer hours, and all shops are open 9am to 5pm Saturday. Except in rural areas, some shops also open 10am to 4pm Sunday. Late-night shopping is usually possible on Thursday or Friday. Some supermarkets are open 24 hours.

PUBLIC HOLIDAYS & SPECIAL EVENTS

Most banks, businesses and a number of museums and other places of interest are closed on public holidays (also known as Bank Holidays): New Year's Day; 2 January (Bank Holiday in Scotland); Good Friday; Easter

Monday (not in Scotland); May Day Bank Holiday (first Monday in May); Spring Bank Holiday (last Monday in May); Summer Bank Holiday (first Monday in August in Scotland, last Monday in August outside Scotland); Christmas Day; and Boxing Day.

There are countless, diverse special events held around the country all year. Even small villages have weekly markets, and many still enact traditional customs and ceremonies, some of which are believed to date back thousands of years.

New Year
Hogmanay Huge street parties in Edinburgh

March
Edinburgh Folk Festival Held in the last week of the month
Oxford/Cambridge University Boat Race Traditional rowing race; River Thames, Putney to Mortlake, London

April
Grand National Famous horse-racing meeting held on the first Saturday of the month; Aintree, Liverpool

May
English FA Cup Final Deciding match in knock-out football tournament; Millennium Stadium, Cardiff (while Wembley in London is under reconstruction)
Glasgow Mayfest High-quality arts festival running for three weeks
Bath International Festival Arts festival; runs for two weeks in late May
Chelsea Flower Show Premier flower show held in the last week of the month; Royal Hospital, London

June
Beating Retreat Military bands and marching held in the first week of the month; Whitehall, London
Derby Week Horse racing and people-watching in the first week of the month; Epsom, Surrey
Trooping the Colour The Queen's birthday parade in mid-June with spectacular pageantry; Whitehall, London
Royal Ascot More horses and hats in mid-June; Ascot, Berkshire
Lawn Tennis Championships Runs for two weeks in late June; Wimbledon, London
Henley Royal Regatta Premier rowing and social event in late June; Henley-on-Thames, Oxfordshire
Glastonbury Festival Enormous, open-air music festival and hippy gathering in late June; Pilton, Somerset

BRITAIN

July

Cowes Week Yachting extravaganza in late July; Isle of Wight

August

Edinburgh Military Tattoo Pageantry and military displays, starting early in the month, running for three weeks

Edinburgh International & Fringe Festivals Premier international arts festivals, starting mid-August, running for three weeks

Notting Hill Carnival Enormous Caribbean carnival held late in the month; London

Reading Festival Three days of outdoor rock and roll late in the month; Reading, Berkshire

September

Royal Braemar Gathering (Highland Games) Kilts, cabers and other Highland paraphernalia, held in early September; Braemar, Aberdeenshire

November

Guy Fawkes Day Held on 5 November in memory of an unsuccessful Catholic coup; bonfires and fireworks around the country

ACTIVITIES
Cycling

There are many places which hire bikes. Prices vary, but you should get a three-speed bike for around £25 per week, or a mountain bike for £60. Book ahead if you want a bike in July or August. Hiring is easiest with a credit card; a signed slip is used in lieu of a large deposit. You will also need ID (a passport will do).

Bicycles can be taken on most rail services, but the regulations are complex and inconsistent so it is essential to check in advance. In some cases it is also necessary to make a reservation. The major coach operators (National Express, Citylink etc) don't carry bikes, but most local bus lines do.

The **Cyclists' Touring Club** (☎ 0870 873 0061; w www.ctc.org.uk; Cotterell House, 69 Meadrow, Godalming, Surrey GU7 3HS) is a national cycling association that can provide a great deal of helpful information for visiting cyclists, including detailed information on a range of routes.

Also worth investigating is the National Cycle Network, a project to create 10,000mi of cycle routes around the UK by 2005. In 2002, 6000mi already had been opened. Nonprofit organisation **Sustrans** (Sustainable transport; ☎ 0117-929 0888; w www.sustrans.org.uk) is the force behind this project and its Official Guide to the National Network (£10.99) details 30 one-day rides.

For more ideas on where to tour check Lonely Planet's Cycling Britain.

Hiking

This is great hiking country. The countryside is crisscrossed by a network of rights of way, or public footpaths, most of them crossing private land. They have existed for centuries and are marked on the excellent Ordnance Survey maps. With the exception of Scotland, you are rarely going to be far away from civilisation, so it's easy to put together walks that connect with public transport and take you from village to village. A tent and cooking equipment aren't always essential but warm waterproof clothing, sturdy footwear and a map and compass are.

For long-distance walks, the best areas include the Cotswolds, the Exmoor National Park, the North York Moors National Park, the Yorkshire Dales National Park, the Lake District, the Pembrokeshire Coast National Park and the Scottish islands. There are many superb long-distance walks in Scotland but, day walks aside, these tend to require more preparation.

The national parks were set up to protect the finest landscapes, but much of the land remains privately owned. It's almost always necessary to get permission from a landowner before pitching a tent.

There are nine national long-distance trails in England, three in Wales, and three in Scotland, created and administered by the relevant countryside commissions (which, along with Aurum Press, publish excellent guides). A number of these are mentioned in this chapter. There are also a growing number of regional routes created by county councils, some of which are well organised and excellent. Finally, there are unofficial long-distance routes, often devised by individuals or groups like the Ramblers' Association. Bear in mind that some walks, particularly along the coast and in the Yorkshire Dales and Lake District, can be very crowded on weekends and in July/August.

The British countryside looks deceptively gentle. Especially in the hills or on the open moors, however, the weather can close in and turn nasty very quickly at any time of the year. It is vital if you're walking in upland areas to carry good maps and a compass (and know how to use them), plus, of course, warm and waterproof clothing.

Those intent on a serious walking holiday should contact the **Ramblers' Association**

BRITAIN

(☎ 020-7339 8500; 🖳 www.ramblers.org.uk; Camelford House, 87-90 Albert Embankment, London SE1 7TW); the group's *Year-book* (£5.99) is widely available and itemises the information available for each walk, the appropriate maps, and nearby accommodation (hostels, B&Bs and bunkhouses).

Lonely Planet's *Walking in Britain* guide details more than a dozen long-distance paths together with a wide selection of shorter walks and day-hikes.

Boating

Even budget travellers should consider the possibility of hiring a canal boat and cruising part of the extraordinary 2000mi network of canals that has survived the railway era.

Especially outside the high season, prices are quite reasonable, ranging from about £350 per week in April to £700 in August for a boat that sleeps four. Try **Alvechurch Boat Centres** (☎ 0121-445 2909) or **Hoseason's Holidays** (☎ 01502-501501).

An annual *Directory* (£4) is published by **Inland Waterways Association** (☎ 01923-711114; PO Box 114, Rickmansworth, Herts WD3 1ZY) which can provide mail-order maps and guides.

ACCOMMODATION

This will almost certainly be your single-largest expense. Even camping can be expensive at official sites. For travel on the cheap, there are really only three options: hostels, B&Bs and some hotels. At mid-range, guest-houses and B&Bs offer good accommodation, often in beautiful old buildings. At the top-end are hotels occupying converted castles and mansions.

TIC Reservations

The TICs can make accommodation bookings. These services are particularly handy for big cities and over weekends and during the summer high season. Bookings can be free, but are usually £3 (£5 in the case of London). In addition you often pay a 10% deposit, which is subtracted from the price.

Camping

Free camping is rarely possible, except in Scotland. Camping grounds vary widely in quality but most have reasonable facilities, although they're often ugly and usually inaccessible unless you have a car or bike. For an

extensive listing, buy *Camping & Caravanning in Britain* (£9.99) published by the **Automobile Association** (☎ 01256-491524); local TICs also have listings. Some YHA hostels cater for campers.

Hikers will occasionally find camping barns – usually converted farm buildings – where you can bunk down for between £3.50 to £5 per night. Bunkhouses (from £7) are similar but have a bit more comfort.

Hostels

Hostelling International/Youth Hostel Association (HI/YHA; advance bookings ☎ 0870 870 8808, 0870 241 2314; 🖳 www.yha.org.uk) membership gives you access to a huge network of hostels throughout England, Wales, Scotland and Ireland.

There are separate, local associations for England/Wales, Scotland, Northern Ireland and Ireland, and each publishes individual accommodation guides. If you're travelling extensively it's essential to get hold of these. Most importantly, they include the (often complicated) days and hours during which the hostels are open, as well as information on prices, facilities and directions to each place.

UK residents can join the YHA – in advance or on arrival at most hostels – for £13 for adults or £6.50 for under-18s. Overseas visitors without an international membership can join through a system of 'welcome stamps', available at most hostels. A £2 stamp is purchased for each of the first six nights, after which you can become a YHA member.

All hostels have facilities for self-catering and some have cheap meals. Advance booking is advisable, especially on weekends, Bank Holidays and at any time over the summer months. Booking policies vary: most hostels accept phone bookings and payment with Visa or MasterCard; some will accept same-day bookings, although they will usually only hold a bed until 6pm; some work on a first-come, first-served basis. Once on the hostelling trail, you can use the YHA's free Book A Bed Ahead scheme to reserve your next night's accommodation at a different hostel – just ask the hostel receptionist to make the necessary phone call. Some hostels have curfews at night and are locked during the day.

Overnight prices are in two tiers: under-18s, with prices from £5.50 to £20, but mostly around £8; and adults, with prices from £7 to £24, but mostly around £11.25. Bear in mind that when you add £3.40 for breakfast, you can get very close to cheap B&B prices. Bed linen is free at hostels in England and Wales but costs 60p in Scotland.

Independent Hostels

Outside London, there are more and more independent backpackers hostels, particularly in the southwest, Scotland and some of the popular hiking regions. This growing network offers the opportunity to escape curfews and daytime closures for a price of around £11 per night in a basic bunkroom. Like youth hostels these are great places to meet other travellers, and they tend to be in town centres rather than out in the sticks. *The Independent Hostel Guide* (£4.95) covers Britain and Ireland, but new places are opening fast so it's always worth asking at the TIC.

Universities

Many British universities offer student accommodation to visitors during the Christmas, Easter and summer holidays. Bed and breakfast will normally cost from £19 to £28 per person. For more information contact the **British Universities Accommodation Consortium** (BUAC; ☎ 0115-846 6444; **w** buac.co.uk).

B&Bs, Guesthouses & Hotels

B&Bs are a great British institution and the cheapest private accommodation you can find. At the bottom end (£15 to £20 per person) you get a bedroom in a normal house, a shared bathroom and an enormous cooked breakfast. Small B&Bs may only have one room to let, and you can really feel like a guest of the family. More upmarket B&Bs have an en suite bathroom and TV in each room. Single rooms are in short supply and many B&B owners would rather not let a room at all than let a single person have it for less than the price of both beds.

Guesthouses, which are often just large converted houses with half-a-dozen rooms, are an extension of the B&B idea. They range from £15 to £50 per night, depending on the quality of the food and accommodation. In general, they tend to be less personal than B&Bs, and more like small budget hotels. Local pubs and inns also often have cheap rooms; they can be good fun since they place you at the hub of the community.

Hotels range from humble pubs to grand old castles. The national tourist boards operate a classification and grading system; participating hotels, guesthouses and B&Bs have a plaque at the front door. If you want to be reasonably confident that your accommodation reaches basic standards of safety and cleanliness, the first classification is 'listed', denoting clean and comfortable accommodation. Better places are indicated by one to five crowns – the more crowns, the more facilities and, generally, the more expensive the room.

In addition to the classifications there are gradings which are perhaps more significant. 'Approved', 'commended' and 'highly commended' gradings reflect a subjective judgment of quality. Bear in mind that some accommodation providers prefer not to pay the TIC to promote them, so there are always more places available than appear in the lists. Unlisted places are often as good as those that are listed, but in big towns it's wise to stick with registered places since some B&Bs and old-style residential hotels now earn their living from accommodating homeless people – not necessarily the atmosphere you'd expect for a holiday.

Rental Accommodation

There has been a big increase in the number of houses and cottages available for short-term rent. Staying in one place gives you an unmatched opportunity to get a real feel for a region. Cottages for four can cost as little as £160 per week; many can be let for three days.

It's often possible to book through TICs, but there are also a number of excellent agencies that can supply you with glossy brochures to help the decision-making process. Outside weekends and July/August, it's not essential to book a long way ahead. Most organisations have agents in North America and Australasia. Among them, **Country Holidays** (☎ 0870 072 3723; *Spring Mill, Earby, Colne, Lancashire BB8 6RN)* has been recommended. **English Country Cottages** (☎ 01328-864041; *Grove Farm Barns, Fakenham, Norfolk NR21 9NB)* is one of the largest agencies.

FOOD

British cuisine used to crop up more often in comedy sketches than on the restaurant review pages but fortunately those days are long gone. You don't have to try hard to find a decent restaurant even in some of the most out-of-the-way places.

Takeaways, Cafés & Pubs

Britain has a full complement of takeaway chains, from McDonald's, Burger King and Pizza Hut to the home-grown and aptly named Wimpy.

The days of the 'greasy spoon' café that used to dispense cheap breakfasts (eggs, bacon and sausages) and English tea (strong, sweet and milky) on every high street look numbered, their place taken by the ubiquitous café/bars, which prefer pasta and pesto to beans and burgers. The Pret A Manger ready-made sandwich chain is also spreading its tentacles out of London, although you'll probably find cheaper sarnies (surprisingly) at Boots – the chemist!

If you're on a tight budget, pubs will often be one of your best sources of cheap nutrition. At the bottom end they're not much different from cafés, while at the expensive end they're closer to restaurants. Chilli con carne or lasagne are often the cheapest offerings on the menu. A filling 'ploughman's lunch' of bread, cheese and pickle costs around £4.50.

Restaurants

In the main towns and cities a cosmopolitan range of cuisines is available; most small towns will have at least Chinese and Indian restaurants. Particularly if you like pizza, pasta and curry, you should be able to get a reasonable main course for about £8 pretty well anywhere. At the other end of the scale there are scores of excellent restaurants serving seafood, roasts and various meats and where main courses start at around £15.

Vegetarians should have little problem finding somewhere to eat.

Vegetarian restaurants have popped up in many towns in recent years and many other restaurants have at least a token vegetarian dish. As anywhere, vegans will find the going tough, however, Indian restaurants offer welcome salvation.

Self-Catering

The cheapest way to eat in Britain is to cook for yourself. Hopefully, however, you won't be forced to the extremes of an Australian backpacker who was arrested and jailed for attempting to cook a Canada goose in Hyde Park.

Good-quality precooked meals are available from supermarkets (Marks & Spencer's are highly regarded).

DRINKS

British pubs generally serve an impressive range of beers – lagers, bitters, ales and stouts. The drink most people from the New World know as beer is actually lager and, much to the distress of local connoisseurs, lagers (including Foster's and Budweiser) now take a huge proportion of the market. Fortunately, the traditional English bitter has made something of a comeback, thanks to the Campaign for Real Ale (CAMRA) organisation. Look for its endorsement sticker on pub windows.

If you've been raised on lager, a traditional bitter or ale is something of a shock – not as cold or as effervescent. Ale is similar to bitter – it's more a regional difference in name than anything else. Stout is a dark, rich, foamy drink; Guinness is the most famous brand.

Don't think of any of these drinks as beers, but as something completely new; if you do, you'll discover subtle flavours that a cold and chemical lager cannot match.

Beers are usually served in pints (from £1.60 to £3), but you can also ask for a 'half' (a half-pint). The stronger brews are usually 'specials' or 'extras'. Beware: potency can vary from around 2% to more than 10% alcohol!

Pubs are allowed to open 11am to 11pm daily, but beware – the bell for last drinks rings out at about 10.45pm. In bigger cities, many pubs and bars have late licences until 2am. Takeaway alcoholic drinks are sold from supermarkets and 'off-licence' shops, but rarely from pubs.

Good wines are widely available and very reasonably priced (except in pubs). Check the supermarkets; an ordinary but drinkable *vin de pays* will cost around £3.

Unfortunately, most restaurants are licensed and their alcoholic drinks, particularly good wines, are always expensive. There are very few BYO restaurants (where you can Bring Your Own bottles for free), although there are a small number in London. Most places charge an extortionate amount of money for 'corkage' – opening your own bottle for you.

ENTERTAINMENT

For many Brits, 'the local' (pub) is still the main focus for a good night out. For the visitor, the country offers some of the world's best drama, dance and music. A visit to a London theatre is a real must. TICs have lists of nightclubs and discos.

SPECTATOR SPORTS

The British are responsible for either inventing or codifying many of the world's most popular spectator sports such as tennis, football (soccer), rugby and golf. To this list add billiards and snooker, lawn bowls, boxing, darts, hockey, squash and table tennis.

The country also hosts premier events for a number of sports, Wimbledon (tennis) and the English FA Cup Final (football) among them. See Public Holidays & Special Events earlier in this section for more details.

SHOPPING

Napoleon once dismissively described the British as a nation of shopkeepers; today, as chains take over the high streets, it would be truer to say that they are a nation of shoppers. Shopping is the most popular recreational activity in the country.

Multinational capitalism being what it is, you can buy few things unique to Britain. On the other hand, if you can't find it for sale in London, it probably doesn't exist.

Although few things are cheap, books and clothing can be good value. Shopping at one of London's street markets, especially on Sunday morning, can be a highlight of your trip. Similarly, trawling the nation's charity shops (second-hand shops where the profit goes to a charity) can be very rewarding.

Check *TNT Magazine* for the names of shipping companies, when you realise you've exceeded your baggage limit. Choose an established company rather than just opting for the cheapest quote if you want to see your stuff again.

Getting There & Away

London is one of the most important transport hubs in the world. As a result, there's an enormous number of travel agencies, some of dubious reliability. All the main 'student' travel services have offices in London; they understand budget travellers and are competitive and reliable. You don't have to be a student to use their services. See under London later in this chapter for details.

Buses are the cheapest, most exhausting method of transport, although discount rail tickets are competitive, and budget flights (especially last-minute offers) can be good value. Shop around. A small saving on the fare may not adequately compensate you for an agonising two days on a bus that leaves you completely exhausted for another two days. When making an assessment don't forget the hidden expenses: getting to/from airports, airport departure taxes and food and drink consumed en route.

See the Getting There & Away chapter at the beginning of this book for information on long-haul flights from Australia, Canada, New Zealand and the USA; the Getting Around chapter for details on Eurail, Inter-Rail, Billet International de Jeunesse (BIJ; international youth) tickets, and other European travel passes; and the Ireland chapter for details of transport to/from Ireland.

AIR

There are international air links with London, Manchester, Newcastle, Edinburgh and Glasgow, but most travellers will find that cheap flights all wind up in one of the five London airports: Heathrow is the largest, followed by Gatwick, Stansted, Luton and London City.

London is an excellent centre for cheap tickets; the best resource is *TNT Magazine*, but Sunday papers also carry travel ads. If you're prepared to shop around and don't mind flying at short notice, you can pick up some bargains, particularly with discount carriers such as easyJet, Ryanair and Go.

Excellent discount charter flights are often available to full-time students aged under 30 and all young travellers aged under 26 (you need an ISIC or youth card), and are available through the large student travel agencies. See Tourist Offices and Travel Agencies under Information in the London section later in this chapter.

Low season one-way/return flights from London bucket shops start at: Amsterdam £20/40, Athens £45/60, Frankfurt £25/45, Istanbul £50/80, Madrid £35/60, Paris £20/40 and Rome £35/65. Official tickets with carriers like British Airways can cost a lot more.

LAND

The Channel Tunnel gives Britain a land link with Europe (albeit rail only), but even without using the tunnel, you can still get to Europe by bus or train – there's just a short ferry ride thrown in as part of the deal. The ferries carry cars and motorcycles.

BRITAIN

Bus

Eurolines (☎ *0870 514 3219;* ⓦ *www.euro lines.com; 52 Grosvenor Gardens, Victoria, London SW1* • *Paris* ☎ *01 49 72 48 00* • *Amsterdam* ☎ *020-560 8788* • *Brussels* ☎ *02-203 07 07* • *Frankfurt* ☎ *069-790 32 40* • *Madrid* ☎ *091-327 1381* • *Rome* ☎ *06-884 08 40),* a division of National Express (the largest UK bus line), has an enormous network of European destinations, including Ireland and Eastern Europe.

You can book through any National Express office, including Victoria coach station in London (which is where Eurolines' buses depart and arrive), and at many travel agencies.

The following one-way/return prices and journey times are representative: Amsterdam (£32/52, 11 hours), Brussels (£32/52, eight hours), Frankfurt (£42/69, 18½ hours), Madrid (£77/89, 27 hours), Paris (£32/52, 10 hours) and Rome (£69/79, 36 hours).

Eurolines Explorer tickets allow travel between 46 major cities and are valid for up to six months. As an example, a 15-day pass costs £90 (€150).

Train

Three options exist for travel between England and Europe: Eurostar, Eurotunnel or train/ferry connections.

Travellers aged under 26 can pick up BIJ tickets which cut train fares by up to 50%. Various agents issue BIJ tickets in London, including **Usit Connections** (☎ *0870 240 1010; 52 Grosvenor Gardens, London SW1; tube Victoria),* which sells Eurotrain (BIJ) tickets. Eurotrain options include circular Explorer tickets, allowing a different route for the return trip: London to Madrid, for instance, includes Barcelona, Paris and numerous other cities. For an extensive trip around Europe, however, the Eurail or Inter-Rail tickets are still better value.

Eurostar The high-speed **Eurostar** (☎ *0870 518 6186;* ⓦ *www.eurostar.com)* passenger train service travels between London and Paris or Brussels via the Channel Tunnel. There are stops in Ashford (England), and in Lille and Calais (France). The London terminal is at Waterloo station. There are between 14 and 20 trains per day from London to Paris (£170 one way, three hours), and from eight to 12 trains daily between London and Brussels (£157, 2¾ hours). Immigration formalities are completed on the train, but British customs are at Waterloo. Buy tickets from travel agents and at major train stations. Holders of BritRail, Eurail and Euro passes are entitled to discounted fares.

Eurotunnel The **Eurotunnel** (☎ *0870 535 3535;* ⓔ *callcentre@eurotunnel.com;* ⓦ *www .eurotunnel.com)* trains carry vehicles, and their passengers or freight, through the Channel Tunnel between terminals at Folkestone in the UK and Calais in France. British and French customs and immigration formalities are carried out before you drive on to the train. The Eurotunnel terminals are clearly signposted and connected to motorway networks. Travel time from motorway to motorway, including loading and unloading, is one hour; the shuttle itself takes 35 minutes. The specially designed shuttle trains run 24 hours, departing up to four times an hour in each direction between 6am and 10pm, and every hour from 10pm to 6am. A car and its passengers costs between £185 and £220, depending on the day and time of travel.

Train & Ferry Connections Rail/ferry links involve trains at either end and a ferry or high-speed catamaran across the Channel. Trains depart from London's Victoria, Liverpool St or Charing Cross stations, depending on which ferry terminal you're heading for. Rail/ferry links include: Charing Cross–Dover–Calais (France); Charing Cross–Folkestone–Boulogne (France); and Liverpool St–Harwich–Hook of Holland (the Netherlands).

Fares from London depend on where you are travelling to in Europe. For example, an adult fare from London to Amsterdam via Harwich and the Stena Line high-speed catamaran costs £25/79 (7¾ hours); youth tickets and passes are considerably lower. For inquiries concerning European trains contact **Rail Europe** (☎ *0870 584 8848; 179 Piccadilly, London W1).*

SEA

There is a bewildering array of alternatives between Britain and mainland Europe. It's impossible to list all the services because of space limitations. See the Ireland chapter for details on links between Britain and Ireland.

Competition from the Channel Tunnel and low-fare airlines has led to mergers of once-competing ferry companies and, in some cases, closures of long-standing cross-Channel routes. The entire market is now so competitive that there are constant special deals. Prices vary widely depending on the time of day or year that you travel. Return tickets may be much cheaper than two one-way fares; on some routes a standard five-day return costs the same as a one-way ticket; and vehicle tickets may also cover a driver and passenger. Unless otherwise noted, the prices quoted for cars don't include passengers.

France

On a clear day, you can see across the Channel. A true budget traveller would obviously swim (the record is seven hours, 40 minutes).

Dover The shortest ferry link to Europe is between Dover and Calais. It is also the most convenient crossing for those who plan onward travel (in Britain) by bus or train.

P&O Stena Line (☎ 0870 600 0600) operates ferries roughly every 45 minutes from Dover to Calais (1¼ hours). It charges one-way foot passengers £26; a car plus two/nine passengers costs from £139/154; motorcycle prices (including driver and passenger) start at £89. Special low-fare offers make a big difference.

Hoverspeed (☎ 0870 240 8070) uses high-speed catamarans, called SeaCats, between Dover and Calais (45 minutes). It charges £24 for either a one-way passenger or for a five-day return. A car plus two/five passengers costs £110/115 for a standard one-way fare, or £137/147 for a five-day return.

Portsmouth Another option to France is a P&O (☎ 0870 242 4999) ferry to/from either Cherbourg (one to five ferries per day) or Le Havre (two to three per day). The day ferries to Cherbourg take 2¾ to five hours; to Le Havre takes 5½ hours. The night crossings are longer, taking seven to eight hours and 7½ hours respectively. One-way foot-passenger fares start at £12, and a car costs from a bargain £15 to a steep £120.

Brittany Ferries (☎ 0870 536 0360) has at least one sailing a day to/from Caen (six hours) and St Malo (8¾ hours).

Belgium, the Netherlands & Germany

There are direct links with Germany but many people prefer to drive to/from the Dutch or Belgian ferry ports.

Dover To Belgium, Hoverspeed (☎ 0870 240 8070) has regular high-speed ferries sailing daily to Ostend (one to two hours depending on the ferry). It charges one-way foot passengers £24; a car plus one passenger costs £104.

Harwich To Hamburg in Germany, DFDS Seaways (☎ 0870 533 3000) has ferries every two days for most of the year (one-way fare in a reclining seat in the low/high season £29/54, 16½ hours).

Stena Line (☎ 0870 570 7070) has high-speed ferries running three times per day to the Hook of Holland in the Netherlands (from £26 one way, 3¾ hours).

Newcastle Another option to the Netherlands is a DFDS Seaways (☎ 0870 533 3000) daily ferry to Amsterdam (one-way fare in the low/high season £39/64, 15 hours).

Spain

From Plymouth, Brittany Ferries (☎ 0870 536 0360) operates one or two ferries a week (from 15 March to 15 November) to Santander on Spain's north coast (£185 for a one-way fare, £525 for a vehicle plus one passenger, 24 hours).

P&O (☎ 0870 242 4999) operates a service between Portsmouth and Bilbao (31 hours) twice a week from February to the end of October at similar rates to Brittany Ferries.

Scandinavia

Until you see the ferry possibilities, it's easy to forget how close Scandinavia and Britain are.

Aberdeen & Lerwick (Shetland) One of the most interesting possibilities is the summer-only link (15 May-early Sept, once a week) between Shetland and Norway (13½ hours) or Shetland to Iceland (via the Faroe Islands, 31 hours). The operator is Smyril Line Shetland (☎ 01595-690845). It works in conjunction with P&O Scottish Ferries (☎ 01224-572615), which has ferries from Aberdeen to Lerwick on Shetland (from £56 one way, Monday to Friday January to September). A one-way ticket for a reclining chair from Aberdeen to Norway or the Faroes in the low/high season costs £97/117, or to Iceland £155/199.

Newcastle Norway's Fjord Line (☎ 0191-296 1313) operates ferries year-round to

Stavanger, Haugesund and Bergen in Norway. These are overnight trips. The high-season fare for a reclining chair is £90; a car and five people costs £345. Bicycles are free.

DFDS Seaways (☎ *0870 533 3000*) operates ferries twice a week to Gothenburg in Sweden (one-way fare in the low/high season £64/134, 25½ hours) via Kristiansand in Norway (£64/119, 17 hours).

Harwich To Denmark, **DFDS Seaways** (☎ *0870 533 3000)* has ferries every second day to Esbjerg (low/high season fare £49/89, 19½ hours).

LEAVING BRITAIN

People taking flights from Britain need to pay an Air Passenger Duty: those flying to countries in the EU will pay £10; those flying beyond it, £20. This is usually factored into the price of your ticket. There's no departure tax if you leave by sea or tunnel.

See Money in the Facts for the Visitor section earlier in this chapter for details about reclaiming VAT when you depart.

Getting Around

Although public transport is generally of a high standard, many travellers will want to explore the national parks and small villages where transport is worst. If time is limited, a car becomes a serious temptation, although with a mix of local buses, the occasional taxi, plenty of time, walking and occasionally hiring a bike, you can get almost anywhere.

Buses are nearly always the cheapest way to get around. Unfortunately, they're also the slowest (sometimes by a considerable margin) and on main routes they are confined to major roads, which screen you from the small towns and landscapes that make travel worthwhile in the first place. With discount passes and tickets (especially Apex), trains can be competitive; they're quicker and often take you through beautiful countryside.

Ticket types and prices vary considerably, with an advance purchase often saving you as much as 50% of the full-price fare.

The BTA's excellent brochure, *Getting About Britain for the Independent Traveller*, gives details of bus, train, plane and ferry transport around Britain and into mainland Europe.

AIR

Most regional centres and islands are linked to London. However, unless you're going to the outer reaches of Britain, in particular northern Scotland, planes (including the time it takes to get to and from airports) are only marginally quicker than trains. Prices are generally higher than 1st-class rail, but see under Getting There & Away in the Scotland section later in this chapter for details of no-frills flights from London to Scotland. Note that UK domestic flights now carry a £10 tax (Air Passenger Duty) each way; it is usually included in the ticket price.

BUS

Road transport in Britain is almost entirely privately owned and run. **National Express** (☎ *0870 580 8080;* ⓦ *www.gobycoach.com*) runs the largest national network – it completely dominates the market and is a sister company to Eurolines – but there are often smaller competitors on the main routes.

In Britain, long-distance express buses are usually referred to as coaches, and in many towns there are separate terminals for coaches and local buses. Over short distances, coaches are more expensive (though quicker) than buses.

For information on the fast-changing and often chaotic timetables you should telephone the national public transport information line, **Traveline** (☎ *0870 608 2608; available 8am-8pm*). If the consultant cannot answer your query they will transfer your call to the relevant county telephone inquiry-line or regional transport company. Before commencing a journey off the main routes it is wise to phone for the latest information. Unless otherwise stated, prices quoted in this chapter are for economy single (one-way) tickets.

Passes & Discounts

The National Express Discount Coach Card allows 30% off standard adult fares. It is available to full-time students, and those aged from 16 to 25 and 50 or over. The cards are available from all National Express agents. They cost £9 and require a passport photo – ISIC cards are accepted as proof of student status and passports for date of birth.

The National Express Travel Pass allows unlimited coach travel within a specified period. It's available to all overseas visitors but it must be bought outside Britain, usually from a

Eurolines agent. An adult/concession for five days costs £68/55, for seven days £100/80, for 14 days £140/110 and for one month £190/150.

National Express Tourist Trail Passes are available to UK and overseas citizens. They provide unlimited travel on all services for two days travel within three consecutive days (£49/39 for an adult/discount-card holder), any five days travel within 10 (£85/69), any seven days travel within 21 (£120/94) and any 14 days travel within 30 (£190/145). The passes can be bought overseas, or from any National Express agent in the UK.

Hop-On Hop-Off Buses

Stray Travel Network (*Slowcoach*; ☎ 020-7373 7737) is an excellent bus service designed especially for those staying in hostels, but useful for all budget travellers. Buses run on a regular circuit between London, Windsor, Bath, Wales, the Lake District, Edinburgh, York, Stratford-upon-Avon and London, calling at hostels. You can get on and off the bus where you like and catch another one as it comes along (at least two times a week and almost daily in peak season).

There are four ticket options: one day costs £34, three days in two months is £109, four days in two months £129 and six days in four months £159. The price includes some activities and visits en route. Tickets are available from branches of STA Travel (see under Travel Agencies in the Facts for the Visitor chapter earlier in this book); look in the *Yellow Pages* for the nearest branch.

Postbus

Royal Mail postbuses provide a reliable service to remote areas and can be useful for walkers. For information and timetables contact **Customer Services** (☎ 01246-546329). Postbuses take four to 10 people, but no bicycles.

TRAIN

Despite the cutbacks of the last decade and the privatisation programme, Britain still has an

---

On the Buses

For all National Express bus information regarding departure times and ticket prices, call ☎ 0870 580 8080. For National Express bus information and ticket booking over the Internet, visit **W** www.gobycoach.com.

---

impressive rail service – if you're using it as a tourist rather than a commuter, that is. There are several particularly recommended trips on beautiful lines through sparsely populated country, the most famous being in Wales and Scotland. The main routes are served by excellent intercity trains that travel at speeds of up to 140mph and whisk you from London to Edinburgh, for example, in just over four hours. Unless otherwise stated, the prices quoted in this chapter are for adult one-way tickets. Unfortunately, Eurail passes are not recognised in Britain. There are local equivalents, but they aren't recognised in Europe.

Rail Privatisation

British Rail is no more. Services are provided by a host of train operating companies (TOCs). A separate company, Railtrack, owns and maintains the track and the stations. For the sake of convenience the British Rail logo and name are still used on direction signs.

The main railcards (which give holders a reduction on fares – see Railcards later in this section) are accepted by all the companies, and travellers are still able to buy a ticket to any destination from any rail station or from authorised travel agents, though travel agents are not able to sell the full range of tickets.

Passengers can travel only on services provided by the company who issued the ticket and each company is able to set whatever fare it chooses. Thus on routes served by more than one operator, passengers can choose to buy a cheaper ticket with a company offering a less frequent/direct service or pay more for a faster (usually Virgin) service. In some cases competing companies use the same route. The era of competition means that companies often have special offers (eg, 'two for the price of one'), or special reductions for tickets bought in advance (see Tickets later in this section).

BritRail Passes

BritRail passes are the most interesting possibility for visitors, but they are *not available in Britain* and must be bought in your country of origin. Contact the BTA in your country for details.

A BritRail Classic pass, which allows unlimited travel, can be bought for eight, 15, 22 or 30 days. An eight-day pass for an adult/youth is US$265/215, a 15-day pass US$399/279, a 22-day pass US$499/355 and a 30-day pass US$599/415.

A BritRail plus Ireland pass for five days in a month costs US$399 or US$569 for 10 days in a month and includes unlimited rail travel in both countries and a return ferry trip.

An even more useful deal is the Flexipass, which allows four days (adult/youth US$235/ 185), eight days (US$339/239) or 15 days (US$515/359) of unlimited travel within two months.

BritRail Pass 'n Drive

BritRail Pass 'n Drive combines a Flexipass (see previous entry) with the use of an Avis rental car for side trips, and the car-rental price is competitive. The package is available in various combinations – a two-day Flexipass plus three days car hire in one month costs US$289 (this price assumes you use a small car). Contact the BTA in your country for details.

Rail Rovers

The domestic versions of these passes are called BritRail Rovers: a seven-day All Line Rover for an adult/youth costs £325/215, and 14 days costs £495/330. There are also regional Rovers and some Flexi Rovers to Wales, the North Country, the northwest coast and Peaks, the southwest, and Scotland. Details have been given in the appropriate sections.

Railcards

Various railcards, available from major stations, give a third off most tickets and are valid for a year.

The Young Person's Railcard (£18) is for people aged from 16 to 25, or for those studying full time. You'll need a passport photo and proof of age (birth certificate or passport) or student status. There are also railcards for seniors (over 60s £18), disabled people (£14) and families (£20).

If you're planning to do a lot of rail travel in the south of England, a Network SouthEast card is well worth considering. This is valid for the region previously known as Network SouthEast London and the entire southeast of England, from Dover to Weymouth, Cambridge to Oxford. It costs £20 and allows one-third off adult fares. Discounts apply to up to three adults travelling together providing a member of the party is a card-holder. Children and young people aged between five and 15 years get a 60% discount. Travel is permitted only after 10am Monday to Friday (and not between 5.30pm and 7.30pm) and at any time

on the weekend. A couple of journeys can pay for the card.

Tickets

Since privatisation the complexity of the ticketing system has significantly increased. Like the airlines, each TOC has its own discount scheme and promotional fares, and the cheapest fares have advance-purchase and minimum-stay requirements, as well as limited availability. You can just roll up to a station and buy a standard one-way or return ticket for any time on the day you want, but this is the most expensive way to go. The price you pay for a ticket depends on the degree of flexibility you require, the availability of cheap tickets and any railcards that you hold. If you don't have one of the passes listed in the previous entries, the cheapest tickets must be bought at least one week in advance and you have to commit yourself to travelling on specified trains. Failure to travel on the specified train will usually mean having to pay a fine; note also that these tickets may not be refundable. Contact **National Rail Enquiries** (☎ 0845 748 4950; w www.nationalrail.co.uk) for timetables, fares and the numbers to ring for credit-card bookings.

The main fare classifications are as follows:

Apex For outward and return journeys not on the same day, but at fixed times and dates; the cheapest long-term return ticket, but must be booked well in advance, and has a limited availability.

Cheap Day Return For outward and return journeys on the same specified day, with restricted outward travel time (eg, only after 9.30am); often costs barely more than a one-way fare; a great deal for day-trippers.

Open Return For outward travel on a stated day and return on any day within a month.

Saver Open return but with no travel during weekday peak-traffic periods.

SuperSaver Open return but with no travel during weekday peak-traffic periods, nor on Friday at any time, nor on certain other high-traffic days (eg, during the Christmas and Easter holidays).

On the Rails

For all train information regarding departure times and ticket prices, call ☎ 0845 748 4950. For train information and ticket booking over the Internet, visit w www.thetrainline.com.

CAR & MOTORCYCLE

There are five grades of road. Motorways are dual or triple carriageway and deliver you quickly from one end of the country to the other. In general, they are not a particularly pleasant experience. You miss the most interesting countryside, and the driving can be very aggressive. Avoid motorways whenever possible, and be very careful if you use them in foggy or wet conditions when it's usually good safety record plummets. Unfortunately, the primary routes (main A roads) are often very similar.

Minor A roads are single carriageway and are likely to be clogged with slow-moving trucks, but life on the road starts to look up once you join the B roads and minor roads. Fenced by hedgerows, these wind through the countryside from village to village. You can't travel fast, but you won't want to.

Americans and Australians will find petrol expensive (around 75p per litre, or £2.85 for a US gallon), but distances aren't great.

Many towns and cities operate handy Park & Ride systems – you park in the designated car park on the edge of town and catch one of the regular P&R buses to the centre. These buses generally run every 10 minutes from about 7am to 6.30pm Monday to Saturday; a day return ticket costs about £1.20.

In the event of a breakdown, 24-hour roadside assistance is offered by the **Automobile Association** (AA; ☎ 0800 887766) or the **Royal Automobile Club** (RAC; ☎ 0800 828282).

Road Rules

Anyone using the roads should get hold of the *Highway Code* (£1.49), which is often available in newsagents. If you're bringing a car from Europe make sure you're adequately insured.

Briefly, vehicles drive on the left-hand side of the road; front seat belts are compulsory and belts must be worn if they are fitted in the back.

The speed limit is 30mph (48km/h) in any built-up areas, 60mph (96km/h) on single carriageways and 70mph (112km/h) on the dual carriageways and motorways; you give way to your right at roundabouts (that is, traffic already on the roundabout has the right of way); and motorcyclists must wear helmets.

A yellow line painted along the edge of the road indicates there are parking restrictions.

The only way to establish the exact restrictions is to find the nearby sign that spells them out. A single line means no parking for at least an eight-hour period between 7am and 7pm, five days a week; a double line means no parking for at least an eight-hour period between 7am and 7pm more than five days a week; and a broken line means there are some restrictions.

Rental

Rates are expensive in the UK; often you will be best off making arrangements in your home country for some sort of package deal. See the introductory Getting Around chapter earlier in this book for more details. The large international rental companies charge from around £160 per week for a small car (Ford Fiesta, Peugeot 106).

Holiday Autos (☎ 0870 400 0000) operates through a number of rental companies and can generally offer excellent deals. A week's all-inclusive hire starts at around £150. For other cheap operators check the ads in *TNT Magazine*. TICs have lists of local car-hire companies, and these are often much cheaper than the major operators.

If you're travelling as a couple or a group, a camper van is worth considering. **Sunseeker Rentals** (☎ 020-8960 5747) has four-berth and two-berth vans from £250 per week (£400 in the high season).

Purchase

In Britain all cars require the following: a Ministry of Transport (MOT) safety certificate (the certificate itself is usually referred to simply as an MOT) valid for one year and issued by licensed garages; full third-party insurance – shop around but expect to pay at least £300; registration – a standard form signed by the buyer and seller, with a section to be sent to the Ministry of Transport; and tax – from main post offices on presentation of a valid MOT certificate, insurance and registration documents. Note that cars that are 25 years or older are tax exempt.

You are strongly recommended to buy a vehicle with valid MOT and tax. MOT and tax remain with the car through a change of ownership; third-party insurance goes with the driver rather than the car, so you will still have to arrange this (and beware of letting others drive the car). For information concerning registering, licensing, insuring and testing

BRITAIN

your vehicle, contact a main post office or the Vehicle Registration Office.

See the introductory Getting Around and Facts for the Visitor chapters earlier in this book for general information on private transport and the paperwork involved.

BICYCLE
See under Activities earlier in this chapter.

HITCHING
If you're not worried about the safety implications, hitching is reasonably easy, except around the big cities and built-up areas, where you'll need to use public transport. It's against the law to hitch on motorways or the immediate slip roads; make a sign and use approach roads, nearby roundabouts, or the service stations.

BOAT
See the individual Getting There & Away and Getting Around sections later in this chapter for ferry information and the Activities section earlier in this chapter for canal boating.

LOCAL TRANSPORT
See the London Getting Around section for information on the famous London taxis and their minicab competitors. In taxis outside London, you could expect to pay £2 flag fall and around £1.10 per mile, which means they are definitely worth considering to get to an out-of-the-way hostel or sight, or the beginning of a walk. If there are three or four people to share the cost, a taxi over a short distance will often be competitive with the cost of a local bus.

ORGANISED TOURS
Since travel is so easy to organise in Britain, there is very little need to consider a tour. Still, if your time is limited and you prefer to travel in a group there are some interesting possibilities; the BTA has information. Also see Hop-on Hop-off Buses earlier in this chapter.

Contiki (☎ 020-7637 0802, fax 7637 2121; w www.contiki.com; Royal National Hotel, Bedford Way, London WC1H 0DG) offers trips aimed at young people. Seven to 16-day tours average around £50 to £55 per day.

Shearings Holidays (☎ 01942-824824; w www.shearingsholidays.com) is the equivalent for mature travellers.

England

Mistake this part of Britain with Scotland or Wales at your peril. The largest part of the island is also the part most linked in people's minds with all things 'British'. For centuries, the English have buried their identity in that of greater Britain, but as Scotland and Wales devolve, the English are rediscovering themselves. The George Cross, the white flag with the red cross, can increasingly be found on display.

London is the heart of England. Other significant English sites include the Cotswolds, Bath, Oxford, the historic southeast, Cambridge, York and the Lake District.

HISTORY
Celts & Romans
England had long been settled by small bands of hunters when, around 4000 BC, a new group of immigrants arrived from Europe. The new arrivals used stone tools, and they were the first to leave enduring marks on the island. They farmed the chalk hills radiating from Salisbury Plain, and began the construction of stone tombs and, around 3000 BC, the great ceremonial complexes at Avebury and Stonehenge.

The next great influx were the Celts, a people from central Europe who had mastered the smelting of bronze and later of iron. They brought two forms of the Celtic language: Gaelic, which is still spoken in parts of Ireland and Scotland, and Brythonic, which was spoken in England and is still spoken in parts of Wales.

In AD 43, the Romans arrived in force and, despite fierce resistance, established themselves in England. The mountains of Wales and Scotland remained Celtic strongholds, but England was a part of the Roman Empire for 350 years. Paved roads radiated from London to important regional centres: Ermine St ran north to Lincoln, York and Hadrian's Wall; and Watling St ran northwest to Chester. Christianity arrived in the 3rd century.

English
By the 4th century the Roman Empire was in retreat, and in 410 the last Roman troops withdrew. The British were left to the tender mercies of the heathen Angles, Jutes and Saxons – Teutonic tribes originating from north of the Rhine. During the 5th century they advanced

across what had been Roman England and by the 7th century they had come to think of themselves collectively as English. The Celts, particularly in Ireland, kept Latin and Roman Christian culture alive.

Vikings & Normans

The English were ill-prepared to meet the challenges posed by the next wave of invaders. The Norwegian Vikings conquered northern Scotland, Cumbria and Lancashire, and the Danes conquered eastern England, making York their capital. Eastern England (north of the Romans' Watling St) was called the Danelaw. They were finally stopped by Alfred the Great, and he and his successors created a tenuously unified country. Danish raids continued, however, and in 1016 the crown was taken by Canute the Great, who was also King of Norway and Denmark.

After a brief period of Danish rule, Edward the Confessor was made king. He had been brought up in Normandy – a Viking duchy in France – alongside his cousin Duke William, the future Conqueror. Edward's death left two contenders for the crown: Harold Godwin, his English brother-in-law, and William, his Norman cousin. In 1066 William, with 12,000 men, and defeated Harold at the Battle of Hastings.

The conquest of England by the Normans was completed rapidly: English aristocrats were replaced by French-speaking Normans, dominating castles were built and the feudal system was imposed.

Middle Ages

In the 12th century, after a disastrous civil war fought over the succession to the crown, Henry II, Count of Anjou, was made king. He had inherited more than half of modern France and clearly surpassed the King of France in the extent of his power.

The struggle to retain this empire was a dominant concern of the Plantagenet and Lancastrian kings leading to the Hundred Years' War, and finally to English defeat. In order to finance these adventures, the Plantagenet kings conceded a considerable amount of power to Parliament, which jealously protected its traditional right to control taxation.

Further disputes over the royal succession allowed Parliament to consolidate its power. The Wars of the Roses, a dynastic struggle between the houses of York and Lancaster, lasted for 30 years. The final victor in 1485 was Henry VII, the first Tudor king.

Tudors & Stuarts

Under Henry VIII, the long struggle of the English kings against the power of the pope came to a head. Parliament made Henry the head of the Church of England (C of E), and the Bible was translated into English. In 1536 the monasteries were dissolved – a largely popular move because the wealthy and often corrupt religious orders were widely resented.

The 16th century was a golden age. Greek learning was rediscovered, the European powers explored the world, trade boomed, Shakespeare wrote his plays, and Francis Bacon laid the foundations for modern science.

An age of religious intolerance was beginning, however, and after Elizabeth I the relationship between Parliament and the autocratic Stuart kings deteriorated. In 1642 the conflict became a civil war. Catholics, traditionalist members of the C of E and the old gentry supported Charles I, whose power base was the north and west. The Protestant Puritans and the new rising merchant class, based in London and the towns of the southeast, supported Parliament.

Parliament found a brilliant leader in Oliver Cromwell; the royalists were defeated and then in 1649 Charles I was executed. Cromwell assumed dictatorial powers, but he also laid the foundation for the British Empire by modernising the army and navy. Two years after his death in 1658, a reconstituted Parliament recalled Charles II from exile.

The Restoration was a period of expansion – colonies stretched down the American coast and the East India Company established its headquarters in Mumbai (Bombay).

Empire & Industry

In the 18th century, the Hanoverian kings increasingly relied on Parliament to govern the kingdom, and Sir Robert Walpole became the first prime minister in all but name.

By 1770 France had ceded all of Canada and surrendered all but two of its trading stations in India, while Captain Cook claimed Australia for Britain in 1778. The empire's first major reverse came when the American colonies won Independence in 1783.

Also in the 1780s were the first developments that would lead to the Industrial Revolution and Britain was its crucible. Canals, trains, coal, water and steam power transformed the means of production and transport, and the rapidly growing towns of the Midlands became the first industrial cities.

By the time Queen Victoria took the throne in 1837, Britain was the greatest power in the world. Its fleets dominated the seas linking an enormous empire, and its factories dominated world trade.

Under Prime Ministers Disraeli and Gladstone, the worst excesses of the Industrial Revolution were addressed, education became universal and the right to vote was extended to most men (women did not get equal voting rights until 1928).

The 20th Century

Victoria died at the very beginning of the new century and the old order was shattered by the Great War (WWI). By the war's end in 1918 a million British men had died and 15% of the country's accumulated capital had been spent.

The euphoria of victory didn't last long. In the late 1920s the world economy slumped, ushering in more than a decade of misery and political upheaval. The Labour Party first came to power in 1924, but lasted less than a year.

On 1 September 1939, Hitler provoked a new war by invading Poland. By mid-1940, most of Europe was either ruled by or under the direct influence of the Nazis, Stalin had negotiated a peace, the USA was neutral, and Britain, under the extraordinary leadership of Winston Churchill, was virtually isolated. Between July and October 1940 the Royal Air Force fought and won the Battle of Britain and Hitler's invasion plans were blocked (43,000 Britons died in the bombing raids of 1940–41).

The postwar years have been challenging. The last of the empire has gained Independence (India in 1947, Malaya in 1957, Kenya in 1963), many traditional industries have collapsed and the nation has had to accept a new role as a partner in the EU. Britain has entered the 21st century as a wealthy and influential country, but it's no longer a superpower and unable to maintain that it's anything more than an island just off mainland Europe.

LONDON

☎ 020 ● pop 7.4 million

If anything is true of London, it is that it's incredibly difficult to sum up. It's been heralded as 'the coolest, hottest city in the world' – the very definition of modern. But you only have to look up at the architecture to see the splendour of a bygone age. The city is a combination of the establishment and the avant-garde. Afternoon tea, pomp and all that was quintessentially English, sits comfortably alongside international cuisine, world music and all that is quintessentially modern.

It's a glorious juxtaposition borne out by the fact that even though you'll be one of some 30 million people who visit London every year, you'll leave feeling as if you've encountered something unique and personal (even if you're no longer on speaking terms with your bank manager!).

There's no denying that London is a tug on the purse strings. Even Londoners think the capital comes with a huge price tag, and unfortunately, the most extortionate prices are slapped on items vital to a traveller's existence – hotels, food and drink. Thankfully, your stay doesn't have to cost the earth and there's plenty to do for free or very little – from big-name museums and galleries, to a stroll in the royal parks or watching Covent Garden's quirky street entertainers.

Equally, there's little point in putting up with the tutting 'locals', the hoards of fellow tourists, and the pollution, if you aren't prepared to splash-out occasionally and soak up London's vibrant culture and nightlife – which, like the city itself, rarely disappoints.

History

Although a Celtic community established itself around a ford across the River Thames, it's the Romans who are credited with the founding of Londinium in AD 43. Despite this first development collapsing – with avenging Britons led by Queen Boadicea burning it to the ground in AD 60 – the Romans returned to the site in AD 200. With proper walled fortifications, a bridge and a population of some 30,000, the 'square mile' finally took on a defined structure and the City of London was born.

Although little trace of the Dark Ages remains, during Viking raids of the 9th century London became a prime target for attack. Focus moved from the then capital, Winchester, to London, and London took on the capital status it still retains today.

Fifty years before the Normans arrived, Edward the Confessor had built his abbey and palace at Westminster, leaving William the Conqueror a legacy of a city that was the richest and largest in its kingdom. William raised

BRITAIN

the White Tower (the core of the Tower of London) and confirmed the city's independence and right to self-government.

With Henry VIII's Reformation and selling of religious houses, London experienced a mini property boom and the population swelled from 50,000 in 1500 to 140,000 in 1600.

The courts of both Henry VIII and Elizabeth I became cultural oases, and theatres, most notably the Globe (1598), sprang up.

Unfortunately, medieval Tudor and Jacobean London were virtually destroyed, first by the Plague of 1665, and then the Great Fire of 1666. This did nothing to halt or discipline the city's growth, however, and provided Christopher Wren with an opportunity to redesign great chunks of London.

By 1720 there were 750,000 inhabitants and London, as the seat of Parliament and focal point for a growing empire, was becoming ever more important. Georgian architects replaced the last of medieval London with their imposing symmetrical architecture and residential squares; the Victorians set about displaying their prosperity and built some of London's greatest landmarks and museums.

The arrival of the Luftwaffe and the dropping of some 18,000 bombs in its WWII campaign left huge swathes of the centre and the East End totally flattened. After the war, ugly housing and low-cost developments were thrown up on the bomb sites. The docks never recovered and the Docklands declined to the point of dereliction, until rediscovery by developers in the 1980s. Since then, the Docklands has boomed, becoming home to a world of twinkling glass office blocks, a flurry of chain-restaurants and pubs, and of course, the much-maligned Millennium Dome.

In 2000, London elected its first true mayor, Ken Livingstone, whose efforts to improve London's transport system continue to fuel debate.

Since then, London has played host to the Queen's Golden Jubilee, royal funerals, and has experienced continued growth and prosperity.

Orientation

Despite London's size, finding your way around isn't as daunting as it first looks. To get any sense of the geography of the place and fully appreciate the idiosyncrasies between the north and south of London's mighty tidal river – the Thames – you'll really need to don your walking shoes. But if you're pressed for time, the temperamental Underground railway system (the 'tube') will become your travelling habitat.

Each line has its own colour, immortalized in the indispensable (though geographically misleading) Underground map. Any train heading from left to right on the map is designated as eastbound; any train heading from top to bottom is southbound.

Most important sights, theatres, restaurants and even some cheap places to stay lie north of the Thames within the reasonably compact rectangle formed by the tube's Circle line (yellow on the tube map and one of the slowest lines on the network).

Once you're back at ground level, you'll probably need to rely on a good street map to get around. The city has had little planning, evolving instead into a jumbled collection of bizarrely postcoded streets and alleyways. Its only saving grace is that it's divided into locally governed districts, making a city as vast as London much easier to explore.

The City & the East Once the site of the original London settled by the Romans, the aptly named City is now London's financial heartland, and despite its position in the southeastern corner of the Circle line, is regarded as the centre of the capital.

It's suit-central during the week and a ghost town at weekends, but has crowd-pulling sights that remain busy year-round. These include the Tower of London and St Paul's Cathedral, Spitalfields market, the Guildhall and the Barbican; you'll need plenty of time to do them justice.

To the east, beyond the Circle line, is the East End; once the exclusive habitat of the cockney and a massive Jewish quarter, now a trendy, multicultural melting pot. Incorporating districts like fashionable Shoreditch and Hoxton, this is a place on the up, and is fascinating for espresso drinking and people-watching.

Further east again lie the Docklands, which has witnessed a renaissance since the early 1980s. Some 100 chic cafés, bars and restaurants lie in the shadow of the majestic Canary Wharf and Heron Quays development. With the Museum of Docklands and Mudchute's city farm, this area is definitely worth a visit, especially if combined with a trip to Greenwich.

The West West of the City, but before the West End proper, are Holborn and Bloomsbury. Holborn (pronounced hoeburn) is Britain's sedate legal nucleus, the home of wigs, gowns and common law. Bloomsbury is still synonymous with the literary and publishing worlds, and is a blue-plaque mecca (used to identify buildings associated with famous people). Besides dozens of specialist shops, this is where you'll find that unrivalled treasure chest – the British Museum.

The West End lies west of Tottenham Court Rd and Covent Garden, and offers an eclectic mix of tourist-trap tack and cultural gastronomy. It includes such magnets as Trafalgar Square, the restaurants and clubs of lively and infamous Soho, the West End cinemas and theatres around Piccadilly Circus and Leicester Square, and the elegant shops of Regent and Bond Sts.

St James's and Westminster, the political hub, lie to the southwest. This is where you'll find Whitehall, No 10 Downing St, the Houses of Parliament, Big Ben, Westminster Abbey, St James's Palace and Buckingham Palace.

To the south of Victoria station lies Pimlico, an altogether uninspiring district if it weren't for its proximity to the Tate Britain Gallery and the lure of some cheap accommodation.

Earl's Court, South Kensington and Chelsea are in the southwest corner formed by the Circle line. Earl's Court, once infamous as Kangaroo Valley, now feels tired and lacklustre.

With Knightsbridge (home to Harrods and Harvey Nichols) just a stone's throw away, South Kensington is much more sophisticated. There's a clutch of world-famous museums (the Victoria & Albert, Science and Natural History), plenty of culture, and some great eateries once you get off Kensington High Street.

Chelsea is home to the 'Sloanes', and in keeping with catering for ladies who lunch, is unsurprisingly chic.

Farther southwest you come to some very comfortable residential districts like Richmond and Chiswick. Sites worth trekking out west for include: Hampton Court Palace, Kew Gardens, Syon House and The Wetlands Centre.

The North With a famous annual carnival to boot, Notting Hill is a lively, cosmopolitan district that gets trendier by the day. The funky Portobello Road market is its main draw and is as diverse as the area itself.

North of Kensington Gardens and Hyde Park, Bayswater and Paddington are tourist ghettos, but there are plenty of restaurants and cheap accommodation.

From west to east, the band of districts to the north of the Central tube-line includes Hampstead, Camden Town, Highgate, Highbury and Islington. Hampstead, with its great views and the marvellous heath, would be an oasis of calm if it weren't for the crowds; Camden Town still retains its alternative charm in its over-populated but must-see markets.

Highbury is synonymous with one thing – Arsenal football club. If football's your thing it's great, otherwise avoid it, especially on match days. Islington went from gritty to trendy in the mid-1990s and Upper Street still boasts one of London's most densely packed collections of eating places.

The South Cross the Thames from central London (via the Millennium Bridge, the similarly designed pedestrian access on the Hungerford Bridge, or the tube's fast Jubilee line) and you encounter one of London's fastest developing areas. The British Airways London Eye observation wheel across from Parliament and the huge Tate Modern gallery on the Thames in Southwark are the most notable of scores of developments that are transforming this once ugly, concrete mass.

Take a walk down the Millennium mile and get your culture fix courtesy of the South Bank Centre or The Dalí Universe. Head further southeast, and you'll reach beautiful Greenwich, home to the *Cutty Sark*, brilliant views, an excellent market and the Prime Meridian.

Notorious for racial problems in the early 1980s, Brixton is London at its most multicultural and still plays host to some of the city's best club-nights.

Maps If you want some clue as to which Station Rd you're in (there are 47 of them), a decent map is vital. Ideally, get a single-sheet map so you can whip it out and see all of central London at a glance; not only will it fare well in a battle with the British weather, but you'll be less of a beacon for pickpockets who can see you're lost.

Lonely Planet's *London City Map* has three separate maps at different scales as well as an inset map of Theatreland and an index. The bound *Mini London A-Z Street Atlas & Index*

BRITAIN

CENTRAL LONDON

CENTRAL LONDON

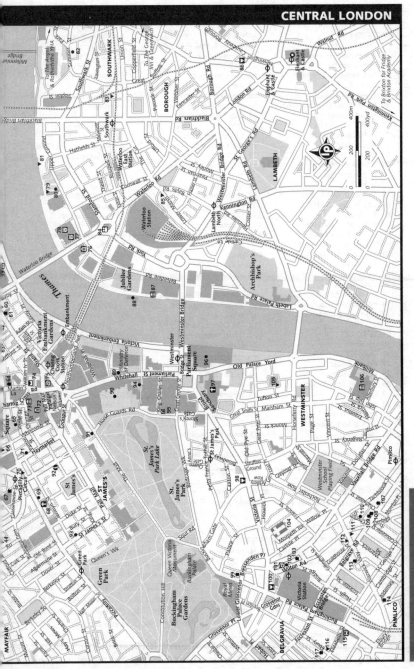

CENTRAL LONDON

PLACES TO STAY
- 2 Ashlee House
- 3 St Pancras YHA Hostel
- 4 The Generator
- 6 Euro Hotel; George Hotel
- 7 John Adams Hall Student Residence
- 11 International Students House
- 12 Indian Student YMCA
- 14 Carr-Saunders Hall
- 15 Hotel Cavendish; Arran House Hotel
- 19 Pickwick Hall
- 21 Academy Hotel
- 24 La Brasserie Town House
- 37 Hazlitt's
- 41 Oxford St YHA Hostel
- 58 City of London YHA
- 61 The Savoy
- 64 St Martin's Lane Hotel
- 67 Regent Palace Hotel
- 99 Rubens at the Palace; 41
- 103 Victoria Park Plaza Hotel
- 107 Victoria Hotel
- 108 Victor Hotel
- 109 Luna-Simone Hotel
- 113 Brindle House Hotel
- 114 Windermere Hotel
- 117 James & Cartref Houses

PLACES TO EAT
- 10 L'etoile Café
- 13 Sardo
- 22 Rasa Sumudra
- 25 Coffee Gallery
- 28 Café des Amis du Vin
- 29 Café Pacifico
- 30 Belgo Centraal
- 31 Food for Thought
- 32 Rock & Sole Plaice
- 39 Star Café
- 40 Soba
- 42 The Garden Café

- 44 Mômo
- 46 Busaba Eathai
- 47 Palms of Goa
- 48 Café Emm
- 50 Pollo; Stockpot
- 52 Yee Tung Chinese Restaurant
- 56 Joe Allen
- 60 Simpson's-in-the-Strand
- 62 Bistro 1
- 63 Rules
- 66 Chuen Cheng Ku
- 70 The Criterion
- 79 Sarnis
- 81 Oxo Tower Restaurant & Brasserie
- 83 Mariterra
- 85 Freshly Maid Café
- 105 Footstool
- 111 UNo 1
- 112 Marmaris
- 116 Ebury Wine Bar & Restaurant

OTHER
- 1 Scala
- 5 Judd Two Books
- 8 London University
- 9 University College Hospital
- 16 Safeway Supermarket
- 17 Fabric
- 18 The Queen's Larder
- 20 British Museum
- 23 Bradley's Spanish Bar
- 26 The End
- 27 Sir John Soane's Museum
- 33 12 Bar Club
- 34 Astoria
- 35 Borderline
- 36 Foyle's
- 38 Pizza Express Jazz Club
- 43 Biblion
- 45 Berwick St Market
- 49 Ronnie Scott's
- 51 Coach & Horses

- 53 The Photographers' Gallery
- 54 Stanfords
- 55 Lamb & Flag
- 57 Courtauld Institute Gallery
- 59 Gilbert Collection
- 65 tkts
- 68 St James's Piccadilly
- 69 Waterstones
- 71 American Express (Main Office)
- 72 National Gallery
- 73 National Portrait Gallery
- 74 Trafalgar Square Post Office
- 75 easyEverything
- 76 Hayward Gallery
- 77 National Film Theatre
- 78 Royal National Theatre
- 80 London Bicycle Tour Company
- 82 Bankside House
- 84 bfi London IMAX Cinema
- 86 Ministry of Sound
- 87 Dalí Universe
- 88 BA London Eye
- 89 Banqueting House
- 90 Horse Guards Parade
- 91 Institute for Contemporary Arts (ICA)
- 92 Britain Visitor Centre; Stanfords
- 93 Thomas Cook (Main Office)
- 94 No 10 Downing St
- 95 Cabinet War Rooms
- 96 Houses of Parliament
- 97 Westminster Abbey
- 98 The Albert
- 100 Pacha London
- 101 easyEverything
- 102 1st Contact; Rapid Visa
- 104 Westminster Cathedral
- 106 Tate Britain
- 110 The Laundrette Centre
- 115 Victoria Coach Station

provides comprehensive coverage of London in a discreet size and has the invaluable tube map on the back.

Throughout this chapter, the nearest tube or main line station has been given with addresses; the Central London map shows the location of tube stations.

Information

Thanks to scores of innovations and good old TICs, information about London is never difficult to find.

Time Out magazine (out Tuesday; £2.20) is a listings guide covering and reviewing everything from clubs, music and theatre events, to films, books and comedy nights. It's highly recommended.

Free magazines are available at most hostels and from pavement bins. *TNT Magazine* (out Monday) and *SA Times* (out Wednesday) covers Australian and South African news and sports results, but are also invaluable for entertainment listings, excellent travel sections and useful classifieds. More difficult to find but well worth a read are *Living Abroad Magazine* (LAM) and the entertainment-focused *Footloose in London*. Both are free.

Tourist Offices London's TICs are extremely helpful and packed to the hilt with useful information. What's more, they aren't just London-focused and can offer practical information and advice on travelling to other destinations. Helpful centres include:

Britain Visitor Centre (1 Regent St SW1Y 4XT). A two-minute walk from Piccadilly Circus, this is a one-stop shop for information about London, with the tourist boards of Wales, Scotland and Ireland providing assistance too. On the ground floor you'll find information desks and a branch of the renowned map shop, Stanfords. The mezzanine level is home to independent agents who can arrange accommodation (for a fee); organise train, bus, air and car travel; and book tours and theatre tickets. It opens 9am to 6.30pm weekdays and 10am to 4pm weekends (9am to 5pm on Saturday from late June to late September). It gets extremely busy and only deals with walk-in customers. If you need more information on Britain or Ireland and can't get to Regent Street, then call the British Tourist Authority (BTA) general inquiries line (☎ 8846 9000).

London Tourist Information Centres There are TICs in the Underground concourse of Heathrow Terminals 1, 2 and 3, in the Arrivals Hall at Waterloo International Terminal and at Liverpool St Underground station. There are also information desks at Gatwick, Stansted and Luton airports. These also only handle walk-ins. The offices are all open at least from 9am to 6pm daily and often much longer in summer. Written inquiries should be sent to the London Tourist Board & Convention Bureau, Glen House, Stag Place, London SW1E 5LT (fax 7932 0222). You can call its recorded information line on ☎ 0906-866 3344, but at 60p a minute it's expensive and can only be dialled within the UK.

Soho Sandwich Company (☎ 7428 9740; 289 Camden High St NW1; tube Camden Town). This is a café and computerised information centre rolled into one. Over a cup of coffee, you can sit at a touch screen and access masses of information on the Camden borough. What's more, if the sun's out, you can go up to the mezzanine level, chill out, and watch life go by on the canal next door. It's open from 8am to 6pm or 7pm daily depending on how busy it is.

Money Banks and ATMs abound across central London. If you must use *bureaux de change*, at least check the commission rates carefully first.

There is a 24-hour *bureau de change* in Heathrow Terminal 3 and various Thomas Cook branches throughout all terminals with extended opening hours. There are also 24-hour bureaus in Gatwick's South and North Terminals and one at Stansted. Luton and London City airports have desks open during operating hours.

American Express (main office ☎ 7930 4411; 6 Haymarket; tube Piccadilly Circus; open for currency exchange 9am-5.30pm Mon-Fri, 9am-4pm Sat & Sun) has currency exchange and open slightly longer hours June to September.

Thomas Cook (main office ☎ 7853 6400; 30 St James's St SW1; tube Green Park; open 9am-5.30pm Mon, Tues, Thur & Fri, 10am-5.30pm Wed) has many branches scattered around central London.

Discounts If you plan to do a lot of sightseeing, the London Pass (one/two/three/six days £22/39/49/69) can be purchased from any London TIC. It's valid for entry to over 60 attractions, but entry to Buckingham Palace isn't valid with a one-day pass.

You can pay a bit extra and get a Zone 1–6 Travelcard included in the price (one/two/three/six days £27/52/68/108), but this must be bought before you arrive in London. To purchase, phone ☎ 0870 242 9988 or log on to w www.londonpass.com.

Post & Communications Unless you specify otherwise, poste restante mail ends up at **Trafalgar Square Post Office** (24-28 William IV St WC2N 4DL; tube Charing Cross). Mail will be held for four weeks and can be collected from 8am to 8pm weekdays and 9am to 8pm on Saturday; ID is required.

CallShop International (181a Earl's Court Rd; tube Earl's Court; open 10am-10.30pm daily) has lower charges than British Telecom (BT) for international calls and also has photocopying and faxing facilities.

Email & Internet Access There are numerous Internet cafés dotted around the capital, but it's often cheaper to head for the huge easyEverything outlets. A £1 voucher will usually buy 40 minutes, with some vouchers being transferable between locations. This gives you the freedom to log on and off as you please, without missing out on a penny of the time you've paid for. All are open 24 hours and locations include:

Kensington (☎ 7938 1814) 160–166 Kensington High St W8; tube High St Kensington

Oxford St (☎ 7491 8986) 358 Oxford St W1; tube Bond St

Tottenham Court Rd (☎ 436 1771) 9–16 Tottenham Court Rd W1; tube Tottenham Court Rd

Trafalgar Square (☎ 7930 4094) 7 The Strand WC2; tube Charing Cross

Victoria (☎ 7233 8456) 9–13 Wilton Rd SW1; tube Victoria

Travel Agencies London has always been a centre for cheap travel. Refer to the Sunday papers (especially the *Sunday Times*), *TNT Magazine* and *Time Out* for listings of cheap flights, but beware of sharks.

Long-standing and reliable firms include:

London Flight Centre (☎ 7727 4290) 47 Notting Hill Gate; tube Notting Hill

STA Travel (☎ 7361 6262) 86 Old Brompton Rd SW7; tube South Kensington

Trailfinders (☎ 7938 3939) 194 Kensington High St W8; tube High St Kensington; for travel centre & 1st- & business-class flights • 215 Kensington High St W8; tube High St Kensington; for transatlantic & European flights

Bookshops All the major chains are good, but Waterstones, Books etc and Borders have particularly strong travel sections. A **Waterstones branch** (☎ 7851 2400; 203-206 Piccadilly W1; tube Piccadilly Circus) is Europe's largest bookshop. Several specialist bookshops are tourist attractions in their own right:

Biblion (☎ 7629 1374) 1–7 Davies Mews W1; tube Bond St – a frequently praised mecca for rare and antiquarian books.

Foyles (☎ 7437 5660) 119 Charing Cross Rd WC2; tube Leicester Square – possibly the most disorganised bookshop in the world offering cheap finds if you're prepared to hunt them down.

Judd Two Books (☎ 7387 5333) 82 Marchmont St WC1; tube Russell Square – excellent for second-hand bargains.

Stanfords (☎ 7836 1321) 12 Long Acre WC2; tube Covent Garden – the largest and best selection of maps and guides in the world.

Travel Bookshop (☎ 7229 5260) 13 Blenheim Crescent W11; tube Ladbroke Grove – claims to be the inspiration for the bookshop in the film *Notting Hill*, which starred Julia Roberts and Hugh Grant. It has all the new guides, plus a selection of out-of-print and antiquarian gems.

Laundry Most hostels provide laundry facilities for a reasonable sum. If they're out of order, there's bound to be a laundrette within walking distance of your accommodation. Opening hours vary but are usually 7am or 8am to 6pm or 7pm for a last wash; a single-load wash and dry will cost between £2.50 and £3. A few options include: **Bobo's Bubbles** (111 Earl's Court Rd SW5; tube Earl's Court); **Laundrette House** (18 London St W2; tube Paddington); and **Laundrette Centre** (Churton St SW1; tube Victoria).

Left Luggage Heathrow, Gatwick and Stansted airports all offer left-luggage facilities operated by private companies in all terminals from £4 a day per bag. At Heathrow these facilities are usually open from 5.30am to 11pm, and at Stansted from 4.30am to midnight. A 24-hour facility is available at Gatwick's South Terminal. Most major train stations and Victoria coach station also have left-luggage facilities, but they can cost you anything from £2 to £8 a day depending on the bag's size and how long it will be left.

Medical & Emergency Services Dial ☎ 999 (free) for fire, police or ambulance. The following hospitals have 24-hour accident and emergency departments:

Charing Cross Hospital (☎ 8846 1234) Fulham Palace Rd W6; tube Hammersmith

Chelsea and Westminster Hospital (☎ 8746 8000) 396 Fulham Rd SW10; tube Fulham Broadway

Royal Free Hospital (☎ 7794 0500) Pond St NW3; tube Belsize Park

University College Hospital (☎ 7387 9300) Grafton Way WC1; tube Euston Square

Drop-in doctor services or MediCentres have opened in several main-line railway terminals but charges can be high. You could try **NHS Direct** (☎ 0845 4647; 24hr service) for help with diagnosis and further advice. Pharmacies display the address of the nearest late-night pharmacy in the windows.

To find an emergency dentist call **Dental Emergency Care Service** (☎ 7955 2186) between 8.45am and 3pm weekdays, or drop in at the **Eastman Dental Hospital** (☎ 7915 1000; 256 Gray's Inn Rd WC1; tube Chancery Lane; open 9am-5pm Mon-Fri).

Visas & Immunisations Several of the companies offering visa and immunisation services advertise in *TNT Magazine*. Charges can differ widely. **Trailfinders** (☎ 7938 3999; 194 Kensington High St W8; tube High St Kensington) has both a visa service and an immunisation centre. There's also an appointment-only Wellbeing Travel Clinic situated at the backpacking equipment shop **Trekmate** (☎ 7370 4228; 137 Earl's Court Rd SW5; tube Earl's Court).

Try **1st Contact** (☎ 0870 727 4384; 6th Floor, Abford House, 15 Wilton Rd SW1; tube Victoria) for another visa service.

Dangers & Annoyances While an empty wallet is more likely to be a result of hiked prices than something more sinister, crime in London shouldn't be downplayed – especially after dark. Your main hazard will be pickpockets, whose haunts include the tube, Oxford St and Leicester Square.

Due care and attention should also be taken when using ATMs, as 'shoulder surfing' (someone watches you type in your pin and later distracts or pickpockets you to get your card) is becoming more common. If you have to use an ATM, try and use those located inside buildings rather than ones on streets.

It goes without saying that women should take particular care if alone after dark, especially on the tube; a walk down Brixton's Coldharbour Lane late at night is not for the faint-hearted! Licensed taxis are probably your safest option.

Food from mobile street carts usually found in the parks, though temptingly cheap, should also be treated warily. The vendors may be unlicensed, have poor hygiene levels and you may be left with a nasty taste in your mouth.

Things to See & Do

The centre of London can easily be explored on foot. The following tour could be covered in a day but doesn't allow time to explore the individual sights in detail; it will, however, introduce you to the West End, the South Bank and Westminster. For most sites, the last entry time has been given rather than the final closing hour.

Start at one of London's most enduring sites – **St Paul's Cathedral** (adult/concession/child £6/5/3), and marvel at Christopher Wren's masterpiece completed in 1710. Admission gains you access to the cathedral plus the dome and crypt. A limited number of guided tours for adult/concession/child costs £2.50/2/1 are also available from 11am Monday to Saturday.

From the Cathedral, walk down to the Thames. Here you can cross the **Millennium Bridge** directly to the **Tate Modern**. It's difficult to decide whether the exhibits housed in this huge old Bankside Power Station are the expressions of very talented or very disturbed minds. Either way, it's worth seeing, even if you come away only appreciating the river views.

Walk west along the river past the **Oxo Tower** and stop at **Gabriel's Wharf** for a delicious toasted panini from **Sarnis** at Unit 10. Continue west and enjoy the many attractions of the **South Bank Centre**. It's difficult to miss the **British Airways London Eye** (☎ 0870 500 0600; adult/concession/child £11.50/10.50/6). Rising 450ft above the Thames, it's the world's largest observation wheel and on a rare, clear day you can see for 25mi. It's very popular whatever the weather and you best book your ride in advance. Some tickets are held back for same-day sale, but beware of the crowds and touts.

Continue under the **Hungerford Bridge** to **County Hall** and visit the famous Mae West Lips Sofa at the **Dalí Universe** (☎ 7620 2720; adult/concession/child £8.50/7.50/4.95). Return to, and cross, the **Hungerford Bridge**, cut through Charing Cross Station and walk east along the Strand to Southhampton St and head north to **Covent Garden piazza**. Once London's fruit and vegetable market, the piazza is now home to a colourful variety of street performers and a million and one tourists.

Leave the piazza walking west on Long Acre. Continue across Charing Cross Rd to **Leicester Square** with its cinemas and statues of Charlie Chaplin and Shakespeare. Note that tkts (see Theatre & Cinema under Entertainment later in this chapter) sells half-price theatre tickets on the day of performance.

Continue along Coventry St to **Piccadilly Circus**, the neon capital of London. Regent St curves from the northwestern corner; at the northeastern corner is Shaftesbury Avenue – a theatre-goer's mecca. This eventually runs back into chaotic **Soho**, where it's cheap eats by day, a vibrant red-light and gay district by night.

Continue west along Piccadilly and ogle another Wren offering, **St James's church**. Buy something quintessentially English at the historic **Fortnum & Mason**, and pop into the **Royal Academy of Arts** across the road, which often has special shows and exhibitions. Detour into the timeless **Burlington Arcade** just after the academy, for some well-heeled shopping.

Return to Piccadilly and continue until you reach St James's St on your left. This runs down to **St James's Palace**, the royal home from 1660 to 1837, until it was judged insufficiently impressive. It's now the home of Prince Charles. Skirt around its eastern side and you'll come to the Mall.

Trafalgar Square is to the east, **Buckingham Palace** (☎ 7321 2233; adult/concession/child/family £11.50/9.50/6/29; open 9.30am-4.15pm daily in summer only) to the west. Don't be surprised if the 19 state rooms remind you of a series of ornate hotel lobbies.

From mid-April to late July the **changing of the guard** happens outside Buckingham Palace at 11.30am daily; the rest of the year (weather permitting) it's at 11.30am on alternate days.

Cross back into St James's Park, an ideal spot for a picnic, and follow the lake to its eastern end. Turn right onto Horse Guards Rd. This takes you past the **Cabinet War Rooms** (adult/concession/child £5.80/4.20/free to under 16s), which gives an extraordinary insight into Sir Winston Churchill's secret operations during WWII.

Continue along Horse Guards Rd and then turn left onto Great George St, which takes you through to stunning Westminster Abbey, the Houses of Parliament and Westminster Bridge. **Westminster Abbey** (adult/concession/child/family £6/3/free to under 11s/12) is so rich in history you will need a few hours to do it justice. The coronation chair, where all but two monarchs since 1066 have been crowned, is behind the altar, and many greats – from Darwin to Chaucer – have been buried here. It also houses the grave of the Unknown Warrior, a place of pilgrimage. Unfortunately the crowds are now so dense that an admission fee is charged to go into any part of the cathedral. The best way to soak in the atmosphere is to attend Evensong, which takes place at 5pm weekdays and 3pm weekends.

The **Houses of Parliament** (☎ 7219 4272) and the clock tower (actually its bell), **Big Ben**, were built in the 19th century in neo-Gothic style. The best way to get into the building is to attend the Commons or Lords visitors' galleries during a parliamentary debate. Phone for information.

Walking away from Westminster Bridge, turn right onto Parliament St, which becomes Whitehall. On your left, the hard-to-see, unspectacular house at **No 10 Downing St** is the official residence of the prime minister.

Farther along on the right is the neoclassical wonder of Inigo Jones' **Banqueting House** (adult/concession/child £4/3/2.50), with its amazing ceiling paintings by Rubens and the story of Charles I's execution to heighten its appeal. Continue past the **Horse Guards**, where you can see a less-crowded changing of the guard at 11am Monday to Saturday, 10am on Sunday.

Finally, you reach **Trafalgar Square** with its many pigeons and Nelson's Column. The **National Gallery** and **National Portrait Gallery**, both free, are on the northern side.

River Tour If walking doesn't seem such a great idea, consider catching a boat from Westminster Pier (beside Westminster Bridge) down the river to **Greenwich**. You'll pass **Shakespeare's Globe Theatre**, the **Tower of London**, and Sir Francis Drakes' reconstructed **Golden Hinde**.

There are a few operators to choose from, but you could try **City Cruises** (☎ 7740 0400; one-way/return £6.30/7.80), which departs every 40 minutes from 10am, June to August; subject to demand May to September. Show your One Day Travelcard and you'll get a third off the fare.

For multilingual commentary try the circular cruise from **Catamaran Cruisers** (☎ 7925 2215; cruise £7). Boats depart roughly hourly from 10.30am. Both operators also offer hop-on/hop-off tickets; all services are significantly reduced during winter.

Greenwich can absorb the best part of a day and needs time to be fully explored. Start with the **Cutty Sark** (☎ 8858 3445; adult/concession/child/family £3.90/2.90/2.90/9.70), the only surviving tea-and-wool clipper and arguably one of the most beautiful ships ever built. Wander around Greenwich's excellent market, then visit the **Queen's House**, a Palladian masterpiece designed in 1616 by Inigo Jones as a retreat for the wife of James I, Queen Anne of Denmark. Britain's famous naval traditions are covered in fascinating fashion at the **National Maritime Museum**. Admission to both is free. The elegant **Old Royal Naval College** (☎ 8269 4747; admission free; open 10am-5pm daily), beside the river, was designed by Wren; its Painted Hall and Chapel are stunning.

Climb the hill behind the museum to the **Royal Observatory**, also free. A brass strip in the courtyard marks the Prime Meridian that divides the world into eastern and western hemispheres while displays show famous timepieces, including those first used to accurately calculate longitude. There are great views over the Docklands.

Walk back down the hill and through the historic Greenwich foot tunnel (near the *Cutty Sark*) to Island Gardens. From here you can catch the Docklands Light Railway (DLR) back to Tower Gateway. Alternatively, you can catch the DLR at the Cutty Sark stop and avoid the tunnel.

At Tower Gateway follow the signs for the **Tower of London** (☎ 7709 0765; *adult/ concession/child/family £11.50/8.75/7.50/ 34; open 9am-5pm Mon-Sat, 10am-5pm Sun*). Home to the dazzling Crown Jewels, Beefeaters and ravens, the Tower has been a fortress, royal residence, prison and place of execution. It's one of London's most popular attractions and in summer, it shows. If you want to avoid the inevitable admission queues, buy your tickets in advance at any Underground station; leave yourself plenty of time to do the sight justice.

For some amazing views of London's skyline, make sure that you stop at the Gothic spires of **Tower Bridge** (☎ 7403 3761; *adult/ concession/child £4.50/3/3; open 9.30am-5pm daily*).

Museums Museums abound in London and it's easy to reach the point of cultural saturation very quickly. Thanks to the great variety, there's bound to be a museum that strikes a chord with you. Listed below are a few that really shouldn't be missed – whatever your taste. They're all free but a donation is advised; special exhibitions will charge.

The **British Museum** (☎ 7323 8299; *Great Russell St WC1; tube Russell Square or Tottenham Court Rd; open 10am-5.30pm Sat-Wed, 10am-8.30pm Thur-Fri*) is arguably London's greatest museum. Its collection of Egyptian, Mesopotamian, Greek and Roman antiquities are unparalleled, and you'll marvel at the architectural wonder of the Great Court. Free gallery tours are available.

The little-known **Sir John Soane's Museum** (☎ 7405 2107; *13 Lincoln's Inn Fields WC2; tube Holborn; open 10am-5pm Tues-Sat*) is a gem. The home of Sir John Soane, an architect by trade, is now an amazing and bizarre collection of antiquities, preserved in

pretty much the same state they were on Soane's death in 1837.

The **Imperial War Museum** (☎ 7416 5320; *Lambeth Rd SE1; tube Lambeth North; open 10am-6pm daily*) is both thought-provoking and moving; the Holocaust Exhibition is especially recommended.

The **Victoria & Albert Museum** (☎ 0870 442 0808; *Cromwell Rd SW7; tube South Kensington; open 10am-5.45pm daily*) has the world's greatest collection of decorative arts dating from 3000 BC to the present day. It also has the best of the museums' cafés.

The **Science Museum** (☎ 0870 870 4868; *Exhibition Rd SW7; tube South Kensington; open 10am-6pm daily*) is ideal for kids, with plenty of interactive, hands-on displays. The post office in the entrance hall is very handy.

A good all-round package, the **Natural History Museum** (☎ 7942 5000; *Cromwell Rd SW7; tube South Kensington; open 10am-5.30pm Mon-Sat, 11am-5.30pm Sun*) consists of a striking facade and interesting galleries. The Darwin Centre, with plant and animal specimens collected by Captain James Cook, is a highlight.

Galleries Visits to the National and Tate Modern galleries are musts, but there are also likely to be interesting exhibitions at the **Hayward Gallery** (☎ 7960 4242; *South Bank Centre, Belvedere Rd SE1; tube Waterloo; adult/concession/child £7/5/free; open 10am-6pm daily*). The innovative **Institute for Contemporary Arts** (ICA; ☎ 7930 3647; *Nash House, The Mall SW1; tube Piccadilly Circus; bar open noon-1am Tues-Sat, noon-10.30pm Mon, noon-11pm Sun*) and the **Royal Academy of Arts** (☎ 7300 5760; *Burlington House, Piccadilly, W1; tube Piccadilly Circus; open 10am-6pm Thur-Sat, 10am-10pm Fri*), both of which have varying admission prices, depending on the exhibition you wish to see, are among many others. Check *Time Out* for current exhibitions.

The **Photographers' Gallery** (☎ 7831 1772; *5 & 8 Great Newport St WC2; tube Leicester Square; admission free; open 11am-6pm Mon-Sat, noon-6pm Sun*) has some amusing, thought-provoking photographs among its innovative collection.

The **National Gallery** (☎ 7747 2885; *Trafalgar Square WC2; tube Charing Cross; admission free; open 10am-6pm daily, to 9pm Wed*) houses 2300 masterpieces from some

CENTRAL WEST LONDON

CENTRAL WEST LONDON

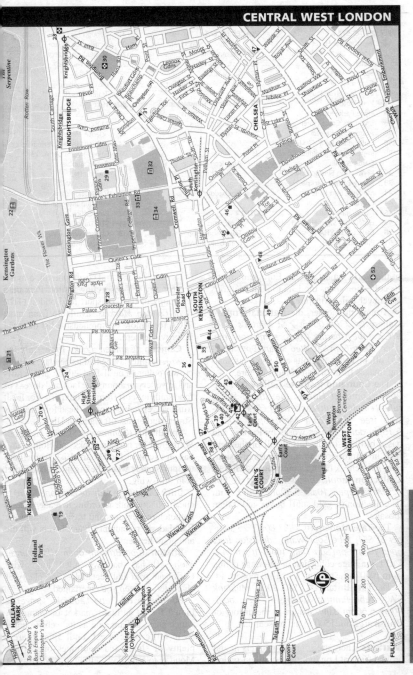

CENTRAL WEST LONDON

PLACES TO STAY	PLACES TO EAT	
6 Westbourne Hotel	2 Sausage & Mash Café;	17 London Flight Centre
8 Norfolk Court & St David's	Makan Café	21 Kensington Palace
Hotel	3 Café Grove	22 Serpentine Gallery
9 Springfield Hotel	7 Satay House	23 Harvey Nichols;
10 Cardiff Hotel	11 Niki Taverna; Laundrette	Fifth Floor
12 Glendale Hyde Park Hotel	House	25 easyEverything
13 Kent Hotel	18 Costas Fish Restaurant	26 Trailfinders (Branch)
14 Hyde Park Hostel	20 Kandy Tea Rooms	30 Harrods
15 Inverness Court Hotel	24 Arcadia; Bellinis	32 Victoria & Albert
16 Abbey Court Hotel	27 Phoenicia	Museum
19 Holland House YHA Hostel	28 Pasha	33 Science Museum
29 Imperial College Prince's	31 Veg Veg	34 Natural History Museum
Gardens Hall	39 American Diner	36 Sainsbury's Supermarket
35 Kensington Europe Hotel	47 Chelsea Kitchen	37 Bobo's Bubbles
38 Barmy Badger Backpackers	48 Lundum's	Laundrette
43 Merlyn Court Hotel	52 Troubadour	40 Trekmate; Wellbeing
44 Curzon House Hotel		Vaccination Clinic
46 Five Sumner Place	OTHER	41 Callshop International
49 Hotel 167; Swiss House Hotel	1 Subterania	42 Post Office
50 Earl's Court YHA Hostel	4 Travel Bookshop	45 STA Travel
51 Philbeach Hotel	5 Portobello Rd Market	53 Chelsea &
		Westminster Hospital

of the world's most prolific European artists. Its collection spans the 13th to 20th centuries and never fails to inspire.

Around the corner, the **National Portrait Gallery** (☎ 7306 0055; 2 St Martin's Place WC2; tube Charing Cross; admission free; open 10am-6pm Sat-Wed, 10am-9pm Thur-Fri) offers Tudor portraits and some fascinating images from British popular culture.

The **Courtauld Institute Gallery** (☎ 7848 2546; Somerset House, the Strand WC2; tube Temple; adult/concession £5/4, admission free 10am-2pm Mon; open 10am-5.15pm daily) houses works by Rubens and has a brilliant room stuffed full of the very best in impressionism and postimpressionism. Also check out the neighbouring **Gilbert Collection** (adult/concession/child £6.50/4.50/free; open 10am-5.30pm daily), with its collection of gold snuff boxes and Italian mosaics.

The **Tate Modern** (☎ 7887 8000; 25 Sumner St SE1; tube Southwark; admission free; open 10am-6pm Sun-Thur, 10am-10pm Fri & Sat) has a huge collection of offerings dating from 1900 to the present. It's called modern art.

The **Tate Britain** (☎ 7887 8000; Millbank SW1; tube Pimlico; admission free; open 10am-5.50pm daily) majors in the history of British art from 1500 to the present day.

Markets There are some 42 markets in and around Central London, representing London

at its most diverse and cosmopolitan; a must-see for any self-respecting visitor. Pick up a free copy of the Transport for London (TfL) *Real London Markets*, available from most TICs, for a more comprehensive list than can be provided here.

Camden (Camden Lock; tube Camden Town), despite having had its heyday, is still a crowd puller. You'll find ethnic arts, crafts and jewellery in among the tack and dozens of food stalls to scoff from at your peril. For fresh fruit and vegetable bargains head for Inverness Street Market just off Camden High St.

Spitalfields (Commercial St; tube Liverpool St) is great for bargain books and clothes, and has an excellent food court. Visit from 10am to 3pm Sunday when the organic food market is in full swing.

Brick Lane (tube Aldgate East; open Sun) is cheap, chaotic and, according to readers, a real hotpotch of treasures and trash. In among the Bangladeshi restaurants, bagel lovers will die and go to heaven.

Brixton (tube Brixton; open 10am-sunset Mon-Sat) has barrows piled high with Caribbean fruit and vegetables, and plenty of characters to keep you entertained.

Portobello Rd (tube Ladbroke Grove) is famed for its antiques market on Saturday, which starts at 8am, and as its website notes 'is in full cardiac arrest' until 5pm. There's plenty of shops and boutiques open from Monday to Saturday, selling a good array of antique jewellery as well as cheap, second-hand clothes.

Other Attractions All visitors, but especially travellers on a tight budget, should make the most of London's glorious parks. A long walk starting at St James's, and continuing through parks Green, Hyde, Kensington, Holland and Regent's will banish any urban blues.

Hyde Park is central London's largest park. Visit the weird yet wonderful **Serpentine Gallery** (☎ 7298 1515; admission free; open 10am-6pm daily), row a boat on the Serpentine, go **horse riding** (☎ 7723 2813), take a dip in the outdoor swimming pool, or heckle the soapbox orators on Sunday at Speakers' Corner (near Marble Arch).

Kensington Palace (☎ 7937 9561; Kensington Gardens W8; tube High St Kensington; State Apartments adult/concession/child/ family £10/7.50/6.50/30; open 10am-5pm daily, Mar-end Oct, to 4pm in winter) was home to the late Princess Diana. Afternoon tea in the **Orangery** is served from 3pm to 6pm and costs from £7.95.

Regent's Park has an **Open Air Theatre** (☎ 7486 2431; open May-Sept) where you can enjoy some interesting interpretations of Shakespeare.

Kew Gardens (☎ 8940 1171; Richmond; tube Kew Gardens; adult/concession/child £6.50/4.50/free), the Royal Botanic Gardens, are a haven of tranquillity amid the urban sprawl. As an alternative to the tube, ferries sail from Westminster Pier from 10.15am (April to October). They take 1¾ hours and 50 one-way/return costs £10.50/16.

Hampton Court Palace (☎ 8781 9500; palace & grounds adult/concession/child/ family £11/8.75/7.25/33, maze only £3; open 10.15am-5.15pm Mon, 9.30am-5.15pm Tues-Sun, to 3.45pm in winter) is Britain's grandest Tudor house. Transformed by Cardinal Wolsey in 1514 and 'adopted' by Henry VIII, it's a beautiful mix of architectural styles from Henry's splendid Great Hall to the State Apartments built by Wren for King William III and Queen Mary II. There are trains every half-hour from Waterloo (£4.70 return), or you can catch a ferry from Westminster Pier. Ferries sail from April to late-September at 10.30am, 11.15am, noon and hourly until 5pm; they take 3½ hours and one way/return costs £12/18.

Tourist Traps London's alternative attractions are long on commercialism and short on culture.

Madame Tussaud's (☎ 0870 400 3000; Marylebone Rd; tube Baker St; admission £12, with London Planetarium adult/ concession/child £14.95/11.70/10.50; for queue-jumping tickets add £2; open from 9.30am) is eminently tacky and permanently crowded; proof that people really, really want to see wax versions of the rich and famous. The queues are horrendous.

Harrods (☎ 7730 1234; 87 Brompton Rd SW1; tube Knightsbridge; open 10am-7pm Mon-Sat) is always busy and will either be your idea of heaven or your living hell. Full of its own importance, it has rules aplenty and five floors of expensive, over-hyped luxuries.

Organised Tours
The **Original Tour London Sightseeing** (☎ 8877 1722) and the **Big Bus Company** (☎ 7233 9533) offer tours of the main sights on double-decker buses that allow you either to go straight round without getting off or to hop-on and hop-off along the way. They're all expensive (around £15) and probably worth considering if you're only going to be in London for a day or two. Most companies can sell you advance tickets to the biggest attractions to save wasting time in queues.

Convenient starting points are in Trafalgar Square in front of the National Gallery and at Marble Arch near Speaker's Corner.

The **Original London Walks** (☎ 7624 3978) offers a range of guided, themed walking tours around the capital that are informative and entertaining. Walks usually last around two hours and cost £5.

Places to Stay
The price of accommodation in London never fails to shock and the cost quickly eats into any budget. To make the most of the cheaper offerings it's wise to book a night or two's accommodation in advance, especially in summer. The official TICs at the airports can arrange last-minute bookings. You can also phone the London Tourist Board's **Acommodation Line** (☎ 7932 2020), or use the private services at Victoria; both services charge £5. It's cheaper to search for accommodation yourself and phone or email hotels direct.

YHA/HI Hostels There are seven hostels in central London that are affiliated with Hostelling International (HI), known as Youth Hostels Association (YHA) in Britain.

Central London's hostels get very crowded in summer. They all take advance bookings by phone (if you pay by Visa or MasterCard), and once you're on the hostelling trail you can use the YHA's free Book A Bed Ahead scheme to book your next hostel bed. They do hold some beds for those who wander in on the day, but come early and be prepared to queue. All offer 24-hour access and some have a *bureau de change* and Internet access. Most have facilities for self-catering and some offer cheap meals.

City of London (☎ 7236 4965, fax 7236 7681; e city@yha.org.uk; 36 Carter Lane EC4; tube St Paul's; B&B adult/child from £24/20) was the old choir-school for nearby St Paul's Cathedral and is an excellent hostel (193 beds). Rooms are mainly four to eight beds, though there are a few singles and twins. There's a licensed cafeteria but no kitchen. Remember, this part of town is pretty quiet outside working hours.

Earl's Court (☎ 7373 7083, fax 7835 2034; e earlscourt@yha.org.uk; 38 Bolton Gardens SW5; tube Earl's Court; adult/child £19/16.75) hostel (159 beds) is a Victorian town house and, like the area it occupies, is shabby but lively. Rooms are mainly six- to 10-bed dorms with communal showers. There's a café, kitchen facilities, foreign exchange and a small garden courtyard for summer barbecues.

Hampstead Heath (☎ 8458 9054, fax 8209 0546; e hampstead@yha.org.uk; 4 Wellgarth Rd NW11; tube Golders Green; B&B adult/child £20.40/18) is a 199-bed hostel situated in a beautiful leafy suburb, if a little isolated. The dormitories are comfortable and each room has a washbasin, some overlooking the pretty garden. There's a licensed café and kitchen.

Holland House (☎ 7937 0748, fax 7376 0667; e hollandhouse@yha.org.uk; Holland Walk, Kensington W8; tube High Street Kensington; B&B adult/child £21/18.75) hostel (201 beds) is built into the Jacobean wing of Holland House in the middle of Holland Park. The location is gorgeous, but care is needed after dark when the park gates shut and access is via a poorly lit side path. The dorms are comfortable and there is a café and kitchen.

Oxford St (☎ 7734 1618, fax 7734 1657; 14 Noel St W1; tube Oxford Circus or Tottenham Court Rd; adult/child in 3- or 4-bed room £22/17.25, in twin room £24) is the most central of the hostels and has 75 beds. While it's clean, its office-block appearance makes it feel cramped and you can kiss goodbye to a good night's sleep. No meals are served but there's a kitchen and you can buy a packed breakfast for £3.40. Laundry and locker facilities are also available.

Rotherhithe (☎ 7232 2114, fax 7237 2919; e rotherhithe@yha.org.uk; 20 Salter Rd SE16; tube Rotherhithe; B&B adult/child £24/20) has 320 beds and is modern and functional. It's right by the River Thames and recommended, but the location is a bit quiet. Most rooms have four or six beds, though there are some doubles; all have a bathroom. There's a bar with a pool table, restaurant, kitchen and laundry.

St Pancras (☎ 7388 9998, fax 7388 6766; e stpancras@yha.org.uk; 79-81 Euston Rd NW1; tube King's Cross St Pancras; B&B adult/child £24/20) is central and although modern, also retains an office-block feel. The area isn't great, but the hostel (152 beds) is ideal for King's Cross station.

Independent Hostels London's independent hostels tend to be more relaxed and cheaper than the YHA's, though you'll have to do a bit of searching for something approaching decent. Expect to pay a minimum of £10 per night in a basic bunk-bedded dormitory, but remember that some don't accept credit cards. Most should have a kitchen, lounge, laundry facilities and if you're lucky, secure lockers (bring your own padlock).

Ashlee House (☎ 7833 9400, fax 7833 9677; e info@ashleehouse.co.uk; 261-265 Gray's Inn Rd WC1; tube King's Cross St Pancras; B&B 4- to 16-bed rooms £15-19, bunk-bed twins £24) has an excellent position next to King's Cross station and is clean and well maintained. Dorm rooms feel cramped, but facilities include laundry and a kitchen, and there's a supermarket within walking distance.

Barmy Badger Backpackers (☎/fax 7370 5213; e barmybadger@hotmail.com; 17 Longridge Rd SW5; tube Earl's Court; B&B dorm beds from £15, twins £17 per person) has a variety of dorms; four-bed ones are en suite. A large kitchen leads to a small courtyard area that catches the sun (when it's shining). Laundry facilities and safety deposit are available.

Curzon House Hotel *(☎ 7581 2116, fax 7835 1319; e info@curzonhousehotel.co.uk; 58 Courtfield Gardens SW5; tube Gloucester Road; B&B 4-/8-bed dorms £18/16, singles/ doubles without bath per person £35/21)* is an excellent find in one of the better parts of Earl's Court. The staff are some of the friendliest you'll meet, and there's a kitchen and cable-TV room on offer.

The Generator *(☎ 7388 7666, fax 7388 7644; e info@the-generator.co.uk; Compton Place, off 37 Tavistock Place WC1; tube Russell Square; B&B 7- to 8-bed dorms £19-21.50, 3- to 6-bed dorms £20-22.50, singles £42, twins £26.50 per person)* can be summed up in one word – loud! It's fun, funky and extremely sociable, and has to be seen to be believed (particularly the decor). Excellent facilities and a bar open until 2am make this immensely popular, so booking's advised.

Hyde Park Inn *(☎ 7229 0000; 48-50 Inverness Terrace W2; tube Queensway; B&B 10-bed dorm £10, singles £28)* is situated in what seems to be hostel central, with a variety of different-sized dorms. The staff are friendly, the place is relaxed and there's a games and pool room, laundry and sofa in the kitchen for the ultimate in laid-back style.

International Students House *(☎ 7631 8310, fax 7631 8315; e accom@ish.org.uk; 229 Great Portland St W1; tube Great Portland St; 6- to 8-bed room without breakfast £11.99, singles/twins without bath but £2 breakfast allowance £31/25; open year-round)* has enamoured readers and has a residential-college feel to it. The single and twin rooms are ordinary but clean, and there's a friendly, relaxed atmosphere.

Pickwick Hall *(☎ 7323 4958; 7 Bedford Place WC1; tube Russell Square; dorm beds £15, doubles £20)* is a stone's throw from the British Museum and offers basic, good-value accommodation. There's a kitchen, laundry and TV lounge.

St Christopher's Inn *(☎ 7407 1856, fax 7403 7715; e bookings@st-christophers.co .uk; 13-15 Shepherd's Bush Green W12; tube Shepherd's Bush; 8-/6-/4-bed dorm £10/17/ 18.50, twin £23)* is lively to say the least, with a bar offering regular entertainment and drinks promotions. There are showers on every floor, laundry and Internet access.

For a rooftop hot tub and sauna, head for **The Village** *(☎ 7407 1856; 163 Borough High St; tube London Bridge)*. We kid you not.

Victoria Hotel *(☎ 7834 3077, fax 7932 0693; e astorvictoria@aol.com; 71 Belgrave Rd SW1; tube Victoria; dorm beds from £15)* is the cleanest and nicest of Astor's hostels, the wooden interior giving it a modern, clean feel. The wooden benches in the eating/cable-TV area are a bit school hallish, but the dorms are comfortable, mixed and have a sink.

Student Accommodation University halls of residence are let to nonstudents during the holidays, usually from the end of June to mid-September and sometimes over the Easter break. They're a bit more expensive than hostels, but you usually get a single room (there are a few doubles) with shared facilities, plus breakfast.

The **London School of Economics and Political Science** *(☎ 7955 7531; Room B508, Page Building, Houghton St, London WC2A 2AE)* lets seven of its halls in summer and a few during Easter. The convenient options are:

Bankside House *(☎ 7633 9877, fax 7574 6730; 24 Sumner St SE1; tube Blackfriars; B&B singles £30, en suite singles/twins/quads £43/58/88)* is only open during the summer months but has an enviable location near the Globe Theatre and Tate Modern. There's a laundry and bar.

Carr-Saunders Hall *(☎ 7580 6338, fax 7580 4718; 18-24 Fitzroy St W1; tube Warren St; B&B singles/twins £27/45)* is in a quiet location and don't be fooled by the dodgy exterior. There's kitchens on each floor, a basement bar, and pool and table tennis tables.

Imperial College of Science, Technology & Medicine *(☎ 7594 9507, fax 7594 9504; e accommodationlink@ic.ac.uk; Watts Way, Prince's Gardens SW7; tube South Kensington; B&B singles/twins without bath £39.50/59; open Easter & July-late Sept)* is huge and, two minutes from some of London's greatest museums – right in the centre of the action.

John Adams Hall *(☎ 7387 4086, fax 7383 0164; e jah@ioe.ac.uk; 15-23 Endsleigh St WC1; tube Euston; singles/doubles from £27/ 48; open Easter & July-Sept)*, belonging to the Institute of Education, is quite a grand residence occupying a row of Georgian houses. Rates vary depending on the time of year.

YMCAs For a list of all YMCA hostels in the Greater London area contact **YMCA England** *(☎ 8520 5599; 640 Forest Rd, London E17 3DZ)*.

BRITAIN

Barbican YMCA (☎ 7628 0697, fax 7638 2420; e Barbicanymca@aol.com; 2 Fann St EC2; tube Barbican; B&B singles/doubles £27.30/42) has 240 beds and is good value for the area.

Indian Student YMCA (☎ 7387 0411, fax 7383 4735; e indianymca@aol.com; 41 Fitzroy Square W1; tube Warren St; B&B dorm bed £20; singles/doubles with shared facilities £34/46) is quiet, but has clean, good-sized rooms, a laundry and sports facilities. The food has been commended by readers.

B&Bs & Hotels Once you've exhausted the hostels, YMCAs and University halls, searching for decent, cheap accommodation in London is like a quest for the holy grail. If you find anything for a basic single/double below £30/50 and with private bathroom below £40/60, you will have done well – this is 'budget' London! For some good deals, you might want to check out w www.lastminute.com. Although the best offers are for the more expensive hotels you can pick up mid-range rooms at up to 50% off. Have a credit card handy.

Once you do find somewhere suitable, don't be afraid to ask for the 'best' price, particularly if you are staying out of high season or for more than a couple of nights. In July, August and September prices can jump by 25% or more, and it's advisable to book ahead. Like hostels, some of the cheaper places either add a surcharge for credit card use or won't accept them at all.

The following listings are arranged by neighbourhood and listed in order of price.

Pimlico & Victoria Victoria may not be the most attractive part of London, but the budget hotels are better value than those in Earl's Court. Pimlico is more residential though convenient for the Tate Britain gallery at Millbank.

Brindle House Hotel (☎ 7828 0057, fax 7931 8805; 1 Warwick Place North SW1; tube Victoria; B&B singles without bath £35-45, doubles with/without bath £48/44, triples £69) is cheap for the area and popular with travellers. The rooms are small but clean, and the staff are helpful.

Luna-Simone Hotel (☎ 7834 5897, fax 7828 2474; 47 Belgrave Rd SW1; tube Victoria; B&B singles/doubles without bath from £40/50, doubles with bath £55-70), in a road stuffed full of varying quality B&Bs, is a shining example of good value simply done. The

rooms are bright, airy and spotlessly clean. Highly recommended.

James House and **Cartref House** (☎ 7730 6176, fax 7730 7637; e jandchouse@cs.com; 108 & 139 Ebury Street SW1; tube Victoria; B&B singles/doubles £52/70, with bath £62/85) are situated across the street from each other and are run by a very friendly couple with a good knowledge of Victoria. The rooms are simple but clean.

Victor Hotel (☎ 7592 958, fax 7592 9854; 51 Belgrave Rd SW1; tube Victoria; B&B en suite singles £50-70, doubles £70-90) makes a good, if slightly more pricey, alternative to the Luna-Simone. It's modern, clean and has reasonably sized rooms. Breakfast is noisily prepared downstairs so avoid rooms near the kitchen if you want a lie in.

Windermere Hotel (☎ 7834 5163, fax 7630 8831; e windermere@compuserve .com; 142-144 Warwick Way SW1; tube Victoria; B&B singles without bath £69, singles/doubles with shower from £84/104) has a number of small but individually designed rooms in a sparkling-white mid-Victorian town house. Ask about special offers.

Victoria Park Plaza (☎ 7666 9000; e info@vpp-sw1.com; 239 Vauxhall Bridge Rd SW1; singles/doubles from £135) has a range of stylish, modern double or twin rooms and doesn't charge extra for single occupancy. There's a gym and it's unsurprisingly popular with business travellers.

Rubens at the Palace (☎ 7834 6600, fax 7233 6037; e bookrb@rchmail.com; 39 Buckingham Palace Rd SW1; tube Victoria; singles/doubles from £170/200) has a brilliant position overlooking the walls of the Royal Mews. Rates don't include breakfast. It's popular with well-heeled overseas visitors who'll also like the super-expensive, extremely classy hotel **41** (☎ 7300 0041) next door.

The West End & Covent Garden Here you're in the centre of the action, but you pay for the convenience.

Regent Palace Hotel (☎ 0870 400 8703, fax 7734 6435; Piccadilly Circus, W1; tube Piccadilly Circus; singles/doubles £64/69 Sun-Thur, weekends £75/89) is ripe for a makeover but ideal for those arriving from Heathrow on the tube. This enormous hotel has basic rooms and rates don't include breakfast.

Hazlitt's (☎ 7434 1771, fax 7439 1524; 6 Frith St W1; tube Tottenham Court Rd;

singles/doubles from £175/195) was built in 1718 and comprises three original Georgian houses. The exquisite, meticulous attention to detail in each of its 23 individually designed rooms is commendable, and you won't find stuffy pretension. Booking is advisable.

St Martins Lane (☎ 7300 5500, fax 7300 5501; 45 St Martin's Lane WC2; tube Leicester Square; doubles from £235) is a late '90s minimalist designer hotel, so cool it doesn't even put its name on display. Every room has floor-to-ceiling windows and a host of snazzy features. It's ultra cool, ultra modern, ultra chic – check out the toilets.

The Savoy (☎ 7950 5492, fax 7950 5482; e reservations@the-savoy.co.uk; Strand WC2; tube Charing Cross; singles/doubles from £290/390) is an English institution still going strong, with rooms offering great views of the Thames (at a price). It stands on the site of the old Savoy Palace, which was burned down during the Peasants' Revolt of 1381.

Bloomsbury & Fitzrovia Bloomsbury is an altogether more sedate, refined district at half the price of the West End. There are lots of places on Gower and North Gower Sts.

La Brasserie Town House (☎ 7636 2731, fax 7580 1028; e Labrasserietownhouse@hot mail.com; 24 Coptic St WC1; tube Tottenham Court Rd; B&B singles/doubles £32/60) is strictly a good French restaurant just off a rather busy street, but its four tidy, stylish rooms and one studio are excellent value.

Hotel Cavendish (☎ 7636 9079, fax 7580 3609; 75 Gower St WC1; tube Goodge Street; B&B singles/doubles without bath £38/48, en suite £45/66) is extremely friendly and the rooms are simple, but clean. The shaded, walled garden makes a pleasant spot for catching some rays.

Arran House Hotel (☎ 7636 2186, fax 7436 5328; e arran@dircon.co.uk; 77-79 Gower St WC1; tube Goodge Street; B&B singles without bath £45, en suite £55, doubles £55-75, triples £73-93) grabs attention with its family-run atmosphere, scrupulous attention to detail and peaceful summer rose garden. The windows are sound-proofed and laundry facilities are also available. Definitely recommended.

Euro Hotel (☎ 7387 4321, fax 7383 5044; e reception@eurohotel.co.uk; 53 Cartwright Gardens WC1; B&B singles/doubles without bath £49/69, with bath £70/89) has a brilliant

position overlooking a tennis court in a leafy crescent. The rooms, decked out with pine furniture, are comfortable if a bit flowery. If it's full, try the slightly more expensive **George Hotel** (☎ 7387 8777; 58-60 Cartwright Gardens WC1) nearby.

Academy Hotel (☎ 7631 4115, fax 7636 3442; 21 Gower St WC1; tube Goodge Street; B&B singles £136, doubles £159-189) is in a rather busy street, although double glazing keeps the noise down. Its 49 individually styled rooms are fresh and pretty, with all the trappings you'd expect at this price.

Chelsea, South Kensington & Earl's Court
Chelsea and South Kensington are close to museums and restaurants, but the cheapest accommodation is in Earl's Court. If you're on a budget, stick to the hostels – the lower end of Earl's Court's hotel market is appalling.

Merlyn Court Hotel (☎ 7370 1640, fax 7370 4986; 2 Barkston Gardens SW5; tube Earl's Court; B&B singles/doubles without bath £35/55, with bath £45/70, triples with/ without bath £75/65) is cheap accommodation, expertly done. It's ideally placed for the tube and the rooms are small but clean. There's a 24-hour laundry service and you'll receive a friendly welcome.

Philbeach Hotel (☎ 7373 1244, fax 7244 0149; 30-31 Philbeach Gardens SW5; tube Earl's Court; B&B singles/doubles without bath £55/70) is a gay-friendly hotel set in the middle of a sweeping crescent. Its 35 rooms are small, but clean and arty, and the onsite bar and restaurant are renowned.

Swiss House Hotel (☎ 7373 2769, fax 7373 4983; e recap@swiss-hh.demon.co.uk; 171 Old Brompton Rd SW5; tube Gloucester Rd; B&B singles £51-89/doubles £71-104) has a modern, relaxed feel with small singles/ doubles offering a variety of private bathroom facilities. Laminated floors and uplighters provide an uncluttered, contemporary edge.

Hotel 167 (☎ 7373 0672, fax 7373 3360; 167 Old Brompton Rd SW5; tube Gloucester Road; B&B singles from £72, doubles £90-99) is small and stylish with beautiful mosaic tiling in the entrance. All rooms have been individually styled and all have a private bathroom.

Five Sumner Place (☎ 7584 7586, fax 7823 9962; e reservations@sumnerplace.com; 5 Sumner Place SW7; tube South Kensington; B&B singles/doubles from £85/130) is part of an impressive, white Victorian terrace on a quiet leafy road. It has 13 traditionally decorated, well-equipped rooms, and there's an attractive, airy breakfast conservatory.

Kensington Europe Hotel (☎ 7598 7979, fax 7598 7981; e book@kensingtoneurope.co .uk; 131-137 Cromwell Rd SW7; tube Gloucester Rd; singles/doubles from £90/115) has 97 good-sized rooms combining contemporary decor with Victorian period features. Purple predominates in the rooms' colour scheme; the stylish approach will appeal to the design-conscious.

Bayswater, Paddington & Notting Hill

This area is stuffed full of hotels to suit every budget and it's not surprising that it's a tourist hub.

Kent Hotel (☎ 402 0254, fax 402 2468; e kenthotel@btinternet.com; 41 Lancaster Gate W2; tube Lancaster Gate; B&B singles without bath £30, en suite singles/doubles £45/60) has 20 simple, clean and functional rooms in a prime location. You'll get plenty of exercise if your room's on the top floor – there's no lift.

Glendale Hyde Park Hotel (☎ 7706 4441, fax 7479 9273; e booking@ghphotel.com; 8 Devonshire Terrace W2; tube Lancaster Gate; en suite singles/doubles £35/45) offers great facilities behind an unassuming exterior. Despite flowery duvets, all 20 rooms have satellite TV, phone and minibar. With free Internet access, this is excellent value.

Norfolk Court & St David's Hotel (☎ 7723 4963, fax 7402 9061; 16-20 Norfolk Square W2; tube Paddington; B&B singles/ doubles without bath £39/59, en suite singles/doubles £49/69) may possibly be the friendliest hotel in London with huge, tasty breakfasts. The rooms are clean and comfortable with some 'interesting' colour schemes.

Cardiff Hotel (☎ 7723 9068, fax 7402 2342; e stay@cardiff-hotel.com; 5-9 Norfolk Square W2; tube Paddington; B&B singles £45-55, doubles £79) is a family-run hotel and its 60 rooms are a good size and neatly decorated. The staff are friendly.

Springfield Hotel (☎ 7723 9898, fax 7723 0874; e info@springfieldhotellondon.co.uk; 154 Sussex Gardens W2; tube Paddington; B&B en suite singles/doubles £50/70) is one of a cluster of hotels separated by a major traffic artery. Despite the inevitable noise, the modern, fresh decor and good room-size give this the edge.

Inverness Court Hotel (☎ 7229 1444, fax 7706 4240; Inverness Terrace W2; tube Queensway; B&B singles/doubles £86/110) is all panelled walls, stained glass and open fires, but only in the entrance hall. This building was reputedly commissioned by Edward VII for his mistress, Lillie Langtry, and it's a shame the grandeur and charm aren't replicated in the majority of the 183 rooms.

Abbey Court (☎ 7221 7518, fax 7792 0858; e info@abbeycourthotel.co.uk; 20 Pembridge Gardens W2; tube Notting Hill Gate; B&B en suite singles/doubles from £105/155) has 22 traditionally decorated rooms, some with Jaccuzi jet baths and four-poster beds. It's elegant and unpretentious and deserving of its many recommendations.

Westbourne Hotel (☎ 7243 6008, fax 7229 7201; e wh@zoohotels.com; 165 Westbourne Grove W1; tube Bayswater; B&B en suite doubles £175-255) bills itself as an 'urban inn' and while a tad overpriced, is a mecca for modern art. Think stylish, almost retro chic, and mull over the prospect of sleeping with the works of Tate Modern–artist Sarah Lucas.

Rental Prices for rental accommodation are high and standards are low. At the bottom end of the market are bedsits, usually with a shared bathroom and kitchen, although some have basic cooking facilities. Expect to pay £70 to £150 per week. The next step up is a studio, normally with a separate bathroom and kitchen for between £90 and £200. One-bedroom flats range from around £120 to £250. Shared houses and flats are the best value, with a bedroom for between £60 and £90 plus bills. Most landlords demand a security deposit (normally one month's rent) plus a month's rent in advance.

For help in finding a flat, take a mate along to viewings and avoid expensive agency fees by sticking to message boards, classifieds and word-of-mouth. Rooms and flats are advertised in *Loot* (£1.40), *Evening Standard* (30p), *TNT* and *Time Out*, but rooms are also posted at w www.thegumtree.com, a site friendly to Aussies, Kiwis and South-Africans. Gay and lesbians could try w www.outlet.co.uk.

Places to Eat

British food has long surpassed its dire reputation and London is no exception. Although kebabs and curries remain a national institution, you'll find food from every corner of the globe – there isn't a country or ethnic group that isn't represented in some way. It all amounts to a feasting opportunity of gastronomic proportions and even the smallest budget will be able to take advantage of lunchtime offers and set dinner menus from a growing collection of good restaurants.

The listings here are in order of price and just scratch the surface. You'll find many other good places near the choices we've listed. If you're self-catering, supermarkets and grocery stores are common everywhere.

Westminster & Pimlico Heavy on hotels, light on restaurants – this part of town is for recliners rather than diners.

UNo 1 (☎ 7834 1001; 1 Denbigh St SW1; tube Victoria) is upmarket dining at mid-range prices. The well-designed, modern interior offers a piece of Italian chic in the middle of suburbia and the food isn't bad either. Pizzas and pastas cost from £5.90 to £11.

Marmaris (☎ 7828 5940; 45 Warwick St SW1; tube Victoria) does excellent deluxe kebabs from £6.75 and Turkish meze from £14 to £17.50 (for a minimum of two). It also has a takeaway next door if you're pressed for time.

Footstool (☎ 7222 2779; St John's, Smith Square SW1; tube Westminster; buffet from £3.50, lunch mains £9.95-11.95, 2-course set dinners £10.95) is in the crypt of an 18th-century baroque church (now a concert hall) and is a favoured lunchtime retreat of MPs. It offers a buffet with soups and a more formal restaurant for à la carte lunches and set dinners on concert evenings.

Ebury Wine Bar & Restaurant (☎ 7730 5447; 139 Ebury St SW1; tube Victoria; meals £15-20) is a favourite with the gastro-media and it's easy to see why. The cosy surroundings prevent pretension and the gourmet food and exotic wines are excellent.

The West End: Piccadilly, Soho & Chinatown These days Soho is London's gastronomic centralis. You'll find plenty of choice along Old Compton and Dean Sts. Gerrard and Lisle Sts form London's Chinatown and offer set-menu bargains.

Pollo (☎ 7734 5917; 20 Old Compton St W1; tube Leicester Square; all dishes under £5) has a massive selection of generous and filling pasta dishes – they're a bargain at £3.

It's intimate, noisy and usually crowded, but brilliant value for money.

Stockpot (☎ 7287 1066; 18 Old Compton St W1; tube Leicester Square; set menu £4.20) is more country kitchen than Italian chic, but is good value with pasta dishes from £3.50.

Garden Café (☎ 7494 0044; 4 Newburgh St W1; tube Oxford Circus) is a yellow-and-pink lunch spot offering simple fare just off famous Carnaby St. Jacket potatoes are a reasonable £3.60, but there's plenty of inexpensive sandwiches and salads on offer too.

Yee Tung Chinese Restaurant (☎ 7437 3870; 20 Gerrard St W1; tube Leicester Square; buffets from £4.90-7.90) is one of many stuff-your-face hang-outs in Chinatown, and despite the dodgy decor does surprisingly edible food. Unlike its neighbours, you won't be hurried out of your seat.

Café Emm (☎ 7437 0723; 17 Frith St W1; tube Tottenham Court Rd; mains £5.50) looks like a dive from the outside but is home to some of the finest-value food in Soho. It's friendly and intimate with generous portions.

Palms of Goa (☎ 7439 3509; 4 Meard St W1; tube Leicester Square; dishes from £5.95) is on a sneaky little back street away from Soho's crowds. The restaurant isn't huge, but the Goan-inspired dishes are recommended.

Star Café (☎ 7437 8778; 22 Great Chapel St W1; tube Tottenham Court Road; open 7am-3.30pm Mon-Fri) is covered floor to ceiling in old signs and posters and is excellent for its fried breakfasts and lunchtime treats. Pasta and hot ciabatta are all around £6.25.

Soba (☎ 734 6400; 38 Poland St W1; tube Oxford Circus) is a funky, long-table, bench-seating affair with stir-fried noodles, soup and rich dishes for around £7; it attracts a mixed crowd.

Chuen Cheng Ku (☎ 7437 1398; 17 Wardour St W1; mains around £6-9, set menu £12; open 11am-midnight daily) has a massive menu and a massive (if somewhat less appealing) interior to match. Simple, Cantonese dim sum served from a trolley makes this an ideal introduction to Chinatown.

Mômo (☎ 7434 4040; 25 Heddon St W1; tube Piccadilly Circus; 4-veg dishes £6, 3-meat & 1-veg £7.50) is a Moroccan kasbah in the middle of the smog. Its adjoining tearoom has an amazing selection of herbal teas and is all cushions, low tables and hypnotic music. It's a touch of the unique that you could sit in all day.

BRITAIN

Busaba Eathai (☎ 7255 8686; 106-110 Wardour St W1; tube Tottenham Court Rd; meals around £20) is Thai with a modern twist. Large wooden tables and low-lit lanterns play home to 'great bowls of fire' that are worth the wait. No smoking and no booking mean inevitable queues.

The Criterion (☎ 7930 0488; 224 Piccadilly W1; tube Piccadilly Circus; dinners around £45 per person, 2-/3-course lunches £14.95/19) transports you to a bygone era with its stunning interior, and is where French nouvelle cuisine meets large-sized meaty portions to die for. Booking is advised.

Covent Garden & the Strand

Covent Garden is packed to the rafters with eateries, and thanks to its proximity to Theatreland has plenty of pre-theatre set-menu deals to take advantage of. The following are all accessible from Covent Garden tube station unless indicated otherwise.

Food for Thought (☎ 7836 0239; 31 Neal St WC2) is a mecca for vegetarians. It has a café-atmosphere upstairs, a restaurant-feel downstairs. Quiches and stir-fried vegetables with rice are moreish and start at around £4.

Bistro 1 (☎ 7379 7585; 33 Southampton St WC2; 2-/3-course set menu £5.90/£6.90) is intimate and does European dishes and Mediterranean specials such as vegetable moussaka expertly. Highly recommended.

Rock & Sole Plaice (☎ 7836 3785; 47 Endell St WC2; open 11.30am-10pm Mon-Sat, noon-9pm Sun) looks like a sweaty 'caff' but tastes like a million dollars. For delicious cod and chips from a British chippy institution, expect to pay £7 – divine.

Belgo Centraal (☎ 7813 2233; 50 Earlham St WC2; Beat the Clock pricing from 5pm-6.30pm) is the flagship of a Belgian moules-and-frites chain, so amusing it has to be seen to be believed. The kilogram pots of mussels (£9.95) are served by Trappist monks – you'll either love it or hate it.

Café Pacifico (☎ 7379 7728; 5 Langley St WC2; mains £9.15-13.75) has been around since the '70s and it looks as if the decor hasn't changed much. Excellent enchiladas (£9.15) washed down with a shot of tequila (£2.70 to £5.75) – perfect.

Café des Amis du Vin (☎ 7379 3444; 11-14 Hanover Place WC2; 2-/3-course set lunches £12.50/15) is a classy French brasserie which doesn't have the pretence of the 'luvvie' Theatreland. Ideal for pre- or post-theatre meals, the grilled goats cheese with black-olive focaccia (£7.50) is succulent.

Simpson's-in-the-Strand (☎ 7836 9112; 100 Strand WC2; mains £16-19.50) has been dishing up large joints of meat on a silver wagon since 1848 (when it was called Simpson's Grand Divan and Tavern). The Sunday roast (three courses £25, from 12.15pm to 2.30pm) comes highly recommended.

Joe Allen (☎ 7836 0651; 13 Exeter St WC2; 2-/3-course pre-theatre dinners £14/16, Sat & Sun brunch £16.50/18.50, 3-course meal £22-27) is a carnivore's heaven with a few vegie options thrown in. The pan-fried sea bass accompanied by live jazz (8pm to 11pm Sunday) in this basement setting is a must.

Rules (☎ 7379 0258; 35 Maiden Lane WC2; 2 courses from 3pm-5pm £19.95) achieves kudos as London's oldest restaurant (1798) and specialises in game from its Pennine estate. The skylights, inscribed with poetry, are fitting for a place frequented by Dickens. Booking is advised.

Bloomsbury

Though usually thought of as B&B land, Bloomsbury has a few reasonably priced restaurants and cafés.

Coffee Gallery (☎ 7436 0455; 23 Museum St WC1; tube Tottenham Court Rd; open 8.30am-6pm Mon-Fri, 11am-7pm Sat & Sun) has a daily changing menu, 90% of which is vegetarian. Pasta dishes are around £4 and salads £4.90. Art of sorts provides the decor, with the 'exhibition' changing monthly.

L'etoile Café (☎ 7387 5400; 45 Fitzroy St W1; tube Warren St; open 6am-4pm Mon-Fri) has a few seats outside but is mainly a takeaway joint. Start the day with a mean full-English breakfast (£5), or enjoy filled ciabatta and bagels (around £3).

Sardo (☎ 7387 2521; 45 Grafton Way W1; tube Warren St) is a trendy little Italian eatery serving pasta dishes from £7.95 to £10.50. It has a good range of specials including proceddu arrostiu (whole suckling pig) – so expensive the price isn't listed on the menu.

Rasa Samudra (☎ 7637 0222; 5 Charlotte St W1; tube Goodge Street; meal around £20 per person) is a bizarre but workable combination of South Indian vegetarian cuisine and fine seafood. The Crab Varuthathu (£12.50) is excellent.

South Bank Reflecting the development of the area itself, this part of town offers a mixed bag of workers' 'caffs' and upmarket refinement.

Freshly Maid Café (☎ 7928 5426; 79 Lower Marsh; tube Waterloo) is officially the fourth-cheapest café in London, and as long as you're not hoping to rest your legs, you'll get decent enough food at bargain prices (burger and chips £1.99).

Mariterra (☎ 7928 7628; 14 Gambia St SE1; tube Southwark; tapas £4-6.50) does excellent Spanish food but is overpopulated with office workers in the early evening. If you can stand the mobile-phone mania, the chorizo and meatballs are recommended.

Oxo Tower (☎ 7401 2255; Queen's Walk SE1; tube Southwark; mains £15.50-26), with its restaurant and cheaper brasserie, offers amazing views over the Thames and decent food. It's pricey, but the ambient blue-neon lighting overhead and excellent roasted sea bass are worth it.

Chelsea, South Kensington & Earl's Court All budgets are well catered for in these areas, just avoid the Sloanes.

At **Chelsea Kitchen** (☎ 7589 1330; 98 King's Rd SW3; tube Sloane Square; set meal £5.50) the decor suggests trucker's café but the food suggests you've found a bargain.

American Diner (☎ 7255 9196; 139 Earl's Court Rd SW5; tube Earl's Court; mains under £5) is a bit tacky with its US-themed decor, but you can't argue with the prices or the real ice-cream milkshakes (£2.40).

Veg Veg (☎ 7584 7007; 8 Egerton Gardens Mews SW2; tube South Kensington) is a small, stylish affair offering Szechuan vegetarian cuisine. The £4.99 all-you-can-eat lunch buffet is excellent and surprisingly filling.

Troubadour (☎ 7370 1434; 265 Old Brompton Rd SW5; tube Earl's Court; mains £7-9) is a café and music venue that's played host to Eric Clapton and the Rolling Stones. The atmosphere is still dark and moody with live music on occasions and good food every day, especially the breakfasts (£4.50).

Lundum's (☎ 7373 7774; 119 Old Brompton Rd SW7; tube Gloucester Rd; 2-/3-course menu £17.25/21.50) is a real treat if you're looking for something different. Fish and open sandwiches are this Danish restaurant's staples, but the speciality – cured duck with mashed potato (£16.50) – is a must.

Kensington & Knightsbridge These cosmopolitan 'villages' still cater for their loyal following of well-heeled foodies, but once you get off High St Kensington there's plenty of choice for all budgets.

Kandy Tea Rooms (☎ 7937 3001; 4 Holland St W8; tube High St Kensington) mixes a small, traditional English tearoom with a touch of the oriental and, bizarrely, it works. Praised by readers, afternoon tea is a snip at £6.70.

Bellini's (☎ 7937 5520; 47 Kensington Court W8; tube High Street Kensington; 2-/3-course set lunch £7.25/8.75) is a stylish blue-and-silver Italian eatery with pavement tables.

Phoenicia (☎ 7937 0120; 11-13 Abingdon Rd W8; tube High St Kensington; set menus from £16.80 minimum of 2 people) is a pricey but highly praised Lebanese place that becomes slightly more affordable at the weekends. Buffet lunches cost £12.95 (Saturday, 12.15pm to 2.30pm) and £14.95 (Sunday, 12.15pm to 3.30pm).

Pasha (☎ 7589 7969; 1 Gloucester Road SW7; tube Gloucester Rd; 2 courses from £18-25) is a romantic Moroccan dining experience in a stunning setting. It's well worth its price tag.

Notting Hill & Bayswater Notting Hill is yet another good eat-out option, with everything from cheap takeaways to good quality restaurants, some quite quirky.

Makan Café (☎ 8960 5169; 270 Portobello Rd W10; tube Ladbroke Grove; mains £5-6) has horrific luminous decor but cheap Malaysian-inspired vegetarian, meat and fish dishes. Daily specials from £3.50 to £4.

Costas (☎ 7727 4310; 18 Hillgate St W8; tube Notting Hill; open noon-2.30pm, 5.30pm-10.30pm Tues-Sat) is a down-to-earth fish and chippy with cod or rock salmon and chips at £6.50. It's ripe for a makeover, but it's still producing some of the best chips in London.

Sausage & Mash Café (☎ 8968 8898; 268 Portobello Rd W10; tube Ladbroke Grove; dishes £7), entertainingly known as 'S & M', does an upmarket version of an English favourite, and it's more appealing than it sounds. It even caters for vegetarians.

Satay House (☎ 7723 6763; 13 Sale Place W2; tube Edgware Rd; mains £5-7) is tacked onto a residential area and is one of the better Malaysian places in the area. Satay is the obvious choice at £5.20.

Café Grove (☎ 7243 1094; 253A Portobello Rd W11; tube Ladbroke Grove; open 9.30am-6pm Mon-Sat, 10am-6pm Sun) has hiked up its prices but still makes an ideal spot to watch the hustle and bustle from its brilliant terrace. Its famed huge breakfasts are now £7.50 for vegies, £8.50 for meaties.

Niki Taverna (☎ 7262 4628; 16-18 London St W2; tube Paddington; mains £7.50-10) has been recommended for its charcoal-grilled Greek cuisine and hefty meat dishes. The *afelia* (pieces of marinated pork; £7.50) is mouthwatering.

Camden Camden is better for its bars, clubs and eclectic nightlife than its eateries, but has a few tantalising options. Unless stated otherwise, our selection can be reached from Camden Town tube stop.

Fresh and Wild (☎ 7428 7575; 49 Parkway NW1) is strictly an organic health-food chain, but does a good line of light bites. Sit among the homeopathy books and enjoy shepherd's pie (£1.99) or more mysterious vegetarian options (£3.49).

Le Montmartre (☎ 7916 0653; 71 Chalk Farm Rd NW1; tube Chalk Farm; 2-/3-course set menu £4.95/6.95 to 6pm) is an intimate, attractive French bistro. The savoury crepes (£5.90) are the cheap alternative at dinner, but the mussels (£7.90) shouldn't be missed.

Mango Rooms (☎ 7482 5065; 10 Kentish Town Rd NW1; mains around £9) is considered by many to offer the best in Caribbean cooking and so many can't be wrong. Funky background music accompanies a 'manana, manana' feel; your tastebuds will go mad for the jerk chicken.

Singapore Sling (☎ 7424 9527; 16 Inverness St NW1; meals £10-15; open 11am-midnight daily) is a restaurant and cocktail bar over four levels that's all ornate-wood decor, water features and ambient music. The food provides a taste of the Far East and its laksa (thick noodle soup) belongs in the highly recommended category.

Islington Islington is stuffed full of eateries, especially on Upper St. If you can't find what you fancy here, your tastebuds must be dead.

Afgan Kitchen (☎ 7359 8019; 35 Islington Green N1; tube Angel; mains from around £5.50) is an old favourite that has first-timers coming back for more. Bland food is spiced up and given a delicious makeover, leaving

you wondering how every other London restaurant gets away with their prices. Booking advised.

Tartuf (☎ 7288 0954; 88 Upper St N1; tube Angel) is Alsatian and proud of it. Modern, upbeat and authentic, you'll love its *tarte flambeés* (French thin-bread pizzas), either savoury (£5 to £6) or sweet (£4).

Bel Mondo (☎ 7704 0383; 47 Cross St N1; tube Angel; mains £9.90-16.90) is set away from the masses on Upper St. Despite its escalope of veal and *tartines* it's unpretentious and the fish dishes are particularly well executed.

East End If your life's in need of spicing up, Brick Lane (dubbed 'Banglatown' on account of being lined with Indian and Bangladeshi restaurants), will become your spiritual home. For those with a more cosmopolitan palette, stick to Hoxton.

Brick Lane Beigel Bake (☎ 7729 0616; 159 Brick Lane E2; tube Shoreditch; open 24hr) provides the ultimate cure for the late-night munchies. You won't find cheaper or fresher bagels anywhere else.

Bengal Cuisine (☎ 7377 8405; 12 Brick Lane E1; tube Aldgate East; mains £4.95-8.95) is praised by all who eat in her for excellent service and authentic taste. Try the Shatkora Chicken (£7.95) for a true taste of Bangladesh.

Viet Hoa (☎ 7729 8293; 70-72 Kingsland Rd E2; tube Old St; meal under £10) serves excellent and authentic Vietnamese dishes. It's always full.

Cantaloupe (☎ 7613 4411; 35 Charlotte Rd EC2; tube Old St; mains £9-13) is a bar (absinthe) and restaurant (Mediterranean fare) that's great if you can find your way to and from the toilets.

Greenwich Beautiful Greenwich is great for finding what you want, fast. Its best eateries are packed into a triangle formed by the Market, Greenwich Church St and Nelson Rd. The Cutty Sark DLR station is convenient for all the places here.

Nelson Rd has a few options that'll suit all budgets. **Bar de Musee** (☎ 8858 4710; mains £11.75-13.50) at No 17 is a sophisticated bistro, all red and arty. Next door at No 15 is **Pistachios** (☎ 8853 0602; open 8am-6pm daily), the ideal place for breakfast (around £4).

Entertainment

By day and by night, London plays host to a lively, vibrant mix of welcome distractions. It's rich in contemporary and classical music, and theatre, and is home to world-renowned venues that live up to their hype. Most charge anywhere from £5 to £15 entry. Note that the last Underground trains leave between 11.30pm and 12.30am, after which you must figure out the night-bus system or take a taxi. For all event listings, check in *Time Out*.

Pubs London is awash in pubs, all of which close at a puritanical 11pm. Unfortunately many are uninspired boozers or charmless chain outlets. However, there are still a few gems to be found.

Albert *(Victoria St SW1; tube St James's Park)* is home to the Division Bell, used to call drinking MPs back to Parliament to vote. It's a popular daytime boozer with plenty of good pub-grub on offer. The Sunday carvery (three courses, £15) is the best value.

Lamb & Flag *(Rose St WC2; tube Covent Garden)* is manic just after office hours, but is loved by all for its family-like quality. Interesting, then, that it used to be called 'The Bucket of Blood'.

Bagley's Spanish Bar *(44 Hanway St W1; tube Tottenham Court Rd)* is more pub-like than its name suggests, with an excellent jukebox and wicked staff.

Coach & Horses *(29 Greek St W1; tube Leicester Square)* is a small, busy pub with excellent beer and a regular band of satisfied customers.

The Queen's Larder *(1 Queen Square WC1; tube Russell Square)*, used by Queen Charlotte to store delicacies for George III, now offers a handy retreat, with outside benches and pub grub.

George Inn *(Talbot Yard, 77 Borough High St SE1; tube London Bridge or Borough)* is London's only surviving galleried coaching inn. It dates from 1676 and is mentioned in Charles Dickens' *Little Dorrit*. Here too is the site of the Tabard Inn where the pilgrims gathered in Chaucer's *Canterbury Tales* before setting out.

The Angel *(101 Bermondsey Wall East SE16; tube Bermondsey)* is a riverside pub dating from the 15th century (though the present building is early 17th century). This is where Captain Cook supposedly prepared for his trip to Australia.

Music & Clubs Major venues for live contemporary music include the **Brixton Academy** *(☎ 7771 2000; 211 Stockwell Rd SW9; tube Brixton)*, **Shepherds Bush Empire** *(☎ 7771 2000; Shepherds Bush Green W12; tube Shepherds Bush)* and **Wembley Arena** *(☎ 8902 0902; Empire Way, Wembley; tube Wembley Park)*.

Smaller places with a more club-like atmosphere that are worth checking out: **12 Bar Club** *(☎ 7916 6989; 22 Denmark Place WC2; tube Oxford Circus)*; **Borderline** *(☎ 7734 2095; Orange Yard, off Manette St WC2; tube Tottenham Court Rd)*; **Garage** *(☎ 7607 1818; 20-22 Highbury Corner N5; tube Highbury & Islington)*, an indie favourite; and **Subterania** *(☎ 8960 4590; 12 Acklam Rd W10; tube Ladbroke Grove)*. Ring ahead to find out which bands are playing.

If you're into DJing, check out some quality mixing at the occasionally free DJ bars. Excellent haunts include: **Bar Vinyl** *(☎ 7682 7898; 6 Inverness St N1; tube Camden Town; open 7pm-11pm Wed-Sun)* and the über-cool **Retreat** *(☎ 7704 6868; 144 Upper St N1; tube Angel; open from 8pm Mon-Sat, from 7pm Sun)*.

Some of the better club venues include: **Fabric** *(☎ 7490 0444; 77a Charterhouse St EC1; tube Farringdon)*, with its bodysonic dancefloor; the multifaceted **Fridge** *(☎ 7326 5100; Town Hall Parade SW2; tube Brixton)*; the famous **Ministry of Sound** *(☎ 7378 6528; 103 Gaunt St SE1; tube Elephant & Castle)*; **Pacha London** *(☎ 7834 4440; Terminus Place SW1; tube Victoria)* for Balearic beats; the eclectic **Scala** *(☎ 7833 2022; 278 Pentonville Rd N1; tube Kings Cross)*; **The End** *(☎ 7419 9199; 16a West Central St WC1; tube Holborn)* owned by The Shamen's Mr C; and the ever-popular gay haunt **Astoria** *(☎ 7434 9592; 157 Charing Cross Rd WC2; tube Tottenham Court Rd)*.

If you're a jazz fan, keep your eye on **Ronnie Scott's** *(☎ 7439 0747; 47 Frith St W1; tube Leicester Square)*, the **Jazz Café** *(☎ 7916 6060; 5 Parkway NW1; tube Camden Town)* and the **Pizza Express Jazz Club** *(10 Dean St W1; tube Tottenham Court Rd)*.

Theatre & Cinema Even if it's not your thing, you'll be surprised by the diversity of London's theatre and musicals scene. It's not all stuffy or over-sentimental, and it's not all avant-garde either. The South Bank's **National Theatre** *(☎ 7452 3000)* is actually three

BRITAIN

theatres in one – the Olivier, Lyttleton and Cottesloe – and puts on consistently good performances, mixing classic and contemporary works. For cheap tickets, queue at the box office from 10am on the day of a performance.

tkts (tube Leicester Square; open 10am-7pm Mon-Sat, noon-3.30pm Sun), on the southern side of Leicester Square, sells half-price tickets (plus £2.50 commission) on the day of performance. The queues can be worse than Harrods' sales. Some theatres and concert halls sell stand-by tickets 90 minutes before performances.

Don't miss a performance at **Shakespeare's Globe Theatre** (☎ 7401 9919; 21 New Globe Walk; tube London Bridge; standing spaces £5, tickets £12-27), the replica of Shakespeare's 'wooden O', which now dominates Bankside. Although there are wooden bench seats in tiers around the stage, many people copy the 17th-century 'groundlings' who stood in front of the stage, moving around as the mood took them. With no roof, the Globe is open to the elements; hence performances are only from May to September.

The **National Film Theatre** (☎ 7928 3232; South Bank Centre; tube Waterloo) screens an impressive range of classic, unusual, experimental and foreign films, or you could try the nearby **bfi London Imax Cinema** (☎ 7902 1234), which is good if you've got kids.

Spectator Sports

Tickets for Premier League football matches start at around £20 and thanks to the popularity of the sport are difficult to come by through official routes.

If you can get a ticket, some of the big teams worth watching are **Arsenal** (☎ 7413 3366), **Chelsea** (☎ 7386 7799) and **Tottenham Hotspur** (☎ 8365 5050).

International fixtures at **Wembley Stadium** (☎ 8900 1234) will cost more once the famous venue recovers from its multimillion pound makeover which is planned for completion in late 2006.

Tickets to rugby union internationals at **Twickenham** (☎ 8831 6666) cost around £30.

The two major venues for cricket are **Lord's** (☎ 7432 1066; St John Rd NW8) and **The Oval** (☎ 7582 7764; Kennington Oval SE11).

Crystal Palace (☎ 8778 0131; tickets from £10) is the venue for important athletics events. Expect to pay a lot more to watch tennis at **Wimbledon** (☎ 8946 2244).

Getting There & Away

As London is Britain's major gateway, Getting There & Away information has been given in the introductory transport sections of this chapter.

Bus Bus travellers will arrive at Victoria coach station, Buckingham Palace Rd, about 10 minutes' walk south of Victoria station.

Train It's probably worth highlighting that each of the 10 (11 if you include King's Cross' separate Thameslink station) main-line stations serve various parts of the UK, so the station you arrive at might not necessarily be the one you'll leave from. The station you'll need will be made clear when you book tickets. TfL has TICs situated at Euston, Paddington and Victoria stations, which can provide timetables, book tickets for immediate or advanced travel, and answer queries. You can also call **National Rail Enquiries** (☎ 0845 748 4950).

Getting Around
To/From the Airports
Transport to and from London's five airports is as follows:

Heathrow The airport (☎ 0870 000 0123) is accessible by bus, Underground (between 5am and 11pm) and main-line train.

The Heathrow Express rail link whisks its passengers from the Paddington station to Heathrow in just 15 minutes. Tickets cost an exorbitant £12 each way. Trains leave every 15 minutes from around 5am to 11.30pm. Many airlines have advance check-in desks at Paddington.

The Underground station for Terminals 1, 2 and 3 is directly linked to the terminus buildings; there's a separate station for Terminal 4. Check which terminal your flight uses when you reconfirm. The adult single fare is £3.60, or you can use an All Zone Travelcard (£5). The journey time from central London is about 50 minutes – allow an hour.

The **Airbus A2** (☎ 0870 575 7757; w www.gobycoach.com) service is prone to traffic congestion. It runs from Heathrow Terminal 4 to King's Cross Cheney Rd every 30 minutes from 5.30am to 9.45pm, and from King's Cross at 4am to 10pm. It takes one hour 40 minutes and costs £8.

All four terminals have left-luggage services run by private companies. Call the main Heathrow number for details.

Gatwick The **Gatwick Express train** (☎ 0870 530 1530) runs nonstop between the main terminal and Victoria station 24 hours daily. One-way fares are £11 and the journey takes about 30 minutes. The **Connex South Central** (☎ 01332-387601) service takes a little longer and costs £8.20.

Both Gatwick's **north and south terminals** (☎ 0870 000 2468) are linked by a monorail; check which terminal your flight uses.

A minicab to or from central London will cost around £35, while a metered black cab costs around £50.

There are luggage storage facilities in both terminals.

London City The **airport** (☎ 7646 0000) is two minutes' walk from the Silvertown & City Airport train station, which is linked by train to Stratford. A frequent shuttle bus also connects the airport with Liverpool St Station (£6, 30 minutes), Canary Wharf DLR and tube (£3, 12 minutes) and Canning Town station (£2, 10 minutes).

Luton The **airport** (☎ 01582-405100) is connected by frequent shuttle bus from the Luton Airport Parkway station. There are several trains (☎ 0845 748 4950) an hour going to/from London through Kings Cross Thameslink station. Fares cost £9.50 and the journey takes about 35 minutes.

Stansted The **airport** (☎ 0870 0000 303) is served by the **Stansted Express** (☎ 0845 730 1530) from Liverpool St station, which costs £11 and takes 45 minutes. The trains depart every 15 minutes.

There's also the **Airbus A6** (☎ 0870 575 7747) service which runs every 20 minutes at peak times, 30 minutes off peak, 24 hours between the airport and Victoria Coach Station. It takes one hour and 45 minutes and costs £8.

Bus & Underground Information regarding the bus or Underground network can be obtained by calling ☎ 7222 1234 or by visiting the TICs at Victoria Coach Station and various tube stations – Heathrow 1, 2 and 3; King's Cross; Liverpool St; Oxford Circus; and Piccadilly Circus. It's well worth asking for one of the free bus maps, particularly if you want to travel by night bus.

Although traffic will make your journey substantially longer than by Underground, the top decks of routes such as the No 11 offer great DIY sightseeing tours, so congested roads shouldn't put you off.

Prices for bus and tube travel depend on how many geographic zones your journey covers. Central London is covered by Zone 1. A ticket good for Zones 1 and 2 should suffice for most visitors. Single journeys on the bus for Zone 1/Zones 1 and 2 costs £1/70p, by tube £1.60/£1.90. You can also buy a book of six single bus tickets (£3.90) from TICs.

Travelcards are the easiest and cheapest option, and they can be used on all forms of transport – trains in London, the DLR, buses and the Tube. A Zones 1 and 2 card costs £5.30 before 9.30am; £4.10 after. Weekly travelcards are also available; they require an ID card with a passport photo (Zones 1 and 2 cost £19.30). If you're in London for only the weekend, the Weekend Travelcard is ideal. Costing £6.10 it is 25% cheaper than buying two separate Off-Peak Day Travelcards. A carnet of Zone 1 tube tickets good for 10 rides costs £11.50.

Times of the last tube trains vary from 11.30pm to 12.30am, depending on the station and line. A reasonably comprehensive network of night buses runs from or through Trafalgar Square (routes are denoted by the letter 'N'); a single Zone 1 fare is £1.50.

DLR & Train The monorail-like, driverless Docklands Light Railway (DLR) links the City at Bank and Tower Gateway with Canary Wharf, Stratford, Beckton, Greenwich and Lewisham. It's a quick, convenient way of seeing what some herald as 'new' London – all gleaming glass, trendy cafés and expensive warehouse apartments. Fares operate the same way as on the tube.

Trains are the primary means of transport to much of London's suburbia. All main line stations interchange with the tube and you can use your Travelcard for any parts of the journey within London.

Taxi The famous **London black cabs** (☎ 7272 0272) can be hailed when the yellow 'for hire' sign is lit. They can carry five people but are not cheap. All fares are metered and this starts running the moment you get in. Surcharges are added for extra passengers, luggage or if it's late at night, and most 'cabbies' expect a tip of 10%.

Minicabs can carry four people and tend to be cheaper than the black cabs. Although they are only supposed to be hired by phone and need a license to operate, hawkers abound in popular spots at night. This makes cabs very easy to find, but as they are unlicensed and generally more interested in money than safety, aren't really worth the potential savings. Women, particularly if alone, are advised to steer clear. They're also unmetered, so make sure you barter hard on a price before you get in.

Small minicab companies are based in particular areas – ask a local for the name of a reputable company, or phone one of the large **24-hour minicab operations** (☎ 7272 2612, 8340 2450, 8567 1111). Women could phone **Lady Cabs** (☎ 7254 3501). Gays and lesbians can choose **Freedom Cars** (☎ 7734 1313).

Car & Motorcycle With congested roads, extortionate parking charges and annoyingly dutiful traffic wardens, London is a driver's nightmare. If you do have to bring a car to the capital, avoid peak hours (7.30am to 9am and 4.30pm to 7pm) and be prepared for a spot of road rage.

Bicycle Cyclists are definitely second-rate citizens in London and you'll need nerves of steel to negotiate the capital's roads. If you fancy a challenge, you can hire bikes at **Bikepark** (☎ 7731 7012; 63 New Kings Rd SW6; tube Parsons Green). The minimum rental charge is £12 for the first day, £6 the second day and £4 for subsequent days. A large deposit is required. You could also try **The London Bicycle Tour Company** (☎ 7928 6838; 1a Gabriel's Wharf SE1; tube Waterloo). A deposit is required by credit card and hire starts at £2.50 an hour or £12 for the first day, with cheaper rates the longer you hire.

Boat There are all sorts of services on the river. See River Tour and Other Attractions under Things to See & Do earlier in this London section. The main starting points are at Embankment Pier and Westminster and Waterloo Millennium Piers. For information call ☎ 7222 1234.

AROUND LONDON

When it isn't plagued by strikes, engineering works or delays, the rail network puts a surprisingly large number of places within day-tripping striking distance. Obvious choices would be the dreaming spires of Oxford or the cultural might of Cambridge, both only an hour away. But even Stratford-upon-Avon, Bath and Brighton are all within easy reach if you want to escape the smog for a day.

Windsor & Eton
☎ 01753

Windsor Castle (☎ 831118; adult/concession/child/family £11.50/9.50/6/29; open from 9.45am daily) is one of three official residences of the Queen and has been home to English sovereigns for over 900 years. It was built in stages between 1165 and the 16th century on chalk bluffs overlooking the Thames; its majesty is still striking.

Inside the castle, St George's Chapel is a masterpiece of perpendicular Gothic architecture. You can also examine Queen Mary's Doll's House and the recently restored State Apartments. The castle can be closed at short notice when members of the royal family are in residence; phone for opening arrangements. In summer, the changing of the guard takes place from Monday to Saturday, weather permitting, at 11am, and on alternate days for the remainder of the year. Admission is cheaper on Sunday when St George's Chapel is closed.

A short walk along Thames St and across the river brings you to another enduring symbol of Britain's class system, **Eton College** (adult/child £3.50/2; open to visitors 2pm-4.30pm during term, from 10.30am Easter & summer holidays), a famous public (meaning private) school that has educated 18 prime ministers and a number of royals. Several buildings date from the mid-15th century, when the school was founded by Henry VI.

Easily accessible from London, Windsor (population 31,000) crawls with tourists. If possible, avoid at weekends. South West Trains operates direct services from London Waterloo to Windsor & Eton Riverside station for £6.30 return.

Hatfield House

Some six miles from St Albans, north of London, Hatfield House (☎ 01707-287010, fax 287033; house & garden adult/child £7/3.50; house open noon-4pm daily Easter Sun-end Sept, gardens open 11am-5.30pm daily) is home to the Marquess of Salisbury and is England's most celebrated Jacobean house – a graceful red-brick and stone mansion full of treasures amid 42 acres of gardens. There are trains from King's Cross Thameslink station.

Southeast England

Due to the proximity to London, the counties of Kent, East and West Sussex and Hampshire are home to a large chunk of the capital's workforce. For this reason there are plenty of fast, regular rail and bus services, making it possible to see the main sights on day trips, though you are advised to avoid visiting at weekends and during school holidays.

The southeast is a region exceptionally rich in beauty and history and it caters to those unshakeable traditional images of England – picturesque villages with welcoming old pubs, spectacular coastlines, impressive castles and magnificent cathedrals. There are also a number of excellent walks along the South and North Downs.

Be warned though – prices for accommodation and food are much higher here than in the northern parts of England.

Orientation & Information

The main roads and railway lines radiate from London like spokes in a wheel, linking the south-coast ports and resorts with the capital. Chalk country runs through the region along two hilly east-west ridges, or 'downs'.

The North Downs curve from Guildford towards Rochester, then to Dover where they become the famous White Cliffs. The South Downs run from north of Portsmouth to end spectacularly at Beachy Head near Eastbourne. Lying between the two is the Weald, once an enormous stretch of forest, now orchards and market gardens.

Getting Around

For information on all public transport options in Kent, East and West Sussex and Hampshire, ring **Traveline** (☎ 0870 608 2608).

Bus Virtually all bus companies accept Explorer tickets, which give unlimited travel for one day and for an adult/concession cost £6/4. They can be bought from bus drivers or bus stations, and are nearly always the best value option if you are travelling extensively.

Train It is possible to do an interesting rail loop from London via Canterbury East, Dover, Ashford, Rye, Hastings, Battle (via Hastings), Brighton, Arundel, Portsmouth and Winchester. If you are considering extensive rail travel, a Network SouthEast Card is essential (see Railcards under Train in the main Getting There & Away section earlier in this chapter).

CANTERBURY
☎ 01227 • pop 36,000

Canterbury's greatest treasure is its magnificent cathedral, the successor to the church St Augustine built after he began converting the English to Christianity in AD 597. In 1170 Archbishop Thomas à Becket was murdered in the cathedral by four of Henry II's knights as a result of a dispute over the church's independence. An enormous cult grew up around the martyred Becket and Canterbury became the centre of one of the most important medieval pilgrimages in Europe, immortalised by Geoffrey Chaucer in the *Canterbury Tales*.

Canterbury was severely damaged during WWII, and parts have been rebuilt insensitively. However, there's still plenty to see and the bustling town centre has a good atmosphere. The place crawls with tourists and there's not much chance of escaping the queues.

Orientation & Information

The centre of Canterbury is enclosed by a medieval city wall and a modern ring road. It's easily covered on foot. The two train stations are both a short walk from the centre. The bus station is just within the city walls at the eastern end of High St.

The **TIC** (☎ 766567, fax 459840; e canter buryinformation@canterbury.gov.uk; 34 St Margaret's St; open 9.30am-5.30pm Mon-Sat & 10am-4pm Sun) is in the heart of town.

For free Internet access (bookings required) head to the **Library** (☎ 463608; High St).

Things to See & Do

The **Canterbury Cathedral** (☎ 762862; adult/concession £3.50/2.50; open 9am-6.30pm Mon-Sat Easter-Sept, 9am-5pm Oct-Easter, shorter hours Sun) was built in two stages between 1070 and 1184, and 1391 and 1505. The cathedral complex can easily absorb half a day. It is a massive rabbit warren of a building, with treasures tucked away in corners and a trove of associated stories, so a tour (£4) is recommended. They take place at 10.30am, noon and 2.30pm Monday to Saturday.

Also not to be missed is the **Roman Museum** (☎ 785575; Butchery Lane; adult/concession £2.60/1.65; open 10am-5pm

Mon-Sat, 1.30pm-5pm Sun June-Oct), built underground around the remains of a Roman town house. Here you can visit the marketplace, smell the odours of a Roman kitchen and handle artefacts. Kids will love it.

Places to Stay

Canterbury Youth Hostel *(☎ 0870 770 5744, fax 0870 770 5745;* e *canterbury@yha.org .uk; 54 New Dover Rd; dorm beds £11.25, twin £32)* is 1mi east of the centre. There is one twin room. Another budget option is the **University of Kent** *(☎ 828000, fax 828019;* e *d.p.smith@ukc.ac.uk; Tanglewood; per person from £19.50, with en suite £27.50; open Apr & June-Sept)*, a 20-minute walk from the centre. Rates include breakfast.

Head to London Rd or New Dover Rd for good-value B&Bs such as **Alverstone House** *(☎/fax 766360; 38 New Dover Rd; singles/ doubles £20/38)* which has large rooms (but no tea- or coffee-making facilities) that look out over a pleasant garden.

Tudor House B&B *(☎ 765650; 6 Best Lane; singles £20, doubles without/with en suite £38/45)*, in a slightly eccentric 450-year-old building, is very good value for somewhere so central. It also offers canoe and bike hire for guests (£10 per day).

Cathedral Gate Hotel *(☎ 464381, fax 462800;* e *cgate@cgate.demon.co.uk; 36 Burgate; singles/doubles £24/37, with en suite £55.50/83.50)* has a superb central location for cathedral gazers. Continental breakfast is included.

Those into four-poster beds and a bygone atmosphere should try the centrally located **County Hotel** *(☎ 766266, fax 451512;* e *reservations@county.macdonald-hotels.co.uk; High St; singles/doubles £80/119)*. A continental/ English breakfast costs £8.50/11.

Places to Eat

There's a Safeway supermarket on the corner of New Dover Rd and Lower Chantry Rd, just southeast of the centre.

The Custard Tart *(☎ 785178; 35a St Margaret's St)* charges from £2.75 for delicious baguettes and sandwiches, or £1.75 if you takeaway. Try to avoid the 1pm lunchtime rush.

Three Tuns Hotel *(☎ 456391; 24 Watling St; pub meals around £4.50)* stands on the site of a Roman theatre and dates from the 16th century. It serves good-value pub grub.

Ha!Ha! *(☎ 379800; 7 St Margaret's St; dishes £7)* is a modern bar doing bistro-style food.

Tapas en las Trece *(☎ 762637; 13 Palace St; tapas from £3.55)* serves mouthwatering Spanish dishes together with good *rioja* and, every third Tuesday, live jazz.

There's a plethora of Italian restaurants in Canterbury – try the **Olive Grove** *(☎ 764388; 12 Best Lane; mains £6.50)* for a casual pizza or pasta meal, or **Tuo e Mio** *(☎ 761471; 16 The Borough; mains £7.50-15.50)* for fine dining.

One of the town's best restaurants is the intimate **Augustine's** *(☎ 453063; 1 Longport; 2-/3-course lunch £9.95/10.95, dinner mains £15)*, located just outside the city walls.

Entertainment

The TIC stocks copies of *W3 – What WhereWhen* – a free leaflet to what's on in Canterbury. The **Miller's Arms** *(☎ 456057; Mill Lane)* is a cosy pub near the old locks. **Caseys** *(☎ 463252; 5 Butchery Lane)* has a large selection of Irish ales and stouts.

Marlowe Theatre *(☎ 787787;* w *www.mar lowetheatre.com; The Friars; box office open 10am-9pm Mon-Sat)* puts on a variety of plays and concerts.

Getting There & Away

Canterbury makes a good base for exploring the eastern and northern coastal areas of Kent, namely Herne Bay and Whitstable, Margate, Broadstairs and Sandwich.

Bus To Canterbury, National Express coaches leave every half-hour from London Victoria (£7.50 one way, £11.50 day return, two hours). **Stagecoach East Kent's** *(☎ 828100)* No 115 bus runs hourly (less on Sunday) from Canterbury to Dover (£3.25/4 one way/return, 30 minutes), Deal, Sandwich, Ramsgate, Broadstairs, Margate, Herne Bay, Whitstable and back to Canterbury.

Train Canterbury East station (for the YHA hostel) is accessible from London's Victoria station, and Canterbury West is accessible from London's Charing Cross and Waterloo stations (£15.90, 1½ hours).

There are regular trains operating between Canterbury East and Dover Priory (£4.40, 45 minutes).

DOVER
☎ 01304 • pop 37,000

Dover may be England's 'Gateway to Europe' but the place has just two things going for it: the famous white cliffs and its spectacular medieval hill-top castle. The foreshore of Dover is basically an enormous, complicated (though well signposted) and unattractive vehicle ramp for the ferries. Everyone's in transit, few stay.

Orientation & Information

Dover is dominated by the looming profile of the castle to the east. The town itself runs back from the sea along a valley formed by the unimpressive River Dour.

Ferry departures are from the Eastern Docks (accessible by bus) below the castle. Dover Priory train station is off Folkestone Rd, a short walk to the west of the town centre. The bus station is on Pencester Rd.

The **TIC** (☎ 205108, fax 225498; e tic@ doveruk.com; Biggin St; open 9am-5.30pm daily) is in the town centre. It has an accommodation and ferry-booking service. Try the **Mangle laundrette** (Worthington St) for laundry.

Things to See & Do

The main attraction, **Dover Castle** (☎ 211067; adult/concession/child £7.50/5.60/3.80; open 10am-6pm daily Apr-Sept, 10am-4pm Oct-Mar) is a well-preserved medieval fortress with spectacular views. The excellent tour of **Hellfire Corner** covers the castle's history during WWII, and takes you through the tunnels that burrow beneath the castle. Admission includes Hellfire Corner.

The **Dover Museum** (☎ 201066; Market Square; £1.75/95p; open 10am-5.30pm daily) is one of the best around and admission includes entry to the Bronze Age Boat Gallery, home to the world's oldest (3600 years) boat.

Places to Stay

Book well ahead if you intend to be here in July and August.

Dover Youth Hostel (☎ 0870 770 5798, fax 0870 770 5799; e dover@yha.org.uk; 306 London Rd; adults/under-18s £11.25/8) is five minutes' walk from Market Square.

There are a few cheap B&Bs on Castle St and Maison Dieu Rd. **East Lee Guest House** (☎ 210176, fax 206705; e eastlee@eclipse .co.uk; 108 Maison Dieu Rd; singles/doubles from £35/50) is friendly and luxurious. **St Martin's Guest House** (☎ 205938, fax 208229; 17 Castle Hill Rd; singles/doubles £38/45) is also highly recommended.

For a sea view and a touch of opulence head to the **Churchill Hotel** (☎ 203633, fax 21 6320; e enquiries@churchill-hotel.com; Waterfront; singles/doubles from £59/79). Breakfast costs £9.

Places to Eat

Dover is short on decent places to eat, so you'll need to look around a bit.

Riveria Coffee House (☎ 201303; 9 Worthington St) is good value with cream teas for £2, or sandwiches and light meals from £1.75. **Jermain's** (☎ 205956; Beaconsfield Rd; meals £4.25) is near the hostel and has a range of traditional lunches. **Curry Garden** (☎ 206357; 24 High St) is a cheap Indian restaurant where prawn korma costs £6.

Gourmets should head to **Cullin's Yard** (☎ 211666; 11 Cambridge Rd; mains £11-13) for seafood or **The Cabin** (☎ 206118; 91 High St; mains £8.25-11.50), an intimate restaurant specialising in traditional English and game dishes (but vegetarians are catered for too).

Getting There & Away

See the Getting There & Away section at the beginning of this chapter for details on ferries to mainland Europe.

Bus To Dover, National Express coaches leave hourly from London Victoria (£9.50 one way, £10.50 day return, 2¼ hours). **Stagecoach East Kent** (☎ 0870 243 3711) has an office on Pencester Rd. Dover to Canterbury (30 minutes) costs £3.25. There's an hourly bus to Brighton but you'll need to change at Eastbourne. An Explorer ticket for £5.30 is better value on this route.

Train There are over 40 trains a day from London Victoria and Charing Cross stations to Dover Priory (£19.15 one way, 1¾ hours).

Getting Around

The ferry companies run complimentary buses every 20 minutes between the docks and train stations. **Central Taxis** (☎ 240441) and **Heritage** (☎ 204420) have 24-hour services. A one-way taxi trip to Folkestone or Deal costs about £10.

BRITAIN

HEVER CASTLE

Idyllic Hever Castle (☎ 01732-865224; adult/ concession/child £8.20/7/4.50; open 11am-5pm daily Mar-late Nov) near Edenbridge, a few miles west of Tonbridge, was the childhood home of Anne Boleyn, mistress to Henry VIII and then his doomed queen. Walking through the main gate into the courtyard of Hever is like stepping onto the set of a period film. It's a truly fairy-tale place and one of the highlights of the area. Restored by the Astor family, it also has magnificent gardens. The nearest train station is Hever, 1mi from the castle itself.

KNOLE HOUSE

In a country that is full of extraordinary country houses, Knole (☎ 01732-450608; adult/ child/family £5.50/2.50/13; open 11am-4pm Wed-Sun, Easter-1 Nov), now a National Trust property, is outstanding. It seems as if nothing substantial has changed since early in the 17th century. Virginia Woolf based the novel Orlando on the history of the house and family.

Knole is 1½mi to the south of Sevenoaks, which is on the rail line from London's Charing Cross to Tonbridge.

LEEDS CASTLE

Near Maidstone in Kent, Leeds Castle (☎ 01622-765400; adult/concession £11/ 9.50; open 10am-5.30pm daily Mar-Oct, 10am-3pm Nov-Feb) is one of the world's most famous and most visited castles. It stands on two small islands in a lake, and is surrounded by a park housing an aviary, a maze and grotto. Unfortunately, it's usually overrun by families and school groups. Also, some of the rooms are closed from time to time for conferences and functions. If you want to be sure of getting your money's worth from the rather high admission price, call ahead.

National Express has a bus from Victoria coach station, leaving at 9am and returning at 3.45pm (1½ hours). It must be prebooked, and combined admission and travel is £15.

BRIGHTON

☎ 01273 • pop 180,000

Brighton is deservedly Britain's number one seaside town – a fascinating mixture of seediness and sophistication. Just an hour away from London by train, it's the perfect choice for day-trippers looking for a drop of froth and ozone.

Londoners have been travelling to Brighton ever since the 1750s, when a shrewd doctor suggested that bathing in, and drinking, the local seawater was good for them. It's still fine to swim here, though a little on the cool side, and the pebble beach comes as a bit of a shock if you're used to fine sand. Drinking the seawater, however, is definitely not recommended.

Brighton has a reputation as the club and party capital of the south. There's a vibrant population of students and travellers, excellent shopping, a terrific arts scene and countless restaurants, pubs and cafés.

During May, Brighton hosts the largest arts festival (☎ 292961; w www.brighton -festival.org.uk) outside Edinburgh. Though it's mostly mainstream, there also are fringe events.

Orientation & Information

Brighton train station is a 15-minute walk north of the beach. The bus station is tucked away in Poole Valley. The interesting part of Brighton is a series of streets north of North St, including Bond, Gardner, Kensington and Sydney Sts.

The TIC (☎ 0906-711 2255; e brighton -tourism@brighton-hove.gov.uk; 10 Bartholomew Square) has maps and copies of magazines such as the Brighton Latest and New Insight (both free) and The List (50p).

Bubbles Laundrette (75 Preston St) can help with laundry requirements. For £2-an-hour Internet access go to Riki-Tik (☎ 683844; 18a Bond St).

Things to See & Do

The Royal Pavilion (☎ 290900; adult/ concession £4.50/3.25; open 10am-5.15pm daily June-Sept, 10am-4.15pm Oct-May) is an extraordinary fantasy: an Indian palace on the outside, a Chinese brothel on the inside, all built between 1815 and 1822 for George IV. The whole edifice is way over the top in every respect and is not to be missed.

The Brighton Museum & Art Gallery (☎ 290900; w www.museums.brighton-hove .gov.uk; entry via Royal Pavilion gardens; admission free; open 10am-7pm Tues, 10am-5pm Wed-Sat, 2pm-5pm Sun) is another must. It reopened in 2002 after a £10 million facelift and houses Art Deco and Art Nouveau furniture, archaeological finds and surrealist paintings (including Salvador Dalí's sofa in the

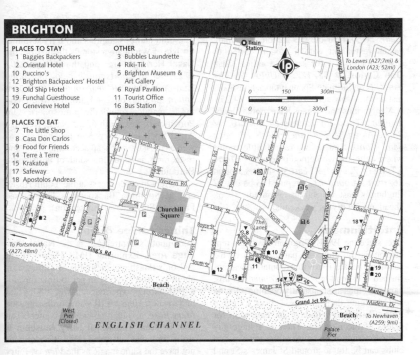

BRIGHTON

PLACES TO STAY
1 Baggies Backpackers
2 Oriental Hotel
10 Puccino's
12 Brighton Backpackers' Hostel
13 Old Ship Hotel
19 Funchal Guesthouse
20 Genevieve Hotel

PLACES TO EAT
7 The Little Shop
8 Casa Don Carlos
9 Food for Friends
14 Terre à Terre
15 Krakatoa
17 Safeway
18 Apostolos Andreas

OTHER
3 Bubbles Laundrette
4 Riki-Tik
5 Brighton Museum &
   Art Gallery
6 Royal Pavilion
11 Tourist Office
16 Bus Station

shape of lips). Nearby **Palace Pier** is the very image of Brighton with fast food, flashing lights and rides. **The Lanes** is a maze of narrow alleyways crammed with antique and jewellery shops, restaurants and bars, south of North St.

Places to Stay

There are loads of accommodation options in Brighton.

Baggies Backpackers (☎ 733740; 33 Oriental Place; dorm beds £12, doubles £25, room-key deposit £5) is more friendly and homy than the other hostels. **Brighton Backpackers** (☎ 777717; e stay@brightonbackpackers.com; 75 Middle St; dorm beds £11, in seafront annexe £12, doubles £30) bills itself as 'England's funkiest hostel' – there's loud music and decor to prove it.

The main cluster of cheap B&Bs is to the east of the Palace Pier, off St James's St. **Funchal Guesthouse** (☎ 603975; 17 Madeira Place; rooms per person from £20) is a cosy, clean establishment. The same can be said of **Genevieve Hotel** (☎ 681653; 18 Madeira Place; rooms per person £25-30).

Puccino's (☎ 204656, fax 206915; 1 Bartholowmews; rooms per person £25-35) is

primarily a café but the friendly owner runs a couple of pleasant B&B rooms located above the café. It's highly recommended.

Oriental Hotel (☎ 205050, fax 821096; e info@orientalhotel.co.uk; 9 Oriental Place; singles Mon-Fri/Sat-Sun £25/35, doubles Mon-Fri/Sat-Sun £57.50/64.50) is a real breath of fresh air among B&Bs. Decorated with bright colours and cool decor, it's very funky. Prices include breakfast.

The **Old Ship Hotel** (☎ 329001, fax 820718; e oldship@paramount-hotels.co.uk; King's Rd; singles/doubles £125/155) is the doyen of Brighton's hotels. In the 1830s, Thackeray stayed there while writing Vanity Fair. Prices can drop to as low as £30 per person off season – ring for the current rates.

Places to Eat

Brighton has many great eating places and a **Safeway** (St James's St) for self-catering.

Apostolos Andreas (☎ 687935; 24 George St; sandwiches £1-1.50) is a popular, tiny coffeehouse with English-style food.

The Little Shop (☎ 325594; 48a Market St, The Lanes) has delicious and chunky sandwiches from £2.35.

BRITAIN

Krakatoa (☎ 719009; 7 Poole Valley; mains £6-9), near the bus station, is a small, casual restaurant with a modern Oriental-fusion menu. It's for serious foodies. **Casa Don Carlos** (☎ 327177; 5 Union St, The Lanes) is an intimate Spanish tapas house and restaurant. A big serve of paella costs £4.25.

Vegetarians and vegans have ample choice including **Food for Friends** (☎ 202310; 17 Prince Albert St, The Lanes; meals £5; open 8am-10pm), a rabbit warren of little rooms where delicious wholefood is served, or **Terre à Terre** (☎ 729051; 71 East St; starters around £6, mains around £12), reputed to be one of England's best vegetarian restaurants (book ahead, especially on weekends).

Entertainment
Ever since the 1960s, Brighton has had a reputation as the club and party capital of the south. In the late 1970s this reputation was enshrined in the cult movie *Quadraphenia*. Pubs, bars and clubs are constantly opening, closing and changing their themes – check *Brighton Latest*, *New Insight* and bar and café walls for places of the moment. There is a huge gay scene in Brighton and most of the gay bars and clubs can be found around St James's St and the Old Steine.

Getting There & Away
National Express coaches leave hourly from London Victoria to Brighton (£8 one way). Stagecoach East Kent bus No 712 runs to Eastbourne from where No 711 connects with Dover. There are twice hourly train services to Brighton from London's Victoria and King's Cross stations (£15.10/15.20 one way/day return, 50 minutes). There are hourly trains to Portsmouth (£12 one way, 1½ hours), and frequent services to Canterbury and Dover.

PORTSMOUTH
☎ 023 • pop 183,000
For much of British history, Portsmouth has been the home of the Royal Navy and it is littered with reminders that this was, for hundreds of years, a force that shaped the world. Portsmouth is still a busy naval base and the sleek, grey killing machines of the 20th century are also very much in evidence.

Unfortunately, Portsmouth is not a particularly attractive city, largely due to WWII bombing, so there is no persuasive reason to stay overnight.

Orientation & Information
The train and bus stations and ferry terminal for Isle of Wight are a stone's throw from the Naval Heritage Area and the TIC (☎ 9282 6722; e tic@portsmouthcc.gov.uk; open 9am-6pm Mon-Sat year-round, 10am-5pm Sun in summer) on The Hard. It's worth having a wander round the atmospheric Old Portsmouth, just south of the Naval Heritage Area. Southsea, where the beaches are, as well as most of the cheap accommodation and restaurants, is about 2mi south of Portsmouth Harbour.

There's Internet access at the Youth Hostel and at Southsea Backpackers Lodge (see Places to Stay later in this section).

Things to See & Do
Portsmouth's centrepiece is the **Naval Heritage Area**. Exploring HMS *Victory*, Lord Nelson's flagship at the Battle of Trafalgar, is about as close as you can get to time travel – a fascinating experience. After 437 years underwater, Henry VIII's favourite ship, the *Mary Rose*, and its time-capsule contents can now be seen. **The Royal Navy Museum** is really for naval buffs, and HMS *Warrior* does not have the same magic as the *Victory*. Entry is around £7 for each ship; alternatively buy a three-for-two ticket (£13.75), which includes the Royal Navy Museum and the **Mary Rose Museum**, or a Passport ticket (£18) valid for all attractions.

Places to Stay
Most budget accommodation is in Southsea. One exception is the **Youth Hostel** (☎ 0870 770 6002; e portsmouth@yha.org.uk; Old Wymering Lane, Cosham; adults/under-18s £10.25/7), about 4mi from the main sights. Bus No 12 operates to Cosham from the harbour bus station. **Portsmouth & Southsea Backpackers Lodge** (☎/fax 9283 2495; 4 Florence Rd, Southsea; dorm beds £10, doubles without/with en suite £22/25) is far more convenient.

Sailmaker's Loft (☎ 9282 3045; e sailmakersloft@aol.com; 5 Bath Square; rooms per person with shared bath/en suite £22/23) is a tasteful B&B run by a retired merchant seaman who can tell you a lot about Portsmouth. There are great views across the harbour.

The greatest range of cheaper B&Bs are in Southsea. **Kilbenny Guesthouse** (☎ 9286 1347; 2 Malvern Rd; rooms per person £20) has clean, large rooms. En suite is a few pounds dearer.

Queen's Hotel *(☎ 9282 2466, fax 9282 19 01; Clarence Parade, Southsea; singles/doubles from £45/65, doubles with sea view £95)* is a large, Edwardian-style hotel with old-world charm.

Places to Eat

Twigs *(☎ 9282 8316; 39 High St)* is a small coffee shop with sandwiches, baguettes and baps (rolls) from £2.40 to £3.75.

Osborne Rd and Palmerston Rd are the main restaurant strips. **Sur la Mer** *(☎ 9287 6678; 69 Palmerston Rd; mains £8-13)* is an intimate but informal French restaurant.

A great place for an outdoor drink or bite to eat is **Still & West** *(☎ 9282 1567; 2 Bath Square; meals £9)*, a pub with a terrace overlooking part of Portsmouth harbour.

Getting There & Away

Bus From London, National Express bus No 30 goes via Heathrow to Portsmouth (£11 one way, £12 day return, 2½ hours). **Stagecoach Coastline** *(☎ 01903-237661)* bus No 700 runs between Brighton and Portsmouth every 30 minutes (£3.40 one way) and Stagecoach bus No 69 runs to/from Winchester hourly from Monday to Saturday.

Train There are over 40 trains a day from London Victoria and Waterloo stations (£20, 1½ hours). There are plenty of trains to/from Brighton (£12, 1½ hours) and Winchester (£7, one hour).

Boat A passenger ferry operated by **Wightlink** *(☎ 0870 582 7744)* goes from The Hard to Ryde pier (15 minutes). It also runs a car-and-passenger ferry (35 minutes) to Fishbourne every half-hour. The day-return fare for an adult/child costs £8.60/4.30. Car fares start at £54 for a day return.

For information on ferries to France and Spain, see Sea in the main Getting There & Away section of this chapter. The Continental Ferryport is north of Flagship Portsmouth.

WINCHESTER
☎ 01962 • pop 37,000

Winchester is a beautiful cathedral city on the River Itchen, interspersed with water meadows. It has played an important role in the history of England, being both the capital of

Saxon England and the seat of the powerful Bishops of Winchester from AD 670. Much of the present-day city dates from the 18th century, and its main attraction is the stunning cathedral. Despite its appeal, Winchester has escaped inundation by tourists, certainly by comparison to nearby Salisbury and to theme parks like Bath and Oxford.

Winchester makes a good base for exploring the south coast (ie, Portsmouth and New Forest) or the country farther west towards Salisbury.

Orientation & Information

The city centre is compact and easily negotiated on foot. The train station is a 10-minute walk to the west of the centre, and the bus and coach station is on Broadway, directly opposite the Guildhall and TIC.

The **TIC** *(☎ 840500; e tourism@winchester.gov.uk; the Guildhall, Broadway; open daily May-Sept)* organises regular guided walking tours (£3/50p) from April to October.

Things to See

One of the most beautiful cathedrals in the country is **Winchester Cathedral** *(suggested donation £2.50)*, a mixture of Norman, Early English and perpendicular styles. The north and south transepts are a magnificent example of pure Norman architecture. There are fascinating 20th-century paintings and sculptures dotted around the place. Cathedral tours are run by enthusiastic local volunteers.

Nearby is **Winchester College** *(☎ 621217; tours of chapel & cloisters at 10.45am, noon, 2.15pm & 3.30pm Mon-Sat, 2.15pm & 3.30pm Sun; adult/concession £2.50/2)*, founded in 1382 and the model for the great public schools of England.

In town it's also worth visiting the **Great Hall**, begun by William the Conqueror and the site of the trial of Sir Walter Raleigh in 1603. It houses **King Arthur's Round Table**, now known to be a fake at 'only' 600 years of age.

Places to Stay

In the heart of town there's the **Youth Hostel** *(☎ 0870 770 6092, fax 0870 770 6093; 1 Water Lane; adults/under-18s £9.50/6.75)* in a beautiful 18th-century water mill.

B&Bs in Winchester tend not to hang signs out the front. You'll have to get a list from the TIC. **East View** *(☎ 862986; 16 Clifton Hill; singles/doubles from £35/45)* is conveniently

BRITAIN

located and there are three small but comfortable rooms with en suites.

Very central and upmarket is the handsome old **Winchester Royal** (☎ 840840, fax 841582; e royal@marstonhotels.com; St Peter St; singles/doubles £99/107).

Places to Eat
For self-catering there's a **Sainsbury's supermarket** (Middle Brook St). At **Presto** (☎ 87 8370; The Square) try an Indian chicken pastie or a huge baguette (£2). **The Cathedral Refectory** (☎ 857258; sandwiches £1.90, cream tea £4.25), near the entrance to the cathedral, is a self-service cafeteria with a pleasant terrace.

Several eateries with outdoor tables are located on The Square. Here too you will find **La Bodega** (☎ 864004; Great Minster St; meals £7-13), an intimate Spanish restaurant that serves excellent tapas (£6.95).

LFR (☎ 872930; 18 Jewry St; mains £7-15) is located in a fine Tudor-style house dating from 1509 and is part of a chain of restaurants specialising in seafood. It's recommended.

Getting There & Away
National Express bus No 32 leaves every two hours from London Victoria via Heathrow (£10.50, one hour). **Stagecoach Hampshire Bus** (☎ 0845 121 0180) has a good network of services linking Salisbury, Southampton, Portsmouth and Brighton. Trains depart about every 15 minutes from London Waterloo (£21.20 one way, one hour), Southampton (£3.80, 18 minutes) and Portsmouth (£7, one hour).

CHANNEL ISLANDS
Across the Channel from Dorset and just off the coast of France lie the small islands of Jersey, Guernsey, Alderney, Sark and Herm. As well as being a tax haven, the Channel Islands are a popular summer-holiday resort for the British. Although there are pleasant beaches, good walks and cycle rides on some islands, and there's the famous **Jersey Zoo** (☎ 01534-860000) started by Gerald Durrell, compared to mainland Britain or the Scottish islands there's really not a lot to see and do. Jersey is the biggest and busiest of the islands, Alderney the most peaceful. There are numerous camping grounds and B&Bs from £18 per person. For more information contact **Jersey Tourism** (☎ 01534-500777, fax 500899;

e info@jersey.com) and, for all the other islands, **Guernsey Tourism** (☎ 01481-723552, fax 714951; e enquiries@guernseytouristboard.com).

Getting There & Away
There are daily flights to the Channel Islands (£105) from a few UK airports on several airlines including **British European** (☎ 0870 567 6676) and **Aurigny Air Services** (☎ 01481-822886).

Condor (☎ 01305-761551) runs ferries from Portsmouth to Jersey (£50 return, 10½ hours) via Guernsey (6½ hours). In addition it has high-speed catamarans running from Weymouth to Jersey (£55 return, 3¼ hours) via Guernsey (two hours), or from Poole to Jersey (£70, four hours).

Southwest England

The counties of Wiltshire, Dorset, Somerset, Devon and Cornwall include some of the most beautiful countryside and spectacular coastline in Britain. They are also littered with the evidence of successive cultures and kingdoms that have been swept away by one invader after another.

The region can be divided between Devon and Cornwall out on a limb in the far west, and Dorset, Wiltshire and Somerset in the east, which are more readily accessible.

In the east, the story of English civilisation is signposted by some of its greatest monuments: the Stone Age left Stonehenge and spellbinding Avebury; the Iron Age Britons left Maiden Castle just outside Dorchester; between them, the Romans and the Georgians created Bath; the legendary King Arthur is said to be buried at Glastonbury; the Middle Ages left the great cathedrals at Exeter, Salisbury and Wells; and the landed gentry left grand houses like Montacute and Wilton.

The east is densely packed with things to see, and the countryside, though varied, is a classic English patchwork of hedgerows, thatch-roofed cottages, stone churches, great estates and emerald-green fields.

Parts of Somerset and Wiltshire, particularly Bath and Salisbury, are major tourist attractions, but are still, unquestionably, worth visiting. You can happily wander Dorset and North Devon without too many plans and without stumbling over too many people.

Devon and particularly Cornwall were once Britain's 'wild west', and smuggling was rife. Until the 18th century there were still Cornish speakers in Cornwall. The 'English Riviera' is almost too popular for its own good. It's wise to steer clear of the coastal towns in July and August, not least because the narrow streets are choked with traffic.

The weather is milder in the southwest year-round and there are beaches with golden sand and surfable surf. Then there are the exquisite villages tucked into unexpected valleys or overlooking beautiful harbours, and lanes squeezed between high hedges.

Some people find Cornwall disappointing, however. Land's End – a veritable icon – has been reduced to an overly commercialised tourist trap, and inland, much of the peninsula has been devastated by generations of tin and china-clay mining. However, many of the coastal villages retain their charm, especially if you visit out of season.

For walkers the region offers great choice – see Activities later for details.

Orientation & Information

The chalk downs centred on Salisbury Plain run across Wiltshire and down through the centre of Dorset to the coast. In the west, Exmoor and Dartmoor dominate the landscape. The railways converge on Exeter, the most important city in the west, then run round the coast to Truro and Penzance. Bristol and Salisbury are also important crossroads.

Among others, there are YHA hostels in and around Dartmoor and Exmoor National Parks, and at Salisbury, Bath, Bristol, Winchester, Exeter, Plymouth, Penzance, Land's End and Tintagel.

Activities

Hiking The southwest has plenty of beautiful countryside, but walks in the Dartmoor and Exmoor National Parks, and round the coastline, are the best known. The barren, open wilderness of Dartmoor can be an acquired taste, but Exmoor covers some of the most beautiful countryside in England, and the coastal stretch from Ilfracombe to Minehead is particularly spectacular. See the individual sections on Dartmoor and Exmoor National Parks later in this chapter for more information.

The South West Coast Path, a long-distance walking route, follows the coastline round the peninsula for 613mi from Poole, near Bournemouth in Dorset, to Minehead in Somerset, giving spectacular access to the best and most untouched sections. However, it is not a wilderness walk – villages are generally within easy reach. It's the longest national trail and completing a section of the path is essential for any keen walker; visiting at busy summer weekends is best avoided.

Another famous walk, the Ridgeway, starts near Avebury and runs northeast for 85mi to Ivinghoe Beacon near Aylesbury. Much of it follows ancient roads over the high open ridge of the chalk downs, before descending to the Thames Valley and climbing into the Chilterns. The western section (to Streatley) can be used by mountain bikes, horses, farm vehicles and recreational 4WDs. For peace and quiet, walk during the week.

Surfing The capital of British surfing is Newquay on the west Cornish coast, and it's complete with surf shops, bleached hair and Kombi vans. The surfable coast runs from Porthleven (near Helston) in Cornwall, west around Land's End and north to Ilfracombe. The most famous reef breaks are at Porthleven, Lynmouth and Millbrook; although good, they are inconsistent.

Cycling Bikes can be hired in most major regional centres, and the infrequent bus connections make cycling more sensible than usual. There's no shortage of hills, but the mild weather and quiet back roads make this excellent cycling country.

Getting Around

Bus Reasonable connections between the main towns, particularly in the east, are provided by National Express buses. However the farther west you go the more dire the situation becomes. Transport around Dartmoor and Exmoor is very difficult in summer, and nigh on impossible at any other time. This is territory that favours those with their own transport. Contact **Traveline** (☎ 0870 608 2608) for information on regional bus services.

Train Train services in the east are reasonably comprehensive, linking Bristol, Bath, Salisbury, Weymouth and Exeter. Beyond Exeter a single line follows the south coast as far as Penzance, with spurs to Barnstaple, Gunnislake, Looe, Falmouth, St Ives and Newquay. For rail information, phone ☎ 0845 748 4950.

BRITAIN

Several regional rail passes are available, including the Freedom of the SouthWest Rover (£71.50 in summer, £61 in winter) which, over 15 days, allows eight days of unlimited travel west of a line drawn through (and including) Salisbury, Bath, Bristol and Weymouth.

SALISBURY
☎ 01722 • pop 37,000

Salisbury is justly famous for its cathedral and its close, but its appeal also lies in the fact that it is still a bustling market town, not just a tourist trap. Markets have been held in the town centre every Tuesday and Saturday since 1361, and the jumble of stalls still draws a large, cheerful crowd.

The town's architecture is a blend of every style since the Middle Ages, including some beautiful, half-timbered black-and-white buildings. It's a good base for visiting the Wiltshire Downs, Stonehenge, Wilton House and Avebury. Portsmouth and Winchester are also easy day trips if you're travelling by rail.

Orientation & Information

The town centre is a 10-minute walk from the train station – walk down the hill and turn right at the T-junction onto Fisherton St. This leads directly into town (which is well signposted). The bus station is just north of the centre of town, along not-so Endless St.

The TIC (☎ 334956; e visitorinfo@salis bury.gov.uk; Fish Row) is behind the impressive 18th-century Guildhall, on the southeastern corner of Market Square.

Things to See

Beautiful St Mary's Cathedral (suggested donation £3.50) is built in a uniform style known as Early English (or Early Pointed). This period is characterised by the first pointed arches and flying buttresses, and has a rather austere feel. The cathedral owes its uniformity to the speed with which it was built. Between 1220 and 1266, over 70,000 tons of stone were piled up. The spire, at 123m, is the highest in Britain.

The adjacent chapter house is one of the most perfect achievements of Gothic architecture. There is plenty more to see in the cathedral close, including two houses that have been restored and two museums. The Salisbury & South Wiltshire Museum (☎ 332151; 65 The Close; admission £3.50) is also worth visiting.

Places to Stay & Eat

Salisbury Youth Hostel (☎ 0870 770 6018, fax 0870 770 6019; e salisbury@yha.org.uk; Milford Hill; adults/under-18s £11.25/8) is an attractive old building, 15-minute's walk from the town centre.

Griffin Cottage (☎ 328259, fax 416928; e mark@brandonsoc.demon.co.uk; 10 St Edmunds Church St; per person £20) is a central, peaceful and comfortable B&B.

The enjoyable Red Lion Hotel (☎ 323334, fax 325756; e reception@the-redlion.co.uk; Milford St; singles/doubles £88/109) claims to be England's oldest purpose-built hotel. It dates back to the 13th century.

Fisherton St, running from the centre to the train station, has Chinese, Thai, Indian and other restaurants. For a casual bite to eat try Cawardine's (☎ 320619, 3 Bridge St), a popular local café big on sandwiches and snacks. Berli's (☎ 328923; 14 Ox Row; meals £4.50-6) is an informal vegetarian restaurant with delicious food and a great view over the Market Square. More upmarket is Le Hérisson (☎ 333471; 90 Crane St; mains £9.50), which caters to carnivores and vegetarians alike. Haunch of Venison (1 Minster St) is a recommended pub that dates from the 16th century.

Getting There & Away

Bus National Express has three buses a day from London via Heathrow to Salisbury (£12, three hours).

There are three unlimited travel tickets available in Wiltshire – Wiltshire Bus Lines (☎ 0845 709 0899) or Wilts & Dorset (☎ 336855) can tell you more. There are daily buses to Avebury and Stonehenge. If you're going through to Bristol or Bath, via Somerset (Wells, Glastonbury) or Gloucestershire (Cotswolds), get the Badgerline Day Explorer ticket (£5.70). Wilts & Dorset run an hourly bus No X6 to Bath (£5.50, 2¼ hours).

Train Salisbury is linked by rail to London Waterloo station (£23.10, two hours), Portsmouth (£11.10, 1¾ hours), Bath (£10, 50 minutes) and Exeter (£20.20, 1¾ hours).

Getting Around

Local buses are reasonably well organised and link Salisbury with Stonehenge (£5.50 return) and Wilton House; phone ☎ 336855 for details. Bikes can be hired from Hayball Cycle Centre (☎ 411378; Winchester St; £10 per day).

STONEHENGE

Stonehenge is the most famous prehistoric site in Europe – a ring of enormous stones (some of which were brought from Wales), built in stages beginning 5000 years ago. Reactions vary; some find that the car park, gift shop and crowds of tourists swamp the monument. Avebury, 18mi to the north, is much more impressive in scale and recommended for those who would like to commune with the ley lines in relative peace.

Stonehenge is 2mi west of Amesbury at the junction of the A303 and A344/A360, and 9mi from Salisbury (the nearest station). Some feel that it's unnecessary to pay the entry fee (£4.40), because you can get a good view from the road and even if you do enter you are kept at some distance from the stones. There are six buses a day from Salisbury (£5.50 return); a Getaway ticket (also £5.50) can be used for the day and is better value.

AVEBURY

☎ 01672 • pop 250

Avebury (between Calne and Marlborough, just off the A4) stands at the hub of a prehistoric complex of ceremonial sites, ancient avenues and burial chambers dating from 3500 BC. In scale the remains are more impressive than Stonehenge, and it's quite possible to escape crowds if you visit outside summer weekends.

In addition to an enormous stone circle, there's Silbury Hill (the largest constructed mound in Europe), West Kennet Long Barrow (a burial chamber) and a pretty village with an ancient church.

Avebury TIC (☎ 01380-729408, fax 73 0319; e alltic@kennet.gov.uk) can help with accommodation. For accommodation within the circle try either **B&B Manor Farm** (☎ 539294; singles/doubles £45/60) or **The Red Lion** (☎ 539266; doubles £60), an atmospheric country pub.

Avebury can be easily reached by frequent buses from Salisbury (Wiltshire Bus No 5, £4, 1½ hours) or from Swindon (No 6, £2, 30 minutes). To travel to/from Bath (£9.40, 1¾ hours) you'll have to change buses at Devizes; check connections (☎ 0845 709 0899).

DORSET

The greater part of Dorset is designated as an area of outstanding natural beauty but, with the exceptions of Poole and Weymouth, it avoids inundation by tourists.

The coast varies from sandy beaches to shingle banks and towering cliffs. Lyme Regis is a particularly attractive spot, made famous as the setting for John Fowles' book *The French Lieutenant's Woman*, and the subsequent film.

For those who've read Thomas Hardy, however, Dorset is inextricably linked with his novels. You can visit his birthplace at Higher Bockhampton, or Dorchester (Casterbridge), the unspoilt market town where he lived. Maiden Castle, the largest Iron Age fort in England, is nearby.

Orientation & Information

Dorchester makes a good base for exploring the best of Dorset, but on the coast colourful Weymouth or quieter Bridport are good alternatives. One of the reasons for Dorset's backwater status is that no major transport routes cross it. A rail loop runs west from Southampton to Dorchester, then north to Yeovil.

There are good TICs in all the main towns.

Places to Stay

There is no YHA hostel in Dorchester or Weymouth but there are hostels in Swanage, Lulworth Cove, Portland and Litton Cheney, all convenient for walkers on the Dorset Coast Path. Dorchester and Lyme Regis have some B&Bs while Weymouth is positively packed with them.

Getting There & Away

There are hourly trains from London to Dorchester (£33.40, 2½ hours) that continue to Weymouth (from Dorchester £2.60, 10 minutes). Trains continue north to Bath and Bristol from Dorchester.

There are also buses on these routes but, although cheaper, they tend to be much slower. Axminster is also a reasonable transport hub.

Getting Around

There are regular buses between Dorchester and Weymouth, Salisbury, Bournemouth and Bridport. Buses also operate regularly between Bridport/Lyme Regis and Axminster. Contact **Southern National** (☎ 01305-783645), **Wilts & Dorset** (☎ 01722-336855) or **Traveline** (☎ 0870 608 2608) for more information.

EXETER

☎ 01392 • pop 102,000

Exeter is the heart of the West Country. It was devastated during WWII and, as a result, first impressions are not particularly inspiring; if you get over these, you'll find a lively university city with a thriving nightlife. It's a good starting point for Dartmoor and Cornwall.

The cathedral is one of the most attractive in England, with two huge Norman towers surviving from the 11th century. From AD 50, when the city was established by the Romans, until the 19th century, Exeter was a very important port, and the waterfront (including a large boat museum) is gradually being restored.

There are a number of highly recommended free tours, which cover both cathedral and town.

Orientation & Information

There are two train stations, but most intercity trains use St David's, which is a 20-minute walk west of the city centre, and Central station. From St David's, cross the station forecourt and Bonhay Rd, climb some steps to St David's Hill and then turn right up the hill for the centre. You'll pass a batch of reasonably priced B&Bs on your right; keep going for three-quarters of a mile, then turn left up High St. The centre of the city is well signposted.

The **TIC** (☎ 265700; e tic@exeter.gov.uk; Civic Centre, Paris St; open 9am-5pm Mon-Sat & 10am-4pm Sun) is just across the road from the bus station, a short walk northeast of the cathedral.

Places to Stay & Eat

Exeter Youth Hostel (☎ 0870 770 5826, fax 0870 770 5827; e exeter@yha.org.uk; 47 Countess Wear Rd; dorm beds £11.40; open year-round, closed Christmas/New Year break) is 2mi southeast of the city towards Topsham. It occupies a large, comfortable house near the river. From High St, catch minibus K or T (10 minutes) and ask for the Countess Wear post office.

Globe Backpackers (☎ 215521, fax 215531; e caroline@globebackpackers.free serve.co.uk; 71 Holloway St; dorm beds £11, doubles £30) is a thankful addition to the budget scene; it has a good vibe and Internet access.

There are several B&Bs on St David's Hill. The welcoming **Kellsmoor** (☎ 211128, fax 211198; e kellsmoor@exeter81.fsnet.co.uk; 81 St David's Hill; singles/doubles £25/45) is the pick of the crop. There's another batch on Blackall Rd (near the prison). **Raffles** (☎/fax

270200; e raffleshtl@btinternet.com; 11 Blackall Rd; singles/doubles £34/50) is another good mid-range option.

The town's top address is the **Royal Clarence Hotel** (☎ 319955, fax 439423; e reservations@regalhotels.co.uk; Cathedral Yard; singles/doubles £105/130), overlooking the cathedral in the heart of town.

Coolings (☎ 434184; 11 Gandy St; mains £6.65) is a busy brasserie on a medieval, pedestrianised street; it's signposted off High St. The **Ship Inn** (☎ 272040; Martin's Lane), down the alley between the cathedral and the High St, was where Sir Francis Drake used to drink. **Herbies** (☎ 258473; 15 North St; mains £5.25-6.50) is a good vegetarian restaurant. Carnivores should be satisfied by the steaks at **Mad Meg's** (☎ 221225; Fore St; mains £5-15). **Michael Caine's** (☎ 310031; mains £16-22) at the Royal Clarence Hotel, does some of the best English fare in town.

Getting There & Away

Bus Nine buses a day run between London, Heathrow airport and Exeter (£18, four hours). From Exeter there are frequent services to Plymouth (£5.35, 1¼ hours) and three direct buses a day to Penzance (£19, 4½ hours). For bus information phone National Express or **Stagecoach** (☎ 01392-427711).

Train For rail information, phone ☎ 0845 748 4950. Exeter is at the hub of lines running from London's Waterloo and Paddington stations (£51, 2¾ hours, hourly), Bristol (£15.60, 1¾ hours), Salisbury (£20.20, 1¾ hours) and Penzance (£19.10, three hours).

The 39mi branch line to Barnstaple (£9.60, 1¼ hours) gives good views of traditional Devon countryside.

PLYMOUTH

☎ 01752 • pop 240,000

Plymouth's renown as a maritime centre was established long before Sir Francis Drake's famous game of bowls on Plymouth Hoe in 1588. Devastated by WWII bombing raids, much of the city is modern but the Old Quarter by the harbour, from where the Pilgrim Fathers set sail for the New World in 1620, has been preserved.

Orientation & Information

The **TIC** (☎ 264849; e barbicantic@plymouth .gov.uk; 9 The Barbican; open 9am-5pm

Mon-Fri) is to the south of the bus station (half-mile) and train station (1mi). To the west is Plymouth Hoe, a grassy park with wide views over the sea.

Places to Stay
The city's only hostel is the welcoming and relatively central **Plymouth Backpackers** (☎ 225158; e *plymback@hotmail.com; 172 Citadel Rd, The Hoe; dorm beds £10)*.

B&Bs cluster round the northwestern corner of the Hoe and are generally good value, from £16.

Try the friendly **Westwinds Guest House** (☎ 601777, fax 662158; e *paul.colman@bt internet.com; 99 Citadel Rd; singles/doubles £18/38, with en suite £28/42)*.

For top-end budgets there's the Victorian **Duke of Cornwall** (☎ 275850, fax 275854; e *dukereservations@hotmail.com; Millbay Rd; singles/doubles from £84.50/99)*.

Getting There & Away
Stagecoach (☎ 01392-427711) has frequent buses to and from Exeter. National Express has direct connections to numerous cities, including London (£23.50, 4½ hours) and Bristol (£21.50, 2½ hours). Trains are faster to London (£65.50, four hours) and Penzance (£10.30, 1½ hours) but more expensive.

DARTMOOR NATIONAL PARK
Although the park is only about 25mi from north to south and east to west, it encloses some of the wildest, bleakest country in England – a suitable terrain for the hound of the Baskervilles (one of Sherlock Holmes' most notorious foes).

The park covers a granite plateau punctuated by distinctive tors, which can look uncannily like ruined castles, and cut by deep valleys known as coombs.

The high moorland is covered by windswept gorse and heather (there are no trees, apart from some limited plantations), and is grazed by sheep and semiwild Dartmoor ponies.

There are several small market towns surrounding the tableland, but the only village of any size on the moor is Princetown, which is not a particularly attractive place.

The countryside in the southeast is more conventionally beautiful, with wooded valleys and thatched villages. This is hiking country par excellence.

Orientation & Information
Dartmoor is accessible from Exeter and Plymouth, and infrequent buses run from these regional centres to the surrounding market towns. There are only two roads across the moor and they meet near Princetown.

The National Park Authority (NPA) has eight information centres in and around the park, or visit the TICs at Exeter and Plymouth before setting off. The **High Moorland Visitor Centre** (☎ 01822-890414; open year-round) is in Princetown. The **Ministry of Defence** (☎ 0800 458468) has three live firing ranges in the northwestern section; phone for an update on firing schedules.

Places to Stay
Most of Dartmoor is privately owned, but the owners of unenclosed moorland don't usually object to backpackers who keep to a simple code: don't camp on moorland enclosed by walls or within sight of roads or houses; don't stay on one site for more than two nights; and leave the site as you found it.

You could also contact the **camping barn network** (☎ 01200-420102; from £3.50 a night).

The **Bellever Youth Hostel** (☎ 0870 770 5692; e *bellever@yha.org.uk)*, Postbridge, is very popular. **Steps Bridge Youth Hostel** (☎ 0870 770 6048, fax 0870 770 6049), near Dunsford between Moretonhampstead and Exeter, is another good option.

B&Bs are plentiful in the larger towns on the edge of the park (like Buckfastleigh, Okehampton and Tavistock). Try the **Old Post House** (☎ 01647-440900; e *stay@theold posthouse.com; 18 Court St, Moretonhampstead; per person including breakfast from £22.50)*. The delightful **Lydgate House** (☎ 01822-880209; e *lydgatehouse@email .com; Postbridge; singles/doubles £35/76)* is smack in the park, has immaculate rooms and does one of Devon's best cream teas.

Getting There & Away
Exeter or Plymouth are the best starting points for the park, but Exeter has the better transport connections to the rest of England. Public transport in and around the park is lousy, so consider hiring a bike (£10 a day) from **Flash Gordon** (☎ 01392-213141) in Exeter.

From Exeter, Stagecoach bus No 359 goes via Steps Bridge to Moretonhampstead. The only bus that actually crosses Dartmoor is First

Western National No 82, running between Exeter and Plymouth via Moretonhampstead, Postbridge and Princetown. It runs daily (three buses each way) from late May to late September; the rest of the year there are weekend services only.

A one-day Rover ticket (£6) allows you to get on and off whenever you like. Outside summer, life becomes considerably more difficult, with infrequent services and changing schedules. Work out roughly what you want to do, then contact the **Devon County Public Transport Help Line** (☎ 01392-382800) or **Traveline** (☎ 0870 608 2608).

SOUTH CORNWALL COAST
Penzance
☎ 01736 • pop 20,000

At the end of the railway line from London, Penzance is a busy little town that has not yet completely sold its soul to tourists. It makes a good base for walking the Coastal Path from Land's End to St Ives, a dramatic 25mi section. There are many cheap farm B&Bs along the way.

The **TIC** (☎ 362207; e pztic@penwith.gov .uk) is just outside the train station.

Places to Stay Situated on the outskirts of town is the **Penzance Youth Hostel** (☎ 0870 770 5992, fax 0870 770 5993; e penzance@yha.org.uk; Castle Horneck, Alverton). Take bus No 5B or 6B from the train station to the Pirate Inn from where it's a half-mile walk. More central is the friendly **Penzance Backpackers** (☎ 363836, fax 363844; e pz backpack@ndirect.co.uk; Alexander Rd; dorm beds £10).

Alexander Rd is lined with mid-range options and here you'll find the pleasant **Dunedin Hotel** (☎ 362652, fax 360497; singles/ doubles £28/42). For old-fashioned comfort and a sea view head to the **Queens Hotel** (☎ 362371, fax 350033; e enquiries@queens -hotel.com; The Promenade; rooms from £55).

Getting There & Away There are four buses a day from Penzance to Bristol via either Newquay or Truro and Plymouth; three direct buses a day to Exeter (£19, 4½ hours); and five buses a day to London and Heathrow (£30.50, 7½ hours).

The train is definitely the civilised, if expensive, way to get to Penzance from London's Paddington station (£61.70, five hours).

There are frequent trains from Penzance to St Ives (£2.90, 20 minutes) or Plymouth (£10.30, two hours).

Land's End
☎ 01736

The coastal scenery on either side of Land's End is some of the finest in Britain, although the development at Land's End itself is shameful. Colourful **Whitesand's Lodge** (☎ 871776; e info@whitesandslodge.co.uk; Sennen village; dorm beds £11, doubles with en suite £51) is on the main road 2mi before Land's End. The closest **Youth Hostel** (☎ 0870 770 5906, fax 0870 770 5907; St Just) is just over 3mi from Land's End or 8mi from Penzance.

The coastal hills between St Just and St Ives, with their dry stone walling, form one of the oldest, most fascinating agricultural landscapes in Britain that still follow an Iron Age pattern. There are numerous prehistoric remains and the abandoned engine houses of old tin and copper mines.

WEST CORNWALL COAST
St Ives
☎ 01736 • pop 9500

St Ives is the ideal to which other seaside towns can only aspire. The omnipresent sea, the harbour, the beaches, the narrow alleyways, steep slopes and hidden corners are captivating, but it gets mighty busy in summer. Artists have long been attracted to St Ives, and in 1993 a branch of London's **Tate Gallery** (☎ 796226) was opened here.

The **TIC** (☎ 796297, fax 798309; e ivtic@ penwith.gov.uk; the Guildhall, Street-an-Pol; open year-round) is a short walk from the train station. There are several surf shops on the Wharf (the street edging the harbour) where it's possible to rent boards.

The busy **St Ives Backpackers** (☎/fax 799444; e st.ives@backpackers.co.uk; Lower Stennack; dorm beds £12) occupies a converted chapel. Of the numerous B&Bs, **Kynance Guest House** (☎ 796636; e enquiries@ kynance24.co.uk; The Warren; per person £23) is a sure bet. For rooms with smashing sea views there's **Pedn-Olva Hotel** (☎ 796222, fax 797710; e pednolva@westcountryhotel rooms.co.uk; Porthminster Beach; singles/ doubles £73/116). Restaurants – both cheap and pricey – congregate around the harbour and on Fore St.

St Ives is easily accessible by train from Penzance (£2.90, 20 minutes) and London (£61.70, five hours) via St Erth.

Newquay
☎ 01637 • pop 14,000

Newquay, the original Costa del Cornwall, was drawing them in long before the British learned to say Torremolinos. There are numerous sandy beaches, several of them right in town (including Fistral Beach for board riders).

The **TIC** (☎ 854020; e info@newquay.co .uk; Marcus Hill) is near the bus station in the centre of town. Several surf shops on Fore St hire fibreglass boards and wetsuits, each around £6 per day.

Newquay has many independent hostels geared up for surfers. **The Original Backpackers** (☎ 874668; 16 Beachfield Ave; dorm beds from £10) is in an excellent central position overlooking Towan Beach. **Home Surf Lodge** (☎ 873387; 18 Tower Rd; dorm beds £10 per night, in summer per week £120) is bigger and brighter. If you're not here to surf, the best place to stay is the palatial **Headland Hotel** (☎ 872211; fax 872212; e office@headland hotel.co.uk; Fistral Beach; singles/doubles from £76/122).

There are four trains a day between Newquay and Par (£4.30, 45 minutes), which is on the London-Penzance line, and numerous buses to Truro.

Tintagel
☎ 01840 • pop 1750

Even the summer crowds and the grossly commercialised village can't destroy the surf-battered grandeur of **Tintagel Head** (admission £3). According to legend the scanty ruins mark the birthplace of King Arthur, hence the plethora of King Arthur teashops etc. It's also worth visiting the picturesque 14th-century **Old Post Office** (admission £2.30). **Tintagel Youth Hostel** (☎ 0870 770 6068, fax 0870 770 6069; Dunderhole Point) is nearly 1mi from the village. Smack in the village is **The Cottage Teashop** (☎ 770639; e cotteashop@ talk21.com; Bossiney Rd; singles/doubles £35/40), a dainty little B&B. For information on irregular bus services, phone **Traveline** (☎ 0870 608 2608).

NORTH DEVON
North Devon is one of the most beautiful regions in England, with a spectacular, largely unspoilt coastline and the superb Exmoor National Park, which protects the best of it.

Barnstaple
☎ 01270 • pop 25,000

Barnstaple is a large town and transport hub, a good starting point for North Devon. There are some handsome old buildings, but there's no reason to stay. Contact the **TIC** (☎ 375000; e info@staynorthdevon.co.uk) for B&Bs.

Barnstaple is at the western end of the Tarka Line railway from Exeter and connects with a number of bus services around the coast. First Red Bus operates service No 310 direct to Lynton, but the most interesting option is the excellent No 300 scenic service that crosses Exmoor from Barnstaple, through Lynton to Minehead (£6 for a one-day Explorer Pass).

Mountain bikes are available from **Tarka Trail** (☎ 324202; £9 per day) in the train station.

Exmoor National Park
Exmoor is a small national park (265 sq mi) enclosing a wide variety of beautiful landscapes. In the north and along the coast the scenery is particularly breathtaking, with dramatic humpbacked headlands giving superb views across the Bristol Channel.

A high plateau rises steeply behind the coast, but is cut by steep, fast-flowing streams. On the southern side the two main rivers, the Exe and Barle, wind their way south along the wooded coombs. Pony herds, descended from ancient hill stock, still roam the commons, as do England's last herds of wild red deer.

There are a number of particularly attractive villages: Lynton/Lynmouth, twin villages joined by a water-operated railway; Porlock, at the edge of the moor in a beautiful valley; Dunster, which is dominated by a castle, a survivor from the Middle Ages; and Selworthy, a National Trust village with many classic thatch-roofed cottages.

For walkers, arguably the best and easiest section of the South West Coast Path is between Minehead and Padstow (sometimes known as the Somerset & North Devon Coast Path).

Orientation & Information Exmoor is accessible from Barnstaple (train from Exeter) and Taunton.

The NPA has five information centres in and around the park, but it's also possible to get information from the TICs at Barnstaple, Ilfracombe, Lynton and Minehead. The **main NPA visitor centre** (☎ 01398-323841; Fore St, Dulverton; open year-round) is between Bampton and Minehead. Other **NPA centres** (Dunster ☎ 01643-821835 • Lynmouth ☎ 01 598-752509) are open from the end of March to November.

Places to Stay There are **YHA hostels** at **Ilfracombe** (☎ 0870 770 5878), **Minehead** (☎ 0870 770 5968), **Lynton** (☎ 0870 770 5942) and **Exford** (☎ 0870 770 5828) in the centre of the park. All these hostels close over winter – phone for opening dates. **Ocean Backpackers** (☎ 01271-867835; 29 St James Place, Ilfracombe; dorm beds £10, doubles £30) is a fine, friendly hostel.

B&Bs are scattered throughout the park but the main swarm is around Lynton/Lynmouth. Try the **Victoria Fernery** (☎ 01598-752440, fax 01598-752396; e enquiries@thefernery .co.uk; Lydiate Lane, Lynton; singles/doubles £20/38) or contact the **Lynton TIC** (☎ 01598-752225) for more suggestions.

Getting There & Away From Exeter catch a Tarka Line train to Barnstaple, from where buses run to Ilfracombe, Lynton and Minehead. See the Exeter and Barnstaple sections earlier in this chapter for more details.

Alternatively, there are buses from Taunton (one hour) to Minehead. Contact **Southern National** (☎ 01823-272033) for details. A timetable covering local public transport is available from TICs, or you can phone **Devon County Public Transport Help Line** (☎ 01392-382800).

BATH
☎ 01255 • pop 85,000
For more than 2000 years Bath's fortune has been linked to its hot springs and tourism. The Romans developed a complex of baths and a temple to Sulis-Minerva. Today, however, Bath's Georgian architecture is an equally important attraction.

Throughout the 18th century, Bath was the most fashionable haunt of English society. Aristocrats flocked here to gossip, gamble and flirt.

Fortunately, they had the good sense and fortune to employ a number of brilliant architects who designed the Palladian terrace that dominates the city.

Like Italy's Florence, Bath is an architectural jewel, with a much-photographed, shop-lined bridge. In high summer the town can seem little more than an exotic shopping mall for wealthy tourists. However, when sunlight brightens the honey-coloured stone, no-one can deny Bath's exceptional beauty.

Orientation & Information
Bath sprawls more than you'd expect (as you'll discover if you stay at the Bath Youth Hostel). Fortunately, the centre is compact and easy to get around, although the tangle of streets, arcades and squares can be confusing. The train and bus stations are both south of the TIC, by the river.

The **TIC** (☎ 477101; e tourism@bathnes .gov.uk; Abbey Chambers, Abbey Churchyard; open 9am-7pm Mon-Sat, 9am-6pm Sun mid-June–mid-Sept; 9am-5pm Mon-Sat, 9am-4pm Sun late Sept-early June) can help with information.

Advance booking of accommodation is essential over Easter, during the Bath International Festival (late May), over summer weekends and throughout July and August.

The best currency exchange is at **Marks & Spencer** (☎ 462591; 16 Stall St).

Click (☎ 481008; 13a Manvers St; open 10am-10pm) provides Internet access (£1 per 20 minutes).

Things to See & Do
Bath was designed for wandering around and you'll need at least a full day. There is a **covered market** next to the Guildhall, and don't miss the maze of **passageways** just north of Abbey Churchyard. Free walking tours (10.30am and 2pm, 10.30am only on Saturday) leave from outside the Pump Room.

Try to see a play at Bath's sumptuous **Theatre Royal** (☎ 448844), which often features shows before their London run.

Bath's **flea market** (☎ 852773; Walcot St; Sat morning) is a popular place for bargain hunters (antiques and clothes).

A convenient starting point for a **walking tour** is **Bath Abbey** (donation £2). Built between 1499 and 1616, it is more glass than stone.

Across the street from Abbey Churchyard (an open square) is the **Pump Room** (☎ 444477), an opulent restaurant that exemplifies the elegant style that once drew the aristocrats.

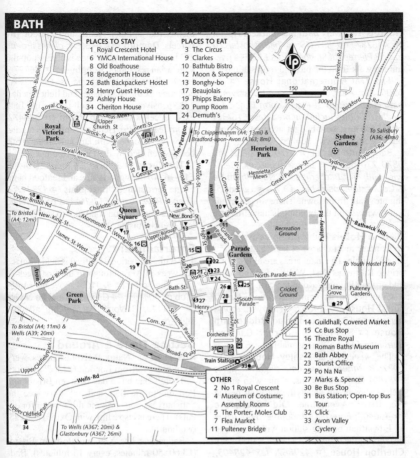

BATH

PLACES TO STAY
1 Royal Crescent Hotel
6 YMCA International House
8 Old Boathouse
18 Bridgenorth House
26 Bath Backpackers' Hostel
28 Henry Guest House
29 Ashley House
34 Cheriton House

PLACES TO EAT
3 The Circus
9 Clarkes
10 Bathtub Bistro
12 Moon & Sixpence
13 Bonghy-bo
17 Beaujolais
19 Phipps Bakery
20 Pump Room
24 Demuth's

14 Guildhall; Covered Market
15 Cc Bus Stop
16 Theatre Royal
21 Roman Baths Museum
22 Bath Abbey
23 Tourist Office
25 Po Na Na
27 Marks & Spencer
30 Be Bus Stop
31 Bus Station; Open-top Bus Tour
32 Click
33 Avon Valley Cyclery

OTHER
2 No 1 Royal Crescent
4 Museum of Costume; Assembly Rooms
5 The Porter; Moles Club
7 Flea Market
11 Pulteney Bridge

Next door, the **Roman Baths Museum** (☎ 477785; admission £8, with Museum of Costume £10.50; open 9am-5pm daily, to 9pm July & Aug) is a series of excavated passages and chambers beneath street level, taking in the sulphurous mineral springs (still flowing after all these years), the ancient central-heating system and the bath itself, which retains its Roman paving and lead base. This is Bath's top attraction and it can get hopelessly overcrowded in summer.

From the Roman Baths, walk north until you hit the main shopping drag, Milsom St, and finally the **Assembly Rooms** and the **Museum of Costume**, a 20-minute walk uphill, which covers fashion from the last four centuries.

Turn left on Bennet St and walk west to the **Circus**, an architectural masterpiece by John Wood the Elder, designed so that a true crescent faces each of its three approaches. Continue to **Royal Crescent**, designed by John Wood the Younger and even more highly regarded than his father's effort. **No 1** (☎ 428126; adult/concession £4/3.50; open 10.30am-5pm, 4pm winter) has been superbly restored to its 1770 glory, down to the minutest detail.

From Royal Crescent, wander back to the Abbey, then keep going east until you find yourself overlooking the formal **Parade Gardens** with the famous view up the Avon to **Pulteney Bridge**, built by Robert Adam and lined with tiny shops. Continue along Great Pulteney St from the bridge and you will reach Sydney Place. Jane Austen lived at No 4 with her parents.

BRITAIN

Places to Stay

Hostels The lively **Bath Backpackers Hostel** (☎ 446787, fax 331319; e bath@hostels.co .uk; 13 Pierrepont St; dorm beds £12) is a five-minute walk from the bus and train stations.

The **YMCA International House** (☎ 32 5900, fax 462065; e reservations@ymca bath.co.uk; Broad St Place; dorm beds £12, singles/doubles including breakfast £16/32) offers the next best budget accommodation, but it's often heavily booked.

Bath Youth Hostel (☎ 0870 770 5688, fax 0870 770 5689; e bath@yha.org.uk; Bathwick Hill; First Badgerline bus No 18 from Be & Cc bus stops; dorm beds £9.75) is a good 25-minute walk from town. There are compensatory views and the building is magnificent.

B&Bs & Hotels Bath's B&Bs are expensive. In summer most charge at least £22/45 for a single/double. The main areas are along Newbridge Rd to the west, Wells Rd to the south and around Pulteney Rd in the east.

Considering its central location, **Henry Guest House** (☎ 424052; 6 Henry St; rooms per person £22) is good value. **Bridgenorth House** (☎ 331186; 2 Crescent Gardens; doubles £44) is also reasonable.

The wisteria-clad **Ashley House** (☎ 42 5027; 8 Pulteney Gardens; singles/doubles £28/55) has eight rooms, some with an attached shower. In an idyllic location beside the River Avon, the **Old Boathouse** (☎ 466407; Forester Rd; doubles £60-70) is an Edwardian boating station within walking distance of the centre. Up a notch is the lovely **Cheriton House** (☎ 429862, fax 428403; e cheriton@which.net; 9 Upper Oldfield Park; doubles from £66-90).

For a true splurge there's the **Royal Crescent Hotel** (☎ 823333, fax 339401; e reservations@royalcrescent.co.uk; 16 Royal Crescent; doubles from £330), a Georgian delight.

Places to Eat

Phipps Bakery (☎ 462483; Kingsmead Square; light lunches £3.50) has excellent filled rolls, vegetable curries and spinach turnovers. There are several fast-food places in this area.

The **Moon & Sixpence** (☎ 460962; 6 Broad St; 2-course lunch £5) is a pleasant pub. Pubs are good bets for cheap evening meals, too.

Clarkes (☎ 444440; 7 Argyle St; mains £8-13) is a cosy wine bar flaunting international cuisine. Nearby, **Bathtub Bistro** (☎ 460593; 2 Grove St; mains £8) serves an array of dishes like spinach, lentil and apricot filo parcels. **Demuth's** (☎ 446059; dishes around £5) in North Parade Passage is a very popular vegetarian restaurant. **Bonghy-bo** (☎ 462276; Upper Borough Walls; mains £4) has an eclectic mix of Asian dishes and light lunches.

Expensive, but very much part of the Bath experience, is the **Pump Room** (☎ 444477; cream teas £6.25). Here one sips one's tea and heaps one's scones with jam and cream while being serenaded by the Pump Room Trio.

The Circus (☎ 318918; 34 Brock St; dishes £11-16.50) does good game and seafood in intimate surroundings. **Beaujolais** (☎ 423417; 5 Chapel Row; mains £13-16) has been around for three decades and continues to serve excellent French cuisine.

Entertainment

The Bath International Festival is held from the last week of May through to the first week of June. **The Porter** (☎ 424104) above the **Moles Club** (☎ 404445; 14 George St) and **Po Na Na** (☎ 401115; 8 North Parade) are all cool nightspots.

Getting There & Around

Bus There are National Express buses every 90 minutes to/from London (£13, 3¼ hours).

There's one bus a day between Bristol and Portsmouth via Bath and Salisbury (see the Salisbury section earlier in this chapter for details). There is also a link with Oxford (£10.25, two hours).

Badgerline bus X39 runs to/from Bristol (£3.60, 50 minutes, every 15 minutes). Badgerline's Day Explorer (£5.70) gives you access to a good network of buses in Bristol, Somerset (Wells, Glastonbury), Gloucestershire (Gloucester via Bristol) and Wiltshire (Lacock, Bradford-on-Avon, Salisbury).

Maps and timetables are available from the **bus station** (☎ 464446).

Train There are numerous services to/from London's Paddington station (£37.50, 1¾ hours). Plenty of trains also run to Bristol (£4.60, 10 to 20 minutes) for onward travel to Exeter, Cardiff or the north. Trains run hourly to Salisbury (£10, 50 minutes).

Bicycle The Bristol & Bath Cycle Walkway is an excellent footpath and cycleway that follows the route of the disused railway. Bikes are available from **Avon Valley Cyclery** (☎ 442442; half-day £9, full-day £14, deposit required).

AROUND BATH
Lacock

Three miles south of Chippenham, Lacock is a classic, dreamy Cotswold village with an **abbey** (☎ 01249-730 227; admission £6; open 11am-5pm except Tues) dating back to the 13th century and, at the entrance to Lacock Abbey, a **museum of photography**. Badgerline bus No 234 (Chippenham to Trowbridge) serves Lacock.

Bradford-on-Avon

Eight miles east of Bath, this beautiful small town has somehow managed to avoid becoming a tourist trap. Its narrow streets tumble down a steep bluff overlooking the Avon. There are good bus connections with Bath, and hourly trains, so the town could easily be used as a base; Bradford's few B&Bs tend to be pricey. Contact the **TIC** (☎ 01225-865797) for more information.

WELLS
☎ 01749 • pop 9500

Wells is a small cathedral city that has kept much of its medieval character; many claim that the cathedral is England's most beautiful, and it is certainly one of the best surviving examples of a full cathedral complex.

Wells is 21mi southwest of Bath on the edge of the Mendip Hills. The **TIC** (☎ 67 2552; e wells.tic@ukonline.co.uk; open 9.30am-5.30pm daily) is in the town hall on the picturesque Market Place. **Bike City** (☎ 67 1711; 31 Broad St) has bicycles for hire at £8.95 a day.

Things to See & Do

The **cathedral** was built in stages from 1180 to 1508 and incorporates several styles. The most famous features are the extraordinary west facade, an immense sculpture gallery with over 300 surviving figures; the interior scissor arches, a brilliant solution to the problem posed by the subsidence of the central tower; the delicate chapter house; and the ancient mechanical clock in the north transept. Try and join one of the free tours.

Beyond the cathedral is the moated **Bishop's Palace** (admission £3.50; open 10.30am-6pm Tues-Fri & Sun, 2pm-6pm June-Sept), with its beautiful gardens; **Market Place** (markets Wed & Sat); and the 14th-century **Vicars' Close**.

Places to Stay & Eat

The nearest YHA hostel is at Street, near Glastonbury, but there are plenty of B&Bs with prices for around £18 per person.

The **Old Poor House** (☎ 675052; per person £25) is a comfortable 14th-century cottage just outside the cathedral precincts.

The Crown (☎ 673457; e reception@crownatwells.co.uk; Market Place; singles/doubles £45/60) is Wells' oldest hotel.

The **City Arms** (☎ 673916; 69 High St; mains around £5) used to be the city jail but now serves good pub grub. Near the bus station the **Good Earth Restaurant** (☎ 678600; 4 Priory Rd) produces excellent home-made soup, pizzas and puddings at reasonable prices.

Getting There & Away

Badgerline operates buses from Bath (No 173, 1¼ hours) and Bristol (No 376, one hour). No 376 from Bristol continues to Yeovil via Glastonbury and Street. No 163 runs from Wells to Bridgwater (for connections to Exmoor) also via Glastonbury and Street.

GLASTONBURY
☎ 01458 • pop 7000

Legend and history combine at Glastonbury to produce an irresistible attraction for romantics and eccentrics of every description. It's a small market town with the ruins of a 14th-century **abbey**, and a nearby **tor** with superb views.

According to various legends, Jesus travelled here with Joseph of Arimathea and the chalice from the Last Supper. It's also the burial place of King Arthur and Queen Guinevere, and the tor is either the Isle of Avalon or a gateway to the underworld. Whatever you choose to believe, a climb to the top of the tor is well worthwhile. Turn right at the top of High St (the far end from the TIC) onto Chilkwell St and then left onto Dod Lane; there's a footpath to the tor from the end of the lane.

The **Glastonbury Festival** (☎ 832020), a three-day festival of theatre, music, circus, mime, natural healing etc, is a massive affair with over 1000 acts. It takes place over three days in late June at Pilton, 8mi from Glastonbury; admission is by advance ticket only (around £100 for the whole festival).

BRITAIN

The **TIC** (☎ 832954; e glastonbury.tic@uk online.co.uk) can supply maps and accommodation information; there are plenty of B&Bs for around £21 per person. The **Glastonbury Backpackers Hostel** (☎ 833353; e backpackers@glastonbury/online.com; Crown Hotel, 4 Market Place; dorm beds £10, doubles £26) has good facilities. Another possibility is **Street Youth Hostel** (☎ 0870 770 6056, fax 0870 770 6057), 4mi south.

There are Badgerline buses from Bristol to Wells, Glastonbury and Street. Glastonbury is only 6mi from Wells, so walking or hitching is feasible. Bus No 163 from Wells continues to Bridgwater, from where there are buses to Minehead (for Exmoor).

BRISTOL
☎ 0117 • pop 415,000

Bristol is by far and away the region's largest and coolest city, home to Massive Attack and Tricky. Approaching through the unlovely southern suburbs, you might wonder what the hell you're getting into, but the centre has some magnificent architecture, docks and warehouses that are being rescued from ruin, and a plethora of bars, pubs and restaurants.

Unlike its glamorous neighbour, the tourist honeypot of Bath, Bristol remains very much a working city where tourism is almost incidental. Consequently, many folk may prefer it. Bristol is most famous as a port, although it is 6mi from the Severn estuary, and it grew rich on the 17th-century trade with the North American colonies and the West Indies (rum, slaves, sugar and tobacco).

It continues to prosper today (although it has had to switch some commodities) and it's an important transport hub, with connections north to the Cotswolds and the Midland cities, west to southern Wales, southwest to Devon and Cornwall, and southeast to Bath (an easy day trip).

Orientation & Information

The city centre lies north of the Floating Harbour – a system of locks, canals and docks fed by the tidal River Avon. The central area is compact and easy to get around on foot, if rather hilly.

The main train station is Bristol Temple Meads, about 1mi to the southeast of the centre, although some trains use Bristol Parkway 5mi to the north, which is accessible from the centre by bus and train.

The bus station is to the north of the city centre.

The **TIC** (☎ 926 0767, fax 9157340, e ticharbourside@bristol-city.gov.uk; Wildscreen Walk, Harbourside; open 10am-6pm daily, to 5pm Nov-Feb) is at Bristol's newly transformed waterfront.

Things to See & Do

The first thing on a visitor's agenda should be a wander around the twisting streets of the old city centre – be sure to take in **St Nicholas Market** – followed by a ferry trip on the Floating Harbour (see Getting Around later in this section).

Close to the TIC is College Green, flanked by impressive council offices and the imposing **Bristol Cathedral**. Up the hill (Park St) there are numerous restaurants, the university and, 1½mi beyond, the genteel suburb of Clifton, which is dominated by fine Georgian architecture. The spectacular **Clifton Suspension Bridge** (☎ 974 4664; adult/concession £2/1.20; visitors centre open 10am-5pm), designed by Brunel and completed in 1864, crosses the equally spectacular Avon Gorge. The suspension bridge is quite a walk from the centre of town – catch bus No 8 from bus stop 'Cu' on Colston Ave, or from Temple Meads station.

Back in the centre, you could visit the **Arnolfini Centre** (☎ 929 9191), an important contemporary-arts complex, or take in a film at the **Watershed Media Centre** (☎ 925 2455), on opposite sides of St Augustine's Reach. Then walk down King St, with its old buildings, now used as restaurants and clubs, and the **Llandoger Trow**, a 17th-century pub reputed to be the Admiral Benbow in Robert Louis Stevenson's *Treasure Island*.

There are numerous other important sights: **St Nicholas Church** with its magnificent 18th-century altarpiece by William Hogarth; the beautiful **Church of St Mary Redcliffe**; the **Maritime Heritage Centre** (☎ 929 1843; admission free; open 10am-5.30pm daily, 10am-4.30pm Nov-Mar) with Brunel's SS *Great Britain* (admission £6.25), the first ocean-going iron ship with a screw propeller; and the **Industrial Museum** (☎ 925 1470; admission free).

Places to Stay

Occupying a converted warehouse right at the waterfront is the excellent **Bristol Youth**

Hostel (☎ 0870 770 5726, fax 0870 770 5727; e bristol@yha.org.uk; 14 Narrow Quay; beds in 4-bed room £12.50, doubles £26-30). Bristol Backpackers (☎ 925 7900; e info@bristolbackpackers.co.uk; 17 St Stephen's St; dorm beds £13) is central and charming.

The university lets out rooms at well located The Hawthorns (☎ 954 5900; e client -services-office@bris.ac.uk; Woodland Rd, Clifton; singles/doubles £50/64). Rates include breakfast.

Most of the cheap B&Bs tend to be a fair distance from the centre, although there is a good town bus service. There are a number of places on Bath Rd (the A4) and Wells Rd (the A37).

Clifton, 1½mi from the centre, is a very attractive suburb but most of the B&Bs here cost £25 per person. The quiet Oakfield Hotel (☎ 973 5556, fax 974 4141; 52 Oakfield Rd; singles/doubles £30/40) is off Whiteladies Rd towards Bristol Parkway train station.

Exuding individuality and modern grandeur, Hotel du Vin (☎ 925 5577, fax 925 1199; The Sugar House, Narrow Lewins Mead; rooms from £115-135) occupies a cluster of stylishly renovated warehouses.

Places to Eat

Bristol is well endowed with restaurants, and most are reasonably priced.

The trendy cafés in the Watershed and Arnolfini arts centres on either side of the Floating Harbour have some delicious dishes for under £4.

The intimate Boston Tea Party (☎ 929 8601; 75 Park Street; sandwiches from £3.20) has a lounge and garden. Park St has several pizza places, but very popular is the nearby Pizza Express (☎ 926 0300; 31 Berkeley Square; pizzas £4.45-7.70). Across the road is the ever-popular Browns (☎ 930 47770; 38 Queen St; mains from £6).

The grand old bank buildings along Corn St now house pubs, café/bars and restaurants, including groovy Toad (☎ 945 9990; 31 Corn St).

There's more sophistication at two designer restaurants on the dockside known as The Grove: Riverstation (☎ 914 4434) and Severnshed (☎ 925 1212). Both have fine cuisine with meals around £13.

The nearby restaurant/bar Aqua (☎ 915 6060; Welshback; mains from £8.50) has a

mouthwatering menu, and Belgo (☎ 905 8000; Queen Charlotte St; mains from £8) provides the mussels to take on its Belgian beers.

Near St Nicholas market, Las Iguanas (☎ 927 6233; 10 St Nicholas St; meals from £7) does Mexican and South American dishes.

At Broadmead shopping centre there is a Tesco supermarket.

Entertainment

There's plenty going on at night, ranging from high culture to low. Get a copy of Venue (£1.90), Bristol and Bath's answer to Time Out.

There are several entertainment options on King St, ranging from Monday jazz at the Old Duke (☎ 927 7137) to theatre in the New Vic (☎ 987 7877).

On St Nicholas St, there's often live music at Las Iguanas (see Places to Eat earlier).

Down an alley off Park St is Folk House (40A Park St), which has regular candlelit jazz, blues and folk.

Clubs come in and out of favour, but those that are in at present include Lakota (☎ 942 6208; Upper York St) and Thekla (☎ 929 3301) on a boat at The Grove.

The legendary Bierkeller (☎ 926 8514; All Saints St; admission between £8-15) has played host to luminaries like the Stone Roses and the Stranglers.

Getting There & Away

Bus Bristol has excellent bus connections. There are hourly National Express buses to London's Victoria coach station (£13, 2½ hours), and Heathrow (£26.50, two hours) and Gatwick (£30, 3¼ hours) airports.

National Express has frequent buses to Cardiff (£5.50, 1¼ hours). There are three buses a day to Barnstaple (£15.50, 2¾ hours), five to Exeter (£10.25, 1¾ hours), four to Penzance (£35, six hours), and daily services to Oxford (£13.50, 2½ hours) or Portsmouth (£15.50, 3¾ hours) via Salisbury (£7.25, two hours).

Badgerline has numerous services per day to/from Bath (£3.60). There are also services to Salisbury and north to Gloucester. A Badgerline Day Explorer ticket costs £5.70. For all bus information including city services, phone Traveline (☎ 0870 608 2608).

Train Bristol is an important rail hub, with regular connections to London's Paddington station (£39.50, 1¾ hours). Most trains (except

BRITAIN

those to the south) use both Temple Meads and Parkway stations. There are frequent links to Bath (£4.60, 10 to 20 minutes), to Cardiff (£8.90, one hour), to Exeter (£15.60, one hour), to Fishguard (£21.50, 3½ hours), to Oxford (£14.50, 1½ hours) and to Birmingham (£21, 1½ hours). Phone ☎ 0845 748 4950 for timetable information.

Getting Around
The nicest way to get around is on the ferry which, from April to September, plies the Floating Harbour. There are a number of stops including Bristol Bridge, the Industrial Museum, the SS *Great Britain* and Hotwells. The **ferry** *(☎ 927 3416)* runs every 20 minutes; a single fare is £1.20, a round trip £5.

Taxis wait at the rank opposite the Hippodrome Theatre in the city centre. The TIC has a list of taxi operators.

There's a good **local bus system** *(☎ 941 2525)*.

Central England

The English heartland covers a vast swathe of territory that includes some of England's highs and lows. Many of the areas around the M1 corridor can look pretty miserable on a wet and windy day, but some of the region's liveliest cities are here such as Nottingham, Leicester, Coventry and Birmingham. What it lacks in prettiness, it makes up for in personality, and there is a real feel to the East Midlands that isn't always found in the tourist meccas of the Cotswolds and the Peak District.

To the west, however, it's a different story. Oxford remains a very beautiful city that is a must for any visitor. The southwest sections of the Chilterns remain largely unspoilt and are accessible to walkers of the Ridgeway.

The Cotswolds, more than any other region, embody the popular image of English countryside. The prettiness can be forced, and the villages are certainly not strangers to mass tourism, but there are also moments when you will be transfixed by the area's beauty. The combination of golden stone, flower-draped cottages, church spires, towering chestnuts and oaks, rolling hills and green, stone-walled fields can be too extraordinarily picturesque to seem quite real.

West again, you reach the Bristol Channel and the wide Severn Valley, a natural border to the counties of Herefordshire and Worcestershire and the region known as the Welsh Marches. Herefordshire and Worcestershire have rich agricultural countryside with orchards and market gardens. The Wye Valley is a famous spot of beauty, popularised by the first Romantic poets in the 18th century.

To the north, Shrewsbury is an attractive town that's well worth a visit, and the Peak District National Park is one of England's most beautiful regions.

Some of Britain's most popular tourist sites are in the southern part of the Midlands, among them Blenheim Palace, Warwick Castle, Stratford-upon-Avon and Oxford.

Orientation & Information
The southern section of this region is cut by two ranges of hills and two major rivers. From east to west, you first meet the chalk ridge of the Chilterns, which runs northeast from Salisbury Plain to Hertfordshire, then come the Thames Valley, the limestone Cotswolds that run north from Bath, and finally the Severn Valley. The Peak District National Park lies in the far north of the Midlands.

Major northbound transport arteries (including the M1 and M40) cross the region, so it's highly likely you'll pass through it at some stage.

Hiking
The best hiking in the southern section of the Midlands is in the Cotswolds, although there are a number of other interesting paths in the region.

The Cotswolds Way, with easy accessibility to accommodation, is the best way to discover the Cotswolds. The path follows the western escarpment overlooking the Bristol Channel for 100mi from Chipping Campden to Bath, but it is quite feasible to tackle a smaller section. Bath is obviously easily accessible, but you'll have to contact the **Gloucestershire inquiry line** *(☎ 01452-425543)* for information about the infrequent buses that run between Chipping Campden and Stratford or Moreton-in-Marsh.

Ordnance Survey/Aurum Press publishes a comprehensive guide to *The Cotswold Way* (£10.99) by Anthony Burton, complete with maps and walking details.

The main walking area in the north of this region is the stunning Peak District National Park.

Getting Around

Bus transport around the region is fairly efficient, and particularly good in the Peak district.

There's also a good network of railway lines; you'll rarely need to resort to buses. See Shrewsbury later in this chapter for details on an interesting rail loop around northern Wales.

OXFORD

☎ 01865 • pop 115,000

It's impossible to pick up any tourist literature about Oxford without reading about its dreaming spires. Like all great cliches it's strikingly apt. Looking across the meadows or rooftops to Oxford's golden spires is certainly an experience to inspire purple prose.

These days, however, Oxford battles against a flood of tourists that can dilute the charm during summer. It is not just a university city, but the home of Morris cars (the plant is now owned by BMW), and Oxford has expanded rapidly in the 20th century. This expansion has created a city with a bustling heart surrounded by sprawling industrial suburbs.

Oxford University is the oldest university in Britain, but no-one can find an exact starting date. It evolved during the 11th century as an informal centre for scholars and students. The colleges began to appear from the mid-13th century onwards. There are now about 14,500 undergraduates and 36 colleges.

Orientation & Information

The city centre is surrounded by rivers and streams on the eastern, southern and western sides, and can easily be covered on foot. **Carfax Tower** (admission £1.20; open daily) at the intersection of Queen St and Cornmarket St/St Aldate's is a useful central marker. The tower is all that remains of St Martin's Church. There's a fine view from the top, which is good for orienting yourself.

The train station is to the west of the city, with frequent buses to Carfax Tower. Alternatively, turn left off the station concourse onto Park End St and it's a 15-minute walk.

The bus station is nearer the centre, on Gloucester Green (there's no green).

A visit to the hectic **TIC** (☎ 726871, fax 240261; e tic@oxford.gov.uk; w www.visit oxford.org; open 9.30am-5pm Mon-Sat year-round, 10am-3.30pm Sun in summer), also on Gloucester Green, is essential. A hefty £3 charge (plus 10% deposit) is made for accommodation bookings.

You need more information than this guide can give if you're going to do the town justice. The *Welcome to Oxford* brochure (£1.30) has a walking tour with college opening times. The TIC has **walking tours** (adult/concession £6/3; 11am and 2pm) of the colleges that last for two hours. **Guide Friday** (☎ 202154) runs a hop-on, hop-off city bus tour every 15 minutes from 9.30am to 7pm in summer (until 4.30pm in winter). It leaves from the train station and tickets cost £9/7.50.

Marks & Spencer (13-18 George St) has the best rates in town for foreign exchange and charges no commission.

For Internet access (£1 for 30 minutes) head to **Mic@s.com** (☎ 726364; 118 High St; open 9am-11pm daily).

Things to See & Do

Colleges You need more than a day to 'do' Oxford, but, at a minimum, make sure you visit Christ Church (with Christ Church Cathedral), Merton and Magdalen (pronounced maudlen) colleges and the Ashmolean Museum. The colleges remain open throughout the year (unlike Cambridge) but their hours vary; many are closed in the morning. Some never admit visitors.

Starting at the Carfax Tower, cross Cornmarket St and walk down the hill, along St Aldate's, to **Christ Church** (☎ 276150; admission £4), perhaps the most famous college in Oxford. The main entrance is beneath Tom Tower, which was built by Christopher Wren in 1680, but the usual visitors entrance is farther down the hill via the wrought-iron gates of the War Memorial Gardens and the Broad Walk facing out over Christ Church Meadow. The college chapel is the smallest cathedral in England, but it is a beautiful example of late Norman (1140–80) architecture.

Return to the Broad Walk, follow the stone wall, then turn left up Merton Grove, through wrought-iron gates, then right onto Merton St. **Merton College** (☎ 276110; admission free) was founded in 1264 and its buildings are among the oldest in Oxford. The present buildings mostly date from the 15th to the 17th centuries. The entrance to the 14th-century Mob Quad, with its medieval library, is on your right.

Turn left onto Merton St, then take the first right onto Magpie Lane, which will take you through to High St with its fascinating mix of architectural styles. Turn right down the hill

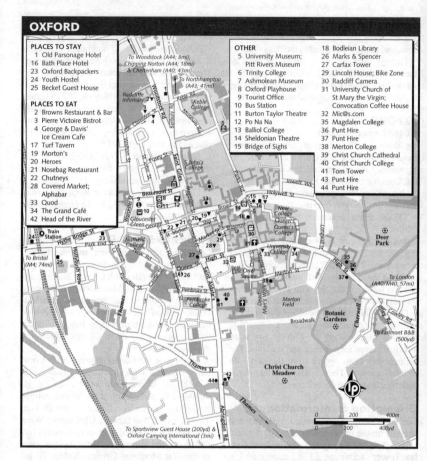

OXFORD

PLACES TO STAY
1 Old Parsonage Hotel
16 Bath Place Hotel
23 Oxford Backpackers
24 Youth Hostel
25 Becket Guest House

PLACES TO EAT
2 Browns Restaurant & Bar
3 Pierre Victoire Bistrot
4 George & Davis'
  Ice Cream Cafe
17 Turf Tavern
19 Morton's
20 Heroes
21 Nosebag Restaurant
22 Chutneys
28 Covered Market;
  Alphabar
33 Quod
34 The Grand Café
42 Head of the River

OTHER
5 University Museum;
  Pitt Rivers Museum
6 Trinity College
7 Ashmolean Museum
8 Oxford Playhouse
9 Tourist Office
10 Bus Station
11 Burton Taylor Theatre
12 Po Na Na
13 Balliol College
14 Sheldonian Theatre
15 Bridge of Sighs
18 Bodleian Library
26 Marks & Spencer
27 Carfax Tower
29 Lincoln House; Bike Zone
30 Radcliff Camera
31 University Church of
  St Mary the Virgin;
  Convocation Coffee House
32 Mic@s.com
35 Magdalen College
36 Punt Hire
37 Punt Hire
38 Merton College
39 Christ Church Cathedral
40 Christ Church College
41 Tom Tower
43 Punt Hire
44 Punt Hire

until you come to **Magdalen** (☎ 276000; admission £2) just before the river on your left. Magdalen is one of the richest Oxford colleges and has the most extensive and beautiful grounds, with a deer park, river walk, three quadrangles and superb lawns. This was CS Lewis' college and the setting for the film *Shadowlands*.

Walk back up High St until you come to the **University Church of St Mary the Virgin** on your right. There's a good view from the **tower**; *(admission £1.60/80p)*. Turn right up Catte St to the distinctive, circular **Radcliffe Camera**, a reading room for the **Bodleian Library** (☎ 277224). Continue up Catte St passing the **Bridge of Sighs** on your right, then turn left onto Broad St. On your left you pass Wren's **Sheldonian Theatre**, and on your right

Trinity and **Balliol** colleges. Turn left at Cornmarket St and you'll be back where you started.

Museums Established in 1683, the **Ashmolean** (☎ 278000; **w** www.ashmol.ox.ac.uk; Beaumont St; donation £3; open 10am-5pm Tues-Sat, 2pm-5pm Sun) is the country's oldest museum and houses extensive displays of European art (including works by Raphael and Michelangelo) and Middle Eastern antiquities.

Housed in a superb Victorian Gothic building, the **University Museum** (☎ 272950; Parks Rd; admission free; open noon-5pm daily) is devoted to natural science. You reach the **Pitt Rivers Museum** (☎ 270927; donation £3; open noon-4.30pm Mon-Sat, 2pm-4.30pm Sun) through the University Museum. The glass cases here are crammed to overflowing with everything from a sailing boat to a gory collection of shrunken South American heads.

Punts From May to September, punts and boats can be hired (£10 per hour, £25 deposit) at Folly Bridge and Magdalen Bridge. There's no better way of letting the atmosphere of Oxford seep in, however the seepage can be dramatic – punting is not as easy as it looks. From Magdalen Bridge, go left for peace and quiet, and right for views back to the colleges across the Botanic Gardens and Christ Church Meadow.

Places to Stay
The **Youth Hostel** (☎ 0870 770 5970, fax 0870 770 5971; e oxford@yha.org.uk; 2a Botley Rd; adults/under-18s in 4- or 6-bed room £18.50/13.75, twin room £41, rates include breakfast) is well located in a new building directly behind the train station. It gets booked up very quickly in summer.

Much less spick-and-span is **Oxford Backpackers** (☎ 721761; 9A Hythe Bridge St; beds in 8- to 18-bed dorms £12, beds in 4-bed dorms £13).

Oxford Camping International (☎ 244088; 426 Abingdon Rd; tent/person £4.50/4.45, backpackers £4.15 including tent site) is roughly 3mi south of the centre near the Park & Ride car park.

B&Bs are expensive and suburban, the two main areas being Abingdon Rd and Cowley/Iffley Rds, both on regular bus routes.

Earlmont (☎ 240236, fax 434903; e beds@earlmont.prestel.co.uk; 322 Cowley Rd; singles/doubles £40/60) is a large and comfortable B&B within walking distance of shops and restaurants.

Sportsview Guest House (☎ 244268, fax 249270; e stay@sportsview-guest-house.free serve.co.uk; 106-110 Abingdon Rd; singles/doubles from £40/62) is clean, quiet and non-smoking. **Becket Guest House** (☎/fax 72 4675; 5 Becket St; singles/doubles from £35/48) is convenient to the train station.

The intimate **Bath Place Hotel** (☎ 243235, fax 791834; e bathplace@compuserve.com; 4-5 Bath Place; singles/doubles £90/95, cottage suite £125/150) occupies a cluster of 17th-century cottages. Another historic gem is the **Old Parsonage Hotel** (☎ 310210, fax 311262; e info@oldparsonage-hotel.co.uk; 1 Banbury Rd; singles/doubles from £130/150).

Places to Eat
There are some excellent sandwich bars throughout the centre and many a student debate has centred on which is best. **Morton's** (☎ 200860; 22 Broad St) can't be faulted for its tasty baguettes and attractive garden; nearby, the relaxed **Heroes** (☎ 723459; 8 Ship St; sandwiches from £2.15) builds sandwiches to order with a fine selection of fillings.

Pubs are also a good bet. There's excellent pub grub at **Turf Tavern** (☎ 243235; 4 Bath Place), a recommended watering hole hidden away down an alley. **Head of the River** (☎ 721600; Folly Bridge) has an ideal location and is very popular.

Self-caterers should visit the **covered market**, near Carfax Tower, for fruit and vegetables. Here too is **Alphabar** (☎ 250499; sandwiches from £2.50; open until 4pm), the place to go for an organic or biodynamic snack or light meal.

Nosebag Restaurant (☎ 203222; 6 St Michael's St; soups £2.75, mains £6.25) has filling soups and a good range of vegetarian choices. **George & Davis' Ice Cream Café** (☎ 516652; 55 Little Clarendon St; open until midnight) serves pizzas and bagels as well as delicious home-made ice cream. At **Convocation Coffee House**, attached to St Mary the Virgin church, soup and a roll costs £3.65.

Chutneys (☎ 724241; 36 St Michael's St) is an Indian restaurant with lunchtime buffets for £7.50.

Browns Restaurant & Bar (☎ 319655; 5 Woodstock Rd; mains £7.50-13.50) is a popular, stylish brasserie.

The Grand Café (☎ 204463; 84 High St) is just that, with divine salads and sandwiches for around £5. **Quod** (☎ 202505; 92 High St; mains £10) is a classy Italian restaurant and worth a splash. For good French cuisine head to **Pierre Victoire Bistrot** (☎ 316616; 9 Little Clarendon St).

Entertainment
Po Na Na (☎ 249171; 13 Magdalen St) is a late-night bar-cum-club. **Oxford Playhouse** (☎ 305305; Beaumont St) has a mixed bag of theatre, dance and music. **Burton Taylor Theatre** (☎ 305350; Beaumont St) has more off-beat productions.

Getting There & Away
Bus Oxford is easily and quickly reached from London, and there are a number of competitive

bus lines on the route. A return ticket from London on the **Oxford Tube** (☎ 772250) costs £9 and is valid two days; the trip to Oxford takes 1¾ hours. It starts at London's Victoria coach station but also stops at Marble Arch, Notting Hill Gate and Shepherd's Bush. The service operates 24 hours a day.

National Express has one service a day to and from Bath (£10, two hours) and Bristol (£13, 2¾ hours), and two services to/from Gloucester (£8.25, 1½ hours) and Cheltenham (£8, one hour). From Bristol there are connections to Wales, Devon and Cornwall. Buses to Shrewsbury, North Wales, York and Durham go via Birmingham.

Oxford Express (☎ 785400) has frequent departures to London (£8.50 one way, 1¾ hours, every 20 to 30 minutes), Heathrow (£11 one way, 1¼ hours, every 30 minutes) and Gatwick (£18, two hours, hourly).

Stagecoach (☎ 772250) runs six buses a day to Cambridge and Stratford.

Train There are very frequent trains from London's Paddington station (£13.70 one way, 1½ hours). Network SouthEast cards apply.

Regular trains run north to Coventry and Birmingham, and northwest to Worcester and Hereford (for Moreton-in-Marsh, Gloucester and Cheltenham in the Cotswolds). Birmingham is the main hub for transport farther north.

To connect with trains to the southwest you have to change at Didcot Parkway (15 minutes). There are plenty of connections to Bath; with a bit of luck the whole trip won't take longer than 1½ hours. Change at Swindon for another line running into the Cotswolds (Kemble, Stroud and Gloucester). For train inquiries, phone ☎ 0845 748 4950.

Getting Around

Local buses and minibuses leave from the streets around Carfax Tower. For information on Stagecoach services phone ☎ 772250.

There are a number of places where you can hire bicycles. **Bike Zone** (☎ 728877; 6 Market St) is central and charges £10 a day or £20 a week.

Salter's Steamers (☎ 243421) offers several interesting boat trips from Folly Bridge between May and September. Punts are available for hire – see Things to See & Do earlier.

BLENHEIM PALACE

Blenheim Palace (☎ 01993-811325; adult/concession £10/7.50; house open 10.30am-5.30pm 11 Mar-31 Oct, park open 9am-4.45pm daily year-round), one of the largest palaces in Europe, was a gift to John Churchill from Queen Anne and Parliament as a reward for his role in defeating Louis XIV. Curiously, the palace was the birthplace of Winston Churchill, who perhaps more than any other individual was responsible for checking Hitler.

Designed and built by Vanbrugh and Hawksmoor between 1704 and 1722, with gardens by Capability Brown, Blenheim is an enormous baroque fantasy, and is definitely worth visiting. Blenheim is just south of the village of Woodstock. Catch a Stagecoach bus (Nos 20a–c) from Gloucester Green in Oxford to the palace's entrance (£3.55 return, every 30 minutes).

STRATFORD-UPON-AVON

☎ 01789 • pop 22,000

Stratford is a pleasant Midlands market town that just happened to be William Shakespeare's birthplace. Due to shrewd management of the cult of Bill, it's now one of England's busiest tourist attractions. Fans can visit several buildings associated with his life, including Shakespeare's Birthplace, New Place, Nash's House, Hall's Croft, Anne Hathaway's Cottage and Mary Arden's House. A passport ticket to all the Shakespearian properties costs adult/concession £12/11.

As it's just beyond the northern edge of the Cotswolds, Stratford makes a handy stopover en route to and from the north. The Royal Shakespeare Company has three theatres here, in addition to its London venues, and there's nearly always something on. Warwick, with its wonderful castle, is just to the north.

Orientation & Information

Stratford is easy to explore on foot. The main street changes names several times as it extends from the river to the train station.

The TIC (☎ 293127; Bridgefoot; open 9am-6pm Mon-Sat & 10.30am-4.30pm Sun) has plenty of information about the sights and the numerous B&Bs. Seeing a production by the **Royal Shakespeare Company** (☎ 403403; W www.rsc.org.uk; tickets £12-42; box office open 9.30am) is definitely worthwhile. Tickets are often available on the day of performance, but get in early. Stand-by tickets (£12) are available to students immediately before performances and there are almost always standing-room tickets (£5).

Places to Stay & Eat

The **Backpackers Hostel** (☎/fax 263838; 33 Greenhill St; dorm beds £12) is centrally located on the road between the train station and the town centre. The **Youth Hostel** (☎ 0870 770 6052, fax 0870 770 6053; e stratford@ yha.org.uk; Hemmingford House, Alveston; adults/under-18s including breakfast £16/ 11.75) is nearly 2mi out of town – from the TIC, cross Clopton Bridge and follow B4086, or take bus No 18 from Bridge St near the TIC.

B&Bs are plentiful just west of the centre on Evesham Place, Grove Rd and Broad Walk. In summer, however, many insist on bookings of at least two nights. Head to the neat **Dylan** (☎ 204819; e thedylan@lineone.net; 10 Evesham Place; per person £25) or the delightful **Twelfth Night** (☎ 414595; 13 Evesham Place; doubles only from £55).

For something more upmarket and central try either **The Payton** (☎ 266442, fax 294410; e info@payton.co.uk; 6 John St; singles/ doubles £45/60), a lovely little guesthouse, or the historic **Shakespeare Hotel** (☎ 0870 400 8182, fax 415411; Chapel St; singles/doubles £125/165).

Sheep St has a fine selection of dining possibilities including **The Vintner** (☎ 297259; 4-5 Sheep St; mains £9-16), a popular wine bar. The nearby **Edward Moon** (☎ 267069; 9 Chapel St; meals around £10) also has imaginative fare. For a cheap snack head to the **Lemon Tree** (☎ 292997; 2 Union St). The **Dirty Duck** (☎ 297312; Waterside) is good for an ale.

Getting There & Away

National Express buses link Birmingham, Stratford, Warwick, Oxford, Heathrow and London.

Phone ☎ 01788-535555 for local bus information. The X20 operates regularly to Birmingham (£3.40, 1¼ hour), the X16 to Warwick (£2.55, 20 minutes) and Coventry (£3.20, 1½ hours), and No 50 to Oxford (change bus at Chipping Norton, £5.25, 2½ hours).

Direct train services to and from London's Paddington station cost £21.50. There are trains to Warwick (£2.70) and Birmingham (£3.70). For further information phone ☎ 0845 748 4950.

COTSWOLDS

The Cotswolds are a range of beautiful limestone hills rising gently from the Thames and its tributaries in the east, but forming a steep escarpment overlooking the Bristol Channel in the west. The hills are characterised by honey-coloured stone villages and a gently rolling landscape. The villages were built on the wealth of the medieval wool trade and are these days extremely popular with tourists.

Orientation & Information

The hills run north from Bath for 100mi to Chipping Campden. The most attractive countryside is bounded in the west by the M5 and Chipping Sodbury, and in the east by Stow-on-the-Wold, Burford, Bibury, Cirencester and Chippenham.

There are train stations at Cheltenham, Kemble (serving Cirencester), Moreton-in-Marsh (serving Stow-on-the-Wold) and Stroud.

Bath, Cheltenham, Stratford-upon-Avon and Oxford are the best starting points for the Cotswolds. Cirencester likes to think of itself as the region's capital.

The TICs in surrounding towns all stock information on the Cotswolds, but those dealing specifically with the region are **Cirencester TIC** (☎ 01285-654180; Market Place) and **Stow-on-the-Wold TIC** (☎ 01451-831082; The Square).

The Cotswolds area is not particularly well served by YHA hostels, but there are countless B&Bs and hotels.

Getting Around

Getting around the Cotswolds by public transport isn't easy. If you're trying anything ambitious, contact the **Gloucestershire inquiry line** (☎ 01452-425543). Bikes can be hired in Bath, Oxford and Cheltenham. **Compass Holidays** (☎ 01242-250642) has bicycles for hire (£12 per day) at Cheltenham station.

Stow-on-the-Wold
☎ 01451 • pop 2000

Stow, as it is known, is one of the most impressive (and visited) towns in the Cotswolds. It's a terrific base if you don't have a vehicle, because several particularly beautiful villages, including the famous Upper and Lower Slaughters, are within a day's walk or cycle ride.

The **Youth Hostel** (☎ *0870 770 6050, fax 0870 770 6051;* e *stow@yha.org.uk; The Square; adults/under-18s £12.75/8.75)* is in a 16th-century building. **Number 9** (☎ *870333; 9 Park St; rooms £70)* is a stylish B&B. At the top-end there's the lovely **Stow Lodge Hotel** (☎ *830485, fax 831671;* e *enquiries@stow lodge.com; The Square; singles/doubles from £74/80).*

Stow can be reached by bus from Moreton-in-Marsh, which is on the main Cotswolds line between Worcester and Oxford. Contact **Pulhams' Coaches** (☎ *820369)* for a timetable.

Cheltenham
☎ 01242 • pop 88,000
Cheltenham is a large and elegant spa town easily accessible by bus and train. The **TIC** (☎ *522878; 77 Promenade)* is helpful. Cheltenham is on the main Bristol–Birmingham train line, and can be reached by train from South Wales, Bath and southwest England, and Oxford (changing at Didcot and Swindon).

BIRMINGHAM
☎ 0121 • pop 1.01 million
Birmingham is Britain's second-largest city, culturally vibrant, socially dynamic but aesthetically challenged. Traditionally it's been thought of as a rather dreary city with no essential sights and not particularly accessible to the short-term visitor. More recently, however, things have looked up, with the restoration of the old canal network and the opening of innumerable restaurants and bars in the Brindleyplace area. The **Museum & Art Gallery** (☎ *303 2834)* has a fine collection of Pre-Raphaelite paintings and overlooks **Victoria** and **Chamberlain Squares**, both of them full of interesting statuary. The old **Jewellery Quarter**, where, surprise, surprise, jewellery was made, is also looking much smarter and houses a couple of interesting small museums.

It's unlikely that you'll want to stay long in Birmingham even now, and a dearth of cheap accommodation in the city centre hardly helps (there's no hostel). However, New St Station and Digbeth St Coach Station are both major transport hubs. If you're passing through it might be worth stepping out to explore for a few hours. Try a balti restaurant for the Midlands' own version of Indian cooking.

The **TIC** (☎ *693 6300; Victoria Square; open daily)* can help with visitor information.

ALTHORP
With the late Diana, Princess of Wales, continuing to attract the public's attention from beyond the grave, the memorial and museum in the grounds of her ancestral home, **Althorp Park** (☎ *0870 167 9000;* w *www.visitalthorp .com; adult/child £10/5; park open 1 July-30 Aug)*, off the A428 northwest of Northampton, remain popular tourist attractions. Ticket prices are hefty (profits go to her Memorial Fund) and numbers are limited so it's wise to book in advance. Incidentally, Althorp should be pronounced altrup!

SHREWSBURY
☎ 01743 • pop 60,000
Shrewsbury is the attractive regional capital of Shropshire, and is famous for its black-and-white, half-timbered buildings. Because there are no vitally important sights, Shrewsbury has been saved from inundation by tourists but it makes a good base for Ironbridge, Stokesay Castle, Shropshire's wonderful walking country, and even Wales. Two famous railways into Wales terminate here and it's possible to do a fascinating circuit of North Wales.

Orientation & Information
The town is strategically sited within a loop of the River Severn. Across the narrow land bridge formed by the loop is the train station, a five-minute walk north of the town centre. The bus station, Smithfield Rd, is central. The **TIC** (☎ *281200; The Square)* shares its premises with a cinema and café.

Things to See & Do
Shrewsbury's main attraction is wandering its **medieval streets** whose names – Butcher Row, Fish St and Milk St – hark back to the days when these trades were conducted here. The **Abbot's House** on Butcher Row is a fine example of the distinctive timber-framed architecture of that time. The TIC organises daily **walking tours** *(adult/concession £2.50/1)* of the town at 2.30pm from May to October.

Rowley's House (☎ *361196; Barker St; admission free; open 10am-5pm daily)* is the town's main museum and features Roman and medieval finds.

Places to Stay & Eat
Shrewsbury Youth Hostel (☎ *0870 770 6030, fax 0870 770 6031;* e *shrewsbury@ yha.org.uk; Abbey Foregate)* is 1mi from the

train and bus stations. Walk down High St, cross English Bridge and veer right when Abbey Foregate splits in two around the abbey.

There are numerous cheap B&Bs in this area including **Prynce's Villa Guest House** (☎ 356217; 15 Monkmoor Rd; per person from £17, rates include breakfast).

Dating from 1460, quaint **Tudor House** (☎ 351735; 2 Fish St; singles/doubles £28/42) is centrally located on a quiet medieval street. A notch up is the **Prince Rupert Hotel** (☎ 499955, fax 357306; e post@prince-ru pert-hotel.co.uk; Butcher Row; singles/doubles £75/95).

Good Life Wholefood Restaurant (☎ 350455; Barracks Passage; open Mon-Sat) is a fantastic place for lunch with decent portions of righteous food, all at very reasonable prices. Also good for a light meal is **Bertie's Coffee House** (☎ 232236; 1 Fish St). **Owen's Café-Bar** (☎ 363633; Butcher Row; mains £8-11) is a trendy eatery. **Peach Tree** (☎ 355055; 21 Abbey Foregate; mains £15) is a great, if expensive, restaurant and bar.

Getting There & Away

Bus There are two or three National Express buses a day to and from London (£14, five hours) via Telford and Birmingham.

For information on transport in Shropshire, contact **Traveline** (☎ 0870 608 2608). Bus No 96 runs every two hours between Shrewsbury and Telford via Ironbridge (35 minutes). Bus No 420 connects Shrewsbury with Birmingham twice daily. Bus No 435 runs regularly to and from Ludlow.

Train Two fascinating small railways terminate at Shrewsbury, in addition to plenty of main-line connections. It's possible to do a highly recommended rail loop from Shrewsbury around North Wales. Timetabling is a challenge so phone ☎ 0845 748 4950 for information. The journey is possible in a day as long as you don't miss any of the connections, but it's much better to allow at least a couple of days as there's plenty to see. The Freedom of North and Mid-Wales Flexi-Rover ticket is the most economical way of covering this route. It costs £29 and allows travel on three days out of seven.

From Shrewsbury you head due west across Wales to Machynlleth (1¼ hours), where you connect with the famous Cambrian Coast Line, which hugs the beautiful coast on its way north to Porthmadog (1½ hours).

At Porthmadog you can pick up the Ffestiniog Railway, a restored narrow-gauge steam train that winds up into Snowdonia National Park to the slate-mining town of Blaenau Ffestiniog (1¼ hours). From Blaenau another small railway carves its way through the mountains and down the beautiful, tourist-infested Conwy Valley to Llandudno (1¼ hours) and Conwy. From there it's a short trip to Chester.

Another famous line, promoted as the Heart of Wales Line, runs southwest to Swansea (four hours), connecting with the main line from Cardiff to Fishguard (six hours).

There are numerous trains to and from London's Euston station (from £13, three hours), and regular links to Chester (£6.30, one hour). There are also regular trains from Cardiff to Manchester via Bristol, Ludlow and Shrewsbury.

AROUND SHREWSBURY
Ironbridge Gorge
☎ 01952
The Silicon Valley of the 1700s, Ironbridge, on the southern edge of Telford, is a monument to the Industrial Revolution. This World Heritage Site was the wonder of its age, developing iron smelting on a scale never seen before – easy transport on the Severn and rich deposits of iron and coal in the gorge itself made it possible.

Ironbridge Gorge Museums (☎ 433522; open daily) comprises nine museums and historic sites strung along the gorge. There's Blists Hill Victorian Town, which re-creates an entire community; the Coalport China Museum, with more than you ever wanted to know about porcelain; the Museum of Iron; the Museum of the Gorge; and, among other sites, the beautiful iron bridge – the world's first. The bridge is close to the TIC and is the best place to start. A passport ticket, allowing entrance to all the museums, for an adult/concession costs £10.50/6.50.

Ironbridge Gorge has two **Youth Hostels** (☎ 0870 770 5882 for both; adults/under-18s £11.25/8) but are open only sporadically – phone ahead. For a B&B with local charm try **Calcutts House** (☎ 882631, fax 882951; e enquiries@calcuttshouse.co.uk; Jackfield; rooms from £39).

From Shrewsbury, bus No 96 runs every two hours to Telford via Ironbridge (35 minutes).

BRITAIN

There are also regular buses from Telford's town centre. Unless you're into walking, you'll need your own transport to get around the sites – it's 3mi from Blists Hill to the Museum of Iron.

PEAK DISTRICT

Squeezed between the industrial Midlands to the south, Manchester to the west and Sheffield to the east, the Peak District seems an unlikely site for one of England's most beautiful regions. Even the name is misleading being derived from the tribes who once lived here, not from the existence of any significant peaks (there are none!). Nonetheless, the 542-sq-mi Peak District National Park is a delight, particularly for walkers and cyclists.

The Peak District divides into the green fields and steep-sided dales of the southern White Peak and the bleak, gloomy moors of the northern Dark Peak. Buxton, to the west, and Matlock, to the east, are good bases for exploring the park, or you can stay right in the centre at Bakewell or Castleton. In May and June the ancient custom of 'well dressing' can be seen at many villages. There are also prehistoric sites, limestone caves, the tragic plague village of Eyam and the fine stately homes of Chatsworth and Haddon Hall.

Castleton and nearby Edale are popular villages on the border between the White and Dark Peaks. From Edale, the Pennine Way starts its 250mi meander northwards. From the town of Castleton, the 25mi Limestone Way is a superb day walk covering the length of the White Peak to Matlock. In addition, a number of disused railway lines in the White Peak have been redeveloped as walking and cycling routes, with strategically situated bicycle-rental outlets at old station sites.

Contact National Park Information Centres (*Edale* ☎ 01433-670207 • *Castleton* ☎ 01433-620679 • *Bakewell* ☎ 01629-813227) for information. The Peak District is packed with hotels, B&Bs, YHA hostels and a collection of **camping barns** (☎ 01629-825850), together with plenty of convivial pubs and good restaurants. Visitors to Bakewell should make sure to sample Bakewell pudding (not tart).

The regular Transpeak bus service cuts right across the Peak District from Nottingham and Derby to Manchester via Matlock, Bakewell and Buxton.

East England

With the exception of the city of Cambridge, most of the eastern counties – Essex, Suffolk, Norfolk, Cambridgeshire and Lincolnshire – have been overlooked by tourists. East Anglia, as the region is often known, has always been distinct, historically separated from the rest of England by the Fens and the Essex forests.

The Fens were strange marshlands that stretched from Cambridge north to The Wash and beyond into Lincolnshire. They were home to people who led an isolated existence among a maze of waterways, fishing, hunting and farming scraps of arable land. In the 17th century, however, Dutch engineers were brought in to drain the fens, and the flat open plains with their rich, black soil were created.

To the east of the fens, Norfolk and Suffolk have gentle, unspectacular scenery that can still be very beautiful. John Constable and Thomas Gainsborough painted in the area known as Dedham Vale, the valley of the River Stour. Villages like East Bergholt, Thaxted and Cavendish are quintessentially English with their beautiful churches and their thatch-roofed cottages.

The distinctive architectural character of the region has been determined by the lack of suitable building stone. Stone was occasionally imported for important buildings, but for humble churches and houses three local materials were used: flint, clay bricks and oak. The most unusual of the three, flint, can be chipped into usable shapes, but a single stone is rarely larger than a fist. Often the flint is used in combination with dressed stone or bricks to form decorative patterns.

More than any other part of England, East Anglia has close links with northern Europe. In the 6th and 7th centuries it was overrun by the Norsemen. From the late Middle Ages, Suffolk and Norfolk grew rich by trading wool and cloth with the Flemish; this wealth built scores of churches and helped subsidise the development of Cambridge. The windmills, the long straight drainage canals and even sometimes the architecture (especially in King's Lynn) call to mind the Low Countries.

Orientation & Information

East Anglia and Lincolnshire are situated to the west of the main northbound transport arteries. The region's southern boundary is the

Thames estuary, and its western boundary (now marked by the M1 and A1) was formed by that huge expanse of almost impenetrable marshland, the Fens. Peterborough, Norwich and Lincoln are the most important cities. Harwich is the main port for ferries to Germany, the Netherlands and Scandinavia.

The **East of England Tourist Board** (☎ 01473-822922) can provide information on the various hostels and many B&Bs.

Activities

Hiking The 94mi Peddars Way and Norfolk Coast Path runs across the middle of Norfolk from Knettishall Heath until it reaches the beautiful north Norfolk coast at Holme-next-the-Sea. It follows this coastline through a number of attractive, untouched villages, like Wells-next-the-Sea, to Cromer. The **Peddars Way and Norfolk Coast Path National Trail Office** (☎ 01328-711533; e peddars.way@ dial.pipex.com; 6 Station Rd, Wells-next-the-Sea, Norfolk NR23 1AE) can supply further information.

Cycling This is ideal cycling country. Where there are hills, they're gentle. Bicycles can be hired cheaply in Cambridge, and the TIC there can suggest several interesting routes.

Boating The Norfolk Broads, a series of inland lakes (ancient flooded peat diggings) to the east of Norwich, are popular with nautical people of every description. Contact **Hoseasons** (☎ 01502-501010) for information about hiring narrow boats, cruisers, yachts and houseboats.

Getting There & Away

Harwich, Norwich, King's Lynn and Cambridge are all easily accessible by train from London.

For details on ferry services from Harwich to the Netherlands, Germany and Scandinavia, see the introductory Getting There & Away section at the beginning of this chapter.

Getting Around

Bus Bus transport around the region is slow and disorganised. For regional timetables and information phone **Traveline** (☎ 0870 608 2608).

Train From Norwich you can catch trains to the Norfolk coast and Sheringham, but there's

an unfortunate gap between Sheringham and King's Lynn (bus or hitch?), which prevents a rail loop back to Cambridge. It may be worth considering Anglia Plus passes that offer three days travel out of seven for £20, one day for £9.

CAMBRIDGE
☎ 01223 • pop 100,000

Cambridge can hardly be spoken of without reference to Oxford – so much so that the term Oxbridge is used to cover them both. The two cities are not just ancient and beautiful university towns; they embody preconceptions and prejudices that are almost mythical in their dimension.

An Oxbridge graduate is popularly characterised as male, private-school educated, intelligent and upper class, but the value judgments attached to the term will very often depend on who is using it.

It can be both abusive and admiring: for some it means academic excellence, for others it denotes an elitist club whose members unfairly dominate many aspects of British life.

Cambridge University is the newer of the two, probably beginning some time in the early 13th century, perhaps a century later than Oxford. There is a fierce rivalry between the two cities and the two universities, and a futile debate over which is best and most beautiful. If you have the time, visit both. Oxford draws many more tourists than Cambridge. Partly because of this, if you only have time for one and the colleges are open, choose Cambridge. Its trump card is the choir and chapel of King's College, which should not be missed by any visitor to Britain. If the colleges are closed (see the following section for opening dates), choose Oxford.

Orientation & Information

Cambridge is 54mi north of London. The central area, which lies in a wide bend of the River Cam, is easy to get around on foot or bike.

The bus station is in the centre of town, but the train station is a 20-minute walk to the southeast. Sidney St, which changes its name many times, is the main shopping street. The most important group of colleges (including King's) and the Backs (the meadows adjoining the Cam) are to the west of Sidney St.

The **TIC** (☎ 322640, fax 457549; e tourism@cambridge.gov.uk; Wheeler St; open 10am-6pm Mon-Sat year-round, 11am-4pm Sun Easter-Sept) organises two-hour walking

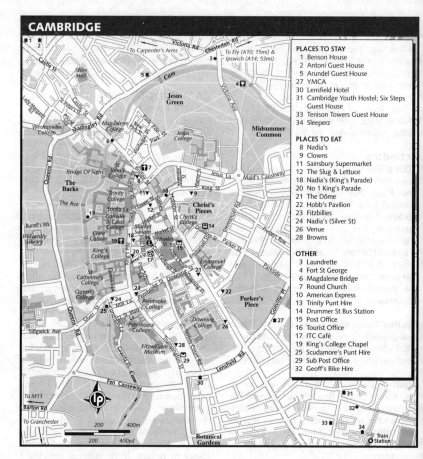

CAMBRIDGE

PLACES TO STAY
1 Benson House
2 Antoni Guest House
5 Arundel Guest House
27 YMCA
30 Lensfield Hotel
31 Cambridge Youth Hostel; Six Steps Guest House
33 Tenison Towers Guest House
34 Sleeperz

PLACES TO EAT
8 Nadia's
9 Clowns
11 Sainsbury Supermarket
12 The Slug & Lettuce
18 Nadia's (King's Parade)
20 No 1 King's Parade
21 The Dôme
22 Hobb's Pavilion
23 Fitzbillies
26 Nadia's (Silver St)
26 Venue
28 Browns

OTHER
3 Laundrette
4 Fort St George
6 Magdalene Bridge
7 Round Church
10 American Express
13 Trinity Punt Hire
14 Drummer St Bus Station
15 Post Office
16 Tourist Office
17 ITC Café
19 King's College Chapel
25 Scudamore's Punt Hire
29 Sub Post Office
32 Geoff's Bike Hire

tours at 1.30pm daily, all year, with more during summer. Group sizes are limited, so buy your ticket in advance (£7.25 including King's college, £6.25 including St John's).

The university has three eight-week terms: Michaelmas (October to December), Lent (mid-January to mid-March) and Easter (mid-April to mid-June). Exams are held from mid-May to mid-June. There's general mayhem for the 168 hours following exams, the so-called May Week. Most colleges are closed to visitors for the Easter term, and all are closed for exams. Precise details of opening hours vary from college to college and year to year, so contact the TIC for up-to-date information.

For Internet access head to **ITC Café** (☎ 377358; 2 Wheeler St), opposite the TIC, which charges £1 for 30 minutes.

Things to See & Do

Cambridge is an architectural treasure house. If you are seriously interested you will need considerably more information than this guide can give, and more than a day.

Starting at Magdalene Bridge, walk south down Bridge St until you reach the unmistakable **Round Church**, one of only four surviving medieval round churches, dating from the 12th century. Turn right down St John's St (immediately across the road), which is named in honour of **St John's College** (on the right). The gatehouse dates from 1510 and on the other side are three beautiful courts, the second and third dating from the 17th century. From the third court, the picturesque **Bridge of Sighs** (not open to the public) crosses the river.

Next door, **Trinity College** (☎ 338400) is one of the largest and most attractive colleges. It was established in 1546 by Henry VIII on the site of several earlier foundations. The Great Court, Cambridge's largest enclosed court, incorporates buildings from the 15th century. Beyond Great Court is Nevile's Court with one of Cambridge's most important buildings on its western side – Sir Christopher Wren's library, built in the 1680s.

Next comes Caius (pronounced keys) College, and then **King's College** (☎ 331100), and its famous chapel, one of Europe's greatest buildings. The reason its late-Gothic style is described as perpendicular is immediately obvious. The chapel was begun in 1446 by Henry VI, but it was not completed until 1545. Majestic as this building is from the outside, its interior, with its breathtaking scale and intricate fan vaulting, makes the greater impact. It comes alive when the choir sings; even the most pagan heavy-metal fan will find choral evensong an extraordinary experience. Admission for adult/concession costs £3.50/2.25.

There are services from mid-January to mid-March, mid-April to mid-June, mid-July to late July, early October to early December, and 24 and 25 December. Evensong is sung during term time at 5.30pm Tuesday to Saturday and at 3.30pm on Sunday.

Continue south on what is now King's Parade and turn right onto Silver St (St Catherine's College is on the corner), which takes you down to the Cam and the hiring point for punts.

Punting along the Backs is at best sublime, but it can also be a wet and hectic experience, especially on a busy weekend. Several companies compete for the trade – the cheapest is **Trinity Punts** (£8/hr; deposits from £30 to £50) behind Trinity College. Punting the 3mi up the river to the idyllic village of Grantchester makes a great day out. Punts hold up to six people. If you do wimp out, the Backs are also perfect for a walk or a picnic – cross the bridge and walk along the river to the right.

Places to Stay
The TIC has an accommodation guide (75p) or you can call its booking service on ☎ 457581.

Cambridge Youth Hostel (☎ 0870 770 5742, fax 0870 770 5743; e cambridge@yha .org.uk; 97 Tenison Rd; adults/under-18s £12.75/8.75), breakfast £3.40 has small dormitories and a restaurant near the train station. It's very popular – book ahead.

The **YMCA** (☎ 356998, fax 312749; e admin@camymca.org.uk; Gonville Place; singles/doubles £23/37, per week £130/224) is closer to the centre and is good value for weekly stays. Breakfast is included.

There are numerous B&Bs at all times, even more during university holidays from late June to late September. Right outside the train station is **Sleeperz** (☎ 304050, fax 357286; e info@sleeperz.com; Station Rd; singles/ twins with shower £35/45, large doubles £55), a converted railway warehouse with attractive minimalist rooms.

There are several B&Bs on Tenison Rd, including the cosy **Tenison Towers Guest House** (☎ 363924, fax 411093; rooms per person from £25) at No 148. **Six Steps Guest House** (☎ 353968, fax 356788; e sara.dias@ ntlworld.com; rooms per person from £28) at No 93 is considerably larger and has big, uncluttered rooms.

The other B&B area is in the north of the city around Chesterton Rd. **Antoni Guest House** (☎ 357444; 4 Huntingdon Rd; rooms per person £20-25) is spacious and comfortable. **Benson House** (☎/fax 311594; 24 Huntingdon Rd) is similarly priced and has well-equipped doubles with showers.

Closer to the city centre and considerably more upmarket is the elegant **Arundel House Hotel** (☎ 367701, fax 367721; e info@arun delhousehotels.com.uk; 53 Chesterton Rd; singles £68-90, doubles £85-115). It overlooks Jesus Green.

Lensfield Hotel (☎ 355017, fax 312022; e reservations@lensfieldhotel.co.uk; 53 Lensfield Rd; singles/doubles £55/75) has well-appointed rooms.

Places to Eat & Drink
Cambridge may be a university town, but tourism is an enormous cash cow, reflected in restaurant prices. There are, however, a number of reasonably priced restaurants, some of which give student discounts.

Nadia's is a small chain of bakeries that are excellent value (eg, sandwich and coffee for £1 before 10.30am). A smoked ham-and-Swiss-cheese baguette is £1.85. There's a **King's Parade branch** (☎ 568334) and a **Silver St branch** (☎ 568335).

Tucked away in a narrow alley is **Rainbow** (☎ 321551; 9A King's Parade; mains from £6.75; closed Sun), a cosy vegetarian/vegan restaurant.

Clowns (☎ 355711; 54 King St; light meals £3-6) is informal, popular with students and good value. The nearby **Slug & Lettuce** (☎ 306051; 41 Green St; mains around £7) is a trendy new café/bar that attracts students galore with its filling burgers, tortillas and pasta dishes.

Hobb's Pavilion (☎ 67480; Park Terrace; open 11am-3pm Tues-Sat) occupies the old cricket pavilion and specialises in filled pancakes.

There's a number of reasonably priced restaurants along Regent and St Andrew's Sts. One of the most pleasant options is **The Dôme** (☎ 313818; 33-34 St Andrew's St; steak sandwich for £7.95), a French-style brasserie with a small garden at the back. There are a few vegetarian meals too.

Fitzbillies (☎ 352500; 52 Trumpington St; closed Sun) is a brilliant bakery/restaurant. The Chelsea buns are an outrageous experience, and so is the chocolate cake beloved by generations of students.

At **Browns** (☎ 461655; 23 Trumpington St; mains from £7.95) the hustle-and-bustle of many diners echoes throughout a large old warehouse. It's highly recommended.

No 1 Kings Parade (☎ 359506; meals around £10) is a vaulted cellar restaurant good for stylish dining.

Venue (☎ 367333; 66 Regent St; mains from £11) goes in for trendiness, with expensive meals served on tables that have to be seen to be believed.

There's a **Sainsbury supermarket** (open daily) on Sidney St.

Fort St George (☎ 354327; Midsummer Common) is a good riverside pub.

Getting There & Away
Cambridge can easily be visited as a day trip from London or en route to the north. It's well served by trains, but not so well by buses.

Bus To London there are hourly National Express buses (£8/8.50 one way/day return, two hours). There are four buses a day to and from Bristol (two stop at Bath). Unfortunately, links to the north aren't very straightforward. To get to Lincoln or York you'll have to change at Peterborough or Nottingham respectively. King's Lynn is also only accessible via Peterborough.

Jetlink (☎ 0870 575 7747) runs buses to all London airports: Stansted (£6/10 one way/return, one hour), Luton (£8/12, 1½ hours),

Heathrow (£16/20, 2¼ hours) and Gatwick (£19/24, 3½ hours) airports.

Stagecoach Express (☎ 01640-676060) goes to Oxford (£5.99, 3½ hours, hourly).

Train There are trains every half-hour from London's King's Cross and Liverpool St stations (£15.10, 45 minutes). Trains from King's Cross run via Hatfield and Stevenage. There are also regular train connections to Bury St Edmunds (£5.80, one hour), Ely (£3.30, 20 minutes) and King's Lynn (£7.50, one hour). There are connections at Peterborough with the main northbound trains to Lincoln, York and Edinburgh. If you want to head west to Oxford or Bath, you'll have to return to London first. For more information, phone ☎ 0845 748 4950.

Getting Around
Cambus (☎ 423553) operates buses around town from Drummer St, including bus No 1 from the train station to the town centre.

If you're staying out of the centre, or plan to wander into the fens (fine flat country for the lazy cyclist), a bicycle can be hired from **Geoff's Bike Hire** (☎ 365629; 65 Devonshire Rd; £7 per day), near the youth hostel.

ELY
☎ 01353 • pop 9000
Ely is set on a low hill that was once an island deep in the watery world of the fens. It is dominated by the overwhelming bulk of Ely Cathedral, a superb example of the Norman Romanesque style, built between 1081 and 1200. Phone the **TIC** (☎ 662062) for places to stay.

There are regular trains from Cambridge (£3.30, 20 minutes).

LINCOLNSHIRE
Lincoln
☎ 01522 • pop 81,500
Since it's not on a main tourist route, many people bypass Lincoln, missing a magnificent 900-year-old cathedral (the third largest in Britain) and an interesting city with a compact medieval centre of narrow, winding streets. The suburbs are unattractive and depressing; however, perhaps because Lincoln escapes the hordes of visitors that places like York attract, the people are particularly friendly.

The **TIC** (☎ 873213; 9 Castle Square) has information on B&Bs; the **Youth Hostel**

☎ 0870 770 5918; 77 South Park; dorm beds £10.25) is excellent.

Lincoln is 132mi from London, with direct bus and rail services.

NORFOLK
Norwich
☎ 01603 • pop 170,000

This ancient capital was for many years larger than London, its prosperity based on trade with the Low Countries. Norwich's medieval centre has been retained along with its castle, cathedral and no fewer than 33 churches. There are numerous B&Bs – contact the **TIC** (☎ 666071; the Guildhall, Gaol Hill) for details. There's also a **Youth Hostel** (☎ 0870 770 5976; 112 Turner Rd; dorm beds £10.25). Direct rail and bus links connect Norwich with Cambridge and London.

King's Lynn
☎ 01553 • pop 37,500

King's Lynn is an interesting old port with some notable buildings, some of which were distinctly influenced by the trading links with Holland. Contact the **TIC** (☎ 763044; Saturday Market Place) for further information. There is a **Youth Hostel** (☎ 0870 770 5902; College Lane; open July & Aug, reduced hours other times). There are regular trains from Cambridge (£7.50, one hour).

SUFFOLK
Harwich
☎ 01255 • pop 15,000

Contact the **TIC** (☎ 506139) if you need a B&B at this typically ugly shipping terminal.

There are numerous trains from Harwich (International Port) to London (Liverpool St station); on some services you will have to change trains at Manningtree or Colchester. Alternatively, you could go north to Norwich, or change for Bury St Edmunds and Cambridge at Ipswich. See the introductory Getting There & Away section at the beginning of this chapter for details on the ferries.

Northeast England

Northeast England is a place of contrasts. Its undulating, spectacular landscape, containing three of England's best national parks, is both romantic and rugged. You can't move for the history, and what this region hasn't witnessed isn't worth knowing. Every inch has been fought over, leaving Scottish-English buffer zones like Berwick-upon-Tweed still unsure of its true identity. The Romans were the first to attempt to delineate a north-south divide in Hadrian's Wall, but skirmishes over land continued well into the 18th century.

Against such a backdrop, grandiose buildings dominate, representing everything that war is not. If you don't leave something of yourself here, you will have failed to truly explore this region's many facets.

Orientation & Information
The dominating geological feature is the Pennine Hills, which form a north-south spine dividing the region from Cumbria and Lancashire in the west.

The major transport routes, both rail and road, basically run east of this spine, northward from York to Newcastle-upon-Tyne and Edinburgh. Newcastle-upon-Tyne is an important ferry port for Scandinavia.

Hiking
This is definite wind-in-your-hair, air-in-your-lungs country – walkers are spoilt for choice. The most famous path is the Pennine Way, which stretches 266mi from Edale in the Peak District to Kirk Yetholm in Scotland. Unfortunately, it's become so popular that it's lost its unspoilt appeal. The quagmire effect in certain sections will leave you feeling more at one with nature than you bargained for.

The Cleveland Way in the North York Moors National Park is another well-worn alternative; the section along the coast is particularly impressive. If you're looking for a place to call your own, head to the Yorkshire Dales; local TICs will offer pearls of wisdom on less well-known tracks.

Getting There & Around
Bus Transport by bus around the region is pitiful. Fortunately, **Traveline** (☎ 0870 608 2608) can provide up-to-the-minute advice on transport for the entire region. There are also some good deals on cheap tickets that make the hassle worthwhile. There are several one-day Explorer tickets; always ask if one might be appropriate. The Explorer North-East is useful, covering a vast area north of York to the Scottish Borders and west to Hawes (in the Yorkshire Dales) and Carlisle. You can purchase the tickets on the buses.

BRITAIN

Train The main-line routes run north to Edinburgh via York, Durham and Newcastle-upon-Tyne and west to Carlisle roughly following Hadrian's Wall.

There are numerous special-price Rover tickets, for single-day travel and longer periods. For example, the North-East Rail Rover allows unlimited travel throughout the North (not including Northumberland). A version allowing travel for any four days out of eight costs £59.

YORK

☎ 01904 • pop 179,305

King George VI declared, 'The history of York is the history of England', and how right he was. It existed before the Romans, but entered the world stage under their rule. In AD 306, Constantine, the first Christian emperor and founder of Constantinople (now Istanbul), was reputedly proclaimed emperor on the site of the cathedral.

In Saxon times, York became an important centre for Christianity – the first church on the site of the current cathedral was built in 627. Danish invaders captured the city in 867, transforming it into an important trading centre and port, the River Ouse providing the link with the sea.

York continued to prosper as a political and trading hub after William the Conqueror's initial 'pacification'. In the 15th and 16th centuries, however, it declined economically. Although it remained the social and cultural capital of the north, it was the arrival of George Hudson and the railway in 1839 that gave York a new lease of commercial life, allowing the development of tourism.

The city walls were built during the 13th century and are among the most impressive surviving medieval fortifications in Europe. They enclose a thriving, fascinating centre that still retains the refinement of an age long since passed. This is typified in the dominating Minster, the largest Gothic cathedral in England.

The crowds are still an ever-present, often suffocating feature; but even they can't detract from a place so imposing, so elegant, so stunningly alive with history.

Orientation & Information

Although it's relatively small, York's streets are a confusing medieval tangle. Bear in mind that *gate* means street, and *bar* means gate.

There are five major landmarks: the walkable 2½mi city wall; the Minster at the northern corner; Clifford's Tower, a 13th-century castle and mound at the southern end; the River Ouse that cuts the centre in two; and the enormous train station outside the western corner.

The main **TIC** (☎ 621756, fax 551801 e tic@york-tourism.co.uk; De Grey Rooms, Exhibition Square; open 9am-6pm Mon-Sat, 9.30am-6pm Sun; 9am-7pm daily July & Aug) is north of the river near Bootham Bar. There's also a small TIC at the train station.

Head to Parliament St for pharmacies, banks and *bureaux de change*.

Discounts If you plan to do a lot of sightseeing, the **York Pass** (£21/31/39 for 1/2/3 days), available from the TIC, allows free entry to over 30 attractions.

Things to See & Do

Thanks to York's rich history, there's loads to see. The Association of Voluntary Guides offers free two-hour **walking tours** every day at 10.15am outside the City Art Gallery in Exhibition Square. Alternatively, follow this introductory ramble, which takes in the main sites but doesn't allow time for thorough exploration.

Start at the main TIC in Exhibition Square and head to **King's Manor**. Follow the path to its left and pass through the stone doorway 800m along. The circular stone wall with arches is the **Multangular Tower**, built by the Romans as part of their ancient fortress. Return to the doorway and follow the path round to the **Yorkshire Museum** (☎ 551800; adult/concession/child/family £3.95/2.95/2.95/11.50). It has an excellent collection of Roman artefacts; the grounds are worth visiting for the ruins of **St Mary's Abbey**.

Return to the entrance of King's Manor, crossing the road to **Bootham Bar** and climb the city wall. Walk northeast along the wall and enjoy beautiful views of the Minster. Leave the walls at Monk Bar – the best preserved of York's medieval gates with its working Porticullis and entertaining **Richard III Museum** (☎ 634191; adult/concession/child £2/1/free) – and walk along Goodramgate taking the first right onto Ogleforth, then left onto Chapter House St.

The **Treasurer's House** (☎ 624247; adult/child/family £3.80/2/9.50; open Apr-Nov) has been restored by the National

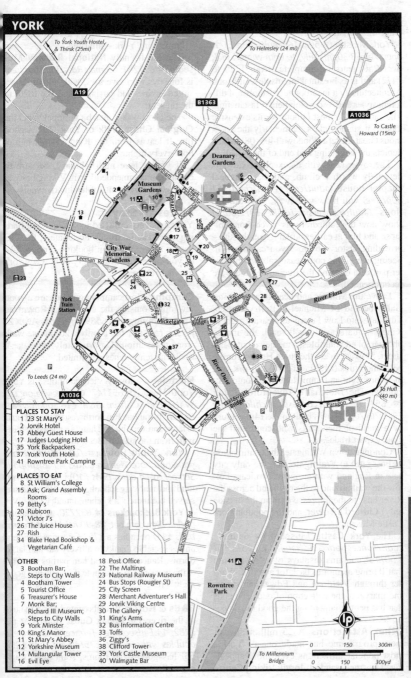

YORK

To York Youth Hostel, & Thirsk (25mi)

To Helmsley (24 mi)

A19

B1363

A1036

To Castle Howard (15mi)

Deanary Gardens

Museum Gardens

City War Memorial Gardens

Leeman Rd

York Train Station

Mickelgate

River Ouse

River Floss

River Foss

To Leeds (24 mi)

A1036

To Hull (40 mi)

Paragon St

Rowntree Park

To Millennium Bridge

PLACES TO STAY
1 23 St Mary's
2 Jorvik Hotel
13 Abbey Guest House
17 Judges Lodging Hotel
35 York Backpackers
37 York Youth Hotel
41 Rowntree Park Camping

PLACES TO EAT
8 St William's College
15 Ask; Grand Assembly Rooms
19 Betty's
20 Rubicon
21 Victor J's
26 The Juice House
27 Rish
34 Blake Head Bookshop & Vegetarian Café

OTHER
3 Bootham Bar; Steps to City Walls
4 Bootham Tower
5 Tourist Office
6 Treasurer's House
7 Monk Bar; Richard III Museum; Steps to City Walls
9 York Minster
10 King's Manor
11 St Mary's Abbey
12 Yorkshire Museum
14 Multangular Tower
16 Evil Eye
18 Post Office
22 The Maltings
23 National Railway Museum
24 Bus Stops (Rougier St)
25 City Screen
28 Merchant Adventurer's Hall
29 Jorvik Viking Centre
30 The Gallery
31 King's Arms
32 Bus Information Centre
33 Toffs
36 Ziggy's
38 Clifford Tower
39 York Castle Museum
40 Walmgate Bar

0   150   300m
0   150   300yd

BRITAIN

Trust. Turn right onto Minster Yard and enter the Minster.

York Minster (☎ 557216; adult/child £3/1; open 7am-8.30pm daily, to 6pm winter) took over 250 years to complete (from 1220 to 1472) and is as breathtaking inside as it is out. Architecturally it incorporates a number of different styles and its development is fascinating. The cathedral is most famous for its extensive medieval stained glass, particularly the enormous Great Eastern Window (1405–08), which depicts the beginning and end of the world.

The tower (£3) with its excellent views is definitely worth a climb, and the octagonal **chapter house** (adult/concession/child £1/80p/free) will blow you away. The **foundations** (adult/concession/child £3/2.60/1) show how the cathedral was saved from collapse and hint at earlier buildings on the site – providing history so close you can smell it. Seeing everything could easily absorb the better part of a day and the free guided tours are recommended.

Leave the Minster and head down Minster Gates behind St Michael-le-Belfry church. Turn left into Low Petergate, bearing right at King's Square and you'll reach the much-photographed **Shambles**, a medieval butcher's street. Stop at No 28, the **Juice House**, for the best smoothies (£1.90 to £3.50) in York, and then turn right and immediately left onto Piccadilly. The **Merchant Adventurers' Hall** (☎ 654818; adult/concession/child/family £2/1.70/70p/5), was built in the 14th century by a guild of merchants who controlled the cloth export trade.

Continue down Walmgate (the continuation of Fossgate) to **Walmgate Bar**, the only city gate in England with an intact barbican. Follow the wall around to the right and across the River Foss to the impressive (from the outside only) **Clifford's Tower**, and the popular York Castle Museum.

The **York Castle Museum** (☎ 653611; adult/concession/child/family £5.95/3.50/3.50/16) contains displays of everyday life that'll bring memories back for any Brit. Wander through Victorian and Edwardian streets and marvel at the collection of odds and ends that has people lamenting the good old days.

Other Attractions A £5 million investment programme has made one of York's most popular attractions even more appealing. The smells-and-all **Jorvik Viking Centre**

(☎ 643211; adult/concession/child/family £6.95/6.10/5.10/21.95) is a re-creation of 10th-century York – hilarious.

The kid-friendly **National Railway Museum** (☎ 621261; Leeman Rd; admission free) is for boys who love toys, with numerous restored engines and carriages from the 1820s to the present.

The ghost walks are a bit gimmicky, but the **Original Ghost Walk of York** (£3) is good fun. It leaves from the King's Arms pub at 8pm every night.

If you're here mid-February, be sure to catch the recommended Jorvik Viking Festival with its re-enactments of landmark events.

Places to Stay

York gets very crowded in summer and finding a bed can be trying. Fortunately, the TIC has an accommodation booking service (£4), or you can check availability at **w** www.york.roomcheck.co.uk.

Camping Most camping grounds are a good few miles outside the centre, but **Rowntree Park Camping** (☎ 658997; Terry Ave; 2-person tent £11.50) is only a 20-minute walk from the station. Unfortunately, you can't book and tent pitches are limited.

Hostels In a lovely Victorian house is **York Youth Hostel** (☎ 653147; e york@yha.org.uk; Water End, Clifton; B&B £16; open year-round). It's about 1mi northwest of the TIC and is large and very busy. There's a riverside footpath from the station. Book in advance.

York Youth Hotel (☎ 625904; e info@yorkyouthhotel.demon.co.uk; 11 Bishophill Senior; co-ed dorm beds £10) is popular with loud and annoying school groups. No meals are served but there's a kitchen, laundry and TV.

York Backpackers (☎ 627720; e yorkbackpackers@cwcom.net; 88-90 Micklegate; dorm beds £11) occupies a 1752 Georgian building and is sociable thanks to a lively bar and large dorms. Raucous stag and hen parties descend at the weekend, so take note if you want a good night's rest.

B&Bs & Hotels With its central position next to the river, the **Abbey Guest House** (☎ 62 7782; 14 Earlsborough Terrace; B&B singles/doubles without bath £25/45, en suite £30/55) has good-sized rooms, some with four-poster beds.

Jorvik Hotel (☎ 653111; 52 Marygate; B&B en suite singles £35-40, doubles £29-32, four-poster £35) has simple, small rooms and a lovely walled garden.

Running along the railway line, you'll find plenty of choice on Bootham Terrace (south of Bootham), but St Mary's running parallel to it, offers a gem. **23 St Mary's** (☎ 622738; B&B en suite singles/doubles £36/70), is a family-run affair with good-sized rooms and friendly hosts.

A classy place is the **Judges Lodging Hotel** (☎ 638733; e judgeshotel@aol.com; 9 Lendal; B&B singles/doubles £75/100) in a Georgian mansion featuring elegant, time-honoured rooms.

Places to Eat

York has a good selection of eating haunts, from the ubiquitous all-you-can-eats, to the ultra chic.

Victor J's (☎ 673788; 1a Finkle St; mains £5-6) is a funky, ambient café/bar selling art, absinthe and munchies.

Vegetarians will love the excellent **Blake Head Bookshop & Vegetarian Café** (☎ 623767; 104 Micklegate; lunch mains £5.90), and the sophisticated **Rubicon** (☎ 676076; 5 Little Stonegate; mains £6-8). Both are recommended.

Ask (☎ 637254; Grand Assembly Rooms) is an average Italian eatery, but it's worth trying just to gawp at the amazing interior. Pizzas and pastas are around £6.

Betty's (☎ 659142; St Helen's Square) is the only place to go for traditional afternoon tea (£10).

St William's Restaurant (☎ 634830; College St; 2-/3-course dinner £13.95/16.95) is part of the 15th-century St William's College and makes an ideal spot to relax after exploring the cathedral. Lunch includes soup (£2.75).

Rish (☎ 622688; 7 Fossgate; 2-/3-course lunch £11/14, dinner mains £13-18) mixes Art Deco with the modern and minimalist, and cooks up food to die for.

Entertainment

Head to **City Screen** (☎ 541155; 13-17 Coney St) for cinema and live music. The limited clubbing 'scene' consists of the locals' favourite, **The Gallery** (Clifford St), the student-orientated **Toffs** (Toft Green) and the small and sweaty **Ziggy's** (Micklegate). This certainly isn't Leeds.

Evil Eye (☎ 640002; above Forever Changes, Stonegate) is chilled with Internet access (£2 per hour) and excellent cocktails (£3.50).

King's Arms on King's Staith, does cheap beer and is the pub that famously floods. Excellent for lounging by the river.

The Maltings (Tanners Moat) below Lendal Bridge, has great beers, friendly locals and a toilet in the corner!

Getting There & Away

Bus The main bus terminal is on Rougier St. National Express buses leave from the train station. There are at least three services a day to London (£19.50, five hours), one to Birmingham (£20, 2½ hours) and one to Edinburgh (£26.50, 5¼ hours).

For information on local buses (to Castle Howard, Helmsley, Scarborough, Whitby etc), call ☎ 551400 or drop into the **Bus Information Centre** (20 George Hudson St). Yorkshire Coastliner has buses to Leeds, Malton and Scarborough.

Train There are numerous trains from London's King's Cross (£63.50, two hours) and on to Edinburgh (£51, 2½ hours).

North-south trains also connect with Peterborough (£36, 1½ hours) for Cambridge and East Anglia. There are a few trains for southwest England, including Oxford, via Birmingham (£53.50, 4¼ hours).

Local trains to/from Scarborough take 45 minutes (£9.30). For Whitby it's necessary to change at Middlesbrough (three hours).

Left luggage has been farmed out to Europcar on platform 1.

Getting Around

You can hire bikes from **Europcar** (☎ 656161) for £7.50 a day. There are plenty of good cycling routes in the environs; the TICs have maps.

AROUND YORK
Castle Howard

Castle Howard (☎ 01653-648333; house & grounds adult/concession/child £8/7/5, gardens & grounds adult/child £5/4; open 10am-last admission 4.30pm daily mid-Mar–early Nov), home to Hollywood films with an intricate history, is difficult to sum up. Not even 'spectacular' does it justice. The house is set in the rolling Howardian Hills and is surrounded by 400 hectares of superb terraces and landscaped grounds; it's imposing, yet strangely tranquil.

It's 15mi north of York off the A64 (4mi) and can be reached by several tours from York – ask at the TIC. Yorkshire Coastliner has a morning bus from York that links Castle Howard and Pickering.

NORTH YORK MOORS NATIONAL PARK

The North York Moors (☎ 01439-770657) carries every texture in its landscape. Vast expanses of rugged heather moorland and rolling hills are offset by dramatic coastline and secluded dales; it's impressive to say the least. If you're a walker, you'll have found your spiritual home. The famous Cleveland Way (110mi) snakes around the edge of the park from Helmsley to Filey, taking in all the contrasting harshness and romanticism. If you don't fancy walking, enjoy nostalgic steam travel on the North Yorkshire Moors Railway (NYMR), which runs up the beautiful wooded Newton Dale from Pickering to Grosmont.

Orientation & Information

The park's western boundary is a steep escarpment formed by the Hambleton and Cleveland Hills; the moors run east-west and stretch along the coast between Scarborough and Staithes. After the open space of the moors, the dales form a gentler, greener landscape, sometimes wooded, often sheltering a beautiful stone village. The coastline is as impressive as any in Britain, and is home to such gems as Robin Hood's Bay and Whitby. The best visitor centre for the park is at **Danby** (☎ 01287-660654; open 11am-4pm daily Nov-Jan & Mar; 10am-5pm daily Apr-Oct & Jan-Feb, 11am-4pm Sat & Sun).

Getting Around

A must for all public transport users is the invaluable *Transport Times for Ryedale District* booklet available from TICs.

The **Moorsbus** (☎ 01845-597426) is a special service that runs daily from mid-July to early September, linking a web of destinations in the Moors.

The **North Yorkshire Moors Railway** (☎ 01751-472508) cuts through the park from Pickering to Grosmont, which is on the Esk Valley line between Whitby and Middlesbrough. It operates from April to early

November (£10 all lines). There are pleasant walks from most of the stations along the line; brochures are available from NYMR shops.

Bicycles can be hired from **Footloose** (☎ 01439-770886; Borogate) in Helmsley from £7.50 a day.

Helmsley & Around
☎ 01439 • pop 1520

What Helmsley lacks in size, it makes up for in charm. It attracts bus loads of tourists (especially on Friday, market day), but unlike Pickering, they seem to melt into the background. Perhaps it's because the **ruined castle** (admission £2.50) like York Minster, is too dignified to be overrun.

The town's main focus is the bustling marketplace, from which everything spills. The **TIC** (☎ 770173; open 9.30am-6pm daily Mar-Oct, 10am-4pm Fri-Sun Nov-Feb) is in the town hall.

Hunters (13 Borogate) arguably does the best sandwiches in Yorkshire.

Duncombe Park and Nunnington Hall are within easy walking distance, but the 13th-century remains of **Rievaulx Abbey** (☎ 798228; admission £3.30) are the highlight. The 3½mi uphill walk from Helmsley along the Cleveland Way is well worth it, but the Moorsbus also runs from the town to the site for the less energetic. The **Rievaulx Terrace & Temples** (admission £3.30) are also recommended for their gorgeous views over the abbey.

There are several camping grounds nearby, but **Foxholme Caravan Park** (☎ 770416; Harome), is only 2mi southeast. Dorm accommodation is available at the excellent and friendly YHA **Helmsley Youth Hostel** (☎/fax 770433; Carlton Lane; £9.50). Opening times vary so phone ahead. The TIC offers a free booking service for B&Bs, with rooms usually around £20.

Scarborough & District has hourly buses (No 128) daily between Helmsley and Scarborough via Pickering (1½ hours).

Pickering
☎ 01751 • pop 6650

Pickering is a terminus for the NYMR and thanks to a grant from the Heritage Lottery Fund, the station has been restored to 1937 glory. Other worthwhile attractions include the impressive ruins of the **motte-and-bailey castle** (admission £2.80), and the 15th-century frescoes of the **Church of St Peter and St Paul.**

The helpful staff at the **TIC** (☎ 473791; *The Ropery; open 9.30am-6pm Mon-Sat & 9.30am-5pm Sun Mar-Oct; 10am-4.30pm Mon-Sat Nov-Feb*) can suggest one of numerous B&Bs and book ahead for free; there are a clutch of decent options on Eastgate. The nearest YHA hostel is the extremely basic **Lockton Youth Hostel** (☎/fax 460376; open *Tues-Sat late Mar-late Sept*) 4mi north. The Yorkshire Coastliner bus No 840 stops in Lockton village.

Pickering can be reached from York and Whitby on Yorkshire Coastliner; from Helmsley and Scarborough on Scarborough & District buses.

Scarborough
☎ 01723 • pop 38,070

With rail links to York, frequent buses west to Pickering and Helmsley, and regular buses to Whitby via Robin Hood's Bay, Scarborough is a good transport hub. Unfortunately, that's all.

The Victorian Grand Hotel and Rotunda Museum hint at a time long since lost to this seaside resort. Its South Bay is full of amusement arcades, tea-dancing pensioners and candy-floss munching toddlers – it's tacky. Despite its views, even the castle is disappointing.

For interesting history, visit the 15th-century **King Richard III** (☎ 375201; *Sandside*) restaurant and ask the owners about the building – it's fascinating stuff.

It's also worth popping along to the **Stephen Joseph Theatre** (☎ 370541; *Westborough*) to catch a play by its artistic director and all-round theatrical guru, Alan Ayckbourn.

If you need to stay, contact the **TIC** (☎ 373333). The YHA **White House Youth Hostel** (☎ 361176; [e] scarborough@yha.org.uk; *Burniston Rd; dorm beds £10.25*) is 2mi north of town; you'll need bus No 12 or 21. It has complex opening times, so ring ahead.

Whitby
☎ 01947 • pop 14,120

If you're lucky enough to catch a sea mist, you'll appreciate exactly why Bram Stoker wrote *Dracula* here. The imposing, evocative ruins of the **abbey** (*admission £3.60*) loom over a seagull-filled harbour, both with an atmosphere all their own. It reveals a town with a split personality, the seaside paraphernalia joined to the stoic by the well-trodden 199 steps. Captain James Cook was apprenticed to

a Whitby shipowner in 1746, and HMS *Endeavour* was built here.

The helpful staff at the **TIC** (☎ 602674; open *9am-6pm daily May-Sept, 10am-4.30pm Oct-Apr*) near the train station books rooms. **Whitby Youth Hostel** (☎ 602878, fax 825146; *dorm beds £10.25*), beside the abbey, has fantastic views. There's also the functional **Harbour Grange Hostel** (☎ 600817; [e] backpackers@harbourgrange.onyxnet.co.uk; *Spital Bridge; dorm beds £10*), on the eastern side of the harbour. Both have curfews of around 11pm. Much more laid-back and friendly is **Whitby Backpackers** (☎ 601794; [e] martin@warrener65.freeserve.co.uk; *28 Hudson St; dorm bed £10*).

There are plenty of B&Bs on the Victorian western side. **Number Seven** (☎/fax 606019; *7 East Crescent; B&B from £20*) is modern, friendly and has good views from some rooms. For pure luxury try the Tudor **Bagdale Hall** (☎ 602958, fax 820714; *1 Bagdale; B&B doubles £45-49, suites per person £59*).

With queues up its steps, the harbour-based **Magpie Café** is still doing the best fish and chips in England.

For excellent coffee in funky surroundings head to **Java** (*2 Flowergate*). Shame the Internet access isn't as sweet tasting – it's an exorbitant £5 an hour.

Consider attempting the 5½mi cliff-top walk south to beautiful Robin Hood's Bay. You'll be rewarded with a delightful old fishing village looking as if it's about to tumble into the sea below. Accommodation is always prebooked; **Boggle Hole YHA Hostel** (☎ 88 0352; *Fylingthorpe; dorm beds £10.25*) is only a further 1½mi-walk south.

There are buses to Whitby from Scarborough and York. There's also the Esk Valley train from Middlesbrough (£6.70, 1½ hours), which connects with the NYMR at Grosmont.

DURHAM
☎ 0191 • pop 81,079

Durham is home to over 1000 years of history and the third-oldest university in England. It's like your favourite grandma – old, endearing and reassuringly familiar. After just five minutes in the city, you'll feel as if you've made an attachment to it. The omnipotence of the Norman cathedral probably has something to do with this – its dramatic position on a wooded promontory, high above a bend in the River Wear, keeps it in constant view.

BRITAIN

Orientation & Information

This compact city is easy to explore. The marketplace, castle and cathedral are on the teardrop-shaped peninsula surrounded by the River Wear. The train station is above and northwest of the cathedral, on the other side of the river. The bus station is also on the western side.

The **TIC** (☎ 384 3720; open 9.30am-5.30pm Mon-Sat, 10am-4pm Sun year-round) is in the Gala building, just off Clayport. It's part of the relatively new Millennium City that has seen a theatre, library and whole host of facilities being added to existing attractions.

Internet access is available at Saints, in the old Market Vaults just off the Marketplace. Rates per hour for members/nonmembers are £3.50/4.50. A one-off membership fee is £1.50.

Things to See & Do

The World Heritage–listed **Durham Cathedral** is an architectural masterpiece. The vast interior is all stocky pillars and intricate stonework archways; the **stunning Galilee Chapel** and a climb up the **tower** (£2) are obligatory. There are tours (£3.50) at 11am and 2.30pm Monday to Saturday, late July to the end of September.

Durham Castle served as the home for the county's Prince-Bishops. These 11th-century bishops lived like kings and had virtual autonomy over the running of what was essentially a buffer-zone between England and Scotland. It's now a university college, and it's possible to stay here during summer holidays. Entry is by guided tour (£3) from Easter to October.

A stroll along the outer river bank is particularly recommended for its excellent views of these two architectural beasts, as is hiring a boat at Elvet Bridge (£2.50 an hour, April to October).

Places to Stay & Eat

Several colleges rent their rooms during the university holidays (Easter and July to September), but if you want to feel like a Prince-Bishop then head straight for the salubrious **University College** (☎ 374 3863; B&B per person without bath £20.50), in the old Durham Castle.

The TIC makes local bookings free, but cheap accommodation is difficult to come by; graduation week in late June should be avoided like the plague. **Mrs Koltai** (☎/fax 386 2026; 10 Gilesgate; singles £16) is still the cheapest. If you're after a quirky building with a touch of

opulence, **Farnley Tower** (☎ 375 0011; e enquiries@farnley-tower.co.uk; The Avenue, B&B singles/doubles £50/68) will measure up.

Most of the eating possibilities are within a short walk of the market square. **Hide** (☎ 384 1999; 39 Saddler St) is a modern café/bar which does 'better-than-bar-quality' food. The grilled chicken tortilla (£5.95) is highly recommended. The **Almshouses** (☎ 386 1054, Palace Green; lunch mains £5) makes an ideal refreshment spot after traipsing around the Cathedral.

Getting There & Away

There are six National Express buses a day to London (£23, 6½ hours), one to Edinburgh (£18.50, 4½ hours), and three to Newcastle-upon-Tyne (£2, 30 minutes). Arriva X1 runs throughout the day (except Sunday) to Newcastle, via Chester-le-Street.

There are numerous trains to York (£14.90, one hour), a good number of which head on to London (£78, three hours) via Peterborough. Frequent trains from London continue through to Edinburgh (two hours).

NEWCASTLE-UPON-TYNE
☎ 0191 • pop 270,500

There's never been a more exciting time to visit Newcastle. Once home to the 'new castle' of Robert Curthose (the eldest son of William the Conqueror) from which the city takes its name, Newcastle's past is chequered. As a medieval walled town it thrived and was later to become the commercial hub of Tyneside, most famous for the mining and exporting of coal. Throughout the 19th century it maintained its industrial ties and the grandeur of the era is still very much in evidence in and around Grainger Street.

With WWII and the general decline of manufacturing, Newcastle struggled to find its niche. It's only recently that the spirit of regeneration has taken hold with visitors being treated to a minicultural revolution.

The Quayside north of the River Tyne and Gateshead Quays to the south have been transformed into airy, stimulating quarters. The tilting Gateshead Millennium Bridge and Music Centre Gateshead are both visually stunning, while the BALTIC Centre for Contemporary Art seems to define modern Newcastle. What's more, the nightlife is definitely on the up too – no-one seems to party like the Geordies.

Orientation & Information

The city centre is surprisingly easy to navigate on foot, and the metro or underground railway (for the YHA hostel and B&Bs) is fast and easy to use. The Central train station is just south of the centre and the coach station is just east. If you get lost, ask for directions to Grey's Monument as it's fairly central.

The friendly, helpful TIC (☎ 277 8006; 132 Grainger St; open 9.30am-5.30pm Mon-Sat, 9.30am-7.30pm Thur & 10am-4pm Sun in summer) also has an office at the train station (closed Sunday). Both offices have a free map, guide and accommodation list. Be sure to pick up the free and indispensable entertainment listings guide *The Crack*. All major banks and *bureaux de change* are dotted around this area.

Internet access is available at **Internet Exchange** (26 Market St) where £1 will get you 30 minutes.

There's a **laundrette** (3 Clayton Rd) about 10 minutes' walk from the Newcastle Youth Hostel (see Places to Stay later).

Things to See & Do

With its five amazing art galleries, the **BALTIC Centre** (☎ 478 1810; Gateshead Quays; admission free) could easily absorb a day. If this appeals, you'll also appreciate Thomas Heatherwick's quirky **Blue Carpet** just outside another cultural oasis, the **Laing Art Gallery** (☎ 232 7734; Higham Place; admission free). The 'carpet' actually comprises purpose-made tiles containing recycled blue-glass shreds – the effect at night is fab. **LIFE** (☎ 243 8210; Times Square; admission £6.95) is ideal for kids, providing a hands-on experience delving into all aspects of life. Both **St Nicholas Cathedral** and **Castle Garth Keep** are also worth visiting.

Further afield, take the metro to nearby Wallsend with its reconstruction of **Segedunum** (☎ 295 5757; admission £3.50), the last outpost of Hadrian's Wall. Alternatively, enjoy river cruises, or walks through the city's parks, particularly Jesmond Dene, off Jesmond Rd.

Places to Stay

Newcastle Youth Hostel (☎ 281 2570; e newcastle@yha.org.uk; 107 Jesmond Rd; dorm beds £11.25; open Feb-Dec, Fri-Sun only Jan) is a five-minute walk from Jesmond metro station. It's clean and comfortable but has no laundry.

North East YWCA (☎ 281 1233; Jesmond House, Clayton Rd; B&B per person £16) accepts male and female guests. Turn left on Osborne Rd from Jesmond station and take the second street on the right.

There are quite a number of B&Bs within easy walking distance of West Jesmond station, mostly along Jesmond and Osborne Rds. The **Portland Guest House** (☎ 232 7868; 134 Sandyford Rd; singles/doubles from £18/36) is on a major traffic artery but has large rooms and is cheap for the area.

For the flash, there's the well-designed and luxurious **Malmaison** (☎ 245 5000; e newcastle@malmasion.com; Quayside; doubles/suites £120/150). The views over the Tyne are worth the price.

Places to Eat & Drink

A cluster of good restaurants can be found around Grey St, among them **eviva** (☎ 241 4565; 11 Grey St; pizza & pasta £3.50; lunch & evenings 5pm-7pm), which is modern, excellent value and has a romantic alcoved lower floor. The bizarrely decorated **JT's** (☎ 222 0659; 6-10 Leazes Park Rd; mains £4-12; open 24hr) does a three-course lunch and an early evening special for £5.99. **Paradiso** (☎ 221 1240; 1 Market Lane; 2-courses £6.95; open 11am-11pm Mon-Sat) is arguably the best Italian eatery in Newcastle; the slightly more pricey **Ichiban** (☎ 261 6946; No 2 Phoenix House, Queen St; set menu from £13 for minimum of 2) is arguably the best Japanese restaurant. Also check out **Bob Trollop** and **Red House** just off the Quayside; both have pub meals for about £5.

Newcastle's nightlife is superb. For bars and late-night drinking head to the Quayside. **Trent House** (1-2 Leazes Lane) with its laid-back feel and free soul-classics jukebox, is more relaxed.

Clubs worth shaking a stick at include the housey **Foundation** (57-59 Melbourne St) and the cheaper, funk and hip-hop pumping **World Headquarters** (7 Marlborough Crescent); membership needed (£1).

Getting There & Away

Bus There are numerous National Express connections with virtually every major city in the country. For local buses around the northeast, don't forget the excellent value Explorer North East ticket, valid on most of the services (£5.50). Bus No 505 serves

Berwick-upon-Tweed and No 685 Hexham and Haltwhistle for Hadrian's Wall (see that section later).

Train There are frequent trains (☎ 0845 748 4950) to Edinburgh (£33.50, 1¾ hours), London (£83, three hours) and York (£15.50, one hour). Berwick-upon-Tweed and Alnmouth (for Alnwick) are also served.

Air Newcastle airport serves Europe, Toronto and Florida, with frequent domestic flights to most UK airports.

Boat Regular ferries link Newcastle with Bergen, Kristiansand, Haugesund and Stavanger (Norway), Gothenburg (Sweden) and Amsterdam. See the Getting There & Away section in this chapter for details.

Getting Around
The excellent metro (underground railway) is quicker and more efficient than local buses. It'll ferry you round the city and out to Tynemouth and Whitley Bay, which are definitely worth a look. Unlimited travel for a day is £3. The service also links up with Newcastle airport and the Ferry Terminal. For advice and information use **Traveline** (☎ 0870 608 2608) or the touch-screen information point at Haymarket bus station.

NORTHUMBERLAND
Northumberland has a haunting beauty about it. It offers a rare opportunity to really get away from everything and everyone, and is refreshingly unspoilt. It claims ownership of more historical sites than any other county in England, many a living testament to England's long, bloody struggle with the Scots.

The most significant is of course, Hadrian's Wall. The brainchild of the Roman Emperor Hadrian in AD 122, it stretches for 73mi from Newcastle to Bowness-on-Solway near Carlisle and was the northern frontier of the empire for almost 300 years. It was abandoned around AD 410, but enough remains to bring the past dramatically alive. After the arrival of the Normans, large numbers of castles and fortified houses (or *peles*) were built. Most have now lapsed into ruin, but others, like Bamburgh and Alnwick, stand perfect and proud.

Northumberland National Park lies north of Hadrian's Wall, incorporating the sparsely populated Cheviot Hills. The walks can be challenging, and cross some of the loneliest parts of England. There are information centres open mid-March to October and at weekends in winter. **Once Brewed** (☎ 01434-344396) and **Rothbury** (☎ 01669-620887) both handle accommodation bookings, while **Ingram** (☎ 01665-578248) has fewer facilities.

Berwick-upon-Tweed & Around
☎ 01289
Berwick-upon-Tweed makes for a good stop-off before heading up to explore Scotland, with good bus and train links to Edinburgh. But once you've marvelled at the views of the River Tweed from the ramparts and stormed the Barracks, there's little to hold the attention. The **TIC** (☎ 330733; 106 Marygate; open 10am-5pm Mon-Sat, 11am-3pm Sun year-round) offers an accommodation booking service for the numerous B&Bs, but by far the cheapest option is **Berwick Backpackers** (331481; 56 Bridge St; dorm beds £10). It's more like being in your own flat than a hostel.

If you want to truly appreciate the area, spend more time exploring Bamburgh and Lindisfarne, making Alnwick your base. Alnwick is a mini York with **Alnwick Castle** (☎ 01665-510777; admission £6.95; open late Mar-late Oct) replacing the Minster as the dominating feature. With its amazing garden, it rose to recent fame in the Harry Potter films – it's fascinating inside and out. The **TIC** (☎ 01665-510665) can book accommodation, but the **Lindisfarne Guest House** (☎ 01665-603430; 6 Bondgate; single without bath £17) is superb.

Bamburgh Castle (☎ 01668-214515) has a dramatic location and lovely sand dunes nearby. Bus No 501 will get you there from Alnwick. **Lindisfarne** was the Anglo-Saxon seat of Christianity, and despite the throngs of tourists, still retains an element of peace and tranquillity. Local TICs have safe-crossing times for the causeway that separates 'Holy Island' from the mainland.

Getting There & Away Berwick is on the main London to Edinburgh line. Phone ☎ 0870 608 2608 for connecting bus services. Monday to Saturday, service No 501 runs to/from Alnwick via Bamburgh.

Hadrian's Wall
The most spectacular section of the wall is between Hexham and Brampton. It's possible to

walk the entire length (allow at least five days), but the first section through Newcastle is pretty uninteresting.

Chesters Roman Fort & Museum (☎ 01434-681379; admission £3) is in a pleasant valley by the River Tyne. There's an interesting museum, an extraordinary bath-house and the remains of a massive bridge.

Housesteads Roman Fort (☎ 01434-344363; admission £3) is the most dramatic, most popular ruin. The well-preserved foundations include the famous latrine and offer gorgeous views over the Northumbrian countryside. It requires an uphill walk to reach them.

Vindolanda Fort & Chesterholm Museum (☎ 01434-344277; admission £3.90), 2½mi south, is an extensively excavated fort and civil settlement with an accompanying museum. The reconstructions will appeal to kids. If you're lucky, you'll catch chatty archaeologists hard at work.

Birdoswald Roman Fort (☎ 016977-47602; admission £3) sits on an escarpment overlooking the picturesque Irthing Valley. It's less inundated with visitors than some of the other sites.

Places to Stay Corbridge, Hexham, Haltwhistle and Brampton make ideal bases for exploring the wall and are plentiful with B&Bs. There's also a number of YHA hostels that are cheap and convenient.

Starting in the east, the **Acomb Youth Hostel** (☎ 01434-602864; dorm beds £7) is about 2½mi north of Hexham and 2mi south of the wall. Catch bus No 880 from Hexham.

Once Brewed Youth Hostel (☎ 01434-344360; dorm beds £11.25) is central for both Housesteads Fort (3mi) and Vindolanda (1mi). It's right next door to the Park Information Centre too. Northumbria bus No 685 (from Hexham or Haltwhistle stations) will drop you at Henshaw, 2mi south; in summer, bus AD122 will drop you at the front door. The nearest train station is Bardon Mill, 2½mi southeast. The walk from here to Housesteads is definitely worth doing.

Greenhead Youth Hostel (☎ 016977-47401; dorm beds £9.50) is a charming chapel conversion 3mi west of Haltwhistle station; it's also served by the trusty bus No 685 and the White Star bus No 185 from Carlisle.

For cheap, basic accommodation with outstanding views try **Bankshead Camping Barn** (☎ 01697-73198; beds £4). It's close to Banks East Turret and is ideal for exploring Lanercost Priory. Bus No 682 drops you outside.

Getting There & Away There are hourly services between Carlisle and Newcastle on **Bus No 685** (☎ 0870 608 2608). The **Newcastle to Carlisle railway line** (☎ 0845 748 4950) has stations at Hexham, Haydon Bridge, Bardon Mill, Haltwhistle and Brampton, but not all trains stop at all stations.

From June to September the special hail-and-ride Hadrian's Wall Bus (AD122) runs between Hexham and Haltwhistle train stations, calling at the main sites. For further information contact **Hexham TIC** (☎ 01434-652220).

Explorer tickets on all bus services cost £5.50, or in summer use the Hadrian's Wall Rail Rover Ticket (£12.50) for travel any two days out of three on trains, the metro and Hadrian's Wall Bus.

YORKSHIRE DALES & AROUND

This is the region that was made famous by James Herriot and the TV series *All Creatures Great and Small*, and it's one of outstanding natural beauty. The lush valleys (dales) topped by craggy limestone cliffs (scars), are zig-zagged by distinctive drystone walls. Amazing limestone 'pavements' shelter beneath famous towering peaks, while deep ravines hide dramatic waterfalls.

The landscape is unique, and you'll find something different around every bend – from the rugged and dramatic, to the sheltered and tranquil. You can't help but be impressed. Unfortunately, like the Lake District, the Dales are a walker's mecca and it can feel extremely crowded in summer. Weekends are worst so it's best to get off the beaten track.

Orientation & Information

The Dales can be broken into northern and southern halves. In the north, the main dales run parallel and east-west and include Wensleydale, beautiful Swaledale and Teesdale.

In the southern half, the north-to-south Ribblesdale with its famous Viaduct is the route taken by the Leeds-Settle-Carlisle (LSC) railway line. Romantic Wharfedale is parallel to the east.

For visitors without transport, the best bet will be those places accessible on the LSC line such as gorgeous Settle, which has many accommodation and hiking choices.

The main **National Park Centre** (☎ 01756-752774; open daily Apr-Oct) is in Grassington, 6mi north of Skipton.

Getting Around

Apart from the Leeds-Settle-Carlisle (LSC) railway line, public transport is a shoddy collection of infrequent services. For general transport information pick up the *Transport Times for Craven District* leaflet from local TICs. The *Dales Buses* timetable is also invaluable. Cycling is probably your best bet; you can hire bikes in Skipton from **The Bicycle Shop** (☎ 01756-794386; 3-5 Water St) for £15 a day.

Skipton

☎ 01756 • pop 13,574

Skipton heralds the gateway to the dales and is a transport hub. Sadly, it lacks the charm of other market towns and once you've raided the **TIC** (☎ 792809; 35 Coach St) and toured the **castle** (admission £4.60), you'll want to be off. It's served by frequent trains from Leeds (30 minutes). A row of decent B&Bs are on Keighley Rd.

Grassington

☎ 01756 • pop 1102

Grassington, arguably the prettiest of the Dales' villages, is home to a combined **National Park Centre and TIC** (☎ 752774; open 10am-5pm daily year-round). It's a good base for walks in Wharfedale. There are a few B&Bs in the village, but the nearest **hostel** (☎ 760232; dorm beds £10.25) is in sleepy Kettlewell 6mi away. Catch the Pride of the Dales bus No 74.

Settle

☎ 01729 • pop 2395

Settle is on the LSC line and shouldn't be missed. It's small but perfectly formed, and a walk to Castleberg rock overhanging the town makes for brilliant views. Also consider the 5mi circular route to the gorgeous Attermire Scar, or check out the chapel of **Giggleswick School** (☎ 893000).

The **TIC** (☎ 825192; open 10am-5pm daily Mar-Oct, 10am-4pm in winter) can supply maps and find rooms. The YHA **Stainforth Youth Hostel** (☎ 823577; e stainforth@yha.org.uk; dorm beds £11.25) is 2mi north. Opening times are complex, so call first.

Haworth

☎ 01535 • pop 2753

Once home to the literary Brontë sisters, Haworth, with its cobbled streets and hillside location, is a gem. Despite being a summer tourist trap, the **Brontë Parsonage Museum** (☎ 642323; admission £4.80) is very interesting. The **TIC** (☎ 642329; Main St) can help with accommodation, but **Haworth YHA** (☎ 642234; Longlands Drive; dorm beds £10.25) is a stately home at budget prices. There are frequent buses from Keighley, which has train connections with Leeds.

Northwest England

The southern part of this region is often dismissed as England's industrial back yard. The dense network of motorways you see on maps gives forewarning of both the level of development and the continuing economic importance of the region, despite the decline of some traditional industries. This said, there are still some beautiful corners, and the larger cities are cultural hubs with a legacy of brilliant Victorian architecture and a population that really know how to have a good time.

This is the working-class heartland of England. There's a big gap between these northern cities and those south of Birmingham. Since the Industrial Revolution created them, life for the inhabitants has often been an uncompromising struggle. The main industrial corridor runs from Merseyside (Liverpool) to the River Humber. The cities of Liverpool and Manchester sprawl into the countryside, burying it under motorways, grim suburbs, power lines, factories and mines. There are, nonetheless, some important exceptions, including walled Chester, which makes a good starting point for North Wales and the Lake District, (the most beautiful corner of England).

MANCHESTER

☎ 0161 • pop 460,000

Best known for the football team Manchester United and for modern music giants Oasis, The Smiths and New Order, Manchester is also a monument to England's industrial history. In the city-centre warehouses and factories rub shoulders with stunning Victorian Gothic buildings and modern apartment blocks, rusting train tracks and motorway overpasses with flashy bars and nightclubs. At the time of research most of Manchester was a construction site, in the final stages of preparation for the 2002 Commonwealth Games. Significant money has been spent on improving major visitor attractions and on opening up and beautifying public spaces. The longer you stay, the more you'll like Manchester. Not many cities in England can rival Manchester for its vibrancy and nightlife, its gay scene and fantastic sports facilities. England's largest student population gives it that extra spark.

Orientation & Information

The centre of Manchester is easy to get around on foot and with the help of the excellent Metrolink tramway. The University of Manchester lies to the south of the city centre (on Oxford St/Rd). To the west of the university is Moss Side, a ghetto with high unemployment and a thriving drug trade – keep clear. Victoria train station caps the city in the north. The TIC (☎ 234 3157; Lloyd St, St Peter Square) is in the town hall extension, with another branch at the Castlefield Urban Heritage Park and at the airport. City Life is the local 'what's on' magazine – a compulsory purchase. For cheap Internet access try easyEverything (☎ 832 9200; St Anne's Square).

Things to See & Do

Castlefield Urban Heritage Park is an extraordinary landscape made up of the remains of ancient Roman fortresses and newly constructed canalside footpaths, pubs, hotels and a YHA hostel. The area also takes in the excellent Museum of Science & Industry (☎ 832 1830; Liverpool Rd; admission free; open 10am-5pm daily).

Dominating Albert Square in the city centre is the enormous Victorian Gothic Town Hall, designed by Albert Waterhouse (of London's Natural History Museum fame) in 1876.

The recently renovated Manchester Art Gallery (☎ 234 1456; cnr Nicholas & Mosley Sts; admission free; open 10am-5pm Tues-Sun) has an impressive collection covering everything from early Italian, Dutch and Flemish painters to Gainsborough, Blake, Constable and the Pre-Raphaelites.

The Lowry is an eye-catching modern construction on Salford Quay. Two theatres and a number of galleries (one devoted to LS Lowry himself) are encapsulated in the complex. The galleries are free to enter. Take the Metrolink to either Broadway or Harbour City.

Places to Stay

Surprisingly, playing host to the 2002 Commonwealth Games hasn't resulted in an increased number or variety of places to stay in Manchester city, however there is a reasonable range of accommodation, but most cheap options are some distance from the city centre. The TIC's free booking service is recommended.

The Youth Hostel (☎ 839 9960; dorm beds adults/under-18s £18.50/13.75), across the road from the Museum of Science & Industry in the Castlefield area (well signposted), has over 140 beds in comfortable four-bed rooms. From mid-June to mid-September, the University of Manchester lets students' rooms to visitors from around £13 per person. Contact St Anselm Hall (☎ 224 7327) or Woolaton Hall (☎ 224 7244).

The Burton Arms Hotel (☎ 834 3455; 31 Swan St; singles/doubles from £25/40) is a traditional pub close to the centre of town. Castlefield Hotel (☎ 832 7073; e info@ castlefield-hotel.co.uk; Liverpool Rd; singles/ doubles £49/59) is in a convenient location close to the Castlefield Heritage Park. The hotel has all the mod cons including a restaurant and bar.

Places to Eat

The most distinctive restaurant zones are Chinatown in the city centre and Rusholme in the south. That said, much of Manchester is experiencing a minigastronomic boom with restaurants and cafés springing up throughout the city centre.

Chinatown is bounded by Charlotte, Portland, Oxford and Mosley Sts, and it has a number of restaurants, not all Chinese, and most not particularly cheap. The most acclaimed is Little Yang Sing (☎ 228 7722; 17 George St; daytime set menu £9.95), which specialises in Cantonese cuisine. You'll pay twice the cost of the daytime set menu in the evening. More affordable is Tampopo (☎ 819 1966; 16 Albert Square; mains around £7), which serves up noodle and rice dishes inspired by Thai, Malaysian and Japanese cuisines.

Dimitri's (☎ 839 3319; Campfield Arcade) serves up a mixture of Greek, Italian and Spanish food with a good vegetarian selection. A lunch will set you back £4.

Rusholme is to the south of the university on Wilmslow Rd, the extension of Oxford

BRITAIN

St/Rd, and has numerous popular, cheap and very good Indian/Pakistani places.

Cafés are big business in Manchester these days, as the ubiquitous chain coffee houses will testify, however if you're looking for something less generic the **Earth Vegetarian Café** (☎ 834 1996; 16-20 Turner St; mains £3-7), in the Northern Quarter, serves up an imaginative vegetarian selection and **Java Coffee Bar** (☎ 236 4003; 8a Oxford Rd; snacks £1.95-4.95) has a good selection of pastries and decent coffee. There are several cafés there in the indoor market of Affleck's Palace.

Entertainment

You will be spoilt for choice in Manchester when it comes to after-dark entertainment. One of the best venues for live jazz, blues and folk is **Band on the Wall** (☎ 832 6625; ticket info 237 5554; 25 Swan St). For rock and pop, including big international acts, check out the **Manchester Academy** (☎ 275 2930; 269 Oxford Rd), part of the University Students Union. Two historic pubs are the **Old Wellington Inn** (☎ 830 1440) and **Sinclairs Oyster Bar** at the top of New Cathedral St.

Mancunians, like hip young things the world over, have taken a strong liking to cocktail and wine bars. One of the first to emerge, **Dry Bar** (☎ 236 9840; 28 Oldham St) is still popular and still cool. **Kro Bar** (☎ 274 3100; 325 Oxford Rd) is a newcomer to the scene and seems to be popular with the punters.

There are several places to drink in Castlefield, including **Barça** (☎ 839 7099) in Catalan Square and **Dukes 92** (☎ 839 8646); both have outdoor seating for sunny days.

Canal St is the centre of Manchester's enormous gay nightlife scene. There are over 20 bars and clubs in the so-called 'Gay Village'. **Paradise Factory** (☎ 273 5422; 114-116 Princess St) is a cutting edge club, with gay nights on the weekend.

Getting There & Away

There are numerous coach links with the rest of the country. National Express operates out of Chorlton St station in the city centre to pretty well anywhere you'll want to go. A return adult/concession ticket from London's Victoria coach station will set you back £25.50/14.40.

Piccadilly is the main station for trains to and from the rest of the country, although Victoria serves Halifax and Bradford. The two are linked by **Metrolink** (☎ 0845 748 4950).

Getting Around

For general inquiries about local transport, including night buses, phone ☎ 228 7811 (open 8am to 8pm daily). A Day Saver ticket for £3 covers travel throughout the Great Manchester area on bus, train and Metrolink. Manchester's Metrolink light-railway (tram) makes frequent connections between Victoria and Piccadilly train stations and G-Mex (for Castlefield). Buy tickets from machines on the platforms.

CHESTER
☎ 01244 • pop 80,000

Despite steady streams of tourists, Chester remains a beautiful town, ringed by an unbroken, red sandstone city wall that dates back to the Romans. The 2mi walk along the top of the wall is the best way to see the town; allow a couple of hours to include detours down to the river and a visit to the cathedral. The eye-catching two-level shopping streets may date back to the post-Roman period and certainly make convenient rainproof shopping arcades.

Orientation & Information

Built in a bow formed by the River Dee, the walled centre is now surrounded by suburbs. The train station is a 15-minute walk from the city centre; go up City Rd, then turn right onto Foregate at the large roundabout. From the bus station, turn left onto Northgate St.

The **TIC** (☎ 402111) is in the town hall opposite the cathedral. **Chester Visitor Centre** (☎ 351609) is just outside Newgate, opposite the Roman amphitheatre. There's another small tourist information office at the train station. The Internet can be accessed at **i-station** (☎ 401680; Rufus Court); £2 for 35 minutes.

Things to See & Do

The present **Chester Cathedral** (☎ 324756; requested donation £2) was built between 1250 and 1540. It retains its fine 12th-century cloister but there were later alterations and a lot of Victorian reconstruction.

The **Dewa Roman Experience** (☎ 343407; Pierpoint Lane; adult/child under 16 £3.95/2.25; open 9am-5pm daily), off Bridge St, gives you a taste for life during Roman times.

Places to Stay & Eat

The **Youth Hostel** (☎ 680056; 40 Hough Green; dorm beds adults/under-18s £14.50/11.25) is 1mi from the centre, on the opposite side from the train station. To get there, head out of town by Grosvenor Rd past the castle on your left, cross the river and turn right at the roundabout.

There are numerous good-value B&Bs along Hoole Rd, the road into the city from the M53/M56. The **Bawn Park Hotel** (☎ 324971), at No 10, is typical with rates starting at £15 per person. Close to the train station, **Ormonde Guest House** (☎ 328816; 126 Brook St) and **Aplas Guest House** (☎ 312401; 106 Brooke St) both have rooms starting at £22. B&Bs can also be found inside the city walls, the **Recorder Hotel** (☎ 326580; 19 City Walls; rooms from £35), overlooking the River Dee, is a perfectly positioned option.

On a sun-soaked afternoon, it's hard to beat the beer garden at **BarsLounge** (cnr Nicholson & Watergate Sts), where food is served till 9pm daily. Good, basic pub food can also be found at **Watergates** (☎ 320515; 11 Watergate St). A good place for a light lunch is **Katie's Tea Rooms** (☎ 400322; 38 Watergate St), which turns into the more upmarket, Italian restaurant I Tre Piani in the evening. **Alexander's Jazz Theatre** (☎ 313400; Rufus Court by Northgate) is a wine, coffee and tapas bar with great music. **Loaf** (☎ 354041; Music Hall passage, St Werburgh St) is a sleek addition to Chester's bar scene.

Getting There & Away
Chester has excellent transport connections, especially to and from North Wales.

Bus National Express has numerous connections with Chester, including Birmingham (£8.25, 2½ hours) and on to London (£15, 5½ hours), Manchester (£4.50, 1¼ hours), Glasgow (£22.50, six hours), Liverpool (£5, one hour) and Llandudno (£5.50, 1¾ hours). For many destinations in the south or east it's necessary to change at Birmingham; for the north, change at Manchester.

For information on local bus services ring **Chester City Transport** (☎ 602666). Local buses leave from Market Square behind the town hall.

Train Any bus from the station goes into the centre. There are numerous trains to Manchester (£8.50, 1½ hours) and Liverpool (£3, 40 minutes); Holyhead (£16.15, two hours), via the North Wales coast, for ferries to Ireland; and London's Euston station (£48, three hours). Phone ☎ 0845 748 4950 for details.

LIVERPOOL
☎ 0151 • pop 510,000
Of all northern England's cities, Liverpool has perhaps the strongest sense of its own identity, an identity which is closely tied up with the totems of the Beatles, the Liverpool and Everton football teams, and the Grand National steeplechase, run at Aintree since 1839.

Architecturally, the city is a striking mix of grandeur and decay, decrepit streets, boarded-up windows and massive cathedrals and imperious buildings. This juxtaposition coupled with the city's dramatic site above the broad Mersey estuary with its shifting light, its fogs, its gulls and its mournful emptiness, creates one of the most arresting sights in Britain.

Liverpool's dramatic economic collapse has given the whole city a sharp edge you'd do well not to explore. But on weekends the centre pumps to music from countless pubs and clubs, a testimony to the city's determinedly vibrant population.

Orientation & Information
Liverpool stretches north-south along the Mersey estuary for more than 13mi. The main visitor attraction is Albert Dock (which is well signposted) to the south of the city centre. The centre, including the two cathedrals to the east, is quite compact (about 1½mi by 1mi).

Lime St, the main train station, is just to the east of the city centre. The National Express coach station is on the corner of Norton and Islington Sts in the north of the city. The bus station is in the centre on Paradise St. The main **TIC** (☎ 0906-680 6886; Queen Square Centre; open 9am-5.30pm Mon-Sat, 10.30am-4.30pm Sun) has a branch at **Albert Dock**. Both can book accommodation and the service is recommended. Log on to the Internet at **Planet Electra** (☎ 708 0303; 38 London Rd) for £2 per 30 minutes.

You're advised to be a bit cautious while in Liverpool. It's best to avoid dark side-streets even in the city centre.

Things to See & Do
The restored **Albert Dock** (☎ 708 8854; open from 10am daily) is, deservedly, Liverpool's number one tourist attraction, housing several outstanding modern museums (the **Merseyside Maritime Museum**, **Museum of Liverpool Life** and **Tate Gallery Liverpool**) as well as shops and restaurants, a branch of the TIC

BRITAIN

and several tacky tourist attractions (the **Beatles Story** is disappointing).

The **Walker Gallery** (☎ 478 4199; *William Brown St*) contains works by Rubens, Rembrant, Poussin and modern British artists. Next door, the **Liverpool Museum** (☎ 478 4399) covers everything from archaeology to natural history. Admission to both attractions is free.

The secret command centre for the Battle of the Atlantic in WWII was buried under yards of concrete beneath an undistinguished building behind the town hall in Rumford Square. At the end of the war the bunker was abandoned, with virtually everything left intact. It's now the **Western Approaches Museum** (☎ 227 2008; *Rumford St; adult/concession £4.75/3.45; open Mon-Thur & Sat Mar-Oct*).

A visit to Liverpool wouldn't be complete without a Beatles tour. There are numerous sites around town associated with the Beatles, all of whom grew up here. Both TICs sell tickets to the **Magical Mystery Tour**, a two-hour bus trip taking in homes, schools, venues, Penny Lane, Strawberry Fields and many other landmarks. It departs from inside the Albert Dock TIC at 3pm/2pm April to October/ November to March and from the main TIC at 2.40pm/1.40pm. Tickets are £10.95, no concessions.

A re-creation of the original music venue where the Beatles made their name, the **Cavern Club** (☎ 236 1964; *10 Mathew St*), hosts live music and DJs and still attracts a big crowd. Phone for opening times.

Places to Stay

The **YHA Liverpool International** (☎ 709 8888; e *liverpool@yha.org.uk; Wapping; dorm beds from £16.85*) is right across the road from Albert Dock. The inconspicuous **Embassie Hostel** (☎ 707 1089; *1 Falkner Square; dorm beds from £12.50*), to the west of the Anglican Cathedral, has excellent facilities and provides free tea, coffee and toast. The new **International Inn** (☎ 709 8135; e *info@internationalinn.co.uk; 4 Hunter St; dorm beds £15*) is in a handy position just off Hardman street, close to the city centre, and is well-equipped with a café, kitchen, laundry and Internet facilities.

There are several central hotels on Mount Pleasant, between the city centre and the Metropolitan Cathedral. The basic **Belvedere** (☎ 709 2356; *beds from £20*), at No 83, is the cheapest. The award-winning **Aachen Hotel** (☎ 709 3477; *singles/doubles £34/40*), at No 89, has comfortable rooms and an all-you-can-eat breakfast. **Feathers Hotel** (☎ 709 9655; *singles/doubles from £34/44*), No 119, is a good mid-range hotel. The upmarket **Britannia Adelphi Hotel** (☎ 709 7200; *fax 708 8326; Ranelagh Place; singles/doubles from £45/60*) was once the world's most luxurious hotel and is still an opulent experience.

Places to Eat

There's a plethora of places to eat down Bold St in the city centre. At the eastern end of this street is **Cafe Tabac** (☎ 709 3735; *mains around £5*), at No 124, a relaxed wine bar that attracts a mixed crowd. **Coffee Union** (☎ 709 9434; *snacks from £1.95*), at No 89, serves cheap snacks and tasty coffee. **Everyman Bistro** (☎ 708 9545; *5 Hope St*), underneath the famous Everyman Theatre, is highly recommended for its variety of good cheap food (pizza slices under £3). There's also a café in the Walker Art Gallery. The restaurants at the Albert Dock are geared towards fine dining.

Entertainment

The entertainment guide *Itchy Liverpool*, £3 from TICs and major bookshops, can point you in the right direction or just wander around Mathew St and southwest to Bold, Seel and Slater Sts and you'll stumble upon an amazing array of clubs and pubs catering to every style you can imagine. The best known of the clubs is **Cream** (☎ 709 1693), off Parr St, a super-club that rings the changes between samba, house and techno. The **Philharmonic Dining Room** (☎ 709 1163; *cnr Hope & Hardman Sts*), built in 1900, is one of Britain's most extraordinary pubs. The interior is resplendent with etched glass, stained glass, wrought iron, mosaics and ceramic tiling. **The Baltic Fleet** (☎ 709 3116; *33 Wapping*), next to the YHA Hostel, pours a superb traditional ale. The pubs around Concert Square, off Wood St, have chairs outside for alfresco imbibing.

Everyman Theatre (☎ 709 4776; *Hope St*) is one of the best repertory theatres in the country.

Getting There & Away

There are National Express services linking Liverpool to most major towns. The journey takes five hours from London (£15). Numerous intercity services run to Lime St station.

Getting Around
Public transport in the region is coordinated by **Merseytravel** (☎ 236 7676). There are various zone tickets, such as the £4.30 ticket for bus, train and ferry (except cruises). These are also sold at post offices.

Bus There are a number of bus companies. Smart Bus Nos 1 and 5 run from Albert Dock through the city centre to the university, and vice versa, every 20 minutes.

Ferry The ferry across the Mersey (£1.20), started 800 years ago by Benedictine monks but made famous by Gerry & the Pacemakers, still offers one of the best views of Liverpool. Boats depart from Pier Head ferry terminal, to the north of Albert Dock and next to the Liver Building. Special one-hour commentary cruises run year-round departing hourly from 10am to 3pm on weekdays and until 6pm on weekends (£3.75). Phone ☎ 630 1030 for more information.

LAKE DISTRICT
The Lake District is arguably the most beautiful corner of England, offering a combination of perfect green dales, rocky mountains and stunning still lakes. The Cumbrian Mountains are not particularly high (none reach 1000m), but they're more dramatic than their height would suggest.

This is Wordsworth country, and his houses, Dove Cottage at Grasmere and Rydal Mount, between Ambleside and Grasmere, are literary shrines.

There are over 10-million visitors a year to the Lake District. The crowds can be so intense over summer that it's probably best to visit weekdays in May and June, or in September and October to experience the Lake District fully.

Orientation & Information
The two principal bases for the Lake District are Keswick in the north (particularly for walkers) and Windermere/Bowness in the south. Kendal, Coniston, Ambleside, Grasmere and Cockermouth are less-hectic alternatives. All these towns have hostels, numerous B&Bs and places to eat.

Ullswater, Grasmere, Windermere, Coniston Water and Derwent Water are usually considered the most beautiful lakes, but they also teem with boats. Wastwater, Crummock

Water and Buttermere are equally spectacular and less crowded.

In general, the mob stays on the A roads, and the crowds thin out west of a line drawn from Keswick to Coniston.

TICs stock a frightening quantity of local guidebooks and brochures and both Windermere and Keswick have decent TICs with free booking services. If you're staying for a few days, buy a copy of *The 12 Best Walks in the Lake District* by Paul Buttle. Those interested in Wordsworth's life might enjoy reading his sister Dorothy's *Grasmere Journals*.

The numerous walking/climbing shops in the region, particularly in Ambleside and Keswick, are good sources of local information. **George Fisher** (☎ 017687-72178; 2 Borrowdale Rd, Keswick) is an excellent shop for stocking up on equipment.

There are almost 30 YHA hostels in the region, many of which can be linked by foot. Contact the **YHA Central Bookings Service** (☎ 01629-581061) for details on the different routes. The YHA also runs a shuttlebus between eight of the Lake District hostels during summer, call ☎ 01539-432304 for more information.

Getting There & Away
National Express buses run from Manchester via Preston (three hours) and on to Keswick and from London via Birmingham and on to Keswick (seven hours). There's a train service from Manchester airport to Windermere (two hours).

For all public transport inquiries contact **Traveline** (☎ 0870 608 2608). There are several important bus services in the Lake District, including bus No 555, which links Lancaster with Carlisle, via Kendal, Windermere, Ambleside, Grasmere and Keswick. No 599 runs between Windermere and Ambleside, via Grasmere, linking up with the ferry service on Windermere. No 505/506, runs from Ambleside to Coniston via Hawkshead. Ask about Day Ranger and Explorer tickets.

Windermere is at the end of a spur off the main railway line between London's Euston station and Glasgow. For Windermere and Kendal, change at Oxenholme.

Getting Around
Walking or cycling are the best ways to get around, but bear in mind that conditions can be treacherous, and the going can be very, very

steep. **Alexander Sports** (☎ 01539-488891; Main Rd, Windermere) rents out bikes for £12 a day.

Windermere & Bowness
☎ 015394 • pop 8500

It's thanks to the railway that the Windermere/Bowness conglomerate is the largest tourist town in the Lake District. At times it feels like a seaside resort. The two towns are quite strung out, with lakeside Bowness a 30-minute downhill walk from Windermere. The excellent **TIC** (☎ 46499; Victoria St, Windermere) is conveniently located near the train station at the northern end of town. For Internet access try **T2** (Lake Rd, Bowness); it's pricey at £3 per half-hour but the delicious home-made pancakes will make you feel better.

Less than two minutes' walk from the train station, **Lake District Backpackers Lodge** (☎ 46374; High St; dorm beds £12) offers beds in small dormitories. **Windermere YHA** (☎ 43543; High Cross, Bridge Lane, Troutbeck) is larger but 2mi from the station. Numerous buses run past Troutbeck Bridge and in summer the hostel sends a minibus to meet trains.

Windermere is wall-to-wall B&Bs, most of them costing about £18 a night. **Brendan Chase** (☎/fax 45638; College Rd; rooms from £20) is comfortable and close to the train station. There's a healthy smattering of cafés and restaurants in both townships. **The Bowness Kitchen** (☎ 45529; 4 Grosvenor Terrace, Bowness) serves tasty toasted sandwiches for £3. For something a little fancier try **Oregano** (☎ 44954; High St, Windemere) where delicious baked salmon will set you back £9.95.

Grasmere
☎ 015394 • pop 2700

Grasmere is a picture-postcard village and a lovely place to stay out of season; in summer it's completely overrun with tourists. Information can be found at the **TIC** (☎ 35245; Red Bank Rd; open 9.30am-5.30pm daily). The homes of poet William Wordsworth are the major attractions here. **Dove Cottage & Museum** (☎ 35544; adult/concession/child £5.50/4.30/2.50; open 9.30am-5.30pm daily; closed 7 Jan-3 Feb) and **Rydal Mount** (☎ 33002; Ambleside; adult/student/child £4/3/1.50; open 9.30am-5.30pm daily, shorter hours in winter) are intriguing time capsules from the poet's life.

Butterlip How Youth Hostel (☎ 35316; [e] grasmere@yha.org.uk; Easedale Rd; dorm beds from £9.25) is just north of the village. The lovely **How Foot Lodge** (☎ 35366) has rooms priced from £20 and is ideal for access to Dove Cottage, which is on the main A591 Kendal–Keswick Rd, just south of Grasmere village. Next door, **Dove Cottage Café & Restaurant** (☎ 35268; mains £4.95-12) serves light snacks throughout the day and switches to à la carte dining in the evening.

Keswick
☎ 017687 • pop 5000

Keswick is an important walking centre, and although the town centre lacks the green charm of Windermere, the lake is beautiful. The **TIC** (☎ 72645), in the middle of the pedestrianised town centre, books accommodation and runs guided tours of the area. Check email at **U-Compute Cyber Café** (☎ 75127; 48 Main St) above the post office.

The **Youth Hostel** (☎ 72484; dorm beds £11.25), a short walk down Station Rd from the TIC, is open most of the year. Station Rd has a number of B&Bs, most charging around £20 per person.

Kendal
☎ 01539

On the eastern outskirts of the Lake District National Park, Kendal is a lively town and makes for a good base from which to explore the region. The **TIC** (☎ 725758; Highgate) is in the Town Hall.

Kendal Youth Hostel (☎ 724066; 118 Highgate; dorm beds adults/under-18s £13/10; open daily mid-Apr–Aug, Tues-Sat Sept-early Apr) is right next door to the **Brewery**, a wonderful arts complex with a theatre, cinema and bar/bistro.

Kendal is on the branch railway line from Windermere to Oxenholme, with connections north to Manchester and south to Lancaster and Barrow-in-Furness.

CARLISLE
☎ 01228 • pop 72,000

For 1600 years, Carlisle defended the north of England, or south of Scotland, depending on who was winning. In 1745 Bonnie Prince Charlie proclaimed his father king at the market cross.

Although the city's character was diminished by industrialisation in the 19th century, it's still an interesting place and makes a useful base for getting to or from Northumberland, Dumfries & Galloway and the Borders (the beautiful Scottish border counties), and the Lake District. It's also the hub for five excellent train journeys.

Orientation & Information
The train station is south of the city centre, a five-minute walk to Greenmarket (the market square) and the **TIC** (☎ 625600), which is inside the old town hall. The bus station is on Lowther St, just one block east of the square.

Things to See & Do
The 11th-century **Carlisle Castle** (☎ 591922; adult/concession/child £3.20/2.40/1.60) is to the north of the cathedral, overlooking the River Eden. The excellent **Tullie House Museum & Art Gallery** (☎ 534781; admission £3.75) reveals the region's fascinating history and hosts changing exhibitions by contemporary artists.

Places to Stay
The University halls double as the **Carlisle Youth Hostel** (☎ 597352; dorm beds £12.50; open early July-early Sept) in the Old Brewery Residences on Bridge Lane.

There are plenty of comfortable B&Bs for around £16, especially along Warwick Rd. The small and friendly **Stratheden** (☎ 520192; rooms £16-20), at No 93, has pleasingly decorated rooms. **Cornerways Guest House** (☎ 521733; from £16), at No 107, is larger.

Getting There & Away
Bus National Express runs services to/from London (6½ hours), Glasgow (two hours) and Manchester (three hours). A Rail Link coach service runs to Galashiels in the Scottish Borders (see the Southeast Scotland section later in this chapter).

Train Carlisle is the terminus for five famous scenic railways; phone ☎ 0845 748 4950 for information. There are 15 trains a day to Carlisle from London's Euston station (four hours). Most of the following lines have Day Ranger tickets that allow you unlimited travel, ask for details.

Leeds-Settle-Carlisle Line (LSC) This famous line cuts southeast across the Yorkshire Dales through beautiful countryside and is one of the great engineering achievements of the Victorian railway age. Several stations make good starting points for walks in the Yorkshire Dales National Park.

Lake District Line This line branches off the main north-south line between Preston and Carlisle at Oxenholme, just outside Kendal, for Windermere. The landscape on the main line is beautiful. The Windermere branch is only about 10mi long but takes nearly half an hour.

Tyne Valley Line This line follows Hadrian's Wall to and from Newcastle. There are fine views; see the Newcastle-upon-Tyne and Hadrian's Wall sections earlier in this chapter.

Cumbrian Coast Line This line follows the coast in a great arc around to Lancaster, with views over the Irish Sea and back to the Lake District. Change at Barrow for trains to Lancaster on the main line. Ulverston, on the line just past Barrow, is the starting point for the Cumbria Way, which traverses the lakes to Carlisle.

Glasgow to Carlisle Line The main route north to Glasgow gives you a glimpse of the grand scale of Scottish landscapes.

Scotland

No visitor to Britain should miss seeing Scotland. Despite its official union with England in 1707, it maintains an independent national identity that goes far beyond the occasional kilt and bagpipes. Similarities and close links exist, but there are also considerable differences.

Scotland is very beautiful and suffers less than England from poor urban planning. The Highlands are extraordinary. It's hardly a secret, but for a region that has some of the world's most dramatic scenery, it's curiously under-appreciated, especially by the English, who don't realise what an extraordinary neighbour they have. The islands – Orkney, Shetland and Inner and Outer Hebrides – are some of the most remote places on earth but Scottish hospitality will make you feel at home.

Scottish urban centres are also quite different. Edinburgh is one of the world's most beautiful cities; energetic Glasgow is a vibrant cultural centre; St Andrews is a beautiful coastal university town; and prosperous Aberdeen surveys the North Sea with a proprietorial interest.

FACTS ABOUT SCOTLAND
History
Celts It's believed that the earliest settlement of Scotland was undertaken by hunters and fishers 6000 years ago. They were followed by

SCOTLAND

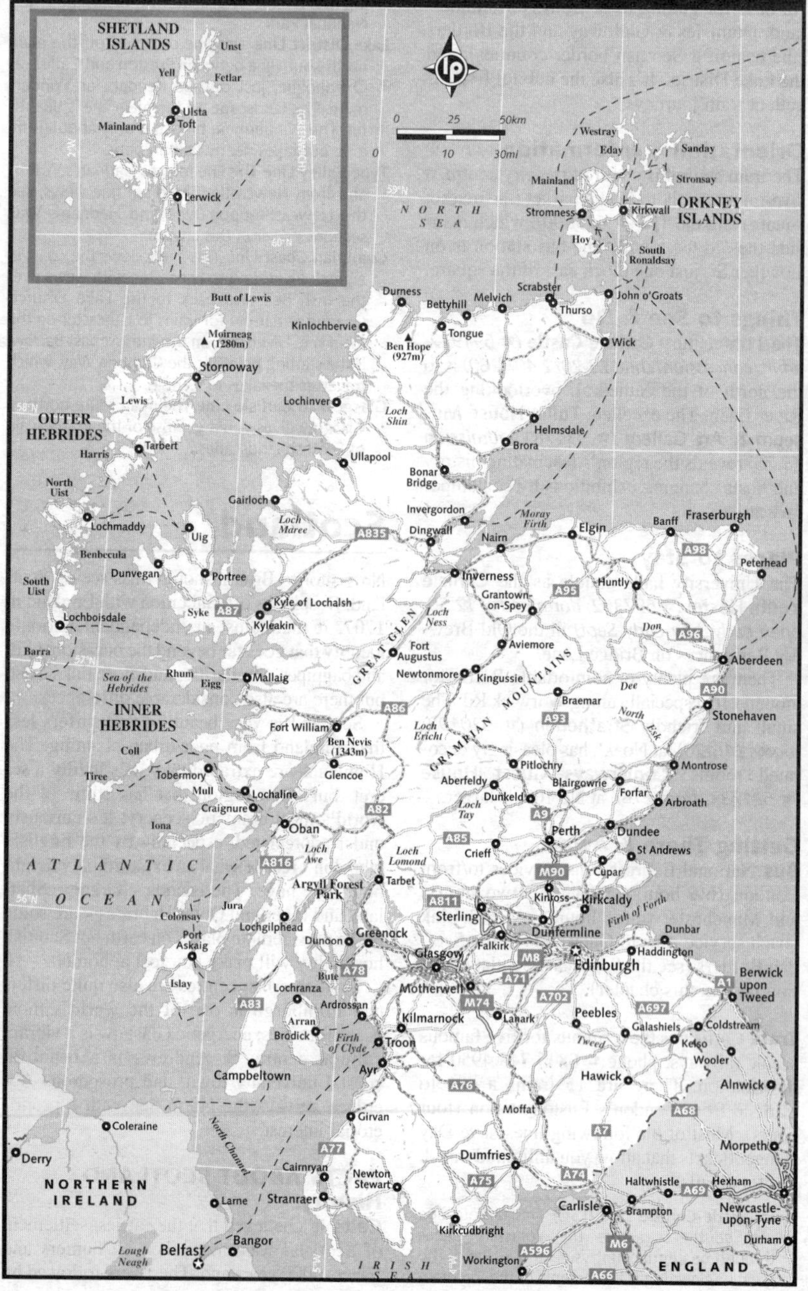
SHETLAND ISLANDS
Unst
Yell
Fetlar
Ulsta
Toft
Mainland
Lerwick
0
25
50km
0
10
30mi
NORTH SEA
Westray
Eday
Sanday
Stronsay
Mainland
ORKNEY ISLANDS
Stromness
Kirkwall
Hoy
South Ronaldsay
Scrabster
Thurso
John o'Groats
Butt of Lewis
Durness
Bettyhill
Melvich
Kinlochbervie
Tongue
Ben Hope (927m)
Moirneag (1280m)
Stornoway
Wick
Lewis
Lochinver
Loch Shin
OUTER HEBRIDES
Helmsdale
Brora
Harris
Tarbert
Ullapool
Bonar Bridge
North Uist
Gairloch
Invergordon
Moray Firth
Loch Maree
A835
Dingwall
Elgin
Banff
Fraserburgh
Lochmaddy
Uig
Nairn
A98
Benbecula
Peterhead
Dunvegan
Portree
Inverness
Huntly
South Uist
Grantown-on-Spey
A95
Syke
A87
Kyle of Lochalsh
Kyleakin
Loch Ness
Don
A96
Lochboisdale
Aviemore
GREAT GLEN
Fort Augustus
Aberdeen
Barra
Rhum
Mallaig
Newtonmore
Kingussie
Sea of the Hebrides
Eigg
GRAMPIAN MOUNTAINS
Dee
A90
Braemar
INNER HEBRIDES
A86
Stonehaven
North Esk
Fort William
Loch Ericht
A93
Ben Nevis (1343m)
Coll
Pitlochry
Montrose
Tiree
Tobermory
Glencoe
Aberfeldy
Blairgowrie
Forfar
Mull
Lochaline
Dunkeld
Craignure
A82
Arbroath
Loch Tay
A9
Iona
Oban
Perth
Dundee
A85
Crieff
St Andrews
Loch Awe
Loch Lomond
A816
ATLANTIC OCEAN
Tarbet
M90
Cupar
Argyll Forest Park
Kinross
Kirkcaldy
A811
Jura
Colonsay
Sterling
Firth of Forth
Lochgilphead
Dunfermline
Dunbar
Port Askaig
Dunoon
Greenock
Falkirk
Glasgow
M8
Edinburgh
Haddington
Islay
Bute
A78
A71
Motherwell
Berwick upon Tweed
A1
Lochranza
A702
A83
Ardrossan
M74
A697
Kilmarnock
Lanark
Peebles
Arran
Galashiels
Coldstream
Brodick
Firth of Clyde
Troon
Tweed
Kelso
Wooler
Ayr
Campbeltown
Hawick
Alnwick
A76
Coleraine
Moffat
A68
Girvan
North Channel
A7
Derry
A77
Morpeth
Dumfries
Cairnryan
NORTHERN IRELAND
Newton Stewart
A75
A74
Haltwhistle
Hexham
A69
Larne
Stranraer
Carlisle
Brampton
Newcastle-upon-Tyne
Kirkcudbright
M6
Durham
Lough Neagh
Belfast
Bangor
Workington
A596
IRISH SEA
A66
ENGLAND

the Picts, whose loose tribal organisation survived to the 18th century in the clan structure of the Highlands. They never bowed to the Romans, who retreated and built the Hadrian and Antonine Walls, defining the north as a separate entity.

The Celtic Gaels (Scotti), arrived from northern Ireland (Scotia) in the 6th century AD. They finally united with the Picts in the 9th century in response to the threat posed by the Scandinavians who dominated the northern islands and west coast. By the time the Normans arrived, most of Scotland was Christian and loosely united under the Canmore dynasty.

Normans The Normans never conquered Scotland, although they wielded a major influence over several weak kings, and the Lowlands (with the most important arable land) were controlled by French-speaking aristocrats from northern England. The Highland clans remained staunchly Gaelic, the Islands maintained close links to Norway, and neither paid much attention to central authority.

Despite almost continuous border warfare, it wasn't until a dispute over the Canmore succession that Edward I attempted the conquest of Scotland. Beginning with the siege of Berwick in 1296, fighting finally ended in 1328 with the Treaty of Northampton, which recognised Robert the Bruce as king of an independent country. Robert, more Norman than Scottish in his ancestry, cemented an alliance with France that would complicate the political map for almost 400 years.

Stuarts In 1371 the kingship passed to the Fitzalan family. The Fitzalans had served William the Conqueror and his descendants as High Stewards, and Stewart (changed to Stuart following Mary's accession) became the dynasty's name.

In 1503 James IV married the daughter of Henry VII of England, the first of the Tudor monarchs, thereby linking the two families. However, this didn't prevent the French from persuading James to go to war against his in-laws; he was killed at the disastrous battle of Flodden Hill (1513) along with 10,000 of his subjects.

By the 16th century, Scotland was a nationalistic society, with close links to Europe and a visceral hatred for the English. It had universities at St Andrews, Glasgow, Edinburgh and Aberdeen (there were only two in England) and a rigorous intellectual climate that was fertile ground for the ideas of the Reformation, a critique of the medieval Catholic church, and the rise of Protestantism.

Mary Queen of Scots In 1542 James V died, leaving his two-week-old daughter Mary to be proclaimed queen. Henry VIII of England decided she would make a suitable daughter-in-law, and his armies ravaged the Borders and sacked Edinburgh in a failed attempt to force agreement from the Scots (the 'Rough Wooing'). At 15, Mary married the French dauphin and duly became Queen of France as well as Scotland; she claimed England, on the basis that her Protestant cousin, Elizabeth I, was illegitimate.

While Catholic Mary was in France, the Scottish Reformation was under way under the leadership of John Knox. In 1560 the Scottish Parliament abolished the Latin mass and the authority of the pope, creating a Protestant church that was independent of Rome and the monarchy.

On the death of her husband, 18-year-old Mary returned to Scotland. She married Henry Darnley and gave birth to a son, but, in a scarcely believable train of events, Darnley was involved in the murder of Mary's Italian secretary Rizzio (rumoured to be her lover). Then Darnley himself was murdered, presumably by Mary and her lover and future husband, the Earl of Bothwell.

Forced to abdicate in favour of her son, James VI, Mary was imprisoned, but escaped and fled to Elizabeth, who, recognising a security risk when she saw one, locked her in the Tower of London. Nineteen years later, at the age of 44, she was beheaded for allegedly plotting Elizabeth's death. When the childless Elizabeth died in 1603, Mary's son united the two crowns as James I of England and James VI of Scotland.

Revolution The Stuarts have become romantic figures, but their royal skills were extremely suspect. When Charles I meddled in religious matters, he provoked the Scots into organising a National Covenant that reaffirmed the total independence of the General Assembly of the Church of Scotland. This led to armed conflict. Civil war between Parliament and the king followed, with the Scottish Covenanters supporting Cromwell in his successful revolution.

In 1660, after Cromwell's death, the Stuart monarchy was restored, but the honeymoon was brief and James II, a Catholic, appeared to set out determinedly to lose his kingdom. Among other poor decisions, he made worshipping as a Covenanter a capital offence.

The English Protestants invited William of Orange, a Dutchman who was James' nephew and married to his oldest Protestant daughter, to take power. In 1689 he landed with a small army; James broke down and fled to France.

In 1692, people were horrified by the treacherous massacre, on English government orders, of MacDonalds by Campbells in Glencoe, for failing to swear allegiance to William. The massacre became Jacobite (Stuart) propaganda that still resonates today.

Union with England In 1707, after complex bargaining (and buying a few critical votes), England's government persuaded the Scottish Parliament to agree to the union of the two countries under a single parliament. The Scots received trading privileges and retained their independent church and legal system.

The decision was unpopular from the start, and the exiled Stuarts promised to repeal it. The situation was exacerbated when Parliament turned to the house of Hanover to find a Protestant successor to Queen Anne. George, the Elector of Hanover, was James I's great-grandson, but he was German and spoke no English.

Scotland was the centre for Jacobitism (Stuart support) and there were two major rebellions – first in 1715, then in 1745 when Bonnie Prince Charlie failed to extend his support beyond the wild, Catholic Highland clans. The Jacobite cause was finally buried at the Battle of Culloden (1746), after which the English set out to destroy the clans, prohibiting Highland dress, weapons and military service.

Scottish Enlightenment & Highland Clearances The old Scotland was already fast disappearing by the mid-18th century. There was strong economic growth and the beginning of industrialisation. Eighteenth-century Scotland was a sceptical and well-educated society. Among other figures, it produced philosopher David Hume, economist Adam Smith, poet Robert Burns and novelist and poet Sir Walter Scott.

In the mid-19th century, overpopulation, the collapse of the kelp industry, the 1840s potato famine and the increased grazing of sheep by the lairds (landowning aristocrats) led to the Highland Clearances. People were driven to the burgeoning slums of the new industrial cities – especially Glasgow and Dundee – and to the four corners of the British Empire.

Modern Scotland By the end of the 19th century the population was concentrated in the grim industrial towns and cities of the Lowlands. Working-class disillusionment led to the development of fierce left-wing politics. After WWI Scotland's ship, steel, coal, cotton and jute industries began to fail, and, though there was a recovery during WWII, since the 1960s they have been in terminal decline.

In the 1970s and 1980s, North Sea oil (Scottish oil, as many will tell you) gave the economy a boost. Despite the bonanza, Thatcherism failed to impress the Scots. From 1979 to 1997, Scotland was ruled by a Conservative government for which the vast majority of Scots didn't vote. Following the Labour Party's 1997 electoral victory, voters in a referendum chose overwhelmingly in favour of the creation of a Scottish Parliament, which began sitting in Edinburgh in 1999. The government, called the Scottish Executive, is a coalition of the Labour Party and Liberal-Democrats, while the Scottish National Party (SNP) is the second largest in Parliament.

Geography & Geology

Scotland covers 30,414 sq mi and can be divided into three areas: Southern Uplands, with ranges of hills bordering England; the Central Lowlands, a triangular slice from Edinburgh and Dundee in the east to Glasgow in the west, containing the majority of the population; and the Highlands and Islands in the north, an area that makes up two thirds of the country. The Highland Boundary Fault, a geological division, runs northeast from Helensburgh (west of Glasgow) to Stonehaven (south of Aberdeen) on the east coast. North of it lie the Highlands and Islands.

Climate

Scotland has a cool temperate climate, with winds from the Atlantic warmed by the Gulf Stream. The east coast tends to be cool and dry, the west coast milder and wetter. The weather changes quickly – a rainy day is often followed by a sunny one and there are wide variations over small distances. May and June are generally the driest months, but expect rain at any time.

Ecology & Environment

Some two-thirds of Scotland is mountain and moorland. Once it was almost entirely covered by the Caledonian forest, but now only 1% remains. The hillsides are kept bare by managed grazing of sheep and deer. In many areas of Scotland you'll notice thick conifer plantations. The Thatcher government encouraged landowners to plant these fast-growing trees, despite serious ecological drawbacks. As well as destroying wildlife habitat, conifers increase soil acidity and may have a detrimental effect on weather patterns. The seas around Scotland have suffered from pollution. Until relatively recently, most Scottish cities discharged untreated waste straight into the sea. If you see a pollution incident, call the emergency number ☎ 0800 807060.

Government & Politics

The Scottish parliament is a single-chamber system with 129 members (known as MSPs) elected through a system of proportional representation, led by a first minister (at the time of writing, Jack McConnell). It sits for four-year terms and is responsible for education, health, housing, transport, economic development and other domestic affairs. The Scottish Executive – composed of the first minister, Scottish minister, junior ministers and Scottish law officers – is the Scottish government, which proposes new laws and deals with the areas of responsibility outlined above, while the body of MSPs constitutes the Scottish legislature, which debates, amends and votes on new legislation. Scotland has four main political parties – the Labour Party, the SNP, the Scottish Conservative and Unionist Party and the Liberal Democrats – and the main struggle for power is between Labour and the SNP.

Population

Scotland has just over five million people, 9% of the UK's total.

Science & Philosophy

The Scots are a particularly ingenious lot. Although Scotland accounts for only 9% of the British population, it has produced more than 20% of Britain's leading scientists, philosophers, engineers and inventors. Scots pioneered the modern disciplines of economics,

sociology, geology, electromagnetic theory, anaesthesiology and antibiotics, and their many inventions include the steam engine, the pneumatic tyre, the telephone and the television.

Language

There are three main languages. Gaelic is spoken by some 80,000 people, mainly in the Highlands and Islands. It's taught in many colleges and some schools and there is now a Gaelic-only school in Glasgow. Lallans or Lowland Scots is spoken in the south. Then there's English, which the Scottish accent can make almost impenetrable to foreigners. Numerous Gaelic and Lallan words linger in everyday English speech. Some common terms you might encounter are:

aye	yes/always
bairn	child
bap	bread roll
ben	mountain
brae	hill
burn	creek
ceilidh	(pronounced kaylee) informal evening of entertainment and dance
croft	small farm
firth	estuary
glen	valley
haar	fog off the North Sea
Hogmanay	New Year's Eve
ken	know
kirk	church
wynd	lane

FACTS FOR THE VISITOR

Planning

When to Go The best time to visit is May to September. April and October are also acceptable weather risks, although many businesses close in October. In summer, daylight hours are long; the midsummer sun sets around 11pm in the Shetland Islands and even in Edinburgh there are seemingly endless evenings.

Edinburgh becomes impossibly crowded during the festivals in August.

In winter the weather's cold and daylight hours are short but Edinburgh and Glasgow are still worth visiting. Though travel in the Highlands can be difficult, roads are rarely closed and Scotland's ski resorts are popular then. Although many facilities close for the season, there's usually one TIC open for an area, and more B&Bs and hotels are staying open year-round. Travel in the islands can be a problem in winter because high winds easily disrupt ferries.

Tourist Offices

The **Scottish Tourist Board/Visit Scotland** *(STB; ☎ 0131-332 2433, fax 315 4545; e info@stb.gov.uk; headquarters 23 Ravelston Terrace, (PO Box 705), Edinburgh EH4 3TP)* deals with postal and telephone inquiries. In London, contact the **STB** *(☎ 020-7930 8661; 19 Cockspur St, London SW1 5BL)*, off Trafalgar Square, for routes, detailed information and reservations.

Most towns have TICs that open 9am to 5pm daily, although in some smaller Highland towns TICs may close on weekends.

Overseas, the **British Tourist Authority** *(BTA; w www.bta.org.uk)* represents STB and stocks masses of information, much of it free.

Visas & Diplomatic Missions

No visas are required if you arrive from England, Wales or Northern Ireland. If you arrive from the Republic of Ireland or any other country, normal British regulations apply (see under Visas in the introductory Facts for the Visitor section earlier in this chapter). Edinburgh has numerous diplomatic missions (check the *Yellow Pages*).

Money

The British currency is the pound sterling and the same currency is valid both sides of the border; however, the Clydesdale Bank, the Royal Bank of Scotland and the Bank of Scotland print their own pound notes. You won't have any trouble changing Scottish notes immediately south of the Scotland-England border, but elsewhere it's best to change them at banks.

You can use MasterCard and Visa in ATMs belonging to the Royal Bank of Scotland, Clydesdale Bank and Bank of Scotland; American Express card-holders can use the Bank of Scotland.

Accommodation for backpackers is more readily available in Scotland than in England, so you can keep sleeping costs right down. Edinburgh and Glasgow are more expensive than most other mainland towns, but prices also rise in remote parts of the Highlands and on the Islands where supplies depend on ferries.

Useful Organisations

Historic Scotland *(HS; ☎ 0131-668 8800; Longmore House, Salisbury Place, Edinburgh EH9 1SH)* manages more than 330 historic sites, including top attractions like Edinburgh and Stirling castles. It offers short-term 'Explorer' membership – three/seven/14 days for £12/17/22.

The **National Trust for Scotland** *(NTS; ☎ 0131-243 9555; 28 Charlotte Square, Edinburgh EH2 4ET)* cares for over 100 properties and 73,340 hectares of countryside. YHA and Scottish Youth Hostel Association (SYHA) members and student-card holders get half-price entry to its properties.

Dangers & Annoyances

Edinburgh and Glasgow are big cities with the usual problems, so normal caution is required.

Highland hikers should be properly equipped and cautious – the weather can become vicious at any time of the year. After rain, peaty soil can become boggy, so always wear stout shoes and carry a change of clothing.

The most infuriating problem facing visitors to the west coast and Highlands, however, is midges. These tiny blood-sucking flies, related to mosquitoes, can be prolific. They're worse in the evenings or in cloudy or shady conditions; their season lasts from late May to mid-September, peaking mid-June to mid-August. Cover up, particularly in the evening; wear light-coloured clothing (midges are attracted to dark colours); and, most importantly, buy a reliable insect repellent.

Another annoying aspect of touring in the Highlands is the sudden appearance and sound of military jets. It's something you never get used to.

Business Hours

Banking hours are normally 9.30am to 4pm weekdays, but in remote areas banks may only open for two or three days. Post offices and shops open 9am to 5.30pm weekdays; post offices close at 1pm Saturday. Shops in small towns sometimes have an early closing day midweek, while in cities there's often late-night shopping until 7pm or 8pm on Thursday or Friday.

Public Holidays & Special Events

Although Bank Holidays are also public holidays in England, in Scotland they only apply to banks and some other commercial offices. Bank Holidays occur at the start of January, Good Friday, the first and last weekend in May, the last weekend in August, St Andrew's

Day (30 November) and Christmas Day and Boxing Day. New Year's Day and Good Friday are general holidays, and Scottish towns normally have a spring and autumn holiday – dates vary.

The Edinburgh International Festival (the world's largest arts festival), the Edinburgh Fringe Festival and the Military Tattoo, take place during August each year.

Activities

One of the most popular outdoor pursuits in Scotland is hiking. Long-distance hiking routes in Scotland include the Southern Upland Way, the West Highland Way, the Fife Coastal Path and the Speyside Way. There's also a network of thousands of miles of paths and tracks. Scotland has a long tradition of relatively free access to open country. Numerous guidebooks are available, including Lonely Planet's *Walking in Scotland*.

Cycling is a popular way to see the lochs, forests, glens and hills of central and southern Scotland. Intrepid (and very fit) cyclists can visit the more remote, but majestic Highlands and mystical Islands.

Scotland has a flourishing skiing industry and the season runs between December and April. There are several resorts of international standard in the Cairngorms (near Aviemore and Braemar) and around Ben Nevis (Scotland's highest mountain, near Fort William). The STB has details.

The north coast of Scotland, from Thurso to Bettyhill, offers some of the best (and coldest) surfing in Britain.

Accommodation

Prices are given per person, per night, unless otherwise noted.

Free wild camping is usually acceptable in unenclosed land, well away from houses and roads. Commercial camping grounds are geared to caravans and vary widely in quality, but usually have tent sites for £4 to £12. The STB's *Scotland: Caravan & Camping* (£3.99), available from TICs, lists many camping grounds. Bothies and camping barns are primitive shelters, often in remote places. They're not locked, there's no charge and you can't book. Users should stay one night only.

There are numerous hostels and B&Bs. The **Scottish Youth Hostel Association** (SYHA; ☎ 01786-891400, fax 891333; w www.syha .org.uk; 7 Glebe Crescent, Stirling FK8 2JA)

produces a free handbook giving details of over 70 hostels, including transport links. Its hostels are generally cheaper and often better than its English counterparts. In big cities costs 50 for adults/children are around £14/12; the rest start at £6.50/5. These are supplemented by independent hostels and bunkhouses, most between £7 and £11. Check out w www.hos tel-scotland.co.uk.

Many Scottish universities offer their student accommodation to visitors during the holidays (late June to late September). B&Bs cost around £18 to £25. TICs have details. B&Bs and small hotels are usually cheaper than their English counterparts and budget-conscious travellers rarely need pay more than £20. The TICs have local booking services (usually £1 or £2) and a Book-a-Bed-Ahead scheme (£3). A 10% deposit is also required for most bookings. The service is worth using in July and August, but isn't necessary otherwise, unless you plan to arrive in a town after business hours (when the local TIC will be closed). If you arrive in the evening without prebooked accommodation, it may still be worth going to the TIC, since many leave a list in the window showing B&Bs.

Food

Scotland's chefs have an enviable range of fresh meat, seafood and vegetables at their disposal. Most restaurants are reasonably good and will cater for vegetarians. In small villages and hotels, alternatives are usually limited, although village bakeries have a good range of pies, cakes and snacks. Almost every town has at least one Chinese or Indian restaurant.

GETTING THERE & AWAY
Air

There are direct services from many European cities to Edinburgh, Glasgow, Dundee, Aberdeen and Inverness, and from North America to Glasgow. New York to Glasgow is around US$650 and takes around 7½ hours.

If you're coming from overseas, it's often more economical to buy a cheap fare to London, then take an internal flight to Scotland. See the introductory Getting There & Away section earlier in this chapter for more information. You shouldn't have to pay more than £150 for a return flight from London to Glasgow or Edinburgh (one hour), but fierce competition between airlines has meant that discount return flights can be as low as £50.

BRITAIN

There are often no-frills special deals from companies like **easyJet** (☎ *0870 600 0000*) and **Ryanair** (☎ *0870 156 9569*).

Land

Bus Long-distance buses (coaches) are usually the cheapest method of getting to Scotland. The main operators are **National Express** (☎ *0870 580 8080;* **w** *www.gobycoach.com*) and its subsidiary **Scottish Citylink** (☎ *0870 550 5050;* **w** *www.citylink.co.uk*), with numerous services from London and other points in England and Wales (see Getting There & Away under Edinburgh or Glasgow later in this chapter for more information).

Fares on the main routes are competitive, with some operators undercutting National Express. **Silver Choice Travel** (☎ *0141-333 1400*) offers the cheapest deal for a return ticket from London to Edinburgh or Glasgow (£24, 9½ hours); the ticket must be bought at least seven days in advance. Cheap tickets sell out quickly so book in advance. See the introductory Getting Around section at the beginning of this chapter for more information.

Train For timetable and fare information throughout the UK call the **National Rail Enquiry Service** (☎ *0845 748 4950*). **Great North Eastern Railway** (GNER; ☎ *0845 722 5225*) runs a regular rail service between London's King's Cross and Edinburgh (4½ to 5½ hours) or from London's Euston or Paddington stations to Glasgow (5½ hours). See the Getting There & Away sections for those cities.

There's a range of fares but you can make considerable savings by planning ahead, even though restrictions will apply to the cheaper ones (eg, travelling off peak). With Virgin Trains the cheapest adult return ticket between London and Edinburgh or Glasgow is the Virgin Value seven-day advance ticket, which costs only £39. This compares with the standard open-return fare of £85.

Car & Motorcycle Edinburgh is 403mi from London and Glasgow is 417mi away. Allow eight hours. The main roads are the M6, A74 and M74 to Glasgow, the A1 and A68 to Edinburgh.

Hitching It's easy enough, though not particularly wise, to hitch to Scotland along the A68 to Edinburgh or the M6 to Glasgow. The coastal routes are scenic but slow.

Sea

For more details on the ferry services listed here, see the introductory Getting There & Away section at the start of this chapter.

Northern Ireland From Northern Ireland the main car-ferry links to Scotland are the Belfast–Stranraer, Larne–Cairnryan and Belfast–Troon crossings operated by **Stena Line** (☎ *028-90 747 747*), **P&O Irish Sea** (☎ *0870 242 4777*) and **SeaCat** (☎ *0870 552 3523*), respectively. It's a high-speed catamaran only between Belfast and Troon. Fares vary widely depending on the season, and there are special deals worth looking out for.

Continental Europe In May 2002, a superfast ferry link between Rosyth (north of Edinburgh) and Zeebrugge (north of Brussels) was established. A one-way ticket for a standard two-bed cabin will set you back £104 and the trip takes approximately 16 hours. Contact **Viamare Travel** (☎ *020-7431 4560*) for details.

Scandinavia From late May to early September, **P&O/Smyril Line** (☎ *01224-572615*) operates a weekly car ferry between Lerwick (Shetland), Tórshavn (Faroe Islands), Seydisfjördur (Iceland), Bergen (Norway) and Hantsholm (Denmark). A special through-fare (one way) from Aberdeen to Bergen via Lerwick on P&O Scottish Ferries and Smyril Line costs from £95/115 per person for a couchette.

GETTING AROUND

If you're not a student, it's worth considering ScotRail's Freedom of Scotland Travelpass, which gives unlimited travel on ScotRail trains and most Caledonian MacBrayne (CalMac) ferries to the west-coast islands, as well as discounts on some other ferry services (see Train later in this section).

Another possibility is Haggis Backpackers, a bus company that runs a jump-on, jump-off circuit from hostel to hostel around the Highlands (see Bus later in this section).

Air

The main domestic operators in Scotland are British Regional Airlines and Loganair/British Airways Express – both fly under the franchise of **British Airways** (☎ *0845 773 3377*). Loganair/British Airways Express operates inter-island flights in Orkney and Shetland.

Highland Airways (☎ 01851-701282) runs a service between Inverness and Stornoway. Most airlines offer a range of tickets, including Apex (which must be booked 14 days in advance) and youth fares (for under 25s).

Bus

Scotland's major bus service is **Scottish Citylink** (☎ 0870 550 5050). There are also smaller regional operators. **Royal Mail postbuses** (☎ 0845 774 0740, outside UK ☎ 012 46-546329) provide a stable, reliable service to remoter areas and can be particularly useful for walkers.

Regional inquiry telephone numbers have been given throughout the text.

The National Express Tourist Trail Pass (see the introductory Getting Around section at the beginning of this chapter) can be used on Scottish Citylink services. Citylink offers a range of discount cards, which give up to 30% off standard adult fares. Cards are available for fulltime students, people aged between 16 and 25, and people aged 50 and over. You'll need a passport photo and proof of ID (ISIC card for student status and passport for proof of age).

Haggis Backpackers (☎ 0131-557 9393; 60 High St, Edinburgh) operates a circuit between hostels in Edinburgh, Pitlochry, Inverness, Loch Ness, Ullapool, Isle of Skye, Fort William, Oban, Loch Lomond and Glasgow, finishing back in Edinburgh. You can hop on and off the minibus wherever and whenever you like, booking up to 24 hours before departure. There's no compulsion to stay in hostels either. Buses depart from Edinburgh on Monday, Wednesday, Friday and Saturday year-round and tickets in high/low season cost £69/55.

Train

ScotRail (☎ 0845 748 4950; w www.scotrail .co.uk) operates Scotland's trains, which travel on some stunning routes, but they're limited and expensive, so you'll probably have to combine rail travel with other modes of transport. The West Highland line through Fort William to Mallaig and the routes from Stirling to Inverness, Inverness to Thurso and Inverness to Kyle of Lochalsh are some of the most scenic in the world.

ScotRail offers a range of good-value passes for train travel in Scotland. You can buy them at BritRail outlets in the USA, Canada and Europe, at the British Travel Centre, Regent St,

London and at train stations throughout Britain. ScotRail's Freedom of Scotland Travelpass and its regional Rover tickets can be bought in Britain, from the British Travel Centre, and from most staffed train stations in Scotland. The pass gives unlimited travel on ScotRail trains, CalMac ferries, Strathclyde Passenger Transport trains and on certain Scottish Citylink coach services; 33% discount on postbuses and selected regional bus routes with Scottish Citylink, Fife Scottish and First Edinburgh; 33% discount on the P&O Orkney (Stromness) to Scrabster ferry; and 20% discount on P&O Aberdeen to Shetland, Aberdeen to Orkney.

The Travelpass in high/low season costs £79/69 for four days travel out of eight consecutive days, for eight days out of 15£99/89.

The Highland Rover ticket covers the West Highlands, northeast coast and the Aberdeen–Inverness–Kyle line and a discount on ferries to Mull and Skye (£49/39 for four out of eight consecutive days). The Central Scotland Rover ticket covers the central area (£29 for three out of seven consecutive days).

Reservations for bicycles are compulsory on many services.

Sometimes the cheap day-return fare is cheaper than the full one-way fare.

Hitching

Hitching is reasonably good in Scotland, with the average wait 30 to 40 minutes. Although the northwest is more difficult because there's less traffic, waits of over two hours are unusual (except on Sunday in 'Sabbath' areas). Public transport isn't scheduled to stop on the A9 (except in villages), though buses will usually stop and rescue you.

Boat

Caledonian MacBrayne (CalMac; ☎ 0870 565 0000; w www.calmac.co.uk) is the most important ferry operator on the west coast, with services from Ullapool to the Outer Hebrides, and from Mallaig to Skye and on to the Outer Hebrides. Its main west-coast port, however, is Oban, with ferries to the Inner Hebridean islands of Coll, Tiree, Lismore, Mull and Colonsay and the Outer Hebridean islands of Barra and South Uist.

CalMac's Island Rover ticket gives unlimited travel on its ferry services, and for eight/15 days costs £43/63, plus £210/315 for a car.

P&O Scottish Ferries (☎ 01224-572615; w www.posf.co.uk) has ferries from Aberdeen and Scrabster to Orkney and from Aberdeen to Shetland. See those sections for details.

EDINBURGH
☎ 0131 • pop 453,430

Edinburgh has an incomparable location, studded with volcanic hills, on the southern edge of the Firth of Forth. Its superb architecture ranges from extraordinary 16th-century tenements to monumental Georgian and Victorian masterpieces. Sixteen thousand buildings are listed as architecturally or historically important, in a city that is a World Heritage Site.

In some ways, however, it's the least Scottish of Scotland's cities partly because of the impact of tourism, partly because of its closeness to England and the links between the two countries' upper classes, and partly because of its multicultural population.

The royal capital since the 11th century, all the great dramas of Scottish history played at least one act in Edinburgh. Even after the union of 1707 it remained the centre for government administration (now the Scottish Executive), the separate Scottish legal system and the Presbyterian Church of Scotland. With devolution and the location of the new Scottish Parliament in Edinburgh, the city once again wields real political power.

History
Castle Rock, a volcanic crag with three vertical sides, dominates the city centre. This natural defensive position was probably the feature that first attracted settlers; it has been fortified since at least AD 600 and there are even older traces of habitation.

The old, walled city grew on the east-west ridge (the Royal Mile, which runs from the Palace of Holyroodhouse to the castle) and south of the castle around Grassmarket. This restricted, defensible zone became a medieval Manhattan, forcing its densely packed inhabitants to build multistoreyed tenements. Even so, the city was sacked by the English seven times.

In the second half of the 18th century a new city was created across the ravine to the north of the old city. Before it was drained, this valley was a lake, now it's the Princes St Gardens, cut but not spoilt by the railway line.

As the population expanded, defence declined in importance, and the thinkers and architects of the Scottish Enlightenment planned to distance themselves from Edinburgh's Jacobite past. Built on a grid, the New Town owes its brilliance to the way that it opens onto the castle, the Old Town and the Firth of Forth, and to the genius of architects like Robert Adams whose gracious, disciplined buildings line the streets.

The population exploded in the 19th century – Edinburgh quadrupled in size to 400,000, not much less than it is today – and the Old Town's tenements were taken over by refugees from the Irish famines. A new ring of crescents and circuses was built south of the New Town, then grey Victorian terraces sprang up. In the 20th century the slums were emptied into new housing estates even farther out, which now fosters severe social problems.

Edinburgh entered a new era following the 1997 referendum in favour of an independent Scottish Parliament, which began functioning in July 1999. The parliament is temporarily housed in the Church of Scotland Assembly Rooms in the Old Town while a modern Parliament building is being constructed at the eastern end of the Royal Mile.

Orientation
The two most distinctive landmarks are Arthur's Seat, the 251m-high rocky peak southeast of the centre and the castle, which dominates Princes St Gardens. The Old and New Towns are separated by Princes St Gardens and Waverley station.

Princes St, the main shopping street, runs along the northern side of the gardens. Buildings are restricted to the northern side of Princes St, which has the usual high-street shops. At the eastern end, Calton Hill is crowned by several monuments including an incomplete war memorial modelled on the Parthenon, and a tower honouring Nelson. The Royal Mile (Lawnmarket, High St and Canongate) is the parallel equivalent in the Old Town.

Information
Tourist Offices The busy main TIC (☎ 473 3800; Waverley Market, 3 Princes St EH2 2QP; open 9am-5pm daily year-round, to 8pm July & Aug) has a **branch** (☎ 338 2167) at Edinburgh airport. Both have Scotland-wide information, and sell the useful Essential Guide to Edinburgh (£1). They also have an accommodation service, but charge £3, so consider using the free accommodation brochure.

CENTRAL EDINBURGH

PLACES TO STAY
6 City Centre Tourist Hostel
20 Edinburgh Backpackers
21 Royal Mile Backpackers
28 Brodies Backpackers
31 High St Hostel
46 Castle Rock Hostel
58 Menzies Guest House
59 Villa Nina
61 Bruntsfield Youth Hostel
62 Salisbury Guest House
63 Casa Buzzo

PLACES TO EAT
7 The Basement
8 Sainsbury's Supermarket
9 Henderson's Salad Table
     Tampopo Noodle &
     Sushi Bar
11 Mussel Inn
32 Black Bo's
35 Biblos
48 Rianma's Pizzas
     Ristorante Gennaro
53 Kebab Mahal
57 Ndebele
60 Parrots

BARS, PUBS & CLUBS
23 Venue Night Club
33 Bannerman's
34 Oxygen
36 The Beat Jazz Restaurant
37 La Belle Angele
38 City Café
52 Bam Bou
56 The Peartree House

OTHER
2 St James Shopping Centre
3 Post Office
4 St Andrew Square
     Bus & Coach Station
5 Scottish National
     Portrait Gallery
10 Thomas Cook
12 easyEverything
13 American Express
14 Royal Scottish Academy
15 National Gallery of Scotland
16 Sir Walter Scott Monument
17 Edinburgh and Scotland
     Information Centre (TIC);
     Waverley Market
18 Airport Bus;
     Tour Bus Departure Point
19 Tattoo Office
22 John Knox House
24 Nelson Monument
25 National Monument
26 New Scottish Parliament
27 Dynamic Earth
29 Museum of Childhood
30 Edinburgh Cycle Hire
39 Fringe Festival Box Office
40 St Giles Cathedral
41 Parliament House
42 Gladstone's Land
43 The Writers' Museum
44 Church of Scotland General
     Assembly Buildings
45 Edinburgh Festival Office
49 Web 13 internet Café
50 Greyfriars Kirk
51 Museum of Scotland
54 Festival Theatre

BRITAIN

Money The TIC *bureau de change* is open the same hours as the TIC. **American Express** (☎ 718 2501; 139 Princes St; open 9am-5.30pm Mon-Wed & Fri, 9.30am-5.30pm Thur, 9am-4pm Sat) can help with currency exchange, as can **Thomas Cook** (☎ 456 7700; 26-28 Frederick St; open 9am-5.30pm Mon-Wed, Fri & Sat, 10am-5.30pm Thur).

Email & Internet Access You can get Net access for £5 per hour at **Web 13 Internet Café** (☎ 229 8883; 13 Bread St; open 9am-10pm Mon-Fri, 9am-8pm Sat, 11am-8pm Sun). At **easyEverything** (☎ 220 3580; 58 Rose St; open 24hr) the charge is around £1 per hour.

Things to See & Do
The best place to start any tour of Edinburgh is **Edinburgh Castle** (☎ 225 9846; adult/concession/child £8/6/2; open 9.30am-6pm daily Apr-Sept, 9.30am-5pm Oct-Mar), which has excellent views overlooking the city.

The castle is the headquarters for the British army's Scottish Division, and is a complex of buildings that were altered many times by war and the demands of the military. The small, 12th-century **St Margaret's Chapel** is the oldest building in Edinburgh. The castle was the seat of Scottish kings, and the royal apartments include the tiny room where Mary Queen of Scots gave birth to the boy who became James VI of Scotland and James I of England. You can also see the **Stone of Destiny**, returned to Scotland in 1996, and the **Scottish Crown Jewels**.

The castle is at the western end of the Royal Mile, which runs down to the Palace of Holyroodhouse. The streetscape is an extraordinary collage of 16th- and 17th-century architecture, and an exploration of the closes and wynds that radiate from it evokes the crowded and vital city of these times.

Gladstone's Land (☎ 226 5856; 477b Lawnmarket; adult/concession £5/3.75; open Apr-Oct) is a townhouse, originally completed in 1620, which has been skilfully restored, giving a fascinating insight into urban life in the past. The **Writers' Museum** (☎ 529 4901; Lady Stair's Close, Lawnmarket; admission free; open 10am-5pm Mon-Sat) contains memorabilia belonging to Robert Burns, Sir Walter Scott and Robert Louis Stevenson.

From the Royal Mile, turn right onto the George IV Bridge, which crosses Cowgate (an ancient, narrow street). Grassmarket, below and to the right, has a number of pubs and restaurants. Continue until you reach the angled intersection with Candlemaker Row and **Greyfriars Kirk** (where the National Covenant was signed) with its beautiful old churchyard; there are views from here across the roofs to the castle.

Return to the Royal Mile and turn right past the much-restored 15th-century **St Giles Cathedral**. At the cathedral's rear is **Parliament House**, now the seat of the supreme law courts of Scotland.

Continue down the Royal Mile over North/South Bridge to the **Museum of Childhood** (☎ 529 4142; 42 High St; admission free; open Mon-Sat) on your right and **John Knox House** (☎ 556 9579; 43-45 High St; adult/concession £2.25/1.75; open Mon-Sat) on your left. The Museum of Childhood has a fascinating collection of toys. John Knox was the fiery leader of the Scottish Reformation.

The **Palace of Holyroodhouse** (☎ 556 7371; admission £6; open daily Apr-Oct except when the Queen is in residence – usually around mid-May or mid-June) at the eastern end of the Royal Mile is a Stuart palace mostly dating from a reconstruction by Charles II in 1671. Holyroodhouse is the official Scottish residence of the British royal family. Visitors only have access to a limited part of the palace.

Close to Holyroodhouse, the new **Scottish Parliament** was in the final stages of construction at the time of writing and was expected to be completed in early 2003. Opposite is the engaging **Dynamic Earth** (☎ 550 7800; Holyrood Rd; adult/concession £7.95/4.50; open daily Apr-Oct, Wed-Sun Nov-Mar) exhibition on the planet's geology and natural history.

From the palace, turn right and climb Abbey Hill (under the railway overpass). Turn left onto Regent Rd, which takes you back to Princes St. On your right you pass **Calton Hill**, worth climbing for its superb views across to the castle.

Continue along Princes St until you get to the extravagant 200ft spire of the **Sir Walter Scott Monument**. A farther 200m along Princes St, on the corner of Princes St and The Mound, the **Royal Scottish Academy** (RSA; ☎ 558 7097; special exhibitions £2-5; open 10am-5pm Mon-Sat, 2pm-5pm Sun) and **National Gallery of Scotland** (☎ 624 6200;

special exhibitions £2-5; same opening hours as RSA) contain collections of paintings, drawings, sculptures and architectural drawings by academy members and European art, from Renaissance to postimpressionism.

Continue west on Princes St and turn right onto Frederick St. Walk until you reach Queen St and at No 1 the **Scottish National Portrait Gallery** (☎ 624 6200; admission free; open 10am-5pm Tues-Sat) contains portraits of famous Scots, from Mary Queen of Scots to Sean Connery.

Special Events

The Edinburgh International Festival is the world's largest, most important arts festival and the world's premier companies play to packed audiences. The Fringe Festival grew up alongside it, presenting the would-be future stars. It now claims to be the largest such event in the world, with over 500 amateur and professional groups presenting every possible kind of avant-garde performance. Just to make sure that every bed within 40mi is taken, the Edinburgh Military Tattoo is held at the same time.

The festivals take place around mid-August, but the Tattoo finishes earlier, so the last week is less hectic. If you want to attend the International Festival, it's necessary to book; the programme, published in April, is available from the **Edinburgh Festival Office** (☎ 473 2000; The Hub, Castlehill, Royal Mile, EH1 2NE). The Fringe Festival is less formal, and many performances have empty seats the day before. Programmes are available from June from the **Fringe Festival Box Office** (☎ 226 0026; 180 High St EH1 1QS). To book the Military Tattoo, contact the **Tattoo Office** (☎ 225 1188; 32 Market St EH1 1QB).

Hogmanay, the Scottish celebration of the New Year, is another major fixture in Edinburgh's festival calendar. Edinburgh is *the* place to be in the New Year and you'll need to book ahead if you want to be part of the fun.

Places to Stay

Edinburgh has numerous accommodation options, but fills quickly over New Year, at Easter and also between mid-May and mid-September. Single rooms are in short supply. Book in advance or use the accommodation services operated by the TIC.

Camping The **Mortonhall Caravan Park** (☎ 664 1533; 38 Mortonhall Gate; sites £9-

13.90; open Mar-Oct) is off Frogston Rd East, 5mi southeast of the centre.

Hostels & Colleges The ever-popular **High St Hostel** (☎ 557 3984; 8 Blackfriars St; dorm beds from £10.50) is comfortable and convenient for Royal Mile tourist attractions, pubs and clubs. Nearby are two quality hostels: **Royal Mile Backpackers** (☎ 557 6120; 105 High St; dorm beds from £10.50) and **Brodies Backpackers** (☎ 556 6770; 12 High St; dorm beds from £9.90). In the shadow of the castle is the excellent **Castle Rock Hostel** (☎ 225 9666; 15 Johnston Terrace; dorm beds from £10.50). **Edinburgh Backpackers Hostel** (☎ 220 1717, for reservations 220 2200; 65 Cockburn St; dorm beds from £12.50) is close to all the action and has a licensed café. **City Centre Tourist Hostel** (☎ 556 8070; 5 West Register St; dorm beds from £12) has an equally good location, behind Princes St and close to the bus station, although you do have to negotiate 77 exhausting steps to reach reception.

There are two good SYHA hostels. **Eglinton Youth Hostel** (☎ 337 1120; 18 Eglinton Crescent; adults/under-18s from £12/10.50) is west of the city centre near Haymarket train station. Walk down Princes St and continue on Shandwick Place, which becomes West Maitland St; veer right at Haymarket along Haymarket Terrace, then turn right onto Coates Gardens, which runs into Eglinton Crescent.

Bruntsfield Youth Hostel (☎ 447 2994; 7 Bruntsfield Crescent; dorm beds from £11.50) has an attractive location overlooking Bruntsfield Links about 2½mi southwest of Waverley train station. Catch bus No 11 or 16 from the garden side of Princes St and get off at Forbes Rd after the gardens on the left.

B&Bs You'll need to hunt around for a good deal in Edinburgh; get the TIC's free accommodation guide and make some phone calls. Outside festival time you should not have any trouble getting something for approximately £20, although it may be a bus-ride away in the suburbs.

Guesthouses are generally £2 or £3 more expensive, and to get a private bathroom you'll have to pay about £25 to £30. The main concentrations are around Pilrig St, Pilrig; Minto St (a southern continuation of North Bridge), Newington; and Gilmore Place and Leamington Terrace, Bruntsfield.

There are two good deals in the New Town: **Dene Guest House** (☎ 556 2700; 7 Eyre Place; rooms from £23.50) and next door **Ardenlee Guest House** (☎ 556 2838; 9 Eyre Place; rooms from £26). Both these places are about 1mi from the city centre.

Pilrig St, off Leith Walk (veer left at the eastern end of Princes St), is a happy hunting ground for guesthouses. **Balmoral Guest House** (☎ 554 1857; rooms from £20), at No 32, has easy access to the city. At No 94, attractive, three-crown **Balquhidder Guest House** (☎ 554 3377; rooms £22-50) has en suite facilities.

There are numerous guesthouses on and around Minto St/Mayfield Gardens in Newington, south of the centre, accessed by plenty of buses. This is the main traffic artery from the south and carries traffic from the A7 and A68. The best places are on the streets on either side of the main road.

Casa Buzzo (☎ 667 8998; 8 Kilmaurs Rd; doubles from £20) is east of Dalkeith Rd. Nonsmoking **Salisbury Guest House** (☎ 667 1264; 45 Salisbury Rd; singles/doubles £30/ 24), 10 minutes from the centre by bus, is quiet and comfortable but closed in January.

Using the same bus stop as for the Bruntsfield Youth Hostel, you can get to **Menzies Guest House** (☎ 229 4629; 33 Leamington Terrace; singles/doubles from £20/28) and **Villa Nina** (☎ 229 2644; 39 Leamington Terrace; singles/doubles from £23/36).

Places to Eat

The wide variety of eating establishments in Edinburgh should keep culinary adventurers happy.

Mussel Inn (☎ 225 5979; 61-65 Rose St; 2-course meal £14.50; open noon-10pm Mon-Sat, 1.30pm-10pm Sun) has a solid reputation as one of the best seafood restaurants in town. **Tampopo Noodle & Sushi Bar** (☎ 220 5254; 25a Thistle St; mains around £8; open noon-3pm & 6pm-9pm Tues-Sat) is a tiny place but it's big on authenticity and flavour.

Highly recommended, **The Basement** (☎ 557 0097; 10a-12a Broughton St; mains from £5.95; open noon-10.30pm daily) changes its lunchtime menu daily but you can rely on the Mexican-influenced fare on weekends and Thai-inspired meals on Wednesdays. **Biblos** (☎ 226 7177; 1a Chambers St; sandwiches from £4, mains from £5.95; open 8am-9pm daily) joins the burgeoning ranks of cool cafés in Edinburgh's centre.

Those staying at Bruntsfield can enjoy the quirky, popular **Parrots** (☎ 229 3252; 3 Viewforth St; open Tues-Sat) off Bruntsfield Place. It has an interesting, 10-page menu with offerings such as haddock-and-spinach hotpot for £7.95.

Khushi's (☎ 556 8996; 16 Drummond St; 2-course meal £7.50; open Mon-Sat) is Edinburgh's original curry house. You can BYO booze, but it takes cash only.

Vegetarians should look for **Henderson's Salad Table** (☎ 225 2131; 94 Hanover St; mains from £4.25; open 8am-10.45pm Mon-Sat), an excellent-value cafeteria-style restaurant; and **Black Bo's** (☎ 557 6136; 57-61 Blackfriars St; 2-course meal £16; open noon-2pm & 6pm-10pm Mon-Sat), which prides itself on inventive offerings like mushroom-and-olive roulade.

Ndebele (☎ 221 1141; 57 Home St, Tollcross; light meals £4-8; open 10am-10pm daily) serves South African specialities.

There are some lively pubs and reasonable restaurants on the northern side of Grassmarket, catering to a mixed crowd. Casual **Ristorante Gennaro** (☎ 226 3706; pizzas & pastas £4.80-7), at No 64, has standard Italian fare. Nearby, **Mamma's Pizzas** (☎ 225 6464; pizzas £3.95-9.95), at No 30, is an informal pizzeria with imaginative pizzas.

The university students' budget favourites can be found between Nicolson St and Bristo Place at the end of the George IV Bridge. **Kebab Mahal** (☎ 667 5214; 7 Nicolson Square; kebabs from £3.25) is a legendary source of cheap sustenance.

For self-caterers, there's a **Sainsbury's** on St Andrew's Square, near the bus station.

Entertainment

The fortnightly magazine List (£1.95), giving full coverage of events in Edinburgh (and Glasgow), is essential if you're staying for a few days.

There are several busy pubs on Grassmarket's northern side, often with live music. Turn up Cowgate, off Grassmarket's southeast, and you reach a couple of good pubs, including the relaxed **Bannerman's** (☎ 556 3254). For the long summer evenings **The Peartree House** (☎ 667 7533; 38 West Nicolson St) has a large outdoor courtyard popular with students.

Jazz lovers will gravitate to **The Beat Jazz Basement** (☎ 225 5209; 1 Chambers St). The Friday-night improvised jazz jam, sponsored by Blue Note records, is popular.

For a mix of music styles, from hip-hop and house to drum 'n' bass and funk, try **Bam Bou** (☎ 556 0200; 66/67 South Bridge) or **La Belle Angele** (☎ 225 7536; 11 Hasties Close).

Fashionable young things can be seen at **Oxygen** (☎ 557 9997; 3-5 Infirmary St), where house beats dominate the decks.

City Café (☎ 220 0125; 19 Blair St) is a cool, 1950s US-style bar and diner with pool tables. **Venue Night Club** (☎ 557 3073; 17 Calton Rd) has dance music on three floors and is worth checking.

Getting There & Away

Air Some 8mi west of the centre, **Edinburgh airport** (☎ 333 1000) services other parts of the UK, Ireland and Europe.

Bus Fares from London are competitive and you may be able to get cheap promotional tickets. National Express and Scottish Citylink are the main operators. The journey time is 9½ to 11¼ hours depending on the route, and the cheapest fare with National Express is £28 return (£24 with Silver Choice).

There are links to cities throughout England and Wales, including Newcastle (£21, 2¾ hours) and York (£28.50, six hours). Scottish Citylink has buses to major towns in Scotland. Most west coast towns are reached via Glasgow to which there are buses every 15 to 20 minutes from Edinburgh (£5 return, 1¼ hours); there are also regular services to Aberdeen (£25, 3¼ hours) and Inverness (£24, four hours).

The bus station is in the New Town, off the southeastern corner of St Andrew Square, north of Princes St.

Train There are up to 20 trains daily from London's King's Cross station (4½ to 5½ hours); apart from Saver fares (as low as £36), which must be booked in advance and can't be changed, they're expensive (see also the introductory Getting There & Away section under Scotland).

ScotRail has two northern lines from Edinburgh: one cuts north across the Grampians to Inverness (£37.10, 3¼ hours) and on to Thurso, the other follows the coast north around to Aberdeen (£44.90, 2½ hours) and on to Inverness.

There are trains every 15 minutes to Glasgow (£7.50 one way, 50 minutes).

For rail inquiries, phone ☎ 0845 748 4950.

Getting Around

To/From the Airport The Lothian Buses Airlink service runs from Waverley Bridge near the train station to the airport, taking 30 minutes and costing £3.30/5 one way/return. A taxi costs around £15 one way.

Bus There are two main bus companies, **Lothian Regional Transport** (LRT; ☎ 555 6363) and **First Edinburgh** (☎ 663 9233). You can buy tickets when you board buses, but you must have the exact change. For short trips in the city, fares are 50p to £1.20. After midnight there are special night buses. The free *Edinburgh Travelmap* shows the most important services and is available from the TIC, or during weekdays contact **Traveline** (☎ 225 3858, 0800 232323).

Bicycle For mountain and hybrid bikes try **Edinburgh Cycle Hire** (☎ 556 5560; e info@ cyclescotland.co.uk; 29 Blackfriars St), which charges £10 to £15 a day, or £50 to £70 a week.

GLASGOW
☎ 0141 • pop 612,000

Glasgow is one of Britain's largest, most interesting cities. It doesn't have the instantly inspiring beauty of Edinburgh, but it does have interesting Georgian and Victorian architecture and some distinguished suburbs of terraced squares and crescents. What makes it appealing is its vibrancy.

Although influenced by thousands of Irish immigrants, this is the most Scottish of cities, with a unique blend of friendliness, urban chaos, black humour and energy. There are some excellent art galleries and museums (most free), numerous good-value restaurants, countless pubs and bars and a lively arts scene.

Glasgow is also close to great scenery – Loch Lomond, the Trossachs and the Highlands to the north, the Hebrides to the west and the rolling hills of southern Scotland to the south.

History

Glasgow grew around the cathedral founded by St Mungo in the 6th century. In 1451 the University of Glasgow was founded – the fourth-oldest university in Britain. Unfortunately,

BRITAIN

with the exception of the cathedral, virtually nothing of the medieval city remains. It was swept away by the energetic people of a new age – the age of capitalism, the Industrial Revolution, and the British Empire.

In the 19th century, Glasgow – transformed by cotton, steel, coal, shipbuilding and trade – justifiably called itself the second city of the empire. Grand Victorian public buildings were built, but the working class lived in ghastly slums.

In the 20th century, Glasgow's port and its engineering industries went into terminal decline. By the early 1970s Glasgow looked doomed, but it has fought back by developing service industries and has rediscovered its rich cultural roots. Certainly there's renewed confidence in the city, but behind the optimism, the standard of living remains low for the UK and life continues to be tough for those affected by relatively high unemployment, inadequate housing and escalating drug problems.

Orientation

The city centre is built on a grid system on the northern side of the River Clyde. The two train stations (Central and Queen St), Buchanan bus station and the TIC are all within a couple of blocks of George Square, the main city square. Running along a ridge in the northern part of the city, Sauchiehall St has a pedestrian mall with numerous high-street shops at its eastern end, and pubs and restaurants to the west. The University of Glasgow and SYHA hostel are northwest of the city centre around Kelvingrove Park. Motorways bore through the suburbs and the M8 slices through the western and northern edges of the centre. Glasgow airport lies 10mi west.

Information

Tourist Offices The main TIC (☎ 204 4400; 11 George Square; open 9am-6pm Mon-Sat Sept-May, 9am-8pm June-Aug, also 10am-6pm Sun) provides a £2 accommodation-booking service. There's another branch (☎ 848 4440) at Glasgow airport.

Money For currency exchange there's American Express (☎ 222 1401; 115 Hope St; open 8.30am-5.30pm Mon-Fri, 9am-2pm Sat). The TIC and the post office, on the corner of Buchanan and St Vincent Sts, both have currency-exchange facilities.

Email & Internet Access You can access the Internet at easyEverything (☎ 222 2364; 57 St Vincent St). The average cost is £1 for 45 minutes.

Things to See & Do

A good starting point is **George Square**, surrounded by imposing Victorian architecture, including the post office, the Bank of Scotland and, along its eastern side, the **City Chambers**. The chambers were built in the 1880s at the high point of the city's wealth; their interior is even more extravagant than their exterior.

The current **Glasgow Cathedral** (☎ 552 6891; open 9.30am-6pm Mon-Sat, 2pm-5pm Sun Apr-Oct & 9.30am-4pm Mon-Sat, 2pm-4pm Sun Nov-Mar) is a direct descendant of St Mungo's simple church.

It was begun in 1238 and is seen as a perfect example of pre-Reformation Gothic architecture. The lower church is reached by a stairway, and its forest of pillars creates a powerful atmosphere around St Mungo's tomb, the focus of a famous medieval pilgrimage that was believed to be as meritorious as a visit to Rome.

Beside the cathedral, the **St Mungo Museum of Religious Life & Art** (☎ 552 2557; admission free; open 10am-5pm Mon-Thur & Sat, 11am-5pm Fri & Sun) is worth visiting. In the main gallery, Dalí's *Christ of St John of the Cross* hangs beside statues of the Buddha and Hindu deities. Outside you'll find Britain's only **Zen garden**.

Opposite the cathedral and St Mungo Museum is **Provand's Lordship** (☎ 553 2557; admission free; open 10am-5pm Mon-Thur & Sat, 11am-5pm Fri & Sat), the oldest dwelling in Glasgow. Built in 1471 as a manse for St Nicholas Hospital it's now a museum with period displays. There's also a medieval herb garden in the grounds.

There are some superb Art Nouveau buildings designed by famous Scottish architect and designer Charles Rennie Mackintosh. In particular, check the **Glasgow School of Art** (☎ 353 4500; 167 Renfrew St; open 10am-7pm Mon-Thur, 10am-5pm Fri, 10am-noon Sat), which has guided tours from Monday to Saturday (adult/concession costs £5/3).

The hugely popular **Kelvingrove Art Gallery & Museum** (☎ 287 2699) will be undergoing a £25.5 million refurbishment during 2003. While the renovations are taking place,

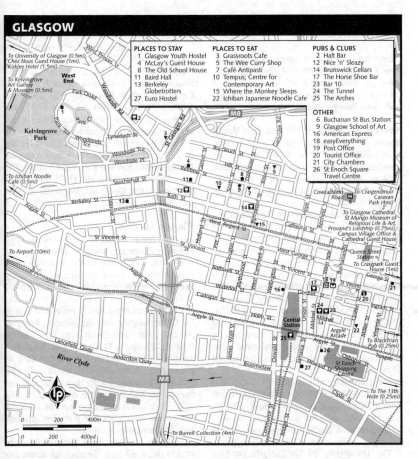

GLASGOW

PLACES TO STAY
1 Glasgow Youth Hostel
4 McLay's Guest House
8 The Old School House
11 Baird Hall
13 Berkeley Globetrotters
27 Euro Hostel

PLACES TO EAT
3 Grassroots Cafe
5 The Wee Curry Shop
7 Café Antipasti
10 Tempus; Centre for Contemporary Art
15 Where the Monkey Sleeps
22 Ichiban Japanese Noodle Cafe

PUBS & CLUBS
2 Halt Bar
12 Nice 'n' Sleazy
14 Brunswick Cellars
17 The Horse Shoe Bar
23 Bar 10
24 The Tunnel
25 The Arches

OTHER
6 Buchanan St Bus Station
9 Glasgow School of Art
16 American Express
18 easyEverything
19 Post Office
20 Tourist Office
21 City Chambers
26 St Enoch Square Travel Centre

the bulk of the world-famous collection will be transferred to the McLellen Galleries in Sauchiehall St. For more information about the Kelvingrove New Century Project, call ☎ 287 2757.

The **Burrell Collection** (☎ 287 2550; admission free; open 10am-5pm Mon-Sat, 11am-5pm Sun), in a superb museum in Pollok Country Park, 3mi south of the city centre, was amassed by a wealthy local before it was given to the city. This idiosyncratic collection includes Chinese porcelain, medieval furniture and paintings by Renoir and Cézanne. Catch a train (for East Kilbride and Kilmarnock, three per hour) from Central station to Pollokshaws West (second station on the light-blue line south), then walk for 10 minutes through the pleasant park.

Special Events

Like Edinburgh, Glasgow has developed several festivals of its own, starting with a two-week **Celtic Connections** (☎ 353 8000) music festival from mid-January. The **West End Festival** (☎ 341 0844) of music and the arts runs for two weeks in mid-June and is Glasgow's biggest festival. The excellent **International Jazz Festival** (☎ 552 3552) is held in early July. **Glasgay** (☎ 334 7126) is a gay performing arts festival, held around October/November.

Places to Stay

Finding a decent B&B in July and August can be difficult, so get into town reasonably early and use the TIC's booking service. Unfortunately, Glasgow's B&Bs are expensive by

BRITAIN

Scottish standards – you may have to pay up to £35 for a single.

Camping The nearest option is **Craigendmuir Caravan Park** (☎ 779 2973; *Campsie View; per tent from £7.50*) 4mi northeast of the city in Stepps, but it's still a 15-minute walk from Stepps station.

Hostels & Colleges The **Glasgow Youth Hostel** (☎ 332 3004; *7 Park Terrace; dorm beds adult/child £12.50/10.50*) has mainly four-bed rooms, many with en suite facilities; book in summer. From Central station take bus No 44 or 59 and ask for the first stop on Woodlands Rd.

Berkeley Globetrotters (☎ 221 7880; *63 Berkeley St, Charing Cross; dorm beds £8.50-10.50, in twin rooms £12.50*) is another option. Phone ahead for bookings; the reception is at No 56 opposite the hostel. Berkeley St is a western continuation of Bath St (one block south of Sauchiehall St). The hostel's just past Mitchell Library Theatre.

The 380-bed **Euro Hostel** (☎ 222 2828; e info@euro-hostels.com; *318 Clyde St; B&B £13.75-25*) is a former student hall of residence. The rooms are en suite, there's 24-hour reception, and Internet access for around £3 per hour.

The **University of Glasgow** (☎ 330 5385; e vacation@gla.ac.uk; *dorm beds day/week from £14/84, B&B per room from £35.50; open mid-Mar–mid-Apr & July-Sept*) has self-catering hostel & B&B accommodation around the city (confirm location when booking).

The **University of Strathclyde** (☎ 553 4148; e rescat@mis.strath.ac.uk; *Cathedral St; open mid-June–Sept*) also seasonally opens its halls of residence to tourists. Its **Campus Village** (☎ 552 0626; *beds from £13.50, B&B singles/doubles £24/40*), opposite Glasgow Cathedral, is open 24 hours. The impressive Art Deco **Baird Hall** (☎ 332 6415; *460 Sauchiehall St; B&B from £16.50*) is looking a little shabby, but offers some accommodation year-round and is in a central location.

B&Bs Renfrew St, north of Sauchiehall St, has several places. **McLay's Guest House** (☎ 332 4796; *264-276 Renfrew St; singles/doubles from £24/40*) is excellent value and well placed for city-centre attractions. The **Old School House** (☎ 332 7600; *194 Renfrew St; singles/doubles from £29/46*) is a

listed building that's not far from the School of Art.

There's a batch of reasonable-value B&Bs east of the Necropolis. **Craigpark Guest House** (☎ 554 4160; *33 Circus Drive; singles/doubles from £18/32*) is an acceptable option. **Cathedral Guest House** (☎ 552 3519; *28 Cathedral Square; singles/doubles from £49/69*) has eight rooms, all en suite. There's also a restaurant serving Scottish cuisine.

In the West End, **Chez Nous Guest House** (☎ 334 2977; *33 Hillhead St; singles/doubles from £18/40*) has some en suite rooms. The recommended **Kirklee Hotel** (☎ 334 5555; *11 Kensington Gate; singles/doubles from £48/64*) is a real treat.

Places to Eat

Glasgow has an excellent range of moderately priced restaurants. Along Sauchiehall St or around the city centre you'll find the ethnic cuisine of your choice. Set lunches offered by many restaurants are usually good value at £4 to £6.

Located inside the newly renovated Centre for Contemporary Art, the bar/café **Tempus** (☎ 332 7959; *350 Sauchiehall St; 2-course meal £12; open 11am-9.30pm Mon-Sat, noon-4pm Sun*) has flavoursome fare such as gorgonzola risotto and an excellent early-bird special – two courses for less than £10 between 5pm and 7pm. **Café Antipasti** (☎ 332 9002; *305 Sauchiehall St; mains £4.25-8.75; open noon-midnight daily*) dishes up standard Italian pizza and pasta dishes.

Towards the West End, **Grassroots Cafe** (☎ 333 0534; *93-97 St Georges Rd; mains £4-8; open 10am-10pm daily*) will keep the herbivores happy. The completely nonsmoking **Ichiban Japanese Noodle Café** (☎ 334 9222; *184 Dumbarton Rd; 2-course meal £10; open noon-10pm Mon-Wed, noon-11pm Thur-Sat & 1pm-10pm Sun*) has a smaller **sister restaurant** (☎ 204 4200; *50 Queen St*) in the city.

The **Wee Curry Shop** (☎ 353 0777; *7 Buccleuch St; mains around £7; open noon-2pm & 5.30pm-10.30pm Mon-Sat*) is popular for its authentic, home-style Indian cooking. There's a great-value two-course lunchtime special for £4.25. You'll need to book.

Where the Monkey Sleeps (☎ 226 3406; *182 West Regent St; open 7am-7pm Mon-Fri, 10am-7pm Sat & noon-6pm Sun*) has delicious soups and sandwiches for those on the run.

Entertainment

Some of the best nightlife in Scotland is found in the pubs, bars and clubs of Glasgow. The *List* (£1.95) is Glasgow's (and Edinburgh's) comprehensive, invaluable fortnightly entertainment guide.

There's no shortage of fun places. The centre is where the club action is focused; West Regent and Bath Sts have a plethora of small, subterranean hang-outs; and Merchant City is full of larger, hipper joints. The West End offers a cool nightlife alternative.

Pubs & Bars In the centre, **Brunswick Cellars** (☎ 572 0016; 239 Sauchiehall St) is a smoky, candlelit, basement bar that's popular with a younger crowd. **Nice 'n' Sleazy** (☎ 333 0900; 421 Sauchiehall St) is not as bad as it sounds; there was no sleaze in sight when we were there, just a laid-back crowd, chilled tunes and cheap drinks.

Bar 10 (☎ 221 8353; 10 Mitchell Lane) is a stylish but unpretentious place (a rare combination) just off Buchanan St.

The Horse Shoe Bar (☎ 229 5711; 17 Drury Lane) has the longest continuous bar in the UK, but its main attraction is the real ale and excellent-value food. **Blackfriars** (☎ 552 5924; 36 Bell St) is relaxed and friendly and there's free jazz on the weekend. In the West End, there are numerous pubs on or around Byres Rd. The **Halt Bar** (☎ 564 1527; 160 Woodlands Rd) is a popular university pub that hasn't been tarted up. There's a great atmosphere and free live music most nights.

Clubs Clubs charge for entry and the price varies from £3 to £7. You might avoid the charge by asking for free club passes at bars that are linked to club nights – often the bars and clubs will share DJs.

The Tunnel (☎ 204 1000; 84 Mitchell St) pumps out hard house to a dressed-up crowd. Friday and Saturday nights at **The 13th Note** (☎ 243 2177; 50-60 King St) are a seriously funky affair. **The Arches** (☎ 221 4001; Midland St, off Jamaica St) keeps its 2000-plus punters on their toes with house, hard house and trance. Howie B and Junior Sanchez were playing while we were in town.

Getting There & Away

Air Ten miles west of the city, **Glasgow International Airport** (☎ 887 1111) handles domestic and international flights.

Bus All long-distance buses arrive and depart from Buchanan bus station. Fares from London are competitive. **Silver Choice** (☎ 01355-230403) offers the best deal at £20/24 for a single/return. Departures are daily at 10pm from both Victoria coach station, London, and Buchanan bus station in Glasgow; the run takes 8½ hours. The service is popular so you'll need to book.

National Express also leaves from Victoria and Buchanan St and has up to five daily services for single/return £26/28.

There are numerous links with other English cities. National Express services include three daily buses from Birmingham (single/return £33.50/36, 5¾ hours), one from Cambridge (£39.50/41, 9¾ hours), numerous from Carlisle (£13/14, two hours), two from Newcastle (£21/22, four hours), and one from York (£23.50/25.50, 7½ hours).

Scottish Citylink has buses to most major towns in Scotland. There are buses every 20 minutes to Edinburgh (£5 return, 1¼ hours); and frequent buses to Stirling (single/return £3.60/5, 45 minutes), Inverness (£14/19.50, from 3½ hours), Oban (£11.20/15, three hours), Aberdeen (£15/21, four hours), Fort William (£11.80/16, three hours) and Skye (£20/27, 6¼ hours).

There's a twice-daily summer service (late May to September) to Stranraer, connecting with the ferry to Belfast (£29/39, six hours).

First Edinburgh (☎ 01324-613777) runs hourly buses to Milngavie (£1.15 one way, 30 minutes), which is the start of the West Highland Way.

Train As a general rule, Central station serves southern Scotland, England and Wales, and Queen St serves the north and east. There are buses every 10 minutes between the two (50p, or free with a through train ticket). There are up to eight direct trains daily from London's Euston station; they're not cheap, but they're quicker (five to six hours) and more comfortable than the bus. There are also up to eight direct services from London's King's Cross. Fares change name and price constantly, but there are usually return fares in the £30 to £40 range.

ScotRail operates the West Highland line north to Oban and Fort William (see those sections later in this chapter) and direct links to Dundee (£19.70 one way), Aberdeen (£28 one way) and Inverness (£30.60 one way). There

BRITAIN

are numerous trains to Edinburgh (£7.50 one way, 50 minutes). For rail inquiries call ☎ 0845 748 4950.

Getting Around
At the **St Enoch Square Travel Centre** (☎ 226 4826; St Enoch Square), **Strathclyde Passenger Transport** (STP; open 8.30am-5.30pm Mon-Sat) provides information on transport in the Glasgow region.

The **Roundabout Glasgow ticket** (adult/concession £3.50/1.75) covers all public transport in the city for a day; it also entitles you to a £1.50 discount on city bus tours.

To/From the Airport There are buses every 15 to 30 minutes from the airport to Buchanan bus station (£2.70, 25 minutes). A taxi costs about £12 to £15.

Bus Bus services are frequent and cheap. You can buy tickets when you board buses, but on some you have to have the exact change. For short trips in the city, fares are 70p. After midnight there are limited night buses from George Square.

Train There's an extensive suburban network; tickets should be bought before travel if the station is staffed, or from the conductor if it isn't. The network connects with the Underground at Buchanan St station. The circular Underground serves 15 stations in the centre and west (north and south of the river) for 90p one way; a Discovery Ticket (£2.50) gives unlimited travel for a day.

SOUTHWEST SCOTLAND
The tourist board bills this region as Scotland's surprising southwest, but it's only surprising if you expect beautiful mountain and coastal scenery to be confined to the Highlands. What's really surprising is that you can escape the crowds that flock to the better known Western Highlands.

Ayrshire, immediately southwest of Glasgow, was the home of Scotland's national poet, Robert Burns, and a major horse-racing hub. Dumfries & Galloway covers the southern half of this western elbow, and is where the coast and mountains approach the grandeur of the north. Warmed by the Gulf Stream, this is the mildest corner of Scotland, and there are some famous gardens. There are many notable historic and prehistoric attractions linked by the

Solway Coast Heritage Trail (information from TICs). Kirkcudbright is a picturesque town that makes a good base. This is excellent cycling and walking country, and it's crossed by the coast-to-coast Southern Upland Way and a number of cycle trails (TICs have brochures).

Orientation & Information
Southern Scotland is divided from east to west by the Southern Uplands. The western coast from Glasgow to Girvan is busy, but south of there, the crowds diminish. Stranraer (with nearby Cairnryan) is the ferry port to Larne and Belfast in Northern Ireland; it's the shortest link from Britain to Ireland, taking less than 2½ hours. The area's SYHA hostels are situated at Ayr, Newton Stewart (Minnigaff), Kendoon, Wanlockhead, and at Lochranza and Whiting Bay on the Isle of Arran.

Getting There & Around
Bus Coaches operated by National Express go from London and Birmingham (via Manchester and Carlisle), and Glasgow/Edinburgh to Stranraer. These coaches service the main towns and villages along the A75 (including Ayr, Dumfries and Newton Stewart). **Stagecoach Western** (☎ 01387-253496) provides local bus services.

Train There are regular services between Glasgow and Ayr (£6.90, 50 minutes) and Glasgow and Stranraer (£14.90, 2½ hours). For inquiries call ☎ 0845 748 4950.

Boat Frequent car and passenger ferries between Stranraer and Belfast in Northern Ireland are operated by **Stena Line** (☎ 0870 570 7070) and between Cairnryan (5mi north of Stranraer) and Larne by **P&O** (☎ 0870 242 4777). **SeaCat** (☎ 0870 552 3523) operates a high-speed catamaran between Troon, to the north of Ayr, and Belfast three times a day.

CalMac (☎ 302166) runs a daily car ferry between Ardrossan and Brodick on Arran (£4.55 for driver and for each passenger, £25.50/31.50 for car low/high season, 55 minutes, four to six daily).

Isle of Arran
☎ 01770 • pop 4800
Described as 'Scotland in miniature' because of its varied scenery, Arran is an hour's ferry ride from Ardrossan, conveniently accessible from Glasgow.

With 10 peaks over 600m, this is excellent walking country. A coastal road right around the island provides good cycling, except on weekends at the height of the tourist season when traffic can be bad. The TIC (☎ 302140), by the pier in **Brodick** (the main town), is open daily and has details of accommodation on the island. There's little in Brodick, although **Brodick Castle** (☎ 302202; adult/concession £6/4.50; open 11am-4.30pm daily Apr-Oct), 2½mi north, is worth visiting.

Head instead for either the peaceful village of **Lochranza**, 14mi north, where **Lochranza Youth Hostel** (☎ 830631; dorm beds £9.25; open Feb-Oct) is a great place to stay or picturesque **Lagg**, 18mi south, where **The Lagg Inn** (☎ 870255; twins/doubles from £32.95) provides excellent rooms and reasonable food.

Stranraer & Cairnryan
☎ 01776 • pop 11,348
Stranraer is more pleasant than the average ferry port, but there's no compelling reason to stay. Make for the south coast (maybe nearby Portpatrick), or Glasgow. The bus and train stations, accommodation and TIC are close to the Stena Sealink and SeaCat terminals. At the **TIC** (☎ 702595; 28 Harbour St) you can make National Express/Citylink bookings. Cairnryan is 5mi north on the eastern side of Loch Ryan (accessed by bus from Stranraer). London to Stranraer by rail is nine hours.

Kirkcudbright
☎ 01557 • pop 3588
Kirkcudbright, with its dignified streets of 17th- and 18th-century merchants houses and its lively harbour, is the ideal base if you wish to explore the beautiful southern coast. There's no SYHA hostel but the **TIC** (☎ 330494; Harbour Square) can provide information about local B&Bs.

SOUTHEAST SCOTLAND
There's a tendency by some to think that the 'real' Scotland only begins north of Perth, but the castles, forests and glens of the Scottish Borders have a romance and beauty of their own. The region survived centuries of war and plunder and was romantically portrayed by Robert Burns and Sir Walter Scott.

Few people pause in their rush to get to Edinburgh, but if you do stop, you'll find the lovely valley of the River Tweed, rolling hills, castles, ruined abbeys and sheltered towns.

The cycling and walking opportunities are excellent. Among many possibilities are the challenging 212mi coast-to-coast **Southern Upland Way** and the 62mi **Tweed Cycleway**, a signposted route between Biggar (on the A702 west of Peebles) to Berwick-upon-Tweed.

Orientation & Information
The Scottish Borders region lies between the Cheviot Hills along the English border, and the Pentland, Moorfoot and Lammermuir Hills, which form the border with Lothian and overlook the Firth of Forth. The most interesting country surrounds the River Tweed and its tributaries.

Getting There & Around
Bus There's a good network of local buses. For those coming from the southwest, **First Borders** (Galashiels ☎ 01896-752237) operates a Rail Link coach service between Carlisle in northwest Cumbria and Galashiels; up to eight a day, Monday to Saturday, three on Sunday (£12 return, two hours).

First Edinburgh (Galashiels ☎ 01896-752237) has numerous buses between Galashiels, Melrose and Edinburgh. Regular First Edinburgh buses run between Berwick-upon-Tweed and Galashiels via Coldstream, Melrose and Kelso. Another useful, frequent service links Jedburgh, Melrose and Galashiels. First Edinburgh's Waverley Wanderer ticket allows a day (£11.50) or week (£28) of unlimited travel around the Scottish Borders and to Edinburgh.

National Express bus No 383 runs twice a day between Chester and Edinburgh via Manchester, Leeds, Newcastle, Jedburgh and Melrose.

Train The main line north from Carlisle skirts the region's west, and the line north from Newcastle/Berwick-upon-Tweed skirts the east along the coast. In between, buses are the only option.

Jedburgh & Around
☎ 01835
The most complete of the ruined Border abbeys is **Jedburgh Abbey** (☎ 863925; adult/child £3.30/1.20; open 9.30am-6.30pm daily Apr-Sept, 9.30am-4.30pm Mon-Sat & 2pm-4.30pm Sun Oct-Mar). In 1566 Mary Queen of Scots arrived in Jedburgh to hold court; after

BRITAIN

hearing that her lover, the Earl of Bothwell, lay wounded at Hermitage Castle she set out on a famously arduous ride of 40mi to visit him. She came back from the ride close to death and was nursed back to health in a Jedburgh house, now a **museum**, that bears her name. The TIC (☎ 863435; Murray's Green; open year-round) can provide further information and can also book accommodation.

Hermitage Castle (☎ 013873-76222; adult/child £2/75p; open 9.30am-6.30pm daily Apr-Sept, 9.30am-4.30pm Mon-Sat & 2pm-4.30pm Sun Oct-Mar), off the B6399 from Hawick, is only accessible if you have transport, but it's well worth a detour; its forbidding architecture bears testimony to the Scottish Borders' brutal history.

Melrose & Around
☎ 01896

Melrose is a small, attractive town 4mi east of Galashiels, and is a popular base for exploring the Borders. The TIC (☎ 822555; open 10am-5pm Mon-Sat & 10am-1pm Sun Sept-June, 9am-6pm Mon-Sat & 10am-5pm Sun July & Aug) is right next to the entrance to the ruined **Melrose Abbey** (☎ 822562; adult/child £3.30/1.20; open 9.30am-6.30pm daily Apr-Sept, 9.30am-4.30pm Mon-Sat & 2pm-4.30pm Sun Oct-Mar), where a casket, believed to contain the heart of Robert the Bruce, is buried.

This is the only Borders town with a convenient Youth Hostel (☎ 822521; open year-round); it overlooks the abbey. The lovely **Braidwood** (☎ 822488; Buccleuch St; rooms £20-23) is warm and welcoming and there are home-made biscuits to boot.

Sir Walter Scott's house, **Abbotsford** (☎ 752043; adult/child £4/2; open 9.30am-5pm daily June-Sept, 9.30am-5pm Mon-Sat & 2pm-5pm Sun Mar-May & Oct), in a beautiful spot 2mi west of Melrose on the banks of the Tweed, has an extraordinary collection of the great man's possessions.

STIRLING
☎ 01786 • pop 37,000

Twenty-six miles north of Glasgow and occupying the most strategically important location in Scotland, Stirling has witnessed many of the struggles of the Scots against the English. The cobbled streets of the attractive Old Town surround the castle. The TIC (☎ 0870 720 0620; 41 Dumbarton Rd; open Mon-Sat) can help

with information. There's a **visitor centre** next to the castle that is open year-round.

The town is dominated by **Stirling Castle** (☎ 450000; adult/concession/child £7/5/2; open daily), perched dramatically on a rock. Mary Queen of Scots was crowned here and it was a favourite royal residence. It's one of Scotland's most interesting castles.

Stirling Youth Hostel (☎ 473442; St John St; dorm beds from £10/8) is central and an excellent place to stay. The independent **Willy Wallace Hostel** (☎ 446773; 77 Murray Place; dorm beds £10) has Internet access and free tea and coffee. The excellent **Forth Guest House** (☎ 471020, fax 447220; 23 Forth Place; B&B £19.50-37.50) is a short walk north from the train station, just off Seaforth Rd.

There are regular buses to Edinburgh, Glasgow and Aberdeen.

ST ANDREWS
☎ 01334 • pop 13,900

St Andrews is a beautiful and unusual seaside town – an eclectic mix of medieval ruins, golf fanatics, coastal scenery, tourist kitsch and a university where wealthy English undergraduates (including the future King of England, Prince William) rub shoulders with Scottish theology students.

Although St Andrews was once the ecclesiastical capital of Scotland, both its cathedral and castle are now in ruins. For most people the town is the home of golf. It's the headquarters of the game's governing body, the Royal & Ancient Golf Club, and home of the world's most famous golf course, the 16th-century Old Course.

Orientation & Information

The most important parts of old St Andrews, lying east of the bus station, are easily explored on foot. The TIC (☎ 472021; 70 Market St; open year-round) has copies of Getting Around Fife, a free guide to public transport.

Things to See

At the eastern end of North St, **St Andrews Cathedral** is the ruined west end of what was once the largest and one of the most magnificent cathedrals in Scotland. Many of the town's buildings are constructed from its stones. **St Andrews Castle & Visitor Centre** (☎ 477196; joint admission with cathedral adult/concession/child £4/3/1.50; open daily) has a spectacular cliff-top location.

Near the Old Course is the **British Golf Museum** (☎ 460046; adult/concession/child £4/3/2; open daily Apr–mid-Oct, Thur-Mon mid-Oct–Mar).

Places to Stay

Just five minutes' walk from the bus station, **St Andrews Tourist Hostel** (☎ 479911; e info@eastgatehostel.com; Inchape House, St Mary's Place; dorm beds from £12) is the only hostel in town so be sure to book ahead in summer.

Two good-value B&Bs are **Abbey Cottage** (☎ 473727; e coull@lineone.net; Abbey Walk; rooms from £19-24), just south of Abbey St, and **Fairnie House** (☎ 474094; e kate@fairniehouse.freeserve.co.uk; 10 Abbey St; rooms £16-30).

Other central B&Bs and hotels line Murray Park and Murray Place; most charge from around £25.

Places to Eat

The Vine Leaf (☎ 477497; 131 South St; 2-course dinner £19.95) serves gourmet seafood, game, Scottish beef and vegetarian meals. **Ziggy's** (☎ 473686; 6 Murray Place; mains £6.95-15.95) is popular with students and has burgers from £4.95 and a good range of Mexican, vegetarian and seafood dishes. **Brambles** (☎ 475380; 5 College St; mains £5.95-12.95) has excellent soups, salads and vegetarian choices. For delicious snacks, try **Fisher & Donaldson** (Church St), which sells a wonderful range of pastries.

Getting There & Away

Stagecoach Fife (☎ 01592-642394) has a half-hourly bus service from Edinburgh to St Andrews (£5.70, two hours) and on to Dundee (£2.40, 30 minutes).

The nearest train station is Leuchars (one hour from Edinburgh), 5mi away on the Edinburgh, Dundee, Aberdeen, Inverness coastal line. Bus Nos X59 and X60 leave every half-hour Monday to Saturday to St Andrews, hourly on Sunday.

EASTERN HIGHLANDS

A great elbow of land juts into the North Sea between Perth and the Firth of Tay in the south, and Inverness and Moray Firth in the north. The Cairngorm Mountains are as dramatic and demanding as any of the Scottish ranges, and the coastline, especially from Stonehaven to

Buckie, is excellent. The valley of the River Dee – the Royal Dee thanks to the Queen's residence at Balmoral – has sublime scenery.

Orientation & Information

The Grampian Mountains march from Oban in a great arc northeastward, becoming the Cairngorm Mountains in this eastern region. Aberdeen is the main ferry port for Shetland, and Inverness is the centre for the northern Highlands. The division between the Eastern and Western Highlands reflects the transport realities – there are few coast-to-coast links between Perth and Inverness.

Getting Around

The main bus and train routes from Edinburgh to Inverness run directly north through Perth, or around the coast to Aberdeen and then northwest and inland back to Inverness.

Bus The main towns are linked by Scottish Citylink. Edinburgh to Inverness via Perth takes four hours (£12.50); to Aberdeen, changing at Dundee, takes four hours (£13.50). There are also regular buses from both cities to Glasgow for much the same price. Aberdeen to Inverness takes three hours for £10 and passes through Elgin.

For detailed information on local bus services, phone **Perth & Kinross** (☎ 0845 301 1130), **Angus** (☎ 01307-461775), **Dundee** (☎ 01382-433125) and **Aberdeenshire & Moray** (☎ 01224-664581).

Train The train journey from Perth to Inverness is one of the most spectacular in Scotland, with a beautiful climb through the Cairngorms from Dunkeld to Aviemore. There are up to 10 trains daily Monday to Saturday, and five on Sunday (2¼ hours). There are many trains from Edinburgh and Glasgow to Aberdeen (2½ hours from Edinburgh) and from Aberdeen to Inverness (2¼ hours). Call **ScotRail** (☎ 0845 748 4950) for information on the various fares available.

Perthshire & Cairngorms

On the direct route from Edinburgh to Inverness, **Perth**, once the capital of Scotland, is an attractive town ringed by castles. Both **Dunkeld** and **Pitlochry** to the north are appealing but touristy villages. **Aviemore** is a touristy town, best used just as a walking base, but it's popular in winter with skiers.

BRITAIN

Aviemore Youth Hostel (*☎ 01479-810345; 25 Grampian Rd; dorm beds from £9; open year-round*) is well set up. Frequent buses and trains service this route.

Grampian Country Coast
Following the coastal route from Perth to Aberdeen and Inverness, you quickly reach **Dundee**, one of Scotland's largest cities. Despite its excellent location, it has suffered from poor modern development and the loss of industries. It's now experiencing a revival and it's worth pausing to visit Captain Scott's Antarctic ship *Discovery*, the Verdant Works Museum and the Dundee Contemporary Arts centre. The **TIC** (*☎ 01382-527527; 21 Castle St; open 9am-5pm Mon-Sat Oct-Apr, 9am-6pm Mon-Sat & noon-4pm Sun May-Sept*) books accommodation.

The Grampian range meets the sea at **Stonehaven**, with its spectacular Dunnottar Castle. Continuing around the coast from Aberdeen there are long stretches of sand, and, on the north coast, some magical fishing villages like **Pennan**.

Buses and trains follow the coast to Aberdeen, then the train cuts inland to Inverness (via Forres). Bus transport around the northeast coast is reasonable.

Grampian Country Inland
The region between Braemar and Huntly and east to the coast is castle country, and includes the Queen's residence at Balmoral. The TICs have information on a Castle Trail, but you really need private transport. **Balmoral Castle** (*☎ 013397-42334; adult/child £4.50/1; open Easter-late July*) attracts large numbers of visitors; it can be reached by the Aberdeen–Braemar bus.

Braemar is an attractive small town surrounded by mountains. There's a helpful **TIC** (*☎ 013397-41600; open year-round*), and the town makes a fine walking base. On the first Saturday in September the town is invaded by 20,000 people for the Braemar Gathering (Highland Games); bookings are essential. There are several B&Bs and two hostels, **Braemar Youth Hostel** (*☎ 013397-41659; 21 Glenshee Rd; dorm beds adults/under-18s £9.25/8*) and **Braemar Bunkhouse** (*☎ 013397-41242; 15 Mar Rd; dorm beds £7-8.50*).

It's a beautiful drive between Perth and Braemar, but public transport is limited. From

Aberdeen to Braemar (£6, 2¼ hours) there are several buses a day operated by **Stagecoach Bluebird** (*☎ 01224-212266*), which travel along the beautiful valley of the River Dee.

Aberdeen
☎ 01224 • pop 211,250
Aberdeen is an extraordinary symphony in grey; almost everything is built of granite. In the sun, especially after a shower of rain, the stone turns silver and sparkles like fairy-lights, but with low grey clouds and rain scudding in off the North Sea it can be a bit depressing.

Aberdeen was a prosperous North Sea trading and fishing port centuries before oil was considered a valuable commodity. Now it services one of the largest oilfields in the world. Start with over 200,000 Scots, add multinational oil workers and a large student population and the result – a thriving nightlife.

Orientation & Information Aberdeen is built on a ridge that runs east-west to the north of the River Dee. Union St, the main shopping street, runs along the crest of this ridge. The train and bus stations are next to each other off Guild St. The **TIC** (*☎ 288828; open year-round*) is next door to the Maritime Museum on Shiprow.

Places to Stay The **Aberdeen Youth Hostel** (*☎ 646988; 8 Queen's Rd; dorm beds adults/under-18s £12.25/10.75; open year-round*) is 1mi west of the train station. Walk east along Union St and take the right fork along Albyn Place until you reach a roundabout; Queen's Rd continues on the western side.

Clusters of B&Bs line Bon Accord St and Springbank Terrace (both close to the centre) and Great Western Rd (the A93, a 25-minute walk). They're more expensive than is usually the case in Scotland. Try **Dunrovin Guest House** (*☎/fax 586081; 168 Bon Accord St; rooms from £17.50*). There are plenty of other alternatives.

Places to Eat & Drink The **Ashvale Fish Restaurant** (*☎ 596981; 42-48 Great Western Rd*) is a fish-and-chip shop well known outside the city, having won several awards. Mushy peas with haddock and chips (from £3.30 takeaway) tastes much better than it sounds.

Lemon Tree (*☎ 621610; 5 West North St; mains £4.25-6.45; open noon-3pm Wed-Sun*), an excellent café/bar attached to the theatre of the same name, does great coffee, meals and cakes. **Nargile** (☎ 636093; 77-79 Skene St; lunch £7.50, dinner £13.50; open noon-3pm & 5.30pm-10.30pm Mon-Thur, noon-3pm & 5.30pm-11pm Fri & Sat) has a reputation as one of the best Turkish restaurants in Scotland – delicious marinated meats and tasty *mezes*.

The **Prince of Wales** (☎ 640597; 7 St Nicholas Lane, off Union St) is a good, traditional pub. There are many others along Union and Belmont Sts, some with live music.

Getting There & Away For transport around the region, see the earlier Getting Around section under Eastern Highlands.

Bus & Train There are daily buses to London with Scottish Citylink, but it's a tedious 12-hour trip. **Stagecoach Bluebird** (☎ 212266) is the major local bus operator. There are numerous trains from London's King's Cross station taking an acceptable seven hours, but they're more expensive than buses.

Ferry The passenger terminal is a short walk east of the train and bus stations. **P&O** (☎ 572615) has daily evening departures Monday to Friday for Lerwick (Shetland). The trip takes 14 hours (20 hours via Orkney). A reclining seat in the low/high season costs £55.50/62, one way. Mid-April to mid-December there are weekly Saturday (plus Tuesday from June to August) departures to Stromness (Orkney); £41.50/45, 10 hours.

WESTERN HIGHLANDS
This is the Highlands of the tour bus, but there are also some unspoilt peninsulas and serious mountains where you can be very isolated. The scenery is unquestionably dramatic; Ben Nevis (1343m) is Britain's highest mountain; brooding Glencoe still seems haunted by the massacre of the MacDonalds; the Cowal and Kintyre peninsulas have a magic of their own; the picture-perfect Isle of Mull is enchanting; and Loch Lomond may be a tourist cliche but is still beautiful.

This area provides challenges for the most experienced and well-equipped mountaineers, rock climbers and walkers, but there are also moderate walks that are quite safe if you're properly equipped. The 95mi **West Highland Way** runs between Fort William and Glasgow.

Orientation & Information
Fort William, at the southern end of the Great Glen, is a major tourist centre, easily reached by bus and train and a good base for the mountains. Oban, on the west coast, is the most important ferry port for boats to the Inner Hebrides (Mull, Coll, Tiree, Colonsay, Jura and Islay) and the Outer Hebridean islands of South Uist and Barra. There's a reasonable scattering of SYHA hostels, including those at Glencoe village, Oban, Tobermory and Crianlarich. There are also independent bunkhouses at Glencoe, Inchree and Corpach.

Getting There & Around
Although the road network is comprehensive and traffic sparse, travel around this region is still difficult – many of the roads are single-track, steep and have hairpin bends.

Bus From Glasgow, Scottish Citylink runs daily connections to Oban (£11.20, three hours), Fort William (£11.80, three hours) and Inverness (£14, 3½ hours).

Train The spectacular West Highland line runs from Glasgow north to Fort William and Mallaig, with a spur to Oban from Crianlarich. There are up to three trains daily from Glasgow to Oban (£15.50, three hours). There are the same number of Glasgow to Fort William trains (£18, 3¼ hours).

Fort William
☎ 01397 • pop 10,774
Fort William is an attractive little town and an excellent base for the mountains.

The town meanders along the edge of Loch Linnhe for several miles. The pedestrianised centre, with its small selection of shops, takeaways and pubs, is easy to get around. The **TIC** (☎ 703781; Cameron Square, open year-round) can help with information.

Popular **Fort William Backpackers' Guest House** (☎ 700711; e fortwilliam@scotlands top-hostels.com; Alma Rd; dorm beds from £10) is a short walk from the train station. Three miles from Fort William, up magical Glen Nevis, there's the **Glen Nevis Youth Hostel** (☎ 702336; dorm beds from £9) and, across the river, **Ben Nevis Bunkhouse** (☎ 702240; e achintee.accom@glennevis .com; Achintee Farm; dorm beds £9.50).

There are several other independent hostels in the area; the TIC has details. Particularly

BRITAIN

favoured by mountain-climbers, **Glencoe Youth Hostel** (☎ *01855-811219; beds from £8.50*), 16mi from Fort William, is a 1½mi walk from the main road, which is the Fort William to Glasgow bus route.

Getting There & Around Scottish Citylink has four daily buses to Glasgow (£11.80, three hours) and two daily buses to Edinburgh (£16.50, 3¼ hours), both via Glencoe, with connections to London. See also the earlier Western Highlands Getting There & Around section.

Oban
☎ 01631 • pop 8517
As the most important ferry port on the west coast, Oban gets inundated with visitors, but it's on a beautiful bay and the harbour is interesting. By Highland standards it's quite large, but you can easily get around on foot.

The bus, train and ferry terminals are together beside the harbour. The **TIC** (☎ *563122; Argyll Square; open year-round, to 9pm July & Aug, closed Sun Oct-May*) is in an old church, one block behind the harbour.

Oban Backpackers Lodge (☎ *562107;* e *oban@scotlands-top-hostels.com; Breadalbane St; dorm beds £9.50-11.50*) is popular. **Oban Youth Hostel** (☎ *562025; Corran Esplanade; dorm beds adults/under-18s £12.25/ 10.75; open year-round*) is north of the train station. The **Corran Hotel** (☎ *566040; 1 Victoria Crescent; beds £13-20*) has wonderful views over the harbour.

For transport options, see the Scotland Getting Around section earlier in this chapter. **CalMac** (☎ *566688*) boats link Oban with the Inner Hebridean islands and South Uist (Lochboisdale) in the Outer Hebrides. Up to seven ferries sail daily to Craignure on Mull (£6.25 return, 45 minutes).

Isle of Mull
pop 2600
It's easy to see why Mull is so popular with tourists. As well as having superb mountain scenery, two castles and a picturesque harbourside village, it's also a charmingly endearing place. About two-thirds of the population is centred on Tobermory, the island's capital, in the north. Craignure, at the southeastern corner, has the main ferry terminal. There are TICs at Craignure (open year-round) and Tobermory. The only bank on the island is at Tobermory.

Campers should head for **Tobermory Camp Site** (☎ *01688-302525;* e *angus.williams@ icscotland.net; Newdale, Dervaig Rd; adult/ child £3.50/2; open Mar-Oct*). The **Tobermory Youth Hostel** (☎ *01688-302481; Main St; dorm beds adults/under-18s £8.75/7.50; open Mar-Oct*) is located right on the waterfront. Eight miles north of Tobermory is the tiny village of **Dervaig** where you'll find the **Bellachroy Hotel & Pub** (☎ */fax 01688-400314; B&B £20-27.50*), an atmospheric 17th-century droving inn. The bar is a focus for local social life and there is often live folk music; they also serve excellent bar meals.

Public transport is limited. **Bowman's Buses** (☎ *01680-812313*) is the main operator, connecting the ferry ports with the main villages.

NORTHERN HIGHLANDS & ISLANDS
Forget castles, forget towns, forget villages. The Highlands and northern Islands are all about mountains, sea, moors, lochs and wide, empty, exhilarating space. This is one of Europe's last great wildernesses, and it's mindblowingly beautiful. The east coast is dramatic, but it's the north and west, where the mountains and sea collide, that exhaust superlatives. Orkney and Shetland are bleak and beautiful, and the Outer Hebrides (Western Isles) are a stronghold of Gaelic culture and the old crofting ways.

Information
The **Highlands of Scotland Tourist Board** (☎ *01997-421160*) publishes free accommodation guides for the Highlands north of Glencoe (including Skye). The **Western Isles Tourist Board** (☎ *01851-703088*) does the same for the Outer Hebrides. There are also separate tourist boards for **Orkney** (☎ *01856-872856;* w *www.visitorkney.com*) and **Shetland** (☎ *01595-693434;* w *www.visitshetland.com*).

Getting There & Around
This is a remote, sparsely populated region, so you need to be well organised and/or have plenty of time if you're relying on public transport. Transport services are drastically reduced after September so double-check timetables. Car rentals are available in Inverness, Oban and Stornoway; if you can get a group together, this can be a worthwhile option.

Air There are daily flights with **British Airways** (☎ 0845 773 3377) and its partners British Regional Airlines and Loganair between Benbecula, Stornoway and Inverness, and between Inverness and the Outer Hebrides. There are also daily scheduled flights from Glasgow to the beach airport at Barra, to Benbecula and to Stornoway on the Outer Hebrides, and regular flights between Glasgow and Inverness and between Edinburgh and Wick.

Bus Wick, Thurso, Ullapool and Kyle of Lochalsh can all be reached by regular buses from Inverness, or from Edinburgh and Glasgow via Inverness or Fort William; contact **Scottish Citylink** (☎ 0870 550 5050) and **Highland Country** (☎ 01847-893123). In the far northwest, however, there's no straightforward link around the coast between Thurso and Ullapool; Highland Country buses and Royal Mail postbuses are the main options.

Train The Highland lines are justly famous. There are two routes from Inverness: up the east coast to Thurso, and west to Kyle of Lochalsh (see Getting There & Away under Inverness later for details). There's also a regular train from Glasgow to Oban, Fort William and Mallaig (for Skye and the Inner Hebrides). Call ☎ 0845 748 4950 for more information.

Ferry Car and passenger ferries to all of the area's major islands are available with **CalMac** (☎ 0870 565 0000), but it can be expensive, especially if you're taking a vehicle. Consider CalMac's Island Rover tickets for unlimited travel between islands for eight or 15 days, or Island Hopscotch tickets that offer various route combinations at reduced rates. Inter-island ferry timetables depend on tides and weather, so check departures with TICs.

Inverness
☎ 01463 • pop 41,800
Inverness, on the Moray Firth, is the capital of the Highlands and the hub for Highlands transport. It's a pleasant place to while away a few days, although it lacks major attractions. In summer it's packed with keen monster hunters on their way to Loch Ness and visitors on their way to Fort William.

Orientation & Information The River Ness flows through the town from Loch Ness to Moray Firth. The bus and train stations, the TIC and the hostels are east of the river, within 10 minutes' walk of each other. The **TIC** (☎ 234353; Castle Wynd; open year-round) is beside the museum, just off Bridge St.

Places to Stay & Eat In peak season it's best to book a bed ahead. The Inverness TIC books accommodation.

Only 10 minutes' walk from the train station and just past the castle is the **Inverness Student Hostel** (☎ 236556; 8 Culduthel Rd; dorm beds £10); this place has the same owner as Edinburgh's High St Hostel – you can make phone bookings from there. It's a friendly, cosy place with a great view. **Ho Ho Hostel** (☎ 221225; 23a High St; dorm beds £8.90-9.90, twin room per person £12) is conveniently positioned, just off the pedestrianised High St.

Along Old Edinburgh Rd and on Ardconnel St are lots of guesthouses and B&Bs, including **Ivybank Guest House** (☎/fax 232796; e ivybank@talk21.com; 28 Old Edinburgh Rd; B&B from £20) and the graceful **Ardconnel House** (☎/fax 240455; 21 Ardconnel St; B&B £20-38).

On Kenneth St, west of the river and adjoining Fairfield Rd, you'll find several B&Bs in the £22 to £40 range.

Near the TIC, the **Castle Restaurant** (☎ 230925; 41 Castle St; mains £4-8) is a traditional café with plentiful food at low prices. **Café 1** (☎ 226200; 75 Castle St; mains £7.50-14.50) is a stylish bistro. **The Phoenix** (☎ 233685; 108 Academy St; bar meals from £4.95) is a comfortable, traditional pub in the city centre.

Getting There & Away See the introductory Getting Around sections for Scotland. Many people take tours from Inverness to Loch Ness, and there's a wide variety costing from £7.50.

Bus The Inverness bus station number is ☎ 233371. Scottish Citylink has bus connections with major centres in England, including London (£28, 13 hours) via Perth and Glasgow. There are numerous daily buses to Glasgow (£14, 3½ hours) and Edinburgh via Perth (£14, four hours). Buses to Aberdeen (£10, three hours) are run by Stagecoach Bluebird.

Two buses run daily to Ullapool (£6, 1½ hours), connecting with the CalMac ferry to

BRITAIN

Stornoway on Lewis (except Sunday). The 2¾-hour ferry trip costs £13.35.

There are three or four daily Scottish Citylink services via Wick to Thurso and Scrabster (£10, three hours) for ferries to Orkney. The Citylink bus leaving Inverness at 1.30pm connects at Wick with a Highland Country service to John o'Groats. There are connecting ferries from John o'Groats to Burwick and Kirkwall (both in Orkney). It costs £16 to John o'Groats, the same price to Kirkwall.

Citylink/Skyeways (☎ 01599-534328) operates three buses a day (two on Sunday) from Inverness to Kyle of Lochalsh and Portree (£12.40, three hours), on Skye.

It's possible to head to the northwest through Lairg. **Stagecoach Inverness** (☎ 239292) has a Monday to Saturday service to Lairg (Sunday in summer). In summer, daily buses run through to Durness. There's also a Monday to Saturday **postbus service** (☎ 01246-546329), travelling Lairg–Tongue–Durness.

Train The standard one-way fare from London costs £90.50 and takes eight hours. There are direct trains from Glasgow (£29.90, four hours), Edinburgh (£30.60, four hours) and Aberdeen (£17.80, 2¼ hours). The onward line from Inverness to Kyle of Lochalsh (£14.70, 2½ hours) offers one of the greatest scenic journeys in Britain and leaves you within walking distance of the pier for buses across the Skye Bridge. The line to Thurso (£12.50, 3½ hours) connects with the ferry to Orkney. There are three trains a day Monday to Saturday on both lines.

John o'Groats

The coast at the island's northeastern tip isn't particularly dramatic, and John o'Groats is little more than an upmarket car park, but there's something inviting about the view across the water to Orkney. **John o'Groats Youth Hostel** (☎ 01955-611424; dorm beds £8.50/7.25; open Apr-Oct) is in Canisbay, 3mi west of John o'Groats. There are up to seven buses daily Monday to Saturday from Wick (£2.50, one hour), via Canisbay, and Thurso (£2.50).

Thurso & Scrabster

Thurso (population 9000) is a fairly large, fairly bleak place looking across Pentland Firth to Hoy, in Orkney. It's the end of the line, both

for the east-coast railway and the big bus lines. For information contact the **TIC** (☎ 01847-892371; Riverside Rd; open Apr-Oct).

The nearby coast has arguably the best, most regular **surf** in Britain. On the eastern side of Thurso, in front of Lord Caithness' castle, there's a right-hand reef break. There's another shallow reef break 5mi west at Brimms Ness.

Sandra's Backpackers (☎/fax 01847-894575; 24-26 Princes St; dorm beds from £7) in Thurso has excellent facilities, including Internet access. There are plenty of B&Bs around town. For a cheap bar meal, try the **Central Hotel** (☎ 01847-893129; Traill St; mains £4-5.80).

Car ferries to Orkney depart from Scrabster, which is a 2mi walk or a £1 bus ride from Thurso.

Orkney Islands
☎ 01856

Just 6mi off the north coast of Scotland, this magical group of islands is known for its dramatic coastal scenery (which ranges from 300m cliffs to white, sandy beaches) and abundant marine-bird life, and for a plethora of prehistoric sites, including an entire 4500-year-old village at **Skara Brae**. If you're in the area around mid-June, don't miss the St Magnus Arts Festival.

Sixteen of these 70 islands are inhabited. **Kirkwall** (population 6100) is the main town, and **Stromness** the major port; both are on the largest island, which is known as Mainland. The land is virtually treeless, but lush and level rather than rugged. The climate, warmed by the Gulf Stream, is surprisingly moderate, with April and May being the driest months. Contact the **TIC** (☎ 872856; 6 Broad St, Kirkwall) for more information.

Places to Stay There's a good selection of cheap B&Bs and numerous hostels.

In Stromness, **Brown's Hostel** (☎ 850661; 45 Victoria St; dorm beds £9) is a very popular hostel, just five-minutes' walk from the ferry. The **Kirkwall Youth Hostel** (☎ 872243; Old Scapa Rd; dorm beds £8.75/7.75) is large and well-equipped.

Getting There & Away There's a car ferry from Scrabster, near Thurso, to Stromness operated by **P&O Scottish Ferries** (☎ 01224-572615). There's at least one departure a day all year, with one-way fares for a passenger/car costing £16.50/51. P&O also sails from Aberdeen (see that section earlier in this chapter).

John o'Groats Ferries (☎ 01955-611353) has a passenger ferry from John o'Groats to Burwick on South Ronaldsay from May to September. A one-way ticket is £16.

Shetland Islands
☎ 01595 • pop 23,000

Sixty miles north of Orkney, the Shetland Islands remained under Norse rule until 1469, when they were given to Scotland as part of a Danish princess' dowry. Even today, these remote, windswept, treeless islands are almost as much a part of Scandinavia as of Britain. Lerwick, the capital, is less than 230mi from Bergen in Norway.

Much bleaker than Orkney, Shetland is famous for its varied bird life, its rugged coastline and 4000-year-old archaeological heritage. There are 15 inhabited islands. **Lerwick** is the largest town on Mainland Shetland, which is used as a base for the North Sea oilfields. Oil has brought a certain amount of prosperity to the islands – there are well-equipped leisure centres in many villages.

Small ferries connect a handful of the smaller islands. Contact the **TIC** (☎ 693434) for information on B&Bs and camping *böds* (barns). You can stay at **Lerwick Youth Hostel** (☎ 692114; *King Harald St; dorm beds from £9.25; open mid-Apr–Sept*).

Getting There & Away There are daily flights with **British Airways** (☎ 0845 773 3377) between Orkney and Shetland. The standard fare is around £100 return.

Newly established **NorthLink Ferries** (☎ 01856 851144; e info@northlinkferries.co .uk) runs a service from Aberdeen to Kirkwall (£40, 5¾ hours) and Scrabster to Stromness (£30, 1½ hours). See Scotland's introductory Getting There & Away section for ferry links to Scandinavia.

North Coast
The coast from Dounreay, with its nuclear power station, west around to Ullapool is nothing short of spectacular. Everything is on a massive scale: vast emptiness, enormous lochs and snowcapped mountains. Unreliable weather and limited public transport are the only drawbacks.

Surveying lovely Torrisdale Bay, the **Bettyhill Hotel** (☎/fax 01641-521352; *Betty-*

hill; beds from £20) has a cosy back-bar that serves cheap meals; the entertaining banter from the bar staff is free.

Durness Youth Hostel (☎ 01971-511244; *Smoo, Durness; beds adults/under-18s from £7.50/6.25)* is backed by the rocky Sutherland hills.

Getting to Thurso by bus or train is no problem, but from there your troubles start. From June to September, **Highland Country Buses** (☎ 01847-893123) runs the Northern Explorer bus once daily (except Sunday) from Thurso to Durness, leaving Thurso at 11.30am (£7.25, 2½ hours). The rest of the year, there are Monday to Saturday services from Thurso to Bettyhill.

The alternative is to come north from Inverness via Lairg. There are trains daily (except Sunday in winter) to Lairg. Monday to Saturday, postbus services operate the Lairg–Tongue and Lairg–Kinlochbervie–Durness routes and from Lairg to Lochinver. There are also services around the coast from Elphin to Scourie, Drumbeg to Lochinver, Shieldaig to Kishorn via Applecross, and Shieldaig to Torridon and Strathcarron, but often with gaps between towns.

Renting cars or hitching are the other options.

West Coast
Ullapool is the most northerly town of any significance and the jumping-off point for the Isle of Lewis. There's more brilliant coast round to Gairloch, along the incomparable Loch Maree and down to the Kyle of Lochalsh and Skye. From there onward you're back in the land of the tour bus; civilisation (and main roads) can be a shock after all the empty space.

Ullapool The pretty fishing village of Ullapool attracts the crowds because it's easily accessible along beautiful Loch Broom from Inverness. The **TIC** (☎ 01854-612135; *6 Argyle St*) is one block inland, but most places are strung along the harbourfront, including **Ullapool Youth Hostel** (☎ 01854-612254; *dorm beds adults/under-18s from £8.50/ 7.25; closed Jan)*; book ahead in Easter and summer. There are a great many B&Bs, including **Sea Breezes** (☎ 01854-612148; *2 West Terrace; singles/doubles from £15/30)*.

See the Inverness Getting There & Away section earlier.

Kyle of Lochalsh Kyle, as it's known, is a small village that overlooks the lovely island of Skye across narrow Loch Alsh. There's a TIC (☎ 01599-534276) beside the seafront car park; the nearest hostels are on Skye.

Kyle can be reached by bus and train from Inverness (see that section earlier), and by direct Scottish Citylink buses from Glasgow (£17.50, 5½ hours), which continue across to Kyleakin (£1.60, 10 minutes), Portree (£7.20, one hour) and on to Uig (£7.90, 1½ hours) for ferries to Tarbert on Harris and Lochmaddy on North Uist.

Isle of Skye
pop 8847
Skye is a large, rugged island, 50mi north to south and east to west. It's ringed by stunning coastline and dominated by the magnificent Cuillin Hills, popular for the sport of 'Munro bagging' – climbing Scottish mountains of 3000ft (914m) or higher. Tourism is a mainstay of the island economy, so you won't escape the crowds until you get off the main roads. You can contact the **Portree TIC** (☎ 01478-612137; Bayfield Rd), for more information.

Places to Stay & Eat There are more than a dozen SYHA and independent hostels on the island and numerous B&Bs. The SYHA hostels most relevant to ferry users are at **Uig** (☎ 01470-542211; dorm beds adults/under-18s from £8.25/7; open Apr-Sept) for the Outer Hebrides; and **Armadale** (☎ 01471-844260; dorm beds adults/under-18s from £8.25/7; open Apr-Sept), for Mallaig. There's also an SYHA hostel at **Kyleakin** (☎ 01599-534585; dorm beds adults/under-18s from £9/6; open year-round).

The pick of the independents is the friendly **Skye Backpackers** (☎/fax 01599-534510; e skye@scotlands-top-hostels.com; Kyleakin; dorm beds £10-12), a short walk from the Skye Bridge; there are some double rooms. **Dunsgiath** (☎ 01478-612851; e stay@dunsgiath.com; The Harbour, Portree; doubles/twins £34/54) is a recommended B&B with a great view across the harbour.

Portree is the main centre on the island and the **Bosville Hotel** (☎ 01478-612846; Bosville Terrace; bar meals £7-12) and **Portree House** (☎ 01478-613713; Home Farm Rd; bar meals £7-12) are two of the best places for a hearty meal. **Granary Bakery** (☎ 01478-612873; Somerled Square; meals £2.95-5.25) serves

tasty takeaway pastries and fresh bread as well as dine-in snacks and meals.

Getting There & Away The bridge toll on the Skye bridge is an exorbitant £4.70 one way per car. There are still two ferries from the mainland to Skye. Mid-July to August, **CalMac** (☎ 0147-844248) operates between Mallaig and Armadale (£2.80 passengers, £15.65 cars, 30 minutes); it's wise to book. There's also a private **Glenelg–Kylerhea service** (☎ 01599-511302) from mid-April to late October (not always on Sunday), taking 10 minutes and costing 70p.

From Uig on Skye, CalMac has daily services to Lochmaddy on North Uist and (except Sunday) to Tarbert on Harris; both destinations take 1¾ hours.

Outer Hebrides (Western Isles)
The Outer Hebrides are bleak, remote and treeless. The climate is fierce – the islands are completely exposed to the gales that sweep in from the Atlantic, and it rains more than 250 days of the year. Some people find the landscape mournful, but others find the stark beauty and isolated world of the crofters strangely unique and captivating.

The islands are much bigger than might be imagined (stretching in a 130mi arc); those that do fall under the islands' spell will need plenty of time to explore. The Sabbath is strictly observed – nothing moves on a Sunday and it can be hard finding anything to eat. Tarbert (Harris) and Lochmaddy (North Uist) are reasonably pleasant villages, but the real attraction lies in the landscape.

See the earlier Skye and Kyle of Lochalsh sections for details of CalMac ferries to Tarbert and Lochmaddy, and the Oban section for ferries to Lochboisdale. All the TICs open for late ferry arrivals in summer but close between mid-October and early April.

Lewis & Harris Lewis (main town Stornoway, reached by ferry from Ullapool) and Harris (Tarbert, by ferry from Uig on Skye) are actually one island with a border of high hills between them. Lewis has low, rolling hills and miles of untouched moorland and freshwater lochs; Harris is rugged, with stony mountains bordered by meadows and sweeping, sandy beaches.

Stornoway (population 8100) is the largest town, but it's not an attractive one. It does have a reasonable range of facilities, including a **TIC** (☎ 01851-703088) and several banks.

The **Stornoway Backpackers Hostel** (☎ 01851-703628; 47 Keith St; dorm beds £9), is a five-minute walk from the ferry and bus station. **Fernlea** (☎ 01851-702125; 9 Matheson Rd; rooms £18-25) is a recommended B&B with en suite facilities, five minutes' walk from the ferry. There's at least one bus a day between Tarbert and Stornoway (except Sunday).

Tarbert has a **TIC** (☎ 01859-502011; open year-round), a Bank of Scotland (no ATM) and two general stores. Between the eastern and western lochs, the **Harris Hotel** (☎ 01859-502154; Tarbert; singles £33.50-43.50, doubles £57-77) has a range of rooms, some en suite. This place also has good-value pub meals (some vegetarian) for £6 to £9. At **Rhenigidale**, there's the SYHA **Rhenigidale Crofters' Hostel** (dorm beds adults/under-18s £6.50/5), 10mi north of Tarbert; a bus can take you to the end of the road at Maraig, but it's a two-hour walk from there; alternatively, walk the whole way – it's a great hike.

North & South Uist North Uist (main town Lochmaddy, reached by ferry from Uig on Skye, or from Tarbert or Leverburgh on Harris), Benbecula (by air from Inverness and Glasgow) and South Uist (Lochboisdale, by ferry from Oban or Mallaig) are joined by a bridge and causeway. These are low, flat, green islands half-drowned by sinuous lochs and open to the sea and sky.

Barra (Castlebay, by ferry from Lochboisdale and, for passengers only, Ludag on South Uist) lies at the southern tip of the island chain and is famous for its wild flowers and glorious white, sandy beaches.

Lochmaddy has a **TIC** (☎ 01876-500321; open Apr–mid-Oct), a Bank of Scotland (no ATM), a post office and a hotel. **Uist Outdoor Centre** (☎ 01876-500480; dorm beds £8-10; open year-round) is popular with groups of outdoor enthusiasts.

There's one postbus a day between Lochmaddy and Lochboisdale, which also has a bank and **TIC** (☎ 01878-700286). In Howmore, 15mi north on the west coast, is the **Howmore Youth Hostel** (dorm beds adults/under-18s £7/5.50; open year-round). There's a bus from Lochboisdale. Barra has a **TIC** (☎ 01871-810336) in Castlebay and about 20 scattered B&Bs, but no hostel.

Wales (Cymru)

There's a remarkably upbeat feeling in Wales today. In 1979 the majority of the people voted against home rule; yet in the 1997 referendum they said yes to a Welsh Assembly, and two years later its first members were elected.

Wales has had the misfortune to be so close to England that it could not be allowed its independence, and yet to be far enough away to be conveniently forgotten.

It sometimes feels rather like England's unloved back yard – a suitable place for mines, pine plantations and nuclear power stations.

It is almost miraculous that anything Welsh should have survived the onslaught of its dominating neighbour, but Welsh culture and language has proved enduring.

Although miles of coastline have been ruined by shoddy bungalows and ugly caravan parks, much of the most attractive countryside is now protected by national parks.

Wales' appeal lies in its countryside – the towns and cities are not particularly inspiring. The best way to appreciate the Great Welsh Outdoors is by walking, cycling, canal boating or hitching, or by some other form of private transport. Hay-on-Wye, Brecon, St David's, Dolgellau, Llanberis and Betws-y-Coed are noteworthy.

Many of Wales' magnificent medieval castles are within a mile of a train station: Caerphilly, north of Cardiff; Kidwelly, north of Llanelli; Harlech, south of Porthmadog; Caernarfon, in the northwest; and Conwy in the north.

FACTS ABOUT WALES
History
The Celts arrived from their European homeland sometime after 500 BC. Little is known about them, although it is to their Celtic forebears that the modern Welsh national characteristics like eloquence, warmth and imagination are attributed to them.

The Romans invaded in AD 43, and for the next 400 years kept close control over the Welsh tribes from their garrison towns at Chester and Caerlon.

From the 5th century to the 11th, the Welsh were under almost constant pressure from the Anglo-Saxon invaders of England. In the 8th century, a Mercian king, Offa, constructed a dyke marking the boundary between the

WALES

To Dublin & Dun Laoghaire (Ireland)

Southport

Formby

Wigan

Wallasey · St Helens

Birkenhead · LIVERPOOL

M56

Isle of Anglesey

Holyhead Bay

Amlwch

ANGLESEY

Llandudno · Colwyn Bay · Rhyl · Prestatyn

Great Orme

Holyhead

Holy Island

Llangefni · Menai Bridge · Beaumaris

Conwy · Abergele · Rhuddlan · Holywell · Flint · Ellesmere Port

Bangor

A55

A55

Dee

M56

A54

Chester

IRISH SEA

Caernarfon · Llanberis · Capel Curig · Llanrwst · CONWY · Denbigh · FLINTSHIRE

DENBIGHSHIRE

CHESHIRE

Caernarfon Bay

Waunfawr · Mt Snowdon (1113m) · Pen-y-Pass · Betws-y-Coed · Ruthin · Brymbo · Wrexham

A487

Horseshoe Pass · WREXHAM · A49

Blaenau Ffestiniog · Corwen

Porthmadog · Ffestiniog · Y-Bala · Llangollen · Oswestry

Llangollen Canal

Criccieth

Lleyn Pennisula · Pwllheli · Harlech

Snowdonia National Park

A470

SHROPSHIRE

Abersoch

GWYNEDD

A494

Llanfyllin · Tanat · A483 · Shrewsbury

Barmouth · Dolgellau

Cain

Dovey

A487

A458 · Welshpool

CARDIGAN BAY

Tywyn

Centre for Alternative Energy

Machynlleth

Vyrnwy

ENGLAND

Church Stretton

Borth

A470

Rheidol · Severn

Llanidloes · Newtown

 Offa's Dyke Path

Bishop's Castle

Aberystwyth

A44

Devil's Bridge

POWYS

A483

Ludlow

Rheidol Falls · Ystwyth

Knighton

Leominster

Aberaeron

New Quay

Tregaron

Llandrindod Wells

Kington

CEREDIGION

Lampeter

HEREFORD SHIRE

To Rosslare (Ireland)

Llanwrtyd Wells

Builth Wells

Cardigan

Pwll Deri

Newcastle Emlyn

Teifi

Hay-on-Wye · Wye · Hereford

Trefin

Fishguard

Preseli Hills

A470

St David's · Pembrokeshire Coast National Park

Newgale

CARMARTHENSHIRE

Gwili

Llandovery

Talgarth

Capel-y-ffin

Pembroke- shire

Carmarthen

Llandeilo

Black Mountain

A40

Brecon

Black Mountains

Haverfordwest · Narberth

National Botanic Gardens of Wales

Libanus

Crickhowell · Abergavenny

St Brides Bay

Milford Haven

Carew Castle

Amroth

Kidwelly

A48

Ammanford

Brecon Beacons National Park

Ebbw Vale · BLAENAU GWENT

MONMOUTH- SHIRE

Pembroke

Tenby

A483

Pontarddulais

Clydach

NEATH & PORT TALBOT

Merthyr Tydfil · Aberdare

Aberaychan

Usk

To Rosslare & Cork (Ireland)

Caldey Island

Llanelli

Carmarthen Bay

RHONDDA CYNON TAFF

Pontypool · Cwmbran · Tintern Abbey

To Cork (Ireland)

Gower Peninsula

Rhossili

SWANSEA

The Mumbles

Swansea · Neath

Pontypridd

Bedwas

Chepstow

Port Talbot

Caerphilly

CAERPHILLY

Newport

Oxwich Bay

M4

Cardiff

BRISTOL CHANNEL

Porthcawl · Bridgend

VALE OF GLAMORGAN

Llandaff

MOUTH OF THE SEVERN

Bristol

Penarth

Clevedon

BRIDGWATER BAY

Cardiff Airport

Barry

Weston- super- Mare

M5

Ilfracombe

Minehead

Burnham

Wells

Glastonbury

Barnstaple

Bridgwater

0   10   20km

0   5   10mi

53°N

52°N

Welsh and the Mercians. Offa's Dyke can still be seen today, in fact you can walk its length.

The Celtic princes failed to unite Wales, and local wars were frequent. However, in 927, faced with the destructive onslaught of the Vikings, the Welsh kings recognised Athelstan, the Anglo-Saxon King of England, as their overlord in exchange for an alliance against the Vikings.

By the time the Normans arrived in England, the Welsh had returned to their warring, independent ways. To secure his new kingdom, William I set up powerful feudal barons along the Welsh borders. The Lords Marcher, as they were known, developed virtually unfettered wealth and power and began to advance on the lowlands of south and Mid-Wales.

Edward I, the great warrior king, finally conquered Wales in a bloody campaign. In 1302 the title of Prince of Wales was given to the monarch's eldest son, a tradition that continues today.

To maintain his authority, Edward built the great castles of Rhuddlan, Conwy, Beaumaris, Caernarfon and Harlech.

The last doomed Welsh revolt began in 1400 under Owain Glyndwr and was crushed by Henry IV. In 1536 and 1543, the Acts of Union made Wales, for all intents and purposes, another region of England.

From the turn of the 18th century, Wales, with its plentiful coal and iron, became the most important source of Britain's pig iron. By the end of the 19th century, almost a third of the world's coal exports came from Wales, and its enormous network of mining villages, with their unique culture of Methodism, rugby and male-voice choirs had developed.

The 20th century, especially the 1960s, '70s and '80s, saw the coal industry and the associated steel industry collapse. Large-scale unemployment persists as Wales attempts to move to more high-tech and service industries. After agriculture, tourism is now the second-most important industry.

In 1997, the people of Wales voted to be governed by a Welsh Assembly rather than from the House of Commons in London. In a self-confident step towards greater political autonomy, the first Assembly was put in place in May 1999 and it now meets in a new Assembly building at Cardiff Bay. The next election is due in mid-2003.

Geography

Wales has two major mountain systems: the Black Mountains and Brecon Beacons in the south, and the more dramatic mountains of Snowdonia in the northwest. The population is concentrated in the southeast along the coast between Cardiff (the capital) and Swansea and the old mining valleys that run north into the Brecon Beacons. Wales is approximately 170mi long and 60mi wide. About 20% of the country is designated as national park.

Population

Wales has a population of 2.9 million, around 5% of the total population of Britain.

Language

Welsh is spoken by 20% of the population, mainly in the north, although a major effort has been made recently to reverse its slide into extinction. Although almost everyone speaks English, there is Welsh TV and radio, a more aggressive education policy and most signs are now bilingual.

At first sight, Welsh looks impossibly difficult to get your tongue around. Once you know that 'dd' is pronounced 'th', 'w' can also be a vowel pronounced 'oo', 'f' is 'v' and 'ff' is 'f', and you've had a native speaker teach you how to pronounce 'll' (roughly 'cl'), you'll be able to ask the way to Llanfairpwllgwyngyll-gogerychwyrndrobwllllantysiliogogogoch (a village in Anglesey reputed to have Britain's longest place name – no joke) and be understood. Try the following (pronunciation in brackets):

Bore da (bora-da)	good morning
Shw'mae (shoo-my)	hello
Peint o gwrw (paint-o-guru)	pint of beer
Diolch (diolkh)	thank you
Da boch (da bokh)	goodbye

FACTS FOR THE VISITOR
Activities

Hiking Wales has numerous popular walks; the most challenging are in the rocky Snowdonia National Park (around Llanberis and Betws-y-Coed) and the grassy Brecon Beacons National Park (around Brecon). There are three official National Trails in Wales – long-distance paths open to walkers, cyclists and horse riders. These are the Pembrokeshire Coast Path, Offa's Dyke Path and Glyndwr's Way.

BRITAIN

Most of the 186mi Pembrokeshire Coast
Path is in the Pembrokeshire Coast National
Park, an area rich in coastal scenery and his-
torical associations.

From Amroth to Cardigan, there are wide,
sandy beaches; rocky, windswept cliffs; and
picturesque villages. Accommodation is
widely available and it is easy to undertake
shorter sections. The walk can be crowded on
summer weekends. The National Park people
publish an accommodation guide (£2.50);
phone ☎ 01437-764636 for further information.

Offa's Dyke Path follows the English/
Welsh border for 168mi from Chepstow on the
River Severn, through the beautiful Wye Val-
ley and Shropshire Hills, ending on the North
Wales coast at Prestatyn. The *Offa's Dyke
Path National Trail* guide, listing accommo-
dation and maps, is available from **Offa's
Dyke Association** (☎ *01547-528753*).

Glyndwr's Way runs for 132mi across
Mid-Wales and back again, from Knighton to
Welshpool via Machynlleth, the ancient cap-
ital of Wales.

See Lonely Planet's *Walking in Britain* for
more information.

Cycling Much of Wales is excellent for cycling. Two of the best known-routes are Lôn
Las Cymru ('the Welsh National Route'),
which takes in 260mi from Holyhead to
Cardiff, and the 227mi Lôn Getaidd ('the
Celtic Trail') from near Chepstow to Fishguard. Pick up the Wales Tourist Board's free
Cycling Wales publication for an introduction
to these and other routes.

For more on cycling see Activities in the
introductory Facts for the Visitor section earlier in this chapter.

Surfing The southwest coast of Wales has a
number of surf spots. From east to west, try
Porthcawl, Oxwich Bay, Rhossili, Manorbier,
Freshwater West and Whitesands.

GETTING AROUND

Distances in Wales are small, but, with the exception of links around the coast, public transport users have to fall back on infrequent and
complicated bus timetables.

Sniff out a copy of *Wales Bus, Rail and
Tourist Map & Guide*, sometimes available
from TICs. This invaluable map lists bus and
train routes, journey times and operators.

Travel Passes

Four excellent passes are available that give
free travel, in designated regions of Wales and
immediately adjacent areas of England, on all
rail routes and nearly all intercity bus routes.
The passes, with high/low season prices (high
season being from late May to late September), are:

Freedom of Wales 15-day Flexipass Fifteen days
 bus travel plus any eight days train travel
 throughout Wales (£92/75)
Freedom of Wales 8-day Flexipass Eight days bus
 travel plus any four days train travel throughout
 Wales (£55/45)
Freedom of South Wales 7-day Flexi-Rover Seven
 days bus travel plus any three days train travel
 in South Wales (£35/30)
**Freedom of North and Mid-Wales 7-day Flexi
 Rover** Any three days out of seven of bus and
 train travel in North and Mid-Wales (£29 year-
 round)

These passes give various discounts including
£1 off at YHA hostels in Wales and free or discounted travel on narrow-gauge railways. They
are sold online at **w** www.walesflexipass.com
or over the counter at most train stations and at
many TICs.

Bus

Some 70 private bus companies operate in
Wales. The biggest intercity operators are Arriva Cymru for the north and west, First
Cymru in the southwest and Stagecoach in the
southeast.

Arriva has a useful daily TrawsCambria
service, known as the 701 (west coast), but
there's only one bus a day each way. It runs
between Cardiff, Swansea, Carmarthen,
Aberystwyth, Porthmadog, Caernarfon, Bangor, Conwy and Llandudno. Cardiff to
Aberystwyth (four hours) costs £10.90;
Aberystwyth to Porthmadog (two hours) is £8.

For all bus information call the UK-wide
public transport information line, **Traveline**
(☎ *0870 608 2608; 8am-8pm*).

Train

Wales has some fantastic train lines, both
main-line services (☎ 0845 748 4950) and
narrow-gauge survivors. Apart from the main
lines along the north and south coasts to the
Irish ferry ports, there are some interesting
lines that converge on Shrewsbury (see
Shrewsbury in the Central England section

earlier in this chapter). The lines along the west coast and down the Conwy valley are exceptional. For details on passes see Travel Passes earlier in this section.

SOUTH WALES

The valleys of the Usk and Wye, with their castles and **Tintern Abbey**, are beautiful, but can be packed with day-trippers. The south coast from Newport to Swansea is heavily industrialised, and the valleys running north into the Brecon Beacons National Park are still struggling to come to grips with the loss of the coal-mining industry.

Even so, the little villages that form a continuous chain along the valleys have their own stark beauty and the people are very friendly. The traditional market town of Abergavenny is also worth a look. The **Big Pit** (☎ 01495-790311; admission free), near Blaenafon, closed as a coal mine in 1980. These days it gives you a chance to experience life underground, and the guided tours by former miners are highly recommended.

The Black Mountains and Brecon Beacons have very majestic, open scenery and their northern flanks overlook some of the most beautiful country in Wales.

Cardiff (Caerdydd)
☎ 029 • pop 285,000

The Welsh are proudly defensive of their capital, which has rapidly been transformed from a dull provincial backwater into a prosperous university city with an increasingly lively arts scene.

If you are planning to explore South Wales, stock up on maps and information from the **TIC** (☎ 2022 7281; e enquiries@cardifftic.co.uk; open daily) at the central train station. Free Internet access is available at **Cardiff Central Library** (☎ 2038 2116; Frederick St).

Cardiff Castle (☎ 2087 8100; Castle St) is worth seeing for its outrageous interior refurbishment. Revamped by the Victorians, it's more Hollywood than medieval. Nearby, the **National Museum & Gallery of Wales** (☎ 2039 7951; Cathays Park) packs in everything Welsh but also includes one of the finest collections of impressionist art throughout Britain. The **Museum of Welsh Life** (☎ 2057 3500; St Fagan's), 5mi from the centre, is a popular open-air attraction with reconstructed buildings and craft demonstrations.

The **Youth Hostel** (☎ 0870 770 5750, fax 0870 770 5751; e cardiff@yha.org.uk; 2 Wedal Rd, Roath Park; dorm beds £14; bus No 80 or 80B) is 2mi from the city centre. The lively **Cardiff Backpacker** (☎ 2034 5577, fax 2023 0404; e cardiffbackpacker@hotmail.com; 98 Neville St, Riverside; dorm beds from £14) is less than 1mi from the train and bus stations.

Austin's Guest House (☎ 2037 7148; e austins@hotelcardiff.com; 11 Coldstream Terrace; singles/doubles £20/39) is a cheap, central B&B. Much nicer is **The Town House** (☎ 2023 9399, fax 2022 3214; e thetownhouse@msn.com; 70 Cathedral Rd). Top billing goes to **St David's Hotel & Spa** (☎ 2045 4045, fax 2031 3075; e reservations@thestdavidshotel.com; Havanna St, Cardiff Bay; singles/doubles £120/150).

National Express has buses to/from London (£15.50, 3¼ hours) or you can do it in two hours by train from London's Paddington station (£36/97 SuperSaver/standard single, hourly).

Swansea (Abertawe)
☎ 01792 • pop 190,000

Swansea is the second-largest town (it would be stretching the definition to call it a city), and the gateway to the **Gower Peninsula** and its superb coastal scenery (crowded in summer). Dylan Thomas grew up in Swansea and later called it an 'ugly, lovely town'. The town's position is certainly lovely, but there's no pressing reason to stay.

For more information, contact the **TIC** (☎ 468321; e tourism@swansea.gov.uk; Plymouth St). Internet access is available at **Swansea public library** (☎ 516757; Alexandra Rd). Moving on west to the Gower Peninsula, the **Youth Hostel** (☎ 0870 770 5998) is a converted lifeboat house, superbly situated right on the beach at Port Eynon. Bus No 18/A covers the 16mi from Swansea.

National Botanic Garden of Wales

Opened in 2000, the **National Botanic Garden of Wales** (☎ 01558-668768; w www.gardenofwales.org.uk; adult/child £6.95/3.50; open 10am-6pm daily Easter-Oct, 10am-4.30pm daily Nov-Easter) is one of Wales' newest attractions. The 72-hectare garden (double the size of London's Kew Gardens) contains the world's largest single-span greenhouse and is home to endangered plants from around the globe. The garden is on the B4310, 7mi east of Carmarthen. First Cymru's bus No 100 (late June to late September) will get you there from Cardiff (£10.50, 1½ hours) or Swansea (£5.25, 40 minutes).

Brecon Beacons National Park

The Brecon Beacons National Park covers 519 sq mi of high bare hills, surrounded on the northern flanks by a number of attractive market towns; Llandovery, Brecon, Crickhowell, Talgarth and Hay-on-Wye make good bases. The railhead is at Abergavenny. A 55mi cycleway/footpath, the Taff Trail, connects Cardiff with Brecon.

There are three mountain ridges in the park: the popular Brecon Beacons in the centre, the Black Mountains in the east and the confusingly named Black Mountain in the west.

The **National Park Visitor Centre** (☎ 01874-623366) is in open countryside near Libanus, 5mi southwest of Brecon. Other information offices are in **Brecon** (☎ 01874-623156), at the Cattle Market Car Park, and in **Llandovery** (☎ 01550-720693; Kings Rd). Both make B&B bookings. The **Monmouthshire & Brecon Canal**, which runs southeast from Brecon, is popular both with hikers (especially the 33mi between Brecon and Pontypool) and canal boaters, and cuts through beautiful country.

Brecon (Aberhonddu)
☎ 01874 • pop 7000

Brecon is an attractive, historic market town, with a **cathedral** dating from the 13th century. The market is held on Tuesdays and Fridays. There's a highly acclaimed jazz festival in August.

The **TIC** (☎ 622485; e brectic@powys .gov.uk) can help with further information. The **Ty'n-y-Caeau Youth Hostel** (☎ 0870 770 5718; e tynycaeau@yha.org.uk) is 3mi from town; ask directions from the TIC. In town there's **B&B Cantre Selyf** (☎ 622904, fax 622315; e cantreselyf@imaginet.co.uk; Lion St; singles/doubles £40/60), a spacious Georgian townhouse with decor that harks back to the 17th century.

Brecon has no train station, but there are regular bus links. **Stagecoach Red & White** (☎ 01685-385539) has regular buses to Swansea and Abergavenny, and to Hereford via Hay-on-Wye.

Hay-on-Wye
☎ 01497 • pop 1600

At the northeastern tip of the Black Mountains there's Hay-on-Wye, an eccentric market village that is now known as the world centre for **second-hand books** – there's over 35 shops and more than one million books, everything from first editions costing £1000 to books by the yard (literally).

Contact the **TIC** (☎ 820144) for information on the excellent restaurants and B&Bs in the neighbourhood. **Capel-y-Ffin Youth Hostel** (☎ 0870 770 5748, fax 0870 770 5749) is 8mi south of Hay on the road to Abergavenny. The walk here from Hay follows part of Offa's Dyke and is highly recommended.

SOUTHWEST WALES

The coastline northeast of St David's to Cardigan is particularly beautiful and, as it is protected by the national park, it remains unspoilt. The Pembrokeshire Coast Path begins at Amroth, north of Tenby, on the western side of Carmarthen Bay and continues to St Dogmaels to the west of Cardigan.

Carmarthen Bay is often referred to as Dylan Thomas Country; **Dylan's boathouse** (☎ 01994-427420; adult/concession £3/2) at Laugharne, where he wrote *Under Milk Wood*, has been preserved exactly as he left it, and it is a moving memorial. Llanstephan has a beautiful Norman castle overlooking sandy beaches. On west-facing beaches, there can be good surf; the **Newgale filling station** (☎ 01437-721398), Newgale, hires the necessary equipment and has daily surf reports.

Irish Ferries (☎ 0990-329129) leave Pembroke Dock for Rosslare in Ireland; ferries connect with buses from Cardiff and destinations east. **Stena Line** (☎ 0990-707070) has ferries to Rosslare from Fishguard; these connect with buses and trains. See the Ireland chapter later in this book for more details.

Pembroke Dock is an unpleasant ferry port and the surrounding region is not particularly inspiring either, although nearby **Pembroke Castle** (☎ 01646-684585), the home of the Tudors and birthplace of Henry VII, is magnificent. Tenby is attractive, however, and Fishguard is surprisingly pleasant.

Pembrokeshire Coast National Park

The national park protects a narrow band of magnificent coastline, broken only by the more dense development around Pembroke and Milford Haven. The only significant inland portion is the Preseli Hills to the southeast of Fishguard. There are National Park Information Centres and TICs at **Tenby** (☎ 01834-842402), **St David's** (☎ 01437-720392) and **Fishguard** (☎ 01348-873484), among others. Get a copy of the free paper, *Coast to Coast*, which has detailed local information. Apart from hostels, there are loads of B&Bs from around £20.

There's quite good public transport in the area (except on Sunday). Around Pembroke the main bus operator is **Silcox Coaches** (☎ 01646-683143), with buses from Pembroke Dock to Tenby; **Richards Bros** (☎ 01239-613756) is the main operator from St David's to Cardigan.

St David's (Tyddewi)

☎ 01437 • pop 1450

The linchpin for the southwest is beautiful St David's, one of Europe's smallest cities. There's a web of interesting streets, and, concealed in the Vale of Roses, beautiful **St David's Cathedral** (☎ 720199; open 8am-6pm Mon-Sat, from 12.45pm Sun). There is something particularly magical about this isolated, secretive, 12th-century building. But it's not an undiscovered secret.

Contact the **TIC** (☎ 720392; e enquiries@ stdavids.pembrokeshirecoast.org.uk: High St) for more information. There are regular **Richards Bros** (☎ 01239-613756) buses to and from Fishguard (45 minutes, every two hours Monday to Saturday). The closest train station to St David's is Haverford West, from where bus No 411 runs hourly into town. There's a stunning section of the coast path between St David's and Fishguard.

There are several handy **youth hostels** but you'll need to ring ahead for opening times: near **St David's** (☎ 0870 770 6042); at **Trefin** (☎ 0870 770 6074), 11mi from St David's; and the superb little **Pwll Deri** (☎ 0870 770 6004), on the cliffs 8mi from Trefin and just over 4½mi from Fishguard.

In the town itself, the cheapest B&B is the bright yellow **Pen Albro** (☎ 721865; 18 Goat St; rooms per person £17). For a B&B with a few more frills head to **The Waterings** (☎ 720876; Anchor Drive; rooms per person £30), not far from the TIC. The town's top address is **Warpool Court Hotel** (☎ 720300, fax 720676; e warpool@enterprise.net; per person £75, or with a sea view £95, rates include breakfast) which is on the road to St Brides Bay.

Fishguard (Abergwaun)

☎ 01348 • pop 3200

Fishguard stands out like a jewel among the depressing ranks of ugly ferry ports. It is on a beautiful bay, and the old part of town – Lower Fishguard – was the location for the 1971 film version of *Under Milk Wood*, which starred Richard Burton and Elizabeth Taylor. The train station and harbour (for ferries to Rosslare) are at Goodwick, a 20-minute walk from the town proper.

The **TIC** (☎ 873484; e fishguard@pem brokeshire.gov.uk; open daily summer) can help with information. The friendly **Hamilton Guest House & Backpackers Lodge** (☎ 874797; 21 Hamilton St; dorm beds £12, doubles £25; open 24hr) is near the TIC. By rail, Fishguard to London is £46 (five hours).

MID-WALES

Most visitors to Wales head either for the easily accessible south or the scenically more dramatic north, leaving the quiet valleys of Mid-Wales to the Welsh.

This is unspoilt walking country – farming land interspersed with bare rolling hills and small lakes. The 120mi **Glyndwr's Way** national trail visits sites associated with the Welsh hero between Knighton (on Offa's Dyke Path) and Welshpool via Machynlleth. Leaflets are available from TICs in the area and are invaluable – route-finding is difficult in places.

Machynlleth is an attractive market town and a good base for exploring Mid-Wales. The **TIC** (☎ 01654-702401; e mactic@mail .powys.gov.uk) dispenses information. The interesting **Centre for Alternative Technology** (☎ 01654-702400; adult/concession £7/5; open 10am-5pm daily) challenges conventional thinking with displays on solar, wind and water generating devices among other green technologies. Kids will also enjoy it.

Aberystwyth, the only place of any size on the west coast, is a remarkably pleasant university town with good transport connections. Contact the **TIC** (☎ 01970-612125; e ab erystwyth.tic@ceredigion.gov.uk) for B&Bs and more information. **Borth Youth Hostel** (☎ 0870 770 5708) is 8mi north of Aberystwyth, near a wide sandy beach.

Steam trains run through the Vale of Rheidol to Devil's Bridge, with spectacular views of the waterfall.

NORTH WALES

North Wales is dominated by the Snowdonia Mountains, which loom over the beautiful coastline. This is the holiday playground for much of the Midlands, so the coast is marred by tacky holiday villages and the serried ranks of caravan parks.

Heading east from Chester, the country is flat, industrialised and uninteresting until you reach Victorian resort, Llandudno – virtually contiguous with Conwy. From Llandudno and Conwy you can catch buses or trains to Betws-y-Coed or Llanberis, the main centres for exploring the Snowdonia National Park. From Betws-y-Coed there's a train to the bleak but strangely beautiful mining town of Blaenau Ffestiniog. One of Wales' most spectacular steam railways runs from Blaenau to the coastal market town of Porthmadog. From Porthmadog you can loop back to Shrewsbury, via Harlech and its castle.

The remote Lleyn Peninsula in the west escapes the crowds to a large extent; start from Caernarfon, with its magnificent castle, or Pwllheli. Near Porthmadog is whimsical Portmeirion, a holiday village built in the Italianate style – it's bizarrely attractive, but crowded in summer. Holyhead is one of the main Irish ferry ports.

The Red Rover day ticket (£4.80) is available on bus Nos 1 to 99 and covers most of the region. For information call **Traveline** (☎ 0870 608 2608).

Holyhead (Caergybi)
☎ 01407 • pop 12,500

Holyhead is a grey and daunting ferry port. Both **Irish Ferries** (☎ 0870 517 1717) and **Stena Line** (☎ 0870 570 7070) run ferries to Dublin. Stena Line also sails to Dun Laoghaire, just outside Dublin.

The **TIC** (☎ 762622; e holyhead.tic@virgin.net) is in ferry terminal 1. In the nearby township there's a batch of B&Bs that are used to dealing with late ferry arrivals. The **Min-y-Don** (☎ 762718; rooms per person £18) is pleasant. The TIC also has a 24-hour information terminal in the train station (next to ferry terminal 1). There are trains to Llandudno (£7.90), Chester (£16.95), Birmingham (£28.60) and London (£58).

Llandudno
☎ 01492 • pop 22,000

Llandudno seethes with tourists in summer. It was developed as a Victorian holiday town and has retained much of its 19th-century architecture and antiquated atmosphere. There's a wonderful **pier and promenade** and donkeys on the beach.

Llandudno is on its own peninsula between two sweeping beaches, and is dominated by the spectacular limestone headland, the **Great Orme**, with the mountains of Snowdonia as a backdrop. The Great Orme, with its tramway (£3.95 return), chair lift (£5 return), superb views and Bronze Age mine, is fascinating.

There are hundreds of guesthouses, but it can be difficult to find somewhere in the peak July/August season. Contact the **TIC** (☎ 87 6413; e llandudno.tic@virgin.net) for more information.

Getting There & Away There are numerous trains and buses between Llandudno and Chester, and between Llandudno and Holyhead.

Buses and trains run between Llandudno Junction, Betws-y-Coed (for Snowdonia National Park) and Blaenau Ffestiniog (for the brilliant narrow-gauge railway to Porthmadog). See the Shrewsbury Getting There & Away section earlier for information on the complete Llandudno, Blaenau, Porthmadog, Dovey Junction, Shrewsbury loop.

Arriva Cymru (No 5/5X) has frequent bus services between Llandudno, Bangor and Caernarfon; there are plenty of buses from Bangor to Holyhead for the ferry.

Conwy
☎ 01492 • pop 3900

Conwy has been revitalised since the through traffic on the busy A55 was consigned to a tunnel, which burrows under the estuary of the River Conwy. It's a picturesque and interesting little town, dominated by superb **Conwy Castle** (adult/concession £3.50/3), one of the grandest of Edward I's castles and a medieval masterpiece.

The **TIC** (☎ 592248; e conwy.tic@virgin.net) is in the Conwy Castle Visitor Centre. Five miles west of Llandudno, Conwy is linked to Llandudno by several buses an hour and a few trains. There are, however, numerous trains from Llandudno to Llandudno Junction, a 15-minute walk from Conwy.

Snowdonia National Park

Although the Snowdonia Mountains are fairly compact, they loom over the coast and are definitely spectacular. The most popular region is in the north around Mt Snowdon, at 1085m the highest peak in Britain south of the Scottish Highlands. Hikers must be prepared to deal with hostile conditions at any time of the year.

There are several **National Park Information Centres** including **Betws-y-Coed** (☎ 01690-710426), **Blaenau Ffestiniog** (☎ 01766-830360), and **Harlech** (☎ 01766-780658). They all have a wealth of information, and all make B&B bookings.

Betws-y-Coed
☎ 01690 • pop 600

Betus (as it is known and pronounced) is a tourist village in the middle of the Snowdonia National Park. Despite bus loads of visitors it just can't help being beautiful. There's nothing to do except go for walks and take afternoon teas, which in this case is enough.

The **TIC** (☎ 710426; e ticbetws@hotmail.com) and the National Park Information Centre share a building near the train station. The nearest hostel is **Capel Curig** (☎ 0870 770 5746), 5mi west, but there are also several other hostels in the Snowdonia area.

B&Bs and hotels are plentiful. The intimate **Henllys Guest House** (☎ 710534, fax 710884; e henllys@betws-y-coed.co.uk; Old Church Rd; rooms per person from £25) is a converted Victorian magistrate's court set next to the Conwy River. Another historic building is the **Royal Oak Hotel** (☎ 710219, fax 710603; e royal-oak@betws-y-coed.co.uk; rooms per person from £35), a former coaching inn right in the heart of the village.

Snowdon Sherpa buses run along the major mountain routes within the national park, with connections to Llandudno from Betws-y-Coed, to Caernarfon from Waunfawr, and to Caernarfon/Bangor from Llanberis. A day ticket costs £2.50.

Llanberis
☎ 01286 • pop 2000

This tourist town lies at the foot of Mt Snowdon and is packed with walkers and climbers. If you're neither, for £18 you can take the **Snowdon Mountain Railway** (☎ 0870 458 0033) for the ride to the top and back. The **TIC** (☎ 870765; e llanberis.tic@gwynedd.gov.uk; 41a High St) is helpful.

The best hostel in the area is the **Pen-y-Pas Youth Hostel** (☎ 0870 770 5990), 6mi up the valley in a spectacular site at the start of one of the paths up Snowdon. Back in Llanberis there are numerous B&Bs and hotels. **Pete's Eats** (☎ 870358) is a warm café opposite the TIC where hikers swap information over large portions of healthy food. In the evenings, climbers hang out in the **Heights** (☎ 871179), a hotel with a pub and restaurant that even has its own climbing wall.

Llangollen
☎ 01978 • pop 2600

In the northeast, 8mi from the border with England, Llangollen is famous for its **International Musical Eisteddfod** (☎ 862001; w www.international-eisteddfod.co.uk). This six-day music, song and dance festival, held in July, attracts folk groups from around the world.

The **TIC** (☎ 860828; e llangollen.tic@virgin.net; Castle St) dispenses information. The town makes an excellent base for outdoor activities – walks to ruined **Valle Crucis Abbey** and the Horseshoe Pass, horse-drawn canal-boat trips, and canoeing on the River Dee. **Plas Newydd** was the 'stately cottage' of the eccentric Ladies of Llangollen, fascinating as much for their unorthodox (for those days, 1780–1831) lifestyle as for the building's striking black-and-white decoration.

The **Llangollen Youth Hostel & Activity Centre** (☎ 0870 770 5932, fax 0870 770 5933; e llangollen@yha.org.uk; Tyndwr Rd) is 1½mi from the centre. Contact the TIC for B&Bs. There are frequent buses from Wrexham, but public transport to Snowdonia is limited.

BRITAIN

France

France has its share of coiffed, caffeinated croissant-munchers with arrogant sneers at the ready. It also has its share of warm-hearted souls who accept that decent human beings may not always speak fluent French. Endearing, delicious, beautiful, diverse and occasionally maddening, France is the 'quoi' in 'je ne sais quoi'.

The largest country in Western Europe, France stretches from the rolling hills of the north to the seemingly endless beaches of the south; from the wild coastline of Brittany to the icy crags of the Alps, with cliff-lined canyons, dense forest and vineyards in between.

Over the centuries, France has received more immigrants than any other country in Europe. From the ancient Celtic Gauls and Romans to the more recent arrivals from France's former colonies in Indochina and Africa, these peoples have introduced their own culture, cuisine and art.

Once on the western edge of Europe, today's France stands firmly at the crossroads: between England and Italy, Belgium and Spain, North Africa and Scandinavia. Of course, this is exactly how the French have always regarded their country – at the very centre of things.

Facts about France

HISTORY
Prehistory to Medieval

Human presence in France dates from the middle Palaeolithic period, about 90,000 to 40,000 years ago. Around 25,000 BC the Stone Age Cro-Magnon people appeared and left their mark in the form of cave paintings and engravings.

The Celtic Gauls moved into what is now France between 1500 and 500 BC. Julius Caesar's Roman legions took control of the territory around 52 BC, and France remained under Roman rule until the 5th century, when the Franks (thus 'France') and other Germanic groups overran the country.

Two Frankish dynasties, the Merovingians and the Carolingians, ruled from the 5th to the 10th centuries. In AD 732, Charles Martel defeated the Moors at Poitiers, ensuring that France would not follow Spain and

At a Glance

- **Paris** – art treasures of the Louvre, walks along the romantic River Seine
- **Normandy** – Mont St-Michel's fascinating narrow streets, Monet's famous home at Giverny
- **Burgundy** – Dijon's medieval and Renaissance architecture, Beaune's spectacular Hôtel-Dieu, plus wine!
- **Provence** – Van Gogh's old haunts in Arles, Avignon's immense Palais des Papes
- **Corsica** – Bonifacio's huge limestone cliffs, Les Calanques mountain trails

Capital	Paris
Population	58.5 million
Official Language	French
Currency	euro
Time	GMT/UTC+0100
Country Phone Code	☎ 33

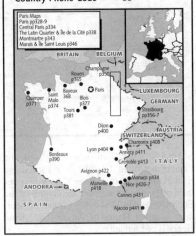

come under Muslim rule. Charles Martel's grandson, Charlemagne, extended the boundaries of the kingdom and was crowned Holy Roman Emperor in AD 800. During the 9th century, the Scandinavian Vikings (the Normans) began raiding France's western coast leading to the foundation of the Duchy of Normandy.

Under William the Conqueror (the Duke of Normandy), Norman forces occupied England

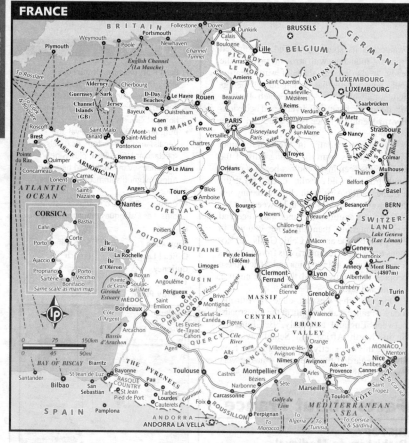

FRANCE

in 1066, making Normandy – and later, the Plantagenet-ruled England – a formidable rival of the kingdom of France. A further one-third of France came under the control of the English Crown in 1154, when Eleanor of Aquitaine married Henry of Anjou (later King Henry II of England).

In 1415, French forces were defeated at Agincourt; in 1420, the English took control of Paris, and two years later King Henry IV of England became king of France. But a 17-year-old peasant girl known to history as Jeanne d'Arc (Joan of Arc) surfaced in 1429 and rallied the French troops at Orléans. She was captured, convicted of heresy and burned at the stake two years later, but her efforts helped to transform the war in favour of the French.

Renaissance & Reformation

The ideals and aesthetics of the Italian Renaissance were introduced in the 15th century, partly by the French aristocracy returning from military campaigns in Italy. The influence was most evident during the reign of François I, and the chateaux of Fontainebleau, near Paris, and Chenonceau in the Loire are both good examples of Renaissance architectural style.

By the 1530s the Protestant Reformation had been strengthened in France by the ideas of the Frenchman John Calvin, an exile in Geneva. The Wars of Religion (1562–98) involved three groups: the Huguenots (French Protestants); the Catholic League, led by the House of Guise; and the Catholic monarchy. The fighting brought the French state close to disintegration. Henry of Navarra, a Huguenot who embraced Catholicism, eventually became King Henry IV. In 1598, he promulgated the Edict of Nantes, which guaranteed the Huguenots many civil and political rights.

Louis XIV & the Ancien Régime

Louis XIV – also known as Le Roi Soleil (the Sun King) – ascended the throne in 1643 at the age of five and ruled until 1715. Throughout his long reign, he sought to extend the power of the French monarchy. He also involved France in a long series of costly wars and poured huge sums of money into his extravagant palace at Versailles.

His successor, Louis XV (r. 1715–74), was followed by the incompetent – and later universally despised – Louis XVI. As the 18th century progressed, new economic and social circumstances rendered the *ancien régime* (old order) dangerously at odds with the needs of the country.

The Seven Years' War (1756–63), which was fought by France and Austria against Britain and Prussia, was one of a series of ruinous wars pursued by Louis XV, culminating in the loss of France's flourishing colonies in Canada, the West Indies and India to the British.

The French Revolution

By the late 1780s, Louis XVI and his queen, Marie-Antoinette, had managed to alienate virtually every segment of society. When the king tried to neutralise the power of reform-minded delegates at a meeting of the Estates General in 1789, the urban masses took to the streets and, on 14 July, a Parisian mob stormed the Bastille prison.

The Revolution began in the hands of the moderate, republican Girondists (Girondins in French), but they soon lost power to the radical Jacobins, led by Robespierre, Danton and Marat, who established the First Republic in 1792. In January 1793, Louis was guillotined in what is now place de la Concorde in Paris. Two months later the Jacobins set up the notorious Committee of Public Safety, which had near-dictatorial control during the Reign of Terror (September 1793 to July 1794).

In the resulting chaos, a dashing young general by the name of Napoleon Bonaparte chalked up a string of victories in the Italian campaign of the war against Austria, and his success soon turned him into an independent political force.

Napoleon

In 1799, when it appeared that the Jacobins were again on the ascendancy, Napoleon assumed power himself. Five years later he had himself crowned Emperor of the French by Pope Pius VII, and the scope and nature of Napoleon's ambitions became obvious to all.

In 1812, in an attempt to do away with his last major rival on the continent, Tsar Alexander I, Napoleon invaded Russia. Although his Grande Armée (Grand Army) captured Moscow, it was wiped out shortly thereafter by the brutal Russian winter. Prussia and Napoleon's other enemies quickly recovered from earlier defeats, and less than two years later the Allied armies entered Paris. Napoleon abdicated and was exiled to his tiny Mediterranean island-kingdom of Elba.

At the Congress of Vienna (1814–15), the Allies restored the House of Bourbon to the French throne. But in March 1815, Napoleon escaped from Elba, landed in southern France and gathered a large army as he marched northward towards Paris. His 'Hundred Days' back in power ended with defeat by the English at Waterloo in Belgium. Napoleon was banished to the remote South Atlantic island of St Helena where he died in 1821.

19th Century

The 19th century was a chaotic one for France. Louis XVIII's reign (1815–24) was dominated by the struggle between extreme monarchists and those who saw the changes wrought by the Revolution as irreversible. Charles X (r. 1824–30) handled the struggle between reactionaries and liberals with great ineptitude and was overthrown in the July Revolution of 1830. Louis-Philippe (r. 1830–48), an ostensibly constitutional monarch of upper bourgeois sympathies and tastes, was then chosen by the parliament to head what became known as the July Monarchy.

Louis-Philippe was in turn ousted in the February Revolution of 1848, in whose wake the Second Republic was established. In the presidential elections which were held that year, Napoleon's undistinguished nephew Louis-Napoleon Bonaparte was overwhelmingly elected. A legislative deadlock led Louis-Napoleon to lead a coup d'etat in 1851, after which he was proclaimed Napoleon III, Emperor of the French.

The second empire lasted from 1852 until 1870, when the Prussian prime minister,

Bismarck, goaded Napoleon III into declaring war on Prussia. Within months the thoroughly unprepared French army had been defeated and the emperor taken prisoner. When news of the debacle reached the French capital, the Parisian masses took to the streets and demanded that a republic be declared – the Third Republic.

WWI

Central to France's entry into WWI was the desire to regain Alsace and Lorraine, lost to Germany in 1871. This was achieved but at immense human cost: of the eight million French men who were called to arms, 1.3 million were killed and almost one million crippled. The war was officially ended by the Treaty of Versailles in 1919, which laid down severe terms (Germany was to pay US$33 billion in reparations).

WWII

During the 1930s the French, like the British, did their best to appease Hitler, but two days after the 1939 German invasion of Poland, the two countries reluctantly declared war on Germany. By June of the following year, France had capitulated. The British forces sent to help the French barely managed to avoid capture by retreating to Dunkirk and crossing the English Channel in small boats.

The Germans divided France into zones of direct occupation (in the north and along the west coast) and a puppet state based in the spa town of Vichy. Both the collaborationist government and French police forces in the German-occupied areas were very helpful to the Nazis in rounding up French Jews and other targeted groups for deportation to concentration camps.

General Charles de Gaulle, France's undersecretary of war, fled to London and set up a French government-in-exile. He also established the Forces Françaises Libres (Free French Forces), a military force dedicated to continuing the fight against Germany. The liberation of France began with the USA, British and Canadian landings in Normandy on D-Day (6 June 1944). Paris was liberated on 25 August.

The Fourth Republic

De Gaulle soon returned to Paris and set up a provisional government, but in January 1946 he resigned as its president, miscalculating

that this move would create a popular outcry for his return. A few months later, a new constitution was approved by referendum. The Fourth Republic was a period of unstable coalition cabinets, characterised by slow economic recovery fuelled by massive US aid, an unsuccessful war to reassert French colonial control of Indochina and an uprising by Arab nationalists in Algeria, whose population included more than one million French settlers.

The Fifth Republic

The Fourth Republic came to an end in 1958; de Gaulle was brought back to power to prevent a military coup and even civil war. He soon drafted a new constitution that gave considerable powers to the president at the expense of the national assembly.

In 1969, de Gaulle was succeeded as president by the Gaullist leader Georges Pompidou, who in turn was followed by Valéry Giscard d'Estaing in 1974. François Mitterrand, a Socialist, was elected president in 1981 and re-elected seven years later. Smooth, irksome Jacque Chirac was elected president in 1995 and re-elected in 2002. In 2002, he won with an overwhelming majority (82% of the vote) after French voters boxed themselves into a corner by setting up National Front rightwinger Jean Marie Le Pen as the only alternative. Le Pen's strongest support is along the Mediterranean coast, in southern Corsica and in pockets of France's northeast.

GEOGRAPHY

France (551,000 sq km) is the third-largest country in Europe, after Russia and Ukraine. It's shaped like a hexagon bordered by either mountains or water, except for the relatively flat, northeast frontier that abuts Germany, Luxembourg and Belgium.

CLIMATE

France has a temperate climate with mild winters, except in mountainous areas and Alsace. The Atlantic impacts on the northwest, bringing high humidity, rain and persistent westerly winds. A pleasant Mediterranean climate extends from the southern coast as far inland as the southern Alps, the Massif Central and the eastern Pyrenees. The down side is the mistral, a cold, dry wind that blows down the Rhône Valley; it's particularly fierce in spring.

The Paris basin records France's lowest rainfall overall (about 575mm a year) but

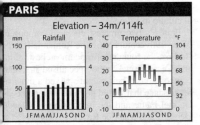

PARIS

Elevation – 34m/114ft

Rainfall

Temperature

JFMAMJJASOND   JFMAMJJASOND

enough erratic showers to keep you on your toes. Paris' average yearly temperature is 12°C, ranging from below zero temperatures in January and days in the mid-30s in August.

ECOLOGY & ENVIRONMENT

France has a rich variety of flora and fauna, including some 113 species of mammals (more than any other country in Europe).

About three-quarters of France's electricity is produced by nuclear power plants. France maintains an independent arsenal of nuclear weapons; in 1992, the government finally agreed to suspend nuclear testing on the Polynesian island of Moruroa and a nearby atoll. However, one last round of tests was concluded in January 1996 before France signed a nuclear test-ban treaty in April 1998.

GOVERNMENT & POLITICS

Despite a long tradition of highly centralised government, the country remains linguistically and culturally heterogeneous. There are even groups in the Basque Country, Brittany and Corsica who still demand complete independence from France.

France has had 11 constitutions since 1789. The present one, instituted by de Gaulle in 1958, established what is known as the Fifth Republic (see the earlier History section). It gives considerable power to the president of the republic.

The 577 members of the national assembly are directly elected in single-member constituencies for five-year terms. The 321 members of the rather powerless Sénat, most of whom serve for nine years, are indirectly elected. The president of France is elected directly for a five-year term (recently reduced from a seven-year term).

Executive power is shared by the president and the council of ministers, whose members, including the prime minister, are appointed by the president but are responsible to parliament.

The president, who resides in the Palais de l'Élysée in Paris, makes all the major policy decisions.

France is a member of the European Union (EU) and one of the five permanent members of the UN Security Council. It withdrew from NATO's joint military command in 1966.

Local Administration

Regional names still exist, but for administrative purposes the country has been divided into units called *départements*, of which there are 96 in metropolitan France and another six abroad. The government in Paris is represented in each department by a *préfet* (prefect). A department's main town, where the departmental government and the prefect are based, is known as a *préfecture*.

ECONOMY

After sluggish growth through much of the 1990s, the French economy has finally started to hum again. Economists are predicting that GDP growth will rebound to 2.6% in 2003 and a couple of years at around 1.5% as money filters through from a trade surplus. Unemployment – which was stuck around 12% in the late 1990s – has dropped to around 9%.

The government has long played a significant interventionist *(dirigiste)* role in the French economy. About 24% of GDP is spent by the state, despite a series of heavyweight privatisations during the 1990s.

Being ignored by waiters may make you doubt it but France is one of the world's most service-oriented countries; the services sector accounts for around 72% of GDP. France is also the largest agricultural producer and exporter in the EU. Nearly one in 10 workers is engaged in agricultural production, which helps to account for the attention given by the government to French farmers during their periodic protests against cheaper imports.

POPULATION & PEOPLE

France has a population of 58.5 million, more than 20% of whom live in the Paris metropolitan area. During the last 150 years France has received more immigrants than any other European country (4.3 million between 1850 and WWI), including significant numbers of political refugees. In the late 1950s and early 1960s, as the French colonial empire collapsed, more than one million French settlers returned to France from Algeria, Morocco, Tunisia and Indochina.

Today, France has approximately five million foreign-born residents. In recent years, there has been a strong racist backlash against France's nonwhite immigrant communities, led by the extreme-right Front National (FN) party. Assaults on Jewish property and people, perpetrated by white and Muslim racists, are also on the rise.

ARTS
Architecture
A religious revival in the 11th century led to the construction of a large number of Romanesque churches, so called because their architects adopted elements from the austere Gallo-Roman buildings, such as round arches and heavy walls.

The Gothic style originated in the mid-12th century in northern France. Gothic structures are characterised by ribbed vaults, pointed arches and stained-glass windows, with the emphasis on space, verticality and light. The invention of the flying buttress meant that greater height and width were now possible. By the 15th century, decorative extravagance ushered in the Flamboyant Gothic style with its characteristic wavy stone carving.

Painting
An extraordinary flowering of artistic talent occurred in France during the late 19th and early 20th centuries. The impressionists, who endeavoured to capture the ever-changing aspects of reflected light, included Édouard Manet, Claude Monet, Edgar Degas, Camille Pissarro and Pierre-Auguste Renoir. They were followed by the postimpressionists, among whose ranks were Paul Cézanne, Paul Gauguin and Georges Seurat. A little later, the Fauves (literally, 'wild beasts'), the most famous of whom was Henri Matisse, became known for their radical use of vibrant colour. In the years before WWI Pablo Picasso, who was living in Paris, and Georges Braque, pioneered cubism, a school of art which concentrated on the analysis of form through abstract and geometric representation.

Music
When French music comes to mind, most of us hear accordions and *chansonniers* (cabaret singers) like Édith Piaf. But at many points in history, France has been at the centre of musical culture in Europe.

France's two greatest classical composers of the 19th century were the Romantic Hector Berlioz, the founder of modern orchestration, and César Franck, who specialised in organ compositions. Their output sparked a musical renaissance that would produce such greats as Gabriel Fauré and the impressionists Claude Debussy and Maurice Ravel.

Jazz hit Paris in the 1920s and has remained popular ever since. Violinists Stéfane Grappelli and Jean-Luc Ponty, and pianist Michel Petrucciani have all left their mark on the world jazz scene.

Popular music has come a long way since the *yéyé* (imitative rock) of the 1960s sung by Johnny Halliday. Evergreen balladeers/folk singers include Francis Cabrel and Julien Clerc. Watch out for rap group IAM and modern troubadours Massilia Sound System from Marseille. New and groovy are the ethereal François Breut and the jazzy Paris Combo. *Sono mondial* (world music) coming out of France includes Algerian *raï*, Senegalese *mbalax* and West Indian *zouk*.

Literature
To get a feel for France and its literature of the 19th century, you might pick up a translation of novels by Victor Hugo (*Les Misérables* or *The Hunchback of Notre Dame*), Stendahl (*The Red and the Black*), Honoré de Balzac (*Old Goriot*), Émile Zola (*Germinal*) or Gustave Flaubert (*A Sentimental Education* or *Madame Bovary*).

After WWII, existentialism emerged – a significant literary movement based upon the philosophy that people are self-creating beings. Its most prominent figures were Jean-Paul Sartre (*Being and Nothingness*), Simone de Beauvoir, and Albert Camus (*The Plague*). De Beauvoir also wrote *The Second Sex*, which has had a profound influence on feminist thinking.

Contemporary authors who enjoy a wide following include Françoise Sagan, Emmanuel Carrère, Michel Houellebecq and Algerian-born Anouar Benmalek.

Cinema
Film is taken seriously as an art form in France. Some of the most innovative and influential filmmakers of the 1920s and '30s were Jean Vigo, Marcel Pagnol and Jean Renoir.

After WWII, a *nouvelle vague* (new wave) of directors burst onto the scene, including Jean-Luc Godard, François Truffaut, and Claude Chabrol.

Contemporary directors of note include Luc Besson *(The Fifth Element, Nikita)*, Claire Denis *(Chocolat, Beau Travail)* and Jean-Pierre Jeunet *(Delicatessen, Amelie)*. The French film industry's main annual event is the Cannes Film Festival held in May.

SOCIETY & CONDUCT

Some visitors to France conclude that it would be a lovely country if it weren't for the French. The following tips might prove useful: never address a waiter or bartender as *garçon* (boy) – *s'il vous plaît* is the way it's done nowadays; avoid discussing money; keep off the manicured French lawns; resist handling produce in markets; and always address people as *Monsieur* (Mr/sir), *Madame* (Mrs) and *Mademoiselle* (Miss) – when in doubt use 'Madame'.

Finally, when you go out for the evening, it's a good idea to follow the local custom of dressing relatively well, particularly in a restaurant.

RELIGION

Some 80% of French people say they are Catholic, but although most have been baptised very few attend church. Protestants, who were severely persecuted during much of the 16th and 17th centuries, now number about one million.

France now has more than five million Muslims, making Islam the second-largest religion in the country. The majority are immigrants (or their offspring) who came from North Africa during the 1950s and 1960s.

There has been a Jewish community in France almost continuously since Roman times. About 75,000 French Jews were killed during the Holocaust. The country's Jewish community now numbers around 700,000.

LANGUAGE

Around 77 million people worldwide speak French as their first language, and various forms of Creole are used in Haiti, French Guiana and southern Louisiana. French was the international language of culture and diplomacy until WWI – in France it tends to be assumed that all decent human beings speak French.

Your best bet is always to approach people politely in French, even if the only words you know are *'Pardon, Monsieur/Madame/ Mademoiselle, parlez-vous Anglais?'* ('Excuse me sir/madam/miss, do you speak English?').

See the Language chapter at the back of this book for pronunciation guidelines and useful words and phrases.

Facts for the Visitor

HIGHLIGHTS
Museums

Many of the country's most exceptional museums are in Paris. Besides the rather overwhelming Louvre, Parisian museums not to be missed include the Musée d'Orsay (late-19th and early-20th-century art), the Pompidou Centre (modern and contemporary art), the Musée Rodin, and the Musée National du Moyen Age (Museum of the Middle Ages) at the Hôtel de Cluny. Other cities known for their museums include Nice, Bordeaux, Strasbourg and Lyon.

Palaces & Chateaux

The royal palace at Versailles is the largest and most grandiose of the hundreds of chateaux located throughout the country. Many of the most impressive ones, including Chambord, Cheverny, Chenonceau and Azay-le-Rideau, are in the Loire Valley around Blois and Tours. The cathedrals at Chartres, Strasbourg and Rouen are among the most beautiful in France.

Beaches

The Côte d'Azur – the French Riviera – has some of the best-known beaches in the world, but you'll also find lovely beaches farther west on the Mediterranean.

SUGGESTED ITINERARIES
Two days
  Paris – the most beautiful city in the world.
One week
  Paris plus a nearby area, such as the Loire Valley, Champagne, Alsace or Normandy.
Two weeks
  As above, plus one area in the west or south, such as Brittany, the Alps or Provence.
One month
  As above, but spending more time in each place and visiting more of the west or south – Brittany, say, or Corsica.

FRANCE

PLANNING
When to Go
France is at its best in spring, though wintry relapses aren't uncommon in April and the beach resorts only begin to pick up in mid-May. Autumn is pleasant, too, but by late October it's a bit cool for sunbathing. Winter is great for snow sports in the Alps and Pyrenees, but Christmas, New Year and the February/March school holidays create surges in tourism. On the other hand, Paris always has all sorts of cultural activities during its rather wet winter.

In summer, the weather is warm and even hot, especially in the south, and the beaches, resorts and camping grounds get packed. Also, millions of French people take their annual month-long *congé* (holiday) in August. Resort hotel rooms and camp sites are in extremely short supply, while in the half-deserted cities many shops, restaurants, cinemas, cultural institutions and even hotels simply shut down. Avoid travelling in France during August.

Maps
For driving, the best road map is Michelin's *Motoring Atlas France* (1:200,000), which covers the entire country. Éditions Didier Richard's series of 1:50,000 trail maps are adequate for most hiking and cycling excursions.

The Institut Géographique National (IGN) publishes maps of France in both 1:50,000 and 1:25,000 scale. Topoguides are booklets for hikers that include trail maps and information (in French) on trail conditions, flora, fauna, villages en route and more.

TOURIST OFFICES
Local Tourist Offices
Every city, town, village and hamlet seems to have either an *office de tourisme* (a tourist office run by some unit of local government) or a *syndicat d'initiative* (a tourist office run by an organisation of local merchants). Both are excellent resources and can almost always provide a local map at the very least. Many tourist offices will make local hotel reservations, usually for a small fee.

Details on local tourist offices appear under Information at the beginning of each city, town or area listing.

Tourist Offices Abroad
The French Government Tourist Offices in the following countries can provide brochures and tourist information.

Australia (☎ 02-9231 5244, fax 9221 8682, e france@bigpond.net.au) 25 Bligh St, 22nd floor, Sydney, NSW 2000
Canada (☎ 514-876 9881, fax 845 4868; e mfrance@attcanada.net) 1981 McGill College Ave, Suite 490, Montreal, Que H3A 2W9
UK (☎ 090-6824 4123, fax 020-7493 6594, e info@mdlf.co.uk) 178 Piccadilly, London W1J 9AL
USA (☎ 212-838 7800, fax 838 7855, e info@ francetourism.com) 444 Madison Ave, New York, NY 10020

VISAS & DOCUMENTS
Citizens of the USA, Canada, Australia and New Zealand, and most European countries can enter France for up to three months without a visa. South Africans, however, must have a visa to visit France (to avoid delays, apply before leaving home).

If you're staying in France for more than three months to study or work, apply to the French consulate nearest where you live for a long-stay visa. If you're not an EU citizen, it's extremely difficult to get a work visa; one of the few exceptions allows holders of student visas to work part-time. Begin the paperwork several months before you leave home.

By law, every person in France, including tourists, must carry identification with them. For visitors, this means a passport. A national identity card is sufficient for EU citizens.

Visa Extensions
Tourist visas *cannot* be extended. However, if you qualify for an automatic three-month stay upon arrival, you'll get another three months if you exit and then re-enter France. At many French borders, though, it's hard to get exit and entry stamps in your passport (even if you want them) so you can more or less stay as long as you like.

EMBASSIES & CONSULATES
French Embassies & Consulates
French embassies abroad include:

Australia (☎ 02-6216 0100, fax 6216 0127, e embassy@ambafrance-au.org) 6 Perth Ave, Yarralumla, ACT 2600
Canada (☎ 613-789 1795, fax 562 3704, e consulat@amba-ottowa.fr) 42 Sussex Drive, Ottawa, Ont K1M 2C9
Germany (☎ 030-206 39000, fax 206 39010, e consulat.berlin@diplomatie.gouv.fr) Pariser Platz 5, 10117 Berlin

taly (☎ 06-686 011, fax 860 1360, e france
-italia@france-italia.it) Piazza Farnese 67,
00186 Rome

Jew Zealand (☎ 04-384 2555, fax 384 2577,
e consulfrance@actrix.gen.nz) Rural Bank
Bldg, 34-42 Manners St, Wellington

pain (☎ 91-423 8900, fax 423 8901) Calle de
Salustiano Olozaga 9, 28001 Madrid

JK (☎ 020-7073 1000, fax 7073 1004, e info
-londres@diplomatie.gouv.fr) 58 Knightsbridge, London SW1X 7JT. Visa inquiries:
☎ 0891-887733

JSA (☎ 202-944 6060, fax 944 6040, e info
-washington@diplomatie.gouv.fr) 4101
Reservoir Rd, NW Washington, DC, 20007

Embassies & Consulates in France

Countries with embassies in Paris include:

Australia (☎ 01 40 59 33 00, fax 01 40 59 33 10,
e information.paris@dfat.gov.au) 4 rue Jean
Rey, 15e (metro Bir Hakeim)

Canada (☎ 01 44 43 29 00, 01 44 43 29 99)
35 ave Montaigne, 8e (metro Franklin D
Roosevelt)

New Zealand (☎ 01 45 01 43 43, fax 01 45 01
43 44, e nzembassy.paris@wanadoo.fr) 7ter
rue Léonard de Vinci, 16e (metro Victor Hugo)

Spain (☎ 01 44 43 18 00, fax 01 47 23 59 55,
e emba.espa@wanadoo.fr) 22 ave Marceau,
8e (metro Alma Marceau)

UK (☎ 01 44 51 31 00, fax 01 44 51 31 27,
e ambassade@amb-grandebretagne.fr) 35 rue
du Faubourg St Honoré, 8e (metro Concorde)

USA (☎ 01 43 12 22 22, fax 01 42 66 97 83,
e citizeninfo@state.gov) 2 rue St Florentin,
1er (metro Concorde)

MONEY
Currency

The official currency of France is the euro.

Cash & Travellers Cheques You often get
a better exchange rate for travellers cheques
than for cash. The most widely accepted ones
are issued by American Express (AmEx) in
US dollars or euros.

Visa (Carte Bleue in France) is more widely
accepted than MasterCard (Eurocard). Visa
card-holders with a PIN can get cash advances
from banks and ATMs nationwide. AmEx
cards aren't very useful, except to get cash at
AmEx offices in big cities or to pay in upmarket shops and restaurants.

Many post offices make exchanges at a good
rate and accept AmEx travellers cheques; there
is 2.5% commission on cash and 1.5% commission on US dollar travellers cheques.

Banque de France no longer offers currency
exchange. Commercial banks usually charge a
stiff €3 to €5 per foreign currency transaction. In larger cities, exchange bureaus are
faster, easier, open longer hours and often give
better rates than the banks.

If your AmEx travellers cheques are lost or
stolen, call ☎ 0800 90 86 00, a 24-hour toll-
free number. For lost or stolen Visa cards, call
☎ 0800 90 11 79.

Costs

If you stay in hostels, buy provisions from grocery stores and don't travel much, it's possible
to survive in France for US$30 a day (US$35
in Paris). A frugal (but less miserable) budget
is more like to be US$55 a day. Eating out,
travelling a lot or treating yourself to France's
many little luxuries can increase this figure
dramatically.

Discounts Museums, cinemas, the SNCF,
ferry companies and other institutions offer
price breaks to people under the age of either
25 or 26, students with ISIC cards (age limits
may apply), and seniors (people over 60 or, in
some cases, 65.) Look for the words *demi-
tarif* or *tarif réduit* (half-price tariff or reduced
rate) on rate charts.

Tipping & Bargaining

It's not necessary to leave a *pourboire* (tip) in
restaurants or hotels; under French law, the bill
must already include a 15% service charge.
However, it's usual to leave €0.50 or €1 for
a casual meal, about €1 per person for a more
formal meal and about 10% of the bill in a
truly posh restaurant. For a taxi ride, the usual
tip is about €1 no matter what the fare (10%
in Paris). You'll rarely have an opportunity to
bargain in France.

Taxes & Refunds

France's VAT (value-added tax, ie, sales tax)
is known in French as TVA *(taxe sur la valeur
ajoutée)*. The TVA is 19.6% on the purchase
price of most goods (and for noncommercial
vehicle rental). Prices that include TVA are
often marked TTC *(toutes taxes comprises)*,
which means 'all taxes included'.

It's possible (though rather complicated) to
get a reimbursement for TVA if you meet several conditions: you are not an EU national and
are over 15 years of age; you have stayed in
France less than six months; you are buying

more than €175 worth of goods (not more than 10 of the same item); and the shop offers *vente en détaxe* (duty-free sales).

To claim a TVA, you fill out an *bordereau de vente* (export sales invoice) when you make your purchase, and this is stamped at your port of exit. The shop then reimburses you – by mail or bank transfer within 30 days – for the TVA you've paid. Note that there's no duty-free shopping within the EU.

POST & COMMUNICATIONS
Postal Rates
La Poste, the French postal service, is fast, reliable and expensive. Postcards and letters up to 20g cost €0.46 within the EU, €0.67 to the USA, Canada and the Middle East, and €0.79 to Australasia. Aerograms cost €0.69 to all destinations. Overseas packages are sent by air only, which is expensive.

Receiving Mail Mail to France *must* include the area's five-digit postcode, which begins with the two-digit number of the department. In Paris, all postcodes begin with 750 and end with the arrondissement number, eg, 75004 for the 4th arrondissement, 75013 for the 13th.

Poste restante mail is held alphabetically by family name, so make sure your last name is written in capital letters. If not addressed to a particular branch, poste restante mail ends up at the town's *recette principale* (main post office). In Paris, this means the **central post office** (☎ 01 40 28 20 00; *52 rue du Louvre, 1er; metro Sentier or Les Halles*). There's a €0.46 charge for every poste restante claimed.

You can also receive mail care of AmEx offices, although if you don't have an AmEx card or travellers cheques there's a €0.76 charge each time you check to see if you have received any mail.

Telephone
Public Telephones Almost all public phones now require *télécartes* (phonecards), which are sold at post offices, *tabacs* (tobacco shops), Paris metro ticket counters and supermarket check-out counters. Cards worth 50/120 units cost €7.50/15. Each unit is good for one three-minute local call. To make a call with a phonecard, pick up the receiver, insert the card and dial when the LCD screen reads *'Numérotez'*. All telephone cabins can take incoming calls; give the caller the 10-digit number written after the words *'ici le'* on the information sheet next to the phone.

Domestic Dialling France has five telephone zones and all the telephone numbers comprise 10 digits. Paris and the Île de France numbers begin with 01. The other codes are ☎ 02 for the northwest; ☎ 03 for the north-east; ☎ 04 for the southeast (including Corsica); and ☎ 05 for the southwest.

Numbers beginning with 0800 are free, but others in the series (eg, 0826) generally cost €0.15 per minute. For directory assistance dial ☎ 12.

International Dialling The international country code for France is ☎ 33. When dialling from abroad, omit the initial '0' at the beginning of 10-digit phone numbers.

To place a direct call, dial ☎ 00 and then the country code, area code and local number. Peak rates are about €0.25 per minute to North America and €0.65 per minute to Asia.

To make a reverse-charge (collect) call *(en PCV)* or person-to-person *(avec préavis)* from France to other countries, just call ☎ 3123 or ☎ 0800 990 011 (for the USA and Canada and ☎ 0800 990 061 for Australia. It's about US$10 for a three-minute call.

For directory inquiries outside France dial ☎ 3212. It costs about €2.25. For information on home-country direct calls, see the Telephones Appendix in the back of this book.

Telephone Cards Lonely Planet's ekno Communication Card is aimed specifically at independent travellers and provides budget international calls, a range of messaging services, free email and travel information – for local calls, you're usually better off with a télécarte (see Public Telephones earlier). You can join online at **w** www.ekno.lonelyplanet .com, or by phone from France by dialling ☎ 08 00 90 08 50. To use ekno in France, dial ☎ 08 00 90 91 18.

Minitel This is a computerised information service peculiar to France. Though useful, it can be expensive to use and the Internet has more or less overtaken it. Minitel numbers consist of four digits (eg, 3611, 3614, 3615) and a string of letters. Most of the terminals in post offices are free for directory inquiries.

Fax

Virtually all French post offices can send and receive domestic and international faxes (*télécopies* or *téléfaxes*). It costs around €1.20/1.60 to send a one-page fax within France/to the USA.

Email & Internet Access

Email can be sent and received at Internet cafés throughout France. La Poste has Internet entries at many post offices around France; a €7 Cybercarte gives you an hour's access, and each €4.50 'recharge' is good for another hour. Commercial Internet cafés charge about €3 for 30 minutes of surfing.

DIGITAL RESOURCES

Useful websites in English include the **Paris Tourist Office** (w *www.paris-touristoffice.com*), and the USA's **French Government Tourist Office** (w *www.francetourism.com*). GuideWeb (w *www.guideweb.com*) has detailed information about selected regions in France. Many towns feature their own websites. Gay and lesbian travellers should check the **Queer Resources Directory** (w *www.france.qrd.org*).

BOOKS

Lonely Planet

Lonely Planet's *France* guide has comprehensive coverage of France and includes chapters on Andorra and Monaco. *Paris Condensed* is a pocket companion with short visits in mind. Regional guides include *Provence & the Côte d'Azur, The Loire, Southwest France, Brittany, Normandy* and *Corsica*. The *French phrasebook* is a complete guide to *la langue française*.

Guidebooks

Michelin's hardcover *Guide Rouge* (red guide) lists mid-range and top-end hotels and rates France's greatest restaurants with the famous stars. Michelin's *guides verts* (green guides) cover all of France in 24 regional volumes (12 in English). The finest general French-language guides are by *Guide Bleu*. Its blue-jacketed all-France and its regional guides provide accurate, balanced information on history, culture and architecture.

Travel

Paul Rambali's *French Blues* is a series of uncompromising yet sympathetic snapshots of modern France. *A Year in Provence* by Peter Mayle is an irresistible account of country life in southern France. *A Moveable Feast* by Ernest Hemingway portrays Bohemian life in 1920s Paris. Henry Miller also wrote some pretty dramatic stuff set in the French capital of the 1930s, including *Tropic of Cancer*. Gertrude Stein's *The Autobiography of Alice B Toklas* is an entertaining account of Paris' literary and artistic circles from WWI to the mid-1930s.

History & Politics

There are many excellent histories of France in English. Among the best is Fernand Braudel's two-volume *The Identity of France*. *France Today* by John Ardagh provides excellent insights into the way French society has evolved since WWII. Both are out of print but available in second-hand stores. *The Days of the French Revolution* by Christopher Hibbert is a highly readable account.

NEWSPAPERS & MAGAZINES

The excellent *International Herald Tribune* is sold at many news kiosks throughout France for €1.85. Other English-language papers you can find include the *Guardian* and *USA Today*. *Newsweek* and *Time* are also widely available.

RADIO & TV

The BBC World Service can be picked up on 195kHz AM as well as 6195kHz, 9410kHz, 9760kHz and 12095kHz short wave. In northern France, BBC for Europe is on 648kHz AM. Top-end hotels often offer cable TV access to CNN, BBC Prime, Sky and other networks. Canal+ (pronounced ka-**nahl**-pluce), a French subscription TV station available in many mid-range hotels, sometimes shows undubbed English movies.

PHOTOGRAPHY & VIDEO

Be prepared to have your camera and film forced through the ostensibly film-safe x-ray machines at airports and when entering sensitive public buildings. Ask to have your film hand-checked, if not your entire camera. Film is widely available, and costs about €5.50/7 for a 36-exposure roll of 100ASA print/slide film, excluding processing.

Note that French videotapes use the Secam system, therefore they cannot be played on many British, Australian or American video cassette recorders.

FRANCE

TIME

France is GMT/UTC plus one hour. Clocks are turned one hour ahead on the last Sunday in March and back again on the last Sunday in September.

LAUNDRY

Self-service *laveries libre service* (laundrettes) generally charge €3.35 to €5 a load and around €0.30 for five minutes of drying. Bring lots of coins as few laundrettes have change machines.

TOILETS

Public toilets are scarce, though small towns often have one near the *mairie* (town hall). In Paris, you're more likely to come upon one of the tan, self-disinfecting toilet pods. Many public toilets cost €0.30 or even €0.50. Except in the most tourist-filled areas, café owners usually allow you to use their toilets provided you ask politely.

WOMEN TRAVELLERS

In general, women need not walk around in fear, although the French seem to have given little thought to sexual harassment – many men tend to stare hard at passing women, for instance. If you're subject to catcalls or hassled on the street, the best strategy is usually to walk on and ignore the comment. Making a cutting retort is ineffective in English and risky in French if your slang isn't proficient.

France's national rape crisis hotline, run by women's organisation **Viols Femmes Informations** (☎ *0800 05 95 95; staffed 10am-7pm Mon-Fri*), can be reached toll free.

GAY & LESBIAN TRAVELLERS

Centre Gai et Lesbien (*CGL; ☎ 01 43 57 21 47; 3 rue Keller, 11e; metro Ledru Rollin; open 4pm-8pm daily*), 500m east of place de la Bastille, is headquarters for numerous organisations. It has a bar, and library among its facilities. Paris' Gay Pride parade is held on the last weekend in June. Gay publications include the monthlies *3 Keller*, *Action* and the newsstand magazine *Têtu*. The monthly *Lesbia* gives a rundown of what's happening around the country.

DISABLED TRAVELLERS

France isn't well-equipped for *handicapés* – kerb ramps are few and far between, older public facilities and budget hotels often lack lifts, and the Paris metro is hopeless. Details of train travel for wheelchair users are available in SNCF's booklet *Guide du Voyageur à Mobilité Réduite*. You can also contact the French rail company **SNCF Accessibilité** (☎ *0800 15 47 53*).

Hostels in Paris that cater to disabled travellers include the Foyer International d'Accueil de Paris Jean Monnet and Centre International de Séjour de Paris Kellermann (see Hostels in the Paris Places to Stay section later).

SENIOR TRAVELLERS

Senior travellers are generally treated with a great deal of respect in France and are entitled to discounts on public transport, museum admission fees and so on, provided they show proof of age. If you're doing a lot of travel, the SNCF's Carte Senior, entitling the holder to further reductions on train travel, may be a good deal.

DANGERS & ANNOYANCES

The biggest crime problem for tourists in France is theft – especially of and from cars. Pickpockets are a problem, and women are a common target because of their handbags. Be especially careful at airports and on crowded public transport in cities.

France's laws regarding even small quantities of drugs are very strict, and the police have the right to search anyone at any time.

The rise in support for the extreme right wing Front National in recent years reflects growing racial intolerance in France. Especially in the south, entertainment places such as bars and discos are, for all intents and purposes, segregated.

BUSINESS HOURS

Most museums are closed on either Monday or Tuesday and on public holidays, though in summer some open daily. Most small businesses open 9am or 10am to 6.30pm or 7pm daily except Sunday and perhaps Monday with a break between noon and 2pm or between 1pm and 3pm. In the south, middle-of-the-day closures are more like siestas and may continue until 3.30pm or 4pm.

Emergency Services

Nationwide emergency numbers are ambulance ☎ 15, fire ☎ 18, and police ☎ 17.

Many food shops open daily except Sunday afternoon and Monday. Most restaurants open only for lunch (noon to 2pm or 3pm) and dinner (6.30pm to about 10pm or 11pm); outside Paris, very few serve meals throughout the day. In August, lots of establishments simply close down for the annual month-long holiday.

Banks open Monday to Friday but may only change money and travellers cheques in the morning (usually 8.45am to 12.15pm).

PUBLIC HOLIDAYS & SPECIAL EVENTS

National *jours fériés* (public holidays) in France include New Year's Day, Easter Sunday and Monday, 1 May (May Day), 8 May (1945 Victory Day), Ascension Thursday, Pentecost/Whit Sunday and Whit Monday, 14 July (Bastille Day), 15 August (Assumption Day), 1 November (All Saints' Day), 11 November (1918 Armistice Day) and Christmas Day.

Some of the biggest and best events in France include: the Festival d'Avignon (early July to early August), with some 300 daily music, dance and drama events; Bastille Day celebrations, on 13 and 14 July; Francofolies, a six-day dance and music festival held in mid-July in La Rochelle, with performers from all over the French-speaking world; the Festival Interceltique, a 10-day Celtic festival in early August held in the Breton town of Lorient; Lyon's Biennale de la Danse/d'Art Contemporain, a month-long festival (from mid-September) that's held in even-numbered years (in odd-numbered years the city holds a festival of contemporary art); the Carnaval de Nice, held in Nice every spring around Mardi Gras (Shrove Tuesday); and the Nice Jazz Festival in July.

ACTIVITIES

The French Alps have some of the finest (and priciest) **skiing** in Europe, however, there are cheaper, low-altitude ski stations in the Pyrenees; w www.skifrance.fr provides information in English about ski resorts, services, conditions and more.

France has thousands of kilometres of **hiking** trails in every region of the country. These include *sentiers de grande randonnée*, long-distance hiking paths with alphanumeric names that begin with the letters GR and are sometimes hundreds of kilometres long (as in Corsica). These paths are run by an organisation called **Fédération Française de Randonnée**

Pédestre *(FFRP;* ☎ *01 44 89 93 93, fax 01 40 35 85 67;* e *info@ffrp.asso.fr)*, which also publishes guides to these routes.

The **Fédération Française de Canoë-Kayak** *(*☎ *01 45 11 08 50;* e *ffck@ffcanoe .asso.fr; 87 quai de la Marne, 94344 Joinville-le-Pont)* can supply information on **canoeing** and **kayaking** clubs around the country. The sports are very popular in the Dordogne (Périgord) area.

The French take their **cycling** very seriously, and parts of the country almost grind to a halt during the annual Tour de France. Lonely Planet's *Cycling in France* is an essential resource when touring. *France by Bike: 14 Tours Geared for Discovery* by Karen and Terry Whitehall is a worthy rival. Some of the best areas for cycling are around the Alpine resorts of Annecy (see The French Alps section later for details) and Chambery. The Loire Valley and the coastal regions such as Brittany, Normandy and the Atlantic Coast offer a wealth of easier options.

Details on places that rent bikes appear at the end of individual city or town listings under Getting Around.

COURSES

For details see Language Courses in the Paris section later. Information on studying in France is available from French consulates and French Government Tourist Offices abroad. In Paris, you might also get in touch with the Ministry of Tourism-sponsored **International Cultural Organisation** *(ICO;* ☎ *01 42 36 47 18, fax 01 40 26 34 45; 55 rue de Rivoli, 1er, BP 2701, 75027 Paris CEDEX; metro Châtelet).*

WORK

All EU citizens are allowed to work in France. For anyone else it's almost impossible, though the government tolerates undocumented workers helping out with agricultural work.

Working as an au pair is very common in France, especially in Paris. Single young people – particularly women – receive board, lodging and a bit of money in exchange for taking care of the kids. Knowing some French may be a prerequisite. For au pair placements contact a French consulate or private agencies such as **Agence Nurse Au Pair Placement** *(NAPP;* ☎ *01 45 00 33 88, fax 01 45 00 33 99;* w *www.napp.fr; 16 rue Le Sueur, Paris 75016).*

FRANCE

ACCOMMODATION
Camping
France has thousands of seasonal and year-round camping grounds. Facilities and amenities, reflected in the number of stars the site has been awarded, determine the price. At the less fancy places, two people with a small tent pay €10 to €15 a night. Campers without a vehicle can usually get a spot, even late in the day, but not in July and August, when most are packed with families.

Refuges & Gîtes d'Étape
Refuges (mountain huts or shelters) are basic dorms operated by national park authorities, the Club Alpin Français and other private organisations. They are marked on hiking and climbing maps. Some open year-round.

In general, refuges have mattresses and blankets but not sheets. Charges average €10 to €16 per night (more in popular areas), and meals are sometimes available. It's a good idea to call ahead and make a reservation.

Gîtes d'étape, which are usually better equipped and more comfortable than refuges, are found in less-remote areas, often in villages. They cost around €9 to €11 per person.

Chambre d'Hôtes
A chambre d'hôte, basically a B&B, is a room in a private house rented to travellers by the night. Breakfast is included.

Hostels
In the provinces, *Auberges de Jeunesse* (hostels) generally charge €9 to €12 for a bunk in a single-sex dorm. In Paris and the Côte d'Azur, expect to pay €15 to €20 a night, including breakfast. In the cities, especially Paris, you'll also find *foyers*, student dorms used by travellers during summer. Most of France's hostels belong to one of three Paris-based organisations:

Fédération Unie des Auberges de Jeunesse
(FUAJ; ☎ 01 44 89 87 27, fax 01 44 89 87 10, ⓦ www.fuaj.org) 27 rue Pajol, 18e, 75018 Paris (metro La Chapelle)

Ligue Française pour les Auberges de la Jeunesse
(LFAJ; ☎ 01 44 16 78 78, fax 01 44 16 78 80) 67 rue Vergniaud, 75013 Paris (metro Glacière)

Union des Centres de Rencontres Internationales de France (UCRIF; ☎ 01 40 26 57 64, fax 01 40 26 58 20, ⓦ www.ucrif.asso.fr) 27 rue de Turbigo, 2e, 75002 Paris (metro Étienne Marcel)

Only FUAJ is affiliated with the Hostelling International (HI) organisation.

Hotels
For two people sharing a room, budget hotels are often cheaper than hostels. Doubles tend to cost only marginally more than singles; most have only one bed *(un grand lit)*. Doubles with two beds usually cost a little more. A half *douche* (shower) can be free or cost between €2 and €3. If you'll be arriving after noon (after 10am at peak times), it's wise to book ahead, though if you phone on the day of your arrival, many will hold a room for you until a set hour. Local tourist offices also make reservations, usually for a small fee. Check whether your hotel is part of the Bon Weekend en Ville scheme whereby one night's stay at the weekend gives you a second night free.

The prices listed in this chapter are high season prices (usually June to August, except in ski areas); discounts of 30% to 50% are possible at other times of year.

FOOD
A fully fledged traditional French dinner – usually begun about 8.30pm – has quite a few distinct courses: an apéritif or cocktail; an *entrée* (first course); the *plat principal* (main course); *salade* (salad); *fromage* (cheese); *dessert*; *fruit* (fruit; pronounced fwee); *café* (coffee); and a *digestif* liqueur.

Restaurants usually specialise in a particular cuisine while brasseries – which look very much like cafés – serve quicker meals of more standard fare (eg, steak and chips/french fries or omelettes). Restaurants tend to open only for lunch (noon to 2pm or 3pm) and dinner (6.30pm to about 10pm or 11pm); brasseries serve meals throughout the day.

Most restaurants offer at least one fixed-price multicourse meal known in French as a *menu*. In general, *menus* cost much less than ordering each dish *à la carte* (separately). Many restaurants close on Sunday (some on Monday too) and it can be genuinely hard to find a place to eat on a Sunday in a provincial French town.

Sitting in a café to read, write or talk with friends is an integral part of everyday life in France. A café located on a grand boulevard will charge considerably more than a place that fronts a side street. Once inside, progressively more expensive tariffs apply at the *comptoir* (counter), in the café itself *(salle)* nd outside on the *terrasse*. The price of drinks goes up at night, usually after 8pm.

DRINKS
Nonalcoholic Drinks

Tap water in France is perfectly safe. Make sure you ask for *une carafe d'eau* (a jug of water) or *de l'eau du robinet* (tap water) or you may get costly *eau de source* (mineral water). A small cup of espresso is called *un café*, *un café noir* or *un express*; you can also ask for a *grand* (large) one. *Un café crème* is espresso with steamed cream. *Un café au lait* is espresso served in a large cup with lots of steamed milk. Decaffeinated coffee is *un café décaféiné* or simply *un déca*.

Other popular hot drinks include *thé* (tea) and if you want milk you ask for *'un peu de lait frais'*; *tisane* (herbal tea); and *chocolat chaud* (hot chocolate).

Alcoholic Drinks

The French almost always take their meals with wine – *rouge* (red), *blanc* (white) or *rosé*. The least-expensive wines cost less per litre than soft drinks. The cheapest wines are known as either *vins ordinaires* or *vins de table* (table wines).

Alcoholic drinks other than wine include apéritifs, such as *kir* (dry white wine sweetened with *cassis* – blackcurrant liqueur), *kir royale* (champagne with cassis), and *pastis* (anise-flavoured alcohol drunk with ice and water); and *digestifs* such as brandy or Calvados (apple brandy). A *demi* of beer (about 250ml) is cheaper *à la pression* (on draught) than from a bottle.

Getting There & Away

AIR

Air France and scores of other airlines link Paris with every part of the globe. Other French cities with international air links (mainly to places within Europe) include Bordeaux, Lyon, Marseille, Nice, Strasbourg and Toulouse. For information on Paris' two international airports, Orly and Roissy-Charles de Gaulle, see Getting There & Away in the Paris section later.

The Internet is the place to find cheap seats on discount airlines – flights between London and Paris are sometimes available for as little as €25 return. Regular tickets with the larger companies are more like €120. One-way discount fares to Paris start at €110 from Rome, €160 from Athens, €140 from Dublin, 220 million Turkish lira from Istanbul, and €110 from Madrid. Student travel agencies can supply details.

In France, inexpensive flights offered by discount airlines and charter clearing houses can be booked through many regular travel agencies – look in agency windows and pamphlets advertising **Go Voyages** (☎ *01 53 40 44 29;* w *www.govoyages.com)* or **Look Voyages** (☎ *01 55 49 49 60, 0825 82 38 23;* w *www.look-voyages.fr)*.

Some reliable travel agency chains include French student travel company **OTU** (☎ *0820 81 78 17;* w *www.otu.fr)* and **Nouvelles Frontières** (☎ *0825 00 08 25;* w *www.nouvelles -frontieres.fr)*.

LAND
Britain

The highly civilised **Eurostar** (*UK:* ☎ *08705 186 186* • *France:* ☎ *0892 35 35 39;* w *www .eurostar.com)* links London's Waterloo Station with Paris' Gare du Nord via the Channel Tunnel, which passes through a layer of impermeable chalk marl 25m to 45m below the floor of the English Channel. The journey takes about three hours (including 20 minutes in the tunnel), not including the one-hour time change. Tickets for people aged 25 and under cost UK£40/69 one way/return; return fares booked 14/seven days ahead cost UK£79/95.

Discount return fares start around UK£60. Student travel agencies often have youth fares not available direct from Eurostar.

Eurotunnel shuttle trains (*UK:* ☎ *08705 35 35 35* • *France:* ☎ *03 21 00 61 00;* w *www .eurotunnel.com)* whisk buses and cars (and their passengers) from near Folkstone to Coquelles (west of Calais) in 35 minutes. Regular one-way fares for a car and its passengers range from UK£147.50 (February and March) to UK£162.50 (July and August). Book at least a day ahead for promotional fares.

Elsewhere in Europe

Bus For details on **Eurolines coach services** (*France:* ☎ *0836 69 52 52;* w *www.euro lines.fr)* linking France with other European countries, see Getting There & Away in the Paris section later in this chapter.

Train Paris, France's main rail hub, is linked with every part of Europe. Depending on where you're coming from, you sometimes have to change train stations in Paris to reach the provinces. For details on Paris' six train stations, see Getting There & Away in the Paris section later.

People aged 25 or under are eligible for at least 20% discounts on most international 2nd-class rail travel; on some routes discounts are limited to night trains. On the super-fast *Thalys* trains that link Paris with Brussels, Amsterdam and Cologne, seniors also get significant discounts.

SEA

Ferry tickets are available from almost all travel agencies.

Britain & the Channel Islands

Hoverspeed (*UK:* ☎ 0870 240 8070 • *France:* ☎ 0800 1211 1211; ⓦ *www.hoverspeed.co .uk*) operates giant catamarans (SeaCats) from Folkestone to Boulogne (55 minutes, 17 daily). Foot passengers are charged UK£24 one way (or return if you come back within five days). Depending on the season, a car with up to five passengers is charged UK£115 to UK£189 one way.

The Dover-Calais crossing is also handled by some car ferries (one to 1½ hours, 15 daily) run by **SeaFrance** (*UK:* ☎ 0870-571 1711 • *France:* ☎ 0803 04 40 45; ⓦ *www.seafrance .com*) and **P&O Stena** (*UK:* ☎ 0870-600 0611 • *France:* ☎ 0802 01 00 20; ⓦ *www.posl .com*). Pedestrians pay UK£17/26 with SeaFrance/P&O Stena; cars are charged UK£130 to UK£170 one way.

If you're travelling to Normandy, the Newhaven–Dieppe route is handled by Hoverspeed's SeaCats (2¼ hours, one to three daily). Poole is linked to Cherbourg by **Brittany Ferries** (*UK:* ☎ 0870-536 0360 • *France:* ☎ 0825 82 88 28; ⓦ *www.brittany-ferries.com*), which has one or two 4¼-hour crossings daily; it also has ferries from Portsmouth to Caen (Ouistreham). On the Portsmouth–Cherbourg route, **P&O Portsmouth** (*UK:* ☎ 0870-598 0555 • *France:* ☎ 0803 01 30 13; ⓦ *www.po portsmouth.com*) has two car ferries daily and, from mid-March to mid-October (UK£117 with car), two faster catamarans daily; the company also links Portsmouth with Le Havre.

If you're going to Brittany, Brittany Ferries links Plymouth with Roscoff (six hours, one

to three daily) from mid-March through mid-November; the company also has services from Portsmouth to Saint Malo (8¾ hours). For information on ferries from Saint Malo to Weymouth, Portsmouth and the Channel Islands, see Getting There & Away in the Saint Malo (Brittany) section later.

Ireland

Irish Ferries (*Ireland:* ☎ 1890 31 31 31 • *Cherbourg, France:* ☎ 02 33 23 44 44; ⓦ *www .irishferries.com*) operates overnight runs from Rosslare to either Cherbourg (19½ hours) or Roscoff (17 hours) between six and 13 times a month. Pedestrians pay €60 to €120 (€48 to €96 for students and seniors). Eurailpass holders are charged 50% of the adult pedestrian fare.

Italy

For information on ferry services between Corsica and Italy, see Getting There & Away in the Corsica section.

North Africa

France's **SNCM** (☎ 0836 67 21 00; ⓦ *www .sncm.fr*) and the **Compagnie Tunisienne de Navigation** (*CTN; Tunis:* ☎ 01-341 777 • *Marseille:* ☎ 04 91 91 55 71) link Marseille with Tunis (about 24 hours, three or four a week). The standard adult fare is TD196/356 one way/return.

Sète, 29km southwest of Montpellier, is linked with the Moroccan port of Tangier (Tanger; 36 hours, five to seven a month) by the **Compagnie Marocaine de Navigation** (*Marseille:* ☎ 04 91 56 40 88 • *Tangier:* ☎ 09-94 40 57; ⓦ *www.comanav.co.ma*). The cheapest one-way berth costs Dh1940. Discounts are available if you're under 26 or in a group of four or more.

Getting Around

AIR

France's long-protected domestic airline industry has been opened up to competition, though Air France still handles the majority of domestic flights.

Full-fare flying within France is extremely expensive, but very significant discounts are available to people aged 12 to 24, couples, families and seniors. Some heavily discounted flights may be cheaper than long-distance rail

FRANCE

travel. Details on the complicated fare structures are available from travel agencies.

BUS

Because the French train network is state-owned and the government prefers to operate a monopoly, the country has only very limited intercity bus service. However, buses (some run by the SNCF, see the following Train section) are widely used for short distances, especially in rural areas with relatively few train lines (eg, Brittany and Normandy).

TRAIN

Eurail and Inter-Rail passes are valid in France.

France's excellent rail network, operated by the **Société Nationale des Chemins de Fer Français** (SNCF; [w] www.sncf.com) reaches almost every part of the country. The most important train lines fan out from Paris like the spokes of a wheel. The SNCF's nationwide telephone number for inquiries and reservations (☎ 0836 35 35 39 in English) costs €0.34 per minute.

The pride and joy of the SNCF is the high-speed TGV ('teh-zheh-veh') network. The TGV Sud-Est and TGV Midi-Mediterranée link Paris' Gare de Lyon with the southeast, including Dijon, Lyon, the Alps, Avignon, Marseille, Nice and Montpellier; the TGV Atlantique Sud-Ouest and TGV Atlantique Ouest link Paris' Gare Montparnasse with western and southwestern France, including Brittany, Tours, La Rochelle, Bordeaux, Biarritz and Toulouse; and the TGV Nord links Paris' Gare du Nord with Arras, Lille and Calais.

Reservation fees are optional unless you're travelling by TGV or want a couchette or special reclining seat. On popular trains (eg, on holiday weekends) you may have to reserve ahead to get a seat. Eurail-pass holders must pay all applicable reservation fees.

Before boarding the train, you must validate your ticket (and your reservation card, if it's separate) by time-stamping it in one of the *composteurs*, the bright orange posts that are located somewhere between the ticket windows and the tracks. Eurail and some other rail passes *must* be validated at a train station ticket window to initiate the period of validity.

Discounts
Passes for Nonresidents of Europe The
France Railpass allows unlimited rail travel within France for to 10 days during the course

of a month. In 2nd class, the three-day version costs US$210 (US$171 each for two people travelling together); each additional day of travel costs US$30. The France Youthpass, available if you're 25 and under, costs US$148 for four days of travel in a month; additional days (up to a maximum of six) cost US$18. **Rail Europe** (USA: ☎ 877-456-RAIL; [w] www .raileurope.com) has details.

Passes for Residents of Europe The Euro Domino France flexipass gives European residents who don't live in France three to eight days of midnight-to-midnight travel over a period of one month.

The youth version (for people 25 and under) costs €84 for three days plus about €15 each additional day; the adult version costs €115 for three days plus about €20 for each additional day.

Other Discounts Discounts of 25% on one-way or return travel within France are available at all train station ticket windows to: people aged 12 to 25 (the Découverte 12/25 fare); one to four adults travelling with a child aged four to 11 (the Découverte Enfant Plus fare); people over 60 (the Découverte Senior fare); and – for return travel only – any two people who are travelling together (the Découverte À Deux fare).

No matter what age you are, the Découverte Séjour excursion fare gives you a 25% reduction for return travel within France if you meet two conditions: the total length of your trip is at least 200km; and you'll be spending a Saturday night at your destination.

The Découverte J30, which must be purchased 30 to 60 days before the date of travel, offers savings of 45% to 55%.

The Découverte J8, which you must purchase at least eight days ahead, gets you 20% to 30% off.

CAR & MOTORCYCLE
Travelling by car or motorcycle is expensive; petrol is costly and tolls add up quickly if you're going cross-country in a hurry. Three or four people travelling together, however, may find that renting a car is cheaper than taking the train.

In the centres of almost all French cities, parking is metered.

Unless otherwise posted, speed limits are 130km/h (110km/h in the rain) on *autoroutes* (dual carriageways/divided highways with names beginning with A); 110km/h (100km/h in the rain) on *routes nationales* (highways with names beginning with N) that have a divider down the middle; and 90km/h (80km/h if it's raining) on nondivided routes nationales and rural highways. When you pass a sign with a place name, you have entered the boundaries of a town or village; the speed limit automatically drops to 50km/h and stays there until you pass an identical sign with a red bar across it.

The maximum permissible blood-alcohol level in France is 0.05%.

Petrol *sans plomb* (unleaded) costs around €1.10 a litre, give or take 10%. *Gasoil* or *gazole* (diesel) is about €0.75 to €1 a litre. Fuel is most expensive at the autoroute rest stops, and tends to be cheapest at the big supermarkets on the outskirts of towns.

If you don't live in the EU and need a car in France (or Europe) for 17 days (or a bit more) to six months, it's *much* cheaper to 'purchase' one from the manufacturer and then 'sell' it back than it is to rent one. The *achat-rachat* (purchase-repurchase) paperwork is not your responsibility.

Both Renault's **Eurodrive** *(USA: ☎ 800-221-1052; w www.eurodrive.renault.com)* and Peugeot's **Vacation Plan/Sodexa** *(USA: ☎ 212-581-3040; w www.sodexa.com)* can give you really good deals that (quite surprisingly) include insurance with no deductible (excess).

HITCHING

Hitching in France can be difficult, and getting out of big cities like Paris, Lyon and Marseille or travelling around the Côte d'Azur by thumb is well nigh impossible.

Remote rural areas are your best bet, but few cars are likely to be going farther than the next large town. Women should never hitch alone.

It's an excellent idea to hold up a sign with your destination followed by the letters *s.v.p.* (for *s'il vous plaît* – 'please'). Some people have reported good luck hitching with truck drivers from truck stops. It's illegal to hitch on autoroutes, but you can stand near the entrance ramps.

FUAJ, the French youth hostel association, has a car-pooling registry that matches drivers and passengers for car journeys within Europe. Check it out at w www.fuaj.org.

Paris

pop 2.2 million
metropolitan area 10.6 million

Paris has almost exhausted the superlatives that can reasonably be applied to a city. Notre Dame and the Eiffel Tower – at sunrise, at sunset, at night – have been described ad nauseam, as have the Seine and the subtle (and not-so-subtle) differences between the Left and Right banks. But what writers rarely capture is the grandness and the magic of strolling along the city's broad, 19th-century avenues leading from impressive public buildings and exceptional museums to parks, gardens and esplanades. Paris is enchanting at any time, in every season.

ORIENTATION

In central Paris (which the French call Intra-Muros – 'within the walls'), the Rive Droite (Right Bank) is north of the Seine, while the Rive Gauche (Left Bank) is south of the river. For administrative purposes, Paris is divided into 20 *arrondissements* (districts) that spiral out from the centre. Paris addresses always include the arrondissement number, listed here after the street address, using the usual French notation, ie, 1er stands for *premier* (1st), 19e for *dix-neuvième* (19th) etc. When an address includes the full five-digit postal code, then the last two digits indicate the arrondissement, eg, 75014 for the 14e.

Maps

Lonely Planet's *Paris City Map* includes central Paris, the Métro, Montmartre, a walking tour and an index of all streets and sights.

INFORMATION
Tourist Offices

Paris' **main tourist office** *(☎ 0836 68 31 12, fax 01 49 52 53 00; e info@paris-touristof fice.com; 127 ave des Champs-Élysées, 8e; metro Georges V; open 9am-8pm daily, 11am-7pm Sun winter ● branches: Gare de Lyon; open 8am-8pm Mon-Sat ● base of Eiffel Tower; open 11am-6pm daily May-Sept)* is the best source of information on what's going on in the city.

For a small fee (€3 for a one-star hotel), the office can find you accommodation in Paris for that night only.

Money

All of Paris' six major train stations have exchange bureaus open seven days a week until at least 7pm. Exchange offices at both airports are open until 10.30pm.

Champs-Élysées (8e) Thanks to fierce competition, the Champs-Élysées is an excellent place to change money. There's a bureau de change inside the tourist office at 127 ave des Champs-Élysées and a Thomas Cook branch next door.

Grands Boulevards (9e) FCO (☎ 01 47 70 02 59, 19 rue du Faubourg Montmartre, metro Grands Blvds) tends to have decent rates and is open 8.30am to 7pm daily.

Notre Dame (4e & 5e) Société Française de Change (☎ 01 43 26 01 84, 21 rue Chanoinesse, metro Cité) has good rates and is open 8.30am to 7pm daily.

Opéra Garnier (9e) Paris' landmark AmEx office (☎ 01 47 77 77 75, metro Auber or Opéra) at 11 rue Scribe, faces the west side of Opéra Garnier. Exchange services are available 9.30am to 6.30pm (to 7pm June to September) Monday to Friday and 9am to 5.30pm Saturday and Sunday.

Post & Communications

Paris' **main post office** (☎ 01 40 28 76 00; 52 rue du Louvre, 1er; metro Sentier or Les Halles; open 24hr) has foreign exchange available during regular post office hours – 8am to 7pm Monday to Friday and to noon on Saturday.

Email & Internet Access

The cheapest Internet cafés are **EasyInternet** (31-37 blvd de Sébastopol, 2e; metro Châtelet-Les Halles • 6 rue de la Harpe, 6e; metro St Michel • 15 rue de Rome, 8e; metro St-Lazare; all open 24hr daily) where you can get a 24-hour Internet access pass for €5. More pleasant, but more expensive is the cool **Web Bar** (☎ 01 42 72 66 55; 32 rue de Picardie, 3e; metro Temple or Républic; open 8.30am-2am daily), which charges €4 for one hour of Internet access.

Also try **Mike's Bike Tours** (24 rue Edgar Faure, 15e) with its English keyboards and a tourist-friendly atmosphere.

Travel Agencies

Nouvelles Frontières (☎ 0825 000 825; 66 blvd St Michel, 6e; metro Luxembourg; open 9am-7pm Mon-Sat) has 15 outlets around the city. **Voyageurs du Monde** (☎ 01 42 86 16 00; 55 rue Ste Anne, 2e; metro Pyramides or Quartre Septembre; open 9.30am-7pm Mon-Sat) is a huge agency.

Bookshops

Famous English-language bookshop **Shakespeare & Company** (☎ 01 43 26 96 50; 37 rue de la Bûcherie, 5e; metro St Michel) is across the Seine from Notre Dame Cathedral.

WH Smith (☎ 01 44 77 88 99; 248 rue de Rivoli; metro Concorde) is the largest English-language bookshop in the city. The mellow, Canadian-run **Abbey Bookshop** (☎ 01 46 33 16 24; 29 rue de la Parcheminerie, 5e; metro Cluny-La Sorbonne) has an eclectic selection of new and used fiction titles. **Les Mots à la Bouche** (☎ 01 42 78 88 30; 6 rue Ste Croix de la Bretonnerie, 4e; metro Hôtel de Ville) is Paris' premier gay bookshop.

Cultural & Religious Centres

The **British Council** (☎ 01 49 55 73 00; 9 rue de Constantine, 7e; metro Invalides) has a library. The **American Church** (☎ 01 40 62 05 00; 65 quai d'Orsay, 7e; metro Invalides) is a place of worship and a community centre for English speakers; its announcement board is an excellent source of information regarding accommodation and employment.

Laundry

The laveries (laundrettes) mentioned here open daily and are near many of the places to stay listed later. **Laverie Libre Service** (7 rue Jean-Jacques Rousseau; metro Louvre Rivoli) is near the BVJ hostel, or there's another **branch** (25 rue des Rosiers; metro St Paul) in the Marais. There's also another **branch** (4 rue Burq, Montmartre; metro Blanche). There's another **laundrette** (216 rue St Jacques; metro Luxembourg) four blocks southwest of the Panthéon. **Lavomatique** (63 rue Monge; metro Monge) is another option. Near Gare de l'Est is the **Lav' Club** (55 blvd de Magenta; metro Gare de l'Est).

Lost Property

Paris' **Bureau des Objets Trouvés** (Lost & Found Office; ☎ 01 55 76 20 20; 36 rue des Morillons, 15e; metro Convention; open 8.30am-5pm Mon, Wed & Fri, 8.30am-8pm Tues & Thur) is the first place to contact. Since telephone inquiries are impossible, the only way to find out if a lost item has been located is to go there and fill in the forms. For items lost on the metro, call ☎ 01 40 30 52 00.

FRANCE

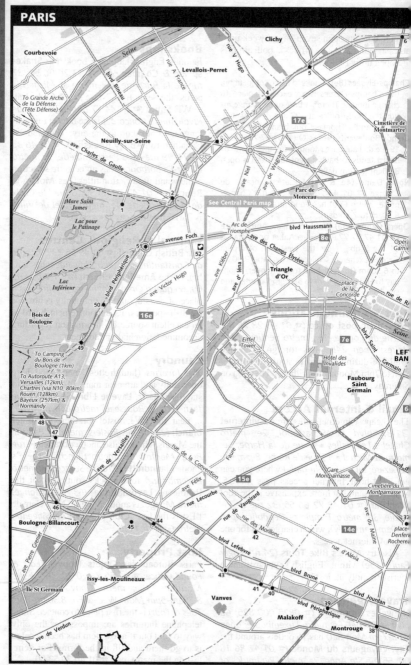

PARIS

Courbevoie

Clichy

Levallois-Perret

Seine

rue V. Hugo

rue A. France

blvd Bineau

To Grande Arche
de la Défense
(Tête Défense)

ave Charles de Gaulle

Neuilly-sur-Seine

Cimetière de
Montmartre

17e

ave Niel

ave de Wagram

rue d'Amsterdam

Parc de
Monceau

Mare Saint
James

1

Lac pour
le Patinage

See Central Paris map

Arc de
Triomphe

blvd Haussmann

Opéra
Garnier

8e

2

51

avenue Foch

52

ave Kléber

ave des Champs Elysées

ave d' Iéna

Triangle
d'Or

place
de la
Concorde

rue de Ri

Lac
Inférieur

ave Victor Hugo

16e

Lou

Seine

50

Eiffel
Tower

blvd Saint

LEF
BAN

Bois de
Boulogne

7e

Germain

Hôtel des
Invalides

6

To Camping
du Bois de
Boulogne (1km)

49

Faubourg
Saint
Germain

To Autoroute A13,
Versailles (12km),
Chartres (via N10, 80km),
Rouen (128km),
Bayeux (257km) &
Normandy

Seine

48

47

ave de Versailles

rue de la Convention

Faure

Gare
Montparnasse

Cimetière du
Montparnasse

15e

ave Félix

rue Lecourbe

rue de Vaugirard

ave du Maine

46

37

Boulogne-Billancourt

44

rue des Morillons

14e

place
Denfert
Rochera

45

42

rue d'Alésia

ave Pierre Grenier

blvd Lefebvre

43

blvd Brune

Île St Germain

Issy-les-Moulineaux

41

40

blvd Jourdan

Vanves

blvd Périphérique

39

38

ave de Verdun

Malakoff

Montrouge

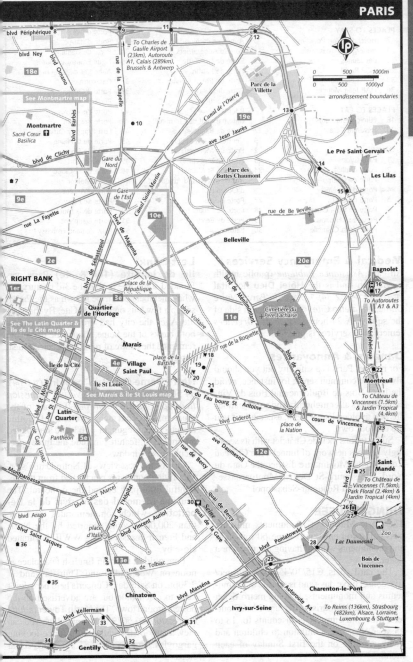

FRANCE

PARIS

PLACES TO STAY	10	Fédération Unie des	31	Porte d'Ivry
7 Hôtel des Trois Poussins		Auberges de Jeunesse	32	Porte d'Italie
21 Auberge Internationale	11	Porte d'Aubervilliers	34	Porte de Gentilly
des Jeunes	12	Porte de la Villette	35	Ligue Française pour les
25 CISP Ravel	13	Porte de Pantin		Auberges de la Jeunesse
33 CISP Kellermann	14	Porte du Pré St Gervais	37	Catacombes
36 FIAP Jean Monnet	15	Porte des Lilas	38	Porte d'Orléans
	16	Gare Routière	39	Porte de Châtillon
PLACES TO EAT		Internationale	40	Porte de Vanves
18 Ethnic Restaurants		(International Bus Terminal)	41	Porte Brancion
20 Havanita Café	17	Porte de Bagnolet	42	Lost Property Office
	19	Centre Gai et Lesbien	43	Porte de la Plaine
OTHER	22	Porte de Montreuil	44	Porte de Sèvres
1 Paris Cycles	23	Porte de Vincennes	45	Paris Heliport
2 Porte Maillot	24	Porte de St Mandé	46	Porte de St Cloud
3 Porte de Champerret	26	Musée des Arts d'Afrique et	47	Porte Molitor
4 Porte d'Asnières		d'Océanie	48	Porte d'Auteuil
5 Porte de Clichy	27	Porte Dorée	49	Porte de Passy
6 Porte de Saint Ouen	28	Porte de Charenton	50	Porte de la Muette
8 Porte de Clignancourt	29	Porte de Bercy	51	Porte Dauphine
9 Porte de la Chapelle	30	Batofar	52	New Zealand Embassy

Medical & Emergency Services

An easy *Assistance Publique* (public health service) to find is the **Hôtel Dieu hospital** (☎ *01 42 34 82 34; 1 place du Parvis Notre Dame, 4e; metro Cité*) on the northern side of the square. A 24-hour *service des urgences* (emergency service) is provided.

Dangers & Annoyances

For its size, Paris is a safe city but you should always use common sense; for instance, avoid the large Bois de Boulogne and Bois de Vincennes parks after nightfall. And some stations are best avoided late at night, especially if you are on your own.

Such stations include Châtelet with its seemingly endless network of tunnels, the Château Rouge in the Montmartre district, the Gare du Nord, Strasbourg-St Denis, Montparnasse-Bienvenüe and Réaumur-Sébastopol.

THINGS TO SEE

The Carte Musées et Monuments museum pass gains you entry into some 60 museums and monuments without having to queue for a ticket.

The card costs €15/30/45 for one/three/five consecutive days and is on sale at the museums and monuments, at some metro ticket windows, at the tourist office and FNAC outlets. Most museums offer discounts for 18 to 25 year olds, free admission to children and many are free on the first Sunday of each month.

Left Bank

Île de la Cité (1er & 4e) Paris was founded sometime during the 3rd century BC when members of a tribe known as the Parisii set up a few huts on Île de la Cité. By the Middle Ages the city had grown to encompass both banks of the Seine, though Île de la Cité remained the centre of royal and ecclesiastical power.

Notre Dame (4e) Paris' cathedral (☎ *01 42 34 56 10; metro Cité or St Michel; admission free; open 8am-6.45pm daily*) is one of the most magnificent achievements of Gothic architecture. Begun in 1163 and completed around 1345, features include the three spectacular rose windows.

One of the best views of Notre Dame's ornate flying buttresses can be had from the delightful little park behind the cathedral. The haunting **Mémorial des Martyrs de la Déportation**, which commemorates the more than 200,000 people deported by the Nazis and French fascists during WWII, is situated close by.

Free **guided tours** in English take place at noon on Wednesday and Thursday and at 2.30pm on Saturday. Concerts held here don't keep to a schedule but are advertised on the posters around town. The **North Tower** (*adult/concession €5.50/3.50*), from which you can view many of the cathedral's fierce-looking gargoyles, can be climbed via long, spiral steps.

Ste Chapelle (1er) The gem-like upper chapel of Ste Chapelle (☎ 01 53 73 78 50; metro Cité; adult/concession €5.50/3.50, combination ticket for Ste Chapelle & Conciergerie €8/5; open 9.30am-6pm daily) is illuminated by a veritable curtain of 13th-century stained glass and is inside the **Palais de Justice** (Law Courts; 4 blvd du Palais, 1er). Consecrated in 1248, Ste Chapelle was built in three years to house a crown of thorns (supposedly worn by the crucified Christ) and other relics purchased by King Louis IX (later St Louis) earlier in the 13th century.

Conciergerie (1er) The Conciergerie was a luxurious royal palace when it was built in the 14th century. During the Reign of Terror (1793–94), it was used to incarcerate 'enemies' of the Revolution before they were brought before the tribunal, which met next door in what is now the Palais de Justice.

Île St Louis (4e) The 17th-century houses of grey stone and the small-town shops lining the streets and quays of Île St Louis create an almost provincial atmosphere, making it a great place for a quiet stroll. On foot, the shortest route between Notre Dame and the Marais passes through Île St Louis. For reputedly best ice cream in Paris, head for **Berthillon** (31 rue St Louis en l'Île).

Latin Quarter (5e & 6e) This area is known as the Quartier Latin because, until the Revolution, all communication between students and their professors here took place in Latin.

While the 5e has become increasingly touristy, there's still a large population of students and academics. Shop-lined **Blvd St Michel**, known as 'Boul Mich', runs along the border of the 5e and the 6e.

Panthéon (5e) A Latin Quarter landmark, the Panthéon (☎ 01 44 32 18 00; metro Luxembourg; adult/concession €7/4.50; open 9.30am-5.45pm daily Apr-Sept, 10am-5.15pm daily Oct-Mar), at the eastern end of rue Soufflot, was commissioned as an abbey church in the mid-18th century. In 1791, the Constituent Assembly converted it into a mausoleum for the 'great men of the era of French liberty'. Some of the permanent residents are Victor Hugo, Voltaire and Jean-Jacques Rousseau.

Sorbonne (5e) Founded in 1253 as a college for 16 poor theology students, the Sorbonne was closed in 1792 by the Revolutionary government but reopened under Napoleon. **Place de la Sorbonne** links blvd St Michel with **Église de la Sorbonne**, the university's domed 17th-century church.

Jardin du Luxembourg (6e) The gardens' main entrance is opposite 65 blvd St Michel. The **Palais du Luxembourg**, fronting rue de Vaugirard at the northern end of the Jardin du Luxembourg, was built for Maria de' Medici, queen of France from 1600 to 1610. It now houses the Sénat, the upper house of the French parliament.

Musée National du Moyen Age (5e) The Museum of the Middle Ages (☎ 01 53 73 78 16; metro Cluny-La Sorbonne; adult/concession €5.50/4; open 9.15am-5.45pm Wed-Mon), also known as the Musée de Cluny, houses one of France's finest collections of medieval art. Its prized possession is a series of six late-15th-century tapestries from the southern Netherlands known as La Dame à la Licorne (The Lady and the Unicorn).

Mosquée de Paris (5e) Paris' ornate central mosque (☎ 01 45 35 97 33; place du Puits de l'Ermite; metro Monge; open 9am-noon & 2pm-6pm Sat-Thur) was built between 1922 and 1926. The mosque complex includes a small souk (marketplace), a salon de thé (tearoom), an excellent couscous restaurant and a hammam (Turkish bath).

The mosque is opposite the **Jardin des Plantes** (Botanical Gardens), which includes a small **zoo** as well as the **Musée d'Histoire Naturelle** (Museum of Natural History; ☎ 01 40 79 30 00; metro Monge; adult/concession €4.57/3.05; open 10am-5pm; Wed-Mon).

Catacombes (14e) In 1785, the bones of millions of Parisians were exhumed from overflowing cemeteries and moved to the tunnels of three disused quarries. One such ossuary is the Catacombes (☎ 01 43 22 47 63; metro Denfert Rochereau; adult/student or senior/child €5/3.30/2.59; open 11am-4pm Tues, 9am-4pm Wed-Sun). During WWII, these tunnels were used by the Résistance as headquarters. The route through the Catacombes begins from the small green building at 1 place Denfert Rochereau. Take a flashlight (torch).

Musée d'Orsay (7e) Musée d'Orsay (☎ *01 40 49 48 48; 1 rue de la Légion-d'Honneur; metro Musée d'Orsay; adult/concession €7/ 5, both €5 Sun; open 10am-6pm Tues-Wed & Fri-Sat, 10am-9.45pm Thur, 9am-6pm Sun, from 9am in summer)* exhibits works of art produced between 1848 and 1914, and is spectacularly housed in a 1900 train station. Tickets are valid all day.

Musée Rodin (7e) The Musée Rodin (☎ *01 44 18 61 10; 77 rue Varenne; metro Varenne; adult/concession €5/3; open 9.30am-5.45pm daily Apr-Sept, 9.30am-4.45pm daily Oct-Mar)* is one of the most pleasant museums in Paris. Visiting just the garden (which closes at 5pm) costs €1.

Invalides (7e) The Hôtel des Invalides *(metro Invalides for Esplanade, metro Varenne or Latour Maubourg for main building)* was built in the 1670s by Louis XIV to provide housing for 4000 *invalides* (disabled veterans). It also served as the headquarters of the military governor of Paris, and was used as an armoury. On 14 July 1789 the Paris mob forced its way into the building and took all 28,000 firearms before heading for the Bastille prison.

The **Église du Dôme**, built between 1677 and 1735, is considered one of the finest religious edifices constructed under Louis XIV. In 1861 it received the remains of Napoleon, encased in six concentric coffins.

The buildings on either side of the **Cour d'Honneur** (Main Courtyard) are home to the **Musée de l'Armée** (☎ *01 44 42 37 72; adult/ concession €6/4.50; open 10am-5pm daily, 10am-6pm in summer)*, a huge military museum that includes the light and airy **Tombeau de Napoléon 1er** (Napoleon's Tomb).

Tour Eiffel (7e) The Tour Eiffel (☎ *01 44 11 23 23; metro Champ de Mars-Tour Eiffel; open 9.30am-11pm daily Sept–mid-June, 9am-midnight mid-June–Aug)* faced massive opposition from Paris' artistic and literary elite when it was built for the 1889 Exposition Universelle (World's Fair), held to commemorate the Revolution. It was almost torn down in 1909 but was spared for practical reasons – it proved an ideal platform for newfangled transmitting antennae. The Eiffel Tower is 320m high, including the television antenna at the very tip.

Three levels are open to the public. The lift (west and north pillars) costs €3.70 for the 1st platform (57m), €6.90 for the 2nd (115m) and €9.90 for the 3rd (276m). Children three to 12 pay €2.10/3.80/5.30 respectively; there are no other discounts. The escalator in the south pillar to the 1st and 2nd platforms costs €3.

Champ de Mars (7e) The Champ de Mars, a grassy park around the Eiffel Tower, was once a parade ground for the 18th-century **École Militaire** (France's military academy) at the southeastern end of the lawns.

Right Bank

Jardins du Trocadéro (16e) The Trocadéro gardens *(metro Trocadéro)*, with its fountain and nearby sculpture park grandly illuminated at night, are across the pont d'Iéna from the Eiffel Tower. The colonnaded Palais de Chaillot was built in 1937 and houses the anthropological and ethnographic **Musée de l'Homme** *(Museum of Mankind; ☎ 01 44 05 72 72; adult/concession €4.57/3.05; open 9.45am-5.15pm Wed-Mon)*; and the **Musée de la Marine** *(Maritime Museum; ☎ 01 53 65 69 69; adult/concession €6.86/5.34; open 10am-5.50pm Wed-Mon)*, known for its beautiful model ships.

Musée National des Art Asiatiques-Guimet (16e) The Guimet Museum (☎ *01 56 52 53 00; 6 place d'Iéna; metro Iéna; adult/concession €7/5; open 10am-6pm Wed-Mon)* displays antiquities and art from throughout Asia.

Louvre (1er) The Louvre Museum (☎ *01 40 20 53 17, recorded message ☎ 01 40 20 51 51; metro Palais Royal-Musée du Louvre; permanent collection admission €7.50, after 3pm & Sun €5; open 9am-6pm Thur-Sun, 9am-9.45pm Mon & Wed)*, constructed around 1200 as a fortress and rebuilt in the mid-16th century as a royal palace, became a public museum in 1793. The collections on display have been assembled by French governments over the past five centuries and include works of art and artisanship from all over Europe as well as important collections of Assyrian, Egyptian, Etruscan, Greek, Coptic, Roman and Islamic art. The Louvre's most famous work is undoubtedly Leonardo da Vinci's *Mona Lisa*.

Ticket sales end 45 minutes before closing time. Admission to temporary exhibits varies.

Tickets are valid for the whole day, so you can leave and re-enter as you please. By advance purchasing your tickets at the *billeteries* (ticket office) at FNAC, or other department stores, for an extra €1.10, you can walk straight in without queuing.

For English-language guided tours (€6/4.50 per adult/concession; 11am, 2pm and 3.45pm most days) and audioguide tours (€5), go to the mezzanine level beneath the glass pyramid.

Place Vendôme (1er) The 44m-high column in the middle of place Vendôme consists of a stone core wrapped in bronze from 1250 cannons captured by Napoleon at the Battle of Austerlitz (1805). The shops here are among Paris' most fashionable and expensive.

Musée de l'Orangerie (1er) This museum (☎ 01 42 97 48 16; metro Concorde), usually home to important impressionist works including a series of Monet's spectacular *Nymphéas* (Water Lilies), is being renovated and is due to reopen at the end of 2004.

Place de la Concorde (8e) This vast, cobbled square between the Jardin des Tuileries and the Champs-Élysées was laid out between 1755 and 1775. Louis XVI was guillotined here in 1793 – as were another 1343 people, including his wife Marie Antoinette, during the next two years. The 3300-year-old Egyptian **obelisk** in the middle of the square was given to France in 1829 by the ruler of Egypt, Mohammed Ali.

La Madeleine (8e) The church of St Mary Magdalene *(metro Madeleine)*, built in the style of a Greek temple, was consecrated in 1842 after almost a century of design changes and construction delays.

Champs-Élysées (8e) The 2km-long ave des Champs-Élysées links place de la Concorde with the Arc de Triomphe. Once popular with aristocrats parading their wealth, it has been partly taken over by fast-food restaurants and overpriced cafés. The nicest bit is the park between place de la Concorde and Rond Point des Champs-Élysées.

Musée du Petit Palais (8e) The Petit Palais (☎ 01 42 65 12 73) is due to reopen in 2003 after refurbishment.

West of the Petit Palais, the **Grand Palais** (☎ 01 44 13 17 17; 3 ave du Général du Eisenhower; admission varies; open 10am-8pm Thur-Mon, 10am-8pm Wed), built for the 1900 World Fair, is now used for temporary exhibitions.

Arc de Triomphe (8e) Paris' second most famous landmark, the Arc de Triomphe (☎ 01 55 37 73 77; metro Charles de Gaulle-Étoile; viewing platform adult/concession €7/4.50; viewing platform open 10am-11pm daily Apr-Sept, 10am-10.30pm Oct-Mar) is 2.2km northwest of place de la Concorde in the middle of place Charles de Gaulle. Also called place de l'Étoile, this is the world's largest traffic roundabout and the meeting point of 12 avenues. Commissioned in 1806 by Napoleon to commemorate his imperial victories, it remained unfinished until the 1830s. An Unknown Soldier from WWI is buried under the arch, his fate and that of countless others like him commemorated by a memorial flame lit each evening at around 6.30pm.

The platform atop the arch is accessed by a lift going up, and by steps heading down. The only sane way to get to the arch's base is via the underground passageways.

The **Voie Triomphale** (Triumphal Way) stretches 4.5km from the Arc de Triomphe along ave de la Grande Armée to the skyscraper district of **La Défense**, known for its landmark, the **Grande Arche** (Grand Arch), a hollow cube (112m to a side).

Centre Georges Pompidou (4e) Thanks in part to its outstanding temporary exhibitions, Centre Pompidou (☎ 01 44 78 12 33; metro Rambuteau or Châtelet-Les Halles) – also known as Centre Beaubourg – is by far the most frequented sight in Paris. **Place Igor Stravinsky**, south of the centre, and the large square to the west attract all kinds of street artists.

The **Musée National d'Art Moderne** (National Museum of Modern Art; adult/concession €5.50/3.50; open 11am-9pm Wed-Mon, 11am-11pm Thur) on the 4th floor displays France's brilliant collection of modern art, from 1905 to the present day. The fee includes admission to Brancusi's studio, reconstructed at the north of the forecourt. The **Bibliothèque Publique d'Information**, a huge, nonlending library, is on the 2nd floor (enter from Rue du Renard).

FRANCE

CENTRAL PARIS

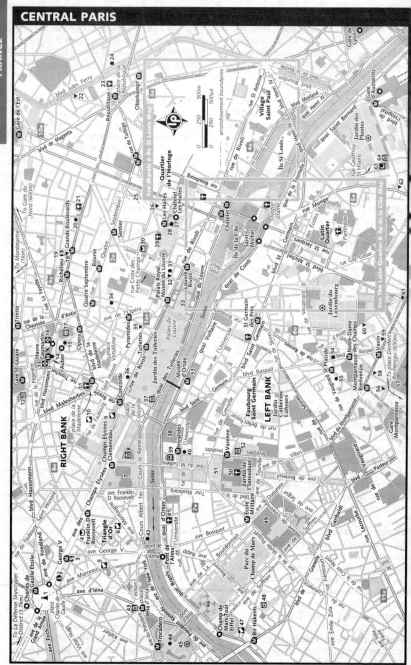

CENTRAL PARIS

Les Halles (1er) Paris' main wholesale food market, Les Halles, occupied this site from the 12th century until 1969, when it was moved out to the suburb of Rungis; a huge underground shopping mall (Forum des Halles) was built in its place. Just north of the grassy area on top of Les Halles is the mostly 16th-century **Église St Eustache**, noted for its wonderful pipe organ.

Hôtel de Ville (4e) Paris' magnificent city hall (☎ 01 42 76 50 49; place de l'Hôtel de Ville; metro Hôtel de Ville) was burned down during the Paris Commune of 1871 and rebuilt (1874–82) in the neo-Renaissance style.

Marais Area (4e) A *marais* (marsh) converted to agricultural use in the 13th century, this area was, during the 17th century – when the nobility erected luxurious but discreet mansions known as *hôtels particuliers* – the most fashionable part of the city. Eventually the marais was taken over by ordinary Parisians and by the time renovation began in the 1960s, it had become a poor but lively Jewish neighbourhood.

In the 1980s the area underwent serious gentrification and today it is the centre of Paris' gay life.

Place des Vosges (4e) Built in 1605 and originally known as place Royal, place des Vosges *(metro Chemin Vert)* is a square ensemble of 36 symmetrical houses. Duels were once fought in the elegant park in the middle. Today, the arcades around place des Vosges are occupied by upmarket art galleries, antique shops and boutiques.

The nearby **Maison de Victor Hugo** (☎ 01 42 72 10 16; adult/concession €3.50/2.50; open Tues-Sun) is where the author lived from 1832 to 1848.

Musée Picasso (3e) The Picasso Museum (☎ 01 42 71 25 21; 5 rue de Thorigny; metro St Paul; adult/concession €5.50/4; open 9.30am-6pm, 9.30am-8pm Thur; closes 5.30pm Oct-Mar) is just northeast of the Marais. Paintings, sculptures, ceramics, engravings and drawings – donated to the French government by the heirs of Pablo Picasso (1881–1973) to avoid huge inheritance taxes – are on display, as is Picasso's personal art collection (Braque, Cézanne, Matisse, Rousseau etc).

Bastille (4e, 11e & 12e) The Bastille is the most famous nonexistent monument in Paris; the notorious prison was demolished shortly after the mob stormed it on 14 July 1789. The site is known as place de la Bastille. The 52m-high **Colonne de Juillet** in the centre was erected in 1830. There's also the new (and rather drab) **Opéra Bastille** (☎ 0836 69 78 68; place de la Bastille; metro Bastille).

Opéra Garnier (9e) Paris' renowned opera house (see Opera & Classical Music under Entertainment later) was designed in 1860 by Charles Garnier. The **ceiling** of the auditorium was painted by Marc Chagall in 1964. The building also houses the **Musée de l'Opéra** (adult/concession €6/4; open 10am-5pm daily).

Montmartre (18e) During the 19th century Montmartre was a vibrant centre of artistic and literary creativity. Today it's an area of mimes, buskers, tacky souvenir shops and commercial artists.

Basilique du Sacré Cœur Sacré Cœur (☎ 01 53 41 89 00; metro Anvers; admission free; open 7am-11pm daily; admission to dome & crypt adult/student €4.50/2.50; dome & crypt open 10am-5.45pm daily) was built to fulfil a vow taken by Parisian Catholics after the disastrous Franco-Prussian War of 1870–71. The funicular up the hill's southern slope costs one metro/bus ticket each way.

Place du Tertre Just west of **Église St Pierre**, place du Tertre is filled with cafés, restaurants, portrait artists and tourists – though the real attractions of the area are the quiet, twisting streets. Look for the **windmills** on rue Lepic and Paris' last **vineyard**, on the corner of rue des Saules and rue St Vincent.

Pigalle (9e & 18e) The area along blvd de Clichy between the Pigalle and Blanche metro stops is lined with sex shops, striptease parlours and bad nightclubs.

Musée de l'Érotisme (Museum of Eroticism; ☎ 01 42 58 28 73; 72 blvd de Clichy; metro Blanche; adult/student €7/5; open 10am-2am daily) tries to raise erotic art, both antique and modern, to a loftier plane – but we know why we visited. The **Moulin Rouge** (☎ 01 53 09 82 82; 82 blvd de Clichy; metro Blanche; tickets from €60), founded in 1889, is known for its thrice-nightly revues of near-naked girls.

Cimetière du Père Lachaise (20e) Père Lachaise Cemetery (☎ 01 55 25 82 10; metro Père Lachaise; admission free; open to at least 5.30pm daily), final resting place of such notables as Chopin, Proust, Oscar Wilde and Édith Piaf, may be the most visited cemetery in the world. The best known tomb is that of 1960s rock star Jim Morrison, lead singer for The Doors, who died in 1971.

Bois de Vincennes (12e) Highlights of this 9.29-sq-km English-style park include the **Parc Floral** (Floral Garden; metro Château de Vincennes); the **Parc Zoologique de Paris** (Paris Zoo; ☎ 01 44 75 20 10; metro Porte Dorée); and the **Jardin Tropical** (Tropical Garden; RER stop Nugent-sur-Marne).

Château de Vincennes (12e) A bona fide royal chateau, the Château de Vincennes (☎ 01 48 08 31 20; metro Château de Vincennes; open 10am-noon & 1pm-5pm daily) is at the northern edge of the Bois de Vincennes. You can walk around the grounds for free, but to see the Gothic **Chapelle Royale** and the 14th-century **donjon** (keep), you must take a tour (in French, with an information booklet in English).

Musée des Arts d'Afrique et d'Océanie (12e) This museum (☎ 01 44 74 84 80; 293 ave Daumesnil; metro Porte Dorée; adult/concession €4.50/3; open 10am-5.30pm Wed-Mon) specialises in art from Africa and the South Pacific.

Bois de Boulogne (16e) The 8.65-sq-km Bois de Boulogne is endowed with meandering trails, forests, cycling paths and belle époque-style cafés. Rowing boats can be rented at the **Lac Inférieur** (metro Ave Henri Martin).

Paris Cycles (☎ 01 47 47 76 50; Rond-Point du Jardin d'Acclimation; metro Les Sablons) rents out bicycles for €5/12 per hour/day.

LANGUAGE COURSES

Alliance Française (☎ 01 45 44 38 28; 101 blvd Raspail, 6e; metro St Placide) offers month-long French courses; it can also help you find a family to stay with. **Accord Language School** (☎ 01 42 36 24 95; 14 blvd Poissonnière, 9e; metro Bonne Nouvelle) gets high marks from students.

ORGANISED TOURS
Bus

From April to late September, RATP's Balabus follows a 50-minute return route from Gare de Lyon to the Grande Arche in La Défense. Buses depart about every 20 minutes; the whole circuit costs three metro/bus tickets. **L'Open Tour** (☎ 01 43 46 52 06) runs open-deck buses along three circuits year-round, allowing you to jump on and off at more than 30 stops. Tickets cost €24/26 for one/two days (€20 if you're holding a Carte Orange, Paris Visite or Batobus pass).

Bicycle

Paris à Vélo C'est Sympa! (☎ 01 48 87 60 01; e info@parisvelosympa.com; 37 blvd Bourdon, 4e; metro Bastille; €30/26 for over/under 26s) offers three-hour bicycle tours on Saturday and Sunday (and weekdays depending on demand). **Mike's Bike Tours** (☎ 01 56 58 10 54; w www.MikesBikeToursParis.com, e info@MikesBikeToursParis.com) head off from the south leg of the Eiffel Tower daily at 11am and 3pm 15 May to 31 August and at 3pm only 1 March to 14 May and 1 September to 15 November (€22). Night tours (€26) leave at 7pm (daily 1 March to 15 November). A guide, bicycle and insurance are included.

Boat

Every 25 minutes, April to early November, the **Batobus river shuttle** (☎ 01 44 11 33 99) docks at eight places including Notre Dame and the Musée d'Orsay. A one-/two-day pass costs €10/12.50 (€5.50/6.50 for children under 12). **Bateaux Mouches** (☎ 01 42 25 96 10, English-language recording ☎ 01 40 76 99 99; metro Alma Marceau) makes a one-hour cruise for €7 (€4 for children four to 12) with commentary. **Vedettes du Pont Neuf** (☎ 01 46 33 98 38; metro Pont Neuf) operates one-hour boat circuits day and night for €9 (€4.50 for under 12s).

PLACES TO STAY
Accommodation Services

OTU Voyages (☎ 01 40 29 12 12; w www .otu.fr; 119 rue St Martin, 4e; metro Rambuteau; open 9.30am-6.30pm Mon-Fri, 10am-5pm Sat), directly across the square from the Centre Pompidou, can find you accommodation for the same or following day for a €3 fee. The staff will give you a voucher to take to the hotel.

The main tourist office (see Information earlier) and its Gare de Lyon annexe can also make same-day bookings.

Camping

Camping du Bois de Boulogne (☎ 01 45 24 30 81, fax 01 42 24 42 95; e resa@mobil home-paris.com; Allée du Bord de l'Eau, 16e; 2 people & tent without/with vehicle from €11/17), at the far western edge of the Bois de Boulogne, is Paris' only camping ground. The Porte Maillot metro stop is linked to the camping ground by RATP bus No 244 (6am to 8.30pm) and, April to October, by privately operated shuttle bus (€1.70).

Hostels

Many hostels allow a three-night maximum stay, especially during summer. Only official *auberges de jeunesse* (youth hostels) require guests to present Hostelling International (HI) cards or equivalent. Curfew – if enforced – tends to be 1am or 2am. Few hostels accept reservations by telephone.

Louvre Area (1er) There are bunks in single-sex rooms at **Centre International BVJ Paris-Louvre** (☎ 01 53 00 90 90; 20 rue Jean-Jacques Rousseau; metro Louvre-Rivoli; dorm beds €26) and rates include breakfast.

Marais (4e) The Maison Internationale de la Jeunesse et des Étudiants (MIJE; ☎ 01 42 74 23 45, fax 01 40 27 81 64; dorm beds/ singles from €23/38) runs three hostels in attractively renovated 17th- and 18th-century Marais residences. Rates include breakfast. **MIJE Maubisson** (12 rue des Barres; metro Hôtel de Ville) is, in our opinion, the best. **MIJE Fourcy** (6 rue de Fourcy; metro St Paul), the largest hostel, and **MIJE Fauconnier** (11 rue du Fauconnier; metro Pont Marie), two blocks south of MIJE Fourcy, are the other options.

Panthéon Area (5e) The clean and friendly **Y&H Hostel** (☎ 01 45 35 09 53, fax 01 47 07 22 24; e smile@youngandhappy.fr; 80 rue Mouffetard; metro Monge; dorm beds/doubles €22/50) is popular with a younger crowd.

11e Arrondissement Breakfast is included in the rates at the **Auberge de Jeunesse Jules Ferry** (☎ 01 43 57 55 60; e auberge@easynet.fr; 8 blvd Jules Ferry; metro

FRANCE

THE LATIN QUARTER & ÎLE DE LA CITÉ

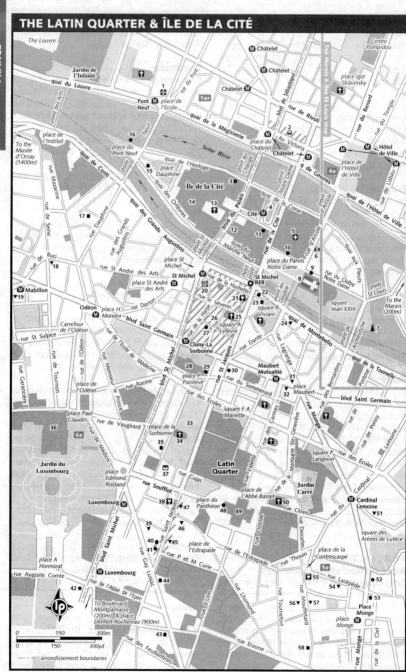

The Louvre

Jardin de l'Infante

quai du Louvre

To the Musée d'Orsay (1400m)

place de l'Institut

place de l'École

Pont Neuf

1er

quai de la Mégisserie

Seine River

quai de Conti

place du Pont Neuf

quai de l'Horloge

place du Châtelet

Châtelet

place Dauphine

Île de la Cité

quai des Orfèvres

Cité

quai du Marché Neuf

quai de la Corse

place du Parvis Notre Dame

Centre Pompidou

place Igor Stravinsky

rue de Rivoli

place de l'Hôtel de Ville

Hôtel de Ville

quai de l'Hôtel de Ville

place St Michel

St Michel

place St André des Arts

Mabillon

Odéon

place H Mondor

blvd saint Germain

Carrefour de l'Odéon

rue St Sulpice

place de l'Odéon

rue de Tournon

place Paul Claudel

rue de Vaugirard

Jardin du Luxembourg

place Edmond Rostand

Luxembourg

place A Honnorat

rue Auguste Comte

To Boulevard Montparnasse (200m) & place Denfert Rochereau (900m)

St Michel RER

place St Séverin

square A Lefèvre

Cluny-La Sorbonne

place P Painlevé

rue des Écoles

square F.A Mariette

place de la Sorbonne

Latin Quarter

rue Cujas

rue Soufflot

place du Panthéon

place de l'Estrapade

rue P et M Curie

Maubert Mutualité

place Maubert

square R Viviani

quai de Montebello

quai de la Tournelle

blvd Saint Germain

square P Langevin

square Ste Geneviève

Jardin Carré

place de l'Abbé Basset

rue Clovis

place de la Contrescarpe

square des Arènes de Lutèce

Cardinal Lemoine

Place Monge

place Monge

rue de la Clef

square Jean XXIII

To the Marais (200m)

quai d'Archevêché

pont St Louis

square R Viviani

arrondissement boundaries

0   150   300m
0   150   300yd

LP

THE LATIN QUARTER & ÎLE DE LA CITÉ

PLACES TO STAY
15 Hôtel Henri IV
17 Hôtel de Nesle
23 Hôtel Esmeralda
35 Hôtel de la Sorbonne
40 Hôtel de Médicis
43 Grand Hôtel du Progrès
44 Hôtel Gay Lussac
53 Hôtel St Christophe
58 Y & H Hostel

PLACES TO EAT
18 Food Shops
19 CROUS
24 Le Grenier de Notre-Dame
26 Restaurants ('Bacteria Alley')
31 Food Shops
32 Fromagerie (Cheese Shop)
39 Douce France Sandwich Bar
45 Food Shops
46 Tashi Delek Tibetan
    Restaurant
47 Perraudin
51 Le Petit Légume
54 Ed l'Épicier Supermarket

56 Le Petit Grec
57 Restaurants

OTHER
1 Samaritaine
   (Department Store)
2 Noctambus (All-Night
   Bus) Stops
3 Conciergerie Entrance
4 Flower Market
5 Hôtel Dieu (Hospital)
6 Société Française de Change
7 Mémorial des Martyrs
   de la Déportation
8 Notre Dame Cathedral
9 Notre Dame Tower Entrance
10 Hospital Entrance
11 Préfecture Entrance
12 Préfecture de Police
13 Sainte Chapelle
14 Palais de Justice &
    Conciergerie
16 Vedettes du Pont Neuf
    (Boat Tours)
20 EasyInternet

21 Caveau de la Huchette
    Jazz Club
22 Shakespeare & Co Bookshop
25 Abbey Bookshop
27 Église Saint Séverin
28 Musée du Moyen Age
    (Thermes de Cluny)
29 Musée du Moyen
    Age Entrance
30 Eurolines Bus Office
33 Sorbonne (University
    of Paris)
34 Église de la Sorbonne
36 Palais du Luxembourg
    (French Senate Building)
37 Post Office
38 Café Oz
41 Laundrette
42 Nouvelles Frontières
48 Panthéon Entrance
49 Panthéon
50 Église Saint Étienne
    du Mont
52 Laundrette
55 La Contrescarpe

République; dorm beds €18 plus €2.90 without HI card).

Clean and friendly **Auberge Internationale des Jeunes** (☎ 01 47 00 62 00, fax 01 47 00 33 16; e aij@aijparis.com; 10 rue Trousseau, 11e; metro Ledru Rollin; dorm beds Nov-Feb €13, Mar-Oct €14) attracts a young crowd and gets full during summer. Rates include breakfast.

12e Arrondissement Breakfast is included in the tariff at **Centre International de Séjour de Paris (CISP) Ravel** (☎ 01 44 75 60 00, fax 01 43 44 45 30; e reservation@cisp.asso.fr; 6 ave Maurice Ravel; metro Porte de Vincennes; beds in 2–4-bed rooms €19.20, singles/doubles €30/48).

13e & 14e Arrondissements The **Foyer International d'Accueil de Paris (FIAP) Jean Monnet** (☎ 01 43 13 17 00, fax 01 45 81 63 91; e fiapadmi@fiap.asso.fr; 30 rue Cabanis; metro Glacière; dorm beds from €22, singles €48.50) has modern rooms, and rates include breakfast. Rooms specially outfitted for handicapés (disabled people) are available. Reservations are accepted.

The **Centre International de Séjour de Paris (CISP) Kellermann** (☎ 01 44 16 37 38, fax 01 44 16 37 39; 17 blvd Kellermann; metro Porte d'Italie; dorm beds/singles

€15.40/22.40) includes sheets and breakfast in its rates. There are facilities for disabled people on the 1st floor. Reservations are accepted up to 48 hours in advance.

Hotels
Marais (4e) The friendly **Hôtel Rivoli** (☎ 01 42 72 08 41; 44 rue de Rivoli; metro Hôtel de Ville; singles without shower from €26, doubles with bath & toilet €48) is still a good deal. **Hôtel de Nice** (☎ 01 42 78 55 29, fax 01 42 78 36 07; 42bis rue de Rivoli; metro Hôtel de Ville; singles/doubles/triples €60/95/115) is a family-run place; some rooms have balconies. **Grand Hôtel Malher** (☎ 01 42 72 60 92, fax 01 42 72 25 37; e gh malher@yahoo.com; 5 rue Malher; metro St Paul; singles/doubles from €103/118) has nice rooms with satellite TV. Rates drop by €20 in the low season.

Bastille (11e) Above the bistro of the same name, **Hôtel Les Sans-Culottes** (☎ 01 49 23 85 80, fax 01 48 05 08 56; 27 rue de Lappe; metro Bastille; singles/doubles €53/61) has nine pleasant rooms with TV.

Notre Dame Area (5e) The **Hôtel Esmeralda** (☎ 01 43 54 19 20, fax 01 40 51 00 68; 4 rue St Julien; metro St Michel; singles €30, doubles with shower & toilet from €60) is a scruffy but well-loved institution. Its simple rooms are booked well in advance.

Panthéon Area (5e) Shabby **Hôtel de Médicis** (☎ 01 43 54 14 66; e hotelmedicis@ aol.com; 214 rue St Jacques; metro Luxembourg; singles/doubles €16/31) has some good-sized but basic rooms. Triples are available too. Much nicer is **Grand Hôtel du Progrès** (☎ 01 43 54 53 18, fax 01 56 24 87 80; 50 rue Gay Lussac; metro Luxembourg; singles/doubles from €27/42, with shower & toilet from €54/56 including breakfast) with good views from some rooms. There are some spacious rooms at older-style **Hôtel Gay Lussac** (☎ 01 43 54 23 96, fax 01 40 51 79 49; 29 rue Gay Lussac; metro Luxembourg; singles/doubles/quads from €55/49/95). **Hôtel St Christophe** (☎ 01 43 31 81 54, fax 01 43 31 12 54; e saintchristophe@wanadoo .fr; 17 rue Lacépède; metro place Monge; singles/doubles €111/123) is a classy small hotel with 31 well-equipped rooms. Wipe off about €10 in low season. **Hotel de la Sorbonne** (☎ 01 43 54 58 08, fax 01 40 51 05 18; e reservation@hotelsorbonne.com; 6 rue Victor Cousin; rooms with shower/bath €79/ 89) is a comfortable place near Boulevard St Michel. Breakfast is €5.

St Germain des Prés (6e) Whimsically decorated **Hôtel de Nesle** (☎ 01 43 54 62 41; e contact@hoteldenesle.com; 7 rue de Nesle; metro Odéon or Mabillon; singles/doubles from €35/69) is hospitable, with a tranquil garden. The well-positioned **Hôtel Henri IV** (☎ 01 43 54 44 53; 25 place Dauphine; metro Pont Neuf; singles/doubles from €22/25, no credit cards) at the western end of Île de la Cité, has adequate rooms (hall showers are €2.50). Book well ahead.

Montmartre (18e) An attractive place is **Hôtel des Arts** (☎ 01 46 06 30 52, fax 01 46 06 10 83; e hotel.arts@wanadoo.fr; 5 rue Tholozé; metro Abbesses; singles/doubles from €64/78), while the **Hôtel de Rohan** (☎ 01 42 52 32 57, fax 01 55 79 79 63; 90 rue Myrha; metro Château Rouge; singles/ doubles €19/23, with shower & toilet €28/ 31) has recently renovated most of its rooms (hall showers €3). The **Hôtel des Trois Poussins** (☎ 01 53 32 81 81, fax 01 53 32 81 82; e h3p@les3poussins.com; 15 rue Clauzel; metro St Georges; singles/doubles from

€120/135) is a lovely hotel due south of place Pigalle. Rooms with kitchen facilities cost an extra €15.

PLACES TO EAT
Restaurants

Except for those in the very touristy areas, most of the city's thousands of restaurants are pretty good value for money.

Forum des Halles There are Lyon-inspired specialities at **Le Petit Mâchon** (☎ 01 42 60 08 06; 158 rue St Honoré; metro Palais Royal; menu €15) bistro. The American bar/ restaurant **Joe Allen** (☎ 01 42 36 70 13; 30 rue Pierre Lescot; metro Étienne Marcel; burgers €12) promises the best burgers in Paris.

Opéra Area (2e & 9e) Although the food is so-so, **Chartier** (☎ 01 47 70 86 29; 7 rue du Faubourg Montmartre; metro Grands Boulevards; mains from €6.25, 3-course menu with wine €13.65) is worth it for the atmosphere and fabulous belle époque dining room.

Marais (4e) Rue des Rosiers (metro St Paul), the heart of the old Jewish neighbourhood, has a few kascher (kosher) restaurants. Paris' best known Jewish (but not kosher) restaurant, founded in 1920, is **Restaurant Jo Goldenberg** (☎ 01 48 87 20 16; mains around €13) at No 7. **Minh Chau** (10 rue de la Verrerie; metro Hôtel de Ville; mains around €4.50) is a tiny but welcoming Vietnamese/ Chinese place with tasty dishes. For vegetarian fare head to **Aquarius** (☎ 01 48 87 48 71; 54 rue Ste Croix de la Bretonnerie; metro Rambuteau; 2-course lunch €11, 3-course dinner €15.40; closed Sun), which has tasty dishes like soy sausages and tofu omelette.

Au Gamin de Paris (☎ 01 42 78 97 24; 51 rue Vieille du Temple; metro St Paul) is a lively restaurant with great salads, steak and pasta. Count on spending at least €15 per person. **Le Colimacon** (☎ 01 48 87 12 01; 44 rue Vieille du Temple; metro St Paul; 2-/3-course menus €14.50/20.70) serves delicious modern French food.

République (10e) On the Canal St Martin, **Chez Prune** (☎ 01 42 41 30 47; 36 rue Beaurepaire, 10e; metro République; lunch around €10) is a hip café with tasty French food.

Bastille (4e, 11e & 12e) The area around Bastille has many ethnic and traditional restaurants. Rue de Lappe, a happening strip since the 17th century, has heaps of eateries and bars. **Havanita Café** (☎ 01 43 55 96 42; mains €10-17), at No 11, is a loud, brassy lounge serving Cuban-inspired food and drinks. For good French food in a charming room try **Les Sans-Culottes** (☎ 01 48 05 42 92; menu €20) at No 27.

Bofinger (☎ 01 42 72 87 82; 5-7 rue de la Bastille; metro Bastille; lunch/dinner menus €20/30; open daily) is a brasserie with an Art Nouveau interior and seafood specialities.

Latin Quarter (4e, 5e & 6e) This area has plenty of good Greek, North African and Middle Eastern restaurants – but avoid rue de la Huchette (aka 'bacteria alley') and its nearby streets, unless you're after shwarma (€4), available at several places.

The Moroccan **Founti Agadir** (☎ 01 43 37 85 10; 117 rue Monge; metro Censier Daubenton; lunch menus €12 & €14) has some of the best couscous, grills and tajines on the Left Bank. Or, if you fancy classics like bœuf bourguignon (€12.20), try **Perraudin** (☎ 01 46 33 15 75; 157 rue St Jacques; metro Luxembourg; open Mon-Fri), a reasonably priced traditional French restaurant.

Le Petit Légume (☎ 01 40 46 06 85; 36 rue des Boulangers; metro Cardinal Lemoine; menus €8, €10.50 & €13) is a great choice for organic vegetarian fare.

Some of the best crepes in Paris are sold at **Le Petit Grec** (68 rue Mouffetard; crepes about €3), which has upgraded from the cart it used to operate across the street. **Tashi Delek** (☎ 01 43 26 55 55; 4 rue des Fossés St Jacques; metro Luxembourg; dinner menus €17.50, vegetarian dishes €6.40-8.40) offers good, cheap, Tibetan fare. **Douce France** (7 rue Royer Collard; metro Luxembourg) is a popular hole-in-the-wall selling great sandwiches for €2.20.

Le Grenier de Notre-Dame (☎ 01 43 29 98 29; 18 rue de la Bûcherie; menu €12) is a vegetarian restaurant with dishes like lasagne and cassoulet.

Montparnasse (6e & 14e) One of many Breton-style creperies along rue d'Odessa and rue du Montparnasse is **Le Flibustier** (☎ 01 43 21 70 03; 20 rue d'Odessa; crepes around €6). **Mustang Café** (☎ 01 43 35 36 12; 84 blvd du Montparnasse; metro Montparnasse-Bienvenüe; platters & chilli from €10; open to 5am) serves passable Tex-Mex.

For innovative food in a traditional setting, try **Le Caméléon** (☎ 01 43 20 63 43; 6 rue de Chevreuse, 6e; metro Vavin); the lobster ravioli (€16) alone is worth a visit.

Montmartre (9e & 18e) Restaurants around place du Tertre tend to be touristy and overpriced – but there are alternatives. An old favourite is **Chez des Fondus** (☎ 01 42 55 22 65; 17 rue des Trois Frères; metro Abbesses; open 7pm-2am daily) where €15 buys an apéritif, wine, and either cheese or meat fondue. **Le Mono** (☎ 01 46 06 99 20; 40 rue Véron; dishes €8-12) serves West African fare.

Le Bateau Lavoir (☎ 01 42 54 23 92; 8 rue Garreau; entrees/mains €7/14) is an atmospheric and traditional French restaurant.

University Restaurants Paris has 17 restaurants universitaires (student cafeterias) run by the **Centre Régional des Œuvres Universitaires et Scolaires** (Crous; ☎ 01 40 51 37 01). Students with ID pay €2.40. Opening times vary, so check the schedule outside any of the following: **Assas** (☎ 01 46 33 61 25; 92 rue d'Assas, 6e; metro Port Royal or Notre Dame des Champs); **Bullier** (☎ 01 43 54 93 38; 39 ave Georges Bernanos, 5e; metro Port Royal); **Châtelet** (☎ 01 43 31 51 66; 10 rue Jean Calvin, 5e; metro Censier Daubenton), just off rue Mouffetard; and **Mabillon** (☎ 01 43 25 66 23; 3 rue Mabillon, 6e; metro Mabillon).

Self-Catering

Supermarkets are always cheaper than small grocery shops. The **Monoprix supermarket** (23 ave de l'Opéra) opposite metro Pyramides is convenient for the Louvre area, or try **Ed l'Épicier** (37 rue Lacépède; metro Monge) if you're in the Latin Quarter. For a different shopping experience altogether, head to **Fauchon** (☎ 01 47 42 91 10; 26 place de la Madeleine; metro Madeleine), Paris' most famous gourmet-food shop.

Food Markets Paris' marchés découverts (open-air markets; open 7am-2pm) pop up in various squares and streets two or three times a week. There are also **marchés couverts** (covered markets; open 8am–about 1pm &

4pm-7pm Tues-Sun). Ask at your hotel for the location of the nearest market.

Notre Dame Area (4e & 5e) There are a number of *fromageries* and **groceries** along rue St Louis en l'Île *(metro Pont Marie)* and place Maubert hosts a **food market** *(open Tues, Thur & Sat)* and various other food shops.

St Germain des Prés (6e) Food shops are clustered on **rue de Seine** and **rue de Buci** *(metro Mabillon)* and at rue St Jacques. The covered **Marché St Germain** *(rue Lobineau)*, just north of the eastern end of Église St Germain des Prés, has a huge array of produce and prepared foods.

Marais (4e) Flo Prestige *(10 rue St Antoine; metro Bastille; open 8am-11pm daily)* has fancy picnic supplies and, more importantly, delectable pastries and baked goods.

Montmartre (18e) Most of the food shops in this area are along rue Lepic and rue des Abbesses, about 500m southwest of Sacré Cœur.

ENTERTAINMENT

It's virtually impossible to sample the richness of Paris' entertainment scene without consulting *Pariscope* (€0.40; includes an English-language insert from Time Out) or *L'Officiel des Spectacles* (€0.35), both published on Wednesday and available at any newsstand. Look out for *LYLO*, a free listings zine.

Tickets

Theatre and concert tickets can be reserved and bought at the ticket outlets in **FNAC stores** (☎ 01 43 42 04 04; 4 place Bastille, 12e; metro Bastille ● ☎ 01 40 41 40 00; 3rd underground level, Forum des Halles shopping mall, 1 rue Pierre Lescot, 1er; metro Châtelet-Les Halles) and in the **Virgin Megastores** (☎ 01 49 53 50 00; 52 ave des Champs-Élysées, 8e; metro Franklin D Roosevelt ● ☎ 01 44 50 03 10; 99 rue de Rivoli, 1er; metro Pont Neuf).

Bars

L'Etoile Manquante (☎ 01 42 72 47 47; 34 rue Vieille du Temple, 4e; metro St Paul) is a gay/mixed bar with funky art. Meals are available. The Anglophone and always crowded **Stolly's** (☎ 01 42 76 06 76; 16 rue de la Cloche Percée, 4e; metro Hôtel de Ville) is on a tiny street just off rue de Rivoli.

De La Ville Café (☎ 01 48 24 48 09; 36 blvd Bonne Nouvelle, 10e; metro Bonne Nouvelle) is a fashionable but welcoming bar. **Café Oz** (☎ 01 43 54 30 48; 18 rue St Jacques; metro Luxembourg) is a casual, friendly pub with Foster's on tap.

Relaxed **La Contrescarpe** (☎ 01 43 36 82 88; 57 rue Lacépède, 5e), on place Contrescarpe, is as nice for morning coffee or cocktail hour.

Clubs & Dance Venues

The clubs and other dancing venues favoured by the Parisian 'in' crowd change frequently, and many are officially private, which means bouncers can deny entry to whomever they don't like the look of. For example, single men may not be admitted; women, on the other hand, get in free some nights.

Favela Chic (☎ 01 40 21 38 14; 18 rue du Faubourg du Temple, 9e; metro Republique; admission free; open 7.30pm-2am Tues-Sat) morphs from a Brazilian restaurant into a heaving dance spot.

Batofar (☎ 01 45 83 33 06; quai de la Gare, 13e; metro Bibliothèque Nationale) is the best known of a number of floating barges, all of which host parties and concerts.

Café de la Danse (☎ 01 47 00 57 59; 5 passage Louis Philippe; metro Bastille) is a good venue with a varied line-up. It's off 21 rue de Lappe. Pick up a programme at Web Bar (see Email & Internet Access earlier).

Jazz

Caveau de la Huchette (☎ 01 43 26 65 05; 5 rue de la Huchette, 5e; metro St Michel; adult/student €10.50/9 Mon-Fri, all €13 Sat-Sun; open 9.30pm-2am, later Sat-Sun) is touristy but still a favourite for live jazz.

Opera & Classical Music

Paris plays host to dozens of concerts each week. The **Opéra National de Paris** (☎ 0892 69 78 68; w www.opera-de-paris.fr) splits its performances between **Opéra Garnier**, its original home built in 1875, and the modern **Opéra Bastille**, which opened in 1989. Both opera houses also stage ballets and concerts. Opera tickets (September to July only) cost €7 to €109; ballets €8 to €67; and concerts €7 to €39. Unsold tickets are offered 15 minutes prior to showtime to students and

MONTMARTRE

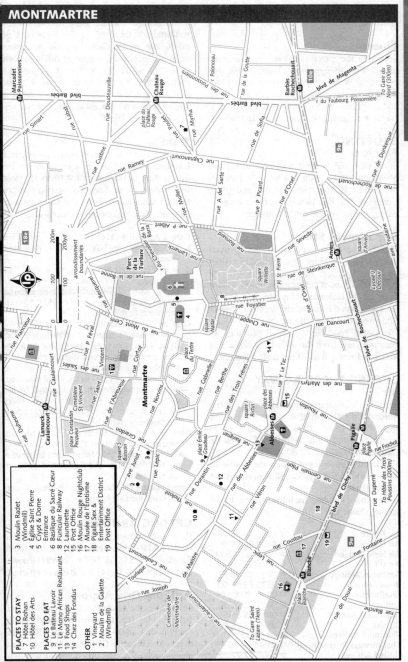

PLACES TO STAY
7 Hôtel Rohan
10 Hôtel des Arts

PLACES TO EAT
9 Le Bateau Lavoir
11 Le Mono African Restaurant
13 Food Shops
14 Chez des Fondus

OTHER
1 Vineyard
2 Moulin de la Galette (Windmill)
3 Moulin Radet (Windmill)
4 Église Saint Pierre
5 Crypt & Dome Entrance
6 Basilique du Sacré Cœur
8 Funicular Railway
15 Post Office
16 Moulin Rouge Nightclub
17 Musée de l'Érotisme
18 Pigalle Sex & Entertainment District
19 Post Office

under 25s for about €15 – ask for the *tarif spécial*.

Cinemas

Going to the movies in Paris is expensive (about €8), though most cinemas give discounts on Wednesday (and sometimes Monday and in the mornings). Check *Pariscope* and *L'Officiel des Spectacles* for listings: 'vo' *(version originale)* indicates subtitled movies.

SHOPPING
Fashion

Some of Paris' fanciest shops are along ave Montaigne and rue du Faubourg St Honoré, 8e; rue St Honoré, 1er and 8e; and place Vendôme, 1er. Rue Bonaparte, 6e, is home to a good choice of mid-range boutiques.

Department Stores

Paris' three main department stores, open 9.30am to 7pm Monday to Saturday (10pm on Thursday), are: **Au Printemps** *(☎ 01 42 82 50 00; 64 blvd Haussmann; metro Havre Caumartin)*; **Galeries Lafayette** *(☎ 01 42 82 36 40; 40 blvd Haussmann; metro Auber or Chaussée)* and **Samaritaine** *(☎ 01 40 41 20 20; metro Pont Neuf)*, which provides an amazing view from the 10th-floor terrace of Magasin Principal at 19 rue de la Monnaie.

GETTING THERE & AWAY
Air

Paris has two major international airports. **Aéroport d'Orly** *(flight & other information ☎ 01 49 75 15 15, 0836 25 05 05)* is 14km south of central Paris. **Aéroport Charles de Gaulle** *(☎ 01 48 62 22 80, 0836 25 05 05)*, also known as Roissy-Charles de Gaulle in the suburb of Roissy, is 23km northeast of central Paris.

Telephone numbers for information at Paris' airline offices are:

Air France	☎ 0836 68 10 48
Air Liberté	☎ 0825 80 58 05
Air New Zealand	☎ 01 40 53 82 23
Air UK	☎ 01 44 56 18 08
American Airlines	☎ 0810 87 28 72
British Airways	☎ 0825 82 54 00
Continental	☎ 01 42 99 09 09
Lufthansa	☎ 0802 02 00 30
Northwest Airlines	☎ 0810 55 65 56
Qantas	☎ 0820 82 05 00
Singapore Airlines	☎ 01 53 65 79 01
Thai Airways International	☎ 01 44 20 70 15
United Airlines	☎ 0801 72 72 72

Bus

The Eurolines terminal **Gare Routière Internationale** *(☎ 0836 69 52 52; Porte de Bagnolet, 20e; metro Gallieni)* is on the eastern edge of Paris. There's a ticket office in town *(☎ 01 43 54 11 99; 55 rue St Jacques, 5e; metro Cluny-La Sorbonne; open 9.30am-6.30pm Mon-Fri, 10am-1pm & 2pm-6pm Sat)*. There is no domestic, intercity bus service to or from Paris.

Train

Paris has six major train stations *(gares)*, each handling traffic to different destinations. For information in English call ☎ 0836 35 35 35 from 7am to 10pm. The metro station attached to each train station bears the same name as the gare. Paris' major train stations are:

Gare d'Austerlitz (13e) Loire Valley, Spain and Portugal and non-TGV trains to southwestern France.

Gare de l'Est (10e) Parts of France east of Paris (Champagne, Alsace and Lorraine), Luxembourg, parts of Switzerland (Basel, Lucerne, Zürich), southern Germany (Frankfurt, Munich) and points farther east.

Gare de Lyon (12e) Regular and TGV Sud-Est trains to places southeast of Paris, including Dijon, Lyon, Provence, the Côte d'Azur, the Alps, parts of Switzerland (Bern, Geneva, Lausanne), Italy and points beyond.

Gare Montparnasse (15e) Brittany and places between (Chartres, Angers, Nantes) and the terminus of the TGV Atlantique serving Tours, Nantes, Bordeaux and other destinations in southwestern France.

Gare du Nord (10e) Northern suburbs of Paris, northern France, the UK, Belgium, northern Germany, Scandinavia, Moscow etc; terminus of the TGV Nord (Lille and Calais), and the Eurostar to London.

Gare St Lazare (8e) Normandy, including Dieppe, Le Havre and Cherbourg.

GETTING AROUND

Paris' public transit system, mainly operated by the **RATP** *(Régie Autonome des Transports Parisiens; ☎ 0836 68 77 14; English information ☎ 0892 68 41 14)* is cheap and efficient.

To/From Orly Airport

Orly Rail is the quickest way to reach the Left Bank and the 16e. Take the free shuttle bus to the Pont de Rungis-Aéroport d'Orly RER station, which is on the C2 line, and get on a train heading into the city. Another fast way into town is the Orlyval shuttle train (€7, 35 to 40 minutes); it stops near Orly-Sud's Porte F and links Orly with the Antony RER station, which is on line B4. Orlybus (€5.50, 30 minutes) takes you to the Denfert-Rochereau metro station, 14e. Air France buses (€7.50) go to/from Gare Montparnasse, 15e (every 15 minutes) along Aérogare des Invalides in the 7e. RATP bus No 183 (one bus/metro ticket) goes to Porte de Choisy, 13e, but is very slow. Jetbus, the cheapest option, links both terminals with the Villejuif-Louis Aragon metro stop (€4.50, 15 minutes). All services between Orly and Paris run every 15 minutes or so (less frequently late at night) from 5.30am or 6.30am to 11pm or 11.30pm. A taxi to/from Orly costs about €45 to €55, plus €0.90 per piece of luggage weighing more than 5kg.

To/From Charles de Gaulle Airport
Roissybus links the city with both of the airport's train stations (€8, 50 minutes). To get to the airport, take any line B train whose four letter destination code begins with E (eg, EIRE). Regular metro ticket windows can't always sell these tickets, so you may have to buy one at the RER station where you board. Trains run every 15 or 20 minutes from 6am to around 11pm.

Air France bus No 2 will take you to Porte Maillot and the corner of ave Carnot near the Arc de Triomphe for €10; bus No 4 to Gare Montparnasse costs €11.50.

The RATP bus No 350 (€3.90 or three bus/metro tickets) links both aérogares with Porte de la Chapelle, 18e, and stops at Gare du Nord and Gare de l'Est, both in the 10e. RATP bus No 351 goes to ave du Trône, on the eastern side of place de la Nation in the 11e and runs every half-hour or so until 8.20pm (9.30pm from the airport to the city). The trip costs €3.90 or three bus/metro tickets.

A taxi to/from Charles de Gaulle costs about €40.

Bus
Short trips cost one bus/metro/RER ticket (see Metro/RER/Bus Tickets later), while longer rides require two. Travellers without tickets can purchase them from the driver. Whatever kind of *coupon* (ticket) you have, you must cancel it in the little machine next to the driver. The fines are hefty if you're caught without a ticket or without a cancelled ticket. If you have a Carte Orange or Paris

Visite pass (see the following Metro & RER section), just show it to the driver – do not cancel it in the machine.

After the metro shuts down at around 12.45am, the Noctambus network (its symbol is a black owl silhouetted against a yellow moon) links the Châtelet-Hôtel de Ville area with most parts of the city. Noctambuses begin their runs from ave Victoria, 4e, between the Hôtel de Ville and place du Châtelet between 1am and 5.30am seven days a week. A single ride costs €2.40 and allows one transfer onto another Noctambus.

Metro & RER
Paris' underground rail network consists of two separate but linked systems: the Métropolitain, known as the metro, which now has 14 lines and more than 300 stations, and the suburban commuter rail network, the RER which, along with certain SNCF lines, is divided into eight concentric zones. The whole system has been designed so that no point in Paris is more than 500m from a metro stop.

How It Works Each metro train is known by the name of its terminus; trains on the same line have different names depending on which direction they are travelling in. On lines that split into several branches and thus have more than one end-of-the-line station, the final destination of each train is indicated on the front, sides and interior of the train cars. In the stations, white-on-blue *sortie* signs indicate exits and black-on-orange *correspondance* signs show how to get to connecting trains. The last metro train sets out on its final run at 12.30am. Plan ahead so as not to miss your connection. The metro starts up again at 5.30am.

Metro/RER/Bus Tickets
The same tickets are valid on the metro, the bus and, for travel within the Paris city limits, the RER's 2nd-class carriages. They cost €1.30 if bought individually and €9.30 (half for children aged four to 11) for a *carnet* of 10. One ticket lets you travel between any two metro stations, including stations outside of the Paris city limits, no matter how many transfers are required. You can also use it on the RER system within zone 1.

For travel on the RER to destinations outside the city, purchase a special ticket *before* you board the train or you won't be able to get out of the station and could be fined. Always

FRANCE

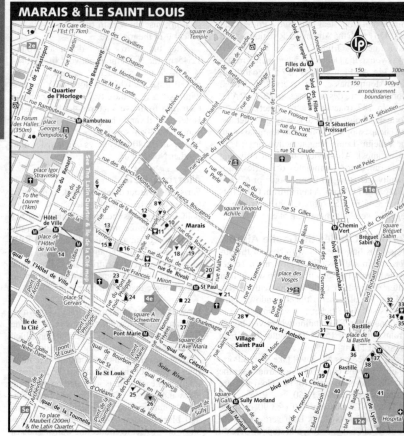

MARAIS & ÎLE SAINT LOUIS

keep your ticket until you reach your destination and exit the station.

The cheapest and easiest way to travel the metro is with a Carte Orange, a bus/metro/RER pass that comes in weekly and monthly versions. You can get tickets for travel in up to eight urban and suburban zones; the basic ticket – valid for zones 1 and 2 – is probably sufficient.

The weekly ticket costs €13.25 for zones 1 and 2 and is valid Monday to Sunday. Even if you'll be in Paris for only three or four days, it may very well work out cheaper than purchasing a carnet (you'll break even at 15 rides) and it will certainly cost less than purchasing a daily Mobilis or Paris Visite pass. The monthly Carte Orange ticket (€44.35 for zones 1 and 2) begins on the first day of each calendar month. Both are on sale in metro and RER stations and at certain bus terminals.

To get a monthly Carte Orange, bring a passport-size photograph of yourself to the ticket counter (automatic photo booths are in most stations). You don't need a photo for a weekly carte.

Mobilis and Paris Visite passes, designed for tourists, are on sale in many metro and train stations and international airports. The Mobilis card (and its *coupon*) allows unlimited travel for one day in two to eight zones (€5 to €17.95). Paris Visite transport passes, which provide discounts on entries to certain museums and activities as well as transport, are valid for one/two/three/five consecutive days of travel in either three, five or eight zones. The one- to three-zone version costs

MARAIS & ÎLE SAINT LOUIS

PLACES TO STAY
15 Hôtel Rivoli
16 Hôtel de Nice
20 Grand Hôtel Malher
22 MIJE Fourcy
23 MIJE Maubisson
27 MIJE Fauconnier
35 Hôtel Les Sans-Culottes

PLACES TO EAT
6 Aquarius Vegetarian
   Restaurant
8 Au Gamin de Paris
9 Le Colimacon
13 Minh Chau
18 Restaurants
19 Restaurant Jo Goldenberg
21 Food Shops

25 Berthillon Ice Cream
26 Food Shops
28 Monoprix Supermarket
30 Bofinger
31 Flo Prestige
32 Restaurants
34 Havanita

OTHER
1 Union des Centres de
   Rencontres Internationales
   de France (UCRIF)
2 Web Bar
3 EasyInternet
4 OTU Voyages
5 Centre Pompidou
7 Musée Picasso
10 Laundrette

11 L'Etoile Manquante
12 Les Mots à la
    Bouche Bookshop
14 Hôtel de Ville
    (City Hall)
17 Stolly's
24 Memorial to the
    Unknown Jewish Martyr
29 Maison de Victor Hugo
33 Café de la Danse
36 Colonne de Juillet
37 FNAC Store NEW;
    ticket office
38 Entrance to Opéra-Bastille
39 Paris à Vélo C'est Sympa!
40 Port de Plaisance
    de Paris Arsenal
41 Opéra-Bastille

€8.35/13.70/18.25/26.65 for one/two/three/five days. Children aged four to 11 pay half-price. They can be purchased at larger metro and RER stations, at SNCF bureaus in Paris and at the airports.

Taxi

The *prise en* charge (flag fall) is €2. Within the city limits, it costs €0.60 per kilometre for travel 7am to 7pm Monday to Saturday (tariff A). At night and on Sundays and holidays (tariff B), it's €1 per kilometre. An extra €2.45 is charged for taking a fourth passenger, but most drivers refuse to take more than three people because of insurance constraints. Luggage more than 5kg costs €0.90 extra and for pick-up from SNCF mainline stations there's a €0.70 supplement. The usual tip is 10% no matter what the fare.

There are 500 *tête de station* (taxi stands) in Paris. Radio-dispatched taxis include **Taxis Bleus** (☎ 01 49 36 10 10) and **G7 Taxis** (☎ 01 47 39 47 39). If you order a taxi by phone, the meter is switched on as soon as the driver gets your call.

Car & Motorcycle

Driving in Paris is nerve-wracking but not impossible. The fastest way to get across Paris is usually via the Périphérique, the ring road that encircles the city.

Street parking can cost €2 per hour; large municipal parking garages charge about €2.50/5/18 for one/two/24 hours.

If you rent a small car (Opel Corsa 1.2) for one day, including insurance and 250km, it will cost about €85, but cheaper deals are often available.

Rental agencies in Paris include:

Avis	☎ 0820 05 05 05, 01 43 48 29 26
Budget	☎ 01 45 44 62 00
Europcar	☎ 0825 35 23 52
Hertz	☎ 01 39 38 38 38
National/Citer	☎ 01 42 06 06 06

Bicycle

There are 130km of bicycle lanes running throughout Paris. Some of them aren't particularly attractive or safe, but cyclists may be fined about €40 for failing to use them. The tourist office distributes a free brochure-map called *Paris à Vélo*.

Paris à Vélo (see Bicycle under Organised Tours earlier) rents bikes for €12.20/30.50 for one/three days. Also try the RATP-sponsored Roue Libre (☎ 0810 44 15 34; 1 passage Mondétour).

Around Paris

The region surrounding Paris is known as the Île de France (Island of France) because of its position between the rivers Aube, Marne, Oise and Seine.

DISNEYLAND PARIS

It took US$4.4 billion to turn beet fields 32km east of Paris into the much heralded Disneyland Paris *(adult/child 3-11 years €39/29 Apr–early Jan, €29/25 early-Jan–Mar; open*

FRANCE

9am-8pm daily, 9am-11pm July-Aug), now the most popular tourist attraction in Europe. Three-day passes are available.

VERSAILLES
pop 95,000

Versailles served as the country's political capital and the seat of the royal court from 1682 until 1789. After the Franco-Prussian War of 1870–71, the victorious Prussians proclaimed the establishment of the German empire from the chateau's Galerie des Glaces (Hall of Mirrors), and in 1919 the Treaty of Versailles was signed in the same room, officially ending WWI.

The chateau can be jammed with tourists, especially on weekends, in summer and most especially on summer Sundays. Arrive early to avoid the queues or beat most of the queues by prebuying or buying a guided tour ticket when you arrive which includes general admission.

Information

The **tourist office** (☎ *01 39 24 88 88;* [e] *tourisme@ot-versailles.fr; 2 bis ave de Paris; open 9am-7pm daily Apr-Oct, 9am-6pm Nov-Mar)* is just north of the Versailles-Rive Gauche train station.

Château de Versailles

The enormous Château de Versailles *(☎ 01 30 83 78 00, 01 30 83 77 77)* was built in the mid-17th century during the reign of Louis XIV (the Sun King). The chateau essentially consists of four parts: the main palace building; the vast 17th-century gardens; the late-17th century Grand Trianon; and the mid-18th century Petit Trianon.

Opening Hours & Tickets The main building opens 9am to 5.30pm (6.30pm April to October) Tuesday to Sunday. Admission to the **Grands Appartements** (State Apartments), including the 73m-long **Galerie des Glaces** (Hall of Mirrors) and the **Appartement de la Reine** (Queen's Suite) costs €7.50 (€5.30 after 3.30pm, free for under 18s). Tickets are on sale at Entrée A (Entrance A) off to the right from the equestrian statue of Louis XIV as you approach the building. You won't be able to visit other parts of the main palace unless you take one of the guided tours (see Guided Tours later). Entrée H has facilities for the disabled, including a lift.

The **Grand Trianon** *(admission €5, €3 reduced rate; admits to Petit Trianon too)* opens noon to 6.30pm daily April to October; the rest of the year it closes at 5.30pm. The **Petit Trianon** is open the same days and hours.

The gardens (€3) are open 8am (9am in winter) to nightfall daily (except if it's snowing). On Saturday, July to September, and Sunday early April to early October, the baroque fountains 'perform' the **Grandes Eaux** *(☎ 01 30 83 78 78; admission €5.50; times vary).*

A 'passport' (€21.20) includes admission to the Chateau, audio tour, the Grand Trianon, Petit Trianon and the garden; it's available from FNAC stores and some SNCF stations.

Guided Tours To make a reservation go to entrées C or D. A one-hour tour costs €4.20 in addition to the regular entry fee; 80-minute audioguide tours are available at entrée A for €3.50.

Getting There & Away

Bus No 171 (€1.30 or one metro/bus ticket, 35 minutes) links Pont de Sèvres in Paris with the place d'Armes and Versailles but it's faster to go by train. Each of Versailles' three train stations is served by RER and/or SNCF trains coming from a different group of Paris stations.

RER line C4 takes you from Paris' Left Bank RER stations to Versailles-Rive Gauche station (€2.20). From Paris, catch any train with a four-letter code beginning with V. There are up to 70 trains daily (around 35 on Sunday), and the last train back to Paris leaves shortly before midnight.

RER line C5 links Paris' Left Bank with Versailles-Chantiers station (€2.20). From Paris, take any train whose code begins with 'S'. Versailles-Chantiers is also served by some three dozen SNCF trains daily (20 on Sunday) from Gare Montparnasse (€2.20, 15 minutes); all trains on this line continue on to Chartres.

From Paris' Gare St Lazare (€3) and La Défense (€2), the SNCF has approximately 70 trains daily to Versailles-Rive Droite, which is 1200m from the chateau. The last train to Paris leaves a bit past midnight.

CHARTRES
pop 42,059

The impressive 13th-century cathedral of Chartres rises spectacularly from the fields

38km southwest of Paris. The amenable town is an easy place to spend a day or two.

Orientation

The medieval sections of Chartres are situated along the Eure River and the hillside to the west. The cathedral is about 500m east of the train station.

Information

The **tourist office** (☎ 02 37 18 26 26; e chartres.tourism@wanadoo.fr) is across place de la Cathédrale from the cathedral's main entrance. The **post office** (place des Épars) handles money exchange.

Cathédrale Notre Dame

There have been churches on this site since the 4th century. The current 13th-century cathedral (☎ 02 37 21 75 02; open 8am-8pm Easter-Oct, 8.30am-7.30pm Nov-Easter, except during services) has a high degree of architectural unity, having been built in 30 years after a Romanesque cathedral on this site was destroyed by fire in 1194.

Unlike so many of its contemporaries, this early Gothic masterpiece has not been significantly modified, apart from its 16th-century steeple.

Fascinating **tours** (☎ 02 37 28 15 58; adults/students €5.50/4) are conducted by Englishman Malcolm Miller from Easter to November; audioguides (€2.50 to €5.65) are available from the cathedral bookshop. The 112m-high **Clocher Neuf** (new bell tower; adult/concession 18-25 years €4/2.50) is well worth the ticket price and the long, spiral climb.

Inside, the cathedral's most exceptional feature is its 172 **stained-glass windows**, most of which are 13th-century originals. The **trésor** (treasury) displays a piece of cloth said to have been worn by the Virgin Mary.

The early-11th century Romanesque **crypt**, the largest in France, can be visited by a half-hour guided tour in French (with a written English translation) for €2.30.

Old City

Streets with buildings of interest include **rue de la Tannerie**, which runs along the Eure, and **rue des Écuyers**, midway between the cathedral and the river.

Église St Pierre (place St Pierre) has a massive bell tower dating from around 1000 and some fine (and often overlooked) medieval stained-glass windows.

Places to Stay

Camping About 2.5km southeast of the train station there's **Les Bords de l'Eure** (☎ 02 37 28 79 43, fax 02 37 23 41 99; 9 rue de Launay; open May-early Sept). Bus No 8 (direction Hôpital) from the train station goes to the Vignes stop.

Hostel The pleasant and calm **Auberge de Jeunesse** (☎ 02 37 34 27 64, fax 02 37 35 75 85; 23 ave Neigre; dorm beds €10.50; reception open 2pm-10pm daily) includes breakfast in its rates. From the train station, take bus No 5 (direction Mare aux Moines) to the Rouliers stop.

Hotels It's fair to say that **Hôtel de l'Ouest** (☎ 02 37 21 43 27, fax 02 37 21 47 80; 3 place Pierre Sémard; singles/doubles from €15/23) is pretty dingy. Better is **Hôtel Jehan de Beauce** (☎ 02 37 21 01 41, fax 02 37 21 59 10; e jehan_de_beauce@club-internet.fr; 19 ave Jehan de Beauce; singles/doubles from €37/45).

Le Boeuf Couronné (☎ 02 37 18 06 06, fax 02 37 21 72 13; 15 place Châtelet; singles/doubles from €26/29) is quiet but central with a decent restaurant.

Places to Eat

Across from the south porch of the cathedral is **Café Serpente** (☎ 02 37 21 68 81; 2 rue du Cloître Notre Dame; mains €13-18). Nearby, **La Vieille Maison** (☎ 02 37 34 10 67; 5 rue au Lait; menus €28 & €45; open Tues-Sat lunch & dinner, Sun lunch only) is a much-lauded restaurant.

Le Vesuve (☎ 02 37 21 56 35; 30 place des Halles; pizzas €6.50-9.50) serves light meals. There's a **Monoprix supermarket** (21 rue Noël Ballay) situated northeast of place des Épars.

Getting There & Around

Train There are three dozen trains daily (20 on Sunday) to/from Paris' Gare Montparnasse (€11.40, 55 to 70 minutes) also stopping at Versailles' Chantiers station (€9.70, 45 to 60 minutes). The last train back to Paris leaves Chartres a bit after 9pm (7.55pm on Saturday, after 10pm on Sunday and holidays).

FRANCE

Champagne

Champagne is a largely agricultural region famed for its sparkling wines.

The town of Épernay is the de facto champagne capital and the best place for *dégustation* (wine tastings).

REIMS
pop 220,000

Reconstructed after wartime, Reims isn't particularly attractive or friendly.

However, it is proud of its champagne heritage and famed cathedral.

Orientation & Information
The commercial centre, northwest of the cathedral, runs along rue Carnot with the train station located across place Drouet d'Erlon, the city's major nightlife centre.

The **tourist office** (☎ 03 26 77 45 25, fax 03 26 77 45 27; W www.tourisme.fr/reims; 2 rue Guillaume de Machault; open 9am-7pm Mon-Sat, 10am-6pm Sun Apr-Sept, 9am-6pm Mon-Sat, 11am-5pm Sun Oct-Mar) exchanges currency at weekends when the **Credit Lyonnais exchange machine** (rue du Trésor) is closed.

There's a **post office** (8 place Drouet d'Erlon; open 8.30am-6pm Mon-Sat, 8am-noon Sun) with Cyberposte; **Clique et Croque** (☎ 02 36 86 93 92; 27 rue de Vesle; open 10.30am-12.30am Mon-Sat, 2pm-9pm Sun) charges €4.50 for one hour online. There is a **laundrette** (59 rue Chanzy; open 7am-9.30pm daily) in town.

Things to See & Do
Reims boasts four Unesco sites: **Cathédrale Notre Dame** (open 7.30am-7.30pm), the **Palais du Tau** (☎ 03 26 47 81 79; 2 place du Cardinal Luçon; adult/concession €5.50/2.50; open Tues-Sun), the **Basilique St-Rémi** (place St Rémi), and nearby **Musée St-Rémi** (☎ 03 26 85 23 36; 53 rue Simon; adult/student €1.52/free; open 2pm-6.30pm daily, 2pm-7pm Sat-Sun).

Of Reims' nine Champagne cellars, four offer guided tours without reservation (tasting session included). **Mumm** (☎ 03 26 49 59 70; 34 rue du Champ de Mars) has €5 tours year-round from 9am to 11am and 2pm to 5pm (closed weekend mornings from November to February); **Taittinger** (☎ 03 26 85 84 33;

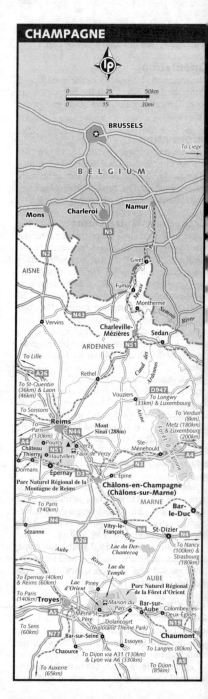

CHAMPAGNE

place Ste Nicaise) has €5.50 tours from
.30am to noon and 2pm to 4.30pm Monday
Friday, 9am to 11am and 2pm to 5pm Sat-
rday and Sunday (closed weekends Decem-
er to February); **Maxim's** (☎ 03 26 82 70
7; 17 rue des Créneaux) has tours daily from
)am to 7pm; and **Piper-Heidsieck** (☎ 03 26
4 43 44; 51 blvd Henry Vasnier) has €6.50
mily tours daily from 9am to 11.45am and
pm to 5.15pm (closed Tuesday and Wednes-
ay during January and February).

Places to Stay
he **Centre International de Séjour** (CIS;
03 26 40 52 60, fax 03 26 47 35 70;
haussée Bocquaise; dorm beds/singles €9/
4 breakfast included) is 1km west of the
athedral in Parc Léo Lagrange. Take bus H to
op Pont De Gaulle. It offers bike hire (half-/
ll day/weekend €7.61/10.65/18.26).

The friendly **Hôtel Alsace** (☎ 03 26 47 44
8, fax 03 26 47 44 52; 6 rue du Général Sar-
il; singles/doubles/quads €22/24/42) is the
est budget option. It offers a fantastic €9.90
nch menu.

On place Drouet d'Erlon, **Grand Hôtel du
ord** (☎ 03 26 47 39 03, fax 03 26 40 92 26;
ngles/doubles €46.50/53.40) at No 75 is an
ld favourite; **Hôtel Crystal** (☎ 03 26 88 44
4; singles/doubles with shower & toilet
38/46) at No 86 has smart rooms off a quiet
ourtyard.

Le Bon Moine (☎ 03 26 47 33 64, fax 03
6 40 43 87; 14 rue des Capucins; singles/
oubles €38/43) is a small but cosy place.

Places to Eat & Drink
Place Drouet d'Erlon is the centre of action.
'Apostrophe (☎ 03 26 79 19 89; menu
13), at No 59, is a brasserie with a literary
heme, **The Glue Pot** (☎ 03 26 47 36 46; plats
8-10) at No 49, is an Irish pub with Tex-
Mex food, and **Waïda** (☎ 03 26 47 44 49;
losed Mon) at No 5, is a great little patisserie
or coffee or snacks.

Le Chamois (☎ 03 26 88 69 75; 45 rue des
Capucins; closed Sun lunch & Wed) has tasty
8/12.50 lunch/dinner menus.

For self-caterers, try the **food market** (place
lu Boulingrin; until 2pm Wed & Sat) and
Monoprix supermarket (1 rue de Talleyrand;
pen 8.30am-9pm Mon-Sat).

Le Kraft (☎ 03 26 05 29 29; 5 rue Salin;
pen until 3am Tues-Sat) is the artistic
ightlife hub.

Getting There & Away
Bus The only way to reach Troyes is by bus.
TransChampagne (STDM; ☎ 03 26 65 17 07)
buses leave from the station (€18.50, two
hours, two to four daily, one on Sunday except
university holiday periods).

Train Reims' **train station** (☎ 08 92 35 35
39) has direct connections to Paris' Gare de
l'Est (€19.10, 1½ hours, up to 18 daily), Épernay (€5, 25 minutes, 13 to 21 daily), Dijon
(€30.40, 3¾ hours, four daily) and Nancy
(€24.60, 2½ hours, two or three daily).

ÉPERNAY
pop 26,000
Épernay, an easy day trip 25km south of
Reims, is home to some of the world's most
famous champagne houses.

Orientation & Information
The mansion-lined ave de Champagne, home
to many of Épernay's champagne houses,
stretches eastward from the town's commercial heart (around place des Arcades). The
tourist office (☎ 03 26 53 33 00, fax 03
26 51 95 22; w www.epernay.net; 7 ave
de Champagne; open 9.30am-12.30pm &
1.30pm-7pm Mon-Sat, 11am-4pm Sun Apr-
Oct, to 5.30pm & closed Sun Oct-Mar) has
details of cellar visits.

Cyberposte and currency exchange are on
offer at the **main post office** (place Hugues
Plomb; open 8am-7pm Mon-Fri, 8am-noon
Sat); **ATMs** line place de la République. Net
café **Icône** (☎ 03 26 55 73 93; 25 rue Hôpital
Auban Moët; open 11am-11pm Mon-Thur,
11am-1am Fri & Sat, 3pm-8pm Sun) charges
€4.57 for one hour online.

There's a **Lavoclair** laundrette (18 rue Jean
Jaures; open 7am-8pm daily).

Champagne Houses
Of Épernay's 13 champagne houses, three
offer guided visits without reservation (including tasting). **Moët & Chandon** (☎ 03 26 51 20
20; 20 ave de Champagne; adult/concession
€7/4) has tours daily from 9.30am to 11.30am
and 2pm to 4.30pm (closed Tuesday and
Wednesday from December to mid-March).
Mercier (☎ 03 26 51 22 22; 68-70 ave de
Champagne; adult/child €6/3) offers tours
daily from 9.30am to 11.30am and 2pm to
4.30pm (5pm weekends and holidays; closed
on Tuesday and Wednesday from December to

February). De Castellane (☎ 03 26 51 19 19; 57 rue de Verdun; adult/child €6/3) has cellar tours (including museum visit) daily from 10am to noon and 2pm to 6pm daily from March to December.

Places to Stay

The Camping Municipal (☎ 03 26 55 32 14; allées de Cumières; per person €12.20; open mid-Apr–Sept) is 2km northwest of the station and poorly served by public transport. Foyer des Jeunes Travailleurs (☎ 03 26 51 62 51, fax 03 26 54 15 60; 2 rue Pupin; dorm beds €11) is the closest hostel.

The smart and friendly Hôtel St Pierre (☎ 03 26 54 40 80, fax 03 26 57 88 68; 1 rue Jeanne d'Arc; rooms from €25) is deservedly the most popular option in town – book ahead. Near the station, Hôtel Le Chapon Fin (☎ 03 26 55 40 03, fax 03 26 54 94 17; 2 place Mendès France; rooms from €34) provides refurbished rooms and an adjoining restaurant.

Places to Eat

Restaurants Place de la République has several cafés with €10 lunchtime menus; try Le Central at No 11 or Le Progrés at No 5. Otherwise head for cheap eats in rue Gambetta. The La Cave à Champagne (☎ 03 26 55 50 70; menus €13-25; closed Wed evening) at No 16 is a cut above with local specialities.

L'Ancêtre (☎ 03 26 55 57 56; 20 rue de la Fauvette; menus €13.30-18.30; open Thur-Tues, closed Tues evening Nov-Mar) serves traditional French cuisine.

Le Darjeeling (☎ 03 26 51 56 80; 32 place des Arcades; closed Sun) is a good spot for a salad (€8) or crepe (€3).

Self Catering Self-caterers can head for the covered market (rue Ste Thibault; open 8am-noon Wed-Sat), the Marché Plus grocery (13 place Hugues Plomb; open 7am-9pm Mon-Sat, 9am-1pm Sun) or nearby Monoprix supermarket (open 9.30am-12.30pm & 2pm-7pm Mon-Sat).

Getting There & Away

The train station (☎ 08 92 35 35 39; place Mendès-France) has direct connections to Paris' Gare de l'Est (€16.50, 1¼ hours, 12 to 15 daily), Reims (€5, 30 minutes, 13 to 21 daily) and Nancy (€21.30, two hours, five daily).

Getting Around

The town centre is easily accessible on foo Rémi Royer (☎ 03 26 55 29 61; 10 plac Hugues Plomb; open 9am-noon & 2pm-7pr Tues-Sat) hires mountain bikes for half-/fu day €11/17.

TROYES
pop 125,000

Troyes, famous for its churches and cut-pric outlet stores, has no champagne cellars. does, however, boast a charming old tow making it the most attractive of the thre Champagne towns.

Orientation & Information

The old town is centred around the 17th century town hall and nearby Église St-Jea with rue Georges Clémenceau and place Ale andre Israël providing the central hub.

The main tourist office (☎ 03 25 82 62 7(fax 03 25 73 06 71; W www.ot-troyes.fr; 1 blvd Carnot; open 9am-12.30pm & 2pm 6.30pm Mon-Sat, closed holidays) is situate to the west, with an annexe (☎ 03 25 73 3 88; rue Mignard; open 9am-8.30pm Mon-Sa July-Sept, 9am-12.30pm & 2pm-6.30pr Oct-June, 10am-noon & 2pm-5pm Sun & holidays, 10am-6.30pm Sun July-Sept) oppo site Église St-Jean. There's a billet commu (combined ticket; adult/child €6/1.50), vali for admission to any four museums.

The post office (place Général Patton open 9am-noon & 1.30pm-6.30pm Mon-Fr 9am-noon Sat) has currency exchange, a does the Credit Agricole opposite. Cyberwa (☎ 03 25 40 86 95; 20 rue Claude Huez charges €3 for one hour online. There's laundrette (9 rue Georges Clemenceau; oper 7.30am-8pm daily).

Things to See & Do

Half-timbered houses line the streets o Troyes' old city, rebuilt after a devastating fir in 1524. Of the nine churches in town, fiv open year-round – ask the tourist office for de tails as opening times vary throughout the year

Museums are free on Wednesday and the first Sunday of the month. In the Quartier de la Cité district, the superb Musée d'Art Moderne (☎ 03 25 76 26 80; place St-Pierre, adult/concession €4.60/0.80; open 11am 6pm Tues-Sun, closed holidays) has works by Matisse, Picasso and Cézanne. The Musée St Loup (☎ 03 25 76 21 68; rue Chrestien de royes; adult/concession €4.60/0.8; open 0am-noon & 2pm-6pm Wed-Mon; closed olidays), comprises natural history, archaeology and fine arts exhibits.

Troyes' famous **magasins d'usine** (factory utlets; open 10am-7pm, closed Mon morng & Sun) attract coachloads of designer argain-hunters. **Marques Avenue** (☎ 08 25 5 86 87) has fashion goods, **McArthur Glen** ☎ 03 25 70 47 10) has fashion and **Marques** ity sports goods.

Places to Stay

Camping Municipal (☎ 03 25 81 02 64; 7 rue oger Salengro; €9.50 per night; open Apr-15 ct) is 3.1km northeast of the train station. ake bus No 1 (direction Pont Ste-Marie) to top Stade de l'Aube. There's also camping at he **Auberge de Jeunesse** (☎ 03 25 82 00 65, ax 03 25 72 93 78; e troyes-rosiers@fuaj.org; chemin Ste Scholastique; dorm beds €8), .5km south of the train station. Take bus No (direction Rosières-Château) to stop Liberté.

Troyes hotels operate the Bon Weekend en ille scheme in winter only. The best spot is he friendly **Hôtel Les Comtes de Champagne** (☎ 03 25 73 11 70, fax 03 25 73 06 02; 6 rue de la Monnaie; singles/doubles with hower & toilet €31/34). If it's full, **Hôtel du** **héâtre** (☎ 03 25 73 18 47, fax 03 25 73 85 73; 35 rue Jules Lebocey; singles/doubles €24/32) is a cheap option in a quiet location.

Hôtel Arlequin (☎ 03 25 83 12 70, fax 03 25 83 12 99; 50 rue Turenne; singles/doubles €30.50/32.50, with shower & toilet €36.50/ 40.50) has smart rooms.

Places to Eat & Drink

Restaurants are found on the pedestrian streets around place Alexandre Israël.

Pizzeria Giuseppino (☎ 03 25 73 92 44; 26 rue Paillot de Montabert; closed lunch Mon & Sun) has good (€10) pizzas. Around the corner, **L'Illustré** (☎ 03 25 40 00 88; 8 rue Champeux) attracts a young crowd. The speciality dish is andouillette (€12.50), a sausage made of pig's intestines – tastier than it sounds.

For snacks or coffee, **Le Potron Minet** (☎ 03 25 73 62 42; 1 cour du Mortier d'Or; open 9am-5pm Mon-Sat, 2pm-7pm Sun; allday menu €12), a rare nonsmoking café, is a mellow spot in a historic courtyard.

For self-caterers, try **Les Halles** (open 8am-12.30pm & 3pm-7pm Mon-Sat, closed Sun afternoon), just off rue de la République or the

Monoprix supermarket (71 rue Émile Zola; open 8.30am-8pm Mon-Sat) with one of the most elaborate shop facades in France.

For a beer, **La Bougnat des Pouilles** (☎ 03 25 73 59 85; 29 rue Paillot de Montabert) has live music and exhibitions.

Getting There & Away

Bus Coach services plug the gaps in Troyes' rail services. **Courriers de l'Aube** in a corner of the train station, has details of buses to Sens (€12.50, two hours).

TransChampagne (STDM; ☎ 03 26 65 17 07) runs two to four buses daily (one on Sunday except during university holiday periods, none on holidays) to Reims (€18.50, two hours). **Les Rapides de Bourgogne** (☎ 03 86 94 95 00) has a 4pm service Monday to Wednesday to Auxerre in Burgundy (€13.20, two hours).

Train The only direct connection to/from Troyes (☎ 08 92 35 35 39) is to Paris' Gare de l'Est (€18.60, 1½ hours, up to 13 daily) and Basel (Bâle in French, €33.40, 3½ hours, three to five daily).

Alsace & Lorraine

The charming Alsace region, long a meeting place of Europe's Latin and Germanic cultures, nestles between the Vosges Mountains and the Rhine River, which marks the Franco-German border.

Most of Alsace became part of France in 1648 (Strasbourg, the region's largest city, retained its independence until 1681) but French rule did little to dampen German enthusiasm for a foothold on the west bank of the Rhine; the region (along with part of Lorraine) was twice annexed by Germany – from the Franco-Prussian War (1871) until the end of WWI, and again between 1940 and 1944.

STRASBOURG
pop 451,000

Strasbourg, just a few kilometres west of the Rhine, is Alsace's intellectual and cultural capital. Towering above the restaurants and pubs of the lively old city is the marvellous cathedral, near which you'll find one of the finest ensembles of museums in France.

When it was founded in 1949, the Council of Europe decided to base itself in Strasbourg as a symbol of Franco-German (as well as pan-European) co-operation. The city is also the seat of the European parliament (the legislative branch of the EU) hence many signs are in French, German and English.

Today, Strasbourg has acquired something of a reputation as a flashpoint for street crime, an issue currently dominating French politics.

Around the tram intersection place de l'Homme-de-Fer, travellers should keep their wits about them – as they should in any European city at night.

Orientation

The train station is 400m west of the Grande Île ('Large Island'), the city centre, which is delimited by the Ill River to the south and the Fossé du Faux Rempart to the north. Place Kléber, the main public square on the Grande Île, is 400m northwest of the cathedral. Grand Rue is the main pedestrian thoroughfare; most nightlife is across the river in the Krutenau quarter.

Information

The **main tourist office** (☎ 03 88 52 28 28, fax 03 88 52 28 29; w www.strasbourg.com; 17 place de la Cathédrale; open 9am-7pm daily) has **branch offices** (☎ 03 88 32 51 49 • ☎ 03 88 61 39 23; both open 9am-12.30pm & 1.45pm-6pm Mon-Sat, 9.30am-12.30pm & 1.15pm-5.30pm Sun) at level 1 in the underground complex beneath the train station and at Pont de l'Europe respectively. Offices exchange money and sell the three-day **Strasbourg Pass** (€9.90), which offers sightseeing discounts.

Post & Communications The **main post office** (5 ave de la Marseillaise; open 8am-noon & 1pm-5.30pm Mon-Fri, 8am-noon Sat) has exchange services and Cyberposte; there's a branch in place de la Cathédrale.

Best Coffee Shop (☎ 03 88 35 10 60; 10 quai des Pêcheurs; open 8am-7pm Mon-Fri, 9.30am-5pm Sat) offers one hour of Internet access for €3 with a compulsory drink. The **L'Utopie** (☎ 03 88 23 89 21; 21 rue du Fossé des Tanneurs), off the cinema-lined rue du 22 Novembre, has the same rate.

Laundry On the Grande Île, there are **laundrettes** at 29 Grand' Rue (open 8am to 8pm) and 15 rue des Veaux (open 8am to 9pm).

Things to See

Grande Île is about bustling public squares and pedestrianised areas with upmarket shopping. Work started on Strasbourg's lacy Gothic cathedral, **Cathédrale Notre Dame** (open 7am-11.30am & 12.40pm-7pm daily), in 1176. The west facade was completed in 1284; the spire (its southern companion was never built) not until 1439. The **astronomical clock** (adult/concession €0.80/0.60) goes through its paces at 12.30pm daily. You can visit the 66m-high **platform** (adult/concession €3/2.30; open 9am-7pm) above the facade (from which the tower and its spire soar another 76m) via 332 steep steps.

Crisscrossed by narrow lanes, canals and locks, **Petite France**, in the southwest corner of the Grande Île, is a fairy-tale area of half-timbered houses.

Tours of the **European parliament** (☎ 03 88 17 20 07) and the **Conseil de l'Europe** (Council of Europe; ☎ 03 88 41 20 29) – both about 2km northeast of the cathedral – have been scaled down for security reasons. Group tours are still possible; phone ahead for reservations.

Place de la Gare hosts a huge flea market every Saturday.

Museums

The outstanding **Musée de l'Œuvre Notre Dame** (3 place du Château; open 10am-6pm Tues-Sun) displays one of France's finest collections of sculpture, including many of the cathedral's original statues. The **Palais Rohan** (2 place du Château; open 10am-6pm Wed-Mon), built between 1732 and 1742 as a residence for the city's princely bishops, now houses three museums (combined ticket €6/3 per adult/concession): the **Musée Archéologique**, **Musée des Arts Décoratifs** and the **Musée des Beaux-Arts**.

The superb **Musée d'Art Moderne et Contemporain** (☎ 03 88 23 31 31; 1 place Hans Jean Arp; adult/concession €4.40/3; open 11am-7pm Tues-Sun, 11am-10pm Thur) has a extensive collection of works from Rodin to Picasso.

The **Musée Alsacien** (23-25 quai Saint-Nicolas; adult/concession €3/1.5; open 10am-6pm Wed-Sun) glimpses Alsatian life throughout history.

Organised Tours

Call to reserve a free brewery tour of **Kronenbourg** (☎ 03 88 27 41 59; 68 route d'Oberhausbergen; tram stop Duc d'Alsace) or **Heineken** (☎ 03 88 19 57 50; 4 rue Saint-Charles; bus No 4 to Schiltigheim Mairie). Both are in suburbs about 2.5km from the city centre.

Strasbourg Fluvial (☎ 03 88 84 13 13; adult/concession €6.40/3.20) boat excursions run all year (duration 70 minutes), leaving from behind Palais Rohan.

Places to Stay

It's *extremely* difficult to find accommodation from Monday to Thursday when the European parliament is in plenary session (one week monthly, except August, and twice in October). Many hotels, however, offer good deals at weekends.

Camping Grassy **Camping de la Montagne Verte** (☎ 03 88 30 25 46; 2 rue Robert Forrer; open Mar-Dec; 2-person sites €10.90) is a not far from the **Auberge de Jeunesse René Cassin** (see Hostels). Rates include breakfast.

Hostels The modern **CIARUS** (☎ 03 88 15 27 88, fax 03 88 15 27 89; 7 rue Finkmatt; bus No 4, 2 or 10 to place de Pierre stop; dorm beds from €16 including breakfast) is about 1km northeast of the train station.

The 286-bed **Auberge de Jeunesse René Cassin** (☎ 03 88 30 26 46, fax 03 88 30 35 16; 9 rue de l'Auberge de Jeunesse; dorm beds €13 including breakfast) is 2km southwest of the train station. Take tram B or C to Montagene Verte stop then bus No 12, 13 or 15 to Auberge de Jeunesse stop.

Hotels Opposite the train station there's the **Hôtel du Rhin** (☎ 03 88 32 35 00, fax 03 88 23 51 92; 7-8 place de la Gare; doubles with washbasin/shower & toilet from €41/58) which has decent but unwelcoming rooms. A better option, a few minutes' walk along rue du Maire Kuss, is refurbished **Le Grillon** (☎ 03 88 32 71 88, fax 03 88 32 22 01; e contact@grillon.com; 2 rue Thiergarten; singles/doubles €38/49), which offers clean rooms, a €6.50 buffet breakfast and Internet access (€1 for 15 minutes).

Opposite, **Hôtel Le Colmar** (☎ 03 88 32 16 89, fax 03 88 21 97 17; 1 rue du Maire Kuss; singles/doubles from €24/27) has cheap, simple rooms.

Rooms at the dark and rustic **Hôtel Patricia** (☎ 03 88 32 14 60, fax 03 88 32 19 08; e hotelpatricia@hotmail.com; 1a rue du Puits; rooms with/without bathroom €29/38) are ordinary but there are great views of Petit France.

The two-star **Hôtel de l'Ill** (☎ 03 88 36 20 01, fax 03 88 35 30 03; 8 rue des Bateliers; singles/doubles €34/40) has a quiet location away from tourist hordes.

Hotel Gutenberg (☎ 03 88 32 17 15, fax 03 88 75 76 67; 31 rue des Serruriers; rooms without/with shower €53/73) is smart with a central location.

Places to Eat

A *winstub* (pronounced **veen**-shtub) is typically Alsacian, serving hearty fare. **Winstub Le Clou** (3 rue du Chaudron; mains from €12-20; closed Wed lunch, Sun & holidays) is a good example.

Rue de l'Écurie is the best spot for cheap eats. It has several decent restaurants offering good value *menus* which (rare for Strasbourg) open on Sunday too.

At No 4, **La Robe des Champs** (☎ 03 88 22 36 82) has huge €10 salads, while **Le Petit Ours** (☎ 03 88 32 13 21) at No 3 has filling lunch options.

Of Petite France's tourist-oriented restaurants **Au Pont St Martin** (15 rue des Moulins; menu €7) has a few vegetarian options.

Visiting dignitaries head for **Au Crocodile** (☎ 03 88 32 13 02; 10 rue de l'Outre; lunch menus from €119) for its two Michelin stars.

Self-service vegetarian-organic food is on offer at **Adan** (☎ 03 88 35 70 84; 6 rue Sédillot; open noon-2pm Mon-Sat); self-caterers head for **Monoprix supermarket** (47 rue des Grandes Arcades; open 8.30am-8pm Mon-Sat).

Try **Café La Chaine d'Or** (134 Grand Rue) to read the papers over a coffee.

Entertainment

Strasbourg's live music venue is **La Laiterie** (☎ 03 88 23 72 37; 13 rue de Hohwald); the **L'Abattoir** (☎ 03 88 32 28 12; 1 quai Charles Altorffer) is the techno club, while **La Salamandre** (☎ 03 88 25 79 42; 3 rue Paul Janet; open 9pm-3am Wed-Sat) has 1980s nights.

Students frequent the **Académie de la Bière** (☎ 03 88 22 38 88; 17 rue Adolphe Seyboth; open 9am-2.30am Mon-Fri, 9am-4am Sat & Sun), which has a daily 6pm to 8pm happy hour and €4 beer cocktails. **The Irish Times** (☎ 03 88 32 04 02; 19 rue St Barbe; open

STRASBOURG

PLACES TO STAY
1 CIARUS Hostel
16 Hôtel du Rhin
17 Hôtel Le Grillon
19 Hôtel Le Colmar
33 Hôtel de l'Ill
39 Hôtel Gutenberg
50 Hôtel Patricia

PLACES TO EAT
26 Au Crocodile
27 Monoprix Supermarket
28 Winstub Le Clou
40 Café La Chaine d'Or
44 Au Pont St Martin
51 Le Petit Ours
52 La Robe des Champs
55 Adan Vegetarian Restaurant

MUSEUMS
35 Palais Rohan (Musée
   Archéologique, Musée des Arts
   Décoratifs & Musée des
   Beaux-Arts)
36 Musée de l'Œuvre Notre Dame
49 Musée d'Art Moderne et
   Contemporain
53 Musée Alsacien

PUBS & CLUBS
31 La Salamandre
32 Rock City
43 The Irish Times
45 Académie de la Bière
47 L'Abattoir

TRAM STOPS
3 Parc du Contades Tram Stop
8 République Tram Stop
13 Ancienne Synagogue
   Les Halles Tram Stop
14 Gare Centrale (Underground
   Tram Stop)
24 Homme de Fer Tram & Bus Hub
29 Gallia Tram Stop
42 Langstross Grand'
   Rue Tram Stop
46 Faubourg National Tram Stop
48 Musée d'Art Moderne
   Tram Stop
56 Porte de l'Hôpital
   Tram Stop

OTHER
2 Église Saint Pierre-
  le-Jeune (Catholic)
4 Synagogue de la Paix

5 US Consulate
6 Église Saint Paul
7 Main Post Office
9 Banque de France
10 Hôtel de Police
11 Laundrette
12 Église Saint
   Pierre-le-Jeune
   (Prostestant)
15 Tourist Office
   Annexe (Galerie
   de l'En-Verre)
18 Velocation Bike Hire
20 Pont Kuss Bus Stop
21 Église Saint Pierre-le-Vieux
   (Catholic & Protestant)
22 Laundrette
23 L'Utopie Internet
25 CTS Bus Information
   Office
30 Best Coffee Shop
34 Strasbourg Fluvial Boat
   Excursions
37 Cathédrale Notre Dame
38 Main Tourist Office
41 German Consulate
54 Eurolines Coach Office
57 Hôpital Civil

To Brasseries
Heineken (1.5km)

To Hautepierre
Maillon Tram
Terminus

To Kronenbourg
brewery (2km)

Place des
Halles
Shopping
Mall

blvd Clemenceau

rue du Fossé des

rue du Faubourg de Pierre

blvd du Président Wilson

rue du Faubourg de Saverne

rue du Marais Vert

Kléber

rue de Pâques

12

13

quai Kellerman

quai Kellermann

Train
Station

place
de la
Gare

14

15

rue Thiergarten

rue Kageneck

rue Kuhn

Public Library

Underground
Tramway

quai de Paris

quai du Vieux

Marché; aux Vins

rue de la Haute Mon

24

rue du Maire Kuss

Saint-Jean

17
18
16

19

pont
Kuss
Desaix

rue du Jeu des Enfants

Place
de l'Homme
de Fer

place
Kléber

25

rue de la Course

20

quai Altorffer

quai Turckheim

21

rue du 21 Novembre

rue du Fossé des Tanneurs

rue des
Francs Bourg

23

rue du Faubourg National

46

22

Sainte-Hélène

rue Sainte Marguerite

45

47

R Adolph Seyboth

quai Adolph Seyboth

rue du Bain aux Plantes

Grand'

rue

43

blvd de Nancy

rue de Rosheim

blvd de Metz

rue Déserte

place Hans Jean Arp

Petite
France

rue des Moulins

ponts
Couverts

rue du
Bouclier

rue Salzmann

rue Saint Martin
du Pont

place
Thor

44

49

48

rue de
Molsheim

Barrage
Vauban

Towers

rue Finkwiller

quai Finkwiller

rue M Luther

blvd de Lyon

rue de Wasselonne

Ill River

Hôtel
du
Département

rue des Glacières

rue Kinchleger

rue d'Obernai

Humann

To La Laiterie
(200m)

To Auberge de Jeunesse
René Cassin (1.2km),
Camping de la Montagne Verte
(1.8km), Airport (12km) & Obernai

rue Sébastopol

STRASBOURG

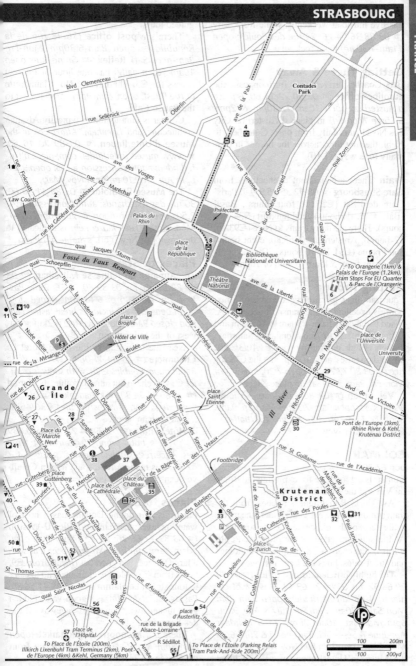

blvd Clemenceau

rue Sellénick

rue Oberlin

ave de la Paix

Contades Park

rue Turenne

quai Zorn

4

3

ave des Vosges

rue du Maréchal Foch

rue Finkmatt

1

Law Courts

2

rue du Général de Castelnau

Palais du Rhin

Préfecture

rue du Général Gouraud

place de la République

ave d'Alsace

quai Jacques Sturm

Fossé du Faux Rempart

quai Schoepflin

Bibliothèque National et Universitaire

5

To Orangerie (1km) & Palais de l'Europe (1.2km), Tram Stops For EU Quarter & Parc de l'Orangerie

6

rue de la Fonderie

Théâtre National

ave de la Liberté

quai de la Nuée Bleue

10

11

quai Lezay-Marnésia

ave de la Marseillaise

7

pont d'Auvergne

quai du Maire Dietrich

place de l'Université

place Broglie

Hôtel de Ville

9

rue Brûlée

Ill River

29

blvd de la Victoire

University

rue de l'Outre

Grande Île

26

rue du Dôme

rue des Juifs

rue du Fail

rue Sainte-Hélène

place Saint Étienne

quai des Pêcheurs

27

Place du Marché Neuf

28

rue des Orfèvres

rue des Hallebardes

rue des Frères

rue des Écrivains

rue des Veaux

30

41

rue Gutenberg

place Gutenberg

38

37

Footbridge

rue St Guillaume

rue de l'Académie

39

rue Mercière

place de la Cathédrale

place du Château

35

Krutenau District

rue de la Manufacture des Tabacs

32

31

40

rue des Serruriers

rue des Vieux Marché aux Poissons

34

36

quai des Bateliers

rue des Bateliers

33

R Ste Catherine

rue des Poules

rue de Zurich

rue Paul Janet

50

rue de la Division Leclerc

rue de l'Ail

rue des Tonneliers

52

51

St-Thomas

quai Saint Nicolas

53

rue des Couples

place de Zurich

rue de Zurich

rue du Jeu de Paume

rue d'Austerlitz

rue des Orphelins

rue Saint Gothard

56

rue des Bouchers

57

place de l'Hôpital

To Place de l'Étoile (200m), Illkirch Lixenbuhl Tram Terminus (2km), Pont de l'Europe (4km) & Kehl, Germany (5km)

rue de la 1ère Armée

54

place d'Austerlitz

rue de Berne

rue de la Brigade Alsace-Lorraine

R Sédillot

55

To Place de l'Étoile (Parking Relais Tram Park-And-Ride 200m)

0   100   200m
0   100   200yd

LP

2pm-1am or 2am Mon-Sat, from noon Sun) has live music at weekends, while **Rock City** (☎ 03 88 36 54 76; 24 rue des Poules; open 11am-1.30am) has a rock vibe.

Getting There & Away
Bus Coaches arrive/depart from opposite the **Eurolines office** (☎ 03 90 22 14 60; 6 place d'Austerlitz; open 10am-12.30pm & 2pm-6.15pm Mon-Fri) in place d'Austerlitz. City bus No 21 runs daily from place Gutenberg to Kehl, the first town across the border in Germany (one way €1.10).

Train There are frequent connections from **Gare Strasbourg** (☎ 08 92 35 35 39) to Paris' Gare de l'Est (€25.50, four hours), Basel (Bâle; €16, 1½ hours) and Frankfurt (€34, two hours). There are daily trains to Nice (€93.30, 12 hours), Amsterdam (€65.80, eight hours) and Prague (€91.10, 10 hours). The ticket office opens from 5.15am to 9pm or 10pm.

Getting Around
Four tram lines form the centrepiece of Strasbourg's excellent public transport network. A, B and C run daily from 4.30am to 12.30am and D runs from 7am to 7pm Monday to Saturday. Tickets (single/day/family pass €1.10/3/3.80) are sold on buses, at tram stops and the **CTS office** (☎ 03 88 77 70 70; open 7.30am-6.30pm Mon-Fri, 9am-5pm Sat) in place Kléber.

Velocation (☎ 03 88 43 64 30; 4 rue de Marie Kuss; open 6am-7.30pm Mon-Fri, 9am-noon & 2pm-7pm Sat & Sun; full/half-day €4.50/3) hires bicycles.

COLMAR
pop 67,000

Colmar is a good base for exploring the Route du Vin and the Massif des Vosges.

Ave de la République stretches from the train station to Musée d'Unterlinden; the medieval streets of the old city are to the southeast. At the southern edge of the old city, **Petite Venise**, with charming half-timbered buildings and street cafés, hugs the Lauch River.

The highly efficient **tourist office** (☎ 03 89 20 68 92, fax 03 89 20 69 14; w www.ot-colmar.fr; 4 rue d'Unterlinden; open 9am-7pm Mon-Sat, 9.30am-2pm Sun July & Aug, 9am-6pm Mon-Sat, 10am-2pm Sun & holidays Apr-June & Sept-Oct, 9am-noon & 2pm-6pm Mon-Sat, 10am-2pm Sun Nov-Mar), opposite the Musée d'Unterlinden, offers free hotel

reservations via email, currency exchange and guided tours.

There's a **post office** (36-38 rue de la République; open 8am-6.30pm Mon-Fri, 8am-noon Sat); **Reflex** (41 Grand-Rue; open 10am-10pm daily) has one hour of Internet access for €3. The **Laverie No 1** laundrette (1 rue Ruest; open 7am-9pm daily) is next to the **Pause Café**.

Colmar is famous for its typically Alsatian architecture and *Issenheim Altarpiece* in the **Musée d'Unterlinden** (☎ 03 89 20 15 50; w www.musee-unterlinden.com; place d'Unterlinden; adult/concession €7/5; open 9am-6pm Apr-Oct, 10am-5pm Nov-Mar).

The **Musée Bartholdi** (☎ 03 89 41 90 60; 30 rue des Marchands; adult/concession €4/2.50; open 10am-noon & 2pm-6pm Wed-Mon, closed Tues Jan & Feb) is dedicated to the creator of New York's *Statue of Liberty*.

Places to Stay
The **Auberge de Jeunesse Mittelhart** (☎ 03 89 80 57 39, fax 03 89 80 76 16; 2 rue Pasteur; bus No 4, 5 or 6 to Pont-Rouge stop; dorm beds €11.50 includes breakfast; reception closed 9am-5pm in winter) is 2km northwest of the train station.

Near the train station, the faded **Hôtel La Chaumière** (☎ 03 89 41 08 99; 74 ave de la République; doubles €28, with shower & toilet €34) is cheap but unremarkable; the **Kyriad** (☎ 03 89 41 34 80; e kyriadcolmar@aol.com; 1 rue de la Gare; singles/doubles €36/45) is a typical chain hotel.

Hôtel Primo (☎ 03 89 24 22 24, fax 03 89 24 55 96; e hotel-primo-99@calixo.net; 5 rue des Ancêtres; singles/doubles/quads €45/52/61) has modern rooms and does a €6 all-you-can-eat breakfast buffet.

Places to Eat
Place de l'Ancienne Douane has a host of watering holes; the **Schwendi Bier-U-Wistub** (☎ 03 89 23 66 26; 23-25 Grand-Rue; open 10am-1am daily), an Alsacian beer hall with a large terrace, is a good bet (meals from €9, beers from €3). Most restaurants tend to cater to tourists but **Le Flamm's** (☎ 03 89 41 56 85; Passage Saint-Martin) is a good-value hidden gem, tucked away down a passageway off rue des Serruriers.

There's a **Monoprix supermarket** (open 8am-8pm Mon-Sat) across the square from the Musée d'Unterlinden.

Getting There & Around

Colmar is served by frequent trains from Strasbourg (€9.10, every 30 minutes). Many Route du Vin and Massif des Vosges destinations are accessible by local bus; ask the tourist office for details. The office also arranges guided Route du Vin **bus tours** in summer (half-/full day €25/35). **Colmarvélo** (place Rapp; open Apr-Oct) hires out bicycles (half-/full day €3/4.50).

Euro Regio (☎ 03 89 24 65 65) runs seven weekday (four Saturday, three Sunday) **buses** to the German university city of Freiburg (€6.15, 1¼ hours).

ROUTE DU VIN

Meandering for some 170km along the eastern foothills of the Vosges, the Alsace Wine Route passes through picturesque villages guarded by ruined castles. Sometimes rather twee, it starts from Marlenheim, about 20km west of Strasbourg, and finishes at Thann, 35km southwest of Colmar.

Riquewihr, **Ribeauvillé** and **Kaysersberg** are perhaps the most attractive villages – they certainly attract tourists. You can walk from village to village through the vineyards but only access the imposing chateau of **Haut-Koenigsbourg**, rebuilt early last century by Emperor Wilhelm II, with your own transport.

MASSIF DES VOSGES

The forests, glacial lakes and tiny villages of the Vosges Mountains are a hiker's paradise, with an astounding 7000km of marked trails. In the winter, the area has 36 modest skiing areas with 170 ski lifts. The Colmar **tourist office** has walking maps.

From the **Route des Crêtes** (Route of the Crests), which begins in Cernay (36km southwest of Colmar), mountaintop lookouts afford spectacular views of the Alsace plain, the Jura and the Schwarzwald (Black Forest) in Germany. The highest point in the Vosges is the dramatic, windblown summit of the 1424m-high **Grand Ballon**.

NANCY

pop 99,351

Nancy has an air of refinement unique in Lorraine, the region that borders Alsace to the west. The gilded **place Stanislas** (the central square) and shop windows filled with fine glassware give the former capital of the dukes of Lorraine an opulent feel.

Orientation & Information

The heart of Nancy is place Stanislas; the train station, at the bottom of busy rue Stanislas, is 800m to the southwest. Nancy is a small town with everything accessible on foot.

The **tourist office** (☎ 03 83 35 22 41, fax 03 83 35 90 10; **e** tourisme@ot-nancy.fr; open 9am-7pm Mon-Sat, 10am-5pm Sun & holidays Apr-Oct, 9am-6pm Mon-Fri, 10am-1pm Sun & holidays Nov-Mar) is inside the **Hôtel de Ville** (place Stanislas). It charges €2 for hotel reservations and offers currency exchange on weekends only. **Banks** line rue des Dominicains.

The **post office** (open 8am-7pm Mon-Fri, 8am-noon Sat) is behind the tourist office on rue Pierre Fourier and has Cyberposte. For a small town, Nancy has an excellent Internet café, **e-café** (☎ 03 83 35 47 34; 11 rue des Quatre-Eglises; open 9am-9pm daily, 9am-8pm Sun), which charges €5.34 for one hour of Internet access and offers student discounts.

The **Laverie de la Source** laundrette opens 7am to 8pm daily.

Things to See

The **Musée de l'École de Nancy** (☎ 03 83 40 14 86; 36-38 rue du Sergent Blandan; bus No 123 to Nancy Thermal stop; adult/concession €4.57/2.29, free Wed to students; open 10.30am-6pm Wed-Sun) is home to a superb collection of works from the Art Nouveau movement.

The renovated **Musée des Beaux-Arts** (Fine Arts Museum; ☎ 03 83 85 30 72; 3 place Stanislas; adult/concession €5.34/3.05, free Wed for students; open 10am-6pm Wed-Mon) is absorbing; **Musée Lorrain** (Lorraine Museum; ☎ 03 83 32 18 74; 64 Grande Rue; adult/concession €3.10/2.30 per museum, €4.40/3.10 both; open 10am-12.30pm & 2pm-6pm Wed-Mon), which comprises both the **Palais Ducal** and **Traditions Polulaires**, less so.

Places to Stay

The 60-bed **Auberge de Jeunesse Remicourt** (☎ 03 83 27 73 67, fax 03 83 41 41 35; 149 rue de Vandœuvre in Villers-les-Nancy; bus No 122 to Grand Corvée stop; dorm beds €9 including breakfast), in an old chateau, is 4km south of the centre.

Two blocks southwest of place Stanislas, **Hôtel de l'Académie** (☎ 03 83 35 52 31, fax 03 83 32 55 78; 7 bis rue des Michottes;

singles/doubles with shower from €22.50/ 25.50) is cheap and welcoming. The two-star **Hôtel des Portes d'Or** (☎ 03 83 35 42 34, fax 03 83 32 51 41; 21 rue Stanislas; singles/ doubles €40/45) has smart rooms with up-holstered doors.

Places to Eat & Drink

Rue des Maréchaux is lined with restaurants; **Le Pitchoun** at No 14 (☎ 03 83 30 45 33; lunch menu €14; open Tues-Sat) is one of the best.

La Romana (☎ 03 83 37 35 43; 10 Grand Rue; open Tues-Sat & Mon dinner) is a friendly, good-value pizzeria.

Self-caterers should head for the **covered market** (place Henri Mangin; open 7am-6pm Tues-Sat) and the **Monoprix supermarket** (open 8.30am-8.30pm Mon-Sat) inside the St Sébastien shopping centre.

For drinks, **cafés** line place Stanislas; the **Blue Note** (3 rue des Michottes; open 11pm-4am Wed-Sun) is a Latin-style club.

Getting There & Away

Gare Nancy (☎ 08 92 35 35 39; place Thiers) has direct services to Strasbourg (€17.30, 80 minutes), Paris' Gare de l'Est (€32.90, 2½ hours), Épernay (€21.30, two hours) and Lyon (€38, four hours).

Far Northern France

Le Nord de France (ⓦ www.cdt-nord.fr) is made up of three historical regions: Flanders (Flandre or Flandres), Artois and Picardy (Picardie). Traditionally an industrial area, this is not one of the best known corners of France but does offer several attractions and excellent dining.

LILLE
pop 1.5 million

Thanks to the Eurostar and other fast rail links, Lille – France's northern metropolis – has become increasingly popular for visitors coming across the Channel and from Belgium to discover Lille's renowned art museums and its attractive old town which is graced with or-nate Flemish-style buildings.

During 2004, Lille (ⓦ www.lille2004.com) will be deemed a European City of Culture with an accompanying programme of cultural events.

Orientation & Information

Lille is centred around place du Général de Gaulle, place du Théâtre, and place Rihour. Vieux Lille (Old Lille) is situated on the north side of the centre. Lille-Flanders train station is about 400m southeast of place du Général de Gaulle; the ultra-modern Lille-Europe train station is 500m further east.

The **tourist office** (☎ 03 20 21 94 21, fax 03 20 21 94 20; ⓦ www.lilletourism.com; place Rihour; open 9.30am-6.30pm Mon-Sat, 10am-noon & 2pm-5pm Sun & holi-days) sells the **Lille Metropole City Pass** (1/2/3 days €14.50/25.15/31.25), which offers free museum entry and use of public transport.

Money, Post & Communications There are **banks** in the three main squares. The **main post office** (8 place de la République; open 8am-7pm Mon-Fri, 8am-noon Sat) has currency exchange and Cyberposte.

Email & Internet Access You can have 30 minutes of Internet access for €3.81 at **Le Smiley** (☎ 03 20 21 12 19; 2 rue Royale) and a happy hour from 7pm to 9pm nightly.

Laundry For laundry there's the **Laverie O'Claire** (57 rue du Molinel; open 7am-7pm daily).

Things to See & Do

On place du Général de Gaulle, the ornate **Vieille Bourse** (Old Stock Exchange) con-sists of 24 buildings around a courtyard; it closes on Monday. Place du Théâtre is dom-inated by the neoclassical **Opéra** and the neo-Flemish **Chambre de Commerce building**. North of place du Général de Gaulle in **Vieux Lille**, restored 17th- and 18th-century houses abound.

Lille's outstanding **Palais des Beaux-Arts** (Fine Arts Museum; ☎ 03 20 06 78 00; place de la République; adult/concession €4.60/3; open 10am-6pm Wed-Sun, 2pm-6pm Mon, closed Tues & bank holidays) is second only to Paris' Louvre for its collection.

The **Musée Charles de Gaulle** is closed until late 2003. The newest arts attraction, the **La Piscine Musée d'Art et d'Industrie** (☎ 03 20 69 23 60; 24 rue des Champs; metro Jean Lebas; admission €3; open 11am-6pm Tues-Thur, 11am-8pm Fri, 1pm-6pm Sat & Sun) is located in the suburb of Roubaix.

Every Sunday from 8am to noon, place Nouvelle Aventure hosts a huge **outdoor market** with everything from food to clothes.

Special Events

The Braderie, a huge flea market, is held on the first weekend of September and attracts large crowds. It is accompanied by a *moules frites* (muscles and fries) eating competition among local restaurants. Hotel prices rise steeply during this time.

Places to Stay

Hostels The modern, 170-bed **Auberge de Jeunesse** (☎ 03 20 57 08 94, fax 03 20 63 98 93; e lille@fuaj.org; 12 rue Malpart; metro République; dorm beds from €11.20 including breakfast; reception closed 11am-3pm; closed 20 Dec–end Jan) is centrally located.

Hotels Near the station, **Hôtel Premiére Classe** (☎ 03 28 36 51 10, fax 03 28 36 51 11; 19 place des Reignuax; 1- to 3-people rooms/quads €37/48) has simple and clean rooms. In the pedestrian centre, the two-star **Hôtel de France** (☎ 03 20 57 14 78, fax 03 20 57 06 01; 10 rue de Béthune; singles/ doubles with washbasin €29/32, with shower & toilet €36.60/42.70) has decent rooms with TVs.

Best Hotel (☎ 03 20 54 00 02, fax 03 20 54 00 06; e besthotel.lille@wanadoo.fr; 66 rue Littré; metro Gambetta; rooms from €39) has the soulless feel of a chain hotel but clean rooms and a decent breakfast buffet (€5.50). For a family atmosphere, chambre d'hôte **chez Quillerou** (☎/fax 03 20 13 76 57; 78 rue Caumartin; metro Gambetta; singles/ doubles €36/46) has three airy rooms in a friendly family home. One has a kitchenette, two are en suite and all have TVs.

Places to Eat

Head for rue Royale or rue de Gand in Vieux Lille for the best eats. **Estaminet 't Rijsel** (☎ 03 20 15 01 59; 25 rue de Gand; 3-course lunch menu €10; open Tues-Sat lunch & dinner) is a hidden gem with excellent Flemish dishes. Booking is essential as it's deservedly popular. **El Koutoubia** (☎ 03 20 55 58 97; 16 rue Royale) does a decent couscous (€12), while **La Pâte Brisée** (☎ 03 20 74 29 00; 63-65 rue de la Monnaie; 1-/2-/3-course menus €7.80/11.10/13.50) has savoury and sweet *tartes* in *menus* that include a drink.

In the pedestrian area, **Brasserie Flore** (☎ 03 20 57 97 07; 11 place Rihour; menus €12.90 & 16; open daily) has good Flemish dishes; **Aux Moules** (☎ 03 20 57 12 46; 34 rue de Béthune; menus €10.50; open noon-6pm Mon-Fri) usually wins the Braderie *moules frites* competition. It opens daily till midnight.

Finally, no visit to Lille is complete without tasting the spiced brown sugar waffles at patisserie **Meert** (27 rue Esquermoise).

Self-Catering Try the lively **Wazemmes food market** (place Nouvelle Aventure; metro Gambetta; open Tues, Thur & Sun), 1.2km southwest of the centre, or **Monoprix supermarket** (31 rue du Molinel; open 8.30am-8.30pm Mon-Sat).

Entertainment

Pubs & Bars A branch of Paris' famous Australian bar, **Café Oz** (☎ 03 20 55 15 15; 33 place Louise de Bettignies) has cheap Foster's and cocktails during happy hour (6pm to 9pm Monday to Saturday).

In Vieux Lille, **Le Balatum** (☎ 03 20 57 41 81; 13 rue de la Barre) is a relaxed place, while the arty **L'Illustration** (☎ 03 20 12 00 90; 18 rue Royale) has regular exhibitions plus speciality local beers (€8).

Le 30 (☎ 03 20 30 15 54; 30 rue de Paris) is a slightly kitsch jazz bar with live music nightly (except Sunday). Most Lille bars close around 2am, leaving the hard core to party on across the border at all-night Belgian clubs.

Getting There & Away

Bus The **Eurolines office** (☎ 03 20 78 18 88; 23 parvis St Maurice; open 9am-7pm Mon-Fri in summer, 9.30am-12.30pm & 1.30pm-6pm Mon-Fri rest of year, Sat 1pm-6pm) has direct buses to Brussels (€7, two hours), London (€35, 5½ hours) and other destinations.

Train Lille has frequent rail links across France. Its two **train stations** (☎ 08 92 35 35 39) are linked by metro line No 2 or a 400m walk.

Gare Lille-Flandres handles regional services including those to Calais (€13.40) and Dunkerque (€11.50), and most of the TGVs to Paris' Gare du Nord (€32.90 to €44.50, one hour, one to two per hour).

Gare Lille-Europe is served by Eurostar trains to London (from €75, two hours, nine to 10 daily) and Brussels (€21.30, 40 minutes, seven to eight daily). It has a **tourist office** with hotel reservation service and an **information office** (*open 5.45am-10pm Mon-Sat, 7.30am-10pm Sun*). Both provide **Thomas Cook** currency exchange.

Getting Around

Transpole (☎ *03 20 40 40 40*) runs Lille's metro, trams and buses. The **information office** (*open 7.30am-6pm Mon-Fri*) in Gare Lille-Flandres sells tickets as do tobacconists. A single journey/daily pass/carnet of 10 €1.15/ 3.35/10. Tickets must be validated before boarding the metro or tram.

CALAIS
pop 78,000

Calais, a grim and desperate town, is only 34km from the English town of Dover. Long a popular port for passenger travel between the UK and continental Europe, the 1994 opening of the Channel Tunnel at Coquelles, 5km southwest of the town centre, heralded the end of its dominance over trans-Channel transport. Calais now relies on the bawdy booze-cruise trade and offers poor value for money – best push on to Lille.

Orientation & Information

Calais is centred around place d'Armes with Calais-Ville train station to the south. The car ferry terminal is 1.7km northeast of place d'Armes; the hoverport 1.5km farther out. The hotels and eateries are located near the harbour off rue Royale.

The **tourist office** (☎ *03 21 96 62 40, fax 03 21 96 01 92; w www.ot-calais.fr; 12 blvd Clémenceau; open 9am-7pm Mon-Sat, 10am-1pm Sun*) fields visitor inquiries.

Banks line rue Royale. The **post office** (*place de Rheims; open 8.30am-6pm Mon-Fri, 9am-noon Sat*) has currency exchange and Cyberposte. **Spicey Café** (☎ *03 21 96 84 20; 68 rue Royale*) charges €4 for one hour of Internet access.

For laundry, **Lavorama** (*open 7am-9pm daily*) is on the eastern side of place d'Armes.

Things to See

A cast of Auguste Rodin's famous bronze statue of six emaciated but proud figures, known in English as **The Burghers of Calais**, stands in front of the Flemish Renaissance-style Hôtel de Ville, which is topped with an ornate 75m clock tower.

Opposite, the **Musée de la Guerre** (☎ *03 21 34 21 57; Parc St Pierre; adult/concession €4.50/3.80; open 10am-5.15pm May-Aug, 11am-4.45pm Apr & Sept, 11am-4.15pm 15 Feb–31 Mar, noon-4.15pm 1 October-15 Nov, closed Tues*) has WWII artefacts housed in a 94m-long concrete bunker.

The **Musée des Beaux-Arts et de la Dentelle** (*Museum of Fine Arts & Lace; ☎ 03 21 46 48 40; 25 rue Richelieu; adult/concession €3/1.50, free Wed; open 10am-noon & 2pm-5.30pm, 10am-6.30pm Sat & Sun; closed Tues, Sun morning & holidays*) traces the history of mechanised lacemaking.

Places to Stay

Camping Municipal (☎ *03 21 97 89 79; ave Raymond Poincaré; bus No 3 from train station to Pluviose stop; sites from €9.15; open year-round*) is grassy but soulless.

The modern **Auberge de Jeunesse** (☎ *03 21 34 70 20, fax 03 21 96 87 80; ave Maréchal De Lattre de Tassigny; bus No 3 to Pluviose stop; 2-bed doubles per person €14.33, singles €16 including breakfast*), also called the Centre Européen de Séjour, is 200m from the beach.

Close to the train station, there's **Hôtel-Pension L'Ovale** (☎/fax *03 21 97 57 00; 38-40 ave Wilson; singles & doubles €25, triples €30.50*) with adequate rooms with private shower and TV receiving UK channels. The central **Hôtel Bristol** (☎/fax *03 21 34 53 24; 15 rue du Duc de Guise; singles & doubles €25, singles/doubles with shower & toilet €31/36, 4-/5-bed rooms €59/70*) has simple rooms.

The family-run **Hôtel Richelieu** (☎ *03 21 34 61 60, fax 03 21 85 89 28; 17 rue Richelieu; singles/doubles/quads €45/46/55 including breakfast*) has quiet rooms with good amenities. Private parking costs €4.

Places to Eat & Drink

Histoire Ancienne (☎ *03 21 34 11 20; 20 rue Royale; menus €10-28; open Tues-Sat, & Mon lunch*) is a cosy bistro. Show a ferry or shuttle ticket for a free bottle of takeaway wine. The rustic **Au Coq d'Or** (☎ *03 21 34 79 05; 31 place d'Armes; menus €10.10-38.30; open Thur-Tues*) serves grilled meat dishes and seafood.

The **Au Tonnaire de Brest** (☎ *03 21 96 95 35; 16 place d'Armes*) is a bright and friendly creperie featuring good value pancakes (€6).

Bouddha Bar (☎ 03 21 34 63 67; 7 rue Royale) is a decent venue for both a beer and a snack.

For self-caterers, place d'Armes is host to a food market on Wednesday and Saturday mornings and the Match supermarket (open to 7.30pm & Sun morning in summer).

Getting There & Away
For details on Channel Tunnel and ferry schedules, see Britain under Land and Sea in the Getting There & Away section.

Bus The express buses of BCD (☎ 03 21 83 51 51) operate from Boulogne to Calais (€6.40, 35 minutes, four on weekdays and two on Saturday) and onto Dunkerque (€7, 45 minutes, nine weekdays and three on Saturday). There's no service on Sunday and holidays.

Train Calais has two train stations: **Gare Calais-Ville** (☎ 08 92 35 35 39) and **Gare Calais-Fréthun**, 10km southwest of town near the Channel Tunnel entrance, connected by Opale Bus No 7 (€1.50).

Calais-Ville handles non-TGV trains to Paris' Gare du Nord (€29.20, three hours, three to six daily), Boulogne (€6.30, 35 minutes, hourly), and Lille-Flandres (€13.40, 1½ hours, seven to 15 daily). Calais-Fréthun handles TGVs only to Paris' Gare du Nord (€34.30, 1½ hours, two daily) and Eurostar to London (from €75, 1½ hours, three or four daily).

Car To reach the Channel Tunnel's vehicle loading area, follow road signs on the A16 to 'Tunnel Sous La Manche'.

Boat P&O Stena and SeaFrance Sealink car ferries to/from Dover dock at the busy Terminal Est, just over 1km northeast of place d'Armes.

P&O Stena's office (☎ 08 20 01 00 20; W www.posl.com; 41 place d'Armes; open 8.30am-6pm Mon-Fri, 8.30am-5pm Sat) sells tickets. SeaFrance Sealink's office (☎ 08 25 04 40 45; W www.seafrance.com; open 9.30am-12.30pm & 1.30pm-6pm Mon-Fri, 9am-12.30pm Sat in summer only) is nearby at No 2.

SeaCats to/from Dover, operated by Hoverspeed (W www.hoverspeed.com), use the hoverport, 3km northeast of the town centre.

Getting Around
Bus To reach the car ferry terminal, free shuttles run by SeaFrance Sealink and P&O Stena stop around the corner from Calais-Ville train station (turn left out of the station) and outside each company's office on place d'Armes. Last buses leave around 9pm.

Hoverspeed runs free buses to the hoverport from the train station roughly 45 minutes before each departure.

DUNKERQUE
pop 209,000
Dunkerque never really recovered from its wartime damage. Unless you're planning to spend time on the beach or join in the Mardi Gras-style carnival, it offers few attractions. It does, however, offer better value than Calais.

Orientation & Information
The train station is 600m southwest of Dunkerque's main square, place Jean Bart. The **tourist office** (☎ 03 28 66 79 21, fax 03 28 63 38 34; W www.ot-dunkerque.fr; rue de l'Amiral Ronarc'h; open 9am-12.30pm & 1.30pm-6.30pm Mon-Fri, 9am-6.30pm Sat, 10am-noon & 2pm-4pm Sun and holidays) is in the town's medieval belfry.

The beach, its waterfront esplanade Digue de Mer and a separate **tourist office** (☎ 03 28 58 10 10, fax 03 28 58 85 29; e eole.dunes deflandre@ot-dunkerque.fr; 48b Digue de Mer; open daily Apr-Oct) with currency exchange are all 2km northeast of the centre in the resort of Malo les Bains – an area popular for beach sports in summer.

Banks surround place de la République with a **Monoprix supermarket** at No 2. There's a **post office** (55 rue Poincaré; open 8.30am-6.30pm Mon-Fri, 8.30am-1pm Sat); **Surf N' Play** (☎ 03 28 66 27 41; place du Minck) offers one hour of Internet access for €4. For laundry, there's **Lav O Clair** (7 bld Paul Verley; open 6am-10pm daily).

Things to See & Do
The **Musée Portuaire** (Harbour Museum; ☎ 03 28 63 33 39; 9 quai de la Citadelle; adult/concession €4/3), housed in a former tobacco warehouse, exhibits the history of Dunkerque port. The **Mémorial du Souvenir** (☎ 03 28 66 79 21; 32 rue des Chantes de France; adult/concession €3.05/2.29) recounts the events of May 1940 that flattened Dunkerque.

La Bazenne (reservations ☎ 03 28 66 79 21; adult/child €7.50/5.50; open daily in summer, Sat & Sun in low season) boat tours depart from place du Minck, touring the third-largest port in France.

Places to Stay & Eat

The **Auberge de Jeunesse** (☎ 03 28 63 36 34, fax 03 28 63 24 54; place Paul Asseman; dorm beds €11.20 including breakfast) is on the beach 3km north of the train station. Take bus No 3 from the station to the 'Piscine' stop. Opposite the tourist office, the two-star **Hôtel du Tigre** (☎/fax 03 28 66 75 17; 8 rue Clemenceau; singles/doubles €30.50/38.10) is the best budget option in town with shower and TV in every room. **Hôtel Eole** (☎ 03 28 69 13 64, fax 03 28 69 52 57; 77-79 Digue de Mer; singles/doubles €30/35, with sea views €34/38) overlooks the beach.

La Fondu (☎ 03 28 63 23 90; 37 rue Bourgogne) has decent menus for €10.50 and €12.15. **Au Petit Pierre** (☎ 03 28 66 28 36; 4 rue Dampierre; menus €14.48-19.06) has regional specialities. For a snack, **Café Boutteau** (☎ 03 28 66 71 81; 19 place Jean Bart) has salads and crepes from €6.

Getting There & Away

BCD (☎ 03 21 83 51 51) runs buses to/from Dunkerque train station to Calais (€7, 45 minutes, nine on weekdays and three Saturday). **Gare Dunkerque** (☎ 08 92 35 35 39) has direct trains to Lille (€11.50, 1¼ hours, 16 daily), Calais (€13.40, 1½ hours, 13 daily) and Paris Gare du Nord by TGV (€32.90, 1½ hours, hourly).

BATTLE OF THE SOMME MEMORIALS

The First Battle of the Somme, the WWI Allied offensive waged in the villages and woodlands northeast of Amiens, was designed to relieve pressure on the beleaguered French troops at Verdun. On 1 July 1916, British, Commonwealth and French troops 'went over the top' in a massive assault along a 34km front. But German positions proved virtually unbreachable, and on the first day of the battle an astounding 20,000 British troops were killed and another 40,000 were wounded. Most casualties were infantrymen mowed down by German machine guns.

By the time the offensive was called off in mid-November, some 1.2 million lives had been lost on both sides. The British had advanced 12km, the French only 8km. The Battle of the Somme has become a metaphor for the meaningless slaughter of war, and its killing fields are a site of pilgrimage.

Commonwealth Cemeteries & Memorials

More than 750,000 soldiers from Canada, Australia, New Zealand, South Africa, the Indian subcontinent, the West Indies and other parts of the British Empire died on the Western Front, two-thirds of them in France. By Commonwealth tradition, they were buried where they fell, in more than 1000 military cemeteries and 2000 civilian cemeteries. Today, hundreds of neatly-tended Commonwealth plots dot the landscape along a wide line running roughly from Albert and Cambrai north via Arras and Béthune to Armentières and Ypres (Ieper) in Belgium. Some 26 memorials (20 of them in France) bear the names of more than 300,000 Commonwealth soldiers whose bodies were never recovered or identified. The French, Americans and Germans reburied their dead in large war cemeteries after the war.

Larger Commonwealth cemeteries usually have a plaque with historical information in English. Touring the area is only really feasible by car or bicycle. Government plans to build a third Parisien airport at Chaulnes (forcing the removal of some Somme memorials) remain hotly contested.

Maps & Brochures Memorials and cemeteries are indicated on Michelin's 1:200,000 scale maps. For more information, contact the **Commonwealth War Graves Commission** (ⓦ www.cwgc.org). You can order a copy of the useful guide *Discover Wartime Memories* from **Eurotunnel** (ⓦ www.eurotunnel.com).

Normandy

Normandy (Normandie) derives its name from the Norsemen (Vikings) who took control of the area in the early 10th century. Modern Normandy is the land of the *bocage*, farmland subdivided by hedges and trees.

ROUEN
pop 107,000
The city of Rouen, for centuries the lowest bridging point on the Seine, is known for its

ROUEN

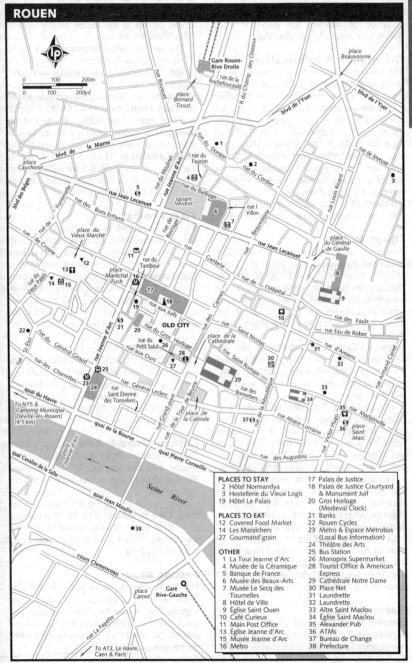

PLACES TO STAY
2 Hôtel Normandya
3 Hostellerie du Vieux Logis
19 Hôtel Le Palais

PLACES TO EAT
12 Covered Food Market
14 Les Maraîchers
27 Gourmand'grain

OTHER
1 La Tour Jeanne d'Arc
4 Musée de la Céramique
5 Banque de France
6 Musée des Beaux-Arts
7 Musée Le Secq des
   Tournelles
8 Hôtel de Ville
9 Église Saint Ouen
10 Café Curieux
11 Main Post Office
13 Église Jeanne d'Arc
15 Musée Jeanne d'Arc
16 Metro

17 Palais de Justice
18 Palais de Justice Courtyard
   & Monument Juif
20 Gros Horloge
   (Medieval Clock)
21 Banks
22 Rouen Cycles
23 Metro & Espace Métrobus
   (Local Bus Information)
24 Théâtre des Arts
25 Bus Station
26 Monoprix Supermarket
28 Tourist Office & American
   Express
29 Cathédrale Notre Dame
30 Place Net
31 Laundrette
32 Laundrette
33 Aître Saint Maclou
34 Église Saint Maclou
35 Alexander Pub
36 ATMs
37 Bureau de Change
38 Prefecture

FRANCE

many spires, church towers and half-timbered houses, not to mention its Gothic cathedral and excellent museums. Rouen can be visited on a day or overnight trip from Paris.

Orientation & Information

The train station (Gare Rouen-Rive Droite) is at the northern end of rue Jeanne d'Arc, the major thoroughfare running south to the Seine.

The **tourist office** (☎ 02 32 08 32 40, fax 02 32 08 32 44; e www.rouen-online.com; 25 place de la Cathédrale; open 9am-7pm Mon-Sat, 9.30am-12.30pm & 2.30pm-6pm Sun May-Sept, 9am-6pm Mon-Sat, 10am-1pm Sun Oct-Apr) is the departure point for guided city tours (adult/concession €6/4) in summer at 2.30pm daily.

Place Net (37 rue de la Republique; open daily) offers Internet access for €6 an hour.

Things to See

Rouen's main street, rue du Gros Horloge, runs from the cathedral to **place du Vieux Marché**, where 19-year-old Joan of Arc was burned at the stake for heresy in 1431. You'll learn more about her life from its stained-glass windows at the adjacent Église Jeanne d'Arc than at the tacky **Musée Jeanne d'Arc** across the square at No 33.

Rouen's **Cathédrale Notre Dame** truly is a masterpiece of French Gothic architecture. There is a guided visit at 3pm daily during the summer months and on weekends during the rest of the year.

The **Musée Le Secq des Tournelles** (rue Jacques Villon; adult/concession €2.30/1.55; open Wed-Mon), opposite 27 rue Jean Lecanuet, is devoted to the blacksmith's craft and displays some 12,000 locks, keys and tongs made between the 3rd and 19th centuries.

The **Musée des Beaux-Arts** (26 bis rue Jean Lecanuet; adult/concession €3/2; open Wed-Sun) facing the square, features some major paintings from the 16th to 20th centuries, including some of Monet's cathedral series.

La Tour Jeanne d'Arc (rue du Donjon), south of the train station, is the tower where Joan of Arc was imprisoned before her execution. There are two **exhibition rooms** (adult/concession €1.50/0.75; open Wed-Mon).

Places to Stay

Camping Municipal (☎ 02 35 74 07 59; rue Jules Ferry; 2 people & tent €9.60; open year-round), in the Déville-lès-Rouen suburb,

is 5km northwest of town. From the Théâtre des Arts or the nearby bus station, take bus No 2 and get off at the mairie (town hall) of Déville-lès-Rouen.

The spotless **Hôtel Normandya** (☎ 02 35 71 46 15; 32 rue du Cordier; singles €19-25, doubles €2 more) is on a quiet street 300m southeast of the train station. Some singles have a shower. The very French **Hostellerie du Vieux Logis** (☎ 02 35 71 55 30; 5 rue de Joyeuse; rooms from €15), 1km east of the train station, has a pleasantly frayed atmosphere and a lovely garden out the back. The **Hôtel Le Palais** (☎ 02 35 71 41 40; 12 rue du Tambour; singles/doubles from €20/25, with shower €25/38) is between the Palais de Justice and the Gros Horloge.

Places to Eat

There's a **covered market** (place du Vieux Marché; open 6am-1.30pm Tues-Sun) for self-catering. The bistro-style **Les Maraîchers** (menus from €15, dinner menus from €16) at No 37 is the pick of the Vieux Marché's many restaurants, with its terrace and varied menus.

Gourmand'grain (☎ 02 35 98 15 74; 3 rue du Petit Salut; menus from €8) behind the tourist office, is a lunchtime vegetarian café.

Entertainment

Café Curieux (3 rue des Fossés Louis VIII; admission €3; open from 9pm Fri & Sat) is a small and intimate nightclub in the heart of the old city. **Alexander Pub** (85 rue Martainville) is a pleasant English-style pub open until 2am daily.

Getting There & Away

The **bus station** (☎ 02 35 52 92 00; 9 rue Jeanne d'Arc) is near the Théâtre des Arts. Buses tend to be slower and more expensive than the train.

There are at least 20 trains daily to/from Paris' Gare St Lazare (€16.50, 70 minutes), as well as services to Caen (€18.20) and Bayeux (€20.60). For train information, call ☎ 08 36 35 35 39.

Getting Around

TCAR operates the local bus network and metro line. The metro links the train station with the Théâtre des Arts before crossing the Seine into the southern suburbs. Bus tickets cost €1.20, or €10 for a magnetic card valid for 10 rides.

FRANCE

BAYEUX

pop 15,000

Bayeux is celebrated for two trans-Channel invasions: the 1066 conquest of England by William the Conqueror (an event chronicled in the Bayeux Tapestry) and the Allied D-Day landings of 6 June 1944; Bayeux was the first town in France to be liberated from the Nazis.

Bayeux is an attractive – though fairly touristy – town with several excellent museums. It's also a good base for the D-Day beaches.

Orientation & Information

The cathedral, Bayeux's central landmark, is 1km northwest of the train station.

The **tourist office** (☎ 02 31 51 28 28, fax 02 31 51 28 29; Pont St Jean; open 9am-noon & 2pm-7pm Mon-Sat, 9am-12.30 & 2pm-6.30pm Sun July & Aug, slightly reduced hours in other months) is just off the northern end of rue Larcher.

Things to See

The world-famous **Bayeux Tapestry** – a 70m-long strip of coarse linen decorated with woollen embroidery – was commissioned by Odo, bishop of Bayeux and half-brother to William the Conqueror, for the consecration of the cathedral in Bayeux in 1077. The tapestry recounts the story of the Norman invasion of 1066 – from the Norman perspective. Halley's Comet, which visited our solar system in 1066, also makes an appearance. The tapestry is housed in the **Musée de la Tapisserie de Bayeux** (rue de Nesmond; adult/student €6.40/2.60; open 9am-6.30pm daily, closed for lunch in low season).

Bayeux's **Cathédrale Notre Dame** is an exceptional example of Norman-Gothic architecture, dating from the 13th century.

The **Musée Mémorial 1944 Bataille de Normandie** (blvd Fabien Ware; adult/student €5.40/2.50), Bayeux's huge war museum, displays a haphazard collection of photos, uniforms, weapons and life-like scenes associated with D-Day and the Battle of Normandy. An excellent 30-minute film is screened in English.

The **Bayeux War Cemetery** (blvd Fabien Ware) is a British cemetery a few hundred metres west of the museum. It's the largest of the 18 Commonwealth military cemeteries in Normandy. Many of the headstones are inscribed with poignant epitaphs.

Places to Stay

Camping Some 2km north of town is **Camping Municipal de Bayeux** (☎/fax 02 31 92 08 43; bus Nos 5 & 6 from train station; sites per tent/person €1.53/2.85; open Mar-Sept), just south of blvd d'Eindhoven.

Hostels The **Family Home hostel and guesthouse** (☎ 02 31 92 15 22, fax 02 31 92 55 72; 39 rue du Général de Dais; dorm beds HI members/nonmembers €16/18), in three old buildings, is an excellent place to meet other travellers. There's a kitchen, or you can have a multicourse French dinner (with wine) for €9.15. The modern, if slightly sterile, **Centre d'Accueil Municipal** (☎ 02 31 92 08 19; 21 rue des Marettes; singles €11.90) is 1km southwest of the cathedral. Singles are good value.

Hotels The old but well-maintained **Hôtel de la Gare** (☎ 02 31 92 10 70, fax 02 31 51 95 99; 26 place de la Gare; singles/doubles from €16/22) is opposite the train station. A few hundred metres north, **Hôtel Le Maupassant** (☎ 02 31 92 28 53; 19 rue St Martin; singles/doubles from €26/33.55) has decent rooms (most with shower). The **Hotel Reine Mathilde** (☎ 02 31 92 08 13; 23 rue Larcher; rooms from €45) is slightly more upmarket, with congenial motel-style rooms and friendly staff.

Places to Eat

There are **food markets** on rue St Jean (Wednesday morning) and on place St Patrice (Saturday morning).

Le Petit Normand (☎ 02 31 22 88 66; 35 rue Larcher; menus from €9; open daily July & Aug, Thur-Sat, & Sun dinner Sept-June) specialises in traditional Norman food and has simple menus.

Le Pommier (☎ 02 31 21 52 10; 38 rue des Cuisiniers; lunch & dinner menus from €11.50; closed Tue & Wed) offers Norman fare at its best, including a vegetarian menu. **Milano** (☎ 02 31 92 15 10; 18 rue St Martin; open daily June-Aug, Mon-Sat Sept-May) serves good pizza from €6 to €10.

Getting There & Away

The **train station office** (☎ 02 31 92 80 50; open 7am-8.45pm daily) sells tickets. Trains serve Paris' Gare St Lazare (€27, via Caen), Cherbourg, Rennes and points beyond.

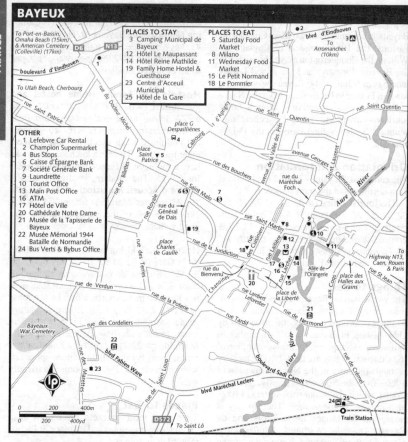

BAYEUX

PLACES TO STAY
3 Camping Municipal de Bayeux
12 Hôtel Le Maupassant
14 Hôtel Reine Mathilde
19 Family Home Hostel & Guesthouse
23 Centre d'Acceuil Municipal
25 Hôtel de la Gare

PLACES TO EAT
5 Saturday Food Market
8 Milano
11 Wednesday Food Market
15 Le Petit Normand
18 Le Pommier

OTHER
1 Lefebvre Car Rental
2 Champion Supermarket
4 Bus Stops
6 Caisse d'Épargne Bank
7 Société Générale Bank
9 Laundrette
10 Tourist Office
13 Main Post Office
16 ATM
17 Hôtel de Ville
20 Cathédrale Notre Dame
21 Musée de la Tapisserie de Bayeux
22 Musée Mémorial 1944 Bataille de Normandie
24 Bus Verts & Bybus Office

D-DAY BEACHES

The D-Day landings were the largest military operation in history. Early on the morning of 6 June 1944, swarms of landing craft – part of a flotilla of almost 7000 boats – ferried ashore 135,000 Allied troops along 80km of beaches north of Bayeux. The landings on D-Day were followed by the 76-day Battle of Normandy that began the liberation of Europe from Nazi occupation.

Things to See

Arromanches In order to unload the vast quantities of cargo necessary for the invasion, the Allies established two prefabricated ports. The remains of one of them, Port Winston, can be seen at Arromanches, a seaside town 10km northeast of Bayeux.

The **Musée du Débarquement** (Landing Museum; ☎ 02 31 22 34 31; adult/concession €6/4; open 9am-7pm daily in summer, 9.30am-12.30pm & 1.30pm-5.30pm in low season) explains the logistics and importance of Port Winston and makes a good first stop before visiting the beaches.

Omaha Beach The most brutal combat of 6 June was fought 20km west of Arromanches at Omaha Beach. Today, little evidence of the war remains except the bunkers and munitions sites of a German fortified point to the west (look for the tall obelisk on the hill).

American Military Cemetery The remains of the Americans who lost their lives during the Battle of Normandy were either sent back to the USA or buried in the American Military Cemetery at Colleville-sur-Mer, containing the graves of 9386 American soldiers and a memorial to 1557 others whose bodies were never found.

Organised Tours

Tours of the D-Day beaches are offered by **Bus Fly** (☎ 02 31 22 00 08), based at the Family Home hostel in Bayeux (see Places to Stay in Bayeux earlier). An afternoon tour to major D-Day sites costs €35/31 per adult/concession, including museum entry fees. There are three other tour operators, all offering their own variations on the war cemetery theme – the tourist office can provide more details.

Getting There & Away

Bus With an office (closed weekends and in July) opposite Bayeaux's train station, **Bus Verts** (☎ 02 31 92 02 92) sends bus No 70 west to the American cemetery at Colleville-sur-Mer and Omaha Beach. Bus No 74 serves Arromanches, and Gold and Juno beaches. In July and August only, Bus No 75 goes to Caen via Arromanches, Gold, Juno and Sword beaches and the port of Ouistreham. There are timetables posted in the train station and at place G Despallières. Canadians wishing to visit the Canadian war cemetery at Courseulles-sur-Mer should consider renting a car, as public transport options are limited.

Car For three or more people, renting a car can actually be cheaper than a tour. **Lefebvre Car Rental** (☎ 02 31 92 05 96; blvd d'Eindhoven) in Bayeux charges €65 per day with 200km free.

MONT ST MICHEL
pop 42

It is difficult not to be impressed by Mont St Michel with its massive abbey anchored at the summit of a rocky island. Around the base are the ancient ramparts and a jumble of buildings that house the handful of people who still live there.

At low tide, Mont St Michel looks out over bare sand stretching into the distance. At high tide – about six hours later – this huge expanse of sand is under water, though only the very highest tides cover the 900m causeway that connects the islet to the mainland. The French government is currently spending millions to restore Mont St Michel to its former glory, so parts of it may be scaffolded.

The Mont's major attraction is the **Abbaye du Mont St Michel** (☎ 02 33 89 80 00; adult/concession €7/4.50; open 9am-5.30pm daily, 9.30am-5pm Oct-Apr), at the top of the Grande rue, up the stairway. It's worth taking the guided tour (in English) included in the ticket price. There are also self-paced evening tours (adult/concession €9/6.50) at 9pm or midnight (except Sunday) of the illuminated and music-filled rooms.

Pontorson The nearest town, Pontorson, is 9km south and the base for most travellers. Route D976 from Mont St Michel runs directly into Pontorson's main thoroughfare, rue du Couësnon.

Information

The **tourist office** (☎ 02 33 60 14 30, fax 02 33 60 06 75; e ot.mont.saint.michel@ wanadoo.fr; open 9am-noon & 2pm-5.45pm Mon-Sat Oct-Easter, 9.30am-noon & 1pm-6.30pm daily Easter-June & Sept, 9am-7pm daily July & Aug) is up the stairs to the left as you enter the Mont St Michel at Porte de l'Avancée.

There's another **tourist office** (open daily; closed Sun in low season) in Pontorson.

Places to Stay

Camping On the road to Pontorson (D976), 2km from the Mont, is **Camping du Mont St Michel** (☎ 02 33 60 09 33, fax 02 33 60 20 02; Route du Mont-St-Michel; sites per tent/person €4.65/3, 2-person bungalows with shower & toilet low/high season €34.60/42.40; open mid-Feb–mid-Nov). It also offers hotel rooms (singles/doubles from €45.60/55) and breakfast.

Hostels Pontorson's **Centre Duguesclin** (☎ 02 33 60 18 65; dorm beds members/nonmembers €8/8.40; closed 10am-6pm, no curfew) operates as a 10-room hostel from Easter to mid-September. The hostel is 1km west of the train station on rue du Général Patton, which runs parallel to the Couësnon River north of rue du Couësnon. The hostel is on the left side in a three-storey stone building opposite No 26.

Hotels Mont St Michel has about 15 hotels but most of them are expensive. The **La Mère**

Poulard (☎ 02 33 60 14 01, fax 02 33 48 52 31; doubles with shower from €95) is the first hotel on the left as you walk up the Grande rue.

In Pontorson, across place de la Gare from the train station, there are a couple of cheap hotels, including **Hôtel de l'Arrivée** (☎ 02 33 60 01 57; 14 rue du Docteur Tizon; rooms without/with shower €15.40/25).

Places to Eat

The tourist restaurants around the base of the Mont have lovely views but tend to be mediocre; *menus* start at about €12. A few places along the Grande rue sell sandwiches, quiches and similar fare. The nearest **supermarket** to the Mont is next to Camping du Mont St Michel on the D976.

In Pontorson, **La Crêperie du Couësnon** (☎ 02 33 60 16 67; 21 rue du Couësnon) has crepes and savoury galettes (€1.50 to €6.10). **La Tour de Brette** (☎ 02 33 60 10 69; 8 rue du Couësnon; menus from €9.80) across from the river, has good *menus*.

Getting There & Away

STN (☎ 02 33 58 03 07) sends bus No 15 from Pontorson's train station to Mont St Michel daily year-round; most of the buses connect with trains to/from Paris, Rennes and Caen.

There are trains to Pontorson from Caen (via Folligny) and Rennes (via Dol). From Paris, take the train to Caen (from Gare St Lazare), Rennes (from the Gare Montparnasse) or direct to Pontorson via Folligny (from the Gare Montparnasse).

Getting Around

Bikes can be rented from **Couësnon Motoculture** (☎ 02 33 60 11 40; 1 bis rue du Couësnon), which charges €7/12 per half-day/day for mountain bikes.

Brittany

Brittany (Bretagne in French, Breizh in Breton), the westernmost region of France, is famous for its rugged countryside and its wild coastline. Traditional costumes, including the extraordinarily tall headdresses worn by the women, can still be seen at *pardons* (religious festivals) and other local festivals.

The indigenous language of Brittany is Breton, which, to the untrained ear, sounds like Gaelic with a French accent. It can sometimes still be heard in western Brittany and especially in Cornouaille, where perhaps one-third of the population understands it.

QUIMPER
pop 63,200

Situated at the confluence of two rivers, the Odet and the Steïr, Quimper (cam-**pair**) has managed to preserve its Breton architecture and atmosphere and is considered by many to be the cultural capital of Brittany. Some even refer to the city as the 'soul of Brittany'.

The Festival de Cornouaille, a showcase for traditional Breton music, costumes and culture, is held here every year between the third and fourth Sundays in July.

Orientation & Information

The old city, largely pedestrianised, is to the west and northwest of the cathedral. The train station is 1km east of the city centre on ave de la Gare; the bus station is to the right as you exit, in the modern-looking building.

The **tourist office** (☎ 02 98 53 04 05, fax 02 98 53 31 33; e office.tourisme.quimper@ ouest-mediacap.com; place de la Résistance open 9am-12.30pm & 1.30pm-6pm Mon-Sat open 9am-7pm July & Aug, 10am-12.45pm & 3pm-5.45pm Sun mid-June–Sept) can help with information.

Cyber Vidéo (51 blvd Kerguélen) has Internet facilities for €4.50 per hour.

Things to See

The old city is known for its centuries-old houses, which are especially in evidence on **rue Kéréon** and around **place au Beurre**.

The **Cathédrale St Corentin** (place Saint-Corentin), built between 1239 and 1515, incorporates many Breton elements, including - on the western facade between the spires – an equestrian statue of King Gradlon, the city's mythical 5th-century founder.

The **Musée Départemental Breton** (1 rue du Roi Gradlon; adult/concession €3.80/ 2.50; open Tues-Sat, & Sun afternoon, to 7pm daily in summer), next to the cathedral in the former bishop's palace, houses exhibits on the history, costumes, crafts and archaeology of the area. The **Musée des Beaux-Arts** (adult/ concession €3.85/2.30; open daily July-Aug, Wed-Mon Sept-June) in the **Hôtel de Ville** (40 place St Corentin) has a wide collection of European paintings from the 16th to early 20th centuries.

QUIMPER

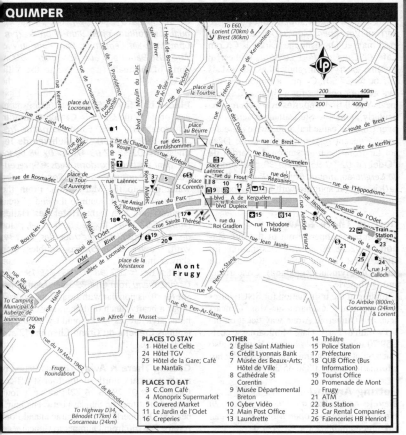

PLACES TO STAY
1 Hôtel Le Celtic
24 Hôtel TGV
25 Hôtel de la Gare; Café
   Le Nantaïs

PLACES TO EAT
3 C.Com Café
4 Monoprix Supermarket
5 Covered Market
11 Le Jardin de l'Odet
16 Creperies

OTHER
2 Église Saint Mathieu
6 Crédit Lyonnais Bank
7 Musée des Beaux-Arts;
   Hôtel de Ville
8 Cathédrale St
   Corentin
9 Musée Départemental
   Breton
10 Cyber Vidéo
12 Main Post Office
13 Laundrette

14 Théâtre
15 Police Station
17 Préfecture
18 QUB Office (Bus
   Information)
19 Tourist Office
20 Promenade de Mont
   Frugy
21 ATM
22 Bus Station
23 Car Rental Companies
26 Faïenceries HB Henriot

Faïenceries HB Henriot (☎ 02 98 90 09 36; rue Haute) has been turning out faïence (glazed earthenware) since 1690. Tours (€3.05/2.30 per adult/concession) of the factory, southwest of the cathedral, are held from 9am to 11.15am and 1.30pm to 4.15pm Monday to Friday (to 4.45pm in July and August).

Places to Stay

It's extremely difficult to find accommodation during the Festival de Cornouaille in late July. The tourist office makes bookings in Quimper (€0.30) and elsewhere in Brittany (€0.76), and has a list of **private rooms**.

Camping Just over 1km west of the old city is **Camping Municipal** (☎ 02 98 55 61 09; ave des Oiseaux; bus No 1 from train station

to Chaptal stop; sites per person/tent €2.90/0.63; open year-round).

Hostels The **Auberge de Jeunesse** (☎ 02 98 64 97 97, fax 02 98 55 38 37; 6 ave des Oiseaux; bus No 1 or 8 to Chaptal stop; dorm beds €8) is about 1km west of the old city.

Hotels The spotless **Hôtel TGV** (☎ 02 98 90 54 00; 4 rue de Concarneau; rooms from €27.50) has large, basic rooms with shower and toilet. The **Hôtel de la Gare** (☎ 02 98 90 00 81; 17 bis ave de la Gare; singles/doubles with shower €31/40, €40/46 during peak periods) offers another option. The **Hôtel Le Celtic** (☎ 02 98 55 59 35; 13 rue Douarnenez; doubles without/with shower €25/30.50) is 100m north of Église St Mathieu.

Places to Eat

There's a **Monoprix supermarket** (quai du Port au Vin; open Mon-Sat) near the **covered market**. Opposite the market is **C.Com Café** (9 Quai du Port au Vin), a cheerful daytime eatery with sandwiches and salads (€2.60 to €7.60). Crepes, a Breton speciality, are your best bet for a cheap and filling meal. You'll find **creperies** everywhere, particularly along rue Ste Catherine across the river from the cathedral. Otherwise there are several decent restaurants on rue Le Déan not far from the train station. **Le Jardin de l'Odet** (☎ 02 98 95 76 76; 39 blvd Amiral de Kerguélen; menus from €19; open Mon-Sat) is a good splurge, with tasty Lyonnais cuisine.

Getting There & Away

Six companies operate out of the **bus station** (☎ 02 98 90 88 89). Destinations include Brest, Pointe du Raz, Roscoff (for ferries to Plymouth, England), Concarneau and Quimperlé.

Inquire at the train station for SNCF buses to Douarnenez, Camaret-sur-Mer, Concarneau and Quiberon. A one-way ticket on the TGV train to Paris' Gare Montparnasse costs €59.70 to €69.80 (4½ hours). You can also reach Saint Malo by train via Rennes. For rail information call ☎ 0836 35 35 35.

Getting Around

Bicycle At **Airbike** (☎ 02 98 90 88 02; 128 ave de la Libération; open Mon-Sat) you can hire mountain bikes for €12 per day.

AROUND QUIMPER
Concarneau
pop 19,500

Concarneau (Konk-Kerne in Breton), 24km southeast of Quimper, is France's third-most important trawler port. Concarneau is slightly scruffy and at the same time a bit touristy, but it's refreshingly unpretentious and is near several decent beaches. The **Ville Close** (walled city), built on a small island measuring 350m by 100m and fortified between the 14th and 17th centuries, is reached via a footbridge from place Jean Jaurès.

Orientation & Information Concarneau curls around the busy fishing port (Port de Pêche), with the two main quays running north-south along the harbour.

The **tourist office** (☎ 02 98 97 01 44, fax 02 98 50 88 81; w www.concarneau.org quai d'Aiguillon; open 9am-noon & 2pm-6pm Mon-Sat Sept-June, 9am-8pm July & Aug, also 9am-noon Sun Apr-June) is 200m north of the main (west) gate to the Ville Close.

Places to Stay & Eat About 600m southeast of the Ville Close is **Camping Moulin d'Aurore** (☎ 02 98 50 53 08; 49 rue de Trégunc; open Apr-Sept). The **Auberge de Jeunesse** (☎ 02 98 97 03 47, fax 02 98 50 87 57; quai de la Croix; dorm beds €9; reception open 9am-noon & 6pm-8pm) is on the water next to the Marinarium. From the tourist office, walk south to the end of quai Peneroff and turn right. **Hôtel des Halles** (☎ 02 98 97 11 41, fax 02 98 50 58 54; place de l'Hôtel de Ville; singles/doubles €32/34, with shower €40/45) has doubles with shower and TV.

L'Escale (☎ 02 98 97 03 31; 19 quai Carnot; menu from €14.20; open Mon-Fri, & Sat lunch) is popular with local Concarnois – it has a hearty lunch or dinner. For excellent home-style crepes, you should try the unpretentious **Crêperie du Grand Chemin** (17 ave de la Gare).

Getting There & Away The bus station is in the car park north of the tourist office. **Caoudal** (☎ 02 98 56 96 72) runs up to four buses daily (three on Sunday) between Quimper and Quimperlé (via Concarneau and Pont Aven). The trip from Quimper to Concarneau costs €4 and takes 30 minutes.

SAINT MALO
pop 52,700

The Channel port of Saint Malo is one of the most popular tourist destinations in Brittany – and with good reason. It has a famous walled city and good nearby beaches, and is an excellent base for day trips to Mont St Michel (see the earlier Normandy section).

Orientation & Information

Saint Malo consists of the resort towns of St Servan, Saint Malo, Paramé and Rothéneuf. The old city is signposted as Intra-Muros ('within the walls') and also known as the Ville Close. It is connected to Paramé by the Sillon Isthmus. The train station is 1.2km east of the old city along ave Louis Martin.

The **tourist office** (☎ 02 99 56 64 48, fax 02 99 56 67 00; e office.de.tourisme.saint -malo@wanadoo.fr; esplanade St Vincent; open 2pm-6pm Mon, 9.30am-12.30pm & 2pm-6pm Tues-Fri, 9.30am-1pm & 2pm-5pm Sat Sept-June, 8.30am-8pm Mon-Sat, 10am-7pm Sun July & Aug) is just outside the old city. **Cybercom** (26 bis blvd des Talards; open 9am-noon & 2pm-6pm Mon-Fri, 9am-noon Sat) charges €1.60/half-hour of web surfing.

Things to See & Do
Old City In August 1944, fighting drove the Germans from Saint Malo and 80% of the old city was destroyed. While the main historical monuments were lovingly reconstructed, the rest of the area was rebuilt in 17th- and 18th-century style. The **ramparts**, built over the course of many centuries, are largely original. They afford superb views in all directions.

The **Musée de la Ville** (adult/concession €4.40/2.20; open 10am-noon & 2pm-6pm daily in summer, Tues-Sun in winter), in the Château de Saint Malo at Porte St Vincent, deals with the history of the city and the Pays Malouin, the area around Saint Malo.

Aquarium Intra-Muros (adult/concession €5.50/4), with more than 100 tanks, is built into the walls of the old city next to place Vauban. Europe's first circular aquarium, **Le Grand Aquarium Saint Malo** (ave Général Patton; adult/concession €12/9) is 1.5km south of the train station. Take bus No 5 from the train station and hop off at the La Madelaine stop.

Île du Grand Bé You can reach the Île du Grand Bé, where the 18th-century writer Chateaubriand is buried, on foot at low tide via the Porte des Bés. Be warned – when the tide comes rushing in, the causeway is impassable for about six hours.

St Servan St Servan's fortress, **Fort de la Cité**, was built in the mid-18th century and served as a German base during WWII. The **Musée International du Long Cours Cap-Hornier** (esplanade Menguy; adult/concession €4.40/2.20, combined ticket with Musée de la Ville €11/5.50; closed Mon low season), housed in the 14th-century Tour de Solidor, has interesting seafaring exhibits.

Beaches To the west, just outside the old city walls, is **Plage de Bon Secours**. The **Grande Plage**, which stretches northeastward from the Sillon Isthmus, is spiked with tree trunks that act as breakers.

Places to Stay
Camping At the northern tip of St Servan is **Camping Municipal Cité d'Aleth** (☎ 02 99 81 60 91; sites 1 or 2 people plus tent €10.50; open year-round), next to Fort de la Cité. In summer take bus No 1; at other times your best bet is bus No 6.

Hostels About 2km northeast of the train station (bus No 5) there's **Auberge de Jeunesse** (☎ 02 99 40 29 80, fax 02 99 40 29 02; 37 ave du Père Umbricht; bus No 2 or 5 from train station; beds per-person in 2–3/5– 6-bed room €14.90/12.20; singles/doubles per person €19.90/14.90; reception open 24hr) where prices include breakfast.

Hotels Across the roundabout from the train station is the **Hôtel de l'Europe** (☎ 02 99 56 13 42; 44 blvd de la République; singles/ doubles from €25/28, with shower & toilet €34/40). Rooms are modern, nondescript and one-third cheaper in winter.

Hôtel Armoricaine (☎ 02 99 40 89 13, fax 02 99 49 46 42; 4 rue du Boyer; rooms from €31) is in the old city. The friendly, family-run **Hôtel Aux Vieilles Pierres** (☎ 02 99 56 46 80; 4 rue des Lauriers; singles/doubles from €24.40/39.65) is in a quiet part of the old city. Hall showers are free.

Places to Eat
Tourist restaurants, creperies and pizzerias are chock-a-block in the area between Porte St Vincent, the cathedral and the Grande Porte, but if you're after better food, and better value, avoid this area completely.

As good as any for seafood is **La Pomme d'Or** (☎ 02 99 40 90 24; 4 place du Poids du Roy; menus €10.80-34). If you overindulge you might consider staying in one of the rooms upstairs (from €45.20). Or try the more intimate **Grain de Sable** (☎ 02 99 56 68 72) at No 2, which serves an excellent fish soup (€4.50). In St Servan, **Crêperie du Val de Rance** (11 rue Dauphine) serves Breton-style crepes and galettes (€1.50 to €6).

Getting There & Away
Bus The bus station, served by several operators, is at esplanade St Vincent. Many of the

FRANCE

SAINT MALO

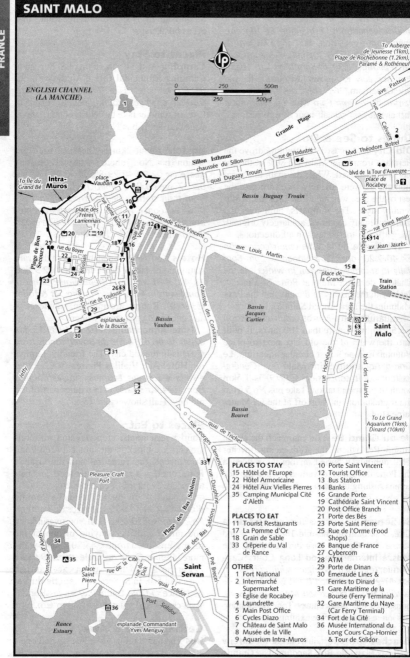

ENGLISH CHANNEL
(LA MANCHE)

To Auberge
de Jeunesse (1km),
Plage de Rochebonne (1.2km),
Paramé & Rothéneuf

Grande Plage

Sillon Isthmus
chaussée du Sillon
quai Duguay Trouin
rue de l'Industrie

blvd Théodore Botrel

blvd de la Tour d'Auvergne
place de
Rocabey

To Île du
Grand Bé

Intra-
Muros

place Vauban

place des
Frères
Lamennais

Bassin Duguay Trouin

esplanade Saint Vincent
ave Louis Martin

rue Sainte Barbe

Plage de Bon Secours

rue du Boyer

rue Broussais

rue de Toulouse

blvd de la République

rue Ernest Renan

av Jean Jaurès

place de
la Grande

Train
Station

Saint
Malo

rue Alphonse Thébault

rue Hochelaga

blvd des Talards

Bassin
Jacques
Cartier

Bassin
Vauban

esplanade
de la Bourse

chaussée des Corsaires

Bassin
Bouvet

To Le Grand
Aquarium (1km),
Dinard (10km)

jetty

Pleasure Craft
Port

Corniche d'Aleth

quai Georges Clemenceau

rue Dauphine

Plage des Bas Sablons

rue des Bas

rue Georges Clemenceau

rue de la Cité
rue du Dick
place
Saint Pierre

Saint
Servan

rue Pré Brécel

quai Solidor

Port Solidor

Rance
Estuary

esplanade Commandant
Yves Menguy

PLACES TO STAY	10 Porte Saint Vincent
15 Hôtel de l'Europe	12 Tourist Office
22 Hôtel Armoricaine	13 Bus Station
24 Hôtel Aux Vielles Pierres	14 Banks
35 Camping Municipal Cité	16 Grande Porte
d'Aleth	19 Cathédrale Saint Vincent
	20 Post Office Branch
PLACES TO EAT	21 Porte des Bés
11 Tourist Restaurants	23 Porte Saint Pierre
17 La Pomme d'Or	25 Rue de l'Orme (Food
18 Grain de Sable	Shops)
33 Crêperie du Val	26 Banque de France
de Rance	27 Cybercom
	28 ATM
OTHER	29 Porte de Dinan
1 Fort National	30 Émeraude Lines &
2 Intermarché	Ferries to Dinard
Supermarket	31 Gare Maritime de la
3 Église de Rocabey	Bourse (Ferry Terminal)
4 Laundrette	32 Gare Maritime du Naye
5 Main Post Office	(Car Ferry Terminal)
6 Cycles Diazo	34 Fort de la Cité
7 Château de Saint Malo	36 Musée International du
8 Musée de la Ville	Long Cours Cap-Hornier
9 Aquarium Intra-Muros	& Tour de Solidor

buses departing from here also stop at the train station.

Courriers Bretons (☎ 02 99 19 70 70) has regular services to regional destinations, including Mont St Michel (€8.80, one hour). The first daily bus to Mont St Michel leaves at 10am and the last one returns around 4.30pm.

TIV (☎ 02 99 40 82 67) has buses to Dinan (€6.40) and Rennes (€9.40). Buses to Dinard run about once an hour until around 7pm.

Train From the **train station** (☎ 0836 35 35 35) there is a direct service to Paris' Gare Montparnasse (€49.60 to €59.80, 3¼ hours). Some go via Rennes (€10.70). There are local services to Dinan (€7.30) and Quimper (€31).

Boat Ferries link Saint Malo with the Channel Islands, Weymouth and Portsmouth in England. There are two ferry terminals: hydrofoils, catamarans and the like depart from Gare Maritime de la Bourse; car ferries leave from the Gare Maritime du Naye. Both are south of the walled city.

From Gare Maritime de la Bourse, **Condor** (☎ 02 99 20 03 00) has catamaran and jetfoil services to Jersey (one-day excursion €46) and Guernsey (€46) from mid-March to mid-November. Condor's service to Weymouth (one way from €46, four hours) operates daily from late May to mid-October – discount prices are sometimes available.

Émeraude Lines (☎ 02 23 18 01 80) has ferries to Jersey, Guernsey and Sark from Gare Maritime du Naye. Service is most regular between late March and mid-November. **Brittany Ferries** (☎ 08 25 82 88 28) has boats to Portsmouth from the Gare Maritime du Naye.

The Bus de Mer ferry (operated by Émeraude Lines) links Saint Malo with Dinard (€3.40/5.40 one way/return, 10 minutes) from April to September. In Saint Malo, the dock is just outside the Porte de Dinan; the Dinard quay is at 27 ave George V.

AROUND SAINT MALO
Dinard
pop 10,400
While Saint Malo's old city and beaches are geared towards middle-class families, Dinard attracts a well-heeled clientele – especially from the UK. Indeed, Dinard has the feel of an early-20th-century beach resort, with its candy-cane bathing tents and carnival rides.

Beautiful seaside trails extend along the coast in both directions from Dinard. The famous **promenade du Clair de Lune** (Moonlight Promenade) runs along the Baie du Prieuré. The town's most attractive walk is the one that links the promenade du Clair de Lune with Plage de l'Écluse via the rocky coast of **Pointe du Moulinet**. Bikes are not allowed.

The **tourist office** (☎ 02 99 46 94 12, fax 02 99 88 21 07; e dinard.office.de.tourime@wanadoo.fr; 2 blvd Féart; open 9am-noon & 2pm-6pm Mon-Sat Sept-June, 9.30am-7.30pm July & Aug) is in the colonnaded building. Staying in Dinard can strain the budget, so consider making a day trip from Saint Malo (see that town's Getting There & Away section earlier for details).

Loire Valley

From the 15th to 18th centuries, the fabled Loire Valley (Vallée de la Loire) was the playground of kings and nobles who expended vast fortunes and the wealth of the nation to turn it into a vast neighbourhood of lavish chateaux. Today, this region is a favourite destination of tourists seeking architectural glories from the Middle Ages and the Renaissance.

The earliest chateaux were medieval fortresses, thrown up in the 9th century to fend of marauding Vikings. As the threat of invasion diminished by the 15th century, chateaux architecture changed: fortresses gave way to pleasure palaces as the Renaissance ushered in whimsical, decorative features. From the 17th century onwards, grand country houses (built in the neoclassical style amid formal gardens) took centre stage.

BLOIS
pop 49,300
The medieval town of Blois (pronounced blwah) was a hub of court intrigue between the 15th and 17th centuries, and in the 16th century served as a second capital of France. Some dramatic events involving some of France's most important kings and historical figures took place inside the outstanding Château de Blois. The old city, seriously damaged by German attacks in 1940, retains its steep, twisting medieval streets.

Several of the Loire Valley's most rewarding chateaux, including Chambord and

Cheverny, are a pleasant 20km-or-so cycle from Blois.

Orientation

Almost everything of interest is within walking distance of the train station, which is at the western end of ave Dr Jean Laigret. The old city is situated south and east of Château de Blois, which towers over place Victor Hugo.

Information

Tourist Offices The tourist office (☎ 02 54 90 41 41, fax 02 54 90 41 49; e blois .tourism@wanadoo.fr; 3 ave Dr Jean Laigret; open 9am-7pm Mon-Sat, 10am-7pm Sun May-Sept, 9am-12.30pm & 2pm-6pm Mon-Sat, 9.30am-12.30pm Sun Oct-Apr) can help with information.

Money & Post The Banque de France (4 ave Dr Jean Laigret; open 9am-12.15pm & 1.45pm-3.30pm Mon-Fri) is one of a number of banks. Several commercial banks face the river along quai de la Saussaye, near Rond Point de la Résistance.

Send mail at the post office (rue Gallois; open 8.30am-7pm Mon-Fri, 8am-noon Sat), which has Cyberposte.

Email & Internet Access You can get speedy Internet connection at Planet Info (☎ 02 54 55 99 41; 1 rue Jeanne d'Arc; open 10am-noon & 2pm-6pm Mon-Fri) for the princely sum of €1.50 for every 10 minutes.

Things to See

Château de Blois Château de Blois (☎ 02 54 74 16 06; adult/concession €6/4) has a compellingly bloody history and an extraordinary mixture of architectural styles. Its four distinct sections are: early Gothic (13th century); Flamboyant Gothic (1498–1503), dating back to the reign of Louis XII; early Renaissance (1515–24), from the reign of François I; and classical (17th century). The chateau also houses an **archaeological museum** as well as the **Musée des Beaux-Arts** (Museum of Fine Arts), both open 9am to noon and 2pm to 5pm from mid-October to mid-March; and 9am to 6.30pm (8pm in July and August) during the rest of the year. The chateau's evening **sound-and-light show** (adult/concession €9.50/4.50) runs May to September. For a chateau visit and show, buy the combination ticket (€11.50/5).

Opposite, there's the **Maison de la Magie** (House of Magic; ☎ 02 54 55 26 26; 1 place du Château; adult/12-17 years/6-11 years €7.30/6.40/5.20; open 10.30am-12.30pm & 2pm-6.30pm daily July-Aug, 10am-noon & 2pm-6pm Tues-Sun Apr-June, 10am-noon & 2pm-6pm Wed-Thur & Sat-Sun Sept-Mar) with magic shows, interactive exhibits and displays of clocks invented by the Blois-born magician Jean-Eugène Robert-Houdin (1805–71), after whom the great Houdini named himself.

Old City Large brown signs in English pinpoint tourist sights around the predominantly pedestrian old city. **Cathédrale St-Louis** is named after an ancestor of Louis XIV, who had it rebuilt after a hurricane in 1678. There's a great view of Blois and the River Loire from the lovely **Jardins de l'Évêché** (Gardens of the Bishop's Palace) behind the cathedral.

The 15th-century **Maison des Acrobates** (House of Acrobats; 3 bis rue Pierre de Blois) is one of Blois' few medieval houses to survive the bombings of WWII. It's named after the cheeky characters carved in its timbers.

Places to Stay

Camping A two-star site in Vineuil is **Camping des Châteaux** (☎ 02 54 78 82 05; 2 adults, tent & car €8; open July-Sept), about 4km south of Blois. There is no bus service from town except in July and August (phone the camp site or the tourist office for details).

Hostels The **Auberge de Jeunesse Les Grouëttes** (☎/fax 02 54 78 27 21; 18 rue de l'Hôtel Pasquier; bus No 4 from place de la République; dorm beds €7; closed 10am-6pm, open Mar–mid-Nov) in Les Grouëts, is 4.5km southwest of Blois train station. Call first – it's often full.

Hotels Near the train station, your best bet is **Hôtel St-Jacques** (☎ 02 54 78 04 15, fax 02 54 78 33 05; 7 rue Ducoux; singles/doubles from €21.50/23, with shower from €26/27.50), which has basic doubles. Opposite at No 6, family-run **Hôtel Le Savoie** (☎ 02 54 74 32 21, fax 02 54 74 29 58; singles/doubles from €36/39) has well-kept rooms with shower, toilet and TV.

North of the old city, 12-room **Hôtel du Bellay** (☎ 02 54 78 23 62, fax 02 54 78 52 04; 12 rue des Minimes; rooms €22.10-24.40, with shower & toilet €30.50) is another option.

BLOIS

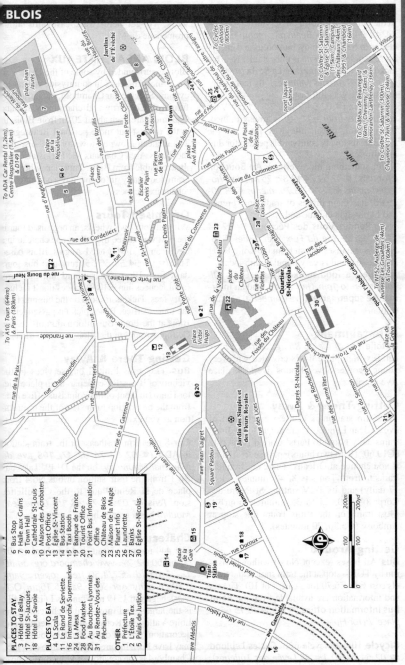

PLACES TO STAY
3 Hôtel du Bellay
17 Hôtel St-Jacques
18 Hôtel Le Savoie

PLACES TO EAT
4 La Scala
11 Le Rond de Serviette
16 Intermarché Supermarket
24 La Mesa
29 Au Bouchon Lyonnais
31 Au Rendez-Vous des Pêcheurs

OTHER
1 Préfecture
2 L'Étoile Tex
5 Palais de Justice
6 Bus Stop
7 Halle aux Grains
8 Town Hall
9 Cathédrale St-Louis
10 Maison des Acrobates
12 Post Office
13 Église St-Vincent
14 Bus Station
15 Taxi Booth
19 Banque de France
20 Tourist Office
21 Point Bus Information Office
22 Château de Blois
23 Maison de la Magie
25 Planet Info
26 Laundrette
27 Banks
30 Église St-Nicolas

FRANCE

Places to Eat
In the old city, **Le Rond de Serviette** (☎ 02 54 74 48 04; 18 rue Beauvoir; menu €7.80) claims to be Blois' most humorous and cheapest restaurant; its *menu* is unbeatable. Nearby, tuck into pasta and pizza at **La Scala** (☎ 02 54 74 88 19; 8 rue des Minimes). Its leafy summer terrace gets full fast.

La Mesa (☎ 02 54 78 70 70; 11 rue Vauvert; menus from €11.50) is a busy Franco-Italian joint, up an alleyway from 44 rue Foulerie. Its lovely courtyard is perfect for dining alfresco.

For something more refined, **Au Bouchon Lyonnais** (☎ 02 54 74 12 87; 25 rue des Violettes; mains €12.10-13.75, menus €18.30-29.90) has main dishes of traditional French and Lyon-style cuisine and *menus*.

Au Rendez-Vous des Pêcheurs (☎ 02 54 74 67 48; 27 rue du Foix; fish dishes €16-22.70) specialises in fish from the Loire River and the sea, and is very popular with locals.

There's a **food market** (place Louis XII; Tues, open to 1pm Thur & Sat), and an **Intermarché supermarket** (ave Gambetta) near the station.

Entertainment
L'Étoile Tex (9 rue du Bourg Neuf) is a busy bar/Tex-Mex place that's crowded with very young people. Several pubs overlook place Ave Maria.

Getting There & Away
The train station is at the western end of ave Dr Jean Laigret. There are up to 16 direct trains daily going to Paris' Gare d'Austerlitz (€19.60, 1½ to two hours), plus several more if you change at Orléans. There are frequent trains to/from Tours (€8, 40 minutes, 11 to 17 daily) and its TGV station, St-Pierre des Corps (€7.70, 25 to 35 minutes, hourly). Most trains on the Blois-Tours line stop at Amboise (€5.30, 20 minutes).

Getting Around
Bus All buses (except No 4) within Blois – run by TUB – stop at the train station and tickets cost €1 (€6.70 for a carnet of 10). Tickets and information are available from the **Point Bus information office** (☎ 02 54 78 15 66; 2 place Victor Hugo).

Bicycle Hire a bicycle from **Cycles Leblond** (☎ 02 54 74 30 13; 44 Levée des Tuileries), which charges upwards of €12.20/80 per day/week. To get here, walk eastwards along promenade du Mail.

BLOIS AREA CHATEAUX
Blois is surrounded by some of the Loire Valley's finest chateaux in countryside perfect for cycling. Spectacular Chambord, magnificently furnished Cheverny and charmingly situated Chaumont are each about 20km from Blois, as is the modest but more personal Beauregard. The chateau-crowned town of Amboise (see the Tours Area Chateaux section) is also easily accessible from Blois. Travellers who try to cram too many into one day risk catching 'chateaux sickness'.

Organised Tours
Without your own wheels, an organised tour is the best way to see more than one chateau in a day. From mid-May to 31 August, Blois-based **TLC** (☎ 02 54 58 55 55) runs two bus tours daily from Blois to Chambord and Cheverny (adult/concession €10/8); prices don't include entry fees. Tickets are sold on the bus and from the tourist office. Buses pick up passengers in Blois at the Point Bus information office (see Getting Around in the Blois section earlier).

Getting There & Away
Bus TLC runs limited bus services in the vicinity of Blois. Buses depart from place Victor Hugo (in front of the Point Bus office) and from the bus station to the left of the train station as you exit.

Car Some 3km northeast of the train station is **ADA** (☎ 02 54 74 02 47; 108 ave du Maréchal Maunoury) on the D149. Take bus No 1 from the train station or bus No 4 from place de la République to the Cornillettes stop. **Avis** (☎ 02 54 74 48 15; 6 rue Jean Moulin) has a branch here.

Château de Chambord
The 440-room Château de Chambord (☎ 02 54 50 50 02; w www.chambord.org; adult/18-25s/child €7/4.50/free; open 9am-6.30pm daily Apr-Sept, 9am-5.15pm Oct-Mar), begun in 1519 by François I (1515–47), is the largest and most-visited chateau in the Loire Valley. Its Renaissance architecture and decoration, grafted onto a feudal ground plan, may have been inspired by Leonardo da Vinci. Chambord is the creation of François I, whose

mblems – a royal monogram of the letter 'F' nd a fierce salamander – adorn parts of the uilding. Beset by financial problems – which ven forced him to leave his two sons unran-omed in Spain – the king managed to keep 800 workers and artisans at work on Cham-ord for 15 years. At one point he demanded hat the Loire River be rerouted so it would ass by Chambord.

The chateau's famed **double-helix stair-case**, attributed by some to Leonardo, consists f two spiral staircases that wind around the ame central axis but never meet. It leads to n Italianate **rooftop terrace**, where you're urrounded by towers, cupolas, domes, chim-eys, dormers and slate roofs with geometric hapes. Visitors already in the chateau can tay 45 minutes after ticket sales end.

Getting There & Away Chambord is 16km ast of Blois and 20km northeast of Cheverny. During the school year, TLC bus No 2 aver-ges three return trips (two on Saturday, one n Sunday) from Blois to Chambord (€3.25, 45 minutes). In July and August, your only bus ption is TLC's guided tour (see Organised Tours earlier in this section).

Getting Around You can rent a bicycle rom the Echapée Belle kiosk, next to Pont St-Michel in the castle grounds (€5.25/12.25/ 21.50 per hour/day/weekend).

Château de Cheverny

The Château de Cheverny (☎ 02 54 79 96 29; e chateau.cheverny@wanadoo.fr; adult/ concession €5.80/4; open 9.15am or 9.30am-5.15pm Apr-June & Sept, to 6.30pm July & Aug, 9.15am or 9.30am-noon & 2.15pm-5.30pm Oct & Mar, to 5pm Nov-Feb), the most magnificently furnished of the Loire Val-ey chateaux and still privately owned, was completed in 1634. Visitors wander through sumptuous rooms outfitted with the finest canopied beds, tapestries, paintings, painted ceilings and walls covered with embossed Córdoba leather. Three dozen panels illustrate the story of Don Quixote in the downstairs dining room.

The lush grounds shelter an 18th-century **Orangerie** where Leonardo da Vinci's Mona Lisa was hidden during WWII. The stables now house a mediocre **Tintin museum** (adult/ concession €10/8.20, includes entry to the château) that might appeal to kids and diehard

fans. The antlers of almost 2000 stags cover the walls of the **Salle des Trophées**, while the ken-nels keep a pack of 100 hunting hounds – their daily meal at 5pm, called the 'Soupe des chiens', is worth a glimpse.

Getting There & Away Cheverny is 16km southeast of Blois and 20km southwest of Chambord.

The TLC bus No 4 from Blois to Ville-franche-sur-Cher stops at Cheverny (€3, 25 to 35 minutes). Buses leave Blois at 12.25pm Monday to Friday. Returning to Blois, the last bus leaves Cheverny at 6.58pm. Departure times can vary and are different on Sunday and holidays; check schedules first.

Château de Beauregard

Built in the 16th century as a hunting lodge for François I, Beauregard (☎ 02 54 70 36 74; adult/student & child €6.50/4.50; open 9.30am-noon & 2pm-5pm or 6.30pm daily Apr-Sept, 9.30am-noon & 2pm-5pm or 6.30pm Thur-Tues Oct-Mar) is most famous for its **Galerie des Portraits**, which displays 327 portraits of notable faces from the 14th to 17th centuries.

Getting There & Away Beauregard is 6km south of Blois or a pleasant 15km cycle ride through forests from Chambord. There's road access to the chateau from the Blois-Cheverny D765 and the D956 (turn left at the village of Cellettes).

The TLC bus from Blois to St-Aignan stops at Cellettes (€1.45), 1km southwest of the chateau, Monday to Friday at 7.50am; and on Wednesday, Friday and Saturday the first bus from Blois to Cellettes leaves at 12.25pm. Unfortunately, there's no afternoon bus back except for the Châteauroux-Blois line oper-ated by **Transports Boutet** (☎ 02 54 34 43 95), which passes through Cellettes around 6pm daily.

Château de Chaumont

Château de Chaumont (☎ 02 54 51 26 26; adult/18-25s/child €5.50/3.50/free; open 9.30am-6.30pm daily mid-Mar–mid-Oct, 10am-4.30pm daily mid-Oct–mid-Mar), set on a bluff overlooking the Loire, resembles a feudal castle. Built in the late 15th century, it served as a booby prize for Diane de Poitier when her lover, Henry II, died in 1559, and hosted Benjamin Franklin several times when he served as ambassador to France after the American Revolution.

Its luxurious **stables** are the most famous feature, but the **Salle du Conseil** (Council Chamber) on the 1st floor, with its majolica tile floor and tapestries, and **Catherine de' Medici's bedroom** overlooking the chapel, are also remarkable.

Getting There & Away Château de Chaumont is 17km southwest of Blois and 20km northeast of Amboise in Chaumont-sur-Loire. The path to the chateau begins at the intersection of rue du Village Neuf and rue Maréchal Leclerc (D751). Trains go from Blois to Onzain (€2.70, 10 minutes, eight or more daily), a 2km walk across the river from the chateau.

TOURS
pop 270,000

Lively Tours has the cosmopolitan and bourgeois air of a miniature Paris, with wide 18th-century avenues and café-lined boulevards. The city was devastated by German bombardment in June 1940, but much of it has been rebuilt since. The French spoken in Tours is said to be the purest in France.

Orientation

Tours' focal point is place Jean Jaurès, where the city's major thoroughfares – rue Nationale, blvd Heurteloup, ave de Grammont and blvd Béranger – join up. The train station is 300m east along blvd Heurteloup. The old city, centred around place Plumereau, is about 400m west of rue Nationale.

Information

Tourist Offices The **tourist office** (☎ 02 47 70 37 37, fax 02 47 61 14 22; e info@ligeris .com; 78-82 rue Bernard Palissy; open 8.30am-7pm Mon-Sat, 10am-12.30pm & 2.30pm-6pm Sun May-Oct, 9am-12.30pm & 1.30pm-6pm Mon-Sat, 10am-1pm Sun Nov-Apr) can help with information.

Money The **Banque de France** (2 rue Chanoineau) is open 8.45am to noon on weekdays. Commercial banks overlook place Jean Jaurès, and ATMs are easily identifiable throughout the city's centre.

Post & Communications The **post office** (1 blvd Béranger; open 8am-7pm Mon-Fri, 8am-noon Sat) has Cyberposte.

Alli@nce Micro (☎ 02 47 05 49 50; 7te rue de la Monnaie), and **Le Cyberspace** (☎ 0. 47 66 29 96; 27 rue Lavoisier; open 2pm 5am) both charge around €4 per hour to sur the web; the latter is housed in a pub.

Things to See

Tours offers lovely quarters for strolling in cluding the **old city** around place Plumereau which is surrounded by half-timbered houses as well as **rue du Grand Marché** and **rue Col bert**. The neighbourhood around the **Cath édrale St-Gatien**, built between 1220 an 1547, is renowned for its 13th- and its 15th century stained glass. Its Renaissance **cloiste** can be visited.

The **Musée de l'Hôtel Goüin** (25 rue du Commerce; adult/concession €3.50/2.60) i an archaeological museum, housed in a splen did Renaissance mansion built around 1510 The **Musée du Compagnonnage** (Guild Museum; 8 rue Nationale; adult/concession €4/ 2.50), overlooking the courtyard of **Abbaye St-Julien**, is a celebration of the skill of the French artisan. The **Musée des Vins de Touraine** (Museum of Touraine Wines; adult/ concession €2.50/2) at No 16 is in the 13th century wine cellars of Abbaye St-Julien.

The **Musée des Beaux-Arts** (Museum o Fine Arts; 18 place François Sicard; adult/ concession €4/2) has a good collection o works from the 14th to 20th centuries.

Most museums in Tours are closed on Tuesday.

Places to Stay

Camping Three-star **Camping Les Rives du Cher** (☎ 02 47 27 27 60; 63 rue de Rochpinard, St-Avertin; sites per tent/person/car €3/3/2; open Apr–mid-Oct), 5km south of Tours, is friendly. From place Jean Jaurès, take bus No 5 to the St-Avertin bus terminal, then follow signs.

Hostels About 500m north of the train station, **Le Foyer** (☎ 02 47 60 51 51, fax 02 47 20 75 20; e fjt.tours@wanadoo.fr; 16 rue Bernard Palissy; singles/doubles €17/26; reception open Mon-Sat) is a workers' dormitory that sometimes has space for travellers.

Hotels Recently spruced up **Hôtel Val de Loire** (☎ 02 47 05 37 86, fax 02 47 64 85 54; 33 blvd Heurteloup; singles/doubles with washbasin & bidet €16.50/26, with shower,

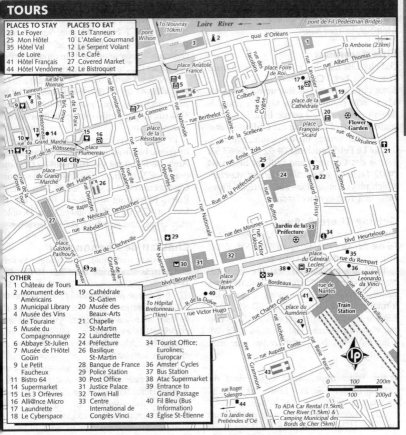

TOURS

PLACES TO STAY
23 Le Foyer
25 Mon Hôtel
35 Hôtel Val de Loire
41 Hôtel Français
44 Hôtel Vendôme

PLACES TO EAT
8 Les Tanneurs
10 L'Atelier Gourmand
12 Le Serpent Volant
13 Le Café
27 Covered Market
42 Le Bistroquet

OTHER
1 Château de Tours
2 Monument des Américains
3 Municipal Library
4 Musée des Vins de Touraine
5 Musée du Compagnonnage
6 Abbaye St-Julien
7 Musée de l'Hôtel Goüin
9 Le Petit Faucheux
11 Bistro 64
14 Supermarket
15 Les 3 Orfèvres
16 Alli@nce Micro
17 Laundrette
18 Le Cyberspace
19 Cathédrale St-Gatien
20 Musée des Beaux-Arts
21 Chapelle St-Martin
22 Laundrette
24 Préfecture
26 Basilique St-Martin
28 Banque de France
29 Police Station
30 Post Office
31 Justice Palace
32 Town Hall
33 Centre International de Congrès Vinci
34 Tourist Office; Eurolines; Europcar
36 Amster' Cycles
37 Bus Station
38 Atac Supermarket
39 Entrance to Grand Passage
40 Fil Bleu (Bus Information)
43 Église St-Étienne

toilet & TV €30/40) has rooms that may be spartan but they're clean and comfortable.

Hôtel Français *(☎ 02 47 05 59 12; 11 rue de Nantes; singles/doubles/triples/quads with washbasin & bidet €20/20/25/29, with shower & TV €25/29/34/37, with shower, TV & toilet €27/33/36/47)* provides a cold welcome but is good for penny-pinchers. A hall shower/breakfast costs €2/5.

Mon Hôtel *(☎ 02 47 05 67 53, fax 02 47 05 21 85; 40 rue de la Préfecture; singles/ doubles from €17/20, with shower & toilet €30/35)* is 500m north of the train station. Cheerful **Hôtel Vendôme** *(☎/fax 02 47 64 33 54; e hotelvendome.tours@wanadoo.fr; 24 rue Roger Salengro; rooms from €20, with shower & toilet from €30.50)* is run by a friendly couple. It has simple but decent rooms.

Places to Eat

In the old city, place Plumereau and rue du Grand Marché are loaded with places to eat. **Le Serpent Volant** *(54 rue du Grand Marché)* is a quintessential French café, while **Le Café** *(39 rue du Dr Bretonneau)* is a contemporary, funky favourite.

L'Atelier Gourmand *(☎ 02 47 38 59 87; 37 rue Etienne Marcel; menu €16)* has the most romantic courtyard terrace. Simple but attractive **Le Bistroquet** *(☎ 02 47 05 12 76; 17 rue Blaise Pascal; menus €10.30/15)* specialises in paella but has French food *menus*. **Les Tanneurs** is a university restaurant-cum-café near the main university building on rue des Tanneurs. To dine you need a student ticket.

Sandwich stalls selling well-filled baguettes and pastries fill the **Grand Passage shopping**

FRANCE

mall *(18 rue de Bordeaux)*. There's a **covered market** *(place Gaston Pailhou; open to 7pm Mon-Sat, to 1pm Sun)*.

Entertainment
Old-city café nightlife is centred around place Plumereau. **Les 3 Orfèvres** *(☎ 02 47 64 02 73; 6 rue des Orfèvres)* has live music starting at 11pm most nights. Student nightlife abounds down tiny rue de la Longue Echelle and the southern strip of adjoining rue Dr Bretonneau.

Live jazz venues include alternative café-theatre **Le Petit Faucheux** *(☎ 02 47 38 67 62; 23 rue des Cerisiers)* and brilliant **Bistro 64** *(☎ 02 47 38 47 40; 64 rue du Grand Marché)*, which plays Latin, blues and *musique Française* in a 16th-century interior.

Getting There & Away
Bus There's a **Eurolines** *(☎ 02 47 66 45 56; 76 rue Bernard Palissy; open Mon-Sat)* ticket office next to the tourist office.

The **Tours bus station** *(☎ 02 47 05 30 49; place du Général Leclerc)*, opposite the train station, serves local destinations. It has an **information desk** *(☎ 02 47 05 30 49; open 7.30am-noon & 2pm-6.30pm Mon-Sat)*. You can visit Chenonceau and Amboise in a day using CAT bus No 10 (study the schedules carefully).

Train Tours train station is on place du Général Leclerc. Several Loire Valley chateaux can be easily accessed by rail.

Paris' Gare Montparnasse is about 1¼ hours away by TGV (€33.50 to €43.60, up to 20 daily), often with a change at St-Pierre des Corps. Other services include to/from Paris' Gare d'Austerlitz (€24.30, 2½ hours), Bordeaux (€35.40, 2½ hours) and Nantes (€23.80, 1½ hours).

Car There's a **Europcar** *(☎ 02 47 64 47 76; 76 blvd Bernard Palissy)* office next to the tourist office.

Getting Around
Bus Local buses are run by **Fil Bleu** *(information office ☎ 02 47 66 70 70; 5 bis rue de la Dolve)*.

Bicycle From April to September, **Amster' Cycles** *(☎ 02 47 61 22 23; fax 02 47 61 28 48; 5 rue du Rempart)* rents road and mountain bikes for €14/54 per day/week.

TOURS AREA CHATEAUX
Several chateaux around Tours can be reached by train, SNCF bus or bicycle. Several companies offer English-language tours of the chateaux – reserve at the Tours tourist office or contact the company directly.

Services Touristiques de Touraine *(STT ☎/fax 02 47 05 46 09; w www.stt-millet.fr)* runs coach tours April to mid-October costing €34 (including admission fees to three to four chateaux).

In summer, you can make an all-day circuit by public bus from Tours to Chenonceaux and Amboise by taking the 10am bus to Chenonceaux (€2.10), then the 12.40pm bus from Chenonceaux to Amboise (€1.05, 25 minutes). Return buses from Amboise to Tours (€2.10) leave at 4.25pm, 5.25pm and 6.20pm. Double-check times and schedules before departing.

Château de Chenonceau
With its stylised moat, drawbridge, towers and turrets straddling the Cher River, the 16th-century Chenonceau *(☎ 02 47 23 90 07; e chateau.de.chenonceau@wanadoo.fr; adult/concession €7.60/6.10; open 9am-4.30pm mid-Nov-Jan, 9am-7pm mid-Mar-mid-Sept)* is everything a fairy-tale castle should be, although its interior is only of moderate interest.

Of the many remarkable women who created Chenonceau, Diane de Poitiers, mistress of King Henri II, planted the garden to the left (east) as you approach the chateau. After Henri's death in 1559, his widow Catherine de Médicis laid out the garden to the right (west) as you approach the castle.

Between 1940 and 1942, the demarcation line between the Vichy-ruled France and the German-occupied zone ran down the middle of the Cher: the castle itself was under direct German occupation, but the southern entrance to the 60m-long **Galerie** was in the area controlled by Marshal Pétain. For many trying to escape to the Vichy zone, this room served as a crossing point.

Getting There & Away The Château de Chenonceau, in the town of Chenonceaux (spelt with an 'x'), is 34km east of Tours, 10km southeast of Amboise and 40km southwest of Blois.

Chenonceaux SNCF train station is in front of the chateau. Between Tours and Chenonceaux there are four to six trains daily (€5.20,

0 minutes); alternatively, trains on the Tours–Vierzon line stop at Chisseaux (€5.20, 14 minutes, six daily), 2km east of Chenonceaux. In summer, take CAT bus No 10 to/from Tours (€2.10, 1¼ hours, one daily).

Château d'Azay-le-Rideau

Built on an island in the Indre River, Azay-le-Rideau (☎ 02 47 45 42 04; adult/concession €5.50/3.50; open 9.30am-6pm Apr-June & Sept, 9am-7pm July & Aug, 10am-12.30pm & 2pm-5.30pm Oct-Mar) is among the most elegant of Loire chateaux. The highlight of the 14 renovated rooms open to the public are a few 16th-century Flemish tapestries, and it's one of the few chateaux that allows picnicking in its beautiful park.

Getting There & Away Azay-le-Rideau, 26km southwest of Tours, is on SNCF's Tours-Chinon line (four or five daily Monday to Saturday, one on Sunday). From Tours, the 30-minute trip (50 minutes by SNCF bus) costs €4.30; the station is 2.5km from the chateau.

Amboise

pop 11,000

Picturesque Amboise, an easy day trip from Tours, is known for its **Château d'Amboise** (☎ 02 47 57 00 98; adult/concession €6.50/5.50; open 9am-noon & 2pm-4.45pm or 5.30pm Nov-Mar, 9am-6.30pm Apr-June, Sept & Oct, 9am-7pm July & Aug), perched on a rocky outcrop overlooking the town. The remains of Leonardo da Vinci (1452–1519), who lived in Amboise for the last three years of his life, are supposedly under the chapel's northern transept.

Inside the chateau walls, opposite 42 place Michel Debré, is the innovative **Caveau des Vignerons d'Amboise**, a wine cellar where you can taste (for free) regional Touraine wines from Easter to October.

Da Vinci, who came to Amboise at the invitation of François I in 1516, lived and worked in **Le Clos Lucé** (☎ 02 47 57 62 88; 2 rue du Clos Lucé; adult/concession €6.50/5.50; open 9am-7pm Mar-June, Sept-Dec, 9am-8pm July & Aug, 9am-5pm Jan, 9am-6pm Feb), a 15th-century brick manor house 500m southeast of the chateau along rue Victor Hugo. The building contains restored rooms and scale models of some 40 of Leonardo's fascinating inventions.

Information Amboise **tourist office** (☎ 02 47 57 09 28, fax 02 47 57 14 35; e tourisme .amboise@wanadoo.fr; open daily Easter-Oct, Mon-Sat Nov-Easter) is next to the river, opposite 7 quai du Général de Gaulle.

Getting There & Away Several daily trains run to Amboise from both Tours (€4.20, 20 minutes) and Blois (€5.40, 20 minutes). From Tours, you can also take CAT bus No 10 (€2.10, 30 to 50 minutes).

Southwestern France

The southwestern part of France is home to a number of diverse regions, ranging from the Bordeaux wine-growing area near the beachlined Atlantic seaboard, to the Basque Country and the Pyrenees mountains in the south. The region is linked to Paris, Spain and the Côte d'Azur by convenient rail links.

NANTES

pop 550,000

The lively and relaxed university city of Nantes, historically part of Brittany, has several fine museums, carefully tended parks and an unbelievable number of inexpensive cafés and restaurants. For centuries, it was a major slave-trading centre between Africa and the Caribbean, and the Edict of Nantes – a landmark royal charter guaranteeing civil rights and freedoms to France's Protestants – was signed here in 1598.

Orientation & Information

The city centre's two main arteries, both served by tram lines, are the north-south, partly pedestrianised cours des 50 Otages (named in memory of 50 people taken hostage and shot by the Germans in 1941) and an east-west boulevard that connects the train station (to the east) with quai de la Fosse (to the west).

The main **tourist office** (☎ 02 40 20 60 00, fax 02 40 89 11 99; w www.nantes-tourism .com; place du Commerce; open 10am-7pm Mon-Sat) is in the Palais de la Bourse. This is a good place to pick up bus/tram and city maps.

Internet cafés are sprinkled throughout this scholarly city. Try **Cyber House** (8 Quai de Versailles; open 2pm-2am Mon-Fri, 3pm-2am Sat), which charges €4.60 per hour.

Things to See & Do

Inside the medieval walls of the **Château des Ducs de Bretagne** (*Chateau of the Dukes of Brittany; ☎ 02 40 41 56 56; admission to grounds free, exhibitions adult/concession €3.10/1.10; open 10am-6pm daily*) is a Renaissance pleasure palace. The building opposite the entrance arch often houses temporary exhibitions (open Wednesday to Monday).

Inside the Flamboyant Gothic **Cathédrale St-Pierre et St-Paul** (*place St-Pierre*), the **tomb of François II** (r. 1458–88), duke of Brittany, and his second wife, Marguerite de Foix, is considered a masterpiece of Renaissance art.

The renowned **Musée des Beaux-Arts** (*☎ 02 40 41 65 65; 10 rue Georges Clemenceau; adult/concession €3.10/1.60; open 10am-6pm Wed-Mon*) has three works by Georges de La Tour. The old-fashioned but excellent **Musée d'Histoire Naturelle** (*Natural History Museum; ☎ 02 40 99 26 20; 12 rue Voltaire; adult/concession €3.10; open 10am-5.30pm Wed-Mon*) features a **vivarium** with live pythons, crocodiles and iguanas.

Places to Stay

Camping A bit over 3km due north of the Gare Centrale is **Camping du Petit Port** (*☎ 02 40 74 47 94, fax 02 40 74 23 06; 21 blvd du Petit Port; tram stop Morrhonnière; 2 adults, tent & car from €9.10; open year-round*).

Hostels Kitchen facilities are on offer at **Auberge de Jeunesse** (*☎ 02 40 29 29 20, fax 02 51 12 48 42; 2 place de la Manu; tram stop Moutonnerie, line 1; dorm beds & breakfast €14.25*) and the reception is staffed from 9am to 11pm. Rooms are plain and well-lit. The 82-bed hostel is 600m east of the train station.

Résidence Porte Neuve (*☎ 02 40 20 63 63, fax 02 40 20 63 79; 7 place Ste-Elisabeth; doubles with breakfast per person €14.40*) is a dormitory for young workers. Reservations are compulsory and places may be hard to come by on weekdays.

Hotels For a great deal try **Hôtel de la Bourse** (*☎ 02 40 69 51 55, fax 02 40 71 73 89; 19 Quai de la Fosse; rooms from €17, with shower & toilet €22*), which has tidy rooms. Hall showers cost €2.20. **Hôtel d'Orléans** (*☎ 02 40 47 69 32; 12 rue du Marais; rooms with shower €26, doubles/quads with shower & toilet €30/39*) is a friendly hotel with bright, quiet rooms. **Hôtel St-Patrick** (*☎ 02 40 48 48 80; 7 rue St-Nicolas; doubles from €22 doubles/quads with shower & toilet €31/44*) welcoming and well-placed, has decent, modern rooms.

Places to Eat

Nantes has an exceptionally varied selection of restaurants. There are dozens of cafés, bars and small restaurants, many of them French regional or ethnic, a couple of blocks west of the chateau in the lively area around rue de la Juiverie, rue des Petites Écuries and rue de la Bâclerie.

Brasserie La Cigale (*4 place Graslin; menu €12-22.90*), an exquisite brasserie, is grandly decorated with 1890s tilework and painted ceilings that mix baroque with Art Nouveau. **Le Guingois** (*3 bis rue de Santeuil; menus €11.15-18.45; open Tues-Sat*) is a real old-time bistro with hearty food. **Le Couscousier** (*6 rue de la Juiverie; mains €9-13; closed Wed*), is a good bet for couscous, and has vegetarian options. **Le Viet Nam** (*☎ 02 40 20 06 26; 14 rue Beauregard; dishes €6-8; closed Sun*) has good Vietnamese/Chinese food.

The small **covered market** (*place du Bouffay*) and the huge **Marché de Talensac** (*rue Talensac*) are open until about 1pm (closed Monday), otherwise there's the **Monoprix supermarket** (*2 rue du Calvaire; open 9am-9pm Mon-Sat*).

Entertainment

Listings of cultural events appear in *Nantes Poche* and *Pil'* (both €0.45). *Le Mois Nantais*, available at the tourist office and tobacconists, has day-by-day details of cultural events.

Cinéma Katorza (*☎ 02 51 84 90 60; 3 rue Corneille*) is a six-screen cinema offering non-dubbed films for a flat fee of €5. **La Maison** (*4 rue Lebrun; open 3pm-2am daily*), a hilarious send-up of a home furnished in very bad taste circa 1970, is a perfect place for a chat, which probably explains its popularity among students.

Getting There & Away

The southbound **bus station** (*☎ 0825 08 71 56*), across from 13 allée de la Maison Rouge, is used by the CTA buses which serve areas of the Loire-Atlantique department south of the Loire River. The northbound **bus office** (*☎ 0825 08 71 56; 1 allée Duquesne*) on cours des 50 Otages, run by Cariane Atlantique, handles buses to destinations north of the Loire.

There's a **Eurolines office** (☎ 02 51 72 02 03; allée de la Maison Rouge; open to 6pm Mon-Fri, to 12.30pm Sat).

The **train station** (☎ 0836 35 35 35; 27 blvd de Stalingrad) is well connected to most of France. Destinations include Paris' Gare Montparnasse (€37.50 to €57.90, 2¼ hours by TGV), Bordeaux (€36.10, four hours), La Rochelle (€22, 1¾ hours), Poitiers (€22, 3¼ hours) and Tours (€23.80, 1½ hours).

Getting Around

The **TAN network**, which has an **information office** (2 allée Brancas, place du Commerce; open Mon-Sat), includes three modern tram lines that intersect at the Gare Centrale (Commerce), the main bus/tram transfer point. Buses run until 9pm. Night services continue until 12.30am, departing from place du Commerce. Bus/tram tickets, sold individually (€1.20) by bus (but not tram) drivers and at tram stop ticket machines, are valid for one hour after being time-stamped for travel in any direction. A ticket journalier, good for 24 hours, costs €3.30; time-stamp it only the first time you use it.

Pierre Qui Roule (☎ 02 40 69 51 01; 14 rue Racine; open 10am-12.30pm & 2pm-7pm; closed Mon morning & Sun) rents out inline skates per half/full day for €6/9.

POITIERS

pop 120,000

Poitiers, the former capital of Poitou, is home to some of France's most remarkable Romanesque churches. It is not a particularly fetching city – it fits very tightly into its hilltop site – but the pedestrian-only shopping precinct has its charms.

In AD 732, somewhere near Poitiers (the exact site is not known), the cavalry of Charles Martel defeated the Muslim forces of Abd ar-Rahman, governor of Córdoba, thus ending Muslim attempts to conquer France.

Orientation & Information

The train station is about 600m west – and down the slope – from the old city and commercial centre, which begins just north of Poitiers' main square, place du Maréchal Leclerc, and stretches northeast to Église Notre Dame la Grande. Rue Carnot heads south from place du Maréchal Leclerc.

The **tourist office** (☎ 05 49 41 21 24, fax 05 49 88 65 84; e acceuil@ot-poitiers.fr;

45 place Charles de Gaulle; open 10am-6pm Mon-Sat Oct-May, 9.30am-7pm Mon-Sat, 10am-6pm Sun June-Sept) is near the Église Notre Dame.

Commercial banks can be found around place du Maréchal Leclerc. The post office is at 21 rue des Écossais. It has Cyberposte.

Cybercafé Poitiers (☎ 05 49 39 51 87; w www.cybercafe-poitiers.fr; 171 Grand'Rue; open 10.30am-8pm Mon-Sat, 4pm-8pm Sun) is east of Église Notre Dame and charges €7.20 per hour.

Things to See

The renowned, Romanesque **Église Notre Dame la Grande** (place Charles de Gaulle; open 8am-7pm daily) is in the pedestrianised old city. It dates from the 11th and 12th centuries except for several of the chapels. The celebrated **west facade** is decorated with three layers of stone carvings based on the Old and New Testaments.

At the northeastern end of rue Gambetta, the Palais de Justice (law courts) occupies a one-time palace of the counts of Poitou and the dukes of Aquitaine. Inside, you can visit the **Salle des Pas-Perdus** (open 9am-6pm Mon-Fri Sept-June, 9am-6pm daily July & Aug), a vast, partly 14th-century hall with three huge fireplaces.

The worthwhile **Musée Ste-Croix** (3 rue Jean Jaurès; adult/child €3.50/free; open 1.15pm-5pm Mon, 10am-noon & 1.15pm-5pm Tues-Fri, 2pm-6pm Sat & Sun Oct-May, 1.15pm-6pm Mon, 10am-noon & 1.15pm-6pm Tues-Fri, 10am-noon & 2pm-6pm Sat & Sun June-Sept) was built atop Gallo-Roman walls that were excavated and left in situ. It has exhibits on the history of Poitou from prehistoric times to the 19th century. Admission here also affords access to the **Musée Rupert de Chièvre** (☎ 05 49 41 07 53; 9 rue Victor Hugo) which displays furniture, paintings and art objects assembled in the 19th century.

Places to Stay

In the unappealing area around the train station, the nine-room hotel above **Bistrot de la Gare** (☎ 05 49 58 56 30; 131 blvd du Grand Cerf; doubles €19.50, with shower €22.50) has mid-sized, spartan doubles. From November to February, reception (at the bar) closes on Sunday.

Hôtel Le Terminus (☎ 05 49 62 92 30, fax 05 49 62 92 40; 3 blvd Pont Achard; doubles *from €46)* is in the two-star category and is a good bet in this area, with spacious, shower-equipped rooms.

Hôtel Jules Ferry (☎ *05 49 37 80 14, fax 05 49 53 15 02; 27 rue Jules Ferry; doubles/quads with basin €22/37, with shower & toilet €33/43)*, a family-run, 25-room hotel with clean, simply furnished rooms, is the best deal in town. It is about 1km south of the train station (go up blvd du Pont Achard and the rue Jean Brunet pedestrian ramp) – best to ring ahead for directions.

Places to Eat

The most promising area for dining is south of place du Maréchal Leclerc, especially rue Carnot. The Grand'Rue also has some good eateries.

La Joyeuse Marmite *(66 Grand'Rue; menu €10; open lunch only Mon-Fri)*, a merry local bistro, serves hearty lunch meals including wine. It's just north of place de la Cathédral.

Le Poitevin (☎ *05 49 88 35 04; 76 rue Carnot; menus €15-35; open Mon-Sat)* serves fine regional cuisine.

The cement-roofed **Marché Notre Dame** *(open until 1pm or 1.30pm Tues-Sat)* is next to Église Notre Dame la Grande. About 200m to the south, the **Monoprix supermarket** *(open 9am-7.30pm Mon-Sat)* is across from 29 rue du Marché Notre Dame (behind the Palais de Justice).

Entertainment

There are many **bars** and **pubs** along rue Carnot and one block north of place du Maréchal Leclerc along rue du Chaudron d'Or.

Getting There & Away

The **train station** *(blvd du Grand Cerf)* has direct links to Bordeaux (€27, 1¾ hours), La Rochelle (€18.70, one hour 20 minutes), Tours (€12.60, one hour 20 minutes) and many other cities. TGV tickets from Paris' Gare Montparnasse (1½ hours) cost around €32. SNCF buses go to Nantes (€22, 3¼ hours).

AROUND POITIERS
Futuroscope

Futuroscope (☎ *05 49 49 30 80;* **w** *www.futuroscope.com; Jaunay-Clan; adult/child 5-12 years €30/22 daily Apr-Sept, €21/16 Mon-Fri Oct-Mar; open 9am or 10am-7pm daily, to 10.30pm or 11pm on show nights)* is a unique cinema theme park with 21 innovative pavilions that make for a hugely entertaining day. There are lakeside laser and firework shows at night on weekends from March to early November and daily from April to August – as a result, closing times range from 7.30pm to 1am. The park may be closed in January. On days when there are laser and fireworks shows, a ticket costs €15/9 if you arrive after 6pm.

The many attractions include the **Tapis Magique** (Magic Carpet), which shows action underfoot – from a bird's-eye perspective – as well as in front of you. At **Le Solido**, the rounded 180° images appear in colour 3-D, through special liquid-crystal glasses. **Le 360°** is a round projection hall with nine screens giving you a 360° view from the centre of the action. The **Cinéma Dynamique** is a virtual-reality roller-coaster ride.

Futuroscope is a little more than 10km north of Poitiers in Jaunay-Clan (take exit No 28 off the A10). TGV trains link the park's TGV station with Paris (€45, 1½ hours, three daily) and Tours (€14, 30 minutes, three daily).

Local **STP buses** (☎ *05 49 44 66 88)* No 16 and 17 (€1.20, 30 minutes) link Futuroscope (Parc de Loisirs stop) with Poitiers' train station (the stop in front of Avis car rental); there are one to two buses every hour from 6.15am until 7.30pm or 9pm.

LA ROCHELLE
pop 120,000

La Rochelle, a lively port city midway down France's Atlantic coast, is popular with the middle-class French families and students on holiday. The ever-expanding Université de La Rochelle, opened in 1993, adds to the city's vibrancy. The nearby Île de Ré is ringed by long, sandy beaches.

Orientation & Information

The old city is north of the Vieux Port (old port), which is linked to the train station – 500m southeast – by ave du Général de Gaulle.

The **tourist office** (☎ *05 46 41 14 68;* **w** *www.ville-larochelle.fr; open 9am-6pm Mon-Sat Oct-May, 9am-8pm Mon-Sat, 11am-5pm Sun June-Sept)* is in Le Gabut, the quarter on the south side of the Vieux Port.

Things to See

To protect the harbour at night and defend it in times of war, a chain used to be stretched between the two 14th-century stone towers at the arbour entrance, the 36m **Tour St Nicolas** and **our de la Chaîne**; the latter houses displays in local history. West along the old city wall is **our de la Lanterne**, long used as a prison. All ree towers are open daily; admission to each osts €4/2.50 per adult/concession (€8.50 for ombined ticket).

The **Musée Maritime Neptunea** (*Bassin es Chalutiers; adult/concession €7.60/5.30*), n excellent maritime museum, is also the pernanent home of Jacques Cousteau's research hip *Calypso*. The entry fee includes tours of a *halutier* (fishing trawler). Next door, the vast **quarium La Rochelle** (☎ 05 46 34 00 00; *assin des Grands Yachts; adult/concession 10/7; open 10am-8pm Oct-Mar, 9am-8pm pr-June & Sept, 9am-11pm July & Aug*) feares some 10,000 of the sea's flora and fauna pecies.

le de Ré

his flat, 30km-long island, fringed by eaches, begins 9km west of La Rochelle. It's onnected to the mainland by a 3km toll ridge.

In July and August, and on Wednesday, veekends and holidays in June, city bus No 1 r 50 (known as No 21 between the train staion and place de Verdun) go to Sablanceaux €2.50, 25 minutes). Year-round, **Rébus** ☎ 05 46 09 20 15 in St Martin de Ré) links .a Rochelle (the train station and place de erdon) with St Martin de Ré and other island owns.

laces to Stay

Camping du Soleil (☎ 05 46 44 42 53; *ave Marillac; bus No 10; open mid-May–midept*), about 1.5km south of the city centre, is ften full.

The **Centre International de Séjour-Auberge de Jeunesse** (☎ 05 46 44 43 11, *fax 5 46 45 41 48; ave des Minimes; dorm beds 12.50*) is 2km southwest of the train station. ake bus No 10 and ask for the Lycée Hôteier stop. Rates include breakfast.

In the pedestrianised old city, the friendly, 24-room **Hôtel Henri IV** (☎ 05 46 41 25 79; *ax 05 46 41 78 64; place de la Caille; rooms rom €34, with shower & toilet €45*) has spaious doubles.

A few blocks from the train station, the 32-room **Terminus Hôtel** (☎ 05 46 50 69 59, *fax 05 46 41 73 12;* e *terminus@cdl lr.com; 7 rue de la Fabrique; singles/doubles*

€31-55/35-60*) offers comfortable doubles, with rates depending on the season. One block north, the 22-room **Hôtel de Bordeaux** (☎ 05 46 41 31 22, *fax 05 46 41 24 43;* e *hbordeaux@free.fr; 43 rue St Nicolas; singles/doubles from €27.50/29, with shower & toilet from €30.50/33*) has quiet, pastel rooms (also at variable rates), and breakfast is included. Near the bus station, **Hôtel de la Paix** (☎ 05 46 41 33 44; *14 rue Gargoulleau; singles/doubles from €40/43, rooms for up to 5 people from €60*) is another pleasant, friendly option.

Places to Eat

The rustic **Le Petit Rochelais** (*25 rue St Jean du Perot; mains from €12.20; open daily July & Aug, Thur-Mon Sept-June*) serves traditional fare in a warm, inviting atmosphere. The bustling **Les Comédiens** (*15 rue de la Chaîne; menus from €10*) derives its name from the theatre above it and serves contemporary French cuisine. There are dozens of other eateries along the northern side of the port and on nearby streets, many specialising in seafood.

Loan Phuong (*quai du Gabut; lunch/dinner buffet €11/12*) has an all-you-can-eat Chinese and Vietnamese buffet. Couscous is on offer at **Shéhérazade** (*35 rue Gambetta; open Tues-Sun, & Mon dinner*).

There's a lively **covered market** (*place du Marché; open 7am-1pm daily*) and a **Prisunic supermarket** (*30 rue du Palais; open Mon-Sat*) in the Old City.

Getting There & Away

Eurolines ticketing is handled by **Citram Littoral** (☎ 05 46 50 53 57; *30 cours des Dames; open Mon afternoon, Tues-Fri, & Sat morning*).

You can take a TGV from Paris' Gare Montparnasse (€50.60 to €61.10, three hours). Other destinations include Bordeaux (€21.10, two hours) and Tours (€29).

Getting Around

The innovative local transport system, **Autoplus** (☎ 05 46 34 02 22), has its main bus hub at place de Verdun. Most lines run until sometime between 7.15pm and 8pm.

Autoplus' *Le Passeur* (€0.60) ferry service links Tour de la Chaîne with the Avant Port. It runs whenever there are passengers – just press the red button on the board at the top of the gangplank – until midnight in summer, and until 10pm at other times.

FRANCE

Les Vélos Jaunes, a branch of the public transport company, will furnish you with a bike (lock included) for free for two hours (€1 per hour after that). Bikes are available daily at **Electrique Autoplus** (place de Verdun; open 7.30am-7pm Mon-Sat, 1pm-7pm Sun). From May to September, the bikes can also be picked up at the Vieux Port (across the street from 11 quai Valin).

The Electrique Autoplus office at place de Verdun also rents electric motorcars with a range of 50km for €10/16 per half-/full day. Electric Barigo scooters cost €6.50/11.

BORDEAUX

pop 735,000

Bordeaux is known for its neoclassical (if a bit grimy) architecture, wide avenues and well-tended public parks. Its cultural diversity (including 60,000 students), excellent museums and untouristy atmosphere make it more than a convenient stop between Paris and Spain. Marketing and exporting of Bordeaux wine are its most important economic activities.

Orientation

Cours de la Marne stretches for about 2km from the train station northwestward to place de la Victoire, which is linked to the tourist office area – 1.5km farther north – by the pedestrians-only rue Ste Catherine. The city centre lies between place Gambetta and the Garonne River. The city's peripheral road is called the *rocade*.

Information

The **main tourist office** (☎ 05 56 00 66 00, fax 05 56 00 66 01; w www.bordeaux -tourisme.com; 12 cours du 30 Juillet; open 9am-7pm Mon-Sat, 9.45am-4.30pm Sun Nov-Apr, 9am-8pm Mon-Sat, 9am-7pm Sun May-Sept or Oct) can help with information.

Money Open 9am to noon from Monday to Friday is **Banque de France** (15 rue de l'Esprit des Lois). There are commercial banks near the tourist office on cours de l'Intendance, rue Esprit des Lois and cours du Chapeau Rouge. **American Express** (☎ 05 56 00 63 36; 14 cours de l'Intendance; open Mon-Fri Oct-May, Mon-Fri, & Sat morning June-Sept) has a branch here.

Post & Communications The **main post office** (37 rue du Château d'Eau; open

8.30am-6.30pm Mon-Fri, 8.30am-12.30pr Sat) and the **branch post office** (place St Pro jet; open to 6.30pm Mon-Fri, to noon Sat both offer currency exchange and Cyberpostes

Cyberstation (☎ 05 56 01 15 15; 23 Cou Pasteur; open 11am-2am Mon-Sat, 2pm-mid night Sun) has Internet access for €2 per hour

Laundry The laundrettes at 5 rue de For daudège and 8 rue Lafaurie de Monbadon ope from 7am to 9pm.

Things to See

The following sights are listed roughly nort! to south. Admission to each museum costs €4 2.50 per adult/concession (free for student and on the first Sunday of the month).

The excellent **Musée d'Art Contemporai** (Museum of Contemporary Art; ☎ 05 56 00 8 50; Entrepôt 7, rue Ferrére; open 11am-6pn Tues-Sun, 11am-8pm Wed, closed Mon) host exhibits by contemporary artists. The **Jardi** **Public**, an 18th-century English-style park, i along cours de Verdun and includes Bor deaux's **botanical garden** and **Musée d'His** **toire Naturelle** (Natural History Museum ☎ 05 56 48 26 37; 5 place Bardineau; open 11am-6pm Mon-Fri, 2pm-6pm Sat & Sun closed Tues).

The most prominent feature of **esplanad** **des Quinconces**, a vast square laid out i 1820, is a towering fountain-monument to the Girondins, a group of moderate and bourgeoi legislative deputies who were executed during the French Revolution.

The neoclassical **Grand Théâtre** (☎ 05 5 00 85 95; place de la Comédie; closed Sun & Mon) was built in the 1770s. **Porte Dijeaux** which dates from 1748, leads from **place** **Gambetta**, which has a garden in the middle to the pedestrianised commercial centre. A few blocks south, the **Musée des Arts Décoratifs** (Museum of Decorative Arts; ☎ 05 56 00 72 50; 39 rue Bouffard; open 2pm-6pm Wed-Mon, temporary exhibits from 11am Mon-Fri, specialises in faïence, porcelain, silverwork glasswork, furniture and the like.

In 1137, the future King Louis VII married Eleanor of Aquitaine in **Cathédrale St André** Just east of the cathedral, there's the 15th century, 50m-high belfry, **Tour Pey-Berland** (place Jean Moulin; adult/concession €3.95/ 2.45; open 10am-6.30pm daily June-Sept, 10am-12.30pm & 2pm-5.30pm daily Oct-May). The **Centre National Jean Moulin**

(Jean Moulin Documentation Centre; ☎ 05 56 79 66 00; admission free; open 11am-6pm Tues-Fri, 2pm-6pm Sat & Sun), facing the north side of the cathedral, has exhibits on France during WWII.

The **Musée des Beaux-Arts** (☎ 05 56 10 20 56; 20 cours d'Albret; open 11am-6pm Wed-Sat) occupies two wings of the 18th-century Hôtel de Ville and houses a large collection of paintings, including 17th-century Flemish, Dutch and Italian works. The outstanding **Musée d'Aquitaine** (☎ 05 56 01 51 00; 20 cours Pasteur; open 11am-6pm Tues-Sun) illustrates the history and ethnography of the Bordeaux area.

The **Synagogue** (rue du Grand Rabbin Joseph Cohen; open 9am-noon & 2pm-4pm Mon-Thur), just west of rue Ste Catherine, and dating from 1882, is a mixture of Sephardic and Byzantine styles. During WWII the Nazis turned the complex into a prison. Ring the bell marked gardien at 213 rue Ste Catherine.

Places to Stay

The small **Camping Beausoleil** (☎ 05 56 89 17 66; 371 cours du Général de Gaulle, Gradignan; open year-round) is the closest to central Bordeaux, 15km southwest of the city centre in the suburb of Gradignan. By bus, take line G to the Beausoleil terminus, or if driving take rocade exit 16.

About 700m west of the train station, the **Auberge de Jeunesse** (☎ 05 56 91 59 51; 22 cours Barbey; members/nonmembers €16/ 17.50) is well-appointed if somewhat cold. Take bus No 7 or 8 from the station, alighting at the Meunier stop.

North of the centre near place de Tourny (from the station take bus No 7 or 8), friendly **Hôtel Touring** (☎ 05 56 81 56 73; fax 05 56 81 24 55; 16 rue Huguerie; singles/doubles with shower from €24.30/29, with shower & toilet €35.10/38.10) has gigantic and spotless rooms. Nearby, **Hôtel Studio** (☎ 05 56 48 00 14, fax 05 56 81 25 71; w www.hotel-bordeaux.com; 26 rue Huguerie) and three affiliated hotels offer charmless singles/doubles with shower, toilet and (in most cases) cable TV starting at an absolute minimum of €16/ 20. The hotel's mini Internet café charges guests €2.25 an hour.

A few blocks southwest of place Gambetta, the quiet **Hôtel Boulan** (☎ 05 56 52 23 62, fax 05 56 44 91 65; 28 rue Boulan;

singles/doubles from €17/20, with shower €20/23) has decent rooms.

Just east of place Gambetta is **Hôtel de la Tour Intendance** (☎ 05 56 81 46 27, fax 05 56 81 60 90; 16 rue de la Vieille Tour; singles €35, doubles €41-52), where you're assured of a warm welcome.

Places to Eat

La Chanterelle (3 rue de Martignac; lunch/ dinner menus €12/16; open Mon, Tues, Fri & Sat, & Wed lunch) serves moderately priced traditional French and regional cuisine. Bistro-style cuisine and southwestern French specialities are on offer at **Claret's** (☎ 05 56 01 21 21; place Camille Julien; lunch menu €10, dinner menus €16 & €20; open Mon-Fri, & Sat dinner). The popular **Le Bistrot d'Édouard** (16 place du Parlement; lunch menu €11 Mon-Sat, dinner menus €16 & €26) purveys French bistro-style meat and fish dishes. There are lots of eateries along nearby rue du Parlement Ste Catherine, rue des Piliers de Tutelle and rue St Rémi.

The **Restaurant Baud et Millet** (19 rue Huguerie; open Mon-Sat) has cheese-based cuisine (most dishes are vegetarian), including an all-you-can-eat raclette for €17.50. Slightly more upmarket is **Restaurant Brasserie V. Hugo** (160 cours Victor Hugo; entrees €6.50-11.50, mains €10-12), where a meal will cost around €25 without wine.

The inexpensive cafés and restaurants around place de la Victoire include the **Cassolette Café** (20 place de la Victoire; small/ large cassolettes €2.20/6.50; open daily), which serves family-style French food on cassolettes (terracotta plates).

There's a **Champion supermarket** (place des Grands Hommes; open Mon-Sat) in the basement of the mirror-plated Marché des Grands Hommes. Near **Marché des Capucins** (open 6am-1pm Tues-Sun), a covered food market just east of place de la Victoire, you'll find super-cheap fruit and vegetable stalls (open to 1pm Mon-Sat) along rue Élie Gintrec.

Entertainment

Cinephiles will love **Cinéma Utopia** (☎ 05 56 52 00 03; 5 place Camille), where new and old films are shown in their original language. A bistro serves a €10 lunch menu and drinks.

Bordeaux has a hopping nightlife scene. **The Down Under** (104 cours Aristide Briand; open 7pm or 8pm-2am daily) is run by a former

FRANCE

BORDEAUX

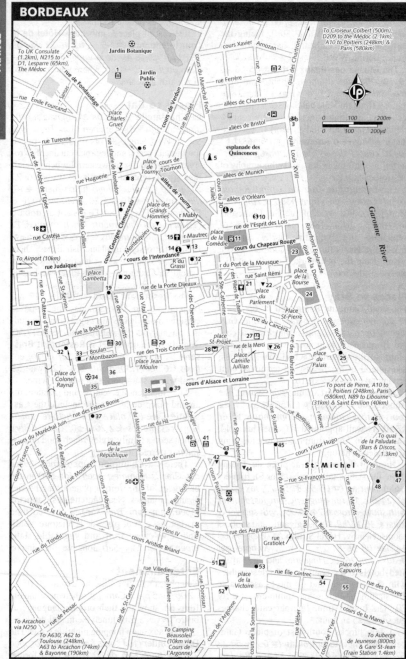

To Croiseur Colbert (500m),
D209 to the Médoc (2.1km),
A10 to Poitiers (248km) &
Paris (580km)

To UK Consulate
(1.2km), N215 to
D1, Lesparre (65km),
The Médoc

Jardin Botanique

Jardin Public

cours Xavier Amozan

rue Ferrère

rue de Fondaudège

rue Emile Fourcand

cours du Marechal Foch

cours du Chartrons

quai des Chartrons

allées de Chartres

place Charles Gruet

rue Turenne

allées de Bristol

esplanade des Quinconces

quai Louis XVIII

allées de Munich

place de Tourny

cours de Tourny/Tournon

allées de Tourny

cours du 30 Juillet

allées d'Orléans

rue Huguerie

place des Grands Hommes

r Mably

cours de l'Esprit des Lois

rue de l'Intendance

place de la Comédie

cours du Chapeau Rouge

rue Mautrec

r du Grassi

R du Grassi

To Airport (10km)

rue Judaïque

place Gambetta

rue de la Porte Dijeaux

r du Port de la Mousque

rue Saint Rémi

place de la Bourse

place du Parlement

Place St-Pierre

rue du Cancéra

rue des Remparts

rue Vital Carles

place St-Projet

place de la Merci

place Camille Jullian

place du Palais

cours d'Alsace et Lorraine

To pont de Pierre, A10 to
Poitiers (248km), Paris
(580km), N89 to Libourne
(31km) & Saint Émilion (40km)

place du Colonel Raynal

cours du Marechal Juin

rue des Freres Bonie

place de la République

rue de Cursol

cours Victor Hugo

St-Michel

To quai
de la Paludate
(Bars & Discos,
1.3km)

cours de la Libération

rue Henri IV

rue des Augustins

rue Gratiolet

place des Capucins

rue Élie Gintrec

place de la Victoire

To Arcachon
via N250

To A630, A62 to
Toulouse (248km),
A63 to Arcachon (74km)
& Bayonne (190km)

To Camping
Beausoleil (10km via
Cours de
l'Argonne)

To Auberge
de Jeunesse (800m)
& Gare St-Jean
(Train Station 1.4km)

Garonne River

0   100   200m
0   100   200yd

BORDEAUX

PLACES TO STAY
8 Hôtel Touring & Hôtel Studio
20 Hôtel de la Tour Intendance
33 Hôtel Boulan

PLACES TO EAT
7 Restaurant Baud et Millet
13 La Chanterelle
16 Champion Supermarket
   (Marché des
   Grands Hommes)
22 Le Bistrot d'Édouard
26 Claret's
42 Restaurant Brasserie V. Hugo
44 Champion Supermarket
52 Cassolette Café
54 Fruit & Vegetable Stalls
55 Marche des Capucins

OTHER
1 Musée d'Histoire Naturelle
2 Musée d'Art Contemporain

3 Bord'Eaux Velos Loisirs
4 Halte Routière (Bus Station)
5 Girondins Fountain-
   Monument
6 Laundrette
9 Tourist Office
10 Banque de France
11 Grand Théâtre
12 American Express
14 Maison du Tourisme
   de la Gironde
15 Église Notre Dame
17 Laundrette
18 Hôtel de Police
19 Porte Dijeaux
21 Calle Ocho
23 Bourse du Commerce
24 Hôtel de la Douane
25 Porte Cailhau
27 Cinéma Utopia
28 Post Office Branch
29 Centre National Jean Moulin

30 Musée des Arts Décoratifs
31 Main Post Office
32 Galerie des Beaux-Arts
34 Jardin de la Mairie
35 Musée des Beaux-Arts
36 Hôtel de Ville
37 Tribunal de Grande Instance
   (Court; 1998)
38 Cathédrale Saint André
39 Tour Pey-Berland (Belfry)
40 Cyberstation
41 Musée d'Aquitaine
43 Laundrette
45 Porte de la
   GrosseCloche
46 Porte des Salinières
47 Église Saint Michel
48 Tour Saint Michel
49 Synagogue
50 Hôpital Saint André
51 The Down Under
53 Porte d'Aquitaine

Aucklander and is a favourite of Anglophones. One of the really hot venues is a Cuban-style bar called **Calle Ocho** (24 rue des Piliers de Tutelle; open 5pm-2am Mon-Sat).

Among the best of the late-late dancing bars is tropical beach-themed **La Plage** (☎ 05 56 49 02 46; 40 quai de la Paludate; open midnight-5am Wed-Sat) along the river east of the train station.

Getting There & Away

Buses to places all over the Gironde and nearby departments leave from the **Halte Routière** (☎ 05 56 43 68 43), in the northeast corner of esplanade des Quinconces; schedules are posted.

Bordeaux's train station, **Gare St Jean** (☎ 0836 35 35 39), is about 3km southeast of the city centre at the end of cours de la Marne. It occasionally has attractive special fares worth asking for. By TGV it takes only about three hours to/from Paris' Gare Montparnasse (€64 to €66.10). The trip to Bayonne (€23) takes 1¾ hours.

BORDEAUX VINEYARDS

The Bordeaux wine-producing region, 1000 sq km in extent, is subdivided into 57 production areas called *appellations*, where the climate and soil impart distinctive characteristics to the wines.

More than 5000 chateaux (also known as *domaines*, *crus* and *clos*) produce the region's highly regarded wines, which are mainly reds. Many smaller chateaux accept walk-in visitors (some are closed during the October grape harvest); the larger and better-known ones usually require that you phone ahead.

Each vineyard has different rules pertaining to tasting – at some it's free, others charge entry fees, and others don't serve wine at all. Look for signs reading *dégustation* (wine tasting), *en vente directe* (direct sales), *vin à emporter* (wine to take away) and *gratuit* (free).

Opposite Bordeaux's main tourist office, the **Maison du Vin de Bordeaux** (☎/fax 05 56 00 22 66; w www.vins-bordeaux.fr; open Mon-Fri year-round, & Sat summer) has details on vineyard visits. It can also supply information on the many local *maisons du vin* (special wine-oriented tourist offices).

From May to October, the Bordeaux tourist office runs five-hour bus tours in French and English to local wine chateaux, with wine tastings included (adult/concession €26/22.50).

ST ÉMILION
pop 2500

The medieval village of St Émilion, 39km east of Bordeaux, is surrounded by vineyards that are renowned for their full-bodied, deeply coloured red wines. The most interesting historical sites – including the **Église Monolithe**, carved out of solid limestone from the 9th to the 12th centuries – can be visited only on the 45-minute guided tours (adult/concession

€5.05/3.05) offered by the **tourist office** (☎ 05 57 55 28 28; place des Créneaux; open daily). The 50 or so wine shops include the co-operative **Maison du Vin** (☎ 05 57 55 50 55; place Pierre Meyrat; open daily), around the corner from the tourist office, which is owned by the 250 chateaux whose wines it sells.

From Bordeaux, St Émilion is accessible by train (€6.80, 35 minutes, two or three daily) and bus (at least once daily, except on Sunday and holidays from October to April). The last train back usually departs at 6.27pm.

THE MÉDOC

Northwest of Bordeaux, along the western shore of the Gironde Estuary, lie some of Bordeaux's most celebrated vineyards. To the west, fine sandy beaches bordered by dunes stretch for some 200km from Pointe de Grave south along the **Côte d'Argent** (Silver Coast) to the Bassin d'Arcachon and beyond. The coastal dunes abut a vast pine forest planted in the 19th century to stabilise the drifting sands.

The most beautiful part of this renowned wine-growing area is north of **Pauillac**, along the D2 and the D204 (towards Lesparre). Vineyards around here include the **Château Lafitte Rothschild** (Paris: ☎ 01 53 89 78 00) and the equally illustrious **Château Mouton Rothschild** (☎ 05 56 73 21 29; admission €5). Both places require advance reservations.

Seaside resorts include the beach resort of **Soulac-sur-Mer** (population 2800), which has the two-star, 13-room **Hôtel La Dame de Cœur** (☎ 05 56 09 80 80; 103 rue de la Plage; singles/doubles/triples from €31/40/46).

The relaxed naturist village of **Euronat** (☎ 05 56 09 33 33, fax 05 56 09 30 27; 🖳 www.euronat.fr; tent sites for 2 people low/high season €8/21, 'ready to live in' tents per week €203-322; open year-round), about 80km north of Bordeaux, covers 3.3 sq km (including 1.5km of dune-lined beachfront). Minimum stay is three nights, and prices vary according to season.

Getting There & Away

The northern tip of the Médoc, Pointe de Grave, is linked to Royan by car ferries. Three to five Citram Aquitaine buses daily connect Bordeaux with Lesparre, Soulac-sur-Mer (two hours) and Point de Grave (€12.80, 2¼ hours). SNCF bus-train combos linking Bordeaux with Margaux, Pauillac (€8.50, one hour), Lesparre, Soulac (€13.20, two hours)

and Pointe de Grave (or nearby Le Verdon, €14.10) run up to five times daily (twice on weekends).

ARCACHON
pop 11,800

The beach resort of Arcachon, in the southwest corner of the triangular **Bassin d'Arcachon** (Arcachon Bay), became popular with bourgeois residents of Bordeaux at the end of the 19th century. Its major attractions are the sandy seashore and the extraordinary, 114m-high **Dune de Pyla**, Europe's highest sand dune, which is 8km south of town.

The flat area that abuts the **Plage d'Arcachon** (the town's beach) is known as the **Ville d'Été** (Summer Quarter). The liveliest section is around **Jetée Thiers**, one of the two piers, which is linked to pine-shaded **Cap Ferret** by boat. The **Ville d'Hiver** (Winter Quarter), on the tree-covered hillside south of the centre, was built about a century ago.

A few kilometres east of Arcachon, the oyster port of **Gujan Mestras** sprawls along 9km of the coastline. Super-fresh and remarkably cheap oysters can be sampled at **Port de Larros**, one of the town's seven ports.

The **tourist office** (☎ 05 57 52 97 97, fax 05 57 52 97 77; 🖳 www.arcachon.com; place Président Roosevelt; open 9am-6.30pm Mon-Sat, 9am-1pm & 2pm-5pm Sun & holidays Apr-Sept, 9am-12.30pm & 2pm-6pm Mon-Sat Oct-Mar, closed Sun & holidays Oct-Mar) is a few hundred metres from the train station.

Places to Stay

The steep, inland side of the Dune de Pyla is gradually burying five large and rather pricey **camping grounds** (2 people & tent from €12.45-22.30; open Apr-Sept).

Hotel rooms are nearly impossible to find in July and August. The 15-room **Hôtel Saint Christaud** (☎/fax 05 56 83 38 53; 8 Allée de la Chapelle; low/high season rooms from €18/30.50) has modern rooms, with rates depending on the season. **La Pergola** (☎ 05 56 83 07 89; 40 cours Lamargue; low/high season rooms from €30/43, with shower €43/74; open Apr-Sept) has good, clean but charmless rooms.

Getting There & Away

Some of the trains from Bordeaux to Arcachon (€8.20, 55 minutes, 11 to 18 daily), which also stop at Gujan Mestras near the Port de

Larros, are coordinated with TGVs from Paris' Gare Montparnasse.

BAYONNE

pop 40,000

Bayonne is the most important city in the French part of the Basque Country (Euskadi in Basque, Pays Basque in French), a region straddling the French-Spanish border.

Its most important festival is the annual Fêtes de Bayonne, beginning on the first Wednesday in August. The festival includes a 'running of the bulls' like Pamplona's, except that here they have cows.

Orientation & Information

The Adour and Nive Rivers split Bayonne into three: St Esprit, north of the Adour; Grand Bayonne, the oldest part of the city, on the west bank of the Nive; and the very Basque Petit Bayonne to its east.

The **tourist office** (☎ 05 59 46 01 46, fax 05 59 59 37 55; e info@bayonne-tourisme .com; place des Basques; open 9am-6.30pm Mon-Fri, 10am-6pm Sat Sept-June, 9am-7pm Mon-Sat, 10am-1pm Sun July & Aug) can help visitors. Its free brochure Fêtes de Bayonne is useful for cultural and sporting events while Fêtes en Pays-Basques, also free, describes the region more generally. The office organises guided tours of the city at 3pm on Saturday (€4.60).

You can log on at **Cyber Net Café** (☎ 05 59 55 78 98; place de la République; open 7am-11pm Mon-Sat, noon-11pm Sun); it charges €4.50 per hour until noon, €6.80 per hour thereafter.

Things to See & Do

Construction of the Gothic **Cathédrale Ste Marie** (place Monseigneur Vansteenberghe) began in the 13th century and was completed in 1451. The entrance to the beautiful 13th-century **cloister** is on place Louis Pasteur.

The **Musée Bonnat** (5 rue Jacques Laffitte; adult/concession €5.50/3; open 10am-12.30pm & 2.30pm-6.30pm Wed-Mon), in Petit Bayonne, has a diverse collection, which includes an entire gallery of paintings by Rubens.

Places to Stay

Camping Try **Camping de Parme** (☎ 05 59 23 03 00; route de l'Aviation; 2 people & tent low/high season €13.40/19.40; open

year-round), 1.25km northeast of Biarritz-La Négresse train station. It's usually booked during July and August.

Hostels The **Auberge de Jeunesse d'Anglet** (☎ 05 59 58 70 00, fax 05 59 58 70 07; e biarritz@fuaj.fr; 19 route des Vignes; tent sites €8.30 per person, B&B €14.90 1st night, €12.20 per night thereafter; open mid-Feb–mid-Nov) in Anglet comes complete with a Scottish pub. Popular with surfers, reservations are essential in summer. You can also pitch a tent here, and rates include breakfast. Membership costs €2.90. There's a minimum one-week stay in July and August, when the hostel is often booked out.

From Bayonne, take bus No 2 to the Cinq-Cantons, then bus No 7 and get off at Moulin Barbot, a 10-minute walk away. From Biarritz, town or station, take bus No 9.

Hotels You can tumble off the train into hyperfriendly **Hôtel Paris-Madrid** (☎ 05 59 55 13 98, fax 05 59 55 07 22; singles from €15, doubles with/without shower from €23/21, quads with shower & toilet from €39), just beside the station. It has singles, pleasant doubles, and big rooms with bathroom and cable TV. Nearby, the **Hôtel Monte Carlo** (☎ 05 59 55 02 68; 1 rue Ste Ursule; basic rooms from €19, 2-4 person rooms €26-39) has simple rooms and larger ones with bathroom for two to four people.

In Petit Bayonne, **Hôtel des Basques** (☎ 05 59 59 08 02; 4 rue des Lisses; rooms with washbasin €21.50-26, with bathroom €28-30.50), in a quiet location on place Paul Bert, has large, pleasant rooms.

The mid-range **Hôtel des Basses-Pyrénées** (☎ 05 59 59 00 29, fax 05 59 59 42 02; 12 rue Tour de Sault; doubles/triples with toilet & shower from €45.73/57.93; closed Jan) is built around a 17th-century tower, and offers private parking.

Places to Eat

Nowhere in town is more Basque than the **Restaurant Euskalduna Ostatua** (61 rue Pannecau; mains €6.80; open lunch Tues-Sat), near Hôtel des Basques, where main dishes are a bargain. Over the Nive River the family-run **Bar-Restaurant du Marché** (39 rue des Basques; open lunch), where the cooking's homy and the owner's wife mothers everyone, will fill you to bursting point for about €12.

The central market **Les Halles** *(open Mon-Sat morning)* is on the west quay (quai Amiral Jauréguiberry) of the Nive River.

Entertainment
The greatest concentration of pubs and bars is in Petit Bayonne, especially along rue Pannecau and quai Galuperie. **Chai Ramina** *(☎ 05 59 50 33 01; 9 rue de la Poissonerie; open 9.30am-8pm Mon-Thur & until 2am Fri & Sat)* is a friendly bar that opens late on Friday and Saturday nights, with a disco next door open until dawn.

Getting There & Away
Bus The ATCRB buses *(☎ 05 59 26 06 99)* that run to St-Jean de Luz (€3.60, 40 minutes, 10 daily) leave from place des Basques with connections for Hendaye (€5.60, one hour). Two Transportes Pesa buses run to Irún and San Sebastián in Spain (€6.20, 1¾ hours, daily except Sunday).

From the train station car park, **RDTL** *(☎ 05 59 55 17 59)* runs services northwards into Les Landes. For beaches north of Bayonne, such as Mimizan Plage and Moliets Plage, get off at Vieux Boucau (€6.40, 1¼ hours). **TPR** *(☎ 05 59 27 45 98)* has three buses daily to Pau (€13.20, 2¼ hours).

Bayonne is one of three hubs in southwest France for Eurolines, and buses stop in place Charles de Gaulle, opposite the **Eurolines office** *(☎ 05 59 59 19 33)* at No 3.

Train The train station is just north of pont St Esprit bridge. TGVs run to/from Paris' Gare Montparnasse (€67.81 to €76.80, five hours). Two classy non-TGV trains go overnight to Paris' Gare d'Austerlitz (€61.50 or €76 with couchette, eight hours).

There's a frequent service to Biarritz (€2, 10 minutes), St-Jean de Luz (€3.80, 25 minutes) and St-Jean Pied de Port (€7.20, one hour), plus the Franco-Spanish border towns of Hendaye (€5.60, 40 minutes) and Irún (€5.90, 45 minutes).

Some other destinations are Bordeaux (€21.30, 2¼ hours, about 12 daily), Lourdes (€16.90, 1¾ hours, six daily) and Pau (€13.10, 1¼ hours, six daily).

BIARRITZ
pop 30,000
The classy coastal town of Biarritz, 8km west of Bayonne, has fine beaches and some of

Europe's best surfing. Unfortunately, it can be a real budget-buster – consider making it a day trip from Bayonne, as lots of French holiday-makers do. Many surfers camp or stay at one of the two excellent youth hostels – in Biarritz and in Anglet (see the Bayonne section earlier).

Biarritz's Festival International de Folklore is held in early July.

Orientation & Information
Place Clemenceau, at the heart of Biarritz, is just south of Grande Plage, the main beach. The **tourist office** *(☎ 05 59 22 37 10, fax 05 59 24 14 19; e biarritz.tourisme@biarritz.tm .fr; 1 square d'Ixelles; open 9am-6pm daily Sept-June, 8am-8pm daily July & Aug)* is one block east of the square. It publishes *Biarritzscope*, a free monthly guide to what's on. In July and August, it has a branch at the train station.

Check your emails at **Génius Informatique** *(☎ 05 59 24 39 07; 60 ave Édouard VII)* for €8 an hour.

Things to See & Do
The **Grande Plage**, lined in season with striped bathing tents, stretches from the Casino Bellevue to the stately Hôtel du Palais. North of the hotel is **Plage Miramar** and the 1834 **Phare de Biarritz**. Beyond this lighthouse the superb surfing beaches of **Anglet** extend for 4km (take bus No 9 from place Clemenceau).

The **Musée de la Mer** *(adult/concession €7.20/4.60)*, Biarritz' sea museum, is on Pointe Atalaye overlooking **Rocher de la Vierge**, an islet reached by a short footbridge which offers sweeping coastal views. The museum has a 24-tank aquarium, including seal and shark pools.

Places to Stay
Camping Some 3km southwest of the centre there's **Biarritz Camping** *(☎ 05 59 23 00 12; 28 rue d'Harcet; bus No 9 to Biarritz Camping stop; 2 people & tent low/high season €13.50/19; open early May–late Sept)*.

Hostels For Biarritz's **Auberge de Jeunesse** *(☎ 05 59 41 76 00, fax 05 59 41 76 07; e aubergejeune.biarritz@wanadoo.fr; 8 rue Chiquito de Cambo; B&B €15.50 1st night, €12.80 thereafter, meals €8)*, follow the railway westwards from the train station for 800m. The otherwise expensive **Hôtel Barnetche** *(☎ 05 59 24 22 25, fax 05 59 24 98 71; 5 ave*

Charles Floquet; dorm beds €20) has dorm bunks.

Hotels Nowhere is cheap in Biarritz, but prices drop by up to 25% outside summer.

In the Vieux Port area is the trim **Hôtel Palym** (☎ 05 59 24 16 56; 7 rue du Port Vieux; rooms with toilet & shower low/high season €40/47). In the centre of town, **Hôtel Au Saint James** (☎ 05 59 24 06 36; 15 rue Gambetta; singles/doubles low season €29/ 37, high season €45/55) has small but charming rooms, with full and half-board available in the hotel restaurant.

Hôtel Etche-Gorria (☎ 05 59 24 00 74; 21 ave du Maréchal Foch; rooms low/high season €31/40, with bathroom €40/45) is an attractive option.

Places to Eat
Popular **Le Bistroye** (☎ 05 59 22 01 02; 6 rue Jean Bart; mains from €7.35; open Mon-Tues, Wed lunch, Thur-Sat) has delicious fare. Next door, **La Mamounia** (☎ 05 59 24 76 08) doles out couscous from €12.50 and other Moroccan specialities from €15.

There are quite a few decent little restaurants around Les Halles, such as **Bistrot des Halles** (☎ 05 59 24 21 22; 1 rue du Centre; 2-course meal about €20). There's a **covered market** (open 7am-1.30pm daily) off ave Victor Hugo.

Entertainment
Popular bar areas include the streets around rue du Port Vieux, the covered market area and around place Clemenceau. Two central discos are **Le Caveau** (4 rue Gambetta) and **Le Flamingo** inside the Casino Bellevue.

Getting There & Away
Most local STAB buses stop beside the Biarritz town hall, from where Nos 1 and 2 go to Bayonne's town hall and station.

Biarritz-La Négresse train station is 3km south of the centre and served by bus Nos 2 and 9. There's a downtown office of **SNCF** (☎ 05 59 24 00 94; 13 ave du Maréchal Foch).

AROUND BIARRITZ
St-Jean Pied de Port
pop 1500
The walled Pyrenean town of St-Jean Pied de Port, 53km southeast of Bayonne, was once the last stop in France for pilgrims heading for

the Spanish pilgrimage city of Santiago de Compostela. Nowadays it's a popular departure point for hikers and bikers but can be hideously crowded in summer. The climb to the 17th-century **Citadelle** merits the effort with fine views.

The **tourist office** (☎ 05 59 37 03 57; place Charles de Gaulle) helps with information. Riverside **Camping Municipal Plaza Berri** (☎ 05 59 37 11 19; ave du Fronton; 2 people & tent €5.50; open Easter–mid-Oct) has tent sites. **Hôtel des Remparts** (☎ 05 59 37 13 79; 16 place Floquet; singles/doubles with bathroom from €34/39) is a cheerful place.

For lunch, **Chez Dédé** (☎ 05 59 37 16 40; menu du pays €10, mains from €8), just inside the porte de France, has as many as seven good value, tasty menus.

Half the reason for coming to St-Jean Pied de Port is the scenic train trip from Bayonne (€7.20, one hour, up to four daily).

LOURDES
pop 15,000
In 1858, 14-year-old Bernadette Soubirous saw the Virgin Mary within a small grotto in a series of 18 visions, later confirmed as bona fide apparitions by the Vatican. This simple peasant girl, who lived out her short life as a nun, was canonised as Ste Bernadette in 1933.

Some five million pilgrims annually, including many seeking cures for their illnesses, converge on Lourdes from all over the world. In counterpoint to the fervent, almost medieval piety of the pilgrims is a tacky display of commercial exuberance.

Orientation & Information
Lourdes' two main east-west streets are rue de la Grotte and, 300m north, blvd de la Grotte. Both lead to the Sanctuaires Notre Dame de Lourdes. The principal north-south thoroughfare connects the train station with place Peyramale and the **tourist office** (☎ 05 62 42 77 40, fax 05 62 94 60 95; e lourdes@sudfr.com; open 9am-7pm Mon-Sat, 10am-6pm Sun Easter–mid-Oct, 9am-5.30pm or 6pm Mon-Sat mid-Oct–Easter).

The office sells the **Visa Passeport Touristique** (€30), allowing entry to five museums in Lourdes.

Things to See
The huge religious complex that has grown around the cave where Bernadette saw the

Virgin, is just west of the town centre. The main Pont St Michel entrance is open from 5am to midnight.

Major sites include the **Grotte de Massabielle**, where Bernadette had her visions, its walls today worn smooth by the touch of millions of hands, the nearby **pools** in which 400,000 people immerse themselves each year; and the **Basilique du Rosaire** (Basilica of the Rosary). You should dress modestly.

From the Sunday before Easter to mid-October, solemn **torch-lit processions** leave nightly at 9pm from the Grotte de Massabielle while the **Procession Eucaristique** (Blessed Sacrament Procession) takes place at 5pm daily.

Places to Stay

Camping Tiny **Camping de la Poste** (☎ 05 62 94 40 35; 26 rue de Langelle; sites per person/tent €2.50/3.60, rooms with/without shower €25/22; open Easter–mid-Oct) is a few blocks east of the tourist office. It is small and friendly, and the rooms, though spartan, are good value.

Hotels Lourdes has plenty of budget hotels. Near the train station is the friendly **Hôtel d'Annecy** (☎ 05 62 94 13 75; 13 ave de la Gare; singles/doubles/triples/quads with washbasin €14/23/27/28, with bathroom €21/29.50/32.50/33.50; open Easter-Oct). In the town centre, **Hôtel St Sylve** (☎/fax 05 62 94 63 48; 9 rue de la Fontaine; singles/doubles €12.50/22, with shower €20/28; open Apr-Oct) has large rooms.

The stylish **Hôtel de la Grotte** (☎ 05 62 94 58 87, fax 05 62 94 20 50; 66 rue de la Grotte; singles/doubles from €61/67; open Apr-Oct) has fine balconies and a gorgeous garden. Its rooms have all mod-cons.

Places to Eat

Restaurants close early in this pious town. **Restaurant Le Magret** (10 rue des Quatre Frères Soulas; menus €13, €23 & €31; open Tues-Sun), opposite the tourist office, has excellent value menus. Next door, **La Rose des Sables** (open Tues-Sun) specialises in couscous (from €11). The **covered market** (place du Champ Commun) is south of the tourist office.

Getting There & Away

Bus The bus station, down rue Anselme Lacadé east of the covered market, serves

regional towns including Pau (€7.20, 1½ hours, four to six daily). SNCF buses to the Pyrenean towns of Cauterets (€5.90, one hour, five daily) and Luz-St-Sauveur (€6.30, one hour, six daily) leave from the train station's car park.

Train The train station is 1km east of the sanctuaries. Trains connect Lourdes with many cities including Bayonne (€16.90, 1¾ hours, up to six daily), Bordeaux (€27.30, 2½ hours, six daily), Pau (€6, 30 minutes, more than 10 daily) and Toulouse (€19.70, 2¼ hours, seven daily). There are five TGVs daily to Paris' Gare Montparnasse (€72.40 to €81.40, six hours) and an overnight train to Gare d'Austerlitz (€66.20, nine hours).

The Dordogne

The Dordogne (better known as Périgord in France) was one of the cradles of human civilisation, and a number of local caves, including the world-famous Lascaux, are adorned with extraordinary prehistoric paintings. The region is also renowned for its cuisine, which makes ample use of those quintessential French delicacies, *truffes du Périgord* (black truffles) and *foie gras*, the fatty liver of force-fed geese.

PÉRIGUEUX
pop 33,000

Founded more than 2000 years ago on a curve in the gentle Isle River, Périgueux has one of France's finest museums of prehistory, the **Musée du Périgord** (22 cours Tourny; adult/concession €3.50/1.75; open Wed-Mon, closed holidays).

The old city, **Puy St Front**, lies between blvd Michel Montaigne and the Isle River. The **tourist office** (☎ 05 53 53 10 63, fax 05 53 09 02 50; e tourisme.perigueux@perigord.tm.fr; 26 place Francheville; open 9am-6.30pm daily mid-June–mid-Sept, other times 9am-1pm & 2pm-6pm Mon-Sat) is next to a fortified, medieval tower called **Tour Mataguerre**.

Places to Stay

Barnabé Plage Campground (☎ 05 53 53 41 45; bus line No 8 to rue des Bains stop; open year-round) is about 2.5km east of the train station along the Isle River.

About 600m south of the cathedral is the **Foyer des Jeunes Travailleurs** (☎ 05 53 53 52

05; rue des Thermes Prolongée; dorm beds
€11.50), just off blvd Lakanal. Rates include
breakfast. Near the train station, the cheapest
hotel is the family-run, 16-room **Hôtel des
Voyageurs** (☎ 05 53 53 17 44; 26 rue Denis
Papin; doubles with/without shower €14/17)
with basic but clean rooms. Reception may be
closed on weekend afternoons (hours posted).

Getting There & Away
The **bus station** (☎ 05 53 08 91 06; place
Francheville), just southwest of the tourist of-
fice, has buses to Sarlat (€8.15, 1½ hours, one
or two daily) via the Vézère Valley town of
Montignac (€5.30, 55 minutes).

The **train station** (☎ 0836 35 35 39; rue
Denis Papin), about 1km northwest of the
tourist office, is served by local bus No 1, 4 and
5. Destinations include Bordeaux (€15.40, 1¼
hours), Les Eyzies de Tayac (€6.10, 30 minutes, two to four daily), Paris' Gare d'Austerlitz (€42.90, four to five hours) and Sarlat
(€11.60).

SARLAT-LA-CANÉDA
pop 10,000
This beautiful town, situated between the Dordogne and Vézère Rivers, is graced by numerous Renaissance-style, 16th- and 17th-century
stone buildings. On Saturday morning there's
a colourful market on place de la Liberté and
along the rue de la République – the edible
(though seasonal) offerings include truffles,
mushrooms, geese and parts thereof.

The main drag is known as rue de la
République where it passes through the heart-
shaped old town. The **tourist office** (☎ 05 53
59 27 67; rue Tourny; e info@ot-sarlat-peri
gord.fr) can organise hotel bookings (€2
within the *département* or €3 outside it).

Places to Stay
The modest but friendly, 15-bed **Auberge de
Jeunesse** (☎ 05 53 59 47 59, 05 53 30 21
27; 77 ave de Selves; tent sites per person
€5, plus €0.50 for 1st night; dorm beds €9,
plus €1 for 1st night; open mid-Mar–Nov)
has cooking facilities. Call ahead to check
availability.

Doubles start at €40 at these two-star
places: **Hôtel de la Mairie** (☎ 05 53 59 05 71;
13 place de la Mairie; closed Jan), located in
the heart of the medieval city; and **Hôtel Les
Récollets** (☎ 05 53 31 36 00, fax 05 53 30 32
26; e otelrecol@aol.com; 4 rue Jean-Jacques

Rousseau), up an alley just west of rue de la
République.

Getting There & Away
There are one or two buses daily (fewer in July
and August) from place de la Petite Rigaudie
to Périgueux (€8, 1½ hours) via the Vézère
Valley town of Montignac (35 minutes).

Sarlat's tiny **train station** (☎ 0836 35 35
39) is linked to Bordeaux (€18.80, 2½ hours),
Périgueux (€11.60) and Les Eyzies de Tayac
(€7.20, 50 minutes, two daily).

VÉZÈRE VALLEY
Périgord's most important prehistoric sites are
about 45km southeast of Périgueux and 20km
northwest of Sarlat in the Vézère Valley,
mainly between Les Eyzies de Tayac and
Montignac. Worthwhile caves not mentioned
here include the **Grotte du Grand Roc** and **La
Roque St Christophe**. For details on public
transport, see Getting There & Away under
Périgueux and Sarlat earlier.

Les Eyzies de Tayac
pop 850
This dull, touristy village offers one of the region's best introductions to prehistory, the
Musée National de la Préhistoire (adult/
concession €4.50/3; open Wed-Mon Sept-
June, daily July & Aug), built into the cliff
above the tourist office. Also of interest is the
Abri Pataud (adult/concession €4.60/2.50;
open Tues-Sun Sept-June, daily July & Aug),
an impressive Cro-Magnon rock shelter in the
cliff face.

The **Grotte de Font de Gaume**, a cave
with 230 remarkably sophisticated poly-
chrome figures of bison, reindeer and other
creatures, and the **Grotte des Combarelles**,
decorated with 600 often-superimposed engravings of animals, are 1km and 3km respectively northeast of Les Eyzies de Tayac on the
D47. Tours cost adult/18–25/under 18s €6/4/
free and must be reserved in advance on ☎ 05
53 06 86 00 (closed Saturday).

Les Eyzies' **tourist office** (☎ 05 53 06 97
05, fax 05 53 06 90 79; open daily Mar-Sept,
Mon-Sat Oct-Feb) is on the town's main street.

Montignac
pop 3100
Montignac, 25km northeast of Les Eyzies,
achieved sudden fame thanks to the **Lascaux
Cave**, 2km to the southeast, discovered in 1940

by four teenage boys who, it is said, were out searching for their dog. The cave's main room and a number of steep galleries are decorated with 15,000-year-old figures of wild oxen, deer, horses, reindeer and other creatures depicted in quite vivid reds, blacks, yellows and browns.

Lascaux has long been closed to the public to prevent deterioration, but you can get a good idea of the original at **Lascaux II** *(open 10am-noon & 2pm-5.30pm Mon-Sat Sept-June, 9am-7pm daily July & Aug; closed 3 weeks in Jan)*, a meticulous replica of the main gallery. The last tour begins about an hour before closing time. Tickets, which from April to October are sold *only* in Montignac (next to the tourist office), cost €7.70 (children €4.50).

SOUTHWEST OF SARLAT

Along the Dordogne River about 15km southwest of Sarlat you'll find a number of lovely towns and spectacular fortified chateaux.

The trapezoid-shaped, walled village of **Domme**, set on a steep promontory high above the river, is one of the few bastides to have retained most of its 13th-century ramparts. The hamlet of **La Roque Gageac** is built halfway up the cliff face on the right bank of the river.

The 12th- to 16th-century **Château de Castelnaud** *(admission €6.40)* has everything you'd expect from a cliff-top castle. The interior is occupied by a **museum of medieval warfare** *(open daily Mar–mid-Nov)*. Across the river – also perched atop a sheer cliff – is Castelnaud's archrival, the dramatic **Château de Beynac** *(admission €6.55; open daily)*.

Quercy

Southeast of the Dordogne department lies the warm and unmistakably southern region of Quercy. The dry limestone plateau in the northeast is covered with oak trees and cut by dramatic canyons created by the serpentine Lot River and its tributaries.

CAHORS
pop 21,432
Cahors, nestled in a bend of the Lot River, is a quiet town with a relaxed Midi atmosphere.

Orientation
The train station is situated about 600m west of north-south oriented blvd Léon Gambetta,

the main commercial thoroughfare. A bit south of the train station is **pont Valentré**, one of France's finest fortified medieval bridges. **Vieux Cahors** is the medieval quarter situated east of blvd Léon Gambetta.

Information
The **tourist office** *(☎ 05 65 53 20 65, fax 05 65 53 20 74; place François Mitterrand; open 9am-12.30pm & 1.30pm-6.30pm Mon-Fri, to 6pm Sat, also Sun & holidays 10am-12.30pm July & Aug)* can help with information.

About 500m south of the train station, the municipal centre **Les Docks** *(430 Allée des Soupirs)* has a **Cuber Café** offering Internet access for €2 per hour from about 2pm to 8pm (until 6pm at weekends, until 10pm or 11pm Wednesday to Friday).

Things to See
The cavernous nave of the Romanesque-style **Cathédrale St Étienne**, consecrated in 1119, is crowned with two 18m-wide cupolas, the largest in France. The heavily mutilated, Flamboyant Gothic **cloître** (cloister) opens May to September.

The small **Musée de la Résistance** *(☎ 05 65 22 14 25; admission free; open 2pm-6pm daily)*, on the north side of place Charles de Gaulle, has exhibits on the Resistance, the concentration camps and the liberation of France.

Places to Stay
The three-star **Camping Rivière de Cabessut** *(☎ 05 56 30 06 30; open Apr-Oct)* is on the left bank of the Lot River about 1km north of pont de Cassebut (the bridge just east of Vieux Cahors).

The **Auberge de Jeunesse** *(☎ 05 65 35 64 71, fax 05 65 35 95 92; 20 rue Frédéric Suisse; dorm beds €8.50, linen €4.50)* is in the same building as the Foyer des Jeunes Travailleurs. Accommodation is in four- to 11-bed rooms. Telephone reservations are advisable.

In Vieux Cahors, **Hôtel de la Paix** *(☎ 05 65 35 03 40, fax 05 65 35 40 88; place des Halles; doubles from €30.50, with shower & toilet €33.60; reception open Mon-Sat, closed holidays)* has basic but clean rooms.

Places to Eat
There are inexpensive restaurants around the **Marché Couvert** *(place des Halles; open 7.30am-12.30pm & 3pm-7pm Tues-Sat, & Sun mornings)*. Nearby is **Le Dousil** *(124 rue*

Nationale; menu €9, mains from €9; closed Mon), an atmospheric restaurant/wine bar featuring regional specialities.

Getting There & Away

The **train station** (☎ 0836 35 35 39; *place de la Gare*) is on the main SNCF line linking Paris' Gare d'Austerlitz (€50.70, 5¼ hours) with Toulouse (€13.80, 1¼ hours). To get to Sarlat-la-Canéda, take a train to Souillac and an SNCF bus from there.

AROUND CAHORS

East of Cahors, the limestone hills between Cahors and Figeac are cut by the dramatic, cliff-flanked Lot and Célé Rivers. The **Grotte de Pech Merle** (☎ 05 65 31 27 05; *open week before Easter–Oct)*, 30km east of Cahors, has thousands of stalactites and dozens of paintings drawn by Cro-Magnon people more than 16,000 years ago. Arrive early as only 700 people per day are allowed to visit.

The village of **St Cirq Lapopie**, 25km east of Cahors, is perched on a cliff 100m above the Lot River. The harmonious riverside town of **Figeac** is on the Célé about 70km northeast of Cahors. Both are linked to Cahors by four to six SNCF buses daily.

Burgundy & the Rhône

DIJON

pop 230,000

Dijon, the prosperous capital of the dukes of Burgundy for almost 500 years, is one of France's most appealing provincial cities, combining elegant Renaissance buildings with a youthful university town feel.

Dijon is a good starting point for visits to the vineyards of the Côte d'Or, arguably the greatest wine-growing region in the world (unless you come from Bordeaux).

Orientation & Information

Ave Maréchal Foch links the train station with the tourist office. Rue de la Liberté, Dijon's main thoroughfare, runs easterly onwards.

The main **tourist office** (☎ 03 80 44 11 44, fax 03 80 42 18 83; w *www.ot-dijon.fr; open 9am-8pm daily May–mid-Oct, 10am-6pm Mon-Sat, 10am-noon & 2pm-6pm Sun & holidays mid-Oct–Apr)* is 300m east of the train

station at place Darcy. The **tourist office annexe** (*34 rue des Forges; open Mon-Sat May–mid-Oct, Mon-Fri mid-Oct–Apr; closed lunchtime)* faces the north side of the Palais des Ducs. Both sell **wine country bus tour** tickets (*half-/full day €45/95).*

Money & Post Rue de la Liberté is lined with **banks**. The **main post office** (*place Grangier; open 8am-7pm Mon-Fri, 8am-noon Sat)* also offers exchange and Cyberposte.

Email & Internet Access Situated in the bus station, **Multi Rezo** (☎ 03 80 42 13 89; *open 10am-midnight Mon-Sat, 2pm-10pm Sun)* charges €1 for 12 minutes of Internet access.

Laundry The **laundrettes** at 41 rue Auguste Comte and Nos 28 and 55 rue Berbisey are open until 8.30pm or 9pm daily.

Things to See

Dijon's major museums open daily, but not on Tuesday (except Musée National Magnin, which closes Monday). Except where noted, entry is free for under 18s and students and, on Sunday, for everyone. The **Dijon Card** (*24/ 48/72hr €8/12/14)*, available at tourist offices, offers museum and transport access.

The **Palais des Ducs et des États de Bourgogne**, once home to the dukes of Burgundy, now houses the **Musée des Beaux-Arts** (☎ 03 80 74 52 09; *adult €3.40; open 9.30am-6pm May-Oct, 10am-5pm Nov-Apr)*, one of France's most renowned fine arts museums.

Many great figures of Burgundy's history are buried in the Burgundian-Gothic **Cathédrale St Bénigne**, built in the late 13th century. Next door, the **Musée Archéologique** (☎ 03 80 30 88 54; *5 rue du Docteur Maret; adult €2.20; open 9am-6pm)* houses rare Gallo-Roman artefacts.

Just off place de la Libération, the **Musée National Magnin** (☎ 03 80 67 11 10; *4 rue des Bons Enfants; adult €3; open 9am-noon & 2pm-6pm)* contains approximately 2000 works of art.

Dijon has been associated with producing the world's finest mustard since the 13th century, a heritage that's celebrated at the **Amora Musée de la Moutarde** (☎ 03 80 44 11 44; *48 quai Nicolas Rodin; 3 guided tours at 3pm Mon-Sat mid-June–mid-Sept, Wed & Sat Oct-May)*. Bookings are mandatory.

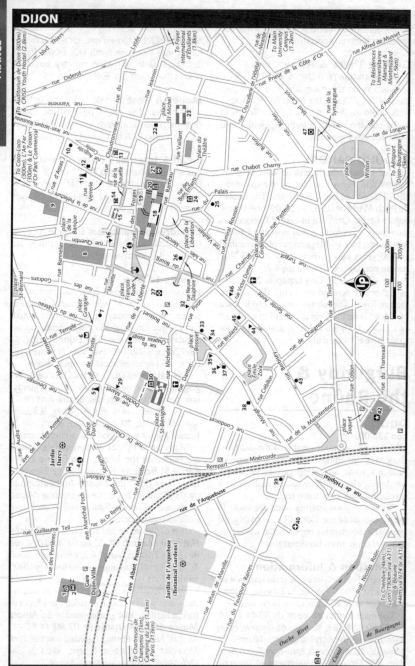

DIJON

DIJON

PLACES TO STAY		OTHER		19	Place des Ducs de Bourgogne
12	Hôtel Le Jacquemart	1	Multi Rezo Internet Centre	20	Musée des Beaux-Arts
22	Hôtel Le Chambellan	2	Intercity Bus Station	21	Opéra de Dijon
26	Hôtel Lamartine	3	Airport Shuttle Stop	23	Église Saint Michel
37	Hôtel Monge	4	Main Tourist Office	24	Musée National Magnin
38	Hôtel Le Sauvage	5	Porte Guillaume	25	Palais de Justice
			(Arc de Triomphe)	27	Dauphine Shopping Centre
PLACES TO EAT		6	Main Post Office	28	Maille
8	Halles du Marché	7	STRD Bus Information	30	Musée Archéologique
16	Chez Nouz		Office	31	Cathédrale Saint Bénigne
29	Restaurant	9	Préfecture	33	Moulot et Petitjean
	Universitaire Maret	10	Laundrette	39	Eurobike
32	Monoprix	11	Hôtel de Ste Seine	40	Hôpital Général
	Supermarket	13	Maison des Cariatides	41	Amora Musée
34	La Dame d'Aquitaine	14	Hôtel de Vogüé		de la Moutarde
35	Alice's	15	Église Notre Dame	42	Hôtel de Police
36	Restaurant Marrakech	17	Tourist Office Annexe	43	Laundrette
44	Crêperie Kerine	18	Palais des Ducs et des	45	Laundrette
46	Le Petit Charlois		États de Bourgogne	47	Synagogue

Places to Stay

Camping The two-star **Camping du Lac** (☎ 03 80 43 54 72; 3 blvd Chanoine Kir; open 8.30am-8pm Apr–mid-Oct) is 1.2km west of the train station; take bus No 12 (direction Fontaine d'Ouche) to stop Hôpital des Chartreux.

Hostels The 260-bed **Centre de Rencontres Internationales et de Séjour de Dijon** (CRISD; ☎ 03 80 72 95 20, fax 03 80 70 00 61; e reservation@auberge-cri-dijon.com; 1 blvd Champollion; dorm beds €17.50 including breakfast) is 2.5km northeast of the centre. Take bus No 5 (direction Épirey) from place Grangier.

Hotels Three blocks south of rue de la Liberté, **Hôtel Monge** (☎ 03 80 30 55 41, fax 03 80 30 30 15; 20 rue Monge; singles/doubles with shower & toilet €32.50/34.50) is a cheap and cheerful option. Further down the road at No 64, **Hôtel Le Sauvage** (☎ 03 80 41 31 21, fax 03 80 42 06 07; singles/doubles with bathroom €43/46) is smarter with tasteful rooms built around a lively courtyard restaurant.

A hidden gem is the **Hôtel Le Jacquemart** (☎ 03 80 60 09 60, fax 03 80 60 09 69; w www.hotel-lejacquemart.fr; 32 rue Verrerie; singles/doubles with washbasin from €25.50/27) with smart, clean rooms.

Just north of Église St Michel, **Hôtel Le Chambellan** (☎ 03 80 67 12 67, fax 03 80 38 00 39; 92 rue Vannerie; rooms with washbasin/shower from €27.45/36.59) has comfortable rooms with a rustic feel.

Hôtel Lamartine (☎ 03 80 30 37 47, fax 03 80 30 03 43; 12 rue Jules Mercier; singles/doubles with washbasin €27.20/30.40), on a narrow street off rue de la Liberté, has clean rooms, although they're a little threadbare.

Places to Eat

Head for rue Monge and rue Berbisey for cheap eats. **Alice's** (☎ 03 80 50 19 51; 2 rue Monge; lunch menus €10) is a nice spot while, at No 20, **Restaurant Marrakech** (☎ 03 80 30 82 69; closed Mon lunch) has tasty couscous (€11 to €16). Going upmarket, **La Dame d'Aquitaine** (☎ 03 80 30 45 65; 23 place Bossuet; lunch/dinner menus with wine €21/35.90; open Tues-Sat & Mon dinner) specialises in Burgundy wines and cuisine.

Breton crepes (€5 to €7) are the speciality at **Crêperie Kerine** (36 rue Berbisey); the small but friendly **Le Petit Charlois** (☎ 03 80 49 81 60) at No 106 has a €14.80 dinner menu including an all-you-can-eat salad buffet.

For cheap student eats, the **Restaurant Universitaire Maret** (3 rue du Docteur Maret; open 11.40am-1.15pm & 6.40pm-8pm Mon-Fri, closed during university holidays) requires student ID for its €2.40 meal tickets (sold on the ground floor weekday lunchtimes).

The **Halles du Marché** (open to 1pm Tues, Thur-Sat) covered market, 150m north of rue de la Liberté, is ideal for picnics, while **Chez Nous** (6 Impasse Quentin), down an alley from the market, serves excellent €7

Burgundian plat du jour from noon in a divey café with an anarchist squat vibe. Get there early.

Monoprix supermarket (open 8.30am-8pm Mon-Sat) is in the Centre Commercial Dauphine off rue Bossuet. **Moulot et Petit-jean** (13 place Brossuet) is a long-established sweet shop; **Maille** (30 rue de la Liberté) has all those essential mustard souvenirs.

Entertainment

The nightlife area can be found north of place de la République with techno club **L'An-Fer** (w www.an-fer.com; 8 rue Marceau; admission €8 with drink after 11pm, €6.50 before, open until 5am Wed-Sat), and the Latin bar/club **Coco-Loco** (18 ave Garibaldi; open until 2am Tues-Sat) the main attractions.

Getting There & Away

Transco buses (☎ 03 80 42 11 00) link the bus station (next to the train station) with winemaking villages along the Côte d'Or via bus No 60 (€6.40 return); No 44 goes direct to Beaune (€6.40).

The train station, **Gare Dijon-Ville** (☎ 08 92 35 35 39) has TGV services to/from Paris' Gare de Lyon (€35.80 to €40.80, 1½ hours). There are non-TGV trains to Lyon (€22.80, two hours) and Nice (€70.40, six hours).

Getting Around

STRD **shuttle buses** (☎ 03 80 30 60 90; €3 ticket bought on the bus), connecting with Buzz flights from London, run from **Dijon-Bourgogne airport** (☎ 03 80 67 67 67) to behind the place Darcy tourist office.

The **STRD office** (place Grangier; open 6.30am-7.15pm Mon-Sat) can provide details of Dijon's urban bus network. A day ticket costs €2.70.

Eurobike (☎ 03 80 45 32 32; 4 rue du Faubourg Raines; half-/full day €9.15/15.25) hires bikes.

CÔTE D'OR

Burgundy's finest vintages come from the vine-covered Côte d'Or, the eastern slopes running for about 60km south from Dijon. The northern section, known as the Côte de Nuits, incorporates Gevrey-Chambertin, Vougeot, Vosne-Romanée and Nuits St Georges, known for their fine reds; the southern section, the Côte de Beaune, includes Pommard, Volnay, Meursault and Puligny-Montrachet.

Beaune
pop 22,000

Beaune, a sleepy little town about 40km south of Dijon, makes for an ideal day trip. It's known for its wine cellars and the **Hôtel-Dieu** France's most opulent medieval charity hospital (adult/concession €5.10/4.10).

The **tourist office** (☎ 03 80 26 21 30, fax 03 80 26 21 39; w www.ot-beaune.fr; place de la Halle; open 9.30am-7pm Mon-Sat, 9.30am-8pm mid-June–mid-Sept, from 10am in winter & 10am-noon & 2pm-5pm Sun year-round), 1km west of the train station, is opposite the Hôtel-Dieu. It sells the **Pass Beaune** (€14.50), which offers a variety of tourist discounts, and advises on visits to caves (wine cellars) offering tours and dégustation, as well as **bus tours** of wine country (lunch/evening €32/34, two hours).

Alternatively, hire bikes from the friendly **Bourgogne Randonnées** (☎ 03 80 22 06 03; ave du 8 Septembre; €15 per day; open 9am-noon & 1.30pm-7pm Mon-Sat, from 10am Sun).

There's a **currency exchange** machine opposite the tourist office that – like most of Beaune – is closed on Monday. Net café **Diz** (☎ 03 80 26 36 01; 28 rue de Lorraine; open 11am-9pm Mon-Sat) has English keyboards and charges €1 for 10 minutes of Internet time.

There are 18 wine cellars in town. The two best known are the **Marché aux Vins** (☎ 03 80 25 08 20; 2 rue Nicolas Rolin), behind the tourist office, offering a daily sampling of 18 wines for €9, and **Patriarche Père et Fils** (☎ 03 80 24 53 78; 5-7 rue du Collège), which has visits (including sampling 13 wines for €9) from 9.30am to 11.30am and 2pm to 5.30pm.

Musée du vin de Bourgogne (☎ 03 80 22 08 19; 6 rue d'Enfer; adult/concession €5.10/3.10; open 9.30am-6pm daily, 9.30am-5pm Jan-Mar) incorporates the Musée Marey and Musée des Beaux Arts.

Places to Stay & Eat The best deal in town is **Hôtel Rousseau** (☎ 03 80 22 13 59; 11 place Madeleine; singles/doubles from €23/29, 5-person room €61.50). It has large, old-fashioned rooms near a tranquil garden and is run by a charismatic woman. Opposite the station, **Hôtel de France** (☎ 03 80 24 10 34, fax 03 80 24 96 78; 35 ave du 8 Septembre; singles/doubles from €43/49) has clean and modern rooms.

Place Madeleine is graced with eateries; many close Sunday and Monday. The best place to eat is **Caves Madeleine** (☎ 03 80 22 93 30; 8 rue du Faubourg Madeleine; menus €12 & €19.20; open noon-2pm & 6pm-9.30pm Mon-Wed, Fri & Sat), a very friendly wine bar, that encourages people to sit together at long tables and chat – ideal for lone travellers.

Restaurant Maxime (3 place Madeleine; menus €13.50-29; open Tues-Sat, & Sun lunch June-Sept; closed Thur Oct-May) offers Burgundy cuisine in a rustic setting.

There's a **Petit Casino supermarket** (6 rue Carnot); café **Jean Ourvois** (8 rue Carnot) is a nice coffee spot.

Getting There & Away Beaune has direct train connections to Dijon (€5.70, 25 minutes, roughly every 40 minutes) and Paris (€38.40, two hours, three daily).

Transco (☎ 03 80 42 11 00) runs bus No 60 through winemaking villages along the Côte d'Or (€3.20) and bus No 44 direct to Beaune (€6.40).

LYON
pop 450,000

Lyon forms part of a prosperous urban area of almost two million people, France's second-largest conurbation. Founded by the Romans more than 2000 years ago, it has spent the last 500 years as a commercial, industrial and banking powerhouse. Lyon boasts outstanding museums, a dynamic cultural life and is among France's greatest gastronomic capitals.

Orientation
The city centre is on the Presqu'île, a peninsula bounded by the Rhône and Saône Rivers. Place Bellecour is 1km south of place des Terreaux and 1km north of place Carnot, next to one of Lyon's train stations, Gare de Perrache. The main station, Gare de la Part-Dieu, is 2km east of the Presqu'île in a commercial district called La Part-Dieu. Vieux Lyon (old Lyon) sprawls across the Saône's west bank but offers little by way of hotels or eateries – unless you're happy paying inflated tourist prices. Overall, Lyon is an easy city to navigate with many attractions within walking distance.

Information
Tourist Offices The efficient **tourist office** (☎ 04 72 77 69 69, fax 04 78 42 04 32;

w www.lyon-france.com; place Bellecour; open 9am-7pm Mon-Sat, 10am-7pm Sun) sells the **Lyon City Card** (1/2/3 days €15/ 25/30), which offers museum entry and use of public transport. Tickets have to be validated before transport use. An **SNCF reservations desk** (2 place Bellecour; open 9am-7pm Mon-Sat) is nearby.

Money There are **Thomas Cook** exchange offices at both train stations; **banks** dot rue Victor Hugo and rue de la République.

Post The **central post office** (10 place Antonin Poncet; open 8am-7pm Mon-Fri, 8am-12.30pm Sat) has exchange and Cyberposte.

Email & Internet Access Specialist travel bookshop and relaxed Internet café **Raconte-Moi La Terre** (☎ 04 78 92 60 20; 38 rue Thomassin) is one of the best traveller resources you could hope to find. It stocks a superb map selection and charges €3.80/6 for 30 minutes/one hour of Internet access (student discounts available).

Connectick (☎ 04 72 77 98 85; 19 quai St Antoine; open 11am-7pm Mon-Sat) charges €7 for one hour online.

Things to See & Do
Vieux Lyon The old city, with its cobble streets, restored houses and famous *traboules* (hidden connecting passageways), lies at the base of Fourvière hill. The area is one of four Lyon sites named as Unesco World Heritage property in 1998.

During summer, guided rooftop tours of the **Basilique Notre Dame de Fourvière** are held daily (Wednesday and Sunday in low season) at 2.30pm and 4pm (adult/concession €4/2.50).

The stuffy **Musée Gadagne** (☎ 04 78 42 03 61; 1 place du Petit Collège; adult/concession €3.80/2; open Wed-Mon) is easily the least compelling of Lyon's museums.

Fourvière Around 2000 years ago, the Romans established the city of Lugdunum on Fourvière's slopes. Today the hill – topped by the **Tour Métallique** (1893), a sort of stunted Eiffel Tower – offers spectacular views of Lyon, its two rivers and, on clear days, Mont Blanc. The easiest way to the top is to ride the funicular railway (between 6am and 10pm) from rue Vieux Lyon station.

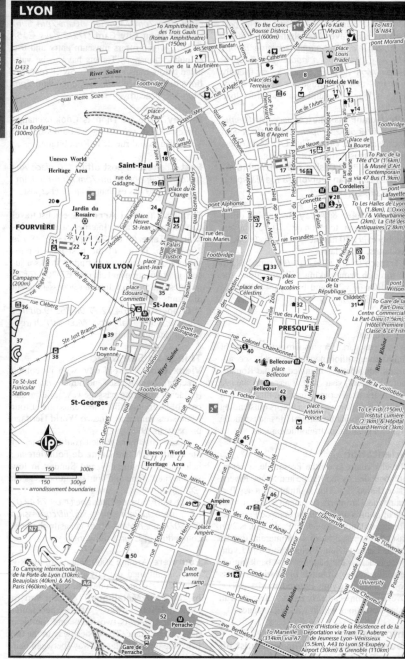

LYON

To Amphithéâtre
des Trois Gauls
(Roman Amphitheatre)
(150m)

To the Croix
Rousse District
(600m)

To Kafé
Myzik

To N83
& N84

pont Morand

rue Romain

rue des Sergent Blandan

rue Ste-Catherine

place
Louis
Pradel

rue Terme

rue de la Martinière

River Saône

Footbridge

quai Pierre Scize

To D433

To La Bodéga
(300m)

place
St-Paul

rue d'Algérie

place des
Terreaux

rue Octavio Mey

quai de la Pêcherie

Hôtel de Ville

rue de l'Arbre

place de
la Bourse

To Parc de la
Tête d'Or (1.6km)
& Musée d'Art
Contemporain
via 47 Bus (1.9km)

Unesco World
Heritage Area

Saint-Paul

rue de Gadagne

place du
Change

rue du
Bât d'Argent

rue Neuve

rue Président Édouard Herriot

rue St-Antoine

rue Mercière

Cordeliers

pont
Lafayette

To Les Halles de Lyon
(1.8km), L'Oxxo
& Villeurbanne
(2km); La Cité des
Antiquaires (2.8km)

FOURVIÈRE

Jardin du
Rosaire

place
Neuve
St-Jean

rue de Boeuf

Montée St-Barthélemy

place
du Change

pont Alphonse
Juin

rue des
Trois Maries

rue Grenette

rue Ferrandière

rue du Palais Grillet

pont
Wilson

To Gare de la
Part-Dieu,
Centre Commercial
La Part-Dieu (1.5km);
Hôtel Première
Classe & Le Fish

VIEUX LYON

Palais
de
Justice

Footbridge

place
Saint-Jean

place des
Célestins

place
des
Jacobins

place
de la
République

rue Childebert

rue du Président Carnot

rue Cléberg

To Campagne
(200m)

Fourvière Branch

Montée

Palais
de
Justice

St-Jean

place
Édouard
Commette

Vieux Lyon

Ste Just Branch

rue du
Doyenné

River Saône

pont
Bonaparte

rue Colonel Chambonnet

rue Émile Zola

rue des Archers

PRESQU'ÎLE

To Le Fish (150m),
Institut Lumière
(2.3km) & Hôpital
Édouard Herriot (3km)

To St-Just
Funicular
Station

St-Georges

Footbridge

quai St-Georges

quai Tilsit

quai du Plat

Bellecour

place
Bellecour

Bellecour

rue A Fochier

rue de la Barre

rue des
Marronniers

place
Antonin
Poncet

pont de la Guillotière

Unesco World
Heritage Area

rue Ste-Hélène

rue Sala

rue Victor Hugo

rue de la Charité

quai Docteur Gailleton

rue Jarente

Ampère

rue des Remparts d'Ainay

place
Ampère

rue Henri IV

rue du Plat

rue d'Enghein

rue Vaubecour

ruee Franklin

River Rhône

University

quai Claude Bernard

quai Pasteur

pont de
l'Université

rue de l'Université

To Camping International
de la Porte de Lyon (10km),
Beaujolais (40km) & A6/
Paris (460km)

place
Carnot
ramp

rue de Condé

rue Duhamel

ave Berthelot

Perrache

Gare de
Perrache

To Marseille
(314km) via A7

To Centre d'Historie de la Résistance et de la
Deportation via Tram T2, Auberge
de Jeunesse Lyon-Vénissieux
(5.5km); A43 to Lyon St-Exupéry
Airport (30km) & Grenoble (110km)

0   150   300m
0   150   300yd
- - - arrondissement boundaries

LYON

PLACES TO STAY		OTHER		31	British Consulate
13	Hôtel Iris	3	Le Voxx	33	Tombé du Ciel
18	Hôtel Ste Paul	4	Le Shamrock	35	Cathédrale Saint Jean
32	Hôtel Élysée	5	Laundrette	36	Musée de la Civilisation
39	Auberge de Jeunesse du	6	Musée des Beaux-Arts		Gallo-Romaine
	Vieux Lyon	7	Branch Post Office	37	Roman Theatres
48	Hôtel d'Ainay	8	Town Hall	38	Minimes Funicular
50	Gîtes de France	9	Skater Statue		Stop
		10	Opéra House	40	SNCF Office
PLACES TO EAT		15	Cinéma Ambience	41	Louis XIV Statue
1	La Randonnée	16	Musée de l'Imprimerie	42	Tourist Office
2	Les Halles de la Martinière	17	Église St-Nizier	44	Central Post Office
	(Covered Food Market)	19	Musée Gadagne	45	Laundrette
11	Bistro Pizay	20	Tour Métallique	47	Musée des Tissus;
12	Café 203	21	Fourvière Funicular Station		Musée des Arts
14	Alyssaar	22	Basilique Notre Dame de		Décoratifs
23	Restaurant de Fourvière		Fourvière	49	Branch Post Office
26	Outdoor Food Market	24	La Tour Rose	51	Police Stations
28	Monoprix Supermarket	25	St James Pub	52	Centre d'Échange;
34	Notre Pain	27	Connectick Internet Centre		Bus Terminal
43	Chabert et Fils	29	TCL Info Office	53	Airport Bus
46	Petit Grain	30	Raconte-Moi La Terre		(Satobus)

Use a bus/metro ticket or buy a €1.20 funicular ticket.

Musée de la Civilisation Gallo-Romaine (☎ 04 72 38 81 90; 17 rue Cléberg; adult/concession €3.80/2.30, free to all Thur; open 9am-12.30pm & 2pm-5pm Tues-Sun) is neighboured by two **Roman theatres** that host rock and classical music concerts during **Les Nuits de Fourvière** (W www.nuits-de-fourviere.org), a summer festival held mid-June to mid-September.

Presqu'île The centrepiece of **place des Terreaux** is a monumental 19th-century fountain by Bartholdi, sculptor of New York's Statue of Liberty. Fronting the square is the town hall (1655). Its south side is dominated by Lyon's **Musée des Beaux-Arts** (Fine Arts Museum; ☎ 04 72 10 17 40; adult/concession €3.80/2; open 10.30am-6pm Wed-Mon), which showcases sculptures and paintings from every period of European art.

The **statue** of a giant on roller skates on place Louis Pradel, northeast of the **opera house**, was sculpted from scrap metal by the Marseille-born sculptor César (1921–98). Skaters buzz around its feet. To the south, **rue de la République** is the main thoroughfare for shops and cinemas.

The **Musée des Tissus** (☎ 04 78 38 42 00; 34 rue de la Charité), where Lyonnais silks are displayed, also houses the **Musée des Arts Décoratifs** (Decorative Arts Museum).

Admission is €4.60/2.30 per adult/concession and both open 10am to 5.30pm Tuesday to Sunday.

The history of printing, a technology established in Lyon in the 1480s, is illustrated by the **Musée de l'Imprimerie** (☎ 04 78 37 65 98; 13 rue de la Poulaillerie; adult/concession €3.80/2; open 9.30am-noon & 2pm-5.30pm Wed-Sun).

Other Attractions The city's main park, **Parc de la Tête d'Or**, sits on the east bank of the Rhône, north of La Part-Dieu. The inspirational **Musée d'Art Contemporain** (Contemporary Art Museum; ☎ 04 72 69 17 18; W www.moca-lyon.org; 81 quai Charles de Gaulle; adult/concession €3.80/2; open noon-7pm Wed-Sun), borders the river and hosts fantastically daring modern art exhibitions. It also houses a multimedia centre devoted to digital art.

The **Institut Lumière** (☎ 04 78 78 18 95; W www.institut-lumiere.org; 25 rue du Premier-Film; adult/concession €5.34/4.42; open 11am-7pm Tues-Sun) brings to life the work of the motion-picture pioneers Auguste and Louis Lumière.

Lyon's role as the centre for the WWII resistance movement is recorded in arguably the city's most important exhibition, the **Centre d'Histoire de la Résistance et de la Deportation** (☎ 04 78 72 23 11; 14 ave Berthelot; adult/concession €3.80/2; open

9am-5.30pm Wed-Sun). Housed in the former Gestapo headquarters where Klaus Barbie operated until 1944, it's a thought-provoking experience.

Places to Stay

Camping Some 10km northwest of Lyon, in Dardilly, there's **Camping International de la Porte de Lyon** (☎ 04 78 35 64 55; 2 people, tent & car €13 per night; open year-round). Bus No 3 or 19 (to Ecully-Dardilly), from Hôtel de Ville metro station, stops at the front.

Hostels In Vieux Lyon, the **Auberge de Jeunesse du Vieux Lyon** (☎ 04 78 15 05 50, fax 04 78 15 05 51; e lyon@fuaj.org; 41-45 montée du Chemin Neuf; dorm beds €12.20 including breakfast; reception open 24hr) requires non-HI affiliates to buy membership (€14.20).

Auberge de Jeunesse Lyon-Vénissieux (☎ 04 78 76 39 23, fax 04 78 77 51 11; e lyon venissieux@fuaj.fr; 51 rue Roger Salengro; dorm beds €11.30 including breakfast; reception open 7.30am-12.30am) is 5.5km southeast of Gare de Perrache in the Vénissieux district. Bus No 35 from place Jean Macé stops outside.

Chambres d'Hôtes B&B-type accommodation around Lyon is arranged by **Gîtes de France** (☎ 04 72 77 17 55, fax 04 78 38 21 15; 1 rue Général Plessier) which has lists of gîtes (self-catering farms and cottages) to rent on a weekly basis; prices range from €50 to €80 per night for two people and includes breakfast.

Hotels Near the station, **Hôtel d'Ainay** (☎ 04 78 42 43 42, fax 04 72 77 51 90; 14 rue des Remparts d'Ainay; singles/doubles €32/34 with shower & TV) has basic but functional rooms.

The best for tasteful budget accommodation is **Hôtel Élysée** (☎ 04 78 42 03 15, fax 04 78 37 76 49; 92 rue du Président Édouard Herriot; singles/doubles from €43/59). It has the bonus of being the only hotel listed here that is in the Bon Weekend en Ville scheme. Just off place des Terraux, **Hôtel Iris** (☎ 04 78 39 93 80, fax 04 72 00 89 91; 36 rue de l'Arbre Sec; singles/doubles €37/40) is dark but centrally located.

In Vieux Lyon, **Hôtel St Paul** (☎ 04 78 28 13 29, fax 04 72 00 97 27; 6 rue Lainerie; rooms from €43) is the pick of the bunch.

Around Gare Part-Dieu, head for **Hôtel Première Classe** (☎ 04 72 36 86 62, fax 04 72 36 89 57; 75 bld Vivek Merle; rooms from €40) for a quick stopover.

Places to Eat

Piggy-part cuisine is the speciality of the traditional Lyonnais bouchon, a small, unpretentious bistro-style restaurant. It's now hard to find genuine bouchons who haven't sold out to coach-party catering but rue des Marronniers and rue Merciére are still good places to look. **Chabert et Fils** (☎ 04 78 37 01 94; 11 rue des Marronniers) has a decent €10.50 lunch menu as does **Bistro Pizay** (☎ 04 78 28 37 26; 4 rue Verdi).

Many restaurants close on Sunday. One of Lyon's hidden gems (open seven days) is the arty **Café 203** (☎ 04 78 28 66 65; 9 rue de Garet; open 7am-midnight Mon-Sat, 3pm-midnight Sun), a buzzy place that's deservedly popular for its excellent €10 set menus. Around the corner, Syrian **Alyssaar** (☎ 04 78 29 57 66; 29 rue du Bât d'Argent) has spicy €12, €14 and €18 menus.

La Randonnée (☎ 04 78 27 86 81; 4 rue Terme) offers vegetarian dishes and lunchtime/evening €6.50/12.5 menus; the Vietnamese **Petit Grain** (☎ 04 72 41 77 85; 19 rue de la Charité) has salad platters from €7.50.

In Vieux Lyon, **Restaurant de Fourvière** (☎ 04 78 25 21 15; 9 place Fourvière) has a €11.50 lunch menu and great panoramic views.

For coffee, **Notre Pain** (☎ 04 78 37 03 16; 1 rue de l'Ancienne Préfecture) is a mellow bakery – get there around opening time (9am) for warm patisserie fresh from the oven.

Self-Catering Fresh produce, cheeses and bread are piled high at the **outdoor morning food market** (quai St Antoine; open Tues-Sun); **Les Halles de la Martinière** (covered food market; 24 rue de la Martinière; closed Sun afternoon & Mon) in the northern Presqu'île is also good for self-caterers.

The **Monoprix supermarket** is at the intersection of rue de la République and rue Grenette.

Entertainment

Rue Ste-Catherine is lined with bars. The long established **Shamrock pub** (☎ 04 78 27 37 82), at No 15, opens late; another popular Irish bar is the **St James pub** (☎ 04 78 37 36 70; 19 rue

Ste Jean) in Vieux Lyon which has an all-night happy hour on Thursday. Nearby, bands play at **Kafé Myzik** (☎ *04 72 07 04 26; 20 Montée St-Sébastien)*, a hole-in-the-wall club.

On the Saône's left bank, bar **Le Voxx** (☎ *04 78 28 33 87; 1 rue d'Algérie)* lures lively bands and patrons. Lively in a seedy late-night dive way is café **Tombé du Ciel** (☎ *04 78 42 69 30; 9 rue du Port du Temple)*.

The city's big night out is the club-on-a-boat **Le Fish** (☎ *04 72 84 98 98; face au 21 quai Victor Augagneur; open 10pm-5am Wed-Sat)*.

Getting There & Away

Bus Intercity and international buses depart from the terminal next to Gare de Perrache. Timetables are available from **TCL information office** (☎ *04 78 71 70 00; open 7.30am-6.30pm Mon-Fri, 9.30am-noon & 1.30pm-7pm Sat)* on the middle level of the Centre d'Échange. Tickets are sold on the bus.

Satobus runs **airport shuttles** (☎ *04 72 68 72 17)* to/from Perrache to Lyon Ste Exupéry airport (€8, one hour, every 20 minutes).

Train Lyon is a major rail hub. There are up to 30 trains daily to/from Paris (€50.30, two hours). Rather confusingly, trains can terminate at either of Lyon's stations. Generally, Part-Dieu (the larger and more blessed with facilities) handles TGV and international traffic, Perrache local trains. Check, however, where trains are stopping as it's a €15 taxi ride between the stations, or a change at Charpennes metro station.

Getting Around

Lyon's efficient and musical metro system has four lines (A to D), running 5am to midnight. Tickets (€1.30) are valid for buses, the funicular and metro for one hour after time-stamping. A carnet of 10 tickets/day pass (€10.40/3.74), can be bought at ticket machines, and at **TCL information offices** (☎ *04 78 71 70 00; Centre d'Échange, 43 rue de la République ● Vieux Lyon metro station)*.

The French Alps

The French Alps truly is one of the most awe-inspiring mountain ranges in the world.

During the summer, visitors can take advantage of many hundreds of kilometres of hiking trails, while the area's ski resorts attract enthusiasts from around the world during the winter.

If you're going to ski or snowboard, expect to pay at least €45 a day (including equipment hire, lifts and transport) at low-altitude stations, which operate from December to March. Larger, high-altitude stations cost €55 to €65 a day. There are good deals in January between the school holiday periods.

CHAMONIX
pop 10,109

Chamonix sits in a valley surrounded by the most spectacular scenery in the French Alps, an area almost Himalayan in its awesome scenery with Mont Blanc soaring almost vertically, 4km above the valley floor.

There are some 330km of hiking trails in the Chamonix area. In winter, the valley provides superb skiing, with dozens of ski lifts and more than 140km of downhill and cross-country ski runs. The population swells to 100,000 in peak season and the town takes on an Ibiza *sur neige* feel, accompanied by giant music festivals.

Information

The **tourist office** (☎ *04 50 53 00 24, fax 04 50 53 58 90;* w *www.chamonix.com; 85 place du Triangle de l'Amitié; open 8.30am-12.30pm & 2pm-7pm daily)* has brochures on ski-lift hours and costs, refuges, camping grounds and parapente schools. In winter it sells a range of ski passes, valid for bus transport and ski lifts in the valley.

The **Maison de la Montagne** *(109 place de l'Église)*, opposite the tourist office, houses the **Office de Haute Montagne** (☎ *04 50 53 22 08; open 9am-noon & 3pm-6pm Mon-Sat)*, which has information and maps for walkers and mountaineers.

There are **money exchange** machines on place Balmat opposite the **post office** *(open 8.30am-noon & 2pm-6pm Mon-Fri, 8.30am-noon Sat)* and ave Michel Croz. The **cyBar** (☎ *04 50 53 64 80; 80 rue des Moulins)* and **El Dorado** *(75 ave de l'Aiguille)* both charge €1 for 10 minutes of Internet access.

Laundry is available (9am to midnight) on rue Joseph Vallot, next to **Garage** nightclub.

Climate Weather bulletins are posted on the window of the tourist office, as well as at the Maison de la Montagne. For a six-day English-language forecast, call ☎ *08 92 70 03 30.*

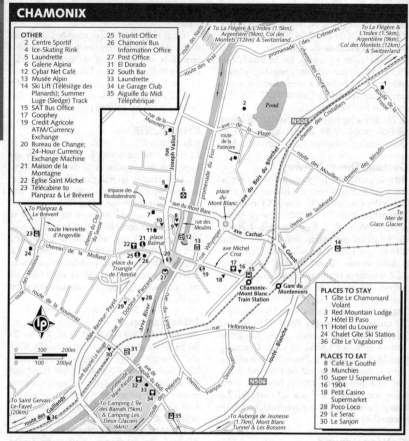

CHAMONIX

OTHER
2 Centre Sportif
4 Ice-Skating Rink
5 Laundrette
8 Galerie Alpina
12 Cybar Net Café
13 Musée Alpin
14 Ski Lift (Télésiège des Planards); Summer Luge (Sledge) Track
15 SAT Bus Office
17 Goophey
19 Credit Agricole ATM/Currency Exchange
20 Bureau de Change; 24-Hour Currency Exchange Machine
21 Maison de la Montagne
22 Église Saint Michel
23 Télécabine to Planpraz & Le Brévent
25 Tourist Office
26 Chamonix Bus Information Office
27 Post Office
31 El Dorado
32 South Bar
33 Laundrette
34 Le Garage Club
35 Aiguille du Midi Téléphérique

PLACES TO STAY
1 Gîte Le Chamoniard Volant
3 Red Mountain Lodge
7 Hôtel El Paso
11 Hotel du Louvre
24 Chalet Gîte Ski Station
36 Gîte Le Vagabond

PLACES TO EAT
8 Café Le Gouthé
9 Munchies
10 Super U Supermarket
16 1904
18 Petit Casino Supermarket
28 Poco Loco
29 Le Serac
30 Le Sanjon

Things to See & Do

The **Musée Alpin** (☎ 04 50 53 25 93; admission €4; open 2pm-7pm June–mid-Oct, 3pm-7pm Christmas-Easter, closed end May & June), just off ave Michel Croz, illustrates the history of Alpine sports.

Aiguille du Midi The Aiguille du Midi (3842m) is a lone spire of rock 8km from the summit of Mont Blanc. The **téléphérique** (€33; operates 6am-4.45pm July & Aug, 8am-3.45pm rest of year) from Chamonix to the Aiguille du Midi, is the highest and probably scariest cable car in the world. Arrive before 9am for better visibility and to avoid the tourist buses.

A ride from Chamonix to the cable car's halfway point, **Plan de l'Aiguille** (2308m) –

an excellent place to start hikes in summer – costs €12/14 one way/return.

Between April and September, you can take a second cable car, depending on the winds, from the Aiguille du Midi across the glacier to **Pointe Helbronner** (3466m) and down to the Italian ski resort of Courmayeur (€79.50 return).

Le Brévent The highest peak on the west side of the valley, Le Brévent (2525m) is known for its views of Mont Blanc. It can be reached from Chamonix by a combination of **téléphérique** and **télécabine** (gondola; ☎ 04 50 53 13 18; €12/15 one way/return; operates 9am-4pm in winter, 8am-5pm rest of year). Hiking trails back to the valley can be picked up at Le Brévent or at the cable car's

...idway station, **Planpraz** (1999m; €8/10 one ...ay/return).

Mer de Glace The second-largest glacier in ...he Alps, Mer de Glace (Sea of Ice) is 14km ...ong, 1950m across at its widest point and up ...o 400m deep. It is a popular tourist destination ...ue to a cog-wheel railway, which has an ...pper terminus at an altitude of 1913m. The ...rain, which runs year-round (weather permit-...ing), leaves from **Gare du Montenvers** (☎ 04 ...0 53 12 54; €10/13 one way/return) in Cha-...nonix. A combined ticket valid for the train, ...he gondola to the ice cave and entry to the ...ave costs €19.60.

Activities

Hiking From mid-June to October, Cha-...nonix has some of the most spectacular hik-...ng trails anywhere in the Alps. The combined ...nap and guide, *Carte des Sentiers du Mont ...Blanc* (Mountain Trail Map, €12.50) is ideal ...or day hikers. Lonely Planet publishes the ...useful *Walking in France*. The **Grand Balcon ...ud** trail, which traverses the Aiguilles ...Rouges (western) side of the valley at about ...000m, offers great views of Mont Blanc and ...he glaciers to the east and south. If you'd pre-...er to avoid 1km of hard uphill walking, take ...ither the Planpraz or La Flégère lift (both €8 ...ne way).

From Plan de l'Aiguille, the midway point ...n the Aiguille du Midi cable car, the Grand ...Balcon Nord takes you to the Mer de Glace, ...rom where you can hike down to Chamonix.

Skiing & Snowboarding The Chamonix ...rea has 140km of marked ski runs, 42km of ...ross-country trails and 64 ski lifts of all sorts. ...Count on paying around €13/60 per day/week ...or regular skis or boots and €20/100 for a ...nowboard. Ask the tourist office for a list of ...lealers.

Places to Stay

Camping There are some 14 camp sites in the ...Chamonix region. In general, camping costs ...€5.50 per person and €4 for a tent site. **L'Île ...des Barrats** *(open May-Sept)* is near the base ...of the Aiguille du Midi cable car. The three-...star **Les Deux Glaciers** *(route des Tissières; ...open mid-Dec–mid-Nov)* is in Les Bossons, ...3km south of Chamonix. To get there, take the ...rain to Les Bossons or Chamonix bus to the ...Tremplin-le-Mont stop.

Refuges The **Mountain refuges** *(€10 per night; open June–mid-Sept)* are accessible to hikers. Easy-to-reach refuges include **Plan de l'Aiguille** (☎ 04 50 53 55 60) at 2308m, the intermediate stop on the Aiguille du Midi cable car, and **La Flégère** (☎ 04 50 53 06 13) at 1877m. You should reserve ahead.

Hostels The **Auberge de Jeunesse** (☎ 04 50 53 14 52, fax 04 50 55 92 34; e chamonix@ fuaj.org; 127 Montée Jacques Balmat; dorm beds €13) is located two train stops before Chamonix at Les Pelérins and operates a free ski shuttle bus. In winter, six-day packages in-cluding bed, food, ski pass and ski hire cost €405 to €440.

The Scottish-run **Red Mountain Lodge** (☎ 04 50 53 94 97; e redmountainlodge@ yahoo.com; 435 rue Joseph Vallot; dorm beds/doubles €16/23 including breakfast; open Apr-Oct only) organises mountain-biking tours. **Gîte Le Vagabond** (☎ 04 50 53 15 43, fax 04 50 53 68 21; 365 ave Ravanel le Rouge; dorm beds €12.50, with half-board €25.76) has a guest kitchen, bar/restaurant with Internet access, a climbing wall and parking.

Further out, **Chalet Gîte Ski Station** (☎ 04 50 53 20 25; 6 Route des Moussoux; dorm beds €10.70; closed 10 May–20 June & 20 Sept–20 Dec) is next to the Planpraz/Le Brévent télécabine station. The semirustic **Gîte Le Chamoniard Volant** (☎ 04 50 53 14 09; 45 Route de la Frasse; €13) is rather cramped on the northeastern outskirts of town. The nearest bus stop is La Frasse.

Hotels The lively **Hôtel El Paso** (☎ 04 50 53 64 20, fax 04 50 53 64 22; e cantina@ cantina.fr; 37 impasse des Rhododendrons; rooms without/with bathroom from €36/43, dorm beds €15, negotiable in low season) has the whole package, incorporating **La Cantina** Tex-Mex restaurant, Internet access and a nightclub.

Hôtel du Louvre (☎ 04 50 53 00 51, fax 04 50 53 70 39; e louvre@wanadoo.fr; 95 im-passe de l'Androsace; singles/doubles €66/54) has dark but clean rooms.

Places to Eat & Drink

Rue des Moulins is the place to go for nightlife. **Munchies** (☎ 04 50 53 45 41) at No 87 has excellent €15 dinner *menus* and is sur-rounded by bars. By the station, **1904** (259 ave Michel Croz) has good €12 lunch *menus*;

Goophey at No 239 is smarter for dinner and drinks.

Le Serac (☎ 04 50 55 88 67; 148 rue du Docteur Paccard) has a €17 walker's *menu*; Le Sanjon (☎ 04 50 53 56 44; 5 ave Ravanel-le-Rouge; open daily) serves €11 *raclette* (a block of melted cheese eaten with potatoes and cold meats) in a picturesque wooden chalet.

For snacks, Poco Loco (47 rue du Docteur Paccard) has hot sandwiches/sweet crepes from €4/3; Le Gouthé (95 rue des Moulins) is an excellent patisserie.

Supermarket Super U (117 rue Joseph Vallot; open 8.15am-7.30pm Mon-Sat, 8.15am-noon Sun) is well-stocked, as is the Petit Casino (ave Michel Croz) near the station.

For après-ski, Cham Sud is the downmarket party zone. There's the Swedish-run South Bar (place de Chamonix Sud) which runs happy-hour promotions and Le Garage (200 ave de l'Aiguille du Midi), a cheesy nightclub, open *very* late.

Getting There & Away

Bus Chamonix' bus station is next to the train station. SAT Autocar (☎ 04 50 53 01 15) has buses to Annecy (€14.45, three hours), Geneva (€29, two hours) and Grenoble (€30, 3½ hours).

Train The Mont Blanc Express from St Gervais takes 30 minutes to Chamonix (stopping at eight towns in the Chamonix Valley) before heading towards Martigny, Switzerland (36km north of Chamonix); change trains at the Swiss border.

Chamonix-Mont Blanc train station (☎ 08 92 35 35 39), on the east side of town, has connections to Paris' Gare de Lyon (€70, up to 10 hours), Lyon (€29, 3½ hours) and Geneva (€15, two hours via St Gervais). Most journeys require a change at St Gervais, which has connections across France.

Getting Around

Bus transport in the valley is handled by Chamonix Bus (☎ 04 50 53 05 55) with an office at place de l'Église opposite the tourist office. The town is easily accessible on foot.

ANNECY

pop 51,000

Annecy, situated at the northern tip of the incredibly blue Lac d'Annecy, is an ideal chill-out spot. Often compared to Bruges or Venice,

it boasts a delightful old town and, although sights are limited, it is steadily acquiring a reputation as an excellent base for water and adrenaline sports.

Orientation & Information

The train and bus stations are 500m northwest of the old city, which is centred around the canalised Thiou River. The modern town centre is between the main post office and the Centre Bonlieu complex. The lake town of Annecy-le-Vieux is just east of Annecy.

The tourist office (☎ 04 50 45 00 33, fax 04 50 51 87 20; ⓦ www.lac-annecy.com; open 9am-6.30pm Mon-Sat May-Sept, 9am-12.30pm & 1.45pm-6pm Mon-Sat Oct-Apr, 9am-12.30pm Sun May-Oct) is situated in the Centre Bonlieu, north of the place de la Libération.

There's a main post office (4 rue des Glières); the Emailerie (☎ 04 50 10 18 91; Faubourg de Annonciades; open 10.30am-12.30pm & 2.30pm-7.30pm Mon-Fri & 2.30pm-7.30pm Sat, 10am-8pm daily June-Aug) has 30 minutes of Internet access for €3.

For laundry, try Lav'Comfort Express (6 rue de la Gare; open 7am-9pm).

Things to See & Do

The Vieille Ville, an area of narrow streets on either side of the Canal du Thiou, retains much of its 17th-century character. On the island in the middle, the Palais de l'Ile (a former prison) houses the Musée d'Histoire d'Annecy et de la Haute-Savoie (adult/concession €3.10/0.80; open 10am-6pm daily June-Sept, 10am-noon & 2pm-6pm Wed-Mon rest of the year).

The Musée d'Annecy (☎ 04 50 33 87 30; adult/concession €4.40/1.50; open 10am-6pm daily June-Sept, 10am-noon & 2pm-6pm Wed-Mon rest of the year), housed in the 16th-century Château d'Annecy overlooking the town, puts on innovative temporary exhibitions.

For adrenaline junkies, adventure sports specialist Takamata (☎ 04 50 45 60 61; ⓦ www.takamaka.fr; 17 Faubourg Sainte Claire) offers a range of activities from canyoning (€45) to tandem paragliding (€80). Mountain bike hire costs €20 per day.

Boat trips on Lake Annecy operated by Compagnie de Navigation (☎ 04 50 51 08 40; 2 place aux Bois; 1/2hr €9.80/12.10) run daily from April to September.

ANNECY

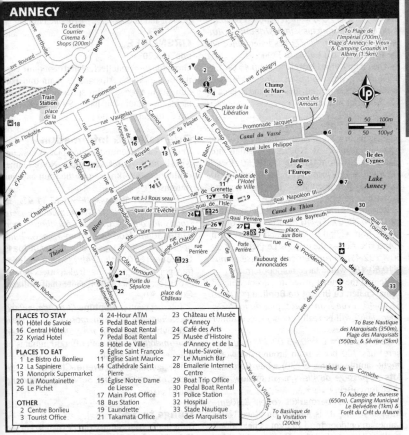

PLACES TO STAY		4	24-Hour ATM	23	Château et Musée
10	Hôtel de Savoie	5	Pedal Boat Rental		d'Annecy
16	Central Hôtel	6	Pedal Boat Rental	24	Café des Arts
22	Kyriad Hotel	7	Pedal Boat Rental	25	Musée d'Histoire
		8	Hôtel de Ville		d'Annecy et de la
PLACES TO EAT		9	Église Saint François		Haute-Savoie
1	Le Bistro du Bonlieu	11	Église Saint Maurice	27	Le Munich Bar
12	La Sapiniere	13	Cathédrale Saint	28	Emailerie Internet
13	Monoprix Supermarket		Pierre		Centre
20	La Mountainette	14	Cathédrale Saint	29	Boat Trip Office
26	Le Pichet	15	Église Notre Dame	30	Pedal Boat Rental
			de Liesse	31	Police Station
OTHER		17	Main Post Office	32	Hospital
2	Centre Bonlieu	18	Bus Station	33	Stade Nautique
3	Tourist Office	19	Laundrette		des Marquisats
		21	Takamata Office		

There's a large **antiques market** held along rue Saint Claire on the last Saturday of the month.

Beaches A free beach, **Plage d'Annecy-le-Vieux**, is 1.5km northeast of the Champ de Mars. Slightly closer to town, next to the casino, is the **Plage de l'Impérial**, which costs €5 and is equipped with changing rooms. Annecy's best swimming beach is the free **Plage des Marquisats**, 1km south of the old city along rue des Marquisats, which also acts as a rollerblading and biking path. Beaches officially open June to September.

Places to Stay

Camping Situated 2.5km south of the train station is **Camping Municipal Le Belvédère** (☎ 04 50 45 48 30, fax 04 50 51 81 62; e camping@ville-annecy.fr; Forêt du Crêt du Maure; 2-person tent sites €17.53) in a shaded forest.

Hostels The **Auberge de Jeunesse** (☎ 04 50 45 33 19, fax 04 50 52 77 52; 4 route du Semnoz; dorm beds €15.60) is 1km south of town in the Forêt du Semnoz. From mid-June to early September only, take bus No 91 (Ligne des Vacances) from the train station for both hostel and camping.

Hotels By far the best bet, and close to the Veille Ville, is the friendly **Central Hôtel** (☎ 04 50 45 05 37; 6 bis rue Royale; rooms without/with shower €30/39.50) in a quiet courtyard behind an enticing bakery. The quirky **Hôtel de Savoie** (☎ 04 50 45 15 45, fax 04 50 45 11 99; e hotel@hotelsavoie.fr; 1 place de St François; singles/doubles with washbasin from €43/77) has its entrance on the left side of the Église St François.

The chain **Kyriad Hôtel** (☎ 04 50 45 04 12; 1 Faubourg des Balmettes; singles/doubles €46/50) has a central location and a decent €6.50 buffet breakfast.

Places to Eat

Rue Faubourg Ste Claire is the best bet for eats and drinks. At No 22, the small but charming **La Montagnette** (☎ 04 50 45 88 78; menu €15; closed Wed, Sat & Sun lunch) has good alpine cuisine. Try the Assiette Savoyarde (€11.43).

Restaurants line the canal; the **La Sapinière** (☎ 04 50 45 97 71; 10 quai de l'Isle) offers salads from €3.50 to €8.90 and crepes from €4 to €8. Across the canal is **Le Pichet** (☎ 04 50 45 32 41; 13 rue Perrière; 3-course menus €10.80-18), with a large outdoor terrace.

Behind the tourist office in a deconstructed alpine chalet, **Le Bistrot de Bonlieu** (☎ 04 50 51 45 40; 1 rue Jean Jaurès; plat du jour €9; open daily) will be really good once customer service improves.

Le Munich (☎ 04 50 45 02 11; quai Perrière) has 300 beers from around the world (eight-sample tasting €9.30) while **Café des Arts** (4 passage de l'Isle) is an mellow arty place for coffee.

Monoprix supermarket (open 8.30am-7.30pm Mon-Sat) is located on place Notre Dame; an outdoor **food market** is held along rue Ste Claire on Tuesday, Friday and Sunday morning.

Getting There & Away

Bus The **bus station** (place de la Gare) is next to the train station. **Voyages Crolard** (☎ 04 50 45 08 12; w www.voyages-crolard.com) has regular services to Bout du Lac at the far southern tip, as well as to Albertville (€7.30, 1¼ hours) and Chamonix (€14.95, 2¾ hours).

Autocars Frossard (☎ 04 50 45 73 90) runs buses to Geneva (€9, 1¼ hours); **Satobus** (☎ 04 72 68 72 17) runs buses to/from Lyon Ste Exupéry airport (adult/concession €30/22.50, two hours).

Train The **train station** (☎ 08 92 35 35 39; place de la Gare) has direct trains to Paris' Gare de Lyon (€57.60, 3½ hours by TGV), Lyon

(€18.50, two hours), Chamonix (€16.80, 2½ hours), and Grenoble (€14.10, one hour).

GRENOBLE
pop 156,203

Grenoble is the intellectual and economic capital of the French Alps and its main transport hub. Set in a broad valley surrounded by spectacular mountains, it has a Swiss feel and a large student population.

Orientation & Information

The old city is centred around place Grenette, with its many cafés, and place Notre Dame. Both are about 1km east of the train and bus stations.

The **tourist office** (☎ 04 76 42 41 41, fax 04 76 00 18 98; w www.grenoble-isere-tourisme.com; 14 rue de la République; open 9am-6.30pm Mon-Sat, 10am-1pm & 2pm-5pm Sun & holidays) sells the **Multipass Grenoble** (€10, valid 24hr), which includes transport and sightseeing. It also offers money exchange, Internet and bike hire (half-/full day €6.10/8.50).

Internet centres **Neptune** (2 rue de la Paix; open 9am-8pm & Sun morning) and **New Age Cyberspace** (16 place Notre Dame; open 7am-midnight daily) both offer 30 minutes of Internet access for €4.

For laundry, try **Laverie Cloîtres** (5 rue Très Cloîtres), or **Libre Service** opposite the tourist office.

Things to See

Built in the 16th century (and expanded in the 19th), **Fort de la Bastille** sits on a hill north of the Isère River, 263m above the old city. The fort affords superb views and is reached via the 685m **téléphérique** (cable car; ☎ 04 76 44 33 65) from quai Stéphane Jay (one way/return €3.80/5.50, students €3/4.40, children €2.40/3.40).

It's a fair old hike down to the poorly signposted **Musée Dauphinois** (☎ 04 76 85 19 01; w www.musee-dauphinois.fr; 30 rue Maurice Gignoux; adults/students €3.20/free, free to everyone the first Sunday of each month; open 10am-7pm Wed-Mon, 10am-6pm Nov-Apr), housed in a 17th-century convent, with displays on the history of the Dauphiné region.

Grenoble's fine-arts museum, the **Musée de Grenoble** (☎ 04 76 63 44 44; 5 place de Lavalette; adult/concession €4/2; open 11am-10pm Wed, 11am-7pm Thur-Sun) has

GRENOBLE

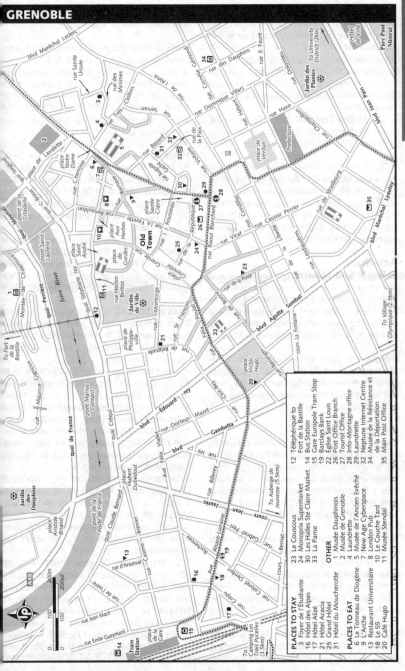

PLACES TO STAY
3 Foyer de l'Étudiante
16 Hôtel des Alpes
17 Hôtel Alizé
21 Hôtel Acacia
25 Grand Hôtel
31 Hôtel du Moucherotte

PLACES TO EAT
6 Le Tonneau de Diogène
7 L'Arche
13 Restaurant Universitaire
18 Le 5B
20 Café Hugo

23 Le Couscous
24 Monoprix Supermarket
30 Les Halles Ste Claire Market
33 La Panse

OTHER
1 Musée Dauphinois
2 Musée de Grenoble
4 Laundrette
5 Musée de l'Ancien Evêché
8 New Age Cyberspace
9 London Pub
10 Le Couche Tard
11 Musée Stendal

12 Téléphérique to
   Fort de la Bastille
14 Bus Station
15 Gare Europole Tram Stop
19 Barclays Bank
22 Église Saint Louis
26 Post Office Branch
27 Tourist Office
28 Info-Montagne office
29 Laundrette
32 Neptune Internet Centre
34 Musée de la Résistance et
   de la Déportation
35 Main Post Office

permanent and visiting collections including works by Matisse, Picasso and Chagall.

The **Musée de la Résistance et de la Déportation** (☎ 04 76 42 38 53; 14 rue Hébert; adult/concession €3.20/1.60; open 9am-6pm Wed-Mon, 10am-6pm Sat & Sun) examines the region's role in the Resistance, and the deportation of Jews from Grenoble to Nazi concentration camps.

The **Musée Stendhal** (☎ 04 76 54 44 14; 1 rue Hector Berlioz; admission free; open 2pm-6pm Wed-Mon) celebrates the writer's life.

The newest attraction, uncovered by excavations, is **Musée de l'Ancien Evêché** (☎ 04 76 03 15 25; w www.ancien-eveche-isere .com; 2 rue Très Cloîtres; adult/concession €3.20/1.60; open 10am-7pm Wed-Mon), which houses the **Baptistére de Grenoble** and traces the history of the region.

Activities
Skiing & Snowboarding There are several low-altitude ski stations near Grenoble, notably Chamrousse (to the southwest), Les Sept-Laux (north east) and Villard-de-Lans (west). The tourist office has comprehensive details; the season runs December to March.

Hiking For good hiking information **Info-Montagne** (☎ 04 76 42 45 90; 3 rue Raoul Blanchard; open Mon-Sat) sells hiking maps and has detailed information about mountain accommodation.

Places to Stay
Camping In Grenoble's western suburb of Seyssins is **Camping Les Trois Pucelles** (☎ 04 76 96 45 73; 58 rue des Allobroges; open year-round). From the train station, take the tram (direction Fontaine) to the Maisonnat stop, then bus No 51 to Mas des Îles and walk east on rue du Dauphiné.

Hostels The **Auberge de Jeunesse** (☎ 04 76 09 33 52, fax 04 76 09 38 99; e grenoble -echirolles@fuaj.org; 10 ave du Grésivaudan; dorm beds €11.90; reception open 7.30am-11pm) is in Échirolles, 5.5km south of the train station. Take bus No 1 from cours Jean Jaurès (direction Pont de Claix) and get off at the Quinzaine stop.

Friendly and central **Foyer de l'Étudiante** (☎ 04 76 42 00 84; 4 rue Ste Ursule; singles/ doubles €14/11 per person, per week €68/53;

open 7am-12.30am) accepts travellers of both sexes from June to September.

Hotels Near the train station, **Hôtel Alizé** (☎ 04 76 43 12 91, fax 04 76 47 62 79; 1 rue Amiral Courbet; rooms with washbasin, shower/toilet €24/29/35) is a good budget option. If it's full, **Hôtel des Alpes** (☎ 04 76 87 00 71, fax 04 76 56 95 45; 45 ave Félix-Viallet; singles/doubles €41/42) has rooms with shower and TV.

In the city centre, a reliable option is the **Hôtel Acacia** (☎ 04 76 87 29 90, fax 04 76 47 21 25; 13 rue de Belgrade; singles/doubles €35/42) for modern, clean rooms. The **Hôtel du Moucherotte** (☎ 04 76 54 61 40; 1 rue Auguste Gaché; singles/doubles from €23.63, 31.10) has a good location but the surroundings are shabby.

Certain three-star hotels, notably **Grand Hôtel** (☎ 04 76 44 49 36, fax 04 76 63 14 06; 5 rue de la République; rooms with shower €61) form part of the Bon Weekend en Ville scheme. The tourist office has more details.

Places to Eat
Many restaurants close Sunday and Monday but **Le Couscous** (☎ 04 76 47 92 93; 19 rue de la Poste; menus €13.59 & 16.62) stays open for filling meals.

Good budget options are **Le 55** (☎ 04 76 46 14 95; 55 ave Alsace Lorraine; menu €9), one block from Barclays Bank, for simple, hearty food, and the **Restaurant Universitaire** (5 rue d'Arsonval; open 11.45am-1.30pm & 6.20pm-7.50pm Mon-Fri mid-Sept–mid-June), which sells tickets for the subsidised student canteen at lunchtime (students/nonstudents €2.40/ 5.03). Students require ID.

La Panse (☎ 04 76 54 09 54; 7 rue de la Paix; lunch menus €12.20-25.15; open noon-1.30pm & 7.15pm-10pm Mon-Sat) and **L'Arche** (☎ 04 76 44 22 62; 4 rue Pierre Duclot; menus lunch/dinner €13/21; open noon-2pm & 7.30pm-10pm) are smart and welcoming.

Le Tonneau de Diogène (☎ 04 76 42 38 40; 6 place Notre Dame; menus from €6.40; open 8.30am-1am) is good value, but service was poor at the time of research. Upstairs its **Librairie le Sphinx** bookshop hosts café philosophie discussion groups – they probably get all metaphysical about the high-tech loo.

For self-caterers, the **Les Halles Ste Claire** food market (open to 1pm daily except Mon)

s near the tourist office, as is the **Monoprix**
supermarket.

For a coffee or snack, you should try **Café**
Hugo *(8 place Victor Hugo)*, and **London Pub**
(11 rue Brocherie) or, for a beer, the **Le Couche**
Tard *(1 rue du Palais)* .

Getting There & Away

Bus The **bus station** (☎ *04 76 87 90 31;*
place de la Gare) is next to the train station.
VFD (☎ *08 20 83 38 33)* has services to
Geneva (€25.50, 2¾ hours), Nice (€52.40,
seven hours), Annecy (€16.60, 1¾ hours) and
to a number of ski resorts. **Intercars** (☎ *04 76*
76 19 77) handles long-haul destinations such
as Barcelona (€45), Budapest (€88), Lisbon
(€139), London (€82), Moscow (€145) and
Prague (€80).

Timed to connect with Buzz flights, shuttle
buses run to/from Grenoble Ste Geoirs airport,
41km northwest of the city, stopping at the bus
station (one way/return €13/20, 45 minutes).

Train The **train station** (☎ *08 92 35 35 39)* is
served by both tram lines (get off at the Gare
Europole stop). There are direct connections to
Paris' Gare de Lyon (€58.80, three hours by
TGV), four trains daily to Turin (€38.90) and
four to Milan (€50.80), plus three trains daily
to Geneva (€18.50).

Getting Around

Satobus (☎ *04 72 68 72 17)* operates buses
to/from the Lyon Ste Exupéry airport (adult/
concession €20/15, one hour).

City buses and trams take the same tickets
(single/carnet of 10 €1.10/8.90), which are
sold by bus (but not tram) drivers and by ticket
machines at tram stops. They must be validated before travel, and remain valid for transfers within one hour but not for return trips.

The Jura

The Jura Mountains, part of the historic
Franche-Comté region, are a range of wooded
hills stretching 360km along the Franco-Swiss
border. The French Jura – the name taken from
a Gaulish word meaning 'forest' – has the
lively student town of Besançon as its capital
and attractive surrounding countryside, yet it's
one of the least explored regions of France.
This could possibly be attributed to the area's
desperately poor public transport network,

which renders it isolated to travellers without
their own transport.

BESANÇON
pop 120,000

Besançon's most famous sons – Victor Hugo,
the author of *Les Misérables*, and the film-
pioneering Lumière brothers – would doubt-
less be proud to see the town today with its
wide green spaces and well-preserved old
town, not to mention the lively nightlife its student population attracts (but not so happy with
onward transport links).

Orientation & Information

Besançon's old city is encased by the curve of
the Doubs River (the Boucle du Doubs) and
dissected by Grande Rue, the pedestrian thoroughfare. To the northwest there's the **tourist**
office (☎ *03 81 80 92 55, fax 03 81 80 58 30;*
w *www.besancon.com; 2 place de la 1ère*
Armée Française; open 9.30am-6.30pm Mon-
Sat, 10am-noon Sun), which has slightly disappointing material, with the train station
further north. The tourist office exchanges currency, as does the main **post office** *(23 rue*
Proudhon; open 8am-7pm Mon-Fri, 8am-
noon Sat). **Banks** line Grand Rue.

At **t@cybernet** (☎ *03 81 81 15 74; 18 rue*
Pontarlier; open 11am-midnight Mon-Sat,
2pm-8pm Sun), 20 minutes of Internet access
costs €1.52.

For laundry there's **Blanc-Matic laundrette**
(14 rue de la Madeleine; open 7am-8pm
daily).

Things to See

The best known attraction is the **citadel** (☎ *03*
81 87 83 33; adult/concession €6.10/4.60;
open 9am-6pm daily Apr-Oct, 9am-7pm July
& Aug, 10am-5pm Wed-Mon Nov-Mar), built
by Vauban for Louis XIV between 1668 and
1711. A steep 15-minute walk from the **Porte**
Noire (Black Gate), it contains three museums:
the **Musée Comtois**, the **Musée d'Histoire**
Naturelle and the **Musée de la Résistance et**
de la Déportation, as well as an **insectarium**,
aquarium, **noctarium** and **parc zoologique**.
In summer, a free shuttle leaves from place
Victor Hugo. Admission includes entry to all
the museums.

The **Musée des Beaux-Arts et d'Archéo-**
logie (☎ *03 81 87 80 49; 1 place de la Révo-*
lution; adult/student €3/free; open 9.30am-
6pm Wed-Mon June-Oct, 9.30am-noon &

2pm-6pm Nov-May), thought to be France's oldest museum, includes works documenting the region's clock-making heritage.

Places to Stay

The **Auberge de Jeunesse Les Oiseaux** *(☎ 03 81 40 32 00, fax 03 81 40 32 01; 48 rue des Cras; singles/subsequent nights €17/15, doubles/subsequent nights €25/23 including breakfast)* is 2km east of the train station. Take bus No 7 (direction Orchamps) from the tourist office to Les Oiseaux.

Opposite the train station, **Hôtel Florel** *(☎ 03 81 80 41 08, fax 03 81 50 44 40; 6 rue de la Viotte; singles/doubles with shower €29/34)* is the best budget option and just a 10-minute walk north of the old city.

Down a quiet alley in the heart of the old city, **Hôtel Regina** *(☎ 03 81 81 50 22, fax 03 81 81 60 20; 91 Grande Rue; singles/doubles €34/43)* is a quiet and cosy two-star place. **Hôtel de Paris** *(☎ 03 81 81 36 56, fax 03 81 61 94 90; e hoteldeparis@hotmail.com; 33 rue des Granges; singles/doubles with bathroom & TV €36.50/46.50)* has 80 smart rooms and private parking.

Places to Eat & Drink

Near Hôtel Florel, **Le Mistigris** *(☎ 03 81 50 22 96; 1 rue Général Roland; open 10am-2pm & 5pm-10pm Tues-Sun)* has a filling €10.70 house speciality, *jambon de montagne*, a slab of ham served with salad and fried potatoes.

For vegetarians, **Crep'corner** *(☎ 03 81 81 81 49; 1 rue Mégevand; open Tues-Sat)* has speciality €6.50 salads and crepes. Rue Bersot is lined with cheap *pizzerias*; try **Trattoria Romana** at No 52 or La Veneziana at No 48.

Students head for the **Boîte á Sandwichs** *(21 rue du Lycée)* for filling €3 to €6 sandwiches, while arty types prefer **Carpe Diem** *(☎ 03 81 83 11 18; 2 place Jean Gigoux; open 7am-1am)*, a small, simple café-restaurant with decent €7 plats du jour.

There's a large **indoor market** *(cnr rue Paris & rue Claude Goudimel; open Tues-Sat)*, a nearby **outdoor market** *(place de la Révolution; open Tues, Fri & Sat)* and a **Monoprix supermarket** *(12 Grand Rue; open 8.30am-8pm Mon-Sat)*.

Les Passagers du Zinc *(☎ 03 81 81 54 70; 5 rue de Vignier; open 5pm-1am Tues-Fri, 5pm-2am Sat & Sun)*, and **Le Casablanca** next door are grungy bar/clubs with live bands and drinks promotions.

Getting There & Away

Bus Buses operated by **Monts Jura** *(☎ 03 81 21 22 38)* depart from the **bus station** *(9 rue Proudhon; open 8am-6.30pm Mon-Fri, 8am-1pm & 2.30pm-5.30pm Sat)*. There are daily connections to Ornans (€3.30, 40 minutes, five daily) Grey (€6.50, one hour, three daily) and Pontarlier (€7.30, one hour, six daily). For bus information, call ☎ 08 25 00 22 44.

Train Both the **Besançon Gare Viotte** *(☎ 08 92 35 35 39)*, 800m up the hill from the city centre at the northwestern end of ave Maréchal Foch, and the **SNCF office** *(44 Grande Rue, open 8.30am-7pm Sun-Fri, 9am-6pm Sat)*, handle information and ticket sales.

Major connections include Paris' Gare de Lyon (€40 to €50, 2½ hours, at least six daily), Dijon (€11.70, one hour, 20 daily), Lyons (€21.90, 2½ hours, at least five daily) and Belfort (€13.80, one hour, 10 daily).

Getting Around

Bus Local buses are run by **CTB** *(☎ 03 81 48 12 12; place du 8 Septembre; open 10am-12.45pm & 1.15pm-7pm Mon-Sat)*. A day ticket/carnet of 10 costs €0.90/7.80. A **city circular bus** links the train station with the centre (single journey €0.91).

AROUND BESANÇON
Saline Royal

Envisaged by 18th-century designer, Claude-Nicolas Ledoux, as the 'ideal city', Saline Royale *(Royal Salt Works; ☎ 03 81 54 45 45, fax 03 81 54 45 46; guided tours adult/concession/family €6.50/4.50/15.60; open 9am-6pm daily June & Sept, 9am-7pm July & Aug, 9am-noon & 2pm-5pm Oct-May)* at Arc-et-Senans, some 30km southwest of Besançon off the N83 to Lyon, is a showpiece of early Industrial Age town planning. It now is a Unesco World Heritage site.

There are six trains daily operating from Besançon (€5.40, 30 minutes) to Arc-et-Senans for day-trippers.

Route Pasteur & Route du Vin

Louis Pasteur (1822–95), the man who invented pasteurisation, lived in **Arbois**; his former laboratory and workshops, **Pasteur's house** *(☎ 03 84 66 11 72; ave Pasteur; admission €5.34; open 9.45am-11.45am & 2.15pm-5.15pm; closed Nov-Mar)*, are a testament to his life's work. The history of Jura ine-making and its trademark 'yellow wine' *in jaune* is recounted at the **Musée de la igne et du Vin** (☎ *03 84 66 40 45; admis- ion €3.30; open 10am-noon & 2pm-6pm Wed-Mon) inside Arbois' medieval Château* écauld.

The **tourist office** (☎ *03 84 66 55 50, fax 3 84 66 25 50; 10 rue de l'Hôtel de Ville)* rranges guided tours and accommodation. he nearest train station for trains from Be- ançon is at Mouchard, 8km north of Arbois €8.60, 1½ hours). This is a difficult day trip vithout a car.

Métabief Mont d'Or

he region's leading cross-country ski resort is 8km south of Pontarlier on the main road to Lausanne in the central part of the Jura range. Lifts operate year-round to the top of Mont l'Or (1463m), the area's highest peak. The re- ort comprises six traditional villages with the nain lift station for downhill skiers located in Métabief itself.

The **tourist office** (☎ *03 81 49 13 81; 1 place de la Mairie)* is in the village of Les Hôpitaux Neufs. The closest **train station** is at Frasne (journey via Mouchard, €13.80, wo hours), from where there are six buses daily that pass through both Métabief and Les Hôpitaux Neufs (€3.30 and €3.50 respec- ively, 50 minutes).

Provence

Provence was settled by the Ligurians, the Celts and the Greeks, but it was after its con- quest by Julius Caesar in the mid-1st century BC that the region really began to flourish.

Many well-preserved amphitheatres, aque- ducts and other buildings from the Roman period can still be seen in Arles and Nîmes (see the Languedoc-Roussillon section later). During the 14th century, the Catholic Church, then led by a series of French-born popes, moved its headquarters from feud-riven Rome to Avignon, thus beginning the most resplen- dent period in that city's history.

MARSEILLE
pop 797,491
The cosmopolitan and much maligned port of Marseille, France's second-largest city and third-most populous urban area, isn't in the least bit prettified for the benefit of tourists. Its urban geography and atmosphere derive from the diversity of its inhabitants, the majority of whom are immigrants (or their descendants) from the Mediterranean basin, West Africa and Indochina. Although Marseille is notorious for organised crime and racial tensions, the city is a vibrant and interesting place to explore.

Orientation
The city's main street, La Canebière, stretches eastward from the Vieux Port. The train and bus stations are north of La Canebière at the top of blvd d'Athènes. The city centre is around rue Paradis, which becomes more fash- ionable as you move south.

Information
The **tourist office** (☎ *04 91 13 89 00, fax 04 91 13 89 20; e accueil@marseille-tourisme .com; 4 La Canebière; open 9am-7pm Mon- Sat, 10am-6pm Sun Oct-June, 9am-7.30pm Mon-Sat, 10am-6pm Sun July-Sept)* is next to the Vieux Port. There are **annexes** *(open Mon-Fri Sept-June, Mon-Sat July & Aug)* at the train station and place des Pistoles.

Info-Café (☎ *04 91 33 74 98; 1 quai de Rive-Neuve; open 9am-10pm Mon-Sat, 2pm- 7pm Sun)* charges €3.60 an hour for Internet access, has more than 50 computer terminals, fast connections, a bar and harbour views.

Dangers & Annoyances Despite its fear- some reputation, Marseille is probably no more dangerous than other French cities. At night it's advisable to avoid the Belsunce area – the neighbourhood southwest of the train station and streets bordering La Canebière.

Things to See & Do
Marseille grew up around the **Vieux Port**, where Greeks from Asia Minor established a settlement around 600 BC. The quarter north of quai du Port (around the Hôtel de Ville) was blown up by the Germans in 1943 and rebuilt after the war. The lively **place Thiars** pedes- trian zone, with its many late-night restaurants and cafés, is south of the quai de Rive Neuve.

For panoramic views and overwrought mid- 19th-century architecture, take Bus No 60 1km south of the Vieux Port to the **Basilique Notre Dame de la Garde**, the city's highest point.

Museums Unless otherwise noted, the mu- seums listed are open 10am to 5pm Tuesday to Sunday, with extended hours in summer;

MARSEILLE

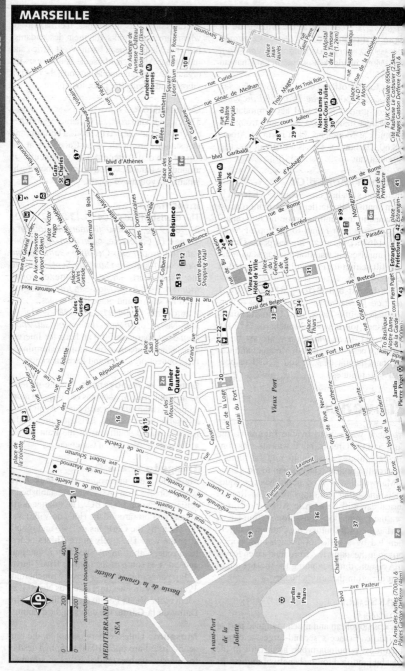

MEDITERRANEAN SEA

Avant-Port de la Joliette

Bassin de la Grande Joliette

Vieux Port

Jardin du Pharo

To Auberge de Jeunesse Château de Bois Luzy (3km)

To Aix-en-Province & Airport (28km)

Autoroute Nord

Gare St-Charles

Canebière-réformés

Belsunce

Noailles

Jules Guesde

Colbert

Joliette

Panier Quarter

Vieux Port-Hôtel de Ville

Estrangin Préfecture

To UK Consulate (650m), Cité Radieuse Le Corbusier (2.5km), Plages Gaston Defferre (4km) &

To Hôpital de la Timone (1.2km)

To Basilique Notre Dame de la Garde

To Anse des Auffes (700m) & Plages Gaston Defferre (4km)

arrondissement boundaries

Jardin Pierre Puget

MARSEILLE

PLACES TO STAY	OTHER		19	Fort Saint Jean
8 Hôtel d'Athènes	1 Passenger Ferry Terminal		20	Hôtel de Ville
10 Hôtel Ozea; Hôtel	(Gare Maritime)		21	La Caravelle
Pied-à-Terre	2 SNCM Ferries Office		24	Espaces Infos RTM
11 Hôtel Lutetia	3 Le Web Bar		25	American Express
22 Hôtel Résidence	4 Bus Station		31	Opéra
du Vieux Port	5 Post Office		32	Tourist Office
	6 Taxi Stand		33	Boats to Château
PLACES TO EAT	7 Tourist Information Annexe			d'If & Îles du Frioul
23 Restaurant	9 Laverie des Allées Laundrette		34	Info-Café
Miramar	12 Musée d'Histoire		35	O'Malleys
26 Marché des	de Marseille		36	Bas Fort Saint Nicolas
Capucins	13 Jardin des Vestiges		37	Fort d'Entrecasteaux
27 Restaurant Antillais	14 Main Post Office			& Fort Saint Nicolas
28 Mosaic La Poudriere	15 Tourist Office Annexe		38	Musée Cantini
29 Le Resto Provençal	16 Centre de la Vieille Charité		39	SNCF Office
30 Le Chalet Berbere	17 Nouvelle Cathédrale		40	Préfecture de Police
43 Fruit & Vegetable	18 Ancienne Cathédrale		41	Préfecture
Market	de la Major		42	Banque de France

ll charge €2 to €3 for admission and admit tudents for half-price. The **Carte Privilèges** €15.25/22.87/30.49 for 1/2/3 days) in-ludes admission to all museums, boat fare to .e Château d'If and all public transport. It's nly a good deal if you are going to visit the slands.

The **Centre de la Vieille Charité** (☎ 04 91 ¶4 58 80; 2 rue de la Charité) is home to Mar-eille's **Museum of Mediterranean Archaeo-ogy** and has superb permanent exhibits on ancient Egypt and Greece. It's in the mostly North African Panier quarter (north of the Vieux Port).

The **Musée Cantini** (☎ 04 91 54 77 75; 19 rue Grignan), off rue Paradis, hosts modern art exhibitions.

Roman history buffs will love the **Musée d'Histoire de Marseille** (☎ 04 91 90 42 22; ground floor, Centre Bourse shopping mall; open noon-7pm Mon-Sat), just north of La Canebière. Its exhibits include the remains of a merchant ship dating to the late 2nd cen-tury AD.

Château d'If Château d'If (☎ 04 91 59 02 30; admission €4; open 9am-7pm Tues-Sun Apr-Sept, 9am-7.30pm Tues-Sun Oct-Mar) is the 16th-century island fortress-turned-prison made infamous by Alexandre Dumas' *The Count of Monte Cristo*. Boats (€8 re-turn; 20 minutes each way) depart from quai des Belges in the Vieux Port and continue to the nearby **Îles du Frioul** (€13 return for both islands).

Cité Radieuse Le Corbusier Finished in 1952, Le Corbusier's apartment building (☎ 04 91 77 14 07; 280 blvd Michelet, 8e; bus No 21 from La Canebière) has been much imitated but rarely with the famous architect's careful dimensions. Ask at the 3rd floor hotel (see Places to Stay) about tours (€5; min-imum 3 people).

Places to Stay

Hostels In the Montolivet neighbourhood, 4.5km east of the city centre, is **Auberge de Jeunesse Château de Bois Luzy** (☎/fax 04 91 49 06 18; Allées des Primevères, 12e; bus No 8 from La Canebière; dorm beds €7.62). HI cards are required.

The **Auberge de Jeunesse de Bonn-eveine** (☎ 04 91 17 63 30, fax 04 91 73 97 23; e ajemb@freesurf.fr; Impasse du Docteur Bonfils, 8e; dorm beds €11.90-16.40; closed Jan) is 4.5km south of the Vieux Port. Take bus No 44 from the Rond-Point du Prado metro stop and get off at place Louis Bonnefon.

Hotels – Train Station Area Two-star **Hôtel d'Athènes** (☎ 04 91 90 12 93, fax 04 91 90 72 03; 37-39 blvd d'Athènes, 1er; rooms with bath/shower & toilet €34.30/38.15) is at the foot of the grand staircase leading from the train station into town. The well-kept rooms are comfortable but can be noisy.

Hotels – Around La Canebière New guests can arrive 24 hours a day at clean, sim-ple **Hôtel Ozea** (☎/fax 04 91 47 91 84; 12 rue

Barbaroux, 1er; doubles without/with shower €23/27; hall shower €3). At night just ring the bell to wake up the night clerk. There are well-kept rooms, but no hall showers, at **Hôtel Pied-à-Terre** (☎ 04 91 92 00 95; 18 rue Barbaroux, 1er; singles/doubles €26.50/20).

More expensive but worth the money is the homy **Hôtel Lutetia** (☎ 04 91 50 81 78, fax 04 91 50 23 52; 38 Allées Léon Gambetta; singles/doubles €40/45, with bath €44/49) with smallish rooms equipped with TV and phone.

Hotels – Elsewhere For water views, try three-star, seven-storey **Hôtel Résidence du Vieux Port** (☎ 04 91 91 91 22, fax 04 91 56 60 88; e hotel.residence@wanadoo.fr; 18 Quai du Port, 1er; singles/doubles €85/100, 5-person apartment €138).

Hôtel Corbusier (☎ 04 91 16 78 00, fax 04 91 16 78 28; e hotelcorbusier@wanadoo.fr; 280 blvd Michelet, 8e; doubles €38) has simple but stylish rooms in a famous apartment block.

Places to Eat
Fresh fruit and vegies are sold at the **Marché des Capucins** (place des Capucins; open Mon-Sat), one block south of La Canebière.

Restaurants along the pedestrianised cours Julien, a few blocks south of La Canebière, offer an incredible variety of cuisines: Antillean, Pakistani, Thai, Lebanese, Tunisian and even French.

The **Restaurant Antillais** (10 cours Julien; mains from €6.50, menu with house wine €16) features West Indian cuisine. **Mosaic La Poudriere** (☎ 04 91 47 48 32; 36-38 cours Julien; dinner menu €14; open 2pm-midnight Mon, 10am-midnight Tues-Sat) is a bar, restaurant and illustrated book store. **Le Resto Provençal** (62 cours Julien; menu €20; open Tues-Sat) does regional French cuisine.

Le Chalet Berbere (☎ 04 96 12 08 47; 94 cours Julien; mains from €7; open Tues-Sun lunch, Mon-Sat dinner) is a small but smart Algerian couscous place.

Restaurants line the streets around place Thiars on the south side of the Vieux Port. Though many offer bouillabaisse, the rich fish stew for which Marseille is famous, you must wander to the other side of the harbour to **Restaurant Miramar** (☎ 04 91 91 10 40; 12 quai du Port) to find the real (and really expensive at €48) thing.

Entertainment
Listings magazines such as *Vox Mag*, *Ventil* and *Cesar* are distributed for free at the tourist office. *Sortir* comes out with the Friday edition of *La Provence* newspaper; look out for *PAF*, a monthly one-page gig guide.

Le Web Bar (☎ 04 96 11 65 11; 114 Rue République; open 10am-2am daily) hosts all kinds of funky music events including brunch concerts.

Atmospheric **La Caravelle** (☎ 04 91 90 36 64; 34 quai du Port) is a jazzy bar with views of the port. On the other side of the water is **O'Malleys Irish pub** (9 quai de Rive Neuve).

Getting There & Away
Bus The **bus station** (☎ 04 91 08 16 40; place Victor Hugo), 150m to the right as you exit the train station, offers services to Aix-en-Provence, Avignon, Cannes, Nice, Nice airport and Orange, among others.

Eurolines (☎ 04 91 50 57 55) has buses to Spain, Italy, Morocco, the UK and other countries. Its counter in the bus station is open from 9am to noon and 2pm to 5.30pm (closed Sunday).

Train Marseille's passenger train station, served by both metro lines, is called **Gare St-Charles** (☎ 0836 35 35 35). Services along Voie (platform A) include a busy ticket office, sparkling **toilets** (admission €0.40, open 6am-midnight daily) and **left luggage** (from €3 per piece for 72hr; open 7.15am-10pm). There's a **tourist information annexe** out the side door at the top of the platform.

From Marseille there are trains to more or less any place in France. Some sample destinations are Paris' Gare de Lyon (€77.10, 3¼ hours by TGV, 18 daily), Avignon via Arles (€17.10, one hour, 20 daily), Lyon (€32.90, 3½ hours), Nice (€25, 1½ hours), Barcelona (€60.40, 8½ hours) and Geneva (€49.50, 6½ hours).

Ferry The **Société Nationale Maritime Corse-Méditerranée** (SNCM; ☎ 08 36 67 95 00, fax 04 91 56 35 86) runs ferries from the *gare maritime* (passenger ferry terminal) at the foot of blvd des Dames. There's also an **SNCM office** (61 blvd des Dames; open Mon-Sat). For ferries to Corsica, Italy and Sardinia call ☎ 0891 701 801, for Algeria and Tunisia call ☎ 0891 702 802.

Getting Around

Bus & Metro Marseille has a trolley bus line and an extensive bus network, operating from 5am to 9pm. Night buses and tram No 68 run from 9pm to 1am (12.30am Saturday and Sunday). Two easy-to-use metro lines run to about 9pm (to 12.30am Friday to Sunday). Tickets (single/carnet of six €1.40/6.50) are valid on all services for one hour. Time-stamp your ticket when you board the bus. For more information, visit the **Espace Infos RTM** (☎ 04 91 91 92 10; 6-8 rue des Fabres).

AROUND MARSEILLE

Aix-en-Provence
pop 134,324

One of the most appealing cities in Provence, Aix owes its atmosphere to the students who make up more than 20% of the population. The city is renowned for its *calissons*, almond-paste confectionery, and for being the birthplace of postimpressionist painter Cézanne. Aix hosts the Festival International d'Art Lyrique each July.

The **tourist office** (☎ 04 42 16 11 61, fax 04 42 16 11 62; e infos@aixenprovencetourism.com; place Général de Gaulle) has walking tour brochures. Aix is easy to see on a day trip from Marseille, and frequent trains (€4.10) make the 35-minute trip.

Things to See The mostly pedestrianised old city is a maze of tiny streets full of ethnic restaurants and specialist food shops, intermixed with elegant 17th- and 18th-century mansions.

Aix also has several interesting museums, the finest of which is the **Musée Granet** (place St Jean de Malte; admission varies; open Wed-Mon). The collection includes paintings from the 16th to 19th centuries, including some lesser known Cézanne works. Slow-moving renovations mean the museum may be only partially open.

Places to Stay About 2km southeast of town is **Camping Arc-en-Ciel** (☎ 04 42 26 14 28; route de Nice; camp sites €17.10; open Apr-Sept) at Pont des Trois Sautets. Take bus No 3 to Les Trois Sautets stop. **Auberge de Jeunesse du Jas de Bouffan** (☎ 04 42 20 15 99, fax 04 42 59 36 12; 3 ave Marcel Pagnol; beds €14 including breakfast & sheets) is almost 2km west of the centre. Rooms are locked between 9am and 5pm.

Take bus line No 4 from La Rotonde to the Vasarely stop. **Hôtel Cardinal** (☎ 04 42 38 32 30, fax 04 42 26 39 05; 24 rue Cardinale; singles/doubles €46/58, self-catering suites €73) has large rooms with shower, toilet and a mix of modern and period furniture. The small self-catering suites are in its annexe at 12 rue Cardinale.

Places to Eat Pop your head into **Les Deux Garçons** (53 cours Mirabeau), the café where everyone from Cézanne to Sartre drank and chatted. **Restaurant Gu et Fils** (3 rue Frédéric Mistral) serves delicious regional meals.

AVIGNON
pop 85,937

Avignon acquired its ramparts and its reputation as a city of art and culture during the 14th century, when Pope Clement V and his court, fleeing political turmoil in Rome, established themselves here. From 1309 to 1377 huge sums of money were invested in building and decorating the popes' palace. Even after the pontifical court returned to Rome amid bitter charges that Avignon had become a den of criminals and brothel-goers, the city remained an important cultural centre.

Today, Avignon maintains its tradition as a patron of the arts, most notably through its annual performing arts festival. The city also has interesting museums, including several across the Rhône in Villeneuve-lès-Avignon.

The world-famous Festival d'Avignon in July attracts hundreds of artists who put on some 300 performances of all sorts each day.

Orientation

The main avenue in the walled city runs northward from the train station to place de l'Horloge; it's called cours Jean Jaurès south of the tourist office and rue de la République north of it. Rue des Teinturiers in the southeastern segment of the walled city is dotted with cool cafés, galleries and shops. The island that runs down the middle of the Rhône between Avignon and Villeneuve-lès-Avignon is known as Île de la Barthelasse.

Information

The helpful **tourist office** (☎ 04 32 74 32 74, fax 04 90 82 95 03; e information@ot-avignon.fr; 41 cours Jean Jaurès; open 9am-6pm Mon-Sat, 10am-5pm Sun Apr-Oct, 9am-7pm Mon-Sat, 10am-5pm Sun July, 9am-6pm

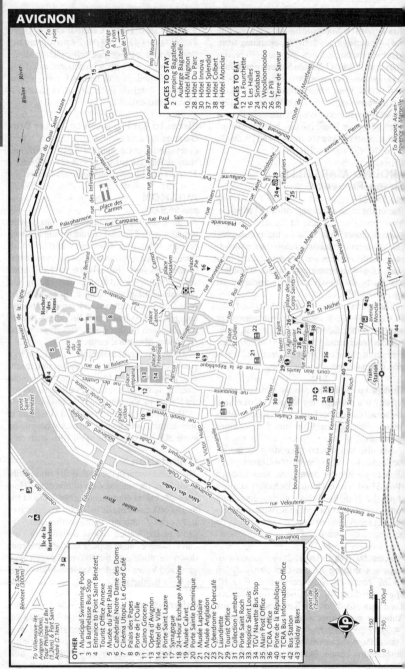

AVIGNON

PLACES TO STAY
2 Camping Bagatelle;
   Auberge Bagatelle
10 Hôtel Mignon
28 Hôtel Du Parc
30 Hôtel Innova
37 Hôtel Splendid
38 Hôtel Colbert
44 Hôtel Monclar

PLACES TO EAT
12 La Fourchette
16 Les Halles
24 Sindabad
25 Woolloomooloo
26 Le Pili
39 Terre de Saveur

OTHER
1 Municipal Swimming Pool
3 La Barthelasse Bus Stop
4 Entrance to Pont Saint Bénézet;
   Tourist Office Annexe
5 Musée du Petit Palais
6 Cathédrale Notre Dame des Doms
7 Cinéma Utopia; Le Grand Café
8 Palais des Papes
9 Porte de l'Oulle
11 Casino Grocery
13 Opéra d'Avignon
14 Hôtel de Ville
15 Porte Saint Lazare
17 Synagogue
18 24-Hour Exchange Machine
19 Musée Calvet
20 Porte Sainte Dominique
21 Musée Lapidaire
22 Musée Angladon
23 Cyberdrome Cybercafé
27 Laundrette
29 Tourist Office
31 Collection Lambert
32 Porte Saint Roch
33 Hospice Saint Louis
34 TGV Navette Bus Stop
35 Main Post Office
36 TCRA Office
40 Porte de la République
41 TCRA Bus Information Office
42 Bus Station
43 Holiday Bikes

Mon-Fri, 9am-5pm Sat, 10am-noon Sun Nov-Mar) is 300m north of the train station. There's an annexe at pont St Bénézet (open April to October).

The **main post office** (cours Président Kennedy) can be accessed via Porte de la République from the train station.

Cyberdrome (☎ 04 90 16 05 15; e cyber drome@wanadoo.fr; 68 rue Guillaume Puy; open 7am-1am) is a decent Internet café which charges €4.60 an hour.

Things to See & Do

Palais des Papes & Around Avignon's leading tourist attraction is the fortified Palace of the Popes (adult/concession €11/7.50 including admission to pont St Bénézet; open 9am-7pm daily Apr-June, 9am-8pm July-Sept, 9.30am-5.45pm Oct-Mar), built during the 14th century. The seemingly endless halls, chapels, corridors and staircases were once sumptuously decorated, but these days they are nearly empty except for a few damaged frescoes.

At the far northern end of place du Palais, the **Musée du Petit Palais** (adult/concession €4.50/2.50; open 9.30am-1pm & 2pm-5.30pm Wed-Mon Oct-May, 10am-1pm & 2pm-6pm Wed-Mon June-Sept) houses an outstanding collection of 13th- to 16th-century Italian religious paintings. Just up the hill there is **Rocher des Doms**, a park offering great views of the Rhône, the pont St Bénézet and Villeneuve-lès-Avignon.

Pont St Bénézet Originally built in the 12th century to link Avignon and Villeneuve-lès-Avignon, this is the **'pont d'Avignon'** (same hours as Palais des Papes) mentioned in the French nursery rhyme. Once 900m long, the bridge was repaired and rebuilt several times until all but four of its 22 spans were washed away in the 17th century.

Museums Housed in an 18th-century mansion, the **Musée Calvet** (☎ 04 90 86 33 84; 65 rue Joseph Vernet; adult/concession €5/3; open Wed-Mon) has a collection of ancient Egyptian, Greek and Roman artefacts as well as paintings from the 16th to 20th centuries. Its annexe, the **Musée Lapidaire** (27 rue de la République; adult/concession €5/3; open Wed-Mon) houses sculpture and statuary from the Gallo-Roman, Romanesque and Gothic periods.

The **Collection Lambert** (☎ 04 90 16 56 20; 5 rue Violette; adult/concession €5/4; open Tues-Sun) is a new contemporary art museum displaying the astonishing collection of art dealer Yvon Lambert.

The **Musée Angladon** (☎ 04 90 82 29 03; 5 rue Laboureur; adult/concession €5/3; open 1pm-6pm Wed-Sun, also Tues mid-June–mid-Oct) was once a private home; now it shows 19th- and 20th-century paintings to the public. It's the only place in the region where you can see a Van Gogh painting.

Villeneuve-lès-Avignon Avignon's picturesque sister city can be reached by foot or bus No 10 from the main post office. A pass for the following attractions costs €6.86.

The **Chartreuse du Val de Bénédiction** (☎ 04 90 15 24 24; 60 rue de la République; adult/concession €5.50/3.50) was once the largest and most important Carthusian monastery in France. The **Musée Pierre de Luxembourg** (☎ 04 90 27 49 66; 3 rue de la République; adult/concession €3/1.90; open Tues-Sun, closed Feb) has a fine collection of religious paintings. The **Tour Philippe le Bel** (☎ 04 32 70 08 57; admission €1.60/0.90), a defensive tower built in the 14th century at what was then the northwestern end of pont St Bénézet, has superb views of Avignon's walled city, the river and the surrounding countryside. Another Provençal panorama can be enjoyed from the 14th-century **Fort St André** (☎ 04 90 25 45 35; adult/concession €4/2.50).

Special Events

The **Festival d'Avignon** (☎ 04 90 14 14 60, fax 04 90 27 66 83; w www.festival-avignon.com) is held every year during the last three weeks of July. Tickets can be reserved from mid-June onwards.

Places to Stay

Camping Three-star **Camping Bagatelle** (☎ 04 90 86 30 39, fax 04 90 27 16 23; Île de la Barthelasse; bus No 10 from main post office to Barthelasse stop; sites per adult/tent €3.78/2.59; reception open 8am-9pm year-round) is an attractive, shaded camping ground just north of pont Édouard Daladier, 850m from the walled city.

Hostels The 210-bed **Auberge Bagatelle** (☎ 04 90 86 30 39, fax 04 90 27 16 23; Île

FRANCE

de la Barthelasse; dorm beds €10.17) is part of a large, park-like area that includes Camping Bagatelle. See the Camping section for bus directions.

Hotels – Within the Walls There are three hotels all close to each other on the same street. **Hôtel Du Parc** *(☎ 04 90 82 71 55, fax 04 90 85 64 86; e hotelsurparc@aol.com; 18 rue Agricol Perdiguier; singles/doubles without shower €29/34, with shower €36/42)* is an option.

Hôtel Splendid *(☎ 04 90 86 14 46, fax 04 90 85 38 55; e contacthotel@infonie.fr; 17 rue Agricol Perdiguier; singles/doubles with shower €34/43, with shower & toilet €36/46)* is a friendly place.

Two-star **Hôtel Colbert** *(☎ 04 90 86 20 20, fax 04 90 85 97 00; e colberthotel@wanadoo.fr; 7 rue Agricol Perdiguier; singles with shower €42, doubles/triples with shower & toilet €52/79)* is the third in the trio.

The always busy **Hôtel Innova** *(☎ 04 90 82 54 10, fax 04 90 82 52 39; e hotel.innova@wanadoo.fr; 100 rue Joseph Vernet; rooms €23-41)* provides comfortable, soundproofed rooms.

Hôtel Mignon *(☎ 04 90 82 17 30, fax 04 90 85 78 46; e hotel.mignon@wanadoo.fr; 12 rue Joseph Vernet; singles/doubles with shower & toilet €37/43)* has spotless rooms with English-language cable TV and decent breakfasts (€4).

Hotels – Outside the Walls The noisy, family-run **Hôtel Monclar** *(☎ 04 90 86 20 14, fax 04 90 85 94 94; e hmonclar84@aol.com; 13 ave Monclar; rooms for 1 or 2 people with shower & toilet from €45, triples/quads from €45/55)* is just across the tracks from the train station. The hotel has its own car park (€4.50) and a pretty back garden.

Places to Eat
For self-catering try **Les Halles food market** *(place Pie; open 7am-1pm Tues-Sun)*.

Le Grand Café *(☎ 04 90 86 86 77; la Manutention, 4 rue des Escaliers Ste Anne; mains around €15; open Tues-Sat)* in the Cinéma Utopia complex is a sophisticated place for a Provençal lunch, dinner or drink.

La Fourchette *(☎ 04 90 85 20 93; 17 rue Racine; menus €21-26; open Mon-Fri)* is a homy Michelin-recommended place. Try the salmon with saffron and lentil salad.

On the other side of town, in a groovy little strip, **Woolloomooloo** *(16 bis rue des Teinturiers; lunch menu €11; open Tues-Sat)* draws a young crowd with its international menu.

Terre de Saveur *(☎ 04 90 86 68 72; 1 rue St Michel; vegetarian lunch menu €13, open 11.30am-2.30pm Tues-Sat, 7pm-9.30pm Fri & Sat)*, just off place des Corps Saints, has vegetarian dishes like *tortilla da quinoa*.

Nearby, **Le Pili** *(☎ 04 90 27 39 53; 34-36 place des Corps Saints; meals about €8)* has good wood-fired pizza and steaks.

Entertainment
Cinéma Utopia *(☎ 04 90 82 65 36; 4 rue des Escaliers Ste Anne; tickets €3-5)* is a student entertainment/cultural centre with a jazz club, café and four cinemas screening nondubbed films. There's an annexe at 5 Rue Figuiere. The tourist office has programmes.

Getting There & Away
Bus The bus station *(☎ 04 90 82 07 35; 5 ave Monclar)* is down the ramp to the right as you exit the train station. The destinations include Aix-en-Provence (€12, 1¼ hours), Arles (€7.80, one hour), Nice (€27), and Marseille (€15.20, 2½ hours). Tickets are sold on the buses.

Train Across blvd St Roch from Porte de la République is the **train station** *(Gare Avignon Centre; ☎ 0893 35 35 35)*. There are frequent trains to Arles (€7, 20 minutes), Nîmes (€35.40, three hours), Nîmes (€7.10, 35 minutes) and Paris (€63.70, three hours via TGV). Most TGV services leave from **Gare Avignon TGV** *(Quartier de Courtine)*, accessible by frequent shuttle bus from outside the main post office. The tourist office has timetables.

Getting Around
TCRA municipal buses operate 7am to about 7.40pm. Tickets cost €1 or €7.80 for a carnet of 10 tickets; they're available from drivers, tabacs and the **TCRA office** *(☎ 04 32 74 18 32; ave de Latre de Tassigny)*.

Holiday Bikes *(☎ 04 90 27 92 61, fax 04 90 95 66 41; e motovelo@provencebike.com; 52 blvd St Roch; open 9am-6.30pm daily)* rents road bikes (€14 per day) and scooters (from €30).

AROUND AVIGNON
Arles
pop 50,467

Arles began its ascent to prosperity in 49 BC when Julius Caesar, to whom the city had given its support, sacked Marseille, which had backed the Roman general Pompey. It soon became a major trading centre and by the late 1st century AD, needed a 20,000-seat amphitheatre and a 12,000-seat theatre. Now known as the **Arènes** and the **Théâtre Antique** respectively, they are still used to stage bullfights and cultural events.

Arles is also known for its **Église St Trophime** and **Cloître St Trophime**. Significant parts of both date from the 12th century and are in the Romanesque style. But the city is probably best known as the place where Van Gogh painted some of his most famous works, including *The Sunflowers*. The **tourist office** (☎ 04 90 18 41 20; e ot-arles@visitprovence .com; esplanade des Lices) can help with information.

There are bus services to Marseille (€14.60, 2½ hours), Aix-en-Provence (€11.40, 1¾ hours) and Avignon (€6, 1½ hours, including a shuttle that connects with the TGV to Lyon and Paris).

Côte d'Azur

The Côte d'Azur, which includes the French Riviera, stretches along France's Mediterranean coast from Toulon to the Italian border. Many of the towns here – budget-busting St Tropez, Cannes, Antibes, Nice and Monaco – have become world-famous through the recreational activities of the tanned and idle rich. The reality is less glamorous, but the Côte d'Azur still has a great deal to attract visitors: sunshine, 40km of beaches, all sorts of cultural activities and, sometimes, even a bit of glitter.

Unless you're camping or hostelling, your best bet is to stay in Nice, which has a generous supply of cheap hotels, and make day trips to other places. Note that theft from backpacks, pockets, cars and even laundrettes is a serious problem along the Côte d'Azur, especially at train and bus stations.

NICE
pop 343,123

Known as the capital of the Riviera, the fashionable yet relaxed city of Nice makes a great base from which to explore the entire Côte d'Azur. The city, which did not become part of France until 1860, has plenty of relatively cheap accommodation and is only a short train or bus ride from the rest of the Riviera. Nice's beach may be nothing to write home about, but the city has some fine museums.

Orientation

Ave Jean Médecin runs from near the train station to place Masséna. Vieux Nice is the area delineated by the quai des États-Unis, blvd Jean Jaurès and the 92m hill known as Le Château. The neighbourhood of Cimiez, home to several very good museums, is north of the town centre.

Information

The **main tourist office** (☎ 04 93 87 07 07, fax 04 93 16 85 16; e info@nicetourism .com; open 8am-7pm Mon-Sat, 9am-6pm Sun; 9am-8pm July-Sept) is at the train station. There's an **annexe** (☎ 04 92 14 48 00; 5 promenade des Anglais; open 9am-6pm Mon-Sat).

The **main post office** (23 ave Thiers) is one block from the train station.

Opposite the train station, **Le Change** (☎ 04 93 88 56 80; 17 ave Thiers; open 7.30am-9pm), to the right as you exit the terminal, has decent rates.

American Express (☎ 04 93 16 53 53; 11 promenade des Anglais; open Mon-Sat) also has currency exchange.

Access the Internet for €5 an hour at **Société Sencom** (☎ 04 97 03 23 10; cnr Paganini & Rue Belgique; open 10am-8pm daily). **Master Home** (☎ 04 93 80 33 82; 11 rue de la Préfecture), a pub in the old town, charges €6 an hour.

Things to See

An excellent-value museum pass (€8/25 for one/seven days), available at tourist offices and participating museums, provides free admission to some 60 Côte d'Azur museums. There's a cheaper one for Nice's museums. Unless otherwise noted, the following museums are open Wednesday to Monday from around 10am to 5pm or 6pm (sometimes with a break for lunch in the off season), and entry is around €4/2 per adult/concession.

The **Musée d'Art Moderne et d'Art Contemporain** (Museum of Modern and Contemporary Art; ave St Jean Baptiste; bus Nos 3, 5, 7, 16 & 17) specialises in conceptual works by

NICE

PLACES TO STAY
6 Hôtel Baccarat
7 Backpackers Chez
   Patrick; Le Faubourg
   Montmartre
10 Hôtel du Piemont
11 Hôtel Belle Meunière
15 Hôtel Les Orangers
18 Le Petit Louvre
25 Hôtel Le Grimaldi
29 Hôtel Négresco;
   Chantecler Restaurant
31 Hôtel Les Mimosas
38 Hôtel Felix
39 Hôtel Little Masséna
45 Boulangerie
48 Hôtel au Picardie

PLACES TO EAT
5 Mondial Buffet
8 Restaurant Le Toscan
53 Nissa Socca
54 Restaurant du Gésu
56 Fruit & Vegetable Market

OTHER
1 Fruit & Vegetable
   Market
2 Musée Chagall
3 Russian Orthodox
   Cathedral of St
   Nicholas
4 Main Tourist Office
9 Société Sencom
   Internet Café
12 Holiday Bikes
13 Le Change
14 Main Post Office
16 Église Notre Dame
17 UK Consulate
19 Post Office
20 Monoprix
   Supermarket
21 Police Headquarters
22 Musée d'Art Moderne
   et d'Art Contemporain
23 Théâtre de Nice
24 24-Hour Currency
   Exchange Machine
26 Airport Buses
27 Public Showers &
   Toilets
28 Airport Buses
30 Laundrette
32 Anglican Church
33 English-American
   Library
34 Post Office Branch
35 American Express
36 Tourist Office Annexe
37 US Consulate
40 Opéra de Nice
41 Flower Market
42 Post Office Branch
43 Palais de Justice
44 Chez Wayne's;
   Master Home
46 Station Centrale
   Terminus
47 Intercity Bus Station
49 William's Pub
50 Jonathan's Live
   Music Pub
51 Johnny's Wine Bar
52 Cathédrale Sainte
   Réparate
55 Église Saint Jacques
   le Majeur
57 Tour Bellanda & Lift
58 Dizzy Club
59 Corsica Ferries
   Ticket Office
60 Buses to City Centre
61 Ferry Terminal;
   SNCM Office

blvd Joseph Garnier — place Général de Gaulle — rue Raiberti
avenue
ave Villermont
ave Raym
To blvd Auguste Reynaud & autoroute A8
Gare du Sud
(for Digne-les-Bains)
rue Clément Roassal
ave Mirabeau
rue Vernier
ave Malaussena
rue Marceau
rue Trachel
blvd Gambetta
blvd du Parc Imperial
ave Nicholas II
Gare Nice Ville
r de Belgique
rue d'Alsace - Lorraine
blvd du Tzaréwich
ave Thiers
Gounod
ave Durante
Paganini
rue d'Angleterre
ave d'Italie
ave Jean Méde
rue de Châteauneuf
ave Berlioz
ave Auber
ave Georges Clemenceau
rue de Russie
rue F Passy
rue Guigla
rue Rossini
ave
rue de
rue Verdi
rue Caffarelli
ave des Fleurs
blvd Victor Hugo
ave Maccarani
ave Alphonse Karr
ave de la Liberté
ave des Orangers
rue du Maréchal Joffre
blvd Gambetta
rue Bottero
blvd François Crosso
rue Dante
rue de Rivoli
rue de la Buffa
rue Meyerbeer
rue Dalpozzo
rue du Congrès
place Grimaldi
rue de la Liberté
Masséna
place Mager
ave de Suède
rue de France
rue Renoir
avenue des Baumettes
rue de France
promenade des Anglais
Baie des Anges (Bay of Angels)
To Cannes
To Musée d'Art Naïf (1.5km) & Airport (5km)
auto route Urbaine Sud

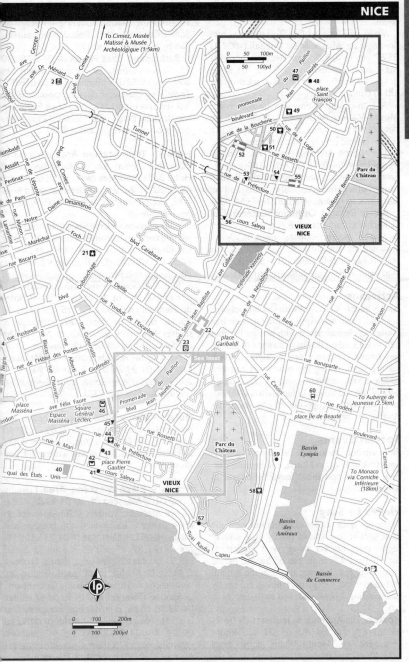

To Cimiez, Musée
Matisse & Musée
Archéologique (1.5km)

0   50   100m
0   50   100yd

47
48
place
Saint
François

promenade

boulevard

rue de la Boucherie

49

50

rue de la Loge

52

51

rue Rossetti

53
54
55

rue de la Préfecture

Parc du
Château

56   cours Saleya

VIEUX
NICE

ave George V

ave Dr Menard

2

blvd de Cimiez

Tunnel

blvd de Cimiez

Cambou

aribaldi

Assalit

Pertinax

de Paris

rue de Lépante

Notre Dame Desambrois

Maréchal Foch

rue Biscarra

blvd Carabacel

21

rue Delille

Dubouchage

rue Tonduti de l'Escarène

blvd

ave Saint Jean Baptiste

ave Galliéni

esplanade Kennedy

ave de la République

rue Barla

22

23

place
Garibaldi

rue Augusta Gal

rue Arson

Parc du
Château

rue Bonaparte

rue Cassini

rue de l'Hôtel des Postes

rue Pastorelli

rue Blacas

rue Gubernatis

rue Alberti

rue Gioffredo

rue Chauvain

place
Masséna

ave Félix Faure

Espace
Masséna

Square
Général
Leclerc

46

45

rue   44

43

42

41

place Pierre
Gautier

cours Saleya

Promenade

blvd Jean Jaurès

du Paillon

See Inset

rue Rossetti

rue de la Préfecture

VIEUX
NICE

60

To Auberge de
Jeunesse (2.5km)

rue Fodéré

place Île de Beauté

Boulevard

Bassin
Lympia

To Monaco
via Corniche
Inférieure
(18km)

59

58

57

Quai Rauba Capeu

Bassin
des
Amiraux

Bassin
du Commerce

61

rue A Mari

quai des États - Unis

40

0   100   200m
0   100   200yd

artists such as Arman and Nice-born Yves Klein.

Vivid paintings of Old Testament scenes dominate the **Musée Marc Chagall** (☎ 04 93 53 87 20; 16 ave Docteur Ménard, opposite No 4; adult/concession €5.50/4). Ask at the ticket counter for your free bus ticket up the hill to Cimiez.

A 17th-century Genoese villa houses the **Musée Matisse** (☎ 04 93 81 08 08; 164 ave des Arènes de Cimiez) in Cimiez. Bus No 15 is convenient; get off at the Arènes stop.

The **Musée Archéologique** (Archaeology Museum; ☎ 04 93 81 59 57; 160 ave des Arènes de Cimiez) and nearby **Gallo-Roman ruins** (which include public baths and an amphitheatre) are next to the Musée Matisse.

Nice's **Russian Orthodox Cathedral of St Nicholas** (admission €2; open Mon-Sat, & Sun afternoon, closed noon-2.30pm), crowned by six onion-shaped domes, was built between 1903 and 1912. Shorts, short skirts and sleeveless shirts are forbidden.

Activities

Nice's **beach** is covered with smooth pebbles, not sand. From mid-April to mid-October, free public beaches alternate with private beaches (€8 to €13 a day) that have all sorts of amenities (mattresses, showers, changing rooms, security etc). Along the beach you can hire paddle boats, sailboards and jet skis, and go parasailing and water-skiing. Showers (€1.80) and toilets (€0.35) opposite 50 promenade des Anglais are open to the public .

Special Events

Parties in Nice include the Festin des Cougourdons (gourd feast) in March, a jiving Jazz Festival in July and the Vineyard Festival in September.

Places to Stay

There are quite a few cheap hotels near the train station and lots of places in a slightly higher price bracket along rue d'Angleterre, rue d'Alsace-Lorraine, rue de Suisse, rue de Russie and rue Durante, also near the station. In summer the inexpensive places fill up in late morning – book your bed by 10am.

Hostels The **Auberge de Jeunesse** (☎ 04 93 89 23 64, fax 04 92 04 03 10; Route Forestière de Mont Alban; dorm beds €13.40; curfew midnight) is 4km east of the

train. It's often full – call ahead. Take bus No 14 from the Station Centrale terminus on Square Général Leclerc, linked to the train station by bus Nos 15 and 17.

Backpackers Chez Patrick (☎ 04 93 80 30 72; 32 rue Pertinax; e chezpatrick@viola.fr; dorm beds €18) is well-managed and friendly. There's no curfew or daytime closure. If it's full, ask downstairs at restaurant **Le Faubourg Montmartre** (☎ 04 93 62 55 03; 32 rue Pertinax; rooms per person about €15).

Hotels – Train Station Area For a cruisy place that attracts lots of young people try **Hôtel Belle Meunière** (☎ 04 93 88 66 15, fax 04 93 82 51 76; 21 ave Durante; dorm beds €13, doubles/triples with bath €79/94.50; open Feb-Nov).

Although the welcome is patchy, there are some excellent balcony rooms at the **Hôtel Les Orangers** (☎ 04 93 87 51 41, fax 04 93 82 57 82; 10bis ave Durante; dorm beds €14, doubles from €34).

Rue d'Alsace-Lorraine is dotted with two-star hotels. One of the cheapest is the **Hôtel du Piemont** (☎ 04 93 88 25 15, fax 04 93 16 15 18; singles/doubles with washbasin & shower from €24.50/28.50), at No 19. The old-fashioned rooms have kitchenettes.

Also in this neighbourhood is **Hôtel Baccarat** (☎ 04 93 88 35 73, fax 04 93 16 14 25; 39 Rue d'Angleterre; dorm beds €14, singles/doubles €29/36).

Hotels – Vieux Nice Opposite the bus station, **Hôtel au Picardie** (☎ 04 93 85 75 51; 10 blvd Jean Jaurès; singles/doubles from €19/24) also has pricier rooms with toilet and shower.

Hotels – Place Masséna Area Friendly **Hôtel Little Masséna** (☎/fax 04 93 87 72 34; 22 rue Masséna; doubles €26-42; reception open to 8pm) has rooms with hotplate and fridge. **Hôtel Les Mimosas** (☎ 04 93 88 05 59, fax 04 93 87 15 65; 26 rue de la Buffa; singles/doubles/triples with shared facilities €30.50/37/48) has clean, good-sized rooms with air-con and a cute sheep dog for company.

Spotless **Hôtel Felix** (☎ 04 93 88 67 73, fax 04 93 16 15 78; rue Masséna; doubles €75) is hard to beat. **Hôtel Le Grimaldi** (☎ 04 93 16 00 24, fax 04 93 87 00 24; e zedde@le -grimaldi.com; 15 Rue Grimaldi; singles/ doubles €80/90) has stylish, cheery rooms.

Hotels – Elsewhere in Town Between the train station and the beach is colourful **Le Petit Louvre** (☎ 04 93 80 15 54, fax 04 93 62 45 08; e petitlouvre@aol.com; 10 rue Emma Tiranty; singles/doubles with shower & toilet €34/43).

The top rooms in town are at *belle epoque* **Hôtel Négresco** (☎ 04 93 16 64 00, fax 04 93 88 35 68; e direction@hotel-negresco.com; 37 promenade des Anglais; rooms without/ with seaview from €213/297).

Places to Eat

In Vieux Nice, there's a **fruit and vegetable market** (cours Saleya; open 6am-5.30pm Tues-Sat, & Sun morning) in front of the préfecture. The no-name **boulangerie** at the south end of rue du Marché is the best place for pizza slices and *michettes* (bread stuffed with cheese, olives, and anchovies).

Near the train station, **Mondial Buffet** (☎ 04 93 16 15 51; 7 ave Thiers) has cheap noodles and rice dishes. In the same vicinity, **Restaurant Le Toscan** (1 rue de Belgique; open Tues-Sat), a family-run Italian place, has large portions of home-made ravioli.

Nearby, **Le Faubourg Montmartre** (☎ 04 93 62 55 03; 32 rue Pertinax; menu €11), beneath the Backpackers Hotel, is frequently crowded. The house speciality is bouillabaisse (€28 for two).

In the old city, **Nissa Socca** (5 rue Ste Reparate; menu €13) is a perennial favourite. Its Niçois specialities include *socca* (chickpea pancakes), *farcis* (stuffed vegetables) and ratatouille.

Restaurant du Gésu (1 place du Jésus; pasta about €7; no credit cards) is local, cheap and loud.

Chantecler (lunch/dinner menus from €40/90) is the much-fêted restaurant at Hôtel Négresco (see Places to Stay earlier).

Entertainment

William's Pub (4 rue Centrale; open Mon-Sat) has live music starting at around 9pm. There's pool, darts and chess in the basement. **Jonathan's Live Music Pub** (1 rue de la Loge) has live music every night in summer. **Chez Wayne's** (☎ 04 93 13 46 99; 15 rue de la Préfecture) is an expat pub with live bands on Friday and Saturday and karaoke on Sunday. Happy hour is 6pm to 9pm.

Local students and backpackers come for the live music and cheap pasta (€7.95) at

Johnny's Wine Bar (1 Rue Rossetti; open Mon-Sat), just east of Cathédrale Ste Réparate.

Down at the port there's **Dizzy Club** (☎ 06 12 16 78 81; 26 quai Lunel; open from 11.30pm Wed-Sun) with an eclectic roster of drum 'n' bass, breakbeat and pure house nights.

Getting There & Away

Air Nice's **airport** (☎ 04 93 21 30 30) is 6km west of the city centre. Bus No 98 runs along the beach between the airport and the city centre (€3.50).

Bus The intercity bus station, opposite 10 blvd Jean Jaurès, is served by around two dozen bus companies. There are slow but frequent services daily until about 7.30pm to Cannes (€5.70, 1½ hours), Antibes (€4.50, 1¼ hours), Monaco (€3.70 return, 45 minutes), and Menton (€4.90 return, 1¼ hours).

Train Nice's main train station, Gare Nice Ville, is 1.2km north of the beach on ave Thiers. There are fast, frequent services (up to 40 daily trains) to points all along the coast, including Monaco (€2.90, 20 minutes), Cannes (€5, 40 minutes) and Marseille (€25.10, 2¾ hours).

About six daily TGVs link Nice with Paris' Gare de Lyon (€80 to €90, six hours; discounts available). SNCF trains go to Spain as well.

Trains for Digne-les-Bains (€17, 3¼ hours) make the scenic trip five times daily from Nice's **Gare du Sud** (☎ 04 93 82 10 17; 4 bis rue Alfred Binet).

Getting Around

Local buses, run by Sunbus, cost €1.30/4 for a single ticket/daily pass (available on the bus). The **Sunbus information office** (☎ 04 93 16 52 10; ave Félix Faure) is at the Station Centrale. From the train station to Vieux Nice and the bus station, take bus No 2, 5 or 17. Bus No 12 links the train station with the beach. Bus Nos 9 and 10 go to the port.

Holiday Bikes (☎ 04 93 16 01 62; 34 ave Auber) rents bicycles (€12 per day) and motor scooters (from €30 per day).

CANNES
pop 67,406
The harbour, the bay, Le Suquet hill, the beachside promenade, and the sun-worshippers

on the beach provide more than enough natural beauty to make Cannes worth at least a day trip. It's also fun watching the rich drop their money with such fashionable nonchalance.

Cannes is renowned for its many festivals, the most famous being the International Film Festival during two weeks in mid-May. Visitors come to Cannes all year long, but the main tourist season runs from May to October.

Orientation

From the train station, follow rue Jean Jaurès west and turn left onto rue Vénizélos, which runs west into the heart of the Vieux Port. Place Bernard Cornut Gentille (formerly place de l'Hôtel de Ville), where the bus station is located, is on the northwestern edge of the Vieux Port. Cannes' most famous promenade, the magnificent blvd de la Croisette, begins at the Palais des Festivals and continues eastward around the Baie de Cannes to Pointe de la Croisette.

Information

The **main tourist office** (☎ 04 93 39 24 53, fax 04 92 99 84 23; e semoftou@palais-fes tivals-cannes.fr; open 9am-7pm Mon-Fri, 10am-6pm Sat & Sun Sept-June, 9am-8pm July & Aug) is on the ground floor of the **Palais des Festivals**. There's an **annexe** (☎ 04 93 99 19 77; open Mon-Fri) at the train station; turn left as you exit the station and walk up the stairs next to Buffet de la Gare.

The main **post office** (22 rue Bivouac Napoléon) is not far from the Palais des Festivals. There are Internet terminals for €4/7 for 30 minutes/one hour at **Mondego Café** (☎ 04 93 68 19 21; 15 square Merimée), opposite Palais des Festivals.

Things to See & Do

Vieux Port Some of the largest yachts you'll ever see are likely to be sitting in the Vieux Port, a fishing port now given over to pleasure craft. The streets around the old port are particularly pleasant on a summer's evening, when the many cafés and restaurants light up the area.

The hill just west of the Vieux Port, **Le Suquet**, affords magnificent views of Cannes. The **Musée de la Castre** (☎ 04 93 38 55 26; Le Suquet; adult/student €3/free; open 10am-1pm & 2pm-5pm Tues-Sun Dec-Oct), housed in a chateau atop Le Suquet, has Mediterranean and Middle Eastern antiquities

as well as objects of ethnographic interest from all over the world.

Beaches Each of the fancy hotels that line blvd de la Croisette has its own private section of the beach. You can pay to roast alongside the hotel guests; a sunlounge at the Hotel Carlton beach starts at €21.

There's a small strip of public sand near the Palais des Festivals. Other free public beaches – the **Plages du Midi** and **Plages de la Bocca** – stretch several kilometres westward from the old port.

Îles de Lérins The eucalyptus and the pine-covered **Île Ste Marguerite**, where the man in the iron mask (made famous in the novel by Alexandre Dumas) was held captive during the late 17th century, is a little more than 1km from the mainland. The island is crisscrossed by many trails and paths.

The smaller **Île St Honorat** is home to Cistercian monks who welcome visitors to their monastery, the ruins of a cloister and the small chapels dotted around the island. Bring a picnic to eat on the rocky shores of this tiny island.

Compagnie Maritime Cannoise (CMC; ☎ 04 93 38 66 33) is among several companies running ferries to Île Ste Marguerite (€8 return, 15 minutes). The ticket offices are at the Vieux Port near the Palais des Festivals. Ferries to St Honorat are less common but you'll find one at the same port. Many companies offer day trips to Monaco and St Tropez (about €27).

Places to Stay

Tariffs can be up to 50% higher in July and August – when you'll be lucky to find a room at any price – than in winter. Hotels are booked up to a year in advance for the film festival.

Hostels The pleasant **Le Chalit** (☎/fax 04 93 99 22 11; e le_chalit@libertysurf.fr; 27 ave du Maréchal Galliéni; dorm beds €20; open year-round no curfew, reception closed 10.30am-5pm) is a five-minute walk northwest of the station.

Hotels The extremely friendly **Hôtel Florella** (☎ 04 93 38 48 11, fax 04 93 99 22 15; e reservations@hotelflorella.com; 55 blvd de la République; singles/doubles/triples/quads

CANNES

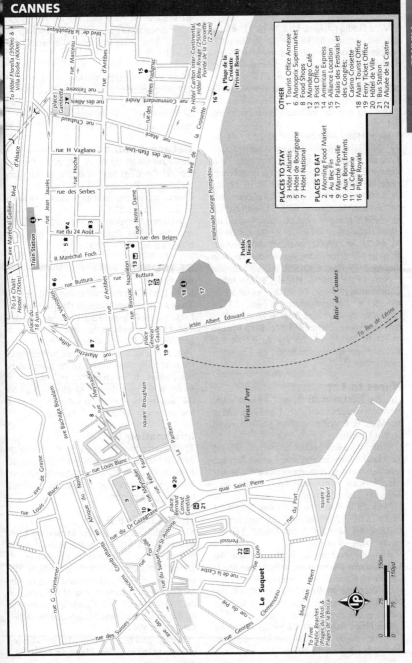

OTHER
1 Tourist Office Annexe
6 Monoprix Supermarket
8 Food Shops
12 Mondego Café
13 Post Office
14 American Express
15 Alliance Location
17 Palais des Festivals et des Congrès; Casino Croisette
18 Main Tourist Office
19 Ferry Ticket Office
20 Bus Station
21 Hôtel de Ville
22 Musée de la Castre

PLACES TO STAY
3 Hôtel Atlantis
5 Hôtel de Bourgogne
7 Hôtel National

PLACES TO EAT
4 Morning Food Market
9 Au Bec Fin
10 Marché Forville
11 Aux Bons Enfants
11 La Crêperie
16 Plage Royale

with shower & toilet €30/35/45/60) is run by an Irish couple.

Villa Elodie *(☎/fax 04 93 39 39 91; e villa elodie@wanadoo.fr; 35 ave de Vallauris; 2-person studio/8-person apartment €39/80)* is about 400m northeast of the train station. There's a two-night minimum and you need to call ahead because there's no reception. To get there, follow blvd de la République for 300m and ave de Vallauris runs off to the right.

Large **Hôtel Atlantis** *(☎ 04 93 39 18 72, fax 04 93 68 37 65; e hotel.atlantis@wanadoo.fr; 4 rue du 24 Août; singles/doubles with TV & shower €55/65)* has access to a private beach. **Hôtel de Bourgogne** *(☎ 04 93 38 36 73, fax 04 92 99 28 41; 11 rue du 24 Août; singles/ doubles with washbasin €24/31, with bath & toilet €45)* is another option, or you could try **Hôtel National** *(☎ 04 93 39 91 92, fax 04 92 98 44 06; e hotelnationalcannes@wanadoo .fr; 8 rue Maréchal Joffre; singles/doubles with shower & TV from €40/55)*.

Next to the famous **Hôtel Carlton Inter-Continental** *(☎ 04 93 06 40 06, fax 04 93 06 40 25; e cannes@interconti.com; 58 La Croisette; rooms/suites from €370/1310)* is the much more affordable **Hôtel Bleu Rivage** *(☎ 04 93 94 24 25, fax 04 93 43 74 92; e bleurivage@wanadoo.fr; 61 La Croisette; rooms from €175)*.

Places to Eat
Morning **food markets** *(open Tues-Sun, daily in summer)* are held on place Gambetta, and at the **Marché Forville** north of place Bernard Cornut Gentille.

There are a few budget restaurants around the Marché Forville and many small (but not necessarily cheap) restaurants along rue St Antoine, which runs northwest from place Bernard Cornut Gentille.

Near the train station is **Au Bec Fin** *(☎ 04 93 38 35 86; 12 rue du 24 Août; menus €18 & 22; open Mon-Fri & Sat lunch)*. Try the lovely *soupe au pistou*.

Another good choice is the popular **Au Bons Enfants** *(80 rue Meynadier; open Mon-Sat; menu €15.50)* with regional dishes.

La Crêperie *(☎ 04 92 99 00 00; 66 rue Meynadier; menu €8.85; open Mon-Sat)* has dozens of buckwheat crepe options.

The **Plage Royale** *(☎ 04 93 38 22 00; La Croisette; menu €22.50)* provides seafood-skewed lunches on the beach.

Getting There & Away
Bus Buses to Nice (€5.10, 1½ hours) and other destinations, most operated by Rapides Côte d'Azur, leave from place Bernard Cornut Gentille.

Train From the **train station** *(☎ 0836 35 35 39)* there are regular services to Nice (€5, 40 minutes), Marseille (€20.90, two hours) and St Raphaël (€5.30, 20 minutes), where you can pick up a bus to St Tropez.

Getting Around
Bus Azur *(☎ 04 93 45 20 08; place Bernard Cornut Gentille)* has an office in the same building as Rapides Côte d'Azur. It serves Cannes and destinations up to 7km from town. Tickets cost €1.22.

Alliance Location *(☎ 04 93 38 62 62; 19 rue des Frères Pradignac)* rents mountain bikes/scooters for €15/26 a day.

ST TROPEZ
pop 19,858
Since 1956 when the small fishing village of St Tropez found fame through the patronage of French actor Brigitte Bardot and her acolytes, things have never been the same. The once iso-lated fishing village now draws in thousands of visitors a year. If you can, come by boat since the road traffic into and out of the town can be horrendous. If watching the rich dining on yachts is not your flute of Moët then head for the backstreets where men still play pétanque and you might spy a famous face or two.

Information
The **tourist office** *(☎ 04 94 97 45 21, fax 04 94 97 82 66; e tourisme@saint-tropez.st; quai Jean Jaurès; open 9.30am-8.30pm July & Aug, hours vary outside high season)* has informa-tion and guided tours.

Things to See & Do
You might care to visit the **Musée de l'An-nonciade** *(place Grammont)*, a disused chapel in the Old Port containing an impressive col-lection of modern art, including works by Ma-tisse, Bonnard, Dufy, Derain and Rouault. The **Musée Naval** in the dungeon of the citadel at the end of Montée de la Citadelle has displays on the town's maritime history and the Allied landings in 1944.

For a decent beach you need to get 4km out of town to the excellent **Plage de Tahiti**.

Places to Stay & Eat

Accommodation isn't cheap, even if you camp. St Tropez's cheapest hotel is the dingy **Hôtel La Méditerranée** (☎ 04 94 97 00 44, fax 04 94 97 47 83; 21 blvd Louis Blanc; singles/doubles €63/99). **Hôtel Le Baron** (☎ 04 94 97 06 57, fax 04 94 97 58 72; e contact@hotel-le-baron.com; 23 rue de l'Aïoli; singles/doubles with bath €69/100) is more classy.

Extremely tasteful is **Café Sud** (☎ 04 94 97 71 72; 12 rue Étienne Berny; mains around €22), tucked down a narrow street off places des Lices. Tables are outside in a star-topped courtyard. Close by, **Bistrot des Lices** (☎ 04 94 55 82 82; 3 places des Lices; mains €18-30) serves traditional Provençal cuisine, including wonderful ratatouille.

Getting There & Away

The **bus station** (ave Général de Gaulle) is on the southwestern edge of town on the main road out of town. Frequent taxi boats run to Port Grimaud nearby and excursion boats run regularly to and from St Maxime and St Raphaël.

MENTON
pop 28,792

Reputed to be the warmest spot on the Côte d'Azur, Menton is encircled by mountains. The town is renowned for lemons and holds a two-week Fête du Citron (Lemon Festival) each year between mid-February and early March. The helpful **tourist office** (☎ 04 92 41 76 76; 8 ave Boyer) is in the Palais de l'Europe.

It's pleasant to wander around the narrow, winding streets of the Vieille Ville (old town) and up to the cypress-shaded **Cimetière du Vieux Château**, with the graves of English, Irish, North Americans, New Zealanders and others who died here during the 19th century. The view alone is worth the climb.

Église St Michel

The grandest baroque church in this part of France sits perched in the centre of the Vieille Ville. The **beach** along the promenade du Soleil is public and, like Nice's, carpeted with smooth pebbles. Better private beaches are found east of the old city in the port area, the main one being **Plage des Sablettes**.

Places to Stay

Camping St Michel (☎ 04 93 35 81 23, fax 04 93 57 12 35; Plateau St Michel; adult/tent/car from €3.20/3.70/3.50; open Apr-Oct) is 1km northeast of the train station up steep steps. Terraced sites are interspersed with olive trees and the facilities are clean. The adjacent **Auberge de Jeunesse** (☎ 04 93 35 93 14, fax 04 93 35 93 07; e menton@fuaj.org; Plateau St Michel; dorm beds €11.34; open Feb-Oct) takes HI members only.

Hôtel St Michel (☎ 04 93 57 46 33, fax 04 93 57 71 19; 1684 promenade du Soleil; rooms from €65) has some rooms overlooking the water.

Getting There & Away

The **bus station** (☎ 04 93 28 43 27) has services to Monaco (€2 return, 30 minutes) and Nice (€4.90 return, 1¼ hours). Take the train to get to Ventimiglia in Italy.

Monaco (Principauté de Monaco)

pop 30,000

The Principality of Monaco, a sovereign state whose territory covers only 1.95 sq km, has been ruled by the Grimaldi family for most of the period since 1297.

Prince Rainier III (born in 1923), whose sweeping constitutional powers make him far more than a figurehead, has reigned since 1949. The citizens of Monaco (Monégasques), of whom there are only 5000 out of a total population of 30,000, pay no taxes.

The official language is French, although efforts are being made to revive the country's traditional dialect.

There are no border formalities and Monaco makes a perfect day trip from Nice.

Orientation

Monaco consists of four principal areas: Monaco Ville, also known as the old city or the Rocher de Monaco, is perched atop a 60m-high crag which overlooks the Port de Monaco; Monte Carlo, which is famed both for its casino and its annual Grand Prix motor race, is north of the harbour; La Condamine is the flat area which surrounds the harbour; and Fontvieille is an industrial area situated southwest of Monaco Ville and the Port de Fontvieille.

FRANCE

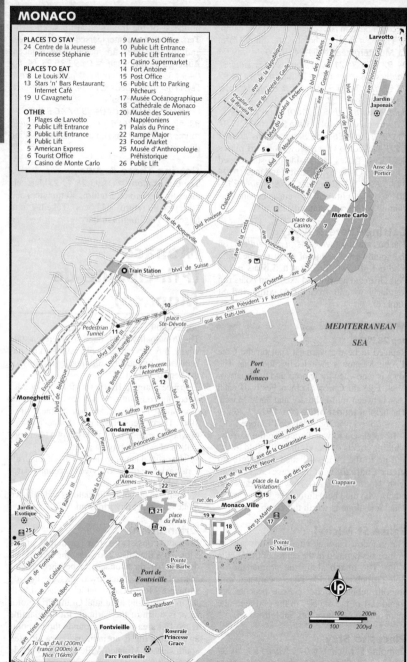

MONACO

PLACES TO STAY
24 Centre de la Jeunesse
   Princesse Stéphanie

PLACES TO EAT
8 Le Louis XV
13 Stars 'n' Bars Restaurant;
   Internet Café
19 U Cavagnetu

OTHER
1 Plages de Larvotto
2 Public Lift Entrance
3 Public Lift Entrance
4 Public Lift
5 American Express
6 Tourist Office
7 Casino de Monte Carlo

9 Main Post Office
10 Public Lift Entrance
11 Public Lift Entrance
12 Casino Supermarket
14 Fort Antoine
15 Post Office
16 Public Lift to Parking
   Pêcheurs
17 Musée Océanographique
18 Cathédrale de Monaco
20 Musée des Souvenirs
   Napoléoniens
21 Palais du Prince
22 Rampe Major
23 Food Market
25 Musée d'Anthropologie
   Préhistorique
26 Public Lift

Larvotto

Jardin
Japonais

Anse du
Portier

Monte Carlo

place du
Casino

Train Station   blvd de Suisse

ave d'Ostende

ave Président J F Kennedy

quai des États-Unis

MEDITERRANEAN

SEA

place
Ste-Dévote

Pedestrian
Tunnel

blvd Rainier III

rue Louise Aurelia

rue Grimaldi

*Port
de
Monaco*

Moneghetti

blvd de Belgique

rue Princesse
Antoinette

rue Louise

blvd Albert 1er

quai Albert 1er

rue Suffren Reymond

Florestine

La
Condamine

rue Princesse Caroline

quai Antoine 1er

ave de la Quarantaine

ave de la Porte Neuve

ave des Pins

place de la
Visitation

Ciappaira

23
place
d'Armes

ave du Pont

22

Jardin
Exotique

blvd Rainier III

rue de la Colle

rue des Remparts

Monaco Ville

place
du Palais

Pointe
St-Martin

Pointe
Ste-Barbe

*Port de
Fontvieille*

des
Sanbarbani

Fontvieille

To Cap d'Ail (200m),
France (200m) &
Nice (16km)

Roseraie
Princesse
Grace

Parc Fontvieille

0   100   200m
0   100   200yd

Information
Tourist Offices The **Direction du Tourisme et des Congrès de la Principauté de Monaco** (☎ 92 16 61 66, fax 92 16 60 00; e dtc@ monaco-tourisme.com; 2a blvd des Moulins; open 9am-7pm Mon-Sat, 10am-noon Sun Oct–mid-June, 8am-8pm daily mid-June–Sept) is across the public gardens from the casino. There's a helpful counter at the train station open the same hours; several tourist office kiosks operate around the principality in summer.

Money Unsurprisingly, there are lots of **banks** in the vicinity of the casino. **American Express** (☎ 93 25 74 45; 35 blvd Princesse Charlotte; open Mon-Fri) is near the main tourist office.

Post & Communications Monégasque stamps are valid only within Monaco, and postal rates are the same as in France. The **main post office** (1 ave Henri Dunant) is inside the Palais de la Scala.

Calls between Monaco and the rest of France are treated as international calls. Monaco's country code is ☎ 377. To call France from Monaco, dial ☎ 00 and France's country code (☎ 33). This applies even if you are only making a call from the east side of blvd de France (in Monaco) to its west side (which is in France)!

Email & Internet Access For Internet access, head to **Stars 'n' Bars** (☎ 97 97 95 95; 6 quai Antoine, 1er; open 11am-midnight Tues-Sun), an American-style bar and restaurant, charging €6 for 30 minutes of web surfing.

Things to See & Do
Palais du Prince The changing of the guard takes place outside the Prince's Palace (adult/concession €6/3; open 9.30am-6.20pm daily June-Oct) daily at 11.55am. About 15 state apartments are open to the public. Guided tours (35 minutes) in English leave every 15 or 20 minutes. Entry to the **Musée des Souvenirs Napoléoniens** – a display of Napoleon's personal effects in the palace's south wing – is €4/2.

Musée Océanographique If you're planning on visiting one aquarium on your whole trip, the world-famous Oceanographic Museum (ave St Martin in Monaco Ville;

adult/concession €11/6; open 9am-7pm daily, 9am-8pm July & Aug), with its 90 seawater tanks, should be it.

Cathédrale de Monaco The unspectacular 19th-century cathedral (4 rue Colonel) has one major attraction – the grave of Grace Kelly (1929–1982). The Hollywood star married Prince Rainier III in 1956, but was killed in a car crash in 1982. The remains of other members of the royal family, buried in the church crypt since 1885, rest behind Princess Grace's tomb.

Jardin Exotique The steep slopes of the wonderful Jardin Exotique (bus No 2 from tourist office to end of line; adult/concession €6.40/3.60) are home to some 7000 varieties of cacti and succulents from all over the world. The spectacular view is worth at least half the admission fee, which also gets you into the **Musée d'Anthropologie Préhistorique** and includes a half-hour guided visit to the **Grottes de l'Observatoire**, a system of caves 279 steps down the hillside.

Places to Stay
Monaco's HI hostel, **Centre de la Jeunesse Princesse Stéphanie** (☎ 93 50 83 20, fax 93 25 29 82; e info@youthhostel.asso.mc; 24 ave Prince Pierre; dorm beds €16) is 120m uphill from the train station. You must be aged between 16 and 31 to stay here. Beds are given out each morning on a first-come, first-served basis, though you can book ahead with a deposit.

The two-star **Hôtel de France** (☎ 93 30 24 64, fax 92 16 13 34; e hotel-france@monte -carlo.mc; 6 rue de la Turbie; singles/doubles €67/85) has rooms with shower, toilet and TV.

Places to Eat
There are a few cheap restaurants in La Condamine along rue de la Turbie. Lots of touristy restaurants can be found in the streets leading off from place du Palais. The flashy **Stars 'n' Bars** (☎ 93 50 95 95; 6 Quai Antoine 1er; open Tues-Sun, food until midnight) does Tex-Mex, burgers and salads.

One of the few affordable restaurants specialising in Monégasque dishes is **U Cavagnetu** (☎ 93 30 35 80; 14 rue Comte Félix-Gastaldi; lunch/dinner menus from €13/18).

If you need to know the prices, you can't afford to eat at Alain Ducasse's landmark

Le Louis XV (☎ 92 16 30 31; place du Casino Monte Carlo).

Getting There & Away

There is no single bus station in Monaco. The intercity buses leave from various points around the city.

The flash **train station** (☎ 0836 35 35 39; ave Prince Pierre) is part of the French SNCF network. There are frequent trains to Menton (€2, 10 minutes), Nice (€2.90, 20 minutes) and Ventimiglia in Italy (€3, 25 minutes).

Languedoc-Roussillon

Languedoc-Roussillon stretches in an arc along the coast from Provence to the Pyrenees. The plains of Bas Languedoc (Lower Languedoc) extend to the coast, where beaches are generally broad and sandy. The wine – Languedoc is France's largest wine-producing area – is red, robust and cheap. Inland you'll find the rugged, sparsely populated mountains of Haut Languedoc (Upper Languedoc), a region of bare limestone plateaus and deep canyons.

Transport is frequent between cities on the plain but buses in the interior are about as rare as camels. For train information throughout the region, ring ☎ 08 36 35 35 35.

MONTPELLIER
pop 229,000

Montpellier is one of the nation's fastest-growing cities. It's also one of the youngest – a quarter of the population are students.

Montpellier hosts a popular theatre festival in June and a two-week international dance festival in June/July.

Orientation & Information

The Centre Historique has at its heart place de la Comédie, a huge pedestrianised square. Westward from it is a series of lanes between rue de la Loge and rue Grand Jean Moulin.

Montpellier's **main tourist office** (☎ 04 67 60 60 60; open 9am-6.30pm Mon-Fri, reduced hours Sat & Sun, later closing in summer) is at the south end of esplanade Charles de Gaulle.

To snack and surf, visit the **Dimension 4 Cybercafé** (11 rue des Balances; open 10am-1am daily). It charges €4 per hour.

Things to See

Musée Fabre (39 blvd Bonne Nouvelle) has one of France's richest collections of French, Italian, Flemish and Dutch works from the 16th century onwards. **Musée Languedocien** (7 rue Jacques Cœur) displays the region's archaeological finds. Both charge €5.50/3 per adult/concession.

Beaches The closest beach is at **Palavas-les-Flots**, 12km south of the city. Take bus No 17 or 28.

Places to Stay

Camping Some 4km south of town there's **L'Oasis Palavasienne** (☎ 04 67 15 11 61; Route de Palavas; bus No 17 to Oasis stop; 2 people & tent low/high season €16.40/24.05; open mid-Apr–Aug).

Hostels The **Auberge de Jeunesse** (☎ 04 67 60 32 22, fax 04 67 60 32 30; e montpellier@fuaj.org; 2 impasse de la Petite Corraterie; dorm beds €8; open mid-Jan–mid-Dec) is just off rue des Écoles Laïques. Take the tram to the Louis Blanc stop.

Hotels Just off place de la Comédie is **Hôtel des Touristes** (☎ 04 67 58 42 37, fax 04 67 92 61 37; 10 rue Baudin; singles/doubles/triples with shower from €24.40/29.75/49.55) with spacious rooms. Friendly **Hôtel des Étuves** (☎/fax 04 67 60 78 19; 24 rue des Étuves; singles/doubles with bathroom from €27.45/33.55) is another option. Close by, the **Hôtel Majestic** (☎ 04 67 66 26 85; 4 rue du Cheval Blanc; singles/doubles €18/23, doubles/triples/quads with bathroom €29/46/53) has basic rooms.

Places to Eat

Eating places abound in Montepellier's old quarter. **Tripti Kulai** (20 rue Jacques Cœur; menus €10.50 & €14.50) is vegetarian. **La Tomate** (6 rue Four des Flammes; menus from €8) does great regional dishes, salads the size of a kitchen, plus dessert.

Entertainment

For a drink, try the bars flanking rue En-Gondeau, off rue Grand Jean Moulin. **Mash Disco Bar** (5 rue de Girone) is a popular student hang-out. For more entertainment options, look out for a free copy of Sortir à Montpellier in restaurants and shops.

Getting There & Away

Montpellier's **bus station** (☎ 04 67 92 01 43) is immediately southwest of the train station, itself 500m south of place de la Comédie.

Rail destinations include Paris' Gare de Lyon (€63.10/77.10 weekdays/weekends, four to five hours by TGV, about 10 daily), Carcassonne (€17.70, 1½ hours, at least 10 daily) and Nîmes (€7.20, 30 minutes, 15 or more daily).

NÎMES

pop 133,000

Nîmes has some of Europe's best-preserved Roman buildings. **Les Arènes** *(the amphitheatre; adult/child €4.50/3.20)*, built around AD 100 to seat 24,000 spectators, is used to this day for theatre performances, music concerts and bullfights.

The rectangular **Maison Carrée** is a well-preserved 1st-century Roman temple which survived the centuries as a meeting hall, private residence, stable, church and archive.

Try to coincide with one of Nîmes' three wild *férias* (festivals) – Féria Primavera (Spring Festival) in February, Féria de Pentecôte (Whitsuntide Festival) in June, and the Féria des Vendanges coinciding with the grape harvest in September.

The **main tourist office** (☎ 04 66 58 38 00; 6 rue Auguste) can help with information.

To check your email, log on at **Netgames** *(25 rue de l'Horloge)*, beside the Maison Carrée, which charges €3 an hour.

Places to Stay

Domaine de la Bastide *(☎/fax 04 66 38 09 21; tent sites for 2 people with car €11.30; open year-round)* is 4km south of town on route de Générac (the D13). Take bus D and get off at La Bastide, the terminus.

Hôtel de la Maison Carrée *(☎ 04 66 67 32 89, fax 04 66 76 22 57; 14 rue de la Maison Carrée; singles/doubles with washbasin €22/26, singles/doubles with bathroom €28-37/34-43, triples/quads €50/53)* is a welcoming, highly recommended place.

Places to Eat

La Truye qui Filhe *(9 rue Fresque; menu €8.40; open noon-2pm Mon-Sat; closed Aug)*, beneath the vaults of a restored 14th-century inn, is a self-service format with a warm atmosphere and a superb-value changing daily *menu*.

Getting There & Away

Bus Nîmes' bus station is beside the train station. Destinations include Pont du Gard (€5.40, 45 minutes, five to six daily), Avignon (€7.10, 30 minutes, 10 or more daily) and Arles (€5.25, 30 to 45 minutes, four to eight daily).

Train The train station is at the southeastern end of ave Feuchères. Destinations include Paris' Gare de Lyon (€62.50, four hours by TGV, seven daily), Avignon (€7.10, 30 minutes, 10 or more daily), Marseille (€15.30, 1¼ hours, 12 daily) and Montpellier (€7.20, 30 minutes, 15 or more daily).

AROUND NÎMES
Pont du Gard

The Roman general Agrippa slung the mighty Pont du Gard over the Gard River around 19 BC. You won't be alone; this three-tier aqueduct, 275m long and 49m high, receives more than two million visitors a year.

There's a tourist kiosk on each bank and a brand new information centre on the left bank, set back from the river.

Buses from Avignon (26km) and Nîmes (23km) stop 1km north of the bridge.

CARCASSONNE
pop 46,250

From afar, the old walled city of Carcassonne looks like a fairy-tale medieval city. Once inside the fortified walls, however, the magic rubs off. Luring some 200,000 visitors in July and August alone, it can be a tourist hell in high summer. Purists may sniff at Carcassonne's 'medieval' Cité – whose impressive fortifications were extensively renovated and rebuilt in the 19th century – but what the heck; it *is* magic, one of France's greatest skylines.

The Ville Basse (lower town), a more modest stepsister to camp Cinderella up the hill, has cheaper eating places and accommodation and also merits a browse.

Orientation & Information

The Aude River separates the Ville Basse from the Cité on its hillock. The **main tourist office** (☎ 04 68 10 24 30) is in the Ville Basse opposite square Gambetta.

Alerte Rouge *(Red Alert; 73 rue Verdun; open 10am-11pm daily)* is an Internet café charging €4.80 per hour.

Things to See

The 1.7km-long double ramparts of **La Cité** (spectacularly floodlit at night) are spiked with 52 witches' hat towers. Within are narrow, medieval streets and the 12th-century **Château Comtal** (Count's Castle), visited by guided tour only (adult/concession €4.50/3.50). A 40-minute tour in English departs up to five times daily, according to season.

Places to Stay

Camping About 2km south of square Gambetta is **Camping de la Cité** (☎ 04 68 25 11 77, fax 04 68 47 33 13; route de St-Hilaire; tent site 2 people & car €12.20-16.80 according to season; open mid-Mar–early Oct). From mid-June to mid-September, bus No 8 connects the camp site with La Cité and the train station.

Hostels In the heart of the Cité, the large, cheery **Auberge de Jeunesse** (☎ 04 68 25 23 16; rue Vicomte Trencavel; dorm beds €12.20 including breakfast) has a snack bar offering light meals and a great outside terrace. The B&B at the **Centre International de Séjour** (☎ 04 68 11 17 00; 91 rue Aimé Ramon; dorm beds €8) in the Ville Basse is another option.

Hotels Handy for the train station is the recommended **Hôtel Astoria** (☎ 04 68 25 31 38; 18 rue Tourtel; singles/doubles from €18/20, with bathroom from €27).

Pricing policy at welcoming **Relais du Square** (☎ 04 68 72 31 72; 51 rue du Pont Vieux; 1- to 3-person room €30) couldn't be simpler; all the large rooms, accommodating one to three people, cost the same, whatever their facilities. So in summer get there early if you want your own bathroom.

Places to Eat

In the Ville Basse, **Le Gargantua** (Mon-Fri menu €10.55, other menus from €21) is the restaurant of Relais du Square. **L'Italia** (32 route Minervoise), handy for the station, is a pizza-plus joint that also does takeaways. Next door is the more stylish **Restaurant Gil** (menus from €14) with Catalan-influenced cuisine.

Getting There & Away

The train station is at the northern end of pedestrianised rue Georges Clemenceau. Carcassonne is on the main line linking Toulouse (€11.70, 50 minutes, 10 or more daily) with

Béziers (€11.10, 50 minutes, five daily) and Montpellier (€17.70, 1½ hours, 10 or more daily).

TOULOUSE
pop 690,000

Toulouse, France's fourth-largest city, is renowned for its high-tech industries, especially aerospace; local factories have built the Caravelle, Concorde and Airbus passenger planes and also the Ariane rocket. Like Montpellier, it's a youthful place with more than 110,000 students – more than any other French provincial city.

Most older buildings in the city centre are in rose-red brick, earning the city its nickname *la ville rose* (the pink city).

Orientation

The heart of Toulouse is bounded to the east by blvd de Strasbourg and its continuation, blvd Lazare Carnot and, to the west, by the Garonne River. Its two main squares are place du Capitole and, 300m eastwards, place Wilson.

Information

The busy **tourist office** (☎ 05 61 11 02 22; open 9am-6pm Mon-Fri, 9am-12.30pm & 2pm-6pm Sat, 9am-12.30pm & 2pm-5pm Sun Oct-Apr, 9am-7pm Mon-Sat, 10am-1pm & 2pm-6.15pm Sun May-Aug) is in the Donjon du Capitole, a 16th-century tower on Square Charles de Gaulle.

Online time at Internet café **Résomania** (85 rue Pargaminières; open until midnight daily) is €3 per hour before noon and €4 between noon and midnight.

Major annual events include the Festival Garonne with riverside music, dance and theatre (July), Musique d'Été with music of all definitions around town (July and August) and Jazz sur Son 31, an international jazz festival (October).

Things to See & Do

Cité de l'Espace Space City (☎ 05 62 71 48 71; adult/concession €12/10) is a truly mind-boggling interactive space museum and planetarium. To get there, take bus No 15 from Allées Jean Jaurès to the end of the line, from where it's a 600m walk.

The **Galerie Municipale du Château d'Eau** (place Laganne; adult/concession €2.30/1.50; open 1pm-7pm Wed-Mon) is a world-class photographic gallery inside a 19th-century

water tower at the western end of pont Neuf,
just across the Garonne River.

Musée des Augustins (21 rue de Metz;
adult/student €2.20/free) has a superb collection of paintings and stone artefacts.

Within the magnificent Gothic **Église des
Jacobins**, the remains of St Thomas Aquinas
(1225–74), an early head of the Dominican
order, are interred on the north side.

The **Basilique St Sernin** is France's largest
and most complete Romanesque structure. It
is topped by a magnificent eight-sided 13th-
century **tower**.

The **Jardin des Plantes** (allée Jules Guesde)
is open until dusk daily. As well as being the
site of the **Natural History Museum**, it has a
fine collection of modern sculpture.

Places to Stay
Camping The oft-packed **Camping de Rupé**
(☎ 05 61 70 07 35; 21 chemin du Pont de
Rupé; 2 people, car & tent €11.50; open
year-round) is 6km northwest of the train station. Take bus No 59 (last departure at
7.25pm) from place Jeanne d'Arc to the Rupé
stop. Camping is allowed from mid-June to
mid-September.

Hotels Avoid the cheap hotels near the train
station; most are fairly sordid.

The exceptionally friendly **Hôtel Beausé-
jour** (☎/fax 05 61 62 77 59; 4 rue Caffarelli;
basic rooms from €20, doubles/triples with
bath €25/33), off Allées Jean Jaurès, is great
value. The **Hôtel Splendid** (☎/fax 05 61 62
43 02; basic rooms from €13.72, singles/
doubles/triples with bath €21.40/24.40/
33.55) is at No 13.

Places to Eat
Fill yourself at lunchtime when there are some
amazing deals. Look around – many places
have lunch menus for €8 to €10. Unmissable
and an essential Toulouse experience are the
small, spartan, lunchtime-only **restaurants** on
the 1st floor of Les Halles Victor Hugo covered market (great in itself for atmosphere and
fresh produce). They serve up generous quantities of hearty fare for €9 to €20.

Place St Georges is almost entirely taken
over by café tables. Both blvd de Strasbourg
and place du Capitole are lined with restaurants and cafés.

Restaurant Saveur Bio (22 rue Maurice
Fonvieille; lunch mixed plate or buffet €8,

menus €19.50) serves tasty vegetarian food
including a great value buffet, and three menus.

Entertainment
For what's on where, pick up a copy of
Toulouse Hebdo (€0.90) or Intramuros (free
from selected restaurants and bars). For life
after dark, ask at the tourist office for its free
listing Toulouse By Night.

The cafés around place St-Pierre beside the
Garonne pull a mainly young crowd. Nearby,
the **Why Not Café** (5 rue Pargaminières) has
a beautiful terrace while **Café des Artistes**
(13 place de la Daurade) is an art-student
hang-out.

Two of the hottest discos near the centre are
La Strada (4 rue Gabriel Péri) and **L'Ubu** (16
rue St-Rome).

Getting There & Away
Bus Toulouse's bus station (☎ 05 61 61 67
67), just north of the train station, serves
mainly regional destinations including Andorra (€20, four hours, one to two daily). For
longer distance travel, both **Intercars** (☎ 05 61
58 14 53) and **Eurolines** (☎ 05 61 26 40 04)
have offices in Toulouse.

Train The train station, Gare Matabiau, is on
blvd Pierre Sémard, about 1km northeast of
the city centre.

Destinations served by multiple daily direct
trains include Bayonne (€31, 3¾ hours), Bordeaux (€26.10, 2½ hours) and Carcassonne
(€11.70, 50 minutes).

The fare to Paris is €56 by Corail (6½
hours, Gare d'Austerlitz) and €70.40 to €80
by TGV (5½ hours, Gare Montparnasse via
Bordeaux).

SNCF (5 rue Peyras) provides information
and ticketing.

Corsica

Corsica (Corse), the most mountainous and
geographically diverse of all the Mediterranean islands, has spent much of its history
under foreign rule. From the 13th century it
remained under Genoese control until the
Corsicans, led by the extraordinary Pasquale
Paoli, declared the island independent in
1755. But France took over in 1769 and has
ruled Corsica since – except in 1794–96,
when it was under English domination, and

during the German and Italian occupation of 1940–43.

The island has 1000km of coastline, soaring granite mountains that stay snowcapped until July, an enormous national park, flatland marshes, an uninhabited desert in the northwest and a 'continental divide' running down the middle of the island.

It's a popular holiday destination for the French and increasingly for foreign travellers who come for its exceptional hiking and diving opportunities.

Dangers & Annoyances In 2002, Corsica gained a smidgeon of administrative autonomy from France and the right to teach Corsican in local schools. That's not enough for the island's small core of committed activists, who continue to agitate for independence. As a traveller, there's no need to be nervous; defaced road signs are the only evidence you're likely to see of civil unrest in Corsica.

AJACCIO
pop 52,850

The port city of Ajaccio (Aiacciu) is the birthplace of Napoleon Bonaparte (1769–1821). It's also a great place to begin a visit to Corsica and a fine place for strolling. The many museums and statues dedicated to Bonaparte speak volumes – not about Napoleon himself, but about how the people of his native town prefer to think of him.

Orientation

Ajaccio's main street is cours Napoléon, which stretches from place du Général de Gaulle northward to the train station and beyond. The old city is south of place Foch. The ferry port is central to both the old and new town.

Information

Tourist Offices The **tourist office** (☎ 04 95 51 53 03, fax 04 95 51 53 01; e ajaccio .tourisme@wanadoo.fr; 1 place Foch; open 8am-7pm Mon-Sat, 9am-1pm Sun Apr-June & Sept-Oct, 8am-8.30pm Mon-Sat, 9am-1pm & 2pm-7pm Sun July-Aug, 8am-6pm Mon-Fri, 8am-noon & 2pm-5pm Sat & Sun Nov-Mar) is boosted by a **chamber of commerce counter** (☎ 04 95 23 56 56; open 6am-10.30pm daily) at the airport.

Gare.Net (☎ 04 95 50 72 79; 2 ave de Paris) charges €5 for an hour's Internet access.

Money & Post Money can be exchanged at the **main post office** (13 cours Napoléon).

Hiking The **Maison d'Information Randonnées** (☎ 04 95 51 79 00, fax 04 95 21 88 17, e infos@parc-naturel-corse.com; 2 rue du sergent Casalonga; open 8.30am-12.30pm & 2pm-6pm Mon-Thur, to 5pm Fri) provides information on the Parc Naturel Régional de la Corse and its hiking trails.

Things to See & Do

Museums The house where Napoleon was born and raised, the **Maison Bonaparte** (☎ 04 95 21 43 89; rue St Charles; adult/ concession €4/2.60; open 10am-noon & 2pm-4.45pm Oct-Mar, 9am-noon & 2pm-6pm Apr-Sept, closed Mon morning year-round), is in the old city. It was sacked by Corsican nationalists in 1793 but rebuilt later in the decade.

The sombre **Salon Napoléonien** (☎ 04 95 21 90 15; 1st floor, Hôtel de Ville, place Foch; admission €2.29; open 9am-11.45am & 2pm-4.45pm Mon-Fri mid-Sept–mid-June, 9am-11.45am & 2pm-5.45pm Mon-Sat mid-June–mid-Sept) exhibits memorabilia of the emperor.

The **Musée A Bandera** (☎ 04 95 51 07 34; 1 rue Général Lévie; adult/concession €3.85/ 2.30; open 9am-7pm Mon-Sat, 9am-noon Sat July-15 Sept, 9am-noon & 2pm-6pm Mon-Sat 16 Sept–June) deals with Corsican military history.

Musée Fesch (☎ 04 95 21 48 17; 50 rue du Cardinal Fesch; adult/concession €5.34/ 3.81; open 1.30pm-6pm Mon, 9am-6.30pm Tues-Thur, 9am-6.30pm & 9pm-midnight Fri, 10.30am-6pm Sat & Sun July-Aug, 1pm-5.15pm Mon, 9.15am-12.15pm & 2.15pm-5.15pm Tues-Sun Apr-June & Sept, 9.15am-12.15pm & 2.15pm-5.15pm Tues-Sat Oct-Mar) houses an awesome assembly of 14th- to 19th-century Italian paintings collected by Napoleon's uncle.

Places to Stay

Camping About 3km north of the town centre, **Camping Les Mimosas** (☎ 04 95 20 99 85, fax 04 95 10 01 77; Route d'Alata; sites per adult/tent/car €4.80/2/2; open Apr-Oct) offers 10% discounts out of season. Take bus No 4 from cours Napoléon to the corner of route d'Alata and chemin des Roseaux, and walk up route d'Alata for 1km.

AJACCIO

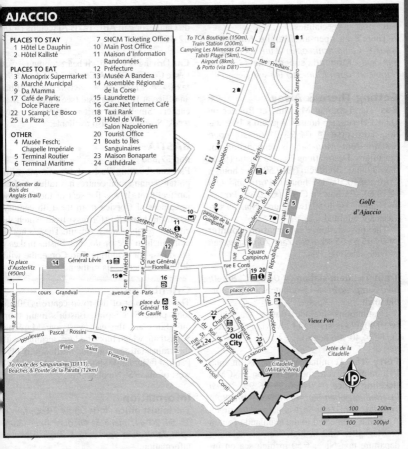

PLACES TO STAY
1 Hôtel Le Dauphin
2 Hôtel Kallisté

PLACES TO EAT
3 Monoprix Supermarket
8 Marché Municipal
9 Da Mamma
17 Café de Paris;
   Dolce Piacere
22 U Scampi; Le Bosco
25 La Pizza

OTHER
4 Musée Fesch;
   Chapelle Impériale
5 Terminal Routier
6 Terminal Maritime

7 SNCM Ticketing Office
10 Main Post Office
11 Maison d'Information
   Randonnées
12 Préfecture
13 Musée A Bandera
14 Assemblée Régionale
   de la Corse
15 Laundrette
16 Gare.Net Internet Café
18 Taxi Rank
19 Hôtel de Ville;
   Salon Napoléonien
20 Tourist Office
21 Boats to Îles
   Sanguinaires
23 Maison Bonaparte
24 Cathédrale

Hotels Efficient **Hôtel Kallisté** (☎ 04 95 51 34 45, fax 04 95 21 79 00; e hotelkalliste@ cyrnos.com; 51 cours Napoléon; singles/ doubles with shower & toilet €56/69) has classy rooms with terracotta tiles. Prices drop by 33% during low season. Breakfast (€6.50) is served in your room.

Only 200m from the ferry terminal, **Hôtel Le Dauphin** (☎ 04 95 21 12 94, fax 04 95 21 88 69; 11 blvd Sampiero; singles/doubles with shower & toilet €49/60) includes breakfast in the price.

Places to Eat

Most of Ajaccio's restaurants are seasonal. Cafés can be found along blvd du Roi Jérôme, quai Napoléon and the north side of place de Gaulle. **Café de Paris** and the neighbouring **Dolce Piacere**, on the west side of place du Général de Gaulle, both have giant terraces with sea views.

The best pizza is served at **La Pizza** (☎ 04 95 21 30 71; 2 rue des Anciens Fosées; pizza €8.50-10.50). Try the quatre saisons, drizzled with chilli-laced olive oil.

Popular **U Scampi** (☎ 04 95 21 38 09; 11 rue Conventionnel Chiappe; menus from €13; open Mon-Thur, Fri lunch & Sat dinner year-round) serves up Corsican specialities – including octopus stew – on a flower-filled terrace. **Le Bosco** (☎ 04 95 21 25 06) shares the same terrace as the Scampi and has the same sort of food, including a €31.25 shellfish platter.

Da Mamma (☎ 04 95 21 39 44; Passage de la Guinguetta; menus from €10.50), tucked away off cours Napoléon, does paella, pasta and Corsican specialities.

There's an open-air **Marché Municipal** *(square Campinchi; open 8am-noon Tues-Sun)* and a **Monoprix supermarket** *(33 cours Napoléon; open Mon-Sat)* for supplies.

Getting There & Away

Bus The Terminal Maritime et Routier on Quai l'Herminier houses Ajaccio's bus station. **Eurocorse** *(☎ 04 95 21 06 30; open 8.30am-4pm Mon-Sat)* is responsible for most lines. Destinations include Bastia (€18, three hours), Bonifacio (€19.50, four hours), Corte (€10.50, 1½ hours), Porto and Ota (€10.50, 2½ hours), Calvi (€22, via Porto), and Sartène (€11.50, two hours). Sunday services are minimal.

The bus station's **information counter** *(☎ 04 95 51 55 45; open 7am-7pm daily)* can provide schedules.

Train The train station *(☎ 04 95 32 80 60; blvd Sampiero)* is a 15-minute walk from the old town.

Destinations include Bastia via Corte (€19.90, 3½ hours) and Calvi via Ponte Leccia (€24.40, 4½ hours).

Ferry The Terminal Maritime is on quai l'Herminier next to the bus station. SNCM's **ticketing office** *(☎ 04 95 29 66 99; 3 quai l'Herminier; open 8am-6pm Mon, 8am-8pm Tues-Fri, 8am-1pm Sat)* is across the street. Ajaccio is connected to the mainland (Toulon or Marseille, €62 in high season, including departure tax; Nice, €50 in high season including departure tax) by at least one daily ferry; the **SNCM bureau** *(open 7am-8pm Mon-Sat)* in the ferry terminal also opens two hours before the scheduled departure time on Sunday.

Corsica Ferries *(☎ 04 95 50 78 82, fax 04 95 50 78 83; w www.corsicaferries.com)* runs cheaper but less frequent services to Ajaccio from Toulon and Nice (€35 in high season, including tax). Its office is at the Terminal Maritime.

Getting Around

Bus Local bus tickets cost €1.15 (€4 to the airport). Pick up maps and timetables at the **TCA Boutique** *(☎ 04 95 23 29 41; 75 cours Napoleon; open 8am-noon & 2.30pm-6pm Mon-Sat)*.

Taxi There's a taxi rank on place du Généra de Gaulle, or call **ABC Taxis Ajacciens** *(☎ 06 62 55 71 38)*.

Car Driving is a good – if heartstopping – way to see Corsica. **Rent A Car** *(☎ 04 95 51 61 81, fax 04 95 21 79 00; w www.rentacar.fr)* has an office at Hôtel Kallisté (see Places to Stay earlier). Small cars start at €49/227 a day/week. Scooters are also available.

BASTIA
pop 37,880

Pleasant, bustling Bastia, Corsica's most important commercial centre, has rather an Italian feel to it. It was the seat of the Genoese governors of Corsica from the 15th century, when the *bastiglia* (fortress) from which the city derives its name was built. There's not all that much to see or do, but Bastia makes a good base for exploring **Cap Corse**, the wild, 40km-long peninsula to the north.

Orientation

The focal point of the town centre is 300m-long place St Nicolas. Bastia's main thoroughfares are the east-west ave Maréchal Sébastiani, which links the ferry terminal with the train station, and the north-south blvd Paoli, a fashionable shopping street one block west of place St Nicolas.

Information

The **tourist office** *(☎ 04 95 54 20 40, fax 04 95 54 20 41; place St Nicolas; open 8am-6pm daily, 8am-8pm July & Aug)* dispenses information.

The **main post office** *(cnr ave Maréchal Sébastiani & blvd Paoli)* is a block west of place St Nicolas.

Le Cyber *(☎ 04 95 34 30 34; 6 rue Jardins; open 9am-late)* provides drinks and snacks as well as Internet access for €3.10 an hour.

Things to See & Do

Bastia's **place St Nicolas**, a palm and plane tree-lined esplanade, was laid out in the late 19th century.

The narrow streets and alleyways of **Terra Vecchia**, which is centred around place de l'Hôtel de Ville, are situated just south. The 16th-century **Oratoire de l'Immaculée Conception** is opposite 3 rue Napoléon and was decorated in rich baroque style in the early 18th century.

The picturesque, horseshoe-shaped **Vieux Port** is between Terra Vecchia and the **Citadelle** and is the most colourful part of Bastia with its crumbling buildings and lively restaurants.

Places to Stay

Camping Small and sweet **Camping Les Orangers** (☎ 04 95 33 24 09; sites per tent/parking/adult €2/1.60/4; open Apr–mid-Oct) is about 4km north of Bastia in Miomo. Take the bus to Sisco from opposite the tourist office.

Hotels Book ahead because Bastia's hotels fill up with business travellers.

The **Hôtel Le Riviera** (☎ 04 95 31 07 16, fax 04 95 34 17 39; 1bis rue du Nouveau Port; doubles with shower & toilet €58) is very close to the ferry. The family-run **Hôtel Central** (☎ 04 95 31 71 12, fax 04 95 31 82 40; e infos@centralhotel.fr; 3 rue Miot; singles/doubles with shower & toilet 40/50, with kitchenette €75/90) has recently renovated its rooms.

Don't be discouraged by the dingy stairs – once you get inside, the rooms are fresh and comfortable at **Hôtel Le Forum** (☎ 04 95 31 02 53, fax 04 95 31 65 60; e hotel_leforum@wanadoo.fr; 20 blvd Paoli; rooms with shower & toilet from €60). Prices drop about €10 outside July and August.

Places to Eat

Cafés and brasseries line the western side of place St Nicolas. There are more restaurants at the Vieux Port, on quai des Martyrs de la Libération and on place de l'Hôtel de Ville in Terra Vecchia, where the **Café Pannini** sells great jumbo sandwiches.

La Barcarolle (☎ 04 95 31 42 45; Corsican menu €19) at the Vieux Port, serves pizzas and seafood dishes.

A delightful **food market** (place de l'Hôtel de Ville; open 8am-1pm Tues-Sun) takes place in Terra Vecchio, and there's also a **Spar supermarket** (cnr rue César Campinchi & rue Capanelle).

Getting There & Away

Air France's fifth-busiest airport, **Aéroport de Bastia-Poretta** (☎ 04 95 54 54 54), is 20km south of the town. Municipal buses to the airport (€8) depart from the roundabout opposite the train station about an hour before each flight (seven to 12 times daily). The tourist office has timetables.

Bus **Rapides Bleus** (☎ 04 95 31 03 79; 1 ave Maréchal Sebastiani) operates buses to Porto-Vecchio (€16.30, three hours) and handles tickets for Eurocorse buses to Corte and Ajaccio. The afternoon bus to Calvi run by **Les Beaux Voyages** (☎ 04 95 65 02 10) leaves from outside the train station.

Train The **train station** (☎ 04 95 32 60 06) is at the northern end of ave Maréchal Sébastiani. Destinations include Corte (€9.40, two hours), Ajaccio (€19.90, 3½ hours) and Calvi via Ponte Leccia (€15, 4½ hours).

Ferry Bastia is linked by ferry to both France and Italy. The ferry terminal is at the eastern end of ave Pietri. **SNCM's office** (☎ 04 95 54 66 81; open 7.15am-6.30pm Mon-Fri, 8am-11.45am Sat) handles ferries to mainland France. The SNCM counter in the ferry terminal opens two hours before each sailing.

Corsica Ferries (☎ 04 95 32 95 95, fax 04 95 32 14 71; 15bis rue Chanoine Leschi; open 8.30am-noon & 2pm-6pm Mon-Sat) runs to Toulon, Nice and Italy. For more Italian destinations, try **Mobylines** (☎ 04 95 34 84 94, fax 04 95 32 17 94; 4 rue du Commandant Luce de Casabianca; open 8am-noon & 2pm-6pm Mon-Fri, 8am-noon Sat), 200m north of place St Nicolas. Mobylines and Corsica Ferries also have ticket windows in the ferry terminal with restricted hours.

Standard fares to/from mainland France are around €30/15 for passengers over/under 25 years of age, including departure tax.

CALVI
pop 6219

Calvi, where Admiral Horatio Nelson lost his eye, serves both as a military town and a rather upmarket holiday resort.

The Citadelle is garrisoned by a crack regiment of the French Foreign Legion, and sits atop a promontory at the western end of a beautiful half-moon-shaped bay.

Orientation

The Citadelle – also known as the Haute Ville (upper town) – is northeast of the port. Blvd Wilson, the main thoroughfare in the Basse Ville (lower town), is up the hill from quai Landry and the marina.

Information

The **tourist office** (☎ 04 95 65 16 67, fax 04 95 65 14 09; open 9am-noon & 2pm-6pm Mon-Sat Oct-May, 8.30am-1pm & 2.30pm-7pm daily June-Sept) is near the marina.

Crédit Lyonnais (7 blvd Wilson; open 8.15am-noon & 2pm-5pm Mon-Fri) is on the same street as the **main post office**, about 100m to the south.

Café de L'Orient (☎ 04 95 65 00 16; quai Landry) has Internet-connected computers for €1 plus €0.10 a minute.

Things to See & Do

The **Citadelle**, set atop an 80m-high granite promontory and enclosed by massive Genoese ramparts, affords great views of the surrounding area. The 13th-century **Église St Jean Baptiste** was rebuilt in 1570; inside is a miraculous ebony icon of Christ. West of the church, a marble plaque marks the site of the house where, according to local tradition, Christopher Columbus was born. Imposing 13th-century **Palais des Gouverneurs** (Governors' Palace) is above the entrance to the citadel. Now known as Caserne Sampiero, it serves as a barracks and mess hall for officers of the French Foreign Legion.

Beaches Calvi's 4km-long beach begins just south of the marina and stretches around the Golfe de Calvi. Other nice beaches, including one at **Algajola**, are west of town. The port and resort town of L'Île Rousse (Isula Rossa) east of Calvi is also endowed with a long, sandy beach with incredibly clean water.

Places to Stay

Camping & Bungalows Just less than 1km southeast of town is **Camping La Clé des Champs** (☎/fax 04 95 65 00 86; e camagni@ wanadoo.fr; route de Pietra Maggiore; sites per adult/tent/car €5.35/1.55/1.55, bungalows per week for 2 people from €185; open Apr-Oct).

Hostels The 130-bed **Auberge de Jeunesse BVJ Corsotel** (☎ 04 95 65 14 15, fax 04 95 65 33 72; ave de la République; dorm beds €20.60; open late Mar–Oct) has beds in two-to eight-person rooms, and rates include a filling breakfast.

Hotels A cheap option is **Hôtel du Centre** (☎ 04 95 65 02 01; 14 rue Alsace-Lorraine; rooms with showers €31-42; open 1 June-Oct). A step up are the deluxe rooms at the **Hôtel Balanea** (☎ 04 95 65 94 94, fax 04 95 65 29 71; e info@hotel-balanea.com; room without/with sea view €81/185). Prices drop about 40% out of season.

Places to Eat

Calvi's attractive marina is lined with pricey restaurants, but there are several budget places on rue Clemenceau, which runs parallel to blvd Wilson. **Best Of**, at the south end of the street, sells good sandwiches (around €4.50).

Quai Landry's line-up of waterfront cafés and nice seafood restaurants includes **Callelu** (☎ 04 95 65 22 18; fish dishes €18.30-20.60).

It doesn't have sea views but **U Fornu** (☎ 04 95 65 27 60; Impasse du blvd Wilson; mains €15-19) has the best Corsican food in town. You'll find it up the stairs next to the Banque Lyonnais on blvd Wilson.

The tiny **Marché Couvert** (open 8am-noon daily) is near Église Ste Marie Majeure. The **Super U supermarket** (ave Christophe Colomb) is south of the town centre.

Getting There & Away

Bus Buses to Bastia are run by **Les Beaux Voyages** (☎ 04 95 65 15 02; place de la Porteuse d'Eau). From mid-May to mid-October **Autocars SAIB** (☎ 04 95 26 13 70) trundles to Porto (€16, 2½ hours) along Corsica's spectacular western coast.

Train Calvi's **train station** (☎ 04 95 65 00 61) is just off ave de la République. From mid-April to mid-October, navettes (one-car trains) make 19 stops between Calvi and L'Île Rousse (€6, 45 minutes).

Ferry SNCM ferries (☎ 04 95 65 01 38) sail to Calvi from Nice and Marseille, but during winter they can be very infrequent. **Corsica Ferries** (☎ 04 95 65 43 21) links Calvi with Nice and Savone, Italy about once a week (more in summer).

PORTO
pop 460

The pleasant seaside town of Porto (Portu), nestled among huge outcrops of red granite and renowned for its sunsets, is an excellent base for exploring some of Corsica's natural wonders. **Les Calanques**, a spectacular mountain landscape of red and orange granite outcrops, towers above the azure waters of the Mediterranean slightly south of Porto along route D81. The **Gorges de Spelunca**, Corsica's most famous river gorge, stretches almost from the town of Ota, 5km east of Porto, to the town of Evisa, 22km away.

Orientation & Information

The marina is about 1.5km downhill from Porto's pharmacy – the local landmark – on the D81. The area, known as Vaïta, is spread out along the road linking the D81 to the marina. The Porto River just south of the marina is linked by an arched pedestrian bridge to a eucalyptus grove and small pebble beach.

The **tourist office** (☎ 04 95 26 10 55, fax 04 95 26 14 25; open 9am-noon & 2pm-6pm Mon-Fri Sept-June, 9am-8pm daily July & Aug) is near the marina. The only ATM between Ajaccio and Calvi is here at Porto – it's outside the post office, halfway between the pharmacy and the marina.

Things to See & Do

A short trail takes you to the 16th-century **Genoese tower** (admission €2.50; open 10am-12.30pm & 3pm-7pm Apr-Oct) on the outcrop above the town.

From March to November, **Nave Va** (☎ 04 95 26 15 16) runs boat excursions (€25.50) to the fishing village of Girolata (passing by the Scandola Nature Reserve), and occasionally to Les Calanques in the evenings (€12).

Places to Stay

Camping Friendly **Funtana al' Ora** (☎ 04 95 26 11 65, fax 04 95 26 10 83; e info@ porto-tourisme.com; sites per tent/person/ car €2.15/5.20/2.15, bungalows per week from €183; open 15 Apr-Oct) is 2km east of Porto on the road to Évisa.

Hostels Nearby, in Ota, **Gîte d'Étape Chez Félix** (☎/fax 04 95 26 12 92) and **Gîte d'Étape Chez Marie** (☎/fax 04 95 26 11 37) both open year-round and charge €11 for a dorm bed.

Hotels There are plenty of hotels in Vaïta and at the marina but most are closed between November and March. One of the best deals is the **Hôtel du Golfe** (☎/fax 04 95 26 13 33; doubles/triples with shower & toilet €40/ 49). **Hôtel Monte Rosso** (☎ 04 95 26 11 50, fax 04 95 26 12 30; doubles with shower & toilet €51) is nearby.

Getting There & Away

Autocars SAIB (☎ 04 95 22 41 99) has two buses daily (Sunday service July to mid-September only) linking Porto and nearby Ota with Ajaccio (€10.50, 2½ hours). From mid-May to mid-October a bus also goes from Porto to Calvi (€16, 2½ hours).

PIANA
pop 428

A good base for walks to Les Calanques, this hillside village has stunning views and a cruisy atmosphere, even when it's overrun by summer hordes.

Places to Stay & Eat

Just 100m south of the centre, **Hôtel Continental** (☎ 04 95 27 89 00, fax 04 95 27 84 71; annexe rooms €45; singles/doubles/triples/ quads €27/33/40/47; open Apr-Sept) has annexe rooms with groovy 1960s furniture and terrific views.

Wonderful **Les Roches Rouges** (☎ 04 95 27 81 81, fax 04 95 27 81 76; singles/doubles/ triples/quads €69/69/84/115; open Apr-Oct) opened in 1912 and has an Agatha Christie atmosphere. It's situated just north of Piana, below the D81.

Le Casanova (☎ 04 95 27 84 20; place de la Coletta) is one of a number of pleasant terrace restaurants in Piana's central plaza.

CORTE
pop 6335

When Pasquale Paoli led Corsica to independence in 1755, he made Corte (Corti), a fortified town at the centre of the island, the country's capital. To this day, the town remains a potent symbol of Corsican independence. In 1765, Paoli founded a national university there, but it was closed when his short-lived republic was taken over by France in 1769. The Università di Corsica Pasquale Paoli was reopened in 1981 and now has approximately 4000 students, making Corte the island's liveliest and least touristy town.

Ringed with mountains, snowcapped until as late as June, Corte is an excellent base for hiking; some of the island's highest peaks rise west of the town.

Information

The **tourist office** (☎ 04 95 46 26 70, fax 04 95 46 34 05; e corte.tourisme@wanadoo.fr; La Citadelle; open 9am-noon & 2pm-6pm

Mon-Fri Oct-Apr, 9.30am-6pm Mon-Sat May-June, 9am-8pm Mon-Sat, 10am-11am & 2pm-7pm Sun July-Aug, 9am-1pm & 2pm-7pm Mon-Sat Sept) has helpful staff.

There are several **banks** with ATMs along cours Paoli. The **post office** (ave Baron Mariani) also has an ATM.

There's Internet access for €3.50 an hour at **Grand Café du Cours** (22 cours Paoli).

Things to See & Do

The **Citadelle**, built in the early 15th century and largely reconstructed during the 18th and 19th centuries, is perched on top of a hill, with the steep and twisted alleyways and streets of the **Ville Haute** and the Tavignanu and Restonica river valleys below.

The **Château** – the highest part, also known as the Nid d'Aigle (Eagle's Nest) – was built in 1419 by a Corsican nobleman and expanded by the French.

Outstanding **Museu di a Corsica** (Musée de la Corse; ☎ 04 95 45 25 45; adult/concession €5.34/3.05; open 10am-6pm Tues-Sun, 10am-8pm July & Aug) houses exhibitions on Corsican folk traditions, crafts, agriculture, economy and anthropology. It also hosts temporary art exhibitions.

The **Gorges de la Restonica**, a deep valley cut through the mountains by the Restonica River, is a favourite with hikers. The river passes Corte, but some of the choicer trails begin about 16km southwest of town at the Bergeries Grotelle sheepfolds.

Places to Stay

Camping Just south of pont Restonica is **Camping Alivetu** (☎ 04 95 46 11 09, fax 04 95 46 12 34; e camping.alivetu@laposte.net; Faubourg de St Antoine; sites per tent/adult/car €6/2.50/2.50; open 1 Apr-15 Oct).

Hostels Very rural and pretty is **Gîte d'Étape U Tavignanu** (☎ 04 95 46 16 85, fax 04 95 61 14 01; chemin de Baliri; dorm beds with breakfast/full pension €14/34.30, camping per tent/adult €1.90/3.80; open year-round). From pont Tavignanu (the first bridge on Allée du Neuf Septembre), walk westward along chemin de Baliri and follow the signs and orange paint splodges (almost 1km). There's parking down below.

Hotels The 135-room **Hôtel HR** (☎ 04 95 45 11 11, fax 04 95 61 02 85; e hr2b@aol.com; 6 allée du 9 Septembre; singles/doubles from €21/25) has clean, utilitarian rooms. **Hôtel de la Poste** (☎ 04 95 46 01 37; 2 place Padoue, rooms with shower/shower & toilet €29/41.50) has spacious and simple rooms with shower.

The atmospheric **Hôtel du Nord et de L'Europe** (☎ 04 95 46 00 68, fax 04 95 46 03 40; e info@hoteldunord-corte.com; 22 cours Paoli; rooms with shower & toilet €55) has recently been renovated.

Places to Eat

Corte's best restaurant is **U Museu** (☎ 04 95 61 08 36; Rampe Ribanella; 2-/3-course menus €11.50/13.60). Tasty local fare includes civet de sanglier aux myrtes sauvages (wild boar stew with myrtle).

Restaurant Le Bip's (☎ 04 95 46 06 26; 14 cours Paoli; menus from €12; open Sun-Fri) is a nice cellar restaurant at the bottom of the flight of stairs beside **Brasserie Le Bip's** (☎ 04 95 46 04 48).

Nearby, **Grand Café du Cours** (22 cours Paoli; open 7am-2am daily) is a cruisy student bar with Internet facilities. It serves light snacks.

There's a **Spar supermarket** (7 ave Xavier Luciani) and a **Casino supermarket** (allée du 9 Septembre).

Getting There & Away

Corte is on Eurocorse's Bastia-Ajaccio route, served by two buses daily in each direction (no Sunday service). The stop is at 3 ave Xavier Luciani where a schedule is posted.

The **train station** (☎ 04 95 46 00 97; open 6.25am-8pm Mon-Sat, 8.50am-11.20am & 3.30pm-8.25pm Sun) is at the eastern end of allée du 9 Septembre.

BONIFACIO
pop 2661

The famed **Citadelle** of Bonifacio (Bunifaziu) sits 70m above the translucent waters of the Mediterranean, atop a long, narrow and easily defensible promontory – 'Corsica's Gibraltar'. On all sides, limestone cliffs sculpted by the wind and the waves drop almost vertically to the sea; the north side looks out on 1.6km-long Bonifacio Sound, at the eastern end of which is the **marina**. The southern ramparts afford views of the coast of Sardinia, 12km away.

Bonifacio was long associated with the Republic of Genoa. The local dialect, which 's unintelligible to other Corsicans, is Genoese and many local traditions (including cooking methods) are Genoa-based.

Information

The **tourist office** (☎ 04 95 73 11 88, fax 04 95 73 14 97; **e** tourisme.bonifacio@wanadoo .fr; 2 rue Fred Scamaroni; open 9am-8pm daily May-Oct, 9am-noon & 2pm-6pm Mon-Fri, 9am-noon Sat Nov-Apr) is in the Citadelle.

The **Société Générale** (38 rue St Érasme; open Mon-Fri), outside the Citadelle, has poor rates, charges €5.30 plus a percentage commission, and has the only ATM in town. In summer, there are exchange bureaus along the marina.

Things to See & Do

Looking down the dramatic cliffs to the sea is a delight; the best views are to be had from **place du Marché** and from the walk west towards and around the cemetery. Don't miss **Porte de Gênes**, which is reached by a tiny 16th-century drawbridge, or the Romanesque **Église Ste Marie Majeure**, the oldest building in Bonifacio. **Rue des Deux Empereurs** (Street of the Two Emperors) is so-called because both Charles V and Napoleon slept there; look for the plaques at Nos 4 and 7. The **Foreign Legion Monument** east of the tourist office was brought back from Algeria in 1963 when that country won its independence.

Places to Stay

The olive-shaded **Camping Araguina** (☎ 04 95 73 02 96, fax 04 95 73 01 92; **e** camping .araguina@wanadoo.fr; ave Sylvère Bohn; sites per person/tent €6.25/1.90, bungalows €53.50; open mid-Mar–Oct) is 400m north of the marina.

In the Citadelle, **Hôtel Le Royal** (☎ 04 95 73 00 51, fax 04 95 73 04 68; rue Fred Scamaroni; rooms from €91.50 Aug, from €68.60 July & Sept, €38.20 Nov-Mar) is a friendly place with restaurant attached.

Near the cemetery at the end of the promontory is **Hôtel Santateresa** (☎ 04 95 73 11 32, fax 04 95 73 15 99; rooms €131); prices are halved in low season.

Places to Eat

In the Citadelle, **Pizzeria-Grill de la Poste** (☎ 04 95 73 13 31; 5 rue Fred Scamaroni) has Corsican dishes, pizza (from €7) and pasta (€8 to €20). **Cantina Doria** (☎ 04 95 73 50 49; 27 rue Doria) is a rustic hole-in-the-wall popular with the locals. The enormous soupe Corse (€6) is enough for two people.

Super Marché Simoni (93 quai Jérôme Comparetti) is at the marina.

Getting There & Away

Bus For buses to Ajaccio via Sartène (€19.50, four hours, two or three daily with some Sunday services) and Porto-Vecchio (€6, 30 minutes, two buses daily, four in summer), there's **Eurocorse** (Bastia ☎ 04 95 31 73 76; 1 Rue du Nouveau Port). All buses leave from the car park next to the Eurocorse kiosk at the east end of the marina.

Ferry From Bonifacio's ferry port, both **Saremar** (☎ 04 95 73 00 96) and **Moby Lines** (☎ 04 95 73 00 29) offer car and passenger ferry service year-round to Santa Teresa (50 minutes, two to seven per day).

Saremar charges €6.71/8.52 for a one-way passenger fare in low/high season while Moby Lines charges €8.50/12. There's an additional €3.10 port tax.

Germany

Few countries in Western Europe have such a fascinating and complicated past as Germany, and much of this history is easily explored by visitors today. It is also a country of sheer beauty, where outdoor activity is a way of life, and there is a huge variety of museums, architecture from many historical periods and heavy emphasis on cultural pursuits. Infrastructure is well organised, there is plenty of accommodation, and the frothy beer, heady wine and hearty food are superb.

Germany's reunification in 1990 was the beginning of yet another intriguing chapter, more than a decade old yet hardly forgotten. Though some cultural, social and economic differences of the formerly separate Germanys still exist, visitors will find that they both have their – significant – charms.

Facts about Germany

HISTORY

Events in Germany have often dominated Europe's history. But for many centuries Germany was a patchwork of semi-independent principalities and city-states, preoccupied with internal quarrels and at the mercy of foreign conquerors. In the 18th and 19th centuries, these squabbling territories gradually came under the control of Prussia, a state created by the rulers of Brandenburg. Germany only became a nation-state in 1871 and, despite the momentous events that have occurred since, many Germans still retain a strong regional identity.

Ancient & Medieval History

Germany west of the Rhine and south of the Main was part of the Roman Empire, but Roman legions never managed to subdue the warrior tribes beyond. As the Roman Empire crumbled, these tribes spread out over much of Europe, establishing small kingdoms. The Frankish conqueror Charlemagne, from his court in Aachen, forged a huge empire that covered most of Christian Western Europe, but it broke up after his death in AD 814.

The eastern branch of Charlemagne's empire developed in AD 962 into the Holy

At a Glance

- **Berlin** – world class museums, bustling bars, pubs and clubs
- **Rügen Island** – rugged chalk cliffs, wind-swept beaches, Romantic spa architecture and tree-lined country roads
- **Munich** – Oktoberfest and boisterous local beer halls
- **Füssen** – King Ludwig's fairy-tale castles Neuschwanstein and Hohenschwangau
- **Bamberg** – stellar local brews, great architecture in a Unesco World Heritage city

Capital	Berlin
Population	82.5 million
Official Language	German
Currency	euro
Time	GMT/UTC+0100
Country Phone Code	☎ 49

GERMANY

Roman Empire, organised under Otto I (Otto the Great). It included much of present-day Germany, Austria, Switzerland and Benelux. The term 'Holy Roman' was coined in an effort to assume some of the authority of the defunct Roman Empire.

The house of Habsburg, ruling from Vienna, took control of the shrinking empire in the 13th century, which became little more than a conglomerate of German-speaking states run by local rulers who paid mere lip service to the Habsburg emperor. A semblance

GERMANY

GERMANY

DENMARK

SWEDEN

COPENHAGEN

Bornholm

NORTH SEA

Sylt Island
Amrum Island
North Frisian Islands

Schleswig

BALTIC SEA

Rügen Island
Sassnitz
Binz

Heide
Kiel
Warnemünde
Stralsund

SCHLESWIG-HOLSTEIN

Rostock

East Frisian Islands

Cuxhaven
Lübeck
Wismar

MECKLENBURG-WESTERN POMERANIA

Wilhelmshaven

Hamburg
Schwerin

HAMBURG

NETHERLANDS

Bremen

Elbe River

BREMEN

POLAND

LOWER SAXONY

SAXONY-ANHALT

BRANDENBURG

Oder

BERLIN

Frankfurt/Oder

Hanover
Potsdam
BERLIN

Hameln
Badenwerder
Goslar

Magdeburg

River

Clausthal-Zellerfeld
Wernigerode
Quedlinburg

Lutherstadt Wittenberg
Dessau

NORTH RHINE-WESTPHALIA

Dortmund

Göttingen
Kassel

Nordhausen

Halle
Leipzig

Meissen

Görlitz

Düsseldorf

THURINGIA

Erfurt
Naumburg
Weimar

Dresden

SAXONY

Cologne
Aachen
Bonn

Marburg
Eisenach

BELGIUM

HESSE

Cochem
Koblenz

Frankfurt/Main

RHINELAND-PALATINATE

Rüdesheim
Wiesbaden
Hanau
Mainz

PRAGUE

LUXEMBOURG

Trier

Würzburg
Bamberg

Marktredwitz

Moselle

SAARLAND

Mannheim
Heidelberg

CZECH REPUBLIC

Saarbrücken

Rothenburg o.d. Tauber

Nuremberg

BAVARIA

Karlsruhe

Dinkelsbühl

Regensburg

Baden-Baden
Stuttgart

Nördlingen

Danube River

Passau

BADEN-WÜRTTEMBERG

Ulm

Augsburg

FRANCE

Freiburg

Rhine River

Munich

AUSTRIA

Donaueschingen

Constance
Lake Constance
Lindau

Füssen
Garmisch-Partenkirchen

Berchtesgaden

Oberstdorf

SWITZERLAND

LIECHTENSTEIN

0   50   100km
0   30   60mi

of unity in northern Germany was maintained by the Hanseatic League, a federation of German and Baltic city-states with Lübeck as its centre. The League began to form in the mid-12th century and dissolved in 1669.

The Reformation

Things would never be the same in Europe after Martin Luther, a scholar from the monastery in Erfurt, nailed his *95 Theses* to the church door in Wittenberg in 1517. Luther opposed the Catholic Church's system involving the selling of so-called 'indulgences', which absolved sinners from temporal punishment. In 1521 he was condemned by the Church and went into hiding in Wartburg Castle in Eisenach. There he translated the Bible from the Greek version into an everyday form of German. This Bible was printed on presses developed by Gutenberg in Mainz and was then read widely to the masses.

Luther's efforts at reforming the Church gained widespread support from merchants, wealthy townsfolk and, crucially, several ambitious German princes. This protest against the established Church began the Protestant movement and the Reformation. The Peace of Augsburg in 1555 declared that the religion of a state would be determined by its ruler.

Meanwhile the established Church, often called the 'Roman' Catholic Church, began a campaign known as the Counter-Reformation to stem the spread of Protestantism.

Thirty Years' War

The tensions between Protestant and Catholic states across Europe led to the catastrophic Thirty Years' War (1618–48). Germany became the battlefield for the great powers of Europe, losing more than one-third of its population and many of its towns and cities. It took the country centuries to recover.

The Peace of Westphalia in 1648 established the rights of both faiths in Germany but also sealed the country's political division. The German-speaking states remained a patchwork of independent principalities within the loose framework of the Holy Roman Empire, but were weakened further by the loss of important territories.

Prussia Unites Germany

During the 18th century the Kingdom of Prussia, with its capital in Berlin, became one of Europe's strongest powers. Thanks to the organisational talents of Friedrich Wilhelm I (the Soldier King) and his son Friedrich II (Frederick the Great), it expanded eastwards at the expense of Poland, Lithuania and Russia.

In the early 19th century, the fragmented German states proved easy pickings for Napoleon. The Austrian emperor, Francis II, relinquished his crown as Holy Roman Emperor in 1806 following his defeat at Austerlitz. But the French never quite managed to subdue Prussia, which became the centre of German resistance. After his disastrous foray into Russia, Prussia led the war that put an end to Napoleon's German aspirations in a decisive battle at Leipzig in 1813.

In 1815 the Congress of Vienna again redrew the map of Europe. The Holy Roman Empire was replaced with a German Confederation of 35 states; it had a parliament in Frankfurt and was led by the Austrian chancellor Klemens von Metternich. The Confederation was shaken by liberal revolutions in Europe in 1830 and 1848, but the Austrian monarchy continued to dominate a divided Germany.

The well-oiled Prussian civil and military machine eventually smashed this arrangement. In 1866, Otto von Bismarck (the Iron Chancellor) took Prussia to war against Austria, and rapidly annexed northern Germany. Another successful war in 1870–71 resulted in Prussia defeating France and seizing Alsace and Lorraine. The Catholic, anti-Prussian states in southern Germany were forced to negotiate with Bismarck, who had achieved his dream of German unity. The Prussian king, Wilhelm I, became *Kaiser* (German emperor).

WWI & the Rise of Hitler

Wilhelm II dismissed Bismarck in 1890, however, Germany's rapid growth overtaxed the Kaiser's political talents and led to mounting tensions with England, Russia and France. When war broke out in 1914, Germany's only ally was a weakened Austria-Hungary.

Gruelling trench warfare on two fronts sapped the nation's resources, and by late 1918 Germany sued for peace. The Kaiser abdicated and escaped to Holland. Anger on the home front, which had been mounting during the fighting and deprivation, exploded when the troops returned home. A full-scale socialist uprising, based in Berlin and led by the Spartacus League, was put down, and its leaders, Karl Liebknecht and Rosa Luxemburg,

GERMANY

were murdered. A new republic, which became known as the Weimar Republic, was proclaimed.

The Treaty of Versailles in 1919 chopped huge areas off Germany and imposed heavy reparation payments. These were impossible to meet, and when France and Belgium occupied the Rhineland to ensure continued payments, the subsequent hyperinflation and miserable economic conditions provided fertile ground for political extremists. One of these was Adolf Hitler.

Led by Hitler, an Austrian drifter and German army veteran, the National (or Nazi) Socialist German Workers' Party staged an abortive coup in Munich in 1923. This landed Hitler in prison for nine months, during which time he wrote *Mein Kampf*.

From 1929 the worldwide economic depression hit Germany particularly hard, leading to massive unemployment, strikes and demonstrations. The Communist Party under Ernst Thälmann gained strength, but wealthy industrialists began to support the Nazis and police turned a blind eye to Nazi street thugs.

The Nazis increased their strength in general elections and in 1933 replaced the Social Democrats as the largest party in the Reichstag (parliament), with about one-third of the seats. Hitler was appointed chancellor and one year later assumed absolute control as *Führer* (leader) of what he called the Third Reich (the 'third empire'; the previous two being the Holy Roman Empire and Wilhelm I's German Empire).

WWII & the Division of Germany

From 1935 Germany began to re-arm and build its way out of depression with strategic public works such as the autobahns. Hitler reoccupied the Rhineland in 1936, and in 1938 annexed Austria and, following a compromise agreement with Britain and France, parts of Czechoslovakia.

All of this took place against a backdrop of growing racism at home. The Nuremburg Laws of 1935 deprived non-Aryans – mostly Jews and Roma (Gypsies) – of German citizenship and many other rights. On 9 November 1938, the horror escalated into the *Reichspogromnacht* (often called *Kristallnacht* or the 'night of broken glass'), in which synagogues and Jewish cemeteries, property and businesses across Germany were desecrated, burnt or demolished.

In September 1939, after signing a pact that allowed both Stalin and himself a free hand in the east of Europe, Hitler attacked Poland which led to war with Britain and France. Germany quickly invaded large parts of Europe but after 1942 began to suffer increasingly heavy losses. Massive bombing reduced Germany's centres to rubble, and the country lost 10% of its population. Meanwhile, Nazi racism was creating unprecedented horrors. 'Concentration camps' were intended to rid Europe of people considered undesirable according to Nazi doctrine, with the resulting extermination of some six million Jews and one million more Roma, communists, homosexuals and others in what has come to be known as 'the Holocaust, history's first 'assembly-line' genocide. Germany accepted unconditional surrender in May 1945, soon after Hitler's suicide.

At conferences in Yalta and Potsdam, the Allies (the Soviet Union, the USA, the UK and France) redrew the borders of Germany, making it around 25% smaller than it had already become after the Treaty of Versailles 26 years earlier. Some 6.5 million ethnic Germans migrated or were expelled to Germany from Eastern Europe, where they had lived for centuries. Germany was divided into four occupation zones, and Berlin was occupied jointly by the four victorious powers.

In the Soviet zone of the country, the communist Socialist Unity Party (SED) won the 1946 elections and began a rapid nationalisation of industry. In June 1948 the Soviet Union stopped all land traffic between Germany's western zones and Berlin. This forced the Western allies to mount a military operation known as the Berlin Airlift, which brought food and other supplies to West Berlin by plane until the Soviets lifted the blockade in May 1949.

In September 1949 the Federal Republic of Germany (FRG) was created out of the three western zones; in response the German Democratic Republic (GDR) was founded in the Soviet zone the following month, with (East) Berlin as its capital.

From Division to Unity

As the West's bulwark against communism, the FRG received massive injections of US capital, and experienced rapid economic development (the *Wirschaftswunder*, or 'economic miracle') under the leadership of Konrad Adenauer. At the same time the

GDR had to pay US$10 billion in war reparations to the Soviet Union and rebuild itself from scratch.

A better life in the west increasingly attracted skilled workers away from the miserable economic conditions in the east. As these were people the GDR could ill afford to lose, in 1961 it built a wall around West Berlin and sealed its border with the FRG. As the Cold War intensified, TV and radio stations in both Germanys beamed programmes heavy with propaganda to the other side.

Coinciding with a change to the more flexible leadership of Erich Honecker in the east, the *Ostpolitik* of FRG chancellor Willy Brandt allowed an easier political relationship between the two Germanys. In 1971 the four occupying powers formally accepted the division of Berlin. Many Western countries, but not West Germany itself, then officially recognised the GDR.

Honecker's policies produced higher living standards in the GDR, yet East Germany barely managed to achieve a level of prosperity half that of the FRG. After Mikhail Gorbachev came to power in the Soviet Union in March 1985, the East German communists gradually lost Soviet backing.

Events in 1989 rapidly overtook the East German government, which resisted pressure to introduce reforms. When Hungary relaxed its border controls in May 1989, East Germans began crossing to the west. Tighter travel controls introduced by the Politburo resulted in would-be defectors taking refuge in the FRG's embassy in Prague. Meanwhile, mass demonstrations in Leipzig spread to other cities of the GDR and Honecker was replaced by his security chief, Egon Krenz, who introduced cosmetic reforms. Then suddenly on 9 November 1989, a Politburo decision to allow direct travel to the west was mistakenly interpreted as the immediate opening of all GDR borders with West Germany. That same night thousands of people streamed into the west past stunned border guards. Millions more followed in the next few days, and dismantling of the Berlin Wall began soon thereafter.

The trend at first was to reform the GDR but, in East German elections held in early 1990, citizens voted clearly in favour of the Christian Democratic Union (CDU), thus paving the way for fast-track reunification. The wartime Allies signed the Two-Plus-Four Treaty which ended the postwar system of occupation zones, and a Unification Treaty was drawn up to integrate East Germany into the Federal Republic of Germany, which came about on 3 October 1990. All-German elections were held on 2 December that year and, in the midst of national euphoria, the CDU-led coalition, which strongly favoured reunification, soundly defeated the Social Democrat opposition, earning the CDU's leader, Helmut Kohl, the moniker of 'unification chancellor'.

The Land in the Middle

In 1998, a coalition of Social Democrats, led by Gerhard Schröder, and Bündnis 90/the Green party took political office from Kohl and the CDU. Schröder and the SDP-Greens coalition narrowly retained office in the 2002 election, although the close result foreshadowed a period of instability.

At reunification, it was said that it would take 10 years to bring the two Germanys to parity, but now it's generally considered that another 10 years will be needed. Unemployment in some eastern states hovers above 20%, there have been occasionally violent attacks on foreigners, and the German 'economic miracle' seems to be losing steam.

Still, Germany, the 'land in the middle', is more confident than it was under division and more democratic, and it has assumed a more assertive role in world affairs, strongly bound to the European Union (EU) but also focusing attention on the East.

GEOGRAPHY

Germany covers 356,866 sq km and can be divided from north to south into several geographical regions.

The Northern Lowlands are a broad expanse of flat, low-lying land that sweeps across the northern third of the country from the Netherlands into Poland. The landscape is characterised by moist heaths interspersed with pastures and farmland.

The complex Central Uplands region divides northern Germany from the south. Extending from the deep schisms of the Rhineland massifs to the Black Forest, the Bavarian Forest, the Ore Mountains and the Harz Mountains, these low mountain ranges are Germany's heartland. The Rhine and Main Rivers, important waterways for inland shipping, cut through the southwest of this region. With large deposits of coal as well as favourable transport conditions, this was one

GERMANY

of the first regions in Germany to undergo industrialisation.

The Alpine Foothills, wedged between the Danube and the Alps, are typified by subalpine plateau and rolling hills, and by moors in eastern regions around the Danube.

Germany's Alps lie entirely within Bavaria and stretch from the large, glacially formed Lake Constance in the west to Berchtesgaden in Germany's southeastern corner. Though lower than the mountains to their south, many summits are well above 2000m, rising dramatically from the Alpine Foothills to the 2966m Zugspitze, Germany's highest mountain.

CLIMATE

German weather can be variable, so it's best to be prepared for many conditions throughout the year. That said, the most reliable weather is from May to October, coinciding with the standard tourist season (except for skiing). The shoulder periods (late March to May and September to October) can bring fewer tourists and surprisingly pleasant weather.

Eastern Germany lies in a transition zone between the temperate maritime climate of Western Europe and the rougher continental climate of Eastern Europe – continental and Atlantic air masses meet here. The mean daily temperature in Berlin is 11°C, the average range of temperatures varying from -1°C in January to 18°C in July. The average annual precipitation is 585mm and there is no special rainy season. Camping season is from May to September.

ECOLOGY & ENVIRONMENT

Germans are fiercely protective of their natural surroundings. Households and businesses participate enthusiastically in waste-recycling programmes. A refund system applies to a wide range of glass bottles and jars, while containers for waste paper and glass can be found in each neighbourhood. Though acid rain is a problem, German forests have lost little of their wonderful fairy-tale charm, whereas in eastern Germany regions around the Oder River and in parts of Mecklenburg and Western Pomerania have retained an intact central European ecosystem.

Energy

Clashes between the police and antinuclear demonstrators in Germany in the 1980s were the most violent and bloody in Europe since the 1968 Paris student riots: armed anarchists,

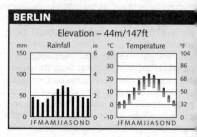

armed police, and committed ordinary Germans were caught between revolutionary intent and a state of siege. In Germany, it was all about shutting down nuclear reactors and preventing new ones being built. Times have changed. Germany still generates about one-third of its energy from its 19 atomic plants but a deal has been struck with the powerful energy lobby to close the plants over the next three decades. In the meantime, nuclear waste remains a sticky, unresolved issue.

FLORA & FAUNA

Few species of flora and fauna are unique to Germany. Unique, however, is the importance Germans place on their forests, the prettiest of which are mixed-species deciduous forests planted with beech, oak, maple and birch. You'll find that many cities even have their own city forest (Stadtwald). Alpine regions bloom in spring with orchids, cyclamen, gentians, edelweiss, and more; and the heather blossom on the Lüneburg Heath, north of Hanover, is stunning in August.

Apart from human beings, common mammals include deer, wild pigs, rabbits, foxes and hares. The chances of seeing any of these in summer are fairly good, especially in eastern Germany. The wild pig population is particularly thriving; some pigs even wander occasionally into the suburbs of Berlin! On the coasts you will find seals and, throughout Germany, falcons, hawks, storks and migratory geese are a common sight.

Berchtesgaden (in the Bavarian Alps), the Wattenmeer parks in Schleswig-Holstein, Lower Saxony and Hamburg, and the Unteres Odertal, which is a joint German-Polish endeavour, are highlights among Germany's dozen or so national parks.

GOVERNMENT & POLITICS

Germany has a very decentralised governmental structure – a federal system based upon regional states. Reunification resulted in eastern Germany's six original (pre-1952) states of Berlin, Brandenburg, Mecklenburg-Vorpommern (Mecklenburg-Western Pomerania), Sachsen (Saxony), Sachsen-Anhalt (Saxony-Anhalt) and Thüringen (Thuringia) all being re-established. In the context of the Federal Republic of Germany they are called *Bundesländer* (federal states).

The Bundesländer in western Germany are Schleswig-Holstein, Hamburg, Niedersachsen (Lower Saxony), Bremen, Nordrhein-Westfalen (North Rhine-Westphalia), Hessen (Hesse), Rheinland-Pfalz (the Rhineland-Palatinate), Saarland, Baden-Württemberg and Bayern (Bavaria). Germans commonly refer to the eastern states as the *neue Bundesländer* (new states) and to the western states as the *alte Bundesländer* (old states).

The Bundesländer have a large degree of autonomy in internal affairs and exert influence on the central government through the *Bundesrat* (upper house). The *Bundestag* (lower house) is elected by direct universal suffrage with proportional representation, although a party must have at least 5% of the vote to gain a seat. In September 1999 the Bundestag resumed sitting in Berlin's restored Reichstag building, transferring the seat of government from Bonn.

Germany's two major parties are the Christian Democrats (CDU, or CSU in Bavaria) and the Social Democrats (SPD). The Free Democrats (FDP), a small but influential liberal party, often holds the balance of power. The Democratic Socialists (PDS), the former East German SED, is a strong force in eastern Germany, whereas the popularity and fortunes of Bündnis 90/the Green party have been mixed in recent years.

ECONOMY

The Marshall Plan helped to produce West Germany's *Wirtschaftswunder* (economic miracle), which in the 1950s and 1960s turned the FRG into the world's third-largest economy. Trade unions and industrial corporations developed a unique economic contract which involves employees in company decisions. Important industries include electrical manufacturing, precision and optical instruments, chemicals and vehicle manufacturing, and environmental technology.

East Germany's recovery was even more remarkable given the wartime destruction, postwar looting by the USSR, loss of skilled labour, and isolation from Western markets. The GDR was by any measure an important industrial nation, with major metallurgical, electrical, chemical and engineering industries. As a result of reunification, many industries were privatised, but others were closed down, causing unemployment and hardship in some regions. Those most affected were women and older workers.

Eastern Germany now has a modern infrastructure, but little is being invested there, and it has been losing population since reunification. About 15 million people currently live in the eastern states. However, with the decline of traditional heavy industries in the region, tourism has become important; the region is also well-placed geographically to gain from restructured Eastern European markets or an expanded EU.

Unemployment remains a major problem throughout Germany, especially in the eastern regions where some 17.5% of the work force is unemployed. The national figure is around 9.5%.

Germany, though slow at first to adapt to the 'new economy' of the 1990s, now has thriving IT, online and telecommunications industries.

Economic growth is slow in comparison to most other European countries, particularly in eastern Germany.

When Germany switched its currency from the hallowed Deutschmark to the forward-thinking euro in 2002, there was supposed to be an even conversion of prices; but many business owners used the opportunity to raise prices, causing a low-level stir.

POPULATION & PEOPLE

Germany has a population of around 82.5 million, making it the most populous in Europe after Russia. Germany's main native minority is the tiny group of Slavonic Sorbs in the eastern states of Saxony and Brandenburg. In political and economic terms, Germany is Europe's most decentralised nation, but considerable variation in population density exists. The Ruhr district in the northern Rhineland has Germany's densest concentration of people and industry, while Mecklenburg-Western Pomerania in the northeastern corner is relatively sparsely settled. About one-third of the population lives in 84 cities, each with more than 100,000 people.

A strong immigrant tradition in Germany dates back to around 1700, when some 30% of Berlin's population consisted of Huguenots who had fled religious oppression in France. Another large wave of immigrants moved to the Ruhr region from Poland in the late 19th century. In effect, immigration compensates for the extremely low birth rate among the established German population.

More than seven million foreigners now live in Germany. Most hail from Turkey, Italy, Greece and the former Yugoslavia, and have arrived as 'guest workers' in the FRG since the early 1960s to work in lower-paid jobs. In 1999 archaic immigration laws dating back to 1913 were changed to make it easier for residents without German ancestry to gain citizenship. This now takes about seven years. Eastern Germany has fewer resident foreigners, though some of the roughly 200,000 workers who arrived in the GDR during the 1980s from 'fraternal socialist' countries remain.

ARTS

Germany's meticulously creative population has made major contributions to international culture. Germans take their *Kultur* so seriously that visitors sometimes wonder how on earth they manage to actually enjoy it. The answer may lie in a German musician's proverb: 'True bliss is absolute concentration'.

Architecture, Painting & Literature

The scope of German art is such that it could be the focus of an entire visit. The arts first blossomed during the Romanesque period (800–1200), of which examples can be found at the Germanisches Nationalmuseum in Nuremberg, Trier Cathedral, the churches of Cologne, the chapel of Charlemagne's palace in Aachen, and the Stiftskirche in Gernrode.

The Gothic style (1200–1500) is best viewed at Freiburg's Münster cathedral, Meissen Cathedral, Cologne's Dom and the Marienkirche in Lübeck. Artists from the Cologne school of painters and sculptor Peter Vischer and his sons produced both Gothic sculpture and innovative paintings featuring rudimentary landscapes. One famous panel painting is a work by Meister Bertram (c. 1340), in Hamburg's Kunsthalle.

The Renaissance came late to Germany but flourished once it took hold. The draughtsman Albrecht Dürer of Nuremberg (1471–1528) was one of the world's finest portraitists, as was the prolific Lucas Cranach the Elder (1472–1553) who worked in Wittenberg (now Lutherstadt Wittenberg) for more than 45 years.

The baroque period brought great sculpture including works by Andreas Schlüter in Berlin. Balthasar Neumann's superb Residenz in Würzburg and the magnificent cathedral in Passau are the foremost examples of baroque architecture.

The Enlightenment During the 18th century, the Saxon court at Weimar attracted some of the major cultural figures of Europe. Among them was Johann Wolfgang von Goethe (1749–1832), the poet, dramatist, painter, scientist, philosopher and perhaps the last European to achieve the Renaissance ideal of excellence in many fields. His greatest work, the drama *Faust*, is a masterful epic of all that went before him, as the archetypal human strives for meaning and knowledge.

Goethe's close friend, Friedrich Schiller (1759–1805), was a poet, dramatist and novelist. His most famous work is the dramatic cycle *Wallenstein*, based on the life of a treacherous general of the Thirty Years' War who plotted to make himself arbiter of the empire. Schiller's other great play, *William Tell*, dealt with the right of the oppressed to rise against tyranny. There are large museums in Weimar dedicated to both Schiller and Goethe.

The 19th & Early 20th Centuries Berlin too produced remarkable individuals, such as Alexander von Humboldt (1769–1859), an advanced thinker in environmentalism through his studies of the relationship of plants and animals to their physical surroundings. His contemporary, the philosopher Georg Wilhelm Friedrich Hegel (1770–1831), created an all-embracing classical philosophy that is still influential today. The neoclassical period in Germany was led by Karl Friedrich Schinkel and the Munich neoclassical school. The romantic period is best exemplified by the paintings of Caspar David Friedrich and Otto Runge.

Art Nouveau also made important contributions to German architecture. Expressionism followed, with great names like Paul Klee and the Russian-born painter Vasili Kandinsky. In 1919, Walter Gropius founded the Bauhaus movement in an attempt to meld theoretical concerns of architecture with the practical problems faced by artists and craftspeople. The Bauhaus flourished in Dessau, but with the arrival of the Nazis, Gropius left for Harvard University.

In the 1920s, Berlin was the theatrical capital of Germany; one of its most famous practitioners was the poet and playwright Bertold Brecht (1898–1956). Brecht introduced Marxist concepts into his plays, and his work was distinguished by the simplicity of its moral parables, its language and its sharp characterisation. Brecht revolutionised the theatre by detaching the audience from what was happening on stage, enabling them to observe the content without being distracted by the form. In 1933 Brecht fled the Nazis and lived in various countries, eventually accepting the directorship of the Berliner Ensemble in East Berlin, where his work has been performed ever since.

One of Brecht's contemporaries was Kurt Weill (A Threepenny Opera), associated with Dessau and Berlin before fleeing the Nazis for New York.

Easily Germany's most famous performer of the 20th century was Marlene Dietrich (1901–1992). The Berlin-born femme fatale started as a silent film star, later moved to Hollywood and refused to return to Germany after Hitler's rise to power. She became an icon for her androgynous getups and erotic overtones, represented by her signature song 'Falling in Love Again', and led a reclusive later life in Paris.

WWII & Beyond During the Third Reich, the arts were devoted mainly to propaganda, with grandiose projects and realist art extolling the virtues of German nationhood. The best-known Nazi-era director was Leni Riefenstahl (1902-). Her Triumph of the Will (1934) won some of filmmaking's highest honours but later rendered her unemployable due to its status as Nazi propaganda. Albert Speer was Hitler's favourite architect, known for pompous neoclassical buildings.

Max Ernst, resident in France and the USA, was an exponent of dada and surrealism who developed the technique of collage.

Postwar literature in both Germanys was influenced by the politically focused Gruppe 47. It included writers such as Günter Grass, winner of the 1999 Nobel Prize for Literature, whose modern classic, Die Blechtrommel (The Tin Drum), humorously follows German history through the eyes of a young boy who refuses to grow. Christa Wolf, an East German novelist and Gruppe 47 writer, won high esteem in both Germanys. Her 1963 story Der geteilte Himmel (Divided Heaven) tells of a young woman whose fiance abandons her for life in the West.

Patrick Süskind's Das Parfum (The Perfume) is the extraordinary tale of a psychotic 18th-century perfume-maker with an obsessive genius. Helden wie wir (Heroes Like Us) by Thomas Brussig, an eastern German, tells the story of a man whose penis brings about the collapse of the Berlin Wall.

Music

Few countries can claim the impressive musical heritage of Germany. A partial list of household names includes Johann Sebastian Bach, Georg Friedrich Händel, Ludwig van Beethoven, Richard Wagner, Richard Strauss, Felix Mendelssohn-Bartholdy, Robert Schumann, Johannes Brahms and Gustav Mahler.

Johann Sebastian Bach (1685–1750) was born at Eisenach into a prominent family of musicians. During his time as court organist at Weimar and city musical director at Leipzig, Bach produced some 200 cantatas, as well as masses, oratorios, passions and other elaborate music for the Lutheran service, as well as sonatas, concertos, preludes and fugues for secular use.

Georg Friedrich Händel (1685–1759) left his native Halle for Hamburg at 18. He composed numerous operas and oratorios, including his masterpiece Messiah (1742). The birthplaces of both Händel and Bach are now large museums.

In 1843, Robert Schumann (1810–56) opened a music school at Leipzig in collaboration with composer Felix Mendelssohn-Bartholdy (1809–47), director of Leipzig's famous Gewandhaus Orchestra. Works by Richard Wagner (1813–83) represent a milestone in European classical music, and no composer since Wagner's time could ignore his attempts to balance all operatic forms to produce a 'total work of art'.

These musical traditions continue to thrive: the Dresden Opera and Leipzig Orchestra are known around the world, and musical performances are hosted almost daily in every major theatre in the country.

Germany has also made a significant contribution to the contemporary music scene,

GERMANY

with Kraftwerk creating the first 'techno' sounds, and through internationally renowned Nina Hagen, Nena, the Scorpions, Die Toten Hosen and Fury in the Slaughterhouse.

You can hear jazz, folk, techno, house and other sounds in clubs in major cities. The Studio for Electronic Music in Cologne and Hamburg's Mojo club are two innovative venues. Traditional German oompah music is still popular with some locals and tourists, while Schlager music, with its treacly lyrics, confounds foreigners with its popularity.

SOCIETY & CONDUCT

The unflattering image of Germans as overly disciplined and humourless is a stereotype. On the whole, you'll find Germans relaxed, personable and interested in enjoying life.

Tradition plays a surprisingly strong role despite, or perhaps because of, the country's modern industrial achievements. Hunters still wear green, many Bavarian women don the *Dirndl* (skirt and blouse), while some menfolk sport the typical Bavarian *Lederhosen* (leather shorts), a *Loden* (short jacket) and felt hat. In contrast, you might hear young Germans dismiss this sort of thing as *typisch deutsch* (typically German), a phrase that usually has negative connotations.

While Germans are generally not prudish or awkwardly polite, formal manners remain important. When making a phone call to anywhere in Germany, you'll find people more helpful if you first introduce yourself by name. Germans sometimes shake hands when greeting or leaving. Hugging and cheek kissing is common between males and females who know one another.

The Holocaust and WWII, while by no means taboo topics, should be discussed with tact and understanding in Germany. In western Germany these themes have been dealt with openly for decades – less so in eastern Germany until reunification – but Germans sometimes feel their country's pre and postwar contributions are under-emphasised against its relatively short period under the Nazis. Germans take great offence at the presumption that fascist ideas are somehow part of or even compatible with their national culture.

RELIGION

Most Germans belong to a church, and there are almost equal numbers of Catholics and Protestants; roughly speaking, the Catholics predominate in the south, Protestants in the north and east. Most citizens pay contributions to their church, which the government collects along with their taxes, but in practice few Germans regularly attend church services.

Despite their bitter historical rivalry, conflict between Catholics and Protestants in Germany is not an issue. In eastern Germany the Protestant Church, which claims support among the overwhelming majority of the population there, played a major role in the overthrow of German communism by providing a gathering place for antigovernment protesters. Active church membership, however, remains lower than in western Germany.

In 1933 some 530,000 Jews lived in Germany. Today that number is around 50,000, with the largest communities in Berlin, Frankfurt and Munich. Their population is growing with the recent influx of Russian Jews. There are also more than 1.7 million Muslims, most of them Turks.

LANGUAGE

It might come as a surprise to learn that German is a close relative of English. English, German and Dutch are all known as West Germanic languages. This means that you already know lots of German words – *Arm, Finger, Gold* – and you'll be able to figure out many of the others, such as *Mutter* (mother), *trinken* (drink), *gut* (good). A primary reason why English and German have grown apart is that when the Normans invaded England in 1066 they brought in many non-Germanic words. For this reason, English has many synonyms, usually with the everyday word being German, and the more literary or specialised one coming from French, eg, 'start' and 'green' as opposed to 'commence' and 'verdant'.

German is spoken throughout Germany and Austria and in much of Switzerland. It is also useful in Eastern Europe, especially with older people. Although you will hear different regional dialects, the official language, *Hochdeutsch*, is universally understood. English is widely understood by young or educated Germans, but as soon as you try to meet ordinary people or move out of the big cities, especially in eastern Germany, the situation is rather different. Your efforts to speak the local language will be appreciated and will make your trip much more enjoyable.

Words that you'll often encounter on maps and throughout this chapter include: *Altstadt* (old city), *Bahnhof* (train station), *Brücke* (bridge), *Hauptbahnhof* (main train station), *Markt* (market, often the central square in old towns), *Platz* (square), *Rathaus* (town hall) and *Strasse* (street). German nouns are always written with a capital letter.

See the Language chapter at the back of the book for pronunciation guidelines and useful words and phrases.

Facts for the Visitor

HIGHLIGHTS
Museums & Galleries
Germany is a museum-lover's dream. Munich features the huge Deutsches Museum, and Frankfurt's Museumsufer (Museum Embankment) has enough museums for any addict. Berlin's Kulturforum and Museumsinsel (Museum Island, still being rebuilt) are home to some astounding works. Dresden's Zwinger and Albertinum are among its chief art museums, while cultural treasures are centred at Nuremberg's Germanisches Nationalmuseum.

Castles
Germany has castles of all periods and styles. If you're into castles, make sure to hit Heidelberg Meissen, Neuschwanstein, Burg Rheinfels on the Rhine River, Burg Eltz on the Moselle, the medieval Königstein and Wartburg Castles, Renaissance Wittenberg Castle, baroque Schloss Moritzburg and the romantic Wernigerode Castle.

Historic Towns
Time stands still in parts of Germany, and some of the best towns in which to find this flavour are Wismar, Goslar and Regensburg. Meissen and Quedlinburg have a fairy-tale air, Weimar has a special place in German culture, and Lübeck is one of Europe's true gems. The *Altstadt* (old district) of many large cities also imparts this historic feel.

Roads & Rivers
Germany has many scenic theme roads, such as those in the Black Forest and the Fairy-Tale Road between Hanau and Bremen. The best way to explore them is by car. Check with local or regional tourist offices for maps and highlights of the route.

Important rivers such as the Rhine, Danube, Moselle and Elbe are well-serviced by boats in summer, and the Rhine and Moselle Rivers are especially suited to combined wine quaffing and cruising.

SUGGESTED ITINERARIES
Depending on the length of your stay, you might want to see and do the following things:

Two days
Depending on where you enter the country, try to spend your days in either Berlin or Munich.
One week
Divide your time between Berlin and Munich, and throw in a visit to Dresden or Bamberg.
Two weeks
Berlin (including Potsdam), Dresden or Bamberg, Munich, Freiburg and the Rhine or Moselle Valley.
One month
Berlin (including Potsdam), Dresden or Bamberg, Meissen, the Harz Mountains, the Rhine or Moselle Valley, Munich, the Alps, Lake Constance, Freiburg or Lübeck.
Two months
As for one month, plus Weimar, Regensburg, Passau, the Romantic Road, Cologne, and the North Frisian Islands.

PLANNING
When to Go
Unless frolicking in winter snow is your thing, Germany is best visited from April to October – July and August tend to have the most visitors. If you don't mind slushy, bitterly cold and bleak weather, a winter visit does have its charms; large cities and the Baltic coast can be blessedly free of tourists. Central Uplands regions, like the Harz Mountains and Black Forest, are good places to hike and relax year-round, especially at the higher altitudes. Bring good winter gear and rain jackets.

Flood Damage
At the time of writing Germany was facing an estimated clean-up bill of around €15 billion following the floods that hit the southern and eastern parts of the country in the summer of 2002. What effect the flood damage will have on travellers is not yet clear; however, visitors to affected regions – particularly the Dresden area – would be well advised to check on the latest situation.

TOURIST OFFICES

German tourist offices are efficient, a mine of information and have useful free maps.

Local Tourist Offices

Before your trip, consult the **German National Tourist Office** (*Deutsche Zentrale für Tourismus, DZT;* ☎ *069-97 46 40, fax 75 19 03;* e *info@d-z-t.com;* w *www.visits-to-Germany .com; Beethovenstrasse 69, 60325 Frankfurt/ Main*). For local information, you can go to the *Verkehrsamt* (tourist office) or *Kurverwaltung* (resort administration), listed for each town.

Tourist Offices Abroad

German National Tourist Office representatives abroad include:

Australia & New Zealand (☎ 02-9267 8148, fax 9267 9035, e gnto@germany.org.au) PO Box A 980, Sydney, NSW 1235
Canada (☎ 416-968 1570, fax 968 1986, e gnto@aol.com) 175 Bloor St East, North Tower, 6th floor, Toronto, Ont M4W 3R8
South Africa (☎ 011-643 1615, fax 484 2750) c/o Lufthansa German Airlines, PO Box 10883, Johannesburg 2000
UK (☎ 020-7317 0908, fax 7495 6129) PO Box 2695, London W1A 3TN
USA (☎ 212-661 7200, fax 661 7174, e gntony@aol.com) 122 East 42nd St, 52nd floor, New York, NY 10168-0072

Other offices are in Amsterdam, Brussels, Copenhagen, Helsinki, Hong Kong, Madrid, Milan, Moscow, Oslo, Paris, São Paulo, Stockholm, Tel Aviv, Tokyo, Vienna and Zürich.

VISAS & DOCUMENTS

Americans, Australians, Britons, Canadians, Israelis, Japanese, New Zealanders and Singaporeans require only a valid passport (no visa) to enter Germany. Citizens of the EU and some other Western European countries can enter on an official identity card. Three months is the usual limit of stay; less for citizens of some developing countries. See Work later in this section for information on work permits.

EMBASSIES & CONSULATES
German Embassies & Consulates

Diplomatic representation abroad includes:

Australia (☎ 02-6270 1911, fax 6270 1951) 119 Empire Circuit, Yarralumla, ACT 2600

Canada (☎ 613-232 1101, fax 594 9330) 1 Waverley St, Ottawa, Ont K2P 0T8
Ireland (☎ 01-269 3011, fax 269 3946) 31 Trimleston Ave, Booterstown, Dublin
New Zealand (☎ 04-473 6063, fax 473 6069) 90-92 Hobson St, Wellington
UK (☎ 020-7824 1300, fax 7824 1435) 23 Belgrave Square, London SW1X 8PZ
USA (☎ 202-298 4000, fax 298 4249) 4645 Reservoir Rd, NW Washington, DC 20007-1998

Embassies & Consulates in Germany

The area code for Berlin is ☎ 030.

Australia (☎ 880 08 80, fax 880 08 80 351) Friedrichstrasse 200, 10117 Berlin
Canada (☎ 20 31 20, fax 20 31 25 90) Friedrichstrasse 95, 10117 Berlin
Ireland (☎ 22 07 20, fax 22 07 22 99) Friedrichstrasse 200, 10117 Berlin
New Zealand (☎ 20 62 10, fax 20 62 11 14) Friedrichstrasse 60, 10117 Berlin
South Africa (☎ 82 52 711, fax 82 66 543) Friedrichstrasse 60, 10117 Berlin
UK (☎ 20 45 70) Wilhelmstrasse 70-71, 10117 Berlin
USA (☎ 238 51 74, fax 238 62 90 1) Neustädtische Kirchstrasse 4-5, 10117 Berlin

CUSTOMS

Most items needed for personal use during a visit are duty free. In Germany, usual allowances apply to duty-free and duty-paid items if you're coming from a non-EU country.

MONEY

The easiest places to change cash in Germany are banks or foreign exchange counters at airports and train stations, particularly those of the Reisebank. Main banks in larger cities generally have money-changing machines for after-hours use, though they don't often give good rates. The Reisebank charges a flat €2.50 to change cash. Some local Sparkasse banks have good rates and low charges.

There are ATMs virtually everywhere in Germany; most accept Visa, MasterCard, American Express (AmEx), Eurocard, and bankcards linked to the Plus and Cirrus networks. Typically, withdrawals over the counter against cards at major banks cost a flat €5 per transaction. Check other fees and the availability of services with your bank before you leave home.

Travellers cheques can be cashed at any bank and the most widely accepted are AmEx,

Thomas Cook and Barclays. A percentage commission (usually a minimum of €5) is charged by most banks on any travellers cheque, even those issued in euros. The Reisebank charges 1% or a minimum of €5 (€2.50 on amounts less than €50) and €3.75 for AmEx. Note that AmEx does not charge commission on its own cheques.

Credit cards are especially useful for emergencies, although they are often not accepted by hotels in the budget category and restaurants outside major cities. Cards most widely accepted for payment for goods and services are Eurocard (linked to Access and MasterCard), Visa and AmEx.

Having money sent to Germany is straightforward, albeit expensive. For emergencies, both Reisebank (Western Union) and Thomas Cook (MoneyGram) offer ready and fast international cash transfers through agent banks, but commissions are costly.

Currency
In 2002, Germany switched from its beloved Deutschmark (DM) to the euro, with a minimum of trauma. See the boxed text 'The Euro' in the earlier Facts for the Visitor chapter.

Costs
A tight budget can easily blow out in Germany. You can minimise costs by staying in hostels or private rooms, eating midday restaurant specials or by self-catering, and by limiting museum visits to days when they are free. Students pay the concession price mentioned in this chapter; the price for children is usually the same or marginally lower (often depending on age). Campers can expect to pay around €7.50 per night, less if there are two of you. Add another €10 for self-catering expenses and a beer or two from the supermarket, and your food, drinks and accommodation costs will be around €17.50 per day. If travelling on a rail pass, but allowing for public transport costs and occasional expenses like toiletries, €22.50 per day should be sufficient. Local public transit passes for tourists often offer discounts to museums and attractions.

Tipping & Bargaining
Apart from restaurants and taxis, tipping is not widespread in Germany. In restaurants, rather than leave money on the table, tip when you pay by stating a rounded-up figure or saying *es stimmt so* (that's the right amount). A tip of 10% is generally more than sufficient. Bargaining is usual only at flea markets.

Taxes & Refunds
Most German goods and services include a value-added tax (VAT, or *Mehrwertsteuer*) of 16% (7% for books and anything else involving copyright). Non-EU residents leaving the EU can have this tax refunded for any goods (not services) they buy.

At Frankfurt airport you should have your luggage labelled at the check-in and then take it to customs in area B6 of terminal 1, level 0.

POST & COMMUNICATIONS
Post
Standard post office hours are 8am to 6pm weekdays and to noon on Saturday. Many train station post offices stay open later or offer limited services outside these hours.

Postal Rates Postcard rates are €0.51 within Europe, €1.02 to North America and Australasia; a 200g letter to anywhere in Europe costs €0.56 and a 50g letter is €1.53. Aerograms to North America and Australia cost €1.02, and 20g letters by air to North America and Australasia cost €1.53. Surface-mail parcels of up to 2kg to Europe/elsewhere cost €7.67/9.71; the airmail cost is €11.71/20.40.

Receiving Mail Mail can be sent *Postlagernde* (poste restante) to the main post office in any city. There's no fee for collection, but German post offices will only hold mail for two weeks.

Telephone
Most pay phones in Germany accept only phonecards, available for €6 and €25 at post offices and some news kiosks, tourist offices and banks. One call unit costs a little more than €0.06 from a private telephone and €0.10 from a public phone. Calling from a private phone is most expensive between 9am and 6pm, when a unit lasts 90 seconds for a city call, 45 seconds for a regional call (up to 50km) and 30 seconds for a Deutschland call (more than 50km) during the peak period. From telephone boxes city calls cost €0.10 per minute. Calls to anywhere else in Germany from a phone box cost €0.20 per minute. Note that calls made to mobile (cell) phones (prefix generally ☎ 016 or 017) cost €0.54 per minute.

To ring abroad from Germany, dial ☎ 00 followed by the country code, area code and number. A three-minute call to the USA from a public phone in Germany at peak time costs €2.70, but you can reduce most international costs substantially by using prepaid private telephone cards.

The country code for Germany is ☎ 49.

Home direct services whereby you reach the operator direct for a reverse charge (collect) call from Germany are only possible to some countries. The prefix is ☎ 0800 followed by the home direct number. For the USA dial ☎ 888 225 5388 (AT&T) or ☎ 888 00 13 (Sprint). For Canada, dial ☎ 080 10 14; Australia, ☎ 080 00 61 (Telstra); and for Britain dial ☎ 080 00 44.

For directory assistance within Germany call ☎ 11833 (☎ 11837 in English); both cost €1 for the first minute and €0.49 after that. International information is ☎ 11834 (€1.48/ first minute, €0.97 after that).

Fax

Most main post offices and main train stations have public fax-phones that operate with a phone card. The regular cost of the call, plus a €1 service charge, will be deducted from your card on connection.

Sending a telegram, though still possible, is costly and slow and has few advantages over using a telephone or fax.

Email & Internet Access

Internet cafés, where you can buy online time and send email, exist in most large cities. Locations change frequently, so check at tourist offices.

The price in an Internet café is anything from around €3 to €10 per hour. If you wish to plug in your own laptop, you'll need a telephone plug adapter. Major Internet service providers have dial-in nodes in Germany. Because these usually vary from town to town, it's best to download a list from your provider before setting out.

DIGITAL RESOURCES

For up-to-date information about Germany on the Net, try the German Information Centre website at ⓦ www.germany-info.org. Most of the information there is in English. The website ⓦ www.visits-to-germany.com is targeted at tourists, while individual cities and regions also have websites.

BOOKS

For a more detailed guide to the country, pick up a copy of Lonely Planet's *Germany*. Lonely Planet also publishes *Bavaria*, and *Berlin* and *Munich* city guides.

The German literary tradition is strong and there are many works that provide excellent background to the German experience. Mark Twain's *A Tramp Abroad* is recommended for his comical observations on German life. For a more modern analysis of the German character and the issues facing Germany, dip into the Penguin paperback *Germany and the Germans* by John Ardagh.

NEWSPAPERS & MAGAZINES

Major British newspapers, the *International Herald Tribune* and *USA Today* are available from news kiosks at major train stations or throughout large cities, as are international editions of *Time*, *Newsweek* and the *Economist*. In smaller towns the choice may be limited.

The most widely read newspapers in Germany are *Die Welt*, *Bild*, *Frankfurter Allgemeine*, Munich's *Süddeutsche Zeitung* and the green-leaning *Die Tageszeitung (Taz)*. Germany's most popular magazines are *Der Spiegel*, *Focus* and *Stern*. *Die Zeit* is a weekly publication about culture and the arts.

RADIO & TV

Germany's two national TV channels are the government-funded ARD and ZDF. They are augmented by a plethora of regional and cable channels. You can catch English-language news and sports programmes (Sky News, CNN and BBC World depending on the region) on cable or satellite TV in many midrange hotels and pensions.

The BBC World Service (on varying AM wavelengths depending on the region) and the Armed Forces Network (AM 873 around Frankfurt) broadcast in English.

LAUNDRY

You'll find a coin-operated *Münzwäscherei* (laundry) in most cities. Average costs are €3.50 per wash, €0.50 for optional spinning, plus €0.50 per 15 minutes for drying. Some camping grounds and a few hostels also have laundry facilities.

If you're staying in a private room, the host may take care of your washing for a reasonable fee. Most major hotels provide laundering services at fairly steep charges.

GERMANY

TOILETS

Finding a public toilet when you need one is usually not a problem in Germany, but it may cost anything from €0.25 to €1 for the convenience. All train stations and large public transit stations have toilets, and at some main stations you can even shower for around €1 to €5. The level of hygiene is usually very high, although some train stations and otherwise nice pubs can be surprisingly grotty. Public toilets also exist in larger parks, pedestrian malls and inner-city shopping areas, where ultra-modern self-cleaning pay toilets (with wide automatic doorways that allow easy wheelchair access) are increasingly being installed. Restaurant and pub owners rarely mind passers-by using their toilet in cases of emergency if you ask first.

WOMEN TRAVELLERS

Women should not encounter particular difficulties while travelling in Germany. Most larger cities have women-only cultural organisations. If you are a victim of harassment or violence, get in touch with **Frauenhaus München** (☎ 089-354 83 11, 24hr service ☎ 089-35 48 30) in Munich, and **LARA – Krisen und Beratungszentrum für vergewaltigte Frauen** (Crisis and Counselling Centre for Raped Women; ☎ 030-216 88 88) in Berlin.

GAY & LESBIAN TRAVELLERS

Germans are generally fairly tolerant of homosexuality, but gays (who call themselves Schwule) and lesbians (Lesben) still don't enjoy quite the same social acceptance as in some other northern European countries. Most progressive are the large cities, particularly Berlin and Frankfurt, where the sight of homosexual couples holding hands is not unusual, although kissing in public is less common. The age of consent is 18 years. Larger cities have many gay and lesbian bars as well as other meeting places for homosexuals. Berlin Pride festival is held in June. Other Pride festivals are held in June in Bielefeld, Bochum, Hamburg, Mannheim and Wurzburg, and in July in Cologne.

DISABLED TRAVELLERS

Germany caters reasonably well to the needs of disabled travellers, with access ramps for wheelchairs and/or lifts in most public buildings, including toilets, train stations, museums, theatres and cinemas. Assistance is usually

Emergency Services

The emergency number for the police is ☎ 110 and the fire brigade/ambulance is ☎ 112. See Car & Motorcycle in the introductory Getting Around section later in this chapter for information regarding roadside assistance in the event of breakdown.

required when boarding any means of public transport in Germany. On Deutsche Bahn (DB) distance services, you can arrange this when buying your ticket.

DANGERS & ANNOYANCES

Although the usual cautions should be taken, theft and other crimes against travellers are relatively rare in Germany. In the event of problems, the police are helpful and efficient.

Africans, Asians and southern Europeans may encounter racial prejudice, especially in eastern Germany where they have been singled out as convenient scapegoats for economic hardship. However, the animosity is usually directed against the immigrants, not tourists.

LEGAL MATTERS

Police in Germany are well trained and usually treat tourists with respect. You are required by law to prove your identity if asked by the police, so always carry your passport, or an identity card if you're an EU citizen.

BUSINESS HOURS

By law, shops in Germany may open from 6am to 8pm on weekdays and until 4pm on Saturday. In practice, however, only department stores and some supermarkets and fashion shops stay open until 8pm; most open at 8am or 9am. Bakeries are open 7am to 6pm on weekdays, until 1pm on Saturday, and some open for the allowable maximum of three hours on Sunday.

Banking hours are generally 8.30am to 1pm and 2.30pm to 4pm weekdays, but many banks remain open all day, and until 5.30pm on Thursday. Government offices close for the weekend at 1pm or 3pm on Friday. Museums are generally closed on Monday; opening hours vary greatly, although many art museums are open later one evening per week.

Restaurants usually open 11am to midnight (the kitchen often closes at 10pm), with

GERMANY

varying *Ruhetage* or closing days. Many restaurants close during the day from 3pm to 6pm. All shops and banks are closed on public holidays.

PUBLIC HOLIDAYS & SPECIAL EVENTS

Germany has many holidays, some of which vary from state to state. Public holidays include New Year's Day; Good Friday to Easter Monday; 1 May (Labour Day); Ascension Day (40 days after Easter); Whit/Pentecost Sunday & Monday (May or June); Corpus Christi (10 days after Pentecost); 3 October (Day of German Unity); 1 November (All Saints' Day); 18 November (Day of Prayer and Repentance); and usually Christmas Eve to the day after Christmas.

There are many festivals, fairs and cultural events throughout the year. The famous and worthwhile ones include:

January
Carnival season (Shrovetide, known as 'Fasching') Many carnival events begin in large cities, most notably Cologne, Munich, Düsseldorf and Mainz; the partying peaks just before Ash Wednesday.

February
International Toy Fair Held in Nuremberg.
International Film Festival Held in Berlin.

March
Frankfurt Music Fair and **Frankfurt Jazz Fair**
Thuringian Bach Festival
Spring Fairs Held throughout Germany.

April
Stuttgart Jazz Festival
Munich Ballet Days
Mannheim May Fair
Walpurgisnacht Festivals Held the night before May Day in the Harz Mountains.

May
International Mime Festival Held in Stuttgart.
Red Wine Festival Held in Rüdesheim.
Dresden International Dixieland Jazz Festival
Dresden Music Festival Held in last week of May into first week of June.

June
Moselle Wine Week Held in Cochem.
Händel Festival Held in Halle.
Sailing regatta Held in Kiel.
Munich Film Festival
International Theatre Festival Held in Freiburg.

July
Folk festivals Held throughout Germany.
Berlin Love Parade
Munich Opera Festival
Richard Wagner Festival Held in Bayreuth.
German-American Folk Festival Held in Berlin.
Kulmbach Beer Festival
International Music Seminar Held in Weimar.

August
Heidelberg Castle Festival
Wine festivals Held throughout the Rhineland area.

September-October
Oktoberfest Held in Munich.
Berlin Festival of Music & Drama

October
Frankfurt Book Fair
Bremen Freimarkt
Gewandhaus Festival Held in Leipzig.
Berlin Jazzfest

November
St Martin's Festival Held throughout Rhineland and Bavaria.

December
Christmas fairs Held throughout Germany, most famously in Munich, Nuremberg, Berlin, Essen and Heidelberg.

ACTIVITIES

Germany, with its rugged Alps, picturesque uplands and fairy-tale forests, is ideal for hiking and mountaineering. Well-marked trails crisscross the country, especially popular areas like the Black Forest, the Harz Mountains, the so-called Saxon Switzerland area and the Thuringian Forest. The Bavarian Alps offer the most inspiring scenery, however, and are the centre of mountaineering in Germany. Good sources of information on hiking and mountaineering are: **Verband Deutscher Gebirgs-und Wandervereine** (*Federation of German Hiking Clubs;* ☎ *0561-93 87 30, fax 938 73 10; Wilhelmshöher Allee 157-159, 34121 Kassel*); and **Deutscher Alpenverein** (*German Alpine Club;* ☎ *089-14 00 30, fax 140 03 98; Von-Kahr-Strasse 2-4, 80997 Munich*).

The Bavarian Alps are the most extensive area for winter sports. Cross-country skiing is also good in the Black Forest and Harz Mountains. Ski equipment starts at around €12 per day, and daily ski-lift passes start at around €13. Local tourist offices are the best sources of information.

Cyclists will often find marked cycling routes, and eastern Germany has much to offer cyclists in the way of lightly travelled back roads, especially in the flat and less-populated north. There's also an extensive cycling trail along the Elbe River. Islands like Amrum and Rügen are also good for cycling. For more details and tips, see Cycling in the Getting Around section later in this chapter.

Railway enthusiasts will be excited by the wide range of excursions on old steam trains organised by the Deutsche Bahn and local services. Ask for the free booklet *Nostalgiereisen* at any large train station in Germany. Historic steam trains ply a 132km integrated narrow-gauge network year-round in the eastern Harz. For more information, see Wernigerode in the Saxony-Anhalt section.

WORK

Germany currently offers limited employment prospects for anyone except computer programmers and software specialists, who can apply for so-called Green Cards, which will allow you to work and live in Germany for a restricted period. EU citizens may work in Germany (with an *EU-Aufenthaltserlaubnis* residency permit), and special conditions apply for citizens of Australia, Canada, Israel, Japan, New Zealand, Switzerland and the USA.

Employment offices (*Arbeitsamt*) have an excellent data bank (SIS) of vacancies, or try major newspapers. Private language-teaching is another option. Street artists and hawkers are widespread in the cities, though these activities are often associated with begging. Numerous approved agencies can help you find work as an au pair.

An organisation that arranges unpaid cooperative work is the **Christlicher Friedensdienst** (☎ 069-45 90 72, fax 46 12 13; e yap-cfd@t-online.de; *Rendeler Strasse 9-11, 60385 Frankfurt/Main*).

ACCOMMODATION

Accommodation in Germany is well organised, though some cities are short on budget hotels; private rooms are one option in such situations. Accommodation usually includes breakfast. Look for signs saying *Zimmer frei* (rooms available) or *Fremdenzimmer* (tourist rooms) in house or shop windows of many towns. If you're after a hotel or especially a private room, head straight for the tourist office and use the room-finding service

(*Zimmervermittlung*), which is free or typically €3. Staff will usually go out of their way to find something in your price range, although telephone bookings are not always available. **TIBS** (☎ 0761-88 58 10, fax 885 81 19; e email@TIBS.de) handles accommodation bookings throughout Germany.

In official resorts and spas, displayed prices usually don't include *Kurtaxe* (resort tax) levies. Tourist offices can also help with farm stays.

Camping

Germany has more than 2000 organised camping grounds. Most are open from April to September, but several hundred stay open throughout the year. Facilities range from primitive to over-equipped. In eastern Germany camping grounds often rent out small bungalows. For camping on private property, permission from the landowner is required. The best overall source of information is the **Deutscher Camping Club** (☎ 089-380 14 20, fax 33 47 37; *Mandlstrasse 28, 80802 Munich*). Local tourist information sources can also help.

Hostels

The **Deutsches Jugendherbergswerk** (*DJH;* ☎ 05231-740 10, fax 74 01 49), or write to: DJH Service GmbH, 32754 Detmold, coordinates all affiliated Hostelling International (HI) hostels in Germany. Almost all hostels in Germany are open all year. Guests must be members of a HI-affiliated organisation, or join the DJH when checking in. The annual fee is €10/17.50 for juniors/seniors, which refers to visitors below/above 26 years old, with hostel cards.

A dorm bed in a DJH hostel ranges from around €12 to €20 for juniors to €15 to €23 for seniors. Camping at a hostel (where permitted) is generally half price. If you don't have a hostel-approved sleeping sheet, it usually costs from €2.50 to €3.50 to hire one (some hostels insist you hire one anyway). Breakfast is always included in the overnight price. Lunch or an evening meal will cost between €3 and €4.50.

Theoretically, visitors aged under 27 get preference, but in practice prior booking or arrival determines who gets rooms, not age. In Bavaria, though, the strict maximum age for anyone, except group leaders or parents accompanying a child, is 26. Check-in hours

GERMANY

vary, but you usually must be out by 9am. You don't need to do chores at the hostels and there are few rules. Most hostels have a curfew, which may be as early as 10pm in small towns. The curfew is rarely before 11pm in large cities; several have no curfew.

DJH's *Jugendgästehäuser* (youth guesthouses) offer some better facilities, freer hours and two- to four-bed dorm rooms from €12.50 to €22.50 per person, which includes sleeping sheet.

Pensions & Guesthouses

Pensions offer the basics of hotel comfort without asking hotel prices. Many of these are private homes with several rooms to rent, often a bit out of the centre of town. Private facilities may or may not be included. Some proprietors are a little sensitive about who they take in and others are nervous about telephone bookings – you may have to give a time of arrival and stick to it (many visitors have lost rooms by turning up late).

Hotels

Cheap hotel rooms are a bit hard to find during summer, but there is usually not much seasonal price variation except in luxury and resort hotels.

The cheapest hotels have only rooms with shared toilets (and showers) in the corridor. Average budget prices are €30 for a single and €45 for a double (without bathroom). Rates almost always include breakfast. This section lists prices for single/double rooms, but many lodgings have larger, less-expensive dorm-style rooms.

Expensive hotels provide few advantages for their upmarket prices. Some city hotels offer weekend packages, while spa towns are nice places to splurge on luxury hotels and healthy pursuits.

Rentals

Renting an apartment for a week or more is a popular form of holiday accommodation in Germany.

Look in newspaper classifieds for *Ferienwohnungen* (sometimes abbreviated to *FeWo*) or *Ferien-Apartments*, or particularly if you want shared accommodation somewhere in an urban centre contact the local *Mitwohnzentrale* (accommodation-finding service). Rates vary widely, but are lower than hotels and decrease dramatically with the length of stay.

FOOD

Germans are hearty eaters and this is truly a meat-and-potatoes kind of country, although vegetarians will usually find suitable restaurants or fast-food places. Restaurants always display their menus outside with prices, but watch for daily or lunch specials chalked onto blackboards. Beware of early closing hours, and of the *Ruhetag* (rest day) at some establishments. Lunch is the main meal of the day; getting a main meal in the evening is never a problem, but you may find that the dish or menu of the day only applies to lunch.

A German breakfast in a pension or hotel is solid and filling. Germans at home might eat their heaviest meal at noon and then have lighter evening fare (*Abendbrot* or *Abendessen*, consisting of cheeses and bread).

Students can eat cheaply (well or badly, depending on the town) at university *Mensa* cafeterias if they can show international student ID. This is not always checked.

Cafés & Bars

Much of the German daily and social life revolves around these institutions, which often serve meals and alcohol as well as coffee. Some attract a young or student crowd, stay open until late and are great places to meet people.

Snacks

If you're on a low budget, you can get a feed at stand-up food stalls (*Schnellimbiss* or *Imbiss*). The food is usually quite reasonable and filling, ranging from döner kebabs (Turkish sandwiches of grilled meat) to Chinese stirfries and traditional German sausages with beer.

Main Dishes

Wurst (sausage), in its hundreds of forms, is by far the most universal main dish. Regional favourites include *Bratwurst* (spiced sausage), *Weisswurst* (veal sausage) and *Blutwurst* (blood sausage). Other popular main dishes include *Rippenspeer* (spare ribs), *Rotwurst* (black pudding), *gegrilltes Fleisch* or *Rostbrätl* (grilled meat), *Putenbrust* (turkey breast) and many forms of *Schnitzel* (breaded pork or veal cutlet). Many restaurants serve at least one fish dish; vegetarian dishes may be harder to find.

Potatoes feature prominently in German meals, either *Bratkartoffeln* (fried), *Kartoffelpüree* (mashed), grated and then Swiss *Rösti* (fried), or as *Pommes Frites* (french fries); a Thuringian speciality is *Klösse*, a ball of mashed and raw potato which is then cooked into a dumpling. A similar Bavarian version is the *Knödel*. In Baden-Württemberg, potatoes are often replaced by *Spätzle*, a local noodle variety.

Mid-priced Italian, Turkish, Greek and Chinese restaurants can be found in every town.

Desserts

Germans are keen on rich desserts. Popular choices are the *Schwarzwälder Kirschtorte* (Black Forest cherry cake), one worthwhile tourist trap, as well as endless varieties of *Apfeltasche* (apple pastry). In the north you're likely to find berry *mus*, a sort of compote. Desserts and pastries are also often enjoyed during another German tradition, the 4pm coffee break.

Self-Catering

It's very easy and relatively cheap to put together picnic meals in any town. Simply head for the local market or supermarket and stock up on breads, sandwich meats, cheeses, wine and beer. Supermarkets such as Penny Markt, Kaiser's, Aldi, Rewe and Plus are cheap and have quite a good range.

DRINKS

Buying beverages in restaurants is expensive. Make a point of buying your drinks in supermarkets if your budget is tight.

Nonalcoholic Drinks

The most popular choices are mineral water and soft drinks, coffee and fruit or black tea. Bottled water almost always comes bubbly (*mit Kohlensäure*) – order *ohne Kohlensäure* if you're bothered by bubbles. Nonalcoholic beers are popular; Löwenbräu makes a nonalcoholic beer that is frequently served on tap in Bavaria.

Alcoholic Drinks

Beer is the national beverage and it's one cultural phenomenon that must be adequately explored. The beer is excellent and relatively cheap. Each region and brewery has its own distinctive taste and body.

Beer-drinking in Germany has its own vocabulary. *Vollbier* is 4% alcohol by volume, *Export* is 5% and *Bockbier* is 6%. *Helles Bier* is light, while *dunkles Bier* is dark. Export is

similar to, but much better than, typical international brews, while the *Pils* is more bitter. *Alt* is darker and more full-bodied. A speciality is *Weizenbier*, which is made with wheat instead of barley malt and served in a tall, 500ml glass with a slice of lemon.

Eastern Germany's best beers hail from Saxony, especially *Radeberger Pils* from near Dresden and *Wernesgrüner* from the Erzgebirge on the Czech border. *Berliner Weisse* is a foaming, low-alcohol wheat beer mixed with woodruff or raspberry syrup. The breweries of Cologne produce *Kölsch*; in Bamberg *Schlenkerla Rauchbier* is smoked to a dark-red colour.

German wines are exported around the world, and for good reason. They are inexpensive and typically white, light and intensely fruity. Wines are usually served in glasses or tiny carafes holding 200ml or 250ml. A *Weinschorle* or *Spritzer* is white wine mixed with mineral water. Wines don't have to be drunk with meals. The Rhine and Moselle Valleys are the classic wine-growing regions. The *Ebbelwei* of Hesse is a strong apple wine with an earthy flavour, and the Saale-Unstrut region around Naumburg in Saxony-Anhalt is famous for tart wines and Rotkäppchen *Sekt* (sparkling wine).

ENTERTAINMENT

The standard of theatre performances, concerts and operas is among the highest in Europe. Berlin is unrivalled when it comes to concerts and theatre and Dresden is famed for its opera.

Tickets can usually be purchased at short notice from tourist offices and directly from box offices.

Pubs & Beer Halls

The variety of pubs in Germany is enormous, ranging from vaulted-cellar bars through to theme pubs, Irish pubs, historic student pubs and clubs offering music or performances. Beer gardens are especially common in the south. It is worth experiencing the raucous atmosphere of a traditional Bavarian beer hall at least once during a visit to Germany.

Nightclubs

Germany's large cities throb with club and disco sounds. Berlin is a world techno capital, but you'll find a variety of lively clubs in most major cities. Posters around clubs, universities and cafés or city listing guides are good information sources.

GERMANY

Cinemas

Germans are avid movie-goers, but foreign films are usually dubbed into German. Original soundtrack versions (identifiable by letter-codes OF, OV or OmU with subtitles) are mostly limited to university towns and bigger cities such as Berlin, Munich, Hamburg and Frankfurt.

SPECTATOR SPORTS

Soccer is by far Germany's most popular sport, and the country will host the 2006 World Cup. Tickets to first-division games, usually played from Friday to Sunday, can be purchased at grounds and outlets. National knockout and European matches are mostly played during the week. The national team made the 2002 World Cup final, only to lose to Brazil. The popularity of tennis has been boosted by the past achievements of Boris Becker and Steffi Graf, and motor racing is a national passion, due in no small part to Michael Schumacher. Exciting winter sports events are held annually in Oberstdorf and Garmisch-Partenkirchen.

SHOPPING

Products made in Germany are rarely cheap, but higher prices generally mean high quality. Worthwhile products include optical lenses, fine crystal glassware (particularly from the Bavarian Forest), fine porcelain (particularly from Meissen) and therapeutic footwear such as the sandals and shoes made by Birkenstock. Excellent art reproductions, books and posters are sold in some museums and speciality shops. Germany's fine regional wines give you a real taste of the country. More predictable souvenirs include colourful heraldic emblems, cuckoo clocks from the Black Forest, Bavarian wooden carvings and traditional Bavarian clothing. Some open-air streetsellers in Berlin offer GDR-era memorabilia, though sometimes of questionable authenticity.

Getting There & Away

AIR

The main arrival and departure points in Germany are Frankfurt, Munich, Düsseldorf and Berlin. Frankfurt is Europe's busiest airport after London's Heathrow. Flights are generally priced competitively among all major airlines, but **Lufthansa** (**w** www.lufthansa.com) offers the most flexibility.

Flights to Frankfurt are usually cheaper than to other German cities. Regular flights from Western Europe to Germany tend to be more expensive than the train or bus. Airline deregulation within Europe has encouraged cheap, no-frills deals, especially between London and Frankfurt, Berlin or Düsseldorf. Ryanair and Buzz are cheap options.

From North America, Lufthansa, United Airlines, Air Canada, Delta Airlines and Singapore Airlines have the most frequent flights. You can often get the best fare by flying another European carrier and changing planes for Germany at their home-country hub. The German charter company LTU makes regular scheduled international flights between North America and Düsseldorf, but these fill up quickly.

Asian carriers offer the cheapest – but often the most indirect – flights from Australia and New Zealand. Qantas and Lufthansa both fly via Asian hubs such as Singapore and Bangkok and continue on to Germany.

Lufthansa has many flights to the Eastern European nations, but the region's national carriers are cheaper.

LAND

Bus

If you're already in Europe, it's generally cheaper to get to/from Germany by bus than it is by train or plane, but you trade price for speed. Return fares are noticeably cheaper than two one-way fares.

Eurolines is a consortium of national bus companies operating routes throughout the continent. Some sample one-way fares and travel times for routes include:

London–Frankfurt	€72	14¼ hours
Amsterdam–Frankfurt	€36	6 hours
Paris–Hamburg	€55	12½ hours
Paris–Cologne	€34	7¼ hours
Prague–Berlin	€35	6½ hours
Barcelona–Frankfurt	€85	20 hours

Eurolines has a youth fare for those aged under 26 that saves around 10%. Tickets can be bought in Germany at most train stations. For detailed information (but not bookings), contact **Deutsche-Touring GmbH** (**☎** 069-79 03 50, fax 790 32 19; Am Römerhof 17, 60486 Frankfurt/Main).

Train

Another good way to get to Germany from elsewhere in Europe is by train. It's a lot more comfortable (albeit more expensive) than the bus.

Long-distance trains between major German cities and other countries are called Euro-City (EC) trains. The main German hubs with the best connections to/from major European cities are Hamburg (Scandinavia); Cologne (France, Belgium and the Netherlands, with Eurostar connections from Brussels or Paris going on to London); Munich (southern and southeastern Europe); and Berlin (Eastern Europe). Frankfurt-am-Main has the widest range of, but not always the quickest, international connections.

Generally the longer international routes are served by at least one day train and often a night train as well. Many night trains only carry sleeping cars, but a bunk is more comfortable than sitting up in a compartment and only adds from €21/14 to the cost of a 2nd-class ticket in four-/six-berth compartments.

Car & Motorcycle

Germany is served by an excellent highway system. If you're coming from the UK, the quickest option is the Channel Tunnel. Ferries take longer but are cheaper. Choices include hovercraft from Dover, Folkestone or Ramsgate to Calais in France. You can be in Germany three hours after the ferry docks.

Within Europe, autobahns and highways become jammed on weekends in summer and before and after holidays. This is especially true where border checks are still carried out, such as going to/from the Czech Republic and Poland.

You must have third-party insurance to enter Germany with a car or motorcycle.

Hitching & Ride Services

Lonely Planet does not recommend hitching, but should you decide to try it you may encounter delays getting to Germany via the main highways as hitching is becoming less popular both for riders and drivers.

Aside from hitching, the cheapest way to get to Germany from elsewhere in Europe is as a paying passenger in a private car. Leaving Germany, or travelling within the country, such rides are arranged by *Mitfahrzentrale* (ride sharing agencies) in many German cities. You pay a reservation fee to the agency and a

share of petrol and costs to the driver. Local tourist offices can direct you to local agencies, or call the city area code and ☎ 194 40 in large German cities. Agencies for major cities are listed in the Getting There & Away sections for each city.

BOAT

If you're heading to or from the UK or Scandinavia, the port options are Hamburg, Lübeck, Rostock, Sassnitz, and Kiel. The Hamburg–Harwich service operates at least three times a week. The Puttgarden–Rodbyhavn ferry is popular with those heading to Copenhagen (see the Hamburg Getting There & Away section for details). In eastern Germany, there are five ferries in each direction daily all year between Trelleborg (Sweden) and Sassnitz near Stralsund (see the Rügen Island section).

There are daily services between Kiel and Gothenburg (Sweden) and Oslo. A ferry between Travemünde (near Lübeck) and Trelleborg (Sweden) runs one to four times daily. Ferries also run several times a week between the Danish island of Bornholm and Sassnitz. Car-ferry service is also good from Gedser (Denmark) to Rostock. Finnjet-Silja runs fast ferries several times a week on the Rostock–Tallin–Helsinki route (23 hours) from June to September. Finnlines has daily sailings from Lübeck to Helsinki. See the Kiel, Rostock, Stralsund and Rügen Island Getting There & Away sections for more details.

DEPARTURE TAX

All security, airport and departure taxes are included in ticket prices. Be aware that some companies in Germany will advertise a flight *excluding* these charges, so check the fine print carefully. There is no departure tax if you depart by sea or land.

Getting Around

AIR

There are lots of flights within the country, but costs can be prohibitive compared to other modes of transport. Lufthansa has the most frequent air services within Germany. Deregulation has brought some competition. **Lufthansa** and **Deutsche BA** (☎ 01805-35 93 32) regularly offer special fares, mostly from around €35 to €105 for the longest routes.

It is also well worth checking with a travel agency for other savers including youth (under 27) fares.

BUS

The bus network in Germany functions primarily in support of the train network, going places where trains don't. Bus stations or stops are usually near the train station in any town. Schedule and route information is usually posted. Consider buses when you want to cut across two train lines and avoid long train rides to and from a transfer point. A good example of this is in the Alps, where the best way to follow the peaks is by bus.

In the Getting There & Away section for each city and town we note any bus services that are useful for reaching other places described in this chapter. **Deutsche Bahn** agencies have information on certain key regional services, otherwise check with tourist offices.

Eurolines operates within Germany as Deutsche-Touring GmbH, a subsidiary of the German Federal Railways (Deutsche Bahn). Eurolines services include the Romantic and Castle Roads buses in southern Germany, as well as organised bus tours of Germany lasting a week or more. See the Frankfurt and Romantic Road sections for details, or contact **Deutsche-Touring GmbH** (☎ 069-79 03 50, fax 790 32 19), in Frankfurt/Main.

TRAIN

Operated almost entirely by the **Deutsche Bahn** (DB), the German train system is arguably the best in Europe.

The trains run on an interval system that means from the busiest to the quietest routes, you can count on service every one or two hours. The schedules are integrated throughout the country so that connections between trains are time-saving and tight, often only five minutes. Of course the obverse of this is that when a train is late (a not uncommon occurrence, especially during busy travel periods) connections are missed and you can find yourself stuck waiting for the next train. If you have to be somewhere at a specified time, put some slack in your itinerary so you won't miss a connection and be really stranded.

Types of Trains

There is rarely ever a need to buy a 1st-class ticket on German trains; 2nd class is usually quite comfortable. German trains fall into specific classifications; supplements (Zuschlag) for faster trains are built into fares:

ICE
The InterCityExpress trains run at speeds up to 280km/h when they use special high-speed tracks. The trains are very comfortable and feature restaurant cars. Main routes link Hamburg to Munich, Cologne to Berlin, Frankfurt to Berlin, Frankfurt to Munich and Frankfurt to Basel, Switzerland.

IC/EC
Called InterCity or EuroCity, these are the premier conventional trains of DB. When trains are crowded, the open-seating coaches are much more comfortable than the older carriages with compartments.

IR
Called InterRegio, these are fast trains that cover secondary routes and usually run at intervals of two hours. For journeys of more than two hours you can usually get to your destination faster by transferring from an IR train to an IC or ICE.

RE
RegionalExpress trains are local trains that make limited stops. They are fairly fast and run at one- or two-hourly intervals.

SE
StadtExpress trains are found in metropolitan areas. They make few stops in urban areas and all stops in rural areas.

RB
RegionalBahn are the slowest DB trains, not missing a single cow town or junction of roads so sit back and enjoy the view.

S-Bahn
These DB-operated trains run frequent services in larger urban areas and sometimes run in tunnels under the city centre. Not to be confused with U-Bahns, which are run by local authorities who don't honour rail passes.

EN, ICN, D
These are night trains, although an occasional D may be an extra daytime train.

Tickets & Reservations

Nearly every DB station offers the option of purchasing tickets with credit cards at ticket machines for longer haul trains; these usually have English-language options, but when in doubt consult at the ticket window. It is always better to buy your ticket before boarding, since buying a ticket or Zuschlag from a conductor carries a penalty (€1.50 to €4.50). If you're really stuck you can *technically* use a credit card to buy a ticket on the train, but you're likely to get a better response, say, if you ask the conductor to launder your dirty clothes. Ticket agents, on the other hand, cheerfully accept credit cards, as do most machines.

On some trains there are no conductors at all, and roving teams of inspectors enforce compliance. If you are caught travelling without a ticket the fine is €30 and they accept *no* excuses.

During peak travel periods, a seat reservation (€2.50) on a long-distance train can mean the difference between squatting near the toilet or relaxing in your own seat. Express reservations can be made at the last minute. If a crowded train is sold out or you don't have a reservation, try the end carriages. Most waiting passengers mill about the middle of platforms like flocks of sheep.

Fares

Standard DB ticket prices are distance-based. You will usually be sold a ticket for the shortest distance to your destination, so if for example you wish to travel from Munich to Frankfurt via Nuremberg (a slightly more expensive route than via Stuttgart), say so when you buy your ticket.

Sample fares for one-way, 2nd-class ICE travel include: Hamburg to Munich €137.80; Frankfurt to Berlin €106.40; and Frankfurt to Munich €75.60. Tickets are good for four days from the day you tell the agent your journey will begin and you can make unlimited stopovers along your route during that time (if you break your journey, it's wise to inform the conductor).

There are hosts of special fares that allow you to beat the high cost of regular tickets. The following are the most popular special train fares offered by DB (all fares are for 2nd class):

BahnCard
A €140/280 card (2nd/1st class) that entitles the owner to half-price travel on all trains (except S-Bahn). It's only worthwhile for extended visits to Germany.

Guten Abend
Literally 'Good Evening' tickets. They are valid for unlimited travel between 7pm and 3am the next day and cost €30 (€36 for ICE). They can offer significant reductions in price. For instance, you can take the 7.15pm ICE from Hamburg to Munich, arriving at 1.26am, for €36 instead of the usual €137.80.

Länder Tickets
Good within individual German states, for up to five people travelling together, or one or

both parents and all their children. Tickets cost €21, and are valid in 2nd class, weekdays from 9am on the first day until 3pm the next day. Other conditions vary by state.

Schönes Wochenende
These cheerful 'Good Weekend' tickets allow unlimited use of trains on a Saturday or Sunday between midnight and 3am the next day, for up to five people travelling together, or one or both parents and all their children for €21. The catch is that they are only good on RE, SE, RB and S-Bahns, so a money-saving trip from Cologne to Dresden can be a 12-hour ordeal of frequent train-changing or an adventure, depending on your outlook. They are best suited to weekend day trips from urban areas.

In addition, ask about various 'Sparpreis' schemes that offer big savings on return tickets if one leg of the journey is on a weekend or a weekend falls between the forward and return trip.

Most ticket agents are quite willing to help you find the cheapest options for your intended trip. For schedule and fare information (available in English), you can call ☎ 01805-99 66 33 from anywhere in Germany (€0.13 per minute).

Rail Passes

Travel agencies outside Germany sell German Rail Passes valid for unlimited travel on all DB trains for a given number of days within a 30-day period. Sample prices per person (in US$), good for 2nd-class travel, are for adults/two adults together/individuals under 26 for five days $202/151.50/156 and for 10 days $316/237/216. There also are 1st-class adult passes available.

The passes also include some ships but not seat reservations. Eurail and Inter-Rail passes are also valid in Germany.

Stations

Almost all train stations have lockers (from €1 depending on size). The few exceptions are noted in the Getting There & Away section for each city or town. Larger stations have DB Service Points counters that offer schedule information and are open long hours. Many have local maps that will help you find the tourist office.

Disabled passengers who need assistance must notify DB in advance of their needs. Train station platforms and the trains themselves are often not easily accessible.

GERMANY

CAR & MOTORCYCLE

German roads are excellent, and motorised transport can be a great way to tour the country. Prices for fuel vary from €1.04 to €1.08 per litre for unleaded regular. Avoid buying fuel at the more expensive autobahn filling stations.

The autobahn system of motorways runs throughout Germany. Road signs (and most motoring maps) indicate national autobahn routes in blue with an 'A' number, while international routes have green signs with an 'E' number. Though efficient, the autobahns are often busy, and resemble life in the fast lane. Tourists often have trouble coping with the very high speeds and the dangers involved in overtaking – don't underestimate the time it takes for a car in the rear-view mirror to close in at 180km/h. Secondary roads (usually designated with a 'B' number) are easier on the nerves and much more scenic, but can be slow going. Most are just two lanes, and you're bound to get stuck behind a lorry, camping caravan or farm vehicle. Hone your passing skills.

Cars are impractical in urban areas. Vending machines on many streets sell parking vouchers which must be displayed clearly behind the windscreen. Leaving your car in a central *Parkhaus* (car park) costs roughly €10 per day or €1.25 per hour.

To find passengers willing to pay their share of fuel costs, drivers should contact the local Mitfahrzentrale (see Hitching & Ride Services in the earlier Getting There & Away section).

Germany's main motoring organisation is the Munich-based **Allgemeiner Deutscher Automobil Club** *(ADAC; ☎ 089-767 60, fax 76 76 28 01)*; it has offices in all major cities. Call the **ADAC road patrol** *(☎ 0180-222 22 22)* if your car breaks down.

Road Rules

Road rules are easy to understand and standard international signs are in use. The usual speed limits are 50km/h in built-up areas (in effect as soon as you see the yellow name board of the town) and 100km/h on the open road. The speed on autobahns is unlimited, though there's an advisory speed of 130km/h; exceptions are clearly signposted. The blood-alcohol limit for drivers is 0.05%. Obey the road rules carefully: the German police are very efficient and issue heavy on-the-spot fines; cameras are in widespread use and notices are sent to the car's registration address wherever that may

be. If it's a rental company, they will bill your credit card.

Rental

Germany's four main rental companies are **Avis** *(☎ 0180-555 77)*, **Europcar** *(☎ 0180-580 00)*, **Hertz** *(☎ 0180-533 35 35)* and **Sixt** *(☎ 0180-526 02 50)*. There are numerous smaller local rental companies – **AutoEurope** *(☎ 0800-822 19 80)* offers some great deals – and there's a new DB Reisebüro car rental programme. For weekend deals, expect to pay €100 to €130 including collision damage waiver. You usually must be at least 21 years of age to hire a car.

Deals that include rental cars with train passes or airline tickets can be excellent value. Check with your travel agent.

Purchase

Due to the costs, paperwork and insurance hassles involved, buying a car in Germany tends to be an unwise option.

BICYCLE

Radwandern (bicycle touring) is very popular in Germany. In urban areas the pavement is often divided into separate sections for pedestrians and cyclists – be warned that these divisions are taken very seriously. Even outside towns and cities there are often separate cycling routes. Favoured routes include the Rhine, Moselle, Elbe and Danube Rivers and the Lake Constance area. Of course, cycling is strictly *verboten* (forbidden) on the autobahns. Hostel-to-hostel biking is an easy way to go, and route guides are often sold at local DJH hostels. There are well-equipped cycling shops in almost every town, and a fairly active market for used touring bikes.

Simple three-gear bicycles can be hired from around €8/32 per day/week, and more robust mountain bikes from €10/48. Rental shops in many cities are noted in the Getting Around sections of the city and town listings. The DB publishes *Bahn&Bike*, an excellent annual handbook covering bike rental and repair shops, routes, maps and other resources.

A separate ticket must be purchased whenever you carry your bike on most trains (generally €3 to €6). Most trains (excluding ICEs) have a 2nd-class carriage at one end with a bicycle compartment.

The central office of Germany's main cycling organisation is **Allgemeiner Deutscher**

Fahrrad Club (ADFC; ☎ 0421-34 62 90, fax 346 29 50; e kontakt@adfc.de) in Bremen.

See also Activities in the earlier Facts for the Visitor section.

HITCHING

Lonely Planet does not recommend *Trampen* (hitching), and it's is absolutely not allowed on autobahns. Mitfahrzentrale ride-share services (see Hitching & Ride Services in the earlier Getting There & Away section) is a cheap, more reliable and safer option.

BOAT

Boats are most likely to be used for basic transport when travelling to or between the Frisian Islands, though tours along the Rhine and Moselle Rivers are also popular. In summer there are frequent services on Lake Constance but, except for the Constance to Meersburg and the Friedrichshafen to Romanshorn car ferries, these boats are really more tourist craft than a transport option. From April to October, excursion boats ply lakes and rivers throughout Germany and on a nice day can be a lovely way to see the country.

LOCAL TRANSPORT

Local transport is excellent within big cities and small towns, and is generally based on buses, Strassenbahn (trams), S-Bahn and/or U-Bahn (underground train system). The systems integrate all forms of transit; fares are determined by the zones or the time travelled, or sometimes both. Multiticket strips or day passes are generally available and offer better value than single-ride tickets. In some cities, tourist offices sell one- to three-day transit passes that also include discounts to attractions. See the individual city and town Getting Around entries in this chapter for details.

Make certain that you have a ticket when boarding – on buses and some trams, you can buy tickets when you board. In some cases you will have to validate it in a little time-stamp machine on the platform or once aboard. Ticket inspections are frequent (especially at night and on holidays) and the fine is a non-negotiable €30 payable on the spot. If you can't pay, the inspector will take your passport until you can.

Bus & Tram

Cities and towns operate their own services that can include buses, trolleybuses and/or trams. Bus drivers usually sell single-trip tickets as a service to forgetful passengers, but these are more expensive than tickets bought in advance. Large cities often have a limited night-bus system operating from about 1am to 4am, when everything else has shut down.

Underground

Larger cities such as Berlin, Hamburg, Munich and Frankfurt have underground metro systems known as the U-Bahn. They have the same ticketing and validation requirements as the local buses and/or trams.

Train

Most large cities have a system of S-Bahn suburban trains. In places like Berlin, Hamburg, Munich and Frankfurt, they also serve the city centre. Tickets on these lines are integrated with other forms of local transport; however train pass-holders can ride S-Bahns (and only S-Bahns!) for free since they are operated by DB.

Taxi

Taxis are expensive and only really needed late, late at night. In fact, given traffic, they can actually take longer than public transport. For fast service, look up 'TaxiRuf' in the local telephone directory to find the nearest taxi rank. Taxis are metered and cost up to €2.30 flag fall and €1.30 per kilometre; higher night tariffs apply.

ORGANISED TOURS

Local tourist offices offer various tour options, from short city sightseeing trips to multiday adventure, spa-bath and wine-tasting packages. Apart from city tours, other good sources for organised tours in and around Germany are Deutsche-Touring and DB.

There are scores of international and national tour operators with specific options. Your travel agent should have some details. Many airlines also offer tour packages with their tickets.

Berlin

☎ 030 • pop 3.45 million

Berlin, Germany's largest city, has more to offer visitors than almost any city in Europe: bustling pubs, peerless cultural life, a worldly-wise, tolerant attitude and an indomitable spirit. No other city has been split by a brutal, impenetrable, 162km wall (torn down in 1990), and no other city has reintegrated so completely or quickly – the construction still continues. Some eastern neighbourhoods near the wall are now centres of artistic and cultural activity, although a few outlying areas, with their grim communist-era high-rise housing, remain as bleak as ever.

The centre of 19th-century Prussian military and industrial might, this great city reached maturity in the 1920s, only to be bombed into rubble in WWII. After hibernating for decades after the war, Berlin is now reassuming its role as the heart of Germany. With hundreds of construction cranes dotting the city, the changes are breathtaking and it is an exciting time to visit Berlin, once again the nation's capital and one of Europe's most dynamic cities.

HISTORY

The first recorded settlement in present-day Berlin was named Cölln (1237) around the Spree River, south of the present-day Museumsinsel (Museum Island), although Spandau to the west, the junction of the Spree and the ponded Havel Rivers, is considered to be older. Medieval Berlin developed on the bank of the Spree around Nikolaikirche and spread northeast towards today's Alexanderplatz. In 1432, Berlin and Cölln, which were linked by the Mühlendamm, merged.

In the 1440s, Elector Friedrich II of Brandenburg established the rule of the Hohenzollern dynasty, which was to last until Kaiser Wilhelm II's escape from Potsdam in 1918. Berlin's importance increased in 1470 when the elector moved his residence here from Brandenburg and built a palace near the present Marx-Engels-Platz.

During the Thirty Years' War, Berlin's population was decimated, but in the mid-17th century the city was reborn stronger than before under the so-called Great Elector Friedrich Wilhelm. His vision was the basis of Prussian power and he sponsored Huguenot refugees seeking princely tolerance.

The Great Elector's son, Friedrich I, the first Prussian king, made fast-growing Berlin his capital, and his daughter-in-law Sophie Charlotte encouraged the development of the arts and sciences and presided over a lively, intellectual court. Friedrich II sought greatness through building and was known for his

political and military savvy. All this led to the city being nicknamed *Spreeathen* (Athens-on Spree).

The Enlightenment arrived with some au thority in the form of the playwright Gotthold Ephraim Lessing, and thinker and publisher Friedrich Nicolai; both helped make Berlin a truly international city.

The 19th century began on a low note with the French occupation of 1806–13, and in 1848 a bourgeois democratic revolution was suppressed, somewhat stifling the political development that had been set in motion by the Enlightenment. The population doubled between 1850 and 1870 as the Industrial Revolution, spurred on by companies such as Siemens and Borsig, took hold. In 1871 Bismarck united Germany under Kaiser Wilhelm I. By 1900, Berlin's population was almost two million.

Before WWI Berlin had become an industrial giant, but the war and its aftermath led to revolt throughout Germany. On 9 November 1918 Philipp Scheidemann, leader of the Social Democrats, proclaimed the German Republic from a balcony of the *Reichstag* (parliament) and hours later Karl Liebknecht proclaimed a free Socialist republic from a balcony of the Berliner Schloss. In January 1919 the Berlin Spartacists, Liebknecht and Rosa Luxemburg were murdered by remnants of the old imperial army, which entered the city and brought the Revolution to a bloody end.

On the eve of the Nazi takeover, the Communist Party under Ernst Thälmann was the strongest single party in 'Red Berlin', having polled 31% of the votes in 1932. Berlin was heavily bombed by the Allies in WWII and during the 'Battle of Berlin' from August 1943 to March 1944, British bombers hammered the city every night. Most of the buildings you see today along Unter den Linden were reconstructed from the ruins. The Soviets shelled Berlin from the east, and after the last terrible battle, buried 18,000 of their own troops.

In August 1945, the Potsdam Conference sealed the fate of the city by finalising plans for each of the victorious powers – the USA, Britain, France and the Soviet Union – to occupy a separate zone. In June 1948 the city was split in two when the three Western Allies introduced a western German currency and established a separate administration in their sectors. The Soviets then blockaded West Berlin, but an airlift by the Western Allies kept the

GREATER BERLIN

city stocked with food and supplies. In October 1949 East Berlin became the capital of the GDR. The construction of the Berlin Wall in August 1961 prevented the drain of skilled labour (between 1945 and 1961 four million East Germans were lured westwards by higher wages and political freedom).

When Hungary breached the Iron Curtain in May 1989, the GDR government was back where it had been in 1961, but this time without Soviet backing. On 9 November 1989 the Wall opened and by 1 July 1990, when the Bundesrepublik's currency was adopted in the GDR, the Wall was being hacked to pieces. The Unification Treaty between the two Germanys designated Berlin the official capital of Germany, and in June 1991 the Bundestag voted to move the seat of government from Bonn to Berlin over the following decade at a cost of €10 billion. A huge consortium of public and private organisations was charged with constructing the heart of a metropolis from scratch.

Finally, in 1999, the federal government moved back to Berlin, with a newly refurbished Reichstag just one of the city's great symbols.

ORIENTATION

Berlin sits in the middle of the region known from medieval times as the Mark and is surrounded by the *Bundesland* (federal state) of Brandenburg. Roughly one-third of the city's municipal area is made up of parks, forests, lakes and rivers. There are more trees here than in Paris and more bridges than in Venice. Much of the natural beauty of rolling hills and quiet shorelines is in the southeast and southwest of the city.

The Spree River winds across the city for more than 30km, from Grosser Müggelsee in the east to Spandau in the west. North and south of Spandau the Havel River widens into a series of lakes from Tegel to Potsdam. A network of canals links the waterways to each other and to the Oder River to the east, and there are beautiful walks along some of them.

Berlin has 23 *Bezirken* (independent administrative districts), although most travellers will end up visiting only the eight 'core' ones. They are (clockwise from the west): Charlottenburg, Tiergarten, Mitte, Prenzlauer Berg, Friedrichshain, Kreuzberg, Schöneberg and Wilmersdorf.

The Wall once ran east of Brandenburger Tor (Brandenburg Gate), and now the gate is a symbol of city unity. From here Unter den Linden, the fashionable avenue of aristocratic old Berlin, and its continuation, Karl-Liebknecht-Strasse, extend eastwards to Alexanderplatz, once the heart of socialist Germany. En route are some of Berlin's finest museums, on Museumsinsel (Museum Island) in the Spree, and the monstrous Fernsehturm (TV Tower, probably Berlin's most useful landmark). The cultural centre is around Friedrichstrasse, which crosses Unter den Linden. South of here, in areas once occupied by the Wall, the former Checkpoint Charlie is now almost lost amid new construction. Some startling new buildings have been built around Potsdamer Platz, which before the war had been the busiest intersection in Europe. A few sections of the Wall have been preserved for public view, but otherwise it is virtually impossible to tell where the historic barrier once stood.

To the west, near Zoo station, you will find the ruin and the modern annexes of Kaiser-Wilhelm-Gedächtnis-Kirche, the shattered memorial church on Breitscheidplatz. A branch of the tourist office and hundreds of shops are situated in the faded Europa-Center at the end of the square farthest from the station. The Kurfürstendamm (known colloquially as the 'Ku'damm') runs 3.5km southwest from Breitscheidplatz. To the northeast, between Breitscheidplatz and the Brandenburger Tor, is Tiergarten, a district named after the vast city park which was once a royal hunting domain. Nearby is another Brobdingnagian work site around the Lehrter Bahnhof, where the Spree has actually been rerouted to allow a vast underground tunnel to create a new central train station in 2007. Just north of the Hackescher Markt Bahnhof stretches the ancient neighbourhood of the Scheunenviertel (barn district). This was a centre of Jewish life before the war and is now home to stylish businesses and residents.

In central Berlin, street numbers usually run sequentially up one side of the street and down the other (important exceptions are Martin-Luther-Strasse in Schöneberg, and Unter den Linden). Number guides appear on most corner street signs. Be aware, too, that a continuous street may change names several times and that on some streets (Pariser Strasse, Knesebeckstrasse) numbering sequences continue after interruptions for squares or plazas.

INFORMATION
Tourist Offices
The main office of **Berlin Tourismus Marketing** (☎ 0190-01 31 16 for information, ☎ 25 00 25 for hotel & event reservations both from inside Germany, ☎ 1805-75 40 40 from outside Germany, fax 25 00 24 24; e hotel-reservation@t-online.de; Budapester Strasse 45; open 8.30am-8.30pm Mon-Sat, 10am-6.30pm Sun) is located at the Europa-Center. This office also handles hotel reservations. There are other branches situated in the southern wing of the Brandenburger Tor (open 9.30am-6pm daily) and at the base of the Fernsehturm (TV Tower) at Alexanderplatz (open 10am-6pm daily). The website is w www.berlin-tourism.de.

The tourist office sells the Berlin-Potsdam Welcome Card (€18), which entitles you to unlimited transport for three days and discounted admission to major museums, shows, attractions, sightseeing tours and boat cruises in both Berlin and Potsdam.

It is also available at hotels and public transport ticket offices.

EurAide (open 8am-noon & 1pm-4pm Mon-Sat), which is located in Zoo station, is an English-language service offering train advice and reservations.

Money
With offices at two locations, **AmEx** (Bayreuther Strasse 37 • Friedrichstrasse 172) cashes its own travellers cheques without charging commission. The Friedrichstrasse office is across from Galeries Lafayette department store. There is an exchange office of **Thomas Cook** (Friedrichstrasse 56, Mitte).

Reisebank (Hardenbergplatz 1; open 7.30am-10pm daily) has an exchange office outside Zoo station. If you show a EurAide coupon you'll pay less commission. There is another branch inside Ostbahnhof.

Post & Communications
The **main post office** (open 8am-midnight Mon-Sat, 10am-midnight Sun) is in Joachimstalerstrasse, one block south of Zoo station. The poste restante service is here; letters should be clearly marked 'Hauptpostlagernd' and addressed to you at 10612 Berlin.

Note that mail will only be held for a two-week period. There are dozens of post offices throughout Berlin with more-restricted opening hours.

Email & Internet Access
With hundreds of terminals for your surfing pleasure, try **Easy Everything** (☎ 88 70 79 70; Kurfürstendamm 224). You could also try the rather smoky **Alpha Café** (☎ 447 90 67; Dunckerstrasse 72, Prenzlauer Berg); take S8 or S10 to Prenzlauer Allee.

Travel Agencies
Travel agencies offering cheap flights advertise in the *Reisen* (travel) classified section (*Kleinanzeigen*) of the city magazines *Zitty* and *Tip*. One of the better discount operators is **Alternativ Tours** (☎ 881 20 89; Wilmersdorfer Strasse 94, Wilmersdorf; U7 to Adenauerplatz), which specialises in a range of unpublished, discounted fares to anywhere in the world.

The following agencies are generally open between 9am and 6pm weekdays and until 1pm Saturday. The most convenient **Atlas Reisewelt branch** (☎ 247 57 60; Alexanderplatz 9) is inside the Kaufhof department store; it's a big chain with several offices around Berlin. **STA Travel** (☎ 28 59 82 64; Gleimstrasse 28, Prenzlauer Berg • ☎ 311 09 50, Goethestrasse 73, Charlottenburg • ☎ 310 00 40; Hardenbergstrasse 9, Charlottenburg) specialises in travel for young people and issues ISIC cards, provided you have proper and recognisable student and personal ID.

Newspapers & Magazines
The bimonthly English-German *Berlin Kalender* (€1.75) has mainstream listings and is available at newsstands, hotels and tourist offices. The magazines *Zitty* (€2.30) and *Tip* (€2.50) offer comprehensive listings (in German only) of all current events, including concerts, theatre, clubs, gallery exhibits, readings, movies etc. Also look for the free *030* (in pubs and cafés), which has the latest club and rave news (in German).

Bookshops
Books in Berlin (☎ 313 12 33; Goethestrasse 69, Charlottenburg) has a good selection of English and American literature. Large German bookshops with decent English-language sections include the vast **Hugendubel** (☎ 21 40 60; Tauentzienstrasse 13, Charlottenburg). **Kiepert** (☎ 31 18 80; Hardenbergstrasse 4-5, Charlottenburg) has many departments, from guidebooks to foreign-language dictionaries. **Europa Presse Center** at ground level in the

GERMANY

Europa-Center has a big range of international papers and magazines.

Laundry

The Schnell & Sauber chain has various **laundrette branches** (*Uhlandstrasse 53 & Leibnizstrasse 72, Charlottenburg • Torstrasse 115, Mitte • Mehringdamm 32, Kreuzberg*); the Kreuzberg branch is situated just outside the Mehringdamm U-Bahn station. Hours are generally from 6am to 11pm, and to wash and dry a load costs about €5.

Medical & Emergency Services

For 24-hour medical aid, advice and referrals, call the **Kassenärztliche Bereitschaftsdienst** (*Public Physicians' Emergency Service; ☎ 31 00 31*). If you need a **pharmacy** after hours, dial ☎ 118 80. For information on where you can find an emergency **dentist** (*Zahnarzt*), dial ☎ 89 00 43 33.

The general emergency number for a **doctor** (*Notarzt*) or **fire brigade** (*Feuerwehr*) throughout Berlin is ☎ 112.

Call ☎ 110 for police emergencies only. Otherwise, there are police stations all over the city, including the upstairs **City Wache** (*Joachimstaler Strasse 15*), south of Ku'damm and near Zoo station. In eastern Berlin, there's a station at Otto-Braun-Strasse 27, northeast of Alexanderplatz.

Police headquarters and the municipal **lost-and-found office** (*☎ 69 95; Platz der Luftbrücke 6*) are beside Tempelhof airport. If you've lost something on public transport, contact the **BVG** (*☎ 25 62 30 40; Potsdamer Strasse 182, Schöneberg*).

Dangers & Annoyances

Berlin is generally safe and tolerant. Walking alone at night on city streets shouldn't be considered a risk, bearing in mind the caveat that there is always safety in numbers in any urban environment. You may want to avoid the area along the Spree south of the Ostbahnhof, until recently the haunt of punks, urban drifters and druggies, although the neighbourhood is rapidly gentrifying. Also use the usual cautions against robberies in the Zoo station area. Some travellers may be put off by graffiti, sometimes found even in upscale neighbourhoods.

THINGS TO SEE & DO

Among Berlin's 170 museums, the **State museums** (denoted in this section by 'SMB')

are among the highlights. Unless otherwise noted, the SMB museums are closed on Monday, admission is by day-pass (€6/3 adult, concession), valid for all SMB museums on that day, and is free the first Sunday of each month. Serious museumgoers may invest in the Drei-Tages-Touristenkarte (€10/5), offering free entry to more than 50 museums during three consecutive days (ask at tourist offices).

Around Alexanderplatz

Soaring above Berlin is the restored 368m **Fernsehturm** (*TV Tower; ☎ 242 33 33; Panoramastrasse 1A; adult/concession €6/3; open 10am-1am daily*) built in 1969. If it's a clear day and the queue isn't too long, it's worth paying the fee to go up the tower or have a drink at the 207m-level Telecafé, which revolves twice an hour. The best thing about the view from the tower is that it is the one place in the city where you can't see it.

On the opposite side of the elevated train station from the tower is **Alexanderplatz** (or, affectionately, 'Alex'), the square named after Tsar Alexander I who visited Berlin in 1805. The area was redesigned several times in the late 1920s but little was ever actually built because of the Depression. It was bombed in WWII and completely reconstructed in the 1960s. The **World Time Clock** (1969) is nearby in case you want to check the time before making a telephone call home.

Museumsinsel

Berlin's famed Museum Island is a scene of heavy construction as its grand buildings are restored. West of the Fernsehturm, on an island between two arms of the Spree River, is the GDR's **Palace of the Republic** (1976), which occupies the site of the bombed baroque Berliner Schloss that was demolished in 1950. During the communist era, the Volkskammer (People's Chamber) used to meet in this monstrosity which faces Marx-Engels-Platz. In 1990 it was discovered that asbestos had been used in the construction and its future has been up in the air ever since.

On the southern side is the former **Staatsrat** (Council of State; 1964) building, with a portal from the old city palace incorporated in the facade. Immediately east are the **Neue Marstall** (New Royal Stables), built at the end of the 19th century, which house the State Archives.

North of Marx-Engels-Platz looms the great neo-Renaissance **Berliner Dom** (1904), the former court church of the Hohenzollern family. The 1930 SMB **Pergamonmuseum** (☎ 20 90 55 55; Am Kupfergraben) is a feast of classical Greek, Babylonian, Roman, Islamic and Oriental antiquity. The world-renowned Ishtar Gate from Babylon (580 BC), the reconstructed Pergamon Altar from Asia Minor (160 BC) and the Market Gate from Greek Miletus (Asia Minor, 2nd century AD) are among the beautiful Middle Eastern artefacts. The SMB **Alte Nationalgalerie** (Old National Gallery; ☎ 20 90 58 01; Bodestrasse 1-3) houses classical sculpture, and paintings by European masters in dozens of tiny galleries. Inside the stairwell is a massive frieze of the great German philosophers, thinkers, writers and patrons. The imposing edifice beside it is Karl Friedrich Schinkel's 1829 neoclassical SMB **Altes Museum** (☎ 20 90 52 01; Am Lustgarten), with its famed rotunda area featuring statues of the Greek divinities, a permanent antiquities display plus special exhibitions. The Museumsinsel's two remaining museums are undergoing badly needed facelifts; the **Bodemuseum** (1904) is closed until mid-2004, and the **Neues Museum** (1855) until 2005.

Nikolaiviertel

The rebuilt 13th-century **Nikolaikirche** stands amid the forced charms of the Nikolaiviertel (Nikolai quarter), conceived and executed under the GDR's Berlin restoration programme. Another medieval church is **Marienkirche** (Karl-Liebknecht-Strasse), which stands across the square from the monumental **Rotes Rathaus** (or Red Town Hall, named for its appearance, not its politics), a neo-Renaissance structure from 1860, which has been proudly restored and is once again the centre of Berlin's municipal government. Across Grunerstrasse, the remains of the bombed-out shell of the late 13th-century **Franciscan Abbey** mark the position of the former Spandauer Tor and the earliest town wall.

Märkisches Ufer

Several interesting sights can be covered from the Märkisches Museum U-Bahn station. The collections of the **Märkisches Museum** (☎ 30 86 60; Am Köllnischen Park 5; adult/concession €4/2, free Wed; open Tues-Sun) cover Berlin's history, art and culture. The

brown bears housed in a pit in the park behind the main museum are the official mascots of the city.

Unter den Linden

A stroll west of Museumsinsel along Unter den Linden takes in the greatest surviving monuments of the former Prussian capital. The **Deutsches Historisches Museum** in a former armoury (Zeughaus; 1706) should have reopened after a renovation by the time you read this, with a collection on German history from AD 900 to the present, under a new glass roof by architect IM Pei.

Opposite the museum is the beautiful colonnaded **Kronprinzenpalais** (Crown Princes' Palace; ☎ 20 30 40; admission free; open Thur-Tues) dating from 1732. Next to the museum is Schinkel's **Neue Wache** (admission free; open daily), an 1818 memorial to the victims of fascism and despotism, which harbours Käthe Kollwitz's sculpture Mother and Her Dead Son. **Humboldt Universität** (1753), the next building situated to the west, was originally a palace of the brother of King Friedrich II of Prussia and was converted to a university in 1810. Take note of the restored equestrian **statue of Friedrich II** in the avenue. Beside this is the enormous **Staatsbibliothek** (State Library; 1914).

Across the street from the university, beside the **Alte Königliche Bibliothek** (Old Royal Library; 1780) with its curving baroque facade, is Wenzeslaus von Knobelsdorff's **Staatsoper** (State Opera; 1743). The square between them, **Bebelplatz**, was the site of the Nazis' first book-burning on 10 May 1933. A poignant, below-ground memorial marks the spot. South of here is the Catholic **St Hedwig Kirche** (1783), partly modelled on Rome's Pantheon.

Just south is Gendarmenmarkt, an elegant square containing a trio of magnificent buildings. The **Deutscher Dom** (German Cathedral; ☎ 22 73 04 31; admission free; open Tues-Sun) at the southern end of the square boasts a museum with an excellent exhibit on German history from 1800 to the present. The **Französischer Dom** (French Cathedral) contains the **Hugenottenmuseum** (Huguenot Museum; ☎ 229 17 60; adult/concession €1.50/1; open Tues-Sun), which covers the French Protestant contribution to Berlin life. The statuesque **Konzerthaus** (Concert Hall) completes the picture.

GERMANY

GERMANY

BERLIN – MITTE & PRENZLAUER BERG

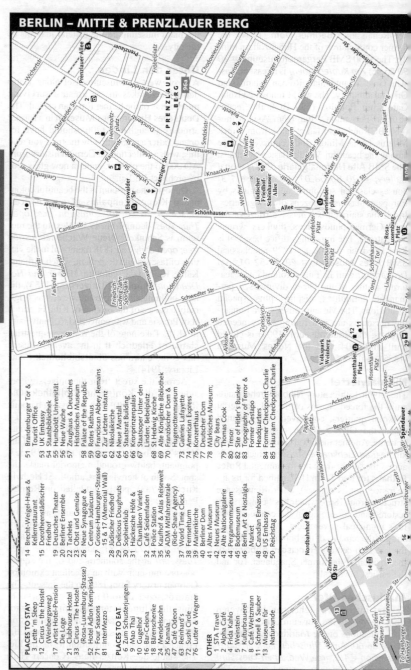

PLACES TO STAY
8 Lette 'm Sleep
12 Circus – The Hostel (Weinbergsweg)
17 Artist Hotel-Pension Die Loge
21 Clubhouse Hostel
33 Circus – The Hostel (Rosa-Luxemburg-Strasse)
52 Hotel Adlon Kempinski
71 Four Seasons
81 InterMezzo

PLACES TO EAT
6 Zum Schusterjungen
9 Mao Thai
10 Gugelhof
16 Bar-Celona
18 Bärenschenke
24 Kamala
47 Café Odeon
63 Reinhard's
72 Sushi Circle
76 Lutter & Wegner

OTHER
1 STA Travel
2 Alpha Café
4 Frida Kahlo
5 Weinstein
7 Kulturbrauerei
8 Café Weitzmann
11 Schnell & Sauber
13 Museum für Naturkunde

14 Brecht-Weigel-Haus & Kellerrestaurant
15 Dorotheenstädtischer Friedhof
19 Deutsches Theater
20 Berliner Ensemble
22 Tacheles
23 Obst und Gemüse
26 Neue Synagoge & Centrum Judaicum
27 Grosse-Hamburger-Strasse 15 & 17 (Memorial Wall)
28 Jüdischer Friedhof
29 Delicious Doughnuts
30 Sophienklub
31 Hackesche Höfe & Chamäleon Varieté
32 Café Seidenfaden
34 Police Station
35 Kaufhof & Atlas Reisewelt
36 ADM Mitfahrzentrale (Ride-Share Agency)
37 World Time Clock
38 Fernsehturm
39 Marienkirche
40 Berliner Dom
41 Altes Museum
42 Neues Museum
43 Alte Nationalgalerie
44 Pergamonmuseum
45 Bodemuseum
46 Berlin Art & Nostalgia Market
48 Canadian Embassy
49 US Embassy
50 Reichstag

51 Brandenburger Tor & Tourist Office
53 UK Embassy
54 Staatsbibliothek
55 Humboldt Universität
56 Neue Wache
57 Zeughaus & Deutsches Historisches Museum
58 Palace of the Republic
59 Rotes Rathaus
60 Franciscan Abbey Remains
61 Zur Letzten Instanz
62 Nikolaikirche
64 Neue Marstall
65 Staatsrat Building
66 Kronprinzenpalais
67 Staatsoper Unter den Linden; Bebelplatz
68 St Hedwig Kirche
69 Alte Königliche Bibliothek
70 Französischer Dom & Hugenottenmuseum
73 Galeries Lafayette
74 American Express
75 Konzerthaus
77 Deutscher Dom
78 Märkisches Museum; City Bears
79 Thomas Cook
80 Tresor
82 Site of Hitler's Bunker
83 Topography of Terror & Former Gestapo Headquarters
84 Former Checkpoint Charlie
85 Haus am Checkpoint Charlie

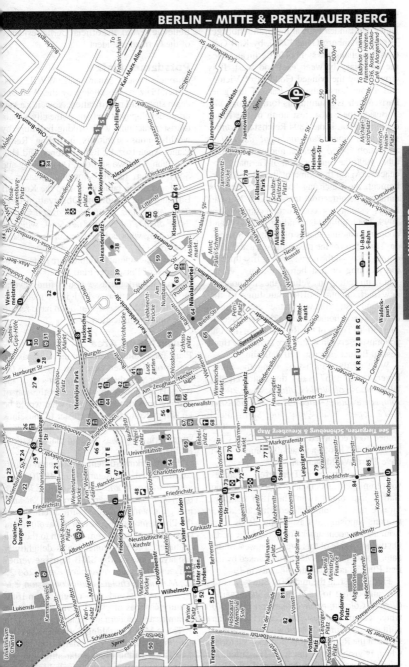

BERLIN – MITTE & PRENZLAUER BERG

See Tiergarten, Schöneburg & Kreuzberg Map

GERMANY

GERMANY

Tiergarten

Unter den Linden ends at the **Brandenburger Tor** (Brandenburg Gate; 1791), by Karl Gotthard Langhans, the symbol of Berlin and once the boundary between east and west. It is crowned by the winged Goddess of Victory and a four-horse chariot. East of the gate, Pariser Platz is resuming its former glory.

Beside the Spree, just north of the Brandenburger Tor, is the 1894 **Reichstag** *(admission free; open 8am-midnight daily, last admission 10pm)* where at midnight on 2 October 1990 the reunification of Germany was enacted. Again the home of the German parliament, the Reichstag has become Berlin's number one attraction, thanks to Sir Norman Foster's stunning reconstruction completed in 1999. The highlight is wending your way (and dodging blinding shards of light on a sunny day) to the top of the gleaming metal and glass dome. To avoid the hordes, arrive first thing in the morning or just before closing. While you're up getting an eyeful of the city, note the new parliamentary office buildings to the north and east; to the west is the Federal Chancellery's new home on the northern edge of Tiergarten. Tours of the Reichstag are free but you must reserve in writing to: Deutscher Bundestag, Besucherdienst, 11011 Berlin.

West of the Reichstag, along the Spree River, is the 1957 **Haus der Kulturen der Welt** *(House of World Cultures; ☎ 39 78 70; John Foster Dulles-Allee 10; adult/concession €4/2; open 10am-9pm Tues-Sun)*, nicknamed the 'pregnant oyster' for its shape. The arched roof collapsed in 1980 but has since been rebuilt. Photo and art exhibitions often have Third World themes.

The huge city park, **Tiergarten**, stretches west from the Brandenburger Tor towards Zoo station and dates from the 18th century. Strasse des 17 Juni (named after the 1953 workers' uprising in East Berlin) leads west from the Brandenburger Tor through the park. On the north side of this street, just west of the gate, is a **Soviet War Memorial** flanked by the first Russian tanks to enter the city in 1945.

Farther west, in the middle of Strasse des 17 Juni and dating to 1873, is the **Siegessäule** *(Victory Column; adult/concession €1/0.50)* which commemorates 19th-century Prussian military adventures. It is crowned by a gilded statue of the Roman victory goddess, Victoria, which is visible from much of Tiergarten. A spiral staircase leads to the top and affords a worthwhile view. Just northeast is **Schloss Bellevue** (1785), the official Berlin residence of the German president.

Potsdamer Platz

Europe's busiest square until WWII, Potsdamer Platz was occupied by the Wall and death strip until reunification. Now, it's a vast urban development and one of the city's main tourist attractions, with striking buildings by world-famous architects including Renzo Piano, Arata Isozaki, Rafael Moneo and Helmut Jahn. The two sections, DaimlerCity and Sony Center, feature shopping, theatres, a hotel and office buildings. Atop the Kollhoff Building is the **Panorama Observation Deck** *(Potsdamer Platz 1; adult/concession €3.50/ 2.50; open 11am-8pm Tues-Sun)*, which is reached by what is billed as Europe's fastest elevator.

The contemporary architecture fest continues west of Potsdamer Platz.

On Tiergartenstrasse you'll find several striking new embassy buildings; many nations that had embassies in Bonn have rebuilt here since reunification.

Kulturforum Area

Plans for a cultural centre in the southeastern corner of Tiergarten were born as early as the 1950s. One of the premier architects of the time, Hans Scharoun, was given the job of coming up with the design of what would be known as Kulturforum, a cluster of museums and concert halls. The first building constructed (in 1961) was the gold-plated **Berliner Philharmonie**.

The **Musikinstrumenten-Museum** *(Musical Instruments Museum; ☎ 25 48 10; Tiergartenstrasse 1; adult/concession €3/1.50; open 9am-5pm Tues-Fri, 10am-5pm Sat-Sun)* in a grand annexe on the northeastern side of the Philharmonie, focuses on the evolution of musical instruments from the 16th to the 20th centuries. The rich collection is delightfully displayed. The nearby SMB **Kunstgewerbemuseum** *(Museum of Applied Art; ☎ 266 29 25; Matthäikirchplatz; adult/concession €3/ 1.50)* shows arts and crafts ranging from 16th-century chalices of gilded silver to Art Deco ceramics and modern appliances.

The SMB **Gemäldegalerie** *(Gallery of Paintings; ☎ 20 90 55 55; Matthäikirchplatz 4-6)* is the Kulturforum's star attraction, focusing on European works from the 13th to the

8th centuries; its 1200-plus collection includes works by Dürer, Rembrandt, Botticelli and Goya.

To the southeast, looking a bit forlorn amid the modern museums, there's the 1846 **St Matthäus Kirche** (☎ 262 12 02; Matthäis-kirchplatz 12; open noon-6pm Tues-Sun). The **bell tower** (admission €1) offers panoramic views. Continue on to the squat SMB **Neue Nationalgalerie** (New National Gallery; ☎ 266 26 51; Potsdamer Strasse 50) for a collection of 19th- and 20th-century paintings and sculptures by Picasso, Klee, Miró and many German expressionists.

Several blocks west, the **Bauhaus Archiv/ Museum für Gestaltung** (Bauhaus Archive/ Museum of Design; ☎ 254 00 20; Klingel-höferstrasse 14; adult/concession €4/2; open 10am-5pm Wed-Mon) is dedicated to artists of the Bauhaus school, who developed the tenets of modern architecture and design. The building is designed by Bauhaus founder Walter Gropius.

Around Oranienburger Tor

Known as the Scheunenviertel, this neighbourhood is one of Berlin's most vibrant. The **Brecht-Weigel Gedenkstätte** (Brecht-Wegel-Haus; ☎ 283 05 70 44; Chausseestrasse 125; adult/concession €3/1.50; open daily, ring for hours & tour info) is where the socialist playwright Bertolt Brecht and his wife Helene Weigel lived from 1948 until his death in 1956. Behind is **Dorotheenstädtischer Friedhof** with tombs of the illustrious, such as philosopher Georg Friedrich Hegel, poet Johannes Becher, and Brecht and Weigel. There are two adjacent cemeteries here; you want the one closer to Brecht's house.

Nearby, the 1810 **Museum für Naturkunde** (Natural History Museum; ☎ 20 93 85 91; Invalidenstrasse 43; adult/concession €2.50/ 1.25; open 9.30am-5pm Tues-Sun) has an impressive dinosaur collection. To the west is the SMB **Hamburger Bahnhof** (☎ 39 78 34 12; Invalidenstrasse 50), a former train station cleverly converted into a top contemporary gallery. Lofty ceilings and streams of natural light make the collection, including works by Warhol, Lichtenstein and Rauschenberg, even more appealing.

If you travel east along Oranienburger Strasse you'll come across the rambling, crumbling **Tacheles** alternative art, culture and entertainment centre. Made famous by post-Wende squatters who gave the former department store a new lease of life, it's run by a self-governed, nonprofit organisation and boasts galleries, a theatre and studios. Not surprisingly, it's under threat from developers but was given a reprieve, supposedly until around 2010.

Don't miss the magnificent **Neue Synagogue**. Built in the Moorish-Byzantine style in 1866, it was desecrated by the Nazis and later destroyed by WWII bombing. It is no longer a functioning synagogue these days, but instead houses the **Centrum Judaicum** (☎ 88 02 83 16; Oranienburger Strasse 28-30; adult/ concession €3/2; open 10am-6pm Sun-Thur, 10am-2pm Fri) with permanent and special exhibitions on Jewish life in Berlin. You may climb the dome for an additional €1.50/1, but it is closed from November to March.

Another legacy of the area's Jewish culture is the **Jüdischer Friedhof** (Jewish Cemetery; Grosse-Hamburger-Strasse). Although some 10,000 people are buried here including Moses Mendelssohn, the revered Enlightenment philosopher, few tombstones survived Nazi destruction in 1942. Across the street, plaques climbing the walls of the courtyard between Grosse-Hamburger-Strasse 15 and 17 identify the buildings' prewar residents; the simplicity is wrenching.

The district's big drawcard is the **Hackesche Höfe** (1907), once owned by a Jewish businessman. This Art Nouveau cluster of buildings with eight interconnected courtyards is filled with galleries, shops, theatres and cafés.

Kreuzberg

Parallel to a section of the Wall is the site of the former SS-Gestapo headquarters, where the open-air **Topography of Terror** (☎ 25 48 67 03; Niederkirchnerstrasse 8; admission free; open 10am-6pm daily in summer, until dusk in winter) exhibition documents Nazi crimes.

Almost nothing remains at the site of the famous **Checkpoint Charlie**, a major crossing between east and west during the Cold War. However, the history of the Wall is commemorated nearby in the **Haus am Checkpoint Charlie** (☎ 253 72 50; Friedrichstrasse 43-45; adult/concession €7/4; open 9am-8pm daily), a fascinating private museum of escape memorabilia and photos.

The longest surviving stretch of the **Berlin Wall** is just west of the Warschauer Strasse terminus of the U1. This 300m section was

GERMANY

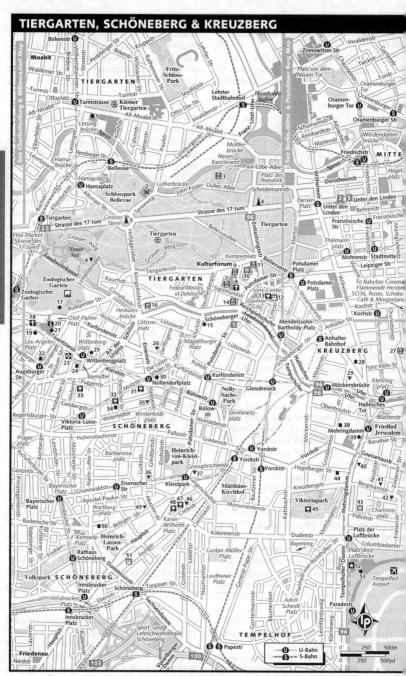

TIERGARTEN, SCHÖNEBERG & KREUZBERG

TIERGARTEN, SCHÖNEBERG & KREUZBERG

PLACES TO STAY		42	Barcomi's		18	Kaiser-Wilhelm-Gedächt-
1	Hotel Tiergarten	46	Pasodoble			niskirche (Memorial Church)
15	Jugendherberge Berlin	49	Don Antonio		19	Hugendubel Bookshop
	International				20	Tourist Office
22	Pension Fischer	**OTHER**			21	Europa-Center
24	Comfort Hotel Auberge	2	Schloss Bellevue		23	KaDeWe Department Store
28	Hotel am Anhalter Bahnhof	3	Haus der Kulturen		25	American Express
34	Hotel Gunia		der Welt		27	Jüdisches Museum
38	Pension Kreuzberg	4	Soviet War Memorial		30	Mann-O-Meter
44	Hotel Transit	5	Siegessäule		31	KitKat Club
50	Studentenhotel Meininger 10	7	Gemäldegalerie		32	Tom's Bar; Hafen
		8	St Matthäus Kirche		33	Connection Disco
PLACES TO EAT		9	Kunstgewerbemuseum		39	Schnell & Sauber
6	Café am Neuen See	10	Berliner Philharmonie		43	Friends of Italian Opera
26	Café Einstein	11	Musikinstrumenten-Museum		45	Golgatha
29	Grossbeerenkeller	12	Cinestar		47	Leuchtturm
35	Tim's Canadian Deli	13	Blu Discothek		48	Café Mirell
36	Ousies Taverna	14	Neue Nationalgalerie		51	Odeon Cinema
37	Tuk-Tuk	16	Bauhaus Archiv/Museum für		52	Police Headquarters
40	Seerose		Gestaltung		53	Municipal Lost & Found
41	Knofi	17	Aquarium			Office

turned over to artists who created the **East Side Gallery**, a permanent open-air art gallery along the side facing Mühlenstrasse.

Be careful when you visit this area as it can be a bit seedy, however, it is improving with gentrification.

Even before it opened in 2001, the zinc-clad shell of the Daniel Libeskind-designed **Jüdisches Museum** (*Jewish Museum;* ☎ 25 99 33 00; Lindenstrasse 9-14; adult/concession €5.50/2.75; open 10am-8pm daily, except Jewish high holidays & Christmas eve) drew thousands of visitors. Now its collection covers 1000 years of Jewish history in Germany in a manner that's both admiring and wistful.

Kurfürstendamm

Once the commercial heart of West Berlin, the 'Ku'damm' is showing a touch of age as creative and commercial energies are focused elsewhere in town. The area around Zoo station can become a stultifying tourist ghetto in summer.

The stark ruins of the **Kaiser-Wilhelm-Gedächtniskirche** (1895) in Breitscheidplatz, engulfed in roaring commercialism, are a world-famous landmark. A British bombing on 22 November 1943 left only the broken west tower standing.

South of Zoo station is the **Erotik-Museum** (☎ 866 06 66; Joachimstalerstrasse 4; adult/concession €5/4; open 9am-midnight daily) a surprisingly highbrow creation of Beate Uhse, the German porno and sex toy queen.

On the other side of Gedächtniskirche rises the **Europa-Center** (1965), a shopping and restaurant complex that's still bustling when other shops are closed. Situated northeast of the Europa-Center is the elephant gate of Germany's oldest **Zoo and Aquarium** (☎ 25 40 10; Budapester Strasse 34; each section adult/concession €7/6, combined ticket €11/8; zoo open 9am-6.30pm or dusk, aquarium open 9am-6pm daily). It is more than 150 years old and contains around 1400 species.

Charlottenburg

Completed in 1699 as a summer residence for Queen Sophie Charlotte, the **Schloss Charlottenburg** (☎ 0331-969 42 02; Luisenplatz; day card adult/concession €7.50/5), is a truly exquisite baroque palace (U-Bahn to Sophie-Charlotte-Platz, then a 15-minute walk north along Schlossstrasse; or take bus No 145 from Zoo station to the door). The palace was bombed in 1943 but has been completely rebuilt. Before the entrance is an equestrian statue of the Great Elector (1620–88), Sophie Charlotte's father-in-law. Along the Spree River behind the palace are extensive French and English **gardens** (admission free).

In the central building below the dome are the former royal living quarters. The winter chambers of Friedrich II, upstairs in the new wing (1746) to the east, are highlights, as well as the **Schinkel Pavilion**, the neoclassical **Mausoleum** and the rococo **Belvedere pavilion**. Huge crowds are often waiting for the guided tour of the palace and it may be difficult to get a ticket, especially on weekends and holidays in summer. If you can't get into the main palace, content yourself with the facades and gardens. A day card is good for all the tours and attractions.

Across the street at the beginning of Schlossstrasse is the SMB **Ägyptisches Museum** (Egyptian Museum; ☎ 34 35 73 11; Schlossstrasse 70). The highlight here is the 14th-century BC bust of Queen Nefertiti. Across the road from the museum is the SMB **Sammlung Berggruen** (☎ 32 69 58 15; Schlossstrasse 1), which is showing a collection called 'Picasso and His Time', on loan until 2006. As well as many Picasso paintings, drawings and sculptures, you'll be treated to the works of Cézanne, Van Gogh, Gauguin, Braque and Klee.

Olympic Stadium

Built by Hitler for the 1936 Olympic Games in which African-American runner Jesse Owens won four gold medals, this 85,000-seat stadium (☎ 301 11 00; Olympischer Platz 3; adult/concession €2.50/1, guided tours €5 per person) is situated southwest of Schloss Charlottenburg. One of the best examples of Nazi-era neoclassical architecture, it's still very much in use – the finals of the 2006 World Cup will be played here. Renovations for the occasion will continue until 2004. Take the U2 to Olympia-Stadion Ost, then it's a 10-minute walk along Olympische Strasse to Olympischer Platz.

Zehlendorf

A mere shadow of their former selves, the **Dahlem Museums** in southwest Berlin (U1 to Dahlem-Dorf, then walk five minutes south on Iltisstrasse) all can be entered at Lansstrasse 8 and each costs €3/1.50 per adult/concession. The SMB **Ethnologisches Museum** (Museum of Ethnology; ☎ 830 14 38) takes you back to the early cultures from around the world. You'll also find the SMB **Museum für Ostasiatische Kunst** (Museum of East Asian Art; ☎ 830 13 82) and SMB **Museum für Indisches Kunst** (Museum of Indian Art; ☎ 830 13 61).

Treptower Park

The city's largest **Soviet Monument** (open daily) is a 1949 grave site built to the heroic style and scale favoured by Stalin – some 5000

Soviet soldiers are buried here. It's a remarkable place, although somewhat faded since its days as a top attraction in East Berlin. The Treptower Park S-Bahn station is served by several lines.

ORGANISED TOURS

Guide yourself for the price of a bus ticket (€2.10) on bus No 100, which passes 18 major sights as it makes its way from Zoo station to Michelangelostrasse in Prenzlauer Berg via Alexanderplatz, providing you with a great overview and cheap orientation to Berlin. The BVG even puts out a special brochure describing the route.

Walking Tours

Among the best walking tours we've ever taken are those by **Berlin Walks** (☎ 301 91 94, ⓦ www.berlinwalks.com), which take between three and four hours and cost €10/7.50 for those over/under 26 (and Berlin-Potsdam Welcome Card holders). The Discover Berlin tour covers the heart of the city and runs twice daily from April to October (once daily the rest of the year). It also offers tours of Third Reich sites and Berlin's Jewish heritage. The walks leave from outside the main entrance of Zoo station at the top of the taxi rank.

Insider Tours (☎ 692 31 49; ⓦ www.insidertour.com) has 3½-hour walking tours of the major sites in the city twice daily from April to October (once daily from November to March). The walks (€12/9) leave from in front of the Reisebank at Zoo station. It also has four-hour bike tours (€20/17, including bikes).

Readers have also written in praise of the knowledge and breadth of **Brewer's Best of Berlin Walking Tour** (☎ 70 13 10 37; ⓦ www.brewersberlin.com). Tours meet opposite the Neue Synagogue in Oranienburger Strasse. The four-hour Classic Berlin tour takes in important sights, while the Total Berlin tour may last 10 hours. Both cost €10.

Cruises

One of the best ways to see Berlin's historic past is by boat. **Reederei Bruno Winkler** (☎ 349 95 95) runs a variety of tours on the Spree. The most popular is a three-hour cruise (€13) that leaves several times a day from mid-March to October. It departs from the Schlossbrücke across the Spree just east of Schloss Charlottenburg.

CHARLOTTENBURG & WILMERSDORF

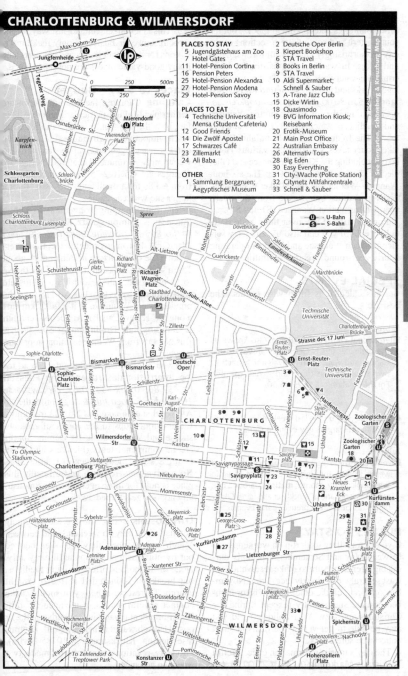

PLACES TO STAY
5 Jugendgästehaus am Zoo
7 Hotel Gates
11 Hotel-Pension Cortina
16 Pension Peters
25 Hotel-Pension Alexandra
27 Hotel-Pension Modena
29 Hotel-Pension Savoy

PLACES TO EAT
4 Technische Universität
   Mensa (Student Cafeteria)
12 Good Friends
14 Die Zwölf Apostel
23 Schwarzes Café
23 Zillemarkt
24 Ali Baba

OTHER
1 Sammlung Berggruen;
   Ägyptisches Museum

2 Deutsche Oper Berlin
3 Kiepert Bookshop
6 STA Travel
8 Books in Berlin
9 STA Travel
10 Aldi Supermarket;
    Schnell & Sauber
13 A-Trane Jazz Club
15 Dicke Wirtin
18 Quasimodo
19 BVG Information Kiosk;
    Reisebank
20 Erotik-Museum
21 Main Post Office
22 Australian Embassy
26 Alternativ Tours
28 Big Eden
30 Easy Everything
31 City-Wache (Police Station)
32 Citynetz Mitfahrzentrale
33 Schnell & Sauber

U — U-Bahn
S — S-Bahn

GERMANY

See Tiergarten, Schöneberg & Kreuzberg Map

Central Berlin may be crowded with roads, office buildings and apartment blocks, but the southeastern and southwestern sections of the city are surprisingly green, with forests, rivers and lakes. In warmer months, tourist boats cruise the waterways, calling at picturesque villages, parks and castles. **Stern und Kreis Schiffahrt** (☎ 536 36 00; w www.sternundkreis.de) operates a number of cruises on the Wannsee and its adjacent waters between April and October. The frequent 7-Seen-Rundfahrt (seven lakes tour) takes you through various Havel lakes (including the Kleiner Wannsee and Glieniecker) lasting two hours (€8). The six-hour Wannsee-Werder tour (€13) takes in Potsdam. These and other tours leave from the docks near S-Bahn station Wannsee (S1 and S7).

For the price of a regular three-zone BVG ticket (€2.40) you can also use the ferry service between Wannsee and Kladow operating hourly year-round, weather permitting.

SPECIAL EVENTS

Berlin's calendar is filled with events. The best are:

February

International Film Festival Berlin Also known as the Berlinale, this is Germany's answer to the Cannes and Venice film festivals and attracts its own stable of stars (few) and starlets (plenty). For information call ☎ 25 48 90.

June

Berlin Pride Held on the last weekend in June, this is by far the largest gay event in Germany.

July

Love Parade The largest techno party in the world wends its way through the streets of Berlin in the middle of the month. It attracts around one million people and is quickly challenging Oktoberfest as Germany's premier party event.

PLACES TO STAY

If you're travelling to Berlin on weekends and between May and September, especially during big events, be sure to make reservations at least several weeks in advance. From November to March, on the other hand, visitor numbers plunge significantly (except during the Christmas and New Year holidays) and you may be able to get very good deals at short notice – be sure to ask.

The city's tourist information office, **Berlin Tourismus Marketing** (BTM; ☎ 25 00 25, fax 25 00 24 24), handles hotel reservations for €3. This is a convenient and fast way to find a room; however BTM can only make reservations for its partner hotels and pensions, and many good-value places are not represented.

Places to Stay – Budget

Camping Camping facilities in Berlin are neither plentiful nor particularly good. All are far from the city centre and complicated to reach without your own transport. They fill up quickly – space gets taken up by caravans – so we strongly recommend that you call ahead. Charges are €5.10/2.35 per adult/child, plus from €3.80 for a small tent site to €6.60 for a larger site with car space.

The only camping convenient to public transport is **Campingplatz Kohlhasenbrück** (☎/fax 805 17 37; Neue Kreisstrasse 36; open Mar-Oct). It's in a peaceful location overlooking the Griebnitzsee in Zehlendorf, about 15km southwest of central Berlin. Take the S7 to Griebnitzsee station, and it's a 10-minute walk. Alternatively, take bus No 118 from the previous stop, Wannsee. If it's full, 2km east along the Teltow Canal at Albrechts-Teerofen is **Campingplatz Dreilinden** (☎ 805 12 01). Bus No 118 from Wannsee station stops here as well.

If you're on a really tight budget, head for the **Internationales Jugendcamp Fliesstal** (☎ 433 86 40, fax 434 50 63; Ziekowstrasse 161; beds €5; open July & Aug). From the U6 Alt-Tegel station take bus No 222 (direction: Lübars) four stops to the corner of Ziekowstrasse and Waidmannsluster Damm. Spaces are in communal tents (blankets and foam mattresses provided); check-in is after 5pm. No reservations are taken and officially this place is only for those aged 14 to 27, but usually nobody gets turned away.

DJH Hostels Berlin's hostels are extremely popular, especially on weekends and between March and October; they are often booked out by noisy school groups until early July. None of the hostels offers cooking facilities, but breakfast is included in the overnight charge. To reserve a bed, you should make contact several weeks in advance (e djh-berlin-brandenburgzr@jugendherberge.de, or post: Deutsches Jugendherbergswerk Zentralreservierung, Kluckstrasse 3, 10785 Berlin). Phone reservations can only be made two weeks in advance.

The only DJH hostel within the city centre is the institutional, 364-bed **Jugendherberge Berlin International** (☎ 261 10 98, fax 265 03 83; Kluckstrasse 3; dorm beds juniors/seniors €18.50/22.60, doubles €23/27.10). It's in Schöneberg, near the Landwehrkanal (U1 to Kurfürstenstrasse). Double rooms and the less-expensive dorm rooms are available.

Jugendherberge am Wannsee (☎ 803 20 34, fax 803 59 08; Badeweg 1; beds juniors/seniors €18/22.10), on the corner of Kronprinzessinnenweg, is pleasantly located on Grosser Wannsee, the lake southwest of the city on the way to Potsdam. The hostel is a 10-minute walk from Nikolassee S-Bahn station (S1 and S7) via the footbridge; turn left at Kronprinzessinnenweg.

Jugendherberge Ernst Reuter (☎ 404 16 10, fax 404 59 72; Hermsdorfer Damm 48-50; beds juniors/seniors €14.40/18) is in the far northwest of Berlin. Take the U6 to Alt-Tegel, then bus No 125 right to the door.

Independent Hostels & Guesthouses

The non-DJH hostels listed following don't have curfews. Rooms do not have private facilities, and breakfast costs extra unless indicated. Some give discounts to students with ID.

In Charlottenburg, **Jugendgästehaus am Zoo** (☎ 312 94 10, fax 312 54 30; Hardenbergstrasse 9a; dorm beds €18, singles/doubles €25/44) is just three blocks from Zoo station and has handsome, wooded communal spaces. Add €3 if you're over 27.

In Mitte, **Circus – The Hostel** (☎ 28 39 14 33, fax 28 39 14 84; e info@circus-berlin.de; Rosa-Luxemburg-Strasse 39 & Weinbergsweg 1a; dorm beds/singles/doubles/triples €14/30/46/60) has two hugely popular, well-run hostels. The newer Weinbergsweg location has a café and bar. You'll find similarly helpful and friendly staff at the **Clubhouse Hostel** (☎ 28 09 79 79, 28 09 79 77; e info@clubhouse-berlin.de; Kalkscheune 4-5; dorm beds/doubles/triples from €14/45/60), near Friedrichstrasse and Tacheles.

In the heart of Prenzlauer Berg's nightlife and across from a park is **Lette 'm Sleep** (☎ 44 73 36 23, fax 44 73 36 25; e info@backpackers.de; Lettestrasse 7; dorm beds €15-19 with linen €3 extra, doubles €48 including linen). Doubles have kitchenettes.

Two moderately priced hotels close to Mehringdamm station in Kreuzberg (U6 or U7) have dorm accommodation. Friendly **Pension Kreuzberg** (☎ 251 13 62, fax 251 06 38; Grossbeerenstrasse 64; dorm beds/singles/doubles €22.50/40/52) has plain rooms and garden views at the back. **Hotel Transit** (☎ 789 04 70, fax 78 90 47 77, e info@hotel-transit.de; Hagelberger Strasse 53-54; dorm beds/singles €19/52/60, including breakfast) is in a former factory teeming with character and, occasionally, school groups. Most rooms have shower but no private toilet.

Hotels In Charlottenburg, there's the **Hotel-Pension Cortina** (☎ 313 90 59, fax 312 73 96; Kantstrasse 140; singles/doubles from €31/50 with shared toilet) with plenty of basic rooms, some with shower. Mitte's **Artist Hotel-Pension Die Loge** (☎/fax 280 75 13; e die-loge@t-online.de; Friedrichstrasse 115; singles/doubles from €40/60) has far more personality than your average hotel, a clientele including actors and artists, and a great deal on rooms with shared bath.

New **InterMezzo** (☎ 22 48 90 96, fax 22 48 90 97; w www.hotelintermezzo.de; Gertrud-Kolmar-Strasse 5; singles/doubles €40/67) is a spotless place between Brandenburger Tor and Potsdamer Platz, exclusively for women (and their children). Most rooms have shower but no toilet. Gay men might try **Hotel Gunia** (☎ 218 59 40, fax 218 59 44; e info@hotelgunia.de; Eisenacher Strasse 10; singles without bath €45, singles/doubles with bath €50/70), offering simple but well-kept rooms near Nollendorfplatz, right in the heart of the gay district.

Readers have written to recommend cheery **Pension Peters** (☎ 312 22 78, fax 312 35 19; e penspeters@aol.com; Kantstrasse 146; singles/doubles from €58/78) for service above the call. Rooms without toilet cost less.

Places to Stay – Mid-Range

In Kreuzberg, **Hotel am Anhalter Bahnhof** (☎ 251 03 42, fax 251 48 97; e hotel-aab@t-online.de; Stresemannstrasse 36; singles/doubles from €45/70 without facilities, €65/90 with facilities) has simple, reasonably priced digs. Schöneberg's **Pension Fischer** (☎ 21 91 55 66, fax 21 01 96 14; e hotelpensionfischer@t-online.de; Nürnberger Strasse 24a; singles/doubles from €60/70) has only recently been handsomely renovated.

GERMANY

In Charlottenburg is **Hotel-Pension Modena** (☎ 885 70 10, fax 881 52 94; *Wielandstrasse 26; singles without bath €41, singles/doubles with bath from €65/95*) in an atmospheric old building. Attractive **Hotel-Pension Alexandra** (☎ 885 77 80, fax 88 57 78 18; e *mail@alexandra-berlin.de; Wielandstrasse 32; singles/doubles €72/82*) has quiet, simple rooms, some with full facilities. The **Hotel-Pension Savoy** (☎ 88 47 16 10, fax 882 37 46, e *info@hotel-pension-savoy.de; Meinekestrasse 4; singles €62-73, doubles €90-109*) is in a beautiful building featuring a muralled, church-like entrance and an antique lift.

Hotel Tiergarten (☎ 39 98 96, fax 39 98 97 35; e *hotel.tiergarten@t-online.de; Alt-Moabit 89; singles/doubles from €77/92*) is a contemporary business-style hotel in a bourgeois 19th-century house. For Internet junkies, *every* room at Charlottenburg's **Hotel Gates** (☎ 31 10 60, fax 312 20 60; e *info@hotel-gates.com; singles/doubles from €95/120*) has its own computer terminal. It's in a historic house with contemporary renovations.

Comfort Hotel Auberge (☎ 235 00 20, fax 23 50 02 99; e *hotel-auberge@t-online.de; Bayreuther Strasse 10; singles/doubles from €104/132*), in an interesting old building in Schöneberg, is a good place with large rooms, or mini-singles for €79.

Places to Stay – Top End

Those holding generous expense accounts might head for **Hotel Adlon Kempinski** (☎ 226 10, toll-free 00800-42 63 13 55, fax 22 61 22 22; *Unter den Linden 77; singles/doubles from €260/310*), which offers front-row vistas of Brandenburger Tor. This replica of the famous historic hotel reopened to great fanfare in mid-1997 after a hiatus of more than half a century. It has lavish rooms, but rates do *not* include the €27 breakfast buffet.

On fashionable Gendarmenmarkt, the **Four Seasons Berlin** (☎ 203 38, toll-free 00800-64 88 64 88, fax 203 61 66; w *www.fourseasons .com; Charlottenstrasse 49; singles/doubles from €280/315*) pampers guests with large, luxurious rooms, sauna and fitness centre.

PLACES TO EAT

Berliners love eating out and have literally thousands of restaurants and cafés to choose from. There's no need to travel far, since every neighbourhood has its own cluster of eateries running the gamut of cuisines and price categories. The blocks around Savigny platz in Charlottenburg, Prenzlauer Berg's Kollwitzplatz, and south of Winterfeldtplatz in Schöneberg are great places to browse for good restaurants with character.

German

In Charlottenburg is the Art Nouveau **Zillemarkt** (☎ 881 70 40; *Bleibtreustrasse 48a, mains €8-12.50*), serving huge portions at fair prices. In Mitte, you can eat like a playwright at the **Kellerrestaurant** (☎ 282 38 43; *Chausseestrasse 125; mains €6-15.50*) in Brecht-Weigel-Haus, which serves up Helene Weigel's Austrian-influenced recipes, or slum like a beer-slogger at **Bärenschenke** (☎ 282 90 78; *Friedrichstrasse 124; mains €3-10*), with a long bar and local specialities. The rustic **Grossbeerenkeller** (☎ 742 39 30; *Grossbeerenstrasse 90; mains €7-14.20*) serves delicious artery-cloggers in Kreuzberg. For hearty home-style basics, head for the corner **Zum Schusterjungen** (☎ 442 76 54; *Danziger Strasse 9; mains €4.50-9*) in Prenzlauer Berg. At the top of the spectrum, there's Gendarmenmarkt's **Lutter & Wegner** (☎ 20 29 54 10; *Charlottenstrasse 56; mains €16-21*), one of Berlin's oldest restaurants and possibly its fanciest.

Asian

Near Savignyplatz in Charlottenburg, the Chinese **Good Friends** (☎ 313 26 59; *Kantstrasse 30; most dishes €6.80-23.50*) is short on decor but big on popularity. In Mitte, **Sushi Circle** (☎ 20 38 79 60; *Französische Strasse 48*) has all-you-can-eat conveyor-belt sushi for €14.90 on weekday evenings.

Tuk-Tuk (☎ 781 15 88; *Grossgörschenstrasse 2; mains €8.50-17.50*) in Schöneberg feels like an intimate bamboo den in Jakarta. For Thai specialities, **Mao Thai** (☎ 441 92 61; *Wörtherstrasse 30; mains €10-19*) in Prenzlauer Berg is pricey but delightful; its less-expensive sister restaurant, which is situated in Mitte, is the rather pleasant cellar **Kamala** (☎ 283 27 97; *Oranienburger Strasse 69; mains around €8.20*).

French

The atmospheric **Gugelhof** (☎ 442 92 29; *Kollwitzplatz cnr Knaackstrasse 37; mains €8-13.40*) serves Alsatian specialities overlooking the square and has a nice wine list. Franco-German **Reinhard's** (☎ 242 52 95;

Poststrasse 28; mains €9-20.50) is an island of sophistication situated in the touristy Nikolaiviertel area.

Italian
Readers have recommended the atmospheric **Die Zwölf Apostel** (12 Apostles; ☎ 312 14 33; Bleibtreustrasse 49; mains €7.50-11; open 24hr), which serves light meals, pastas, insalate and large, brick-oven pizzas named for Matthew, Thomas et al. Busy **Ali Baba** (☎ 881 13 50; Bleibtreustrasse 45; mains €3-10.50) is nearby and, situated in Schöneberg, there's **Don Antonio** (☎ 78 71 56 00; Akazienstrasse 24; mains €3-12.60); both serve individual pizzas starting at €3 in a cosy atmosphere.

Mediterranean
Highly recommended is the Greek **Ousies Taverna** (☎ 216 79 57; Grunewaldstrasse 16; mains €4.90/14.60) in Schöneberg, where the atmosphere is as boisterous as the waiters. In Kreuzberg, **Knofi** (☎ 694 58 07; Bergmannstrasse 98) is a takeaway shop with lavish displays of Greek, Italian and Turkish specialities.

North American
Never mind that we've always associated delis with New York; **Tim's Canadian Deli** (☎ 21 75 69 60; Maassenstrasse 14; dishes €3-19.50) in Schöneberg has great bagels for breakfast (from €0.80), sandwiches, burgers and steaks for later in the day, and a diverse crowd all day.

Spanish
Bar-Celona (☎ 282 91 53; Hannoversche Strasse 2; tapas €2.50-9, mains €11-18.50) is a friendly, well-regarded tapas bar near Brecht-Weigel Haus. On a pretty block in Schöneberg, **Pasodoble** (☎ 784 52 44; Crellestrasse 39; tapas €1.80-7, mains €7-12.20) offers tapas, tortillas, paellas and some Mexican specialities.

Vegetarian
Homy **Seerose** (☎ 69 81 59 27; Mehringdamm 47; mains €4.20-6.20) in Kreuzberg (U6 or U7 to Mehringdamm) has takeaway or eat-in choices. Most Asian restaurants will make vegetarian dishes too, including several Indian places on Goltzstrasse, south of Winterfeldtplatz in Schöneberg.

Cafés
The number and variety of cafés in Berlin is astonishing. They're wonderful places to relax over a cup of coffee and some cake, while ploughing through a newspaper or chatting with friends. Many of these places also honour the great Berlin tradition of serving breakfast all day, and some serve more-elaborate meals.

The elegant **Café Einstein** (☎ 261 50 96; Kurfürstenstrasse 58; mains €5-21.50) is a Viennese-style coffee house in a rambling villa. The more rock-and-roll **Schwarzes Café** (☎ 313 80 38; Kantstrasse 148; dishes €4.50-9; open 24hr) in Charlottenburg is not far from Zoo station. Footpath benches at **Mendelssohn** (☎ 281 78 59; Oranienburger Strasse 39; mains €7-13.20) are pleasant places to slurp Milchkaffee and to people-watch on a sunny morning. Mains include steaks and salads. **Barcomi's** (☎ 694 81 38; Bergmannstrasse 21; baked goods from around €1) in Kreuzberg is a hole-in-the-wall loved by locals for coffee and bagels.

Beneath the S-Bahn near Museumsinsel, **Café Odéon** (☎ 208 26 00; Georgenstrasse, S-Bahn arch 192; dishes €1.80-6.90) serves light meals like quiche lorraine and vegetable lasagne. The walls are plastered with old-time, enamelled advertising signs. Balmy summer nights are the best time to be at the **Café am Neuen See** (☎ 254 49 30; Lichtensteinallee 1; dishes €3-11.50), in Tiergarten park. Service in the beer garden is pretty slow, but that just gives you more time for people-watching and enjoying the view over the lake.

Student Cafeterias
Anyone, student or not, may eat at the 1st-floor **Technische Universität Mensa** (Hardenbergstrasse 34; 3-course lunch €3-5 for students, add about €2 for nonstudents; open 11am-2.30pm), three blocks from Zoo station. The **Humboldt Universität Mensa** (Unter den Linden 6) in Mitte has the same hours, and similar prices, and can be found by entering the main portal, then taking the first door on your left, turning right at the end of the corridor and following your nose.

Snacks & Fast Food
Berlin is paradise for snackers on the go, with Turkish (your best bet), Wurst, Greek, Italian, Chinese – you name it – available at Imbiss (snack) stands throughout the city. The good areas to look are along Budapester Strasse in

GERMANY

Tiergarten, the eastern end of Kantstrasse near Zoo station, on Wittenbergplatz in Schöneberg, on Alexanderplatz in Mitte and around Schlesisches Tor station in the Kreuzberg district.

Self-Catering

To prepare your own food, there are the discount Aldi, Lidl or Penny Markt **supermarket** chains, which have outlets throughout Berlin. There are also **farmers' markets** around town, the most famous (though not necessarily cheapest) of which is held on Wednesday and Saturday on Schöneberg's Winterfeldtplatz. Snootier self-caterers should not miss the food floor of **KaDeWe** (see Shopping later in this section).

ENTERTAINMENT

Berliners take culture and fun seriously. The options are almost daunting and are always changing, so don't be surprised if the places we list are a bit different by the time you get to them. Put your faith in word-of-mouth tips for the most up-to-date, cutting-edge scenes.

For fancy, fairly upmarket venues, go to Savignyplatz and side streets like Bleibtreustrasse and northern Grolmannstrasse in Charlottenburg.

Kreuzberg – around Mehringdamm, Gneisenaustrasse and Bergmannstrasse – is alternative albeit with some trendy touches, while Kreuzberg along Oranienstrasse and Wiener Strasse has a grungy and slightly edgy feel. Around Winterfeldtplatz in Schöneberg, you will find few tourists and plenty of the 30-something brigade with alternative lifestyles and young families.

In the eastern districts, the nightlife is far more earthy and experimental. New bars and restaurants open, bringing previously dull streets to life, seemingly overnight. The most dynamic scenes are in Prenzlauer Berg and Friedrichshain, where the feel is energetic and slightly gritty. More established are the nightclubs and cafés/pubs in Mitte along Oranienburger Strasse, Rosenthaler Platz, Hackescher Markt and adjacent streets in the Scheunenviertel area.

Pubs & Bars

Gentrifying Kreuzberg is **Morgenland** (☎ 611 31 83; Skalitzer Strasse 35), which is good for long conversations at oddly shaped designer tables. A longtime hang-out is **Flammende**

Herzen (Flaming Hearts; ☎ 615 71 02; Oranienstrasse 170), which is dark, knick knack-filled and, occasionally, gay.

Plenty of popular cafés/pubs with outdoor tables during the warm weather are clustered around Kollwitz-Platz and Helmholtz-Platz in Prenzlauer Berg, including the contemporary **Café Weitzmann** (Husemannstrasse 2), the Mexican-themed **Frida Kahlo** (☎ 445 70 16; Lychener Strasse 37) and the cosy wine bar **Weinstein** (☎ 441 18 42; Lychener Strasse 33). Dark and retro, **Astro** (☎ 29 66 16 15; Simon-Dach-Strasse 40) is a bar in a relatively gritty section of Friedrichshain that's developing into party central. In Schöneberg are lots of interesting pubs and cafés around Akazienstrasse and on lovely Crellestrasse, including the inexpensive, tropical **Café Mirell** (☎ 782 04 57; Crellestrasse 46) and the **Leuchtturm** (Lighthouse; Crellestrasse 41), which features walls plastered in kitsch oil paintings. **Obst und Gemüse** (☎ 282 96 47; Oranienburger Strasse 49) in Mitte is a hip and popular bar.

Berliner Kneipen

Typical Berlin pubs have their own tradition of hospitality: good food (sometimes rustic daily dishes or stews), beer, humour and Schlagfertigkeit (quick-wittedness). In Charlottenburg, **Dicke Wirtin** (☎ 314 49 52; Carmerstrasse 9) is an earthy place and sports bar off Savignyplatz. Historic **Zur letzten Instanz** (The Final Authority; ☎ 242 55 28; Waisenstrasse 14) in Mitte claims traditions dating back to the 1600s and is next to a chunk of medieval town wall.

Beer Gardens

As soon as the last winter storms have blown away, pallid Berliners reacquaint themselves with the sun. The open-air **Golgatha** (☎ 785 24 53; Viktoriapark) in Kreuzberg is an institution (enter off Katzbachstrasse). In the southwestern district of Zehlendorf is **Loretta am Wannsee** (☎ 803 51 56; Kronprinzessinenweg 260), a huge garden with seating for more than 1000 (S-bahn to Wannsee).

Clubs

Berlin has a reputation for unbridled and very late nightlife. Not much starts before 11pm at the earliest, though there's a growing trend for 'after-work' clubs and raves, so those hip, hard-working, hard-clubbing types don't have to kiss their partying lifestyle goodbye. Cover charges (when they apply) range from €2.50 to €10 and usually don't include a drink.

Berlin *is* techno music and you'll be hard pressed to find a nightclub that plays anything else. One of the oldest techno temples is Mitte's **Tresor** (☎ 609 37 02; *Leipziger Strasse 126a*), housed inside the actual money vault of a former department store. It also has a summer beer garden.

Also very popular is **Delicious Doughnuts** (☎ 28 09 92 74; *Rosenthaler Strasse 9*), an acid jazz club in Mitte. **SO 36** (☎ 61 40 13 07; *Oranienstrasse 190*) in Kreuzberg is one of Berlin's longest-running techno nightclubs with theme nights including punk and gay and lesbian. In Friedrichshain, **Matrix** (☎ 29 49 10 47; *Warschauer Platz 18*) has several dance floors situated beneath U-Bahn arches; it attracts young techno-ravers.

Technoed-out? At Mitte's **Sophienklub** (☎ 282 45 52; *Sophienstrasse 6*), you'll hear Brazilian, house, reggae, but *no* techno. The hot-spot on busy Potsdamer Platz is **Blu** (☎ 25 59 30 30; *Marlene-Dietrich-Platz 4*), with three floors of dancing, plus city views.

A great example of Berlin's wilder side is the **KitKat Club** (*Bessemerstrasse 2-14*) in Tempelhof-Schöneberg. On Friday and Saturday nights you only get in wearing your 'sexual fantasy outfit' (meaning erotic or basically no clothes!), and women choose who's admitted.

The nightclubs around the Ku'damm are generally avoided by most Berliners. Places tend to be packed with tourists, especially German high-school kids, who usually disappear with the last U-Bahn train. Typical is **Big Eden** (☎ 882 61 20; *Kurfürstendamm 202*).

Gay & Lesbian

Pardon our presumption, but if you're reading this, you probably don't need to be told that Berlin is about the gayest city in Europe. *Anything* goes, and we can just scratch the surface; for more specialised listings, consult the gay and lesbian freebie *Siegessäule* or the strictly gay *Sergej* magazine, or contact **Mann-O-Meter** (☎ 216 80 08; *Bülowstrasse 106*) in Schöneberg.

Hafen (☎ 214 11 18; *Motzstrasse 19*), near Nollendorfplatz, is full of gay yuppies fortifying themselves before they move next door to the legendary **Tom's Bar** (☎ 213 45 70; *Motzstrasse 19*), with its famous dark and active cellar. The multiroomed **Connection**

(☎ 218 14 32; *Fuggerstrasse 33*) is the biggest and arguably the busiest gay nightclub in the city.

Interesting places in Kreuzberg include the over-the-top, kitschy **Roses** (☎ 615 75 70; *Oranienstrasse 187*), as well as the **Schoko-Café** (☎ 615 15 61; *Mariannenstrasse 6*), which is a convivial meeting place for lesbians. Alcohol-free **Café Seidenfaden** (☎ 283 27 83; *Dircksenstrasse 47*) is a pleasant lesbian café near Häckische Höfe.

Jazz

The **A-Trane** (☎ 313 25 50; *Bleibtreustrasse 1; admission €5-10*) in Charlottenburg, is still *the* place in Berlin for jazz. There is a cover charge but on some nights (usually Tuesday and Wednesday) admission is free. **Quasimodo** (☎ 312 80 86; *Kantstrasse 12a*) has live jazz, blues or rock acts in the basement every night. The stylish café on the ground floor is a good place for a preshow drink.

Classical Music

The **Berliner Philharmonie** (☎ 25 48 81 32; *Herbert-von-Karajan Strasse 1*) is famous for its supreme acoustics. All seats are excellent, so just take the cheapest. The lavish **Konzerthaus** (☎ 25 00 25; *Gendarmenmarkt*) in Mitte is home to the renowned Berlin Symphony Orchestra.

Cinemas

Films cost as much as €9, and foreign films are usually dubbed into German. If the film is shown in the original language with German subtitles, it will say 'OmU' on the advertisement. If the film is screened in the original language without German subtitles, it will say 'OF' or 'OV'.

Cinemas with frequent original-language showings include the new **Cinestar** (☎ 26 06 62 60; *Potsdamer Strasse 4*) at Potsdamer Platz, the **Odeon** (☎ 78 70 40 19; *Hauptstrasse 116*) – take the U4 to Innsbrucker Platz or S1, S45 or S46 to Schöneberg – and the **The Babylon** (☎ 61 60 91 93; *Dresdner Strasse 126*) in Kreuzberg.

Theatre

Berlin has around 150 theatres, so there should be something for everybody. In the former eastern section, they cluster around Friedrichstrasse; in the western part they're concentrated along Ku'damm. The historic

GERMANY

Deutsches Theater (☎ 25 00 25; *Schumann-strasse 13a*) offers both classic and modern productions. Situated nearby, the **Berliner Ensemble** (☎ 282 31 60; *Bertolt-Brecht-Platz 1*) performs works by Brecht and other 20th-century Europeans. **Friends of Italian Opera** (☎ 691 12 11; *Fidicinstrasse 40*) in Kreuzberg is Berlin's only regular English-language theatre venue.

Opera

The **Staatsoper Unter den Linden** (☎ 20 35 34 55; *Unter den Linden 5-7*) in Mitte, hosts lavish productions with international talent in an exquisite building dating from 1743.

The **Deutsche Oper Berlin** (☎ 343 84 01; *Bismarckstrasse 35, Charlottenburg*) has classical works of mostly Italian and French composers, plus contemporary works.

Cabaret

A number of venues are trying to revive the lively and lavish variety shows of 1920s Berlin. Programmes include dancers, singers, jugglers, acrobats and other entertainers, who each perform a short piece. Expect to pay at least €12. Don't confuse cabaret with *Kabarett*, political and satirical revues.

Chamäleon Varieté (☎ 282 71 18; *Rosenthalerstrasse 40-41*) in the Hackesche Höfe in Mitte, has a variety show which includes comedy and slapstick, juggling acts, singing and more.

Cultural Centres

The hottest venue in Prenzl'berg is the **Kulturbrauerei** (*Culture Brewery;* ☎ 441 92 69; *Knaackstrasse 97*), a renovated 8000 sq metre space where artists from around the world work. It attracts people from all walks of life with galleries, cinemas and events as diverse as post-Love Parade raves and poetry readings.

SHOPPING

Berlin's decentralised character is reflected in the fact that it doesn't have a clearly defined shopping artery like London's Oxford Street or New York's Fifth Avenue. Rather, the numerous shopping areas are in various neighbourhoods, many of which have a local speciality and 'feel'. For art galleries and *haute couture*, for instance, you should head for posh Charlottenburg, while multiethnic Kreuzberg is known for its eclectic second-hand and junk stores.

The closest Berlin gets to an international shopping strip is the area along Kurfürstendamm and its extension, Tauentzienstrasse. The star of this area is **KaDeWe** (*Tauentzienstrasse 21*). This is truly one of Europe's grand department stores, the Harrods of Germany. Every year, about 30 million shopping fetishists have a field day on its top floors. The gourmet food halls located on the 6th floor are extraordinary.

The Wilmersdorfer Strasse stop of the U7 will put you in the thick of pedestrian streets filled with affordable shops and department stores patronised by real Berliners. Much more upmarket is the chic indoor shopping complex outside the U6 Französische Strasse in Mitte. Anchored by **Galeries Lafayette**, a branch of the famous Parisian department store, it is connected by an underground tunnel to smallish malls filled with international designer boutiques.

Markets

The **Berlin Art and Nostalgia Market** (*open 8am-5pm Sat & Sun*) is held at the northeastern end of Museumsinsel. The selection here is heavy on collectibles, books, ethnic crafts and possibly authentic GDR memorabilia. From U/S-Bahn station Friedrichstrasse, walk east along Georgenstrasse for about 10 minutes.

GETTING THERE & AWAY
Air

There are few direct flights to Berlin from overseas and, depending on the airline you use, you're likely to fly first into another European city like Frankfurt, Amsterdam, Paris or London and catch a connecting flight from there.

For now, Berlin has three airports. **Tegel** (TXL) primarily serves destinations within Germany and Europe, while **Schönefeld** (SXF) mostly operates international flights to/from Europe, Asia, Africa and Central America. Eventually, Tegel will close, leaving a revamped and expanded Schönefeld as Berlin's airport hub. Close-in **Berlin-Tempelhof** (THF) became famous as the landing hub for Allied airlifts during the Berlin blockade of 1948–49. However, as Schönefeld expands, Tempelhof's future is, shall we say, up in the air.

Bus

Berlin is well connected to the rest of Europe by long-distance bus. Most buses arrive at and depart from the **Zentraler Omnibusbahnhof**

(ZOB; ☎ 302 53 61; Masurenalee 4-6) in Charlottenburg, opposite the stately Funkturm radio tower (U2 to Kaiserdamm or S45 to Witzleben). Tickets are available from many travel agencies in Berlin or at the bus station.

Train

ICE and IC trains have hourly services to every major city in Germany. There are night trains to the capitals of most major central European countries.

That said, until the opening of the huge new, centralised Lehrter Bahnhof (scheduled for 2007; the current station is just for local trains), visitors may find train services to and from Berlin confusing.

Zoo station is the principal station for long-distance travellers going to/from the west. It has scores of lockers (from €1) and a large Reisezentrum (reservation and information office). Ostbahnhof (the former main station) is gaining importance as the train system is revised, while Lichtenberg station in the east generally handles trains to/from the old east and countries beyond, as well as night trains.

Many trains serving Zoo station also stop at Ostbahnhof (the former main train station) and may also stop at Friedrichstrasse and Alexanderplatz. Check your schedules carefully and be aware that you may need to switch stations, usually easily done via S-Bahn. The S5 and S7 travel directly between Zoo and Lichtenberg (35 to 45 minutes); several additional lines serve the rest.

Conventional train tickets to and from Berlin are valid for all trains on the S-Bahn, which means that you can use your train ticket to ride the S-Bahn to/from your train station.

Hitching

Lonely Planet does not encourage hitching for all the obvious reasons. Having said that, if you do want to hitch a ride, it's best to head to one of the service areas on the city autobahns. If your destination is Leipzig, Nuremberg, Munich and beyond, make your way to the Dreilinden service area on the A115. Take the U1 to Krumme Lanke, then bus No 211 to Quantzstrasse, then walk down to the rest area. For Dresden, take the S9 or the S45 to Altglienicke and position yourself near the autobahn on-ramp. Those headed to Hamburg or Rostock should go to the former border checkpoint Stolpe by catching the U6 to Alt-Tegel and then bus No 224 to Stolpe.

Mitfahrzentralen (ride-share agencies) organise lifts and charge a fixed amount payable to the driver, plus commission ranging from €6 for short distances to €10.50 for longer trips (including outside Germany). Some sample fares (including commission) are Leipzig €13.50, Hanover €17, Frankfurt/Main, Munich or Cologne €28.50. **ADM Mitfahrzentrale** (☎ 194 40) has two branches: at Zoo station on the Vinetastrasse platform of the U2 (open 9am-8pm Mon-Fri & 10am-6pm Sat & Sun), and in the Alexanderplatz U-Bahn station as you cross from U2 to U8 (open 10am-6pm Mon-Fri, 11am-4pm Sat & Sun). Another agency is **Citynetz** (☎ 194 44; Joachimstalerstrasse 17).

GETTING AROUND

Ongoing construction in central Berlin has the expected effect on traffic flow. Gridlock, mysteriously rerouted roads and sudden dead ends that weren't there yesterday are among the obstacles you'll have to navigate when driving through the core districts.

However, Berlin's public transport system is excellent, so use it. Roughly one billion passengers each year ride the huge network of U-Bahn and S-Bahn trains, buses, trams and ferries which extends pretty much into every corner of Berlin and the surrounding areas.

To/From the Airport

Tegel airport is connected by bus No 109 to Zoo station (€2.10), a route that travels via Kurfürstendamm and Luisenplatz.

JetExpress Bus TXL (€3.10) goes via Unter den Linden, Potsdamer Platz and the Reichstag. The trip between the airport and the western centre takes around 30 minutes. A taxi between Tegel and Zoo station costs about €19.

Schönefeld airport is easily reached in 30 minutes by **Airport Express** trains leaving from Zoo station every 30 minutes. The train also stops at the rest of the stations along the central train line including Friedrichstrasse and Ostbahnhof. The station is about 300m from the terminal and is connected by a free shuttle bus. A taxi to Zoo station costs between €25 and €35.

Close-in Tempelhof airport is reached by the U6 (Platz der Luftbrücke) and by bus No 119 from Kurfürstendamm via Kreuzberg. A taxi to/from Zoo station will cost about €16.

GERMANY

Public Transport

Berlin's public transport system offers services provided by **Berliner Verkehrsbetriebe** (BVG; ☎ 194 49), which operates the U-Bahn, buses, trams and ferries; and the **Deutsche Bahn** (DB; ☎ 01805-99 66 33, call cost €0.12 per min) which runs the S-Bahn and regional RE, SE and RB trains (rail pass-holders can use the DB trains for free). Since the system is jointly operated, one type of ticket is valid on all forms of transport (with the few exceptions noted following). BVG has information kiosks at major entry points, which also sell tickets and passes. For information on S-Bahn, RE and RB connections, visit the Reisezentrum office inside Zoo station.

Greater Berlin is divided into three tariff zones: A, B and C. Tickets are valid in at least two zones (AB or BC), or in all three zones. Unless you're venturing to Potsdam or the very outer suburbs, you'll only need the AB ticket. Taking a bicycle in specially marked carriages of the S-Bahn or U-Bahn costs €1.25 (free if you hold a monthly ticket). On the U-Bahn, bikes are allowed only between 9am and 2pm and from 5.30pm to closing time on weekdays (any time on weekends). The following types of tickets and passes are available:

Ganzstrecke (Entire Route System) – This ticket (€2.40) also allows unlimited travel for two hours, but in all three zones (ABC). It's also valid on RE, SE and RB trains.

Kurzstrecke (Short Trip) – This ticket (€1.20) allows you to travel any three stops by U-Bahn or S-Bahn or six stops by bus or tram.

Langstrecke (Long Trip) – With this ticket (€2.10) you can travel on all forms of public transport (except RE, SE and RB trains) for two hours within two of the three zones (AB or BC) with unlimited transfers.

Tageskarte (Day Pass) – This ticket gives you unlimited travel until 3am the following day and costs only €6.10 (zones AB or BC) or €6.30 (zones ABC).

Bus drivers sell single and day tickets, but tickets for U/S-Bahn trains and other multiple day tickets must be purchased in advance.

Most types of tickets are available from vending machines (which feature instructions in English) in U/S-Bahn stations. Tickets must be stamped (validated) in a red or yellow machine (Entwerter) at the platform entrances to U/S-Bahn stations, at bus stops before boarding, or as you enter the bus or tram. If you're using a timed ticket like the Langstrecke, validate it just as your train or bus arrives to ensure full value. If you're caught without a ticket (or with an unvalidated one), there's a €30 on-the-spot fine.

The most efficient way to travel around Berlin is by U/S-Bahn. A network of some 30 tram lines crisscross the entire eastern half of Berlin. There's also bus service throughout the city, but if you need to travel across town in a hurry, don't take the bus! Traffic congestion can slow your journey. Bus and tram stops are marked with a large 'H' and the name of the stop.

Services operate from 4am until just after midnight, but most S-Bahns continue to operate hourly between midnight and 4am on Saturday and Sunday. Some 70 bus lines operate between 1am and about 4am (Nachtbus), when regular service resumes. Buses leave from the major nightlife areas like Zoo station, Hackescher Markt in Mitte and Nollendorfplatz in Schöneberg, and cover the entire Berlin area, including the outer districts. Normal fares apply.

Car & Motorcycle

You'll soon want to ditch your wheels in Berlin. Garage parking is expensive (about €1 to €1.50 per hour), but it'll often be your only choice if you want to be near the main shopping areas or attractions. Free street parking, while impossible to find in these central areas, is usually available in residential streets, especially in the eastern districts. If you're staying at a hotel, keep in mind that most don't have their own garages.

Taxi

Taxi stands with call columns are located beside all main train stations and throughout the city. Basic fare flag fall is €2.50; then it's €1.53 per kilometre for the first 7km and €1.02 thereafter; short trips (less than 2km) cost €3. If you order a taxi by phone (☎ 194 10, 21 01 01, 21 02 02), flag fall goes up to €3.

Bicycle

Fahrradstation is the largest bike-rental agency with branches all over the city, including at the **left-luggage office** (☎ 29 74 93 19) in Zoo station. Bikes cost from €10 a day with a €50 deposit.

Brandenburg

The state of Brandenburg surrounds the city-state of Berlin and is a flat region of lakes, marshes, rivers and canals. In 1618, the electors of Brandenburg acquired the eastern Baltic duchy of Prussia, eventually merging the two states into a powerful union called the Kingdom of Prussia. By 1871, this kingdom brought all the German states under its control, leading to the establishment of the German Empire.

Many Berliners will warn you about the 'Wild East', advising you not to stray too far afield in what they consider to be a backward and sometimes violent region. But Brandenburgers, ever *korrekt* in the Prussian style, sniff and say that's what they'd expect from a bunch of loud-mouthed and brash upstarts like the Berliners. However, there are still occasional violent attacks against African and Asian foreigners in some small Brandenburg towns. In 1996 the dichotomy was set in stone when a referendum to merge Brandenburg with the city-state of Berlin failed at the polls.

POTSDAM
☎ 0331 • pop 130,500

Potsdam, on the Havel River just beyond the southwestern tip of Greater Berlin, is the capital of Brandenburg state. During the mid-18th century Friedrich II (Frederick the Great, 1740–86) built many of those marvellous palaces in Sanssouci Park, to which visitors flock today.

In April 1945, British bombers attacked Potsdam, devastating much of the historic centre including the City Palace on Alter Markt. However, parts of downtown have been pleasantly restored, and most of the palaces in the park escaped undamaged. The Allies chose Schloss Cecilienhof for the Potsdam Conference of August 1945, which set the stage for the division of Berlin and Germany into occupation zones.

Only 24km from central Berlin and easily accessible by S-Bahn, Potsdam is an ideal day trip.

Orientation & Information
Potsdam's main train station and last stop for the S-Bahn from Berlin is Potsdam Hauptbahnhof. From here, it is about a 3km walk over the Lange Brücke (long bridge) and through the town centre to the gates of Sanssouci Park; two other stations are closer to Sanssouci but not as conveniently reached. You can also take a bus or tram (see Getting Around later in this section).

The town centre provides an interesting mix of newly restored buildings exuding charm, bad GDR-era architecture, and some old classics that have been mouldering away for decades.

Potsdam-Information (☎ 27 55 80, fax 27 55 99; Friedrich-Ebert-Strasse 5; open 9am-7pm Mon-Fri, 9am-4pm Sat & Sun Apr-Oct, 10am-6pm Mon-Fri, 10am-2pm Sat & Sun Nov-Mar) is situated beside the Alter Markt. **Sanssouci-Information** (☎ 969 42 02; An der Historischen Mühle; w www.spsg.de), near the old windmill northwest of Schloss Sanssouci, has details on the palaces in the park and is usually open the same hours as the Schloss.

The Berlin-Potsdam Welcome Card (€18) gets you here on public transport and offers discounts to some attractions.

Sanssouci Park
This large park (*admission free; open dawn-dusk daily*) contains palaces and outbuildings which all keep separate hours and charge separate admission prices. A ticket valid for two consecutive days offers admission to all the park sites (Premium Tageskarte) including the tour of Schloss Sanssouci. It costs €15 and must be purchased at Schloss Sanssouci. A two-day ticket to all the other park sites (Tageskarte) is sold for €12 at other venues. Note that some sites have different days of closure.

Covering the entire circuit of sites means walking several kilometres. Begin your tour of the park with Georg Wenzeslaus von Knobelsdorff's **Schloss Sanssouci** (*adult/concession €8/5; tours depart 9am-5pm Tues-Sun Apr–mid-Oct & 9am-4pm Tues-Sun Nov-May*), the celebrated 1747 rococo palace with glorious interiors. You have to take the guided tour (around 40 minutes), so arrive early and avoid weekends and holidays, or you may not get in. They're usually sold out by 2.30pm, even in the shoulder seasons. Tours are in German, but guides have text in English.

The late-baroque **Neues Palais** (1769), the summer residence of the royal family, is one of the most imposing buildings in the park

GERMANY

GERMANY

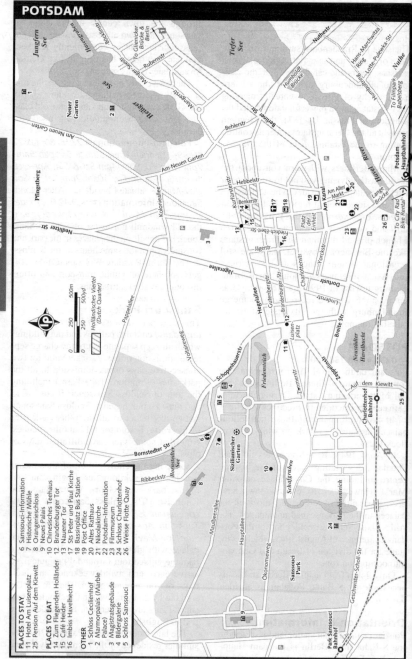

POTSDAM

PLACES TO STAY
11 Hotel Am Luisenplatz
25 Pension Auf dem Kiewitt

PLACES TO EAT
14 Zum Fliegenden Holländer
15 Café Heider
16 Imbiss Havelhecht

OTHER
1 Schloss Cecilienhof
2 Marmorpalais (Marble Palace)
3 Magistratsgebäude
4 Bildergalerie
5 Schloss Sanssouci
6 Sanssouci-Information
7 Historische Mühle
8 Orangerieschloss
9 Neues Palais
10 Chinesisches Teehaus
12 Brandenburger Tor
13 Nauener Tor
17 Sts Peter und Paul Kirche
18 Bassinplatz Bus Station
19 Post Office
20 Altes Rathaus
21 Nikolaikirche
22 Potsdam-Information
23 Filmmuseum
24 Schloss Charlottenhof
26 Weisse Flotte Quay

Holländisches Viertel
(Dutch Quarter)

Sanssouci Park

d the one to see if your time is limited. It eps the same hours as the Schloss but oses on Friday instead of Monday.

The following sites are closed on Monday d 15 October to 15 May. The **Bildergalerie** 764) contains an extensive collection of 7th-century paintings. The Renaissance-yle **Orangerieschloss** (1864) was built as guesthouse for foreign royalty. Although 's the largest palace on the grounds, it is not e most interesting. The **Schloss Charlot-nhof** (1826) is a must and can be visited on 30-minute German-language tour. How-er, the exterior is more interesting than the terior.

Take some time to wander around the royal ounds and use up some film on the **Chine-sches Teehaus** (1757).

ltstadt

rom the baroque **Brandenburger Tor** (1770) Luisenplatz at the western end of the old wn, pedestrian Brandenburger Strasse runs st to **Sts Peter und Paul Kirche** (Sts Peter d Paul Church; 1868). Northwest of here ere's the 1755 **Nauener Tor** *(Nauen Gate; iedrich-Ebert-Strasse)*, another monumental ch. North of the church, the **Holländisches iertel** (Dutch Quarter) features some 134 bled red-brick houses built for Dutch work-s in the 1730s.

Southeast of central Platz der Einheit is the reat neoclassical dome of Schinkel's **Niko-aikirche** (1850) on Alter Markt. On the east-n side of the square is Potsdam's 1753 **Altes athaus** *(Old Town Hall; adult/concession 2/1; open 10am-6pm Tues-Sun)*, which ow contains several art galleries.

West of the Alter Markt and housed in the **Marstall**, the former royal stables designed y Knobelsdorff in 1746, is the **Filmmuseum** ☎ 271 81 12; Breite Strasse; adult/concession 2/1; open 10am-6pm daily). It contains ex-ibits on the history of the UFA and DEFA novie studios in nearby Babelsberg and some xcellent footage from Nazi-era and postwar ommunist propaganda films.

Neuer Garten, the winding lakeside park on e west bank of the Heiliger See, northeast of e city centre, is home to **Schloss Cecilien-of** *(admission €2; open daily)*, an English-tyle country manor. This was the site of the 945 Potsdam Conference. The park is also ome to the lovely **Marmorpalais** (Marble alace; 1792).

Filmpark Babelsberg

This theme park *(August-Bebel-Strasse; adult/ concession/child €15/14/9; open 10am-6pm Mar-Oct)* is on the site of the UFA Studios, Germany's one-time response to Hollywood, east of the city centre (enter from Gross-beerenstrasse). This is where silent movie epics such as Fritz Lang's *Metropolis* were made, along with some early Greta Garbo films. For a look behind the scenes you can take the commercial, and expensive, tour.

Cruises

Weisse Flotte *(☎ 275 92 10)* operates boats on the Havel River and the lakes around Pots-dam, departing regularly from April to early October from the dock below the Hotel Mer-cure near Lange Brücke. There are frequent boats to Wannsee (€9.50 return).

Places to Stay & Eat

Potsdam's proximity to Berlin and the dearth of cheap accommodation make staying over-night an unappealing option. However, should you end up here for the night, **Pension Auf dem Kiewitt** *(☎ 90 36 78, fax 967 87 55; Auf dem Kiewitt 8; singles/doubles €48/69)* is kindly despite the GDR high-rises surrounding it. **Hotel am Luisenplatz** *(☎ 97 19 00, fax 971 90 19; e info@hotel-luisenplatz.de; singles/ doubles from €79/109)* is just west of the centre and run by a friendly Dutchman.

For breakfast, lunch or dinner try the clas-sic **Café Heider** *(☎ 270 55 96; Friedrich-Ebert-Strasse 29; dishes €4.80-9.80)*, a lively meeting and eating place adjacent to Nauener Tor. In the Dutch Quarter, **Zum Fliegenden Holländer** *(☎ 27 50 30; Benkertstrasse 5; mains €8-15.50)* has German cooking and reasonable lunch specials.

Brandenburger Strasse has several nice cafés, shops and snack shops (we like **Imbiss Havelhecht** at No 25 for fishy snacks); there's also good people-watching.

Getting There & Away

Potsdam Hauptbahnhof is just southeast of the town centre across the Havel River. Two other stations, Charlottenhof and Sanssouci, are closer to Sanssouci Park but are not served by the Regional Express (RE) or S-Bahn Nos 3 and 7, which is how most people get here from Berlin.

Potsdam Hauptbahnhof is also served by ICE and IC trains linking Berlin with points

GERMANY

west, so you can stop off on your way to or from the big metropolis.

Getting Around

Bus No 695 goes past Schloss Sanssouci, the Orangerieschloss and the Neues Palais, from the south exit of Potsdam Hauptbahnhof. Change to bus No 692 to Schloss Cecilienhof. To reach Schloss Charlottenhof and the Neues Palais, take bus No 606; tram No 610 is also good for the former.

City Rad (☎ 620 06 06) rents bikes from the shopping centre beneath Potsdam Hauptbahnhof, from €13 per day.

SACHSENHAUSEN CONCENTRATION CAMP

In 1936 the Nazis opened a 'model' concentration camp near the town of Oranienburg, about 35km north of Berlin. By 1945 about 220,000 men from 22 countries had passed through the gates of Sachsenhausen labelled, as at Auschwitz in southwestern Poland, *Arbeit Macht Frei* (Work Makes Free); about 100,000 died here. After the war, the Soviets and the communist leaders of the GDR used the camp for *their* undesirables.

Plan on spending at least two hours at Sachsenhausen (☎ 03301-20 02 00; admission free; open 8.30am-6pm daily Apr-Sept, 8.30am-4.30pm daily Oct-Mar), which is quite easily reached from Berlin. Among the many museums and monuments within the triangular-shaped, walled grounds are **Barracks 38 and 39**. Rebuilt after an arson attack by neo-Nazis in 1992, they contain excellent displays of the camp's history. At the front gate you may rent a chilling audio guide in English (€2.50), and an **information office** sells maps, brochures and books, including several useful English-language guides.

From Berlin take the S1 to Oranienburg (€2.40, 40 minutes). The camp is an easy 2km northeast of the station. Follow Stralsunder Strasse north and turn east (right) onto Bernauer Strasse. After about 600m turn left at Strasse der Einheit and then right on Strasse der Nationen to the camp entrance.

Saxony

The Free State of Saxony (Sachsen) is the most densely populated and industrialised region in eastern Germany. Germanic Saxon tribes originally occupied large parts of north western Germany, but in the 10th century they expanded southeastwards into the territory of the pagan Slavs.

The medieval history of the various Saxon duchies and dynasties is complex, but in the 13th century the Duke of Saxony at Wittenberg obtained the right to participate in the election of Holy Roman emperors. Involvement in Poland weakened Saxony in the 18th century, and ill-fated alliances, first with Napoleon and then with Austria, led to the ascendancy of Prussia over Saxony in the 19th century.

In the south, Saxony is separated from Czech Bohemia by the Erzgebirge, eastern Germany's highest mountain range. The Elbe River cuts northwest from the Czech border through a picturesque area known as 'Saxon Switzerland' towards the capital, Dresden. Leipzig, a great educational and commercial centre on the Weisse Elster River, rivals Dresden in historic associations. Quaint little towns like Görlitz and Meissen punctuate this colourful, accessible corner of Germany.

DRESDEN
☎ 0351 • pop 463,000

In the 18th century the Saxon capital Dresden was famous throughout Europe as 'the Florence of the north'. During the reigns of Augustus the Strong (r. 1694–1733) and his son Augustus III (r. 1733–63), Italian artists, musicians, actors and master craftsmen, particularly from Venice, flocked to the Dresden court. The Italian painter Canaletto depicted the rich architecture of the time in many paintings which now hang in Dresden's Alte Meister Gallery, alongside countless masterpieces purchased for Augustus III with income from the silver mines of Saxony.

In February 1945 much of Dresden was devastated by Anglo-American fire-bombing raids. At least 35,000 people died at a time when the city was jammed with refugees and the war was almost over. This horrific attack is the basis for the book *Slaughterhouse Five* by Kurt Vonnegut, who was a POW in Dresden at the time. Quite a number of Dresden's great baroque buildings have been restored, but the city's greatest architectural masterpiece, the Frauenkirche, is still in the midst of a laborious and enormously expensive reconstruction.

The Elbe River cuts a curving course between the low, rolling hills. In spite of modern rebuilding in concrete and steel, this city

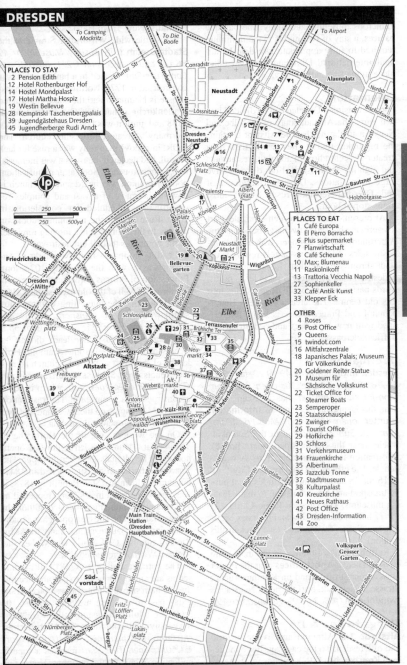

DRESDEN

PLACES TO STAY
2 Pension Edith
12 Hotel Rothenburger Hof
14 Hostel Mondpalast
17 Hotel Martha Hospiz
19 Westin Bellevue
28 Kempinski Taschenbergpalais
39 Jugendgästehaus Dresden
45 Jugendherberge Rudi Arndt

PLACES TO EAT
1 Café Europa
3 El Perro Borracho
6 Plus supermarket
7 Planwirtschaft
8 Café Scheune
10 Max; Blumenau
11 Raskolnikoff
13 Trattoria Vecchia Napoli
27 Sophienkeller
32 Café Antik Kunst
33 Klepper Eck

OTHER
4 Roses
5 Post Office
9 Queens
15 twindot.com
16 Mitfahrzentrale
18 Japanisches Palais; Museum für Völkerkunde
20 Goldener Reiter Statue
21 Museum für Sächsische Volkskunst
22 Ticket Office for Steamer Boats
23 Semperoper
24 Staatsschauspiel
25 Zwinger
26 Tourist Office
29 Hofkirche
30 Schloss
31 Verkehrsmuseum
34 Frauenkirche
35 Albertinum
36 Jazzclub Tonne
37 Stadtmuseum
38 Kulturpalast
40 Kreuzkirche
41 Neues Rathaus
42 Post Office
43 Dresden-Information
44 Zoo

GERMANY

invariably wins visitors' affections. With its numerous museums and many fine baroque palaces, a stay of two nights is the minimum required to fully appreciate Dresden. Its annual International Dixieland Festival takes place in the first half of May.

Orientation

For most visitors, Dresden can be divided into two parts: the Altstadt south of the Elbe and Neustadt to the north. The Altstadt contains the big-ticket tourist sites, while there is a greater concentration of lodging, restaurants and nightlife in Neustadt. Both districts have large train stations, Dresden Hauptbahnhof and Dresden-Neustadt respectively; most trains stop at both.

At present most of Dresden's priceless art treasures are housed in two large buildings, the Albertinum and the Zwinger, which are at opposite sides of Dresden's largely restored Altstadt. From the Dresden Hauptbahnhof, the pedestrian mall of Prager Strasse leads northwards past some classic GDR monoliths into this old centre. The area around the Hauptbahnhof and Prager Stasse is being redeveloped with new high-rises and pedestrian and traffic underpasses.

Information

Dresden-Information (*☎ 49 19 20, fax 49 19 21 16; Prager Strasse 10; open 9am-7pm Mon-Fri, 9am-4pm Sat*) has its main office near the Hauptbahnhof and an **information counter** (*open 10am-6pm Mon-Fri, 10am-4pm Sat, Sun & holidays*) in the Schinkelwache near the Semperoper (opera house). Information is also available at **w** www.dresden.de. The offices sell the Dresden-City-Card (€16 for 48 hours) which includes local public transport and free admission to many leading museums. The Dresden-Regio-Card (€25 for 72 hours) does all that and includes Meissen and Saxon Switzerland (see later in this section).

Reisebank has a branch in the main train station. There are **post offices** near the Prager Strasse tourist office and on Köningsbrücker Strasse in Neustadt. Surf the net at Neustadt's **twindot.com** (*☎ 802 06 02; Alaunstrasse 19*).

Things to See & Do

Altstadt The Altmarkt area is the historic hub of Dresden. To the east you'll see the rebuilt **Kreuzkirche** (1792), famous for its boys'

choir, and in the distance the 1912 **Neues Rathaus** (New Town Hall).

Cross the wide Wilsdruffer Strasse to the **Stadtmuseum** (*City History Museum; ☎ 49 86 60; adult/concession €2/1; open 10am-6pm Tues-Sun*) located in a building that was constructed in 1776. Northwest up Landhausstrasse is Neumarkt and the site of the ruined **Frauenkirche** (Church of Our Lady) built in 1738 and, until it was badly bombed in 1945, Germany's greatest Protestant church. The GDR, in a move many say was a ruse for lack of will, had declared the ruins a war memorial to remain untouched. Soon after reunification, popular opinion was heard and the church is now in the midst of a vast and complex reconstruction scheduled for completion in 2006. Ruse or not, the remaining rubble on display to the southeast is a moving reminder of the bombings that all but destroyed it.

Leading northwest from Neumarkt is Augustusstrasse, with the stunning 102m-long **Procession of Princes** porcelain mural covering the outer wall of the old royal stables. Here you'll also find the interesting **Verkehrsmuseum** (*Museum of Transport; ☎ 864 40; adult/concession €2/1; open 10am-5pm Tues-Sun*). Augustusstrasse leads directly to Schlossplatz and the baroque Catholic **Hofkirche** (1755). Just south of the church there's the Renaissance **Schloss** (*adult/concession €2.60/1.50; open Tues-Sun*), which is being reconstructed as a museum. The restoration work is advancing, and the tower and a palace exhibit are now open to the public.

On the western side of the Hofkirche is Theaterplatz, with Dresden's glorious opera house, the neo-Renaissance **Semperoper**. The first opera house on the site opened in 1841, but burned down in 1869. Rebuilt in 1878, it was again destroyed in 1945 and reopened in 1985 after the communists invested millions in the restoration. The Dresden opera has a tradition going back 350 years, and many works by Richard Strauss, Carl Maria von Weber and Richard Wagner premiered here.

The baroque **Zwinger** (1728) and its museums are among Dresden's stars and occupy the southern side of Theaterplatz. You can buy a day pass to all these museums for €6.10/3.60 per adult/concession, otherwise they have individual admissions. The **Historisches Museum** (*Rüstkammer; adult/concession €1.50/1; open Tues-Sun*) features a superb collection of ceremonial weapons. Housed in opposite corners of the complex with separate entrances are the **Mathematisch-Physikaler Salon** (adult/concession €1.50/1; open Fri-Wed) displaying scientific instruments and timepieces, the **Museum für Tierkunde** (Zoological Museum; adult/concession €3/1.50; open Wed-Mon), with natural history exhibits, and the **Porcelain Collection**, which should have reopened by the time you read this.

East of the Augustusbrücke is the **Brülsche Terrasse**, a pleasant elevated riverside promenade with the overwrought moniker 'the Balcony of Europe'. At the eastern end is the **Albertinum** (1885). Here you will find the **Gemäldegalerie Alte Meister** (open Tues-Sun), which boasts Raphael's *Sistine Madonna*, **Gemäldegalerie Neue Meister** (open Wed-Mon), with renowned 19th- and 20th-century paintings, and the **Grünes Gewölbe** (Green Vault; open Wed-Mon), hosting a collection of jewel-studded precious objects. Eventually the Grünes Gewölbe will be relocated to its original site in the Schloss. You can visit all three with a combined ticket (adult/concession €4.50/2.50).

Southeast of the Altstadt is the Grosser Garten, enchanting in summer and home to a fine **zoo** (☎ 471 80 60; Tiergartenstrasse 1; adult/concession €5/3; open daily) with more than 400 species. In the garden's northwestern corner are the **Botanical Gardens** (admission free). The hothouse is especially lovely during a freezing Dresden winter. And for a glimpse of Dresden's newest architectural marvel, check out the glass-enclosed **VW factory**, opened 2001, north of the zoo at Lennéstrasse and Stübelallee.

Neustadt This is an old part of Dresden largely untouched by wartime bombings. After unification it became the centre of the city's alternative scene and is now the centre of Dresden's nightlife.

The **Goldener Reiter** statue (1736; under repair during our visit) of Augustus the Strong stands at the northern end of the Augustusbrücke, leading to Hauptstrasse, a (largely GDR-era) pedestrian mall. At the mall's northern end, on Albertplatz, there's an evocative marble monument to the poet Schiller. Just west is Königstrasse, lined with genteel renovated buildings and high-end shops. Other museums near the Goldener Reiter include the **Museum für Sächsische**

Volkskunst (Museum of Saxon Folk Art; Grosse Meissner Strasse 1; adult/concession €1.50/1; open Tues-Sun), and the **Japanisches Palais** (1737), with the famous **Museum für Völkerkunde** (Ethnological Museum; ☎ 81 44 50; Palaisplatz; adult/concession €2/1; open Sat-Thur).

Neustadt is also where you'll find Dresden's greatest variety of dining and nightlife, mostly northeast of Albertplatz.

Elbe River Excursions

From March through November, **Sächsische Dampfschifffahrts GmbH** (☎ 86 60 90), which prides itself on having the world's oldest and largest fleet of paddle-wheel steamers, has frequent excursions on the Elbe River. A one-hour tour costs €10/5 per adult/child. You can also use the boats to reach Pillnitz Palace (€8.50/13 one way/return, 1¾ hours) and even as far as lovely Meissen (€10.50/15 one way/return, two hours). Schedules vary and you may need to book, so check with the ticket office, in a small glass building on the waterfront just east of Augustusbrücke.

Places to Stay

The **tourist office** (☎ 49 19 22 22 for bookings) can arrange **private rooms** for a €3 fee.

Camping The closest place to pitch your tent is **Camping Mockritz** (☎ 471 52 50; open Mar-Dec), 5km south of the city. Take the frequent Mockritz bus from behind the Dresden train station. It has bungalows, but like the camping ground they're often full in summer.

Hostels In a former Communist Party training centre, **Jugendgästehaus Dresden** (☎ 49 26 20, fax 492 62 99; Maternistrasse 22; dorm beds juniors/seniors without bath €17.50/21, with bath €19.70/23.20) is a 15-minute walk northwest of the Hauptbahnhof (or take tram No 7, 9, 10 or 26 to the corner of Ammonstrasse and Freiberger Strasse). The non-DJH **Jugendherberge Rudi Arndt** (☎ 471 06 67, fax 472 89 59; Hübnerstrasse 11; beds juniors/seniors €16.80/19.50) is a 10-minute walk south of the Hauptbahnhof in a residential neighbourhood.

In Neustadt are two hostels enjoyed by readers; their prices exclude breakfast. **Hostel Mondpalast Dresden** (☎/fax 804 60 61; e mondpalast@t-online.de; Katherinenstrasse 11-13; dorm beds €13, singles/doubles

GERMANY

€23/34) is in the centre of Neustadt's nightlife. **Die Boofe** (☎ 801 33 61, fax 801 33 62; ⓔ info@boofe.com; Hechtstrasse 10; beds from €14.50 per person) had just moved to a new location north of Neustadt station. It has a sauna and was installing a courtyard garden during our visit.

Hotels Average hotel rates in Dresden are among the highest in Germany, with few genuine budget places near the centre. Pickings south of the Elbe are especially slim.

Pension Edith (☎/fax 802 83 42; Priesnitzstrasse 63; singles/doubles €41/61), in a quiet backstreet, has rooms with private shower; it only has a few, so you need to book well ahead. **Hotel Rothenburger Hof** (☎ 88 12 60, fax 812 62 22; ⓔ kontakt@dresden -hotel.de; Rothenburger Strasse 15-17; singles/doubles from €64/85) is clean and bright and boasts a good restaurant. **Hotel Martha Hospiz** (☎ 817 60, fax 817 62 22, ⓔ marthahospiz.dresden@t-online.de; Nieritzstrasse 11; singles/doubles from €72/102) is cosy, well-kept and a few minutes' walk from Neustadt's high-end Königstrasse.

The **Westin Bellevue** (☎ 805 17 33, fax 805 17 49, ⓔ hotelinfo@westin-bellevue.de; Grosse Meissner Strasse 15; rooms from €102, excluding breakfast) has nice business-standard accommodation and awesome Altstadt views from rooms facing the Elbe. King of the hill is the **Kempinski Taschenberg-palais** (☎ 491 20, fax 491 28 12, ⓔ reserva tion@kempinski-dresden.de; Taschenberg 3; singles/doubles from €250/280, excluding breakfast), next to the Schloss, with palais-tial rooms, spa and fitness facilities and crisp service.

Places to Eat

Head straight to Neustadt for food and fun – few of Altstadt's culinary options match its archi-cultural wonders.

Raskolnikoff (Böhmische Strasse 34; mains €3-12) serves dishes from the four corners of central Europe. Alaunstrasse has loads of Italian places including comfortable **Trattoria Vecchia Napoli** (☎ 802 90 55; Alaunstrasse 33; mains €4.50-14.90), where wood-oven baked pizzas and enticing pastas demand to be washed down with red wine.

You'll also find many late-night restaurant-bars nearby. Some long-standing favourites include the **Planwirtschaft** (☎ 801 31 87;

Louisenstrasse 20; mains €6.50-12.50), with a beer cellar and some Saxon dishes; **Café Scheune** (☎ 802 66 19; Alaunstrasse 36, mains €6.30-10) with a rock-and-roll setting and popular Indian food; and the **Café Europa** (☎ 804 48 10; Königsbrücker Strasse 68; mains €4-18.20; open 24hr). **El Perro Borracho** (☎ 803 67 23; Alaunstrasse 70; dishes €2.80-10.20) serves tapas and other Spanish fare in an avant-garde courtyard.

You really don't need help in choosing a place near Altstadt's Brühlsche Terrace as long as you're happy with high prices, marginal food and excellent people-watching. **Café Antik Kunst** (☎ 498 98 36; Terrassengasse) is an exception; sit amid antique art and furniture and drink good coffee. On the next corner, **Klepper Eck** (☎ 496 51 23; Münzgasse 10; mains €6.50-18.80) is well-regarded for Saxon cooking. Otherwise in Altstadt, hotels offer your best restaurant options, or families might enjoy **Sophienkeller** (☎ 49 72 60; Taschenberg 3; mains €9-16.50), a theme restaurant decorated like an 18th-century fair.

Popular Neustadt cafés include **Max** (☎ 563 59 96; Louisenstrasse 65) and **Blumenau** (☎ 802 65 02; Louisenstrasse 67) next door. You'll find several fast-food options on Prager Strasse and around the transit hub at Postplatz; there are several supermarkets in Neustadt, including a **Plus** at Königsbrückerstrasse south of Louisenstrasse.

Entertainment

Sax (€1.25) is a comprehensive German-language listings guide available at newsstands throughout the city.

Dresden is synonymous with opera performances at the **Semperoper**. Dresden's two other great theatres are the **Staatsschauspiel** (☎ 491 35 55), also near the Zwinger, and the **Staatsoperette** (☎ 207 99 29; Pirnaer Landstrasse 131) in Leuben in the far east of the city. Tickets for all three theatres can be bought from Dresden-Information, or an hour before each performance at the appropriate theatre's box office. Tickets for the Semperoper usually sell out well in advance. Many theatres close from mid-July to the end of August.

A variety of musical events are presented in the austere **Kulturpalast** (☎ 486 60; Schlossstrasse 2). **Jazzclub Tonne** (☎ 802 60 17; Königstrasse 15; admission €6-10) has live jazz five nights per week.

For a drink, the choices in the café-laden blocks around Alaunstrasse and Louisen-strasse are many and change frequently (see also Places to Eat earlier). Gay visitors might start at the cocktail bar **Roses** (☎ 802 42 64; Jordanstrasse 10) or amid a young-ish crowd at the club **Queens** (☎ 803 16 50; Görlitzer-strasse 3). *Gegenpol* magazine has gay and lesbian listings.

Getting There & Around

Dresden airport is 9km from the city centre. A new S-Bahn line connects both main stations with the airport (€1.50, 15 minutes from Neustadt, 20 minutes from Hauptbahnhof). From either station you have easy access to local transport.

Hourly trains link Dresden to the Berlin-Ostbahnhof (€30.60, two hours) and Leipzig (ICE: €24, 1¼ hours; IR: €16.80, 1¾ hours), where you can connect to major cities all over Germany. IR trains running every two hours to Hanover (€54.40, 4½ hours) allow more connection possibilities. There's a **Mitfahrzen-rale** (☎ 194 40; Dr.-Friedrich-Wolfsstrasse 2) across from Neustadt station.

For travel on Dresden's local transit, a single-trip ticket is €1.50, a day ticket is €4 and a weekly ticket is €13. Regional day tickets cost €8.

AROUND DRESDEN
Schloss Pillnitz

From 1765 to 1918, Schloss Pillnitz was the summer residence of the kings and queens of Saxony. The most romantic way to get to this palace, on the Elbe about 10km southeast of Dresden, is on one of Dresden's old steamers. Otherwise, take tram No 9 or 14 to the end of the line, then walk a few blocks down to the riverside and cross the Elbe on the small ferry, which operates year-round. Bus No 83 also gets you almost to the palace. There's a museum (☎ 261 32 60; adult/concession €1.50/1; open 9.30am-5.30pm Tues-Sun May–mid-Oct), but the gardens (which stay open until 8pm) and the palace exterior with its Oriental motifs are far more interesting than anything inside.

Schloss Moritzburg

This palace (☎ 035207-87 30; adult/concession €4.10/2.60; open 10am-4pm daily) rises impressively from its lake 14km northwest of Dresden. Erected as a hunting lodge for the Duke of Saxony in 1546, Moritzburg was completely remodelled in baroque style in 1730 and has an impressive interior. You can catch a bus or train from Dresden-Hauptbahnhof.

Meissen
☎ 03521 • pop 32,000

Just 27km northwest of Dresden, Meissen is a perfectly preserved old German town and the centre of a rich wine-growing region. Augustus the Strong of Saxony created Europe's first porcelain factory at the Albrechtsburg palace in 1710. Meissen straddles the Elbe, with the old town on the western bank and the train station on the eastern bank. The train-pedestrian bridge behind the station is the quickest way across (and presents a picture-postcard view). From the bridge, continue up Obergasse then bear right through Hahnemannsplatz and Rossplatz to Markt, the town's central square.

There you'll find **Meissen-Information** (☎ 03521-419 40, fax 41 94 19; Markt 3; open 10am-6pm Mon-Fri, 10am-4pm Sat & Sun Apr-Oct, 10am-5pm Mon-Fri, 10am-3pm Sat Nov-Mar). Also on Markt are the restored **Rathaus** (1472) and the 15th-century **Frauenkirche** (☎ 45 38 32; open 10am-noon, 1pm-5pm daily May-Oct). The church's 1549 **tower** (adult/concession €1/0.50), with a porcelain carillon that chimes every quarter-hour, is well worth climbing for fine views of the Altstadt; pick up the key in the church or from the adjacent *Pfarrbüro* (parish office).

Various steeply stepped lanes lead up to **Albrechtsburg** (☎ 45 24 90; adult/concession €2/1.50; open daily). Its towering medieval Dom with its altarpiece by Lucas Cranach the Elder, is visible from afar. Beside the cathedral is the remarkable 15th-century Albrechtsburg **castle** (adult/concession €3.50/2.50; open daily 1 Feb-9 Jan). Constructed with an ingenious system of internal arches, it was the first palace-style castle built in Germany.

Meissen has long been famous for its china-ware, with its trademark blue crossed-swords insignia. The **porcelain factory** (☎ 46 87 00; Talstrasse 9; open daily) is now 1km southwest of town. There are often long queues for the workshop demonstrations (admission €3), but you can view the fascinating porcelain collection in the **museum** (adult/concession €4.50/4) at your leisure.

Campingplatz Waldbad (☎ 035243-360 12; adult/child/car €4/3/5) is in Niederau, 8km from Meissen. The **Pension Burkhardt**

GERMANY

(☎ 45 81 98, fax 45 81 97; Neugasse 29; singles/doubles from €25/50) has attractive rooms with full facilities. Hotel-restaurant **Burgkeller** (☎ 414 00, fax 414 04; e burgkell er@meissen-hotels.com; Domplatz; singles/ doubles from €60/100) offers unparalleled city views from atop Albrechtsburg. At **Gold-ener Löwe** (☎ 441 10; Heinrichsplatz 6; mains €6.75-15.25) you can sit on the square and people-watch. Around the Markt are grocers, bakers, eiscafés and butchers selling snacks.

Half-hourly S-Bahns travel to Meissen from both Dresden train stations (€4.40, 40 minutes), but it's far nicer, between May and September, to travel by steamer (see Cruises in the earlier Dresden section).

Sächsische Schweiz

'Saxon Switzerland' is only a quick jaunt from Dresden, near the Czech border, but feels continents away. This national park's central attraction, **Bastei**, has breathtaking outcrops that recall New Mexico, towering 305m above the Elbe River and connected by a series of footbridges.

Berghotel Bastei (☎ 035024-77 90, fax 77 94 81; w www.bastei-berghotel.de; singles/ doubles €44/82) is surprisingly pleasant for a former GDR holiday lodge. In the nearby town of Lohmen, the **tourist office** (☎ 03501-58 10 24, fax 58 10 25; Basteistrasse 79) can help book private rooms from about €15 per person, or try in the poky little spa town of Bad Schandau at its **tourist office** (☎ 035022-900 31, fax 900 34; e info@bad-schandau.de).

LEIPZIG
☎ 0341 • pop 437,000

Since the discovery of rich silver mines in the nearby Erzgebirge (Ore Mountains) in the 16th century, Leipzig has enjoyed almost continual prosperity. Today Leipzig is a major business and transport centre, and the second-largest city in eastern Germany. It has a strong cultural tradition and offers plenty for book and music lovers, particularly Bach, as well as pub-crawlers.

Since medieval times Leipzig has hosted annual trade fairs, and during the communist era these provided an important exchange window between East and West. After unification, the city built a new ultramodern fairground. Leipzig, never as heavily bombed as nearby Dresden, has undergone a restoration and construction boom that has brought new life to

many fine old buildings. Still, you might find these structures adjacent to crumbling prewar grand dames and GDR era monstrosities.

Orientation

With 26 platforms, the imposing Leipzig train station (1915) is Europe's largest. It has been lavishly renovated and houses many shops and restaurants. To reach the city centre, cross Willy-Brandt-Platz; the central Markt square is just a couple of blocks southwest. Ring roads surround the centre, more or less where the city walls once stood.

Information

Leipzig-Information (☎ 710 42 60, fax 710 42 71; w www.leipzig.de; Richard-Wagner-Strasse 1; open 9am-7pm Mon-Fri, 9am-4pm Sat, 9am-2pm Sun) is directly opposite the train station. You can buy the Leipzig Card here (one/three days €9.90/21) for unlimited local transport and discounts at attractions and some restaurants.

There is a **Reisebank** at the Hauptbahnhof. There's also a main **post office** (Augustusplatz 1). Sip coffee and watch your dirty clothes spin at the laundrette-café **Maga Pon** (Gottschedstrasse 3). You can surf the Internet at **Le Bit** (☎ 998 20 20; Friedrich-List-Platz), east of the Hauptbahnhof, for €3 per hour.

Things to See & Do

The Renaissance **Altes Rathaus** (1556) on Markt is one of Germany's most beautiful town halls. Behind it is the **Alte Börse** (1687), with a monument to Goethe (1903) in front. The former Leipzig University law student called the town a 'little Paris' in his drama Faust. **Nikolaikirche** (☎ 960 52 70; Nikolaikirchhof 3), between Markt and Augustusplatz, dates back to 1165. It has a truly remarkable interior and was the local meeting point of the 'Gentle Revolution' that helped overthrow the Communist regime.

Just southwest of Markt is the 13th-century **Thomaskirche** (☎ 960 28 55; Thomaskirchhof 18), with Bach's tomb in front of the altar. Bach worked in Leipzig from 1723 until his death in 1750, and the St Thomas Boys' Choir, which he once led, is still going strong. Opposite the church is the **Bach Museum** (☎ 964 41 33; Thomaskirchhof 16; adult/concession €3/2; open 10am-5pm daily).

To the south, **Neues Rathaus**, with its impressive 108m tower, was completed in 1905

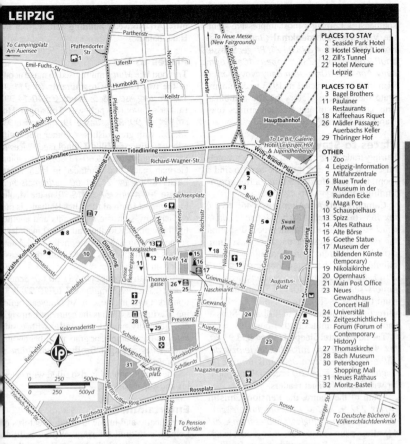

LEIPZIG

PLACES TO STAY
2 Seaside Park Hotel
8 Hostel Sleepy Lion
12 Zill's Tunnel
22 Hotel Mercure
   Leipzig

PLACES TO EAT
3 Bagel Brothers
11 Paulaner
   Restaurants
18 Kaffeehaus Riquet
26 Mädler Passage;
   Auerbachs Keller
29 Thüringer Hof

OTHER
1 Zoo
4 Leipzig-Information
5 Mitfahrzentrale
6 Blaue Trude
7 Museum in der
   Runden Ecke
9 Maga Pon
10 Schauspielhaus
13 Spizz
14 Altes Rathaus
15 Alte Börse
16 Goethe Statue
17 Museum der
   bildenden Künste
   (temporary)
19 Nikolaikirche
20 Opernhaus
21 Main Post Office
23 Neues
   Gewandhaus
   Concert Hall
24 Universität
25 Zeitgeschichtliches
   Forum (Forum of
   Contemporary
   History)
27 Thomaskirche
28 Bach Museum
30 Petersbogen
   Shopping Mall
31 Neues Rathaus
32 Moritz-Bastei

GERMANY

although its origins date back to the 16th century. North along Dittrichring is the former East German *Stasi* (secret police) headquarters, diagonally opposite the Schauspielhaus. Now it houses the **Museum in der Runden Ecke** (☎ 961 24 43; *admission free; open 10am-6pm daily*), outlining Stasi methods of investigation and intimidation – some appalling, some worthy of Inspector Clouseau. A new museum, **Zeitgeschichtliches Forum** (*Forum of Contemporary History*; ☎ 222 00; *Grimmaishce Strasse 6; admission free; open 9am-6pm Tues-Fri, 10am-6pm Sat & Sun*), gives a history of the GDR that's both factfilled and wrenching.

Across the street are the temporary quarters of the best of Leipzig's fine museums, **Museum der bildenden Künste** (*Museum of Fine Arts;* ☎ 21 69 90; *Grimmaische Strasse 1-7; adult/concession €2.50/1.25*), until a new building is completed, scheduled for late 2003. It has an excellent collection of old masters.

Wide Augustusplatz, three blocks east of Markt, is ex-socialist Leipzig, with the squat **universität** (university; 1975) and space-age **Neues Gewandhaus** concert hall (1983) juxtaposed with the functional **Opernhaus** (*opera house; 1960*). Leipzig's dazzling **Neue Messe** (*trade fairgrounds*) are 5km north of the train station (take tram No 16).

Leipzig has long been a publishing and library centre, and the **Deutsche Bücherei** (*German Library;* ☎ 227 13 24; *Deutscher Platz 1; admission free; open 9am-4pm Mon-Sat*), houses millions of books (including most titles published in German since 1913) as well as a book and printing museum. Farther to the southeast is Leipzig's most impressive sight, the **Völkerschlachtdenkmal** (Battle of Nations Monument; ☎ 878 04 71; Prager Strasse; adult/concession €3/2; open 10am-6pm daily Apr-Oct, 10am-4pm daily Nov-Mar), a 91m monument erected in 1913 to commemorate the decisive victory by the combined Prussian, Austrian and Russian armies over Napoleon's forces here in 1813.

Places to Stay

During trade fairs many of Leipzig's hotels raise their prices and it can be hard to find a room. Leipzig-Information runs a free **room-finding service** (☎ 710 42 55).

Campingplatz Am Auensee (☎ 465 16 00, fax 465 16 17; Gustav-Esche-Strasse 5; adult/child €4/3) is in a pleasant wooded spot on the city's northwestern outskirts (take tram No 11 to Wahren; from here it's an eight-minute walk). The **Jugendherberge** (☎ 245 70 11, fax 245 70 12; Volksgartenstrasse 24; juniors/seniors €14.30/17) is about 3km from the centre. Take tram No 17, 27 or 31 (direction: Schönefeld) to Löbauer Strasse and walk five minutes farther north.

The new **Hostel Sleepy Lion** (☎ 993 94 80, fax 993 94 82; e info@hostel-leipzig.de; Käthe-Kollwitz-Strasse 3; dorms from €14, singles/doubles €24/36) is central and popular with Lonely Planet readers.

South of the centre, the **Pension Christin** (☎/fax 232 93 66; e pension-christin@gmx.de; Kochstrasse 4; singles/doubles from €29/41) offers plain but spotless rooms on a handsome side street. Rooms with private facilities cost more. Take tram No 10 or 11 to Kochstrasse. **Zill's Tunnel** (☎ 960 20 78, fax 960 19 69; e info@zillstunnel.de; Barfussgässchen 9; doubles from €67) is a real find; a couple of lovely rooms with private facilities above Leipzig's pub district.

Stay amid what's often called Leipzig's second best art collection at **Galerie Hotel Leipziger Hof** (☎ 697 40, fax 697 41 50; Hedwigstrasse 1-3; singles/doubles from €55/65), about 1.2km east of the centre. Or sleep like a politburo member at the GDR-era **Hotel Mercure Leipzig** (☎ 214 60, fax 960 49 16; e mercure_leipzig@t-online.de; Augustusplatz 5-6; singles/doubles from €61/77), with large rooms. The **Seaside Park Hotel** (☎ 985 20, fax 98 57 50; e seaside-hotels@regionett.de; Richard-Wagner-Strasse 7; singles/doubles from €78/93) occupies a nifty Art Nouveau building across from the Hauptbahnhof.

Places to Eat

Try food like Mutti (mum) used to make at one of the two **Paulaner restaurants** (☎ 211 3 15; Klostergasse 3 & 5; mains €5.40-14.90). Luther's favourite pub was **Thüringer Hof** (☎ 994 49 99; Burgstrasse 19; mains €6.90-13.15), with great dishes. Another place with a long tradition is **Zill's Tunnel** (see Places to Stay earlier; mains €6.60-13.60), with typical German specialities. Founded in 1525, **Auerbachs Keller** (☎ 21 61 00; Grimmaische strasse 3-4; mains €7.10-18.90) in the Mädler Passage just south of the Altes Rathaus, is one of Germany's classic restaurants and another for those on the Goethe trail. Faust includes a scene in which Mephistopheles and Faust carouse with students here before they leave riding on a barrel.

Kaffeehaus Riquet (☎ 961 00 00; Schuhmachergässchen 1; mains €7.10-10.80) is an upmarket café in a superb Art Nouveau building. Barfussgässchen is the centre of Leipzig's exaggeratedly named **pub mile**, with casual cafés and restaurants, or grab quick bagels and sandwiches at **Bagel Brothers** (cnr Brühl & Nikolaistrasse).

The Hauptbahnhof is also filled with eateries and supermarkets.

Entertainment

Live theatre and music are major features of Leipzig's cultural offerings. With a tradition dating back to 1743, the **Neues Gewandhaus** (☎ 127 02 80; Augustusplatz 8) has Europe's longest established civic orchestra; one of its conductors was the noted composer Felix Mendelssohn-Bartholdy. Leipzig's modern **Opernhaus** is just across the square. The **Schauspielhaus** (☎ 126 81 68; Bosestrasse 1), a few blocks west of Markt, mixes classic theatre with modern works.

Moritz-Bastei (☎ 70 25 90; Universitätsstrasse 9), spread over three underground floors, has live music or disco most nights, but in summer it really comes into its own as a cultural venue. **Spizz** (☎ 960 80 43; Markt 9) is a trendy café by day and slick drinking and dancing venue by night. Both of these clubs have music ranging from rock to jazz. **Blaue Trude** (☎ 212 66 79; Katharinenstrasse 17) is Leipzig's current gay club.

Getting There & Away

Leipzig is linked by fast and frequent trains to all major German cities, including Dresden (€24, 1¼ hours), Berlin (€33.40, 1¾ hours) and Munich (€76, five hours). Major car rental agencies are at the Hauptbahnhof. Ride sharers can visit the **Mitfahrzentrale** (☎ 194 40; Goethestrasse 7-10).

Getting Around

Trams are the main form of public transport in Leipzig, with the most important lines running via Willy-Brandt-Platz in front of the Hauptbahnhof. A 15-minute ticket in the inner city is €1 while a one-hour ticket on the whole system is €1.30. Strip tickets valid for four rides are €4/4.90 for short/long trips. Day tickets are €4.

GÖRLITZ

☎ 03581 • pop 63,000

Situated 100km east of Dresden on the Neisse River, Görlitz emerged from WWII with its beautiful old town undamaged. The town was split in two, however, under the Potsdam Treaty, which used the Neisse as the boundary between Germany and Poland. The Polish part of Görlitz was renamed Zgorzelec. The town is an important border stop between the two countries.

Görlitz's Renaissance and baroque architecture is better preserved than that of any city its size in Saxony. Of particular interest are the **Rathaus** (1537), the **Peterskirche** (1497) and the 16th-century **Dreifaltigkeitskirche** on Obermarkt. The **tourist office** (☎ 475 70, fax 47 57 27; Obermarkt 29; open 9am-6.30pm Mon-Fri, 10am-4pm Sat, 10am-1pm Sun) has a free room-finding service.

The **DJH hostel** (☎ 40 65 10, fax 66 17 75; e jugendherbergegoerlitz@t-online.de; Goethestrasse 17; juniors/seniors €12.50/15) is south of the station. **Gästehaus Lisakowski** (☎ 40 05 39, fax 31 30 19; Landeskronstrasse 23; singles/doubles €23/46) offers simple rooms near the train station and is a 10-minute walk from the centre. **Hotel Tuchmacher** (☎ 473 10, fax 47 31 79; w www.tuchmacher .de; Peterstrasse 8; singles/doubles from €79/ 105) is a delightful, top-end place in the old town. **Zum Flyns** (☎ 40 06 97; Langenstrasse 1; mains €6.50-14.50) serves local specialities amid vaulted ceilings and tiny nooks. There are a number of fast-food options in the Strassburg Passage shopping centre.

Frequent trains run to/from Dresden (€14.80, 1½ hours). There are a few nonstop trains daily to/from Berlin (€30, three hours). Not surprisingly, Görlitz is an important stop to/from Poland.

Thuringia

The state of Thuringia (Thüringen) occupies a basin cutting into the heart of Germany between the Harz Mountains and the hilly Thuringian Forest. The Germanic Thuringians were conquered by the Franks in AD 531 and converted to Christianity by St Boniface in the 8th century. The Duke of Saxony seized the area in AD 908 and for the next 1000 years the region belonged to one German principality or another. Only in 1920 was Thuringia reconstituted as a state with something approaching its original borders. Under the communists it was again split into separate districts, but since 1990 it has been a single unit once again.

ERFURT

☎ 0361 • pop 215,000

This trading and university centre, founded as a bishop's residence by St Boniface in AD 742, is the lively capital of Thuringia. Erfurt was only slightly damaged during WWII and boasts numerous burgher town houses, churches and monasteries gracing the surprisingly well-preserved medieval quarter. Mindless graffiti has unfortunately become an all-too-common sight in the city; nonetheless this is a charming and often fascinating destination.

In April 2002 Erfurt became the unlikely focus of worldwide grief when a disgruntled former student shot dead 16 people and himself at a local high school.

Orientation & Information

Bahnhofstrasse leads north from the train station to Anger, a large square in the heart of the city. Continue straight ahead, following tram tracks along Schlösserstrasse to Fischmarkt. The friendly and efficient **tourist office** (☎ 664 00; Benediktsplatz 1; e service@erfurt -tourist-info.de; open 10am-7pm Mon-Fri, 10am-4pm Sat & Sun Apr-Dec, 10am-6pm Mon-Fri, 10am-4pm Sat & Sun Jan-Mar) is just east of Fischmarkt and the Rathaus. It sells the three-day Erfurt Card (€14), which allows unlimited use of public transport and entry to museums.

GERMANY

GERMANY

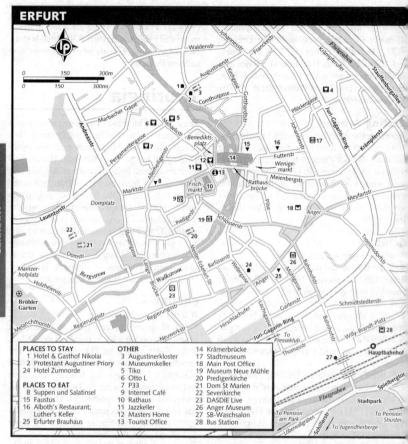

ERFURT

| 0 | 150 | 300m |
| 0 | 150 | 300mi |

PLACES TO STAY	OTHER	14 Krämerbrücke
1 Hotel & Gasthof Nikolai	3 Augustinerkloster	17 Stadtmuseum
2 Protestant Augustiner Priory	4 Museumskeller	18 Main Post Office
24 Hotel Zumnorde	5 Tiko	19 Museum Neue Mühle
	6 Otto L	20 Predigerkirche
PLACES TO EAT	7 P33	21 Dom St Marien
8 Suppen und Salatinsel	9 Internet Café	22 Severikirche
15 Faustus	10 Rathaus	23 DASDIE Live
16 Alboth's Restaurant;	11 Jazzkeller	26 Anger Museum
Luther's Keller	12 Masters Home	27 SB-Waschsalon
25 Erfurter Brauhaus	13 Tourist Office	28 Bus Station

There's a **Reisebank** at Erfurt's Haupt-bahnhof, and the main **post office** is on Anger. The laundrette **SB-Waschsalon** (*Bahnhof-strasse 22*) is conveniently located below the rail bridge. The **Internet Café** (*Fischmarkt 5*) charges €4 per hour.

Things to See & Do
The numerous interesting backstreets and laneways in Erfurt's surprisingly large Altstadt make this a fascinating place to explore on foot. Pick up the tourist office's *A Tour of the Historical City* booklet (€1.50), which has a map and good descriptions of numbered sights.

Don't miss the 13th-century Gothic **Dom St Marien** and **Severikirche**, which stand together on a hillock dominating the central square of

Domplatz. The wooden stools (1350) and stained glass (1410) in the choir, and figures on the portals, make the cathedral one of the richest medieval churches in Germany.

Around Fischmarkt you will find numerous historical buildings. The eastbound street beside the town hall leads to the medieval restored **Krämerbrücke** (1325), which is lined on each side with timber-framed shops. This is the only such bridge north of the Alps. Further north, on the same side of the River Gera, is **Augustinerkloster** (☎ 576 60; Augustiner-strasse 10; adult/concession €3.50/2.50; open 9am-noon, 2pm-5pm Mon-Sat, from 11am Sun Apr-Oct & 10am-noon, 2pm-4pm Mon-Sat, from 11am Sun Nov-Mar), a late-medieval monastery that was home to Luther early in the 16th century.

Although Erfurt's main attraction is its magnificent Altstadt buildings, it also has some interesting museums. The **Anger Museum** (☎ 562 33 11; Anger 18; adult/concession €1.50/0.75; open 10am-6pm Tues-Sun) has regional medieval art, frescoes and faience; the **Stadtmuseum** (☎ 562 48 88; Johannesstrasse 169; adult/concession €1.50/0.75; open 10am-6pm Tues-Sun) focuses mainly on Erfurt's Stone Age and medieval history; whereas the **Museum Neue Mühle** (☎ 646 10 59; Schlösserstrasse 25a; adult/concession €1.50/.75; open 10am-6pm Tues-Sun) is an old streamside millhouse (the last of some 60 water mills that Erfurt once had) with working machinery dating from the early 1880s.

Places to Stay

Erfurt's **Jugendherberge** (☎ 562 67 05, fax 562 67 06; e jh-erfurt@djh-thueringen.de; Hochheimer Strasse 12; juniors/seniors €15/18) is southwest of the centre. Take tram No 5 from Erfurt train station to Steigerstrasse, then it's a five-minute walk.

The tourist office arranges private accommodation from around €20/40 for doubles/singles (plus a booking fee of 10%).

Pension Schuster (☎ 373 50 52; Rubenstrasse 11; rooms €40 with bathroom) has sunny, spotless rooms just a 10-minute walk from the train station. Stay among the nuns at the historic **Protestant Augustiner Priory** (☎ 57 66 00, fax 576 60 99; e AK-efurt@augustinerkloster.de; Augustinerstrasse 10; singles/doubles €40/70), which offers fully renovated but simple lodgings. Nearby, the **Hotel & Gasthof Nikolai** (☎ 59 81 70, fax 59 81 71 20; e info@hotel-nikolai-erfurt.com; Augustinerstrasse 30; singles/doubles from €65/84) has charming rooms with varnished furniture.

Top of the scale is **Hotel Zumnorde** (☎ 568 00, fax 568 04 00; e info@hotel-zummnorde.de; Anger 50-51; singles/doubles with bathroom €98/118) with large and comfortable rooms.

Places to Eat

Erfurt has a lively restaurant and eatery scene. **Suppen und Salatinsel** (Marktstrasse 45; dishes €2-7) is a simple place that serves up soups, vegetarian fare and German goodies like Bratwurst. **Erfurter Brauhaus** (☎ 562 58 27; Anger 21; mains €5-10) is a microbrewery that serves its own beer, and has a good

selection of regional specialities. **Faustus** (☎ 540 09 54; Wenigemarkt 5; mains €7-17), at the foot of the Krämerbrücke, adds an international flavour to its mostly German menu.

Descend into the middle ages at **Luther Keller** (☎ 568 82 05; Futterstrasse 15-16; mains €8-12) where there's cheap, traditional food, lusty wenches and tankards of frothy brew. Sharing this address is **Alboth's Restaurant** (☎ 568 82 07; mains €10-24), which is the total opposite – refined, intimate and expensive.

Entertainment

There are several small bars like **Otto L** (Pergamentergasse 30) and **Tiko** (Michaelistrasse 35) huddled throughout the Andreasviertel, northwest of Fischmarkt. The focus here is **P33** (Pergamentergasse 33), a popular live music venue that attracts a student crowd. **Masters Home** (Michaelistrasse 48) is a stylish bar with a lively mixed clientele, while nearby the **Jazzkeller** (Fischmarkt 12-13) makes Thursday night its own with live jazz from 8.30pm. Try **Museumskeller** (Juri-Gargarin-Ring 140a) for rock music, **DASDIE Live** (Marstallstrasse 12) for Kabarett and variety, and for Latin and blues venture out to **Presseklub** (Dalbersweg 1). The tourist office sells the monthly Erfurt Magazine (€0.50), which outlines entertainment happenings in the city.

Getting There & Away

Every two hours a direct IR train connects Frankfurt (€37, 2½ hours) and Erfurt. The same train goes to/from Berlin (€49, 3½ hours) and to/from Weimar (€4, 15 minutes) and Eisenach (€15.20, 27 minutes). Cheaper but slower regional trains also run to/from Weimar and Eisenach. ICE trains go to/from Leipzig (€23.60, 1¾ hours) every two hours.

WEIMAR

☎ 03643 • pop 62,000

Not a monumental city nor a medieval one, Weimar appeals to more refined tastes. As a repository of German humanistic traditions it is unrivalled. Many famous people lived and worked in Weimar, including Lucas Cranach the Elder, Johann Sebastian Bach, Friedrich Schiller, Johann Wolfgang von Goethe, Franz Liszt, Walter Gropius, Wassily Kandinsky, and Paul Klee. From 1919 to 1925 it was the focal point of the Bauhaus movement, which laid the foundations of modern architecture, and today

GERMANY

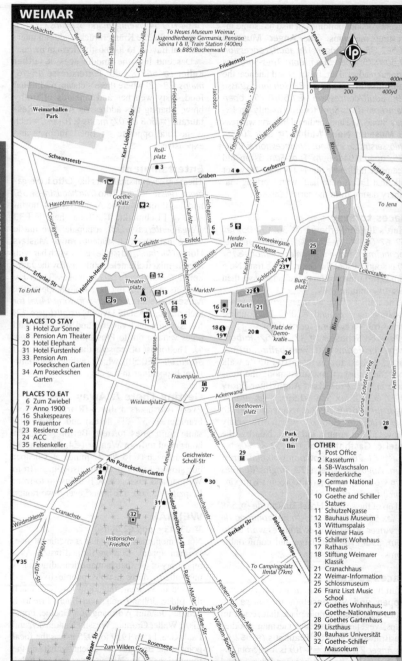

WEIMAR

To Neues Museum Weimar,
Jugendherberge Germania, Pension
Savina I & II, Train Station (400m)
& B85/Buchenwald

Weimarhallen
Park

GERMANY

PLACES TO STAY
3 Hotel Zur Sonne
8 Pension Am Theater
20 Hotel Elephant
31 Hotel Furstenhof
33 Pension Am
   Poseckschen Garten
34 Am Poseckschen
   Garten

PLACES TO EAT
6 Zum Zwiebel
7 Anno 1900
16 Shakespeares
19 Frauentor
23 Residenz Cafe
24 ACC
35 Felsenkeller

OTHER
1 Post Office
2 Kasseturm
4 SB-Waschsalon
5 Herderkirche
9 German National
   Theatre
10 Goethe and Schiller
   Statues
11 SchutzeNgasse
12 Bauhaus Museum
13 Wittumspalais
14 Weimar Haus
15 Schillers Wohnhaus
17 Rathaus
18 Stiftung Weimarer
   Klassik
21 Cranachhaus
22 Weimar-Information
25 Schlossmuseum
26 Franz Liszt Music
   School
27 Goethes Wohnhaus;
   Goethe-Nationalmuseum
28 Goethes Gartenhaus
29 Liszthaus
30 Bauhaus Universität
32 Goethe-Schiller
   Mausoleum

s a centre for architecture, music and media
tudies. Weimar's rich contribution to the con-
inent's cultural life was recognised in 1999
when it was named European City of Culture.

Weimar is also known as the place where
he German republican constitution was draft-
d after WWI (hence, the 1919–33 Weimar
Republic). The ruins of the Buchenwald con-
entration camp, near Weimar, are haunting
vidence of the terrors of the Nazi regime (see
he Around Weimar section later).

Orientation & Information

The centre of town is just west of the Ilm River
nd a 20-minute walk south of the Haupt-
ahnhof. Buses run fairly frequently between
he station and Goetheplatz, from where it's a
hort walk east along small streets to Herder-
latz or Markt.

The tourist office **Weimar-Information**
☎ 240 00; e tourist-info@weimar.de; Markt
0; open 9.30am-6pm Mon-Fri, 9.30am-4pm
at, 9.30am-3pm Sun Apr-Oct, 10am-6pm
Mon-Fri, 10am-2pm Sat & Sun Nov-Mar) is
very helpful. There is a smaller **tourist office**
☎ 24 00 45; open 10am-8pm daily) inside
he Hauptbahnhof. Both offices sell the three-
lay Weimar Card (€10), providing entry to
most of Weimar's museums, unlimited travel
on city buses and other benefits.

Most of Weimar's museums and many cul-
ural activities are managed by a trust foun-
lation, the **Stiftung Weimarer Klassik** (☎ 54
51 02; Frauentorstrasse 4; e info@weimar
klassik.de).

There's a central **post office** (cnr Heinrich-
Heine-Strasse & Schwanseestrasse). Unfortunately, at present there's no public Internet
access in Weimar, but for laundry services
head to Graben 47.

Things to See & Do

Except where otherwise noted, attractions are
closed on Monday.

A good place to begin your visit is on
Herderplatz. The **Herderkirche** (1500) has an
altarpiece (1555) by Lucas Cranach the Elder,
who died before he could finish it. His son,
Lucas Cranach the Younger, completed the
work and included a portrait of his father (to
the right of the crucifix, between John the Baptist and Martin Luther).

A block east of Herderplatz towards the Ilm
River is Weimar's main art museum, the
Schlossmuseum (☎ 54 60; Burgplatz 4;

adult/concession €4/2.50; open 10am-6pm
Tues-Sun Apr-Oct, 10am-4.30pm Tues-Sun
Nov-Mar). The large collection, with master-
pieces by Cranach, Dürer and others, occupies
three floors of this castle, formerly the resi-
dence of the Elector of the Duchy of Saxony-
Weimar. North of the centre, the **Neues
Museum Weimar** (☎ 54 60; Weimarplatz;
adult/concession €3/2; open 10am-6pm
Tues-Sun Apr-Oct, 10am-4.30pm Tues-Sun
Nov-Mar) houses, among other pieces, one of
Germany's most important private collections
of contemporary art.

Platz der Demokratie, with the renowned
music school founded in 1872 by Franz Liszt,
is south of the Schlossmuseum. This square
spills into Markt, where you'll find the neo-
Gothic **Rathaus** (1841), and the **Cranachhaus**,
in which Lucas Cranach the Elder spent his
last two years before his death in 1553. West
of Markt via some narrow lanes is Theaterplatz, with **Goethe and Schiller statues**
(1857), and the **German National Theatre**,
where the constitution of the Weimar Republic was drafted in 1919. Opposite the theatre
on this same square is the **Bauhaus Museum**
(☎ 54 51 02; Theaterplatz; adult/concession
€3/2; open 10am-6pm Tues-Sun Apr-Oct,
10am-4.30pm Tues-Sun Nov-Mar), which
documents the evolution of this influential
artistic and architectural movement. Nearby,
Weimar Haus (☎ 90 18 90; Schillerstrasse
16-18; adult/concession €6.50/5.50; open
10am-8pm daily Apr-Sept, 10am-6pm daily
Oct-Mar) offers a modern multimedia take on
5000 years of history.

Houses & Tombs From Theaterplatz, the
elegant Schillerstrasse curves its way around
to **Schillers Wohnhaus** (☎ 54 51 02; Schillerstrasse 12; adult/concession €3.50/2.50;
open 9am-6pm Wed-Mon Apr-Oct, 9am-
4pm Wed-Mon Nov-Mar). Schiller lived in
Weimar from 1799 to 1805. Goethe, his contemporary, spent the years 1775 to 1832 here.
Goethes Wohnhaus (☎ 54 51 02; Frauenplan
1; adult/concession €6/4.50; open 9am-6pm
Tues-Sun Apr-Oct, 9am-4pm Tues-Sun Nov-
Mar), where the immortal work Faust was
written, is nearby. Attached to the house is the
Goethe-Nationalmuseum (☎ 54 51 02;
Frauenplan 1; adult/concession €2.50/2;
open 9am-6pm Tues-Sun Apr-Oct, 9am-4pm
Tues-Sun Nov-Mar) with exhibits on Schiller,
Goethe and their life and times.

The **Liszthaus** (☎ 54 51 02; *Marienstrasse 17; adult/concession €2/1.50; open 9am-1pm, 2pm-6pm Tues-Sun Apr-Oct, 10am-1pm, 2pm-4pm Tues-Sun Nov-Mar*) is by the edge of Park an der Ilm. Liszt resided in Weimar during 1848 and from 1869 to 1886, and here he wrote his *Hungarian Rhapsody* and *Faust Symphony*. In the yellow complex across the road from the Liszthaus, Walter Gropius laid the groundwork for modern architecture. The buildings themselves, erected by the famous architect Henry van de Velde between 1904 and 1911, now house Weimar's **Bauhaus Universität**.

The tombs of Goethe and Schiller lie side by side in a neoclassical crypt in the **Historischer Friedhof** (Historical Cemetery), two blocks west of the Liszthaus.

Parks & Palaces Weimar boasts three large parks, each replete with monuments, museums and attractions. The most accessible is **Park an der Ilm**, running along the eastern side of Weimar and containing **Goethes Gartenhaus** (☎ 54 51 02; *Park an der Ilm; adult/concession €2.50/2; open 9am-6pm Tues-Sun Apr-Oct, 10am-4pm Tues-Sun Nov-Mar*). Goethe himself landscaped the park.

On Theaterplatz you'll find the **Wittumspalais** (*Widow's Palace;* ☎ 54 51 02; *adult/concession €3.50/2; open 9am-6pm Tues-Sun Apr-Oct, 10am-4pm Tues-Sun Nov-Mar*), the former residence of Duchess Anna Amalia who, after acquiring it in 1774, held meetings of the round table with court personalities, literary figures, scholars and artists, making the baroque palace the focus of intellectual life in Weimar.

Places to Stay
For a flat fee of €2.50 the tourist office arranges private rooms (from about €20 per person).

Camping The closest camping ground is **Campingplatz Ilmtal** (☎ 802 64; *Oettern; person/vehicle/site €3/5/2; open Apr-Nov*), at Oettern in the scenic Ilm Valley, 7km southeast of Weimar.

Hostels Weimar has four DJH hostels, but the most central are **Jugendherberge Germania** (☎ 85 04 90, fax 85 04 91; e *jh-germania@djh-thueringen.de; Carl-August-Allee 13*) in the street running south (downhill) from the

station, and **Am Poseckschen Garten** (☎ 85 07 92, fax 85 07 93; e *jh-posgarten@djh-thueringen.de; Humboldtstrasse 17*) near the Historischer Friedhof. Both charge €15/18 for juniors/seniors.

Pensions & Hotels Cheapest of the pensions is **Am Poseckschen Garten** (☎ 51 12 39; e *koenig-weimar@t-online.de; Am Poseckschen Garten 1; singles/doubles €18/34*) which has reasonable rooms. **Pension Savina II** (☎ 866 90, fax 86 69 11; e *savina@pension-savina.de; Meyerstrasse 60; singles/doubles with shower & toilet €40/70*) is a comfortable option near the train station. Its sister **Savina** (☎ 866 90, fax 86 69 11; e *savina@pension-savina.de; Rembrandtweg 13; singles/doubles with shared facilities €34/52*) is more basic. **Pension Am Theater** (☎ 889 40, fax 88 94 32; *Erfurterstrasse 10; singles/doubles with bathroom €45/65*) is about the friendliest accommodation you'll find anywhere. And the rooms aren't bad either.

The tastefully restored **Hotel Furstenhof** (☎ 83 32 31, fax 83 32 32; e *furstenhofweimar@t-online.de; Rudolf-Breitscheid-Strasse 2; singles/doubles from €52/80*) has small and comfortable rooms. The **Hotel Zur Sonne** (☎ 80 04 10, fax 86 29 32; *Rollplatz 2; singles/doubles from €51/77*) offers good value for money in a central location.

At historic **Hotel Elephant** (☎ 80 20, fax 80 26 10; e *elephant.weimar@arabellasheraton.com; Markt 19; singles/doubles from €179/205*) a night of luxury awaits, followed by an exorbitant €18 breakfast.

Places to Eat
ACC (☎ 85 11 61; *Burgplatz 2; mains €6-10*) is an alternative little place with an interesting menu and a palatable price range. Next door, **Residenz Cafe** (☎ 594 08; *Grüner Markt 4, dishes €4-15*) is a bit glitzier; it serves Thuringian specialities like *Braeti* (pig's neck steak in beer and mustard) and vegetarian dishes.

In a restored late 19th-century winter garden, **Anno 1900** (☎ 90 35 71; *Geleitstrasse 12a; mains €6-11*) pulls a good crowd with its well-priced pastas, steaks, fish and vegetarian. Everything is in its place at **Frauentor** (☎ 51 13 22; *Schillerstrasse 2; mains €8-17*), a simple and intimate place with an international menu. **Zum Zwiebel** (☎ 50 23 75; *Teichgasse 6; mains €6-13*) serves hearty regional dishes, while classy **Shakespeares** *(☎ 90 12 85; Windischenstrasse 4-6; mains €13-16)* has acclaimed gourmet cuisine and hosts live performances in its Othello Theatre.

Southwest of the centre, the ever-popular **Felsenkeller** *(☎ 85 03 66; Humboldstrasse 37; mains €6-13)* has brewed its own Felsenbräu since 1889, and serves it liberally with cheap, traditional German food.

Entertainment

The **German National Theatre** *(☎ 75 53 34; Theaterplatz)* is the main stage for Weimar's cultural activities, including Goethe's theatrical works. Tickets for it and other events can be bought at the tourist office.

The **Kasseturm** *(Goetheplatz 1)*, a beer cellar in a round tower, has live music, disco or cabaret most nights. The **SchutzeNgasse** *(Schutzengasse 2)* is a relaxed bar that packs in the student crowd.

Getting There & Away

There are frequent direct IR trains to Berlin-Zoo (€38.40, three hours) via Naumburg and Halle, and to Frankfurt/Main (€40, three hours) via Erfurt and Eisenach. ICE trains go to Dresden (€37, two hours) and Leipzig (€21.20, one hour).

AROUND WEIMAR
Buchenwald

The **Buchenwald museum and concentration camp** *(☎ 43 02 00; Ettersburg Hill; admission free; open 9.45am-6pm Tues-Sun May-Sept, 9.45am-5pm Tues-Sun Oct-Apr)* is 10km north of Weimar. You first pass the memorial with mass graves of some of the 56,500 WWII victims from 18 nations, including German antifascists, Jews, and Soviet and Polish prisoners of war. The concentration camp and museum are 1km beyond the memorial. Many prominent German communists and Social Democrats, Ernst Thälmann and Rudolf Breitscheid among them, were murdered here. On 11 April 1945, as US troops approached, the prisoners rebelled at 3.15pm (the clock tower above the entrance still shows that time), overcame the SS guards and liberated themselves.

After the war the Soviet victors turned the tables by establishing Special Camp No 2, in which thousands of (alleged) anticommunists and former Nazis were worked to death.

Last entry is 45 minutes before closing. Bus No 6 runs via Goetheplatz and Weimar train station to Buchenwald roughly every 40 minutes.

EISENACH

☎ 03691 • pop 44,000

The birthplace of Johann Sebastian Bach, Eisenach is a small picturesque city on the edge of the Thuringian Forest. Its main attraction is the Wartburg castle, from where the landgraves (German counts) ruled medieval Thuringia. Luther went into hiding here under the assumed name of Junker Jörg after being excommunicated and put under a papal ban.

Information

Eisenach-Information *(☎ 194 33; Markt 2; e tourist-info@eisenach-tourist.de; open 10am-6pm Mon, 9am-6pm Tues-Fri, 10am-2pm Sat & Sun)* is friendly and well-organised. Its three-day Classic-Card (€14) provides free admission to the castle, most museums and use of public transport.

Wartburg

Superb **Wartburg** *(☎ 770 73; tour adult/ concession €6/3; open 8.30am-5pm Mar-Oct, 9am-3.30pm Nov-Feb)*, on a forested hill overlooking Eisenach, is world famous, with a Unesco World Heritage Site designation to prove it. Luther translated the New Testament from Greek into German while in hiding here (1521–22), thus making an enormous contribution to the development of the written German language. You can only visit the castle's interior with a guided tour (most of the tours are in German), which includes the museum, Luther's study room and the amazing Romanesque great hall; arrive early to avoid the crowds. Guided tours in English are only possible by prior reservation (at least two weeks beforehand in summer) through **Wartburg-Information** *(☎ 770 73; Am Schlossberg 2)*. A free English-language leaflet set out in the sequence of the tour is available.

Between April and October there's a shuttle bus running up to the castle; it leaves from the terminal in front of the train station roughly every hour (€1.60 return). Alternatively, you can walk the 2km.

Places to Stay & Eat

The nearest camping ground is the **Camping-platz Altenberger See** *(☎ 21 56 37, fax 21 56 07; Neubau 24; site/person €3/4)*, 7km south of town in Wilhelmsthal. **Jugendherberge**

Artur Becker (☎ 74 32 59, fax 74 32 60; e jh -eisenach@djh-thueringen.de; Mariental 24; juniors/seniors €14/17) is in the valley below Wartburg. Take bus No 3 to Liliengrund.

Eisenach-Information has an extensive list of hotels and private rooms from €15, and offers free reservations. Gasthof Storchenturm (☎ 73 32 63, fax 73 32 65; Georgenstrasse 43; beds €18 per person, groups of 4 or more €15.50) has bare, clean rooms with facilities. Pension Mahret (☎ 74 27 44, fax 750 33; e pension.mahret@t-online.de; Neustadt 30; singles/doubles €35/52) offers pleasant self-contained apartments near the town centre.

The 18th-century Thüringer Hof (☎ 280, fax 28 19 00; e eisenach@steigenberger.de; Karlsplatz 11; singles/doubles with breakfast €92/107) provides plush rooms with attractive town views.

In a cave-like cellar, Brunnenkeller (☎ 21 23 58; Markt 13; dishes €6-8) has a cosy feel and cheap Thuringian specialities. Kartoffelhaus (Sophienstrasse 44) offers all things potato for around €8.

Getting There & Away
Use the frequent RB/RE services to Erfurt (€8.10, 50 minutes) and Weimar (€10.70, 70 minutes) rather than the IC as they are far cheaper and take only a few minutes longer. IR services run direct to Frankfurt/Main (€29) and ICE to Berlin-Zoo (€56.60).

Saxony-Anhalt

The state of Saxony-Anhalt (Sachsen-Anhalt) comprises the former East German districts of Magdeburg and Halle. Originally part of the duchy of Saxony, medieval Anhalt was split into smaller units by the sons of various princes. In 1863 Leopold IV of Anhalt-Dessau united the three existing duchies, and in 1871 his realm was made a state of the German Reich. Today, it is Germany's poorest state, with unemployment hovering at more than 20%.

The mighty Elbe flows northwest across Saxony-Anhalt, past Lutherstadt-Wittenberg, Dessau and Magdeburg on its way to the North Sea at Hamburg. Halle and Naumburg are on the Saale River south of Magdeburg.

The Harz Mountains fill the southwestern corner of Saxony-Anhalt and spread right across Lower Saxony to Goslar (see the Harz Mountains map in the Lower Saxony section). Historical Harz towns like Quedlinburg and Wernigerode are highly recommended, and Dessau and Lutherstadt-Wittenberg are gaining visitors for lovers of the Bauhaus and Luther; the state's two largest cities, Halle and Magdeburg, are of limited interest.

MAGDEBURG
☎ 0391 • pop 250,000
Magdeburg, on the Elbe River, is situated at a strategic crossing of transport routes from Thuringia to the Baltic and Western Europe to Berlin. It was severely damaged by wartime bombing and became an unfortunate example of GDR post-war reconstruction; recent building has helped it regain some charm. The main reason for visiting Magdeburg, the capital of Saxony-Anhalt, is for its splendid churches and Gothic cathedral.

Orientation & Information
From the broad square in front of the train station, take Ernst-Reuter-Allee east towards the Elbe. After two large blocks, turn left (north) into Breiter Weg to Alter Markt. Tourist Information Magdeburg (☎ 540 49 01, fax 540 49 10; e info@magdeburg-tourist.de; Julius-Bremer-Strasse 10; open 10am-6pm Mon-Fri, 10am-1pm Sat) is just north of Alter Markt, though there was talk that it might move.

Things to See & Do
The centre of the old town is Alter Markt, with a copy of the bronze Magdeburger Reiter (Magdeburg Rider; 1240) said to be Otto the Great, in front of the high-Renaissance Rathaus (1698). Just east there's the Johanniskirche (☎ 540 21 26; Johannisbergstrasse 1; admission €1; open 10am-8pm Tues-Sun May-Sept, 10am-4pm Tues-Sun Oct-Apr); destroyed in the war, it was proudly reconstructed in 1999. To the south, Magdeburg's oldest building, the 12th-century Romanesque convent Kloster Unser Lieben Frauen, is now a museum (☎ 540 61 64; Regierungstrasse 4-6; adult/concession €2/1; open 10am-5pm Tues-Sun); you can enter the cloister and church for free. A little farther south is the soaring Gothic Dom (cathedral; ☎ 543 24 14; Am Dom 1; open 10am-4pm Mon-Sat, 11.30am-4pm Sun), said to be the oldest on German soil. The cathedral, the second tallest in Germany after Cologne, has evocative and moody cloisters.

Places to Stay & Eat

The simple but pleasant **Campingplatz Bar-leber See** (*π/fax 50 32 44; adult/child/car €1.50/1/1.70*) is 8km north of town at a lake. Take tram No 10 to the last stop. The DJH **Jugendgästehaus Magdeburg** (*π 53 21 01, fax 53 21 02; e JH-Magdeburg@sjh-sachsen-anhalt.de; Leiterstrasse 10; beds juniors/seniors €18/20.70*) is a little austere but very central. You can book private rooms from around €20 through Tourist Information Magdeburg. **Hotel Stadtfeld** (*π 50 77 60, fax 506 66 99; Maxim-Gorki-Strasse 31/37; singles/doubles from €40/50*) is a good mid-priced option above an apartment building. **Geheimer Rat** (*π 738 02, fax 738 05 99; e geheimer-rat@t-online.de; Goethestrasse 38; singles/doubles from €72/85*) is a very professional operation, on a park-like street west of the centre.

Zum Paulaner (*π 543 88 13; Einsteinstrasse 13; mains €8.50-13.50*) serves hearty Bavarian chow and beer in a rather elegant quarter of town. Down the block, **Athen** (*π 544 09 66; Schleinufer 14; mains €5.30-13.50*) is a popular Greek place with reasonable plate dinners. You'll find plenty of **fast-food** options in the Allee Center off Ernst-Reuter-Allee.

Getting There & Away

There are frequent regional trains operating to/from Berlin-Zoo (€20.40, 1½ hours) and trains to Leipzig (€17.20, 1½ hours), Hanover (€23.80, 1½ hours) and Quedlinburg (€10.70, 1¼ hours). Change trains in Halberstadt if heading for Wernigerode (€12.40, 1¼ hours).

QUEDLINBURG

π 03946 • pop 26,000

One of Germany's true gems, Quedlinburg dates back more than 1000 years. It once exercised considerable power in German affairs through a collegiate foundation for widows and daughters of the nobility. Almost all buildings in the centre are half-timbered, street after cobbled street of them, earning Quedlinburg the honour of being a Unesco World Heritage Site.

Orientation & Information

The centre of the old town is a 10-minute walk from the train station down Bahnhofstrasse. There is a **Quedlinburg-Information** (*π 90 56 24, fax 90 56 29; e q.t.m@t-online.de; Markt 2; open 9am-7pm Mon-Fri, 10am-3pm Sat & Sun Apr-Oct, 9.30am-6pm Mon-Fri, 10am-4pm Sat Nov-Mar*).

Things to See & Do

The Renaissance **Rathaus** (1615) on Markt has its own Roland statue (1426), however, the real focal point for visitors is the hill just southwest with the old castle district, known as **Schlossberg**. The area features the 1129 Romanesque **Church of St Servatii** (*Dom; π 70 99 00; Am Dom; adult/concession €3/2; open 10am-6pm Tues-Fri, 10am-4pm Sat, noon-6pm Sun May-Oct & 10am-4pm Mon-Sat, noon-4pm Sun Nov-Apr*), with a 10th-century crypt and priceless reliquaries and early Bibles. In 1938 SS meetings were held in the Dom – a 'Germanic solemn shrine'. On a more contemporary note, try visiting **Lyonel-Feininger-Galerie** (*π 22 38; Finkenherd 5a; adult/concession €6/3; open 10am-6pm Tues-Sun Apr-Oct, 10am-5pm Tues-Sun Nov-Mar*) where you can view brilliant works by this Bauhaus artist who fled the Nazis then settled in America.

For hiking, take a bus or train 10km southwest to Thale, the starting point for hikes along the lovely Bode Valley in the Harz Mountains. From here it's just a short walk to Hexentanzplatz, the site of a raucous celebration during *Walpurgisnacht* every 30 April, believed in German folklore to be the night of a witches' sabbath. Also worthwhile is a visit to Gernrode and its delightful **Church of St Cyriakus**, just 8km south of Quedlinburg.

Places to Stay & Eat

Hotel and private rooms can be booked free of charge through Quedlinburg-Information. The central **Familie Klindt** (*π 70 29 11; Hohe Strasse 19; without/with breakfast €12/16 per person*) is a great deal, with comfy rooms. **Hotel am Dippeplatz** (*π 77 14 11, fax 77 14 47; Breite Strasse 16; singles/doubles from €49/59*) is bright and clean. **Hotel Theophano** (*π 963 00, fax 96 30 36; e theophano@t-online.de; Markt 13/14; singles/doubles from €62/93*) is top of the range, a gracious 350-year-old building with an upmarket restaurant.

Kartoffelhaus No 1 (*π 70 83 34; Breite Strasse 37; mains €5.10-11.60*) serves filling meals and snacks for all budgets. Enter off Klink. **Brauhaus Lüdde** (*π 70 52 06; Blasiistrasse 14; dishes €8.50-14.50*) has hearty pub food and brews its own pilsener, *Altbier*, and the sweetish low-alcohol *Pubarschknall*.

Getting There & Away

You can change trains in Magdeburg (€10.70, 1¼ hours) for long-distance routes. To Wernigerode (€6.60, one hour), trains connect via Halberstadt.

WERNIGERODE

☎ 03943 • pop 35,000

Wernigerode is flanked by the foothills of the Harz Mountains. A romantic ducal castle rises above the old town, which contains some 1000 half-timbered houses from five centuries in various states of repair. Summer throngs of tourists have brought cash that has all but erased any trace of the old GDR. The century-old steam-powered, narrow-gauge Harzquerbahn runs a gorgeous 60km route south through the Harz Mountains to Nordhausen and also to Brocken, the highest mountain in northern Germany (1142m).

Orientation & Information

From the Bahnhofsplatz, Rudolf-Breitscheid-Strasse leads southeast to Breite Strasse, which runs southwest to Markt, the old town centre. The **tourist office** (☎ 194 33, fax 63 20 40; Nicolaiplatz 1; open 9am-7pm Mon-Fri May-Sept, 9am-6pm Mon-Fri Nov-Apr, 10am-3pm Sat & Sun year-round) is near Markt.

Things to See & Do

It's nice to wander along the streets of the medieval old town centre. The **Rathaus** (1277) on Markt, with its pair of pointed black-slate towers, is a focal point. From here it's just a short climb to the neo-Gothic **castle**. First built in the 12th century, the castle has been renovated and enlarged over the centuries and got its current fairy-tale facade from Count Otto of Stolberg-Wernigerode in the 19th century. The castle's **museum** (adult/concession €4/3.50; open 10am-6pm daily May-Oct, 10am-4pm Tues-Fri, 10am-6pm Sat & Sun Nov-Apr) has a nice chapel and hall.

Activities

There are plenty of short walks and day hikes nearby. The beautiful deciduous forest behind the castle is highly recommended. The more serious might tackle the 30km route (marked by blue crosses) from Mühlental southeast of

the town centre to Elbingerode, Königshütte, with its 18th-century wooden church, and the remains of medieval Trageburg castle at Trautenstein. The tourist office can make suggestions and you'll need a good topographic map for some of them.

Wernigerode is the major northern terminus for steam train services throughout the Harz Mountains and Hochharz National Park. For information contact **Harzer Schmalspurbahnen** (☎ 55 80; Marktstrasse 3).

Services to Brocken from Wernigerode cost €14/22 one way/return (1¾ hours), and those to Nordhausen-Nord €8/14 (three hours). There is a three-day steam-train pass for €35/17.50 (adult/child) and a one-week pass for €70/35.

Places to Stay & Eat

Wernigerode has a new DJH **Jugendherberge** (☎ 60 61 76, fax 60 61 77; e JH-Wernigerode@djh-sachsen-anhalt.de; Am Eichberg 5; juniors/seniors €15/17.70) with a disco and sauna. It's a 35-minute walk from the centre.

Rooms booked through the tourist office's free room-finding service cost around €25. The central **Hotel zur Tanne** (☎ 63 25 54, fax 67 37 35; Breite Strasse 57-59; singles/doubles from €41/49) has basic rooms. **Pension Schweizer Hof** (☎/fax 63 20 98; Salzbergstrasse 13; singles/doubles from €35/50) is quiet and away from the centre, catering to hikers. **Gothisches Haus** (☎ 67 50, fax 67 55 37; e gothisches-haus@tc-hotels.de; Marktplatz 2; singles/doubles from €82/98) on the Markt, is the place to splurge. It also has a ritzy restaurant.

Altwernigerode Kartoffelhaus (☎ 94 92 90; Marktstrasse 14; dishes €2.50/14.50) serves well-priced traditional and potato dishes. **Restaurant Am Nicolaiplatz** (☎ 63 23 28; Breite Strasse 17; mains €6.90-13.50) is a local favourite for regional specialities. There are lots of cafés around the Markt.

Getting There & Away

There are frequent trains to Goslar (€6.60, 40 minutes), Hanover (€18.60, two hours) and Halle (€16, 1¼ hours). Change trains in Halberstadt for Magdeburg (€12.40, 1¼ hours), from where you can catch longer-distance trains. See also the Getting Around section under Western Harz Mountains in Lower Saxony.

DESSAU

☎ 0340 • pop 87,000

The Bauhaus school – a cradle of contemporary design – was born in Weimar but became synonymous with Dessau when Walter Gropius moved the school here in 1925. The school languished under the Nazis and GDR, but recent renovations of key Bauhaus sites have put this ancient ducal city on tourist maps. These Bauhaus buildings can be seen in a few hours, but many visitors spend the night between days cycling along the Elbe, or in the adjacent Dessau-Wörlitz Garden Realm.

Orientation & Information

Dessau's well-equipped tourist office (☎ 204 22 42; w www.dessau.de; Zerbsterstrasse 4) is in the Rathaus, a 10-minute walk southeast of the Hauptbahnhof via Antoinettenstrasse, crossing Kavalierstrasse and a pedestrian district. Bauhaus sites begin about a five-minute walk west of the Hauptbahnhof.

Things to See & Do

The **Bauhausgebäude** (Bauhaus Building; ☎ 650 82 51; Gropiusallee 38; open 10am-6pm Tues-Sun) is a touchstone of modern architecture, with three glass and concrete sections, galleries and a 'form follows function' interior. It was being renovated as we went to print, but open to visitors. The **Meisterhäuser** (Masters' Houses; Ebertallee; open 10am-6pm Tues-Sun mid-Feb–Oct, 10am-5pm Nov–mid-Feb) are three restored homes that Gropius built for important Bauhaus teachers including Lyonel Feininger, Wassily Kandinsky and Paul Klee. You can see their studio and living spaces; the interior of the Kandinsky/Klee Haus is painted some 170 colours, while the Feiningerhaus is home to the Kurt-Weill-Zentrum, dedicated to the life of this noted Dessau-born theatrical composer (A Threepenny Opera, the song Mack the Knife).

A combination card for all these sites costs €7.50/5.50 (adult/concesion); it's €4/3 for the Bauhausgebäude or the Meisterhäuser alone.

Ask at the tourist office for detailed information on the lovely, green Dessau-Wörlitz Garden Realm, including the fairytale Schloss Wörlitz (1769–73).

Places to Stay & Eat

The **Jugendherberge** (☎/fax 61 94 52; Waldkaterweg 11; juniors/seniors €11.50/14.20) is in a wooded spot situated 3km west of the Hauptbahnhof.

Hotel-Pension an den 7 Säulen (☎ 61 96 30, fax 61 96 22; Ebertallee 66; singles/doubles from €41/62) is well-kept, across from the Masters' Houses and popular with cyclists. The swish, Bauhaus-influenced **Hotel Fürst Leopold** (☎ 251 50, fax 251 51 77; e reservierung@hotel-fuerst-leopold.de; Friedensplatz; singles/doubles from €100/130) is a one-minute walk from the Hauptbahnhof and overlooks a park. Ask about the weekend deals.

Rub elbows with Bauhaus students at the fun **Cafe im Bauhaus** (☎ 650 84 44; Gropiusallee 38; dishes €2.60-8). **Kornhaus** (☎ 640 41 41; Kornhausstrasse 146; mains €6.90-8.40) combines the best of Bauhaus design with modern German cooking; its terrace is great for coffee and cake overlooking the Elbe. **Zum Alten Dessauer** (☎ 220 59 09; Lange Gasse 16; mains €7.40-14.80) is a friendly brewery-pub in the city centre.

Getting There & Away

Dessau is easily reached by fast train from Berlin (€16.80, 1¾ hours), Leipzig, Magdeburg and Halle (all €8.10, 40 minutes), and Lutherstadt Wittenberg (€5.50, 30 minutes). There's a Dessau exit from the A9 autobahn.

LUTHERSTADT WITTENBERG

☎ 03491 • pop 53,000

Wittenberg is where Luther did most of his work, including launching the Protestant Reformation in 1517, which changed the face of Europe. Ever quotable, Luther hurled vitriol at the corrupt church in Rome, even calling the Vatican a 'gigantic, bloodsucking worm'. The town's a must for anyone interested in the great man; it can be seen in a day from Berlin but is worth a longer look.

Orientation & Information

Hauptbahnhof Lutherstadt Wittenberg is a 15-minute walk from the tourist office, through the city centre. Go under the tracks and on to Collegienstrasse.

Wittenberg-Information (☎ 49 86 10, fax 49 86 11; e wb_info@wittenberg.de; Schlossplatz 2; open 9am-6pm Mon-Sat, 11am-4pm Sun Mar-Oct, 10am-4pm Mon-Sat, 11am-3pm Sun Nov-Feb) is very well organised and offers an excellent audio guide to the town (€5).

Things to See & Do

The **Lutherhaus** (☎ *420 30; Collegienstrasse 54; adult/concession €5/3*) is a Reformation museum inside Lutherhalle, a former monastery. It contains an original room furnished by Luther in 1535. He stayed here in 1508 while teaching at Wittenberg University and made the building his home for the rest of his life after returning in 1511.

The large altarpiece in **Stadtkirche St Marien** (☎ *40 44 15; Jüdenstrasse 35; admission free; open 9am-5pm Mon-Sat, 11.30am-5pm Sun May-Oct, 10am-4pm Mon-Sat, 11.30am-4pm Sun Nov-Apr*) was created jointly by Renaissance painter Lucas Cranach the Elder and his son in 1547. It shows Luther, his friend and supporter Melanchthon and other Reformation figures, as well as Cranach the Elder himself, in Biblical contexts. Luther preached in this church and was married here; the town recalls the nuptials in a festival each June. The **Luthereiche** (*Luther's Oak; cnr Lutherstrasse & Am Bahnhof*) is the site where Luther burnt the papers that threatened his excommunication.

Imposing monuments to both Luther and Melanchthon stand in front of the impressive **Altes Rathaus** (1535) on Markt. Also on Markt, the **Cranachhaus** is where painter Louis Cranach the Elder lived and worked; there's also the **Galerie im Cranachhaus** (☎ *420 19 17; Markt 4; adult/concession €2/1; open 10am-5pm Thur, 10am-6pm Tues, Wed & Fri, 1pm-5pm Sat & Sun*).

At the western end of town is the **Schloss** (1499) with its huge, rebuilt church onto the door Luther allegedly nailed his *95 Theses* on 31 October 1517. His tombstone is below the pulpit, and Melanchthon's is opposite.

Places to Stay & Eat

Camping ground **Bergwitzsee** (☎ *034921-282 28; e info@Bergwitzsee.de; adult/child/car €2.50/1/2*) is some 11km south of town on Lake Bergwitz. There are hourly trains. The often-mobbed **Jugendherberge** (☎ *40 32 55, fax 40 94 22; e Jugendherberge@wittenberg.de; Schloss; beds juniors/seniors €12/14.70*) is situated upstairs in the Schloss (sheets €3.50).

Wittenberg-Information finds private rooms from €25 per person. The **Hotel-Garni Am Schwanenteich** (☎ *41 10 34, fax 40 28 07; Töpferstrasse 1; singles/doubles from €31/59*) is central and has charming staff. For a

room with a brew **Im Beyerhof** (☎ *43 31 30, fax 43 31 31; Markt 6; singles/doubles €50/70*) has comfy accommodation located above a brewery. For a stylish upmarket option try the **Best Western Stadtpalais** (☎ *42 50, fax 42 51 00; e info@stadtpalais.bestwestern.de; Collegienstrasse 56-57; singles/doubles from €86/107*).

Most of the town's food options face Collegienstrasse. One block north, **Schlossfreiheit** (☎ *40 29 80; Coswigerstrasse 24; mains €6.25-10.50*) serves theme dishes including *Lutherschmaus*, duck in a peppery sultana sauce.

Getting There & Away

Wittenberg is on the main train line between Berlin (€23.60, one hour) and Leipzig (€15.80, 30 minutes) and has direct trains to/from Dessau (€5.50, 30 minutes) and Halle (€9, one hour). Be sure you buy tickets to 'Lutherstadt Wittenberg', as there is another town, Wittenberge, in eastern Germany.

HALLE

☎ 0345 • pop 262,000

The former state capital and largest city in Saxony-Anhalt, Halle was the centre of the GDR chemical industry – with all that implies. But it also has a 500-year-old university, a nice old castle and some other cultural attractions worth a visit.

Orientation & Information

To walk to the city centre from the Hauptbahnhof, head through the underpass and down pedestrian Leipziger Strasse, past the 15th-century Leipziger Turm to Markt, Halle's central square. **Halle Tourist** (☎ *47 23 30, fax 472 33 33; open 10am-6pm Mon-Fri, 10am-2pm Sat*) is in the elevated gallery built around the 1506 Roter Turm on the Markt.

Things to See & Do

The Markt has a statue (1859) of the great composer Georg Friedrich Händel, born in Halle in 1685. The four tall towers of the 1529 **Marktkirche** (☎ *517 08 94; An der Marienkirche 1; admission free; open 10am-noon, 3pm-5pm Mon-Sat, 3pm-5pm Wed, 11am-noon Sun*) loom above the square; you can climb one for a view of the city. Don't miss the exquisitely decorated Gothic interior.

The **Händelhaus** (☎ *50 09 00; Grosse Nikolai Strasse 5-6; adult/concession €2.60/1.80;*

open daily) was the composer's birthplace and now houses a major collection of musical instruments. Nearby is the imposing 15th-century **Schloss Moritzburg** (☎ 212 55 90; Friedemann-Bach-Platz 5; adult/concession €4/2, free Tues; open 11am-8.30pm Tues, 10am-6pm Wed-Sun), a former residence of the archbishops of Magdeburg and now a museum of 19th- and 20th-century art, including GDR art and some impressive German expressionist works. Fans of the Fab Four will appreciate the Continent's only **Beatles Museum** (☎ 290 39 00; Alter Markt 12; adult/child €3/2; open 10am-6pm Wed-Sun, closed September); it's also a great example of historic warehouse architecture. If you're walking from the Hauptbahnhof, note the graffiti art in the underpass. It's legal, encouraged and sometimes pretty skillful, though that does not explain the graffiti throughout much of the rest of the city. Also note the goofy GDR workers' monument, **Die Fäuste** (The Fists; Riebeck Platz), looking like a pulled tooth.

Places to Stay & Eat
The municipal **Am Nordbad Campingplatz** (☎ 523 40 85; Am Nordbad 12; site/person/car €1/4/2; open early May-late Sept) is near the Saale River; take tram No 2 or 3 to Am Nordbad. **Jugendherberge** (☎ 202 47 16, fax 202 51 72; e jh-halle@djh-sachsen-anhalt .de; August-Bebel-Strasse 48a; beds juniors/seniors €13.50/16.20) is central.

The tourist office can find private rooms from €15.50 per person. **Pension Am Alten Markt** (☎ 521 14 11, fax 523 29 56; Schmeerstrasse 3; singles/doubles €48/65) is small but very central; rooms have shower and toilet. **Hotel Dorint Charlottenhof** (☎ 292 30, fax 232 31 00; w www.dorint.de/halle; Dorotheenstrasse 12; singles/doubles from €105/110) has the cure for the post-GDR blues with modern rooms in a shopping complex.

Drei Kaiser (☎ 203 28 68; Bergstrasse 1; mains €7.50-15.90) near Schloss Mortizburg, has a genteel atmosphere and fine German and international cuisine. There are cheap eats throughout town and some handsome pubs on Sternstrasse.

Getting There & Away
Several trains per hour go to/from Leipzig (€7, 30 minutes). Direct IR trains go to/from Berlin-Zoo (€24.60, two hours).

NAUMBURG
☎ 03445 • pop 32,000
Naumburg is one of those pretty little medieval towns for which Germany is so famous. It is strategically located inbetween Halle/Leipzig and Weimar, in the very scenic Saale-Unstrut wine country. It can be hurriedly seen in a two-hour break between trains but really deserves a day.

Orientation & Information
The main train station (Naumburg/Saale) is 1.5km northwest of the old town. Out of the station take Markgrafenweg to Rossbacher Strasse, then turn left and walk to Bauernweg, which heads up the hill. From here, follow the curving road to the cathedral. Markt, the central square, is a five-minute walk from the cathedral along the pedestrian quarter. Alternatively, bus Nos 1 and 2 run frequently from the train station to Markt or to the nearby Theaterplatz.

Naumburg's helpful **tourist office** (☎ 20 16 14, fax 26 60 47; e stadt.naumburg@t-online .de; Markt 6; open 9am-6pm Mon-Fri, 9am-4pm Sat all year, also 10am-1pm Sun Apr-Oct) offers the excellent *A Walk Through Town* brochure (free).

Things to See & Do
In the ancient western quarter of town stands the magnificent late-Romanesque/early-Gothic **Dom Sts Peter and Paul** (☎ 23 01 10; Domplatz 16-17; adult/concession/student €4/3/2; open 9am-6pm Mon-Sat, noon-6pm Sun Apr-Sept, shorter hours Oct-Mar) filled with art treasures such as the famous 13th-century statues of Uta and Ekkehard in the west choir. Don't miss the 1972 bronze handrails on the stairs to the east choir. Naumburg's picturesque **Rathaus** (1528) and the Gothic **Stadtkirche St Wenzel** (☎ 30 84 01; Topfmarkt; admission free; open 10am-noon & 2pm-5pm Apr-Oct, hours vary Nov-Mar), built between 1218 and 1523, rise above Markt. Friedrich Nietzsche enthusiasts will want to make a pilgrimage to **Nietzsche-Haus** (☎ 20 16 38; Weingarten 18; adult/concession €1.50/1; open 2pm-5pm Tues-Fri, 10am-4pm Sat & Sun), the existentialist's one-time home.

Naumburg is an ideal base for **hiking, cycling, kayaking** and **winery touring** throughout the Saale-Unstrut region. The tourist office has information.

Places to Stay & Eat

Campingplatz Blütengrund (☎ 20 27 11, fax 20 05 71; adult/child/car €4/1.50/2), 1.5km northeast of Naumburg, is at the confluence of the Saale and Unstrut Rivers and has a popular swimming facility. The rather institutional **Jugendherberge** (☎ 70 34 22, fax 77 95 60; e JH-Naumburg@djh-sachsen-anhalt.de; Am Tennisplatz 9; juniors/seniors €16.50/18.70) is up a hill 1.5km south of the town centre. Subtract €3 if you bring your own linen.

The tourist office organises private rooms; expect to pay around €15 per person for somewhere central. The friendly **Zur Alten Schmiede** (☎ 243 60, fax 24 33 66; e Hotel _Zur_Alten_Schmiede@t-online.de; Lindenring 36-37; singles/doubles from €44/57) is just outside the Altstadt, while **Hotel Stadt Aachen** (☎ 24 70, fax 24 71 30; e Hotel-Stadt-Aachen@t-online.de; Markt 11; singles/doubles €50/70) is Naumburg's central, establishment choice.

Both of these hotels have top-notch restaurants. **Alt Naumburg** (☎ 20 42 95; Marienplatz 13; mains €4.90/12.40) is a relaxing place for a beer or coffee and cake on the square.

Getting There & Away

Frequent IR trains stop at Naumburg to/from Frankfurt (€45.60, 3½ hours), Berlin (€32.60, 2½ hours), Leipzig (€12.40, 45 minutes) and Weimar (€6.60, 30 minutes).

Mecklenburg-Western Pomerania

The state of Mecklenburg-Western Pomerania (Mecklenburg-Vorpommern) is a low-lying, postglacial region of lakes, meadows, forests and Baltic Sea (Ostsee) beaches, stretching across northern Germany from Schleswig-Holstein to Poland. Most of the state is historic Mecklenburg; only the island of Rügen and the area from Stralsund to the Polish border traditionally belong to Western Pomerania, or Vorpommern.

In 1160 the Duke of Saxony, Heinrich (Henry the Lion), Christianised the region and made the local Polish princes his vassals. Germanisation gradually reduced the Slavonic element, and in 1348 the dukes of Mecklenburg became princes of the Holy Roman Empire.

Sweden entered the scene during the Thirty Years' War (1618–48). In 1867 the whole region joined the North German Confederation and, in 1871, the German Reich.

Offshore islands like Poel and Hiddensee are largely untouched, while others, including Rügen, are popular resorts. Just keep in mind the very short swimming season (July and August usually).

SCHWERIN
☎ 0385 • pop 105,000

Surrounded by lakes, Schwerin is one of eastern Germany's most genteel and picturesque towns. The town gets its name from a Slavic castle known as Zaurin (animal pasture) on the site of the present Schloss. This former seat of the Grand Duchy of Mecklenburg – now the capital of Mecklenburg-Western Pomerania – is an interesting mix of renovated 16th- and 17th-century half-timbered houses and 19th-century architecture.

Orientation & Information

Down the hill east of the Hauptbahnhof there's the Pfaffenteich, the rectangular lake whose southern end is at the beginning of Schwerin's main street, Mecklenburgstrasse. Markt is southeast of here. Farther southeast, around Alter Garten on Schweriner See, are the monumental Marstall (the former royal stables), the Schloss (ducal castle), and museums, parks, tour boats and other treats. Marienplatz, the major shopping and transit centre, is about a five-minute walk to the west.

Schwerin-Information (☎ 592 52 13, fax 55 50 94; e stadtmarketing-schwerin@t-on line.de; Am Markt 10; open 9am-6pm Mon-Fri, 10am-4pm Sat, 10am-2pm Sun) sells the Schwerin-Ticket, covering local transport and discounted admissions for €6/4 per adult/child (€8/5 for two days).

Things to See & Do

Above the **Markt** rises the tall 14th-century Gothic **Dom** (☎ 56 50 14; Am Dom 1; adult/concession €1/0.50; open 11am-5pm Mon-Sat, noon-5pm Sun May-Oct, shorter hours Nov-Apr); you can climb the 219 steps up the 19th-century **church tower** (an additional €1) for the view. The cathedral is a wonderful example of north German red and glazed-black brick architecture.

Southeast of Alter Garten, over a causeway, there's the neo-Gothic **Schloss** (☎ 56 57 38;

SCHWERIN

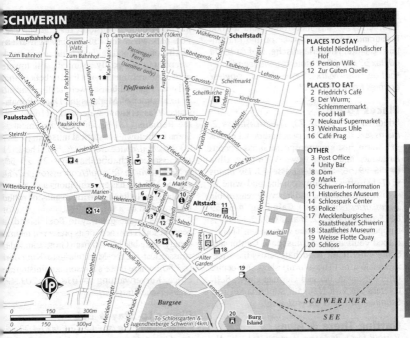

PLACES TO STAY
1 Hotel Niederländischer Hof
6 Pension Wilk
12 Zur Guten Quelle

PLACES TO EAT
2 Friedrich's Café
5 Der Wurm; Schlemmermarkt Food Hall
7 Neukauf Supermarket
13 Weinhaus Uhle
16 Café Prag

OTHER
3 Post Office
4 Unity Bar
8 Dom
9 Markt
10 Schwerin-Information
11 Historisches Museum
14 Schlosspark Center
15 Police
17 Mecklenburgisches Staatstheater Schwerin
18 Staatliches Museum
19 Weisse Flotte Quay
20 Schloss

GERMANY

Lennéstrasse 1; adult/concession €4/2.50; open 10am-6pm Wed-Sun Apr-Oct, 10am-5pm Wed-Sun Nov-Mar), with superb interiors and lake country views. It's connected to the **Schlossgarten** by another causeway. On the city side of Alter Garten is the **Staatliches Museum** (☎ 595 80; Alter Garten 3; adult/concession €3/2; open 10am-8pm Tues, 10am-6pm Wed-Sun Apr-Oct, 10am-6pm Tues-Sun Nov-Mar), with an excellent collection of works by old Dutch masters.

The dramatic cream-coloured building next to the museum is the **Mecklenburgisches Staatstheater Schwerin** (State Theatre). There is also a **Historisches Museum** (☎ 59 38 10; Grosser Moor 38; adult/concession €1.50/1; open 10am-6pm Tues-Sun).

Town **markets** are held on Schlachtermarkt, behind the Rathaus, from Tuesday to Saturday. At No 3, on the same square, stands the building that housed a synagogue until Nazi atrocities of 1938.

Cruises

From May to September, excursion boats operate every 30 minutes on the Schweriner See. They depart from the **Weisse Flotte** (☎ 55 77 70) quay near the Staatliches Museum, and 1½-hour cruises cost €9.50. There is a reduced schedule in March, April and early October.

Places to Stay

There's a nifty computerised accommodation system in front of the Hauptbahnhof. You'll find lists and locations of hotels and pensions with available rooms, and a free phone for calling the place of your choice.

Campingplatz Seehof (☎ 51 25 40, fax 581 41 70; e info@fereinparkseehof.de; 2-person sites €17.50) is 10km north of Schwerin on the western shore of Schweriner See (take bus No 8 from the train station). It gets crowded in summer. **Jugendherberge Schwerin** (☎ 326 00 06, fax 326 03 03; Waldschulweg 3; beds juniors/seniors €14.30/17) is lakeside, about 4km south of the city centre (take bus No 14 from Marienplatz).

Schwerin-Information can book private rooms from about €25 per person. Tiny, central **Pension Wilk** (☎ 550 70 24; Buschstrasse 13; €18 per person) has basic rooms without private facilities (breakfast €5 extra). The following include breakfast and private facilities. Historic **Zur Guten Quelle** (☎ 56 59 85, fax

500 76 02; Schusterstrasse 12; singles/doubles from €51/70) has nice rooms and a good restaurant. An upscale place on the Pfaffenteich is **Hotel Niederländischer Hof** (☎ *59 11 00, fax 591 10 99;* e *hotel@niederlaendischer -hof.de; Karl-Marx-Strasse 12-13; singles/ doubles from €90/118).*

Places to Eat
Friedrich's (☎ *55 54 73; Friedrichstrasse 2; mains €8.90-12.50)* serves traditional dishes in a warm, historic atmosphere; it has a popular terrace and water views. **Weinhaus Uhle** (☎ *56 29 56; Schusterstrasse 13-15; mains €11-17)* offers quality cuisine and wine in stylish surroundings, and has very reasonable *Tageskartes* (set *menus*). **Café Prag** (☎ *56 59 00; Schlossstrasse 17; mains €6.10-10.40)* is a popular coffee and cake destination. There's a food court in the **Schlosspark Center** and **Schlemmermarkt food hall** across the street in Der Wurm (The Worm) shopping centre offers cheap Asian and German chow. Self-caterers can visit **Neukauf supermarket** *(cnr Schmiedestrasse & Buschstrasse).*

Getting There & Away
Various fast trains serve Rostock (€12.40, 1¼ hours), Stralsund (€22.40, 2½ hours) and Hamburg (€17.60, 1¼ hours). Frequent trains go to/from Wismar (€5.50, 30 minutes). Most travel to/from Berlin (€33.40, two hours) requires a change at Wittenberge or Ludwigslust.

WISMAR
☎ 03841 • pop 47,500
Wismar, about halfway between Rostock and Lübeck, became a Hanseatic trading town in the 13th century. For centuries Wismar belonged to Sweden, and traces of Scandinavian rule can still be seen (and heard). It's less hectic than Rostock or Stralsund and is a pretty little town worth seeing for its historic centre and crumbling architectural gems.

Information
Wismar-Information (☎ *194 33, fax 251 30 91;* e *touristinfo@wismar.de; Am Markt 11; open 9am-6pm daily)* is very helpful.

Things to See & Do
Of the three great red-brick churches that once climbed above the rooftops, it was only **St Nikolai** *(donation €1)* that survived the Anglo-American bombing raids during WWII

intact. The massive red shell of **St Georgenkirche** is under long-term restoration. Cars now park where the 13th-century **St Marienkirche** once stood, although the great brick steeple (1339), partly restored, still towers above. Apart from this, it's hard to believe that Wismar's gabled houses were badly bombed.

In a corner of Markt is the Dutch Renaissance **Wasserkunst** waterworks (1602) and the **Rathaus** (1819), where its basement is home to the town's **historical museum** (☎ *251 30 96; adult/concession €1/0.50).* The 1571 Renaissance **Schabbellhaus** (☎ *28 23 50; Schweinsbrücke 8; adult/concession €2/1),* near St Nikolai, has art exhibitions and special displays, including a horrific display of rotted teeth yanked by a local dentist.

Wismar is the gateway to **Poel Island**, a beach resort renowned for its preserved natural beauty. Take bus No 430 from Grossschmiedestrasse, just off the Marktplatz, to Kirchdorf (€1.90), where there's a resort administration office, **Kurverwaltung** (☎ *038 425-203 47; Wismarsche Strasse 2).*

Places to Stay & Eat
Ostsee-Camping (☎ *64 23 77, fax 64 23 74; Am Strand 19c;* w *www.ostee-camping.de; tent site with adult/child/car €4/2.50/6 in summer, less rest of year)* is by the beach in Zierow, 9km northwest of Wismar. Among its other charms, it has a beer garden. Take route B105 or bus No 401. The **Jugendherberge** (☎ *326 80, fax 32 68 68; Juri-Gagarin-Ring 30a;* e *jh-wismar@t-online.de; beds juniors/ seniors €16/19)* is a 15-minute walk from the centre in Friedenshof or can be reached with bus D from the main train station.

Wismar-Information arranges private rooms from €13 per person. The central, charming **Pension Chez Fasan** (☎ *21 34 25, fax 20 22 85; Bademutterstrasse 19; beds €21 per person)* offers good value (breakfast €4 extra).

New Orleans Hotel (☎ *268 60, fax 26 86 10; Runde Grube 3; singles/doubles from €49/72)* is a modern hotel and restaurant on the waterfront with nice sized rooms with facilities; some with harbour views. **Steigenberger Hotel Stadt Hamburg** (☎ *23 90, fax 23 92 39;* e *info@steigenberger-wismar.de; Am Markt 24; singles/doubles from €82/ 104)* has pleasant rooms in a beautifully renovated building on the Markt.

A string of restaurants and bars line the car-free quarter near Alter Hafen. **Brauhaus am**

Lohberg (☎ 25 02 38; Am Lohberg; mains €3-16.50) brews its own beer and serves traditional dishes in a historic building. **To'n Zägenkrog** (☎ 28 27 16; Ziegenmarkt 10; mains €4-11.50) is filled with maritime mementoes and serves excellent fish dishes. In town, you'll find Mecklenburg specialities at **Zum Weinberg** (☎ 28 35 30; Hinter dem Rathaus 3; mains €5.30-15), while **Alter Schwede** (☎ 28 35 52; Alter Markt 18; mains €7-15) is an upmarket option located in Wismar's oldest burgher house.

Busy town **markets** (Am Markt) are held on Tuesday, Thursday and Saturday. On Saturday, a lively fish market takes place at the Alter Hafen fishing harbour.

Getting There & Away
Regional trains run to/from Rostock every hour (€8.10, 1¼ hours) and regularly to/from Schwerin (€5.50, 30 minutes). Connect in Bad Kleinen for trains to Lübeck (€10.70, 1¼ hours).

ROSTOCK & WARNEMÜNDE
☎ 0381 • pop 210,000
Rostock, the largest city in lightly populated northeastern Germany, is a major Baltic port and ship-building centre. In the 14th and 15th centuries Rostock was an important Hanseatic city trading with Rīga, Bergen and Bruges. Rostock University, founded in 1419, was the first in northern Europe.

The years after reunification were difficult in Rostock – unemployment soared and neo-Nazis engaged in attacks on foreign workers, bringing national and worldwide condemnation. Now, however, the city centre along Kröpeliner Strasse and the former dock area on the Warnow River have been redeveloped into pleasant pedestrian quarters. Rostock hosts the **IGA** (International Garden Show; ⓦ www.iga.de) from April to October 2003, cause for more, er, sprucing up.

Rostock's chief suburb is the beach resort and fishing village of Warnemünde, 12km north. In winter this popular getaway offers a picturesque alternative as a place to stay, while on warm days it is jammed with Berlin's fun-seekers. The IGA site is between central Rostock and Warnemünde.

Orientation & Information
Rostock-Information (☎ 194 33, 381 22 22, fax 381 26 01; ⓔ touristinfo@rostock.de; Neuer Markt 3-8; open 10am-6pm Mon-Fri, 10am-4pm Sat & Sun May-Sept, closed weekends Oct-Apr) is about 1.5km from the Hauptbahnhof (tram No 11 or 12). The tourist office sells the 48-hour Rostock Card (€8), which entitles holders to a free walking tour (in German), various reductions for sights and performances, and free public transport (including the S-Bahn to/from Warnemünde). Rostock's **post office** is in the same building. Web information on Rostock is available at ⓦ www.rostock.de.

Things to See & Do
Rostock's splendid 13th-century **Marienkirche** (☎ 45 33 25; Am Ziegenmarkt; adult/concession €1/0.50; open 10am-5pm Mon-Sat, 11.15am-5pm Sun), survived WWII unscathed. This huge brick edifice contains a functioning astronomical clock (1472), a Gothic bronze baptismal font (1290), a Renaissance pulpit (1574) and a baroque organ (1770). For a bird's-eye view of town, visit the **Petrikirche** (☎ 211 01; Alter Markt; open 10am-5pm daily Apr-Oct, 10am-4pm Mon-Fri Nov-Mar) and scale the stairs or take the lift up the tower (€2).

Kröpeliner Strasse, a broad pedestrian mall lined with 15th- and 16th-century burgher houses, runs west from the **Rathaus** on Neuer Markt to the 14th-century **Kröpeliner Tor** (☎ 45 41 77; Kröpeliner Strasse; adult/concession €3/1; open 10am-6pm Wed-Sun), near a stretch of old city wall. Halfway along, off the southwestern corner of Universitätsplatz, is the **Kloster 'Zum Heiligen Kreuz' Museum** (☎ 20 35 90; Klosterhof; adult/concession €2/1; open 10am-6pm Tues-Sun) situated in an old convent (1270).

The city will permanently move its interesting **Schifffahrtsmuseum** (shipping museum) to the IGA site.

At Warnemünde's north end, a broad, sandy beach stretches west from the **lighthouse** (1898). It's chock-a-block with bathers on hot summer days, and its promenade makes for a nice stroll.

Places to Stay
Both Rostock-Information and Warnemünde-Information can book private rooms from €15 per person, plus a €2.50 fee. After hours, you can call ☎ 194 14 for a recorded message (in German only) about vacant hotel rooms.

GERMANY

The new **Jugendherberge** (☎ 54 81 70, fax 548 17 23; Parkstrasse 47, Warnemünde; e jh-warnemuende@t-online.de; juniors/ seniors €19.30/23.30) is a two-minute walk to the beach and sporting activities.

The small **City-Pension** (☎ 459 07 04, fax 25 22 60; Krönkenhagen 3; singles/doubles from €44/67) is central, quiet and homy with rooms with facilities, near the Warnow River. **Courtyard by Marriott** (☎ 497 00, fax 497 07 00; Schwaansche Strasse 6; w www.court yard.com; rooms from €80) offers plenty of comfort off Universitätsplatz. The upmarket **Steigenberger Hotel Sonne** (☎ 497 30, fax 497 33 51; e info@hotel-sonne-rostock.de; singles/doubles from €99/127) is Rostock's premier downtown hotel, with a contemporary gabled facade.

In Warnemünde finding good, cheap accommodation is easy in winter, and it makes a wonderful alternative to Rostock. In summer, however, rooms in Warnemünde are as scarce as hen's teeth.

Places to Eat
Kölsch-& Altbierhaus (☎ 490 38 62; Wokrenter Strasse 36; dinner mains €5-14) has a good pub atmosphere – lunches and pub selections are cheaper. Down the hill, **Zur Kogge** (☎ 493 44 93; Wokrenter Strasse 27; mains €7.65-14.30) is a seafood place with a seafaring feel, plus some meat and veg selections. If you're looking to explore Rostock's Swedish heritage, **Tre Kronor** (☎ 490 42 60; Lange Strasse 11; mains €7.50-15.80) serves salmon, reindeer and elk. **Fast food** is available in the Rostocker Hof shopping centre, off Universitätsplatz.

In Warnemünde, along Alter Strom, the picturesque fishing harbour, stallholders sell the daily catch – fresh, smoked or in bread rolls...it's delicious! There are also loads of fish restaurants. A couple of blocks to the west, **Salsalitos** (☎ 519 35 65; Am Leucht turm 9; mains €7.50-15) pulls a young crowd in the evenings for expensive Mexican.

Getting There & Away
There are hourly trains from Wismar (€8.10, 1¼ hours), and frequent trains to/from Berlin-Zoo (€33.40, 2¾ hours), Stralsund (€10.70, one hour), Schwerin (€12.40, 1¼ hours) and Hamburg (€28, 2¼ hours).

Vehicle-passenger ferries cross to Trelleborg (Sweden) and Gedser (Denmark) from Rostock Seaport (bus No 19 or 20). **Scand lines** (☎ 01805-722 63 54 637, call cost €0.12 per min; w www.scandlines.de) has services daily between Rostock and Trelleborg for €14 to €19 per passenger (5¾ hours). Trips to Gedser cost €5 to €8 per person and take up to two hours. **TT-Line** (☎ 040-360 14 42, fax 360 14 07; w www.TTLine.de) departs from Rostock for Trelleborg several times daily using fast and slow boats. The crossing takes three to six hours and costs average €40; costs vary by season and boat.

Getting Around
Tageskarte (day tickets) cost €3.15. For two zones (covering Rostock and Warnemünde), single rides cost €1.70, or €0.90 within either zone. The double-decker S-Bahn north to Warnemünde departs from Rostock Hauptbahnhof every 15 minutes during the day, every 30 minutes in the evenings, and hourly from midnight to dawn.

STRALSUND
☎ 03831 • pop 61,500
Stralsund, an enjoyable city on the Baltic Sea north of Berlin, is almost completely surrounded by lakes and the sea, which once contributed to its defence. It was a Hanseatic city in the Middle Ages and later formed part of the Duchy of Pommern-Wolgast. From 1648 to 1815 it was under Swedish control. Today it's an attractive, historic town with fine museums and buildings, pleasant walks and a restful, uncluttered waterfront. The island of Rügen is just across the sound, the Strelasund, and in summer the ferry to Hiddensee Island leaves from here.

Orientation & Information
Stralsund's Altstadt is compact and easily walkable. It's connected by causeways to its surrounds; the main train station is across the Tribseer Damm causeway to the west, with Rügen to the east. Neuer Markt is the southwestern hub, and the bus station is a few blocks south, past the Marienkirche. You'll find the **post office** (Neuer Markt) opposite the Marienkirche.

Stralsund Tourismuszentrale (☎ 246 90; Alter Markt 9; e info@stralsund-tourismus .de; open 9am-7pm Mon-Fri, 9am-2pm Sat, 10am-2pm Sun May-Sept & 9am-5pm Mon-Fri, 10am-2pm Sat Oct-Apr) is near the northern focus of the old town. Here you can pick

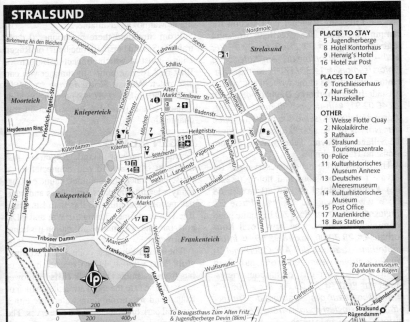

STRALSUND

PLACES TO STAY
5 Jugendherberge
8 Hotel Kontorhaus
9 Herwig's Hotel
16 Hotel zur Post

PLACES TO EAT
6 Torschliesserhaus
7 Nur Fisch
12 Hansekeller

OTHER
1 Weisse Flotte Quay
2 Nikolaikirche
3 Rathaus
4 Stralsund Tourismuszentrale
10 Police
11 Kulturhistorisches Museum Annexe
13 Deutsches Meeresmuseum
14 Kulturhistorisches Museum
15 Post Office
17 Marienkirche
18 Bus Station

GERMANY

up a pamphlet guide to the city's Gothic architecture (€0.50).

Things to See & Do

On Alter Markt is the medieval **Rathaus**, where you can stroll through the vaulted and pillared structures and around to the impressive **Nikolaikirche** (☎ 29 71 99). The 14th-century **Marienkirche** (☎ 29 35 29; Neuer Markt; open 10am-noon Mon-Sat, 2pm-4pm Sat, 11.30am-noon Sun) is a massive red-brick edifice typical of north German Gothic architecture.

You can climb the 350 steps of the **tower** (admission €2), on a daunting network of steep ladders, for a sweeping view of Stralsund. Ask at the tourist office about **organ recitals** and chamber music at these churches, especially in summer.

There are two excellent museums on Mönchstrasse. **Deutsches Meeresmuseum** (German Oceanographic Museum; ☎ 265 00; Katharinenberg 14-20; adult/concession €4.50/3; open 9am-6pm daily July & Aug, 10am-5pm Sept-June), is an oceanic complex and aquarium in a 13th-century convent church. Some aquariums contain tropical fish

and coral, while others display creatures of the Baltic and North Seas.

The **Kulturhistorisches Museum** (Cultural History Museum; ☎ 287 90; Mönchstrasse 25-27; adult/concession €3/1.50; open 10am-5pm Tues-Sun) has a large collection housed in the cloister of an old convent (and an annexe for local history at Böttcherstrasse 23; one ticket admits you to both). It's affiliated with the **Marinemuseum** (Naval Museum; ☎ 29 73 27; Sternschanze 10; adult/concession €3/1.50; open Tues-Sun), on the island of Dänholm, off the B96 towards Rügen, covering the colourful history of Baltic seafaring, with some cool equipment in the yard.

Many fine buildings have been restored on the showpiece **Mühlenstrasse** near Alter Markt. The old harbour is close by and you can stroll along the sea wall, then west along the waterfront park for a great view of Stralsund's skyline.

Cruises

There are short crossings to Altefähr (on Rügen; adult/child €1.50/0.75 one way) as well as one-hour harbour cruises from May to October (€5/3).

Places to Stay

See the following Rügen Island section for camping grounds. The excellent Stralsund **Jugendherberge** (☎ 29 21 60, fax 29 76 76; e jh-stralsund@t-online.de; Am Kütertor 1; juniors/seniors €14.30/17) is in the 17th-century waterworks at the western edge of the Altstadt. **Jugendherberge Devin** (☎ 49 02 89, fax 40 02 91; e jh-devin@djh-mv.de; Strand-strasse 219; juniors/seniors €14.30/17; open Mar-Nov) is by the sea, 8km east of town in the village of Devin. Take bus No 3 from Stralsund Hauptbahnhof.

The tourist office handles reservations for private rooms, pensions and hotels (€2.50 fee). **Herwig's Hotel** (☎ 266 80, fax 26 68 23; w www.herwigs.de; Heilgeiststrasse 50; singles/doubles from €50/70) has quite good rooms with facilities. The new **Hotel Kontorhaus** (☎ 28 90 00, fax 28 98 09; e info@kontorhaus-stralsund.de; Am Querkanal 1; singles/doubles from €55/65) has flash rooms and flashier city or harbour views. **Hotel zur Post** (☎ 20 05 00, fax 20 05 10; e info@hotel-zur-post-stralsund.de; Tribseer Strasse 22; singles/doubles from €60/75) is historic, central and stylish.

Places to Eat

Torschliesserhaus (☎ 29 30 32; Am Kütertor; mains €7.40-14.90) is a cosy pub in the old gatekeeper's house next to the youth hostel. Less-expensive pub grub is available. **Nur Fisch** (☎ 28 85 95; Heilgeiststrasse 92; mains €7.20-19.50) is a daytime bistro specialising in its namesake. The **Hansekeller** (☎ 70 38 40; Mönchstrasse 48; mains €7-12.30) serves hearty regional dishes in a vaulted cellar. The brewhouse **Zum Alten Fritz** (☎ 25 55 00; Greifswalder Chausee 84-85; mains €7.20-15.10) is worth the trek out of town (take bus No 3 from the main train station), with good beer and some tasty and well-priced dishes. There's also a selection of imbisse (snack stands) around Apollonienmarkt.

Getting There & Away

Frequent IR trains operate to/from Rostock (€10.70, 50 minutes), Berlin (€35, three hours), Schwerin (€22.40, two hours) and Hamburg (€38.20, 3¼ hours).

International trains between Berlin and Stockholm or Oslo use the car ferry connecting Sassnitz Mukran harbour on Rügen Island with Trelleborg and Malmö (Sweden). Two or three daily connections to Stockholm (changing at Malmö) are available.

From Stralsund there are about 20 daily trains to Sassnitz (€8.10, one hour) on Rügen Island, most of which connect at Bergen for Binz (€8.10, one hour). In summer you can also catch **Weisse Flotte ferries** (☎ 0180-321 21 50, call cost €0.18 per min) to Hiddensee Island (see that entry later in this chapter).

RÜGEN ISLAND

Germany's largest island, Rügen is just northeast of Stralsund and connected by a causeway. Once the summer haunt of Germany's leading thinkers, politicoes and businesspeople (including no less than Einstein), it fell on hard times during the War and GDR eras, but since German reunification it's being resurrected.

The island's highest point is the **Königs-stuhl** (king's throne, 117m), reached by car or bus from Sassnitz. The **chalk cliffs** that tower above the sea are the main attraction. Much of Rügen and its surrounding waters are either national park or protected nature reserves. The **Bodden** inlet area is a bird refuge popular with bird-watchers. **Kap Arkona**, on Rügen's north shore, is famous for rugged cliffs and two lighthouses.

The main resort area is in eastern Rügen, around the towns of Binz, Sellin and Göhren. A lovely hike from Binz to Sellin skirts the cliffs above the sea through beech and pine forest and offers great coastal views. Another destination is **Jagdschloss Granitz** (1834), also surrounded by lush forest, and Prora, up the coast from Binz, is the site of a 2km-long workers' retreat built by Hitler before the war, now housing several museums.

Tourismus Verband Rügen (☎ 03838-807 70; Am Markt 4) in Bergen, the administrative centre, publishes a huge booklet listing all accommodation on the island and other useful information. Otherwise, Rügen has dozens of tourist offices, both municipal and private. We've found **Tourismusgesellschaft Binz** (☎ 038393-134 60; e tourismusag@binz.de; Hauptstrasse 1, Binz) to be especially helpful.

Places to Stay & Eat

Rügen has 21 **camping grounds** – the largest concentration of them is at Göhren. Also popular are **Fereinwohnungen**, longer-term apartment rentals.

Rügen's **Jugendherberge** (☎ 038393-325 97, fax 325 96; e jugendherberge-binz@t-on line.de; Strandpromenade 35; beds juniors/ seniors €18.30/22.30) is across from the beach in Binz.

Binz is also the island's top resort, with lodgings known for their distinctive *Bäder-arkitektur* (spa architecture) of whitewashed wooden balconies. The **Hotel Villa Neander** (☎ 038393-42 90, fax 529 99; e glasner@ binz.de; Hauptstrasse 16; rooms from €41 per person) has warm rooms and friendly owners. **Deutsche Flagge** (☎ 038393-460, fax 462 99; Schillerstrasse 9; singles/doubles €55/80) has comfortable accommodation.

Fischmarkt (☎ 038393-38 14 43; Strandpromenade 41, Binz; mains €12-17.50) has an upscale atmosphere and fish fondue. At **Lohme** (☎ 038302-9221; Dorfstrasse 35, Lohme), on the island's north side, you can dine on regional specialities while watching the sun set over Kap Arkona.

Getting There & Away

Local trains run almost hourly from 8am to 9pm between Stralsund and Sassnitz (€8.10, one hour) or Binz via Bergen (€8.10, one hour). A historic and fun narrow-gauge train links Putbus to Göhren via Binz.

Fares for Baltic ferries vary with the season. **Scandlines** (☎ 01805-722 63 54 637, call cost €0.12 per min; w www.scand lines.de) runs five passenger-vehicle ferries daily from Sassnitz Mukran ferry terminal, 5km south of town, to/from Trelleborg (Sweden; €10 to €15 one way). Cars are €83 to €104, including all passengers. Scandlines also has at least two services weekly to/from Ronne on Bornholm (€12 to €17, daily in summer) in Denmark.

To reach the ferries by train, make sure the train goes to Sassnitz Mukran station. Otherwise, you can either catch a bus or walk from Sassnitz.

HIDDENSEE ISLAND

Hiddensee is a narrow 17km-long island off Rügen's west coast, north of Stralsund. No cars are allowed on Hiddensee and there are no camping grounds or hostels. The **tourist office** (☎ 038300-642 26; e insel.information@ t-online.de; Norderende 162; open 7am-5pm Mon-Fri year-round, 10am-noon Sat May-Sept) in Vitte, has accommodation information and a free booking service.

Weisse-Flotte Ferries (☎ 0180-321 21 50, call cost €0.18 per min) runs frequent services from Schaprode on Rügen's west coast to Hiddensee (€6.50/11.50 one way/return to Neuendorf, €8/13.50 to Kloster and Vitte). Buses link Schaprode to Bergen, which is on the main Rügen train line. Summer ferries also link Hiddensee with Stralsund (€8/14.50).

Bavaria

For many visitors to Germany, Bavaria (Bayern) is a microcosm of the whole country. Here you will find fulfilled the German stereotypes of *Lederhosen*, beer halls, oompah bands and romantic castles.

Bavaria was ruled for centuries as a duchy under the line founded by Otto I of Wittelsbach, and eventually graduated to the status of kingdom in 1806. The region suffered amid numerous power struggles between Prussia and Austria and was finally brought into the German Empire in 1871 by Bismarck. The last king of Bavaria was Ludwig II (1845–86), who earned the epithet the 'mad king' due to his obsession for building fantastic fairy-tale castles at enormous expense. He was found drowned in Starnberger See in suspicious circumstances and left no heirs.

Bavaria draws visitors all year. If you only have time for one part of Germany after Berlin, this is it. Munich, the capital, is the heart and soul. The Bavarian Alps, Nuremberg and the medieval towns on the Romantic Road are other important attractions.

MUNICH
☎ 089 • pop 1.3 million

Munich (München) is the Bavarian mother lode. But this beer-quaffing, sausage-eating city can be as cosmopolitan as anywhere in Europe. Munich residents have figured out how to enjoy life and are perfectly happy to show outsiders, as a visit to a beer hall will confirm. There's much more to Munich, however, than beer. Decide on one of the many fine museums and take a leisurely look.

Munich has been the capital of Bavaria since 1503, but really achieved prominence under the guiding hand of Ludwig I in the 19th century. It has endured many turbulent times, but the 20th century was particularly rough. The city almost starved during WWI, the Nazis got their start here in the 1920s and

WWII brought bombing and more than 6000 civilian deaths. Today it is the centre of Germany's burgeoning high-tech industries and boasts lower unemployment than many other regions.

Orientation

The main train station is just west of the centre. Although there is extensive public transport, old-town Munich is enjoyable for walking. From the station, head east along Bayerstrasse, through Karlsplatz, and then along Neuhauser Strasse and Kaufingerstrasse to Marienplatz, the hub of Munich.

North of Marienplatz are the Residenz (the former royal palace), Schwabing (the famous student section) and the parklands of the Englischer Garten. East of Marienplatz is the Platzl quarter for beer houses and restaurants, as well as Maximilianstrasse, a fashionable street that is ideal for simply strolling and window-shopping.

Information

Tourist Offices The main branch of the tourist office (☎ 23 33 03 00; e tourismus@ ems.muenchen-tourist.de; Hauptbahnhof; open 8am-8pm Mon-Sat, 10am-6pm Sun) is at the main train station, to the right as you exit via the eastern entrance. Its room-finding service is free and you must apply in person; call ☎ 23 33 03 00 or write to: Fremdenverkehrsamt München, D-80313 München. There's another branch (Marienplatz; open 10am-8pm Mon-Fri, 10am-4pm Sat) beneath the Neues Rathaus. Both offices sell the Munich Welcome Card (€15.50), which allows three days unlimited travel on public transport, plus discounts for many museums, galleries and other attractions.

EurAide (☎ 59 38 89; e euraide@compu serve.com; Hauptbahnhof; open 7.45am-12.45pm & 2pm-4pm daily May-Oct, 8am-noon & 1pm-4pm Sat & Sun Nov-Mar), near platform 11 at the main train station, is an excellent source of information in English. The office gives advice on local and European train travel, and its room-finding service (€4 per booking) is at least as skilful as the tourist office's.

Yet another useful office is the **Jugendinformationszentrum** (Youth Information Centre; ☎ 51 41 06 60; Paul-Heyse-Strasse 22; open noon-6pm Mon-Fri, to 8pm Thur). It has a wide range of information for young people as well as an extensive library of periodicals and cheap Internet access.

The excellent Young People's Guide (€0.50) is available from information offices. The English-language monthly Munich Found (€3) is also useful (find it at English bookstores, cafés and restaurants) as is the annual Visitors' Guide (free), which is published by the same organisation and available at the tourist offices. There is a useful website at w www.munich-tourist.de.

Money Reisebank has two offices at the main train station; if you show a EurAide newsletter, The Inside Track, your commission will be 50% cheaper. You can also use AmEx (Promenadeplatz 6) and Thomas Cook (Kaiserstrasse 45, Schwabing).

Post & Communications Munich's main post office (Bahnhofplatz 1) is open from 8am to 8pm weekdays and until noon Saturday. The poste restante address is: Hauptpostlagernd (Poste Restante), Bahnhofplatz 1, 80074 München.

Sharing the post office building is **easyEverything** (Bahnhofplatz 1; open 24hr), part of a chain of Internet cafés. It costs €2 for 80 minutes online, has hundreds of terminals and is normally packed with cyber surfers.

At **Savic Internet Point** (☎ 55 02 89 88; Schillerstrasse 17), you can download, print files and burn CDs. It costs €3 an hour.

Travel Agencies In the main train station there's **ABR Reisebüro** (☎ 120 40).

Bookshops The best travel bookshop in town is **Geobuch** (Rosental 6), opposite Viktualienmarkt. The widest cultural book range is available at **Hugendubel** (Marienplatz), with a good selection of Lonely Planet guides and tons of English-language offerings. **Anglia English Bookshop** (Schellingstrasse 3) is overflowing with English titles.

Laundry Close to the Hauptbahnhof is **City SB-Waschcenter** (Paul-Heyse-Strasse 21; open 7am-11pm daily) where loads cost €4.

Medical & Emergency Services Medical help is available at the **Home Medical Service** (☎ 55 17 71, 724 20 01). For **ambulances** call ☎ 112. There is an English-speaking **pharmacy** at the main train station, as well as a police station (*emergency number* ☎ *110*) on the Arnulfstrasse side.

Dangers & Annoyances Munich residents love to stroll in the evening, so walking around the city centre feels pretty safe. The usual precautions apply in regard to staggering drunks from the beer halls, and you need to be wary of pickpockets around the touristy areas, near the Hauptbahnhof, and during major festivals like Oktoberfest and the *Christkindlmarkt* (Christmas Market). A common trick is to steal your gear if you strip off in the Englischer Garten (don't let that stop you, just watch your stuff!)

Things to See & Do

Except where otherwise noted, museums and galleries are closed on Monday.

The pivotal **Marienplatz** is a good starting point. Dominating the square is the towering neo-Gothic **Neues Rathaus** (*Marienplatz*), with its incessantly photographed **Glockenspiel** (carillon) which performs at 11am and noon (also at 5pm from May to October), bringing the square to an expectant standstill. Two important churches are on this square: **Peterskirche** and, behind the Altes Rathaus, the **Heiliggeistkirche**. Head west along shopping street Kaufingerstrasse to the late-Gothic **Frauenkirche** (*Church of Our Lady*; ☎ *42 34 57; Frauenplatz; tower adult/concession €3/1.50*), the landmark church of Munich. Go inside and join the hordes wandering in stupefied awe at the grandeur of the place, or climb the tower for majestic views of Munich. Continue west to the large, grey **Michaelskirche** (☎ *609 02 24; Kaufingerstrasse*), Germany's grandest Renaissance church.

Farther west is the **Richard Strauss Fountain** and then the medieval **Karlstor**, an old city gate. Double back towards Marienplatz and turn right onto Eisenmannstrasse, which becomes Kreuzstrasse and converges with Herzog-Wilhelm-Strasse at the medieval gate of **Sendlinger Tor**. Go down the left side of the shopping street Sendlinger Strasse to the **Asamkirche** (*Sendlinger Strasse 34*), a remarkable church designed by brothers Cosmas Damian and Egid Quirin Asam. It shows a rare unity of style, with scarcely a single unembellished surface.

Continue along Sendlinger Strasse and turn right on Hermann-Sack-Strasse to reach the **Stadtmuseum** (☎ *233; St-Jakobs-Platz 1;* *adult/concession €2.50/1.50; open 10am-6pm Tues-Sun*), where the outstanding exhibits cover beer brewing, fashion, musical instruments, photography and puppets.

Palaces The huge **Residenz** (*Max-Joseph-Platz 3*) housed Bavarian rulers from 1385 to 1918 and features more than 500 years of architectural history. Apart from the palace itself, the **Residenzmuseum** (☎ *29 06 71; enter from Max-Joseph-Platz 3; adult/concession €4/2; open 9am-6pm Tues-Sun, 9am-8pm Thur*) has an extraordinary array of 100 rooms containing the Wittelsbach house's belongings, while in the same building, the **Schatzkammer** (☎ *29 06 71; enter from Max-Joseph-Platz 3; adult/concession €4/2; open 9am-6pm Tues-Sun, 9am-8pm Thur*) exhibits a ridiculous quantity of jewels, crowns and ornate gold.

If this doesn't satisfy your passion for palaces, visit **Schloss Nymphenburg** (☎ *17 90 80; adult/concession €3.60/2.60, museum & gallery €7.70/6.15; open 9am-6pm Tues-Sun, 9am-8pm Thur*) northwest of the city centre via tram No 17 from the main train station. This was the royal family's equally impressive summer home. The surrounding park is worth a long, regal stroll.

Deutsches Museum A vast science and technology museum (☎ *217 91; Theresienhöhe 14a; adult/concession €6/4, planetarium €1.50 extra; open 9am-5pm Tues-Sun*), this is like a combination of Disneyland and the Smithsonian Institution all under one huge roof that covers 13km of corridors on eight floors. You can explore anything from the depths of coal mines to the stars, but it's definitely too large to see everything so pursue specific interests. It can be reached via the S-Bahn to Isartor or tram No 18 to Deutsches Museum.

Other Museums The **Glyptothek** (☎ *28 61 00; Königsplatz 3; adult/concession €3/1.75; open 10am-5pm Tues-Sun, 10am-8pm Thur*) and **Antikensammlungen** (☎ *59 83 59; Königsplatz 1; adult/concession €3/1.75; open 10am-5pm Tues-Sun, 10am-8pm Wed*) have some of Germany's best antiquities. To visit both is €5.

Bayerisches Nationalmuseum (☎ *211 24 01; Prinzregentenstrasse 3; adult/concession €3.10/1.80; open 9.30am-5pm Tues-Sun*) houses an impressive collection of Bavarian and southern German artefacts.

GERMANY

CENTRAL MUNICH (MÜNCHEN)

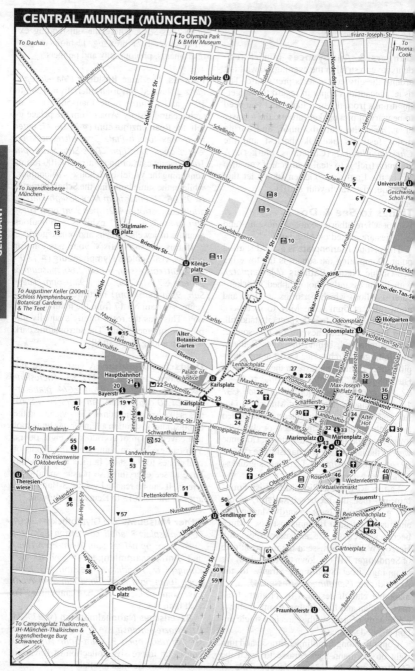

To Dachau

To Olympia Park
& BMW Museum

Franz-Joseph-Str

To Thoma Cook

Nordendstr

Masannstr

Schleissheimer Str

Josephsplatz Ⓤ

Isabellastr

Türkenstr

Joseph-Adalbert-Str

Schellingstr

3 ▼

2

Kreitmayrstr

Hessstr

Schellingstr

Theresienstr Ⓤ

Theresienstr

Arcostr

Barer Str

Annalienstr

4 ▼

5 ▼

6 ▼

Universität Ⓤ

Geschwister-Scholl-Pla

7 ●

To Jugendherberge
München

🏛 8

🏛 9

Lämmerstr

Gabelsbergerstr

🏛 10

Schönfeldst

🏧 13

Stiglmaier-platz Ⓤ

Brienner Str

🏛 11

Königs-platz Ⓤ

🏛 12

Von-der-Ta-Si

Seidlstr

To Augustiner Keller (200m),
Schloss Nymphenburg,
Botanical Gardens
& The Tent

Marsstr

Türkenstr

Oskar-von-Miller-Ring

Odeonsplatz ☸ Hofgarten

14 ● ● 15

Hirtenstr

Karlstr

Ottostr

Maximiliansplatz

Odeonsplatz Ⓤ

Hofgarten Str

Arnulfstr

Elisenstr

Alter Botanischer Garten

Theatinerstr

Residenzstr

Marstallpl

Lenbachplatz

27 ● 28

Promenadeplatz

35 🏛

Hauptbahnhof

Palace of Justice

Karlsplatz Ⓤ

Maxburgstr

Löwengrube

Max-Joseph-Platz

36

20 ℹ 21 ℹ

✉ 22 Schützenstr

26 ✝

Schäfflerstr

Dienerstr

Maximilianstr

Bayerstr

Karlsplatz

23 ●

25 ✝

Neuhauser Str

30 ✝

29

31 ✝

Landschaftr

34 ✝

Alter Hof

39 ✝

16 ●

19 ℹ

17 ●

18 ●

Adolf-Kolping-Str

24

Herzogspitalstr

Eisenmannstr

Kaufinger Str

32 ✝ 33 ℹ

Weinstr

Marienplatz ✝ 🏛

43 🏛

Marienplatz Ⓤ

Schwanthalerstr

Senefelderstr

Schwanthalerstr

🏛 52

Altheimer Eck

Hochbrückenstr

44

Rosenstr

42

Sparkassenstr

41

40

55 ●

● 54

Goethestr

Landwehrstr

53

Josephspitalstr

48 ▼

45

Rindermarkt

46 ✝

Tal

Westenriederstr

To Theresienwiese
(Oktoberfest)

Schillerstr

Oberanger

49 ✝

47

Rosental

Viktualienmarkt

Theresien-wiese Ⓤ

Pettenkoferstr

51

50 ●

Unterer Anger

Frauenstr

Rumfordstr

Uhlandstr

Paul-Heyse-Str

56

Nussbaumstr

Sendlinger Tor Ⓤ

Blumenstr

Müllerstr

Reichenbachplatz

Cornelstr

Reichenbachstr

Kleinzstr

Buttermelcherstr

🏛 64

🏛 63

▼ 57

Lindwurmstr

61 ●

Fraunhoferstr

Klenzestr

Gärtnerplatz

Basdstr

Hackenstr

58 ●

Thalkirchner Str

60 ▼

59 ▼

🏛 62

Goethe-platz Ⓤ

Fraunhoferstr Ⓤ

Erhardtstr

To Campingplatz Thalkirchen,
JH-München-Thalkirchen &
Jugendherberge Burg
Schwaneck

Kapuzinerstr

Pestalozzistrasse

Ohlmüllerstr

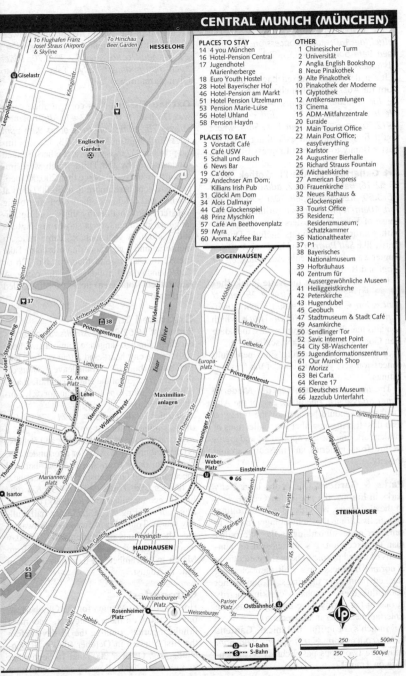

CENTRAL MUNICH (MÜNCHEN)

PLACES TO STAY
14 4 you München
16 Hotel-Pension Central
17 Jugendhotel
     Marienherberge
18 Euro Youth Hostel
28 Hotel Bayerischer Hof
46 Hotel-Pension am Markt
51 Hotel Pension Utzelmann
53 Pension Marie-Luise
56 Hotel Uhland
58 Pension Haydn

PLACES TO EAT
3 Vorstadt Café
4 Café USW
5 Schall und Rauch
6 News Bar
19 Ca'doro
29 Andechser Am Dom;
     Killians Irish Pub
31 Glöckl Am Dom
34 Alois Dallmayr
44 Café Glockenspiel
48 Prinz Myschkin
57 Café Am Beethovenplatz
59 Myra
60 Aroma Kaffee Bar

OTHER
1 Chinesischer Turm
2 Universität
7 Anglia English Bookshop
8 Neue Pinakothek
9 Alte Pinakothek
10 Pinakothek der Moderne
11 Glyptothek
12 Antikensammlungen
13 Cinema
15 ADM-Mitfahrzentrale
20 Euraide
21 Main Tourist Office
22 Main Post Office;
     easyEverything
23 Karlstor
24 Augustiner Bierhalle
25 Richard Strauss Fountain
26 Michaelskirche
27 American Express
30 Frauenkirche
32 Neues Rathaus &
     Glockenspiel
33 Tourist Office
35 Residenz;
     Residenzmuseum;
     Schatzkammer
36 Nationaltheater
37 P1
38 Bayerisches
     Nationalmuseum
39 Hofbräuhaus
40 Zentrum für
     Aussergewöhnliche Museen
41 Heiliggeistkirche
42 Peterskirche
43 Hugendubel
45 Geobuch
47 Stadtmuseum & Stadt Café
49 Asamkirche
50 Sendlinger Tor
52 Savic Internet Point
54 City SB-Waschcenter
55 Jugendinformationszentrum
61 Our Munich Shop
62 Morizz
63 Bei Carla
64 Klenze 17
65 Deutsches Museum
66 Jazzclub Unterfahrt

GERMANY

North of the city, auto-fetishists can thrill to the **BMW Museum** (☎ *38 22 33 07; Petuelring 130; adult/concession €2.75/2; open 9am-5pm Tues-Sun).* Take the U3 to Olympiazentrum.

It's a delightfully mixed bag at the **Zentrum für Aussergewöhnliche Museen** *(Centre for Unusual Museums;* ☎ *290 41 21; Westenriederstrasse 26; adult/concession €4/2.50; open 10am-6pm Tues-Sun),* where you'll find displays on everything from the Easter Bunny to Austrian Empress Elisabeth.

Art Galleries The **Alte Pinakothek** (☎ *23 80 52 16; Barer Strasse 27; adult/concession €5/3.50, free Sun; open 10am-5pm Tues-Sun, 10am-10pm Thur)* is a veritable treasure house of European masters from the 14th to 18th centuries. Highlights include Dürer's Christ-like *Self Portrait* and his *Four Apostles*, Rogier van der Weyden's *Adoration of the Magi* and Botticelli's *Pietà*.

Immediately north is the **Neue Pinakothek** (☎ *23 80 51 95; Barer Strasse 29; adult/concession €5/3.50, free Sun; open 10am-5pm Wed-Sun, 10am-10pm Thur),* which contains mainly 19th-century works, including Van Gogh's *Sunflowers,* and sculpture.

A combined card costing €8/5 per adult/concession gets you into both of the previous listings.

The huge new **Pinakothek der Moderne** *(Barer Strasse 40),* one block east of the Alte Pinakothek, should be open by the time you read this. It brings together four collections of modern art, graphic art, applied art and architecture from galleries and museums around the city.

Parks & Gardens One of the largest city parks in Europe, the Englischer Garten, west of the city centre, is a great place for strolling, especially along the Schwabinger Bach. In summer, nude sunbathing is the rule rather than the exception. It's not unusual for hundreds of naked people to be in the park during a normal business day, with their clothing stacked primly on the grass. If they're not doing this, they're probably drinking merrily at one of the park's three **beer gardens** (see Entertainment later in this section).

Munich's beautiful **Botanical Gardens** *(adult/concession €3/2; open 9am-6pm daily)* are two stops past Schloss Nymphenburg on Tram 17.

Olympiaturm If you like heights, then go up the lift of the 290m Olympiaturm (tower) situated in the Olympia Park complex (☎ *67 24 14; adult/concession €2.80/1.70; tower open 9am-midnight daily).* Take the U3 to Olympiazentrum.

Dachau The first Nazi concentration camp was Dachau (☎ *08131-17 41; Alte-Roemer-Strasse 75; admission free; open 9am-5pm Tues-Sun),* built in March 1933. Jews, political prisoners, homosexuals and others deemed 'undesirable' by the Third Reich were imprisoned in the camp. More than 200,000 people were sent here; more than 30,000 died at Dachau and countless others died after being transferred to other death camps. An English-language documentary is shown at 11.30am and 3.30pm. A visit includes camp relics, a memorial and a very sobering museum. Take the S2 to Dachau and then bus No 726 or 724 (Sunday and holidays) to the camp. A Gesamtnetz (total area) ticket (€9) is needed for the trip.

Organised Tours
Radius (☎ *55 02 93 74; Arnulfstrasse 3)* runs excellent English-language tours: a two-hour walk of the city heart, and a tour of the Third Reich sites (both €9). Tours leave from its office near track 30 at the Hauptbahnhof. It also offers five-hour trips to Dachau for €18, including transport.

Munich Walk Tours (☎ *0171-274 02 04)* offers similar options at similar prices, plus a royal castle tour of the Residenz and Schloss Nymphenburg for €18/16 for over/under 26s. Tours run daily from April to October and meet under the Glockenspiel on Marienplatz.

Mike's Bike Tours (☎ *25 54 39 87)* runs highly recommended (and leisurely) city cycling tours in English (€22/33 for half-/full-day tours). Tours depart from the archway at the Altes Rathaus on Marienplatz. Half-day tours (four hours) run at least once daily from March to November; all-day tours run from June to August.

Oktoberfest
Hordes come to Munich for the Oktoberfest, one of the Continent's biggest, and most drunken, parties, running the 15 days before the first Sunday in October (that's 20 September to 5 October 2003 and 18 September to 3 October 2004). Reserve accommodation

well ahead and go early in the day so you can grab a seat in one of the hangar-sized beer 'tents'. The action takes place at the Theresienwiese grounds, about a 10-minute walk southwest of the main train station. While there is no entrance fee, those €6 1L steins of beer add up fast.

Places to Stay

Munich can be jammed with tourists year-round. Without reservations you may have to throw yourself at the mercy of the tourist office or EurAide room-finding services (see Tourist Offices under Information earlier).

Camping The most central camping ground is **Campingplatz Thalkirchen** (☎ 723 17 07, fax 724 31 77; Zentralländstrasse 49; tent/person €3.60/4.40, heated cabin €10.50 per person), southwest of the city centre. Take the U3 to Thalkirchen and then bus No 57 (about 20 minutes). This place is closed from November to mid-March.

Youth Hostels Munich's youth hostels that are DJH and HI affiliated do not accept guests over age 26, except group leaders or parents accompanying a child.

The **Jugendherberge München** (☎ 13 11 56, fax 167 87 45; e jhmuenchen@djh-bayern.de; Wendl-Dietrich-Strasse 20; dorm beds €19.20) is northwest of the centre (U1 to Rotkreuzplatz). It lacks atmosphere, but has plenty of beds. Also fairly close is the modern **JH München-Thalkirchen** (☎ 723 65 50, fax 724 25 67; e jhmuenchen-thalkirchen@djh .de; Miesingstrasse 4; dorm beds €19.20). Take the U3 to Thalkirchen, then follow the signs. Cheaper is the **Jugendherberge Burg Schwaneck** (☎ 74 48 66 70, fax 74 48 66 80; e info@jugendherberge-burgschwaneck.de; Burgweg 4-6; dorm beds €15.50), in a superb old castle; take the S7 to Pullach, then it's a 10-minute walk.

The **Tent** (☎ 141 43 00, fax 17 50 90; e see-you@the-tent.com; In den Kirschen 30; bed in main tent €9, camp site €5.50) is a fun and cheap summer option. This mass camp is open from June to September, and has a beer garden and no curfew. Take Tram 17 to the Botanic Gardens then follow the signs.

Other Hostels Close to the Hauptbahnhof, the **Euro Youth Hotel** (☎ 59 90 88 11, fax 59 90 88 22; e info@euro-youth-hotel.de; Senefelderstrasse 5; dorm beds €17.50, singles/doubles without bathroom €45/72) is a backpacker favourite, though the bathrooms could use a scrub. There are wool-fibre pillows and cotton sheets at ecologically correct **4 you München** (☎ 55 21 60, fax 55 21 66 66; e info@the4you.de; Hirtenstrasse 18; dorm beds under/over 27s €16.50/17.50, singles/doubles with breakfast €43.50/68.50). This has a hostel section downstairs and a guesthouse upstairs.

Women under 26 can try the pleasant **Jugendhotel Marienherberge** (☎ 55 58 05, fax 55 02 82 60; e invia-marienherberge@t-on line.de; Goethestrasse 9; dorm beds €17, singles/doubles €25/40).

Hotels There are plenty of fairly cheap, if scruffy, places near the station. One of the better deals is tidy **Hotel Pension Central** (☎ 543 98 46, fax 543 98 47; e pensioncentral@t-on line.de; Bayerstrasse 55; singles/doubles with breakfast €34/40). Similar but more worn is **Pension Marie Luise** (☎ 55 25 56 60, fax 55 45 56 66; e comfort-hotel-andi@t-online.de; Landwehrstrasse 35; singles/doubles €30/45), but you don't get breakfast.

Close to the Goetheplatz U-Bahn station, **Pension Haydn** (☎ 53 11 19, fax 54 40 48 27; Haydnstrasse 9; singles/doubles from €35/50) is a pleasant surprise. Beneath the shabby facade it's spotless, friendly and cheap.

There's an old-fashioned feel at **Hotel Pension Utzelmann** (☎ 59 48 89, fax 59 62 28; Pettenkoferstrasse 6; singles/doubles with breakfast €33/53) in an attractive building in a quiet street. Near the Viktualienmarkt, **Hotel-Pension am Markt** (☎ 22 50 14, fax 22 40 17; e hotel-am-markt.muenchen@t-on line.de; Heiliggeiststrasse 6; singles/doubles with breakfast from €38/68) has a pleasant feel and lovely rooms.

One of the classier (and friendlier) hotels in town is **Hotel Uhland** (☎ 54 33 50, fax 54 33 52 50; e hotel_uhland@compuserve.com; Uhlandstrasse 1; singles/doubles from €64/77), near the Oktoberfest site. Behind a beautiful neo-Renaissance facade you'll find all the mod cons and an inspirational breakfast buffet.

Hotel Bayerischer Hof (☎ 212 00, fax 212 09 06; e info@bayerischerhof.de; Promenadeplatz 2-6; singles/doubles from €182/232) is all marble, gold leaf and bustling efficiency, and won't leave you much change from a week's pay.

GERMANY

Places to Eat

At **Viktualienmarkt**, just south of Marien-platz, you can put together a picnic feast to take to the Englischer Garten. More prosperous picnickers might prefer the legendary **Alois Dallmayr** (Dienerstrasse 14), one of the world's greatest (and priciest) delicatessens, with an amazing range of exotic foods imported from every corner of the earth.

Student card-holders can fill up for around €2 in any of the university **Mensas** (Leopold-strasse 13 • Arcistrasse 17 • Helene-Mayer-Ring 9). If your sightseeing timetable is tight, you can pick up some cheap Italian from the window at the **Ca'Doro** (Bayerstrasse 31; pizza pieces €1.90).

South of the Hauptbahnhof, the **Café Am Beethovenplatz** (Goethenstrasse 51; dishes €7-10) is a casual hang-out with no airs and graces. It also serves great, affordable food.

For hearty Bavarian chow at its best, slip behind the Frauenkirche to **Andechser Am Dom** (☎ 29 84 81; Weinstrasse 7; mains €9-14). If that's packed (probable), try nearby **Glöckl Am Dom** (☎ 291 94 50; Frauenplatz 9; mains €5-13), a medieval Bratwurst house where they serve up your sausages and sauer-kraut on pewter plates.

The sprawling **Ratskeller** (☎ 219 98 90; Marienplatz 8; mains €11-19), in the cellar beneath the Neues Rathaus, has an extensive menu with dishes like Scottish salmon and hickory-smoked trout. South of Sendlinger Tor, **Myra** (☎ 26 01 83 84; Pestalozzistrasse 32; mains €10-19) has a menu of meat, seafood, vegetarian dishes infused with a Turk-ish tang, and an awe-inspiring cocktail list.

The stylish **Prinz Myschkin** (☎ 26 55 96; Hackenstrasse 2; mains €9-13) provides a spirited cosmopolitan vegetarian menu, and a tasty selection of pizza and pasta.

Cafés Most of Munich's café culture centres on Schwabing, the university haunt. Here you'll find plenty of snug little spots filled with laid-back laureates and lively lingo.

For the ultimately cool hang-out, head to unpretentious **Schall und Rauch** (Schelling-strasse 22), where ciggies are smoked and the problems solved over coffee. To chill out even more, grab your book and join the mellow gang around the corner at **Café USW** (Turken-strasse 55).

Nearby, **Vorstadt Café** (Turkenstrasse 83) is busy and trendy, while at the modern **News Bar** (Amalienstrasse 54), an entire wall is dedi-cated to the latest magazines and newspapers (some in English).

In the Altstadt, a window seat at **Café Glockenspiel** (Marienplatz 28) is a much-sought, if ambitious, goal – here you can view the café's namesake at eye level. **Stadt Café** (St-Jakobsplatz 1), at the Stadtmuseum, has funky decor and an intellectual crowd, while south of Sendlinger Tor, cramming 30 people into a shoebox isn't easy, so the coffee must be good at the tiny **Aroma Kaffee Bar** (Pestalozzi-strasse 24).

Entertainment

Beer Halls & Beer Gardens Beer drink-ing is an integral part of Munich's entertain-ment scene. Germans drink an average of 130L of the amber liquid each per year, while Munich residents manage to drink much more than this!

Several breweries run their own beer halls, so try at least one large, frothy, 1L mug (called a *Mass*) of beer before heading off to another hall. Most famous is the enormous **Hof-bräuhaus** (Am Platzl 9). A tourist trap it may be, but it's still a rollicking good time – singing, drinking and general merriment is en-couraged. Less prominent but no less enjoy-able is the **Augustiner Bierhalle** (Neuhauser Strasse 27), an authentic example of an old-style Munich beer hall, filled with laughter, smoke and clinking glasses.

On a summer day there's nothing better than sitting and sipping among the greenery at one of Munich's beer gardens. In the Eng-lischer Garten is the classic **Chinesischer Turm** beer garden, although the nearby **Hir-schau** beer garden on the banks of Kleinhes-seloher See is less crowded. The **Augustiner Keller** (Arnulfstrasse 52), five minutes from the Hauptbahnhof, has a large and leafy beer garden. Its beer hall is a fine place when the weather keeps you indoors.

Pubs & Clubs Munich has no shortage of lively pubs and clubs. The *Young People's Guide* (see the earlier Information section) keeps abreast of the hot spots to party. **Klenze 17** (Klenzestrasse 17) has a great crowd and an extensive whisky selection, while in a cellar behind the Frauenkirche, **Killians Irish Pub** (Frauenplatz 11) is a cosy, casual drinking hole. If you can get past the goons at the door, **P1** (Prinzregentenstrasse 1) is a classy club with a high celebrity quotient. In northern Schwabing, **Skyline** (*Leopoldstrasse 82*) plays hip-hop on the top floor of the Hertie department store.

Performing Arts, Cinemas & Jazz Munich is one of the cultural capitals of Germany; the publications listed in the earlier Information section can guide you to the best events. The **Nationaltheater** (☎ 21 85 19 20; *Max-Joseph-Platz 2*) is the home of the Bavarian State Opera and the site of many cultural events (particularly during the opera festival in July). You can buy tickets at the box office or book by telephone.

You can catch films in English at **Cinema** (☎ 55 52 55; *Nymphenburger Strasse 31*).

Munich's hot jazz scene is led by **Jazzclub Unterfahrt** (☎ 448 27 94; *Kirchenstrasse 42-44*), near the Max-Weber-Platz U-Bahn station. It has live music every night from 7.30pm, and open jam sessions on Sunday night.

Gay & Lesbian Much of Munich's gay and lesbian nightlife is in the area just south of Sendlinger Tor, especially around Gärtnerplatz. *Our Munich* is a monthly guide to gay and lesbian life, and is available at **Our Munich Shop** (☎ 26 01 85 03, *Müllerstrasse 36*). Resembling a Paris bar, **Morizz** (*Klenzestrasse 43*) is a popular haunt for gay men, serving food and cocktails and cranking up later in the night. **Bei Carla** (*Buttermelcherstrasse 9*) is an exclusively lesbian bar-café with a friendly atmosphere and lots of regulars.

Shopping

Christkindlmarkt (*Marienplatz*) in December is large and well stocked but often expensive, so buy a warm drink and just wander around. A huge flea market, the **Auer Dult** (*Mariahilfplatz*), has great buys and takes place during the last weeks of April, July and October.

Getting There & Away

Air Munich is second in importance only to Frankfurt for international and national connections. Flights will take you to all major destinations worldwide. Main German cities are serviced by at least half a dozen flights daily.

Train Train services to/from Munich are excellent. There are rapid connections at least every two hours to all major cities in Germany, as well as frequent EC trains to other European cities such as Innsbruck (two hours), Vienna (five hours), Prague (six hours), Zürich (4¼ hours), Verona (5½ hours) and Paris (eight hours).

High-speed ICE services from Munich include Frankfurt (€75.60, 3½ hours), Hamburg (€127, six hours) and Berlin (€142.40, 6½ hours).

Bus Munich is linked to the Romantic Road by the Deutsche-Touring (also known as the Europabus) Munich-Frankfurt service (see Getting Around in the following Romantic Road section). Inquire at **Deutsche-Touring** (☎ 545 87 00, fax 54 58 70 21; e *service@deutsche-touring.com*), near platform 26 of the main train station, about its international services to destinations such as Prague and Budapest. Buses stop along the northern side of the train station.

Car & Motorcycle Munich has autobahns radiating outwards on all sides. Take the A9 to Nuremberg, the A92 to Passau, the A8 east to Salzburg, the A95 to Garmisch-Partenkirchen and the A8 west to Ulm or Stuttgart. The main rental companies have counters together on the second level of the main train station. For arranged rides, the **ADM-Mitfahrzentrale** (☎ 194 40; *Lämmerstrasse 6*) is near the main train station. Destinations and sample charges (including booking fees) include: Berlin €32, Frankfurt €25 and Hamburg €39.

Getting Around

To/From the Airport Munich's gleaming Flughafen Franz Josef Strauss is connected by the S8 and the S1 to Marienplatz and the main train station (€8). The service takes 40 minutes and runs every 20 minutes from 4am until around 12.30am.

The airport bus also runs at 20-minute intervals from Arnulfstrasse on the north side of the main train station (€9, 45 minutes) between 6.50am and 7.50pm. Forget taxis (at least €50!).

Public Transport Getting around is easy on Munich's excellent public transport network (MVV). The system is zone-based, and most places of interest to tourists (except Dachau and the airport) are within the 'blue' inner zone (*Innenraum*). MVV tickets are valid for the S-Bahn, U-Bahn, trams and buses, but must be validated before use. The U-Bahn

GERMANY

stops operating around 12.30am on weekdays and 1.30am on weekends, but there are some later buses and S-Bahns. Rail passes are valid only on the S-Bahn.

Kurzstrecke (short rides) cost €1 and are good for no more than four stops on buses and trams and two stops on the U and S-Bahns. Longer trips cost €2. It's cheaper to buy a strip-card of 10 tickets *(Mehrfahrtenkarte)* for €9 and stamp one strip per adult on short rides, two strips for longer rides in the inner zone. *Tageskarte* (day passes) for the inner zone cost €4.50, while three-day tickets cost €11, or €15 for two adults.

Taxi Taxis are expensive (€2.50 flag fall, plus €1.30 per kilometre) and not much more convenient than public transport. For a radio-dispatched taxi dial ☎ 216 10.

Car & Motorcycle It's not worth driving in the city centre – many streets are pedestrian only. The tourist office has a map that shows city parking places (€1.50 or more per hour).

Bicycle Pedal power is popular in relatively flat Munich. **Radius Bike Rental** (☎ 59 61 13) rents out two-wheelers from €14/43 per day/week.

AUGSBURG
☎ 0821 • pop 262,000

Originally established by the Romans, Augsburg later became a centre of Luther's Reformation and is now a lively provincial city crisscrossed by small streams. For some it will be a day trip from Munich, for others it's an ideal base (especially during Oktoberfest) or a gateway to the Romantic Road.

Augsburg's tourist offices are at Bahnhofstrasse 7 (☎ 502 07 22), open 9am to 6pm weekdays; and at Rathausplatz (☎ 502 07 35), open 9am to 6pm weekdays and 10am to 4pm Saturday (to 1pm Sunday). Both keep slightly shorter hours in winter.

Things to See & Do
The onion-shaped towers of the modest, 16th-century **St Maria Stern Kloster** in Elias-Holl-Platz started a fashion that spread throughout southern Germany. More impressive are those on the **Rathaus**, the adjacent **Perlachturm** and the soaring tower of **St Ulrich und Afra Basilika** (on Ulrichsplatz near the southern edge of the old town). **Dom Mariae Heimsuchung**, on

Hoher Weg north of Rathausplatz, is more conventionally styled. One of Luther's more colourful anti-papal documents was posted here after he was run out of town in 1518. Dramatist Bertolt Brecht's family home was on the stream and is now the **Bertolt-Brecht-Gedänkstätte** (☎ 324 27 79; *Am Rain 7, adult/concession €1.50/1; open 10am-4pm Wed-Sun*), a museum dedicated to Brecht and the work of young artists.

Places to Stay & Eat
Campingplatz Augusta (☎ 70 75 75, fax 70 58 83; e *info@campingplatz-augusta.de; Mülhaserstrasse 54b; tent/car/person €3/3/4*) is 7km northeast of the centre (bus No 23 to the terminus then a 2km walk). Augsburg's seedy **DJH Hostel** (☎ 339 09, fax 15 11 49; e *jugendherberge@kvaugsburg-stadt.bvk .de; Beim Pfaffenkeller 3; dorm beds from €12.30*), just east of St Mary's Cathedral, needs a serious spruce-up, but its beds are cheap.

Jakoberhof (☎ 51 00 30, fax 15 08 44; *Jakobstrasse 39-41; singles/doubles €25/ 32.50*) is a simple place with a good Bavarian restaurant downstairs. Modern **Dom Hotel** (☎ 34 39 03, fax 34 39 32 00; e *info@dom hotel-augsburg.de; Frauentorstrasse 8; singles/doubles €63/73 with breakfast*) has attractive rooms, a pool and a sauna.

Der Andechser (☎ 349 79 90; *Johannisgasse 4; mains €5-12*) is cosy, affordable and serves hearty German fare. Tucked in behind the Rathaus is **Die Ecke** (☎ 51 06 00; *Elias-Holl-Platz 2; mains €18-26*), one of Augsburg's best (and most expensive) restaurants.

Getting There & Away
Trains between Munich and Augsburg are frequent (€9, 40 minutes). Regular ICE/IC trains also serve Ulm (€12.40, 50 minutes), Stuttgart (€33.80, 1½ hours) and Nuremberg (€19.20, 1½ hours). Connections to/from Regensburg take two hours via Ingolstadt. The Deutsche-Touring Romantic Road bus stops at the train station.

ROMANTIC ROAD
Originally conceived as a way of promoting tourism in western Bavaria, the popular Romantic Road (Romantische Strasse) links a series of picturesque Bavarian towns and cities.

The road runs north-south through western Bavaria, from Würzburg to Füssen near the

Austrian border, passing through Rothenburg ob der Tauber, Dinkelsbühl and Augsburg. The main places for information about the Romantic Road are the tourist offices in Würzburg and Augsburg.

Locals get their cut of the Romantic Road hordes through, among other things, scores of good-value private accommodation offerings. Look for the 'Zimmer Frei' signs and expect to pay around €15 to €25 per person. Tourist offices are efficient at finding accommodation in almost any price range. DJH hostels listed in this section only accept people aged under 27.

Getting There & Away

In the north of the Romantic Road route, Würzburg is well-served by trains. To start at the southern end, take the hourly RE train from Munich to Füssen (€18.20, two hours). Rothenburg is linked by train to Würzburg, Nuremberg and Munich via Steinach. To reach Dinkelsbühl, take a train to Ansbach and from there a frequent bus onwards. Nördlingen has train connections to Stuttgart and Munich.

There are four daily buses between Füssen and Garmisch-Partenkirchen (€7; all stop at Hohenschwangau and Oberammergau), as well as several connections between Füssen and Oberstdorf (€8.10; via Pfronten). Deutsche-Touring runs a daily 'Castle Road' coach service in each direction between Mannheim and Rothenburg via Heidelberg (€29, 5½ hours).

Getting Around

It is possible to do this route using train connections, local buses or by car (just follow the brown 'Romantische Strasse' signs), but most train pass-holders prefer to take the Deutsche-Touring (also known as Europabus) bus. From April to October Deutsche-Touring runs one coach daily in each direction between Frankfurt and Munich (12 hours), and another in either direction between Dinkelsbühl and Füssen (4½ hours). The bus makes short stops in some towns, but it's both silly and mind-numbing to do the whole trip in one go, since you can break the journey at any point and continue the next day (reserve a seat for the next day as you disembark).

The full fare from Frankfurt to Füssen is €74 (change buses at Rothenburg). Eurail and German Rail passes are valid and Inter-Rail pass-holders receive a 50% discount, as do those over 60, while those under 26 save 10%.

Tickets are available for short segments and reservations are only necessary on summer weekends. Bike transport is €6 for up to 12 stops. For detailed information and reservations, you should contact **Deutsche-Touring GmbH** (☎ 069-79 03 50, fax 790 32 19; e service@deutsche-touring.com; Am Römerhof 17, 60486 Frankfurt/Main).

With its gentle gradients and ever-changing scenery, the Romantic Road makes a good bike trip. **Radl-Tours** (☎ 09341-53 95) offers nine-day cycling packages from Würzburg to Dinkelsbühl from €398.

Rothenburg ob der Tauber
☎ 09861 • pop 12,000

Visit Rothenburg and it's soon obvious why this charmingly preserved medieval town is continually under siege from tourists. Granted 'free imperial city' status in 1274, it's an enchanting place of twisting cobbled lanes and strikingly pretty architecture enclosed by towered stone walls. The town's museums only open in the afternoon from November to March. There's a **tourist office** (☎ 404 92; e info@rothenburg.de; Markt 1; open 9am-6pm, with a 1hr break at noon Mon-Fri, 10am-3pm Sat May-Oct & 9am-5pm Mon-Fri, 10am-1pm Sat Nov-Apr).

Things to See The **Rathaus on Markt** was commenced in Gothic style in the 14th century but completed in Renaissance style. The **tower** (€1) gives a majestic view over the town and the Tauber Valley. According to legend, the town was saved during the Thirty Years' War when the mayor won a challenge by the Imperial general Tilly and downed more than 3L of wine at a gulp. The **Meistertrunk** scene is re-enacted by the clock figures on the tourist office building (eight times daily in summer).

The **Puppen and Spielzeugmuseum** (Doll and Toy Museum; ☎ 73 30; Hofbronnengasse 13; adult/concession €4/2.50; open 9.30am-6pm Mar-Dec, 11am-5pm Jan & Feb) is the largest private doll and toy collection in Germany. The **Reichsstadt Museum** (☎ 93 90 43; Klosterhof 5; adult/concession €3/1.50; open 10am-5pm Apr-Oct, 1pm-4pm Nov-Mar), in the former convent, features the superb Rothenburger Passion in 12 panels (by Martinus Schwarz, 1494) and the Judaica room, with a collection of gravestones with Hebrew inscriptions. Get a gruesome glimpse of the past at the **Krimminalmuseum** (☎ 53 59; Burggasse

3-5; adult/concession €3.20/1.70; open 10am-5pm Apr-Oct, 1pm-4pm Nov-Mar), which houses all manner of devices with which to torture and shame medieval miscreants.

Places to Stay & Eat Camping options are 1km to 2km or two north of the town walls at Detwang, west of the road on the river. There are signs to **Tauber-Romantik** (☎ 61 91, fax 868 99; Detwang 39; tent/person €4/3.75), open from Easter to late October. Rothenburg's jammed **Youth Hostel** (☎ 941 60, fax 94 16 20; e jhrothenburg@djh.bayern.de; Mülacker 1; dorm beds €15.10) is housed in two enormous renovated old buildings in the south of the old town.

Das Lädle (☎/fax 61 30; e das-laedle-pension-hess@t-online.de; Spitalgasse 18; singles/doubles €22/40 with breakfast) is a good budget option, with casual, comfortable rooms in a central location.

There are bright, spotless lodgings at **Gasthof Butz** (☎ 22 01; e gasthofbutz@rothenburg.com; Kapellenplatz 4; singles/doubles €37/73). **Reichs Küchenmeister** (☎ 97 00, fax 869 65; e hotel@reichskuechenmeister.com; Kirchplatz 8-10; singles/doubles from €57/67) is a quality top-end choice, with a popular restaurant downstairs (mains €8 to €21).

Vine-covered and impossibly cosy, **Altfrankische Weinstube** (☎ 64 04; Klosterhof 7; mains €6-13) is justifiably popular, with a varied and well-priced menu and fantastic atmosphere.

Resist the temptation to try a *Schneeball*, a crumbly ball of bland dough with the taste and consistency of chalk – surely one of Europe's worst 'local specialities'.

Dinkelsbühl
☎ 09581 • pop 11,500

South of Rothenburg, Dinkelsbühl is another walled town of cobbled streets. It celebrates the **Kinderzeche** (Children's Festival) in mid-July, commemorating a legend from the Thirty Years' War that the town's children successfully begged the invading Swedish troops to leave Dinkelsbühl unharmed. The hour-long walk around the town's **walls** and its almost 30 **towers** is the scenic highlight. There's a **tourist office** (☎ 902 40; e touristik.service@dinkelsbuehl.de; Marktplatz 1; open 9am-6pm Mon-Fri, 10am-4pm Sat, 10am-1pm Sun; closed 1pm-2pm Sat).

DCC-Campingplatz Romantische Strasse (☎ 78 17, fax 78 48; Kobeltsmühle 2; tent person €6/4) is open all year. Dinkelsbühl' **Youth Hostel** (☎ 95 09, fax 48 74; e bayheimer@t-online.de; Koppengasse 10; dorm beds €11.20) is super cheap. The **Fränkische Hof** (☎ 579 00, fax 57 90 99; Nördlinge Strasse 10; singles/doubles from €34/57) i a good budget option. The ornate facade o **Deutsches Haus** (☎ 60 59, fax 98 51 79 11 Weinmarkt 3; singles/doubles from €75. 115) is one of the town's attractions. The hote features a cosy restaurant serving Franconiar dishes for around €12.

Nördlingen
☎ 09081 • pop 20,000

Nördlingen is encircled by its original 14th-century walls and lies within the basin of the **Ries**, a huge crater created by a meteor more than 15 million years ago. The crater is one of the largest in existence (25km in diameter, and the **Rieskrater Museum** (☎ 273 82 20 Eugene-Shoemaker-Platz 1; adult/concession €3/1.50; open 10am-noon & 1.30pm-4.30pm Tues-Sun) gives details. For a bird's-eye view of the town, climb the tower of **St Georg Kirche**. You'll find the **tourist office** (☎ 43 80; e verkersamt@noerdlingen.de, Marktplatz 2) very helpful. The **Youth Hostel** (☎/fax 27 18 16; Kaiserwiese 1; dorm beds €11.25) is a signposted 10-minute walk from the centre. **Altreuter Garni** (☎ 43 19, fax 97 97; Markt 11; singles/doubles with bath & toilet €38/52) has simple, pleasant rooms.

Füssen
☎ 08362 • pop 14,000

Just short of the Austrian border, Füssen has a monastery, a castle and splendid baroque architecture, but it is primarily visited for the two castles in nearby Schwangau associated with King Ludwig II. There's a **tourist office** (☎ 938 50; e tourismus@fuessen.de; Kaiser-Maximillian-Platz 1; open 8.30am-6pm Mon-Fri, 10am-noon Sat).

Neuschwanstein & Hohenschwangau Castles
The castles provide a fascinating glimpse into the king's state of mind (or lack thereof). Hohenschwangau (☎ 811 27; adult/concession €7/6, combination €13/11; open 9am-6pm daily, 9am-8pm Thur Apr-Oct, 10am-4pm daily Oct-Apr) is where Ludwig lived as a child, but more interesting

s the adjacent Neuschwanstein (☎ 810 35; same hours & prices as Hohenschwangau), his own creation (albeit with the help of a theatrical designer). Although it was unfinished when he died in 1886, there is plenty of evidence of Ludwig's twin obsessions: swans and Wagnerian operas. The sugary pastiche of architectural styles reputedly inspired Disney's Fantasyland castle. There's a great view of Neuschwanstein from the Marienbrücke (bridge) over a waterfall and gorge just above the castle. From here you can hike the Tegelberg for even better vistas.

Take the bus from Füssen train station (€2.80 return), share a taxi (☎ 77 00; €8.50) or walk the 5km. The only way to enter the castles is with a 35-minute guided tour, which can be purchased from the ticket centre at Alpseestrasse 12, near Hohenschwangau. Go early to avoid the massive crowds.

Places to Stay & Eat The **Youth Hostel** (☎ 77 54, fax 27 70; e jhfuessen@djh-bayern .de; Mariahilferstrasse 5; dorm beds €13.30) is a signposted 10-minute walk from the train station.

A pavillion near the tourist office has a computerised list of vacant rooms in town; the cheapest are private rooms at around €12 per person. **Hotel Filser** (☎ 912 50, fax 915 73; Saulingerstrasse 3; singles/doubles €49/86) is a quiet, comfortable place with clean rooms, a good restaurant downstairs (mains €7 to €15) and a health spa in the basement. Central **Sonne Café** (Reichenstrasse 37; dishes €3-15) has great baguettes, salads and schnitzels. There are light bites at the cosy **Downtown Bistro-Café** (Hinteregasse 29; dishes €3-5).

WÜRZBURG
☎ 0931 • pop 130,000

Surrounded by forests and vineyards, the charming city of Würzburg straddles the upper Main River. Rebuilt after bombings late in the war, Würzburg is a centre of art, beautiful architecture and delicate wines.

The **tourist office** (☎ 37 23 98; e tourismus@wuerzburg.de; Oberer Markt), in the rococo masterpiece Haus zum Falken, is open 10am to 6pm weekdays and to 2pm weekends (closed Sunday November to April). In the same building, the **Stadtbücherei** (☎ 37 34 38) provides 10 minutes of Internet access for €0.50.

Things to See & Do

The magnificent, sprawling **Residenz** (☎ 35 51 70; Balthasar-Neumann-Promenade; adult/concession €4/3; open 9am-6pm daily, 9am-8pm Thur Apr-Oct, 10am-4pm Oct-Mar), a baroque masterpiece by Neumann, took a generation to build and is well worth the admission. The open **Hofgarten** at the back is a favourite spot. The **Dom St Kilian** interior and the adjacent **Neumünster** in the old town continue the baroque themes of the Residenz.

Neumann's fortified **Alter Kranen** (old crane), which serviced a dock on the riverbank south of Friedensbrücke, is now the **Haus des Frankenweins** (☎ 390 11 11; Kranenkai 1), where you can taste Franconian wines (for around €3 per glass).

The fortress **Marienberg**, across the river on the hill, is reached by crossing the 15th-century stone **Alte Mainbrücke** (bridge) from the city and walking up Tellstiege, a small alley. It encloses the **Fürstenbau Museum** (☎ 438 38; adult/concession €3/1.50; open 9am-6pm Tues-Sun Apr-Oct, 10am-4pm Tues-Sun Oct-Mar) featuring the episcopal apartments, and the regional **Mainfränkisches Museum** (☎ 430 16; adult/concession €3/1.50; open 10am-6pm Tues-Sun Apr-Sept, 10am-4pm Tues-Sun Oct-Mar). See both on a combined card (€4). For a dizzy thrill, look down the well in the courtyard. For a simple thrill, wander the walls enjoying the panoramic views.

Places to Stay & Eat

Kanu-Club (☎ 725 36; Mergentheimer Strasse 13b; tent/person €3.50 each) is a camping ground on the west bank of the Main; take tram No 3 or 5 to Jugendbühlweg. **Jugendgästehaus Würzburg** (☎ 425 90, fax 41 68 62; e jhwuerzburg@djh-bayern.de; Burkarderstrasse 44; dorm beds €17.70) is below the fortress (tram No 3 or 5 from the train station).

Simple and friendly **Pension Spehnkuch** (☎ 547 52, fax 547 60; e spehnkuch@web.de; Röntgenring 7; singles/doubles/triples from €29/52/75) has spotless rooms and welcoming hosts. **Hotel Alter Kranen** (☎ 351 80, fax 500 10; e mail@hotel-alter-kranen.de; Kärrnergasse 11; singles/doubles €60/80) offers lovely lodgings overlooking the river and fort. Breakfast is included. For a treat, try **Schloss Steinburg** (☎ 970 20, fax 971 21; e hotel@steinburg.com; Auf dem

GERMANY

Steinburg; singles/doubles from €80/120) in a gorgeous castle with majestic town views.

Just south of the Friedensbrücke, **Pane e Vino** *(Dreikronenstrasse 2; dishes €6-15)* is a sunny lunch spot with views of vine-covered hills. It serves up fresh pastas for around €8. Insanely popular **Bürgerspital** *(☎ 35 28 80; Theaterstrasse 19; mains €5-18)* is in a labyrinthine former medieval hospice; the atmosphere, food and the local wines are all first class.

Getting There & Away

Würzburg is two hours by frequent RE trains from Frankfurt (€19.20) and one hour from Nuremberg (€14.40). It's a major stop-off for the ICE trains on the Hamburg-Munich line. It is also on the Deutsche-Touring Romantic Road bus route (2½ hours to/from Rothenburg by bus). The main bus station is next to the train station off Röntgenring.

BAMBERG
☎ 0951 • pop 70,000

Tucked away from the main routes in northern Bavaria, Bamberg is practically a byword for magnificence – an untouched monument to the Holy Roman Emperor Heinrich II (who conceived it), to its prince-bishops and clergy and to its patriciate and townsfolk. It is a fun and beautiful town recognised by Unesco as a World Heritage Site.

The **tourist office** *(☎ 87 11 61; e info@ bamberg.de; Geyerswörthstrasse 3)* is situated on an island in the Regnitz River. It's open 9am to 6pm weekdays and 9am to 3pm Saturday (plus 10am to 2pm Sunday from May to October).

Things to See & Do

Bamberg's main appeal is its fine buildings; their sheer number, their jumble of styles and the ambience this helps create. Most attractions are spread either side of the Regnitz River, but the colourful **Altes Rathaus** is actually in it, precariously perched on its own islet. The princely and ecclesiastical district is centred on Domplatz, where the Romanesque and Gothic **cathedral**, housing the statue of the chivalric king-knight, the *Bamberger Reiter*, is the biggest attraction. Above Domplatz is the former Benedictine monastery of St Michael, at the top of Michaelsberg. The **Kirche St Michael** is a must-see for its baroque art and the herbal compendium painted on its ceiling.

The garden terraces afford another marvellou[s] overview of the city's splendour. There is als[o] the **Fränkisches Brauereimuseum** *(☎ 530 16 Michaelsberg 10f; adult/concession €2/1.5(; open 1pm-5pm Wed-Sun Apr-Oct)*, whic[h] shows how the monks brewed their robu[st] *Benediktiner Dunkel* beer.

Places to Stay & Eat

You can camp at **Campingplatz Insel** *(☎ 56[3] 20, fax 563 21; e campinginsel@web.de; Ar[?] Campingplatz 1; tent/person €6/3.50)*. **Jugendherberge Wolfsschlucht** *(☎ 560 02[?] fax 552 11; e jh-bamberg@stadt.bamber[g] .de; Oberer Leinritt 70; dorm beds €14.60)* i[s] on the river's west bank, and is closed from mid-December to mid-January; take bus N° 18 to Rodelbahn, walk northeast to the river bank, then turn left.

Gasthof Fässla *(☎ 265 16, fax 20 19 8[9] e kaspar_schultz@t-online.de; Hallstadte[r] Strasse 174; singles/doubles €34/52)* offers [a] drinker's dream – a bed in a brewery. Th[e] rooms are large, clean and comfy. The quiet **Barock Hotel** *(☎ 540 31, fax 540 21; Vordere[r] Bach 4; singles/doubles with bathroom from €57/80)*, near the Dom, offers lovely room[s] in a quiet spot. **Wirsthaus zum Schlenkerl[a]** *(Dominikanerstrasse 6; mains €7-12)* ha[s] been brewing its extraordinary *Rauchbie[r]* since 1678. The dark-red concoction with [a] smoky flavour accompanies a menu of Fran[-] conian specialities. Nearby, the **Fränkische[s] Gästhaus** *(Obere Sandstrasse 1; mains €5-15)* serves hearty mains and excellent Brat[-] wurst on outdoor tables.

Getting There & Away

There are hourly RE and RB trains to/from both Würzburg (€14) and Nuremberg (€9) taking one hour. Bamberg is also served by ICE trains running between Munich (€45.20 2½ hours) and Berlin (€68.80, 4½ hours) every two hours.

NUREMBERG
☎ 0911 • pop 500,000

Nuremberg (Nürnberg) is the largest city o[f] the Franconia region of northern Bavaria. Though the flood of tourists to this historica[l] town never seems to cease – especially during its world-famous Christmas market – it's still worth the trip. Nuremberg played a major role during the Nazi years and during the war crimes trials afterwards. The city was rebuilt

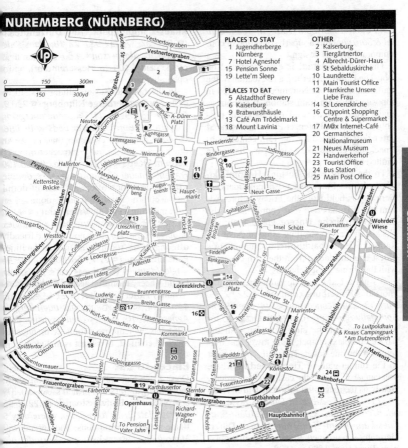

NUREMBERG (NÜRNBERG)

PLACES TO STAY
1 Jugendherberge Nürnberg
7 Hotel Agneshof
15 Pension Sonne
19 Lette'm Sleep

PLACES TO EAT
5 Alstadthof Brewery
6 Kaiserburg
9 Bratwursthäusle
13 Café Am Trödelmarkt
18 Mount Lavinia

OTHER
2 Kaiserburg
3 Tiergärtnertor
4 Albrecht-Dürer-Haus
8 St Sebalduskirche
10 Laundrette
11 Main Tourist Office
12 Pfarrkirche Unsere Liebe Frau
14 St Lorenzkirche
16 Citypoint Shopping Centre & Supermarket
17 M@x Internet-Café
20 Germanisches Nationalmuseum
21 Neues Museum
22 Handwerkerhof
23 Tourist Office
24 Bus Station
25 Main Post Office

after Allied bombs reduced it to rubble on 2 January 1945.

Orientation & Information

The main train station is just outside the city walls of the old town. The main artery, the mostly pedestrian Königstrasse, takes you through the old town and its major squares. The main **tourist office** (☎ 233 61 32; e tourismus@nuernberg.de; Königstrasse 93; open 9am-7pm Mon-Sat) is near the train station. A smaller **branch** (☎ 233 61 35; Hauptmarkt 18; open 9am-6pm Mon-Sat, 10am-4pm Sun May-Sept) operates on the city's main square. Both offices sell the two-day Kultour Ticket (€14.50), available to visitors staying one night. It provides free public transport, and entry to most museums and attractions.

The main **post office** (Bahnhofplatz 1) is by the station and a **Reisebank** operates inside the station. There's a central **laundrette** (Fünferplatz 2). **M@x Internet-Cafe** (☎ 23 23 84; Färberstrasse 11) offers one hour of surfing for €2.50.

Things to See & Do

The spectacular **Germanisches Nationalmuseum** (☎ 133 10; Kartäusergasse 1; adult/concession €4/3, free 6pm-9pm Wed; open 10am-5pm Tues-Sun, 10am-9pm Wed) is the most important general museum of German culture. It displays works by German painters and sculptors, an archaeological collection, arms and armour, musical and scientific instruments and toys. Close by, the sleek and harmonious **Neues Museum** (☎ 24 02 00;

Luitpoldstrasse 5; adult/concession €3.50/
2.50; open 10am-8pm Tues-Fri, 10am-6pm
Sat & Sun) contains a superb collection of contemporary art and design.

The scenic **Altstadt** is easily covered on
foot. The **Handwerkerhof**, a re-creation of the
crafts quarter of old Nuremberg, is walled in
opposite the main train station. It's about as
quaint (read 'over-priced') as they can possibly make it. On Lorenzer Platz there's the **St
Lorenzkirche**, noted for the 15th-century tab-
ernacle that climbs like a vine up a pillar to the
vaulted ceiling.

To the north is the bustling **Hauptmarkt**,
where the most famous Christkindlesmarkt in
Germany is held from the Friday before Advent to Christmas Eve. The church here is the
ornate **Pfarrkirche Unsere Liebe Frau**; the
clock's figures go strolling at noon. Near the
Rathaus is **St Sebalduskirche**, Nuremberg's
oldest church (dating from the 13th century),
with the shrine of St Sebaldus.

It's not a bad climb up Burgstrasse to the
enormous **Kaiserburg complex** (☎ 22 57 26;
Burg 13; adult/concession €5/4; open 9am-
6pm daily Apr-Sept, 10am-4pm Oct-Mar) for
a good view of the city. You can visit the
palace complex, chapel, well, tower and museum on the one ticket. The walls spread west
to the tunnel-gate of **Tiergärtnertor**, where
you can stroll behind the castle to the gardens.
Nearby is the renovated **Albrecht-Dürer-Haus**
(☎ 231 25 68; Albrecht-Dürer-Strasse 39;
adult/concession €4/2; open 10am-5pm
Tues-Sun, 10am-8pm Thur), where Dürer,
Germany's renowned Renaissance draughtsman, lived from 1509 to 1528.

Nuremberg's role during the Third Reich is
well known. The Nazis chose this city as their
propaganda centre and for mass rallies, which
were held at **Luitpoldhain**, a (never completed) sports complex of megalomaniac proportions. After the war, the Allies deliberately
chose Nuremberg as the site for the trials of
Nazi war criminals. A new museum called
Dokumentationzentrum (☎ 231 56 66; Bay-
ernstrasse 110; adult/concession €5/2.50;
open 9am-6pm Mon-Fri, 10am-6pm Sat &
Sun) opened in 2002 in the north wing of the
massive Congress Hall. The upper level
houses a permanent exhibition, Fascination
and Terror, dealing with the causes, relationships and consequences of the Nazi regime,
and its links with Nuremberg. Take tram No 9
to Luitpoldhain.

Places to Stay
Knaus-Campingpark 'Am Dutzendteich
(☎ 981 27 17, fax 981 27 18; Hans-Kalb
Strasse 56; site/person €4.50/5) is southeas
of the centre (U1 to Messezentrum), and i
open all year.

In the historic Kaiserstallung next to th
castle, **Jugendherberge Nürnberg** (☎ 230 9
60, fax 23 09 36 11; e jhnuernberg@dj
-bayern.de; Burg 2; dorm beds with line
€17.70) has more character than most. An
other good and central backpacker option i
Lette'm Sleep (☎ 99 28 128, fax 99 28 13C
Frauentormauer 42; dorm beds €13, double
from €22), which offers a choice of dormi
tory accommodation or double rooms.

Family-run **Pension Vater Jahn** (☎ 44 4:
07, fax 43 15 236; Jahnstrasse 13; singles
doubles from €25/39) is no-frills and friendly
offering clean rooms with shared facilities
Pension Sonne (☎ 22 71 66; Königstrasse 45
singles/doubles with breakfast €30/50) ha
bright, cheery rooms up a steep flight of stairs

Sunny **Hotel Agneshof** (☎ 21 44 40, fax 2
44 41 44; e info@agneshof-nuernberg.de
Agnesgasse 10; singles/doubles from €90,
105) has welcoming rooms with an extr
touch of comfort. Breakfast is included.

Places to Eat
Don't leave Nuremberg without trying its fa
mous Bratwurstl (small grilled sausages). The
best place is the **Bratwursthäusle** (☎ 22 76 95
Rathausplatz 2; 10 for €8.30), where they'r
flame-grilled, scrumptious, and served wit
Meerettich (horseradish) and Kartoffelsala
(potato salad).

Kaiserburg (☎ 22 12 16; Obere Krämers-
gasse 20; mains €8-17) is steeped in medieva
ambience and has a Franconian/internationa
menu.

Nearby, there's the sprawling **Alstadtho**
(☎ 22 43 27; Bergstrasse 19; light meals €6-
9), a brewery, café, theatre and bar all throwr
together.

On an island in the Pegnitz River, **Café Am
Trödelmarkt** (☎ 20 88 77; Trödelmarkt 42,
salads & light snacks €5-10) is in a plum position, with views of the water, the ducks, the
houses and the three bridges. **Mount Lavinia**
(☎ 22 70 09; Jakobsplatz 22; mains €12-16,
is a superb little Ceylon-Thai restaurant decorated with grass matting and stencilled cloth.
It serves up delicious spicy concoctions to
make you sweat.

Getting There & Around

IC trains run hourly to/from Frankfurt (€37.20, 2¼ hours) and Munich (€38, 1½ hours). IR trains run every two hours to Stuttgart (€28, two hours) and ICE trains every two hours to Berlin Ostbahhof (€78.20, five hours). Several daily EC trains travel to Vienna (seven hours) and Prague (5½ hours). Buses to regional destinations leave from the station just east of the main train station.

Tickets on the bus, tram and U-Bahn system cost €1.35/1.75 for each short/long ride in the central zone. A day pass is €3.50.

REGENSBURG

☎ 0941 • pop 143,000

On the Danube River, Regensburg has relics of all periods, yet lacks the packaged feel of some other German cities. It escaped the carpet bombing, and here, as nowhere else in Germany, you enter the misty ages between the Roman and the Carolingian.

From the main train station, you walk up Maximillianstrasse for 10 minutes to reach the centre. There's a **tourist office** (☎ 507 44 10; e tourismus@info.regensburg.baynet.de; open 8.30am-6pm Mon-Fri, 9am-4pm Sat, 9.30am-4pm Sun) in the Altes Rathaus. **Surf City** (Speichergasse 1) charges €3 for 30 minutes on the Internet.

Things to See

Dominating the skyline are the twin spires of the Gothic **Dom St Peter** (☎ 597 10 02; Domplatz; admission free; tours in German adult/concession €2.50/1.50; tours 10am, 11am, 2pm Mon-Fri, noon, 2pm Sun May-Nov, 11am Mon-Fri, noon Sun low season) built during the 14th and 15th centuries from unusual green limestone. It has striking original stained-glass windows above the choir on the eastern side. The **Altes Rathaus** was progressively extended from medieval to baroque times and remained the seat of the Reichstag for almost 150 years. Guided tours in English (€2.50; 3pm Mon-Sat May-Sept) are available through the tourist office. The **Roman wall**, with its **Porta Praetoria** arch, follows Unter den Schwibbögen onto Dr-Martin-Luther-Strasse.

Lavish **Schloss Thurn und Taxis** (☎ 504 81 33; Emmeramsplatz 6; adult/concession for all three €10/8.50; open 11am-5pm Mon-Fri, 10am-5pm Sat & Sun Apr-Oct, 10am-5pm Sat & Sun Nov-Mar) is near the train station and is divided into three separate sections: the castle proper (Schloss), the monastery (Kreuzgang) and the royal stables (Marstall). Nearby is **St Emmeram Basilika** (Emmeramplatz 3; admission free), a baroque masterpiece containing untouched Carolingian and episcopal graves and relics.

Places to Stay & Eat

Campers can head to **Azur-Camping** (☎ 27 00 25, fax 29 94 32; Weinweg 40; site/person €5.50/4.50). Bus No 6 from the train station goes to the entrance.

The **Youth Hostel** (☎ 574 02, fax 524 11; e jhregensburg@djh-bayern.de; Wöhrdstrasse 60; dorm beds €16.60) can be reached on bus No 3 to the Eisstadion stop.

Central **Hotel Am Peterstor** (☎ 545 45, fax 545 42; Fröliche-Türken-Strasse 12; singles/doubles €40/50) is good value, with clean, basic rooms. The attractive **Bischofshof Hotel** (☎ 584 60, fax 584 61 46; e info@hotel-bischofshof.de; Krauterermarkt 3; singles/doubles from €67/119) has pleasant rooms, some overlooking a pretty courtyard. On warm nights and sunny days, the courtyard accommodates the hotel's quality restaurant.

Wok House (☎ 56 73 34; Obermünsterplatz 2; mains €6-8) is an above-average Asian place, while by far the best spot for a snack of Bratwurstl in bread is the **Historische Wurstküche** (Thundorferstrasse; €6), on the banks of the roaring Danube.

Getting There & Away

Regensburg is on the train line between Nuremberg (€19, one hour) and Austria and there are EC/IC trains in both directions every two hours, as well as RB/RE trains to Munich (€19.20, 1½ hours). EC/IC services run every two hours to Passau (€20.20, one hour). Regensburg is a major stop on the Danube bike route.

PASSAU

☎ 0851 • pop 51,000

As it exits Germany for Austria, the Danube River flows through the lovely baroque town of Passau, where it is joined by the Inn and Ilz Rivers. Passau is not only at a confluence of inland waterways, but also forms the hub of long-distance cycling routes.

The main **tourist office** (☎ 95 59 80; e tourist-info@passau.de; Rathausplatz 3; open 8.30am-6pm Mon-Fri, 9.30am-3pm Sat

GERMANY

& Sun Easter–mid-Oct, 8.30am-5pm Mon-Thur, 8.30am-4pm Fri mid-Oct–Easter) is in the Altstadt. The **regional tourist centre** (same contact details; Bahnhofstrasse 36), virtually opposite the train station, is useful for information about bicycle and boat travel along the Danube.

Things to See & Do

You'll notice that the Italian-baroque essence has not doused the medieval feel as you wander through the narrow lanes, tunnels and archways of the old town and monastic district to Ortspitze, where the rivers meet. The 13th-century **Veste Oberhaus** (☎ 49 33 50; Oberhaus 125; adult/concession €4/2.50; open 9am-5pm Mon-Fri, 10am-6pm Sat & Sun, closed Nov-Mar) has a museum and views over the city from the castle tower. Imposing cathedral **Dom St Stephan** (Domplatz; concerts adult/concession €3/1, evening €5/3), built between 1680 and 1890, houses the world's largest church organ (17,774 pipes). From May to October there are acoustically stunning daily half-hour concerts at noon and at 7.30pm Thursday. The glockenspiel in the colourful **Rathaus** chimes several times daily and wall markings show historical flood levels.

Places to Stay & Eat

There's camping at **Zeltplatz Ilzstadt** (☎ 414 57; Halser Strasse 34; person €5), over the Ilz River bridge on bus No 1, 2, 3 or 4. Passau's **Youth Hostel** (☎ 49 37 80, fax 49 37 820; e jhpassau@djh-bayern.de; Veste Oberhaus 125; dorm beds juniors only €14.10) is situated in the castle across the Danube. Take bus No 1, 2 or 4.

In the shape of a supine sleeper, modern **Rotel Inn** (☎ 951 60, fax 95 16 100; e info@rotel.de; singles/doubles €25/30) is on the river near the train station. **Pension Rössner** (☎ 931 350, fax 931 3595; e info@pension-roessner.de; Braugasse 19; singles with bathroom from €35/50) is ideally situated in the Altstadt. It has basic, clean rooms. Nestled beneath the castle, **Hotel Schloss Ort** (☎ 340 72, fax 318 17; e info@schlosshotel-passau.de; Im Ort 11; singles/doubles from €49/78) has lovely timber-floored rooms with four-poster beds. Its downstairs restaurant has a cosy open fire and a shiny suit of armour.

For cheap eats, there's a large **marketplace** (Ludwigstrasse 16), complete with fruit stalls, meat and fish stands. **Zum König** (☎ 93 10 60;

Rindermarkt 2; mains €8-13) is a cosy spot with a varied international menu, including some Balkan specialities.

Getting There & Away

RE and RB trains run direct to/from Munich (€27, two hours), Regensburg (€16.60, one hour) and EC trains to Nuremberg (€34.40, two hours). EC trains also serve Austria, including Linz (2¼ hours) and Vienna (three hours). From May through October **Wurm + Köck** (☎ 92 92 92; Höllgasse 26), sails down the Danube to Linz (€21, five hours) twice daily.

BAVARIAN ALPS

While not quite as high as their sister summits farther south in Austria, the Bavarian Alps (Bayerische Alpen) rise so abruptly from the rolling hills of southern Bavaria that their appearance seems all the more dramatic. Stretching westward from Germany's southeastern corner to the Allgäu region near Lake Constance, the Alps take in most of the mountainous country fringing the southern border with Austria.

Activities

The Bavarian Alps are extraordinarily well organised for outdoor pursuits, with skiing, snowboarding and hiking being the most popular. The ski season usually runs from mid-December to April. Ski gear is available for hire in all the resorts, with the lowest daily/weekly rates including skis, boots and stocks at around €12/48 (downhill), €7/32 (cross-country) and €16/57 (snowboard). Five-day skiing courses start at around €100.

During the warmer months, the activities include hiking, canoeing, rafting, biking and paragliding.

Accommodation

Most of the resorts have plenty of reasonably priced guesthouses and private rooms, though it's still a good idea to reserve accommodation. Tourist offices can help you find a room; otherwise look out for 'Zimmer Frei' signs. In most resorts a local tax (or Kurtaxe, usually an extra €1.80 per night) is levied, although this usually gives free local transport and other deals. Be warned that rates can be higher in July and August, and that hotel and pension owners may not be keen to let rooms for short stays.

Getting Around

While the public transport network is very good, the mountain geography means there are few direct routes between main centres; sometimes a short cut via Austria is quicker (such as between Füssen and Oberstdorf). Road rather than rail routes are often more practical. For those driving, the German Alpine Road (Deutsche Alpenstrasse) is a scenic way to go, though obviously much slower than the autobahns and highways that fan out across southern Bavaria.

Regional RVO bus passes giving free travel on the network between Füssen, Garmisch and Mittenwald are excellent value (☎ 089-55 16 40); the day pass is €7 and a pass for five days' travel within one month costs €22.50.

Berchtesgaden
☎ 08652 • pop 8200

Berchtesgaden is perhaps the most romantically scenic place in the Bavarian Alps. To reach the centre from the train station, cross the footbridge and walk uphill up Bahnhofstrasse. The helpful tourist office (☎ 96 70; e info@berchtesgaden.de; Königsseer Strasse 2) is just across the river from the train station at Königsseer Strasse 2. It's open 8am to 6pm weekdays and 8am to 5pm Saturday (plus 9am to 3pm Sunday from mid-June to September). Outside these months, it's open 8am to 5pm weekdays and 9am to noon Saturday.

Things to See & Do A tour of the Salzbergwerk (☎ 600 20; Bergwerkstrasse 83; adult/concession €12/6.50; open 9am-5pm May–mid-Oct; 12.30pm-3.30pm Mon-Sat mid-Oct–Apr) combines history with a carnival (rides and games to amuse you). Visitors descend into the salt mine for a 1½-hour tour.

Nearby Obersalzberg is a deceptively innocent-looking place with a creepy legacy as the second seat of government for the Third Reich. Hitler, Himmler, Goebbels and the rest of the Nazi hierarchy all maintained homes here. The Dokumentation Obersalzberg museum (☎ 94 79 60; Salzbergstrasse 41; adult/concession €2.50/1.50; open 9am-5pm Tues-Sun May-Nov, 10am-3pm Tues-Sun Nov-May) documents the evil bunch's time in the area (don't miss the photo of the fun-loving Führer relaxing in Lederhosen), as well as the horrors their policies produced, through photos, audio and film. Ask for the free brochure in English (the explanatory captions and audio are in German). The admission fee also gets you into the eerie Hitler's bunker. Catch bus No 9538 (€3.70 return) from the Nazi-constructed Berchtesgaden train station to Obersalzberg-Hintereck. Take the first major street on the right after alighting from the bus and follow it for five minutes.

Kehlstein (☎ 29 69; admission €12; buses run 7.40am-4.25pm; open May-Oct) is a spectacular meeting house built for, but seldom used by, Hitler. Despite its reputation as the 'Eagle's Nest', it's a popular destination. The views are stunning and the history is bracing. Entry includes transport on special buses which link the summit with Hintereck/Obersalzberg as well as the 120m lift through solid rock to the peak. Alternatively you can make the steep ascent or descent on foot in two to three hours.

The best way to see Obersalzberg and Kehlstein is with Eagle's Nest Tours (☎ 649 71; €35), which has English-language tours lasting four hours and covering the entire history of the area during WWII.

You can forget the horrors of war at the Königssee, a beautiful alpine lake situated 5km south of Berchtesgaden (and linked by hourly buses in summer). There are frequent boat tours across the lake to the quaint chapel at St Bartholomä (€10.50), or all the way to Obersee (€13.50).

The wilds of Berchtesgaden National Park unquestionably offer some of the best hiking in Germany. A good introduction to the area is a 2km path up from St Bartholomä beside the Königssee to the Watzmann-Ostwand, a massive 2000m-high rock face where scores of ambitious mountaineers have died.

Berchtesgaden has five major skiing resorts, and you can buy five-day lift passes that cover them all (€98). Rossfeld is the cheapest for day passes (€13), while Götschen, with a permanent half-pipe, is the destination for snowboarders (€20 per day).

Places to Stay & Eat Of the five camping grounds in the Berchtesgaden area, the nicest are up at Königssee: Grafenlehen (☎ 41 40; site/person €5.11/4.35) and Mühleiten (☎ 45 84; site/person €5.11/4.35). The pleasant Youth Hostel (☎ 943 70, fax 94 37 37; e jhberchtesgaden@djh-bayern.de; Gebirgsjägerstrasse 52; dorm beds €13.10) is closed in November and December. Take bus No 9539 to Jugendherberge.

GERMANY

Lovely **Hotel Watzmann** (☎ 20 55, fax 51 74; Franziskanerplatz 2; singles/doubles from €28/50) is decorated in traditional upper-Bavarian style, and has comfortable rooms and an excellent outdoor terrace with top food (mains €9 to €11).

You'll get a warm welcome at **Hotel Floriani** (☎ 660 11, fax 634 53; Königsseer Strasse 37; singles/doubles from €33/56), which has cheerful, vista-flooded rooms. If you have an itch for schnitzel, head to **Alt Berchtesgaden** (☎ 45 19; Bahnhofstrasse 3; schnitzel €4.99), with 15 varieties to choose from.

Getting There & Away Both RB and RE trains run to Munich and cost €24.80.

Garmisch-Partenkirchen
☎ 08821 • pop 27,000

The combined towns of Garmisch and Partenkirchen were merged by Hitler for the 1936 Winter Olympics. Munich residents' favourite getaway spot, this often-snooty, year-round resort is also a big draw for skiers, snowboarders, hikers and mountaineers.

The huge **ski stadium** outside town hosted the Olympics. From the pedestrian Am Kurpark, walk up Klammstrasse, cross the tracks and veer left on the first path to reach the stadium and enjoy the spectacular views. The **tourist office** (☎ 18 07 00; e tourist-info@garmisch-partenkirchen.de; Richard Strauss Platz 2; open 8am-6pm Mon-Sat, 10am-noon Sun) is in the centre of town.

About 20km north of Garmisch is over-touristed **Oberammergau**. The town becomes a focus of world attention every 10 years when many of the local populace perform day-long Passion plays. The next series of performances, which date back to the 17th century, will be held in 2010.

An excellent short hike from Garmisch is to the **Partnachklamm gorge**, via a winding path above a stream and underneath the waterfalls. You take the Graseck cable car and follow the signs.

An excursion to the **Zugspitze** summit, Germany's highest peak (2963m), is the most popular outing from Garmisch. There are various ways up, including a return trip by rack-railway (just west of the main train station), summit cable car and Eibsee cable car for €42, or you can scale it in two days. For detailed information concerning guided hiking

or mountaineering courses, check with **Bergsteigerschule Zugspitze** (☎ 589 99; Am Gudiberg 7, Garmisch).

Garmisch is bounded by four separate ski areas – **Zugspitze plateau** (the highest) **Alpspitze/Hausberg** (the largest), **Eckbauer** (the cheapest) and **Wank** (the most evocative despite its name). Day ski passes range from €16 for Eckbauer to €33 for Zugspitze. The Happy Ski Card covers all four areas and is valid for a minimum of three days (€77). A web of cross-country ski trails runs along the main valleys.

Flori Wörndle (☎ 583 00) has ski-hire outlets at the Alpspitze and Hausbergbahn lifts. For detailed skiing information and instruction (downhill), contact the **Skischule Garmisch-Partenkirchen** (☎ 49 31; Am Hausberg 4), or (cross-country) the **Skilanglaufschule** (☎ 1516; Olympia-Skistadion).

Places to Stay & Eat The closest camping ground, **Zugspitze** (☎ 31 80, fax 94 75 94; Greisener Strasse 4, Grainau; tent/person/vehicle €3/5/3) is along highway B24. Take the blue-and-white bus (outside the train station and left across the street) towards Eibsee.

The **Youth Hostel** (☎ 29 80, fax 585 36, e jhgarmisch@djh-bayern.de; Jochstrasse 10; dorm beds €15.10), situated in the suburb of Burgrain, is closed from mid-November to Christmas. From the train station take bus No 3 or 4 to the Burgrain stop.

Sunny **Gästehaus Becherer** (☎ 547 57, fax 73 07 17; Hollentalstrasse 4; singles/doubles with bathroom & breakfast €29/46) offers a warm welcome and spotless comfort. Near the train station, **Hotel Schell** (☎ 95 750, fax 95 7540; e hotel-schell@hotel-schell.de; Partnachauenstrasse 3; singles/doubles from €23/46) is another good option. Neither will mind if you only stay one night.

Quality **Hotel Zugspitze** (☎ 90 10, fax 90 13 33; e info@hotel-zugspitze.de; Klammstrasse 19; singles from €72/97) has a lovely feel, and cosy timber-lined rooms.

Café Mukkefuck (☎ 73 440; Zugspitzstrasse 3; meals €6-12) has a double-take name, an outdoor courtyard and a tasty array of light meals. Work up your hunger with the hour's climb to **St Martin Am Grasberg** (☎ 49 70; Am Grasberg; mains €7-15), an eatery perched in the mountains northwest of the centre that boasts spectacular views.

GERMANY

Getting There & Away Garmisch is serviced from Munich by hourly trains (€14, 1½
hours). Trains from Garmisch to Innsbruck
(1½ hours) pass through Mittenwald (€3.10,
20 minutes). RVO bus No 1084, from in front
of the train station, links Garmisch with Füssen (€7, two hours) four times daily via Oberammergau. There is a daily bus to Oberstdorf
(€16).

Mittenwald
☎ 08823 • pop 8500
Mittenwald is a less-hectic alternative to the
nearby Garmisch-Partenkirchen. The **tourist
office** (☎ 339 81; e kurvewaltung@mitten
wald.de; Dammkarstrasse 3) is open 8am to
noon and 1pm to 5pm weekdays, and 10am to
noon on weekends.

Popular local hikes with cable-car access
go to Wank (1780m), Mt Karwendel (2384m)
and Wettersteinspitze (2297m). The Karwendel ski area has the longest run (7km) in Germany. Combined day ski passes covering the
Karwendel and nearby Kranzberg ski areas
cost €24. For ski hire and instruction, you
should contact **Erste Skischule** (☎ 35 82;
Bahnhofsplatz).

The closest camping ground is **Am Isarhorn** (☎ 52 16, fax 80 91; e camping@mitt
enwald.de; Isarhorn 4; site/adult/car €4/
4.50/6.70), 3km north of town off the B2
highway. The **Youth Hostel** (☎ 17 01, fax 29
07; e jhmittenwald@djh-bayern.de; Buck-
elwiesen 7; beds €13.10) is in a beautiful,
isolated spot, some 4km outside Mittenwald.
There's no bus service and the walk takes
about one hour.

Gästehaus Sonnenheim (☎ 82 47, fax 25
28; e sonnenheim@mittenwald.de; Dammk-
karstrasse 5; singles/doubles with bathroom
& breakfast from €41.50/78) has classy
rooms lined with honey-coloured timber. **Die
Alpenrose** (☎ 92 700, fax 37 20; e alpen-
rose.mittenwald@t-online.de; Obermarkt 1;
basic singles €28, singles/doubles from €44/
85) offers cramped but otherwise comfortable
lodgings. There's a cosy restaurant downstairs
with filling fare (mains €8 to €10) and live
Bavarian music. **Hochland Restaurant-Café**
(Albert-Schott-Strasse 5; mains €8-17) has an
eat-on-the-street courtyard, and fresh fish and
steak dishes.

For information on getting to/from Mittenwald, see the earlier Garmisch-Partenkirchen
entry.

Oberstdorf
☎ 08322 • pop 10,400
Over in the western part of the Bavarian Alps,
Oberstdorf is a car-free resort. Like Garmisch,
it is surrounded by towering peaks and offers
superb hiking.

The main **tourist offic**e (☎ 70 00; e info@
oberstdorf.de; Marktplatz 7) is open from
8.30am to 6pm weekdays and 9.30am to noon
Saturday. There's another office near the train
station (☎ 70 02 17; Bahnhofplatz 3); both
offer a convenient room-finding service.

For an exhilarating day **hike**, ride the
Nebelhorn cable car to the upper station then
walk down via the Gaisalpseen, two lovely
alpine lakes. In-the-know skiers value Oberstdorf for its friendliness, its lower prices and
generally uncrowded pistes. The village is surrounded by several ski areas: the **Nebelhorn**,
Fellhorn/Kanzelwand and **Söllereck**. Combined daily/weekly ski passes that include all
three areas (plus the adjoining Kleinwalsertal
lifts on the Austrian side) cost €30/160. For
ski hire and tuition, try the Neue Skischule,
which has convenient outlets at the valley stations of the Nebelhorn (☎ 27 37) and Söllereck
(☎ 51 54) lifts.

Oberstdorf's barren **camping ground** (☎ 65
25, fax 80 97 60; e camping-oberstdorf@
t-online.de; Rubingerstrasse 16; tent/person/
car €2.60-4.60/4.60-5.10/2.60) is 2km north
of the station beside the train line, and open all
year. The **Youth Hostel** (☎ 22 25, fax 804 46;
e jhoberstdorf@djh-bayern.de; Kornau 8;
beds €14.10), sits on the outskirts of town near
the Söllereck chairlift; take the Kleinwalsertal
bus to the Reute stop.

Gästehaus Geiger (☎ 98 84 70, fax 804 98,
e gabi_geiger@t-online.de; Am Frohmarkt 5;
singles with breakfast €25/50) is small and
friendly, with pleasant rooms. For the more in-
dulgent, **Hotel Traube** (☎ 46 48, fax 31 68;
e hotel-traube@hotel-traube.de; Hauptstrasse 6; singles/doubles from €66.50/122)
has delightful rooms with four-poster beds and
a large Bavarian-style restaurant downstairs
(mains €10 to €20). **Paulaner Bräu** (☎ 96
760; Kirchstrasse 1; meals €7.50) has a similar menu, but is simpler and cheaper.

There are hourly RB trains to/from Immen-
stadt where you connect to Lindau (€13.50,
two hours) and Munich (€24, 2½ hours; IR
train). Direct RE trains to/from Ulm run hourly
(€17.80, 1¾ hours). On weekdays, several bus
connections to Füssen go via Pfronten (€8.10).

GERMANY

Baden-Württemberg

Baden-Württemberg is one of Germany's main tourist regions. With recreational centres such as the Black Forest and Lake Constance, medieval towns like Heidelberg and the health spa of Baden-Baden, it's one of the most varied parts of Germany.

The prosperous modern state of Baden-Württemberg was created in 1951 out of three smaller regions: Baden, Württemberg and Hohenzollern. Baden was first unified and made a grand duchy by Napoleon, who was also responsible for making Württemberg a kingdom in 1806. Both areas, in conjunction with Bavaria and 16 other states, formed the Confederation of the Rhine under French protection. Baden and Württemberg both sided with Austria against Prussia in 1866, but were ultimately drafted into the German Empire in 1871.

STUTTGART
☎ 0711 • pop 590,000

Stuttgart enjoys the status of being Baden-Württemberg's state capital and the hub of its industries. At the forefront of Germany's economic recovery from the ravages of WWII, Stuttgart started life less auspiciously in AD 950 as a horse stud farm. About 80% of the city centre was destroyed in the war, but there are still some fine historical buildings left, along with huge expanses of parkland, vine-covered hills and an air of relaxed prosperity.

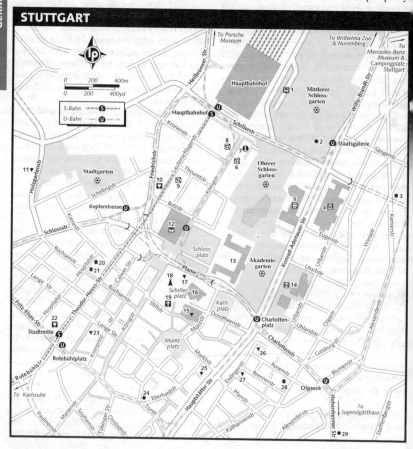

STUTTGART

Information

The **tourist office** (☎ 22 280; e info@stuttgart-tourist.de; Königstrasse 1a; open 9.30am-8.30pm Mon-Fri, 9.30am-6pm Sat, 10.30am-6pm Sun Mar-Oct, same hours Nov-Apr except 1pm-6pm Sun) is opposite the main train station and on the main pedestrian strip. Room reservations can be made here for no fee. The office sells the three-day StuttCard (€14), which allows free public transport and free entry to some museums.

There's a main **post office** (Bolzstrasse 3). You'll find a **Reisebank** at the main train station, and there's a convenient (if expensive) **laundry** (Hohenheimer Strasse 33). **Surf Inn** (Königstrasse 6), situated on the top floor of the Kaufhof department store, charges €1.50 for 30 minutes on the Internet. **Cyberb@r** (Königstrasse 27-29) in the Karstadt building opposite, charges €2.50. **Netbox** (Lautenschlager Strasse 21) is free.

Things to See & Do

The tower at the main train station sports the three-pointed star of the Mercedes-Benz. It's also an excellent vantage point for the sprawling city and surrounding hills, and is reached via a lift (elevator; free; open 10am-10pm Tues-Sun).

Stretching southwest from the Neckar River to the city centre is the **Schlossgarten**, an extensive strip of parkland divided into three sections (Unterer, Mittlerer and Oberer), complete with ponds, swans, street entertainers and modern sculptures. At their northern edge the gardens take in the **Wilhelma** zoo and botanical gardens (☎ 540 20; Neckarstrasse; adult/concession €9/4.50; open 8.15am-6pm May-Aug, 8.15am-5.30pm Apr & Sept, 8.15am-5pm Mar & Oct, 8.15am-4pm Nov-Feb). At their southern end they encompass the

sprawling baroque **Neues Schloss** and the Renaissance **Altes Schloss**, which houses a **regional museum** (☎ 279 34 00; Schillerplatz 6; adult/concession €2.60/1.50; open 10am-5pm Wed-Sun, 10am-1pm Tues).

Next to the Altes Schloss is the city's oldest square, Schillerplatz, with its monument to the poet **Schiller** and the 12th-century **Stiftkirche**. Adjoining the park you'll find the **Staatsgalerie** (☎ 212 40 50; Konrad-Adenauer-Strasse 30; adult/concession €4.50/2.50; open 10am-6pm daily, 10am-9pm Thur) housing an excellent collection from the Middle Ages to the present.

Next door there's the **Haus der Geschichte** (House of History; ☎ 212 39 50; Urbansplatz 2; admission €3), which opened in late 2002. This ia an eye-catching post-modern museum which covers the past 200 years of the Baden-Württemburg area in film, photography, documents and multimedia.

In the Mittlerer Schlossgarten, is the **Carl Zeiss Planetarium** (shows from 10am & 3pm Tues-Fri, plus 8pm Wed & Fri, 2pm, 4pm & 6pm Sat & Sun; adult/concession €5/3).

Motor Museums The motor car was first developed by Gottlieb Daimler and Carl Benz at the end of the 19th century. The impressive **Mercedes-Benz Museum** (☎ 172 25 78; Mercedesstrasse 137; admission free; open 9am-5pm Tues-Sun) is in the suburb of Bad-Cannstatt; take S-Bahn No 1 to Neckarstadion. Mercedes-Benz also runs free weekday tours of its Sindelfingen plant, but you must reserve a spot in advance (☎ 07031-907 04 03; children under 6 not allowed). For even faster cars, cruise over to the **Porsche Museum** (☎ 911 56 85; Porschestrasse 42; admission free; open 9am-4pm Mon-Fri, 9am-5pm Sat & Sun); take S-Bahn No 6 to

GERMANY

STUTTGART

PLACES TO STAY
3 DJH Youth Hostel
20 Museumstube
21 Gasthof Alte Mira
28 Der Zauberlehrling

PLACES TO EAT
11 University Mensa
15 Markthalle
17 Alte Kanzlei
23 Calwer Eck Bräu
25 iden

26 Zur Kiste
27 Bovie

OTHER
1 Bus Station
2 Carl Zeiss Planetarium
4 Staatsgalerie
5 Staatstheater
6 Cyberb@r; Karstadt
7 Tourist Office
8 Surf Inn; Kaufhof

9 Netbox
10 Palast de Republic
12 Main Post Office
13 Neues Schloss
14 Haus der Geschichte
16 Altes Schloss
18 Schiller Statue
19 Stiftkirche
22 Bar Code
24 Hans-im-Glück Platz
29 Laundrette

Neuwirtshaus. Sadly, neither place offers free samples.

Places to Stay

You can camp at **Campingplatz Stuttgart** (☎ 55 66 96, fax 55 74 54; e info@camping platz-stuttgart.de; Mercedesstrasse 40; site/person €4.10/4.60), beside the river and 500m from the Bad Cannstatt S-Bahn station. It's a steep climb to the **DJH Hostel** (☎ 24 15 83, fax 236 10 41; e info@jugendherberge -stuttgart.de; Haussmannstrasse 27; juniors/seniors €13.35/16.05), which is a signposted 15-minute walk from the train station.

You might prefer the spacious, bright non-DJH **Jugengästehaus** (☎ 24 11 32, fax 236 11 10; e JGH.Stuttgart@internationaler -bund.de; Richard-Wagner-Strasse 2; singles/doubles/triples €21/36/48). Take the U15 to Bubenbad.

Gasthof Alte Mira (☎ 222 95 02, fax 222 95 03 29; e altemira@web.de; Büchenstrasse 24; singles/doubles from €31/52) offers clean, simple rooms with shared facilities. Around the corner, **Museumstube** (☎/fax 29 68 10; Hospitalstrasse 9; singles/doubles €32/50) offers similar lodgings.

For a splurge, don't go anywhere but **Der Zauberlehrling** (☎ 237 77 70, fax 237 77 75; e contact@zauberlehrling.de; Rosenstrasse 38; singles/doubles without breakfast from €117/200). This innovative place has nine distinctly different thematic rooms that marry ultra-contemporary design with tasteful old-fashioned touches.

Places to Eat

Pack a picnic at the **Markthalle** (Dorotheen-strasse 4; open 7am-6.30pm Mon-Fri, 7am-4pm Sat), an excellent Art Nouveau-style market that's jam-packed with fresh fare. Alternatively, fill up for around €2.50 at the university **Mensa** (Holzgartenstrasse 11), which has a downstairs cafeteria for the un-educated masses. Vegetarians (and those who have overdosed on German sausages) can try **iden** (Eberhardtsrasse 1), which serves cheap, self-serve salad (€1.50), 100g of vegetarian lasagne (€1.50) and soup (€2.50).

Alte Kanzlei (☎ 29 44 57; Schillerplatz 5b; dishes €6-10) is excellent for a sunny lunch, with pastas, wraps and salads.

Stuttgart is a great place to sample Swabian specialities such as *Spätzle* (like doughy pasta) and *Maultaschen* (similar to ravioli).

The best spot is cosy **Zur Kiste** (☎ 24 40 02, Kanalstrasse 2; mains €8-15) in the Bohnen-viertel (Bean Quarter). This is Stuttgart's oldest restaurant and its delicious menu really packs 'em in. Two blocks down **Bovie** (☎ 23 37 78; Eslinger Strasse 8; €9-16) is friendly and casual, and provides an inspiring international selection with Swabian influences. **Calwer Eck Bräu** (☎ 22 24 94 40; Calwer-strasse 31; mains €9-12) brews its own beer and serves top-notch regional fare.

Entertainment

Lift Stuttgart is a comprehensive guide to local entertainment and events (€1).

Home of the famous Stuttgart Ballet, the **Staatstheater** (☎ 20 20 90; Oberer Schloss-garten 6) holds regular symphony, ballet and opera performances.

The grandly-named **Palast de Republic** (Friedrichstrasse 27), is a tiny bar that pulls a huge crowd of laid-back footpath drinkers. There are several funky drinking holes around Hans-im-Glück-Platz, a small square that's often packed with party-goers. Nearby, **Bar Code** (Theodore-Heuss-Strasse 30) is a cool modern bar with a young crowd. For leafy fun, there's a **beer garden** in the Mittlerer Schlossgarten, northeast of the main train station.

Getting There & Around

Stuttgart's international airport is south of the city and is served by S2 and S3 trains (30 minutes from the main train station). There are frequent train departures for all major German and many international cities. ICE trains run to Frankfurt (€45.20, 1½ hours), Berlin (€127.00, 5½ hours) and Munich (€44.60, two hours). Regional and long-distance buses leave from the station next to the main train station.

One-way fares on Stuttgart's public transport network are €1.10/5.30 for short/long trips. A four-ride strip ticket costs €5.80 and a central zone day pass is €4.70.

AROUND STUTTGART
Tübingen
☎ 07071 • pop 8000

This gentle, picturesque university town is a perfect place to spend a day wandering winding alleys and enjoying the views of half-timbered houses and old stone walls. On **Marktplatz**, the centre of town, is the 1435

Rathaus with its ornate baroque facade and astronomical clock. The nearby late-Gothic **Stiftkirche** *(Am Holz-markt)* houses the tombs of the Württemberg dukes and has excellent medieval stained-glass windows. From the heights of the Renaissance **Schloss Hohentübingen** *(Burgsteig 11)*, now part of the university, there are fine views over the steep, red-tiled rooftops of the old town. The **tourist office** (☎ 913 60; **e** *mail@tuebingen-info.de; An der Neckarbrücke; open 9am-7pm Mon-Fri, 9am-5pm Sat all year & 2pm-5pm Sun May-Sept)* is beside the bridge.

The **DJH hostel** (☎ 230 02, fax 250 61; *Gartenstrasse 22/2; juniors/seniors €14.90/ 17.60)* has a delightful location by the river. Attractive **Hotel Am Schloss** (☎ 929 40, fax 92 94 10; **e** *info@hotelamschloss.de; Burgsteige 18; singles/doubles with breakfast €51/76)* has simple and pleasant rooms. Its restaurant, *Maultaschen*, is a local institution. **Al Dente Spaghetteria** (☎ 251 57; *Clinicumsgasse 20; dishes €6-10)* serves superb pasta in a sunny little nook.

There are regular RE trains between Tübingen and Stuttgart (€9; one hour).

HEIDELBERG
☎ 06221 • 140,000
The French destroyed Heidelberg in 1693; they may have been the last visitors to dislike this charming town on the Neckar River. Its magnificent castle and medieval town are irresistible drawcards for most travellers in Germany. Mark Twain began his European travels here and recounted his comical observations in *A Tramp Abroad*. Britain's JMW Turner loved Heidelberg and it inspired him to produce some of his finest landscape paintings.

Heidelberg's sizable student population (attending the oldest university in the country) makes it a lively city. But be warned; this place is chock-a-block with tourists during July and August, so try to avoid coming then or you might start to empathise with the French...

Orientation & Information
Heidelberg's captivating old town starts to reveal itself about a 15-minute walk west of the main train station, along the Kurfürsten-Anlage. Hauptstrasse is the pedestrian way leading eastwards through the heart of the Altstadt from Bismarckplatz via Marktplatz to Karlstor.

The main **tourist office** (☎ 194 33; **e** *cvb@ heidelberg.de; Willy-Brandt-Platz 1; open 9am-7pm Mon-Sat all year plus 10am-6pm Sun Apr-Nov)* is outside the train station. There are smaller, independent offices at the funicular train station near the castle and on Neckarmünzplatz that keep reduced hours. The €12 Heidelberg Card offers unlimited public transport and free admission to many sights.

There's a post office branch to the right as you leave the train station – the main office is on Sophienstrasse near the Altstadt. You'll find a **Reisebank** in the train station. **Office Shop GmbH** *(Plock 85)* charges €1.30 for 15 minutes on the Internet. **Waschsalon Wojtala** *(Kettergasse 17)* is a convenient, if expensive, laundry, charging €8 to wash and dry. **Schnell & Sauber Waschcenter** *(Poststrasse 44)* charges €3.50 per wash.

Things to See & Do
Heidelberg's imposing **Schloss** (☎ 53 84 14; *admission free to grounds, adult/concession €2/1 to castle; open 8am-5.30pm daily)* is one of Germany's finest examples of grand Gothic-Renaissance architecture. The building's half-ruined state actually adds to its romantic appeal. Seen from anywhere in the Altstadt, this striking red-sandstone castle dominates the hillside. The entry fee covers the castle, the **Grosses Fass** (Great Vat), an enormous 18th-century keg capable of holding 221,726L, and **Deutsches Apothekenmuseum** (German Pharmaceutical Museum).

You can take the funicular railway to the castle from lower Kornmarkt station *(adult/ concession €3/2 return)*, or enjoy an invigorating 10-minute walk up steep, stone-laid lanes. The funicular continues up to the **Königstuhl**, where there's a TV and lookout tower *(adult/concession €5.10/3.60 return, including a castle stop)*.

Dominating Universitätsplatz are the 18th-century **Alte Universität** and the **Neue Universität**. Nearby there's the **Studentenkarzer** *(student jail; ☎ 54 21 63; Augustinergasse 2; adult/concession €2.50/2; open 10am-noon & 2pm-5pm Tues-Sat Apr-Oct, 10am-2pm Tues-Fri Nov-Mar)*. From 1778 to 1914 this jail was used for uproarious students. Sentences (usually two to 10 days) were earned for heinous crimes such as drinking, singing and womanising (no word as to whether 'manising' was *verboten*). The **Marstall** is the

GERMANY

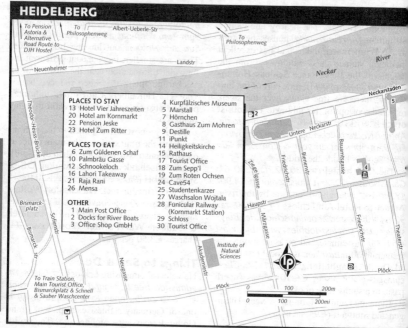

HEIDELBERG

PLACES TO STAY
13 Hotel Vier Jahreszeiten
20 Hotel am Kornmarkt
22 Pension Jeske
23 Hotel Zum Ritter

PLACES TO EAT
6 Zum Güldenen Schaf
10 Palmbräu Gasse
12 Schnookeloch
16 Lahori Takeaway
21 Raja Rani
26 Mensa

OTHER
1 Main Post Office
2 Docks for River Boats
3 Office Shop GmbH

4 Kurpfälzisches Museum
5 Marstall
7 Hörnchen
8 Gasthaus Zum Mohren
9 Destille
11 iPunkt
14 Heiligkeitskirche
15 Rathaus
17 Tourist Office
18 Zum Sepp'l
19 Zum Roten Ochsen
24 Cave54
25 Studentenkarzer
27 Waschsalon Wojtala
28 Funicular Railway
   (Kornmarkt Station)
29 Schloss
30 Tourist Office

---

former arsenal, now a student mensa. The **Kurpfälzisches Museum** (*Palatinate Museum;* ☎ 58 34 02; *Hauptstrasse 97; adult/ concession €2.50/1.50; open 10am-5pm Tues-Sun, 10am-9pm Wed*) contains paintings, sculptures and the jawbone of the 600,000-year-old Heidelberg Man.

A stroll along the **Philosophenweg**, north of the Neckar River, gives a welcome respite from Heidelberg's tourist hordes.

Places to Stay

Finding any accommodation in Heidelberg's high season can be difficult. Arrive early in the day or book ahead.

Camping Haide (☎ 21 11, fax 71 959; *Ziegelhäuser Landstrasse, Haide; site/person €3/4.60*) is in a pretty spot on the river. Take bus No 35 to Orthopädische Klinik. The local **DJH hostel** (☎ 41 20 66, fax 40 25 59; e jh -heidelberg@t-online.de; *Tiergartenstrasse 5; juniors/seniors €13.35/16.05*) is across the river from the train station. From the station or Bismarckplatz, take bus No 33 towards Ziegelhausen.

Labyrinthine backpacker favourite **Pension Jeske** (☎ 237 33, fax 65 91 23; *Mittelbadgasse 2; dorm beds €20, doubles from €50*) has new owners, beds and bathrooms, but is still the cheapest in the Altstadt. Quaint, friendly **Pension Astoria** (☎ 40 29 29; *Rahmengasse 30; singles/doubles from €40/65*) has comfy rooms with character. It's north of the river, across Theodor-Heuss-Brücke.

Amiable **Hotel am Kornmarkt** (☎ 243 25, fax 282 18; *Kornmarkt 7; singles/doubles without bathroom €50/98*) has pleasant, spacious rooms and a superb breakfast buffet. There are newly renovated lodgings at **Hotel Vier Jahreszeiten** (☎ 241 64, fax 16 31 10; e info@4-jahreszeiten.de; *Haspelgasse 2; singles/doubles from €80/100*), where the great Goethe himself reputedly once slumbered.

The ornate **Hotel Zum Ritter** (☎ 13 50, fax 13 52 30; e info@ritter-heidelberg.de; *Hauptstrasse 178; singles/doubles €92/155*) is close to the cathedral, and provides grand accommodation.

Places to Eat

The **Mensa** (*Univsersitätsplatz; meals for students/guests €2/3*) has budget feeds whether you're the studious type or not. There are two decent, cheap Indian takeaways in the

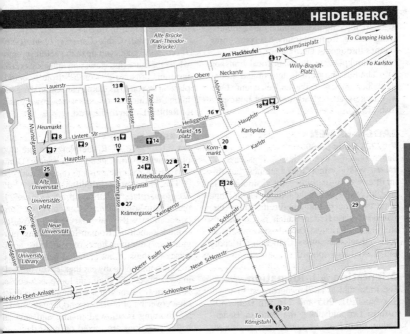

HEIDELBERG

Altstadt: **Raja Rani** (*Mittelbadgasse 5*) and **La-hori** (*Heiliggeiststrasse 9a*). Both will sell curries, tandoori and other spicy favourites from around €3.

You can grab a feed at many student pubs (see Entertainment later) for around €8. In a dimly-lit stone tunnel adorned with blackened wood and heavy chains, medieval **Palmbräu Gasse** (☎ 285 36; *Hauptstrasse 185; mains €8-16*) wins hands down for atmosphere, service and food. Dialect for 'mosquito hole', **Schnookeloch** (☎ 13 80 80; *Haspelgasse 8; mains €7-20*) defies its name, with an inviting and insect-free atmosphere and a good German/Italian menu. **Zum Güldenen Schaf** (☎ 208 79; *Hauptstrasse 115; lunch €7-17, dinner €14-23*) is pricey, however, the spread is great.

Entertainment

This being a university town, you won't have to go far to find a happening backstreet bar. Tiny **Hörnchen** (*Heumarkt*) is the perfect place to start an evening out; it's laid-back, intimate and friendly. In contrast, nearby **Gasthaus Zum Mohren** (*Untere Strasse 5-7*) is loud, proud and crowded – watch for presumptuous,

tip-hungry bar staff. At the **Destille** (*Untere Strasse 16*), there's an eclectic mix of loud chat, louder music and board games. Also popular is modern **iPunkt** (*Untere Strasse 30*). Heidelberg's famous historic student pubs **Zum Roten Oschen** (*Hauptstrasse 213*) and **Zum Sepp'l** (*Hauptstrasse 217*) don't get much more than a tourist trade these days.

For live jazz and blues, head to **Cave54** (*Krämergasse 2*), an underground stone cellar that oozes character, and once hosted Louis Armstrong. It's big on Thursday, Friday and Saturday.

Getting There & Around

Heidelberg is on the Castle Road route from Mannheim to Nuremberg. From mid-May until the end of September Deutsche-Touring has a daily coach service, with one bus in either direction between Heidelberg and Rothenburg ob der Tauber (€29, five hours); contact **Deutsche-Touring GmbH** (☎ 089-59 38 89, fax 550 39 65; e service@deutsche-touring.com; Am Römerhof 17, 60486 Frankfurt/Main).

There are hourly ICE/IC trains which operate to/from Frankfurt (€22.80, one hour),

Stuttgart (€19.60, 40 minutes) and Munich (€53.40, three hours). Mannheim, 12 minutes to the west by frequent trains, has connections to cities throughout Germany.

Bismarckplatz is the main local transport hub. The bus and tram system in and around Heidelberg is extensive and efficient. One-way tickets are €1.80 and a 24-hour pass costs €5.90.

BADEN-BADEN
☎ 07221 • pop 50,000
Baden-Baden's natural hot springs have attracted visitors since Roman times, but this small city only really became fashionable in the 19th century when the likes of Victor Hugo came to bathe in and imbibe its therapeutic waters. Today Baden-Baden is Germany's premier (and ritziest) health spa and offers many other salubrious activities in a friendly and relaxed atmosphere.

Orientation & Information
The train station is 7km northwest of town. Bus Nos 201, 205 and 216 run frequently to/from Leopoldsplatz, the heart of Baden-Baden. From here, Sophienstrasse leads eastwards to the more historic part of town. North of Sophienstrasse are the baths, the Stiftskirche and the Neues Schloss. Across the river to the west you will find the Trinkhalle (pump room) and the tourist office, and past Goetheplatz both the Kurhaus and Spielhalle (casino).

The tourist office (☎ 27 52 00; e info@ baden-baden.com; Kaiserallee 3; open 10am-5pm Mon-Sat, 2pm-5pm Sun) is in the Trinkhalle; collect some information and sample the local drop. There is a spa Kurtaxe (visitors' tax) of €2.50, entitling you to a Kurkarte from your hotel that brings various discounts. The tax doesn't apply to those staying at the hostel.

Things to See & Do
The ancient Römische Badruinen (Roman Bath Ruins; Römerplatz 1; admission free) are worth a quick look, but for a real taste of Baden-Baden head for the ornate and grand Trinkhalle (Kaiserallee 3). You can have a free drink of the spa water piped in hot from the ground. Next door is the 1820s Kurhaus, which houses the opulent casino (☎ 210 60; Kaiserallee 1; guided tours adult/child €4/2; tours 9.30am-noon daily) where Dostoyevsky

was inspired to write The Gambler. Call ahead to arrange a tour in English.

The Merkur Cable Car (€4; open 10am-10pm daily) takes you up to the 660m summit where there are fine views and numerous walking trails (bus No 204 or 205 from Leopoldplatz takes you to the cable-car station). A good hiking-driving tour is to the wine-growing area of Rebland, 6km to the west.

Spas
On either side of Römerplatz are the two places where you can take the waters. Don't leave town without a visit to one or both.

The 19th-century Friedrichsbad (☎ 27 59 20; Römerplatz 1; bathing programme €21; open 9am-10pm Mon-Sat, noon-8pm Sun) is decadently Roman in style and provides a muscle-melting Roman-Irish bathing programme. Your three hours of humid bliss comprises 16 steps of hot and cold baths, saunas, steam rooms and showers that leave you feeling scrubbed, sparkling and loose as a goose. An extra €8 gets you a soap-and-brush massage covering almost every nook and cranny. No clothing is allowed inside, and several bathing sections are mixed on most days, so leave your modesty at the reception desk. Modern Caracalla-Therme (☎ 27 59 40; Römerplatz 11; €11 for 2hr; open 8am-10pm) is a vast complex of outdoor and indoor pools, hot and cold-water grottoes and many more delights. You must wear a bathing costume and bring your own towel.

Places to Stay & Eat
The closest camping ground is Campingplatz Adam (☎ 07223-231 94; Campingplatzstrasse 1, Bühl-Oberbruch; tent/person €8/6.50) about 12km outside town.

Baden-Baden's DJH hostel (☎ 522 23, fax 600 12; e info@jugend herberge-baden-baden.de; Hardbergstrasse 34; juniors/seniors €13.35/16.05) is situated 3km northwest of the centre; take bus No 201 to Grosse Dollenstrasse then walk for 10 minutes.

The tourist office has a free room reservation service.

Central Hotel Zur Altstadt (☎ 30 22 80, fax 302 28 28; Baldreitstrasse 1; singles/doubles with bathroom from €34/64) is a good deal, with rooms that are both pleasant and ample.

Lovely Holland Hotel Sophienpark (☎ 35 60, fax 35 61 21; e info@holland-hotel-sophienpark.de; Sophienstrasse 14; singles/

doubles from €110/165) has its own park, and bright and sunny rooms with a touch of luxury.

For a light bite, head to **Leo's** (☎ 380 81; Luisenstrasse 8; meals €8), a trendy spot with outdoor tables as well as tasty, well-presented dishes. Ambient **Rathausglöckl** (☎ 906 10; Steinstrasse 7; mains €8-17) serves excellent regional fare in a historic setting.

Getting There & Away
Baden-Baden is on the busy Mannheim-Basel train line. Fast trains in either direction stop every two hours. Frequent local trains serve both Karlsruhe and Offenburg, from where you can make connections to much of Germany.

BLACK FOREST
Home of the cuckoo clock, the Black Forest (Schwarzwald) gets its name from the dark canopy of evergreens. The fictional Hansel and Gretel encountered their wicked witch in these parts, but modern-day hazards are more likely to include packs of tourists piling out of buses. However, a 20-minute walk from even the most crowded spots will put you in quiet countryside dotted with huge traditional farmhouses and patrolled by amiable dairy cows.

Orientation & Information
The Black Forest is east of the Rhine between Karlsruhe and Basel. It's roughly triangular in shape, about 160km long and 50km wide. Baden-Baden, Freudenstadt, Titisee and Freiburg act as convenient information posts for Black Forest excursions. Even smaller towns in the area generally have tourist offices.

Freudenstadt is a good place for information on the northern section. Its **tourist office** (☎ 07441-86 40; e touristinfo@freudenstadt .de; open 9am-6pm Mon-Fri, 10am-2pm Sat & Sun Mar-Nov, 10am-5pm Mon-Fri, 10am-1pm Sat & Sun Dec-Feb) is on Am Marktplatz. Titisee's **tourist office** (☎ 07651-980 40; e touristinfo@titisee.de; Strandbadstrasse 4; open 8am-noon & 1.30pm-5.30pm Mon-Fri all year, 10am-noon Sat & Sun May-Oct), situated inside the Kurhaus, also covers the southern Black Forest. The Feldberg **tourist office** (☎ 07655-80 19; e tourist-info@ feldbergschwarzwald.de; Kirchgasse 1; open 8am-5.30pm Mon-Fri all year & Sat Jun-Sept, Sun July-Aug) also supplies ski information.

Things to See
Enjoying the natural countryside will be the main focus, although you can take a plunge in a lake or down a ski slope, or lose yourself in shops full of cuckoo clocks.

Roughly halfway between Baden-Baden and Freudenstadt – along the Schwarzwald-Hochstrasse (Black Forest Highway) – the first major tourist sight is the **Mummelsee**, south of the Hornisgrinde peak. It's a small and deep lake steeped in folklore (legend says an evil sea king inhabits the depths).

Farther south, **Freudenstadt** is mainly used as a base for excursions into the countryside, however the central marketplace, the largest in Germany, is worth a look.

The area between Freudenstadt and Freiburg is cuckoo-clock country, a name that takes on new meaning when you see the prices people are willing to pay. A few popular stops are **Schramberg**, **Triberg** and **Furtwangen**. In Furtwangen, visit the **Deutsches Uhrenmuseum** (German Clock Museum; ☎ 07723-92 01 17; Gerwigstrasse 11; adult/concession €3/2.50; open 9am-6pm daily, 10am-6pm Nov-Mar) for a look at the traditional Black Forest skill of clock-making.

Titisee boasts its namesake natural lake where you can take a soothing **cruise** (€4; 25min) or rent a boat in summer. The engines are all electric to preserve the lake's serenity.

Activities
Summer With more than 7000km of marked trails, the possibilities are, almost literally, endless. Hiking maps are everywhere and any tourist office can set you off on anything from easy one-hour jaunts to multiday treks. Three classic long-distance **hiking trails** run south from the northern Black Forest city of Pforzheim as far as the Swiss Rhine: the 280km Westweg to Basel; the 230km Mittelweg to Waldhut-Tiengen; and the 240km Ostweg to Schaffhausen.

The southern Black Forest, especially the area around the 1493m Feldberg summit, offers some of the best hiking; small towns like Todtmoos or Bonndorf serve as useful bases for those wanting to get off the more heavily trodden trails. The 10km **Wutachschlucht** (Wutach Gorge) outside Bonndorf is justifiably famous. You can also try windsurfing, boating or swimming on the highland lakes, though some may find the water a bit cool. Titisee boasts several beaches.

GERMANY

GERMANY

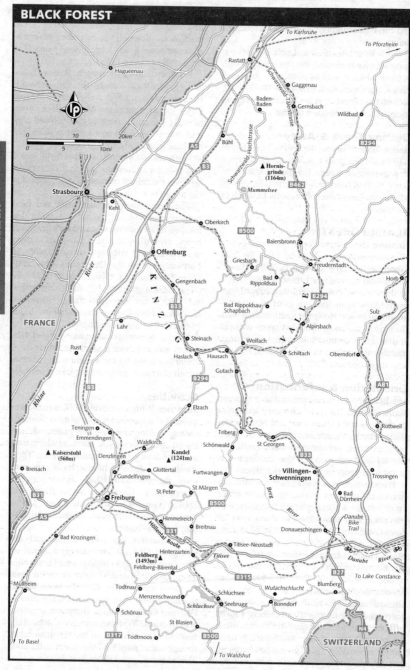

BLACK FOREST

Winter The Black Forest ski season runs from late December to March. While there is some good downhill skiing, the Black Forest is more suited to cross-country skiing. The Titisee area is the main centre for winter sports, with uncrowded downhill runs at **Feldberg** *(day passes €20; rental equipment available)* and numerous graded cross-country trails. In midwinter, ice skating is also possible on the Titisee and the Schluchsee. For winter sports information, check with the Feldberg or Titisee tourist offices.

Places to Stay
Away from the major towns you can find scores of simple guesthouses where the rates are cheap and the welcome warm. The Black Forest is also good for longer stays, with holiday apartments and private rooms available in almost every town.

Camping It's only natural that a forest would have plenty of excellent camping. Facilities include **Campingplatz Wolfsgrund** *(☎ 07656-573; site/person €5-6/4.25-4.75)* on the Schluchsee and **Terrassencamping Sandbank** *(☎ 07651-82 43, fax 82 86; Seerundweg; site/person €5-6.50/3.25-4.25)*, one of four camping grounds on the Titisee.

Hostels The DJH net is extensive in the southern Black Forest but limited in the north. Some convenient hostels are in: **Freudenstadt** *(☎ 07441-77 20; e info@jugendherberge-freudenstadt.de; Eugen-Nägele-Strasse 69)*; **Triberg** *(☎ 07722-41 10; e info@jugendherberge-triberg.de; Rohrbacher Strasse 3)*; and **Zuflucht** *(☎ 07804-611; e info@jugendherberge-zuflucht.de; Schwarzwaldhochstrasse)*. All of them charge €13.35/16.05 for juniors/seniors.

Hotels & Pensions Lodges may outnumber cows (but not cuckoo clocks) in the Black Forest and there are some good deals for basic rooms. Tourist offices can also direct you to private rooms from about €16 per person. In Freudenstadt there's **Gasthof Pension Traube** *(☎ 07441-91 74 50, fax 853 28; Markt 41; singles/doubles €30/57)*, with simple rooms. Triberg's attractive **Hotel Pfaff** *(☎ 07722-44 79, fax 78 97; e hotel-pfaff-triberg@t-online.de; Hauptstrasse 85; singles/doubles with bathroom €38/66)* offers comfortable

lodgings near the waterfall. At Titisee, **Hotel Sonneneck** *(☎ 07651-82 46, fax 881 74; Parkstrasse 2; singles/doubles €44/88)* provides spacious comfort as well as an excellent restaurant downstairs. In neighbouring Neustadt, **Hotel Adler-Post** *(☎ 07651-50 66, fax 37 29; Hauptstrasse 16; singles/doubles from €49/83)* has charming rooms furnished in period style; the price includes use of the luxurious indoor pool, sauna and solarium. **Berggasthof Wasmer** *(☎ 07676-230, fax 430; An der Wiesenquelle 1; singles/doubles from €23/46)* in Feldberg offers small, comfortable timber-lined rooms.

Places to Eat
Regional specialities include *Schwarzwälderschinken* (ham), which is smoked and served in a variety of ways. Rivalling those ubiquitous clocks in fame (but not price), *Schwarzwälderkirschtorte* (Black Forest cake) is a chocolate and cherry concoction. Restaurants are often expensive, therefore a picnic in the woods makes both fiscal and scenic sense. Most hotels and guesthouses have restaurants serving traditional hearty German fare.

Getting There & Away
The Mannheim to Basel train line has numerous branches that serve the Black Forest. Trains for Freudenstadt and the north leave from Karlsruhe. Triberg is on the busy line linking Offenburg and Constance. Titisee has frequent services from Freiburg with some trains continuing to Feldberg and others to Neustadt, where there are connections to Donaueschingen.

Getting Around
The rail network is extensive and where trains don't go, buses do. However travel times can be slow and service infrequent, so check the schedules at bus stops, which are usually located outside train stations, or consult with the tourist offices. There's a variety of group and multiday deals valid on trains and buses and sold from ticket machines at the stations. To reach Feldberg, take one of the frequent buses from the train stations in Titisee or Bärental. Drivers will enjoy flexibility in an area that really rewards it. The main tourist road is the Schwarzwald-Hochstrasse (B500), which runs from Baden-Baden to Freudenstadt and from Triberg to Waldshut. Other thematic roads

with maps provided by tourist offices include Schwarzwald-Bäderstrasse (spa town route), Schwarzwald-Panoramastrasse (panoramic view route) and Badische Weinstrasse (wine route).

FREIBURG
☎ 0761 • pop 200,500

The gateway to the southern Black Forest, Freiburg im Breisgau is a fun place, thanks to the city's large and thriving university community. Ruled for centuries by the Austrian Habsburgs, Freiburg has retained many traditional features, although major reconstruction was necessary following severe bombing damage during WWII. The monumental 13th-century cathedral is the city's key landmark but the real attractions are the vibrant cafés, bars and street-life, plus the local wines. The best times for tasting are early July for the four days of *Weinfest* (Wine Festival), or early August for the nine days of *Weinkost* (loosely meaning 'wine as food').

Orientation & Information

The city centre is a convenient 10-minute walk from the train station. Walk east along Eisenbahnstrasse to the tourist office, then continue through the bustling pedestrian zone to Münsterplatz, dominated by the red stone cathedral.

The **tourist office** (☎ 388 18 80; e *tourist ik@fwt-online.de; Rotteckring 14; open 9.30am-8pm Mon-Fri, 9.30am-5pm Sat, 10am-noon Sun May-Oct & 9.30am-6pm Mon-Fri, 9.30am-2pm Sat, 10am-noon Sun Nov-Apr*) has piles of information on the Black Forest.

The main post office is at Eisenbahnstrasse 58–62, while Volksbank Freiburg is opposite the train station. The **PingWing Internet Center** (*Niemensstrasse 3*) is pretty central and charges €1.20 per 15 minutes. **Wash & Tours** (*Salzstrasse 22; wash €3*) is a combined laundry and Internet café.

Things to See & Do

The major sight in Freiburg is the 700-year-old **Münster** (*Cathedral; Münsterplatz; steeple adult/child €1.30/0.80; open 9.30am-5pm Mon-Sat, 1pm-5pm Sun Easter-Oct & 10am-4pm Tues-Sat, 1pm-5pm Sun Nov-Easter*), a classic example of both high and late-Gothic architecture which looms over Münsterplatz,

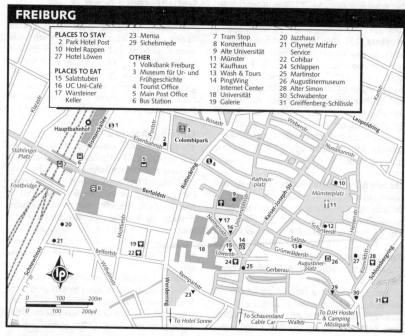

FREIBURG

PLACES TO STAY	23 Mensa	7 Tram Stop	20 Jazzhaus
2 Park Hotel Post	29 Sichelsmiede	8 Konzerthaus	21 Citynetz Mitfahr
10 Hotel Rappen		9 Alte Universität	Service
27 Hotel Löwen	OTHER	11 Münster	22 Cohibar
	1 Volksbank Freiburg	12 Kaufhaus	24 Schlappen
PLACES TO EAT	3 Museum für Ur- und	13 Wash & Tours	25 Martinstor
15 Salatstuben	Frühgeschichte	14 PingWing	26 Augustinermuseum
16 UC Uni-Café	4 Tourist Office	Internet Center	28 Alter Simon
17 Warsteiner	5 Main Post Office	18 Universität	30 Schwabentor
Keller	6 Bus Station	19 Galerie	31 Greiffenberg-Schlössle

Freiburg's market square. Check out the stone and wood carvings, the stained-glass windows and the western porch. Ascend the tower to the stunning pierced spire for great views of Freiburg and, on a clear day, the Kaiserstuhl and the Vosges. South of the Münster stands the picturesque **Kaufhaus**, the 16th-century merchants' hall.

The bustling **university quarter** is northwest of the Martinstor (one of the old city gates).

Freiburg's main museum, the **Augustinermuseum** (☎ 201 25 31; Salzstrasse 32; adult/concession €2/1; open 10am-5pm Tues-Sun) has a fine collection of medieval art. The **Museum für Ur- und Frühgeschichte** (Museum of Pre- & Early History; ☎ 201 25 71; Rotteckring 5; admission free; open 10am-5pm Tues-Sun) is in Columbipark; it has, among other things, lots of pots.

The popular trip by cable car to the 1286m **Schauinsland** peak is a quick way to reach the Black Forest highlands (one way/return €6.60/10.20, concession €3.60/5.60; open 9am-5pm daily). Numerous easy and well-marked trails make the Schauinsland area ideal for day walks. From Freiburg take tram No 4 south to Günterstal and then bus No 21 to Talstation. The five-hour hike from Schauinsland to the Untermünstertal offers some of the best views with the fewest people; return to Freiburg via the train to Staufen and then take the bus.

Places to Stay
Pleasant **Camping Möslepark** (☎ 729 38, fax 775 78; e campingfreizeit@aol.com; Waldseestrasse 77; tent/person €2.10-2.60/5) is open all year. Take tram No 1 to Stadthalle (direction: Littenweiler), turn right under the road, go over the train tracks and follow the bike path. The modern **DJH Hostel** (☎ 675 65, fax 603 67; e jh-freiburg@t-online.de; Karthäuserstrasse 151; juniors/seniors €14.90/17.60) isn't very convenient. Take tram No 1 to Römerhof (direction: Littenweiler) then follow the signs down Fritz-Geiges-Strasse.

A 10-minute walk south of the centre, friendly **Hotel Sonne** (☎ 40 30 48, fax 409 88 56; Basler Strasse 58; singles/doubles €35/52) has decent, simple rooms and a magnificent breakfast buffet. **Hotel Löwen** (☎ 331 61, fax 362 38; Herrenstrasse 47; singles/doubles €35/80) offers clean, basic rooms in a busy part of the Altstadt.

Charming **Hotel Rappen** (☎ 313 53, fax 38 22 52; e rappen@t-online.de; Münsterplatz 13; singles/doubles from €55/70) has lovely rooms with close-up views of the Münster. **Park Hotel Post** (☎ 38 54 80, fax 316 80; e park-hotel-post-freiburg@t-online.de; Eisenbahnstrasse 35-37; singles/doubles €89/114) is an attractive option, with harmoniously hued rooms near Columbipark.

Places to Eat
Being a university town, Freiburg virtually guarantees cheap eats and boasts a lively restaurant scene. University-subsidised **Mensas** (Rempartstrasse 18 • Hebelstrasse 9a) have salad buffets and other filling fodder. You may be asked to show student ID.

Most of the student bars serve good, cheap meals for between €3 and €8 (see Entertainment later). **UC Uni-Café** (☎ 38 33 55; Niemensstrasse 7; meals €3-7) is a popular hang-out that serves light bites on its highly-visible outdoor terrace. **Warsteiner Keller** (☎ 329 29; Niemensstrasse 13; meals €7.50) is a bar/café that oozes atmosphere, and has an excellent range of cheap chow. At the self-serve **Salatstuben** (Löwenstrasse 1; 100g salad €1.20, hot meal €4.10) there's a great range of cheap vegetarian dishes.

For something more substantial, try the cosy **Sichelschmiede** (☎ 350 37; Insel 1; mains around €12), in the eastern Altstadt.

Entertainment
The Freiburg **Konzerthaus** (☎ 388 85 52; Konrad-Adenauer-Platz 1) hosts an impressive range of orchestral performances, while nearby the **Jazzhaus** (☎ 34 973; Schnewlinstrasse 1) has live jazz every night, and hosts many touring acts. Admission starts at €6, depending on who's playing.

Schlappen (Lowenstrasse 2) is where it happens with the student crowd on most nights. It's a large, sprawling bar with a lively vibe, a budget menu and late closing. **Galerie** (Milchstrasse 7) is an intimate watering hole with a nice courtyard and cheap Spanish eats. Mellow and candlelit **Cohibar** (Milchstrasse 9) is a nearby cocktail bar that doesn't close till 3am on weekends. **Alter Simon** (Konviktstrasse 43) has a laid-back feel, and provides a good stopover on your way back from the **Greiffenberg-Schlössle** (Schlossbergring 3), a hilltop beer garden with stunning views over the town.

GERMANY

Getting There & Around

Freiburg is situated on the Mannheim-Basel train corridor and is served by numerous ICE and EC trains in both directions. The trains to Titisee leave every 30 minutes (€9). The regional bus station is next to Track 1. For ride-sharing information contact the **Citynetz Mitfahr-Service** (☎ 194 44; Belfortstrasse 55).

Single rides on the efficient local bus and tram system cost €1.75. A 24-hour pass costs €4.60. Trams depart from the bridge over the train tracks.

DANUBE RIVER

The Danube (Donau), one of Europe's great rivers, rises in the Black Forest. In Austria, Hungary and Romania it is a mighty, almost intimidating, waterway, but in Germany it's narrower and more tranquil, making it ideal for hiking and biking tours. In fact, Donaueschingen is the gateway to the **Donauradwanderweg** (Danube Bike Trail), a beautiful and level trail that stretches 583km east through cities that include Ulm and Regensburg, to Passau on the Austrian border. From there you can continue on to Vienna and beyond.

The booklet *Donauradwanderführer* provides maps and descriptions of the German route and is available from bookshops and tourist offices for €10.

To exploit its location at the source of the Danube, **Donaueschingen** boasts the Donauquelle (Danube Source) monument in the park of the Fürstenberg Schloss. However, the river really begins 1km east where two tributaries – the Brigach and the Breg – meet at a site dominated by a charmless highway bridge.

Donaueschingen's **tourist office** (☎ 0771-85 72 21; Karlstrasse 58; open 9am-6pm Mon-Fri, 10am-noon Sat Apr-Oct, 9am-5pm Mon-Fri Nov-Mar) provides heaps of information on Danube cycling. **Josef Rothweiler** (☎ 0771-131 48; Max-Egan-Strasse 11) rents bikes from €6.50 per day. Trains runs to/from Offenburg (€13.50), Constance (€12.40) and Neustadt (€5.50) in the Black Forest.

ULM

☎ 0731 • pop 165,000

A city well worth a visit, Ulm is famous for its Münster tower, the highest cathedral spire in Europe. It's also the birthplace of Albert Einstein. It was a trading city in the 12th century and barges with local goods floated down the Danube as far as the Black Sea.

Greater Ulm is actually two cities in two *Länder* (states), a situation that dates back to Napoleon's influence on the region: he decreed that the middle of the river would divide Baden-Württemberg and Bavaria.

On the southern side of the Danube, the Bavarian city of Neu Ulm is bland and modern. On the other side is Ulm, with the main attractions. Ulm is a hub for frequent fast trains to Lindau, Munich, Stuttgart and the north.

Orientation & Information

Ulm's **tourist office** (☎ 161 28 30; e info@tourismus.ulm.de; Münsterplatz; open 9am-6pm Mon-Fri, 9am-1pm Sat all year, plus 10.30am-2.30pm Sun May-Oct) is very helpful. **Albert's Café** (Kornhausplatz 5) offers free Internet access.

Things to See & Do

The main reason for coming to Ulm is to see the huge **Münster** (Cathedral; Münsterplatz; steeple climb adult/concession €3/2; open 9am-5pm Sept-May, longer hours June-Aug) famous for its 161m-high steeple, the tallest in the world. Though begun in 1377, it took more than 500 years for the entire structure to be completed. Climbing to the third gallery via the 768 spiralling steps yields great views and a dizzy head. A stained-glass window above the entrance recalls the Holocaust.

Schwörmontag (Oath Monday), held on the second-last Monday in July, has been going on since 1397. After the mayor makes an oath, at the **Schwörhaus** (Oath House), the populace moves down to **Fischerviertel**, a charming old quarter built around streams flowing into the Danube, for a raucous procession of rafts and barges. Later, all-night parties take place on the town's streets and squares. The next day is a local holiday as everybody sleeps it off.

Places to Stay & Eat

The **DJH hostel** (☎ 38 44 55, fax 38 45 11; e jh-ulm@t-online.de; Grimmelfinger Weg 45; juniors/seniors €13.35/16.05) can be reached by taking the S1 to Ehinger Tor, then bus No 4 or 8 to Schulzentrum; from here it's a five-minute walk. Over in Neu-Ulm is the **Rose** (☎ 778 03, fax 977 17 68; e u.hilpert@t-online.de; Kasernstrasse 42a; singles/doubles €22/44) with tidy, spacious rooms and friendly hosts. Near the Münster, **Hotel Bäumle** (☎ 622 87, fax 602 26 04; Kohlgasse 6; singles/doubles from €30/45) is terrific value, with lovely timber-lined rooms, and a snug **downstairs restaurant** *(mains €7-14)* with regional fare. In a charmingly crooked historic half-timbered building, there's **Hotel Schiefes Haus** *(☎ 96 79 30, fax 967 93 33; Schwörhausgasse 6; singles/doubles €100/ 130)* which offers pleasant rooms. **Drei Kannen** *(☎ 677 17; Hafenbad 31; mains €4-11)* brews its own dark beer and serves hearty German tucker in its sunny courtyard.

LAKE CONSTANCE
Lake Constance (Bodensee) is a perfect cure for travellers stranded in landlocked southern Germany. Often jokingly called the 'Swabian Ocean', this giant bulge in the sinewy course of the Rhine offers a choice of water sports, relaxation or cultural pursuits. The lake itself adds special atmosphere to the many historic towns around its periphery, which can be explored by boat or bicycle and on foot.

The lake's southern side belongs to Switzerland and Austria, where the snow-capped mountain tops provide a perfect backdrop when viewed from the northern (German) shore. The German side of Lake Constance features three often-crowded tourist centres in Constance, Meersburg and the island of Lindau. It's essentially a summer area, when it abounds with liquid joy, and is too often foggy, or at best hazy, in winter.

Cycling
A 270km international bike track circumnavigates Lake Constance through Germany, Austria and Switzerland, tracing the often steep shoreline beside vineyards and pebble beaches. The route is well signposted, but you may want one of the many widely sold cycling maps. The tourist booklet *Rad Urlaub am Bodensee* lists routes, rental places and a wealth of other information for the region. In Constance, **Velotours** *(☎ 07531-982 80; Fritz-Arnold-Strasse 2b; bike rental €11/ 52 daily/weekly)* rents out bikes and organises cycling tours.

Accommodation
The lake's popularity pushes up accommodation prices; fortunately excellent hostel and camping facilities exist around the lake. During summer the hostels roar with mobs, so call ahead.

See tourist offices for apartments and private rooms away from the tourist mobs (and often set among vineyards overlooking the lake).

Getting There & Around
Constance has train connections every one to two hours to Offenburg (€25.40) and Stuttgart (€34). Meersburg is easily reached by bus No 7395 from Friedrichshafen (€6.40, every 30 minutes), or by **Weisse Flotte** *(☎ 07531-28 13 98)* boats from Constance (€3.40, several times daily in season). The Constance to Meersburg **car ferry** *(☎ 07531-80 36 66; person/bicycle/car €1.40/0.75/4.65)* runs every 15 minutes all year from the northeastern Constance suburb of Staad. Lindau has trains to/from Ulm (€17.80), Munich (€28) and Bregenz (€2.10), where you can connect to the rest of Austria.

Trains link Lindau, Friedrichshafen and Constance, and buses fill in the gaps. By car, the B31 hugs the northern shore of Lake Constance, but it can get rather busy. The most enjoyable, albeit slowest, way to get around is on the Weisse Flotte boats which, from Easter to late October, call several times a day at the larger towns along both sides of the lake; there are discounts for rail pass-holders. The **Erlebniskarte** *(3/7/14 days €47/60/87)* is a handy pass that allows free boat travel and free access to a host of activities around the lake. The seven-day **Bodensee-Pass** *(€30)* gives half-price fares on all boats, buses, trains and mountain cableways on and around Lake Constance (including its Austrian and Swiss shores).

CONSTANCE
☎ 07531 • pop 76,000
The town of Constance (Konstanz) achieved historical significance in 1414 when the Council of Constance convened to try to heal huge rifts in the Church. The consequent burning at the stake of the religious reformer Jan Hus as a heretic, and the scattering of his ashes over the lake, failed to block the impetus of the Reformation.

In the west, Constance straddles the Swiss border, a good fortune that spared it from Allied bombing in WWII. The **tourist office** *(☎ 13 30 30; e info@ti.konstanz.de; Bahnhofplatz 13; open 9am-6.30pm Mon-Fri, 9am-4pm Sat, 10am-1pm Sun Apr-Oct, 9.30am-12.30pm & 2pm-6pm Mon-Fri Nov-Mar)* is 150m to the right from the train station exit.

Things to See & Do

The city's most visible feature is the Gothic spire of the cathedral, added only in 1856 to a church that was started in 1052, which gives excellent views over the old town. Visit the old **Niederburg** quarter or relax in the parklands of the **Stadtgarten**. If you have time, head across to **Mainau Island** (☎ 30 30; adult/concession €10/5; open 7am-8pm mid-Mar–Nov, 9am-6pm Nov–mid-Mar), with its baroque castle set among vast and gorgeous gardens that include a butterfly house. Take bus No 4 or a Weisse Flotte boat from the harbour behind the station. Five public beaches are open from May to September, including the Strandbad Horn with shrub-enclosed nude bathing. Take bus No 5 or walk for 20 scenic minutes around the shore.

Places to Stay & Eat

Campingplatz Bruderhofer (☎ 313 88, fax 313 92; Fohrenbülweg 50; person €3.50) is a lovely spot to camp. Take bus No 1 to the auto ferry terminal, then walk south along the shore for 10 minutes. Stay in a converted water tower at the **DJH Hostel** (☎ 322 60, fax 311 63; e jh-konstanz@t-online.de; Zur Allmannshöhe 16; juniors/seniors €14.90/17.60). Take bus No 1 or 4 from the station to the Jugendherberge stop.

Central **Pension Gretel** (☎ 45 58 25, fax 99 12 54; e rezeption@hotel-gretel.de; Zollernstrasse 6-8; singles/doubles from €36/64) has basic but decent rooms. **Hotel Barbarossa** (☎ 12 89 90, fax 12 89 97 00; e wieder mann@barbarossa-hotel.com; Obermarkt 8-12; singles/doubles from €38/85) is a charming old place with period furniture and creaky floors. There's also a **restaurant** (mains €10-19) downstairs with local specialities.

Latinos (☎ 173 99; Am Fischmarkt; all-you-can-eat €7.80) serves an eclectic mix of Mexican food, sushi and barbecue spare ribs. The **Restaurant Elefanten** (☎ 221 64; Salmannsweilergasse 34; mains €10-21) offers a cosy dining room, an international menu and elephant-sized serves.

MEERSBURG

☎ 07532 • pop 5200

Across the lake from Constance, enchanting Meersburg boasts winding cobblestone streets, vine-patterned hills and a sunny lakeside promenade. Its helpful **tourist office** (☎ 43 11 10; e info@meersburg.de; Kirchstrasse 4; open 9am-6.30pm Mon-Fri, 10am-2pm Sat May-Sept, 9am-noon & 2pm-4.30pm Mon-Fri Oct-Apr) is in the Altstadt.

Steigstrasse is lined with delightful half-timbered houses, each boasting a gift shop. The 11th-century **Altes Schloss** (☎ 800 00; adult/concession €5.50/4; open 9am-6.30pm daily May-Oct, 10am-6pm Nov-Apr) is the oldest structurally intact castle in Germany. Baroque **Neues Schloss** (☎ 41 40 71; adult/concession €4/3; open 10am-1pm & 2pm-6pm daily) houses the town's art collection.

Meersburg is a good base for watery pursuits and is popular with windsurfers. **Rudi Thum's** (☎ 73 11) at the yacht harbour, rents out equipment and offers sailing courses.

With no DJH hostel or handy camping grounds, cheap accommodation is hard to find. Not far from the town centre, brand-new **Pension Schönblick** (☎ 97 50, fax 16 57; Von Lassberg-Strasse 8; singles/doubles from €45/85) offers large rooms with contemporary stylings. The historic **Hotel Weinstube Löwen** (☎ 430 40, fax 43 04 10; e info@hotel-loewen-meersburg.de; Marktplatz 2; singles/doubles from €67/105) has pretty rooms with views of the cobbled streets.

There's no shortage of gastronomic options on the promenade, with dozens of cafés and restaurants jostling for attention; meals average about €11. You can eat cheap soups, pastas and pizzas at **Schlossplatz Café** (Schlossplatz 11; dishes around €6), or try the expensive international spread at historic **Winzerstube Zum Becher** (☎ 075 32; Hollgasse 4; mains from €12).

LINDAU

☎ 08382 • pop 26,000

Most of the German part of Lake Constance lies within Baden-Württemberg, but Lindau in the east is just inside Bavaria, near the Austrian border. The **tourist office** (☎ 26 00 30; e info@lindau-tourismus.de; Ludwigstrasse 68; open 9am-6pm Mon-Fri all year, plus 10am-2pm Sat Apr-Oct) is directly opposite the train station.

Connected to the nearby lakeshore by bridges, key sights of this oh-so-charming island town are muralled **Altes Rathaus** (Reichsplatz), the **city theatre** (Barfüsser-platz) and the harbour's **Seepromenade**, with its Bavarian Lion monument and lighthouse. When the haze clears, the Alps provide a stunning backdrop for a zillion photos.

Lindau's water isn't as crowded as the land. **Windsurf-Schule Kreitmeir** (☎ 233 30; *Strandbad Eichwald*) has a windsurfing school and equipment rental. For boat rental contact **Grahneis** (☎ 55 14).

Pleasant **Park Camping Lindau am See** (☎ 722 36; e info@park-camping.de; *Fraunhoferstrasse 20; tent/person €2.50/5.50*) is on the foreshore 3km southeast of Lindau. The rather posh **DJH Hostel** (☎ 96 71, fax 96 71 50; e jhlindau@djh-bayern.de; *Herbergsweg 11; dorm beds €17.20*) is only open to under 27s. For both, take bus No 1 or 2 to the bus station, then bus No 3.

On the island, family-run **Pension Noris** (☎ 36 45, fax 10 42; *Brettermarkt 13; singles/ doubles from €30/62*) is basic and clean. **Alte Post** (☎ 934 60, fax 93 46 46; e info@ alte-post-lindau.de; *Fischergasse 3; singles/ doubles from €44/67*) has beautifully maintained rooms and a Bavarian/Austrian restaurant (mains €7 to €17). Five-star **Bayerischer Hof** (☎ 91 50, fax 91 55 91; e bayerischerhof-lindau@t-online.de; *Seepromenade; singles/ doubles from €103/135*) has the best views in town. **Gasthaus zum Sünfzen** (*Maximilianstrasse 1; dishes from €7*) is a popular island institution.

FRIEDRICHSHAFEN
☎ 07541 • pop 56,400

Friedrichshafen, the largest and most 'central' city on the lake's northern shore, has its **tourist office** (☎ 300 10; *Bahnhofplatz 2*) near the Stadtbahnhof train station. Count Zeppelin built his first explodable cigar-shaped airships here. This is commemorated in the town's **Zeppelin Museum** (☎ 380 10; *Seestrasse 22; adult/concession €6.50/3; open 10am-6pm Tues-Sun all year, 10am-5pm Nov-Mar*). The **DJH hostel** (☎ 724 04, fax 749 86; e jh-friedrichschafen@t-online.de; *Lindauer Strasse 3; juniors/seniors €14.90/17.60*) is a 15-minute walk from the harbour.

Rhineland-Palatinate

Rhineland-Palatinate (Rheinland-Pfalz) has a rugged topography characterised by thinly populated mountain ranges and forests cut by deep river valleys. Created after WWII from parts of the former Rhineland and Rhenish Palatinate regions, its turbulent history resulted in the area being settled by the Romans and later hotly contested by the French and a variety of German states. The state capital is Mainz.

This land of wine and great natural beauty reaches its apex in the enchanted Moselle Valley towns like Cochem, and along the heavily touristed Rhine, where verdant hillside vineyards twine around the foundations of noble castles and looming medieval fortresses.

THE MOSELLE VALLEY

Exploring the vineyards and wineries of the Moselle (Mosel) Valley is an ideal way to get a taste of German culture and people – and, of course, the wonderful wines. Take the time to slow down and do some sipping. (But don't take it too slow as most wineries close from November to March.)

The Moselle is bursting at the seams with historical sites and picturesque towns built along the river below steep rocky cliffs planted with vineyards (they say locals are born with one leg shorter than the other so that they can easily work the vines). It's one of the country's most romantically scenic regions, with stunning views rewarding the intrepid hikers who brave the hilly trails. Tourist offices sell good maps showing trails and paths, and usually have tips on short hikes.

There are camping grounds, hostels and rooms with classic views all along the Moselle Valley. Many wine-makers also have their own small pensions and, as usual, local tourist offices operate well-organised room-finding services. In May, on summer weekends or during the local wine harvest (mid-September to mid-October), accommodation is hard to find.

Getting There & Away

The most scenic section of the Moselle Valley runs 195km northeast from Trier to Koblenz; it's most practical to begin your Moselle Valley trip from either of these two hubs. If you have private transport and are coming from the north, however, you might head up the Ahr Valley and cut through the scenic Eifel Mountain area between the A61 and A48.

Getting Around

It is not possible to travel the length of the Moselle River via rail. Local and fast trains run every hour between Trier and Koblenz (€16, 1½ hours), but the only riverside stretch

GERMANY

of this line is between Cochem and Koblenz. Apart from this run – and the scenic Mosel-weinbahn line taking tourists between Bullay and Traben-Trarbach (€2.50, 20 minutes) – travellers must use buses, ferries, bicycles, or cars to travel between Moselle towns.

Moselbahn (☎ 0651-14 77 50) runs eight buses on weekdays (fewer on weekends) between Trier and Bullay (three hours each way). It's a very scenic route, following the river's winding course and passing through numerous quaint villages along the way. Buses leave from outside the train stations in Trier, Traben-Trarbach and Bullay. Frequent buses operate between Kues (Alter Bahnhof) and the Wittlich main train station (€3.60, 30 minutes one way), and connect with trains to Koblenz and Trier.

A great way to explore the Moselle in the high season is by boat. Just make sure you have enough time to relax and enjoy the languorous pace; getting from Koblenz to Trier using scheduled ferry services takes two days. Between early May and mid-October, **Köln-Düsseldorfer (KD) Line** (☎ 0221-208 8318) ferries sail daily between Koblenz and Cochem (€20.20 one way, 4½ hours), and the **Gebrüder Kolb Line** (☎ 02673-15 15) runs boats upriver from Cochem to Trier and back via Traben-Trarbach and Bernkastel. Various smaller ferry companies also operate on the Moselle. Eurail and German Rail passes are valid for all normal KD Line services, and travel on your birthday is free. There are numerous other possible excursions, ranging from short return cruises to multiday wine-tasting packages.

The Moselle is a popular area among cyclists, and for much of the river's course there's a separate 'Moselroute' bike track. **Touren-Rad** (☎ 0261-911 60 16; Hohenzollernstrasse 127), six blocks from the main train station in Koblenz, rents quality mountain and touring bicycles from €6 to €10 per day. It has a deal with the rental shop at Trier's main **train station** (☎ 0651-14 88 56), so you can pick up or return bikes at either. In Bernkastel, **Fun-Bike Team** (☎ 06531-940 24; Schanzstrasse 22) rents standard bikes from €8 per day.

Koblenz
☎ 0261 • pop 109,000
While not to be compared with Trier or Cochem, Koblenz is a nice enough place to spend around half a day or so. The **tourist office**

(☎ 30 38 80; e info@koblenz-touristik.de; Bahnhofsplatz) is in front of the Hauptbahnhof.

Things to See The Deutsches Eck is a park at the sharp confluence of the Rhine and Moselle Rivers dedicated to German unity. Immediately across the Rhine is the impressive **Festung Ehrenbreitstein fortress** (☎ 974 24 45; adult/concession €1.10/0.50), which houses both the DJH hostel and the rather staid **Landesmuseum** (☎ 970 30; adult/concession €2/1.50).

South of Koblenz, at the head of the beautiful Eltz Valley, **Burg Eltz** (☎ 02672-95 05 00; open daily Apr-Nov) is not to be missed. Towering over the surrounding hills, this superb medieval castle has frescoes, paintings, furniture and ornately decorated rooms. Burg Eltz is best reached by train to Moselkern, from where it's a 50-minute walk up through the forest. Alternatively, you can drive via Münster-Maifeld to the nearby car park. Entry is allowed only with regular guided tours (adult/concession €5/3), but the **Schatzkammer** (treasure chamber; adult/concession €2/1) can be visited without one.

Places to Stay & Eat The camping ground **Rhein Mosel** (☎/fax 827 19; open Apr–mid-Oct), is on Schartwiesenweg at the confluence of the Moselle and Rhine Rivers opposite the Deutsches Eck. The daytime passenger ferry across the Moselle puts the camping ground within a five-minute walk of town.

Koblenz has a wonderful **DJH hostel** (☎ 97 28 70; e jh-koblenz@djh-info.de; dorm beds €14.20-17.50) housed in the old Ehrenbreitstein fortress, but it's advisable to book ahead in summer. From the main train station take bus No 7, 8 or 9; there's also a chairlift (€4/6 up/return) from Ehrenbreitstein station by the river. **Hotel Jahn van Werth** (☎ 365 00, fax 365 06; van Werth Strasse 9; singles/doubles €23/44, with bath €41/62) offers good value and basic rooms.

Altenhof and the area around Münzplatz in the Altstadt offer many good eating options. **Café Miljöö** (☎ 142 37; Gemüsegasse 8-10) does light dishes in a pleasant café atmosphere till late.

Cochem
☎ 02671 • pop 5300
This pretty picture-postcard German town has narrow alleyways and one of the most

beautiful castles in the region. It's also a good base for hikes into the hills. The staff are very helpful in Cochem's **tourist office** (☎ 600 40; e verkehrsamt.Cochem@lcoc .de; Endertplatz) next to the Moselbrücke bridge.

Things to See For a great view, head up to the **Pinnerkreuz** with the chairlift on Endert- strasse (€4). The stunning **Reichsburg Castle** (☎ 255; open 9am-5pm daily mid-Mar–mid- Nov) is just a 15-minute walk up the hill from town. There are regular daily tours (adult/ concession €3/1.60) and English translation sheets are available.

Cochem's **HH Hieronimi** (☎ 221; Stadion- strasse 1-3), just across the river is a friendly, family-run winery that offers tours for €5, in- cluding two tastings, a bottle of its own wine and a souvenir glass. Also in Cochem there's **Weingut Rademacher** (☎ 41 64; Pinner- strasse 10), diagonally behind the train station, where you can tour its winery and cellar (an old WWII bunker) for €5/6.80 with four/six wine tastings.

Places to Stay & Eat Lodging options in Cochem are copious. The riverside **Camping- platz Am Freizeitszentrum** (☎ 44 09; Sta- dionstrasse; tent/person/car €4/4/6.50) is downstream from the northern bridge; it's open from eight days before Easter to the end of October. Cochem's **DJH hostel** (☎ 86 33; e jh-cochem@djh-info.de; Klottener Strasse 9; dorm beds €16.10-21.20) was closed for renovation at the time of our visit; they expect to open again in April 2003. The large **Hotel Noss** (☎ 36 12, fax 53 66; Moselpromenade 17; singles/doubles €44/86) is on the water- front and has quite good rooms with shower and toilet.

A cheap fast-food choice is **Kochlöffel** (Am Markt 10), where you can eat well for less than €5 (chicken halves €2.50). **Zom Stüffje** (☎ 72 60; Oberbachstrasse 14; mains €8-18) is a traditional eating house.

Bernkastel-Kues
☎ 06531 • pop 7500
The twin town of Bernkastel-Kues is at the heart of the middle Moselle region. On the right bank, Bernkastel has a charming **Markt**, a romantic ensemble of half-timbered houses with beautifully decorated gables. For a primer on the local vino, try Bernkastel's **Weingut Dr**

Willkomm (☎ 80 54; Gestade 1). Located in a lovely old arched cellar, the winery also distils its own brandy. For a more thorough course, head across the river to Kues' **Vinothek** (☎ 41 41; Cusanusstrasse 2; admission €1.50, ad- mission with tastings €9), where €9 entitles you to taste as much or as little of the 130 wines and sparkling wines from the Moselle- Saar-Ruwer growing region as you wish. The **tourist office** (☎ 40 23; Am Gestade 6) is on the Bernkastel side.

The **Campingplatz Kueser Werth** (☎ 82 00; Am Hafen 2) has pleasant tent sites by the river. The **DJH hostel** (☎ 23 95; e jh-bernkas tel-kues@djh-info.de; Jugendherbergsstrasse 1; dorm beds €12.30) is near the castle. **Hotel Bären** (☎ 95 04 40, fax 950 44 46; singles/ doubles €38/88) has first-rate, modern rooms, some with river views.

Traben-Trarbach
☎ 06541 • pop 5800
Full of fanciful Art Nouveau villas, the smart double town of Traben-Trarbach is a welcome relief from the 'romantic-half-timbered-town' circuit. Pick up a map at the **tourist office** (☎ 839 80; e info@traben-trarbach.de; Bahn- strasse 22), a five-minute walk south of Tra- ben's train station.

For camping, there's the **Rissbach** (☎ 31 11; Rissbacher Strasse 170; open Apr–mid- Oct). The **DJH hostel** (☎ 92 78; e jh-traben -trarbach@djh-info.de; Hirtenpfad 6; dorm beds €14.60-17.90) has small and modern dorms.

The **Central-Hotel** (☎ 62 38; Bahnstrasse 43; singles/doubles €33/60) is clean, friendly and provides a good breakfast and rooms with toilet and shower.

Unusual and popular with the locals, the restaurant **Alte Zunftscheune** (☎ 97 37; Neue Rathausstrasse) serves steak with horseradish sauce, salad and fried potato for €14.

TRIER
☎ 0651 • pop 100,000
Trier is touted as Germany's oldest town. Al- though settlement of the site dates back to 400 BC, Trier itself was founded in 15 BC as Au- gusta Treverorum, the capital of Gaul, and was second in importance only to Rome in the Western Roman Empire. You'll find more Roman ruins here than anywhere else north of the Alps. There's a university too, and the city is quite lively.

GERMANY

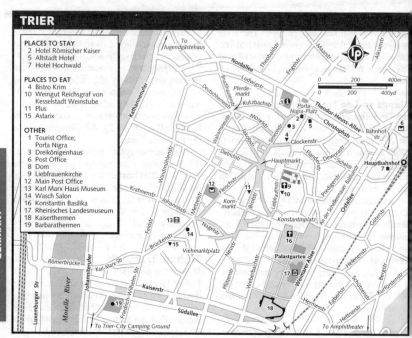

TRIER

PLACES TO STAY
2 Hotel Römischer Kaiser
5 Altstadt Hotel
7 Hotel Hochwald

PLACES TO EAT
4 Bistro Krim
10 Weingut Reichsgraf von
   Kesselstadt Weinstube
11 Plus
15 Astarix

OTHER
1 Tourist Office;
   Porta Nigra
3 Dreikönigenhaus
6 Post Office
8 Dom
9 Liebfrauenkirche
12 Main Post Office
13 Karl Marx Haus Museum
14 Wasch Salon
16 Konstantin Basilika
17 Rheinisches Landesmuseum
18 Kaiserthermen
19 Barbarathermen

Orientation & Information

From the main train station head west along Bahnhofstrasse and Theodor-Heuss-Allee to the Porta Nigra, where you'll find Trier's **tourist office** (☎ 97 80 80; e info@tit.de; open 9am-6pm Mon-Sat, 10am-3pm Sun Apr-Oct, 10am-5pm Mon-Sat Nov-Mar). It has a free and efficient room-finding service. Ask here about daily guided **city walking tours** in English (€6), and the three-day Trier-Card (€9), a combined ticket for the city's main sights, museums and public transport. From Porta Nigra, walk along Simeonstrasse's pedestrian zone to Hauptmarkt, the heart of the old city. Most of the sights are within this area of roughly one sq km. There's a convenient and cheap **Wasch Salon laundrette** (Brücken-strasse 19-21). The **main post office** is near the station.

Things to See

The town's chief landmark is the **Porta Nigra** (adult/concession €2.10/1.60; open 9am-6pm daily Apr-Sept, till 9am-5pm Oct-Mar), the imposing city gate on the northern edge of the town centre, which dates back to the 2nd century. The interesting **Rheinisches Landesmuseum** (Weimarer Allee 1; admission €5.50; open 9.30am-5pm Tues-Fri, 10.30am-5pm Sat & Sun) has works of art dating from Paleolithic, Roman and modern times.

Trier's massive Romanesque **Dom** shares a 1600-year history with the nearby and equally impressive **Konstantin Basilika**. Also worth visiting are the ancient **Amphitheater**, the **Kaiserthermen** and **Barbarathermen** (Roman baths). The early-Gothic **Dreikönigenhaus** (Simeonstrasse 19) was built around 1230 as a protective tower; the original entrance was on the second level, accessible only by way of a retractable rope ladder.

History buffs and nostalgic socialists can visit the **Karl Marx Haus Museum** (☎ 97 06 80; Brückenstrasse 10; adult/concession €2/1; open daily), in the house where a star was born (but don't expect to view anything particularly revolutionary).

Places to Stay

The municipal camping ground **Trier-City** (☎ 869 21; Luxemburger Strasse 81; tent/ person/car €4/6/4; open Apr-Oct) is nicely positioned beside the Moselle River. The DJH

Jugendgästehaus (☎ 14 66 20; e jh-trier@ djh-info.de; An der Jugendherberge 4; dorm beds/doubles/singles €16/21/29 per person) is also down by the riverside.

Hotel Hochwald (☎ 758 03, fax 743 54; Bahnhofplatz 5; singles €26, singles/doubles with bath €36/60) is opposite the train station and has austere but clean rooms. **Altstadt Hotel** (☎ 480 41, fax 412 93; Am Porta-Nigra-Platz; singles/doubles from €66/96) in the centre, has spacious rooms. **Hotel Römischer Kaiser** (☎ 977 00, fax 97 70 99; Am Porta-Nigra-Platz 6; singles/doubles from €67/98) is across the road and offers even better rooms.

Places to Eat

Trier is a great place to sample some Franco-German cooking. The bustling **Bistro Krim** (☎ 739 43; Glockenstrasse 7) offers generous Mediterranean-inspired dishes at affordable prices. There are also several set menus such as its two-course 'Mediterranean' menu for €14.80. **Astarix** (☎ 722 39; Karl-Marx-Strasse 11) is a favourite student hang-out back in an arcade that serves large salads and main dishes for under €6 (open till late). The weinstube of the **Weingut Reichsgraf von Kesselstadt** (☎ 411 78; Liebfrauenstrasse 10; mains from €7) offers a limited menu and superlative wines in a casual outdoor setting beside the Liebfrauenkirche.

Plus (Brotstrasse 23) is a central supermarket. The narrow Judengasse, near Markt, has several bars and cafés for tipples and nibbles, whereas a slicker crowd gravitates towards a cluster of bars on Viehmarktplatz.

Getting There & Away

Trier has hourly local and fast trains to Saarbrücken (€12.40, 1½ hours) and Koblenz (€15.60, 1½ hours), as well as services to Luxembourg (€7.40, 45 minutes) and Metz (in France; €18.20, 2½ hours). For information on river ferries, see Getting There & Away in the previous Moselle Valley section.

RHINE VALLEY – KOBLENZ TO MAINZ

A trip along the Rhine is on the itinerary of most travellers. The section between Mainz and Koblenz offers the best scenery, especially the narrow tract downriver from Rüdesheim. Spring and autumn are the best times to visit; in summer it's over-run and in

winter most towns go into hibernation. For information on Koblenz, see the previous Moselle Valley section.

Activities

The Koblenz-to-Mainz section of the Rhine Valley is great for wine tasting, with Bacharach, 45km south of Koblenz, being one of the top choices for sipping. For tastings in other towns, ask for recommendations at the tourist offices or just follow your nose.

Though the trails here may be a bit more crowded with day-trippers than those along the Moselle, hiking along the Rhine is also excellent. The slopes and trails around Bacharach are justly famous.

Getting There & Away

Koblenz and Mainz are the best starting points. The Rhine Valley is also easily accessible from Frankfurt on a long day trip, but that won't do justice to the region.

Getting Around

Each mode of transport on the Rhine has its own advantages and all are equally enjoyable. Try combining several of them by going on foot one day, cycling the next, and then taking a boat for a view from the river. The **Köln-Düsseldorfer (KD) Line** (☎ 0221-208 83 18) earns its bread and butter on the Rhine, with many slow and fast boats daily between Koblenz and Mainz. The most scenic stretch is between Koblenz and Rüdesheim; the journey takes about four hours downstream, about 5½ hours upstream (€23.20). See Getting Around in the previous Moselle Valley section for information about concessions. Boats stop at many riverside towns along the way.

Train services operate on both sides of the Rhine River, but are more convenient on the left bank. You can travel nonstop on IC/EC trains or travel by regional RB or SE services.

Touring the Rhine Valley by car is also ideal. The route between Koblenz and Mainz is short enough for a car to be rented and returned to either city. There are no bridge crossings between Koblenz and Rüdesheim, but there are several ferry crossings.

Mainz

☎ 06131 • pop 183,000

A 30-minute train ride from Frankfurt, Mainz has an attractive old town. Though it can't compare to the compact beauty of the nearby towns along the Rhine, Mainz impresses with its massive **Domstrasse** (*cathedral; admission free; open daily*) and the **St Stephanskirche** (*Weissgasse 12; admission free; open daily*), with stained-glass windows by Marc Chagall. Mainz's museums include the **Gutenberg Museum** (☎ 26 40; *Liebfrauenplatz 5; adult/concession €3/1.30; open Tues-Sun*), which contains two precious copies of the first printed Bible. For more information on attractions in Mainz, visit the **tourist office** (☎ 28 62 10; **e** tourist@info-mainz.de; *Brückenturm am Rathaus*). **C@fé Enterprise** (*Bilhildisstrasse 2*), on Münsterplatz in Mainz, has Internet facilities.

If you are staying overnight, try the **Jugendgästehaus** (☎ 853 32; **e** jh-mainz@djh-info.de; *Otto-Brunfels-Schneise 4; beds €16.10-21.20*); take bus No 62, 63 or 92 towards Weisenau. The **Hotel Stadt Coblenz** (☎ 22 76 02, fax 22 33 07; *Rheinstrasse 499; singles/doubles without bath €42/55, with bath €52/68*) has hostel-quality rooms (ask for one away from the street).

The **Augustiner Keller** (☎ 22 26 62; *Augustinerstrasse 26; mains €6-14*) serves tasty Alsatian-style pizzas in a homy, old-fashioned setting.

St Goar/St Goarhausen
☎ 06741 • pop 3500

Where the slopes along the Rhine aren't covered with vines, you can bet they built a castle. One of the most impressive is **Burg Rheinfels** (☎ 383; *adult/concession €4/2; open 9am-5pm daily Apr-Oct, 10am-4pm Sat & Sun in good weather Nov-Mar*) in St Goar. An absolute must-see, the labyrinthine ruins reflect the greed and ambition of Count Dieter V of Katzenelnbogen, who built the castle in 1245 to help levy tolls on passing ships. You will need a torch (flashlight) to explore the more removed of the castle's spooky corridors. Across the river, just south of St Goarshausen, is the Rhine's most famous sight, the **Loreley Cliff**. Legend has it that a maiden sang sailors to their deaths against its base. It's worth the trek to the top of the Loreley for the view, but try to get up there early in the morning before the hordes ascend.

For camping, **Campingplatz Loreleyblick** (☎ 20 66; *tent sites €2.20, plus €3 per person; open Mar-Oct*) is on the banks of the Rhine, opposite the legendary rock. St Goar's

Jugendherberge (☎ 388; **e** jh-st-goar@djh-info.de; *Bismarckweg 17; dorm beds €11.80*) is right below the castle. More restful accommodation can be found at **Knab's Mühlenschänke** (☎ 16 98, fax 16 78; *Gründelbachtal 73; singles/doubles €25/48*) about 1.5km north of St Goar. You can sip the house wine here in a rural atmosphere. The **Schlosshotel Rheinfels** (☎ 80 20, fax 80 28 02; *singles/doubles from €85/128*) in the castle is the top address in town, with rooms and a fine restaurant with prices to match.

Bacharach
☎ 06743 • pop 2400

The town of Bacharach hides its not inconsiderable charms behind a time-worn wall and is therefore easily bypassed.

Walk beneath one of its thick arched gateways, however, and you'll find yourself in a beautifully preserved medieval village. Drop by the **tourist office** (☎ 91 93 03; *Oberstrasse 45; open 9am-5pm Mon-Fri, 10am-4pm Sat Apr-Oct*) for information on Bacharach's sights and lodging.

The **Sonnenstrand** (☎ 17 52; *tent/person/car €3/4.20/5.50; open Apr–mid-Oct*) offers riverside camping just 500m south of the centre. Bacharach's **Jugendherberge** (☎ 12 66; **e** jh-bacharach@djh-info.de; *dorm beds €14.20-17.50*) is a legendary facility housed in the Burg Stahleck castle. In town, **Irmgaard Orth** (☎ 15 53; *Spurgasse 2; singles/doubles €18/34*) offers good budget rooms.

Kurpfälzische Münze (☎ 13 75; *Oberstrasse 72; dishes €7-20*) serves traditional dishes, including game. **Zum Grünen Baum** (☎ 12 08; *Oberstrasse 63; mains from €7*) is wonderful place to sample the region's abundance of top-notch wines.

Rüdesheim
☎ 06722 • pop 10,360

Rolling drunk on tourism, this town is worth a visit only if you are studying mass tourism at its worst, or seeking out the bucolic paths in the hills above. Avoid eating anywhere in Rüdesheim's Drosselgasse, an oversold row of touristy shops and restaurants. Instead, get some perspective on the area by taking the **Weinlehrpfad** walking route from above the touristy main drag. It leads through vineyard slopes to the **Brömserburg**, an old riverside castle that houses an interesting **wine museum** (*adult/concession €3/2*).

The **Jugendherberge** (☎ 27 11; e *ruede sheim@djh-hessen.de; Am Kreuzberg; dorm beds juniors/seniors €12/14.70)* is about a 30-minute walk from the train station. The large **Parkhotel Deutscher Hof** (☎ 30 16, fax 17 17; e *info@parkhotel-ruedesheim.de; Rheinstrasse 21-23; singles/doubles €50/74)* is nicely situated along the river.

Saarland

In the late 19th century, Saarland's coal mines and steel mills fuelled the burgeoning German economy. Since WWII, however, the steady economic decline of coal and steel has made Saarland the poorest region in western Germany. Though distinctly German since the early Middle Ages, Saarland was ruled by France for several periods during its turbulent history. Reoccupied by the French after WWII, it only joined the Federal Republic of Germany in 1957, after the population rejected French efforts to turn it into an independent state.

SAARBRÜCKEN
☎ 0681 • pop 185,000

Saarbrücken, capital of Saarland, has an interesting mixed French and German feel. While lacking in major tourist sights, this city is a matter-of-fact place where people go about their daily business and where tourists are treated as individuals. It's also an easy base for day trips to some of the beautiful little towns nearby, such as Ottweiler, Saarburg, Mettlach and St Wendel.

Orientation & Information

The main train station is in the northwestern corner of the old town, which stretches out on both sides of the Saar River. The **tourist office** (☎ 93 80 90; Reichsstrasse 1; open 9am-6pm Mon-Fri, 10am-12.30pm & 1pm-6pm Sat) is directly in front of the station.

The **Reisebank** in the main train station is open daily. There's also a **post office** here and another in the city centre at Dudweilerstrasse 17. There is a laundry **Waschhaus** (Nauwieserstrasse 22; open 8am-10pm daily).

Things to See & Do

Start your visit by strolling along the lanes around lively **St Johanner Markt** in the central pedestrian zone. A flea market is held here every second Saturday from April to November. Not far away beside the Saar River are the **Saarländische Staatstheater** *(Schillerplatz 1)*, a neoclassical structure built by the Nazis, and the two buildings of the **Saarland-Museum** *(Bismarckstrasse 11-19 • Karlstrasse 1; adult/concession €1.50/1; open Tues-Sun)*. The modern gallery on Bismarckstrasse is the more interesting of the two, displaying pieces by Picasso, Otto Dix, and other renowned 20th-century artists. The best bet for contemporary art is the **Stadtgalerie Saarbrücken** (☎ 93 68 30; St Johanner Markt 24; admission free), a playful, fascinating gallery dedicated to cutting-edge works.

Cross the 1549 **Alte Brücke** (Old Bridge) to the **Schloss Saarbrücken**, the former palace on Schlossplatz designed by King Wilhelm Friedrich's court architect, Friedrich Joachim Stengel, in the 18th century. A 1989 facelift by Gottfried Böhm gives the building a distinctly sinister, Darth Vader-ish appearance.

There are several museums located around Schlossplatz; the most interesting being the **Abenteuer Museum** *(Adventure Museum; adult/concession €3/2; open 9am-1pm Tues & Wed, 3pm-7pm Thur & Fri)*, with a hotchpotch of weird souvenirs and photos collected since 1950 by solo adventurer extraordinaire, Heinz Rox-Schulz.

The nearby **Ludwigsplatz**, a baroque square that is also the work of Stengel, is dominated by the Lutheran **Ludwigskirche**. It is often closed, but you can peer through the glass doorway.

Places to Stay & Eat

The **Campingplatz Saarbrücken** (☎ 517 80; Am Spicherer Berg; tent sites €6, plus €4 per person) is on the French border, south of the city; take bus No 42 to Spicherer Weg from where it's a five-minute walk. The excellent **Jugendherberge** (☎ 330 40, fax 37 49 11; Meerwiesertalweg 31; dorm beds/twins €16.10-21.20 per person) is a 30-minute walk northeast of the train station. Or take bus No 49 or 69 to Prinzenweiher. Beds are in four-person dorms, or two-person rooms.

Hotel zur Klause (☎ 92 69 60, fax 926 96 50; Deutschherrnstrasse 72; singles/doubles €36/62) is one of the cheapest in the city. **Hotel Stadt Hamburg** (☎ 330 53, fax 37 43 30; Bahnhofstrasse 71-73; singles/doubles €49/78) has clean rooms. **Hotel im Fuchs** (☎ 93 65 50, fax 936 55 36; Kappenstrasse 12;

GERMANY

singles/doubles €57/81) has nice rooms with facilities.

In Saarbrücken's eateries, your taste buds get to visit France while enjoying hearty German servings. **Gasthaus Zum Stiefel** (☎ 93 54 50; Am Stiefel 2; restaurant mains from €9) is in an old brewery just off St Johanner Markt. It has an upmarket restaurant at the front specialising in fine meat and fish dishes. The pub out the back (enter from Froschengasse) has house beers on tap and serves less expensive food. Also try some of the other bistros and fast-food places along Froschengasse.

You'll find many restaurants and student pubs along the streets running off Max-Ophüls-Platz. The **Café Kostbar** (Nauwieserstrasse 19), situated in an attractive backstreet courtyard, has well-priced set menus from €6.50. **Tomate 2** (Schlossstrasse 2; dishes €7-14) is a Mediterranean-style bistro across the river, near Schlossplatz.

Getting There & Away

There are frequent trains to the connecting cities of Mannheim (€18.60, 2¼ hours), Koblenz (€28, 2½ hours), Mainz (€23.40, two hours) and Frankfurt (€30.80, 2½ hours), as well as services across the border to Metz.

Hesse

The Hessians, a Frankish tribe, were among the first to convert to Lutheranism in the early 16th century. Apart from a brief period of unity in that same century under Philip the Magnanimous, Hesse (Hessen) remained a motley collection of principalities and, later, of Prussian administrative districts until proclaimed a state in 1945. Its main cities are Frankfurt, Kassel and the capital, Wiesbaden.

As well as being a transport hub, the very un-German city of Frankfurt can also be used as a base to explore some of the smaller towns in Hesse. The beautiful Taunus and Spessart regions offer quiet village life and hours of scenic walks.

FRANKFURT/MAIN

☎ 069 • pop 650,000

They call it 'Bankfurt', 'Mainhattan' and much more. It's on the Main (pronounced 'mine') River, and is generally referred to as Frankfurt-am-Main, or Frankfurt/Main, since there is another large city called Frankfurt

(Frankfurt an der Oder) which is near the Polish border.

Frankfurt/Main is the financial and geographical centre of western Germany, as well as the host of important trade fairs. Thanks to generous funding in the 1980s and early 1990s, Frankfurt also has some excellent museums.

It is Germany's most important transport hub for air, train and road connections so you'll probably end up here at some point. Don't be surprised if you find this cosmopolitan melting pot much more interesting than you had expected.

Orientation

The airport is 11 minutes by train southwest of the city centre. The Hauptbahnhof is on the western side of the city, but within walking distance of the old city centre.

The safest route to the city centre through the sleazy train station area is along Kaiserstrasse. This leads to Kaiserplatz and then to a large square called An der Hauptwache. The area between the former lockup (Hauptwache), and the Römerberg, in the tiny vestige of Frankfurt's original old city, is the centre of Frankfurt. The Main River flows just south of the Altstadt, with several bridges leading to one of the city's livelier areas, Sachsenhausen. Its northeastern corner, behind the youth hostel (see Places to Stay later in this section), is known as Alt-Sachsenhausen and is full of quaint old houses and narrow alleyways.

Information

Tourist Offices Frankfurt's most convenient **tourist office** (☎ 21 23 88 00; open 8am-5pm Mon-Fri, 9am-6pm Sat, Sun & holidays) is in the main hall of the train station. For its efficient room-finding service there's a charge of €2.50.

In the centre of the city, the **Römer tourist office** (☎ 21 23 88 00; Römerberg 27; open 9.30am-5.30pm Mon-Fri, 10am-4pm Sat & Sun) occupies the northwest corner of the Römerberg square. Another conveniently located branch is the **CityInfo Zeil** (☎ 21 23 88 00; cnr Zeil & Stiftstrasse; open 10am-6pm Mon-Fri, 10am-4pm Sat & Sun), where you can reserve rooms and pick up city maps and brochures.

The head office of the **German National Tourist Office** (☎ 974 64, fax 75 19 03; **w** www.deutschland-tourismus.de; Beethovenstrasse 69), is a good place to contact if you're still planning your trip to Germany; it has brochures on all areas of the country.

One- and two-day Frankfurt cards (€7.50/11) give 50% reductions on admission to all of the city's important museums, the airport terraces, the zoo and Palmengarten, as well as unlimited travel on public transport.

Money The main train station has a branch of the **Reisebank** *(open 6.30am-10pm daily)*, near the southern exit at the head of platform No 1. There are banks and numerous ATMs at the airport, including a **Reisebank** *(Terminal 1, arrival hall B; open 6am-11pm daily)*.

AmEx and **Thomas Cook** are situated opposite each other on Kaiserstrasse at Nos 10 and 11 respectively.

Post & Communications The **main post office** *(Zeil 90)* is on the ground floor of the Karstadt department store (standard shop hours). Inside the Hauptbahnhof there is a **post office** *(open 7am-7.30pm Mon-Fri, 8am-4pm Sat)*. The airport **post office** *(open 7am-9pm daily)* is in the waiting lounge, departure hall B.

Email & Internet Access Directly across from the train station, **Telebistro** *(☎ 61 99 11 87; Poststrasse 2)* charges €2.10 for 30 minutes online.

Bookshops Between the Hauptwache and Rathenauplatz, **Hugendubel** *(Beibergasse)* stocks Lonely Planet guides and has a café downstairs. The **British Bookshop** *(Börsenstrasse 17)* provides a wide range of English-language fiction and nonfiction.

Laundry The Waschcenter chain in Frankfurt has a **laundrette** *(Wallstrasse 8)* in Sachsenhausen. In Bockenheim, the **SB-Waschcenter** *(Grosse Seestrasse 46)* is another option.

Medical Services The **Uni-Klinik** *(☎ 630 10; Theodor Stern Kai; open 24hr)* is in Sachsenhausen. For medical queries, contact the 24-hour **doctor** service on ☎ 192 92.

Dangers & Annoyances The area around the main train station is a base for Frankfurt's sex and illegal drug trades. Frequent police patrols of the station and the surrounding Bahnhofsviertel keep things under control, but it's advisable to exercise 'big city' sense.

Things to See & Do
About 80% of the old city was wiped off the map by two Allied bombing raids in March 1944, and postwar reconstruction was subject to the demands of the new age. Rebuilding efforts were more thoughtful, however, in the **Römerberg**, the old central area of Frankfurt west of the cathedral, where restored 14th- and 15th-century buildings provide a glimpse of the beautiful city this once was. The old town hall, or **Römer**, is in the northwestern corner of Römerberg and consists of three 15th-century houses topped with Frankfurt's trademark stepped gables.

East of Römerberg, behind the Historischer Garten (Historical Garden), which has the remains of Roman and Carolingian foundations, is the **Dom**, the coronation site of Holy Roman emperors from 1562 to 1792. It's dominated by the elegant 15th-century Gothic **tower** (completed in the 1860s) – one of the few structures left standing after the 1944 raids. The small **Wahlkapelle** (Voting Chapel) on the cathedral's southern side is where the seven electors of the Holy Roman Empire chose the emperor from 1356 onwards; the adjoining **choir** has beautiful wooden stalls.

Anyone with an interest in German literature should visit **Goethe Haus** *(☎ 13 88 00; Grosser Hirschgraben 23-25; adult/concession €5/3; open 9am-6pm Mon-Fri Apr-Sept, 9am-4pm Mon-Fri Oct-Mar, 10am-4pm Sat & Sun all year)*. Johann Wolfgang von Goethe was born in this house in 1749.

A little bit farther afield, there's the botanical **Palmengarten** *(Siesmayerstrasse; adult/concession €3.50/1.50)* as well as the creative **Frankfurt Zoo** *(Alfred-Brehm-Platz 16; adult/concession €5.50/2.50)*, both good places to unwind. It is also a nice 40-minute walk east along the south bank of the Main River to the **lock** in Offenbach – just before it there's a good beer garden.

There's a great **flea market** along Museumsufer between 8am and 2pm every Saturday.

Museums Most of Frankfurt's museums are closed on Monday and offer free entry on Wednesday. Unless otherwise indicated, the ones below are open 10am to 5pm Tuesday to Sunday (to 8pm Wednesday).

The **Museum für Moderne Kunst** *(☎ 21 23 04 47; Domstrasse 10; adult/concession €5/2.50)* north of the cathedral, features works of modern art by Joseph Beuys, Claes Oldenburg

CENTRAL FRANKFURT

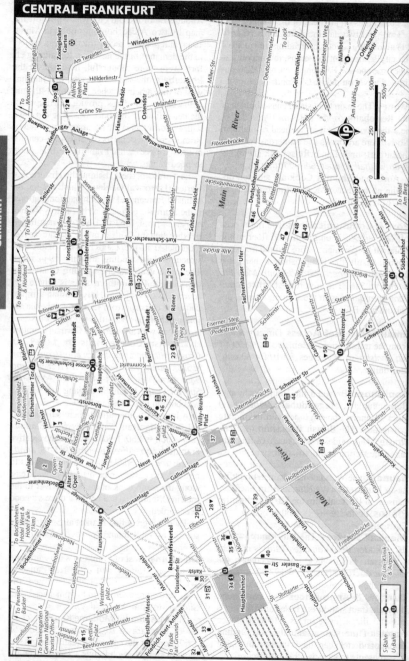

CENTRAL FRANKFURT

PLACES TO STAY
1 Hotel-Pension Gölz; Hotel Beethoven
12 Hotel Am Zoo
15 Hotel-Pension Bruns
19 Hotel-Garni Diplomat
27 Steinberger Frankfurter Hof
30 Hotel Carlton; Concorde Hotel
32 Hotel Glockshuber
33 Hotel Topas
35 Hotel Münchner Hof
36 Hotel Eden
40 Hotel Wiesbaden
41 Hotel Tourist
46 Haus der Jugend

PLACES TO EAT
3 Blaubart Gewölbekeller
18 Kleinmarkthalle
20 Metropol

28 India Curry House
39 Ginger Brasserie
48 Fichte-Kränzi
50 HL Supermarket
51 Zum Gemalten Haus

OTHER
2 Alte Oper (Old Opera House)
4 British Bookshop
5 Turm-Palast Cinema
6 The Cave
7 Sinkkasten
8 CityInfo Zeil
9 Main Post Office; Karstadt Department Store
10 Zum Schwejk
11 Zoo
13 Hugendubel
14 Jazzkeller
16 American Express

17 U60311
21 Dom
22 Museum für Moderne Kunst
23 Römer Tourist Office
24 Cooky's
25 Goethe Haus
26 Thomas Cook
29 English Theater
31 Telebistro
34 Tourist Office
37 Städtische Bühnen/ Frankfurter Oper
38 Jüdisches Museum
42 ADM-Mitfahrzentrale
43 Städelsches Kunstinstitut
44 Deutsches Filmmuseum
45 Museum für Angewandte Kunst
47 Waschcenter
49 Stereo Bar

GERMANY

and many others. Also on the north bank there's the **Jüdisches Museum** (Jewish Museum; ☎ 21 23 50 00; adult/concession €2.60/1.30, free Sat).

Numerous museums line the south bank of the Main River along the so-called **Museumsufer** (Museum Embankment). Pick of the crop is the **Städelsches Kunstinstitut** (☎ 605 09 80; Schaumainkai 63; adult/concession €6/5; open to 8pm Thur), with a world-class collection of paintings by artists from the Renaissance to the 20th century, including Botticelli, Dürer, Van Eyck, Rubens, Rembrandt, Vermeer, Cézanne and Renoir. Other highlights include the **Deutsches Filmmuseum** (☎ 21 23 88 30; Schaumainkai 41; adult/concession €2.50/1.30; open 2pm-8pm Sat); and the fascinating, design-oriented **Museum für Angewandte Kunst** (Museum of Applied Arts; ☎ 21 23 40 37; Schaumainkai 17; admission €5).

Places to Stay

Camping The most recommended camping ground is **Campingplatz Heddernheim** (☎ 57 03 32; An der Sandelmühle 35; tent sites €3.50, plus €5.20/4.50 per person/car; open year-round) in the Heddernheim district northwest of the city centre. It's a 15-minute ride on the U1, U2 or U3 from the Hauptwache U-Bahn station – get off at Heddernheim.

Hostels The big, bustling and crowded **Haus der Jugend** (☎ 610 01 50, fax 61 00 15 99; Deutschherrnufer 12; beds under/over 20

years €14.50/18; curfew 2am) is within walking distance of the city centre and Sachsenhausen's nightspots. From the train station take bus No 46 to Frankensteinerplatz, or take S-Bahn No 2, 3, 4, 5 or 6 to Lokalbahnhof, then walk north for 10 minutes. Check-in begins at 1pm (postcode for bookings: 60594 Frankfurt/Main).

Hotels & Pensions In this city, 'cheap' can mean paying more than €60 for a spartan double room. During the many busy trade fairs even that price is unrealistic, with scarce rooms commanding a 50% to 200% premium.

Predictably, most of Frankfurt's budget accommodation is in the sleazy Bahnhofsviertel which surrounds the station. **Hotel Eden** (☎ 25 19 14, fax 25 23 37; Münchener Strasse 42; singles/doubles €45/60) has fairly reasonable rooms with toilet and shower. **Hotel Münchner Hof** (☎ 23 00 66, fax 23 44 28; Münchener Strasse 46; singles/doubles €49/65) has fairly good basic offerings with toilet and shower. **Hotel Carlton** (☎ 23 20 93, fax 23 36 73; Karlstrasse 11; singles/doubles €57/73) and the neighbouring **Concorde Hotel** (☎ 242 42 20, fax 24 24 22 88; Karlstrasse 9; singles/ doubles €50/65) both have rooms with facilities. **Hotel Tourist** (☎ 23 30 95/96/97, fax 23 69 86; Baseler Strasse 23-25; singles/doubles €55/75) is similar. **Hotel Wiesbaden** (☎ 23 23 47, fax 25 28 45; Baseler Strasse 52; singles/doubles from €65/75) is one of the better options in the area.

Hotel Glockshuber (☎ 74 26 28, fax 74 26 29; Mainzer Landstrasse 120; singles/doubles from €35/60), north of the main train station, is another pleasant option. **Hotel Topas** (☎ 23 08 52, fax 238 05 82 60; Niddastrasse 88; singles/doubles €64.50/68) has quite nice rooms with bathroom.

Sachsenhausen has few budget places. **Hotel Am Berg** (☎ 61 20 21, fax 61 51 09; Grethenweg 23; singles/doubles without bath from €33/55, doubles with bath from €70), in the quiet backstreets a few minutes' walk southeast from Südbahnhof, has rooms with and without bathroom, and several more expensive choices.

Some of the best pensions are in Frankfurt's posh Westend. **Pension Backer** (☎ 74 79 92, fax 74 79 00; Mendelssohnstrasse 92; singles/doubles €25/40) has basic rooms. **Hotel-Pension Bruns** (☎ 74 88 96, fax 74 88 46; singles/doubles without bath €40/50, with bath €50/65) at No 42 has simple rooms in a spacious house. The pleasant **Hotel-Pension Gölz** (☎ 74 67 35, fax 74 61 42; e info@hotel-goelz.de; Beethovenstrasse 44; singles/doubles with bath €45/70) has basic rooms.

The **Hotel Beethoven** (☎ 74 60 91, fax 74 84 66; e mail@hotelbeethoven.de; Beethovenstrasse 44; singles/doubles with bath €70/145) has newly renovated rooms.

In Bockenheim, **Hotel West** (☎ 247 90 20, fax 707 53 09; Gräfstrasse 81; singles/doubles €60/80) has quite good rooms with facilities. **Hotel Falk** (☎ 70 80 94, fax 70 80 17; Falkstrasse 38a; singles/doubles €89/109), in a quiet but still central neighbourhood, is one notch higher.

East of Konstablerwache there's the friendly **Hotel-Garni Diplomat** (☎ 430 40 40, fax 430 40 22; Ostendstrasse 24-26; singles/doubles €50/70) which has passable rooms a short walk from the Ostend S-Bahn station. The **Hotel am Zoo** (☎ 94 99 30, fax 94 99 31 99; e Hotel-am-Zoo@t-online.de; Alfred-Brehm-Platz 6; singles/doubles €72/106) is a reasonable option.

The quality **Steigenberger Frankfurter Hof** (☎ 215 02, fax 21 59 00; e frankfurter-hot@steigenberger.de; Am Kaiserplatz; singles/doubles Mon-Fri €335/385, Sat & Sun €160/210) has rates during the week that exclude breakfast, however, it's a far better bet on the weekend when there are special rates that include breakfast.

Places to Eat

The area around the main train station has lots of ethnic eating options. Baseler Strasse in particular has a Middle Eastern tone. **India Curry House** (Weserstrasse 17; mains from €5) has savoury kormas and curries. The pan-Asian **Ginger Brasserie** (Windmühlstrasse 14; mains €10-17) has everything Eastern on the menu from Sichuan to sushi, tandoori to Thai.

Known to the locals as Fressgass (Munch-Alley), the Kalbächer Gasse and Grosse Bockenheimer Strasse area, between Opernplatz and Börsenstrasse, has some medium-priced restaurants and fast-food places with outdoor tables in summer. **Blaubart Gewölbekeller** (Kaiserhofstrasse 18; mains from €6) serves well-priced hearty dishes in a beer cellar atmosphere. It's also a lively place to drink until late. The **Kleinmarkthalle** off Hasengasse, is a great produce market with loads of fruit, vegetables, meats and hot food. **Metropol** (Weckmarkt 13-15; mains from €7.20), near the Dom, serves up well-priced and filling salads, casseroles and the like until late, but the service is notoriously slow.

Apple-wine taverns are a Frankfurt eating and drinking tradition. They serve *Ebbelwoi* (Frankfurt dialect for *Apfelwein*), an alcoholic apple cider, along with local specialities like *Handkäse mit Musik* (literally, 'hand-cheese with music'). This is a round cheese soaked in oil and vinegar and topped with onions; your bowel supplies the music. Some good Ebbelwoi are situated in Alt-Sachsenhausen – the area directly behind the DJH hostel – which bulges with eateries and pubs. The **Fichte-Kränzi** (Wallstrasse 5; mains around €8) is highly recommended for its friendly atmosphere and well-priced food. It also serves beer. **Zum Gemalten Haus** (Schweizer Strasse 67; mains from €7) is a lively place full of paintings of old Frankfurt. The **Zur Sonne** (☎ 45 93 96; Berger Strasse 312; open from 4pm daily), in Bornheim, is authentic and has a gorgeous yard for summer tippling. Take the U-4 to Bornheim-Mitte.

Wallstrasse and the surrounding streets in Alt-Sachsenhausen also have lots of ethnic mid-priced restaurants.

Another good place for ravenous hunters and gatherers is the cosmopolitan Berger Strasse and Nordend areas north of the Zeil. **Eckhaus** (Bornheimer Landstrasse 45; meals from €6) is a relaxed restaurant and bar that serves well-priced salads and main dishes in he evening. For both of these, take the U-4 to Merianplatz. **Strandcafé** *(Koselstrasse 46; dishes under €13)* serves delicious felafel and salads and other Middle Eastern dishes in a pleasant atmosphere; take the U-5 to Musterschule. **Grössenwahn** (☎ 59 93 56; *Lenaustrasse 97)* is a truly wonderful upmarket pub where, if you choose carefully, you can eat for less than €15. Take the U-5 to Glauburgstrasse. Follow Lenaustrasse north until you think you've reached the end – and keep going north.

In Bockenheim, **Stattcafé** *(Grempstrasse 21; dishes from €6)* offers vegetarian and meat dishes, as well as good coffee and cakes. **Pielok** *(Jordanstrasse 3; mains around €7)* looks like your grandmother had a hand in the decorations; it's cosy and the food is traditional, filling and very popular with students.

Fresh produce **markets** are held 8am to 6pm on Thursday and Friday at Bockenheimer Warte and Südbahnhof respectively. There is a **supermarket** in the basement of Karstadt on Zeil. An **HL supermarket** is situated in the basement of Woolworths on Schweizer Strasse in Sachsenhausen.

Entertainment

Ballet, opera and theatre are strong features of Frankfurt's entertainment scene. For information and bookings, ring **Städtische Bühnen** (☎ 134 04 00; *Willy-Brandt-Platz)*, or the **Karstadt concert and theatre-booking service** (☎ 29 48 48; *Zeil 90; commission charged)*. *Journal Frankfurt* (€1.50) and *Fritz* have good listings in German of what's on in town.

The **Turm-Palast** (☎ 28 17 87; *Am Eschenheimer Turm)* is a multiscreen cinema showing films in English. English-language plays and musicals are staged every evening (except Monday) by the **English Theater** (☎ 24 23 16 20; *Kaiserstrasse 52)*.

Frankfurt also has a couple of very good jazz venues. **Blues & Beyond** (☎ 46 99 09 87; *Berger Strasse 159)* is a small venue for blues and jazz bands; the **Jazzkeller** (☎ 28 85 37; *Kleine Bockenheimer Strasse 18a)* gets top acts. **Sinkkasten** (☎ 28 03 85; *Brönnerstrasse 5)* has a mix of acoustic shows and 1980s-themed dance nights. **Mousonturm** (☎ 40 58 95 20; *Waldschmidtstrasse 4)*, in a converted soap factory in Bornheim, offers arty rock, dance performances and politically oriented cabaret.

The Cave *(Brönnerstrasse 11)* is a club that spins goth and features occasional live concerts; **U60311** *(Rossmarkt)* has techno and house music; **Cooky's** *(Am Salzhaus 4)* stays open until the wee hours, delivering a winning combination of hip-hop and house nights and live indie bands; **Stereo Bar** *(Abtgässchen 7)*, in Sachsenhausen, has a 1970s feel. A popular gay bar is **Zum Schwejk** *(Schäffergasse 20)*, while **Harvey's** *(Friedberger Platz)*, a restaurant and bar, is a favoured meeting place for Frankfurt's gay and lesbian yuppies.

Getting There & Away

Air Germany's largest airport is **Flughafen Frankfurt/Main** (☎ 69 01), with the highest freight and second-highest passenger turnover in Europe. This high-tech town has two terminals linked by an elevated railway. Departure and arrival halls A, B and C are in Terminal 1, with Lufthansa flights handled in hall A; halls D and E are in the new Terminal 2. The airport train station has two sections: platforms 1 to 3 (below Terminal 1, hall B) handle regional and S-Bahn connections, whereas IR, IC and ICE connections are in the long-distance train station. Signs point the way. Hourly IC or EC trains go to Cologne (€33.80, two hours) and Nuremberg (€38.80, 2½ hours) and ICEs run to/from Hamburg on weekdays (€100, four hours).

Bus Long-distance buses leave from the southern side of the main train station, where there's a **Deutsche Touring/Eurolines office** (☎ 79 03 50; *Mannheimer Strasse 4)* that handles bookings. It handles most European destinations; the most interesting possibility is the Romantic Road bus (see the Bavaria section earlier in this chapter). Also see the introductory Getting There & Away section.

Train The Hauptbahnhof handles more departures and arrivals than any other station in Germany. For rail information, call ☎ 01805-99 66 33. The **DB Lounge** *(open 6am-11pm daily)* above the information office is a comfortable retreat for anyone with a valid train ticket.

Car Frankfurt features the famed Frankfurter Kreuz, the biggest autobahn intersection in the country. All main car rental companies have offices in the main hall of the train station and at the airport.

The **ADM-Mitfahrzentrale** (☎ *194 40; Baselerplatz*), is a three-minute walk south of the train station. A sample of fares (including fees) is: Berlin €29, Hamburg €28, Cologne €14, Dresden €27 and Munich €22.

Getting Around

To/From the Airport The S-Bahn's S8/S9 train runs every 15 minutes between the airport and Frankfurt Hauptbahnhof (11 minutes), usually continuing via Hauptwache and Konstablerwache to Offenbach; a fixed fare of €5.90 applies. Taxis (about €25 and taking 30 minutes without traffic jams) or the frequent airport bus No 61 (from Südbahnhof; €3.10) take longer.

Public Transport Frankfurt's excellent transport network (RMV) integrates all bus, tram, S-Bahn and U-Bahn lines. Single or day tickets can be purchased from automatic machines (press the flag button for explanations in English) at almost any stop. Press *Einzelfahrt Frankfurt* for destinations in zone 50, which takes in most of Frankfurt (a plane symbol indicates the button for the airport). Peak period short-trip tickets (*Kurzstrecken*) cost €1.05, single tickets cost €1.60 and a *Tageskarte* (24-hour ticket) is €4.35 without a trip to the airport and €6.65 with an airport trip.

Car Traffic flows smoothly in Frankfurt, but the extensive system of one-way streets can be extremely frustrating. You might want to park your vehicle in an outlying area or one of the many car parks and proceed on foot or by public transport.

Taxi They are slow compared with public transport and expensive at €2.05 flag fall plus a minimum of €1.48 per kilometre. There are numerous taxi ranks throughout the city, or you can book a cab (☎ 23 00 01, 25 00 01, 54 50 11).

MARBURG
☎ 06421 • pop 77,000

Situated 90km north of Frankfurt, Marburg is known for its charming Altstadt with the splendid **Elizabethkirche** and **Philipps-Universität**, Europe's very first Protestant university, which was founded in 1527. Wander up to the museum in the **castle**, from where there are nice views of the old town.

Places to Stay & Eat

Marburg's **DJH hostel** (☎ *234 61*; e *ma burg@djh-hessen.de; Jahnstrasse 1; juniors/ seniors €16.50/19.20*) is about a 10-minute walk upstream along the river from Rudolfsplatz in the Altstadt. For other budget accommodation drop in at the **tourist office** (☎ *99 12 23*; e *mtm@marburg.de; Pilgrimstein 26*); it has a free room-finding service. The **Barfuss** (☎ *253 49; Barfüsserstrasse 33*) is a very lively eatery with moderately priced food.

North Rhine-Westphalia

The North Rhine-Westphalia (Nordrhein-Westfalen) region was formed in 1946 from a hotchpotch of principalities and bishoprics, most of which had belonged to Prussia since the early 19th century. One-quarter of Germany's population lives here. The Rhine-Ruhr industrial area is Germany's economic powerhouse and one of the most densely populated conurbations in the world. Though the area is dominated by bleak industrial centres connected by a maze of train lines and autobahns, some of the cities are steeped in history and their attractions warrant an extensive visit.

COLOGNE
☎ 0221 • pop 1 million

Located at a major crossroads of European trade routes, Cologne (Köln) was an important city even in Roman times. It was then known as Colonia Agrippinensis, the capital of the province of Germania, and had no fewer than 300,000 inhabitants. In later years it remained one of northern Europe's main cities (the largest in Germany until the 19th century), and it is still the centre of the German Roman Catholic church. Almost completely destroyed in WWII, it was quickly rebuilt and many of its old churches and monuments have been meticulously restored.

It's worth making the effort to visit this lively, relaxed city, especially for its famous cathedral, interesting museums and vibrant nightlife.

Orientation

Situated on the Rhine River, the skyline of Cologne is dominated by the cathedral. The pedestrianised Hohe Strasse runs straight through the middle of the old town from north to south and is Cologne's main shopping street. The main train station is just north of the cathedral. The main bus station is just behind the train station, on Breslauer Platz.

Maps The DB Service Point has useful free maps of the central area and the tourist office sells an excellent map (€2) with a street key.

Information

Tourist Offices The helpful **tourist office** (☎ 22 12 33 45; **e** koelntourismus@stadt-koeln.de; Unter Fettenhennen 19; open 8am-9pm Mon-Sat, 9.30am-7pm Sun & holidays May-Oct, 8am-9pm Mon-Sat, 9.30am-7pm Sun & holidays Nov-Apr) is opposite the cathedral's main entrance. Browse through the guide booklets before deciding which one to buy. Monatsvorschau, the monthly what's-on booklet, is a good investment at €1.20. The room-finding service (€3) is a bargain when the city is busy with trade fairs, however, note that you cannot book by telephone.

Money There is a **Reisebank** (open 8am-10pm daily) situated at the train station. There is an office of **AmEx** (Burgmauer 14) and a **Thomas Cook** (Burgmauer 4) near the tourist office.

Post & Communications The **post office** (open 6am-10pm Mon-Sat, 7am-10pm Sun) is in Ludwig im Bahnhof bookshop near track 6 inside the main train station.

Email & Internet Access At **Future Point** (☎ 206 72 51; Richmodstrasse 13; open 8am-1am Mon-Sat, 10am-1am Sun), the charge is €1.50 per 30 minutes online.

Bookshops Inside the main train station, **Ludwig im Bahnhof** stocks the international press and also has Lonely Planet titles.

Laundry There is an **Eko-Express Waschsalon** (cnr Händelstrasse & Richard-Wagner-Strasse; open Mon-Sat).

Medical & Emergency Services The police are on ☎ 110; for **fire and ambulance** call ☎ 112. An on-call **doctor** can be contacted on ☎ 192 92.

Things to See

Cologne has a large town centre and the cathedral (Dom) is its heart, soul and tourist draw. Combined with the excellent museums next door, plan to spend at least one full day inside and around the Dom.

Dom Head first to the southern side of the Dom (open 7am-7.30pm daily) for an overall view. The structure's sheer size, with spires rising to 157m, is overwhelming. Building began in 1248 in the French Gothic style. The huge project was stopped in 1560 but started again in 1842, in the style originally planned, as a symbol of Prussia's drive for unification. It was finally finished in 1880. Miraculously, it survived WWII's heavy night bombing intact.

When you reach the transept you'll be overwhelmed by the sheer size and magnificence of it all. The five **stained-glass windows** along the north aisle depict the lives of the Virgin and St Peter. Behind the high altar you can see the **Magi's Shrine** (c. 1150–1210), believed to contain the remains of the Three Wise Men, which was brought to Cologne from Milan in the 12th century. On the south side, in a chapel off the ambulatory, is the 15th-century **Adoration of the Magi altarpiece**. Guided tours in English are held at 10.30am and 2.30pm Monday to Saturday (at 2.30pm only on Sunday) and cost €4/2 per adult/concession; meet inside the main portal. Tours in German are more frequent and cost €3/2.

For a fitness fix, climb 509 steps up the Dom's south tower to the base of the stupendous **steeples** (adult/concession €2/1; open 9am-5pm daily Mar-Sept, 9am-4pm Oct-Feb), which towered over all of Europe until the Eiffel Tower was erected. Look at the 24-tonne **Peter Bell**, the largest working bell in the world, on your way up. At the end of your climb, the view from the vantage point, 98.25m up, is absolutely stunning; on a clear day you can see all the way to the Siebengebirge Mountains beyond Bonn. The cathedral **treasury** (adult/concession €4/2; open 10am-6pm daily) has a small but valuable collection of reliquaries. Cologne's archbishops are interred in the crypt.

Other Churches Many other churches are worth a look, particularly Romanesque ones that have been restored since WWII bombing. The most handsome from the outside is **Gross St Martin**, near Fischmarkt, while the most

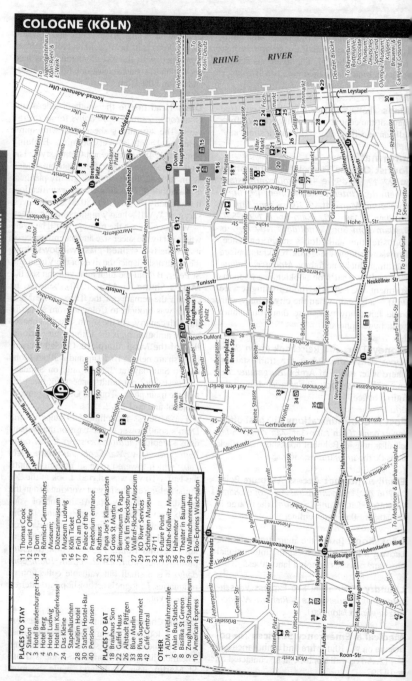

COLOGNE (KÖLN)

PLACES TO STAY
2 Station
3 Hotel Brandenburger Hof
4 Hotel Berg
5 Hotel Ludwig
7 Hotel Im Kupferkessel
24 Das Kleine
   Stapelhäuschen
28 Maritim Hotel
30 Station Hostel-Bar
40 Pension Jansen

PLACES TO EAT
18 Brauhaus Sion
22 Gaffel Haus
26 Altstadt Päffgen
33 Blue Marlin
38 Plus Supermarket
42 Café Central

OTHER
1 ADM Mitfahrzentrale
6 Main Bus Station
8 Basilika St Gereon
9 Zeughaus/Stadtmuseum
10 American Express
11 Thomas Cook
12 Tourist Office
14 Dom
   Römisch-Germanisches
   Museum;
   Diözesanmuseum
15 Museum Ludwig
16 Köln Ticket
17 Früh am Dom
19 Palace of the
   Praetorium entrance
20 Rathaus
21 Papa Joe's Klimperkasten
23 Gross St Martin
25 Biermuseum & Papa
   Joe's Em Streckstrump
27 Wallraf-Richartz-Museum
29 KD River Services
31 Schnütgen Museum
32 4711
34 Future Point
35 Käthe-Kollwitz Museum
36 Hahnentor
37 Theater in Bauturm
39 Wallmachenreuther
41 Eko-Express Waschsalon

stunning interior is that of the **Basilika St Gereon** *(Christophstrasse)*, with its incredible four-storey **decagon** *(open 9am-12.30pm & 1.30pm-6pm Mon-Fri, Sat morning & Sun afternoon)*; enter from Gereonkloster.

Museums Next to the cathedral there's the **Römisch-Germanisches Museum** *(Roman Germanic Museum; Roncalliplatz 4; adult/concession €4/2; open 10am-5pm Tues-Sun)*, which displays artefacts from all aspects of the Roman settlement in the Rhine Valley. The highlights are the giant Poblicius grave monument and the Dionysos mosaic around which the museum was built.

The **Wallraf-Richartz-Museum** *(Martinstrasse 39; adult/concession €6.60/4.10; open 10am-6pm Wed-Fri, 10am-8pm Tues, 11am-6pm Sat & Sun)* has a fantastic collection that includes paintings by Rubens, Rembrandt and Monet. The **Museum Ludwig** *(Bischofsgartenstrasse 1; adult/concession €7.70/4.10; open 10am-6pm Wed-Fri, 10am-8pm Tues, 11am-6pm Sat & Sun)* uses natural light to brilliant effect, displaying prime pieces from Kirchner, Kandinsky and Max Ernst, as well as pop-art works by Rauschenberg and Andy Warhol. The building also houses a unique photography collection from the former Agfa Museum in Leverkusen.

The former church of St Cecilia houses the **Schnütgen Museum** *(Cäcilienstrasse 29; adult/concession €2.50/1.25; open 10am-5pm Tues-Fri, 11am-5pm Sat & Sun)*, an overwhelming display of church riches, including many religious artefacts as well as early ivory carvings. At the **Diözesanmuseum** *(Roncalliplatz; admission free; open Fri-Wed)* you can see religious treasures.

The multimedia **Deutsches Sport- und Olympia-Museum** *(Rheinaufen 1; adult/concession €4/2; open 10am-6pm Tues-Fri, 11am-7pm Sat & Sun)* is a great place to find out all about the history of sport from ancient times to the present day.

Other museums worth visiting are **Käthe Kollwitz Museum** *(Neumarkt 18-24; adult/concession €2.50/1)*, with some fine sculpture and graphics by this acclaimed socialist artist; the **Zeughaus** *(Zeughausstrasse)*, restored as the **Stadtmuseum** *(adult/concession €3.60/2)*, with a model of Cologne and a good armoury collection; and the **Chocolate Museum** *(Rheinauhafen 1a; adult/concession €5.50/3)*, on the river in the Rheinauhafen near the Altstadt, where you will learn everything about the history of making chocolate – as if you cared beyond the taste (all closed Monday).

Activities

Guided Tours The summer daily **city tour** in English lasts two hours; the bus departs from the tourist office at 10am, 12.30pm and 3pm (at 11am and 2pm from November to March). The cost is a steep €14. You can also make day trips to nearby cities with **KD River Cruises** (see Getting There & Away later in this section). A trip down the Rhine to Bonn is €10.40 and to Koblenz it's €32.80 one way.

Historical Walks You can give yourself a free tour of ancient and medieval Cologne by walking around its restored monuments with a free city-sights map from the tourist office. If you walk west from the Dom along Komödienstrasse over Tunisstrasse, you'll reach the Zeughaus museum, the Burgmauer side of which was built along the line of the **Roman wall**.

Continue west until you find a complete section of the north wall, which leads to a corner tower standing among buildings on the street corner at St-Apern-Strasse. One block south of here is another tower ruin near Helenenstrasse.

You can also take a lift down and walk through the **Roman sewer** to view the remains of the **palace of the Praetorium** *(adult/concession €1.50/0.75; open Tues-Sun)* under the medieval town hall (the entry is located on Kleine Budengasse). The **Rathaus** *(open 7.30am-4.15pm Mon-Thur, 7.30am-12.15pm Fri)* is open for viewing; the facades, foyer and tower have been restored.

The city's medieval towers and gates complement its Romanesque churches. The Bayenturm on the Rhine bank at the eastern end of Severinswall was completely rebuilt, but along the street to the west the vine-bedecked Bottmühle and the mighty main south gate of Severinstor have more of the original basalt and tuff stones.

To the northwest along Sachsenring is the vaulted Ulrepforte tower-gate and a section of wall with two more towers.

North of the city centre is the gate of Eigelsteintor on Eigelstein, suspended from which is a boat from the MS *Schiff Cöln*, which sank off Heligoland in 1914. The main west gate, Hahnentor, is at Rudolfplatz.

Special Events

Try to visit Cologne during the wild and crazy period of the Cologne Carnival (Karneval), rivalled only by Munich's Oktoberfest. People dress in creative costumes, clown suits, as popular personalities and whatever else their alcohol-numbed brains may invent. The streets explode with activity on the Thursday before the seventh Sunday before Easter. On Friday and Saturday evening the streets pep up, Sunday is like Thursday and on Monday *(Rosenmontag)* there are formal and informal parades, and much spontaneous singing and celebrating.

Places to Stay

Cheap accommodation in Cologne is not plentiful, but there are a couple of good pensions around the city, and you should be able to get private rooms unless there's a trade fair on.

Camping The most convenient camping ground is **Campingplatz der Stadt Köln** *(☎ 83 19 66; tent sites €4, plus €4 per person; open Easter–mid-Oct)* on Weidenweg in Poll, 5km southeast of the city centre. Take U16 to Marienburg and cross the Rodenkirchener bridge. **Campingplatz Berger** *(☎ 39 22 11; Uferstrasse 71; tent sites €4.50/6 per person/ car; open all year)* is 7km southeast of the city in Rodenkirchen. Take the U16 to Heinrich-Lübke-Ufer and from there bus No 130.

Hostels Cologne has two DJH hostels. The bustling **Jugendherberge Köln-Deutz** *(☎ 81 47 11; e jh-koeln-deutz@djh-rheinland.de; Siegesstrasse 5a; dorm beds juniors/seniors €17/19.50)* in Deutz is a 15-minute walk east from the main train station over the Hohenzollernbrücke, or three minutes from Bahnhof Köln-Deutz (sometimes called the Messe-Osthallen. The more pleasant **Jugendgästehaus Köln-Riehl** *(☎ 76 70 81; e jh-koeln -riehl@djh-rheinland.de; An der Schanz 14; rooms €21-34 per person)* is north of the city and has one- to six-bed rooms. Take the U15 or U16 to Boltensternstrasse. The backpackers hostel **Station** *(☎ 912 53 01; fax 912 53 03; e station@hostel-cologne.de; Marzellen-strasse 44-48; dorm beds €14, singles €25)* is an easy walk from the main train station.

Station Hostel+Bar *(☎ 221 23 02 47; e station2@hotel-cologne.de; Rheingasse 34-6; dorm beds €16.50, singles €25)*, the hostel's other branch, is closer to Cologne's pubs.

Hotels & Pensions Accommodation prices in Cologne increase by at least 20% when fairs are on. If you have private transport, inquire about parking – a night in a car park will set you back €15 or more (and not all of them operate 24 hours). The tourist office has a room-finding service that can help with hotel rooms in the lower price range.

Pension Jansen *(☎/fax 25 18 75; Richard-Wagner-Strasse 18; singles/doubles from €31/62)* provides basic rooms and is convenient to the restaurant quarter of town. **Hotel Im Kupferkessel** *(☎ 13 53 38, fax 12 51 21, Probsteigasse 6; singles/doubles from €26/ 49)* has recently remodelled rooms just a 15-minute walk west of the train station.

A lot of other budget and mid-range hotels cluster in the streets just north of the main train station. **Hotel Brandenburger Hof** *(☎ 12 28 89, fax 13 53 04; Brandenburger Strasse 2; singles/doubles without bath from €27/48, with bath €50/75)* has basic rooms. **Hotel Berg** *(☎ 12 11 24, fax 139 00 11; e hotel@ hotel-berg.com; Brandenburger Strasse 6; singles/doubles without bath from €41/49, with bath €62/72)* has fairly good rooms and offers Internet access. **Hotel Ludwig** *(☎ 16 05 40, fax 16 05 44 44; e hotel@hotelludwig .com; Brandenburger Strasse 22-24; singles/ doubles €70/110)* is a fairly good option in the mid-price range, with decent rooms; some have a view to the Dom and there are also weekend deals.

Das Kleine Stapelhäuschen *(☎ 257 77 77, fax 257 42 32; e stapelhaeuschen@compu serve.com; Fischmarkt 1-3; singles/doubles from €38.50/64, with bath €51/90)*, in the middle of the Altstadt, has pleasant rooms. Catering largely to a trade fair and business clientele is the **Maritim Hotel** *(☎ 202 70, fax 202 78 26; e info.kol@maritim.de; Heumarkt 20; singles/doubles from €145/169)*.

Places to Eat

Cologne's beer halls serve cheap and filling (though often bland) meals to go with their home brew (see Beer Halls under Entertainment later).

Brauhaus Sion *(Unter Taschenmacher 9)* is a big beer hall, packed most nights and for good reason: you'll eat your fill for well under €15, including a couple of beers. **Altstadt Päffgen** *(Heumarkt 62; dishes around €8)* at the northern end of the Heumarkt is more up-market but authentic. The **Gaffel Haus** *(Alter Markt 20-22)* is another nice place to eat and sample the local concoction. The **Blue Marlin** *(Wolfstrasse 4)* does delicious sushi from €8 for eight pieces or from €1.10 a piece.

The Belgisches Viertel (Belgian Quarter) around and west of Hahnentor is packed with restaurants of all descriptions. You'll find a couple of moderately priced Asian eating houses on Händelstrasse.

Café Central *(Jülicher Strasse 1)*, on the corner of Händelstrasse, is open till late and has an adjoining restaurant called **o.T.** *(mains €6.50-9.50)*; the café itself does breakfast and light dishes.

To put together a picnic, visit a **market**; the biggest is held on Tuesday and Friday at the Aposteln-Kloster near Neumarkt. The super-market **Plus** *(Aachener Strasse 64)* is in the Belgisches Viertel.

Entertainment

Evenings and weekends in the Altstadt are like miniature carnivals, with bustling crowds and lots to do.

Papa Joe's Klimperkasten *(Alter Markt 50)* is a lively jazz pub with a wonderful pianola. **Papa Joe's Em Streckstrump** *(Buttermarkt 37)* is more intimate. **Metronom** *(☎ 21 34 65; Weyerstrasse 59)*, near the Kwartier Latäng (Latin Quarter), is Cologne's most respected evening bar for jazz enthusiasts, with live performances mainly weekdays.

Wallmachenreuther *(Brüsseler Platz 9)* is an off-beat bar in the Belgisches Viertel that also serves food. The gay scene also centres on the Belgisches Viertel.

E-Werk *(☎ 96 27 90; Schanzenstrasse 37)*, in a converted power station in Mülheim, is Cologne's usual venue for rock concerts. It turns into a huge techno club on Friday and Saturday nights.

Köln Ticket *(☎ 28 02 80; Roncalliplatz)*, next to the Römisch-Germanisches Museum, has tickets and information on classical music and theatre performances in town. **Theater am Bauturm** *(☎ 52 42 42; Aachener Strasse 24)* is one of Cologne's more innovative theatres.

Beer Halls As in Munich, beer in Cologne reigns supreme. There are more than 20 local breweries, all producing a variety called *Kölsch*, which is relatively light and slightly bitter. The breweries run their own beer halls and serve their wares in skinny glasses holding a mere 200ml, but you'll soon agree it's a very satisfying way to drink the stuff. See Places to Eat earlier for other suggestions. **Früh am Dom** *(Am Hof 12-14)* is famous for its own-brew beer; the **Biermuseum** *(Buttermarkt 39)* – beside Papa Joe's – has 18 varieties on tap. **Küppers Brauerei** *(☎ 934 78 10; Alteburger Strasse 157)* is in Bayenthal, south of the city (take the U16 to Bayenthalgürtel). It has a nice beer garden and there's also a beer museum which you can visit if you call ahead.

Shopping

A good Cologne souvenir might be a small bottle of *eau de Cologne*, which is still produced in its namesake city. The most famous brand is called 4711, after the house number where it was invented. There's still a **perfumery and gift shop** *(cnr Glockengasse & Schwertnergasse)* by that name. Try to catch the Glockenspiel, with characters from Prussian lore parading above the store hourly from 9am to 9pm.

Getting There & Away

Air Cologne/Bonn airport has many connections within Europe and to the rest of the world. For detailed flight information phone ☎ 02203-40 40 01/02.

Bus Deutsche Touring's **Eurolines** *(☎ 13 52 52)* offers overnight trips to Paris (€34, 6½ hours). The office is at the main train station at the Breslauer Platz exit.

Train There are frequent services operating to both nearby Bonn (€7, 18 minutes) and Düsseldorf (€8.10, 20 minutes) as well as to Aachen (€10.70, one hour). Frequent direct IC/EC (€47.80, 3¼ hours) and ICE (€53.40, 2¾ hours) trains go to Hanover. There are ICE links with Frankfurt/Main (€39, 2¼ hours) and Berlin (€97.60, 4½ hours). The Thalys high-speed train connects Paris and Cologne via Aachen and Brussels (€74.60/67.10 weekdays/weekends, four hours, seven times daily), with only a small discount for rail pass-holders!

Car The city is on a main north-south autobahn route and is easily accessible for drivers and hitchhikers. The **ADM Mitfahrzentrale** (☎ 194 40; Maximinen Strasse 2) is near the train station.

Boat An enjoyable way to travel to/from Cologne is by boat. **KD River Cruises** (☎ 208 83 18; Frankenwerft 1) has its headquarters in the city, and has services all along the Rhine.

Getting Around

To/From the Airport Bus No 170 runs between Cologne/Bonn airport and the main bus station every 15 minutes from 5.30am to 11.20pm daily (€4.80, 20 minutes).

Public Transport Cologne offers a convenient and extensive mix of buses, trams and local trains – trams go underground in the inner city, and trains handle destinations up to 50km around Cologne. Ticketing and tariff structures are complicated. The best ticket option is the one-day pass: €5.15 if you're staying near the city (one or two zones); €8.25 for most of the Cologne area (four zones); and €11.50 including Bonn (seven zones). Single city trips cost €1.20 and 1½-hour two-zone tickets are €1.90.

Taxi To order a taxi call ☎ 194 10 or ☎ 28 82.

AROUND COLOGNE
Bonn
☎ 0228 • pop 293,000

This friendly, relaxed city on the Rhine south of Cologne became West Germany's temporary capital in 1949 and is mainly an administrative centre now that the seat of government and embassies are in Berlin. Settled in Roman times, Bonn was the seat of the electors of Cologne in the 18th century, and some of their baroque architecture survived the ravages of WWII and the postwar demand for modern government buildings. Organise a day trip out here and to the nearby spa town of Bad Godesberg. Classical music buffs can pay homage to Bonn's most famous son – Ludwig van Beethoven.

The **tourist office** (☎ 77 50 00, 194 33, fax 77 50 77, e bonninformation@bonn.de; open 9am-6.30pm Mon-Fri, 9am-4pm Sat, 10am-2pm Sun) is behind the Karstadt department store in Windeckstrasse, a three-minute walk along Poststrasse from the Hauptbahnhof.

Bonn is a city that lives and breathes Beethoven. You can visit the **Beethoven-Haus** (☎ 981 75; Bonngasse 20; adult/concession €4/3; open 10am-6pm Mon-Sat Apr-Oct, 10am-5pm Mon-Sat Nov-Mar, 11am to 4pm Sunday all year), where the composer was born in 1770. The house contains much memorabilia concerning his life and music, including his last piano, specially made with an amplified sounding board to accommodate his deafness. The annual Beethoven Festival takes place in September/October.

The **Münsterbasilika** (Münsterplatz) has a splendid interior and honours Sts Cassius and Florentius, two martyred Roman officers who became the patron saints of Bonn.

Bonn also boasts several interesting museums. The **Frauenmuseum** (☎ 69 13 44; Im Krausfeld 10; adult/concession €8/5; open 2pm-6pm Tues-Sat, 11am-6pm Sun) promotes and exhibits art created by women in an environment that combines history, mythology and contemporary artistic expressions. Take bus No 625, 626, 627 or 635 to Kaiser-Karl-Ring.

The **Haus der Geschichte der Bundesrepublik Deutschland** (FRG History Museum; ☎ 916 50; Willy-Brandt-Allee 14; admission free; open 9am-7pm Tues-Sun) covers the history of Germany from 1945; it is part of the **Museumsmeile**, a row of four museums that also includes the **Museum Alexander Koenig** (☎ 912 20; Willy-Brandt-Allee 160), a natural history museum; the **Kunstmuseum** (☎ 77 62 60; Friedrich-Ebert-Allee 2) with its collection of 20th-century art; and exhibitions at the **Kunst- und Ausstellungshalle der Bundesrepublik Deutschland** (☎ 917 12 00; Friedrich-Ebert-Allee 2).

There are frequent trains to Cologne in the north and to Koblenz (€15.40, 30 minutes) in the south. See the earlier Cologne Activities section for river cruises to/from Bonn. The Bonn transit system is linked with Cologne's and a one-way train ride between the two cities costs only €7 (see the earlier Cologne Getting Around section for passes covering both).

DÜSSELDORF
☎ 0211 • pop 571,000

Though not particularly strong in historical sights, this elegant and wealthy capital of North Rhine-Westphalia is, however, an important centre for fashion and commerce, and a charming example of big-city living along the Rhine River.

Information

The **tourist office** (☎ 17 20 20; e tourist@ duesseldorf.de; open 8am-8pm Mon-Sat, 4pm-8pm Sun) is opposite the main exit of the train station towards the northern end of Konrad-Adenauer-Platz. The **main post office** is across the street. The **Reisebank** (open to 10pm Mon-Fri, until 9pm Sat & Sun) is in the train station's main hall. There's a convenient **SB Waschsalon laundry** (Charlottenstrasse 87).

Email & Internet Access Internet Café World (Worringer Platz 21), three blocks north of the train station, charges €2 for 30 minutes online.

Things to See & Do

To catch a glimpse of Düsseldorf's swish lifestyle, head for the famed Königsallee, or 'Kö', with its stylish (and pricey) boutiques and arcades. Stroll north along the Kö to the **Hofgarten**, a large park in the city centre.

The city has several interesting museums. These include the **Kunstmuseum Düsseldorf** (☎ 899 24 60; adult/concession €4/2; open 10am-6pm Tues-Sun) at Ehrenhof north of the Oberkasseler Brücke, with a comprehensive European collection, and the incorporated **Glasmuseum Hentrich** (open 10am-6pm Tues-Sun). The quite expansive modern art collection in the **Kunstsammlung Nordrhein-Westfalen** is displayed in two different galleries: **K20** (☎ 838 11 30; Grabbeplatz 5; adult/concession €6.50/4.50; open 10am-6pm Tues-Fri, 11am-6pm Sat & Sun) features works by 20th-century masters; **K21** (☎ 838 16 00; Ständehausstrasse 1; adult concession €6.50/4.50) specialises in art from 1990 onwards. A combined ticket to both costs €10/8.

The **Goethe-Museum Düsseldorf** (☎ 899 62 62; Jacobistrasse 2; adult/concession €2/1; open 11am-5pm Tues-Fri & Sun, 1pm-5pm Sat) in Schloss Jägerhof, pays tribute to the life and work of one of Europe's great men of letters. The large collection includes books, first drafts, letters, medals and more. Any German-literature buff will also want to visit **Heinrich-Heine-Institut** (Bilker Strasse 12-14; adult/concession €2/1; open 11am-5pm Tues-Fri & Sun, 1pm-5pm Sat), which documents this Düsseldorfer's career, or his house at Bolkerstrasse 53, now a literary pub.

On Marktplatz, the restored **Rathaus** looks out onto the **statue of Prince Elector Johann Wilhelm**, known in local speech as 'Jan Wellem'. He lies buried in the ornate early-baroque **St Andreas Kirche** (cnr Kay-und-Lore-Lorentz-Platz & Andreasstrasse), now in the care of a Dominican monastery. Another church worth visiting is the 13th-century **St Lambertus Basilika** (Stiftsplatz).

Nearby, the reconstructed **Schlossturm** of the long-destroyed Residenz stands on Burgplatz as a forlorn reminder of the Palatine elector's glory. In summer, the town's youth congregate on the steps below the tower. From here the pedestrian-only **Rheinuferpromenade** provides perfect strolling along the river. **Schloss Benrath** (☎ 899 72 71; open daily), a late-baroque pleasure palace with a park, located 12km south of the city, makes for a lovely excursion. Take tram No 701 from Jan-Wellem-Platz.

Places to Stay

There are two camping grounds relatively close to the city. **Campingplatz Nord Unterbacher See** (☎ 899 20 38; tent sites €5.50, plus €3.25/4 per person/car; open 4 Apr-27 Sept) is at Kleiner Torfbruch in Düsseldorf-Unterbach (take S-Bahn No 7 to Eller, and then bus No 735 to Seeweg). **Camping Oberlörick** (☎ 59 14 01; tent sites €4, plus €3/4.50 per person/car; open all year) is at Lutticherstrasse, just beside the Rhine in Düsseldorf-Lörick (U-Bahn No 70, 74 or 76 to Löricker Strasse, and then bus No 833 to Strandbad Lörick). The trek to the Altstadt is particularly inconvenient from either camping ground.

The **Jugendgästehaus** (☎ 55 73 10, fax 57 25 13; e jgh-duesseldorf@t-online.de; Düsseldorfer Strasse 1; dorm beds €20.20) is in posh Oberkassel across the Rhine from the Altstadt. It also has some private rooms. Take U-Bahn No 70, 74, 75, 76, or 77 from the main train station to Luegplatz. From there it's a short walk.

Düsseldorf frequently hosts trade shows that inflate its already high hotel and pension prices. The tourist office can help with finding big discounts offered by many of the comfortable business hotels on weekends and when no fair is in town. It levies €4 for bookings made on the day of check-in, otherwise it's €5.

Hotel Komet (☎ 17 87 90, fax 178 79 50; e info@hotelkomet.de; Bismarckstrasse 93; singles/doubles €33/44) provides reasonable

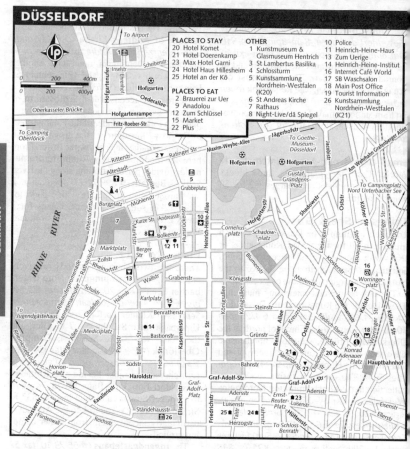

DÜSSELDORF

PLACES TO STAY
20 Hotel Komet
21 Hotel Doerenkamp
23 Max Hotel Garni
24 Hotel Haus Hillesheim
25 Hotel an der Kö

PLACES TO EAT
2 Brauerei zur Uer
9 Anadolou
15 Zum Schlüssel
15 Market
22 Plus

OTHER
1 Kunstmuseum &
  Glasmuseum Hentrich
3 St Lambertus Basilika
4 Schlossturm
5 Kunstsammlung
  Nordrhein-Westfalen
  (K20)
6 St Andreas Kirche
7 Rathaus
8 Night-Live/dä Spiegel

10 Police
11 Heinrich-Heine-Haus
13 Zum Uerige
14 Heinrich-Heine-Institut
16 Internet Café World
17 SB Waschsalon
18 Main Post Office
19 Tourist Information
26 Kunstsammlung
  Nordrhein-Westfalen
  (K21)

rooms including bathroom. The **Hotel Haus Hillesheim** (☎ 38 68 60, fax 386 86 33; e rezeption@hotel-hillesheim.de; Jahnstrasse 19; singles/doubles without bath €40/55, with bath €60/70) is a good value option. **Hotel Doerenkamp** (☎ 32 80 11, fax 13 45 82; Stresemannstrasse 25; singles/doubles €60/80) has fine rooms with facilities (ask for a quiet one), and pet rabbits to thrill the kids.

Hotel an der Kö (☎ 37 10 48, fax 37 08 35; Talstrasse 9; singles/doubles €78/87) has nice bright rooms with all facilities. **Max Hotel Garni** (☎ 38 68 00, fax 386 80 22; e info@max-hotelgarni.de; Aderstrasse 65; singles/doubles €115/140) has colourful, unique rooms with toilet and shower. Call before arriving.

Places to Eat

Brauerei zur Uer (Ratinger Strasse 16) is a rustic place to fill up for less than €10. Ratinger Strasse is also home to a couple of other pub-style places where you can eat and drink. **Zum Schlüssel** (Bolkerstrasse 43-47; dishes €5-11) is popular for beer, but also has good food. **Anadolou** (Mertensgasse 10; mains from €4) serves delicious Anatolian sit-down and takeaway food including vegetarian dishes.

You can replenish supplies at the supermarket **Plus** (Stresemannstrasse 31), near Hotel Doerenkamp. A fresh produce **market** (open Mon-Sat) is held on Karlplatz.

Entertainment

Besides walking and museum-hopping, one of the best things to do in Düsseldorf is (surprise!)

drink beer. There are lots of bars (for drinking and eating) in the Altstadt, affectionately referred to as the 'longest bar in the world'. On evenings and weekends, the best places overflow onto the pedestrian-only streets. Favoured streets include Bolkerstrasse, Kurze Strasse, and Andreasstrasse as well as the surrounding side streets.

The beverage of choice is Alt beer, a dark and semisweet brew typical of Düsseldorf. Try Gatzweilers Alt in **Zum Schlüssel** (see Places to Eat earlier). Spartan **Zum Uerige** (*Berger Strasse*) is the only place where you can buy Uerige Alt beer. It's €1.40 per 250ml glass, and the beer flows so quickly that the waiters just carry around trays and give you a glass when you're ready (and sometimes even when you're not!). **Night-Live** (*Bolkerstrasse 22*) has live bands; it's upstairs from the **dä Spiegel**, itself a popular bar.

Getting There & Away
Düsseldorf's Lohausen airport (S-Bahn trains run every 20 minutes between the airport and the main train station) is busy with many national and international flights. Düsseldorf is part of a dense S-Bahn and train network in the Rhine-Ruhr region and there are regular IC/EC services to/from Hamburg (€63.20, 3¾ hours), ICE services to Hanover (€48.80, 2¾ hours) and Frankfurt (€47.20, 2½ hours), trains to Cologne (€6.60, 30 minutes) and most other major German cities.

Getting Around
As Düsseldorf is very spread out, it's easiest to get around by public transport. Buy your ticket from one of the orange machines at stops, although bus drivers will sell singles, and validate it before boarding. A short-trip ticket up to 1.5km (destinations are listed on the machines) costs €2. A single ticket for zone A, which includes all of Düsseldorf proper, is €3.30. Better value is the 24-hour *Tages-Ticket* for €12, valid for up to five people in zone A.

AACHEN
☎ 0241 • pop 244,000
Aachen was famous in Roman times for its thermal springs. The great Frankish conqueror Charlemagne was so impressed by their revitalising qualities that he settled here and made it the capital of his kingdom in AD 794. Ever since, Aachen has held special significance

among the icons of German nationhood. It is now an industrial and commercial centre and is home to the country's largest technical university.

Orientation
Aachen's compact old centre is contained within two ring roads that roughly follow the old city walls. The inner ring road, or Grabenring, changes names – most ending in 'graben' – and encloses the old city proper. To get to the tourist office from the Hauptbahnhof, turn left on leaving the main entrance, cross Römerstrasse, follow Bahnhofstrasse north and then go left along Theaterstrasse to Kapuzinergraben. Pick up an excellent free city map from the DB Service Point counter in the train station.

Information
The efficient **tourist office** (☎ 180 29 60/1; **e** *mail@aachen-tourist.de; Kapuzinergraben; open 9am-6pm Mon-Fri, 9am-2pm Sat, 10am-2pm Sun*) is at Atrium Elisenbrunnen. The **Sparkasse bank** (*Lagerhausstrasse 12; open 8.30am-4.30pm Mon-Wed, 8.30am-5.30pm Thur, 8.30am-4pm Fri*) is one block west of the train station. Three blocks northwest from there is the **main post office** (*An den Frauenbrüdern 1*). The bus station is at the northeastern edge of Grabenring on the corner of Kurhausstrasse and Peterstrasse.

Email & Internet Access Surf until late at **The Web** (*Kleinmarschierstrasse 74-76*), where 30 minutes of Internet time costs €2.

Things to See & Do
Dom Aachen's drawing card is its cathedral Dom (*Kaiserdom or Münster; open 7am-7pm daily*). The cathedral's subtle grandeur, its historical significance and interior serenity make a visit almost obligatory – it's a Unesco World Heritage Site. No fewer than 30 Holy Roman emperors were crowned here from 936 to 1531.

The heart of the cathedral is a Byzantine-inspired **octagon**, built on Roman foundations, which was the largest vaulted structure north of the Alps when consecrated as Charlemagne's court chapel in AD 805. He lies buried here in the golden **shrine**, and the cathedral became a site of pilgrimage after his death, not least for its religious relics. The Gothic **choir** was added in 1414; its massive stained-glass windows are impressive even though some date from after WWII. The octagon received its **folded dome** after the city fire of 1656 destroyed the original tent roof. The **western tower** dates from the 19th century.

Worth noting is the huge brass **chandelier**, which was added to the octagon by Emperor Friedrich Barbarossa in 1165; the **high altar** with its 11th-century gold-plated Pala d'Oro (altar front) depicting scenes of the Passion; and the gilded copper ambo, or **pulpit**, donated by Henry II. Unless you join up with a German-language tour (€2), you'll only catch a glimpse of Charlemagne's white-marble **throne** on the upper gallery of the octagon on the western side, where the nobles sat.

The entrance to the **Domschatzkammer** *(cathedral treasury; adult/concession €2.50/ 2; open 10am-1pm Mon, 10am-6pm Tues, Wed & Fri-Sun, 10am-9pm Thur)*, with one of the richest collections of religious art north of the Alps, is on nearby Klostergasse. The entrance fee includes a pamphlet.

Other Attractions North of the cathedral, the 14th-century **Rathaus** *(adult/concession €1.50/0.75; open 10am-5pm Mon-Fri, 10am-1pm & 2pm-5pm Sat & Sun)* overlooks Markt, a lively gathering place in summer, with its fountain statue of Charlemagne. The eastern tower of the Rathaus, the Granusturm, was once part of Charlemagne's palace. History buffs will be thrilled by the grand Empire Hall upstairs, where Holy Roman emperors enjoyed their coronation feasts.

Foremost among Aachen's worthwhile museums is the **Ludwig Forum for International Art** *(☎ 180 70; Jülicherstrasse 97-109; adult/ concession €3/1.50; open 10am-4pm Tues & Thur, 10am-7.30pm Wed & Fri, 11am-4.30pm Sat & Sun)* with works by Warhol, Lichtenstein, Baselitz and others.

Thermal Baths Aachen was known for its thermal springs as early as Roman times, and the 8th-century Franks called the town 'Ahha', which is supposed to mean water. A visit to the city-owned **Carolus Thermen** *(☎ 18 27 40; Passstrasse 79)* costs €8 for two hours (€15 with the sauna), or €14 for up to five hours of splashy activity (€24 with sauna). It's in the city garden, northeast of the centre.

Places to Stay
The nearest camping ground is **Hoeve de Gastmolen** *(☎ 0031-433 06 57 55; tent sites,*

including 1 car, €7, plus €2.50 per person) in the Dutch town of Vaals, about 6km outside Aachen at Lemierserberg 23. Take bus No 15 or 65 and get off at the 'Heuvel' stop.

The DJH **Jugendgästehaus** *(☎ 71 10 10; Maria-Theresia-Allee 260; dorm beds €20.50, singles/doubles €33.80/38.80)* is 4km southwest of the train station on a hill overlooking the city. Take bus No 2 to Ronheide, or bus No 12 to the closer Colynshof at the foot of the hill.

Hotels & Pensions The tourist office can arrange private rooms (in person only) from €13.50 to €64, but ask for something within walking distance of the city centre. To arrange a room in advance, call Aachen's room reservation line weekdays on ☎ 180 29 50/1.

Hotel Marx *(☎ 375 41, fax 267 05, e info@hotel-marx.de; Hubertusstrasse 33-35; singles/doubles €34/62, with bath from €49/67)* offers good cheap rooms but you'll have to perform your ablutions acrobatically in the basin. The central **Hotel Drei Könige** *(☎ 483 93, fax 361 52; Büchel 5; singles/ doubles €35/55, with shower & toilet €60/ 75)* has a few rather basic rooms. **Hotel am Marschiertor** *(☎ 319 41, fax 319 44; e hotel .marschiertor@t-online.de; Wallstrasse 1-7; singles/doubles from €62/75)*, near the train station, has nice rooms (breakfast €8.50 extra). The historic hotel **Dorint Select Quellenhof** *(☎ 913 20, fax 913 21 00; e info .aahque@dorint.com; Monheimsallee 52; singles/doubles €170/195)* near the city park, charges an extra €19 for breakfast.

Places to Eat
Being a university town, Aachen is full of spirited cafés, restaurants and pubs, especially along Pontstrasse, referred to by locals as the 'Quartier Latin'. **Café Kittel** *(Pontstrasse 39; mains around €6)* is a cosy hang-out with a lively garden area. It serves reasonably priced light meals, including vegetarian dishes. **Gaststätte Labyrinth** *(Pontstrasse 156-158; dishes €7-11)* is a rambling beer-hall type place that lives up to its name and serves good, filling meals.

Alt Aachener Kaffeestuben *(Büchel 18)* is a coffee house (where wine also is served) with old-world charm that does a traditional lunchtime dish for €7. **Plus** *(Bahnhofstrasse 18)* is a fairly centrally situated supermarket for self-caterers.

Entertainment

The best source of information on bars, clubs and restaurants in Aachen and the Maas-Rhine region is the free *Euroview* guide in English – the tourist office keeps copies. **Domkeller** *(Hof 1)* has been a student pub since the 1950s and usually features jazz or blues on Monday. **B9** *(Blondelstrasse 9)* is one club that attracts a young crowd. The style changes nightly. **Club Voltaire** *(Friedrichstrasse 9)* attracts an older, mixed crowd. The **City Theatre** *(☎ 478 42 44; Theaterplatz)* has concerts and opera most nights; **Aachen Ticket** *(☎ 180 29 65)* in the tourist office has information and sells tickets.

Getting There & Away

Aachen is well served by road and rail. There are fast trains almost every hour to Cologne (€10, 43 minutes) and Liège (€9.90, 40 minutes). The high-speed Thalys passes through seven times daily on its way to Brussels and Paris. There's also a frequent bus service to Maastricht (€5, 55 minutes).

Getting Around

Aachen's points of interest are clustered around the city centre, which is covered easily on foot. Those arriving with private transport can park their cars in one of the many car parks. City bus tickets bought from the driver cost €1.20. A 24-hour Familienkarte und Gruppenkarte is valid for up to five people and costs €4.85. You can buy it on buses and from machines and outlets.

Bremen

The federal state of Bremen covers only the 404 sq km comprising the two cities of Bremen (the state capital) and Bremerhaven. In medieval times Bremen was Europe's northernmost archbishopric. The city was ruled by the Church until joining the Hanseatic League in the 14th century. Controlled by the French from 1810 to 1813, Bremen went on to join the German Confederation in 1815. In 1871 the city was made a state of the German Empire. In 1949 Bremen was officially declared a state of the Federal Republic of Germany.

BREMEN

☎ 0421 • pop 550,000

Bremen is, after Hamburg, the most important harbour in Germany, even though the open sea lies 113km to the north. Its Hanseatic past and congenial Altstadt area around Am Markt and Domsheide make it an enjoyable place to explore on foot, and Bremen's vibrant student population ensures the fun continues long after dark.

Orientation & Information

The heart of the city is Am Markt, but its soul is the port. The **tourist office** *(☎ 30 80 00; e btz@bremen-tourism.de; open 9.30am-6.30pm Mon-Wed, 9.30am-8pm Thur & Fri, 9.30am-4pm Sat & Sun)* is before the main train station. There is also a booth at the Rathaus opposite the smaller of the main Altstadt churches, Unser Lieben Frauen Kirche. **City walks** (English explanations provided) leave at 2pm daily from the tourist office at the station (€6). A Bremen tourist card (from €8.50 for two days) offers unlimited public transport and substantial discounts on city sights.

There's a **Reisebank** inside the train station. The **main post office** is also on Domsheide and there's another one near the train station. For more information visit the city's website at w www.bremen-tourism.de.

Things to See & Do

Around Am Markt don't miss the splendid and ornate **Rathaus**, the cathedral **St-Petri-Dom**, which has a tower **lookout** *(admission €1; open Easter-Oct)* and **museum** *(adult/concession €1.50/1)* For general gawking and climbing, the Dom, lookout, and museum are open 10am to 5pm Monday to Friday, 10am to 2pm Saturday and 2pm to 5pm Sunday. The lookout, though is only open half the year. There's also the large statue of **Roland**, Bremen's sentimental protector, which was erected in 1404.

Walk down **Böttcherstrasse**, a must-see recreation of a medieval alley, complete with tall brick houses, shops, galleries, restaurants and three **museums** *(adult/concession combined ticket €6/3; open 11pm-6pm Tues-Sun)*. The **Paula Modersohn-Becker Museum**, at No 8, has works by its namesake contemporary painter, and varied exhibits of the **Bernhard Hoetger Collection**; Hoetger's striking sculptures grace much of the Böttcherstrasse. The **Museum im Roselius-Haus** is at No 6, with a collection of paintings and applied arts from the 12th through to the 19th centuries. The **Glockenspiel**, active in summer hourly from

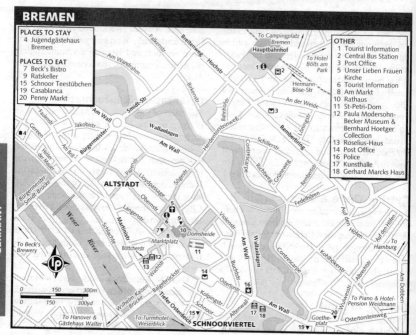

BREMEN

PLACES TO STAY
4 Jugendgästehaus Bremen

PLACES TO EAT
7 Beck's Bistro
9 Ratskeller
15 Schnoor Teestübchen
19 Casablanca
20 Penny Markt

OTHER
1 Tourist Information
2 Central Bus Station
3 Post Office
5 Unser Lieben Frauen Kirche
6 Tourist Information
8 Am Markt
10 Rathaus
11 St-Petri-Dom
12 Paula Modersohn-Becker Museum & Bernhard Hoetger Collection
13 Roselius-Haus
14 Post Office
16 Police
17 Kunsthalle
18 Gerhard Marcks Haus

noon to 6pm (in winter at noon, 3pm and 6pm), plays an extended tune between rooftops and an adjacent panel swivels to reveal a rotating cast of fearless explorers, from Leif Erikson to Charles Lindbergh.

The nearby **Schnoorviertel** area features fishing cottages that are now a tourist attraction, with shops, cafés and tiny lanes.

An excellent walk around the Altstadt is along the **Wallanlagen**, peaceful parks stretching along the old city walls and moat. Backing onto the parkland is Bremen's **Kunsthalle** (*adult/concession €5/2.50; open 10am-5pm Wed-Sun, 10am-9pm Tues*) art gallery. **Gerhard Marcks Haus** (*adult/concession €3.50/ 2.50; open 10am-6pm Tues-Sun*) contains a good collection which spans the breadth of sculpting history, including works by the museum's namesake. Both museums are closed on Monday.

Beck's Brewery Tours of Beck's Brewery (☎ 50 94 55 55; Am Deich 18-19) are available (take tram No 1 or 5 from the train station to Westerstrasse). German-language tours are run hourly from 10am to 5pm Tuesday to Saturday, to 3pm Sunday, and tours in English are

at 1.30pm on the same days. Tours cost €3 and include a tasting.

One good reference around which to frame a Bremen trip is the **Fairy-Tale Road** between Hanau, the birthplace of the Brothers Grimm, and Bremen (see Fairy-Tale Road in the Lower Saxony section later in this chapter).

Places to Stay

The closest camping ground is **Campingplatz Bremen** (☎ 21 20 02; Am Stadtwaldsee 1; tent sites €4, plus €4/2 per person/car). Take tram No 6 from the train station to the Klagenfurter Strasse stop.

Jugendgästehaus Bremen (☎ 17 13 69, fax 17 11 02; Kalkstrasse 6; beds juniors/seniors €17/19.70) is across the river from Beck's Brewery. Take tram No 3 or 5 from the train station to Am Brill.

The friendly **Hotel Garni Gästehaus Walter** (☎ 55 80 27, fax 55 80 29; Buntentorsteinweg 86-88; singles/doubles from €25/40) has pleasant rooms, some with shower and toilet. Take tram No 4 or 5 from the main train station. **Hotel-Pension Weidmann** (☎ 498 44 55; Am Schwarzen Meer 35; singles/doubles €21/41) provides basic accommodation. Take tram No 2 from Domsheide or No 10 from the station. The Art Nouveau **Hotel Bölts am Park** (☎ 34 61 10, fax 34 12 27; Slevogtstrasse 23; singles/doubles from €35/75) has very nice rooms with facilities. You get a pretty nifty view at the **Turmhotel Weserblick** (☎ 94 94 10, fax 949 41 10; Osterdeich 53; singles/doubles €67/82).

Places to Eat
A prowl around Ostertorsteinweg (near Am Dobben) will offer all sorts of gastronomic possibilities. **Casablanca** (Ostertorsteinweg 59; mains €5-12) is known for its breakfasts; it also has cheap pastas and soups. **Piano** (Fehrfeld 64), just east of Am Dobben, serves huge Mediterranean-inspired salads and tasty baked casseroles for around €5.50 to €7.50.

The long courtyard of Auf den Höfen, north of Ostertorsteinweg, has several restaurants and bars and serves as one of the epicentres of Bremen's nightlife. **Zum Hofheurigen** serves schnitzel to an older crowd for around €10. **Savarin** serves good casseroles by candlelight for around €6; **2Raum Lounge** is an achingly hip, minimalist bar/restaurant that offers a limited menu starting at €6.50.

On Markt, **Beck's Bistro** (Markt 9; lunch specials around €8) has traditional dishes à la carte, and lunch specials. **Schnoor Teestübchen** (Wüstestätte 1; lunch dishes around €6) specialises in tea and cakes, but it also serves vegetarian soups and quiche in a low-ceilinged, hobbit-like setting. Bremen's **Ratskeller** has 650 varieties of wine but no Beck's beer.

The **Penny Markt** (Ostertorsteinweg) is one convenient supermarket.

Getting There & Away
There are frequent regional and IC trains servicing Hamburg (€16.80, one hour). There are hourly IC trains to Cologne (€46.60, three hours). A couple of ICE trains run direct to Frankfurt (€88.40, 3½ hours) and Munich (€124, six hours) daily. Change trains in Hanover for Berlin (€135, 3½ hours). For Amsterdam (€54, four hours), you change in Osnabrück.

Getting Around
To get to Am Markt follow the tram route from directly in front of the train station. The tourist office stocks good public transport

maps. Short trips on buses and trams cost €1.85, a four-trip transferable ticket is €5.60 and a day pass is €4.50.

Lower Saxony

Lower Saxony (Niedersachsen) has much to offer, and it's a quick train ride or autobahn drive from the tourist centres down south. The scenic Harz Mountains, the old student town of Göttingen, and the picturesque towns along the Fairy-Tale Road are the most popular tourist attractions. British occupation forces created the federal state of Lower Saxony during 1946, when the states of Braunschweig (Brunswick), Schaumburg-Lippe and Oldenburg were amalgamated with the Prussian province of Hanover.

HANOVER
☎ 0511 • pop 523,000
Hanover (Hannover), the capital of Lower Saxony, has close links with the English-speaking world. In 1714, the eldest son of Electress Sophie of Hannover, a granddaughter of James I of England and VI of Scotland, ascended the British throne as King George I. This Anglo-German union lasted through several generations until 1837. Savaged by heavy bombing in 1943, Hanover was rebuilt into a prosperous city known throughout Europe for its trade fairs.

Information
The **tourist office** (☎ 16 84 97 11; Ernst-August-Platz 2; open 9am-6pm Mon-Fri, 9am-2pm Sat) is next to the main post office and near the main train station. The Hannover-Card, which entitles you to unlimited public transport and discount admission to museums and other attractions, costs €8 for one day or €12 for three days.

Things to See & Do
One way to pick out most city sights on foot is to follow the numbered attractions with the help of the Red Thread Guide (€2) from the tourist office. The chief attractions are the glorious parks of the **Herrenhäuser Gärten** (☎ 16 84 77 43; open from 9am all year, closing coincides with sunset), especially the baroque **Grosser Garten** and the **Berggarten** (admission €3; open to 8pm in summer), with its newly installed rainforest exhibit, the

GERMANY

GERMANY

Regenwald Haus (adult/concession €9/6). The gardens also include two museums: **Fürstenhaus** (adult/concession €3.30/1.50; open Tues-Sun) shows how royalty lived in the 1700s; and the **Wilhelm-Busch-Museum** (adult/concession €4.50/2.50; open Tues-Sun) of caricature and satirical art contains the work of Wilhelm Busch and others. To reach the gardens, take tram No 4 or 5.

Sprengel Museum (☎ 16 84 38 75; Kurt-Schwitters-Platz; adult/concession €3.50/1.80; open Tues-Sun, to 8pm Tues) exhibits contemporary works, the highlights being Picasso and Max Beckmann. **Niedersächsisches Landesmuseum** (☎ 980 75; Willy-Brandt-Allee 5; adult/concession €3/1.50; open Tues-Sun) has displays of natural history and European paintings.

At Am Markt in the old town is the 14th-century **Marktkirche**. Apart from its truncated tower, it is characteristic of the northern red-brick Gothic style; the original stained-glass windows are particularly beautiful. The **Altes Rathaus** – across the marketplace – was built in various sections over a century. Around **Burgstrasse** some of the half-timbered town houses remain, as well as the **Ballhof** (Ballhofstrasse), originally built for badminton-type games of the 17th century, but nowadays offering theatrical plays.

On Breite Strasse near the corner of Osterstrasse, the ruin of the **Aegidienkirche** – smashed in 1943 – is an eloquent memorial; the peace bell inside is a gift from one of Hanover's sister-cities, Hiroshima.

Places to Stay

The tourist office only offers a private room-finding service during trade fairs but will arrange a hotel room year-round for €6.50. The **Jugendherberge** (☎ 131 76 74, fax 185 55; Ferdinand-Wilhelm-Fricke-Weg 1; dorm beds juniors/seniors €13.50/16) is 3km out of town. Take the U3 or U7 from Hauptbahnhof to Fischerhof, then cross the river on the Lodemannbrücke bridge and turn right.

Hotel Flora (☎ 38 39 10, fax 383 91 91; Heinrichstrasse 36; singles/doubles from €36/62, with bath €46/72) provides pleasant rooms. **Hotel Gildehof** (☎ 36 36 80, fax 30 66 44; Joachimstrasse 6; singles/doubles €41/65, with bath €57/75) has clean rooms, some with bathroom. The restaurant downstairs serves well-priced traditional dishes. **Hotel am Thielenplatz** (☎ 32 76 91, fax 32 51 88; e hotel.am.thielenplatz@t-online.de; Thielenplatz 2; singles/doubles from €45/68) is centrally located. The **Hotel Alpha** (☎ 34 15 35; Friesenstrasse 19; singles/doubles €79/99) offers rooms with all facilities. **Congress Hotel am Stadtpark** (☎ 280 50, fax 81 46 52; e info@congress-hotel-hannover.de; Clausewitzstrasse 6; singles/doubles from €96/166) gets congress and trade fair visitors.

Places to Eat

The Altstadt area behind Marktkirche has plenty of well-priced restaurants offering German cuisine. The food hall **Markthalle** (cnr Karmarschstrasse & Leinestrasse) is a gourmand's paradise – it roughly keeps normal shop hours and has lots of budget ethnic food stalls, some vegetarian offerings and fresh produce. The Hanover institution **Brauhaus Ernst August** (Schmiedestrasse 13a; mains €5-17) brews its own Hannöversch beer and also serves German dishes. Thai restaurant **Sawaddi** (☎ 34 43 67; Königstrasse 7; mains about €11) is behind the train station; its all-you-can-eat lunch buffet is good value.

Getting There & Away

Hanover's spruced-up train station is a major hub. ICE trains to/from Hamburg (€34.40, 1½ hours), Munich (€110, 4½ hours), Frankfurt (€72, 2½ hours) and Cologne (€53.40, 2¾ hours) leave hourly, and every two hours to Berlin-Zoo (€51.80, 1¾ hours). A web of regional services fills in the gaps locally.

Getting Around

The city centre is fairly compact and can be easily covered on foot. Single journeys on the combined tram/U-Bahn system for one zone cost €1 and day passes cost €3.10. The S5 connects the airport with the fairgrounds via the main train station in 25 minutes. For the Messe, the U8 also runs to Messe Nord from the main train station.

AROUND HANOVER
Hildesheim
☎ 05121 • pop 103,000

When a 1945 bombing raid destroyed the city centre of Hildesheim, the town responded in then-typical fashion – it replaced many of the damaged age-old buildings with modern, 'German Post-War Hideous' concrete structures. What makes Hildesheim worth a day trip, though, is what happened next – a town movement forced the city's leaders to tear down the ugly new buildings and painstakingly reconstruct the town's historic heart according to the original plans (at fantastic expense). As a result, Hildesheim boasts two Unesco World Heritage Sites and some of the most authentic (if not authentically old) examples of Gothic and late Gothic architecture in Germany.

The **tourist office** (☎ 179 80; e tourist -info@hildesheim.com; Rathausstrasse 18-20) is 750m south of the train station. Stop by and pick up a copy of *Hildesheimer Rosenroute* (€1), a guide to the city's buildings and their history.

The town's jewel is the **Hildesheimer Dom** (Domhof; admission free), which contains the priceless **Bernward bronze doors** and the elegant **Column of Christ**, both dating back to the early 1000s. In the cathedral's cloister blooms the **Thousand-Year-Old Rosebush** (adult/concession €0.50/0.30), alleged to be the same one that Ludwig the Pious hung his gear on in AD 815. Other reconstructed churches of note include the Romanesque **St Michaeliskirche** (Michaelisplatz; admission free) and the Gothic **St Andreaskirche** (Andreasplatz; admission free). If you're looking for a way to work off the calories from that lunchtime schnitzel, you can climb the 364 steps of the St Andreaskirche's **tower** (adult/concession €1.50/1) for a breathtaking view over the city.

The **Roemer- Und Pelizaeusmusuem** (Am Steine 1-2; adult/concession €6/5; open 9am-6pm daily) has one of Europe's best collections of Egyptian art and artefacts.

The picturesque Lappenberg neighbourhood south of the city centre is an ideal place for a stroll. The former **Jewish Quarter** is the oldest area of the town, and is home to a moving **memorial** (Gelber Stern) to the synagogue that was burned down here on Kristallnacht in 1938.

There are frequent trains to Hanover (€5.50, 30 minutes), as well as ICE trains to Göttingen (€11.60, 25 minutes).

FAIRY-TALE ROAD

The Fairy-Tale Road (Märchenstrasse), so called because of the number of legends and fairy tales that sprang from this region, is well worth a day or two. The route begins at Hanau and runs to Kassel and Göttingen, passes near Hanover and ends in Bremen.

The stretch between Hanover and Göttingen is the most historical section of the route. Among the most interesting towns here are Hamelin (Hameln) of Pied Piper fame, Bodenwerder where the great adventurer Baron von Münchhausen made his home, and the surprising town of Bad Karlshafen.

Information

Every town, village and hamlet along the Fairy-Tale Road has an information office of some sort. The **Fremdenverkehrsverband Weserbergland-Mittelweser E.V.** (☎ 930 00, fax 93 00 33; Deisterallee 1) in Hamelin is the best place to obtain brochures on activities and sights all along the middle Weser. Weserdampfschiffahrt GmbH ferries is in the same building.

In Hamelin there is a **tourist office** (☎ 95 78 23; Deisterallee 1); in Bodenwerder there is a **tourist office** (☎ 405 41; Weserstrasse 3); and in Bad Karlshafen it is in the **Kurverwaltung** (☎ 99 99 24) by the 'harbour'.

The telephone area codes are Hamelin ☎ 05151, Bodenwerder ☎ 05533 and Bad Karlshafen ☎ 05672.

Things to See

Hamelin Among the most interesting sights is the **Rattenfängerhaus** (Rat Catcher's, aka Pied Piper's, House; Osterstrasse), the old town's main street, built at the beginning of the 17th century. On the Bungelosenstrasse side is an inscription that tells how, in 1284, 130 children of Hamelin were led past this site and out of town by a piper wearing multi-coloured clothes, never to be seen again. Also have a look at the Rattenfänger **Glockenspiel** at the Weser Renaissance **Hochzeitshaus** at the Markt end of Osterstrasse (daily at 1.05pm, 3.35pm and 5.35pm). More of the story is at the museum in the ornate **Leisthaus** (adult/concession €3/1.50; open Tues-Sun).

For the other beauties of Hamelin – restored 16th- to 18th-century half-timbered houses with inscribed dedications – stroll through the southeastern quarter of the old town, around the Alte Marktstrasse and Grossehofstrasse areas or Kupferschmiedestrasse.

Bodenwerder The **Rathaus** (Münchhausen-platz 1) is said to be the house in which the legendary Baron von Münchhausen was born. The baron became known for telling outrageous tales, the most famous of which was how he rode through the air on a cannonball. This very cannonball is in a room dedicated to the baron in the Rathaus. Also interesting is the statue of the baron, riding half a horse, in the garden outside the Rathaus. This was, of course, another of his stories.

There is a rather pleasant **walking track** along the Weser River in both directions from Bodenwerder.

Bad Karlshafen After passing through the towns like Hamelin and Bodenwerder, the last thing you expect is this whitewashed, meticulously planned, baroque village. Originally the city was planned with an impressive harbour and a canal connecting the Weser River with the Rhine in the hope of diverting trade away from Hanover and Münden in the north. The plans were laid by a local earl with help from Huguenot refugees. The earl's death in 1730 prevented completion of the project, but even today his incomplete masterpiece and the influence of the Huguenots is too beautiful to miss.

Places to Stay & Eat

In Hamelin the camping ground **Fährhaus an der Weser** (☎ 611 67; tent sites €6, plus €4 per person) is on Uferstrasse, across the Weser River from the old town and a 10-minute walk north. Also in Hamelin, there's the **DJH hostel** (☎ 34 25; Fischbeckerstrasse 33; dorm beds juniors/seniors €12.30/15); in Bodenwerder the **DJH hostel** (☎ 05533-26 85; Richard-Schirrmann-Weg; dorm beds juniors/seniors €12.30/15); and in Bad Karlshafen the hostel is **Hermann Wenning** (☎ 338, fax 83 61; Winnefelderstrasse 7; dorm beds juniors/seniors €13.50/16.20).

Hotel Altstadtwiege (☎ 05151-278 54; Neue Marktstrasse 10; singles/doubles from €33/75) is in Hamelin. **Hotel-Garni Christinenhof** (☎ 950 80, fax 436 11; Alte Marktstrasse 18, Hamelin; singles/doubles from €66/95) offers stylish rooms. The **Gaststätte Rattenfängerhaus** in the Rat Catcher's House, serves main courses averaging €12.

Getting Around

The easiest way to follow the Fairy-Tale Road is by car. There are frequent regional trains operating between Hanover and Hamelin (€8.10, 45 minutes). From Hamelin's train station, direct bus No 520 follows the Weser River to Holzminden via Bodenwerder

several times daily. Bus No 221 from Holzminden (board at Hafendamm) runs to Höxter bus station, which connects with bus No 220 to Bad Karlshafen, from where trains go to Göttingen.

GÖTTINGEN
☎ 0551 • pop 130,000

This leafy university town is an ideal stopover on your way north or south; it's on the direct train line between Munich and Hamburg. Though small, Göttingen is lively, mostly because of its large student population. A legion of notables, including Otto von Bismarck and the Brothers Grimm, studied and worked here, and the university has produced more than 40 Nobel Prize winners.

Information

The **main tourist office** (☎ 49 98 00; e tourismus@goettingen.de; Markt 9; open 9.30am-6pm Mon-Fri, 10am-4pm Sat & Sun in summer, 9.30am-1pm & 2pm-6pm Mon-Fri, 10am-1pm Sat in winter) is in the old Rathaus. There's a **post office** just to the left (north) and another in the Altstadt at Groner Strasse 15–17. There is a **Waschcenter laundry** (Ritterplan 4). Check your email at **Computerwerk** (Düsterestrasse 20), where 30 minutes of Internet time costs €2.

Things to See

The tourist office sells the excellent brochure *Göttingen Komplett* for €2.50. At Markt, don't miss the **Great Hall** in the Rathaus where colourful frescoes cover every centimetre of wall space. Just outside, students and a colourful assortment of harmless punk rockers mill about the **Gänseliesel** fountain, the town's symbol. The bronze beauty has a reputation as 'the most kissed girl in the world' because every student who obtains a doctor's degree must then plant a kiss on her cheek.

The 15th-century **Junkernschänke** (Barfüsserstrasse 5), with its colourful carved facade, is the most stunning of the town's half-timbered buildings. A walk on top of the old **town wall** along Bürgerstrasse takes you past **Bismarckhäuschen** (admission free; open 10am-1pm Tues, 3pm-5pm Wed, Thur & Sat), a modest building where the Iron Chancellor lived in 1833 during his wild student days, and the pretty **Botanical Gardens**.

Places to Stay

Camping am Hohen Hagen (☎ 05502-21 47; tent sites €3, plus €5 per person; open all year) is about 10km west of town in Dransfeld (bus No 120). To reach the **Jugendherberge** (☎ 576 22, fax 438 87; Habichtsweg 2; dorm beds juniors/seniors €14.80/20.70) from the train station main entrance take bus No 6 to the Jugendherberge stop.

The friendly **Hotel Garni Gräfin von Holtzenorff** (☎ 639 87, fax 63 29 85; Ernst-Ruhstrat-Strasse 4; singles/doubles €26/45, with bath €45/65) has basic rooms. Take bus No 13 to Florenz-Sartorius-Strasse. **Berliner Hof** (☎ 38 33 20, fax 383 32 32; e info@ berlinerhof.de; Weender Landstrasse 43; singles/doubles €36/52) is located directly across from the university. The **Hotel Kasseler Hof** (☎ 720 81, 770 34 29; Rosdorfer Weg 26; singles/doubles from €34/67, with bath €52/85), on the edge of the old town, has simple rooms. **Hotel Central** (☎ 571 57, fax 571 05; Jüdenstrasse 12; singles without bath from €40, singles/doubles with bath €52/80) is conveniently situated in the middle of town.

Places to Eat

Nikolaistrasse and Goethe Allee offer loads of takeaway options. The **Mensa Am Turm** (Gosslerstrasse 12b), just east of campus, is the most pleasant of the dirt-cheap student cafeterias in town; lunches cost €4 or less. There's another more convenient Mensa on Wilhelmsplatz. **Salamanca** (Gartenstrasse 21b; mains €5-10; open from 6pm Mon-Fri, from 1pm Sat & Sun) offers tasty, well-priced food in a prototypical leftist 20-something café. **Diwan** (Rote Strasse 11) is a good Turkish restaurant in the mid-price range. **La Hacienda** (☎ 531 13 39; Weender Landstrasse 23) serves delicious Mexican food and drinks in a lively atmosphere. Make sure you reserve ahead for dinner on weekends.

Plus (cnr Prinzenstrasse & Stumpfebiel) is a convenient supermarket.

Entertainment

Göttingen's bars and clubs give this small university town a lively, big-city atmosphere. **Apex** (Burgstrasse 46) is a nice place for a nibble and drink. The **Irish Pub** (Mühlenstrasse 4) offers a few dishes and has live music. The salsa, hip-hop, and funk dance nights at the **Blue Note** (Wilhelmsplatz 3) are popular with students and nonstudents alike; **Tangente** (☎ 463 76; Goetheallee 8a) gets an older student crowd. The **Sechs Million Dollar Club** (Neustadt 1) has a cool and retro feel and stiff cocktails. Tiny **Elektroosho** (Weender Strasse 38), Göttingen's hippest dance club, specialises in house music. Things don't get started there until late.

Getting There & Away

Hourly ICE trains pass through on their way to/from Hanover (€26.20, 30 minutes), Berlin (€62.60, 2¼ hours), Hamburg (€53, two hours), Frankfurt (€48.20, two hours) and Munich (€92.60, 4½ hours). Direct RB trains depart every two hours from Göttingen for Goslar in the Harz Mountains (€12.40, 1¼ hours).

GOSLAR

☎ 05321 • pop 48,000

Goslar is a centre for Harz Mountains tourism, but this 1000-year-old city with its beautifully preserved half-timbered buildings has plenty of charm in its own right. The town and the nearby Rammelsberg Mine is listed as a World Heritage Site by Unesco.

Information

The **tourist office** (☎ 780 60; e goslarinfo@ t-online.de; Markt 7; open 9.15am-6pm Mon-Fri, 9.30am-4pm Sat, 9.30am-2pm Sun May-Oct, 9.15am-5pm Mon-Fri, 9.30am-2pm Sat Nov-Apr) can help when the area's accommodation is packed. For information on the Harz Mountains go to **Harzer Verkehrsverband** (☎ 340 40, fax 34 04 66; e info@harzinfo.de; Marktstrasse 45; open 8am-4pm Mon-Thur, 8am-1pm Fri).

Things to See & Do

The **Marktplatz** has several photogenic houses. The one opposite the Gothic **Rathaus** has a chiming clock depicting four scenes from the history of mining in the area. It struts its stuff at 9am, noon, 3pm and 6pm. The **market fountain** dates from the 13th century and is crowned by an eagle.

Usually jammed with tour-bus visitors, the **Kaiserpfalz** (Kaiserbleek 6; adult/concession €4.50/2.50; open daily) is a reconstructed Romanesque 11th-century palace. Just below there's the restored **Domvorhalle** which displays the 11th-century 'Kaiserstuhl' throne, used by German emperors. At the **Rammelsberger Bergbaumuseum** (adult/concession

GERMANY

€8.50/5.50; open 9am-6pm daily), about 1km south of the town centre on Rammelsberger Strasse, you can delve into the 1000-year mining history of the area and descend into the shafts on a variety of tours.

Places to Stay

The pretty **Jugendherberge** (☎ 222 40, fax 413 76; Rammelsberger Strasse 25; dorm beds juniors/seniors €15.40/18.10) is situated behind the Kaiserpfalz (take bus No 803 to Theresienhof from the train station). It is often full of high-school students.

Another option is **Hotel und Campingplatz Sennhütte** (☎ 225 02; Clausthaler Strasse 28; tent sites €2.50, plus €3.30/2 per person/car, singles/doubles from €20/40; open Fri-Wed), 3km south on Route B241. Take bus No 803 from the train station to Sennhütte. There are also several clean, simple rooms with nice views and you'll find lots of trails nearby.

The tourist office can help with room bookings, especially on busy weekends and in summer. **Gästehaus Schmitz** (☎ 234 45, fax 30 60 39; Kornstrasse 1; singles/doubles €30/40, apartments from €30) offers the best value with bright, cheerful rooms. **Gästehaus Verhoeven** (☎ 238 12; Hoher Weg 12; singles/doubles from €32/50, with bath €42/58) has clean and simple rooms. The upmarket **Hotel Kaiserworth** (☎ 70 90, fax 70 93 45; e hotel@kaiserworth.de; Markt 3; singles/doubles from €49/99) is in a magnificent 500-year-old building.

Places to Eat

The **Altdeutsches Kartoffelhaus** (Breite Strasse) in the Kaiserpassage shopping arcade offers generous portions of potato dishes for between €4 and €11. **Brauhaus Wolpertinger** (Marstallstrasse 1; mains €5-15) is a restaurant with whimsical decor. **Didgeridoo** (Hoher Weg 13; mains €7-10) specialises in well-priced kangaroo burgers and barbecue meals (and has some good Australian wines). **Restaurant Aubergine** (☎ 421 36; Marktstrasse 4; mains €18-36) has delicious Mediterranean cuisine.

Getting There & Away

Goslar is regularly connected by train to Göttingen (€12.40, 1¼ hours), Hanover (€12.40, one hour) and Wernigerode (€5.50, 30 minutes). For information on getting to/from the eastern Harz region, see Getting Around in the following Western Harz Mountains section and the Getting There & Away sections under Quedlinburg and Wernigerode earlier in this chapter.

WESTERN HARZ MOUNTAINS

Known mostly to Germans and Scandinavians, the Harz Mountains (Harzgebirge) don't have the dramatic peaks and valleys of the Alps, but they offer a great four-seasons sports getaway without some of the Alpine tackiness and tourism. Silver, lead and copper mines in the area have been largely exhausted, and many can now be visited.

Orientation & Information

Pick up the booklet Der Harz (€3), available at any tourist office in the Harz and at many hotels. For weather reports and winter snow information (in German), contact the **Harzer Verkehrsverband** (☎ 05325-340 40) in Goslar.

The **Goslar tourist office** has information on the Harz Mountains. Hahnenklee has a **tourist office** (☎ 05325-510 40; Kurhausweg 7); in Bad Harzburg there is a **tourist office** (☎ 05322-753 30; Herzog-Wilhelm-Strasse 86); and in Clausthal-Zellerfeld there is a **tourist office** (☎ 05323-810 24; Bahnhofstrasse 5a).

Things to See

Hahnenklee is proud of its Norwegian-style **'stave' church**, but most remarkable is Clausthal-Zellerfeld's 17th-century wooden church **Zum Heiligen Geist** (Hindenburgplatz), built to accommodate more than 2000 worshippers! Nearby, the technical university's **mineral collection** (Römerstrasse 2a; admission €1.50) is one of the largest in Germany.

For a fine view, take the **Bergbahn** car up to the castle ruins above Bad Harzburg (€2/3 one way/return, less with resort card). The embarkation point is 2km uphill from the train station, so you can promenade among German wealth and ambition and check the array of furs and other luxury goods flaunted in this health resort.

Activities

Despite 500km of groomed **hiking trails**, the beauty of the National Park Harz hasn't suffered. Maps and information are abundant, and most of the hikes are less than 10km. Trails through wildly romantic Okertal (just outside

Goslar), and the 15km to Hahnenklee from Goslar, are especially picturesque. From the cable-car station in Bad Harzburg, paths lead to Sennhütte (1.3km), Molkenhaus (3km) and to the scenic Rabenklippe (7km) overlooking the Ecker Valley. All have restaurants; a blackboard inside the cable-car station indicates the ones that are open. From Bad Harzburg you can also pick up the medieval Kaiserweg route, which joins the Goetheweg to Torfhaus (11km) and the Brocken (7km from Torfhaus).

Cycling is popular in summer among those seeking a hilly challenge, and in winter the Harz Mountains offers excellent conditions for **cross-country skiing**. Snow enthusiasts will find **downhill skiing** conditions average, but slopes can be quite good in Hahnenklee, St Andreasberg and Braunlage. Rental equipment is easy to find. Both downhill and cross-country gear start at about €15 a day. Tourist offices in most towns keep a list of places that hire bikes and ski equipment.

The Harz Mountains also has a healthy number of spa towns where **spa activities** are offered. Most spa towns have indoor swimming facilities and all have *Kurzentren* (spa centres) that offer massages and other physical therapies to soothe an aching body after an all-too-brisk hike, ride or ski through hilly terrain.

Places to Stay
Many of the 30 or so camping grounds in the Harz Mountains are open all year – pick up the free *Der Harz Camping* brochure at local tourist offices. There is no shortage of budget rooms in hotels and pensions. Tourist offices in each town have useful listings and can help with bookings. For extended stays ask about apartments or holiday homes, which become good deals when staying a week or more. In spa resorts you will pay about a €2 *Kurtaxe* (resort tax) per day on hotel accommodation (less in hostels and at camping grounds).

Hahnenklee Around 2km north of Hahnenklee there's the **Campingplatz am Kreuzeck** (☎ 05325-25 70; *tent sites* €5.50, *plus* €3.50 *per person*). To get there, take bus No 830 from Goslar or Hahnenklee. The **Jugendherberge** (☎ 05325-22 56, *fax* 35 24; *Hahnenkleer Strasse 11; juniors/seniors* €12.30/15) is near the Bockswiese bus stop (same bus) on the road from Goslar.

Bad Harzburg Between Goslar and Bad Harzburg, on the L501 (bus No 810 or 871 to Campingplatz stop) is **Harz-Camp Göttingerode** (☎ 05322-812 15; *Kreisstrasse 66; tent sites* €5, *plus* €4.40 *per person*). Rustic youth hostel **Braunschweiger Haus** (☎ 05322-45 82, *fax* 18 67; *Waldstrasse 5; juniors/seniors* €16/20) has one-, two-, and three-bed rooms. Take bus No 873 from the train station to the Lärchenweg stop.

Clausthal-Zellerfeld Around 1km west of Zellerfeld there's **Campingplatz Waldweben** (☎ 05323-817 12; *Spiegeltaler Strasse 31; tent sites* €4.80, *plus* €3.50 *per person*). The **Jugendherberge** (☎ 05323-842 93, *fax* 838 27; *Altenauer Strasse 55; juniors/seniors* €12.30/15) is in the forest about 2km from town; take bus No 831 to the Jugendherberge stop. The hostel is usually closed on the first weekend of the month from mid-September to mid-May.

Getting Around
Frequent regional trains link Goslar with Wernigerode. Four direct trains depart daily for Göttingen via Bad Harzburg. Bus No 877 shuttles several times daily between Bad Harzburg and Wernigerode (just under one hour; €3). It stops on the far side of Am Bahnhofsplatz at Bad Harzburg train station and next to the main station in Wernigerode.

Bus No 861 runs between Goslar and Altenau, while Nos 830 and 831 connect Goslar with Clausthal-Zellerfeld (No 830 via Hahnenklee on alternating hours).

Hamburg

☎ 040 • pop 1.7 million
The first recorded settlement on the present site of Hamburg was the moated fortress of Hammaburg, built in the first half of the 9th century. The city that developed around it became the northernmost archbishopric in Europe, to facilitate the conversion of the northern peoples.

The city was burned down many times, but in the 13th century it became the Hanseatic League's gateway to the North Sea and was second in importance and influence only to Lübeck. With the decline of the Hanseatic League in the 16th century, Lübeck faded into insignificance but Hamburg continued to thrive.

GERMANY

Hamburg strode confidently into the 20th century but WWI stopped all trade and most of Hamburg's merchant shipping fleet (almost 1500 ships) was forfeited to the Allies as reparation payment. In WWII, more than half of Hamburg's residential areas and port facilities were demolished and 55,000 people killed in the Allied air raids that spawned such horrific firestorms.

Today this is a sprawling port city and a separate state of Germany, with a stylish shopping district, numerous waterways (with more bridges than Venice), and even a beach (in Blankenese, which is one of Germany's most exclusive suburbs).

Orientation

The Hauptbahnhof is very central, near Aussenalster lake and fairly close to most of the sights. These are south of Aussenalster and north of the Elbe River, which runs all the way from the Czech Republic to Hamburg before flowing into the North Sea. The city centre features the Rathaus and the beautiful Hauptkirche St Michaelis. The port is west of the city centre, facing the Elbe.

Information

The small **tourist office** (☎ 30 05 12 00; e info@hamburg-tourism.de; open 7am-11pm daily) is in the main train station at the Kirchenallee exit and offers limited brochures and a room-finding service (€4). It has great hours and friendly staff. There's also a **tourist office** (open 8am-8pm Mon-Sat, 8am-7pm Sun Apr-Sept, 10am-5.30pm daily Oct-Mar) at St Pauli harbour, between piers 4 and 5. View its official website at w www.hamburg-tourism.de.

Both tourist offices stock the Hamburg Card, which offers unlimited public transport and free or slightly discounted admission to many attractions, museums and cruises. The 'day card' is valid on the day of purchase and costs €6.80 (single) or €12.70 (groups of up to five people). The 'multiday card' is valid on the day of purchase and the following two days (€14/22.50). An even better deal is the Power Pass, which gives steep discounts to anyone under 30 for a mere €6.70 (extendable for an extra €3 per day).

Money There is a **Reisebank** (open 7.30am-10pm daily) above the Kirchenallee exit of the main train station, and others at Altona train station (open Mon-Sat) and in terminal 4 at the airport (open 6am-10pm daily).

Post & Communications There's a small **post office** (open 8am-8pm Mon-Fri, 9am-6pm Sat, 10am-6pm Sun) with a poste-restante service (four weeks for international mail) near the Kirchenallee exit of the train station. There is a main **post office** (cnr Dammtorstrasse & Stephansplatz) close to the Stephansplatz U-Bahn stop.

Email & Internet Access On the 3rd floor of the Karstadt department store, **Cyberb@r** (Mönchebergstrasse 16) charges €1.50 for 30 minutes online.

Newspapers & Magazines For cultural events and lifestyle information, look for the weekly magazines Szene (€2.50) and Oxmox (€1.50), and the monthly Prinz (€1).

Bookshops There are guidebooks in English at **Dr Götze Land & Karte** (Alstertor 14-18) which claims to be the biggest specialist map and travel bookshop in Europe. The branch of **Thalia Bücher** (Grosse Bleichen 19) has a large selection of English-language books and some guidebooks. Second-hand books can be bought at the **English Bookstore** (Stresemannstrasse 169; S-Bahn to Holstenstrasse).

Laundry The Schnell & Sauber chain has a **laundrette** (Nobistor 34) in St Pauli, and another outlet at Neuer Pferdemarkt 27 (U3 to Feldstrasse).

Medical & Emergency Services For an **ambulance** call ☎ 112. A **medical** emergency service is available on ☎ 22 80 22. For urgent **dental** treatment call ☎ 33 11 55. The **police** emergency number is ☎ 110; there is one station in St Georg at Steindamm 82 and another in St Pauli at Spielbudenplatz 31, on the corner of Davidstrasse.

Dangers & Annoyances Overall, Hamburg is a very safe city, but you should take special care in the seedy drug and prostitution area near the Hauptbahnhof.

Things to See & Do

Altstadt Much of Hamburg's old city centre was lost in WWII, but it's still worth a walking tour. The area is laced with wonderful canals (called 'fleets') running from the Alster lakes to the Elbe.

The Altstadt is centred on Rathausmarkt, where the large **Rathaus** and the huge clock tower overlook the lively square. This is one of the most interesting city halls in Germany, and the 35-minute tour is worthwhile at €1/0.50 per adult/concession. It's in English hourly from 10.15am to 3.15pm Monday to Thursday, to 1.15pm Friday to Sunday. The building has 647 rooms – six more than Buckingham Palace.

It is a moving experience to visit the remaining tower of the devastated **St-Nikolai-Kirche**, now an antiwar memorial, nearby on Ost-West-Strasse. From there, walk a few blocks west to the baroque **Hauptkirche St Michaelis** and take the lift up the **tower** (adult/concession €2.50/1.25; open 10am-6pm daily Apr-Oct, 10am-5pm Nov-Mar), enter through portal No 3, for a great view of the city and the port. Inside, the beautiful interiors and the crypt (a donation of €1.25 is requested) are open for viewing.

Port After exploring the Altstadt, stroll down to one of the busiest ports in the world. It boasts the world's largest carpet warehouse complex, while the Free Port Warehouses stockpile goods from all continents.

The **port cruises** are touristy but still worthwhile. There are many options; for details see Organised Tours later in this section.

If you're in the port area early on a Sunday (5am to 10am, October to March from 7am), head for **Fischmarkt** (Fish Market) in St Pauli, right on the Elbe. Hamburg's oldest market (established 1703) is popular with locals and tourists alike and everything under the sun is sold here. Cap your morning with a visit to the live music session at the **Fischauktionshalle** (Fish Auction Hall; Grosse Elbstrasse 9).

Reeperbahn Among Hamburg's biggest tourist attractions is the famous Reeperbahn red-light district. It is 600m long and is the heart of the St Pauli entertainment district, which includes shows, bars, cabarets, clubs, theatres and a casino. In recent years, the Reeperbahn sex establishments have been gradually moving over for popular restaurants and bars, with a dwindling number of peep shows and sex shops plying a 'traditional' trade.

If you go to one of these haunts, make sure you understand costs beforehand. Ask for the price list if it's not posted by the entrance. Entry is sometimes free or €2 to €5, but there will likely be a minumum purchase of €25 or more – enough for a campari and soda in some places. On **Grosse Freiheit**, Safari is one of the more famous clubs. Notorious **Herbertstrasse** is where prostitutes pose in windows offering their wares. It is fenced off at each end and men under 18 and women are not allowed in. Ironically, hustling is much more aggressive on the surrounding regular streets.

Other Attractions Hamburg's **Kunsthalle** (Glockengiesserwall) has old masters and a large collection of German paintings from both the 19th and 20th centuries. Contemporary art is housed next door in the modern **Galerie der Gegenwart** (adult/concession for both museums €7.50/5; both open 10am-6pm Tues-Sun, 10am-9pm Thur). The waxworks museum **Panoptikum** (Spielbudenplatz 3; adult/concession €4/2.50; open 11am-9pm Mon-Fri, 11am-midnight Sat, 10am-9pm Sun early Feb–mid-Jan) is kitschy fun; don't miss the gruesomely realistic syphilitic hands in the 'medical history' wing.

Harry's Hamburger Hafen Basar (Bernhard-Nocht-Strasse 89-91; admission €2.50) is a fascinating 'shop'. It's the life's work of Harry, a bearded character known to seamen all over the world, who for decades bought trinkets and souvenirs from sailors and others. Now run by Harry's daughter, the shop has a wealth of curiosities and the entry fee is refunded with a €5 purchase. The **Erotic Art Museum** (Nobistor 10a; adult/concession €8/5; open 10am-midnight Sun-Thur, 10am-1am Fri & Sat) contains some 1800 paintings, drawings and sculptures by artists from Delacroix to Picasso.

The viewing deck of Hamburg's **TV Tower** (Lagerstrasse 2-8) was closed indefinitely for renovations at the time of our visit, but you can still bungee jump off the 130m-high platform (€99), Germany's tallest jump. Call ☎ 089-60 60 89 23 for bookings. From the free fall, you'll see the adjacent sprawling gardens of **Planten un Blomen**, a gorgeous landscaped city park with a large Japanese garden.

Organised Tours

Basic city sightseeing **bus tours** in English operate at least twice daily from April to October,

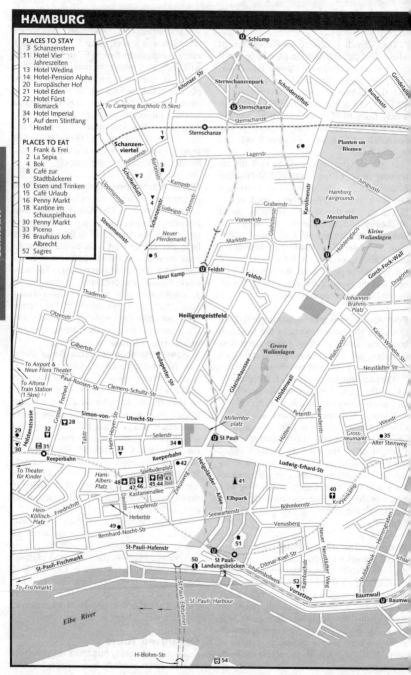

HAMBURG

PLACES TO STAY
3 Schanzenstern
11 Hotel Vier Jahreszeiten
13 Hotel Wedina
14 Hotel-Pension Alpha
20 Europäischer Hof
21 Hotel Eden
22 Hotel Fürst Bismarck
34 Hotel Imperial
51 Auf dem Stintfang Hostel

PLACES TO EAT
1 Frank & Frei
2 La Sepia
4 Bok
8 Café zur Stadtbäckerei
10 Essen und Trinken
15 Café Urlaub
16 Penny Markt
30 Penny Markt
33 Piceno
36 Brauhaus Joh. Albrecht
52 Sagres

GERMANY

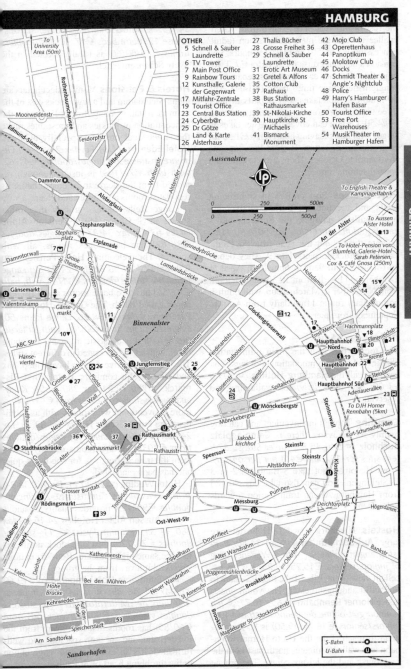

OTHER
5 Schnell & Sauber Laundrette
6 TV Tower
7 Main Post Office
9 Rainbow Tours
12 Kunsthalle; Galerie der Gegenwart
17 Mitfahr-Zentrale
19 Tourist Office
23 Central Bus Station
24 Cyberb@r
25 Dr Götze Land & Karte
26 Alsterhaus
27 Thalia Bücher
28 Grosse Freiheit 36
29 Schnell & Sauber Laundrette
31 Erotic Art Museum
32 Gretel & Alfons
35 Cotton Club
37 Rathaus
38 Bus Station Rathausmarket
39 St-Nikolai-Kirche
40 Hauptkirche St Michaelis
41 Bismarck Monument
42 Mojo Club
43 Operettenhaus
44 Panoptikum
45 Molotow Club
46 Docks
47 Schmidt Theater & Angie's Nightclub
48 Police
49 Harry's Hamburger Hafen Basar
50 Tourist Office
53 Free Port Warehouses
54 MusikTheater im Hamburger Hafen

GERMANY

and every 30 minutes from 9.30am to 4.45pm
the rest of the year. They leave from Kirchenallee next to the main train station (adult/
concession €12/6.50) and last 1¾ hours; you
can add a harbour cruise for an extra €7. Two-
hour 'Fleet' (inner canal) **cruises** depart from
Jungfernstieg three times daily (€14/7). The
50-minute Alster lakes tour departs at least
three times daily from Jungfernstieg and costs
€9/4.50. Or you can cover the Alster lakes in
stages with boats leaving hourly; it's €1.50 for
each stop or €7 return. Both of these operate
from April to October. There are also canal and
special summer cruises.

Port Cruises Port cruises in sightseeing
boats and the unusual **Barkassen** wooden
boats built to navigate the Speicherstadt's
canals (adult/concession €8.50/4.50; 1hr)
operate throughout the year from St Pauli-
Landungsbrücken, piers 1 to 9. They depart
half-hourly from 9am to 6pm from April to
October, and hourly from 10.30am to 3.30pm
from November to March. Tours with English
commentary run at 11am daily from April to
September from pier 1.

Places to Stay
The tourist office at the main train station
charges €4 for accommodation bookings. You
can also call the **Hamburg-Hotline** (☎ 30 05
13 00; 8am-8pm daily) for availability and
reservations.

Camping Though inconvenient and catering
mainly for caravans, there is **Campingplatz
Buchholz** (☎ 540 45 32; Kieler Strasse 374;
tent sites €7-10, plus €4/4 per person/car).
From Hauptbahnhof take S-Bahn No 2 or 3
to Stellingen. You can also take bus No 183
from Hamburg-Altona train station towards
Schnelsen.

Hostels Hamburg's two DJH hostels are
large. **Auf dem Stintfang** (☎ 31 34 88; e jh
-stintfang@t-online.de; Alfred-Wegener-Weg
5; juniors/seniors €15.25/19.25) has an excellent view of the Elbe. Take the U/S-Bahn to
St Pauli-Landungsbrücken. The youth guesthouse **Horner Rennbahn** (☎ 651 16 71; e jgh
-hamburg@t-online.de; Rennbahnstrasse 100;
juniors/seniors €16.75/19.50) is less convenient to reach. Take the U3 to Horner Rennbahn and walk 10 minutes north past both the
racecourse and the leisure centre. The private

hostel **Schanzenstern** (☎ 439 84 41, fax 439
34 13; e info@schanzenstern.de; Bartels-
strasse 12; dorm beds €17, singles/doubles/
triples €35/50/60) is ideally located in the
lively Schanzenviertel.

Hotels & Pensions Many budget hotels are
along Steindamm and a few blocks east of the
main train station along Bremer Reihe, but the
concentration of junkies and prostitutes make
the streets feel unsafe, especially at night.
Hotel Eden (☎ 24 84 80, fax 24 15 21; Ell-
menreichstrasse 20; singles/doubles €41/62,
with bath €72/103) is just far enough removed from the sleaze to be comfortable; its
renovated rooms are simple and clean.
   Lange Reihe is less grubby than other
streets in St Georg. **Hotel-Pension Alpha**
(☎ 24 53 65, fax 24 37 94; singles/doubles
€36/62) has bare-bones rooms, all with
shower. The welcoming **Hotel-Pension von
Blumfeld** (☎ 24 58 60, fax 24 32 82; Lange
Reihe 54; singles/doubles €31/46, with bath
€41/56) has nice basic rooms and a friendly
parrot called Jakob. The **Galerie-Hotel Sarah
Petersen** (☎/fax 24 98 26; Lange Reihe 50;
singles/doubles from €45/65, with all facilities €70/85) is a classic art-scene Hamburg
hotel, with rooms decorated in different styles.
The most expensive rooms have video, fax
and other useful comforts. **Hotel Fürst Bismarck** (☎ 280 10 91, fax 280 10 96; Kirchenallee 49; singles/doubles from €61/100) is
more conventional with rooms with all facilities. The **Europäischer Hof** (☎ 24 82 48, fax
24 82 47 99; Kirchenallee 45; singles/doubles
from €103/133) has rooms directly across
from the train station; ask for one that's quiet
and has been renovated.
   Hotel Wedina (☎ 24 30 11, fax 280 38 94;
e info@wedina.de; Gurlittstrasse 23; singles/
doubles €90/105) provides quality, spacious
rooms. **Aussen Alster Hotel** (☎ 24 15 57, fax
280 32 31; Schmilinskystrasse 11; singles/
doubles €79/128), just one block north, offers the same high standard. Both are in quiet
streets a bit away from the grunge.
   The family-run **Hotel Imperial** (☎ 319 60
21, fax 31 56 85; e info@hotel-imperial
-hamburg.de; Millerntorplatz 3-5; singles/
doubles weekdays €50/77, weekends from
€60/85) has rooms that face away from the
Reeperbahn, and are both spacious and well-
furnished. It's an excellent mid-range option
in the throbbing heart of St Pauli.

Hotel Vier Jahreszeiten (☎ 349 40, fax 34 94 26 00; e vier-jahreszeiten@hvj.de; Neuer ungfernstieg 9-14; singles/doubles from €175/225) is Hamburg's premier address for big spenders.

Places to Eat

Hauptbahnhof Area Kantine im Schauspielhaus (Kirchenallee; lunches €6) downstairs in the Deutsches Schauspielhaus, is one of the best kept secrets in this part of town, with plain but filling lunches. The student **Café Urlaub** (Lange Reihe 63; dishes around €7; open until 2am), which is open from breakfast until late, is a good eating and drinking option. Here you can find good salads and pasta dishes. **Cafe Gnosa** (Lange Reihe 93; mains from €6.20) is especially popular among gays and lesbians. It has good lunch specials, wonderful home-made cakes, and is nice for an evening meal or drink. The upmarket bistro **Cox** (☎ 24 94 22; Lange Reihe 68; mains around €16), with its stylish, Continental decor and friendly staff, is a great place to spend an hour or three.

Gänsemarkt & Around You'll find a wide choice around Gänsemarkt and Jungfernstieg near the Binnenalster lake. **Essen und Trinken** (Gänsemarkt 21) is a food hall in an arcade where you can choose from Asian, Mediterranean and German cuisine at budget prices. **Café zur Stadtbäckerei** is a bakery which also supplies shoppers and workers with warm drinks and filling, tasty snacks. **Brauhaus Joh. Albrecht** (Adolfsbrücke 7; dishes less than €10) is a bustling microbrewery with a few canal-side tables.

Schanzenviertel The lively Schanzenviertel neighbourhood lies west of the TV Tower and north of St Pauli (take the U-Bahn or S-Bahn to Sternschanze) and is shared by students and immigrants. Lots of cosy cafés and restaurants string along Schanzenstrasse and Susannenstrasse; **Frank and Frei** on the corner of the two, is a student hang-out offering a small menu. **La Sepia** (Schulterblatt 36; dishes around €13) provides terrific seafood in a Mediterranean atmosphere, at times with live music. The main outpost of **Bok** (Schanzenstrasse 27; mains around €8) draws a young crowd with an array of Thai, Korean and Japanese dishes. A delicious 18-piece Bento II sushi platter costs €32.

St Pauli/Port Area There is a cluster of good Portuguese and Spanish restaurants situated along Ditmar-Koel-Strasse and Reimarus-Strasse near St Pauli Landungsbrücken. **Sagres** (Vorsetzen 52; mains €10) specialises in fresh-off-the-boat fish dishes and is always packed. Just off the Reeperbahn, **Piceno** (Hein-Hoyer-Strasse 8) is good for Italian fare at reasonable prices in a cosy, relaxed atmosphere.

Self-Catering Head for one of the **Penny Markt** budget groceries. There's one on Baumeisterstrasse, one on the corner of Lange Reihe and Schmilinskystrasse to the east of the main train station, and one near the corner of Königstrasse and Holstenstrasse at the western end of the Reeperbahn. Really good fresh fare is offered at Grossneumarkt on market days (Wednesday and Saturday).

Entertainment

The jazz scene in Hamburg is hot. Hip **Mojo Club** (☎ 43 52 32; w www.mojo.de; Reeperbahn 1) should absolutely not be missed by aficionados of jazz or avante garde music, or by anyone else for that matter who has more than a passing interest in music. The **Cotton Club** (☎ 34 38 78; Alter Steinweg 10) has more traditional jazz flavours. Get there before 8.30pm if you've reserved seats.

The **English Theatre** (☎ 227 70 89; Lerchenfeld 14) is good for a language fix; **Theater für Kinder** (☎ 38 25 38; Max-Brauer-Allee 76) in Altona is great for kids – its language is more international. The small cinema **Abaton** (☎ 41 32 03 20; Allende-Platz 3) screens English-language films.

Hamburg has an excellent alternative and experimental theatre scene. **Kampnagelfabrik** (☎ 27 09 49 49; Jarrestrasse 20-24) is a good place to start. Take bus No 172 or 173 from U-Bahn station Mundsburg. **Schmidt Theater** (☎ 31 77 88 99; Spielbudenplatz 27) is much loved for its wild variety shows and a casual atmosphere.

Musicals are big in Hamburg. Catch them at the **Neue Flora Theater** (cnr Alsenstrasse & Stresemannstrasse; S-Bahn to Holstenstrasse) and **MusikTheater im Hamburger Hafen** (Norderelbstrasse 6; shuttle service from Pier 1 of St Pauli Landungsbrücken), which was showing The Lion King on our visit. Tickets, which start at around €26, can be reserved at the tourist offices or on the hotline ☎ 30 05 13 00.

For central theatre or concert bookings, go to the **Theaterkasse** (☎ 35 35 55) in the basement of the Alsterhaus shopping complex on Grosse Bleichen.

Not surprisingly, St Pauli is the flash point for nightclubs. **Angie's Nightclub** (☎ 31 77 88 16; Spielbudenplatz 27-28) is a classy, sweaty local favourite for dancing to live music. For indie oddities, cool 1960s London soul and dub music, head to the **Molotow Club** (☎ 31 08 45; Spielbudenplatz 5). **Docks** (☎ 31 78 83 11; Spielbudenplatz 19) sometimes has live bands; as does the hip **Grosse Freiheit 36** (Grosse Freiheit 36). At **Gretel & Alfons** across the street, you can have a drink where the Beatles once quaffed.

Getting There & Away

Air Hamburg's international airport (☎ 50 75 25 57) in Fuhlsbüttel has frequent flights to domestic destinations as well as cities in Scandinavia and elsewhere in Europe.

Bus International destinations that aren't served directly by train from Hamburg, such as Amsterdam (€44.50, 6½ hours) and London (€61.50, 17½ hours), are served by Euro-lines buses.

A good option for getting to London is **Rainbow Tours** (☎ 32 09 33 09, fax 32 09 30 99; Gänsemarkt 45), which offers return trips without an overnight stay from €55 – a cheap way to get to London, even if you don't use the return portion of the ticket. The central bus station is southeast of the main train station on Adenauerallee.

Train Hamburg's Hauptbahnhof is one of the busiest in Germany, although it does not handle all the through traffic. There are frequent RE/RB trains to Lübeck (€9, 45 minutes) and Kiel (€15.20, 1¼ hours), various services to Hanover (€26.50, 1½ hours) and Bremen (€16, 1¼ hours), as well as ICE trains to Berlin (€51.40, 2½ hours) and Frankfurt/Main (€98.20, 3½ hours). Almost hourly trains depart for Copenhagen (4½ hours). There are overnight services to Munich, Vienna and Paris as well as Zurich via Basel. Hamburg-Altona is quieter but has a monopoly on some services to the north. Carefully read the timetables when booking to/from Hamburg stations or you could finish up at the wrong station at the wrong time. Hamburg-Harburg handles some regional services (for instance to/from Cuxhaven, the main port for Heligoland).

Car & Motorcycle The autobahns of the A1 (Bremen-Lübeck) and A7 (Hanover-Kiel) cross south of the Elbe River. Hamburg's only **Mitfahr-Zentrale** (☎ 194 40; Ernst-Merck-Strasse 8) is near the train station. Sample one-way prices are Cologne €24, Frankfurt/Main €28, Amsterdam €33 and Berlin €17.

Ferry Hamburg is 20 hours by car ferry from the English port of Harwich. **DFDS Seaways** (☎ 389 03 71, fax 38 90 31 20) runs services at least three times a week in either direction. The Fischereihafen terminal is at Van-der-Smissen-Strasse 4, about 1km west of the Fischmarkt (S1 to Königstrasse, or bus No 383 to/from Altona station). It is open 10am to 4.30pm weekdays, just before departure at weekends (exchange money before you reach the terminal or on board). The one-way passenger fare to Harwich ranges from €35 to €319, depending on the season, the day of the week and cabin comforts. A car costs an extra €25 to €128 and a bicycle will cost €2.

Scandlines (☎ 01805-72 26 35 46 37; Ⓦ www.scandlines.com) operates a busy car and passenger ferry from the German harbour town of Puttgarden to Rodby in Denmark, which leaves every half-hour 24 hours a day and takes 45 minutes. The cost is €60 each way for a car including up to five people all year. A bicycle costs €7, including one person. A single passenger pays €3 (€6 mid-June to August) each way. If you're travelling by train, the cost of the ferry is included in your ticket.

Getting Around

To/From the Airport A taxi from the main train station costs around €30 (one easy number to use is ☎ 21 12 11). A better airport option is to take the U1 from the main train station to Ohlsdorf and from there the No 110 express bus (€2.20). Airport buses (€4.25) make the 25-minute trip to the airport from the train station every 25 minutes between 5am and 9.20pm.

Public transport buses, the U-Bahn and the S-Bahn operate in Hamburg. A day pass for travel after 9am in most of Hamburg is €4.25 (€6.85 if you include the surrounding area) and there are various family passes. Single journeys cost €1.40 for the city tariff area, €2.20 for the city and surrounding area, and

€3.60 within the outer tariff area. Children pay a basic €0.80. For the Schnellbus or 1st-class S-Bahn the day supplements are €1.05. A three-day travel-only pass is €12.25, and weekly cards range from €12.50 to €26.30 depending on your status and the distance you want to travel (check the diagrams with the oval-shaped zones marked in yellow). From midnight to dawn the night-bus network takes over from the trains, converging on the main metropolitan bus station at Rathausmarkt. For transport options with a Hamburg Card see the earlier Information section.

Hamburg's bicycle tracks are extensive and reach almost to the centre of the city.

Schleswig-Holstein

Schleswig-Holstein is Germany's northern-most state and borders Denmark at the southern end of the Jutland Peninsula. Among the many attractions here are the North Frisian Islands and the historical city of Lübeck.

Schleswig and Holstein began breaking away from Denmark with the help of Sweden in the mid-17th century, a process which took until 1773.

When Holstein joined the German Confederation in 1815, Denmark attempted to lure Schleswig back to the motherland.

Three wars were fought over the region between Germany and Denmark: the first in 1848–50; a second in 1864; and a third in 1866, when Bismarck annexed it to unify Germany. Under the Treaty of Versailles in 1919, North Schleswig was given to Denmark. Finally, in 1946, the British military government formed the state of Schleswig-Holstein from the Prussian province of the same name.

LÜBECK
☎ 0451 • pop 215,000
Medieval Lübeck was known as the Queen of the Hanseatic League, as it was the capital of this association of towns that ruled trade on the Baltic Sea from the 12th to the 16th centuries. This beautiful city, with its red-stone buildings, is a highlight of the region and well worth taking the time to explore.

Orientation & Information
Lübeck's old town is set on an island ringed by the canalised Trave River, a 15-minute walk east from the main train station. To get there,

just take Konrad-Adenauer-Strasse across the pretty Puppenbrücke (Doll Bridge) to Holstentor, the city's western gateway. Then follow Holstenstrasse east from An der Untertrave to Kohlmarkt, from where Breite Strasse leads north to Markt and the historic Rathaus.

Lübeck-Information (☎/fax 122 54 19; Breite Strasse 62; open 9.30am-6pm Mon-Fri, 10am-2pm Sat & Sun) is near the Rathaus. Both city tourist offices run a room-finding service. The private room-finding office (☎ 86 46 75, fax 86 30 24) at the train station charges €3 (free if reserved by phone). See w www.Luebeck-info.de.

The Lübeck Happy Day Card entitles you to unlimited travel and discounts on cruises, museums, cinema and other attractions. It costs €5 for 24 hours and €10 for three days and is available at tourist offices, hotels, youth hostels and museums.

The central post office (Königstrasse 46) is across from the Katarinenkirche. For Internet access, visit PC & Internet Café (Am der Untertrave 103) near the Holstentor. There's a police station situated near the youth hostel at Mengstrasse 20.

Things to See & Do
The landmark Holstentor (☎ 122 41 29; adult/concession €5/3; open Tues-Sun), a fortified gate with huge twin towers, serves as the city's symbol as well as its museum, but for a literary kick, visit the recently refurbished Buddenbrookhaus (Mengstrasse 4; adult/concession €4.10/2.60; open daily), the family house where Thomas Mann was born and which he made famous in his novel Buddenbrooks. The literary works and philosophical rivalry of the brothers Thomas and Heinrich are commemorated here. The must-see Marienkirche (Markt) contains a stark reminder of WWII; a bombing raid brought the church bells crashing to the stone floor and the townspeople have left the bell fragments in place, with a small sign saying: 'A protest against war and violence'. Also on Markt is the imposing Rathaus which covers two full sides of the square. It can be toured with a guide – three times on weekdays – for €2.60/1.50 per adult/concession.

Lübeck's Marionettentheater (Puppet Theatre; ☎ 700 60; cnr Am Kolk & Kleine Petersgrube; open Tues-Sun) is a must. Usually there is a daily afternoon performance for children (3pm) and an evening performance for adults only on Saturday, however, the schedule varies. Afternoon seats cost €4 and evening seats €8 to €11 depending on the play. It's best to book ahead. **Museum für Puppentheater** (☎ 786 26; Am Kolk 14; adult/student/child €3/ 2.50/1.50; open 10am-6pm daily), a survey of all types of dolls and puppetry, is just around the corner from the theatre.

The tower lift at the partly restored **Petri-kirche** (adult/concession €2/1.20; open 9am-7pm daily May-Oct, closed Jan & Feb) affords a superb view over the Altstadt. It is usually open the listed hours above and shorter hours in other months.

Places to Stay

The nearest camping ground is **Campingplatz Schönböcken** (☎ 89 30 90; Steinrader Damm 12; tent site/person/car €3.50/4.50/1; open Apr-Oct) in a western suburb of Lübeck. The tourist office can help with information on camping grounds in the nearby coastal resort of Travemünde.

Lübeck has two DJH hostels. The **Jugend-gästehaus Lübeck** (☎ 702 03 99; Mengstrasse 33; dorm beds juniors/seniors €17.40/20.10, singles/twins €25.60 per person) is clean, comfortable and well situated in the middle of the old town, a 15-minute walk from the train station. The **Jugendherberge 'Vor dem Burgtor'** (☎ 334 33, fax 345 40; Am Gertru-denkirchhof 4; juniors/seniors €15.40/ 18.10) is a little outside the old town. Take bus No 1, 3, 11, 12 or 31 to Gustav-Radbruch-Platz. The YMCA's centrally located **Sleep-Inn** (☎ 719 20, fax 789 97; Grosse Petersgrube 11; dorm beds €10, doubles €30, apartments €32 per person; open mid-Jan–mid-Dec) charges €4 extra for breakfast and €4.50 extra for sheets.

The **Hotel Stadt Lübeck** (☎ 838 83, fax 86 32 21; Am Bahnhof 21; singles/doubles €43/ 63) is just outside the main train station. Fairly good rooms come with shower and toilet. The **Klassik Altstadt Hotel** (☎ 720 83, fax 737 78; e info@klassik-hotel.de; Fischergrube 52; singles/doubles €44/105, suites €123) is convenient and pleasant. The **Mövenpick Hotel** (☎ 150 40, fax 150 41 11; Willy-Brandt-Allee 1-3; singles €95-165, doubles €115-185) is opposite the Holstentor.

Places to Eat

The best eating and drinking options are in the area directly east of the Rathaus. The fun

Tipasa (Schlumacherstrasse 12-14; main from €4.40) serves everything from tandoor to tacos. It's also a great place to eat and drink in the evening. **Hieronymus** (☎ 706 30 17; Fleischhauerstrasse 81; mains €4.50-19.40) is a relaxed and rambling restaurant which is spread over three floors of a 15th-century building. Most dishes on the creative menu are quite filling. The lunch specials are good value. The **Schiffergesellschaft** (Breite Strasse 2; mains from €14.80) has a unique maritime atmosphere.

Save room for a dessert or a snack of marzi-pan, which was invented in Lübeck (local legend has it that the town ran out of flour during a long siege and resorted to grinding almonds to make bread). **JG Niederegger** (Breite Strasse 89), a shop and café directly opposite the Rathaus, is Lübeck's mecca of marzipan. The supermarket **Sky** (Sandstrasse 24) is conveniently located near Kohlmarkt.

Getting There & Away

Lübeck is close to Hamburg, with at least one train every hour (€9, 45 minutes). There are also frequent services to Kiel (€12.40, 1¼ hours) and Schwerin (€10.70, 1¼ hours). Trains to/from Copenhagen also stop here.

The central bus station is next to the main train station. Services to/from Wismar stop here, as well as Autokraft buses to/from Hamburg, Schwerin, Kiel, Rostock and Berlin.

Getting Around

Frequent double-decker buses run to Travemünde (€3.50, 45 minutes) from the central bus station. City buses also leave from here; a single journey costs €1.35.

KIEL

☎ 0431 • pop 246,000

Kiel, the capital of Schleswig-Holstein, was seriously damaged by Allied bombing during WWII, but is now a vibrant and modern city. At the end of a modest firth, it has long been one of Germany's most important Baltic Sea harbours and was the host of Olympic sailing events in 1936 and 1972.

Orientation & Information

Kiel's main street is Holstenstrasse, a colourful pedestrian street near the fjord. It runs north-south from the Nikolaikirche to Sophienhof, a large indoor shopping mall connected to the main train station by an overpass.

The **tourist office** (☎ 67 91 00; e info@kiel tourist.de; Andreas-Gayk-Strasse 31; open am-6.30pm Mon-Fri all year, 9am-1pm Sat Oct-Apr, 9am-4.30pm Sat May-Sept) is a northern extension of Sophienblatt and just five minutes by foot from the main train station. **Cyber Treff** (Bergstrasse 17) is a good place to surf the Web until late. See w www kiel-tourist.de.

Things to See & Do

Kiel's most famous attraction is the **Kieler Woche** (Kiel Week) in the last full week in June, a festival revolving around a series of yachting regattas attended by more than 4000 of the world's sailing elite and half a million spectators. Even if you're not into sailing, the atmosphere is electric – just make sure you book a room in advance if you want to be in on the fun.

To experience Kiel's love for the sea in a less energetic fashion, take a ferry ride to the village of **Laboe** at the mouth of the firth. Ferries leave hourly from Bahnhofbrücke pier behind the train station. They take around one hour to reach Laboe, hopping back and forth across the firth along the way. In Laboe, you can visit the **U995**, a wartime U-boat, on the beach, which is now a **technical museum** (adult/concession €2.10/1.50; open daily). Nearby is the **Marine-Ehrenmal** (Naval Memorial; adult/concession €2.80/1.80; open daily) with a navigation museum.

Kiel is also the point at which the shipping canal from the North Sea enters the Baltic Sea. Some 60,000 ships pass through the canal every year, and the **locks** (Schleusen; ☎ 360 30; adult/concession €1.50/1) at Holtenau, 6km north of the city centre, are worth a visit. There's an admission fee to the viewing platform; tours of the locks are at 9am, 11am, 1pm and 3pm daily (adult/concession €2.30/1.50).

The open-air **Schleswig-Holstein Freilichtmuseum** (☎ 65 96 60; adult/concession €4.50/2.50; open 9am-6pm daily Apr-Oct, 11am-4pm Sun Nov-Mar) in nearby Molfsee (take Autokraftbus No 501) is also worth seeing. More than 60 historical houses typical of the region have been relocated here, giving you a thorough introduction to the northern way of life.

Places to Stay

Kiel's **Campingplatz Falckenstein** (☎ 39 20 78; Palisadenweg 171; tent sites €4.90-7.50,

plus €4.35/1.90 per person/car; open Apr-Oct) is in the northern suburb of Friedrichsort. The **Jugenherberge** (☎ 73 14 88, fax 73 57 23; Johannesstrasse 1; juniors/seniors €14.90/16.90) is in the suburb of Gaarden. You can walk across the pretty drawbridge behind the train station, or take the Laboe ferry to Gaarden, from where it's a 10-minute walk; or take bus No 11 from the main train station to Kieler Strasse.

The tourist office charges €2.50 for accommodation bookings and stocks an excellent free brochure listing private rooms and apartments.

The **Hotel Runge** (☎ 733 33 96, 73 19 92; Elisabethstrasse 16; singles/doubles €34/56, with shower & toilet €46/61) in Gaarden is one of the area's cheapest options. Take bus No 11 or 12 to Augustern from the main train station. The central **Hotel Schweriner Hof** (☎ 614 16, fax 67 41 34; Königsweg 13; singles €36, singles/doubles with shower & toilet €57/77) provides good rooms. **Muhl's Hotel** (☎ 997 90, fax 997 91 79; Lange Reihe 5; singles/doubles €57/77) is central and has nice rooms with facilities. The **Steigenberger Hotel Conti-Hansa** (☎ 511 50, fax 511 54 44; Schlossgarten 7; singles/doubles €135/160) has standard rooms.

Places to Eat

The **Ratskeller** (Fleethörn 9; mains €8.40-17.90) in the Rathaus serves typical German cuisine with an emphasis on fish.

The **Klosterbrauerei** (Alter Markt 9; lunch specials €7.40) is a private brewery with good beer, well-priced food and a great atmosphere. You'll find lots of cheap takeaway options in the Turkish quarter around the hostel in Gaarden. **Ça va** (Holtenauer Strasse 107; dishes from €5.50) is a popular gay café-bar that does light dishes in the evening (open late).

Getting There & Away

There are regional buses to/from Lübeck, Schleswig and Puttgarden from the bus station on Auguste-Viktoria-Strasse, just north of the main train station. Numerous RE trains run every day between Kiel and Hamburg-Altona or Hamburg Hauptbahnhof (€15.20, 1¼ hours). The trains to Lübeck leave every hour (€12.40, 1¼ hours). For ride-sharing, you should contact **ADM Mitfahrzentrale** (☎ 194 40; Sophienblatt 52a).

The daily Kiel-Gothenburg ferry (13½ hours) leaves from Schwedenkai and is run by **Stena Line** (☎ *0431-90 99*; **w** *www.stena line.de*). One-way passenger prices go from €38 to €74 depending on the season.

Color Line ferries (☎ *730 03 00*; **w** *www .colorline.com*) run direct to/from Kiel and Oslo daily (19½ hours). Noncabin space is only available from mid-June to mid-August (€64/72 during the week/weekend). Otherwise, basic double cabins cost from €84 to €116 per person depending on the season. There are 50% off-peak student concessions. Ferries depart from the Norwegenkai across the fjord in Gaarden (use the footbridge).

Getting Around

City buses leave from Sophienblatt, in front of the train station. To get to the North-Baltic Sea Canal and the locks, take bus No 11 to Wik; the locks are about a five-minute walk from the terminus.

NORTH FRISIAN ISLANDS

Sylt ☎ 04651 • pop 21,600
Amrum ☎ 04682 • pop 2100

The Frisian Islands reward those who make the trek with sand dunes, sea, pure air and, every so often, sunshine. Friesland covers an area stretching from the northern Netherlands along the coast up into Denmark. North Friesland (Nordfriesland) is the western coastal area of Schleswig-Holstein up to and into Denmark. The sea area forms the National Park of Wattenmeer, and the shifting dunes, particularly on the islands of Amrum, Föhr and Langeness, are sensitive and cannot be disturbed; paths and boardwalks are provided for strolling. The most popular of the North Frisian Islands is the glamorous resort of Sylt, which gets very crowded from June to August; the neighbouring islands of Föhr and Amrum are far more relaxed and less touristy.

Orientation & Information

The excellent **tourist office** (☎ *99 88*; open *9am-6pm Mon-Fri, 9am-4.30pm Sat all year, 9am-2pm Sun June-Sept*) is inside Westerland's train station on Sylt and can help with information and accommodation. **Sylt Marketing** (☎ *820 20*, fax *82 02 22*; *Stephanstrasse 6*), near the Westerland Rathaus, and **Sylt Tourismus Zentrale** (☎ *60 26*, fax *281 80*; *Keitumer Landstrasse 10b*) just outside of town in Tinnum, are other

useful sources of information. On Amrum the friendly **tourist office** (☎ *940 30*) is at the harbour car park. The spa administrations **Kurverwaltungen** at the various resorts are also useful sources of information.

All communities charge visitors a so-called *Kurtaxe*, a resort tax of about €3 a day, depending on the town and the season. Paying the tax gets you a *Kurkarte* which you need on Sylt even just to get onto the beach. Day passes are available from kiosks at beach entrances, but if you're spending more than one night, your hotel can obtain a pass for you for the length of your stay (not included in the room rate).

Things to See

Nature is the prime attraction on the North Frisian Islands; the different moods of the rough North Sea and the placid Wattenmeer lend the region its unique character. Beautiful dunes stretch out for kilometres, red and white cliffs border wide beaches, and bird lovers will be amply rewarded. The reed-roofed *Friesenhäuser* is typical of the region. But, of course, civilisation has also taken hold here, especially in Westerland on Sylt. After WWII the German jet-set invaded the island, which explains the abundance of luxury homes, cars and expensive restaurants, particularly around Kampen.

On Amrum, you'll find signs of traditional Frisian life around the village of **Nebel**. The **lighthouse** (*adult/concession €2/0.50*; *open 8.30am-12.30pm Mon-Fri Apr-Oct, 8.30am-12.30pm Wed Nov-Mar*), the tallest in northern Germany at 63m, affords a spectacular view of the dunes from the southwest of the island and over to the islands of Sylt, Föhr and Langeness.

Activities

In Westerland, a visit to the indoor water park and health spa **Sylter Welle** (☎ *99 82 42*; open *10am-9pm or 10pm daily*) is fun, especially when it's too cold for the beach. It includes saunas, solariums, a wave pool and a slide (€8.70, €12.80 with sauna; no time limit). For a real thrill, though, visit one of Sylt's **beach saunas** – the tourist office can point you in the right direction.

Heiko's Reitwiese (☎ *56 00*) in Westerland on Sylt, and **Reiterhof Jensen** (☎ *20 30*) on Amrum offer **horse riding**. One of several excellent **hikes** on Amrum (8km return) is from

Is nothing sacred? Mime artist posing in front of Sacré Cœur, Paris, France.

The mighty neo-Renaissance Berliner Dom, viewed from the Altes Museum, Berlin, Germany

Fun for all the family, Cologne Carnival, Germany

Swans and Wagnerian operas inspired the design of Neuschwanstein, near Füssen, Germany

Sun decoration, Sanssouci Park, Potsdam, Germany

Leisure time on Marienplatz, Munich, Germany

Colourful rides at Munich's Oktoberfest

Norddorf along the beach to the tranquil Odde nature reserve. The tourist office can help with information on guided hikes in summer across the Watt to Föhr. The flat terrain of the islands is also suited to **cycling**. On Amrum, the tourist office keeps a list of rental places. In Westerland on Sylt, **Fahrrad am Bahnhof** (☎ 58 03) is conveniently situated at the train station (€5 per day).

Places to Stay

Low-budget accommodation is hard to find on the islands, but the tourist offices can help with private rooms from €20 per person. Another option may be to rent an apartment, which can cost as little as €45 in the low season and around €85 in the high season. Unless it's a particularly slow time proprietors may be reluctant to rent for fewer than three days.

Sylt It has seven camping grounds. **Campingplatz Kampen** (☎ 420 86; Möwenweg 4; tent/person/car sites €4.50/3.50/1.50; open Easter-Oct) is set beautifully amid dunes near the small town of Kampen. In Hörnum, there's the **Jugendherberge** (☎ 88 02 94, fax 88 13 92; Friesenplatz 2) in the south of the island. There's also a **Jugendherberge** (☎ 87 03 97, fax 87 10 39) in List. Both charge €13.30/16 for juniors/seniors and neither is very central, but bus services bring you near.

Hotel Garni Diana (☎ 988 60, fax 98 86 86; Elisabethstrasse 19; singles/doubles €41/72, with bath €46/87) has basic rooms near the beach. The delightful **Landhaus Nielsen** (☎ 986 90, fax 98 69 60; Bastianstrasse 5; doubles €65/75) has lower winter prices.

Amrum At the northern edge of Wittdün is **Campingplatz Schade** (☎ 22 54; tent sites €4, plus €5 per person). The **Jugendherberge** (☎ 20 10, fax 17 47; Mittelstrasse 1; beds juniors/seniors €13.30/16) has 218 beds but it's best to book ahead, even in the low season. The historic **Hotel Ual Öömrang** (☎ 836, fax 14 32; Bräätlun 4; singles/doubles €51/102; open Mar-Dec) has a sauna.

Places to Eat

Sylt Picnics are a fine option on the islands. On Westerland, pick up groceries and fresh-baked bread at **Spar** (Sandstrasse 24) near the Sylter Welle. **Toni's Restaurant** (Norderstrasse 3; dishes from €5.80-12.80) serves good, inexpensive fare; it also has a pleasant garden. **Blum's** (Neue Strasse 4; mains from €8) has soup from €4.35, main dishes and some of the freshest fish in town. The **Alte Friesenstube** (☎ 12 28; Gaadt 4) is in a cosy 17th-century building. It specialises in northern German and Frisian cooking but you can expect to pay around €35 per person for a three-course meal with wine. Kampen's **Kupferkanne** (☎ 410 109) in Stapelhooger Wai is a beautiful stop during a bike tour. You'll end up paying €8 for a giant cup of coffee and a slice of cake with cream, but the view of the Wattenmeer is free.

List's harbour sports a number of colourful kiosks. **Gosch** prides itself on being Germany's northernmost fish kiosk, and is an institution well known beyond Sylt.

Amrum Amrum has only a few restaurants and many of them close in the low season. The **Hotel Ual Öömrang** (dishes around €14) serves filling traditional dishes. The **Haus Burg**, built on an old Viking hill-fort above the eastern beach at Norddorf, has a teahouse atmosphere and home-made cakes.

Note that restaurants can close as early as 7pm in the low season.

Getting There & Away

Sylt Sylt is connected to the mainland by a scenic train-only causeway right through the Wattenmeer. Around seven trains leave from Hamburg-Hauptbahnhof daily for Westerland (€33, 3¼ hours). If you are travelling by car, you must load it onto a train in the town of Niebüll near the Danish border. There are about 26 crossings in both directions every day and no reservations can be made. The cost per car is a shocking €77 return, but that includes all passengers.

Amrum To get to Amrum and the island of Föhr, you must board a ferry in Dagebüll Hafen. To get there, take the Sylt-bound train from Hamburg-Altona and change in Niebüll. In summer, there are also some through trains. A day-return from Dagebüll costs €17.50, which allows you to visit both islands. If you stay overnight, return tickets cost €18.20 (bicycle €4). The trip to Amrum takes around two hours, stopping at Föhr on the way.

There are daily flights between Westerland airport and Hamburg, Munich and Berlin, and several flights weekly from other German cities.

Getting Around

Sylt's two north-south bus lines run every 20 to 30 minutes, and three other frequent lines cover the rest of the island. There are seven price zones, costing from €1.30 to €5.60. Some buses have bicycle hangers. On Amrum, a bus runs from the ferry terminal in Wittdün to Norddorf and back every 30 to 60 minutes, depending on the season. The slow, fun inter-island options are the day-return cruises to Föhr (Wyk) and Amrum (Wittdün) from the harbour at Hörnum on Sylt. Day-return cruises through shallow banks that attract both seals and sea birds are offered by **Adler-Schiffe** (☎ 04651-836 10 28 in Westerland; €18.50). Bicycles are an extra €5. WDR ferries also run on day-return trips in the summer from Wittdün on Amrum to Föhr (€6.70/3.40 per adult/concession) and the two nearby islands of Hallig Hooge and Nordmarsch-Langeness (€8.70/4.40 per adult/concession).

HELIGOLAND
☎ 04725 • pop 1650

Not technically part of the Frisian Islands, Heligoland (Helgoland) is 70km out to sea and is a popular day trip from the islands. Oddly, Heligoland is economically not part of the EU and therefore it remains a duty-free port.

Because of the North Sea's strong currents and unpredictable weather, however, the passage will be most enjoyed by people with iron stomachs.

From April through September, **WDR ferries** (☎ 01805-08 01 40) sail from Hörnum or Sylt at least twice weekly and from Amrum and Dagebüll (all €26 to €42.50 day return).

Seasick crowds flock like lemmings to this unlikely chunk of red rock sticking up out of the sea. It was used as a submarine base in WWII, and it's still possible to tour the strong bunkers and underground tunnels. The island was heavily bombed and all of the houses are new. Take a walk along Lung Wai ('long way'), filled with duty-free shops, and then up the stairway of 180 steps to Oberland for what view there is.

There's also a scenic trail around the island. Small boats run from Heligoland to neighbouring **Düne**, a tiny island filled with beaches and nudists.

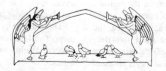

Greece

The first travel guide to Greece was written 1800 years ago by the Greek geographer and historian Pausanias, so the tourism industry isn't exactly in its infancy.

The country's enduring attraction is its wonderful archaeological sites; those who travel through Greece journey not only through the landscape but also through time, witnessing the legacy of Europe's greatest ages – the Mycenaean, Minoan, classical, Hellenistic and Byzantine.

You cannot wander far in Greece without stumbling across a broken column, a crumbling bastion or a tiny Byzantine church, each perhaps neglected and forgotten but still retaining an aura of its former glory.

Greece's culture is a unique blend of East and West, inherited from the long period of Ottoman rule, which is apparent in its food, music and traditions. The mountainous countryside is a walker's paradise crisscrossed by age-old donkey tracks leading to stunning vistas.

The magnetism of Greece is also due to less tangible attributes – the dazzling clarity of the light, the floral aromas that permeate the air, the spirit of places – for there is hardly a grove, mountain or stream which is not sacred to a deity, and the ghosts of the past still linger.

Then again, many visitors come to Greece simply to get away from it all and relax in one of Europe's friendliest and safest countries.

Facts about Greece

HISTORY

Greece's strategic position at the crossroads of Europe and Asia has resulted in a long and turbulent history.

During the Bronze Age, which lasted from 3000 to 1200 BC in Greece, the advanced Cycladic, Minoan and Mycenaean civilisations flourished. The Mycenaeans were eventually swept aside in the 12th century BC and replaced by the Dorians, who introduced Greece to the Iron Age. The next 400 years are often referred to as the Dark Ages, a period about which very little is known. Homer's *Odyssey* and *Iliad* were composed at this time.

At a Glance

- **Athens** – lively tavernas, the most famous monument in the ancient world: the Acropolis
- **Olympia** – nostalgic birthplace of the Olympic games, nestled among pine trees on the banks of the River Kladeos
- **Delphi** – awe inspiring ruins, home of the Delphic oracle
- **Zagoria** – fairy-tale land of slate and stone villages, the base for trekking the Vikos Gorge
- **Rhodes** – fortress city built by the Knights of St John, largest inhabited medieval town in Europe

Capital	Athens
Population	10.9 million
Official Language	Greek
Currency	euro
Time	GMT/UTC+0200
Country Phone Code	☎ 30

By 800 BC, when Homer's works were first written down, Greece was undergoing a cultural and military revival with the evolution of the city-states, the most powerful of which were Athens and Sparta. Greater Greece – Magna Graecia – was created, with southern Italy as an important component. The unified Greeks repelled the Persians twice, at Marathon (490 BC) and Salamis (480 BC).

GREECE

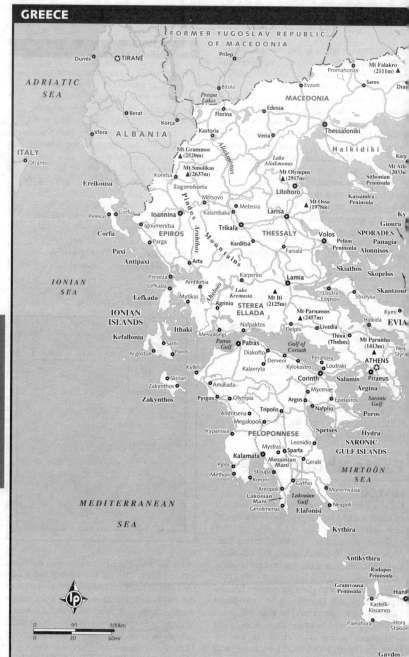

GREECE

FORMER YUGOSLAV REPUBLIC
OF MACEDONIA

Durrës
TIRANE
Prilep
Promahonas
Mt Falakro
(2111m)

ADRIATIC
SEA
Bitola
Prespa
Lakes
Evzoni
MACEDONIA
Seres
Drar

Berat
Florina
Edessa

Korça
Kastoria
Veria
Thessaloniki

Vlora
ALBANIA
Halkidiki
Kary

ITALY
Mt Grammos
(2520m)
Lake
Aliakmonas
Mt Ath
(2033m

Otranto
Mt Smolikas
(2637m)
Mt Olympus
(2917m)
Sithonian
Peninsula

Ereikousa
Konitsa
Zagorohoria
Litohoro
Kassandra
Peninsula

Metsovo
Meteora
Mt Ossa
(1978m)

Pelekas
Corfu
Ioannina
Kalambaka
Larisa
Gioura

Corfu
Igoumenitsa
EPIROS
Trikala
THESSALY
Volos
SPORADES
Ky

Paxi
Parga
Karditsa
Pelion
Peninsula
Panagia

Antipaxi
Arta
Farsala
Alonnisos

Preveza
Karpenisi
Skiathos
Skopelos

IONIAN
SEA
Amfilohia
Lamia
Skantzour

Lefkada
Mytikas
Lake
Kremasta
Mt Iti
(2125m)
Loutra
Edipsou
Strofylia

Lefkada
Agrinio
STEREA
ELLADA
Mt Parnassos
(2457m)
Kymi
Halkida
EVIA

IONIAN
ISLANDS
Ithaki
Nafpaktos
Delphi
Livadia

Kefallonia
Messolongi
Patras
Gulf of
Corinth
Thiva
(Thebes)
Mt Parnitha
(1413m)

Sami
Poros
Patras
Gulf
Diakofto
Perahora
Nea
Styra

Argostoli
Kyllini
Kalavryta
Derveni
Xylokastro
Loutraki
ATHENS

Skinari
Amaliada
Mycenae
Corinth
Salamis
Piraeus

Zakynthos
Pyrgos
Olympia
Argos
Epidavros
Aegina
Saronic
Gulf

Zakynthos
Andritsena
Tripolis
Nafplio
Poros

Megalopoli
PELOPONNESE
Spetses
Hydra

Kyparissia
Mystras
Leonidio
SARONIC
GULF ISLANDS

Kalamata
Sparta
Geraki

Pylos
Messinian
Mani
MIRTOÖN
SEA

Methoni
Stoupa
Koroni
Gythio

Areopoli
Lakonian
Gulf
Monemvasia

Lakonian
Mani
Neapoli

MEDITERRANEAN
Gerolimenas
Elafonisi

SEA
Kythira

Antikythira

Rodopos
Peninsula

Gramvousa
Peninsula
Han

Kastelli-
Kissamos

Paleohora
Hora
Sfakior

Gavdos

0   50   100km
0   30   60mi

GREECE

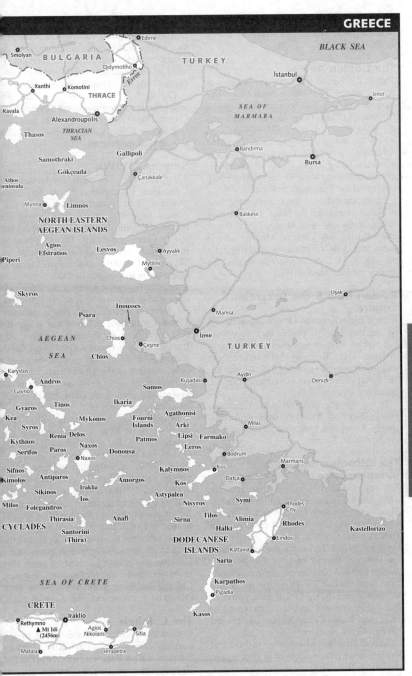

BLACK SEA

Smolyan

BULGARIA

Edirne

TURKEY

İstanbul

İzmit

Didymotiho

Xanthi   Komotini

THRACE

Erros

SEA OF
MARMARA

Kavala

Alexandroupolis

Bandırma

Bursa

THRACIAN
SEA

Thasos

Gallipoli

Samothraki

Çanakkale

Gökçeada

Athos
eninsula

Balıkesir

Myrina   **Limnos**

**NORTH EASTERN
AEGEAN ISLANDS**

Agios
Efstratios   **Lesvos**

Ayvalık

Piperi

Mytilini

Uşak

Skyros

Inousses

Manisa

Psara

Chios   İzmir   **TURKEY**

AEGEAN

Çeşme

SEA   **Chios**

Karystos

Kuşadası   Aydın   Denizli

Andros

Gavrio

Samos

Gyaros   **Tinos**

Ikaria

Kea

Agathonisi

Syros   **Mykonos**   **Fourni
Islands**   **Arki**   Milas

Kythnos   **Renia Delos**   **Patmos**   **Lipsi Farmako**

Serifos   **Paros**   **Naxos**   **Leros**

Sifnos   **Naxos**   **Donousa**   Bodrum   Marmaris

Kimolos   **Antiparos**   **Kalymnos**   Kos

Sikinos   **Amorgos**   **Kos**   Datça

Iraklia   **Astypalea**

Milos   **Folegandros**   **Ios**   **Nisyros**   **Symi**   Rhodes
City

CYCLADES   **Thirasia**   **Anafi**   **Sirna**   **Tilos**   **Alimia**   **Rhodes**

**Santorini
(Thira)**   **Halki**   **Kastellorizo**

**DODECANESE
ISLANDS**   Kattavia   Lindos

Saria

SEA OF CRETE

Karpathos

Pigadia

CRETE   Iraklio

Rethymno ▲ Mt Idi
(2456m)   Agios
Nikolaos   Sitia   **Kasos**

Matala   Ierapetra

Victory over Persia was followed by a period of unparalleled growth and prosperity known as the classical (or golden) age.

The Golden Age

This is the period when the Parthenon was commissioned by Pericles, Sophocles wrote *Oedipus the King*, and Socrates taught young Athenians to think. The golden age ended with the Peloponnesian War (431–404 BC), in which the militaristic Spartans defeated the Athenians. So embroiled were they in this war that they failed to notice the expansion of Macedonia under King Philip II, who easily conquered the war-weary city-states.

Philip's ambitions were surpassed by those of his son Alexander the Great, who marched triumphantly into Asia Minor, Egypt, Persia and what are now parts of Afghanistan and India. In 323 BC he met an untimely death at the age of 33, and his generals divided his empire between themselves.

Roman Rule & the Byzantine Empire

Roman incursions into Greece began in 205 BC, and by 146 BC Greece and Macedonia had become Roman provinces. After the subdivision of the Roman Empire into eastern and western empires in AD 395, Greece became part of the eastern (Byzantine) Empire, based at Constantinople.

In the centuries that followed, Venetians, Franks, Normans, Slavs, Persians, Arabs and, finally, Turks took their turns to chip away at the Byzantine Empire.

The Ottoman Empire & Independence

The end of the Byzantine Empire came in 1453, when Constantinople fell to the Turks. Most of Greece soon became part of the Ottoman Empire. Crete was not captured until 1670, leaving Corfu as the only island never occupied by the Turks. By the 19th century the Ottoman Empire had become the 'sick man of Europe'. The Greeks, seeing nationalism sweep through Europe, fought the War of Independence (1821–32). The great powers – Britain, France and Russia – intervened in 1827, and Ioannis Kapodistrias was elected the first Greek president.

Kapodistrias was assassinated in 1831 and the European powers stepped in once again, declaring that Greece should become a

monarchy. In January 1833, Otho of Bavaria was installed as king. His ambition, called the Great Idea, was to unite all the lands of the Greek people to the Greek motherland. In 1862 he was peacefully ousted and the Greeks chose George I, a Danish prince, as king.

During WWI, Prime Minister Venizelos allied Greece with France and Britain. King Constantine (George's son), who was married to the Kaiser's sister Sophia, disputed this and left the country.

Smyrna & WWII

After the war, Venizelos resurrected the Great Idea. Underestimating the new-found power of Turkey under the leadership of Atatürk, he sent forces to occupy Smyrna (the present-day Turkish port of İzmir), which had a large Greek population. The army was repulsed and many Greeks were slaughtered. This led to a brutal population exchange between the two countries in 1923.

In 1930 George II, Constantine's son, was reinstated as king and he appointed the dictator General Metaxas as prime minister. Metaxas' grandiose ambition was to take the best aspects from Greece's ancient and Byzantine past to create a Third Greek Civilisation. What he actually created was more a Greek version of the Third Reich. His chief claim to fame is his celebrated *okhi* (no) to Mussolini's request to allow Italian troops into Greece in 1940.

Despite Allied help, Greece fell to Germany in 1941. Resistance movements polarised into royalist and communist factions, leading to a bloody civil war that lasted until 1949. The country was left in chaos. More people were killed in the civil war than in WWII, and 250,000 people were left homeless. The sense of despair became the trigger for a mass exodus. Almost a million Greeks headed off in search of a better life elsewhere, primarily to Australia, Canada and the USA. Villages – whole islands even – were abandoned as people gambled on a new start in cities such as Melbourne, Toronto, Chicago and New York. While some have drifted back, the majority have stayed away.

The Colonels

Continuing political instability led to the colonels' coup d'etat in 1967. King Constantine (son of King Paul, who succeeded George II) staged an unsuccessful counter-coup, and then fled the country. The colonels' junta distinguished itself by inflicting appalling brutality, repression and political incompetence upon the Greek people. In 1974 they attempted to assassinate Cyprus' leader, Archbishop Makarios. When Makarios escaped, the junta replaced him with the extremist Nikos Samson, prompting Turkey to occupy North Cyprus. The continued Turkish occupation of Cyprus remains one of the most contentious issues in Greek politics. The junta, now discredited, had little choice but to hand back power to civilians. In November 1974 a plebiscite voted against restoration of the monarchy, and Greece became a republic. An election brought the right-wing New Democracy (ND) party into power.

The Socialist 1980s

In 1981 Greece entered the then EC (European Community, now the EU). Andreas Papandreou's Panhellenic Socialist Movement (Pasok) won the next election, giving Greece its first socialist government. Pasok promised the removal of US air bases and withdrawal from NATO, which Greece had joined in 1951. Instead Papandreou presided over seven years of rising unemployment and spiralling debt.

He was forced to step aside in 1989 while an unprecedented conservative and communist coalition took over to investigate a scandal involving the Bank of Crete. Papandreou and four ministers were ordered to stand trial, and the coalition ordered fresh elections in October 1990.

The 1990s

The elections brought the ND party back to power with a majority of two. Tough economic reforms introduced by Prime Minister Konstantinos Mitsotakis soon made his government unpopular. By late 1992, allegations emerged about the same sort of corruption and dirty tricks that had brought Papandreou unstuck. Mitsotakis himself was accused of having a secret hoard of Minoan art, and he was forced to call an election in October 1993.

Greeks again turned to Pasok and the ailing Papandreou, who eventually had been cleared of all charges. He had little option but to continue with the austerity programme begun by Mitsotakis, quickly making his government equally unpopular.

Papandreou was forced to step down in January 1996 after a lengthy spell in hospital.

His departure produced a dramatic change of direction for Pasok, with the party abandoning its leftist policies and electing experienced economist and lawyer Costas Simitis as its new leader. Cashing in on his reputation as the Mr Clean of Greek politics, Simitis romped to a comfortable majority at a snap poll called in October 1996.

His government has since been focused almost exclusively on the push for further integration with Europe. Simitis's prime goal of admission to the euro club was achieved in January 2001 when the EU agreed that Greece had met the economic requirements for monetary union. Greece duly adopted the euro as its currency in 2002.

Simitis was rewarded with a further four-year mandate in April 2000, but was suffering a serious mid-term popularity slump at the time of research. Newspaper polls in May 2002 showed Pasok trailing the opposition ND party by more than 7%. The next election is due before April 2004.

Foreign Policy

Greece's foreign policy is dominated by its extremely sensitive relationship with Turkey, its giant Muslim neighbour to the east.

After decades of constant antagonism, these two uneasy NATO allies were jolted to their senses (literally) by the massive earthquake which devastated the İzmit area of western Turkey in August 1999. According to geologists, the quake moved Turkey 1.5m closer to Greece. It had the same effect on the Greek people, who urged their government to join the rescue effort. Greek teams were among the first on the scene, where they were greeted as heroes. The Turks were quick to return the favour after the Athens quake which followed on 7 September 1999. The relationship has continued to blossom, despite the occasional hiccup, and at the time of research the two countries were discussing a joint bid to stage the 2008 European soccer championships.

While Turkey remains the country's top priority, Greece has also had its hands full in recent years coping with events to the north precipitated by the break-up of former Yugoslavia and the collapse of the communist regimes in Albania and Romania.

GEOGRAPHY

Greece consists of the southern tip of the Balkan Peninsula and about 2000 islands,

GREECE

only 166 of which are inhabited. The land mass is 131,900 sq km and Greek territorial waters cover a further 400,000 sq km.

Most of the country is mountainous. The Pindos Mountains in Epiros are the southern extension of the Dinaric Alps, which run the length of former Yugoslavia. The range continues down through central Greece and the Peloponnese, and re-emerges in the mountains of Crete. Less than a quarter of the country is suitable for agriculture.

GEOLOGY

Greece lies in one of most seismically active regions in the world, recording over 20,000 earthquakes in the last 40 years. Fortunately, most of them are very minor – detectable only by sensitive seismic monitoring equipment. The reason for all this activity is that the eastern Mediterranean lies at the meeting point of three continental plates: the Eurasian, African and Arabian. The three grind away at each other constantly, generating countless earthquakes as the land surface reacts to the intense activity beneath the earth's crust.

The system has two main fault lines. The most active is the North Aegean Fault, which starts as a volcano-dotted rift between Greece and Turkey, snakes under Greece and then runs north up the Ionian and Adriatic coasts. Less active but more dramatic is the North Anatolian Fault that runs across Turkey, which is renowned for major tremors like the 7.4 monster that struck more than 40,000 dead in western Turkey in August 1999. Seismologists maintain that activity along the two fault lines is not related.

CLIMATE

Greece's climate is typically Mediterranean with mild, wet winters followed by very hot, dry summers.

There are regional variations. The mountains of northern Greece have a climate similar to the Balkans, with freezing winters and very hot, humid summers, while the west coast and the Ionian Islands have the highest rainfall.

Mid-October is when the rains start in most areas, and the weather stays cold and wet until February – although there are also plenty of winter days with clear blue skies and sunshine. Crete stays warm the longest and you can swim off its southern coast from mid-April to November.

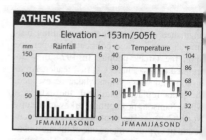

ATHENS
Elevation – 153m/505ft

ECOLOGY & ENVIRONMENT

Greece is belatedly becoming environmentally conscious; regrettably, it is often a case of closing the gate after the horse has bolted. Deforestation and soil erosion are problems that go back thousands of years. Olive cultivation and goats have been the main culprits, but firewood gathering, shipbuilding, housing and industry have all taken their toll.

Forest fires are also a major problem, with an estimated 25,000 hectares destroyed every year. The 2000 season was one of the worst on record, particularly in the Peloponnese and on the island of Samos. Epiros and Macedonia in northern Greece are the only places where extensive forests remain.

General environmental awareness remains at a depressingly low level, especially where litter is concerned. The problem is particularly bad in rural areas, where roadsides are strewn with soft drink cans and plastic packaging hurled from passing cars. Environmental education has begun in schools, but it will be some time before community attitudes change.

The news from the Aegean Sea is both good and bad. According to EU findings, it is Europe's least-polluted sea – apart from areas immediately surrounding major cities. Like the rest of the Mediterranean, the Aegean has been overfished.

FLORA & FAUNA

The variety of flora in Greece is unrivalled in Europe. The wildflowers are spectacular. They continue to thrive because much of the land is too poor for agriculture and has escaped the ravages of modern fertilisers. The best places to see the dazzling array of wildflowers are the mountains of Crete and the southern Peloponnese.

You won't encounter many animals in the wild, mainly due to the macho Greek habit of blasting to bits anything that moves. Wild boar are still found in reasonable numbers in the north and are a favourite target for hunters. Squirrels, rabbits, hares, foxes and weasels are all fairly common on the mainland; less common is the cute European suslik – a small ground squirrel. Reptiles are well represented. Snakes include several viper species, which are poisonous.

Bird-watchers have more chance of coming across something unusual than animal-spotters. Lake Mikri Prespa in Macedonia has the richest colony of fish-eating birds in Europe, while the Dadia Forest Reserve in Thrace numbers such majestic birds as the golden eagle and the giant black vulture among its residents.

Endangered Species

The brown bear, Europe's largest land mammal, still survives in very small numbers in the mountains of northern Greece, as does the grey wolf.

Europe's rarest mammal, the monk seal, was once very common in the Mediterranean Sea, but is now on the brink of extinction in Europe. There are about 400 left in Europe, half of which live in Greece. There are about 40 in the Ionian Sea and the rest are found in the Aegean.

The waters around Zakynthos are home to the last large sea turtle colony in Europe, that of the loggerhead turtle (*Careta careta*). The **Sea Turtle Protection Society of Greece** (☎/fax 21 0523 1342; e stps@compulink .gr; Solomou 57, Athens 104 32) runs monitoring programmes and is always looking for volunteers.

National Parks

Visitors who expect Greek national parks to provide facilities on par with those in countries such as Australia and the USA will be very disappointed. Although they all have refuges and some have marked hiking trails, Greek national parks have little else in the way of facilities.

The most visited parks are Mt Parnitha, just north of Athens, and the Samaria Gorge on Crete. The others are Vikos-Aoös and Prespa national parks in Epiros; Mt Olympus on the border of Thessaly and Macedonia; and Parnassos and Iti national parks in central Greece.

If you want to see wildlife, the place to go is the Dadia Forest Reserve in eastern Thrace.

There is also a National Marine Park off the coast of Alonnisos, and another around the Bay of Laganas area off Zakynthos.

GOVERNMENT & POLITICS

Since 1975, democratic Greece has been a parliamentary republic with a president as its head of state. The president and parliament, which has 300 deputies, have joint legislative power. Prime Minister Costas Simitis heads a 43-member cabinet.

ECONOMY

Traditionally, Greece has been an agricultural country, but the importance of agriculture in the economy is declining. Tourism is by far the biggest industry; shipping comes next.

POPULATION & PEOPLE

The 2001 census recorded a population of 10,964,080. Women outnumber men by more than 200,000. Greece is now a largely urban society, with 68% of people living in cities. By far the largest city is Athens, with more than 3.7 million people in the greater Athens area, which includes Piraeus (171,000). Other major cities are: Thessaloniki (750,000), Patras (153,300), Iraklio (127,600), Larisa (113,400) and Volos (110,000). Less than 15% of the population live on the islands. The most populous are Crete (537,000), Evia (209,100) and Corfu (107,592).

Contemporary Greeks are a mixture of all of the invaders who have occupied the country since ancient times. There are a number of distinct ethnic minorities: about 300,000 ethnic Turks in Thrace; about 100,000 Britons; about 5000 Jews; Vlach and Sarakatsani shepherds in Epiros; Roma (Gypsies); and, recently, a growing number of Albanians.

ARTS

The arts have been integral to Greek life since ancient times. In summer, Greek dramas are staged in the ancient theatres where they were originally performed.

The visual arts follow the mainstream of modern European art, and traditional folk arts such as embroidery, weaving and tapestry continue.

The *bouzouki* (a stringed instrument similar to a mandolin) is the most popular musical instrument, but each region has its own special instruments and sounds. *Rembetika* music, with its themes of poverty and suffering, was

GREECE

banned by the junta, but is now enjoying a revival. Rembetika is the music of the working classes and has its roots in the sufferings of the refugees from Asia Minor in the 1920s. Songs are accompanied by bouzouki, guitar, violin and accordion.

The blind bard Homer composed the narrative poems *Odyssey* and *Iliad*. These tales of the Trojan War and the return to Greece of Odysseus, King of Ithaki, link together the legends sung by bards during the dark age.

Plato was the most devoted pupil of Socrates, writing down every dialogue he could recall between Socrates, other philosophers and the youth of Athens. His most widely read work is the *Republic*, where it argues that the perfect state could only be created with philosopher-rulers at the helm.

Nikos Kazantzakis, author of *Zorba the Greek* and numerous other novels, plays and poems, is the most famous of 20th-century Greek novelists. The Alexandrian, Constantine Cavafy (1863–1933), revolutionised Greek poetry by introducing a personal, conversational style. He is considered to be the TS Eliot of Greek literary verse. Poet George Seferis (1900–71) won the Nobel Prize for literature in 1963, and Odysseus Elytis (1911–96) won the same prize in 1979.

Theophilos (1866–1934) is famous for his primitive style of painting. The country's most famous painter was a young Cretan called Domenikos Theotokopoulos, who moved to Spain in 1577 and became known as the great El Greco.

SOCIETY & CONDUCT

Greece is steeped in traditional customs. Name days (celebrated instead of birthdays), weddings and funerals all have great significance. On someone's name day there is an open house and refreshments are served to well-wishers who stop by with gifts. Weddings are highly festive with dancing, feasting and drinking sometimes continuing for days.

If you want to bare all, other than on a designated nude beach, remember that Greece is a conservative country, so take care not to offend the locals.

MYTHOLOGY

The myths are accounts of the gods whom the Greeks worshipped and heroes idolised in ancient times. The main characters are the 12 principle deities, who lived on Mt Olympus –

which the Greeks thought to be at the exact centre of the world.

The supreme deity was Zeus, who was also god of the heavens. He was the possessor of an astonishing libido and mythology is littered with his offspring. Zeus was married to his sister, Hera, who was the protector of women and the family. She was able to renew her virginity each year by bathing in a spring. She was the mother of Ares, the god of war, and Hephaestus, god of the forge.

Demeter was the goddess of earth and fertility, while the goddess of love (and lust) was the beautiful Aphrodite. The powerful goddess of wisdom and guardian of Athens was Athena, who is said to have been born (complete with helmet, armour and spear) from Zeus' head.

Poseidon, the brother of Zeus, was god of the sea and preferred his sumptuous palace in the depths of the Aegean to Mt Olympus. Apollo, god of the sun, was also worshipped as the god of music and song. His twin sister, Artemis, was the goddess of childbirth and the protector of suckling animals.

Hermes, messenger of the gods, completes the first 11 – the gods whose position in the pantheon is agreed by everyone. The final berth is normally reserved for Hestia, goddess of the hearth. She was too virtuous for some, who promoted the fun-loving Dionysos, god of wine, in her place.

Other gods included Hades, the god of the underworld; Pan, god of the shepherds; Asclepius, the god of healing; and Eros, the god of love.

Heroes such as Heracles and Theseus were elevated almost to the ranks of the gods.

RELIGION

About 97% of Greeks nominally belong to the Greek Orthodox Church. The rest of the population is split between the Roman Catholic, Protestant, Evangelist, Jewish and Muslim faiths. While older Greeks and those in rural areas tend to be deeply religious, most young people are decidedly more interested in the secular.

LANGUAGE

Greeks are naturally delighted if you can speak a little of their language, but you don't need to be able to speak Greek to get around. English is almost a second language, especially among younger people. You'll also find many Greeks have lived abroad, usually in Australia or the USA, so even in remote villages there are invariably one or two people who can speak English.

See the Language chapter at the back of this book for pronunciation guidelines and useful Greek words and phrases.

Transliteration

Travellers in Greece will frequently encounter confusing and seemingly illogical English transliterations of Greek words. Transliteration is a knotty problem – there are six ways of rendering the vowel sound 'ee' in Greek, and two ways of rendering the 'o' sound and the 'e' sound.

This guidebook has merely attempted to be consistent within itself, not to solve this long-standing difficulty.

As a general rule, the Greek letter gamma (g) appears as a 'g' rather than a 'y'; therefore it's *agios*, not ayios. The letter delta (d) appears as 'd' rather than 'dh', so it's *domatia*, not dhomatia. The letter phi (f) can be either 'f' or 'ph'. Here, we have used the general rule that classical names are spelt with a 'ph' and modern names with an 'f' – so it's Phaestos (not Festos), but Folegandros, not Pholegandros. Please bear with us if signs in Greek don't agree with our spelling. It's that sort of language.

Facts for the Visitor

HIGHLIGHTS
Islands

Many islands are overrun with visitors in summer. For tranquillity, head for the lesser-known islands, such as Kassos, Sikinos and Kastellorizo. If you enjoy mountain walks, Crete, Lesvos, Naxos and Samos are ideal destinations.

Museums & Archaeological Sites

Greece has more ancient sites than any other country in Europe. It's worth seeking out some of the lesser lights where you won't have to contend with the crowds that pour through famous sites, such as the Acropolis, Delphi, Knossos and Olympia.

The counrty's leading museum is the National Archaeological Museum in Athens, which houses Heinrich Schliemann's finds from Mycenae, and Minoan frescoes from Akrotiri on Santorini (Thira). The Thessaloniki Museum contains treasures from the graves of the Macedonian royal family, and the Iraklio Museum houses a vast collection from the Minoan sites of Crete.

Visiting the museums and sites is free for card-carrying students and teachers from EU countries. An International Student Identification Card (ISIC) gets non-EU students a 50% discount.

Historic Towns

Two of Greece's most spectacular medieval cities are in the Peloponnese. The ghostly Byzantine city of Mystras, west of Sparta, clambers up the slopes of Mt Taygetos, its winding paths and stairways leading to deserted palaces and churches. In contrast, Byzantine Monemvasia is still inhabited, but is equally dramatic and full of atmosphere.

There are some stunning towns on the islands. Rhodes is the finest surviving example of a fortified medieval town in Europe, while Naxos' *hora* (main village or town) is a maze of narrow, stepped alleyways of whitewashed Venetian houses, their tiny gardens ablaze with flowers.

SUGGESTED ITINERARIES

Depending on the length of your stay, you might want to see and do the following:

Two days
Spend the time in Athens seeing its museums and ancient sites.

One week
Spend one day in Athens, two days in the Peloponnese visiting Nafplio or Mycenae and Olympia, and four days in the Cyclades.

Two weeks
Spend two days in Athens, two days in the Peloponnese, and two days in central Greece visiting Delphi and Meteora. Follow up with a week of island-hopping through the Cyclades.

One month
Spend two days in Athens, two days in the Peloponnese and then catch an overnight ferry from Patras to Corfu for two days. Head to Ioannina and spend two days exploring the Zagorohoria villages of northern Epiros before spending three days travelling back to Athens via Meteora and Delphi. Take a ferry from Piraeus to Chios and spend two weeks island-hopping your way back through the northeastern Aegean Islands, the Dodecanese and the Cyclades.

GREECE

PLANNING
When to Go
Spring and autumn are the best times to visit. Outside the major cities, winter is pretty much a dead loss – unless you're going to take advantage of the cheap skiing. The islands go into hibernation between late November and early April. Hotels and restaurants are closed, and buses and ferries operate on drastically reduced schedules.

The cobwebs are dusted off in time for Easter, and conditions are perfect until the end of June. Everything is open, public transport operates normally, but the crowds have yet to arrive. From July until mid-September, it's on for young and old as northern Europe heads for the Mediterranean en masse. If you want to party, this is the time to go. The flip side is that everywhere is packed out, and rooms can be hard to find.

The pace slows down again by about mid-September, and conditions are ideal once more until the end of October.

Maps
Unless you are going to trek or drive, the free maps given out by the tourist offices will probably suffice. The best motoring maps are produced by local company Road Editions, which also produces a good trekking series.

What to Bring
In summer, bring light cotton clothing, a sun hat and sunglasses; bring sunscreen, too, as it's expensive in Greece. In spring and autumn, you will need light jumpers (sweaters) and thicker ones for the evenings. In winter, thick jumpers and a raincoat are essential.

You will need to wear sturdy walking shoes for trekking in the country, and comfortable shoes are a better idea than sandals for walking around ancient sites. An alarm clock for catching early-morning ferries, a torch (flashlight) and a small day-pack will also be useful.

TOURIST OFFICES
The Greek National Tourist Organisation (GNTO) is known as EOT in Greece. There is either an EOT office or a local tourist office in almost every town of consequence and on many of the islands. Most do no more than give out brochures and maps. Popular destinations have tourist police, who can often help in finding accommodation.

Local Tourist Offices
The EOT main tourist office (☎ 21 0331 0561/0562, fax 21 0325 2895; e info@ gnto.gr; w www.gnto.gr; Amerikis 2, Athens 105 64) helps with information. Other tourist offices are listed throughout this chapter.

Tourist Offices Abroad
Australia (☎ 02-9241 1663) 51–57 Pitt St, Sydney, NSW 2000
Canada (☎ 416-968 2220) 91 Scollard St, Toronto, Ontario M5R 1G4
(☎ 514-871 1535) 1170 Place Du Frere Andre, Montreal, Quebec H3B 3C6
France (☎ 1-42 60 65 75) 3 Ave de l'Opéra, Paris 75001
Germany (☎ 069-236 561) Neue Mainzerstrasse 22, 60311 Frankfurt
(☎ 089-222 035) Pacellistrasse 5, 2W 80333 Munich
(☎ 040-454 498) Neurer Wall 18, 20254 Hamburg
(☎ 030-217 6262) Wittenbergplatz 3A, 10789 Berlin 30
Italy (☎ 06-474 4249) Via L Bissolati 78-80, Rome 00187
(☎ 02-860 470) Piazza Diaz 1, 20123 Milan
Japan (☎ 03-350 55 917) Fukuda Bldg West, 5th Floor 2-11-3 Akasaka, Minato-ku, Tokyo 107-0052
UK (☎ 020-7734 5997) 4 Conduit St, London W1R ODJ
USA (☎ 212-421 5777) Olympic Tower, 645 Fifth Ave, New York, NY 10022
(☎ 312-782 1084) Suite 160, 168 North Michigan Ave, Chicago, IL 60601
(☎ 213-626 6696) Suite 2198, 611 West 6th St, Los Angeles, CA 92668

VISAS & DOCUMENTS
Nationals of Australia, Canada, EU countries, Israel, New Zealand and the USA are allowed to stay in Greece for up to three months without a visa. For longer stays, apply at a consulate abroad or at least 20 days in advance to the **Aliens Bureau** (☎ 21 0770 5711; Leoforos Alexandras 173, Athens) at Athens Central Police Station. Elsewhere in Greece, apply to the local police authority.

In the past, Greece has refused entry to those whose passport indicates that they have visited Turkish-occupied North Cyprus, although there are reports that this is less of a problem now. To be on the safe side, however, ask the North Cyprus immigration officials to stamp a piece of paper rather than your passport. If you enter North Cyprus from the Greek Republic of Cyprus, no exit stamp is put in your passport.

Driving Licence & Permits
Greece recognises all national driving licences, provided the licence has been held for at least one year. It also recognises an International Driving Permit, which should be obtained before you leave home.

Discount Cards
A Hostelling International (HI) card is of limited use in Greece. The only place you will be able to use it is at the Athens International Youth Hostel (see Places to Stay under Athens, later).

The most widely recognised (and thus the most useful) form of student ID is the International Student Identity Card (ISIC). Holders qualify for half-price admission to museums and ancient sites and for discounts at some budget hotels and hostels.

See Senior Travellers, later in this chapter, for more information.

EMBASSIES & CONSULATES
Greek Embassies Abroad
Greece has diplomatic representation in the following countries:

Australia (☎ 02-6273 3011) 9 Turrana St, Yarralumla, ACT 2600
Canada (☎ 613-238 6271) 76–80 Maclaren St, Ottawa, Ontario K2P 0K6
France (☎ 01-47 23 72 28) 17 Rue Auguste Vaquerie, 75116 Paris
Germany (☎ 0228-83010) An Der Marienkapelle 10, 53 179 Bonn
Italy (☎ 06-854 9630) Via S Mercadante 36, Rome 3906
Japan (☎ 03-340 0871/0872) 3-16-30 Nishi Azabu, Minato-ku, Tokyo 304-5853
New Zealand (☎ 04-473 7775) 5–7 Willeston St, Wellington
South Africa (☎ 12-437 351/352) 1003 Church St, Hatfield, Pretoria 0028
Turkey (☎ 312-436 8860) Ziya-ul-Rahman Caddesi 9–11, Gazi Osman Pasa 06700, Ankara
UK (☎ 020-7229 3850) 1A Holland Park, London W11 3TP
USA (☎ 202-939 5818) 2221 Massachusetts Ave NW, Washington, DC 20008

Foreign Embassies in Greece
The following countries do have diplomatic representation in Greece:

Australia (☎ 21 0645 0404) Dimitriou Soutsou 37, Athens 115 21
Canada (☎ 21 0727 3400) Genadiou 4, Athens 115 21

France (☎ 21 0361 1663) Leoforos Vasilissis Sofias 7, Athens 106 71
Germany (☎ 21 0728 5111) Dimitriou 3 & Karaoli, Kolonaki 106 75
Italy (☎ 21 0361 7260) Sekeri 2, Athens 106 74
Japan (☎ 21 0775 8101) Athens Tower, Leoforos Messogion 2-4, Athens 115 27
New Zealand (☎ 21 0687 4701) Kifissias 268, Halandri 152 32; honorary consulate
South Africa (☎ 21 0680 6645) Kifissias 60, Maroussi, Athens 151 25
Turkey (☎ 21 0724 5915) Vasilissis Georgiou 8, Athens 106 74
UK (☎ 21 0723 6211) Ploutarhou 1, Athens 106 75
USA (☎ 21 0721 2951) Leoforos Vasilissis Sofias 91, Athens 115 21

CUSTOMS
Duty-free allowances in Greece are the same as for other EU countries. Import regulations for medicines are strict; if you are taking medication, make sure you get a statement from your doctor before you leave home. It is illegal, for example, to take codeine into Greece. The export of antiques is prohibited. You can bring as much foreign currency as you like, but if you want to leave with more than US$1000 in foreign banknotes the money must be declared on entry.

MONEY
Banks will exchange all major currencies, in either cash or travellers cheques and also Eurocheques. Post offices charge less commission than banks, but won't cash travellers cheques.

All major credit cards are accepted, but only in larger establishments. You'll find ATMs everywhere, particularly in tourist areas.

Currency
Greece adopted the euro at the beginning of 2002, and the Greek drachma disappeared at the end of February after a two-month period of dual circulation. Most people appear to welcome the change, although older people have struggled to adapt.

The only place that will now convert outstanding drachma into euro is the Bank of Greece, and only at its central offices in major cities such as Athens, Patras and Thessaloniki. The Athens branch is at Panepistimiou 15, near Syntagma.

Costs
Greece is still a cheap destination by northern European standards, but it is no longer

dirt-cheap. A rock-bottom daily budget would be €25. This would mean hitching, staying in youth hostels or camping, staying away from bars, and only occasionally eating in restaurants or taking ferries. Allow at least €50 per day if you want your own room and plan to eat out regularly as well as seeing the sights. If you really want a holiday – comfortable rooms and restaurants all the way – you will need closer to €100 per day.

Your money will go a lot further if you travel in the quieter months. Accommodation, which eats up a large part of the daily budget, is generally about 25% cheaper outside the high season. There are fewer tourists around and more opportunities to negotiate even better deals.

Tipping & Bargaining

In restaurants the service charge is included on the bill, but it is the custom to leave a small tip – just round off the bill. Accommodation is nearly always negotiable outside peak season, especially if you are staying more than one night. Souvenir shops are another place where substantial savings can be made. Prices in other shops are normally clearly marked and non-negotiable.

Taxes & Refunds

Value-added tax (VAT) varies from 15% to 18%. A tax-rebate scheme applies at a restricted number of shops and stores; look for a Tax Free sign in the window. You must fill in a form at the shop and then present it with the receipt at the airport on departure. A cheque will (hopefully) be sent to your home address.

POST & COMMUNICATIONS
Post

The postal rate for postcards and airmail letters is €0.60 to all destinations. Post within Europe takes five to eight days and to the USA, Australia and New Zealand, nine to 11 days.

Post offices are usually open from 7.30am to 2pm. In major cities they stay open until 8pm and are also open 7.30am to 2pm on Saturday. Do not wrap up a parcel until it has been inspected at the post office. Some tourist shops also sell stamps, but with a 10% surcharge.

Mail can be sent poste restante to any main post office and is held for up to one month.

Your surname should be underlined and you will need to show your passport when you collect your mail. Parcels are not delivered in Greece – they must be collected from a post office.

Telephone & Fax

The phone system is modern and efficient. All public phone boxes use phonecards, sold at Organismos Tilepikoinonion Ellados (OTE) offices and *periptera* (street kiosks). The cards cost €2.95 for 1000 units, €5.60 for 2000 units, €12.35 for 5000 units, and €24.10 for 10,000 units. The 1000-unit cards are widely available at *periptera*, corner shops and tourist shops; the others can be bought at OTE offices.

It's also possible to use these phones using a growing range of discount-card schemes, such as Kronokarta and Teledome, which involve dialling an access code and then punching in your card number. The cards come with instructions in Greek and English. They are easy to use and buy double the time.

It is no longer possible to use public phones to access other national card schemes, such as Telstra Australia's Telecard, for international calls. These calls can be made from private digital phones, but the time you spend on the phone is also charged at local call rates. It's better to use Kronokarta or Teledome.

If you're calling Greece from abroad, the country code is ☎ 30. If you need to make an international call from Greece, the international access code is ☎ 00.

Main city post offices have fax facilities.

Email & Internet Access

Greece was slow to embrace the wonders of the Internet, but is now striving to make up for lost time. Internet cafés are springing up everywhere, and are listed under Information for cities and islands where available. Charges differ radically – from less than €3.50 per hour in big cities up to €15 per hour on Mykonos.

There has also been a huge increase in the number of hotels and businesses using email, and addresses have also been listed in this chapter where available.

DIGITAL RESOURCES

There has also been a huge increase in the number of websites providing information about Greece.

A good place to start is the 500 Links to Greece listed at **w** www.viking1.com/corfu/link.htm. It has links to a huge range of sites covering everything from accommodation to Zeus. One site that it doesn't provide a link to, however, is **w** www.greektravel .com, the front door for an assortment of interesting sites by Matt Barrett.

The Greek Ministry of Culture has put together an excellent site ath at **w** www.culture .gr, which has loads of information about museums and ancient sites. Other websites include **w** www.gogreece.com/travel and **w** www.aegean.ch. You'll find more specialist websites listed through the chapter.

BOOKS
Lonely Planet
Lonely Planet's *Greece* contains more comprehensive information on the areas covered by this chapter, as well as coverage of less-visited areas, particularly in central and northern Greece. The *Greek Islands* guide is especially tailored for island-hoppers. If you want to concentrate on specific regions, pick up Lonely Planet's guides to *Athens*, *Corfu & the Ionians*, *Crete* and *Rhodes & the Dodecanese*. *Peloponnese* will be published in 2003.

Travel
The ancient Greek traveller Pausanias is acclaimed as the world's first travel writer. His *Guide to Greece* was written in the 2nd century AD and even now makes fascinating reading.

History
A Traveller's History of Greece by Timothy Boatswain & Colin Nicholson is probably the best choice for the layperson who wants a good general reference.

General
There are numerous books to choose from if you want to get a feel for the country. *Zorba the Greek* by Nikos Kazantzakis may seem an obvious choice, but read it and you'll understand why it's the most popular of all Greek novels translated into English.

English writer Louis de Bernières has become almost a cult figure following the success of *Captain Corelli's Mandolin*, which tells the emotional story of a young Italian army officer sent to the island of Kefallonia during WWII.

Athenian writer Apostolos Doxiadis has charmed critics the world over with his latest novel, *Uncle Petros and Goldbach's Conjecture*, an unlikely blend of family drama and mathematical theory.

NEWSPAPERS & MAGAZINES
The weekly *Athens News* (€1.50) appears on Friday with an assortment of news, local features and entertainment listings. The Athens edition of the *International Herald Tribune* (€1.60) carries an eight-page English translation of the popular Greek daily *Kathimerini*.

Foreign newspapers are widely available, although only between April and October in smaller resort areas.

RADIO & TV
There are plenty of radio stations to choose from, especially in Athens, but not many broadcast in English. If you have a short-wave radio, the best frequencies for the World Service are 618, 941 and 1507MHz.

The nine TV channels generate nine times as much rubbish as one channel. You'll find the occasional American action drama in English (with Greek subtitles). Reality show junkies will find local versions of shows such as Big Brother and Survivor.

PHOTOGRAPHY
Major brands of film are widely available, but quite expensive outside major towns and on the islands.

Never photograph military installations or anything else with a sign forbidding pictures.

TIME
Greece is two hours ahead of GMT/UTC, and three hours ahead on daylight-saving time, which begins at 12.01am on the last Sunday in March when clocks are put forward one hour. Clocks are put back an hour at 12.01am on the last Sunday in September.

Out of daylight-saving time, at noon in Greece it is also noon in İstanbul, 10am in London, 2am in San Francisco, 5am in New York and Toronto, 8pm in Sydney and 10pm in Auckland. Note: These times do not make an allowance for daylight saving in other countries.

LAUNDRY
Large towns and some islands have laundrettes. They charge from €8 to €10 to wash

GREECE

and dry a load. Hotel managers and room owners will usually provide you with a wash-tub if requested.

TOILETS

You'll find public toilets at all major bus and train stations, but they are seldom very pleasant. You will need to supply your own paper. In town, a café is the best bet, but the owner won't be impressed if you don't at least buy something.

Greek plumbing cannot handle toilet paper; always put it in the bin provided.

WOMEN TRAVELLERS

Many foreign women travel alone in Greece. Hassles occur, but they tend to be a nuisance rather than threatening. Violent offences are very rare. Women travelling alone in rural areas are usually treated with respect. In rural areas it's sensible to dress conservatively; it's perfectly OK to wear shorts, short skirts etc in touristy places.

GAY & LESBIAN TRAVELLERS

In a country where the church still plays a major role in shaping society's views on issues such as sexuality, it should come as no surprise that homosexuality is generally frowned upon. Although there is no legislation against homosexual activity, it is wise to be discreet and to avoid open displays of togetherness.

However, this has not prevented Greece from becoming a popular destination for gay travellers. Athens has a busy gay scene, but most people head for the islands – Mykonos and Lesvos in particular. Paros, Rhodes, Santorini (Thira) and Skiathos also have their share of gay hang-outs.

DISABLED TRAVELLERS

If mobility is a problem, the hard fact is that most hotels, museums and ancient sites are not wheelchair accessible.

SENIOR TRAVELLERS

Elderly people are shown great respect in Greece. There are some good deals available for EU nationals. For starters, those over 60 qualify for a 50% discount on train travel plus five free journeys per year. Take your ID card or passport to a Greek Railways (OSE) office and you will be given a Senior Card. Pensioners also get a discount at museums and ancient sites.

DANGERS & ANNOYANCES

Greece has the lowest crime rate in Europe. Athens is developing a bad reputation for petty theft and scams, but elsewhere crimes are most likely to be committed by other travellers.

Emergency Services

The emergency number for the police is ☎ 100, tourist police ☎ 171, fire brigade ☎ 199, and ambulance (Athens only) ☎ 166. The Europe-wide emergency telephone number ☎ 112 can also be used. See Car & Motorcycle in the introductory Getting Around section later in this chapter for information on assistance in the event of breakdown.

LEGAL MATTERS

Greek drug laws are the strictest in Europe. There is no distinction between possession and pushing. Possession of a small amount of marijuana is likely to land you in jail.

BUSINESS HOURS

Banks are open from 8.30am to 2.30pm Monday to Thursday, and 8.30am to 2pm Friday. Some city banks also open from 3.30pm to 6.30pm and on Saturday morning. Shops are open from 8am to 1.30pm and 5.30pm to 8.30pm on Tuesday, Thursday and Friday, and 8am to 2.30pm on Monday, Wednesday and Saturday, but these times are not always strictly adhered to. *Periptera* are open from early morning to midnight. All banks and shops, and most museums and archaeological sites, close during public holidays.

PUBLIC HOLIDAYS & SPECIAL EVENTS

Public holidays are as follows:

New Year's Day 1 January
Epiphany 6 January
First Sunday in Lent February
Greek Independence Day 25 March
Good Friday/Easter Sunday March/April
Spring Festival/Labour Day 1 May
Feast of the Assumption 15 August
Okhi Day 28 October
Christmas Day 25 December
St Stephen's Day 26 December

Easter is Greece's most important festival, with candle-lit processions, feasting and firework displays. The Orthodox Easter is 50 days after the first Sunday in Lent.

There are a number of cultural festivals that are also held during the summer months. The most important is the Athens Festival, when plays, operas, ballet and classical music concerts are staged at the Theatre of Herodes Atticus. The festival also features performances of ancient Greek dramas at the Theatre of Epidavros in the Peloponnese.

ACTIVITIES
Windsurfing
Sailboards are widely available for hire, priced from €12. The top spots for windsurfing are Hrysi Akti on Paros, and Vasiliki on Lefkada, which is reputedly one of the best places in the world to learn.

Sailing
Sailing facilities are harder to find, although the same locations recommended previously for windsurfing are all also ideal for sailing.

Hrysi Akti on Paros and Mylopotas Beach on Ios are two of the best locations. Hire charges for Hobie Cats (catamarans) range from €20 to €25.

Skiing
Greece offers some of the cheapest skiing in Europe. There are 16 resorts dotted around the mainland, most of them in the north. They have all the basic facilities and are a pleasant alternative to the glitzy resorts of northern Europe.

The season depends on snow conditions but runs approximately from January to the end of April. You'll find information about the latest snow conditions on the Internet at w www.snowreport.gr.

Hiking
The mountainous terrain of the Greek countryside is perfect for trekkers who want to get away from the crowds. The popular routes are well marked and well maintained, including the E4 and E6 trans-European treks, which both end in Greece.

A number of companies run organised treks. **Trekking Hellas** (☎ 21 0323 4548, fax 21 0325 1474; e trekking@compulink.gr; w www.trekking.gr; Filellinon 7, Athens 105 57) operates treks on the islands as well as on the mainland, while **Alpin Club** (☎ 21 0729 5486, fax 21 0721 2773; e alpinclub@inte net.gr; w www.alpinclub.gr; Mihalakopoulou 39, Athens 115 28) concentrates on the Peloponnese and central Greece.

LANGUAGE COURSES
If you are serious about learning Greek, an intensive course at the start of your stay is a good way to go about it. Most of the courses are in Athens and are covered under Athens, later in this chapter. More information about courses is available from EOT offices and Greek embassies.

WORK
Your best chance of finding work is to do the rounds of the tourist hotels and bars at the beginning of the season. The few jobs available are hotly contested, despite the menial nature of the work and dreadful pay. EU nationals don't need a work permit, but everyone else does.

ACCOMMODATION
There is a range of accommodation in Greece to suit every taste and pocket. All places to stay are subject to strict price controls set by the tourist police. By law, a notice must be displayed in every room, which states the category of the room and the price for each season. If you think you've been ripped off, contact the tourist police. Prices quoted in this book are for the high season, unless otherwise stated. Prices are about 40% cheaper between October and May.

Camping
Greece has almost 350 camping grounds, and a lot of them in great locations. Standard facilities include hot showers, kitchens, restaurants and minimarkets – and often a swimming pool. Prices vary according to facilities, but reckon on €4.50 per adult and €3 for a small tent.

Refuges
Greece has 55 mountain refuges, which are listed in the booklet *Greece Mountain Refuges & Ski Centres*, available free of charge at EOT and EOS (Ellinikos Orivatikos Syndesmos, the Greek Alpine Club) offices.

Hostels
You'll find youth hostels in most major towns and on half a dozen islands. The only place affiliated to Hostelling International (HI) is the excellent **Athens International**

GREECE

Youth Hostel (☎ *21 0523 4170*); see Places to Stay under Athens, later.

Most other youth hostels throughout Greece are run by the **Greek Youth Hostel Organisation** (☎ *21 0751 9530, fax 21 0751 0616; e y-hostels@otenet.gr; Damareos 75, Athens 116 33*). There are affiliated hostels in Athens, Olympia, Patras and Thessaloniki on the mainland, and on the islands of Crete and Santorini (Thira). Most charge €7 to €8, and you don't have to be a member to stay in any of them.

Domatia

Domatia are the Greek equivalent of the British bed and breakfast, minus the breakfast. Once upon a time, *domatia* consisted of little more than spare rooms that families would rent out in summer to supplement their income. Nowadays many of these *domatia* are purpose-built appendages to the family house. The rates start at about €18/25 for singles/doubles.

Hotels

Hotels in Greece are classified as deluxe, A, B, C, D or E class. The ratings seldom seem to have much bearing on the price, but expect to pay €18/25 for singles/doubles in D and E class, and anything from €35/45 to €60/80 for singles/doubles in a decent C-class place with private bathroom.

Some places are classified as pensions and are rated differently. Both are allowed to levy a 10% surcharge for stays of less than three nights, but they seldom do. It normally works the other way – you can bargain a cheaper rate if you're staying more than one night.

Apartments

Self-contained family apartments are available in some hotels and *domatia*, particularly on the islands.

Houses & Flats

For long-term rental accommodation in Athens, you can check the advertisements in the English-language newspapers. In rural areas, ask around in tavernas.

FOOD

If Greek food conjures up an uninspiring vision of lukewarm *mousakas* collapsing into a plate of olive oil, take heart – there's a lot more on offer.

Snacks

Greece has a great range of fast-food options for the inveterate snacker. Foremost among them are the *gyros* and the *souvlaki*. The gyros is a giant skewer laden with seasoned meat that grills slowly as it rotates, the meat being steadily trimmed from the outside. Souvlaki are small, individual kebabs. Both are served wrapped in pitta bread with salad and lashings of *tzatziki* (a yogurt, cucumber and garlic dip). Other snacks are pretzel rings, *spanakopitta* (spinach and cheese pie) and *tyropitta* (cheese pie).

Starters

Greece is famous for its appetisers, known as *mezedes* (literally, 'tastes'; *meze* for short). Standards include tzatziki, *melitzanosalata* (aubergine or eggplant dip), *taramasalata* (fish-roe dip), *dolmades* (stuffed vine leaves), *fasolia* (beans) and *oktapodi* (octopus). A selection of three or four starters represents a good meal and can be a very good option for vegetarians.

Main Dishes

You'll find *mousakas* (layers of aubergine and mince, topped with bechamel sauce and baked) on every menu, alongside a number of other taverna staples. They include *moschari* (oven-baked veal and potatoes), *keftedes* (meatballs), *stifado* (meat stew), *pastitsio* (baked dish of macaroni with minced meat and bechamel sauce) and *yemista* (either tomatoes or green peppers stuffed with minced meat and rice). Most mains cost between €4 and €8.

The most popular fish are *barbouni* (red mullet) and *sifias* (swordfish), but they don't come cheap. Prices start at about €10 for a serve. *Kalamaria* (fried squid) is readily available and cheap at about €4.50.

Fortunately for vegetarians, salad is a mainstay of the Greek diet. The most popular is *horiatiki salata*, normally listed on English menus as Greek or country salad. It's a mixed salad comprising cucumbers, peppers, onions, olives, tomatoes and feta (sheep's- or goat's-milk white cheese).

Desserts

Turkish in origin, most Greek desserts are variations on pastry soaked in honey. Popular ones include *baklava* (thin layers of pastry filled with honey and nuts) and *kadaïfi* (shredded wheat soaked in honey).

GREECE

Restaurants

There are several varieties of restaurants. An *estiatorio* is a straightforward place with a printed menu. A taverna is often cheaper and more typically Greek, and you'll probably be invited to peer into the pots. A *psistaria* specialises in charcoal-grilled dishes. *Ouzeria* (ouzo bars) often have such a range of *mezedes* that they can be regarded as eating places.

Kafeneia

Kafeneia are the smoke-filled cafés where men gather to drink coffee, play backgammon and cards and engage in heated political discussion. They are a bastion of male chauvinism. Female tourists tend to avoid them, but those who venture in invariably find they are treated courteously.

Self-Catering

Buying and preparing your own food is easy – every town of consequence has a supermarket, as well as fruit and vegetable shops.

DRINKS
Nonalcoholic Drinks

Bottled mineral water is cheap and available everywhere, as are soft drinks and packaged juices.

Alcoholic Drinks

Greece is traditionally a wine-drinking society. If you're spending a bit of time in the country, it's worth acquiring a taste for retsina (resinated wine). The best (and worst) flows straight from the barrel in the main production areas of Attica and central Greece, but it's available by the bottle everywhere. Greece also produces a large range of regular wines from traditional grape varieties.

Mythos and Alpha are two Greek beers to look out for. Amstel is the most popular of several northern European beers produced locally under licence. You can expect to pay about €0.80 in a supermarket, or €1.50 in a restaurant for a beer. The most popular aperitif is the aniseed-flavoured ouzo.

ENTERTAINMENT

The busy nightlife is a major attraction for many travellers. Nowhere is the pace more frenetic than on the islands in high season. Discos abound in all resort areas and Ios and Paros especially are famous for their raging discos and bars. If you enjoy theatre and classical music, Athens and Thessaloniki are the places to be.

Greeks are great film-goers. Cinemas show films in the original language (usually English) with Greek subtitles.

SPECTATOR SPORTS

Greek men are sports mad. Basketball has almost overtaken soccer as the main attraction. If you happen to be eating in a taverna on a night when a big match is being televised, expect indifferent service.

SHOPPING

Greece produces a vast array of handicrafts, including woollen rugs, ceramics, leather work, hand-woven woollen shoulder bags, embroidery, copperware and carved-wood products.

Getting There & Away

AIR

There are no less than 16 international airports in Greece, but most of them handle only summer charter flights to the islands. Eleftherios Venizelos International Airport in Athens handles the vast majority of international flights, including all intercontinental flights. Athens has regular scheduled flights to all the European capitals. Thessaloniki is also well served.

Most flights are with the national carrier, Olympic Airways, or the flag carrier of the country concerned.

Departure Tax

The airport tax is €12 for passengers travelling to destinations within the EU, and €22 for other destinations. It applies to travellers aged over five, and is paid when you buy your ticket, not at the airport.

Travellers using Athens airport must fork out an additional €10.30 for the privilege of using the swish new terminal, as well as a security charge of €1.29. These charges apply to all passengers aged over two, and are paid when you buy your ticket.

The USA & Canada

Olympic Airways has daily flights to Athens from New York and up to three a week from

Boston. Delta also has daily flights from New York. Apex fares range from US$960 to US$1550. It's worth shopping around for cheaper deals from major European airlines.

You should be able to get to Athens from Toronto and Montreal for about C$1150 or from Vancouver for C$1500. Olympic has up to five flights a week to Athens from Toronto via Montreal.

Australia
Olympic flies to Athens twice a week from Sydney via Melbourne. Fares range from A$1695 to A$2400.

Europe
Flying is the fastest, easiest and cheapest way of getting to Greece from northern Europe. What's more, scheduled flights are so competitively priced that it's hardly worth hunting around for charter cheapies.

Olympic Airways and British Airways both offer 30-day return tickets from London for about UK£240 (midweek departures) in high season, as well as returns to Thessaloniki for about UK£225.

At the time of writing, the cheapest fares were being offered by **EasyJet** (☎ 0870 600 0000), which had flights from London (Stansted) to Athens from UK£69 one way.

Charter flights from London to Athens are readily available for around UK£99/189 one way/return in high season, dropping to UK£79/129 in low season. Fares are about UK£109/209 to most island destinations in high season. Similar deals are available from charter operators throughout Europe.

Athens is a good place to buy cheap air tickets. Examples of one-way fares include London (€75), Madrid (€220), Paris (€165) and Rome (€125).

LAND
Northern Europe
Overland travel between northern Europe and Greece is virtually a thing of the past. Buses and trains can't compete with cheap air fares, and the turmoil in the former Yugoslavia has cut the shortest overland route. All bus and train services now go via Italy and take the ferries over to Greece.

Unless you have a Eurail pass, travelling to Greece by train is prohibitively expensive. Greece is part of the Eurail network, and passes are valid on the ferries operated by Adriatica di Navigazione and Hellenic Mediterranean Lines from Brindisi to Corfu, Igoumenitsa and Patras.

Neighbouring Countries
The Hellenic Railways Organisation (OSE) has buses from Athens to İstanbul (€67.50, 22 hours) at 7pm from Thursday to Tuesday, and to Tirana (€35.20, 21 hours) at 7pm daily.

There are daily trains between Athens and İstanbul for €58.70, leaving from Larisis station at 11.15pm. The trip takes 23 hours.

The crossing points into Turkey are at Kipi and Kastanies, the crossings into the Former Yugoslav Republic of Macedonia (FYROM) are at Evzoni and Niki, and the Bulgarian crossing is at Promahonas. All are open 24 hours a day. The crossing points to Albania are at Kakavia and Krystallopigi.

If you want to hitchhike to Turkey, look for a through-ride from Alexandroupolis because you cannot hitchhike across the border.

SEA
Departure Tax
Port taxes are €5.50 to Italy and €8.80 to Turkey, Cyprus and Israel.

Italy
The most popular crossing is from Brindisi to Patras (18 hours), via Corfu (nine hours) and Igoumenitsa (10 hours). There are numerous services. Deck-class fares start at about €35 one way in low season and €45 one way in high season. Eurail pass-holders can travel free with Blue Star Ferries and Hellenic Mediterranean. You still need to make a reservation and pay port taxes.

There are also ferries to Patras from Ancona, Bari, Trieste and Venice, stopping at either Corfu or Igoumenitsa on the way. In summer you can get ferries from Bari and Brindisi to Kefallonia.

Turkey
There are five regular ferry services between the Greek Islands and places in Turkey, these are between: Lesvos–Ayvalık, Chios–Çeşme, Samos–Kuşadası, Kos–Bodrum and Rhodes–Marmaris. All are daily services in summer, dropping to weekly in winter. Tickets must be bought a day in advance and you will be asked to hand over your passport. It will be returned on the boat.

Cyprus & Israel

Salamis Lines and Poseidon Lines operate services from Piraeus to the Israeli port of Haifa, via Rhodes and Lemessos (formerly Limassol) on Cyprus. Deck-class fares from Piraeus are €70.50 to Lemessos and €106 to Haifa.

Students and travellers aged under 30 qualify for a 20% discount on these fares.

Getting Around

AIR

Most domestic flights are operated by **Olympic Airways** (W www.olympic-airways .gr) and its offshoot, Olympic Aviation. They offer a busy schedule in summer with flights from Athens to 25 islands and a range of mainland cities. Sample fares include Athens to Iraklio for €89, Athens to Rhodes for €96 and Athens to Santorini (Thira) for €84. There are also flights from Thessaloniki to the islands. It is advisable to book at least two weeks in advance, especially in summer. Services to the islands are fairly skeletal in winter. **Aegean Airlines** (W www.aegeanair.com) provides competition on a few major routes.

These fares include the €12 tax on domestic flights, paid when you buy your ticket.

BUS

Buses are the most popular form of public transport. They are comfortable, they run on time and there are frequent services on all the major routes. Almost every town on the mainland (except in Thrace) has at least one bus a day to Athens. Local companies can get you to all but the remotest villages. Reckon on paying about €4 per hour of journey time. Sample fares from Athens include €28 to Thessaloniki (7½ hours) and €12.25 to Patras (three hours). Tickets should be bought at least an hour in advance to ensure a seat.

Major islands also have comprehensive local bus networks. In fact, every island with a road has a service of some sort, but they tend to operate at the whim of the driver.

TRAIN

Trains are generally looked on as a poor alternative to bus travel. The main problem is that there are only two main lines: to Thessaloniki and Alexandroupolis in the north,

and to the Peloponnese. In addition there are a number of branch lines, such as the Pyrgos–Olympia line and the spectacular Diakofto–Kalavryta mountain railway.

If there are trains going in your direction, they are a good way to travel. Be aware that there are two distinct levels of service: the painfully slow, dilapidated trains that stop at all stations, and the faster, modern intercity trains.

The slow trains represent the cheapest form of transport. It may take five hours to crawl from Athens to Patras, but the 2nd-class fare is only €5.30. Intercity trains do the trip in 3½ hours for €10, which is still cheaper than the bus.

Inter-Rail and Eurail passes are valid in Greece, but you still need to make a reservation. In summer, make reservations at least two days in advance.

CAR & MOTORCYCLE

Car is a great way to explore areas that are off the beaten track. Bear in mind that roads in remote regions are often poorly maintained. You'll need a good road map.

You can bring a vehicle into Greece for four months without a carnet – if you have a Green Card (international third-party insurance).

Average prices for fuel are €0.70 to €0.82 per litre for super, €0.68 to €0.80 for unleaded and €0.65 to €0.75 for diesel.

Most islands are served by car ferries. Sample fares for small cars from Piraeus include €65 to Crete and €78 to Rhodes.

The Greek automobile club, ELPA, offers reciprocal services to members of other national motoring associations. If your vehicle breaks down, dial ☎ 104.

Road Rules

Greek motorists are famous for ignoring the road rules, which is probably why the country has one of the highest road-fatality rates in Europe. No casual observer would ever guess that it is compulsory to wear seat belts in the front seats of vehicles, nor that it is compulsory to wear a crash helmet on motorcycles of more than 50cc – always insist on a helmet when renting a motorcycle.

The speed limit for cars is 120km/h on toll roads, 90km/h outside built-up areas and 50km/h in built-up areas. For motorcycles, the speed limit outside built-up areas is 70km/h. Speeding fines start at €60.

GREECE

Drink-driving laws are strict; a blood alcohol content of 0.05% incurs a penalty and over 0.08% is a criminal offence.

Rental

Car hire is expensive, especially from the multinational hire companies. High-season weekly rates with unlimited mileage start at about €380 for the smallest models, dropping to €300 in winter – and that's without tax and extras.

You can generally do much better with local companies. Their advertised rates are about 25% lower and they're often willing to bargain.

Mopeds, however, are cheap and available everywhere. Most places charge about €15 per day.

Warning If you plan to hire a motorcycle or moped, check that your travel insurance does cover you for injury resulting from motorcycle accidents. Many policies don't.

Lonely Planet receives a lot of letters complaining about companies hiring out poorly maintained machines. Most insurance policies won't pay out for injuries caused by defective machines.

BICYCLE

Cycling is becoming a popular way to visit Greece. Bicycles are an ideal way to explore some of the larger islands, and are carried free on ferries. The Peloponnese is another favourite destination, but you need strong leg muscles to tackle some of the mountainous terrain.

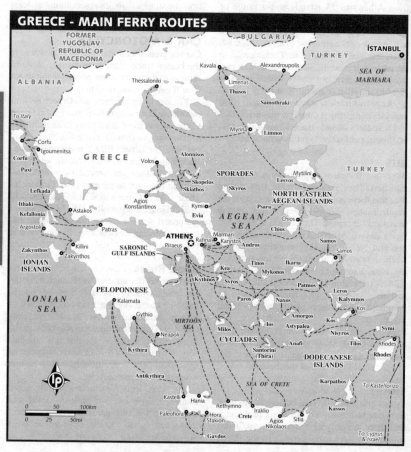

GREECE - MAIN FERRY ROUTES

You can hire bicycles, but they are not nearly as widely available as cars and motorcycles. Prices range from about €5 to €15, depending on the age and style of bike and the location.

HITCHING

The further you are from a city, the easier hitching becomes. Getting out of major cities can be hard work, and Athens is notoriously difficult. In remote areas, people may stop to offer a lift even if you aren't hitching.

BOAT
Ferry

Every island has a ferry service of some sort. They come in all shapes and sizes, from the state-of-the-art 'superferries' that run on the major routes to the ageing open ferries that operate local services to outlying islands.

The hub of the vast ferry network is Piraeus, the main port of Athens. It has ferries to the Cyclades, Crete, the Dodecanese, the Saronic Gulf Islands and the northeastern Aegean Islands. Patras is the main port for ferries to the Ionian Islands, while Volos and Agios Konstantinos are the ports for the group of islands called Sporades.

Some of the smaller islands are virtually inaccessible during winter, when schedules are cut back to a minimum. Services start to pick up in April and are running at full steam from June to September.

Fares are fixed by the government. The small differences in price you may find between ticket agencies are the result of some agencies sacrificing part of their designated commission to qualify as a 'discount service'. The discount offered seldom amounts to much. Tickets can be bought at the last minute from quayside tables set up next to the boats. Prices are the same, contrary to what you will be told by agencies.

When buying your ticket, unless you specify otherwise, you will automatically be sold deck class, which is the cheapest fare. Sample fares from Piraeus include €17.30 to Mykonos and €21 to Santorini (Thira).

Hydrofoil

Hydrofoils offer a faster alternative to ferries on some routes, particularly to islands close to the mainland. They take half the time, but cost twice as much. Most routes operate only during high season.

Catamaran

High-speed catamarans have become an important part of the island travel scene. They are just as fast as hydrofoils, if not faster, and are much more comfortable. They are also much less prone to cancellation in rough weather.

Yacht

It's hardly a budget option, but *the* way to see the islands is by yacht. There are many places to hire boats, both with and without a crew. If you want to go it alone, two crew members must have sailing certificates. Prices start at about US$1500 per week for a four-person boat. A skipper is an extra US$800 per week.

LOCAL TRANSPORT

You'll find taxis almost everywhere. Flag fall is €0.75, followed by €0.23 per kilometre in towns and €0.46 per kilometre outside towns. The rate doubles from midnight to 5am. There's a surcharge of €0.90 from airports and €0.60 from ports, bus stations and train stations. Luggage is €0.30 per item over 10kg.

Taxis in Athens and Thessaloniki often pick up extra passengers along the way (yell out your destination as they cruise by; when you get out, pay what's on the meter, minus what it read when you got in, plus €0.75).

In rural areas taxis don't have meters, so make sure you agree on a price with the driver before you get in.

ORGANISED TOURS

Greece has many companies which operate guided tours, predominantly on the mainland, but also on larger islands. The major operators include CHAT, Key Tours and GO Tours, which are all based in Athens. It is cheaper to travel independently – tours are only worthwhile if you have extremely limited time.

STREET NAMES

Odos means street, *plateia* means square and *leoforos* means avenue. These words are often omitted on maps and other references, so we have done the same throughout this chapter, except when to do so would cause confusion.

Athens Αθήνα

☎ 21 • pop 3.7 million

Ancient Athens ranks alongside Rome and Jerusalem for its glorious past and its influence

ATHENS

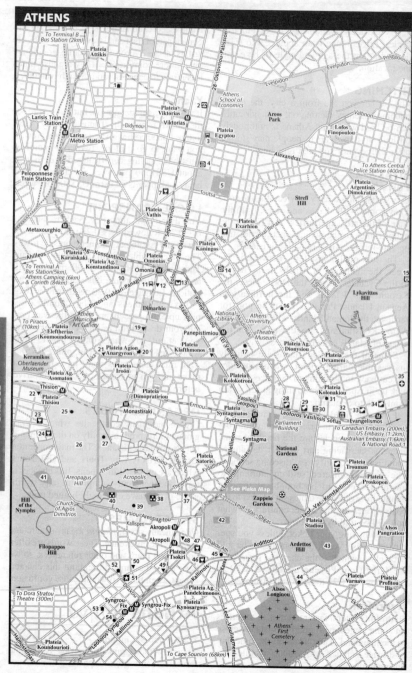

GREECE

ATHENS

PLACES TO STAY
1 Hostel Aphrodite
8 Athens International Youth Hostel
20 Hotel Cecil
52 Art Gallery Hotel
53 Marble House Pension

PLACES TO EAT
12 Marinopoulos (Supermarket)
18 Vasilopoulou (Supermarket)
19 Fruit & Vegetable Market
21 Embros
22 To Steki tou Elia
37 Daphne Restaurant
48 Oinomageireion ton Theon
49 To 24 Hours
50 Veropoulos (Supermarket)

OTHER
2 OTE Main Office
3 Mavromateon Bus Terminal
4 Museum Internet Café
5 National Archaeological Museum
6 AN Club
7 Rodon Club
9 OSE Office
10 Bus No 051 to Bus Terminal A
11 Bus No 049 to Piraeus
13 Athens' Central Post Office
14 Bits and Bytes Internet Café
15 Lykavittos Theatre
16 Hellenic American Union
17 OSE Office
23 Stavlos
24 To Lizard
25 Temple of Hephaestus
26 Ancient Agora
27 Church of the Holy Apostles
28 French Embassy
29 Italian Embassy
30 Benaki Museum
31 British Council
32 Goulandris Museum of Cycladic & Ancient Greek Art
33 German Embassy
34 British Embassy
35 Evangelismos Hospital
36 Turkish Embassy
38 Theatre of Dionysos
39 Stoa of Eumenes
40 Theatre of Herodes Atticus
41 Hill of the Pnyx Theatre
42 Temple of Olympian Zeus
43 Roman Stadium
44 Athens Centre
45 Key Tours Office & Terminal
46 Granazi Bar
47 Lamda Club
51 Tourist Police
54 Olympic Airways Head Office

on Western civilisation, but the modern city is a place that few people fall in love with.

However inspiring the Acropolis might be, most visitors have trouble coming to terms with the surrounding urban sprawl, the appalling traffic congestion and the pollution. Most stop no longer than is required to take in the two main attractions: the Acropolis and the treasures of the National Archaeological Museum.

The city's well-publicised deficiencies are coming under the spotlight as never before as it struggles to prepare to host the 2004 Olympic Games. Progress has been exasperatingly slow, and some major public works projects have been scaled back before leaving the drawing board. The International Olympic Committee, however, remains publicly optimistic that preparations are almost on track.

Culturally, Athens is a fascinating blend of East and West. King Otho and the middle class that emerged after independence may have been intent on making Athens a European city, but the influence of Asia Minor is everywhere – the coffee, the kebabs, the raucous street vendors and the colourful markets.

ORIENTATION

Although Athens is a huge, sprawling city, nearly everything of interest to travellers is located within a small area bounded by Omonia Square (Plateia Omonias) to the north, Monastiraki Square (Plateia Monastirakiou) to the west, Syntagma Square (Plateia Syntagmatos) to the east and the Plaka district to the south. The city's two major landmarks, the Acropolis and Lykavittos Hill, can be seen from just about everywhere in this area.

Syntagma is the heart of modern Athens. Flanked by luxury hotels, banks and fast-food restaurants, the square is dominated by the old royal palace – home of the Greek parliament since 1935.

Omonia has developed a sorry reputation for sleaze in recent years, but this is set to change with the announcement of plan to transform Plateia Omonias from a traffic hub into an expanse of formal gardens. This is guaranteed to create traffic chaos, since all the major streets of central Athens meet here. Panepistimiou (El Venizelou) and Stadiou run parallel southeast to Syntagma, while Athinas leads south to the market district of Monastiraki. Monastiraki is in turn linked to Syntagma by Ermou – home to some of the city's smartest shops – and Mitropoleos.

Mitropoleos skirts the northern edge of Plaka, the delightful old quarter which was virtually all that existed when Athens was declared the capital of independent Greece. Its labyrinthine streets are nestled on the northeastern slope of the Acropolis, and most of the city's ancient sites are close by. It may be touristy, but it's the most attractive and interesting part of Athens and the majority of visitors make it their base.

Streets are clearly signposted in Greek and English. If you do get lost, it's very easy to find help. A glance at a map is often enough to draw an offer of assistance. Anyone you ask will be able to direct you to Syntagma (say **syn**-tag-ma).

INFORMATION
Tourist Offices
Athens' main **EOT tourist office** (☎ 21 0331 0561/0562, fax 21 0325 2895; e info@ gnto.gr; Amerikis 2; open 9am-4pm Mon-Fri) is close to Syntagma. It has a useful free map of Athens, as well as information about public transport in Athens, including ferry departures from Piraeus.

The airport also has an **EOT office** (☎ 21 0353 0445; open 9am-7pm daily).

The **tourist police** (☎ 21 0920 0724; Veikou 43, Koukaki; trolleybus No 1, 5 or 9 from Syntagma; open 24hrs) also has a 24-hour **information service** (☎ 171).

Money
Most of the major banks have branches around Syntagma, which are open from 8am to 2pm Monday to Thursday and 8am to 1.30pm Friday. The **National Bank of Greece** (cnr Karageorgi Servias & Stadiou) is open extended hours for foreign-exchange dealings only: 3.30pm to 6.30pm Monday to Thursday; 3pm to 6.30pm on Friday; 9am to 3pm on Saturday; and 9am to 1pm on Sunday. It also has an ATM.

For money exchange try **American Express** (AmEx; ☎ 21 0324 4975; Ermou 2) or **Eurochange** (☎ 21 0322 0155; Karageorgi Servias 4), which has an office nearby. It changes Thomas Cook travellers cheques without commission.

Acropole Foreign Exchange (Kydathineon 23; open 9am-midnight daily) is in Plaka. The banks at the airport are open from 7am to 9pm. The airport also has several ATMs.

Post & Communications
Athens Central Post Office (Eolou 100, Omonia) is where mail addressed to poste restante will be sent unless specified otherwise; its postcode is 102 00. If you're staying in Plaka, it's best to get mail sent to the Syntagma post office (postcode 103 00) on the corner of Plateia Syntagmatos and Mitropoleos. Both are open 7.30am to 8pm

Monday to Friday, 7.30am to 2pm Saturday, and 9am to 1.30pm Sunday. Parcels over 2kg going abroad must be posted from the **parcels office** (Stadiou 4) in the arcade. They should not be wrapped until they've first been inspected.

The city's main **OTE telephone office** (28 Oktovriou-Patission 85) is open 24 hours.

Email & Internet Access
Internet cafés are popping up like mushrooms all over Athens. Most charge from €4 to €6 per hour of computer time, whether you log on or not. They include:

Bits and Bytes Internet Café Akadimias 78, Exarhia; open 24 hours
Museum Internet Café Oktovriou-Patission 46, Omonia (next to the National Archaeological Museum); open 9am to 3am daily
Plaka Internet World Pandrosou 29, Monastiraki; open 11am to 11pm daily
Skynet Internet Centre Cnr Voulis & Apollonos, Plaka; open 9am to 11pm Monday to Saturday
Sofokleous.com Internet Café Stadiou 5, Syntagma (behind Flocafé); open 10am to 10pm Monday to Saturday, 1pm to 9pm Sunday

Travel Agencies
The bulk of the city's travel agencies are around Plateia Syntagmatos, particularly in the area just south of the square on Filellinon, Nikis and Voulis.

Reputable agencies include **STA Travel** (☎ 21 0321 1188, 21 0321 1194; e statravel@robissa.gr; Voulis 43) and **USIT-Etos Travel** (☎ 21 0324 0483, fax 21 0322 8447; e usit@usitetos.gr; Filellinon 7). Both these places also issue ISIC cards.

Bookshops
There are several good English-language bookshops around the city centre. The biggest, with two branches, is **Eleftheroudakis Books** (Panepistimiou 17 • Nikis 20). Others include **Pantelides Books** (Amerikis 11), and **Compendium Books** (Nikis 28). Compendium also has a second-hand books section.

Cultural Centres
The **British Council** (☎ 21 0369 2314; Plateia Kolonakiou 17) and the **Hellenic American Union** (☎ 21 0362 9886; Massalias 22) hold frequent concerts, film shows, exhibitions and the like. Both also have libraries.

Laundry
Plaka has a convenient **laundrette** *(Angelou Geronta 10)*, just off Kydathineon, near the outdoor restaurants.

Medical & Emergency Services
For emergency medical treatment, ring the **tourist police** *(☎ 171)* and they'll tell you where the nearest hospital is. Hospitals give free emergency treatment to tourists. For hospitals with outpatient departments on duty, call ☎ 106. For first-aid advice, ring ☎ 166. You can get free dental treatment at the **Evangelismos Hospital** *(Ipsilandou 45)*.

Dangers & Annoyances
Athens has its share of petty crime.

Pickpockets A major problem in Athens are pickpockets. Their favourite hunting grounds are the metro system and the crowded streets around Omonia, particularly Athinas. The Sunday market on Ermou is another place where it pays to take extra care of your valuables.

Taxi Touts Working in league with some overpriced C-class hotels around Omonia, some taxi drivers have become a problem. The scam involves taxi drivers picking up late-night arrivals, particularly at the airport and Bus Terminal A, and persuading them that the hotel they want to go to is full. The taxi driver will pretend to phone the hotel of choice, announce that it's full and suggest an alternative. You can ask to speak to your chosen hotel yourself, or insist on going where you want.

Bar Scams Lonely Planet receives a steady flow of letters warning about bar scams, particularly around Syntagma. The most popular version runs something like this: friendly Greek approaches solo male traveller and discovers that the traveller knows little about Athens; friendly Greek then reveals that he, too, is from out of town. Why don't they go to this great little bar that he's just discovered and have a beer? They order a drink, and the equally friendly owner then offers another drink. Women appear, more drinks are provided and the visitor relaxes as he realises that the women are not prostitutes, just friendly Greeks. The crunch comes at the end of the evening when the traveller is presented with an exorbitant bill and the smiles disappear. The con men who cruise the streets playing the role of the friendly Greek can be very convincing – some people have been taken in more than once.

ACROPOLIS
Most of the buildings now gracing the Acropolis *(combined site & museum admission €12; site open 8am-6.30pm daily, museum open 8am-6.30pm Tues-Sun, noon-6.30pm Apr-Oct; site & museum open 8am-2.30pm daily Nov-Mar)* were commissioned by Pericles during the golden age of Athens in the 5th century BC. The site had been cleared for him by the Persians, who destroyed an earlier temple complex on the eve of the Battle of Salamis.

The entrance to the Acropolis is through the **Beule Gate**, a Roman arch that was added in the 3rd century AD. Beyond this is the **Propylaia**, the monumental gate that was the entrance to the city in ancient times. It was damaged by Venetian bombing in the 17th century, but it has since been restored. To the south of the Propylaia is the small, graceful **Temple of Athena Nike**, which is not accessible to visitors.

Standing supreme over the Acropolis is the monument which more than any other epitomises the glory of ancient Greece – the **Parthenon**. Completed in 438 BC, this building is unsurpassed in grace and harmony. To achieve perfect form, its lines were ingeniously curved to counteract unharmonious optical illusions. The base curves upward slightly towards the ends, and the columns become slightly narrower towards the top, with the overall effect of making them both look straight.

Above the columns are the remains of a Doric frieze, which was partly destroyed by Venetian shelling in 1687. The best surviving pieces are the controversial Elgin Marbles,

Admission

The €12 admission charge buys a collective ticket that also gives entry to all the other significant ancient sites: the Ancient Agora, the Roman Agora, the Keramikos, the Temple of Olympian Zeus and the Theatre of Dionysos. The ticket is valid for 48 hours, otherwise individual site fees apply.

GREECE

carted off to Britain by Lord Elgin in 1801. The Parthenon, dedicated to Athena, contained an 11m-tall gold-and-ivory statue of the goddess completed in 438 BC by Phidias of Athens (only the statue's foundations exist today).

To the north is the **Erechtheion** and its much-photographed Caryatids, the six maidens who support its southern portico. These are plaster casts – the originals (except for the one taken by Lord Elgin) are in the site's **museum**.

SOUTH OF THE ACROPOLIS

The importance of theatre in the life of the Athenian city-state can be gauged from the dimensions of the enormous **Theatre of Dionysos** (entrance: Dionysiou Areopagitou; admission €2; open 8am-7pm Tues-Fri, 8.30am-3pm Sat-Sun Apr-Oct, 8.30am-3pm daily Nov-Mar), just south of the Acropolis. Built between 342 and 326 BC on the site of an earlier theatre, in its time it could hold 17,000 people spread over 64 tiers of seats, of which about 20 tiers survive.

The **Stoa of Eumenes**, built as a shelter and promenade for theatre audiences, runs west from the Theatre of Dionysos to the **Theatre of Herodes Atticus**, which was built in Roman times. It is used for performances during the Athens Festival, but is closed at other times.

TEMPLE OF OLYMPIAN ZEUS

Begun in the 6th century BC, this massive temple (admission €2; open 8.30am-3pm Tues-Sun) took more than 700 years to complete. Emperor Hadrian eventually finished the job in AD 131. It was the largest temple in Greece, impressive for the sheer size of its 104 **Corinthian columns** (17m high with a base diameter of 1.7m). The site is just southeast of Plaka, and the 15 remaining columns are a useful landmark.

ROMAN STADIUM

The stadium, east of the Temple of Olympian Zeus, hosted the first Olympic Games of modern times in 1896. It was originally built in the 4th century BC as a venue for the Panathenaic athletic contests. The seats were rebuilt in Pentelic marble by Herodes Atticus in the 2nd century AD, and faithfully restored in 1895.

ANCIENT AGORA

The agora (admission €4; open 8am-7pm daily Apr-Oct, 8.30am-3pm Tues-Sun Nov-Mar) was the marketplace of ancient Athens and the focal point of civic and social life. Socrates spent much time here expounding his philosophy. The main monuments are the well-preserved **Temple of Hephaestus**, the 11th-century **Church of the Holy Apostles** and the reconstructed **Stoa of Attalos**, which houses the site's museum.

ROMAN AGORA

The Romans built their agora (admission €2; open 8.30am-2.30pm Tues-Sun) just west of its ancient counterpart. Its principle monument is the wonderful **Tower of the Winds**, built in the 1st century BC by a Syrian astronomer named Andronicus. Each side represents a point of the compass, and has a relief carving depicting the associated wind.

MUSEUMS

Athens has no less than 28 museums, displaying everything from ancient treasures to old theatre props. You'll find a complete list at the tourist office. These are the highlights:

National Archaeological Museum

This is the undoubted star of the show – the most important museum (28 Oktovriou-Patission 44; admission €6; open 12.30pm-7pm Mon, 8am-7pm Tues-Sun Apr-Oct, 10.30am-5pm Mon, 8.30am-3pm Tues-Sun Nov-Mar) in Greece, with finds from all the major sites. The crowd-pullers are the magnificent, exquisitely detailed gold artefacts from Mycenae and spectacular Minoan frescoes from Santorini (Thira), which are here until a suitable museum is built on the island.

Benaki Museum

This museum (cnr Vasilissis Sofias & Koumbari; admission €5.90; open 9am-5pm Mon, Wed, Fri & Sat, 9am-midnight Thur, 9am-3pm Sun) houses the collection of Antoine Benaki, the son of an Alexandrian cotton magnate named Emmanual Benaki. The collection includes ancient sculpture, Persian, Byzantine and Coptic objects, Chinese ceramics, icons, two El Greco paintings and a superb collection of traditional costumes.

Goulandris Museum of Cycladic & Ancient Greek Art

This private museum (Neofytou Douka 4; admission €2.95; open 10am-4pm Mon &

GREECE

Wed-Fri, 10am-3pm Sat) was custom-built to display a fabulous collection of Cycladic art, with an emphasis on the early Bronze Age. Particularly impressive are the beautiful marble figurines. These simple, elegant forms, mostly of naked women with arms folded under their breasts, inspired 20th-century artists such as Brancusi, Epstein, Modigliani and Picasso.

LYKAVITTOS HILL
Pine-covered Lykavittos is the highest of the eight hills dotted around Athens. From the summit there are all-embracing views of the city, the Attic basin and the islands of Salamis and Aegina – pollution permitting of course.

The open-air Lykavittos Theatre, northeast of the summit, is used for concerts in summer.

The southern side of the hill is occupied by the posh residential suburb of Kolonaki. The main path to the summit starts at the top of Loukianou, or you can take the funicular railway from the top of Ploutarhou (€2/4 single/return, 9.15am to 11.45pm daily).

CHANGING OF THE GUARD
Every Sunday at 11am a platoon of traditionally costumed *evzones* (guards), accompanied by a band, marches down Vasilissis Sofias to the Tomb of the Unknown Soldier located in front of the parliament building on Syntagma.

LANGUAGE COURSES
Try the **Athens Centre** (☎ 21 0701 2268, fax 21 0701 8603; e athenscr@compulink.gr; w www.athenscentre.gr; Arhimidous 48, Mets), or the **Hellenic American Union** (☎ 21 0362 9886, fax 21 0363 3174; e vioannou@hau.gr; w www.hau.gr; Massalias 22, Kolonaki) for language courses.

ORGANISED TOURS
Hop In Sightseeing (☎ 21 0428 5500; Zanni 29, Piraeus), **Key Tours** (☎ 21 0923 3166; Kallirois 4); **CHAT Tours** (☎ 21 0322 3137; Stadiou 4); and **GO Tours** (☎ 21 0322 5951; Voulis 31-33) are the main organised-tour operators – you'll see their brochures everywhere, offering similar tours and prices. They include a half-day sightseeing tour of Athens (€29.35), which does nothing more than point out all the major sights, and Athens by Night (€40), which takes in a *son et lumière*

(sound-and-light show) before taking in a taverna dinner with folk dancing.

Every hotel mentioned later in the Places to Stay section handles bookings for at least one of the tour companies. Some offer substantial discounts for hotel clients. You will be told of your pick-up point when you book.

HELLENIC FESTIVAL
The annual Hellenic Festival is the city's most important cultural event, running from mid-June to late September. It features a line-up of international music, dance and theatre at the Theatre of Herodes Atticus. The setting is superb, backed by the floodlit Acropolis. Information and tickets are available from the **Athens Festival Box Office** *(Stadiou 4)*. You'll find details of events on the Internet at w www.greekfestival.gr.

PLACES TO STAY
Camping
The closest camping ground is **Athens Camping** (☎ 21 0581 4114, fax 21 0582 0353; Athinon 198), 7km west of the city centre on the road to Corinth. There are several camping grounds southeast of Athens on the coast road to Cape Sounion.

Hostels
There are a few places around town making a pitch for the hostelling market by tagging 'youth hostel' onto their name. There are some dreadful dumps among them.

There is only one youth hostel worth knowing about, the excellent HI-affiliated **Athens International Youth Hostel** (☎ 523 4170, fax 523 4015; e info2002yh@yahoo.com; Victor Hugo 16; dorm beds HI members €8.40). Location is the only drawback, otherwise the place is almost too good to be true. The spotless rooms, each with bathroom, sleep two to four people. You need to become a HI member to stay here; if you're not a member the joining fee is €12.35, or it's €2.05 for a daily stamp.

Hotels
Athens is a noisy city and Athenians keep late hours, so an effort has been made to select hotels in quiet areas. Plaka is the most popular place to stay, and it has a good choice of accommodation right across the price spectrum. Rooms fill up quickly during July and August, so it's wise to make a reservation.

Plaka Most backpackers head to the **Student & Travellers' Inn** (☎ 21 0324 4808, fax 21 0321 0065; e students-inn@ath.forth net.gr; Kydathineon 16; dorm beds €18, singles/doubles with shared bathroom €32/42, singles/doubles with private bathroom €36/52). Facilities include a courtyard with big-screen TV, Internet access and a travel service.

Festos Youth & Student Guest House (☎ 21 0323 2455, fax 21 0321 0907; e con solas@hol.gr; Filellinon 18) is the main budget alternative.

Plaka also has some good mid-range accommodation.

Acropolis House Pension (☎ 21 0322 2344, fax 21 0322 6241; Kodrou 6-8; singles/doubles with bathroom from €49.50/66) occupies a beautifully preserved 19th-century house.

Hotel Adonis (☎ 21 0324 9737, fax 21 0323 1602; Kodrou 3; singles/doubles from €39/55.70), opposite the Acropolis House Pension, is a comfortable modern hotel with air-con rooms. It has good views of the Acropolis from the 4th-floor rooms and from the rooftop bar.

Monastiraki The friendly and family-run **Hotel Tempi** (☎ 21 0321 3175, fax 21 0325 4179; e tempihotel@travelling.gr; Eolou 29; singles with shared bathroom €28, doubles/triples with private bathroom €42/50) is a quiet place on the pedestrian precinct part of Eolou. Rooms at the front overlook a small square with a church and a flower market. It has a small communal kitchen where guests can prepare breakfast.

Hotel Cecil (☎ 21 0321 7909, fax 21 0321 8005; e cecil@netsmart.gr; Athinas 39; singles/doubles with bathroom €50/70.50) occupies a fine old classical building with beautiful high, moulded ceilings. It looks immaculate after a complete refit, and rates include breakfast.

Koukaki It isn't exactly backpacker territory, but **Marble House Pension** (☎ 21 0923 4058, fax 21 0922 6461; Zini 35A; singles/doubles without bathroom €27/35; singles/doubles with bathroom €32/41), on a quiet cul-de-sac off Zini, is one of Athens' better budget hotels. All rooms have a bar fridge, ceiling fans and safety boxes for valuables, and air-con is available.

Art Gallery Hotel (☎ 21 0923 8376, fax 21 0923 3025; e ecotec@otenet.gr; Erehthiou 5; singles/doubles/triples with bathroom €58.60/70.40/84.50) is a friendly place that's always brimming with fresh flowers.

Omonia Area There are dozens of hotels around Omonia, but most of them are either bordellos masquerading as cheap hotels or are uninspiring, overpriced C-class places.

Hostel Aphrodite (☎ 21 0881 0589, fax 21 0881 6574; e hostel-aphrodite@ath .forthnet.gr; Einardou 12; dorm beds €17, singles/doubles/triples with shared bathroom €30/40/54; singles/doubles with private bathroom €32/42) is a fair way north of Omonia, but it's only 10 minutes from the train stations. It offers Internet access and there's a bar.

PLACES TO EAT
Plaka

For most people, Plaka is the place to be. It's hard to beat the atmosphere of dining out beneath the floodlit Acropolis. You do, however, pay for the privilege – particularly at the many outdoor restaurants around the square on Kydathineon. The best of this bunch is **Byzantino** (☎ 21 0322 7368; Kydathineon 20; mains €3.50-12), which prices its menu more reasonably and is popular with Greek family groups.

Eden Vegetarian Restaurant (☎ 21 0324 8858; Lyssiou 12; mains €8-12; open Wed-Mon) is one of only two vegie restaurants, which are thin on the ground in Athens. The Eden has been around for years, substituting soya products for meat in tasty vegetarian versions of mousakas and some other Greek favourites.

Daphne Restaurant (☎ 21 0322 7971; Lysikratous 4; meals around €30; open from 7pm nightly) is the place to head for a real treat. It's an exquisitely restored 1830s neo-classical mansion decorated with frescoes from Greek mythology. The menu includes regional specialties, such as rabbit cooked in mavrodaphne wine.

South of the Acropolis

Oinomageireion ton Theon (☎ 21 0924 3721; Makrigianni 23-27; mains €4-9) is a new place just five minutes' walk from Plaka. It's got a great selection of meze, priced from €2, as well as tasty versions of favourites such

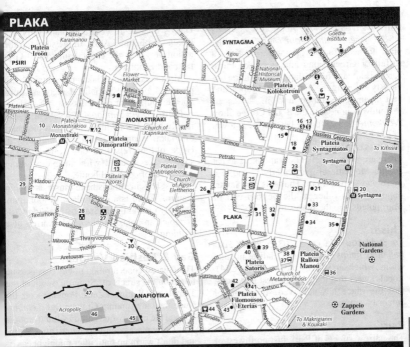

PLAKA

PLAKA

PLACES TO STAY
- 9 Hotel Tempi
- 38 Festos Youth & Student Guest House
- 39 Hotel Adonis
- 40 Acropolis House Pension
- 42 Student & Travellers' Inn

PLACES TO EAT
- 7 Brazil Coffee Shop
- 11 Thanasis
- 12 Savas
- 24 Furin Kazan Japanese Fast-Food Restaurant
- 30 Eden Vegetarian Restaurant

OTHER
- 1 Bank of Greece
- 2 Eleftheroudakis Books
- 3 Pantelides Books
- 4 EOT Main Tourist Office
- 5 Athens Festival Box Office
- 6 Parcels Office
- 8 Sofokleous.com Internet Café
- 10 Athens Flea Market
- 13 Plaka Internet World
- 14 Athens Cathedral
- 15 Eleftheroudakis Books
- 16 Eurochange
- 17 National Bank of Greece
- 18 American Express
- 19 Parliament Building
- 20 Bus E95 to Airport
- 21 USIT-Etos Travel
- 22 Bus No 040 to Piraeus
- 23 Syntagma Post Office
- 25 Skynet Internet Centre
- 26 National Welfare Organisation Shop
- 27 Tower of the Winds
- 28 Roman Agora
- 29 Stoa of Attalos
- 31 STA Travel
- 32 Compendium Books
- 33 Trekking Hellas
- 34 Olympic Airways Branch Office
- 35 CHAT Tours Terminal
- 36 Bus No 024 to Bus Terminal B
- 37 Trolley-bus Stop for Plaka
- 41 Acropole Foreign Exchange
- 43 Laundrette
- 44 Brettos
- 45 Acropolis Museum
- 46 Parthenon
- 47 Erechtheion

GREECE

as beef *stifado* and *mousakas*. There are good views of the Acropolis from the window seats.

To 24 Hours (☎ 21 0922 2749; *Syngrou 44; mains €4-6.50*) is a great favourite with Athenian night owls. As the name suggests, it's open 24 hours. It calls itself a *patsadiko*, which means that it specialises in *patsas* (tripe soup), but it always has a wide selection of taverna dishes.

Syntagma

Fast food is the order of the day around busy Syntagma with an assortment of Greek and international offerings.

Furin Kazan Japanese Fast-Food Restaurant (☎ 21 0322 9170; Apollonos 2; mains €5-16; open 11am-11pm Mon-Sat) is the place to head for anyone suffering from a surfeit of Greek salad and souvlaki. Furin Kazan is always full of Japanese visitors, obviously enjoying the food at the cheapest and best Japanese restaurant in town.

Follow your nose to the **Brazil Coffee Shop** (Voukourestiou 2) for the best coffee in town.

Monastiraki

There are some excellent cheap places to eat around Monastiraki, particularly if you're a gyros and souvlaki fan. **Thanasis** and **Savas**, opposite each other at the bottom end of Mitropoleos, are the places to go.

Thisio

To Steki tou Elia (☎ 21 0345 8052; Epahalkou 5; mains €4.50-6) specialises in lamb chops, which are sold by the kilogram (€14). Locals swear that they are the best in Athens, and the place has achieved some sort of celebrity status.

Psiri

The narrow streets of Psiri, just northwest of Monastiraki, are now dotted with numerous trendy ouzeris, tavernas and music bars, particularly the central area between Plateia Agion Anargyron and Plateia Iroön.

Embros (☎ 21 0321 3285; Plateia Agion Anargyron 4; meze €3.50-12) is a popular spot to try with seating in the square and a choice of about 20 mezedes.

Self-Catering

The following are among the main **supermarkets** in central Athens:

Marinopoulos Athinas 60, Omonia • Kanari 9, Kolonaki
Vasilopoulou Stadiou 19, Syntagma
Veropoulos Parthenos 6, Koukaki

You'll find the best selection of fresh produce at the **fruit and vegetable market** on Athinas.

ENTERTAINMENT

The weekly Athens News carries a 16-page entertainment guide listing weekly events, while the Kathimerini supplement that accompanies the International Herald Tribune has daily listings.

Discos & Bars

Discos operate in central Athens only between October and April. In the summer, the action moves to the coastal suburbs of Glyfada and Ellinikon.

Most bars around Plaka and Syntagma are places to avoid, especially if there are guys outside touting for customers.

Brettos (Kydathineon 41), a delightful, old family-run place, which is right in the heart of Plaka, is one bar that's recommended. Huge old barrels line one wall, and the shelves are stocked with an eye-catching collection of coloured bottles.

Most bars in Athens have music as a main feature. Thisio is a good place to look, particularly on Iraklidon. **Stavlos** (Iraklidon 10) occupies an amazing old rabbit warren of a building.

Gay & Lesbian Venues

The greatest concentration of gay bars is to be found on the streets off Syngrou, south of the Temple of Olympian Zeus. Popular spots include the long-running **Granazi Bar** (Lembesi 20) and the more risqué **Lamda Club** (Lembesi 15). These places don't open until after 10pm, and don't warm up until after midnight.

To Lizard (Apostolou Pavlou 31), in Thisio, is a party venue which operates Friday to Sunday nights from 11pm. The crowd is mostly lesbian, with a few gays and the occasional straight.

Rock & Jazz

Rodon Club (Marni 24), north of Omonia, hosts touring international rock bands, while local bands play at the **AN Club** (Solomou 20, Exarhia).

Folk Dancing

Dora Stratou Dance Company (☎ 21 0921 6650; tickets €11.75) performs at its theatre on Filopappos Hill at 10.15pm every night from mid-May to October, with additional performances at 8.15pm on Wednesday. Filopappos Hill is west of the Acropolis, off Dionysiou Areopagitou. Bus No 230 from Syntagma will get you there.

Sound-&-Light Show

Athens' endeavour at this spectacle is not one of the world's best. There are shows in English every night at 9pm from April to October at the theatre on the **Hill of the Pnyx**

Domed church, Santorini, Greece

Softly hued Venetian buildings and a waterfront location, Hania, Crete

The Doric columns and entablature of the Tholos at Delphi, Greece

Rembetika rhythms, Athens

OK, who's got the pump? Tour group in historic Munich, Germany.

The handiwork of frisky Finn McCool – Giant's Causeway, County Antrim, Northern Ireland

Brightly painted houses in a village on the 'Ring of Beara', County Cork, Ireland

Picnic on an alpine plain, Umbria, Italy

Magnificent Cinque Terre coastline, Liguria, Italy

Part of the spectacular Dolomites, Italy

☎ 21 0322 1459; tickets €8.80). The Hill of the Pnyx is opposite Filopappos Hill, and the show is timed so that you can cross straight to the folk dancing.

SPECTATOR SPORTS

Almost half of the 18 soccer teams in the Greek first division are based in Athens or Piraeus. The most popular are Panathinaikos (Athens) and Olympiakos (Piraeus).

SHOPPING

The **National Welfare Organisation shop** (cnr Apollonos & Ipatias, Plaka) is a good place to go shopping for handicrafts. It has top-quality goods and the money goes to a good cause – the organisation was formed to preserve and promote traditional Greek crafts.

For some serious bargaining, check out the famous **Flea Market**, west of Monastiraki metro station.

GETTING THERE & AWAY

Air

Athens is served by Eleftherios Venizelos International Airport at Spata, 27km east of Athens.

Facilities at the new airport, named in honour of the country's leading 20th-century politician, are immeasurably better than at the city's former airport at Ellinikon. Where Ellinikon was shabby and outdated, the new airport gleams. Built by a German consortium, everything is absolutely state of the art. It also has good selection of cafés, and some very reasonably priced eating places.

For Olympic Airways flight information ring ☎ 21 0936 3363; for all other airlines ring ☎ 21 0969 4466/4467. The head office of **Olympic Airways** (☎ 21 0926 7251/4) is at Leoforos Syngrou Andrea 96. The most central **Olympic Airways branch office** (☎ 21 0926 7444, international ☎ 21 0926 7489) is at Filellinon 13, just off Plateia Syntagmatos.

Bus

Athens has two main intercity bus stations. EOT gives out schedules for both stations detailing departure times, journey times and fares.

Terminal A (Kifissou 100), northwest of Omonia, has departures to the Peloponnese, the Ionian Islands and western Greece. To get to Terminal A, take bus No 051 from the junction of Zinonos and Menandrou, near Plateia Omonia. Buses run every 15 minutes from 5am to midnight.

Terminal B (off Liossion) is north of Omonia and has departures to central and northern Greece, as well as to Evia. To get to Terminal B, take bus No 024 from outside the main gate of the National Gardens on Amalias. EOT misleadingly gives the terminal's address as Liossion 260, which turns out to be a small workshop. Liossion 260 is where you should get off the bus. Turn right onto Gousiou and you'll see the terminal at the end of the road.

Buses for Attica leave from the Mavromateon bus terminal at the junction of Alexandras and 28 Oktovriou-Patission.

Train

Athens has two train stations, about 200m apart on Deligianni, approximately 1km northwest of Omonia. Trains to the Peloponnese leave from the Peloponnese station, while trains to the north leave from Larisis station – as do all international services.

Services to the Peloponnese include eight trains to Patras, four of which are intercity express (€10, 3½ hours), while services north include 10 trains a day to Thessaloniki, five of which are intercity express (€27.60, six hours). The 7am service from Athens is express right through to Alexandroupolis, arriving at 7pm. There are also trains to Volos and Halkida in Evia. The easiest way to get to the stations is on metro Line 2 to Larisa, outside Larisis station. The Peloponnese station is across the footbridge at the southern end of Larisis station. Tickets can be bought at the stations, or at **OSE offices** (Sina 6 • Karolou 1).

Car & Motorcycle

National Rd 1 is the main route north from Athens. It starts at Nea Kifissia. To get there from central Athens, take Vasilissis Sofias from Syntagma and follow the signs. National Rd 8, which begins beyond Dafni, is the road to the Peloponnese; take Agiou Konstantinou from Omonia.

The northern reaches of Syngrou, just south of the Temple of Olympian Zeus, are packed solid with car-rental firms.

Hitching

Athens is the most difficult place in Greece to hitchhike from. Your best bet is to ask the truck drivers at the Piraeus cargo wharves. Otherwise, for the Peloponnese, take a bus from Panepistimiou to Dafni, where National Rd 8 begins. For northern Greece, take the metro to Kifissia, then a bus to Nea Kifissia and walk to National Rd 1.

Ferry

See Piraeus, later in this chapter, for information on ferries travelling to and from the islands.

GETTING AROUND
To/From the Airport

There are two special express-bus services operating between the airport and the city, as well as a service between the airport and Piraeus.

Bus service E94 operates between the airport and the eastern terminus of Metro Line 3 at Ethniki Amyna. According to the official timetable there are departures every 16 minutes between 6am and midnight. The journey takes about 25 minutes.

Service E95 operates between the airport and Plateia Syntagmatos. This line operates 24 hours a day with services approximately every 30 minutes. The bus stop is outside the National Gardens on Amalias on the eastern side of Plateia Syntagmatos. The journey takes between an hour and 90 minutes, depending on traffic conditions.

Service E96 operates between the airport and Plateia Karaïskaki in Piraeus. This line also operates 24 hours, with services approximately every 40 minutes.

Tickets for all these services cost €2.95. The tickets are valid for 24 hours, and can be used on all forms of public transport in Athens – buses, trolleybuses and the metro.

Taxi fares vary according to the time of day and level of traffic, but you should expect to pay €15 to €20 from the airport to the city centre, and €20 to €25 from the airport to Piraeus, depending on traffic conditions. Neither trip should take longer than an hour.

Bus & Trolleybus

Blue-and-white suburban buses operate from 5am to midnight. Route numbers and destinations, but not the actual routes, are listed on the free EOT map. The map does, however, mark the routes of the yellow trolleybuses, making them easy to use. They also run from 5am to midnight.

There are special buses that operate 24 hours a day to Piraeus. Bus No 040 leaves from the corner of Syntagma and Filellinon and No 049 leaves from the Omonia end of Athinas. The buses run every 20 minutes from 6am to midnight, and then hourly until 6am.

Tickets for all these services cost €0.45 and must be purchased before you board – either from a ticket booth or from a *periptero*. The same tickets can be used on either buses or trolleybuses and must be validated as soon as you board. The penalty for travelling without a validated ticket is €17.60.

Metro

The opening of the first phase of the long-awaited new metro system has transformed travel around central Athens. Coverage is still largely confined to the city centre, but that's good enough for most visitors. The following is a brief outline of the three lines that make up the network:

Line 1 This line is the old Kifissia–Piraeus line. Until the opening of lines 2 and 3, this was the metro system. It is indicated in green on maps and signs. Useful stops include Piraeus (for the port), Monastiraki and Omonia (city centre), Plateia Viktorias (National Archaeological Museum) and Irini (Olympic Stadium). Omonia and Attiki are transfer stations with connections to Line 2. Monastiraki will eventually become a transfer station with connections to Line 3.

Line 2 This line runs from Sepolia in the northwest to Dafni in the southeast. It is indicated in red on maps and signs. Useful stops include Larisa (for the train stations), Omonia, Panepistimiou and Syntagma (city centre) and Akropoli (Makrigianni). Attiki and Omonia are transfer stations for Line 1, while Syntagma is the transfer station for Line 3.

Line 3 This line runs northeast from Syntagma to Ethniki Amyna. It is indicated in blue on maps and signs. Useful stops are Evangelismos (for the museums on Vasilissis Sofias) and Ethniki Amyna (buses to the airport). Syntagma is the transfer station for Line 2.

Travel on lines 2 and 3 costs €0.75, while Line 1 is split into three sections: Piraeus–Monastiraki, Monastiraki–Attiki and Attiki–Kifissia. Travel within one section costs €0.60, and a journey covering two or more sections costs €0.75. The same conditions apply everywhere though: tickets must be validated at the machines at platform entrances before travelling. The penalty for travelling without a validated ticket is €23.50.

The metro operates from 5am to midnight. Trains run every three minutes during peak periods, and every 10 minutes at other times.

Taxi

Athenian taxis are yellow. The flag fall is €0.75, and there's an additional surcharge of €0.60 from ports and train and bus stations, as well as a €0.90 surcharge from the airport. After that, the day rate (tariff 1 on the meter) is €0.23/km. The rate doubles between midnight and 5am (tariff 2 on the meter). Baggage is charged at the rate of €0.30 per item over 10kg. The minimum fare is €1.50, which covers most journeys in central Athens.

Around Athens

PIRAEUS Πειραιάς

☎ 21 • pop 171,000

Piraeus has been the port of Athens since classical times. These days it's little more than an outer suburb of the space-hungry capital, linked by a mish-mash of factories, warehouses and apartment blocks. The streets are every bit as traffic-clogged as in Athens, and behind the veneer of banks and shipping offices most of Piraeus is pretty seedy. The only reason to come here is to catch a ferry or hydrofoil.

Orientation & Information

Piraeus consists of a peninsula surrounded by harbours. The most important of them is the

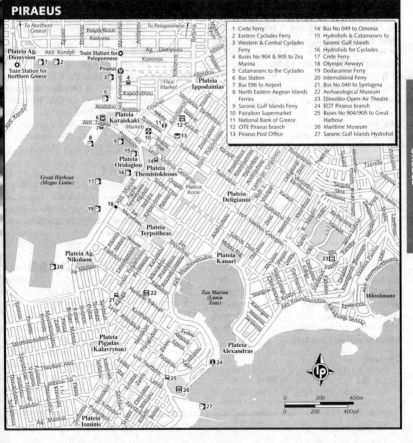

PIRAEUS

1 Crete Ferry
2 Eastern Cyclades Ferry
3 Western & Central Cyclades Ferry
4 Buses No 904 & 905 to Zea Marina
5 Catamarans to the Cyclades
6 Bus Station
7 Bus E96 to Airport
8 North Eastern Aegean Islands Ferries
9 Saronic Gulf Islands Ferry
10 Pairaikon Supermarket
11 National Bank of Greece
12 OTE Piraeus branch
13 Piraeus Post Office
14 Bus No 049 to Omonia
15 Hydrofoils & Catamarans to Saronic Gulf Islands
16 Hydrofoils for Cyclades
17 Crete Ferry
18 Olympic Airways
19 Dodacanese Ferry
20 International Ferry
21 Bus No 040 to Syntagma
22 Archaeological Museum
23 Dimotiko Open-Air Theatre
24 EOT Piraeus branch
25 Buses No 904/905 to Great Harbour
26 Maritime Museum
27 Saronic Gulf Islands Hydrofoil

GREECE

Great Harbour (Megas Limin). All ferries leave from here, as do hydrofoil and catamaran services to Aegina and the Cyclades. There are dozens of shipping agencies around the harbour, as well as banks and a post office.

Zea Marina (Limin Zeas), on the other side of the peninsula, is the main port for hydrofoils to all the Saronic Gulf Islands, except for Aegina. Northeast of here is the picturesque Mikrolimano (Small Harbour), which is lined with countless fish restaurants. There's an **EOT office** (☎ 21 0452 2586) at Zea Marina.

Getting There & Away

Bus There are two 24-hour bus services between central Athens and Piraeus. Bus No 049 runs from Omonia to the Great Harbour, and bus No 040 runs from Syntagma to the tip of the Piraeus peninsula. No 040 is the service to catch for Zea Marina – get off at the Hotel Savoy on Iroön Polytehniou – and leave plenty of time as the trip can take over an hour in bad traffic. The fare is €0.45 for each service. There are no intercity buses to or from Piraeus.

E96 buses to the airport leave from the southern side of Plateia Karaïskaki.

Metro The fastest and most convenient link between the Great Harbour and Athens is the metro. The station is close to the ferries, at the northern end of Akti Kalimassioti. There are metro trains every 10 minutes from 5am to midnight.

Train All services to the Peloponnese from Athens start and terminate at Piraeus, although some schedules don't mention it. The station is next to the metro.

Ferry The following information is a guide to departures between June and mid-September. Schedules are similar in April, May and October, but are radically reduced in winter – especially to smaller islands. The main branch of EOT in Athens has a reliable schedule, which is updated weekly.

Cyclades
There are daily ferries to Amorgos, Folegandros, Ios, Kimolos, Kythnos, Milos, Mykonos, Naxos, Paros, Santorini (Thira), Serifos, Sifnos, Sikinos, Syros and Tinos; two or three ferries a week to Iraklia, Shinoussa, Koufonisi, Donoussa and Anafi; none to Andros or Kea.

Crete
There are two boats a day to Iraklio; daily services to Hania and Rethymno; and three week to Agios Nikolaos and Sitia.
Dodecanese
There are daily ferries to Kalymnos, Kos, Leros, Patmos and Rhodes; three a week to Karpathos and Kassos; and weekly services to the other islands.
Northeastern Aegean Islands
There are daily ferries to Chios, Lesvo (Mytilini), Ikaria and Samos; and two a week to Limnos.
Saronic Gulf Islands
There are daily ferries to Aegina, Poros, Hydra and Spetses year-round.

The departure points for the ferry destination are shown on the map of Piraeus. Note that there are two departure points for Crete. Check where to find your boat when you buy your ticket. See Boat under Getting Around, earlier in this chapter, and the Getting There & Away sections for each island, for more details.

Hydrofoil & Catamaran Minoan Line operates Flying Dolphins (hydrofoils) and high-speed catamarans to the Cyclades from early April to the end of October, and year round services to the Saronic Gulf Islands.

All services to the Cyclades and Aegina leave from Great Harbour. Some services to Poros, Hydra and Spetses also leave from here, but most leave from Zea Marina.

Getting Around
Local bus Nos 904 and 905 run between the Great Harbour and Zea Marina. They leave from the bus stop beside the metro at Great Harbour, and drop you by the maritime museum at Zea Marina.

The Peloponnese
Η Πελοπόννησος

The Peloponnese is the southern extremity of the rugged Balkan peninsula. It's linked to the rest of Greece only by the narrow Isthmus of Corinth, and this has long prompted some people to declare the Peloponnese to be more an island than part of the mainland. It technically became an island after the completion of the Corinth Canal across the isthmus in 1893, and it is now linked to the mainland only by road and rail bridges.

The Peloponnese is an area rich in history. The principal site is Olympia, which is the birthplace of the Olympic Games, but there are many other sites which are worth seeking out. Epidavros, Corinth and Mycenae in the northeast are all within easy striking distance of the pretty Venetian town of Nafplio.

In the south are the magical old Byzantine towns of Monemvasia and Mystras. The rugged Mani Peninsula is famous for its spectacular wild flowers in spring, as well as for the bizarre tower settlements sprinkled across its landscape.

PATRAS Πάτρα
☎ 261 • pop 153,300

Patras is Greece's third-largest city and the principal port for ferries to Italy and the Ionian Islands. It's not particularly exciting and most travellers hang around only long enough for transport connections.

Orientation & Information

The city is easy to negotiate and is laid out on a grid stretching uphill from the port to the old *kastro* (castle). Most services of importance to travellers are to be found along the waterfront, which is known as Othonos Amalias, in the middle of town, and Iroön Politehniou to the north. The train station is right in the middle of town on Othonos Amalias, and the main bus station is close by.

The **EOT office** (☎ 261 062 0353) is inside the port fence, off Iroön Politehniou, and the **tourist police** (☎ 261 045 1833) are upstairs in the embarkation hall.

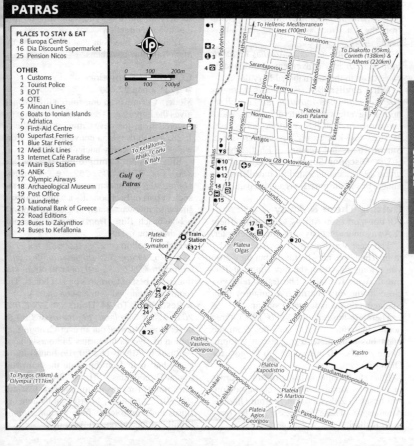

PATRAS

PLACES TO STAY & EAT
8 Europa Centre
16 Dia Discount Supermarket
25 Pension Nicos

OTHER
1 Customs
2 Tourist Police
3 EOT
4 OTE
5 Minoan Lines
6 Boats to Ionian Islands
7 Adriatica
9 First-Aid Centre
10 Superfast Ferries
11 Blue Star Ferries
12 Med Link Lines
13 Internet Café Paradise
14 Main Bus Station
15 ANEK
17 Olympic Airways
18 Archaeological Museum
19 Post Office
20 Laundrette
21 National Bank of Greece
22 Road Editions
23 Buses to Zakynthos
24 Buses to Kefallonia

To Hellenic Mediterranean Lines (100m)
Ioanninon
To Diakofto (55km), Corinth (138km) & Athens (220km)

To Ketallonia, Ithaki, Corfu & Italy

Gulf of Patras

Plateia Trion Symahon
Train Station
Plateia Olgas

Plateia Vasileos Georgiou

To Pyrgos (98km) & Olympia (111km)

Plateia Kapodistrio

Plateia 25 Martiou

Plateia Agios Georgiou

Kastro

GREECE

The **National Bank of Greece** (Plateia Trion Symahon) has a 24-hour ATM.

You can send mail at the **post office** (cnr Zaïmi & Mezonos). There's an **OTE telephone office** opposite the tourist office at the port. For Internet access, try **Internet Café Paradise** (Zaïmi 7; open 5am-1am daily).

Road Editions (Agiou Andreou 50) stocks a large range of Lonely Planet guides as well as maps and travel literature.

Things to See & Do
There are great views of Zakynthos and Kefallonia from the Byzantine **kastro**, which is reached by the steps at the top of Agiou Nikolaou.

Places to Stay & Eat
Pension Nicos (☎ 261 062 3757; cnr Patreos & Agiou Andreou 121; singles/doubles/triples with bathroom €18/30/40), just up from the waterfront, is where most travellers head.

Europa Centre (Othonos Amalias 10; meals from €3.50) is a convenient cafeteria-style place close to the international ferry dock.

Nitro English Bar (Pantanasis 9; mains €7.50-10.50; open 1pm until late) is well set up for travellers with Internet access and a shower room. You'll find daily specials, such as steak-and-kidney pie or shepherd's pie, Sunday roasts and a choice of English beers.

Dia Discount Supermarket (Agiou Andreou 29) is ideally located for travellers planning to buy a few provisions and keep moving.

Getting There & Away
For transport from Athens, see Getting There & Away under that city earlier in this chapter.

The best way to travel to Athens is by train. The buses may be faster, but they drop you a long way from the city centre at Terminal A on Kifissou. The trains take you close to the city centre, five minutes from Syntagma on the new metro system.

There are buses to Athens (€12.25, three hours) that run every 30 minutes from the main bus station, with the last at 9.45pm. There are also 10 buses a day to Pyrgos (for Olympia).

Buses to Kefallonia leave from the corner of Othonos Amalias and Gerokostopoulou, and buses to Zakynthos leave from Othonos Amalias 58. These services travel by ferry from Kyllini.

There are nine trains a day to Athens. Four are slow trains (€5.30, five hours) and five are intercity express trains (€10, 3½ hours) The last intercity train leaves at 6.30pm. Trains also run south to Pyrgos and to Kalamata.

There are daily ferries to Kefallonia (€10, 2½ hours), Ithaki (€10.90, 3¾ hours) and Corfu (€17.90, seven hours). Services to Italy are covered under Getting There & Away at the start of this chapter. Ticket agencies line the waterfront.

DIAKOFTO–KALAVRYTA RAILWAY
This spectacular rack-and-pinion line climbs up the deep gorge of the Vouraikos River from the small coastal town of **Diakofto** to the mountain resort of **Kalavryta**, 22km away. It is a thrilling journey, with dramatic scenery all the way. There are four trains a day in each direction.

Diakofto is one hour east of Patras on the main train line to Athens.

CORINTH Κόρινθος
☎ 2741 • pop 27,400
Modern Corinth is an uninspiring town which gives the impression that it has never quite recovered from the devastating earthquake of 1928. It is, however, a convenient base from which to visit nearby ancient Corinth.

Blue Dolphin Campground (☎ 2741 025 766, fax 2741 085 959; e skoupos@otenet.gr) is about 4km west of town near the ancient port of Lecheon. It's a well-organised site with its own stretch of Gulf of Corinth pebble beach. Buses from Corinth to Lecheon can drop you here.

Hotel Apollon (☎ 2741 022 587, fax 2741 083 875; Pirinis 18; singles/doubles with bathroom €23.50/35.20), near the train station, is the best of Corinth's budget hotels. The rooms are equipped with air-con and TV.

Restaurant To 24 Hours (☎ 2741 083 201; Agiou Nikolaou 19; mains €3.50-8) never closes, turning out an ever-changing selection of taverna favourites 24 hours a day.

Buses to Athens (€5.70, 1½ hours) leave every half-hour from opposite the train station at Dimocratias 4. This is also the departure point for buses to ancient Corinth (€0.80, 20 minutes, hourly) and Lecheon. Buses to Nafplio leave from the junction of Ethnikis Antistaseos and Aratou.

There are 14 trains a day to Athens, five of which are intercity services. There are also trains to Kalamata, Nafplio and Patras.

ANCIENT CORINTH & ACROCORINTH

The ruins of ancient Corinth (admission €4; open 8am-7pm May-Oct, 8am-5pm Nov-Mar) lie 7km southwest of the modern city. Corinth (Κόρινθος) was one of ancient Greece's wealthiest and most wanton cities. When Corinthians weren't clinching business deals, they were paying homage to Aphrodite in a temple dedicated to her, which meant they were frolicking with the temple's sacred prostitutes. The only ancient Greek monument remaining here is the imposing **Temple of Apollo**; the others are Roman. Towering over the site is Acrocorinth (admission free; open 8am-6pm daily), the ruins of an ancient citadel built on a massive outcrop of limestone.

NAFPLIO Ναύπλιο
☎ 2752 • pop 11,900

Nafplio ranks as one of Greece's prettiest towns. The narrow streets of the old quarter are filled with elegant Venetian houses and neoclassical mansions.

The **municipal tourist office** (☎ 2752 024 444; 25 Martiou; open 9am-1.30pm & 4.30pm-9pm daily) is about as unhelpful as tourist offices get.

The bus station is on Syngrou, the street which separates the old town from the new. There are hourly buses to Athens (€8.50, 2½ hours) via Corinth, as well as services to Argos (for Peloponnese connections), Mycenae and Epidavros.

Palamidi Fortress
There are terrific views of the old town and the surrounding coast from this magnificent hill-top fortress (admission €4; open 8am-6.45pm Apr-Oct, 8am-5pm Nov-Mar), built by the Venetians at the beginning of the 18th century. The climb is strenuous – there are almost 1000 steps – so start early and take water with you.

Places to Stay
The cheapest rooms are in the new part of town along Argous, the road to Argos.

Hotel Argolis (☎/fax 2752 027 721; Argous 32; singles/doubles with bathroom

€18/25) is a good place to start. It normally discounts rooms to a bargain €8/16 for singles/doubles. If you're arriving by bus, ask to be let off at the Thanasenas stop, which is right opposite the hotel.

Most people prefer to stay in the old town, which is the most interesting place to be. Unfortunately, there is very little budget accommodation here.

Dimitris Bekas (☎ 2752 024 594; Efthimiopoulou 26; singles/doubles/triples with shared bathroom €15/21/24) offers top value for a great location above the church on the slopes of the Akronafplia. The rooftop terrace has great views over the old town.

Pension Marianna (☎ 2752 024 256, fax 2752 021 783; e petros4@otenet.gr; Potamianou 9; singles/doubles/triples with bathroom €40/50/60), nearby, also has great views. The rooms have air-con and TV, and prices include breakfast.

Hotel Epidauros (☎/fax 2752 027 541; Kokinou 2; doubles with bathroom €35.20) is a good fallback if the above are full. There is a selection of rooms here and at the co-owned **Hotel Tiryns** (☎ 2752 021 020) nearby.

Places to Eat
Mezedopoleio O Noulis (☎ 2752 025 541; Moutzouridou 21; meze €1.50-7.35) serves a fabulous range of meze which can easily be combined into a meal. Check the saganaki flambé, ignited with Metaxa (brandy) as it reaches your table.

Taverna O Vassilis (☎ 2752 025 334; Staikopoulou 20-24; mains €4-8.50) is a popular family-run place at the heart of the restaurant strip on Staikopoulou. It has a large choice of starters, and a good selection of mains – including a very tasty rabbit stifado for €4.85.

EPIDAVROS Επίδαυρος
The crowd-puller at this site is the huge and well-preserved **Theatre of Epidavros** (admission €6; open 8am-7pm daily Apr-Oct, 8am-5pm daily Nov-Mar), but don't miss the more peaceful **Sanctuary of Asclepius** nearby. Epidavros was regarded as the birthplace of Asclepius, the god of healing, and the sanctuary was once a flourishing spa and healing centre.

You can enjoy the theatre's astounding acoustics first-hand during the Epidavros Festival from mid-June to mid-August.

There are two buses a day from Athens (€8.40, 2½ hours,), as well as four a day from Nafplio (€2, 40 minutes).

MYCENAE Μυκήνες

Mycenae (admission €6; open 8am-7pm daily Apr-Oct, 8am-5pm daily Nov-Mar) was the most powerful influence in Greece for three centuries until about 1200 BC. The rise and fall of Mycenae is shrouded in myth, but the site was settled as early as the sixth millennium BC. Historians are divided as to whether the city's eventual destruction was wrought by invaders or internal conflict between the Mycenaean kingdoms. Described by Homer as 'rich in gold', Mycenae's entrance, the **Lion Gate**, is Europe's oldest monumental sculpture.

Excavations have uncovered the palace complex and a number of tombs. The so-called **Mask of Agamemnon**, discovered by Heinrich Schliemann in 1873, now holds pride of place at the National Archaeological Museum in Athens along with other finds from the site.

Most people visit on day trips from Nafplio, but there are several hotels in the modern village below the site. The **Belle Helene Hotel** (☎ 2751 076 225, fax 2751 076 179; Christou Tsounta; singles/doubles €26.40/ 38.15), on the main street, is where Schliemann stayed during the excavations.

There are buses to Mycenae from Argos and Nafplio.

SPARTA Σπάρτη
☎ 2731 • pop 14,100

The bellicose Spartans sacrificed all the finer things in life to military expertise and left no monuments of any consequence. Ancient Sparta's forlorn ruins lie amid olive groves at the northern end of town. Modern Sparta is a neat, unspectacular town, but it's a convenient base from which to visit Mystras.

Sparta is laid out on a grid system. The main streets are Palaeologou, which runs north-south through the town, and Lykourgou, which runs east-west. The **tourist office** (☎ 2731 024 852; open 8am-2.30pm Mon-Fri) is in the town hall on Plateia Kentriki.

Camping Paleologou Mystras (☎ 2731 022 724; open year-round), 2km west of Sparta on the road to Mystras, is a well-organised site with good facilities, including a swimming pool. Buses to Mystras can drop you there.

Hotel Cecil (☎ 2731 024 980, fax 2731 081 318; Palaeologou 125; singles/doubles with bathroom €30/40) is a family-run place and one of the many good hotels back in town. Rooms here have TV.

Restaurant Elysse (☎ 2731 029 896; Palaeologou 113; mains €4.50-8.80) offers Lakonian specialties such as chicken bardouniotiko, which is chicken cooked with onions and feta cheese.

The bus station is at the eastern end of Lykourgou. There are 10 buses a day that go to Athens (€12.65, four hours), three that go to Monemvasia and two to Kalamata. There are also frequent buses to Mystras (€0.80, 30 minutes).

MYSTRAS Μυστράς

Mystras (admission €5; open 8am-6pm Apr-Oct, 8am-3.30pm Nov-Mar), 7km from Sparta, was once the shining light of the Byzantine world. Its ruins spill from a spur of Mt Taygetos, and are crowned by a mighty fortress built by the Franks in 1249. The streets of Mystras are lined with palaces, monasteries and churches, most of them dating from the period between 1271 and 1460, when the town was the effective capital of the Byzantine Empire.

MONEMVASIA Μονεμβασία
☎ 2732

Monemvasia is no longer an undiscovered paradise, but mass tourism hasn't lessened the impact of one's first encounter with this extraordinary old town – nor the thrill of exploring it.

Monemvasia occupies a great outcrop of rock that rises dramatically from the sea opposite the village of Gefyra. It was separated from the mainland by an earthquake in AD 375 and access is by a causeway from Gefyra. From the causeway, a road curves around the base of the rock for about 1km until it comes to a narrow L-shaped tunnel in the massive fortifying wall. You emerge, blinking, into the **Byzantine town**, hitherto hidden from view.

The cobbled main street is flanked by stairways leading to a complex network of stone houses with tiny walled gardens and courtyards. Signposted steps lead to the ruins of the **fortress** built by the Venetians in the 16th century. The views are great, and there is the added bonus of being able to explore the

Byzantine **Church of Agia Sophia**, perched precariously on the edge of the cliff.

There is no budget accommodation in Monemvasia, but there are *domatia* in Gefyra, as well as cheap hotels.

Hotel Monemvasia (☎ 2732 061 381, fax 2732 061 707; singles/doubles with bathroom €25/38) is a small modern hotel 500m north of Gefyra on the road to Molai. It has large balconies looking out to Monemvasia, and prices include breakfast.

If your budget permits, treat yourself to a night in one of the beautifully restored traditional settlements in Monemvasia. **Malvasia Guest Houses** (☎ 2732 061 113, fax 2732 061 722; singles/doubles from €35/40) has a wide choice of rooms, and prices include breakfast.

Taverna O Botsalo is the place to go for a hearty meal in Gefyra, while **To Kanoni**, on the right of the main street in Monemvasia, has an imaginative menu.

There are four buses a day to Athens (€18.65, six hours), travelling via Sparta, Tripolis and Corinth.

In July and August, there are at least two hydrofoils a day to Piraeus via the Saronic Gulf Islands.

GYTHIO Γύθειο
☎ 2733 • pop 4900

Gythio, once the port of ancient Sparta, is an attractive fishing town at the head of the Lakonian Gulf. It is the gateway to the rugged Mani Peninsula to the south.

The main attraction is the picturesque islet of **Marathonisi**, linked to the mainland by a causeway. According to mythology this islet is ancient Cranae, where Paris (a prince of Troy) and Helen (the wife of Menelaus of Sparta) consummated the love affair that sparked the Trojan War. An 18th-century tower on the islet has been turned into a **museum** of Mani history.

Meltemi Camping (☎ 2733 022 833) is the pick of the sites along the coast south of town. Buses to Areopoli can drop you there.

You'll find plenty of *domatia* signs around town. They include **Xenia Rooms to Rent** (☎ 2733 022 719; singles/doubles with bathroom €15/20), opposite the causeway to Marathonisi. **Saga Pension** (☎ 2733 023 220, fax 2733 024 370; singles/doubles €25/30), nearby, is another good choice and rooms have TV.

The waterfront is lined with countless fish tavernas with similar menus. For something completely different, head inland to the tiny **General Store & Wine Bar** (☎ 2733 024 113; Vasileos Georgiou 67). It has an unusually imaginative menu featuring such dishes as orange-and-pumpkin soup (€3.50) and fillet of pork with black pepper and ouzo (€11).

There are five buses a day to Athens (€15.10, 4¼ hours) via Sparta (€2.60, one hour), five to Areopoli (€1.70, 30 minutes), two to Gerolimenas (€3.70, 1¼ hours), and one to the Diros Caves (€2.30, one hour).

ANEN Lines operates ferries to Kastelli–Kissamos on Crete (€15.60, seven hours) via Kythira (€7.10, 2½ hours), three times a week between June and September. The schedule is subject to constant change, so check with **Rozakis Travel** (☎ 2733 022 207, fax 2733 022 229; e rosakigy@otenet.gr) before coming here to catch a boat.

THE MANI
The Mani is divided into two regions, the Lakonian (inner) Mani in the south and Messinian (outer) Mani in the northwest below Kalamata.

Lakonian Mani
☎ 2733

The Lakonian Mani is wild and remote, and its landscape is dotted with the dramatic stone-tower houses that are a trademark of the region. The houses were built as refuges from the clan wars of the 19th century. The best time to visit is in spring, when the barren countryside briefly bursts into life with a spectacular display of wild flowers.

The region's principal village is **Areopoli**, about 30km southwest of Gythio. There are a number of fine towers on the narrow, cobbled streets of the old town at the lower end of the main street, Kapetan Matepan.

Just south of here are the magnificent **Diros Caves** (admission €10.90; open 8am-5.30pm June-Sept, 8am-2.30pm Oct-May), where a subterranean river flows.

Gerolimenas, 20km further south, is a tiny fishing village built around a sheltered bay. **Vathia**, a village of towers built on a rocky peak, is 11km southeast of Gerolimenas. Beyond Vathia, the coastline is a series of rocky outcrops sheltering pebbled beaches.

Most of the accommodation in the Lakonian Mani is found in Areopoli.

Tsimova Rooms (☎ 2733 051 301; singles/doubles €22/36) has cosy rooms tucked away behind the Church of Taxiarhes on Kapetan Matepan.

Pyrgos Kapetanakas (☎ 2733 051 233, fax 2733 051 401; singles/doubles €30/45) occupies the tower house built by the powerful Kapetanakas family at the end of the 18th century. It's signposted to the right at the bottom of Kapetan Matepan.

Nicola's Corner Taverna (☎ 2733 051 366; Plateia Athanaton; mains €3-6.50) is a popular spot on the central square with a good choice of tasty taverna staples.

Hotel Akrotenaritis (☎ 2733 054 205; singles/doubles €18/35), in Gerolimenas, is a good budget option. Also in Gerolimenas, **Hotel Akrogiali** (☎ 2733 054 204, fax 2733 054 272; singles/doubles from €25/36) has a great setting overlooking the bay on the way into town. Both of these hotels have restaurants.

Areopoli is the focal point of the local bus network. There are four buses a day to Gythio and Sparta, two to Gerolimenas and Itilo, and one to Diros Caves. Crossing to the Messinian Mani involves changing buses at Itilo.

Messinian Mani
☎ 2721

The Messinian Mani runs north along the coast from Itilo to Kalamata. The beaches here are some of the best in Greece, set against the dramatic backdrop of the Taygetos Mountains.

Itilo, the medieval capital of the entire Mani area, is split by a ravine that is the traditional dividing line between inner and outer Mani.

The picturesque coastal village of **Kardamyli**, 37km south of Kalamata, is a favourite destination for trekkers. It's well set up, with a network of colour-coded trails that crisscross the foothills of the Taygetos Mountains behind the village. Many of the walks incorporate the spectacular Vyros Gorge. If you plan to trek, strong, good-quality footwear is essential and make sure that you take plenty of water.

Stoupa, 10km south of Kardamyli, has a great beach and is a popular package destination in summer.

Kardamyli has a good choice of accommodation to suit all budgets, starting with several domatia.

Olympia Koumounakou (☎ 2721 073 623; singles/doubles €20/25) is a good place to try; it's signposted opposite the post office.

Anniska Apartments (☎/fax 2721 073 600; studios/apartments from €61.50/91.50) has a range of spacious, well-appointed studios and apartments. The studios sleep two people, while the larger apartments accommodate up to four people.

The popular **Taverna Perivolis** is one of nine tavernas around the village.

There are two buses a day from Kalamata to Itilo, stopping at Kardamyli and Stoupa.

OLYMPIA Ολυμπία
☎ 2624

The site of ancient Olympia lies 500m beyond the modern town, surrounded by the foothills of Mt Kronion. There is a well-organised **municipal tourist office** (open 9am-9pm daily June-Sept, 8am-2.45pm Mon-Sat Oct-May) on the main street, which also changes money.

In ancient times, Olympia was a sacred place of temples, priests' dwellings and public buildings, as well as being the venue for the quadrennial Olympic Games. The first Olympics were staged in 776 BC, reaching the peak of their prestige in the 6th century BC. The city-states were bound by a sacred truce to stop fighting for three months and compete.

The **site** (admission €6 site only, €9 site & museum; open 8am-7pm daily Apr-Oct, 8am-5pm Mon-Fri, 8.30am-3pm Sat-Sun Nov-Mar) is dominated by the immense, ruined **Temple of Zeus**, to whom the games were dedicated. There's also a **museum** (admission €6), north of the archaeological site, which keeps similar hours.

There are three good camping grounds to choose from.

Camping Diana (☎ 2624 022 314), 250m west of town, is the most convenient. It has excellent facilities and a pool.

Youth hostel (☎ 2624 022 580; Praxitelous Kondyli 18; dorm beds €7) has free hot showers. There are two more good budget options around the corner on Stefanopoulou: **Pension Achilleys** (☎ 2624 022 562; Stefanopoulou 4; singles/doubles with shared bathroom €15/20) and **Pension Posidon** (☎ 2624 022 567; Stefanopoulou 9; singles/doubles with bathroom €18/28).

Taverna To Steki tou Vangeli (Stefanopoulou 13; mains €4-6.50) represents better value than most of the tavernas around town.

There are four buses a day to Olympia from Athens (€19.05, 5½ hours) and regular buses to Pyrgos, 24km away on the coast.

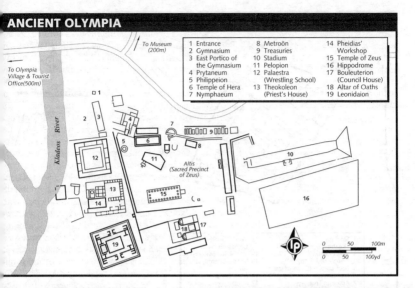

ANCIENT OLYMPIA

1 Entrance	8 Metroön	14 Pheidias'
2 Gymnasium	9 Treasuries	Workshop
3 East Portico of	10 Stadium	15 Temple of Zeus
the Gymnasium	11 Pelopion	16 Hippodrome
4 Prytaneum	12 Palaestra	17 Bouleuterion
5 Philippeion	(Wrestling School)	(Council House)
6 Temple of Hera	13 Theokoleon	18 Altar of Oaths
7 Nymphaeum	(Priest's House)	19 Leonidaion

Central Greece

Central Greece has little going for it in terms of attractions – with the notable exceptions of Delphi and surroundings.

DELPHI Δελφοί
☎ 2265 • pop 2400

Like so many of Greece's ancient sites, the setting at Delphi – overlooking the Gulf of Corinth from the slopes of Mt Parnassos – is stunning. The Delphic oracle is thought to have originated in Mycenaean times, when the earth goddess Gaea was worshipped here.

By the 6th century BC, Delphi had become the Sanctuary of Apollo and thousands of pilgrims came to consult the oracle, who was always a peasant woman of 50 years or more. She sat at the mouth of a chasm which emitted fumes. These she inhaled, causing her to gasp, writhe and shudder in divine frenzy. The pilgrim, after sacrificing a sheep or goat, would deliver a question, and the priestess' incoherent mumbling was then translated by a priest. Wars were fought, voyages embarked upon, and business transactions undertaken on the strength of these prophecies.

Orientation & Information
The bus station, post office, OTE, National Bank of Greece and tourist office (☎ 2265

082 900; Vasileon Pavlou 44; open 7.30am-2.30pm Mon-Fri) are all on modern Delphi's main street, Vasileon Pavlou. The ancient site is 1km east of modern Delphi.

Sanctuary of Apollo
The Sacred Way leads up from the entrance of the site to the Temple of Apollo (admission €6 site only, €9 site and museum; open 7.30am-7.15pm Mon-Fri, 8.30am-2.45pm Sat, Sun & public holidays). It was here that the oracle supposedly sat, although no chasm, let alone vapour, has been detected. The path continues to the theatre and stadium. Opposite this sanctuary is the Sanctuary of Athena (admission free) and the much-photographed Tholos, a 4th-century BC columned rotunda of Pentelic marble.

Places to Stay & Eat
There are lots of hotels in the modern town, catering for the many tour groups that stop overnight.

Hotel Tholos (☎/fax 2265 082 268; Apollonos 31; singles/doubles with bathroom €15/30; open daily April-Nov, Fri & Sat only Dec-Mar) is great value for rooms with air-con and TV.

Hotel Parnassos (☎ 2265 082 321; Vasileon Pavlou & Frederikis 32; singles/doubles €30/38) is another good choice, and rates include buffet breakfast.

GREECE

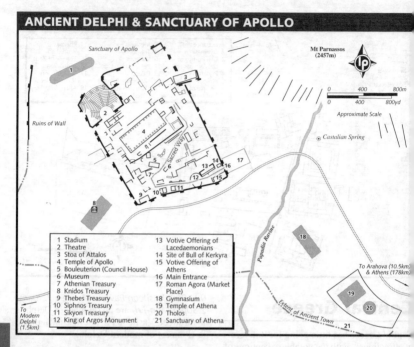

ANCIENT DELPHI & SANCTUARY OF APOLLO

1 Stadium	13 Votive Offering of
2 Theatre	Lacedaemonians
3 Stoa of Attalos	14 Site of Bull of Kerkyra
4 Temple of Apollo	15 Votive Offering of
5 Bouleuterion (Council House)	Athens
6 Museum	16 Main Entrance
7 Athenian Treasury	17 Roman Agora (Market
8 Knidos Treasury	Place)
9 Thebes Treasury	18 Gymnasium
10 Siphnos Treasury	19 Temple of Athena
11 Sikyon Treasury	20 Tholos
12 King of Argos Monument	21 Sanctuary of Athena

Taverna Vakhos (☎ 2265 083 186; Apollonos 31; mains €4.80-10.50), next to the Hotel Tholos, turns out tasty taverna dishes such as lamb in lemon sauce with rice and potatoes (€5.60).

Getting There & Away
There are five buses a day to Delphi from Athens (€10.20, three hours).

METEORA Μετέωρα
☎ 2432
Meteora is an extraordinary place. The massive, sheer columns of rock that dot the landscape were created by wave action millions of years ago. Perched precariously atop these seemingly inaccessible outcrops are stunning monasteries that date back to the late 14th century. Each monastery is built around a central courtyard in the centre of which stands the main church.

Meteora is just north of the town of Kalambaka, on the Ioannina-Trikala road. The rocks behind the town are spectacularly floodlit at night. **Kastraki**, which is 2km from Kalambaka, is a charming village of red-tiled houses just west of the monasteries.

Things to See
There were once monasteries on each of the 24 pinnacles, but only six are still occupied. They are **Megalou Meteorou** (Grand Me-teora, open 9am-1pm & 3pm-6pm Wed-Mon), **Varlaam** (open 9am-1pm & 3.30pm- 6pm Sat-Thur), **Agiou Stefanou** (open 9am-1pm & 3pm-5pm daily), **Agias Triados** (Holy Trinity, open 9am-5pm Fri-Wed), **Agiou Nikolaou** (open 9am-5pm daily) and **Agias Varvaras Rousanou** (open 9am-6pm Thur-Tues). Admission is €2 for each monastery; free for Greeks.

Meteora is best explored on foot, following the old paths where they exist. Allow a whole day to visit all of the monasteries, and take food and water. Women must wear skirts that reach below their knees, men must wear long trousers, and arms must be fully covered.

Places to Stay & Eat
Kastraki is the best base for visiting Meteora. **Vrachos Camping** (☎ 2432 022 293), on the edge of the village, is excellent.

There are several **domatia** in town, charging from €20/30 for singles/doubles.

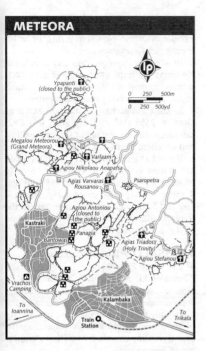

METEORA

Ypapanti
(closed to the public)

0   250   500m
0   250   500yd

Megalou Meteorou
(Grand Meteoro)

Varlaam

Agiou Nikolaou Anapafsa

Agias Varvaras
Rousanou

Psaropetra

Agiou Antoniou
(closed to
the public)

Kastraki

Bantowas

Panagia

Agias Triados
(Holy Trinity)

Agiou Stefanou

Vrachos
Camping

Kalambaka

To
Ioannina

Train
Station

To
Trikala

Hotel Sydney *(☎/fax 2432 023 079; singles/doubles with bathroom €25/30)*, on the road into town from Kalambaka, has comfortable rooms.

In Kalambaka, **Koka Roka Rooms** *(☎ 2432 024 554; doubles with bathroom €30)*, is a popular travellers place; the taverna downstairs is good value. Telephone for a lift from the bus or train station.

Getting There & Away

There are hourly buses to Trikala and two a day to Ioannina. Local buses shuttle constantly between Kalambaka and Kastraki; five a day continue to Metamorphosis.

Trikala is the region's major transport hub. It has eight buses a day which run to Athens (€18.20, 5½ hours).

There are trains between Kalambaka and Volos. These trains connect with services from Athens and Thessaloniki at Paleofarsalos.

Northern Greece

Northern Greece covers the regions of Epiros, Thessaly, Macedonia and Thrace. It includes some areas of outstanding natural beauty, such as the Zagoria region of northwestern Epiros.

IGOUMENITSA Ηγουμενίτσα
☎ 2665 • pop 6800

Igoumenitsa, opposite the island of Corfu, is the main port of northwestern Greece. Few people stay here any longer than it takes to buy a ticket out. The bus station is on Kyprou. To get there from the ferries, follow the waterfront (Ethnikis Antistasis) north for 500m and turn up El Venizelou. Kyprou is two blocks inland and the bus station is on the left.

If you get stuck for the night, you'll find signs for **domatia** around the port. The D-class **Egnatia** *(☎ 2665 023 648; Eleftherias 2; singles/doubles with bathroom €30/40)* has comfortable rooms.

Alekos *(☎ 2665 023 708; Ethnikis Andistasis 84; mains €3.5-5.50)*, 500m north of the Corfu ferry quay, does fine *mousakas* (€3.80) and other taverna favourites.

Bus services include nine buses a day to Ioannina (€6.20, two hours), and four a day to Athens (€28.45, 8½ hours).

There are international ferry services to the Italian ports of Ancona, Bari, Brindisi, Trieste and Venice. Ticket agencies are opposite the port.

Ferries to Corfu (€4.20, 1½ hours) operate every hour between 5am and 10pm.

IOANNINA Ιωάννινα
☎ 2651 • pop 90,000

Ioannina is the largest town in Epiros, sitting on the western shore of Lake Pamvotis. In Ottoman times, it was one of the most important towns in the country.

The town centre is around Plateia Dimokratias where the main streets of the new town meet. All facilities of importance to travellers are nearby.

The **EOT office** *(☎ 2651 041 142; Dodonis 39; open 7.30am-2.30pm & 5.30pm-8.30pm Mon-Fri, 9am-1pm Sat)* is about 600m south of Plateia Dimokratias.

Robinson Travel *(☎ 2651 074 989; e activities@robinson.gr; 8th Merarhias Gramou 10)* is an outfit that specialises in treks in the Zagoria region.

There are lots of Internet cafés in town, including **Armos Internet Café** *(2651 071 488; Harilaou Trikoupi 40)*, 300m west of Plateia Dimokratias.

The **old town** juts out into the lake on a small peninsula. Inside the impressive fortifications lies a maze of winding streets flanked by traditional Turkish houses.

The **Nisi** (island) is a serene spot in the middle of the lake, with four monasteries set among the trees. Ferries (€0.80) to the island leave from just north of the old town. They run half-hourly in the summer and hourly in winter.

Most travellers end up staying either at the no-frills **Agapi Inn** (☎ 2651 020 541; Tsirigoti 6; doubles €18) near the bus station, or at the co-owned **Hotel Paris** (singles/doubles €20/30) next door.

There are several restaurants outside the entrance to the old town. **To Manteio Psistaria** is recommended.

Aegean Airlines and Olympic Airways both fly twice a day to Athens, and Olympic has a daily flight to Thessaloniki.

The main bus terminal is 300m north of Plateia Dimokratias on Zossimadon, the northern extension of Markou Botsari. Services include 12 buses a day to Athens (€24.85, seven hours), nine to Igoumenitsa, five to Thessaloniki and three to Trikala via Kalambaka.

ZAGORIA & VIKOS GORGE
☎ 2653

The Zagoria (Ζαγόρα) region covers a large expanse of the Pindos Mountains north of Ioannina. It's a wilderness of raging rivers, crashing waterfalls and deep gorges. Here, snowcapped mountains rise out of dense forests and the remote villages that dot the hillsides are famous for their impressive grey-slate architecture.

The fairytale village of **Monodendri** is the starting point for treks through the dramatic **Vikos Gorge**, with its awesome sheer limestone walls. It's a strenuous 7½-hour walk from Monodendri to the twin villages of **Megalo Papingo** and **Mikro Papingo**. The trek is very popular and the path is clearly marked. Ioannina's EOT office has more information.

Other walks start from **Tsepelovo**, near Monodendri.

There are some wonderful places to stay, but none of them are particularly cheap.

The options in Monodendri include cosy **To Kalderimi** (☎ 2653 071 510; doubles €35). **Haradra tou Vikou** (☎ 2653 071 559)

specialises in fabulous *pittes* (pies). Try its excellent cheese pies (*tyropitta*), or wild-greens pies (*hortopitta*).

In Megalo Papingo, you can check out **Xenonas Kalliopi** (☎/fax 2653 041 081; singles/doubles €34/42). It also has a small restaurant-bar serving meals and pittes.

Mikro Papingo has the pleasant **Xenonas Dias** (☎ 2653 041 257, fax 2653 041 892; doubles €36). Its restaurant serves breakfast and excellent meals.

Buses to the Zagoria leave from the main bus station in Ioannina. There are buses to Monodendri Monday to Friday at 6am and 4.15pm; to Tsepelovo on Monday, Wednesday and Friday at 6am and 3pm; and to the Papingo villages on Monday, Wednesday and Friday at 6am and 2.30pm.

THESSALONIKI Θεσσαλονίκη
☎ 231 • pop 750,000

Thessaloniki, also known as Salonica, is Greece's second-largest city. It's a bustling, sophisticated place with good restaurants and a busy nightlife. It was once the second city of Byzantium, and there are some magnificent Byzantine churches, as well as a scattering of Roman ruins.

Orientation

Thessaloniki is laid out on a grid system. The main thoroughfares – Tsimiski, Egnatia and Agiou Dimitriou – run parallel to Nikis, on the waterfront. Plateias Eleftherias and Aristotelous, both on Nikis, are the main squares. The city's most famous landmark is the White Tower (which is no longer white) at the eastern end of Nikis.

The train station is on Monastiriou, the westerly continuation of Egnatia beyond Plateia Dimokratias, and the airport is 16km to the southeast.

Information

The **EOT office** (☎ 231 027 1888; Plateia Aristotelous 8; open 8.30am-8pm Mon-Fri, 8.30am-2pm Sat) can help with inquiries, or try the **tourist police** (☎ 231 055 4871; Dodekanisou 4, 5th floor; open 7.30am-11pm daily).

There are numerous banks around the city centre, all with ATMs. The **National Bank of Greece** (Tsimiski 11) is open Saturday and Sunday for currency exchange; there are other branches elsewhere.

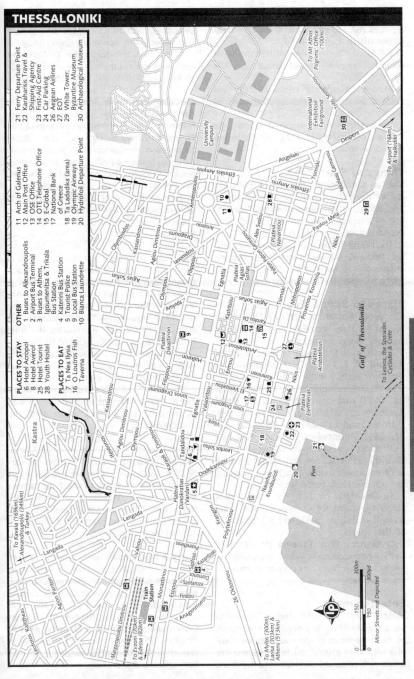

THESSALONIKI

PLACES TO STAY
6   Hotel Acropol
8   Hotel Averof
25 Hotel Tourist
28 Youth Hostel

PLACES TO EAT
7   Ta Nea Ilysia
16 O Loutros Fish
    Taverna

OTHER
1   Buses to Alexandroupolis
2   Airport Bus Terminal
3   Buses to Athens,
    Igoumenitsa & Trikala
    Bus Station
4   Katerini Bus Station
5   Tourist Police
9   Local Bus Station
10 Bianca Laundrette
11 Arch of Galerius
12 Main Post Office
13 OSE Office
14 OTE Telephone Office
15 E-Global
17 National Bank
    of Greece
18 Ta Ladadika (area)
19 Olympic Airways
20 Hydrofoil Departure Point
21 Ferry Departure Point
22 Karaharisis Travel &
    Shipping Agency
23 First-Aid Centre
24 Car Parking
26 Aegean Airlines
27 EOT
29 White Tower;
    Byzantine Museum
30 Archaeological Museum

GREECE

Send mail at the **main post office** (*Aristotelous 26*), and make calls at the **OTE telephone office** (*Karolou Dil 27*).

E-Global (*Vas Irakliou 40*) is the most central of the city's many Internet cafés. It's open 24 hours.

Bianca Laundrette (*Antoniadou*), just north of the Arch of Galerius, charges €6 to wash and dry a load.

For medical attention you should try the **first-aid centre** (☎ *231 053 0530; Navarhou Koundourioti 6*).

Things to See

The **archaeological museum** (*admission €4.40; open 8am-7pm Tues-Fri, 12.30pm-7pm Mon*), at the eastern end of Tsimiski, houses a superb collection of treasures from the royal tombs of Philip II.

The **White Tower** is the city's most prominent landmark. It houses a **Byzantine Museum** (*admission free; open 8am-2.30pm Tues-Sun*), which has splendid frescoes and icons.

Places to Stay & Eat

The **youth hostel** (☎ *231 022 5946; Alex Svolou 44; dorm beds €8*) is extremely basic and hard to recommend.

The best budget hotel in town is **Hotel Acropol** (☎ *231 053 6170; Tandalidou 4; singles/doubles with shared bathroom €16/20.50*), on a quiet side street off Egnatia. You'll find similar prices at the **Hotel Averof** (☎ *231 053 8498; Leontos Sofou 24*).

Hotel Tourist (☎ *231 027 0501; fax 231 022 6865; Mitropoleos 21; singles/doubles €60/80.50*) is a big step up from these. Hotel Tourist is a fine old neoclassical hotel, which has comfortable rooms with TV and air-con, and prices include buffet breakfast.

Ta Nea Ilysia (☎ *231 053 6996; Leotos Sofou 17; mains €4-6*), opposite the Hotel Averof, is a popular place with a good choice of daily specials.

O Loutros Fish Taverna (☎ *231 022 8895; M Koundoura 5; fish dishes €6-9*) has not lost its cult following despite its move to a new location.

Entertainment

Mylos (☎ *231 052 5968; Andreou Georgiou 56; admission free*) is a huge old mill which has been converted into an entertainment complex with an art gallery, restaurant, bar and live music club (classical and rock). To get there,

follow 26 Oktovriou southwest from Plateia Dimokratias; Andreou Georgiou is on the right after about 700m, opposite a small park.

Music bars abound in the Ta Ladadika area, with the main emphasis on music and all kinds of draught and bottled beer.

Getting There & Away

Air Olympic Airways and Aegean Airlines both have seven flights a day to Athens (€96). **Olympic Airways** (☎ *231 036 8666; Navarhou Koundourioti 1-3*) also has daily flights to Ioannina, Lesvos and Limnos; three weekly to Corfu, Iraklio and Mykonos; and two weekly to Chios, Hania and Samos. **Aegean Airlines** (☎ *231 028 0050; Venizelou 2*) also has two flights a day to Iraklio on Crete, and daily flights to Lesvos, Rhodes and Santorini.

Bus There are several bus terminals, most of them near the train station. Buses to Athens, Igoumenitsa and Trikala leave from Monastiriou 65 and 67; buses to Alexandroupolis leave from Koloniari 17; and buses to Litihoro (for Mt Olympus) leave from the Katerini bus station, Promitheos 10. Buses to the Halkidiki Peninsula leave from Karakasi 68 (in the eastern part of town; it's marked on the free EOT map). To get there, take local bus No 10 from Egnatia to the Botsari stop.

The **OSE** (*Aristotelous 18*) has two buses a day to Athens from the train station, as well as international services to İstanbul and Tirana (Albania).

Train There are nine trains a day to Athens, five of which are intercity express services (€27.60, six hours). There are also five trains to Alexandroupolis, two of which are express services (€16.20, 5½ hours). All international trains from Athens stop at Thessaloniki. You can get more information from the OSE office or from the train station.

Ferry & Hydrofoil There's a Sunday ferry to Lesvos, Limnos and Chios throughout the year. In summer there are at least three ferries a week to Iraklio (Crete), stopping in the Sporades and the Cyclades on the way. There are also daily hydrofoils to Skiathos, Skopelos and Alonnisos. **Karaharisis Travel & Shipping Agency** (☎ *231 052 4544, fax 231 053 2289; Navarhou Koundourioti 8*) handles tickets for both ferries and hydrofoils.

Getting Around
There is no bus service from the Olympic Airways office to the airport. Take bus No 78 from the train station (€0.50). A taxi from the airport costs about €8.

HALKIDIKI Χαλκιδική
Halkidiki is the three-pronged peninsula southeast of Thessaloniki. It's the main resort area of northern Greece, with superb sandy beaches right around its 500km of coastline. **Kassandra**, the southwestern prong of the peninsula, has surrendered irrevocably to mass tourism. The **Sithonia Peninsula**, the middle prong, is not as over-the-top and has some spectacular scenery.

Mt Athos
Halkidiki's third prong is occupied by the all-male Monastic Republic of Mt Athos (also called the Holy Mountain), where monasteries full of priceless treasures stand amid an impressive landscape of gorges, wooded mountains and precipitous rocks.

Obtaining a four-day visitors permit involves a bit of work. Start early, because only 10 foreign adult males may enter Mt Athos per day and there are long waiting lists in summer. You can start the process from outside Thessaloniki, but you will have to pass through Thessaloniki anyway to pick up your reservation.

You must first book a date for your visit with the **Mount Athos Pilgrims' Office** (☎ 231 083 3733, fax 231 086 1611; Leoforos Karamanli 14; open 8.30am-1.30pm & 6pm-8pm Mon, Tues, Thur & Fri), just east of the International Exhibition Fairground in Thessaloniki. Call first and make a telephone booking.

Letters of recommendation are no longer required, but you must declare your intention to be a pilgrim. You need to supply a photocopy of your passport details and, if you are Orthodox, a photocopied certificate showing your religion.

You must then call at the Pilgrims' Office in person to collect the forms confirming your reservation. You can then proceed from Thessaloniki to the port of Ouranoupolis, which is the departure point for boats to Mt Athos, where you will be given your actual permit.

Armed at last with your permit, you can explore, on foot, the 20 monasteries and dependent religious communities of Mt Athos. You can stay only one night at each monastery.

MT OLYMPUS Ολυμπος Ορος
☎ 2352
Mt Olympus is Greece's highest and mightiest mountain. The ancients chose it as the abode of their gods and assumed it to be the exact centre of the earth. Olympus has eight peaks, the highest of which is Mytikas (2917m). The area is popular with trekkers, most of whom use the village of **Litohoro** as a base. Litohoro is 5km inland from the Athens-Thessaloniki highway.

The **EOS office** (☎ 2352 084 544; Plateia Kentriki; open 9am-1pm & 6pm-8.30pm Mon-Fri, 9am-1pm Sat) has information on the various treks and conditions.

The main route to the top takes two days with a stay overnight at one of the refuges on the mountain. Good protective clothing is essential, even in summer.

Hotel Markisia (☎ 2352 081 831; Dionysou 5; singles/doubles with bathroom €20.50/23.50) is a good, clean budget choice.

Hotel Enipeas (☎ 2352 084 328, fax 2352 081 328; Plateia Kentriki; doubles/triples €32.30/38.20) is a cheery place and has the best views of Olympus.

Olympus Taverna (Agiou Nikolaou) serves standard fare at reasonable prices.

There are four **refuges** (open May-Sept) on the mountain at altitudes ranging from 940m to 2720m.

There are eight buses a day to Litohoro from Thessaloniki (€6.10, 1½ hours), and three from Athens (€24.80, 5½ hours).

ALEXANDROUPOLIS
Αλεξανδρούπολη
☎ 2551 • pop 37,000
Dusty Alexandroupolis doesn't have much going for it, but if you're going to Turkey or Samothraki, you may end up staying overnight here.

Hotel Lido (☎ 2551 028 808; Paleologou 15; singles/doubles without bathroom €16.20/22; singles/doubles with bathroom €22/27), one block north of the bus station, is a great budget option.

Neraïda Restaurant (☎ 2551 022 867; Plateia Polytehniou; mains €5-7) has a good range of local specialities.

GREECE

Olympic Airways and Aegean Airlines both have two flights a day to Athens (€79.55) from the airport which is 7km west of town. There are five trains and six buses (€20) a day to Thessaloniki. There's also a daily train and a daily OSE bus to İstanbul.

In summer there are at least two boats a day to Samothraki, dropping to one boat a day in winter. There are also hydrofoils to Samothraki and Limnos.

Saronic Gulf Islands Νησιά του Σαρωνικού

The Saronic Gulf Islands are the closest island group to Athens. Not surprisingly, they are a very popular escape for residents of the congested capital. Accommodation can be hard to find between mid-June and September, and at weekends year-round.

AEGINA Αίγινα
☎ 2297 • pop 11,000

Aegina is the closest island to Athens and is a popular destination for day-trippers. Many make for the lovely **Temple of Aphaia** (admission €4; open 8am-7pm daily Apr-Oct, 8am-5pm Nov-Mar), a well-preserved Doric temple 12km east of Aegina town. Buses from Aegina town to the small resort of **Agia Marina** can drop you at the site.

Most travellers prefer to stay in Aegina town, where the **Hotel Plaza** (☎ 2297 025 600; singles/doubles €25/28) has rooms overlooking the sea.

POROS Πόρος
pop 4000

Poros is a big hit with the Brits, but it's hard to work out why. The beaches are nothing to write home about and there are no sites of significance. The main attraction is pretty Poros town, draped over the Sferia Peninsula. Sferia is linked to the rest of the island, known as Kalavria, by a narrow isthmus. Most of the package hotels are here. There are a few *domatia* in Poros town, signposted off the road to Kalavria.

The island lies little more than a stone's throw from the mainland, opposite the Peloponnese village of Galatas.

HYDRA Ύδρα
☎ 2298 • pop 3000

Hydra is the island with the most style and is famous as the haunt of artists and jet-setters. Its gracious stone mansions are stacked up the rocky hillsides that surround the fine natural harbour. The main attraction is peace and quiet. There are no motorised vehicles on the island – apart from a garbage truck and a few construction vehicles.

Accommodation is expensive, but of a high standard.

Pension Theresia (☎ 2298 053 984, fax 2298 053 983; singles/doubles with bathroom €30/45) has clean, comfortable rooms with small communal kitchens. It's about 300m from the harbour on Tombazi.

Hotel Miranda (☎ 2298 052 230, fax 2298 053 510; e mirhydra@hol.gr; doubles with bathroom from €54) is a good spot for a minor splurge. It was once the mansion of a wealthy Hydriot sea captain.

SPETSES Σπέτσες
☎ 2298 • pop 3700

Pine-covered Spetses is perhaps the most beautiful island in the group. It also has the best beaches, so it's packed with package tourists in summer. The **old harbour** in Spetses town is a delightful place to explore.

Cyclades Κυκλάδες

The Cyclades, named after the rough circle they form around Delos, are quintessential Greek Islands with brilliant white villages, dazzling light and azure waters.

Delos, the most important historic island of the group, is uninhabited. The inhabited islands of the archipelago are Mykonos, Syros, Tinos, Andros, Paros, Naxos, Ios, Santorini (Thira), Anafi, Amorgos, Sikinos, Folegandros and the tiny islands of Koufonisi, Shinousa, Iraklia and Donousa, lying east of Naxos.

Some of the Cyclades, such as Mykonos, Ios and Santorini (Thira), have seized tourism, stuffing their coastlines with bars and their beaches with sun lounges. Others, such as Anafi, Sikinos and the tiny islands east of Naxos, are little more than clumps of rock, each with a village, secluded coves and curious tourists.

To give even the briefest rundown on every island is impossible in a single chapter.

For more detailed information, check out Lonely Planet's *Greek Islands* guide.

History
The Cyclades enjoyed a flourishing Bronze Age civilisation (3000 to 1100 BC), more or less concurrent with the Minoan civilisation.

By the 5th century BC, the island of Delos had been taken over by Athens.

Between the 4th and 7th centuries AD, the islands, like the rest of Greece, suffered a series of invasions and occupations. During the Middle Ages they were raided by pirates – hence the labyrinthine character of their towns, which was meant to confuse attackers. On some islands the whole population would move into the mountainous interior to escape the pirates, while on others they would brave it out on the coast. Hence on some islands the hora is on the coast, and on others, it is inland.

The Cyclades became part of independent Greece in 1827.

MYKONOS Μύκονος
☎ 2289 • pop 6170
Polished Greek island perfection, Mykonos is perhaps the most visited – and expensive – of the archipelago. It has the most sophisticated nightlife and is a mecca for gay travellers.

Orientation & Information
There is no tourist office. The **tourist police** (☎ 2289 022 482) are at the port, in the same building as the **hotel reservation office** (☎ 2289 024 540), which has free tourist maps, the **Association of Rooms and Apartments** (☎/fax 2289 026 860) and the **camping information office** (☎ 2289 022 852).

Island Mykonos Travel (☎ 2289 022 232; e islandmykonos@1net.gr) on Taxi Square, where the port road meets the town, is a hectic but quite helpful agency with tourist and travel information. The **post office** is near the southern bus station. **Double Click** (*Florou Zouganeli*), which is off Taxi Square, has rather expensive Internet access.

Things to See
Summer crowds consume the island's capital and port, shuffling through snaking streets of chic boutiques and blinding white walls with balconies of cascading flowers.

The most popular beaches are **Platys Gialos** (wall-to-wall sun lounges), the often nude

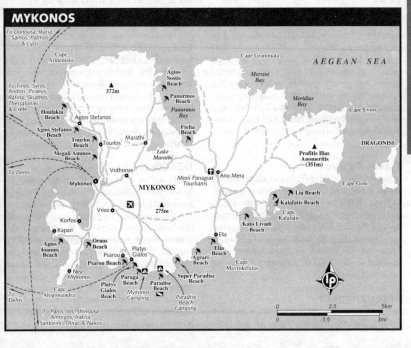

Paradise Beach and mainly gay Super Paradise, Agrari and Elia. The less squashy ones are Panormos, Kato Livadi and Kalafatis.

But wait, there's culture, too – the amazing World Heritage–listed ancient site on nearby Delos (see Delos, later).

Places to Stay
Paradise Beach Camping (☎ 2289 022 852; e paradise@paradise.myk.forthnet.gr; camping per person/tent €7/3.50, sleeping bag area €7) is skin-to-skin mayhem in summer bursting with facilities as well as a party atmosphere.

Mykonos Camping (☎/fax 2289 024 578; e info.mykcamp.gr; camping per person/tent €7/3.50), near Platys Gialos beach, also parties. Minibuses from both meet the ferries and buses jog regularly into town.

Rooms fill up quickly in high season so it's wise to go with the first domatia owner who accosts you. Outside July and August, rooms are cheap as chops.

Kalogera is a good street for mid-range lodgings such as Hotel Philippi (☎ 2289 022 294, fax 2289 024 680; singles/doubles/triples €35/56/67) with spacious rooms and garden.

Rooms Chez Maria (☎ 2289 022 480; doubles/triples with bathroom €80/90), near Hotel Philippi, has quaint rooms and an elegant restaurant.

Hotel Delos (☎ 2289 022 517, fax 2289 022 312; doubles with bath €80), where the waves lap gently outside, offers sparkling doubles on the harbourfront walk into town.

Hotel Apollon (☎ 2289 022 223, fax 2289 024 456; doubles with bathroom €62) is further along the harbour and has an old-world charm.

Places to Eat
Seduce someone over dinner in Little Venice on the western waterfront – it's bound to work.

Busy Niko's Taverna, near the Delos quay, serves good seafood. Sesame Kitchen, behind the maritime museum, is a vegetarian's friend. Popular with locals are intimate Avra (cnr Kalogera & Florou Zouganeli) for gourmet Greek food or Antonini's Taverna on Taxi Square.

Entertainment
For house and Latin vibes, there's the chic Bolero Bar, off Malamatenias, or the flirty Anchor Bar, off Matogianni. Rhapsody in Little Venice is the place to chill.

For a huge night, it's Space Dance near the post office or Cavo Paradiso, 300m above Paradise Beach, world-famous for raves that attract top DJs. A 24-hour bus transports clubbers in summer.

Porta, Kastro Bar, Icaros, Manto and Pierro's are among popular gay spots.

Getting There & Away
There are daily flights from Mykonos to Athens (€75) and to Santorini (Thira; €58). In summer, there are flights to and from Rhodes and Thessaloniki. Visit Island Mykonos Travel for schedules (see under Orientation & Information, earlier).

In winter, ferry services sleep most days and from July to September, the Cyclades are vulnerable to the meltemi, a fierce northeasterly wind that culls ferry schedules. Otherwise, there are daily ferries to Mykonos from Piraeus (€17). From Mykonos, there are daily ferries and hydrofoils to most Cycladic islands, three services weekly to Crete, and less-frequent services to the northeastern Aegean Islands and the Dodecanese. For schedules, ask at the waterfront travel agencies.

Getting Around
The northern bus station is near the port, behind the OTE office. It serves Agios Stefanos, Elia, Kalafatis and Ano Mera. The southern bus station, southeast of the windmills, serves Agios Ioannis, Psarou, Platys Gialos, Ornos and Paradise Beach.

In summer, caïques (small fishing boats) from Mykonos town and Platys Gialos putter to Paradise, Super Paradise, Agrari and Elia Beaches.

DELOS Δήλος
Southeast of Mykonos, the uninhabited island of Delos (admission €5; open 9am-3pm Tues-Sun) is the Cyclades' archaeological jewel. According to mythology, Delos was the birthplace of Apollo – the god of light, poetry, music, healing and prophecy. The island flourished as an important religious and commercial centre from the 3rd millennium BC, reaching its apex of power in the 5th century BC.

To the north of the island's harbour is the Sanctuary of Apollo, containing temples dedicated to him, and the Terrace of the Lions.

These proud beasts were carved in the 7th century or early 6th century BC using marble from Naxos to guard the sacred area. The original lions moved to the island's museum to avoid ageing; youthful replicas remain on the site. The **Sacred Lake** (dry since 1926) is where Leto supposedly gave birth to Apollo. The **museum** is east of this section.

South of the harbour is the **Theatre Quarter** where private houses were built around the **Theatre of Delos**. East of here are the **Sanctuaries of the Foreign Gods**. Climb up **Mt Kynthos** (113m) for a spectacular view of Delos and the surrounding islands.

Excursion boats leave Mykonos for Delos (€6 return, 30 minutes) between 9am and 12.50pm. To appreciate the site, invest in a guidebook or guided tour. **Meridian** *(☎ 2289 024 702)* offers a 3½-hour tour (€28.50).

PAROS Πάρος

☎ 2284 • pop 9591

Paros is an attractive island with softly contoured and terraced hills that culminate in Mt Profitis Ilias. It has fine swimming beaches and is famous for its pure white marble from which the *Venus de Milo* was created.

Orientation & Information

Paros' main town and port is Parikia, on the west coast. Agora, also known as Market St, is Parikia's main commercial thoroughfare running from the main square, Plateia Mavrogenous (opposite the ferry terminal).

There is no tourist office, but travel agencies oblige with information. The post office is on the waterfront, to the north of the pier.

Opposite the ferry quay, to the left, is Memphis.net Internet café, or there's funky **Cyber Cookies** *(Market St)*. An excellent website is W www.parosweb.com.

Things to See & Do

One of the most notable churches in Greece is Parikia's **Panagia Ekatontapyliani** *(Our Lady of the Hundred Gates; open 7am-9pm daily)* for its beautiful, ornate interior. Visitors must dress modestly (ie, no shorts).

On the northeast coast, **Naoussa** is still a sweet fishing village, despite a deluge in tourism, and there's good swimming nearby: **Kolimvythres** has Wild West rock formations; tiny **Monastiri** has a pumping beach bar; and **Santa Maria**, a dive-instruction centre.

PAROS & ANTIPAROS

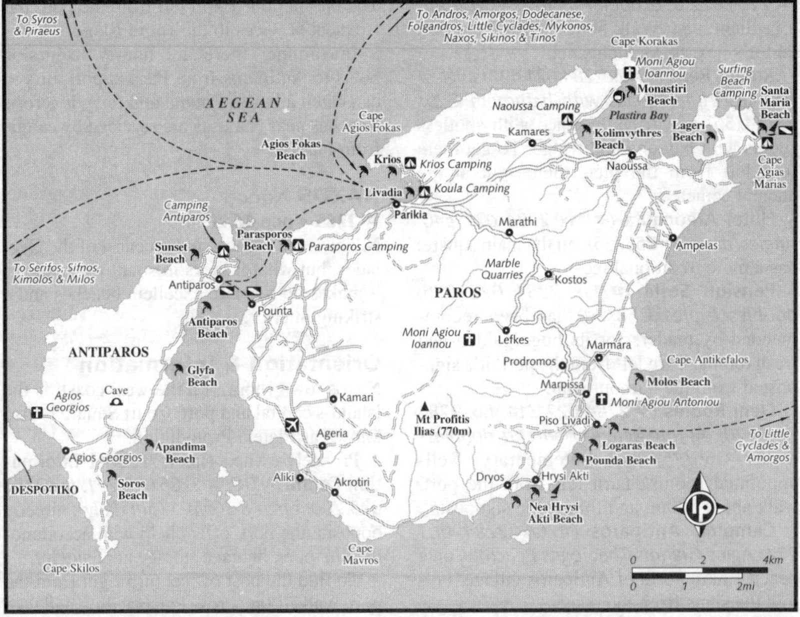

Take a bus to the peaceful inland villages of **Lefkes**, **Marmara** and **Marpissa** for walks through unspoilt hilly terrain and Kodak opportunities. The **Moni Agiou Antoniou** (Monastery of St Anthony), on a hill above Marpissa, offers soaring views.

You can visit the **marble quarries** by taking the bus to Marathi but the steep walk and marble powder may trouble those with respiratory conditions.

Less than 2km from Paros, the small island of **Antiparos** has fantastic beaches which has made it wildly popular. The chief attraction is its **cave** (admission €2; open 9.30am-3.30pm daily), which is considered to be one of Europe's best.

Places to Stay

There's loads of camping on Paros but it's away from the action. **Koula Camping** (☎ 2284 022 081) is on Livadia beach. **Parasporas** (☎/fax 2284 022 268) and **Krios Camping** (☎ 2284 021 705) are near Parikia.

Head to Naoussa for **Naoussa Camping** (☎ 2284 051 565), or **Surfing Beach** (☎ 2284 052 491) on Santa Maria Beach. There's a bus service in summer between Parikia and Naoussa, and some owners greet the ferries.

Back in Parikia, Mike at **Rooms Mike** (☎ 2284 022 856; doubles/triples €30/45) is a brilliant host. Walk 50m left from the port and it's next to Memphis.net.

Rooms Rena (☎/fax 2284 021 427; singles/doubles/triples/quads with bathroom €29/38/44/55) is a friendly place with spotless rooms with balcony and fridge. To get there turn left from the pier, then right at the ancient cemetery.

Hotel Argonauta (☎/fax 2284 021 440; singles/doubles €53/65), on the main square, has a more traditional feel.

Pension Sofia (☎/fax 2284 022 085; doubles/triples €58/70) has been recommended by readers for its huge garden and fresh rooms. Turn left from the port; it's signposted from the harbourfront.

Eleni Rooms (☎ 2284 022 714, fax 2284 024 170; e info@eleni-rooms.gr; doubles/triples €55/75) has contemporary, well-appointed rooms. Turn left from the port, walk about 500m, and follow the signposts.

Camping Antiparos (☎/fax 2284 061 221; Agios Giannis Theologos Beach) is on a beach 1.5km north of Antiparos village. Follow the signs from the quay.

Places to Eat

On Plateia Mavrogenous, trust **Zorba's** gyros for a quick fix, or **Restaurant Argonauta** for tasty Greek fare in cheery surrounds. **Ephesus**, on the street behind the yacht marina, is dip delicious.

Entertainment

Mellow **Pirate** jazz-and-blues bar is tucked away in the old town. The far southern end of Parikia's waterfront has **Pebbles** bar for classical music, and **Mojo** and **Black Bart's** for upbeat vibes. Further along you'll find **The Dubliner** (three bars in one) and **Sex Club**, for dancing, not topless Playboy bunnies.

Pounda Beach has two rave clubs; **Pounda Beach Club** and **Viva Pounda**.

Getting There & Away

There is one flight daily to and from Athens (€69.75). Paros is a major ferry hub with daily connections to Piraeus (€16), frequent ferries and daily catamarans to Naxos, Ios, Santorini (Thira) and Mykonos, and less-frequent ones to Amorgos. The Dodecanese and the northeastern Aegean Islands (via Syros) are also well serviced from here.

Getting Around

The bus station, 100m left from the port, has frequent services to the entire island.

In summer there are hourly excursion boats to Antiparos from Parikia port, or you can catch a bus to Pounta and ferry it across. Beaches near Naoussa are serviced by caïque from Parikia.

NAXOS Νάξος
☎ 2285 • pop 16,703

Naxos is the biggest and greenest of the Cyclades, but what it lacks in small-town allure, it makes up for with excellent beaches and a striking interior.

Orientation & Information

Naxos town (hora), on the west coast, is the island's capital and port. Court Square is also known as Plateia Protodikiou.

Privately-owned **Naxos Tourist Information Centre** (NTIC; ☎ 2285 025 201, fax 2285 025 200; open 8.30am-11pm daily), directly opposite the port, offers help with accommodation, tours, luggage storage and laundry.

To find the post office, turn right from the port, walk 700m, cross Papavasiliou and take the left branch where the road forks. Reliable Internet access is at **Rental Centre** (*Court Square*) and the cool **M@trix Cyber Café**, off Court Square, towards the police station.

Things to See & Do

Naxos town twists and curves up to a crumbling 13th-century **Kastro** and well-stocked **archaeological museum** (*admission €3; open 8.30am-3pm Tues-Sun*).

The town beach of **Agios Georgios** is a 10-minute walk from town; turn right from the port. Beyond it, wonderful sandy beaches as far as **Pyrgaki Beach** become progressively less crammed. **Agia Anna Beach** is a sublime 3km stretch.

A day trip to **Apollonas** on the north coast reveals a dramatic landscape. The **Tragaea**

region is a vast Arcadian olive grove with tranquil villages in valleys and dome churches atop rocky crests.

Filoti, the largest settlement, perches on the slopes of **Mt Zeus** (1004m). It's a tough three-hour trail to the summit.

In Apollonas you'll find the mysterious 10.5m **kouros** (naked male statue), constructed circa 7th century, lying abandoned and unfinished in an ancient marble quarry.

The old village of **Apiranthos** is a gem, with paved marble streets and few tavernas.

There are a string of **minor islands** off the east coast of Naxos also known as the **Little Cyclades**. Only four are inhabited: Donousa, Shinousa, Iraklia and Ano Koufonisi. Intrepid visitors will find few amenities on these, but each has some *domatia*. They are served by

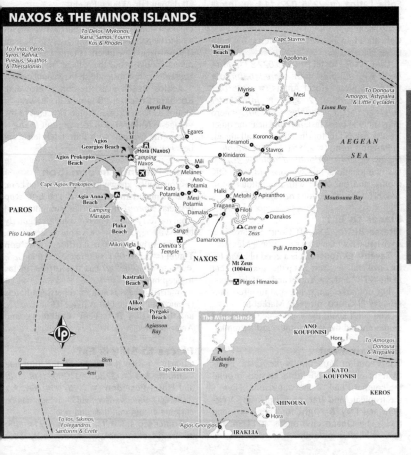

two to three ferries per week from Piraeus via Naxos, some of which continue to Amorgos.

Places to Stay

Camping Maragas (☎/fax 2285 042 552; e maragas@naxos-island.com), on Agia Anna Beach 8km from town, is a lovely place with a café and bar and huge rooms available.

Camping Naxos (☎ 2285 023 500) is in a lonely spot, 1km south of Agios Georgios Beach.

Both Camping Maragas and Naxos have ferry pick-ups – or take the bus.

Studios Stratos (☎/fax 2285 025 898; doubles/triples with bathroom €35/45), in the back streets around Agios Georgios, has immaculate, lovingly decorated rooms with mini kitchen. The combined **Hotel Galini & Sofia Latina** (☎ 2285 022 114; e info@ hotelgalini.com; doubles with bathroom €50), next to the town hall, has great views. Call ahead to be met at the ferry for both these places.

Dionyssos Hostel (☎ 2285 022 331; dorm beds €7, doubles with shared bathroom €30) and pretty **Hotel Anixis** (☎ 2285 022 932, fax 2285 022 112; e info@hotel anixis.gr; singles/doubles €40/50), where rates include breakfast, is found near the quiet Kastro; ask NTIC for directions or call ahead.

Pension Irene (☎ 2285 023 169; doubles/ triples €30/40 • doubles/triples €36/50) has two locations in town, one old, with OK rooms, and one new, with a fabulous pool. Ask NTIC for directions or call ahead.

Places to Eat

Picasso Bistro, 20m off Court Square, is a stylish place which does sensational Mexican.

Taverna O Apostolis is a good place to try for ouzo and *mezedes*; go up the street adjacent to the NTIC and Zas Travel and spot the signs.

For upmarket ambience and inspired sunsets, try **El Greco**, off New Market St.

You can't avoid the waffles, ice cream and crepes around the waterfront – just surrender.

Entertainment

The **Venetian Museum** by the Kastro holds twilight concerts. Nightlife clusters around the southern end of the waterfront. There's the tropical **Med Bar**, crowd-pleasing **Veggera** and **Day & Night** for Greek pop and rock. The **Ocean** club opens at 11pm, but goes wild after midnight.

Getting There & Around

Naxos has six flights weekly to Athens (€70.40). There are daily ferries to Piraeus (€16.35) and good ferry and hydrofoil connections to most Cycladic islands. Boats go once a week to Crete, Thessaloniki and usually Rhodes, and to Samos two to three times per week. Check with travel agencies.

Buses travel to most villages regularly (including Apollonas and Filoti) and the beaches towards Pyrgaki. The bus terminal is in front of the port. Car and motorcycle rentals are off Court Square.

IOS Ιος

☎ 2286 • pop 2000

In high season, Ios is the spoilt brat of the islands with little to offer beyond beach baking all day and drinking all night.

The island is reasonably popular with the older set – anyone over 25 – but the two groups tend to be polarised. The young stay in the hora (Ios town) and the others at Ormos port. Non-ravers should avoid the village from June to September. The locals wish they could, too.

Gialos Beach near the port is crowded. **Koubara Beach**, a 20-minute walk west of Gialos, is less crazy. Stumble 1km east of the village to **Milopotas** to recover, but **Manganari** is the magnet, with four sandy crescent beaches on the south coast.

Orientation & Information

Ios town, also known as 'the village' or hora, is 2km inland from the port. The **bus stop** (Plateia Emirou) in Ormos is straight ahead from the ferry quay. The bus trundles regularly to the village, otherwise it's a nasty, steep hike.

There is no EOT tourist office, but **Acteon Travel** (☎ 2286 091 343, fax 2286 091 088; e acteon@otenet.gr) has five offices in Ios to keep busy.

Internet access is scattered between hotels (Francesco's, Far Out Village Hotel), cafés and bars (Fun Pub, Café Cyclades), and Acteon Travel.

Places to Stay & Eat

Clearly visible just right of the port are **Camping Ios** (☎ 2286 091 050; tents €8) and **Hotel Poseidon** (☎ 2286 091 091, fax 2286 091 969; doubles €67), which has an enticing communal area and pool.

Francesco's (☎/fax 2286 091 223; e fragesco@otenet.gr; dorm beds €15, doubles with bathroom €50), in the village, is a lively meeting place with superlative views from its terrace bar.

Milopotas Beach parties hard from noon until midnight with up to 3000 people.

Camping Stars (☎ 2286 091 302; tents €7.50, bungalows with bathroom per person €19) has a pool, bar and live music.

Far Out Camping Club (☎ 2286 091 468; e camping@faroutclub.com; camping per person €8, bungalows & dorms per person €18) has tons of facilities and bungy jumping. Next door, **Far Out Village Hotel** (☎ 2286 092 305; doubles €82) is less hyper.

In Ormos, **Café Cyclades** does pricey Mexican. In the village, **The Nest** is the cheapest taverna for hungry backpackers, or try **Ali Baba's** near the gym for huge meals and funky ambience. **Lord Byron Taverna** and **Pithari** are cosy nooks for Greek fare. For decent seafood, try **Filippos** on the road between the port and Koubara Beach.

Entertainment

At night, the village erupts with bars to explore and you'll have to elbow your way nicely to the other side. Perennial favourites

include **Red Bull**, **Slammers** and **Blue Note**. Opposite the central car park, **Sweet Irish Dreams** is a crowd pleaser with table dancing. For clubbing you could head to a place called **Scorpions**.

Getting There & Around

Mercifully, Ios has daily connections to Piraeus (€16.50) and there are frequent hydrofoils and ferries to the major Cycladic islands. For schedules, visit Acteon Travel (see under Orientation & Information, earlier).

There are buses every 20 minutes between the port, the village and Milopotas Beach until early morning, and two to three per day to Manganari Beach (45 minutes).

SANTORINI (THIRA)
Σαντορίνη (Θήρα)
☎ 2286 • pop 9360

Around 1450 BC, the volcanic heart of Santorini (Thira) exploded and sank, leaving an extraordinary landscape. Today, the startling sight of the submerged caldera almost encircled by sheer cliffs remains – this is certainly the most dramatic sights of all the islands. It's possible that the catastrophe destroyed the Minoan civilisation, but neither this theory nor the claim that the island was part of the lost continent of Atlantis has been proven.

Orientation & Information

The capital, Fira, perches on top of the caldera on the west coast. The port of Athinios is 12km away.

The bus station and taxi station are located just south of Fira's main square Plateia Theotokopoulou.

There is no EOT tourist office or tourist police but there are several travel agencies on the square and the helpful **Dakoutros Travel** (☎ 2286 022 958, fax 2286 022 686), which is opposite the taxi station.

The post office is one block south of the taxi station. The best-value Internet café on the square is **PC Club**, above Santo Volcano Tours & Travel, or **Espresso Caffe**, up the steps opposite the taxi station.

Fira

The shameless commercialism of Fira has not quite reduced its all-pervasive dramatic aura. The best of the town's museums is the exceptional **Museum of Prehistoric Thira**

GREECE

(admission free; open 8.30am-3pm Tues-Sun), which has wonderful displays of artefacts predominantly from ancient Akrotiri. To get there, walk south from the main square, past the bus station and take the next street on the right. The **Megaron Gyzi Museum** (adult/student €2.50/1; open 10.30am-1.30pm & 5pm-8pm Mon-Sat, 10.30am-4.30pm Sun), behind the youth hostel and Catholic monastery, houses local memorabilia, including photographs of Fira before and after the 1956 earthquake.

Around the Island

Excavations in 1967 uncovered the remarkably well-preserved Minoan settlement of **Akrotiri** with its remains of two- and three-storey buildings, and evidence of a sophisticated drainage system. Until a new shelter to protect the ruins is complete (around 2007), artefacts have been moved to the Museum of Prehistoric Thira. Without a guided tour, the site is just rubble. Dakoutros Travel conducts tours for €20.

Moni Profiti Ilia, a monastery built on the island's highest point, can be reached along a path from the site of **Ancient Thira**; the walk takes about one hour.

The flawless village of **Oia** (pronounced ee-ah), famed for its postcard sunsets, is less hectic than Fira and a must visit. Its caldera-facing tavernas are dreamy spots for brunch.

Santorini's **beaches** of black volcanic sand sizzle – beach mats are essential. **Kamari**, **Perissa** and **Monolithos** get crowded but those near Oia are quieter. **Red Beach**, a 15-minute walk from Akrotiri, is very popular.

Of the surrounding islets, only **Thirasia** is inhabited. At **Palia Kameni** you can bathe in hot springs and on **Nea Kameni** you can clamber around on volcanic lava. A six-hour tour to these three islands by caïque or glass-bottomed boat costs €17. Tickets are available from most travel agencies.

Places to Stay

You should beware the aggressive accommodation owners who meet boats and buses and claim that their rooms are in Fira town when they're actually in Karterados; a 20-minute walk or short bus ride into town. Ask to see a map to check their location. Dakoutros Travel can help with a range of accommodation in Fira (and Oia) and organises pick-ups from its office.

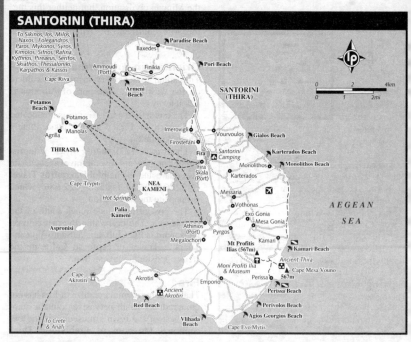

SANTORINI (THIRA)

Santorini Camping (☎ 2286 022 944; e santocam@otenet.gr; camping per person/ tent €6/3), 400m east of the main square, has a restaurant and swimming pool.

Thira Hostel (☎ 2286 023 864; dorm beds €11, doubles/triples with bathroom €35/40), 200m north of the square, is a spacious, run-down old monastery. Some may enjoy its decaying appeal! It also has a cheap restaurant.

Pension Petros (☎ 2286 022 573, fax 2286 022 615; doubles €60) is centrally located, 250m east of the square. Its owners meet the ferries.

Hotel Olympia (☎ 2286 022 213, fax 2286 022 498; doubles/triples €73/82) in Karterados has lovely rooms overlooking a pool.

Hotel Hellas (☎ 2286 023 555, fax 2286 023 840; doubles €79) at the top end of town, is roomy with relaxing rural and sea views and an edgeless pool.

Astir Thira Hotel (☎ 2286 022 585, fax 2286 022 525; e astir-h@hol.gr; doubles €120), about 500m from Fira on the main road, is an upmarket option with some caldera views and breakfast is included. Call ahead to be claimed at the ferry.

Places to Eat

Effusive **Mama's Cyclades** up the top end of town past the youth hostel offers a hearty breakfast. On the square, **Lucky's Souvlakis** cares for the budget conscious. You'll find excellent-value meals at **Naoussa** on Erythrou Stavrou, which is not far from the cable-car station, and **Stani Taverna**, next to the Koo Club. **Koukoumavlos**, below the Orthodox cathedral, wins the fine-dining prize.

One must sunset-sip at bars overlooking the caldera; hang the expense!

Entertainment

Bars and clubs are clustered along one street, Erythrou Stavrou. From the main square, facing north, turn left at George's Snack Corner, then take the first right.

Koo Club, **Enigma** and **Murphys** are all big. The dimly lit **Kira Thira Jazz Bar** is a cosy alternative. The **Dubliner Irish Pub**, next to the youth hostel, rocks till late.

Getting There & Away

There are regular flights to Athens (€78.40), Rhodes (€80.40), Mykonos (€57.40) and Iraklio (Crete; €59.40). Book through the travel agencies on the main square.

There are daily ferries to Piraeus (€23.90), daily connections in summer to Mykonos, Ios, Naxos, Paros and Iraklio, and three ferries per week to Anafi, Sikinos, Folegandros, Sifnos, Serifos, Kimolos and Milos.

Getting Around

Large ferries use Athinios port, where they are met by buses (€1.20) and taxis. Small boats use Fira Skala port, where the mode of transport is by donkey or by cable car (€3); otherwise it's a clamber up 600 steps.

There are daily boats from Athinios and Fira Skala to Thirasia and Oia. The islets surrounding Santorini (Thira) can be visited only on excursion from Fira.

Buses go frequently to Oia, Kamari, Perissa, Akrotiri, Ancient Thira and Monolithos. Port buses usually leave Fira, Kamari and Perissa 90 minutes to an hour before ferry departures.

Crete Κρήτη

Crete, Greece's largest island, hosts a quarter of all visitors to the country. All of Crete's major towns are on the northern coast and it's here that the package-tourism industry thrives. You can escape the hordes by visiting the undeveloped western coast or by heading into the villages. The mountainous interior offers rigorous trekking and climbing. Crete is also the best place in Greece to buy high-quality, inexpensive leather goods.

For more detailed information, see Lonely Planet's Crete.

History

Crete was the birthplace of Minoan culture, Europe's first advanced civilisation, which flourished from 2800 to 1450 BC. Very little is known of Minoan civilisation, which came to an abrupt end, possibly destroyed by Santorini's volcanic eruption.

Later, Crete passed from the warlike Dorians to the Romans, and then to the Genoese, who in turn sold it to the Venetians. Under the Venetians, Crete became a refuge for artists, writers and philosophers who fled Constantinople after it fell to the Turks. Their influence inspired the young Cretan painter Domenikos Theotokopoulos, who moved to Spain and there won immortality as the great El Greco.

GREECE

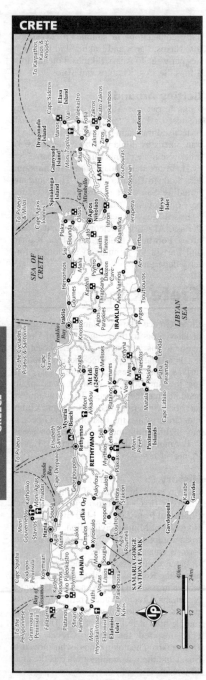

The Turks finally conquered Crete in 1670. It became a British protectorate in 1898 after a series of insurrections and was united with independent Greece in 1913. There was fierce fighting during WWII when a German airborne invasion defeated Allied forces in the 10-day Battle of Crete. An active resistance movement drew heavy reprisals from the German occupiers.

IRAKLIO Ηράκλειο
☎ 281 • pop 127,600

Iraklio, Crete's capital, is a noisy, polluted, unavoidable transport hub and it's the main connection to the Cyclades. Apart from the city's archaeological museum and proximity to Knossos, there's no reason to linger here.

Information

There is no EOT tourist office but the **tourist police** (☎ 281 028 3190; Dikeosynis 10; open 7am-10pm) are helpful with maps and information.

Banks, travel agencies and Olympic Airways are on 25 Avgoustou. There's a central **post office** (Plateia Daskalogiani) and Internet access is available at **Cyber SportC@fe** (25 Avgoustou).

Washsalon (Handakos 18) laundrette also has luggage storage. A wash and dry will cost you €6.

Archaeological Museum

Iraklio's archaeological museum (adult/student €6/3; open 12.30pm-7pm Mon, 8am-7pm Tues-Sun) has an outstanding collection, second only to the national museum in Athens.

Places to Stay

Beware of taxi drivers who tell you that the pension of your choice is a dud; they're being paid commission by the big hotels.

Rent Rooms Hellas (☎ 281 028 8851; Handakos 24; dorm beds €8; doubles/triples €27/34) is the best budget choice and popular with backpackers. It's clean, with packed dorms, a rooftop bar and a bargain breakfast.

Near the old harbour and bus stations is a cluster of decent mid-range hotels.

Hotel Lena (☎ 281 022 3280; Lahana 10; singles with bathroom €32, doubles without bathroom €33) has large, dull rooms, while nearby **Ilaira Hotel** (☎ 281 0227103; Epimenidou 1; singles/doubles €35/42) has compact ones and nice views from the rooftop bar.

Hotel Mirabello (☎ *281 028 5052;* e *mirabhot@otenet.gr; Theotokopoulou 20; singles with shared bathroom €28, doubles with bathroom €46)* is clean and comfortable.

Hotel Kastro (☎ *281 028 4185;* e *info@kastro-hotel.gr; Theotokopoulou 22; singles/doubles with bathroom €55/75)* is remarkable value for its sleek, new, renovated interior. It won't be long before prices here take a hike.

Places to Eat

There's a bustling, colourful **market** all the way along 1866 for self-caterers.

Giakoumis Taverna is the best of a bunch of cheap tavernas in the area around 1866.

Ippokampos Ouzeri, on the waterfront, offers a full range of well-priced *mezedes*.

Pagopeion, by Agios Titos church, is a super-cool café and bar with exceptional food at OK prices. (Check out the toilets!)

Getting There & Away

It's easy to leave Iraklio. There are several flights a day to Athens and, in summer, daily

flights from Iraklio to Thessaloniki, and three flights a week to Rhodes and Santorini (Thira).

There are daily ferries to Piraeus (€24), as well as boats most days to Santorini (Thira) that continue on to other Cycladic islands. In summer, a boat sails twice weekly from Iraklio to Marmaris in Turkey, via Rhodes. For boat schedules, the **Skoutelis Travel Bureau** (☎ *281 028 0808, fax 281 033 2747; 25 Avgoustou 20)* seems friendly, or try some of the other agencies on this strip.

Iraklio has two bus stations. Bus Station A, just inland from the new harbour, serves eastern Crete (Agios Nikolaos, Ierapetra, Sitia, Malia and the Lasithi Plateau). The Hania and Rethymno terminal is opposite Bus Station A, across the street. Bus Station B, 50m beyond the Hania Gate, serves the southern route (Phaestos, Matala, Anogia). For more information, visit the **long-distance bus website** (w *www.ktel.org).*

Getting Around

In Iraklio, Bus No 1 travels to and from the airport (€0.60) every 15 minutes between 6am and 11pm. It stops at Plateia Eleftherias, across the road from the archaeological museum.

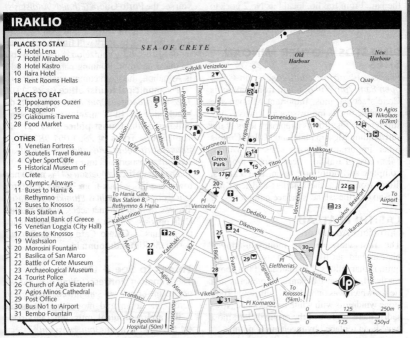

IRAKLIO

PLACES TO STAY
6 Hotel Lena
7 Hotel Mirabello
8 Hotel Kastro
10 Ilaira Hotel
18 Rent Rooms Hellas

PLACES TO EAT
2 Ippokampos Ouzeri
15 Pagopeion
25 Giakoumis Taverna
28 Food Market

OTHER
1 Venetian Fortress
3 Skoutelis Travel Bureau
4 Cyber SportC@fe
5 Historical Museum of Crete
9 Olympic Airways
11 Buses to Hania & Rethymno
12 Buses to Knossos
13 Bus Station A
14 National Bank of Greece
16 Venetian Loggia (City Hall)
17 Buses to Knossos
19 Washsalon
20 Morosini Fountain
21 Basilica of San Marco
22 Battle of Crete Museum
23 Archaeological Museum
24 Tourist Police
26 Church of Agia Ekaterini
27 Agios Minos Cathedral
29 Post Office
30 Bus No1 to Airport
31 Bembo Fountain

GREECE

The car- and motorcycle-rental outlets are mostly along 25 Avgoustou.

KNOSSOS Κνωσός

Five kilometres south of Iraklio, Knossos (adult/concession €6/3; open noon-7pm Mon, 8am-7pm Tues-Sun Apr-Oct), is the most famous of Crete's Minoan sites and is the inspiration for the myth of the Minotaur. According to legend, King Minos of Knossos was given a bull to sacrifice to the god of Poseidon, but decided to keep it, as you would. This enraged Poseidon, who punished the king by causing his wife Pasiphae to fall in love with the animal. The result of this odd union was the Minotaur – half-man and half-bull – who lived in a labyrinth beneath the king's palace, munching on youths and maidens.

In 1900, the ruins of Knossos were uncovered by Arthur Evans. Although archaeologists tend to disparage Evans' reconstruction, the buildings – an immense palace, courtyards, private apartments, baths, lively frescoes and more – give a fine idea of what a Minoan palace might have looked like.

A whole day is needed to see the site and a guidebook is essential. Arrive early to avoid the jam. From Iraklio, local bus No 2 goes to Knossos (€0.80) every 10 minutes from Bus Station A; it also stops on 25 Avgoustou.

PHAESTOS & OTHER MINOAN SITES

Phaestos (Φαιστός; adult/concession €4/2; open 8am-7pm daily), 63km from Iraklio, is Crete's second-most important Minoan site and, while not as impressive as Knossos, it's still worth a visit for its stunning views of the surrounding Mesara plain and Mt Idi. Crete's other important Minoan sites are Malia, 34km east of Iraklio where there is a palace complex and adjoining town, and Zakros, 40km from Sitia, the smallest and least impressive of the island's palace complexes.

LASITHI PLATEAU

Οροπέδιο Λασιθίου

The first view of this mountain-fringed plateau, laid out like an immense patchwork quilt, is marvellous. The plateau, 900m above sea level, is a vast expanse of orchards and fields, which was once dotted with some 1000 stone windmills with white canvas sails. Now, sadly, there are few of the originals left; most have been replaced by mechanical pumps.

The **Dikteon Cave** (admission €4; open 8.30am-2.30pm Mon, 8am-7pm Tues-Sun), is where, according to mythology, the Titan Rhea hid the newborn Zeus from Cronos, his offspring-gobbling father.

The cave of stalagmites and stalactites is just outside the small village of Psyhro, which is the best place to stay. Try **Hotel Dias** (☎ 2844 031 207; Agios Georgios; doubles with bathroom €16). On the main street, **Stavros** and **Platanos** tavernas serve decent food at OK prices.

There are daily buses to the area from Iraklio (€4.55, two hours) and three a week from Agios Nikolaos.

RETHYMNO Ρέθυμνο

☎ 2831 • pop 24,000

Rethymno's gracious old quarter of crumbling Venetian and Turkish buildings radiates magic – and package tourists who crowd its long, sandy beachfront.

Orientation & Information

Rethymno's bus station is at the western end of Igoumenou Gavriil. To reach the old quarter, follow Igoumenou east for 700m until you see the **Porto Guora** (Ethnikis Andistasis), which is the remnant of a Venetian defensive wall and gate. Turn left and you're there. Those arriving by ferry will find the old quarter dead ahead. El Venizelou is the main strip by the waterfront. Running parallel behind it is Arkadiou, the main commercial street.

The **municipal tourist office** (☎ 2831 029 148; open 8am-2.30pm Mon-Fri) is on the beach side of El Venizelou, in the same building as the **tourist police** (☎ 2831 028 156). **Ellotia Tours** (☎ 2831 051 981; e elotia@ret.forthnet.gr; Arkadiou 155) will answer all transport and tour inquiries.

The **post office** (Moatsou 21) is in the new town, one block back from **Plateia Martyron** (cnr Igoumenou Gavriil & Ethnikis Andistasis). There's 24-hour Internet access at **G@meNet-Café** opposite Plateia Martyron, or you could try upstairs at **Galero Café** (Plateia Rimini), beside the **Rimondi fountain**.

Things to See & Do

The **Venetian Fortress** (admission €2.90; open 9am-6pm Tues-Sun) affords great views across the town and mountains. Opposite is the **archaeological museum** (admission €1.50; open 8.30am-3pm Tues-Sun).

The **historical and folk art museum** *(Vernardou; admission €3; open 9.30am-2.30pm & 6pm-9pm Mon-Sat)* proudly displays Cretan crafts.

Happy Walker *(☎/fax 2831 052 920; e hapwalk@hol.gr; w www.happywalker.nl; Tombazi 56)* is worth a visit for its programme of daily walks in the countryside (from €25 per person).

Places to Stay
Elisabeth Camping *(☎ 2831 028 694; camping per person/tent €6.30/4.20)* is situated on Mysiria Beach, 4km east of town, and it is accessible by the bus that goes to and from Iraklio. From Hania, take the bus that services the beach hotels.

Youth hostel *(☎ 2831 022 848; e reservations@yhrethymno.com; Tombazi 45; dorm & roof beds €6)* is a well-run place with crowded dorms.

Olga's Pension *(☎ 2831 028 665; Souliou 57; singles/doubles/triples with bathroom €30/35/45)* is central with colourful, cosy rooms of intriguing taste and a wild rooftop garden.

Garden House *(☎ 2831 028 586; Nikiforou Foka 82; doubles/triples €35/50)* is a romantic, old, Venetian place which has average rooms but excellent ambience.

Rent Rooms Sea Front *(☎ 2831 051 981, fax 2831 051 062; e elotia@ret.forthnet.gr; Arkadiou 159; singles/doubles €24/35)* is ideally positioned with beach views and spacious rooms.

Places to Eat
Taverna Kyria Maria *(Diog Mesologiou 20)* is tucked behind the Rimondi fountain under a lush canopy.

Gounakis Restaurant & Bar *(Koroneou 6)* has live Cretan music and reasonably priced food.

East of the Rimondi fountain, Arabatzoglou and Radamanthios have upmarket eateries of bewitching ambience. Check out the intimate **Avli**, cave-like **Castelo Taverna** and **Taverna Larenzo**.

Getting There & Away
Ferries travel daily from Piraeus to Rethymno (€24). For schedules and other details, visit **ANEK** *(Arkadiou 250)* by the old Venetian harbour or Ellotia Tours (see Orientation & Information, earlier).

Buses depart regularly to Iraklio (€5.90, 1½ hours), Hania (€5.30, one hour), Agia Galini, Moni Arkadiou and Plakas.

HANIA Χανιά
☎ 2821 • pop 65,000
Lovely Hania, the old capital of Crete, lures tourists in droves with its softly hued Venetian buildings and snug location near idyllic beaches and a glorious mountain interior.

Orientation & Information
Hania is a place to amble wide-eyed for a couple of days, enjoying its vital signs and plotting side trips.

There is no EOT tourist office but you can try the **tourist police** *(2821 053 333; Kydonias 29; open 7.30am-2.30pm Mon-Fri)*, near Plateia 1866. Send your mail at the **central post office** *(Tzanakaki 3)*.

Vranas Studios *(Agion Deka)* has a comfortable Internet setup, or try **N@ftilos Internet Café** for cool ambience. It's next to the food market; walk up the steps off Mousouron.

Laundry Express Fidias *(Sarpaki)* is next to Pension Fidias; a wash and dry costs €6.

Things to See & Do
The **archaeological museum** *(Halidon 30; admission €1.50; open 8.30am-3pm Tues-Sun)* used to be the Venetian Church of San Francesco, until the Turks made it into a mosque.

Places to Stay
Camping Hania *(☎ 2821 031 138; camping per person/tent €5/3.50)* is 3km west of town on the beach. Jump on a Kalamaka bus from Plateia 1866.

Pension Fidias *(☎ 2821 052 494; Sarpaki 6; dorm beds/doubles/triples €8/15/21)*, behind the Orthodox Cathedral, is still the budget choice and renovations are planned.

Vranas Studios *(☎/fax 2821 058 618; Agion Deka; doubles €55-60, triples €70)* has superior, contemporary studios.

For rooms with character, wander through the ancient Venetian buildings around the old harbour. Friendly **Casa Dell Amore** *(☎ 2821 086 206; Theotokopoulou 52; doubles €45-50)* has cute, loft-style rooms of quirky design.

Ifigenia II *(☎ 2821 094 357, fax 2821 036 104; Angelou 18; doubles €35-40)* has a range of excitingly eccentric rooms, some with four-poster beds.

GREECE

Rooms for Rent George (☎ 2821 088 715; Zambeliou 30; singles/doubles/triples €15/24/33) is an atmospheric relic.

Places to Eat

The **food market** off Plateia Markopoulou is self-caterers' paradise.

To Ayho Toy Kokkopa (Agion Deka), beneath Vranas Studios, does crisp salads and sandwiches.

For alfresco dining, try romantic **Tsikoydadiko** in an ancient Venetian courtyard, or the preserved ruins at classy **Tholos Restaurant**; both serve local cuisine at reasonable prices.

Suki Yaki and **Chin Chin** offer a refreshing change with Thai and Chinese meals, respectively.

Entertainment

Many restaurants play live Cretan music bu **Café Kriti** is the authentic experience.

Harbour tavernas are packed at sunset After dark, **Neorio Café**, **Bora Bora** and **Cocktails Galini** attract a younger crowd. Fo shots and dancing on the bar, it's **Nota-Bene**

Getting There & Away

If you must leave Hania, there are severa flights a day to Athens and two flights a week to Thessaloniki.

There are daily ferries to Piraeus (€22 from the port of Souda, 10km east of town The travel agencies on Halidon can help with all schedules and ticketing.

Frequent buses plough daily to Iraklio Rethymno and Kastelli–Kissamos; buses run

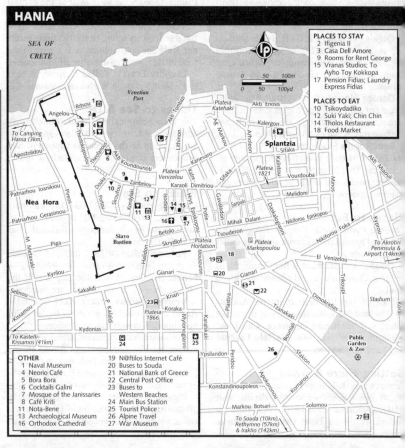

HANIA

SEA OF
CRETE

PLACES TO STAY
2 Ifigenia II
3 Casa Dell Amore
9 Rooms for Rent George
15 Vranas Studios; To
   Ayho Toy Kokkopa
17 Pension Fidias; Laundry
   Express Fidias

PLACES TO EAT
10 Tsikoydadiko
12 Suki Yaki; Chin Chin
14 Tholos Restaurant
18 Food Market

OTHER
1 Naval Museum
4 Neorio Café
5 Bora Bora
6 Cocktails Galini
7 Mosque of the Janissaries
8 Café Kriti
11 Nota-Bene
13 Archaeological Museum
16 Orthodox Cathedral
19 N@ftilos Internet Café
20 Buses to Souda
21 National Bank of Greece
22 Central Post Office
23 Buses to
   Western Beaches
24 Main Bus Station
25 Tourist Police
26 Alpine Travel
27 War Museum

ess-frequently to Paleohora, Omalos, Hora
Sfakion and Elafonisi from the main bus
station on Kydonias.

Buses for Souda (the port) leave frequently
from outside the food market. Buses for the
beaches west of Hania leave from the southeastern corner of Plateia 1866.

THE WEST COAST

This is Crete's least-developed coastline. At
Falasarna, 16km west of Kastelli–Kissamos,
there's a magnificent sandy beach and a few
tavernas and *domatia*. There are buses to
Falasarna in summer from Kastelli–Kissamos
and Hania.

Further south, you can wade out to more
beaches from the shallow waters surrounding
superb Elafonisi islet. Travel agencies in Hania
and Paleohora run excursions to the area.

SAMARIA GORGE
Φαράγγι της Σαμαριάς
Samaria Gorge (☎ 2825 067 179; admission
€3.50; open 6am-3pm daily May–mid-Oct)
is one of Europe's most spectacular gorges.
Rugged footwear, food, water and sun protection are essential for this strenuous six-
hour trek, which is not recommended for
inexperienced walkers. You can do the walk
independently by taking the Omalos bus from
the main bus station in Hania (€5, one hour,
three daily) to the head of the gorge at Xylo-
skalo and walking the length of the gorge
(16km) to Agia Roumeli, from where you
take a boat to Hora Sfakion (€4.40, two
daily) and then a bus back to Hania (€5.10;
two hours; four daily). Too much? You could
join one of the easier daily excursions from
Hania that walk about 4km into the gorge.
Check out the travel agencies on Halidon in
Hania for information.

LEFKA ORI Λευκά Όρη
Crete's rugged 'White Mountains' are south
of Hania. Alpine Travel (☎ 2821 050 939,
fax 2821 053 309; e info@alpine.gr; Shopping Centre, Bldg C, 2nd floor, Bouniali 11-
19), in Hania, offers excellent one- to 15-day
trekking programmes from €58 per person,
as well as trail advice.

Trekking Plan (☎/fax 2821 060 861;
e sales@cycling.gr, w www.cycling.gr), based
in Agia Marina 8km west of Hania next to
Santa Marina Hotel, has mountain biking,
trekking and mountaineering tours.

PALEOHORA & THE SOUTHWEST COAST
☎ 2823
Paleohora (Παλαιοχώρα), discovered by
hippies back in the 1960s, is a relaxing, if
overrated resort favoured by backpackers.
There's a welcoming tourist office (☎ 2823
041 507) three blocks south of the bus stop.
Some tour companies offer dolphin watching.

Further east, along Crete's southwest
coast, are the resorts of Sougia, Loutro (the
least developed) and Hora Sfakion.

Camping Paleohora (☎ 2823 041 120;
camping per person/tent €4/3) is 1.5km
northeast of town, near the pebble beach.
There's also a restaurant and nightclub here.

Homestay Anonymous (☎ 2823 042 098;
singles/doubles/triples €12/17/20), in Paleohora, is a great place for backpackers with its
warm service and communal kitchen.

Oriental Bay Rooms (☎ 2823 041 076;
doubles/triples with bathroom €36/39) is
comfy; it's at the north end of the pebble beach.

Domatia and tavernas dot the harbourfront. Readers recommend Calypso near
the pebble beach. Near the sandy beach, try
The Third Eye for vegetarian, or The Small
Garden for international fare.

There are at least five buses daily between
Hania and Paleohora (€5, 1¼ hours). No
road links the coastal resorts but if you can't
swim (kidding) daily boats from Paleohora to
Elafonisi, Agia Roumeli and Hora Sfakion
connect the resorts in summer.

Coastal paths lead from Paleohora to
Sougia and from Agia Roumeli to Loutro.
Both walks take a hefty six to seven hours.

SITIA Σητεία
☎ 2843 • pop 9000
Back on the northeastern coast, package
tourism gathers momentum as it advances
eastwards, reaching a crescendo in Agios
Nikolaos. Attractive Sitia, on a hotel-lined
bay flanked by mountains, is an easy place to
unwind and has good connections to the
Dodecanese islands.

The main square, Plateia El Venizelou, is
at the northern end of Karamanli.

The municipal tourist office (open 9am-
2.30pm & 5.30pm-8.30pm Mon-Fri) is on
the waterfront just before the town beach.
Tzortzakis Travel Agency (☎ 2843 025 080;
e tzortzakis@sit.forthnet.gr; Kornarou 150)
is good for tickets and accommodation ad-

vice. The **post office** *(Dimokratou)* is off El Venizelou.

The ferry port is about 800m away, signposted from the square.

There is no shortage of *domatia* behind the waterfront but if you're desperate, the shabby **youth hostel** (☎ 2843 028 062; *dorms €6*) is 400m from the square on the road to Iraklio.

Hotel Arhontiko (☎ 2843 028 172; *Kondylaki 16; doubles/triples €23/27.60*) is a basic hotel, but it's immaculate. To find it, walk towards the ferry quay along El Venizelou, turn left up Filellinon and then right onto Kondylaki.

Hotel Apollon (☎ 2843 028 155, fax 2843 026 598; *Kapetan Sifis 28; singles/doubles/triples €27.70/30.80/37*) is in a central position, 150m up Kapetan Sifis from the harbourfront, on your right.

Just inland, **Kali Kardia** *(Foundalidhou 22)* and the harbourside **O Mixos** *(Kornarou 15)* are popular tavernas with the locals. At the port end of Kornarou, you'll find **Murphy's Irish Pub**.

At the time of writing, Sitia's domestic airport was closed for a runway extension. It normally receives one to two flights per week from Athens. There are daily ferries from Piraeus to Sitia (€24), three ferries per week to Rhodes and four to Karpathos. In summer, there's one ferry per week to Santorini (Thira). Visit Tzortzakis Travel Agency for tickets and schedules.

There are five buses daily to Ierapetra, and five to Iraklio, via Agios Nikolaos. In peak season, there are four buses daily to Vaï Beach.

AROUND SITIA

The reconstructed **Moni Toplou** *(admission €2.50; open 9am-1pm & 2pm-6pm daily)*, 15km from Sitia, houses some beautifully intricate icons and relics. To get there, take a Vaï bus from Sitia, get off at the fork for the monastery and plod the last 4km.

Vaï Beach, famous for its palm trees, is 26km from Sitia and worth the trip.

Dodecanese
Δωδεκάνησα

The Dodecanese are more verdant and mountainous than the Cyclades and have comparable beaches. Here, you get a sense of Greece's proximity to Asia. Ancient temples, massive crusader fortifications, mosques and imposing Italian-built neoclassical buildings stand juxtaposed, vestiges of a turbulent past.

There are 16 inhabited islands in the group; the most visited are Rhodes, Kos, Patmos and Symi.

RHODES Ρόδος

According to mythology, the sun god Helios chose Rhodes as his bride and bestowed light, warmth and vegetation upon her. The blessing seems to have paid off, for Rhodes produces more flowers and sunny days than most Greek Islands.

The ancient sites of Lindos and Kamiros are legacies of Rhodes' importance in antiquity. In 1291, the Knights of St John, having fled Jerusalem under siege, came to Rhodes and established themselves as masters. In 1522, Süleyman I, sultan of the Ottoman Empire, staged a massive attack on the island and took Rhodes City. The island, along with the other Dodecanese islands, then became part of the Ottoman Empire.

In 1912 it was the Italians' turn and in 1944 the Germans took over. The following year Rhodes was liberated by British and Greek commandos. In 1948 the Dodecanese became part of Greece. These days, tourists rule.

Rhodes City
☎ 2241 • pop 43,500

Rhodes' capital and port is Rhodes City, on the northern tip of the island. Almost everything of interest lies in the old town, enclosed within massive walls. The main thoroughfares are Sokratous, Pythagora, Agiou Fanouriou and Ipodamou, with a clump of spaghetti streets in between. The new town to the north is a monument to package tourism.

The main port, Commercial Harbour, is east of the old town, and north of here is Mandraki Harbour, the supposed site of the Colossus of Rhodes, a giant bronze statue of Apollo (built in 292–280 BC) – one of the Seven Wonders of the World. The statue stood for a mere 65 years before being toppled by an earthquake.

Orientation & Information The EOT **tourist office** (☎ 2241 023 255; **e** eot-rodos@ otenet.gr; *cnr Makariou & Papagou; open 8.30am-2.30pm Mon-Fri*) is next door to the **tourist police** (☎ 2241 027 423; *open 7.30am-9pm daily*). In summer there is also a **municipal tourist office** (☎ 2241 035 945; *Plateia Rimini; open 8am-9pm daily*).

For ticketing and tour information, see **Triton Holidays** (☎ 2241 021 690; e info@tritondmc.gr; *1st floor, Plastira 9*) in the new town. To get there turn left after the **National Bank of Greece** (Mandraki Harbour). In the old town, try **Castellania Travel** (☎ 2241 075 860; e castell@otenet.gr) which faces the clock tower in front of the Castellania Fountain. It's tucked in the right-hand back corner of the square.

Send mail at the **main post office** (*Mandraki Harbour*). There is a tiny Internet café in the old town, **Cosmonet** (*Plateia Martyron Evreon*), on the west corner of the square, or in the new town, **Minoan Internet Café** (*Iroön Politehniou 13*) has 20 computers.

Things to See & Do The old town is reputedly the world's finest surviving example of medieval fortification. The 12m-thick walls are closed to the public but you can take a **guided walk** (€6; *2.45pm Tues & Sat*) along them starting in the courtyard of the Palace of the Knights.

Odos Ippoton (Avenue of the Knights) is lined with magnificent medieval buildings, the most magnificent of which is the **Palace of the Knights** (*Ippoton; admission €6; open 12.30pm-7pm Mon, 8am-7pm Tues-Sun*), restored, but never used, as a holiday home for Mussolini.

The 15th-century Knight's Hospital now houses the **archaeological museum** (*Plateia Mousiou; admission €4; open 8.30am-7pm Tues-Sun*). It's a splendid building, restored

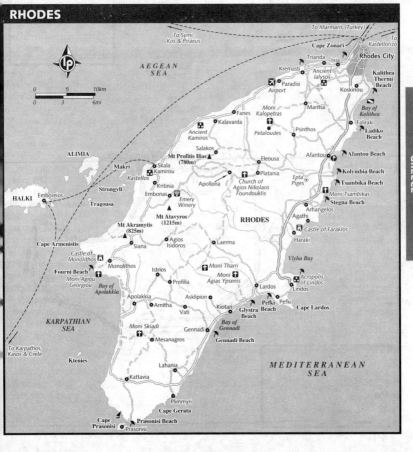

RHODES

To Symi, Kos & Piraeus

To Marmaris (Turkey)

To Kastellorizo

AEGEAN SEA

Cape Zonari

Trianda   Ixia   **Rhodes City**

Kremasti

Ancient Ialysos

Kalithea Thermi Beach

Paradisi Airport

Koskinou

0   5   10km
0   3   6mi

Moni Kalopetras

Maritsa

Bay of Kalithea

Fanes

Kalavarda

Petaloudes

Psinthos

Faliraki

Ladiko Beach

Ancient Kamiros

Salakos

Eleousa

Afantou

Afantou Beach

ALIMIA

Mt Profitis Ilias (780m)

Platania

Kolymbia Beach

Makri

Skala Kamirou

Apollona

Church of Agios Nikolaos Foundouklis

Epta Piges

Tsambika Beach

Moni Tsambikas

Stegna Beach

Kastellos

Strongyli

Kritinia

Embonas

Emery Winery

Arhangelos

Agathi

HALKI   Emboreios

Tragousa

Mt Atavyros (1215m)

RHODES

Castle of Faraklos

Mt Akramytis (825m)

Agios Isidoros

Laerma

Haraki

Cape Armenistis

Siana

Vlyha Bay

Castle of Monolithos

Monolithos

Istrios

Moni Tharri

Moni Agias Ypsenis

Acropolis of Lindos

Fourni Beach

Moni Agiou Georgiou

Bay of Apolakkia

Profilia

Lardos

Lindos

Apolakkia

Asklipion

Pefki Beach   Pefki

Arnitha

Vati

Kiotari

Glystra Beach

Cape Lardos

KARPATHIAN SEA

Moni Skiadi

Mesanagros

Gennadi

Bay of Gennadi

Gennadi Beach

To Karpathos, Kasos & Crete

Ktenies

Lahania

MEDITERRANEAN SEA

Kattavia

Plimmyri

Cape Gerata

Cape Prasonisi   Prasonisi Beach

Prasonisi

GREECE

RHODES CITY

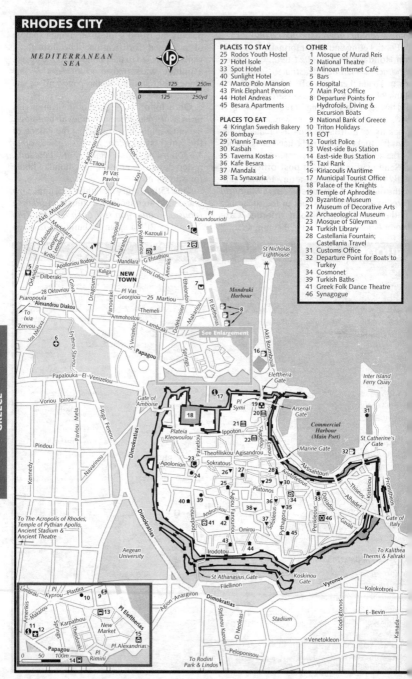

MEDITERRANEAN SEA

PLACES TO STAY
25 Rodos Youth Hostel
27 Hotel Isole
33 Spot Hotel
40 Sunlight Hotel
42 Marco Polo Mansion
43 Pink Elephant Pension
44 Hotel Andreas
45 Besara Apartments

PLACES TO EAT
4 Kringlan Swedish Bakery
26 Bombay
29 Yiannis Taverna
30 Kasbah
35 Taverna Kostas
36 Kafe Besara
37 Mandala
38 Ta Synaxaria

OTHER
1 Mosque of Murad Reis
2 National Theatre
3 Minoan Internet Café
5 Bars
6 Hospital
7 Main Post Office
8 Departure Points for
  Hydrofoils, Diving &
  Excursion Boats
9 National Bank of Greece
10 Triton Holidays
11 EOT
12 Tourist Police
13 West-side Bus Station
14 East-side Bus Station
15 Taxi Rank
16 Kiriacoulis Maritime
17 Municipal Tourist Office
18 Palace of the Knights
19 Temple of Aphrodite
20 Byzantine Museum
21 Museum of Decorative Arts
22 Archaeological Museum
23 Mosque of Süleyman
24 Turkish Library
28 Castellania Fountain;
   Castellania Travel
31 Customs Office
32 Departure Point for Boats to
   Turkey
34 Cosmonet
39 Turkish Baths
41 Greek Folk Dance Theatre
46 Synagogue

NEW TOWN

St Nicholas Lighthouse

Mandraki Harbour

Pl Koundourioti

Pl Vas Pavlou

Pl Vas Georgiou

See Enlargement

Inter Island Ferry Quay

Eleftheria Gate

Pl Symi

Arsenal Gate

Commercial Harbour (Main Port)

St Catherine's Gate

Marine Gate

Plateia Kleovoulou

Ippoton

Theofiliskou Agisandrou

Apolonion

Sokratous

Platonos

Gate of Italy

Aegean University

To The Acropolis of Rhodes, Temple of Pythian Apollo, Ancient Stadium & Ancient Theatre

St Athanasius Gate

Koskinou Gate

To Kalithea Thermi & Faliraki

Filellinon

Vyronos

Kolokotroni

E-Bevin

Stadium

To Rodini Park & Lindos

Venetokleon

Peloponisou

GREECE

Pl Kyprou
Pl Plastira
Pl Eleftherias
New Market
Pl Alexandrias
Pl Rimini
Papagou

by the Italians, with an impressive collection that includes the ethereal marble statue, the *Aphrodite of Rhodes*.

The 18th-century **Turkish Baths** (*Plateia Arionos; admission €1.50; open 11am-6pm Wed-Fri, 8am-6pm Sat*) – signposted from Ipodamou – offers a rare opportunity to bathe Turkish-style in Greece. Bring your own soap and towel.

Places to Stay The EOT can help with accommodation in the new town, but get there early; they're frantic in summer.

Rodos Youth Hostel (☎ 2241 030 491; Ergiou 12; roof/dorm beds €6/8, doubles with/without bathroom €22/18), off Agio Fanouriou in the old town, has a lovely garden but lumpy mattresses. Ask about the new studios out the back.

Sunlight Hotel (☎/fax 2241 021 435; Ipodamou 32; doubles/triples with bathroom €40/45) is above sociable Stavros Bar; rooms have a fridge.

Hotel Andreas (☎ 2241 034 156; e an dreasch@otenet.gr; Omirou 28D; rooms €33-59) has small, pleasant rooms with varied facilities and terrific views from its terrace.

You'll find fresh, basic rooms at **Pink Elephant Pension** (☎/fax 2241 022 469; e pinkelephantpension@yahoo.com; Timaxida; doubles €32-53), signposted off Irodotou, and **Spot Hotel** (☎ 2241 034 737; e spothot@otenet.gr; Perikleous 12; singles/doubles/triples with bathroom €35/44/68).

Hotel Isole (☎ 2241 020 682; e hotel isole@hotmail.com; Evdoxou 75; doubles with bathroom €47-73) has cheerful rooms off a central lounge area and some remarkable views (check the attic!).

Besara Apartments (☎/fax 2241 031 012; Sofokleous 11; 2-person/4-person apartments €25/35) has large, self-contained apartments set around a lovely courtyard.

Marco Polo Mansion (☎/fax 2241 025 562; e marcopolomansion@hotmail.com; Agiou Fanouriou 40-42; rooms €60-140) is just the place to indulge yourself in one of its exotic theme rooms (featured in glossy magazines). Breakfast is included and there's a sophisticated café and courtyard downstairs.

Places to Eat Away from the venues with tacky photo menus, you'll find some good eateries.

You could check out **Kringlan Swedish Bakery** (*I Dragoumi 14*) in the new town for exceptional sandwiches and light snacks.

Taverna Kostas (*Pythagora 62*), **Yiannis Taverna** (*Platanos*) and **Ta Synaxaria** (*Aristofanous*) are authentic Greek places with family service.

If you're tired of Greek food, there are some excellent options.

Kasbah (*Platanos 4*) serves some huge Moroccan-influenced meals in a refined atmosphere.

Mandala (*Sofokleous*) is very relaxed, with a healthy choice of stir-fries and pasta.

Bombay (*Agiou Fanouriou*) serves a tasty, rather than authentic version of Indian in enticing surrounds.

Entertainment The **Greek Folk Dance Theatre** (☎ 2241 029 085; *Andronikou; adult/concession €12/8; performances from 9.20pm Mon, Wed & Fri*) gives a first-rate show. Go Zorba!

The old town has some classy, less-chaotic bars for a cruisy night out, as well as leafy squares with live Greek music. In the new town, the drink-till-you-drop crowd goes bar hopping on Orfanidou in the city's northwest where there's a bar for every nationality.

Around the Island

The **Acropolis of Lindos** (*admission €6; open 12.30pm-7pm Mon, 8am-7pm Tues-Sun*), 47km from Rhodes City, is Rhodes' most important ancient city and is spectacularly perched atop a 116m-high rocky outcrop. Below the site is Lindos town, a tangle of streets with elaborately decorated 17th-century houses. It's beautiful but tainted by tourism. The bus to Lindos (€3.20) departs from Rhodes City's east-side station.

The extensive ruins of **Kamiros** (*admission €3; open 8.30am-7pm Tues-Sun*), an ancient Doric city on the west coast, are well preserved, with the remains of houses, baths, a cemetery and a temple, but the site should be visited as much for its lovely setting on a gentle hillside overlooking the sea.

Between Rhodes City and Lindos the **beaches** are choked. If you prefer space, venture south to the bay of Lardos. Even further south, between Genardi and Plimmyri, you'll find good stretches of deserted sandy beach. Forget the southwestern coast; beaches tend to be pebbly and the sea choppy.

GREECE

Getting There & Away

There are daily flights from Rhodes to Athens (€110) and Karpathos (€29). In summer there are regular flights to Iraklio, Mykonos, Santorini (Thira) and Kastellorizo. Contact Triton Holidays or Castellania Travel (see Orientation & Information under Rhodes City, earlier).

There are daily ferries from Rhodes to Piraeus (€29). Most sail via the Dodecanese north of Rhodes, but at least three times a week there is a service via Karpathos, Crete and the Cyclades. The EOT gives out a schedule. Kiriacoulis Maritime holds the hydrofoil schedules.

Excursion boats (€18 return) and hydrofoils (€12, one way) trip daily to Symi. Ferries travel less often (€8, one way). Similar services also run to Kos, Kalymnos, Nisyros, Tilos, Patmos and Leros.

Between April and October, there are regular boats from Rhodes to Marmaris in Turkey (€36, one way). There is an additional US$15 Turkish port tax each way.

From April to August, there are regular ferries to Israel (€100) via Cyprus (€71). Prices do not include foreign port tax. For information, contact Triton Holidays, Castellania Travel, or other travel agencies in the New Market area.

Getting Around

There are frequent buses between the airport and Rhodes City's west-side bus station (€2). Or you could catch a taxi for about €13.

Rhodes City has two bus stations. The **west-side bus station**, next to the New Market, serves the airport, the west coast, Embona and Koskinou; the **east-side bus station** (Plateia Rimini) serves the east coast and the inland southern villages. The EOT has a schedule.

Car- and motorcycle-rental outlets compete for business in Rhodes City's new town on and around 28 Oktovriou – so try to bargain.

Cars are forbidden in most of the old town but there are small car parks around the periphery.

KARPATHOS Κάρπαθος
☎ 2245 • pop 5323

Soothing Karpathos lies midway between Crete and Rhodes. It's a scenic, hype-free place with a cosy port.

The main port and capital of Karpathos is Pigadia.

Two main thoroughfares run parallel to the waterfront, Apodimon Karpathion and 28 Oktovriou. The bus stop is on the corner of Dimokratias and 28 Oktovriou. A booth on the harbourfront serves as municipal tourist office. There's no tourist police. **Possi Holidays** (☎ 2245 022 627, fax 2245 022 252, Apodimon Karpathion) can suggest local tours and handles travel arrangements. The Pavilion Hotel (see its entry, later in this section) has Internet access.

Karpathos has lovely **beaches**, particularly **Apella**, **Kyra Panagia**, **Lefkos** on the west coast and **Ammoöpi**, 8km south of Pigadia.

The northern village of **Olymbos** was isolated until 1980 when the first road and electricity arrived! Locals wear traditional outfits and the facades of houses are decorated with bright plaster reliefs.

Accommodation owners usually meet the boats.

Christina's Rooms (☎ 2245 022 045; 28 Oktavriou; doubles/triples with bathroom €27/30), 20m from the bus stop, has large rooms and free Sunday dinners.

Ask for the 'traditional' room at **Elias Rooms** (☎ 2245 022 446; e eliasrooms@hotmail.com; doubles/triples €303).

Pavilion Hotel (☎ 2245 022 059; e pavilion@inkarpathos.com; double studios €56.50) has well-appointed studios; walk east on Apodimon Karpathion and turn left up Georgio Louziou to get there.

Head for **Taverna Karpathos** near the quay for fresh seafood or **Annemoussa** for decent Italian. There are also two nightclubs and a groovy lounge bar here.

Karpathos has two daily flights to Rhodes (€29) and three a week to Athens (€92.30).

There are three ferries a week to Rhodes (€14.50) and four to Piraeus (€26.30), via the Cyclades and Crete.

There are daily excursion boats from Pigadia to Apella and Kyra Panagia Beaches and the small port of Diafani; a free bus goes to Olymbos from Diafani. Local buses drop you at Lefkos and Ammoöpi Beaches.

SYMI Σύμη
☎ 2246 • pop 2332

Symi town is extremely attractive, with pastel-coloured neoclassical mansions surrounding the harbour and hills. The island is swamped by day-trippers from Rhodes; it's worth staying over to enjoy Symi in cruise control.

The town is divided into Gialos, the harbour, and the tranquil horio above it, accessible by taxi, bus, or 360 steps from the harbour.

There is no tourist office or tourist police. The best source of information is the free and widely available English-language *Symi Visitor*, which includes maps of the town.

There is a tiny Internet café at Roloi Bar, on the street behind Vapori Bar.

Excursion boats to other parts of the island also run guided walks. **Kalodoukas Holidays** (☎ 2246 071 077; e information@ kalodoukas.gr) has a book of trails that you can do independently. An excellent website is w www.symivisitor.com.

Budget accommodation is scarce but digs in the village are cheaper; ask at Kalodoukas Holidays.

Catherinettes Rooms & Studios (☎/fax 2246 072 698; e marina-epe@rho.forth net.gr; doubles €54) in Gialos has airy rooms with ornate ceilings; prices include breakfast.

Located in the two streets opposite the excursion boats, **Hotel Albatros** (☎ 2246 071 829, fax 2246 072 257; e fabienne@ otenet.gr; doubles €50) and **Hotel Kokona** (☎ 2246 071 549, fax 2246 072 620; doubles €50) both have spotless, bright doubles.

From the ferry dock, the bulk of restaurants are to the left, past the central square. **Meraklis** is a cheap and cheery taverna. **Sunflower** offers excellent sandwiches and savoury vegetarian. **Tholos**, a five-minute walk past the clock tower, is a shaded, harbourside taverna with imaginative pickings.

Up in the Horio, **Kali Strata Bar** (Kali Strata) provides perfect sunset moments. A few steps up, **To Klima** creates Greek with a twist, while **Giorgio's Taverna** offers classics.

There are frequent ferries and hydrofoils between Rhodes and Kos that also call at Symi, as well as less-frequent services to Tilos, Nisyros, Kalymnos, Leros and Patmos.

The bus and taxi stop is at the east end of the harbour, past the restaurants.

For tickets and tour information, see Kalodoukas Holidays in Gialos, or the horio. There's an ANEK booth opposite the quay.

KOS Κως
☎ 2242 • pop 26,379

Kos is the birthplace of Hippocrates, the father of medicine, but that's as Greek as this place

gets. With its ruins and Turkish buildings on a backdrop of pretty palm-lined streets, neon cafés, pulsing clubs and tourist trains, Kos town exudes an aura of mini Las Vegas. It's well located for day trips to several islands and Turkey.

Orientation & Information
Kos town, on the northeast coast, is the main town and port. The **municipal tourist office** (☎ 2242 024 460; e dotkos@hol.gr; open 8am-8.30pm Mon-Fri, 8am-3pm Sat), on the waterfront just past the police station, provides maps and accommodation information. The post office is on Vasileos Pavlou. The **tourist police** (☎ 2242 022 444) and regular police are housed together, just opposite the quay.

To get to the **bus station** (Kleopatras) walk 350m up Vasileos Pavlou from the harbourfront and turn right.

Café Del Mare (Megalou Alexandrou 4) is the best-equipped Internet café.

Things to See & Do
The focus of the **archaeological museum** (Plateia Eleftherias; admission €3; open 8am-2.30pm Tues-Sun) is sculpture from excavations around the island. The **ancient agora**, with the ruins of the **Shrine of Aphrodite** and **Temple of Hercules**, is just off Plateia Eleftherias. It's free but has zero data.

On a pine-clad hill, 4km from Kos town, stand the extensive ruins of the renowned healing centre of **Asklipion** (admission €4; open 8.30am-6pm Tues-Sun), where Hippocrates practised medicine.

Further south is **Kefalos Bay** a long stretch of beach swamped in sun lounges and rippling with water sports.

Places to Stay & Eat
Kos Camping (☎ 2242 023 910; camping per adult/tent €6/3.50) is 3km along the eastern waterfront, with good shade and a minimart. Hop on any of the buses from the harbourfront going to Agios Fokas.

Pension Alexis (☎ 2242 028 798, fax 2242 025 797; Irodotou 9; doubles/triples with shared bathroom €26/32) is a convivial place. It's noisy here, but Alexis is an admirable host. To find it, turn right from the port and walk about 300m to the port police, turn left and then take the first right.

GREECE

Hotel Afendoulis (☎ 2242 025 321; Evripilou 1; doubles/triples with bathroom €36/45) is a superior hotel with well-kept rooms in a quieter area. Turn left from the ferry, walk about 500m to Evripilou and turn right.

Hotel Kamelia (☎ 2242 028 983; e kamelia.hotel@hotmail.com; Artemisias 3; singles/doubles/triples with bathroom €26.50/ 44/53) has neat rooms with TV and garden views, and breakfast is included. To get there, turn left from the ferry, past the police, turn right up Korai, then left onto Artemisias.

Among the glut of uninspired tourist tavernas, **Filoxenia Taverna** (cnr Pindou & Alikarnassou) and **Barba's Grill**, opposite Hotel Afendoulis, are happy exceptions. Classy **Platanos**, by the Hippocrates tree, is top notch and top dollar.

Entertainment
There are a dozen discos and clubs catering to the different music moods of the crowd around the streets of Diakon and Nafklirou. Head for **Kalua**, 400m past the ferry quay, for foam parties and dance mania.

Getting There & Away
There are daily flights to Athens (€80.40) from Kos' international airport.

There are frequent ferries from Rhodes that continue on to Piraeus (€29.75), via Kalymnos, Leros and Patmos, and less-frequent connections to Nisyros, Tilos, Symi, Samos and Crete. Daily excursion boats visit Nisyros, Kalymnos, Patmos and Rhodes.

In summer, ferries depart daily for Bodrum in Turkey (€15 one way, €25 return). Port tax costs €10.

For tickets and scheduling information, visit the efficient **Exas Travel** (☎ 2242 029 900; e exas@exas.com; Antinavarhou Ioannini).

Getting Around
Next to the tourist office is a blue mini-train that leaves hourly for Asklipion (€3) and a mini-green train that does city tours (€2).

Buses for Agios Fokas leave from opposite the town hall on the harbourfront; all other buses (including those to Kefalos Bay) leave from the bus station on Kleopatras.

PATMOS Πάτμος
☎ 2247 • pop 2663
Starkly scenic Patmos gets crowded duing summer but somehow remains remarkably tranquil. Orthodox and Western Christians have long made pilgrimages to this holy island for its World Heritage–listed sites. ▶ entices the visitor to linger.

Orientation & Information
The **tourist office** (open 8am-1pm & 4pm-6pm Mon-Fri), post office and police station are in the white building at the island's port and capital of Skala. Buses leave regularly for the hora, 4.5km inland. **Blue Bay Hotel** 200m left from the port (facing inland), has limited Internet access.

Things to See & Do
The **Cave of the Apocalypse** (admission free; open 8am-1.30pm Mon-Sat, 8am-1.30pm Sun, 4pm-6pm Tues, Thur & Sun) where St John wrote the divinely inspired Book of Revelations, is halfway between the port and hora. Take a bus or make the pilgrimage via the **Byzantine path**. To do this, walk up the Skala-Hora road and take the steps to the right 100m beyond the far side of the football field. The path begins opposite the top of the steps.

The **Monastery of St John the Theologian** (admission monastery/treasury free/€5), which is open the same hours as the cave, exhibits monastic treasures: early manuscripts, embroidered robes, incredible carvings and an El Greco painting. Dress modestly (ie, no shorts) for the holy sites.

Patmos' coastline provides secluded coves, mostly with pebble beaches. The best is **Psili Ammos**, in the south, reached by excursion boat from Skala port.

Places to Stay & Eat
Stefanos Camping (☎ 2247 031 821) is on Meloi Beach, 2km northeast of Skala.

Try **Travel Point Holidays** (☎ 2247 032 801; e info@travelpoint.gr; w www.travelpoint.gr), an accommodation-finding service on the road to the hora, for budget pensions such as **Pension Maria Paskeledi** (☎ 2247 032 152, fax 2247 033 346; doubles/triples with bathroom €32/45).

Hotel Delfini (☎ 2247 032 060, fax 2247 032 061; doubles/triples €52/68), to the left of the port, has gentle views and rooms include breakfast.

There is a cluster of mid-range hotels about 700m to the right of the port, including one called **Hotel Australis** (☎ 2247 031 576, *fax 2247 032 284; doubles/triples with bathroom €56/66)*, with a prolific garden.

Grigoris Taverna, which is opposite the port's passenger-transit gate, is popular, or enjoy refined ambience and tangy Indonesian at **GiaGia**, next to Hotel Delfini. Further along, **Café Aman** offers excellent salads and pastas in a breezy setting.

Getting There & Away

Frequent ferries travel between Patmos and Piraeus (€20.40), and to Rhodes (€17) via Leros, Kalymnos and Kos. Visit **GA Ferries**, inland from the central square, for schedules. In summer, there are daily Flying Dolphin hydrofoils to Leros, Kalymnos, Kos, Rhodes, Fourni, Ikaria, Agathonisi and Samos. See **Apollon Travel** on the waterfront, near the quay, for bookings.

Northeastern Aegean Islands

There are seven major islands in this ne-glected group: Chios, Ikaria, Lesvos, Lim-nos, Samos, Samothraki and Thasos. The distance between them makes island hopping tricky but these neighbours reward explo-ration with wonderful hiking, crowd-free beaches and unique villages.

SAMOS Σάμος
☎ 2273 • pop 32,000

Samos was an important centre of Hellenic culture and is reputedly the birthplace of the philosopher and mathematician Pythagoras. Lush and humid, its powerful mountains are skirted by forested hills.

Orientation & Information

Samos has three ports: Vathy (Samos town), Karlovasi on the north coast and Pythagorio on the southeast coast.

Pretty Pythagorio, where you'll disembark if you've come from Patmos, is small and touristy. Its cordial **municipal tourist office** *(Lykourgou Logotheti)* is two blocks from the waterfront on the main street. Busy Vathy, 20 minutes away, is dreary but cheaper.

Vathy's useless EOT is in a side street one block north of the main square, Plateia Pythagorou. The competing travel agencies directly opposite the port help with travel, excursions, accommodation and luggage storage. Try **By Ship Travel** *(☎ 2273 025 065, fax 2273 028 570)*.

Diavlos NetCafé *(Themistoklous Sofouli 160)* is on the waterfront, 250m from Plateia Pythagorou, next to the police station.

Things to See & Do

Pythagorio's **Evpalinos Tunnel** *(adult/student €4/2; open 8.45am-2.45pm Tues-Sun)*, built

GREECE

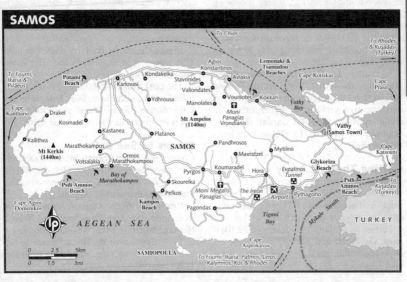

SAMOS

in the 6th century BC, is a 1km tunnel dug by political prisoners and used as an aqueduct to bring water from the springs of Mt Ampelos. Part of it can still be explored. It's 2km north of Pythagorio but there's no bus access.

Vathy's **archaeological museum** *(adult €3; open 8.30am-3pm Tues-Sun)*, by the municipal gardens, is first rate. The highlight is a 4.5m male kouros statue.

The captivating villages of **Vourliotes** and **Manolates** on the slopes of imposing Mt Ampelos, northwest of Vathy, provide excellent walking territory and there are many marked pathways.

Choice beaches, **Kampos** and **Psili Ammos**, are along the southwest coast in the Marathokampos area.

Places to Stay & Eat

In Pythagorio, **Pension Sydney** *(☎ 2273 061 733; Pythagora; doubles with bathroom €30)* and **Pension Boulas** *(☎ 2273 061 277; Despoti Kyrillon; doubles with bathroom €29.50)*, both off Lykourgou Logotheti, offer simple, central rooms.

Pythagoras Hotel *(☎ 2273 028 601; e smicha@otenet.gr; doubles/triples/quads €26/33/36)* in Vathy is a friendly, great-value place with uplifting views. Facing inland, the hotel is 500m to the left of the quay. Call ahead for pick-up on arrival.

Pension Vasso *(☎/fax 2273 023 258; doubles/studios €35/75)*, where rooms include minikitchen, or **Hotel Samos** *(☎ 2273 028 377; e hotsamos@otenet.gr; singles/doubles €37/46.50)*, where room rates include breakfast, are two places to try for more modern facilities.

In Vathy, **La Casa** on the waterfront, 400m past the square, and **Taverna Petrino** behind Hotel Samos present tempting variety and attentive service. In Pythagorio, you could try Asian **Oriental Garden** *(Odyessa Orologa)*, or **Taverna Ta Platania** on leafy Plateia Irinis.

Getting There & Away

There's a daily flight to Athens (€66.45) from the airport at Pythagorio, and three a week to Thessaloniki (€71.50). The travel agencies opposite the port handle tickets.

Ferries leave daily for Piraeus (€22.10) – most via Paros and Naxos, and some via Mykonos – and Ikaria, but only two a week visit Chios (€9.25). Daily hydrofoils ski to

Patmos (€11.68), carrying on to Leros, Kalymnos and Kos.

There are daily boats to Kuşadası (for Ephesus) in Turkey (€30, one way; plus port taxes for Greece €8.80 and Turkey €13).

Getting Around

Pythagorio's **bus stop** *(Lykourgou Logotheti)* is on the main street, about 300m from the waterfront heading inland, on your left.

To get to Vathy's bus station, follow the waterfront and turn left onto Lekati, 250m south of Plateia Pythagorou (just before the police station).

You can get to most of the island's villages and beaches by bus, except Manolates. Agios Konstantinos, 4km away, is its closest bus stop.

CHIOS Χίος

☎ 2271 • pop 54,000

Chios has not courted tourism because of its thriving shipping and mastic industries (mastic produces the resin used in chewing gum). The chief attraction lies in exploring its undulating interior and distinct villages.

Orientation & Information

Chios town, the main port, is unattractive and noisy. It is, however, a good base for day trips to Turkey.

The **municipal tourist office** *(☎ 2271 044 389; e infochio@otenet.gr; Kanari 18; open 7am-10pm daily)* is on the main street that runs from the waterfront to Plateia Vounakiou, the main square.

Manos Centre, by the ferry dock, can help with transport arrangements and with some accommodation.

The **post office** *(Rodokanaki)* is one block back from the waterfront. Slick **Enter Internet Café** *(Aigaiou)* is visible upstairs on the southern waterfront; enter from the side street.

Things to See & Do

Compelling **Philip Argenti Museum** *(admission free; open 8am-2pm Mon-Fri, 5pm-7.30pm Fri, 8am-12.30pm Sat)* contains the treasures of the wealthy Argenti family.

Nea Moni *(New Monastery; admission free; open 9am-1pm Tues-Sun)*, now World Heritage listed, is 14km west of Chios town and reveals some of the finest Byzantine art in the country, with mosaics dating from the 11th century.

The ghost village of **Anavatos**, 10km from Nea Moni and built on a precipitous cliff, bears testament to the tragedy of 1822, when the inhabitants perished during an uprising against Turkish rule.

Pyrgi, 24km southwest of Chios town, is one of Greece's most extraordinary villages. The facades of the town's dwellings are decorated with intricate grey and white geometric patterns and motifs.

The tiny medieval town of **Mesta**, 10km from Pyrgi and nestled within fortified walls, has two ornate churches and cobbled streets connected by overhead arches that lead to an enchanting square of tavernas laced with birdsong.

Places to Stay
The tourist office gives out a practical accommodation guide for the town and villages.

Chios Rooms (☎ 2271 020 198; Leoforos Aigaiou; singles/doubles with shared bathroom €20/25, doubles with bathroom €30), on the waterfront at the opposite end of the harbour from the ferry dock, has bright, airy rooms in a building that oozes rustic charm.

Hotel Kyma (☎ 2271 044 500; e kyma@ chi.forthnet.gr; Evgenias Chandris 1; singles/doubles/triples with bathroom €53/68/85), around the corner from Chios Rooms, has well-appointed suites and prices include breakfast.

Places to Eat
Ouzeri Theodosiou's delectable *mezedes* are recommended by locals. It's 50m to the right of the ferry disembarkation point.

Taverna Hotzas, 15 minutes' walk from the town crush, has excellent food and ambience. To find it, walk up Kanari which becomes Aplotarias. At the fork, take Stefanou Tsouri, then turn right onto Kondyli G.

Bella Visa is a sleek place that serves sublime Italian. It's on the waterfront past Hotel Kyma.

Getting There & Away
Moving on, there are daily flights from Chios to Athens (€62), three flights weekly to Thessaloniki (€60) and two to Lesvos (€28.30).

Ferries sail daily to Piraeus (€19.40), via Lesvos (€11.20), and once a week to Thessaloniki (€28), via Lesvos and Limnos.

There are two ferries per week to Samos (€10.25). In summer, there are daily boats to the wealthy island of Inousses to the east, and several to quiet Psara, west of Chios.

Daily boats travel to Çeşme in Turkey (€30, one way; Turkish port tax €8.80). The waterfront travel agencies handle bookings.

Getting Around
There are two bus stations. Blue buses go regularly to local villages and Karfas and Kontari Beaches, and leave from the right side (coming from the waterfront) of Plateia Vounakiou, by the garden. Green long-distance buses to Pyrgi and Mesta leave from the station one block back to the left of Plateia Vounakiou. In summer, only one to two green buses per week go to Anavatos via Nea Moni.

Rent a Car (☎ 2271 029 300), just down from Hotel Kyma, quotes fair rates.

LESVOS (MYTILINI)
Λέσβος (Μυτιλήνη)
Fertile Lesvos is the third-largest Greek island. It has always been a centre of philosophy and artistic achievement and still attracts creative types on sabbatical. Spoil yourself with its prized olive oil, ouzo, sardines and therapeutic hot springs.

An excellent source of information on the island is w www.greeknet.com.

Mytilini
☎ 2251 • pop 23,970
The capital and main port, Mytilini, is a large, dreary working town. The **tourist police** (2251 022 776) are at the entrance to the quay. The **EOT** (☎ 2251 042 511; open 9am-1pm Sun-Fri), 50m up Aristarhou by the quay, offers brochures and maps, but is too busy for tourists! **Manos Centre** (☎ 2251 048 124; Kountourioti 47), 400m from the ferry on the waterfront, is the choice for travel arrangements.

Things to See & Do Mytilini's museums are exceptional. The neoclassical **archaeological museum** (admission €3; open 8.30am-7pm Tues-Sun) has a fascinating collection from Neolithic to Roman times. The **new archaeological museum** (same admission & hours) displays spectacular mosaics from ancient households. Both are on 8 Noemvriou, signposted from the ferry.

GREECE

Theophilos Museum (*admission €2; open 9am-2.30pm & 6pm-8pm Tues-Sun*), 4km from Mytilini in Varia village, is a shrine to the prolific folk painter, Theophilos.

Five kilometres from Mytilini are the **Loutra Yera hot springs** (*admission €2.50; open 7am-8pm daily*).

Places to Stay Central, budget choices are **Arion Rooms** (☎ 2251 042 650; Arionos 4; doubles €25) for basic rooms with mythical frescoes and **Alkaios Rooms** (☎/fax 2251 047 737; Alkaiou 16; doubles €24) in an old mansion. To get there, face inland from the waterfront and take Alkaiou to the right of Therapon church; Arion is on the first left, Alkaios is another 100m straight ahead.

Pelagia Koumniotou Rooms (☎ 2251 020 643; Terseti 6; doubles €25) has pleasant rooms with mod cons. Terseti is 250m up 8 Noemvriou, past the museums, on your left.

Getting There & Away There are daily flights to Athens (€78) and to Thessaloniki (€80), five per week to Limnos (€36.25) and two per week to Chios (€28.25); but don't rush to leave.

In summer, there are daily boats to Piraeus (€24), some via Chios, Mykonos and Syros, and one boat per week to Thessaloniki (€28).

There are four ferries per week to Ayvalik in Turkey (€38 one way, €45 return, including taxes). Stop by Manos Centre for ticketing and schedules.

Getting Around Mytilini has two bus stations. For local buses, walk about 400m from the ferry to the harbour station where buses leave regularly for Loutra Yera and Varia.

For long-distance buses, walk 600m from the ferry along the waterfront to El Venizelou and turn right until you reach Agia Irinis park which is next to the station. There are regular services in summer to Mithymna, Petra, Agiasos, Skala Eresou, Mantamados and Agia Paraskevi.

For car hire, try **Samiotis Tours** (*Kountourioti 43*) on Mytilini's waterfront, or wait until you get to Mithymna for more competitive rates.

Mithymna
☎ 2253 • pop 1333

The gracious, preserved town of Mithymna (known by locals as Molyvos) is 62km north

of Mytilini. Cobbled streets canopied by flowering vines are lined with cosy tavernas and genteel stone cottages. You'll be tempted never to leave this scenic place.

Orientation & Information From the bus stop, walk straight ahead towards the town to a fork in the road. Take the right fork onto 17 Noemvriou, the main thoroughfare, or continue straight ahead to reach the colourful fishing port.

The **municipal tourist office** (☎ 2253 071 347; open 9am-3.30pm daily) is 50m from the bus stop. There are three Internet cafés and an open-air cinema along the port road.

Things to See & Do The noble **Genoese castle** (*admission €2; open 8am-7pm Tues-Sun*) hosts a drama festival in summer.

Eftalou hot springs (*admission €2.50; open 9am-1pm & 3pm-7pm Mon-Sat*), 3km from town on the beach, is a tiny bathhouse with a whitewashed dome and steaming, pebbled pool.

Mithymna Beach gets crowded. Nearby Eftalou, **Skala Sykaminias** and **Petra** are better options.

Places to Stay & Eat There are over 50 *domatia* in Mithymna. Those nearest the port bars can ruin your sleep in high season, otherwise 17 Noemvriou is a good place to start. The tourist office also offers accommodation advice.

Nassos Guest House (☎ 2253 071 432; e nassosguesthouse@hotmail.com; doubles with shared bathroom €29) is an airy, friendly, traditional place with communal kitchen and rapturous views. To get there, head up 17 Noemvriou and take the second right (a sharp switchback).

At the end of the port road, elegant **Onap** has a varied, tempting menu. Next door, busy **Captain's Table** does Greek fare with flair. Upstairs at **Dilino** is ideal for breakfast.

Entertainment Head up the port road for action. For cruisy blues and nightcaps, drop by **Pirates Café**. **Café Del Mare** and **Christine's Bar** are good primers for a big night out at **Med Bar** dance club.

Getting Around In the summer, buses go regularly to Petra Beach and Eftalou. Excursion boats leave the port daily for Skala

Sykaminias. For more information, Faonas Travel at the port has schedules.

Competitive car- and scooter-hire outlets line the port road.

Around the Island

East of Mithymna, the traditional picturesque villages surrounding **Mt Lepetymnos** (Sykaminia, Mantamados and Agia Paraskevi) are worth your time.

The southwestern beach resort of **Skala Esrou**, built over ancient Eresos, is the birthplace of sensuous Sappho (c. 630 BC), one of the great poets of ancient Greece.

It has become a popular destination for lesbians who come on a kind of pilgrimage to honour her.

Southern Lesvos is dominated by **Mt Olympus** (968m) and the very pretty day-trip destination of **Agiasos** which has good artisan workshops.

Local clubs, sponsored by the government, have established a network of gentle **walking trails** around the island that traverse olive groves and landscapes featuring water mills, stone bridges, and olive presses. The EOT in Mytilini has a map of the trails.

See Getting Around under Mytilini for transport information.

Sporades Σποράδες

The Sporades group comprises the lush, pine-forested islands of Skiathos, Skopelos and Alonnisos, and far-flung Skyros, off Evia.

The main ports for these islands are Volos and Agios Konstantinos on the mainland.

SKIATHOS Σκιάθος
☎ 2427 • pop 4100

Crowded and expensive with a happening nightlife, Skiathos has a universal beach-resort feel but no charm. There are loads of good beaches awash with water sports on the south coast, particularly Koukounaries.

Orientation & Information

There is a tourist-information booth to the left as you leave the port. Harried travel agencies along the waterfront spit out tour and travel information.

Skiathos town's main thoroughfare is Papadiamanti, running inland opposite the port. Here you'll find the post office, **tourist police**

(☎ 2427 023 172) and Draft-Net Internet café. Internet Zone Café is up Evangelistrias, which is on your right just before you reach the post office. The bus stop is at the far end of the harbour; turn right from the ferry.

Nightlife sprawls along Politehniou; to find it, turn left off Papadiamanti and walk 70m up Evangelistrias.

Places to Stay & Eat

There is a **Rooms to Let** bookings kiosk on the waterfront. Package-tour operators book accommodation solid for July and August when *domatia* owners drop value for money. Off peak, rooms are up to 50% cheaper.

Camping Koukounaries (☎ 2427 049 250; *camping per person/tent €6/3*) is 30 minutes away by bus at Koukounaries Beach.

Hotel Karafelas (☎ 2427 021 235, fax 2427 023 307; *singles/doubles with bathroom €30/53*), in town at the end of Papadiamanti on your left, has generous rooms with balconies.

Hotel Marlton (☎ 2427 022 552, ☎/fax 2427 022 878; *doubles/triples with bathroom €40/48*) is friendly and has fresh, pine-furnished rooms. To get there from Papadiamanti, turn right onto Evangelistrias and walk 50m.

Pension Vasiliki (☎ 2427 022 549, fax 2427 021 978; *doubles/triples with bathroom €45/55*) has rooms with TV and is in a quiet part of town off Evangelistrias, opposite Taverna Ilias. Follow the signs to the taverna.

On the waterfront, **Zio Peppe**'s yummy pizza cures hangovers. **Ta Psaradiki Ouzeri** by the fish market is the seafood winner.

On Papadiamanti, try reasonably priced **Niko's Café Bar**, or the slightly upmarket **Gerania**.

Scandinavian **Restaurant Bonaparte** (*Evangelistrias*), left off Papadiamanti, offers pricier taste sensations.

Getting There & Away

In summer, there are five flights per week from Athens to Skiathos (€69.35) and one a week to Skyros (€34.55).

There are frequent ferries to the mainland ports of Volos (€11) and Agios Konstantinos (€10.10), and frequent hydrofoils each day to Skopelos (€8.80) and Alonnisos (€12). In summer, there are two boats a week to Thessaloniki.

GREECE

Getting Around

Crowded buses ply the south-coast road between Skiathos town and Koukounaries every 20 minutes, stopping at all the beaches along the way.

Many of the south-coast beaches are only accessible by caïque from the port.

SKOPELOS Σκόπελος
☎ 2424 • pop 5000

Skopelos has the appeal of a mountain-lake resort with its thick forests of scruffy pine and pebbled beaches of jade green.

Orientation & Information

There is no tourist office or tourist police in Skopelos town, but **Thalpos Leisure & Services** (☎ 2424 022 947; e thalpos@ otenet.gr) on the waterfront is handy for accommodation and tours. It's a few doors past Pension Kir Sotos on the 1st floor.

The post office is elusive. Walk up the road opposite the port entrance, take the first sharp left, the first right, the first left, and it's on the right. To get to **Click & Surf Internet Café** (Doulidi) walk up the road opposite the port entrance, take the third left and walk a further 100m. The bus station is next to the port.

Things to See & Do

Attractive **Skopelos town**, with its dazzling white, hillside homes, is a maze of narrow streets and stairways where the kissing balconies of cascading flowers and bright window shutters burst with colour. Take time to wander. You'll find stone churches with glittering interiors tucked around many corners.

Glossa, the island's other inland town, is quite ordinary but it's a pleasant drive there with marvellous views.

Velanio Beach is the island's nudie spot. Pebbled **Panormos Beach**, with its sheltered emerald bay surrounded by pine forest, is superb. The 2km stretch of **Milia Beach**, a few kilometres further on, is considered the island's best.

Thalpos Leisure & Services and **Madro Travel** (☎ 2424 022 145; e enquiries@ madrotravel.com) offer boat excursions and walking tours. Madro is at the end of the northern waterfront, about 70m before the church.

Places to Stay

In high season, rooms are engulfed by package tourists so it pays to sift through the domatia owners who meet the boats. Thalpos Leisure & Services has an accommodation-finding service. Opposite the port entrance, the Rooms & Apartments Association of Skopelos has a brochure of domatia, but doesn't make bookings.

Pension Kir Sotos (☎ 2424 022 549, fax 2424 023 668; doubles/triples with bathroom €35/49), in the middle of the waterfront, has big rooms in an enchanting building. There's also a communal kitchen and courtyard.

Pension Soula (☎ 2424 022 930, 2424 024 631; doubles/studios from €24/27), a 10-minute walk out of town, is a welcoming place with airy rooms; you'll awake in rural bliss to donkeys braying and birdsong. To find it, walk left from the port and turn left at Hotel Amalia. Follow the road, bearing right after about 200m; it's on your right.

Hotel Ionia (☎ 2424 022 568, fax 2424 023 301, e hotelionia@vol.forthnet.gr; singles/doubles/triples with bathroom €35/60/70) has all mod cons, bright wall murals and a pool; prices include breakfast. Facing inland, take the road to the right of Pension Kir Sotos. It's a steep hike of about 300m. The road veers slightly right then bears left the last 120m; it's on your left.

Places to Eat

Zio Peppe, on the waterfront, is the best place for a pizza fix.

Taverna Fikinas has imaginative dishes; follow the signs from the middle of the waterfront – getting there is a treasure hunt!

The Garden, on the road to Pension Soula (see Places to Stay, earlier), offers superb dining and service in an elegant garden.

Entertainment

On the same strip as Click & Surf Internet Café (see Orientation & Information, earlier) you'll find the crowd-pleasing **Dancing Club Kounos**, **Panselinos** for Greek rembetika music, and **Metro Club** for Greek pop and rock.

For a sultry mood, it's **La Costa** bar, opposite the bus station, or the so-laid-back-it's-falling-over **Platanos Jazz Bar** at the northern end of the waterfront.

Getting There & Away

In summer, there are daily ferries to Volos (€10.60) and Agios Konstantinos (€25.40)

GREECE

that also call at Skiathos. Flying Dolphin hydrofoils dash several times a day to Skiathos, Alonnisos, Volos and Agios Konstantinos. All boats leave from the same port, but in rough weather may depart from Agnontas Beach, southwest of town. Most hydrofoils also call in at Loutraki, the port below Glossa. For schedules and tickets, see **Kosifis Travel** opposite the port.

There are frequent buses from Skopelos town to Glossa, stopping at all beaches along the way.

ALONNISOS Αλόννησος
☎ 2424 • pop 3000

Green, serene Alonnisos is the least visited of the Sporades. The area surrounding the island has been declared a marine park and has the cleanest waters in the Aegean.

The restful port village of Patitiri has two main thoroughfares; facing inland from the ferry quay, Pelasgon is to the left and Ikion Dolopon is to the far right.

There is no tourist office or tourist police but the post office, police and Internet access at Il Mondo Café are on Ikion Dolopon. The bus stop is on the corner of Ikion Dolopon and the waterfront.

The tiny hora, **Old Alonnisos**, is a few kilometres inland. Its streets sprout a profusion of plant life, alluring villas of eclectic design and dramatic vistas.

Alonnisos is ideal for walking. Waterfront travel agencies offer guided tours, or there's an excellent trail guide called *Alonnisos on Foot: A Walking & Swimming Guide* by Bente Keller & Elias Tsoukanas which is available at newsstands for €9.

Patitiri Beach is OK for a dip; **Kokkinokastro** and **Hrysia Milia**, on the east coast, are better.

The **Rooms to Let service** (☎/fax 2424 065 577), right of the quay, books accommodation all over the island.

Camping Rocks (☎ 2424 065 410) is a shady, basic site. It is a steep hike about 1.5km from the port; go up Pelasgon and take the first road on your left.

Ikaros Camping (☎ 2424 065 258) is smaller than Camping Rocks and is on the beach at the tiny fishing village of Steni Vala.

Villa Gallini (☎ 2424 065 573, fax 2424 065 094; doubles/triples with bathroom €45/72) has exceptional rooms, a pool and bar. It's 400m up Pelasgon on your left.

Haravgi Hotel (☎ 2424 065 090, fax 2424 065 189; doubles/studios €58/70) has sensational views over Patitiri and rooms have minikitchen. To get there take the first left up Pelasgon, and then turn left again.

Fantasia House (☎ 2424 065 186; doubles €35) in Old Alonnisos has sweet rooms and a verdant terrace. From the bus stop, it's on the road towards town.

In Patitiri, **To Kamaki Ouzeri** and **Kavari Ouzeri** on Ikion Dolopon offer delectably prepared fare. Get there early!

Cruisy **Café Dennis**, near the quay, and **Rahati** (signposted from Ikion Dolopon) with its moody interior and shady terrace, are the places to sip and lounge.

In the hora, **Azzurro** café has sublime views, and **Astrofengia**, signposted from the bus stop, serves scrumptious alternative fare.

There are daily ferries from Alonnisos to Volos, and two a week to Agios Konstantinos, via Skiathos and Skopelos. Flying Dolphin hydrofoils travel several times a day to Volos and Agios Konstantinos and between the islands.

The local bus runs to the hora every hour and to Steni Vala twice a day.

Car- and scooter-hire outlets are on Pelasgon and Ikion Dolopon, but only one main road spans the island! In summer, taxi boats leave Patitiri every morning for the east-coast beaches.

Ionian Islands
Ιόνια Νησιά

The Ionian Islands stretch down the western coast of Greece from Corfu in the north to remote Kythira, which is off the southern tip of the Peloponnese.

CORFU Κέρκυρα
pop 107,592

Corfu is the most important island in the group and has the largest population.

Corfu Town
☎ 2661 • pop 36,000

The old town of Corfu, wedged between two fortresses, occupies a peninsula on the island's east coast. The narrow alleyways of high-shuttered tenements in mellow ochres and pinks are an immediate reminder of the town's long association with Venice.

Orientation & Information The town's old fortress (Palaio Frourio) stands on an eastern promontory, separated from the town by an area of parks and gardens known as the Spianada. The new fortress (Neo Frourio) lies to the northwest. Ferries dock at the new port, just west of the new fortress. The **long-distance bus station** (Avrami) is inland from the port.

The **EOT office** (☎ 2661 037 520; Rizospaston Voulefton) is between OTE and the post office, or try the **tourist police** (☎ 2661 030 265; Samartzi 4). All major Greek banks are in town, including the **National Bank of Greece** (cnr Voulgareos & Theotoki).

Things to See The **archaeological museum** (Vraili 5; admission €3; open 8.30am-3pm Tues-Sun) houses a collection of finds from Mycenaean to classical times. The star attraction is the pediment from the Temple of Artemis, decorated with gorgons.

The **Church of Agios Spiridon**, Corfu's most famous church, has an richly decorated interior. Pride of place is given to the remains of St Spiridon, displayed in a silver casket; four times a year it is paraded around town.

Places to Stay & Eat Near the fruit and vegetable market, **Hotel Hermes** (☎ 2661 039 268, fax 2661 031 747; G Markora 14; singles/doubles with shared bathroom €26.40/30.80, singles/doubles with private bathroom €30.80/38.15) has a certain shabby charm and is popular with backpackers.

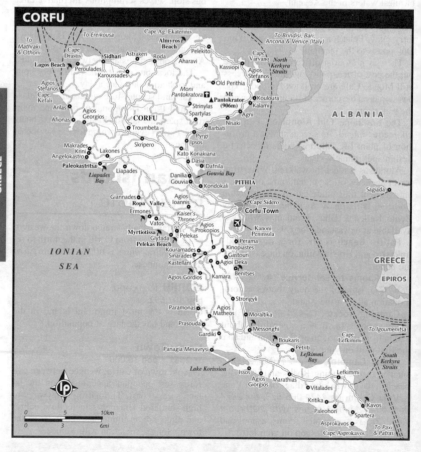

Hotel Konstantinopoulis (☎ 2661 048 716, fax 2661 048 718; Zavitsianou 11; singles/doubles €52.80/70.50) has a great position overlooking the old harbour.

Hrysomalis (☎ 2661 030 342; Nikiforou Theotaki 6; mains €5), near the Spianada, is one of Corfu's oldest restaurants. It's a no-frills place that turns out excellent staples.

Around the Island

Hardly anywhere in Corfu hasn't made a play for the tourist dollar, but the north is over the top. The only real attraction there is the view from the summit of **Mt Pantokrator** (906m), Corfu's highest mountain. There's a road to the top from the village of **Strinila**.

The main resort on the west coast is **Paleokastritsa**, built around a series of pretty bays. Further south, there are good beaches around the small village of **Agios Gordios**. Between Paleokastritsa and Agios Gordios is the hilltop village of **Pelekas**, supposedly the best place on Corfu to watch the sunset.

Places to Stay

Pink Palace (☎ 2661 053 103/4, fax 2661 053 025; e pink-palace@ker.forthnet.gr; rooms from €22 per person), a huge complex of restaurants, bars and budget rooms that tumbles down a hillside outside Agios Gordios, is where most backpackers head. Rates include bed, breakfast and dinner. Debauchery is the main item on the menu for those who want to party hard.

Getting There & Away

Three flights daily to Athens are offered by both **Olympic Airways** (☎ 2661 038 694; Polila 11, Corfu town) and **Aegean Airlines** (☎ 2661 027 100). Olympic also flies to Thessaloniki three times a week.

There are daily buses to Athens (€27.90, 11 hours) and Thessaloniki (€25.70, nine hours) from the Avrami terminal in Corfu town. Fares include the ferry to Igoumenitsa.

There are hourly ferries to Igoumenitsa (€4.10, 1½ hours) and a daily ferry to Paxoi. In summer, there are daily services to Patras (€17.90, 10 hours) on the international ferries that call at Corfu on their way from Italy.

Getting Around

Buses for villages close to Corfu town leave from Plateia San Rocco. Services to other destinations leave from the station on Avrami.

ITHAKI Ιθάκη
• pop 3100

Ithaki (ancient Ithaca) is the fabled home of Odysseus, the hero of Homer's *Odyssey*, who pined for his island during his journeys to far-flung lands. It's a quiet place with some isolated coves. From the main town of Vathy you can walk to the **Fountain of Arethousa**, the fabled site of Odysseus' meeting with the swineherd Eumaeus on his return to Ithaki. Take water with you, as the fountain dries up in summer.

Ithaki has daily ferries to the mainland ports of Patras and Astakos, as well as daily services to Kefallonia and Lefkada.

KEFALLONIA Κεφαλλονιά
• pop 32,500

After years of drifting along in relative obscurity, quiet Kefallonia found itself thrust into the international spotlight following the success of Louis de Bernières' novel *Captain Corelli's Mandolin*.

Publicity reached fever pitch in the summer of 2001 with the release of the movie that starred Nicholas Cage, Penelope Cruz and John Hurt.

Visitors who come to the island's capital, Sami, hoping to wander the old Venetian streets depicted in the movie, will be disappointed to learn that it was all a cleverly constructed set. The originals were destroyed by a major earthquake in 1953.

Kefallonia is the largest of the Ionians, and tourism remains fairly low key outside the resort areas near the capital and on the beaches in the southwest. Public transport is very limited, apart from regular services between Argostoli and the main port of Sami, 25km away on the east coast.

There's an **EOT** (☎ 2671 022 248) on the waterfront in Argostoli.

Kyknos Studios (☎ 2671 023 398, fax 025 943, M Geroulanou 4; double studios €35.20), in Argostoli close to the main square, Plateia Vallianou, is a good place to check out.

Hotel Melissani (☎/fax 2674 022 464; singles/doubles €38.20/49.90), in Sami, is a pleasant older-style hotel offering such comforts as TV and fridge. It's signposted from the eastern end of the waterfront.

Captain's Table (☎ 2671 023 896; Rizospaston 3; mains €5-15), near Kyknos Studios, is one of Argostoli's top restaurants and the place to go for a splurge.

Delfinia (☎ 2674 022 008; mains €4-10.50) is a popular waterfront spot favoured by local diners.

There is a daily flight to Athens from the airport, which is 9km south of Argostoli. There are daily ferries from Sami to Patras (€10, 2½ hours), as well as from Argostoli and the southeastern port of Poros to Kyllini in the Peloponnese. There are also ferry connections to the islands of Ithaki, Lefkada and Zakynthos.

ZAKYNTHOS Ζάκυνθος
pop 32,560
Zakynthos, or Zante as it is also known, is a beautiful island surrounded by great beaches – so it's hardly surprising that the place is completely overrun by package groups. Its capital and port, Zakynthos town, is an imposing old Venetian town that has been painstakingly reconstructed after being levelled by an earthquake in 1953.

Some of the best beaches are around the huge **Bay of Laganas** in the south, which is where endangered loggerhead turtles come ashore to lay their eggs in August – at the peak of the tourist invasion. Conservation groups are urging people to stay away and the Greek government has declared this area a National Marine Park. There are regular ferries between Zakynthos and Kyllini in the Peloponnese.

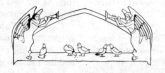

Ireland

Ireland is one of Western Europe's least populated, least industrialised and, in a word, least 'spoilt' countries. It also has one of the longest and most tragic histories in Europe.

That long history is easy to trace through Stone Age passage tombs and ring forts, medieval monasteries and castles, and the stately homes and splendid Georgian architecture of the 18th and 19th centuries. The tragic side is almost as easy to spot; the reminders of Ireland's long and difficult relationship with Britain are ubiquitous.

This chapter covers the independent Republic of Ireland plus Northern Ireland, which forms part of the United Kingdom (UK).

WHAT'S IN A NAME?

The northeastern corner of Ireland is part of the UK and its official name is Northern Ireland. It is also referred to as 'the North', or Ulster, a reference to the historical province of Ulster that was ceded to Britain following the partition of Ireland in 1921. The rest of Ireland is known as the Republic of Ireland, although on your travels you may hear it referred to as Éire, the Irish Republic, the Republic, Southern Ireland or 'the South'.

Facts about Ireland

HISTORY
Celts & Vikings

Fierce Celtic warriors probably reached Ireland from mainland Europe around 300 BC and were well ensconced by 100 BC. Christian monks, including St Patrick, arrived in Ireland around the 5th century AD and, as the Dark Ages enveloped Europe, Ireland became an outpost of European civilisation. A land of saints, scholars and missionaries, its thriving monasteries produced beautiful illuminated manuscripts, some of which survive to this day.

From the end of the 8th century, the rich monasteries were targets for raids by Vikings until they, too, began to settle. At the height of their power the Vikings ruled Dublin, Waterford and Limerick, but they were eventually defeated by the legendary Celtic hero Brian Ború, the king of Munster, at the battle of Clontarf in 1014.

At a Glance

- **Dublin** – Georgian architecture and great Guinness
- **Kilkenny** – pretty, medieval streets and lively festivals
- **Killarney National Park** – evocative still loughs and misty mountains
- **Aran Islands** – windswept and starkly beautiful, magical Stone Age forts
- **Giant's Causeway** – the country's most spectacular rock formation

Capital	Dublin (Ire), Belfast (NI)
Population	3.9 million (Ire), 1.6 million (NI)
Official Language	English, Irish Gaelic
Currency	euro (Ire), 1 British pound (£) = 100 pence (NI)
Time	GMT/UTC+0000
Country Phone Code	☎ 353 (Ire), ☎ 44 28 (NI)

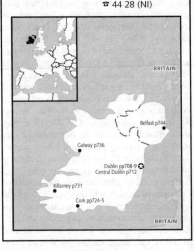

The British Arrive

In 1169 the Norman conquest of England, by then more than a century old, spread to Ireland when Henry II, fearful of the growing power of the Irish kingdoms, dispatched his forces to the island – the legendary figure Strongbow among them. Yet, just as the Vikings had first raided then settled and assimilated, so did the

Anglo-Norman intruders. Over the centuries, English control gradually receded to an area around Dublin known as 'the Pale'.

In the 1500s, the Protestant Henry VIII moved once again to enforce English control over his unruly neighbour, but real entanglement in Irish affairs was left to his daughter and successor, Elizabeth I. Under Elizabeth the oppression of the Catholic Irish got seriously underway. Huge swathes of Irish land were confiscated and given to trustworthy Protestant settlers, sowing the seeds of the divided Ireland that exists today. The English forces put down a series of rebellions and in 1607 the disheartened Irish lords departed for France in the 'Flight of the Earls'.

In 1641 a Catholic rebellion in Ulster led to violent massacres of Protestant settlers. Later in the decade, the English Civil War ended in victory for Oliver Cromwell and defeat for the Catholic sympathiser Charles I. Once again the English turned their attention to Ireland. In 1649 Cromwell began a two-year rampage through the country, leaving a trail of blood and smoke behind him.

In 1685 James II (a Scotsman) became King, but angered his English Protestant subjects with his outspoken Catholicism, and was forced to flee the country. He intended to raise an army in Ireland and regain his throne, which had been handed over to the Protestant William of Orange (a Dutchman) and his wife Mary (James' daughter). In March 1689 James landed from France at Kinsale, near Cork, and marched north. Unfortunately for James, William of Orange landed in 1690 at Carrickfergus, just north of Belfast. William's victory at the ensuing Battle of the Boyne on 12 July 1690 was a turning point, and is commemorated to this day by northern Protestants as a pivotal triumph over 'popes and popery'.

By the early 18th century, the dispirited Catholics in Ireland held less than 15% of the land and suffered brutal restrictions in employment, education, land ownership and religion. An organisation known as the United Irishmen, originally formed by Belfast Presbyterians, began agitating for Irish civil rights under the leadership of a young Dublin Protestant and republican, Theobald Wolfe Tone (1763–98). The group started out with high ideals of bringing together men of all creeds to reform and reduce England's power in Ireland. However, its attempts at gaining power through straightforward politics were fruitless,

and when war broke out between Britain and France, the United Irishmen tried to organise a French invasion of Ireland. In 1796 a French fleet with thousands of troops approached Bantry Bay in County Cork, but was repelled by poor weather. Tone was captured by the British and committed suicide after he sailed with a second failed invasion fleet a few years later.

Ireland's Protestant gentry, alarmed at the level of unrest, sought the security of closer ties with Britain. In 1800 the Act of Union was passed, joining Ireland politically with Britain. The Irish parliament duly voted itself out of existence and around 100 of the Irish MPs moved to the House of Commons in London.

In the first half of the 19th century Daniel O'Connell (1775–1847) seemed to be succeeding in moving Ireland towards greater independence by peaceful means. In 1828 O'Connell stood for a seat representing County Clare in the British parliament, even though being a Catholic meant that he could not legally take the seat. O'Connell won easily and, rather than risk a Catholic rebellion, the British parliament passed the 1829 Act of Catholic Emancipation, allowing Catholics limited voting rights and the right to be elected as MPs. After this great victory, O'Connell settled down to the business of securing further reforms. He died just as Ireland was suffering its greatest tragedy.

Introduced from South America, the easily grown potato was the staple food of a rapidly growing but desperately poor Irish population. From 1800 to 1840 the population had rocketed from four to eight million, but successive failures of the potato crop, caused by a blight between 1845 and 1851, resulted in the mass starvation and emigration known as Ireland's Great Famine.

During these years there were excellent harvests of other crops such as wheat, but these were too expensive for the poor to purchase. Inadequate and ill-conceived relief schemes from Britain and the Irish ruling classes, many of whom profited from inflated food prices, were a national disgrace. As a result, about one million people died from disease or starvation – some of them buried in mass graves, others left to rot in the fields where they had dropped. Another million emigrated, and migration continued to reduce the population during the next 100 years.

IRELAND

Counties

1 Derry	9 Sligo	17 Meath	25 Tipperary
2 Antrim	10 Mayo	18 Louth	26 Ladis
3 Tyrone	11 Roscommon	19 Offaly	27 Kilkenny
4 Fermanagh	12 Galway	20 Kildare	28 Carlow
5 Armagh	13 Longford	21 Dublin	29 Wicklow
6 Down	14 Cavan	22 Clare	30 Cork
7 Donegal	15 Monaghan	23 Kerry	31 Waterford
8 Leitrim	16 Westmeath	24 Limerick	32 Wexford

In the late 19th and early 20th centuries, the British parliament began to contemplate Irish home rule, but WWI interrupted the process. Ireland might still have moved, slowly but peacefully, towards some sort of accommodation but for a bungled uprising in 1916. Though it is now celebrated as a glorious bid for freedom, the so-called Easter Rising was, in fact, heavy with rhetoric, light on planning and lacking in public support. The British response was just as badly conceived. After the insurrection had been put down, a series of trials and executions (15 in all) transformed the ringleaders from troublemakers to martyrs, rousing international support for Irish independence.

The Road to Independence
In the 1918 general election, Irish republicans stood under the banner of Sinn Féin ('We Ourselves' or 'Ourselves Alone') and won a majority of the Irish seats. Ignoring London's parliament, where technically they were supposed to sit, the newly elected Sinn Féin deputies, many of them veterans of the 1916 Easter Rising, declared Ireland independent and formed the first Dáil Éireann (Irish assembly or lower house), led by Eamon de Valera. The British had by no means conceded independence, however, and confrontation was inevitable.

The Anglo–Irish War (1919–21) pitted Sinn Féin and its military wing, the Irish Republican Army (IRA), against the British. The increasingly brutal responses of Britain's hated Black and Tans infantry further roused anti-British sentiment, and atrocity was met with atrocity. This was the period when Michael Collins came to the fore, a charismatic and ruthless leader who masterminded the IRA's campaign of violence against the British (while serving as finance minister in the new Dáil).

After months of negotiations in London, Michael Collins and Arthur Griffith led the delegation that signed the Anglo–Irish Treaty on 6 December 1921. The treaty gave 26 counties of Ireland independence and allowed six largely Protestant counties in Ulster the choice to opt out (a foregone conclusion).

The treaty was ratified by the Dáil in January 1922, but passions were so inflamed that within weeks a civil war broke out. At issue was not so much the future of Protestant Ulster, but rather that, under the Anglo–Irish Treaty, the British monarch remained the (nominal) head of the new Irish Free State and Irish MPs

were required to swear allegiance. To de Valera and many Irish Catholics, these compromises were a betrayal of IRA and republican principles. In the violence that followed, Michael Collins was assassinated in Cork by anti-Treaty forces, while the Free State government briefly imprisoned de Valera.

By 1923 the civil war had ground to a halt, and for nearly 50 years development in the Republic of Ireland was slow and relatively peaceful. After boycotting the Dáil for a number of years, de Valera founded a new party called Fianna Fáil (Warriors of Ireland), which won a majority in the 1932 election. De Valera introduced a new constitution in 1937 that abolished the oath of British allegiance and claimed sovereignty over the six counties of Ulster. In 1948 the Irish government declared the country a republic and, in 1949, left the British Commonwealth.

The Troubles
While the Anglo-Irish Treaty granted independence to 26 counties, six counties in the north were governed by a Northern Irish parliament sitting at Stormont, near Belfast, from 1920 until 1972.

The Protestant majority made sure that its rule was absolute by systematically excluding Catholics from power. This led to the formation of an initially nonsectarian civil rights movement in 1967 to campaign for fairer representation for Northern Irish Catholics. In January 1969 civil rights marchers walked from Belfast to Derry to demand a fairer division of jobs and housing. Just outside Derry a Protestant mob attacked mostly Catholic marchers. Further marches and protests and violence followed. Far from keeping the two sides apart, Northern Ireland's mainly Protestant police force, the Royal Ulster Constabulary (RUC), was becoming part of the problem.

Finally, in August 1969 British troops were sent into Derry and (two days later) Belfast to maintain law and order. Though the Catholics initially welcomed it, the army soon came to be seen as a tool of the Protestant majority. The peaceful civil rights movement lost ground and the IRA, which had been hibernating, found itself with new and willing recruits for an armed independence struggle.

Thus the so-called Troubles rolled back and forth throughout the 1970s and into the 1980s. Passions reached fever pitch in 1972 when 13 unarmed Catholics were shot dead by British troops in Derry on 'Bloody Sunday' (30 January). Then in 1981 IRA prisoners in Northern Ireland went on a hunger strike to demand the right to be recognised as political prisoners (rather than as terrorists). Ten of them fasted to death, the best known being an elected MP, Bobby Sands.

The waters were further muddied by the IRA splitting into 'official' and 'provisional' wings, from which sprang even more violent republican organisations. Protestant paramilitary organisations such as the Ulster Volunteer Force (UVF) sprang up in opposition to the IRA and its splinter groups, and violence was met with violence.

Giving Peace a Chance

In 1985 the Anglo–Irish Agreement gave the Dublin government an official consultative role in Northern Irish affairs for the first time. The Downing St Declaration of December 1993, signed by Britain and the Republic, moved matters forward, with Britain declaring it had no 'selfish, economic or military interest' in preserving the division of Ireland.

In August 1994 a 'permanent cessation of violence' by the IRA, announced by Sinn Féin's leader Gerry Adams, offered the almost unimagined prospect of peace in Ulster. When Protestant paramilitary forces responded with their own cease-fire in October 1994, most British troops were withdrawn to barracks and roadblocks were removed.

In 1995 the British and Irish governments published two 'framework documents' to lay the groundwork for all-party peace talks. The subsequent negotiations stalled when Britain's Conservative prime minister, John Major, refused to allow all-party talks to start until the IRA decommissioned its weapons. An IRA bomb in the Docklands area of London shattered the negotiations in February 1996. In June 1996, with the IRA's refusal to restore its cease-fire, 'all-party' talks on Ulster's future convened without Sinn Féin.

The peace process regained momentum with the landslide victory in May 1997 of Tony Blair's Labour Party, its massive majority enabling it to act with a freer hand than the previous Conservative government. In June 1997 Britain's new Northern Ireland Secretary, Dr Mo Mowlam, promised to admit Sinn Féin to all-party talks following any new cease-fire. Encouraged by this, the IRA declared another cease-fire on 20 July 1997.

To worldwide acclaim these talks produced the Good Friday Agreement on 10 April 1998. This complex agreement allows the people of Northern Ireland to decide their political future by majority vote, and commits its signatories to 'democratic and peaceful means of resolving differences on political issues'. It established a new Northern Irish parliament and high-level political links between the Republic and Northern Ireland. In May 1998, the agreement was approved by 71% of the voters in referendums held simultaneously on both sides of the Irish border. However, despite these moves towards peace, later that year a bomb planted by the 'Real IRA' killed 28 people in Omagh.

Since the Good Friday Agreement the peace process has stopped and started, with the new parliament being suspended then reinstated, largely over wrangles about how and when the IRA should 'decommission' its weapons stockpiles, an unknown quantity of which it has voluntarily 'put beyond use'.

Despite these significant gestures, power-sharing in Stormont was strained in 2002 by some serious sectarian skirmishes and the theft of intelligence documents from Castlereagh Police Station. Sinn Féin, meanwhile, refused to give evidence to the US congress about the arrest of three Irish Republicans in Columbia who were allegedly paid to advise on terror tactics to rebel forces there.

Nevertheless, there's an underlying sense of optimism in Ireland, the island. An apology in the summer of 2002 from the IRA to non-combatants affected by its actions during the troubles, although dismissed as posturing by hard-line loyalists, was yet another example of a gesture that would have been unimaginable a few years ago.

Although it often seems bickering of one sort or another will continue forever, most agree (with fingers crossed perhaps) that the 'war' is over.

GEOGRAPHY & ECOLOGY

Ireland is divided into 32 counties: 26 in the Republic and six in Northern Ireland. The island measures 84,421 sq km (about 83% is the Republic) and stretches 486km north to south and 275km east to west. The jagged coastline extends for 5631km. The midlands of Ireland are flat, generally rich farmland with huge swaths of brown peat (which is rapidly being depleted for fuel).

IRELAND

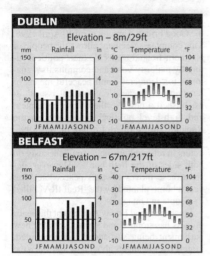

Carrantuohill (1038m) on the Iveragh Peninsula, County Kerry, is the highest mountain on the island. The Shannon River, the longest in Ireland, flows for 259km before emptying into the Atlantic west of Limerick.

Ireland's rivers and lakes are well stocked with fish, such as salmon and trout, and the island is home to some three dozen mammal species, including the Irish hare and Irish stoat. The Office of Public Works (OPW) maintains five national parks and 75 nature reserves in the Republic; the National Trust oversees 26 nature reserves in Northern Ireland.

CLIMATE

Ireland has a relatively mild climate with a mean annual temperature of 10°C. In January and February, average temperatures range from 4°C to 7°C. Average maximums in July and August are from 14°C to 16°C. June, July and August are the sunniest months; December and January are the gloomiest. The sea around Ireland is surprisingly warm for the latitude, due to the influence of the Gulf Stream. Snow is relatively scarce – perhaps one or two flurries in winter in higher areas.

It can rain a lot in Ireland. Annual rainfall is about 1000mm.

GOVERNMENT & POLITICS

The Republic of Ireland has a parliamentary system of government. The lower house of parliament (Oireachtas) or Dáil has 166 members elected by a system of proportional representation. The prime minister's official title is Taoiseach (pronounced tea shock); the current Taoiseach is Bertie Ahern. The 60-strong upper house is known as the Seanad (Senate), and basically it rubber-stamps Dáil legislation. The president (an tuachtaran) of Ireland is elected for seven years. Though the post lacks political power and is limited to two terms, Mary Robinson, the president from 1991 to 1997, injected a healthy dose of liberalism into an otherwise highly conservative political structure. The current president is Mary McAleese.

The main political parties in the Republic are Fianna Fáil, which fell just short of securing an overall majority in the May 2002 general election, and Fine Gael. The Labour Party is the third-largest party. Lesser but still influential players include the Liberal Progressive Democrats (which split from Fianna Fáil in the mid-1980s but with whom Fianna Fáil has since formed coalitions) and the Green Party; both held six seats each in the May 2002 elections. Sinn Féin, the only party to contest elections on both sides of the border, won five seats.

Northern Ireland, governed from London since its ineffective parliament at Stormont was abolished in 1972, elected a new parliament in 1998 as part of the Good Friday Agreement. Northern Ireland's main Protestant parties are the Ulster Unionist Party (UUP) led by David Trimble, and Ian Paisley's hard-line Democratic Unionist Party (DUP). Catholic parties are John Hume's moderate Social Democratic and Labour Party (SDLP), and Sinn Féin, the political wing of the IRA led by Gerry Adams. At present, Trimble is the First Minister of the new Northern Ireland parliament.

ECONOMY

Although small, the Irish economy is one of Europe's most buoyant, although inflation is higher than the European average at between 4% and 5%. Exports, mainly to Britain, the European Union (EU) and the USA, continue at record levels, although the rapid annual economic growth rates it experienced in the 1990s slowed somewhat in 2001 to around 6%. Ireland is a major exporter of computer hardware and software, and information technology is now contributing more to the economy than agriculture. Continuing economic growth has reduced unemployment to historic lows of 4% or less, although wages are still below EU standards.

Northern Ireland's shipbuilding and other great industrial activities have declined dramatically, but new industries have developed and, of course, the region is heavily supported financially by Britain. Almost 30% of the working population is employed in one way or another by the government. Northern Ireland's unemployment rate has been dropping and now sits below 5%.

The cease-fire and the Good Friday Agreement have delivered a substantial dividend in the shape of a tourism boom, especially from Britain and the Republic. Foreign investment has reached record levels.

POPULATION & PEOPLE

The total population of Ireland is around 5.5 million: 3.9 million in the Republic and 1.6 million in Northern Ireland. Prior to the 1845–51 Great Famine, the population was around eight million; death and emigration reduced it to around six million, and emigration continued at a high level for the next 100 years. It wasn't until the 1960s that Ireland's population finally began to recover.

Lately, economic migrants including relatively wealthy Western European nationals and poorer migrants from elsewhere have also been having a minor but palpable impact on the population.

ARTS
Music

Traditional Irish music – played on instruments such as the *bodhrán* (a flat, goatskin drum), *uilleann* (or 'elbow') pipes, flute and fiddle – is an aspect of Irish culture that visitors are most likely to encounter. Almost every town and village in Ireland seems to have a pub renowned for its traditional music. Of the Irish music groups, perhaps the best-known are the Chieftains, the Dubliners, Altan, De Danann and the wilder Pogues. Among popular Irish singers/musicians who have made it on the international stage are Van Morrison, Enya, Sinéad O'Connor, Bob Geldof, U2, the Cranberries and, more recently, The Corrs, Boyzone and Ash.

Literature

The Irish have made an enormous impact on world literature. Important writers include Jonathan Swift, Oscar Wilde, WB Yeats, George Bernard Shaw, James Joyce, Sean O'Casey, Samuel Beckett and, more recently, Roddy Doyle, whose *Paddy Clarke Ha Ha Ha* won the Booker Prize in 1993. The Ulster-born poet Séamus Heaney was awarded the Nobel Prize for Literature in 1995. Earlier Irish Nobel laureates include Shaw (1925), Yeats (1938) and Beckett (1969). Presently Frank McCourt is a world favourite with his autobiographical *Angela's Ashes* and *'Tis*.

Architecture

Ireland is packed with archaeological sites, prehistoric graves, ruined monasteries, crumbling fortresses, abandoned manor houses and many other firm reminders of its long and usually dramatic history. You may encounter the following terms on your travels:

cashel – a stone ring fort or *rath*

dolmen – a portal tomb or Stone Age grave consisting of stone 'pillars' supporting a stone roof or capstone

ogham stone – a memorial stone of the 4th to 9th centuries, marked on its edge with groups of straight lines or notches to represent the Latin alphabet

passage tomb – a megalithic mound-tomb with a narrow stone passage which leads to a burial chamber

ring fort or *rath* – a circular fort, originally constructed of earth and timber, but later made of stone

round tower – a tall tower or belfry built as a lookout and place of refuge from the Vikings

SOCIETY & CONDUCT

The Irish are an easy-going, loquacious, fun-loving people. They are used to tourists and there are few social taboos. In Northern Ireland people discuss the Troubles more openly than before but it can still be a sensitive topic of discussion. Do not take humorous Irish scepticism or sarcasm too seriously.

Immigration is starting to have an impact, particularly in the larger towns and cities, although Irish society remains fairly homogeneous. Many Irish people have had relatively little experience with those of different races, cultures and sexual orientations. Many, especially those in the countryside, tend to be socially conservative.

RELIGION

Religion has always played a pivotal role in Irish history. Almost everybody is either

IRELAND

Catholic or Protestant, with the Republic 95% Catholic and Northern Ireland about 60% Protestant. The Jewish community in Ireland is tiny but long-established.

The Catholic Church has always opposed attempts to liberalise laws governing contraception, divorce and abortion. Today, condom machines can be found in all parts of Ireland and divorce is legal, but abortion remains illegal in the Republic. The Catholic Church's once considerable political and social power in the Republic is waning owing to increased secularism and to the waves of sexual and physical abuse scandals that have convulsed the Church during the past decade.

LANGUAGE

Officially the Republic is bilingual. English is spoken throughout the island, but there are still parts of western and southern Ireland, known as the Gaeltacht, where Irish is still the native language.

A Celtic language closely related to Scottish Gaelic (and less so to Welsh), it's an attractive but difficult tongue with a unique orthographic (spelling) system. For example, 'mh' is pronounced like 'v', 'bhf' is a 'w', and 'dh' is like 'g'.

Facts for the Visitor

HIGHLIGHTS
Scenery, Beaches & Coastline

There's a lot of natural beauty in Ireland, but among the best is the scenery around the Ring of Kerry, the Beara and Dingle Peninsulas, the barren stretches of the Burren, the rocky Aran Islands, and the Glens of Antrim in Northern Ireland.

Favourite stretches of coast include the Cliffs of Moher, the Connemara and Donegal coasts, and the Causeway Coast of Northern Ireland.

Museums & Castles

In Dublin, Trinity College's Old Library with the ancient *Book of Kells* is a must-see, and there are extensive collections at the National Museum and National Gallery. Belfast has the Ulster Museum and, just outside the city, the Ulster Folk Museum.

Ireland is littered with castles and ancient ring forts. The Stone Age forts on the Aran Islands are of particular interest. Prime examples

of castles can be found at Kilkenny, Blarney and, in Northern Ireland, Carrickfergus and Dunluce.

Religious Sites

The passage tomb at Newgrange, near Dublin, is the most impressive relic of pre-Christian Ireland. Early Christian churches and ruined monastic sites, some well over 1000 years old, are scattered throughout Ireland. Glendalough and the Rock of Cashel are recommended. If the weather allows, the tiny early-Christian monastery atop the jagged isle of Skellig Michael is an amazing place to visit.

SUGGESTED ITINERARIES

Depending on the length of your stay, you might want to see and do the following things:

Two days
Visit Dublin and perhaps one place nearby – Powerscourt and Glendalough to the south, or Newgrange to the north.

One week
Visit Dublin, Glendalough, Kilkenny, the Burren and Galway.

Two weeks
As for one week, plus the Ring of Kerry (Iveragh Peninsula), Killarney and Cork.

One month
With your own car you can cover all the main attractions around the coast. This is more difficult to achieve in the same time by bicycle or on public transport.

PLANNING
When to Go

The tourist season begins the weekend before the much-celebrated St Patrick's Day (17 March) and is in full swing from Easter onward.

In July and August the crowds are at their biggest and that's when prices are at their highest. Weekends in Dublin are busy year round. Many tourist facilities close or have shorter opening hours in the quieter winter months.

Maps

There are many good-quality maps of Ireland, including the Lonely Planet *Dublin City Map*, Michelin *Ireland Motoring Map* No 923 (1:400,000) and Ordnance Survey's (OS) four Ireland *Holiday Maps* (1:250,000). The more detailed OS *Discovery* series (1:50,000) covers the entire country with 89 maps.

What to Bring

The Irish climate is changeable and even at the height of summer be prepared for cold weather and sudden rainfall. A raincoat and/or umbrella is an absolute necessity.

Walkers should be particularly well prepared if they are crossing the open country. Otherwise, Ireland presents few surprises. Dress is usually casual even in the cities.

TOURIST OFFICES

The Irish tourist board, Bord Fáilte (pronounced bord fawlcha), and the Northern Ireland Tourist Board (NITB) operate separate offices, although they share some marketing and a helpful website (**W** www.tourismire land.com). Both are usually well organised and helpful, though Bord Fáilte will not provide any information on places (such as B&Bs and camping grounds) that it has not approved.

Every town big enough to have half-a-dozen pubs will certainly have a tourist office, although the smaller ones close during winter. Most will find you a place to stay for a fee of €2 to €4.

Tourist Offices Abroad

Overseas offices of Bord Fáilte include:

Australia (☎ 02-9299 6177) 5th floor, 36 Carrington St, Sydney, NSW 2000
Canada (☎ 416-487 3335) 120 Eglinton Ave East, Suite 500, Toronto, Ont M5P 1E2
Netherlands (☎ 020-504 0689) Spuistraat 104, 1012 VA Amsterdam
New Zealand (☎ 09-379 8720) Dingwall Bldg, 87 Queen St, Auckland 1
UK (☎ 020-7493 3201) Ireland House, 150 New Bond St, London W1Y OAQ
USA (☎ 1800 223 6470) 345 Park Ave, New York, NY 10154

Tourist information for Northern Ireland abroad is usually handled by the British Tourist Authority (BTA), though there are a few offices of the NITB:

Canada (☎ 1800 223 6470) 2 Bloor St West, Suite 1501, Toronto, Ont M4W 3E2
New Zealand (☎ 09-977 2255) 18 Shortland St, Private Bag 92136, Auckland 1
UK (☎ 0800 039700) British Travel Centre, 12 Lower Regent St, London SW1Y 4PQ
USA (☎ 800-233 6470) 551 5th Ave, Suite 701, New York, NY 10176

VISAS & DOCUMENTS

For citizens of the EU and most other Western countries, no visa is required to visit either the Republic or Northern Ireland. EU nationals are allowed to stay indefinitely, while other visitors can usually remain for three to six months.

UK nationals born in Britain or Northern Ireland do not need a passport, but it's advisable to carry some form of identification.

EMBASSIES & CONSULATES
Irish Embassies & Consulates

Irish diplomatic offices overseas include:

Australia (☎ 02-6273 3022) 20 Arkana St, Yarralumla, ACT 2600
Canada (☎ 613-233 6281) 130 Albert St, Ottawa, Ontario, K1A OL6
Japan (☎ 03-3263 0695) 2-10-7 Kojimachi, Chiyoda-ku, Tokyo 102
New Zealand (☎ 09-302 2867) 6th floor, 18 Shortland St, 1001 Auckland
South Africa (☎ 012-342 5062) Tubach Centre, 1234 Church St, 0083 Colbyn, Pretoria
UK (☎ 020-7235 2171) 17 Grosvenor Place, London SW1X 7HR
USA (☎ 202-462 3939) 2234 Massachusetts Ave NW, Washington, DC 20008. In addition there are consulates in Boston, Chicago, New York and San Francisco.

Foreign Embassies in Ireland

Foreign embassies in Dublin include:

Australia (☎ 01-676 1517) 2nd floor, Fitzwilton House, Wilton Terrace, Dublin 2
Canada (☎ 01-478 1988) 65-68 St Stephen's Green, Dublin 2
France (☎ 01-260 1666) 36 Ailesbury Rd, Dublin 4
New Zealand (☎ 01-660 4233) 37 Leeson Park, Dublin 6
UK (☎ 01-205 3700) 29 Merrion Rd, Dublin 4
USA (☎ 01-668 9946) 42 Elgin Rd, Dublin 4

In Northern Ireland, nationals of most countries other than the USA should contact their embassy in London.

USA (☎ 028-9032 8239) Queens House, 14 Queen St, Belfast, BT1 6EQ

MONEY
Currency

In 2002 the Irish Republic exchanged its pounds or punts, for the new Europe-wide currency the euro (€), which is divided into 100

IRELAND

cents. The British pound sterling (£) is still the Northern Irish currency and is divided into 100 pence (p). Banks offer the best exchange rates. Exchange bureaus are open longer than banks, but the rates are not as good and the commission higher. Most post offices provide currency-exchange facilities.

In Northern Ireland several banks issue their own Northern Irish pound notes, which are equivalent to sterling but not readily accepted in Britain. Many Northern Irish shops and businesses accept payment in euros.

Most major currencies and types of travellers cheques are readily accepted in Ireland. Eurocheques can also be cashed here.

Costs

Ireland is an expensive place, marginally more costly than Britain, but prices vary around the island. Many places to stay, particularly hostels (but also hotels and some B&Bs) have low- and high-season prices. Some, mainly in Dublin, have higher weekend rates. Entry prices to sites and museums are usually 20% to 50% lower for children, students and senior citizens (OAPs).

For the budget traveller, €60 per day should cover hostel accommodation, getting around and a meal in a restaurant leaving just enough for a pint at the end of the day.

ATMs & Credit/Charge Cards

Major credit cards, particularly Visa and MasterCard, are widely accepted, even at B&Bs. You can obtain cash advances on your card from banks and from automatic teller machines (ATMs). Even small towns have ATMs that accept foreign cards affiliated with the Cirrus, Plus and Maestro networks.

Tipping

Fancy hotels and restaurants usually add a 10% or 15% service charge onto the bill. Simpler places usually do not add service; if you decide to tip, just round up the bill (or add 10% at most). Taxi drivers do not have to be tipped, but if you're feeling flush 10% is more than generous.

Consumer Taxes

Value-added tax (VAT) of 20% applies to most goods and services in Ireland. EU residents are not entitled to VAT refunds. Other visitors can claim back VAT on purchases that are being taken out of the EU. The stores that display Cashback stickers will give you a voucher that can be refunded at most of the international airports or stamped at ferry ports and mailed back for a refund.

POST & COMMUNICATIONS
Post

The post offices (An Post) throughout the Republic are open from 9am (9.30am Tuesday and Wednesday) to 5.30pm Monday to Friday, and from 9am to 1pm Saturday; smaller offices close for lunch.

Letters weighing less than 25g cost €0.38 to Britain, €0.44 to EU countries and €0.57 outside Europe.

Post-office hours and postal rates in Northern Ireland are the same as in Britain. Mail can be addressed to poste restante at post offices, but is officially held for only two weeks. Writing 'hold for collection' on the envelope may help.

Telephone

Phonecards are almost essential these days in the Republic, where Eircom sells Callcards of 10/20/50 units for €2.50/4.50/10.20. Post offices also sell the Swift low-cost international phone cards for €7/15/25/30.

In Northern Ireland, the telephone booths (boxes) that accept the British Telecom (BT) phonecards are few and far between outside Belfast. International calls can be dialled directly from pay phones.

See the Telephones appendix at the back of this book for information about making international calls to or from the Republic or Northern Ireland (ie, the UK). The important difference is that to call Northern Ireland from the Republic, you do not use ☎ 0044 as for the rest of the UK. Instead, you dial ☎ 048 and then the local number.

The mobile (cell) phone network in Ireland runs on the GSM 900/1800 system compatible with the rest of Europe and Australia, but not the USA. It's also possible to buy pay-as-you-go phones on arrival for around €50.

Direct Home Calls You can dial direct to your home country operator and then reverse charges (collect) or charge the call to a local phone-credit card. From the Republic, dial the following codes then the area code and number you want. Your home-country operator will come on the line before the call goes through:

Australia	☎ 1800 5500 61 + number
France	☎ 1800 5500 33 + number
New Zealand	☎ 1800 5500 64 + number
UK BT	☎ 1800 5500 44 + number
USA AT&T	☎ 1800 5500 00 + number
USA MCI	☎ 1800 5510 01 + number
USA Sprint	☎ 1800 5520 01 + number

Reverse-charge calls can also be made from the North using the same numbers as from the UK.

Fax, Telegraph, Email & Internet Access

Faxes can be sent from specialist offices. To send international telegrams, phone ☎ 196 in the Republic or ☎ 0800 190190 in Northern Ireland. Internet access is available in almost every town, with typical hourly rates of about €6 per hour.

DIGITAL RESOURCES

Your first stop should be the award-winning **Lonely Planet site** (**w** www.lonelyplanet.com). For an overview of travelling and tourism throughout Ireland you can try **Dublin Tourism** (**w** www.visitdublin.com), the **Bord Fáilte** (**w** www.ireland.travel.ie) or the **Northern Irish Tourism Board** (**w** www.discovernorthernireland.com).

Useful travel websites for the south and north respectively are: **CIE Group** (**w** www.cie.ie) and **Translink** (**w** www.translink.co.uk). The site for the **Irish Government** is **w** www.gov.ie and for the **Northern Ireland Office** it's **w** www.nio.gov.uk. The *Irish Times* (**w** www.irish-times.ie) has an award-winning site with news and arts features.

BOOKS

Lonely Planet's *Ireland*, *Dublin*, *Dublin Condensed* and *Walking in Ireland* guides offer comprehensive coverage of the island and its most visited city.

One of the better books about Irish history is *The Oxford Companion to Irish History* (1998) edited by SJ Connolly.

NEWSPAPERS

The main papers in the Republic are the Dublin-based *Irish Times* and *Irish Independent*, and the *Irish Examiner*. In Northern Ireland there's the *Belfast Telegraph*, the Sinn Féin-published *An Phoblacht Rebublican News* and staunchly Protestant *News Letter* tabloid. British newspapers are available, as

are the *International Herald Tribune* and *USA Today*.

RADIO & TV

Ireland has two state-controlled television channels (RTÉ 1 and Network 2) and three radio stations. Northern Ireland's two TV channels are BBC Northern Ireland and Ulster Television. With the correct aerial, Britain's BBC and other stations can now be picked up throughout most parts of the country. Raidió na Gaeltachta (92.5/96 FM or 540/828/963 MW) is the national Irish-language service.

PHOTOGRAPHY

Ireland and its people are very photogenic, but the sky is often overcast, so photographers should bring high-speed film (eg, 200 or 400 ASA). A roll of 24-exposure print film costs around €9 (or about £5.50) to process.

TIME

Ireland is on the same time as Britain and advances the clock by one hour from late March to late October. During the summer months it stays light until after 10pm.

LAUNDRY

Most towns have several laundrettes, usually with an attendant who washes, dries and neatly folds your clothes for around €9. Hostel laundries are usually good value.

TOILETS

Public toilets in the Republic are often marked *fir* for men and *mná* for women.

WOMEN TRAVELLERS

Women travellers will find Ireland a blissfully relaxing experience, with little risk of hassle on the street or anywhere else. Nonetheless, walking alone at night, especially in certain parts of Dublin, is unwise. Hitching is not recommended, even though it's probably safer than anywhere else in Europe.

There's little need to worry about what you wear in Ireland. Nor is finding contraception the problem it once was, although anyone on the pill should bring adequate supplies with them.

GAY & LESBIAN TRAVELLERS

Despite the decriminalisation of homosexuality for people over the age of 17 (Northern

IRELAND

Ireland in 1982 and the Republic in 1993), gay life is generally neither acknowledged nor understood. Only Dublin and, to a certain extent, Belfast and Cork have open gay communities. The *Gay Community News*, a free tabloid published monthly in Dublin, is available at bars and cafés or by subscription to GCN (☎ 01-671 0939/9076; e info@gcn.ie; w www.gcn.ie; Unit 2, Scarlet Row, Temple Bar, Dublin 8). The bi-monthly events magazine *In Dublin* (w www.indublin.ie) has a gay and lesbian section with club and resource-centre listings. Information is also available from the following:

Northern Ireland Gay Rights Association (Nigra; ☎ 028-9066 4111) PO Box 44, Belfast
Outhouse Community Centre (☎ 01-873 4932; e info@outhouse.ie) 105 Capel St, Dublin 1

DISABLED TRAVELLERS

Guesthouses, hotels and sights throughout Ireland are increasingly being adapted for people with disabilities. Bord Fáilte's various accommodation guides indicate which places are wheelchair accessible, and the NITB publishes *Accessible Accommodation in Northern Ireland*. Comhairle publishes detailed accessibility information in the Republic and Northern Ireland.

Comhairle (☎ 01-874 7503; w www.com hairle.ie) 44 North Great George's St, Dublin 1
Disability Action (☎ 028-9049 1011; w www .disabilityaction.org) 2 Annadale Ave, Belfast BT7 3JH

DANGERS & ANNOYANCES

Ireland is probably safer than most countries in Europe, but the usual precautions should be observed. Drug-related crime is on the increase, and Dublin has its fair share of pickpockets. Look after your belongings when visiting pubs and cafés.

Dublin is notorious for car break-ins and petty theft. Car theft is also a problem in Belfast. Cyclists should lock their bicycles and be cautious about leaving bags attached.

BUSINESS HOURS

Offices are open 9am to 5pm Monday to Friday, shops a little later. On Thursday and/or Friday, shops stay open later. Many are also open on Saturday. In winter, tourist attractions are often open shorter hours, fewer days per

---

Emergency Services

The emergency number in both the Republic and Northern Ireland is ☎ 999. For roadside assistance in the event of breakdown phone the Automobile Association (Republic: ☎ 1800-667788, Northern Ireland: ☎ 0800 887766). In Northern Ireland, Royal Automobile Club members can phone ☎ 0800 828282.

---

week or may be shut completely. In Northern Ireland some tourist attractions are closed or Sunday morning.

PUBLIC HOLIDAYS & SPECIAL EVENTS

Public holidays in Ireland (IR), Northern Ireland (NI) or both are: New Year's Day; S Patrick's Day (17 March); Easter (March April); May Holiday (IR; first Monday ir May); May Bank Holidays (NI; first and las Mondays in May); June Bank Holiday (IR first Monday in June); Orangemen's Day (NI 12 July, or 13th if 12th is a Sunday); Augus Holiday (IR; first Monday in August); Augus Bank Holiday (NI; last Monday in August) October Holiday (IR; last Monday in October) Christmas Day; St Stephen's Day/Boxing Day

The All-Ireland hurling and football finals both take place in Dublin in September. There are some great regional cultural events around the island, like the Galway Arts Festival in late July. In Dublin, Leopold Bloom's Joycean journey around the city is marked by various events on Bloomsday (16 June). The Dublin International Film Festival in April is also a highlight. In Northern Ireland, July is marching month and every Orangeman in the country hits the streets on the 'glorious 12th'. Other events include the Ould Lammas Fair at Ballycastle during August, and the Belfast Festival at Queen's in November.

ACTIVITIES

Ireland is a great place for outdoor activities, and the tourist boards put out a wide selection of information sheets covering bird-watching (the Hook area of County Wexford), surfing (great along the west coast), scuba diving, hang-gliding, trout and salmon fishing, ancestor tracing, horse riding, sailing, canoeing and many other activities.

Walking is particularly popular although, as usual, you must come prepared for wet weather. There are now well over 20 way-marked trails, varying in length from the 26km Cavan Way to the 900km Ulster Way.

WORK

At present Ireland is good for casual employment and many pubs and restaurants advertise positions in their windows. Citizens of EU countries can work in Ireland without special papers. For information contact an Irish embassy or consulate in your own country.

ACCOMMODATION

Bord Fáilte's dedicated guides to camping grounds, B&Bs, hotels etc cost €3 and €4. There are also many excellent places that aren't 'tourist-board approved'. NITB publishes free B&B and hotel guides, while its camping and caravanning guide costs £0.50.

Bord Fáilte offices book local accommodation for a fee of €1.50 (or €2.54 to book in another town). This can be handy when it may take numerous phone calls to find a free room. The NITB provides a similar booking service. Accommodation for the Republic and the North may also be booked online, via the **Gulliver booking service** (W www.gulliver.ie). A deposit of 10% and a €4 fee is payable.

All accommodation prices in this chapter are high-season rates (generally June to August); at other times of year, subtract 15% to 25% from the listed prices.

Camping

Camping grounds are not as common in Ireland as elsewhere in Europe, but there are still plenty of them around. Some hostels also have space for tents. At the commercial camping grounds, costs are typically €9 to €14 for a tent and two people.

Hostels

There are plenty of hostels in Ireland, but in summer they can be heavily booked. They do also come and go (for example, Waterford and Limerick had no hostels at the time of writing), so check ahead.

An Óige (meaning 'youth'), the Irish branch of Hostelling International (HI), has 31 hostels scattered around the country, and there are another 10 in Northern Ireland administered by Hostelling International Northern Ireland (HINI). These hostels are open to members of HI, members of An Óige/HINI (annual membership €15/£10), or to any

overseas visitor for a small additional nightly charge.

Two other hostel associations offering accommodation include the Independent Holiday Hostels (IHH), a cooperative group with about 140 hostels in both Northern Ireland and the Republic; and the Independent Hostels Owners (IHO) association, with more than 100 members around Ireland.

From June to September nightly costs at most hostels are about €20, except for the more expensive hostels in Dublin, Belfast and a few other places. Rates are cheaper in the low season.

An Óige (☎ 01-830 4555; e mailbox@anoige .ie; W www.irelandyha.org) 61 Mountjoy St, Dublin 7

Hostelling International Northern Ireland (HINI; ☎ 048-9031 5435; W www.hini.org.uk) 22-32 Donegall Rd, Belfast

Independent Holiday Hostels (IHH; ☎ 01-836 4700; e info@hostels-ireland.com; W www .hostels-ireland.com) 57 Gardiner St Lower, Dublin 1

Independent Hostels Owners in Ireland (IHO; ☎ 073-30130; W holidayhound.com/ihi) Dooey Hostel, Glencolumbcille, County Donegal

B&Bs

The bed and breakfast is as Irish a form of accommodation as there is. It sometimes seems that every other house is a B&B, and you'll stumble upon them in the most unusual and remote locations. Typical costs are around €30 per person a night, though more-luxurious B&Bs can cost from €45 per person. Most B&Bs are small, so in summer they can quickly fill up. Irish B&B breakfasts almost inevitably include 'a fry', which means fried eggs, bacon, sausages, the ubiquitous black pudding (a blood sausage), as well as toast and butter.

FOOD

Traditional meals (like Irish Stew, often found in pubs) are hearty and cheap. Fast food is everywhere, from traditional fish and chips to more recent arrivals like burgers, pizzas and kebabs. A bowl of the day's soup and some excellent soda or brown bread can be a cheap lunch. Seafood, long neglected in Ireland, is often excellent, especially in the west, and there are some good vegetarian restaurants.

IRELAND

DRINKS

In Ireland a drink means a beer, either lager or stout. Stout is usually Guinness, the famous black beer of Dublin, although in Cork it can mean a Murphy's or a Beamish. If you have not developed a taste for stout, a wide variety of lagers are available, including Harp and Smithwicks (don't pronounce the 'w'!). Simply asking for a Guinness will get you a pint (570ml, €3 to €4 in a pub). If you want a half-pint (285ml, around €2), ask for a 'glass' or a 'half'.

In the Republic, pub hours (last orders) are 10.30am to 11.30pm Monday to Wednesday, 10.30am to 12.30am Friday and Saturday, and 12.30pm to 11pm Sunday. In Northern Ireland, pub hours are 11.30am to 11pm Monday to Saturday; 12.30pm to 2pm and 7pm to 10pm Sunday.

ENTERTAINMENT

Listening to traditional music in a pub while nursing a Guinness is a popular form of entertainment in Ireland. If someone suggests visiting a pub for its good 'crack' (from the Irish *craic*), it means a good time, convivial company, sparkling conversation and scintillating music. Music sessions usually begin at around 9pm or 9.30pm at pubs. Theatre is also popular.

A useful website for what's happening in Ireland is at **w** www.entertainmentireland.ie, which has reviews, festival information and listings for music, clubs, theatre, exhibitions and comedy.

SHOPPING

Clothing, especially anything hand-knitted or woven in wool, is the most authentically Irish purchase. Celtic-inspired jewellery and fine Waterford crystal and glassware are also popular buys.

Getting There & Away

AIR

Aer Lingus is the Irish national airline with international connections to other countries in Europe and to the USA.

Budget airline Ryanair is the next largest Irish carrier, with many routes to Europe and the USA.

Britain

Competition is fierce on UK/Irish routes, so prices are keenly competitive. Dublin, Shannon and Cork are linked by a variety of airlines to many cities in Britain, including London's five airports. There are also flights to various regional cities in the Republic of Ireland. A number of budget airlines, including Ryanair and EasyJet, offer advance-purchase fares for £50 or less, but they are limited and must be booked well in advance. Ryanair has some of the best deals to Ireland from London's Stansted airport, sometimes as low as £20 one way. A late-booked standard return is likely to cost £100 or more.

Other cities with direct flights from London include Cork, Shannon, Kerry, Knock and Waterford.

Belfast is also linked with several cities in Britain, including London (Heathrow), via regular British Airways services. Other UK airlines operating services to Ireland include **British Midland** (☎ 0870-607 0555) and **British European** (☎ 0870-567 6676).

Continental Europe

Dublin is connected with other major centres in Europe; there are also flights to Cork, Shannon and Belfast. Fares from Paris to Belfast or Dublin range from €150 to €550, sometimes more in peak times. From Paris, Frankfurt and Brussels, Ryanair flies to Dublin and/or Shannon. EasyJet flies between Amsterdam and Belfast.

The USA

Aer Lingus (from New York and other centres) and Delta (from Atlanta) fly direct to Dublin and Shannon. Because competition on flights to London is fierce, it can be cheaper to fly to London first. During the summer high season, the return fare between New York and Dublin with Aer Lingus is around US$850, though advance-purchase fares sit just less than US$650 return. In the low season, discount return fares from New York to London are about US$500, and in the high season between US$600 and US$700.

Australia & New Zealand

Advance-purchase excursion fares from Australia or New Zealand to Britain (see the Britain chapter) can have a return flight to Dublin tagged on at no extra cost. Return fares from Australia vary from around A$1500 (low season) to A$2200 (high season), but special deals are often available.

LAND

Because of cheap flights, getting to Ireland by land (including ferry) is not very popular. Bus Éireann and National Express operate services direct from London and other UK centres to Dublin, Belfast and other cities. For details in London, contact **Eurolines** (☎ 0870-514 3219) or **National Express** (☎ 0870-580 8080); they share a website at **w** www.goby coach.com. London to Dublin by bus takes about 12 hours and costs £20/37 one way/ return. To Belfast it's 13 hours and slightly more expensive.

SEA

There's a great variety of ferry services from Britain and France to Ireland. Prices vary drastically, depending on season, time of day, day of the week and length of stay. One-way fares for an adult foot passenger can be as little as £20, but nudge close to £50 in summer. For a car plus driver and up to four adult passengers, prices can range from £130 to £210.

There are often special deals, discounted return fares and other money savers that are worth investigating.

Britain

There are ferry services from Scotland (Cairnryan, Troon and Stranraer), England (Fleetwood, Heysham, Mostyn and Liverpool), Wales (Fishguard, Holyhead, Pembroke and Swansea) and the Isle of Man (Douglas) to ports in the Republic (Dublin, Cork, Rosslare Harbour and Dun Laoghaire) and Northern Ireland (Belfast and Larne).

Following is a list of shipping lines:

Irish Ferries
   (☎ 0870-517 1717) For ferry services from Holyhead to Dublin (3¼ hours), and Pembroke to Rosslare Harbour (1¾ to four hours by ferry).
Isle of Man Steam Packet Company and SeaCat Services
   (☎ 0870-552 3523) For catamaran services from Douglas (Isle of Man) to Belfast (2¾ hours, May to September) and Dublin (2¾ hours, May to September); Liverpool to Dublin (3¾ hours); and Heysham (four hours), and Troon (2½ hours) to Belfast.
Norse Merchant Ferries
   (☎ 028-9077 9090) For ferry services from Liverpool to Belfast (8½ hours).

P&O European Ferries
   (☎ 0870-242 4777) For services from Cairnryan to Larne (one hour by fast ferry, 1¾ hours by ferry), Fleetwood to Larne (eight hours by ferry), and Mostyn (near Chester) to Dublin (six hours by ferry).
Stena Line
   (☎ 0870-570 7070) For services from Holyhead to Dublin (3¼ hours by fast ferry) and Dun Laoghaire (1¾ hours by fast ferry), Fishguard to Rosslare Harbour (3½ hours by ferry, 1¾ hours by catamaran), and Stranraer to Belfast (3¼ hours by ferry, 1¾ hours by catamaran).
Swansea Cork Ferries
   (☎ 01792-456116) For services from Swansea to Ringaskiddy (10 hours, mid-May to mid-September).

France

Eurail passes are valid for ferry crossings between Ireland and France on Irish Ferries only; Inter-Rail passes give reductions of 75%.

Irish Ferries runs from Roscoff and Cherbourg to Rosslare Harbour, April to January, taking 14 and 18½ hours respectively.

Brittany Ferries *(Cork: ☎ 021-27 7801; **w** www.brittanyferries.com)* sails from Roscoff to Cork once weekly, the trip taking 14 hours (Friday from Roscoff, Saturday from Cork) from April to the end of September. The trip takes 14 hours.

Getting Around

Travelling around Ireland looks very simple, as the distances are short and there's a dense network of roads and railways. But in Ireland, from A to B is seldom a straight line, and public transport can be expensive (particularly trains), infrequent or both. For these reasons having your own transport – car or bicycle – can be a major advantage.

PASSES & DISCOUNTS

Eurail passes are valid for train travel in the Republic of Ireland but not in Northern Ireland and entitle you to a reduction on Bus Éireann's three-day Irish Rambler tickets. They are also valid on some ferries between France and the Republic. Inter-Rail passes offer a 50% reduction on train travel within Ireland and discounts on some ferries to/from France and Britain.

For €10 students can have a Fairstamp affixed to their ISIC card by any usit CAMPUS agency. This gives a 50% discount on Iarnród

IRELAND

Éireann (Irish Rail) services. Irish Rambler tickets are available from Bus Éireann for bus-only travel in the Republic. They cost €45 (for travel on three out of eight consecutive days), €100 (eight out of 15 days) or €145 (15 out of 30 days).

For train-only travel within the Republic, the Irish Explorer ticket (€98) is good for five travel days out of 15. In Northern Ireland, the Freedom of Northern Ireland pass allows unlimited travel on Ulsterbus and Northern Irish railways for one day (£11), three days (£27.50) or seven consecutive days (£40). The Irish Rover ticket combines services with Bus Éireann and Ulsterbus for three days (€60), eight days (€135) or 15 days (€195).

BUS

Bus Éireann (☎ 01-836 6111; W www.bus eireann.ie) is the Republic's national bus line, and it operates services all over the Republic and into Northern Ireland. Fares are much cheaper than regular rail fares. Returns are usually only slightly more expensive than one-way fares, and special deals (eg, same-day returns) are often available. Most inter-city buses in Northern Ireland are operated by Ulsterbus.

TRAIN

Iarnród Éireann (☎ 01-836 3333), the Republic of Ireland's railway system, operates trains on routes that fan out from Dublin. Distances are short in Ireland and fares are often twice as expensive as the bus, but travel times can be dramatically reduced. As with buses, special fares are often available, and a mid-week return ticket is often not much more than the single fare. First-class tickets cost from €5 to €10 more than the standard fare for a single journey.

Northern Ireland Railways (☎ 028-9089 9411) has four routes from Belfast, one of which links up with the Republic's rail system.

CAR & MOTORCYCLE

The **Automobile Association** (AA; • Dublin: ☎ 01-677 9481 • Cork: ☎ 021-50 5155; breakdowns: Republic: ☎ 1800-667788, Northern Ireland: ☎ 0800 887766) has various offices. In Northern Ireland, members of the **Royal Automobile Club** (RAC; information: ☎ 028-9033 1133, breakdowns: ☎ 0800 82 8282) can phone for assistance.

Road Rules

As in Britain, driving is on the left and you should only overtake (pass) to the right of the vehicle ahead of you. The driver and front-seat passengers must wear safety belts; in Northern Ireland passengers in the rear must also wear them. Motorcyclists and their passengers must wear helmets; headlights should be dipped. Minor roads can be potholed and narrow, but the traffic is rarely heavy except through popular tourist or busy commercial towns.

Speed limits in both Northern Ireland and the Republic appear in kilometres, miles or both, and are generally the same as in Britain: 112km/h (70mph) on the motorways, 96km/h (60mph) on other roads and 48km/h (30mph) or as signposted in towns. On quiet, narrow, winding rural roads it's simply foolish to speed. Ireland's blood-alcohol limit is 0.08% and strictly enforced.

Parking in car parks or other specified areas in Ireland is regulated by the 'pay and display' tickets or disc parking. Available from news-agencies, discs are good for one hour and usually cost around €0.80 each. In Northern Ireland beware of the Control Zones in town centres where, for security reasons, cars absolutely must not be left unattended. Double yellow lines by the roadside mean no parking at any time; single yellow lines warn of restrictions, which will be signposted.

Rental

Car rental in Ireland is expensive so you will often be better off booking a package deal from your home country. In high season it's wise to book ahead. In the low season prices are generally around 25% cheaper and there are often special deals. There may be an extra daily fee if you go across the border to either Northern Ireland or the Republic.

People under 21 are not allowed to hire a car; for the majority of rental companies you must be at least 23 and have had a valid driving licence for at least one year. Some companies will not rent to those over 70 or 75. Your own local licence is usually sufficient to hire a car for up to three months.

In the Republic, typical weekly high-season rental rates – with insurance, collision-damage waiver, VAT and unlimited distance – start from €300 for a small car (Ford Fiesta) and range up to €450 for a larger car (Ford Mondeo). In Northern Ireland similar cars would cost about 10% less.

International rental companies such as Avis, Budget and Hertz have offices all over Ireland. There are many Dublin-based operators with rates from as low as €230 per week, including **Murray's Europcar** (☎ 01-614 2800), **Argus Rent-A-Car** (☎ 01-490 4444) and **Malone Car Rental** (☎ 01-670 7888).

BICYCLE

A large number of visitors explore Ireland by bicycle. Although the distances are relatively short, the weather is often rainy, and the most interesting parts of Ireland can be very hilly. Despite these drawbacks, it's a great place for bicycle touring, and facilities are good.

You can either bring your bike with you on the ferry or plane, or rent one in Ireland. Typical rental costs are €10 to €20 a day or to €70 to €80 a week. Bags and other equipment can also be rented. **Raleigh Rent-a-Bike** (☎ 01-465 9659; Unit 1, Finches Park, Longmile Rd, Dublin 12) has dozens of outlets around the country, some of which offer one-way rentals for €80 a week.

Bicycles can be transported on some Bus Éireann and Ulsterbus routes; the charges vary. By train the costs start from €2.25 for a one-way journey, depending on the distance.

HITCHING

While we don't recommend hitching – it's never entirely safe in any country – hitching in Ireland is commonplace and generally hassle-free. The major exceptions are in busy tourist areas where the competition from other hitchers is stiff and the cars are often full. In the Republic there are usually large numbers of local people on the road who use hitching as an everyday means of travel.

Women should travel with someone else (even though many local women appear to hitch alone).

If you feel at all doubtful about an offered ride, turn it down.

ORGANISED TOURS

Bord Fáilte has details of general tour operators and specialist companies that provide angling, walking, cycling and cultural holidays, and tours for the disabled. Ulsterbus and Bus Éireann run day trips to major tourist sites.

Tír na nÓg Tours (☎ 01-836 4684; e info@tirnanogtours.com; 57 Gardiner St Lower, Dublin 1) specialises in off-the-tourist-trail tours. Prices start at €127 (for three days)

and include transport, accommodation and site entry fees.

CIE Tours International (☎ 01-703 1888) runs several tours from four to 10 days around Ireland.

Rail Tours Ireland (☎ 01-856 0045), with a desk in the Dublin Tourism Centre, uses the rail network for its guided tours, making stops that synchronise with the train timetable. Day tours start from around €29.

Dublin

☎ 01 • pop 1,122,600

Dublin (Baile Átha Cliath) is Ireland's capital and its largest, most cosmopolitan city. Although one of the smallest capitals in the EU, Dublin is a bustling place that is growing at a furious pace.

Although it's far from being Europe's most elegant city, Dublin has been busy sprucing itself up and making the most of its physical charms. Those returning to the city after a few years should be favourably struck by the vibrantly painted buildings, the new walkway along the river Liffey and the ever-growing numbers of smart restaurants and bars.

In recent years the city has become popular with party goers, many of them British groups on stag and hen parties, which can make the city centre a boisterous place at weekends and accommodation can be difficult to find.

In spite of the rapid pace of development, Dublin remains a city of character and characters. Its rich literary past seems to bump against you at every corner, much of it associated with Dublin's many excellent pubs. A good number of them remain classic, unreconstructed Dublin boozers, where regulars happily enjoy a blether over a leisurely pint of Guinness.

Orientation

Dublin is neatly divided by the Liffey River into the more affluent 'south side' and the grubbier, less prosperous 'north side'.

North of the river important landmarks are O'Connell St, the major shopping thoroughfare, and Gardiner St, with its many B&Bs and guesthouses. Pedestrianised Henry St, running west off O'Connell St, is the main shopping area.

Immediately south of the river is the bustling, sometimes raucous, Temple Bar district, Dame St, Trinity College and just below

DUBLIN

PLACES TO STAY
1 Marian Guesthouse
2 Fatima House
3 Carmel House
4 Harvey's
5 An Óige Dublin International Youth Hostel
6 Frederick Budget Accomodation
7 Waverly House
8 Barry's Hotel; Castle Hotel
9 Belvedere Hotel
12 Charles Stewart
13 Mount Eccles Court
16 Park House B&B; Gardiner Lodge
17 Backpackers Ireland; Eurohostel; Abraham House
18 Marlborough Hostel
28 Globetrotters Tourist Hostel; Townhouse
29 Jacob's Inn
35 Wynn's Hotel Dublin
40 Litton Lane Hostel
41 Abbey Court Hostel
42 Arlington House
48 Four Courts Hostel
51 Brewery Hostel
57 Avalon House
68 Le Miridien Shelbourne

PLACES TO EAT
25 Bewley's Oriental Café
27 101 Talbot
39 Epicurean Food Hall
45 Winding Stair Bookshop & Café
58 Wagamama
60 Rajdoot Tandoori
62 Café Java
64 La Stampa
70 Unicorn Cafe Restaurant

PUBS
19 Patrick Conway's Pub
24 Slatterys
43 Pravda
47 John Mulligan's
63 John Kehoe's
71 O'Donoghue's
72 Doheny & Nesbitt
73 James Toner's

OTHER
10 The Hugh Lane Gallery
11 Dublin Writers Museum
14 James Joyce Centre
15 Gate Theatre
20 Laundry Shop
21 Imax Cinema; Virgin Multiplex; UGC Multiplex
22 The Chimney
23 Old Jameson Distillery

26 Dublin Bus; Bus Éireann
30 Busáras (Central Bus Station)
31 Rail Tours Ireland; Tír na nÓg Tours
32 Abbey Theatre; Peacock Theatre
33 Laughter Lounge
34 Iarnród Éireann (Irish Railways Office)
36 Global Cyber Café
37 Eason & Son
38 General Post Office (GPO)
44 Well Women Clinic
46 Usit Campus Travel Office
49 Christ Church Cathedral
50 Dublinia; Synod Hall
52 Eastern Health Board
53 Guinness Storehouse
54 Viking Splash Tours
55 St Patrick's Cathedral
56 Marsh's Library
59 Gaiety Theatre
61 Post Office
65 National Museum
66 National Gallery
67 Natural History Museum
69 Irish Ferries

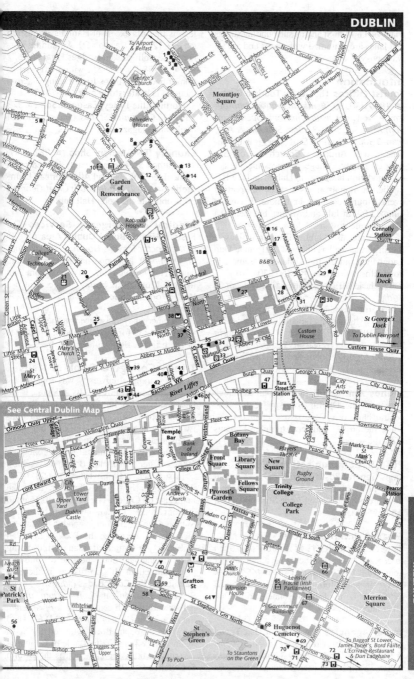

DUBLIN

To Airport & Belfast

St George's Church

Mountjoy Square

Belvedere House

Garden of Remembrance

Rotunda Hospital

Diamond

College of Technology

Cathedral

B&B's

Connolly Station

Inner Dock

Custom House

St George's Dock
To Dublin Ferryport

Custom House Quay

St Mary's Church

St Mary's Abbey

River Liffey

See Central Dublin Map

George's Quay

City Arts Centre

City Quay

Tara Street Station

Ormond Quay Upper

Wellington Quay

Temple Bar

Bank of Ireland

Botany Bay

Essex Quay

Front Square

Library Square

New Square

Players Theatre

Lord Edward St

City Hall

Dame St

College Green

Trinity College

Rugby Ground

Pearse Station

Upper Yard Lower Yard

Dublin Castle

St Andrew's Church

Provost's Garden

Fellows Square

College Park

Nassau St

Iveagh Trust

St Patrick's Park

St Ann's Church

Mansion House

Schoolhouse

Leinster House (Irish Parliament)

Merrion Square

Government Buildings

Grafton St

St Stephen's Gm North

Huguenot Cemetery

St Stephen's Green

To PoD

To Stauntons on the Green

To Baggot St Lower,
James Toner's, Bord Fáilte,
L'Ecrivain Restaurant
& Dun Laoghaire

IRELAND

it, the lovely St Stephen's Green. The pedestrianised Grafton St and its surrounding streets and lanes are crammed with shops and are always busy.

Information

Tourist Offices The **Dublin Tourism Centre** (☎ 1850 230330; e information@dublintourism.ie, w www.visitdublin.com; open 9am-7pm Mon-Sat, 9am-3.30pm Sun July & Aug, 9am-5.30pm Mon-Sat Sept-June) is in the desanctified **St Andrew's Church** (Suffolk St), west of Trinity College. Services include accommodation bookings in Dublin and the Republic, car rentals, maps, tickets for sporting events, tours, concerts and more. It can be jammed full in July and August, but there is a pleasant café upstairs.

There are also Dublin Tourism offices at the airport as well as on the waterfront at Dun Laoghaire, and all three share the same 24-hour information line (☎ 1850 230 330).

The head office of **Bord Fáilte** (Baggot St Bridge; open 9.30am-5pm Mon-Fri) has an information desk and, although it is less conveniently situated, it is much less crowded.

The **NITB** (☎ 679 1977; w discovernorthernireland.com; 16 Nassau St; open 9.15am-5.30pm Mon-Fri, 10am-5pm Sat) office offers information and booking services.

Money American Express has an exchange bureau in the Dublin Tourism Centre. The central bank offers the best exchange rates, while the airport and ferry terminal bureaus offer the worst.

Post & Communications Dublin's famous **General Post Office** (GPO; O'Connell St) is north of the river. South of the river there are post offices on Anne St South and St Andrew's St.

Email & Internet Access To go online, **Planet Cyber Cafe** (13 St Andrew's St; open to at least 10pm daily) charges about €5 per hour. **Does Not Compute** (☎ 670 4464; Essex St West), and **Global Internet Café** (☎ 878 0295), just north of the O'Connell Bridge, are other alternatives.

Travel Agencies The office of **Usit Travel** (☎ 679 8833; 19 Aston Quay; open 9.30am-6.30pm Mon-Wed & Fri, 9.30am-8pm Thur, 9.30am-5pm Sat) is near O'Connell Bridge.

Bookshops Directly opposite Trinity College is Eason's excellent **Hanna's Bookshop** (☎ 677 1255; 1 Dawson St). Around the corner is the well-stocked **Hodges Figgis** (☎ 677 4754; 56-58 Dawson St), with a large selection of books on things Irish. Facing it across the road is **Waterstone's** (☎ 679 1415).

North of the Liffey, **Eason & Son** (☎ 873 3811; 40 O'Connell St) has a big selection of books and magazines.

Laundry The **Laundry Shop** (☎ 872 3541; 191 Parnell St) is conveniently located north of the river. The cheerful **All American Laundrette** (☎ 677 2779; 40 South Great George's St) is opposite the Long Hall pub.

Medical & Emergency Services The **Eastern Health Board Dublin Area** (☎ 679 0700; Doctor Stevens Hospital, 138 Thomas St, Dublin 8), just opposite Heuston Station, can advise you on a suitable doctor from 9am to 5pm Monday to Friday. There is also a **Well Women clinic** (☎ 872 8051; 35 Lower Liffey St).

For emergency assistance you should phone ☎ 999 or ☎ 112 for *gardai* (police), ambulance or fire brigade. Both numbers are free.

Trinity College & Book of Kells

Ireland's premier university was founded by Queen Elizabeth I in 1592. Its full name is the University of Dublin, but Trinity College is the institution's sole college. Until 1793 Trinity's students were all Protestants, but today the majority of its 9500 students are Catholic. Women were first admitted to the college in 1903 – earlier than at most British universities.

In summer, **walking tours** (☎ 608 1827) depart regularly from College St (from the main gate on College Green) from 10.15am to 3.40pm Monday to Saturday, and noon to 3pm Sunday. The €8.50 tour is good value since it includes the fee to see the *Book of Kells*, an elaborately illuminated manuscript dating from around AD 800, and one of Dublin's prime attractions. It's on display in the **East Pavilion of the Colonnades** (adults €7; open 9.30am-5pm Mon-Sat, noon-4.30pm Sun) together with the 9th-century *Book of Armagh*, the even older *Book of Durrow* (AD 675) and the harp of Brian Ború, who led the Irish against the Vikings in the Battle of Clontarf.

Trinity's other big attraction is the **Dublin Experience** (☎ 608 1688; €4.20 or €10 with joint admission to the Book of Kells), a 45-minute audiovisual introduction to the city. It's open from mid-May to October and shows take place daily on the hour from 10am to 5pm.

Museums

Among the highlights of the exhibits at the impressive **National Museum** (☎ 667 7444; Kildare St; admission free; open 10am-5pm Tues-Sat, 2pm-5pm Sun) are the superb collection of Bronze Age, Iron Age and medieval gold objects in the treasury, the skeleton of a once-tall, mighty Viking and the slighter but incredibly well-preserved 'Bog Body'. Other exhibits focus on the Viking period, the 1916 Easter Rising and the struggle for Irish independence. The nearby **Natural History Museum** (☎ 677 7444; Merrion St; admission free; open 10am-5pm Tues-Sat, 2pm-5pm Sun) is basically a gruesome treasure house of slaughtered and stuffed fauna.

The small **Dublin Civic Museum** (☎ 679 4260; 58 William St South; admission free; open 10am-6pm Tues-Sat, 11am-2pm Sun) offers random artefacts and curiosities from Dublin's long and tumultuous history, including the stone head from Lord Nelson's Pillar on O'Connell St, which was blown up by the IRA in 1966.

Dublin Writers Museum (☎ 872 2077; 18-19 Parnell Square; admission €5.50; open 10am-5pm Mon-Sat, 11am-5pm Sun), north of the river, celebrates the city's long and continuing role as a literary centre, with displays on Joyce, Swift, Yeats, Wilde, Beckett and others. The nearby **James Joyce Centre** (35 North Great George's St; admission €4.50) is a must for avid Joyceans.

Galleries

The **National Gallery** (☎ 661 5133; Merrion Square West; admission free; open 9.30am-5.30pm Mon-Wed, Fri & Sat, 9.30am-8.30pm Thur, noon-5pm Sun) has a fine collection with a strong Irish content. Don't miss the impressive new Millennium wing, which focuses on contemporary Irish art. There are guided tours on Saturday (3pm) and Sunday (2pm, 3pm and 4pm).

On Parnell Square, north of the river, **The Hugh Lane Gallery** (☎ 874 1903; admission free; open 9.30am-5pm or 6pm Tues-Sat, 9.30am-5pm Sun) has works by contemporary Irish artists, as well as retrospectives and a large impressionist collection.

The **Irish Museum of Modern Art** (IMMA; admission free; open 10am-5.30pm Tues-Sat, noon-5.30pm Sun), at the old Royal Hospital Kilmainham, is renowned for its conceptual installations and temporary exhibits.

In Temple Bar, around Meeting House Square, is the **National Photographic Archive** (☎ 603 0200) and the **Gallery of Photography** (☎ 671 4654). In fact, in and around Meeting House Square is a cauldron of cultural activities, which includes the **Irish Film Archive**, the multimedia centre **Arthouse**, galleries, studios, an excellent **Irish Film Centre** (☎ 679 5744) showing a good selection of independent films. For information call the **Temple Bar Culture Line** (☎ 671 5717).

Christ Church Cathedral & Around

Christ Church Cathedral (Christ Church Place; admission €3; open 9.45am-5pm Mon-Sat) was a simple structure of wood until 1169, when the present stone church was built. In the south aisle is a monument to the 12th-century Norman warrior Strongbow. Note the church's precariously leaning north wall (it's been that way since 1562).

Next door and connected to the Cathedral by an elegant arched walkway **Dublinia** (☎ 679 4611; admission €5.75 or €7 joint admission to the Cathedral; open 10am-5pm daily Apr-Sept, 11am-4pm Mon-Sat Oct-Mar) tells the story of the city from Medieval times to the Reformation. There's some interesting detail, although the dioramas and bewigged dummies look a bit tired.

St Patrick's Cathedral & Around

A church was on the site of St Patrick's Cathedral (St Patrick's Close; admission €3.50; open 9am-6pm daily, closed during times of worship) as early as the 5th century, but the present building dates from 1191. Satirist Jonathan Swift, author of Gulliver's Travels, was the most famous dean of St Patrick's from 1713 to 1745. Swift and his beloved companion 'Stella' (Esther Johnson) are both interred here.

Swift apparently suffered the indignity of being dug up later for his death mask to be taken, and it's on display just south of the cathedral in the not-to-be-missed **Marsh's Library** (☎ 454 3511; admission €2.50; open 10am-12.45pm & 2pm-5pm Mon, Wed-Fri, 10.30am-12.45pm Sat). Dating from 1701, this lovely building boasts some

IRELAND

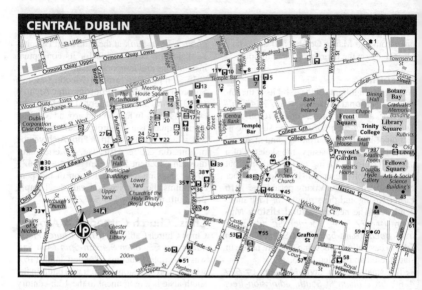

CENTRAL DUBLIN

rare manuscripts. The friendly librarians are full of interesting facts about the library.

Dublin Castle

Though much of it has been rebuilt over the centuries, Dublin Castle (☎ 677 7129; admission €3.35 by guided tour only; open 10am-5pm Mon-Fri, 2pm-5pm Sat & Sun), more a palace than a castle, dates back to the 13th century, when it was the centre of British power. The city got its modern name from the *dubh linn* (black pool) beneath the castle gardens. There's not much to see, since many of the castle's rooms are reserved for government functions.

Guinness Brewery

The excellent Guinness Storehouse (☎ 453 8364; Market St; bus No 51B or 78A from Aston Quay, No 123 from O'Connell St; adult/concession €12/8; open 9.30am-5pm daily) sits in the midst of the malty fug of the mighty Guinness brewery southeast of the city centre. The production and marketing processes of Dublin's world-famous black stuff are presented with sensory verve inside the seven floors of this impressively converted former fermentation plant. The city views from the glass-walled bar at the top are unbeatable on a clear day and you won't get better Guinness anywhere than the complementary pint served at the end of the tour.

Kilmainham Gaol

The grey, sombre Kilmainham Gaol (☎ 453 5984; Inchicore Rd; bus No 51B, 79 or 79A from Aston Quay; admission €4.40; open 9.30am-4.45pm daily Apr-Sept, 9.30am-4pm Mon-Fri, 10am-4.45pm Sun Oct-Mar), some way from the city centre, played a key role in Ireland's struggle for independence and was the site of mass executions following the 1916 Easter Rising. The tour includes a great audiovisual introduction to the prison from its opening in 1796 until its closure in 1924.

Other Attractions

Dublin's finest Georgian architecture, including its famed doorways, is found around the handsome St Stephen's Green and Merrion Square, both of which are prime picnic spots whenever the sun shines.

The 1815 General Post Office (GPO) building on O'Connell St is an important landmark, both physically and historically. During the 1916 Easter Rising the Irish Volunteers used the GPO as a base for attacks against the British army. After a fierce battle the GPO was almost totally destroyed. Upon surrendering, the leaders of the Irish rebellion and 13 others were taken to Kilmainham Gaol and executed.

The Old Jameson Distillery (☎ 807 2355; Bow St; €6.50; tours from 9am to 5.30pm daily), north of the Liffey, has displays on the

IRELAND

CENTRAL DUBLIN

whiskey-making process as well as whiskey tastings.

At the back of the distillery is **The Chimney** (☎ 817 3838; Smithfield Village; admission €6; open 10am-5.30pm Mon-Sat, 11am-5.30pm Sun), an old distillery chimney topped by a modern glass deck offering impressive views down onto the city.

Organised Tours

Gray Line (☎ 676 5377), with a kiosk at the Dublin Tourism Centre, **Irish City Tours** (☎ 872 9010) and **Dublin Bus** (☎ 873 4222) run a variety of coach tours in and around Dublin, including frequent daily hop-on hop-off services from €10 that complete 1½-hour city circuits with commentary. For a fun amphibious version, don a lifejacket and jump aboard one of the **Viking Splash Tours'** (☎ 855 3000; admission €13) WWII landing craft for an 80-minute tour departing from Bull Alley St, beside St Patrick's Cathedral Gardens. With luck you'll also be taught the Viking roar.

It's certainly worth considering one of the many walking tours and pub crawls of the city. Among the best are **The Dublin Literary Pub Crawl** (☎ 670 5602), on which you will be accompanied by actors performing pieces from Irish literature; and the well-reviewed **1916 Rebellion Walking Tour**

(☎ 676 2493), which visits key sites in the rebellion.

There's also the **Musical Pub Crawl** (☎ 478 0193); **The Walk Macabre** (☎ 677 1512) for tales of horror from Dublin's past; and the more scholarly 'seminar on the street' **Historical Walking Tours of Dublin** (☎ 878 0227). Each lasts about two hours and costs around €10. Bookings can be made via Dublin Tourism, hostels or by calling direct.

Places to Stay

At weekends and other unexpected times Dublin can be bedless for a radius of up to 60km. So we recommend advance reservations, even for hostels. Don't forget that the Dublin Tourism offices can find and book accommodation for €2.50 plus a deposit of 10% for the first night's stay.

Hostels – North of the Liffey A stone's throw from the Busáras bus and Connolly train stations is the 212-bed **Jacobs Inn** (☎ 855 5660; 21-28 Talbot Place; dorm beds from €16/18 Fri/Sat, doubles/triples/quads per person from €36/32/30), which has a café and cooking facilities.

Gardiner St Lower has three places worth considering. At No 47, the welcoming IHH **Globetrotters Tourist Hostel** (☎ 873 5893; dorm beds low/high season €16.50/21.50) is

IRELAND

a modern, secure place. Rates include a full Irish breakfast. The IHH **Abraham House** (☎ 855 0600; dorm beds from €12, doubles from €75, or €96 weekends) is at No 82. **Brown's Hostel** at No 90 (☎ 855 0034; dorm beds from €20) is smart and modern, offering Internet access and a light breakfast, but no self-catering.

If you don't mind street noise, the pleasant and central **Abbey Court Hostel** (☎ 878 0700; 29 Bachelor's Walk; dorm beds from €26, doubles €88) overlooks the Liffey River and has new facilities, good security and a friendly vibe. Just around the corner and off the main road, the **Litton Lane Hostel** (☎ 872 8389; 2-4 Litton Lane; dorm beds from €16) is a former recording studio. Groups or couples might find the hostel's nearby one- and two-bedroom self-catering apartments nearby, from €63 per night, cost effective.

IHH **Marlborough Hostel** (☎ 874 7629; 81-82 Marlborough St; dorm beds from €14/16.50 weekends, private rooms €51) is friendly, but offers austere dorms and can be noisy.

IHH **Mount Eccles Court** (☎ 873 0826; 42 Great George's St North; dorm beds from €14, doubles €60 plus €3 weekend supplement) is a sprawling 100-bed hostel in an old Georgian townhouse. A light breakfast is included.

Charles Stewart (☎ 878 0350; 5-6 Parnell Square East, singles/doubles/triples €32/89/120) offers decent mid-range accommodation with an Irish breakfast thrown in.

An Óige's creaking 363-bed **Dublin International Youth Hostel** (☎ 830 1766; 61 Mountjoy St; dorm beds from €19, €22 on weekends, twins/triples €57/81.90) was due for a massive, and much overdue, €5 million re-fit in early 2003, which should transform it. Although the hostel is safe, after dark it's an unsavoury walk from the city centre. From Dublin airport, bus No 41A stops on Dorset St Upper, a short walk away. Rates include a light breakfast.

Hostels – South of the Liffey One of the best hostels south of the river is the friendly, smart 230-bed **Four Courts Hostel** (☎ 672 5839; 15-17 Merchant's Quay; dorms/twins from €16.50/64) occupying a handsome Georgian mansion facing the Liffey.

The big IHH **Kinlay House** (☎ 679 6644; 2-12 Lord Edward St; beds in 4-bed dorms €22.50, singles/doubles €36/57), beside

Christ Church Cathedral, is central, but dorms need updating and can be noisy. Continental breakfast is included and cooking facilities are available. Couples or groups of three might consider **Harding Hotel** next door (see Hotels later in this section).

IHH's **Avalon House** (☎ 475 0001; 55 Aungier St; dorm beds weekdays/weekends €15/17, twins €32/35) is a popular place in a renovated Georgian building nicely positioned just west of St Stephen's Green. It has some cleverly designed rooms with mezzanine levels. Beds are in standard dorms, and rates include continental breakfast.

Just north of Trinity College, the pleasant **Ashfield House** (☎ 679 7734; 19-20 D'Olier St; dorm beds weekdays/weekends €17/17, singles/doubles €50/80) has all the amenities of a semideluxe hotel, but fills up quickly. Breakfast is included.

Although staying in the Temple Bar district is fun and convenient, street noise is a serious drawback. A good choice is the IHH **Barnacles Temple Bar House** (☎ 671 6277; 19 Temple Lane; dorm beds from €16.50, doubles & twins from €74). **Oliver St John Gogarty Hostel** (☎ 671 1822; 18-21 Anglesea St; dorm beds from €23, twins €56) adjoins a boisterous pub but is surprisingly quiet.

The IHH **Brewery Hostel** (☎ 453 8600; 22-23 Thomas St; dorm beds from €20, doubles from €75) is close to the Guinness Brewery and has top-drawer facilities, including a secure car park, although the neighbourhood is scruffy and is a fair way from the centre.

B&Bs If you want something close to the city centre, Gardiner Sts Upper and Lower are the places to look. They're not the prettiest parts of Dublin and can be noisy, but they are relatively cheap.

Harvey's (☎ 874 8384; 11 Gardiner St Upper; singles/doubles €40/45) is a friendly place. There are several more B&Bs nearby, including **Flynn's B&B** (☎ 874 1702) at No 15, **Carmel House** (☎ 874 1639) at No 16 and **Fatima House** (☎ 874 5410) at No 17. The cheapest is **Marian Guest House** (☎ 874 4129; rooms per person sharing €27, or singles €30) at No 21.

Nicer B&Bs along Gardiner St Lower include **Gardiner Lodge** (☎ 836 5229; singles/twins €45/50) and the highly recommended

Townhouse (☎ 878 8808; e gtrotter@indigo ie; singles/twins €55/88) joined to Globe-trotters hostel at No 47–48.

Hardwicke St, only a short walk from Gardiner St Upper, has a few B&Bs including the Joycean haunt **Waverley House** (☎ 874 6132; singles/doubles €30/64) at No 4, which was then known as 'The Boarding House'.

Hotels Sister to next-door Kinlay House, **Harding Hotel** (☎ 679 6500; e harding .hotel@usitworld.com; Fishamble St; singles/ twins or triples €60/90) offers good value for groups of three. Nearby, the **Jury's Inn Christ-church** (☎ 454 0000; e jurysinnchrist church@ jurysdoyle.com; rooms weekdays/weekends €96/105) offers the smart, standard rooms expected of this chain.

Two top-tier hotels overlook leafy St Stephen's Green: **Stauntons on the Green** (☎ 478 2300; 83 St Stephens Green South; singles/doubles €96/150) and Dublin's most exclusive hotel, **Le Meridien Shelbourne** (☎ 663 4500; 27 St Stephens Green North; singles/doubles high season €320/360). Breakfast is not included.

North of the Liffey, the pleasant, modern **Frederick Budget Accommodation** (☎ 878 6689; 48 Hardwicke St; singles/doubles from €40/60) is not quite a hostel, and has en-suite rooms with TVs.

The **Arlington Hotel** (☎ 804 9100; 23-25 Bachelor's Walk; singles/doubles weeknights €99/150, weekends €129/160) is a stylish Georgian inn overlooking the river. **Wynn's Hotel Dublin** (☎ 874 5131; 35-39 Abbey St Lower; singles/doubles €83/121) is an older hotel with plenty of charm, though the facilities are basic.

Belvedere Hotel (☎ 874 1413; 5 Gt Denmark St; singles/doubles €76/127) has recently refurbished en-suite rooms. Nearby, **Barry's Hotel** (☎ 874 9407; 1-2 Gt Denmark St) and the slightly smarter **Castle Hotel** (☎ 874 6949) next door are older but cheaper, and both charge €55 for singles and €110 for doubles.

Places to Eat

Around Temple Bar The Temple Bar district holds probably the largest and best concentration of restaurants in Dublin – there's a great range of cuisine from posh French fare to late night beer-session ballast. Generous, cheap portions of pizza and pasta are on offer at **Da Pino** (38-40 Parliament St; mains around €10). At the other end of Parliament St, **Zaytoon's** (cnr Essex St & Parliament St; mains €7) serves tasty, flat breads, kebabs and Iranian dishes in smart café-style surroundings. **Les Frères Jacques** (☎ 679 4555; 74 Dame St; mains from €30) is one of Temple Bar's fancier (and pricier) French restaurants. The **Mermaid Café** (70 Dame St; mains from €18) is renowned for creative seafood dishes and decadent desserts. The interior is dull at **Gruel** (☎ 670 7119; 68a Dame St; mains around €5), but the sandwiches and lovely home-made desserts are far from it.

The breakfast/brunch menu at the smart **Elephant & Castle** (18 Temple Bar; open to midnight Fri & Sat, to 11.30pm Sun-Thur) is imaginative and offers diner-type food. **The Chameleon** (1 Fownes St; open evenings), just off Wellington Quay, specialises in Indonesian dishes such as rijstaffel from €20 and gado gado. The small **Cafe Irie** (upstairs at 12 Fownes St) is good for cheap, tasty sandwiches and snacks. **La Paloma** (Asdill's Row), around the corner from the Quays Bar, has a wide range of Spanish tapas from €4.

Although it's not in Temple Bar proper, **Leo Burdock's** (2 Werburgh St) serves Dublin's best takeaway fish and chips. Weather permitting, nearby St Patrick's cathedral is a good place to eat them.

Around Grafton St Popular **Café Java** (5 Anne St South) does good brunches and lunches at around €8. **Cornucopia** (19 Wicklow St; dishes under €9; open Mon-Sat) is a justly popular vegie wholefood café, catering for special diets with all sorts of creative concoctions. **Aya** (☎ 677 1544; Clarendon St; mains around €11) is a smart, conveyor-belt sushi place.

Blazing Salads (42 Drury St; open Mon-Sat) offers crunchy, inventive takeaway salads for around €3 to €5.

Large helpings and late opening hours are the selling points at **Trocadero** (3 St Andrew's St; mains €14-20).

Rajdoot Tandoori (26-28 Clarendon St), in the Westbury Centre behind the Westbury Hotel, has superb tandoori dishes from €15.

Yamamori (71-72 Great George's St South) serves sushi and delicious Japanese noodle soups from €8. In similar vein, **Wagamama** (King St South; mains €9) serves cheap noodles and ramen in modern surroundings.

IRELAND

The stylish **Odessa Lounge & Grill** (☎ *670 7634; 13-14 Dame Court; mains €13-20)*, next to the Rí Rá dance club, is a great option for steaks, pre-clubbing cocktails and Sunday brunch.

La Stampa (☎ *677 8611; 35 Dawson St; mains around €20; open lunch-late)* serves European cuisine in an attractive Georgian dining area.

Some of Dublin's best (and priciest) restaurants are situated further south around St Stephen's Green. The smart **Unicorn Café Restaurant** (☎ *676 2182; 12b Merrion Court, Merrion Row; pasta dishes €12, mains €20-30)*, near O'Donoghue's pub, is a very popular Italian place with locals. For an expensive treat, try the French **L'Ecrivain** (☎ *661 1919; 109 Lower Baggot St; 3-course lunch & early evening/dinner €30/50)*. The à la carte menu is pricey.

North of the Liffey Although fast-food chains and cafés are well represented north of the Liffey, especially on O'Connell St, you won't find many good full-service restaurants. A major exception is **101 Talbot** (*mains €9-17; open evenings only Tues-Sat)*, strangely enough at 101 Talbot St. It does adventurous pastas and interesting mains. The lovely, upmarket **Chapter One** (☎ *873 2266; mains around €20)* is downstairs from the Dublin Writers Museum.

Cafés There are three branches of **Bewley's Oriental Cafés** (*full meals up to €8)* around the centre. Bewley's, something of a Dublin institution, has above-average cafeteria-style breakfasts (€6), sandwiches (to €5) and full meals, and you can sit all day reading the paper without feeling guilty. The 78 Grafton St branch is the flagship, open to 1am daily (to 7pm Sunday). Drama lovers might try the €10 lunchtime soup and sandwich theatre performance at the Theatre Cafe upstairs. The branch at 11–12 Westmoreland St is open to 9pm daily. There is a smaller branch north of the Liffey at 40 Mary St.

The **Winding Stair Bookshop & Café** (*Ormond Quay Lower)*, north of the Liffey opposite Ha'penny Bridge, is a rambling bookshop with teas, pastries and sandwiches.

The excellent **Epicurean Food Hall** (*open 8.30am-7pm Mon-Sat, 10am-6pm Sun)*, with entrances on Lower Liffey and Middle Abbey Sts, has several good delis celebrating world food from Japanese to Eastern European, plus several cafés.

Entertainment

For events, reviews and club listings, get a free copy of the fortnightly *Event Guide* (ⓦ www.eventguide.ie), available from music venues, cafés, hostels etc.

The **Temple Bar Music Centre** (☎ *670 9202; Curved St)* is a venue to watch. There is music seven days a week, with something to suit most tastes.

Pubs Dublin has some 850 pubs, so there's no possibility of being caught too far from a Guinness should a terrible thirst strike. The Temple Bar district is crammed with pubs that feature live music. Notables here include the **Temple Bar** (*Temple Lane)*, the restored **Oliver St John Gogarty Bar** (*57-58 Fleet St)*, the **Quays Bar** overlooking Temple Square, and the **Auld Dubliner** (*24-25 Temple Bar)*.

Other atmospheric spots for a pint include the **Stag's Head** (*Dame Court)* a classic Dublin boozer, **The Long Hall** (*South Great George's St)*, the **Palace Bar** (*Fleet St)*, **John Kehoe's** (*Anne St South)*, **John Mulligan's** (*8 Poolbeg St)*, **Grogan's Castle Lounge** (*cnr William & Castle Sts)*, and **James Toner's** and **Doheny & Nesbitt** (*Baggot St)* – also popular for lunch.

Pubs with live music from blues to rock to traditional Irish include the **International Bar** (*23 Wicklow St)*; touristy but still atmospheric **O'Donoghue's** (*15 Merrion Row)*.

North of the river on Capel St, **Slatterys** is a busy music pub. **Patrick Conway's Pub** (*70 Parnell St)* has atmosphere and music some nights.

Hipster spots include **Front Lounge** (*Parliament St)*, **The Globe** and **Hogan's** (*Great George's St South)*, and the northside's USSR-style **Pravda** (*Liffey St)*. **Cocoon** (*Hibernian St)* is another pre-club flocking place for the beautiful people.

Clubs Venues, clubnights and tastes change in Dublin's thriving club scene, so it's a good idea to check club listings or just ask around. Some stayers include **Rí Rá** (*Dame Court)*, which is cheesy but friendly with funk leanings, and the legendary 'Place of Dance' – **PoD** (*35 Harcourt St)*. **Switch** (☎ *670 7655; 11 Eustace St)* is a small, relaxed place boasting some accomplished local DJs.

Theatre & Classical Music The famous **Abbey Theatre** (☎ 878 7222) and the smaller **Peacock Theatre** are on Abbey St Lower near the river. The **Gate Theatre** (☎ 874 4045; *Parnell Square East*) is yet another venue. The **Olympia Theatre** (☎ 677 7744; *Dame St*) has plays and international music acts, and there's also the **Gaiety Theatre** (☎ 677 1717; *King St South*). The **Laughter Lounge** (*Abbey St Middle*) has stand-up comedy most nights.

Concerts take place at the **National Concert Hall** (☎ 671 1888; *Earlsfort Terrace*), just south of St Stephen's Green.

Cinema The excellent **Irish Film Centre** (*IFC*; ☎ 679 5744; *6 Eustace St*) has two screens in the Temple Bar showing off-beat and art films. It also has a decent bar, a café and bookshop. North of the river, the Parnell Centre, at the west end of Parnell St, has a **UGC** (☎ info/bookings 872 8400, 872 8444) multiscreen cinema showing all the mainstream releases.

Getting There & Away
Air For flight information contact **Aer Lingus** (*reservations:* ☎ 886 8888, *flight information:* ☎ 886 6705) or **Ryanair** (*reservations/flight information:* ☎ 0818-303030).

Bus At Bus Éireann's central bus station, just north of the Liffey on Store St, is **Busáras** (☎ 836 6111; **w** *www.buseireann.ie*). Standard one-way fares from Dublin include Cork (€17.10, 3½ hours, every two hours from 8am to 6pm), Galway (€11.40, 3¾ hours, five daily), and Rosslare Harbour (€12.70, three hours, six daily). Buses to Belfast depart from the Busáras up to seven times a day Monday to Saturday (three times on Sunday) and cost €16.50.

Slightly cheaper private bus companies have many services daily to Galway, but are less frequent to other locations. Try **City Link** (☎ 626 6888).

Train Just north of the Liffey is **Connolly station** (☎ 836 6222), the station for Belfast, Derry, Sligo, other points north and Wexford. **Heuston station**, south of the Liffey and well west of the centre, is the station for Cork, Galway, Killarney, Limerick, Waterford and most other points to the west, south and southwest. For travel information and tickets, contact the **Iarnród Éireann Travel Centre** (☎ 836 6222;

w *www.irishrail.ie; 35 Abbey St Lower*). Regular one-way fares from Dublin include Belfast (€26.60, 2¼ hours, six daily), Cork (€44.40, 3¼ hours, up to eight daily) and Galway (€20.90, three hours, four daily).

Boat There are two direct services from Holyhead on the northwestern tip of Wales – one to Dublin Port and the other to Dun Laoghaire at the southern end of Dublin Bay. **Stena Line** (☎ 204 7777), in Dun Laoghaire, and **Irish Ferries** (*office/information line:* ☎ 638 3333, 661 0715; **w** *www.irishferries.com; 2-4 Merrion Row*) are the main carriers. See the Getting There & Away section earlier in this chapter for more details.

Getting Around
To/From the Airport Around 10km north of the centre, **Dublin airport** (☎ 814 1111) has an Airlink Express service to/from Busáras and to/from Heuston train station for €4.50 (both 30 to 40 minutes). Alternatively, the slower (one hour) bus Nos 41 and 41A (the latter on weekends only) cost €1.40. A taxi to the centre should cost about €16.50.

To/From the Ferry Terminals Buses go to Busáras from the **Dublin Ferryport terminal** (☎ 855 2296; *Alexandra Rd*) after all ferry arrivals. Buses also run from Busáras to meet all of the ferry departures. To travel between Dun Laoghaire's ferry terminal and Dublin, take bus No 46A to Fleet St in Temple Bar, bus No 7 to Eden Quay, or bus No 7A or 8 to Burgh Quay. Alternatively, take the Dublin Area Rapid Transport (DART) rail service to Pearse station (for south Dublin) or Connolly station (for north Dublin).

Local Transport Contact **Dublin Bus** (*Bus Átha Cliath*; ☎ 873 4222; *59 O'Connell St*). Buses cost €0.75 for one to three stages, up to a maximum of €1.65. These tickets give you two trips valid for a month, and single fares can be bought on the bus.

One-day passes cost €4.50 for bus, or €7.20 for bus and DART. Late-night **Nitelink** buses (€4 to €6) operate from the College St/Westmoreland St/D'Olier St triangle, south of the Liffey, until 3am on Friday and Saturday nights.

DART provides quick rail access to the coast as far north as Howth (€1.50) and south to Bray (€1.70). Pearse station is handy for central Dublin. Bicycles cannot be taken on the DART, but may travel on suburban trains.

Taxis in Dublin are expensive, and flag-fall costs €2.50. You could try **National Radio Cabs** (☎ 677 2222).

Car All the major companies have offices at Dublin airport and in the city centre. Three of the cheaper options are **Murray's Europcar** (☎ 614 2800); **Argus Rent-A-Car** (☎ 490 4444; **w** www.argusrentals.com), with a desk at the Dublin Tourism Centre; and **Malone Car Rental** (☎ 670 7888; 26 Lombard St East). The cheapest rates are around €230 per week.

Bicycle Most rental places open during high season. Daily rental costs around €14 per day. Try **Dublin Bike Tours** (☎ 670 0899; Lord Edward St) near Kinlay House.

AROUND DUBLIN
Dun Laoghaire
☎ 01

Dun Laoghaire (pronounced dun leary), only 13km south of central Dublin, is a popular resort and a busy harbour with ferry connections to Britain. The B&Bs are slightly cheaper than in central Dublin, and the fast and frequent rail connections make it convenient to stay out here.

On the southern side of the harbour is the **Martello Tower**, where James Joyce's epic novel *Ulysses* opens. It now houses the **James Joyce Museum** (☎ 280 9265; admission €5.50; open 10am-1pm & 2pm-5pm Mon-Sat, 2pm-6pm Sun early Apr-Oct). If you fancy a cold saltwater dip, Dun Laoghaire's famous **Forty Foot** bathing place is here also.

Bus No 7, 7A or 8 or the DART rail service (€1.50, 20 minutes), will take you from Dublin to Dun Laoghaire.

Places to Stay About 1km south of the DART station is the friendly B&B, **Innisfree** (☎ 280 5598, fax 280 3093; **e** djsmyth@clubi .ie; 31 Northumberland Ave; singles/doubles from €30/45).

Further east, the Rosmeen Gardens area is packed with B&Bs. To get there, walk south along George's St, the main shopping street; Rosmeen Gardens is the first street after Glenageary Rd Lower, directly opposite People's Park.

Malahide Castle
☎ 01

Despite the vicissitudes of Irish history, the Talbot family managed to keep Malahide Castle (☎ 846 2184; admission €5.50; open 10am-5pm Mon-Sat year-round, 11am-8pm/ 11am-5pm Sun summer/winter) under its control from 1185 through 1973. The castle is packed with furniture and paintings, and Puck, the family ghost, is still in residence. The extensive **Fry Model Railway** (☎ 846 3779; admission €5.50) in the castle grounds covers 240 sq metres and re-creates Ireland's rail and public transport system (it's better than it sounds). The railway has similar opening hours to the castle. Combined admission tickets are available.

To reach Malahide, take bus No 42 from beside Busáras, or a Drogheda-bound suburban train or DART from Connolly station. Malahide is 13km northeast of Dublin.

Newgrange
☎ 041

The Boyne Valley boasts the finest **Celtic passage-tomb** (admission €5) in Europe, a huge flattened mound faced with quartz and granite at Newgrange on the N51. The tomb is believed to date from around 3200 BC, predating the great pyramids of Egypt by some six centuries. You can follow a guide down the narrow passage to the tomb chamber about one-third of the way into the colossal mound. Around 8am on the mornings on and around the winter solstice, the rising sun's rays shine directly down the long passage and illuminate the tomb chamber for 17 minutes. Tours leave from the **Brú na Bóinne visitor centre** (☎ 988 0300), 2km west of Donore, from 9am to 7pm June to September, 9am to 6.30pm May, and 9am to 5.30pm the rest of the year. If you have time, a visit to the recently excavated and reopened **Knowth tombs** nearby (combined Newgrange/Knowth admission €8) is also well worthwhile.

The Southeast

COUNTY WICKLOW

County Wicklow, less than 20km south of Dublin, has three contenders for the 'best in Ireland': best garden (at Powerscourt), best monastic site (at Glendalough) and best walk (the Wicklow Way). Its main towns, many of them dormitory communities for Dublin, hug the coast south of the capital. Pleasant seaside resorts and beaches sit between Bray and Arklow, especially at Brittas Bay. West towards Sally Gap and due south from here is a striking, sparsely populated mountainous wasteland, which includes the black waters of Lough Tay.

Powerscourt

In 1974, after major renovations, the 18th-century mansion at Powerscourt Estate was burned to the ground when a bird's nest in a chimney caught fire. One wing of the building remains, now internally revamped with exhibition room, café and shop, but people come for the 19th-century, 20-hectare formal gardens. There are five strollable terraces extending for more than 500m down to Triton Lake, with views east to the Great Sugar Loaf Mountain.

The estate (☎ 01-204 6000; admission to gardens & visitor centre €8, to gardens alone €5.50; estate open 9.30am-5.30pm daily Feb-Oct, 9.30am-4.30pm Nov-Jan) is situated 500m south of Enniskerry's main square and about 22km south of Dublin. In winter admission prices are lower. Bus No 44 runs regularly from Hawkins St in Dublin to Enniskerry.

From the estate, a scenic 6km trail leads to Powerscourt Waterfall (admission €3.50; open daily 9.30am-7pm summer, to dusk in winter), at 130m the highest in Ireland. You can reach the waterfall by road (5km), following signs from the estate entrance.

Glendalough

☎ 0404

Haunting Glendalough (Gleann dá Loch), pronounced glen-da-lock, is one of the most historically significant monastic sites in Ireland and is quite simply one of the loveliest spots in the country, nestling as it does between two lakes at the foot of a deep valley.

It was founded in the late 6th century by St Kevin, an early Christian bishop who established a monastery on the Upper Lake's south shore. It is said that St Kevin stood in one of the lakes long enough for birds to nest in his hands and made his bed in the hollow of a tree.

During the Middle Ages, when Ireland was known as 'the island of saints and scholars', Glendalough became a monastic city catering to thousands of students and teachers. The site is entered through the only surviving monastic gateway in Ireland.

The **Glendalough Visitor Centre** (☎ 45325; admission €2.50; open 9.30am-5.15pm daily), opposite the Lower Lake car park (free), overlooks a round tower, a ruined cathedral and the tiny Church of St Kevin. It has historical displays and a good 20-minute audio-visual. From here a trail leads 1km west to the panoramic Upper Lake, with a car park (€2) and more ruins nearby.

Visitors swarm to Glendalough in summer so the secret is to arrive early and/or to stay late, as the site is free and open 24 hours. The lower car park gates are locked when the visitor centre closes.

Places to Stay An Óige's recently renovated **Glendalough Hostel** (☎ 45342; e glen daloughyh@ireland.com; dorm beds up to €22; open year-round), 600m west of the visitor centre, has excellent facilities.

If you like the quiet life, consider the hermitages or **Glendlough Cillíns** (☎ 45777; St Kevin's Parish Church; huts €35, minimum 2-night stay). Designed for those in need of a contemplative retreat atmosphere, these are modest one-person, self-catering dwellings. The Glendalough area also has plenty of moderately priced B&Bs.

Getting There & Away Buses operate daily to Glendalough from outside Dublin's College of Surgeons, across from St Stephen's Green. Contact **St Kevin's Bus Service** (☎ 01-281 8119). Buses leave daily at 11.30am and 6pm, returning to Dublin at 4.15pm.

It's recommended to stay the night and return on the 7.15am or 9.45am service (9.45am only on weekends). The one-way/return fare is €5.10/14.

The Wicklow Way

Running for 132km, from County Dublin through to County Carlow, the Wicklow Way is the most popular of Ireland's long-distance walks. The route is clearly signposted and is documented in leaflets and guidebooks; one of the better ones is The Complete Wicklow Way by JB Malone. Much of the trail traverses countryside above 500m, so pack boots with grip, a walking stick and clothing for Ireland's fickle weather.

The most attractive section of the walk is from Enniskerry to Glendalough (three days).

Knockree Hostel (☎ 01-286 4036; dorm beds €12) is 7km out of Enniskerry.

WEXFORD
☎ 053 • pop 44,000

Little remains of Wexford's Viking past – apart from its narrow streets and name, Waesfjord, or 'Ford of Mud Flats'. Cromwell was in one of his most destructive moods when he included Wexford on his 1649–50 Irish tour, destroying the churches and 'putting to the sword' three-quarters of the town's 2000 inhabitants.

Wexford is a convenient stopover for those travelling to France or Wales via the Rosslare Harbour ferry port, 21km southeast of Wexford.

Orientation & Information

The train and bus stations are at the northern end of town, on Redmond Place. Follow the Slaney River 700m south along the waterfront quays in order to reach the **tourist office** (☎ 23111; The Crescent; open 9am-6pm Mon-Sat Mar-Oct, 9.30am-5.30pm Nov-Feb). The curiously tight North Main and South Main Sts are a block inland and parallel to the quays.

The main post office is northwest of the tourist office, between the quays and Nth Main St on Anne St. Wash your clothes at **Padraig's Laundry**, next to the hostel. Internet access is available for €5 per hour at the **Westgate Computer Centre** (☎ 46291; Westgate Yard, Westgate).

Things to See & Do

Of the six original town gates it's just the 14th-century **West Gate** (Slaney St) that survives. Nearby there's **Selskar Abbey** which was founded by Alexander de la Roche in 1190 after a crusade to the Holy Land. Its present ruinous state is a result of Cromwell's visit in 1649. The **Bullring** (cnr Cornmarket & North Main St) was the site of one of Cromwell's massacres, but it gets its name from the now-defunct sport of bull-baiting. Today a market is held on Friday and Saturday mornings.

About 5km northwest of Wexford, beside the Dublin–Rosslare (N11) road at Ferrycarrig, the **Irish National Heritage Park** (☎ 20733; admission €7; open 9.30am-6.30pm daily Mar-Nov, 9.30am-5.30pm Dec-Feb) is an outdoor theme park that re-creates dwellings and life in the Stone Age to the early Norman

period. Last admission is at 5.30pm. Taxis from town cost about €5.

Places to Stay

The **Ferrybank Camping & Caravan Park** (☎ 43274; tent sites €10-14; open Easter-late Sept) is close to town across the river.

The IHH **Kirwan House** (☎ 21208; e kir wanhostel@eircom.net; 3 Mary St; dorm beds from €12, private rooms €16) is a small and friendly hostel with Internet access. From the tourist office, go right at Henrietta St, then right at South Main St, take a quick left at Allen St, right at High St and left at Mary St.

The **Blue Door** (☎ 21047; e bluedoor@in digo.ie; doubles from €60), opposite White's Hotel, is a clean, friendly, tastefully decorated B&B with en suite and TV.

The Talbot Hotel (☎ 22566; e talbotwx@ eircom.net; singles/doubles €95/150) is the town's best-equipped hotel. It has a decent leisure centre and a pool.

There's a row of better quality B&Bs in handsome period houses, near the station on Auburn Terrace along Redmond Rd, including **McMenamin's** (☎ 46442; e mcmem@indigo .ie) and **O'Brien's** (23605; e mary@obrien sauburnhouse.com). Both charge around €30 per person.

Places to Eat

North and South Main Sts have something for most tastes, including a delicious range of picnic supplies at **Greenacres Food Hall** (54 North Main St) and pub grub at **Tim's Tavern** (51 South Main St).

The upmarket **La Riva** (The Crescent) serves tasty-sounding modern European cuisine and has a good wine list. There's a **Tesco** in the Crescent. **Finegan's Bar** (74 Sth Main St) is a smartly furnished bar with some good outdoor seating and a decent snack menu.

Entertainment

Many of Wexford's pubs are strung along North and South Main Sts. Just around the corner is the small **Thomas Moore Tavern** (Cornmarket), where the poet's mother was born, although it's not always open during the day. For music try **Wren's Nest** (Customs House Quay), **Mooney's** (12 Commercial Quay), **Tack Room** (South Main St) or the tiny **Crown Bar** (Monck St). **The Sky and the Ground**, on the far end of South Main St, is one of the town's most popular bars and often hosts traditional music.

Wexford hosts the country's biggest opera festival in late October and theatre and dance are performed year-round at the **Wexford Arts Centre** (☎ 23764; Cornmarket).

Getting There & Away

On the Dublin–Rosslare line is Wexford's **O'Hanrahan train station** (☎ 22522; w www .irishrail.ie), which is served by three trains daily in each direction; the three-hour trip to Dublin costs €14.60. There are also trains to Rosslare Harbour (€4.45, 30 minutes, three daily). **Bus Éireann** (☎ 33114) runs from the train station to Rosslare Harbour (€3.35, 25 minutes, every 45 minutes, 10 on Sundays), Dublin (€10.15, 2¼ hours, 10 daily, eight Sundays) and beyond.

ROSSLARE HARBOUR
☎ 053

Rosslare Harbour has frequent ferry services to France and Wales (see the Getting There & Away section earlier in this chapter). There is no reason to linger at Rosslare Harbour, so catch the first bus or train to Wexford or beyond. The bus and train stations are just outside. If you do stay, An Óige's **Rosslare Harbour Hostel** (☎ 33399; Goulding St; dorm beds from €11.50) is across the park at the back of the Hotel Rosslare, just uphill from the ferry terminal. It opens both early and late for ferry departures. The **tourist office** (☎ 33622) is in Kilrane 500m from Rosslare Port on the N25.

See the earlier Dublin Getting There & Away section for transport details.

WATERFORD
☎ 051 • pop 44,000

Waterford (Port Láirge) is a busy port and modern commercial centre, retaining vestiges of its Viking and Norman past in its narrow streets and old town walls.

Strongbow took the city in 1170, and in later centuries it was the most powerful political centre in Ireland.

Today Waterford is famed for its crystal but little else, apart from a few lively pubs. It's an unlovely town with little to offer beyond a couple of mildly interesting heritage sites. Travellers on a budget should also consider avoiding Waterford as all its hostels had shut at the time of writing.

Orientation & Information

The main shopping street runs directly back from the Suir River, beginning as Barronstrand St and changing names as it runs south to intersect with Parnell St, which runs northeast back up to the river, becoming The Mall on the way. Reginald's Tower (at the top of The Mall) and the Clocktower (at the top of Barronstrand St) are handy landmarks.

The **tourist office** (☎ 87 5823; The Granary, 41 Merchant's Quay; open 9am-5pm Mon-Sat Nov-Mar, 9am-6pm Mon-Sat Apr-Oct, also 11am-5pm Sun July & Aug) is near the river. Hidden away in Parnell Court, off Parnell St, is **Voy@ger Internet Café** (☎ 84 3843; open 10am-7pm Mon-Sat). The laundrette **Duds 'n' Suds** is next to a big grey church on Parnell St.

Waterford Crystal Factory

The **visitor centre** (☎ 33 2500; open 8.30am-4pm daily, shorter hours out of season) is 2km out on the road to Cork (N25). A guided tour (€6) takes you through the factory, where you can see big-cheeked glass blowers and fragile exhibits. Public transport runs from the top of the mall at Broad St to the factory every 10 minutes (€2 return).

Other Attractions

The **old quarter** is good for a stroll. Several handsome sections of the old city wall still stand, including **Reginald's Tower** on the corner of The Mall and Parade Quay. The tower, built in 1003, has a **museum** (admission €1.90; open Easter-Oct). Around the corner there's the ruin of the **French Church** (1240).

On Merchants Quay, **The Granary** (☎ 30 4500; admission €6; open 9.30am-9pm daily June-Aug, 10am-5pm Sept-May) is a sleekly redesigned grain house containing the tourist office and the Waterford Treasures, an impressive exhibition documenting Waterford's 1000-year history.

The lovely interior of the neo-classical Georgian **Christ Church Cathedral** (Cathedral Square; admission €3) is worth a visit. Look out for the tomb of former Lord Mayor James Rice.

Places to Stay

There's no hostel accommodation in Waterford. The **Mayor's Walk House** (☎ 85 5427; Mayor's Walk; singles/twins €22/40) is a

IRELAND

cheap, basic, but friendly B&B near the police station.

The Mall and Parnell St have several cheap B&Bs, but traffic noise can be a problem. You could try **Derrynane House** (☎ 87 5179; 19 The Mall; singles/doubles €25/50). Attractively positioned and quieter, near the Christ Church Cathedral, is **Beechwood** (☎ 87 6677; 7 Cathedral Square; €22 per person).

Places to Eat

Haricot's Wholefood (11 O'Connell St; dishes €7-11) serves generous portions of vegetarian and meat dishes. The chocolate cake is a gooey delight. Nearby, **Full of Beans** (35 O'Connell St) serves vegie snacks, fresh juices and coffee. **Cafe Luna** (John St) is popular after pub-closing time. In the lanes of the old quarter, **The Wine Vault** (2 High St; mains around €15) serves great food and wines. There are a couple of **supermarkets** in the City Square shopping centre.

Entertainment

The venerable **T & H Doolan** (32 George's St) is packed on weekends, hosts some good traditional musicians and is popular with tourists. **Geoff's** (John St) is also popular. Just up the street at the junction with Manor Rd, **Peig's Bar** has music sessions.

Garter Lane Art Centre (☎ 85 5038; 22a O'Connell St) hosts contemporary and cutting edge films and exhibitions, and stages plays.

Getting There & Away

Waterford Airport (☎ 87 5589) is 7km south of the city at Killowen. **Euroceltic Airways** (☎ 87 5020) has two daily flights (one way €139 to €227) to Luton airport, outside London.

The **train station** (☎ 87 3401) is across the river from the town centre.

There are regular rail connections to Dublin (€17.10, 2½ hours, four daily), Rosslare Harbour (€8.20, 80 minutes, twice daily), Kilkenny and Wexford.

Bus Éireann (☎ 87 9000) has a new depot opposite the tourist office and sends buses to Dublin (€8.85), Wexford (€9.75), Rosslare Harbour (€11.60) and Cork (€12.70). **Rapid Express Coaches** (☎ 01-679 1549; Olympia Court, Parnell St) runs several services daily to Dublin and Dublin airport for €10 and €14. Services leave from Parnell St.

Getting Around

BnB Cycles (☎ 87 0356, 22 Ballybricken), up Patrick St and past the police station, rents bikes for €14 per day.

KILKENNY

☎ 056 • pop 18,696

Kilkenny (Cill Chainnigh) is perhaps the most attractive large town (in fact it's officially a city) in the country. Even though Cromwell ransacked it during his 1650 campaign, Kilkenny retains some of its medieval ground plan, particularly the narrow streets. There's an excellent selection of eating, drinking and accommodation options, and a vibrant arts and music scene. Overlooking a sweeping bend in the river, and nestling in expansive grounds, Kilkenny Castle is a must for visitors.

Orientation & Information

Most places of interest can be found on or close to Parliament St and its continuation (High St), which runs parallel to the Nore River; and along Rose Inn St, which changes its name to John St, and leads away from the river to the northeast. The **tourist office** (☎ 51500; Shee Alms House, Rose Inn St; open Mon-Sat year-round) is a short walk from the castle. Internet access is plentiful and the **Kilkenny E-centre** (☎ 60093; 26 Rose St) is central.

Kilkenny Castle

Stronghold of the powerful Butler family, Kilkenny Castle (☎ 21450; open 10am-7pm daily in summer, shorter hours rest of year) has a history dating back to 1172 when the legendary Anglo-Norman Strongbow erected a wooden tower on the site.

The **Long Gallery**, with its vividly painted ceiling and extensive portrait collection of Butler family members over the centuries, is quite remarkable. Guided castle-tours are compulsory and cost €4.40.

The castle also hosts contemporary art exhibitions in the **Butler Gallery** (admission free), which is open whenever the castle is.

St Canice's Cathedral

The approach on foot from Parliament St leads over Irishtown Bridge and up **St Canice's Steps**, which date from 1614. Around the cathedral (admission €3) is a **round tower** (which you can climb for €2). Although the present cathedral dates from 1251, it has a much lengthier history and it contains some remarkable tombs and monuments that are decoded on a board in the south aisle.

Other Attractions

Rothe House *(Parliament St; admission €3; open 10.30am-5pm Mon-Sat, 3pm-5pm Sun Apr-Oct, 1pm-5pm Mon-Sat, 3pm-5pm Sun Nov-Mar)* is a restored Tudor house dating from 1594. Its original owner, the wealthy John Rothe, lived here with his wife and 12 children.

Tynan walking tours *(☎ 63955)* has one-hour tours of Kilkenny, taking in some of the more interesting sites. The tours cost €5 and leave from the tourist office several times a day throughout the year.

Places to Stay

The small **Tree Grove Caravan & Camping Park** *(☎ 70302; 2-person tent sites without/ with car €11/13)* is 1.5km south of Kilkenny on the New Ross (R700) road.

The IHH **Kilkenny Tourist Hostel** *(☎ 63541; 35 Parliament St; open year-round; dorm beds from €12, twins €31)* is central and has helpful staff.

Rose Inn *(☎ 70061; 9 Rose Inn; dorm beds/ rooms €13/20)*, just opposite the tourist office, is good value, central and throws in a light breakfast.

Well worth the hassle of getting there is An Óige's **Foulksrath Castle Hostel** *(☎ 67674; dorm beds €11)*. It's beautifully situated in a stout 16th-century Norman castle 13km north of Kilkenny in Jenkinstown, near Ballyragget (watch for the sign) overlooking some pretty countryside. **Buggy's Buses** *(☎ 41264)* has a service between The Parade in Kilkenny and the hostel (€2.50, 20 minutes), leaving at 11.30am and 5.30pm Monday to Saturday. Taxis cost about €8.

There are plenty of B&Bs, especially south of the city along Patrick St and north of the city on Castlecomer Rd. The central **Bregagh Guesthouse** *(☎ 22315; Dean St; rooms per person from €38)* is near St Canice's Cathedral with comfortable en suite rooms.

The Kilford Arms *(☎ 61018; e kilford arms@indigo.ie; John St; rooms weekdays/ weekends per person €35/60)* provides good, large and new hotel rooms at B&B prices on weekdays.

Lacken House *(☎ 61085; e info@lacken house.ie; Dublin Rd; B&B doubles from €110)* is a comfortable, upmarket B&B just out of town and runs its own superior restaurant.

Places to Eat

The Kilkenny Design Centre *(☎ 22118; Castle Yard; mains around €6; closed evenings)* is one of Kilkenny's best all round lunch spots. Opposite the castle, it offers cheap, home-cooked food in appealing and spacious surroundings.

Jacob's Cottage *(☎ 71888; 1 Ormonde St; mains around €20)* is situated inside the Hibernian Hotel and serves imaginative fish and Irish dishes.

Ristorante Rinuccini *(☎ 61575; e info@ rinuccini.com; 1 The Parade; mains €12-22)* is an upmarket Italian opposite the castle.

Key Largo *(1-2 Canal Square; mains around €10)* provides less outstanding Italian fare, but it overlooks the river and offers reasonable value.

Lacken House (see Places to Stay) has expensive but celebrated food and a €36 set menu. **Dunn's Stores** on St Kieran's St is Kilkenny's most convenient supermarket.

Entertainment

The best pub in town for traditional Irish music is **Maggie's** *(St Keiran St)*. Other regular traditional music joints include **Ryan's** *(Friary St)* and **John Cleere's**, on Parliament St, which also has a theatre out the back staging occasional comedy and more contemporary bands.

The Pumphouse is popular with travellers and locals alike. **The Marble City Bar** *(66 High St)* is a tastefully modernised bar with a good atmosphere.

The **Watergate Theatre** *(☎ 61674; Parliament St)* hosts musical and theatrical productions throughout the year.

Getting There & Around

McDonagh train station *(☎ 22024; Dublin Rd)* is east of the town centre via John St. Four trains a day (five on Monday and Friday, three on Sunday) link Dublin's Heuston station to Kilkenny (€15.80) and then on to Waterford (€6.90).

Bus Éireann *(☎ 051-87 9000)* operates out of the train station. There are six buses a day (five on Sunday) to Dublin (€8.85), three to Cork (€13.95), up to six to Galway (€19.05) and one or two to Wexford, Waterford and Rosslare Harbour.

JJ Wall *(☎ 21236; 88 Maudlin St)* rents bikes for €15 a day (plus €40 deposit) from April to August.

IRELAND

AROUND KILKENNY
Kells Priory

Only 13km south of Kilkenny, Kells Priory is one of Ireland's most impressive and romantic monastic sites. Set by rolling fields and a babbling brook, the earliest remnants of the priory date from the late 12th century, with the bulk of the present ruins from the 15th century. Extraordinarily, it's free and there are no set opening hours, which makes it ideal for a private monastic adventure and a great picnic destination. Unfortunately, unless you've got a car, the site is difficult to get to. A taxi will cost approximately €16 from Kilkenny.

CASHEL
☎ 062

The **Rock of Cashel** (☎ 61437), in the town of Cashel 18km north of Cahir, is one of Ireland's most striking archaeological sites. On the outskirts of town rises a huge lump of limestone bristling with ancient fortifications. Mighty stone walls encircle a complete round-tower, a roofless abbey and the country's finest 12th-century **Romanesque chapel** (admission €4.40; open 9am-3.45pm daily Oct–mid-March, 9am-4.45pm mid-March–June, 9am-6.45pm summer).

If you choose to stay the night, try the IHH **Cashel Holiday Hostel** (☎ 62330; 6 John St; dorm beds €11.45, doubles from €60). The **tourist office** (☎ 61333) is in the town hall, on Cashel's main street. Six buses on line 8 (Dublin to Cork) pass through Cashel daily.

The Southwest

CORK
☎ 021 • pop 180,000

Cork (Corcaigh), the Irish Republic's second-largest city, is a lively, friendly place increasingly rivalling Dublin as a place to party, but without the capital's sometimes edgy feel. Home to a major university, Cork prides itself on a great mix of pubs, cafés and restaurants, and a love of the arts.

The Cork International Jazz Festival and the International Film Festival both take place in October.

Cork has long been a significant city in Ireland, not least during the Anglo-Irish War. The Black and Tans were at their most brutal in

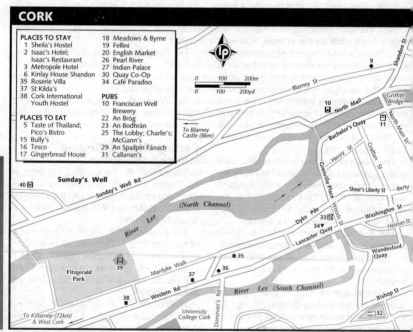

CORK

PLACES TO STAY
1 Sheila's Hostel
2 Isaac's Hotel;
   Isaac's Restaurant
3 Metropole Hotel
6 Kinlay House Shandon
35 Roserie Villa
37 St Kilda's
38 Cork International
   Youth Hostel

PLACES TO EAT
5 Taste of Thailand;
   Pico's Bistro
15 Bully's
16 Tesco
17 Gingerbread House
18 Meadows & Byrne
19 Fellini
20 English Market
26 Pearl River
27 Indian Palace
30 Quay Co-Op
34 Café Paradiso

PUBS
10 Franciscan Well
   Brewery
22 An Bróg
23 An Bodhrán
25 The Lobby; Charlie's;
   McGann's
29 An Spailpin Fánach
31 Callanan's

Cork. The city was also a centre for the civil war that followed independence (Irish leader Michael Collins was ambushed and killed nearby). Today Cork is noted for its hurling and Gaelic-football teams, and its fierce rivalry with Dublin.

Orientation & Information

The city centre is an island between two channels of the Lee River. Oliver Plunkett St and the curve of St Patrick's St are the main shopping/eating/drinking areas. The train station and several hostels are north of the river; MacCurtain St and Glanmire Rd Lower are the main thoroughfares there.

The **tourist office** (☎ 425 5100; Grand Parade; open 9.15am-5.30pm Mon-Sat Oct-May, 9am-6pm daily June-Sept, 9am-7pm Mon-Fri, 9am-6pm Sat & Sun July & Aug) is helpful. There is a **post office** (Oliver Plunkett St).

Internet access is available at the **Internet Exchange** (☎ 425 4666; 5 Wood St; open 10am-midnight daily). There are **laundrettes** at 14 MacCurtain St (across from Isaac's Hostel), and on Western Rd opposite the gates of University College Cork.

Things to See

Cork's notable churches include the fairytale riot of spires and buttresses of the 1879 Protestant **St Finbarr's Cathedral**, south of the centre; particularly impressive are the huge pulpit and colourful chancel ceiling. North of the river there's a fine view from the tower of the 18th-century **St Anne's Church, Shandon** (☎ 450 5906; admission €5; open 10am-5pm Mon-Sat). Admission lets you climb the tower, ring the Shandon Bells and watch an audiovisual presentation about the Shandon area.

Cork Public Museum (☎ 427 0679; admission free Mon-Fri, €1.50 Sun afternoon) should be worth a visit when it opens its new €1.8 million extension. Two permanent displays will trace Cork's history from prehistory to the present, including the city's role in the fight for independence.

Cork City Gaol (☎ 430 5022; admission €5; open 9.30am-6pm daily Mar-Oct, shorter hours Nov-Feb) received its first prisoners in 1824 and its last in 1923, including many prominent independence fighters. The impressive 35-minute taped tour around the restored cells is worthwhile. The gaol is off Sunday's Well Rd.

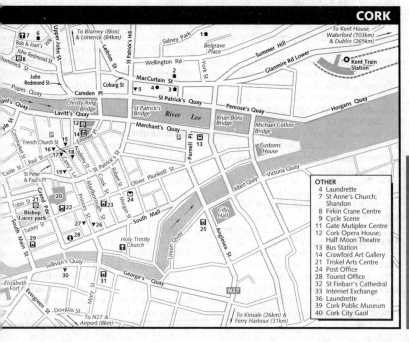

CORK

OTHER
4 Laundrette
7 St Anne's Church; Shandon
8 Firkin Crane Centre
9 Cycle Scene
11 Gate Mutiplex Centre
12 Cork Opera House; Half Moon Theatre
13 Bus Station
14 Crawford Art Gallery
21 Triskel Arts Centre
27 Post Office
28 Tourist Office
32 St Finbarr's Cathedral
33 Internet Exchange
36 Laundrette
39 Cork Public Museum
40 Cork City Gaol

IRELAND

The brick, glass and steel **Crawford Art Gallery** (*☎ 427 3377; admission free; open 10am-5pm Mon-Sat*) is an impressive example of cutting-edge architecture blending into an existing 18th-century building. The permanent collection has works by Irish artists like Jack Yeats and Seán Keating, as well as works of the British Newlyn and St Ives schools. There are also contemporary shows and retrospectives. The gallery café is a good place to stop for a snack or drink.

Places to Stay

Hostels Back from MacCurtain St and off Wellington Rd, is the clean, busy and friendly **Sheila's Hostel** (*☎ 450 5562;* e *info@ sheilashostel.ie; 4 Belgrave Place; dorm beds/ doubles from €12/36*). Facilities include a laundry, café, foreign exchange, bike hire and sauna.

Behind St Anne's Church is the modern **Kinlay House Shandon** (*☎ 450 8966; Bob & Joan's Walk; dorm beds €11, doubles €40*). Beds are in basic mixed dorms of up to 12 people. A light breakfast is included.

Out by the university, to the west of the centre, the An Óige **Cork International Youth Hostel** (*☎ 454 3289; 1-2 Western Rd; dorm beds weekdays/weekends €15/17, twins €37*) has had an expensive make-over. Bus No 8 from the bus station stops outside the hostel.

B&Bs & Hotels Glanmire Rd Lower, a short distance east of the train station, is lined with economical B&Bs. **Kent House** (*☎ 450 4260; singles/doubles from €28/52*) at No 47 is clean and cheap, although the rooms are small.

Isaac Hotel (*☎ 450 0011;* e *cork@isaacs .ie; 48 MacCurtain St; singles/doubles from €70/110*) is a pleasant place and groups and families might find the Isaac's adjoining apartments economical.

On the opposite side of town, Western Rd also has plenty of more-exclusive (and expensive) B&Bs, including **St Kilda's** (*☎ 427 3095;* e *gerald@stkildas.com; singles/doubles €50/ 76*), a big blue house with its own car park. **Roserie Villa** (*☎ 427 2958;* e *info@roserie villa.com; singles/doubles €45/57*), on nearby Mardyke Walk, is pleasant and clean.

The old-world **Metropole Hotel** (*☎ 450 8122, fax 450 6450;* e *info@greshamho tels.com; MacCurtain St; singles/doubles from €85/100*) has undergone a refurbishment in recent times.

Places to Eat

For self-catering, head straight for the well-stocked food stalls inside the **English Market**, off the western end of St Patrick's St. There's also a **Tesco** on Paul St.

Between St Patrick's St and the pedestrianised Paul St are several narrow lanes packed with restaurants. For coffee and light meals, try the popular **Gingerbread House**, which also does cheap breakfasts, or **Fellini**, with its French film paraphernalia. Both are on Carey's Lane.

Meadows & Byrne (*French Church St*) is often full; and trendy, mid-range **Bully's** (*40 Paul St*) has candles and low lighting, tasty pizzas and pasta.

Princes St is a haven of ethnic cuisine. There's authentic Chinese at mid-range **Pearl River**, and delicious (if expensive) Indian at the adjacent award-winning **Indian Palace**.

For vegetarians, **Café Paradiso** (*Lancaster Quay; open Tues-Sat*), opposite Jury's Hotel, has friendly staff, good coffee and inventive dishes. The popular **Quay Co-Op** (*24 Sullivan's Quay; evening menus from €10; open Mon-Sat*) also caters for vegetarians. It has soups from €4 and more-elaborate evening menus.

Isaac's Restaurant (*☎ 450 3805; MacCurtain St; mains around €14*) – not run by the hotel to which it's attached – offers terrific food, friendly service, great atmosphere and good wines. Nearby, **Taste of Thailand** (*8 Bridge St; 3-course dinner before 7pm €16*) offers Thai cuisine. A few doors down **Pico's Bistro** offers a two-course early dinner for €15.

Entertainment

In Cork locally brewed Murphy's is supposedly the stout of choice, not Guinness. Entertainment in Cork goes further than pints though; *Cork's List*, a free fortnightly publication available from pubs, cafés and the like, lists it all.

On Union Quay **The Lobby**, **Charlie's** and **McGann's** are all side by side, and at least one of them has live music (from rock to traditional) most nights.

An Bodhrán (*42 Oliver Plunkett St*) regularly features music, as does **An Bróg** at No 78. More subdued is **An Spailpín Fánach** (*28 South Main St*), with traditional music four nights a week. For a real Cork drinking experience visit tiny **Callanan's** on Georges Quay.

The splendid new **Franciscan Well Brewery** (☎ *421 0130; 14b North Mall*) serves its own ales brewed in the gleaming copper vats behind the bar and a fine selection of guest ales, lagers and stouts. It also has a beer garden.

Cork's cultural institutions include the **Gate Multiplex Cinema** (☎ *427 9595; North Main St*), **Cork Opera House** (☎ *427 0022; Emmet Place*), the **Half Moon Theatre** (☎ *427 0022*) behind it, hosting live bands and dance music, and the **Triskel Arts Centre** (*Tobin St*), just off South Main St, an important venue for films, theatre, music, and other media arts.

The **Firkin Crane Centre** (☎ *450 7487; Eason's Hill*), occupying Cork's old butter weighing house near St Anne's church, is a respected venue for national and international contemporary dance (and occasionally ballet) companies.

Getting There & Away

Cork Airport (☎ *431 3131*) is 8km south of the city on the N27. There are direct flights into Dublin, London, Manchester, Exeter, Jersey, Paris, Rennes and Amsterdam.

The **bus station** (☎ *450 8188; cnr Merchants Quay & Parnell Place*) is east of the centre. You can get to almost anywhere in Ireland from Cork: Dublin (€17.10, 3½ hours, six daily), Killarney (€11.80, two hours, 11 daily), Waterford, Wexford and more.

Cork's **Kent train station** (☎ *450 6766; Glanmire Rd Lower*) is across the river. Trains go to Dublin (€44.40), Kilkenny (€30.40) and Galway (€40).

Cork's ferry terminal is at Ringaskiddy, about 15 minutes by car southeast of the city centre along the N28. **Bus Éireann** runs frequent daily services to the terminal (45 minutes). Details of ferries are listed in the Getting There & Away section earlier in this chapter.

Getting Around

Buses leave the bus station for the airport (€3.15) four times daily from April to September. Parking discs (€0.75) are on sale at newsagencies.

Hire a bike for €20 per day from **Cycle Scene** (☎ *430 1183; 396 Blarney St*).

AROUND CORK
Blarney
☎ 021

Just northwest of Cork, Blarney (An Bhlarna) is a village with one reason to visit – the tall imposing walls of 15th-century **Blarney Castle** (☎ *438 5252; admission €5.50; open 9am-6.30pm or 7pm Mon-Sat, or to sunset in winter, 9.30am-5.30pm Sun*). If you don't mind putting your lips where millions have also been, you can kiss the castle's legendary **Blarney Stone** on the high battlements and get the 'gift of the gab'. It was Queen Elizabeth I, exasperated with Lord Blarney's ability to talk endlessly without ever actually agreeing to her demands, who invented the term. Bending over backwards to kiss the sacred rock requires a head for heights, although there's someone there to hold you in position.

There are myriad B&Bs surrounding the castle including **The White House** (☎ *438 5338; e info@thewhitehouseblarney.com*), plus the basic, unaffiliated **Blarney Tourist Hostel** (☎ *438 5580; dorm beds €10, doubles €25*), a few kilometres west on the road to Killarney.

Buses run regularly from the Cork bus station (€2.50 return, 30 minutes).

Cobh
☎ 021 • pop 6771

The small town of Cobh (pronounced cove) is worth a day trip from Cork for its picture-postcard looks and rich maritime history which is celebrated in the excellent **Cobh, The Queenstown Story** (☎ *481 3591; admission €5; open 10am-6pm daily Apr-Nov, 10am-5pm Dec-Mar*) heritage centre in the town's picturesque old train station. It tells the story of the migrants who sailed from here and of the town's links with the *Titanic* and the *Lusitania*. The old Cunard buildings in town have been converted into a pub and restaurant.

Cobh is 24km southeast of Cork reached via the N25 or by car ferry from Passage West. Hourly trains (€3, 30 minutes) also connect with Cork.

Kinsale
☎ 021 • pop 2237

Kinsale (Cionn tSáile) is the quintessential Irish seaside town. People come for the coastal scenery and for the town's reputation (perhaps overrated) as Ireland's gourmet capital.

The **tourist office** (☎ *477 2234; 1 Pier Rd; open 9.30am-5.30pm Mar-Oct, 9am-7pm July-Aug*) can help with visitor inquiries.

Southeast of Kinsale, a scenic 2.5km walk from the town centre, stand the stout ruins of the 17th-century **Charles Fort** (☎ *477 2263;*

IRELAND

admission €3.10; open 10am-6pm daily mid-Mar–Oct, Sat & Sun Nov-Feb). Built in the 1670s, it's one of the best-preserved star forts in Europe. On a sunny day the views from the hill-top battlements are lovely.

Buses connect Kinsale with Cork (€5.90 return, 45 minutes) at least nine times Monday to Saturday and three times on Sundays, and stop near the tourist office. To head west by bus you'll have to go back to Cork.

Places to Stay To get to the friendly, modern hostel at the **Castlepark Marina Centre** (☎ 477 4959; dorm beds €15, doubles €45; open mid-Mar–Oct), walk from the tourist office for 20 minutes along Pier Rd to the Trident Hotel. From here, ferries run to the hostel June to September on the hour, starting at 8am. Alternatively, take a cab (€6 to €7) or call and ask nicely for a pick-up. There's an on-site café and a pleasant pub next door. The **Cork Dive Centre** (☎ 431 2510) also runs diving trips from here.

B&Bs in town are pricey. Two of the good ones in handsome Georgian houses are the friendly **Captain's Quarters** (☎ 477 4549; e captquarters@eircom.net; 5 Denis Quay; singles/doubles from €51/68) and the sumptuously decorated **Chart House** (☎ 477 4568; e charthouse@eircom.net; 6 Denis Quay; singles/doubles from €45/90).

Places to Eat The Mango Tree Cafe serves cheap snacks. Some of the upmarket places, like **Max's Wine Bar** (☎ 477 2443) and **Cottage Loft** (☎ 477 2803), both on Main St, serve close-to-affordable lunches and early-evening meals. If you really want to push the boat out, the **Vintage Restaurant** (☎ 477 2502; 50 Main St; mains around €25) is one of Kinsale's best and most creative places. The **SuperValu** supermarket is on Pearse St.

WEST COUNTY CORK

Travelling west by public transport from Cork can be tough. There are at least two daily bus services (more in summer) connecting towns. The trick is to plan ahead at Cork, have the timetables committed to memory, and be prepared to change buses and backtrack.

Baltimore, Sherkin & Clear Islands
☎ 028

Just 13km down the Ilen River from Skibbereen, sleepy Baltimore has a population of around 200 that swells enormously during summer. The small **tourist office** (☎ 21766) at the harbour opens in high season. The **Baltimore Diving Centre** (☎ 20300) arranges diving expeditions.

Baltimore has plenty of B&Bs, plus the excellent IHH **Rolf's Hostel** (☎ 20289; dorm beds from €12, doubles €44); follow the signs up a hill about 700m east of town. Whether or not you are staying, Rolf's cheap, terrific café and restaurant is the place to eat in town.

Baltimore's main attraction is its proximity to Cape Clear Island, or Cape Clear as the locals prefer to call it, the most southerly point of Ireland (apart from Fastnet Rock, 6km to the southwest). Clear Island is a Gaeltacht area with about 150 Irish-speaking inhabitants, one shop and three pubs. From June to September, **ferries** (☎ 39135) leave Baltimore (weather permitting) at 11am, 2.15pm and 7pm Monday to Saturday and at noon, 2.15pm, 5pm and 7pm on Sunday. In July and August there is an extra service at 11am (noon on Sunday). At other times of year boats leave Monday to Saturday at 2.15pm. The trip takes 45 minutes and the return fare is €12, with no extra charge for bikes. In summer, boats to Clear Island also leave from Schull (see the Mizen Head Peninsula section).

There is a **camping ground** (☎ 39119; tent sites per person €4; open June–mid-Sept) signposted from the shop. An Óige's basic **Cape Clear Island Hostel and Adventure Centre** (☎ 39198; dorm beds members/non-members €10/12; open June-Sept) is a short walk from the pier and offers kayaking, snorkelling and archery. Further up the road is the friendly **Ard Na Goithe B&B** (☎ 39160; €28 per person).

If Cape Clear seems a long ride, consider heading to tiny Sherkin Island, its friendly neighbour just across the water from Baltimore. It offers a couple of convivial pub/restaurants, several decent B&Bs, a few good beaches and apparently one elderly resident who has never left the island.

Ferries leave 10 times daily in summer and reasonably frequently in winter (☎ 20218 for winter times). Try the **Jolly Roger Tavern** for fresh mussels and a great atmosphere. **Horseshoe Cottage B&B** (☎ 20598; e info@sherkintefl.com) is homy and provides great bay views.

izen Head Peninsula
028

izen Head is a scenic alternative to the bet-known and much more touristy Ring of rry and Dingle Peninsula to the north.

At least two buses a day leave Cork (via ibbereen) for the small village of **Schull** at e foot of Mt Gabriel (407m). In summer, hull's pubs and restaurants are packed with urists, but the rest of the year it's blissfully iet.

Schull Backpackers' Lodge (☎ 28681; lla Rd; dorm beds €18, doubles from €33) excellent and offers diving and bike hire. If u're headed to Clear Island, note that **boats** 39153) also leave from Schull's pier from id-June to mid-September at 11.30 am, 3pm d return at 5.30pm. The return fare is €12.

The road west from Schull leads to the all village of **Goleen**, home to a few cafés d pubs. From Goleen, one road leads to Bar-ycove Beach and onwards to the small vil-ge of **Crookhaven**, with its handful of B&Bs d pubs.

The other road leads south, to **Mizen Head** d its 1910 **signal station** (admission €4.45; en daily Apr-Oct, Sat & Sun Nov-Mar), w a **visitors centre** (☎ 35115), which is on small island connected to the mainland by m-high suspension bridge. From here it's ssible to look down on pounding seas, strik-g layered rock formations and maybe the ld seal. It's a great place to just to come and and and experience the mighty Atlantic inds and seas as they strike land.

antry
027 • pop 2936

amed for its mussels and wedged between lls and the waters of Bantry Bay, Bantry's ajor attraction is colourful old **Bantry House** 50047; admission to gardens and house 9.50, gardens only €4; both open 9am-6pm aily, closed Nov-Mar), superbly situated verlooking the bay. The gardens are beauti-lly kept, and the house is noted for its French nd Flemish tapestries. In the courtyard a rench Armada exhibit recounts France's iled 1796 attempt to aid the Irish indepen-ence struggle.

Bantry's **tourist office** (☎ 50229; open Mar-Nov) is on the east end of Wolfe Tone quare. Frequent buses to Cork (three daily), Killarney, Glengarriff and beyond stop just off e main square at Barry Murphy's pub.

The IHH **Bantry Independent Hostel** (☎ 51050; Bishop Lucey Place; dorm beds/doubles €10/24) is just off Glengarriff Rd, about 600m northeast of the town centre. The **Small Independent Hostel** (☎ 51140; dorm beds €11) is shabby but well located on the harbour's north bank. There are plenty of B&Bs in Bantry, including a few around Wolfe Tone Square.

The place to go to for those famous mus-sels is undoubtedly **O'Connor's Seafood Res-taurant** (☎ 50221; Wolfe Tone Square). A cheaper dining option is a few doors along at the **Brick Oven Pizza Restaurant**.

The Beara Peninsula
☎ 027

From Bantry, the N71 follows the coast northwest to Glengarriff from where the R572 runs southwest to the Beara Peninsula, a wild, handsome, rocky landscape that's ideal for exploring by foot or bike. The Beara is far less on the tourist trail than the Ring of Kerry or the Dingle and is a great place to spend a few relaxing days. It's possible to drive the 137km 'Ring of Beara' in one day although that would be missing the point. If you're driving or cycling (leg power permitting) don't miss the beautiful Healy Pass.

Walkers might like to tackle ruggedly beau-tiful Hungry Hill, made famous by Daphne DuMaurier's book of the same name, just out-side the pleasant fishing town of Castletown-bere, itself a good place to stop for a bite or a pint.

Coming from Glengarriff, the first village on the peninsula is **Adrigole**, a tiny hamlet with lots of rocks and **Hungry Hill Lodge** (☎ 60228; e info@hungryhilllodge.com; tent sites €6, dorm beds from €11, doubles from €28). It has new facilities, bike hire, boat trips, diving and a café.

Other peninsula hostels include **Beara Hos-tel** (☎ 70184; tent sites €5.50, dorm beds €10.50), 3km west of Castletownbere, and the **Garranes Hostel** (☎ 73147; dorm beds €10.50), between Castletownbere and Alli-hies, which has a breathtaking location perched high above Bantry Bay. The atmosphere is quiet and meditative here, appropriately so as it's owned by the **Dzogchen Buddhist retreat** (☎ 73032) next door. Guests have the option of joining daily meditation sessions. Given the re-flective atmosphere, this is not a place to come to party.

IRELAND

In the lovely, sleepy village of **Allihies** is the delightful, modern IHH **Village Hostel** (☎ 73107; dorm beds €12.50; open all year). The pub next door is a great place to sit out and survey the bay below on a fine day. Among the surrounding copper mines is An Óige's **Allihies Hostel** (☎ 73014; dorm beds €11; open June-Sept). An Óige's **Glanmore Lake Lodge** (☎ 064-83181; dorm beds €12; open Easter-Sept) is in an old schoolhouse 5km from Lauragh nestling in stunning Healy Pass.

The West Coast

KILLARNEY
☎ 064 • pop 7250

By the time you reach Killarney (Cill Airne) you will have seen plenty of touristy Irish towns, but nothing will prepare you for a Killarney summer weekend chock-a-block with tour coaches. Cynics may find Killarney little more than a charmless and pricey Irish theme-park. Still, with a national park and three lakes on its doorstep, there are easy escapes for walkers and cyclists. Killarney is also a convenient base for touring the Ring of Kerry (see that section later in this chapter).

Information

Killarney's **tourist office** (☎ 31633; Beech Rd; open 9.15am-1pm & 2pm-5.30pm Mon-Sat Sept-May, 9am-6pm Mon-Sat, 10am-6pm Sun June-Aug) is busy. Send mail at the **main post office** (New St). **Gleeson's Laundrette** is behind the Spar supermarket where Plunkett St meets College St. **Web Talk** (High St) and the newer **Ri-Ra** (Plunkett St) provide daily Internet access.

Around Town

Most of Killarney's attractions are just outside the town, not actually in it. The 1855 **St Mary's Cathedral** (Cathedral Place) is worth a look, as is the **National Museum of Irish Transport** (admission €4; open 10am-6pm daily Apr-Oct), set back from East Avenue Rd. The latter has an interesting assortment of old cars, bicycles and automotive smells.

Killarney National Park

The picture perfect backdrop of mountains (well, big hills) beyond town are in fact part of Killarney's huge 10,236 hectare national park. Within the park there are beautiful Lough

Leane, Muckross Lake and the Upper La[ke]. There's a pedestrian entrance immediately o[p]posite St Mary's Cathedral, and a drivers e[n]trance off the N71.

As well as ruins and ex-gentry housing, [the] park offers rewards exploring by foot, bike [or] boat. There are plenty of options to last a d[ay] or longer. The *Killarney Area Guide* has so[me] ideas.

The restored 14th-century **Ross Cast[le]** (admission €3.80) is a 2.5km walk from [St] Mary's Cathedral. Hour-long **cruises of Loug[h] Leane** leave the castle daily in summer; ma[ke] bookings at the tourist office. From late Se[p]tember to May boats depart on weekends on[ly].

Inisfallen Island, Lough Leane's largest, [is] where the 13th-century *Annals of Inisfall[en]* were written. The annals, now in the Bodlei[an] Library at Oxford, remain a vital source of [in]formation about early Irish history. From Ro[ss] Castle you can hire a boat and row to the isla[nd] to inspect the ruins of a 12th-century orato[ry].

The core of Killarney National Park [is] **Muckross Estate** (admission €5; open da[ily] year-round), donated to the government [in] 1932 by Arthur Bourn Vincent. The estate [is] 5km from Killarney and you can walk arou[nd] the estate's rooms, and view their faded 19t[h] century fittings.

Gap of Dunloe

In summer the Gap, a heather-clad valley [at] the foot of Purple Mountain (832m), is Killa[r]ney tourism at its worst. Rather than payi[ng] more than €50 for a one-hour horse-and-tra[p] ride through the Gap, consider hiring a bi[ke] and cycling to Ross Castle. From here take [a] boat across to Lord Brandon's Cottage a[nd] cycle down through the Gap and back in[to] town via the N72 and a path through the go[lf] course. Including bike hire, this should co[st] you about €23. The 1½-hour boat ride alo[ne] justifies the trip.

Places to Stay

Wherever you stay, book ahead from June [to] August.

Camping About 1.5km along the Cork roa[d] (N22) is **Fleming's White Bridge Caravan [&] Camping Park** (☎ 31590) while **Flesk Muc[k]ross Caravan Park** (☎ 31704) is 1.5km out o[n] the Kenmare road (N71). Tent sites at both a[re] €6.50 per person and are available mid-Mar[ch] to October.

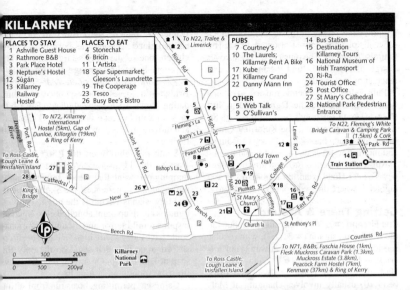

KILLARNEY

PLACES TO STAY
1 Ashville Guest House
2 Rathmore B&B
3 Park Place Hotel
8 Neptune's Hostel
12 Súgán
13 Killarney Railway Hostel

PLACES TO EAT
4 Stonechat
6 Bricín
11 L'Artista
18 Spar Supermarket; Gleeson's Laundrette
19 The Cooperage
23 Tesco
26 Busy Bee's Bistro

PUBS
7 Courtney's
10 The Laurels; Killarney Rent A Bike
17 Kube
21 Killarney Grand
22 Danny Mann Inn

OTHER
5 Web Talk
9 O'Sullivan's
14 Bus Station
15 Destination Killarney Tours
16 National Museum of Irish Transport
20 Ri-Ra
24 Tourist Office
25 Post Office
27 St Mary's Cathedral
28 National Park Pedestrian Entrance

Hostels Just off Park Rd and closest to the bus and train station is the modern and well-equipped **Killarney Railway Hostel** (☎ 35299; e railwayhostel@eircom.net; dorm beds/ doubles €12/36).

Off New St, in the town centre, Bishop's Lane will lead you to the **Neptune's Hostel** (☎ 35255; dorm beds from €11, singles/ doubles €32/34).

The small, friendly **Súgán** (☎ 33104; Lewis Rd; dorm beds €12) has a big kitchen, a cosy dining room, bikes for hire and a rack of guitars, but there are only two toilets and an outdoor shower. An Óige's large **Killarney International Hostel** (☎ 31240; e anoige@ killarney.iol.net; dorm beds/doubles €12/44) is an excellent bet apart from its location about 4km west of town. It offers plenty of double rooms and a pick-up from the train station. The huge 18th-century house it occupies sits in well-tended grounds with lakes and woods. Even more remote, the IHH **Peacock Farm Hostel** (☎ 33557; dorm beds from €10; open Apr-Sept) is a quiet rural oasis with impressive views, 7km away in Gortdromakiery. Call to arrange a free pick-up.

B&Bs In high season finding a room can be tricky, so it's worth paying the booking fee and letting the tourist office do the hunting. Within easy walking distance of the centre of town on Rock Rd is **Ashville Guest House** (☎ 36405; doubles from €56) and **Rathmore B&B** (☎ 32829; doubles from €56) next door.

The Muckross road is also lined with B&Bs. **Fuschia House** (☎ 33743; e fuschiahouse@ eircom.net; Muckross Rd; singles/doubles €65/100) is a big, beautifully furnished place.

The recently refurbished **Park Place Hotel** (☎ 31058, fax 30266; High St; doubles €90) is a reasonably located mid-range hotel.

Places to Eat

It's easy to eat badly or expensively in Killarney and sometimes both. The exceptions include **L'Artista** (☎ 38744; Bohereen Cael; mains €8) tucked away from the high street, a cosy Italian with very reasonably priced pizza and pasta.

The Cooperage (☎ 37716; Old Market Lane; mains around €15) succeeds very well with an imaginative menu of modern European cuisine. **Busy Bee's Bistro** next door is cheap and cheerful.

Duck down Flemings Lane, off High St, to the appealing **Stonechat**, which has a good choice of home-made soups, sandwiches and cakes and a courtyard if the weather is kind.

The inviting **Bricín** (High St; lunch specials €8, mains €20), situated above a craft shop, does seafood and stews. It also has vegetarian options. **Tesco** is near the tourist office on Beach St.

IRELAND

Entertainment

Killarney has plenty of music pubs, but much of what's played is tourist-oriented, like at **The Laurels** *(Main St)*. The musical part (€6 cover charge) is actually behind the main pub and reached by a side alley.

Pubs with more authentic music and often a better buzz include the **Danny Mann Inn** *(New St)* and **Courtney's**, just off the High St. But the most popular is the **Killarney Grand** *(Main St)*, which has nights of poetry readings, and interesting takes on the traditional thing.

Kube *(East Avenue Rd)* beneath the Killarney Towers Hotel is an ultra-modern bar and nightclub where dressed-up locals go to party.

Getting There & Around

Bus Éireann *(☎ 30011)* operates from outside the small train station *(☎ 31067)*, with regular services to Cork (€11.90), Galway (via Limerick, €17.10), Dublin (€19) and Rosslare Harbour (€20.20). Travelling by train to Cork (€17.70) usually involves changing at Mallow, but there is a direct route to Dublin (€45) via Limerick Junction.

In the same lane as Neptune's Hostel is **O'Sullivan's** *(☎ 31282)*, which rents bikes for €12 per day. **Killarney Rent A Bike** *(☎ 32578)* beside The Laurels pub rents bikes for €10.

THE RING OF KERRY
☎ 066

The Ring of Kerry, a 179km circuit around the Iveragh Peninsula featuring dramatic coastal scenery, clearly is one of Ireland's premier tourist attractions.

Most travellers tackle the Ring by bus on a guided day trip from Killarney. The tourist coaches approach the Ring in an anticlockwise direction and in summer it's hard to know which is more unpleasant – driving/cycling behind the buses or travelling in the opposite direction and meeting them on blind corners.

Eliminate some of these frustrations by leaving the main highway. The **Ballaghbeama Pass** cuts across the peninsula's central highlands and has spectacular views and remarkably little traffic.

The shorter **Ring of Skellig**, at the end of the peninsula, has fine views of the Skellig Rocks and is less touristy. You can forgo roads completely by walking the **Kerry Way**, which winds through the Macgillycuddy's Reeks mountains past Carrantuohill (1038m), Ireland's highest mountain.

Things to See

Daniel O'Connell (see History in the Fact about Ireland section) was born near **Cahirciveen**, one of the Ring's larger towns. The excellent **Barracks Heritage Centre** *(☎ 94. 2777; admission €4; open Mar-Sept)* of Bridge St occupies what was once an intimidating Royal Irish Constabulary (RIC) barracks. Exhibits focus on Daniel O'Connell and moving material on the local impact of the famine.

South of Cahirciveen the R565 branches west to the 11km-long **Valentia Island**, a jumping-off point for one of Ireland's most unforgettable experiences: the **Skellig Rocks**, two tiny islands 12km off the coast. The vertiginous climb up uninhabited Skellig Michael inspires a mild terror and an awe that monks could have clung to life in the meagre beehive-shaped stone huts that stand on the only flat strip of land on top. On a clear day the views from the summit are astounding.

Calm seas permitting, boats run from spring to late summer from Portmagee, just before the bridge to Valentia, to Skellig Michael. The standard fare is €32 return. Booking is essential; contact **Joe Roddy** *(☎ 947 4268)* or **Des Lavelle** *(☎ 947 6124)*.

The worthwhile **Skellig Experience Centre** *(☎ 947 6306; admission €4.40; open daily Mar-Oct)*, on Valentia Island across from Portmagee, has exhibits on the life and times of the monks who lived on Skellig Michael from the 7th to the 12th centuries.

The pretty pastel-coloured town of **Kenmare** is an excellent alternative base for exploring the Ring of Kerry. Kenmare is somewhat touristy, but it's nothing like Killarney.

Places to Stay

It's wise to book your next night as you make your way around the Ring; some places are closed out of season, others fill up quickly. Ring of Kerry hostels typically charge €11 to €14 for dorm beds.

Cycling hostel-to-hostel around the Ring, there's the IHH **Laune Valley Farm** *(☎ 976 1488)*, 2km east of Killorglin; the IHO **Caitin Baiters Hostel** *(☎ 947 7614)* in Kells; the meagre IHH **Sive Hostel** *(☎ 947 2717)* in Cahirciveen; IHO **Ring Lyne Hostel** *(☎ 947 6103)* in Chapeltown; the large **Royal Pier Hostel** *(☎ 947 6144)* in Knightstown on Valentia Island; and the An Óige **Baile an Sceilg** *(☎ 947 9229)* in Ballinskelligs.

An Óige's **Black Valley Hostel** (☎ 064-4712; open Mar-end Oct), in the Macgilly-uddy's Reeks mountains, is a good starting point for walking the Kerry Way.

Getting There & Around

If you're not up to cycling, **Bus Éireann** (☎ 064-30011) has a Ring of Kerry bus service daily from mid-May through mid-September. In June, buses leave Killarney at 8.30am, 1.30pm and 3.45pm (at 9.40am and noon on Sunday), and stop at Killorglin, Glenbeigh, Kells, Cahirciveen, Waterville, Caherdaniel and Sneem, before returning to Killarney (the 3.45pm service terminates at Waterville.)

Travel agencies in Killarney, including **Destination Killarney Tours** (☎ 064-32638; East Avenue Rd), offer daily tours of the Ring for about €20. Hostels in Killarney arrange tours for around €16.

THE DINGLE PENINSULA
☎ 066

The Dingle Peninsula is far less crowded and just as beautiful as the Ring of Kerry, with narrow roads that discourage heavy bus traffic.

The region's main hub, Dingle Town (An Daingean), is a workaday fishing village with a dozen good pubs. The western tip of the peninsula, noted for its extraordinary number of ring forts and high crosses, is predominantly Irish-speaking.

Dingle Town

In the winter of 1984 fisherfolk noticed a solitary bottlenose dolphin that followed their vessels and sometimes leapt over their boats. **Boats** (☎ 915 2626) leave Dingle's pier for a one-hour trip to find Fungie the dolphin. The cost is €10 (free if Fungie doesn't show, but he usually does). You can swim with him for €18; wetsuit hire is extra. **Tour boats** (☎ 915 2199) also leave from the harbour for the Blasket Islands.

Dingle Oceanworld (☎ 915 2111; open daily), opposite the harbour, has a walk-through tunnel and touch pool for €7.50. You can ride a horse through the peninsula with **Dingle Horse Riding** (☎ 915 2199).

East of Dingle Town

From Tralee the N86 heads west along the coast. The 'quick' route to Dingle Town is southwest from Camp via Anascaul and the N86. The scenic route follows the R560

northwest and crosses the wildly scenic **Connor Pass** (456m).

West of Dingle Town

From Dingle follow signs for the 'Slea Head Drive', a scenic coastal stretch of the R559. To the southwest, **Slea Head** offers some of the peninsula's best views.

Ferries (☎ 915 6422) run from Dunquin to the bleak, now uninhabited (since 1953) **Blasket Islands** (€20 return, 20 minutes), off the tip of the peninsula. Dunquin's excellent and architecturally splendid **Blasket Centre** (☎ 915 6444; admission €3.10; open daily Easter-Sept) focuses on the lives of the islanders, many of them celebrated musicians, story-tellers and writers.

Places to Stay

The going rate for a dorm bed in and around Dingle is €12 to €15.

In Dingle Town, the inviting **Grapevine Hostel** (☎ 915 1434; Dykegate St) has beds in dorms and four-bed rooms. Its owner was due to open a budget hotel at the time of research. For a more rural setting, try the popular **Rainbow Hostel** (☎ 915 1044), 1km west of town (call for free pick-up from the bus stop); camping is also available. East along the Tralee road, the IHH **Ballintaggart Hostel** (☎ 915 1454), in a spacious 19th-century house, has a free shuttle service to/from town, plus bike hire.

There are plenty of B&Bs in town, including the **Captain's House** (☎ 915 1531; e captigh@eircom.net; singles/doubles from €50/70) and **Marina Lodge** (☎ 915 0800; e din glemarinalodge@eircom.net; doubles €70) near the pier.

Hostels east of Dingle include the IHH **Fuchsia Lodge** (☎ 915 7150; open year-round), in Anascaul; and IHH **Connor Pass Hostel** (☎ 713 9179; open mid-Mar–Nov) in Stradbally.

West of Dingle, look for An Óige's **Dunquin Hostel** (☎ 915 6121; open year-round) near the Blasket ferry, the pleasant **Ballybeag Hostel** (☎ 915 9876; e balybeag@iol.ie) in Ventry and the IHO **Black Cat Hostel** (☎ 915 6286; open year-round) in Ballyferriter.

Getting There & Around

Buses stop outside the car park at the back of the Super Valu store in Dingle Town. Buses for Dingle Town leave Tralee four times daily from Monday to Saturday. Two buses

IRELAND

daily depart from Killarney for Dingle in the summer. Note that there are few services on Sunday.

There are several bike-rental places in Dingle. **Paddy Walsh** (☎ 915 2311; *Dykegate St)* is near the Grapevine Hostel and has bikes for €7.

LIMERICK

☎ 061 • pop 79,000

Limerick (Luimneach) is the Irish Republic's third-largest city with a reputation as one of Ireland's dullest tourist spots. Matters have improved in recent years with better restaurants and a lively music scene. The jewel in Limerick's tarnished crown is the delightful Hunt Museum. Budget travellers should note that at the time of writing all of Limerick's hostels had closed and B&B options were not great. In short, if you're pressed for money or time, skip Limerick.

Orientation & Information

The main street through town changes name from Rutland St to Patrick St, O'Connell St, The Crescent and Quinlan St as it runs south. The train and bus station are situated to the southeast, off Parnell St.

The **tourist office** (☎ 31 7522; *Arthur's Quay; open Mon-Sat low season, Mon-Sun summer)* is near the Shannon River. There is Internet access at **Webster's** (☎ 31 2066; *Thomas St)* and a **laundrette** at 19 Ellen St.

Things to See

Across the Shannon is the sturdy but underwhelming **King John's Castle** (☎ 41 1201; *admission €6.65; open year-round)*. The adjacent **Limerick Museum** (☎ 41 7826; *open 10am-1pm & 2.15pm-5pm Tues-Sat)* is cluttered and unimaginative, but is far more interesting if you read the old letters. A short walk south is Limerick's oldest building, the 12th-century **St Mary's Cathedral** (*admission €2 donation)*.

Continue south on Bridge St to the fascinating **Hunt Museum** (*Rutland St; admission €5.70; open 10am-5pm Mon-Sat, 2pm-5pm Sun)*, which features contemporary art shows, 2000 artefacts and a superb collection of Bronze Age, Celtic and medieval treasures. Half the fun of a visit to this museum is in opening the drawers, in which much of the collection is kept, to discover random treasures within.

Places to Stay

There are cheap, but fairly grim, B&Bs on Davis St, directly opposite the train station. **Alexandra** (☎ 31 8472; *6 Alexandra Terrace singles/doubles from €25/40)* off O'Connell Ave is a welcoming place. **Cruises House** (☎ 31 5320; [e] cruiseshouse@tinet.ie; *Denmark St; singles/doubles €50/76, light breakfast included)* is impersonal but it's central. **Hanratty's Hotel** (☎ 41 0999; *5 Glentworth St; singles/doubles €60/80)* is central and comfortable.

Places to Eat

There is a **Tesco** supermarket in the Arthur's Quay Shopping Centre beside the tourist office. For good coffee and snacks, try **Java's - The Beat Café** (*5 Catherine St)*, near the corner of Thomas St. **La Romana** (*O'Connell St)*, between Cecil and Shannon Sts, does mostly pasta for around €11. Open when its museum namesake is, **The Hunt Museum Restaurant** has views of the Shannon and is highly recommended for lunch.

Getting There & Away

Bus Éireann (☎ 31 3333) services operate from Colbert train station. There are regular bus connections to Dublin (€13.30), Cork, Galway, Killarney (€12.40) and other centres. By **train** (☎ 31 5555) it costs €33.60 to Dublin and (€17.70) to Cork. Specials are often available for early trains to Dublin.

Shannon airport (☎ 47 1444), 24km from Limerick, handles domestic and international flights.

Getting Around

Buses connect the airport with the bus and train station for €4.70. There are also direct buses from the airport to Dublin.

Emerald Alpine Cycles (☎ 41 6983; *1 Patrick St)* hires bikes for €20 per day.

THE BURREN

County Clare's greatest attraction is the haunting Burren, a harsh and bleakly beautiful stretch of country. *Boireann* is Irish for 'Rocky Country', and the name is no exaggeration. One of Cromwell's generals concluded that in the Burren there was 'neither water enough to drown a man, nor a tree to hang him, nor soil enough to bury him'.

Despite its unwelcoming look, the Burren is an area of major interest, with many ancient

olmens, ring forts, round towers and high
rosses. There's also some stunning scenery, a
ood collection of hostels and some of Ire-
and's best music pubs.

Tim Robinson's excellent *Burren Map &
Guide* is available at bookshops or tourist
offices. From Galway, both **Lally Coaches**
(☎ 091-56 2905) and **O'Neachtain Tours**
(☎ 091-55 3188) arrange guided bus tours to
he Burren and Cliffs of Moher (see the fol-
owing Doolin section) for €25, leaving the
Galway tourist office at 10am daily and re-
urning by 5.30pm. **Rambler Guided Walks**
(☎ 091-58 2525) explores the Burren by bus
nd foot.

Doolin
☎ 065
Tiny Doolin, famed for its music pubs, is a
convenient base for exploring the Burren and
he awesome Cliffs of Moher. It's also a gateway for boats to Inisheer, the easternmost and
mallest of the Aran Islands. In summer it can
be difficult to get a bed in Doolin, so book
head. Some of the hostels and **Doolin Bike
Rental** rent bikes for around €8 a day plus
deposit.

Doolin's popularity among holidaymakers
rom all over the world has soared over the
past few years, and at night the three pubs are
packed with an appreciative cosmopolitan
crowd. Doolin attracts a good standard of
musicians playing mainly traditional Irish
music.

Places to Stay & Eat Down by the harbour
s **O'Connors Riverside Camping & Caravan
Park** (☎ 707 4314; *sites per tent €6-7, per
person €3; open May-Sept*). Both the **Aille
River** and **Rainbow** hostels allow camping for
around €6 per person.

Doolin's hostels charge around €11 for
dorm beds. **Paddy Moloney's Doolin Hostel**
(☎ 707 4006; *doubles €33*), a large but basic
IHH hostel in the lower village, offers two
doubles, but eternally slamming doors makes
t noisy.

The upper village has three IHH hostels: 16-
bed **Rainbow Hostel** (☎ 707 4415; e *rain
bowhostel@eircom.net*), which also has some
cheap B&B rooms, the 30-bed **Aille River
Hostel** (☎ 707 4260), and 24-bed **Flanagan's
Village Hostel** (☎ 707 4564). Aille River, in
a converted farmhouse, is the nicest of the
bunch.

There are plenty of B&Bs, including the excellent, modern and spacious **Doolin Activity
Lodge** (☎ 707 4888; e *info@doolinlodge
.com*), which also has good value self-catering
apartments.

Doolin's three pubs serve basic, cheap pub
food. Alternatively, try the **Doolin Cafe** or the
more upmarket **Anne's Organic Restaurant**.

Getting There & Away There are direct
buses to Doolin from Limerick, Ennis, Galway
and even Dublin; the main Bus Éireann stop is
across from Paddy Moloney's Doolin Hostel.
See the Aran Islands section later in this chapter for information on ferries to and from the
islands.

Cliffs of Moher
About 8km south of Doolin are the towering
Cliffs of Moher (*admission free; always open*),
at 203m one of Ireland's most famous natural
features. In summer the cliffs are overrun by
day-trippers, so consider staying in Doolin and
hiking along the Burren's quiet country lanes
where the views are just as good and crowds
are never a problem. Either way, be careful
walking along these sheer cliffs, especially in
wet or windy weather.

Near the **Cliffs of Moher visitor centre**
(☎ 065-708 1171; *open daily*) is **O'Brien's
Tower**. Apparently, local landlord Cornelius
O'Brien (1801–57) raised it to impress 'lady
visitors'. Today's visitors pay €1.50 to climb
the tower. From here walk south or north and
the crowds soon disappear.

There is a **shop/café** adjacent to the visitor
centre, and it costs €2 to use the car park.

GALWAY
☎ 091 • pop 57,000
The city of Galway (Gaillimh) is a pleasure,
with its narrow streets, fast-flowing river, ramshackle shop-fronts, and good restaurants and
pubs. On weekends people come from as far as
Dublin for the nightlife, and during the city's
festivals the streets are bursting. Galway is also
a departure point for the rugged Aran Islands.

Orientation & Information
Galway's tightly packed town-centre is spread
evenly on both sides of the Corrib River. The
bus and train stations are within a stone's
throw of Eyre Square.

The **tourist office** (☎ 56 7700; *Forster St;
open 9am-5.45pm Mon-Fri, 9am-12.45pm*

IRELAND

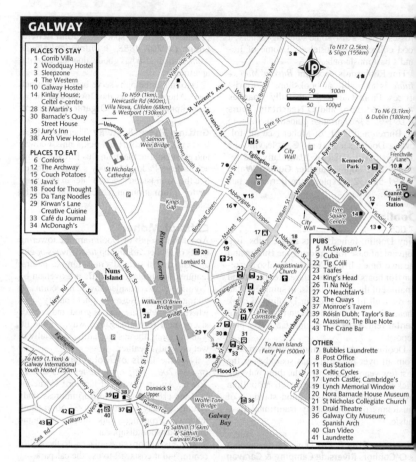

GALWAY

PLACES TO STAY
1 Corrib Villa
2 Woodquay Hostel
3 Sleepzone
4 The Western
10 Galway Hostel
14 Kinlay House; Celtel e-centre
28 St Martin's
30 Barnacle's Quay Street House
35 Jury's Inn
38 Arch View Hostel

PLACES TO EAT
6 Conlons
12 The Archway
15 Couch Potatoes
16 Java's
18 Food for Thought
25 Da Tang Noodles
29 Kirwan's Lane Creative Cuisine
33 Café du Journal
34 McDonagh's

PUBS
5 McSwiggan's
9 Cuba
22 Tig Cóilí
23 Taafes
24 King's Head
26 Ti Na Nóg
27 O'Neachtain's
32 The Quays
37 Monroe's Tavern
39 Róisín Dubh; Taylor's Bar
42 Massimo; The Blue Note
43 The Crane Bar

OTHER
7 Bubbles Laundrette
8 Post Office
11 Bus Station
13 Celtic Cycles
17 Lynch Castle; Cambridge's
19 Lynch Memorial Window
20 Nora Barnacle House Museum
21 St Nicholas Collegiate Church
31 Druid Theatre
36 Galway City Museum; Spanish Arch
40 Clan Video
41 Laundrette

Sat, extended hours peak season, open daily Easter-Sept) is a short way off Eyre Square. In summer there can be a long wait to make accommodation bookings.

Send mail at the **main post office** *(Eglington St)*. You can do your washing at **Bubbles laundrette** *(Mary St)* and there's another laundrette across the river on Dominick St. Nearby, at **Clan Video** you can access the Internet, although **Celtel e-centre** near the entrance to Kinlay House, has better facilities. The cathedral car park, just east of the Corrib offers a better deal on parking than buying discs.

Things to See

Galway is a great place to simply wander around and the *Galway Guide*, available from

the tourist office, points out many of the city's curiosities.

Eyre Square is the uninspired focal point of the eastern part of the city centre.

In the centre of the square is **Kennedy Park** honouring a visit by John F Kennedy in 1963. To the north of the square is a controversial statue to the Galway-born writer and hell raiser Pádraic O'Conaire (1883–1928). Southwest of the square, **St Nicholas Collegiate Church** *(Shop St)* dates from 1320 and has several interesting tombs.

Also on Shop St, parts of **Lynch Castle**, now a bank, date back to the 14th century. Lynch, so the story goes, was a mayor of Galway in the 15th century who, when his son was condemned for murder, personally acted as hangman, since nobody else was willing to do the job. The stone facade that is the **Lynch Memorial Window** (*Market St*) marks the spot of the sorrowful deed.

Across the road, in the Bowling Green area, is the **Nora Barnacle House Museum** (☎ 56 4743; *admission €2; open Mon-Sat June, July & Aug*), the former home of the wife and lifelong muse of James Joyce. The small museum is dedicated to the couple.

Little remains of Galway's old city walls apart from the **Spanish Arch**, right beside the river mouth. Next to the arch is the small and unimpressive **Galway City Museum** (*admission €2; open 10am-1pm & 2pm-5pm Mon-Sat, closed Mon & Tues in winter*).

Special Events
The **Galway Arts Festival** (W *www.galwayartsfestival.com*) in July is a huge event.

Places to Stay
Camping On the coast just west of Salthill, off Salthill Road, is **Salthill Caravan Park** (☎ 52 3972; *2-person tent €12, open Apr-Sept*).

Hostels There are plenty of hostels in and around Galway. All are open year-round except for the An Óige hostel. It's wise to pre-book your hostel if you plan on staying during summer, festivals and on weekends.

Sleepzone (☎ 56 6999; e *info@sleepzone.ie; Bóthar na mBán, Wood Quay; dorm beds/singles/doubles from €18/50/56*) is Galway's newest and by far its best hostel. The facilities are excellent, including laundry, secure parking, Internet access and safety deposit boxes. A light breakfast is included.

The cheerful 50-bed **Galway Hostel** (☎ 56 6959; *dorm beds/doubles €15/25*) is on Frenchville Lane. The prices include a light breakfast.

The IHH **Kinlay House** (☎ 56 5244; *dorm beds/singles/doubles from €14.50/38/43*), just off Eyre Square, is well equipped and offers a light breakfast. **Barnacle's Quay Street House** (☎ 56 8644; *10 Quay St; dorm beds €18*) is an always-busy IHH property with 98 beds in the heart of town, but is noisy and has meagre washroom facilities.

Near the Salmon Weir Bridge, **Corrib Villa** (☎ 56 2892; *4 Waterside St; dorm beds €15*) is in a three-storey townhouse with good kitchen facilities and power-showers, but cramped dorms. The independent **Woodquay Hostel** (☎ 56 2618; *23-24 Wood Quay; dorm beds €15*) has a decent kitchen and eating area but cramped washrooms and rickety bunks.

On the other side of the river is the **Arch View Hostel** (☎ 58 6661; *cnr Upper & Lower Dominick Sts; dorm beds €9*), the cheapest, but perhaps the scruffiest hostel in Galway.

Continue northwest from Upper Dominick St along Henry and St Helen Sts, then turn left onto St Mary's Rd to reach An Óige's 200-bed **Galway International Youth Hostel** (☎ 52 7411; *open late June-Aug; dorm beds €12.70*). It's on the St Mary's College campus; ring before you make the journey out there. Bus No 1 leaves for the college from Eyre Square.

B&Bs & Hotels Expect to pay €30 to €40 per person for B&B accommodation in Galway. There are not many around the city centre, but it's worth trying small but popular **St Martin's** (☎ 56 8286; *2 Nuns Island St; singles/doubles €35/64*), situated on the Corrib. **The Western** (☎ 56 2834; e *info@thewestern.ie; 33 Prospect Hill; singles/doubles €40/70*), with off-street parking just off Eyre Square, is another reasonable option.

Otherwise, Newcastle Rd, a 10-minute walk west of the river, has a few choices including **Villa Nova** (☎ 52 4849; *40 Lower Newcastle Rd; singles/doubles €33/50*).

The **Jury's Inn** (☎ 56 6444; *Quay St; high season room only rate €94*) hotel is central.

Places to Eat
Among old books and library lighting, **Café du Journal** (*Quay St*) serves light but filling meals and good espresso. For bagels, large sandwiches and desserts, daily to midnight, head to **Java's** (*Abbeygate St Upper*). Across the road **Couch Potatoes** has big spuds stuffed with all manner of fillings for about €6.

Food for Thought (*Abbeygate St Lower*) is a budget wholefood restaurant that also serves vegie options, chicken and fish. Nobody does fish and chips better than **Conlons** (*Eglington St; from €7*).

Da Tang Noodles (*Middle St*) serves up Japanese-style noodle soups, meat and vegie meals.

McDonagh's (*Quay St; lunch specials from €8, mains from €16*) is excellent for seafood, and terrific fish and chips.

Kirwan's Lane Creative Cuisine (☎ 56 8266) at the end of Kirwan's Lane serves modern Irish cuisine and could happily sit in any stylish area of New York or London, with comparable prices.

The Archway (☎ 56 3693; Victoria Place) is a top-notch restaurant which serves mainly French cuisine and offers reasonable value set menus.

There are branches of **Dunnes** and **Supervalu** in the Eyre Square shopping centre. **Cambridge's**, next door to Lynch's Castle, is a decent grocer, deli and off-licence.

Entertainment

The weekly *Galway Edge* has listings of what's on in and around Galway. It is available free from hostels, cafés and pubs.

Galway has dozens of good pubs, among them **O'Neachtain's** (17 Upper Cross St), which is more than 100 years old. Nearby, **Ti Na Nóg** is new, plays loud music and has big TV screens attracting a young crowd and sports fans.

King's Head (High St), a little farther north, has music most nights in summer. Almost next door, the enormously popular and much recommended **Taafes** is a music and sports bar. Just across the way, **Tigh Cóilí** (Mainguard St) is a small, snug pub with music year-round.

McSwiggan's (Daly's Place; meals from €12) is big, always busy, and has good meals. **The Quays** (Quay St) draws a crowd on weekends and in summer, and has an eclectic mix of music.

Across the river the choice spot for traditional music is **Monroe's Tavern** (cnr Dominick St Upper & Fairhill St). The nearby **Róisín Dubh** is good for alternative music and often has international acts. **Taylor's Bar** next door and, around the corner, **The Crane Bar** (Sea Rd), have music in summer. **Massimo** and **The Blue Note**, both on William St West, both favour dance music with DJs.

The small **Druid Theatre** (☎ 56 8617; Chapel Lane) puts on two or three, often experimental, productions per year. **Cuba**, at the northwestern edge of Eyre Square, is a large bar, nightclub, live music and comedy venue.

Getting There & Away

The **bus station** (☎ 56 2000) is situated just behind the Great Southern Hotel, off Eyre Square, and next to the Ceannt train station (☎ 56 4222). Bus Éireann operates services to Doolin (€10.70), Dublin (€11.40), Killarney (€17.10), Limerick, Sligo and beyond.

The Dublin services operate up to eight times daily.

Private bus companies, generally a bit cheaper than Bus Éireann, also operate from Galway. **Bus Nestor** (☎ 1800 42 4248) run five buses a day (seven on Friday) to Dublin's Tara St (€10) DART station via Dublin airport (€15). **Citylink Express** (☎ 56 4163) has similar deals.

From Galway there are four or more trains to and from Dublin (€20.90 one way, €29.20 Friday to Sunday; 2¾ hours). Connections with other train routes can be made at Athlone.

Getting Around

Celtic Cycles (☎ 56 6606; Queen St) rent bikes for €13/64 a day/week.

ARAN ISLANDS
☎ 099

In recent years the windswept, starkly beautiful Aran Islands have become one of western Ireland's major attractions. Apart from natural beauty, the Irish-speaking islands have some of the country's oldest Christian and pre-Christian ruins.

On the islands, particularly on tiny **Inisheer** the Irish passion for stone walls is almost absurd, with countless kilometres of stone wall separating even the tiniest patches of rocky land. Inhospitable though these rocky patches may appear, the islands were settled at a much earlier date than the mainland, since agriculture was easier to pursue here than in the densely forested Ireland of the pre-Christian era.

There are three main islands in the group, all inhabited year-round. Most visitors head for long and narrow (14.5km by a maximum 4km) **Inishmór** (or Inishmore). The land slopes up from the relatively sheltered northern shores of the island and plummets on the southern side into the raging Atlantic. **Inishmaan** and **Inisheer** are much smaller and receive far fewer visitors.

Although day trips to the islands are feasible, Inishmór alone is worth a few days of exploration. The islands can get crowded at holiday times (St Patrick's Day, Easter) and in July and August, when accommodation is at a premium and advance reservations are advised.

Orientation & Information

The **tourist office** (☎ 61263) operates year-round on the waterfront at Kilronan, the arrival point and major village of Inishmór. You can change money there and at some of the local shops. About 200m to the north is a small post office and a Wednesday-only branch of the Bank of Ireland.

There's Internet access at the **Ionad Árann** heritage centre, but there are no ATMs on the islands, although a couple of stores on Inishmór offer cash advances on credit cards.

JM Synge's *The Aran Islands* is the classic account of life on the islands and is readily available in paperback. A much less accessible (but more recent) tribute to the islands is mapmaker Tim Robinson's *Stones of Aran*. For detailed exploration, pick up a copy of his *The Aran Islands: A Map and Guide*.

Getting There & Away

Air If time is important or if seasickness is a concern on the often-rough Atlantic, you could fly to the islands and back with **Aer Árann** (☎ 091-59 3034) for €44. Flights operate to all three islands at least four times a day (hourly in summer) and take less than 10 minutes. The mainland departure point is Connemara regional airport at Minna, near Inverin, 38km west of Galway. A connecting bus from outside the Galway tourist office costs €3 one way.

Boat Inishmór is served year-round by **Island Ferries** (*Galway:* ☎ 091-56 8903; *adults/students* €19/15 *return*) and the trip takes around 40 minutes. Unfortunately the boat leaves from Rossaveal, 37km west of Galway. It's an extra €4 to catch an Island Ferries bus from outside the tourist office in Galway. Ferry tickets cost €15 from the Galway tourist office. Buses leave 1½ hours before ferry departure time and are scheduled to meet arriving ferries. If you have a car you can go straight to Rossaveal.

From April to October, Island Ferries sails daily to Inishmór at 10.30am, 1.30pm and 6.30pm; from November to March times are 10.30am and 5.30pm. Direct services to Inisheer and Inishman leave at 10.30am and 6.30pm from April to October and at 10.30am and 5.30pm from November to March.

Inishmor Ferries (☎ 091-56 6535) also runs similar services four times daily from Rossaveal at 10.30am, 1pm, 5pm and 6pm for most of the year and three daily from November to March at 10.30am, 1pm and 6pm.

Between June and September, **O'Brien's Shipping** (☎ 091-56 7676) sails direct daily

to the islands from Galway's docks (the trip costs €15.10 return). The 46km sea crossing takes 1½ hours, which can be a bit hard on sensitive stomachs.

Another option is to leave from Doolin in County Clare (see The Burren section earlier in this chapter). **Doolin Ferries** (*Doolin:* ☎ 065-707 4455; **w** www.doolinferries.com) operates some services from mid-April to September and runs to all three islands at least once daily from mid-May to the end of August: Doolin-Inisheer (€18.90 return, 30 minutes), Doolin-Inishmaan (€22.70 return, 40 minutes) and Doolin-Inishmór (€22.20 return, 55 minutes). Be aware that the ferry does not always call at Inishmaan or Inisheer if it has a full load of passengers for Inishmór.

Inter-island services are extremely limited in winter.

Getting Around

Inisheer and Inishmaan are small enough to explore on foot, but on larger Inishmór, bikes are definitely the way to go. **Aran Cycle Hire** (☎ 61132), just up from Kilronan's pier, charges €10 per day. The islands are tough on bikes, so check your cruiser carefully before renting it.

Plenty of small operators offer island bus tours for around €10.

Inishmór

The 'Big Island' has four impressive stone forts of uncertain age, though 2000 years is a good guess. Halfway down the island and about 8km west of Kilronan, semicircular **Dún Aengus** (☎ 61008; admission €1.25; open 10am-6pm summer, 10am-4pm rest of year), perched terrifyingly on the edge of the sheer southern cliffs, is the best known of the four. It's an amazing place, but take great care near the cliff edge as there are no guard rails. If you see only one sight on Inishmór, let it be Dún Aengus.

About 1.5km north is **Dún Eoghanachta**, while halfway back to Kilronan is **Dún Eochla**; both are smaller but perfectly circular ring forts. Directly south of Kilronan and dramatically perched on a promontory is another fort, **Dún Dúchathair**.

Ionad Árann (☎ 61355; admission €3.50; open 10am-5pm daily Apr-Oct, 10am-7pm June-Aug), just off the main road leading out of Kilronan, introduces the landscape and traditions of the islands. Robert Flaherty's 1934 film *The Man of Aran* is shown three times daily.

Places to Stay & Eat Hostels charge €10 to €15 for dorm beds and most of them are open year-round.

In Kilronan, the modern, justly popular **Kilronan Hostel** *(☎ 61255)*, also known as Tí Joe Mac's Hostel, is a short walk from the pier. A light breakfast is included. **St Kevin's Hostel** *(open summer)*, between Tí Joe Mac's and the Spar supermarket, is a bit run down; inquire at the **Dormer House B&B** *(☎ 61125)* opposite. **The Artist's Hostel Lodge** *(☎ 61457)* is just out of town.

A few kilometres northwest of Kilronan, the IHO **Mainistir House Hostel** *(☎ 61169, 61322)* needs redecorating but does excellent breakfasts and has transport that meets the ferry.

The numerous B&Bs that are in and around Kilronan include the large **Dormer House** *(☎ 61125; rooms per person from €20; open year-round)*, behind Tí Joe Mac's. **Tí Eithne** *(☎ 61303)* charges €19 per person sharing or €25 for a single. The upmarket **Pier House** *(☎ 61417; e pierh@iol.ie)* charges €45 per person.

Eating options are not great. **Mainistir House Hostel** has a great-value evening 'almost vegie' buffet (bookings essential). **The Bayview Guesthouse** has a café. The **Aran Fisherman Restaurant** is open year-round, although the food's nothing special.

Inishmaan

The least visited of the three islands is Inishmaan (Inis Meáin, or 'Middle Island'). High stone walls border its fields, and it's a delight to wander along the lanes and take in some of the tranquillity. The main archaeological site here is **Dún Chonchúir**, a massive oval-shaped stone-fort built on a high point and offering good views of the island.

Places to Stay There are no hostels on Inishmaan, but B&Bs are relatively cheap, at about €25 per person. Try **Angela Faherty's** *(☎ 73012; open Mar-Oct)* in Creigmore, about 500m northwest of the pier.

Inisheer

The smallest island, only 8km off the coast from Doolin, is Inisheer (Inis Oírr, or 'Eastern Island'). The 15th-century **O'Brien Castle**

(Caislea'n Uí Bhriain) overlooks the beach and harbour.

Places to Stay The **Inisheer Camp Site** *(☎ 75008; tent sites €3.15; open May-Sept)* is by the Strand and has basic facilities. **Brú Radharc Na Mara** *(☎ 75087, 75024; e maire .serraigh@oceanfree.net)* is an IHH hostel near the pier and offers private rooms and B&B accommodation (next door) for €25 per person. **Ard Mhuire** *(☎ 75005)* has pleasant rooms for €25.

CONNEMARA
☎ 095

The northwest corner of County Galway is the wild and barren region known as Connemara. It's a stunning patchwork of bogs, lonely valleys, pale-grey mountains and small lakes that shimmer when the sun shines. Connemara's isolation has allowed Irish to thrive and the language is widely spoken here; the lack of English signposting can be a little confusing at times.

By car or bicycle the most scenic routes through Connemara are Oughterard–Recess (via the N59), Recess–Kylemore Abbey (via the R344) and the Leenane–Louisburgh route (via the R335). From Galway, **Lally Coaches** *(☎ 091-56 2905)* and **O'Neachtain Tours** *(☎ 091-55 3188)* and, from Clifden, **Michael Nee Coaches** *(☎ 095-51082)*, arrange day-long tours of Connemara for around €25.

Things to See

Aughanure Castle *(☎ 55 2214; admission €2.50; open daily mid-June–mid-Sept)*, 3km east of Oughterard, is a 16th-century tower house on a rocky outcrop overlooking Lough Corrib.

Just west of **Recess** (Straith Salach) on the N59, the turn north at the R334 takes you through the stunning Lough Inagh Valley. At the end of the R334 is the equally scenic **Kylemore Abbey** *(☎ 41146; admission €5; some sections open daily year-round)* and its adjacent lake. The neo-Gothic 19th-century abbey is run by nuns.

From Kylemore you can take the N59 east to Leenane (An Líonán), then detour north on the R335 to Louisburgh and onwards to Westport (see the following Westport section); or you can travel 17km southwest along the N59 to **Clifden** (An Clochán), Connemara's largest town. Clifden is quiet, pleasant and has a few good pubs and restaurants. The **Clifden Walking Centre** (☎ 21379; *Island House, Market St*) runs guided walking trips for around €20.

Places to Stay

Oughterard has numerous B&Bs and a good hostel. **Canrawer House Hostel** (☎ 55 2388; *dorm beds from €11*) is a very good, attractive place at the Clifden end of town, just over 1km down a signposted turning. It has bike hire. In town the **Jolly Lodger** (☎ 55 2682) has cheap B&B from €22 per person.

An Óige's excellent **Ben Lettery Hostel** (☎ 51136; *dorm beds €12; open Easter-Sept*) is on the N59 halfway between Recess and Clifden.

In Clifden, the IHH **Clifden Town Hostel** (☎ 21076; *Market St; dorm beds/doubles €12/32*) is in the centre of town. The IHH/IHO **Brookside Hostel** (☎ 21812; *Hulk St; dorm beds/doubles €11.50/30; open Jan-Oct*) is down by the Owen Glin River.

The **Arch B&B** (☎ 22241), opposite the Clifden Town Hostel, offers B&B for €25. Just out of town is the lovingly restored and tastefully furnished **Mallmore House** (☎ 21460; e *mall more@indigo.ie; doubles €60*).

Getting There & Away

Buses link Clifden with Galway via Oughterard and Maam Cross, or via Cong and Leenane. In summer there are three express buses a day to/from Galway.

WESTPORT

☎ 098

Westport (Cathair na Mairt) is a popular stop on the way to/from Sligo or Donegal. It has a pleasant main street and a handful of good pubs.

North over the River Carrowbeg, there's a small **tourist office** (☎ 25711; *open year-round Mon-Sat summer, Mon-Fri winter*).

Things to See

Westport's major attraction, **Croagh Patrick**, about 7km west of the town, is the hill from which St Patrick performed his snake expulsion (Ireland has been serpent-free ever since). Climbing the 765m peak is a ritual for thousands of pilgrims on the last Sunday of July.

Places to Stay

There are two IHH hostels: the **Old Mill Hostel** (☎ 27045; *dorm beds €12*) in a courtyard

off James St, and the almost-luxurious **Club Atlantic Holiday Hostel** (☎ 26644; *Altamount St; dorm beds/doubles €11.50/30; open Mar-Oct*) near the train station.

Getting There & Away

There are bus connections to Belfast, Cork, Galway, Limerick, Shannon, Sligo and Waterford. Buses depart from Mill St. The **train station** (☎ 25253; *Altamount St*) is southeast of the town centre. There are three daily rail connections to Dublin (3½ hours) via Athlone.

The Northwest

County Sligo and County Donegal comprise Ireland's rural northwestern corner.

The coastal scenery is unparalleled, yet the region's distance from Dublin (and the lack of convenient rail links) keeps crowds to a minimum. Tourism in the northwest, especially County Donegal, is extremely seasonal, and many attractions and tourist offices close from October to March.

SLIGO

☎ 071 • pop 18,000

William Butler Yeats (1865–1939) was educated in Dublin and London, but his poetry is muddied with the county of his mother's family. He returned to Sligo (Sligeach) many times, and there are plentiful reminders of his presence in this sleepy (some would say boring) town and in the rolling green hills around it.

The **tourist office** (☎ 61201; *Temple St; open Mon-Fri year-round, also Sat & Sun July & Aug*) is just south of the centre. The **main post office** (*Wine St*) is east of the train and bus station. **Cygo Internet Café** (*19 O'Connell St*) has Internet access.

Things to See

Sligo's two major attractions are outside town. **Carrowmore**, 5km to the southwest, is the site of a **megalithic cemetery** (☎ 61534; *admission €1.90; open Easter-end Oct*) with more than 60 stone rings, passage tombs and other Stone Age remains. It's the largest Stone Age necropolis in Europe.

If it's a fine day don't miss the hill-top cairn-grave **Knocknarea**, a few kilometres northwest of Carrowmore. About 1000 years younger than Carrowmore, the huge cairn is

IRELAND

said to be the grave of the legendary Maeve, 1st century AD Queen of Connaught. Several trails lead to the 328m summit, which commands amazing views over the surrounding country and shore.

Places to Stay & Eat

The IHH **White House Hostel** (☎ 45160; Markievicz Rd; dorm beds €10) is just north of the town centre. About 1km north east of the centre is the comfortable **Harbour House** (☎ 71547; e harbourhouse@eircom.ie; Finisklin Rd; dorm beds/twins €15/36). Facilities include bike hire, family rooms, laundry. A light breakfast is included. **The Railway Hotel** (☎ 44530; 1 Union Place; dorm beds/doubles €10/26) is a small, recently refurbished place with free tea and coffee.

Sligo's less expensive B&Bs are on the various approaches to town. **Renate House** (☎ 62014; Upper John St; singles/doubles from €33/48) in the centre is a small B&B.

Bar Bazzar: Coffee Culture (Market St), near the monument, has coffee, snacks and second-hand books. **Bistro Bianconi** (44 O'-Connell St; meals around €16) serves decent Italian dishes, as well as salads and pizzas at around €11.

Daravogue (Rear, 15-16 St Stephens St) overlooking the river and bridge serves good pasta and pizza.

Getting There & Around

Bus Éireann (☎ 60066) has four services a day to/from Dublin (€12.20, four hours). There's also a Galway–Sligo–Donegal–Derry service at least three times daily. Buses operate from below the train station (☎ 69888), which is just west of the centre along Lord Edward St. Trains leave four times a day for Dublin via Boyle, Carrick-on-Shannon and Mullingar.

Hire a bike from **Gary's Cycles** (☎ 45418; Lower Quay St).

DONEGAL
☎ 073 • pop 3000

Donegal Town (Dún na nGall) is not the major centre in County Donegal, but it's a pleasant and laid-back place and well worth a visit.

The triangular Diamond is the centre of Donegal; a few steps south along the Eske River is the **tourist office** (☎ 21148; open Mon-Fri June-Sept).

Donegal Castle (admission €3.80; open daily Mar-Oct), on a rocky outcrop over the

Eske River, stands in ruins but is impressive all the same. Notice the floral decoration on the corner turret and the decorated fireplace on the 1st floor.

Places to Stay & Eat

The comfortable IHH/IHO **Donegal Town Independent Hostel** (☎ 22805; tent sites per person €5, dorm beds €10.50, private rooms per person €12; open year-round) is 1km northwest of town on the Killybegs road (N56).

An Óige's **Ball Hill Hostel** (☎ 21174; dorm beds €11; open Easter-Sept and weekends rest of the year) has a beautiful setting at the end of a quiet road, on the shores of Donegal Bay. To get here, take the Killybegs road (N56) and, 5km out, look for the signs on the left-hand side of the road. The location is pretty remote, so stock up on food before arriving.

The **Blueberry Tearoom** (meals from €8) is busy and often smoky, but has good meals. The **Atlantic Restaurant** (Main St) and **Errigal Restaurant** farther east are inexpensive, with meals from €7.

Getting There & Away

From Donegal **Bus Éireann** (☎ 21101) connections go to Derry, Enniskillen and Belfast to the north; Sligo and Galway to the west; and Limerick and Cork to the south. The bus stop is on the Diamond, outside the Abbey Hotel. **McGeehan's Coaches** (☎ 075-46150) does a Donegal-Dublin return trip three times a day (more in summer) departing from the police station opposite the tourist office.

AROUND DONEGAL

The awe-inspiring cliffs at **Slieve League**, dropping 300m straight into the Atlantic Ocean, are a recommended side trip from Donegal. To drive to the cliff edge, take the Killybegs–Glencolumbcille road (R263) and, at Carrick, take the turn-off signposted 'Bunglas'. Continue beyond the narrow track signposted for Slieve League (this trail is good for hikers) to the one signposted for Bunglas. Starting from Teelin, experienced walkers can spend a day walking via Bunglas and the somewhat terrifying One Man's Path to Malinbeg, near Glencolumbcille.

If you're walking, a convenient base is the IHH's **Derrylahan Hostel** (☎ 38079; e derrylahan@eircom.net; tents €5, dorm beds/doubles €10/28; open year-round), 2km southeast of Carrick and 3km northwest of

Kilcar. There's a small food shop. Call for free pick-up from Kilcar or Carrick. The remote **Dooey Hostel** *(☎ 30130; tents €5, dorm beds/twins €10/22)* at tiny Glencolumbcille is built into the hillside and has great views down onto the sea.

McGeehan's Coaches *(☎ 075-46150)* serves Carrick and Kilcar once daily (more frequent in summer) on its Dublin–Donegal–Glencolumbcille route. Otherwise, there are daily Bus Éireann coaches from Donegal to Killybegs, with onward buses to Kilcar and Carrick.

Northern Ireland

☎ 028

More than 25 years of internal strife has seriously affected tourism in Northern Ireland. Though this was understandable in the dark days of the late 1960s and early 1970s, wanton violence was never a serious threat to visitors here. In 1995, following the declaration of the first IRA cease-fire, the numbers of visitors from abroad jumped dramatically. Although numbers fell in 1996 after hostilities resumed, ratification in 1998 of the Good Friday Agreement provided a dose of positive international press, and the tourism figures are recovering.

The accent here is distinctly different, the currency is pounds sterling, petrol is pricier and distances are measured in miles; otherwise, cross-border differences are insignificant. If anything, the Northern Irish people are friendlier to foreign visitors than their counterparts in the Republic, perhaps to compensate for years of bad publicity.

Northern Ireland has plenty going for it: the Causeway Coast road, the Glens of Antrim, the old walls of Derry, cosmopolitan Belfast. But even with the coming of peace and the end of military roadblocks, signs of the Troubles can't be ignored: the street murals in Belfast and Derry, shuttered shopfronts, fortified police stations and sporadic unrest are still as much a part of Northern Ireland as green fields and smoke-filled pubs.

BELFAST
pop 279,240

There's been a real buzz about Belfast (Béal Feirste) in recent years as it tentatively recovers from 30 years of sectarian violence

and the dwindling of its once mighty industrial base.

Walking its handsome Victorian town hall square, its lovely Botanic Gardens or past the smart and extensive new waterfront developments, today there's little sign of the daily tension once engendered by bomb threats and army check points.

Belfast has so far reaped the dividend of the peace process and massive inward investment has seen the creation of new entertainment venues and upmarket hotels. In 2002 more was to come as the British government handed over former army and security service property for redevelopment.

Belfast has not shaken its past altogether, however. You'll still see armoured vans patrolling past fortified police stations, the buzz of surveillance helicopters overhead and the ubiquitous murals and propaganda in certain areas. Sporadic rioting (away from the city centre) and sectarian gangsterism still form a dark, and largely unseen, backdrop to growing prosperity and optimism here.

None of this will impact on the visitor though and Belfast really is a friendly city and safer crimewise than many European cities. Forget the received image of the place and you'll discover a city boasting great pubs and bars, an increasingly good selection of restaurants and citizens that know how to party.

Orientation & Information
The city centre is a compact area with the imposing City Hall as the central landmark. Belfast's principal shopping district is north of the square.

To the south lies the Golden Mile, which is a restaurant- and pub-filled stretch of Dublin Rd, Shaftesbury Square, Bradbury Place and Botanic Ave. To the east, most of Belfast's smart new hotel, leisure and arts developments line the banks of the Laggan. The charming, warren of streets of the up-and-coming Cathedral Quarter are a short walk north of the city centre.

The **Belfast Welcome Centre** *(☎ 9024 6609, fax 9031 2424;* **w** *www.gotobelfast .com; 47 Donegall Place)* is efficient and extremely helpful. **Bord Fáilte** *(☎ 9032 7888; 53 Castle St)* has information on the Irish Republic. **Hostelling International Northern Ireland** *(HINI; ☎ 9032 4733; 22-32 Donegall Rd)* has its offices at the Belfast International Youth Hostel.

IRELAND

BELFAST

PLACES TO STAY
1 The Linen House Hostel
23 Jury's Inn
36 Belfast International
   Youth Hostel; HINI
44 Arnie's Backpackers
45 The Ark
46 Botanic Lodge Guesthouse
47 Holiday Inn Express
49 Queen's House
54 Pearl Court House
55 Windermere Guesthouse
57 Liserin Guesthouse

PLACES TO EAT
3 Duke of York
4 Ba Soba
5 Nick's Warehouse
9 White's Tavern
11 Tesco
16 Kitchen Bar
17 Bittle's Bar
27 Flannigan's;
   Crown Liquor Saloon
29 Café Aero
31 Wetherspoon's
33 La Belle Epoque
39 Cayenne
41 The Other Place
43 Villa Italia
47 Café Renoir
53 Café Conor

PUBS
6 Milk Bar
8 John Hewitt
20 Apartment
22 Red Bar
26 Robinsons; Fibber Magee's
28 Beaten Docket
30 Limelight
32 Elbow
40 Empire Music Hall
42 The Globe
58 Botanic
59 Eglantine Inn

OTHER
2 Shankill Rd Taxi Stand
7 Albert Memorial Clocktower
10 Main Post Office; Citybus
   & Living History Tours
12 Bord Fáilte
13 Falls Rd Taxi Stand
14 Usit Now
15 The Belfast Welcome Centre
18 Laganside Buscentre
19 Waterfront Hall; Car Park
21 Ticket Kiosk
24 Grand Opera House
25 Europa Buscentre
34 Bronco's Web Café
37 Post Office
38 The Globe Laundry
39 Civic Arts Theatre
50 McConvey Cycles
51 Queen's Film Theatre
52 Ulster Museum
56 Laundrette

Send mail at the **main post office** *(Castle Place)* or the smaller **branch** at the top end of Botanic Ave by Shaftesbury Square. There's a **laundrette** *(160 Lisburn Rd)* in the university area, or try **The Globe Laundry** *(37 Botanic Ave)*. Access the Internet at **Bronco's Web Café** *(122 Great Victoria St)*.

Around the City

At the northeastern corner of **City Hall** (1906) there's a statue of Sir Edward Harland – the Yorkshire-born engineer who founded Belfast's Harland & Wolff shipyards – whose famous yellow twin cranes **Samson and Goliath** tower above the city. The yard's most famous construction was the ill-fated *Titanic*, the 'unsinkable' boat that sank in 1912. A memorial to the disaster and its victims stands on the east side of City Hall.

City Hall is fronted by an especially dour statue of Queen Victoria. To the northeast – between High St and Queen's Square – the queen's consort, Prince Albert, also makes his Belfast appearance at the slightly leaning **Albert Memorial Clocktower** (1867).

Across from the Europa Hotel, the famed **Crown Liquor Saloon** *(Great Victoria St)* was built by Patrick Flanagan in 1885 and displays Victorian architecture at its most extravagant. The snugs are equipped with bells that were once connected to a board behind the bar, enabling drinkers to demand more drink without leaving their seats. The Crown was lucky to survive a 1993 bomb that devastated the (now fully restored) **Grand Opera House** across the road.

Museums & Gardens

The **Ulster Museum** *(☎ 9038 3000; admission free other than some major exhibitions; open 10am-5pm Mon-Fri, 1pm-5pm Sat, 2pm-5pm Sun)*, in the **Botanic Gardens** *(open 8am-sunset)* near the university, has excellent exhibits on Irish art, wildlife, dinosaurs, steam and industrial machines, and more. The gardens themselves are well worth a wander. The grand glass Palm House contains a luxuriant riot of greenery.

W5 *(☎ 9046 7700; 2 Queen's Quay)* is a science 'discovery centre' with some impressive interactive exhibits, which include a laser harp, a lie detector and a wind tunnel.

The **Belfast Zoo** *(☎ 9077 6277; Antrim Rd; admission £6; open 10am-5pm daily Apr-Sept, 10am-3.30pm Sat-Thur, 10am-2.30pm*

Fri Oct-Mar) is exceptionally good with large animal enclosures. The penguin pool, with its underwater viewing-platform, is especially popular.

Falls & Shankill Rds

The Catholic Falls Rd and the Protestant Shankill Rd have been battlefronts since the 1970s. Even so, these areas are quite safe and worth venturing into, if only to see the large **murals** expressing local political and religious passions. King Billy riding to victory in 1690 on his white steed, and hooded IRA gunmen are two of the more memorable images.

If you don't fancy a fully organised tour (see Organised Tours later), the best way to visit the sectarian zones of the Falls and Shankill Rds is by what is known locally as the 'people taxi'. These former black London cabs run a bus-like service up and down their respective roads from terminuses in the city. Shankill Rd taxis go from North St, and Falls Rd taxis from Castle St. The Falls Rd taxis occupy the first line at the Castle St taxi park, with signs up in Gaelic. They're used to doing tourist circuits of the Falls and typically charge around £8 per person (cabs hold up to five people) for a one-hour tour that takes in the main points of interest. **The Belfast Welcome Centre** (see Orientation & Information earlier) has leaflets on the cab tours.

Ulster Folk & Transport Museum

Belfast's biggest tourist attraction also is one of the finest museums in Northern Ireland *(☎ 9042 8428; joint admission £5; open roughly 10am-5pm Mon-Sat, 11am-5pm Sun, with longer hours in summer and shorter hours in winter)* 11km northeast of the centre beside the Bangor road (A2) near Holywood. The 30 buildings on this 60-hectare site range from urban terrace homes to thatched farm cottages. A bridge crosses the A2 to the Transport Museum, which contains various Ulster-related vehicles including a prototype of the vertical take-off and landing (VTOL) aircraft.

From Belfast take Ulsterbus No 1 or any Bangor-bound train that stops at Cultra station.

Organised Tours

A 3½-hour **Citybus tour** *(☎ 9045 8484; tour £9)* covers all the main sights. It begins at Castle Place outside the main post office Monday to Saturday at 11am from early May to the end of September. The popular Living History

IRELAND

tour takes in Belfast's Troubles-related sights. Tours leave Castle Place daily at 1pm from May to September. Tickets cost £9 and the tour lasts 2½ hours. Both tours are offered off-season, but are subject to demand.

Black Taxi Tours (☎ 9064 2264) runs daily and is a more organised version of the 'people taxi'. Included is an even-sided account of the Troubles in a refreshingly down-to-earth way. Prices are £8 per person based on four sharing.

There are a number of walking tours on offer, including the two-hour **Bailey's Historical Pub Tour** (☎ 9268 3665). It costs £6, and begins at Flannigan's (above the Crown Bar on Great Victoria St) on Thursday at 7pm and Saturday at 4pm.

Special Events

For three weeks in late October and early November, Belfast hosts the UK's second largest arts festival at the **Festival at Queen's** (☎ 9066 7687), in and around Queen's University. Also worth checking out is the new-ish **Cathedral Quarter Arts Festival** (**w** www.cqaf.com) in early May, which has been attracting a good range of writers, comedians, musicians and artists and theatre productions. The **Summerfest** (☎ 9032 0202), also held in May, offers classical music, community events and the Lord Mayor's Show.

Places to Stay

Camping The only camping option in the Belfast area is **Jordanstown Lough Shore Park** (☎ 86 3133; sites £7), 8km to the north on Shore Rd (A2) in Newtownabbey. There's a two-night maximum stay.

Hostels The friendly, if scruffy, **Arnie's Backpackers** (☎ 9024 2867; 63 Fitzwilliam St; dorm beds £7-8.50) has small dorms, laundry and cooking facilities, and two attention-seeking dogs. However, with only 22 beds, demand for space far exceeds supply.

The HINI **Belfast International Youth Hostel** (☎ 9031 5435; **w** www.belfasthostel.com; 22-32 Donegall Rd; dorm beds up to £9, private/twin rooms £16/24) is large (112 beds), modern and very clean. There's a laundry and small café and kitchen.

The Ark (☎ 9032 9626; 18 University St; dorm beds £8.50-9.50, twins per person £16) has 31 beds in four- or six-bed dorms. The bunks are squeaky. At the other (north) end of the central city area is **The Linen**

House Hostel (☎ 9058 6400; 18-20 Kent St; dorm beds £6.50-8.50, singles/doubles £15/24), which is scruffy and well past its prime and probably only remains popular owing to its location near the city centre and the increasingly cool Cathedral Quarter.

Queen's Elms (☎ 9038 1608; 78 Malone Rd; rooms UK/international/nonstudents £8.50/10/12.40, twins £44.40; open June-end Sept), run by the university, offers excellent accommodation. There are cooking and laundry facilities.

B&Bs The **Belfast Welcome Centre** (☎ 9024 6609) makes B&B reservations for a minimal fee; credit-card bookings can be made over the phone. Many B&Bs are in the university area, which is close to the centre, safe and well-stocked with restaurants and pubs. Botanic Ave, Malone Rd, Wellington Park and Eglantine Ave are good hunting grounds.

The clean and friendly **Queen's House** (☎ 9028 2091; **e** queenshouse127@hotmail.com; 127 University St; singles/doubles £20/40), opposite the Holiday Inn Express, is good value, with a weekly rate of £100 per person.

The **Botanic Lodge Guesthouse** (☎ 9032 7682; 87 Botanic Ave; singles/doubles £25/40) has TV in all rooms. Also in the popular university area, **Windermere Guesthouse** (☎ 9066 2693; Wellington Park; rooms per person £24) has small but comfy rooms overlooking a quiet street.

The **Pearl Court House** (☎ 9066 6145; **e** pearlcourtgh@hotmail.com; 11 Malone Rd; singles/doubles £26/48) offers basic accommodation, or you could try **Liserin Guesthouse** (☎ 9066 0769; 17 Eglantine Ave; singles/doubles with shower & TV £22/40).

Hotels At the **Holiday Inn Express** (☎ 9031 1909, fax 9031 1910; 106a University St; rooms £60, weekends per night £55), rates include continental breakfast. Its weekend rate is great value.

In the city centre, **Jury's Inn** (☎ 9053 3500; College Square; triples weekends/weekdays £60/71) is a moderately priced three-star hotel.

Places to Eat

Pubs The **Duke of York** (lunches around £5.50) is not only a great old-fashioned Belfast boozer, it also serves sandwiches starting from £1.50 and excellent solid lunches. It's hidden away down Commercial Court, off Donegall St, and has faded signs directing the way.

Bittle's Bar is a small pub entered from 70 Upper Church Lane. It specialises in traditional dishes like sausages and *champ* (an Ulster speciality of mashed potatoes and spring onions).

White's Tavern (Wine Cellar entry between Rosemary and High Sts) is one of Belfast's most historic taverns and a popular lunchtime meeting spot. **Kitchen Bar** *(Victoria Square)* is another popular lunch spot.

Above the Crown Liquor Saloon, **Flannigan's** (☎ 9027 9901) does cheap, hearty pub grub as well as mammoth, cheap breakfasts for around £5.

The huge new **Wetherspoon's** *(Bedford St; mains around £5)*, almost opposite Ormeau Ave, has some very cheap lunch deals.

Restaurants Decent places are opening in the city centre all the time and around the Cathedral Quarter, although the greatest concentration of budget restaurants is along the Golden Mile from Dublin Rd south to University Rd and Botanic Ave.

Ba Soba (☎ 9058 686; 38 Hill St; mains around £5-7.50), around the corner from St Anne's Cathedral, is a smart new noodle restaurant from the Wagamama mould.

Nick's Warehouse (☎ 9043 9690; 34-39 Hill St; meals £7-14), across from Ba Soba, is a lovely bustling place with a varied menu, great seafood, a buzzing atmosphere and a good wine list. **Tesco** (Royal Ave) is a short walk west of the Cathedral quarter.

Central places include **Cafe Aero** (☎ 9024 4844; 44 Bedford St; mains from £6) is a small, bright new place with an inventive menu; and **La Belle Epoque** (61 Dublin Rd; lunch specials £6.25; open Mon-Sat), which serves basic French fare. The smart **Cayenne** (☎ 9033 1532; 7 Shaftesbury Square; 2-/3-course set lunch £10/23, 3-course set dinner £26), owned by feted TV chef Paul Rankin, has a reputation for great food.

Around the university and golden mile, **Villa Italia** (37-41 University Rd; open dinner only), a vibrant Italian restaurant and pizzeria, is perennially popular.

Botanic Ave has lots of cafés. **The Other Place** (79 Botanic Ave) is lively and good for coffee. **Cafe Renoir** (95 Botanic Ave) serves freshly baked bread and cake, wraps, appealing vegie options and good coffee, making this small modern chain a lunchtime winner.

Cafe Conor (11a Stranmillis Rd), formerly the studio of artist William Conor, makes a lovely, light-filled spot for a coffee or post-Ulster Museum meal.

Entertainment

Belfast's main guide to what's on is the *Big List*, available at cafés, pubs or online at **w** www.thebiglist.co.uk.

A few years ago the city centre's pubs and clubs were packed at lunch and empty or closed in the evenings, but this is rapidly changing and there's far more going on in the centre at night. The pubs along the Golden Mile are abuzz after dark most nights.

Two great Belfast city centre institutions are **Robinsons** (Great Victoria St) with its many bars and, connected directly through double doors, **Fibber Magee's** (Blackstaff Square), which often has live music.

Across the road the rowdy **Beaten Docket** (Great Victoria St) is also busy at night. The legendary **Crown Liquor Saloon** (Great Victoria St) is a splendid place with fine, ostentatious late-Victorian architecture and discreet panelled snugs. Prop up the long bar though and you'll really appreciate the magnificence of the place.

Several smart, dressy new places include **Apartment** (Donegall Square West), overlooking Donegall Square City Hall, and the nearby **Red Bar** (cnr Linenhall St & Donegall Square South) attracting a younger professional crowd.

The student-filled **Globe** (formerly the Elms; 36 University Rd) has a good atmosphere, but can get packed. Further south and facing each other across Malone Rd are the **Eglantine Inn** and the **Botanic**, the 'Egg and Bott'. Of the two, the Botanic is probably the more beloved by students past and present. It can be a bit of a meat market, but the atmosphere is good. If you crave a quiet pint try the **Elbow** (Dublin Rd).

Limelight (17 Ormeau Ave) is a stayer in the Belfast nightclub and live music world. **Empire Music Hall** (42 Botanic Ave), a barnlike pub inside a former church, has live music three nights a week and a stand-up comedy night. Larger classical and pop music events are staged at the impressive **Waterfront Hall** (☎ 9033 4455; 2 Lanyon Place).

The **Milk Bar** (☎ 9027 8876; Tomb St) attracts top-name electronica DJs and has music nightly. The **John Hewitt** (☎ 9023 3768; 51

Donegall St) in the nearby Cathedral Quarter is a lively and pleasant place for pre-clubbing drinks.

The **Queen's Film Theatre** (☎ *toll free 0800-328 28 11; University Square Mews)* has independent, classic, cult and arthouse films. There's often a musical, opera or ballet on at the **Grand Opera House** (☎ *9024 1919)*, and something less formal at the **Civic Arts Theatre** (☎ *9031 6900; Botanic Ave)*.

The new **Odyssey complex** (☎ *9073 9074;* W *www.odysseyarena.com; Queen's Quay Rd)*, across the river from the Seacat Terminal, contains Belfast's **IMAX** cinema (☎ *9078 4000, 9045 2515)*.

Getting There & Away

There's a **Usit Now office** (☎ *9032 4073; 13b Fountain Centre)* in College St. For security reasons there are no left-luggage facilities at Belfast train or bus stations. For all Ulsterbus, Northern Ireland Railways (NIR) and local bus information call ☎ 9089 9411. Rail and bus information is also available from **Translink** (☎ *9066 6630;* W *www.translink.co.uk)*.

Air There are flights from some regional airports in Britain to the convenient **Belfast city airport** (☎ *9093 9093; Airport Rd)*, but everything else goes to **Belfast international airport** (☎ *9448 4848)*, 30km north of the city in Aldergrove by the M2.

Bus Belfast has two separate bus stations. The smaller of the two is the **Laganside Buscentre** *(Oxford St)*, near the river, with bus connections to counties Antrim, Down and Derry. Buses to everywhere else in Northern Ireland, the Republic, the international airport and the Larne ferries, leave from the bigger **Europa Buscentre** *(Glengall St)*. Regional bus timetables are free at the bus stations.

There are seven daily Belfast–Dublin buses (five on Sunday) that take about three hours and start at £10.30 one way. For connections to Derry and Donegal, contact the **Lough Swilly Bus Company** (☎ *7126 2017)* in Derry.

Train Belfast has two main train stations – **Great Victoria St**, next to the Europa Buscentre, and the **Belfast Central** *(East Bridge St)*, east of the city centre.

Destinations served from Belfast Central include Derry and Dublin. Dublin–Belfast trains

(£20/30 one way/return, two hours) run up to six times a day (three on Sunday). From Belfast Central a free (with your bus or train ticket) Centrelink bus to Donegall Square in the city centre leaves every 10 minutes. A local train also connects with Great Victoria St.

Great Victoria St station has services to Derry and Larne Harbour.

For tickets and information contact **NIR** (☎ *9089 9411; open 9am-5pm Mon-Fri, 9am-noon Sat)* at Great Victoria St station.

Boat See the Getting There & Away section at the beginning of this chapter for more details on ferries to/from Northern Ireland.

From Belfast there are three main ferry routes connecting Belfast to Stranraer, Liverpool and the Isle of Man.

Belfast's ferry terminal, on Donegall Quay a short walk north of the city centre, is used by boats to Troon, Heysham and the Isle of Man.

Norse Merchant Ferries (☎ *9077 9090)* to Liverpool leave from Victoria terminal, 5km north of central Belfast; take a bus from Europa Buscentre or catch a taxi (£7 to £10). Stena Line services to Stranraer leave from nearby Corry Rd.

Getting Around

Airbus buses link Belfast international airport with the Europa Buscentre every 30 minutes (£5, 35 minutes). A taxi costs about £20.

The Belfast city airport is only 6km northeast of the centre, and you can cross the road from the terminal to the Sydenham Halt station, from which trains run to Botanic station for less than £1.

A short trip on a bus costs £0.50 to £0.90. Most local bus services depart from Donegall Square, near the City Hall, where there is a ticket kiosk.

If you're driving, be fastidious about where you park; car theft is a serious problem here. The tourist office has a free leaflet showing all the multistorey car parks.

McConvey Cycles (☎ *9033 0322; 182 Ormeau Rd)* rents bikes for £10 a day or £40 a week. A £50 deposit is required.

THE BELFAST–DERRY COASTAL ROAD

Ireland isn't short of fine stretches of coast, but the Causeway Coast stretching from Portstewart in County Derry to Ballycastle in County Antrim, and the Antrim Coast stretching from

Ballycastle to Belfast, taking in the striking rock formations of the Giant's Causeway, are as magnificent as they come.

From late May to late September, Ulsterbus' Antrim Coaster bus No 252 operates twice daily (except Sunday) between Belfast and Coleraine (four hours), stopping at all the main tourist sights. An open-topped Bushmills Bus (No 177) runs from the Giant's Causeway to Coleraine five times daily in July and August. The trip takes just over an hour. Bus No 162 runs year-round along the Antrim coast between Larne and Cushendun.

Carrickfergus

Only 13km northeast of Belfast is Carrickfergus and its impressive Norman **castle** (☎ 9335 1273; admission £2.70; open 10am-6pm Mon-Sat, 2pm-6pm Sun Apr-Sept, 10am-4pm Mon-Sat Oct-Mar), which was built in 1180 by John de Courcy and overlooks the harbour where William III landed in 1690. A small museum documents the castle's long history (it was occupied up until 1928).

There are no hostels in Carrickfergus; the cheapest B&B is **Langsgarden** (☎ 9336 6369; 70-72 Scottish Quarter; singles/doubles £18/20).

Glens of Antrim

Between Larne and Ballycastle, the nine Glens of Antrim are extremely picturesque stretches of woodland and downland where streams cascade into the sea. The picture-perfect port of **Cushendall** has been dubbed the 'Capital of the Glens', while **Glenariff**, a few kilometres to the south, lays claim to the title 'Queen of the Glens'. Between Cushendun and Ballycastle, eschew the main A2 road for the narrower and more picturesque B92, and take the turn-off down to sweeping Murlough Bay.

A good bet for a budget bed, and possibly a bedtime story, is at the modern **Ballyeamon Camping Barn** (☎ 2175 8699, 07703 440558; W www.taleteam.demon.co.uk; dorm beds £8) near Cushendall on the B14. The proprietor is a professional storyteller.

Ballycastle

Ballycastle, where the Atlantic Ocean meets the Irish Sea, is a quiet harbour town and a natural base for exploring the coasts to the west or south.

The IHH/IHO **Castle Hostel** (☎ 2076 2337; 62 Quay Rd; dorm beds £7) is just past the Marine Hotel. It's clean, welcoming and spacious. The IHO **Ballycastle Backpackers** (☎ 2076 3612; 4 North St; dorm beds £6) is near the waterfront and the main bus stop.

Carrick-a-Rede Island

The 20m **rope bridge** (admission free; open April-Sept, closed during strong winds), connecting Carrick-a-Rede Island to the mainland, is fun to stagger across, swaying some 25m above pounding waves. The island is the site of a salmon fishery and a nesting ground for gulls and fulmars. It's free to cross the bridge, but parking costs £3; it's a 1.25km walk from there to the bridge.

Giant's Causeway

Chances are you've seen pictures of the Giant's Causeway (Clochán an Aifir), Northern Ireland's main tourist attraction. The hexagonal basalt columns, all 38,000 of them (that's counting the ones under the water), are amazingly uniform. According to one of the legends that claim to explain the causeway's existence, the giant in question, Finn McCool, fancied a female giant on the Scottish island of Staffa and built some stepping stones to the island where similar rock formations are found.

The more prosaic explanation is that lava erupted from an underground fissure and crystallised some 60 million years ago. The phenomenon is quite clearly explained in the **Causeway Visitors Centre** (☎ 2073 1855) by a new exhibition and audiovisual for £1.50.

It costs nothing to make the pleasant 1.5km pilgrimage to the actual site, although car parking is an exorbitant £5. About four buses a day (more in summer and fewer on Sunday) between Portrush and Ballycastle pass by the Giant's Causeway.

To reach the causeway itself, take one of two circular footpaths, which start from outside the visitors centre. For the less mobile or the downright lazy, a minibus shuttles from the Visitors Centre to the Causeway for £0.80 one way or £1.20 return.

It's worth walking on the path about 1.5km further east to some more striking rock formations and cliff vistas. Landslides have closed the path here, but it is worth peeping past the fencing for some lovely views.

A recommended walk is from the Giant's Causeway 16km east along the coast (not the highway), past Dunseverick Castle to the beach at Whitepark Bay. Be careful if you

IRELAND

walk this route, however, as the windy clifftop conditions have been known to send walkers over the edge. A great place to crash at the end is the terrific, modern HINI **Whitepark Bay Hostel** (☎ 2073 1745; dorm beds from £11, singles/twins from £13/26; open year-round), with bay views and smart en-suite dorms and rooms.

Bushmills

Bushmills, 4km southwest of the Giant's Causeway, is a small town off the A2 between Portrush and Ballycastle. The town itself is a tad dull; the real attraction, 500m south of the main square, is the **Old Bushmills Distillery** (☎ 2073 3272; admission £4). After a noisy tour of the industrial process (it's quieter on weekends, when production is halted), there's a whiskey-tasting session.

From April to October distillery tours leave every 20 to 30 minutes from 9.30am to 4pm daily (Sunday from noon). In the low season, tours leave weekdays at 10.30am, 11.30am, 1.30pm, 2.30pm and 3.30pm.

The town also boasts an excellent new HINI **Bushmills Hostel** (☎ 2073 1222; 49 Main St; dorm beds £12) and makes a good base for visits to the Causeway Coast.

Dunluce Castle

Abandoned back in 1641, the ruins of 14th-century Dunluce Castle (☎ 2073 1938; admission £1.50; open 10am-5.30pm Mon-Sat, 2pm-6pm Sun Apr-Sept, 10am-4pm Mon-Sat, 2pm-4pm Sun Oct-Mar), between Bushmills and Portrush, is dramatically sited right on the cliff edge – so close, in fact, that its kitchen once collapsed into the sea. Perched 30m above the sea, the castle was of obvious military value, and there are extensive remains inside the walls, giving a good idea of life here.

Portstewart, Portrush & Downhill

These seaside resorts are only a few kilometres apart. The pleasant Portstewart has a slightly decayed, early 20th century feel to it, while Downhill boasts a lovely long stretch of beach.

Portstewart's **Causeway Coast Hostel** (☎ 7083 3789; 4 Victoria Terrace; dorm beds £7, private rooms £17) is at the eastern end of town.

Harder to get to, but well worth the effort, is the lovely independent **Downhill Hostel** (☎ 7084 9077; e downhillhostel@hotmail .com; 12 Mussenden Rd, Downhill; dorm

beds/doubles £7.50/20), a friendly place with open fires, and a good library of books and vinyl in a solid converted period house overlooking the beach. Pick-ups can be arranged from Castlerock train station. The No 134 bus also passes nearby on its way between Coleraine and Limavady. Bring supplies as there are no shops in Downhill.

DERRY
pop 72,330

Derry or Londonderry? Even choosing what you call Northern Ireland's second largest city can be a political statement. In practice it's better known as Derry, whatever your politics.

Doire, the original Irish name, means 'oak grove', and the 'London' prefix was added after settlers from London Guilds, the companies that built the city walls, were granted much of the land in the area by James I.

In the 1960s, great resentment at the long-running domination and gerrymandering of the city council by Protestants boiled over in the (Catholic-dominated) civil rights marches of 1968. Simultaneously, perceived attacks by the RUC on the Catholic Bogside district began, leading to days of rioting. The British government decided that open warfare could only be prevented by military intervention, and on 14 August 1968 British troops entered Derry. In January 1972, 'Bloody Sunday' resulted in the deaths of 14 unarmed Catholic civil rights marchers in Derry at the hands of the British army, an event that marked the beginning of the Troubles in earnest. At the time of writing the lengthy inquiry into the events of Bloody Sunday was continuing in Derry's Guildhall.

Today Derry is as safe to visit as anywhere else in Northern Ireland.

The arts are alive, and festivals, such the Foyle Film Festival, draw crowds from everywhere. Halloween is widely and enthusiastically celebrated.

Orientation

The old centre of Derry is the small, walled city on the west bank of the River Foyle. The heart of the walled city is The Diamond, intersected by four main roads: Shipquay St, Ferryquay St, Bishop St Within and Butcher St. The Catholic Bogside area is below the walls to the northwest. To the south is a Protestant estate known as the Fountain. The Waterside district across the river is mostly Protestant.

Information

Derry's **NITB tourist office** (☎ 7126 7284) and **Bord Fáilte** (☎ 7136 9501) share an impressive, modern stone office just outside the walled city at the **Tourist Information Centre** (44 Foyle St). Together they cover the whole of Ireland, are tirelessly helpful and are open 9am to 5pm Monday to Friday year-round. The NITB office has extended hours in summer and opens on Saturday from mid-March to June and is open all week from July to September.

The **main post office** (Custom House St) is just north of the Tower Museum.

At **Central Library** (☎ 7127 2300; 35 Foyle St) you can access the Internet free until 1pm (£2.50 per hour after). It's wise to book ahead. **Wringers Laundrette** (☎ 7126 6006; 141 Strand Rd) has a snack bar and offers cheap deals for students.

Things to See

Until the mid-1990s, the presence of the army and protective iron gates made Derry's magnificent **city walls** hard to appreciate. The gates are still there, but now they're open and it's possible to walk all around the walls, built between 1613 and 1618. They're about 8m high, 9m thick, and go around the old city for a length of 1.5km. A major highlight for the traveller, and a must-walk, the gates give an excellent overview of Bogside (itself worth a closer look on foot) and its defiant **murals**, one notably proclaiming 'You Are Now Entering Free Derry'. From the city walls between Butcher's Gate and the army barracks, you can see many of the in-your-face building-side murals.

Just inside Coward's Bastion to the north, O'Doherty's Tower is home to the excellent **Tower Museum** (☎ 7137 2411; admission £4.20; open 10am-5pm Tues-Sat Sept-June, 10am-5pm Mon-Sat, 2pm-5pm Sun July & Aug), which traces the story of Derry from the days of St Columbcille to the present.

The fine red-brick **Guildhall**, just outside the city walls, was originally built in 1890 and is noted for its stained-glass windows. There's no access while the Bloody Sunday inquiry is being held here, but you can sneak into the foyer to take a peek at the windows.

Austere **St Columb's Cathedral** (admission £1) dates from 1628 and stands at the southern end of the walled city, off Bishop St Within. It's £2 extra if you want to take photos.

Organised Tours

Both **Derry City Guided Walking Tours** (☎ 7127 1996; 11 Carlisle Rd) and the **Derry Visitor & Convention Bureau**, in the Tourist Information Centre (☎ 7126 7284), have walking tours of the City Walls and around for £4.

Places to Stay

There are only two hostels in Derry, so consider booking ahead. The larger of the two is the HINI **Derry City Hostel** (☎ 7128 0280; 6 Magazine St; dorm beds £10-13, doubles £35), in the walled city near Butcher's Gate, just 150m from the bus station.

Not as formal is **Steve's Backpackers** (☎ 7137 7989; 4 Asylum Rd; dorm beds/private rooms per person £9/12; open year-round), a small, basic but friendly hostel north of the walled city. From Butchers Gate follow Waterloo St until it turns into Strand Rd, walk for about 500m and turn left onto Asylum Rd. There is no checkout time, a light breakfast and free Internet access are included in rates, and the fifth night is free.

Within walking distance of the bus station is the friendly **Acorn House** (☎ 7127 1156; 17 Aberfoyle Terrace, Strand Rd; singles/doubles from £20/32). **Clarence House** (☎ 7126 5342; e clarencehouse@zoom.co.uk; 15 Northland Rd; singles/doubles £19/50) is a friendly place in a pleasant period house with good (and varied) buffet breakfasts.

The **City of Derry Travelodge** (☎ 1800 709 709; 22-24 Strand Rd; rooms from £42) offers reasonable central accommodation.

Places to Eat

Just outside the Ferryquay Gate, southeast of the walled city, modern **Fitzroy's** has entrances at 3 Carlisle Rd and 2–4 Bridge St, and moves from cool café to sophisticated mains at night. **The Sandwich Company** (The Diamond) is handy for a simple lunch or coffee break. Just opposite, the new Wetherspoon's-owned **The Diamond** serves very good-value pub grub until 10pm nightly.

In the made-for-tourists **Craft Village** (Shipquay St), **Thran Maggies** (mains from £4.95; open to at least 9.15pm) serves cheap, basic Irish dishes and is one of the few places to eat in the walled city after dark. Whenever it's sunny the outdoor tables are packed.

The Strand Bar (Strand Rd; meals from £8.95), about 200m from the northern corner of the walled city, has meals upstairs, along with a pub, nightclub and live music. **Indigo** (☎ 7127 1011; 27 Shipquay St; mains £4.50) is a modern café/restaurant serving cuisine from around the world.

Tesco has a large supermarket in the Quayside Shopping Centre on Strand Rd.

Entertainment

Derry's liveliest pubs are those situated along Waterloo St: **The Gweedore Bar**; **Tracy's**; and **Peadar O'Donnell's**, which is good for traditional music. **McGinley's** (Foyle St) also has live music six nights a week. The **Metro Bar** (3-4 Bank Place), just inside the walls, is Derry's trendiest (and most crowded) pub.

There are several theatres in Derry, with something for most tastes. The newest and spiffiest is **The Millennium Forum** (☎ 7126 4455; W www.millenniumforum.co.uk; New Market St) with several performance spaces used for theatre, dance, musicals, comedy and concerts.

The **Orchard Gallery** (☎ 7126 9675; Orchard St) has contemporary art shows with works from Ireland and elsewhere. **The Verbal Arts Centre** (☎ 7126 6946; Stable Lane), near Bishop's Gate, focuses on the literary tradition of Derry and its surrounds.

The Nerve Centre (☎ 7126 0562; W www .nerve-centre.org.uk; 7-8 Magazine St) is a multimedia venue with music, art-house cinema and café and bar. It also has workshops and studios for the development of creative technologies, including animation, film and music.

Getting There & Away

City of Derry airport (☎ 7181 0784) is about 13km east of Derry along the A2. Ryanair flies twice daily to Stanstead airport (outside London) and British Airways flies to Dublin, Glasgow and Manchester.

The **Ulsterbus station** (☎ 7126 2261) is just outside the city walls, on Foyle St near the Guildhall. There are frequent services between Belfast and Derry. Bus No 212, the Maiden City Flyer, is the fastest (1¾ hours); a one-way ticket costs £7.80. There are also semifrequent connections to Portrush and Portstewart. Each day at 9am a bus leaves Derry for Cork in the Republic, arriving at 7.15pm. Bus Éireann has a Derry–Galway service three times daily, via Donegal and Sligo.

Lough Swilly Bus Service (☎ 7126 2017), with an office upstairs at the Ulsterbus station, serves County Donegal across the border and has an £22 eight-day unlimited travel offer from May to September.

Air Porter Buses (☎ 7126 9996) run seven daily services (four at weekends) between Belfast airport and Derry for £15.

Derry's **Waterside train station** (☎ 9066 6630) lies across the Foyle River from the centre, but is connected to it by a free Linkline bus. There are seven trains daily to Belfast (three on Sunday; three hours) via Portrush.

ENNISKILLEN & LOUGH ERNE

Enniskillen, the main town of County Fermanagh, is handy for activities on Upper and Lower Lough Erne. Enniskillen itself is bland, with only one notable sight – **Enniskillen Castle** (☎ 6632 5000; admission £2; castle & museums open 10am-5pm Tues-Fri, 2pm-5pm Mon year-round, also 2pm-5pm Sat May-Sept, 2pm-5pm Sun Jul & Aug), home to the Fermanagh History & Heritage Centre and a museum dedicated to the Royal Inniskilling Fusiliers.

The town centre is on an island in the Erne River, which connects the upper and lower lakes. The very helpful **tourist office** (☎ 6632 3110; Wellington Rd; open daily Easter-Sept, Mon-Fri Oct-Easter) is about 100m from the centre; staff are knowledgeable about **boating** and **fishing** on Lough Erne.

Between May and September – from the Round 'O' Jetty at Brook Park – the **MV Kestrel** waterbus (☎ 6632 2882) operates 1½-hour tours (£7) of the lower lough, which includes a visit to **Devenish Island**, with its 9th-century church and one of the best round-towers in Ireland.

At White Island, close to the eastern shore of the lough, there's a line of eight mysterious statues, dating from around the 6th century. From April to September, a ferry runs across to White Island from the Castle Archdale marina, 20km north of Enniskillen on the Kesh road. The return fare is £3.

Marble Arch Caves (☎ 6634 8855; admission £6; open 10am-4.30pm daily mid-Mar–Sept), 16km southwest of Enniskillen via the A4 and A32, is Ireland's most extensive cave network. The 1½-hour tours are popular and it's wise to book ahead.

If you're driving through County Fermanagh to/from Derry, don't miss the excellent

Ulster-American Folk Park (☎ 8224 3292; admission £4; open daily Apr-Sept, 10.30am-3.30pm Mon-Fri Oct-Mar) on the A5 in Castletown, 8km northwest of Omagh. This open-air museum has impressive life-size exhibits: a forge, weaver's cottage, 19th-century Ulster street, and an early street from the US state of Pennsylvania (where many Ulster emigrants settled).

Places to Stay
In Enniskillen there is hostel-style accommodation and a camp site at **Lakeland Canoe Centre** (☎ 6632 4250; tent sites/dorm beds £10), on Castle Island, which is reached by free ferry from the Fermanagh Lakeland Forum southeast of the tourist office (press the bell on the jetty or call to be picked up). The brand new **Bridges Hostel** (☎ 6634 0110; e info@hini.org.uk) was due to open in 2002 in the Bill Clinton Building in the centre of Eniskillen. The HINI **Castle Archdale Youth Hostel** (☎ 6862 8118; open Mar-Oct) is 19km northwest of Enniskillen near the White Island ferry.

Rossole House B&B (☎ 6632 3462; 85 Sligo Rd; doubles £40), on the edge of town, is pleasantly located overlooking a lake with its own rowing boat.

Getting There & Around
Enniskillen's **Ulsterbus station** (☎ 6632 2633; Shore Rd) is across from the tourist office. There are up to 10 services a day to Belfast via Dungannon (two hours). Buses also run to Derry (3¼ hours) and Cork (11¼ hours) via Omagh (one hour). From Omagh, there are express buses to Dublin.

Bicycles can be hired at the Lakeland Canoe Centre for about £10 a day.

IRELAND

Getting There & Around

Places to Stay

Italy

Tell people you're going to Italy and they'll sigh, even if they haven't been there. A place of myth, history, artistic achievement, romantic imagery and all manner of cliches, it stirs peoples hearts with both its simplicity and complexity. As Luigi Barzini wrote in *The Italians*: 'Italy is still a country of limitless opportunities. It offers stage settings for all kinds of adventures, licit or illicit loves, the study of art, the experience of pathos, the weaving of intrigues. It can be gay, tragic, mad, pastoral, archaic, modern, or simply *dolce*.' Many come to Italy to escape their daily lives and to feel more alive in the process. Soak up what's on offer – this is a country that understands, or seems to. However, if you're after efficient bureaucracy or sensitive urban planning outside of city centres, look elsewhere.

Facts about Italy

HISTORY
The traditional date for the founding of Rome by Romulus is 753 BC, but the country had already been inhabited for thousands of years. Palaeolithic Neanderthals lived in Italy during the last ice age more than 20,000 years ago, and by the start of the Bronze Age, around 2000 BC, the peninsula had been settled by several Italic tribes.

From about 900 BC the Etruscan civilisation developed, until these mysterious people dominated the area between the Arno and Tiber Valleys. After the foundation of Rome, Etruscan civilisation continued to flourish until the end of the 3rd century BC, when the Romans overwhelmed the last Etruscan city.

The Roman Republic
The new Roman republic, after recovering from the invasion of the Gauls in 390 BC, began its expansion into southern Italy. Rome claimed Sicily following the Second Punic War against Hannibal in 241 BC, after his crossing of the Alps. Rome defeated Carthage in 202 BC and a few years later claimed Spain and Greece.

Expansion & Empire
In the 1st century BC, under Julius Caesar, Rome conquered Gaul and moved into Egypt.

At a Glance

- **Rome** – phenomenal concentration of history, legend, monuments and artistic treasures
- **Venice** – wandering narrow streets, gondala rides along winding canals
- **Florence** – cradle of the Renaissance, with easy daytrips to the Tuscany countryside
- **Amalfi Coast** – dramatic cliffs, clear blue water, hillside villages
- **Mt Etna, Sicily** – hikes up one of the world's most active volcanoes (and Europe's largest)

Capital	Rome
Population	57.8 million
Official Language	Italian
Currency	euro
Time	GMT/UTC+0100
Country Phone Code	☎ 39

After Caesar's assassination by Brutus on the Ides of March in 44 BC, a power struggle began between Mark Antony and Octavius, leading to the deaths of Antony and Cleopatra in Egypt in 31 BC and the establishment of the Roman Empire in 27 BC. Octavius, who had been adopted by Julius Caesar as his son and heir, took the title of Augustus Caesar and became the first emperor. Augustus ruled for 45 years, a period of great

ITALY (ITALIA)

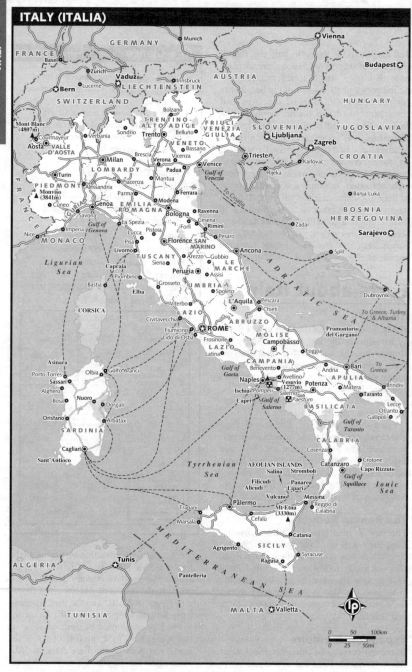

advancement in engineering, architecture, administration and literature.

The Eastern & Western Empires

By the end of the 3rd century, the empire had grown to such an extent that Emperor Diocletian divided it between east and west for administrative purposes. His successor, Constantine, declared religious freedom for Christians and moved the seat of power to the eastern capital, Byzantium, which he renamed Constantinople. During the 4th century, Christianity was declared the official state religion and grew in power and influence.

By the early 5th century, German tribes had entered Rome, and in 476 the Western Roman Empire ended when the German warrior, Odoacer, deposed the emperor and declared himself ruler of Italy. The south and Sicily were dominated by Arab raiders until the Normans invaded in 1036.

The City-States & the Renaissance

The Middle Ages in Italy were marked by the development of powerful city-states in the north. This was the time of Dante, Petrarch and Boccaccio, Giotto, Cimabue and Pisano.

In the 15th century the Renaissance, which began in Florence, spread throughout the country, fostering genius of the likes of Brunelleschi, Donatello, Bramante, Botticelli, da Vinci, Masaccio, Lippi, Raphael and Michelangelo.

By the early 16th century much of the country was under Spanish rule. This lasted until 1713 when, following the War of Spanish Succession, control of Italy passed to the Austrians. After the invasion by Napoleon in 1796 a degree of unity was introduced into Italy, for the first time since the fall of the Roman Empire.

The Risorgimento

In the 1860s Italy's unification movement (The Risorgimento) gained momentum, and in 1861 the Kingdom of Italy was declared under the rule of King Vittorio Emanuele. Venice was wrested from Austria in 1866 and Rome from the papacy in 1870.

Mussolini & WWII

In the years after WWI, Italy was in turmoil. In 1921 the Fascist Party, formed by Benito Mussolini in 1919, won 35 of the 135 seats in parliament. In October 1921, after a period of considerable unrest and strikes, the king asked Mussolini to form a government, whereupon he became prime minister with only 7% representation in parliament.

Mussolini formed the Rome-Berlin axis with Hitler in 1936 and Italy entered WWII as an ally of Germany in June 1941. After a series of military disasters and an invasion by the Allies in 1943, the king led a coup against Mussolini and had him arrested. After being rescued by the Germans, Mussolini tried to govern in the north, but was fiercely opposed by Italian partisans, who killed him in April 1945.

The Italian Republic

In 1946, following a referendum, the constitutional monarchy was abolished and the republic established. Italy was a founding member of the European Economic Community in 1957 (forerunner of the European Union; EU) and was seriously disrupted by terrorism in the 1970s, thanks to the Red Brigades, who kidnapped and assassinated Prime Minister Aldo Moro in 1978.

In the decades following WWII, Italy's national government was dominated by the centre-right Christian Democrats, usually in coalition with other parties (excluding the Communists). Italy enjoyed significant economic growth in the 1980s, but the 1990s heralded a period of crisis for the country, both economically and politically.

The 1990s to the Present

Against the backdrop of a severe economic crisis, the very foundations of Italian politics were shaken by a national bribery scandal known as *tangentopoli* (bribesville). Investigations eventually implicated thousands of politicians, public officials and businesspeople, and left the main parties in tatters after the 1992 elections, effectively demolishing the centre of the political spectrum.

After a period of right-wing government, elections in 1996 brought a centre-left coalition known as the Olive Tree to power. A programme of fiscal austerity was ushered in to guarantee Italy's entry into Europe's economic and monetary union (EMU), which occurred in 1998. The current (since 2001) prime minister is Silvio Berluschoni, a controversial (to put it mildly) right-wing politico, whose party, 'Forza Italia', has proved popular in many quarters with its desire to make Italian bureaucracy (at the expense of state welfare) more efficient. He also owns *a lot* of the Italian media, which is a sore point for a great many people.

The Mafia

The 1990s saw Italy moving more decisively against the Sicilian Mafia (known in Sicily as *Cosa Nostra* – 'Our Thing'), prompted by the 1992 assassinations of prominent anti-Mafia judges Giovanni Falcone and Paolo Borsellino, which saw many Sicilians publicly protesting against the dishonourable conduct of the 'Men of Honour'. The testimonies of several *pentiti* (informers), led to important arrests – most notably of the Sicilian godfather, Salvatore 'Toto' Riina (serving a life sentence). The man believed to have taken power after Riina's arrest, Giovanni Brusca, was arrested in May 1996 and implicated in the aforementioned murders. He was imprisoned for 30 years in 1999. Subsequent high-profile arrests (such as Pietro Aglieri in 1997) have undoubtedly dented the Mafia's confidence, but this is an entrenched system, and the battle is both international and far from won.

GEOGRAPHY

The boot-shaped country, incorporating the islands of Sicily and Sardinia, is bound by the Adriatic, Ligurian, Tyrrhenian and Ionian Seas, which all form part of the Mediterranean Sea. About 75% of the Italian peninsula is mountainous, with the Alps dividing the country from France, Switzerland and Austria, and the Apennines forming a backbone which extends from the Alps into Sicily. There are four active volcanoes: Stromboli and Vulcano (in the Aeolian Islands), Etna (Sicily) and Vesuvius (near Naples).

CLIMATE

Italy lies in a temperate zone, but the climates of the north and south vary. Summers are uniformly hot, but are often extremely hot and dry in the south. Winters can be severely cold in the north – particularly in the Alps and the Po Valley – whereas they are mild in the south, Sicily and Sardinia.

ECOLOGY & ENVIRONMENT

The countryside can be dramatically beautiful, but the long presence of humans on the peninsula has had a significant impact on the environment. Aesthetically the result is not always displeasing – much of the beauty of Tuscany, for instance, lies in the interaction of olive groves with vineyards, fallow fields and stands of cypress and pine. Centuries of tree clearing, combined with illegal building have also led to extensive land degradation and erosion. The alteration of the environment, combined with the Italians' passion for hunting, has led to many native animals and birds becoming extinct, rare or endangered. Under progressively introduced laws, many animals and birds are now protected.

There are over 20 national parks in Italy. Among the most important are the Parco Nazionale del Gran Paradiso and the Parco Nazionale dello Stelvio, both in the Alps, and the Parco Nazionale d'Abruzzo.

Central and southern Italy are sometimes subject to massive earthquakes. A series of quakes devastated parts of the Appenine areas of Umbria and the Marches in September 1997.

GOVERNMENT & POLITICS

For administrative purposes Italy is divided into 20 regions, each of which have some degree of autonomy. The regions are then subdivided into provinces and municipalities.

The country is a parliamentary republic, headed by a president who appoints the prime minister. The parliament consists of a senate and chamber of deputies, which have equal legislative power. The national government is in Rome. Two-thirds of both houses are elected on the basis of who receives the most votes in their district (basically the same as the first-past-the-post system). The old (pre-1994) system produced unstable coalition governments, with 53 governments in 48 years between the declaration of the republic and the introduction of electoral reforms.

ECONOMY

Italy is the fifth-largest economy in the world, thanks to the 1980s. However, the severe economic crisis of 1992–93 prompted a

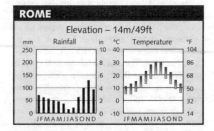

ROME
Elevation – 14m/49ft

succession of governments to pull the economy into line with Draconian measures, such as the partial privatisation of the huge public sector and reduced public spending.

Despite years of effort and the expenditure of trillions of lire for many years, a noticeable gap still exists between Italy's north and south. Italy's richest regions (Piedmont, Lombardy, Veneto and Emilia-Romagna) are northern, and its poorest (Calabria, Campania and Sicily) are southern.

POPULATION & PEOPLE

The population of Italy is 57.8 million. Surprisingly, the country has the lowest birthrate in Europe. Foreigners may like to think of Italy as a land of passionate, animated people who gesticulate wildly, love to eat, drive like maniacs and hate to work. However, it takes more than a holiday to understand Italy's vigorous, remarkably diverse inhabitants. Overall, people remain fiercely protective of regional dialects and cuisine.

ARTS
Architecture, Painting & Sculpture

Italy has often been called a living museum and it's not necessary to enter a gallery to appreciate the country's artistic wealth – it is everywhere as you walk through Florence, Venice, Siena, Rome, Naples or Palermo. In the south of Italy and in Sicily, where Greek colonisation preceded Roman domination, there are important Greek archaeological sites such as the temples at Paestum, south of Salerno, and Agrigento in Sicily. Pompeii and Herculaneum give an idea of how ancient Romans actually lived.

Byzantine mosaics adorn churches found throughout Italy, most notably at Ravenna, in the Basilica of San Marco in Venice, and in Palermo.

The 15th and early 16th centuries in Italy saw one of the most remarkable explosions of artistic and literary achievement in recorded history – the Renaissance. Patronised mainly by the Medici family in Florence and the popes in Rome, painters, sculptors, architects and writers flourished and many artists of genius emerged. The High Renaissance (about 1490–1520) was dominated by three men: Leonardo da Vinci (1452–1519), Michelangelo Buonarrotti (1475–1564) and Raphael (1483–1520).

The baroque period (17th century) was characterised by sumptuous, often fantastic architecture and richly decorative painting and sculpture. In Rome there are innumerable works by the great baroque sculptor and architect Gianlorenzo Bernini (1598–1680) and many works by Michelangelo Merisi da Caravaggio (1573–1610).

Neoclassicism in Italy produced the sculptor, Canova (1757–1822). Of the modern artists, Amedeo Modigliani (1884–1920) is perhaps the most famous. The early 20th century produced an artistic movement known as the Futurists, who rejected the sentimental art of the past and were infatuated by new technology, including modern warfare. Fascism produced its own style of architecture, characterised by the EUR satellite city and the work of Marcello Piacentini (1881–1960).

Music

The realms of opera and instrumental music have seen Italian artists take a dominant place. Antonio Vivaldi (1675–1741) created the concerto in its present form. Verdi, Puccini, Bellini, Donizetti and Rossini, composers from the 19th and early 20th centuries, are all stars of the modern operatic era. Tenor Luciano Pavarotti (1935–) has recently had his crown as 'King of Mother's Day CD Sales' taken by Andrea Bocelli (1958–), who soared to international stardom in the 1990s.

Literature

Before Dante wrote his *Divina Commedia* (Divine Comedy) and confirmed vernacular Italian as a serious medium for poetic expression, Latin was the language of writers. Among the greatest writers of ancient Rome were Cicero, Virgil, Ovid and Petronius.

A contemporary of Dante was Petrarch (1304–74). Giovanni Boccaccio (1313–75), author of the *Decameron,* is considered the first Italian novelist. *The Prince* by Machiavelli, a purely political work, has proved a lasting Renaissance work.

Italy's richest contribution to modern literature has been in the novel and short story. Southerner Carlo Levi based *Christ Stopped at Eboli* on his experiences in Basilicata. Leonardo Sciascia's taut writings on Sicilian themes posed as many questions as they appeared to answer. Umberto Eco's best-known work *The Name of the Rose* is a high-brow murder mystery of the first order.

Theatre

At a time when French playwrights ruled the stage, the Venetian Carlo Goldoni (1707–93) attempted to bring Italian theatre back into the limelight with the *commedia dell'arte*, the tradition of improvisational theatre. Sicilian Luigi Pirandello (1867–1936), author of *Six Characters in Search of an Author*, won the Nobel Prize in 1934. Modern Italian theatre's most enduring representative is actor/director Dario Fo, who won the Nobel Prize in 1998.

Cinema

In the 1940s Roberto Rossellini produced the neorealist masterpiece *Rome Open City* starring Anna Magnani. Vittorio de Sica directed the 1948 classic *Bicycle Thieves*. Schooled with the masters of neorealism, Federico Fellini took the creative baton from them and carried it into the following decades, with films such as *La Dolce Vita*. Michelangelo Antonioni's career reached a climax with 1967's *Blow-up*. Bernardo Bertolucci's international hits include *Last Tango in Paris, The Last Emperor, Stealing Beauty* and *Besieged*. Franco Zeffirelli's most-recent film was *Tea with Mussolini* (1998). Other notable directors include the Taviani brothers, Giuseppe Tornatore, Nanni Moretti and Roberto Benigni, director of the Oscar-winning *Life is Beautiful* (1998). One recent film that proved wildly popular in Italy and abroad is Gabriele Muccino's *L'Ultimo Bacio* (2001), which tells the story of a group of young Italian men grappling with life's and love's big questions.

SOCIETY & CONDUCT

It is difficult to make blanket assertions about Italian culture, because Italians have lived together as a nation for little over 100 years. Prior to unification, the peninsula was long subject to a varied mix of masters and cultures. This lack of unity contributed to the survival of local dialects and customs. Even today many Italians tend to identify more strongly with their region, or home town, than with the nation. An Italian is first and foremost a Tuscan or Sicilian, or even a Roman or Neapolitan.

In some parts of Italy, especially in the south, women might be harassed if they wear skimpy or see-through clothing. Modest dress is expected in all churches. Those that are major tourist attractions, such as St Peter's in Rome, strictly enforce dress codes (no hotpants, low-cut tops, bare shoulders or see-through garments – this goes for you too ladies).

RELIGION

Around 85% of Italians profess to be Catholic. The remaining 15% includes about 800,000 Muslims, 500,000 evangelical Protestants, 200,000 Jehovah's Witnesses and smaller communities of Jews, Waldenses and Buddhists.

LANGUAGE

English is most widely understood in the north, particularly in major centres such as Milan, Florence and Venice. Staff at most hotels and restaurants usually speak a little English, but you will be better received if you attempt to communicate in Italian.

Italian, a Romance language, is related to French, Spanish, Portuguese and Romanian. Modern literary Italian developed in the 13th and 14th centuries, predominantly through the works of Dante, Petrarch and Boccaccio, who wrote chiefly in the Florentine dialect. Although many dialects are spoken in everyday conversation, so-called standard Italian is the national language of schools, media and literature, and is understood throughout the country.

Many older Italians still expect to be addressed by the third-person formal, ie, *Lei* instead of *Tu*. It is not polite to use the greeting *ciao* when addressing strangers, unless they use it first; use *buongiorno* and *arrivederci*.

See the Language chapter at the back of this book for pronunciation guidelines and useful words and phrases.

Facts for the Visitor

HIGHLIGHTS

Coming up with a top 10 list for Italy is no easy task, given the wealth of must-see sights. Bearing that in mind, you could try the following:

1. Italian food and wine
2. Florence
3. Ancient ruins of Rome, Pompeii and Paestum
4. Venice
5. Siena
6. The Amalfi Coast
7. The Cinque Terre
8. The Aeolian Islands
9. The Dolomites
10. Palermo's mosaics and architecture

SUGGESTED ITINERARIES
Depending on the length of your stay, you might want to see and do the following things:

Two days
Visit Rome to see the Forum, the Colosseum, St Peter's Basilica and the Vatican museums.

One week
Visit Rome and Florence, with detours in Tuscany to Siena and San Gimignano. Or visit Rome and Naples, with detours to Pompeii, Vesuvius and the Amalfi Coast.

Two weeks
As above, plus Bologna, Verona, Ravenna and at least three days in Venice.

One month
Visit Rome, Florence, Venice and Naples, and explore the north, centre and south in greater detail, with stays in Liguria, Tuscany, Umbria, the Dolomites, Campania, Apulia, Basilicata, Sicily and Sardinia.

PLANNING
When to Go
The best time to visit Italy is in the off season, particularly April to June and September to October, when the weather is good, prices are lower and there are fewer tourists. During July and August (the high season) it is very hot, prices are inflated, the country swarms with tourists, and hotels by the sea and in the mountains are usually booked out. Note that many hotels and restaurants in seaside areas close down for the winter months.

Maps
Michelin map No 988 (1:1,000,000) covers the entire country. There is also a series of area maps at 1:400,000 – Nos 428 to 431 cover the mainland, No 432 covers Sicily and No 433 Sardinia.

If you're driving, note that Michelin's *Atlante Stradale e Turistico* (€18) is scaled at 1:300,000 and includes 74 town maps.

What to Bring
A backpack is a big advantage in Italy, but if you plan to use a suitcase and portable trolley, be warned about endless flights of stairs at some train stations and in many smaller medieval towns, as well as petty thieves who prey on tourists who have no hands free because they are carrying too much luggage. A small pack (with a lock) for use on day trips and for sightseeing is preferable to a handbag or shoulder bag, particularly in southern cities, where motorcycle bandits operate. A money-belt is essential in Italy, particularly in the south and Sicily, but also in major cities where groups of dishevelled-looking women and children prey on tourists with bulging pockets.

In the more mountainous areas the weather can change suddenly, even in high summer, so remember to bring at least one item of warm clothing. Most importantly, bring a pair of hardy, comfortable, worn-in walking shoes. In many cities, pavements are uneven and often made of cobblestones.

TOURIST OFFICES
Local Tourist Offices
There are three main categories of tourist office in Italy: regional, provincial and local. Their names vary throughout the country. Provincial offices are sometimes known as the Ente Provinciale per il Turismo (EPT) or, more commonly, the Azienda di Promozione Turistica (APT). The Azienda Autonoma di Soggiorno e Turismo (AAST) and Informazioni e Assistenza ai Turisti (IAT) offices usually have information only on the town itself. In some of the very small towns and villages the local tourist office is called a Pro Loco, and is often little more than a room with a desk. At most offices you should be able to get an *elenco degli alberghi* (list of hotels), a *pianta della città* (town map) and information on the major sights. Staff speak English in larger towns, but in the more out-of-the-way places it's Italian only. Tourist offices are generally open 8.30am to 12.30pm or 1pm and 3pm to 7pm Monday to Friday and on Saturday morning. Hours are usually extended in summer.

The Centro Turistico Studentesco e Giovanile (CTS) has offices all over Italy and specialises in discounts for students and young people, but is also useful for travellers of any age looking for cheap flights and sightseeing discounts. It is linked with the International Student Travel Confederation. You can get a student card here if you have documents proving that you are a student.

Tourist Offices Abroad
Information about Italy can be obtained at **Italian State Tourist Offices** *(ENIT;* w *www .enit.it)* throughout the world, including:

Australia
(☎ 02-9262 1666, fax 9262 5745) c/o Italian Chamber of Commerce, Level 26, 44 Market St, Sydney, NSW 2000

Canada
(☎ 416-925 4882, fax 925 4799) Suite 907, South Tower, 175 Bloor St East, Toronto, Ontario M4W 3R8

UK
(☎ 020-7355 1557, fax 7493 6695, e enit lond@globalnet.co.uk) 1 Princes St, London W1R 9AY

USA
Chicago: (☎ 312-644 0996, fax 644 3019, e enitch@italiantourism.com) Suite 2240, 500 North Michigan Ave, Chicago, IL 60611
Los Angeles: (☎ 310-820 1898, fax 820 6357, e enitla@earthlink.net) Suite 550, 12400 Wilshire Blvd, Los Angeles, CA 90025
New York: (☎ 212-245 5095, fax 586 9249, e enitny@italiantourism.com) Suite 1565, 630 Fifth Ave, New York, NY 10111

Sestante CIT (Compagnia Italiana di Turismo), Italy's national travel agency, also has offices throughout the world (known as CIT outside Italy). It can provide extensive information on Italy, as well as book tours and accommodation. It also makes train bookings. Offices include:

Australia
Melbourne: (☎ 03-9650 5510) Level 4, 227 Collins St, Melbourne, VIC 3000
Sydney: (☎ 02-9267 1255) Level 2, 263 Clarence St, Sydney, NSW 2000

Canada
Montreal: (☎ 514-845 9101, toll-free ☎ 800-361 7799) Suite 901, 666 Sherbrooke St West, Montreal, Quebec H3A 1E7
Toronto: (☎ 905-415 1060, toll-free ☎ 800-387 0711) Suite 401, 80 Tiverton Court, Markham, Ontario L3R 0G4

France
(☎ 01 44 51 39 51) 5 Blvd des Capucines, Paris 75002

UK
(☎ 020-8686 0677, 8686 5533) Marco Polo House, 3–5 Lansdowne Rd, Croydon, Surrey CR9 1LL

USA
(☎ 212-730 2121) Level 10, 15 West 44th St, New York, NY 10036

VISAS & DOCUMENTS

EU citizens require only a national identity card or a passport to stay in Italy for as long as they like and since Italy is now a member of the Schengen Area, EU citizens can enter the country without passport controls.

Citizens of many other countries including the USA, Australia, Canada and New Zealand, do not need to apply for visas before arriving in Italy if they are entering the country as tourists only. If you are entering the country for any reason other than tourism, you should insist on having your passport stamped. Visitors are technically obliged to report to a *questura* (police headquarters) if they plan to stay at the same address for more than one week, to receive a *permesso di soggiorno* – in effect, permission to remain in the country for a nominated period up to the three-month limit. Tourists who are staying in hotels or youth hostels are not required to do this since proprietors need to register their guests with the police. A permesso di soggiorno only becomes a necessity (for non-EU citizens) if you plan to study, work (legally) or live in Italy.

EMBASSIES & CONSULATES
Italian Embassies & Consulates
Italian diplomatic missions abroad include:

Australia
Embassy: (☎ 02-6273 3333, fax 6273 4223, e ambital2@dynamite.com.au) 12 Grey St, Deakin, ACT 2601
Consulate: (☎ 03-9867 5744, fax 9866 3932, e itconmel@netlink.com.au) 509 St Kilda Rd, Melbourne, VIC 3004
Consulate: (☎ 02-9392 7900, fax 9252 4830, e itconsyd@armadillo.com.au) Level 45, Gateway, 1 Macquarie Place, Sydney, NSW 2000

Canada
Embassy: (☎ 613-232 2401, fax 233 1484, e ambital@italyincanada.com) Level 21, 275 Slater St, Ottawa, Ontario K1P 5H9
Consulate: (☎ 514-849 8351, fax 499 9471, e cgi@italconsul.montreal.qc.ca) 3489 Drummond St, Montreal, Quebec H3G 1X6
Consulate: (☎ 416-977 1566, fax 977 1119, e consolato.it@toronto.italconsulate.org) 136 Beverley St, Toronto, Ontario M5T 1Y5

France
Embassy: (☎ 01 49 54 03 00, fax 01 45 49 35 81, e ambasciata@amb-italie.fr) 7 rue de Varenne, Paris 75007
Consulate: (☎ 01 44 30 47 00, fax 01 45 25 87 50, e italconsulparigi@mailcity.com) 5 Blvd Emile Augier, Paris 75116

New Zealand
Embassy: (☎ 04-473 5339, fax 472 7255, e ambwell@xtra.co.nz) 34 Grant Rd, Thorndon, Wellington

UK
Embassy: (☎ 020-7312 2200, fax 7312 2230, e emblondon@embitaly.org.uk) 14 Three Kings Yard, London W1Y 4EH
Consulate: (☎ 020-7235 9371, fax 7823 1609) 38 Eaton Place, London SW1X 8AN

USA

Embassy: (☎ 202-612 4400, fax 518 2154)
3000 Whitehaven St NW, Washington DC
20008
Consulate: (☎ 310-826 6207, fax 820 0727,
e cglos@conlang.com) Suite 300, 12400
Wilshire Blvd, West Los Angeles, CA 90025
Consulate: (☎ 212-7737 9100, fax 249
4945, **e** italconsulnyc@italconsulnyc.org)
690 Park Ave, New York, NY 10021

Embassies & Consulates in Italy

The headquarters of most foreign embassies
are in Rome, although there are generally
British and US consulates in other major
cities. The following addresses and phone
numbers are for Rome:

Australia
(☎ 06 85 27 21) Via Alessandria 215, 00198

Canada
(☎ 06 44 59 81) Via G B de Rossi 27, 00161

France
Embassy: (☎ 06 68 60 11) Piazza Farnese 67,
00186
Consulate: (☎ 06 68 80 21 52) Via Giulia
251, 00186

Germany
(☎ 06 49 21 31) Via San Martino della
Battaglia 4, 00185

New Zealand
(☎ 06 441 71 71) Via Zara 28, 00198

UK
(☎ 06 42 20 00 01) Via XX Settembre 80a,
00187

USA
(☎ 06 4 67 41) Via Veneto 119a, 00187

For a complete list of all foreign embassies in
Rome and other major cities throughout Italy,
look in the local telephone book under *ambasciate* or *consolati*, or ask for a list at the
tourist office.

CUSTOMS

As of 1 July 1999, duty-free sales within the
EU were abolished. Under the single market,
goods bought in and exported within the EU
incur no additional taxes, provided duty has
been paid somewhere within the EU and the
goods are for personal consumption.

Travellers coming from outside the EU, on
the other hand, can import, duty-free: 200
cigarettes, 1L of spirits, 2L of wine, 60mls of
perfume, 250mls of *eau de toilet,* and other
goods up to a total value of €175; anything
over this limit must be declared on arrival and
the appropriate duty paid (it is advisable to
carry all receipts).

MONEY

A combination of travellers cheques and
credit cards is the best way to take your
money. If you buy travellers cheques in euro
there should be no commission charged for
cashing them. There are exchange offices at
all major airports and train stations, but it is
advisable to obtain a small amount of euro
before arriving from a noneuro country to
avoid problems and queues at the airport and
train stations.

Major credit cards (eg, Visa, MasterCard
and American Express), are widely accepted in
Italy and can be used for purchases or payment
in hotels and restaurants (although smaller
places might not accept them). They can also
be used to get money from ATMs *(bancomats)*
or, if you don't have a PIN, over the counter in
major banks, including Banca Commerciale
Italiana, Cassa di Risparmio and Credito Italiano. If your credit card is lost, stolen or swallowed by an ATM, you can make a toll-free
telephone call to have it cancelled. To cancel a
MasterCard the number in Italy is ☎ 800-87 08
66 or make a reverse-charge call to St Louis is
in the USA (☎ 314-275 66 90). To cancel a
Visa card in Italy, phone ☎ 800-87 72 32. The
toll-free emergency number to report a lost or
stolen American Express (AmEx) card varies
according to where the card was issued. Check
with AmEx in your country or contact **American Express** *(☎ 06 7 22 82)* in Rome, which
has a 24-hour card-holders' service.

The fastest way to receive money is
through **Western Union** *(toll-free ☎ 800-01
38 39)*. This service functions in Italy through
the Mail Boxes Etc chain of stores, which you
will find in the bigger cities. The sender and
receiver have to turn up at a Western Union
outlet with passport or other form of ID and
the fees charged for the virtually immediate
transfer depend on the amount sent.

Currency

Italy's currency since 2002 is the euro. See
the boxed text 'The Euro' in the introductory
Facts for the Visitor chapter. A good website
for exchange rates is **w** www.oanda.com.

Remember that, as with other continental
Europeans, Italians indicate decimals with
commas and thousands with points.

Costs

A *very* prudent traveller could get by on €45
per day, but only by staying in youth hostels,

eating one meal a day (at the hostel), buying a sandwich or pizza by the slice for lunch and minimising the number of galleries and museums visited, since the entrance fee to most major museums is cripplingly expensive at around €4.50. You can save on transport costs by buying tourist or day tickets for city bus and underground services. When travelling by train, you can save money by avoiding the fast Eurostars, which charge a *supplemento rapido*. Italy's railways also offer a few cut-price options for students, young people and tourists for travel within a nominated period (see the introductory Getting Around section later in this chapter for more information).

Museums and galleries usually give discounts to students, but you will need a valid student card, which you can obtain from CTS offices if you have documents proving you are a student. Other discounts are offered to EU citizens aged between 18 and 25 (around 50%). EU citizens under 18 and over 65 years of age are generally admitted free of charge.

A basic breakdown of costs during an average day could be: accommodation €15 (youth hostel) to €40; breakfast (coffee and croissant) €1.75; lunch (sandwich and mineral water) €3.20; daily public transport ticket €6; entry fee for one museum €4.50 to €6.50; a sit-down dinner €8 to €25.

Tipping & Bargaining

You are not expected to tip on top of restaurant service charges, but it is common practice among Italians to leave a small amount, say around 10%. In bars they will leave any small change as a tip. You can tip taxi drivers if you wish but it's not obligatory.

Bargaining is common throughout Italy in the various flea markets, but not normally in shops. You can try bargaining for the price of a room in a *pensione* (small hotel), particularly if you plan to stay for more than a few days or out of season.

POST & COMMUNICATIONS
Post

Stamps (*francobolli*) are available at post offices and authorised tobacconists (look for the official *tabacchi* sign: a big 'T', often white on black). Since letters often need to be weighed, what you get at the tobacconist's for international airmail will occasionally be an approximation of the proper rate. Main post offices in the bigger cities are generally open from around 8am to 6pm. Many open on Saturday morning, too.

Mail is divided into three zones: zone 1 (Italy, Europe and the Mediterranean Basin) zone 2 (Africa, Asia and the USA) and zone 3 (Oceania). *Posta Ordinaria* (ordinary post – not used much anymore) for letters and postcards up to 20g costs €0.41 (zone 1) and €0.52 (zones 2 and 3).

Posta prioritaria (priority post) for postcards and letters up to 20g costs €0.62 (zone 1) and €0.77 (zones 2 and 3). Using this service, mail is supposed to reach its destination within three days for Europe, five days for the Mediterranean Basin, five to six days for the USA, and eight days for South America, Canada, Africa, Asia, Australia and New Zealand.

Registered mail in Italy is known as *raccomandato,* insured mail as *assicurato* and express post as *postacelere.*

Telephone & Fax

Italy's country code is ☎ 39. Area codes are an integral part of the telephone number, even if you're dialling a local number.

Local and long-distance calls can be made from public phones, or from a Telecom office. Italy's rates, particularly for long-distance calls, are among the highest in Europe. Most public phones accept only phonecards, sold in denominations of €2.50, €5 and €25 at tobacconists and newsstands, or from Telecom vending machines. Local calls from a public phone cost around €0.10 for three minutes. Off-peak hours for domestic calls are between 10pm to 8am. For international calls it's 10pm to 8am and all Sunday.

To make a reverse-charge (collect) call from a public phone, dial ☎ 170. For European countries call ☎ 15. All operators speak English. Numbers for this Home Country Direct service are displayed in the early pages of Italian phone books and include: Australia (☎ 172 10 61, Telstra), Canada (☎ 172 10 01, Teleglobe), New Zealand (☎ 172 10 64), UK (☎ 172 00 44) and USA (☎ 172 10 11, AT&T). For international directory inquiries call ☎ 176.

International faxes can cost €3.50 for the first page and €2 per page thereafter. You can transmit faxes from specialist fax/photocopy shops, post offices, Internet cafés and from some tabacchi.

mail & Internet Access

aly has a growing number of Internet cafés, here you can send and receive email or surf e Net for around €2 to €5 an hour.

DIGITAL RESOURCES

here is an Italy page at Lonely Planet's website at w www.lonelyplanet.com. The following are just a few of the huge number of seful websites for travellers to Italy.

CTS at w www.cts.it has useful information mostly in Italian) from Italy's leading student avel organisation; w www.beniculturali.com s a good cultural site that has museum information and online reservation options. Nature overs can get Italian national park information t w www.parks.it.

The Vatican is represented at w www.vatican va, which has detailed information about atican City, including virtual tours of the ain monuments and the museums. If you're ooking for train information, visit w www s-on-line.com, for details about timetables nd services.

BOOKS

'or a more comprehensive guide to Italy, ick up a copy of Lonely Planet's *Italy*. If ou want to concentrate on specific regions, ick up Lonely Planet's *Rome, Florence, 'enice, Tuscany, Milan, Turin & Genoa* and *icily* guides. Also useful are the *Italian hrasebook, World Food Italy, Rome City 1ap* and *Florence City Map*. If you're a hiking enthusiast, a good companion is Lonely 'lanet's *Walking in Italy*.

For a potted history of the country, try the *Concise History of Italy* by Vincent Cronin. *A History of Contemporary Italy: Society and Politics 1943–1988* by Paul Ginsborg is well vritten and absorbing. Luigi Barzini's classic *The Italians* is a great introduction to Italian people and culture, while *Excellent Cadavers: The Mafia and the Death of the First Italian Republic* by Alexander Stille is a hocking and fascinating account of the Mafia in Sicily.

Interesting introductions to travelling in taly include *A Traveller in Italy* by HV Morton, who also wrote similar guides to Rome and southern Italy.

NEWSPAPERS & MAGAZINES

Major English-language newspapers available n Italy are the *Herald Tribune*, the English *Guardian*, the *Times* and the *Telegraph*. *Time* magazine, *Newsweek* and the *Economist* are available weekly.

TIME

Italy is one hour ahead of GMT/UTC, and two hours ahead during summer. Daylight-saving time starts on the last Sunday in March, when clocks are put forward an hour. Clocks are put back an hour on the last Sunday in September. Remember to make allowances for daylight-saving time in your own country. Note that Italy operates on a 24-hour clock.

LAUNDRY

Coin laundrettes, where you can do your own washing, can be found in most of the main cities and towns, although they are scarce in Italy's south. A load will cost around €3.10. Many camping grounds have laundry facilities.

WOMEN TRAVELLERS

Italy is not a dangerous country for women, but women travelling alone may find themselves recipients of unwanted attention from men. Most of the attention falls into the nuisance category and it is best simply to ignore the catcalls, hisses and whistles. However, women touring alone should use common sense. Avoid walking alone in dark and deserted streets and look for centrally located hotels that are within easy walking distance of places where you can eat at night. In the south the often-persistent attention paid to women travelling alone can border on the very intrusive, particularly in the bigger cities. Women should never hitchhike alone.

GAY & LESBIAN TRAVELLERS

Homosexuality is legal in Italy and generally well tolerated in major cities, although overt displays of affection might get a negative response in smaller towns and villages, particularly in the south. The age of consent for men and women is 16.

The national organisation for gays (men and women) is **Arcigay** (☎ 051 649 30 55, fax 051 528 22 26; w www.arcigay.it; Via Don Minzoni 18) in Bologna.

DISABLED TRAVELLERS

The Italian travel agency CIT can advise on hotels that have special facilities. The UK-based **Royal Association for Disability and**

ITALY

Rehabilitation (Radar, ☎ 020-7250 3222; W www.radar.org.uk; 12 City Forum, 250 City Rd, London EC1V 8AF), publishes a useful guide called Holidays & Travel Abroad: A Guide for Disabled People.

SENIOR TRAVELLERS
Senior travellers who plan on using the train as their main mode of transport should look into the Carta Argento (€25), which gives the over-60s reductions of up to 40% on full-price train fares.

DANGERS & ANNOYANCES
Theft is the main problem for travellers in Italy, mostly in the form of petty thievery and pickpocketing, especially in the bigger cities. Although not something you should be particularly worried about, a few precautions are necessary to avoid being robbed. Carry your valuables in a moneybelt and avoid flashing your dough in public. Pickpockets operate in crowded areas, such as markets and on buses headed for major tourist attractions.

Watch out for groups of kids that have a dishevelled look, as many can be lightning fast as they empty your pockets. Motorcycle bandits are a minor problem in Naples, Rome, Palermo and Syracuse. If you are using a shoulder bag, make sure that you wear the strap across your body and have the bag on the side away from the road.

Never leave valuables in a parked car – in fact, try not to leave anything in the car if you can help it.

It is a good idea to park your car in a supervised car park if you are leaving it for any amount of time. Car theft is a major problem in Rome and Naples.

BUSINESS HOURS
Business hours can vary from city to city, but generally shops and businesses are open 8.30am to 1pm and 5pm to 7.30pm Monday to Saturday, and some are also open on Sunday morning. Banks are generally open 8.30am to 1.30pm and from 2.30pm to 4.30pm Monday to Friday, but hours vary between banks and cities. Large post offices are open 8am to 6pm or 7pm Monday to Saturday. Most museums close on Monday, and restaurants and bars are required to close for one day each week.

Opening times were liberalised under new trading hours laws that went into effect in April 1999, although Italians tend to value their time off and are not necessarily rushing to keep their shops open throughout the week.

PUBLIC HOLIDAYS & SPECIAL EVENTS
Italy's national public holidays include: 6 January (Epiphany), Easter Monday, 25 April (Liberation Day), 1 May (Labour Day), 15 August (Ferragosto or Feast of the Assumption), 1 November (All Saints' Day), 8 December (Feast of the Immaculate Conception), 25 December (Christmas Day), and 26 December (Feast of St Stephen).

Individual towns also have public holidays to celebrate the feasts of their patron saints. Some of these are the Feast of St Mark in Venice on 25 April; the Feast of St John the Baptist on 24 June in Florence, Genoa and Turin; the Feast of St Peter and St Paul in Rome on 29 June; the Feast of St Rosalia in Palermo on July 15; the Feast of St Januarius in Naples on 19 September; and the Feast of St Ambrose in Milan on 7 December.

Annual events in Italy worth keeping in mind include:

Carnevale During the 10 days before Ash Wednesday, many towns stage carnivals (one last binge before Lent!). The one held in Venice is the best known, but there are also others, including a Viareggio in Tuscany and Ivrea near Turin.

Holy Week There are important festivals during this week everywhere in Italy, in particular the colourful and sombre traditional festivals of Sicily. In Assisi the rituals of Holy Week attract thousands of pilgrims.

Scoppio del Carro Literally 'Explosion of the Cart', this colourful event held in Florence in Piazza del Duomo on Easter Sunday features the explosion of a cart full of fireworks and dates back to the Crusades. If all goes well, it is seen as a good omen for the city.

Corso dei Ceri One of the strangest festivals in Italy, this is held in Gubbio (Umbria) on 15 May, and features a race run by men carrying enormous wooden constructions called ceri, in honour of the town's patron saint, Sant'Ubaldo.

Emergency Services
Nationwide emergency numbers are carabinieri (police with military and civil duties) ☎ 112, police ☎ 113, fire brigade (Vigili del Fuoco) ☎ 115, Automobile Club d'Italia (ACI) ☎ 116, ambulance ☎ 118.

◀ **Palio** On 2 July and 16 August, Siena stages this extraordinary horse race in the town's main piazza.

ACTIVITIES
Hiking
It is possible to go on organised treks in Italy, but if you want to go it alone you will find that trails are well marked and there are plenty of refuges in the Alps, in the Alpi Apuane in Tuscany and in the northern parts of the Apennines. The Dolomites provide spectacular walking and trekking opportunities. On Sardinia, head for the coastal gorges between Dorgali and Baunei. Sicily's Mt Etna is also a popular hiking destination.

Skiing
The numerous excellent ski resorts in the Alps and the Apennines usually offer good skiing conditions from December to April.

Cycling
This is a good option if you can't afford a car but want to see the more isolated parts of the country. Classic cycling areas include Tuscany and Umbria.

ACCOMMODATION
The prices mentioned here are intended as a guide only. There is generally a fair degree of fluctuation throughout the country, depending on the season. Prices usually rise by 5% to 10% each year, although sometimes they remain fixed for years, or even drop.

Camping
Facilities throughout Italy are usually reasonable and vary from major complexes with swimming pools, tennis courts and restaurants, to simple camping grounds. Average prices are around €6 per person and €6 or more for a site. Lists of camping grounds in and near major cities are often available at tourist information offices.

The Touring Club Italiano (TCI) publishes an annual book on all camping sites in Italy, *Campeggi e Villaggi Turistici* (€18). Free camping is forbidden in many of the more beautiful parts of Italy, although the authorities seem to pay less attention in the off season.

Hostels
Hostels in Italy are called *ostelli per la gioventú* and are run by Associazione Italiana Alberghi per la Gioventú (AIG), which is affiliated with Hostelling International (HI). Prices, including breakfast, range from €10 to €15. Closing times vary, but are usually from 9am to 3pm or 5pm and curfews are around midnight. Men and women are often segregated, although some hostels also have family accommodation.

An HI membership card is not always required, but it is recommended that you have one. Membership cards can be purchased at major hostels, from CTS offices and from AIG offices throughout Italy. Pick up a list of all hostels in Italy, with details of prices, locations etc from the **AIG office** (☎ 06 487 11 52, fax 06 488 04 92; Via Cavour 44, Rome; open 9am-5pm Mon-Fri).

Pensioni & Hotels
Establishments are required to notify local tourist boards of prices for the coming year and by law must then adhere to those prices (although they do have two legal opportunities each year to increase charges). If tourists believe they are being overcharged, they can make a complaint to the local tourist office. The best advice is to confirm hotel charges before you put your bags down, since many proprietors employ various methods of bill padding. These include a compulsory breakfast (up to €7.75 in the high season) and compulsory half or full board, although this can often be a good deal in some towns.

The cheapest way to stay in a hotel or pensione is to share a room with two or more people: the cost is usually no more than 15% of the cost of a double room for each additional person. Single rooms are uniformly expensive in Italy (from around €30) and quite a number of establishments do not even bother to cater for the single traveller.

There is often no difference between an establishment that calls itself a pensione and one that calls itself an *albergo* (hotel); in fact, some use both titles. *Locande* (similar to pensioni) and *alloggi*, also known as *affittacamere*, are generally cheaper, but not always.

Rental Accommodation
Finding rental accommodation in the major cities can be difficult and time-consuming and you will often find the cost prohibitive, especially in Rome, Florence, Milan and Venice. Major resort areas, such as the Aeolian Islands and the Alps offer rental accommodation

that's reasonably priced and readily available. Many tourist offices will provide information by mail, fax or email.

One organisation that organises expensive but charming villas and houses in Tuscany, Umbria, Veneto, the Amalfi Coast, Sicily and Rome is Cuendet. Write to **Cuendet & Cie spa** (☎ *0577 57 63 30, fax 0577 30 11 49;* Ⓦ *www.cuendet.com; Strada di Strove 17, 53035 Monteriggioni, Siena).* CIT offices throughout the world also have lists of villas and apartments for rent in Italy.

Agriturismo

This is basically a farm holiday and is becoming increasingly popular in Italy. Traditionally, the idea was that families rented out rooms in their farmhouses. For detailed information on all facilities in Italy contact **Agriturist** (☎ *06 685 23 42;* Ⓦ *www.agriturist.it; Corso Vittorio Emanuele 101, 00186 Rome).* It publishes *Agriturist* (€14), which lists establishments throughout Italy.

Refuges

Before you go hiking in any part of Italy, obtain information about refuges *(rifugi)* from the local tourist offices. Some refuges have private rooms, but many offer dorm-style accommodation, particularly those that are more isolated. Average prices are from €10 to €25 per person for B&B. A meal costs around the same as at a trattoria. The locations of refuges are marked on good hiking maps and most open only from late June to September. The alpine refuges of CAI (Italian Alpine Club) offer discounts to members of associated foreign alpine clubs.

FOOD & DRINKS

Eating is one of life's great pleasures for Italians. Cooking styles vary notably from region to region and significantly between the north and south. In the north the food is rich and often creamy; in central Italy the locals use a lot of olive oil and herbs and regional specialities are noted for their simplicity, fine flavour and the use of fresh produce. As you go further south the food becomes hotter and spicier and the *dolci* (cakes and pastries) sweeter and richer.

Vegetarians will have no problems eating in Italy. Most eating establishments serve a selection of *contorni* (vegetables prepared in a variety of ways).

If you have access to cooking facilities buy fruit and vegetables at open-air markets and salami, cheese and wine at *alimentari* or *salumerie* (a cross between a grocery store and a delicatessen). Fresh bread is available at a *forno* or *panetteria.*

Restaurants are divided into several categories. A *tavola calda* (literally 'hot table') usually offers inexpensive, pre-prepared meat, pasta and vegetable dishes in a self-service style. A *rosticceria* usually offers cooked meats, but also often has a larger selection of takeaway food. A pizzeria will of course serve pizza, but usually also a full menu. An *osteria* is likely to be either a wine bar offering a small selection of dishes, or a small *trattoria.* Many of the establishments that are in fact restaurants *(ristoranti)* call themselves trattoria and vice versa for reasons best known to themselves.

Most eating establishments charge a *coperto* (cover charge) of around €1 to €2, and a *servizio* (service charge) of 10% to 15%. Restaurants are usually open for lunch from 12.30pm to 3pm, but will rarely take orders after 2pm. In the evening, opening hours vary from north to south. In the north they eat dinner earlier, usually from 7.30pm, but in Sicily you will be hard-pressed to find a restaurant open before 8.30pm, and you'll be dining alone before about 9.30pm. Restaurants rarely stay open after 11.30pm.

A full meal will consist of an antipasto, which can vary from *bruschetta*, a type of garlic bread with various toppings, to fried vegetables, or *prosciutto e melone* (ham wrapped around melon). Next comes the *primo piatto*, a pasta dish or risotto, followed by the *secondo piatto* of meat or fish. Italians often then eat an *insalata* (salad) or contorni and round off the meal with dolci and *caffé*, often at a bar on the way home or back to work. In this chapter, we've costed eating out as a meal for one person with a first course, second course, some wine and a side dish or desert.

Italian wine is justifiably world-famous. Fortunately, wine is reasonably priced, so you will rarely pay more than €7.75 for a bottle of very drinkable wine and as little as €3.10 will still buy something of reasonable quality. Try the famous chianti and *brunello* in Tuscany, but also the *vernaccia* of San Gimignano, the *barolo* in Piedmont, the *lacrima christi* or *falanghina* in Naples and the *cannonau* in Sardinia. Beer is known as *birra* and the cheapest local variety is Peroni.

ENTERTAINMENT

Italians have a great appreciation of entertainment, so visitors can indulge themselves with opera, theatre, classical music recitals, rock concerts and traditional festivals. Major entertainment festivals are also held, such as the Festival of Two Worlds in June/July at Spoleto, Umbria Jazz in Perugia in July, Rome's Estate Romana in July, and the Venice Biennale every odd-numbered year. Operas are performed in Verona and Rome throughout summer (for details see Entertainment under both cities) and at various times of the year throughout the country, notably at the opera houses in Milan and Rome.

SPECTATOR SPORTS

Soccer (calcio) is the national passion and there are stadiums in all the major towns. If you'd rather watch a game than visit a Roman ruin, check newspapers for details of who's playing where, although tickets for the bigger matches can be hard to find. The Italian Formula One Grand Prix races are held at Monza, just north of Milan in September. The San Marino Grand Prix is held at Imola in May. Good luck finding a ticket, though.

SHOPPING

Italy is synonymous with elegant, fashionable and high-quality clothing, leather goods, glass and ceramics. The problem is that most are very expensive. However, if you happen to be in the country during the summer sales in July and August and the winter sales in January and February, you can pick up some incredible bargains.

Getting There & Away

AIR

Although paying full fare to travel by plane in Europe is expensive, there are various discount options, including cut-price fares for students and people aged under 26. There are also stand-by fares, which are usually around 60% of the full fare. Several airlines offer cut-rate fares on legs of international flights between European cities. These are usually the cheapest fares available, but the catch is that they are often during the night or very early in the morning, and the days on which you can fly are severely restricted. Some examples of high-season Alitalia fares at the time of writing are: Rome–Paris €311 return; Rome–London €271 return; and Rome–Amsterdam €311 return.

Another option is to travel on charter flights. Try **Charter Flight Centre** (☎ 020-7828 1090; w charterflights.co.uk; 19 Denbigh St, London SW1), which specialises in such flights and also organises some regular scheduled flights.

Look in the classified pages of the London Sunday newspapers for information on other cheap flights. **STA Travel** (☎ 020-7361 6161, toll-free ☎ 0870-160 05 99; 86 Old Brompton Rd, London SW7 3LQ), has occasional specials and can help with student fares. Within Italy, information on discount fares is available from CTS and Sestante CIT offices (see Tourist Offices in the Facts for the Visitor section, earlier in this chapter).

LAND

If you are travelling by bus, train or car to Italy it will be necessary to cross various borders, so remember to check whether you require visas for those countries before leaving home.

Bus

Eurolines (w www.eurolines.com) is the main international carrier in Europe, with representatives in Italy and throughout the continent. In Italy the main bus company operating this service is **Lazzi** (☎ 055 35 10 61; Piazza Adua 1, Florence • ☎ 06 884 08 40; Via Tagliamento 27b, Rome). Buses leave from Rome, Florence, Milan, Turin, Venice and Naples, as well as numerous other Italian towns, for major cities throughout Europe including London, Paris, Barcelona, Madrid, Amsterdam, Budapest, Prague, Athens and Istanbul. Some ticket prices are Rome–Paris €82 (€148 return), Rome–London €116 (€179 return) and Rome–Barcelona €102 (€183 return).

Train

Eurostar (ES) and Eurocity (EC) trains run from major destinations throughout Europe direct to major Italian cities. On overnight hauls you can book a cuccetta (known outside Italy as a couchette or sleeping berth, and worth booking!).

Travellers aged under 26 can take advantage of the Inter-Rail Pass, Eurail Pass Youth and Europass Youth. For price and also purchasing details, visit the website at **w** www .eurail.com.

You can book tickets at train stations or at CTS, Sestante CIT and most travel agencies. Eurostar and Eurocity trains carry a supplement (determined by the distance you are travelling and the type of train).

Car & Motorcycle
Travelling with your own vehicle certainly gives you more flexibility. The drawbacks in Italy are that cars can be inconvenient in larger cities where you'll have to deal with heavy traffic, parking problems, the risk of car theft, the exorbitant price of petrol and toll charges on the autostrade.

If you want to rent a car or motorcycle, you will need a valid EU driving licence, an International Driving Permit, or your driving permit from your own country. If you're driving your own car, you'll need an international insurance certificate, known as a Carta Verde (Green Card), which can be obtained from your insurer.

Hitching
Hitching is never safe in any country and we don't recommend it. Your best bet is to inquire at hostels throughout Europe, where you can often arrange a lift. **The International Lift Centre** (☎ 055 28 06 26) in Florence and **Enjoy Rome** (☎ 06 445 18 43) might be able to help organise lifts. Note that it is illegal to hitch on the autostrade.

SEA
Ferries connect Italy to Spain, Croatia, Greece, Turkey, Tunisia and Malta. There are also services to Corsica (from Livorno) and Albania (from Bari and Ancona). See Getting There & Away under Brindisi (for ferries to/from Greece), Ancona (to/from Greece, Albania and Croatia), Venice (to/from Greece) and Sicily (to/from Malta and Tunisia).

Getting Around

AIR
Travelling by plane is expensive within Italy and it makes much better sense to use the efficient and considerably cheaper rail and bus services. The domestic airlines include Alitalia, Meridiana and Air One. The main airports are in Rome, Pisa, Milan, Bologna, Genoa, Turin, Naples, Catania, Palermo and Cagliari, but there are other, smaller airports throughout Italy. Domestic flights can be booked directly with the airlines or through Sestante CIT, CTS and other travel agencies.

Alitalia offers a range of discounts for students, young people and families, and for weekend travel.

BUS
Numerous bus companies operate within Italy. It is usually necessary to make reservations only for long trips, such as Rome–Palermo or Rome–Brindisi. Otherwise, just arrive early enough to claim a seat.

Buses can be a cheaper and faster way to get around if your destination is not on major rail lines, for instance from Umbria to Rome or Florence, and in the interior areas of Sicily and Sardinia.

TRAIN
Travelling by train in Italy is simple, relatively cheap and generally efficient. The Ferrovie dello Stato (FS) is the partially privatised state train system and there are many private train services throughout the country.

There are several types of trains: Regionale (R), which usually stop at all stations and can be very slow; interRegionale (iR), which run between the regions; intercity (IC) or Eurocity (EC), which service only the major cities; and Eurostar Italia (ES), which serves major Italian and European cities.

To go on the Intercity, Eurocity and Eurostar Italia trains, you have to pay a *supplemento,* an additional charge determined by the distance you are travelling and the type of train.

All tickets *must* be validated in the yellow machines at the entrance to all platforms at train stations.

It is not worth buying a Eurail or Inter-Rail pass if you are going to travel only in Italy. The FS offers its own discount passes for travel within the country. These include the Carta Verde for those aged between 12 and 26 years. It costs €26, is valid for one year, and entitles you to a 20% discount on all train travel. You can also buy a *biglietto chilometrico* (kilometric ticket), which is valid for two months and allows you to cover 3000km, with a maximum of 20 trips. It costs €181/117 for 1st/2nd class travel and you must pay the supplement if you catch an Intercity or Eurostar train. The main attraction of this ticket is that it can be used by up to five people, either singly or together.

Some examples of 2nd-class fares (including IC supplement) are Rome–Florence for €21.95 and Rome–Naples €16.53.

CAR & MOTORCYCLE

Roads are generally good throughout the country and there is an excellent system of autostrade (freeways). The main north–south link is the Autostrada del Sole, which extends from Milan to Reggio di Calabria (called the A1 from Milan to Naples and the A3 from Naples to Reggio).

In Italy people drive on the right-hand side of the road and pass on the left. Unless otherwise indicated, you must give way to cars coming from the right. It is compulsory to wear seat belts if they are fitted to the car (front seat belts on all cars and back seat belts on cars produced after 26 April 1990). If you are caught not wearing your seat belt, you will be required to pay an on-the-spot fine of €30.

Wearing a helmet is compulsory for every motorcycle and moped rider and passenger – although you won't necessarily see this.

Some of the Italian cities, including Rome, Bologna, Florence, Milan and Turin have introduced restricted access to both private and rental cars in their historical centres. The restrictions, however, do not apply to vehicles with foreign registrations. *Motorini* (mopeds) and scooters (such as vespas) are able to enter the zones without any problems.

Speed limits, unless otherwise indicated by local signs, are: on autostrade 130km/h, on nonurban roads 110km/h; on secondary nonurban highways 90km/h; and in built-up areas 50km/h.

Petrol prices are high in Italy – around €1.05 per litre. Petrol is called *benzina,* unleaded petrol is *benzina senza piombo* and diesel is *gasolio.*

The blood-alcohol limit is 0.08% and there are now random breath tests.

BOAT

Navi (large ferries) service the islands of Sicily and Sardinia, and *traghetti* (smaller ferries) and *aliscafi* (hydrofoils) service areas such as Elba, the Aeolian Islands, Capri and Ischia. The main embarkation points for Sicily and Sardinia are at Genoa, La Spezia, Livorno, Civitavecchia, Fiumicino and Naples.

Tirrenia Navigazione is the major company servicing the Mediterranean and it has offices throughout Italy. Most long-distance services travel overnight and all ferries carry vehicles (bicycles are free of charge).

BICYCLE

Bikes are available for rent in many Italian towns – and cost around €10 a day or €60 a week. Bicycles can travel in the baggage compartment of some Italian trains (but not on the Eurostars or Intercity trains).

Rome

postcode 00100 • pop 2.65 million

A phenomenal concentration of history, legend and monuments coexist in chaotic harmony in Rome, as well as an equally phenomenal concentration of people busily going about their everyday lives.

Rome's origins date to a group of Etruscan, Latin and Sabine settlements on the Palatine, Esquiline, Quirinal and surrounding hills, but it is the legend of Romulus and Remus (the twins raised by a she-wolf), which has captured the popular imagination. The myth says Romulus killed his brother during a battle over who should govern, and then established the city on the Palatine (Palatino), one of the famous Seven Hills of Rome. From the legend grew an empire that eventually controlled almost the entire world known to Europeans at the time.

In Rome there is visible evidence of the two great empires of the Western world: the Roman Empire and the Christian Church. On the one hand is the Forum and Colosseum, and on the other St Peter's and the Vatican. In between, in almost every piazza, lies so many layers of history that what you see is only the tip of the iceberg – this is exemplified by St Peter's Basilica, which stands on the site of an earlier basilica built by the Emperor Constantine over the necropolis where St Peter was buried.

ORIENTATION

Rome is a vast city, but the historical centre is relatively small. Most of the major sights are west – and within walking distance – of the central train station, Stazione Termini. Lonely Planet's *Rome City Map* is handy to have, with detailed maps of central Rome and

ROME (ROMA)

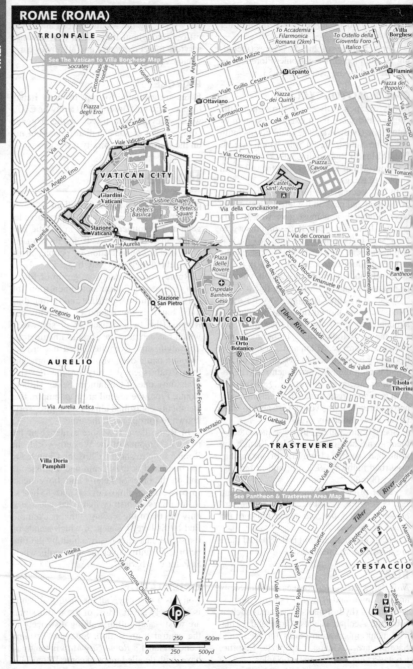

ITALY

ROME (ROMA)

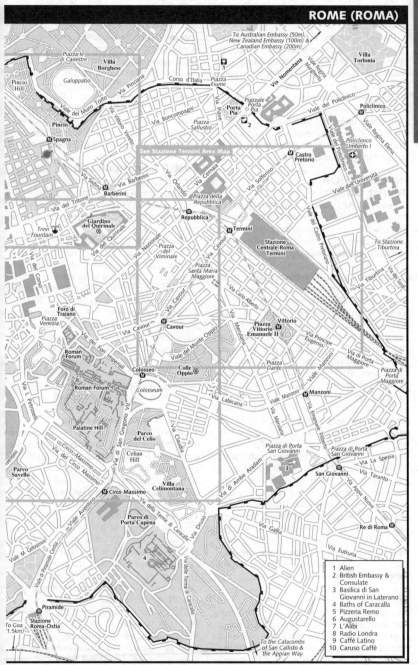

To Australian Embassy (50m),
New Zealand Embassy (100m) &
Canadian Embassy (200m)

Piazza le
di Canestre

Villa
Borghese

Galoppatio

Pincio Hill

Via Pinciana

Corso d'Italia

Piazza
Fiume

Via Nomentana

Villa
Torlonia

Viale del Policlinico

Policlinico

Viale del Muro Torto

Pincio

Vittorio Veneto

Via Boncompagni

Piazzale
Porta
Pia

Porta
Pia

Via Regina Margherita

Spagna

Via Piave

Piazza
Sallustio

Via Sistina

Via Barberini

Barberini

Via del Tritone

Via Sistina

Giardino
del Quirinale

Trevi
Fountain

Via del Quirinale

Via Nazionale

Piazza
del
Viminale

See Stazione Termini Area Map

Via Cernaia

Via Orlando

Piazza della
Repubblica

Via Solferino

Repubblica

Termini

Via del Castro Pretorio

Castro
Pretorio

Viale Regina Elena

Policlinico
Umberto I

Viale dell'Università

To Stazione
Tiburtina

Stazione
Centrale-Roma
Termini

Via Tiburtina

Via dei Sardi

Foro di
Traiano

Piazza
Venezia

Via dei Fori Imperiali

Via Cavour

Piazza
Santa Maria
Maggiore

Via Cavour

Cavour

Via Carlo Alberto

Colosseo

Colle
Oppio

Viale del Monte Oppio

Via Metulana

Piazza
Vittorio
Emanuele II

Vittorio

Via Principe
Eugenio

Via di Porta
Maggiore

Piazza di
Porta
Maggiore

Roman
Forum

Roman Forum

Via di San Gregorio VII

Colosseum

Via Labicana

Piazza
Dante

Viale Manzoni

Viale Manzoni

Manzoni

Via Emanuele Filiberto

Palatine Hill

Circo Massimo

Via del Circo Massimo

Parco
del Celio

Via Claudia

Celian
Hill

Piazza di Porta
San Giovanni

Piazza di Porta
San Giovanni

San Giovanni

Via La Spezia

Via Taranto

Via Appia Nuova

Parco
Savello

Villa
Celimontana

Circo Massimo

Via di Amba Aradam

Re di Roma

Parco di
Porta Capena

Via delle Terme di Caracalla

Via Druso

Via delle Terme di Caracalla

Via Gallia

Via Eutruria

Viale Aventino

Viale M Gelsomini

Viale di Piramide Cestia

Piramide

Stazione
Roma-Ostia

To Goa
(1.5km)

To the Catacombs
of San Callisto &
the Appian Way

1 Alien
2 British Embassy &
  Consulate
3 Basilica di San
  Giovanni in Laterano
4 Baths of Caracalla
5 Pizzeria Remo
6 Augustarello
7 L'Alibi
8 Radio Londra
9 Caffé Latino
10 Caruso Caffé

historical areas, a Metropolitana map and walking tour.

Plan an itinerary if your time is limited. Many of the major museums and galleries open all day until 7pm or 8pm. Many museums are closed on Monday, but it is a good idea to check.

The main bus terminus is in Piazza del Cinquecento, directly in front of the train station. Many intercity buses arrive and depart from the Piazzale Tiburtina, in front of the Stazione Tiburtina, accessible from Termini on the Metropolitana Linea B.

INFORMATION
Tourist Offices
There is an **APT tourist information office** (☎ 06 48 90 63 00; open 8am-9pm daily) at Stazione Termini. It's in the central causeway and has multilingual staff, as well as some 'roaming' staff who may approach you in the station (ID is visible).

There is a great **APT main office** (☎ 06 36 00 43 99; Via Parigi 5; open 9am-7pm Mon-Sat). Walk northwest from Stazione Termini, through Piazza della Repubblica. Via Parigi runs to the right from the top of the piazza, about a five-minute walk from the station. The office has information on hotels and museum opening hours and entrance fees. Staff can also provide maps and printed information about provincial and intercity bus services.

Another good source of information and assistance is **Enjoy Rome** (☎ 06 445 18 43, fax 06 445 68 90; w www.enjoyrome.com; Via Marghera 8a; open 8.30am-7pm Mon-Sat & 8.30am-2pm Sun), five minutes walk to the northeast of the station. It's a privately run tourist office that offers a free hotel-reservation service. The English-speaking staff can also organise alternative accommodation such as apartments. They have extensive up-to-date information about Rome and you can book great three-hour walking tours that cover all sorts of interests and are conducted by native-English speakers or art and history specialists.

Money
Banks are open 8.45am to 1.30pm and usually from 2.45pm to 4pm Monday to Friday. You will find banks and exchange offices at Stazione Termini. There is also an exchange office (Banco di Santo Spirito) at Fiumicino

airport, to your right as you exit from the customs area.

Numerous other exchange offices are scattered throughout the city, including **American Express** (☎ 06 676 41; Piazza di Spagna 38) and **Thomas Cook** (☎ 06 482 81 82; Piazza Barberini 21).

Otherwise, go to any one of the dozens of banks in the city centre. Credit cards can also be used in automatic teller machines (ATMs), known as bancomats, to obtain cash 24 hours a day. You'll need a PIN from your bank.

Post & Communications
The **main post office** (Piazza San Silvestro 19; open 8.30am-6.30pm Mon-Fri & 8.30am-1pm Sat) is off Via del Tritone. Fermo posta (poste restante) is available here, although the postcode is 00186.

The **Vatican post office** (☎ 06 69 88 34 06; Piazza di San Pietro (St Peter's Square); open 8.30am-6pm Mon-Fri & 8.30am-1pm Sat) offers a faster and more reliable service (no fermo posta though).

There is a small Telecom office at Stazione Termini, from where you can make international calls direct or through an operator. Another office is near the station, on Via San Martino della Battaglia opposite Hotel Lachea-Dolomiti. International calls can easily be made with a phonecard (scheda telefonica) from any public phone. These can be bought at tobacconists and newspaper stands.

Email & Internet Access
There are dozens of Internet cafés scattered throughout the city. The biggest and most convenient is **easyEverything** (Via Barberini 2), which has hundreds of terminals, opens 24 hours daily and charges around €1 for 30 minutes, depending on the time of day.

Travel Agencies
There is an office of Italy's national tourist agency, **Sestante CIT** (☎ 06 46 20 31 44; Piazza della Repubblica 65), where you can make bookings for planes, trains and ferries. The staff speak English and there's information on fares for students and young people, plus tours of Rome and surrounds.

The student tourist centre, **CTS** (☎ 06 462 04 31; w www.cts.it; Via Genova 16), off Via Nazionale, offers similar services. It can make hotel reservations, and focuses on the discount- and student-travel market.

Bookshops

Feltrinelli International (☎ 06 482 78 78; Via Orlando 84) has literature and travel guides in several languages. **The Anglo-American Book Company** (☎ 06 679 52 22; Via della Vite 27), off Piazza di Spagna, has an excellent selection of literature and travel guides. The English-speaking **Economy Book & Video Center** (☎ 06 474 68 77; Via Torino 136), off Via Nazionale, has both new and second-hand books (travel guides included).

Laundry

Bolle Blu (Via Palestra 59; open 8am-10pm daily) is a coin laundrette near the train station, and costs €3.10 for a 7kg wash (soap included). Near the Vatican, **Onda Blu** (Via degli Scipioni 35) keeps the same hours as Bolle Blu and charges €3.10 for a 16kg wash with soap.

Medical & Emergency Services

Emergency medical treatment is available in the *pronto soccorso* (casualty section) at public hospitals, including **Ospedale San Gallicano** (☎ 06 588 23 90; Via di San Gallicano 25/a, Trastevere), which specialises in skin and venereal diseases; **Ospedale San Giacome** (☎ 06 362 61; Via Canova 29) near Piazza del Popolo; and **Policlinico Umberto I** (☎ 06 499 71; Via del Policlinico 155), which is close to Stazione Termini. Rome's paediatric hospital is **Bambino Gesú** (☎ 06 68 59 23 51; Piazza di Sant'Onofrio 4) on the Janiculum (Gianicolo) Hill. From Piazza della Rovere (on the Lungotevere near St Peter's) head uphill along Via del Gianicolo. The hospital is at the top of the hill.

There is a **24-hour pharmacy** (☎ 06 488 00 19; Piazza dei Cinquecento 51) near Stazione Termini. All pharmacies should post a list in their windows of others open at night nearby.

The **police headquarters** (questura; ☎ 06 468 61; Via San Vitale 11; open 24hr daily) is where thefts can be reported. Its **Foreigners Bureau** (Ufficio Stranieri; ☎ 06 46 86 29 77; Via Genova 2) is around the corner. For immediate police attendance call ☎ 113.

Dangers & Annoyances

Thieves are active in the areas in and around Stazione Termini, at major sights such as the Colosseum and Roman Forum, and on crowded buses such as the No 64 from Stazione Termini to St Peters, although police activity seems to have reduced the problem in recent years. For more comprehensive information on how to avoid being robbed, see Dangers & Annoyances earlier in this chapter.

THINGS TO SEE & DO

It would take years to explore every corner of Rome, months to begin to appreciate the incredible number of monuments, and weeks for a thorough tour of the city. You can, however, cover most of the important monuments in five days, or three at a minimum. Entry to various attractions is free for EU citizens aged under 18 and over 65, and half-price for EU citizens aged between 18 and 25 plus those from countries with reciprocal arrangements, teachers at state schools and many university students. Cumulative tickets represent good value for money, especially to full-fare payers. A good one to pick is the €20 ticket which covers the Museo Nazionale Romano, Colosseum, Palatine Hill, Baths of Caracalla and more. These tickets can be purchased at the sites they cover, or by calling ☎ 06 39 96 77 00. You can also visit the website W www.archeorm.arti.beniculturali.it for details.

Piazza del Campidoglio

Designed by Michelangelo in 1538, the piazza is on the Capitolino (Capitoline Hill), the most important of Rome's seven hills. Formerly the seat of the ancient Roman government, it is now the seat of Rome's municipal government. The facades of the three palaces that border the piazza were also designed by Michelangelo. A modern copy of the bronze equestrian statue of Emperor Marcus Aurelius stands at its centre; the original is now on display in the ground-floor portico of the Palazzo Nuovo (also called Palazzo del Museo Capitolino). This and the Palazzo dei Conservatori make up the **Musei Capitolini** (☎ 06 67 10 20 71; admission €6.20; open 9am-8pm Tues-Sun), well worth visiting for their collections of ancient Roman sculpture, including the famous *Capitoline Wolf*, an Etruscan statue dating from the 6th century BC.

Walk to the right of the Palazzo del Senato to see a panorama of the Roman Forum. Walk to the left of the same building to reach the ancient Roman **Carcere Mamertino**, where it's believed St Peter was imprisoned. The **Chiesa di Santa Maria d'Aracoeli** is between the Campidoglio and the Monumento

Vittorio Emanuele II at the highest point of the Capitoline Hill. It is built on the site where legend says the Tiburtine Sybil told the Emperor Augustus of the coming birth of Christ.

Piazza Venezia

This piazza is overshadowed by a neoclassical monument dedicated to Vittorio Emanuele II, often referred to by Italians as the *macchina da scrivere* (typewriter) due to its appearance. Built to commemorate Italian unification, the piazza incorporates the **Altare della Patria** and the tomb of the unknown soldier, as well as the **Museo del Risorgimento**. Also in the piazza is the 15th-century **Palazzo Venezia**, which was Mussolini's official residence and now houses a museum.

Roman Forum & Palatine Hill

The commercial, political and religious centre of ancient Rome, the Roman Forum (☎ 06 699 0110; admission to Forum free, to Palatine Hill with Colosseum €8; open 9am-1hr before sunset), stands in a valley between the Capitoline and Palatine (Palatino) hills. Originally marshland, the area was drained during the early republican era and became a centre for political rallies, public ceremonies and senate meetings. Its importance declined along with the empire after the 4th century, and the temples, monuments and buildings constructed by successive emperors, consuls and senators over a period of 900 years fell into ruin, eventually to be used as pasture.

The area was systematically excavated in the 18th and 19th centuries, and excavations are continuing. You can enter the Forum from Via dei Fori Imperiali, which leads from Piazza Venezia to the Colosseum.

As you enter the Forum, to your left is the **Tempio di Antonino e Faustina**, erected by the senate in AD 141 and transformed into a church in the 8th century. To your right are the remains of the **Basilica Aemilia**, built in 179 BC and demolished during the Renaissance, when it was plundered for its precious marble. The Via Sacra, which traverses the Forum from northwest to southeast, runs in front of the basilica. Towards the Campidoglio is the **Curia**, once the meeting place of the Roman senate and converted into a Christian church in the Middle Ages. The church was dismantled and the Curia restored in the 1930s. In front of the Curia is the **Lapis Niger**, a large piece of black marble that legend says covered the grave of Romulus. Under the Lapis Niger is the oldest-known Latin inscription, dating from the 6th century BC.

The **Arco di Settimo Severo** was erected in AD 203 in honour of this emperor and his sons, and is considered one of Italy's major triumphal arches. A circular base stone beside the arch marks the *umbilicus urbis*, the symbolic centre of ancient Rome. To the south is the **Rostrum**, used in ancient times by public speakers and once decorated by the rams of captured ships.

South along Via Sacra is the **Tempio di Saturno**, one of the most important temples in ancient Rome. Eight granite columns remain. The **Basilica Giulia**, in front of the temple, was the seat of justice, and nearby is the **Tempio di Giulio Cesare** (Temple of Julius Caesar), which was erected by Augustus in 29 BC on the site where Caesar's body was burned and Mark Antony read his famous speech. Back towards the Palatine Hill is the **Tempio dei Castori**, built in 489 BC in honour of the Heavenly Twins, or Dioscuri. It is easily recognisable by its three remaining columns.

In the area southeast of the temple is the **Chiesa di Santa Maria Antiqua**, the oldest Christian church in the Forum. It is closed to the public. Back on Via Sacra is the **Case delle Vestali**, home of the virgins who tended the sacred flame in the adjoining **Tempio di Vesta**. If the flame went out, it was seen as a bad omen. The next major monument is the vast **Basilica di Costantino**. Its impressive design inspired Renaissance architects. The **Arco di Tito**, at the Colosseum end of the Forum, was built in AD 81 in honour of the victories of the emperors Titus and Vespasian against Jerusalem.

From here climb the Palatine, where wealthy Romans built their homes and legend says that Romulus founded the city. Archaeological evidence shows that the earliest settlements in the area were on the Palatine. Like the Forum, the buildings of the Palatine fell into ruin and in the Middle Ages the hill became the site of convents and churches. During the Renaissance, wealthy families established gardens here. The Farnese gardens were built over the ruins of the Domus Tiberiana.

Worth a look is the impressive **Domus Augustana**, which was the private residence of the emperors; the **Domus Flavia**, the residence of Domitian; the **Tempio della Magna Mater**, built in 204 BC to house a black stone connected with the Asiatic goddess Cybele; and the **Casa di Livia**, thought to have been the house of the wife of Emperor Augustus, and decorated with frescoes.

Colosseum

Originally known as the Flavian Amphitheatre, Rome's best-known monument *(☎ 06 700 42 61; admission with Palatine Hill €8; open 9am-1hr before sunset)* was begun by Emperor Vespasian in AD 72 in the grounds of Nero's Golden House, and completed by his son Titus. The massive structure could seat 80,000 and featured bloody gladiatorial combat and wild beast shows that resulted in thousands of human and animal deaths.

In the Middle Ages the Colosseum became a fortress and was later used as a quarry for travertine and marble for the Palazzo Venezia and other buildings. Restoration works have been under way since 1992. Avoid having your photo taken with the muscly dudes dressed as gladiators unless you want to spend most of your time in Rome arguing about their extortionate demands for money.

Arch of Constantine

On the west side of the Colosseum is the triumphal arch built to honour Constantine following his victory over his rival Maxentius at the battle of Milvian Bridge (near the present-day Zona Olimpica, northwest of the Villa Borghese) in AD 312. Its decorative reliefs were taken from earlier structures.

Baths of Caracalla

The huge Terme di Caracalla complex *(☎ 06 575 86 26; Viale delle Terme di Caracalla 52; admission €5; open 9am-1hr before sunset Tues-Sun & 9am-2pm Mon)*, covering 10 hectares, could hold 1600 people and included shops, gardens, libraries and entertainment. Begun by Antonius Caracalla and inaugurated in AD 217, the baths were used until the 6th century.

Some Significant Churches

Down Via Cavour from Stazione Termini is the massive **Basilica di Santa Maria Maggiore**, built in the 5th century. Its main baroque facade was added in the 18th century, preserving the 13th-century mosaics of the earlier facade. Its bell tower is Romanesque

and the interior is baroque. There are 5th-century mosaics decorating the triumphal arch and nave.

Follow Via Merulana to reach **Basilica di San Giovanni in Laterano**, Rome's cathedral. The original church was built in the 4th century, the first Christian basilica in Rome. Largely destroyed over a long period of time, it was rebuilt in the 17th century.

Basilica di San Pietro in Vincoli, just off Via Cavour, is worth a visit because it houses Michelangelo's *Moses* and his unfinished statues of Leah and Rachel, as well as the chains worn by St Peter during his imprisonment before being crucified, hence the church's name.

Chiesa di San Clemente *(Via San Giovanni in Laterano)*, near the Colosseum, defines how history in Rome exists on many levels. The 12th-century church at street level was built over a 4th-century church that was, in turn, built over a 1st-century Roman house containing a temple dedicated to the pagan god Mithras.

Santa Maria in Cosmedin, northwest of **Circus Maximus**, is regarded as one of the finest medieval churches in Rome. It has a seven-storey bell tower and its interior is heavily decorated with Cosmatesque inlaid marble, including the beautiful floor. The main attraction for masses of tourists is, however, the **Bocca della Veritá** (Mouth of Truth). Legend has it that if you put your right hand into the mouth and tell a lie, it will snap shut.

Baths of Diocletian

Started by Emperor Diocletian, these baths *(☎ 06 488 05 30; Viale E De Nicola 79; admission €5; open 9am-7.45pm Tues-Sun)* were completed in the 4th century. The complex of baths, libraries, concert halls and gardens covered about 13 hectares and could house up to 3000 people. After the aqueduct that fed the baths was destroyed by invaders in AD 536, the complex fell into decay. Parts of the ruins are now incorporated into the Basilica di Santa Maria degli Angeli.

Basilica di Santa Maria degli Angeli

Designed by Michelangelo, this church *(open 7.30am-6.30pm Mon-Sat & 8am-7.30pm Sun)* incorporates what was the great central hall and *tepidarium* (lukewarm room) of the original baths. During the following centuries

ITALY

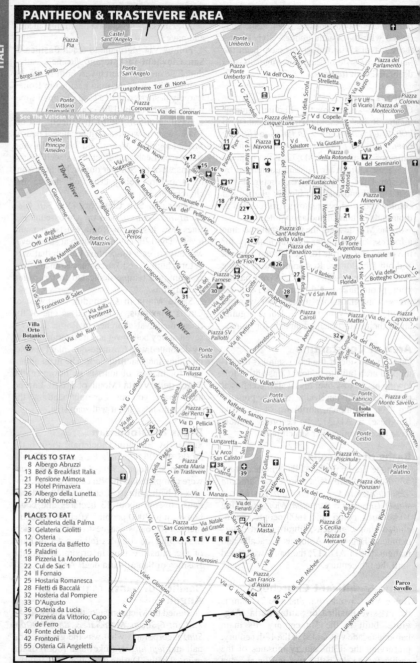

PANTHEON & TRASTEVERE AREA

PLACES TO STAY
8   Albergo Abruzzi
13 Bed & Breakfast Italia
21 Pensione Mimosa
23 Hotel Primavera
26 Albergo della Lunetta
27 Hotel Pomezia

PLACES TO EAT
2   Gelateria della Palma
3   Gelateria Giolitti
12 Osteria
14 Pizzeria da Baffetto
15 Paladini
18 Pizzeria La Montecarlo
24 Il Fornaio
25 Cul de Sac 1
27 Hostaria Romanesca
28 Filetti di Baccalà
32 Hosteria dal Pompiere
33 D'Augusto
36 Osteria da Lucia
37 Pizzeria da Vittorio; Capo de Ferro
40 Fonte della Salute
42 Frontoni
55 Osteria Gli Angeletti

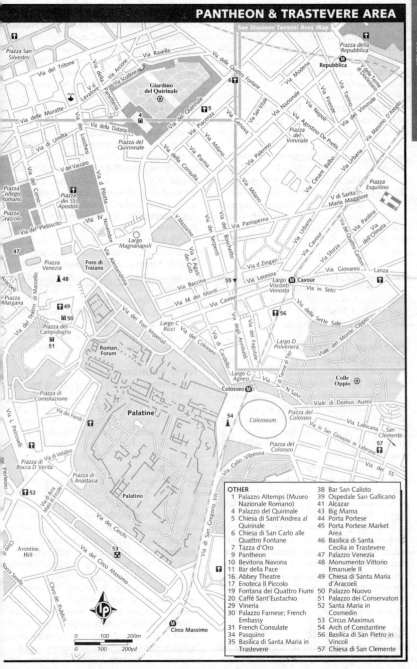

PANTHEON & TRASTEVERE AREA

See Stazione Termini Area Map

OTHER
1 Palazzo Altemps (Museo Nazionale Romano)
4 Palazzo del Quirinale
5 Chiesa di Sant'Andrea al Quirinale
6 Chiesa di San Carlo alle Quattro Fontane
7 Tazza d'Oro
9 Pantheon
10 Bevitoria Navona
11 Bar della Pace
16 Abbey Theatre
17 Enoteca Il Piccolo
19 Fontana dei Quattro Fiumi
20 Caffé Sant'Eustachio
29 Vineria
30 Palazzo Farnese; French Embassy
31 French Consulate
34 Pasquino
35 Basilica di Santa Maria in Trastevere

38 Bar San Calisto
39 Ospedale San Gallicano
41 Alcazar
43 Big Mama
44 Porta Portese
45 Porta Portese Market Area
46 Basilica di Santa Cecilia in Trastevere
47 Palazzo Venezia
48 Monumento Vittorio Emanuele II
49 Chiesa di Santa Maria d'Aracoeli
50 Palazzo Nuovo
51 Palazzo dei Conservatori
52 Santa Maria in Cosmedin
53 Circus Maximus
54 Arch of Constantine
56 Basilica di San Pietro in Vincoli
57 Chiesa di San Clemente

his work was drastically changed and little evidence of his design, apart from the great vaulted ceiling of the church, remains. An interesting feature of the church is a double meridian in the transept, one tracing the polar star and the other telling the precise time of the sun's zenith.

Museo Nazionale Romano

This museum (☎ 06 683 37 59; Piazza Sant' Apollinare 44; admission €5; open 9am-7.45pm Tues-Sun), located in three separate buildings, houses an important collection of ancient art, including Greek and Roman sculpture. The museum is largely housed in the restored 15th-century Palazzo Altemps, near Piazza Navona. It contains numerous important pieces from the Ludovisi collection, including the Ludovisi Throne. Another part of the same museum (☎ 06 48 90 35 00; Largo di Villa Peretti 1; admission €6; open 9am-7.45pm Tues-Sun), is in the Palazzo Massimo alle Terme, just off Piazza dei Cinquecento. It contains a collection of frescoes and mosaics from the Villa of Livia, excavated at Prima Porta, and a knockout numismatic (coin) collection.

Piazza di Spagna & Spanish Steps

This piazza, church and famous staircase (Scalinata della Trinitá dei Monti) have long provided a major gathering place for foreigners and locals alike. Built with a legacy from the French in 1725, but named after the Spanish Embassy to the Holy See, the steps lead to the church of Trinitá dei Monti, which was built by the French.

In the 18th century beautiful Italians gathered there, hoping to be chosen as artists' models, and there are still plenty of beauties of both sexes to cast your eye over, although they're well aware of this. To the right as you face the steps is the house where Keats spent the last three months of his life in 1821. In the piazza is the boat-shaped fountain of the **Barcaccia**, believed to be by Pietro Bernini, father of the famous Gian Lorenzo. One of Rome's most elegant and expensive shopping streets, **Via Condotti**, runs off the piazza towards Via del Corso.

Piazza del Popolo

This vast and impressive piazza was laid out in the 16th century and redesigned in the early 19th century by Giuseppe Valadier. The piazza is also home to Santa Maria del Popolo, where two magnificent Caravaggio paintings (one of St Peter and one of St Paul) are housed. The piazza is at the foot of the **Pincio Hill**, from where there is a wonderful panoramic view of the city, especially in the early hours.

Villa Borghese

This beautiful park was once the estate of Cardinal Scipione Borghese. His 17th-century villa houses the **Museo e Galleria Borghese** (☎ 06 32 81 01; admission €6.50, plus €1.03 booking fee; open 9am-9pm Tues-Sat), a collection of important paintings and sculptures gathered by the Borghese family. Reservations are essential. Just outside the park is the **Galleria Nazionale d'Arte Moderna** (☎ 06 32 29 81; Viale delle Belle Arti 131; admission €6.50; open 8.30am-7.30pm Tues-Sun). The important Etruscan museum, **Museo Nazionale Etrusco di Villa Giulia** (admission €4; open 8.30am-7.30pm Tues-Sun), is along the same street in Piazzale di Villa Giulia, in the former villa of Pope Julius III.

You can hire bicycles at the top of the Pincio Hill or near the Porta Pinciana entrance to Villa Borghese, where there is also a small amusement park that might excite the kids.

Trevi Fountain

The high-baroque Fontana di Trevi was designed by Nicola Salvi in 1732. Its water was supplied by one of Rome's earliest aqueducts. The famous custom is to throw a coin into the fountain (over your shoulder while facing away) to ensure your return to Rome.

Pantheon

The Pantheon (Piazza della Rotonda; admission free; open 8.30am-7.30pm Mon-Sat, 9am-6pm Sun), is the best preserved building of ancient Rome. The original temple was built in 27 BC by Marcus Agrippa, son-in-law of Emperor Augustus, and dedicated to the planetary gods. Although the temple was rebuilt by Emperor Hadrian, Agrippa's name remains inscribed over the entrance.

Over the centuries the temple was consistently plundered and damaged. The gilded-bronze roof tiles were removed by an emperor of the eastern empire, and Pope Urban VIII had the bronze ceiling of the portico melted down to make the canopy over the main altar of St Peter's and 80 cannons for

Castel Sant'Angelo. The Pantheon's extraordinary dome is considered the most important achievement of ancient Roman architecture. In 608 the temple was consecrated to the Virgin and all martyrs.

The Italian kings Vittorio Emanuele II and Umberto I and the painter Raphael are buried there.

Piazza Navona

This vast and beautiful square, lined with baroque palaces, was laid out on the ruins of Domitian's stadium and features three fountains, including Bernini's masterpiece, the **Fontana dei Quattro Fiumi** (Fountain of the Four Rivers), in its centre. Take time to relax on one of the stone benches or the expensive cafés and watch the artists who gather in the piazza to work.

Campo de' Fiori

This is a lively piazza where a flower and vegetable market is held every morning except Sunday. Now lined with bars and trattorias that get packed at night, the piazza was a place of execution during the Inquisition.

The **Palazzo Farnese** (Farnese Palace), in the piazza of the same name, is just off Campo de' Fiori. A magnificent Renaissance building, it was started in 1514 by Antonio da Sangallo, work was carried on by Michelangelo and it was completed by Giacomo della Porta. Built for Cardinal Alessandro Farnese (later Pope Paul III), the palace is now the French embassy. The piazza has two fountains, which were enormous granite baths taken from the Baths of Caracalla.

Via Giulia

This elegant street was designed by Bramante, who was commissioned by Pope Julius II to create a new approach to St Peter's. It is lined with Renaissance palaces, antique shops and art galleries.

Trastevere

You can wander through the narrow medieval streets of this area which, despite the many foreigners who live here, retains the air of a typical Roman neighbourhood. It is especially beautiful at night and is a wonderful area for bar-hopping or a meal.

Of particular note here is the **Basilica di Santa Maria in Trastevere**, in the lovely piazza of the same name. It is believed to be the oldest church dedicated to the Virgin in Rome. Although the first church was built on the site in the 4th century, the present structure was built in the 12th century and features a Romanesque bell tower and facade, with a mosaic of the Virgin. Its interior was redecorated during the baroque period, but the vibrant mosaics in the apse and on the triumphal arch date from the 12th century. Also take a look at the **Basilica di Santa Cecilia in Trastevere**.

Gianicolo

The top of the Gianicolo (Janiculum), the hill between St Peter's and Trastevere, offers a stirring panoramic view of Rome.

Catacombs

There are several catacombs in Rome, consisting of miles of tunnels carved out of volcanic rock, which were the meeting and burial places of early Christians in Rome. The largest are along Via Appia Antica, just outside the city and accessible Metropolitana Linea A to Colli Albani, then bus No 660. The **Catacombs of San Callisto** (admission €5; open 8.30am-noon & 2.30pm-5pm Thur-Tues Mar-Jan) and **Catacombs of San Sebastiano** (admission €5; open 8.30am-noon & 2.30pm-5pm Mon-Sat 10 Dec–10 Nov) are almost next to each other on Via Appia Antica. Admission to each is with a guide only.

Vatican City

After the unification of Italy, the papal states of central Italy became part of the new kingdom of Italy, causing a considerable rift between church and state. In 1929, Mussolini, under the Lateran Treaty, gave the pope full sovereignty over what is now called the Vatican City.

The **tourist office** (☎ 06 69 88 16 62; Piazza San Pietro; open 8.30am-7pm Mon-Sat) is to the left of the basilica. Guided tours of the Vatican City gardens (€10) can be organised here. In the same area is the **Vatican post office** (☎ 06 69 88 34 06; open 8am-7pm Mon-Fri & 8.30am-6pm Sat), which is said to offer a much more reliable service than the normal Italian postal system.

The city has its own postal service, newspaper, radio station, train station and army of Swiss Guards kitted out in uniforms designed by Michelangelo.

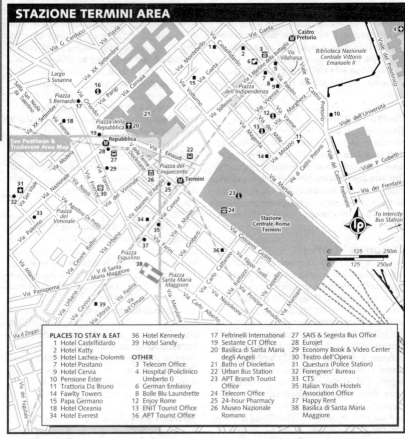

STAZIONE TERMINI AREA

PLACES TO STAY & EAT	36 Hotel Kennedy	17 Feltrinelli International	27 SAIS & Segesta Bus Office
1 Hotel Castelfidardo	39 Hotel Sandy	19 Sestante CIT Office	28 Eurojet
2 Hotel Katty		20 Basilica di Santa Maria	29 Economy Book & Video Center
5 Hotel Lachea-Dolomiti	OTHER	degli Angeli	30 Teatro dell'Opera
7 Hotel Positano	3 Telecom Office	21 Baths of Diocletian	31 Questura (Police Station)
9 Hotel Cervia	4 Hospital (Policlinico	22 Urban Bus Station	32 Foreigners' Bureau
10 Pensione Ester	Umberto I)	23 APT Branch Tourist	33 CTS
11 Trattoria Da Bruno	6 German Embassy	Office	35 Italian Youth Hostels
14 Fawlty Towers	8 Bolle Blu Laundrette	24 Telecom Office	Association Office
15 Papa Germano	12 Enjoy Rome	25 24-hour Pharmacy	37 Happy Rent
18 Hotel Oceania	13 ENIT Tourist Office	26 Museo Nazionale	38 Basilica di Santa Maria
34 Hotel Everest	16 APT Tourist Office	Romano	Maggiore

St Peter's Basilica & Square The most famous church in the Christian world, **St Peter's** *(San Pietro; open 7am-7pm daily Apr-Sept, 7am-6pm daily Oct-Mar)* stands on the site where St Peter was buried. The first church on the site was built during Constantine's reign in the 4th century, and in 1506 work was started on a new basilica, designed by Bramante.

Although several architects were involved in its construction, it is generally held that St Peter's owes its grandeur and power to Michelangelo, who took over the project in 1547 at the age of 72 and was particularly responsible for the design of the dome. He died before the church was completed. The cavernous interior contains numerous treasures, including Michelangelo's superb *Pietá*,

sculpted when he was only 24 years old and the only work to carry his signature (on the sash across the breast of the Madonna). It's protected by bulletproof glass.

Bernini's huge, baroque *Baldacchino* (a heavily sculpted bronze canopy over the papal altar) stands 29m high and is an extraordinary work of art. Another point of note is the red porphyry disc near the central door, which marks the spot where Charlemagne and later emperors were crowned by the pope.

Entrance to Michelangelo's soaring dome is to the right as you climb the stairs to the atrium of the basilica. Make the entire climb on foot for €4, or pay €5 and you take the elevator for part of the way.

Dress rules and security are stringently enforced – no shorts, miniskirts or sleeveless tops, and be prepared to have your bags searched. Prams and strollers must be left in a designated area outside the basilica.

Bernini's **Piazza San Pietro** (St Peter's Square) is rightly considered a masterpiece. Laid out in the 17th century as a place for Christians of the world to gather, the immense piazza is bound by two semicircular colonnades, each of which is made up of four rows of Doric columns. In the centre of the piazza is an obelisk that was brought to Rome by Caligula from Heliopolis (in ancient Egypt). When you stand on the dark paving stones between the obelisk and either of the fountains, the colonnades appear to have only one row of columns.

The Pope usually gives a public audience at 10am every Wednesday in the Papal Audience Hall or St Peter's Square. You must make a booking, in person or by fax to the **Prefettura della Casa Pontifica** (☎ 06 69 88 46 31, fax 06 69 88 38 65), on the Monday or Tuesday before the audience between 9am and 1pm. Go through the bronze doors under the colonnade to the right as you face the basilica.

Vatican Museums From St Peter's follow the wall of the Vatican City (to the right as you face the basilica) to the museums *(admission €10, free last Sun of month; open 8.45am-4.45pm Mon-Fri, 8.45am-1.45pm Sat & last Sun of month)*. The museums are closed Sunday and public holidays, but open on the last Sunday of every month (queues are always very long). Guided visits to the Vatican gardens cost €10 and can be booked by calling ☎ 06 69 88 44 66.

The Vatican museums contain an incredible collection of art and treasures collected by the popes, and you will need several hours (at least) to see the most important areas and museums. The Sistine Chapel comes towards the end of a full visit; otherwise, you can walk straight there and then work your way back through the museums.

The **Museo Pio-Clementino**, containing Greek and Roman antiquities, is on the ground floor near the entrance. Through the tapestry and map galleries are the **Stanze di Rafaello**, once the private apartments of Pope Julius II, decorated with frescoes by Raphael. Of particular interest is the magnificent **Stanza della Segnatura**, which features Raphael's masterpieces *The School of Athens* and *Disputation on the Sacrament*.

From Raphael's rooms, go down the stairs to the sumptuous **Appartamento Borgia**, decorated with frescoes by Pinturicchio, then go down another flight of stairs to the **Sistine Chapel**, the private papal chapel built in 1473 for Pope Sixtus IV. Michelangelo's wonderful frescoes of the *Creation* and *Last Judgment* have been superbly restored to their original brilliance. It took Michelangelo four years, at the height of the Renaissance, to paint the *Creation*; 24 years later he painted the extraordinary *Last Judgment*. The other walls of the chapel were painted by artists including Botticelli, Ghirlandaio, Pinturicchio and Signorelli. To best enjoy the frescoes on the ceiling, a pocket mirror is recommended so that you don't have to strain your neck.

ORGANISED TOURS

Enjoy Rome (☎ 06 445 18 43, fax 06 445 68 90; **w** www.enjoyrome.com; Via Marghera 8a), offers excellent walking or bicycle tours of Rome's main sights from €13 (aged under 26) and €19 (over 26) per person and a bus tour for Pompeii. **ATAC** bus No 110 leaves daily every half-hour between 10am and 6pm (from 9am to 8pm in summer) from Piazza dei Cinquecento, in front of Stazione Termini, for a 90-minute tour of the city. Tickets cost €7.75 (€12.91 if you want to hop on and off). Night tours start at 8pm (9pm in summer). You can also do a basilica tour, which leaves every half-hour from 10.30am to 2.30pm (to 3pm in summer).

Through Eternity Rome (☎ 06 700 93 36, 06 347 336 52 98; **w** www.througheternity .com) has numerous walking tours from €20 per person with an emphasis on storytelling, plus it gets rave reviews from many travellers.

SPECIAL EVENTS

Although Romans desert their city in summer, particularly in August when the weather is relentlessly hot, cultural and musical events take place. The Comune di Roma coordinates a diverse series of concerts, performances and events throughout summer under the general title Estate Romana (Roman Summer). The series usually features major international performers. Details are published in Rome's daily newspapers.

A jazz festival is held in July and August in the Villa Celimontana, which is a park on top of the Celian Hill (access from Piazza della Navicella).

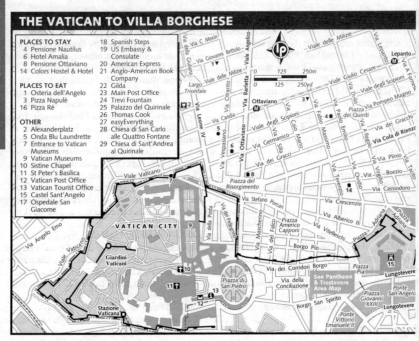

THE VATICAN TO VILLA BORGHESE

PLACES TO STAY
4 Pensione Nautilus
6 Hotel Amalia
8 Pensione Ottaviano
14 Colors Hostel & Hotel

PLACES TO EAT
1 Osteria dell'Angelo
3 Pizza Napulè
16 Pizza Ré

OTHER
2 Alexanderplatz
5 Onda Blu Laundrette
7 Entrance to Vatican
   Museums
9 Vatican Museums
10 Sistine Chapel
11 St Peter's Basilica
12 Vatican Post Office
13 Vatican Tourist Office
15 Castel Sant'Angelo
17 Ospedale San
   Giacome

18 Spanish Steps
19 US Embassy &
   Consulate
20 American Express
21 Anglo-American Book
   Company
22 Gilda
23 Main Post Office
24 Trevi Fountain
25 Palazzo del Quirinale
26 Thomas Cook
27 easyEverything
28 Chiesa di San Carlo
   alle Quattro Fontane
29 Chiesa di Sant'Andrea
   al Quirinale

The Festa de' Noantri is held in Trastevere in the last two weeks of July in honour of Our Lady of Mt Carmel.

At Christmas the focus is on the many churches of Rome, each setting up its own nativity scene. Among the most renowned is the 13th-century crib at Santa Maria Maggiore. During Holy Week, at Easter, the focus is again religious and events include the famous procession of the cross between the Colosseum and the Palatine on Good Friday, and the Pope's blessing of the city and the world in St Peter's Square on Easter Sunday.

The Spanish Steps become a sea of pink azaleas during the Spring Festival in April. Around mid-April, Italian Cultural Heritage Week sees many galleries, museums and tourist attractions open free of charge.

PLACES TO STAY
Camping
About 15 minutes from the centre by public transport is the **Village Camping Flaminio** (☎ 06 333 14 29; Via Flaminia Nuova 821; per person/tent €9.50/12). Tents and good bungalows are available for rent (although there's a fairly frustrating 4pm check-in and

10am check-out for bungalows). You can catch the Metropolitana Linea A from Termini station to Flaminio and change to the Prima Porta Linea, getting off at the Due Ponti station (request stop, so ring the bell), which is 100m from the camp site.

Hostels
HI Ostello della Gioventu Foro Italico (☎ 06 323 62 67; e aig.sedenazionale@uni.net; Viale delle Olimpiadi 61; dorm bed €15) has over 300 beds and opens from 7am to midnight. Take Metropolitana Linea A to Ottaviano, then bus No 32 to Foro Italico. The head office of the **Italian Youth Hostel Association** (☎ 06 487 11 52; w www.ostellion line.org; Via Cavour 44, 00184 Rome; open 9am-5pm Mon-Fri) has information about the hostels in Italy. You can also join HI here.

B&Bs
This type of accommodation in private houses is a relatively recent addition to Rome's accommodation options for budget travellers.

Bed & Breakfast Italia (☎ 06 68 80 15 13, fax 06 687 86 19; e info@bbitalia.it; Corso Vittorio Emanuele II 282; singles/doubles

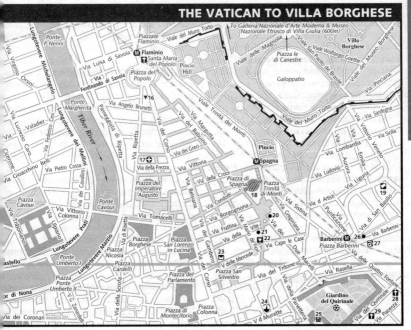

THE VATICAN TO VILLA BORGHESE

per person per night without bath from €28/23, with bath €41/36) is one of several B&B networks and offers central rooms.

Hotels & Pensioni

North of Stazione Termini To reach the pensioni in this area, head to the right as you leave the train platforms onto Via Castro Pretorio. The excellent and frequently recommended **Fawlty Towers** (☎ 06 445 48 02; Via Magenta 39; dorm bed €18, with bath €23) offers hostel-style accommodation and lots of information about Rome. Added bonuses are the sunny terrace and lack of curfew.

Nearby in Via Palestro are several reasonably priced hotels. **Hotel Cervia** (☎ 06 49 10 57, fax 06 49 10 56; e hotelcervia@wnt.it; Via Palestro 55; dorm bed €20, singles without bath €35) has tidy rooms and a ground floor location. **Hotel Katty** (☎ 06 444 12 16; Via Palestro 35; singles/doubles without bath €47/62, with bath €73/83-93) has basic rooms and some other, better ones, plus a friendly owner who'll chat your ear off. Around the corner is the clean and comfy **Pensione Ester** (☎ 06 495 71 23; Viale Castro Pretorio 25; doubles without bath €52).

Hotel Positano (☎ 06 49 03 60; e info@ hotelpositano.it; Via Palestro 49; dorm bed €20, singles/doubles/triples with bath €70/ 105/140) is a flashier option, with very pleasant air-con rooms with TV, fridge and phone (not for dorms though).

Two good hotels, Lachea and Dolomiti, are in the same building, with the same charming management and good prices – **Hotel Lachea-Dolomiti** (☎ 06 495 72 56; e lachea@hotel -dolomiti.it, e dolomiti@hotel-dolomiti.it; Via San Martino della Battaglia 11; singles/ doubles/triples without bath €47/68/73, with bath €68/104/124) has large, quiet, spotlessly clean rooms with all mod-cons.

Papa Germano (☎ 06 48 69 19; e info@ hotelpapagermano.com; Via Calatafimi 14a; singles/doubles without bath €47/68, with bath 62/93) is one of the more popular two-star places in the area.

Hotel Castelfidardo (☎ 06 446 46 38, fax 06 494 13 78; e castelfidardo@italmarkey .it; Via Castelfidardo 31; singles/doubles/ triples without bath €42/60/77, with bath €52/70/93) is a well-run and frequently recommended place with lovely rooms and a 5% discount for cash payments.

South of Stazione Termini This area is a bit seedier, but prices remain the same. As you exit to the left of the station, follow Via Gioberti to Via G Amendola, which becomes Via F Turati. This street, and the parallel Via Principe Amedeo, harbours a concentration of budget pensioni, so you should easily find a room. The area improves as you get closer to the Colosseum and Roman Forum.

On Via Cavour, the main street running southwest from the piazza in front of Termini, is **Hotel Everest** (☎ 06 488 16 29; Via Cavour 47; singles/doubles with bath €80/120), with clean and pleasant rooms. **Hotel Sandy** (☎ 06 488 45 85; Via Cavour 136; dorm bed €18) has dorms with lockers, no curfew, not-great bathrooms and a party atmosphere for the young crowd.

Better-quality hotels in the area include **Hotel Oceania** (☎ 06 482 46 96, fax 06 488 5586; e hoceania@tin.it; Via Firenze 38; singles/doubles with bath €104/135) with a warm welcome and smart rooms. **Hotel Kennedy 2** (☎ 06 446 53 73, fax 06 446 54 17; e hotelkennedy@micanet.it; Via F Turati 62; singles/doubles with bath €88/155) has good rooms and a handy location, although some corners are a little worn.

City Centre On a square just off Via Vittorio Emanuele II, **Hotel Primavera** (☎ 06 68 80 31 09, fax 06 686 92 65; Piazza San Pantaleo 3; doubles with/without bath €115/95) has clean and plain doubles only available. The **Albergo Abruzzi** (☎ 06 679 20 21; Piazza della Rotonda 69; singles/doubles without bath €65/73-95) overlooks the Pantheon – which explains the noise. Rooms are adequate and bookings here are essential year-round.

Pensione Mimosa (☎ 06 68 80 17 53, fax 06 683 35 57; e hotelmimosa@tin.it; Via Santa Chiara 61; singles/doubles without bath €77/93, with bath €93/108), off Piazza della Minerva, has rooms of varying quality and a great location. Service varies, too, depending on who's at the front desk.

Albergo della Lunetta (☎ 06 686 10 80, fax 06 689 20 28; Piazza del Paradiso 68; singles/doubles/triples without bath €52/83/115, with bath €62/109/145) is a solid, decent choice. You'll definitely need to reserve in advance, or check for cancellations.

Hotel Pomezia (☎/fax 06 686 13 71; Via dei Chiavari 12; singles/doubles without

bath €50/85, with bath €105/205), is welcoming and well-kitted out, and includes breakfast in the rates, which can drop by 30% in the low season.

Near St Peter's & the Vatican Bargains are rare in this area, but it is comparatively quiet and reasonably close to the main sights. Bookings are a necessity, as rooms are often filled with people attending conferences and so on at the Vatican. The simplest way to reach the area is on the Metropolitana Linea A to Ottaviano. Bus No 64 from Termini stops at St Peter's.

A long-standing bargain in the area is **Pensione Ottaviano** (☎ 06 39 73 72 53; e gi.costantini@agora.stm.it; Via Ottaviano 6; dorm bed €18, doubles/triples without bath €62/70), near Piazza Risorgimento, with simple rooms and English-speaking staff. A classy new cheaper-end addition is **Colors Hostel & Hotel** (☎ 06 687 40 30; Via Boezio 31; dorm bed €18.50, doubles with/without bath €83/76). It has tidy rooms, great management and cooking facilities. **Pensione Nautilus** (☎ 06 324 21 18; Via Germanico 198; singles/doubles without bath €52/79, with bath €78/93) offers basic, tidy rooms, although things can seem a little dark at times. **Hotel Amalia** (☎ 06 39 72 33 56, fax 06 39 72 33 65; e hotelamalia@iol.it; Via Germanico 66; singles/doubles without bath €70/100, with bath €130/196-210) has quite swanky, sunny rooms and breakfast is included.

PLACES TO EAT

Rome bursts at the seams with trattorias, pizzerias and restaurants – and not all of them are overrun by tourists or are frighteningly expensive. Eating times are generally from 12.30pm to 3pm and 8pm to 11pm. Most Romans head out for dinner about 9pm, so arrive earlier to claim a table. Prices in this guide reflect the cost per person for two courses with wine, plus a dessert or side dish.

Antipasto dishes in Rome are particularly good and many restaurants allow you to make your own mixed selection. Typical pasta dishes include *bucatini all'Amatriciana* (large, hollow spaghetti with a salty sauce of tomato and bacon), *penne all'arrabbiata* (penne with a hot sauce of tomatoes, peppers and chilli) and *spaghetti carbonara* (pancetta, eggs and cheese). Romans also love dishes prepared with offal – try *paiata* (pasta with veal intestines). *Saltimbocca alla Romana* (slices of veal and ham) is a classic meat dish, as is *straccetti con la rucola,* fine slices of beef tossed in garlic and oil and topped with fresh rocket. In winter you can't go past *cariofi alla Romana* (artichokes stuffed with garlic and mint or parsley).

Good options for cheap, quick meals are the hundreds of bars, where *panini* (sandwiches) cost €1.20 to €2.60 if taken *al banco* (at the bar), or takeaway pizzerias, usually called *pizza a taglio,* where a slice of freshly cooked pizza, sold by weight, can cost as little as €1.10. Bakeries are numerous and are another good choice for a cheap snack.

Try **Paladini** *(Via del Governo Vecchio 29)* for sandwiches, and **Il Fornaio** *(Via Baullari 6)* for mouth-watering pastries and bread.

There are numerous outdoor **markets**, notably the lively and colourful daily market in Campo de' Fiori. Other, cheaper food markets are held in Piazza Vittorio Emanuele, near the station, and off Viale delle Millizie, north of the Vatican. There's a well-stocked **24-hour supermarket** underneath the main concourse of Stazione Termini, which is handy for self-caterers.

Restaurants, Trattorias & Pizzerias

The restaurants near Stazione Termini are generally to be avoided if you want to pay reasonable prices for halfway-decent food. The side streets around Piazza Navona and Campo de' Fiori harbour many budget trattorias and pizzerias, and the areas of San Lorenzo (to the east of Termini, near the university) and Testaccio (across the Tiber near Piramide) are popular local eating districts. Trastevere offers an excellent selection of rustic eating places hidden in tiny piazzas, and pizzerias where it doesn't cost the earth to sit at a table on the street.

City Centre The **Pizzeria La Montecarlo** *(☎ 06 686 18 77; Vicolo Savelli 12; meal about €11)* has paper sheets for tablecloths, a high turnover (queues form around 9.30pm) and a long list of tasty pizzas.

Pizza Ré *(☎ 06 321 14 68; Via di Ripetta 13; meal about €15)* gets packed despite its size (and with good reason) by lovers of Naples-style pizza. It's a swanky-looking place, too.

Wondering whether there are any great geniuses left in Rome? Yes, they're making pizza at **Pizzeria da Baffetto** *(☎ 06 686 16 17; Via del Governo Vecchio 114; pizza about €7),* a Roman institution. Expect to join a queue and share a table if you arrive after 9pm. Farther along the street is an **osteria** *(Via del Governo Vecchio 18; meal about €13),* where you can eat an excellent lunch in simple surrounds, with locals who know that it's best to arrive before 1pm if the tum's rumbling. Back along the street towards Piazza Navona is **Cul de Sac 1** *(☎ 06 68 80 10 94; Piazza Pasquino 73; meal about €15),* a wine bar which also has great meals, including hearty soups.

Hostaria Romanesca *(☎ 06 686 40 24; Piazza Capo de' Fiori; meal about €17)* is tiny, so arrive early in winter and get your fill of the generous pasta dishes. In summer there are numerous tables outside.

In cod we trust, and just off Campo de' Fiori is **Filetti di Baccalá** *(☎ 06 686 40 18; Largo dei Librari 88; meal about €9),* which serves only deliciously deep-fried cod fillets in cheap and cheerful surrounds.

In the Jewish quarter, just off Piazza delle Cinque Sole is **Hostaria dal Pompiere** *(☎ 06 686 83 77; Via Santa Maria de Caldari 38; meal about €22),* which has a tastefully subdued decor and some of the best *spaghetti alle vongole* you'll ever try.

West of the Tiber On the west bank of the Fiume Tevere (Tiber River), good-value restaurants are concentrated in Trastevere and the Testaccio district, past the Piramide metro stop. Many of the establishments around St Peter's and the Vatican are geared for tourists and can be very expensive. There are, however, some good options. Try **Pizza Napul'è** *(☎ 06 63 23 10 05; Viale Giulio Cesare 91; meal about €12)* or the handy and inexpensive **Osteria dell'Angelo** *(Via G Bettolo 24),* along Via Leone IV from the Vatican City, where you can gorge on cheap pasta for about €4 after a visit to the Vatican.

In Trastevere, try **Frontoni** *(Viale di Trastevere 54),* near Piazza Mastai, for fantastic panini. **D'Augusto** *(Piazza dei Renzi 15; meal about €15),* just around the corner from the Basilica di Santa Maria in Trastevere (turn right as you face the church and walk to Via della Pelliccia), is a very popular cheap eating spot. The food might be OK at best, but the atmosphere, especially in summer with tables outside in the piazza, is traditionally Roman. **Osteria da Lucia** *(Vicolo del Mattinato 2; meal about €20)* is more expensive, but the food is much better, the owners are lovely, and on sunny days you'll sit beneath the neighbours' washing.

For a good pizza dinner, try **Pizzeria da Vittorio** *(Via San Cosimato 14; meal about €15)*. You'll have to wait for an outside table if you arrive after 8.30pm, but the atmosphere is great, and the bruschetta is worth trying too. Next door is **Capo de Ferro**, where the meals are about the same price and the same Trastevere atmosphere is available.

You won't find a cheaper, noisier, more chaotic pizzeria in Rome than **Pizzeria Remo** *(Piazza Santa Maria Liberatrice 44; meal about €10)* in Testaccio, when Friday and Saturday nights are filled with party types. **Augustarello** *(Via G Branca 98; meal about €15)*, off the piazza, specialises in the very traditional Roman fare of offal dishes, which taste better than it sometimes sounds.

Between Termini & the Forum If you have no option but to eat near Stazione Termini, try to avoid the tourist traps offering overpriced full menus. **Trattoria da Bruno** *(☎ 06 49 04 03; Via Varese 29; meal about €18)* has good food and service, with what looks like a torture rack hanging from the ceiling. Just off Via Cavour is **Osteria Gli Angeletti** *(☎ 06 474 33 74; Via dell'Angeletto 3; meal about €17)*, an excellent little restaurant with prices at the higher end of the budget range, but imaginative dishes that break out of the spag bog/gnocchi pesto/lasagne tourist-menu trap.

Gelati
Both **Gelateria Giolitti** *(Via degli Uffici del Vicario 40)* near the Pantheon and **Gelateria della Palma** *(Via della Maddalena 20)* just around the corner have a huge selection of flavours and get big crowds – get the *fichi* (fig) or pistacchio at Della Palma dribbling down your chin. In Trastevere, **Fonte della Salute** *(Via Cardinale Marmaggi 2-6)* also has excellent gelati.

ENTERTAINMENT
Rome's best entertainment guide is the weekly *Roma C'è* (€1.03), available at all newsstands. It has an English-language section. *La Repubblica* and *Il Messagero* are daily newspapers with cinema, theatre and concert listings.

Wanted in Rome is a fortnightly magazine for Rome's English-speaking community (€0.75). It has good cultural listings and is available at outlets including the **Economy Book & Video Center** *(Via Torino 136)*, and at newsstands in the city centre, including Largo Argentina.

Cafés & Bars
Remember that prices skyrocket in bars as soon as you sit down, particularly near major tourist attractions. The same cappuccino taken at the bar will cost less – but passing an hour or so watching the world go by over a cappuccino, beer or wine in a beautiful location can be hard to beat, and despite what you may have heard, Italians do it too.

For great coffee head for **Tazza d'Oro** *(Via degli Orfani)* just off Piazza della Rotonda; and **Caffé Sant'Eustachio** *(Piazza Sant'Eustachio 82)*, where you might want to pipe up if you don't want any sugar in your espresso. Try the *granita di caffé* at either one in summer.

Campo de' Fiori is a popular spot to bar-hop and socialise for foreigners and locals alike. **Vineria** *(☎ 06 68 80 32 68; Campo de Fiori 15)*, has a tempting selection of wine and beer, plus outdoor tables in warm weather. **Bar della Pace** *(Via della Pace 3-7)* is big with the trendy crew, and you can see why, as it's pretty damn schmick. **Bevitoria Navona** *(☎ 06 68 80 10 22; Piazza Navona 72)* has wine by the glass and makes for a charming early evening spot to have a drink (inside or out). In Trastevere, the slacker-alternative set chooses to hang at **Bar San Calisto** *(Piazza San Calisto)*, and it's easy to see why – drinks aren't extortionate and the clientele is frequently interesting for people watchers. Near Piazza Navona **Abbey Theatre** *(Via del Governo Vecchio 51)* is a popular and relatively intimate Irish pub, which means you can get Guinness and Kilkenny on tap. Also on Via del Governo Vecchio, at No 74, is the small-but-perfectly-formed **Enoteca Il Piccolo**, with a smattering of wines by the glass and a quiet, low-key atmosphere.

Nightclubs
Among the more interesting and popular Roman live music clubs is **Radio Londra** *(☎ 06 575 00 44; Via di Monte Testaccio*

67), in the Testaccio area. On the same street are the more sedate music clubs **Caruso Caffé** at No 36 and **Caffé Latino** at No 96, both generally offering jazz or blues, with some Latin DJ-ing thrown in for dancing. More jazz and blues can be heard at **Alexanderplatz** *(☎ 06 39 74 21 71; Via Ostia 9)* and **Big Mama** *(☎ 06 581 25 51; Via San Francesco a Ripa 18)* in Trastevere.

Roman discos are pants-wettingly expensive. Expect to pay up to €20 to get in, which may or may not include one drink. Popular stayers include **Alien** *(☎ 06 841 22 12; Via Velletri 13),* for those who like the more mainstream end of house and techno, **Goa** *(☎ 06 574 82 77; Via Libetta 13)* with a groovy ethnic decor and glam crowd but a distant location near metro stop Garbatella, and **Gilda** *(☎ 06 679 73 96; Via Mario de' Fiori 97),* which attracts a slightly older crowd. The best gay disco (according to many) is **L'Alibi** *(☎ 06 574 34 48; Via di Monte Testaccio 44).*

Cinema
There are a handful of cinemas in Trastevere that show English-language movies. There are daily shows at **Pasquino** *(☎ 06 580 36 22; Piazza Sant'Egidio),* just off Piazza Santa Maria. **Alcazar** *(☎ 06 588 00 99; Via Merry del Val 14)* shows English-language films on Monday.

Exhibitions & Concerts
From December to June, opera is performed at the **Teatro dell'Opera** *(☎ 06 48 16 02 55, toll-free ☎ 800 01 66 65; Piazza Beniamino Gigli).* A season of concerts is held in October and November at the **Accademia di Santa Cecilia** *(☎ 06 68 80 10 44; Via della Conciliazione 4)* and the **Accademia Filarmonica Romana** *(Teatro Olimpia, Piazza Gentile da Fabriano 17).*

SHOPPING
It is probably advisable to stick to window-shopping in the expensive Ludovisi district, the area around Via Veneto. Many shops are in Via Sistina and Via Gregoriana, heading towards the Spanish Steps. Via Condotti and the parallel streets heading from Piazza di Spagna to Via del Corso are lined with very expensive clothing and footwear boutiques, as well as shops selling accessories. This is label heaven for the seriously fashion-conscious. Via del Corso itself offers good shopping, with

a mix of moderately expensive and cheaper high-street knock-off fashions.

It is cheaper, but not as interesting, to shop along Via del Tritone and Via Nazionale. There are some interesting second-hand clothes shops along Via del Governo Vecchio.

If clothes don't appeal, wander through the streets around Via Margutta, Via Ripetta, Piazza del Popolo and Via Frattina to look at the art galleries, artists' studios and antiquarian shops. Antique shops line Via Coronari, between Piazza Navona and Lungotevere di Tor di Nona.

Everyone flocks to the famous Porta Portese market every Sunday morning. Hundreds of stalls selling anything you can imagine (doll parts and broken typewriters anyone?) line the streets of the Porta Portese area parallel to Viale di Trastevere, near Trastevere. Take time to rummage through the piles of clothing and bric-a-brac and you will find some incredible bargains. Catch tram No 8 from Largo Argentina and get off near Ospedale San Gallicano on Viale di Trastevere (it's a 10-minute ride).

The market on Via Sannio, near Porta San Giovanni, sells new and second-hand clothes and shoes at bargain prices in the morning from Monday to Saturday.

GETTING THERE & AWAY
Air
The main airline offices are in the area around Via Veneto and Via Barberini, north of Stazione Termini. Qantas, British Airways and Alitalia are all on Via Bissolati. Cathay Pacific, Singapore Airlines and Thai International Airways are on Via Barberini. The main airport is Leonardo da Vinci, at Fiumicino (see Rome's Getting Around section, later).

Bus
The main terminal for intercity buses is in Piazzale Tiburtina, in front of the Stazione Tiburtina. Catch the Metropolitana Linea B from Termini to Tiburtina. Buses connect with cities throughout Italy. Numerous companies, some of which are listed here, operate these services. For information about which companies operate services to which destinations and from where, go to the APT office, or Enjoy Rome (see Tourist Offices, earlier in this chapter). There are ticket offices for all of the companies at Tiburtina station. Cotral (also known as Linee Laziali)

buses, which service Lazio, depart from numerous points throughout the city, depending on their destinations.

Some useful bus lines are:

Cotral (☎ 800 43 17 84) Via Volturno 65; services throughout Lazio
Lazzi (☎ 06 884 08 40) Via Tagliamento 27b; services to other European cities (with Eurolines) and northern and central Italy
Marozzi information at Eurojet (☎ 06 474 28 01), Piazza della Repubblica 54; services to Bari, Brindisi, Sorrento, the Amalfi Coast and Pompeii, as well as to Matera in Basilicata
SAIS & Segesta (☎ 06 481 96 76) Piazza della Repubblica 42; services to Sicily
SENA information at Picarozzi (☎ 06 440 44 95), Via Guido Mazzoni; services to Siena
SULGA information at Trioviaggi (☎ 06 440 27 38), Circumvallazione Nomentana, or Sulga Perugia (☎ 075 575 96 41); services to Perugia, Assisi and Romagna

Train

Almost all trains arrive at and depart from Stazione Termini. There are regular connections to all major cities in Italy and throughout Europe. For train **timetable information** (☎ 848 88 80 88; open 7am-9pm), call or go to the information office at the station (English is spoken). Timetables can be bought at most newsstands in and around Termini and are particularly useful if you are travelling mostly by train. Services at Termini include telephones, money exchange (see Information earlier), tourist information, post office, shops and **luggage storage** (open 7am-midnight daily; €3.10 per piece first 5hr, €0.52 per hr per piece thereafter). Note that some trains depart from the stations at Ostiense and Tiburtina.

Car & Motorcycle

The main road connecting Rome to the north and south is the Autostrada del Sole (A1), which extends from Milan to Reggio di Calabria. On the outskirts of the city it connects with the Grande Raccordo Anulare (GRA), the ring road encircling Rome. If you are entering or leaving Rome, use the Grande Raccordo and the major feeder roads that connect it to the city; it might be longer, but it is simpler and faster. If you're approaching from the north, take the Via Salaria, Via Nomentana or Via Flaminia exits. From the south, Via Appia Nuova, Via Cristoforo Colombo and Via del Mare (which connects Rome to the Lido di

Ostia) all provide reasonably direct routes into the city. The A12 connects the city to both Civitavecchia and Fiumicino airport.

Car rental offices at Stazione Termini in Rome include **Avis** (☎ 06 481 43 73), **Hertz** (☎ 06 474 03 89) and **Maggiore** (☎ 06 488 00 49). All have offices at both airports. **Happy Rent** (☎ 06 481 81 85; w www.happyrent.com; Via Farini 3), rents scooters (from €38 per day).

Boat

Tirrenia and the Ferrovie dello Stato (FS) ferries leave for various points in Sardinia (see Sardinia's Getting There & Away section) from Civitavecchia. A Tirrenia fast ferry leaves from Fiumicino, near Rome, and Civitavecchia in summer only. Bookings can be made at the Sestante CIT, or any travel agency displaying the Tirrenia or FS sign. You can also book directly with **Tirrenia** (☎ 06 42 00 98 03; Via San Nicola da Tolentino 5, Rome); or at the Stazione Marittima (ferry terminal) at the ports. Bookings can be made at Stazione Termini for FS ferries.

GETTING AROUND
To/From the Airport

The main airport is **Leonardo da Vinci** (flight information ☎ 06 65 95 36 40) at Fiumicino. Access to the city is via the Leonardo Express train service (follow the signs to the station from the airport arrivals hall), which costs €8.78 one way. The train arrives at and leaves from platform Nos 25–29 at Termini. The trip takes 35 minutes. The first train leaves the airport for Termini at 6.37am and the last at 11.37pm. Another train makes stops along the way, including at Trastevere and Ostiense, and terminates at Stazione Tiburtina (€4.65). The trip takes about 50 minutes. A night bus runs every 45 minutes from Stazione Tiburtina to the airport from 12.30am to 3.45am, stopping at Termini at the corner of Via Giolitti about 10 minutes later. The airport is connected to Rome by an autostrade, accessible from the Grande Raccordo Anulare (ring road).

Taxis are prohibitively expensive from the airport (at least €45).

The other airport is **Ciampino**, which is used for most domestic and international charter flights. Blue Cotral buses (running from 6.50am to 11.40pm) connect with the Metropolitana (Linea A at Anagnina), where you can catch the subway to Termini or the

Vatican. But if you arrive very late at night, you could end up being forced to catch a taxi. A metropolitan train line, the FM4, connects Termini with the Ciampino airport and Albano Laziale. The airport is connected to Rome by Via Appia Nuova.

Bus

The city bus company is **ATAC** *(information in English ☎ 800 43 17 84; open 8am-6pm)*. Details on which buses head where are available at the ATAC information booth in the centre of Piazza dei Cinquecento. Another central point for main bus routes in the centre is Largo Argentina, on Corso Vittorio Emanuele south of the Pantheon. Buses run from 5.30am to midnight, with limited services throughout the night on some routes. A fast tram service, the No 8, connects Largo Argentina with Trastevere, Porta Portese and the suburb of Monte Verde.

Rome has an integrated public transport system, so you can use the same ticket for the bus, Metro, tram and the suburban railway. Tickets cost €0.77 and are valid for 75 minutes. They must be purchased *before* you get on the bus and validated in the orange machine as you enter. The fine for travelling without a ticket is €51, to be paid on the spot, and there is no sympathy for 'dumb tourists' or non-Italian speakers. Tickets can be purchased at any tobacconist, newsstand, metro station or at the main bus terminals. Daily tickets cost €3.10 and weekly tickets cost €12.40.

The new, private **'J' buses** *(☎ 800 07 62 87)* cover some routes of interest to tourists (J2, J4, J5), and you can buy tickets on board, although they are more expensive than ATAC buses. Tickets cost €1 for 75 minutes, €2.45 per day and €9.30 per week. They can also be purchased at tobacconists and newsstands.

Metropolitana

The Metropolitana (Metro) has two lines, A and B. Both pass through Stazione Termini. Take Linea A for Piazza di Spagna, the Vatican (Ottaviano) and Villa Borghese (Flaminio), and Linea B for the Colosseum, Circus Maximus and Piramide (for Testaccio and Stazione Ostiense). Tickets are the same as for city buses (see Bus earlier in this section). Trains run approximately every five minutes between 5.30am and 11.30pm (12.30am on Saturday).

Taxi

Taxis are on radio call 24 hours a day in Rome. **Cooperativa Radio Taxi Romana** *(☎ 06 35 70)* and **La Capitale** *(☎ 06 49 94)* are two of the many operators. Major taxi ranks are at the airports, Stazione Termini and Largo Argentina in the historical centre (look for the orange-and-black taxi signs). There are surcharges for luggage (€1.03 per item), night service (€2.58), Sunday and public holidays (€1.03) and travel to/from Fiumicino airport (€7.23/5.94). The flagfall is €2.32 (for the first 3km), then €0.62 for every kilometre. There is a €2.58 supplement from 10pm to 7am, and €1.03 from 7am to 10pm on Sunday and public holidays.

Car & Motorcycle

Negotiating Roman traffic by car is difficult enough, but you are in for enormous stress if you ride a motorcycle or vespa. Keep your wits about you and say a prayer. Pedestrians should watch out for motorcycles, which never seem to stop at red lights.

If your car goes missing after being parked illegally, check with the **traffic police** *(☎ 06 676 91)*. It will cost about €100 to get it back, plus your parking fine.

A major parking area close to the centre is at the Villa Borghese. Entrance is from Piazzale Brasile at the top of Via Veneto. There is a supervised car park at Stazione Termini. There are large car parks at Stazione Tiburtina and Piazza dei Partigiani at Stazione Ostiense (both accessible to the centre of Rome by the Metro). A new car park at St Peter's station opened in 2002, and holds 144 cars (Metropolitana Linea A). See the preceding Getting There & Away section for information about car and scooter rental.

Around Rome

OSTIA ANTICA

The Romans founded this port city at the mouth of the Tiber in the 4th century BC and it became a strategically important centre of defence and trade. It was populated by merchants, sailors and slaves, and the ruins of the city provide a fascinating contrast to a place such as Pompeii. Ostia Antica was abandoned after barbarian invasions and the appearance of malaria, but Pope Gregory IV re-established the city in the 9th century.

The Rome APT office or Enjoy Rome can provide information about the ancient city, or call the ticket office on ☎ 06 56 35 80 99.

Of particular note in the excavated city (☎ 06 56 35 80 99; admission €4; open 8.30am-4pm Tues-Sun winter, to 6pm summer) are the mosaics of the **Terme di Nettuno** (Baths of Neptune); a **Roman theatre** built by Augustus; the **forum** and **temple**, dedicated to Jupiter, Juno and Minerva; and **Piazzale delle Corporazioni**, with the offices of Roman merchants, distinguished by mosaics depicting their trades.

To get to Ostia Antica take the Metropolitana Linea B to Magliana and then the Ostia Lido train (getting off at Ostia Antica). By car, take the SS8bis (aka Via del Mare) or Via Ostiense.

TIVOLI
postcode 00019 • pop 53,000

Set on a hill by the Anio River, Tivoli was a resort town of the ancient Romans and became popular as a summer playground for the Renaissance wealthy. Today it draws people for the terraced gardens and fountains of the Villa d'Este and the ruins of Villa Adriana, built by the Roman emperor Hadrian.

The local **tourist office** (☎ 0774 33 45 22) is in Largo Garibaldi near the Cotral bus stop.

Things to See

Hadrian built his spectacular summer villa, **Villa Adriana** (☎ 0774 53 02 02; admission €6.20; open 9am-1hr before sunset daily), in the 2nd century AD. It was successively plundered by barbarians and Romans for building materials and many of its original decorations were used to embellish the Villa d'Este. However, enough remains to give an impression of the incredible size and magnificence of the villa. Give yourself about four hours to wander through the vast ruins.

Highlights include La Villa dell'Isola (the Villa of the Island) where Hadrian spent his pensive moments, the Imperial Palace and its Piazza d'Oro (Golden Square), and the floor mosaics of the Hospitalia.

The Renaissance **Villa d'Este** (admission €6.20; open 9am-1hr before sunset Tues-Sun) was built in the 16th century for Cardinal Ippolito d'Este on the site of a Franciscan monastery. The villa's wonderful gardens are decorated with numerous fountains, which are its main attraction.

Getting There & Away

Tivoli is about 40km east of Rome and accessible by Cotral bus. Take Metropolitana Linea B from Stazione Termini to Ponte Mammolo; the bus leaves from outside the station every 20 minutes. The bus also stops near the Villa Adriana, about 1km from Tivoli. Otherwise, catch local bus No 4 from Tivoli's Piazza Garibaldi to Villa Adriana.

TARQUINIA
postcode 01016 • pop 15,300

Believed to have been founded in the 12th century BC and to have been the home of the Tarquin kings, who ruled Rome before the creation of the republic, Tarquinia was an important economic and political centre of the Etruscan League. The major attractions here are the painted tombs of its *necropoli* (burial grounds), although the town itself is quite pretty. There is a **IAT tourist information office** (☎ 0766 85 63 84; Piazza Cavour 1, open 9am-1pm Mon-Sat).

Things to See

The 15th-century Palazzo Vitelleschi houses the **Museo Nazionale Tarquiniense** (admission €4 or €6.50 with Necropolis; open 8.30am-7.30pm Tues-Sun) and an excellent collection of Etruscan treasures, including frescoes from the tombs. Keep an eye out for a few red-and-black plates featuring acrobatic sex acts. There are also numerous sarcophagi found in the tombs. The **necropolis** (open 8.30am-6.30pm Tues-Sun) is a 15- to 20-minute walk away (or catch one of four daily buses). Ask at the tourist office for directions. The tombs are richly decorated with frescoes, although many have deteriorated.

Places to Stay & Eat

Tarquinia has limited accommodation, so it is best visited as a day trip from Rome. If you must stay (especially at weekends), remember to book in advance. The nearest camp site is **Tusca Tirrenica** (☎ 0766 86 42 94; Viale Nereidi) 5km from the town and by the water. **Hotel San Marco** (☎ 0766 684 22 34, fax 0766 84 23 06; Piazza Cavour 10; singles/doubles with bath €52/68) is the closest spot to the sights and transport and has pleasing rooms.

For a meal try **Trattoria Arcadia** (Via Mazzini 6; meal about €15), a friendly joint with good *salsicce* (sausages), near the museum.

Getting There & Away

To get there, take a Cotral bus (roughly every 15 minutes) to Civitavecchia from Via Lepanto in Rome, near the Metropolitana Linea A Lepanto stop, and change for a regular service to Tarquinia (every 45 minutes or so).

CERVETERI

Ancient Caere was founded in the 8th century BC by the Etruscans, enjoying great prosperity as a maritime centre from the 7th to 5th centuries BC. The drawcards now are the tombs known as *tumoli,* great mounds with carved stone bases. Treasures taken from these tombs can be seen in the Vatican Museums, the Villa Giulia Museum and the Louvre. There is a **Pro Loco tourist office** (*Piazza Risorgimento 19*).

Once inside the main necropolis area, **Banditaccia** (☎ *06 994 00 01; Via del Necropoli; admission €4.20; open 9am-7pm Tues-Sun summer; to 4pm winter*), it's a good idea to follow the recommended routes in order to see the best-preserved tombs. Banditaccia is accessible by local bus (summer only) from the main piazza in Cerveteri, but it is also a pleasant 3km walk west from the town.

Cerveteri is accessible from Rome by Cotral bus from Via Lepanto, outside the Lepanto stop on Metropolitana Linea A.

Northern Italy

Italy's affluent north is capped by the Alps and bound by the beaches of Liguria and the lagoons of Venice, with the gently undulating Po River plain at its heart. Venice is the jewel in the crown, but gems are to be found throughout Piedmont, Lombardy, Emilia-Romagna and the Veneto.

GENOA

Postcode 16100 • pop 628,800

Genoa is aristocratic, seedy, grandiose and dingy. Still a busy port, and regional capital of Liguria, it retains an exuberance that its most famous son, Christopher Columbus (1451–1506), would surely recognise. From murky streets around the port to grand thoroughfares and noble palaces, Genoa, the once mighty maritime republic, is a compelling city worthy of its historical title, La Superba.

Recent events have, however, left a bloody mark as the city hit the headlines as host of the G8 summit in the summer of 2001. Violent rioting culminated in police shooting dead a 23-year-old demonstrator.

Orientation

Most trains stop at Genoa's two main stations, Principe and Brignole. The area around Brignole is closer to the city centre and a better bet for accommodation than Principe, which is closer to the port, an area that women travelling alone should avoid at night.

From Brignole walk straight ahead along Via Fiume to get to Via XX Settembre and the historical centre. Walking around Genoa is easier than using the local ATM bus service, but most useful buses stop outside both stations.

Information

On the waterfront there is an **IAT information kiosk** (☎ *010 24 87 11, fax 010 246 76 58; open 9am-1pm & 2pm-6pm daily*) opposite the aquarium. There are further branches at Stazione Principe (*open 9.30am-1pm & 2.30pm-6pm Mon-Sat*), Stazione Marittima, whose opening hours are based on ship arrival and departure times, and at the airport (*open 9.30am-12.30pm & 1.30pm-5.30pm Mon-Sat*). **Genova Informa** (*Piazza Matteotti; 9am-8pm daily*) also provides information.

The **main post office** (*Via Dante 4a*), is just off Piazza de Ferrari while the **Telecom office** (*Piazza Verdi; open 8am-9pm daily*) is to the left of Stazione Brignole as you approach it on foot. For Internet access try **Internet Point** (*Via di Ravecca 39*) where an hour online costs €6.20.

East of the city centre is **Ospedale San Martino** (☎ *010 55 51; Via Benedetto XV*).

Things to See & Do

Genoa claims to have the biggest historical centre in Europe and any tour of the city should start in the backstreets around the old port, which teem with activity, some of it nefarious, most of it entertaining. Search out the 12th-century, black-and-white marble **Cattedrale di San Lorenzo** and the huge **Palazzo Ducale** in Piazza Matteotti.

The palaces of the Doria family, one of the city's most important families in the 14th and 15th centuries, can be found in **Piazza San Matteo**. Further grand palaces line **Via Garibaldi**, several of which are open to the public and contain art galleries, including the 16th-century **Palazzo Bianco** and the

ITALY

17th-century **Palazzo Rosso**. Italian and Flemish Renaissance works are displayed in **Galleria Nazionale di Palazzo Spinola** *(Piazza Superiore di Pelliceria 1; admission €4; open 8.30am-7.30pm Tues-Sat, 1pm-8pm Sun)*.

Genoa's star attraction is, however, its **aquarium** *(Ponte Spinola; admission €11.60; open 9.30am-7.30pm Mon-Wed & Fri, 9.30am-10pm Thur, 9.30am-8.30pm Sat & Sun)*, on the waterfront. Europe's biggest, it is well worth a visit.

Places to Stay

The HI **Ostello Genova** *(☎ 010 242 24 57;* e *hostelge@iol.it; Via Costanzi 120; B&B €13-18)* in Righi, is just outside Genoa. Evening meals cost €7.25. To get there catch bus No 40 from Stazione Brignole.

On the 3rd floor of a gracious old palazzo near Stazione Brignole, **Carola** *(☎ 010 839 13 40; Via Gropallo 4; singles/doubles/ triples without bath €26/42/57, doubles/ triples with bath €52/68)* offers simple rooms and a warm welcome. A few doors up at No 8, **Albergo Rita** *(☎/fax 010 87 02 07; singles/doubles/triples without bath €31/ 47/60, doubles/triples with bath €52/70)* has pleasant-enough rooms. Tucked away in the historic centre, **Hotel Major** *(☎ 010 247 41 74, fax 246 98 98; Via Garibaldi; singles/ doubles without bath €31/41, with bath €41/52)* is a tight squeeze, but the owners are friendly.

Splash out a little at **Hotel Bel Soggiorno** *(☎ 010 54 28 80, fax 010 58 14 18; Via XX Settembre 19; singles/doubles with bath €73/93)*, where the rooms are all chintz and chandeliers.

One of the city's grandest establishments is the **Bristol Palace** *(☎ 010 59 25 41, fax 010 56 17 56; Via XX Settembre 35; singles/ doubles with bath €171/243)*, which has all the trimmings.

Places to Eat

Don't leave town without trying *pesto genovese*, *pansoti* (ravioli in walnut sauce), *farinata* (a Tuscan torte made with chickpea flour) and, of course, focaccia. Plenty of shops sell sandwiches and pizza by the slice in the Brignole and port areas. For seafood, head to the **Via Sottoripo arcades** on the waterfront; at No 113 you'll pay €5 for a bag of freshly fried calamari and zucchini.

The basic **Trattoria Da Maria** *(Vico Test d'Oro 14; meal about €7)*, off Via XX Aprile, is something of an institution, wher good, cheap food is served in an amiabl chaotic environment.

Hidden away in the old town, **La Sant** *(Vico degli Orefici 5; set menu €10.50* specialises in Ligurian cooking.

Entertainment

The Genoa Theatre Company performs at th **Politeama Genovese** *(☎ 010 839 35 89)* an the **Teatro di Genova** *(☎ 010 534 22 00* **Teatro della Tosse in Sant'Agostino** *(☎ 01* 247 07 93; Piazza R Negri 4)* has a season c diverse shows from January to May. Oper buffs should head to **Teatro Carlo Felic** *(☎ 010 58 93 29)*, near Piazza De Ferrari.

Getting There & Away

Air There are regular domestic and als international connections from **Cristofor Colombo airport** *(☎ 010 601 54 10; Sestr Ponente)*, 6km west of the city. **The Volabu** *(☎ 558 24 14)* airport bus service (line N 100) leaves from Piazza Verdi, just outsid Stazione Brignole, and also stops at Stazion Principe. Service is half-hourly from 5.30am to 11pm (€2.05, 25 minutes).

Bus There are buses for Rome, Florence Milan and Perugia which leave from Piazz della Vittoria, south of Stazione Brignole Eurolines coaches leave from the same pi azza for Barcelona, Madrid and Paris. Boo at **Geotravels** *(☎ 010 58 71 81)* in the piazza

Train Genoa is connected by train to majo cities. For train information call ☎ 848 8 80 88.

Boat The city's busy port is a major em barkation point for ferries to Sicily, Sardini and Corsica. Major companies are **Corsic Ferries** *(☎ 019 21 55 11)* in Savona; **Mob Lines** *(☎ 010 254 15 13)* at Ponte Asserat for Corsica; **Tirrenia** *(☎ 199 12 31 99, 80 82 40 79)* at the Stazione Marittima, Pont Colombo (for Sicily and Sardinia); an **Grandi Navi Veloci** and **Grandi Traghett** *(☎ 010 58 93 31; Via Fieschi 17)* for Sar dinia, Sicily, Malta and Tunisia. For more in formation, see the Getting There & Awa sections under Sicily and Sardinia, and in th Corsica section in the France chapter.

ITALY

RIVIERA DI LEVANTE

The Ligurian coast from Genoa to La Spezia (on the border with Tuscany) is quite spectacular, rivalling the Amalfi Coast in its beauty. Summer here can be trying, so try to go in spring and autumn when the weather is more amenable to walking and the smaller crowds to sightseeing.

To explore the region, your best bet is to use either Santa Margherita Ligure in the north as a base or, further south, La Spezia. Tourist information is available in Santa Margherita at the IAT tourist office (☎ 0185 28 74 85, fax 0185 28 30 34; Via XXV Aprile 4) in the town centre, and in La Spezia near the waterfront at the IAT tourist office (☎ 0187 77 09 00, fax 0187 77 09 08; Via Mazzini 45).

Things to See & Do

From pretty Santa Margherita Ligure you can explore the nearby resorts of **Portofino**, a haunt of the rich and famous, and **Camogli**, a fishing village turned resort town. The medieval Benedictine monastery of **San Fruttuoso** is a 2½-hour hilly walk from Camogli or Portofino, with sensational views along the way; you may want to catch the ferry back.

Farther south, there are the five tiny coastal villages of the **Cinque Terre** national park – Riomaggiore, Manorola, Corniglia, Vernazza and Monterosso. All are easily reached by train from La Spezia. They are linked by a 12km path known as the *Via dell'Amore* (Lovers' Lane). The remarkable scenery is well worth the €3 toll.

Places to Stay & Eat

Santa Margherita's **Nuova Riviera** (☎/fax 0185 28 74 03; e info@nuovariviera.com; Via Belvedere 10; singles/doubles with bath €75/90) is a lovely family-run hotel not far from the sea. Nearby, **Albergo Annabella** (☎ 0185 28 65 31; Via Costasecca 10; singles/doubles without bath €43/75) has large, airy rooms.

The orderly and well-run **Ostello 5 Terre** (☎ 0187 92 02 15; e ostello@cdh.it; Via B Riccobaldi 21; dorm bed €19) in Manorola offers an evening meal for €11; be sure to book well ahead.

In La Spezia, **Albergo Parma** (☎ 0187 74 30 10, fax 0187 74 32 40; Via Fiume 143; singles/doubles without bath €25/42, with bath €32/57) has decent rooms opposite the station, while up a notch, the three-star **Hotel**

Astoria (☎ 0187 71 46 55, fax 0187 71 44 25; Via Roma 139; singles/doubles with bath €62/110) offers comfortable rooms and an abundant breakfast.

In Santa Margherita, **Caffè del Porto** (Via Bottaro 32; meal about €20) is a charming spot to while away the lunchtime torpor. The many good trattorias in La Spezia's include **La Tavernetta** (Via Fiume 57; meal about €18), and **I Gabbiani** (Molo Italia; meal around €15), a restaurant floating in the port.

Getting There & Away

The entire coast is served by train and all points are accessible from Genoa. Buses leave from Santa Margherita's Piazza Martiri della Libertà for Portofino.

In the summer, **Servizio Marittimo del Tigullio** (☎ 0185 28 46 70) runs ferries from Santa Margherita to Portofino, San Fruttuoso and the Cinque Terre. From La Spezia there are numerous ferry routes along the coast, but for the Cinque Terre a cheaper option is a *biglietto giornaliero Cinque Terre* (a one-day rail pass; €5.20) valid for unlimited travel between Monterosso and La Spezia.

TURIN

postcode 10100 • pop 898,400

More noted for its factories than its palaces, Turin is, in fact, a rather grand old city. Formerly the capital of Italy (until 1945) and seat of the House of Savoy, it feels like a place that was once great but that still counts. This is thanks to the Agnelli family, their industrial creation Fiat, and the most loved/hated football team in Italy, Juventus. Towering buildings line the busy boulevards in this baroque city, which will host the Winter Olympics in 2006.

Orientation & Information

The Porta Nuova train station is the point of arrival for most travellers. To reach the city centre, cross Corso Vittorio Emanuele II and walk straight ahead through the grand Carlo Felice and San Carlo piazzas until you come to Piazza Castello. If arriving on foot from the station, the spire of the Mole Antonelliana will be on your right as you enter Piazza Castello. There is a **tourist office** (☎ 011 53 51 81, fax 011 53 00 70; e info@turismotorino.org; Piazza Castello 161; open 9.30am-7pm Mon-Sat, 9.30am-3pm Sun) and there are also branches at the Porta Nuova train station

ITALY

(☎ 011 53 13 27, fax 011 561 70 95; open 9.30am-7pm Mon-Sat, 9.30am-3pm Sun) and the airport (☎ 011 567 81 24).

Things to See

Museum enthusiasts should consider the *Torino Card*, a 48-hour pass valid for all public transport in the city and many of the city's museums. It costs €14.

Start at Piazza San Carlo, which is known as Turin's drawing room and is capped by the baroque churches of **San Carlo** and **Santa Cristina**. Nearby, the majestic **Piazza Castello** features the sumptuous **Palazzo Madama**, home to the **Museo Civico d'Arte Antica** and the 17th-century **Palazzo Reale** (Royal Palace) where the gardens were designed in 1697 by Louis le Nôtre, better known for his work at Versailles.

Not far away in the **Cattedrale di San Giovanni Battista**, west of the Palazzo Reale, lies one of the Catholic Church's great curiosities, the **Turin Shroud**, the linen cloth claimed to have been used to wrap the crucified Christ. Carbon dating seems to have scotched this theory, showing the cloth to be 13th century, but the faithful continue to come. The shroud is only brought out a few times a year, but there is a reasonable copy on display in the cathedral. For enthusiasts, the **Museo della Sindone** (*Museum of the Shroud; Via San Domenico 28; admission €5.50; open 9am-noon & 3pm-7pm daily*) will answer most questions.

Turin's enormous **Museo Egizio** (☎ 011 561 77 76; Via Accademia delle Scienze 6; admission €6.50; open 8.30am-7.30pm Tues-Sun) is considered one of the best museums of ancient Egyptian art after those in London and Cairo.

Places to Stay & Eat

Turin has plenty of cheap, if a little rundown, accommodation.

In the hills east of the River Po there is **Campeggio Villa Rey** (☎ 011 819 01 17; Strada Superiore Val San Martino 27; per person/tent €3.65/6; open Mar-Oct) and **Ostello Torino** (☎ 011 660 29 39; Via Alby 1; dorm bed €12). To get to the hostel, catch bus No 52 from Porta Nuova station (No 64 on Sunday). An evening meal costs €8.

The one-star **Canelli** (☎ 011 54 60 78; Via San Dalmazzo 5b; singles/doubles without bath €14/19, singles/doubles/triples with bath €22/30/38) is reminiscent of a dusty university faculty building – all yellowing corridors and torn posters. Near the static the two-star **Bologna** (☎ 011 562 02 90, fax 011 562 01 93; Corso Vittorio Emanuele 60; singles/doubles with bath €55/76) is deservedly popular. In a great location, **Sa Carlo** (☎ 011 562 78 46, fax 011 53 86 5. Piazza San Carlo 197; singles/doubles with out bath €35/55, with bath €59/70) ha rooms with old-world style. Up the luxur scale, **Dogana Vecchia** (☎ 011 436 67 5. fax 011 436 71 94; Via Corte D'Appello singles/doubles with bath €83/104) continues to offer elegant rooms today as it di to the likes of Verdi and Mozart.

For a lunchtime bite try **La Grangia** (Vi Garibaldi 21; meal about €7) and mingle wi the city centre crowd. During the evening, th pizzas at **Pizzeria alla Baita dei 7 Nani** (Vi A Doria 5; pizza meal about €10) are soughi after. For gelati and chocolate you're spoile for choice, but the ice cream at **Caffè Fior** (Via Po 8) was good enough for the father c Italian unification, Cavour.

Getting There & Away

Turin is serviced by **Caselle international ai port** (☎ 011 567 63 61), with flights to Euro pean and national destinations. **Sadem** (☎ 01 300 01 66) buses run to the airport every 4 minutes from the corner between Via Sacc and Corso Vittorio Emanuele II, on the wes ern side of Porta Nuova train station. Intercit national and international buses terminate the bus terminal on Corso Castelfidard Buses serve the Valle d'Aosta, most of th towns and ski resorts in Piedmont and majc Italian cities. Regular trains connect wi Milan, Aosta, Venice, Genoa and Rome.

Getting Around

The city is well serviced by a network c buses and trams. A map of public-transpo routes is available at the station informatic office.

MILAN

postcode 20100 • pop 1.3 million

Milan, a self-styled sophisticated city, is a about money, looks and shopping. Capital c Italy's finance and fashion industries, th surprisingly scruffy city offers the best i Italian theatre, nightlife and clothes – and n a lot else.

Its origins are believed to be Celtic, but it was conquered by the Romans in 222 BC and became a major trading and transport centre. From the 13th century the city flourished under the rule of two powerful families: the Visconti, followed by the Sforza.

Milan closes down almost completely in August, when most of the city's inhabitants take their annual holidays.

Orientation

From Milan's central train station (Stazione Centrale), it's easy to reach the centre of town on the efficient underground railway (known as the Metropolitana Milanese, or MM). The city of Milan is huge, but most sights are in the centre. Use the Duomo (cathedral) and the Castello Sforzesco as your points of reference; the main shopping areas and sights are around and between the two.

Information

Tourist Offices The main branch of the APT tourist office (☎ 02 72 52 43 00, fax 02 72 52 43 50; Via Marconi 1; open 8.45am-1pm & 2pm-6pm Mon-Fri, 9am-1pm & 2pm-5pm Sat & Sun), is in Piazza del Duomo, where you can pick up the useful city guides *Hello Milano* and *Milano Mese*, and the excellent map *Milan is Milano*. The branch office (☎ 02 72 52 43 60; Stazione Centrale; open 9am-6.30pm Mon-Sat, 9am-12.30pm & 1.30pm-5pm Sun), near the Telecom office, has useful listings in English posted outside. There are also APT branches at Linate and Malpensa airports.

Foreign Consulates Diplomatic representation in Milan includes: Australia (☎ 02 77 70 42 17; Via Borgogna 2), Canada (☎ 02 675 81; Via Vittor Pisani 19), France (☎ 02 655 91 41; Via Mangili 1), the UK (☎ 02 72 30 01; Via San Paolo 7) and the USA (☎ 02 29 03 51; Via P Amedeo 2/10).

Money Banks in Milan open 8.30am to 1.30pm and 2.45pm to 3.45pm Monday to Friday. On Piazza Duomo, Banca Ponti at No 19 has an ATM, and there are exchange offices open daily at Stazione Centrale. There is an American Express office (☎ 02 720 03 694; Via Brera 3; open 9am-5.30pm Mon-Fri).

Post & Communications The main post office (Via Cordusio 4; open 8am-7pm Mon-Fri, 8.30am-12pm Sat) is off Via Dante, near Piazza del Duomo. There are also post offices at the station and at Linate airport.

The somewhat squalid **Telecom office** (open 8am-9.30pm daily) on the upper level of Stazione Centrale, has international telephone directories, while the **office** (open 8am-9.30pm daily) in the Galleria Vittorio Emanuele II has Internet access (€0.10 for 70 seconds), a fax machine and phonecards.

The **Hard Disk Café** (Corso Sempione 44) was Milan's first Internet café and is one of Europe's biggest. **Terzomillennio** (Via Lazzaretto 2) is a more modest outfit, charging €1 for five minutes and €3.50 for half an hour.

Bookshops There's a good selection of English-language books at the **American Bookstore** (Via Campiero 16).

Laundry The **Lavanderia Self-Service** (Via Tadino 4; open 7.30am-9.30pm daily) charges €3.10 for a small load, and €6.10 for a mega-load of washing.

Medical & Emergency Services For an ambulance call ☎ 118. The public hospital, **Ospedale Maggiore Policlinico** (☎ 02 550 31; Via Francesco Sforza 35) is close to the centre, and there is an all-night **pharmacy** (☎ 02 669 07 35) in Stazione Centrale.

The **questura** (police headquarters; ☎ 02 622 61; Via Fatebenefratelli 11) is situated near the **Ufficio Stranieri** (Foreigners' Office; ☎ 02 622 61; Via Montebello 26) where English is spoken. For lost property call the **Milan City Council** (☎ 02 54 66 81 18; Via Friuli 30).

Dangers & Annoyances Milan's main shopping areas are popular haunts for groups of thieves, who are lightning-fast. They use a technique of waving cardboard or newspaper in your face to distract you while they head for your pockets or purse. Be particularly careful in the piazza in front of the Stazione Centrale.

Things to See & Do

Start with the extraordinary **Duomo**, the city's unique landmark. Looking like the backdrop to an animated fairy tale, the cathedral was commissioned in 1386 to a lunatic French-Gothic design and finished 600 years later. The resulting spiky marble facade is an unforgettable mass of statues, pinnacles and

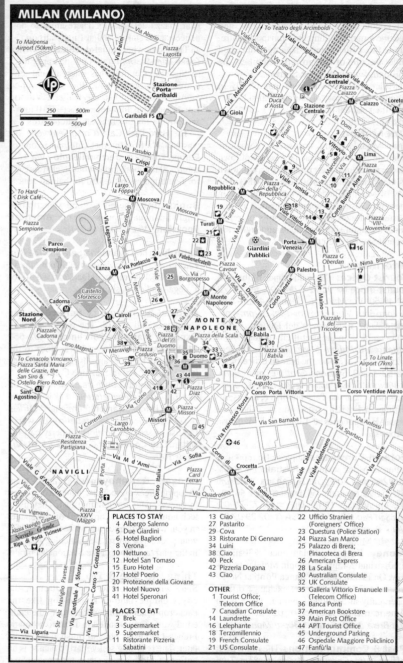

MILAN (MILANO)

PLACES TO STAY
4 Albergo Salerno
5 Due Giardini
6 Hotel Bagliori
8 Verona
10 Nettuno
12 Hotel San Tomaso
15 Euro Hotel
17 Hotel Poerio
20 Protezione della Giovane
31 Hotel Nuovo
41 Hotel Speronari

PLACES TO EAT
2 Brek
3 Supermarket
9 Supermarket
11 Ristorante Pizzeria
     Sabatini

13 Ciao
27 Pastarito
29 Cova
33 Ristorante Di Gennaro
34 Luini
38 Ciao
40 Peck
42 Pizzeria Dogana
43 Ciao

OTHER
1 Tourist Office;
     Telecom Office
7 Canadian Consulate
14 Laundrette
16 Lelephante
18 Terzomillennio
19 French Consulate
21 US Consulate

22 Ufficio Stranieri
     (Foreigners' Office)
23 Questura (Police Station)
24 Piazza San Marco
25 Palazzo di Brera;
     Pinacoteca di Brera
26 American Express
28 La Scala
30 Australian Consulate
32 UK Consulate
35 Galleria Vittorio Emanuele II
     (Telecom Office)
36 Banca Ponti
37 American Bookstore
39 Main Post Office
44 APT Tourist Office
45 Underground Parking
46 Ospedale Maggiore Policlinico
47 Fanfù'la

pillars. The view from the roof is also quite memorable (stairs €3.50, lift €5).

Back on solid ground, join the throngs and take a *passeggiata* (stroll) through the magnificent **Galleria Vittorio Emanuele II** to **La Scala**, the world's most-famous opera house, which is currently closed for a makeover. (See Entertainment later for more details.)

At the end of Via Dante is the immense **Castello Sforzesco** *(admission free; open 9.30am-5.30pm Tues-Sun)*, originally a Visconti fortress and entirely rebuilt by Francesco Sforza in the 15th century. Its museum collections include furniture, artefacts and sculpture, notably Michelangelo's unfinished *Pietà Rondanini*.

Nearby on Via Brera is the 17th-century **Palazzo di Brera**, home to the **Pinacoteca di Brera** *(admission €6.20; open 8.30am-7.15pm Tues-Sun)*. This gallery's vast collection includes Mantegna's masterpiece, the *Dead Christ*.

To view Leonardo da Vinci's *Last Supper* in the **Cenacolo Vinciano** *(☎ 02 89 42 11 46; Piazza Santa Maria delle Grazie 2; admission €6.50; open 8am-7.30pm Tues-Sun)* you'll need to phone to make a booking.

Special Events

St Ambrose's Day (7 December) is Milan's major festival, with celebrations at the Fiera di Milano (MM1: stop Amendola Fiera).

Places to Stay

Hostels The HI-run **Ostello Piero Rotta** *(☎/fax 02 39 26 70 95; Viale Salmoiraghi 1; dorm bed €16; closed 9am-3.30pm, curfew 12.30am)* is northwest of the city centre. Take the MM1 to the QT8 stop. **Protezione della Giovane** *(☎ 02 29 00 01 64; Corso Garibaldi 123; beds €22)* is run by nuns for single women aged 16 to 25 years. Prebooking is required.

Hotels Milan's hotels are among the most expensive and heavily booked in Italy, largely due to trade fairs held in the city, so book in advance. There are numerous budget hotels around Stazione Centrale, but the quality varies.

Stazione Centrale & Corso Buenos Aires
One of Milan's nicest one-star hotels is **Due Giardini** *(☎ 02 29 52 10 93, fax 02 29 51 69 33; Via B Marcello 47; singles/doubles with* bath €55/85)*, which has rooms overlooking a tranquil back garden (a rarity in central Milan). To get there turn right off Via D Scarlatti, which is to the left as you leave the station.

On busy Via Dom Vitruvio, off Piazza Duca d'Aosta, there are many hotels, some of them less than enticing. **Albergo Salerno** *(☎/fax 02 204 68 70; doubles with/without bath €77/60)* at No 18, is, however, a good option with clean, simple rooms.

Nettuno *(☎ 02 29 40 44 81; Via Tadino 27; singles/doubles/triples without bath €34/52/70, with bath €47/70/88)* is a modest outfit with some of the cheapest rates around. Near Piazza della Repubblica, you might be able to bargain the rates down at **Verona** *(☎ 02 66 98 30 91; Via Carlo Tenca 12; singles/doubles with bath €70/110)*, depending on the time of year.

Just off Corso Buenos Aires, the friendly **Hotel San Tomaso** *(☎ 02 29 51 47 47; e hotelsantomaso@tin.it; Viale Tunisia 6; singles/doubles/triples without bath €41/72/100, doubles with bath €82)* provides a TV and phone in every room. On the other side of Corso Buenos Aires, in a quiet(ish) street **Hotel Poerio** *(☎ 02 29 52 28 72; Via Poerio; singles without bath €31, singles/doubles with bath €42/62)* offers rooms at the basic end of the basic scale.

Closer to the centre, off Piazza G Oberdan, **Euro Hotel** *(☎ 02 20 40 40 10, fax 02 29 40 06 74; e eurohotel.viasirtori@tin.it; Via Sirtori 26; singles/doubles/triples €98/149/195)* provides modern rooms with shower, satellite TV and breakfast.

For some three-star comfort, try **Hotel Bagliori** *(☎ 02 29 52 68 84, fax 02 29 52 68 42; e hotelbagliori@tin.it; Via Boscovich 43; singles/doubles with bath €124/176)* with its pretty little walled garden.

City Centre Right in the heart of things, near Piazza del Duomo (for which read handy but noisy), **Hotel Speronari** *(☎ 02 86 46 11 25, fax 02 72 00 31 78; Via Speronari 4; singles/doubles/triples without bath €47/73/88, with bath €62/104/130)* has decent-enough rooms.

Hotel Nuovo *(☎ 02 86 46 05 42, fax 02 72 00 17 52; Piazza Beccaria 6; singles/doubles without bath €31/51, doubles/triples with bath €93/124)*, just off Corso Vittorio Emanuele II and the Duomo, is a good deal with cheap rates and simple rooms.

Places to Eat
There are plenty of fast-food outlets and sandwich bars in the station and Duomo areas, extremely popular during the lunchtime rush.

Restaurants If you're looking for a traditional trattoria, try the side streets south of the station and along Corso Buenos Aires.

Around Stazione Centrale Anything but traditional, **Ciao outlet** *(Corso Buenos Aires 7; meal about €7)* is part of a self-service chain (there are a multitude of others, including those surrounding the Duomo and at Via Dante 5), but the food is pretty good and relatively cheap. The **Brek** chain is a similar but slightly more-expensive alternative.

Ristorante Pizzeria Sabatini *(☎ 02 29 40 28 14; Via Boscovich 54; pizza meal about €15)*, around the corner from Corso Buenos Aires, is a large and characterless place that nevertheless churns out tasty pizzas. Pasta is also available.

City Centre The **Ristorante Di Gennaro** *(☎ 02 805 61 08; Via Santa Radegonda 14; pizza from €5)* is reputed to be one of the city's first pizzerias, and the pizzas and focaccias are good. **Pizzeria Dogana** *(☎ 02 805 67 66; cnr Via Capellari & Via Dogana; pizza from €5, meal about €26)* serves standard dishes within spitting distance of the Duomo.

Near La Scala, **Pastarito** *(☎ 02 86 22 10; Via Verdi 6; pasta meal about €10)* makes up for its lack of atmosphere with huge portions and reliable quality.

Cafés & Sandwich Bars The popular fast-food outlet **Luini** *(Via Santa Radegonda 16)*, just off Piazza del Duomo, is a meeting point for students skipping school. You won't, however, find many screaming teenagers in **Cova** *(Via Monte Napoleone 8)*, established in 1817 and one of Milan's grander tearooms. The best gourmet takeaway is **Peck** *(Via Spadari 7-9)*, a three-storey temple to luxury food.

Self-Catering There are two **supermarkets** at Stazione Centrale, one on the upper level and one on the western side, as well as those close by at Via D Vitruvio 32 and Via Casati 30.

Entertainment
Music, theatre and cinema dominate Milan's entertainment calendar. The opera season at La Scala runs from 7 December through to July, but due to restoration work, performances are being staged at the modern **Teatro degli Arcimboldi** *(☎ 02 887 91; Viale dell' Innovazione)* in the city's northern reaches. The **box office** *(☎ 02 72 00 37 44)* has also been transferred, to the subterranean pedestrian passage in the Duomo underground station. The restoration project is due for completion in December 2004.

Nightlife of the pub/club variety is centred on, but not limited to, Brera and further south, Navigli. Try **Fanfù'la** *(Ripa di Porta Ticinese 37)*, which is fun and, on Friday nights, heaving. Alternatively, and in an altogether quieter area, **Lelephante** *(Via Melzo 22)* is a darkly coloured bar ideal for discussing the woes of the world.

For football fans a visit to the **San Siro**, official name Stadio Olympico Meazza, is nothing short of a pilgrimage. Home to AC Milan and Inter, ticket prices start at around €15. They can be bought at branches of Cariplo (AC Milan) and Banca Popolare di Milano (Inter) banks.

Shopping
Looking good is an obsession, and power shopping is serious business in Milan; but it's not cheap. Hit the main streets behind the Duomo around Corso Vittorio Emanuele II for clothing, footwear and accessories, or dream on and window-shop for designer fashions in Via Monte Napoleone, Via della Spiga and Via Borgospesso.

The areas around Via Torino, Corso Buenos Aires and Corso XXII Marzo are less expensive. **Markets** are held around the canals (southwest of the centre), notably on Viale Papiniano on Tuesday and Saturday morning. A **flea market** *(Viale Gabriele d'Annunzio)* is held each Saturday, and there's an **antique market** *(Via Fiori Chiari)* in Brera every third Saturday of the month.

Getting There & Away
Air Most international flights use **Malpensa airport**, about 50km northwest of Milan. Domestic and a few European flights use **Linate airport**, about 7km east of the city. For arrivals or departures for either airport call **flight information** *(☎ 02 74 85 22 00)*.

Bus Milan's stations are scattered throughout the city, although some international and national bus operators use Piazza Castello as a terminal. Check with the APT.

Train Regular trains go from Stazione Centrale to Venice, Florence, Bologna, Genoa, Turin and Rome, as well as major cities throughout Europe. For **timetable information** (☎ 848 88 80 88; open 7am-9pm) call or go to the busy office in Stazione Centrale (English is spoken). Regional trains stop at Stazione Porta Garibaldi and Stazione Nord in Piazzale Cadorna on the MM2 line.

Car & Motorcycle Milan is the major junction of Italy's motorways, including the Autostrada del Sole (A1) to Rome, the Milan–Turin (A4), the Milan–Genoa (A7) and the Serenissima (A4) for Verona and Venice, and the A8 and A9 north to the lakes and the Swiss border.

All these roads meet with the Milan ring road, known as the Tangenziale Est and Tangenziale Ovest (the east and west bypasses). From here follow the signs to the centre. The A4 in particular is an extremely busy road, where an accident can hold up traffic for hours. In winter all roads in the area become extremely hazardous because of rain, snow and fog.

Getting Around
To/From the Airport STAM airport shuttle buses leave for Linate airport from Piazza Luigi di Savoia, on the east side of Stazione Centrale, every 30 minutes from 5.40am to 9.35pm (€1.81). You can also use the local ATM bus No 73 from Piazza San Babila (€1, 20 minutes).

For Malpensa airport, the Malpensa Shuttle and Malpensa Bus Express both depart from Piazza Luigi di Savoia every 20 minutes between 4.30am and 12.15am (€4.13 to €5.16 depending on which operator you use, 50 to 60 minutes). Buses link the airports hourly from 8am to 9.30pm.

The Malpensa Express train connects Malpensa airport with Cadorna underground station in the centre of Milan. Trains depart from Cadorna from 5.50am to 8.20pm, after which buses take over until 11.10pm. Tickets cost €9.30 and the journey takes 40 minutes.

Bus & Metro Milan's public transport system is extremely efficient, with underground (MM), tram and bus services. Tickets are €1,

valid for one underground ride and/or 75 minutes on buses and trams. You can buy tickets in the MM stations, as well as at authorised tobacconists and newsstands.

Taxi If you try to hail a taxi in the street it won't stop – head for the taxi ranks, all of which have telephones, or call a radio taxi company. Numbers include: ☎ 02 40 40, 02 52 51, 02 53 53, 02 83 83, 02 85 85.

Car & Motorcycle Entering central Milan by car is a hassle. The city is dotted with expensive car parks (look for the blue sign with a white 'P'). A cheaper alternative is to use one of the supervised car parks at the last stop on each MM line. In the centre there are private garages that charge around €3 per hour. If your car is clamped or towed away call the **Polizia Municipale** (☎ 02 772 72 59). Hertz, Avis, Maggiore and Europcar all have offices at Stazione Centrale.

MANTUA
postcode 24100 • pop 48,000
Mantua is a pretty-enough town on the shores of Lake Superior. Closely associated with the Gonzaga family, who ruled from the 14th to 18th centuries, its sumptuous palaces were built on a grand scale. Popular with day trippers, the town is a traditional stronghold of Umberto Bossi's separatist *Lega Nord* party.

Information
The **APT tourist office** (☎ 0376 32 82 53, fax 0376 36 32 92; e aptmantova@iol.it; Piazza Andrea Mantegna 6; open 8.30am-12.30pm & 3pm-6pm Mon-Sat, 9.30am-12.30pm Sun) is a 10-minute walk from the station along Corso Vittorio Emanuele, which becomes Corso Umberto 1.

Things to See
Piazza Sordello is surrounded by impressive buildings, including the eclectic **cattedrale**, which combines a Romanesque tower, baroque facade and Renaissance interior. But the piazza is dominated by the massive **Palazzo Ducale** (admission €6.50; open 8.45am-7.15pm Tues-Sun), former seat of the Gonzaga family. The palace has some 500 rooms and 15 courtyards, but its showpieces are the Gonzaga apartments and art collection, and the **Camera degli Sposi** (Bridal Chamber), with frescoes by Mantegna.

Down by the lake the Gonzaga's lavishly decorated summer palace, **Palazzo del Tè** (admission €8; open 9am-6pm Tues-Sun & 1pm-6pm Mon) was completed in 1534.

Places to Stay & Eat

You can pitch a tent 7km from town at **Agriturismo Facchini** (☎ 0376 44 87 63; per person €6) or a little closer at **Agricampeggio Corte Chiara** (☎ 0376 39 08 04; person/tent €6/6). In town, opposite the train station, **Albergo ABC** (☎ 0376 32 33 47; Piazza Don Leoni 25; singles/doubles with bath €62/83) has rooms with breakfast included. Further up the price scale **Due Guerrieri** (☎ 0376 32 15 33, fax 0376 32 96 45; Piazza Sordello 52; singles/doubles with bath €67/104) is centrally located.

For a casual pizza head for **Il Girasole** (☎ 0376 22 58 80; pizza about €6) in the elegant Piazza Erbe. **La Masseria** (☎ 0376 36 53 03; Piazza Broletto 8; pizza €7, pasta €7.50) has a good reputation and an interesting menu. For finer dining, **Ristorante Pavesi** (☎ 0376 32 36 27; Piazza delle Erbe 13; set menu €34) is your place.

Getting There & Away

Mantua is accessible by train and bus from Verona (about 40 minutes), and by train from Milan and Bologna with a change at Modena.

VERONA

postcode 37100 • pop 256,100

Verona is widely regarded as one of Italy's most beautiful cities, and justifiably so. Forever associated with Romeo and Juliet, the city was an important Roman centre long before the Della Scala (also known as the Scaligeri) family took the reins in the 13th and 14th centuries, a period noted for the savage family feuding on which Shakespeare based his tragedy.

Orientation & Information

Buses leave for the historical centre from outside the train station (see Getting Around, later); otherwise, it's a 20-minute walk, heading right to leave the bus station, crossing the river and walking along Corso Porta Nuova to Piazza Brà.

The main **APT tourist office** (☎ 045 806 86 80; e info@tourism.verona.it; Via degli Alpini 9; open 9am-6pm Mon-Sat, 9am-2pm Sun), faces Piazza Brà. There are also branches at the train station (☎ 045 800 08 61;

open 9am-6pm Mon-Sat) and airport (☎ 045 861 91 63; open 11am-5pm Mon-Sat) in the arrivals hall.

The **post office** (Piazza Viviani) is central, while Internet access is available at **Internet Train** (☎ 045 801 33 94; Via Roma 19) where 15 minutes costs €1.50.

Things to See & Do

Piazza Brà's stunning pink marble Roman amphitheatre, known as the **Arena**, dates from the 1st century and is the third largest in existence. It is now Verona's opera house.

Walk along Via Mazzini to Via Cappello and **Casa di Giulietta** (Juliet's House), where the balcony overlooks a courtyard covered with lovers' graffiti. Further along the street is **Porta Leoni**, one of the gates to the old Roman Verona; **Porta Borsari**, the other city gate, is north of the Arena at Corso Porta Borsari.

Piazza delle Erbe The former site of the Roman forum, Piazza delle Erbe is lined with marble palaces and filled with market stalls selling the usual tourist tat. Just off the square is the elegant, and much quieter, **Piazza dei Signori**, flanked by the medieval town hall, the Renaissance **Loggia del Consiglio** and the Della Scala (Scaligeri) residence, partly decorated by Giotto and nowadays known as the **Governor's Palace**. Take a look at the **Duomo** (Via Duomo), for its Romanesque main doors and Titian's glorious *Assumption*.

Places to Stay & Eat

The excellent **Ostello Villa Francescatti** (☎ 045 59 03 60, fax 045 800 91 27; Salita Fontana del Ferro 15; B&B €12.50) offers an evening meal for €7.50. An HI or student card is necessary. To get there catch bus No 73 from the station.

Pensione al Castello (☎/fax 045 800 44 03; Corso Cavour 43; singles/doubles without bath €52/83, with bath €88/99) is a stone's throw from the river; the entrance is around the corner.

Albergo Ciopeta (☎ 045 800 68 43; e ciopeta@iol.it; Vicolo Teatro Filarmonico 2; singles/doubles without bath €44/73), just off Piazza Brà, has air-conditioned rooms.

Hidden in a side street near Piazza delle Erbe, **Hotel Mazzanti** (☎ 045 800 68 13, fax 045 801 12 62; Via Mazzanti 6; singles/doubles €61/98 with bath) provides simple rooms, although some are a little poky.

Hotel All'Antica Porta Leona (☎ 045 59 54 99, fax 045 59 52 14, e htlanticaportaleona@ tiscalinet.it; Corticella Leoni 3; singles/doubles about €91/129) smacks of faded elegance.

Boiled meats are a Veronese speciality, as is the crisp Soave white wine. The Castello, Ciopeta and Mazzanti hotels all have reasonable restaurants. At the Mazzanti save room for the tiramisu, as it's devilishly good. To get away from the crowds, cross the river and try the **Trattoria All'Isolo** (☎ 045 59 42 91; Piazza dell'Isolo 5a; set menu €12) where they have an interesting boiled meat dish. For pizza on the hoof you'll find no bigger or better slice than at **Pizza Doge** (Via Roma 21b; pizza slice about €3.50).

Entertainment

Verona hosts musical and cultural events throughout the year, culminating in a season of opera and drama from July to September at the **Arena** (tickets from €21.50). There is a lyric-symphonic season in winter at the 18th-century **Teatro Filarmonico** (☎ 800 28 80; Via dei Mutilati 4). For more information go online at w www.arena.it, or ask at the tourist office. Booking is through the **box office** (☎ 045 800 51 51; Via Dietro Anfiteatro 6b), or website.

Getting There & Away

The **Verona-Villafranca airport** (☎ 045 809 56 66) is 16km outside town and accessible by bus and train.

The main bus station is in the piazza in front of the train station, known as Porta Nuova. Buses leave for surrounding areas, including Mantua, Ferrara and Brescia.

Verona is on the Brenner Pass railway line to Austria and Germany, and is directly linked by train to Milan, Venice, Florence and Rome.

The city sits at the intersection of the Serenissima A4 (Milan–Venice) and the Brennero A22 autostrade.

Getting Around

The APT airport bus (€4.20) departs from outside the train station every 20 minutes. Bus Nos 11, 12, 13 and 14 (Nos 91, 92 and 98 on Sunday), connect the station (bus stop A) with Piazza Brà, and Nos 72 and 73 go to Piazza delle Erbe.

If you arrive by car, there's a free car park situated in Via Città di Nimes (near the train station) – a good bet, as parking in the centre is limited.

PADUA

postcode 35100 • pop 211,500

There is one compelling reason to come to Padua and, although thousands of pilgrims would disagree, it is not to visit the tomb of St Anthony. Rather it's to marvel at Giotto's recently restored frescoes in the Cappella degli Scrovegni (Scrovegni Chapel), considered by many one of the world's greatest works of figurative art. Masterpieces apart, Padua is a lively city thanks to its university, one of the oldest in Europe, and, as is the norm in these parts, it is porticoed and pretty.

Orientation & Information

It's a 15-minute walk from the train station to the centre of town, or you can take bus Nos 3 or 8 along Corso del Popolo (which becomes Corso Garibaldi).

There is an **IAT tourist office** (☎ 049 875 20 77, fax 049 875 50 08; open 9.15am-6.30pm Mon-Sat, 9am-12.30pm Sun) at the station; another in the centre (☎ 049 876 79 27, fax 049 836 33 16; Galleria Pedrocchi; 9am-12.30pm & 3pm-7pm Mon-Sat), and a third in Piazza Del Santo (☎ 049 875 30 87; opening hours variable, Apr-Oct).

The **post office** (Corso Garibaldi 33) is on the main road from the station to the centre.

Things to See

If you're planning a couple of days in the city the padovacard is a good investment. Giving significant reductions on museum entry and free transport, it is valid for one adult and one child under 12, and costs €13.

The **Cappella degli Scrovegni** (☎ 049 201 00 20; w www.cappelladegliscrovegni.it; Piazza Eremitani 8; admission €11; open 9am-6pm Mon-Fri, 9am-1pm Sat) houses Giotto's emotionally charged frescoes. Painted between 1303 and 1305, the transcendent 38 panels depict the life of Christ. Booking is now required, and it's advisable to reserve a few days in advance. The ticket also gives access to the **Musei Civici agli Eremitani** (open 9am-6pm Tues-Sun winter, to 7pm spring to autumn) next door to the chapel.

Thousands of pilgrims arrive in Padua every year to visit the **Basilica di Sant'Antonio** (St Anthony's Basilica) in the hope that St Anthony, patron saint of Padua and of lost things, will help them find whatever it is they are looking for. The saint's gaudy tomb is in the basilica, along with artworks including the 14th-century frescoes and bronze sculptures by Donatello which adorn the high altar. Donatello's bronze equestrian statue, known as the *Gattamelata* (Honeyed Cat), is outside the basilica.

Nature lovers shouldn't miss Padua's botanical gardens, **Orto Botanico** *(Via Orto Botanico 15; admission €2.58; open 9am-1pm & 3pm-6pm Mon-Sat Apr-Oct, 9am-1pm Nov-Mar)*, which date from 1545 and contain many rare plants.

Places to Stay & Eat

Padua has no shortage of budget hotels, but they fill up quickly in summer. The non-HI **Ostello della Città di Padova** *(☎ 049 875 22 19, fax 049 65 42 10; Via A Aleardi 30; dorm B&B €15.50)* is a five-minute bus ride from the station. Take bus No 3, 8 or 12 to Prato della Valle and then ask.

The shockingly pink **Junior** *(☎ 049 61 17 56; Via Faggin 2; singles/doubles with bath €37/70)* is in a flowery residential street and has simple rooms. The two-star **Sant'Antonio** *(☎ 049 875 13 93, fax 875 25 08; Via Santo Fermo 118; singles/doubles with bath €57/74)*, near the river, provides comfortable rooms with TV and phone. Not a stone's throw from the basilica, **Al Fagiano** *(☎/fax 049 875 00 73; Via Locatelli 45; singles/doubles/triples with bath €52/73/83)* offers large and airy rooms.

Fight through the lunchtime frenzy at **Dalla Zita** *(Via Gorizia 16; panini from €2.30)*, off Piazza Pedrocchi, where the menu of more than 100 sandwich fillings completely covers the walls. **Birroteca da Mario** *(Via Breda 3; pizza from €3.40)*, off Piazza della Frutta, is a good choice for a pub-style snack. **Trattoria al Pero** *(☎ 049 875 87 94; Via Santa Lucia 72; meal about €16)*, attracts a mix of locals and tourists and serves the most enormous plate of fried fish. Daily **food markets** are held in Piazza delle Erbe and Piazza della Frutta.

Getting There & Away

Padua is directly linked by train to Milan, Venice and Bologna, and is easily accessible from most other major cities. Regular buses serve Venice, Milan, Trieste and surrounding towns. The **bus terminal** *(Piazzale Boschetti)* is off Via Trieste, near the train station. There is a large public car park in Prato della Valle, a massive piazza near the Basilica del Santo.

VENICE
postcode 30100 • pop 272,100

Venice is extraordinary. In no other city is fantasy and reality so artfully combined – picture delivery boats vying for space with gondolas or a €20 bill for afternoon tea in Piazza San Marco (St Mark's Square). Ever since Casanova set the romance myth rolling, travellers, writers and even dictators have been beguiled by La Serenissima (the Most Serene Republic); Byron waxed lyrical, Henry James commented, and Napoleon described San Marco's as the finest drawing room in Europe.

The secret to discovering its beauty is to *walk*. Parts of Dorsoduro and Castello see few tourists even in the high season (July to September), and it's here that you'll appreciate just how seductive Venice can be. It's easy to happily lose yourself for hours in the narrow winding streets between the Accademia and the train station, where the signs pointing to San Marco and the Rialto never seem to make any sense – but who's complaining?

The islands of the lagoon were first settled during the barbarian invasions of the 5th and 6th centuries AD, when the people of the Veneto sought refuge in this marshy region, gradually building the city on a raft of wooden posts driven into the subsoil. Following centuries of Byzantine rule, Venice evolved into a republic ruled by a succession of doges (chief magistrates) and enjoyed a period of independence that lasted 1000 years. It was the point where east met west, and the city grew in power to dominate half the Mediterranean, the Adriatic and the trade routes to the Levant. It was from Venice that Marco Polo set out on his voyage to China in 1271.

Today, Venice is increasingly being left to the tourists – the regular floods (caused by high tides) and sky-high property prices make it a difficult place to live. Most of the 'locals' live in industrial Mestre, which is linked to the city by the 4km-long bridge across the lagoon.

Orientation

Venice is built on 117 small islands and has some 150 canals and 400 bridges. Only three bridges cross the Canal Grande (Grand Canal): the Rialto, the Accademia and, at the train station, the Scalzi. The city is divided into six *sestieri* (quarters): Cannaregio, Castello, San Marco, Dorsoduro, San Polo and Santa Croce. A street can be called a

VENICE (VENEZIA)

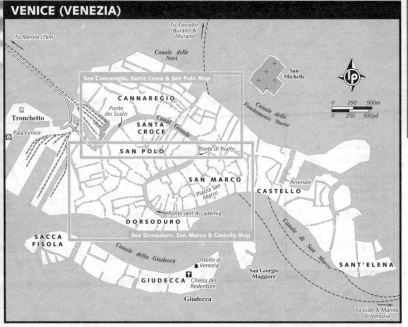

calle, ruga or salizzada; a street beside a canal is a *fondamenta*; a canal is a *rio*; and a quay is a *riva*. The only square in Venice called a *piazza* is San Marco – all the others are called *campo*.

If all that isn't confusing enough, Venice also has its own style of street numbering. Instead of a system based on individual streets, each sestiere has a long series of numbers, so addresses become virtually meaningless to anyone who's not a Venetian postie. There are no cars in the city and all public transport is via the canals, on *vaporetti* (water buses). To cross the Grand Canal between the bridges, use a *traghetto* (basically a public gondola, but much cheaper). Signs will direct you to the various traghetto points. Of course, the other mode of transportation is *a piedi* (on foot).

To walk from the *ferrovia* (train station) to San Marco along the main thoroughfare, Lista di Spagna (whose name changes several times), will take a good half-hour – follow the signs to San Marco. From San Marco the routes to other main areas, such as the Rialto, the Accademia and the ferrovia, are well signposted but can be confusing, particularly in the Dorsoduro and San Polo areas.

The free tourist office map is not great so it's worth buying the yellow street-referenced *Venezia* map published by FMB.

Information

Tourist Offices Central Venice has three **APT tourist office branches**: at the train station *(open 8am-8pm daily)*; at Piazza San Marco 71f *(open 9.45am-3.15pm Mon-Sat)* and the Venice Pavilion *(open 10am-6pm daily)* on the waterfront next to the Giardini Ex Reali (turn right from San Marco). There are also offices at **Piazzale Roma** *(open 8am-8pm daily)*, the Lido and airport. Pick up the useful guide *Un Ospite di Venezia*. For telephone information there is a central number, ☎ 041 529 87 11.

Visitors aged between 14 and 29 can buy a **Rolling Venice card** *(☎ 899 90 90 90)* for €2.58, which offers significant discounts on food, accommodation, shopping, transport and entry to museums. It is available from various outlets; check at the tourist offices for details. City planners have also introduced the Venice Card, a multipurpose pass for museums, public transport, car parks and restrooms. It comes in two forms, one costing €7

ITALY

CANNAREGIO, SANTA CROCE & SAN POLO

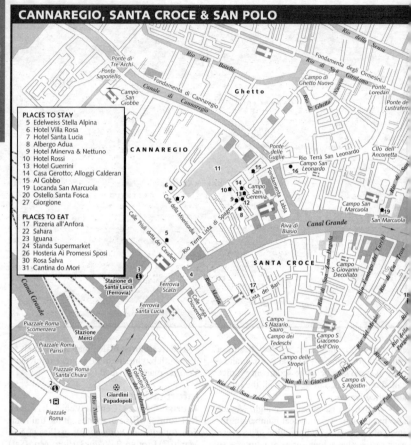

PLACES TO STAY
5 Edelweiss Stella Alpina
6 Hotel Villa Rosa
7 Hotel Santa Lucia
8 Albergo Adua
9 Hotel Minerva & Nettuno
10 Hotel Rossi
13 Hotel Guerrini
14 Casa Gerotto; Alloggi Calderan
15 Al Gobbo
19 Locanda San Marcuola
20 Ostello Santa Fosca
27 Giorgione

PLACES TO EAT
17 Pizzeria all'Anfora
22 Sahara
23 Iguana
24 Standa Supermarket
26 Hosteria Ai Promessi Sposi
30 Rosa Salva
31 Cantina do Mori

and the other €16. For more information go online at �owww.venicecard.it.

Foreign Consulates The **British consulate** (☎ 041 522 72 07) is in the Palazzo Querini near the Accademia, Dorsoduro 1051.

Money Most of the main banks have branches in the area around the Rialto and San Marco. The **American Express office** (☎ 041 520 08 44; Salizzada San Moisè 1471; open 9am-5.30pm Mon-Fri, 9.30am-12.30pm Sat & Sun) will exchange money without charging commission (exit from the western end of Piazza San Marco onto Calle Seconda dell'Ascensione). There's an ATM for card-holders. Additionally, there's a **Thomas Cook** (☎ 041 522 47 51; Piazza San Marco 141; open 9am-

7pm Mon-Sat, 9.30am-5pm Sun) and, at the train station, a **change office** (open 7am-9pm daily) on the main concourse opposite platform four.

Post & Communications The main **post office** (Salizzada del Fontego dei Tedeschi), near the Ponte di Rialto (Rialto Bridge) is on the main thoroughfare to the train station. Stamps are sold at windows No 1 to No 4 in the central courtyard.

There are several Telecom offices in the city, including those at the post office, near the Rialto and on Strada Nova.

Log on at **Nethouse** (☎ 041 277 11 90; Campo Santo Stefano 2967; open 24hr), which has 60 screens, printing and fax. Rates are €3 for 20 minutes or €9 per hour. **Netgate**

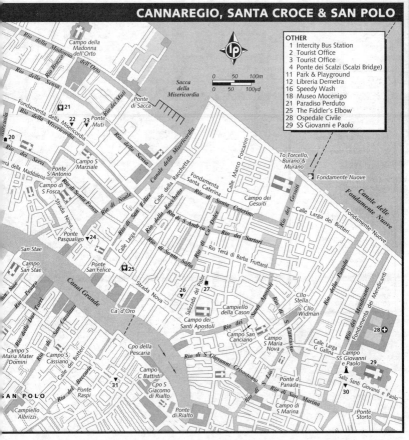

CANNAREGIO, SANTA CROCE & SAN POLO

OTHER
1 Intercity Bus Station
2 Tourist Office
3 Tourist Office
4 Ponte dei Scalzi (Scalzi Bridge)
11 Park & Playground
12 Libreria Demetra
16 Speedy Wash
18 Museo Mocenigo
21 Paradiso Perduto
25 The Fiddler's Elbow
28 Ospedale Civile
29 SS Giovani e Paolo

(☎ 041 244 02 13; Calle dei Preti Crosera 3812, Dorsoduro; open 10.15am-8pm Mon-Fri, 10.15am-10pm Sat & 2.15pm-10pm Sun) offers 11 minutes for €1.29 and one hour for €3.99.

Bookshops English-language guidebooks and general books on Venice are available at **Studium** (cnr Calle de la Canonica) behind the Basilica di San Marco, on the way from San Marco to Castello. **Libreria Demetra** (Campo San Geremia 282, Cannaregio) is open until midnight Monday to Friday.

Laundry At the self-service **Speedy Wash** (Via Cannaregio 1520; open 9am-10pm daily) you can wash 8kg for €4.50. Drying is a further €3.

Medical & Emergency Services If you need a hospital, there is the **Ospedale Civile** (☎ 041 529 41 11; Campo SS Giovanni e Paolo). The **questura** (police headquarters; ☎ 041 271 55 11; Fondamenta di San Lorenzo 5056) is in Castello. An emergency service in foreign languages is run by the carabinieri; call ☎ 112.

Things to See & Do
Before you visit Venice's principal monuments, churches and museums, you should catch the No 1 vaporetto along the Grand Canal, lined with Gothic, Moorish, Renaissance and rococo palaces. Then you can stretch your legs by taking a long walk: start at **San Marco** and either delve into the tiny lanes of tranquil **Castello** or head for the

ITALY

DORSODURO, SAN MARCO & CASTELLO

PLACES TO STAY
2 Hotel Ai Tolentini
9 Foresteria Valdese
12 Locanda Silva; Locanda Canal
13 Hotel Noemi
14 Locanda Casa Petrarca
23 Casa Peron
24 Hotel Dalla Mora
26 Albergo Antico Capon
36 Hotel Galleria
55 Hotel ai Do Mori
61 Hotel Doni
62 Londra Palace

PLACES TO EAT
4 Bar ai Nomboli
5 Trattoria alla Madonna
6 Antica Carbonera
11 Cip Ciap
15 Pasticceria Marchini
19 Da Silvio
21 Arca
27 Mega 1 Supermarket
28 Bar DuChamp
29 Il Doge
30 L'Incontro
32 Osteria ai 4 Ferri
33 Gelati Nico
41 Vino Vino
47 Caffè Florian
52 Caffè Quadri
60 Al Vecio Penasa

Ponte dell'Accademia (Accademia Bridge) to reach the narrow streets and squares of **Dorsoduro** and **San Polo**.

Remember that most, but not all, museums are closed on Monday.

Piazza & Basilica di San Marco San Marco's dreamlike, 'can this be real' quality has you pinching yourself no matter how many times you visit. The piazza is enclosed by the basilica and the elegant arcades of the **Procuratie Vecchie** and **Procuratie Nuove**. While you're standing gob-smacked you might be lucky enough to see the bronze *mori* (Moors) strike the bell of the 15th-century **Torre dell'Orologio** (clock tower).

With its spangled spires, Byzantine domes and facade of mosaics and marble, the **Basilica**

di San Marco (St Mark's Basilica) is the Western counterpart of Constantinople's Santa Sophia. The elaborately decorated basilica was built to house the body of St Mark, stolen from its burial place in Egypt by two Venetian merchants and carried to Venice in a barrel of pork. The saint has been reburied several times in the basilica (at least twice the burial place was forgotten) and his body now lies under the high altar. The present basilica was built in the 11th century and is richly decorated with mosaics, marbles and sculpture, as well as a jumble of looted embellishments over the ensuing five centuries. The bronze horses prancing above the entrance are replicas of the famous statues liberated in the Sack of Constantinople in 1204. The originals can be seen in the basilica's **Galleria** (admission €1.55).

DORSODURO, SAN MARCO & CASTELLO

OTHER	
1 Intercity Bus Station	39 Chiesa di Santa Maria della Salute
3 Frari	40 Legatoria Piazzesi
7 Ponte di Rialto (Rialto Bridge)	42 American Express
8 Main Post Office;	43 Tourist Office; Venice Pavilion
Telecom Office	44 Libreria Nazionale Marciana
10 Questura (Police Station)	45 Museo Archeologico
16 Nethouse	46 Campanile (Bell Tower)
17 Palazzo Grassi	48 Procuratie Nuove
18 Netgate	49 Tourist Office
20 Cafe Noir	50 Museo Correr
22 Cafe Blue	51 Procuratie Vecchie
25 Il Caffe	53 Thomas Cook
31 Annelie Pizzi e Ricami	54 Torre dell'Orologio
34 Galleria dell'Accademia	(Clock Tower)
35 British Consulate	56 Studium Bookshop
37 Ponte dell'Accademia	57 Basilica di San Marco
(Accademia Bridge)	58 Palazzo Ducale
38 Collezione Peggy Guggenheim	59 Ponte dei Sospiri
	(Bridge of Sighs)

Don't miss the **Pala d'Oro** *(admission €1.55)*, a stunning gold altarpiece decorated with silver, enamels and precious jewels. It is behind the basilica's altar.

The 99m freestanding **campanile** *(bell tower; admission to top €6)* dates from the 10th century, although it suddenly collapsed on 14 July 1902 and had to be rebuilt.

Palazzo Ducale The official residence of the doges and the seat of the republic's government, this palace *(admission €9.50; open 9am-7pm daily Apr-Oct, 9am-5pm daily Nov-Mar)*, also housed many government officials and the prisons. The original palace was built in the 9th century and later expanded, remodelled and given a Gothic tracery facade. Visit the **Sala del Maggior Consiglio** to see the paintings by Tintoretto and Veronese. The ticket office closes 1½ hours before palace closing time and the admission ticket also covers entry to the nearby Museo Correr, Biblioteca Marciana and Museo Archeologico. For an additional €6 you can extend the ticket to cover the Palazzo Mocenigo (San Stae area), and Burano and Murano museums.

The **Ponte dei Sospiri** (Bridge of Sighs) connects the palace to the old dungeons. The bridge evokes romantic images, possibly because of its association with Casanova, a native of Venice who spent time in the cells.

Galleria dell'Accademia The Academy of Fine Arts *(admission €6.50; open 8.15am-7.15pm Tues-Sun, 8.15am-2pm Mon)* traces the development of Venetian art, and includes masterpieces by Bellini, Titian, Carpaccio, Tintoretto, Giorgione and Veronese.

For a change of pace, and style, visit the nearby **Collezione Peggy Guggenheim** *(admission €8; open 10am-6pm Wed-Fri, Sun & Mon, 10am-10pm Sat, early Apr–end Oct)* displayed in the former home of the American heiress. The collection runs the gamut of modern art from Bacon to Pollock, and the palazzo is set in a sculpture garden where Miss Guggenheim and her many pet dogs are buried.

Churches Venice has many gorgeous churches, and most of them boast an art treasure or two. The **Chiesa del Redentore** (Church of the Redeemer) on Giudecca Island was built by Palladio to commemorate the end of the great plague of 1576, and is the scene of the annual Festa del Redentore (see Special Events, later). Longhena's **Chiesa di Santa Maria della Salute** guards the entrance to the Grand Canal and contains works by Tintoretto and Titian. Be sure to visit the great Gothic churches **SS Giovanni e Paolo**, with its glorious stained-glass windows, and the **Frari**, home to Titian's tomb and his uplifting *Assumption*. Entry to the latter is €2, or you can buy the Chorus Pass (€8), which gets you into 15 of the city's most famous churches.

The Lido This thin strip of land, east of the centre, separates Venice from the Adriatic and is easily accessible by vaporetto Nos 1, 6, 14, 61 and 82. Once *the* most fashionable beach resort – and still very popular – it's almost impossible to find a space on its long beach in summer.

Islands The island of **Murano** is the home of Venetian glass. Tour a factory for a behind-the-scenes look at its production, or visit the Glassworks Museum to see some exquisite historical pieces. **Burano**, still today a relatively sleepy fishing village, is renowned for its lace and pastel-coloured houses. **Torcello**, the republic's original island settlement, was abandoned due to malaria. Just about all that remains on the hauntingly deserted island is the Byzantine cathedral, its exquisite mosaics intact. Excursion boats travel to the three islands from San Marco (€15 return). Vaporetto No 12 goes to all three from Fondamenta Nuove.

Gondolas Ask yourself what price for romance, and the rather alarming answer is €62

(€77.45 after 8pm) for a 50-minute ride. These are the official rates and are valid for the gondola (which can carry six people), not per person.

Organised Tours

A popular new choice is to pick up an individual handheld audio-guide, which has commentaries on the city's major sights. They are available from the Pavilion tourist office (see Tourist Offices under Information earlier) and cost from €3.60 for an hour to €15.50 for two days. You'll have to leave your passport as a deposit until you return the guide. The **Associazione Guide Turistiche** *(☎ 041 520 90 38; Castello 5327)*, arranges group tours in various languages.

Special Events

The major event of the year is Venice's famed Carnevale, held during the 10 days before Ash Wednesday, when Venetians don spectacular masks and costumes for what is literally a 10-day street party. At its decadent height in the 18th century, the Carnevale lasted for six months!

The Venice Biennale, a major exhibition of international visual arts, is held every odd-numbered year, and the Venice International Film Festival is held every September at the Palazzo del Cinema, on the Lido.

The Festa del Redentore (Festival of the Redeemer), held on the third weekend in July, features a spectacular fireworks display. The Regata Storica, a gondola race on the Grand Canal, is held on the first Sunday in September.

Places to Stay

Venice is the most expensive city in Italy, so be prepared. The average cost of a basic single/double room without bath in a one-star hotel is around €45/70. Prices skyrocket in peak periods (Christmas, Carnevale, Easter etc), but do drop at other times of the year. It is always advisable to book in advance, but if you arrive with nothing lined up, try the **Associazione Veneziana Albergatori** *(☎ 800 84 30 06)* which runs a hotel-reservation office at the train station.

Camping Litorale del Cavallino, northeast of the city on the Adriatic coast, has numerous camping grounds, many with bungalows. The tourist office has a full list. Try **Marina di Venezia** *(☎ 041 530 09 55, fax 041 96 60*

36; e camping@marinadivenezia.it; Via
Montello 6, Punta Sabbioni; per person/tent
€7.50/19; open mid-Apr–end Aug).

Hostels The HI **Ostello di Venezia** (☎ 041
523 82 11, fax 041 523 56 89; Fondamenta
delle Zitelle 86; dorm bed €16) is on the
island of Giudecca. It is open to members
only, although you can buy a card there.
Evening meals are available for €7.75 and
curfew is 11.30pm. Take vaporetto No 41, 42
or 82 from the station and get off at Zitelle.

Foresteria Valdese (☎/fax 041 528 67 97;
Castello 5170; dorm bed €20, doubles without bath €54, with bath €70) has a number
of dormitory and double-room options. Follow Calle Lunga from Campo Santa Maria
Formosa.

Students will feel at home at **Ostello
Santa Fosca** (☎ 041 71 57 75; e cpu@
iuav.unive.it; Cannaregio 2372; dorm bed
€18, singles/doubles without bath €21),
which is less than 15 minutes from the station
through Campo Santa Fosca; check-in is
between 5pm and 8pm daily.

Hotels Not surprisingly, bargain hotels are
few and far between in Venice.

Cannaregio The two-star **Edelweiss Stella
Alpina** (☎ 041 71 51 79, fax 041 72 09 16;
e stelalpina@tin.it; Calle Priuli detta dei
Cavalletti 99d; singles/doubles without bath
€62/104, with bath €130/171), down the
first street on the left after the Scalzi church,
has decent rooms. The next street on the left
is Calle della Misericordia, with two recommended hotels. **Hotel Santa Lucia** (☎ 041 71
51 80, fax 041 71 06 10; e hotelstlucia@
libero.it; singles/doubles without bath €60/
70, doubles/triples/quads with bath €110/
140/170) at No 358 has a friendly owner and
all rates include breakfast. At No 389, **Hotel
Villa Rosa** (☎/fax 041 71 65 69; e villarosa@
ve.nettuno.it; singles/doubles/triples/quads
with bath €82/113/142/165) is pretty and
pink with pleasant, well-furnished rooms.

On Lista di Spagna, the main drag, **Albergo Adua** (☎ 041 71 61 84, fax 041 244
01 62; singles/doubles without bath €70/
75, with bath €100/114) at No 233a has
simple rooms. Across the road at No 230,
Hotel Minerva & Nettuno (☎ 041 71 59 68;
e lchecchi@tin.it; singles/doubles without
bath €50/61, with bath €58/92) has mod-

est rooms. **Hotel Rossi** (☎ 041 71 51 64, fax
041 71 77 84; e rossihotel@interfree.it;
Calle de la Procuratie singles/doubles/
triples/quads with bath €65/89/108/126) is
just off Lista di Spagna (via a Gothic archway) down a tiny side street. Rooms are clean
and straightforward. On the same street, the
two-star **Hotel Guerrini** (☎ 041 71 53 33, fax
041 71 51 14; singles/doubles with bath
€140/150) has well-appointed rooms.

Around the corner, **Casa Gerotto and Alloggi Calderan** (☎/fax 041 71 53 61; Campo
San Geremia 283; dorm bed €20, singles/
doubles/triples without bath €36/62/83,
with bath €46/88/108) has something for
everyone in a pleasantly ramshackle atmosphere. **Al Gobbo** (☎ 041 71 50 01, fax 041 71
47 65; singles/doubles without bath €52/75,
with bath €78/93), at No 312 in the same
campo, is somewhat gloomy inside but has an
enthusiastic owner. Recently opened and situated not two yards from the Grand Canal,
Locanda San Marcuola (☎ 041 71 60 48, fax
041 275 92 17; e info@casanmarcuola.com;
singles/doubles with bath €120/130) has
classy rooms with Venetian decor.

For a multistar splurge the 15th-century
Giorgione (☎ 041 522 58 10, fax 041 523 90
92; Calle Larga dei Proverbi 4587; doubles
from €230), just off Campo dei SS Apostoli,
has the lot.

San Marco Although this is the most touristy
area of Venice, it has some surprisingly good-
quality pensioni. **Hotel Noemi** (☎ 041 523 81
44; e info@hotelnoemi.com; Calle dei Fabbri 909; doubles with/without bath €139/
87) is somewhat characterless but only a few
steps from Piazza San Marco.

Locanda Casa Petrarca (☎ 041 520 04
30; Calle delle Schiavine 4386; singles without bath €44, doubles with/without bath
€110/88) is run by a chatty English-speaking
lady full of useful tips.

Just off Piazza San Marco and up some
alarmingly steep stairs, **Hotel ai Do Mori**
(☎ 041 520 48 17, fax 041 520 53 28; Calle
Larga San Marco 658; doubles with/without
bath €129/87) has some rooms with views
of St Mark's Basilica.

Castello This atmospheric area is to the east
of Piazza San Marco and is far less touristy.
Locanda Silva (☎ 041 522 76 43, fax 041
528 68 17; Fondamenta del Rimedio 4423;

singles/doubles without bath €47/78, with bath €67/104) has rather basic rooms and **Locanda Canal** (☎ 041 523 45 38, fax 041 241 91 38; doubles with/without bath €110/83), next door at No 4422c, is much the same. To get there, head off from Campo Santa Maria Formosa towards San Marco.

Hotel Doni (☎/fax 041 522 42 67; Calle del Vin 4656; singles/doubles without bath €50/80, doubles with bath €105) gives pride of place to a room with an original fresco.

Live like a doge at the **Londra Palace** (☎ 041 520 05 33, fax 041 522 50 32; Riva degli Schiavoni 4171; doubles from €370) right on the waterfront.

Dorsoduro, San Polo & Santa Croce Off Fondamenta Tolentini heading down from the station, **Hotel Ai Tolentini** (☎ 041 275 91 40, fax 041 275 32 66; Corte dei Amai 197g; singles/doubles with bath €70/120) has reasonable rooms and a helpful owner. At the characterful **Casa Peron** (☎/fax 041 71 10 38; Salizzada San Pantalon 84; singles/doubles without bath €45/70, with bath €85) you may well be met by a huge green parrot. To get here from the station, cross Ponte dei Scalzi and follow the signs to San Marco and Rialto till you reach Rio delle Muneghette, then cross the wooden bridge. Nearby, **Hotel Dalla Mora** (☎ 041 71 07 03, fax 041 72 30 06; [e] hoteldallamora@ libero.it; Santa Croce 42a; singles/doubles/ triples/quads with bath €57/88/108/129) is on a small canal just off Salizzada San Pantalon and is justifiably popular.

In one of the liveliest squares in Venice, **Albergo Antico Capon** (☎/fax 041 528 52 92; Campo Santa Margherita 3004b; singles/ doubles with bath €88) provides airy rooms.

The pick of the one-stars **Hotel Galleria** (☎ 041 523 24 89, fax 041 520 41 72; [e] galleria@tin.it; Dorsoduro 878a; singles/ doubles without bath €62/93, doubles with bath €104) has elegant rooms in a 17th-century palace facing the Grand Canal at Ponte dell'Accademia.

Mestre An economical but drab alternative to staying in Venice is to stay in Mestre. There are a number of good hotels as well as plenty of cafés and places to eat around the main square. If you're travelling by car, the savings on car-parking charges are considerable. The two-star **Albergo Roberta** (☎ 041 92 93 55,

fax 041 93 09 83; Via Sernaglia 21; singles/ doubles with bath €68/104) includes breakfast in the rates and the one-star **Albergo Giovannina** (☎ 041 92 63 96, fax 041 538 84 42; Via Dante 113; singles without bath €36, doubles with bath €72) is decent enough.

Places to Eat

Wherever you choose to eat in Venice it will be expensive, but quality can vary greatly, so sniff around and be selective.

Bars serve a wide range of panini, *tramezzini* (sandwiches) and rolls with every imaginable filling. They cost from €2 if you eat them standing at the bar. Head for one of the many *bacari* (traditional wine bars), for wine by the glass *(ombra)* and interesting bite-sized snacks *(cicheti)*. The staples of the Veneto region's cucina are rice and beans. Try the *risi e bisi* (risotto with peas), followed by a glass of *fragolino*, the Veneto's fragrant strawberry wine.

Restaurants Avoid the tourist traps around San Marco and near the train station, where prices are high and the quality is poor.

Cannaregio Tucked away down a tiny alleyway is **Hosteria Ai Promessi Sposi** (☎ 041 522 86 09; Calle De L'Oca 4367; meal about €20) where the mixed fish antipasti is a thing of wonder. It's all shuffling efficiency here as the old boys bring your food between sips. Winning a growing reputation is **Sahara** (☎ 041 72 10 77; Fondamenta della Misericordia; meal about €19) where you can feast on genuine Syrian grub. A few doors down, **Iguana** (☎ 041 71 35 61; meal about €11) represents Venice's Tex-Mex scene.

Around San Marco & Castello The popular bar/osteria **Vino Vino** (☎ 041 523 70 27; San Marco 2007; meal about €17) is at Ponte Veste near Teatro La Fenice. Wine is sold by the glass. **Antica Carbonera** (☎ 041 22 54 79; Calle Bembo; meal about €30), on the continuation of Calle dei Fabbri, is an old trattoria which offers atmosphere in return for euros. It isn't cheap. Just off Campo Santa Maria Formosa and over Ponte del Mondo Novo, **Cip Ciap** (pizza slice €2.30) provides welcome sustenance.

Dorsoduro, San Polo & Santa Croce This is the best area for small, authentic trattorias and pizzerias. The pizzas are usually good at **Pizzeria all'Anfora** (☎ 041 524 03 25; pizza from €4.80), across the Ponte dei Scalzi from the station at Lista dei Bari 1223.

L'Incontro (☎ 041 522 24 04; Rio Terrà Canal 3062a; meal about €26), between Campo San Barnaba and Campo Santa Margherita, serves regional fare.

Cantina do Mori (Sottoportego dei do Mori), off Ruga Rialto, is a small, very popular wine bar that also serves sandwiches. The pricey **Trattoria alla Madonna** (☎ 041 21 01 67; Calle della Madonna 594; meal about €31), two streets west of the Rialto, specialises in seafood.

The bustling **Arca** (☎ 041 524 22 36; Calle San Pantalon 3757; set menu €13, pizza from €5), past Campo San Pantalon, has a warm and lively feel and opposite is **Da Silvio** (☎ 041 20 58 33; Calle San Pantalon 3748), which offers more or less the same dishes at the same prices.

If you're looking for a typical osteria try **Osteria ai 4 Ferri** (☎ 041 520 69 78; Calle Lunga San Barnaba; meal about €17), off Campo San Barnaba. You'll need to book.

Cafés & Bars If you can cope with paying at least €7 for a cappuccino, spend an hour or so sitting at an outdoor table in Piazza San Marco, listening to the orchestra at either **Caffè Florian** or **Caffè Quadri**. For a cheaper alternative, try Campo Santa Margherita's **Bar DuChamp**, a student favourite where panini cost about €1.30 and there's Tetley on tap.

Bar ai Nomboli (cnr Calle dei Nomboli & Rio Terrà dei Nomboli), between Campo San Polo and the Frari, has a huge selection of sandwiches, while in the Castello area you can choose from an extensive range of cheap panini at the bar **Al Vecio Penasa** (Calle delle Rasse 4585).

Gelati & Pastries Some of the best gelati in Venice continue to be served at **Gelati Nico** (Fondamenta Zattere ai Gesuati 922). Join the locals along the fondamenta or take a seat at an outside table. **Il Doge** (Campo Santa Margherita) also has excellent ice cream. A popular place for cakes and pastries is **Pasticceria Marchini** (Calle del Spezier 2769), just off Campo Santo Stefano, where the display of goodies is, to put it mildly, tempting. **Rosa Salva** (Campo SS Giovanni e Paolo) is frequented by locals for its gelati and pastries.

Self-Catering For fruit and vegetables, as well as delicatessens, head for the **market** in the streets on the San Polo side of the Rialto Bridge, or on the Rio Terrà San Leonardo in Cannaregio. There's a **Mega 1** supermarket just off Campo Santa Margherita and a **Standa** supermarket on Strada Nova.

Entertainment

The free weekly booklet Un Ospite di Venezia has entertainment listings, or you can buy a copy of the monthly Venezia News from newsagents for €2.07. The tourist office also has brochures listing events for the entire year.

Venice lost its opera house, the magnificent Teatro La Fenice, to a fire in January 1996. Reconstruction continues, and in the interim performances are held at **PalaFenice** (☎ 041 78 65 11), a tentlike structure on the car-park island of Tronchetto.

Major art exhibitions are held at **Palazzo Grassi** (San Samuele vaporetto stop), and smaller exhibitions at various venues in the city throughout the year.

For less highbrow pursuits, in Cannaregio, **Paradiso Perduto** (Fondamenta della Misericordia 2539; happy hour 6.30pm-7.30pm) has live music and sangria. And where would Venice be without the Irish pub? We'll never know because **The Fiddler's Elbow** (Corte dei Pali 3847) does the job. In Dorsoduro, there's **Café Blue** (Salizzada San Pantalon 3778), a pub-like drinking den near trendy Campo Santa Margherita, or **Café Noir** (Calle San Pantalon 3805), a laid-back, student hang-out. On Campo Santa Margherita, **Il Caffè** is perennially popular.

Shopping

For many visitors, Venice is synonymous with elaborate glassware. There are several workshops and showrooms in Venice, particularly in the area between San Marco and Castello and on the island of Murano. If you're interested in buying, shop around because quality and prices can vary dramatically.

Venice is a trinket box of jewellery, crystals, grotesque Carnevale masks and bronze lions. You'll find them in shops throughout the city. Lace is another characteristic product of the Venetian lagoon, produced mainly on the island of Burano and available in Venice at **Annelie Pizzi e Ricami** (Calle Lunga San Barnaba 2748). Marbled paper and luscious velvet fabrics are other Venetian specialities. Window-shop at Venice's oldest traditional papermaking establishment, **Legatoria Piazzesi** (Campiello della Feltrina 2551c, San Marco), where the high quality is matched by the high prices.

For designer-label clothing, shoes, accessories and jewellery, head for the narrow streets between San Marco and the Rialto, particularly the Merceria and the area around Campo San Luca. Luxury items can be found in the area near La Fenice.

Getting There & Away

Air Some 12km from Venice is **Marco Polo airport** (☎ 041 260 61 11, flight info ☎ 041 260 92 60) which services domestic and European flights. The Alilaguna service from St Mark's costs €9.81. From Piazzale Roma there are also **ATVO buses** (☎ 041 520 55 30) for €2.70 or the ACTV city bus No 5 for €0.77. The official rate for a water taxi from St Marks is €44.95.

Bus The ACTV buses (☎ 899 90 90 90) leave from Piazzale Roma for surrounding areas including Mestre and Chioggia, a fishing port at the southernmost point of the lagoon. Buses also go to Padua and Treviso. Tickets and information are available at the office in Piazzale Roma.

Train The train station, **Stazione Santa Lucia** (☎ 848 88 80 88), is directly linked to Padua, Verona, Trieste, Milan and Bologna, and so is easily accessible for Florence and Rome. You can also head to major points in France, Germany, Austria, Switzerland, Slovenia and Croatia. The Venice Simplon Orient Express runs between Venice and London, via Innsbruck, Zurich and Paris, twice weekly. Ask at any travel agent or phone the headquarters in London (☎ 020 7805 5100).

Boat You can catch ferries to Greece four times a week in winter and daily in summer from **Minoan Lines** (☎ 041 240 71 01; Porto Venezia, Zona Santa Marta). High-season tickets cost from €72 one way.

Getting Around

Once you cross the bridge from Mestre, cars must be left at the car park on the island of Tronchetto or at Piazzale Roma (cars are allowed on the Lido – take car ferry No 17 from Tronchetto). The car parks are not cheap at around €18 a day. A cheaper alternative is to leave the car at Fusina, near Mestre, and catch the vaporetto No 16 to Zattere and then the No 82 either to Piazza San Marco or the train station. Ask for information at the tourist office just before the bridge to Venice.

As there are no cars in Venice, vaporetti are the city's mode of public transport. From Piazzale Roma, vaporetto No 1 zigzags its way along the Grand Canal to San Marco and then to the Lido. There is the faster No 82 if you are in a hurry to get to St Mark's. The No 12 vaporetto leaves from Fondamenta Nuove for the islands of Murano, Burano and Torcello. A full timetable is available at vaporetto ticket offices (€0.50). A single ticket costs €3.10 (plus €3.10 for luggage), even if you only ride to the next station; a return is €5.16. A 24-hour ticket is €9.30 for unlimited travel, a 72-hour ticket is €18.08 (worthwhile) and a one-week ticket costs €30.99.

Water taxis are exorbitant, with a set charge of €13.94 for a maximum of seven minutes, then €0.25 every 15 seconds. It's an extra €4.13 if you phone for a taxi, and various other surcharges add up to make taking a gondola ride seem cheap.

FERRARA
postcode 44100 • pop 131,600

Ferrara's wonderfully evocative medieval centre retains much of the character of its heyday when, as seat of the Este family (1260–1598), the town was a force to be reckoned with. The imposing **Castello Estense** attests to this and remains the dominant landmark in this charming town.

Information

The **tourist information office** (☎ 0532 20 93 70; e infotur.comfe@fe.nettuno.it; open 9am-1pm & 2pm-6pm Mon-Sat, 9.30am-1pm & 2pm-5.30pm Sun) is inside the **Castello Estense**.

Things to See

The small historical centre encompasses medieval Ferrara, to the south of the **Castello Estense**. The castle – complete with moat and drawbridges – was begun by Nicolò II d'Este in 1385. It is partly open to the public and has a suitably chilling atmosphere.

The pink-and-white striped cathedral, the **Duomo**, dates from the 12th century, with

Gothic and Renaissance additions and an unusual triple facade. Its museum has a superb collection of Renaissance art. The Renaissance Palazzo dei Diamanti, along Corso Ercole I d'Este, contains the **Pinacoteca Nazionale** (*☎ 0532 20 58 44; admission €4; open 9am-2pm Tues, Wed, Fri & Sat, 9am-7pm Thur, 9am-1pm Sun*) and exhibitions of modern art.

The **Palazzo Schifanoia** (*☎ 0532 20 99 88; Via Scandiana 23; admission €4.20; open 9am-6pm Tues-Sun*) is one of the city's earliest major Renaissance buildings and another of the Este palaces. It features the 'Room of the Months', decorated with Ferrara's finest Renaissance frescoes.

Special Events
Every May since 1289, Ferrara has celebrated the Palio, considered the oldest in Italy, which culminates in a horse race between the eight town districts. Less dramatic is the Buskers Festival held in August, which attracts street performers from all over the world.

Places to Stay & Eat
Ferrara is a cheap alternative to Bologna, and can be used as a base for visiting Venice. Hidden in the cobbled streets, **Albergo Centro Storico** (*☎ 0532 20 33 74; Via Vegri 15; singles/doubles without bath €26/36*) has basic rooms. South of the cathedral is the modest **Pensione Artisti** (*☎ 0532 76 10 38; Via Vittoria 66; singles without bath €21, doubles with/without bath €52/37*). Better rooms are available at the two-star **Albergo Nazionale** (*☎ 0532 20 96 04; Corso Porta Reno 32; singles/doubles with bath €42/63*). Nearby **Hotel Corte Estense** (*☎ 0532 24 21 68, fax 0532 24 21 76; e info@corteestense.it; Via Correggiari 4/a; singles/doubles/triples with bath €73/124/166*) has a beautiful internal courtyard and free parking for its guests.

Pizzeria il Ciclone (*☎ 0532 21 02 62; Via Vignatagliata 11; pizza from €5.15, meal about €17*) serves local specialities. Closer to the cathedral, **Il Brindisi** (*☎ 0532 20 91 42; Via Adelardi 11; set menu from €10.30*) claims to be the oldest **hosteria** in the world, dating back to the 15th century. Next door at **Pappagallo** (*☎ 0532 20 47 96; meal about €8*) meals are self-service. In the medieval quarter, **Locanda degli Eventi** (*☎ 0532 76 13 47; Via Mayr Carlo 21; meal about €20*) is a quaint local trattoria.

Getting There & Away
Ferrara is on the Bologna–Venice train line, with regular trains to both cities. It is 40 minutes from Bologna and 1½ hours from Venice. Regular trains also run directly to Ravenna. Buses run from the train station to Modena (also in the Emilia-Romagna region).

BOLOGNA
postcode 40100 • pop 380,300
Bologna is vibrant, beautiful and red. And there can't be many cities where the predominant colour of the architecture so accurately reflects the traditional politics of its citizens. The regional capital of Emilia-Romagna, Bologna is home to the oldest university in Europe and its large student population gives the city much of its dynamism.

But it is food for which Bologna is most famous. Other than the eponymous spaghetti bolognese, known as *spaghetti al ragù*, the Bolognese have gifted the world with tortellini, lasagne and mortadella.

Information
The main **IAT tourist office** (*fax 051 23 14 54; Piazza Maggiore 1; open 9am-8pm daily*) is complemented by branch offices at the train station (*open 8.30am-7.30pm Mon-Sat*) and airport (*open 8am-8pm Mon-Sat, 9am-3pm Sun*). All telephone queries are now dealt with by a centralised **Call Center** (*☎ 051 24 65 41; lines open 9am-7pm Mon-Sat*).

The **main post office** is in Piazza Minghetti.

Log on at the Internet café **Net Arena** (*☎/fax 051 22 08 50; Via de' Giudei 3b*) for €3.10 per hour.

Medical & Emergency Services
In a medical emergency call ☎ 118, or **Ospedale Maggiore** (*☎ 051 647 81 11*). For the police go to the **questura** (*police headquarters; ☎ 051 640 11 11; Piazza Galileo 7*).

Things to See & Do
The porticoed streets of Bologna are ideal for a stroll. The best starting point is the traffic-free centre formed by **Piazza Maggiore**, the adjoining **Piazza del Nettuno** and **Fontana del Nettuno** (Neptune's Fountain), sculpted in bronze by the French artist who became known as Giambologna, and **Piazza di Porta Ravegnana**, with its two leaning towers to rival Pisa's (originally there were 42).

ITALY

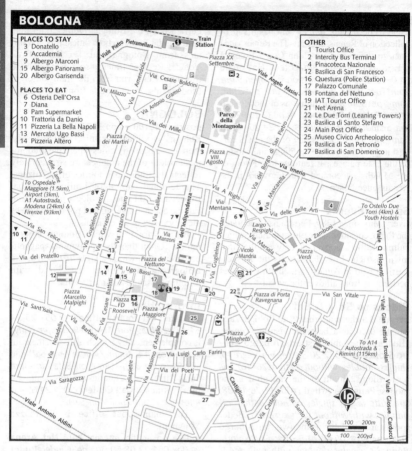

BOLOGNA

PLACES TO STAY
3 Donatello
5 Accademia
9 Albergo Marconi
15 Albergo Panorama
20 Albergo Garisenda

PLACES TO EAT
6 Osteria Dell'Orsa
7 Diana
8 Pam Supermarket
10 Trattoria da Danio
11 Pizzeria La Bella Napoli
13 Mercato Ugo Bassi
14 Pizzeria Altero

OTHER
1 Tourist Office
2 Intercity Bus Terminal
4 Pinacoteca Nazionale
12 Basilica di San Francesco
16 Questura (Police Station)
17 Palazzo Comunale
18 Fontana del Nettuno
19 IAT Tourist Office
21 Net Arena
22 Le Due Torri (Leaning Towers)
23 Basilica di Santo Stefano
24 Main Post Office
25 Museo Civico Archeologico
26 Basilica di San Petronio
27 Basilica di San Domenico

The **Basilica di San Petronio** in Piazza Maggiore is dedicated to the city's patron saint, Petronius. It was here that Charles V was crowned emperor by the pope in 1530. The incomplete red-and-white marble facade displays the colours of Bologna, and the chapels inside contain notable works of art. The adjacent **Palazzo Comunale** (town hall) is a huge building combining several architectural styles in remarkable harmony. It features a bronze statue of Pope Gregory XIII (a native of Bologna, and the creator of the Gregorian calendar), an impressive staircase attributed to Bramante and Bologna's collection of art treasures.

The **Basilica di Santo Stefano** is a medieval religious complex of four churches (originally there were seven) and includes the 11th-century Chiesa del Crocefisso, which houses the bones of San Petronio.

The **Basilica di San Domenico**, erected in the early 16th century, houses the elaborate sarcophagus of St Dominic, the founder of the Dominican order. The chapel was designed by Nicoló Pisano and its shrine features figures carved by a young Michelangelo.

The **Museo Civico Archeologico**, **Pinacoteca Nazionale** and French Gothic **Basilica di San Francesco** are also well worth a visit.

Places to Stay

Budget hotels in Bologna are difficult to come by and finding a single room can be a nightmare, so always book in advance.

A good option is the HI **Ostello Due Torri** (☎/fax 051 50 18 10; Via Viadagola 5; dorm *bed €12)*. Take bus No 93 or 20b from Via Irnerio (off Via dell'Indipendenza south of the station), and ask the bus driver where to alight.

Right in the historic centre, **Albergo Garisenda** (☎ *051 22 43 69, fax 051 22 10 07; Via Rizzoli 9, Galleria del Leone 1; singles/ doubles/triples without bath €42/62/83)* has some rooms overlooking the two towers and the busy Via Rizzoli. Slightly further out, **Albergo Marconi** (☎ *051 26 28 32; Via G Marconi 22; singles/doubles without bath €34/ 53, with bath €43/68)* provides functional but plain rooms. **Albergo Panorama** (☎ *051 22 18 02; Via Livraghi 1; singles/doubles/ triples/quads without bath €47/62/78/88)* has light and airy rooms. **Accademia** (☎ *051 23 23 18, fax 051 26 35 90; Via delle Belle Arti 6; singles/doubles €82/113)* offers good two-star rooms and a grumpy owner. Closer to the station the three-star **Donatello** (☎ *051 24 81 74, fax 051 24 47 76; Via dell'Indipen- denza 65; singles/doubles €60/80)* gives discounts if there are no trade fairs on.

Places to Eat

Pizzeria La Bella Napoli (☎ *051 55 51 63; Via San Felice 40; pizza from €5)* serves pop- ular and reasonably priced pizzas. A few doors away **Trattoria da Danio** (☎ *051 55 52 02; Via San Felice 50a; meal about €15)* is a pearl, full of large locals who like their food. **Pizzeria Altero** *(Via Ugo Bassi 10; pizza slice from €1)* is the place for a quick lunchtime bite. For more of a pub feel, join the students at the **Osteria Dell'Orsa** (☎ *051 23 15 76; Via Mentana 1G; panini from €4, mains about €7)* in the university quarter. **Diana** (☎ *051 23 13 02; Via dell'Indipendenza 24a; meal about €36)* has waiters in white jackets.

Shop at **Mercato Ugo Bassi** *(Via Ugo Bassi 27; open Mon-Sat)*, a covered market offering all the local fare, or at supermarket **Pam** *(Via Marconi 28a)*.

Getting There & Away

Bologna's **Guiglielmo Marconi airport** (☎ *051 647 96 15)* is northwest of the city.

On land, Bologna is a major transport junc- tion and trains from all over the country stop here. National and international coaches to major cities depart from the terminal in Piazza XX Settembre, around the corner from the train station in Piazza delle Medaglie d'Oro.

The city is linked to Milan, Florence and Rome by the A1 (Autostrada del Sole). The A13 heads directly for Venice and Padua, and the A14 goes to Rimini and Ravenna.

Getting Around

Traffic is restricted in the city centre, so it's best to park at one of the many public car parks outside the city walls. The bus system is efficient; to get to the city centre from the train station take bus No 25 or 27.

RAVENNA

postcode 48100 • pop 138,900

Ravenna's exquisite mosaics, relics of the time it was capital of the Western Roman Empire and western seat of the Byzantines, are the big drawcards. But Ravenna is also the last resting place of Dante, who died here in 1321. Easily accessible from Bologna, this perfectly manicured, stress-free town, is worth a day trip at the very least.

Information

There is an **IAT tourist office** (☎ *0544 354 04, fax 0544 48 26 70; Via Salara 8; open 8.30am-6pm Mon-Sat, until 7pm Apr-Oct, 10am-4pm Sun)*. For all things medical try **Ospedale Santa Maria delle Croci** (☎ *0544 40 91 11; Via Missiroli 10)*.

Things to See

The pick of Ravenna's mosaics are found in the **Basilica di Sant'Apollinare Nuovo**, the **Basilica di San Vitale**, the **Mausoleo di Galla Placidia** (these are the oldest) and the **Battis- tero Neoniano**. These buildings are all in the town centre and an admission ticket to the four, as well as to the **Museo Arcivescovile**, costs €6. The mosaics in the **Basilica di Sant' Apollinare in Classe**, 5km away, are also no- table. To get there take bus No 4 or 44 from the train station. **Dante's Tomb** is open to the public daily and is free.

Special Events

Ravenna hosts a music festival from late June to early August, featuring world-renowned artists, while an annual theatre and literature festival is held in September in honour of Dante. In winter, opera and dance are staged at the **Teatro Alighieri** *(box office ☎ 0544 24 92 44; Piazza Garibaldi 5)*.

Places to Stay & Eat

The HI **Ostello Dante** (☎ *0544 42 11 64; Via Aurelio Nicolodi 12; B&B €12.50, family*

ITALY

rooms per person €14) is 1km out of town. Take bus No 1 from Viale Pallavacini, to the left of the train station. **Al Giaciglio** (☎/fax 0544 394 03; Via Rocca Brancaleone 42; singles/doubles without bath €30/42, with bath €36/51) has very blue rooms and a restaurant with a set menu for €12.20. Two-star **Ravenna** (☎ 0544 21 22 04, fax 0544 21 20 77; Via Maroncelli 12; singles/doubles with bath €42/62), provides anonymous rooms just outside the train station. In the heart of the city's historic centre, the three-star **Hotel Centrale Byron** (☎ 0544 334 79, fax 0544 341 14; Via IV Novembre 14; singles/doubles with bath from €53/83) offers all the mod cons and a chatty owner.

For a quick lunch, you could try the **Bizantino** self-service restaurant in the city's fresh-produce market in Piazza Andrea Costa. There is a fixed menu for €7.30, excluding drinks, but it is only open Monday to Friday. **Cá de Vén** (☎ 0544 301 63; Via Corrado Ricci 24; meal about €25) offers regional dishes and wine in monastic surroundings.

Getting There & Away
Ravenna is accessible by train from Bologna, sometimes involving a change at Castel Bolognese. The trip takes around 1½ hours.

Getting Around
Cycling is a popular way to get around, especially as there are no hills anywhere in sight. Rental is €7.75 per day or €1.03 per hour from COOP San Vitale, Piazza Farini, outside the station. The tourist office also has some bikes to lend in spring and summer. They don't charge, but phone ahead to check availability.

SAN MARINO
postcode 47890 • pop 28,000
The world's oldest surviving republic, San Marino was founded in AD 300 by a stonemason said to have been escaping religious persecution; at least according to one legend. The tiny state (only 61 sq km) is an unashamed tourist trap but offers splendid views of the mountains and coast. You can wander along the city walls and visit the two fortresses.

The **tourist office** (☎ 0549 88 29 98; Contrada Omagnano 20; open 8.30am-6.30pm daily) is in the Palazzo del Turismo. San Marino is accessible from Rimini by bus.

The Dolomites

The limestone Dolomites stretch across Trentino-Alto Adige and into the Veneto. Characterised by the reddish glow of the rock formations which jut into the sky like jagged teeth, this spectacular Alpine region is the Italians' favoured area for skiing and, in summer, hiking.

Information
Information about Trentino-Alto Adige can be obtained in Trent (Trento) at the **APT del Trentino** (☎ 0461 83 90 00, fax 0461 26 02 45; e info@trentino.to; Via Romagnosi 11); in Rome (☎ 06 36 09 58 42, fax 06 320 24 13; Via del Babuino 20); and in Milan (☎ 02 86 46 12 51, fax 02 72 00 21 88; Piazza Diaz 5). Bolzano's **tourist office** (☎ 0471 30 70 00; e info@bolzano-bozen.it; Piazza Walther 8) also has information on the region.

The **APT Dolomiti** (☎ 0436 32 31/2/3, fax 0436 32 35) at Cortina can provide details on trekking and skiing in the Veneto.

Skiing
The Dolomites' numerous ski resorts range from expensive and fashionable Cortina d'Ampezzo in the Veneto to family-oriented resorts such as those in the Val Gardena in Trentino-Alto Adige. All the resorts have helpful tourist offices with information on facilities, accommodation and transport.

The high season is from Christmas to early January and from early February to April, when prices increase considerably. A good way to save money is to buy a *settimana bianca* (literally, 'white week'), package-deal that covers accommodation, food and ski passes for seven days. They are available from travel agencies throughout Italy.

If you want to go it alone, invest in a ski pass. Most resort areas offer their own passes for unlimited use of lifts at several resorts for a nominated period. Prices vary depending on the resort but expect to pay around €123 to €154 for six days.

The **Superski Dolomiti pass** (w www.dolomitisuperski.com), which allows access to 464 lifts and 1220km of ski runs in 12 valleys for six days, costs €175.

The average cost of ski and boot hire in the Alps is around €15 a day for downhill and €10 for cross-country.

Trekking

Without doubt, the Dolomites provide the most breathtaking opportunities for walking in the Italian Alps – from a half-day stroll with the kids to demanding treks that require mountaineering skills. The walking season runs from the end of June to the end of September. Alpine refuges *(rifugi)* usually close around 20 September.

Buy a map of the hiking trails with Alpine refuges marked. The best are the Tabacco 1:25,000 series, which are widely available at bookshops throughout the region. Lonely Planet's *Walking in Italy* outlines several treks in detail and the *Italy* guide also details some suggested hikes.

Hiking trails are generally well marked with numbers on red-and-white painted bands on trees and rocks along the trails, or by numbers inside different-coloured triangles for the Alte Vie (the four High Routes through the Dolomites that link a chain of rifugi and can take up to two weeks to walk – the APT in Trent has details).

Recommended hiking areas include:

Alpe di Siusi A vast plateau above the Val Gardena, at the foot of the spectacular Sciliar.

Cortina area Featuring the magnificent Parco Naturale di Fanes-Sennes-Braies.

Pale di San Martino Accessible from San Martino di Castrozza.

Warning Remember that even in summer the weather is extremely changeable in the Alps; although it might be sweltering when you set off, you should be prepared for very cold and wet weather on even the shortest of walks. Essentials include good-quality, worn-in walking boots, an anorak or pile/wind jacket, a lightweight backpack, a warm hat and gloves, a waterproof poncho, light food and plenty of water.

Getting There & Away

The region has an excellent public transport network – the two principal bus companies are SAD (☎ 800 84 60 409) in Alto Adige and the Veneto, and Atesina in Trentino. There's a network of long-distance buses operated by a number of companies (eg, Lazzi, SITA, Sena, STAT and ATVO) connecting the main towns and ski resorts with major cities such as Rome, Florence, Venice, Bologna, Milan and Genoa. Information is available from tourist offices and *autostazioni* (bus stations) in the region. For long-distance travel information, try **Lazzi Express** (☎ 06 884 08 40; *Via Tagliamento 27b*) in Rome, and (☎ 055 28 71 18; *Piazza Stazione 47r*) in Florence. There is a **SITA office** (☎ 055 29 49 55; *Via Santa Caterina da Siena 15*) in Florence.

Getting Around

If you are planning to hike in the Alps during the warmer months, you'll find that hitching is no problem, especially near the resort towns. The areas around the major resorts are well serviced by local buses, and tourist offices will be able to provide information on routes. During winter, most resorts have 'ski bus' shuttle services from the towns to the main ski facilities.

CORTINA D'AMPEZZO
postcode 32043 • pop 6570

The ski resort for Italy's beautiful people, Cortina is excruciatingly fashionable and correspondingly expensive. It is also one of the best equipped and most picturesque resorts in the Dolomites. The area is very popular for trekking and climbing, with well-marked trails and numerous rifugi.

The **main APT tourist office** (☎ 0436 32 31/32/33) has information on Cortina's accommodation options. **International Camping Olympia** (☎/fax 0436 50 57; *per person/tent & car €7.50/9; open year-round*) is 3.5km north of Cortina at Fiames. **Casa Tua** (☎ 0436 22 78; e info@casatuacortina.com; *Zuel 100; rooms per person €34-50*) in Cortina has varying rates, depending on the season. SAD buses connect Cortina with Bolzano, via Dobbiaco; ATVO with Venice, and Zani with Milan and Bologna.

CANAZEI
postcode 38032 • pop 1780

Set in the Fassa Dolomites, the resort of Canazei has more than 100km of trails and is linked to the challenging network of runs known as the **Sella Ronda**. Canazei also offers cross-country and summer skiing on Marmolada, which at 3342m is the highest peak in the Dolomites.

Spend a cheap night at the Marmolada **camping ground** (☎ 0462 60 16 60; *per person/tent €7.75/7.75; open year-round*), or contact the **APT tourist office** (☎ 0462 60 11 13, fax 0462 60 25 02; *Via Roma 34*) for further details on accommodation. The resort is accessible by Atesina bus from Trent and SAD bus from Bolzano.

VAL GARDENA

This is one of the most popular skiing areas in the Alps, due to its reasonable prices and first-class facilities. There are superb walking trails in the Sella Group and the Alpe di Siusi. The Vallunga, behind Selva, is great for family walks and cross-country skiing.

The valley's main towns are Ortisei, Santa Cristina and Selva, all offering plenty of accommodation and easy access to runs. Each town has a **tourist office** *(Ortisei: ☎ 0471 79 63 28, fax 0471 79 67 49; Santa Cristina: ☎ 0471 79 30 46, fax 0471 79 31 98; Selva: ☎ 0471 79 51 22, fax 0471 79 42 45)*, which all have extensive information on accommodation and facilities. Staff speak English and will send details on request. The Val Gardena is accessible from Bolzano by SAD bus, and is connected to major Italian cities by coach services (Lazzi, SITA and STAT).

SAN MARTINO DI CASTROZZA
postcode 38058 • pop 700

Located in a sheltered position beneath the Pale di San Martino, this resort is popular among Italians and offers good ski runs, as well as cross-country skiing and a toboggan run. The **APT office** *(☎ 0439 76 88 67, fax 0439 76 88 14)* will provide a full list of accommodation. **Hotel Suisse** *(☎ 0439 680 87; Via Dolomiti 1; B&B from €30)* is a pleasant one-star option. Buses travel regularly from Trent, Venice and Padua.

Central Italy

Miraculously, the rolling green landscape and soft golden light of Tuscany, and rugged hill towns of Umbria and the Marches (Le Marche) seem virtually unchanged today. In each of the regions there is a strong artistic and cultural tradition and the smallest medieval town can harbour a masterpiece or two.

FLORENCE
postcode 50100 • pop 375,500

Italy has been successfully selling itself on the back of Florence for centuries. And although everything they claim is true – it is a beautiful city with an artistic heritage unrivalled anywhere else in the world – it can also be dis-

heartening. For most of the year, you're more likely to overhear conversations in English than in Italian, and, especially in summer, the heat, car fumes and crowds can be stifling. But, gripes apart, Florence remains one of the most enticing cities in Italy. Cradle of the Renaissance, home of Dante, Machiavelli, Michelangelo, the Medici and Carlo Collodi (the bloke who created Pinocchio), the wealth of history, art and culture continues to overwhelm.

Florence was founded as a colony of the Etruscan city of Fiesole in about 200 BC and later became the strategic Roman garrison settlement of Florentia. In the Middle Ages the city developed a flourishing economy based on banking and commerce, which sparked a period of building and growth previously unequalled in Italy. It was a major focal point for the Guelph and Ghibelline struggle of the 13th century, which saw Dante banished from the city. But Florence truly flourished in the 15th century under the Medici, reaching its cultural, artistic and political height as it gave birth to the Renaissance.

The Grand Duchy of the Medici was succeeded in the 18th century by the House of Lorraine (related to the Austrian Habsburgs). Following unification, Florence was the capital of the new kingdom of Italy from 1865 to 1871. During WWII parts of the city were destroyed by bombing, including all of the bridges except the Ponte Vecchio, and in 1966 a devastating flood destroyed or severely damaged many important works of art.

Orientation

Whether you arrive by train, bus or car, the main train station, Santa Maria Novella, is a good reference point. Budget hotels and pensioni are concentrated around Via Nazionale to the east of the station, and Piazza Santa Maria Novella to the south. The main thoroughfare to the centre is Via de' Panzani and then Via de' Cerretani, about a 10-minute walk. You'll know you've arrived when you first glimpse the Duomo.

Once at Piazza del Duomo you will find Florence easy to negotiate, with most of the major sights within easy walking distance. Many museums are closed on Monday, but you won't waste your time by just strolling through the streets. Take the city ATAF buses for longer distances such as to Piazzale Michelangelo or the nearby suburb of Fiesole, both of which offer panoramic views of the city.

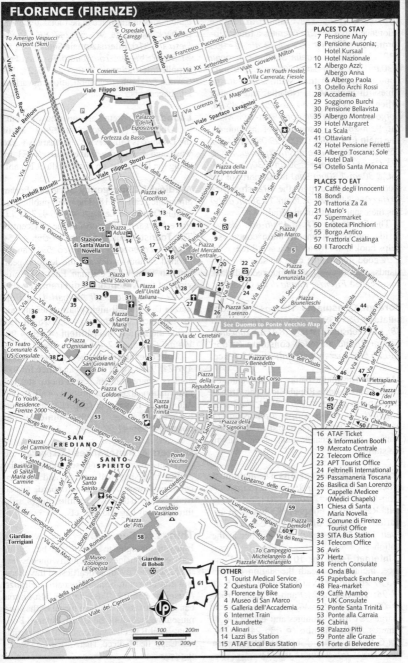

FLORENCE (FIRENZE)

PLACES TO STAY
7 Pensione Mary
8 Pensione Ausonia;
 Hotel Kursaal
10 Hotel Nazionale
12 Albergo Azzi;
 Albergo Anna
 & Albergo Paola
13 Ostello Archi Rossi
28 Accademia
29 Soggiorno Burchi
30 Pensione Bellavista
35 Albergo Montreal
39 Hotel Margaret
40 La Scala
41 Ottaviani
42 Hotel Pensione Ferretti
43 Albergo Toscana; Sole
46 Hotel Dali
54 Ostello Santa Monaca

PLACES TO EAT
17 Caffè degli Innocenti
18 Bondi
20 Trattoria Za Za
21 Mario's
47 Supermarket
50 Enoteca Pinchiorri
55 Borgo Antico
57 Trattoria Casalinga
60 I Tarocchi

OTHER
1 Tourist Medical Service
2 Questura (Police Station)
3 Florence by Bike
4 Museo di San Marco
5 Galleria dell'Accademia
6 Internet Train
9 Laundrette
11 Alinari
14 Lazzi Bus Station
15 ATAF Local Bus Station
16 ATAF Ticket
 & Information Booth
19 Mercato Centrale
22 Telecom Office
23 APT Tourist Office
24 Feltrinelli International
25 Passamaneria Toscana
26 Basilica di San Lorenzo
27 Cappelle Medicee
 (Medici Chapels)
31 Chiesa di Santa
 Maria Novella
32 Comune di Firenze
 Tourist Office
33 SITA Bus Station
34 Telecom Office
36 Avis
37 Hertz
38 French Consulate
44 Onda Blu
45 Paperback Exchange
48 Flea-market
49 Caffè Mambo
51 UK Consulate
52 Ponte Santa Trinitá
53 Ponte alla Carraia
56 Cabiria
58 Palazzo Pitti
59 Ponte alle Grazie
61 Forte di Belvedere

See Duomo to Ponte Vecchio Map

To Amerigo Vespucci
Airport (5km)

To HI Youth Hostel;
Villa Camerata; Fiesole

To Youth
Residence
Firenze 2000

To Teatro
Comunale &
US Consulate

To Campeggio
Michelangelo &
Piazzale Michelangelo

ARNO

0   100   200m
0   100   200yd

Information

Tourist Offices The Comune di Firenze (Florence City Council) operates a **tourist information office** (☎ 055 21 22 45, fax 055 238 12 26; Piazza della Stazione 4; open 8.30am-7pm Mon-Sat, 8.30am-1.30pm Sun), opposite the main train station, next to the Chiesa di Santa Maria Novella; and another **office** (☎ 055 234 04 44, fax 055 226 45 24; Borgo Santa Croce 29r; open 9am-7pm Mon-Sat, 9am-2pm Sun) southeast of the Duomo. The **main APT office** (☎ 055 29 08 32/33, fax 055 276 03 83; e infoturismo@provincia.fi.it; Via Cavour 1r; open 8.30am-6.30pm Mon-Sat, 8.30am-1.30pm Sun) is just north of the Duomo. At the airport the **branch office** (☎/fax 055 31 58 74; 7.30am-11.30pm daily) has the usual wealth of material.

The **Consorzio ITA** (8.45am-8pm daily), inside the station on the main concourse, helps book hotel rooms for a small fee.

A good map of the city, on sale at newsstands, is the one with the white, red and black cover called Firenze: Pianta della Città.

Foreign Consulates There is a **US consulate** (☎ 055 239 82 76; Lungarno Vespucci 38), a **UK consulate** (☎ 055 28 41 33; Lungarno Corsini 2) and a **French consulate** (☎ 055 230 25 56; Piazza Ognissanti 2) in Florence.

Money The major banks are concentrated around Piazza della Repubblica. The **American Express office** (☎ 055 509 81; Via Dante Alighieri 22r; open 9am-5.30pm Mon-Fri, 9.30am-12.30pm Sat) is near the Duomo. Be wary of poor exchange rates at facilities in the station.

Post & Communications The **main post office** (Via Pellicceria 3; open 8.15am-7pm Mon-Fri, 8.15am-12.30pm Sat) is off Piazza della Repubblica. For phones, there is an unstaffed **Telecom office** (Via Cavour 21r; open 7am-11pm daily), and another at the station.

Internet Train has 10 branches in Florence, including beneath the station (☎ 055 239 97 20), just off Via Nazionale (☎ 055 21 47 94; Via Guelfa 24r) and in Santa Croce (☎ 055 263 85 55; Via dei Benci 36). It charges €1 for 10 minutes and €2.30 for 30 minutes. **Caffè Mambo** (☎ 055 247 89 94; Via G Verdi 49) has a separate Internet area and charges €1.30 for 15 minutes.

Bookshops A selection of new and second-hand books in English can be found at the **Paperback Exchange** (☎ 055 247 81 54; Via Fiesolana 31r). **Internazionale Seeber** (☎ 055 21 56 97; Via de' Tornabuoni 70r) and **Feltrinelli International** (☎ 055 21 95 24; Via Cavour 12r) both stock publications in various languages.

Laundry Laundrettes are fairly easy to come by. **Onda Blu** (Via degli Alfani 24r), east of the Duomo, is self-service and charges €3 to wash and €3 to dry. Save yourself €1 by using the laundrette on Via Guelfa at No 55r.

Medical & Emergency Services For an ambulance call ☎ 118. The main public hospital is **Ospedale Careggi** (☎ 055 427 71 11; Viale Morgagni 85), north of the city centre. The **Tourist Medical Service** (☎ 055 47 54 11; Via Lorenzo il Magnifico 59) can be phoned 24 hours a day and the doctors speak English, French and German. First aid is provided at the **Misericordia di Firenze** (☎ 055 21 22 22; Vicolo degli Adimari 1) just off Piazza Duomo. All-night pharmacies include the **Farmacia Comunale** (☎ 055 28 94 35), inside the station; and **Molteni** (☎ 28 94 90; Via dei Calzaiuoli 7r) in the city centre.

At the **questura** (police headquarters; ☎ 055 497 71; Via Zara 2) there is an office for foreigners where you can report thefts etc. For information about lost property call ☎ 055 328 39 42. But if you suspect your car has been towed away, try the **municipal car pound** (☎ 055 41 57 81).

Dangers & Annoyances Pickpockets are active in crowds and on buses: beware of the groups of dishevelled women and children carrying newspapers and cardboard, whose trick is to distract you while others rifle through your bag and pockets.

Things to See & Do

Enjoying the sights in Florence can be a 'grin-and-bear-it' business, as lengthy queues test the patience of even the heartiest of travellers. But don't despair, because by calling **Firenze Musei** (☎ 055 29 48 83, fax 26 44 06) you can book tickets in advance for all of the state museums, including the Uffizi, Palazzo Pitti, Museo del Bargello, Galleria dell'Accademia and Cappelle Medicee. There is a €1.55 booking fee.

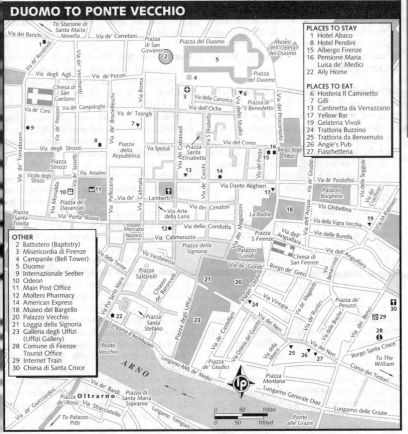

DUOMO TO PONTE VECCHIO

PLACES TO STAY
1 Hotel Abaco
8 Hotel Pendini
15 Albergo Firenze
16 Pensione Maria
   Luisa de' Medici
22 Aily Home

PLACES TO EAT
6 Hosteria Il Caminetto
7 Gilli
13 Cantinetta da Verrazzano
17 Yellow Bar
19 Gelateria Vivoli
24 Trattoria Buzzino
25 Trattoria da Benvenuto
26 Angie's Pub
27 Fiaschetteria

OTHER
2 Battistero (Baptistry)
3 Misericordia di Firenze
4 Campanile (Bell Tower)
5 Duomo
9 Internazionale Seeber
10 Odeon
11 Main Post Office
12 Molteni Pharmacy
14 American Express
18 Museo del Bargello
20 Palazzo Vecchio
21 Loggia della Signoria
23 Galleria degli Uffizi
   (Uffizi Gallery)
28 Comune di Firenze
   Tourist Office
29 Internet Train
30 Chiesa di Santa Croce

Duomo With its nougat facade and skyline-dominating dome, the Duomo is one of Italy's most famous monuments, and the world's fourth-largest cathedral. Named the Cattedrale di Santa Maria del Fiore, the breathtaking structure was begun in 1294 by the Sienese architect Arnolfo di Cambio but took almost 150 years to complete.

The Renaissance architect Brunelleschi won a public competition in 1420 to design the enormous dome, the first of its kind since antiquity. The octagonal dome is decorated with frescoes by Vasari and Zuccari, and stained-glass windows by Donatello, Paolo Uccello and Lorenzo Ghiberti. The marble facade is a 19th-century replacement of the unfinished original, which was pulled down in the 16th century. For a bird's-eye view of Florence, climb to the top of the **cupola** (admission €6; open 8.30am-7pm Mon-Fri, 8.30am-5.40pm Sat).

Giotto designed and began building the graceful **campanile** (bell tower; admission €6; open 8.30am-7.30pm daily) next to the cathedral in 1334, but died before it was completed. Standing at 82m, the climb to the top is a tough one.

The Romanesque **battistero** (baptistry; admission €3, open noon-6pm Mon-Sat, 8.30am-1.30pm Sun), believed to have been built between the 5th and 11th centuries on the site of a Roman temple, is the oldest building in Florence. Dante was baptised here, and it is particularly famous for its gilded-bronze doors. The celebrated *Gates of Paradise* by Lorenzo Ghiberti face the Duomo to the east;

Ghiberti also designed the north door. The south door, by Andrea Pisano, dates from 1336 and is the oldest. Most of the doors are copies – the original panels are being removed for restoration and placement in the Museo dell'Opera del Duomo.

Galleria degli Uffizi (Uffizi Gallery) The Palazzo degli Uffizi *(admission €8; open 8.15am-6.50pm Tues-Sun)*, built by Vasari in the 16th century, houses the single greatest collection of Italian and Florentine art in existence. Bequeathed to the city by the Medici family in 1743, it contains some of the world's most-recognisable Renaissance paintings.

The gallery's inordinate number of masterpieces include 14th-century gems by Giotto and Cimabue; Botticelli's *Birth of Venus* and *Allegory of Spring* from the 15th century; and works by Filippo Lippi, Fra Angelico and Paolo Uccello. *The Annunciation* by Leonardo da Vinci is also here, along with Michelangelo's *Holy Family,* Titian's *Venus of Urbino* and renowned works by Raphael, Andrea del Sarto, Tintoretto and Caravaggio.

Piazza della Signoria & Palazzo Vecchio Designed by Arnolfo di Cambio and built between 1298 and 1340, Palazzo Vecchio *(admission €5.70; open 9am-7pm Tues, Wed & Sat, 9am-11pm Mon & Fri, 9am-2pm Thur, in summer, otherwise 9am-7pm Mon-Wed & Fri-Sat, 9am-2pm Thur)* is the traditional seat of the Florentine government. In the 16th century it became the ducal palace of the Medici (before they moved to the Palazzo Pitti), and was given an interior facelift by Vasari. Visit the Michelozzo courtyard just inside the entrance and the lavishly decorated apartments upstairs.

The palace's turrets, battlements and bell tower form an imposing backdrop to Piazza della Signoria, scene of many pivotal political events in the history of Florence, including the execution of the religious and political reformer Savonarola; a bronze plaque marks the spot where he was burned at the stake in 1498. The **Loggia della Signoria**, which has recently been thoroughly cleaned up and stands at right angles to the Palazzo Vecchio, displays sculptures such as Giambologna's *Rape of the Sabine Women.* Cellini's famous *Perseus* has, however, been relocated to the Uffizi. The statue of *David* is a fine copy of Michelangelo's master-piece; the original was installed on the site in 1504, and is now safely indoors in the Galleria dell'Accademia.

Ponte Vecchio This famous 14th-century bridge, lined with gold and silversmiths' shops, was the only one to survive Nazi bombing in WWII. Originally, the shops housed butchers, but when a corridor along the 1st floor was built by the Medici to link the Palazzo Pitti and Palazzo Vecchio, it was ordered that goldsmiths rather than noisome butchers should trade on the bridge.

Palazzo Pitti This immense and imposing palazzo was built for the Pitti family, great rivals of the Medici, who moved in a century later. The **Galleria Palatina** *(Palatine Gallery; admission €6.50; open 8.15am-6.50pm Tues-Sun)* has works by Raphael, Filippo Lippi, Titian and Rubens, hung in lavishly decorated rooms. The gallery and gloriously (some might say ridiculously) over-the-top **royal apartments** can be visited on the same ticket and keep the same hours. The palace also houses the **Museo degli Argenti** (Silver Museum), the **Galleria d'Arte Moderna** (Modern Art Gallery) and the **Galleria del Costume** *(Costume Gallery; all three museums open 8.15am-1.50pm Tues-Sat)*.

Don't leave without visiting the Renaissance **Giardino di Boboli** *(Boboli Gardens; admission €2)*, with grottoes, fountains, leafy walkways and panoramic city views.

Museo del Bargello The medieval **Palazzo del Bargello** *(Via del Proconsolo 4; admission €4; open 8.15am-5pm Tues-Sun)* should not be missed. With a bloody history as the seat of the chief magistrate and, later, as a police station, the palace now houses Florence's rich collection of sculpture. Here you'll marvel at Michelangelo's *Bacchus*, Donatello's bronze *David*, Giambologna's *Mercury* and works by Benvenuto Cellini.

Galleria dell'Accademia Arguably the most famous sculpture in the Western world, Michelangelo's *David* is housed in this gallery *(Via Ricasoli 60; admission €6.50; open 8.15am-6.50pm Tues-Sun)*, as are four of the artist's unfinished *Slaves*. Early Florentine works are on show in the gallery upstairs.

Museo di San Marco This museum *(admission €4; open 8.15am-1.50pm Mon-Fri, 8.15am-6.50pm Sat, 8.15am-7pm Sun)*, pays homage to the work of Fra Angelico, who decorated many of the cells in this former Dominican convent with sublime frescoes and lived here from 1438 to 1455. Don't miss the peaceful cloisters (depicted in his *Annunciation*). The monastery also contains works by Fra Bartolomeo and Ghirlandaio, as well as the cell of the monk Savonarola.

Basilica di San Lorenzo & Cappelle Medicee (Medici Chapels) The basilica was built by Brunelleschi in the early 15th century for the Medici and includes his mathematically precise **Sagrestia Vecchia** (Old Sacristy), with sculptural decoration by Donatello. The cloister leads to the **Biblioteca Laurenziana**, the huge library built to house the Medici collection of some 10,000 manuscripts is entered via Michelangelo's flowing Mannerist stairway.

The **Cappelle Medicee** *(admission €6; open 8.15am-5pm Mon-Sat, 8.15am-5pm 1st, 3rd & 5th Sun of the month, otherwise 8.15am-1.50pm Sun)* are around the corner in Piazza Madonna degli Aldobrandini. The **Cappella dei Principi**, sumptuously decorated with marble and semiprecious stones, was the principal burial place of the Medici grand dukes. The incomplete **Sagrestia Nuova** was Michelangelo's first architectural effort, and contains his *Medici Madonna*, *Night & Day* and *Dawn & Dusk* sculptures, which adorn the Medici tombs.

Other Attractions The Tuscan Gothic **Chiesa di Santa Maria Novella** was constructed for the Dominican Order during the 13th and 14th centuries; its white-and-green marble facade was designed by Alberti in the 15th century. The church features Masaccio's *Trinity*, a masterpiece of perspective, and is decorated with frescoes by Ghirlandaio (who was perhaps assisted by a very young Michelangelo). **Cappella di Filippo Strozzi** has frescoes by Filippino Lippi, and those in the cloisters are by Paolo Uccello.

Head up to **Piazzale Michelangelo** for unparalleled views of Florence. To get there from the city centre, cross the Ponte Vecchio, turn left and walk along the river, then turn right at Piazza Giuseppe Poggi; if you're tired of walking, take bus No 13 from the station.

Cycling
No churches and no museums is the promise of **I Bike Italy** *(☎ 055 234 23 71; W www .ibikeitaly.com)* on its single and two-day guided bike rides (and walking tours) in the countryside around Florence. It supplies all the gear and English-speaking guides. The Fiesole ride costs US$70, Chianti US$85 and Siena US$280 (two days; price includes meals and accommodation).

Special Events
Major festivals include the Scoppio del Carro (Explosion of the Cart), held in front of the Duomo on Easter Sunday; and, on 24 June, the Festa di San Giovanni (Feast of St John, Florence's patron saint) and lively Calcio Storico, which features football matches played in 16th-century costume. Maggio Musicale Fiorentino, Italy's longest-running music festival, runs from April to June. For more information call the **Teatro Comunale** *(☎ 800 11 22 11)*.

Places to Stay
Always ask the full price of a room before putting your bags down as hotels and pensioni in Florence are becoming increasingly expensive and are notorious for bill-padding, particularly in summer. Prices listed here are for high season.

Camping The **Campeggio Michelangelo** *(☎ 055 681 19 77, fax 055 68 93 48; Viale Michelangelo 80; per person/tent €7.50/ 4.80)* is near Piazzale Michelangelo. Take bus No 13 from the station. **Villa Camerata** *(☎ 055 60 14 51; Viale Augusto Righi 2-4; per person/tent €6/5)* is next to the HI hostel of the same name (see the following section). **Campeggio Panoramico** *(☎ 055 59 90 69, fax 055 591 86; Via Peramonda 1; per person/tent €8.50/14)*, in Fiesole, also has bungalows. Take bus No 7 from the station.

Hostels The HI **Ostello Villa Camerata** *(☎ 055 60 14 51, fax 055 61 03 00; Viale Augusto Righi 2-4; dorm bed €15; closed 9am-2pm)* is beautifully situated. Dinner costs €8 and there is a bar. Take bus No 17, which leaves from the right of the station as you exit the platforms and takes about a half-hour. It is open to HI members only and reservations can be made by mail (essential in summer).

The private **Ostello Archi Rossi** (☎ *055 29 08 04, fax 055 230 26 01; Via Faenza 94r; dorm bed €16)* is another good option for a bed in a six- or nine-bed dorm. **Ostello Santa Monaca** (☎ *055 26 83 38; Via Santa Monaca 6; dorm bed €15.50)* is a 20-minute walk from the station: go through Piazza Santa Maria Novella, along Via de' Fossi, across the Ponte alla Carraia, directly ahead along Via de' Serragli, and Via Santa Monaca is on the right. Further west, **Youth Residence Firenze 2000** (☎ *055 233 55 58;* e *european@dada.it; Viale Raffaello Sanzio 16; doubles with bath from €62)* lacks atmosphere and is not cheap, but its warm indoor pool is a big plus.

Hotels With more than 150 budget hotels in Florence, there is usually a room available somewhere, but, it is still a good idea to book. You should arrive by late morning to claim your room.

Around the Station Recently renovated **Pensione Bellavista** (☎ *055 28 45 28, fax 055 28 48 74; Largo Alinari 15; singles/doubles without bath €50/80, doubles with bath €90)*, at the start of Via Nazionale, has bright rooms and a loo with a view. **Albergo Azzi** (☎/fax *055 21 38 06; Via Faenza 56; singles without bath €42, doubles with/without bath €78/62)* is one of three basic hotels in the same building; upstairs are **Albergo Anna** and **Paola**.

Across Via Nazionale, the easy to miss **Soggiorno Burchi** (☎ *055 41 44 54; Via Faenza 20; doubles with/without bath €60/50)* is a private house with old-fashioned rooms. Nearby at the **Hotel Nazionale** (☎ *055 238 22 03, fax 055 238 17 35; Via Nazionale 22; singles/doubles without bath €47/75, with bath €57/85)* some rooms have the dream view of the Duomo. A few doors up at No 24, **Pensione Ausonia** (☎ *055 49 65 47, fax 055 462 66 15; singles/doubles without bath €48/82, singles/doubles/triples/quads with bath €62/116/143/170)* can cater to most requests and is run by a helpful couple; downstairs in their two-star **Hotel Kursaal** (☎ *055 49 63 24; doubles without bath €90)*, prices are the same except for the doubles without bath, and rooms have balcony, air-con and satellite TV. **Pensione Mary** (☎/fax *055 49 63 10; Piazza dell'Indipendenza 5; singles/doubles without bath €52/73, with*

bath *€68/93)* is a little scruffy and the owner laid-back to the point of indifference.

Closer to the station, the two-star **Accademia** (☎ *055 29 34 51, fax 055 21 97 71;* e *info@accademiahotel.net; Via Faenza 7; singles/doubles with bath €90/150)* is housed in an 18th-century palace, replete with magnificent stained-glass doors and carved wooden ceilings.

Around Piazza Santa Maria Novella Via della Scala, which runs northwest off the piazza, is lined with pensioni. **La Scala** (☎ *055 21 26 29; singles without bath €52, doubles with/without bath €88/77)* at No 21 is a cheerfully unpretentious place. A few doors down, at No 25, **Hotel Margaret** (☎ *055 21 01 38; singles without bath €50, doubles with/without bath €90/70, triples with bath €120)* has newly refurbished rooms, as does **Albergo Montreal** (☎ *055 238 23 31, fax 055 28 74 91; singles/doubles without bath €40/60, doubles/triples/quads with bath €75/100/120)* at No 43.

At **Sole** (☎/fax *055 239 60 94; Via del Sole 8; singles without bath €38, singles/doubles/triples with bath €46/77/104)*, ask for a quiet room as the street below can be noisy. **Albergo Toscana** (☎/fax *055 21 31 56; singles/doubles with bath €70/114)*, in the same building, has pretty rooms.

Moving north, the family-run **Hotel Pensione Ferretti** (☎ *055 238 13 28, fax 055 21 92 88; Via delle Belle Donne 17; singles/doubles/triples without bath €46/74/97, with bath €57/93/116)* has comfortable rooms and a charming address. The much recommended **Hotel Abaco** (☎ *055 238 19 19, fax 055 28 22 89; Via dei Banchi 1; singles without bath €60, doubles with/without bath €85/70)* offers 13th-century Florentine decor and double glazing; one room even has a fireplace.

Ottaviani (☎ *055 239 62 23, fax 055 29 33 55; Piazza Ottaviani 1; singles without/with bath €59/69, doubles without bath €59)*, just off Piazza Santa Maria Novella, has reasonable rates with breakfast included.

The Duomo to Ponte Vecchio This area is a 15-minute walk from the station and is right in the heart of old Florence. One of the best deals in town is the small **Aily Home** (☎ *055 239 65 05; Piazza Santo Stefano 1; singles/doubles without bath €25/40)*, overlooking the river. **Albergo Firenze** (☎ 055 21 42 03, fax 055 21 23 70; Piazza dei Donati 4; singles/doubles with bath €62/83), just south of the Duomo, offers simple rooms, while those at **Pensione Maria Luisa de' Medici** (☎/fax 055 28 00 48; Via del Corso 1; doubles with/without bath €82/67) are large enough to cater for up to five people. Further east **Hotel Dali** (☎/fax 055 234 07 06; Via dell'Oriuolo 17; singles without bath €40, doubles with/without bath €75/60) has sunny rooms and free parking for guests.

Up several notches, the **Hotel Pendini** (☎ 055 21 11 70, fax 055 28 18 07; Via degli Strozzi 2; singles/doubles with bath €110/150, family suite €280) is just around the corner from Piazza della Repubblica. On the 4th floor, it has a distinctly chintzy feel. A family suite accommodates four.

Villas Experience life in an old villa at **Bencistà** (☎/fax 055 591 63; Via Benedetto da Maiano 4; singles/doubles €160/176), about 1km from Fiesole in the hills overlooking Florence.

Places to Eat

Tuscan cuisine is based on the quality of its ingredients and the simplicity of its recipes. At its most basic, how can you beat a thick slice of crusty bread drizzled with olive oil and downed with a glass of Chianti? Local specialities include *ribollita*, a very filling soup of vegetables and white beans, and *bistecca alla Fiorentina* (steak Florentine), usually served in slabs sufficient for two. At the time of writing the steak has become something of a political hot potato with EU lawmakers arguing over its legal status. A ban imposed following the mad cow disease scare technically means that it can not be served, however, you will find that this decree is not always followed. Use your judgment and buon appetito.

You can stock up on supplies at the **food market** (open 7am-2pm Mon-Sat) in San Lorenzo or at the **supermarket** on the western side of the train station, or east of Piazza Duomo at Via Pietrapiana 94.

Restaurants – City Centre A popular place for pizza is the **Yellow Bar** (☎ 055 21 17 66; Via del Proconsolo 39r; pizza meal about €10) which has plenty of seating but is still usually full. At **Trattoria Buzzino** (☎ 055 239 80 13; Via dei Leoni 8; meal €25, tourist menu €13) you'll be served hearty food, possibly by the waiter whose technique bears more than a passing resemblance to that of Basil Fawlty's hapless help Manuel. If, however, you're after a quieter affair, try **Trattoria da Benvenuto** (☎ 055 21 48 33; Via Mosca 16r; meal about €24) where the food and prices are reasonable. At No 35r on the same street, **Angie's Pub** has a huge list of panini from €2.50 and refreshingly cold beer and **Fiaschetteria** (Via dei Neri 17r; pasta from €3.50) offers good value for money.

At **Hosteria Il Caminetto** (☎ 055 239 62 74; Via dello Studio 34r; meal about €30), you can eat on the vine-covered terrace, but you'll pay for your proximity to the Duomo. On the other hand at **Enoteca Pinchiorri** (☎ 055 24 27 77; Via Ghibellina 87; meal about €93), you'll just pay, a lot, for its famed nouvelle cuisine.

Restaurants – Around San Lorenzo Tiny but popular **Mario's** (Via Rosina 2r; meal around €10; open lunch only), near the Mercato Centrale, serves delicious pasta. Around the corner at Piazza del Mercato Centrale 24, **Trattoria Za Za** (☎ 055 21 54 11; meal about €20) is another favourite, with outdoor seating and an imaginative menu. **Bondi** (Via dell'Ariento 85) specialises in focaccia and pizza slices from €1.55.

Restaurants – in the Oltrarno A bustling place popular with the locals is **Trattoria Casalinga** (☎ 055 21 86 24; Via dei Michelozzi 9r; meal about €16) where the food is great and the pace frenetic. **I Tarocchi** (☎ 055 234 39 12; Via de' Renai 16; pizza from €5, meal about €13) serves good pizza and huge portions of pasta. In trendy Piazza Santo Spirito, **Borgo Antico** (☎ 21 04 37; meal about €22) is a cool summer spot for alfresco dining.

Cafés & Snack Bars Perhaps the city's grandest café is the wonderfully intact *belle époque* **Gilli** (Piazza della Repubblica). If you can't resist the bountiful display of mouthwatering sweet and savoury delights, you'll save cash, if not calories, by both eating and drinking at the bar.

Caffè degli Innocenti (Via Nazionale 57), near the Mercato Centrale, has a good selection of panini and cakes for around €1.55 to €2.85. The streets between the Duomo and the Arno harbour many pizzerias where you can buy cheap takeaway pizza by the slice.

The **Cantinetta da Verrazzano** (Via dei Tavolini 18r) wine bar/café is a tight fit. All hanging hams and dark wood, this is the place to sip that Chianti.

Gelati South of Via Ghibellina, **Gelateria Vivoli** (Via dell'Isola delle Stinche 7) is widely considered the city's best. Don't be surprised to find a queue.

Entertainment

Listings to look out for include the bimonthly *Florence Today* and the monthly *Florence Information*, which should be available at tourist offices. *Firenze Spettacolo,* the definitive monthly entertainment guide, is sold at newsstands for €1.55.

Concerts, opera and dance are performed year-round at the **Teatro Comunale** (Corso Italia 16). For reservations contact the **box office** (☎ 800 11 22 11).

Original language films are screened at the **Odeon** (☎ 055 21 40 68; Piazza Strozzi; tickets €7.20), on Monday and Tuesday.

For a pint head to **The William** (Via Magliabechi 7r), which is lively and loud, or across the river to the tiny **Cabiria** bar in Piazza Santo Spirito, itself a good place to hang out, especially in summer.

A more sedate pastime is the evening *passeggiata* (stroll) in Piazzale Michelangelo, overlooking the city.

Shopping

The main shopping area is between the Duomo and the Arno, with boutiques concentrated along Via Roma, Via dei Calzaiuoli and Via Por Santa Maria, leading to the goldsmiths lining the Ponte Vecchio. Window-shop along Via de' Tornabuoni, where top designers such as Gucci, Ferragamo and Prada hawk their wares.

Smell the leather at the **open-air market** (open Mon-Sat) in the streets surrounding San Lorenzo where leather goods, clothing and jewellery are often cheap but sometimes of dodgy quality. You can bargain, but not if you use a credit card. The **flea market** (Piazza dei Ciompi; open daily), off Borgo Allegri and north of Santa Croce, is not as extensive but there are often great bargains.

Florence is renowned for its beautifully patterned paper, which is stocked in the many *cartolerie* (stationer's shops) throughout the city and at the markets. Lovers of Florentine velvet cushions, tapestries and decorative tassels should head for **Passamaneria Toscana** (Piazza San Lorenzo 12r).

Getting There & Away

Air Florence is served by two airports, Amerigo Vespucci and Galileo Galilei. **Amerigo Vespucci** (☎ 055 306 15, flight information ☎ 055 306 13 00/02), 5km north-west of the city centre, serves domestic and European flights. **Galileo Galilei** (☎ 050 84 92 02) is just under an hour away from Florence near Pisa, but is one of northern Italy's main international and domestic airports.

Bus The **SITA** bus station (☎ 800 37 37 60; Via Santa Caterina da Siena 17) is just west of the train station. Buses leave for Siena, San Gimignano and Volterra. **Lazzi** (☎ 055 35 10 61; Piazza Adua 1), next to the station, runs services to Rome, Pistoia and Lucca.

Train Florence is on the main Rome–Milan line. Many of the trains are the fast Eurostars, for which booking is necessary. Regular trains also go to/from Venice (three hours) and Trieste. For train information ring ☎ 848 88 80 88.

Car & Motorcycle Florence is connected by the Autostrada del Sole (A1) to Bologna and Milan in the north and Rome and Naples to the south. The Firenze–Mare motorway (A11) links Florence with Prato, Pistoia, Lucca, Pisa and the Versilia coast, and a *superstrada* (dual carriageway) joins the city to Siena. Exits from the autostrade into Florence are well signposted, and either one of the exits marked 'Firenze nord' or 'Firenze sud' will take you to the centre of town. There are tourist information offices on the A1 both to the north and south of the city.

Getting Around

To/From the Airport Regular trains to Pisa airport leave from platform five at Santa Maria Novella station daily from 6.46am to 5pm; journey time is 1½ hours. Check your bags in at the **air terminal** (☎ 21 60 73) near platform five, at least 15 minutes before train departure time.

You can get to Amerigo Vespucci airport by the Vola in Bus shuttle service which departs from the SITA coach depot in Via Santa Caterina da Siena every half-hour between 6am and 11.30pm. The journey takes about 25 minutes and tickets, which can be bought on the bus, cost €4.

Bus ATAF buses service the city centre and Fiesole. The terminal for the most useful buses is in a small piazza to the left as you go out of the station onto Via Valfonda. Bus No 7 leaves from here for Fiesole and also stops at the Duomo. Tickets must be bought before you get on the bus and are sold at most tobacconists and newsstands or from automatic vending machines at major bus stops (€1 for one hour, €1.80 for three hours, €4 for 24 hours).

Car & Motorcycle If you're spending the day in Florence, there are several car parks dotted around the city centre. A good choice is Fortezza da Basso, which costs €1.05 per hour. Further details are available from **Firenze Parcheggi** (☎ 055 500 19 94).

To rent a car, try **Hertz** (☎ 055 239 82 05; Via M Finiguerra 33r), or **Avis** (☎ 055 21 36 29; Borgo Ognissanti 128r). For bikes and scooters try **Alinari** (☎ 055 28 05 00; Via Guelfa 85r), or **Florence by Bike** (☎/fax 055 48 89 92; Via Zanobi 120/122r), which also runs bike tours.

Taxi You can find taxis outside the station, or call ☎ 055 4798 or ☎ 055 4390 to book one.

PISA
postcode 56100 • pop 92,000

No city in Italy can lay claim to as beautiful a construction cock-up as Pisa. Its leaning tower is one of the must-see sights in Italy and a godsend to producers of tourist kitsch. Once a maritime power to rival Genoa and Venice, Pisa has an important university and was the home of Galileo Galilei (1564–1642). It was devastated by the Genoese in the 13th century, and its history eventually merged with that of Florence, its bigger neighbour up the River Arno. The city today retains its charm despite the many day-trippers.

Orientation & Information
The focus for visitors is the Campo dei Miracoli, a 1.5km walk from the train station across the Arno. Bus No 3 will save you the sweat. The medieval town centre around

Borgo Stretto is a kilometre or so from the station.

There are several **APT tourist information offices**: at the station (☎ 050 4 22 91; open 9am-7pm Mon-Fri, 9.30am-3.30pm Sun), the airport, and west of Campo dei Miracoli (☎ 050 56 04 64; Via Carlo Cammeo 2; 9am-6pm Mon-Sat, 10.30am-4.30pm Sun).

Internet access is available at **InternetSurf** (Via Carducci 5) near Campo dei Miracoli, where 15 minutes costs €0.50.

Things to See & Do
The Pisans can justly claim that their **Campo dei Miracoli** (Field of Miracles) is one of the most beautiful squares in the world, whether by day or by night. A welcome expanse of well-kept lawns provides the perfect setting for the dazzling white marble cathedral, baptistry and bell tower – all of which lean to varying degrees.

The striped Pisan-Romanesque **cathedral** (admission €2), begun in 1063, has a graceful facade of tiered arches and a cavernous column-lined interior. The transept's bronze doors, facing the leaning tower, are by Bonanno Pisano, while the 16th-century bronze doors of the main entrance are by Giambologna. The cathedral's cupcake-like **battistero** (baptistry; admission €5), which was started in 1153 and took two centuries to complete, contains a pulpit sculpted by Nicola Pisano.

The *campanile*, better known as the **Leaning Tower** (Torre Pendente; admission €15), found itself in trouble from the start, because of the marshy nature of the land on which it was built. Its architect, Bonanno Pisano, managed to complete only three of the tower's eventual seven tiers before it started to tilt. It continued to lean by an average 1mm a year, and today is almost 4.1m off the perpendicular despite 11 years of ground-levelling work. It is now open to the public, but visits are limited to groups of 30 people, so entry times are staggered and waits inevitable.

To save on admission to the Campo's monuments and museums, you can choose from a number of ticket options; for example, entry to one museum and one monument costs €5, two museums and the cathedral €8. Admission to the Leaning Tower, however, is always separate.

After taking in the Campo dei Miracoli, wander down Via Santa Maria, along the

Arno and into the Borgo Stretto to explore the old city, which includes the impressive Piazza dei Cavalieri.

Places to Stay & Eat

Pisa has a range of reasonably priced hotels. Many of the budget places double as residences for students during the school year, so it can sometimes be difficult to find a cheap room.

The non-HI **Ostello per la Gioventù** (☎/fax 050 89 06 22; Via Pietrasantina 15; dorm bed €15) is closed during the day between 9am and 6pm. Take bus No 3 from the station. **Albergo Serena** (☎/fax 050 58 08 09; Via Cavaica 45; singles/doubles without bath €28/41) is tucked away near Piazza Dante Alighieri and provides simple rooms. The three-star **Hotel di Stefano** (☎ 050 55 35 59, fax 050 55 60 38; Via Sant'Apollonia 35; singles/doubles without bath €45/60, singles/doubles/triples/quads with bath €70/85/110/120) offers tastefully decorated rooms and a lovely breakfast terrace. Just outside the station, **Albergo Milano** (☎ 050 231 62, fax 050 442 37; Via Mascagni 14; singles/doubles without bath €37/47, doubles/triples/quads with bath €65/87/97) is a modest but welcoming joint.

Splash out with a view of the Arno at the grand **Royal Victoria** (☎ 050 94 01 11, fax 050 94 01 80; Lungarno Pacinotti 12; singles/doubles with bath €87/102), which dates from 1839.

Being a university town, Pisa has a number of cheap eating places. For a whopping great pizza **Pizzeria Del Borgo** (Vicolo del Tinti 15; pizza meal about €11.50) just off Via Oberdan, is just the job; plus one of the waiters does impressions. **Antica Trattoria il Campano** (☎ 050 58 05 85; Vicolo Santa Margherita; meal about €25) serves Tuscan grub in a medieval atmosphere. In the same price range **Spaghetteria alle Bandierine** (☎ 050 50 00 00; Via Mercanti 4; meal about €20) has a rustic feel and continues to win plaudits for its seafood. Head to **La Bottega del Gelato** (Piazza Garibaldi) and join the queue for gelati, or for fruit try the open-air food **market** (Piazza delle Vettovaglie), off Borgo Stretto.

Getting There & Away

The airport, with domestic and European flights, is only a few minutes away by train,

or by bus No 3 from the station. **Lazzi** (☎ 050 462 88) buses run to Florence via Lucca; somewhat surprisingly, there's an original Keith Haring mural opposite its office in Piazza Vittorio Emanuele. **CPT** (☎ 050 50 55 11) operates buses to Livorno via Tirrenia. Pisa is linked by direct train to Florence, Rome and Genoa. Local trains head for Lucca and Livorno.

SIENA
postcode 53100 • pop 54,000

To bypass Siena would be to miss one of Italy's most captivating towns. Built on three hills and surrounded by medieval ramparts, its labyrinthine centre is jam-packed with majestic Gothic buildings in various shades of the colour known as burnt sienna; it's also usually crammed to bursting with visitors.

According to legend, Siena was founded by the sons of Remus (one of the founders of Rome). In the Middle Ages the city became a free republic, but its success and power led to serious rivalry with Florence, both politically and culturally. Painters of the Sienese School produced significant works of art, and the city was home to St Catherine and St Benedict.

Siena is divided into 17 *contrade* (districts) and each year 10 are chosen to compete in the Palio, a tumultuous horse race and pageant held in the shell-shaped Piazza del Campo on 2 July and 16 August.

Orientation

Leaving the train station, cross the concourse to the bus stop opposite and catch bus No 3, 9 or 10 to Piazza Gramsci, then walk into the centre along Via dei Termini (it takes about 10 minutes to reach Piazza del Campo). Visitors' cars are not allowed into the medieval centre.

Information

At the **APT office** (☎ 0577 28 05 51, fax 0577 27 06 76; e aptsiena@siena.turismo.toscana.it; Piazza del Campo 56; open 8.30am-7.30pm Mon-Sat, 9am-3pm Sun), grab the useful guide Terre di Siena and a map of the town.

The **post office** (Piazza Matteotti 1) is to the north of the centre, while to phone you can use the **Telecom offices** (Via dei Termini 42 • Via di Città 113).

Check your email at the **Internet Train** (Via di Città 121), which has 20 screens. For 15 minutes you'll pay €1.55, for one hour €5.16.

SIENA

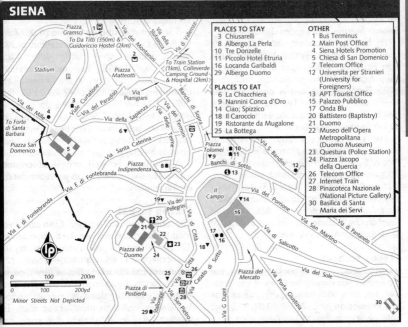

PLACES TO STAY
3 Chiusarelli
8 Albergo La Perla
10 Tre Donzelle
11 Piccolo Hotel Etruria
16 Locanda Garibaldi
29 Albergo Duomo

PLACES TO EAT
6 La Chiacchiera
9 Nannini Conca d'Oro
14 Ciao; Spizzico
18 Il Caroccio
19 Ristorante da Mugalone
25 La Bottega

OTHER
1 Bus Terminus
2 Main Post Office
4 Siena Hotels Promotion
5 Chiesa di San Domenico
7 Telecom Office
12 Universita per Stranieri (University for Foreigners)
13 APT Tourist Office
15 Palazzo Pubblico
17 Onda Blu
20 Battistero (Baptistry)
21 Duomo
22 Museo dell'Opera Metropolitana (Duomo Museum)
23 Questura (Police Station)
24 Piazza Jacopo della Quercia
26 Telecom Office
27 Internet Train
28 Pinacoteca Nazionale (National Picture Gallery)
30 Basilica di Santa Maria dei Servi

0   100   200m
0   100   200yd
Minor Streets Not Depicted

It's €6 to wash and dry up to 7kg at **Onda Blu** *(Via Casato di Sotto 17)*.

For an ambulance, call ☎ 118. The **public hospital** *(☎ 0577 58 51 11; Viale Bracci)* is just north of Siena at Le Scotte and the **questura** *(police headquarters; ☎ 0577 20 11 11; Via del Castoro 23)* is near the Duomo.

Things to See

Siena's uniquely shell-shaped **Piazza del Campo** (known simply as Il Campo) has been the city's focus since the 14th century. The piazza's sloping base is formed by the nobly proportioned **Palazzo Pubblico** *(Town Hall; admission €6.50; open 10am-7pm daily mid-Mar–end Oct, 10am-5.30pm end Nov–mid-Feb, 10am-6.30pm rest of the year)*, which is also known as Palazzo Comunale, considered one of Italy's most graceful Gothic buildings. Its Sienese art treasures include Simone Martini's *Maestà* and Ambrogio Lorenzetti's *Allegories of Good & Bad Government*. Paying an extra €5.50 you can enter the 102m-high **Torre del Mangia** (bell tower). A combined ticket costs €9.50.

The spectacular **Duomo** is another Gothic masterpiece, and one of the most enchanting cathedrals in Italy. Begun in 1196 and largely completed by 1215, extravagant plans for further construction were stymied by the arrival of the Black Death in 1348. Its black-and-white striped marble facade has a Romanesque lower section, with carvings by Giovanni Pisano, and the inlaid-marble floor features 56 panels depicting biblical stories. The marble and porphyry **pulpit** was carved by Nicola Pisano, father of Giovanni; other artworks include a bronze statue of St John the Baptist by Donatello, and statues of St Jerome and Mary Magdalene by Bernini.

A door in the north aisle leads to the **Libreria Piccolomini** *(admission €1.50)*, built by Pope Pius III to house the magnificent illustrated books of his uncle, Pope Pius II. It features frescoes by Pinturicchio and a Roman statue of the Three Graces.

The **Museo dell'Opera Metropolitana** *(Duomo Museum; admission €5.50; open 9am-7.30pm daily mid-Mar–Sept, 9am-6pm daily Oct, 9am-1.30pm daily Nov–mid-Mar)* is in Piazza del Duomo. Its many works of art formerly adorned the cathedral, including the *Maestà* by Duccio di Buoninsegna and the 12 marble statues by Giovanni Pisano, which once graced the Duomo's facade; other works include those by Ambrogio Lorenzetti, Simone Martini and Taddeo di Bartolo.

The **battistero** (baptistry; admission €2.50; open 9am-7.30pm daily mid-Mar–Sept, 9am-6pm daily Oct, 10am-1pm & 2.30pm-5pm daily Nov–mid-Mar) behind the cathedral, has a Gothic facade and is decorated with 15th-century frescoes. The highlight is the font by Jacopo della Quercia, with sculptures by Donatello and Ghiberti.

The 15th-century Palazzo Buonsignori houses the **Pinacoteca Nazionale** (National Picture Gallery; admission €4; open 8.15am-7.15pm Tues-Sat, 8.30am-1.30pm Mon, 8.15am-1.15pm Sun), whose Sienese masterpieces include Duccio di Buoninsegna's *Madonna dei Francescani, Madonna col Bambino* by Simone Martini and a series of Madonnas by Ambrogio Lorenzetti.

Places to Stay

It is always advisable to book in advance, but for August and during the Palio, it's imperative. For help with bookings try **Siena Hotels Promotion** (☎ 0577 28 80 84; e info@hotelsiena.com; Piazza San Domenico 2).

Colleverde camping ground (☎ 0577 28 00 44, fax 0577 33 32 98; per person/tent €7.75/7.75; open late Mar-early Nov) is 2km north of the historic centre at Strada di Scacciapensieri 47 (take bus No 3 from Piazza Gramsci).

Guidoriccio hostel (☎ 0577 522 12; Via Fiorentina; B&B €16.50) is about 3km out of the centre in Stellino. An evening meal costs €9. Take bus No 3 from Piazza Gramsci.

In the heart of the old town, **Tre Donzelle** (☎ 0577 28 03 58, fax 0577 22 39 33; Via delle Donzelle 5; singles/doubles without bath €31/44, doubles with bath €57) offers no-frills rooms. Nearby, the two-star **Piccolo Hotel Etruria** (☎ 0577 28 80 88, fax 0577 28 84 61; Via delle Donzelle 3; singles without bath €39, singles/doubles/triples/quads with bath €44/73/96/119) has large rooms and a 12.30am curfew. Space is of a premium at **Albergo La Perla** (☎ 0577 471 44; Via delle Terme 25; singles/doubles with bath €50/65) where it can get a little claustrophobic. Behind the town hall, **Locanda Garibaldi** (☎ 0577 28 42 04; Via Giovanni Dupré 18; doubles/triples/quads with bath €70/89/108) had a makeover recently so the rooms are in good nick. Its

small trattoria is reasonably priced with the set menu costing €15.

The three-star **Albergo Duomo** (☎ 0577 28 90 88, fax 0577 430 43; Via Stalloreggi 38; singles/doubles/triples/quads with bath €104/130/171/186) has quite pleasant rooms, some with views of the Duomo. The charming **Chiusarelli** (☎ 0577 28 05 62, fax 0577 27 11 77; Viale Curtatone 15; singles/doubles with bath €73/109) is well placed for drivers being near the Stadio Comunale car park, but it can get noisy on match days (usually Sunday).

Agriturismo is well organised around Siena. The tourist office can provide a list of establishments.

Places to Eat

The ubiquitous self-service **Ciao** and fast food **Spizzico** are right on the Campo at No 77. For a more sophisticated meal, try **Il Caroccio** (☎ 4 11 65; Via Casato di Sotto 32; meal about €30) where the quality food is complemented by an enormous wine list. The **Ristorante da Mugalone** (☎ 0577 28 32 35; Via dei Pelligrini 8; meal about €25) is another good establishment for sampling local specialities.

Tiny **La Chiacchiera** (☎ 0577 28 06 31, Costa di Sant'Antonio 4; meal about €18), off Via Santa Caterina, has a rustic feel with wooden stools and handwritten menus and is ideal for lunch.

There are several trattorias further north, in a quieter neighbourhood. **Da Titti** (☎ 0577 480 87; Via di Camollia 193; meal about €15) is one, serving standard Tuscan grub in simple surroundings.

Supermarket **La Bottega** (Via di Città 152-6) is centrally located, as is **Nannini Conca d'Oro** (Banchi di Sopra 22), one of Siena's finest cafés and a good place to stock up on *panforte*.

Getting There & Away

Regular Tra-In buses run from Florence to Siena, arriving at Piazza Gramsci. Buses also go to San Gimignano, Volterra and other points in Tuscany, and there's a daily bus to Rome. For Perugia, buses leave from the train station.

Siena is not on a main train line, so from Rome it is necessary to change at Chiusi and from Florence at Empoli, making buses a better alternative.

ITALY

SAN GIMIGNANO
postcode 53037 • pop 7100

In a region noted for its beauty, San Gimignano still manages to stand out. Characterised by its huge pockmarked towers, and in recent times by the sheer numbers of tourists, this tiny town is perched on a hill deep in the Tuscan countryside. Of an original 72 towers built as fortified homes for the town's 11th-century feuding families, 13 remain.

A veritable magnet for visitors, the best time to visit is during the week, preferably in deepest mid-winter. The Pro Loco **tourist information office** (☎ 0577 94 00 08; e prolocsg@ tin.it; Piazza del Duomo 1; open 9am-1pm & 3pm-7pm daily, to 6pm in winter) is in the town centre.

Things to See & Do
Climb San Gimignano's tallest tower, **Torre Grossa**, off Piazza del Duomo, for a memorable view of the Tuscan hills. The tower is reached from within the **Palazzo del Popolo**, which houses the **Museo Civico**, featuring Lippo Memmi's 14th-century *Maestà*. The **Duomo**, known also as the Collegiata, has a Romanesque interior, frescoes by Ghirlandaio in the **Cappella di Santa Fina** and a particularly gruesome *Last Judgment* by Taddeo di Bartolo. The city's most-impressive piazza is **Piazza della Cisterna**, named for the 13th-century well at its centre.

Places to Stay & Eat
San Gimignano offers few options for budget travellers. The nearest camping ground is **Il Boschetto di Piemma** (☎ 0577 94 03 52, fax 0577 94 19 82; per person/tent €4.70/5; open Easter-15 Oct), about 3km from San Gimignano at Santa Lucia. There is a bus service to the site. At the time of writing the youth hostel was closed with no scheduled reopening date, so for a cheap bed your best bet is the **Foresteria Monastero di San Girolamo** (☎ 0577 94 05 73; Via Folgore 32; B&B €25).

Hotels in town are expensive but there are numerous rooms for rent in **private homes**, and agriturismo is well organised in this area. For information, contact the tourist office. If you can afford a spacial treat, soak up the medieval ambience at **Hotel La Cisterna** (☎ 0577 94 03 28, fax 0577 94 20 80; Piazza della Cisterna 24; singles/doubles with bath €68/100).

For a plate of pasta and sip of the local wine, **Il Castello** (☎ 0577 94 08 78; Via del Castello 20; pastas about €5.50) is as good a spot as any. A fresh-produce **market** is held on Thursday morning in Piazza del Duomo.

Getting There & Away
Regular buses link San Gimignano with Florence and Siena. They arrive at Porta San Giovanni (timetables are posted outside the tourist office). Enter through the Porta and continue straight ahead to reach Piazza del Duomo.

CERTALDO
postcode 50052 • pop 15,800

Located in the Val d'Elsa between Florence and Siena, this small medieval town is definitely worth a visit. Giovanni Boccaccio, one of the fathers of the Italian language, was born here in 1313.

Fattoria Bassetto (☎ 0571 66 83 42; e bassetto@dedalo.com; dorm bed €21, room €36), 2km east of the town on the road to Siena, is in a former 14th-century Benedictine convent, surrounded by a garden with swimming pool.

Umbria

Umbrians like to think of their hilly region as the green heart of Italy. Characterised by its many medieval hill towns, it is noted for its Romanesque and Gothic architecture. Towns such as Assisi, Gubbio, Spello, Spoleto, Todi and Orvieto are accessible by bus or train from Perugia, the region's capital.

PERUGIA
postcode 06100 • pop 158,200

Perugia is a well-preserved medieval hill town that offers sweeping panoramas at every turn. Best known for its University for Foreigners, established in 1925, which attracts thousands of international students, the city is also famous for the Umbria Jazz Festival in July, and for chocolate.

Highlights, or lowlights, of Perugia's history, bloody even by medieval standards, include the vicious internal feuding of the Baglioni and Oddi families, wars waged against neighbours and the death of at least two popes. However, art and culture have thrived: it was the home of the painter Perugino, and Raphael, his student, also worked here.

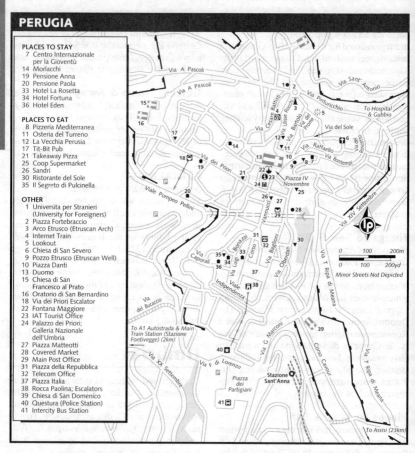

PERUGIA

PLACES TO STAY
7 Centro Internazionale per la Gioventù
14 Morlacchi
19 Pensione Anna
20 Pensione Paola
33 Hotel La Rosetta
34 Hotel Fortuna
36 Hotel Eden

PLACES TO EAT
8 Pizzeria Mediterranea
11 Osteria del Turreno
12 La Vecchia Perusia
17 Tit-Bit Pub
21 Takeaway Pizza
25 Coop Supermarket
26 Sandri
30 Ristorante del Sole
35 Il Segreto di Pulcinella

OTHER
1 Università per Stranieri (University for Foreigners)
2 Piazza Fortebraccio
3 Arco Etrusco (Etruscan Arch)
4 Internet Train
5 Lookout
6 Chiesa di San Severo
9 Pozzo Etrusco (Etruscan Well)
10 Piazza Danti
13 Duomo
15 Chiesa di San Francesco al Prato
16 Oratorio di San Bernardino
18 Via dei Priori Escalator
22 Fontana Maggiore
23 IAT Tourist Office
24 Palazzo dei Priori; Galleria Nazionale dell'Umbria
27 Piazza Matteotti
28 Covered Market
29 Main Post Office
31 Piazza della Repubblica
32 Telecom Office
37 Piazza Italia
38 Rocca Paolina; Escalators
39 Chiesa di San Domenico
40 Questura (Police Station)
41 Intercity Bus Station

Orientation & Information

Perugia's hub is the old town's main drag, Corso Vannucci, running north-south from Piazza Italia, through Piazza della Repubblica and ending at Piazza IV Novembre and the Duomo.

The **IAT tourist office** (☎ 075 573 64 58, fax 075 573 93 86; e info@iat.perugia.it; Piazza IV Novembre 3; open 8.30am-1.30pm & 3.30pm-6.30pm Mon-Sat, 9am-1pm Sun) is opposite the Duomo. The main **post office** is in Piazza Matteotti and **Internet Train** (Via Ulisse Rocchi 30) has cheap Internet access.

The monthly magazine Viva Perugia: What, Where, When (€0.52 at the newsstands) has events listings and other useful information for travellers.

Things to See

Perugia's austere **Duomo** has an unfinished facade in red-and-white marble, while inside are frescoes and decorations by artists from the 15th to 18th centuries, as well as the Virgin Mary's wedding ring, which is unveiled every 30 July. The **Palazzo dei Priori**, nearby on Corso Vannucci, is a rambling 13th-century palace which houses the impressively frescoed **Sala dei Notari** and the **Galleria Nazionale dell'Umbria**, with works by Perugino and Fra Angelico. Between the two buildings, in Piazza IV Novembre, is the 13th-century **Fontana Maggiore**, designed by Fra Bevignate in 1278 and carved by Nicola and Giovanni Pisano.

At the other end of Corso Vannucci is the **Rocca Paolina** (Paolina Fortress), the ruins of a massive 16th-century fortress. Built by Pope Paul III over a medieval quarter formerly inhabited by some of Perugia's most powerful families, notably the Baglioni, the fortress was destroyed by the Perugians after Italian unification in 1860. A series of escalators pass through the underground ruins, which are often used to host exhibitions.

Raphael's fresco *Trinity with Saints*, some say his first, can be seen in the **Chiesa di San Severo**, on Piazza San Severo, along with frescoes by Perugino.

Etruscan remains in Perugia include the **Arco Etrusco** (Etruscan Arch), near the university, and the **Pozzo Etrusco** (Etruscan Well), near the Duomo.

Places to Stay

Perugia has a good selection of reasonably priced hotels, but you could have problems if you arrive unannounced in July or August.

Centro Internazionale per la Gioventù (☎/fax 075 572 28 80; e ostello@ostello .perugia.it; Via Bontempi 13; dorm bed €12; closed 9.30am-4pm daily; closed mid-Dec–mid-Jan) is a well-located non-HI place. Sheets (for the entire stay) are an extra €1.50. Its TV room has a frescoed ceiling and the terrace has some of Perugia's best views.

Pensione Anna (☎/fax 075 573 63 04; Via dei Priori 48; singles/doubles without bath €30/46, with bath €40/62), off Corso Vannucci, is full of character and antiques, while the two-star **Morlacchi** (☎/fax 075 572 03 19; Via Tiberi 2; singles without bath €40, singles/doubles with bath €51/60) nearby is a little smarter but similarly priced.

Pensione Paola (☎ 075 572 38 16; Via della Canapina 5; singles/doubles without bath €28/42) is down the escalator from Via dei Priori, and offers eight rooms with the use of a kitchen. Off the Piazza Italia end of Corso Vannucci, **Hotel Eden** (☎ 075 572 81 02, fax 075 572 03 42; Via Cesare Caporali 9; singles/doubles with bath €36/57) is excellent value with its blazingly white minimalist rooms. Around the corner at the elegant **Hotel Fortuna** (☎ 075 572 28 45, fax 075 573 50 40; Via Bonazzi 19; singles/doubles with bath €79/114) the rooms are wonderful. And, in a similar price-range, **La Rosetta** (☎/fax 075 572 08 41; Piazza Italia 19; singles/doubles with bath €76/115) provides palatial period-detailed rooms.

Places to Eat

Being a student town, Perugia offers many budget eating options. Good places for pizza include **Tit-Bit Pub** (☎ 075 573 54 97; Via dei Priori 105; pizza meal about €10); **Il Segreto di Pulcinella** (☎ 075 573 62 84; Via Larga 8; pizza from €5.50); and **Pizzeria Mediterranea** (☎ 075 572 63 12; Piazza Piccinino 11/12; pizza from €4.20). There's also a tiny but popular **pizza takeaway** (Via dei Priori 3), near the Duomo.

Osteria del Turreno (☎ 075 572 19 76; Piazza Danti 16; meal about €10) serves panini as well as simple, hearty fare. **La Vecchia Perusia** (☎ 075 572 59 00; Via Ulisse Rocchi 9; meal about €20) is a little more pricey, specialising in local cuisine. For unforgettable panoramic views and an equally stunning antipasto spread, head for **Ristorante del Sole** (☎ 075 573 50 31; Via Oberdan 28; meal about €25).

Sandri (Corso Vannucci 32), by now a Perugian institution, has the best cakes in town, as well as free chocolate nibbles at the bar. To buy your own supplies of chocolate and other edibles there's a **Coop supermarket** (Piazza Matteotti 15), near the **covered market**.

Getting There & Away

Perugia is not on the main Rome–Florence railway line, but there are some direct trains from both cities. Most services require a change, either at Foligno (from Rome) or Terontola (from Florence). Intercity buses leave from Piazza dei Partigiani (at the bottom of the Rocca Paolina escalators) for Rome, Fiumicino airport, Florence, Siena and towns throughout Umbria, including Assisi, Gubbio and nearby Lake Trasimeno. Timetables for trains and buses are available from the tourist office.

Getting Around

The main train station is a couple of kilometres downhill from the historical centre. Catch any bus heading for Piazza Italia. Tickets cost €0.80 and can be bought from the ticket office on your left as you leave the station.

Most of the historical centre is closed to normal traffic, but tourists are allowed to drive to their hotels. It is probably wiser, however, not to do this, as driving in central Perugia is a nightmare. The solution is to park at one of the large car parks downhill, and take the pedestrian elevator up to the old centre. There is a supervised car park at Piazza dei Partigiani, from where you can catch the Rocca Paolina escalator to Piazza Italia, and there are two major car parks at the foot of the Via dei Priori escalator.

ASSISI
postcode 06081 • pop 25,500

Birthplace and spiritual home of the animal world's favourite saint, Assisi is a major port of call for millions of visitors who swarm to retrace the footsteps of St Francis. Somehow this small town perched halfway up Mt Subasio manages to cope while maintaining an air of tranquillity, particularly in the lanes off the central streets.

In September 1997, a strong earthquake rocked the town, causing considerable damage to the upper church of the Basilica di San Francesco (St Francis' Basilica), but five years on and it's business as usual, with little sign remaining of any damage.

The APT **tourist office** (☎ 075 81 25 34; e info@iat.assisi.pg.it; Piazza del Comune; open 8am-2pm & 3pm-6pm Mon-Fri, 9am-1pm & 3pm-6pm Sat, 9am-1pm Sun) has plenty of useful information.

Things to See

If you're coming to Assisi to visit the religious sites, which you almost certainly are, look the part, as dress rules are applied rigidly – absolutely no shorts, miniskirts or low-cut dresses or tops are allowed.

The **Basilica di San Francesco** is composed of two churches, one built on top of the other. The lower church is decorated with frescoes by Simone Martini, Cimabue and a pupil of Giotto, and contains the crypt where St Francis is buried. The Italian Gothic upper church has a stone-vaulted roof, and was decorated by the great painters of the 13th and 14th centuries, in particular Giotto and Cimabue. The frescoes in the apse and entrance received the most damage in the 1997 earthquake.

The impressively frescoed 13th-century **Basilica di Santa Chiara** (St Clare's Basilica) contains the remains of St Clare, friend of St Francis and the founder of the Order of Poor Clares.

For spectacular views of the valley below, head to the massive 14th-century **Rocca Maggiore** fortress. You'll easily be able to spot the huge **Basilica di Santa Maria degli Angeli**, built around the first Franciscan monastery. St Francis died in its **Cappella del Transito** in 1226.

Places to Stay & Eat

Assisi is well geared for tourists and there are numerous budget hotels and *affittacamere* (rooms for rent). Peak periods, when you will need to book well in advance, are Easter, August and September, and the Feast of St Francis on 3 and 4 October. The tourist office has a full list of affittacamere and religious institutions.

The small HI **Ostello della Pace** (☎/fax 075 81 67 67; Via Valecchi 177; B&B €13) is on the bus line between Santa Maria degli Angeli and Assisi. The non-HI hostel **Fontemaggio** (☎ 075 81 36 36, fax 075 81 37 49; Via Eremo delle Carceri 8; dorm bed €18.50) also has camping facilities. From Piazza Matteotti, at the far end of town from the basilica, it's a 30-minute uphill walk along Via Eremo delle Carceri.

Heading into town from Piazza Matteotti you'll pass **Pensione La Rocca** (☎/fax 075 81 22 84; Vicolo della Fortezza; singles/doubles with bath €33.50/40) in a quiet corner. Some of its sunny rooms have views of the valley below. In the heart of town, the three-star **Dei Priori** (☎ 075 81 22 37, fax 075 81 68 04; e hpriori@tiscalinet.it; Corso Mazzini 15; singles/doubles with bath €77/114, superior doubles €150) has stylish carpeted rooms.

For a cheap slice of pizza, head for **Pizza Vincenzo**, just off Piazza del Comune at Via San Rufina 1a. A good self-service place in the same area is **Il Foro Romano** (Via Portico 23). **Il Pozzo Romano** (☎ 075 81 30 57; Via Santa Agnese 10; set menu €12.50), off Piazza Santa Chiara, serves simple dishes and is good value for money. To dine under ancient architraves try **Dal Carro** (☎ 075 81 33 07; Vicolo dei Nepis 2; set menu €12.50), off Corso Mazzini, where the pasta dishes win good reviews. If you want to splash out, the stylish **Medio Evo** (☎ 81 30 68; Via Arco dei Priori 4; meal about €30) is one of Assisi's top restaurants.

Getting There & Away

Buses connect Assisi with Perugia, Foligno and other local towns, leaving from Piazza Matteotti. Buses for Rome and Florence leave from Piazzale dell'Unità d'Italia. Assisi's train station is in the valley, in the suburb of Santa Maria degli Angeli. It's on the same line as Perugia and a shuttle bus runs between Piazza Matteotti and the station.

ANCONA

postcode 60100 • pop 98,100

Ancona, a largely unattractive and industrial port city in the Marches, is unlikely to be high on your wish list, but you may well find yourself here waiting for a ferry to Croatia, Greece or Turkey.

The easiest way to get from the train station to the port is by bus No 1. The main **APT office** (☎ *071 35 89 91, fax 071 358 99 29;* e *aptancona@tin.it; Via Thaon de Revel 4; open 9am-2pm & 3pm-6pm Mon-Fri, 9am-1pm & 3pm-6pm Sat, 9am-1pm Sun; opening hours shorter in winter)* is out of the way. Stazione Marittima is home to a **branch office** (☎ *071 20 11 83),* which opens in the summer months.

For postal matters go to the **main post office** (*Largo XXIV Maggio; open 8.15am-7pm Mon-Sat)* and for the Internet try **Internet Point** (*Corso Carlo Alberto 82).*

Places to Stay & Eat

If you're stuck here, there are a couple of options for dining and accommodation. Many backpackers choose to bunk down at the ferry terminal, although the city has many cheap hotels. The relatively new **Ostello della Gioventú** (☎/fax *071 422 57; Via Lamaticci 7; dorm bed €12)* is not far from the train station, while for a bite to eat the **Caffé Lombardo** (*Corso Giuseppe Mazzini 130; sandwiches from €2.60)* is a popular spot. **Osteria del Pozzo** (☎ *071 207 39 69; Via Bonda 2; meal about €16),* just off Piazza del Plebiscito, also serves good food at reasonable prices.

Getting There & Away

Buses depart from Piazza Cavour for towns throughout the Marches region. Rome is served by **Marozzi** (☎ *071 280 23 98).* Ancona is on the Bologna–Lecce train line and thus easily accessible from major towns throughout Italy. It is also linked to Rome via Foligno.

Ferry operators have information booths at the ferry terminal, off Piazza Kennedy. Most lines offer discounts on return fares. Prices listed here are for one-way deck class in high season.

Companies include **Superfast** (☎ *071 207 02 40)* to Patras in Greece (€78), **Minoan**

Lines (☎ *071 20 17 08)* to Igoumenitsa and Patras (€68) and **Adriatica** (☎ *071 20 49 15)* to Durrës in Albania (€86) and to Split in Croatia (€47).

URBINO

postcode 61029 • pop 6000

This town in the Marches can be difficult to reach but, as the pride of the Marches, it is worth the effort. Birthplace of Raphael and Bramante, Urbino is still a centre of art, culture and learning.

The **IAT tourist office** (☎ *0722 26 13, fax 0722 24 41; Piazza Duca Federico 35; open 9am-1pm Mon-Sat)* is conveniently situated in the centre of town.

To stock up on cash the **Banca Nazionale del Lavoro** (*Via Vittorio Veneto)* has an ATM, as do most banks spread about the town centre. There is a **main post office** (*Via Bramante 18)* and **Telecom offices** (*Via Puccinotti 4 • Piazza San Francesco 1).*

Things to See

Urbino's main sight is the dominating **Palazzo Ducale** (*admission €4.15; open 8.30am-7.15pm Tues-Sun, 8.30am-2pm Mon),* designed by Laurana and completed in 1482. The best view is from Corso Garibaldi to the west, from where you can appreciate the size of the building and see its towers and loggias. Enter the palace from Piazza Duca Federico and visit the **Galleria Nazionale delle Marche**, featuring works by Raphael, Paolo Uccello and Verrocchio. Also visit the **Casa di Raffaello** (*admission €2.60; Via Raffaello 5),* where the artist Raphael was born, and the **Oratorio di San Giovanni Battista** (*admission €1.55),* with 15th-century frescoes by the Salimbeni brothers.

Places to Stay & Eat

Urbino is a major university town and most cheap beds are taken by students during the school year. The tourist office has a full list of affittacamere. You could try **Pensione Fosca** (☎/fax *0722 32 96 22; Via Raffaello 61; singles/doubles without bath €21/35)* with its simple rooms.

There are numerous bars around Piazza della Repubblica in the town centre and near the Palazzo Ducale which sell good panini. Go to **Pizzeria Galli** (*Via Vittorio Veneto 19),* for takeaway pizza by the slice, or sit down at **Ristorante Da Franco** (☎ *0722 24 92; Via* del Poggio 1; meal about €10), which has a good value for money self-service section.

Getting There & Away

There is no train service to Urbino, but it is connected by Soget and Bucci buses Monday to Friday to cities including Ancona, Pesaro and Arezzo. There is a bus link to the train station at the town of Fossato di Vico, on the Rome–Ancona line, or take a bus to Pesaro which is on the Bologna-Lecce line. There are also buses to Rome twice a day. All buses arrive at Piazza Mercatale, down Via Mazzini from Piazza della Repubblica. The tourist office has timetables for all bus services.

Southern Italy

Although noticeably poorer than the north, the land of the *mezzogiorno* (midday sun) is rich in history and cultural traditions. The attractions of the area are straightforward: the people seem more passionate; myths, legends and history are intertwined; and the food is magnificent. Campania, Apulia and Basilicata are relatively untouristed in many parts and Naples is like no other city on earth.

NAPLES

postcode 80100 • pop 1.5 million

Beautifully positioned on the Bay of Naples and overshadowed by Mt Vesuvius, the capital of the Campania region, is one of the most densely populated cities in Europe. Love it or hate it, Naples is a truly unforgettable city, with an energy that will either sweep you along or swamp you.

Orientation

Both the Stazione Centrale and the main bus terminal are just off the vast Piazza Garibaldi. Naples is divided into *quartieri* (districts). The main shopping thoroughfare into the historical centre, Spaccanapoli, is Corso Umberto I, which heads southwest from Piazza Garibaldi to Piazza Bovio. West on the bay are Santa Lucia and Mergellina, both fashionable and picturesque and quite a contrast with the chaotic historical centre. In the hills overlooking the bay is the Vomero district, a natural balcony across the city and bay to Vesuvius.

Information

Tourist Offices The **EPT office** (☎ 081 26 87 79; open 8am-8pm Mon-Sat, 8am-2pm Sun) at the train station, will make hotel bookings and has information on the region. Ask for *Qui Napoli* (Here Naples), published monthly in English and Italian, which lists events in the city, as well as information about transport and other services.

There's a good **AAST office** (☎ 081 552 33 28; open 9am-8pm Mon-Sat, 9am-3pm Sun) in Piazza del Gesú Nuovo. There is a student travel centre, **CTS** (☎ 552 79 60; Via Mezzocannone 25).

Money There are plenty of foreign-exchange booths throughout the city, which often offer lower rates than the banks. Banks with ATMs are plentiful, too. **Every Tour** (☎ 081 551 85 64; Piazza Municipio 5) is the agency for American Express.

Post & Communications The **main post office** (Piazza G Matteotti; open 8.15am-7pm Mon-Sat), is off Via Armando Diaz. There is a **Telecom office** (Via A Depretis 40; open 9am-1pm & 2pm-5.30pm Mon-Fri). **Aexis Telecom** (Piazza Gesú Nuovo 52; open 8am-10pm daily) has phones, faxes and Internet access (€3 per hour).

Laundry Near Montesanto metro station, **My Beautiful Laundrette** (Via Montesanto 2) charges €3.10 for a 6kg wash and €3.10 for drying.

Medical & Emergency Services For an ambulance call ☎ 081 752 06 96 or ☎ 112. Each city district has a Guardia Medica (after hours medical service); check in *Qui Napoli* for details. The **Ospedale Loreto-Mare** (☎ 081 254 27 01; Via A Vespucci) is on the waterfront, near the station. There's a **pharmacy** (open 8am-8pm daily) in the central station.

The **questura** (police station; ☎ 081 794 11 11; Via Medina 75) is just off Via A Diaz, and has an office for foreigners where you can report thefts and so on. To report a stolen car call ☎ 081 794 14 35.

Dangers & Annoyances The city's home-grown mafia, the Camorra, is a pervasive local force, but one that won't affect you as a tourist. However, the petty crime rate in Naples is very

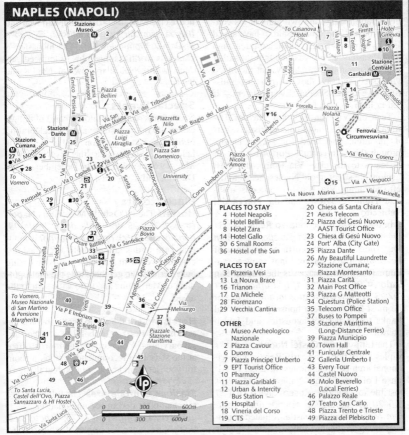

NAPLES (NAPOLI)

PLACES TO STAY
4 Hotel Neapolis
5 Hotel Bellini
8 Hotel Zara
14 Hotel Gallo
30 6 Small Rooms
36 Hostel of the Sun

PLACES TO EAT
3 Pizzeria Vesi
13 La Nouva Brace
16 Trianon
17 Da Michele
26 Fiorenzano
29 Vecchia Cantina

OTHER
1 Museo Archeologico
Nazionale
2 Piazza Cavour
6 Duomo
7 Piazza Principe Umberto
9 EPT Tourist Office
10 Pharmacy
11 Piazza Garibaldi
12 Urban & Intercity
Bus Station
15 Hospital
18 Vineria del Corso
19 CTS

20 Chiesa di Santa Chiara
21 Aexis Telecom
22 Piazza del Gesú Nuovo;
AAST Tourist Office
23 Chiesa di Gesú Nuovo
24 Port' Alba (City Gate)
25 Piazza Dante
26 My Beautiful Laundrette
27 Stazione Cumana;
Piazza Montesanto
31 Piazza Carità
32 Main Post Office
33 Piazza G Matteotti
34 Questura (Police Station)
35 Telecom Office
37 Buses to Pompeii
38 Stazione Marittima
(Long-Distance Ferries)
39 Piazza Municipio
40 Town Hall
41 Funicular Centrale
42 Galleria Umberto I
43 Every Tour
44 Castel Nuovo
45 Molo Beverello
(Local Ferries)
46 Palazzo Reale
47 Teatro San Carlo
48 Piazza Trento e Trieste
49 Piazza del Plebiscito

high, and bag-snatchers and pickpockets abound. Car theft is also a major problem. Keep your wits about you at night near the station, Piazza Dante, the area west of Via Toledo and as far north as Piazza Caritá.

Naples' legendary traffic means you need the power of prayer when crossing roads.

Things to See & Do
If it's still available, a good investment is the **Napoli artecard** (☎ 800 60 06 01; **w** www .napoliartecard.com) which gives access to six museums at reduced rates and public transport for €13. You can buy it at the airport, train and metro stations, as well as at selected museums.

Spaccanapoli, the historic centre of Naples, is a great place to start your sight-

seeing. From the station and Corso Umberto I turn right onto Via Mezzocannone, which will take you to Via Benedetto Croce, the bustling main street of the quarter. To the left is spacious Piazza del Gesú Nuovo, with the 15th-century rusticated facade of **Chiesa di Gesú Nuovo** and the 14th-century **Chiesa di Santa Chiara**, restored to its original Gothic-Provençal style after it was severely damaged by bombing during WWII. The beautifully tiled **Chiostro delle Clarisse** (Nuns' Cloisters; admission €3.10; open 9.30am-1pm & 2pm-5.30pm Mon-Fri, 9.30am-1pm Sat) are also worth visiting.

The **Duomo** has a 19th-century facade but was built by the Angevin kings at the end of the 13th century, on the site of an earlier basilica. Inside is the **Cappella di San Gennaro**, which contains the head of St Januarius (the city's patron saint) and two vials of his congealed blood. The saint is said to have saved the city from plague, volcanic eruptions and other disasters. Every year the faithful gather to pray for a miracle, namely that the blood will liquefy and save the city from further disaster (see under Special Events, later) – if you're in town, don't miss it.

Turn off Via Duomo onto **Via dei Tribunali**, one of the more characteristic streets of the area, and head for Piazza Dante, through the 17th-century **Port'Alba**, one of the gates to the city. Via Roma, the most fashionable street in old Naples, heads to the left (becoming Via Toledo) and ends at Piazza Trento e Trieste and the **Piazza del Plebiscito**.

In the piazza is the **Palazzo Reale** (☎ 081 794 40 21; admission €4.50; open 9am-8pm Thur-Tues), the former official residence of the Bourbon and Savoy kings, now a museum. Just off the piazza is the **Teatro San Carlo** (☎ 081 797 21 11, box office ☎ 081 797 23 31; w www.teatrosancarlo.it), one of the most-famous opera houses in the world thanks to its perfect acoustics and lavish interior.

The 13th-century **Castel Nuovo** overlooks Naples' ferry port. The early-Renaissance triumphal arch commemorates the entry of Alfonso I of Aragon into Naples in 1443. It is possible to visit the **Museo Civico** (☎ 081 795 20 03; admission €5.50; open 9am-7pm Mon-Sat) in the castle. Situated southwest along the waterfront at Santa Lucia is the **Castel dell'Ovo**, originally a Norman castle, which is surrounded by a tiny fishing village, the **Borgo Marinaro**.

The **Museo Archeologico Nazionale** (☎ 081 44 01 66; Piazza 17; admission €6.50; open 9am-8pm Wed-Mon), north of Piazza Dante, contains one of the most important collections of Greco-Roman artefacts in the world, mainly the rich collection of the Farnese family, and the art treasures discovered at Pompeii and Herculaneum. Don't forget to book a (free) tour to see the *gabinetto segreto* (secret cabinet) to see some of the racier artworks, which may well leave your cheeks (facial) flushed.

Catch the Funicolare Centrale (funicular), on Via Toledo, to the relative tranquility of **Vomero** and the Certosa di San Martino, a 14th-century Carthusian monastery, rebuilt in the 17th century in Neapolitan-baroque style. It houses the **Museo Nazionale di San Martino** (Piazza San Martino 5; admission €6; open 8.30am-7.30pm Tues-Sun). The monastery's church is worth visiting, plus its terraced gardens, with spectacular views of Naples and the bay.

Special Events
Neapolitans really get into the spirit of things, especially religious festivals. The celebration of St Januarius, the patron saint of the city, is held three times a year (the first Sunday in May, 19 September and 16 December) in the Duomo, and it's a must-see.

Places to Stay
Hostels The HI **Ostello Mergellina Napoli** (☎ 081 761 23 46; Salita della Grotta 23; dorm bed €13.50; open year-round) is modern, safe and soulless, with breakfast included. Even with 200 beds, it fills up during busy periods. To get there take the Metropolitana to Mergellina and follow the sign to the hostel.

Hotels Most of the cheap hotels are near the station and Piazza Garibaldi in a rather unsavoury area. You can ask the tourist office at the station to recommend or book a room for you (let them know your budget though).

Stazione Centrale Area The following are safe and offer decent accommodation.

Hotel Zara (☎ 081 28 71 25; e hotelzar@tin.it; Via Firenze 81; singles/doubles/triples without bath €26/47/73, doubles/triples with bath €57/83) is clean, welcoming and has a kitchen.

Hotel Ginevra (☎ 081 28 32 10, fax 081 554 17 57; e info@hotelginevra.it; Via Genova 116; singles/doubles/triples/quads without bath €25/40/66/65, with bath €40/50/70/80), near the station, is reliable and well-kept.

The **Casanova Hotel** (☎ 081 26 82 87; Corso Garibaldi 333; singles/doubles without bath €18/39, with bath €26/52) sounds like a brothel, but it's quiet, safe and friendly in a good way.

Hotel Gallo (☎ 081 20 05 12, fax 081 20 18 49; Via Spaventa 11; singles/doubles/triples with bath €57/83/109), to the left of the train station, has nice clean rooms with breakfast.

Around Spaccanapoli The excellent **6 Small Rooms** (☎ 081 790 13 78; e info@ at6smallrooms.com; Via Diodato Lioy 18; dorm bed €15) is a friendly and sociable hostel, with cheery rooms, spacious kitchen (breakfast included) and great word-of-mouth from many travellers. Ask about the 'beer witch' if you're feeling thirsty.

Hotel Bellini (☎ 081 45 69 96, fax 081 29 22 56; Via San Paolo 44; singles/doubles with bath €42/68) has well-appointed rooms with TV, fridge and phone, and a central location.

Hotel Neapolis (☎ 081 442 08 15, fax 081 442 08 19; e informazioni@hotelneapolis .com; Via San Francesco del Giudice 13; singles/doubles/triples/quads with bath €73/ 114/124/145) is a swanky new hotel in the old quarter, with excellent rooms with all amenities, including personal computers.

Stazione Marittima Area The new **Hostel of The Sun** (☎/fax 081 420 63 93; w www .hostelnapoli.com; Via Melsurgo 15; dorm bed €16, doubles with/without bath €61/ 45) is close to the port, but on the 7th floor. It's tidy and laundry facilities are available.

Vomero Just near the funicular station, **Pensione Margherita** (☎ 081 556 70 44; Via D Cimarosa 29; singles/doubles with bath €32/58) is a decent place (some rooms have bay views). Initially you'll need a coin for the lift.

Places to Eat

Naples is the home of pasta and pizza. A true Neapolitan pizza, topped with fresh tomatoes, oregano, basil and garlic, will leave other pizzas looking decidedly wrong. Try *calzone*, a stuffed version of pizza, or *mozzarella in carozza* (mozzarella deep-fried in bread), which is sold at street stalls, along with *misto di frittura* (deep-fried vegetables). Don't leave town without trying the *sfogliatelle* (light, flaky pastry filled with ricotta).

Restaurants There are numerous places to eat in and around Naples' centre.

City Centre Reputedly the best pizza in Naples (and therefore the world) is at **Da Michele** (☎ 081 553 92 04; Via Cesare Sersale 1; pizza €5-7). You can test this by taking a number and waiting for a bubbling,

sizzling masterpiece. **Trianon** (☎ 081 553 94 26; Via Pietro Colletta 46; pizza €5-10) near Via Tribunali, is also great, with a wider selection and marble-topped tables. **La Nouva Brace** (☎ 081 26 12 60; Via Spaventa 14; tourist menu €8.50) is very easy on the pocket, and has tasty local dishes, plus poetry (in dialect) on the walls. **Vecchia Cantina** (☎ 081 552 02 26; Via San Nicola alla Carita; meal about €12) has a convivial atmosphere with great pasta dishes (the pasta with zucchini is delicious – €4.50). **Pizzeria Vesi** (Via Tribunali 388; pizza €4.50-12) is a homy, good-value place in the old quarter, with locals flocking to enjoy both sit-down and takeaway delights.

Mergellina & Vomero Neapolitans often head for the area around Piazza Sannazzaro, southwest of the centre (handy to the HI hostel), for pizza. **Pizzeria da Pasqualino** (☎ 081 68 15 24; Piazza Sannazzaro 79; meal about €17) has outdoor tables (a tad noisy at times) and serves well-liked pizza, seafood and yummy tidbits for snackers. In Vomero, **Cantina di Sica** (☎ 081 556 75 20; Via Bernini 17; meal about €20) has excellent local dishes – try the *spaghetti alle vongole e pomodorini* (spaghetti with clams and cherry tomatoes).

Food Stalls Heavenly fried goodies are on offer at bargain prices at **Fiorenzano** (Piazza Montesanto). Naples has many **alimentari** (grocery shops) and **food stalls** scattered throughout the city.

Entertainment

The monthly *Qui Napoli* and the local newspapers are the only real guides to what's on. In May the city organises Maggio dei Monumenti, with concerts and cultural events (mostly free) around town. Ask at the tourist office for details. The **Teatro San Carlo** (☎ 081 797 21 11, box office ☎ 081 797 23 31; w www.teatrosancarlo.it; tickets from €8) has year-round performances of opera, ballet and concerts and is definitely worth visiting.

There are a handful of good **bars** in Piazza Gesú Nuovo, which go off on weekend nights and then provide daytime coffee to ease the hangover.

Vineria del Corso (Via Paladino 8a) is a great little bar, with good lighting, charming decor and low-key electronica played at a polite volume. The wine list's good, too.

Getting There & Away

Air Some 5km northeast of the city centre, **Capodichino airport** (☎ 081 789 61 11, ☎ 800 88 87 77; *Viale Umberto Maddalena*) has connections to most Italian and several European cities. Bus No 14 or 14R leaves from Piazza Garibaldi every 30 minutes for the airport (20 minutes).

Bus There are buses that leave from Piazza Garibaldi, just outside the train station, for destinations including Salerno, the Amalfi Coast, Caserta and Bari, Lecce and Brindisi in Apulia. Signage is limited, so you might have to ask at the booths to get the necessary information.

Train Naples is a major rail-transport centre for the south, and regular trains for most major Italian cities arrive and depart from the Stazione Centrale. There are over two dozen trains daily for Rome.

Car & Motorcycle Driving in Naples is not recommended. The traffic is chaotic, car and motorcycle theft is rife, and the street plan does not lend itself to easy navigation. However, the city is easily accessible from Rome on the A1. The Naples–Pompeii–Salerno road (A3) connects with the coastal road to Sorrento and the Amalfi Coast.

Boat *Traghetti* (ferries), *aliscafi* (hydrofoils) and *navi veloci* (fast ships) leave for Sorrento and the islands of Capri, Ischia and Procida from Molo Beverello, in front of Castel Nuovo. Some hydrofoils leave for the bay islands from Mergellina, and ferries for Ischia and Procida also leave from Pozzuoli. All operators have offices at the various ports from which they leave.

Hydrofoils cost around double the price of ferries but take half the time.

Tirrenia (☎ 199 12 31 99) operates ferries to Palermo and Cagliari while **Siremar** (☎ 081 580 03 40, 199 12 31 99) services the Aeolian Islands. Ferries leave from the Stazione Marittima on Molo Angioino, next to Molo Beverello (see the Getting There & Away sections under Sicily and Sardinia). **SNAV** (☎ 081 761 23 48) runs regular ferries and, in summer, hydrofoils to the Aeolian Islands.

Getting Around

You can make your way around Naples by bus, tram, Metropolitana (underground) and funicular. City buses leave from Piazza Garibaldi in front of the central station bound for the centre of Naples and Mergellina. Tickets cost €0.77 for 1½ hours (€2.32 for 24 hours) and are valid for buses, trams, the Metropolitana and funicular services. Useful buses include No 14 or 14R to the airport; the R1 to Piazza Dante; the R3 to Mergellina; and No 110 from Piazza Garibaldi to Piazza Cavour and the archaeological museum. Tram No 1 leaves from east of Stazione Centrale for the city centre. To get to Molo Beverello and the ferry terminal from the train station, take bus No R2 or the M1.

The Metropolitana station is downstairs at the train station. Trains head west to Mergellina, stopping at Piazza Cavour, Piazza Amedeo and the funicular to Vomero, and then head on to the Campi Flegrei and Pozzuoli. Another line, still under construction in parts, will connect Piazza Garibaldi, the cathedral, Piazzas Bovio, Carità and Dante, the Museo Archeologico Nazionale and Piazza Vanvitelli.

The main funicular connecting the city centre with Vomero is the Funicolare Centrale in Piazza Duca d'Aosta, next to Galleria Umberto I, on Via Toledo.

The Ferrovia Circumvesuviana operates trains for Herculaneum, Pompeii and Sorrento. The station is about 400m southwest of Stazione Centrale, in Corso Garibaldi (take the underpass from Stazione Centrale). The Ferrovia Cumana and the Circumflegrea, based at Stazione Cumana in Piazza Montesanto, operate services to Pozzuoli, Baia and Cumae every 20 minutes.

AROUND NAPLES

From Naples it's only a short distance to the **Campi Flegrei** (Phlegraean Fields) of volcanic lakes and mud baths, which inspired both Homer and Virgil in their writings. Unavoidably part of suburban Naples today, the area is dirty and overdeveloped, but still worth a half-day trip. The Greek colony of **Cumae** is certainly worth visiting, particularly to see the Cave of the Cumaean Sybil, home of one of the ancient world's greatest oracles. Also in the area is **Lake Avernus**, the mythical entrance to the underworld, and **Baia** with its submerged Roman ruins visible from a glass-bottomed boat.

Reached by CPTC bus from Naples' Piazza Garibaldi or by train from the Stazione Centrale is the wonderful **Palazzo Reale** (☎ 0823 44 74 47; admission €6.50; open 9am-7pm Tues-Sun) at Caserta, AKA Reggia di Caserta. Built in the 18th century under the Bourbon king Charles III, this imposing 1200-room palace is set in elegant gardens.

Pompeii & Herculaneum

Buried under a layer of lapilli (burning fragments of pumice stone) during the devastating eruption of Mt Vesuvius in AD 79, **Pompeii** (☎ 857 53 47; Via Villa dei Misteri 2; admission €10, with Herculaneum €18 for 3 days; open 8.30am-7.30pm Apr-Oct & 8.30am-5pm Nov-Mar) provides a truly fascinating insight into the lives of ancient Romans. Once a resort town for wealthy Romans, the vast ruins include impressive temples, a forum, one of the largest-known Roman amphitheatres, and streets lined with shops and luxurious houses. Many of the site's original mosaics and frescoes are housed in Naples' Museo Archeologico Nazionale (see Things to See & Do under Naples, earlier). The exception is the Villa dei Misteri, where the frescoes remain in situ. Various houses and shops are closed, and details are provided at the entrance to the site. Bring a hat or umbrella, depending on the weather.

There are **tourist offices** (☎ 081 850 72 55; Via Sacra 1) in the new town, and just outside the excavations (toll-free ☎ 800 01 33 50; Piazza Porta Marina Inferiore 12), near the Porta Marina entrance. Both offer information, notes on guided tours and a simple map.

Catch the Ferrovia Circumvesuviana train from Naples and get off at the Pompeii Scavi-Villa dei Misteri stop; the Porta Marina entrance is nearby.

Herculaneum (Ercolano; Corso Resina; admission €10, with Pompeii €18 for 3 days; open 8.30am-7.30pm, last entrance 6pm, Apr-Oct, 8.30am-5pm, last entrance 3.30pm, Nov-Mar) is closer to Naples and is also a good point from which to visit Mt Vesuvius. Legend says the city was founded by Hercules. First Greek, then Roman, it was also destroyed by the AD 79 eruption, buried under mud and lava. Most inhabitants of Herculaneum had enough warning and managed to escape. The ruins here are smaller and the

buildings, particularly the private houses, are remarkably well preserved. Here you can see better examples of the frescoes, mosaics and furniture that used to decorate Roman houses.

Herculaneum is also accessible on the Circumvesuviana train from Naples (get off at Ercolano Scavi; €1.55 one way). If you want to have a look into the huge crater of Mt Vesuvius, catch the **Trasporti Vesuviani bus** (☎ 081 739 28 33) from in front of the Ercolano Scavi train station or from Pompeii's Piazza Anfiteatro. The return ticket costs €3.10 from Ercolano and €5.16 from Pompeii. The first bus leaves Pompeii at 9.30am and takes 40 minutes to reach Herculaneum. You'll then need to walk about 1.5km to the summit, where you must pay €5.16 to be accompanied by a guide to the crater. The last bus returns to Pompeii from Herculaneum's Quota 1000 car park at 3pm, and there are only three buses to the crater (from Pompeii at 9.30am, 11am and 12.10pm).

SORRENTO
postcode 80067 • pop 17,450
A resort town in a beautiful area, summer sees Sorrento overcrowded with middle-aged, middle-class, middle-brow tourists and the trinket shops that cater to them. However, it is handy to the Amalfi Coast and Capri, and pleasant out of season.

Orientation & Information
The centre of town is Piazza Tasso, a short walk from the train station along Corso Italia. The very helpful **AAST tourist office** (☎ 081 807 40 33; w www.sorrento tourism.it; Via Luigi de Maio 35; open 8.45am-7pm Mon-Sat) is inside the Circolo dei Forestieri complex.

There is a **post office** (Corso Italia 210) and **Telecom telephone office** (Piazza Tasso 37). The **Deutsche Bank** (Piazza Angelina Laura) has an ATM.

Internet access is available at **Blu Online** (Via Fuorimura 20), near the train station, for €5 per hour.

For medical emergencies contact the **Ospedale Civile** (☎ 081 533 11 11).

Places to Stay & Eat
Camping grounds include **Nube d'Argento** (☎ 081 878 13 44, fax 081 807 34 50; Via del Capo 21; camp site per person/tent €8.50/12), which is the closest to the action.

ITALY

Head south along Corso Italia, then follow Via Capo.

Ostello delle Sirene (☎ *081 807 29 25; Via degli Aranci 156; dorm bed without bath €14, with bath €16)*, near the train station, is a good option, with breakfast included.

Hotel Nice (☎ *081 878 16 50, fax 081 878 30 86; Corso Italia 257; singles/doubles with bath €52/65)* has pleasant rooms, but traffic noise is a problem.

Pensione Linda (☎ *081 878 29 16; Via degli Aranci 125; singles/doubles with bath €26/47)* is a charming place with sweet service and bargain rates.

Self-Service Angelina Lauro (☎ *081 807 40 97; Piazza Angelina Lauro 39; meal about €6)* offers a cheap feed. **Giardinello** (☎ *081 878 46 16; Via dell'Accademia 7; pizza about €5-6)* has a good menu and friendly service, plus a nice courtyard for summer dining. The **supermarket** *(Corso Italia 223)* has plenty of groceries.

Getting There & Away
Sorrento is accessible from Naples on the Circumvesuviana train line. SITA buses leave from outside the train station for the Amalfi Coast. Hydrofoils and ferries leave from the port, along Via de Maio and down the steps from the tourist office, for Capri and Napoli and Ischia. The tourist office hands out comprehensive timetables.

In summer, traffic is heavy along the coastal roads to Sorrento.

CAPRI
postcode 80073 • pop 7250
This beautiful island, an hour by ferry from Naples, retains the mythical appeal that attracted Roman emperors, including Augustus and Tiberius, who built 12 villas here. Very popular in summer, Capri wears its jet-set exclusivity well, like a cashmere sweater jauntily tied over bronzed shoulders. A short bus ride takes you to Anacapri, the town uphill from Capri, which also has accommodation. The island, famous for its grottoes, is also a good place for walking. There are **tourist offices** at Marina Grande (☎ *081 837 06 34; open 8.30am-8.30pm daily)*, where boats arrive; in Piazza Umberto I (☎ *081 837 06 86; open 8.30am-8.30pm daily)* in the centre of town; and in Anacapri (☎ *081 837 15 24; Piazza Vittoria 4)*. Online information can be found at **w** www.capri.it.

Things to See & Do
There are boat tours of the grottoes, including the famous **Grotta Azzurra** (Blue Grotto). Boats leave from Marina Grande and a return trip costs €14.10 (which includes the cost of a motorboat to the grotto, rowing boat into the grotto and entrance fee). On Sunday and public holidays it's a ludicrous €30. It's cheaper to catch a bus from Anacapri (although the rowboat and entrance fee still cost €8.10). You can swim into the grotto before 9am and after 5pm, but do so only in company and when the sea is very calm. You can walk to most of the interesting points on the island. Sights include the **Giardini d'Augusto**, in the town of Capri, and **Villa Jovis** *(admission €2; open 9am-1hr before sunset daily)*, the ruins of one of Tiberius' villas, along the Via Longano and Via Tiberio. The latter is a one-hour walk uphill from Capri. The beautiful **Villa San Michele** (☎ *081 837 14 01; Viale Axel Munthe; admission €5; open 9am-6pm daily May-Sept, 9.30am-5pm Mar-Apr & Oct, 10.30am-3.30pm Nov-Feb)* at Anacapri was the home of Swedish writer Dr Axel Munthe.

Places to Stay & Eat
Stella Maris (☎ *081 837 04 52, fax 081 837 86 62; Via Roma 27; singles/doubles without bath €45/80)*, just off Piazza Umberto I, is right in the noisy heart of town.

In Anacapri, there is the above-average **Loreley** (☎ *081 837 14 40, fax 081 837 13 99; Via G Orlandi 16; singles/doubles with bath €67/108)*, with low-season reductions available.

In Capri, **La Cisterna** (☎ *081 837 56 20; Via M Serafina 5; meal about €15)* is a good spot to assuage hunger pains. In Anacapri, **Il Saraceno** (☎ *081 837 20 99; Via Trieste e Trento 18; meal about €17)* has a lovely family atmosphere and great home-made *limoncello* (lemon liqueur).

Getting There & Away
Getting to Capri is no problem, as there are hydrofoils and ferries virtually every hour from Naples' Molo Beverello and Mergellina, especially in summer. The Naples daily *Il Mattino* has all sailing times.

Several companies make the trip. Try **Caremar** (☎ *081 551 38 82)*, which runs ferries/fast ferries for €5.42/10.33 one way from Beverello; and **NLG** (☎ *081 552 72 09)*, also in Beverello (hydrofoils €11 one way).

Getting Around

From Marina Grande, the funicular directly in front of the port takes you to the town of Capri, which is at the top of a steep hill some 3km from the port up a winding road. Tiny local buses connect the port with Capri, Anacapri and other points around the island. Tickets for the funicular and buses (buy on board) cost €1.30 each trip or €6.71 per daily ticket.

AMALFI COAST

The 50km-stretch of the Amalfi Coast attracts the world's wealthy in summer and prices skyrocket. Nevertheless, it's a coastline and landscape of inspiring natural beauty, which is more than can be said for the summer hordes. Visit in spring or autumn and you'll find reasonably priced accommodation and a peaceful atmosphere.

There are **tourist information offices** in the individual towns, including in Positano (☎ 089 87 50 67; Via Saracino 2; open 8am-2pm Mon-Sat year-round & 3.30pm-8pm July-Aug), and Amalfi (☎ 089 87 11 07; Corso Roma 19; open 8.30am-1.30pm & 3pm-5.30pm Mon-Fri, 8.30am-12.30pm Sat), on the waterfront.

Positano

postcode 84017 • pop 3900

This is the most beautiful and fashionable town on the coast, with corresponding prices for the most part.

Villa delle Palme (☎ 089 87 51 62; Via Pasitea 134; doubles with bath €78) is a very good English-speaking hotel, with the usual mod-con suspects in all rooms. Next door is the great pizzeria **Il Saraceno d'Oro** (pizza about €6), which is a cut above most of the tourist-trap joints in town.

Around Positano

The hills behind Positano offer some great walks; the tourist office at Positano may have a brochure listing options, and you can buy walking guides in town. Visit **Nocelle**, a tiny, isolated village above Positano, accessible by walking track from the end of the road from Positano. Have lunch at **Trattoria Santa Croce** (☎ 089 81 12 60; meal about €20), which has panoramic views. It opens for lunch and dinner in summer, but at other times, telephone and check in advance. Nocelle is accessible by local bus from Positano, via Montepertuso.

On the way from Positano to Amalfi is the town of **Praiano**, which is not as scenic but has more budget options, including the only camping ground on the Amalfi Coast. **La Tranquillitá** (☎ 089 87 40 84; e contraq@ contraqpraiano.com; €13 per person per camp site, double bungalows €43 per person) has a pensione, bungalows and a small camping ground. Rates for the double bungalows include breakfast. The SITA bus stops outside.

Amalfi

postcode 84011 • pop 5520

One of the four powerful maritime republics of medieval Italy, Amalfi is a popular tourist resort. It has an impressive **Duomo**, and nearby is the **Grotta dello Smeraldo**, a rival to Capri's Grotta Azzurra.

In the hills behind Amalfi is delightful **Ravello**, accessible by bus from Amalfi and worth a visit to see the magnificent 11th-century **Villa Rufolo** (admission €4; open 9am-6pm daily), once the home of popes and later of the German composer Wagner. The 20th-century **Villa Cimbrone** is set in beautiful gardens, which end at a terrace offering a spectacular view of the Gulf of Salerno. There are numerous walking paths in the hills between Amalfi and Ravello. Pick up Strade e Sentieri (€6.50), a guide to walks in the area.

Places to Stay & Eat The HI **Ostello Beato Solitudo** (☎/fax 089 82 50 48; Piazza G Avitabile 4; dorm bed €9.50) is in Agerola San Lazzaro, a village just 16km west of Amalfi. Regular buses leave from Amalfi throughout the day, the last departing at about 8.45pm.

For a room in Amalfi try **Pensione Proto** (☎ 089 87 10 03, fax 089 873 61 80; Via dei Curiali 4; singles/doubles without bath €44/ 70), which has clean, decent rooms. The delightful **Hotel Lidomare** (☎ 089 87 13 32, fax 089 87 13 94; e lidomare@amalfi coast.it; Largo Duchi Piccolomini 9; singles/ doubles with bath €39/88) has romantic rooms and kind service. Just follow the signs from Piazza del Duomo.

Pizzeria al Teatro (Via E Marini 19; pizza about €7) offers good food in attractive surrounds. Follow the signs to the left from Via Pietro Capuana, the main shopping street off Piazza del Duomo. There's a **minimarket** next to Pensione Proto. The best pastries are nibbled at **Pasticceria Andrea Pansa** (Piazza Duomo 40), an old-fashioned place with luxe charm.

Getting There & Away

Bus The Amalfi Coast is accessible by regular SITA buses, which run between Salerno (a 40-minute train trip from Naples) and Sorrento (accessible from Naples on the Circumvesuviana train line). Buses stop in Amalfi at Piazza Flavio Gioia, from where you can catch a bus to Ravello.

Car & Motorcycle The narrow, spectacular and tortuous coastal road is clogged with traffic in summer – be prepared for delays. Things are quieter at other times. **Sorrento Rentacar** (☎ 081 878 13 86; Corso Italia 210a, Sorrento) rents scooters and cars.

Boat Hydrofoils and ferries also service the coast between April and mid-September daily, leaving from Salerno and stopping at Amalfi and Positano. There are also boats between Positano and Capri.

PAESTUM
postcode 84063

The sight that launched a 1000 postcards – the three Greek temples standing in fields of red poppies are well worth making an effort to visit. The **temples** (admission €4.50; open 9am-1hr before sunset daily), just south of Salerno, are among the world's best-preserved monuments of the ancient Greek world and a Unesco World Heritage Site. A **tourist office** (☎ 0828 81 10 16; open 9am-2pm daily) and an interesting **museum** (☎ 0828 81 10 23; admission €4.50; open 9am-7pm daily, closed 1st & 3rd Mon of month) are at the site.

Paestum is accessible from Salerno by CSTP bus No 34 from Piazza della Concordia, or by train. Buses are frequent from Monday to Saturday and almost nonexistent on Sunday.

MATERA
postcode 75100 • pop 57,300

This ancient city of the Basilicata region still trades on haunting images of a peasant culture that existed until the 1960s. Its famous sassi (the stone houses built in the two ravines that slice through the city) were home to more than half of Matera's population until the 1950s, when the local government built a new residential area just out of Matera and relocated 15,000 people. The wards are now a Unesco World Heritage Site – a far cry from the days when Matera struggled against poverty and malaria. Francesco Rosi's excellent film Cristo si é Fermato a Eboli (Christ Stopped at Eboli) is a poignant illustration of what life was like in Basilicata.

There's a **tourist office** (☎ 0835 33 19 83; Via de Viti De Marco 9; open 9am-1pm Mon-Sat & 4pm-6.30pm Mon & Thur), off the main Via Roma. **Itinera** (☎/fax 0835 26 32 59; e arrtir@tin.it) can organise guided tours in English for up to 10 people (two to three hours) for €60. **Sassi Urban Network** (SUN; ☎ 0835 31 98 06; Via Casalnuovo 15) organises visits to the sassi churches (from €2.10) and also provides maps. Its information offices are to be found scattered all through the wards.

Things to See

The two main sassi wards, known as **Barisano** and **Caveoso**, had no electricity, running water or sewerage until well into the 20th century. The oldest sassi are at the top of the ravines, and the dwellings that appear to be the oldest were established in the 20th century. As space ran out in the 1920s, the population turned troglodyte, and started moving into hand-hewn or natural caves. The sassi zones are accessible from Piazza Vittorio Veneto and Piazza del Duomo in the centre of Matera. Be sure to see the rock churches, **Santa Maria d'Idris** and **Santa Lucia alla Malve**, both with well-preserved Byzantine frescoes. The 13th-century Apulian-Romanesque **cathedral**, overlooking Sasso Barisano, is also worth a visit.

Parts of the wards have been restored and some people have moved back to the area. Excavations in Piazza Vittorio Veneto have revealed the ruins of parts of **Byzantine Matera**, including a castle and a rock church decorated with frescoes. Worth visiting is **Casa Grotta di Vico Solitario** (☎ 0835 31 01 18; Piazza San Pietro Caveoso; admission €1.50), an authentic sassi dwelling (English brochures available).

Places to Stay & Eat

Accommodation is best booked in advance. **Albergo Roma** (☎/fax 0835 33 39 12; Via Roma 62; singles/doubles without bath €21/31) has simple rooms but a central location.

Sassi Hotel (☎ 0835 33 10 09, fax 0835 33 37 33; e hotelsassi@virgilio.it; Via San Giovanni Vecchio 89; dorm bed €15.50, singles/doubles with bath €52/78) is the most atmospheric place to stay, as it's in – you guessed it – the sassi.

L'Osteria (☎ 0835 33 33 95; Via Fiorentini 58; meal about €14) is a tiny place with mouth-watering local dishes. There's a **fresh produce market** near Piazza V Veneto, on Via A Persio.

Getting There & Away
SITA buses connect Matera with Taranto and Metaponto. The town is on the private Ferrovie Apulo–Lucane train line, which connects with Bari, Altamura and Potenza. There are also three Marozzi buses a day between Rome and Matera (€30). Buses arrive in Piazza Matteotti, a short walk down Via Roma to the town centre. Buy tickets at **Biglietteria Manicone** (☎ 0835 332 86 21; Piazza Matteoti 3).

APULIA
The province of Apulia, the thin heel of the Italian peninsula, has long been dismissed as a rural backwater with endemic poverty, and it still retains a sense of isolation from the rest of Italy. Yet for centuries, the 400km-long coastline was fought over by virtually every major colonial power, from the Greeks to the Spanish – all intent on establishing a strategic foothold in the Mediterranean. Each culture left its distinctive architectural mark, still in evidence today, albeit often crumbling.

Brindisi
postcode 72100 • pop 93,020
The highlight of no-one's trip to Italy, Brindisi swarms with travellers in transit, as this is the major embarkation point for ferries to Greece (bring a pack of playing cards!). Most backpackers gather at the train station or at either of the two ports. The train station and the old port are connected by Corso Umberto I – which becomes Corso Garibaldi (pedestrianised) – a five-minute walk. The new port, known as Costa Morena, is 7km from the train station, with free bus connections linking the two (see Boat under Getting There & Away, later).

There is a helpful **EPT tourist information office** (☎ 0831 56 21 26; Lungomare Regina Margherita 43). Be mindful of your possessions (and not just around locals), especially in the area around the train station and the ports.

The best-value accommodation here is the non-HI **Babilonia Hostel** (☎ 0831 41 31 23; e hostelbrandisi@hotmail.com; Via Brandi 2; dorm bed €12), about 2km out of town and is definitely recommended if you have time to kill. Take bus No 3 from Via Cristoforo Colombo near the train station, or call and ask Francesco to pick you up. Turn left off Corso Umberto I onto Via S Lorenzo da Brindisi to get to the bog-standard but inexpensive **Hotel Venezia** (☎ 0831 52 75 11; Via Pisanelli 4; singles/doubles without bath €13/25).

There's a **supermarket** (Piazza Cairoli 30), between the train station and the old port, plus a morning **market** in Piazza Mercato, behind the post office. **La Bruschetta** (Via Colonne 30; meal about €21) is a decent spot to grab a good lunch or dinner.

Getting There & Away Marozzi runs several buses a day to/from Rome's Stazione Tiburtina, leaving from Viale Arno. **Appia Travel** (☎ 0831 52 16 84; Viale Regina Margherita 8-9) sells tickets (€34; nine hours). There are rail connections to major cities in northern Italy, as well as to Bari, Lecce, Ancona, Naples and Rome.

Boat Ferries leave Brindisi for Greek destinations including Corfu, Igoumenitsa, Patras and Kefallonia. Major ferry companies are **Hellenic Mediterranean Lines** (HML; ☎ 0831 52 85 31; Corso Garibaldi 8); **Blue Star** (☎ 0831 51 44 84; Corso Garibaldi 65); **Italian Ferries** (☎ 0831 59 08 40; Corso Garibaldi 96); and **Med Link Lines** (☎ 0831 52 76 67; Corso Garibaldi 49).

HML is the most expensive, but also the most reliable. HML also officially accepts Eurail and Inter-Rail passes, which means you pay only €12 to travel deck class. If you want to use your Eurail or Inter-Rail pass, it is important to reserve some weeks in advance in summer. Even with a booking in summer, you must still go to your boat company's embarkation office (ask them for details when you buy) to have your ticket checked.

Discounts are available for travellers under 26 years of age and holders of some Italian rail passes. Note that fares and services increase in July and August. Full prices in the 2002 high season for deck class were: HML to Corfu, Igoumenitsa, Kefallonia or Patras €46 (€37 return); Med Link to Patras €45 (€36 return); Blue Star to Corfu and Igoumenitsa €48.

Bicycles can be taken aboard free, but the average high-season fare for a motorcycle is €18 and for a car around €48. A good website for trip planning is w www.ferries.gr, which has details of fares and timetables from Brindisi to Greece in English. Be wary of any too-good-to-be-true offers from fly-by-night operators claiming your Eurail and Inter-Rail pass is accepted by them or invalid with anyone else. We get numerous letters from travellers who have been stung for two lots of ferry tickets.

The port tax is €6, payable when you buy your ticket. It is essential to check in at least two hours prior to departure. To get to the new port of Costa Morena from the train station take the free Portabagagli bus, which departs a handy two hours before boat departures.

Lecce

postcode 73100 • pop 97,450

If baroque means 'architectural marzipan' to you, you're in for a sweet surprise in Lecce. The style here is so refined and particular to the city that Italians call it Barocco Leccese (Lecce baroque), and the city is known as the 'Florence of the South'. The numerous bars and restaurants are a pleasant discovery in such a small city, thanks to the students from Lecce's university.

There is a dozy **APT information office** (☎ 0832 24 80 92; Via Vittorio Emanuele 24) near Piazza Duomo. Take bus No 1, 2 or 4 from the station to the town centre, or a five-minute walk.

Things to See & Do The most famous example of Lecce baroque is the **Basilica di Santa Croce**. Artists worked for 150 years to decorate the building, creating an extraordinarily ornate facade. In the **Piazza del Duomo** are the 12th-century **cathedral** (completely restored in the baroque style by Giuseppe Zimbalo of Lecce) and its 70m-high **bell tower**; the **Palazzo del Vescovo** (Bishop's Palace); and the **Seminario**, with its elegant facade and baroque well in the courtyard. The piazza is particularly beautiful at night, when the lights really show the buildings at their best. In Piazza Sant'Oronzo are the remains of a **Roman amphitheatre**.

Places to Stay & Eat Camping facilities abound in the province of Salento. **Torre Rinalda** (☎ 0832 38 21 62, fax 0832 38 21 65; e info@torrerinalda.it; camp sites up to €33.50), near the sea at (you guessed it) Torre Rinalda, is accessible by STP bus from the terminal in Lecce's Via Adua. Given the prices it's best to be in a group.

Lecce's **Hotel Cappello** (☎ 0832 30 88 81; Via Montegrappa 4; singles/doubles with bath €28/44) is near the station and 'un buon mercato' (a good price). For a taste of faded glory, try **Grand Hotel** (☎ 0832 30 94 05; Viale Quarta 28; singles/doubles with bath €48/84) just near the train station.

Ristorante Re Idomeneo (Via Libertini 44; meal about €13) is near Piazza del Duomo and has hearty, inexpensive pasta dishes, beloved by locals. **Fiaschetteria** (Via d'Aragone 2; meal about €12) is just near Chiesa di San Matteo and serves tasty local dishes with excellent bread.

Entertainment For a small, seemingly sedate town, Lecce has some great little bars in its historic centre. Try **Caffe Letterario** (Via Paladini 46), where you can enjoy wine by the glass in colourful surrounds.

Getting There & Away STP buses connect Lecce with towns throughout the Salentine peninsula, leaving from Via Adua. Lecce is directly linked by Ferrovie delfo Stato (FS) train to Brindisi, Bari, Rome, Naples and Bologna. The Ferrovie del Sud Est (FSE) runs trains to major points in Apulia.

Sicily

Sicily is a land of Greek temples, Norman churches and fortresses, Arab domes, Byzantine mosaics and splendid baroque architecture. Its landscape, dominated by the volcano Mt Etna (3330m) on the east coast, ranges from fertile coast to mountains in the north to a vast, dry plateau at its centre.

With a population of about 5,070,000 people, Sicily has a mild climate in winter and a relentlessly hot summer. The best times to visit are in spring and autumn, when it's warm but quieter.

Most ferries from Italy arrive at Sicily's capital, Palermo, which is convenient as a jumping-off point. If you're short on time, spend a day in Palermo and then perhaps head for Taormina, Syracuse or Agrigento.

The Mafia remains a powerful force in Sicily, despite taking a hammering from the authorities throughout the 1990s. But the 'men of honour' are not interested in your travellers cheques, so you won't be in a *Godfather*-style shoot-out.

Getting There & Away

Air There are flights from major cities in Italy and throughout Europe to Palermo and Catania. The easiest way to get information is from any Sestante CIT or Alitalia office.

Bus & Train Bus services from Rome to Sicily are operated by **Segesta/Interbus** (☎ 091 616 90 39, Palermo ☎ 616 79 19, Rome ☎ 06 481 96 76), which has departures from Rome's Piazza Tiburtina. Buses service Messina (€27, 9¼ hours), Catania (€30, 11 hours) Palermo (€35, 12 hours) and Syracuse (€32.50, 11½ hours).

One of the cheapest ways to reach Sicily is to catch a train to Messina. The cost of the ticket covers the 3km-ferry crossing from Villa San Giovanni (Calabria) to Messina.

Boat Sicily is accessible by ferry from Genoa, Livorno, Naples, Reggio di Calabria and Cagliari, and also from Malta and Tunisia. The main companies servicing the Mediterranean are **Tirrenia** (Palermo ☎ 091 602 11 11, Rome ☎ 06 42 00 98 03) and **Grimaldi** (Palermo ☎ 091 58 74 04, Genoa ☎ 010 2 54 65), which runs Grandi Navi Veloci. Prices are determined by season and are highest from July to September. Timetables can change each year and it's best to check at a travel agency that takes ferry bookings. Book well in advance during summer, particularly if you have a car.

At the time of writing, high-season fares for a *poltrona* (airline-type chair on a ferry) were Genoa–Palermo (€100, 20 hours) and Livorno–Palermo (€94, 17 hours) with Grimaldi's Grandi Navi Veloci, and Naples–Palermo (€45, 9¾ hours) and Cagliari–Palermo (€39, 13½ hours) with Tirrenia.

Virtu Ferries (Ⓦ www.virtuferries.com) serves Sicily-Malta. For information on ferries going from the mainland directly to Lipari, see Getting There & Away under Aeolian Islands later in this chapter.

Getting Around

Bus is the most common (and often the most convenient) mode of public transport in Sicily. Numerous companies run services between

Syracuse, Catania and Palermo, as well as to Agrigento and towns in the interior. The coastal train service between Messina and Palermo and Messina to Syracuse varies between efficient and reliable, to delayed and unpredictable.

PALERMO
postcode 90100 • pop 680,000

An Arab emirate and later the seat of a Norman kingdom, Palermo was once regarded as the grandest and most beautiful city in Europe. Today, parts of it are in a remarkable state of decay, due to neglect and heavy bombing during WWII, yet enough evidence remains of its golden days to make Palermo one of the most fascinating cities in Italy. Thankfully, some much-needed EU funds are actually beginning to make it to the areas that need it too.

Orientation

Palermo is a large but easily manageable city. The main streets of the historic centre are Via Roma and Via Maqueda, which extend from the central station to Piazza Castelnuovo, a vast square in the modern part of town.

Information

Tourist Offices There is a main **APT tourist office** (☎ 091 58 38 47; Piazza Castelnuovo 34; open 8.30am-2pm & 2.30pm-6pm Mon-Fri). There are branch offices at the Stazione Centrale (☎ 091 616 59 14), with the same opening hours as the main office, and at the airport (☎ 091 59 16 98; open 8am-midnight Mon-Fri, 8am-8pm Sat & Sun).

Money There is an **exchange office** (open 8am-8pm daily) at the Stazione Centrale. American Express is represented by **Ruggieri & Figli** (☎ 091 58 71 44; Via Emerico Amari 40), near the Stazione Marittima. Otherwise, there is no shortage of banks with ATMs in the city.

Post & Communications There is a **main post office** (Via Roma 322; open 8.30am-6.30pm Mon-Sat), which also has a fax service. The main (and grotty) **Telecom telephone office** (Piazza G Cesare; open 8am-9.30pm daily) is opposite the station. You can use the Internet (€3.10 per hour), send faxes and make calls at **Aexis Telecom** (Via Maqueda 347).

ITALY

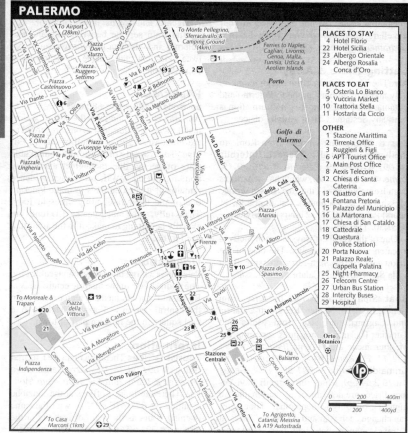

PLACES TO STAY
4 Hotel Florio
22 Hotel Sicilia
23 Albergo Orientale
24 Albergo Rosalia
     Conca d'Oro

PLACES TO EAT
5 Osteria Lo Bianco
9 Vucciria Market
10 Trattoria Stella
11 Hostaria da Ciccio

OTHER
1 Stazione Marittima
2 Tirrenia Office
3 Ruggieri & Figli
6 APT Tourist Office
7 Main Post Office
8 Aexis Telecom
12 Chiesa di Santa
     Caterina
13 Quattro Canti
14 Fontana Pretoria
15 Palazzo del Municipio
16 La Martorana
17 Chiesa di San Cataldo
18 Cattedrale
19 Questura
     (Police Station)
20 Porta Nuova
21 Palazzo Reale;
     Cappella Palatina
25 Night Pharmacy
26 Telecom Centre
27 Urban Bus Station
28 Intercity Buses
29 Hospital

Medical & Emergency Services For an ambulance call ☎ 091 30 66 44. There is a public hospital, **Ospedale Civico** (☎ 091 666 11 11; Via Carmelo Lazzaro). A night pharmacy, **Lo Cascio** (☎ 091 616 21 17; Via Roma 1), is near the train station. The **questura** (police headquarters; ☎ 091 21 01 11; Piazza della Vittoria) is open 24 hours a day. You can also call the **Ufficio Stranieri** (Foreigners Office; ☎ 091 651 43 30; Piazza della Vittoria). If your car has been towed away, call ☎ 091 656 97 21 to find out where to collect it.

Dangers & Annoyances Contrary to popular opinion, Palermo is not a hotbed of thievery, but you will have to watch your valuables, which may attract pickpockets and bag snatchers. The historical centre can be a little dodgy at night, especially for women walking alone. Travellers might also wish to avoid walking alone in the area northeast of the station, between Via Roma and the port (although there is safety in numbers).

Things to See
The intersection of Via Vittorio Emanuele and Via Maqueda marks the **Quattro Canti** (four corners of historical Palermo). The four 17th-century Spanish baroque facades are each decorated with a statue. Nearby Piazza Pretoria has **Fontana Pretoria**, a beautiful fountain created by Florentine sculptors in the 16th century and once known as the Fountain of Shame because of its nude figures. Also in the piazza are the baroque **Chiesa di Santa Caterina** and the **Palazzo**

del **Municipio** (town hall). Just off this piazza is Piazza Bellini and Palermo's famous
church, **La Martorana** (☎ 091 616 1692; admission free; open 8am-1pm & 3.30-5.30pm
Mon-Sat), with a beautiful Arab-Norman bell
tower and Byzantine mosaics inside. Next to
it is the Norman **Chiesa di San Cataldo** (admission free; open 9am-3.30pm Mon-Fri,
9am-1pm Sat & Sun), which mixes Arab and
Norman styles. It's easily recognisable by its
red domes, although the interior is very plain.

The huge **cattedrale** (☎ 091 33 43 76;
Corso Vittorio Emanuele; admission free;
open 7am-7pm Mon-Sat, 8am-1.30pm &
4pm-7pm Sun), although modified many
times over the centuries, retains some vestiges of Norman architecture. At Piazza Indipendenza is **Palazzo Reale**, also known as
the Palazzo dei Normanni, now the seat of the
government. Step inside to see the **Cappella
Palatina** (☎ 091 705 48 79; admission free;
open 9am-11.45am & 3pm-4.45pm Mon-
Fri, 9am-11.45am Sat, 9am-9.45am & noon-
12.45pm Sun), a truly jaw-dropping example
of Arab-Norman architecture, built during the
reign of Roger II and lavishly decorated with
Byzantine mosaics. King Roger's former
bedroom, **Sala di Ruggero** (☎ 091 705 70
03; admission free; open 9am-noon Mon, Fri
& Sat), is decorated with 12th-century mosaics. It is possible to visit the room only with
a guide (free). Go upstairs from the Cappella
Palatina.

Don't forget to take bus No 389 from Piazza Indipendenza to the nearby town of
Monreale to see the magnificent mosaics
in the world-famous 12th-century **Duomo**
(☎ 091 640 44 13; admission free; open 8am-
6pm daily), plus its **cloisters** (admission
€4.50; open 9am-7pm Mon-Sat).

Places to Stay
The best camping ground is **Trinacria** (☎/fax
091 53 05 90; Via Barcarello 25; per per-
son/camp site per night €4.10/7.5), at Sfer-
racavallo by the sea. Catch bus No 628 from
Piazzale Alcide de Gasperi, which can be
reached by bus No 101 or 107 from the station.

Casa Marconi (☎ 091 645 11 16, fax 091
657 03 10; e casamarconi@iol.it; Via Mon-
fenera 140; singles & doubles with bath €26
per person) offers cheap, good-quality rooms.
To get there, take bus No 246 from the station.
Get off at Piazza Montegrappa; the hostel is a
short walk from there.

Near the train station, the basic, anecdote-
inducing **Albergo Orientale** (☎ 091 616 57
27; Via Maqueda 26; singles/doubles without bath €21/31), has a decaying palazzo
courtyard entrance and no heating in winter.
Lifestyles of the Rich & Famous it ain't, but
it's cheap and close to the action. Around the
corner is sweet and spotless **Albergo Rosalia
Conca d'Oro** (☎ 091 616 45 43; Via Santa
Rosalia 7; singles/doubles without bath €27/
40), which is a tad more upmarket.

Hotel Sicilia (☎/fax 091 616 84 60; Via
Divisi 99; singles/doubles with bath €39/
62), on the corner of Via Maqueda, has
decent rooms and friendly management,
although it can get noisy.

Hotel Florio (☎/fax 091 609 08 52; Via
Principe di Belmonte 33; singles/doubles
with bath €45/65) is a new and appealing addition to Palermo's accommodation options,
and it's in a nice part of town, too.

Places to Eat
A popular Palermitan dish is pasta con le
sarde (pasta with sardines, fennel, peppers,
capers and pine nuts). Locals are late eaters
and restaurants rarely open for dinner before
8.30pm.

Osteria Lo Bianco (Via E Amari 104; meal
about €12), at the Castelnuovo end of town,
serves tasty staples amid bright lights, wood
panelling, plastic and warm smiles. The
wonderful **Trattoria Stella** (Via Alloro 104) is
in the La Kalsa quarter. Try the pesce spada
(swordfish) and listen to the lilting Arabic-
influenced songs coming out of the kitchen.
Hostaria da Ciccio (Via Firenze 6; meal
about €16) is worth trying, although it can
seem a little quiet.

Palermo has numerous open-air markets,
but the best two are the **Vucciria** held in the
narrow streets between Via Roma, Piazza
San Domenico and Via Vittoria Emanuele
Monday to Saturday, and **Il Ballaro**, held in
the Albergheria quarter, off Via Maqueda.
There's a wealth of fruit and vegetables,
seafood and dairy to choose from, and the
atmosphere is unbeatable.

Getting There & Away
Air The Falcone–Borsellino airport at Punta
Raisi, 32km west of Palermo, serves as a terminal for domestic and European flights. For
information on domestic and international
flights, ring **Alitalia** (☎ 848 96 56 43).

Bus The main (intercity) terminal for destinations throughout Sicily and the mainland is in the area around Via Paolo Balsamo, to the right (east) as you leave the station. Offices for the various companies are all in this area, including **SAIS Trasporti** (☎ 091 616 11 41; Via Balsamo 16), **SAIS Autolinee** (☎ 091 616 60 28; Via Balsamo 18) and **Segesta** (☎ 091 616 90 39; Via Balsamo 26).

Train Regular trains leave from the Stazione Centrale for Milazzo, Messina, Catania, Syracuse and Agrigento as well as for nearby towns such as Cefalú. Direct trains go to Reggio di Calabria, Naples and Rome.

Boat The **Tirrenia office** (☎ 091 602 11 11) is at the port. Boats leave from the port (Molo Vittorio Veneto) for Sardinia and the mainland (see the introductory Sicily Getting There & Away section).

Getting Around

Taxis to the airport cost upwards of €38. The cheaper option is to catch one of the regular blue Prestia e Comande buses, which leave from outside the station roughly every 45 minutes from 5am to 10.45pm. The trip takes one hour and costs €4.65. There's also a train service from the airport to Stazione Centrale between 5.40am and 10.40pm (€4.13). Most of Palermo's buses stop outside or near the train station. Bus No 101 or 107 runs along Via Roma from the train station to near Piazza Castelnuovo in a loop. Bus No 139 goes from the station past the port. You must buy tickets before you get on the bus; they cost €0.77 (for 1½ hours) or €2.58 (24 hours).

AEOLIAN ISLANDS

Also known as the Lipari Islands, the seven islands of this archipelago just north of Milazzo are volcanic in origin. They range from the well-developed tourist resort of Lipari and the understated jet-set haunt of Panarea, to the rugged Vulcano, the spectacular scenery of Stromboli (and its fiercely active volcano), the fertile vineyards of Salina, and the solitude of Alicudi and Filicudi, which remain relatively undeveloped. The islands have been inhabited since the Neolithic era, when migrants sought the valuable volcanic glass, obsidian. The Isole Eolie (Aeolian Islands) are so named because the ancient Greeks believed they were the home of Aeolus, the god of wind. Homer wrote of them in the *Odyssey*.

Information

The main **AAST tourist information office** (☎ 090 988 00 95; Via Vittorio Emanuele 202; open 8am-2pm Mon-Sat & 4.30pm-7.30pm Mon-Fri) for the islands is on Lipari. Other offices are open on Vulcano, Salina and Stromboli during summer.

Things to See & Do

On **Lipari** visit the **castello** (citadel; admission €4.50; open 9am-1.30pm & 3pm-7pm Mon-Sat), with its archaeological park and museum. You can also go on excellent walks on the island. Catch a local bus from Lipari town to the hill-top village of Quattrocchi for a great view of Vulcano. The tourist office has information on boat trips and excursions to the other islands.

Vulcano, with its pungent sulphurous odour (you get used to it), is a short boat trip from Lipari. The main volcano, Vulcano Fossa, is still active, although the last recorded period of eruption was 1888–90. You can make the one-hour hike to the crater, or take a bath in the therapeutic hot muds.

Stromboli is the most spectacular of the islands. Climb the volcano (924m) at night to see the Sciara del Fuoco (Trail of Fire) – lava streaming down the side of the volcano, and the volcanic explosions from the crater. Many people make the trip (four to five hours) without a guide during the day, but at night you should go with a guided group. Contact **AGAI** (☎ 090 98 62 11; Piazza San Vincenzo), to organise a guide (they only depart if groups are large enough) or the privately owned **Strómbolania information office** (☎ 090 98 63 90; open 9am-noon & 3pm-8pm Easter-Sept) under the Ossidiana Hotel at Scari port, which can help organise climbs, plus other island tours.

Places to Stay & Eat

Camping facilities are available on Salina and Vulcano. Most accommodation in summer is booked out well in advance on the smaller islands, particularly on Stromboli, and many places close during winter.

Lipari The best place to go for accommodation is Lipari, which has numerous budget hotels, *affittacamere* (private room rentals) and apartments. From here the other islands are easily accessible by regular hydrofoil. Accommodation touts at Lipari port are worth checking because offers are usually genuine. The island's camping ground, **Baia Unci** (☎ 090 981 19 09; e baiaunci@tin.it; €7.75/14 per person/camp site), is at Canneto, about 3km out of Lipari town.

Diana Brown (☎ 090 981 25 84, fax 090 981 32 13; e dbrown@netnet.it; Vico Himera 3; singles/doubles with bath €62/68) has great well-appointed rooms with a homy feel. She can also arrange excursions around the islands.

Da Bartolo (☎ 090 981 17 00; Via Garibaldi 53; meal about €25) is a good choice for seafood and pasta dishes. At **Nenzyna** (Via Roma 2; meal about €20) you'll find a tiny, aqua-coloured dining area where your seafood desires will be more than satisfied.

Stromboli Popular **Casa del Sole** (☎ 090 98 60 17; Via Soldato Cincotta; singles/doubles without bath €21/42), on the road to the volcano, has decent rooms and a good kitchen.

In splurge territory is **La Sirenetta** (☎ 090 98 60 25, fax 98 61 24; e lasirenetta@ netnet.it; Via Marina 33; singles/doubles with bath €99/212, half-board €132), perfectly located at Ficogrande in front of **Strómbolicchio**, a towering rock rising out of the sea at San Vincenzo. The hotel has a panoramic terrace with a great restaurant.

Vulcano For a pleasant pensione try **Pensione La Giara** (☎ 090 985 22 29; Via Provinciale 18; B&B €58 per person with bath; closed late Oct–early Apr), which has good rooms and staggering discounts outside of August.

Alicudi & Filicudi If you want seclusion, head for Alicudi or Filicudi. The former offers **Ericusa** (☎ 090 988 99 02, fax 090 988 96 71; Via Regina Elena; doubles €62, half-board €60 per person) while Filicudi has the truly delightful **La Canna** (☎ 090 988 99 56, fax 090 988 99 66; e vianast@tin.it; Via Rosa 43; singles/doubles with bath €39/78; half-board €68 per person). There are restaurants at both these hotels.

Getting There & Away
Ferries and hydrofoils leave for the islands from Milazzo (easily reached by train from Palermo and Messina) and all ticket offices are along Corso dei Mille at the port. SNAV runs hydrofoils (€10 one way). Siremar also has hydrofoils, but its ferries are half the price. If arriving at Milazzo by train, you will need to catch a bus to the port. Giunta buses from Milazzo stop at the port. SNAV also runs hydrofoils between the islands and Palermo (summer only).

You can travel directly to the islands from the mainland. Siremar runs regular ferries from Naples, and SNAV runs hydrofoils from Naples (see the Naples Getting There & Away section, earlier in this chapter), Messina and Reggio di Calabria. Occasionally the sea around the islands can be rough and sailings are cancelled, especially in winter.

Getting Around
Regular hydrofoil and ferry services operate between the islands. Both Siremar and SNAV have booths at Lipari's port, where you can get full timetable information.

TAORMINA
postcode 98039 • pop 10,700
Spectacularly located on a hill overlooking the sea and Mt Etna, Taormina was long ago discovered by the European jet set, which has made it one of the more expensive and touristy towns in Sicily. Its magnificent setting, its Greek theatre and the nearby beaches remain as seductive now as they were for the likes of Goethe and DH Lawrence. The **AAST tourist office** (☎ 0942 2 32 43; w www.taormina-ol .it; open 9am-2pm & 4pm-7pm Mon-Sat) in Palazzo Corvaja, just off Corso Umberto, has extensive information on the town.

Things to See & Do
The **Greek theatre** (admission €4.50; open 9am-6.30pm daily) was built in the 3rd century BC and later greatly expanded and remodelled by the Romans. Concerts, theatre and festivals are staged here in summer and there are wonderful views of Mt Etna. From the beautiful **Villa Comunale** (also known as Trevelyan Gardens) there's a panoramic view of the sea. Along Corso Umberto is the **Duomo**, with a Gothic facade. The postcard-perfect local beach is **Isola Bella**, accessible by funivia (cable car), which costs €2.70 return.

Trips to Mt Etna can be organised through **CST** (☎ 0942 262 60 88; Corso Umberto 101).

Places to Stay & Eat

Bare-bones style **Campeggio San Leo** (☎ 0942 2 46 58; Via Nazionale; €4.20/14.50 per person/camp site per night) is accessible from the train station by the bus to Taormina – ask the driver to drop you off.

The tourist office has a list of affittacamere in Taormina. **Odyssey Youth Hostel B&B** (☎ 0942 2 45 33, fax 0942 2 32 11; w www.taorminaodyssey.it; Via G Martino 2; dorm bed €15.50) is a friendly, small place, with pleasant rooms. To get here, follow the signs from Porta Messina along Via Cappuccini and head down Via Fontana Vecchia (about 10 minutes).

The HI **Ostello della Gioventu 'Ulisse'** (☎ 0942 2 31 93; Vicolo San Francesco di Paola 9; dorm bed €14.50) is reasonable enough, although restrictions on kitchen use and hot water plus a daytime lockout and curfew make it a bit of a pain, but rates include breakfast.

Pensione Svizzera (☎ 0942 2 37 90; e svizzera@tao.it; Via Pirandello 26; singles/doubles/triples/quads with bath €52/72/108/120), on the way from the bus stop to the town centre, is a delightful place to treat yourself (or someone else).

Gambero Rosso (Via Naumachie 11; pizza €4.65-8) has smart service and nice outdoor seating. **Mamma Rosa** (Via Naumachie 10; pizza €5.20-7.20) has standard dishes and expensive seafood, but then again, eating in Taormina is rarely cheap! For a good, stiff drink **Arco Rosso** (Via Naumachie 7) can't be beaten.

There's a **Standa supermarket** (Via Apollo Arcagetta 19), near the Ulisse hostel and Porta Catania.

Getting There & Away

Bus is the easiest way to get to Taormina. SAIS buses leave from Messina, Catania and also from the airport at Catania. Taormina is on the main train line between Messina and Catania, but the station is on the coast and regular buses will take you to Via Pirandello, near the centre; services are reduced on Sunday.

MT ETNA

Dominating the landscape in eastern Sicily between Taormina and Catania, Mt Etna (3330m) is Europe's largest live volcano. It has four live craters at its summit and its slopes are littered with crevices and extinct cones. Eruptions of slow lava flows can occur, but are not really dangerous. Etna's most recent eruption was in 2001, which destroyed large parts of its surroundings. You can climb to the summit (about a seven-hour hike), but the handiest way is to take the 4WD minibus with **SITAS** (☎ 095 91 11 58) from the Rifugio Sapienza (the south side), or with **Le Betulle/STAR** (☎ 095 64 34 30) from Piano Provenzana (the north side). Both companies charge €38.

Mt Etna is best approached from Catania by **AST bus** (☎ 095 746 10 96), which departs from Via L Sturzo (in front of the train station) at about 8am, leaving from Rifugio Sapienza at about 4.45pm (€4.65 return). The private **Circumetnea train line** (☎ 095 54 12 50) circles Mt Etna from Catania to Giarre-Riposto. It starts from Catania just near Stazione Borgo, Via Caronda 352a (take a metro train from Catania's main train station, or any bus going up Via Etnea and get off at the metro stop named 'Borgo'). From Taormina, you can take an FS train to Giarre, where you can catch the Circumetnea.

In Catania, **Natura e Turismo** (NeT; ☎ 095 33 35 43; e natetur@tin.it; Via Quartararo 11) organises tours of the volcano with a volcanologist or expert guide.

A handy accommodation option in Catania is **Agora Hostel** (☎ 095 723 30 10; e agorahostel@hotmail.com; Piazza Curro 6; dorm bed €15.50, doubles without bath €48), which has regular parties and is close to La Pescheria market, making it good for self-caterers. The cheap dinners here get good reviews.

SYRACUSE

postcode 96100 • pop 125,700

Once a powerful Greek city to rival Athens, Syracuse (Siracusa) is one of the highlights of a visit to Sicily. Founded in 743 BC by colonists from Corinth, it became a dominant sea power in the Mediterranean, prompting Athens to attack the city in 413 BC. Syracuse was the birthplace of the Greek mathematician and physicist Archimedes, and Plato attended the court of the tyrant Dionysius, who ruled from 405 to 367 BC.

Orientation & Information

The main sights are in two areas: on the island of Ortygia and at the archaeological park 2km across town. There are two tourist information

ITALY

offices: an **AAT** (☎ 0931 46 42 55; Via Maestranza 33; open 8.30am-1.30pm & 2pm-5pm Mon-Fri, 8.30am-1.30pm Sat) on Ortygia, and an **APT** (☎ 0931 6 77 10; Via San Sebastiano 45; open 8.30am-1.30pm & 2pm-5pm Mon-Fri, 8.30am-1.30pm Sat).

Ortygia
The island of Ortygia has eye-catching baroque palaces and churches. The **Duomo** was built in the 7th century on top of the Temple of Athena, incorporating most of the original columns in its three-aisled structure. The splendid **Piazza del Duomo** is lined with baroque palaces. Walk down Via Picherali to the waterfront and the **Fonte Aretusa** (Fountain of Arethusa), a natural freshwater spring. According to Greek legend, the nymph Arethusa, pursued by the river-god Alpheus, was turned into a fountain by the goddess Diana. Undeterred, Alpheus turned himself into the river that feeds the spring.

Neapolis-Parco Archeologico
To get to this archaeological zone (☎ 0931 6 62 06; admission €4.50; open 9am-1hr before sunset daily), catch bus No 1 or 2 from Riva della Posta on Ortygia. The main attraction here is the 5th-century BC **Greek theatre**, its seating area carved out of solid rock. Nearby is the **Orecchio di Dionisio**, an artificial grotto in the shape of an ear that the tyrant of Syracuse, Dionysius, used as a prison. The impressive 2nd-century **Roman amphitheatre** is well preserved.

The excellent **Museo Archeologico Paolo Orsi** (☎ 0931 46 40 22; admission €4.50; open 9am-1pm Tues-Sat), about 500m east of the archaeological zone, off Viale Teocrito, contains Sicily's best-organised and most interesting archaeological collection.

Places to Stay
Camping facilities are at **Agriturist Rinaura** (☎ 0931 72 12 24; €5/4 per person/camp site), about 4km from the city on the SS115, near the sea. Catch bus No 21 or 22 from Corso Umberto.

Fancy **Hotel Gran Bretagna** (☎ 0931 6 87 65, fax 0931 46 21 69; Via Savoia 21; singles/doubles/triples/quads with bath €69/96/120/140), just off Largo XXV Luglio on Ortygia, has lovely rooms.

Hotel Aretusa (☎/fax 0931 2 42 11; Via Francesco Crispi 75; singles/doubles without bath €27/42, with bath 32/48) is close to the train station and has clean, albeit spartan, rooms.

Hotel Milano (☎ 0931 6 69 81; Corso Umberto 10; singles/doubles without bath €19/37, with bath €37/66) has a little more on offer, such as TV and fridge, and is closer to Ortygia.

Places to Eat
Ortygia is the best area for eating in Syracuse. Try **Pizzeria Nonna Margherita** (☎ 0931 6 53 64; Via Cavour 12; pizza €2.60-11.40), a casual place with great pizza – from simple, tasty Neapolitan to more elaborate affairs.

At **Pasticceria Tipica Catanese** (Corso Umberto 46) you can try scrumptious Sicilian sweets while planning your next trip to the dentist.

There is an open-air, fresh-produce **market** in the streets behind Riva della Poata, until 1pm Monday to Saturday. There are **alimentari** and **supermarkets** along Corso Gelone.

Getting There & Away
Interbus (☎ 0931 6 67 10) buses leave from near the office at Via Trieste 28 (just behind Riva della Posta) for Catania, Palermo, Enna and surrounding towns. The service for Rome also leaves from here, connecting with the Rome bus at Catania. **AST** (☎ 0931 4 62 71) buses service the town and the surrounding area from Riva della Posta. Syracuse is easy to reach by train from Messina and Catania.

AGRIGENTO
postcode 92100 • pop 55,500
Founded in approximately 582 BC as the Greek Akragas, Agrigento is today a pleasant medieval town, but the Greek temples in the valley below are the real reason to visit. The Italian novelist and dramatist Luigi Pirandello (1867–1936) was born here, as was the Greek philosopher and scientist Empedocles (c. 490–430 BC).

There's an **AAST tourist office** (☎ 0922 2 04 54; Via Cesare Battisti 15; open 9am-2pm Mon-Fri).

Things to See & Do
Agrigento's **Valley of the Temples** (admission €4.50, with museum €6; Collina dei Templi open 8.30am-9pm, Tempio di Giove area open 8.30am-6.30pm) is one of the major Greek archaeological sights in the

world. Its five main Doric temples were constructed in the 5th century BC and are in various states of ruin because of earthquakes and vandalism by early Christians. In an area known as the 'Collina dei Templi', you'll find the only temple to survive relatively intact – the **Tempio della Concordia**, which was transformed into a Christian church. The **Tempio di Giunone**, a short walk uphill to the east, has an impressive sacrificial altar.

The **Tempio di Ercole** is the oldest of the structures. Across the main road which divides the valley is the massive **Tempio di Giove**, one of the most imposing buildings of ancient Greece. Although now completely in ruins, it used to cover an area measuring 112m by 56m, with columns that were 18m high. **Telamoni**, colossal statues of men, were also used in the structure. The remains of one of them are in the fine **Museo Archeologico** *(admission €4.50, with temples €6; open 9am-1.30pm & 2pm-7.30pm Tues-Sat, 9am-1.30pm Sun & Mon)*, just north of the temples on Via dei Templi. Close by is the **Tempio di Castore e Polluce**, which was partly reconstructed in the 19th century. The temples are lit up at night. To get to the temples from the town, catch bus No 1, 2 or 3 from the train station.

Places to Stay & Eat

The friendly **Bella Napoli** *(☎ 0922 2 04 35; Piazza Lena 6; singles/doubles/triples with bath €22/54/75)*, off Via Bac Bac at the end of Via Atenea, has clean, comfortable rooms. Good simple food can be had at **La Forchetta** *(Piazza San Francesco 9; meal about €13)*.

Getting There & Away

Intercity buses leave from Piazza Rosselli, just off Piazza Vittorio Emanuele, for Palermo, Catania and surrounding towns.

Sardinia

The second-largest island in the Mediterranean, Sardinia (Sardegna) was colonised by the Phoenicians and Romans, followed by the Pisans, Genoese and last but not least, the Spaniards. It is often said that the Sardinians (known on the island as Sardi) were never really conquered – they simply retreated into the hills. Despite this, their hospitality is noticeable.

The landscape of the island ranges from the 'savage, dark-bushed, sky-exposed land' described by DH Lawrence, to the beautiful gorges and valleys near Dorgali and the unspoiled coastline between Bosa and Alghero. Try to avoid the island in August, when the weather is hot and there are too many tourists.

Getting There & Away

Air There are airports at Cagliari, Olbia, Alghero and Arbatax–Tortoli which link Sardinia with major Italian and European cities. For information contact Alitalia or the Sestante CIT, or CTS offices in all major towns.

Boat The island is accessible by ferry from Genoa, Livorno, Fiumicino, Civitavecchia, Naples, Palermo, Trapani, Bonifacio (Corsica) and Tunis. The departure points in Sardinia are Olbia, Golfo Aranci and Porto Torres in the north, Arbatax on the east coast and Cagliari in the south.

The main company, Tirrenia, runs a service between Civitavecchia and Olbia, Arbatax or Cagliari, and between Genoa and Porto Torres, Olbia, Arbatax or Cagliari. There are fast ferries between Fiumicino and Golfo Aranci/Arbatax and Civitavecchia and Olbia (both summer only). The national railway, Ferrovie dello Stato (FS), also runs a service between Civitavecchia and Golfo Aranci. **Moby Lines** (Ⓦ *www.mobylines.it, Italian only)* and **Sardinia Ferries** (Ⓦ *www .sardiniaferries.com)*, which is also known as Elba and Corsica Ferries, both operate services from the mainland to Sardinia, as well as to Corsica and Elba. They depart from Genoa, Livorno, Civitavecchia and arrive at Olbia, Cagliari or Golfo Aranci. **Grandi Navi Veloci** (Ⓦ *www.gnv.it)* runs a service between Genoa and Olbia (from June to September) or Porto Torres (year-round). Most travel agencies in Italy have brochures on the various companies' services.

Timetables change and prices fluctuate with the season. Prices for a poltrona on Tirrenia ferries in the 2002 high season were: Genoa to Cagliari (€54, 20 hours); Genoa to Porto Torres or Olbia (€46, 13 hours); Naples to Cagliari (€41, 16¼ hours); Palermo to Cagliari (€39, 13½ hours); Civitavecchia to Olbia, (€25, eight hours); and Civitavecchia to Cagliari (€41, 14½ hours). The cost of taking a small car from Civitavecchia to Cagliari in the high season was €78. A motorcycle (over 200cc) costs €40 year-round for the same trip.

Getting Around

Bus The two main bus companies are the state-run ARST, which operates extensive services throughout the island, and privately owned PANI, which links main towns.

Train The main FS train lines link Cagliari with Oristano, Sassari and Olbia. The private railways that link smaller towns throughout the island can be *very* slow. However, the *Trenino Verde* (little green train), which runs from Cagliari to Arbatax through the Barbagia, is a very relaxing and lovely way to see part of the interior (see Getting There & Away under Cagliari, later in this chapter).

Car & Motorcycle The best way to explore Sardinia properly is by road. Rental agencies are listed under Cagliari and some other towns around the island.

Hitching Away from the main towns, hitchhiking can be laborious because of light traffic. Women definitely should not hitchhike alone in Sardinia.

CAGLIARI
postcode 09100 • pop 163,000
This attractive, friendly city offers a beautifully preserved medieval section, the delightful beach of Poetto, and salt lakes with a population of pink flamingoes.

Orientation
If you arrive by bus, train or boat, you will find yourself at the port area of Cagliari. The main street along the harbour is Via Roma, and the old city stretches up the hill behind it to the castle. Most of the budget hotels and restaurants are in the area near the port, normally not a great place in most cities, but perfectly safe and pleasant here.

Information
Tourist Offices There is an **AAST** information office (☎ 070 66 92 55; Piazza Matteotti 9; open 8.30am-7.30pm Mon-Fri & 8.30am-1.30pm Sat). There are also information offices at the airport and in the Stazione Marittima.

The **Ente Sardo Industrie Turistiche office** (ESIT; ☎ 070 6 02 31, 800 01 31 53; Via Goffredo Mameli 97; open 9am-6pm Mon-Sat) has information on the whole island.

Post & Communications The main post office (☎ 070 6 03 11; Piazza del Carmine 27) is up Via La Maddalena from Via Roma. The **Telecom office** (Via G M Angioj 6) is north of Piazza Matteotti. You can use the Internet at **Web Travel Point** (☎ 070 65 93 07; Via Maddalena 34) for €2.60 for 30 minutes.

Laundry There's a **coin-operated laundry** (Corso Vittorio Emanuele 232; open 9am-9pm) that costs €3 per 7kg load (extra for drying).

Medical & Emergency Services For medical attention go to the **Ospedale San Giovanni di Dio** (☎ 070 66 32 37; Via Ospedale). For police help, go to the **questura** (police headquarters; ☎ 070 6 02 71; Via Amat 9).

Things to See
The **Museo Archeologico Nazionale** (☎ 070 65 59 11; Piazza Arsenale; admission €4; open 9am-8pm Tues-Sun), in the Citadella dei Musei, has a fascinating collection of Nuraghic bronzes. These bronzes are objects found in stone constructions all over Sardinia (there are about 7000), a legacy of the island's native culture.

It's enjoyable to wander through the medieval quarter. The Pisan-Romanesque **Duomo** (☎ 070 66 38 37; Piazza Palazzo) was built in the 13th century and has an interesting Romanesque pulpit.

There are good sea and city views from **Bastione di San Remy** in Piazza Costituzione, in the town's centre. It once formed part of the fortifications of the old city.

The Pisan **Torre di San Pancrazio** (Piazza Indipendenza; open 9am-5pm Tues-Sun) is also worth a look. The **Roman amphitheatre** (Viale Buon Cammino; open 9am-5pm Tues-Sun) is considered the most important Roman monument in Sardinia. During summer opera is performed here.

A day on the **Spiaggia di Poetto**, east of the centre is well-spent and you can wander across to the salt lakes to see the flamingoes.

Special Events
The Festival of Sant'Efisio, a colourful festival mixing the secular and the religious, is held annually for four days from 1 May.

ITALY

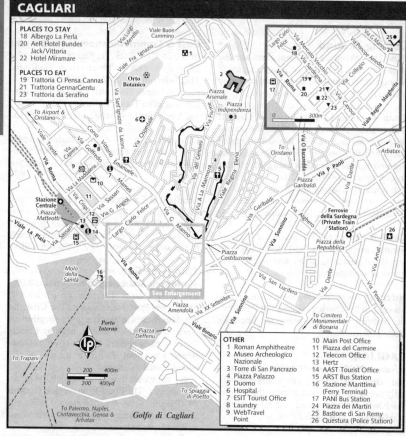

CAGLIARI

PLACES TO STAY
18 Albergo La Perla
20 AeR Hotel Bundes
   Jack/Vittoria
22 Hotel Miramare

PLACES TO EAT
19 Trattoria Ci Pensa Cannas
21 Trattoria GennarGentu
23 Trattoria da Serafino

OTHER
1 Roman Amphitheatre
2 Museo Archeologico
   Nazionale
3 Torre di San Pancrazio
4 Piazza Palazzo
5 Duomo
6 Hospital
7 ESIT Tourist Office
8 Laundry
9 WebTravel
   Point
10 Main Post Office
11 Piazza del Carmine
12 Telecom Office
13 Hertz
14 AAST Tourist Office
15 ARST Bus Station
16 Stazione Marittima
   (Ferry Terminal)
17 PANI Bus Station
24 Piazza dei Martiri
25 Bastione di San Remy
26 Questura (Police Station)

Places to Stay & Eat

There are numerous hotels near the port. Worth a stay is **AeR Hotel Bundes Jack/Vittoria** (☎/fax 070 66 79 70; Via Roma 75; singles/doubles with bath €43/63), with lovely, spotless rooms and a warm welcome. **Hotel Miramare** (☎/fax 070 66 40 21; Via Roma 59; singles/doubles without bath €32/42, with bath €37/47) has OK rooms. **Albergo La Perla** (☎ 070 66 94 46; Via Sardegna 18; singles/doubles/triples without bath €30/39/53) has a few different retro decorating styles in evidence, but it's decent.

Reasonably priced trattorias can be found in the area behind Via Roma, particularly around Via Sardegna and Via Cavour. **Trattoria da Serafino** (Via Lepanto 6; meal about €12), on the corner of Via Sardegna, has very good food at excellent prices. **Trattoria GennarGentu** (☎ 070 67 20 21; Via Sardegna 60; meal about €13) is a friendly place. Try the spaghetti bottarga (spaghetti with dried tuna roe) for a true Sardinian flavour. **Trattoria Ci Pensa Cannas** (Via Sardegna 37; meal about €12) is cheap and cheerful. Via Sardegna also has **grocery shops** and **bakeries**.

Getting There & Away

Air Some 8km northwest of the city at Elmas is **Cagliari's airport**. ARST buses leave regularly from Piazza Matteotti to coincide with flight arrivals and departures. The **Alitalia office** (☎ 070 24 00 79, 147 86 56 43) is at the airport.

Bus & Train Departing from Piazza Matteotti are **ARST buses** (☎ 070 409 83 24, 800 86 50 42) servicing nearby towns, the Costa del Sud and the Costa Rei. **PANI buses** (☎ 070 65 23 26) leave from Stazione Marittima for towns such as Sassari, Oristano and Nuoro. The main train station is also in Piazza Matteotti. Regular trains leave for Oristano, Sassari, Porto Torres and Olbia. The private **Ferrovie della Sardegna** (FdS; ☎ 070 49 13 04) train station is in Piazza della Repubblica. For information about the *Trenino Verde* which runs along a scenic route between Cagliari and Arbatax, contact ESIT (see Tourist Offices under Information earlier in this section), or the FdS directly (☎ 58 02 46). The most interesting and picturesque section of the route is between Mandas and Arbatax.

Boat Ferries arrive at the port adjacent to Via Roma. Bookings for Tirrenia can be made at the Stazione Marittima in the port area (☎ 070 66 60 65). See the introductory Sardinia Getting There & Away section for more details.

Car & Motorcycle For rental cars or motorcycles try **Hertz** (☎ 070 66 81 05; Piazza Matteotti 1), which also has a branch at the airport; or **Autonoleggio Cara** (☎ 070 66 34 71), which can deliver your scooter or bike to your hotel.

CALA GONONE
postcode 08022 • pop 1000

This attractive seaside resort is an excellent base from which to explore the coves along the eastern coastline, as well as the Nuraghic sites and rugged terrain inland. Major points are accessible by bus and boat, but you'll need a car to explore.

Information
There is a **Pro Loco office** (☎ 0784 9 36 96; Viale del Blu Marino) where you can pick up maps, a list of hotels and information (generally from May to September). There is also a good **tourist office** (☎ 0784 9 62 43; Via Lamarmora 181; open 9am-1pm & 3.30pm-7pm Mon-Fri). Also in Dorgali, **Coop Ghivine** (☎/fax 0784 9 67 21; w www.ghivine.com; Via Montebello 5) organises excellent guided treks in the region from €30 per person.

Things to See & Do
From Cala Gonone's tiny port, catch a boat (€7) to the **Grotta del Bue Marino** (admission €5.50), where a guide will take you on a 1km walk to see vast caves with stalagmites, stalactites and lakes. Sardinia's last colony of monk seals once lived here, but have not been sighted in years. Boats also leave for **Cala Luna**, an isolated beach where you can spend the day by the sea or take a walk along the fabulous gorge called **Codula di Luna**. However, the beach is packed with day-tripping tourists in summer. The boat trip to visit the grotto and beach costs around €18.

A **walking track** along the coast links Cala Fuili, about 3.5km south of Cala Gonone, and Cala Luna (about two hours, one way).

If you want to descend the impressive **Gorropu Gorge**, ask for information from the team of expert guides based in Urzulei – **Societá Gorropu** (☎ 0782 64 92 82, 0347 775 27 06; e francescomurru@virgilio.it). They also offer a wide range of guided walks in the area at competitive prices. It is necessary to use ropes and harnesses to traverse the Gorropu Gorge; however, when it doesn't rain too much, it is possible to walk for about 1km into the gorge from its northern entrance.

Places to Stay
Camping Gala Gonone (☎ 0784 9 31 65, fax 0784 9 32 55; w www.campingcalagonone .it; Via Collodi; camp sites per person €15, 4-bed bungalows €110; open Apr-Oct) has good-quality camping facilities, including a pool and restaurant.

Hotels include the attractive **Piccolo Hotel** (☎ 0784 9 32 32; Via Cristoforo Colombo 32; singles/doubles with bath €32/53) near the port, and **Pop Hotel** (☎ 0784 9 31 85, fax 0784 9 31 58; e lfancel@box1.tin.it; singles/doubles with bath €57/93), which is right on the water and has a restaurant.

Getting There & Away
Catch a PANI bus to Nuoro from Cagliari, Sassari or Oristano and then take an ARST bus to Cala Gonone (via Dorgali). If you are travelling by car, you will need a proper road map of the area.

ALGHERO
postcode 07041 • pop 40,600

A highly popular tourist resort, Alghero is on the island's west coast, an area known as the

Coral Riviera. The town is a good base from which to explore the magnificent coastline linking it to Bosa in the south, and the famous Grotte di Nettuno (Neptune's Caves) on the Capocaccia to the north. The best time to visit is in spring or autumn, when the hordes are yet to arrive, or have long gone.

Orientation & Information

The **train station** (*Via Don Minzoni*), is some distance from the centre, and is connected by a regular bus service to the centre of town.

The very helpful **AAST tourist office** (☎ 079 97 90 54; *Piazza Porta Terra 9; open 8am-8pm Mon-Sat*) is near the port and just across the gardens from the bus station. The old city and most hotels and restaurants are in the area west of the tourist office.

There is a **main post office** (*Via XX Settembre 108*). There is a bank of **public telephones** (*Via Vittorio Emanuele*) at the opposite end of the gardens from the tourist office.

In an emergency ring the police on ☎ 113; for medical attention ring ☎ 079 98 71 61, or go to the **Ospedale Civile** (☎ 079 99 62 33; *Via Don Minzoni*).

Things to See & Do

The narrow streets of the old city and around the port are worth exploring. The most interesting church here is the **Chiesa di San Francesco** (*Via Carlo Alberto; open 9am-noon & 4pm-7pm daily*). The city's **cathedral** has been ruined by constant remodelling, but its bell tower remains a fine example of Gothic-Catalan architecture.

Near Alghero at the beautiful **Capocaccia** are the **Grotte di Nettuno**, accessible by boat (€10, hourly 8am to 7pm June to September, four daily April to May and October) from the port, or three times a day by the FS bus from Via Catalogna (€3.25 return, 50 minutes, 1 June to 30 September).

If you have your own transport, don't miss the **Nuraghe di Palmavera** (☎ 079 95 32 00; *admission €2.05*), about 10km out of Alghero on the road to Porto Conte. The site features a ruined palace dating from around 1100 BC and about four dozen huts.

The coastline between Alghero and Bosa is picturesque. Rugged cliffs fall down to solitary beaches, and near **Bosa** is one of the last habitats of the griffon vulture. The best way to see the coast is by car or motorcycle. If you want to rent a bicycle (from €9 per day) or motorcycle (from €70) to explore the coast, try **Cicloexpress** (☎ 079 98 69 50; *Via Garibaldi*) at the port.

Special Events

In summer Alghero stages the Estate Musicale Algherese (Alghero's Summer Music Festival) in the cloisters of the church of San Francesco, Via Carlo Alberto. A festival complete with fireworks display, is held on 15 August for the Feast of the Assumption.

Places to Stay & Eat

Finding a room in August without a reservation from months ago is a nightmare. At other times of the year you'll be fine. Camping facilities include **Calik** (☎/fax 079 93 01 11; ⊛ *www.campeggiocalik.it; open 1 Jun-30 Sept; camp site per person €12*) in Fertilia, which is about 6km out of town on the SS127bis. The HI **Ostello dei Giuliani** (☎/fax 079 93 03 53; ⓔ *ostellodeigiuliani@ticalinet.it; Via Zara 1; dorm bed €10; open year-round*) is also in Fertilia and is in good condition. Take the hourly bus 'AF' from Via Catalogna to Fertilia. Breakfast is included in the rates and a meal costs €7.75.

In the old town is the excellent **Hotel San Francesco** (☎/fax 079 98 03 30; ⓔ *hotsfran@tin.it; Via Ambrogio Machin 2; singles/doubles with bath €43/75*), with a charming cloistered courtyard shared with the church of the same name.

A popular eating choice is stone-ceilinged **Trattoria Il Vecchio Mulino** (☎ 079 97 72 54; *Via Don Deroma 7; meal about €12*), with a good range of pizza. For coffee, wine and cake, head to **Caffe Costantino** (*Piazza Civica 30*).

Getting There & Away

Alghero is accessible from Sassari by train or bus. The main bus station is on Via Catalogna, next to the public park. **ARST** (☎ 079 95 01 79) buses leave for Sassari and Porto Torres. **FdS buses** (☎ 079 95 04 58) also service Sassari, Macomer and Bosa. **PANI buses** (☎ 079 23 69 83) serve Cagliari, Nuoro and Macomer from Sassari.

Liechtenstein

Blink and you might miss Liechtenstein; the country measures just 25km from north to south and an average of 6km from west to east. In some ways you could be forgiven for mistaking it for a part of Switzerland. The Swiss franc is the legal currency, all travel documents valid for Switzerland are also valid for Liechtenstein, and the only border regulations are on the Austrian side. Switzerland also represents Liechtenstein abroad, subject to consultation.

But a closer look reveals that Liechtenstein is quite distinct from its neighbour. Ties with Switzerland began only in 1923 with the signing of a customs and monetary union. Before that, it had a similar agreement with Austria-Hungary. Although Liechtenstein shares the Swiss postal system, it issues its own postage stamps. Unlike Switzerland, Liechtenstein joined the United Nations (UN; 1990) and, in 1995, the European Economic Area (EEA). Despite going separate ways over the EEA issue, the open border between Liechtenstein and Switzerland remains intact. Liechtenstein has no plans to seek full EU membership.

Liechtenstein is a prosperous country, with a high standard of living and the wealthiest royal family in Europe. In 2000 its unemployment rate was a measly 1.1% – 290 people!

Facts about Liechtenstein

Liechtenstein was created by the merger of the domain of Schellenberg and the county of Vaduz in 1712 by the powerful Liechtenstein family. It was a principality under the Holy Roman Empire from 1719 to 1806 and, after a spell in the German Confederation, it achieved full sovereign independence in 1866. A modern constitution was drawn up in 1921, but even today the prince retains the power to dissolve parliament and must approve every act before it becomes law. Prince Franz Josef II was the first ruler to live in the castle above the capital city of Vaduz. He died in 1989 after a reign of 51 years, and was succeeded by his son, Prince Hans-Adam II, who has since clashed with the government over his proposed constitutional reforms that would limit government power.

At a Glance

- **Vaduz** – 400km-worth of hiking trails through stunning Alpine scenery
- Sending postcards home stamped by the country's postal service

Capital	Vaduz
Population	32,860
Official Language	German
Currency	1 Swiss franc (Sfr) = 100 centimes
Time	GMT/UTC+0100
Country Phone Code	☎ 423

Liechtenstein has no military service and its minuscule army (80 men!) was disbanded in 1868. It is best known for wine production, postage stamps, dentures (an important export) and its status as a tax haven. In 2000, Liechtenstein's financial and political institutions were rocked by allegations that money laundering was rife in the country.

In response to international outrage, banks agreed to stop allowing customers to bank money anonymously.

Despite its small size, Liechtenstein has two political regions (upper and lower) and three distinct geographical areas: the Rhine Valley in the west, the edge of the Tirolean Alps in the southeast, and the northern lowlands. The population is 32,860, a third of which are foreign residents.

LIECHTENSTEIN

By road, route 16 from Switzerland passes through Liechtenstein via Schaan and terminates at Feldkirch. The N13 follows the Rhine along the Swiss/Liechtenstein border; minor roads cross into Liechtenstein at each motorway exit.

Getting Around

Postbus travel within Liechtenstein is cheap and reliable; all fares cost Sfr2.40 or Sfr3.60, and a weekly/monthly pass is only Sfr10/20 (half-price for students and seniors).

The only drawback is that some services finish early; the last of the hourly buses from Vaduz to Malbun, for example, leaves at 6.20pm. Grab a timetable from the post office.

Vaduz

pop 4930

Although it's the capital of Liechtenstein, Vaduz is little more than a village. Two adjoining streets – Äulestrasse and pedestrian-only Städtle – enclose the centre of town. Everything of importance is within this small area, including the bus station.

Liechtenstein Tourism (☎ 239 63 00; e touristinfo@liechtenstein.li; Städtle 37; open 8am-noon & 1.30pm-5.30pm Mon-Fri year-round, 10am-noon & 1.30pm-4pm Sat Apr-Oct, 10am-noon & 1.30pm-5pm Sun May-Sept) has plenty of useful information (ask for the Liechtenstein in Figures brochure); for Sfr2, staff will stamp your passport with a souvenir entry stamp.

Send postcards at the **main post office** (Äulestrasse 38; open 7.45am-6pm Mon-Fri, 8am-11am Sat), which has the same postal rates as Switzerland.

The **Telecom FL shop** (☎ 237 74 74; Austrasse 77; open 9am-noon & 1.30pm-6.30pm Mon-Fri, 9am-1pm Sat), 1km south of Vaduz, provides free Internet access.

For medical attention, contact the hospital, **Liechtensteinisches Landesspital** (☎ 235 44 11; Heiligkreuz 25).

Facts for the Visitor

See the Switzerland chapter for practical details not covered here.

Liechtenstein's telephone country code is ☎ 423, and there are no regional telephone codes.

Getting There & Away

Liechtenstein has no airport (the nearest is in Zürich), and only a few trains stop within its borders, at Schaan. Getting there by postbus is easiest. There are usually three buses an hour from the Swiss border towns of Buchs (Sfr2.40) and Sargans (Sfr3.60) that stop in Vaduz. Buses run every 30 minutes from the Austrian border town of Feldkirch; you sometimes have to change at Schaan to reach Vaduz (the Sfr3.60 ticket is valid for both buses).

Things to See & Do

Many tourists come to Liechtenstein for the stamps – a stamp in the passport and stamps on a postcard for the folks back home. But it's also worthwhile heading for the hills, with some 400km of **hiking trails** through Alpine scenery; see the tourist office for the *Liechtenstein Hiking Map* 1:25,000 (Sfr15.50).

Although the **castle** is not open to the public, you can climb the hill for a closer look. There are views of Vaduz and the mountains, and a network of marked walking trails along the ridge.

Liechtenstein Kunstmuseum (☎ 235 030 00; w www.kunstmuseum.li; *Städtle 32; adult/student/child Sfr8/5/5; open 10am-5pm Tues-Wed & Fri-Sun, 10am-8pm Thur)* houses the national art collection in a rather sleek modern building, with works from the 16th to 18th centuries from the prince's private collection.

Philatelists will lick their lips in anticipation of the **Postage Stamp Museum** (☎ 236 61 05; *Städtle 37; admission free; open 10am-noon & 1pm-5pm daily)*, which exhibits 300 frames of national stamps issued since 1912. The **National Museum** *(Städtle 43)* reopens – after major renovations – in spring 2003.

Look out for processions and fireworks on 15 August, Liechtenstein's national holiday. The bands performing at the **Little Big One** (w www.littlebigone.com) open-air music festival sweep into town on the third June weekend.

Places to Stay

The country's minute dimensions mean you can base yourself anywhere and still be within easy cycling or postbus distance of the centre. Ask the tourist office for a list of private rooms and chalets outside Vaduz.

Triesenberg, on a hillside terrace overlooking the Rhine Valley, has **Camping Mittagspitz** (☎ 392 26 86; *adult/child/tent/car Sfr8.50/4/5/4, dorm beds for adult/child Sfr22/13)*. The **SYHA hostel** (☎ 232 50 22, fax 232 58 56; e schaan@youthhostel.ch; *Untere Rütigasse 6; dorm beds from Sfr28.60, doubles without/with toilet Sfr74.20/86.20; open mid-Mar–Nov)* is in a quiet rural setting between Vaduz and nearby Schaan. Take the postbus to the Muhleholz stop; it's a five-minute walk (signposted) from there.

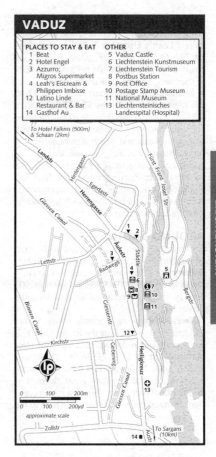

VADUZ

PLACES TO STAY & EAT	OTHER
1 Beat	5 Vaduz Castle
2 Hotel Engel	6 Liechtenstein Kunstmuseum
3 Azzurro;	7 Liechtenstein Tourism
Migros Supermarket	8 Postbus Station
4 Leah's Eiscream &	9 Post Office
Philippen Imbisse	10 Postage Stamp Museum
12 Latino Linde	11 National Museum
Restaurant & Bar	13 Liechtensteinisches
14 Gasthof Au	Landesspital (Hospital)

Another cheapie outside Vaduz is **Hotel Falknis** (☎ 232 63 77; *Landstrasse 92; singles/doubles Sfr55/110)*, a 20-minute walk from the centre (or take the postbus). There's a pub below and basic rooms with hall showers above.

Gasthof Au (☎ 232 11 17, fax 232 11 68; *Austrasse 2; singles/doubles Sfr60/96, with bathroom Sfr80/120)*, on the main road into town, has rudimentary rooms and a garden restaurant.

Places to Eat

Pedestrian-only Stadtle street has a clutch of pavement restaurants and cafés. Popular options include **Hotel Engel** *(Städtle 13)*, with standard international fare; and **Beat** *(Städtle 5)*, a stylish eatery for local suits.

For an odd but delicious mix of authentic Philippino dishes and home-made ice cream, there's **Leah's Eiscream & Philippen Imbiss** (☎ 232 72 00; Städtle 28; dishes Sfr9.50, ice cream from Sfr2; open 10am-7pm daily, later in summer), behind the Kunstmuseum.

Latino Linde Restaurant & Bar (☎ 233 10 05; Kirchstrasse 2; dishes Sfr17.50-25; open 8.30am-11pm Mon-Thur, 8.30am-midnight Fri, 4pm-midnight Sat) is a local haunt with bamboo screens and South American rugs. It serves burgers and Tex-Mex snacks.

For a quick bite, there's **Azzurro** (☎ 232 48 18; open 8am-7pm Mon-Fri, 8am-6pm Sat, 10am-6pm), next to the **Migros** supermarket. Azzurro is a stand-up eatery with kebabs and small pizzas from Sfr7.50.

AROUND VADUZ

Northern Liechtenstein is dotted with small communities with a gentle pace of life. **Schellenberg** has a Russian monument, commemorating the night in 1945 when a band of 500 heavily armed Russian soldiers crossed the border.

Triesenberg is on a terrace above Vaduz and has great views over the Rhine Valley. It has a pretty onion-domed church and the **Heimatmuseum** (☎ 262 19 26; adult/student Sfr2/1; open 1.30pm-5.30pm Tues-Sat year-round, 2pm-5pm Sun June-Aug), devoted to the Walser community, whose members came from Switzerland's Valais to settle here in the 13th century. Apparently, the Walser dialect is still spoken here. **Balzers**, in the extreme south of the country, is dominated by the soaring sides of Gutenberg Castle (not open to public).

MALBUN

Liechtenstein's ski resort, Malbun, perches at 1600m in the southeast. It has some good **mountain runs** for novices (as well as two ski schools) and more difficult runs. A one-day pass for all the ski lifts costs Sfr35 (students/seniors Sfr29). Skis, shoes and poles cost Sfr43 for a day, and can be hired from the **sports shop** (☎ 263 37 55).

During summer, skis give way to mountain boots as the **hiking** fraternity hits town. Worthwhile treks include the Panorama and Furstin-Gina paths, which start and finish in Malbun. See birds of prey at close quarters at **Galina Hotel** (☎ 263 34 24; adult/child Sfr6/3), which runs a 40-minute falconry show at 3pm daily during summer.

The road from Vaduz terminates at Malbun. The **tourist office** (☎ 263 65 77; open 9am-noon & 1.30pm-5pm Mon-Fri, 9am-noon & 1pm-4pm Sat, closed mid-Apr–May & Nov–mid-Dec) is by the first bus stop.

The village has eight hotels, each with a restaurant, including the **Alpenhotel Malbun** (☎ 263 11 81, fax 263 96 46; singles/doubles from Sfr45/90) and **Turna** (☎ 265 50 40, fax 265 50 41; e turna@adon.li; singles/doubles Sfr70/110).

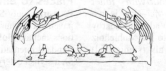

Luxembourg

The Grand Duchy of Luxembourg (Luxemburg, Lëtzebuerg) has long been a transit land. For centuries ownership passed from one superpower to another; and for decades travellers wrote it off as merely an expensive stepping stone to other destinations.

It's true that this tiny country is more a tax shelter for financial institutions than a budget haven for travellers, but many miss the best by rushing through. Beautiful countryside is dotted with feudal castles, deep river valleys and quaint wine-making towns, while the capital, Luxembourg City, is often described as the most dramatically situated in Europe.

Facts about Luxembourg

HISTORY

Luxembourg's history reads a little like the fairy tale its name evokes. More than 1000 years ago, in 963, a count called Sigefroi (or Siegfried, Count of Ardennes) built a castle high on a promontory, laying the foundation stone of the present-day capital and the beginning of a dynasty which spawned rulers throughout Europe.

By the end of the Middle Ages the strategically placed, fortified city was much sought after – the Burgundians, Spanish, French, Austrians and Prussians all waging bloody battles to conquer and secure it. Besieged, devastated and rebuilt more than 20 times in 400 years, it became the strongest fortress in Europe after Gibraltar, hence its nickname, 'Gibraltar of the north'.

Listed as a French 'forestry department' during Napoleon's reign, it was included in the newly formed United Kingdom of the Netherlands, along with Belgium, in 1814. It was cut in half 16 years later when Belgium severed itself from the Netherlands and Luxembourg was split between them. This division sparked the Grand Duchy's desire for independence and in 1839 the Dutch portion became present-day Luxembourg. Later, after the country declared itself neutral, many of the fortifications were dismantled.

Luxembourg rode on the wealth of its iron-ore deposits during much of the 20th century.

When this industry slumped in the mid-1970s, Luxembourg not only survived but prospered by introducing favourable banking and taxation laws, which made it a world centre of international finance. Now home to some key European Union (EU) institutions, the Grand Duchy entered the 21st century with one of Europe's healthiest economies.

GEOGRAPHY

On the maps of Europe, Luxembourg commonly gets allocated a 'Lux' tag – and even that abbreviation can be too big to fit the space it occupies on the map between Belgium, Germany and France. At only 82km long, 57km wide, and riddled with rivers, its 2586 sq km are divided between the forested Ardennes

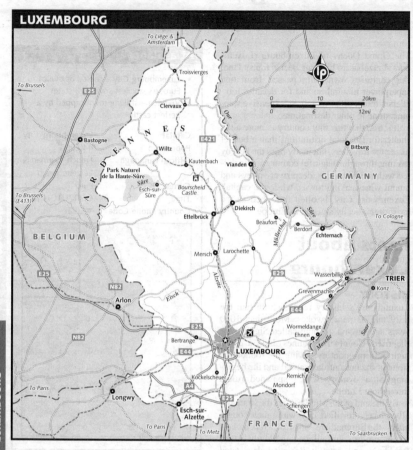

LUXEMBOURG

To Liège & Amsterdam

Troisvierges

To Brussels

Clervaux

Bastogne

A R D E N N E S

Wiltz

Kautenbach

Park Naturel de la Haute-Sûre

Esch-sur-Sûre

Bourscheid Castle

Vianden

Bitburg

GERMANY

Diekirch

Ettelbrück

Beaufort

Berdorf

Echternach

To Cologne

BELGIUM

To Brussels (E411)

Mersch

Larochette

Eisch

Alzette

Müllerthal

Sûre

Wasserbillig

Grevenmacher

Konz

TRIER

Arlon

Bertrange

LUXEMBOURG

Kockelscheuer

Wormeldange

Ehnen

Moselle

Saar

To Paris

Longwy

Esch-sur-Alzette

Remich

Mondorf

Schengen

FRANCE

To Paris

To Metz

To Saarbrücken

highlands to the north, and farming and mining country to the south.

CLIMATE

Luxembourg has a temperate climate with warm summers and cold winters – it's especially cold in the Ardennes, which sometimes gets snow. The sunniest months are May to August, although April and September can be fine also. Precipitation is spread evenly over the year.

ECOLOGY & ENVIRONMENT

About a third of Luxembourg is covered by forests which are home to wild boar, fox and deer. The main environmental concerns are air and water pollution in urban areas.

Luxembourg has no national parks. The so-called Parc Naturel de la Haute-Sûre (Upper Sûre Nature Park) in the country's northwest is a group of communes which have banded together to promote and protect their region. The **Maison du Parc** (☎ 89 93 31 1; 15 Rte de Lultzhausen; open 10am-noon & 2pm-6pm Mon, Tues & Fri, 2pm-6pm Sat & Sun),

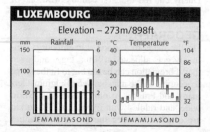

LUXEMBOURG

Elevation – 273m/898ft

Rainfall

Temperature

J F M A M J J A S O N D

about 500m from the village of Esch-sur-Sûre, is the park's impressive information centre-cum-museum.

GOVERNMENT & POLITICS

One of Europe's smallest sovereign states, Luxembourg is a constitutional monarchy headed by Grand Duke Henri. He took over the throne in 2000 following the abdication of his then 79-year-old father, Grand Duke Jean, who had ruled since 1964. In time-honoured Luxembourg tradition, the throne is passed to the oldest male in the royal family.

The main political parties are the Christian-Social, Democratic and Workers-Socialist. The prime minister, Jean-Claude Jüncker, of the Christian-Social party has led the government since 1995.

ECONOMY

Luxembourg's strong economy rides on its banking and insurance sectors. Agriculture and the steel and tourism industries are also important. GDP in 2000 was US$15.9 billion. Unemployment is one of the lowest in Europe at 2.5%.

POPULATION & PEOPLE

Luxembourg's 440,000 inhabitants are a confident and proud lot who have no problem with the fact that they live in a seriously diminutive country. A motto occasionally seen carved in stone walls sums up the people's character: *Mir wëlle bleiwe wat mir sin* – We want to remain what we are.

ARTS

Few Luxembourgers are internationally known in the arts, which is probably why Edward Steichen, one of the pioneers of American photography, is held in such high regard in his native land.

The expressionist painter Joseph Kutter introduced modern art to Luxembourg. Roger Manderscheid is a contemporary author who writes in Letzeburgesch, the national language.

RELIGION

Christianity was established early, and today Catholicism reigns supreme. More than 95% of the population are Roman Catholic, with the church influencing many facets of life, including politics, the media and education. About 3% of the population are Protestant or Jewish.

LANGUAGE

There are three official languages in Luxembourg – French, German and Letzeburgesch. The latter is most closely related to German and it was proclaimed as the national tongue in 1984. English is widely spoken in the capital and by the younger people around the countryside.

Luxembourgers speak Letzeburgesch to each other but generally switch to French when talking to foreigners. A couple of Letzeburgesch words often overheard are *moien* (good morning/hello) and *äddi* (goodbye). Like French speakers, Luxembourgers say *merci* for 'thank you'. In the business world, politics, the judiciary and the press, French or German are mainly used. For a rundown on these two languages, see the Language chapter at the back of this book.

Facts for the Visitor

HIGHLIGHTS

Luxembourg's highlights include: strolling along the capital's Chemin de la Corniche; spending a lazy afternoon visiting wineries along the Moselle Valley; hiking in the Müllerthal region and taking in the expansive view from Bourscheid Castle.

SUGGESTED ITINERARIES

Depending on the length of your stay, you might want to see and do the following things (although if you're relying on public transport, you will need a few more days to cover these areas):

Two days
Spend one day in Luxembourg City and the other in either Echternach or Vianden.

One week
Spend two days in Luxembourg City, two days exploring the centre and north (Vianden, Clervaux or Diekirch), two days in the Müllerthal region (Echternach and Beaufort) and a day along the Moselle Valley.

PLANNING
When to Go

The countryside in spring is a riot of wildflowers and blossoms, summer is the warmest time and, in autumn, wine-making villages are celebrating their grape harvests. For weather considerations, see the Climate section earlier in this chapter.

LUXEMBOURG

Maps

Good road maps include those published by Geoline (scale: 1:140,000) and Michelin (No 924; scale: 1:150,000).

TOURIST OFFICES
Local Tourist Offices

The Office National du Tourisme headquarters (☎ 42 82 82 1, fax 42 82 82 38; e info@ont.lu; PO Box 1001, L-1010, Luxembourg City) will send you information.

Tourist Offices Abroad

Luxembourg tourist offices abroad include:

UK (☎ 020-7434 2800, fax 020-7734 1205, e tourism@luxembourg.co.uk) 122 Regent St, London W1B 5SA

USA (☎ 212-935 88 88, fax 212-935 58 96, e luxnto@aol.com) 17 Beekman Place, New York, NY 10022

VISAS & DOCUMENTS

Visitors from many countries need only a valid passport for three-month visits. Visa requirements are basically the same as for entering The Netherlands (see the Facts for the Visitor section in that chapter for more details).

EMBASSIES & CONSULATES
Luxembourg Embassies

In countries where there is no representative, contact the Belgian or Dutch diplomatic missions. Luxembourg embassies include:

UK (☎ 020-7235 6961, fax 7235 9734) 27 Wilton Crescent, London SW1X 8SD

USA (☎ 202-265 41 71/72, fax 328-82 70) 2200 Massachusetts Ave, NW Washington, DC 20008

Embassies in Luxembourg

The nearest Australian, Canadian and New Zealand embassies are in Belgium (see the Facts for the Visitor section in the Belgium chapter). The following embassies are all in Luxembourg City:

Belgium (☎ 44 27 46 1, fax 45 42 82) 4 Rue des Girondins, L-1626

France (☎ 45 72 71 1, fax 45 72 71 227) 8b Blvd Joseph II, L-1840

Germany (☎ 45 34 45 1, fax 45 56 04) 20-22 Ave Émile Reuter, L-2420

Ireland (☎ 45 06 10, fax 45 88 20) 28 Route d'Arlon, L-1140

Netherlands (☎ 22 75 70, fax 40 30 16) 5 Rue CM Spoo, L-2546

UK (☎ 22 98 64, fax 22 98 67) 14 Blvd Roosevelt, L-2450

USA (☎ 46 01 23, fax 46 14 01) 22 Blvd Emmanuel Servais, L-2535

CUSTOMS

Petrol, alcohol, tobacco and perfume products are relatively cheap throughout Luxembourg and people from neighbouring countries often come here to stock up.

The usual allowances apply to duty-free goods if you are coming from a non-EU country and to duty-paid goods if you're arriving from within the EU.

MONEY
Currency

The unit of currency is the euro. Banks are the main exchange bureaus and charge a minimum of €3.70 commission. All major credit cards are commonly accepted; ATMs are at Findel airport and in the train station at Luxembourg City.

Costs

Prices are slightly more expensive than Belgium, though petrol is cheaper.

Those really keen on exploring the Grand Duchy should consider the Luxembourg Card. Valid from Easter to 31 October, it gives free admission to 40 attractions throughout the country plus unlimited use of public transport. It's available from tourist offices and some hotels and costs €9/16/22 for an adult for one/two/three days; family cards cost €18/32/44.

Many museums offer a concession price for children.

Tipping & Bargaining

Tipping is not obligatory and bargaining is downright impossible.

Taxes & Refunds

Value-added tax (abbreviated in French as TVA) is calculated at 15%, except for hotel, restaurant and camping ground prices, which enjoy only a 3% levy.

The procedure for claiming the tax back is tedious unless you buy from shops affiliated with the Tax Cheque Refund Service. These shops will give you a stamped Tax Refund Cheque which can be cashed at your port of exit.

POST & COMMUNICATIONS
Post

Post offices (except in Luxembourg City) are open 9am to 5.30pm Monday to Friday. It costs €0.52 to send a letter (under 20g) within Europe and €0.74 outside. Mail to Australia, Canada, New Zealand and the USA takes at least a week. To the UK and within Europe, it'll take around two or three days. There's a €0.45 fee (sometimes waived) for poste restante – letters should be addressed to: Post Office, Poste Restante, L-1118 Luxembourg 2.

Telephone

For making international telephone calls to Luxembourg, the country code is ☎ 352. To telephone abroad, the international access code is ☎ 00 (see the Telephone Appendix). There are no telephone area codes in Luxembourg.

Local telephone calls are time-based and cost a minimum of €0.12. International phone calls can be made using €3.10, €6.20 or €13.65 phonecards. The cost of a three-minute phone call in peak time to the USA is €2.80. Numbers prefixed with ☎ 0800 are toll-free numbers.

Mobile phone users will find Luxembourg works on GSM 900/1800, which is compatible with elsewhere in Europe and Australia but not with the North American GSM 1900 or the system used in Japan.

Fax

Faxes can be sent (and received) from post offices and cost €3.95 for the first page to the UK or USA, plus €0.37 for each additional page. To Australia the prices are €4.95/0.62 respectively. It costs €2.45 to receive a fax.

Email & Internet Access

Public Internet access facilities are limited to Internet cafés in Luxembourg City. Expect to pay €1.25 to €3 per half hour.

DIGITAL RESOURCES

Upcoming tourist events in Luxembourg City are listed on the city's website (W www.luxembourg-city.lu/touristinfo). General information on weather, cinema listings, regional events etc is at W www.luxweb.lu.

BOOKS

For a humorous look at Luxembourg ways, get hold of *How to Remain What You Are* by George Müller, a Luxembourg psychologist.

An excellent multilingual publication for walkers is *182 x Luxembourg*, which describes 182 hiking trails; *40 Cycle Routes* is the cyclist's equivalent. Both are published by Éditions Guy Binsfeld and are widely available in bookstores.

NEWSPAPERS & MAGAZINES

The *Lëtzebuerger Journal* and *Luxemburger Wort* are the two main daily newspapers. The weekly English-language *Luxembourg News* (€0.50) gives local news and has entertainment listings. Foreign newspapers and magazines are readily available.

RADIO & TV

Den Neie Radio (DNR; 102.9kHz) concentrates on both classical music and news. Radio Lëtzebuerg (RTL; 93.3kHz) plays commercial pop. There's a plethora of international TV stations from which to choose. RTL, one of the main national stations, broadcasts in Letzeburgesch from 7pm to 1am.

TIME

Luxembourg operates on Central European Time. Noon in Luxembourg is 3am in San Francisco, 6am in New York and Toronto, 11am in London, 9pm in Sydney and 11pm in Auckland. The 24-hour clock is commonly used. Daylight-saving comes into effect at 2am on the last Sunday in March – clocks are moved forward an hour. They're moved back an hour at 2am on the last Sunday in October.

LAUNDRY

Most larger towns have a self-service *laverie*. A 5kg wash and dry costs about €8.50.

TOILETS

Public toilets are not common. Those that have an attendant charge €0.50; those that don't are usually ill-kept and best avoided.

WOMEN TRAVELLERS

Women should face few problems travelling around Luxembourg. However, in the event of attack, contact the women's crisis organisation **Waisse Rank** (☎ 40 20 40; *84 Rue Adolphe Fischer, Luxembourg City*).

GAY & LESBIAN TRAVELLERS

Luxembourg's national homosexual and lesbian organisation is **Rosa Lëtzebuerg** (☎ 021 41 28 12; *252 Ave Gaston Diderich, L-1420*

Luxembourg-Belair). Attitudes to homosexuality are quite relaxed and in Luxembourg City
you'll find a couple of gay bars. The age of
consent is 16. Luxembourg Pride is a small
festival held in mid-June.

DISABLED TRAVELLERS

Disabled travellers will find little joy getting
around Luxembourg – lifts are not commonplace, ramps are few and pavements are uneven. For information it's best to contact
Info-Handicap *(☎ 36 64 66, fax 36 08 85; 20
Rue de Contern, L-5955 Itzig).*

SENIOR TRAVELLERS

Only Luxembourg citizens are entitled to discounts for seniors on local transport. Most
museums offer the elderly a 10% discount.

TRAVEL WITH CHILDREN

Kids usually enjoy exploring any old castle, a
boat trip on the Moselle and riding the toy
train in Luxembourg City.

DANGERS & ANNOYANCES

Travellers will find Luxembourg a safe country to travel around.

LEGAL MATTERS

Should you need (free) legal advice, contact
the **Service d'Accueil et d'Information
Juridique** *(☎ 22 18 46; 12 Côte d'Eich, Luxembourg City).*

BUSINESS HOURS

Trading hours are 9am to 5.30pm weekdays
(except Monday when some shops open about
noon), and a half or full day on Saturday.
Many shops close for lunch between noon and
2pm. Banks have shorter hours: 8.30am to
4.30pm Monday to Friday and, in the capital,
on Saturday mornings – country branches
close for lunch.

PUBLIC HOLIDAYS & SPECIAL EVENTS

Public holidays include New Year's Day,
Easter Monday, May Day (1 May), Ascension
Day, Whit Monday, National Day (23 June),
Assumption Day (15 August), All Saints' Day
(1 November) and Christmas Day.

For a small country, Luxembourg is big on
festivals. Pick up the tourist office's monthly
Agenda brochure for local listings. The biggest
national events are Carnival, held six weeks

Emergency Services

In the event of an emergency, call ☎ 113 for
the police or ☎ 112 for medical assistance. In
the event of a car/motorcycle breakdown
contact the Automobile Club of Luxembourg
(☎ 45 00 45).

---

before Easter, and Bonfire Day (Bürgsonn-
deg), one week later. National Day is held on
23 June, however festivities take place on the
evening of 22 June.

In July, the Festival Européen de Théâtre en
Plein Air et de Musique transforms the town
of Wiltz into an open-air stage for theatre, jazz
and classical music.

ACTIVITIES

With a 5000km network of marked walking
paths, the Grand Duchy is a hiker's haven.
National routes are indicated by yellow signposts. Tracks, marked by white triangles, connect the 11 Hostelling International (HI)
hostels. Most bookshops sell hiking maps (see
the Books section earlier) and local tourist offices always stock regional walking maps.

WORK

Seasonal grape picking is possible in the
Moselle Valley for about six weeks from mid-
September. No permit is needed, but the work
is popular with locals.

ACCOMMODATION

During summer it's wise to reserve all accommodation. The national tourist office provides
free hotel, B&B, camping and farm-stay brochures, and staff will book accommodation for
a €0.50 fee.

Camping grounds are abundant, although
mainly in the central and northern regions.
There are three categories of camping grounds
but the bulk fall into the well-equipped 'Category 1' – expect to pay between €3 and €5
per adult. In general, children are charged half
the adult rate, and a tent site is equivalent to an
adult rate.

There are 11 hostels operated by **Hostelling
International** *(HI; ☎ 26 29 35 00, fax 26 29
35 03; **e** information@youthhostels.lu;
24-26 Place de la Gare, Galerie Kons, L-1616
Luxembourg City).* Most close irregularly
throughout the year, so ring ahead. The nightly
dorm rate, including breakfast and sheets,

varies from €13.60 to €15.50 for members; nonmembers must buy a 'welcome stamp' (€2.75 per night) for the first six nights after which they become an HI member. Many hostels offer single/double rooms for a supplement of €7.50/2.50 per person.

B&Bs are rare in the country and there are none in Luxembourg City. The few you'll find dotted around the countryside go for between €18 and €22 per person. The cheapest hotels in the country charge €25/40 for a basic single/double room with breakfast; mid-range hotels start at €65/80.

FOOD & DRINKS

Luxembourg's cuisine is similar to that of Belgium's Wallonia region – plenty of pork, freshwater fish and game meat – but with a German influence in local specialities like liver dumplings with sauerkraut. The national dish is *judd mat gaardebounen* (smoked pork with beans). Strict vegetarians will find little joy. A *plat du jour* (dish of the day) in the cheapest café costs about €6. Beer, both local (Mousel) and Belgian, is plentiful, and the Moselle Valley white wines are drinkable.

ENTERTAINMENT

Nightlife outside Luxembourg City is very tame. In summer terrace cafés take over town squares and are the place for people-watching, especially during local festivals. Cinemas generally screen films in their original language with French, and sometimes German, subtitles.

SHOPPING

White wines and local liqueurs (made from plums, pears, nuts and cherries) are popular purchases. Look for the Marque Nationale label, which indicates quality vintages. Those into china and crystal will be acquainted with the local manufacturer, Villeroy & Boch.

Getting There & Away

AIR

The international airport, Findel, is 6km east of the capital, and is serviced by frequent buses (see the Luxembourg City Getting Around section). The national carrier, **Luxair** (*main office* ☎ *47 98 1, arrivals/departures* ☎ *4798 50 50*), flies to a number of European destinations, including London, Paris and Frankfurt. Its main office is at the airport. The €2.97 departure tax when leaving Findel is included in ticket prices.

LAND
Bus

Note that Eurolines buses do not pass through Luxembourg.

Train

The Benelux Tourrail pass (see the Belgium Getting Around section) costs €174/116 for a 1st/2nd-class ticket for people over 26 years and €87 (2nd-class only) for those 26 years and under. It's also valid for travelling on national (CFL) buses.

Train services include to Brussels (€24 for a one-way 2nd-class ticket, 2¾ hours, hourly), Amsterdam (€42.80, 5½ hours, hourly), Paris (€39.20, four hours, six trains per day) and Trier in Germany (€7.40, 40 minutes, 11 per day). The **station office** (☎ *49 90 49 90; open 24hr*) is in Luxembourg City.

Car & Motorcycle

The E411 is the major route to Brussels; the A4 leads to Paris and the E25 to Metz; the main route to Germany is the E44 via Trier.

RIVER

From Easter to September it's possible to take a cruise boat from points along the Moselle to destinations in Germany (Remich to Trier costs €11.50 and takes 4¼ hours). See the Moselle Valley section for more details.

Getting Around

BUS & TRAIN

Unlike its Benelux partners, Luxembourg does not have an extensive rail system, so getting around once you leave the main north-south train line can take time. The bus network (operated by CFL) is comprehensive and the fare system for both train and bus is simple: €1.10 for a 'short' trip of about 10km or less (this ticket is valid for one hour) or €4.40 for a 2nd-class unlimited day ticket (known as a *Billet Reseau*), which is also good for travelling on inner-city buses. It's valid from the time of purchase until 8am the next day. A book of 10 short-trip tickets costs €8.80 and a book of five Billet Reseau costs €17.60.

LUXEMBOURG

More information can be obtained from either the **CFL bus information kiosk** (☎ 49 90 55 44) or **train information office** (☎ 49 90 49 90), both inside the Luxembourg City train station.

In most train stations, you'll find either a luggage room (€3 per article for 24 hours) or luggage lockers (€2 to €4 for 48 hours).

CAR & MOTORCYCLE
Road rules are easy to understand and standard international signs are in use. The blood-alcohol limit for drivers is 0.08%. The speed limit on motorways is 120km. Fuel prices are among the cheapest in Western Europe: lead-free/diesel costs €0.80/0.65 per litre (leaded petrol is virtually impossible to find). For all other motoring information, contact the **Club Automobile de Luxembourg** (☎ 45 00 45 1; 54 Route de Longwy, L-8007 Bertrange).

Car rental start at €75 per day (including insurance, VAT and unlimited kilometres) for a small Peugeot.

BICYCLE
Cycling is a popular pastime. Bikes can be hired for €20/37.50/75 per day/weekend/week in Luxembourg City. It costs €1.10 to take your bike on a train.

HITCHING
Hitching is not common. Note that it is illegal on motorways.

BOAT
Special train-boat-bus combo tickets (€10.30) are available on weekends (Easter until 30 September) to tour the Moselle Valley. From Luxembourg City, take the train to Wasserbillig, then a boat to Remich and return to the capital by bus. For details ask at the luggage office at the train station in Luxembourg City.

See the Moselle Valley section for more information on passenger boat services.

LOCAL TRANSPORT
Luxembourg City has a good local bus network. Elsewhere there is little public transport besides taxis. Taxis cost €0.80 per kilometre plus a 10% night surcharge; 25% extra on Sunday.

ORGANISED TOURS
A half-day trip by bus from Luxembourg City takes in Vianden and the Müllerthal region. It

runs on Saturday and Sunday only from late April to early October and costs €15/11 for adults/children; for details ask the tourist office for the *Sightseeing Luxembourg* brochure.

Luxembourg City

pop 82,000

Strikingly situated high on a promontory overlooking the Pétrusse and Alzette Valleys, the Grand Duchy's 1000-year-old capital is a composed blend of old and new. One of Europe's financial leaders, it's a wealthy city with an uncommonly tranquil air and unusually clean streets. The historical value of the city's remaining fortifications and older quarters were acknowledged in 1994 when Unesco added them to its World Heritage List.

Orientation
The city centre has three main sections – the largely pedestrianised old town, the train station area and the Grund. The old town is northwest of the valleys and based around two large squares – Place d'Armes and Place Guillaume II. To the south – across Pont Adolphe and Pont Passerelle, two impressive bridges that span the Pétrusse Valley – is the train station quarter. The station itself is 1.25km from Place d'Armes. The Grund – or lower town – is a picturesque, cobblestoned quarter built well below the fortifications and is now home to some brisk nightlife. Across the Alzette Valley rise the modern towers of the European Centre (Centre Européen) on the Kirchberg Plateau.

Information
Tourist Offices The **Luxembourg City tourist office** (☎ 22 28 09, fax 46 70 70; e touristinfo@luxembourg-city.lu; Place d'Armes; open 9am-7pm Mon-Sat, 10am-6pm Sun Apr-Sept; 9am-6pm Mon-Sat, 10am-6pm Sun Oct-Mar) hands out free city maps, a comprehensive walking tour pamphlet and the handy *Bonjour Luxembourg*, a weekly events guide.

The **national tourist office** (☎ 42 82 82 20, fax 42 82 82 30; e info@ont.lu; open 9am-7pm Mon-Sat, 9am-12.30pm & 1.45pm-7pm Sun June-Sept; 9.15am-12.30pm & 1.45pm-6pm daily Oct-May) is inside the train station. It provides city and national information and reserves rooms.

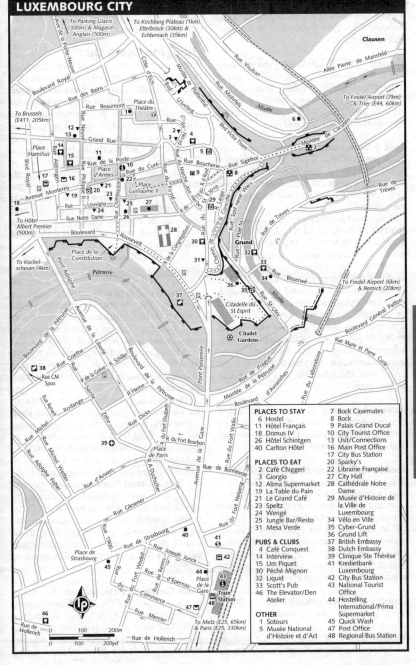

LUXEMBOURG CITY

Clausen

To Parking Glacis (300m) & Magasin Anglais (500m)

To Kirchberg Plateau (1km), Ettelbrück (30km) & Echternach (35km)

To Findel Airport (7km) & Trier (E44, 60km)

To Brussels (E411, 205km)

Place Hamilius

To Hôtel Albert Premier (500m)

To Kockel-scheuer (4km)

Grund

Citadelle du St Esprit

Citadel Gardens

To Findel Airport (6km) & Remich (20km)

Place de la Constitution

Pétrusse

Rue CM Spoo

Place de la Gare

Place de Strasbourg

To Metz (E25, 65km) & Paris (E25, 330km)

Train Station

Rue de Hollerich

| 0 | 100 | 200m |
| 0 | 100 | 200yd |

PLACES TO STAY
6 Hostel
11 Hôtel Français
18 Domus IV
26 Hôtel Schintgen
40 Carlton Hôtel

PLACES TO EAT
2 Café Chiggeri
3 Giorgio
12 Alima Supermarket
19 La Table du Pain
21 Le Grand Café
23 Speltz
24 Wengé
25 Jungle Bar/Resto
31 Mesa Verde

PUBS & CLUBS
4 Café Conquest
14 Interview
15 Um Piquet
30 Péché Mignon
32 Liquid
33 Scott's Pub
46 The Elevator/Den Atelier

OTHER
1 Sotours
5 Musée National d'Histoire et d'Art
7 Bock Casemates
8 Bock
9 Palais Grand Ducal
10 City Tourist Office
13 Usit/Connections
16 Main Post Office
17 City Bus Station
20 Sparky's
22 Librairie Française
27 City Hall
28 Cathédrale Notre Dame
29 Musée d'Histoire de la Ville de Luxembourg
34 Vélo en Ville
35 Cyber-Grund
36 Grund Lift
37 British Embassy
38 Dutch Embassy
39 Clinique Ste Thérèse
41 Kredietbank Luxembourg
42 City Bus Station
43 National Tourist Office
44 Hostelling International/Prima Supermarket
45 Quick Wash
47 Post Office
48 Regional Bus Station

LUXEMBOURG

There are interactive touch screens for national information at Findel airport, the Luxembourg City train station and at the main highway entrances.

Money The Kredietbank Luxembourg (*Place de la Gare*), next to the station, is a convenient bank. Outside banking hours, the exchange offices (with poorer rates) are open at the train station (8.30am to 9pm daily) and at the airport (6am to 10pm daily).

Post & Communications Send mail at the main post office (*25 Rue Aldringen; open 7am-7pm Mon-Fri, 7am-5pm Sat*). There's a post office branch (*38 Place de la Gare; open 6am-7pm Mon-Fri, 6am-noon Sat*) near the train station.

For Internet access, there are a few options. Sparky's (*☎ 26 20 12 23; 11a Ave Monterey; open 8am-8pm Mon-Fri, 11am-8pm Sat*) is a smoky bar with a handful of terminals for €0.10 per minute. For a bit more atmosphere head to Café Chiggeri (*☎ 22 82 36; 15 Rue du Nord; open to 1am Mon-Fri, to 3am Sat & Sun*). This stylish café has just one computer terminal and charges €2.50 per half hour. A new option in the Grund is Cyber-Grund (*☎ 262 39 55; 2 Rue St Ulric; open noon-2pm & 5pm-9pm Tues-Fri, 2pm-5pm Sat*), a non-profit organisation working to revitalise the Grund area which has Net access for €1.25 per half hour.

Travel Agencies Recommended travel agencies include Sotours (*☎ 46 15 14 1; 15 Place du Théâtre*) and Usit/Connections (*☎ 22 99 33; 70 Grand Rue*).

Bookshops The Librairie Française (*☎ 22 00 67; 1 Place d'Armes; open 11.30am-6pm Mon, 9am-6pm Tues-Sat*) has travel guides, maps and a good selection of books on Luxembourg. Magasin Anglais (*☎ 22 49 25; 16 Ave Victor Hugo; open 10am-6pm Tues-Fri, 10am-5pm Sat, 10am-1pm Sun*), an all-round 'English' shop (magazines, Hobnob biscuits, English-language books, videos etc), is a 15-minute walk northwest of Place d'Armes.

Laundry The Quick Wash (*Place de Strasbourg*) is open Monday to Saturday.

Medical Services In the case of a medical emergency or if you need a pharmacy outside normal working hours call ☎ 112. For a hospital, head to Clinique Ste Thérèse (*☎ 49 78 81; Rue Ste Zithe*).

Things to See & Do

Luxembourg is best covered on foot; indeed, the city seems made for leisurely wandering.

From Place d'Armes, head south down Rue Chimay to Place de la Constitution for excellent views over the Pétrusse Valley and the spectacular bridges that span it. Sitting firmly in the background on Place de la Constitution is Cathédrale Notre Dame, the city's main church. Architecturally it's an ugly hotchpotch but it's worth a peek to see the nation's most revered idol, the *Lady Comforter of the Afflicted*, a small, elaborately dressed statue of the Virgin and child. East along the Blvd Roosevelt, the gardens which cover the 17th-century Citadelle du St Esprit offer superb panoramas up both valleys and over the Grund district which lies directly below.

The Grund is easily reached by a free lift dug in the cliff here at Place du St Esprit.

Follow the natural curve north to the Chemin de la Corniche, a pedestrian promenade hailed as 'Europe's most beautiful balcony', which winds along to the Bock, the cliff on which Count Sigefroi built his mighty fort. The castle and much of the fortifications were dismantled between 1867 and 1883 following the treaty of London.

There's little left – the main attractions are the view and the nearby entrance to the Bock Casemates, a 23km network of underground passages spared from destruction because of its delicate position in relation to the town.

From the Bock, it's a short walk west to Rue du Marché aux Herbes where you'll find the Palais Grand Ducal (*adult/concession €5.45/2.75; open 15 Jul-31 Aug*). Originally a town hall, the palace was built in the 1570s during Spanish rule and later expanded; the royal family took up residence here at the end of the 19th century. The nearby Place Guillaume II is lined with formal government edifices.

Bock Casemates This honeycomb of damp, rock rooms (*☎ 22 28 09; Montée de Clauson; adult/concession €1.75/1; open 10am-5pm daily Mar-Oct*) was carved out under the Bock. Long ago, it housed bakeries, slaughterhouses and thousands of soldiers; during

WWI and WWII it was used as a bomb shelter for 35,000 people.

Museums The **Musée d'Histoire de la Ville de Luxembourg** (☎ 47 96 30 61; 14 Rue du St Esprit; adult/concession €5/3.75; open 10am-6pm Tues-Sun, 10am-8pm Thur) is a state-of-the-art complex covering the history of the city. Take the glass elevator between the six floors to appreciate the rocky geology of this part of the old town.

The **Musée National d'Histoire et d'Art** (☎ 47 93 30 1; Place Marché aux Poissons; admission €5; open 10am-5pm Tues-Sun) contains a mixture of Roman and medieval relics, fortification models and art from the 13th century up to the present day. The museum has received a major makeover which was completed in late 2002.

Organised Tours

Take a guided walk to discover the city's many nooks and crannies or a theme walk such as following in the footsteps of Sebastien Vauban (1633–1707), a French military engineer and marshal. The tourist office has details on all possibilities.

The *Pétrusse Express* is a toy train that runs from Place de la Constitution down to the Grund.

It operates daily from Easter to 31 October and costs €6.50/4.25. Alternatively, Sales-Lentz operates 2¼-hour city bus trips for €12/6; inquiries and bookings can be made at the tourist office.

Special Events

Two festivals are worth catching are: Octave, a Catholic pilgrimage held from the third to fifth Sunday after Easter, which climaxes with a street parade headed by the Grand Duke; and Schueberfouer, a fortnight-long fun fair in late August, during which decorated sheep take to the streets.

Places to Stay

Luxembourg City has a dearth of cheap options as most accommodation here is geared for business travellers.

Camping About 4km south of the city there's **Kockelscheuer** (☎ 47 18 15, fax 40 12 43; 22 Route de Bettembourg; bus No 2 from train station; open Easter-31 Oct), situated in (wait for it) Kockelscheuer.

Hostels The HI **hostel** (☎ 22 68 89, fax 22 33 60; e luxembourg@youthhostels.lu; 2 Rue du Fort Olizy; dorm beds €15.50, singles/doubles €23/36; open year-round) is in a valley below the old city. Bus No 9 from the airport or train station stops nearby, otherwise it's a 30-minute walk from the station.

Hotels The big, old **Carlton Hôtel** (☎ 29 96 60, fax 29 96 64; e carlton@pt.lu; 9 Rue de Strasbourg; singles/doubles €24/41, with shower €44/49) has clean rooms; breakfast is €4 extra. **Hôtel Schintgen** (☎ 22 28 44, fax 46 57 19; e schintgen@pt.lu; 6 Rue Notre Dame; singles/doubles/triples from €65/80/87) is well located and has decent rooms.

An enticing mid-range option available is the **Hôtel Français** (☎ 47 45 34, fax 46 42 74; e hfinfo@pt.lu; 14 Place d'Armes; singles/doubles from €94/122). It's small, modern, superbly sited and dotted with *objets d'art* – all in all a winning combination. **Domus IV** (☎ 46 78 78 1, fax 46 78 79; e info@domus.lu; 37 Ave Monterey; single or double rooms Sun-Thur from €112, Fri & Sat €104) has gaily decorated, innovative rooms, some with kitchenette. Breakfast is included on Friday and Saturday nights; the rest of the week it costs €10 per person.

One of the city's most charming hotels is **Hotel Albert Premier** (☎ 44 24 42 1, fax 44 74 41; w www.albert1er.lu; 2a Rue Albert 1er; rooms €198-347). About 750m due west of Place d'Armes, it has 10 opulent rooms – all individually styled.

Places to Eat

Restaurants The **Jungle Bar/Resto** (☎ 22 58 12; 32 Place Guillaume II; meals from €12; open to 11pm) is good for those on a tight budget. It's relatively cheap, has terrace tables overlooking one of the city's main squares and serves interesting French/African cuisine. **Le Grand Café** (☎ 47 14 36; 9 Place d'Armes; mains €16-22) is a lively establishment with an eclectic line-up of meals. It's popular with tourists and locals alike. **Giorgio** (☎ 22 38 18; 11 Rue du Nord; pizzas €8-11) is one of the Grand Duchy's best-known pizzerias and prices are reasonable.

The only purely vegetarian option is **Mesa Verde** (☎ 46 41 26; 11 Rue du St Esprit; lunch Wed & Thur €11-17; dinner Tues-Sat €17-25), an exotically colourful restaurant that's often full. **Wengé** (☎ 26 20 10 58; 15

*Rue Louvigny; 2-course/3-course menu €25/
32, mains €23-28; open 8am-7pm Mon-Sat,
dinner Wed & Fri)* is a vibrant shop-cum-
restaurant and an absolute must for serious
foodies.

One of the best addresses in town is **Speltz**
(☎ 47 49 50; 8 Rue Chimay; mains €25-30).
Seafood and French *haute cuisine* are the
staples in this formal establishment.

Cafés A convivial café-cum-bakery with
nonsmoking surroundings is **La Table du Pain**
*(☎ 24 16 08; 19 Ave Monterey; open 7am-
7pm daily)*. It covers two floors, has a pleasant terrace section and serves salads (€11) and
half-baguette sandwiches (€4).

The **Café Chiggeri** *(☎ 22 82 36; 15 Rue du
Nord; mains €10-14)* draws a hip crowd with
its fine range of international meals, including
vegetarian fare.

Self-Catering For picnic supplies, try either
the **Prima supermarket** *(Galerie Kons, opposite the train station)* or the **Alima supermarket** *(Rue Neuve)*.

Entertainment

The Grund area is one of the most popular
nightlife spots and, when the cliffs are lit up
in summer, it's a pleasant stroll down to the
taverns (open from about 5pm to 1am) which
huddle here. **Liquid** *(Rue de Trèves)* has a
great line-up of international beers and occasional live music. **Scott's Pub** *(Rue Bisserwé)* is popular with lovers of loud blues
and rock on weekends; it's calmer during the
week.

In the old centre, **Pêché Mignon** *(17 Rue
du St Esprit)* is a trendy café with musical and
literary evenings. The raw **Interview** *(19 Rue
Aldringen)* is popular with a younger crowd
while the nearby **Um Piquet** *(30 Rue de la
Poste)* has a cosier feel. The city's gay scene
revolves around the lively **Café Conquest**
(7 Rue du Palais de Justice; closed Sun).
A nightclub worth checking is **The Elevator**
(54 Rue de Hollerich), part of Den Atelier, a
popular venue for local and visiting bands.

Getting There & Away

For information on international flights and
train services, see Getting There & Away at
the beginning of this chapter. Turn left as you
leave the train station to find CFL buses
heading to towns within Luxembourg.

Getting Around

To/From the Airport Bus No 9 (three services hourly) connects Findel airport with the
HI hostel, Place Hamilius in the old town and
the train station; it costs €1 (luggage €1).
Alternatively the Luxair bus (€3.75) picks up
at the station and Place Hamilius. A taxi to
Findel costs about €17.50.

Bus City buses depart from in front of the
train station and from Place Hamilius in the
old town. Free bus route maps are handed out
at the tourist office. For ticket information see
the Getting Around section earlier in this
chapter.

Car Street parking is difficult to find. The
cheapest car park is Glacis, about 800m northwest of Place d'Armes.

From here a free minibus (every 10 minutes
from 8am to 6pm Monday to Saturday) shuttles commuters to Place Hamilius in the old
town centre.

For car rental try **Autolux** *(☎ 22 11 81; 33
Blvd Prince Henri)* or **Avis** *(☎ 43 51 71)*,
Budget *(☎ 43 75 75)* and **Hertz** *(☎ 43 46 45)*
in Findel airport.

Bicycle Rent a bike from **Vélo en Ville** *(☎ 47
96 23 83; 8 Rue Bisserwé)* for €5 per hour or
€12.50/20 per half-day/day (20% off the day
rental rate for under 26s).

Around Luxembourg City

MOSELLE VALLEY

Less than half an hour's drive east of the
capital, the Luxembourg section of the
Moselle Valley is one of Europe's smallest
wine regions.

More than a dozen towns line the **Route du
Vin** (Wine Road), which follows the Moselle
from Wasserbillig, through the region's capital at Grevenmacher, past the popular, waterfront playground of Remich, to the small,
southern border town of Schengen.

There are only two tourist offices en route:
the **Grevenmacher tourist office** *(☎ 75 82
75; 10 Route du Vin; open 8am-noon &
2pm-5pm Mon-Fri)*, and the **Remich tourist
office** *(☎ 69 84 88; Esplanade; open 9am-
5pm daily July-Aug)*.

Things to See & Do

Wine tasting is the obvious attraction and there are several *caves* (cellars) where you can sample the fruity, white vintages. Try the **Caves Bernard-Massard** (☎ 75 05 45 1; 8 Rue du Pont, Grevenmacher) or **St Martin** (☎ 69 97 74; Route de Stadtbredimus, Remich) which have tours for €2.50 and €2.23 respectively. Both are open daily from April to October.

From Easter to September, it's possible to enjoy a **cruise** on the Moselle on the *Princesse Marie-Astrid*. It calls in at Schengen, Remich, Wormeldange, Grevenmacher and Wasserbillig, before continuing to Trier and Bernkastel in Germany. A sample fare is €7.50/11.50 one way/return between Remich and Wasserbillig (three hours). For more details contact **Entente Touristique de la Moselle Luxembourgeoise** (☎ 75 82 75; 10 Route du Vin, Grevenmacher). Also check out the train-boat-bus combo from Luxembourg City (see Boat in the Getting Around section for details).

Special Events

The wine festivals start in August and climax with November's 'New Wine' festival in Wormeldange; each village celebrates nearly all stages of the wine-making process.

Places to Stay & Eat

Next to the butterfly garden in Grevenmacher, there's **Camping Route du Vin** (☎ 75 02 34; Route du Vin; open Apr-Sept).

Remich has several riverfront hotels. The cheapest is **Beau Séjour** (☎ 23 69 81 26, fax 23 66 94 82; 30 Quai de la Moselle; singles/doubles with shared toilet from €33/52, with private facilities €47/70).

Bamberg's (☎ 76 00 22, fax 76 00 56; e bamberg@pt.lu; Route du Vin; singles/doubles €62/87) in the village of Ehnen is best known for its restaurant (delicious French and seafood cuisine) but it also has well-priced accommodation.

Getting There & Away

The region is difficult to explore without your own transport. Trains stop at Wasserbillig only. The buses from Luxembourg City go to Grevenmacher (twice daily) from where there are connections to other towns.

CENTRAL LUXEMBOURG

While there's not much to keep you in central Luxembourg, the area can make a good

exploration base. The town of **Ettelbrück** is the nation's central rail junction and from here it's easy to get a train to the nearby town of **Diekirch**, which is home to the country's main wartime museum.

The Diekirch **tourist office** (☎ 80 30 23; e tourisme@diekirch.lu; 3 Place de la Libération; open 9am-noon & 2pm-5pm Mon-Fri, 2pm-4pm Sat Sept-June, 9am-5pm Mon-Fri, 10am-noon & 2pm-4pm Sat & Sun July-15 Aug) is a 10-minute walk from the station.

Things to See & Do

Diekirch's **Musée National d'Histoire Militaire** (☎ 80 89 08; 10 Rue Barnertal; adult/concession €5/3; open 10am-6pm daily Apr-Nov, 2pm-6pm daily Nov-Mar) details the 1944 Battle of the Bulge and the liberation of Luxembourg by US troops. Its excellent collection of wartime artefacts is well presented.

With a car, it's worth taking the winding drive northwest of Diekirch to the 1000-year-old **Bourscheid Castle** (☎ 99 05 70; admission €3/1.50; open daily Apr-Oct, Sat & Sun Nov-Mar). It's situated on a plateau and has vast views over farmland and the Sûre River.

Places to Stay

Diekirch offers a decent choice of accommodation but if you're looking for hostel accommodation you'll need to stay in Ettelbrück.

Diekirch's **Camping de la Sûre** (☎ 80 94 25; 34 Route de Gilsdorf; open Apr-Sept) is by the river. The Ettelbrück **hostel** (☎ 81 22 69, fax 81 69 35; e ettelbruck@youthhostels .lu; Rue G D Joséphine-Charlotte; open Feb-Dec) is a 20-minute walk from the station. **B&B Weber-Posing** (☎ 80 32 54, fax 26 80 06 54; 74 Rue Principale; rooms per person €18), in Gilsdorf, about 2km west from central Diekirch, has large, old-fashioned rooms. **Hiertz** (☎ 80 35 62, fax 80 88 69; 1 Rue Clairefontaine; singles/doubles €57/72) in the heart of Diekirch has decent rooms and one of the region's best restaurants – try the seven-course *menu de dégustation* for €69.

Getting There & Away

Hourly trains from Luxembourg City to Ettelbrück take 30 minutes; to Diekirch, it takes 40 minutes.

MÜLLERTHAL

The Müllerthal region lies northeast of the capital, based around the old, Christian town of

Echternach. The area is riddled with fascinating sandstone plateaus and is often referred to as *Petite Suisse* (Little Switzerland) due to its extensive woodlands. Outdoor enthusiasts love this area – it's great for hiking, cycling and rock climbing, and is one of Luxembourg's prime tourist spots.

The Echternach **tourist information office** (☎ 72 02 30; *Porte St Willibrord; open 9am-noon & 2pm-5pm Mon-Fri Sept-June, 9am-noon & 2pm-5pm daily July & Aug*) is in front of the basilica. There are smaller offices in the villages of **Beaufort** (☎ 83 60 99; *87 Grand Rue*) and **Berdorf** (☎ 79 06 43; *7 An der Laach*).

Things to See & Do

If you happen to be in Echternach on Whit Sunday, look out for the handkerchief pageant in honour of St Willibrord, a missionary who died in the town centuries ago. If not, you can visit the **basilica**, the country's most important religious building, where St Willibrord's remains lie in a white, marble sarcophagus. Behind the basilica, there's a **Benedictine abbey**.

Immediately west of Echternach, walking paths wind through wonderful rocky chasms and past waterfalls to **Berdorf**, situated on the tableland 6km away, and on to the hidden **Beaufort castle** (*adult/concession €2/1.25; open 9am-6pm daily Apr-Oct*).

Places to Stay

Camping grounds are abundant throughout this region, and the loveliest ones are away from the towns. If you're stuck for transport, **Camping Officiel** (☎ 72 02 72; *5 Route de Diekirch*), is about 200m from Echternach's bus station. In Beaufort is the **Camping um Bierg** (☎ 83 60 70; *110 Grand Rue; open year-round*).

There are two **hostels** (☎ 72 01 58, fax 72 87 35; e echternach@youthhostels.lu; *9 Rue André Duchscher, Echternach* ● ☎ 83 60 75, fax 86 94 67; e beaufort@youthhostels.lu; *6 Rue de l'Auberge, Beaufort; dorms €13.60*). The Echternach hostel is particularly nice and is right in the heart of the town.

Hotels are plentiful in Echternach. **Aigle Noir** (☎ 72 03 83, fax 72 05 44; *54 Rue de la Gare; singles/doubles €32.50/40*), about 40 steps from the bus station, has basic accommodation. **Hôtel Le Pavillon** (☎ 72 98 09, fax 72 86 23; e diedling@pt.lu; *2 Rue de la Gare; singles/doubles Oct-Apr €50/65, May-Sept*

€55/70) is a sweet little corner hotel with 10 well-equipped rooms.

Getting There & Away

Only buses connect Echternach with Luxembourg City – the trip takes 40 minutes. From Echternach, buses head out to other towns.

THE ARDENNES

The Grand Duchy's northern region is known as the Luxembourg Ardennes. It's spectacular country – winding valleys with fast-flowing rivers cut deep through green plateaus crowned by castles. Of the three main towns, Clervaux, in the far north, is the most accessible; while Vianden, in the east, is arguably Luxembourg's most touristy town. To the west is Wiltz, the nominal capital of the Ardennes. It's best visited in July when the Grand Duchy's biggest musical event – an open-air festival of theatre, jazz and classical music – takes over the otherwise quiet little town. Near Wiltz, the tiny hamlet of Esch-sur-Sûre attracts a staggering number of tourists simply because of its picturesque location.

Clervaux

Clervaux's **tourist office** (☎ 92 00 72; *open 2pm-5pm Mon-Fri Easter-June, 9.45am-11.45am & 2pm-6pm daily July-Aug, 9.45am-11.45am & 1pm-5pm Sept & Oct*) is ensconced in its castle.

The town has two main sights: its feudal **castle**, in the town centre, and the turreted **Benedictine abbey**, high in the forest above. The castle houses Edward Steichen's famous photography collection, *Family of Man* (☎ 92 96 57; *adult/concession €3.75/2; open 10am-6pm Tues-Sun Mar-Dec, 10am-6pm daily Apr-Sept*). It's well worth seeing.

Vianden

Vianden's **tourist office** (☎ 83 42 57; *1a Rue du Vieux Marché; open 8am-6pm daily Apr-Oct, 9am-noon & 1pm-5pm Mon-Fri Nov-Mar*) is in the lower part of town, down by the river.

The town's most noted feature is its impeccably restored **chateau** (☎ 83 41 08; *adult/concession €4.50/3.50; open 10am-4pm daily Oct-Mar, 10am-6pm daily Apr-Sept*). The chateau's striking position can be photographed from the **télésiège** (*chairlift; tickets €4.20; operates 10am-5pm daily Easter–mid-Oct*), which climbs the nearby hill.

The **Maison de Victor Hugo** (*☎ 478 66 16; 37 Rue de la Gare; adult/concession €3/2; open 11am-5pm Tues-Sun July-Aug, Easter & Christmas holidays*), across the river from the tourist office, was home to author Victor Hugo during his exile from France between 1870 and 1871. It opened as a museum in 2002 and houses memorabilia related to his time here.

Wiltz

The **tourist office** (*☎ 95 74 44; open 10am-6pm daily June-Aug, 10am-5pm Mon-Sat Sept-May*) is in the chateau.

Built on the side of a small plateau, Wiltz is more spacious, but less picturesque, than Clervaux or Vianden. It's divided in two: the Ville Haute (High Town), where most of the sights are found, is situated on a crest, while the Ville Basse and the train station flank the river below.

The rather sterile **chateau** (*☎ 95 74 42; adult/concession €1.50/0.75; open 10am-noon & 1.30pm-5.30pm daily June-Aug*) sits on the edge of the Ville Haute and is home to an exhibition about the 1944 Battle of the Bulge. Nearby, on the main road to the Ville Basse, is an unusual stone-sculpted tower. This **memorial** commemorates those who died or were sent to concentration camps as a result of a national strike in 1942, called to protest the Nazi's introduction of conscription.

Esch-sur-Sûre

The tiny village of Esch-sur-Sûre is off the Wiltz-Ettelbrück road. It's built on a rocky peninsula skirted by the Sûre River and is lorded over by steep cliffs and a ruined castle. It's all very picturesque and, in summer, tourists come here in droves.

A worthwhile detour is to the **Maison du Parc Naturel** (see Ecology & Environment earlier in this chapter), which contains a wonderful working collection of old looms and other textile-making machines, as well as environmental displays.

Places to Stay

Clervaux In Clervaux the closest camping ground is **Camping Officiel** (*☎ 92 00 42; 33 Klatzewé; open Apr-Oct*). There's no hostel in Clervaux; the nearest hostel is in Wiltz (see the following section). The **Hôtel du Parc** (*☎ 92 06 50, fax 92 10 68; e hduparc@pt.lu; 2 Rue du Parc; singles/doubles from €44/70*) occupies an old mansion and has seven presentable rooms.

Vianden There are several camping grounds in Vianden. **Op dem Deich** (*☎ 83 43 75; open Easter-Sept*) is on the river to the south of town, about 200m from the bus station.

Vianden's **hostel** (*☎ 83 41 77, fax 84 94 27; e vianden@youthhostels.lu; 3 Montée du Château; dorm beds €13.60*) is nestled in the shadow of the chateau. It has rooms with between two and 16 beds.

There are heaps of hotels, many open from Easter to October only. The most expensive ones line the Grand Rue.

For something cheaper try the friendly **Auberge de l'Our** (*☎ 83 46 75, fax 84 91 94; 35 Rue de la Gare; singles/doubles from €24/40, doubles with private bathroom €50*). It's by the river and has bright rooms.

Wiltz The **Camping Kaul** (*☎ 95 03 59 1; Rue Jos Simon; open Apr-Oct*) is about 800m from the train station. The **hostel** (*☎ 95 80 39, fax 95 94 40; e wiltz@youthhostels.lu; 6 Rue de la Montagne; dorm beds €13.60*) is a 1km climb from the train station, behind the Ville Haute.

The most engaging hotel is **Aux Anciennes Tanneries** (*☎ 95 75 99; e tannerie@pt.lu; 42a Rue Jos Simon; singles/doubles from €70/75*) situated in the Ville Basse. It provides modern rooms overlooking a babbling stream, and there also is an excellent restaurant.

Getting There & Away

There are trains every two hours to Clervaux from Luxembourg City (one hour). To reach Vianden, take the Luxembourg City–Ettelbrück train and then catch a connecting bus.

In order to get to Wiltz (1½ hours) you take the Luxembourg City–Clervaux train to Kautenbach, and another train from there.

The Netherlands

A small country with a big reputation for liberalism, the Netherlands swims in a sea of familiar images. A land of bikes, dikes, blazing flower fields, mills and few hills – these quintessential images of the Netherlands do exist outside the major cities and the once-radical, still exuberant, capital of Amsterdam.

While Amsterdam tops most travellers' itineraries, there is plenty to entice you away from the 'anything goes' capital. The historic cities of Leiden, Haarlem and Delft, cosmopolitan Rotterdam, the lively student towns of Groningen and Maastricht, and the vast stretches of beach on the northern islands, are good reasons to venture beyond Amsterdam. The countryside's endlessly flat landscape is also a cyclist's nirvana, where you'll discover a hard-fought-for land with proud and friendly people.

Facts about the Netherlands

HISTORY

You can't talk about the Netherlands' early history without mentioning Belgium and Luxembourg in the same breath: the three were known as the Low Countries until the 16th century, when today's Netherlands' boundaries were roughly drawn. Originally the land was inhabited by tribal groups: the Germanic Batavi drained the sea lagoons while the Frisii lived on mounds in the remote north.

In the late 16th century, the region's northern provinces united to fight the Spanish. Led by Prince William of Orange, the Revolt of the Netherlands lasted 80 years, ending in 1648 with a treaty that recognised the 'United Provinces' as an independent republic. As part of the deal, the Schelde River was closed to all non-Dutch ships. This destroyed the trade of the largest port at that time, Antwerp, but ensured the prosperity of its rival, Amsterdam.

Amsterdam stormed onto the European scene in what was the province of Holland's most glorified period: the Golden Age, which ran from about 1580 to 1740. The era's wealth was generated by the Dutch East India Company, which sent ships to the Far East in search of spices and other exotic goods, while colonising the Cape of Good Hope and Indonesia and

establishing trading posts throughout Asia. Later the West Indies Company sailed to West Africa and the Americas, creating colonies in Surinam, the Antilles and New Amsterdam (today's New York).

Meanwhile, Amsterdam's bourgeoisie indulged in fine, gabled canal houses, and paintings of themselves and the remains of last night's dinner. This stimulated the arts and brought renown to painters such as Rembrandt.

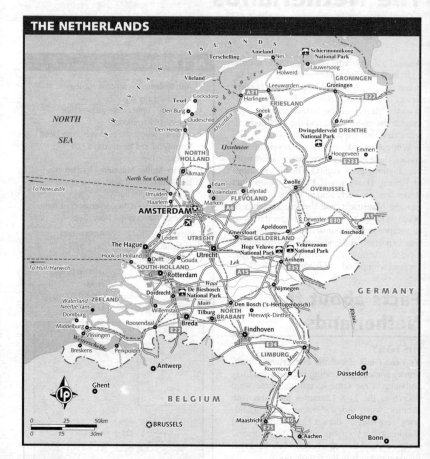

THE NETHERLANDS

But it didn't last. In 1795 the French invaded and Napoleon appointed his younger brother Louis as king. When the largely unpopular French occupation ended, the United Kingdom of the Netherlands – incorporating Belgium and Luxembourg – was born. The first monarch, King William I of Orange, was crowned in 1814, and the House of Orange rules to this day. In 1830 the Belgians rebelled and became independent, and Luxembourg was split between Belgium and the Netherlands. Nine years on, the Dutch portion gained independence and became Luxembourg.

While the Netherlands stayed neutral in WWI, it was unable to do so in WWII. The Germans invaded on 10 May 1940, obliterating much of Rotterdam in a bombing blitz four days later. Although a sound Dutch resistance

movement formed, only a minority of the country's Jews survived the war.

In 1949, despite military attempts to hold on to Indonesia, the colony won independence. Surinam followed much later, gaining a peaceful handover of sovereignty in 1975. The Antilles still has close ties with the Netherlands but is self-ruled.

In 1953 one of the country's worst disasters hit when a high spring tide and a severe storm breached the dikes in Zeeland, drowning 1835 people. To ensure the tragedy would never be repeated, under the Delta Plan a network of dams and dikes was constructed (see the Delta Region section later in this chapter).

The social consciousness of the 1960s found fertile ground in the Netherlands, especially in Amsterdam, which became the radical heart of Europe. The riotous squatter's movement stopped the demolition of much cheap inner-city housing, the lack of which is a problem that has continued into the 21st century.

The Netherlands is very much a part of the EU, and it was in Maastricht that members of the European community gathered in 1992 to sign the treaty which created the EU.

GEOGRAPHY
Bordered by the North Sea, Belgium and Germany, the Netherlands occupies 33,920 sq km. It is largely artificial, its lands reclaimed from the sea over many centuries and the drained polders protected by dikes. More than 50% of the country is situated below sea level. Only in the southeast Limburg province will you find hills.

The southwest province of Zeeland is the combined delta area of the Schelde, Maas, Lek and Waal Rivers.

The Lek and Waal are branches of the Rhine, carrying most of its water to the sea – the mighty Rhine itself peters out in a pathetic little stream (the Oude Rijn, or Old Rhine) at the coast near Katwijk.

CLIMATE
The Netherlands has a temperate maritime climate with cool winters and mild summers. The wettest months are July and August, though precipitation is spread fairly evenly throughout the year. The sunniest months are May to August, and the warmest are June to September. Because it's such a flat country, wind has free reign – something you'll soon notice if you're cycling.

ECOLOGY & ENVIRONMENT
On the whole, the Dutch public takes environmental issues – such as pollution – very seriously, and sound legislation was introduced to help preserve and protect the environment.

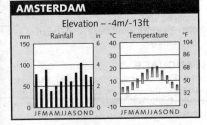

The nation's most pressing environmental problems are water and air pollution, and the contamination of groundwater by high levels of nitrates and phosphates used in agriculture.

There are 15 national parks dotted around the countryside. As you'd expect in a nation of this size, they're not enormous, but invaluable for preserving fauna and flora. The Hoge Veluwe and nearby Veluwezoom were the first parks to be declared in the 1930s. Other major parks are Schiermonnikoog (5400 hectares; mainly dunes), Biesbosch (7100 hectares; wetlands) and Dwingelderveld (3600 hectares; heather fields).

GOVERNMENT & POLITICS
Against the European trend, the Netherlands developed from a republic to a constitutional monarchy, headed today by Queen Beatrix who took over from her mother, Juliana, in 1980. Until 2001, the country's political scene was often compared with the physical landscape – flat and often dull – with coalition governments pursuing policies of compromise. The three main parties have traditionally been the socialist PvdA, the conservative Liberal VVD and the Catholic-Protestant CDA. However, the right-wing politician Pim Fortuyn added an edge to political debate with his anti-immigration views and the country was left shell-shocked when he was shot dead nine days before the May 2002 election. His party, Lijst Pim Fortuyn (LPF), went on to win the second-largest number of seats in the election, behind the CDA. The CDA's leader, Jan Peter Balkenende, is the new prime minister.

The country consists of 12 provinces, including Flevoland, which only came into existence in 1967 after it had been claimed from the sea. The province of Holland was split into North Holland (capital: Haarlem) and South Holland (capital: The Hague) during the Napoleonic era. The Catholic portion of the population lives mainly in the southeastern provinces of North Brabant and Limburg. The province of Zeeland gave New Zealand its name (Australia once was known as New Holland).

ECONOMY
Despite its small size, the Netherlands has a strong economy. The GDP figure in 1999 was US$372 billion, and unemployment in early 2002 was a very low 2.4%. The Netherlands is a leader in service industries such as banking;

THE NETHERLANDS

electronics (Philips) and multimedia (Polygram); and has a highly developed horticultural industry (bulbs and cut flowers). Agriculture plays an important role, particularly dairy farming and glasshouse fruits and vegetables. Rotterdam harbour, which handles the largest shipping tonnage in the world, is vital to the economy, as are the country's large supplies of natural gas in the northeast.

POPULATION & PEOPLE

Western Europe's most densely populated country has 16.11 million people, and a lot of Frisian cows, in its small area. This concentration is intensified in the Randstad, the western hoop of cities which includes Amsterdam, The Hague and Rotterdam.

ARTS

Over the centuries the Netherlands has produced some of the most influential painters in the world. The earliest artist of note was Hieronymus Bosch (1450–1516), whose macabre paintings are full of religious allegories. The greatest artist of 17th-century Dutch painting was Rembrandt (1606–69), who excelled in religious art, portraiture, landscapes and still life, ie, all the categories of paintings popular at the time.

Other notable painters of this golden age were Frans Hals (1582–1666), master of portraits, and Jan Vermeer (1632–75), who meticulously crafted balanced compositions of scenes from ordinary life.

The country's best-known 19th-century painter was Vincent van Gogh (1853–90), whose short but productive painting career ended when he committed suicide to escape mental illness. Van Gogh's early and sombre works were painted in his homeland, and they stand in stark contrast to the frenzied paintings he produced during his last few years in France.

In the 20th century Piet Mondrian (1872–1944), with his abstract rectangular compositions, was one of the leading exponents of the De Stijl movement, while the prints of Maurits Escher (1902–72), depicting impossible images, continue to fascinate mathematicians.

The Netherlands shines internationally in other artistic fields, including jazz (The Hague hosts the world's largest jazz festival each summer) and dance. The latter is highlighted by the respected Nationaal Ballet company and the Nederlands Danstheater, known for its innovative modern dance.

Though relatively little Dutch literature has been translated into English you can find some classic tales such as *Max Havelaar* by Eduard D Dekker, better known as Multatuli. Noted contemporary authors include Harry Mulisch *(The Assault)* and Cees Nooteboom *(A Song of Truth and Semblance* and *In the Dutch Mountains).*

The Diary of Anne Frank, an autobiography written by a Jewish teenager, movingly describes life while hiding in Nazi-occupied Amsterdam.

Two Dutch films have won an Oscar for best foreign film – *De Aanslag* (The Assault) by Fons Rademakers in 1986, and *Karakter* (Character) by Mike Van Diem in 1997. The 1973 film, *Turks Fruit*, by Paul Verhoeven, is also well-known internationally.

SOCIETY & CONDUCT

The Dutch are well known for their tolerance, which perhaps has stemmed from *verzuiling* (pillarisation). This is the custom of dividing society into compartments or pillars which, although separate from each other, support society as a whole. In this way any group that demands a place in society can have it, and the balance is kept by an overall attitude of 'agreeing to disagree'.

It's customary to greet shopkeepers and bar/café owners when entering their premises.

In the red-light districts, 'No photo' stickers often adorn windows and should be taken seriously.

RELIGION

The number of former churches that now house art galleries is the most obvious sign of today's attitude to religion – and art. Around 41% of the population doesn't identify with any religion. Catholics are the largest religious grouping, accounting for 31% of the population more than 18 years old. The Dutch Reformed Church, to which half the population belonged 100 years ago, attracts about 21% today, though it's still the official church of the royal family.

LANGUAGE

Most English speakers use the term 'Dutch' to describe the language that's spoken in the Netherlands, and 'Flemish' for the language spoken in the northern half of Belgium and a tiny northwestern corner of France. Both are in fact the same language – the correct term is Netherlandic, or *Nederlands*, a West Germanic language spoken by about 25 million people worldwide.

The people of the northern Fryslân (Friesland) province speak their own language. Although Frisian is actually the nearest relative of the English language, you won't make much sense of it when you hear it spoken.

The differences between Dutch and Flemish (*Vlaams*), in their spoken as well as written forms, are similar to those between UK and North American English.

Like many other languages, Netherlandic gives its nouns genders. There are three genders: masculine, feminine (both with *de* for 'the') and neuter (with *het*). Where English uses 'a' or 'an', Netherlandic uses *een* (pronounced *ern*), regardless of gender.

Netherlandic also has a formal and informal version of the English 'you'. The formal version is *U* (written with a capital letter and pronounced *ü*), the informal version is *je* (pronounced *yer*).

As a general rule, people who are older than you should still be addressed with *U*. See the Language chapter at the back of the book for pronunciation guidelines and useful words and phrases.

Facts for the Visitor

HIGHLIGHTS

After Amsterdam, the Keukenhof gardens (see The Randstad section) are a must, especially for flower aficionados, while anyone into a bit of dirt should investigate *wadlopen* – mud-flat walking (see The North section).

Museum and cycling buffs will be in their element throughout the Netherlands – a visit to the Kröller-Müller Museum (see the Arnhem & the Hoge Veluwe section) superbly combines the two.

Amsterdam's Rijksmuseum and Van Gogh Museum shouldn't be missed, and Holland's second city Rotterdam is a showcase of modern architecture with cultural influences from around the world.

Groningen is a fun university town, while Maastricht's medieval streets and great nightlife make a winning combination. The island of Texel provides a relaxing break from the cities.

SUGGESTED ITINERARIES

Depending on the length of your stay, you might want to see and do the following:

Two days
Visit Amsterdam.

One week
Spend two days in Amsterdam, one day each in The Hague, Delft, Leiden (visiting the Keukenhof gardens in season), and the remaining two days visiting Rotterdam and the Kinderdijk windmills.

Two weeks
Spend three days in Amsterdam, one day each in Haarlem, Delft, Hoge Veluwe National Park, Den Bosch, and Groningen, and two days each in Rotterdam, Leiden (including the Keukenhof gardens), and Maastricht.

One month
This should give you enough time to have a look around most of the country or spend more time in places along the way.

PLANNING
When to Go

Spring is the ideal time to visit, as there's less chance of rain and the bulbs are in bloom – daffodils from early to late April, and tulips from late April to mid-May.

Maps

The Lonely Planet *Amsterdam City Map* is plastic-coated to make it rainproof and has a handy street index. Excellent road maps of the Netherlands include those produced by Michelin (scale: 1:400,000) and the ANWB (scale: 1:300,000). The ANWB also puts out provincial maps detailing cycling paths and picturesque road routes (scale: 1:100,000).

TOURIST OFFICES
Local Tourist Offices

The ubiquitous VVV (the national tourist organisation) sells brochures on everything and maps for everywhere. Its offices are generally open 8am or 9am to 5pm or 6pm Monday to Friday, and 10am to 4pm Saturday, and sometimes on Sunday as well. Staff will book accommodation and the fee can range from nothing to €12 per booking. In larger cities, and during July and August, opening hours are extended. Most VVV offices have telephone numbers prefixed by ☎ 0900 (these numbers cost about €0.55 per minute) and are answered by recorded messages in Dutch – wait for the message to end to be answered personally.

The **Netherlands Board of Tourism** (*NBT;* [e] *info@nbt.nl; Vlietweg 15, Postbus 458, 2260 MG Leidschendam*) takes postal and email inquiries only.

Tourist Offices Abroad
NBT has offices in other countries, including the following:

Belgium (☎ 02-543 0800, [e] info@nbt.be) Louizalaan 89, 1050 Brussels
Canada (☎ 416-363 1577) 25 Adelaide St East, Suite 710, Toronto, Ont M5C 1Y2
France (☎ 01 43 12 34 27, [e] balie@hollande-tourisme.fr) 9 rue Scribe, 75008 Paris
Germany (☎ 0221-9257 1727) Friesenplatz 1, Postfach 270580, 50672 Cologne 1
Japan (☎ 03-3222 1112) NK Shinwa Bldg 5F, 5-1 Kojimachi, Chiyoda-ku, Tokyo 102-0083
UK (☎ 020-7539 7950, [e] information@nbt.org.uk) PO Box 30783, London, WC2B 6DH
USA (☎ 212-370 7360, [e] info@goholland.com) 355 Lexington Ave, New York, NY 10017

VISAS & DOCUMENTS
Travellers from Australia, Canada, Israel, Japan, New Zealand, the USA and many other countries need only a valid passport (no visa) for a stay of up to three months. EU nationals can enter for three months with just their national identity card or a passport expired for no more than five years. Nationals of most other countries need a so-called Schengen Visa, valid for 90 days. After three months, extensions can be sought through the Vreemdelingenpolitie (Aliens' Police), but you'll need a good reason for an extension to be granted.

EMBASSIES & CONSULATES
Dutch Embassies & Consulates
Dutch embassies and consulates abroad include the following:

Australia (☎ 02-6273 3111) 120 Empire Circuit, Yarralumla, Canberra, ACT 2600
Canada (☎ 613-237 5030) Suite 2020, 350 Albert St, Ottawa, Ont K1R 1A4
New Zealand (☎ 04-471 6390) 10th floor, Investment House, Cnr Ballance & Featherston Sts, Wellington
UK (☎ 020-7590 3200) 38 Hyde Park Gate, London SW7 5DP
USA (☎ 202-244 5300) 4200 Linnean Ave, NW Washington, DC 20008

Embassies & Consulates in the Netherlands
Embassies (in The Hague) and consulates (in Amsterdam) of other countries in the Netherlands include:

Australia (☎ 070-310 82 00) Carnegielaan 4, 2517 KH The Hague
Belgium (☎ 070-312 34 56) Alexanderveld 97, 2584 DB The Hague
Canada (☎ 070-311 16 00) Sophialaan 7, 2514 JP The Hague
France (☎ 070-312 58 00) Smidsplein 1, 2514 BT The Hague
  Consulate: (☎ 020-530 69 71) Vijzelgracht 2, 1017 HR Amsterdam
Germany (☎ 070-342 06 00) Groot Hertoginnelaan 18, 2517 EG The Hague
  Consulate: (☎ 020-673 62 45) De Lairessestraat 172, 1075 HM Amsterdam
Ireland (☎ 070-363 09 93) Dr Kuyperstraat 9, 2514 BA The Hague
New Zealand (☎ 070-346 93 24) Carnegielaan 10, 2517 KH The Hague
UK (☎ 070-427 04 27) Lange Voorhout 10, 2514 ED The Hague
  Consulate: (☎ 020-676 43 43) Koningslaan 44, 1075 AE Amsterdam
USA (☎ 070-310 92 09) Lange Voorhout 102, 2514 EJ The Hague
  Consulate: (☎ 020-575 53 09) Museumplein 19, 1071 DJ Amsterdam

CUSTOMS
In the Netherlands, the usual allowances apply to duty-free goods if you are coming from a non-EU country and to duty paid goods if you're arriving from within the EU.

MONEY
The Netherlands is participating in the euro, the European single currency (see the Exchange Rates section in the introductory Facts for the Visitor chapter).

Exchanging Money
Banks and post offices stick to official exchange rates and charge a fair commission, as does the national exchange organisation, De Grenswisselkantoren (GWK; literally 'The Border Exchange Offices'). You'll find GWK branches at all major border posts and train stations, open 7am or 8am to 8pm or 10pm daily and longer hours at Amsterdam's Centraal Station and Schiphol airport. For ease of use and low transaction costs though, nothing beats ATMs which you'll find as soon as you

land at Schiphol airport and at Centraal Station in Amsterdam.

In larger cities there are many private exchange bureaus that close late but generally demand high commissions or offer lousy rates. Although all major credit cards are recognised, the Netherlands is still very much a cash-based society.

Costs

Staying at hostels and eating in cheap cafés, and going to the occasional museum, you'll be looking at spending at least €35 a day; €50 would be more comfortable. If you want to stay in a mid-range hotel, eat out each day, take in a couple of museums, and travel around the country you'll need at least €100 a day.

Avid museum goers should buy the Museumjaarkaart (Museum Year Card) that gives free entry into more than 400 museums and art galleries. It costs €35 (and €15 for those aged under 25) and is issued at participating museums (you'll need a passport photo). Most museums mentioned in this chapter are free with the Museumjaarkaart. Almost all museums offer concession prices for children and over 65s, and occasionally to students as well.

Tipping & Bargaining

Tipping is not compulsory, but 'rounding up' the bill is always appreciated in taxis, restaurants and pubs with table or sidewalk service. Forget about bargaining, though the Dutch themselves get away with it at flea markets.

Taxes & Refunds

The value-added tax (BTW in Dutch) is calculated at 19% for most goods, except consumer items like food, for which you pay 6%. Travellers from non-EU countries can have it refunded on goods totalling more than €175 providing they're bought from one shop on one day and are exported within three months.

To claim back the tax, ask the shop owner to provide an export certificate when you make the purchase. When you leave for a non-EU country, get the form endorsed by Dutch customs, then send the certificate to the supplier, who in turn refunds the tax by cheque or money order. If you want the tax before you leave the country, it's best to buy from shops affiliated with the Tax Cheque Refund Service. These shops will give you a stamped Tax Refund Cheque which can be cashed at your port of exit (but because of red tape, you'll lose about 5% of the refund). You'll need to show the customs officers the goods, the bill and your passport.

POST & COMMUNICATIONS
Post

In general, post offices are open 9am to 5pm or 6pm Monday to Friday (though Monday is often a late start), and until 1.30pm Saturday. Postcards to anywhere cost €0.54. Letters cost €0.39 within the Netherlands, €0.54 for up to 20g within Europe, and €0.75 outside Europe. Mail generally takes about five to six days to the USA and Canada, six to 10 days to Australia and New Zealand, and two to three days to the UK.

Telephone

For making international telephone calls to the Netherlands, the country code is ☎ 31. To telephone abroad, the international access code is ☎ 00 (see the Telephones appendix at the back of this book).

Local telephone calls are time-based – the minimum charge from a KPN-Telecom public phone is €0.10, then approximately €0.20 per minute. The telephone numbers prefixed with ☎ 0900 are more expensive (between €0.45 and €1.45 per minute). Numbers starting with ☎ 0800 are free calls, and those prefixed with ☎ 06-2, 06-5 or ☎ 06-6 are mobile (cell) and pager numbers. In local telephone books, similar surnames are listed alphabetically by address, not by initials.

Telephones take €5 and €10 phonecards and, sometimes, credit cards. Coin-operated telephones are rare. International calls can be made from public phones and post offices, using phonecards designed specifically for international calls. Alternatively, you can use a Lonely Planet eKno Communication Card; see the Lonely Planet website (**w** www.lonely planet.com) for details.

For travellers with mobile phones, the Netherlands uses GSM 900/1800, which is compatible with the rest of Europe and Australia but not with the North American GSM 1900 or the system used in Japan.

Fax

International faxes can be sent (but not received) from post offices. Within the Netherlands and Europe there is a basic charge of €2.50 plus €0.50 per page; for outside Europe it's €5, plus €1 per page.

THE NETHERLANDS

Kinko's (☎ 020-589 09 10, fax 589 09 20; Overtoom 62, Amsterdam • ☎ 010-411 63 44, fax 213 19 40; Vasteland 92, Rotterdam; both open 24hr daily) charges €1.13/1.60 per page for sending faxes within/outside Europe, and €0.45 per page to receive a fax.

Email & Internet Access

There are plenty of Internet cafés in Amsterdam and at least one in most major towns. The local *bibliotheek* (library) in most towns is a reliable option for Internet access at reasonable rates.

DIGITAL RESOURCES

The Dutch are digital-media leaders. The best place to start a virtual visit to the Netherlands is the websites of the **Netherlands Board of Tourism** (W *www.visitholland.com)* and the **Amsterdam city site** (W *www.amsterdam.nl)*.

BOOKS

Lonely Planet's *The Netherlands* guide is a must for those travellers intending in-depth exploration. If you're concentrating on the capital, there's the Lonely Planet *Amsterdam* city guide or *Amsterdam Condensed*, which has all the essentials for a weekend break and fits easily in your pocket.

For a humorous look at Dutch ways, pick up *The UnDutchables* by the non-Dutch Colin White & Laurie Boucke or, more seriously, *Culture Shock! Netherlands* by Hunt Janin.

Girl with a Pearl Earring by Tracey Chevalier provides an insight into Dutch life in the 17th century.

NEWSPAPERS & MAGAZINES

There's no English-language newspaper, but international papers and magazines are easy to find. The largest national newspaper is *De Telegraaf*.

RADIO & TV

London's BBC radio World Service can be tuned to 648kHz medium wave. Cable TV has reached most homes, meaning that there's no shortage of English-language programmes on Dutch TV.

TIME

The Netherlands is in the Central European Time zone. Noon is 11am in London, 6am in New York, 3am in San Francisco, 6am in Toronto, 9pm in Sydney, and 11pm in Auckland.

The 24-hour clock is commonly used. On the last Sunday in March, daylight-saving time comes into effect at 2am, when clocks are moved an hour forward, and ends at 2am on the last Saturday in October, when they're moved an hour back again.

LAUNDRY

Self-service laundrettes are rare and often no more than a few machines put aside for do-it-yourselfers in staffed laundries. A 5kg wash costs an average of €6 to €8 including drying.

TOILETS

Public toilets are not abundant, which is why most people tend to duck into a café, pub or department store. Toilet attendants require tips of €0.35 to €0.50.

WOMEN TRAVELLERS

The women's movement has a strong foothold and women travellers will find *vrouwen* (women's) cafés, bookshops and help centres in many cities. **Het Vrouwenhuis** (*Women's House;* ☎ 020-625 20 66; e *info@vrouwen huis.nl; Nieuwe Herengracht 95, 1011 RX Amsterdam)* is well known.

Unwanted attention from men is not a big problem in the Netherlands. However, in the unlikely event of a rape or an attack, the **De Eerste Lijn** (*☎ 020-613 02 45; open 10.30am-11pm Mon-Fri, 4pm-11pm Sat & Sun)* is an Amsterdam-based help line.

GAY & LESBIAN TRAVELLERS

The Netherlands has long had the reputation of being the most liberal country in Europe where attitudes to homosexuality are concerned. The age of consent is 16, discrimination on the basis of sexual orientation is illegal, and gay and lesbian couples can legally marry. Most provincial capitals have at least one gay and lesbian bar or café, as well as a branch of COC, a gay and lesbian information service. In Amsterdam, contact **COC** (*☎ 020-626 30 87; Rozenstraat 14)*.

If you're interested in information on gay or lesbian venues, the best place to start is the **Gay & Lesbian Switchboard** (*☎ 020-623 65 65; help line staffed 2pm-10pm daily)*, an Amsterdam-based information and help line. *Gay & Night* and *Gay News* are available free at the COC and bars (but cost €3 in newsagencies) and list gay hotels and bars throughout the Netherlands. The Amsterdam

Pride parade is held on the first weekend of August.

DISABLED TRAVELLERS

Travellers with a mobility problem will find the Netherlands reasonably well equipped to meet their needs. Many government buildings, museums, hotels and restaurants have lifts and/or ramps. Many trains and some taxis have wheelchair access, and most train stations have lifts and a toilet for the handicapped. You can call (☎ 030-230 55 66) in advance of your journey to arrange assistance.

For the visually impaired, train timetables are published in Braille. For more information contact the **Nederlands Instituut voor Zorg & Welzijn** (☎ 030-230 66 03, fax 231 96 41; W www.nizw.nl; Postbus 19152, 3501 DD Utrecht).

SENIOR TRAVELLERS

Senior travellers should have few problems in the Netherlands. Many buildings have lifts or ramps, and public transport is accessible. Most museums offer discounts to over 65s.

TRAVEL WITH CHILDREN

The Dutch are pretty relaxed where kids are concerned and you'll find plenty to occupy children. Popular activities include biking in the countryside, visiting Amsterdam's Vondelpark or the Tropenmusem, the windmill museum in Leiden, or heading to the beach in the Frisian Islands.

DANGERS & ANNOYANCES

The number of tales of travellers in Amsterdam having their wallets swiped could fill a book. Pickpockets often use distraction as their key tool, so keep your hands on your valuables, especially at Centraal Station in Amsterdam, the post office and other tourist strongholds. Cyclists should also beware: the stolen bicycle racket is rife. Locals use two chains to lock up their bikes, and even that's no guarantee.

LEGAL MATTERS

Police in the Netherlands are generally polite and helpful. If you've broken the law, they can hold you for six hours for questioning. Should you need legal assistance, the **Buro voor Rechtshulp** (☎ 020-520 51 00; Spuistraat 10, Amsterdam) can give free legal advice during business hours.

Emergency Services

In the event of an emergency, the national telephone number for police, ambulance and fire brigade is ☎ 112.

Despite popular belief to the contrary, drugs are illegal. Possession of more than 5g of marijuana or hash can, strictly speaking, get you a large fine and/or land you in jail – hard drugs can definitely land you in jail. Small amounts of 'soft' drugs for personal use are generally, though not officially, tolerated, but could complicate matters if you're already in trouble with the police over something else. Don't buy drugs from street dealers – you'll end up getting ripped off or mugged.

BUSINESS HOURS

The working week starts leisurely at around lunchtime on Monday. For the rest of the week most shops open at 8.30am or 9am and close at 5.30pm or 6pm, except Thursday when many close at 9pm, and on Saturday at 5pm. In Amsterdam and tourist centres you will find many shops open on Sunday, too. Supermarkets often have extended trading hours.

Banks are generally open 9am to 4pm or 5pm Monday to Friday. Many museums are closed on Monday.

PUBLIC HOLIDAYS & SPECIAL EVENTS

Public holidays are held on New Year's Day, Good Friday, Easter Sunday and Monday, Queen's Day (30 April), Ascension Day, Whit Sunday and Monday, Christmas Day and Boxing Day.

The Holland Festival brings many of the top names in music, opera, dance and theatre to Amsterdam for performances throughout June. Another big event in Amsterdam is Koninginnedag (Queen's Day), the 30 April national holiday held on the birthday of former Queen Juliana. On this day the whole central city becomes a huge street-market/party where people sell whatever they've dug out of their attics.

ACTIVITIES

Cycling, windsurfing, sailing, boating and hanging out at the beach are popular Dutch pastimes, especially in the waterlogged provinces of Fryslân and Zeeland.

THE NETHERLANDS

WORK

Australian, New Zealand, Canadian and US citizens are legally allowed to work in the Netherlands, but there is a mound of red tape to get through beforehand, and the bottom line is that you must be filling a job that no EU national has the skill to do, which is a pretty tough call. Illegal jobs (working 'in the black') are also very rare these days, although some travellers still manage to pick up work in the bulb fields near Leiden. Another possibility, though available only to Australian, New Zealand and Canadian citizens aged between 18 and 30, is to apply for a one-year working holiday permit at your local Dutch embassy or consulate.

ACCOMMODATION

Rarely cheap and often full, accommodation is best booked ahead, especially in Amsterdam or in the Randstad during the Keukenhof season. You can book hotel accommodation (no deposit required) through the **Netherlands Reservation Centre** (W www.hotelres.nl), or via **Amsterdam Reservation Center** (☎/fax 777 000 888; e reservations@amsterdam tourist.nl).

Once you're in the country, the VVV tourist offices and the GWK money exchange offices usually handle bookings for a fee.

Camping grounds are copious but prices vary – on average €4.50/4/2.50 per adult/tent/car. The NBT has a selective list of sites, or there's the ANWB's annual camping guide (€11), both available from some VVVs or bookshops.

The country's official hostel organisation is the **Nederlandse Jeugdherberg Centrale** (NJHC; ☎ 020-551 31 55, fax 639 01 99; W www.njhc.org; Prof Tulpstraat 2, 1018 HA Amsterdam). Rooms in dorms cost between €16.50 and €28, with a €2.50 discount for members. Some hostels have private rooms – expect to pay between €20 and €27 for a single and €40 and €75 for a double. In Amsterdam you'll find similarly priced unofficial hostels.

B&Bs start at €17 per person a night. Local VVVs have lists, or you can book through **Bed & Breakfast Holland** (☎ 020-615 75 27, fax 669 15 73; W www.bbholland.com; Theophile de Bockstraat 3, 1058 TV Amsterdam). If you use this organisation, you must book a minimum of two nights and there's a €5 booking fee, plus an extra €5 for each place you stay.

Hotels start at €25/50 for basic single/double rooms, with continental breakfast included. In the mid-range, prices start from €70/90, and at the top-end the sky's the limit. Prices are usually the same for the calendar year, though they occasionally rise in the high season (roughly 15 March to 15 November).

FOOD

While gastronomical delights are not a Dutch forte, you won't go hungry. And what the traditional cuisine lacks in taste sensation, it makes up for in quantity. Thanks also to sizable Indonesian, Surinamese and Turkish communities (and to the culinary revolution that has taken over both Amsterdam and Rotterdam in recent rimes) there are spicy and interesting options. Vegetarians will find that many *eetcafés* (eating pubs) have at least one meat-free dish.

Snacks

On the savoury side, the national fast-food habit is *frites* – chips or french fries – usually sold from a *frituur* (chip shop). *Kroketten*, or croquettes (crumbed fried concoctions), are sold hot from vending machines; *broodjes* (open sandwiches) are everywhere; and mussels, raw herrings and deep-fried fish are popular coastal snacks.

As for sweets, *appelgebak* (apple pie) ranks up there with frites, while *poffertjes* (miniature pancakes sprinkled with icing sugar) are surefire tourist food, as are *pannekoeken* (pancakes) and *stroopwafels* (hot wafers glued together with syrup).

Main Dishes

Dinner traditionally comprises thick soups and meat, fish or chicken dishes fortified with potatoes. Most restaurants have a *dagschotel* (dish of the day) for between €8 and €15, while *eetcafés* serve meals or cheap snacks. Otherwise, the Indonesian *rijsttafel* (rice table) of boiled rice with oodles of side dishes costs about €24 per person and is worth a try, as are Zeeland mussels, best during months with an 'r' in their name (or so local tradition has it).

Self-Catering

The national Albert Heijn chain has saturated the country with supermarkets.

DRINKS

Tap water in the Netherlands is fine for drinking. Beer is the staple alcoholic drink, served cool and topped by a two-finger-thick head of froth (a sight that can horrify Anglo-Saxon drinkers). Popular brands include Heineken and Amstel. Many Belgian beers – such as Duvel and Westmalle Triple – have become immensely popular in the Netherlands, and are reasonably priced.

Dutch *genever* (gin) is made with juniper berries; a common combination, known as a *kopstoot* (head butt), is a glass of genever with a beer chaser.

There are plenty of indigenous liqueurs, including *advocaat* (a kind of eggnog) and the herb-based Beerenburg.

ENTERTAINMENT

You'll rarely have to search for nightlife. Bars and cafés abound, from popular footpath terraces to old brown cafés thick with conversation and smoke. In summer, parks come alive with festivals while city squares reverberate with the sounds of street musicians. Movies screen in their original language with Dutch subtitles.

SHOPPING

Diamonds and flowers are Dutch specialities, the latter cheap and plentiful all year. For flower bulbs, it's easiest to buy through one of the specialist mail-order companies. They'll handle all the red tape, including the 'health certificate' many countries require for importing bulbs.

Getting There & Away

AIR

The Netherlands has just one main international airport, Schiphol, 18km southwest of central Amsterdam. It's one of Western Europe's major international hubs, and it services flights from airlines worldwide as well as the national carrier, KLM-Royal Dutch Airlines. Most foreign airlines have offices in Amsterdam (see the Amsterdam Getting There & Away section). The airport is linked directly to the Dutch rail network. Schiphol airport tax is always included in the price of a plane ticket – there's no other departure tax to pay. There is also an airport in Eindhoven which Ryanair, among others, flies into.

LAND

Bus

Eurolines is the main international bus company servicing the Netherlands. It has regular buses from Amsterdam to a crop of European destinations, as well as to Scandinavia and North Africa.

Depending on the service, there are stops in Breda, Rotterdam, The Hague and Utrecht. Eurolines buses cross the Channel either on ferries departing from Calais in France or via the Eurotunnel. Members of Hostelling International (HI) get a 10% discount on Eurolines tickets.

For more detailed information, see the Amsterdam (or other relevant city) Getting There & Away section.

Train

Nederlandse Spoorwegen *(NS; Netherlands Railways; international train information & reservations:* ☎ 0900-92 96, €0.25 per minute*)* operates regular and efficient train services to all neighbouring countries.

The main line south from Amsterdam passes through The Hague and Rotterdam and on to Antwerp (€26.10, two hours, hourly) and Brussels (€29.50, 2¾ hours, hourly) in Belgium. The line southeast runs to Cologne (€45.30, 2¾ hours, every two hours) and farther into Germany.

The line east goes to Berlin, with a branch north to Hamburg. All these fares are one way in 2nd class; travellers aged under 26 get a 25% discount (bring your passport). The *Weekendretour* (weekend return) ticket gives a 40% discount on return fares to Belgium or Germany when travelling between Friday and Monday.

The high-speed **Thalys** (w www.thalys .com) train operates five times per day between Amsterdam and Paris-Nord (€78/67 on weekdays/weekends, 4¼ hours). Those aged under 26 get a 45% discount and seniors with a Railplus card are entitled to a discount on return fares, though you need to book well in advance.

The UK The only train-ferry route is via Hook of Holland (Hoek van Holland) near Rotterdam to Harwich in England and on to London's Liverpool St station. The Channel is crossed using Stena Line's high-speed vessel *Stena HSS*. The fare is €82/41 for adults/ children and the total journey takes six hours.

Alternatively, you can get a train to Brussels and connect there with Eurostar trains which operate through the Channel Tunnel. From Amsterdam, the one-way trip to London's Waterloo station takes about six hours and costs from €114, or €54 for those under 26. There are nine services per day.

Car & Motorcycle

The main entry points from Belgium are the E22 (Antwerp–Breda) and the E25 (Liège–Maastricht).

From Germany there are many crossings, but the main links are the E40 (Cologne–Maastricht), the E35 (Düsseldorf–Arnhem) and the A1 (Hanover–Amsterdam). For details about car ferries from England, see the following section.

SEA

Three companies operate car/passenger ferries between the Netherlands and England. For information on a train-ferry combination, see the earlier Train section. Most travel agencies have information on the following services.

Stena Line (☎ *UK 08705-707 070;* **w** *www .stenaline.com*) is the operator of the high-speed *Stena HSS* from Hook of Holland to Harwich (3¾ hours). Return fares for a car with up to five passengers range from £120 to £200. Foot-passenger tickets start at £50.

P&O/North Sea Ferries (☎ *UK 08701-296 002;* **w** *www.ponsf.com*) runs an overnight boat (14 hours) between Europoort (near Rotterdam) and Hull. The basic one-way rates start from £71/58/46/64 for an adult/student/child/car.

Return fares start from £104 per adult plus £135 for a car. The prices include a cabin (no seat option available).

DFDS Seaways (☎ *UK 08705-333 000;* **w** *dfdsseaways.co.uk*) sails daily from Ijmuiden (near Amsterdam) to Newcastle. The journey takes 15 hours. Return fares start at £114 per adult plus £110 for a car and include reclining seats (cabins extra).

RIVER

Several companies offer return-trip riverboat cruises from either Rotterdam or Arnhem along the Schelde to Belgium (four to six days) or via the Rhine and Moselle Rivers to Germany (eight to 14 days). Most travel agencies have brochures.

Getting Around

The Netherlands' public transport system is excellent. For all national train/bus/tram information, call ☎ 0900-92 92 (€0.50 per minute).

BUS

Buses are used for regional transport rather than for long distances, which are better travelled by train. They provide a vital service, especially in parts of the north and east, where trains are less frequent or nonexistent. The national *strippenkaart* (see Local Transport later in this section) is used on many regional buses.

TRAIN

NS trains are fast and efficient, with at least one InterCity train every 15 minutes between major cities, and half-hourly trains on branch lines. Most train stations have small/large luggage lockers that cost from €2/4 respectively for 24 hours.

If you're returning on the same day, it's cheaper to buy a *dagretour* (day return) rather than two single tickets.

There's a melange of discount fares but you'd have to live on the trains to make most of them worthwhile. A One-Day Ticket gives you unlimited 2nd-/1st-class travel and costs €35.60/55.20. With this ticket you can also buy a Public Transport Day Card for €4 that gives unlimited use of city buses, trams and metros. If a couple of you are travelling around the country, the Summer Tour can be good value. It entitles adults to three days' travel within 10 days for €45/59 for one/two persons. If you're travelling with children, there's a €1 Railrunner ticket that gives one day's unlimited travel.

CAR & MOTORCYCLE

Foreign drivers need a Green Card as proof of insurance. As far as road rules go, you should stick to the right and give way to the right (unless signs or traffic signals indicate otherwise). Watch out for cyclists – they're abundant. Speed limits are 30km/h throughout town residential areas, 50km/h in built-up areas, 80km/h in the country, 100km/h on the major through roads and 120km/h on motorways. The maximum permissible blood-alcohol concentration is 0.05%. For other motoring information, contact the **Royal Dutch Touring**

Association *(ANWB; ☎ 020-673 08 44; Museumplein 5, 1071 DJ Amsterdam)*.

BICYCLE
With 10,000km of cycling paths, a *fiets* (bicycle) is *the* way to go. The ANWB publishes cycling maps for each province. Major roads have separate bike lanes, and, except for the motorways, there's virtually nowhere bicycles can't go. That said, in places such as the Delta region and along the coast you'll need muscles to combat the North Sea headwinds. To take a bicycle on a train (not allowed in peak hours) costs €6 for a *dagkaart* (day card). While about 85% of the population own bikes and there are more bikes than people, they're also available for hire. In most cases you'll need to show your passport, and leave an imprint of your credit card or a deposit (from €25 to €100). Private operators charge about €7.50/ 30 per day/week. Hire shops at train stations charge about €5.50/25. You must return the bike to the same station.

Alternatively, it can work out much cheaper to buy a second-hand bike from a street market for upwards of €15, though bear in mind it's probably part of the stolen bike racket.

HITCHING
Hitching is no longer common in the Netherlands and it is illegal on motorways. Be wary of the usual dangers and risks.

BOAT
Ferries connect the mainland with the five Frisian Islands (see The North section later for details) and are also used as road connections in Zeeland.

LOCAL TRANSPORT
Bus & Tram
Buses and/or trams run in most cities, and Amsterdam and Rotterdam have metro systems.

Fares operate nationally. Buy a *strippenkaart* (strip card), which is valid throughout the country, and stamp off a number of strips depending on how many zones you cross. The ticket is then valid on all buses, trams, metro systems and city trains for an hour, or longer depending on the number of strips you've stamped. Around central Amsterdam, for example, you'll use two strips – one for the journey plus one for the zone. A zone farther will cost three strips, and so on. When riding on trams there may be a conductor, otherwise it's

up to you to stamp your card. On the buses the drivers stamp strips as you get on. Bus and tram drivers sell two-strip cards for €1.40. More economical are 15-/45-strip cards for €5.90/17.40, which you must purchase in advance at train or bus stations, post offices, or some VVV offices. Otherwise you can invest in a *dagkaart*, available in some large cities.

Connexion *(☎ 0900 92 92)* operates most inter-city and local buses.

Taxi
Usually booked by phone (officially you're not supposed to wave them down on the street), taxis also hover outside train stations and hotels and cost roughly €10 for 5km. There are also *treintaxis* (train taxis) which charge a flat rate of €3.50 per person to anywhere within a certain radius (it varies from city to city) of the train station. You can buy your *treintaxi* voucher at most train stations. They do not operate in Amsterdam, The Hague, Rotterdam or from Schiphol airport.

ORGANISED TOURS
It's possible to whip through windmills, visit cheese markets and take in nearby towns all in a day trip from Amsterdam (see Around Amsterdam for details). Local tourist offices can advise on bus, canal, bike or walking tours available in their own town or city.

Amsterdam

☎ 020 • pop 731,000

Personal freedom, liberal drug laws, the gay centre of Europe – these are images that have been synonymous with the Dutch capital since the heady 1960s and 1970s when it was Europe's most radical city.

While the exuberance has dimmed somewhat since then, tolerance is still a guiding principle that even serious social problems such as a chronic housing shortage have failed to dent. Just as enduring has been the rich and lively mix of the historical and contemporary that you'll experience when exploring the many museums, relaxing in the canal-side cafés or enjoying summer-time open-air entertainment.

Orientation
By capital-city standards, Amsterdam is small. Its major sights, accommodation and nightlife

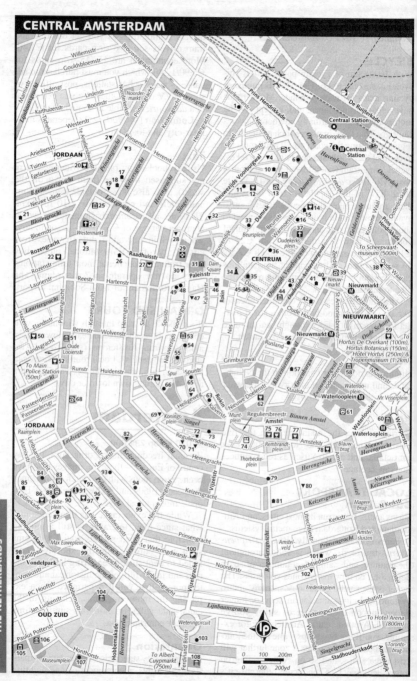

CENTRAL AMSTERDAM

CENTRAL AMSTERDAM

PLACES TO STAY
- 10 Flying Pig Downtown Hostel
- 15 The Greenhouse Effect
- 17 Canal House Hotel
- 18 Hotel Toren
- 21 Hotel van Onna
- 26 Hotel Pax
- 35 NH Grand Hotel Krasnapolsky
- 41 The Shelter
- 42 Zosa
- 57 City Hostel Stadsdoelen
- 81 Seven Bridges
- 85 Quentin Hotel
- 95 Hans Brinker Hostel
- 98 City Hostel Vondelpark
- 101 Hotel Prinsenhof

PLACES TO EAT
- 2 Bolhoed
- 3 Pancake Bakery
- 4 Dorrius
- 19 Christophe
- 23 Koh-I-Noor
- 28 Villa Zeezicht
- 30 Albert Heijn Food Plaza
- 32 La Strada
- 38 Hemelse Modder
- 40 Albert Heijn Supermarket
- 47 Supper Club
- 64 Vlaams Frites Huis
- 69 Albert Heijn Supermarket
- 70 Le Pêcheur
- 71 Rose's Cantina
- 72 Gary's Muffins
- 80 Tempo Doeloe
- 82 Metz & Co Café
- 92 Shoarma/Felafel Eateries
- 95 Bojo
- 102 Pata Negra

ENTERTAINMENT
- 1 Rokerij
- 12 In de Wildeman
- 14 Getto
- 20 Café 't Smalle
- 22 COC Café
- 50 Saarein II
- 52 La Tertulia
- 59 Bimhuis
- 61 Het Muziektheater
- 62 Café de Jaren
- 67 Hoppe
- 74 Tuschinskitheater
- 75 Escape
- 76 Café-Restaurant De Kroon
- 77 Vivelavie
- 78 iT
- 83 Boom Chicago
- 84 Melkweg
- 86 Café Americain
- 89 Stadsschouwburg
- 90 The Bulldog
- 97 Jazz Café Alto
- 99 Paradiso

OTHER
- 5 The Internet Cafe
- 6 Thomas Cook
- 7 Tourist Office; GVB
- 8 Rijwielshop
- 9 Sexmuseum
- 11 Yellow Bike
- 13 easyEverything
- 16 Prostitution Information Centre
- 24 Westerkerk
- 25 Anne Frankhuis
- 27 Main Post Office
- 29 Magna Plaza
- 31 Koninklijk Paleis
- 33 American Express

- 34 Nationaal Monument
- 36 Condomerie Het Gulden Vlies
- 37 Oude Kerk
- 39 In de Waag
- 43 Cannabis College
- 44 Hash Marihuana Hemp Museum
- 45 Rent-a-Bike Damstraat
- 46 Eurolines Amsterdam
- 48 De Bierkoning
- 49 Vrolijk Bookshop
- 51 Woonbootmuseum
- 53 Amsterdams Historisch Museum
- 54 Schuttersgalerij
- 55 Begijnhof
- 56 The Book Exchange
- 58 Rembrandthuis
- 60 Joods Historisch Museum
- 63 American Book Centre
- 65 Waterstones Bookshop
- 66 Kilroy Travels
- 68 Openbare Bibliotheek
- 73 Bloemenmarkt
- 79 Bridge of 15 Bridges
- 87 Thomas Cook
- 88 Amsterdam Uit Buro
- 91 Tourist Office
- 93 Clean Brothers Laundry
- 94 Conscious Dreams
- 100 French Consulate
- 103 Playground
- 104 Rijksmuseum
- 105 Stedelijk Museum
- 106 Van Gogh Museum
- 107 Royal Dutch Touring Association (ANWB)
- 108 Heineken Experience

---

are scattered around a web of concentric canals known as the canal belt, which gives the city an initially confusing, yet ultimately orderly and unique feel. The centre, easily and enjoyably covered on foot, has two main parts: the old, medieval core and the 'newer', 17th-century canal-lined quarters that surround it. Corked to the north by Centraal Station, the old city centre is encased by the Kloveniers-burgwal and Singel canals. After Singel come Herengracht, Keizersgracht and Prinsengracht, the newer canals dug to cope with Amsterdam's Golden Age expansion. The city's central point is Dam Square, a five-minute walk straight down Damrak from Centraal Station. Main streets bisect the canal belt like spokes in a wheel.

Information

Tourist Offices There are three offices of the **VVV** (☎ 0900-400 40 40, €0.55 per minute from 9am-5pm Mon-Fri; e info@amsterdamtourist.nl) around the town. The two busiest are **Centraal Station** (platform 2; open 8am-8pm Mon-Sat, 9am-5pm Sun) and **Stationsplein 10** (open 9am-5pm daily). There's a third tourist office at **Leidseplein** (open 9am-5pm daily). During the peak summer months, opening hours may be extended. There's also an office at **Schiphol airport** (open 7am-10pm daily).

The VVVs sell a one-/two-/three-day Amsterdam Pass (€26/36/46) that gives free entry to several museums and discounts on canal boats and restaurants; you have to really pack

THE NETHERLANDS

things in to make it a worthwhile investment though.

Money There is an (almost) 24-hour **GWK office** *(open midnight-10.30pm)* at Schiphol airport. The main **branch** *(☎ 627 27 31; open 7am-10.45pm daily)* is at Centraal Station, and there's another **GWK office** *(open 8am-11pm daily)* next to the VVV at Leidseplein. Otherwise, there is a throng of midnight-trading bureaux de change along Damrak and Leidsestraat, but expect to pay higher commissions unless you really shop around. The main post office also handles foreign exchange at reasonable rates.

There are ATMs at Schipol airport and Centraal Station and bank ATMs are sprinkled liberally around the city.

American Express *(lost or stolen cards: ☎ 504 80 00, travellers cheques: ☎ 0800-022 01 00; Damrak 66)* and **Thomas Cook** *(☎ 620 32 36; Damrak 1-5 • ☎ 626 70 00; Leidseplein 31a; lost or stolen cheques: ☎ 0800-022 86 30)* are centrally located.

Post & Communications The **main post office** *(☎ 330 05 55; Singel 250)* has an ATM and fax facilities.

Email & Internet Access In a 15th-century building, **In de Waag** *(☎ 422 77 72; Nieuwmarkt 4)* has one computer with free Internet access, though you must buy a drink. Alternatively, book a free session at **Openbare Bibliotheek** *(Public Library; ☎ 523 09 00; Prinsengracht 587; open 1pm-9pm Mon, 10am-9pm Tues-Thur, 10am-5pm Fri & Sat, 1pm-5pm Sun).*

The **Internet Cafe** *(☎ 627 10 52; Martelaarsgracht 11; open 9am-1am Sun-Thur, 9am-3am Fri & Sat)*, close to Centraal Station, charges €1 for 20 minutes, plus compulsory drink purchase.

easyEverything *(W www.easyeverything .com; Damrak 33; €1/5/8 for 20min/24hr/ 7 days; open 7.30am-9.30pm)* has all the ambience of a student examination hall, however, it does offer reasonable rates for longer-term use.

Travel Agencies Amsterdam is an important European centre for cheap fares to anywhere in the world. Shop around (especially along the Rokin) or try **Kilroy Travels** *(☎ 524 51 00; W www.kilroytravels.com; Singel 143).*

Bookshops A specialist in English-language books is **Waterstones** *(☎ 638 38 21; Kalverstraat 152)*, which has plenty of guides, maps and novels, including some translated Dutch literature. Other recommended bookshops include the **American Book Centre** *(☎ 625 55 37; Kalverstraat 185)*, which gives 10% discounts to students; **Book Exchange** *(☎ 626 62 66; Kloveniersburgwal 58)*, a rabbit warren of second-hand books; and **Vrolijk** *(☎ 623 51 42; Paleisstraat 135)*, which is a lesbian and gay bookshop.

Laundry Try **Clean Brothers** *(☎ 622 02 73; Kerkstraat 56; open 7am-9pm daily for self-service wash €4, 9am-7pm Mon-Sat for service €7.50 wash/dry/fold).*

Medical & Emergency Services The **Central Doctors Service** *(☎ 0900-503 20 42)* handles 24-hour medical, dental and pharmaceutical emergencies and inquiries. The closest hospital to the centre is **Onze Lieve Vrouwe Gasthuis** *(☎ 599 91 11; 1e Oosterparkstraat 279)*, near the Tropenmuseum. The national emergency number is ☎ 112, or contact the **main police station** *(☎ 559 91 11; Elandsgracht 117).*

Things to See & Do
The best place to start a walking tour is **Dam Square** (the 'Dam'), where the Amstel River was dammed in the 13th century, giving the city its name. Today it's the crossroads for the crowds surging along pedestrianised Kalverstraat and Nieuwendijk shopping streets, and the pivotal point for trips to some of the interesting outer quarters. Here too is the **Nationaal Monument**, a 22m-high obelisk dedicated to those who died in WWII and, on the western side, the **Koninklijk Paleis** (Royal Palace), which is occasionally used by the royal family (and is often open to the public – check with the VVV).

Heading west from Dam Square along the Raadhuisstraat, you'll cross the main canals to the **Westerkerk**, with its 85m tower, the highest in the city. In the church's shadow stands a **statue of Anne Frank**, the young Jewish diarist who hid for years with her family in a nearby house, only to be tragically discovered near the end of WWII. Across Prinsengracht from here spreads the **Jordaan**, an area built up in the 17th century to house the city's lower class. Revived in the 1960s as a student ghetto, today its many renovated gabled houses sit atop canal-front cafés in Amsterdam's trendiest quarter.

South from the Dam along NZ Voorburgwal, the quaint **Spui Square** acts as a facade to hide one of the inner city's most tranquil spots, the **Begijnhof**. Such *hofjes*, or groupings of almshouses, were built throughout the Low Countries during the Middle Ages to house Catholic women, the elderly and poor.

From the Begijnhof you can walk though the **Schuttersgalerij** (Civic Guard Gallery), a glass-covered passageway adorned with enormous group portraits of dignitaries from the 16th to 18th centuries, to the **Amsterdams Historisch Museum**.

Continuing southwest from Spui, Leidsestraat ends where the city's nightlife takes off at **Leidseplein**. From there it is simply a few minutes' walk southeast past **Vondelpark** (a summer-long entertainment venue) to the ever-inundated **Museumplein** where you'll find the Rijksmuseum, Van Gogh Museum and Stedelijk Museum (see the following section). Follow Singelgracht two blocks east to get to the **Heineken Experience** (see the following section). Across the canal is a rare sight that will delight one- to 12-year-olds – a huge outdoor **playground**.

Back across the canals at the northern end of Vijzelstraat, the **Muntplein tower** denotes the colourful **Bloemenmarkt** (flower market). To the southeast is **Rembrandtplein**, one of the nightlife hubs, and the **'Bridge of 15 Bridges'**, so called because from here you can see 15 bridges (they're best viewed at night when lit up). Farther north, the sleaze of the **red-light district** extends along the parallel OZ Voorburgwal and OZ Achterburgwal canals past **Oude Kerk**, the city's oldest church, to **Zeedijk**, once the heroin nerve centre. It's been given a face-lift in the last decade, however, plenty of drugs are still going down in the alleys leading to the stark **Nieuwmarkt**.

Southeast of here is the city's Jewish quarter, or **Jodenhoek**, and the **Joods Historisch Museum**. The nearby Rembrandthuis and Waterlooplein market attract hordes. Farther east, the **Hortus Botanicus** (Botanical Garden) is home to the world's oldest potplant.

Museums & Galleries If you intend visiting more than a handful of Amsterdam's museums and galleries, then it's worth buying the Museumjaarkaart (see Money in the earlier Facts for the Visitor section in this chapter).

Rijksmuseum (☎ 674 70 00; Stadhouderskade 42; **w** www.rijksmuseum.nl; adult/child €8.50/free; open 10am-5pm daily), in a palatial 19th-century building, boasts the Netherlands' largest art collection, concentrating on Dutch artists from the 15th to 19th centuries and housing Rembrandt's famous *Night Watch*. Most of the museum will be closed from October 2003 until 2006, though the popular Dutch masters works will still be displayed in the southern wing.

The **Van Gogh Museum** (☎ 570 52 00; Paulus Potterstraat 7; **w** www.vangoghmuseum.nl; adult/child €7/2.25; open 10am-6pm daily) boasts the world's largest collection of Vincent's works. Highlights include the dour *Potato Eaters*, the famous *Sunflowers* and the ominous *Wheatfield with Crows*, one of his last paintings. Check the museum website for special events during 2003, the 150th anniversary of Van Gogh's birth.

Anne Frankhuis (☎ 556 71 00; Prinsengracht 263; adult/child €6.50/3; open 9am-9pm daily Apr-Aug, 9am-7pm Sept-Mar) is arguably the city's most famous canal house; come either early, or late, in the day, to avoid the queues. Anne wrote her famous diary here, and excerpts from it are used to describe the persecution of the Jews during WWII.

For a wider picture, the **Joods Historisch Museum** (☎ 626 99 45; Jonas Daniël Meijerplein 2-4; tram No 9 from Centraal Station; adult €5, child €1.50-2.50; open 11am-5pm daily) details Jewish society and has a children's museum which will keep kids over six entertained.

Rembrandthuis (☎ 520 04 00; Jodenbreestraat 4-6; metro to Waterlooplein; adult/student/child €7/5/1.50; open 10am-5pm Mon-Sat, 1pm-5pm Sun) has sketches by the master in his former home, which has been restored to its 17th-century glory.

Amsterdams Historisch Museum (☎ 523 18 22; Kalverstraat 92; adult/child €6/3; open 10am-5pm Mon-Fri, 11am-5pm Sat & Sun), in a former orphanage, explores the city's rich history via an impressive collection of paintings, models and archaeological finds.

The highlight of the excellent **Scheepvaartmuseum** (Shipping Museum; ☎ 523 22 22; Kattenburgerplein 1; bus No 22; adult/child €7/4; open 10am-5pm daily mid-June–mid-Sept; 10am-5pm Tues-Sat rest of year) is the superb replica of the 18th-century East Indiaman, *Amsterdam*, moored alongside. It also houses one of the largest collections of maritime memorabilia in the world and traces the history of Dutch seafaring.

Tropenmuseum *(Museum of the Tropics; ☎ 568 82 15; Linnaeusstraat 2; tram No 9 or bus No 22 from Centraal Station; adult/child €6.80/3.40; open 10am-5pm daily)*, in a grand 1920s building, has exhibitions offering insight into African, Asian and Latin American lifestyles.

For a peek at life on a houseboat, head to the *Hendrika Maria* in the **Woonbootmuseum** *(Houseboat Museum; ☎ 427 07 50; Prinsengracht opposite No 296; adult/child up to 150cm €2.50/2.05; open 11am-5pm Wed-Sat Mar-Oct, 11am-5pm Fri-Sun Nov-Feb)*.

Beer production stopped in 1988 but the **Heineken Experience** *(☎ 523 96 66; Stadhouderskade 78; admission €5; open 10am-6pm Tues-Sun)*, in a 135-year-old former brewery building, still attracts beer buffs for its self-guided tours that end with three glasses of beer.

The **Prostitution Information Centre** *(☎ 420 73 28; Enge Kerksteeg 3; open 11am-7.30pm Tues, Wed, Fri & Sat)*, run by a former prostitute, provides intelligent information about the red-light district as well as souvenirs and supplies. The **Hash Marihuana Hemp Museum** *(☎ 623 59 61; OZ Achterburgwal 148; admission €5.60; open 11am-10pm daily)* sounds more interesting than it is. Just down the road and more informative is the **Cannabis College** *(☎ 423 44 20; OZ Achterburgwal 124; admission free)*, with its own cannabis indoor garden. The **Sexmuseum** *(☎ 622 83 76; Damrak 18; admission €2.50 over 16s only; open 10am-11.30pm daily)* is worth a visit for its eclectic collection of pornographic material, from Roman stone phalluses to 1870 studio photos of graphic sex.

Markets Most street markets are open 9am or 10am to 5pm daily, except Sunday. The biggest flea market is **Waterlooplein**, good for cheap bikes and locks. The **Bloemenmarkt** *(Singel)* is a floating flower market, established in 1862.

Albert Cuypmarkt at Albert Cuypstraat, four blocks south of the Heineken Experience museum, is Amsterdam's busiest and liveliest market, with lots of multicultural food and general goods.

Organised Tours
Yellow Bike *(☎ 620 69 40; Nieuwezijds Kolk 29)* organises bicycle tours of the city (€17, three hours) or a countryside tour taking in a windmill and clog factory (€22.50, six hours). Tours run from April to November only.

Several companies organise bus tours (3½ hours) around Amsterdam for €15 to €25; ask at the VVV for details.

Places to Stay
Amsterdam is popular all year but in peak times it's overrun – bookings are essential.

Camping The closest camping ground is **Vliegenbos** *(☎ 636 88 55, fax 632 27 23; Meeuwenlaan 138; tent/person/car €7.10/7.50/7; open Apr-Sept)*, a few minutes from Centraal Station on bus No 32.

Hostels & Youth Hotels All the hostels mentioned have Internet facilities.

Accurately advertised as the 'cheapest B&B in town', **The Shelter** *(☎ 625 32 30, fax 623 22 82; e reservations@city.shelter.nl; Barndesteeg 21; dorm beds €15; midnight curfew Mon-Thur, 1am Fri & Sat)* is a Christian hostel in the red-light district. It has clean, single-sex dorms, free email access, and huge 'Jesus Loves You' signs.

The bustling NJHC **City Hostel Stadsdoelen** *(☎ 624 68 32, fax 639 10 35; Kloveniersburgwal 97; dorm beds €20.65; open 24hr)*, near the red-light district, has 20-bed single-sex and mixed dorms, free lockers and a no-smoking policy.

Flying Pig Downtown *(☎ 420 68 22; w www.flyingpig.nl; Vossiusstraat 46; singles/doubles €36/72; dorm beds €19-25, queen-size dorm beds €28-37; open 24hr)* takes some advance bookings (via Internet only), but most of the beds are for those who turn up on the day. The rooms are cramped but you can't beat the location.

NJHC **City Hostel Vondelpark** *(☎ 589 89 99, fax 589 89 55; w www.njhc.org/vondelpark; Zandpad 5; dorm beds €22-28, doubles €76; open 24hr)* is one of Europe's largest hostels with 475 beds. The rooms are sunny, and all feature bathrooms and well-spaced bunks. There are lifts, a bar, two restaurants and bike-hire facilities.

In the 550-bed **Hans Brinker Hotel** *(☎ 622 06 87, fax 638 20 60; w www.hans-brinker .com; Kerkstraat 136-138; dorm beds €21-24;*

doubles €70; open 24hr) there are corridors of spartan rooms. Smoking is allowed and there's a nightly disco in the busy bar.

Hotels The following rates, unless stated otherwise, include breakfast.

Hotel Hortus (☎ 625 99 96, fax 625 39 58; **w** www.hotelhortus.com; Plantage Parklaan 8; singles/doubles/triples €25/50/75) is full of young, happy stoners who love that cooked breakfast and huge TV screen. It's the luck of the draw if you get a shower in your room.

Hotel Pax (☎ 624 97 35; Raadhuisstraat 37; singles/doubles/triples from €39/65/110) is a good budget option on hotel-lined Raadhuisstraat run by two friendly brothers.

Hotel Prinsenhof (☎ 623 17 72, fax 638 33 68; **e** info@hotelprinsenhof.com; Prinsengracht 810; singles/doubles from €40/60, doubles with bathroom €80) is in a beautiful old canal house and has spacious rooms and a nifty electric luggage hoist.

In the Jordaan, efficient **Hotel van Onna** (☎ 626 58 01; **w** www.netcentrum.com/onna; Bloemgracht 104; singles/doubles €40/80), on a pretty canal, has simple, tidy rooms. Bring your ear plugs if night-time church bells are likely to keep you awake.

The Greenhouse Effect (☎ 623 74 62, fax 624 49 74; **w** www.the-greenhouse-effect.com; Warmoesstraat 55; singles/doubles from €50/75) is one for smokers: you get a discount on your dope and drinks in the café downstairs, and the themed rooms are well-worn but trippy – try your own Red Light room or some Turkish Delight.

Quentin Hotel (☎ 626 21 87, fax 622 01 21; Leidsekade 89; singles/doubles €35/75, with bath €75/90) has bright and spacious rooms with wooden furniture and white linen, and is a favourite of lesbians, and musicians and actors performing close by. Its breakfast is €7.

The sophisticated **Seven Bridges** (☎ 623 13 29; Reguliersgracht 31; singles/doubles from €100/110) has nine tastefully decorated rooms and the rare treat of having breakfast in your room served on fine china.

The more sophisticated **Zosa** (☎ 330 62 41, fax 330 62 42; **e** info@zosa-online.com; Kloveniersburgwal 20; singles/doubles €110/135) is a modern hotel featuring six superbly designed rooms – check out the tranquil Zen room or the exotic Middle Eastern room. Breakfast is €9.

The incredibly quiet **Canal House Hotel** (☎ 622 51 82, fax 624 13 17; **e** info@canalhouse.nl; Keizersgracht 148; singles/doubles/triples €140/150-190/210) has 26 rooms, all furnished in an ornate, 17th-century style with antiques at every turn; there's a no children under 12 policy. The breakfast room with grand piano overlooks the garden.

Hotel Toren (☎ 622 60 33, fax 626 97 05; **e** hotel.toren@tip.nl; Keizersgracht 164; singles/doubles/triples with bathroom from €140/155/185) is a plushly decorated 17th-century canal house which boasts modern touches like spas in all bathrooms. Breakfast is €12.

NH Grand Hotel Krasnapolsky (☎ 554 91 11, fax 622 86 07; **e** nhkrasnapolsky@nh-hotels.nl; Dam 9; doubles €230-325), on Dam Square, is one of the city's historic showpieces. All 468 rooms are stylishly furnished. Ask about the daily specials that can reduce the room price. Breakfast in the 19th-century winter garden breakfast room costs €19.

Places to Eat
Dutch cuisine isn't the world's most exciting, however, if you tire of it, there are plenty of other tasty choices. All of the listings included in this section are open daily unless otherwise specified.

Restaurants For classy Dutch, try **Dorrius** (☎ 620 05 00; Nieuwezijds Voorburgwal 5; mains average €22; open 6pm-10.30pm) with its old-world surroundings.

Supper Club (☎ 638 05 13; Jonge Roelensteeg 21; 5-course set meal €60; open 8pm-midnight) is an ultra-trendy restaurant in one big, stark, white room where you recline and eat, Roman-style. It's great theatre, but average food and service.

There are inexpensive, authentic **Chinese** and **Thai eateries** at Nieuwmarkt, and **Surinamese cafés** near Albert Cuypmarkt. Greek and Italian cuisine compete fiercely with steakhouses and Dutch fare in the streets off Leidseplein.

Beautifully tiled **Pata Negra** (☎ 422 62 50; Utrechtsestraat 124; tapas around €4.50; open noon-11.30pm) has fine tapas and a fun, boisterous crowd on weekends.

Pancake Bakery (☎ 625 13 33; Prinsengracht 191; mains around €9; open noon-9pm) is one of the best places to get delicious, filling pancakes in a very Dutch environment.

Bojo (☎ 622 74 34; Lange Leidsedwars-straat 51; mains around €9; open 5pm-2am Mon-Thur & Sun, 5pm-4am Fri & Sat), a busy, Indonesian eatery with tasty, generous serves, is one of the few places open until the early hours of the morning.

The interior might be gaudy but the Indian food at **Koh-I-Noor** (☎ 623 31 33; Wester-markt 29; mains around €12.50; open 5pm-11.30pm) is as good as it gets in Amsterdam.

La Strada (☎ 625 02 76; Nieuwezijds Voor-burgwal 93-95; mains around €12; open 4pm-1am Wed-Sun) attracts a mixed lesbian, gay and straight crowd with its pleasant ambi-ence and Euro-style food.

Bolhoed (☎ 626 18 03; Prinsengracht 60-62; mains around €12.50, 3-course meal €19; open noon-10pm) is a colourful vege-tarian haunt which serves excellent organic and vegan food.

Popular with the gay community, **Hemelse Modder** (☎ 624 32 03; Oude Waal 9-11; mains around €16; 3-course meal €26; open 6pm-10.30pm) offers stylish, modern dining. Don't miss the restaurant's namesake choco-late mousse.

Rose's Cantina (☎ 625 97 97; Reguliers-dwarsstraat 40; mains around €16; open 5pm-11pm) is a big and lively ever-popular Mexican restaurant where the huge portions are washed down with margaritas.

Tempo Doeloe (☎ 625 67 18; Utrechtse-straat 75; mains around €19; open 7pm-1am Sun-Thur, 7pm-3am Fri & Sat) is considered a top Indonesian restaurant; expect plenty of spice and book ahead.

Le Pêcheur (☎ 624 31 21; Reguliersdwars-straat 32; mains around €22; open noon-2.30pm Mon-Fri, 6pm-10.30pm Mon-Sat) is a stylish seafood restaurant with a beautiful courtyard and fantastic fish.

For French haute cuisine, go to **Chris-tophe** (☎ 625 08 07; Leliegracht 46; mains around €35; open 6.30pm-10.30pm Tues-Sat). A Michelin star, refined modern decor and dishes such as roasted lobster combine to make this a flash dining experience.

Cafés & Snacks For late-night munchies, try **Gary's Muffins** (☎ 420 24 06; Reguliers-dwarsstraat 53; open noon-2am Sun-Thur, noon-4am Fri & Sat); the chocolate brownie is delicious.

For the best apple cake in town head to **Villa Zeezicht** (☎ 626 74 33; Torensteeg 7; open

8am-9.30pm Mon-Fri, 9am-9.30pm Sat & Sun) where the generous serves go for €2.50.

Metz & Co (☎ 520 70 48; Leidsestraat 34) is a chic department store with a 6th-floor **café** (rolls/sandwiches average €8.50; open 10.30am-6pm Mon-Sat, 10.30am-9pm Thur, 12.30pm-5pm Sun) and a superb view.

Fast Food Amsterdam's favourite fries ven-dor is the hole-in-the-wall **Vlaams Frites Huis** (Voetboogstraat 33; open to 6pm daily) – the green peppercorn sauce is a winner.

There's a clutch of little **shoarma/felafel eateries** situated on Leidsestraat. Most are open until about 4am and do excellent felafels for about €4.

Self-Catering Albert Heijn supermarkets predominate and are dotted around the town. They include large **Albert Heijn Food Plaza** (NZ Voorburgwal 226; open 8am-10pm Mon-Sat, 11am-7pm Sun) and the **Albert Heijn supermarkets** at both Nieuwmarkt 18 and Koningsplein 6.

Entertainment

The infamous 'smoking' coffee shops and red-light district live on, and the zillions of cafés, bars and nightclubs give the city a constant vi-tality. There's also top notch classical music, theatre and ballet.

Pick up the monthly Day to Day guide from the VVV or from the **Amsterdam Uit Buro** (AUB; ☎ 0900-01 91; Leidseplein 26) for de-tails of what's on.

The gay nightlife is centred on Reguliers-dwarsstraat, Kerkstraat, Warmoesstraat, and the streets off Rembrandtplein.

Free gay Amsterdam maps are available from the COC (see the Gay & Lesbian Trav-ellers section earlier in this chapter) as is Gay & Night magazine.

Pubs/Cafés Pubs, bars, brown cafés, cafés – call them what you like, but places to drink abound. They're usually open daily until 1am, and 2am on Friday and Saturday nights.

For the friendly and intimate atmosphere of the old brown café, try **Hoppe** (☎ 420 44 20; Spui 18) where beers have been downed for more than 300 years.

In de Wildeman (☎ 638 23 48; Kolksteeg 3) attracts beer connoisseurs with its menu of more than 200 beers; it also has a nonsmoking section.

In the Jordaan, the gorgeous **Café 't Smalle** (☎ 623 9617; Egelantiersgracht 12) dates back to the 18th century and it has a tiny floating terrace.

Café-Restaurant De Kroon (☎ 625 2011; Rembrandtplein 17) is a classy and grand café overlooking Rembrandtplein from a covered terrace.

The huge **Café de Jaren** (☎ 625 57 71; Nieuwe Doelenstraat 20) has a great sun deck and English-language newspapers.

The **Café Americain** (☎ 556 32 32; American Hotel, Leidsekade 97; open 11am-11pm daily) with its Art Deco interior, is the oldest (1902) and the most stylish grand café in Amsterdam.

Saarein II (☎ 623 49 01; Elandsstraat 119; open Tues-Sun), in a café dating to the early 1600s, is a favourite meeting place for lesbians, as is the lively **Vivelavie** (☎ 624 01 14; Amstelstraat 7).

COC Café (☎ 623 40 79; Rozenstraat 14) holds gay, lesbian and mixed club nights every weekend.

Getto (☎ 421 5151; open 4pm-1am Tues-Sat, 4pm-midnight Sun) is a fun and gay bar-restaurant with nightly entertainment (tarot readers, DJs, cocktail happy hours).

Live Music Amsterdam's main jazz venue is **Bimhuis** (☎ 623 13 61; Oude Schans 73; tickets average €12) and it attracts both local and international greats. It's moving to the Eastern Docklands in early 2004 (west of the ship passenger terminal).

Jazz Café Alto (☎ 626 32 49; Korte Leidsedwarsstraat 115; open 9pm-3am Sun-Thur, 9pm-4am Fri & Sat) is a cosy brown café attracting fans of live jazz and blues.

Legendary **Melkweg** (Milky Way; ☎ 531 81 81; Lijnbaansgracht 234a) is a cinema, theatre, and music venue that moves from late until early with live rock, reggae and African rhythm. Equally hallowed **Paradiso** (☎ 626 45 21; Weteringschans 6), a former church, has been the city's premier rock venue since the 1960s.

'Smoking' Coffee Shops You'll have little difficulty pinpointing the 350-odd coffee shops where the trade is marijuana and hash rather than tea and tart.

One of the most famous, and expensive, is **The Bulldog** (☎ 627 19 08; Leidseplein 13-17) with five branches around town. **La Tertulia** (cnr Prinsengracht & Oude Looiersstraat) is candid and colourful, and run by a mother-and-daughter. **Rokerij** (Singel 8) has cool African and South American vibes and has opened another two branches. The **Hortus De Overkant** (☎ 422 19 49; Nieuwe Herengracht 71) has well-priced hash and grass in a bright, modern environment.

Nightclubs The trendy **Escape** (Rembrandtplein 11) is capable of drawing 2000 people on a Saturday night with top DJs and house music. **iT** (Amstelstraat 24; open 11pm-4am or 5am Thur-Sun) is the largest gay/mixed nightclub – there's usually a queue. On Saturday night it's gay only.

The club at the **Hotel Arena** (☎ 694 74 44; Gravesandestraat 51) offers up rock, house and techno on Friday and Saturday nights.

Cinema The Art Deco **Tuschinskitheater** (☎ 0900-93 63; Reguliersbreestraat 26) is Amsterdam's cinematic showpiece screening mainstream blockbusters.

Theatre & Dance Premier performing arts venues are the **Stadsschouwburg** (☎ 624 23 11; Leidseplein 26; most tickets from €19) for large-scale productions, dance and musicals in the city's most beautiful theatre; and the **Het Muziektheater** (☎ 551 89 11; Waterlooplein 22; tickets from €11), home of the renowned Netherlands Opera and National Ballet.

The comedy club **Boom Chicago** (☎ 423 01 01; Leidseplein 12; tickets €18.50) conducts both stand-up and improvised performances in English reflecting on life in the Netherlands.

Shopping
Shopping in Amsterdam, a free publication available at the VVV, gives an overview of where to find what.

Serious Funshopping Amsterdam, available for €9 from the VVV, gives a snapshot of the most zany options.

Interesting shops include **Condomerie Het Gulden Vlies** (☎ 627 41 74; Warmoesstraat 141), which is well situated for its trade; **Conscious Dreams** (☎ 626 69 07; Kerkstraat 93), selling magic mushrooms and aphrodisiacs; **De Bierkoning** (☎ 625 23 36; Paleisstraat 125), with hundreds of Belgian, German, English and Dutch beers, glasses, mugs and books; and **Magna Plaza** (Nieuwezijds Voorburgwal), a grand 19th-century building with more than 40 upmarket, fashion, gift and jewellery stores.

Getting There & Away

Air Amsterdam has long been known for its cheap air tickets (see Travel Agencies under Information earlier in this section). The airline offices in Amsterdam include **British Airways** (☎ 346 95 59), **KLM** (☎ 474 77 47) and **Qantas** (☎ 023-569 82 836).

Bus Eurolines operates from Amstel Station. Tickets can be bought at the Eurolines office there or in central Amsterdam (☎ 560 87 88; *Rokin 10*). There are buses to London (€55, 10 to 11 hours, four daily), with passengers also collected at Utrecht, The Hague, Rotterdam and Breda. Other Eurolines services include Antwerp (€15, three hours), Brussels (€15, four hours), Copenhagen (€75, 13 hours) and Paris (€39, eight hours).

Train The international information and reservations office at Centraal Station is open 6.30am to 10pm daily; for international information call ☎ 0900-92 96 or go to the information centre on platform 2A. For national information, ask at the ticket windows or call ☎ 0900-92 92.

For fares and journey times to other destinations in the Netherlands, check the Getting There & Away sections in those places. For information on trains to neighbouring countries, including a train/ferry service to London, see the Getting There & Away section earlier in this chapter.

Car Local companies usually have the cheapest car rental – about €40 per day plus kilometre fees.

Among many car-rental companies, there are **Avis** (☎ 683 60 61; *Nassaukade 380*), **Diks Autohuur** (☎ 662 33 66; *Van Ostadestraat 278*), **Europcar** (☎ 683 21 23; *Overtoom 197*) and **Budget** (☎ 612 06 66; *Overtoom 121*).

Ferry For details of a train-ferry service to the UK, see the Getting There & Away section earlier in this chapter.

Getting Around

To/From the Airport There are trains every 10 minutes between Schiphol and Amsterdam Centraal Station (€2.90, 20 minutes). Taxis cost about €40.

Bus, Tram & Metro Amsterdam's comprehensive public transport network is operated by the **Gemeentevervoerbedrijf** (*GVB; open 7am-9pm Mon-Fri, 8am-9pm Sat & Sun*), which has an information office next to the VVV in Stationsplein. Pick up the free transport map and *Tourist Guide to Public Transport Amsterdam*.

Buses, trams and the metro use strip cards (see Local Transport in the Getting Around section earlier in this chapter), or you can buy one-day cards for €5.20. Weekly tickets for one zone cost €8.90. All services run from about 5am or 6am until midnight, when the more limited night buses takes over.

The Circle Tram 20 is designed to meet the needs of tourists and operates from 9am to 7.30pm daily, departing every 12 minutes from Centraal Station.

For all information, ring the national public transport number (☎ 0900-92 92).

Taxi & Watertaxi Both are expensive, but **watertaxis** (*information & bookings:* ☎ 530 10 90), with their half-hourly/hourly rental fee of €70/120, are prohibitively so – much more so than **road taxis** (☎ 677 77 77).

Car & Motorcycle A 17th-century city enmeshed by waterways is hardly the place for motorised transport.

Anticar feelings are strong and the city council has done much to restrict access and parking. The *Amsterdam by Car* leaflet, free from the VVV, pinpoints parking areas and warns of dire penalties (a wheel clamp and a €65 fine) for nonconformists. If you bring your car, the best place to park is the 'Transferium' parking garage at Amsterdam Arena stadium, which charges €5.70 per day and includes two return metro tickets to the city centre (20 minutes).

Motorcycles can usually be parked on footpaths providing they don't obstruct pedestrians, but security is a big problem with any parked vehicle, irrespective of the time of day. For any queries, contact the **Parking Control Department** (☎ 553 03 33).

Bicycle Tram tracks and the other 600,000 bikes are the only real obstacle to cycling. It's advisable to book rental bikes ahead in summer. Try **Rent-a-Bike Damstraat** (☎ 625 50 29; *Damstraat 20-22*), which charges €7/31 per day/week plus a €25 deposit or credit card imprint; or the **Rijwielshop** (☎ 624 83 91), to the left just out of Centraal Station, which charges €5.70 per day with a €100 deposit or credit card imprint.

Canal Boat, Bus & Bike

Canal cruises (about €8 an hour) leave from in front of Centraal Station, along Damrak and Rokin and near the Rijksmuseum. They are very touristy, but they also are a great way to see the city from a different perspective; night cruises are especially enchanting, as many of the bridges are illuminated and the whole scene takes on something of an unreal quality.

If you want to travel around by boat, the **Canal Bus** (☎ 623 98 86) stops at the tourist enclaves situated between Centraal Station and the Rijksmuseum, and has a day ticket for €12.50. The **Museumboot** (☎ 530 10 90) offers a €13.50 day ticket, good for unlimited travel.

In summer, **canal 'bikes'** (☎ 626 55 74) can be hired from kiosks at Centraal Station and Leidseplein for €6 per person.

AROUND AMSTERDAM

Bus tours to nearby sights can be booked through the VVV or GWK, and include trips to Aalsmeer, Alkmaar (about €28), The Hague, Delft and Fryslân via the Afsluitdijk (about €28).

The world's biggest **flower auction** is held Monday to Friday at **Aalsmeer** (☎ 0297-39 39 39; bus No 172 from Centraal Station; adult/child €4/3.50), south of Amsterdam. Bidding starts early, so make sure to arrive between 7.30am and 9am.

To get to the once typical, but now tourist-filled, fishing village of **Volendam**, take bus No 110 from Centraal Station (35 minutes). To the similar village and former island of **Marken**, now connected to the mainland by a dike, get bus No 111 (45 minutes) or go to Volendam and take the ferry.

The **Alkmaar cheese market**, staged at 10am every Friday from April to September in the town's main market square, attracts droves.

Arrive early if you want to get more than a fleeting glimpse of the famous round cheeses being weighed and whisked away. There are two trains per hour from Centraal Station (€5.40, 30 minutes) and it's a 15-minute walk at the other end.

The Randstad

The Netherlands' most densely populated region, the Randstad (literally, 'Urban Agglomeration') spreads in a circle from Amsterdam and incorporates The Hague, Rotterdam and Utrecht, and smaller towns like Haarlem, Leiden, Delft and Gouda. Its many sights are highlighted by the bulb fields that explode into intoxicating colours between March and May.

HAARLEM

☎ 023 • pop 147,873

Haarlem is a small but vibrant town, with a wealth of historic buildings and posh shops. The Haarlem **VVV** (☎ 0900-616 16 00, fax 534 05 37; e info@vvvzk.nl; Stationsplein 1; open 9.30am-5.30pm Mon-Fri, 10am-2pm Sun Oct-Mar, 10am-4pm Apr-Sept) is next to the train station.

Frans Hals Museum (☎ 511 5775; Groot Heiligland 62; adult/child €5.40/free; open 11am-5pm Tues-Sat, noon-5pm Sun), featuring portraits by the master himself as well as other great artists, is a must-see for fans of Dutch painting. The **Teyler Museum** (☎ 531 9010; Spaarne 16; adult/child €4.50/1; open 10am-5pm Tues-Sat, noon-5pm Sun) is the country's oldest museum (1778), housing an eclectic mix of fossils, mineral crystals, scientific gadgets and artwork, including drawings by Michelangelo and Raphael. Also worth a look is the Gothic cathedral **St Bavo** (☎ 553 20 40; Grote Markt; adult/child €2/1; open 10am-4pm Mon-Sat), which houses the stunning Müller organ played by Handel and the 10-year-old Mozart. **Molen de Adrian** (☎ 545 02 59; Papentorenvest 1a; adult/child €2/1; open 10am-4pm Fri-Sun) is Haarlem's newest attraction, a reconstructed 18th-century windmill, with a modern feel, and knowledgeable volunteers can show you around.

From Amsterdam, there are trains every 15 minutes to Haarlem (€2.90, 15 minutes).

KEUKENHOF

Near the town of Lisse between Haarlem and Leiden is the Keukenhof (☎ 0252-46 55 55; w www.keukenhof.nl; adult/child €11/5.50; open late Mar-late May), which is the world's largest garden. Attracting a staggering 800,000 people in a mere eight weeks every year, its beauty is something of an enigma, combining nature's talents with artificial precision to

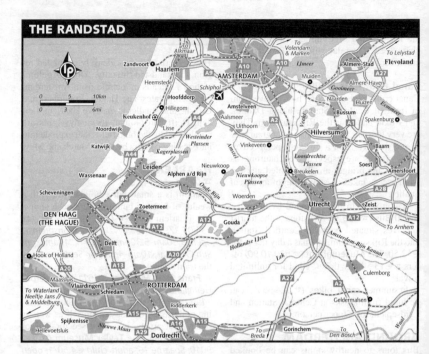

THE RANDSTAD

create a garden where millions of bulbs – tulips, daffodils and hyacinths – bloom every year, perfectly in place and exactly on time.

From Amsterdam, the Keukenhof can be reached either by a bus tour or by train to Leiden, from where you pick up bus No 54 (a bus/entrance pass is €15).

LEIDEN
☎ 071 • pop 118,500

Home to the country's oldest university, Leiden is an effervescent town with an intellectual aura generated largely by 15,000 students who live here. The university was a well-deserved present to the town from William of Orange for withstanding a long Spanish siege in 1574; one-third of the townsfolk starved before the Spaniards retreated on 3 October, now the date of Leiden's biggest festival. Encircled by canals, bursting with cafés and restaurants, and with miles of car-free paved walkways, it's a very civilised place to kick back in.

Orientation & Information
Most of the sights are situated within a network of central canals, about a 10-minute walk from the train station.

The helpful **VVV** (☎ 0900-222 23 33, fax 516 12 27; e leiden@hollandrijnland.nl; Stationsweg 2d; open 9.30am-6pm Mon-Fri, 10am-4.30pm Sat) can provide walking-tour booklets which will guide you through the town's many **hofjes** (almshouses) and another booklet covering the trail of Rembrandt who was born here.

The **main post office** (Schipholweg 130) is about 300m northeast of the station, or there's a **central branch** (Breestraat 46). For €4, **Wash Queen** (Morsstraat 50) will wash and dry your laundry within an hour.

For Internet access head to the **Centrale Bibliotheek** (library; ☎ 514 99 43; Nieuwstraat 4; €2.30 per 30min; open 1pm-5pm Sun-Mon, 11am-5pm Tues-Sat, also 7pm-9pm Mon, Wed & Thur).

Things to See & Do
Canal cruises (☎ 513 49 38; Beestenmarkt; adult/child €4.40/2.50; daily Apr-Sept, weather dependent Oct-Mar) cut a lap of the town and offer a taped commentary.

The **Rijksmuseum van Oudheden** (National Museum of Antiquities; ☎ 516 31 63; Rapenburg 28; adult/child €6/5.50; open

LEIDEN

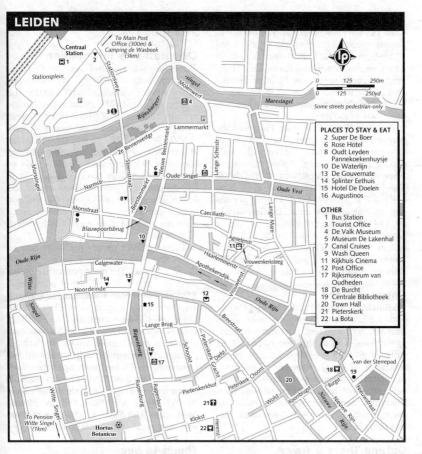

PLACES TO STAY & EAT
2 Super De Boer
6 Rose Hotel
8 Oudt Leyden
   Pannekoekenhuysje
10 De Waterlijn
13 De Gouvernate
14 Splinter Eethuis
15 Hotel De Doelen
16 Augustinos

OTHER
1 Bus Station
3 Tourist Office
4 De Valk Museum
5 Museum De Lakenhal
7 Canal Cruises
9 Wash Queen
11 Kijkhuis Cinema
12 Post Office
17 Rijksmuseum van
   Oudheden
18 De Burcht
19 Centrale Bibliotheek
20 Town Hall
21 Pieterskerk
22 La Bota

10am-5pm Tues-Fri, noon-5pm Sat & Sun) tops Leiden's list of museums. Its striking entrance hall contains an Egyptian temple and it displays its ancient Egyptian, Greek, Near East and Dutch collections with style.

The 17th-century **Museum De Lakenhal** (Cloth Hall; ☎ 516 53 60; Oude Singel 28; adult/child €4/free; open 10am-5pm Tues-Sat, noon-5pm Sun) houses works by old masters and the 1st floor has been restored to how it would have looked during the heady era when Leiden was at the peak of its cloth trade prosperity.

Leiden's landmark windmill, **De Valk** (Falcon; ☎ 516 53 53; Binnenvestgracht 1; adult/child €2.50/1.50; open 10am-5pm Tues-Sat, 1pm-5pm Sun) will blow away notions that windmills were a Dutch invention.

Places to Stay

Camping De Wasbeek (☎ 301 13 80; Wasbeeklaan 5b; adult/tent/car €2.50/2.50/1.20; open mid-Apr–mid-Oct) is at Warmond, a few kilometres north of Leiden.

Pension Witte Singel (☎ 512 45 92, fax 514 28 90; e wvandriel@pension-ws.demon.nl; Witte Singel 80; singles/doubles from €31/46.50), on a peaceful canal south of the centre, is a 25-minute walk from the station.

Rose Hotel (☎ 514 66 30, fax 521 70 96; Beestenmarkt 14; singles/doubles €50/80) is basic and popular with young travellers.

Some rooms have their own private art collection in the stately **Hotel De Doelen** (☎ 512 05 27, fax 512 84 53; e hotel@de doelen.com; Rapenburg 2; singles/doubles from €65/85).

THE NETHERLANDS

Places to Eat
Oudt Leyden Pannekoekenhuysje (☎ 513 31 44; Steenstraat 51; mains around €7; open 11am-9pm Mon-Sat, 2pm-9pm Sun) does enormous pancakes in a traditional Dutch café. Predominantly vegetarian **Splinter Eethuis** (☎ 514 95 19; Noordeinde 30; mains around €11; open 5pm-9.30pm Thur-Sun) has organic two-course meals.

De Waterlijn (☎ 512 12 79; Prinsessekade 5; mains around €3; open 10am-10pm daily) is a floating café that's popular with locals craving a coffee or cake. Behind that austere black door is the **Augustinos** (☎ 516 2336; Rapenburg 24; mains around €4; open 5.30pm-8.15pm Mon-Fri). It's hugely popular with students so book ahead. **De Gouvernate** (☎ 514 88 18; Kort Rapenweg 17; mains around €25; open 5.30pm-10.30pm) has excellent traditional Dutch food with French touches. Self-caterers will find a **Super De Boer** supermarket opposite the train station.

Entertainment
De Burcht (☎ 514 23 89; Burgsteeg 14; open 5pm-1.30am Mon-Thur, 4pm-3am Fri, 2pm-3am Sat, 2pm-2am Sun) is a literary bar next to the remains of a 12th-century citadel. **La Bota** (☎ 514 63 40; Herensteeg 9; mains around €10; meals 5pm-10pm, bar until midnight) is a friendly and down-to-earth student pub, which is good for a meal and a beer. **Kijkhuis Cinema** (☎ 566 15 85; Vrouwenksteeg 10; admission €6-7) has an alternative film circuit.

Getting There & Away
There are trains operating every 15 minutes to Amsterdam (€6.10, 35 minutes), to Haarlem (€4.40, 30 minutes, every seven minutes), to The Hague (€2.50, 15 minutes, every four minutes) and to Schiphol (€4.40, 17 minutes, every 15 minutes).

THE HAGUE
☎ 070 • pop 445,000

The Hague – Den Haag in Dutch – is the country's seat of government and the residence of the Dutch royal family. It is officially known as 's-Gravenhage (The Count's Domain). The city has a refined air, created by the many stately mansions and palatial embassies that line its green boulevards. The city is known for its prestigious art galleries, a huge jazz festival held annually near the seaside suburb of Scheveningen, and the miniature town of Madurodam.

Orientation & Information
Trains stop at Station Hollands Spoor (HS), a 20-minute walk south of the city, or at Centraal Station, five minutes from the centre. The area between Spui and Centraal Station has experienced a massive face-lift in order to create a prestigious commercial and residential area.

VVV (☎ 0900-340 35 05, fax 352 0426; e info@vvvscheveningen.nl; Koningin Julianaplein 30; open 9am-5.30pm Tues-Sat all year, plus 10am-2pm Sun July & Aug) has a free monthly magazine detailing events and action around town and organises a two-hour guided tour of the city's architecture every Saturday from May to August (adult/child €20/free).

There's a **GWK money exchange bureau** (open 8am-9pm Mon-Sat, 9am-5pm Sun) in Centraal Station. The **main post office** (Kerkplein 6; open 7.30am-6.30pm Mon-Wed, 7.30am-8pm Thur, 7.30am-6pm Fri, 7.30am-4pm Sat) has the longest opening hours in the Netherlands. There's a **laundry** (Theresiastraat 250) to the east behind Centraal Station.

Internet users should head to the atmospheric **Café Tweeduizendvijf** (☎ 364 40 94; Denneweg 7f; €1 for 15min; open 8am-1am Sun-Wed, 9am-2am Thur-Sat); or to the bank of terminals at the **Centrale Bibliotheek** (☎ 353 44 55; Spui 68; €1.50 for 30min; open 10am-9pm Mon-Fri, 11am-5pm Sat all year, plus noon-5pm Sun Sept-Apr).

Things to See
The showpiece museum is the **Mauritshuis** (☎ 302 34 35; Korte Vijverberg 8; adult/child €7/free; open 10am-5pm Tues-Sat, 11am-5pm Sun), an exquisite 17th-century mansion packed with superb Dutch and Flemish masterpieces, including works by Vermeer and Rembrandt.

Admirers of De Stijl, particularly Piet Mondrian, won't want to miss the **Gemeentemuseum** (Municipal Museum; ☎ 338 11 11; Stadhouderslaan 41; tram No 17 or bus No 14; adult/child €6.80/2.25; open 11am-5pm Tues-Sun).

The parliamentary buildings, or **Binnenhof** (Inner Court; ☎ 364 61 44; Binnenhof 8a; tour adult/child €5/4.30; open 10am-3.45pm Mon-Sat), have long been the heart of Dutch politics, although nowadays the

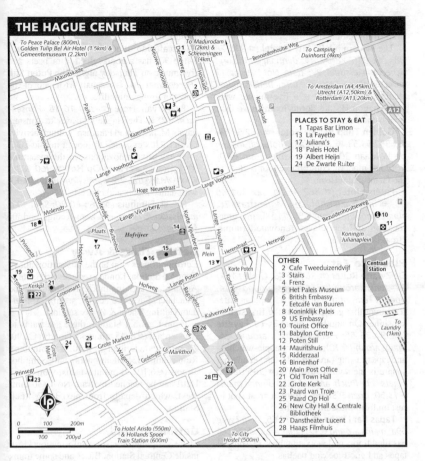

THE HAGUE CENTRE

To Peace Palace (800m),
Golden Tulip Bel Air Hotel (1.5km) &
Gemeentemuseum (2.2km)

To Madurodam
(2km) &
Scheveningen
(4km)

To Camping
Duinhorst (4km)

To Amsterdam (A4,45km),
Utrecht (A12,50km) &
Rotterdam (A13,20km)

A12

Mauritskade

Nieuwe Schoolstr

Dennweg

Hooistr

Benoordenhoutse Weg

Koningskade

Parkstr

Noordeinde

Kazernestr

Lange Voorhout

Lange Voorhout

Molenstr

Kneuterdijk

Hoge Nieuwstraat

Lange Vijverberg

Korte Vijverberg

Lange Houtstr

Lange

Bezuidenhoutseweg

Koningin
Julianaplein

Plaats

Buitenhof

Hofvijver

Herenstraat

Hereng

Plein

Hoogstr

Prinsestr

Kerkpl

Groenmarkt

Venestr

Hofweg

Lange Poten

Korte Poten

Korte Houtstr

Centraal
Station

Nieuwstr

Kalvermarkt

To
Laundry
(1km)

Grote Markt

Spui

Gedempte Gr

Markthof

Grote
Markt

Wagenstr

Prinsegr

To Hotel Aristo (550m)
& Hollands Spoor
Train Station (600m)

To City
Hostel (500m)

0   100   200m
0   100   200yd

PLACES TO STAY & EAT
1 Tapas Bar Limon
13 La Fayette
17 Juliana's
18 Paleis Hotel
19 Albert Heijn
24 De Zwarte Ruiter

OTHER
2 Cafe Tweeduizendvijf
3 Stairs
4 Frenz
5 Het Paleis Museum
6 British Embassy
7 Eetcafé van Buuren
8 Koninklijk Paleis
9 US Embassy
10 Tourist Office
11 Babylon Centre
12 Poten Still
14 Mauritshuis
15 Ridderzaal
16 Binnenhof
20 Main Post Office
21 Old Town Hall
22 Grote Kerk
23 Paard van Troje
25 Paard Op Hol
26 New City Hall & Centrale
   Bibliotheek
27 Danstheater Lucent
28 Haags Filmhuis

parliament actually meets in a building outside the Binnenhof. One-hour tours take in the 13th-century Ridderzaal (Knight's Hall) and depart from the visitors centre in the Binnenhof.

There are three royal palaces but the only one you can visit is the 18th-century **Het Paleis Museum** (☎ 362 40 61; *Lange Varhout 74; adult/child €5.70/free; open 11am-5pm Tues-Sun)*, which stages temporary art exhibitions.

Home of the International Court of Justice, the **Peace Palace** *(Vredepaleis; Carnegieplein; tram No 17 or bus No 4 from Centraal Station; adult/child €3.50/1.80; tours 10am-5pm Mon-Fri)* can be visited by guided tours only, which must be booked – inquire at the VVV.

Everything that's quintessential Netherlands is in the tiny 'town' of **Madurodam** *(☎ 416 24 00; w www.madurodam.nl; George Maduroplein 1; tram Nos 1 & 9 or bus No 22 from Centraal Station; admission €10; open 9am-6pm daily Sept-Feb, 9am-8pm Mar-June, 9am-11pm July & Aug)*. Delighting tourists and kids for 50 years now, it's clever but a bit bizarre when you can so easily see the real thing.

Places to Stay
Camping Duinhorst *(☎ 324 22 70, fax 324 6053; e info@duinhorst.nl; Buurtweg 135; bus No 43; tent/adult €2.30/4.55; open Apr-Sept)* is east of Scheveningen.

The **Hotel Aristo** *(☎/fax 384 04 01; Stationsweg 139; doubles with/without bath*

€48/34) has clean, simple rooms and is only 50m from Station HS.

The modern NJHC **City Hostel** (☎ 315 78 88, fax 315 78 77; e denhaag@njhc.org; Scheepmakerstraat 27; tram No 1, 9 or 12 from Centraal Station; dorm beds/singles/ doubles €23/47/61) is a five-minute walk from Station HS; all dorms/rooms have their own bathroom.

Golden Tulip Bel Air Hotel (☎ 352 53 54, fax 352 53 53; e info@belairhotel.nl; Johann de Wittlaan 30; singles/doubles from €80/ 100) has modern, comfortable rooms close to the Gemeentemuseum.

Paleis Hotel (☎ 362 46 21, fax 361 45 33; e info@paleishotel.nl; Molenstraat 26; singles/doubles from €95/115) is in a great location and has classy renovated rooms. Breakfast is €10.

Places to Eat

De Zwarte Ruiter (☎ 364 95 49; Grote Markt 27; lunch around €4, mains around €14; open 11am-1am daily) is a popular café/ restaurant that gets packed at the first sign of sunshine. On another square is **La Fayette** (☎ 392 36 55; Plein 15; lunch around €5; mains around €10), great for people-watching and tapas-tasting (around €4). On yet another square is the stylish **Juliana's** (☎ 365 02 35; Plaats 11; lunch around €8, dinner mains €13.50; open 9.30am-11pm), a great spot to rest up from museum traipsing.

Tapas Bar Limon (☎ 356 14 65; Denneweg 59a; mains around €12; tapas around €3.50) has tiled floors and wooden tables, reasonable tapas and good-looking paellas.

Self-caterers should head to **Albert Heijn** (Torenstraat 27).

Entertainment

Although it's more a city for fine dining than partying, there are a few lively cafés, and in the second week of July the North Sea Jazz Festival considerably invigorates the music scene. Most bars are open until 1am or 2am, except Sunday when The Hague is dead.

If you're into ballet, catch a performance by the world-renowned Nederlands Danstheater in the **Danstheater Lucent** (☎ 360 49 30; w www.ldt.nl; Spui; tickets around €18). There are no performances in July and August.

Frenz (☎ 362 6657; Kazernestraat 106), a gay bar flying the rainbow flag, has a DJ Friday and Saturday nights. Close by is **Stairs**

(☎ 364 81 91; Nieuwe Schoolstraat 21), a gay bar/disco.

Eetcafé van Buuren (☎ 345 98 22; Noordeinde 90) has a good selection of beers and live music on Thursday night. The **Poten Still** (Herenstraat 15) is a small Irish pub in the midst of grungy nightlife.

Paard van Troje (☎ 360 16 18; Prinsegracht 12) is The Hague's answer to Amsterdam's Melkweg and Paradiso 'cultural activity centres'. It's expected to reopen in mid-2003 after extensive renovations. In the meantime it's operating as **Paard Op Hol** (☎ 360 1838; Grote Markstrat 25; admission around €6), with dance nights and concerts.

Haags Filmhuis (☎ 365 60 30; Spui 191; admission €7) screens both foreign and art movies.

Getting There & Away

Eurolines buses stop at the bus station above Centraal Station. London services originate in Amsterdam, arriving in The Hague about one hour later. For more details, see the Amsterdam Getting There & Away section.

From Centraal Station, there are trains to Amsterdam (€8, 45 minutes), Gouda (€3.90, 20 minutes), Leiden (€2.50, 15 minutes), Rotterdam (€3, 20 minutes) and Schiphol airport (€6.10, 40 minutes). Just 9km away, Delft can be reached by tram No 1 (30 minutes), which departs from next to Centraal Station.

Getting Around

There's a public transport information kiosk inside Centraal Station. Buses and some trams leave from above Centraal Station, while other trams take off from the side. Tram No 8 goes to Scheveningen via the Peace Palace, while tram Nos 1 and 9 follow Nieuwe Parklaan past Madurodam to the coast. Tram No 9 links Centraal Station and HS.

DELFT
☎ 015 • pop 96,000

Delft's old town centre exudes old world charm, with its narrow, brick-paved and canal-lined streets – though it's harder to appreciate in summer when hordes of tourists descend. Delftware, the town's world-famous blue-and-white pottery is everywhere; originally duplicated from Chinese porcelain by 17th-century artisans, some of it is now (ironically) mass-produced in China.

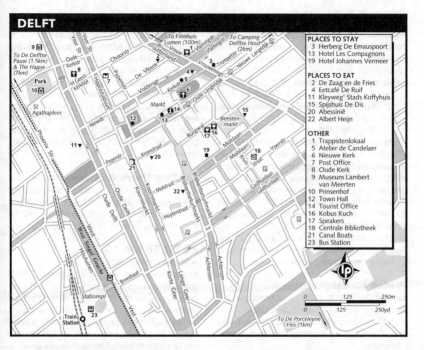

DELFT

PLACES TO STAY
3 Herberg De Emauspoort
13 Hotel Les Compagnons
19 Hotel Johannes Vermeer

PLACES TO EAT
2 De Zaag en de Fries
4 Eetcafé De Ruif
11 Kleyweg' Stads Koffyhuis
15 Spijshuis De Dis
20 Abessinië
22 Albert Heijn

OTHER
1 Trappistenlokaal
5 Atelier de Candelaer
6 Nieuwe Kerk
7 Post Office
8 Oude Kerk
9 Museum Lambert van Meerten
10 Prinsenhof
12 Town Hall
14 Tourist Office
16 Kobus Kuch
17 Speakers
18 Centrale Bibliotheek
21 Canal Boats
23 Bus Station

Orientation & Information

The train and neighbouring bus station are a 10-minute stroll from the central Markt. **VVV** (☎ 213 01 00, fax 215 86 95; ⓦ www.delft .com; Markt 85; open 9am-5.30pm Mon-Sat all year, plus 11am-3pm Sun in summer) will book accommodation. The **post office** (Hippolytusbuurt) has an ATM, and the **Centrale Bibliotheek** (library; ☎ 212 34 50; Kruisstraat 71) has Internet access for €2.40 per hour.

Things to See & Do

See the delftware artisans at work at the central studio and shop **Atelier de Candelaer** (☎ 213 18 48; Kerkstraat 14; open 9am-5.30pm Mon-Fri, 9am-5pm Sat, 9am-4.30pm Sun, closed Sun in winter). Outside the city centre, **De Porceleyne Fles** (☎ 251 20 30; Rotterdamseweg 196; bus No 63, 121 or 129 from train station; guided tours adult/child €2.50/0.50; open 9am-5pm Mon-Sat, 9.30am-5pm Sun, closed Sun in winter) has been producing delftware since 1653. **Museum Lambert van Meerten** (☎ 260 23 58; Oude Delft 199; adult/child €2.50/2; open 10am-5pm Tues-Sat, 1pm-5pm Sun) has a fine collection of porcelain

tiles and delftware dating back to the 16th century.

The 14th-century **Nieuwe Kerk** (Markt; adult/concession €2/0.75; open 9am-6pm Mon-Sat Nov-Mar, 11am-4pm Mon-Fri, 11am-5pm Sat Apr-Oct) houses the crypt of the Dutch royal family as well as the ornate mausoleum of William of Orange. The Gothic **Oude Kerk** (Heilige Geestkerkhof; admission included in Niewe Kerk ticket), with a distinctive 2m tilt in its tower, houses the (very plain) plaque of Delft artist Johannes Vermeer.

The **Prinsenhof** (St Agathaplein 1; adult/concession €3.50/3; open 10am-5pm Tues-Sat, 1pm-5pm Sun) is where William of Orange held court until he was assassinated here in 1584 – you can still see the bullet holes. It now houses a rich collection of mostly 17th-century art.

Canal boat trips (☎ 212 63 85; Koornmarkt; adult/child €4.50/3; mid-Mar–mid-Oct) include informative and a tad quirky 45-minute tours.

Places to Stay

Delftse Hout (☎ 213 00 40, fax 213 12 93; ⓔ info-delftsehout@tours.nl; Korftlaan 5; bus

THE NETHERLANDS

No 64 from station; tent site for 2 people €22, huts for up to 4 people €30; open all year) is a neat camping ground opposite a large park and a 15-minute walk from the city centre.

Hotel Les Compagnons (☎ 215 82 55, fax 212 01 68; Markt 61; singles & doubles €65) has pink decor, hard towels and customer service is yet to arrive, but it has clean rooms overlooking the Markt.

Herberg De Emauspoort (☎ 219 02 19, fax 214 82 51; e emauspoort@emauspoort.nl; Vrouwenregt 11; singles/doubles & caravans €72.50/82.50) has warmly furnished rooms and two cosy, Roma-style (gypsy) caravans.

Hotel Johannes Vermeer (☎ 212 64 66, fax 213 48 35; e hotelvermeer@hotelnet.nl; Molslaan 18; singles/doubles €97.50/109.50) has tastefully decorated rooms and is one for Vermeer fans – prints of his works are everywhere including the stunning breakfast room.

Places to Eat

Eetcafé De Ruif (☎ 214 22 06; Kerkstraat 23, mains around €14; open 5.30pm-9.30pm daily) is a rustic café with a popular bar. Try the salmon, cod and lobster tails wrapped in filo pastry.

The bustling **Kleyweg' Stads Koffyhuis** (☎ 212 46 25; Oude Delft 133; mains around €4; open 9am-7pm Mon-Fri, 9am-6pm Sat) sells award-winning sandwiches, as well as tasty soups and pancakes, and has a magazine table.

De Zaag en de Fries (☎ 213 70 15; Vrouw Juttenland 17; mains around €14; open 5.30pm-9pm Wed-Sun) is an ever-popular vegetarian restaurant. Make sure to get there early or book.

Abessinië (☎ 213 52 60; Kromstraat 21; mains around €12; open 5pm-10pm daily) serves up tasty African fare amid a vibrant atmosphere.

Spijshuis De Dis (☎ 213 17 82; Beestenmarkt 36; mains around €16; open 5pm-9.30pm Thur-Mon) serves up Dutch dishes including the house speciality, De Bokkepot, a stew of rabbit, chicken and beef in mushroom and beer sauce.

Albert Heijn Supermarket (Brabantseturfmarkt 41; open 8am-8pm Sat-Thur, 8am-9pm Fri) should provide all that self-caterers need.

Stock up on local produce at Thursday's **market** at the Markt.

Entertainment

Speakers (☎ 212 44 46; Burgwal 45; open until at least 2am; admission around €7) is big and multilevel and has jazz, rock, comedy and DJs on different nights. For a slightly more quiet haunt head around the corner to **Kobus Kuch** (Beestenmarkt 1; open until 2am). Beer connoisseurs should aim for the cosy **Trappistenlokaal** (Vlamingstraat 4; open until 2am). And for something different, the **Filmhuis Lumen** (☎ 214 02 26; Doelenplein 5) shows alternative films.

Getting There & Away

It's 14 minutes by train to Rotterdam (€2.50), and 10 to The Hague (€1.90). Tram No 1 leaves for The Hague (30 minutes) every 15 minutes from in front of the train station.

ROTTERDAM
☎ 010 • pop 593,000

Rotterdam is not your quintessential Dutch city. Bombed to oblivion on 14 May 1940, its centre is ultra-modern, with mirrored skyscrapers and some extraordinarily innovative buildings. The city prides itself on this experimental architecture, as well as having the world's largest port. The nightlife is good, a large immigrant community adds life and there are some excellent museums.

Orientation & Information

Rotterdam is a sprawling city by Dutch standards; its hub is the pedestrianised shopping streets based around Lijnbaan.

VVV (☎ 414 00 00, fax 413 31 24; e info@vvv.rotterham.nl; Coolsingel 67; open 9.30am-6pm Mon-Thur & Sat, 9.30am-9pm Fri) sells the Rotterdam Card (one/three days €25/49.50), providing entry to things to see, and discounted accommodation.

Use-It (☎ 240 91 58, fax 240 91 59; e use-it@jip.org; Conradstraat 2; open 9am-5pm Tues-Sat mid-Sept–mid-May, 9am-6pm Tues-Sun mid-May–mid-Sept) is situated next to Central Station and is a tourist service aimed at budget travellers. Its services include free day lockers, email access, and information concerning budget hotels and accommodation discounts.

The **main post office** (Coolsingel 42) is opposite the VVV and there's Internet access at the library (☎ 281 61 00; €3.40 per hour; open 10am-8pm Mon-Fri, 10am-5pm Sat all year, 11am-5pm Sun Sept-May).

Things to See & Do

Rotterdam's sights are situated within a region which is bordered by the old town of Delfshaven, the Maas River and the Blaak district.

The city's many museums are lorded over by the **Boijmans van Beuningen** (☎ 441 94 00; Museumpark 18; tram No 4 & 5, metro to Eendrachtsplein; adult/child €6/free; open 10am-5pm Tues-Sat, 11am-5pm Sun), a rich gallery of 14th-century to contemporary art. It has a superb Old Masters collection including work by Bosch, van Eyck and Rembrandt, and also houses work by Monet, van Gogh, Mondrian and Dali.

Het Schielandshuis (☎ 217 67 67; Korte Hoogstraat 31; metro to Beurs; adult/child €2.70/1.35; open 10am-5pm Tues-Fri, 11am-5pm Sat & Sun) was the only central 17th-century building to survive the German bombing blitz. It's now a museum housing a rather eclectic mix of exhibits including some footage of the bombardment.

Spido (☎ 275 99 88; adult/child €7.75/ 4.75; 1¼-hour tour; open 9.30am-5pm daily Apr-Sept, 11am-3.30pm daily Oct, 11am-3.30pm Thur-Sun Nov-Mar) runs harbour cruises, and also operates some day trips in summer. Departure is from Leuvehoofd (take the metro to Leuvehaven).

Euromast (☎ 436 48 11; Parkhaven 20; tram No 6 or 9 or metro to Dijkzigt; adult/ child €7.50/5; open 10am-5pm Oct-Mar, 10am-7pm Apr-Sept, 10am-10.30pm Thur-Sat Jul & Aug), a 185m tower, dominates the Rotterdam skyline and has great views of the city; kids will enjoy the space flight scenario to get to the top.

Kijkkubus (Cube Houses; ☎ 414 22 85; Overblaak 70; metro to Blaak; adult/child €1.75/1.25; open 11am-5pm daily) is a cube-shaped display house that was, during its time, an innovative 1970s response to traditional architecture.

Delfshaven, Rotterdam's old town, is most famous for its **Oude Kerk** (Aelbrechtskolk 20; metro to Delfshaven), where those Pilgrim Fathers prayed before setting sail to the New World.

Kunsthal (☎ 440 03 01; Westzeedijk 341; tram No 5 or 8; adult/child €6.50/3.50; open 10am-5pm Mon-Sat, 11am-5pm Sun) is the city's premier venue for temporary art exhibitions; it's well worth checking what they've got on.

Places to Stay

Stadscamping (☎ 415 34 40, fax 437 32 15; Kanaalweg 84; bus No 33; tent/adult/car €3.50/4.50/2.50) is a 40-minute walk northwest of the station.

The **NJHC hostel** (City Hostel Rotterdam; ☎ 436 57 63, fax 436 55 69; w www.njhc .org/rotterdam; Rochussenstraat 107; metro to Dijkzigt; dorm beds from €19; singles/ doubles €28.25/47) offers a bar and fairly basic rooms, and is a 20-minute walk from the station.

The friendly **Hotel Bienvenue** (☎ 466 93 94, fax 467 74 75; Spoorsingel 24; singles/ doubles & apartments from €43/70) is the pick of the budget hotels; it's close to a small park, overlooks a canal, and is two blocks straight up the canal from the rear entrance of Centraal Station.

Hotel Bazar (☎ 206 51 51, fax 206 51 59; Witte de Withstraat 16; tram No 5 from CS; singles/doubles from €60/65), in the heart of town, has rooms decked out in Middle Eastern and South American style and a fantastic restaurant (see Places to Eat).

Romantics might enjoy a night at the luxury **Hotel New York** (☎ 439 05 00, fax 484 27; e info@hotelnewyork.nl; Koninginnenhoofd 1; singles/doubles with harbour views from €139/155). This was the headquarters of the Holland-America shipping line and is known for its views, café, and boat taxi that takes guests across the Nieuwe Maas to the centre.

Places to Eat

Wester Paviljoen (☎ 436 26 45; Nieuwe Binnenweg 136; mains around €11; open 8am-1am or 2am daily) is a large, smoky café with a down-to-earth atmosphere, and a great outside terrace.

Restaurant Bazar (☎ 206 51 51; Witte de Withstraat 16; mains around €9; open 10am-1am or 2am Mon-Fri, noon-2am Sat, noon-11.30pm Sun) is where the decor and excellent food transports you away to a Middle Eastern bazaar, and it's just as crowded.

Café 't Bolwerk (☎ 414 73 03; Gelersekade 1c; mains around €16; open 11.30am-4am Sun-Thur, 11.30am-6am Fri & Sat) is on the ground floor of the historic White House tower on Oude Haven. It's popular with the after-work crowd; dancing starts around midnight.

De Pannenkoekenboot (☎ 436 72 95; Parkhaven; adult/child €12/7; 2-4 1½-hour trips daily Wed, Fri, Sat & Sun, Sept-June; 4

THE NETHERLANDS

trips daily, Wed-Sun, Jul & Aug) cruises around the harbour (while you eat as many pancakes as you like (the record is 14!). Kids love the room full of plastic balls.

Tampopo Noodle Bar *(☎ 225 15 22; Gravendijkwal 128; mains around €14)* is a trendy, stylish Asian restaurant with a good reputation.

Self-caterers can have a break from Albert Heijn and stock up at **Volume Markt supermarket** *(Nieuwe Binneweg 30a)*.

Entertainment

Check the monthly *R'uit* guide (free from the VVV and cafés) for listings of what's on. The many terrace cafés on Stadhuisplein and at Oude Haven near the Kijk-Kubus are popular. Smokers can indulge in one of the many coffeeshops on Nieuwe Binneweg.

Getting There & Away

Eurolines buses stop at Conradstraat (to the right as you leave the train station) where there is a **Eurolines office** *(☎ 412 44 44)* at No 20. Services to London leave from Amsterdam, arriving in Rotterdam 1½ hours later (€55/83 one way/return, 8½ hours).

If you're under 26 tickets on the Eurostar to London via Brussels cost €54 return. For those over-26s, fares start at €116 return.

Trains run every 15 minutes to Amsterdam (€10.80, one hour), Delft (€2.50, 10 minutes), The Hague (€3.40, 20 minutes) and Utrecht (€7, 40 minutes). Half-hourly services run to Middelburg (€15.60, 1½ hours), Gouda (€3.40, 18 minutes) and Hook of Holland (€3.90, 30 minutes).

For information on the ferries from Hook of Holland and Europoort to England, see the Getting There & Away section at the beginning of this chapter. P&O/North Sea Ferries' bus leaves at 4pm daily from Conradstraat (next to Centraal Station) to connect with the ferry at Europoort.

Getting Around

Trams leave from in front of the train station; the metro from underneath. Both run until about midnight; on Friday and Saturday, night buses then take over. A one-/two-day public transport card costs €6/9.

AROUND ROTTERDAM

The **Kinderdijk**, the Netherlands' picture-postcard string of 19 working windmills, sits between Rotterdam and Dordrecht near Alblasserdam. On Saturday afternoons in July and August the mills' sails are set in motion for a spectacular sight. One windmill is open daily from 1 April to 30 September – get the metro to Zuidplein then bus No 154 (1¼ hours).

GOUDA

☎ 0182 • pop 73,000

Say 'Dutch cheese', and most people will think Gouda (or Edam). This pretty little town, 25km northeast of Rotterdam, is well known for its cheese market, held at 10am every Thursday morning in July and August. Enormous rounds of cheese – some weighing up to 25kg – are brought to the Markt where they're weighed and sold. For more information, contact the **VVV** *(☎ 0900-468 32 888, fax 0182-583 210; Markt 27; open 9am-5pm Mon-Sat, plus noon-5pm Sun Jun-Aug)*.

Regular trains connect Gouda with Rotterdam (€3.80, 18 minutes) and Amsterdam (€8.50, one hour).

UTRECHT

☎ 030 • pop 236,000

Lorded over by the Dom, the country's tallest church tower, Utrecht is an antique frame surrounding an increasingly modern interior. Its 14th-century sunken canals, once-bustling wharfs and cellars now brim with chic restaurants and cafés, and the large student population add plenty of buzz to the city. You see none of this when arriving at the train station, which is behind Hoog Catharijne, the Netherlands largest indoor shopping centre and a modern monstrosity.

Information

VVV *(☎ 0900-128 87 32, call cost €0.50 per min; fax 236 00 37; e info@vvvutrecht.nl; Vinkenburgstraat 19; open 9.30am-6.30pm Mon-Wed & Fri, 9.30am-9pm Thur, 9.30am-5pm Sat; plus 10am-2pm Sun May-Sept)* is a 10-minute walk east from the train station.

Time2Surf *(Oudegracht 112)* has 150 terminals and charges €2.50 per hour, or try the centrally located **library** *(☎ 286 18 00; Oudegracht 167; open 1pm-9pm Mon, 11am-6pm Tues-Fri, 10am-2pm Sat)*, where the charge is €1.20 per 30 minutes.

Things to See & Do

You can see for kilometres from the 112m-high **Dom Tower** *(adult/child €6/3; open*

10am-5pm Mon-Sat, noon-5pm Sun) once you make the 465 steps to the top.

Museum Van Speelklok tot Pierement (☎ 231 27 89; Buurkerkhof 10; adult/child €6/4; open 10am-5pm Tues-Sat, noon-5pm Sun) has a colourful collection of musical clocks and street organs from the 14th century onwards, demonstrated with gusto on hourly tours.

Het Catharijneconvent Museum (Nieuwegracht 63; adult/child €6/3; open 10am-5pm Tues-Fri, 11am-5pm Sat & Sun) winds through a 15th-century convent and features the country's largest collection of medieval Dutch art.

Canal cruises (☎ 272 0111; cnr Oudegracht & Lange Viestrasse; 1hr cruise adult/child €6/4.50; 11am-6pm daily all year) are also available for half and full days.

Places to Stay

Camping De Berekuil (☎ 271 38 70; Arjënslaan 5; tent site €4, plus €4 per person; bus No 57 from station; open all year) is 1.5km from the centre.

Strowis Hostel (☎ 238 02 80, fax 241 54 51; e info@strowis.nl; Boothstraat 8; dorm beds €11-13.50, doubles €41), in a lovingly restored 17th-century building, has friendly, helpful staff, free email access and bike hire. It's a 15-minute walk from Centraal Station or take bus No 3, 4, 8 or 11 to Janskerkhof.

Hotel Kay (☎ 271 21 24, fax 273 40 58; Wittevrouwensingel 44; singles/doubles €72/85) is overpriced for its basic rooms, but is one of the few cheaper options going in the city centre.

Tulip Inn (NH Centre Utrecht Hotel; ☎ 231 31 69, fax 231 01 48; e nhcentre.utrecht@nh-hotels.nl; Janskerkhof 10; singles/doubles from €111/143) is a comfortable central hotel with a lively, atmospheric café (see Places to Eat).

Grand Hotel Karel V (☎ 233 75 55, fax 233 75 00; e info@karelv.nl; Geertebolwerk 1; singles/double from €195/220), in a lavishly converted 14th-century building, is in a class of its own. You're unlikely to want anything here. Breakfast is €17.50.

Places to Eat

Acu (☎ 231 45 90; Voorstraat 71; 3-course meal €6; open 5pm-2am Sun-Thur, 9am-4am Fri & Sat; meals 6pm-7.30pm Sun-Thur), around the corner from the Strowis Hostel,

has good vegetarian food, as well as live music after 10pm.

Surinaams Javaans Restaurant (☎ 231 92 72; Wittevrouwenstraat 22; mains around €13; open 4pm-10pm Tues-Sun) is an Indonesian restaurant which is usually packed with locals.

The Oudegracht is lined with outdoor restaurants and cafés.

The best of the bunch is **Oudaen** (☎ 231 18 64; Oudegracht 99; mains around €16; open 10am-10pm Mon-Sat), set in a restored 13th-century banquet hall – and it also brews its own beer.

Broers (Tulip Inn; ☎ 234 34 06; Janskerkhof 9; mains average €18; open 9am-midnight Mon-Sat, 10am-midnight Sun) sprawls stylishly over several rooms and has good views out on the streets and square.

Shoarma (pitta-bread) eateries are plentiful along Voorstraat and for self-caterers, there's an **Albert Heijn** Supermarket in Hoog Catharijne (the huge shopping centre next to the train station).

Getting There & Around

Connexion buses stop at the back of the train station; there's a ticket office there or they can be purchased on the bus.

As Utrecht is the national rail hub, there are frequent trains to Amsterdam (€8, 30 minutes), Arnhem (€5.30, 40 minutes), Gouda (€4.40, 22 minutes), Maastricht (€19.70, two hours), Rotterdam (€7, 40 minutes) and The Hague (€8, 45 minutes).

Buses leave from underneath Hoog Catharijne (the shopping complex adjoining the train station).

Arnhem & the Hoge Veluwe

☎ 026 (Arnhem)   ☎ 031 (Hoge Veluwe)
• pop 134,650

About an hour's drive east of Amsterdam, the Hoge Veluwe is the Netherlands' best-known national park and home of the prestigious Kröller-Müller Museum.

To the south, there's the town of Arnhem which was the site of fierce fighting between the Germans and British and Polish airborne troops during the failed Operation Market Garden in WWII.

HOGE VELUWE

Stretching for nearly 5500 hectares, the Hoge Veluwe National Park (☎ 859 16 37; Apeldoornseweg 250; ⓦ www.hogeveluwe.nl; combined park/museum ticket adult/child €10/5; plus cars €5; park open 9am-5.30pm daily Nov-Mar, 8am or 9am-sunset daily Apr-Oct, visitors centre open 10am-5pm daily) is a mix of forests and woods, shifting sands and heathery moors. It's home to red deer, wild boar, moufflons (a Mediterranean goat), and **Kröller-Müller Museum** (☎ 859 10 41; open 10am-5pm Tues-Sun) with its world-class collection of Van Gogh paintings, as well as the works of Picasso, Renoir and Manet.

The park is best seen on foot or bicycle – the latter are available free of charge at the park entrances or from the visitors centre inside the park.

To get to the park, take bus No 107 from Stationsplein in Arnhem (four times daily from 1 April to 30 October).

ARNHEM

Arnhem is a bland, uninspiring town but the closest base to the nearby war museum and the national park.

VVV (☎ 0900-202 40 75, fax 442 26 44; ⓔ info@vvvarnhem.nl; Willemsplein 8) is one block left out of Arnhem's train station. Buses leave from the right as you exit the station. The town's pedestrianised centre, based around the well-hidden Korenmarkt, is a five-minute walk from the station.

Things to See

In Arnhem itself, the main attraction is the **Museum voor Moderne Kunst** (Modern Art Museum; ☎ 351 24 31; Utrechtseweg 87; adult/child €5/free; open 10am-5pm Tues-Fri, 11am-5pm Sat & Sun), which boasts a commanding spot overlooking the Rhine. It exhibits mostly Dutch artists, and about half the work is by women. It's a 10-minute walk from the station.

Outside the town is Oosterbeek's wartime **Airborne Museum Hartenstein** (☎ 333 77 10; Utrechtseweg 232; trolleybus No 1 from Arnhem station; adult/child €4/3; open 10am-5pm Mon-Sat Apr-Oct, 11am-5pm Mon-Sat Nov-Mar, plus noon-5pm Sun year-round) which has a film and audiovisual show that does an excellent job of explaining the battle of Arnhem.

Places to Stay & Eat

Hostel Alteveer Arnhem (☎ 442 01 14, fax 351 48 92; ⓔ arnhem@njhc.org; Diepenbrocklaan 27; dorm beds/singles/doubles €22.10/30.05/53.30) is north of town, a 10-minute ride on bus No 3.

Pension Parkzicht (☎ 442 06 98, fax 443 62 02; Apeldoornsestraat 16; singles/doubles €25/50) has basic rooms and is a 10-minute walk from the station.

De Campaen (☎ 443 66 06, mobile 06 517 14 274; ⓔ reijmers@planet.nl; singles/doubles €37/58) is a beautifully restored wood-lined boat with cosy cabins. It's moored on the Rhine and is a 10-minute walk from the station. Book ahead as it's sometimes used for charter trips.

Almost opposite the train station is **Hotel Haarhuis** (☎ 442 74 41, fax 442 74 49; Stationsplein 1; singles/doubles from €92/147), a chain hotel with comfortable rooms.

Terrace cafés rim the Korenmarkt and the **Wampie** (☎ 445 6705; Korenmarkt 18; lunch around €3.50; open 10am-1am Mon-Fri, 10am-2am Sat & Sun) has been operating for more than 30 years and is in one of the oldest buildings (1899).

Getting There & Away

Trains to Amsterdam (€11.80, 65 minutes, every 15 minutes) and Rotterdam (€14.40, 1¼ hours, every five minutes) go via Utrecht (€8, 40 minutes, every 10 minutes), while the line south passes Den Bosch (€8, 45 minutes, every five minutes) and continues to Maastricht (€17, two hours).

The Delta Region

The Netherlands' aptly named province of Zeeland (Sea Land) makes up most of the Delta region. Spread over the southwest corner of the country, it was until recent decades a solitary place, where isolated islands were battered by howling winds and white-capped seas, and where little medieval towns, nestled somewhere in a protected nook, were seemingly lost in time. But after the 1953 flood (see the History section at the beginning of this chapter) came the decision to defend Zeeland from the sea – and thus bring it into the present day.

One by one the islands were connected by causeways and bridges, and the Delta Project (see the later Around Middelburg section) became a reality.

MIDDELBURG
☎ 0118 • pop 45,000

Middelburg is the long-time capital of Zeeland. It makes for a pleasant overnight stop and has a handful of worthy sights. VVV (☎ 65 99 00, fax 65 99 10; e vvvmid@zeelandnet.nl; Nieuwe Burg 40; open 9.30am-5.30pm Mon-Fri, 9.30am-5pm Sat, noon-3pm Sun) has a free brochure about attractions which includes discount passes.

Things to See & Do

Near the VVV is the Gothic **Stadhuis** (Town Hall; ☎ 67 54 52; guided tours adult/child €2.75/2.25; open 11am-5pm Mon-Sat, noon-5pm Sun Apr-Oct), which, like much of the central district, was destroyed during the 1940 German blitz that flattened Rotterdam. Dating back to the mid-15th century, it was convincingly restored and has several sumptuous ceremonial rooms.

A few streets away is the huge complex of the **Abdij** (Abbey; ☎ 61 35 96; open 11am-5pm Mon-Sat, noon-5pm Sun Apr-Oct), housing three churches and two museums; you can also climb the 91m tower **Lange Jan** (adult/child €2.25/1.60). For an insight into the province's history, visit the **Zeeuws Museum** (Zeeland Museum; ☎ 62 66 55; closed for renovations until July 2003) inside the Abbey.

Places to Stay & Eat

The nearest NJHC hostel, **Kasteel Westhove** (☎ 58 12 54, fax 58 33 42; e domburg@njhc .org; Duinvielweg 8; dorm beds €22.90; open mid-Mar–mid-Oct), is inside a medieval castle, complete with moat, about 15km west between the villages of Domburg and Oostkapelle. From Middelburg station, take the hourly bus No 53.

Hotel Roelant (☎ 62 76 59, fax 62 89 73; Koepoortstraat 10; singles/doubles €60/70) has functional rooms, a pleasant garden and an excellent restaurant. Across from the station, **Grand Hotel du Commerce** (☎ 63 60 51, fax 62 64 00; e info_ducommerce@fletcher.nl; Loskade 1; singles/doubles €60/80) has small, nicely furnished rooms.

Vriend Schap (☎ 62 89 89; Markt 75; mains around €7; lunch 11.30am-5pm daily) is one of several cafés excellent for people-watching. **De Mug** (☎ 61 48 51; Vlasmarkt 54; mains around €16.50; open 4pm-11pm daily) is justifiably famous for its menu of dishes prepared with unusual Dutch beers.

Getting There & Away

Trains run hourly to Amsterdam (€23.80, 2½ hours) and Rotterdam (€13.20, 1½ hours).

AROUND MIDDELBURG

The disastrous 1953 flood was the impetus for the Delta Project, in which the southwest river deltas were blocked using a network of dams, dikes and a remarkable 3.2km storm-surge barrier. Lowered only in rough conditions, this barrier was built following environmental opposition to plans to dam the Eastern Schelde (Oosterschelde). It can be dropped during abnormally high tides but generally remains open to allow normal tidal movements and the survival of the region's shellfish.

Finished in 1986, the project is explained at **Waterland Neeltje Jans** (☎ 0111-65 27 02; adult/child €11/8.50 Apr-Oct, €7.50/5 Nov-Mar; open 10am-5.30pm Apr-Oct, 10am-5pm Wed-Sun Nov-Mar), in the Delta Expo, an excellent museum and visitors centre with a model showing how it all works. Next to the storm-surge barrier's command centre is a theme park (good for bored kids), with all sorts of water slides and pools operating in summer. There's also a dolphin rehabilitation centre (though they're not always there), and a theme-park type display on whales inside the belly of one. To get there from Middelburg, take bus No 104 (€5.90 or combined bus/admission ticket €15, 30 minutes, twice hourly). If you are driving or hitching, head onto the N57 in the direction of 'Burgh-Haamstede'. From Rotterdam, take the metro to Spijkenesse Centraal and then bus No 104 (2¼ hours in total).

The North

The Netherlands' northern region is made up of several provinces, including Fryslân and Groningen, and is capped by the Frisian (or Wadden) Islands, a group of five islands which are popular escapes for stressed southerners. The region's shores are washed by the shallow Waddenzee, home to a small number of seals and the unique Dutch sport of wadlopen (see the Groningen section).

Even to the Dutch, the lake-land province of Fryslân is a bit 'different' from the rest of the

THE NETHERLANDS

Netherlands. Here the people have their own flag, anthem and language – Frysk (Frisian). The province's name was officially changed from Friesland to Fryslân (as it is spelt in Frysk) in 1996.

AFSLUITDIJK

The impressively engineered 30km-long Afsluitdijk, or 'Enclosing Dyke', connects the provinces of North Holland and Fryslân and transformed the old Zuiderzee (South Sea) into the IJsselmeer lake when it was completed in 1932. Driving along the dike's A7 motorway, you'll pass the Stevinsluizen, sluices named after the 17th-century engineer Henri Stevin, who first mooted the idea of reclaiming the Zuiderzee. There's also a memorial to Cornelis Lely who came up with the blueprint for the dike but died in 1929 before his project was completed.

Tours to Fryslân from Amsterdam usually take in the Afsluitdijk. Otherwise, without your own wheels, you can cross it on the hourly bus No 350 from Alkmaar to Leeuwarden (€14.40).

LEEUWARDEN
☎ 058 • pop 90,500
The capital of Fryslân, Leeuwarden is a pleasant enough place; there are some quiet old streets for wandering and just enough action to provide interest. The city developed from three *terp* (artificial dwelling mound) settlements used as homes by the first Frisians in the 15th century. Its most famous daughter is WWI spy Mata Hari.

VVV (☎ 0900-202 40 60, fax 234 75 51; e vvvleeuwarden@vvvleeuwarden.nl; Sophialaan 4; open 9am-5.30pm Mon-Fri, 10am-4pm Sat) sells a city map with three walking tours (€1.15).

Fries Museum (☎ 255 55 00; Turfmarkt 11; adult/child €5/2.50, free Wed; open 11am-5pm Tues-Sun) traces the development of Frisian culture and has a huge collection of silver, as well as a look at Mata Hari's life in Leeuwarden and as a dancer of notoriety in Paris.

Pottery lovers will adore the **Princessehof** (☎ 212 74 38; Grote Kerkstraat 11; adult/child €5/2.50; open 11am-5pm Tues-Sun), the national museum for ceramics, with an impressive collection of Dutch, Asian and Middle Eastern tiles and other works.

Hotel De Pauw (☎ 212 36 51, fax 216 07 93; Stationsweg 10; singles/doubles from €27/47), close to the train and bus stations, has birds chirping in the foyer and simple rooms that are faded but comfortable.

Het Stadhouderlijk Hof (☎ 216 21 80, fax 216 38 90; e info@stadhouderlijkhof.nl; Hofplein 29; singles/doubles per room €90) was once the home of local royalty and the hotel still exudes that air. Breakfast is €12.50.

From Amsterdam there are hourly trains to Leeuwarden (€22.40, 2¼ hours), or you can take bus No 350 from Alkmaar across the Afsluitdijk.

GRONINGEN
☎ 050 • pop 175,000
This lively provincial capital has been an important trading centre since the 13th century. Its prosperity increased with the building of the country's second university in 1614 and, later, the discovery of natural gas. **VVV** (☎ 0900-202 30 50, fax 311 38 55; e info@vvvgroningen.nl; Grote Markt 25; open 9am-6pm Mon-Wed & Fri, 9am-8pm Thur, 10am-5pm Sat, plus 11am-5pm Sun July & Aug) provides free bookings for Groningen hotels.

The city's colourful and inspired **Groninger Museum** (☎ 366 65 55; Museumeiland 1; adult/child €6/3; open 10am-5pm Tues-Sun) has an exquisite collection of silver tea and coffee pots, works by Groningen artists and a kaleidoscope of temporary exhibitions.

Groningen is the best place to arrange **wadlopen**, a serious pastime – strenuous and at times dangerous – involving kilometres-long, low-tide walks in mud that can come up to your thighs. To get into the thick of it, contact **Wadloopcentrum** (☎ 0595-528 300; e info@wadlopen.com; walks from €7.30-30) at Pieterburen to the north of town.

The clean **Simplon Jongerenhotel** (☎ 313 52 21, fax 360 31 39; e simplon-jongeren hotel@xs4all.nl; Boterdiep 73-72; bus No 1 from train station; dorm beds/singles/doubles with shared bathrooms from €10.20/24.95/38.85) is a hostel with themed rooms and huge dorms, just outside the city centre.

Hotel de Ville (☎ 318 12 22, fax 318 17 77; e hotel@deville.nl; Oude Boteringestraat 43; singles/doubles from €95/100) is luxuriously comfortable. Breakfast in the sunroom or garden is €10.

Granny's (☎ 318 91 17; A-Kerkhof 43) is a café/bakery devoted to all things apple and has good pies, juice and coffee. The **De Kostery** (☎ *314 19 78; Grote Markt)* has location, location, location in a corner of the 16th-century Martinikerk and serves an assortment of sandwiches and soups.

Every hour, trains depart from Amsterdam to Groningen (€26.10, 2½ hours), as well as from Groningen to Leeuwarden (€12.50, 50 minutes).

TEXEL
☎ 0222 • pop 13,000

Texel island's 30km of beach can seem overrun all summer but even more so in June when the world's largest catamaran race is staged here. The biggest village is Den Burg, where you'll find the **VVV** (☎ *31 28 47, fax 31 41 29;* e *info@texel.net; Emmalaan 66; open 9am-6pm Mon-Fri, 9am-5pm Sat; until 9pm Fri Apr-Oct, plus 10am-1.30pm Sun July & Aug).* It makes accommodation bookings for a hefty €12 and sells good maps of the island (€3).

There are 11 camping grounds including **De Krim** (☎ *39 01 11; fax 39 01 21;* e *info@krim.nl; Roggeslootweg 6; tent site & up to 4 adults €25.50; open all year),* a five-star place in Cocksdorp, which also has hiking huts. The main NJHC hostel is **Panorama** (☎ *31 54 41, fax 31 38 89; Schansweg 7, Den Burg; dorm beds/triples €20.95/66.60)* in a delightful thatched house. **Hotel de Lindeboom Texel** (☎ *31 20 41, fax 31 05 17;* e *info@lindeboomtexel.nl; Groeneplaats 14, Den Burg; singles/doubles €60/120)* is a pleasant option on the main square; some of the rooms have the biggest bathrooms you'll see in the Netherlands.

Kids will love the **Maritime & Beach-combers Museum** (☎ *31 49 56; Barentszstraat 21, Oudeschild; adult/child €4.10/2.05; open 10am-5pm Tues-Sat, plus Mon July & Aug).* There's lots of junk from sunken ships to check out and a windmill with maritime display where you can play at steering ferries; there's serious stuff for big people, too.

Trains from Amsterdam to Den Helder (€10.80, 1¼ hours) and buses from Leeuwarden (€11.80, 1¾ hours, bus No 350 and change at Den Oever, hourly) are met by a bus that whips you to the awaiting, hourly Teso car ferry (☎ *36 96 00; adult/child return €4/2, cars/bicycles €38/2.70).* The trip takes 20 minutes. It's worthwhile buying the €3.50 bus ticket for all day travel available at the ferry terminal or on the bus.

AMELAND
☎ 0519 • pop 3400

Ameland has four quaint villages and a distinct holiday feel. Nes is the prettiest and the best preserved village and is home to the **VVV** (☎ *54 65 46, fax 54 29 32;* e *vvv@ameland.nl; Bureweg 2; open 9am-12.30pm & 1.30pm-6pm Mon-Fri, 10am-3.30pm Sat),* which can book accommodation in hotels and apartments for a fee.

Camping Duinoord (☎ *54 20 70, fax 54 21 46;* w *www.duinoord.net; Jan van Eijckweg 4; tent/adult €2.60/4.10)* is 2km from Nes and one of six camping grounds in the area. The **NJHC Waddencentrum Ameland** (☎ *55 53 53, fax 55 53 55;* e *ameland@njhc.org; Oranjeweg 59; bus No 130 from ferry or Nes; dorm beds/singles/doubles €19.80/26.05/49.70)* is by the beach and below the lighthouse at Hollum. **Hotel Restaurant de Jong** (☎ *54 20 16, fax 54 20 24; Reeweg 29; singles/doubles from €30/60)* has simple but pleasant rooms in the heart of Nes.

From Leeuwarden, take bus No 66, which meets the ferry at Holwerd (nine strip tickets, 40 minutes). On weekdays there are six boats a day; weekends have four (hourly services from 1 June to 31 August). Return trips cost €10.40/5.30 per adult/child, €4.75 for bikes, and cars start at €68. The journey takes 45 minutes.

The Southeast

Sprinkled with woods, heather and the odd incline, the Netherlands' southeastern corner is made up of the North Brabant and Limburg provinces. Its two main towns, Den Bosch and Maastricht, are intimate and energetic.

DEN BOSCH
☎ 073 • pop 127,200

Den Bosch, officially known as 's-Hertogenbosch (The Duke's Forest), is the capital of North Brabant. The town's pedestrianised centre is based around the Markt, a 10-minute walk east of the train station; it's one of the best signposted towns throughout the Netherlands.

VVV (☎ *0900-112 23 34, fax 612 89 30; Markt 77;* e *info@vvvs_hertogenbosch.nl; open 1pm-6pm Mon, 9am-6pm Tues, Wed & Fri, 9am-9pm Thur, 9am-5pm Sat)* is housed in the town's oldest building.

Things to See

St Janskathedraal *(Choorstraat 1; admission free; open 9.30am-4pm daily Nov-Mar, 8am-5pm Apr-Oct)* is the finest Gothic church in the Netherlands. The cathedral is a few minutes' walk from the Markt at the end of Kerkstraat, the main shopping thoroughfare.

Noordbrabants Museum *(Verwersstraat 41; adult/child €5.70/3; open 10am-5pm Tues-Fri, noon-5pm Sat & Sun)* features exhibits about Brabant life and art from earlier times. It has a roomful of works by Bosch and a few early Van Gogh paintings.

Canal Trips run by Stichting Binnendieze *(☎ 613 50 98; 50min trip adult/child €5/2.50; open 2pm-5.20pm Mon, 10am-5.20pm Tues-Sun mid-Apr–Nov)* are more personalised and up-close than the norm, taking you in small boats under canal houses perched on bridges.

Places to Stay & Eat

Hotel Terminus *(☎ 613 06 66, fax 613 07 26; Boschveldweg 15; singles/doubles/triples €26.50/50/72)* is close to the station and has decent rooms and a great bar. The **Euro Hotel** *(☎ 613 77 77, fax 612 87 95; e eurohotel@ bestwestern.nl; singles/doubles €60/75)* has standard business rooms and friendly staff.

There's a line-up of cafés alongside the cathedral. **Café Cordes** *(☎ 612 42 24; Parade 4)* is one of the better ones. **Javaanse Jongens Eetcafé** *(☎ 613 41 07; Korte Putstraat 27; mains around €16)* has good Indonesian food and a decor of carved wooden tigers; it's the first in a street of quality restaurants. The beautifully tiled **Bakkerij Bert van Haren** *(☎ 613 44 81; Hinthamerstraat 89)* sells the local sweet *Bossche Bol*, a huge chocolate-coated ball filled with deliciously sweet cream.

Getting There & Away

Trains operate quite regularly to Amsterdam (€10.80, one hour, two per hour) via Utrecht (€6.10, 30 minutes, six per hour), and to Arnhem (€8, 45 minutes, three per hour) and Maastricht (€15.60, 1½ hours, hourly).

MAASTRICHT
☎ 043 • pop 120,000

The Netherlands' oldest city, Maastricht sits at the bottom end of the thin finger of land that juts down between both Belgium and Germany – and is influenced by them both. The capital of the largely Catholic Limburg province, its history stretches back to 50 BC,

when the Romans set up camp on a bank of the Maas River. Today, spanning both banks, this lively city has a reputation even in its own country as being a little foreign.

Orientation & Information

The west bank of the Maas is the city's main hub; here you'll find the old centre, largely pedestrianised, with shops, restaurants, hotels and churches.

On the east bank there's the Wyck, an area of 17th-century houses, intimate cafés and bars and, further south, Céramique, the modern showpiece quarter.

The particularly helpful **VVV** *(☎ 325 21 21; cnr Kleine Staat & Jodenstraat; open 9am-5pm or 6pm Mon-Sat Nov-Apr, plus 11am-3pm Sun May-Oct)* offers guided walks in summer (€3) and has a brochure on self-guided walks (€1) for the rest of the year.

There's a **GWK money exchange office** *(open 8am-10pm Mon-Fri, 9am-5pm Sat, 9am-10pm Sun)* at the train station, and in the centre, the **main post office** *(Grote Staat 5)*. There's a (serviced) laundry, **Wasserij Huysmans** *(Boschstraat 82; same day wash & dry €8.90; open 8.30am-4pm Mon-Fri)*. For Internet access go to the **Stadsbibliotheek** *(library; ☎ 350 56 00; Ave Céramique 50; Internet card €2, then €1.50 per hour; open 10.30am-5pm Mon, Wed & Thur, 10.30am-8.30pm Tues & Fri, 10am-3pm Sat, 1pm-5pm Sun)*.

Things to See & Do

The premier museum **Bonnefanten** *(☎ 329 01 90; Ave Céramique 250; adult/child €7/6; open 11am-5pm Tues-Sun)* features contemporary art by Limburg artists and medieval sculpture.

The main basilica in town is 10th-century **Sint Servaasbasiliek** *(Keizer Karelplein, Vrijthof; adult/child €2/0.50; open 10am-5pm daily Sept-June, 10am-6pm July & Aug)*. It's barn-like and somewhat stark, but has a rich treasure house of religious artefacts.

Farther south, on the Onze Lieve Vrouweplein, is **Onze Lieve Vrouwebasiliek** *(treasury; adult/child €1.60/0.45; church open 9am-5.30pm daily, treasury open 10am-5pm daily)*, a smaller Gothic structure where you can light candles or explore the treasury.

Stiphout Cruises *(☎ 351 53 00; Maasboulevard 81; 50min city tour adult/child €5.50/3.50)* can also drop you at the St

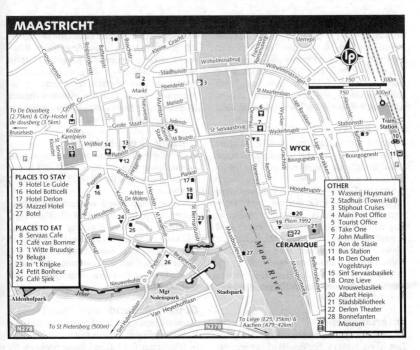

MAASTRICHT

PLACES TO STAY
9 Hotel Le Guide
16 Hotel Botticelli
17 Hotel Derlon
25 Mazzel Hotel
27 Botel

PLACES TO EAT
8 Servaas Cafe
12 Café van Bomme
13 't Witte Bruudsje
19 Beluga
23 In 't Knijpke
24 Petit Bonheur
26 Café Sjiek

OTHER
1 Wasserij Huysmans
2 Stadhuis (Town Hall)
3 Stiphout Cruises
4 Main Post Office
5 Tourist Office
6 Take One
7 John Mullins
10 Aon de Stasie
11 Bus Station
14 In Den Ouden Vogelstruys
15 Sint Servaasbasiliek
18 Onze Lieve Vrouwebasiliek
20 Albert Heijn
21 Stadsbibliotheek
22 Derlon Theater
28 Bonnefanten Museum

Pietersberg fort for a tour of the caves there for an extra €2.75.

Places to Stay

The closest camping ground is the posh **De Dousberg** (☎ 343 21 71, fax 343 05 56; e dousbergcamping@dousberg.nl; Dousbergweg 102; tent/adult €4.40/4.05; open Mar-Oct) with access to swimming pools and tennis courts.

The camping ground is 700m from the **NJHC City-Hostel de Dousberg & Budget-Hotel de Dousberg** (☎ 346 67 77, fax 346 67 55; e dousberghotel@dousberg.nl; Dousbergweg 4; dorm beds/singles/doubles €18/46.50/53.50). In the same building with the same reception, they offer functional rooms. Bus No 11 (two per hour) runs to the front door and on to the camping ground. At night a Call-Bus from the station will get you there.

Botel (☎ 321 9023; Maasboulevard 95; singles/doubles €34/51) has compact rooms on an old boat on the Maas.

Hotel Le Guide (☎ 321 61 76, fax 325 99 13; Stationsstraat 17a; singles/doubles with bathroom €55/65) has basic rooms with plastic tulips and is close to the station.

Hotel Botticelli (☎ 352 63 00, fax 352 63 36; e reception@botticellihotel.nl; Papenstraat 11; singles/doubles from €91.35/94), in a restored 18th-century wine merchant's mansion, has a lavish Romanesque feel. Breakfast costs €12.50.

Mazzel Hotel (☎ 326 30 75, fax 326 30 04; Achter de Molens 15; singles/doubles 95/110) is a newish hotel with old wooden furnishings and a smart look.

Recently renovated **Hotel Derlon** (☎ 321 67 70, fax 325 19 33; e derlon@hospitality.nl; Onze Lieve Vrouweplein 6; singles/doubles €210/260) has stylish rooms decorated with modern art, many overlooking one of the city's oldest squares.

Places to Eat

Thanks mainly to the gastronomic influences of its Belgian and German neighbours, Maastricht ranks highly among the Dutch where cuisine is concerned.

In the centre, Platielstraat is lined with restaurants and cafés. The **Café van Bommel** (☎ 321 44 00; Platielstraat 15; lunch around €6; kitchen open 11am-6pm daily), in a 17th-century building, is one of the best.

THE NETHERLANDS

For cheap, filling and tasty food, **'t Witte Bruudsje** (☎ 321 0057; Platielstraat 12; open 10am-2am Sun-Thur, 10am-3am Fri & Sat) has fresh salads, sandwiches and tapas.

Café Sjiek (☎ 321 01 58; St Pieterstraat 13; mains around €13; kitchen open 5pm-11pm daily) is a smoky, atmospheric eetcafé packed with locals who reckon it's got the best food in town.

In 't Knijpke (☎ 321 65 25; St Bernardusstraat 13; mains around €12; kitchen open 6pm-10pm daily) is a restaurant/cheese cellar/film theatre rolled into one; its fire is popular in winter.

Servaas Café (☎ 321 76 69; Cöversplein 10; mains around €12; kitchen open 11am-9pm daily) has a relaxed ambience and great Belgian food. A good option for French food is **Petit Bonheur** (☎ 321 51 09; Achter de Molens 2; mains around €18; open 6pm-10pm daily). For top-class riverside dining try **Beluga** (☎ 321 33 64; 12 Plein 1992; mains average €35; open noon-1.30pm Tues-Fri, 7pm-10pm Tues-Sat).

Entertainment

All the cafés mentioned stay open until 1am or 2am serving drinks. For details of music, concerts and films pick up the weekly *Week In Week Uit*, available in many cafés. If the weather is good, Vrijthof is taken over by people-watching terrace cafés. **In Den Ouden Vogelstruys** (☎ 32 11 48 88; Vrijthof 15; open 9.30am-2am daily) is housed in the oldest building (1309).

Across the river in Wyck, there are plenty of rustic cafés including **Take One** (☎ 321 64 23; Rechtstraat 28; open 4pm-10pm Wed-Mon), a beer specialist's haven; and **John Mullins** (☎ 350 01 41; Wijckerbrugstraat 50; open until 2am or 3am) has music, atmosphere and smooth Guinness. **Derlon Theater** (☎ 350 71 71; Plein 1992) in Ceramiqué has drama and music performances.

Getting There & Away

Within the Netherlands, the major train lines include those to Amsterdam (€25, 2½ hours, hourly) and to Den Bosch (€23.80, 1½ hours, hourly).

Major international connections include those to Liège in Belgium (€9.10, 30 minutes, one train per hour), Cologne in Germany (€23.60, 1½ hours, hourly), and Luxembourg City (€34.50, three hours, hourly).

For national information phone ☎ 0900-92 92; and for international information phone ☎ 0900-92 96.

Getting Around

Stadsbus buses run local routes, as do Call-Buses (evening minibuses that must be booked by telephone). For information or bookings on either, call ☎ 350 57 07.

The main bus station is situated next to the train station.

Bikes can be hired at **Aon de Stasie** (☎ 321 11 00; Stationsplein 26; bike hire from €7 per day; open 6am-noon daily), a bike shop on the left as you exit the train station.

Portugal

Spirited yet unassuming, Portugal has a dusty patina of faded grandeur; the quiet remains of a far-flung colonialist realm. Even as it flows towards the economic mainstream of the European Union (EU) it still seems to gaze nostalgically over its shoulder and out to sea.

For visitors, this far side of Europe offers more than beaches and port wine. Beyond the crowded Algarve, one finds wide appeal: a simple, hearty cuisine based on seafood and lingering conversation, an enticing architectural blend wandering from the Moorish to Manueline to surrealist styles, and a changing landscape that occasionally lapses into impressionism. Like the *emigrantes* (economically inspired Portuguese who eventually find their way back to their roots), *estrangeiros* (foreigners) who have tasted the real Portugal can only be expected to return.

Facts about Portugal

HISTORY

The early history of Portugal goes back to the Celts who settled the Iberian Peninsula around 700 BC. A subsequent pattern of invasion and reinvasion was established by the Phoenicians, Greeks, Romans and Visigoths.

In the 8th century the Moors crossed the Strait of Gibraltar and commenced a long occupation that introduced Islamic culture, architecture and agricultural techniques to Portugal. The Moors were ejected in the 12th century by powerful Christian forces in the north of the country who mobilised attacks against them with the help of European Crusaders.

In the 15th century Portugal entered a phase of conquest and discovery inspired by Prince Henry the Navigator. Explorers such as Vasco da Gama, Ferdinand Magellan and Bartolomeu Diaz discovered new trade routes and helped create an empire that, at its peak, extended to Africa, Brazil, India and the Far East. This period of immense power and wealth ended in 1580 when Spain occupied the Portuguese throne. The Portuguese regained it within 90 years, but their imperial momentum had been lost.

At a Glance

- **Lisbon** – medieval quarter, Art Deco cafés, Europe's largest Oceanarium
- **Sintra** – romantic villas, palaces, museums and gardens
- **Lagos** – picturesque and vibrant beach packed with restaurants and bars
- **Serra da Estrela** – rough and ready landscape of traditional settlements, high peaks and excellent walks
- **Peneda-Gerês** – popular national park with countless outdoor activities and rural accommodation

Capital	Lisbon
Population	10 million
Official Language	Portuguese
Currency	euro
Time	GMT/UTC+0100
Country Phone Code	☎ 351

At the close of the 18th century Napoleon mounted several invasions of Portugal, but was eventually trounced by the troops of the Anglo-Portuguese alliance.

A period of civil war and political mayhem in the 19th century culminated in the abolition of the monarchy in 1910 and also the founding of a democratic republic.

A military coup in 1926 set the stage for the dictatorship of António de Oliveira Salazar, who clung to power until his death in

PORTUGAL

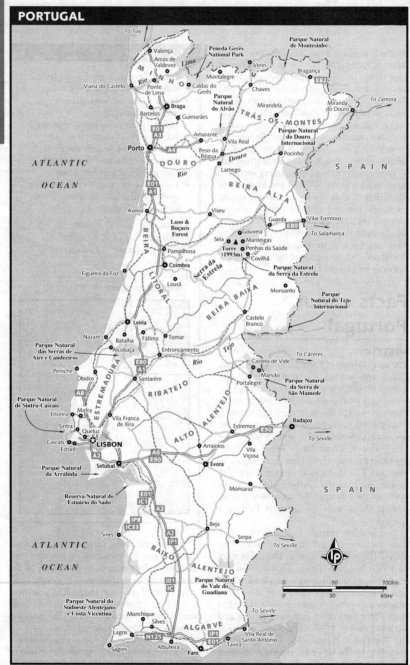

1968. General dissatisfaction with his regime and a ruinous colonial war in Africa led to the so-called Revolution of the Carnations, a peaceful military coup on 25 April 1974.

The granting of independence to Portugal's African colonies in 1974–75 produced a flood of nearly a million refugees into the country. The 1970s and early 1980s saw extreme swings between political right and left, and strikes over state versus private ownership.

Portugal's entry into the EU in 1986 and its acceptance as a member of the European Monetary System in 1992 secured a measure of stability, although the 1990s were troubled by recession, rising unemployment and continuing backwardness in agriculture and also education.

Expo '98 triggered vast infrastructure projects and launched Portugal into a new era of economic success, furthered by Porto's status as a European Capital of Culture in 2001 and is set to be boosted again in 2004 by Portugal's role as host of the European football championships.

GEOGRAPHY & GEOLOGY

Portugal is about twice the size of Switzerland, just 560km from north to south and 220km from east to west.

The northern and central coastal regions are densely populated. The northern interior is characterised by lush vegetation and mountains; the highest range, the Serra da Estrela, peaks at Torre (1993m). The south is more sparse and, apart from the mountainous backdrop of the Algarve, flatter and drier.

CLIMATE

Midsummer heat is searing in the Algarve and Alentejo, and in the upper Douro Valley, but tolerable elsewhere. The north is rainy and chilly in winter. Snowfall is common in the Serra da Estrela. See the Climate Chart in this section.

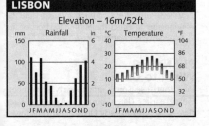

LISBON
Elevation – 16m/52ft

ECOLOGY & ENVIRONMENT

Portugal has one international-standard national park (70,290-hectare Peneda-Gerês), 12 *parques naturais* (natural parks, of which the biggest and best known is 101,060-hectare Serra da Estrela), nine nature reserves and several other protected areas. The government's **Instituto da Conservação da Natureza** *(ICN; Information Division; ☎ 213 523 317; Rua Ferreira Lapa 29-A, Lisbon)* manages them all, though information is best obtained from each park's headquarters.

GOVERNMENT & POLITICS

Portugal has a Western-style democracy based on the Assembleiada República, which is a single-chamber parliament with 230 members and an elected president. The two main parties are the Socialist Party (Partido Socialista; PS) and the right-of-centre Social Democratic Party (Partido Social Democrata; PSD). Other parties include the Communist Party (PCP) and the new Left Bloc (BE). In April 2002 the PSD, under Durão Barroso, commenced a four-year term of office.

ECONOMY

After severe economic problems in the 1980s, Portugal tamed inflation to around 2% thanks largely to infrastructure investment and privatisation, but the shaky early days of life in the euro currency zone have seen the country's annual growth rate dip to around 1.5% and inflation rise to almost 3%. Agriculture plays a decreasing role compared with industry and services (eg, telecommunications, banking and tourism). Portugal benefits from low labour costs, a young population and massive EU funding.

POPULATION & PEOPLE

Portugal's population of 10 million does not include the estimated three million Portuguese living abroad as migrant workers.

ARTS
Music

The best-known form of Portuguese music is the melancholy, nostalgic songs called *fado*, popularly considered to have originated with the yearnings of 16th-century sailors. Much on offer to tourists in Lisbon is overpriced and far from authentic. The late Amália Rodrigues was the star of Portuguese *fado*; her recordings are available in most Portuguese record shops.

PORTUGAL

Literature

In the 16th century, Gil Vicente, master of farce and religious drama, set the stage for Portugal's dramatic tradition. Later in that century Luís de Camões wrote *Os Lusíadas,* an epic poem celebrating the age of discovery (available in translation as *The Lusiads*). Camões is considered Portugal's national poet.

Two of Portugal's finest writers of the 20th century are poet-dramatist Fernando Pessoa (1888–1935), author of the 1934 *Message*; and the 1998 Nobel Prize-winning novelist José Saramago, whose novels (notably *Baltasar and Blimunda* and *The Year of the Death of Ricardo Reis*) weave together the real and imaginary. Others to try are Eça de Queiroz *(The Maias)* and Fernando Namora *(Mountain Doctor)*. A contemporary Portuguese 'whodunnit', close to the political bone, is *The Ballad of Dog's Beach* by José Cardoso Pires.

Architecture

Unique to Portugal is Manueline architecture, named after its patron King Manuel I (1495–1521). It symbolises the zest for discovery of that era and is characterised by boisterous spiralling columns and nautical themes.

Crafts

The most striking Portuguese craft is the decorative blue and white *azulejo* tiles based on Moorish techniques of the 15th century. Superb examples are to be seen all over the country. Lisbon has its own *azulejo* museum.

SOCIETY & CONDUCT

Despite prosperity and foreign influence, the Portuguese have kept a firm grip on their culture. Folk dancing remains the pride of villages everywhere, and local festivals are celebrated with gusto. TV soccer matches, a modern element of male Portuguese life, ensure the continuation of the traditional long lunch break.

The Portuguese tend to be very friendly but socially conservative: win their hearts by dressing modestly outside of the beach resorts, and by greeting and thanking them in Portuguese. Shorts and hats are considered offensive inside churches.

RELIGION

Portugal is 99% Roman Catholic, with fewer than 120,000 Protestants and also around 5000 Jews.

LANGUAGE

Like French, Italian, Spanish and Romanian, Portuguese is a Romance language, derived from Latin. It's spoken by over 10 million people in Portugal and 130 million in Brazil, and is the official language of five African nations. Nearly all turismo staff speak English. In Lisbon, Porto and the Algarve it's easy to find English-speakers, but they are rare in the countryside, and among older folk. In the north, you'll find returned emigrant workers who speak French or German.

See the Language Guide at the back of the book for pronunciation guidelines and useful words and phrases. For more, pick up Lonely Planet's *Portuguese phrasebook*.

Facts for the Visitor

HIGHLIGHTS

Tops for scenery are the mountain landscapes of Peneda-Gerês National Park and the Serra da Estrela. Architecture buffs should visit the monasteries at Belém and Batalha, and the palaces of Pena (Sintra) and Buçaco. Combining the best of both worlds are Portugal's old walled towns such as Évora and Marvão. In Lisbon don't miss the Museu Calouste Gulbenkian, and Europe's largest Oceanarium.

SUGGESTED ITINERARIES

Depending on the length of your stay, you might want to see and do the following:

Two days
Lisbon
One week
Devote four or five days to Lisbon and Sintra and the rest to Óbidos and Nazaré.
Two weeks
As for one week, plus two days in Évora and the rest in the Algarve (including one or two days each in Tavira, Lagos and Sagres).
One month
As above, plus a day each in Castelo de Vide and Marvão, two in Coimbra, five in the Douro Valley (Porto plus a Douro River cruise) and the remainder in either the Serra da Estrela or the Peneda-Gerês National Park.

PLANNING
When to Go

Peak tourist season is June to early September. Going earlier (late March or April) or later (late September to early October) affords fewer crowds, milder temperatures, spectacular foliage, and seasonal discounts, including up to 50% for accommodation (prices in this chapter are for peak season). The Algarve tourist season lasts from late February to November.

Maps

Michelin's No 940 *Portugal; Madeira* map is accurate and useful even if you're not driving. Maps by the Automóvel Club de Portugal (ACP) are marginally less detailed but more current. For maps and information on the national and natural parks it's best to visit the information offices at or near each park, though even here trekkers will find little of use.

Topographic maps are published (and sold) by two mapping agencies in Lisbon: the civilian **Instituto Português de Cartográfia e Cadastro** (☎ 213 819 600, fax 213 819 697; e ipcc@ipcc.pt; Rua Artilharia Um 107), and the military **Instituto Geográfico do Exército** (☎ 218 505 300, fax 218 532 119; e igeoe@igeoe.pt; Avenida Dr Alfredo Bensaúde). **Porto Editora** (Praça Dona Filipa de Lencastre 42, Porto) stocks the (better) military versions.

TOURIST OFFICES
Local Tourist Offices

Called *postos de turismo* or just *turismos*, local tourist offices are found throughout Portugal and offer information, maps and varying degrees of assistance.

Tourist Offices Abroad

Portuguese tourist offices operating abroad under the administrative umbrella of Investimentos, Comércio e Turismo de Portugal (ICEP) include:

Canada Portuguese Trade & Tourism Commission (☎ 416-921-7376, fax 921-1353, e iceptor@idirect.com) Suite 1005, 60 Bloor St West, Toronto, Ontario M4W 3B8
Spain Oficina de Turismo de Portugal (☎ 91 761 7230, fax 570 2270, e turismo-portugal@icep.net) Paseo de la Castellana 141-17D, 28046 Madrid
UK Portuguese Trade & Tourism Office (☎ 020-7494 1441, fax 7494 1868, e iceplondt@aol.com) 22–25a Sackville St, London W1X 1DE
USA Portuguese National Tourist Office (☎ 212-354 4403, fax 764 6137, e tourism@portugal.org) 4th floor, 590 Fifth Ave, New York, NY 10036-4704

VISAS & DOCUMENTS
Visas

No visa is required for any length of stay by nationals of EU countries. Those from Canada, Israel, Australia, New Zealand and the USA can stay up to 60 days in any half-year without a visa. Others, including nationals of South Africa, need visas (and should try to get them in advance) unless they're spouses or children of EU citizens.

Portugal is a signatory of the Schengen Convention on the abolition of mutual border controls (see Visas in the introductory Facts for the Visitor chapter), but unless you're a citizen of the UK, Ireland or a Schengen country, you should check visa regulations with the consulate of each Schengen country you plan to visit. You must apply in your country of residence.

Outside Portugal, visa information is supplied by Portuguese consulates. In Portugal, you can contact the **Foreigners Registration Service** (Serviço de Estrangeiros e Fronteiras; ☎ 213 585 545; Rua São Sebastião da Pedreira 15, Lisbon; open 9am-noon & 2pm-4pm Mon-Fri) for information.

EMBASSIES & CONSULATES
Portuguese Embassies & Consulates

Portuguese embassies abroad include:

Australia (☎ 02-6290 1733) 23 Culgoa Circuit, O'Malley, ACT 2606
Canada (☎ 613-729-0883) 645 Island Park Dr, Ottawa, Ont K1Y 0B8
France (☎ 01 47 27 35 29) 3 Rue de Noisiel, 75116 Paris
Ireland (☎ 01-289 4416) Knocksinna House, Foxrock, Dublin 18
Spain (☎ 91 561 78 00) Calle Castello 128, 28006 Madrid
UK (☎ 020-7235 5331) 11 Belgrave Square, London SW1X 8PP
USA (☎ 202-328 8610) 2125 Kalorama Rd NW, Washington, DC 20008

Embassies & Consulates in Portugal

Foreign embassies in Portugal include:

Australia
    Embassy: (☎ 213 101 500) Avenida da Liberdade 200, Lisbon
Canada
    Embassy & Consulate: (☎ 213 164 600) Avenida da Liberdade 196, Lisbon
    Consulate: (☎ 289 803 757) Rua Frei Lourenço de Santa Maria 1, Faro

France
Embassy: (☎ 213 939 100) Santos o Velho 5, Lisbon
Consulate: (☎ 226 094 805) Rua Eugénio de Castro 352, Porto
Ireland
Embassy: (☎ 213 929 440) Rua da Imprensa à Estrela 1, Lisbon
Spain
Embassy: (☎ 213 472 381) Rua do Salitre 1, Lisbon
Consulate: (☎ 225 101 685) Rua de Dom João IV 341, Porto
Consulate: (☎ 251 822 122) Avenida de Espanha, Valença do Minho
Consulate: (☎ 281 544 888) Avenida Ministro Duarte Pacheco, Vila Real de Santo António
UK
Embassy: (☎ 213 924 000) Rua de São Bernardo 33, Lisbon
Consulate: (☎ 226 184 789) Avenida da Boavista 3072, Porto
Consulate: (☎ 282 417 800) Largo Francisco A Maurício 7, Portimão
USA
Embassy: (☎ 217 273 300) Avenida das Forças Armadas, Lisbon

New Zealand has an **honorary consul** in Lisbon (☎ *213 509 690; open 9am-1pm Mon-Fri)*; the nearest **embassy** is in Rome (☎ *39-6-440 29 28).*

CUSTOMS

The duty-free allowance for travellers over 18 years old from non-EU countries is 200 cigarettes or 50 cigars, 1L of spirits or 2L of wine. EU nationals can import 800 cigarettes, 200 cigars, 10L of spirits, 20L of fortified wine or 110L of beer – assuming they can carry it all.

Duty free shopping at Portuguese airports is no more, but see Taxes & Refunds later in this chapter for information about sales-tax refunds.

MONEY
Currency

In January 2002 the euro, subdivided into 100 cêntimos, became the official unit of currency in Portugal. Prices are written with the € sign in front of the figure, eg, one euro 50 cêntimos is €1.50. See the boxed text 'The Euro' in the introductory Facts for the Visitor chapter.

There is no limit on the importation of currency. If you leave Portugal with more than

€12,470 you must prove that you brought in at least this much.

Exchanging Money

Portuguese banks can change most foreign cash and travellers cheques but charge a commission of around €12.50. Better deals for travellers cheques are at private exchange bureaus in Lisbon, Porto and tourist resorts.

Better value (and handier) are the 24-hour Multibanco ATMs at most banks. Exchange rates are reasonable and normally the only charge is a handling fee of about 1.5% to your home bank. Few tourist centres have automatic cash-exchange machines.

Major credit cards – especially Visa and MasterCard – are widely accepted by shops, hotels and a growing number of guesthouses and restaurants.

Costs

Portugal remains one of the cheapest places to travel in Europe. On a rock-bottom budget – using hostels or camping grounds, and mostly self-catering – you can squeeze by on US$20 to US$25 a day. With bottom-end accommodation and cheap restaurant meals, figure around US$30. Travelling with a companion and taking advantage of the off-season discounts (see When to Go earlier in this section), two can eat and sleep well for US$60 to US$70 per day. Outside major tourist areas, and in low season, prices dip appreciably.

Concessions are often available on admission fees, etc, if you're aged over 65, under 26 or hold a student card.

Tipping & Bargaining

A reasonable restaurant tip is 10%. For a snack, a bit of loose change is sufficient. Taxi drivers appreciate 10% of the fare, and petrol station attendants €0.50 to €1.

Good-humoured bargaining is acceptable in markets but you'll find the Portuguese tough opponents! Off season, you can sometimes bargain down the price of accommodation.

Taxes & Refunds

IVA is a sales tax levied on a wide range of goods and services; in most shops it's 17%. Tourists from non-EU countries can claim an IVA refund on goods from shops belonging to the Global Refund network. The minimum purchase for a refund is €60 in any one shop. The shop assistant fills in a cheque for the refund (minus an administration fee). When you leave Portugal you present goods, cheque and your passport at customs for a cash, postal-note or credit-card refund.

This service is available at Lisbon, Porto and Faro airports (postal refund only at Faro). If you're leaving overland, contact customs at your final EU border point, or call **Global Refund** (*Lisbon:* ☎ 218 463 025).

POST & COMMUNICATIONS
Post
Postcards and letters up to 20g cost €0.28 within Portugal, €0.46 to Spain, €0.54 to European destinations and €0.70 worldwide. For delivery to North America or Australasia allow eight to 10 days; to Europe four to six.

For parcels, 'economy air' (or surface air-lift, SAL) costs about a third less than airmail and usually arrives a week or so later. The main post offices in Lisbon and Porto are open into the evening and at weekends but charge €0.32 for each item claimed. Most major towns have a post office with *posta restante* service.

Addresses in Portugal are written with the street name first, followed by the building address and often a floor number with a symbol, eg, 15-3. An alphabetical tag on the address, eg, 2-A, indicates an adjoining entrance or building. R/C (*rés do chão*) refers to the ground floor.

Telephone
Aside from a few assistance numbers, domestic numbers have nine digits, all of which must be dialled from any location.

Local calls from public coin telephones start at €0.20, but the machines are often broken, especially in big cities, swallowing your cash without allowing you a call. It's easier to buy a PT (Portugal Telecom) phonecard (in €3, €6 or €9 denominations) or a discount card, such as the onicard, offering the option of dialling from any fixed-line phone. Both are available from newsagents, tobacconists, post or telephone offices.

Domestic charges drop by 50% from 9pm to 9am on weekdays, and all day Saturday and Sunday. International charges drop by around 10% to 25% from 9pm to 9am, and 20% to 50% during the weekend. Hotels typically charge over *three times* the economy rate!

A three-minute direct-dial (IDD) evening/weekend call from Portugal using an onicard

costs about €0.51 within the EU, €0.42 to the USA or Canada, and €0.87 to Australia or New Zealand.

To call Portugal from abroad, dial the international access code, then ☎ 351 (the country code for Portugal) and the number. From Portugal, the international access code is ☎ 00. For operator assistance or to make a reverse-charge (collect) call from Portugal, dial ☎ 171. For domestic inquiries, dial ☎ 118; for numbers abroad, dial ☎ 177. Multilingual operators are available.

For more information on telephoning in Europe, see the Telephones Appendix at the back of this book.

Fax
Post offices operate a domestic and international service called Corfax, costing €2.70 for the first page sent within Portugal and €4.25 for international destinations. Some private shops offer much cheaper services.

Email & Internet Access
Many towns have a branch of the Instituto Português da Juventude or IPJ, a state-funded youth-centre network. Most of these offer free Internet access during certain hours. Some municipal libraries also have free access. Some newer youth hostels have access for around €2.50 per hour. Internet cafés in bigger towns charge €1.50 to €4 per hour.

DIGITAL RESOURCES
Three useful websites on Portugal are: **A Collection of Home Pages about Portugal** (Ⓦ *www.well.com/user/ideamen/portugal .html*), **Portugal.com** (Ⓦ *www.portugal.com*) and **Portugal Info** (Ⓦ *www.portugal-info .net*).

BOOKS
Rose Macaulay's *They Went to Portugal* and *They Went to Portugal Too* follow a wide variety of visitors from medieval times to the 19th century. Marion Kaplan's *The Portuguese: The Land and Its People* offers a fine overview of Portugal and its place in the modern world.

Walkers and car tourers should pack the *Landscapes of Portugal* series by Brian & Aileen Anderson, including books on the Algarve, Sintra/Estoril and the Costa Verde. More detailed is *Walking in Portugal* by Bethan Davies and Ben Cole.

PORTUGAL

NEWSPAPERS & MAGAZINES

Portuguese-language newspapers include the dailies *Diário de Notícias*, *Público* and *Jornal de Notícias*, and weeklies *O Independente* and *Expresso*. For entertainment listings, check local dailies or seasonal cultural-events calendars from tourist offices.

English-language newspapers published in Portugal include *The News*, with regional editions featuring local news and classified pages, and *Anglo-Portuguese News*. Newspapers and magazines from abroad are widely available in major cities and tourist resorts.

RADIO & TV

Portuguese radio is represented by the state-owned stations *Antena 1, 2* and *3*, by *Rádio Renascença* and by a clutch of local stations. BBC World Service is at 12.095MHz or 15.485MHz short-wave, but reception is poor.

Portuguese TV includes state-run channels RTP-1 (or Canal 1) and RTP-2 (or TV2) and two private channels, SIC and TVI. Soaps *(telenovelas)* take up the lion's share of broadcasting time.

TIME

Portugal conforms to GMT/UTC, like Britain. Clocks advance an hour on the last Sunday in March and go back on the last Sunday in October.

LAUNDRY

There are *lavandarias* everywhere, most specialising in dry-cleaning *(limpeza à seco)*. They'll often do wash-and-dry *(lavar e secar)* too, though it may take a day or two. Expect €7.50 to €12.50 for a 5kg load.

TOILETS

The rare public toilets are of the sit-down variety, generally clean and usually free. Coin-operated toilet booths are increasingly common in bigger cities. Most people, however, go to the nearest café for a pastry or drink and use the facilities there.

WOMEN TRAVELLERS

Outside Lisbon and Porto, an unaccompanied foreign woman is an oddity, and older people may fuss over you as if you were in need of protection. Women travelling on their own or in small groups report few hassles, although in Lisbon and Porto, women should be cautious after dark. Hitching anywhere in the

country is not recommended for solo women in Portugal.

GAY & LESBIAN TRAVELLERS

In this predominantly Catholic country, there is little understanding or acceptance of homosexuality. But Lisbon has a flourishing gay scene, with an annual Gay Pride Festival (around 28 June) and a **Gay & Lesbian Community Center** *(Centro Comunitário Gay e Lésbico de Lisboa;* ☎ *218 873 918; Rua de São Lazaro 88; open 5pm-9pm daily)*. For information on gay-friendly bars, restaurants and clubs in Lisbon and Porto, check the websites **W** www.ilga-portugal.org and **W** www.portugalgay.pt.

DISABLED TRAVELLERS

The **Secretariado Nacional de Rehabilitação** *(☎ 217 936 517, fax 217 965 182; Avenida Conde de Valbom 63, Lisbon)* publishes the Portuguese-language *Guia de Turismo* with sections on barrier-free accommodation, transport, shops, restaurants and sights in Portugal. It's available at its offices or at Turintegra.

Turintegra, a part of the **Cooperativa Nacional Apoio Deficientes** *(CNAD;* ☎*/fax 218 595 332; Praça Dr Fernando Amado, Lote 566-E, 1900 Lisbon)* keeps a keener eye on developments and arranges holidays and transport for disabled travellers.

SENIOR TRAVELLERS

Travellers 60 and over can receive discounts of up to 50% at many of Portugal's attractions. Domestic rail travel is half-price for senior travellers on weekdays and those with a Rail Plus Card (to qualify you have to be a holder of a senior citizens railcard at home) can benefit from up to 25% off the price of journeys across international borders. In the UK, passes are available from larger stations.

DANGERS & ANNOYANCES

The most widespread crime against foreigners is theft from rental cars, followed by pick-pocketing, and pilfering from camping grounds. On the increase are armed robberies, mostly in the Algarve, Estoril Coast, parts of Lisbon and a few other cities. But with the usual precautions (use a money belt or something similar, bag your camera when not in use and don't leave valuables in cars or tents) there's little cause for worry. For peace of mind take out travel insurance.

Emergency Services

The national emergency number is ☎ 112 for police, fire and medical emergencies anywhere in Portugal. See Car & Motorcycle in the introductory Getting Around section later in this chapter for information regarding roadside assistance in the event of breakdown.

Avoid swimming on beaches that are not marked as safe: Atlantic currents are notoriously dangerous (and badly polluted near major cities).

BUSINESS HOURS

Most banks are open 8.30am to 3pm weekdays. Most museums and other tourist attractions are open 10am to 5pm weekdays but are often closed at lunchtime and all day Monday. Shopping hours generally extend from 9am to 7pm on weekdays, and 9am to 1pm on Saturday. Lunch is given lingering and serious attention between noon and 3pm.

PUBLIC HOLIDAYS & SPECIAL EVENTS

Public holidays in Portugal include:

New Year's Day 1 January
Carnival Shrove Tuesday; February/March
Good Friday and the following Saturday
    March/April
Liberty Day 25 April
May Day 1 May
Corpus Christi May/June
National Day 10 June
Feast of the Assumption 15 August
Republic Day 5 October
All Saints' Day 1 November
Independence Day 1 December
Feast of the Immaculate Conception
    8 December
Christmas Day 25 December

Portugal's most interesting cultural events include:

Holy Week Festival Easter week in Braga features colourful processions, including Ecce Homo, with barefoot penitents carrying torches.
Festas das Cruzes Held in Barcelos in May, the Festival of the Crosses is known for processions, folk music and dance, and regional handicrafts.
Feira Nacional da Agricultura In June, Santarém hosts the National Agricultural Fair, with bullfighting, folk singing and dancing.

Festa do Santo António The Festival of Saint Anthony fills the streets of Lisbon on 13 June.
Festas de São João Porto's big street bash is the St John's Festival, from 16 to 24 June.
Festas da Nossa Senhora da Agonia Viana do Castelo's Our Lady of Suffering Festival, for three days, including the weekend nearest to 20 August, is famed for folk arts, parades and fireworks.

ACTIVITIES

Off-road cycling (BTT; *bicyclete tudo terrano*, all-terrain bicycle) is booming in Portugal, with bike trips on offer at many tourist destinations (see Tavira, Setúbal, Évora and Peneda-Gerês National Park).

Despite some fine rambling country, walking is not a Portuguese passion. Some parks are establishing trails, though, and some adventure travel agencies offer walking tours (see Lisbon, Serra da Estrela, Monchique, Porto and Peneda-Gerês National Park).

Popular water sports include surfing, windsurfing, canoeing, white-water rafting and water-skiing. For information on some local specialists see Lagos, Sagres, Tavira, Coimbra and Peneda-Gerês National Park.

Alpine skiing is possible at Torre in the Serra da Estrela usually from January through to March.

The Instituto Português da Juventude (see Travel Agencies under Lisbon for contact details) offers holiday programs for 16- to 30-year-olds (visitors too), including BTT, canoeing and rock climbing. Private organisations offering the same activities plus trekking, horse-riding, caving and hydrospeed (running white-water without a boat) are listed under Lisbon, Porto and Peneda-Gerês National Park.

COURSES

Interlingua in Portimão (☎/fax 282 416 030; e interlingua@mail.telepac.pt) runs a two-hour fun course in Portuguese language basics for €20. Longer courses are offered by **Centro de Línguas** (☎/fax 282 761 070; e cll@mail.telepac.pt) in Lagos; **Cambridge School** (☎ 213 124 600, fax 213 534 729; e cambridge@mail.telepac.pt) in Lisbon, with Porto and Coimbra branches too; the Lisbon-based **IPFEL** (☎ 213 154 116, fax 213 154 119; e instituto@ipfel.pt), with a Porto branch; and **CIAL-Centro de Linguas** (Lisbon: ☎ 217 940 448, fax 217 960 783; e portuguese@cial.pt • Porto: ☎ 223 320 269 • Faro: ☎ 289 807 611).

ACCOMMODATION

Most tourist offices have lists of accommodation to suit a range of budgets, and can help you find and book it. Although the government uses stars to grade some types of accommodation, criteria seem erratic.

Camping

Camping is popular, and easily the cheapest option. The multilingual, annually updated *Roteiro Campista* (€4.90), sold in larger bookshops, contains details of nearly all Portugal's camping grounds. Depending on the season and facilities, most prices per night run to about €1 to €3 per adult, €1.50 to €3 for a small tent and €1 to €3 per car. A number of camping grounds close in low season.

Hostels

Portugal has 41 *pousadas da juventude* (youth hostels), all part of the Hostelling International (HI) system. Low rates are offset by segregated dorms, midnight curfews and partial daytime exclusion at most (but not all) of them.

In high season, dorm beds cost €9.50 to €15, and most hostels offer basic doubles for €23 to €30 (without bath) or €26.50 to €42 (with). Bed linen and breakfast are included. Many hostels have kitchens where you can do your own cooking, plus TV rooms and social areas.

Advance reservations are essential in summer. Most hostels will call ahead to your next stop at no charge, or you can pay €1.50 per set of bookings (with three days' notice) through the country's central HI reservations office, **Movijovem** (☎ *213 524 072, fax 213 596 001; e reservas@movijovem.pt; Avenida Duque d'Ávila 137, Lisbon*).

If you don't already have a card from your national hostel association, you can pay a €2 supplement per night (and have a one or six night or a year-long 'guest card').

Private Rooms

Another option is a private room *(quarto particular)*, usually in a private house, with shared facilities. Home-owners may approach you at the bus or train station; otherwise watch for 'quartos' signs or ask at tourist offices. Rooms are usually clean, cheap (€25 to €50 for a double in summer) and free from hostel-style restrictions. A variant is a rooming house *(dormida)*, where doubles are about €25. You may be able to bargain in the low season.

Guesthouses

The most common types of guesthouse, the Portuguese equivalent of B&Bs, are the *residencial* and the *pensão*. Both are graded from one to three stars, and the best are often cheaper and better run than some hotels. High-season pensão rates for a double start from around €30; a residencial, where breakfast is normally included, is a bit more. Many have cheaper rooms with shared bath.

Hotels

The government grades hotels with one to five stars. For a high-season double expect €55 up to as much as €250. *Estalagem* and *albergaria* refer to upmarket inns. Prices drop spectacularly in low season. Breakfast is usually included.

Other Accommodation

Pousadas de Portugal are government-run former castles, monasteries or palaces, often in spectacular locations. For details contact tourist offices, or **Pousadas de Portugal** (☎ *218 442 001, fax 218 442 085; Avenida Santa Joana Princesa 10, 1749 Lisbon*).

Private counterparts are operated under a scheme called Turismo de Habitação and a number of smaller schemes (often collectively called 'Turihab'), which allow you to stay in anything from a farmhouse to a manor house; some also have self-catering cottages. The tourist offices can tell you about local Turihab properties.

A double in high season costs a minimum of €82 and up to €182 in a Pousada de Portugal, but it costs between €60 and €100 in a Turihab property.

FOOD

Eating and drinking get serious attention in Portugal. Fast-food is largely ignored in favour of leisurely dining.

The line between snacks and meals is blurred. Bars and cafés offer snacks or even a small menu. For full meals try a *casa do pasto* (a simple, cheap eatery), *restaurante, cervejaria* (bar-restaurant) or *marisqueira* (seafood restaurant). Lunchtime typically lasts from noon to 3pm, evening meals from 7pm to 10.30pm.

The *prato do dia* (dish of the day) is often a bargain at around €4.50; the *ementa turística* (tourist menu) rarely is. A full portion or *dose* is ample for two decent appetites;

a *meia dose* (half-portion) is a quarter to a third cheaper. The *couvert* – the bread, cheese, butter, olives and other titbits at the start of a meal – costs extra.

Common snacks are *pastéis de bacalhau* (codfish cakes), *prego em pão* (meat and egg in a roll) and *tosta mista* (toasted cheese and ham sandwich). Prices start around €1.20.

Seafood offers exceptional value, especially *linguado grelhado* (grilled sole), *bife de atum* (tuna steak) and the omnipresent *bacalhau* (dried cod) cooked in dozens of ways. Meat is hit-or-miss, but worth sampling are local *presunto* (ham), *borrego* (roast lamb) and *cabrito* (kid). Main-dish prices start around €5.

Cafés and *pastelarias* (pastry shops) offer splendid desserts and cakes – try a delicious *pastel de nata* (custard tart). Cheeses from Serra da Estrela, Serpa and the Azores are good but pricey.

Local markets offer fresh seafood, vegetables and fruit. Big cities have grocery shops *(minimercadoes)* and many now have vast *hipermercados*.

DRINKS
Coffee is a hallowed institution with its own nomenclature. In Lisbon, a small black espresso is known as a *bica*, and elsewhere simply as a *café*. Half-and-half coffee and milk is *café com leite*. For coffee with lots of milk at breakfast, ask for a *galão*. Tea *(chá)* comes with lemon *(com limão)* or with milk *(com leite)*. Fresh orange juice is common. Mineral water *(água mineral)* is carbonated *(com gás)* or still *(sem gás)*.

Local beers *(cerveja)* include Sagres in the south and Super Bock in the north. A 20cL draught is called *um imperial*; *uma garrafa* is a bottle.

Portuguese wine *(vinho)* offers great value in all varieties: red *(tinto)*, white *(branco)* and semi-sparkling young *(vinho verde)*, which is usually white. The rarer red isn't quite as good. Restaurants often have quaffable *vinho da casa* (house wine) for as little as €1.99 per 350ml jug. You can please the most discerning taste buds for under €5 a bottle. Port, synonymous with Portugal, is produced in the Douro Valley east of Porto and drunk in three forms: ruby, tawny and white.

ENTERTAINMENT
Portugal has many local festivals and fairs, often centred on saints' days and featuring music, dance, fireworks, parades, handicraft fairs or animal markets. See Public Holidays & Special Events earlier.

Fado, the melancholy Portuguese equivalent of the blues (see Music under Facts about Portugal), is offered in *casas de fado* in Lisbon, Coimbra and Porto. More conventional bars, pubs and clubs abound in Lisbon, Porto and the Algarve.

Some bigger towns sponsor summer cultural programs, especially music (rock, jazz and classical) and dance. Ask at tourist offices for free what's-on publications, or see the local newspaper for listings.

Cinemas cost around €4 a ticket, with prices often reduced once weekly to lure audiences from their homes. Foreign films are usually subtitled.

SPECTATOR SPORTS
Football (soccer) dominates the sporting scene. The season lasts from August to May and most villages and towns have a team. The three best are Lisbon's Benfica and Sporting, and Porto's FC Porto. Ask the tourist office about forthcoming matches. Football fever will peak in 2004 when Portugal hosts the European football championships.

Bullfighting remains popular despite pressure from international animal-rights activists. The season runs from March to October. Portuguese rules prohibit a public kill, though bulls are often dispatched in private afterwards. In Lisbon, bullfights are held at Campo Pequeno on Thursday. Less touristy versions can be seen at the June agricultural fair in Vila Franca de Xira and Santarém.

SHOPPING
Leather goods, especially shoes and bags, are good value, as are textiles such as lace and embroidered linen. Handicrafts range from inexpensive pottery and basketwork to substantial purchases like Arraiolos rugs, filigree jewellery and made-to-order *azulejos*.

Getting There & Away

AIR
BA and TAP Air Portugal have daily direct flights from London to Lisbon; they also go to Porto and Faro. On most days there are direct

PORTUGAL

links to Lisbon and Porto from Frankfurt, Paris, Amsterdam, Brussels and Madrid.

From the UK, high-season London–Faro return fares start about UK£110 with no-frills carrier **Go** (☎ *0870 607 6543*). London–Porto via a third-country carrier can be as low as UK£150, and charter fares to Lisbon or Faro start about UK£180. **TAP** (☎ *0845-601 0932*) offers youth/student fares for year-long trips, but the best deals are with agencies such as **Trailfinders** (☎ *020-7937 1234*) and **STA** (☎ *020-7361 6161*).

France has frequent Portugal connections at reasonable prices. **TAP** (☎ *08 02 31 93 20*) and **Air France** (☎ *08 20 82 08 20*) have youth/student fares but you're better off with agencies like **usit Connection** (☎ *01 43 29 69 50*) or **Wasteels** (☎ *01 43 62 30 20*).

For prices from Portugal, ask youth travel agencies **Tagus** (*Lisbon:* ☎ *213 525 986* • *Porto:* ☎ *226 094 146*) or **Wasteels** (*Lisbon:* ☎ *218 869 793* • *Porto:* ☎ *225 194 230*). **TAP** (☎ *808 205 700*) and **BA** (☎ *808 200 125*) can be contacted at local rates from anywhere in Portugal.

LAND
Bus

Portugal's main Eurolines agents are **Internorte** (*Porto:* ☎ *226 052 420*), **Intercentro** (*Lisbon:* ☎ *213 571 745*) and **Intersul** (*Faro:* ☎ *289 899 770*), serving north, central and southern Portugal, respectively.

UK-based **Busabout** (☎ *020-7950 1661*) is a Europe-wide hop-on-hop-off coach network with stops at hostels and camping grounds, and passes that let you travel as much as you want within a set period. Its stops in Portugal are in Lisbon and Lagos.

Spain Spanish connections of **Eurolines** (*Madrid:* ☎ *915 063 360*) include Madrid–Lisbon (€35.45), Madrid–Porto (€34.25), Seville–Lisbon (€31.25) and Barcelona–Lisbon (€71.92), all going at least three times weekly.

Spanish operators with Portugal links **ALSA** (*Madrid:* ☎ *902 42 22 42*), with twice-daily Madrid–Lisbon services; and **Damas** (*Huelva:* ☎ *959 25 69 00*), running twice daily from Seville to Faro via Huelva, jointly with the Algarve line EVA. Three times weekly, **Transportes Agobe** (☎ *958 63 52 74*) runs from Granada via Seville and the Algarve to Lisbon, Coimbra and Porto.

The UK & France A variety of services are available from **Eurolines** (*UK:* ☎ *08705-143219* • *France:* ☎ *083 669 52 52*) in London (Victoria coach station) via the Channel ferry, with a 7½-hour stopover and change of coach in Paris. These include at least four weekly to Porto (40 hours); and five to Lisbon (42 hours), both UK£82/€134 one way from London/Paris.

The independent line **IASA** (*Paris:* ☎ *01 43 53 90 82* • *Porto:* ☎ *225 373 205* • *Lisbon:* ☎ *213 143 979*) runs three coaches weekly on four routes: Paris–Viana do Castelo; Paris–Braga; Paris–Porto; and Paris–Coimbra–Lisbon. A one-way/return fare to Lisbon is €84/152.

Train

Spain The main rail route is Madrid–Lisbon on the *Talgo Lusitânia* via Valência de Alcántara. The nightly express takes 9½ hours, and a 2nd-class reserved seat costs €46.28 for a sleeper berth €65.51.

Badajoz–Elvas–Lisbon is tedious (one regional services daily) but the scenery is grand. There are no direct southern trains: from Seville you can ride to Huelva (three daily), catch a bus for Ayamonte, change buses to cross the border to Vila Real de Santo António then catch one of the frequent trains to Faro and Lagos.

The daily Paris–Lisbon train (see UK & France following) goes via Salamanca, Valladolid, Burgos, Vitória and San Sebastian.

The UK & France In general, it's only worth taking the train from the UK if you can use under-26 rail passes such as Inter-Rail (see the Getting Around chapter located at the beginning of this book).

All services from London to Portugal go via Paris, where you change trains (and stations) for the *TGV Atlantique* to Irún in Spain (change trains again). From Irún there are two standard routes: the *Sud-Expresso* across Spain to Coimbra in Portugal, where you can continue to Lisbon or change for Porto; and an express service to Madrid, changing there to the overnight *Lusitânia* to Lisbon. Change at Lisbon for the south of Portugal.

Buying a one-way, 2nd-class, adult/youth London–Lisbon ticket (seat only) for the cheapest route, via the channel ferry, costs UK£102/87; allow at least 30 hours. Tickets for this route are available from bigger train stations or from **Trains Europe** (☎ 020 8699 3654). The Eurostar service to Paris via the Channel Tunnel cuts several hours off the trip but bumps up the cost. Ring **Rail Europe** (☎ 08705-848 848) for details.

Car & Motorcycle

The quickest routes from the UK are by ferry via northern Spain: from Portsmouth to Bilbao with **P&O Stena Line** (☎ 08706-003300), or, between March and November, from Plymouth to Santander with **Brittany Ferries** (☎ 08705-360360).

Alternatively, motor through France via Bordeaux, and through Spain via Burgos and Salamanca.

DEPARTURE TAX

Airport taxes for return flights between Portugal and other European countries range from about €17 for Spain to UK£22/€34 for the UK.

Getting Around

AIR

Flights within Portugal are poor value unless you have a youth/student card. Both **PGA Portugália Airlines** (Lisbon: ☎ 218 425 559) and **TAP** (☎ 808 205 700) have multiple daily Lisbon–Porto and Lisbon–Faro links, for €102.08; Portugália offers a 50% youth discount. TAP has a daily Lisbon–Faro service connecting with its international arrivals and departures at Lisbon.

BUS

A welter of regional bus companies together operate a network of comfortable, direct inter-city *expressos*, fast regional *rápidas*, and *carreiras*, which stop at every crossroad. Local weekend services can thin out to nothing, especially up north and when school is out.

A Lisbon–Porto express (3½ hours) costs €12.50 and Lisbon–Faro (under five hours) costs €14. A youth card should get you a discount of about 20%.

TRAIN

Caminhos de Ferro Portugueses (CP), the state railway company, operates three main services: *rápido* or *intercidade* (IC on timetables), *inter-regional* (IR) and *regional* (R). *Intercidade* and *interregional* tickets cost at least twice the

price of regional services, with reservations either mandatory or recommended. A special fast IC service called Alfa links Lisbon, Coimbra and Porto. If you can match your itinerary and pace to a regional service, rail travel is cheaper, if slower, than by bus.

Sample 2nd-class IC/Alfa fares include €14.10/19 for Lisbon–Porto. The IC fare for Lisbon–Faro is €11.30 and for Lisbon–Coimbra it's €10.30.

Children aged four to 11 and adults over 65 travel at half-price. Youth-card holders get 30% off R and IR services (except at weekends). There are also family discounts. One-/two-/three-week tourist tickets (*bilhetes turísticos*) at €100/170/250 are good for 1st-class travel, but worthwhile only if you're practically living on Portuguese trains.

Frequent train travellers may want to buy the *Guia Horário Oficial* (€1.75), with all domestic and international timetables, from ticket windows at most stations.

CAR & MOTORCYCLE

ACP (Automóvel Clube de Portugal; head office: ☎ 213 180 100, fax 213 180 227; Rua Rosa Araújo 24, Lisbon; emergency help numbers for southern Portugal: ☎ 219 429 103 • northern Portugal: ☎ 228 340 001), Portugal's representative for various foreign car, motorcycle and touring clubs, provides medical, legal and breakdown assistance for members. **ACP Insurance** (☎ 217 991 200) can advise members on car and motorcycle insurance. But anyone can get road information and maps from its head office (see above).

Petrol is pricey, eg, €0.89 and up for 1L of 95-octane unleaded fuel (sem chumbo), which is readily available.

Road Rules

There are indeed rules, although Portuguese drivers are among Europe's most accident-prone. While city driving (and parking) is hectic, rural roads have surprisingly little traffic. EU subsidies have paid for upgrades of the road system, and there are now long stretches of motorway, some of them toll roads.

Driving is on the right. Speed limits for cars and motorcycles are 50km/h in cities and public centres, 90km/h on normal roads and 120km/h on motorways (but 50, 70 and 100km/h for motorcycles with sidecars). Drivers and front passengers in cars must wear seat belts. Motorcyclists and passengers must wear helmets, and motorcycles must have headlights on day and night.

Drink-driving laws are strict here, with a maximum legal blood-alcohol level of 0.02%.

Car Rental

Portugal has dozens of local car-rental firms, many offering lower daily rates than international firms. To rent a small car for a week in high season, budget for about UK£200 from the UK or at least €225 from Portugal (with tax, insurance and unlimited mileage). However, fly-drive packages from international firms or TAP Air Portugal can be good value. You must be at least 25 and have held your licence for over a year (some companies allow younger drivers at higher rates).

BICYCLE

A growing number of towns have bike rental outfits (€7.50 to €17.50 a day). If you're bringing your own machine, pack plenty of spares. Bicycles can no longer be taken with you on trains, although most bus lines will accept them as accompanied baggage, subject to space and sometimes for an extra fee.

LOCAL TRANSPORT

Except in Lisbon or Porto there's little reason to take a municipal bus. Lisbon's metro system is handy for getting around the city centre and out to Parque das Nações, the former Expo site (see the Lisbon section for details). Porto is building its own underground system.

Taxis are good value over short distances, especially for two or more people, and are plentiful in towns. Most are metered and the clock starts at €1.50, plus €1.75 for luggage, and increases at around €0.35 per kilometre. Fares increase by around 20% at night, at weekends and if your trip leaves the city limits.

Enthusiasts for stately progress shouldn't miss the trams in Lisbon and Porto, an endangered species, and the *elevadores* (funiculars and elevators) of Lisbon, Bom Jesus (Braga) and Nazaré. Commuter ferries cross the Rio Tejo all day to/from Lisbon.

ORGANISED TOURS

Gray Lines (☎ 213 522 594, fax 213 560 668; Avenida Praia da Vitória 12-B, Lisbon) organises multiday coach tours throughout Portugal, through local agents or upper-end tourist hotels. The **AVIC coach company** (☎ 258 806 180; Avenida dos Combatentes 206, Viana do Castelo) offers short tours of the Douro and Lima Valleys. **Miltours** (☎ 289 890 600; Veríssimo de Almeida 14, Faro) has day trips in the Algarve and elsewhere.

Among unusual offerings by UK agencies are an art and history tour in May by **Martin Randall Travel** (☎ 020-8742 3355) and wine tours by **Arblaster & Clarke** (☎ 01730-893344). UK agency **Explore Worldwide** (☎ 01252-760000) offers Portugal hiking holidays, while **Ramblers Holidays** (☎ 01707-331133) offers more sedate walking tours. For references to the adventure-travel specialists within Portugal, see Activities under Facts for the Visitor in this chapter.

Lisbon

pop 720,000

Although it has the crowds, noise and traffic of a capital city, Lisbon's low skyline and breezy position beside the Rio Tejo (River Tagus) lend it a small, manageable feel. Its unpretentious atmosphere, pleasant blend of architectural styles and diverse attractions appeal to a wide range of visitors. Furthermore, Lisbon (Lisboa to the Portuguese) is one of Europe's most economical destinations.

ORIENTATION

Activity centres on the Baixa district, focused at Praça Dom Pedro IV, known by all as the Rossio. Just north of the Rossio is Praça dos Restauradores, at the bottom of Avenida da Liberdade, Lisbon's park-like 'main street'. West of the Rossio it's a steep climb to the Bairro Alto district, traditional centre of Lisbon's nightlife. East of the Rossio, it's another climb to Castelo de São Jorge and the adjacent Alfama district, a maze of ancient lanes. Several kilometres west is Belém with its cluster of attractions. Parque das Nações, the former Expo '98 site with its grand Oceanarium, lies on the revamped northeastern waterfront.

INFORMATION
Tourist Offices

Turismo de Lisboa's new main office **Lisboa Welcome Center** (☎ 210 312 810, fax 210 312 899; Praça do Comércio; open 9am-8pm daily) deals specifically with Lisbon inquiries.

A **tourist office** (☎ 213 463 314, fax 213 468 772; Palácio Foz on Praça dos Restauradores; open 9am-8pm daily), run by ICEP, the national tourist organisation, deals only with national inquiries.

There are several **Ask Me Lisboa kiosks** *(Rua Augusta* ☎ *213 259 13 • Palácio Foz* ☎ *213 463 314 • Mercado da Ribeira* ☎ *213 225 128 • Santa Apolónia train station* ☎ *218 821 604 • Belém* ☎ *213 658 435 • airport* ☎ *218 450 660; open 6am-midnight daily).* All have free maps and the bimonthly *Follow me Lisboa,* listing sights and current events. All sell the Lisboa Card, good for unlimited travel on nearly all city transport and free or discounted admission to many museums and monuments; a 24-/48-/72-hour card costs €11.25/18.50/23.50.

Money

Banks with 24-hour cash-exchange machines are at the airport, Santa Apolónia train station and Rua Augusta 24. A better deal is the exchange bureau **Cota Câmbios** *(Rossio 41; open 8.30am-10pm daily).* Nearly every bank has an ATM machine.

Top Tours *(☎ 213 108 800; Avenida Duque de Loulé 108; open Mon-Fri)* offers holders of American Express cards or travellers cheques commission-free currency exchange, help with lost cards or cheques and holding/ forwarding of mail and faxes.

Post & Communications

The **central post office** *(Praça dos Restauradores; open 10am-10pm Mon-Fri, to 6pm Sat & Sun)* receives Posta Restante addressed to Central Correios, Terreiro do Paço, 1100 Lisboa. For telecommunications, there's a **telephone office** *(Rossio 68; open to 11pm daily),* and another **post and telephone office** in *(Praça do Comércio),* open weekdays only.

Email & Internet Access

There's Internet access at **Lisboa Welcome Center** *(☎ 210 312 810; Praça do Comércio, 2nd floor; open 9am-8pm daily)* for €2.50 per half-hour. **Portugal Telecom's Hiper Net** *(☎ 213 582 841; Avenida Fontes Pereira de Melo 38; open 9am-9pm Mon-Fri)* charges €1 per half-hour; 30 minutes at **Espaço Ágora** *(☎ 213 940 170, Rua Cintura, Armazém 1),* behind Santos train station, open 2pm to 1am daily, costs €1.50. It's €2.50 per half-hour at the **Web Café bar** *(☎ 213 421 181; Rua do Diário de Notícias 126; 4pm-2am daily)* and the airport **PostNet** boasts 24-hour access at €1.50 for 30 minutes.

Travel Agencies

Trusty youth-travel agencies are **Tagus** *(☎ 213 525 986, fax 213 532 715; Rua Camilo Castelo Branco 20);* and **Wasteels** *(☎ 218 869 793, fax 218 869 797; Rua dos Caminhos do Ferro 90),* by Santa Apolónia train station.

Cabra Montêz *(☎ 918 200 143,* e *cabra montez@ip.pt)* organises biking, walking, horse riding and karting within the wider Lisbon area.

The **Instituto Português da Juventude** *(IPJ;* ☎ *218 920 800, fax 218 920 808;* e *ipj .infor@mail.telepac.pt,* w *www.sej.pt; Via de Moscavide)* is a youth network offering information resources, courses and holiday programs for 16- to 30-year-olds.

Bookshops

The city's biggest bookseller is **Livraria Bertrand**, whose main shop is at Rua Garrett 73. **Diário de Notícias** *(Rossio 11)* has a modest range of guides and maps. **Livraria Buchholz** *(Rua Duque de Palmela 4)* specialises in Portuguese, English, French and German literature.

Cultural Centres

The hours that the library at the **British Council** *(☎ 213 924 160; Rua de São Marçal 174; open 2pm-6.30pm Mon-Sat)* opens in the morning seem to vary, so it's best to turn up in the afternoon. The **Institut Franco-Portugais de Lisbonne** *(☎ 213 111 400; Avenida Luis Bivar 91)* has cultural events and a library open weekdays 1pm to 8pm. The library at the **Goethe Institut** *(☎ 218 824 511; Campo dos Mártires da Pátria 37)* is open 11am to 7pm Tuesday to Friday (3pm to 8pm Wednesday).

Laundry

Head to self-service **Lava Neve** *(Rua da Alegria 37; open 10am-1pm Mon-Sat & 3pm-7pm Mon-Fri)* to do your washing.

Medical & Emergency Services

The **British Hospital** *(☎ 213 955 067, 213 976 329; Rua Saraiva de Carvalho 49)* has English-speaking staff.

Dangers & Annoyances

Take normal precautions against theft, particularly on rush-hour transport. At night avoid wandering alone in the Alfama and Cais do Sodré districts. A tourist-oriented,

LISBON

PLACES TO STAY
15 Residencial Lisbonense
19 Pousada da Juventude
26 Lisboa Camping Parque Municipal
30 Hotel Presidente
40 Casa de São Mamede

PLACES TO EAT
13 Bella Italia III
50 A Cápsula

OTHER
1 Ask Me Lisboa
2 Vasco da Gama Tower
3 Sony Plaza
4 FIL (Feira Internacional de Lisboa)
5 Atlântico (Multipurpose) Pavilion
6 Oceanarium
7 Mafrense Bus Station
8 Colombo Shopping Centre; Cinema
9 US Embassy
10 Centro de Arte Moderna
11 Museu Calouste Gulbenkian
12 Secretariado Nacional de Rehabilitação
14 Arco do Cego: Rede Expressos & EVA Bus Station
16 Movijovem
17 Institut Franco-Portugais de Lisbonne
18 Foreigners Registration Service
20 Hiper Net
21 Museu Nacional do Azulejo

22 Instituto da Conservação da Natureza (ICN)
23 Tagus Travel Agency
24 Top Tours
25 Instituto Português de Cartográfia e Cadastro (IPCC)
27 Amoreiras Shopping Centre; Cinema
28 Automóvel Clube de Portugal (ACP)
29 Livraria Buchholz
31 Canadian Embassy
32 Instituto Português da Juventude (IPJ)
33 Goethe Institut
34 Lux Fragil
35 Wasteels
36 Ask Me Lisboa
37 Feira da Ladra (Flea Market)
38 Igreja da São Vicente de Fora
39 Casa do Fado
41 British Hospital
42 UK Embassy & Consulate
43 Discoteca A Lontra
44 Irish Embassy
45 French Embassy & Consulate
46 Espaço Ágora
47 Museu Nacional de Arte Antiga
48 Dock's Club
49 Tejo Bike
51 Mosteiro dos Jerónimos
52 Museu da Marinha
53 Ask Me Lisboa
54 Centro Cultural de Belém & Museu do Design
55 Torre de Belém

RIO TEJO

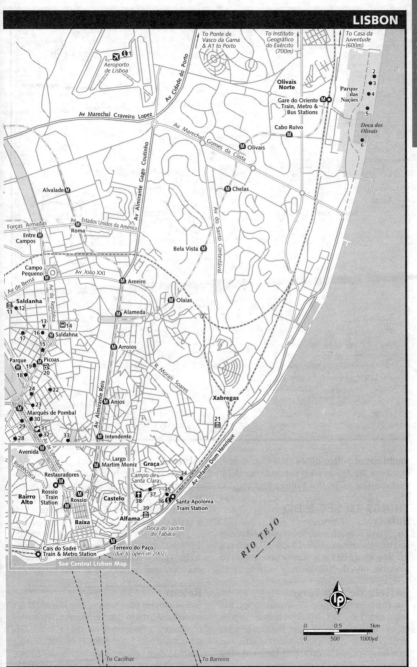

LISBON

To Ponte de
Vasco da Gama
& A1 to Porto

To Instituto
Geográfico
do Exército
(700m)

To Casa da
Juventude
(600m)

Av Cidade do Porto

Aeroporto
de Lisboa

2
3
4
5

Olivais
Norte

Parque
das
Nações

Gare do Oriente
Train, Metro &
Bus Stations

Av Marechal Craveiro Lopez

Av Marechal Gomes da Costa

Cabo Ruivo

Doca dos
Olivais

6

Olivais

Av Almirante Gago Coutinho

Alvalade

Chelas

Av Estados Unidos da América

Forças Armadas

Av do Santo Contestaval

Roma

Entre
Campos

Bela Vista

Campo
Pequeno

Av João XXI

Av de Berna

Areeiro

Av da República

Saldanha

Olaias

11 12

13

14

Alameda

16

17

Saldanha

15

Arroios

Parque

19

Picoas

R Morais Soares

18

20

Xabregas

24

22

23

21

Av Almirante Reis

Anjos

Marquês de Pombal

29

30

31

32

33

28

Intendente

Avenida

Largo
Martim Moniz

Graça

Av Infante Dom Henrique

Politécnica

34

Restauradores

Campo de
Santa Clara

Bairro
Alto

Rossio Train
Station

Rossio

Castelo

35

37

Santa Apolónia
Train Station

38

36

Baixa

Alfama

39

Doca do Jardim
do Tabaco

Cais do Sodré
Train & Metro Station

Terreiro do Paço
(due to open in 2002)

RIO TEJO

See Central Lisbon Map

0   0.5   1km
0   500   1000yd

To Cacilhas

To Barreiro

PORTUGAL

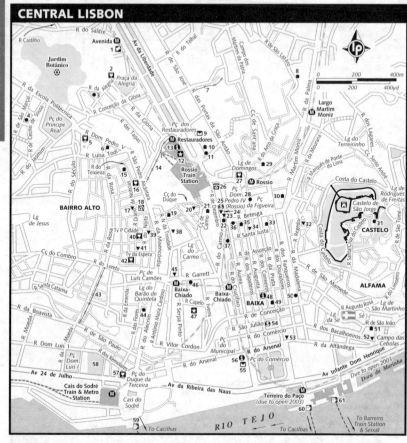

CENTRAL LISBON

multilingual police office (☎ 213 466 802; *Praça dos Restauradores*) is beside the ICEP tourist office in the Foz Cultura building.

THINGS TO SEE & DO
Baixa

The Baixa district, with its imposing squares and straight streets, is ideal for strolling. From the Rossio, ascend at a stately pace by lift or funicular into the surrounding hilly districts.

Castelo de São Jorge

The castle, dating from Visigothic times, has been tarted up but still commands superb views. Take bus No 37 from Rossio, or tram No 28, which clanks up steep gradients and incredibly narrow streets from Largo Martim Moniz.

Alfama

Though increasingly gentrified and full of tourist restaurants, this ancient district below the castle is a fascinating maze of alleys. The terrace at **Largo das Portas do Sol** provides a great viewpoint.

The **Casa do Fado** (*Largo do Chafariz de Dentro 1; adult/concession €2.50/1.25; open 10am-1pm & 2pm-5.30pm daily*) offers an excellent audiovisual look at *fado's* history.

Belém

In this quarter 6km west of the Rossio, don't miss the **Mosteiro dos Jerónimos** (*Jerónimos Monastery; admission to cloisters €3, free Sun morning; open 10am-5pm Tues-Sun*), dating from 1496, a soaring extravaganza of Manueline architecture and the city's finest sight.

CENTRAL LISBON

PLACES TO STAY		45	Café A Brasileira		28	Carris Kiosk

PLACES TO STAY
6 Pensão Londres
10 Pensão Imperial
15 Pensão Globo
19 Pensão Duque
21 Hospedaria Bons Dias
22 Pensão Santo Tirso
29 Pensão Residencial Gerês
30 Pensão Residencial Alcobia
33 Pensão Norte
35 Pensão Arco da Bandeira
49 Pensão Prata
51 Pensão São João da Praça;
     Sé Guest House

PLACES TO EAT
17 Stravaganza
20 Restaurante O Sol
23 Café Nicola
24 Pingo Doce Supermarket
32 São Cristóvão
34 Nilo
38 Cervejaria da Trindade
39 Restaurante Sinal Vermelho
41 Restaurante A Primavera

45 Café A Brasileira
52 Solar do Vez
53 Martinho da Arcada

OTHER
1 Spanish Embassy
2 Hot Clube de Portugal
3 Lava Neve
4 British Council
5 Pavilhão Chinês Bar
7 Elevador de Lavra
8 Gay & Lesbian Community
   Centre
9 Central Post & Telephone
   Office
11 ABEP Ticket Kiosk
12 Tourist Police Post
13 ICEP National Tourist Office &
   Turismo de Lisboa
14 Elevador da Glória
16 Solar do Vinho do Porto
18 Web Café
25 Cota Câmbios
26 Telephone Office
27 A Ginjinha

28 Carris Kiosk
31 Largo das Portas do Sol
36 Diário de Notícias
37 Elevador de Santa Justa
40 Adega Machado (Casa de Fado)
42 Adega do Ribatejo
   (Casa de Fado)
43 Elevador da Bica
44 Fabrica Sant'Ana
46 Livraria Bertrand
47 Police Sation
48 Ask Me Lisboa
50 Santos Ofícios
54 24-Hour Cash Exchange
   Machine
55 Post and Telephone Office
56 Lisboa Welcome Center
57 Ó Gilins Irish Pub
58 Mercado da Ribeira;
   Ask Me Lisboa
59 Cais do Sodré Car Ferry
   Terminal
60 Cais de Alfândega Ferry
   Terminal
61 Terreiro do Paço Ferry Terminal

Sitting obligingly in the river a 10-minute walk away is the Manueline **Torre de Belém**, *the* tourist icon of Portugal; the tower's admission and opening times are the same as for the monastery.

Beside the monastery is the **Museu da Marinha** *(Maritime Museum; admission €3; open 10am-6pm Tues-Sun, to 5pm winter)*, a collection of nautical paraphernalia. The brilliant **Museu do Design** *(adult/student €3/1.50; open 11am-7.15pm daily)* is in the Centro Cultural de Belém, opposite.

To reach Belém take the train, or bus No 43, from Cais do Sodré, or tram No 15 from Praça da Figueira.

Other Museums

These museums are open 2pm to 6pm Tuesday and 10am to 6pm Wednesday to Sunday:

The **Museu Calouste Gulbenkian** is considered Portugal's finest museum. Allow several hours to view its treasures, including paintings, sculptures and also jewellery. The adjacent **Centro de Arte Moderna** exhibits a cross section of modern Portuguese art. Entry to each costs €3 (free to students, children and seniors, and to all on Sunday). Take the metro to São Sebastião.

One of Lisbon's most attractive museums is the **Museu Nacional do Azulejo** *(National Azulejos Museum; admission €2.50)* in the

former convent of Nossa Senhora da Madre de Deus. Take bus No 104 from Praça do Comércio (weekdays) or No 59 from Rossio (weekends).

The **Museu Nacional de Arte Antiga** *(Antique Art Museum; Rua das Janelas Verdes; bus No 40 or 60 or tram No 15 from Praça da Figueira; adult/student €3/1.50, admission free Sun morning)* houses the national collection of works by Portuguese painters.

Parque das Nações

The former Expo '98 site, a revitalised 2km-long waterfront area in the northeast, has a range of attractions, notably a magnificent **Oceanarium** *(adult/senior & child under 16 €9.50/8.50; open 10am-7pm daily)*, which is Europe's largest. Take the metro to Oriente station, an equally impressive Expo project.

ORGANISED TOURS

Carris *(☎ 966 298 558)* offers tours by open-top bus (€13) or tram (€16) from Praça do Comércio. **Transtejo** *(☎ 218 820 348)* runs cruises on the Tejo for €15/8 (adult/senior and child) from the Terreiro do Paço ferry terminal.

PLACES TO STAY
Camping

Lisboa Camping Parque Municipal *(☎ 217 623 100; Parque Florestal de Monsanto; bus*

PORTUGAL

No 43 from Cais do Sodré) is 6km northwest of the Rossio.

Hostels

The **pousada da juventude** (☎ 213 532 696; Rua Andrade Corvo 46; open 24hr daily) is central. The closest metro station is Picoas, or take bus No 46 from Santa Apolónia station or Rossio. The newer **casa da juventude** (☎ 218 920 890; Via de Moscavide) is 1km north of Gare do Oriente. Take bus No 44 from Praça dos Restauradores or Oriente to the Avenida da Boa Esperança roundabout; the hostel is 250m down the road. Reservations at both hostels are essential.

Hotels & Guesthouses

In high season – and for central hotels at any time – advance bookings are imperative.

Baixa & Restauradores There are adequate doubles at **Pensão Santo Tirso** (☎ 213 470 428; Praça Dom Pedro IV 18, 3rd floor; doubles around €40), as is the case at **Pensão Prata** (☎ 213 468 908; Rua da Prata 71, 3rd floor; doubles with/without bath €30/25) and **Pensão Arco da Bandeira** (☎ 213 423 478; Rua dos Sapateiros 226, 4th floor).

Slightly pricier are **Pensão Duque** (☎ 213 463 444; Calçada do Duque 53) and **Pensão Norte** (☎ 218 878 941; Rua dos Dourados 159, 2nd floor).

More salubrious, with doubles around €35 to €40, are **Pensão Imperial** (☎ 213 420 166; Praça dos Restauradores 78, 4th floor) and friendly **Hospedaria Bons Dias** (☎ 213 471 918; Calçada do Carmo 25, 5th floor). Rates at old-fashioned **Pensão Residencial Alcobia** (☎ 218 865 171, fax 218 865 174; Poço do Borratém 15; doubles with/without bath €45/38) include breakfast. Brighter **Pensão Residencial Gerês** (☎ 218 810 497, fax 218 882 006; Calçada do Garcia 6; rooms €45) offers rates without breakfast.

Bairro Alto & Rato Near the Elevador da Glória is pleasant **Pensão Globo** (☎ 213 462 279; Rua do Teixeira 37; doubles without bath from €30). **Pensão Londres** (☎ 213 462 203; Rua Dom Pedro V 53; doubles from around €40) has spacious rooms, the upper ones with great views. Elegant, old **Casa de São Mamede** (☎ 213 963 166, fax 213 951 896; Rua Escola Politécnica 159; doubles €80) has rooms with bath and breakfast.

Marquês de Pombal & Saldahna The **Residencial Lisbonense** (☎ 213 544 628; Rua Pinheiro Chagas 1; doubles with bath €40) offers doubles with breakfast. A three-star hotel with four-star facilities is **Hotel Presidente** (☎ 213 173 570, fax 213 520 272; Rua Alexandre Herculano 13; doubles €102).

Alfama Behind the cathedral, the popular **Pensão São João da Praça** (☎ 218 862 591, fax 218 880 415; Rua São João da Praça 97, 2nd floor) and its 1st-floor neighbour, genteel **Sé Guest House** (☎ 218 864 400), have doubles from €45 to €65, with breakfast.

PLACES TO EAT

There are dozens of restaurants and cafés in the Baixa (best for lunchtime bargains) and Bairro Alto (pricier evening venues). A trendier restaurant and bar zone is riverside **Doca de Santo Amaro**, near Alcântara-Mar station. The main market, **Mercado da Ribeira**, is near Cais do Sodré station and the most centrally located supermarket is **Pingo Doce** just off the Rossio on Rua de Dezembro.

Baixa & Alfama

Minimalist **Nilo** (☎ 213 467 014; Rua dos Correeiros 217) is one of many reasonably priced places along Rua dos Correeiros. **Restaurante O Sol** (☎ 213 471 944; Calçada do Duque 23; set meals around €5) serves vegetarian cuisine in a great location.

Among several restaurants with outdoor seating in lower Alfama, **Solar do Vez** (☎ 218 870 794; Campo das Cebolas 48; mains €6-8) has a simplicity that's appealing. **São Cristóvão** (☎ 218 885 578; Rua de São Cristóvão 30; mains €4-5) dishes up aromatic Cape Verdean dishes.

For coffee or a meal, try Art Deco **Café Nicola** (☎ 213 460 579; Rossio 24) or 18th-century **Martinho da Arcada** (☎ 218 879 259; Praça do Comércio 3). The literary pedigree of Art Nouveau **Café A Brasileira** (☎ 213 469 547; Rua Garrett 120) is symbolised by the bronze figure of Fernando Pessoa outside.

Bairro Alto & Saldanha

Tiny **Restaurante A Primavera** (☎ 213 420 477; Travessa da Espera 34; mains €7-10) has a family ambience. **Restaurante Sinal Vermelho** (☎ 213 461 252; Rua das Gáveas 89; mains €8.50-11.50) is one of Lisbon's best (great desserts).

Chic **Stravaganza** *(213 468 868; Rua do Grémio Lusitano 18)* offers innovative Italian dishes – try spaghetti Mafioso (€8.50). The converted convent **Cervejaria da Trindade** *(☎ 213 423 506; Rua Nova da Trindade 20-C; mains from €7)* is adorned with *azulejos*.

Bright and cheerful **Bella Italia III** *(☎ 213 528 636; Avenida Duque d'Ávila 40-C)* is a pastelaria-cum-restaurant, with pizzas and half-portions of Portuguese fare for under €5.

Belém
A row of attractive restaurants with outdoor seating in Belém includes **A Cápsula** *(☎ 213 648 768; Rua Vieira Portuense 72)*, serving classics such as pork Alentejana (€7.50).

ENTERTAINMENT
For listings, pick up the free bi-monthly *Follow me Lisboa* or quarterly *Lisboa Step By Step* from the tourist office, or *Público* from a newsstand.

Music & Bars
Many *casas de fado* (which are also restaurants) produce pricey, inferior *fado* and have a minimum charge of around €16. In the Bairro Alto, try professional **Adega Machado** *(☎ 213 224 640; Rua do Norte 91)* or simpler **Adega do Ribatejo** *(☎ 213 468 343; Rua Diário de Notícias 23)*.

The **Hot Clube de Portugal** *(☎ 213 467 369; Praça da Alegria 39; open 10pm-2am Tues-Sat)* is part of a thriving live jazz scene.

Ó Gilíns Irish Pub *(☎ 213 421 899; Rua dos Remolares 8-10; open 11am-2am)* has live music Friday and Saturday evenings.

Clubs come and go. Stalwart **Lux Fragil** *(☎ 218 820 890; Avenida Infante Dom Henrique, Cais da Pedra à Santa Apolónia; open midnight-5am)* remains. Riverside options include: **Dock's Club** *(☎ 213 950 856; Rua da Cintura do Porto de Lisboa 226; open to 6am Tues-Sat)*.

The African music scene (predominantly Cape Verdean) centres around Rua de São Bento; **Discoteca A Lontra** *(☎ 213 691 083; Rua de São Bento 155; open to 4am Tues-Sun)* is popular.

For a taste of real – though hardly undiscovered – Lisbon sip a sticky glass of *ginjinha* (cherry liquor) outside **A Ginjinha** *(Largo de Domingos; open 9am-10.30pm)*, by the Rossio. Peruse the lengthy port wine list at snooty **Solar do Vinho do Porto** *(☎ 213 475*

707; Rua de São Pedro de Alcântara 45; open 2pm-midnight Mon-Sat)*; or for cocktails in quirky surrounds ring the bell at **Pavilhão Chinês** *(☎ 213 424 729; Rua Dom Pedro V 89; 6pm-2am Mon-Sat, from 9pm Sunday)*.

Cinemas
Lisbon has dozens of cinemas, including multiscreen ones at **Amoreiras** *(☎ 213 878 752)* and **Colombo** *(☎ 217 113 222)* shopping complexes. Tickets cost €4 (€3.50 Monday).

SPECTATOR SPORTS
Lisbon's football teams are Benfica and Sporting. Ask the tourist office about fixtures and tickets. Bullfights are staged at Campo Pequeno between April and October. Tickets are available at **ABEP ticket agency** *(Praça dos Restauradores)*.

SHOPPING
For *azulejos*, try posh **Fabrica Sant'Ana** *(Rua do Alecrim 95)* or **The Museu Nacional do Azulejo**. **Santos Ofícios** *(Rua da Madalena 87)* has an eclectic range of Portuguese folk art. On Tuesday and Saturday, visit the **Feira da Ladra** *(Campo de Santa Clara)*, a huge open-air market in the Alfama.

GETTING THERE & AWAY
Air
Lisbon is connected by daily flights to Porto, Faro and many European centres (see the introductory Getting There & Away and Getting Around sections of this chapter). For arrival and departure information call ☎ 218 413 700.

Bus
A dozen different companies, including **Renex** *(☎ 222 003 395)*, operate from Gare do Oriente. The **Arco do Cego terminal** is the base for **Rede Expressos** *(☎ 707 223 344)* and **EVA** *(☎ 213 147 710)*, whose networks cover the whole country.

Train
Santa Apolónia station *(☎ 218 816 121)* is the terminus for northern and central Portugal, and for all international services (trains also stop en route at the better-connected Gare do Oriente). Cais do Sodré station is for Belém, Cascais and Estoril. Rossio station serves Sintra.

Barreiro station, which is across the river, is the terminus for southern Portugal; connecting ferries leave frequently from the pier at Terréiro do Paço.

The north–south railway line, over the Ponte de 25 Abril, goes to suburban areas and will eventually carry on further to southern Portugal.

Ferry

Cais da Alfândega is the terminal for several ferries, including to Cacilhas (€0.55), a transfer point for some buses to Setúbal. A car (and bike) ferry runs from Cais do Sodré terminal.

GETTING AROUND
To/From the Airport

The AeroBus runs every 20 minutes from 7.45am to 8.45pm, taking 30 to 45 minutes between the airport and Cais do Sodré, including a stop by the ICEP tourist office. A €2.30/5.50 ticket is good for one/three days on all buses, trams and funiculars. Local bus Nos 44, 45 and 83 also run near the ICEP tourist office; No 44 links the airport with Gare do Oriente too. A taxi into town is about €10, plus €1.75 if your luggage needs to go in the boot.

Bus & Tram

Two-journey bus and tram tickets are €0.93 from Carris kiosks, most conveniently at Praça da Figueira and the Santa Justa Elevador, or €0.90 per ride from the driver. A one-/four-/seven-day Passe Turístico, valid for trams, buses and the metro, costs €2.55/9.25/13.10.

Buses and trams run from 6am to 1am, with some night services. Pick up a transport map, *Planta dos Transportes Públicas da Carris*, from tourist offices or Carris kiosks.

Wheelchair users can call the **Cooperativa Nacional Apoio Deficientes** (☎ 218 595 332) for assistance to hire adapted transport. The clattering, antediluvian trams *(eléctricos)* are an endearing component of Lisbon; try No 28 to Alfama from Largo Martim Moniz.

Metro

The metro is useful for hops across town and to the Parque das Nações. Individual tickets cost €0.55; a *caderneta* of 10 tickets is €4.50. A day ticket *(bilhete diário)* is €1.40. The metro operates from 6.30am to 1am. Beware of rush-hour pickpockets.

Taxi

Lisbon's plentiful taxis are best hired from taxi ranks. Some at the airport are less than scrupulous. From the Rossio to Belém is around €5 and to the castle about €3.50.

Car & Bicycle

Car rental companies in Lisbon include **Avis** (☎ 800 201 002), **Europcar** (☎ 218 410 163) and the cheaper **Rupauto** (☎ 217 933 258, fax 217 931 768). **Tejo Bike** (☎ 218 871 976), 300m east of Belém, rents bicycles for €4 an hour to ride along the waterfront.

Around Lisbon

SINTRA
pop 20,000

If you take only one trip from Lisbon, make it Sintra. Beloved by Portuguese royalty and English nobility, its thick forests and startling architecture provide a complete change from Lisbon. The **tourist office** (☎ 219 231 157, fax 219 235 176; Praça da República 23), in the historic centre, sells tourist day passes (€7).

At weekends and during the annual July music festival, expect droves of visitors. In high season book accommodation ahead.

Things to See

The Manueline and Gothic **Palácio Nacional de Sintra** (☎ 219 106 840; adult/student €3/1.50; open 10am-5pm Thur-Tues), dominates the town with its twin chimneys and Moorish origins.

One of Sintra's best museums is the **Museu do Brinquedo** (☎ 219 242 172; Rua Visconde de Monserrate; adult/concession €3/1.50; open 10am-6pm Tues-Sun), with 20,000 toys from around the world.

An easy 3km climb from the centre leads to ruined **Castelo dos Mouros** (open 9am-6pm daily) providing fine views. Twenty minutes on is the exuberantly romantic **Palácio da Pena** (☎ 219 105 340; open 10am-4pm Tues-Sun), built in 1839. Cars are prohibited; Stagecoach bus No 434 (€3) runs regularly from the station via the tourist office. Rambling **Monserrate Gardens** (☎ 219 237 300; open 10am-5pm daily) are 4km from town. A ticket for all three costs €5/3.50 for adult/concession.

En route to the gardens is an extraordinary, mystical mansion, **Quinta da Regaleira** (☎ 219 106 650; adult/concession €9.98/4.99; open 10am-6pm daily, to 3.30pm in winter). Visits must be pre-arranged.

The **Sintrolândia** (*Granja do Marquês, 5km northeast of Sintra*), which promises to be a huge tourism and leisure complex, had not opened as we went to press. Check at the tourist office for details.

Places to Stay

The best camping ground is **Camping Praia Grande** (☎ 219 290 581), on the coast 11km from Sintra and linked by frequent buses. A **pousada da juventude** (☎ 219 241 210) is at Santa Eufémia, 4km from the centre; note that reservations are essential.

Residencial Adelaide (☎ 219 230 873; *Rua Guilherme Gomes Fernandes 11; doubles from €25*), a 10-minute walk from the station, has reasonable doubles. The tourist office has a list of private rooms at a similar price. Across the tracks is friendly **Piela's** (☎ 219 241 691; *Rua João de Deus 70; rooms €25-50*), which is due to move in 2003 to Avenida Desiderio Cambournac 1–3.

Places to Eat

Close to the tourist office is **Tulhas** (☎ 219 232 378; *Rua Gil Vicente 4-6*), whose hits include bacalhau with cream €6.75. Simple **A Tasca do Manel** (☎ 219 230 215; *Largo Dr Vergílio Horta 5; mains around €6*) serves standards. **Restaurante Parreirinha** (☎ 219 231 207; *Rua João de Deus 41; mains €6-7*) has great grilled fish. Cavernous, classy **Xentra** (☎ 219 240 759; *Rua Consiglieri Pedroso 2-A; snacks €2-3, mains around €8*) has a similarly elegant bar (until 2am).

Getting There & Away

The Lisbon–Sintra railway terminates in Estefânia, 1.5km northeast of the town's historic centre. Sintra's bus station, and another train station, are a further 1km east in the new-town district of Portela de Sintra. Frequent shuttle buses run to the historic centre from the bus station.

Trains run every 15 minutes from Lisbon's Rossio station. Buses run regularly from Sintra to Estoril and Cascais.

Getting Around

A taxi to Pena or Monserrate costs around €10 return. Horse-drawn carriages are a romantic alternative: expect €55 to get to Monserrate and back. Old trams run from Ribeira de Sintra (1.5km from the centre) to Praia das Maças, 12km to the west.

CASCAIS
pop 30,000

Cascais, *the* beach resort west of Lisbon, is packed in summer. The **tourist office** (☎ 214 868 204; *Rua Visconde de Luz 14*) has accommodation lists and bus timetables; there's also a **tourist police post** (☎ 214 863 929).

Ciber Forum (☎ 214 868 311; *Rua da Bela Vista 126; open to 8pm daily, to 11pm Fri & Sat*) has Internet access at €2.50 per half-hour and a courtyard café.

Things to See & Do

Two kilometres east of Cascais, **Estoril** is an old-fashioned resort with Europe's biggest **casino** (*open 3pm-3am daily*). Praia Tamariz beach has an ocean swimming pool.

The sea roars into the coast at **Boca do Inferno** (Hell's Mouth), 2km west of Cascais. Spectacular **Cabo da Roca**, Europe's westernmost point, is 16km from Cascais and Sintra (served by buses from both towns). Wild **Guincho** beach, 3km from Cascais, is a popular surfing venue.

Transrent (☎ 214 864 566; *Centro Commercial Cisne, Avenida Marginal*) rents cars, bicycles and motorcycles.

Places to Stay & Eat

Camping Orbitur do Guincho (☎ 214 871 014, fax 214 872 167) is 7km from Cascais near Guincho beach. **Residencial Avenida** (☎ 214 864 417; *Rua da Palmeira 14; doubles without bath €30*) is another option. The tourist office can recommend private rooms from around €30. Fairytale **Casa da Pergola** (☎ 214 840 040, fax 214 834 791; *Avenida Valbom 13; doubles from €92*) has a beautiful garden.

A Económica (☎ 214 833 524; *Rua Sebastião J C Melo 35; mains €5-7*) serves standards. Try octopus rice (€5.50) at **A Tasca** (*Rua Afonso Sanches 61*).

Getting There & Away

Trains run frequently to Estoril and Cascais from Cais do Sodré station in Lisbon.

SETÚBAL
pop 110,000

This refreshingly untouristy city, an easy 50km south of Lisbon, has fine beaches and seafood restaurants, and is a good base for exploring nearby Parque Natural da Arrábida and Reserva Natural do Estuário do Sado.

The **tourist office** (☎/fax 265 534 402; *Praça do Quebedo*) is a five-minute walk east from the **bus station** (*Avenida 5 de Outubro*). There's also a **regional tourist office** (☎ 265 539 130, fax 265 539 127; *Travessa Frei Gaspar 10*).

The **Instituto Português da Juventude** (*IPJ*; ☎ 265 534 431; *Largo José Afonso*) has free Internet access for limited periods on weekdays. **Sobecome** (☎ 265 521 150; *Avenida Luisa Todi 333, 1st floor; open 10am-2am daily*) charges €2.50 for 30 minutes.

Things to See

The town's main cultural attraction is the 15th-century **Igreja de Jesus** (*Praça Miguel Bombarda*), with early Manueline decoration inside. The **Galeria da Pintura Quinhentista** (*admission free; open 9am-noon & 2pm-5pm Tues-Sat*), which is around the corner, displays a renowned collection of 16th-century paintings.

Good **beaches** west of town include Praia da Figueirinha (accessible by bus in summer). Across the estuary at Tróia is a more developed beach, plus the ruins of a Roman settlement. On the ferry trip across you may see some of the estuary's 30 or so bottle-nosed dolphins.

Activities

SAL (☎ 265 227 685) organises walks from €5 per person. For jeep safaris, hiking and biking in the Serra da Arrábida, or canoe trips through the Reserva Natural do Estuário do Sado, contact **Planeta Terra** (☎ 919 471 871; *Praça General Luís Domingues 9*). **Vertigem Azul** (☎ 265 238 000; *Avenida Luísa Todi 375*) offers dolphin-spotting as well as canoeing trips.

Places to Stay & Eat

A municipal **camping ground** (☎ 265 522 475) is located about 1.5km west of town. The **pousada da juventude** (☎ 265 534 431; *Largo José Afonso*) has doubles with bath, and dorm beds.

Crumbling **Residencial Todi** (☎ 265 220 592; *Avenida Luísa Todi 244; doubles with/without bath €20/15*) is basic. **Pensão Bom Regresso** (☎ 265 229 812; *Praça de Bocage 48; doubles €25*) overlooks the square. **Residencial Bocage** (☎ 265 543 080, fax 265 543 089; *Rua São Cristóvão 14; doubles €44.90*) is smarter.

Cheaper restaurants east of the regional tourist office include **Triângulo** (☎ 265 233 927; *Rua Arronches Junqueiro 72*). Seafood places line the western end of Avenida Luísa Todi; friendly **Casa do Chico** (☎ 265 239 502) at No 490 is less touristy than most. Popular **Restaurante Antóniu's** (☎ 265 523 706; *Rua Trabalhadores do Mar 31*) is also recommended.

Getting There & Away

Buses leave frequently from Lisbon's Gare do Oriente and from Cacilhas, a short ferry ride from Lisbon's Cais de Alfândega. Ferries shuttle across the estuary to Tróia regularly; the tourist office has the latest timetable.

The Algarve

Boisterous and full of foreigners, the Algarve is about as far from traditional Portugal as one can get. The focus is on Albufeira and Lagos, with sun, sand and golf (and surfing along the west coast) the draw cards, but there are other attractions: the forested slopes of Monchique, the fortified village of Silves and windswept, historic Sagres. The district capital and largest town is Faro.

Information

Expat-oriented, English-language newspapers with entertainment information include the *Algarve News,* and *Algarve Resident.*

Dangers & Annoyances Theft is a problem in the Algarve. Don't leave anything valuable in your vehicle, tent or on the beach.

Swimmers should be aware of dangerous currents, especially on the west coast. Beaches are marked by coloured flags: red means no bathing, yellow means yes to wading but no to swimming, green means anything goes.

Shopping

Few souvenirs are made in the Algarve, but woollens (cardigans and fishing pullovers) and Moorish-influenced ceramics are good value. Algarviana is a local *amaretto* (bitter almond liqueur), and the bottled waters of Monchique are sold everywhere.

Getting Around

Rede Expressos and EVA together run an efficient network of bus services throughout

THE ALGARVE

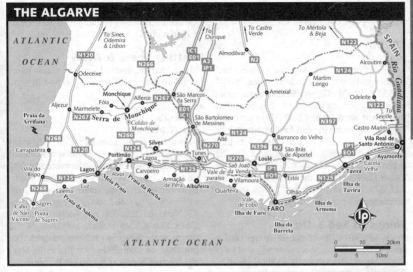

the Algarve. The IP1/EO1 superhighway, to run the length of the coast, is nearly complete. Bicycles, scooters and motorcycles can be rented everywhere; see town listings.

FARO
pop 45,000

Pleasantly low-key Faro is the main transport hub and commercial centre. The **tourist office** (☎ 289 803 604; Rua da Misericórdia) has leaflets on just about every Algarve community.

Things to See & Do

The palm-clad **waterfront** around Praça de Dom Francisco Gomes has pleasant cafés. Faro's beach, **Praia de Faro** (Ilha de Faro) is 6km southwest of the city; take bus No 16 from opposite the bus station. Less crowded is the unspoilt **Ilha Desserta** in the nature park **Parque Natural da Ria Formosa** (☎ 917 811 856; lagoon tours available). Access is by ferry June to mid-September from Cais da Porta Nova.

At Estói, 12km north of Faro, the romantically ruined **Estói Palace** has a surreal garden of statues, balustrades and *azulejos*; take the Faro to São Brás de Alportel bus, which goes via Estói.

Places to Stay & Eat

The **municipal camping ground** (☎ 289 817 876; Praia de Faro) is big and cheap. The **pousada da juventude** (☎ 289 826 521; Rua da Polícia de Segurança Pública 1) has dorm beds and rooms.

Residencial Adelaide (☎ 289 802 383, fax 289 826 870; Rua Cruz dos Mestres 7; doubles from €45) is a friendly budget pensão. Aptly-named, friendly **Pensão Residencial Centro** (☎ 289 807 291; Largo Terreiro do Bispo 10; doubles €40) is spotless.

Lively **Sol e Jardim** (☎ 289 820 030; Praça Ferreira de Almeida 22) serves good grilled squid (€7.49). **A Velha Casa** (☎ 289 824 719; Rua do Pé da Cruz 33, mains €6-7) has good charcoal-grilled meat and fish.

Getting There & Away

Faro airport has both domestic and international flights (see the introductory Getting There & Away section of this chapter).

From the bus station, which is just west of the centre, there are at least a six daily express coaches to Lisbon (about four hours) and frequent buses to other coastal towns.

The train station is a few minutes' walk west of the bus station. Four trains run daily to Lisbon (Barreiro), and about a dozen to Albufeira and ten to Portimão.

Getting Around

The airport is 6km from the centre. The Aero-Bus runs into town in summer only (free to those with airline tickets). Bus Nos 14 and 16 run into town until 9pm (but infrequently in winter). A taxi costs about €7.50.

TAVIRA
pop 12,000

Tavira is one of the Algarve's oldest and handsomest towns. The **tourist office** (☎ 281 322 511; Rua da Galeria 9) dispenses information. Bicycles and scooters can be rented from **Loris Rent** (☎ 964 079 233) next door. For walking or biking call **Exploratio** (☎ 919 338 226). To sail contact **Clube Náutico** (☎ 281 326 858). Jose Salvador Rocha organises diving trips (☎ 939 017 329). **Cyber Café**, opposite the bus station, (☎ 281 325 375; Rua dos Pelames 1) has Internet access for €2 per half-hour.

Things to See & Do
In the old town the **Igreja da Misericórdia** has a striking Renaissance doorway and interior azulejos. From there, it's a short climb to the **castle** dominating the town.

Ilha da Tavira, 2km from Tavira, is an island beach connected to the mainland by ferry. Walk 2km along the river to the ferry terminal at Quatro Águas or take the (summer only) bus from the bus station.

For a look at the old Algarve, take a bus to nearby **Cacela Velha**, an unspoilt hamlet 8km from Tavira. Another worthwhile day trip is to the fishing centre of **Olhão**, 22km west of Tavira.

Places to Stay & Eat
Ilha da Tavira has a **camping ground** (☎ 281 324 455), which is open July to September, when ferries operate (dates vary). **Pensão Residencial Lagoas** (☎ 281 322 252; Rua Almirante Cândido dos Reis 24; doubles €38) has character and a pretty roof terrace; centrally located **Residencial Imperial** (☎ 281 322 234; Rua José Pires Padinha 24; doubles €40) provides breakfast; and smart **Pensão Residencial Princesa do Gilão** (☎ 281 325 171; Rua Borda de Água de Aguiar 10; rooms €60) overlooks the river.

Budget restaurants along the riverside Rua Dr José Pires Padinha include **A Barquinha** (☎ 281 322 843) at No 142. **Cantinho do Emigrante** (☎ 281 323 696; Praça Dr Padinha 27) also has good-value fare. **Restaurante Bica** (☎ 281 332 483), below Residencial Lagoas, has delicious specials such as sole with orange for €10.

Good seafood lunches are up for grabs in Olhão, in the many restaurants that line Rua 5 de Outubro.

Getting There & Away
Some 15 trains and at least six express buses run daily between Faro and Tavira (30 to 50 minutes).

LAGOS
pop 20,000

This tourist resort has some of the Algarve's finest beaches. Of the two **tourist offices**, the new municipal **Posto de Informação** (☎ 282 764 111; Largo Marquês de Pombal; 10am-6pm Mon-Sat) is the more convenient, the other (☎ 282 763 031; open 9.30am-12.30pm & 2pm-5.30pm Mon-Fri, sometimes Sat & Sun) is 1km northeast of the centre, at the Situo São João roundabout. The **pousada da juventude** (see Places to Stay) has Internet access at €1.50 per half-hour.

Things to See & Do
In the old town, the **municipal museum** houses an assortment of exhibits from archaeological finds to ecclesiastical treasures. The adjacent **Igreja de Santo António** has some intricate baroque woodwork.

The beach scene includes **Meia Praia**, a vast strip to the east; and to the west **Praia da Luz** and the more secluded **Praia do Pinhão**.

Blue Ocean (☎ 282 782 718) organises diving, kayaking and snorkelling safaris. On the seaside promenade, local fishermen offer motorboat jaunts to the nearby grottoes. For horse riding in the Algarve interior ring **Tiffany's** (☎ 282 697 395).

Places to Stay
The camping ground is **Trindade** (☎ 282 763 893), 200m south of the town walls. The **pousada da juventude** (☎ 282 761 970; Rua Lançarote de Freitas 50) is another choice.

Residencial Marazul (☎ 289 769 749; Rua 25 de Abril 13; doubles from €55) has smart rooms. **Private rooms** are plentiful, for around €35 to €50.

Places to Eat
A Gamba (☎ 282 760 453; Rua Conselheiro Joaquim Machado 5) serves good traditional fare for around €5 to €7. A favourite with locals is **Restaurante Bar Barros** (☎ 282 762 276; Rua Portas de Portugal 83), where

creamy grilled scabbard fish costs €6.73. **Mullens** (☎ 282 761 281; *Rua Cândido dos Reis 86*) is a wood-panelled pub with good food.

Getting There & Away
Bus and train services depart frequently for other Algarve towns and around six times daily to Lisbon; by train, change at Tunes for Lisbon.

Getting Around
You can rent bicycles, mopeds and motorcycles from **Motoride** (☎ 289 761 720; *Rua José Afonso 23*), or agents in town. Expect to pay about €5 a day for a mountain bike or €30 for a motorbike.

MONCHIQUE
pop 6840
This quiet highland town in the forested Serra de Monchique offers a quiet alternative to the discos and beach life on the coast.

Things to See & Do
Monchique's **Igreja Matriz** has an amazing Manueline portal, its stone seemingly tied in knots! Follow the brown pedestrian signs up from the bus station, around the old town's narrow streets.

Caldas de Monchique, 6km south, is a revamped but still charming hot-spring hamlet. Some 8km west is the Algarve's 'rooftop', the 902m **Fóia** peak atop the Serra de Monchique, which has terrific views through a forest of radio masts.

Monchique's **tourist office** (☎ 289 911 189) is in the square where the bus stops. Ring **Alternativtour** (☎ 282 420 800) for bike and walking tours. For horse riding in the mountains contact **Casa Sesmaria** (☎ 282 912 511; *experienced riders only*).

Places to Stay & Eat
Residencial Estrela de Monchique (☎ 282 913 111; *Rua do Porto Fundo 46; doubles €50*) is central. **Restaurante A Charrete** (☎ 282 912 142; *Rua Dr Samora Gil 30*) is the best in town – try the hearty beans with cabbage (€6.98).

Getting There & Away
Over a dozen buses run daily from Lagos to Portimão, from where five to nine services run daily to Monchique.

SILVES
pop 10,500
Silves was the capital of Moorish Algarve, rivalling Lisbon for influence. Times are quieter now, but the huge castle is well worth a visit.

The **tourist office** (☎ 289 442 255; *Rua 25 de Abril; open Mon-Fri & Sat morning*) is closed out of season.

Places to Stay & Eat
Try **Residencial Sousa** (☎ 282 442 502; *Rua Samoura Barros 17; doubles €30*) or **Residencial Ponte Romana** (☎ 282 443 275; *doubles €30*) beside the old bridge.

Restaurante Rui (☎ 282 442 682; *Rua C Vilarinho 27*), Silves' best fish restaurant, serves a memorable *arroz de marisco* (shellfish rice; €23.50 for two). For cheaper meals, try the **riverfront restaurants** opposite the old bridge.

Getting There & Away
Silves train station is 2km from town; trains from Lagos (35 minutes) stop nine times daily (from Faro, change at Tunes), to be met by local buses. Six buses run daily to Silves from Albufeira (40 minutes).

SAGRES
pop 2500
Sagres is a small, windy fishing port perched on dramatic cliffs in Portugal's southwestern corner. The **tourist office** (☎ 282 624 873; *Rua Comandante Matoso; open Mon-Fri & Sat morning*) is just beyond Praça da República. **Turinfo** (☎ 282 620 003; *Praça da República; open daily*) rents cars and bikes, books hotels and arranges jeep and fishing trips.

Things to See & Do
In the **fort**, on a wide, windy promontory, Henry the Navigator established his school of navigation and primed the explorers who later founded the Portuguese empire.

You can hire windsurfers at sand-dune fringed **Praia do Martinhal**; another option is the beach at the village of **Salema**, 17km east.

No Sagres visit would be complete without a trip to **Cabo de São Vicente** (Cape St Vincent), 6km to the west. A solitary lighthouse stands on this barren cape, Europe's southwesternmost point.

Places to Stay & Eat
Parque de Campismo Sagres (☎ 282 624 351) is 2km from town, off the Vila do Bispo

road. Many Sagres folk rent **rooms** for around €25 a double. Good-value traditional dishes can be had at **Restaurante A Sagres** at the roundabout before the village, and at **cafés** in Praça da República.

Getting There & Away
Frequent buses run daily to Sagres from Lagos (45 to 65 minutes), fewer on Sunday. Three continue out to Cabo de São Vicente on weekdays.

Central Portugal

Central Portugal, good for weeks of desultory rambling, deserves more attention than it receives. From the beaches of the Costa de Prata to the lofty Serra da Estrela and the sprawling Alentejo plains, it is a landscape of extremes.

Some of Portugal's finest wines come from the Dão region, while further south, the hills and plains are studded with cork oaks. The mountainous centre is dotted with fortresses and walled cities with cobbled streets, clean air and grand panoramas.

ÉVORA
pop 50,000
One of Portugal's architectural gems and a Unesco World Heritage Site, the walled town of Évora is the capital of Alentejo province, a vast landscape of olive groves, vineyards and wheat fields. The town's charm lies in the narrow streets of the well-preserved inner town.

Orientation & Information
The focal point is Praça do Giraldo, from where you can wander through backstreets until you meet the city walls. An annotated map is available from the **tourist office** (☎ 266 702 671; Praça do Giraldo 73). For other guides and maps go to **Nazareth bookshop** (Praça do Giraldo 46).

Outside the tourist office is an automatic cash-exchange machine. **Oficin@ bar** (☎ 266 707 312; Rua da Moeda 27) offers Internet access for €1.50 per half hour.

Things to See & Do
The **Sé** (Largo do Marquês de Marialva; admission to cloisters & museum €3; both open Tues-Sun), Évora's cathedral, has

cloisters and a fine museum of ecclesiastical treasures.

The **Museu de Évora** (admission €1.50) features fantastic 16th-century Portuguese and Flemish painting. Opposite is the Roman-era **Temple of Diana**, subject of Évora's top-selling postcard.

The **Igreja de São Francisco** (adult/concession €1/0.50), south of Praça do Giraldo, includes the ghoulish Capela dos Ossos (Chapel of Bones), constructed with the bones and skulls of several thousand people.

Places to Stay
Accommodation gets tight in summer, so book ahead.

There's an **Orbitur camping ground** (☎ 266 705 190), 2km south of town (buses to Alcaçovas stop there), and also a **pousada da juventude** (☎ 266 744 848; Rua Miguel Bombarda 40).

For good **private rooms** try (☎ 266 702 453; Rua Romão Ramalho 27; doubles from €35). **Residencial O Alentejo** (☎ 266 702 903; Rua Serpa Pinto 74; doubles €40) and charismatic **Pensão Policarpo** (☎/fax 266 702 424; Rua da Freiria de Baixo 16; rooms €43) are also recommended. **Residencial Solar Monfalim** (☎ 266 750 000; Largo da Misericórdia 1; doubles from €60) is a mini-palace.

Places to Eat
O Portão (☎ 266 703 325; Rua do Cano 27; mains €4.25-6.25), by the aqueduct, is a popular budget choice. Pretty **Café Restaurant O Cruz** (☎ 266 747 228; Praça 1 de Maio 20) has traditional fare, such as sausage and bean stew (€4.99).

Jovial **Taberna Tipica Quarta-Feira** (☎ 266 707 530; Rua do Inverno 16) specialises in fabulous creamed spinach and pork dishes (around €10). **Pane & Vino** (☎ 266 746 960; Páteo do Salema 22) has great pasta and pizzas. **O Jovem** (☎ 266 701 180) at No 9 has half-portions of pork Alentejana (with clams) for €5.

Entertainment
Student hang-outs include several bars northwest of the centre: **Club Dezasseis** (☎ 266 706 559; Rua do Escrivão da Câmara 16); **Diplomata Pub** (☎ 266 705 675; Rua do Apóstolo 4), with frequent live music; and characterful **Pub O Trovador** (☎ 266 707 370; Rua da Mostardeira 4). **Côdeas**

ÉVORA

PLACES TO STAY
10 Pensão Policarpo
13 Residencial O Alentejo
19 Residencial Solar Monfalim
21 Pousada da Juventude
22 Private Rooms (Quartos)

PLACES TO EAT
4 O Portão
6 Taberna Tipica Quarta-Feira
17 Pane & Vino
18 O Jovem
23 Café Restaurant O Cruz

OTHER
1 Club Dezasseis
2 Diplomata Pub
3 Pub O Trovador
5 Côdeas
7 Post & Telephone Office
8 Temple of Diana
9 Museu de Évora
11 Sé (Cathedral)
12 Nazareth Bookshop
14 Oficin@
15 Tourist Office
16 Policarpo
20 Hospital
24 Igreja de São Francisco

(☎ 266 709 343; Rua do Cano 11) has live jazz Wednesday, Friday and Saturday.

Getting There & Away

Évora has six weekday express coach connections to Lisbon (1¾ hours) and two to Faro (four hours), departing from the station off Avenida Túlio Espanca (700m southwest of the centre). Fast trains run from Lisbon (2½ hours, three daily).

Getting Around

Bike Lab (☎ 266 735 500) rents bicycles for €10 per day. **Policarpo** (☎ 266 746 970, fax 266 746 984; e viagenspolicarpo@ip.pt; Alcárcova de Baixo 43) organises city tours and jaunts to megaliths and other nearby attractions.

MONSARAZ
pop 100

This walled village high above the plain is well worth the trip for its medieval atmosphere, clear light and magnificent views. Of architectural interest is the **Museu de Arte Sacra**, probably a former tribunal, with a rare 15th-century fresco. The **castle's** parapets have the best views.

Places to Stay & Eat

Several places along the main Rua Direita have doubles for around €30 to €50. The **tourist office** (☎ 266 557 136) on the main square has details of Turihab and other elegant places. There are several tourist-geared restaurants, but eat before 8pm: the town goes to bed early.

Getting There & Away

On weekdays only, buses run to/from Reguengos de Monsaraz (35 minutes, two to four daily), which is connected to Évora (one hour, six daily). The last one going back from Monsaraz leaves at 5.30pm.

ESTREMOZ
pop 15,460

The Estremoz region is dominated by mounds of marble from its quarries. The town's architectural appeal lies in its elegant, gently deteriorating buildings, which are liberally embellished with marble.

Information

The **tourist office** (☎ 268 333 541, fax 268 334 010; Largo da República 26) is just south of the main square (known as the Rossio).

Things to See & Do

The upper Estremoz area is crowned by the 14th-century **Torre de Menagem** with panoramic views, and now a luxury pousada. Opposite is the **Museu Municipal** (admission €0.99; open Tues-Sun), specialising in pottery figurines.

The focus of the lower town is the Rossio, with a lively **market** on Saturday morning. The nearby **Museu Rural** (admission €1; open Mon-Sat) is a charming one-room museum of rural Alentejan life. The bell-tower of the **Museu de Arte Sacra** (admission €1; open 9.30am-noon Sun-Fri & 2pm-5.30pm daily summer, 10am-noon Sun-Fri & 2.30pm-5.30pm daily winter) offers great views of the Rossio.

Vila Viçosa, another marble town 17km from Estremoz, is centred on the **Palácio Ducal** (admission €5 plus €2.99 for armoury museum; open Tues-Sun), ancestral home of the dukes of Bragança, and full of period furnishings and artwork.

Places to Stay & Eat

Try friendly **Pensão-Restaurante Mateus** (☎ 268 322 226; Rua Almeida 41; doubles €40). Nearby **Adega do Isaías** (☎ 268 322 318; Rua Almeida 21; mains €6.50-8) serves great grills.

Getting There & Away

Estremoz is linked to Évora by four local buses (1¼ hours) and two *expressos* (45 minutes), Monday to Saturday. Daily *expressos*

include at least two to Portalegre (one hour) and five to Elvas (50 minutes).

CASTELO DE VIDE & MARVÃO
pop 4000

From Portalegre it's a short hop to **Castelo de Vide**, noted for its picturesque houses clustered below a castle. Highlights are the **Judiaria** (Old Jewish Quarter) in a network of well-preserved medieval backstreets, and the view from the castle. Try to spend a night here or in **Marvão**, a mountaintop medieval walled village (population 190) 12km from Castelo de Vide, with grand views across Spain and Portugal.

Information

The **tourist offices** (☎ 245 901 361, fax 245 901 827; Rua de Bartolomeu Álvares da Santa 81, Castelo de Vide • ☎ 245 993 886, fax 245 993 526; Largo de Santa Maria, Marvão) can help with accommodation.

Getting There & Away

On weekdays only, three buses run from Portalegre to Castelo de Vide (20 minutes) and two to Marvão (45 minutes). One daily bus links the two villages (with a change at Portagem, a junction 5km from Marvão).

NAZARÉ
pop 16,000

This once-peaceful 17th-century fishing village was 'discovered' by tourism in the 1970s. Fishing skills and distinctive local dress have gone overboard and in high season it's a tourist circus, but the beautiful coastline and fine seafood still make it worthwhile.

The **tourist office** (☎ 262 561 194; open 10am-10pm daily high season) is at the end of Avenida da República.

Things to See & Do

Lower Nazaré's beachfront retains a core of narrow streets now catering to tourists. The cliff-top, O Sítio, is reached by a vintage funicular railway, and the view is superb.

The beaches attract huge summer crowds. Beware of dangerous currents – the tourist office can advise on which beaches are safe.

Two of Portugal's architectural masterpieces are within easy reach of Nazaré. The immense **Mosteiro de Santa Maria de Alcobaça** (☎ 262 505 120; adult/concession

€3/1.50, church admission free; open 9am-7pm daily, to 5pm winter) at Alcobaça, dates from 1178. Batalha's colossal Gothic **Mosteiro de Santa Maria de Vitória** (☎ 244 765 497; adult/concession admission to Cloisters & Unfinished Chapels €3/1.50; open 9am-6pm daily, to 5pm winter), dating from 1388, is home to the tomb of Henry the Navigator.

Places to Stay & Eat

Two camping grounds are the well-equipped **Vale Paraíso** (☎ 262 561 800) off the Leiria road, and an **Orbitur** (☎ 262 561 111) off the Alcobaça road, both 2.5km from Nazaré. Many townspeople rent out **rooms**; doubles start from €35. Seafront **Pensão Beira Mar** (☎ 262 561 358; Avenida da República 40; doubles from €50) has great showers.

Seafront restaurants are expensive. For cheaper fare in simple surroundings, try **Casa Marques** (☎ 262 551 680; Rua Gil Vicente 37). Friendly **A Tasquinha** (☎ 262 551 945; Rua Adrião Batalha 54) does good grilled squid (€7). Family-run **Casa Bizarro** (☎ 262 552 981; Rua António Carvalho Laranjo 25) has an impressive arroz do marisco (seafood rice) for €9.48.

Getting There & Away

The nearest train station, 6km away at Valado, is connected to Nazaré by frequent buses. Nazaré has numerous bus connections to Lisbon, Alcobaça, Óbidos and Coimbra.

ÓBIDOS

pop 600

This charming walled village is one of the prettiest (and most touristy) in Portugal. Highlights include the **Igreja de Santa Maria**, with fine azulejos, and **views** from the walls. The **tourist office** (☎ 262 959 231; Rua Direita) is near the town gate.

Places to Stay & Eat

Private rooms are available for around €35 a double. Among several Turihab properties is romantic **Casa do Poço** (☎ 262 959 358; Travessa da Mouraria; doubles around €58). **Pastelaria da Moura** (☎ 262 959 151; Rua Josefa de Óbidos; doubles from €40) has good rooms just inside the walls.

Café-Restaurante 1 de Dezembro (☎ 262 959 298), next to the Igreja de São Pedro, has pleasant outdoor seating. Gorgeous **O Barco**

(262 950 925; Largo Dr João Lourenço; mains €10-15) offers classy modern Portuguese fare and is a reader favourite. There's a small **grocery** just inside the town gate.

Getting There & Away

There are regular buses from Lisbon, directly (two hours) or via Caldas da Rainha, 10 minutes away. From the train station, down the hill outside the walls, there are five services daily to Lisbon (four of which involve a change at Cacém).

TOMAR

pop 17,000

Home to the outstanding Unesco-listed **Convento de Cristo**, the former headquarters of the Knights Templar, Tomar is a gem. Cradling the monastery's southern walls is the impressive 17th-century **Aqueduto de Pegões** (aquaduct), beyond which extends the **Mata Nacional dos Sete Montes** (Seven Hills National Forest). Tomar's **tourist office** (☎ 249 322 427; Avenida Dr Cândido Madureira) can help with accommodation and provide town and forest maps.

Places to Stay & Eat

Local camping grounds include **Camping Redondo** (☎/fax 249 376 421, e hansfromme@hotmail.com; Poço Redondo), which boasts a swimming pool.

Pensão Residencial União (☎ 249 323 161; Rua Serpa Pinto 94; doubles with bath and breakfast from €32.50) is central.

Ivy-clad **Casinha d'Avó Bia** (☎ 249 323 828; Rua Dr Joaquim Jacinto 16; mains €6.50-10) makes delicious seafood açorda (bread stew). **Snack Bar dos Moinhos** (Rua dos Moinhos 81; mains €4-6.50) has good-value Portuguese standards.

Getting There & Away

There are at least four express buses daily to Lisbon and three to Nazaré. There are eight to 16 trains to/from Lisbon daily.

COIMBRA

pop 150,000

Coimbra is famed for its 13th-century university, and for its role as a centre of culture and art, complemented in recent times by industrial development.

The **regional tourist office** (☎ 239 855 930, fax 239 825 576; Largo da Portagem) has pamphlets and cultural-events information, but a **municipal tourist office** (☎ 239 832 591; Praça Dom Dinis), and another **tourist office** (☎ 239 833 202; Praça da República) are more useful. **Esp@ço Internet** (Praça 8 de Maio; open 10am-8pm Mon-Fri, to 10pm weekends) has free Internet access for 30 minutes.

Coimbra's annual highlight is Queima das Fitas, a boozy week of *fado* and revelry that begins on the first Thursday in May, when students celebrate the end of the academic year.

Things to See & Do
Lower Coimbra's main attraction is the **Mosteiro de Santa Cruz** (☎ 239 822 941; Rua Visconde da Luz) with its ornate pulpit and medieval royal tombs. The new **elevator** by the market (operates daily; tickets from booth or kiosks; single €1.15) eases the sweltering summer climb to the upper town. At the top visit the **old university** with its baroque library and Manueline chapel, and the **Machado de Castro Museum** (☎ 239 823 727; Largo Dr José Rodrigues), with a fine collection of sculpture and paintings. The lively back alleys of the university quarter are filled with student hang-outs.

At **Conimbriga**, 16km south of Coimbra, are the well-preserved ruins of a Roman town (open 10am-8pm daily summer, 10am-6pm daily winter), including mosaic floors, baths and fountains. There's a good **site museum** (adult/concession €3/1.50; open 10am-1pm & 2pm-6pm Tues-Sun) with a restaurant. Frequent buses run to Condeixa, 2km from the site; direct buses depart at 9.05am or 9.35am (only 9.35am at weekends) from the **AVIC terminal** (Rua João de Ruão 18) returning at 1pm and 6pm (only 6pm at weekends).

O Pioneiro do Mondego (☎ 239 478 385; open 8am-10am, 1pm-3pm & 8pm-10pm daily Apr-Oct) rents kayaks at €15 for paddling the Rio Mondego. A free minibus takes you to Penacova for the 25km river journey.

Places to Stay
For Coimbra's **pousada da juventude** (☎ 239 822 955; Rua António Henriques Seco 12-14), take bus No 7 from outside the Astoria hotel on Avenida Emídio Navarro 50m south of Coimbra A train station.

Pensão Lorvanense (☎ 239 823 481; Rua da Sota 27; doubles €25) is near Coimbra A. **Pensão Santa Cruz** (☎ 239 826 197; Praça 8 de Maio; doubles €25) is opposite the Mosteiro. **Pensão Residencial Larbelo** (☎ 239 829 092, fax 239 829 094; Largo da Portagem 33; doubles including breakfast €33) is very central.

Friendly **Pensão Flôr de Coimbra** (☎ 239 823 865, fax 239 821 545; Rua do Poço 5; doubles with shower €30) has a small daily (except Sunday) vegetarian menu. **Residência Coimbra** (☎ 239 837 996, fax 239 838 124; Rua das Azeiteiras 55; doubles with bath €40) throws in breakfast.

Near the university, Dutch-run **Casa Pombal Guesthouse** (☎ 239 835 175, fax 239 821 548; Rua das Flores 18; doubles with/ without bath €44/38) has more expensive rooms with a bird's-eye view, and the rates include a huge breakfast.

Places to Eat
Head to the lanes west of Praça do Comércio, especially Rua das Azeiteiras, for cheap eats or try central **O Cantinho das Escadas** (☎ 239 820 578; Rua do Gato 29), by the steps, where traditional dishes of the day are €4. **Restaurante Democrática** (☎ 239 823 784; Travessa da Rua Nova; some half-portions under €4) has Portuguese standards.

The self-service **Restaurante Jardim da Manga** (☎ 239 829 156; basic dishes from €4.25; open Sun-Fri) is behind the fountains at the back of the Mosteiro de Santa Cruz. **Zé Manel** (☎ 239 823 790; Beco do Forno 12; open Mon-Fri, Sat lunch) has crazy decor and huge servings (half-portions from €6.25); arrive before 8pm to beat the crowds.

East of the university, **Bar-Restaurante ACM** (☎ 239 823 633; Rua Alexandre Herculano 21A; dishes from €4; open Sun-Fri) serves plain fare. Northwest of Praça da República, sample fruity Brazilian dishes at **Zé Carioca** (☎ 239 835 450; Avenida Sá da Bandeira 89; mains €9-15). Downstairs behind the **Centro de Juventude** (Rua Pedro Monteiro 73; mains under €5) you'll find a clean canteen with lots of salads.

Vaulted **Café Santa Cruz** beside the Mosteiro de Santa Cruz is great for coffee breaks.

Entertainment
Bar Diligência (☎ 239 827 667; Rua Nova 30) and **Boémia Bar** (☎ 239 834 547; Rua do

Cabido 6) are popular *casas de fado*. **Café-Galeria Almedina** (☎ *239 836 192; Arco de Almedina)* offers *fado* and other live sounds. A good dance bar is **Aqui Há Rato** *(Largo da Sé Velha 20)*. Two fashionable discos are **Vinyl** (☎ *239 404 047; Avenida Afonso Henriques 43)* and **Via Latina** (☎ *239 833 034; Rua Almeida Garrett 1)*.

Getting There & Away
At least a dozen buses and as many trains run daily from Lisbon and Porto, plus frequent express buses from Faro and Évora, via Lisbon. The main long-distance train stations are Coimbra B, 2km northwest of the centre, and central Coimbra A (on timetables this is called just 'Coimbra'). Most long-distance trains call at both. Other useful connections are to Figueira da Foz and to Luso/Buçaco (from Coimbra A).

LUSO & THE BUÇACO FOREST
pop 2000
A walker's paradise, the Buçaco Forest was chosen as a retreat by 16th-century monks and has remained relatively untouched ever since. It begins about 1km from the spa resort of Luso, where the **tourist office** (☎/fax *231 939 133; Avenida Emídio Navarro)* has good maps and leaflets about trails and the forest's 700-plus tree and shrub species.

Places to Stay & Eat
The Luso tourist office has lists of **private rooms** that cost around €20. Prices at the nearby **Astória** (☎ *231 939 182; Avenida Emídio Navarro; doubles €32.50)* include breakfast. Hearty meals are available at **Restaurante O Cesteiro** (☎ *231 939 360)* on the N234, which is 500m north from the tourist office.

The elegant five-star **Palace Hotel do Buçaco** (☎ *231 930 101, fax 231 930 509; singles/doubles from €145/170)*, a former royal hunting lodge in the forest, is as fine an expression of Manueline style as any in Portugal. The equally elegant **restaurant** offers set menus for €40.

Getting There & Away
Four buses daily go to Luso/Buçaco from Coimbra and Viseu (two at weekends). Just one train, departing around 10.30am from Coimbra B, provides enough time to take a day trip.

SERRA DA ESTRELA
The forested Serra da Estrela is Portugal's highest mainland mountain range (1993m), and the core of a designated *parque natural*. With its outlying ranges it almost stretches across Portugal, and offers some of the country's best hiking.

Orientation & Information
The best place for information on the Parque Natural da Serra da Estrela is the **main park office** (☎ *275 980 060, fax 275 980 069; Manteigas)*; other offices can be found at Seia, Gouveia and Guarda. Other good sources for regional information are the local **tourist offices** *(Guarda* ☎ *271 205 530; Covilhã* ☎ *275 319 560)*.

The park administration publishes *À Descoberta da Estrela*, a walking guide with maps and narratives. Park offices and some tourist offices sell an English edition (€4.25), plus a detailed topographic map of the park (€5.50).

Places to Stay
The **pousada da juventude** (☎ *275 335 375, fax 275 335 109; Penhas da Saúde)*, 10km above Covilhã, offers meals (or you can cook your own), dorms and a few functional doubles. Buses come from Covilhã twice daily in August only, and hitching is fairly safe and easy. The only other options are your feet or bike, or a taxi (about €8). This makes a good base for excursions.

Guarda also has a **pousada da juventude** (☎/fax *271 224 482)*, and Seia, Gouveia, Guarda and Covilhã have some modestly priced **guesthouses**. Central Manteigas tends to be pricey.

Getting There & Away
Several buses run daily from Coimbra, along the park's perimeter to Seia, Gouveia, Guarda or Covilhã, plus others from Porto and Lisbon to Guarda and Covilhã. Twice-daily IC trains link Lisbon and Coimbra to Guarda, while two daily IC trains run from Lisbon to Covilhã on the Lisbon–Paris line.

Getting Around
No buses cross through the park, although you can go around it: Seia–Covilhã takes two hours via Guarda. At least one or two buses link Seia, Gouveia and Guarda every day, and considerably more run between Guarda and Covilhã.

The North

Many visitors are surprised to discover Portugal's northern tier, with its wine country, forests, mountainous Peneda-Gerês National Park and a strand of undeveloped beaches. The urban scene focuses on Porto, with the town's medieval centre by the Rio Douro. Within easy reach of Porto there are three historical cities: Braga, the country's religious heart; the finely situated Viana do Castelo; and Guimarães, the self-proclaimed birthplace of Portugal.

PORTO
pop 300,000

Porto (only foreigners call it Oporto) is Portugal's second-largest city, and the centre of the port-wine trade. Its reputation as an industrial centre belies considerable charm; indeed its old centre has been declared a Unesco World Heritage Site.

Orientation

The city clings to the north bank of the Rio Douro, spanned by five bridges. On the far bank is Vila Nova de Gaia, home to the port wine lodges, a major attraction.

Central Porto's axis is Avenida dos Aliados. Major shopping areas are eastward around the Bolhão Market and Rua Santa Catarina, home to the glassy shopping complex Via Catarina, and westward along Rua dos Clérigos. At the southern end of Avenida dos Aliados, Praça da Liberdade and São Bento train station are major local bus hubs. Another is Jardim da Cordoaria (called Jardim de João Chagas on some maps), about 400m westward.

The picturesque Ribeira district lies along the waterfront, in the shadow of the great Ponte de Dom Luís I bridge.

Information

Tourist Offices The main **municipal tourist office** (☎ 223 393 470, fax 223 323 303; Rua Clube dos Fenianos 25; open 9am-5.30pm Mon-Fri, weekends 9am-4.30pm Oct-June, 9am-7pm daily July-Sept) is next door to the **tourist police** office. There's also a smaller **tourist office** (☎ 222 009 770; Rua Infante Dom Henriques 63; open 9am-5.30pm Mon-Fri).

There's also a national **ICEP tourist office** (☎ 222 057 514, fax 222 053 212; Praça Dom João I 43; open 9am-7pm Mon-Fri, 9.30am-3.30pm Sat & Sun).

Money Banks with ATMs and exchange desks are everywhere. Better rates for travellers cheques are at the exchange bureaus **Portocâmbios** (Rua Rodrigues Sampaio 193), and **Intercontinental** (Rua de Ramalho Ortigão 8). **Top Tours** (☎ 222 074 020, fax 222 074 039; Rua Alferes Malheiro 96) is Porto's American Express representative.

Post & Communications The main post office (the place for poste-restante mail) is across Praça General Humberto Delgado from the main tourist office. There's a **telephone office** (Praça da Liberdade 62; open 10am-10pm daily). Faxes can be sent from the post office, and domestic ones from the telephone office.

Email & Internet Access At well-equipped **Portweb** (☎ 222 005 922; Praça General Humberto Delgado 291) access costs a bargain €0.50 per hour from 9am to 4pm daily, and a still reasonable €1.20 from 4pm to 2am.

Travel Agencies Youth-oriented agencies include **Tagus** (☎ 226 094 146, fax 226 094 141; Rua Campo Alegre 261), and **Wasteels** (☎ 225 194 230, fax 225 194 239; Rua Pinto Bessa 27/29) near Campanhã station. See also Top Tours listed under Money earlier.

Local adventure-tour operators with northern Portugal experience include **Montes d'Aventura** (☎ 228 305 157, fax 228 305 158) for trekking, cycling and canoeing, and **Trilhos** (☎ 225 020 740; fax 225 504 604) for canyoning and hydrospeed.

Laundry Laundry and dry-cleaning services are available at **Lavandaria Olímpica** (Rua Miguel Bombarda) and **Lavandaria 5 à Sec** (Central Shopping centre). **Lavandaria São Nicolau** (Rua Infante Dom Henrique) is a cheaper municipal service. All are closed on Sunday, though.

Medical Services & Emergency There are English-speaking staff at **Santo António Hospital** (☎ 222 077 500; Largo Prof Abel Salazar). For police help contact the **tourism police office** (☎ 222 081 833; Rua Clube dos Fenianos 11; open 8am-2am daily).

Things to See & Do

The riverfront **Ribeira** district is the city's heart, with narrow lanes, grimy bars, lovely restaurants and river cruises.

The 225 steps of the **Torre dos Clérigos** *(Rua dos Clérigos; admission €1; open 10am-noon & 2pm-5pm daily)* lead to the best panorama of the city.

The **Sé** *(☎ 222 059 028; admission €1.25; open 9am-12.30pm, 2.30pm-5.15pm daily, closed Sun morning)*, the cathedral dominating Porto, is worth a visit for its mixture of architectural styles and ornate interior.

The **Soares dos Reis National Museum** *(☎ 223 393 770; Rua Dom Manuel II 44; admission €2.99; open 10am-12.30pm Wed-Sun & 2pm-6pm daily)* offers masterpieces of 19th- and 20th-century Portuguese painting and sculpture.

Porto's finest new museum is the **Serralves Museum of Contemporary Art,** *(☎ 226 156 500; Rua Dom João de Castro 210; admission €3.99; open 10am-7pm Tues-Wed & Fri-Sun, 10am-10pm Thur).*

The **Museu do Carro Eléctrico** *(Tram Museum; ☎ 226 158 185; Alameda Basílio Teles 51; admission €1.75; open 10am-12.30pm & 2.30pm-6pm Tues-Fri, 3pm-7pm Sat-Sun)*, is a cavernous old tram warehouse with dozens of restored cars.

Bustling **Bolhão market** *(open to 5pm Mon-Fri, to 1pm Sat)*, east of Avenida dos Aliados, sells everything from seafood to flowers and pots.

Across the river in Vila Nova de Gaia, of the two dozen **port-wine lodges** offering tours and tastings (daily, fewer on Sunday), **Taylors** *(☎ 223 719 999)* stands out. The **tourist office** *(☎ 223 773 080)* has details. Or select from a huge port-wine list at the **Solar do Vinho do Porto** *(☎ 226 094 749; Rua Entre Quintas 220; bar open 11am-midnight Mon-Sat)*, in Porto.

Special Events

Porto's big festivals are the Festa de São João (St John's Festival) in June and the international film festival Fantasporto in February. Also worth catching are the Celtic music festival in April-May, and the rock festival in August.

Places to Stay

Camping Four kilometres northwest of the centre is **Camping da Prelada** *(☎ 228 312 616; Rua Monte dos Burgos; bus No 54 from Praça de Liberdade or bus No 6 from Jardim da Cordoaria).*

Three camping grounds near the sea in Vila Nova de Gaia are **Campismo Salgueiros** *(☎ 227 810 500, fax 227 718 239; Praia de Salgueiros)*, **Campismo Marisol** *(☎ 227 135 942, fax 227 126 351; Praia de Canidelo)* and **Campismo Madalena** *(☎ 227 122 520, fax 227 122 534; Praia da Madalena)*. Bus No 57 runs to all of them from São Bento station.

Note that the sea is far too polluted for swimming.

Hostels The fine **pousada da juventude** *(☎ 226 177 257, fax 226 177 247; Rua Paulo da Gama 551)* is 4km west of the centre. Reservations are essential. Take bus No 35 from Praça da Liberdade or No 1 from São Bento station.

Guesthouses Porto's cheapest guesthouses are around Praça da Batalha, east and uphill from São Bento station, but there are more salubrious parts of town. Down towards the river, **Pensão Astória** *(☎ 222 008 175; Rua Arnaldo Gama 56; doubles from €30)* has elegant old doubles, some with river views, and breakfast is included.

Doubles with shower at central **Residencial União** *(☎ 222 003 078; Rua Conde de Vizela 62)* start at €30, and €25 at **Pensão Porto Rico** *(☎ 223 394 690; Rua do Almada 237)*. **Pensão Mira Norte** *(☎/fax 222 001 118; Rua de Santa Catarina 969; doubles €30)* is well placed for shopaholics as is **Solar Residencial São Gabriel** *(☎ 222 005 499, fax 223 323 957; Rua da Alegria 98; doubles €44.50)*, where breakfast is included. **Pensão Chique** *(☎ 222 009 011; Avenida dos Aliados 206; doubles €40)* also includes breakfast in its rates. Or try friendly **Residencial Vera Cruz** *(☎ 223 323 396, fax 223 323 421; Rua Ramalho Ortigão 14; doubles €45)*. **Pensão Pão de Açucar** *(☎ 222 002 425, fax 222 050 239; Rua do Almada 262; doubles with shower from €75)* has handsome rooms with breakfast; a booking is essential.

Near the university, **Pensão Estoril** *(☎ 222 002 751, fax 222 082 468; Rua de Cedofeita 193)* and the better-value **Pensão São Marino** *(☎ 223 325 499; Praça Carlos Alberto 59)* offer doubles with shower and breakfast from €38.

PORTO

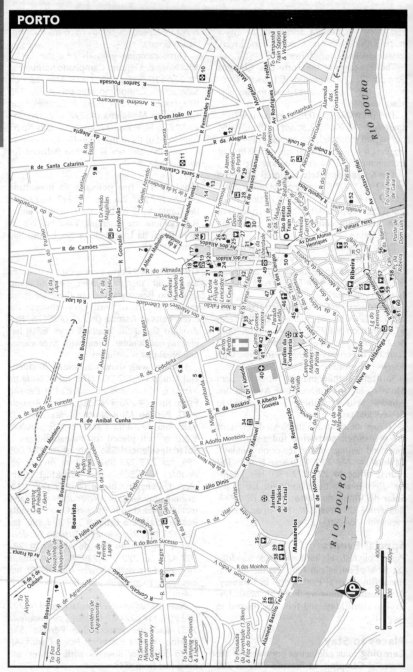

PORTO

PLACES TO STAY
6 Pensão Estoril
9 Pensão Mira Norte
12 Solar Residencial São Gabriel
21 Residencial Vera Cruz
22 Pensão São Marino
23 Pensão Porto Rico
24 Pensão Pão de Açucar
25 Pensão Chique
48 Residencial União
52 Pensão Astória

PLACES TO EAT
29 Café Majestic
31 Café Embaixador
33 Restaurante Romão
41 Restaurante A Tasquinha
43 Café Ancôra Douro
56 Casa Filha da Mãe Preta
58 Pub-Petisqueira O Muro

OTHER
1 STCP Kiosk
2 Instituto Português da Juventude
3 Usit Tagus
4 Internorte Tickets and Buses
5 Lavandaria Olimpica
7 Top Tours & American Express
8 REDM; AV Minho; Carlos Soares Tickets & Buses
10 Central Shopping
11 Via Catarina
13 STCP Kiosk
14 Bolhão Market
15 Casa Januário
16 Main Post Office
17 Town Hall
18 Main Municipal Tourist Office; Tourism Police
19 Portweb
20 Intercontinental Exchange
26 Portocambios Exchange
27 Café Concerto
28 Rodonorte Bus Station
30 National (ICEP) Tourist Office
32 Livraria Porto Editora
34 Soares dos Reis National Museum
35 Solar do Vinho do Porto
36 Museu do Carro Eléctrico
37 Maré Alta
38 Club Mau-Mau
39 Mexcal
40 Santo António Hospital
42 Garrafeira do Carmo
44 Cordoaria Bus Stand
45 Casa Oriental
46 Torre dos Clérigos
47 Renex Tickets and Buses
49 Telephone Office
50 STCP Kiosk
51 Rede Expressos Bus Station
53 Sé
54 Ryan's Irish pub
55 Academia
57 Meia-Cave
59 Municipal Tourist Office
60 Arte Facto
61 Lavandaria São Nicolau
62 Tram Terminus

Places to Eat

The self-service mezzanine at central **Café Embaixador** *(☎ 222 054 182; Rua Sampaio Bruno 5; open 7am-10pm Mon-Fri, from 8am Sat-Sun)* has good-value grills and salads and there's a handy supermarket in Via Caterina on Rua Santa Catarina.

Near the university, cosy **Restaurante A Tasquinha** *(☎ 223 322 145; Rua do Carmo 23)* has well-executed regional dishes – try the *rojões* (€7.50) a Minho speciality pork dish. Casual **Restaurante Romão** *(☎ 222 005 639; Praça Carlos Alberto 100; half-portions €5-6)* has northern specialities such as tripe and roast kid. A lively student haunt at lunchtime is **Café Ancôra Douro** *(☎ 222 003 749; Praça de Parada Leitão 49; mains €2.50-6)*.

An exception to the Ribeira's many overpriced, touristy eateries is **Pub-Petisqueira O Muro** *(☎ 222 083 426; Muro dos Bacalhoeiros 88; open noon-2am daily)*, with decor from dried bacalhau to Che Guevara, and good *feijoado de marisco* (a rich bean and seafood stew) for €4.50. **Casa Filha da Mãe Preta** *(☎ 222 055 515; Cais da Ribeira 40; most mains under €10)* has good views of the Douro.

Café Majestic *(☎ 222 003 887; Rua Santa Catarina 112)* is an extravagant Art Nouveau relic with expensive coffees and afternoon teas.

Entertainment

Lively pubs in the Ribeira include **Academia** *(☎ 222 005 737; Rua São João 80)*, **Ryan's Irish Pub** *(☎ 222 005 366; Rua Infante Dom Henrique 18)* and **Meia-Cave** *(☎ 223 323 214; Praça da Ribeira 6)*. A useful central bar is **Café Concerto** *(☎ 223 392 208; Praça Dom João I)* atop Teatro Rivoli.

A newer generation of clubs in the riverfront area called Massarelos, 2km west of the Ribeira, includes **Mexcal** *(☎ 226 009 188)*, **Club Mau-Mau** *(☎ 226 076 660; Rua da Restauração)* and **Maré Alta** *(☎ 226 162 540; Rua do Ouro)*. All are on the No 1 bus line from São Bento station.

Shopping

Port is, naturally, a popular purchase. Shops with a broad selection include knowledgeable **Garrafeira do Carmo** *(Rua do Carmo 17)*; **Casa Januário** *(Rua do Bonjardim 352)*; and **Casa Oriental** *(Campo dos Mártires de Pátria 111)*. Other good buys are shoes and gold-filigree jewellery. For handicrafts, visit **Arte Facto** *(Rua da Reboleira 37; open Tues-Sun)* in the Ribeira.

Getting There & Away

Air Porto is connected by daily flights from Lisbon and London, and almost-daily direct links from other European centres (see the introductory Getting There & Away and Getting Around sections of this chapter). For flight information call ☎ 229 413 260.

Bus For Lisbon and the Algarve the choice is **Renex** (☎ 222 003 395; *Rua das Carmelitas 32; open 24hr*). From a terminal at Rua Alexandre Herculano 370, **Rede Expressos** (☎ 222 052 459) goes all over Portugal. Three companies operate from or near Praceto Régulo Magauanha, off Rua Dr Alfredo Magalhães: **REDM** (☎ 222 003 152) goes to Braga; **AV Minho** (☎ 222 006 121) to Viana do Castelo; and **Carlos Soares** (☎ 222 051 383) to Guimarães. **Rodonorte** (☎ 222 004 398; *Rua Ateneu Comércial do Porto 19*) departs from its own terminal, mainly to Vila Real and Bragança.

Northern Portugal's main international carrier is **Internorte** (see the introductory Getting There & Away section of this chapter), whose coaches depart from the **booking office** (☎ 226 093 220, fax 226 099 570; *Praça da Galiza 96*).

Train Porto is a northern Portugal rail hub with three stations. Most international trains, and all intercidade links, start at Campanhã, 2km east of the centre. Interregional and regional services depart from either Campanhã or the central **São Bento station** (*information: ☎ 225 364 141 8am-11pm daily*) – bus Nos 34 and 35 run frequently between these two.

At São Bento you can book tickets to any destination from any Porto station.

Getting Around
To/From the Airport The AeroBus (☎ 808 200 166) runs between Avenida dos Aliados and the airport via Boavista every half-hour from 7am to 6.30pm. The €2.50 ticket, purchased on the bus, also serves as a free bus pass until midnight of the day you buy it.

City bus Nos 56 and 87 run about every half-hour until 8.30pm to/from Jardim da Cordoaria, and until about 12.30am to/from Praça da Liberdade.

A taxi costs around €12.50 plus a possible €1.50 baggage charge.

Bus Central hubs of Porto's extensive bus system include Jardim da Cordoaria, Praça da Liberdade and São Bento station (Praça Almeida Garrett). Tickets are cheapest from STCP kiosks (eg, opposite São Bento station,

beside Bolhão market and at Boavista) and many newsagents and tobacconists: €0.50 for a short hop, €0.70 to outlying areas or €1.70 for an airport return trip. Tickets bought on the bus are always €1. There's also a €2 day pass available.

Tram Porto has one remaining tram, the No 1E, trundling daily from the Ribeira to the coast at Foz do Douro.

Metro Work has begun on Porto's own 'underground', a combination of upgraded and new track that will reach Campanhã, Vila Nova de Gaia and several coastal resorts to the north.

Taxi To cross town, expect to pay about €4. An additional charge is made to leave the city limits, including across the Ponte Dom Luís I to Vila Nova de Gaia.

ALONG THE DOURO
The Douro Valley is one of Portugal's scenic highlights, with 200km of expansive panoramas from Porto to the Spanish border. In the upper reaches, port-wine vineyards wrap around every hillside.

The river, tamed by eight dams and locks since the late 1980s, is navigable right across Portugal. Highly recommended is the train journey from Porto to Peso da Régua (about a dozen trains daily, 2½ hours), the last 50km clinging to the river's edge; four trains continue daily to Pocinho (4½ hours). **Douro Azul** (☎ 223 393 950, fax 223 402 510) and other companies run one- and two-day river cruises, mostly from March to October. Cyclists and drivers can choose river-hugging roads along either bank, although they're crowded at weekends.

The elegant, detailed colour map *Rio Douro* (€3) is available from Porto bookshops.

VIANA DO CASTELO
pop 18,000
This attractive port at the mouth of the Rio Lima is renowned for its historic old town and its folk traditions. The **tourist office** (☎ 258 822 620, fax 258 827 873; *Rua Hospital Velho*) has information on festivals and the region in general.

In August Viana hosts the Festas de Nossa Senhora da Agonia (see the Facts for the Visitor section at the start of this chapter for details).

Things to See

The town's focal point is Praça da República, with its delicate fountain and elegant buildings, including the 16th-century **Misericórdia**.

Atop Santa Luzia Hill, the **Templo do Sagrado Coração de Jesus** offers a grand panorama across the river. A funicular railway climbs the hill from 9am to 6pm (hourly in the morning, half-hourly in the afternoon) from behind the train station.

Places to Stay

Viana's **pousada da juventude** (☎ 258 800 260, fax 258 820 870; Rua da Argaçosa) is about 1km east of the town centre.

Pensão Vianense (☎ 258 823 118; Avenida Conde da Carreira 79) and **Casa de Hóspedes Guerreiro** (☎ 258 822 099; Rua Grande 14) have plain doubles with shared facilities from €25. **Pensão Dolce Vita** (☎ 258 824 860; Rua do Poço 44; doubles €30) is central. Or try **Pensão-Restaurant Alambique** (☎ 258 823 894; Rua Manuel Espregueira 88; doubles with bath and breakfast €35).

Porto's tourist office also has listings of **private rooms**.

Places to Eat

Most pensões have good restaurants, open to nonguests. **A Gruta Snack Bar** (☎ 258 820 214; Rua Grande 87) has lunchtime salads for under €5. **Adega do Padrinho** (☎ 258 826 954; Rua Gago Coutinho 162; half-portions around €7.50) offers traditional dishes like octopus rice. Seafood is pricey, but try the cervejaria part of **Os Três Arcos** (☎ 258 824 014; Largo João Tomás da Costa 25; half-portions from €3.50). Viana's **Restaurante** (☎ 258 824 797; Rua Frei Bartolomeu dos Mártires 179; half-portions €5-9), near the fish market, specialises in bacalhau, in all its forms.

Getting There & Away

Half a dozen express coaches go to Braga and to Porto every day (fewer at weekends), with daily express services on to Coimbra and Lisbon. Daily train services run north to Spain and south to Porto and Lisbon.

BRAGA

pop 80,000

Crammed with churches, Braga is considered Portugal's religious capital. During Easter week, huge crowds attend its Holy Week Festival.

The **tourist office** (☎ 253 262 550; Praça da República) can help with accommodation and maps.

Things to See & Do

In the centre of Braga is the **Sé** (admission to treasury museum & several tomb chapels €2), an elegant cathedral complex.

At Bom Jesus do Monte, a hilltop pilgrimage site 5km from Braga, is an extraordinary stairway, the **Escadaria do Bom Jesus**, with allegorical fountains, chapels and a superb view. Buses run frequently from Braga to the site, where you can climb the steps or ascend by funicular railway.

It's an easy day-trip to **Guimarães**, considered the cradle of the Portuguese nation, with a medieval town centre and a palace of the dukes of Bragança.

Places to Stay

The **pousada da juventude** (☎ 253 616 163; Rua de Santa Margarida 6) is a 10-minute walk from the city centre. A bargain in the centre is **Hotel Francfort** (☎ 253 262 648; Avenida Central 7; doubles from €25), with well-kept old rooms. **Grande Residência Avenida** (☎ 253 609 020, fax 253 609 028; Avenida da Liberdade 738; doubles with/ without bath €37/30) offers good value. **Hotel Residencial Dona Sophia** (☎ 253 263 160, fax 253 611 245; Largo de São do Souto 131; singles/doubles €49.88/59.86 with breakfast) has smart rooms.

Places to Eat

Lareira do Conde (☎ 253 611 340; Praça Conde de Agrolongo 56) specialises in inexpensive grills, including ox (€8.75). Around the corner from the bus station, **Retiro da Primavera** (☎ 253 272 482; Rua Gabriel de Castro 100; half-portions under €4) has good fare. Rustic **Taberna do Felix** (☎ 253 617 701; Praça Velha 17; dishes from €6.75) has tasty arroz de pato (duck rice). Classy **Restaurante Pópulo** (☎ 253 215 147; Praça Conde de Agrolongo 116; mains €8-13) offers rich duck, veal and pork dishes.

For people-watching over coffee or beer, settle down at **Café Vianna** (Praça da República).

Getting There & Away

The motorway from Porto puts Braga within easy day-trip reach. Intercidade trains arrive twice daily from Lisbon, Coimbra and Porto, and there are daily connections north to Viana do Castelo and Spain. Daily bus services link Braga to Porto and Lisbon.

PENEDA-GERÊS NATIONAL PARK

This wilderness park along the Spanish border has spectacular scenery and a wide variety of fauna and flora. Portuguese day-trippers and holiday-makers tend to stick to the main villages and camping areas, leaving the rest of the park to hikers.

The park's main centre is **Vila do Gerês** (or Caldas do Gerês, or just Gerês), a sleepy, hot-spring village.

Orientation & Information

Gerês' **tourist office** (☎ 253 391 133, fax 253 391 282) is in the colonnade at the upper end of the village. For park information go around the corner to the **park office** (☎ 253 390 110 • head office: ☎ 253 203 480, fax 253 613 169; Avenida António Macedo, Braga).

Other park offices are at Arcos de Valdevez, Montalegre. All have a map of the park (€2.64) with some roads and tracks (but not trails) marked, and a free English-language booklet on the park's features.

Activities

Hiking A long-distance footpath is being developed, mostly following traditional roads or tracks between villages where you can stop for the night. Park offices sell map-brochures (€0.50) for the route available so far.

Day hikes around Gerês are popular; at weekends and all summer the Miradouro walk at **Parque do Merendas** is crowded. A more strenuous option is the old Roman road from Mata do Albergaria (10km up-valley from Gerês by taxi or hitching), past the **Vilarinho das Furnas** reservoir to Campo do Gerês. More distant destinations include **Ermida** and **Cabril**, both with simple cafés and accommodation.

Guided walks are organised by **PlanAlto** (☎/fax 253 351 005) at Cerdeira Camping Ground in Campo do Gerês, and **Trote-Gerês** (☎/fax 253 659 860) at Cabril.

Cycling Mountain bikes can be hired from **Água Montanha Lazer** (☎ 253 391 779, fax 253 391 598; e aguamontanha@mail.telepac .pt) in Rio Caldo, **Pensão Carvalho Araújo** (☎ 253 391 185) in Gerês, or PlanAlto.

Horse Riding The national park operates **horse riding facilities** (☎ 253 390 110) from beside its Vidoeiro camping ground, near Gerês. Trote-Gerês also has horses for hire.

Water Sports Rio Caldo, 8km south of Gerês, is the base for water sports on the Caniçada reservoir. Água Montanha Lazer rents canoes and other boats. For paddling the Salamonde reservoir, Trote-Gerês rents canoes from its camping ground at Cabril.

Gerês' **Parque das Termas** (admission €1) has a swimming pool, open for €3.50/5 on weekdays/weekends.

Organised Tours

Agência no Gerês (☎ 253 391 141), at Hotel Universal in Gerês, runs two- to 5½-hour minibus trips around the park in summer, for around €5.50 per person.

Places to Stay

The **pousada da juventude** (☎/fax 253 351 339) and **Cerdeira Camping Ground** (☎/fax 253 351 005) at Campo do Gerês make good hiking bases. Trote-Gerês runs its own **Parque de Campismo Outeiro Alto** (☎/fax 253 659 860) at Cabril. The park runs a **camping ground** (☎ 253 391 289) 1km north of Gerês at Vidoeiro, and others at Lamas de Mouro and Entre-Ambos-os-Rios.

Gerês has plenty of pensões, although many are block-booked by spa patients in summer. Try **Pensão da Ponte** (☎ 253 391 121; doubles with/without bath from €40/ 20) beside the river. **Pensão Adelaide** (☎ 253 390 020, fax 253 390 029; doubles with bath from €35) is at the top of the hill.

Trote-Gerês runs the comfortable **Pousadinha de Paradela** (☎ 276 566 165; doubles from €25) in Paradela.

Places to Eat

Most Gerês pensões serve hearty meals, to guests and nonguests. There are several **restaurants**, plus shops in the main street for picnic provisions. The **Cerdeira Camping Ground** at Campo do Gerês has a good-value restaurant.

Getting There & Away

From Braga, at least six coaches daily run to Rio Caldo and Gerês, and seven to Campo do Gerês (fewer at weekends). Coming from Lisbon or Porto, change at Braga.

Spain

Spain is a land of majesty and madness, where ghosts of a legendary past stalk the earth and seemingly every day is devoted to a frenzied, unrelenting quest for bliss. The clashes, conflicts and combinations that shaped Spain's chequered history have given rise to a culture painted in the brightest of colours and steeped in the most vivacious of traditions.

Indeed, Spaniards approach life with such exuberance that visitors have to stop and stare. In almost every city, the nightlife will outlast the foreigners. And just when the bewildered traveller appears to have come to terms with the pace, they are surrounded by the beating drums of a fiesta, with day and night turning into a blur of dancing, laughing, eating and drinking.

This apparently single-minded pursuit of joy actually arises from a syncretic blend of influences – a mixture reflected by Spain's wealth of historical sights. Long a meeting point (and battleground) for myriad civilisations, the country brims over with remnants of a chaotic, glorious past. Fascinating prehistoric displays beckon the traveller at archaeological museums in Teruel and Madrid. Segovia's magnificent aqueduct, Tarragona's seaside amphitheatre and the buried streets of Roman Caesaraugusta (under modern-day Zaragoza) number among several reminders of the classical period. After Roman times, the Moorish era left the most powerful cultural and artistic legacy, focused on Granada's Alhambra, Córdoba's mosque and Seville's *alcázar* (fortress) but apparent in monuments throughout much of the country. Christian Spain saw the construction of hundreds of impressive castles, cathedrals, monasteries, palaces and mansions, which today stand as romantic, mist-kissed tributes to the Middle Ages.

The rise of the Spanish empire engendered the flowering of Spain's devotion to the arts, evident today in its abundance of world-class museums. These include Madrid's Prado and Thyssen-Bornemisza museums, Figueres' idiosyncratic Dalí museum, Barcelona's mesmerising Picasso and Miró galleries, and (most recently) Bilbao's glorious addition to the Guggenheim family.

Spain's cultural pluralism is mirrored in its very geography, among the most diverse in

At a Glance

- **Beaches** – isolated spots on Menorca and the Costa de la Luz, and the famed (and more crowded) Costa Brava and Costa Blanca
- **Madrid** – Spain's capital, filled with museums, parks and buzzing nightlife
- **Barcelona** – stylish, dynamic with heaps to do: Gaudí monuments, medieval Barri Gòtic and fiestas
- **Seville** – home of the Alcázar and a hub for flamenco, bullfighting and fiestas
- **Granada** – showcase of Andalucía's Muslim past, backed by snowcapped Sierra Nevada

Capital	Madrid
Population	40 million
Official Language	Spanish (Castilian)
Currency	euro
Time	GMT/UTC+0100
Country Phone Code	☎ 34

Europe. The landscape varies from soaring mountains to arid plains to idyllic beaches – often within just a few kilometres. Holidaymakers enjoy the uncanny predictability of sunshine on the Mediterranean coast from April to October. More active beachgoers take advantage of the chillier surf strips of western Andalucía or the País Vasco (Basque

Country). Elsewhere, hikers and climbers enjoy good summer weather and spectacular scenery in the more secluded coves of Galicia, in the Pyrenees or the mountains of Andalucía.

All these facets combine to render Spain one of Europe's most sublime, inspiring destinations. It doesn't matter how high your expectations are for the country: they will be surpassed.

Facts about Spain

HISTORY
Ancient History

Located at the crossroads between Europe and Africa, the Iberian Peninsula has long been a target for invading peoples and civilisations. From around 8000 to 3000 BC pioneers from North Africa known as the Iberians crossed the Strait of Gibraltar and settled the peninsula. Around 1000 BC Celtic tribes entered northern Spain, while Phoenician merchants were establishing trading settlements along the Mediterranean coast. They were followed by Greeks and Carthaginians, who arrived around 600 to 500 BC.

The Romans arrived in the 3rd century BC but took two centuries to subdue the peninsula. Although Christianity came to Spain during the 1st century AD, it was initially opposed by the Romans leading to persecution and martyrdom. In AD 409 Roman Hispania was invaded by Germanic tribes, and by 419 the Christian Visigoths, another Germanic

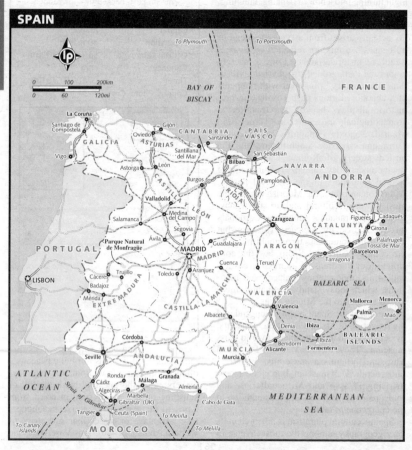

people, had established a kingdom that lasted until 711, when the Moors – Muslim Berbers and Arabs from North Africa – crossed the Strait of Gibraltar and defeated Roderic, the last Visigoth king.

Muslim Spain & the Reconquista

By 714 the Muslim armies had occupied the entire peninsula, apart from some northern mountain regions. Muslim dominion was to last almost 800 years in parts of Spain. In Islamic Spain (known as 'al-Andalus') arts and sciences prospered, new crops and agricultural techniques were introduced, and palaces, mosques, schools, public baths and gardens were built.

In 722 a small army under the Visigothic leader Pelayo inflicted the first defeat on the Muslims (known to Christians as *moros*, or Moors) at Covadonga in northern Spain. This marked the beginning of the Reconquista, the spluttering reconquest of Spain by the Christians. By the early 11th century, the frontier between Christian and Muslim Spain stretched from Barcelona to the Atlantic.

In 1085 Alfonso VI, king of León and Castile, took Toledo. This prompted the Muslim leaders to request help from northern Africa, which arrived in the form of the Almoravids. They recaptured much territory and ruled it until the 1140s. The Almoravids were followed by the Almohads, another North African dynasty, which ruled until 1212. But by the mid-13th century, the Christians had taken most of the peninsula except for the state of Granada.

In the process the kingdoms of Castile and Aragón emerged as Christian Spain's two main powers, and in 1469 they were united by the marriage of Isabel, princess of Castile, and Fernando, heir to Aragón's throne. Known as the Catholic Monarchs, they united Spain and laid the foundations for the Spanish golden age. They also revived the notorious Inquisition, which expelled and executed thousands of Jews and other non-Christians. In 1492 the last Muslim ruler of Granada surrendered to them, marking the completion of the Reconquista.

The Golden Age

Also in 1492, while searching for an alternative passage to India, Christopher Columbus stumbled on the Bahamas and claimed the Americas for Spain. This sparked a period of exploration and exploitation that was to yield Spain enormous wealth while destroying the ancient American empires. For three centuries, gold and silver from the New World were used to finance the rapid expansion and slow decline of the Spanish empire.

In 1516 Fernando was succeeded by his grandson Carlos, of the Habsburg dynasty. Carlos was elected Holy Roman Emperor in 1519 and ruled over an empire that included Austria, southern Germany, the Netherlands, Spain and the American colonies. He and his successors were to lead Spain into a series of expensive wars that ultimately bankrupted the empire. In 1588 Sir Francis Drake's English fleet annihilated the mighty Spanish Armada. The Thirty Years' War (1618–48) saw Spain in conflict with the Netherlands, France and England. By the reign of the last Habsburg monarch, Carlos II (1655–1700), the Spanish empire was in decline.

The 18th & 19th Centuries

Carlos II died heirless. At the end of the subsequent War of the Spanish Succession (1702–13), Felipe V, grandson of French king Louis XIV, became the first of Spain's Bourbon dynasty. A period of stability, enlightened reforms and economic growth ensued, ended by events following the French Revolution of 1789.

When Louis XVI was guillotined in 1793, Spain declared war on the French republic, but then turned to alliance with France and war against Britain, in which the Battle of Trafalgar (1805) ended Spanish sea power. In 1807–08 French troops entered Spain and Napoleon convinced Carlos IV, the Spanish king, to abdicate. In his place Napoleon installed his own brother Joseph Bonaparte. The Spaniards retaliated with a five-year war of independence. In 1815 Napoleon was defeated by Wellington, and a Bourbon, Fernando VII, was restored to the Spanish throne.

Fernando's reign was a disastrous advertisement for monarchy: the Inquisition was re-established, liberals and constitutionalists were persecuted, free speech was repressed, Spain entered a severe recession and the American colonies won their independence. After Fernando's death in 1833 came the First Carlist War (1834–39), fought between conservative forces led by Don Carlos, Fernando's brother, and liberals who supported the claim of Fernando's daughter Isabel (later

Isabel II) to the throne. In 1868 the monarchy was overthrown during the Septembrina Revolution and Isabel II was forced to flee. The First Republic was declared in 1873, but within 18 months the army had restored the monarchy, with Isabel's son Alfonso XII on the throne. Despite political turmoil Spain's economy prospered in the second half of the 19th century, fuelled by industrialisation.

The disastrous Spanish-American War of 1898 marked the end of the Spanish empire. Spain was defeated by the USA and lost its last overseas possessions – Cuba, Puerto Rico, Guam and the Philippines.

The 20th Century
The early 20th century was characterised by military disasters in Morocco and growing instability as radical forces struggled to overthrow the established order. In 1923, with Spain on the brink of civil war, Miguel Primo de Rivera made himself military dictator, ruling until 1930. In 1931 Alfonso XIII fled the country, and the Second Republic was declared.

Like its predecessor, the Second Republic fell victim to internal conflict. The 1936 elections split the nation in two, with the Popular Front (an uneasy alliance of leftist parties) on one side and the right-wing Nationalists (an alliance of the army, Church and the fascist-style Falange Party) on the other.

Nationalist plotters in the army rose against the government in July 1936. During the subsequent Spanish Civil War (1936–39), the Nationalists, led by General Francisco Franco, received heavy military support from Nazi Germany and fascist Italy, while the elected Republican government received support only from Russia and, to a lesser degree, from the International Brigades, made up of foreign leftists.

By 1939 Franco had won and an estimated 350,000 Spaniards had died. After the war, thousands of Republicans were executed, jailed or forced into exile. Franco's 35-year dictatorship began with Spain isolated internationally and crippled by recession. It wasn't until the 1950s and 1960s, when the rise in tourism and a treaty with the USA combined to provide much-needed funds, that the country began to recover. By the 1970s Spain had the fastest-growing economy in Europe.

Franco died in 1975, having named Juan Carlos, the grandson of Alfonso XIII, as his successor. King Juan Carlos is widely credited with having overseen Spain's transition from dictatorship to democracy. The first elections were held in 1977, a new constitution was drafted in 1978, and a failed military coup in 1981 was seen as a futile attempt to turn back the clock. Spain joined the European Community in 1986 and celebrated its return to the world stage in style in 1992, with Expo '92 in Seville and the Olympic Games in Barcelona.

Spain Today
In 1996 the centre-right Partido Popular (Popular Party; PP), led by José María Aznar, won a plurality in parliament and began a programme of economic decentralisation and liberalisation. In 1997 Spain became fully integrated in the North Atlantic Treaty Organisation (NATO), and in 1999 it met the criteria for launching the euro, the new European currency.

By the time of the 2000 general election, Spain enjoyed the fastest-growing economy in the EU. The torrid economic pace gained widespread support for Aznar's policies, leading to an absolute majority in both parliamentary houses for his PP. Aznar has since continued his programme of labour-market reform and promotion of competition.

Spain assumed the rotating presidency of the EU moments before 1 January 2002, thus presiding over the Euro zone's official transition to the new cash currency.

GEOGRAPHY & ECOLOGY
Spain is probably Europe's most geographically diverse country, with landscapes ranging from the near-deserts of Almería to the green, Wales-like countryside and deep coastal inlets of Galicia, and from the sun-baked plains of Castilla-La Mancha to the rugged mountains of the Pyrenees.

The country covers 84% of the Iberian Peninsula and spreads over some 505,000 sq km, more than half of which is high tableland, the *meseta*. This is supported and divided by several mountain chains. The main ones are the Pyrenees, along the border with France; the Cordillera Cantábrica, backing the northern coast; the Sistema Ibérico, from the central north towards the middle Mediterranean coast; the Cordillera Central, from north of Madrid towards the Portuguese border; and three east-west chains across Andalucía, one of which is the highest range of all – the Sierra Nevada.

The major rivers are the Ebro, Duero, Tajo (Tagus), Guadiana and Guadalquivir, each draining a different basin between the mountains and all flowing into the Atlantic Ocean (except for the Ebro, which reaches the Mediterranean Sea).

CLIMATE

The *meseta* and Ebro basin have a continental climate: scorching in summer, cold in winter, and always dry. Madrid regularly freezes from December through February, and temperatures climb above 30°C in July and August. The Guadalquivir basin in Andalucía is only a little wetter and positively broils in high summer, with temperatures in Seville that kill people every year. This area doesn't get as cold as the *meseta* in winter.

The Pyrenees and the Cordillera Cantábrica backing the Bay of Biscay coast bear the brunt of cold northern and northwestern airstreams. Even in high summer you never know when you might get a shower. The Mediterranean coast and Balearic Islands get a little more rain than Madrid, and the southern coast can be even hotter in summer. The Mediterranean also provides Spain's warmest waters (reaching 27°C or so in August), and you can swim as early as April or even late March in the southeast.

In general you can rely on pleasant or hot temperatures just about everywhere from April to early November (plus March in the south, but minus a month at either end on the northern and northwestern coasts). Snowfalls in the mountains start as early as October and some snow cover lasts all year on the highest peaks.

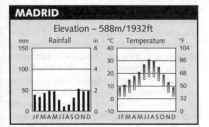

FLORA & FAUNA

The brown bear, wolf, lynx and wild boar all survive in Spain, although only the boar exists in healthy numbers. Spain's high mountains harbour the goat-like chamois and Spanish ibex (the latter is rare) and big birds of prey such as eagles, vultures and the lammergeier. The marshy Ebro delta and Guadalquivir estuary are important for waterbirds, among them the spectacular greater flamingo. Many of Spain's 5500 seed-bearing plants occur nowhere else in Europe because of the barrier of the Pyrenees. Spring wildflowers are magnificent in many country and hilly areas.

The conservation picture has improved by leaps and bounds in the past 25 years and Spain now has 25,000 sq km of protected areas, including 10 national parks. But overgrazing, reservoir creation, tourism, housing developments, agricultural and industrial effluent, fires and hunting all still threaten plant and animal life.

GOVERNMENT & POLITICS

Spain is a constitutional monarchy. The 1978 constitution restored parliamentary government and grouped the country's 50 provinces into 17 autonomous communities, each with its own regional government. Since 1996 Spain has been governed by the right-of-centre Partido Popular (PP), led by José María Aznar, which unseated the long-standing centre-left PSOE party. With a strong mandate from the people in the 2000 elections, the PP enjoys popularity never before seen for a conservative party in democratic Spain.

Spain's government has long been embroiled in a campaign against the Basque separatist movement of ETA (see the País Vasco, Navarra & Aragón section later in this chapter). Although ETA's support and funding has dried up somewhat in recent years, it has pressed on with its agenda, most recently detonating two car bombs in Madrid on 1 May 2002.

ECONOMY

Spain experienced an amazing economic turnabout in the 20th century, raising its living standards from the lowest in Western Europe to a level comparable to the rest of the continent. Recession hit in the early 1990s, although an initially slow recovery sped up by the end of the decade. At 15%, unemployment is among the highest in Western Europe.

Service industries employ over six million people and produce close to 60% of the country's GDP. The arrival of over 50 million tourists every year brings work to around 10% of the entire labour force. Industry accounts for about one-third of both work-force and GDP, but agriculture accounts for only 4% of GDP compared with 23% in 1960, although it employs one in 10 workers.

POPULATION & PEOPLE

Spain has a population of 40 million, de-scended from all the many peoples who have settled here over the millennia, among them Iberians, Celts, Romans, Jews, Visigoths, Berbers and Arabs. The biggest cities are Madrid (three million), Barcelona (1.5 million), Valencia (746,610) and Seville (702,520). Each region proudly preserves its own unique culture, and some – Catalunya and the País Vasco in particular – display a fiercely independent spirit.

ARTS
Cinema

Early Spanish cinema was hamstrung by a lack of funds and technology, and perhaps the greatest of all Spanish directors, Luis Buñuel, made his silent surrealist classics *Un Chien Andalou* (1928) and *L'Age d'Or* (1930) in France. However, he returned to Spain to make *Tierra sin Pan* (Land Without Bread; 1932), a film about rural poverty in Las Hurdes area of Extremadura.

Franco's regime saw strict censorship, but satirical and uneasy films such as Juan Antonio Bardem's *Muerte de un Ciclista* (Death of a Cyclist; 1955) and Luis Berlanga's *Bien-venido Mr Marshall* (Welcome Mr Marshall; 1953) still managed to appear. Carlos Saura, with films like *Ana y los Lobos* (Anna and the Wolves; 1973), and Victor Erice, with *El Espiritu de la Colmena* (Spirit of the Beehive; 1973) and *El Sur* (The South; 1983), looked at the problems of young people scarred by the Spanish Civil War and its aftermath.

After Franco, Pedro Almodóvar broke away from this serious cinema dwelling on the past with humorous films set amid the so-cial and artistic revolution of the late 1970s and 1980s, notably *Mujeres al Borde de un Ataque de Nervios* (Women on the Verge of a Nervous Breakdown; 1988). In 1995 Ken Loach produced a moving co-production on the Spanish Civil War, *Tierra y Libertad* (Land and Freedom).

Painting

The golden age of Spanish art (1550–1650) was strongly influenced by Italy, but the great Spanish artists developed their talents in unique ways. The giants were Toledo-based El Greco (originally from Crete) and Diego Velázquez, perhaps Spain's most revered painter. Both excelled with insightful portraits. Francisco Zurbarán and Bartolomé Esteban Murillo were also prominent. The genius of the 18th and 19th centuries was Francisco Goya, whose versatility ranged from unflat-tering royal portraits and anguished war scenes to bullfight etchings.

Catalunya was the powerhouse of early-20th-century Spanish art, engendering the hugely prolific Pablo Picasso (born in An-dalucía), the colourful symbolist Joan Miró, and Salvador Dalí, who was obsessed with the unconscious and weird. Works by these and other major Spanish artists can be found in galleries throughout the country.

Architecture

Spain's earliest architectural relics are the prehistoric monuments on Menorca. Re-minders of Roman times include the ruins of Mérida and Tarragona, and Segovia's amaz-ing aqueduct. The Muslims left behind some of the most splendid buildings in the entire Islamic world, including Granada's delight-ful Alhambra, Córdoba's mosque and Seville's alcázar – the latter is an example of *mudéjar* architecture, the name given to Moorish work done throughout Christian-held territory.

The first main Christian architectural movement was Romanesque, in the north in the 11th and 12th centuries. Surviving mani-festations include countless lovely country churches and several cathedrals, notably that of Santiago de Compostela. Later came the many great Gothic cathedrals (such as Toledo, Barcelona, León, Salamanca and Seville) of the 13th to 16th centuries, as well as Renais-sance styles, such as the plateresque work so prominent in Salamanca and the austere work of Juan de Herrera, responsible for El Escor-ial (see the Around Madrid section). Spain then followed the usual path to baroque (17th and 18th centuries) and neoclassicism (19th century) before Catalunya produced its start-ling modernist (roughly Art Nouveau) move-ment around the turn of the 20th century, of which Antoni Gaudí's Sagrada Família church is the most stunning example. More recent architecture is likely to excite only specialists.

Literature

One of the earliest works of Spanish literature is the *Cantar de mío Cid* (Song of My Cid), an anonymous epic poem describing the life of El Cid, an 11th-century Christian knight. Miguel de Cervantes' novel *Don Quixote de la Mancha* is the masterpiece of the literary flowering of the 16th and 17th centuries, as well as one of the world's great works of fiction. The playwrights Lope de Vega and Pedro Calderón de la Barca were also leading lights of the age.

The next high point, in the early 20th century, grew out of the crisis of the Spanish-American War that spawned the intellectual 'Generation of '98'. Philosophical essayist Miguel de Unamuno was prominent, but the towering figure was poet and playwright Federico García Lorca, whose tragedies *Bodas de Sangre* (Blood Weddings) and *Yerma* (Barren) won international acclaim before he was murdered in the Civil War for his Republican sympathies.

Camilo José Cela, author of the civil-war-aftermath novel *La Familia de Pascal Duarte* (The Family of Pascal Duarte), won the 1989 Nobel Prize for literature. Juan Goytisolo is probably the major contemporary writer; his most approachable work is his autobiography, *Forbidden Territory*. There has been a proliferation of women – particularly feminist writers – during the past 25 years, among whose prominent representatives are Adelaide Morales, Ana María Matute and Rosa Montero.

SOCIETY & CONDUCT

Most Spaniards are economical with etiquette, but this does not signify unfriendliness. They're gregarious people, on the whole very tolerant and easy-going towards foreigners. It's not easy to give offence. However, obviously disrespectful behaviour, including excessively casual dress in churches, won't go down well.

Siesta

Contrary to popular belief, most Spaniards do not sleep in the afternoon. The siesta is generally devoted to a long, leisurely lunch and lingering conversation. Then again, if you've stayed out until 5am...

Flamenco

Getting to see real, deeply emotional flamenco can be hard, as it tends to happen semispontaneously in little bars. Andalucía is its traditional home. You'll find plenty of clubs there and elsewhere offering flamenco shows; these are generally aimed at tourists and are expensive, but some are good. Your best chance of catching the real thing is probably at one of the flamenco festivals in the south, usually held in summer.

RELIGION

Only about 20% of Spaniards are regular churchgoers, but Catholicism is deeply ingrained in the culture. As the writer Unamuno said, 'Here in Spain we are all Catholics, even the atheists'.

Many Spaniards have a deep-seated scepticism of the Church; during the Civil War, churches were burnt and clerics shot because they represented repression, corruption and the old order.

LANGUAGE

Spanish, or Castilian *(Castellano)*, as it is often and more precisely called, is spoken by just about all Spaniards, but there are also three widely spoken regional languages. Catalan (another Romance language, closely related to Spanish and French) is spoken by about two-thirds of people in Catalunya and the Balearic Islands and half the people in the Valencia region; Galician (another Romance language that sounds like a cross between Spanish and Portuguese) is spoken by many in the northwest; and Basque (of mysterious, non-Latin origin) is spoken by a minority in the País Vasco and Navarra.

English isn't as widely spoken as many travellers seem to expect. In the principal cities and tourist areas it's not too difficult to find people who speak at least some English, though generally you'll be better received if you at least try to communicate in Spanish.

See the Language chapter at the back of the book for pronunciation guidelines and useful words and phrases.

Facts for the Visitor

HIGHLIGHTS
Beaches

It's still possible to have a beach to yourself in Spain, although summertime makes the task tricky. Such gems as the beaches of Cabo Favàritx in Menorca and some of the secluded

SPAIN

coves on Cabo de Gata in Andalucía are bound to be quiet. There are also good, relatively uncrowded beaches on the Costa de la Luz, between Tarifa and Cádiz. On the Galician coast, between Noia and Pontevedra, are literally hundreds of beaches where even in mid-August you won't feel claustrophobic.

Museums & Galleries

Spain has some of the world's finest art galleries. The Prado in Madrid has few rivals, and there are outstanding galleries in Bilbao, Seville, Barcelona, Valencia and Córdoba. Fascinating smaller galleries, such as the Dalí museum in Figueres and the abstract art museum in Cuenca, also abound. Tarragona and Teruel have great archaeological museums.

Buildings

Don't miss Andalucía's Muslim-era gems – Granada's Alhambra, Seville's alcázar and Córdoba's Mezquita – or Barcelona's extraordinary Sagrada Família. The fairy-tale alcázar in Segovia has to be seen to be believed.

For even more exciting views, and loads of medieval ghosts, visit the ruined castle in Morella, Valencia province, or fast-forward to 1997 and hit Bilbao's spectacular Guggenheim museum, whose wavy exterior steals the show from the contemporary art within.

Scenery

Outstanding mountain scenery and highly picturesque villages characterise the Pyrenees and Picos de Europa in the north and parts of Andalucía, such as the Alpujarras. On the coasts, the rugged inlets of Galicia and stark, hilly Cabo de Gata, Andalucía, stand out.

SUGGESTED ITINERARIES

If you want to whizz around as many places as possible in a limited time, the following itineraries might suit you:

Two days
  Fly to Madrid, Barcelona or Seville, or nip into Barcelona or San Sebastián overland from France.
One week
  Spend two days each in Barcelona, Madrid and Seville, allowing one day for travel.
Two weeks
  As above, plus San Sebastián, Toledo, Salamanca or Cuenca, Granada or Córdoba, and maybe Cáceres or Trujillo if you're feeling frisky.

One month
  As above, plus some of the following: side trips from the cities mentioned above; an exploration of the north, including Santiago de Compostela and the Picos de Europa; visits to Teruel, Mallorca, Formentera, Segovia and Ávila, or some smaller towns and more remote regions such as Northeast Extremadura or Cabo de Gata.

PLANNING
When to Go

For most purposes the ideal months to visit Spain are May, June and September (plus April and October in the south). At these times you can rely on good weather, yet avoid the extreme heat and crush of Spanish and foreign tourists in July and August, when temperatures may climb to 45°C in parts of Andalucía and Madrid is unbearably hot and almost deserted.

The summer overflows with festivals, including Sanfermines (think Pamplona's running of the bulls) and Semana Grande all along the northern coast (dates vary from place to place), but there's no shortage of excellent festivals during the rest of the year.

Winter brings unceasing rains (except when it snows) to the north. Madrid regularly freezes from December through February. At these times Andalucía is the place to be, with temperatures reaching the mid-teens in most places and there's good skiing in the Sierra Nevada.

Maps

Some of the best maps for travellers are published by Michelin, which produces a 1:1,000,000 *Spain & Portugal* map and six 1:400,000 regional maps. The country map doesn't show railway lines, but the regional maps do.

What to Bring

You can buy anything you need in Spain, but some articles, such as sunscreen, are more expensive than elsewhere. Books in English tend to be expensive and hard to find outside main cities.

A pair of strong shoes and a towel are essential. A moneybelt or shoulder wallet can be useful in big cities. Bring sunglasses if glare gets to you. If you want to blend in, pack more than T-shirts, shorts and runners (sneakers) – Spaniards are quite dressy, and many tourists look like slobs to them.

TOURIST OFFICES

Most towns and large villages of any interest have an *oficina de turismo* (tourist office). These will supply you with a map and brochures with basic information on local sights, attractions, accommodation, history etc. Staffs are generally helpful and often speak some English. A **nationwide phone line** (☎ 901 30 06 00; *open 9am-6pm daily*) offers information in English.

Tourist Offices Abroad

Spain has tourist information centres in 29 countries, including the following:

Canada (☎ 416-961 3131; e toronto@tour spain.es) 2 Bloor St W, 34th floor, Toronto, Ontario M4W 3E2

France (☎ 01-45 03 82 57; e paris@tourspain .es) 43 Rue Decamps, 75784 Paris, Cedex 16

Portugal (☎ 01-21 354 1992; e lisboa@tour spain.es) Avenida Sidónio Pais 28 3 Dto, 1050-215 Lisbon

UK (☎ 020-7486 8077, brochure request ☎ 090-6364 0630 at UK£0.60 a minute; e londres@ tourspain.es) 22–23 Manchester Square, London W1M 5AP)

USA (☎ 212-265 8822; e oetny@tourspain.es) 666 Fifth Ave, 35th floor, New York, NY 10103

VISAS & DOCUMENTS

Citizens of EU countries can enter Spain with their national identity card or passport. UK citizens must have a full passport, not just a British visitor passport. Non-EU nationals must take their passport.

EU, Norway and Iceland citizens do not need a visa. Nationals of Australia, Canada, Israel, Japan, New Zealand, Switzerland and the USA need no visa for stays of up to 90 days but must have a passport valid for the whole visit. This 90-day limit applies throughout the EU, so don't overstay your time in the EU. South Africans are among nationalities that do need a visa.

It's best to obtain the visa in your country of residence. Single-entry visas are available in flavours of 30-day and 90-day, and there's a 90-day multiple-entry visa, too, though if you apply in a country where you're not resident the 90-day option may not be available. Multiple-entry visas will save you a lot of time and trouble if you plan to leave Spain (say to Gibraltar or Morocco), then re-enter it.

Spain is one of the Schengen Area countries; the others are Portugal, Italy, France, Germany, Austria, the Netherlands, Belgium, Luxembourg, Sweden, Finland, Denmark and Greece. A visa for one Schengen country is valid for the others. Compare validity, prices and permitted entries before applying. Schengen countries theoretically have done away with passport control on travel between them.

Stays of Longer than 90 Days

EU, Norway and Iceland nationals planning to stay in Spain more than 90 days are supposed to apply during their first month in the country for a residence card. This is a lengthy, complicated procedure; if you intend to subject yourself to it, consult a Spanish consulate before you go to Spain, as you'll need to take certain documents with you.

Other nationalities on a Schengen visa are flat out of luck when it comes to extensions. For stays of longer than 90 days you're supposed to get a residence card. This is a nightmarish process, starting with a residence visa issued by a Spanish consulate in your country of residence; start the process well in advance.

EMBASSIES & CONSULATES
Spanish Embassies & Consulates

Spanish embassies include:

Australia (☎ 02-6273 3555;
    e embespau@mail.mae.es) 15 Arkana St, Yarralumba, ACT 2600
    Consulates in Brisbane, Melbourne, Perth and Sydney
Canada (☎ 613-747 2252;
    e spain@DocuWeb.ca) 74 Stanley Ave, Ottawa, Ontario K1M 1P4
    Consulate in Montreal (☎ 514-935 5235)
    Consulate in Toronto (☎ 416-977 1661)
France (☎ 01 44 43 18 00;
    e ambespfr@mail.mae.es) 22 Avenue Marceau, 75381 Paris, Cedex 08
Portugal (☎ 01-347 2381;
    e embesppt@mail.mae.es) Rua do Salitre 1, 1250 Lisbon
UK (☎ 020-7235 5555;
    e espemblon@espemblon.freeserve.co.uk) 39 Chesham Place, London SW1X 8SB
    Consulates in Belfast, Edinburgh, Liverpool and Manchester
USA (☎ 202-452 0100) 2375 Pennsylvania Ave NW, Washington, DC 20037
    Consulates in Albuquerque, Atlanta, Baltimore, Boston, Chicago, Cincinnati, Corpus Christi, Dallas, El Paso, Honolulu, Houston, Kansas City, Los Angeles, Miami, New Orleans, New York, Saint Louis, San Antonio, San Diego, San Francisco and Seattle

SPAIN

Embassies & Consulates in Spain

Some 70 countries have embassies in Madrid, including:

Australia (☎ 91 441 93 00) Plaza del Descubridor Diego de Ordás 3-28003, Edificio Santa Engrácia 120

Canada (☎ 91 431 43 00) Calle de Núñez de Balboa 35

France (☎ 91 423 89 00) Calle de Salustiano Olózaga 9

Germany (☎ 91 557 90 00) Calle de Fortuny 8

Ireland (☎ 91 576 35 00) Paseo de la Castellana 36

Japan (☎ 91 590 76 00) Calle de Serrano 109

Morocco (☎ 91 563 10 90) Calle de Serrano 179
Consulate: (☎ 91 561 21 45) Calle de Leizaran 31

New Zealand (☎ 91 523 02 26) Plaza de la Lealtad 3

Portugal (☎ 91 561 78 00) Calle de Pinar 1
Consulate: (☎ 91 445 46 00) Calle Martínez Campos 11

UK (☎ 91 700 82 00) Calle de Fernando el Santo 16
Consulate: (☎ 91 308 52 01) Edificio Colón, Calle del Marqués Ensenada 16

USA (☎ 91 587 22 00) Calle de Serrano 75

CUSTOMS

From outside the EU you are allowed to bring in duty-free one bottle of spirits, one bottle of wine, 50mL of perfume and 200 cigarettes. From within the EU you can bring 2L of wine *and* 1L of spirits, with the same limits on the rest. Duty-free allowances for travel between EU countries were abolished in 1999.

MONEY
Currency & Exchange Rates

Like in the rest of the euro zone, Spain's currency is now the euro (€). See Money in the introductory Facts for the Visitor chapter for more information on this sparkly new medium of exchange, including exchange rates.

Banks mostly open 8.30am to 2pm Monday to Friday and 8.30am to 1pm Saturday and tend to give better exchange rates than do currency-exchange offices. Travellers cheques attract a slightly better rate than cash. ATMs accepting a wide variety of cards are common.

Costs

Spain is one of Western Europe's more affordable countries. If you are particularly frugal, it's possible to scrape by on €20 to €30 a day. This would involve staying in the cheapest possible accommodation, avoiding eating in restaurants or going to museums or bars, and not moving around too much. Places such as Madrid, Barcelona, Seville and San Sebastián will place a greater strain on your moneybelt.

A more reasonable budget would be €50 a day. This would allow you €20 for accommodation, €20 for meals, €2 for public transport and €5 for entry fees to museum, sights or entertainment...and a bit left over for a drink or two and intercity travel.

Students (and sometimes seniors) are entitled to discounts of up to 50% on admission fees and about 30% on transportation.

Tipping & Bargaining

In restaurants, prices include a service charge, and tipping is a matter of personal choice – most people leave some small change, and 5% is plenty. It's common to leave small change in bars and cafés. The only places in Spain where you are likely to bargain are markets and, occasionally, cheap hotels, particularly if you're staying for a few days.

Consumer Taxes & Refunds

In Spain, VAT (value-added tax) is known as *impuesto sobre el valor añadido* (IVA). On accommodation and restaurant prices, there's a flat IVA of 7%, which is usually, but not always, included in quoted prices. To check, ask if the price is 'con IVA' (with VAT).

On retail goods, alcohol, electrical appliances etc IVA is 16%. Visitors are entitled to a refund of IVA on any item costing more than €90 that they are taking out of the EU. Ask the shop for a Europe Tax-Free Shopping Cheque when you buy, then present the goods and cheque to customs when you leave. If they can't offer a cheque, get an official receipt with the business's address and a description of the item purchased. Customs stamps the cheque and you then cash it at a booth with the 'Cash Refund' sign. There are booths at all main Spanish airports; at the border crossings at Algeciras, Gibraltar and Andorra; and at similar points throughout the EU.

POST & COMMUNICATIONS
Post

Main post offices in provincial capitals are usually open about 8.30am to 8.30pm Monday to Friday and about 9am to 1.30pm Saturday.

Stamps are also sold at *estancos* (tobacco shops with the 'Tabacos' sign in yellow letters on a maroon background). A standard airmail letter or card costs €0.25 within Spain, €0.50 to the rest of Europe, and €0.75 to the rest of the world.

Mail to/from Europe normally takes up to a week, and to North America, Australia or New Zealand around 10 days, but there may be some unaccountable long delays.

Poste-restante mail can be addressed to you at either *poste restante* or *lista de correos*, the Spanish name for it, at the city in question. It's a fairly reliable system, although mail may well arrive late. Unfortunately, American Express (AmEx) no longer offers free client mail service.

Common abbreviations used in Spanish addresses are 1, 2, 3 etc, which mean 1st, 2nd and 3rd floor, and 's/n' *(sin número)*, which means that the building has no number.

Telephone & Fax

Area codes in Spain are an integral part of the phone number; all numbers are nine digits long, without area codes.

Blue public pay phones are common and easy to use. They accept coins, phonecards *(tarjetas telefónicas)* and, in some cases, credit cards. Phonecards come in 1000 and 2000 ptas denominations and are available at main post offices and *estancos*. (At the time of research prices were still given in pesetas. Future new cards should be in denominations of €5, €10 and €20.)

A one-minute call from a pay phone costs €0.06 within a local area, €0.13 to other places in the same province, €0.16 to other provinces, or €0.18 to another EU country or the USA. Australia and Asia can be reached for €0.93 per minute. Plans are under way to equalise international rates.

Provincial and interprovincial calls, except those to mobile phones, are around 50% cheaper between 8pm and 8am weekdays and all day Saturday and Sunday; local and international calls are around 10% cheaper between 6pm and 8am and all day Saturday and Sunday.

International reverse-charge (collect) calls are simple to make: from a pay phone or private phone, dial ☎ 900 99 00 followed by ☎ 61 for Australia, ☎ 44 for the UK, ☎ 64 for New Zealand, ☎ 15 for Canada, and for the USA ☎ 11 (AT&T) or ☎ 14 (MCI).

Most main post offices have a fax service, but you'll often find cheaper rates at shops or offices with 'Fax Público' signs.

Email & Internet Access

Internet-access points have sprouted up everywhere in major Spanish cities and towns. Larger cities even sport 24-hour Internet cafés. Charges for an hour online range anywhere from €0.50 to €4.

DIGITAL RESOURCES

There are thousands of websites devoted to travelling in Spain, and a search on ⓦ www .google.com will bring up many useful ones. Spain's official tourist site is at ⓦ www.tour spain.es. The British embassy maintains an excellent site at ⓦ www.britishembassy .org.uy/dslc/Websites.htm, with a list of links to Spanish press and cultural sites. For cultural and practical information on the country (eg, lists of festivals, types of accommodation) check out ⓦ www.okspain.org. Although ⓦ www.spainview.com is aimed at journalists and editors, it offers links to a wealth of information on the country.

BOOKS

The New Spaniards by John Hooper is a fascinating account of modern Spanish society and culture. For a readable and thorough, but not overlong, survey of Spanish history pick up *The Story of Spain* by Mark Williams.

Classic accounts of life and travel in Spain include Gerald Brenan's *South from Granada* (1920s), Laurie Lee's *As I Walked Out One Midsummer Morning* (1930s), George Orwell's *Homage to Catalunya* (the Civil War) and James Michener's *Iberia* (1960s). Among the best of more recent books are *Homage to Barcelona* by Colm Toíbín; *Spanish Journeys* by Adam Hopkins; and *Cities of Spain* by David Gilmour.

Of foreign literature set in Spain, Ernest Hemingway's Civil War novel *For Whom the Bell Tolls* is a must. *The Sun Also Rises* is partly set in Pamplona.

If you're planning in-depth travels in Spain, get a hold of Lonely Planet's *Spain*.

NEWSPAPERS & MAGAZINES

The major daily newspapers in Spain are solidly liberal *El País*, conservative *ABC*, and *El Mundo*, which specialises in breaking political scandals. There's also a welter of regional dailies, some of the best coming out of Barcelona, the País Vasco and Andalucía.

International press, such as the *International Herald Tribune*, *Time* and *Newsweek*, and daily papers from Western European countries reach major cities and tourist areas on the day of publication; elsewhere they're harder to find and arrive a day or two later.

RADIO & TV

Numerous radio stations occupy the FM band. You'll hear a substantial proportion of British and American music. The national pop/rock station, RNE 3, has well-varied programming.

Spaniards are Europe's greatest TV watchers after the British, but they do a lot of this watching in bars and cafés, which makes it more of a social activity. Most TVs receive six channels: two state-run (TVE1 and La2), three privately run (Antena 3, Tele 5 and Canal6), and one regional channel. Apart from news, TV seems to consist mostly of game and talk shows, sports, soap operas, sitcoms, and English-language films dubbed into Spanish.

PHOTOGRAPHY & VIDEO

Main brands of film are widely available and processing is fast and generally efficient. A roll of print film (36 exposures, 100 ISO) costs about €4 and can be processed for about €10, though there are often better deals if you have two or three rolls developed together. The equivalent in slide film is around €6 plus the same for processing. Nearly all pre-recorded videos in Spain use the PAL system common to Western Europe, South Asia and Australia. These won't work on most video players in France, North America and Japan.

TIME

Spain is one hour ahead of GMT/UTC during winter, and two hours ahead from the last Sunday in March to the last Sunday in September.

LAUNDRY

Self-service laundrettes are rare. Laundries (*lavanderías*) are common but not particularly cheap. They will usually wash, dry and fold a load for €8 to €10.

TOILETS

Public toilets are not very common in Spain. The easiest thing to do is head for a café. It is polite to buy something in exchange for using their toilets.

WOMEN TRAVELLERS

As almost everywhere, women should be ready to ignore stares, catcalls and unnecessary comments. However, Spain has one of the lowest incidences of reported rape in the developed world, and physical harassment is relatively infrequent.

The **Asociación de Asistencia a Mujeres Violadas** (☎ 91 574 01 10; *Calle de O'Donnell 42 bajo, Madrid; open 10am-2pm & 4pm-7pm Mon-Fri, recorded message at other times*) offers advice and help to rape victims and can provide details of similar centres in other cities, though only limited English is spoken.

GAY & LESBIAN TRAVELLERS

Attitudes towards gays and lesbians are pretty tolerant, especially in the cities. Madrid, Barcelona, Sitges, Ibiza and Cádiz all have active gay and lesbian scenes. A good source of information on gay and lesbian places and organisations throughout Spain is **Coordinadora Gai-Lesbiana** (☎ 93 298 00 29, fax 93 298 06 18; **W** *www.co gailes.org; Carrer de Finlandia 45, E08014 Barcelona*). In Madrid, the equivalent is **Cogam** (☎/fax 91 522 45 17, toll-free throughout Spain ☎ 900 601 601 6pm-10pm daily; Calle del Fuencarral 37, 28004 Madrid).

DISABLED TRAVELLERS

Spain is an increasingly wheelchair-friendly country to visit. Spanish tourist offices in other countries can provide a basic information sheet with some useful addresses, and give information on accessible accommodation in specific places. **Inserso** (☎ 91 347 88 88; *Calle de Ginzo de Limea 58, 28029 Madrid)* is the government department for the disabled, with branches in all of Spain's 50 provinces.

You'll find some wheelchair-accessible accommodation in main centres, but many budget establishments lack lifts and ramps. Most Hostelling International–affiliated youth hostels are suitable for wheelchair users.

SENIOR TRAVELLERS

Veterans of life will find Spain a welcoming and accessible destination. There are reduced prices for people aged over 60, 63 or 65 (depending on the place) at some attractions and occasionally on transport.

USEFUL ORGANISATIONS

The travel agency **TIVE** *(☎ 91 543 74 12, fax 91 544 00 62; Calle de Fernando El Católico 88, Madrid)* has offices in major cities throughout Spain. It specialises in discounted tickets and travel arrangements for students and young people.

DANGERS & ANNOYANCES

In large cities, keep valuables close and wear a moneybelt or neck pouch. Always beware of pickpockets and bag-snatchers. Muggings have been on the rise recently in Barcelona, so take extra care in that city.

It's a good idea to take your car radio and any other valuables with you any time you leave your car, leaving nothing at all visible within. In youth hostels, don't leave belongings unattended, as there is a high incidence of theft.

LEGAL MATTERS

Spaniards no longer enjoy liberal drug laws. No matter what anyone tells you, it is not legal to smoke dope in public bars. There is a reasonable degree of tolerance when it comes to people having a smoke in their own home, but not in hotel rooms or guesthouses.

If arrested in Spain you have the right to an attorney and to know the reason you are being held. You may also request to make a phone call.

BUSINESS HOURS

Generally, people work Monday to Friday from 9am to 2pm and then again from 4.30pm or 5pm for another three hours. Shops and travel agencies are usually open these hours on Saturday, too, though some may skip the evening session. Museums all have their own unique opening hours; major ones tend to open for something like normal business hours (with or without the afternoon break), but often have their weekly closing day on Monday, not Sunday.

Emergency Services

The emergency number for the police, medical and fire services is ☎ 112. You can also call the police direct on ☎ 091. See Car & Motorcycle in the introductory Getting Around section later in this chapter for information regarding roadside assistance in the event of breakdown.

PUBLIC HOLIDAYS & SPECIAL EVENTS

Spain has at least 14 official holidays a year, some observed nationwide, some very local. When a holiday falls close to a weekend, Spaniards like to make a *puente* (bridge), taking the intervening day off, too. The holidays listed following are observed virtually everywhere:

New Year's Day 1 January
Epiphany or Three Kings' Day (when children receive presents) 6 January
Good Friday before Easter Sunday
Labour Day 1 May
Feast of the Assumption 15 August
National Day 12 October
All Saints' Day 1 November
Feast of the Immaculate Conception 8 December
Christmas 25 December

The two main periods when Spaniards go on holiday are Semana Santa (the week leading up to Easter Sunday) and the month of August. At these times accommodation in resorts can be scarce and transport heavily booked, but other cities are often half-empty.

Fiestas & Festivals

Spaniards indulge their love of colour, noise, crowds and partying at innumerable local fiestas and *ferias* (fairs); even small villages will have at least one, probably several, during the year. Many fiestas are based on religion. Local tourist offices can always supply detailed information.

Among festivals to look out for are La Tamborada in San Sebastián (20 January), when the whole town dresses up and goes berserk; *carnaval*, a time of fancy-dress parades and merrymaking celebrated around the country about seven weeks before Easter (wildest in Cádiz and Sitges); Valencia's week-long mid-March party, Las Fallas de San José, with all-night dancing and drinking, first-class fireworks and processions; Semana Santa, with its parades of holy images and huge crowds, notably in Seville; Seville's Feria de Abril, a week-long party held in late April, a kind of counterbalance to the religious peak of Semana Santa; Sanfermines, with the running of the bulls, in Pamplona in July; Semana Grande, another week of heavy drinking and hangovers, all along the northern coast during the first half of August; and Barcelona's week-long party, the Festes de la Mercè, around 24 September.

SPAIN

ACTIVITIES
Surfing & Windsurfing
The País Vasco has good surf spots, including San Sebastián, Zarauz and the legendary left at Mundaca, among others. Tarifa, Spain's southernmost point, is a windsurfer's heaven, with constant breezes and long, empty beaches.

Skiing
In Spain, skiing is cheap, and facilities and conditions are good. The season runs from December to May. The most accessible resorts are in the Sierra Nevada (very close to Granada), the Pyrenees (north of Barcelona) and in the ranges north of Madrid. Contact tourist offices in these cities for information. Affordable day trips can be booked through travel agents.

Cycling
Bike touring isn't as common as in other parts of Europe because of deterrents such as the often-mountainous terrain and summer heat. It's a more viable option on the Balearic Islands than on much of the mainland, although plenty of people get on their bikes in spring and autumn in the south. Mountain biking is increasingly popular, and areas such as Andalucía and Catalunya have many good tracks. Finding bikes to rent is a hit-and-miss affair, so it's best to bring your own.

Hiking
Spain is a trekker's paradise, so much so that Lonely Planet has published a guide to some of the best treks in the country, *Walking in Spain.* See also the Mallorca and Picos de Europa sections of this chapter. Walking country roads and paths, between settlements, can also be highly enjoyable and a great way to meet the locals.

Two organisations publish detailed close-up maps of small parts of Spain. The CNIG covers most of the country in 1:25,000 (1cm to 250m) sheets, most of which are recent. The CNIG and the Servicio Geográfico del Ejército (SGE; Army Geographic Service) each publish a 1:50,000 series; the SGE's tends to be more up to date, as the maps were published in the mid-1980s. Also useful for hiking and exploring some areas are the *Guía Cartográfica* and *Guía Excursionista y Turística* series published by Editorial Alpina. The series combines information booklets in Spanish (or sometimes Catalan) with detailed maps at scales ranging from 1:25,000 to 1:50,000, well worth their price (around €4). You may well find CNIG, SGE and Alpina publications in local bookshops, but it's more reliable to get them in advance from specialist map or travel shops like Altaïr and Quera in Barcelona.

If you fancy a really long walk, there's the Camino de Santiago. This route, which has been followed by Christian pilgrims for centuries, can be commenced at various places in France. It then crosses the Pyrenees and runs via Pamplona, Logroño and León all the way to the cathedral in Santiago de Compostela. There are numerous guidebooks explaining the route, and the best map is published by CNIG.

COURSES
The best place to take a language course in Spain is generally at a university. Those with the best reputations include Salamanca, Santiago de Compostela and Santander. It can also be fun to combine study with a stay in one of Spain's most exciting cities, such as Barcelona, Madrid or Seville. There are also hundreds of private language colleges throughout the country; the **Instituto Cervantes** (☎ *020-7235 0353; 102 Eaton Square, London SW1 W9AN; in Spain ☎ 91 436 76 00;* e *informa@cervantes.es; Palacio de la Trinidad, Calle Francisco Silvela 82, Madrid)* can send you lists of these and of universities that run courses. Some Spanish embassies and consulates also can provide information.

Other courses available in Spain include art, cookery and photography. Spanish tourist offices can help with information.

WORK
EU, Norway and Iceland nationals are allowed to work in Spain without a visa, but if they plan to stay more than three months, they are supposed to apply within the first month for a residence card (see Visas & Documents earlier in this chapter). Virtually everyone else is supposed to obtain, from a Spanish consulate in their country of residence, a work permit and, if they plan to stay more than 90 days, a residence visa. These procedures are even more difficult.

That said, quite a few people do manage to work in Spain one way or another – although with Spain's unemployment rate running at around 15%, don't rely on it. Teaching English is an obvious option. A TEFL certificate will be a big help. Another possibility is gaining summer work in a bar or restaurant in a tourist resort, quite a lot of which are run by foreigners.

ACCOMMODATION
Camping
Spain has more than 800 camping grounds. Facilities and settings vary enormously and grounds are officially rated from 1st class to 3rd class. You can expect to pay around €4 each per person, car and tent. Tourist offices can direct you to the nearest camping ground. Many are open all year, though quite a few close from around October to Easter. With certain exceptions (such as many beaches and environmentally protected areas) it is legal to camp outside camping grounds. You'll need permission to camp on private land.

Hostels
Spain's youth hostels (albergues juveniles) are often the cheapest place to stay for lone travellers, but two people can usually get a double room elsewhere for a similar price. With some notable exceptions, hostels are only moderate value. Many have curfews or are closed during the day, or they lack cooking facilities (if so they usually have a cafeteria). They can be short on privacy and are often heavily booked by school groups. Most are members of the country's Hostelling International (HI) organisation **Red Española de Albergues Juveniles** (REAJ; ☎ 91 347 77 00, fax 91 401 81 60; Calle de José Ortega y Gasset 71, 28006 Madrid).

Prices often depend on the season or whether you're aged under 26; typically you pay €10 or more. Some hostels require HI membership; others may charge more if you're not a member. You can buy HI cards for €15 at virtually all hostels.

Pensiones, Hostales & Hotels
Officially, all the establishments are either hotels (from one to five stars), hostales (one to three stars) or pensiones. In practice, there are all sorts of overlapping categories, especially at the budget end of the market. In broad terms, the cheapest are usually fondas and casas de huéspedes, followed by pensiones. All these normally have shared bathrooms and

singles/doubles for €10/15 to €20/25. Some hostales and hostal-residencias come in the same price range, but others have rooms with private bathrooms costing anywhere up to €65 or so. A double in a three-star hotel will run over €100. The luxurious state-run paradores, often converted historic buildings, cost upwards of €200.

Room rates vary by season. It is noted in the individual city sections later in this chapter where seasonal variations are particularly large. July and August, Semana Santa and sometimes Christmas and New Year are the highest seasons. At other times prices in many places go down by 5% to 25%. In many cases you have to add 7% IVA.

FOOD
It's a good idea to reset your stomach's clock in Spain, unless you want to eat alone or with other tourists. Most Spaniards start the day with a light breakfast (desayuno), perhaps coffee with a tostada (piece of buttered toast) or pastel (pastry). Churros con chocolate (long, spiral-shaped deep-fried doughnuts with thick hot chocolate) are a delicious start to the day and unique to Spain.

Lunch (almuerzo or comida) is usually the main meal of the day, eaten between about 1.30pm and 4pm. The evening meal (cena) is usually lighter and may be eaten as late as 10pm or 11pm. It's common (and a great idea!) to go to a bar or café for a snack around 11am and again around 7pm or 8pm.

Spain has a huge variety of local cuisines. Seafood as well as meat is prominent almost everywhere. One of the most characteristic dishes, from the Valencia region, is paella – rice, seafood, the odd vegetable and often chicken or meat, all simmered up together, traditionally coloured yellow with saffron. Another dish, of Andalucían origin, is gazpacho, a soup made from tomatoes, breadcrumbs, cucumber and/or green peppers, eaten cold. Tortillas (omelettes) are an inexpensive stand-by and come in many varieties. Jamón serrano (cured ham) is a treat for meat-eaters.

Cafés & Bars
If you want to follow Spanish habits, you'll be spending plenty of time in cafés and bars, almost all of which offer a range of tapas. These saucer-sized minisnacks are part of the Spanish way of life and come in infinite

varieties, from calamari rings to potato salad to spinach with chickpeas to a small serving of tripe. A typical tapa costs €0.50 to €2 (although sometimes they will come free with your drinks), but check before you order because some are a lot dearer. A *ración* is a meal-sized serving of these snacks; a *media ración* is a half *ración*.

The other popular snacks are *bocadillos*, long filled white bread rolls. Spaniards eat so many bocadillos that some cafés sell nothing else. Try not to leave Spain without sampling a *bocadillo de tortilla de patata*, a roll filled with potato omelette.

You can often save 10% to 20% by ordering and eating food at the bar rather than at a table.

Restaurants

Throughout Spain there are plenty of restaurants serving good, simple food at affordable prices, often featuring regional specialities. Many restaurants offer a *menú del día* – the budget traveller's best friend. For around €5 to €10 you typically get a starter, a main course, dessert, bread and wine – often with a choice of two or three dishes for each course. The *plato combinado* is a near relative of the menú. Such 'combined plates' may include steak and egg with chips and salad, or fried squid with potato salad. You'll pay more for your meals if you order à la carte but the food will be better.

Vegetarian Food

Finding vegetarian fare can be a headache. It's not uncommon for 'meatless' food to be flavoured with meat stock. But in larger cities and important student centres there's a growing awareness of vegetarianism, so that if there isn't a vegetarian restaurant, there are often vegetarian items on menus. A good vegetarian snack at almost any place with bocadillos or sandwiches is a bocadillo (or sandwich) *vegetal*, which has a filling of salad and, often, fried egg (*sin huevo* means 'without egg').

Self-Catering

Every town of any substance has a *mercado* (food market). These are fun and of great value. Even big eaters should be able to put together a filling meal of bread, *chorizo* (spiced sausage), cheese, fruit and a drink for €3 or less. If you shop carefully you can eat three healthy meals a day for as little as €5.

DRINKS

Coffee in Spain is strong. Addicts should specify how they want their fix: *café con leche* is about 50% coffee, 50% hot milk; *café solo* is a short black; *café cortado* is a short black with a little milk.

The most common way to order a beer (*cerveza*) is to ask for a *caña*, which is a small draught beer. *Corto* and, in the País Vasco, *zurrito* are other names for this. A larger beer (about 300mL) is often called a *tubo* or, (in Catalunya) a *jarra*. All these words apply to draught beer (*cerveza de barril*) – if you just ask for a cerveza you're likely to get bottled beer, which is more expensive.

Wine (*vino*) comes in white (*blanco*), red (*tinto*) or rosé (*rosado*). *Tinto de verano*, a kind of wine shandy, is good in summer. There are also many regional grape specialities, such as *jerez* (sherry) in Jerez de la Frontera and *cava* (a sparkling wine) in Catalunya. *Sangría*, a sweet punch made of red wine, fruit and spirits, is refreshing and very popular with tourists.

The cheapest drink of all is, of course, water. To specify tap water (which is safe to drink almost everywhere), just ask for *agua del grifo*.

ENTERTAINMENT

Spain has some of the best nightlife in Europe; wild and *very* late nights, especially on Friday and Saturday, are an integral part of the Spain experience. Many young Spaniards don't even think about going out until midnight or so. Bars, which come in all shapes, sizes and themes, are the main attractions until around 2am or 3am. Some play great music that will get you hopping before you move on to a disco till 5am or 6am. Discos are generally expensive (think covers of €15 to €30), but not to be missed if you like to splurge. Spain's contributions to modern dance music are *bakalao* and *makina*, kinds of frenzied (150bpm to 180bpm) techno.

The live-music scene is less exciting. Spanish rock and pop tends to be imitative, though the bigger cities usually offer a reasonable choice of bands. See the earlier Society & Conduct section for information on flamenco.

Cinemas abound and are good value, though foreign films are usually dubbed into Spanish. To see a film in its original language, look for the 'VO' marking (for *versión original*).

SPECTATOR SPORTS

The national sport is *fútbol* (soccer). The best teams to see for both crowd support and skill level are usually Real Madrid and FC Barcelona, although the atmosphere can be electric anywhere. The season runs from September to May.

Bullfighting is enjoying a resurgence despite continued pressure from international animal-rights activists. It's a complex activity that's regarded as much as an art form as a sport by aficionados. If you decide to see a *corrida de toros* visit from March to October. Madrid, Seville and Pamplona are among the best places to catch a bullfight.

SHOPPING

Many of Spain's best handicrafts are fragile or bulky and inconvenient unless you're going straight home. Pottery comes in a great range of attractive regional varieties. Some lovely rugs and blankets are made in places such as the Alpujarras and Níjar in Andalucía. There's some pleasing woodwork available, too, such as Granada's marquetry boxes and chess sets. Leather jackets, bags and belts are quite good value in many places.

Getting There & Away

AIR

Spain has many international airports, including Madrid, Barcelona, Bilbao, Santiago de Compostela, Seville, Málaga, Almería, Alicante, Valencia, Palma de Mallorca, Ibiza and Maó (Menorca). In general, the cheapest destinations are Málaga, the Balearic Islands, Barcelona and Madrid.

Australia

In general, the best thing to do is to fly to London, Paris, Frankfurt or Rome, then make your way overland. Alternatively, some flight deals to these centres include a couple of short-haul flights within Europe, and Madrid and Barcelona are usually acceptable destinations for these. Some round-the-world (RTW) fares include stops in Spain. STA Travel should be able to help you out with a good price. Generally speaking, a return fare to Europe for under A$1700 is too good to pass up.

The USA & Canada

Return fares to Madrid from Miami, New York, Atlanta or Chicago range from US$700 to US$850 on Iberia or Delta. From the west coast or Canada you are usually looking at about US$100 more. Sales can slash prices down to US$500 or even lower.

The UK

Scheduled flights to Spain are generally expensive, but with the huge range of charter, discount and low-season fares, it's often cheaper to fly than to take a bus or train. Check the travel sections of *TNT* or *Time Out* magazines or the weekend newspapers. Sample destinations from London include Madrid (UK£110 in low season with short notice), Barcelona (UK£130), Ibiza (UK£119) and Málaga (UK£110).

Leaving Spain

For northern Europe, check the ads in local English-language papers in tourist centres such as the Costa del Sol, the Costa Blanca and the Balearic Islands. You may pick up a one-way fare to London for under €90. The youth and student travel agency TIVE (see Useful Organisations earlier in the Facts for the Visitor section of this chapter) and the general travel agency Halcón Viatges, both with branches in most main cities, have some good fares. Generally you're looking at around €95 to €110 one way to London, Amsterdam or Paris, and at least €300 to the USA.

Departure taxes on flights out of Spain, which vary, are factored directly into tickets.

LAND

Bus

There are regular bus services to Spain from all major centres in Europe, including Lisbon, London and Paris. In London, **Eurolines** (☎ *0870-514 3219*) has services at least three times a week to Barcelona (UK£90 one way, 23 to 25 hours), Madrid (UK£80 one way, at least 27 hours) and Málaga (UK£80 one way, 34 hours). Tickets are sold by major travel agencies, and people aged under 26 and senior citizens qualify for a 10% discount. There are also bus services to Morocco from some Spanish cities.

Train

Reaching Spain by train is more expensive than by bus unless you have a rail pass, though fares for those under 26 come close to the bus price. Normal one-way fares from London (using the ferry across the Channel, not Eurostar) to Madrid (via Paris) are under UK£110. For more details, contact the **Rail Europe Travel Centre** (☎ 08705-848848) in London or a travel agent. See the introductory Getting Around chapter for more on rail passes and train travel through Europe.

Car & Motorcycle

If you're driving or riding to Spain from England, you'll have to choose between going through France (check visa requirements) or taking a direct ferry from England to Spain (see the following section). The cheapest way is to take one of the shorter ferries from England to France, then a quick drive down through France.

SEA
The UK

There are two direct ferry services. **Brittany Ferries** (☎ 0870-536 0360 in Britain) runs Plymouth-Santander ferries twice weekly from about mid-March to mid-November (24 hours), and a Portsmouth-Santander service (30 hours), usually once a week, in other months. **P&O European Ferries** (☎ 08702-424999 in Britain) runs Portsmouth-Bilbao ferries twice weekly, on Monday and Thursday, almost year-round (35 hours). Prices on all services are similar: one-way passenger fares range from about UK£50 in winter to UK£90 in summer (cabins extra); a car and driver costs from UK£160 to UK£275, or you can take a vehicle and several passengers for UK£250 to UK£400.

Morocco

Ferry services between Spain and Morocco include Algeciras-Tangier, Algeciras-Ceuta, Gibraltar-Tangier, Málaga-Melilla, Almería-Melilla and Almería-Nador. Those to and from Algeciras are the fastest, cheapest and most frequent, with over 20 ferries a day to Ceuta (€13, 1½ hours) and 14 to Tangier (€14, 2½ hours). Hydrofoils make the same trip in half the time for about 75% more. Taking a car to Ceuta/Tangier costs €60/70.

You can buy tickets at Algeciras' harbour, but it's more convenient to go to one of the many agencies on the waterfront. The price doesn't vary, so just look for the place with the shortest queue.

Don't buy Moroccan currency until you reach Morocco, as you will get ripped off in Algeciras.

Getting Around

Students and seniors are eligible for discounts of 30% to 50% on almost all types of transportation within Spain.

AIR

Spain has four main domestic airlines: **Iberia** (☎ 902 40 05 00), **Air Europa** (☎ 902 40 15 01) and **Spanair** (☎ 902 13 14 15). They and a couple of smaller airlines compete to produce some fares that can make flying worthwhile if you're in a hurry, especially for longer or return trips.

The return fare between Madrid and Barcelona can be as high as €150. To Palma de Mallorca, Santiago de Compostela or Málaga you are looking at around €200 return. All these fares can be cut in half if you comply with certain restrictions.

Among travel agencies, **TIVE** (see Useful Organisations, earlier in this chapter) and **Halcón Viatges** (see Travel Agencies under Barcelona later in this chapter) are worth checking for fares. There are some useful deals if you're under 26 (or, in some cases, over 63).

BUS

Spain's bus network is operated by dozens of independent companies and is more extensive than its train system, serving remote towns and villages as well as the major routes. The choice between bus and train depends on the particular trip you're taking; for the best value, compare fares, journey times and frequencies each time you move. Buses to/from Madrid are often cheaper than (or barely different from) cross-country routes. For instance Seville to Madrid costs €15, while the shorter Seville-Granada trip is €15.50.

Many towns and cities have one main bus station where most buses arrive and depart, and these usually have an information desk giving information on all services. Tourist offices can also help with information but don't sell tickets or list prices, as a rule.

TRAIN

Trains are mostly modern and comfortable, and late arrivals are now the exception rather than the rule. The main headache is deciding how to get the best value.

RENFE (**w** *www.renfe.es*) the national railway company, runs numerous types of train, and travel times can vary a lot on the same route. So can fares, which may depend not just on the type of train but also the day of the week and time of day. RENFE's website is a great resource for schedule and fare information.

Regionales are all-stops trains (think cheap and slow). *Cercanías* provide regular services from major cities to the surrounding suburbs and hinterland, sometimes even crossing regional boundaries.

Among long-distance *(largo recorrido)* trains, the standard daytime train is the *diurno* (its night-time equivalent is the *estrella*). Quicker is the InterCity (mainly because it makes fewer stops), while the *Talgo* is fastest and dearest.

Best of all is the AVE high-speed service that links Madrid and Seville in just 2½ hours. The *Talgo 200* uses part of this line to speed down to Málaga from Madrid. The *Euromed* is an AVE-style train that speeds south from Barcelona to Valencia and Alicante. A *Tren Hotel* is a 1st-class sleeper-only express.

There's also a bewildering range of accommodation types, especially on overnight trains (fares quoted in this chapter are typical 2nd-class seat fares). Fortunately ticket clerks understand the problem and are usually happy to go through a few options with you. The cheapest sleeper option is usually a *litera*, a bunk in a six-berth 2nd-class compartment.

You can buy tickets and make reservations at stations, RENFE offices in many city centres and travel agencies that display the RENFE logo.

Train Passes

Rail passes are valid for all RENFE trains, but Inter-Rail users have to pay €9.50 supplements on Talgo and InterCity services, and on the high-speed AVE service (Madrid-Seville). All pass-holders making reservations for long-distance trains pay a fee of about €5.

RENFE's Tarjeta Turística (also known as the Spain Flexipass) is a rail pass for non-Europeans, valid for three to 10 days' travel in a two-month period. In 2nd class, three days costs US$155, and 10 days is US$365. It can be purchased from agents outside Europe, or at a few main train stations and RENFE offices in Spain.

CAR & MOTORCYCLE

If you're driving or riding around Spain, consider investing €5 in the *Michelin Atlas de Carreteras España Portugal*. It's a handy atlas with detailed road maps as well as maps of all the main towns and cities. Most travel stores and petrol stations will carry it.

Spain's roads vary enormously but are generally quite good. Fastest are the *autopistas*, multilane freeways between major cities. On some, mainly in the north, you have to pay hefty tolls (from the French border to Barcelona, for example, it's about €12). Minor routes can be slow going but are usually more scenic. Petrol is expensive, at around €0.85 for a litre of unleaded.

The head office of the Spanish automobile club is **Real Automovil Club de España** (*RACE*; ☎ *91 434 11 22*; **e** *inforace@race.es*; *Avenida Ciudad de Barcelona 132, Madrid*). For the RACE's 24-hour, nationwide, on-road emergency service, call toll free ☎ 900 11 22 22.

Road Rules

Driving in Spain is not too bad, and locals respect road rules. Speed limits are 120km/h on the autopistas, 90km/h or 100km/h on other country roads and 50km/h in built-up areas. The maximum allowable blood-alcohol level is 0.05%. Seat belts must be worn, and motorcyclists must always wear a helmet and keep headlights on day and night.

Trying to find a parking spot in larger towns and cities can be a nightmare. Spanish drivers park anywhere to save themselves the hassle of a half-hour search, but *grúas* (tow trucks) will tow your car if given the chance. The cost of bailing out a car can be as high as €100.

Remember that Spanish cities do not have US-style parking meters at every spot. Instead, if you park in a blue zone from around 8am to 8pm, you have to obtain a ticket from a street-side meter, which may be several blocks away. You then display the ticket from your dashboard until your time runs out (expiration time is written on the ticket).

Rental

Rates vary widely from place to place. The best deals tend to be in major tourist areas, including at their airports. At Málaga airport you can rent a small car for under €120 a week. More generally, you're looking at up to

€50 for a day with unlimited kilometres, plus insurance, damage waiver and taxes. Hiring for several days can bring the average daily cost down a lot – a small car for a week might cost under €140. Local companies often have better rates than the big firms.

BICYCLE
See Cycling under Activities earlier in this chapter.

HITCHING
Although we don't recommend it, it's still possible to thumb your way around parts of Spain, but large doses of patience and common sense are necessary. Women should avoid hitching alone. Hitching is illegal on autopistas and difficult on major highways. Your chances are better on minor roads, although the going can still be painfully slow.

BOAT
For information on ferries to, from and between the Balearic Islands, see that section later in this chapter.

LOCAL TRANSPORT
In many Spanish towns you will not need to use public transport, as transport terminals and accommodation are centralised and within walking distance of most tourist attractions.

Most towns in Spain have an effective local bus system. In larger cities, these can be complicated, but tourist offices can tell you which buses you need. Barcelona and Madrid both have efficient underground systems that are faster and easier to use than the bus systems.

Taxis are still pretty cheap. If you split a cross-town fare between three or four people, it can be a decidedly good deal. Rates vary slightly from city to city: in Barcelona, they cost €1.30 flag fall, plus about €1 per kilometre; in Madrid they're a bit more expensive (€1.35 flag fall). There are supplements for luggage and airport trips.

Madrid

pop 3 million
One of the most appealing aspects about Madrid is that, despite being the country's capital, there is a friendly neighbourhood feel about the place. Right in the city centre you

find quaint family-owned shops, bars packed with locals and an overall lack of the stress levels on the street that you find in most cities this size. There is also plenty to do and see, including a remarkable collection of museums and galleries, beautiful parks and gardens, and a vibrant nightlife with, reputedly, more bars per square metre than any other city in Europe.

ORIENTATION
The most interesting part of Madrid lies between Parque del Retiro in the east and Campo del Moro in the west. These two parks are more or less connected by Calle de Alcalá and Calle Mayor, which meet in the middle at Puerta del Sol. Calle Mayor passes the historic main square, Plaza Mayor, on its way from Puerta del Sol to the Palacio Real in front of Campo del Moro.

The main north-south thoroughfare is Paseo de la Castellana, which runs (changing names to Paseo de los Recoletos and finally Paseo del Prado) all the way from Chamartín train station in the north to Madrid's other big station, Atocha.

INFORMATION
Tourist Offices
The **Oficina Municipal de Turismo** (☎ 91 588 16 36, fax 91 366 54 77; **e** munemad rid@infoturismo.es; Plaza Mayor 3; metro Sol; open 10am-8pm Mon-Sat, 10am-2pm Sun) is conveniently situated in the city's emblematic main square. The additional tourist information offices include those located at **Chamartín train station** (☎ 91 315 99 76; open 8am-8pm Mon-Sat, 8am-2pm Sun), **Barajas airport** (☎ 91 305 86 56; open 8am-8pm daily), and **Mercado Puerta de Toledo** (☎ 91 364 18 76; Ronda de Toledo 1; open 9am-8pm Mon-Sat, 9am-2pm Sun). There is also a multilingual local information hotline on ☎ 010.

Money
Large banks such as Caja de Madrid usually have the best rates, but check commissions. Banks usually open 8.30am to 2pm weekdays and, during the winter months, to 1pm on Saturday. **American Express** (☎ 91 527 03 03; open 24hr; ☎ 900 99 44 26 for replacing lost travellers cheques; Plaza de las Cortes 2; metro Banco de España; open 9am-5.30pm Mon-Fri, 9am-noon Sat) is reasonably priced.

If you're desperate, there are plenty of *bureaux de change* around Puerta del Sol and Plaza Mayor, which have the predictable rip-off rates but are often open until midnight.

Post & Communications

The **main post office** (☎ 91 521 6500; *Plaza de la Cibeles; metro Banco de España*) is in the gigantic Palacio de Comunicaciones. **Poste restante** (*lista de correos; open 8am-9.30pm Mon-Fri, 8.30am-2pm Sat*) is at windows 17 to 20. Don't forget your passport.

Telefónica (☎ 91 522 39 14; *Gran Vía 30; metro Gran Vía; open 10am-10pm daily*) has phone books for the whole country and cabins where you can make calls in relative peace.

Email & Internet Access

Internet connections are available at dozens of cafés, as well as at such Net centres as **Navegaweb**, part of the 'Telefónica' centre (see earlier), which charges €1.80 an hour; **WEC** (☎ 91 429 16 90; *Calle de Atocha 45; metro Antón Martín; open 10am-10pm daily*) at €2.40 an hour; and **ONO** (☎ 91 547 47 71; *Gran Vía 59; metro Gran Vía; open 24hr*), with varying rates depending on the time.

Travel Agencies

For cheap travel tickets try **Viajes Zeppelin** (☎ 91 542 51 54; *Plaza de Santo Domingo 2; metro Santo Domingo*). If you are under 25 or a student, check out **TIVE** (☎ 91 543 74 12; *Calle de Fernando el Católico 88; metro Moncloa*) or the **Instituto de la Juventud** (☎ 91 347 77 00; *Calle de José Ortega y Gasset 71; metro Lista*) – both open 9am to 1pm Monday to Friday.

Bookshops

La Casa del Libro (☎ 91 521 21 13; *Gran Vía 29-31*) is massive and the largest of the three branches in town, with a good selection of books in English and other languages. For more English books, as well as videos and a children's section, go to **Booksellers** (☎ 91 442 79 59; *Calle de José Abascal 48; metro Alonso Cano*). **Desnivel** (☎ 91 429 97 40; *Plaza Matute 6; metro Huertas*) specialises in walking, climbing and adventure guides, and has a large selection of maps.

Laundry

Laundrettes are hard to find. Two that are still in business are **Lavomatique** (*Calle de Cervantes 1; metro Antón Martín; open 9am-8pm Mon-Sat*) and **Lavandería Alba** (☎ 91 522 44 63; *Calle del Barco 26; metro Gran Vía; open 9am-9pm Mon-Sat*).

Medical & Emergency Services

If you have a minor medical problem and speak some Spanish (or are good at gesticulating), ask a pharmacist's advice. There are several 24-hour pharmacies, including **Farmacia del Globo** (☎ 91 369 20 00; *Plaza de Antón Martín 46; metro Antón Martín*). For more serious problems, head for the nearest emergency health centre – **Casa de Socorro** (☎ 91 588 96 60; *Calle Navas de Tolosa 10; metro Callao*) is the most convenient if you are in the centre. You can also get help at the **Anglo-American Medical Unit** (☎ 91 435 18 23; *Calle del Conde de Aranda 1; metro Retiro*). For an ambulance, call ☎ 061, or Cruz Roja on ☎ 91 522 22 22.

In the case of an emergency see the boxed text 'Emergency Services' near Dangers & Annoyances in the Facts for the Visitor section earlier in this chapter.

THINGS TO SEE & DO
Museo del Prado

The city is elite among Europe's art capitals with three major museums, including the Prado (☎ 91 330 29 00; *Paseo del Prado s/n; adult/student €3/1.50, admission free 2.30pm-7pm Sat & all day Sun; open 9am-7pm Tues-Sat, 9am-2pm Sun & holidays*), the best-known and largest of the trio. The main emphasis is on Spanish, Flemish and Italian art from the 15th to 19th centuries, and one of its strengths lies in the generous coverage given to certain individual geniuses, such as three of the Spanish greats, Goya, Velázquez and El Greco.

Of Velázquez' works, it's *Las Meninas* that most people come to see. This masterpiece depicts maids of honour attending the daughter of King Felipe IV, and Velázquez himself painting portraits of the queen and king (through whose eyes the scene is witnessed). It takes pride of place in room 12 on the 1st floor, the focal point of the Velázquez collection.

Virtually the whole southern wing of the 1st floor is given over to Goya. His portraits, in rooms 34 to 38, include the pair *Maja Desnuda* and *Maja Vestida*; legend has it that the woman depicted here is the Duchess of Alba, Spain's richest woman in Goya's time. Goya was commissioned to paint her portrait by her

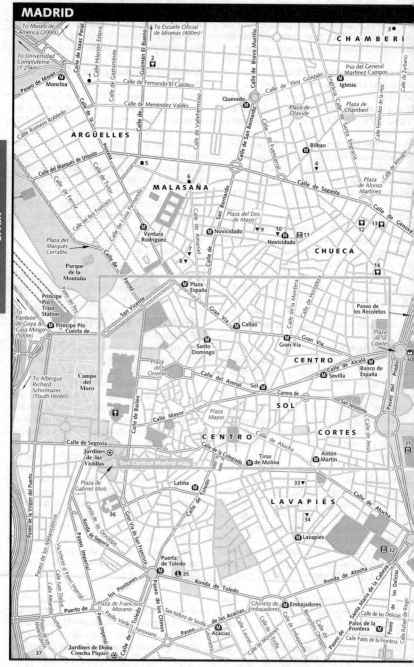

MADRID

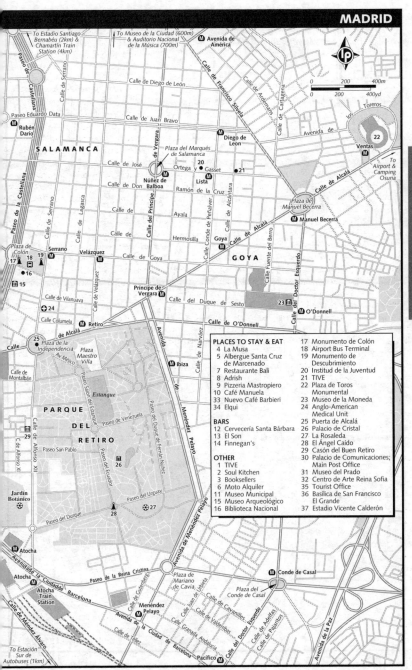

MADRID

To Estadio Santiago
Bernabéu (2km) &
Chamartín Train
Station (4km)

To Museo de la Ciudad (600m)
& Auditorio Nacional
de la Música (700m)

Avenida de
América

Paseo de la Castellana

Calle de Serrano

Calle de Diego de León

Calle de Francisco Silvela

Calle de Ardemans

Calle de Cartagena

Toreros

Paseo Eduardo Data

Rubén
Darío

Calle de Juan Bravo

Plaza del Marqués
de Salamanca

SALAMANCA

Calle de Serrano

Calle de Lagasca

Calle de José

Calle de Don Balboa

Núñez de
Balboa

Plaza de
Vergara

Diego de
León

20
Ortega y ● Gasset
Lista
Ramón de la Cruz

●21

Calle de Alcántara

Calle de Alcalá

Plaza de)
Manuel Becerra

Manuel Becerra

Ventas

To
Airport &
Camping
Osuna

22

Calle del Príncipe

Ayala

Hermosilla

Goya

Calle de Conde de Peñalver

GOYA

Calle Fuente del Berro

Calle del Doctor Esquerdo

Plaza de
Colón

Serrano

17   18
19

●16

15

Calle de Velázquez

Velázquez

Calle de Goya

Príncipe de
Vergara

Calle del Duque de Sesto

23

O'Donnell

Calle de Vilanueva

24

Calle Columela

Retiro

Calle de O'Donnell

Calle
de Alcalá

25
Plaza de la
Independencia

Calle de
Montalbán

Av Mejico

Plaza
Maestro
Villa

Avenida

Calle de Narváez

Ibiza

Estanque

C de Alfonso XII

PARQUE

Paseo de Venezuela

Paseo del Duque de Fernán Núñez

Paseo del Salón del Estanque

DEL

29

Paseo San Pablo

RETIRO

26

Jardín
Botánico

28

Paseo del Ecuador

27

Paseo del Duque

Paseo del Uruguay

Atocha

Atocha

Atocha
Train
Station

Avenida de Menéndez Pelayo

Avenida de la Ciudad de Barcelona

Paseo de la Reina Cristina

Plaza de
Mariano
de Cavia

Calle de Gutenberg

Menéndez
Pelayo

Calle de Juan de Urbieta

Plaza del
Conde de Casal

Conde de Casal

Calle de Cavanilles

Avenida de la Ciudad de Barcelona

Calle del Doctor Esquerdo

Calle Granada

Andalucía

Calle de Valderibas

Calle de Adelfas

Avenida de la Paz

To Estación
Sur de
Autobuses (1km)

Calle de Méndez Álvaro

Calle de Teller

Pacífico

Calle de Pajaritos

LP

0   200   400m
0   200   400yd

SPAIN

PLACES TO STAY & EAT
4 La Musa
5 Albergue Santa Cruz
   de Marcenado
7 Restaurante Bali
8 Adrish
9 Pizzeria Mastropiero
10 Café Manuela
33 Nuevo Café Barbieri
34 Elqui

BARS
12 Cervecería Santa Bárbara
13 El Son
14 Finnegan's

OTHER
1 TIVE
2 Soul Kitchen
3 Booksellers
6 Moto Alquiler
11 Museo Municipal
15 Museo Arqueológico
16 Biblioteca Nacional

17 Monumento de Colón
18 Airport Bus Terminal
19 Monumento de
    Descubrimiento
20 Institud de la Juventud
21 TIVE
22 Plaza de Toros
    Monumental
23 Museo de la Moneda
24 Anglo-American
    Medical Unit
25 Puerta de Alcalá
26 Palacio de Cristal
27 La Rosaleda
28 El Ángel Caído
29 Casón del Buen Retiro
30 Palacio de Comunicaciones;
    Main Post Office
31 Museo del Prado
32 Centro de Arte Reina Sofia
35 Tourist Office
36 Basílica de San Francisco
    El Grande
37 Estadio Vicente Calderón

SPAIN

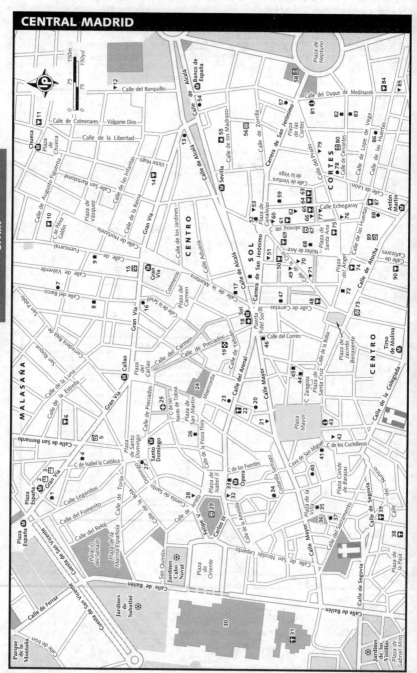

CENTRAL MADRID

husband and ended up having an affair with her, so painted an extra portrait for himself. In room 39 are Goya's great war masterpieces, crowned by *El Dos de Mayo 1808* (2 May 1808) and, next to it, *Los Fusilamientos de Moncloa*, in which he recreates the pathos of the hopeless Madrid revolt against the French. There are more Goya works in rooms 66 and 67 on the ground floor.

Other well-represented artists include El Greco, the Flemish masters Hieronymus Bosch and Peter Paul Rubens, and the Italians Tintoretto, Titian and Raphael.

Entry to the Prado is free on some national holidays. Tickets include entrance to the Casón del Buen Retiro, a subsidiary to the east, that contains 19th-century works.

Centro de Arte Reina Sofía

This museum (☎ 91 467 50 62; *Calle Santa Isabel 52; adult/student €3/1.50, admission free 2.30pm-7pm Sat & Sun; open 10am-9pm Mon & Wed-Sat, 10am-2.30pm Sun)* houses a superb collection of predominantly Spanish modern art. The exhibition focuses on the period 1900 to 1940 and includes Picasso's famous *Guernica*, his protest at the German bombing of the Basque town of Guernica during the Spanish Civil War in 1937.

Guernica was painted in Paris. Picasso insisted that it stay outside Spain until Franco and his cronies were gone and democracy had been restored. It was secretly brought to Spain in 1981 and moved here from the Casón del Buen Retiro in 1992.

The museum also contains further works by Picasso, while room 9 is devoted to Salvador Dalí's surrealist work and room 13 contains a collection of Joan Miró's late works, characterised by their remarkable simplicity.

Museo Thyssen-Bornemisza

This museum (☎ 91 420 39 44; *Paseo del Prado 8; adult/student €5/3; open 10am-7pm*

SPAIN

CENTRAL MADRID

PLACES TO STAY		
1	Hostal Residencia Buenos Aires	
4	Hostal El Pinar	
8	Hotel Laris	
9	Hostal Ginebra	
17	Hostal Centro Sol	
26	Hostal Paz	
33	Hostal Oriente	
34	Hostal Mairu	
41	Hostal La Macarena	
44	Hostal Santa Cruz	
45	Hostal Comercial	
46	Hostal Riesco	
47	Hostal El Pilar	
52	Hotel Asturias	
59	Hotel Santander	
68	Hostal Rodriguez	
72	Hostal Persal	
82	Hostal Dulcinea	
83	Hostal Gonzalo	

PLACES TO EAT	
12	El Pepinillo de Barquillo
21	Comme Bio
28	Restaurante La Paella Real
32	Café del Real
42	Restaurante Sobrino de Botín
49	La Casa del Abuelo
51	Museo del Jamón
53	La Finca de Susana
60	Ducados Café
62	El Jaraíz
66	La Trucha
70	La Trucha

71	Las Bravas
76	El Salón de Prado
77	Cervecería La Cañita
79	Tocorora
85	Maceira

BARS & CLUBS	
6	Morocco Disco
10	Cruising
11	Rimmel
14	Bar Cock
48	Torero
50	Alhambra
61	O'Neills
63	Carbones
64	Los Gabrieles
65	Viva Madrid
69	Suristán
74	Café Central
75	Cervecería Alemana
84	Los Gatos
87	Café Populart
90	Casa Patas

OTHER	
2	Princess Cinema
3	Renior Cinema
5	ONO
7	Lavandería Alba
13	Edificio Metropolis
15	Telefónica/Internet Centre
16	La Casa del Libro
18	Police Station
19	El Corte Inglés Department Store

20	Chocolatería de San Ginés
22	Iglesia de San Ginés
23	Jamoneria Ferpal
24	Monasterio de las Descalzas Reales
25	Casa de Socorro (Emergency Health Centre)
27	Viajes Zeppelin
29	Teatro Real
30	Palacio Real
31	Catedral de Nuestra Señora de la Almudena
35	Torre de los Lujanes
36	Ayuntamiento
37	Casa de Cisneros
38	Iglesia de San Andrés
39	Iglesia de San Pedro
40	Mercado de San Miguel
43	Tourist Office
54	RENFE Train Booking Office
55	Police Station
56	Teatro de la Zarzuela
57	American Express
58	Museo Thyssen-Bornemisza
67	Teatro de la Comedia
73	Teatro Calderón
78	Lavomatique
80	Casa de Lope de Vega
81	Tourist Office
86	Convento de las Trinitarias
88	Desnivel
89	WEC

Tues-Sun) is almost opposite the Prado. Purchased by Spain in 1993 for over US$300 million (a snip), this extraordinary collection of 800 paintings was formerly the private collection of the German-Hungarian family of magnates, the Thyssen-Bornemiszas. Starting with medieval religious art, it moves on through Titian, El Greco and Rubens to Cézanne, Monet and Van Gogh, then from Miró, Picasso and Gris to Pollock, Dalí and Lichtenstein, thereby offering one of the best and most comprehensive art-history lessons you'll ever have. The separate temporary exhibitions generally cost more.

Palacio Real

Madrid's 18th-century Palacio Real *(☎ 91 542 00 59; Plaza de Oriente; metro Opera; adult/student €6/3, admission free Wed for EU citizens; open 9.30am-6pm Mon-Sat, 9am-2.30pm Sun & holidays May-Sept; 9.30am-5pm Mon-Sat, 9am-2pm Sun & holidays Oct-Apr)* is a lesson in what can happen if you give your interior decorators a free hand. You'll see some of the most elaborately decorated walls and ceilings imaginable, including the sublime Throne Room (and other rooms of more dubious merit). This over-the-top palace hasn't been used as a royal residence for some time and today is used only for official receptions and, of course, tourism.

The first series of rooms you strike after buying your ticket is the Farmacia Real (Royal Pharmacy), an unending array of medicine jars and stills for mixing royal concoctions. The Armería Real (Royal Armoury) is a shiny collection of mostly 16th- and 17th-century weapons and royal suits of armour. Elsewhere are a good selection of Goyas, 215 absurdly ornate clocks from the Royal Clock Collection and five Stradivarius violins, still used for concerts and balls. Most of the tapestries in the palace were made in the Royal Tapestry Factory. All the chandeliers are original and no two are the same.

Monasterio de las Descalzas Reales

This monastery *(Convent of the Barefoot Royals; ☎ 91 542 00 59; Plaza de las Descalzas; adult/student €5/4, admission free Wed for EU citizens; open 10.30am-12.45pm Tues-Sat, 4pm-5.30pm Tues-Thur & Sat, 11am-1.45pm Sun & holidays)* was founded in 1559 by Juana of Austria, daughter of the

Spanish King Carlos I, and became one of Spain's richest religious houses thanks to gifts from noblewomen. Much of the wealth came in the form of art; on the obligatory guided tour you'll be confronted by a number of tapestries based on works by Rubens and a wonderful painting entitled *The Voyage of the 11,000 Virgins*.

Panteón de Goya

This little church *(☎ 91 542 07 22; Glorieta de San Antonio de la Florida 5; metro Príncipe Pío; adult/student €2/1, admission free Wed & Sun; open 10am-2pm Tues-Sun year-round, 4pm-8pm Tues-Fri Sept-June)* contains not only Goya's tomb, directly in front of the altar, but also one of his greatest works – the entire ceiling and dome – beautifully painted with religious scenes. The images on the dome depict the miracle of St Anthony.

Museo Arqueológico

This museum *(☎ 91 577 79 12; Calle de Serrano; adult/student €3/1.50, admission free Sun & 2.30pm-8.30pm Sat; open 9.30am-8.30pm Tues-Sat, 9.30am-2pm Sun)* traces the history of the peninsula from prehistoric cave paintings to the Iberian, Roman, Carthaginian, Greek, Visigothic, Moorish and Christian eras. Exhibits include mosaics, pottery, fossilised bones and a partial reconstruction of the prehistoric Altamira cave paintings.

Other Museums

Madrid is museum mad. Examples include: the **Museo Municipal**, with assorted art, including some Goyas, and some beautiful old maps, scale models, silver, porcelain and period furniture; the **Museo de la Moneda**, which follows the history of coinage in great detail and contains a mind-boggling collection of coins and paper money; the **Museo de América**, with stuff brought from the Americas between the 16th and 20th centuries; and even the **Museo de la Ciudad**, perfectly described by one traveller as 'a must for infrastructure buffs!', which rather dryly traces the growth of Madrid. Check the tourist office's *Madrid* brochure for more details.

Real Jardín Botánico

The ideal way to end a cultural overdose day is a stroll through this beautiful eight-hectare botanical garden *(admission €1.50; open 10am-dark daily)* next door to the Prado.

Parque del Retiro

This is another great place to bench-sit or stroll. Time it right and you may even catch a puppet show during the summer.

Walk along **Paseo de las Estatuas**, a path lined with statues originally from the Palacio Real. It ends at a lake overlooked by a **statue of Alfonso XII**. There are rowing boats for rent at the northern end when the weather is good.

Perhaps the most important, and certainly the most controversial, of the park's other monuments is **El Ángel Caído** (The Fallen Angel). First-prize winner at an international exhibition in Paris in 1878, this is said to be the first ever statue dedicated to the devil.

You should also visit some of the park's gardens, such as the exquisite **La Rosaleda** (*rose garden*), and the **Chinese Garden** on a tiny island near the Fallen Angel. The all-glass **Palacio de Cristal** in the middle of the park frequently stages modern-art exhibitions.

Campo del Moro

This stately garden is directly behind the Palacio Real, and the palace is visible through the trees from just about all points. A couple of fountains and statues, a thatch-roofed pagoda and a carriage museum provide artificial diversions, but nature is the real attraction.

El Rastro

If you get up early on a Sunday morning, you'll find the city almost deserted, until you get to **El Rastro** (*metro Latina*). The market spreads along and between Calle de Ribera de Curtidores and Calle de los Embajadores. It's one of the biggest flea markets you'll ever see, where you find almost anything, from hippie threads to the kitchen sink. It's also said to be the place to go if you want to buy your car stereo back. Watch your pockets and bags.

ORGANISED TOURS

You can pick up a **Madrid Vision bus** (☎ 91 779 18 88) around the centre of Madrid up to 10 times a day. A full return trip costs €9.60 and you can hop on and off at any of 20 clearly marked stops. Taped commentaries in four languages, including English, are available, and the bus stops at several major monuments, including the Prado and near Plaza Mayor. **Descubre Madrid** is a walking tour with several itineraries available. Check at the tourist office at Plaza Mayor 3 for exact times and routes.

SPECIAL EVENTS

Madrid's major fiesta celebrates its patron saint, San Isidro Labrador, throughout the third week of May. There are free music performances around the city and one of the country's top bullfight seasons at the Plaza Monumental de las Ventas. The Malasaña district, already busy enough, has its biggest party on 2 May, and the Fiesta de San Juan is held in the Parque del Retiro for the seven days leading up to 24 June. The city now sashays through the hottest months and there are plenty of people around to enjoy the consecutive festivals of La Paloma, San Cayetano and San Lorenzo in August. The last week of September is Chamartín's Fiesta de Otoño (Autumn Festival), about the only time you would go to Chamartín other than to catch a train.

PLACES TO STAY

Finding a place to stay in Madrid is never really a problem. However, it is obviously wise to book ahead. In general, you won't have to leave credit card details.

Camping

There is one camping ground within striking distance of central Madrid. To reach **Camping Osuna** (☎ 91 741 05 10; *Avenida de Logroño; camp sites per person €5, the same price per tent/car*), which is near the airport, take metro No 5 or bus No 101 to Canillejas (the end of the line), from where it's about 500m.

Hostels

There are two HI youth hostels in Madrid. **Albergue Richard Schirrman** (☎ 91 463 56 99; *metro El Lago, bus No 33 from Plaza Ópera; dorm beds for under/over 26 €8/12*) is in the Casa de Campo park. B&B is available. This is a seedy area at night, so try and time your arrival during the day.

Albergue Santa Cruz de Marcenado (☎ 91 547 45 32; *Calle de Santa Cruz de Marcenado 28; metro Argüelles, bus Nos 1, 61 & Circular; dorm beds for under/over 26 €8/12*), has rooms for four to eight people. B&B costs the same as in Albergue Richard Schirrman. It's one of the few Spanish hostels in HI's International Booking Network.

Hostales & Hotels

There is an excellent range of accommodation in Madrid. At the budget end, *hostales* and *pensiones* tend to cluster in three or four parts of the city and the price-to-quality ratio is fairly standard. In August you may get a better deal because of the heat, although the city doesn't empty as it once did, due to the influx of visitors and air-con systems.

Around Plaza de Santa Ana Santa Ana is cleaned up and humming, so budget places are starting to disappear. Close to Sol and within walking distance of the Prado museum and Atocha train station, there are countless bars, cafés and restaurants here attracting every class of clientele.

Just off the square, **Hostal Rodriguez** (☎ 91 522 44 31; Nuñez de Arce 9, 3rd floor; doubles with/without bath €40/37) has clean and comfortable rooms.

West off the square, **Hostal Persal** (☎ 91 369 46 43, fax 91 369 19 52; e hostalper sal@mad.servicom.es; Plaza del Ángel 12; singles/doubles €60/75) provides understated luxury with pleasant comfortable en suite rooms and all the extras, including TV, phone and a bumper breakfast.

There are small but cute rooms at **Hostal El Pilar** (☎ 91 531 26 26; Calle Carretas, 13; doubles from €44); try for one overlooking the church.

In the same mid-range bracket, **Hostal Gonzalo** (☎ 91 429 27 14, fax 91 420 20 07; Calle de Cervantes 34; singles/doubles €35/43) is in sparkling nick. Rooms have own shower and TV. The staff will take a few euros off the bill if you stay at least three days. Across the road **Hostal Dulcinea** (☎ 91 429 93 09, fax 91 369 25 69; e donato@teleline.es; Calle de Cervantes 19; singles/doubles €36/42) has well-maintained if simply furnished rooms.

Around Puerta del Sol & Plaza Mayor You can't get more central than Plaza Puerta del Sol. This and Plaza Mayor, Madrid's true heart, are not major budget accommodation areas but, if you're euro-economising, there are a few good options tucked away among the cafés, bars and souvenir shops.

The pick of the cheaper bunch is **Hostal Comercial** (☎ 91 522 66 30; Calle Esparteros 12; singles/doubles €30/35) with bath, TV and balcony. Right on the square, **Hostal Riesco** (☎ 91 522 26 92; Calle de Correo 2, 3rd floor; singles/doubles €33/41) is a natty little place but may require earplugs on a Saturday night. **Hostal Santa Cruz** (☎ 91 522 24 41; Plaza de Santa Cruz 6; singles/doubles from

€24/36) is bright and smart, in a prime location. A great old building, **Hotel Asturias** (☎ 91 429 66 76, fax 91 429 49 36; e ast urias@chh.es; Calle Sevilla 2; singles/doubles €78/103) combines upmarket convenience with old-world chintz, with the added plus of a lively bar, popular with the locals.

There's a cosy overstuffed sofa feel at **Hotel Santander** (☎ 91 429 95 51, fax 91 369 10 78; Calle Echegaray 1; doubles with bath €60) and this street is buzzing with plenty of bar choices. Just off Plaza Mayor in a tastefully revamped old building, **Hostal La Macarena** (☎ 91 365 92 21, fax 91 366 61 11; Cava de San Miguel 8; singles/doubles €57/73) has excellent rooms with bath, TV and phone – pricey but worth it. **Hostal Centro Sol** (☎ 91 522 15 82, fax 91 522 57 78; Carrera de San Jerónimo 5; singles/doubles €46/54) offers smallish rooms but TV, phone, heating, air-con, minibar, even a hair-dryer.

Around Gran Vía The hostales on and around Gran Vía tend to be a little more expensive, so it's worth shopping around.

A good budget choice is **Hostal El Pinar** (☎ 91 547 32 82; Calle de Isabel la Católica 19; singles/doubles without bath from €19/31), which has a certain old-fashioned charm. The **Hostal Residencia Buenos Aires** (☎ 91 542 01 02, fax 91 542 24 66; Gran Vía 61; doubles from €48) is shiny smart with all mod cons, plus a cafeteria.

Calle de Fuencarral is similarly choked with hostales and pensiones, especially at the Gran Vía end. **Hostal Ginebra** (☎ 91 532 10 35; Calle de Fuencarral 17; singles/doubles with bath €32/40) is a reliable choice not far from Gran Vía. All rooms have both TV and phone, and some have a private balcony.

Hotel Laris (☎ 91 521 46 80, fax 521 46 85; Calle del Barco 3; doubles €63) has been nicely reformed and provides all the extras.

Around Ópera The tiny **Hostal Paz** (☎ 91 547 30 47; Calle Flora 4; singles/doubles €20/30) looks pretty grim from the outside but the cheap rooms inside are reasonable, if a little cramped. Quietly tucked away, **Hostal Mairu** (☎ 91 547 30 88; Calle del Espejo 2; singles/doubles with bath from €22/33) is well priced and some rooms include a small fridge. **Hostal Oriente** (☎/fax 91 548 03 14; Calle del Arenal 23; singles/doubles from €33/51) is a pleasant mid-range choice.

Rental

Many of the *hostales* mentioned above will do a deal on long stays. You can also check the rental pages of *Segundamano* magazine or notice boards at universities, the Escuela Oficial de Idiomas and cultural institutes such as the British Council or Alliance Française.

PLACES TO EAT

Madrid heaves with an infinite number of bars and restaurants, ranging from intimate tapas bars shoe-horned into tiny spaces to cavernous old *mesones* (taverns) with smoke-blackened walls, antique furniture and lip-smacking traditional food. Around Santa Ana it doesn't seem to matter that the sea is more than a pebble's throw away: there are plenty of excellent seafood restaurants. One of the best is **Maceira** (☎ 91 429 42 93; *Calle de Jesús 7; metro Antón Martín; open lunch only*), tucked away from the main tourist hubbub. Splash (or slurp) your *pulpo a la gallega* (octopus in paprika and oil) down with a crisp white Ribeiro.

In **La Casa del Abuelo** (☎ 91 432 28 40; *Calle de la Victoria 14; metro Sol*), on a backstreet southeast of Puerta del Sol, you can sip a *chato* (small glass) of the heavy El Abuelo red wine while munching on heavenly king prawns, grilled or with garlic. Next, duck around the corner to **Las Bravas** (☎ 91 532 26 20; *Callejón de Álvarez Gato; metro Sol*) for a *caña* (glass of draught beer) and the best *patatas bravas* (fried potatoes with spicy tomato sauce) in town.

La Trucha (☎ 91 532 08 90; *Calle de Núñez de Arce 6; metro Sol; open Tues-Sat*) is one of Madrid's great tapas bars. It's just off Plaza de Santa Ana, and there's another at Calle de Manuel Fernández y González 3. You can eat at the bar or in the restaurant.

For crusty old men in flat caps, check out the all-time local **Cervecería La Cañita** (☎ 91 429 04 61; *Calle Echegaray 20; metro Sol*), which serves tasty tapas from €2. A few doors away **El Jaraíz** (☎ 91 369 48 10; *Calle Echegaray 12*) is upmarket, serving trendy tapas such as Roquefort and dates accompanied by goblets of wine. Something of an institution is **Museo del Jamón**, a Miss Piggy nightmare with hundreds of hams swinging from the ceiling. There are 10 branches in town, including at Carrera de San Jerónimo 6.

Everything Cuban is still pretty cool and **Tocorora** (☎ 91 369 40 00; *Calle del Prado 3; metro Antón Martín*) is top banana with

black beans, tamales, fried yucca, avocado salad and umpteen makes of rum.

La Finca de Susana (☎ 91 369 35 57; *Calle de Arlabán 4; metro Sevilla*) hums with young couples and atmosphere, and dishes up Spanish-with-a-twist fare for around €12.

Vegetarians often have to make do with a plate of chips and salad in Spain, but Madrid offers a few safe ports. **Elqui** (☎ 91 468 04 62; *Calle de Buenavista 18; metro Antón Martín; open for lunch until 4pm Tues-Sun, dinner Fri & Sat*) is a self-service buffet-style restaurant for piling up your plate. **Comme Bio** (☎ 91 354 63 00; *Calle Mayor 30; metro Sol*) is excellent and inexpensive, with a health-food shop out front where you can stock up on muesli bars to go.

Around Plaza Mayor

You know you're getting close to Plaza Mayor when you see signs in English saying 'Typical Spanish Restaurant' and 'Hemingway Never Ate Here'. Nevertheless, when the sun's shining (or rising), there's not a finer place to be than at one of the outdoor cafés in the plaza.

Calle de la Cava San Miguel and Calle de Cuchilleros are packed with *mesones* that are fun for tapas hopping, if you can pay a little more. Splendid **Restaurante Sobrino de Botín** (☎ 91 366 42 17; *Calle de los Cuchilleros 17; metro Sol; set menu €30*) is one of Europe's oldest restaurants (established 1725), with loads of atmosphere despite the tourists.

Other Areas

Just about anywhere you go in central Madrid, you can find cheap restaurants with reasonable, filling food.

Casa Mingo (☎ 91 547 79 18; *Paseo de la Florida 34; metro Príncipe Pío*), near the Panteón de Goya, is a bustling great place for chicken and cider. A full roast bird, salad and bottle of cider – enough for two – comes to around €12.

If you're after paella at all costs, head for **Restaurante La Paella Real** (☎ 91 542 09 42; *Calle de Arrieta 2; metro Opera; paella for two from €23*) just off Plaza de Oriente, which does a whole range of rice-based dishes. For more unconventional dishes (and decor), try **El Pepinillo de Barquillo** (☎ 91 310 25 46; *Calle del Barquillo 42; metro Chueca*), with its giant pickle hanging from the ceiling and dishes that range from snails and spaghetti to vegie plates with panache.

SPAIN

SPAIN

In the Malasaña area a couple of blocks from Plaza del Dos de Mayo, **La Musa** (☎ 91 448 75 58; Calle Manuela Malasana 18; metro Bilbao) is stylish and arty, dishing up nouvelle-style Spanish food at affordable prices. For more mainstream fare, head for **Pizzeria Mastropiero** (Calle de San Vicente Ferrer 34) on the corner of Calle del Dos de Mayo. This is a justifiably popular Argentine-run joint where you can get pizza by the slice.

The Plaza de España area is a good hunting-ground for non-Spanish food, though prices tend to be higher. **Restaurante Bali** (☎ 91 541 91 22; Calle de San Bernardino 6; metro Plaza España) has spicy Indonesian food at around €20 for two, while the **Adrish**, across the street at No 1, is a good Indian restaurant, but typically spiced down for the Spanish palate.

Cafés

Madrid has many fine places for a coffee and light bite, ranging from sumptuously elegant with chandeliers and palms, to small and smoky refuges for writing that epic love letter. Historic, elegant **El Salón del Prado** (☎ 91 429 33 61; Calle del Prado 4; metro Antón Martín) also has chamber music concerts on Thursday nights. There's a crumbling romantic feel about **Nuevo Café Barbieri** (☎ 91 527 36 58; Calle del Ave María 45; metro Lavapiés), with its Art Deco light fixtures and red velvet decor. Local artists exhibit at **Café Manuela** (☎ 91 531 70 37; San Vicente Ferrer 11; metro Tribunal), which also has a piano, board games and Belle Époque detailing. **Café del Real** (Plaza de Isabel II; metro Ópera) has a cosy touch of faded elegance – good for breakfast and busy at night, too. In the centre, **Ducados Café** (☎ 91 360 00 89; Plaza de Canalejas 3; metro Sol) has bare brick and beams, and serves up Tex-Mex and a good *tosta* (bite-size toast with topping) choice along with head-spinning cocktails, and coffees.

ENTERTAINMENT

A copy of the weekly *Guía del Ocio* (€1 at newsstands) will give you a good rundown of what's on in Madrid. Its comprehensive listings include music gigs, art exhibitions, cinema, TV and theatre. It's very handy even if you can't read Spanish.

Bars

The epicentres of Madrid's nightlife are the Santa Ana–Calle de las Huertas area and the Malasaña-Chueca zone north of Gran Vía. The latter can be a bit druggy late at night.

The bars on Plaza de Santa Ana are where *el todo* Madrid seem to start their evening out. **Cerverceria Alemana** (☎ 91 429 70 33; Plaza de Santa Ana 6) appeals to travellers as well with its beer served in steins and low-key feel. There's not much elbow-room at **Viva Madrid** (☎ 91 429 36 40; Calle de Manuel Fernández y González 7) at weekends, but take a look at its tiles and heavy wooden ceilings. On the same street, **Carbones** (open until 4am) is a busy place with good mainstream music on the jukebox. **Los Gabrieles** (☎ 91 429 62 61; Calle Echegaray 17) is a dazzling tiled bar with a huge history, serving as a meeting point for the beautiful people of Spain's *movida*.

Café Populart (☎ 91 429 84 07; Calle de las Huertas 22) often has music, generally jazz or blues. For more jazz with your drinks, **Café Central** (☎ 91 369 41 43; Plaza del Ángel 10) is another good choice. Just at the bottom of Huertas is the amiable **Los Gatos** (☎ 91 429 30 67; Calle de Jesús 2), a lively local haunt.

In Malasaña, **Cervecería Santa Bárbara** (Plaza de Santa Bárbara 8) is a classic Madrid drinking house and a good place to kick off a night out. If you fancy some salsa with your cerveza head for **El Son** (☎ 91 308 04 29; Calle Fernando V1 21), a Latino music bar.

Irish pubs are very popular in Madrid: two good ones are **O'Neill's** (☎ 91 521 20 30; Calle Principe 12) and **Finnegan's** (☎ 91 310 05 21; Plaza de las Salesas 9).

Calle de Pelayo Campoamor is lined with an assortment of bars, graduating from hi-octane rock bars at the northern end to the gay bar centre at the southern Chueca area. **Rimmel** (Calle de Luis de Góngora 4) and **Cruising** (☎ 91 521 51 43; Calle de Pérez Galdós 5) are among the more popular gay haunts. The latter has a dark room and puts on occasional shows.

Raising many a schoolgirl titter, the quaintly named **Bar Cock** (☎ 91 532 67 37; Calle de la Reina 16) once served as a discreet salon for high-class prostitution. The ladies in question have gone but this popular bar is still plush and atmospheric.

Live Music & Discos

If you like the skirt-swirling Spanish sound, head for **Alhambra** (☎ 91 521 07 08; Calle Victoria 9) in Santa Ana, which gathers speed at around 11pm. **Morocco** (☎ 91 531 31 77;

Calle del Marqués de Leganés 7) in Malasaña is still a popular stop on the Madrid disco circuit. It gets going about 1am.

Near Plaza de Santa Ana, Calle de la Cruz has a couple of good dance spaces; try to pick up fliers for them before you go – they may save you queuing. **Suristán** at No 7 is a buzzing nightclub dedicated to world music with a colourful, multiethnic clientele and modest cover charge. **Torero** at No 26 has Latin music upstairs and disco house downstairs.

Soul Kitchen *(Calle Fernandez de los Rios 67)* is bigger and badder than ever with the latest hip-hop, reggae and house tracks.

Madrid's not the best where authentic flamenco is concerned, although **Casa Patas** *(☎ 91 369 04 96; Calle de Cañizares 10)* hosts recognised masters of flamenco song, guitar and dance. Bigger flamenco names also play some of Madrid's theatres – check listings.

Cinemas
With tickets around €5, cinemas are reasonably priced. Films in their original language (with Spanish subtitles) are usually marked VO. A good part of town for these is on and around Calle de Martín de los Heros and Calle de la Princesa, near Plaza de España. Check the **Renoir**, **Alphaville** and **Princesa** complexes.

Classical Music, Theatre & Opera
There's plenty happening, except in the height of summer. The city's grandest stage, **Teatro Real** *(☎ 91 516 06 06; Plaza de Isabel 11)*, is for opera. If you can't get in here, the **Teatro Calderón** *(☎ 91 369 14 34; Calle de Atocha 18)* plays second fiddle. Beautiful old **Teatro de la Comedia** *(☎ 91 521 49 31; Calle del Príncipe 14)*, home to the Compañía Nacional de Teatro Clásico, stages gems of classic Spanish and European theatre. The **Centro Cultural de la Villa** *(☎ 91 575 60 80)*, under the waterfall at Plaza de Colón, stages everything from classical concerts to comic theatre, opera and even classy flamenco. Also important for classical music is the **Auditorio Nacional de Música** *(☎ 91 337 01 40; Avenida del Príncipe de Vergara 146; metro Cruz del Rayo)*.

SPECTATOR SPORTS
Spending an afternoon or evening at a football (soccer) match provides quite an insight into Spanish culture. Tickets can be bought on the day of the match, starting from around €15, although big games may be sold out. Real Madrid's home is the huge **Estadio Santiago Bernabeu** *(metro Santiago Bernabeu)*. Atlético Madrid plays at **Estadio Vicente Calderón** *(metro Pirámides)*.

Bullfights take place most Sundays between March and October – more often during the festival of San Isidro Labrador in May – and in summer. Madrid has Spain's largest bullring, the **Plaza de Toros Monumental de Las Ventas** *(☎ 91 726 48 00; metro Ventas)*, and a second bullring by metro Vista Alegre. Tickets are best bought in advance, from agencies or at the rings, and cost up to €12.

SHOPPING
If you're self-catering, follow the shopping baskets to the nearest market. In the centre, **Mercado San Miguel** *(Plaza de San Miguel)* has a good choice of fruit and veg. Pick up your deli items from the mouthwatering display at **Jamonería Ferpal** *(Calle Arenal 7)*. For big-time shopping, El Corte Inglés has a branch on Calle de Preciados with a good size supermarket, albeit pricey. The cheaper hypermarkets are on the outskirts of town. Forgetting food, the most famous market is **El Rastro** (see Things to See & Do earlier in this Madrid section).

For more serious retail therapy, head for Calle de Serrano, a block east of Paseo de la Castellana. Calle del Almirante, off Paseo de Recoletos, has a wide range of engaging, less mainstream shops. For musical instruments, hunt around the area near the Palacio Real. For leather, try the shops on Calle del Príncipe and Gran Vía, or Calle de Fuencarral for shoes. For designer clothing, go to the Chueca area.

GETTING THERE & AWAY
Air
Scheduled and charter flights from all over the world arrive at Madrid's **Barajas airport** *(☎ 902 35 35 70)*, 16km northeast of the city. With nowhere in Spain more than 12 hours away by bus or train, domestic flights are generally not good value unless you're in a burning hurry. Nor is Madrid the budget international flight capital of Europe. That said, you *can* find bargains to popular destinations such as London, Paris and New York. To get an idea of domestic fares, see the Getting Around section earlier in this chapter. See also Travel Agencies under Information earlier in this Madrid section.

SPAIN

Airline offices in Madrid include:

Air France (☎ 91 330 04 12, bookings ☎ 90 111 22 66) Torre de Madrid, Plaza de España 18
American Airlines (☎ 91 453 14 00) Calle de Orense 4
British Airways (☎ 91 387 43 00 or ☎ 902 11 13 33) Calle de Serrano 60
Iberia (☎ 91 587 75 36, bookings ☎ 902 40 05 00) Calle de Velázquez 130
Lufthansa (☎ 902 22 01 01) Calle del Cardenal Marcelo Spinola 2

Bus

There are eight bus stations dotted around Madrid, serving different bus companies. Tourist offices can tell you which one you need. Most buses to the south, and some to other places (including a number of international services), use the **Estación Sur de Autobuses** (☎ 91 468 42 00; Calle de Méndez Álvaro; metro Méndez Álvaro).

Train

Atocha train station, south of the centre, is used by most trains to/from southern Spain and many destinations around Madrid. Some trains from the north also terminate here, passing through **Chamartín**, the other main station (in the northern part of the city), on the way.

RENFE's (☎ 91 328 90 20; open 9.30am-8pm Mon-Fri) main office is on Calle de Alcalá 44.

For fares to Madrid from other towns, see Getting There & Away under those towns.

Car & Motorcycle

Madrid is surrounded by two ring-road systems, the older M-30 and the M-40, considerably further out (a third, the M-50, is under construction). Roads in and out of the city can get pretty clogged around 8am to 10am, 4pm to 5pm and 8pm to 9pm, and on Sunday night.

Car-rental companies in Madrid include **Avis** (☎ 91 547 20 48), **Atesa** (☎ 902 10 01 01), **Europcar** (☎ 91 541 88 92) and **Hertz** (☎ 91 542 58 03). All these have offices at the airport, in the city centre and often at the main train stations. Highway robbery on hire cars leaving the airport is a problem, so be careful.

You can rent motorbikes from **Moto Alquiler** (☎ 91 542 06 57; Calle del Conde Duque 13), but it's pricey, starting at €35 per day for a 50cc Vespa. Rental is from 8am to 8pm and you have to leave a refundable deposit of around €300 on your credit card.

GETTING AROUND
To/From the Airport

The metro runs right into town from the airport, at the upper level of the T2 terminal. Alternatively, an airport bus service runs to/from an underground terminal in Plaza de Colón every 12 to 15 minutes. The trip takes 30 minutes in average traffic and costs €2.50. Note that a taxi between the airport and city centre should cost no more than €20. This is a common rip-off route.

Bus & Metro

In general, the very efficient underground (metro) system is faster and easier than city buses for getting around central Madrid. Trains run from 6.30am to 1.30am.

Bus route maps are available from tourist offices. Night owls may find the 20 bus lines, running from midnight to 6am, useful. They run from Puerta del Sol and Plaza de la Cibeles.

A single ride costs €0.95. A 10-ride Metrobus ticket (€5) can be used on buses and the metro.

Taxi

Madrid's taxis are inexpensive by European standards. They're handy late at night, although in peak hours it's quicker to walk or get the metro. Flag fall is €1.35, after which you are charged by time, so avoid rush-hour.

Car & Motorcycle

There's little point subjecting yourself to Madrid's traffic just to move from one part of the city to another, especially during peak hours. Most on-street parking spaces in central Madrid are designated for people with special permits, but almost everybody ignores this – ignoring the 12,000-plus parking tickets slapped on vehicles every day. But you risk being towed if you park in a marked no-parking or loading zone, or if you double-park. There are plenty of car parks across the city, costing about €1.75 an hour.

AROUND MADRID
El Escorial

The extraordinary 16th-century monastery-palace complex of San Lorenzo de El Escorial (adult/student €6/3 with an additional €1 for a guided tour; open 10am-6pm Tues-Sun Apr-Sept, 10am-5pm Tues-Sun Oct-Mar) lies one hour northwest of Madrid, just outside the town of the same name.

El Escorial was built by Felipe II, king of Spain, Naples, Sicily, Milan, the Netherlands and large parts of the Americas, to commemorate his victory over the French in the battle of St Quentin (1557) and as a mausoleum for his father Carlos I, the first of Spain's Habsburg monarchs. Felipe began searching for a site in 1558, deciding on El Escorial in 1562. The last stone was placed in 1584, and the next 11 years were spent on decoration. El Escorial's austere style, reflecting not only Felipe's wishes but also those of architect Juan de Herrera, is loved by some, hated by others. Either way, it's a quintessential monument of Spain's golden age.

Almost all visitors to El Escorial make it a day trip from Madrid.

Information You can get information on El Escorial from tourist offices in Madrid, or from the local **tourist office** (☎ 91 890 53 13; Calle de Floridablanca 10; open 10am-2pm & 3pm-5pm Mon-Fri, 10am-2pm Sat) close to the monastery.

Things to See Above the monastery's main gateway, on its western side, stands a **statue of San Lorenzo** holding a symbolic gridiron, the instrument of his martyrdom (he was roasted alive on one). Inside, across the Patio de los Reyes, stands the restrained **basílica**, a cavernous church with a beautiful white-marble crucifixion by Benvenuto Cellini, sculpted in 1576. At either side of the altar stand bronze statues of Carlos I and his family (to the left), and Felipe II with three of his four wives and his eldest son (on the right).

The route you have to follow leads first to the **Museo de Arquitectura**, detailing in Spanish how El Escorial was constructed, and the **Museo de Pintura**, with 16th- and 17th-century Spanish, Italian and Flemish fine art. You then head upstairs to the richly decorated **Palacio de Felipe II**, in one room of which the monarch died in 1598; his bed was positioned so that he could watch proceedings at the basilica's high altar. Next you descend to the **Panteón de los Reyes**, where almost all Spain's monarchs since Carlos I, and their spouses, lie in gilded marble coffins. Three empty sarcophagi await future arrivals. Backtracking a little, you find yourself in the **Panteón de los Infantes**, a larger series of chambers and tunnels housing the tombs of princes, princesses and other lesser royalty.

Finally, the **Salas Capitulares** in the southeast of the monastery house a minor treasure trove of El Grecos, Titians and other masters.

When you emerge, it's worth heading back to the entrance, where you can gain access to the **biblioteca** (library), once one of Europe's finest and still a haven for some 40,000 historical and valuable books.

Getting There & Away The Herranz bus company has a service every 10 minutes from 10am to 11pm from No 3 bus stop at the Moncloa metro station in Madrid to San Lorenzo de El Escorial (€2.50 one way). Only about 10 buses run on Sunday and during holidays.

Up to 20 sluggish *cercanías* trains (line C-8a) serve El Escorial from Atocha station (via Chamartín) in Madrid (€3). Seven of these go on to Ávila. Local buses will take you the 2km from the train station up to the monastery.

Castilla y León

The one-time centre of the mighty Christian kingdom of Castile, Castilla y León abounds in romantic mist-enshrouded ruins, convoluted medieval districts and delightful hamlets. Segovia and Ávila provide impressive reminders of antiquity, León and Burgos sport magnificent cathedrals, and Salamanca boasts an intellectual, artsy vibe and fine nightlife.

SEGOVIA
pop 54,040
Segovia's diminutive ridge-top old city and awe-inspiring Roman aqueduct make for a worthwhile day trip from Madrid or a useful launching pad for explorations further into the region. Originally a Celtic settlement, the town was conquered by the Romans around 80 BC. Segovia passed through Visigoth and Moor hands before finally being conquered by Castile in the 11th century.

Both the **main tourist office** (☎ 921 46 03 34; Plaza Mayor) and the **branch tourist office** (☎ 921 46 29 14; Plaza del Azuguejo), beside the aqueduct, are open daily.

Things to See
The first thing you'll notice is the 1st-century AD **aqueduct** stretching over 800m away from the old town's eastern end. Its 163 arches reach up to 29m high, all without the aid of a drop of mortar.

SPAIN

At the heart of the old city is the 16th-century Gothic **cathedral** *(admission €2)* on the pretty Plaza Mayor. Its sombre interior is anchored by an imposing choir and enlivened by about 20 chapels. The Capilla del Cristo del Consuelo houses a remarkable Romanesque doorway preserved from the original church.

Rapunzel towers, turrets topped with slate witch's hats and a deep, dark moat render the **alcázar** *(admission €3)* a most memorable monument. A 15th-century fairy-tale castle, perched on a craggy cliff top at the old city's western end – it was virtually destroyed by fire in 1862. The current structure is an evocative, over-the-top reconstruction of the original. Don't leave without climbing the Torre de Juan II for magnificent views.

Places to Stay
About 2km along the road to La Granja is **Camping Acueducto** *(☎ 921 42 50 00; €4 per person or car; open Apr-Sept)*.

Pensión Aragón *(☎ 921 46 09 14; Plaza Mayor 4; singles/doubles/quads €13/24/26)* is small, clean and characterless but the cheapest place in town. Far more pleasant (but still small) is **Hostal Plaza** *(☎ 921 46 03 03; fax 921 46 03 05; Calle del Cronista Lecea 11; singles/doubles €34/40)*. Also central is **Hostal Juan Bravo** *(☎ 921 43 55 21; Calle de Juan Bravo 12)*, with similar prices.

Outside the old town, but close to the aqueduct, is the spick-and-span **Hostal Don Jaime** *(☎ 921 44 47 87; Calle de Ochoa Ondategui 8; singles/doubles €25/41)*, where the doubles also have TV.

Places to Eat
The simple **Bar Ratos** *(Calle de los Escuderos; bocadillos €3)* makes generously stuffed sandwiches. **Cueva de San Esteban** *(Calle de Valdeláguila 15; set lunch €6)* has delicious lunch menús. A good place to sample Segovia's speciality – *cochinillo asado* (roast suckling pig) – is the timber-laden dining room of **Mesón José María** *(Calle del Cronista Lecea 11; suckling pig ración €5.50)*, a favourite among Segovians.

For meatless fare, try **La Almuzara** *(Marqués del Arco 3; vegie plato combinado €7; open for lunch Wed-Sun, dinner Tues-Sun)*.

Getting There & Around
Up to 30 buses daily run to Madrid (€5, 1½ hours); others serve Ávila and Salamanca.

The bus station is 500m south of the aqueduct, just off Paseo Ezequiel González. Trains to Madrid leave every two hours (€4.50, 1¾ hours). The station is southeast of town; take bus No 2 to the centre.

AROUND SEGOVIA
In the mountain village of San Ildefonso de la Granja, 12km southeast of Segovia, lie the royal palace and glorious gardens of **La Granja**, a Spanish version of Versailles built by Felipe V in 1720. The 300-room Palacio Real, restored after a fire in 1918, is impressive. You can visit about half of the rooms, including the **Museo de Tapices** *(Tapestry Museum; admission €5)*. A highlight of the **gardens** *(admission €2.50)* are the 28 fountains. Buses run regularly from Segovia to San Ildefonso.

About 50km northwest of Segovia, **Castillo de Coca** is well worth a visit. This all-brick castle was built in 1453 by the powerful Fonseca family. **Guided tours** costing €2.50 operate daily. Up to five buses daily make the trip from Segovia.

ÁVILA
pop 47,970
Impressive Ávila is one of the world's best-preserved walled cities. Constructed during the 11th and 12th centuries, its imposing *muralla* (rampart) consists of no fewer than eight monumental gates and 88 towers.

At 1130m Ávila is also the highest city in Spain – and the birthplace of St Teresa of Ávila, a 16th-century mystical writer and reformer of the Carmelite order. Less emphasised is that Tomás de Torquemada orchestrated the most brutal phase of the Spanish Inquisition here, sending off 2000 people to be burnt at the stake in the late 15th century.

The folks at the **tourist office** *(☎ 920 21 13 87; Plaza de la Catedral 4; open daily)* are far more friendly than Torquemada.

Things to See & Do
Of Ávila's many convents, museums and monuments, the **cathedral** *(admission €2.50; open daily)* is perhaps the most interesting. Not merely a house of worship, it was also an ingenious fortress: its stout granite apse forms the central bulwark in the eastern wall of the town, which was the most open to attack and hence the most heavily fortified.

Around the western side, the main facade conceals the Romanesque origins of what is essentially the earliest Gothic church in Spain. You can catch a peek inside for free, but proceeding to the inner sanctum – plus the cloister, sacristy and small museum – requires the entrance fee.

Just outside the walls, the Romanesque **Basílica de San Vicente** *(admission €1.50; open daily)* is striking. Gothic modifications in granite clash with the warm sandstone of the 11th-century Romanesque original.

About 500m east of the old town, the **Monasterio de Santo Tomás** *(admission €1; open daily)* is thought to be Torquemada's burial place. Built hastily in 1482 as a royal residence, it is formed by three interconnecting cloisters and the church.

The **Convento de Santa Teresa** *(admission free; open daily)* was built in 1636, over the saint's birthplace. The room where she was purportedly born is now a gold-smothered chapel. The souvenir shop next door gives access to a room crammed with relics, including Teresa's ring finger (complete with ring).

Los Cuatro Postes, a lookout point around 1km west of the city gates on the Salamanca road, has the best view of the city and its perfectly preserved walls.

Places to Stay
The well-maintained rooms at **Hostal Jardín** *(☎ 920 21 10 74; Calle de San Segundo 38; singles/doubles from €24/34)* come with shared bath and TV. **Hostal El Rastro** *(☎ 920 21 12 18; Plaza del Rastro 1; singles/doubles €27/34)* boasts harshly lit quarters and a good restaurant. More comfortable is **Hostal San Juan** *(☎ 920 25 14 75; Calle de los Comuneros de Castilla 3; singles/doubles €26/34)*, where rooms are sparkly clean and happily orange.

Places to Eat
Pleasant **Posada de la Fruta** *(Plaza de Pedro Dávila 8; bar plates €3-6, meals €10-13)* serves cheap and informal meals in its bar/cafeteria and more substantial fare in its traditional dining room. **Siglo Doce**, just inside Puerta de los Leales, has good bocadillos for €3. **El Rincón de Jabugo** *(Calle de San Segundo 30; salads & pasta €5)* offers solid Italian fare.

Café del Adarve *(Calle de San Segundo 50)* is a hip hang-out and good place for a drink, as is the wine and tapas bar **Bodeguita de San Segundo**, across the street.

Restaurante Los Leales *(Plaza de Italia 4; set menu €8)* offers a filling menú.

Getting There & Away
Buses to Madrid leave up to eight times on weekdays, down to three on the weekend (€5.50, 1½ hours), while Segovia is served up to seven times on weekdays (€5, one hour) and Salamanca four times (€4.50, 1½ hours). There are up to 30 trains a day to Madrid (€5.50, 1½ hours); trains to Salamanca cost the same.

The bus and train stations are, respectively, 700m and 1.5km east of the old town. Bus No 1 links the train station with the old town.

BURGOS
pop 166,250
God has been kind to Burgos, blessing it with one of Spain's greatest Gothic cathedrals as well as a couple of notable monasteries. Unfortunately, the attitude of its citizenry occasionally reflects the town's cold climate.

Information
The **regional tourist office** *(☎ 947 20 31 25; Plaza de Alonso Martínez 7; open Mon-Sat)* and a **branch tourist office** *(☎ 947 28 88 74; Paseo de Espolón; open Mon-Sat)*, inside the Teatro Principal, are well staffed and helpful. The main **post office** is on Plaza del Conde de Castro. **Ciber-Café Cabaret** *(Calle de la Puebla 21)* provides Internet access for €5 an hour.

Things to See
It is difficult to imagine that on the site of the majestic 1261 Gothic **cathedral** *(cloister & treasures admission €3.50)* there once stood a modest Romanesque church. Twin towers, each representing 84m of richly decorated fantasy, lord over this truly dizzying masterpiece. Inside, the highlight is the Escalera Dorada (Gilded Staircase) by Diego de Siloé. El Cid lies buried beneath the central dome.

The **Monasterio de las Huelgas** *(admission €5; open Tues-Sun)* is Burgos' most interesting monastery. About a half-hour's walk west of the centre along the southern bank of the Río Arlanzón, it was founded in 1187 by Eleanor of Aquitaine and is still home to 35 Cistercian nuns. The highlights of the guided tour include Las Claustrillas, an elegant

SPAIN

Romanesque cloister, and a museum with preserved garments once worn by Eleanor and other medieval royals.

About 3.5km east of the centre, the **Cartuja de Miraflores** is a functioning Carthusian monastery rich in treasure. The walk along the Río Arlanzón is pleasant. Alternatively, you could take the 'Fuentes Blancas' bus (which makes the trip from the centre six times daily).

Places to Stay & Eat
Camping Fuentes Blancas (☎/fax 947 48 60 16; €3.50 per person or vehicle; open Apr-Sept) is 4km from the centre on the road to the Cartuja de Miraflores. You can take the 'Fuentes Blancas' bus (see earlier) to get here.

Bright, clean, large, gregariously sociable – it's all part of the package at **Pensión Peña** (☎ 947 20 62 23; Calle de la Puebla 18; singles/doubles €11/18). **Hostal Joma** (☎ 947 20 33 50; Calle de San Juan 26; singles/doubles €12/20) isn't terribly friendly but is cheap and in the heart of the action. **Hotel Norte y Londres** (☎ 947 26 41 25; Plaza Alonso Martínez 10; singles/doubles €41/58), is a tremendous value, with enormous, comfortable rooms.

Cervecería Morito (Calle de la Sombrerería) is popular with locals for its cheap drinks and cheap hot dishes. **Royal** (Huerto del Rey 23; dishes under €5) serves a wide range of salads, burgers and sandwiches.

Getting There & Away
The bus station is at Calle de Miranda 3. Continental Auto runs up to 12 buses daily to Madrid (€12). Buses also run to most major Spanish cities as well as France.

The train station is in a little enclave south of the river, west of the city centre. Trains to Madrid depart up to seven times daily (€12, four hours) and to Bilbao six times (€14, three hours). Others go to León, Salamanca and other major cities.

SALAMANCA
pop 158,520
Storied Salamanca presents fairy-tale sights by day and hopping action at night. It's one of Spain's most inspiring cities, both in the beauty of its architecture and its modern, laid-back lifestyle. Year round, its countless bars, cafés and restaurants are jam-packed with students and young visitors from around the world.

Information
The **municipal tourist office** (☎ 923 21 83 42; Plaza Mayor; open daily), concentrates on city information. A **branch tourist office** (☎ 923 26 85 71; Casa de las Conchas; open Mon-Fri & Sat morning) focuses on the wider region.

The **post office** is on Gran Vía 25. For Internet access try **Campus Cibermático** (Plaza Mayor 10). A coin-operated **laundrette** tries to hide in an arcade off Pasaje Azafranal.

Things to See
One of the joys of Salamanca is simply wandering the streets. At the heart of the old centre is the harmonious **Plaza Mayor** (1755), designed by José Churriguera, which is ringed by medallions of sundry famous figures; until the 19th century, bullfights took place here.

Salamanca's **university** was founded in 1218. Its main facade on Calle de los Libreros is a tapestry in sandstone, bursting with images of mythical and historical figures, including a famously elusive frog. Join the throngs trying to find the little creature.

Brace yourself for the **Catedral Nueva** (New Cathedral). This incredible Gothic structure, completed in 1733, took 220 years to build. With its intricate carvings and detailed relief, it's a wonder they did it so fast. From inside you can enter the adjacent **Catedral Vieja** (Old Cathedral; admission €2.50). A Romanesque construction begun in 1120, it's a bit of a hybrid, with some Gothic elements; the ribbed cupola shows a Byzantine influence.

Other major sights include the **Convento de San Esteban** (admission €1.50; open daily) and **Convento de las Dueñas** (admission €1.50; open daily). The 15th-century **Casa de las Conchas** (open daily), named for the scallop shells clinging to its facade, is a symbol of Salamanca.

Places to Stay
Salamanca is always in season, so book ahead. The central HI **Albergue Juvenil** (☎ 923 26 91 41, fax 923 21 42 27; e est erra@mmteam.disbumad.es; Calle Escoto 13-15; dorm beds €12) has standard bunks. Rates include linen and breakfast.

Hotel Los Ángeles (☎ 923 21 81 66; Plaza Mayor 10; singles/doubles €13/27) has low-frills rooms with washbasins and shared bath. A favourite of young people is tiny, hospitable **Pensión Las Vegas** (☎ 923 21 87 49;

e lasvegas@iponet.es; Calle de Meléndez 13; singles/doubles €12/18). Rooms at **Pensión Feli** (☎ 923 21 60 10; Calle de los Libreros 58; singles/doubles €12/24) are homey.

For more comfort, try **Le Petit Hotel** (☎ 923 60 07 73; Ronda de Sancti-Spíritus 39; singles/doubles €35/43), whose small but tidy rooms have phone, TV and bath. **Hotel La Perla Salamantina** (☎ 923 21 76 56, fax 923 27 22 53; Calle de Sánchez Barbero 7; singles/doubles €51/65) has lovely rooms with all the conveniences.

Places to Eat

For good and filling breakfasts, hit **Café Unamuno** (Calle Zamora 55; breakfast €2.50). **MusicArte Café** (Plaza del Corrillo 22; sandwiches €2, pizza €8) is a hip hang-out.

El Patio Chico (Calle de Meléndez 13; tapas €3, set menu €10) is a lively place for filling tapas. At **Café El Ave** (Calle de los Libreros 24; meals €5) you can eat at budget prices. Sample aromatic paella at bustling **El Bardo** (Calle de la Compañia 8; paella €7). **El Grillo Azul** (Calle Grillo 1; set menu €8) offers cheap all-veg fare in an elegant setting.

La Regenta (Calle de Espoz y Mina 19-20) is a candlelit café with velvet curtains, polished antiques and substantial cakes.

Entertainment

Salamanca, with its myriad bars, is the perfect after-dark playground. A drink at **Tío Vivo** (Calle de Clavel 3) is a must, if only to experience the whimsical decor. A long-time favourite is **El Gran Café Moderno** (Calle

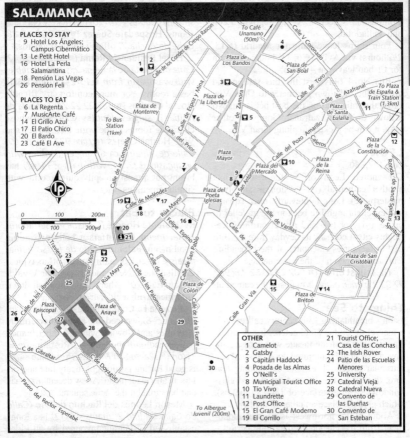

Gran Vía 75), resembling an early-20th-century Parisian street. **El Corrillo** (Calle de Meléndez 8) is great for a beer and (sometimes) live jazz. **O'Neill's** (Calle de Zamora 14) and **The Irish Rover** are Irish pubs.

Capitán Haddock is a surprisingly romantic haunt with a muted nautical theme, in a courtyard off Calle Consejo. A popular bar is **Gatsby** (Calle de Bordadores 18).

Discos include **Camelot** (Calle de la Compañía), inside a convent, and **Posada de las Almas** (Plaza de San Boal), a fantasy world inhabited by life-sized papier-mâché figures.

Getting There & Around

Salamanca's bus station is about 1km northwest of Plaza Mayor. AutoRes has frequent express services to Madrid (€15, 2½ hours), as well as a few nonexpress buses. Other destinations served regularly include Santiago de Compostela, Cáceres, Ávila, Segovia, León and Valladolid.

Four trains leave daily for Madrid (€13, 2½ hours) via Ávila (€6, 1¾ hours). A train for Lisbon leaves at 4.40am.

Bus No 4 runs past the bus station and around the old town perimeter to Gran Vía. From the train station, the best bet is bus No 1 down Calle de Azafranal. Going the other way, it can be picked up along Gran Vía.

LEÓN
pop 137,380

Oft-ignored León offers more than just another cathedral (its version is simply a masterpiece). Long boulevards, open squares and excellent nightlife beckon the traveller to pause a day or two and reflect on the once-mighty city. León saw its heyday from the 10th to 13th centuries as capital of the expanding Christian kingdom of the same name.

The **tourist office** (☎ 987 23 70 82, fax 987 27 33 91; open daily) is opposite the cathedral.

Things to See

León's breathtaking 13th-century **cathedral** is a marvel of Gothic architecture. It has an extraordinarily intricate facade with a rose window, three richly sculptured doorways and two muscular towers. The most outstanding feature, though, is the 128 radiant stained-glass windows (with a surface of 1800 sq metres), which give the place an ethereal quality.

About 500m northwest is a great monument from the earlier Romanesque period –

the **Real Basílica de San Isidoro**. It contains the **Panteón Real** (admission €3), where Leónese royalty lie buried beneath a canopy of some of the finest frescoes in all of Spain.

The last in León's trio of major sights is the **Hostal de San Marcos**, at the end of the Gran Vía de San Marcos. This former pilgrim's hospital, with its golden-hued 100m-long facade (1513), now houses a parador (luxury hotel) and the **Museo de León** (admission €1.50; open Tues-Sun).

Antoni Gaudí designed the **Casa de Botines** (Plaza de San Marcelo), although it's rather conservative by his standards.

Places to Stay

Spartan quarters are the hallmark of **Hostal Jalisco** (☎ 987 22 64 44; Avenida de Roma 18; singles/doubles €13/20). Friendly **Pensión Berta** (☎ 987 25 70 39; Plaza Mayor 8; singles/doubles €15/20) has rickety but clean rooms. **Hospedaje Suárez** (☎ 987 25 42 88; Calle de Ancha 7) offers similar standards.

Hotel Residencia Reina (☎ 987 20 52 12; Calle de Puerta de la Reina 2; singles/doubles with washbasin from €15/24) offers small, basic rooms. For more comfort, try friendly **Hostal Londres** (☎ 987 22 22 74; Avenida de Roma 1; singles/doubles €24/30), whose charming rooms come with TV, shower and WC. **Hostal Orejas** (☎/fax 987 25 29 09; Calle de Villafranca 6; singles/doubles with washbasin €27/34, with bath €34/47) has bright but almost creepily quiet rooms with similar amenities.

Places to Eat

Restaurante Honoré (Calle de los Serradores 4; set menu €7) offers a belly-expanding good menú. **Palomo** (Calle de la Escalerilla; meals €10-20), on a tiny street, offers typical Castilian fare. Next door is popular **Vivaldi** (meals €10-20), where you can wash down your meal with a cider from Asturias.

Pizzeria La Competencia (Calle Mulhacín; pizzas €5-8), wedged into a tight street, offers tasty pies and flowing wine. Another branch has opened on Rebolledo Az. **Restaurante El Tizón** (Plaza de San Martín 1; set lunch €11) is good for big portions of meaty fare and offers an abundant menú. A few decent pizzerias and bars inhabit the same square.

Mesón Leonés del Racimo de Oro (Calle de Caño Badillo 2; mains €8-12) is a long-established restaurant favoured by an older

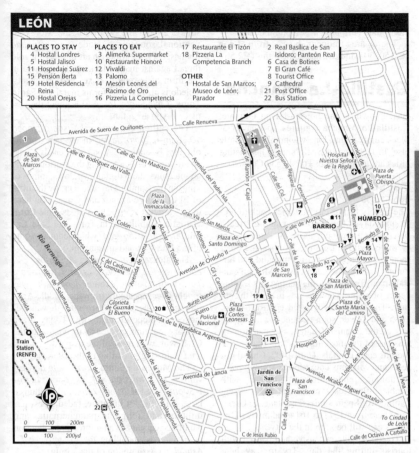

LEÓN

PLACES TO STAY
4 Hostal Londres
5 Hostal Jalisco
11 Hospedaje Suárez
15 Pensión Berta
19 Hotel Residencia
    Reina
20 Hostal Orejas

PLACES TO EAT
3 Alimerka Supermarket
10 Restaurante Honoré
12 Vivaldi
13 Palomo
14 Mesón Leonés del
    Racimo de Oro
16 Pizzeria La Competencia

17 Restaurante El Tizón
18 Pizzeria La
    Competencia Branch

OTHER
1 Hostal de San Marcos;
    Museo de León;
    Parador

2 Real Basílica de San
    Isidoro; Panteón Real
6 Casa de Botines
7 El Gran Café
8 Tourist Office
9 Cathedral
21 Post Office
22 Bus Station

SPAIN

crowd. **Alimerka** *(Avenida Roma 2)* is a well-stocked supermarket.

Entertainment
León's nocturnal activity flows thickest in the aptly named **Barrio Húmedo** *(Wet Quarter)*, the crowded tangle of lanes leading south off Calle de Ancha. Outside of the Barrio, **El Gran Café** *(Calle de Cervantes)* is a classy and popular spot, but there are plenty of other possibilities along this street, as well as on Calle de Fernando Regueral and Calle de Sacramento.

Getting There & Away
Alsa has up to 12 buses daily to Madrid (€17, 3½ hours) and A Coruña (€17, six hours). Other destinations include Bilbao, Burgos, Salamanca and San Sebastián.

Up to 10 trains daily leave for Madrid (€28, 4½ hours), and three go to Barcelona (€40, 10½ hours). Plenty of trains head west to A Coruña (€25, 6½ hours) and east to Burgos (€16, 1½ hours).

AROUND LEÓN
An extravagant example of Antoni Gaudí's work is in **Astorga**, 47km southwest of León. The playful **Palacio Episcopal** (1889) integrates nearly all of Gaudí's stylistic hallmarks, including storybook turrets, frilly facades and surprising details. Inside is the **Museo de los Caminos** *(admission €2.50)*, with moderately interesting Roman artefacts and religious art. Tickets are also good for the cathedral museum next door. Both are open Tuesday to Saturday and Sunday morning. The cathedral has

a striking facade of caramel-coloured sandstone and is dripping in sculptural detail.

There are frequent buses from León (€2.50, 30 minutes), and some trains (€2.50).

Castilla-La Mancha

Best known as the home of Don Quixote, Castilla-La Mancha conjures up images of bleak empty plains, lonely windmills and little else. In fact, two of Spain's most fascinating cities are located here: Toledo and Cuenca.

TOLEDO
pop 69,450

The history of this city stretches back to pre-Roman days. The narrow, winding streets, perched on a small hill above the Río Tajo, are crammed with museums, churches and other monumental reminders of a splendid and turbulent past. As the main city of Muslim central Spain, Toledo was the peninsula's leading centre of learning and the arts in the 11th century. The Christians wrested control of it in 1085 and Toledo soon became the headquarters of the Spanish Church. For centuries it was one of the most important of Spain's numerous early capitals. Until 1492, Christians, Jews and Muslims coexisted peaceably here. Its unique architectural combinations, with Arabic influences everywhere, are a strong reminder of Spain's mixed heritage. El Greco lived here from 1577 to 1614 and many of his works can still be seen in the city.

Toledo is quite expensive and packed with tourists during the day. Try to stay here overnight, when you can really appreciate the spark and soul of the city.

Information

The **main tourist office** (☎ 925 22 08 43, fax 925 25 26 48) is just outside Toledo's main gate, the Puerta Nueva de Bisagra, at the northern end of town. A smaller information office is open in the *ayuntamiento* (town hall), across from the cathedral. You can connect to the Internet at **Scorpions** (☎ 925 21 25 56; Calle Matías Moreno 10; open 12.30pm-2am) for €2.20 an hour; it's located close to the San Juan de los Reyes monastery.

Things to See & Do

Toledo has lots to see. As well as the historical sights, its tourist shops are fun, many reflecting the city's swashbuckling past with suits of armour and swords for sale. More conventional souvenirs include *damasquinado* (damascene), the Moorish art of inlaying gold thread against matte black steel, available in the form of jewellery, boxes and ornaments. Toledo is also famous for its marzipan. **Santo Tomé** (*Calle Santo Tomé 5*) is about the best place if you are a fan.

The **cathedral** (*Cardenal Cisneros; open 10.30am-6.30pm daily*), in the heart of the old city, is stunning. You could easily spend an afternoon here, admiring the glorious stone architecture, stained-glass windows, tombs of kings in the Capilla Mayor and art by the likes of El Greco, Velázquez and Goya. You have to buy a ticket to enter four areas – the **Coro, Sacristía, Capilla de la Torre** and **Sala Capitular** (*admission €5*), which contain some of the finest art and artisanship.

The **alcázar** (*Calle Cuesta de Carlos V, 2; admission €2, free Wed; open 9.30am-2pm Tues-Sun*), Toledo's main landmark, was fought over repeatedly from the Middle Ages through to the Civil War, when it was besieged by Republican troops. Today it's a military museum, created by the victors of the Civil War, with most of the displays – which are fascinating – relating to the 1936 siege.

The **Museo de Santa Cruz** (*Calle de Cervantes 3; admission €1.50; open 10am-6.30pm Tues-Sat, 10am-2pm Sun*) contains a large collection of furniture, faded tapestries, military and religious paraphernalia, and paintings. Upstairs is an impressive collection of El Grecos, including the masterpiece *La Asunción* (Assumption of the Virgin).

In the southwestern part of the old city, the queues outside an unremarkable church, the **Iglesia de Santo Tomé** (*Plaza del Conde; admission €1.50; open 10am-6pm daily winter, 10am-7pm daily summer*), indicate there must be something special inside. That something is El Greco's masterpiece *El Entierro del Conde de Orgaz*. The painting depicts the burial of the Count of Orgaz in 1322 by San Esteban (St Stephen) and San Agustín (St Augustine), observed by a heavenly entourage, including Christ, the Virgin, John the Baptist and Noah.

The so-called **Casa y Museo de El Greco** (*Calle de Samuel Leví; admission €1.50; open 10am-2pm & 4pm-6pm Mon-Sat, 10am-2pm Sun*), in Toledo's former Jewish quarter, contains the artist's famous *Vista y*

Plano de Toledo, plus about 20 of his minor works. Although El Greco certainly lived in Toledo, it is unlikely he ever lived here.

At the time of research, the nearby **Sinagoga del Tránsito** was closed for restoration. Check at the tourist office for an update.

Toledo's other synagogue, **Santa María La Blanca** *(Calle de los Reyes Católicos 4; admission €1.50; open 10am-2pm & 3.30pm-6pm daily)*, a short way north, dates back to the 12th century.

A little further north lies one of the city's most visible sights, **San Juan de los Reyes**, the Franciscan monastery and church founded by Fernando and Isabel. The prevalent late Flemish-Gothic style is tarted up with lavish Isabelline ornamentation and counterbalanced by mudéjar decoration. Outside hang the

chains of Christian prisoners freed after the fall of Granada in 1492.

Places to Stay

The nearest camping ground is **Camping Circo Romano** *(☎ 925 22 04 42; Avenida de Carlos III 19)*, but a notch up, category-wise, is **Camping El Greco** *(☎ 925 22 00 90)*, which is well signposted 2.5km southwest of town. Both are open year-round.

Cheap accommodation is not easy to come by and is often full, especially from Easter to September. Toledo's HI hostel, **Residencia Juvenil de San Servando** *(☎ 925 22 45 54, fax 925 21 39 54; beds for under/over 26 €10/13, including breakfast)*, is a place beautifully located in the Castillo de San Servando, a castle that started life as a Visigothic

SPAIN

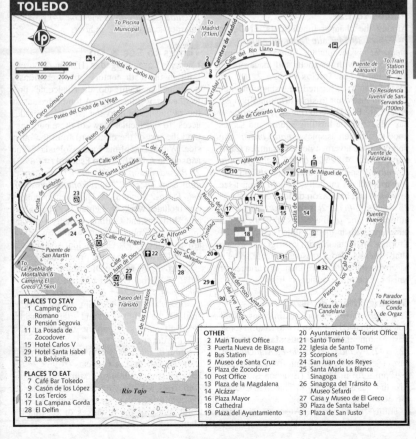

TOLEDO

PLACES TO STAY
1 Camping Circo Romano
8 Pensión Segovia
11 La Posada de Zocodover
15 Hotel Carlos V
29 Hotel Santa Isabel
32 La Belviseña

PLACES TO EAT
7 Café Bar Tolsedo
9 Casón de los López
12 Los Tercios
17 La Campana Gorda
28 El Delfin

OTHER
2 Main Tourist Office
3 Puerta Nueva de Bisagra
4 Bus Station
5 Museo de Santa Cruz
6 Plaza de Zocodover
10 Post Office
13 Plaza de la Magdalena
14 Alcázar
16 Plaza Mayor
18 Cathedral
19 Plaza del Ayuntamiento
20 Ayuntamiento & Tourist Office
21 Santo Tomé
22 Iglesia de Santo Tomé
23 Scorpions
24 San Juan de los Reyes
25 Santa María La Blanca Sinagoga
26 Sinagoga del Tránsito & Museo Sefardí
27 Casa y Museo de El Greco
30 Plaza de Santa Isabel
31 Plaza de San Justo

monastery. **La Belviseña** (☎ 925 22 00 67; Cuesta del Can 5; rooms per person €10) is basic but among the best value (if you can get in). Pleasant **Pensión Segovia** (☎ 925 21 11 24; Calle de los Recoletos 2; singles/doubles €14.50/ 19.50) has simple, clean rooms.

Appealing new **La Posada de Zocodover** (☎ 925 22 15 71; Calle Condonerias 6; doubles with bath €37.50) has just seven exquisite rooms that get snapped up fast. Comfortable and chic, **Hotel Santa Isabel** (☎/fax 925 25 31 36; Calle de Santa Isabel 24; singles/ doubles €28/42) is well placed near the cathedral, yet away from the tourists. Choose a room with a view of the cathedral at **Hotel Carlos V** (☎ 925 22 21 00, fax 925 22 21 05; Calle Trastamara 1; singles/doubles €76/ 113), which is inching into the luxury bracket with antiques and old-fashioned service.

Places to Eat
Among the cheaper lunch spots, **El Delfín** (☎ 925 21 38 14; Calle Taller del Moro 1; set menu €6) is acceptable, if unexciting. Similarly priced with spaghetti and macaroni on the menu is **Los Tercios** (☎ 925 22 05 50; Plaza Solarejo 2) located on a shady plaza.

If you just want to sip a drink and people-gaze, **Café Bar Tolsedo** (Plaza de Zocodover) has tables on the bustling square and serves good tapas, such as spicy patatas bravas. An unpretentious tavern-style restaurant, **La Campana Gorda** (☎ 925 21 01 46; Calle Hombre de Palo 13) specialises in roast meats and fish, and football on the telly. Toledo's must-see restaurant and bar **Casón de los López** (☎ 925 25 47 74; Sillería 2; closed Sun dinner) is housed in one of the city's most beautiful buildings, with antiques, vaulted ceilings, even a former small chapel with its original baroque altar. There's also a reasonable café, plus a basement bar with more than 90 varieties of whisky. One of the owners is Irish.

Getting There & Away
To reach most major destinations from Toledo, you need to backtrack to Madrid (or at least Aranjuez). Toledo's **bus station** (☎ 925 22 36 41; Avenida de Castilla-La Mancha) has buses (€3.50) every half-hour from about 6am to 10pm to/from Madrid (Estación Sur). The Aisa line has a service from Toledo to Cuenca at 5.30pm Monday to Friday.

Trains from Madrid (Atocha) are more pleasant than the bus, but there are only nine daily. The first from Madrid departs at 7.05am, the last from Toledo at 8.58pm (€5 one way). Toledo's **train station** (☎ 902 24 02 02) is on Calle Paseo de la Rosa, 400m east of the Puente de Azarquiel.

Bus No 5 links the train and bus stations with Plaza de Zocodover.

CUENCA
pop 46,490
Cuenca's setting is hard to believe. The high old town is cut off from the rest of the city by the Júcar and Huécar Rivers, sitting at the top of a deep gorge. Most of its famous monuments appear to teeter on the edge – making them a photographer's delight.

The **tourist office** (☎/fax 902 10 01 31; e ofi.turismo@aytocuenca.org; Plaza Mayor 1), just before the arches of the main square, is especially helpful. **Big Play** (☎ 969 23 69 28; Avenida Castillo de la Mancha 14) provides Internet access for €2 an hour.

Things to See & Do
Cuenca's **Casas Colgadas** (Hanging Houses), built in the 15th century, are precariously positioned on a cliff top, their balconies projecting out over the gorge. A footbridge across the ravine leading to the parador provides access to spectacular views of these buildings (and the rest of the old town) from the other side. Within one of the Casas Colgadas is the **Museo de Arte Abstracto Español** (☎ 969 21 29 83; admission €1.50; open 11am-2pm & 4pm-6pm Tues-Fri, 11am-2pm & 4pm-8pm Sat, 11am-2.30pm Sun). This exciting collection includes works by Fernando Zobel, Sempere, Millares and Chillida. Initially a private initiative of Zobel to unite works by fellow artists of the 1950s Generación Abstracta, it now holds works up to the present day.

Nearby is the **Museo Diocesano** (☎ 969 22 42 10; Calle del Obispo Valero 2; admission €1; open 11am-2pm & 4pm-6pm Tues-Fri, 11am-2pm & 4pm-8pm Sat, 11am-2.30pm Sun). Of the religious art and artefacts inside, the 14th-century Byzantine diptych is the jewel in the crown.

South of Plaza Mayor in a former convent is the **Museo de Las Ciencias** (☎ 969 24 03 20; admission free; open 10am-2pm & 4pm-7pm Tues-Sat, Sun morning). This science museum's displays range from a time machine to the study of the resources of Castilla-La Mancha.

On Plaza Mayor you'll find Cuenca's strange **cathedral**. The lines of the unfinished facade are Norman-Gothic and reminiscent of French cathedrals, but the stained-glass windows look like they'd be more at home in the abstract art museum.

As you wander the old town's beautiful streets, check the **Torre de Mangana**, the remains of a Moorish fortress in a square west of Calle de Alfonso VIII, overlooking the plain below.

Places to Stay & Eat

Up at the top of the *casco* (old town) is the budget winner **Pensión La Tabanqueta** (☎ 969 21 12 90; Calle de Trabuco 13; doubles from €30). Ask for a room with views of the Júcar gorge and check out the lively bar downstairs.

Costing more but elegantly sumptuous **Leonor de Aquitania** (☎ 969 22 19 78; Calle San Pedro 60; singles/doubles €64/81) has a sister hotel **Cueva del Fraile**, which is a few kilometres out of town and has definite rustic appeal, as well as the added perk of a swimming pool.

At the edge of the gorge with drop-dead views, the tastefully converted 17th-century former convent **Posada de San José** (☎ 969 21 13 00, fax 923 03 65; e info@posadasanjose.com; Calle Julián Romero 4; doubles from €60) makes for an evocative romantic retreat with every room different but tastefully done.

Most restaurants and cafés around Plaza Mayor are better for a drink and people watching than for good-value eating, although **Taberna el Botijo** is of a higher standard. A decent establishment for solid La Manchan food is the **Restaurante Los Arcos 11** (☎ 969 21 38 06; Calle Severo Catalina 1) with some interesting dishes priced from €5. For superb cheeses and local wines to take away, **La Alacena** delicatessen (Alfonso V111 32) is worth seeking out.

Getting There & Away

There are up to nine buses a day to Madrid (€8.50 to €10, 2½ hours), and daily buses to Barcelona, Teruel and Valencia. There are five trains a day direct to Madrid (€8.50, 2½ hours), which arrive at Atocha train station. There are also four trains a day to Valencia.

Bus No 1 or 2 from near the bus and train stations will take you up to Plaza Mayor in the old town.

Catalunya

Many Catalans bristle at the idea of being lumped together with 'ordinary' Spaniards, maintaining that their corner of the universe is a little closer to heaven. And with its soaring peaks, tranquil coastal resorts, sleepy small towns and exuberant capital, modern-day Catalunya may well lay claim to being its own world. Whether or not one sympathises with Catalan separatists, one must admit that the region offers a culture and lifestyle that sets it apart from the rest of Spain.

BARCELONA
pop 1.5 million

Until the 1990s, Barcelona remained a well-kept secret among Western European backpackers. The 1992 Olympic Games served as the town's coming-out party, stylishly introducing this first-class city to the world. Today, folks come from all corners of the globe to marvel at Barcelona's transcendent modernist architecture, to visit its top-shelf museums and to roam the streets of its old quarter.

No-one should come to Barcelona and miss the visionary creations of Antoni Gaudí, including the Sagrada Família church and Parc Güell. Visitors can further indulge by spending days admiring the works of Pablo Picasso and Joan Miró and spending nights in debauched frenzy, winding their way through the city's myriad bars and clubs. And whether it's midday or midnight, Barcelona's famed street, La Rambla, presents a never-ending stream of hawkers, musicians, beggars, backpackers and villains – nonstop entertainment for the privileged and destitute alike.

Orientation

Barcelona's main square, Plaça de Catalunya, is a good place to get your bearings. The main tourist office is right here, and La Rambla extends southwards. Most travellers base themselves in Barcelona's old city (Ciutat Vella), the area bordered by the Port Vell (south), Plaça de Catalunya (north), Ronda de Sant Pau (west) and Parc de la Ciutadella (east).

La Rambla, the city's best-known boulevard, runs through the heart of the old city down to the harbour. On the eastern side is the medieval quarter (Barri Gòtic), and on the west the seedy Barri Xinès. North of the old city is the gracious neighbourhood of L'Eixample, where you'll find the best of Barcelona's modernist architecture.

One of the best maps of Barcelona is Lonely Planet's very own *Barcelona* City Map. Other good maps are available from the tourist office (see Information following).

Information

Tourist Offices The main tourist office in town is the **Centre d'Informació Turisme de Barcelona** (☎ 906 30 12 82; ⓦ *www.barcel onaturisme.com; Plaça de Catalunya 17-S; open 9am-9pm daily*), which is actually underground. Ask here for city maps, lists of attractions and handy discount cards (such as the Barcelona Card and ArTicket) that let you into select locations for reduced admission fees.

Handy offices are located at Estació Sants, the main train station, and at the EU passengers arrivals hall at the airport and both open daily (mornings only on Sunday and holidays).

Money Banks usually have the best rates for cash and travellers cheques; hours are usually 8am to 2pm Monday to Friday. Both **American Express offices** (*Passeig de Gràcia 101; La Rambla dels Capuxtins 74; open 9.30am-6pm Mon-Fri, 10am-noon Sat*) offer reasonable rates. For after-hours, currency-exchange booths throng La Rambla.

Post & Communications The **main post office** (*Plaça d'Antoni López; open 8am-9.30pm Mon-Sat*) is open for most services, including poste restante (*lista de correos*).

Email & Internet Access There are dozens of places to check your emails. Both **EasyEverything** (*La Rambla*), at €0.50 to €2 an hour, and **Conéct@te** (*Carrer d'Aragó 283*), at €1.50 an hour, are open 24 hours, although you might not want to wander too close to unshowered Internet users at 4am.

Travel Agencies Youth and student air, train and bus tickets can be purchased at **USIT Unlimited** (☎ 93 412 01 04; Ronda de l'Universitat 16). There's a branch in the **Turisme Juvenil de Catalunya office** (*Carrer de Rocafort 116-122*). **Halcón Viatges** (☎ 902 30 06 00; Carrer de Pau Claris 108) is a reliable chain of travel agents.

Bookshops In the Barri Gòtic, **Quera** (*Carrer de Petritxol 2*) specialises in maps and guides. **Próleg** (*Carrer de la Dagueria 13*) is a good women's bookshop.

In L'Eixample, **Altaïr** (*Carrer de Balmes 71*) is a superb travel bookshop. **Librería Francesa** (*Passeig de Gràcia 91*) has French-language books and **Come In** (*Carrer de Provença 203*) is good for novels and books on Spain, as well as dictionaries.

Laundry Two good self-service laundrettes are **Lavomatic** (*Carrer del Consolat de Mar 43-45*) and **Wash 'N Dry** (*Carrer Nou de la Rambla 19*). Cleaning and drying a large load should cost about €6.

Emergency The **Guàrdia Urbana** (*City Police;* ☎ 092; La Rambla 43) has a station opposite Plaça Reial. For an ambulance or emergency medical help call ☎ 061. **Hospital Creu Roja** (☎ 93 300 20 20; Carrer del Dos de Maig 301) has an emergency room. For 24-hour tourist assistance in English, call ☎ 93 344 13 00. There are 24-hour pharmacies at Carrer d'Aribau 62, Passeig de Gràcia 26 and La Rambla 98.

Dangers & Annoyances Watch your pockets, bags and cameras on the train to and from the airport, on La Rambla, in Barri Gòtic south of Plaça Reial and in Barri Xinès – especially at night. These last two areas have been somewhat cleaned up in recent years but pickpockets, bag-snatchers and intimidating beggars still stalk the unsuspecting. Be wary when walking in deserted areas, even strolling in parks during the daytime, as violent muggings of have been on the rise recently.

La Rambla

The best way to introduce yourself to Barcelona is by a leisurely stroll from Plaça de Catalunya down La Rambla, the magnificent boulevard of a thousand faces. This long strip, shaded by leafy trees and varied buildings, is an ever-changing blur of activity, lined with newsstands, bird and flower stalls and cafés. It's populated by artists, buskers, human statues, shoe-shine merchants, beggars and a constant stream of people promenading.

About halfway down La Rambla is the wonderful **Mercat de la Boqueria**, which is worth visiting just for the sights and sounds, but is also a good place to stock up on fresh fruit, vegetables, nuts, bread and pastries. Just off La Rambla, further south, **Plaça Reial** used to be a seedy square of ill repute, but it's now quite pleasant, with numerous cafés and bars and a couple of music clubs. Just off the other side of La Rambla is Gaudí's moody **Palau Güell** (*Carrer Nou de la Rambla 3-5; admission €3; open 10am-6.30pm Mon-Sat*), a house built by Gaudí in the late 1880s for his patron, the industrialist Eusebi Güell.

Down at the end of La Rambla stands the **Monument a Colom**, a statue of Columbus atop a tall pedestal. A small lift will take you to the top (admission €1.80). Just west, in the beautiful 14th-century Royal Shipyards, is the **Museu Marítim** (*admission €5.50; open 10am-7pm daily*), with an impressive array of boats, models, maps and more. If you like the sea and boats, you won't be disappointed.

Barri Gòtic

The Gothic Quarter's centrepiece is its serene **cathedral** (*open 8.30am-1.30pm daily, 4pm-7.30pm Mon-Fri, 5pm-7.30pm Sat & Sun*). Be sure to visit the lovely, verdant cloister. Each Sunday at noon, crowds gather in front of the cathedral to dance the Catalan national dance, the *sardana*. Just to the east is the fascinating **Museu d'Història de la Ciutat** (*City History Museum; admission €3.50; open 10am-2pm & 4pm-8pm Tues-Sat, 10am-2pm Sun, no afternoon break June-Sept*), composed of several buildings around **Plaça del Rei**, the palace courtyard of the medieval monarchs of Aragón. From the chapel, climb the multitiered Mirador del Rei Martí for good views. The museum also includes a remarkable subterranean walk through excavated portions of Roman and Visigothic Barcelona.

A few minutes' walk west of the cathedral, **Plaça de Sant Josep Oriol** is a sometime hang-out for bohemian musicians and buskers. The plaza is surrounded by cafés and towards the end of the week becomes an outdoor art and craft market in summer.

Waterfront

For a look at the modern face of Barcelona, take a stroll along the once-seedy waterfront. From the bottom of La Rambla you can cross the Rambla de Mar footbridge to the **Moll d'Espanya**, a former wharf in the old harbour, Port Vell. There you'll find **L'Aquàrium** (*admission €11; open 9.30am-9pm or later daily*), one of Europe's best (and more expensive) aquariums. Northeast of Port Vell, on the far side of the fishing-oriented La

Barceloneta area, the city **beaches** begin. Along the beachfront, after 1.3km you'll reach **Vila Olímpica**, site of the 1992 Olympic village, which is fronted by impressive **Port Olímpic**, a large marina with dozens of overpriced, touristy bars and restaurants. Don't come here to hobnob with locals.

La Sagrada Família

Gaudí's life masterpiece (*cnr Carrer de Sardenya & Carrer de Mallorca; metro Sagrada Família; admission €6, with tour €9; open 9am-8pm daily Apr-Sept, 9am-6pm daily Oct-Mar*) is Barcelona's most famous building and has the potential to stir the soul. Construction began in 1882 and is proceeding at a suitably otherworldy pace. The church is not yet half-built, and it's anyone's guess whether it will be finished by 2082. Some feel that it should not be completed but rather left as a monument to the master, whose career was cut short when he was hit by a tram in 1926.

Today there are eight towers, all over 100m high, with 10 more to come – the total representing the 12 Apostles, four Evangelists and the mother of God, plus the tallest tower (170m) standing for her son. Although La Sagrada Família is effectively a building site, the awesome dimensions and extravagant yet careful sculpting make it Barcelona's greatest highlight. The northeastern Nativity Facade was done under Gaudí's own supervision; the very different northwestern Passion Facade has been built since the 1950s.

You can climb high inside some of the towers by spiral staircases for a vertiginous overview of the interior and a panorama to the sea, or you can opt out and take a lift for €2 some of the way up.

Passeig de Gràcia

Many of Barcelona's finest modernist buildings are along the aptly named Passeig de Gràcia in L'Eixample. Gaudí's beautifully coloured **Casa Batlló** (*Passeig de Gràcia 43*) beckons onlookers from afar, while his greystone **La Pedrera** (*Passeig de Gràcia 92; admission €6; open 10am-8pm daily, guided visits 6pm Mon-Fri, 11am Sat & Sun*) ripples around the corner of Carrer de Provença. Don't miss its surreal roof, which features some truly bizarre chimney pots.

Next door to Casa Batlló is **Casa Amatller** (*Passeig de Gràcia 41*), by another leading modernist architect, Josep Puig i Cadafalch.

SPAIN

SPAIN

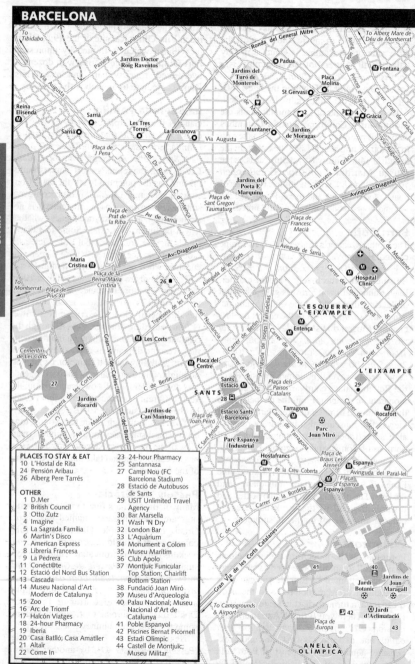

BARCELONA

PLACES TO STAY & EAT
10 L'Hostal de Rita
24 Pensión Aribau
26 Alberg Pere Tarrés

OTHER
1 D.Mer
2 British Council
3 Otto Zutz
4 Imagine
5 La Sagrada Família
6 Martin's Disco
7 American Express
8 Librería Francesa
9 La Pedrera
11 Conéct@te
12 Estació del Nord Bus Station
13 Cascada
14 Museu Nacional d'Art
   Modern de Catalunya
15 Zoo
16 Arc de Triomf
17 Halcón Viatges
18 24-hour Pharmacy
19 Iberia
20 Casa Batlló; Casa Amatller
21 Altaïr
22 Come In

23 24-hour Pharmacy
25 Santannasa
27 Camp Nou (FC
   Barcelona Stadium)
28 Estació de Autobusos
   de Sants
29 USIT Unlimited Travel
   Agency
30 Bar Marsella
31 Wash 'N Dry
32 London Bar
33 L'Aquàrium
34 Monument a Colom
35 Museu Marítim
36 Club Apolo
37 Montjuïc Funicular
   Top Station; Chairlift
   Bottom Station
38 Fundació Joan Miró
39 Museu d'Arqueologia
40 Palau Nacional; Museu
   Nacional d'Art de
   Catalunya
41 Poble Espanyol
42 Piscines Bernat Picornell
43 Estadi Olímpic
44 Castell de Montjuïc;
   Museu Militar

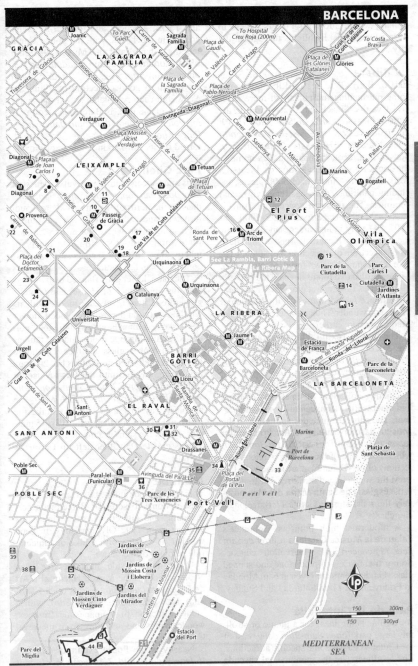

BARCELONA

GRÀCIA

Joanic

To Parc Güell

Carrer de Sardenya

Sagrada Família

Plaça de Gaudí

To Hospital Creu Roja (200m)

Gran Via de les Corts Catalanes

To Costa Brava

LA SAGRADA FAMÍLIA

5

Plaça de la Sagrada Família

Carrer de València

Carrer d'Aragó

Plaça de les Glòries Catalanes

Glòries

Travessera de Gràcia

Passeig de Sant Joan

Plaça de Pablo Neruda

Verdaguer

Avinguda Diagonal

Monumental

Av Meridiana

C dels Almogàvers

6

Diagonal

Plaça de Joan Carlos I

7   9

8

L'EIXAMPLE

Plaça Mossèn Jacint Verdaguer

Carrer de Sardenya

C de Pallars

Carrer de València

Carrer d'Aragó

Tetuan

C de la Marina

Marina

Bogatell

Diagonal

Passeig de Gràcia

11

Girona

Plaça de Tetuan

El Fort Pius

12

Provença

10

Passeig de Gràcia

22

Carrer de Balmes

21

17

20

Gran Via de les Corts Catalanes

Ronda de Sant Pere

Arc de Triomf

16

Vila Olímpica

Parc Carles I

Plaça del Doctor Lefamendi

19

18

Urquinaona

See La Rambla, Barri Gòtic & La Ribera Map

13

Parc de la Ciutadella

23

24

Urquinaona

14

Ciutadella

25

Catalunya

Universitat

LA RIBERA

15

Jardines d'Atlanta

Jaume I

Estació de França

Carrer del Doctor Aiguader

Ronda del Litoral

Urgell

BARRI GÒTIC

Barceloneta

Parc de la Barconeleta

Gran Via de les Corts Catalanes

Liceu

LA BARCELONETA

Ronda de Sant Pau

Sant Antoni

EL RAVAL

Rambla de Santa Mònica

SANT ANTONI

30

31

32

Marina

Platja de Sant Sebastià

Drassanes

Ronda del Litoral

Port de Barcelona

Poble Sec

35

34

33

Paral·lel (Funicular)

Avinguda del Paral·lel

36

Plaça del Portal de la Pau

POBLE SEC

Parc de les Tres Xemeneies

Port Vell

Port Vell

Jardins de Miramar

39

38

37

Jardins de Mossèn Costa i Llobera

Carretera de Miramar

Jardins de Mossèn Cinto Verdaguer

Jardins del Mirador

Estació del Port

44

21

MEDITERRANEAN SEA

Parc del Migdia

0   150   300m

0   150   300yd

SPAIN

Check here for tickets to the Ruta del Modernism, which allows sightseers access to over 50 modernist highlights throughout the city.

La Ribera

East of Barri Gòtic lies La Ribera, home to some outstanding museums and more modernist works. Smack-dab in its centre is the **Museu Picasso** (Carrer de Montcada 15-19; admission €4.50, free first Sun of month; open 10am-8pm Tues-Sat, 10am-3pm Sun), housed in a medieval mansion. It's home to the most important collection of Picasso's work in Spain – more than 3000 pieces, including paintings, drawings, engravings and ceramics. The museum concentrates on Picasso's Barcelona periods (1895–1900 and 1901–04) early in his career, and shows how the precocious Picasso learned to handle a whole spectrum of subjects and treatments before developing his own forms of expression. There are also two rooms devoted to Picasso's 1950s series of interpretations of Velázquez' masterpiece *Las Meninas* (see the Museo del Prado entry under Things to See & Do in the Madrid section, earlier).

The **Museu Textil i d'Indumentària** (Textile & Costume Museum; combined ticket with Museu Barbier-Mueller d'Art Precolombí €3.50; open 10am-8pm Tues-Sat, 10am-3pm Sun), opposite the Museu Picasso, has a fascinating collection of tapestries, clothing and other textiles from centuries past and present. The entry fee includes admission to the **Museu Barbier-Mueller d'Art Precolombí** (open 10am-8pm Tues-Sat, 10am-3pm Sun), which holds one of the most prestigious collections of pre-Columbian art in the world.

At the southern end of Carrer de Montcada is the **Església de Santa Maria del Mar**, probably the most stonily Gothic of Barcelona's churches.

A modernist high point is Montaner's **Palau de la Música Catalana** (Carrer de Sant Pere 11) concert hall, a marvellous concoction of tile, brick, sculpted stone and stained glass. Guided tours are given at 6am Monday to Friday and at 11am Saturday and Sunday.

Parc de la Ciutadella

As well as being ideal for a picnic or stroll, this large park (open 8am-9pm daily) east of the Ciutat Vella has some specific attractions. The headliners are the monumental **cascada** (waterfall), a dramatic combination of statuary, rocks, greenery and thundering water created in the 1870s, with the young Gaudí lending a hand, and the **Museu Nacional d'Art Modern de Catalunya** (admission €3; open 10am-7pm Tues-Sat, 10am-2.30pm Sun), with a good collection of 19th- and early-20th-century Catalan art. At the southern end of the park is Barcelona's **zoo** (admission €10; open 10am-5pm daily winter, longer hours as the weather gets nicer), famed for its still-kicking albino gorilla.

Parc Güell

This man-meets-nature marvel (admission free; open 9am-6pm winter, up to 9pm summer) in the north of the city is where Gaudí turned to landscape gardening. It's a strange, enchanting place where the artist's passion for natural forms took flight to the point where the artificial seems almost less contrived than the natural.

The main, lower gate, flanked by buildings with the appearance of Hansel and Gretel's gingerbread house, sets the mood, with its winding paths and carefully tended flower beds, skewed tunnels with rough stone columns resembling tree roots, and the famous dragon of broken glass and tiles. The house in which Gaudí lived most of his last 20 years has been converted into the **Casa-Museum Gaudí** (admission €3; open 10am-8pm daily Apr-Sept, 10am-6pm Sun-Fri Oct- Mar). The simplest way to Parc Güell is to take the metro to Lesseps and then walk 10 to 15 minutes; follow the signs heading northeast along Travessera de Dalt, then left up Carrer de Larrard.

Montjuïc

This hill overlooking the city from the southwest is home to some of Barcelona's best museums and attractions, some fine parks and the main 1992 Olympic sites. In good weather, it's well worth a hike or funicular ride, if only for the views.

On the northern side, the impressive Palau Nacional houses the **Museu Nacional d'Art de Catalunya** (admission €4.50; open 10am-7pm Tues-Sat, 10am-2.30pm Sun), with a great collection of Romanesque frescoes, woodcarvings and sculpture from medieval Catalunya.

Nearby is the **Poble Espanyol** (Spanish Village; adult/child 7-14 years & student

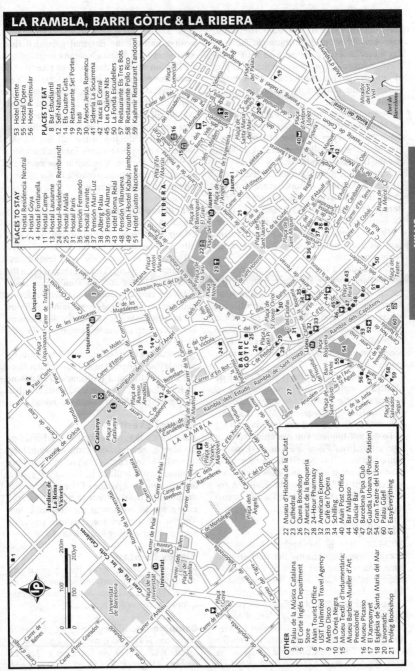

LA RAMBLA, BARRI GÒTIC & LA RIBERA

PLACES TO STAY
1   Hostal Residencia Neutral
2   Hostal Goya
4   Hostal Fontanella
11 Hostal Campi
13 Hostal Lausanne
24 Hostal-Residencia Rembrandt
25 Hostal Maldà
31 Hostal Paris
35 Pensión Fernando
36 Hostal Levante
37 Pensión Mari-Luz
38 Alberg Palau
39 Pensión Alamar
43 Hotel Roma Reial
48 Pensión Villanueva
49 Youth Hostel Kabul; Jamboree
51 Hotel Cuatro Naciones
53 Hotel Oriente
55 Hostal Opera
56 Hostal Peninsular

PLACES TO EAT
8   Bar Estudiantil
12 Self-Naturista
14 Els Quatre Gats
19 Restaurante Set Portes
29 Irati
30 Mesón Jesús Romescu
41 Sidrería La Socarrena
42 Tasca El Corral
45 Les Quinze Nits
50 La Fonda Escudellers
57 Restaurante Els Tres Bots
58 Restaurante Pollo Rico
59 Kashmir Restaurant Tandoori

OTHER
3   Palau de la Música Catalana
5   El Corte Inglés Department
    Store
6   Main Tourist Office
7   VSIT Unlimited Travel Agency
9   Metro Disco
10 La Oveja Negra
15 Museu Tèxtil i d'Indumentària;
    Museu Barbier-Mueller d'Art
    Precolombí
16 Museu Picasso
17 El Xampanyet
18 Església de Santa Maria del Mar
20 Lavomatic
21 Pròleg Bookshop
22 Museu d'Història de la Ciutat
23 Cathedral
26 Quera Bookshop
27 Mercat de la Boqueria
32 24-Hour Pharmacy
33 American Express
34 Café de l'Opera
40 Schilling
44 Main Post Office
46 Bar Malpaso
47 Glaciar Bar
52 Barcelona Pipa Club
54 Guàrdia Urbana (Police Station)
60 Gran Teatre del Liceu
61 Palau Güell
    EasyEverything

SPAIN

€7/3.50, free after 9pm Sun & Tues-Thur; open 9am-8pm Mon, 9am-2am Tues-Thur, 9am-4am Fri & Sat, 9am-midnight Sun), by day a tour group's paradise with craft workshops, souvenir shops and creditable copies of famous Spanish architecture. After dark it becomes a nightlife jungle, featuring bars and restaurants galore.

Downhill eastwards of the Palau Nacional, the **Museu d'Arqueologia** (admission €2.50; open 9.30am-7pm Tues-Sat, 10am-2.30pm Sun) has a good collection from Catalunya and the Balearic Islands.

Above the Palau Nacional is the Anella Olímpica (Olympic Ring), where you can swim in the Olympic pool, the **Piscines Bernat Picornell** (limited tickets €8; open 7am-midnight Mon-Fri, 7am-9pm Sat, 7.30am-4.30pm Sun) and wander into the main **Estadi Olímpic** (admission free; open 10am-6pm daily).

The **Fundació Joan Miró** (admission €7; open 10am-7pm or 8pm Tues, Wed, Fri & Sat, 10am-9.30pm Thur, 10am-2.30pm Sun & holidays), a short distance downhill eastwards of the Estadi Olímpic, is one of the best modern-art museums in Spain. Aside from many works by Miró, there are both permanent and changing exhibitions of other modern art.

At the top of Montjuïc is the **Castell de Montjuïc**, with a military museum (€2.50 includes castle admission; open 9.30am-4.30pm Tues-Sun Nov–mid-Mar, 9.30am-7pm mid-Mar–Oct) and great views.

To get to Montjuïc you can either walk or take a bus from Plaça d'Espanya (Espanya metro station). Bus No 61 from here links most of the main sights and ends at the foot of a chairlift (€3.50) up to the castle. A funicular railway (€1.50) from Parallel metro station also runs to the chairlift.

Tibidabo

At 542m, this is the highest hill in the wooded range that forms the backdrop to Barcelona. It's a good place for long walks along winding roads, some fresh air and, if the air's clear, 70km views. At the top are the **Temple del Sagrat Cor**, a church topped by a giant Christ statue, and the **Parc d'Atraccions** (admission €17), a somewhat kitschy funfair. A short distance along the ridge is the 115m-high **Torre de Collserola** (observation deck €4.50; open 11am-2.30pm Wed-Fri

winter, up to 8pm summer, 11am-6pm or 8pm Sat & Sun) telecommunications tower, with a hair-raising external glass lift that skyrockets you 560m above sea level.

The fun way to Tibidabo is to take the U7 suburban train from Plaça de Catalunya to Avinguda de Tibidabo (€1, 10 minutes), then hop on the *tramvia blau* (€2) across the road, which will take you up to the foot of the Tibidabo funicular railway. The funicular climbs to the church at the top of the hill for €2. All these run every 30 minutes from at least 9am to 9.30pm. The funicular and amusement park are open weekends only outside of the summer months (June to September).

Organised Tours

The **Bus Turístic** (☎ 93 423 18 00) service covers two circuits (24 stops) linking virtually all the major tourist sights. Tourist offices and many hotels have leaflets explaining the system. Tickets, available on the bus, are €14 for one day's unlimited rides, €18 for two consecutive days. Service is about every 20 minutes from 9am to 9.30pm. Tickets entitle you to substantial discounts on entry fees and tickets to more than 20 sights along the route.

A **walking tour** (€7) of the Ciutat Vella on Saturday and Sunday mornings departs from the Centre Oficina d'Informació de Turisme de Barcelona on Plaça de Catalunya (English at 10am, Spanish and Catalan at noon).

Special Events

Barcelona's biggest festival is the Festes de la Mercè, several days of merrymaking around 24 September, including *castellers* (human-castle builders), dances of giants, and *correfocs* – a parade of firework-spitting dragons and devils. Throughout the year, the city is apt to go nuts at the drop of a hat. Tourist offices can help but can't predict soccer victories over Real Madrid.

Places to Stay

Finding a place to sleep isn't particularly cheap or easy between Semana Santa and October. Unless you're willing to canvass hostels, it's wise to book ahead.

Camping   The closest camping ground to Barcelona is **El Toro Bravo** (☎ 93 637 34 62, fax 93 637 21 15), on Carretera C-246. **La Ballena Alegre** (☎ 93 658 05 04, fax 93 658

05 75) 2km further, is also pleasant, and there are several more camping grounds down that highway. All charge upwards of €20 per site. Ask at the tourist office for transportation information.

Hostels A handful of places in Barcelona provide dormitory accommodation. For two people they're not great value, but they're certainly good places to meet other travellers. All require you to rent sheets (€1 to €3) if you don't have them (or a sleeping bag).

Grungy, happy **Youth Hostel Kabul** (☎ 93 318 51 90; Plaça Reial 17; dorm beds €12-18) is a rough-and-ready place with no curfew and a party-hearty atmosphere. This is where youth come from all over Western Europe to get some...exposure to Spanish culture. No card is needed. Security is slack, but there are safes available for your valuables. Bookings are not taken.

Not as loud or social is the HI **Alberg Palau** (☎ 93 412 50 80; Carrer del Palau 6; dorm beds €13; open 7am-midnight daily), with just 40 places. Rooms resemble university dorms; rates include breakfast and also kitchen use. No card is needed.

Alberg Mare de Déu de Montserrat (☎ 93 210 51 51, fax 93 210 07 98; Passeig Mare de Déu del Coll 41-51; dorm beds for ISIC or IYTC card holders & under 25s/all others €15/20, including breakfast), with 180 beds, is the biggest and most comfortable hostel, but it's 4km north of the centre. A hostel card is needed. It's closed during the day and you can't get in after 3am. The hostel is a 10-minute walk from Vallcarca metro or a 20-minute ride from Plaça de Catalunya on bus No 28.

The HI **Alberg Pere Tarrés** (☎ 93 410 23 09, fax 93 419 62 68; Carrer de Numància 149; metro Les Corts; dorm beds €14-16), about a five-minute walk from the metro, has 90 beds, which range in price depending on age and hostel-card possession. It has a kitchen, but it's closed during the day and you can't get in after 2am.

Pensiones & Hostales Most of the cheaper options are scattered through the old city on either side of La Rambla. Generally, the areas closer to the port and on the western side of La Rambla are seedier and cheaper, and as you move north towards Plaça de Catalunya standards (and prices) rise.

Hostal Maldà (☎ 93 317 30 02; Carrer del Pi 5; singles/doubles €9/18), upstairs in an arcade, is about as cheap as you'll find. It's a rambling family-run establishment that shelters cosy rooms and an adorable little kitten. Rambling **Hostal Paris** (☎ 93 301 37 85, fax 93 412 70 96; Carrer del Cardenal Casañas 4; singles from €22, doubles with bath €40) caters to backpackers. It can be slightly dingy and more than a bit unfriendly, but it's central and reasonable. The simple dorm-style **Pensión Mari-Luz** (☎ 93 317 34 63; Carrer del Palau 4; beds €12-15, doubles €36-40) is brighter and more sociable.

Pensión Alamar (☎ 93 302 50 12; Carrer de la Comtessa de Sobradiel 1; singles/doubles €18/36) is fantastic value. It's a good place for lone travellers to meet other wanderers in a tranquil setting. **Hostal Levante** (☎ 93 317 95 65, fax 93 317 05 26; w www.hostallevante.com; Baixada de Sant Miquel 2; singles/doubles €24/46, with bath €27/52) is a plain family-run place in a quiet location. Ask about apartments for longer stays.

If you want a nice double on Plaça Reial, head to **Pensión Villanueva** (☎/fax 91 301 50 84; Plaça Reial 2; singles €12-18, doubles €20-35); rates depend on the season.

Hostal Fontanella (☎/fax 93 317 59 43; Via Laietana 71; singles/doubles €26/41, with bath €32/55) is a warm, immaculate place, with 10 smallish rooms. An excellent deal is the friendly **Hostal Campi** (☎/fax 93 301 35 45, fax 93 301 41 33; e hcampi@terra.es; Carrer de la Canuda 4; singles/doubles €20/38, doubles with bath €45), with roomy doubles.

Up near Plaça de Catalunya is the solid **Hostal Lausanne** (☎ 93 302 11 39; Avinguda del Portal de l'Àngel 24, 1st floor; singles/doubles from €22/42), with good security and slightly dingy rooms (doubles are spiffier).

Hostal-Residencia Rembrandt (☎/fax 93 318 10 11; Carrer Portaferrissa 23; singles/doubles €25/42, doubles with bath €42) offers rooms ranging from acceptable to stylish. Reservations are accepted only for stays of longer than three nights.

Busy **Hostal Ópera** (☎ 93 318 82 01; Carrer de Sant Pau 20; singles/doubles €31/50) offers spotless, bright rooms with own baths. **Pensión Fernando** (☎/fax 93 301 79 93; Carrer de Ferran 4; beds €15, doubles with/without bath €51/36) is a friendly place with a sunny rooftop terrace.

A few cheapies are spread strategically across L'Eixample, to the north of Plaça de Catalunya. **Hostal Goya** (☎ 93 302 25 65, fax 93 412 04 35; e goya@cconline.es; Carrer de Pau Claris 74; singles/doubles €27/45, with bath €32/55) has several beautifully renovated rooms. The **Pensión Aribau** (☎ 93 453 11 06; Carrer d'Aribau 37; singles/doubles €28/42, doubles with bath €50) offers reasonable rooms. The singles come with TV, while many doubles have shower, toilet, TV and even a fridge.

A leafier location is **Hotel Residencia Neutral** (☎/fax 93 487 68 48; Rambla de Catalunya 42; doubles with bath €45), a happy, bustling place that has friendly management.

Hotels Once-grand **Hotel Peninsular** (☎ 93 302 31 38, fax 93 412 36 99; Carrer de Sant Pau 34; singles/doubles €45/65) offers bare rooms that don't quite live up to the impressive foyer and central atrium. Higher up the scale, but good value, is **Hotel Roma Reial** (☎ 93 302 03 66; Plaça Reial 11; singles/doubles €50/65), which offers mod cons but tiny rooms.

If you want to be on La Rambla, try **Hotel Cuatro Naciones** (☎ 93 317 36 24, fax 93 302 69 85; La Rambla 40; doubles €76). A century ago this was Barcelona's top hotel; today its rooms are merely adequate. For more flair, head to **Hotel Oriente** (☎ 93 302 25 58, fax 93 412 28 19; La Rambla 45-47; e horiente@husa.es; singles/doubles €86/125), which offers beautiful, spacious quarters.

Places to Eat

They don't want you to find them, but supermarkets do exist in Barcelona. A convenient one in the old quarter is **Dia**, right next to Pensión Alamar (see under Pensiones & Hostales in Places to Stay earlier).

The greatest concentration of cheap restaurants is within walking distance of La Rambla. There are a few good-value places on Carrer de Sant Pau, west off La Rambla. **Kashmir Restaurant Tandoori** (Carrer de Sant Pau 39; most dishes €5) does tasty curries and biryanis. **Restaurante Pollo Rico** (Carrer de Sant Pau 31; chicken dishes or omelette €5) serves tasty main dishes with chips, bread and wine. **Restaurante Els Tres Bots** (Carrer de Sant

Pau 42; set menu €6) is grungy but cheap, with a good selection of Spanish staples.

There are lots more places in Barri Gòtic. **Self-Naturista** (Carrer de Santa Anna 13; set menu €6.50), a bright self-service vegetarian restaurant, does tasty, fresh dishes. **Mesón Jesús Romescu** (Carrer dels Cecs de la Boqueria 4; set menu €11) is a cosy, homey place that serves piping-hot Spanish dishes.

Carrer de la Mercè, running roughly west from the main post office, is a good place to find little northern Spanish cider houses. **Tasca El Corral** (Carrer de la Mercè 19) and **Sidrería La Socarrena** (Carrer de la Mercè 21) are both worth checking. A Basque favourite is **Irati** (Carrer del Cardenal Cassanyes 17; tapas around €4). Enjoy a range of mouthwatering tapas and a zurrito of beer or six.

For something a bit more upmarket, **Les Quinze Nits** (Plaça Reial 6) and **La Fonda Escudellers** (Carrer dels Escudellers) are two stylish bistro-like restaurants under the same management, with a big range of good Catalan and Spanish dishes at reasonable prices. This results in long queues in summer and on the weekend. Three courses with wine and coffee will cost about €20 at either.

Carrer dels Escudellers, Plaça Reial and La Rambla itself also have a couple of good night-time takeaway felafel joints at around €2.50 a serving.

To impress your date, head for **Restaurante Set Portes** (☎ 93 319 30 33; Passeig d'Isabel II 14; paella €16), a classic dating from 1836 and specialising in paella. It's essentiul to book. Another famous institution is **Els Quatre Gats** (Carrer Montsió 3), Picasso's former hang-out. The standard café fare costs about 50% more than it should, but it's worth it for the bohemian ambience.

L'Eixample has a few good restaurants to offer as well. **Bar Estudiantil** (Plaça de la Universitat; plats combinats €4) does economical combination plates (eg, chicken, chips and eggplant). It's open until late into the night and is a genuine student hang-out. **L'Hostal de Rita** (Carrer d'Aragó 279; set menu €7, mains €5-8), a block east of Passeig de Gràcia, is an excellent, ultrapopular mid-range restaurant with a four-course lunch menú and à la carte mains available.

Entertainment

Barcelona's entertainment bible is the weekly publication *Guía del Ocio* (€1 at newsstands).

Its excellent listings (in Spanish) include films, theatre, music and art exhibitions. Gay and lesbian options have their own special section, labelled 'El Ambiente'.

The tourist office can provide information on current festivals, concerts and other performances.

Bars Barcelona's multifarious bars are at their busiest from about 11pm to 2am or 3am, especially Thursday to Saturday.

Café de l'Òpera (*La Rambla 74*), opposite the Liceu opera house, is the liveliest place on a very lively street. It gets packed with all and sundry at night. Glaciar (*Plaça Reial 3*) is busy with a young crowd of foreigners and locals. Tiny Bar Malpaso (*Carrer d'En Rauric 20*), just off Plaça Reial, plays great Latin and African music. Another hip low-lit place with a more varied (including gay) clientele is the relaxed Schilling (*Carrer de Ferran 23*).

El Xampanyet (*Carrer de Montcada 22*), near the Museu Picasso, is a small place specialising in *cava* (Catalan sparkling wine) and good tapas.

West of La Rambla, La Oveja Negra (*Carrer de les Sitges 5*) is a noisy, barn-like tavern with a young crowd. Hidden away on a side street is Bar Marsella (*Carrer de Sant Pau 65*), specialising in absinthe (*absenta* in Catalan), a potent but mellow beverage with supposed narcotic qualities.

If by 2.30am you still need a drink and don't want to get funky at a disco, your best bet is London Bar (*Carrer Nou de la Rambla 36; open until about 5am Mon-Sat*), which sometimes has live music.

Lesbian bars are clustered in Sarrià, north of the city centre. Try friendly, intimate D.Mer (*Carrer de Plató 13*) or the more girly Imagine (*Carrer de Marià Cubí 4*). Gay men can try Santannasa (*Carrer de Aribau 27*), which sports a cute dance floor.

Live Music & Discos Many music places have dance space, and some discos have bands around midnight or so, to pull in some clientele before the real action starts about 3am. If you go for the band, you can normally stay for the disco at no extra cost and avoid bouncers' whims about what you're wearing, your measurements etc. Count on €2 to €6 for a beer in any of these places. Cover charges can be anything from zero to €25, which may include a drink.

Barcelona Pipa Club (*Plaça Reial 3; cover €7*) has jazz Thursday to Saturday around midnight (ring the bell to get in). Jamboree (*Plaça Reial 17; cover €9*) has jazz and funk, and a disco later, from about 1.30am. Club Apolo (*Carrer Nou de la Rambla 113; cover around €15*) has live world music several nights a week, followed by live salsa or a varied disco.

Manhattanites might feel comfortable at chic Otto Zutz (*Carrer de Lincoln 15*). Wear your bestest, blackest outfit.

Mirablau (*Plaça Dr Andrau; open until 5am*), at the foot of the Tibidabo funicular, is a bar with great views and a small disco floor.

The two top gay discos are Metro (*Carrer de Sepúlveda 185*) and Martin's (*Passeig de Gràcia 130*). Metro attracts some lesbians and straights as well as gay men; Martin's is strictly boys only.

Cinemas For films in their original language (with Spanish subtitles), check listings for those marked VO (*versión original*). A ticket is usually €5 or more, but many cinemas reduce prices on Monday or Wednesday. Check the *Guía del Ocio* for cinema listings.

Classical Music & Opera The Gran Teatre del Liceu (☎ 93 485 99 00; ⓦ www.liceu barcelona.com; La Rambla 51-59) opera house, gutted by fire in 1994, is still being rebuilt but is open for business. Call or check the website for information on opera, dance and concerts.

There are other fine theatres, among them the lovely Palau de la Música Catalana (☎ 93 295 72 00; ⓦ www.palaumusica.org; Carrer de Sant Francesa de Paula 2), the city's chief concert hall.

Getting There & Away

Air Barcelona's airport, 14km southwest of the city centre at El Prat de Llobregat, caters to international as well as domestic flights. It's not a European hub, but you can often dig up specials and cheap youth fares.

Airlines include Iberia (☎ 902 40 05 00; Passeig de Gràcia 30), Spanair (24hr ☎ 902 13 14 15) and Air Europa (☎ 902 40 15 01); the latter two airline offices are at the airport.

Bus The terminal for virtually all domestic and international buses is the Estació del Nord (☎ 93 265 65 08; Carrer d'Alí Bei 80;

metro Arc de Triomf; information desk open 7am-9pm daily). A few international buses leave from Estació d'Autobuses de Sants, beside Estació Sants train station.

Several buses a day go to most main Spanish cities, including Madrid (€22, seven to eight hours), Zaragoza (€10, 4½ hours), Valencia (€24, 4½ hours) and Granada (€54, 13 to 15 hours). Buses run several times a week to London, Paris (€80) and other European cities.

Train Virtually all trains travelling to and from destinations within Spain stop at **Estació Sants** (metro Sants-Estació); many international trains use **Estació de França** (metro Barceloneta).

For some international destinations you have to change trains at Montpellier or the French border. There are direct trains daily to Paris, Zürich and Milan.

Daily trains run to most major cities in Spain. To Madrid there are seven trains a day (€42, 6½ to 9½ hours), to San Sebastián two (€31, eight to 10 hours), to Valencia 10 (€32, as little as three hours on high-speed Euromed train) and to Granada (€46, eight hours).

Tickets and information are available at the stations or from the RENFE office in **Passeig de Gràcia station** *(Passeig de Gràcia; open 7am-10pm Mon-Sat, till 9pm Sun).*

Car & Motorcycle Tolls on the A-7 autopista to the French border are over €12. The N-II to the French border and the N-340 southbound from Barcelona are toll-free but slower. The fastest route to Madrid is via Zaragoza on the A-2 (around €20), which heads west off the A-7 south of Barcelona, then the toll-free N-II from Zaragoza.

Getting Around

To/From the Airport Trains link the airport to Estació Sants and Catalunya station on Plaça de Catalunya every half-hour. They take 15 to 20 minutes and a ticket is €2. The A1 Aerobús does the 40-minute run between Plaça de Catalunya and the airport every 15 minutes, or every half-hour at weekends. The fare is €3.50. A taxi from the airport to Plaça de Catalunya is around €15 to €20.

Bus, Metro & Train Barcelona's metro system spreads its tentacles around the city in such a way that most places of interest are within a 10-minute walk of a station. Buses and suburban trains are needed only for a few destinations.

A single metro, bus or suburban train ride costs €1, but a T-1 ticket, valid for 10 rides, costs only €5.50, while a T-DIA ticket gives unlimited city travel in one day for €4.

Car & Motorcycle While traffic flows smoothly thanks to an extensive one-way system, navigating can be frustrating. Parking a car is also difficult and, if you choose a parking garage, quite expensive (over €20 per day). It's better to ditch your car and rely on public transport.

Taxi Barcelona's black-and-yellow taxis are plentiful, reasonably priced and handy for late-night transport. Flag fall is €1.30, after which it's about €1 per kilometre.

MONESTIR DE MONTSERRAT

Unless you are on a pilgrimage, the prime attraction of Montserrat, 50km northwest of Barcelona, is its incredible setting. The Benedictine Monastery of Montserrat sits high on the side of an 1236m-high mountain of truly weird rocky peaks, and it's best reached by cable car. The monastery was founded in 1025 to commemorate an apparition of the Virgin Mary on this site. Pilgrims still come from all over Christendom to pay homage to the Black Virgin (La Moreneta), a 12th-century wooden sculpture of Mary, regarded as Catalunya's patroness.

Montserrat's **information centre** *(☎ 93 877 77 77; open 10am-6pm daily)* is to the left along the road from the top cable-car station. It has a couple of good free leaflets and maps on the mountain and monastery.

Things to See & Do

If you are making a day trip to Montserrat, come early. Apart from the monastery, exploring the mountain is a treat.

On the plaza in front of the monastery's basilica is the two-part **Museu de Montserrat** *(admission €4; open 10am-6pm Mon-Fri, 9.30am- 6.30pm Sat & Sun)* which has an excellent collection ranging from an Egyptian mummy to art by El Greco and Picasso.

Opening times for when you can file past the image of the Black Virgin, high above the main altar of the 16th-century **basílica**, vary according to season. The Montserrat Boys'

Choir (Escolania) sings in the basilica Monday to Sunday at 1pm and 7pm, except in July. The church fills up quickly, so try to arrive early.

You can explore the mountain above the monastery on a web of paths leading to small chapels and some of the peaks. The **Funicular de Sant Joan** (€3.50 return) will lift you up the first 250m from the monastery.

Places to Stay & Eat
There are several accommodation options (all ☎ 93 877 77 01) at the monastery. The cheapest rooms are in the **Cel.les Abat Olibia** (double apartments high season €23-25), blocks of simple apartments, with showers, for up to 10 people. Overlooking Plaça de Santa Maria is the luxurious and excellent-value **Hotel Abat Cisneros** (singles/doubles €24/44, high season €41/76).

The Cisneros offers probably the finest dining on the mountain. Its delicious four-course Catalan menú costs about €18. Otherwise, restaurant options are bland and uninspiring. Snack bars and cafeterias line the road approach to the monastery, and a few shops by the basilica offer cheap snacks.

Getting There & Away
Trains run from Plaça d'Espanya station in Barcelona to Aeri de Montserrat up to 18 times a day (most often on summer weekdays), a 1½-hour ride. Return tickets for €20 include the cable car between Aeri de Montserrat and the monastery.

There's also a daily bus to the monastery from Estació d'Autobuses de Sants in Barcelona at 9am (plus one at 8am in July and August) for a return fare of €10. It returns at 5pm.

COSTA BRAVA
The Costa Brava ranks with Spain's Costa Blanca and Costa del Sol among Europe's most popular holiday spots. It stands alone, however, in its spectacular rugged scenery and proximity to northern Europe, both of which have sent prices skyrocketing in the area.

The main jumping-off points for the Costa Brava are the inland towns of Girona ('Gerona' in Castilian) and Figueres. Both are on the A-7 autopista and the toll-free N-II highway, which connect Barcelona with France. Along the coast, the most appealing resorts are (from north to south) Cadaqués,

L'Escala (La Escala), Tamariu, Llafranc, Calella de Palafrugell and Tossa de Mar.

Tourist offices along the coast are very helpful, with information on accommodation, transport and other things. There are branches in **Girona** (☎ 972 22 65 75), **Figueres** (☎ 972 50 31 55), **Palafrugell** (☎ 972 30 02 28) and **Cadaqués** (☎ 972 25 83 15).

Coastal Resorts & Islands
The Costa Brava (Rugged Coast) is all about picturesque inlets and coves. Beaches tend to be small and scattered. Some longer beaches at places like L'Estartit and Empúries are worth visiting off-season, but there has been a tendency to build tall buildings wherever engineers think it can be done. Fortunately, in many places it just can't.

Cadaqués, about one hour's drive east of Figueres at the end of an agonising series of hairpin bends, is perhaps the most picturesque of all Spanish resorts. It's haunted by the memory of former resident Salvador Dalí, whose name adorns several establishments. Cadaqués is short on beaches, so people spend a lot of time sitting at waterfront cafés or wandering along the beautiful coast. About 10km northeast of Cadaqués is **Cap de Creus**, a rocky peninsula with a single restaurant atop a craggy cliff. This is paradise for anyone who likes to scramble around rocks risking life and limb with every step.

Further down the coast, past L'Escala and L'Estartit, is Palafrugell, itself a few kilometres inland with little to offer, but near three gorgeous beach towns that have to be seen to be believed. The most northerly of these, **Tamariu**, is also the smallest, least crowded and most exclusive. **Llafranc** is the biggest and busiest, and has the longest beach. **Calella de Palafrugell**, with its truly picture-postcard setting, is never overcrowded and always relaxed. If you're driving down this coast, it's worth stopping at some of these towns, particularly out of season.

For a spectacular stretch of coastline, take a drive north from Tossa de Mar to San Feliu de Guíxols. There are 360 curves in this 20km stretch of road, which, with brief stops to take in the scenery, can take a good two hours.

Among the most exciting attractions on the Costa Brava are the **Illes Medes**, off the coast from the package resort of L'Estartit. These seven islets and their surrounding coral reefs, with a total land area of only 21.5 hectares, have been declared a natural park to protect their extraordinarily diverse flora and fauna. Almost 1500 different life forms have been identified on and around the islands. You can arrange glass-bottom boat trips and diving.

Museums & Historical Attractions

When you have had enough beach for a while, make sure you put the **Teatre-Museu Dalí** (*Plaça Gala i Salvador Dalí; admission €9; open 9am-7.15pm daily July-Sept, 10.30am-5.15pm daily June, 10.30am-5.15pm Tues-Sun Oct-May*), in Figueres, at the top of your list. This 19th-century theatre was converted by Dalí himself and houses a huge and fascinating collection of his strange creations. Queues are long on summer mornings.

Girona sports a lovely though tiny medieval quarter centred on a Gothic cathedral. For a stroll through antiquity, check out the ruins of the Greek and Roman town of **Empúries**, 2km from L'Escala.

Places to Stay & Eat

Most visitors to the Costa Brava rent apartments. If you are interested in renting your own pad for a week or so, contact local tourist offices in advance. Seaside restaurants provide dramatic settings but often at high prices.

Figueres Reasonable rooms with bath can be found at **Pensión Isabel II** (*☎ 972 50 47 35; Carrer de Isabel II 16; singles/doubles €21/26*). A little grungier but still solid is **Pensión Mallol** (*☎ 972 50 22 83; Carrer de Pep Ventura 9; singles/doubles €15/25*). Avoid sleeping in Figueres' Parc Municipal – people have been attacked here at night.

Restaurant Versalles (*Carrer de la Jonquera; platos combinados €5*) is at a sociable location away from the noise and high prices of the main plaza.

Girona Eight kilometres south of town is **Camping Can Toni Manescal** (*☎ 972 47 61 17*). **Alberg de Joventut** (*☎ 972 21 80 03; Carrer de Ciutadans 9; beds €12*) offers standard HI fare. **Pensión Viladomat** (*☎ 972 20 31 76; Carrer dels Ciutadans 5; doubles €31*) has comfortable rooms.

Dine on Girona's own Rambla for good people-watching. **Arts Café** (*La Rambla 23*) offers a mellow atmosphere and a good range of cheap snacks.

Cadaqués At the top of the town as you head towards Cabo de Creus is **Camping Cadaqués** (*☎ 972 25 81 26, fax 972 159 383*). A room in town is probably better value. **Hostal Marina** (*☎ 972 25 81 99; Carrer de Riera 3; singles/doubles €19/36, high season €25/49*) has fresh, bright rooms.

Around Palafrugell There are camping grounds at all three of Palafrugell's satellites, all charging similar hefty rates. In Calella de Palafrugell, try **Camping Moby Dick** (*☎ 972 61 43 07*); in Llafranc, **Camping Kim's** (*☎ 972 30 11 56*); and in Tamariu, **Camping Tamariu** (*☎ 972 62 04 22*).

Hotel and pensione rooms are relatively thin here, as many people come on package deals and stay in apartments. In Calella de Palafrugell, the friendly **Hostería del Plancton** (*☎ 972 61 50 81; rooms €15; open June-Sept*) is one of the best deals on the Costa Brava. **Residencia Montaña** (*☎ 972 30 04 04; Carrer de Cesàrea 2; rooms €52, July-Aug €88*), in Llafranc, is not a bad deal as long as you stay away during the high season. In Tamariu, **Hotel Sol d'Or** (*☎ 972 62 01 72; Carrer de la Riera 18; doubles with bath €45*) is near the beach.

Numerous food stalls and cafés cluster in all three towns.

Getting There & Away

A few buses run daily from Barcelona to Tossa del Mar, L'Estartit and Cadaqués for a couple of euros, but for the small resorts near Palafrugell you need to get to Girona first. Girona and Figueres are both on the railway connecting Barcelona to France. The dozen or so trains daily from Barcelona to Portbou at the border all stop in Girona, and most in Figueres. The fare from Barcelona to Girona is €5, to Figueres €6.

Getting Around

There are two or three buses a day from Figueres to Cadaqués and three or four to L'Escala. Figueres' bus station is across the road from the train station.

Several buses daily run to Palafrugell from Girona (where the bus station is behind the train station), and there are buses from Palafrugell to Calella de Palafrugell, Llafranc and Tamariu. Most other coastal towns (south of Cadaqués) can be reached by bus from Girona.

TARRAGONA
pop 115,150

Tarragona's relaxed, backwards-gazing nature makes a perfect contrast to the frenetic, modern city life of Barcelona. Founded in 218 BC, the town was for a long time the capital of much of Roman Spain, and Roman structures figure among its most important attractions. A medieval cathedral and 17th-century British additions to the old city walls provide evocative representations of other historical periods. And Tarragona's archaeological museum is one of the most interesting in Spain.

For those who don't want to be too *tranquilo*, Tarragona's large student population and constant stream of travellers ensures a lively beach scene. Spain's answer to Disneyland, Port Aventura, is just a few kilometres south of town.

Orientation & Information

Tarragona's main street is Rambla Nova, which runs northwest from a cliff top overlooking the Mediterranean. A couple of blocks east, and parallel to Rambla Nova, is Rambla Vella, which marks the old town.

The **main tourist office** (☎ 977 25 07 95; *Carrer Major 39; open Mon-Sat & Sun morning*) and **regional tourist office** (*Carrer de Fortuny 4; open Mon-Sat*) offer maps and lists of accommodation.

The Old City & Around

The **Museu d'Història de Tarragona** (*admission to each site €2; open 9am-8pm*

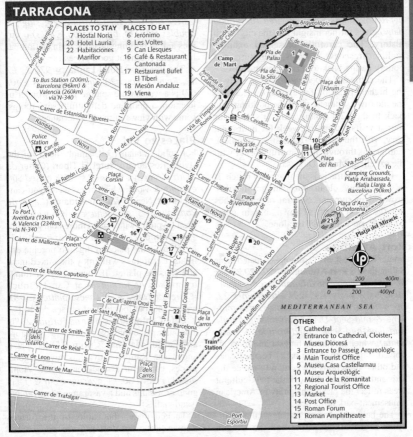

TARRAGONA

PLACES TO STAY
7 Hostal Noria
20 Hotel Lauria
22 Habitaciones Mariflor

PLACES TO EAT
6 Jerónimo
8 Les Voltes
9 Can Llesques
16 Café & Restaurant Cantonada
17 Restaurant Bufet El Tiberi
18 Mesón Andaluz
19 Viena

OTHER
1 Cathedral
2 Entrance to Cathedral, Cloister; Museu Diocesá
3 Entrance to Passeig Arqueològic
4 Main Tourist Office
5 Museu Casa Castellarnau
10 Museu Arqueològic
11 Museu de la Romanitat
12 Regional Tourist Office
13 Market
14 Post Office
15 Roman Forum
21 Roman Amphitheatre

MEDITERRANEAN SEA

Tues-Sat, 10am-2pm Sun) comprises four separate Roman sites around the city, plus the 14th-century noble mansion now serving as the **Museu Casa Castellarnau** *(Carrer dels Cavallers 14)*. A good place to start is the **Museu de la Romanitat** *(Plaça del Rei)*, which includes part of the vaults of the Roman circus, where chariot races were held.

Nearby and close to the beach is the well-preserved **Roman amphitheatre**, where the gladiators battled each other (or unlucky souls were thrown to wild animals) to the death. On Carrer de Lleida, a few blocks west of Rambla Nova, are the remains of a **Roman forum**. The **Passeig Arqueològic** *(open until midnight)* is a peaceful walkway along a stretch of the old city walls, which are a combination of Roman, Iberian and 17th-century British efforts.

Tarragona's **Museu Arqueològic** *(Plaça del Rei 5; admission €2.50, free Tues; open daily)* gives further insight into the city's rich history. The carefully presented exhibits include frescoes, mosaics, sculpture and pottery dating back to the 2nd century BC.

The **cathedral** *(open daily)* sits grandly at the highest point of Tarragona, overlooking the old town. Some parts of the building date back to the 12th century AD. It's open for tourist visits during the week for hours that vary with the season (longest in summer). Entrance is through the beautiful cloister with the excellent Museu Diocesà.

Platja del Miracle is the main city beach. It is reasonably clean but can get terribly crowded in summer. Several other beaches dot the coast north of town, but in good weather you will never be alone.

Port Aventura

Some 7km west of Tarragona, situated near Salou, there's Port Aventura (☎ 902 20 22 20; ⓦ www.universalmediterranea.com; adult/child 5-12 years €31/23, after 7pm €22; open 10am-8pm daily Semana Santa–mid-June & mid-Sept–Dec, 10am-midnight daily mid-June–mid-Sept, closed from Jan-Semana Santa), which is Spain's biggest and most involved funfair-adventure park. Themed rides and other attractions are certain to entice the kids and teenagers, although the faux-cultural areas reflect the plastic insipidity of American amusement-park influence.

The hair-raising experiences available include a virtual submarine and the Dragon Khan, claimed to be Europe's biggest roller coaster.

Trains run to Port Aventura's own station, about a 1km walk from the site, several times a day from Tarragona and Barcelona (€8 return).

Places to Stay

Camping Tàrraco (☎ 977 29 02 89) is near Platja Arrabassada, off the N-340 road 2km northeast of the centre. There are more, better camping grounds on Platja Larga, a couple of kilometres further on. A good option is **Camping Playa Large** (☎ 977 20 79 52; sites €3-4 per person).

If you intend to stay in Tarragona in summer, call ahead to book a room. **Hostal Noria** (☎ 977 23 87 17; Plaça de la Font 53; singles/doubles €17/29) is decent value but is often full. **Habitaciones Mariflor** (☎ 977 23 82 31; Carrer del General Contreras 29; singles/doubles €13/24, high season €17/3) occupies a drab building near the train station but has clean rooms at good prices.

The three-star **Hotel Lauria** (☎ 977 23 67 12; Rambla Nova 20; singles/doubles €40/57) is a worthwhile splurge with a wonderful location, a pool and delightfully airy rooms, some with views of the Mediterranean.

Places to Eat

For solid Catalan food, simply head for the stylish **Restaurant Bufet El Tiberi** (Carrer de Martí d'Ardenya 5; buffet €9-10; closed Sun evening & Mon), which offers an all-you-can-eat buffet. Nearby **Mesón Andaluz** (Carrer de Pons d'Icart 3; set menu €9) is a backstreet local favourite with a good three-course menú.

Jerónimo (Plaça de la Font 6; meat platter €15) is the place to dig into porcine delights. Carnivores will enjoy the mixed meat and sausage platter. If cheese is your thing, try a *taula de formatges* at **Can Llesques** (Carrer de Natzaret 6; cheese platter €7-8), a pleasant spot looking onto Plaça del Rei.

Café Cantonada (Carrer de Fortuny 23) is a popular place for tapas; next door, **Restaurant Cantonada** (dishes from €5) has pizza and pasta. Rambla Nova has several good places, either for a snack or a meal. **Viena** (Rambla Nova 50; sandwiches from €1) has good croissants and a vast range of *entrepans* (sandwiches).

Tucked under the vaults of the former Roman circus, **Les Voltes** (Carrer de Trinquet

Vell 12; set menu €9) is a little overpriced, but the menú is decent value.

Getting There & Away
The train station is southwest of the old town, on the coast. Over 20 regional trains a day run from Barcelona to Tarragona (€4, one to 1½ hours). There are about 12 trains daily from Tarragona to Valencia (€11.50, two to 3½ hours). To Madrid (€40, six hours) there are four trains each day via Zaragoza.

The bus station is on Avinguda Roma, just off Plaça Imperial Tarraco. Buses run to regional cities, such as Barcelona (€3) and throughout Spain, including Madrid (€23).

Balearic Islands

pop 878,630
The Balearic Islands of Mallorca, Menorca, Ibiza and Formentera all share a language – Catalan. In other ways, however, they are quite different, ranging from the culture and sophistication of the grand old city of Palma (Mallorca) to the hedonistic foam-soaked fun of an Ibizan disco.

Despite the annual invasion of several million tourists, the islands have maintained strong links with their cultural identity and their past. Beyond the bars and beaches are Gothic cathedrals, Stone Age ruins and Moorish remains, as well as simple fishing villages, endless olive groves and orange orchards.

Most place names and addresses are given in Catalan. High-season prices are quoted here. Out of season, you will often find things are much cheaper and accommodation especially can be as much as half the rates quoted below. However, as many places close from October to May, always double-check before turning up with your bags.

Getting There & Away
Air Scheduled flights from the major cities on the Spanish mainland are operated by several airlines, including Iberia, Air Europa and Spanair.

Standard one-way fares from Barcelona are not great value, hovering around €49 to Palma de Mallorca and more to the other islands. At the time of writing, the cheapest return fare available was €83 with Spanair. Cheap charter flights to the mainland are increasingly rare.

Interisland flights are expensive (given the flying times involved), with Palma to Maó or Ibiza costing €87/137 one way/return.

Boat The major ferry company for the islands is **Trasmediterránea** *(information & ticket purchases* ☎ 902 45 46 45; *w* www.trasmediterranea.es)*, with offices in (and services between) Barcelona (☎ 93 295 90 00), Valencia (☎ 963 67 65 12), Palma de Mallorca (☎ 971 40 50 14), Maó (☎ 971 36 60 50) and Ibiza city (☎ 971 31 51 00).

The duration time of the services varies dramatically, depending on the type of ferry. The maximum time is given here, but always check whether there is a faster ferry (such as a catamaran) available. At the time of writing, the fast ferry service from Palma was out of service for repairs for an indefinite period. Scheduled services are: Barcelona-Palma/Palma-Barcelona (eight hours, up to 13 services weekly); Palma-Maó/Maó-Palma (four hours, two services weekly); Valencia- Palma/Palma-Valencia (eight hours, seven services weekly); Palma-Ibiza/Ibiza-Palma (five hours, two services weekly). Prices quoted below are the one-way fares during summer; low- and mid-season fares are considerably cheaper.

Fares from the mainland to any of the islands are €45.50 for a Butaca Turista (seat) and €63 for the same class on a catamaran; a berth in a cabin ranges from €80 (four-share) to €162 (single cabin) per person. Taking a small car costs €126, or there are economy packages (Paquete Ahorro) available.

Interisland services (Palma–Ibiza city and Palma–Maó) both cost €25 for a Butaca Turista, and €69 for a small car. Ask, too, about economy packages.

Another company, **Balearia** (☎ 902 16 01 80; *w* www.balearia.com), operates three daily ferries from Dénia (on the coast between Valencia and Alicante) to Ibiza (from €44 one way, three hours). There are also services between Valencia and Palma (from €46 one way, six hours) and between Ibiza and Palma (€35, two hours).

Iscomar (☎ 902 11 91 28) has from one to four daily car ferries (depending on the season) between Ciutadella on Menorca and Port d'Alcúdia on Mallorca, as well as between Palma and Dénia and Ibiza and Dénia. **Cape Balear** (☎ 902 10 04 44) operates up to three daily fast ferries to Ciutadella from

Cala Ratjada (Mallorca) in summer for around €48 return. The crossing takes 75 minutes.

MALLORCA

Mallorca is the largest of the Balearic Islands. Most of the five million annual visitors to the island are here for the three *s* words: sun, sand and sea. There is, however, far more to see here, including the capital city Palma de Mallorca, with its medina-like backstreets, flanked by sun-baked ochre buildings and fanciful Gaudí/Gothic cathedral.

West of the city, the shoreline bubbles up into low, rocky hills while, at Cala Major, grand old mansions and Miró's house are a world away from the thumping nightlife of the Brit resorts.

Orientation & Information

Palma is on the southern side of the island, on a bay famous for its brilliant sunsets. The Serra de Tramuntana mountain range, which runs parallel with the northwestern coastline, is trekkers' heaven. Mallorca's best beaches are along the northern and eastern coasts, along with most of the big tourist resorts.

All of the major resorts have at least one tourist office. Palma has four, including the **main tourist office** (☎ 971 71 22 16, fax 971 72 12 51; ⓦ www.balearia.com; Plaça de la Reina) Other locations include Plaça d'Espanya (☎ 971 75 43 29), Carrer Sant Domingo 11 (☎ 971 72 40 90) and at the airport. Palma has several Internet centres, including **Big Byte** (☎ 971 71 17 54; Carrer Apuntadores 6; open 10am-midnight daily) at €2.50 an hour.

SPAIN

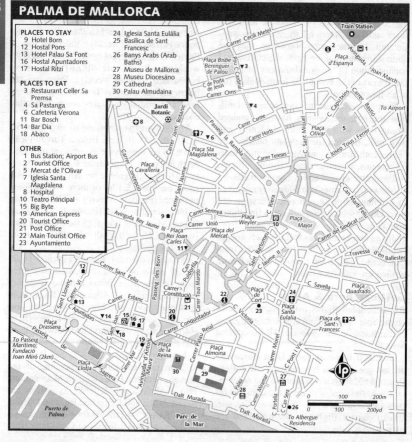

PALMA DE MALLORCA

PLACES TO STAY
9 Hotel Born
12 Hostal Pons
13 Hotel Palau Sa Font
16 Hostal Apuntadores
17 Hostal Ritzi

PLACES TO EAT
3 Restaurant Celler Sa Premsa
4 Sa Pastanga
6 Cafeteria Verona
11 Bar Bosch
14 Bar Dia
18 Abaco

OTHER
1 Bus Station; Airport Bus
2 Tourist Office
5 Mercat de l'Olivar
7 Iglesia Santa Magdalena
8 Hospital
10 Teatro Principal
15 Big Byte
19 American Express
20 Tourist Office
21 Post Office
22 Main Tourist Office
23 Ayuntamiento

24 Iglesia Santa Eulália
25 Basílica de Sant Francesc
26 Banys Àrabs (Arab Baths)
27 Museu de Mallorca
28 Museu Diocesáno
29 Cathedral
30 Palau Almudaina

Things to See & Do

Overlooking Palma and its port, like a grand old dame, is the enormous **cathedral** *(Plaça Almoina; admission €3.50)*. It houses an excellent museum, and some of the interior features were designed by Antoni Gaudí.

In front of the cathedral is the **Palau Almudaina** *(admission €3)*, the one-time residence of the Mallorcan monarchs. Inside is a collection of tapestries and artworks. It's not really worth the entry fee unless this is seriously your thing.

Instead, visit the rich and varied **Museu de Mallorca** *(Carrer Portella 5; admission €2; open 10am-2pm & 5pm-7pm Tues-Sat, Sun morning)*.

Also near the cathedral are the interesting **Museu Diocesáno** and the **Banys Árabs** *(Arab Baths; Carrer Can Sera 7; open 9.30am-8pm daily)*, the only remaining monument to the Muslim domination of the island. Also worth visiting is the collection of the **Fundació Joan Miró** *(Carrer Joan de Saridakis 29; open 10am-6pm Tues-Sat, Sun morning)* housed in the artist's one-time home and studio, 2km west of the centre in Cala Major.

Mallorca's northwestern coast is a world away from the high-rise tourism on the other side of the island. Dominated by the Serra de Tramuntana mountains, it's a beautiful region of olive groves, pine forests and small villages with stone buildings; it also has a rugged and rocky coastline.

There are a couple of highlights for drivers: the hair-raising road down to the small port of **Sa Calobra** and the amazing trip along the peninsula leading to the island's northern tip, **Cap Formentor**.

If you don't have wheels, take the **Palma to Sóller train** (for details see Getting Around later in this section). It's one of the most popular and spectacular excursions on the island. Sóller is also the best place to base yourself for trekking. It is a relatively easy three-hour return walk from here to the beautiful, if heritaged, village of **Deiá,** where Robert Graves, poet and author of *I Claudius*, lived most of his life. The tourist office's *Hiking Excursions* brochure covers 20 of the island's better walks or, for more detailed information, see Lonely Planet's *Walking in Spain*.

Most of Mallorca's best beaches have been consumed by tourist developments, although there are exceptions. The lovely **Cala Mondragó** on the southeastern coast is backed by just a couple of *hostales* while, a little further south, the attractive port town of **Cala Figuera** and nearby **Cala Santanyi** beach have both escaped many of the ravages of mass tourism. There are also some good quiet beaches near the popular German resort of **Colonia San Jordi**, particularly **Ses Arenes** and **Es Trenc**, both a few kilometres back up the coast towards Palma.

Places to Stay

Palma The cluttered 19th-century charm of **Hostal Pons** *(☎ 971 72 26 58; Carrer Vi 8; singles/doubles €16/32)* overcomes its limitations (spongy beds, only one bathroom). **Hostal Apuntadores** *(☎ 971 71 34 91; e apuntadores@ctv.es; Carrer Apuntadores 8; dorm beds €14, singles/doubles €21/33, doubles with bath €37)* has a 7th-floor terrace with a view of the city, and a lively downstairs bar-restaurant where you can get cheap meals and chat with other travellers. **Hostal Ritzi** *(☎ 971 71 46 10; doubles without bath €23, with shower only €34, with bath & shower €49)*, next door to Hostal Apuntadores, needs a lick of paint, but is very central, with good security and satellite TV in the communal sitting room.

The superb **Hotel Born** *(☎ 971 71 29 42, fax 971 71 86 18; e hotel_born@hotmail .com; Carrer Sant Jaume 3; singles/doubles up to €65/91)* in a restored 18th-century palace has a classic Mallorcan patio. Even older, the 14th-century **Hotel Palau Sa Font** *(☎ 971 71 22 77, fax 971 71 26 18; e info@ pauausafont.com; Carrer Apuntadores 38; singles/doubles from €90/132)* is German-owned, and is a hotel with cutting-edge modern decor and class.

Other Areas After Palma, you should head for the hills. In Deiá, there is the exquisite **S'Hotel D'es Puig** *(☎ 971 63 94 09, fax 971 63 92 10; e puig@futurnet.es; singles/ doubles with breakfast €69/103)* in the middle of the village, while **Hostal Miramar** *(☎ 971 63 90 84; singles/doubles with breakfast €29/57)*, overlooking the town, is very good value. In nearby Fornalutx, said to be the prettiest village on the island, **Cán Verdera** *(☎ 971 63 82 03, fax 971 63 81 09; e can verdera@ctv.es; doubles up to €168)* is serious splurge time, housed in an old stone building with original beams, new pool and great views. Beside the train station in Sóller, the down-to-earth **Hotel El Guía** (☎ 971 63 02 27; singles/doubles with breakfast €44/ 65) has pleasant rooms.

If you want to stay on the southeastern coast, the large **Hostal Playa Mondragó** (☎ 971 65 77 52; Cala Mondragó; rooms per person €11) has B&B rates. At Cala Figuera, **Hostal Cán Jordi** (☎ 971 64 50 35; singles/ doubles from €24/33) is justifiably popular.

You can also sleep cheaply at several quirky old monasteries around the island with prices typically under €18 per person. The tourist offices have a list (see Orientation & Information earlier in this section).

Places to Eat

For Palma's best range of eateries, wander through the maze of streets between Plaça de la Reina and the port. Carrer Apuntadores is lined with restaurants, including seafood and Italian, and an inexpensive takeaway **Bar Dia** (☎ 971 71 62 64) at number 18. Around the corner is the incredible **Abaco** (☎ 971 71 59 11; Carrer Sant Joan 1), the bar of your wildest dreams (with the drinks bill of your darkest nightmares).

For the cost-conscious, **Cafeteria Verona** (☎ 971 71 28 34; Carrer Convento de Santa Magdalena; set menu €6; open lunch only) is a check-cloth, bistro-style place serving local and international food. Up the road **Bar Bosch** (☎ 971 72 11 31; Plaça Rei Joan Carlos) is in a prime people-watching spot and good for sandwiches and snacks.

Rumbling tummies should head for **Restaurant Celler Sa Premsa** (☎ 971 72 35 29; Plaça del Bisbe Berenguer de Palou 8; set menu €9), a cavernous, atmospheric place with enormous portions of stolid local fare. For vegetarian food, try **Sa Pastanga** (☎ 971 71 44 47; Carrer Sant Elies 6; set menu €9), serving simple delicious dishes.

Getting Around

Bus No 25 runs every 20 minutes between the airport and Plaça Espanya in central Palma (€2.50, 20 minutes). Alternatively, a taxi will cost around €14.

Most parts of the island are accessible by bus from Palma. Buses generally depart from or near the bus station at Plaça Espanya – the tourist office has details. Mallorca's two train lines also start from Plaça Espanya. One goes to the inland town of Inca and the other goes to Sóller (€2.50 one way, or €4.50 for the

Parada Turística), both highly picturesque jaunts; check at the tourist office for times.

The best way to get around the island is by car – it's worth renting one just for the drive along the northwestern coast. There are about 30 rental agencies in Palma (and all the big companies have reps at the airport). If you want to compare prices, check the many harbourside offices along Passeig Marítim.

IBIZA

Once a hippie hideaway, but now much more mainstream 'hip', Ibiza ('Eivissa' in Catalan) is best known for its extraordinary clubbing scene.

The flip side is very different, particularly in the rural villages in the south. Here the women wear long black skirts and wide straw hats and – forget the nudist beaches – the only traffic stoppers are the goatherds.

Orientation & Information

The capital, Ibiza (Eivissa) city, is on the southeastern side of the island. This is where most travellers arrive (by ferry or air; the airport is to the south) and it's also the best base. The next largest towns are Santa Eulària des Riu on the eastern coast and Sant Antoni de Portmany on the western coast, the latter best avoided unless you are seriously into discos and getting drunk. Other big resorts are scattered around the island.

In Ibiza city, the **tourist office** (☎ 971 30 19 00, fax 971 30 15 62; e promocio@ cief.es) is opposite the Estación Marítima. There are numerous cafés where you can go online but not many, aside from **Wash and Dry.Com** (☎ 971 39 48 22; Avinguda Espanya 53), where you can do a load of washing as well as access the Net.

Things to See & Do

Shopping seems to be a major pastime in Ibiza city. The port area of **Sa Penya** is crammed with funky and trashy clothes boutiques and arty-crafty market stalls. From here you can wander up into **D'Alt Vila**, the atmospheric old walled town, with its up-market restaurants, galleries and the **Museu d'Art Contemporani**. There are fine views from the walls and from the **cathedral** at the top, and the **Museu Arqueològic** next door is worth a visit.

The heavily developed **Platja de ses Figueretes** beach is a 20-minute walk south of Sa Penya – you'd be better off taking the half-hour bus ride (€1.50) south to the beaches at **Ses Salines**.

Away from the coach tours, Ibiza has numerous unspoiled and relatively undeveloped beaches. On the northeastern coast, **Cala de Boix** is the only black-sand beach on the islands, while further north are the lovely beaches of **S'Aigua Blanca**. On the northern coast near Portinatx, **Cala Xarraca** is in a picturesque, secluded bay and, near Port de Sant Miquel, is the attractive **Cala Benirras**. On the southwestern coast, **Cala d'Hort** has a spectacular setting overlooking two rugged rock-islets, Es Verda and Es Verdranell.

Places to Stay

Ibiza City There are several *hostales* in the streets around the port, although in midsummer cheap beds are scarce. On the waterfront **Hostal-Restaurante La Marina** (☎ 971 31 01 72, fax 971 31 48 94; Carrer Barcelona 7; singles/doubles €55/75) has sunny doubles with harbour views.

One of the best choices is **Casa de Huéspedes La Peña** (☎ 971 19 02 40; Carrer de la Virgen 76; doubles around €30; open June-Oct) at the far end of Sa Penya. There are 13 simple and tidy doubles with shared bathrooms. **Hostal Parque** (☎ 971 30 13 58; Plaça del Parque 4; singles/doubles with bath €48/72) has a revamped new look, but is on one of the liveliest squares so can be noisy. If you can afford it, the delightful **La Ventana** (☎ 971 39 08 57; Sa Carrossa 13; doubles up to €125) has wrought-iron four-poster beds, simple yet stylish decor and fantastic terrace views of the old castle walls.

Other Areas One of the best of Ibiza's camping grounds is **Camping Cala Nova** (☎ 971 33 17 74), 500m north of the resort town of Cala Nova and close to a good beach.

If you want luxury, with gymnasium, pool, sauna and sun terrace, **Can Curreu** (☎ 971 33 52 80, fax 971 33 52 80; e curreu@ibiza-hotels.com; doubles from €195) near Santa Eulais is a gorgeous small hotel. For sand between the toes, **Pensión Sa Plana** (☎ 971 33 50 73; doubles with breakfast from €45) is near the S'Aigua Blanca beaches and has a pool. Or you could stay by the black-sand beach at Cala Boix, at the cliff-top **Hostal Cala Boix** (☎ 97133 52 24; rooms per person €17), with breakfast included in the rates.

Places to Eat

Start your evening out with a drink at one of the bars lining the lively Plaça del Parque. **Herry's Bar** does a great tomato and olive oil tostada tapa. For something more substantial, **L'Absinthe** across the way, is woody and rustic, with some innovative salads and pasta dishes. Carnivorous folk may prefer the meaty menu and tapas at around €3 at **Viejo Almacen** (☎ 971 31 44 32; Azara 5). Hang out with the local fishermen at no-frills **La Estrella** (Plaça San Antonio Riquer; sandwiches, hot dogs, burgers €2.50-3), or eat Andalucían-style fare at **La Oliva** (☎ 971 30 57 52; Calle Santa Cruz), which has a pretty patio and excellent fish soup. A hip place for a coffee and coñac is **Café Libro Azul** (☎ 971 39 23 80; Calle Cayetano Soler), which doubles as a bookshop and plays suitably laid-back jazz.

Just within the old town walls, **El Portalón** (☎ 971 30 39 01; Plaça Desamparados 1) serves classy French cuisine, while the heady views from **Plaça del Sol** on the square of the same name are in surprising contrast to the down-to-earth menu, which includes filled baked potatoes, a welcome change from chips.

Entertainment

Ibiza's summer nightlife is renowned. At night, wander the fashion-catwalk of cobbled streets where designer chic couples and seriously studded swingers dodge the outrageous PR performers hired by the discos to attract dusk-to-dawn clubbers. Dozens of bars keep Ibiza city's port area jumping until the early hours – particularly on Carrer de Barcelona and Carrer de Garijo Cipriano. After they wind down, you can continue on to one of the island's world-famous discos – if you can afford the around €30 entry, that is. There's a handy 'Discobus' service that operates nightly from midnight until 6am doing circuits between the major discos, the bars and hotels in Ibiza city, Platja d'en Bossa, San Rafael and San Antonio. The big names are **Pacha**, on the northern side of Ibiza city's port; **Privilege** and **Amnesia**, both 6km out on the road to Sant Antoni; **El Divino**, across the water from the town centre (hop on one of its boats); and **Space**, south of Ibiza city in Platja d'En Bossa.

Getting Around

Buses run between the airport and Ibiza city hourly (€1.50); a taxi costs around €12.

SPAIN

Buses to other parts of the island leave from the series of bus stops along Avenida d'Isidoro Macabich. Pick up a timetable from the tourist office (see Orientation & Information earlier in this section).

If you want to get to some of the more secluded beaches you will need to rent wheels. In Ibiza city, **Autos Isla Blanca** (☎ 971 31 54 07; Carrer de Felipe II) will hire out a Renault Twingo for €103 for three days all-inclusive, or a scooter for around €28 a day.

FORMENTERA

A short boat ride south of Ibiza, Formentera is the smallest and least developed of the four main Balearic Islands. That said, the island is attracting an increasing number of package tourists, particularly from Germany, so it lacks the tranquillity that made it such a hippie haven some thirty years ago. There are some excellent short walking and cycling trails, however, and most of the time it is still possible to spread a towel out on the beach without kicking sand over your neighbour.

Orientation & Information

Formentera is about 20km from east to west. Ferries arrive at La Savina on the northwestern coast; the **tourist office** (☎ 971 32 20 57, fax 971 32 38 25; w www.illadeformen tera.es) is behind the rental agencies you'll see when you disembark. Three kilometres south is the island's pretty capital, Sant Francesc Xavier, where you'll find a pharmacy, several banks and a good-sized supermarket for your picnic supplies. From here, the main road runs along the middle of the island before climbing to the highest point (192m). At the eastern end of the island is the Sa Mola lighthouse. Es Pujols is 3km east of La Savina and is the main tourist resort where most of the *hostales* are located (and the only place with any nightlife to speak of).

Things to See & Do

Some of the island's best and most popular beaches are the beautiful white strips of sand along the narrow promontory, which stretches north towards Ibiza. A 2km walking trail leads from the La Savina–Es Pujols road to the far end of the promontory, from where you can wade across a narrow strait to **S'Es-palmador**, a privately owned uninhabited islet with beautiful, quiet beaches. If you don't fancy the paddle, there are regular boat rides. Along Formentera's southern coast, **Platja de Migjorn** is made up of numerous coves and beaches. Tracks lead down to these off the main road. On the western coast is the lovely **Cala Saona** beach.

The tourist office's *Green Tours* brochure outlines 19 excellent walking and cycling trails in five languages that take you through some of the island's most scenic areas.

Places to Stay & Eat

Camping is not allowed on Formentera. Sadly, the coastal accommodation places mainly cater to German and British package-tour agencies and are overpriced and/or booked out in summer. In Es Pujols you could try **Hostal Tahiti** (☎ 971 32 81 22; singles/ doubles €58/72; open May-Sept), with B&B available. One of the few hotels open year-round **Hostal Bellavista** (☎ 971 32 70 16; singles/doubles €54/66) has sea views and a handy terrace bar. If you prefer peace and quiet, you are better off in Es Caló. **Fonda Rafalet** (☎ 971 32 70 16; singles/ doubles in Aug €39/58; open Apr-Oct) has good rooms on the waterfront or, across the road, there is the tiny and simple **Casa de Huéspedes Miramar** (☎ 971 32 70 60; rooms per person €30; open May-Sept).

Perhaps the best budget bet is to base yourself in one of the small inland towns and bike it to the beaches. In Sant Ferrán de ses Roques (1.6km south of Es Pujols), popular **Hostal Pepe** (☎ 971 32 80 33; singles/doubles €24/ 37) offers rooms with bath and the price includes breakfast. Aside from the inevitable tourist-orientated restaurants serving over-priced egg-and-chip style food, there are some excellent seafood restaurants on the island. Many of the hostales also have bars/restaurants typically serving fairly uninspired but cheap meals. In Es Pujols, **S'Avaradero** on the seafront (☎ 971 32 90 43; Avenida Miramar 32-36) serves great seafood and Argentinean-style meat dishes. Also on the beach, **Bar Restaurant Flipper** (☎ 971 18 75 96; Playa Mitjorn, Arenals) is good for fresh fish and typical island dishes. Try the *arroz a la marinera* for a real taste of Formentera.

Wind up the evening with a blast of good music at the **Blue Bar** (☎ 971 18 70 11; Playa Mitjorn km 8), open until 4am. For tapas and local wine, **Bar Sa Barraca** (☎ 971 32 80 27; Avenida Miramar, Es Pujols) is good while, among the plethora of pizzerias, **El Gatto E La**

Volpe (☎ *971 32 91 00; Carretera Punta Prima, Es Pujols*) is better than most.

Getting There & Away
There are 20 to 25 ferries daily between Ibiza city and Formentera. The trip takes around half an hour and prices between the various companies are fiercely competitive, but cost around €10 one way.

Getting Around
A string of rental agencies lines the harbour in La Savina. Bikes start at €5 a day (€6 for a mountain bike) and scooters start at €17 and head up to €25 for more powerful motorbikes. A regular bus service connects all the main towns.

MENORCA
Although Menorca is the second largest Balearic island, it is the least overrun. In 1993, the island was declared a Biosphere Reserve by Unesco, with the aim of preserving important environmental areas, such as the Albufera d'es Grau wetlands and its unique collection of archaeological sites.

Orientation & Information
The capital, Maó (Mahón in Spanish), is at the eastern end of the island. Its busy port is the arrival point for most ferries and Menorca's airport is 7km southwest. The main road runs down the middle of the island to Ciutadella, Menorca's second-largest town, with secondary roads leading north and south to the resorts and beaches.

The **main tourist office** (☎ *971 36 37 90, fax 971 35 45 30;* w *www.caib.es; Plaça de S'Esplanada 40*) is in Maó. There is a second **tourist office** (☎ *971 38 26 93; Plaça la Catedral s/n*) in Ciutadella. During the summer there is an additional office at the airport. There are **post offices** in Maó (*Carrer del Bon Aire*) and Ciutadella (*Pio V1 4*).

Things to See & Do
Maó and Ciutadella are both harbour towns, and from either place you'll have to commute to the beaches. Maó absorbs most of the tourist traffic. While you're here, you can take a boat cruise around its impressive harbour and sample the local gin at the **Xoriguer distillery** (*open 8.30am-7pm Mon-Fri, 9am-1pm Sat*). Ciutadella, with its smaller harbour and historic buildings, has a more distinctively

Spanish feel about it. Follow the shopping baskets to the colourful market on Plaça Llibertat, surrounded by lively tapas bars.

In the centre of the island, the 357m-high **Monte Toro** has great views of the whole island and, on a clear day, you can see as far as Mallorca.

With your own transport and a bit of footwork, you'll be able to discover some of Menorca's off-the-beaten-track beaches. North of Maó, a drive across a lunar landscape leads to the lighthouse at **Cabo de Favàritx**. If you park just before the gate to the lighthouse and climb up the rocks behind you, you'll see a couple of the eight beaches that are just waiting for scramblers such as yourself to grace their sands.

On the northern coast, the picturesque town of **Fornells** is on a large bay popular with windsurfers. Further west, at the beach of Binimella, you can continue to the unspoilt **Cala Pregonda**, which is a good 20-minute walk from the nearest parking spot.

North of Ciutadella is **La Vall** (€4.50 per car), another stretch of untouched beach backed by a private nature park. On the southern coast are two good beaches either side of the Santa Galdana resort – Cala Mitjana to the east and Macarella to the west. Menorca's beaches aren't its only attractions. The interior of the island is liberally sprinkled with reminders of its rich and ancient heritage. Pick up a copy of the tourist office's *Archaeological Guide to Menorca*.

Places to Stay & Eat
Menorca's two **camping grounds** (*open summer only*) are near the resorts of **Santa Galdana** (☎ *971 37 30 95*), about 8km south of Ferreries, and **Son Bou** (☎ *971 37 26 05*), south of Alaior.

Maó and Ciutadella both have a handful of good budget options. In Maó, **Hostal Orsi** (☎ *971 36 47 51; Carrer de la Infanta 19; singles/doubles with bath €21/42*) is run by a Glaswegian and an American, who are a mine of information. It's bright, clean and well located. If you are not economising with your euros, **Hotel del Almirante** (☎ *971 36 27 00, fax 36 27 04;* e *hotel.almirante@ menorca.net; singles/doubles €52/83*) is a magnificent Georgian-style mansion and a former residence of Nelson's second-in-command at Trafalgar. Really, the potted aspidistras say it all.

SPAIN

In Ciutadella **Hostal Oasis** (☎ 971 38 21 97; Carrer Sant Isidre 33; doubles only €42) has homey rooms around a central courtyard and restaurant, so lots of atmosphere, but it can be noisy at night.

Ciutadella's port is also lined with restaurants and you won't have any trouble finding somewhere to eat. **Cappuccino Menorca** (☎ 971 35 66 20; Moll de Llevant) is a classy place for a light meal, cocktail or coffee. After dinner, check out **Jazzbah**, a hip little music bar. In Maó port, **Latitud 40** (☎ 971 36 41 76; Moll de Llevant 265) is a popular bar-restaurant with the boating fraternity if you're looking for a job scrubbing decks. **Casanova** (☎ 971 35 41 69; Puerto de Mahon 15) is a good pizza place.

Getting Around

From the airport, a taxi into Maó costs around €7.50; there are no buses.

TMSA (☎ 971 36 03 61) runs six buses a day between Maó and Ciutadella (€3.50), with connections to the major resorts on the southern coast. In summer there are also daily bus services to most of the coastal towns from both Maó and Ciutadella.

If you're planning to hire a car, rates vary seasonally from around €24 to €48 a day; during the summer, minimum hire periods sometimes apply. In Maó, places worth trying include **Autos Valls** (☎ 971 36 84 65; Plaça d'Espanya 13) and **Autos Isla** (☎ 971 36 65 69; Avinguda de Josep Maria Quadrado 28). **Just Bicicletas** (☎ 971 36 47 51; Andén de Llevant 35-36) hires out mountain bikes (€6 per day). At **Motos Gelabert** (☎ 971 36 06 14; José Anselmo Clavé) you can rent a scooter from €15 a day.

Valencia

Although perhaps best known for the package resorts of the Costa Blanca, this region also includes Spain's lively third-largest city, Valencia, and some rare undiscovered secrets if you penetrate inland.

VALENCIA
pop 746,610

Valencia is a vibrant city, its old quarter brimming with gracious baroque-fronted houses and its streets buzzing with life until the early hours – especially during the country's wildest party: Las Fallas de San José (mid-March), an exuberant blend of fireworks, music, all-night partying and over 350 *fallas*, giant sculptures that all go up in flames on the final night.

Orientation

The action part of the city is oval, bounded by the old course of the Turia River and the sickle-shaped inner ring road of Calles Colón, Játiva and Guillem de Castro. These trace the walls of the old city, demolished in 1865 as – believe it or not – a job-creation project that dismantled one of the major monuments on the Mediterranean coastline.

Within the oval are three major squares: Plazas del Ayuntamiento, de la Reina (also known as Plaza de Zaragoza) and de la Virgen.

Information

There is a **main tourist office** (☎ 963 98 64 22, fax 963 98 64 21; e touristinfo.valencia@turisme.m400.gva.es; Calle Paz 48; open 10am-6.30pm Mon-Fri, 10am-2pm Sat) in the centre. Three smaller ones are at the train station, town hall and Teatro Principal.

Among several Internet cafés in town is **Jump** (☎ 963 80 50 34; Calle Albacete 8), just south of the Plaza del Ayuntamiento; it charges €1.50 an hour.

Things to See & Do

Located in the dried-up bed of the city's Turia River, the aesthetically stunning, ultramodern **Ciudad de las Artes y las Ciencias** (information & reservations ☎ 902 100 031) includes the Hemisfèric (a planetarium, IMAX cinema and laser show), interactive science museum, aquarium and open-air auditorium.

The **Museo de Bellas Artes** (Fine Arts Museum; admission free; open 10am-2.15pm & 4pm-7.30pm Tues-Sat, 10am-7.30pm Sun) ranks among Spain's best, with works by El Greco, Goya, Velázquez, Ribera and Ribalta.

The **Instituto Valenciano de Arte Moderno** (IVAM; admission €2, free Sun), beside Puente de las Artes, houses an impressive permanent collection of 20th-century Spanish art. Valencia's cathedral boasts three magnificent portals – one Romanesque, one Gothic and one baroque. Climb the Miguelete bell-tower (admission €1.50) for a sweeping view of the sprawling city.

The baroque **Palacio del Marqués de Dos Aguas** (Calle del Poeta Querol) is fronted by

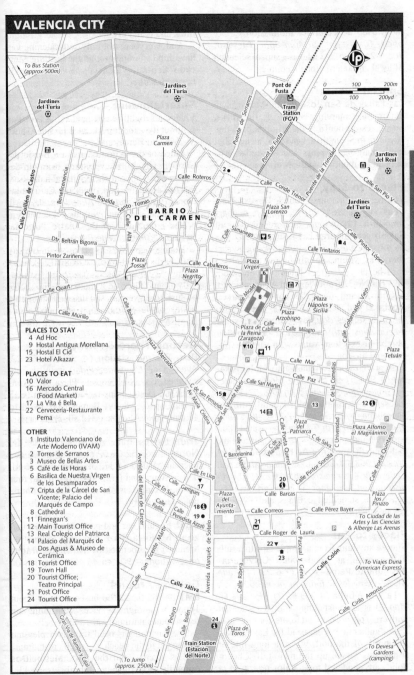

VALENCIA CITY

To Bus Station
(approx 500m)

Jardines
del Turia

Jardines
del Turia

Pont de
Fusta

Tram
Station
(FGV)

Jardines
del Real

Plaza
Carmen

Calle Roteros

Calle Conde Trénor

Calle San Pío V

Puente de Serranos

Pont de Fusta

Puente de la Trinidad

Calle Ripalda

Santo Tomas

Calle Serranos

Plaza San
Lorenzo

Jardines
del Turia

BARRIO
DEL CARMEN

Calle Samaniego

Calle Pintor López

Dtr. Beltrán Bigorra

Alta

Calle Trinitarios

Pintor Zariñena

Plaza
Tossal

Plaza
Negrito

Calle Caballeros

Plaza
Virgen

Calle Gobernador Viejo

Calle Quart

Bolsería

Calle Miclet

Plaza
Nápoles y
Sicilia

Calle Murillo

Plaza
Arzobispo

Plaza
Tetuán

Calle
Cabillars

Calle Milagro

Plaza de
la Reina
(Zaragoza)

Calle Mar

Mercado

Calle Paz

C. de las Comedias

Calle San Martin

Av. María Cristina

C. de San Fernando

Calle San Vicente Martir

Calle
del
Patriarca

Plaza Alfonso
el Magnánimo

Plaza
los
Pinazo

Plaza Alfonso
el Magnánimo

C. de
Vilaragut

C. de Salvá

C. Universidad

Calle Poeta Quintana

Calle Poeta Querol

Avenida del Barón de Cárcer

Calle En Llop

Calle En Sanç

Calle Garrigues

Calle
Padila

Calle
Periodista Azzati

Calle de Moratín

Calle Barcelonina

Plaza
del
Ayuntamiento

Calle Barcas

Calle Correos

Calle Pérez Bayer

Calle Pintor Sorolla

To Ciudad de las
Artes y las Ciencias
& Alberge Las Arenas

Calle San Vicente Martir

Calle Marqués de Sotelo

Calle Roger de Lauria

Calle Pascual y Genís

To Viajes Duna
(American Express)

Calle Ribera

Calle Colón

To Devesa
Gardens
(camping)

Calle Játiva

Calle Pelayo

Calle Bailén

Train Station
(Estación
del Norte)

Plaza de
Toros

Calle Cirilo Amorós

Gran Vía de Ramón y Cajal

To Jump
(approx. 250m)

SPAIN

N

LP

0   100   200m
0   100   200yd

PLACES TO STAY
4 Ad Hoc
9 Hostal Antigua Morellana
15 Hostal El Cid
23 Hotel Alkazar

PLACES TO EAT
10 Valor
16 Mercado Central
   (Food Market)
17 La Vita é Bella
22 Cervecería-Restaurante
   Pema

OTHER
1 Instituto Valenciano de
   Arte Moderno (IVAM)
2 Torres de Serranos
3 Museo de Bellas Artes
5 Café de las Horas
6 Basílica de Nuestra Virgen
   de los Desamparados
7 Cripta de la Cárcel de San
   Vicente; Palacio del
   Marqués de Campo
8 Cathedral
11 Finnegan's
12 Main Tourist Office
13 Real Colegio del Patriarca
14 Palacio del Marqués de
   Dos Aguas & Museo de
   Cerámica
18 Tourist Office
19 Town Hall
20 Tourist Office;
   Teatro Principal
21 Post Office
24 Tourist Office

an extravagantly sculpted facade. It houses the **Museo de Cerámica** *(admission €2.50; open 10am-2pm & 4pm-8pm Tues-Sat, 10am-2pm Sun)*, which has a superb selection of local and international ceramics.

Special Events

Las Fallas de San José in mid-March is an exuberant, anarchic swirl of fireworks, music, festive bonfires and all-night partying. If you're in Spain then, head for Valencia, but don't plan on sleeping – accommodation is booked up months in advance.

Places to Stay

The nearest camping ground, **Devesa Gardens** *(☎/fax 961 61 11 36; open year-round)*, is 13km south of Valencia near El Saler beach. **Alberge Las Arenas** *(☎/fax 963 56 42 88; Calle Eugenia Viñes 24; open year-round)* is within squinting view of Malvarrosa beach and offers Internet connection; take bus No 32 from Plaza del Ayuntamiento.

Central and near the covered market, **Hostal El Cid** *(☎ 963 92 23 23; Calle Cerrajeros 13; singles/doubles without bath €12/24, doubles with bath €32)* is a steep stair climb but excellent value with satellite TV, bath and air-con.

Near Plaza del Ayuntamiento, **Hotel Alkazar** *(☎ 963 51 55 51; Calle Mosén Femades 11; singles/doubles with bath €48/52)* is very pleasant and comfortable. **Hostal Antigua Morellana** *(☎/fax 963 91 57 73; Calle en Bou 2; doubles with bath €42)* in a renovated 18th-century building has cosy rooms. North of the cathedral, the owner of **Ad Hoc** *(☎ 963 91 91 40, fax 963 91 36 67; e adhoc@nixo.net; Calle Boix 4; singles/doubles €89/110 with discounts at weekends)* is in the art business, hence the stencilled ceilings and fabulous colour scheme.

Places to Eat

Choose anything from a simple tapa to a full-blown meal at good value **Cervecería-Restaurante Pema** *(☎ 963 56 22 14; Calle Mosén Femades 3; lunch menu €6.50)*.

La Vita é Bella *(☎ 963 52 21 31; Calle En Llop 4)* is an outstanding Italian restaurant with crisp pizza crust and to-die-for tiramasu.

For authentic paella, head for Las Arenas, just north of the port, where a long line of restaurants serves up the real stuff. Chocoholics are pandered to at **Valor** *(Plaza de la Reina 20)*, where chocolate is served in cups, thick and delicious.

And everyone, not only self-caterers, can have fun browsing around the bustling **Mercado Central**, Valencia's *modernista*-style covered market.

Entertainment

Valencia's nightlife is legendary, as is its gay community – the third largest in Spain, after Madrid and Barcelona.

Much of the action centres on Barrio del Carmen, which has everything from hip designer bars to gloomy heavy-metal hang-outs. For real sophistication, check out **Café de las Horas** *(Calle Conde de Almodóvar 1)*, north of Plaza de la Virgen, with its plush interior, or the programme of the **Teatro Principal** *(☎ 963 51 00 51; Calle Barcas 15)*.

Younger groovers head for the university 2km east (€3.50 by taxi from the centre). Along Avenida Blasco Ibáñez and particularly around Plaza de Xuquer there are scores of dusk-to-dawn bars and discos. **Finnegan's** *(Plaza de la Reina)*, an Irish pub, draws English-speakers.

Getting There & Away

Bus The bus station *(☎ 963 49 72 22; Avenida de Menéndez Pidal)* is by the old riverbed. Bus No 8 goes to Plaza del Ayuntamiento. Destinations include: Madrid (€18 to €20, up to 12 daily), Barcelona (€18, up to 12 daily) and Alicante (€12.50, 2¼ hours).

Train Express trains run from **Estación del Norte** *(☎ 963 52 02 02 or ☎ 902 24 02 02)* to/from Madrid (€37, 3½ hours, up to 10 daily), Barcelona (€29 to €32, three to four hours, 12 daily) and Alicante (€9, two hours, up to eight daily).

Boat Regular car and passenger ferries that go to Mallorca, Ibiza and, less frequently, Menorca are operated by **Trasmediterránea** *(reservations ☎ 902 45 46 45)*.

Getting Around

EMT *(☎ 963 52 83 99)* buses run until about 10pm, with night services continuing on seven routes until around 1am.

The smart high-speed tram is a pleasant way to get to the beach, the paella restaurants of Las Arenas and the port. Metro lines primarily serve the outer suburbs.

INLAND VALENCIA
Morella
pop 2720

Perched on a hill top, crowned by a castle and completely enclosed by a wall over 2km long, the fairy-tale town of Morella, in the north of the Valencia region, is one of Spain's oldest continually inhabited towns.

The **tourist office** (☎/fax 964 17 30 32; open 10am-2pm & 4pm-7pm daily) is just behind the Torres de San Miguel, which flank the main entrance gate.

Things to See & Do Morella's **castle**, although in ruins, remains imposing and gives breathtaking views of the town and surrounding countryside. You can visit the **castle grounds** (admission €2; open 10.30am-7.30pm daily).

The old town itself is easily explored on foot. Four small **museums** (admission for each museum €1-2), set in the towers of the ancient walls, have displays on local history, photography, folklore and the 'age of the dinosaurs' – with fossils of dinosaurs found in the region.

Places to Stay & Eat The cheapest option is friendly **Fonda Moreno** (☎ 964 16 01 05; Calle de San Nicolás 12; doubles €35), which has six quaint and basic doubles. Its upstairs restaurant provides a hearty menú for €6.

Freshly refurbished **Hostal El Cid** (☎ 964 16 01 25; Puerta de San Mateo 2; singles/doubles €21/37) has spruced up rooms with bath and good views.

Hotel Cardenal Ram (☎ 964 17 30 85; Cuesta de Suñer 1; singles/doubles €37.50/59), occupying a 16th-century cardinal's palace, has rooms with all facilities.

Restaurante Vinatea (☎ 964 16 07 44; Calle Blasco de Alagón 17; set menu €6; open Tues-Sun) does excellent tapas, plus a menú that is rich in local dishes.

Getting There & Away The bus company **Autos Mediterráneo** (☎ 964 22 05 36) runs two buses daily, from Monday to Saturday to/from both Castellón and Vinarós.

Guadalest

A spectacular route runs west from just south of Calpe (see its individual entry later in this section) to the inland town of **Alcoy**, famous for its Moros y Cristianos fiesta in April. About halfway to Alcoy, stop at the old Muslim settlement of **Guadalest**, dominated by the Castillo de San José and besieged these days by coach parties from the coast.

Elche (Elx)
pop 198,190

Just 20km southwest of Alicante, Elche is famed for its extensive palm groves, planted by the Muslims, but, aside from these, it's a fairly dreary town, only warranting a day trip.

Visit the **Huerto del Cura** (€2; open 9am-6pm daily), with its tended lawns, colourful flower beds and a freakish eight-pronged palm tree. The gardens are opposite the hotel of the same name. Try to time your visit to coincide with the **Misteri d'Elx**. This extraordinary two-part medieval mystery play and lyric drama is fittingly performed in the Basílica de Santa María on 14 and 15 August (with public rehearsals the three previous days).

ALICANTE (ALACANT)
pop 283,240

Alicante is an underrated city with most tourists heading straight for the Costa Blanca beaches. Yet there's an appealing faded grandeur about the place, particularly around the old quarter, overlooked by the majestic limestone cathedral. The nightlife is also equal to that of any self-respecting Andalucían city, particularly during the Fiesta de Sant Joan, 24 June, when Alicante stages its own version of Las Fallas (see Special Events under the Valencia city section earlier in this chapter).

Alicante has five tourist offices but the most central is the **main tourist office** (☎ 965 20 00 00; e turismo@alicante-ayto .es; Rambla de Méndez Núñez 23; open 10am-7pm Mon-Fri, 10am-2pm Sat). You can connect to the Internet at **Up Internet** (☎ 965 20 05 77; Angel Lozano 10; open 10am-2am daily) for €1.50 an hour.

Things to See & Do

The **Castillo de Santa Bárbara** (admission free), a 16th-century fortress, overlooks the city. Take the lift (€2.50 return), reached by a footbridge opposite Playa del Postiguet, or walk via Avenida Jaime II or Parque de la Ereta.

The **Museo de la Asegurada** (Plaza Santa María; admission free; open 10am-2pm & 5pm-9pm June-Sept; 10am-2pm & 4pm-8pm

SPAIN

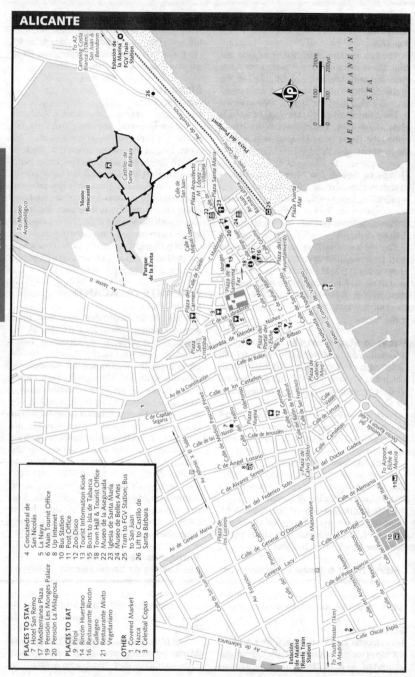

ALICANTE

PLACES TO STAY
7   Hotel San Remo
17 Mediterranea Plaza
19 Pensión Les Monges Palace
20 Pensión La Milagrosa

PLACES TO EAT
9   Piripi
14 Rincón Huertano
16 Restaurante Rincón Gallego
21 Restaurante Mixto Vegetariano

OTHER
1   Covered Market
2   Nazca
3   Celestial Copas
4   Concatedral de San Nicolás
5   La Naya
6   Main Tourist Office
8   Up Internet
10 Bus Station
11 Post Office
12 Zoo Disco
13 Tourist Information Kiosk
15 Boats to Isla de Tabarca
18 Town Hall & Tourist Office
22 Museo de la Asegurada
23 Iglesia de Santa María
24 Museo de Belles Artes
25 Tram to FGV Station; Bus to San Juan
26 Lift to Castillo de Santa Bárbara

Oct-May; closed Sun & Mon afternoon) houses an excellent collection of modern art, including works by Dalí, Miró and Picasso.

The **Museo Arqueológico** *(Plaza Gómez Ulla s/n; adult/student €6/3; open 10am-2pm & 5pm-9pm June-Sept; 10am-2pm & 4pm-8pm Oct-May; closed Sun & Mon afternoon)* houses an excellent collection of Roman and medieval antiquities. The emphasis is on local painters at the **Museo de Bellas Artes** *(Calle Gravina; admission free; open 10am-2pm & 5pm-9pm June-Sept; 10am-2pm & 4pm-8pm Oct-May; closed Sun & Mon afternoon)*, which has recently moved to this suitably eye-catching 18th-century mansion.

Playa del Postiguet This is the closest beach to Alicante. Larger and less crowded beaches are at **Playa de San Juan**, easily reached by bus Nos 21 and 22.

Most days, **Kontiki** *(☎ 965 21 63 96)* runs boat trips (€13 return) to the popular **Isla de Tabarca**, an island which boasts excellent snorkelling and scuba diving from quiet beaches.

Places to Stay

About 10km north of Alicante, **Camping Costa Blanca** *(☎ 965 63 06 70; outside Campello, 200m from the beach)* has a good pool. The youth hostel, **La Florida** *(☎ 965 11 30 44; Avenida de Orihuela 59)*, 2km west of the centre, is open year-round but has limited spaces during the winter months.

At the outstanding **Pensión Les Monges Palace** *(☎ 965 21 50 46, fax 965 14 71 89; Calle de Monges 2)* rooms range from €22 for a single with washbasin and shower to €78 for a luxurious double with jacuzzi.

Pensión La Milagrosa *(☎ 965 21 69 18; Calle de Villavieja 8; rooms per person €15)* has clean, basic rooms and a small guest kitchen. **Hotel San Remo** *(☎ 965 20 95 00; Calle Navas; singles/doubles €39.50/54)* on a busy shopping street has pleasant rooms with full bathroom. **Mediterránea Plaza** *(☎ 965 21 01 88, fax 965 20 67 50; Plaza del Ayuntamiento 6; doubles €104)* is a sparkling new marble-clad hotel on this historic city plaza.

Places to Eat

Restaurante Rincón Gallego *(☎ 965 14 00 14; Plaza del Ayuntamiento 7; daily menu €11.50)* is popular with locals and has a vast choice of the traditional Galícian *raciónes*. Nearby, **Restaurante Mixto Vegetariano** *(Plaza de Santa María 2; set menu €6)* is a simple hole-in-the-wall place with vegetarian menús. **Rincón Huertano** *(☎ 965 14 04 57; Plaza Portal de Elche 4)* serves old-style traditional cuisine, such as rice and snails.

Highly regarded **Piripi** *(☎ 965 22 79 40; Calle Oscar Esplá 30)* is the place for stylish tapas or fine rice and seafood dishes. Expect to pay about €30 for a three-course meal.

Entertainment

Alicante's nightlife zone clusters around the cathedral, where there is a good choice of early evening bars. Later on, look out for **Celestial Copas**, **La Naya**, **Nazca** and **Zoo** discos. In summer, the disco scene at Playa de San Juan is thumping. There are also hundreds of discos in the coastal resorts between Alicante and Dénia.

Getting There & Away

There are daily services from the bus station on Calle de Portugal to Almería (€16, 4½ hours), Valencia (€12, 2¼ hours), Barcelona (€28, eight hours), Madrid (€31.50, 4¼ hours) and towns along the Costa Blanca.

From the train station on Avenida de Salamanca, there's a frequent service to Madrid (€28, four hours), Valencia (€8.50 to €19, two hours) and Barcelona (€39, five hours).

From Estación de la Marina, the Ferrocarriles de la Generalitat Valenciana (FGV) station at the northeastern end of Playa del Postiguet, a narrow-gauge line follows an attractive coastal route northwards as far as Dénia (€6) via Playa de San Juan (€1), Benidorm (€3) and Calpe (€4).

COSTA BLANCA

The Costa Blanca (White Coast), one of Europe's most popular tourist regions, has its share of concrete jungles, particularly around Benidorm, which resembles a Las Vegas skyline from a distance. But if you're looking for a rollicking nightlife, good beaches and a suntan, you won't be disappointed. Accommodation is almost impossible to find during the coach-tour months of July and August.

Xàbia
pop 24,650

In contrast to the comparatively Spanish resort of Dénia, 10km northwest, over two-thirds of

SPAIN

annual visitors to Xàbia (Jávea) are foreigners, so it's not the greatest place to brush up your Spanish. This laid-back resort is in three parts: the old town (3km inland), the port and the beach zone of El Arenal, lined with pleasant bar-restaurants.

Camping Xàbia (☎ 965 79 10 70) is just over 1km from El Arenal. The port area is pleasant and has some reasonably priced *pensiones*. In the old town, **Hostal Levante** (☎ 965 79 15 91; Calle Maestro Alonso 5; singles/doubles €15/30, rooms with shower/bath €28/36) has basic rooms.

Calpe (Calp)

Calpe, 22km northeast of Benidorm, is dominated by the Gibraltaresque **Peñon de Ilfach** (332m), a giant molar protruding from the sea. The climb towards the summit is popular – while you're up there, enjoy the seascape and decide which of Calpe's two long sandy beaches you want to laze on.

Camping Ilfach and **Camping Levante**, both on Avenida de la Marina, are a short walk from Playa Levante. **Pensión Céntrica** (☎ 965 83 55 28; Plaza de Ilfach; double rooms with washbasin €22) just off Avenida Gabriel Miró, is squeaky clean.

Benidorm

pop 57,230

Benidorm succumbed to cheap package tourism (nearly five million visitors annually) several decades ago. About the only things going for it now are the 5km of (crowded) white beaches and a high-spirited nightlife with more karaoke bars per square metre than anywhere else in Spain.

Almost everyone here is on a package deal and there's no truly budget accommodation. **Hostal Santa Faz** (☎ 965 85 40 63; Calle Sant Faz 18; singles/doubles €42/60) has attractive rooms with full bathroom. Deprived Brits may want to stop by the oldest chippy in Benidorm, **Rayťs** (San Vicente 4), which has been serving fish and chips for over 20 years.

Andalucía

The stronghold of the Muslims in Spain for nearly eight centuries, Andalucía is an incomparably beautiful province, peppered with Moorish reminders of the past: the magnificent Alhambra in Granada, the timeless elegance of Córdoba's Mezquita and the whitewashed villages nestling in ochre hills. The regional capital, Seville, is one of the country's most exciting cities.

Away from the cities and resorts, Andalucía is relatively untainted by tourists. Its scenery ranges from semideserts to lush river valleys to gorge-ridden mountains. Its long coastline stretches from the remote beaches of Cabo de Gata, past the crowds of the Costa del Sol, to come within 14km of Africa at Tarifa before opening up to the Atlantic Ocean with the long sandy beaches of the Costa de la Luz. A couple of good websites for general information about Andalucía are **W** www .andalucia.org and **W** www.andalucia.com.

SEVILLE

pop 702,520

It's hard to describe Seville without slipping into superlative overdose. If you want to inhale some authentic ¡Olé! essence, this is the place. Seville is a Spanish cliche of flamenco, tapas bars, strolling guitarists and the bullfight. If this wasn't enough, there is the marvellous exuberance of the people. Seville's air of contentment is well founded. An important and prosperous centre in Muslim times and later in the 16th and 17th centuries, the city took the world stage more recently when it hosted its Expo in 1992. Although the architectural legacy and infrastructure from this Expo come nowhere near matching that of Seville's 1929 World's Fair, the hi-tech new bridges and few remaining pavilions add an upbeat modern dimension to the city.

Seville is quite an expensive place, so it's worth planning your visit carefully. In July and August, the city is stiflingly hot and it's a two-hour drive to the nearest beach. The best time to come is during the unforgettable Easter week and April *feria* (see Special Events later in this section), although rooms then (if you can get one) cost close to double the regular rates.

Information

There is a **main tourist office** (☎ 954 22 14 04, fax 954 22 97 53; **e** otsevilla@turismo -andaluz.com; Avenida de la Constitución 21; open 9am-7pm Mon-Fri, 10am-7pm Sat, 10am-2pm Sun). It's always extremely busy, so you might be better off trying the other **tourist offices** (☎ 954 23 44 65; Paseo de las Delicias 9; open 8.30am-2.45pm Mon-Fri) and (☎ *954 50 56 00; Calle de Arjona 28; open 8am-8.45pm Mon-Fri, 8.30am-2.30pm Sat & Sun)*. Pick up a copy of the monthly freebie *The Tourist*, which includes a map of Seville and lots of restaurants and what's-on type of info in English.

Seville has heaps of public Internet/email services. A typical rate is €2.50 an hour. One reasonably central place is **Cibercenter** (☎ *954 22 88 99; Calle Julio César 9; open 10am-10pm Mon-Sat, 4pm-10pm Sun)*. **Librería Beta** *(Avenida de la Constitución 9 & 27)* has guidebooks and novels in English. **Lavandería Roma** *(Calle de Castelar 2C; open Mon-Sat)* will wash, dry and fold a load of washing for €6.

Things to See & Do
Cathedral & Giralda Seville's massive cathedral *(Calle Alemanes; adult/student & pensioner €6/1.50, admission free Sun; open 11am-5pm Mon-Sat, 2.30pm-6pm Sun)*, one of the biggest in the world, was built on the site of Muslim Seville's main mosque between 1401 and 1507. The structure is primarily Gothic, though most of the internal decoration is in later styles. The adjoining tower, La Giralda, was the mosque's minaret and dates from the 12th century. The puff-you-out climb to the top is worth it for the stunning panoramic views of the city. One highlight of the cathedral's lavish interior is Christopher Columbus' supposed tomb inside the southern door (no-one's 100% sure that his remains didn't get mislaid somewhere in the Caribbean). The four crowned sepulchre-bearers represent the four kingdoms of Spain at the time of Columbus' sailing. The entrance to the cathedral and La Giralda is the Puerta del Perdón on Calle Alemanes.

Alcázar Seville's alcázar *(admission €5, students & pensioners free; open 9.30am-5pm Tues-Sat, 9.30am-1.30pm Sun & holidays)*, a residence of Muslim and Christian royalty for many centuries, was founded in AD 913 as a Muslim fortress. It has been adapted by Seville's rulers in almost every century since, which makes it a mishmash of styles but adds to its fascination. The highlights are the **Palacio de Don Pedro**, exquisitely decorated by Muslim artisans for the Castilian King Pedro the Cruel in the 1360s, and the large, immaculately tended **gardens**, the perfect place to ease your body and brain.

Walks & Parks To appreciate fully **Barrio de Santa Cruz**, the old Jewish quarter immediately east of the cathedral, you need to head for the tangle of narrow streets and plazas east of the main Calle Mateus Gago artery. There's no better place to get lost. A more straightforward walk is along the **riverbank**, where the 13th-century Torre del Oro contains a small, crowded maritime museum. Nearby is Seville's famous bullring, the **Plaza de Toros de la Real Maestranza**, one of the oldest in Spain (begun in 1758). Interesting tours (€3) are given in English and Spanish about every 20 minutes from 9.30am to 2pm and 3pm to 6pm or 7pm daily (bullfight days 10am to 3pm).

South of the centre is **Parque de María Luisa** with its maze of paths, its tall trees, flowers, fountains and shaded lawns. Be sure to seek out the magnificent **Plaza de España** with its fountains, canal and a simply dazzling semicircle of *azuelejo* (ceramic tile) clad buildings.

Museums The **Archivo de las Indias** *(admission free; open 10am-1pm Mon-Fri)*, beside the cathedral, houses over 40 million documents dating from 1492 through to the decolonisation of the Americas. At the time of writing, it was temporarily closed for refurbishment.

The **Museo de Bellas Artes** *(Plaza del Museo; adult/student €1.50/1, EU citizens free; open Tues-Sun)* has an outstanding, beautifully housed collection of Spanish art, focusing on Seville artists like Bartolemé Esteban Murillo and Francisco Zurbarán.

Organised Tours
River cruises by **Cruceros Turísticos** *(€12, one hour)* operate at least hourly from 11am to 7pm from the Torre del Oro. There are also night cruises with open bar for €24. A daily walking tour of the city leaves from the main tourist office on Avenida de la Constitución at 2.45pm daily and costs €9/6 per adult/student. You can also buy a special **tapas route** coupon book for €27, listing the best-known bars. It works out cheaper to go *solo*.

Special Events
The first of Seville's two great festivals is Semana Santa, the week leading up to Easter Sunday. Throughout the week, long processions of religious brotherhoods, dressed in

SEVILLE

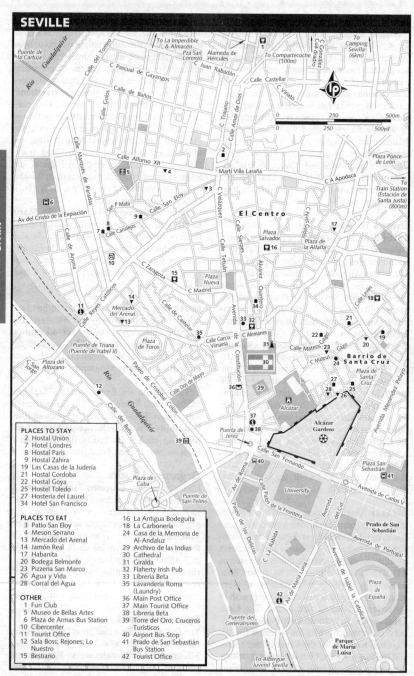

PLACES TO STAY
2 Hostal Unión
7 Hotel Londres
8 Hostal Paris
9 Hostal Zahira
19 Las Casas de la Judería
21 Hostal Cordoba
22 Hostal Goya
25 Hostel Toledo
27 Hosteria del Laurel
34 Hotel San Francisco

PLACES TO EAT
3 Patio San Eloy
4 Meson Serrano
13 Mercado del Arenal
14 Jamón Real
17 Habanita
20 Bodega Belmonte
23 Pizzeria San Marco
26 Agua y Vida
28 Corral del Agua

OTHER
1 Fun Club
5 Museo de Bellas Artes
6 Plaza de Armas Bus Station
10 Cibercenter
11 Tourist Office
12 Sala Boss; Rejones; Lo Nuestro
15 Bestiario

16 La Antigua Bodeguita
18 La Carbonería
24 Casa de la Memoria de Al-Andaluz
29 Archivo de las Indias
30 Cathedral
31 Giralda
32 Flaherty Irish Pub
33 Librería Beta
35 Lavandería Roma (Laundry)
36 Main Post Office
37 Main Tourist Office
38 Librería Beta
39 Torre del Oro; Cruceros Turísticos
40 Airport Bus Stop
41 Prado de San Sebastián Bus Station
42 Tourist Office

strange penitents' garb with tall, pointed hoods, accompany sacred images through the city, watched by huge crowds. The Feria de Abril, a week in late April, is a welcome release after this solemnity: the festivities involve six days of music, dancing, horse-riding and traditional dress on a site in the Los Remedios area west of the river, plus daily bullfights and a general city-wide party.

Places to Stay

Summer prices given here can come down substantially from October to March.

Camping Sevilla (☎ 954 51 43 79; €3 per person), 6km out on the N-IV towards Córdoba, has good rates for two people with a car and tent, and runs a shuttle bus to/from Avenida de Portugal in the city.

Seville's hostel, **Albergue Juvenil Sevilla** (☎ 955 05 65 00; Calle Isaac Peral 2; bus No 34; beds for under/over 26 €8.50/11.50 with breakfast), has 277 places, all in twins or triples. It's about 10 minutes south by bus from opposite the main tourist office.

Accommodation in Barrio de Santa Cruz includes no-frills **Hostal Toledo** (☎ 954 21 53 35; Calle Santa Teresa 15; doubles from €26) and the more spacious, central and more costly **Hostal Goya** (☎ 954 21 11 70; Calle Mateos Gago 31; singles/doubles from €37/47). Freshly refurbished with light wood and a lick of paint, **Hostal Cordoba** (☎ 954 22 74 98; Calle Farnesio 12; singles/doubles €30/60) is well priced. Costing lots more, **Hostería del Laurel** (☎ 954 22 02 95; e host-laurel@eintec.es; Plaza de los Venerables 5; singles/doubles €64/90) is a fabulous, cosy hotel. Bright and cheery **Hotel San Francisco** (☎ 954 50 15 41; Alvarez Quintero 38; singles/doubles from €55/68) is close to the cathedral, and delightful **Las Casas de la Judería** (☎ 954 41 51 50, fax 954 42 21 70; e judería@zoom.es; Callejón de Dos Hermanas 7; singles/doubles from €88/132) is justifiably pricey. The rooms are in small Andalucían-style houses set around patios and fountains.

The area north of Plaza Nueva is well situated for shops, as well as the sights. No-frills **Hostal Unión** (☎ 954 22 92 94; Calle Tarifa 4; singles/doubles €27/36) has nine good clean rooms. **Hotel Londres** (☎ 954 50 27 45; Calle Pedro Martir 1; singles/doubles €38/48) is in a gracious old house with a tiled lobby and pleasant rooms. A few doors down, **Hostal Paris** (☎ 954 22 98 61; fax 95 421 96 45; singles/doubles €38/52) has a light, cheery interior. Located smack-bang in the centre of one of the city's most attractive pedestrian streets **Hotel Zahira** (☎ 954 22 10 61, fax 954 21 30 48; Calle San Eloy 43; singles/doubles €32/45) is sparkling clean and comfortable.

Places to Eat

The Barrio de Santa Cruz provides a wonderful setting for restaurants, although you can expect to pay slightly more. The cool courtyard at **Corral del Agua** (☎ 954 22 48 42; Callejodel Agua 6; fish dishes around €9) is an ideal summer spot for enjoying excellent fish dishes. On the corner, **Agua y Vida** (☎ 954 56 04 71; Callejón del Agua 8; tapas €1.50) has a good choice of tapas, including spinach and chickpeas as a rare vegan option. In the same area **Pizzeria San Marco** (☎ 954 56 43 90; Calle Mesón del Moro 6; open Tues-Sun) was once a Moorish bathhouse and does highly popular pizzas and pastas for around €5. Bullfighting is the decor theme at **Bodega Belmonte** (☎ 954 21 40 14; Calle Mateos Gago 24) and you'll find interesting bits of the beast on the menu. Calle Santa María La Blanca has several places with outdoor tables. At **Casa Fernando** there's plenty of sandwich choice for under €1.50.

West of Avenida de la Constitución, **Jamón Real** (☎ 954 56 39 98; Calle Pastor y Landero) specialises in Extremadura cuisine, such as migas (fried breadcrumbs) with pork and ham for €5. Further north, bright, busy **Patio San Eloy** (☎ 954 22 11 48; Calle de San Eloy 9; tapas €1.50) is known for its fino (sherry) bar and montaditos (multitiered sandwiches). **Meson Serrano** (☎ 954 21 82 99; Calle Alfonso XII 8) has an outside tiled terrace, excellent tapas and more substantial fare. Cuban and vegetarian cuisine is the deal at **Habanita** (☎ 606 71 64 56; Calle Golfo 3) in the buzzy Alfafa district.

Mercado del Arenal (Calle Pastor y Landero) is the main food market in the centre and also has stalls selling bread and drinks.

Entertainment

Seville's nightlife is among the liveliest in Spain. On fine nights throngs of people block the streets outside popular bars. As in most places in Spain, the real action begins around midnight on Friday and Saturday.

Drinking & Dancing Until about 1am, Plaza Salvador has several popular watering-holes, including **La Antigua Bodeguita** at No 6 with outdoor barrel tables for checking out the crowd.

There are some hugely popular bars around the cathedral, including **Flaherty Irish Pub** (*Calle Alemanes 7*) with regular, live Celtic music. The crowds from about midnight around Calle de Adriano, west of Avenida de la Constitución, have to be seen to be believed. Busy music bars around here include **Bestiario** (*Calle Zaragoza s/n*), which is more spacious and modern than some. Nearby on Calle García Vinuesa and Calle Dos de Mayo are some quieter *bodegas* (traditional wine bars), some with good tapas, that attract an older crowd.

Plaza de la Alfalfa is another good area; there are some great tapas bars east along Calle Alfalfa and at least five throbbing music bars north on Calle Pérez Galdós. The **Fun Club** (*Alameda de Hércules 86; open Thur-Sun*) is a small, busy dance warehouse – live bands play some nights. Several good pub-like bars line the same street a little further north. **El Corto Maltés** is a more laid-back drinking den, while **Tetería Platea** at No 87 is a Moroccan-style teahouse with lots of kick-back space and Arabic music.

In summer there's a lively scene along the eastern bank of the Río Guadalquivir, which is dotted with temporary bars. On the far bank, **Sala Boss**, **Rejones** and **Lo Nuestro**, side by side on Calle del Betis, all play good music year-round, attracting an interesting mix of students and travellers.

Flamenco Seville is arguably Spain's flamenco capital and you're most likely to catch a spontaneous atmosphere (of unpredictable quality) in one of the bars staging regular nights of flamenco with no admission fee. These include the sprawling **La Carbonería** (*Calle Leviés 18*), thronged nearly every night from about 11pm to 4am. More tourist-orientated with classes available for the intrepid is the new **Casa de la Memoria de Al-Andaluz** (☎ 954 56 06 70; *Calle Ximenez de Enciso 28*), with flamenco at 9pm costing €11.

Spectator Sports

The bullfight season runs from Easter to October, with fights most Sundays about 6.30pm,

and every day during the Feria de Abril and the preceding week. The bullring is on Paseo de Cristóbal Colón. Tickets start at around €9 or €18, depending on who's fighting.

Getting There & Away

Air There's quite a range of domestic and international flights at **Seville airport** (☎ 954 44 90 00). **Air Europa** (☎ 954 44 91 79) flies to Barcelona from €95.

Bus Buses to Extremadura, Madrid, Portugal and Andalucía west of Seville leave from the **Plaza de Armas bus station** (☎ 954 90 80 40). Numerous daily buses run to/from Madrid (€15, six hours); to/from Lisbon there are eight direct buses a week (€30, eight hours). Daily buses run to/from places on the Algarve, such as Faro, Albufeira and Lagos.

Buses to other parts of Andalucía and eastern Spain use **Prado de San Sebastián bus station** (☎ 954 41 71 11). Daily services include nine or more each to Córdoba (€9, 1¾ hours), Granada (€15.50, three hours) and Málaga (€13.50, 2½ hours).

Train Seville's Santa Justa train station is 1.5km northeast of the centre on Avenida Kansas City.

To/from Madrid, there are 18 superfast AVE trains each day, covering the 471km in just 2½ hours and costing €62.50 in the cheapest class (turista); a few other trains take 3¼ to 3¾ hours for €52.

Other daily trains include about 20 to Córdoba (€7 to €9, 45 minutes with AVE trains to 1¼ hours) and three or more each to Granada (€17, three hours) and Málaga (€13, 2½ hours). For Lisbon (€99, 16 hours) you must change at Madrid.

Getting Around

The airport is 7km from the centre, off the N-IV Córdoba road. **Amarillos Tour** (☎ 902 21 03 17) runs buses to/from Puerta de Jerez in the city at least nine times daily (€2). Bus No C1, in front of Santa Justa train station, follows a clockwise circuit via Avenida de Carlos V, close to Prado de San Sebastián bus station and the city centre; No C2 does the same route anticlockwise. Bus No C4, south down Calle de Arjona from Plaza de Armas bus station, goes to Puerta de Jerez in the centre; returning, take No C3.

CÓRDOBA

pop 314,030

Roman Córdoba was the capital of Baetica province, covering most of Andalucía. Following the Muslim invasion in AD 711 it soon became the effective Islamic capital on the peninsula, a position it held until the Córdoban Caliphate broke up after the death of its ruler Al-Mansour in 1002. Muslim Córdoba at its peak was the most splendid city in Europe and its Mezquita (Mosque) is one of the most magnificent of all Islamic buildings. From the 11th century Córdoba was overshadowed by Seville and in the 13th century both cities fell to the Christians in the Reconquista.

Córdoba's Moorish legacy lives on in the winding alleys, archways and flower-filled patios of the old quarter. The best time to visit is from about mid-April to mid-June, when the weather is warm – but not too warm – and the city stages most of its annual festivals.

Orientation

Immediately north of the Río Guadalquivir is the old city, a warren of narrow streets surrounding the Mezquita. Around 500m north of here is Plaza de las Tendillas, the main square of the modern city.

Information

The helpful **regional tourist office** (☎ 957 47 12 35; Calle de Torrijos 10; open 9.30am-6pm Mon-Fri, 10am-7pm Sat, 10am-2pm Sun Mar-Oct; open until 6pm Mon-Fri Nov-Feb) faces the Mezquita. The **municipal tourist office** (☎ 957 20 05 22; Plaza de Judá Leví) is a block west of the Mezquita.

Connect to the Internet at **Ch@t Is** (☎ 957 48 50 24; Calle Claudio Marcelo 15; open 10am-10pm) near the Plaza de las Tendillas for €1.80 an hour.

Things to See & Do

The inside of the famous **Mezquita** (admission €6.50; open 10am-7.30pm Mon-Sat, 2pm-7.30pm Sun & holidays Apr-Sept; 10am-5.30pm Mon-Sat, 2pm-5.30pm Sun & holidays Oct-Mar), which was begun by emir Abd ar-Rahman I in AD 785 and enlarged by subsequent generations, is a mesmerising sequence of two-tier arches amid a thicket of columns. From 1236 the mosque was used as a church and in the 16th century a cathedral

was built right in its centre – somewhat wrecking the effect of the original Muslim building, in many people's opinion.

The Judería, Córdoba's medieval Jewish quarter northwest of the Mezquita, is an intriguing maze of narrow streets and small plazas. Don't miss the beautiful little **Sinagoga** (Calle Judíos; admission €0.30, EU citizens free; open 10am-7pm Tues-Sun), one of Spain's very few surviving medieval synagogues. Nearby are the **Casa Andalusí** (Calle Judíos 12; admission €2.50; open 10.30am-8pm Mon-Sat), a commercialised, yet still interesting, 12th-century house with exhibits on Córdoba's medieval Muslim culture, and the **Museo Taurino** (Bullfighting Museum; Plaza de Maimónides; admission €3; open 10am-2pm & 5.30pm-7.30pm Tues-Sat), celebrating Córdoba's legendary matadors such as El Cordobés and Manolete.

Southwest of the Mezquita stands the **Alcázar de los Reyes Cristianos** (Castle of the Christian Monarchs; admission €2; open 10am-2pm & 5.30pm-7.30pm Tues-Sat), with large and lovely gardens.

The **Museo Arqueológico** (Plaza de Jerónimo Páez 7; admission €1.50, EU citizens free; open 9am-8pm Wed-Sat, 3pm-8pm Tues) is also worth a visit. On the southern side of the river, across the **Puente Romano**, is the **Torre de la Calahorra** (admission €3.50; open 10am-2pm & 4.30pm-8.30pm daily) with a museum highlighting the intellectual achievements of Islamic Córdoba, with excellent models of the Mezquita and Granada's Alhambra.

Places to Stay

Most people look for lodgings close to the Mezquita. Córdoba's excellent youth hostel, **Albergue Juvenil Córdoba** (☎ 957 29 01 66; bed for under/over 26 €10/13), is perfectly positioned on Plaza de Judá Leví. It has no curfew and breakfast is included in the rates.

Many Córdoba lodgings are built around charming patios. One such place is friendly and central **Hostal Deanes** (☎ 957 29 37 44, fax 957 42 17 23; Calle Deanes 6; singles/doubles €24/31), which has the added plus of a tapas bar styled for the locals, rather than tourists. There are some good places to the east, away from the tourist masses. **Hostal La Fuente** (☎ 957 48 78 27, fax 957 48 78 27; e terra.es; Calle San Fernando 51; singles/doubles €24/42) has compact rooms around

SPAIN

CÓRDOBA

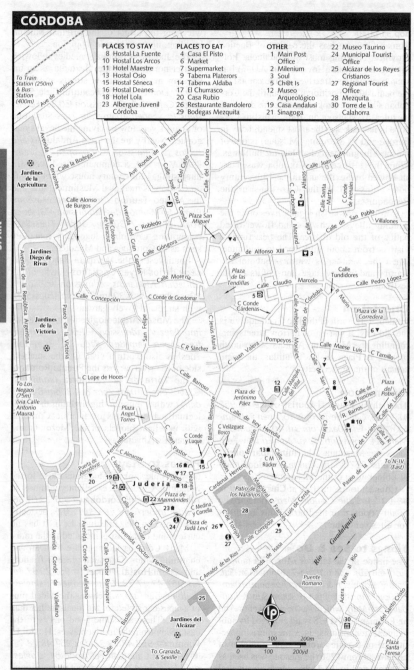

PLACES TO STAY
8 Hostal La Fuente
10 Hostal Los Arcos
11 Hotel Maestre
13 Hostal Osio
15 Hostal Séneca
16 Hostal Deanes
18 Hotel Lola
23 Albergue Juvenil Córdoba

PLACES TO EAT
4 Casa El Pisto
6 Market
7 Supermarket
9 Taberna Plateros
14 Taberna Aldaba
17 El Churrasco
20 Casa Rubio
26 Restaurante Bandolero
29 Bodegas Mezquita

OTHER
1 Main Post Office
2 Milenium
3 Soul
5 Ch@t Is
12 Museo Arqueológico
19 Casa Andalusí
21 Sinagoga
22 Museo Taurino
24 Municipal Tourist Office
25 Alcázar de los Reyes Cristianos
27 Regional Tourist Office
28 Mezquita
30 Torre de la Calahorra

a large patio. Pretty **Hostal Osio** (☎/fax 957 48 51 65; **e** hostalosio@iepana.es; Calle Osio 6; singles/doubles €20/40) has pine furnishings, two patios and good views – try for room 10 overlooking the adjacent convent. **Hostal Los Arcos** (☎ 957 48 56 43 or ☎ 957 486 011; Calle Romero Barros 14; singles/doubles with bath €20/31) has rooms similarly set around a pretty patio. **Hotel Maestre** (☎ 957 47 24 10, fax 957 47 53 95; Calle Romero Barros 4; singles/doubles €29/48) is a small bright hotel with a dash of Spanish chic. The management runs a cheaper hostal next door.

Just north of the Mezquita, the charming **Hostal Séneca** (☎/fax 957 47 32 34; Calle Conde y Luque 7; singles/doubles without bath €25/32, with bath €31/39) has rooms with rates that include breakfast. It's advisable to phone ahead.

Lord it up at fabulous **Hotel Lola** (☎ 957 20 03 05, fax 957 42 20 63; **e** hotel@hotel conencantolola.com; Calle Romero 3; doubles from €108) with its charming *típico* Córdoban decor.

Places to Eat

Handy **Taberna Aldaba** (☎ 957 48 60 06; Velázquez Bosco 8) near the Mezquita has good tapas deals, such as four plus a cerveza for €7. **Restaurante Bandolero** (Calle de Torrijos 6; media raciónes €2.50-5), across from the great mosque, provides *media raciónes* and à la carte; expect to pay up to €10 for three courses with drinks. **Casa Rubio** (☎ 957 42 08 53; Puerta Almodóvar 5) in the Judería serves tasty tapas, such as fried aubergine slices with honey, and good main dishes for around €5. **El Churrasco** (☎ 957 29 08 19; Calle Romero 16; set menu €20) is one of Córdoba's very best restaurants. The food is rich and service attentive.

Taberna Platerors (☎ 957 47 00 42; Calle de San Francisco 6; raciónes €3) is a large patio tavern and restaurant serving solid home-style Córdoban fare. There's a general food **market** on Calle de San Fernando. For gourmet products and olive-oil and fino tasting, head for **Bodegas Mezquita** (Corregidor Luis de la Cerda 13). **Casa El Pisto** (Taberna San Miguel; Plaza San Miguel 1; media raciónes €2.50-5; open Mon-Sat) is a particularly atmospheric old watering-hole with a good range of tapas, *media ración* and *ración*.

Entertainment

Córdoba's livelier bars are scattered around the north and west of town. **Casa El Pisto** (see the preceding Places to Eat section) is one. **Soul** (Calle Alfonso XIII 3; open until 3am daily) attracts a studenty/arty crowd and **Milenium** (Calle Alfaros 33) may have live bands a couple of nights a week. **Magister** (Calle Morería) brews its own tasty beer (around €1.50 a glass). Just beyond the Jardines de la Victoria, **Los Negaos** (Calle Magistral Seco de Herrara 6) has weekly concerts; look for the flyers around town.

Getting There & Away

The train station on Avenida de América, and the **bus station** (☎ 957 40 40 40; Plaza de las Tres Culturas) behind it, are about 1km northwest of Plaza de las Tendillas. At least 10 buses a day run to/from Seville (€8) and five or more to/from Granada (€9.50), Madrid (€10) and Málaga (€9.50), among many other destinations.

About 20 trains a day run to/from Seville (€6.50 to €13, 45 minutes to 1¼ hours). Options to/from Madrid range from several AVEs (€36.50 to €43, 1¾ hours) to a middle-of-the-night estrella service (€23, 6¼ hours).

GRANADA
pop 243,340

From the 13th to 15th centuries, Granada was capital of the last Muslim kingdom in Spain and the finest city on the peninsula. Today it has the greatest Muslim legacy in the country and one of the most magnificent buildings on the continent – the Alhambra. Southeast of the city, the Sierra Nevada mountain range (mainland Spain's highest and the location of Europe's most southerly ski slopes) and the Alpujarras valleys, with their picturesque, mysterious villages, are well worth exploring if you have time to spare.

Information

Granada has a **main tourist office** (☎ 958 24 71 28; Plaza de Mariana Pineda 10; open 9.30am-7pm Mon-Fri, 10am-2pm Sat). The more central **regional tourist office** (☎ 958 22 10 22; Corral del Carbón, Calle Libreras 2) opens the same hours but is tiny and usually crowded.

Navegaweb (Calle Reyes Católicos 55; open 10am-11pm daily) offers Internet access for a reasonable €1.05 an hour.

SPAIN

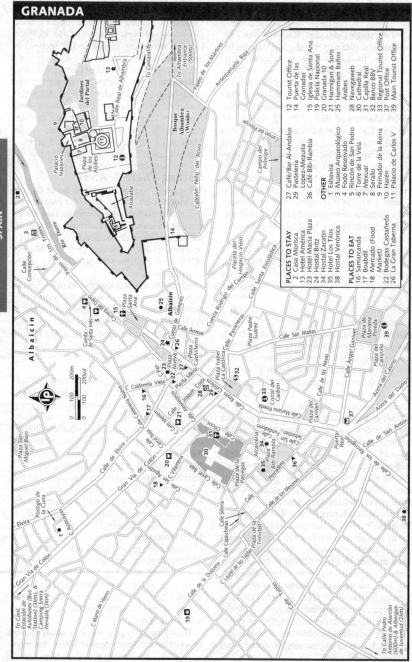

GRANADA

PLACES TO STAY
12 Casa Morisca
13 Hotel América
23 Hotel Macía Plaza
24 Hostal Britz
34 Hostal Zacatín
35 Hotel Los Tilos
38 Hostal Verónica

PLACES TO EAT
16 Samarcanda
17 Boabdil
18 Mercado (Food Market)
22 Bodegas Castañeda
26 La Gran Taberna
27 Café/Bar Al-Andalus
29 Pastelería Lopez-Mezquita
36 Café Bib-Rambla

OTHER
1 Eshavira
3 Museo Arqueológico
4 Fodo Reservado
5 Rincón de San Pedro
6 Torre de la Vela
7 Mexuar
8 Serallo
9 Peinador de la Reina
10 Harén
11 Palacio de Carlos V
12 Tourist Office
14 Puerta de las Granadas
15 Iglesia de Santa Ana
19 Policía Nacional
20 Granada 10
21 Hannigan & Sons
25 Hammam Baños Árabes
28 Navegaweb
30 Cathedral
31 Capilla Real
32 Banco BBV
33 Regional Tourist Office
37 Post Office
39 Main Tourist Office

Things to See

Alhambra One of the greatest accomplishments of Islamic art and architecture, the Alhambra *(adult/EU citizen €7/5; open 8.30am-8pm daily Mar-Apr, 8.30am-6pm daily Nov-Feb)* is simply breathtaking. Much has been written about the Alhambra's fortress, palace, patios and gardens, but nothing can really prepare you for what you will see. It is becoming increasingly essential to book in advance, whatever the time of year. You can reserve via any branch of the Banco Bilbao Viscaya (BBV), including the Granada branch on Plaza Isabel la Católica or by calling ☎ 902 22 44 60 from within Spain and paying by credit card. Alternatively see ⓦ www.decompras.bbv.es for choosing the time and day you wish to visit.

The **Alcazaba** is the Alhambra's fortress, dating from the 11th to the 13th centuries. There are spectacular heady views from the tops of the towers. The **Palacio Nazaries** (Nasrid Palace), built for Granada's Muslim rulers in their 13th- to 15th-century heyday, is the centrepiece of the Alhambra. The beauty of its patios and intricacy of its stucco and woodwork, epitomised by the Patio de los Leones (Patio of the Lions) and Sala de las Dos Hermanas (Hall of the Two Sisters), are stunning. Don't miss the **Generalife**, the soul-soothing palace gardens – a great spot to relax and contemplate the the Alhambra from a little distance.

Other Attractions Explore the narrow, hilly streets of the **Albaicín**, the old Moorish quarter across the river from the Alhambra and head for the **Mirador de San Nicolas** – a steep climb, but worth it for the views. On your way, stop by the **Museo Arqueológico** *(Archaeological Museum; Carrera del Darro)* at the foot of the Albaicín. Another enjoyable area for strolling is around **Plaza de Bib-Rambla**, looking in at the **Capilla Real** *(Royal Chapel; Calle Oficios)*, in which Fernando and Isabel, the Christian conquerors of Granada in 1492, are buried. Next door to the chapel is Granada's **cathedral**, which dates in part from the early 16th century.

Pamper yourself with a visit to the new Arab baths, **Hammam Baños Árabes** *(☎ 958 22 99 78; Calle Santa Ana 16; open 10am-midnight daily)*, which offer a range of treatments and an on-going cultural programme in fabulous surroundings.

Places to Stay

Camping Sierra Nevada *(☎ 958 15 00 62; Avenida de Madrid 107; open year-round)*, 200m from the Estación de Autobuses, is the closest camping ground to the centre. Granada's modern youth hostel, **Albergue de Juventud** *(☎ 958 27 26 38 or ☎ 958 00 29 00; Calle Ramón y Cajal 2; dorm beds for under/over 26 €13/17)* is 1.7km west of the centre and a 600m walk southwest of the train station. Most of the year, bed and breakfast is offered at the listed rate.

Right on the bustling Plaza Nueva (well placed for the Alhambra and Albaicín), **Hostal Britz** *(☎/fax 958 22 36 52; Cuesta de Gomérez 1; singles/doubles €17/26.50, doubles with bath €37)* provides bright comfortable rooms, some with balconies. Across the square, tastefully renovated **Hotel Macía Plaza** *(☎ 958 22 75 36, fax 958 28 55 91; ⓔ maciaplaza@maciahoteles.com; singles/doubles €42/63)* has very pleasant rooms. For a night to remember, **Casa Morisca** *(☎ 958 22 11 00, fax 958 21 57 96; ⓔ casamorisca@terra.es; Cuesta de la Victoria 9; doubles from €108)* has Alhambra views and fabulous Moorish-inspired decor with central patio, wooden ceilings and rich tilework.

The Plaza Bib-Rambla area is another with plenty of choice. Good value, no frills **Hotel Los Tilos** *(☎ 958 26 67 12; Plaza Bib-Rambla; singles/doubles with bath €41/62 including breakfast)* overlooks a daily flower market and has superb views from a 4th-floor terrace. **Hostal Zacatín** *(☎ 958 22 11 55; Calle Ermita 11; singles/doubles €20/29)* is a hospitable, simple place. South of the cathedral **Hostal Verónica** *(☎ 958 25 81 45; Calle Angel 17; singles/doubles €19.50/35.50)* is small and friendly.

Hotel América *(☎ 958 22 74 71, fax 958 22 74 70; Calle Real de Alhambra 53; doubles with breakfast €110; open Mar-Oct)* has a magical position within the walls of the Alhambra; you need to reserve well ahead.

Places to Eat

Popular **Bodegas Castañeda** *(☎ 958 22 32 22; Calle Almireceros 1)* is an unpretentious local bar-restaurant serving classic tapas and interesting quasi-international fare. Nearby **Café/Bar Al-Andalus** *(☎ 958 22 67 30; Calle Elivira; meat mains around €6)* has good cheap Arabic food, such as felafel in pitta bread and kebabs.

La **Gran Taberna** (☎ 958 22 88 46; Plaza Nueva 12) is a traditional-style bodega with untraditional inexpensive tapas such as trout with cottage cheese.

Most of the city's **teterías** (Arabic-style teahouses) are located on a picturesque pedestrian street (Calle Calderería Nueva) west of Plaza Nueva, and are expensive but can be enjoyable. The **Samarcanda** around the corner (☎ 958 21 00 14; Calle Calderería Vieja 3) has tasty Lebanese dishes.

Café Bib-Rambla (Plaza Bib-Rambla) is great for a breakfast of chocolate and churros (spiral-shaped doughnuts). **Boabdil** (☎ 958 22 81 36; Hospital de Peregrines 2; daily menu from €5) is a kitchen-sink-informal restaurant with good basic food.

For fresh fruit and vegies, there is the large covered **mercado** (market; Calle San Agustín). Indulge in a home-made meringue at **Pastelería Lopez-Mezuíta** (Reyes Católicos 39), one of the best cafés and cake shops in Grenada town.

Entertainment

Nightlife in the Albaicín centres on Carrera del Darro, with several bars and clubs within a few doors of each other, including **Rincón de San Pedro** (Carrera del Darro 12) and **Fodo Reservado** (Santa Inés 4), just around the corner.

For foot-tapping live jazz, head for **Eshavira** (Postigo de la Cuna 2), where there is the occasional impromptu flamenco evening. Those suffering from draught-Guinness deprivation should check out **Hannigan & Sons** Irish pub (Cetti Meriem 1). With a tad more sophistication than most, **Granada 10** (Calle Cárcel Baja) near the cathedral attracts a smarter set, while **Cool** (Calle Dr. Guirao) is the city's largest disco with three massive dance floors.

During the evening, coachloads of tourists descend on the Sacromonte caves to see overpriced and contrived flamenco shows. You will find that the impromptu flamenco put on at the annual ferias and fiestas is far more rewarding.

Getting There & Away

Granada's **bus station** (☎ 958 18 54 80; Carretera de Jaén s/n) is 3km northwest of the centre. Catch a No 3 bus to reach the centre. At least nine daily buses serve Madrid (€12, five to six hours), while others run to

Barcelona, Valencia and destinations across Andalucía.

The **train station** (☎ 958 27 12 72; Avenida de Andaluces) is about 1.5km west of the centre. Of the two trains daily to Madrid, one takes 9½ hours overnight (€22), the other six hours (€23). To Seville, there are three trains a day (from €15, three hours). For Málaga and Córdoba, you have to change trains in Bobadilla. There's one train daily to Valencia and Barcelona.

COSTA DE ALMERÍA

The coast east of Almería city in eastern Andalucía is perhaps the last section of Spain's Mediterranean coast where you can have a beach to yourself (not in high summer, admittedly). This is Spain's sunniest region – even in late March it can be warm enough to strip off and take in the rays.

The most useful **tourist offices** are in Almería (☎ 950 62 11 17), San José (☎ 950 38 02 99) and Mojácar (☎ 950 47 51 62).

Things to See & Do

The **alcazaba**, an enormous 10th-century Muslim fortress, is the highlight of Almería city. In its heyday the city was even more important than Granada.

The best thing about the region is the wonderful coastline and semidesert scenery of the **Cabo de Gata** promontory. All along the 50km coast from El Cabo de Gata village to Agua Amarga, some of the most beautiful and empty beaches on the Mediterranean alternate with precipitous cliffs and scattered villages. Roads or paths run along or close to this whole coastline. The main village is laid-back **San José**, with excellent beaches, such as **Playa de los Genoveses** and **Playa de Mónsul** within 7km heading southwest. **Mojácar**, 30km north of Agua Amarga, is a white town of Muslim origin, with cube-shaped houses perched on a hill 2km from the coast. Although a long resort strip, Mojácar Playa is still a pretty place and it's not hard to spend time here, especially if you fancy a livelier summer beach scene than Cabo de Gata offers.

Places to Stay & Eat

Almería The oldest hotel in town and still family-run, **La Perla** (☎ 950 23 88 77, fax 950 27 58 16; Plaza del Carmen 7; doubles from €48) still exudes a certain old-world charm.

Cabo de Gata In high summer it's a good idea to ring ahead about accommodation, as some places fill up. In San José there is **Camping Tau** (☎ 950 38 01 66; open Apr-Sept) and the friendly non-HI youth hostel **Albergue Juvenil de San José** (☎ 950 38 03 53; Calle Montemar s/n; bunk beds €8.50; open Apr-Sept). **Hostal Bahía** (☎ 950 38 03 07; Calle Correo; singles/doubles €35/42) has attractive rooms with bath. **Restaurante El Emigrante** across the road does good fish and meat mains for around €6 to €9.

Mojácar The better-value places are mostly up in the old town. **Hostal La Esquinica** (☎ 950 47 50 09; Calle Cano 1; singles/doubles €20/24) is cheap and cheerful. Charming **Hostal Mamabel's** (☎ 950 47 24 48; Calle Embajadores 5; doubles from €60) has eight big rooms with sea views and bath (one circular!), and a good restaurant. Newer **Hotel Simon** (☎ 950 47 87 69, fax 950 47 87 69; e hotelsimon@interbook.net; Cruce de la Fuente; doubles with bath from €40) has a slick, high standard. **Restaurante El Viento del Desierto** (Plaza del Frontón; mains €5-6) is good value and serves the best steamed mussels in town. **Tito's Beach Bar** (☎ 950 61 50 30; Paseo del Mediterráneo 2) has good music and an excellent Mexican restaurant with garden Margarita Bar next door.

Getting There & Away
Almería has an international and domestic airport and is accessible by bus and train from Madrid, Granada and Seville, and by bus only from Málaga, Valencia and Barcelona. Buses run from Almería bus station to El Cabo de Gata village and (except nonsummer Sundays) to San José. Mojácar can be reached by bus from Almeriá, Murcia, Granada and Madrid.

MÁLAGA
pop 534,200
Although Málaga is still largely ignored by the sun and sand seekers who head straight for the Costa del Sol, the city is well worth a visit. There's plenty to see and savour here, ranging from its Moorish monuments to arguably the best fried fish in Spain.

Orientation
Málaga is situated at the mouth of the Guadalmedina River. The central thoroughfare is the Alameda Principal, which continues eastward as the tree-lined Paseo del Parque and westward as Avenida de Andalucía.

Information
The **main tourist office** (☎ 952 21 34 45; Pasaje Chinitas 4; open 10am-6.30pm Mon-Fri, 10am-2pm Sat) is located in one of the city's most historic areas. The **municipal tourist office** (☎ 952 60 44 10; Avenida de Cervantes 1) is near the park. There are additional information kiosks near the train station and in the centre. **Ciber Málaga Café** (Avenida de Andalucía 11) is open from 10am until late and offers Internet access for €2.50 an hour.

Things to See & Do
The historic core of the city lies around the cathedral: a web of narrow cobbled streets lined with faded ochre-coloured buildings, interspersed with small squares, tapas bars, old-fashioned shops and cafés.

The city's history is colourfully diverse. A **Roman amphitheatre** is currently under excavation but can be plainly viewed near the Alcazaba's main entrance on Calle Alcazabilla. The **Alcazaba** fortress and palace (☎ 952 21 60 05; admission free; open 9am-8pm Tues-Sun summer, 9am-7pm Tues-Sun winter) dates from the 8th century and has recently undergone extensive restoration. The cherry on the cake is the hill top **Castillo Gibralfaro** (admission free; open 9am-7pm daily). It's quite a hike, but well worth it for the views. The **cathedral** (admission €1.80; open Mon-Sat 10am-6.45pm) has a peculiar lopsided look with one unfinished tower but is being restored and the entrance is magnificent. Check it out from one of the pavement cafés across the way. After a succession of delays, and a fire, the long-awaited **Picasso Museum** is scheduled to open in October 2003. Meanwhile, art buffs can make do with the house where Picasso was born, **Casa Natal** (☎ 952 06 02 15; Plaza de la Merced 15; open 11am-2pm & 5pm-8pm Mon-Sat, Sun morning).

Places to Stay
Málaga is short on accommodation, so book ahead. The picturesque small **Hotel Venecía** (☎ 952 21 36 36; Alameda Principal 9; singles/doubles €58/72) is in a great central location. A cheaper option is **Pensión Córdoba** (☎ 952 21 44 69; Calle Bolsa 9; singles/doubles without bath €18/28), a humble friendly place.

SPAIN

Hotel Carlos V (☎ 952 21 51 20; Calle Císter 10; singles/doubles €24/46) near the cathedral has been refurbished. The smartest by far is **Hotel Larios** (☎ 952 22 22 00; Marquées de Larios 2; doubles from €81) with its steel, grey and beige interior.

Places to Eat

For affordable eats, head for the tapas bars. A good place to start is the spit 'n' sawdust **Antigua Casa de Guardia** (☎ 952 21 46 80; Alameda Principal 18), which is the oldest bar in town; try the fresh prawns. The nearby **Restaurante El Compá** (☎ 952 06 07 10; Calle La Bolsa 7) is fronted by an excellent tapas bar, while the restaurant specialises in rice and fish dishes. Málaga's most famous tapas bar is the tiny **Bar Logueno** (Marín García s/n), where tapas start at €1.50 and there are 75-plus varieties to choose from. For that special seafood moment, **El Morata** (☎ 952 29 26 45; Calle Paseo Pedregal 13) is just one of several excellent fish restaurants in the Pedregalejo area, 4.5km east of the centre.

Entertainment

Serious party time starts late around Calle Granada and Plaza de la Merced. **ZZ Pub** (Calle Tejón y Rodriguez) has live music on Monday and Thursday. **Warner Bar** (Plaza de los Martinez) is good for a little frenetic air punching, while **Doctor Funk** (Calle José Denis Belgrano 19), just off Calle Granada, is a heaving reggae club shoe-horned into a small smoky space. There are several teterías (Arabic-style teahouses) in town, including **Barrakis** (Calle Horno) near the Plaza de la Constitucíon, housed in a former 14th-century Arab bakery.

Getting There & Away

Málaga airport has a good range of domestic as well as international flights. Trains and buses run every half-hour from the airport to the city centre The city is also linked by train and bus to all major Spanish centres. The bus and train stations are around the corner from each other, 1km west of the city centre.

TORREMOLINOS
pop 43,610

Torremolinos is trying hard to shed its image as a spam-and-chips resort by pumping money into landscaping and more upmarket

tourist facilities and restaurants. Surprisingly, there is still a relatively untainted old part of town with local bars frequented by old men who play dominoes and drink anís.

The **tourist office** (☎ 952 37 95 12; Plaza de la Independencia; open 9am-1.30pm Mon-Fri) is in the centre. From July to September there are additional tourism booths on the beachfront.

Things to See & Do

If you're travelling family-style, there's no shortage of laid-on entertainment. **Tivoli World** (☎ 952 44 28 48; Arroyo de la Miel; admission €4; open 10am-6pm daily) is the Costa del Sol's biggest theme park with tiny-tot rides, as well as concerts, restaurants and bars. A better than average aquarium, **Sea Life** (☎ 952 56 01 50; Benalmádena Port; adult/child €8/5; open 10am-8pm) has an educational 'touch pool' for young children. Other attractions around town include an equestrian show, birds of prey exhibition, water park and various sea-sports. Pick up the respective flyers at the tourist office.

Places to Stay & Eat

For basic comforts in the old part of town, **Hostal Castilla** (☎ 952 38 10 50; Calle Manila 3; singles/doubles with shared bath €18/36) is good value. Nearer to the beach, **Hotel Cabello** (☎ 952 38 45 05; Calle Chiriva; singles/doubles €55/60) is located in the former fishing village of La Carihuela. The best seafood restaurants are here, too, including **El Roqueo** (☎ 91 238 49 46; Carmen 35) – try the gambas pil-pil (prawns in chilli sauce). Back in town, a rare vegetarian restaurant, **Albahaca** (☎ 952 05 12 06; Calle Doña Maria Barrabino 11), offers a four-course menu for €6.

Getting There & Away

Trains to/from Málaga and Fuengirola run every half-hour from 6am to 10.30pm stopping at the airport. The bus station is on Calle Hoyo and there are services to all the major Costa del Sol resorts, as well as to Ronda, Cádiz and Granada, several times a day.

FUENGIROLA
pop 50,260

Fuengirola is 18km via autovia from Torremolinos and, in spite of the annual tide of tourists who come here to sun-flop on the beach, remains essentially a Spanish working town. It's not a pretty place, having suffered from greedy developers and political corruption, but the beach is pleasant, and there's a vast choice of shops, restaurants and bars.

Fuengirola's annual fair at the beginning of October is one of the biggest and best on the Costa del Sol. Aside from then, accommodation is plentiful, although the faceless highrise hotels on the beachfront tend to be block-booked in advance by tour companies. *Hostales* include the spick-and-span **Hostal Italia** (☎ *952 47 41 93, fax 952 47 11 40; Calle de la Cruz 1; singles/doubles €39/26*) near the main plaza, and the new **Hostal Santa Fe** (☎ *952 47 41 81; singles/doubles/ triples €21/30/36*) in Los Boliches. There are plenty of budget restaurants and bars here, mainly crammed into the pedestrian quarter, east of the church square. Bar **Tu Casa** (☎ *952 46 33 32; Calle Marconi 22*) attracts a lively crowd of resident and visiting expats and holds regular pool tournaments.

Getting There & Away
There are half-hourly trains to Málaga, with stops including Torremolinos and the airport. There are also regular buses to Marbella, Mijas and major Andalucían cities leaving the main bus station on Calle Alfonso X111.

MARBELLA
pop 110,850
Marbella is this Costa's classiest resort. The inherent wealth glitters most brightly along the Golden Mile, a tiara of star-studded clubs, restaurants and hotels that stretches from Marbella to Puerto Banus, where black-tinted-window Mercs slide along a quayside of jaw-dropping luxury yachts.

The main **tourist office** is on Glorieta Fontanilla (☎ *952 77 14 42; open 9.30am-9pm Mon-Fri, 10am-2pm Sat*). A second **tourist office** (☎ *952 82 35 50; open 9am-9pm Mon-Fr, 9am-2pm Sat*) is located on the northern side of Plaza de los Naranjos.

Things to See & Do
The old part of Marbella around the Plaza de los Naranjos is very pretty, duly reflected by the drink prices at the gourmet cafés. Nearby on the Plaza de la Iglesia is the 16th-century **Iglesia de Nuestra Señora de la Encarnación** and, a few paces east, the **Museo del Grabado Español Contemporáneo** (☎ *952 82 50 35;*

Calle Hospital Bazán; admission €2.50; open 10am-2pm & 5.30pm-8.30pm Mon-Fri) houses works by Picasso, Miró and Dalí. The only **Bonsai Museum** (☎ *952 86 29 26; adult/child €3/ 2.50; open 10.30am-1.30pm & 4pm-7pm daily*) in Spain is in Parque de la Represa.

Places to Stay & Eat
The old town has several reasonable *hostales*. Cheery **Hostal La Luna** (☎ *952 82 57 78; Calle Luna 7; singles/doubles €30/40*) has balconied rooms and a pretty patio. Equally good value is **Hostal La Pilarica** (☎ *952 77 42 52; Calle San Cristóbal 31; singles/doubles €21/36*). Definitely in the splash-your-cash category is the **Castillo de Monda** (☎ *952 45 71 42, fax 952 45 73 36; doubles from €110*), a restored Moorish castle that crowns the whitewashed *pueblo* of Monda, 14km north of Marbella.

The self-important but excellent **Finca Besaya** (☎ *952 86 56 30; Urb. Rio Verde Alto; dinner only*) has a classy fixed price menu for €42. For more affordable eats, head for the tapas bars in the old town. **Quernecia** (*Calle Tetuan 9*) is always packed with locals – a good sign. Tapas cost from €1.50, and include small taster dishes of paella and couscous.

Getting There & Away
The **bus station** (☎ *952 76 44 00; Calle Trapiche*) is a good half-hour hike from the hub of town, although some buses still stop in Calle Ricardo Soriano in the centre. Buses from the station run a regular service to Málaga, Fuengirola, La Línea, Algeciras, Cádiz, Seville and Granada.

RONDA
pop 34,210
One of the prettiest and most historic towns in Andalucía, Ronda is a world apart from the nearby Costa del Sol. The town straddles the savagely deep El Tajo gorge, at the heart of some lovely hill country dotted with white villages.

The **regional tourist office** (☎ *952 87 12 72; Plaza de España 1*) has lots of interesting information on the area.

Things to See & Do
Ronda is a pleasure to wander around, but during the day you'll have to contend with busloads of day-trippers from the coast.

The **Plaza de Toros** (1785) is considered the home of bullfighting and is a mecca for aficionados; inside is the small but fascinating **Museo Taurino** (admission €2.50). Vertiginous cliff-top views open out from the nearby Alameda del Tajo park.

The 18th-century **Puente Nuevo** (New Bridge), an amazing feat of engineering, crosses the 100m-deep gorge to the originally Muslim old town (La Ciudad), which is littered with ancient churches, monuments and palaces. At the **Casa del Rey Moro** (Calle Santo Domingo 17; admission €4; open daily), you can climb down the La Mina, a Muslim-era stairway cut inside the rock right to the bottom of the gorge. Try not to miss the **Iglesia de Santa María la Mayor**, a church whose tower was once the minaret of a mosque; the **Museo del Bandolero** (Calle Armiñán 29), dedicated to the banditry for which central Andalucía was once renowned; or the beautiful **Baños Arabes** (Arab Baths; open Wed-Sun).

Places to Stay & Eat
Camping El Sur (☎ 952 87 59 39) is a good small site 2km out on the Algeciras road.

Pleasant **Hotel Morales** (☎/fax 952 87 15 38; Calle Sevilla 51; singles/doubles €21/ 39) has nice rooms with bath and friendly informative owners.

Alavera de los Baños (☎/fax 952 87 91 43; e alavera@ctv.es; singles/doubles with breakfast €42/58) is a small German-run hotel next to the 13th-century Arab baths. There are some excellent old-style tapas bars among the nondescript international restaurants, including **Marisquería Paco** (Plaza del Socorro), which is good for seafood, and **Bodega La Giralda** (Calle Nueva 19), a great spot for wine downed with olives, cheese and *chorizo* tapas.

Getting There & Away
Several buses run daily to Seville (€7.50, 2½ hours), Málaga (€6.50, two hours) and Cádiz. One goes to Algeciras (€6) Monday to Friday. The bus station is on Plaza Concepción García Redondo.

A few direct trains go to Granada (€11, 2¼ hours), Málaga (€7, two hours), Algeciras, Córdoba and Madrid. For Seville, and further trains to/from the above destinations, change at Bobadilla or Antequera. The station is on Avenida de Andalucía.

ALGECIRAS
pop 105,070
Algeciras, an unattractive industrial and fishing town between Tarifa and Gibraltar, is the major port linking Spain with Morocco. Keep your wits about you, and ignore offers from the legions of money-changers, drug-pushers and ticket-hawkers. The **tourist office** (☎ 956 57 26 36; Calle Juan de la Cierva; open 9am-2pm Mon-Fri) is near the port.

If you need a room, there's loads of budget accommodation in the streets behind Avenida de la Marina, the street the port is on. Beware early-hours market noise, though. Friendly **Hostal González** (☎ 956 65 28 43; Calle José Santacana 7; singles/doubles €15/24) has good, clean rooms with bath.

Getting There & Away
Bus About 400m inland from the port, **Comes** (Calle San Bernardo) runs frequent buses to/from La Línea, and several daily to/from Tarifa, Cádiz and Seville. **Portillo** (Avenida Virgen del Carmen 15), 200m north of the port, runs buses to/from Málaga, the Costa del Sol and Granada. **Bacoma**, inside the port, runs buses to/from Barcelona, Valencia, France, Germany and Holland.

Train Direct daily trains run to/from Madrid and Granada, passing through Ronda and through Bobadilla, where you can change for Málaga, Córdoba and Seville.

Boat Frequent ferries to/from Tangier, in Morocco, and Ceuta, the Spanish enclave on the Moroccan coast, are operated by **Trasmediterránea** (☎ 902 45 46 45), **Euro-Ferrys** (☎ 956 65 11 78) and other companies. Usually at least 20 daily go to Tangier and 40 or more to Ceuta. From late June to September there are ferries almost around the clock. Buy your ticket in the port or at agencies on Avenida de la Marina – prices are the same. To Tangier, adults pay €14 one way (2½ hours). To Ceuta, it's €13 by ferry (1½ hour). Cars cost €69. **Buquebus** (☎ 902 41 42 42) crosses to Ceuta in 30 minutes for €17.50 (cars €58.50).

CÁDIZ, TARIFA & THE COSTA DE LA LUZ
The historic port of Cádiz has a well-aged atmosphere with backstreets flanked by magnificent 18th-century buildings interspersed with

elegant squares fringed by lofty palm trees. The best time to visit is during the February **Carnaval**, close to Rio in terms of outrageous exuberance. Ninety kilometres to its southeast is windy Tarifa, perched at continental Europe's most southerly point and with a lively windsurfing scene. Between the two places stretch the long, sandy beaches of the Costa de la Luz (Coast of Light), where stuck-in-a-time-warp villages, such as Los Caños de Meca, Zahara de los Atunes and Bolonia have fairly plentiful mid-range accommodation – they're unfortunately a little hard to reach without your own wheels.

Things to See & Do
Cádiz The **Museo de Cádiz** (open 9am-2pm Wed-Sat, 2.30pm-8pm Tues, 9.30am-2.30pm Sun) has a magnificent collection of archaeological remains, as well as a fine art collection. The **Castillo de Santa Catalina** (open daily) dates from 1598 and the large 18th-century **cathedral** (admission €1.50; open 9am-8pm Wed-Sat, 2.30pm-8pm Tues, 9.30am-2.30pm Sun) is the city's most striking landmark. The city's lively central market is on Plaza de las Flores, the former site of a Phoenician temple. From Cádiz you can visit the historic sherry-making towns of El Puerto de Santa María and Jerez de la Frontera by bus or train (or boat, to El Puerto).

Tarifa A 10km-long beach beloved of windsurfers, **Playa de los Lances** stretches northwest from Tarifa. For **windsurf rental** and classes try places along here, such as **Club Mistral** at the Hurricane Hotel or **Spin Out Surf Base** in front of Camping Torre de la Peña II (€48 for two hours' tuition). In Tarifa town, enjoy exploring the winding old streets and visit the castle, **Castillo de Guzmán**, dating from the 10th century.

Places to Stay & Eat
Cádiz's excellent independent youth hostel **Quo Qádiz** (☎/fax 956 22 19 39; Calle Diego Arias 1; beds per person from €6) has accommodation with rates that include breakfast. **Hostal Bahía** (☎ 956 25 90 61; Calle Plocia 5; singles/doubles €41/52) is a winner, just off the bustling main square. Plaza de San Juan de Dios and the Plaza de Mina areas are full of varied places to eat.

In Tarifa, a good choice is bright and central **Hostal Alborada** (☎ 956 68 11 40; Calle San José 52; doubles with bath €37.50). There are plenty of eating options on and near the central Calle Sancho IV El Bravo.

Getting There & Away
The main bus station is on Plaza de Hispanidad, near Plaza de España. There are regular buses to/from Algeciras (€8, 2¾ hours), Seville (€9, 1½ hours), Cordoba (€15, 4½ hours), Málaga (€14.50, five hours), as well as to Ronda and Tarifa. Up to 15 daily trains chuff to/from Seville (€8, two hours), with others heading for Córdoba and beyond.

Gibraltar

pop 27,030
The British colony of Gibraltar occupies a huge lump of limestone, almost 5km long and over 1km wide, near the mouth of the Mediterranean. Gibraltar has certainly had a rocky history: it was the bridgehead for the Muslim invasion of Spain in AD 711 and Castile didn't finally wrest it from the Muslims until 1462. In 1704 an Anglo-Dutch fleet captured Gibraltar. Spain gave up military attempts to regain it from Britain after the failure of the Great Siege of 1779–83, but after 300 years of concentrated Britishness, both Britain and Spain are now talking about joint Anglo-Spanish sovereignty – much to the ire of the Gibraltarians.

Gibraltar is like 1960s Britain on a sunny day. It's both old-fashioned and safe, attracting coachloads of day trippers from the Costa del Sol who come here to be reassured by the helmet-wearing policemen, the double-decker buses, the bangers and mash, and Marks & Spencer.

Information
To enter Gibraltar you need a passport or EU national identity card. EU, US, Canada, Australia, New Zealand, Israel, South Africa and Singapore passport-holders are among those who do *not* need visitor's visas for Gibraltar, however, anyone who needs a visa for Spain should have at least a double-entry Spanish visa if they intend to return to Spain from Gibraltar.

Gibraltar has a helpful tourist office right at the border. There is also a **main tourist office** (☎ 45000; Duke of Kent House, Cathedral Square; open 9am-5.30pm Mon-Fri) and

SPAIN

another office located at Casemates (☎ 74982; open 9.30am-5.30pm Mon-Fri, 10am-4pm Sat & Sun).

The currency is the Gibraltar pound or pound sterling. Change any unspent Gibraltar pounds before you leave. You can always use euros. At the time of writing, the exchange rate is €1 to £0.70.

To phone Gibraltar from Spain, the telephone code is ☎ 9567; from other countries dial the international access code, then ☎ 350 and the local number.

Things to See & Do

Central Gibraltar is nothing special – you could almost be in Bletchley or Bradford – but the **Gibraltar Museum** (Bomb House Lane; admission £2; open 10am-6pm Mon-Fri, 10am-2pm Sat) has an interesting historical, architectural and military collection, and includes a Muslim-era bathhouse.

The large **Upper Rock Nature Reserve** (admission £7/1.50 adult/vehicle; open 9.30am-7pm daily), covering most of the upper rock, has spectacular views and several interesting spots to visit.

The rock's most famous inhabitants are its colony of **Barbary macaques**, the only wild primates (apart from *Homo sapiens* football supporters) in Europe. Some of these hang around the **Apes' Den** near the middle cable-car station, others can often be seen at the top station or Great Siege Tunnels.

Other attractions include **St Michael's Cave**, a large natural grotto renowned for its stalagmites and stalactites and the **Great Siege Tunnels**, a series of galleries hewn from the rock by the British during the Great Siege to provide new gun emplacements. Worth a stop on the way down to the town from here are the **Gibraltar, a City under Siege** exhibition and the **Tower of Homage**, part of Gibraltar's 14th-century Muslim castle.

From about April to September, several boats make daily **dolphin-watching trips** of about two hours (£12 to £15 per person) from Watergardens Quay or adjacent Marina Bay.

Places to Stay

Emile Youth Hostel (☎ 51106; Montagu Bastion, Line Wall Rd; dorm beds £12) has 43 places in two- to eight-bunk rooms and rates include continental breakfast.

The **Queen's Hotel** (☎ 74000; 1 Boyd St; singles/doubles with bath £39/46) offers a

20% student discount. All rates include English breakfast. **Cannon Hotel** (☎/fax 51711; 9 Cannon Lane; singles/doubles £42/48) has decent rooms with bath. Rates include an English breakfast.

Places to Eat

Most pubs do British pub meals. The **Star Bar** (Parliament Lane) has a traditional Sunday roast for £4.95. At **The Market Tavern** (1 Waterport Market Place) you can have a choice of four different breakfasts (including Scottish and vegetarian).

For a restaurant meal, the chic **House of Sacarello** (57 Irish Town; specials £5.75-6.10) is a good bet, with tasty soups around £2 and some excellent daily specials. The Indian food at **Maharajah** (5 Tuckey's Lane) is spicy and good.

Getting There & Away

GB Airways (☎ 79300, UK ☎ 0345-222111) flies daily to/from London. Return fares from London range from around £175 to £400, depending on the season.

There are no regular buses to Gibraltar, but La Línea bus station is only a five-minute walk from the border.

To take a car into Gibraltar you need an insurance certificate, registration document, nationality plate and driving licence. You do *not* have to pay any fee, despite what con artists might try to tell you.

Getting Around

The frequent bus Nos 3, 9 and 10 run direct from the border into town.

All of Gibraltar can be covered on foot, but there are other options. Weather permitting, the **cable car** (£5/7 one way/return) leaves its lower station on Red Sands Rd every few minutes from 9.30am to 5.15pm Monday to Saturday. For the Apes' Den, disembark at the middle station.

Extremadura

Extremadura, a sparsely populated tableland bordering Portugal, is far enough from the most beaten tourist trails to give you a genuine sense of exploration, something that *extremeños* themselves have a flair for. Many epic 16th-century *conquistadores*, including Francisco Pizarro (who conquered the Incas) and Hernán Cortés (who did the same to the Aztecs), sprang from this land.

Trujillo and Cáceres are the two not-to-be-missed old towns, and Mérida has Spain's biggest collection of Roman ruins. A spot of hiking, or just relaxing, in the valleys of Northeast Extremadura makes the perfect change from urban life. If you can, avoid June to August, when Extremadura becomes *uncomfortably* hot.

TRUJILLO
pop 9260

Trujillo can't be much bigger now than in 1529, when its most famous son Francisco Pizarro set off with his three brothers and a few local buddies for an expedition that culminated in the bloody conquest of the Inca empire three years later. Trujillo is blessed with a broad and fine Plaza Mayor, from which rises its remarkably preserved old town, packed with aged buildings exuding history. If you approach from the Plasencia direction you might imagine that you have driven through a time warp into the 16th century. There is a **tourist office** (☎ 927 32 26 77; Plaza Mayor) and you can connect to the Internet at **Ciberalia** (Calle Tiendas 18) for €2 an hour.

Things to See

A **statue of Pizarro**, by American Charles Rumsey, dominates the Plaza Mayor. On the plaza's southern side, the **Palacio de la Conquista** (closed to visitors) sports the carved images of Francisco Pizarro and the Inca princess Inés Yupanqui.

Two noble mansions you *can* visit are the 16th-century **Palacio de los Duques de San Carlos** (Plaza Mayor; admission €1.20) and **Palacio de Juan-Pizarro de Orellana**, through the alley in the plaza's southwestern corner.

Up the hill, the **Iglesia de Santa María la Mayor** (admission €1.50) is an interesting hotchpotch of 13th- to 16th-century styles, with some fine paintings by Fernando Gallego of the Flemish school. Higher up, the **Casa-Museo de Pizarro** (admission €1.50) has informative displays (in Spanish) on the lives and adventures of the Pizarro family. At the top of the hill, Trujillo's **castillo** is an impressive structure, primarily of Moorish origin with a **hermitage** (admission €1.50) within, which has recently opened to the public.

Places to Stay & Eat

Plaza Mayor Pension (☎ 619 54 46 56; Plaza Mayor 6; doubles with bath €30) has bright tile and pale wood decor, with rooms overlooking the square. **Pension Roque** (☎ 927 32 23 13; Calle Domingo de Ramos 30; doubles with/without bath €24/21) is both quiet and pleasant with lots of communal space. **Hostal La Cadena** (☎ 927 32 14 63; Plaza Mayor 8; doubles from €37) is in a tastefully restored 16th-century building with a handy tapas bar and restaurant. The gorgeous **Parador**, housed in a former convent (☎ 927 32 13 50, fax 927 32 13 66; e trujillo@parador.es; Calle Santa Beatriz da Silva 1; doubles from €92), is positioned around a central courtyard with fountains, arches and pillars. The Spanish king apparently enjoys the stewed lambs tails served here. You can, too – for a regal sum.

Don't miss **Restaurante La Troya** (☎ 927 23 13 64; Plaza Mayor 10; set menu €15) if you're a meat eater. The food isn't cheap, but portions are gigantic and it will save you from eating much else for the next few days. There are great tapas here, too. Elsewhere **Cafetería Nuria** (Plaza Mayor; dishes from €5) has various dishes. At **La Victoria** (Plaza Mayor 20) you can have a dozen frogs' legs for €10, or choose from more conventional, inexpensive dishes. **Café/Bar Escudo** (Plaza de Santiago) serves good tapas from €1.80. After dinner check out the stylish **La Albadia** club on Calle Garcia, which for this neck of the woods seems surprisingly hip.

Getting There & Away

The **bus station** (☎ 927 32 12 02; Carretera de Mérida) is 500m south of Plaza Mayor. At least six buses run daily to/from Cáceres (€2.50, 45 minutes), Badajoz (€7.50, 2½ hours) and Madrid (€13, four hours), and four or more to/from Mérida (€6, 1¼ hours).

CÁCERES
pop 82,030

Cáceres is larger than Trujillo and has an even bigger old town, created in the 15th and 16th centuries. This is so perfectly preserved, it can seem lifeless at times, until you gaze skywards, that is, and see the vast colony of storks that perch on every worthwhile vertical protuberance. The old town is worth two visits – one by day to look around and one by night to soak up the atmosphere of the accumulated ages.

There is a **tourist office** (☎ *927 24 63 47; Plaza Mayor; open 9.30am-2pm & 4pm-7.30pm Mon-Fri, 9.30am-2pm Sat & Sun).* **Ciberjust** *(Calle Diego Maria Crehuet 7)* is a good Internet café.

Things to See

The old town is still surrounded by walls and towers raised by the Almohads in the 12th century. Entering it from Plaza Mayor, you'll see ahead the fine 15th-century **Iglesia de Santa María**, Cáceres' cathedral.

Many of the old city's churches and imposing medieval mansions can be admired only from outside, but you *can* enter the good **Museo de Cáceres** *(Plaza de Veletas; admission €2, EU citizens free; open 9.30am-2.30pm Tues-Sat, 10.15am-2.30pm Sun),* housed in a 16th-century mansion built over a 12th-century Moorish cistern *aljibe*, the museum's prize exhibit. Also worth a look is the **Casa-Museo Árabe Yussuf Al-Borch** *(Cuesta del Marqués 4; admission €2; open 10.30am-2pm & 6pm-8pm daily),* a private house decked out with Oriental and Islamic trappings to capture the feel of Moorish times. The **Arco del Cristo** at the bottom of this street is a Roman gate.

Places to Stay

The best area to stay is around recently pedestrianised Plaza Mayor, although it gets noisy at the weekend. **Pensión Márquez** (☎ *927 24 49 60; Calle de Gabriel y Galán 2; doubles €20),* just off the low end of the plaza, is a friendly place with clean rooms. **Residencia Zurbarán** (☎ *927 21 04 52; Calle Roso de Luna 11; doubles €30)* is comfortable and bright. **Hotel Iberia** (☎ *927 24 82 00, fax 927 24 09 26; Calle Pintores 2; doubles €51)* is in a sumptuous former palace.

Places to Eat

Cafetería El Puchero *(Plaza Mayor 33)* is a popular hang-out with a huge variety of eating options, from good bocadillos (around €2.80) and *raciónes* to à-la-carte fare. Across the square, **Dehesa** is a notch up, price-wise, but the tapas and house wine are classy and good.

Sabor a Mistura (☎ *927 24 52 31; Calle Pintores 32)* on the main shopping street is good for light lunches, while the **Corregidor** (☎ *927 24 48 78; Calle Moret 7)* dishes up tasty local cuisine and is a good breakfast spot.

Meson Restaurante Asador *(Calle Moret 34; set menu €14)* serves good traditional *extremeño* food.

Getting There & Away

Bus Minimum daily services from the **bus station** (☎ *927 23 25 50)* include at least six to Trujillo (€3) and Madrid (€11.50, 3½ hours); five each to Mérida (€4, 1¼ hours) and to Plasencia; three each to Salamanca (€10.50, three to four hours), Seville via Zafra (€11, four hours) and two to Badajoz.

Train Three to five trains a day run to/from Madrid (from €14.50, 3½ to five hours) and Mérida (one hour) and two or three each to/from Plasencia (1¼ hours), Badajoz (two hours) and Barcelona. The single daily train to Lisbon (from €28, six hours) leaves in the middle of the night.

MÉRIDA
pop 51,060

Once the biggest city in Roman Spain, Mérida is home to more ruins of that age than anywhere else in the country. The **tourist office** (☎ *924 31 53 53; Avenida de José Álvarez Saenz de Buruaga)* is by the gates to the Roman theatre. **MGK** (☎ *924 30 40 72; Calle José Ramon; open 10.30am-2pm & 5pm-9pm)* is a funky Internet café that charges €1.50 an hour.

Things to See

For €7/3.50 per adult/student & over 65 you can get a ticket that gives you entry to the **Teatro Romano**, **Anfiteatro**, the **Casa del Anfiteatro**, the **Casa Romana del Mithraeo**, the **Alcazaba**, **Iglesia de Santa Eulalia** and the **Arqueológica de Moreria**. Admission to just the Teatro Romano and Anfiteatro is €2.50. The theatre was built in 15 BC and the gladiators' ring, or Anfiteatro, seven years later. Combined they could hold 20,000 spectators. Various other reminders of imperial days are scattered about town, including the **Puente Romano**, at 792m one of the longest bridges the Romans ever built.

Places to Stay & Eat

Pensión El Arco (☎ *924 31 83 21; Calle de Miguel de Cervantes 16; singles/doubles without bath €12/22)* is great value and deservedly popular with backpackers. **Hostal Nueva España** (☎ *924 31 33 56; Avenida de*

Extremadura 6; doubles €36) is in a pleasant old house with all mod cons a short walk from the centre.

Casa Benito *(Calle de San Francisco)* is a great old-style wood-panelled bar and restaurant that's decked with bullfighting memorabilia, serving local fare at reasonable prices – try the grilled mushrooms with garlic and parsley.

Restaurante Rafael *(☎ 924 31 87 52; Santa Eulalia 13; set menu €8)*, with tables on a pedestrian street, does a good *montado de lomo* (pork loin) and other traditional dishes. Cavernous **Cafeteria Via Flavia** *(☎ 924 30 15 50; Plaza de España; set menu €7)* is packed with locals at the street-level tapas. A more formal restaurant upstairs serves good meat and fish dishes, as well as Extremadura specials, such as *migas* (fried breadcrumbs) with garlic and pork.

Getting There & Away
From the **bus station** *(☎ 924 37 14 04)* at least seven daily buses run to Badajoz (€4), Seville (€9.50 to €10) and Madrid (from €16.50), and at least four to Cáceres (€4) and Trujillo (€5).

At least four trains run a day to Badajoz, and two or more to Cáceres, Ciudad Real and Madrid (€18, five to six hours).

NORTHEAST EXTREMADURA
From Plasencia the green, almost Eden-like, valleys of La Vera, Valle del Jerte and Valle del Ambroz stretch northeast into the Sierra de Gredos and its western extensions. Watered by rushing mountain streams called *gargantas*, and dotted with medieval villages, these valleys offer some excellent walking routes and attract just enough visitors to provide a good network of places to stay.

Information
The Editorial Alpina booklet *Valle del Jerte, Valle del Ambroz, La Vera* includes a 1:50,000 map of the area showing walking routes. Try to get it from a map or bookshop before you come; if not, the tourist office in Cabezuela del Valle may have copies.

There are **tourist offices** at Plasencia (☎ 927 42 21 59), Jaraíz de la Vera (☎ 927 17 05 87), Jarandilla de la Vera (☎ 927 56 04 60), Cabezuela del Valle (☎ 927 47 25 58) and Hervás (☎ 927 47 36 18). Most sizable villages have banks.

Things to See & Do
La Vera About halfway up the valley, **Cuacos de Yuste** has its share of narrow village streets with half-timbered houses leaning at odd angles. Up a side road, 2km northwest, is the **Monasterio de Yuste**, to which in 1557 Carlos I, once the world's most powerful man, retreated for his dying years. Guided tours in Spanish of the simple royal chambers and the monastery church are €1.

The road continues past the monastery to **Garganta la Olla**, another typically picturesque village, from where you can head over the 1269m **Puerto del Piornal** pass into the Valle del Jerte.

Jarandilla de la Vera is a bigger village, with a 15th-century fortress-church on the main square (below the main road) and a parador occupying a castle-palace where Carlos I stayed while Yuste was being readied for him. Of the longer hikes, the Ruta de Carlos V (see the following Valle del Jerte section) is one of the most enticing.

Valle del Jerte This valley grows half of Spain's cherries and turns into a sea of white at blossom time in April. **Piornal**, high on the southern flank, is a good base for walks along the Sierra de Tormantos. In the bottom of the valley, **Cabezuela del Valle** has a particularly medieval main street. A 35km road crosses from just north of here over the 1430m Puerto de Honduras pass to Hervás in the Valle del Ambroz. For hikers, the PR-10 trail climbs roughly parallel, to the south. From **Jerte** you can walk into the beautiful **Parque Natural de la Garganta de los Infiernos**.

Tornavacas, near the head of the valley, is the starting point of the **Ruta de Carlos V**, a 28km marked trail following the route by which Carlos I (who was also Carlos V of the Roman Empire) was carried over the mountains to Jarandilla. It can be walked in one long day just as Carlos' bearers did.

Valle del Ambroz Towards the head of the valley, **Hervás**, a small pleasant town, has the best surviving 15th-century Barrio Judío (Jewish quarter) in Extremadura, where many Jews took refuge in hope of avoiding the Inquisition.

Places to Stay & Eat
There are **camping grounds** – many with fine riverside positions – in several villages,

SPAIN

including Cuacos de Yuste, Hervás, Jarandilla de la Vera and Jerte. Most only open from March/April to September/October. There are free *zonas de acampada*, camping areas with no facilities, at Garganta la Olla and Piornal.

In Plasencia, **Hostal La Muralla** (☎ 927 41 38 74; Calle de Berrozana 6; singles/doubles €17/28) is modern and comfortable and located near the main plaza, which is good for bars and atmosphere. On the main road in Cuacos de Yuste, **Pensión Sol** (☎ 927 17 22 41; doubles €62) has good rooms as well as a restaurant. In Jarandilla de la Vera, **Hostal Jaranda** (☎ 927 56 02 06; Avenida de Soledad Vega Ortiz 101; singles/doubles with breakfast €30/52), on the main road, has rooms with bath and an excellent-value three-course menú with wine for €7.50.

In Piornal, **Pensión Los Piornos** (☎ 927 47 60 55; Plaza de las Eras; doubles €30) is near the bus stop and also has apartments available for longer lets.

In Cabezuela del Valle, the good **Hotel Al-jama** (☎ 927 47 22 91; Calle de Federico Bajo s/n; singles/doubles €21/23), almost touching the church across the street, has pretty good rooms. There are numerous places to eat and drink on nearby Calle del Hondón. **Hostal Puerto de Tornavacas** (☎ 927 19 40 97; singles/doubles €24/31), a couple of kilometres up the N-110 from Tornavacas, is an inn-style place with rooms, and also a restaurant specialising in *extremeño* food.

Getting There & Away

Your own wheels are a big help but, if you do use buses, you can walk over the mountains without worrying about how to get back to your vehicle! The following bus services run Monday to Friday, with much-reduced services on the weekend.

A Mirat bus from Cáceres and Plasencia to Talayuela stops at the villages on the C-501 in La Vera. One or two Mirat buses run from Plasencia to Garganta la Olla and Losar de la Vera. From Estación Sur de Autobuses in Madrid, Doaldi runs daily buses to La Vera.

From Plasencia, a daily bus heads for Piornal, and four a day run up the Valle del Jerte to Tornavacas.

Los Tres Pilares runs two buses between Plasencia and Hervás. Enatcar has a few services between Cáceres, Plasencia and Salamanca via the Valle del Ambroz, stopping at Empalme de Hervás junction, 2km from town.

Galicia, Asturias & Cantabria

Verdant Galicia has been spared the mass tourism that crowds other parts of Spain. Its often wild coast is indented with majestic estuaries – the Rías Altas and Bajas – that hide some of Spain's prettiest and least-known beaches and coves. Inland are rolling green hills dotted with bucolic farmhouses. In winter, Galicia can be freezing, but in summer it boasts one of Europe's most agreeable climates (although into every visit a little rain will probably fall).

The coasts of the still greener and even more inspiring Asturias and Cantabria regions, east of Galicia, are dotted with fine sandy beaches and some agreeable villages and towns. Inland are the beautiful Picos de Europa, with some of Spain's best walking.

SANTIAGO DE COMPOSTELA
pop 93,380

This hauntingly beautiful small city marks the end of the Camino de Santiago, a name given to several major medieval pilgrim routes from as far away as France. Today, avid walkers and cyclists join the faithful in crossing the country to attend mass at Santiago's cathedral. Thanks to its university, Santiago is a lively city almost anytime, but it's at its most festive around 25 July, during the Feast of Santiago. The **regional tourist office** (☎ 981 58 40 81; Rúa do Vilar 43; open daily) can provide a good map and accommodation advice. Get your Internet fix at **Cyber Nova 50** (50 Rúa Nova), for €1.20 an hour.

Things to See & Do

The goal of the Camino de Santiago is the **cathedral** on magnificent **Praza do Obradoiro**. Under the main altar lies the supposed tomb of Santiago Apóstol (St James the Apostle). It's believed that the saint's remains were buried here in the 1st century AD and rediscovered in 813. Santiago was to become the patron saint of the Christian Reconquista, his tomb attracting streams of pilgrims from all over Western Europe. The cathedral is a superb Romanesque creation of the 11th to 13th centuries, with later decorative flourishes, and its *pièce de résistance* is the Pórtico de la Gloria inside the western facade.

Santiago's compact old town is a work of art, and a walk around the cathedral will take you through some of its most inviting squares. Also take a stroll in the beautifully landscaped **Carballeira de Santa Susana** park southwest of the cathedral.

Just northeast of the old city, off Porta do Camino, an impressive old convent houses the **Museo do Pobo Galego** (admission free; open Mon-Sat), covering Galician life from fishing through music and crafts to traditional costume.

Places to Stay & Eat

Santiago is jammed with cheap *pensiones*, but many are full with students. The attractive **Hostal Pazo e Agra** (☎ 981 58 90 45; Rúa da Calderería 37; singles/doubles €17/26) lacks amenities, but offers warm, inviting rooms in a spotless old house. Inquire at Restaurante Zingara; Rúa de Cardenal Payá 16. Popular little **Hostal Suso** (☎ 981 58 66 11; Rúa do Vilar 65; doubles €30) has comfortable modern rooms with bath. **Hotel Real** (☎ 981 56 92 90; Rúa da Calderería 49;

singles/doubles €43/58) provides diminutive but comfortable and well-laid-out quarters with all the trimmings.

A couple of medium-priced places that shelter some of Santiago's best cuisine are **Restaurante Entre Rúas** and **Restaurante A Tulla**, hidden away in the tiny square on the lane Entrerúas. You should get away with spending under €10.

Highly popular **La Bodeguilla de San Roque** (Rúa de San Roque 13; salads & egg dishes €5) offers excellent, eclectic and moderately priced fare, including enormous salads and good *revolto* (scrambled-egg) concoctions.

Entertainment

For traditional Celtic music, Galician-style (sometimes live), head for **Café das Crechas** (Via Sacra 3). **Paraíso Perdido**, on the tiny square of Entrealtares, is one of Santiago's oldest bars. **Bar-Tolo** (Rúa de Abril Ares 8) is a popular new joint. The local drinking and dancing scene is centred in the new town, especially around Praza Roxa (about 800m southwest of the cathedral). Head down there via Rúa de Franco, which offers many bars to

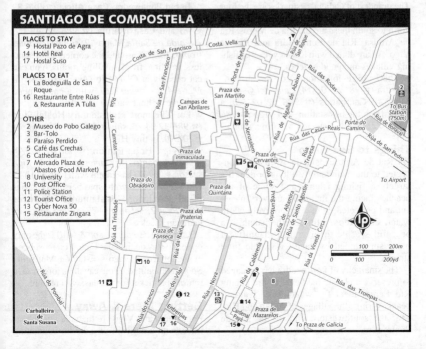

prep you for the disco scene. **Black** (*Avenida de Rosalía de Castro s/n*) is a popular disco. For more of a Latin American touch, look in at **Guayaba** (*Rúa de Frei Rodendo Salvado 16*).

Getting There & Away
Lavacolla airport, 11km southeast of Santiago, caters to some international flights, plus direct flights to Madrid and Barcelona.

Santiago's **bus station** (*Rúa de Rodriguez Viguriis*) is just over 1km northeast of the cathedral and is connected by city bus No 10 to Praza de Galicia, on the southern edge of the old town. Castromil runs regular services to A Coruña and to Vigo via Pontevedra. Dainco runs two buses to Salamanca and one to Cádiz. Alsa has one or more to Madrid (nine hours).

The train station is 600m south of the old town at the end of Rúa do Horreo (city bus Nos 6 and 9 from near the station go to Praza de Galicia). Up to four trains a day run to Madrid (€36, eight to 11 hours), and frequent trains head to A Coruña (€3.50, one hour), Pontevedra (€3.50, one hour) and Vigo (€4, two hours).

RÍAS BAJAS
The grandest of Galicia's estuaries are the four Rías Bajas, on its west-facing coast. From north to south these are the Ría de Muros, Ría de Arousa, Ría de Pontevedra and Ría de Vigo. All are dotted with low-key resorts, fishing villages and good beaches.

There are regional tourist offices in **Pontevedra** (☎ 986 85 08 14; *Calle del General Mola 3*); **Cambados** (☎ 986 52 07 86), a block from the bus station; and **Vigo** (☎ 986 43 05 77), by the Estación Marítima (port).

Things to See & Do
On Ría de Arousa, **Isla de Arousa** is connected to the mainland by a long bridge. It's largely a fishing island, and some of the beaches facing the mainland are very pleasant and protected, with comparatively warm water. **Cambados**, a little further south, is a peaceful seaside town with a magnificent plaza surrounded by easily walkable little streets.

The small city of **Pontevedra** has managed to preserve a classic medieval centre edging Río Lérez, ideal for wandering. Tranquil beaches fringe the villages of **Aldán** and **Hío**, near the southwestern end of the Ría de Pontevedra.

Vigo, Galicia's biggest city, is a disappointment given its wonderful setting, although its small, tangled old town is worth a brief wander if you have to stop here for some reason.

The Rías Bajas' best beaches are on the **Islas Cíes**, off the end of the Ría de Vigo. One of the three islands is off-limits for conservation reasons. The other two, Isla del Faro and Isla de Monte Agudo, are linked by a white sandy crescent, together forming a 9km breakwater in the Atlantic. You can visit the islands only from Easter to mid-September, and numbers are strictly limited. Boats from Vigo cost €13 return. From mid-June they go daily; before that, only at the weekend.

Places to Stay & Eat
An expensive **camping ground** opens in summer on Isla de Arousa. In Cambados, **Hostal Pazos Feijoo** (☎ 986 54 28 10; *Calle de Curros Enríquez 1B; doubles €32*), near the waterfront in the newer part of town (one street from the bus station), offers agreeable rooms with bath. The Praza de Fefiñáns swarms with **restaurants** serving good local Albariño wine (and decent food).

In old Pontevedra, **Casa Alicia** (☎ 986 83 70 79; *Avenida de Santa María 5; doubles €18*) and **Casa Maruja** (☎ 986 85 49 01; *Avenida de Santa María 12; singles/doubles from €15/25*), around the corner, sport spotless, inviting, fresh-smelling rooms. You can eat cheaply at **O' Merlo** (*Avenida de Santa María 4; set menu €6*), with a cheap menú and an excellent variety of dishes.

For a bit more seclusion, try **Hostal Stop** (☎ 986 32 94 75; *singles/doubles in summer €20/30*), in tiny Hío.

In Vigo, **Hotel Pantón** (☎ 986 22 42 70; *Rúa de Lepanto 18; singles/doubles in high season €25/37*) has rooms with bath and TV. Old Vigo is laced with tapas bars and eateries of all descriptions. **Restaurante Fay-Bistes** (*Rúa Real 7; set lunch €7*) offers delicious Galician snacks.

Camping (*€6 per person & tent*) is the only option to stay on the Islas Cíes. You must book at the office in Vigo's Estación Marítima. Spots are limited. You can then organise a return boat ticket for the days you require.

Getting There & Away
Pontevedra and Vigo are the area's transport hubs, with a network of local buses fanning

out from them. Both are well served by buses and trains from Santiago de Compostela and A Coruña, and Vigo has services from more distant places, such as Madrid and Barcelona, as well as Iberia flights from those cities. Two trains a day run from Vigo to Porto in Portugal (3½ hours).

A CORUÑA
pop 239,430

A Coruña (La Coruña in Castilian) is an attractive port city with decent beaches and a wonderful seafront promenade, the Paseo Marítimo. A tourist information kiosk, on the waterfront where the Paseo Marítimo meets Avenida de la Marina, dispenses information. The **Ciudad Vieja** (Old Town) is huddled on the headland north of the port, while the most famous attraction, the **Torre de Hércules** (Tower of Hercules; admission €3; open daily), a lighthouse originally built by the Romans, caps the headland's northern end. The northwestern side of the isthmus joining the headland to the mainland is lined with sandy **beaches**, more of which stretch along the 30km sweep of coast west of the city.

Calle de Riego de Agua, a block back from Avenida de la Marina on the southern side of the isthmus, is a good spot to find lodgings. **Pensión La Alianza** (☎ 981 22 81 14; Calle de Riego de Agua 8; singles/doubles €16/39) has basic rooms but super-friendly management. A step up is **Hostal La Provinciana** (☎ 981 22 04 00, fax 981 22 04 40; Rúa Nueva 9; singles/doubles €24/32), down the street and around a corner, with absolutely enormous rooms and bathrooms.

Calle de la Franja, a block inland from Riego de Agua, has several good places to eat. **Casa Santiso** (Calle de la Franja 26; set lunch €7.50) offers an economical set lunch.

Daily trains and buses run to Santiago de Compostela, Vigo, Santander, León, Madrid and Barcelona.

RÍAS ALTAS

Northeast of A Coruña stretches the alternately pretty and awesome coast of the Rías Altas. The region boasts some of the most dramatic scenery in Spain and beaches that in good weather are every bit as inviting as those on the better-known Rías Bajas. Spots to head for include the medieval towns of **Betanzos**, **Pontedeume** and **Viveiro** (all with budget accommodation), the tremendous

cliffs of **Cabo Ortegal** and the **beaches** between there and Viveiro. Buses from A Coruña and Santiago de Compostela will get you into the area. After that you'll need local buses and the occasional walk or lift.

PICOS DE EUROPA

This small region straddling Asturias, Cantabria and Castilla y León includes possibly the finest walking country in Spain. The spectacular mountain and gorge scenery ensures a continual flow of visitors from all over Europe and beyond. The Picos begin only 20km from the coast and are little more than 40km long and 25km wide. They comprise three limestone massifs: the eastern Macizo Ándara, with a summit of 2444m, the western Macizo El Cornión, rising to 2596m, and the central Macizo Los Urrieles, reaching 2648m.

The Picos constitute a national park, with a **main information office** (☎ 985 84 86 14; Casa Dago, Avenida de Covadonga 43) in Cangas de Onís. Plenty of information on walks is available here and at several other tourist and information offices around the Picos. Trekkers will find Lonely Planet's Walking in Spain useful. Good maps available locally are Adrados Ediciones' Picos de Europa (1:80,000) and Picos de Europa Macizos Central y Oriental and Picos de Europa Macizo Occidental (1:25,000).

The main access towns for the Picos are Cangas de Onís, Arenas de Cabrales and Potes. A good starting point for walks is **Lago Enol**, a lake 7km up from Covadonga, above Cangas de Onís in the northwestern Picos. Another, though without public transport, is **Sotres** in the northeast.

Places to Stay & Eat

You can camp free near Lago de Enol. In Sotres, **Pensión La Perdiz** (☎ 985 94 50 11; singles/doubles with bath €25/30) offers comfortable rooms. **Casa Cipriano** (☎ 985 94 50 24), across the road, is a little more expensive but also has a good restaurant. The good clean **Albergue Peña Castil** (☎ 985 94 50 70; dorm beds €9-12) offers bunks and a decent restaurant.

In Espinama (for a southern approach), the attractive **Hostal Puente Deva** (☎ 942 73 66 58; singles/doubles €25/40) has well-decked-out rooms and a typical Spanish restaurant.

Cangas de Onís, Arenas de Cabrales and Potes all have a range of accommodation.

SPAIN

Getting There & Away

From the roads encircling the Picos, three main routes lead into the heart of the mountains: from Cangas de Onís to Covadonga and Lago Enol, from Arenas de Cabrales to Poncebos and Sotres, and from Potes to Espinama and Fuente Dé.

A few buses from Santander, Oviedo and León serve the three main access towns. Buses also run from Cangas de Onís to Covadonga, from Covadonga to Lago de Enol (July and August only), and from Potes to Espinama and Fuente Dé (late June to mid-September).

SANTANDER
pop 185,230

Santander, capital of Cantabria, is a modern, cosmopolitan city with wide waterfront boulevards, leafy parks and crowded beaches. The city gears up to party hard during late July's Semana Grande fiesta. Be sure to book in advance from mid-July to late August for accommodation all along the north coast. The **city tourist office** (☎ 942 20 30 00) is in the harbourside Jardines de Pereda, and the **regional office** (☎ 942 31 07 08; *Plaza Porticada 5*) is nearby.

Santander's main attractions are its beaches and its bars. As you round the town to the main beach, El Sardinero, on bus No 1 from the central post office, you'll notice all manner of fun-seekers around, with surfers out in force by mid-March, despite the cold. The streets behind El Sardinero are lined with some of Spain's most expensive real estate.

Places to Stay

Camping Bellavista (☎ 942 39 15 30; *Avenida del Faro s/n; open year-round*) is out near the lighthouse about 1.5km beyond El Sardinero beach.

Many rates quoted here can rise by 50% to 100% in midsummer. **Pensión La Porticada** (☎ 942 22 78 17; *Calle Méndez Núñez 6; singles/doubles €25/32, high season €34/45*), near the train and bus stations and ferry dock, has reasonable rooms, some with bay views. It's a loud, bustling location. Nearby and much snazzier is **Hotel México** (☎ 942 21 24 50, fax 942 22 92 38; *Calle Calderón de la Barca 3; singles/doubles €50/74*).

Pensión La Corza (☎ 942 21 29 50; *Calle Hernán Cortés 25; singles/doubles from €18/33*) is nicely located on a pleasant square, Plaza de Pombo. Rooms are sizable and quirk-

ily furnished. Just behind Playa del Sardinero, a splendid choice is **Hostal Carlos III** (☎/fax 942 27 16 16; *Avenida de la Reina Victoria 135; singles/doubles €31/44, high season €48/63*), with bright, spacious rooms and all the mod cons.

Places to Eat

The older part of town has lots of highly atmospheric old *mesones*, which here refers to traditional wine bars that also serve food. **Mesón Goya** (*Calle Daóiz y Velarde 25; salmon or beef €6*) is typical and one of the more economical places to eat in. A cavernous classic is the slightly more expensive **Bodegas La Conveniente** (*Calle Gómez Oreña 9*). Nearby, **Bar Cañadio** (*Plaza de Cañadio; raciónes €5, mains from €10*) serves first-class seafood and local specialities, with tapas in the bar and main dishes in its restaurant.

Near El Sardinero, **La Cañia** (*Calle Joaquin Costa 45; set menu €9.50*) serves up an excellent lunch.

Entertainment

In the old town; Calle Río de la Pila – and to a marginally lesser extent Plaza de Cañadio – teems with bars of all descriptions. In summer, there's quite a good scene along the main drag by El Sardinero.

Getting There & Away

Santander is one of the major entry points to Spain, thanks to its ferry link with Plymouth, England (see Getting There & Away at the start of this chapter).

The ferry terminal and train and bus stations are all in the centre of Santander, within 300m of each other. Several daily buses head east to Bilbao, San Sebastián (€11, two hours) and Irún, and west to Oviedo (€11) and Gijón. Some stop at smaller places along the coast. Six a day go to Madrid (€21) via Burgos. Others run to Pamplona, Zaragoza, Barcelona, Salamanca and elsewhere.

Trains to Bilbao (€6, 2½ hours) and Oviedo are run by **FEVE**, a private company that does not accept rail passes. From Oviedo FEVE continues into northeastern Galicia. Trains to Madrid, Castilla y León and the rest of Galicia are run by RENFE, so rail passes are valid. To Madrid there are three trains most days (from €31, 5½ to nine hours), which go via Ávila.

Galleria Umberto I, Naples, Italy

A carriage parked outside Rome's ancient Colosseum, Italy

Pardon the pun, here's a nun on the run, Rome, Italy

Swiss Guard, Vatican, Rome

Piazza San Marco, Venice, Italy

Children in period costume are part of Milan's lively Carnivale

Place d'Armes, Luxembourg City

Royal castle above Vaduz, Liechtenstein

One of Amsterdam's 600,000 bikes rests against a colourful mural, the Netherlands

Tulips from Amsterdam? Actually they're from the Keukenhof gardens, near Lisse, the Netherlands.

SANTILLANA DEL MAR
pop 3930

Among the good, sandy beaches and appealing villages along the Cantabrian and Asturian coasts, the least missable destination in the region is the marvellously preserved medieval village of Santillana del Mar, 30km west of Santander.

The Romanesque carvings in the cloister of the **Colegiata de Santa Julia** *(admission €2.50; open Tues-Sun)* are Santillana's finest works of art. There's also a **Museo de la Inquisición** *(Inquisition Museum; admission €3.50)*, with an alarming collection of instruments of torture and death.

Two kilometres southwest of Santillana are the world-famous **Cuevas de Altamira**, full of wonderful 14,000-year-old Stone Age animal paintings. A maximum of 20 people a day are allowed into the caves, and the waiting list is years long. For those who can't wait so long, the new **Museo de la Cuevas** *(admission €2.50; open Tues-Sat)* offers a full-scale replica of the caves and the art within.

Places to Stay & Eat
Santillana has heaps of accommodation but few of great value. An excellent choice is **Hospedaje Octavio** *(☎ 942 81 81 99; Plaza Las Arenas 4; singles/doubles €24/36)*, where charming rooms have timber-beam ceilings and private baths. **Casa Cossío** *(set menu €8)*, about the nearest restaurant to the Colegiata, serves a wide range of fare.

Getting There & Away
Several daily buses call in at Santillana en route between Santander and San Vicente de la Barquera, further west.

País Vasco, Navarra & Aragón

The Basque people have lived in Spain's País Vasco (Basque Country, 'Euskadi' in the Basque language), Navarra and the adjoining Pays Basque in southwestern France for thousands of years. They have their own ancient language (Euskara), a distinct physical appearance, a rich culture and a proud history.

Along with this strong sense of identity has come, among a significant percentage of Basques in Spain, a desire for independence.

The Basque nationalist movement was born in the 19th century. During the Franco years the Basque people were brutally repressed, and Euskadi ta Askatasuna (ETA; Basque Homeland and Freedom), a separatist movement, began its activities. With Spain's changeover to democracy in the late 1970s, the País Vasco was granted a large degree of autonomy, but ETA has pursued its violent campaign. ETA has recently been declared a terrorist organisation by the EU, and efforts to eliminate its sources of funding and political support are under way. Supporters of the movement see ETA as a freedom-fighting organisation that has been forced to resort to the only effective means of garnering international attention for its cause.

Although occasional regional instability may be a deterrent to tourism, the País Vasco is a beautiful region. Although the area around Bilbao is heavily industrialised, the region shelters a spectacular coastline, a green and mountainous interior and the elegance of San Sebastián and Bilbao's Guggenheim museum. Another great reason to visit is to sample the delights of Basque cuisine, considered by most non-Catalans to be the best in Spain.

Southeast of the País Vasco, Navarra and Aragón reach down from the Pyrenees into the drier southern lands. Navarra also has a high Basque population, and you're likely to hear Basque spoken in the streets of its capital, Pamplona – home of the famous Sanfermines festival, with its running of the bulls.

The Aragón Pyrenees offer the best walking and skiing on the Spanish side of this mountain range, with over half a dozen decent ski resorts. The most spectacular walking is in the Parque Nacional de Ordesa y Monte Perdido, whose main access point is the village of Torla. During Easter week and from July to September you are forbidden to drive the few kilometres from Torla into the park. Instead, a shuttle-bus service for a maximum 1800 people a day is provided. There's no limit on walking into the park. For the best weather (and most tourist company), visit from late June to mid-September.

SAN SEBASTIÁN (DONOSTIA)
pop 181,060

San Sebastián ('Donostia' in Basque) is a stunning city. Long famed as a ritzy resort for wealthy Spaniards, it has also been a stronghold of Basque nationalist feeling since well before Franco. The surprisingly relaxed town curves around the beautiful Bahía de la Concha. A proud Basque community takes fierce care of its town, making sure that the streets are clean, drugless and prostitute-free. Those who live here consider themselves the luckiest people in Spain, and after spending a few days on the perfect crescent-shaped beaches in preparation for the wild evenings, you may begin to understand why.

Information
The **municipal tourist office** (☎ 943 48 11 66, Boulevard Reina Regente 3; open Mon-Sat, Sun morning) can point you to accommodation and sightseeing options. Look for the **main post office** (Calle de Urdaneta) behind the cathedral. **Donosti-Net** (Calle de Embeltrán 2), in the Parte Vieja (Old Town), is a good Internet café. **Lavomatique** (Calle de Iñigo 14) is a rarity in Spain – a good self-service laundrette. A full load of washing and drying costs about €6.

Things to See
The **Playa de la Concha** and **Playa de Ondarreta** are among the most beautiful city beaches in Spain, although both get rather crowded. You can reach **Isla de Santa Clara**, in the middle of the bay, by boat from the harbour. In summer, you can also swim out to rafts anchored in the bay. The Playa de la Zurriola (also known as 'Playa de Gros'), east of the Río Urumea, is less crowded and popular with both swimmers and surfers.

San Sebastián's revamped **Aquarium** (admission €8; open 10am-10pm daily summer, 10am-8pm daily winter) has 10 large tanks teeming with tropical fish, morays, sharks and other finned creatures. There are also exhibits on pirates, Basque explorers and related themes. The nearby **Museo Naval** (admission €1.50; open Tues-Sun) is interesting, too, providing a more in-depth look at Basque seafaring traditionas, but you need to read Spanish to fully appreciate the displays.

Museo de San Telmo (Plaza de Zuloaga; admission free; open 10.30am-1.30pm & 4pm-8pm Tues-Sat, 10.30am-1.30pm Sun), in a 16th-century monastery, has a varied collection with a heavy emphasis on Basque paintings. A highlight is the chapel, whose lavish wall frescoes chronicle Basque history.

Overlooking Bahía de la Concha from the east is **Monte Urgull**, topped by low castle walls and a statue of Christ that enjoys sweeping views. It takes 30 minutes to walk up – a stairway starts from Plaza de Zuloaga in the old town.

The views from the summit of Monte Igueldo are better still. You can save your legs by catching the funicular (€1.50 return) to the **Parque de Atracciones**, an amusement park. At the foot of the hill, at Punta Torrepea, right in the bay, is Eduardo Chillida's abstract iron sculpture *Peine de los Vientos* (Comb of the Winds).

Places to Stay
As in much of northern Spain, rooms are hard to find in July and August, when prices can double, so book ahead. Be aware of huge seasonal price differences.

Camping Igueldo (☎ 943 21 45 02; hourly bus No 16; open year-round) is out beyond Monte Igueldo but connected to the city centre by bus. The HI-run **Albergue La Sirena** (☎ 943 31 02 68, fax 943 21 40 90; w www.paisvasco.com/albergues; Paseo de Igueldo 25; dorm beds €13 including breakfast; curfew midnight Mon-Fri, 2am Sat & Sun) offers standard bunks.

In the lively Parte Vieja, consider yourself lucky to score a room at the super-friendly **Pensión San Lorenzo** (☎ 943 42 55 16; Calle de San Lorenzo 2; singles/doubles €24/48), which offers recently renovated, nicely decorated rooms with bath. Internet access is available. Also good and gleaming is **Pensión Loinaz** (☎ 943 42 67 14; Calle de San Lorenzo 17; rooms €12-15 per person).

Pensión Aussie (☎ 943 42 28 74; Calle San Jerónimo 23; beds €15 year-round) works much like a hostel. Two- to four-bed rooms house backpackers from the world over. The affable owner is a good source of information on the town. **Pensión San Vicente** (☎ 943 42 29 77; Calle San Vicente 7; singles/doubles €18/24) offers rather barebone rooms. A kitchen is available for use off-season.

The area near the cathedral is more peaceful than the Parte Vieja. **Pensión La Perla** (☎ 943 42 81 23; Calle de Loyola 10; singles/ doubles €24/29, high season €40) has excellent rooms with shower and WC; some overlook the cathedral. Also recommended is **Pensión Añorga** (☎ 943 46 79 45; Calle de Easo 12; singles/doubles €24/30), with plain, clean rooms that have shared baths.

SPAIN

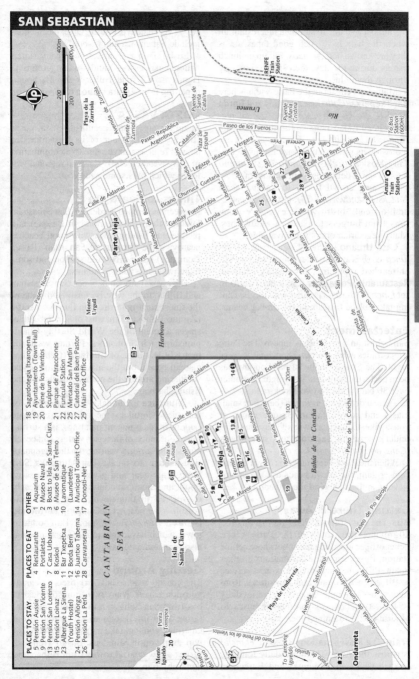

SAN SEBASTIÁN

SPAIN

PLACES TO STAY
5 Pensión Aussie
9 Pensión San Vicente
13 Pensión San Lorenzo
15 Pensión Loinaz
15 Albergue La Sirena (Youth Hostel)
24 Pensión Añorga
26 Pensión La Perla

PLACES TO EAT
4 Restaurante Portaletas
7 Casa Urbano
8 Koskol
11 Bar Txepetxa
12 Borda Berri
16 Juantxo Taberna
28 Caravanserai

OTHER
1 Aquarium
2 Museo Naval
3 Boats to Isla de Santa Clara
6 Museo de San Telmo
10 Lavomatique (Laundrette)
14 Municipal Tourist Office
17 Donosti-Net

18 Sagardotegia Itxaropena
19 Ayuntamiento (Town Hall)
20 Peine de los Vientos Sculpture
21 Parque de Atracciones
22 Funicular Station
25 Mercado San Martín
27 Catedral del Buen Pastor
29 Main Post Office

Places to Eat

It's almost a shame to sit down in a restaurant when the bars have such good tapas, or as they are known here, *pintxos*. Fill up on lunch menús during the day, then snack your way through the night.

Many bars cluster in the Parte Vieja, where **Bar Txepetxa** *(Calle Pescadería 5)* and **Borda Berri** *(Calle Fermín Calbetrón 12)* are recommended. Also here is **Juantxo Taberna** *(Calle de Embeltrán 6; bocadillos €2)*, famous for its cheap, super-sized sandwiches. Tiny **Koskol** *(Calle de Iñigo 5; set menu €6.50)* has a delicious, generous menú.

A young crowd flocks to **Caravanserai** *(snacks & sandwiches €3)*, next to the cathedral, a trendy bistro whose extensive menu runs from burgers to pasta to sandwiches. Many vegetarian options are available.

Casa Urbano *(Calle 31 de Agosto 17; set lunch €20)* is an upmarket choice with a well-entrenched reputation for quality seafood. **Restaurante Portaletas** *(Calle del Puerto 8; set lunch €15-20)* is popular with locals. Dining takes place beneath heavy timber beams.

Entertainment

San Sebastián's nightlife is superb. The Parte Vieja comes alive at around 8pm nearly every night. The Spanish habit of bar-hopping has been perfected here, and you might encounter over 30 bars within a two-block radius.

Typical drinks are a *zurrito* (beer in a small glass) and *txacolí* (a tart Basque wine). If you'd like to have a swig of Basque *sidra* (cider), head for **Sagardotegia Itxaropena** *(Calle de Embeltran 16)*.

When the Parte Vieja quietens down around 1am or 2am, the crowd heads to Calle de los Reyes Católicos, behind the cathedral.

Getting There & Away

Bus The **bus station** *(Plaza de Pío XII)* is a 20-minute walk south of the Parte Vieja; ticket offices are along the streets north of the station. Buses leave for destinations all over Spain. PESA has half-hourly express service to Bilbao (€7.50, one hour), while La Roncalesa goes to Pamplona up to 10 times daily (€4.50, two hours). Continental buses to Madrid (€25) run nine times daily.

Train The **RENFE station** *(Paseo de Francia)* is across the river. There are daily trains to Madrid (€30, eight hours) and Barcelona (€31, 8½ hours). Several trains run to Paris (€77) via Hendaye, France. Other destinations include Salamanca and Lisbon.

Eusko Tren is a private company (international passes not valid) running trains to Hendaye (€2) and Bilbao (€6, 2¾ hours) departing from **Amara station** *(Calle de Easo)*.

COSTA VASCA

Spain's rugged and beautiful Costa Vasca (Basque Coast) is one of its least touristed coastal regions, maybe due to a combination of rainy weather, chilly seas and regional violence which puts some people off.

Things to See & Do

Between the French border and San Sebastián, **Fuenterrabia** ('Hondarribia' in Basque) is a picturesque fishing town with good beaches nearby, while **Pasajes de San Juan** (Pasaia Donibane) has a pretty old section and some mouthwatering-fish restaurants.

The coastal stretch between San Sebastián and Bilbao to the west is considered some of the finest **surfing** territory in Europe. **Zarauz** (Zarautz), about 15km west of San Sebastián, stages a round of the World Surfing Championship each September. Further west, the pretty little village of **Guetaria** (Getaria) has a small beach, but the main attraction is just wandering around the narrow streets and the fishing harbour.

Mundaca (Mundaka), 12km north of Guernica (Gernika – the town Picasso made famous in his poignant painting), is a surfing town. For much of the year, surfers and beach bums hang around waiting for the legendary 'left-hander' to break. The **Mundaka Surf Shop** rents gear and gives surfing lessons. Food and accommodation are hopelessly overpriced in this town, even in the off-season. Your best bet is **Camping Portuondo** (☎/fax 94 687 77 01), about 1km south of town, which has lovely terraced grounds and also rents bungalows.

Getting Around

The coastal road is best explored by car. If you don't have your own transport, take a bus from San Sebastián to Zarauz and Guetaria, or from Bilbao to Guernica. From Guernica you can take a bus to Bermeo that will drop you in Mundaca. Eusko Tren also serves a few coastal towns from Bilbao and San Sebastián.

BILBAO (BILBO)
pop 353,940

Once the ugly industrial heart of the north, Bilbao has spruced itself up and now boasts a prettified downtown area. The friendly denizens of the **main tourist office** (☎ 944 79 57 60, Paseo Arenal 1) will be pleased to point out the city's attractions. There's also an **information kiosk** (open Tues-Sun) by the Guggenheim museum. For Internet access, go to **Láser Bilbao** (Calle de Sendeja 5), which charges €3 an hour, in the old quarter.

In 1997 Bilbao created for itself a tourist gold mine – the US$100 million **Museo Guggenheim de Arte Contemporáneo** (admission €7; open 10am-8pm Tues-Sun Sept-June, 10am-8pm daily July & Aug). Designed by US architect Frank Gehry, this fantastical, swirling structure was inspired in part by the anatomy of a fish and the hull of a boat – both allusions to Bilbao's past and present economy. The interior makes wonderful use of space, with light pouring in through a central glass atrium of cathedral proportions. The permanent exhibit of modern and contemporary art is still small but growing; it includes works by the likes of Picasso, Piet Mondrian and Wassily Kandinsky. All the other galleries are used for high-calibre temporary exhibits. Arrive early and ask about free guided English-language tours.

Some 300m up the street, the excellent **Museo de Bellas Artes** (admission €4.50; open Tues-Sun) boasts works by El Greco, Velázquez and Goya, as well as 20th-century masters such as Gauguin. Basque artists are shown as well.

Places to Stay & Eat
Albergue Bilbao Aterpetxea (☎ 944 27 00 54, fax 944 27 54 79; w albergue.bilbao.net; Carretera Basurto-Kastrexana Errep 70; bus No 58; dorm beds €11-13 with breakfast) is a 10-minute direct bus ride away from the centre. Rooms are bright, bland and boring. Bring your hostel card.

Pensión Méndez (☎ 944 16 03 64; Calle de Santa María 13; singles/doubles €36/48) is central and comfy but can be a bit noisy. **Hostal La Estrella** (☎ 944 16 40 66; Calle de María Múñoz 6; singles/doubles €35/51) offers fetching, brightly painted rooms with bathroom.

Las Siete Calles (Seven Streets), the nucleus of Bilbao's old town, brims with tapas bars and restaurants. **Rio-Oja** (Calle de Perro 6; raciónes €5) is among the many places for cheap food and drink. **Café Boulevard** (Calle de Arenal 3; breakfasts €2, meals €6), Bilbao's oldest coffeehouse (1871), nearby, has full meals and tapas at wallet-friendly prices. The gorgeously decked-out **Café Iruña** (Calle de Colón Larreátegui; set menus €8) is Bilbao's most celebrated café, with ornate artwork and a rich history.

Getting There & Away
Buses to Madrid (€22) and Barcelona (€24) depart from the huge **Termibus** (metro San Mamés) lot in the southwestern corner of town. Cities throughout the region and the country are served from here.

Four daily trains to Madrid (€28, 6¼ hours) and two to Barcelona (€31, nine hours) leave from the RENFE's central **Abando station**. FEVE runs trains from here to towns in Asturias, Cantabria and Galicia. The Eusko Tren station with regional services picks up passengers from the metro station off Plaza Nueva.

P&O European Ferries leave for Portsmouth from Santurtzi, about 14km northwest of Bilbao. The voyage takes about 35 hours from England and 29 hours the other way. See the Getting There & Away section at the beginning of this chapter for details.

PAMPLONA (IRUÑA)
pop 186,250

The madcap festivities of Sanfermines in Pamplona ('Iruña' in Basque) run from 6 to 14 July. They are characterised by nonstop partying and, of course, the running of the bulls. The safest place to watch the *encierro* (running) is on TV. If this is far too tame for you, see if you can sweet-talk your way on to a balcony in one of the streets where the bulls run. The bulls are let out at 8am, but if you want to get a good vantage point you will have to be there before the sun also rises.

If you visit at any other time of year, you'll find a pleasant and modern city, with lovely parks and gardens, and a compact old town with a lively bar and restaurant scene.

Don't expect the overworked **tourist office** (☎ 948 20 65 40; Plaza San Francisco; open Mon-Sat, Sun morning) to be of much help during Sanfermines. Internet access is available at **Kura.net** (Calle de Curia 15) at €3 per hour.

Places to Stay & Eat

The nearest camping ground is **Camping Ez-caba** (☎ 948 33 03 15), 7km north of the city. It fills up a few days before Sanfermines. A bus service (direction Arre/Oricain) runs four times daily from Calle de Teovaldos (near the bullring).

For Sanfermines you need to book months in advance (and pay as much as triple the regular rates). During the festival, beds are also available in *casas particulares* (private houses) – check with the tourist office or haggle with the locals waiting for you at the bus and train stations. Otherwise, join the many who sleep in one of the parks, plazas or shopping malls. There's a left-luggage office *(consigna)* at the bus station, but don't count on much space being available during Sanfermines.

Pamplona's old centre is filled with cheap *pensiones* offering basic singles/doubles for around €15/30.

The contenders include **Fonda Aragonesa** (☎ 948 22 34 28; Calle San Nicolás 32), **Habitaciones Otano** (☎ 948 22 50 95; Calle San Nicolás 5) as well as the slightly superior **Camas Escaray Lozano** (☎ 948 22 78 25; Calle Nueva 24), which is near the tourist office. If you need all the comforts, try **Hostal Bearan** (☎ 948 22 34 28, fax 948 22 43 02; Calle San Nicolás 25; singles/doubles €32/38; during Sanfermines over €100).

Two excellent tapas bars are **Baserri** (Calle San Nicolás 32) and **Otano**, across the street. Nearby is the vegetarian **Restaurante Sarasate** (Calle San Nicolás 19), with some inventive lunch options.

Bar Anaitasuna (Calle de San Gregorio 58; platos combinados €6, set lunch €8.50) has uncluttered, modern decor and is busy from breakfast up to midnight. The fare is typical and cheap, if not terribly inspired.

Getting There & Away

The **bus station** (Avenida de Yangüas y Miranda) is a five-minute walk south of the old town. There are 10 buses daily to San Sebastián (€5.50) and eight to Bilbao (€10). Four daily head for Madrid (€21) and two to Barcelona (€28).

Although Pamplona is located on the San Sebastián–Zaragoza railway line, the station is awkwardly situated northwest of town. If you arrive this way, catch bus No 9 to the centre of town.

ZARAGOZA

pop 610,980

Zaragoza, proud capital of once-mighty Aragón and home to half of its 1.3 million people, is often said to be the most Spanish city of all. Once the important Roman city of Caesaraugusta, and later a Muslim centre for four centuries, it is today primarily a hub of industry and commerce, but with a lively and interesting old heart on the southern side of the Río Ebro.

The **city tourist office** (☎ 976 39 35 37; Plaza del Pilar; open daily) is housed in a surreal-looking glass cube.

Things to See

Zaragoza's focal point is the riverside **Plaza de Nuestra Señora del Pilar** (Plaza del Pilar for short). Dominating the northern side is the **Basílica de Nuestra Señora del Pilar**, a 17th-century church of epic proportions. People flock to its Capilla Santa to kiss a piece of marble pillar believed to have been left by the Virgin Mary when she appeared to Santiago in a vision here in AD 40.

At the plaza's southeastern end is **La Seo** (admission €1.50), Zaragoza's brooding 12th- to 16th-century cathedral. Its northwestern facade is a mudéjar masterpiece. The interior underwent careful restoration from 1980 to 1998 and once again proudly displays an impressive 15th-century main altarpiece in coloured alabaster.

The odd trapezoid structure in front of La Seo is the outside of a remarkable museum housing the **Foro de Caesaraugusta** (admission €2; open 10am-2pm & 5pm-8pm Tues-Sat, 10am-2pm Sun). About 70m below modern ground level you can visit the remains of shops, porticoes and a great sewerage system, all brought to life by an audiovisual show.

A little over 1km west of the plaza, the **Palacio de la Aljafería** (admission €2; open 10am-2pm Tues-Sun & 4pm-6pm Tues, Wed & Sat), today housing Aragón's *cortes* (parliament), is Spain's greatest Muslim building outside Andalucía. It was built as the palace of the Muslim rulers who held the city from 714 to 1118. The inner Patio de Santa Isabel displays all the geometric mastery and fine detail of the best Muslim architecture. The upstairs palace, added by the Catholic monarchs Fernando and Isabel in the 15th century, boasts some fine mudéjar decoration.

ZARAGOZA

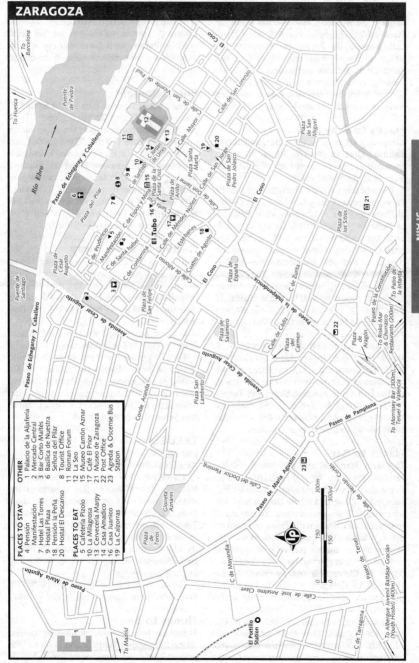

SPAIN

PLACES TO STAY
4 Pensión Manifestación
7 Hotel Las Torres
9 Hostal Plaza
18 Pensión la Peña
20 Hostal El Descanso

PLACES TO EAT
5 Cafetería Pizolo
10 La Milagrosa
14 Cervecería Marpy
16 Casa Amadico
19 La Calzorras

OTHER
1 Palacio de la Aljafería
2 Mercado Central
3 Bar Corto Maltés
6 Basílica de Nuestra Señora del Pilar
8 Tourist Office
11 Roman Forum
12 La Seo
15 Museo Camón Aznar
17 Café El Prior
21 Museo de Zaragoza
22 Post Office
23 Agreda & Oscense Bus Station

Zaragoza has some good museums. Three of them, the **Museo Camón Aznar** *(Calle de Espoz y Mina 23; admission €1; open Tues-Sat)*, **Museo de Zaragoza** *(Plaza de los Sitios; admission free; open Tues-Sat)* and **Patio de la Infanta** *(admission free; open Mon-Sat & Sun morning)*, have good collections of work by Francisco Goya, who was born 30km south at Fuendetodos in 1746.

Places to Stay

Zaragoza's HI hostel is the **Albergue Juvenil Baltasar Gracián** *(☎ 976 30 66 90; Calle Franco y López 4; dorm beds €9-12 with breakfast; open Sept-July)*.

The cheapest rooms elsewhere are in El Tubo, the maze of busy lanes and alleys south of Plaza del Pilar. A basic choice is **Pensión La Peña** *(☎ 976 29 90 89; Calle Cinegio 3; singles/doubles €10/20)*, with a cute little *comedor* (dining room). Another reasonable cheapie is **Pensión Manifestación** *(☎ 976 29 58 21; Calle Manifestación 36; singles/doubles €15/24)*, which should boast fully renovated rooms by 2003. Bright **Hostal El Descanso** *(☎ 976 29 17 41; Calle de San Lorenzo 2; singles/doubles €12/22)* is a great-value place.

Perfectly located **Hostal Plaza** *(☎ 976 29 48 30, fax 976 39 94 06; Plaza del Pilar 14; singles/doubles €39/51)* has large rooms with showers. Those overlooking the plaza are the best value in town. **Hotel Las Torres** *(☎ 976 39 42 50, fax 976 39 42 54; Plaza del Pilar 11; singles/doubles €39/49)* offers the usual two-star range of conveniences.

Places to Eat

Cafetería Pizolo *(Calle Prudencio; platos combinados from €5; open until 1am or 2am daily)* serves decent *platos combinados*. Cheery **La Milagrosa** *(Calle Don Jaime I 43; set menu €7)* serves *raciónes* and inexpensive breakfasts. The small plazas and narrow streets southwest of La Seo host some brilliant tapas bars, among them the inexpensive seafood spot **Casa Amadico** *(Calle Jordán de Urríes 3)*, **Cervecería Marpy** *(Plaza Santa Marta 8)*, **La Calzorras** *(Plaza de San Pedro Nolasco)* and also **Casa Juanico** *(Calle Santa Cruz 21)*.

For classier restauranting, head for Calle Francisco Vitoria, 1km south of Plaza del Pilar. **Risko Mar** *(Calle Francisco Vitoria 16; set menu €35)* is a fine fish restaurant with an excellent *menú* (minimum two people). Across the street, **Churrasco** *(Calle Francisco Vitoria 21; set menu €10)* is another Zaragoza institution, with a wide variety of meat and fish and an excellent-value three-course lunch.

Entertainment

There's no shortage of bars in and around El Tubo. At **Bar Corto Maltés** *(Calle del Temple 23)* all the barmen sport the *corto maltés* (sideburns). **Café El Prior** *(Calle Santa Cruz)* is a good place for a little dancing in the earlier stages of a night out. However, much of the late-night action takes place about 1km further southwest, on and around Calle Doctor Cerrada. A good place to start is the Irish bar **Morrissey** *(Gran Vía 33)*, which often has live bands Thursday to Saturday.

Getting There & Away

Bus stations are scattered all over town; tourist offices can tell you what goes where from where. The Agreda company runs to most major Spanish cities from Paseo de María Agustín 7. Tickets to both Madrid and Barcelona cost €11.

Oscense buses head towards the Pyrenees from the Agreda bus station, too.

Up to 15 trains daily run from El Portillo station to both Madrid (€28, three to 4½ hours) and Barcelona (€28, 3½ to 5½ hours). Some Barcelona trains go via Tarragona. Trains also run to Valencia via Teruel, and to San Sebastián via Pamplona.

TERUEL
pop 30,790

Aragón's hilly deep south is culturally closer to Castilla-La Mancha or the backlands of Valencia than to some other regions of the state. A good stop on the way to the coast from Zaragoza or Cuenca is the town of Teruel, which has a flavour all its own thanks to four centuries of Muslim domination in the Middle Ages and some remarkable mudéjar architecture dating from after its capture by the Christians in 1171.

Get the skinny at the **tourist office** *(☎ 978 60 22 79; Calle Tomás Nogués 1)*.

Things to See

Teruel has four magnificent mudéjar towers, on the cathedral of **Santa María** (12th to 13th centuries) and the churches of **San Salvador**

(13th century), **San Martín** and **San Pedro** (both 14th century). These, and the painted ceiling inside Santa María, are among Spain's best mudéjar architecture and artisanry. Note the complicated brickwork and colourful tiles on the towers, so typical of the style. A guided tour of the cathedral (€2) provides a great introduction to the city's history.

The **Museo Provincial de Teruel** (*Plaza Padre Polanco; admission free; open 10am-2pm & 4pm-9pm Tues-Fri, 10am-2pm Sat & Sun*) is well worth a visit, mainly for its fascinating archaeological section.

Places to Stay & Eat
Fonda del Tozal (*☎ 978 60 10 22; Calle del Rincón 5; singles/doubles €10/20*) inhabits an amazing rickety old house run by a friendly family. Most of the rooms have cast-iron beds, enamelled chamber pots and exposed ceiling beams. In winter, you might prefer **Hostal Aragón** (*☎ 978 60 13 87; Calle de Santa María 4; singles/doubles €15/22,* with bath €24/35), which is also charming but offers luxuries such as heating. Both of these places are just a couple of minutes' walk from the cathedral.

Teruel is famed for its ham. If you can't fit a whole leg in your luggage, at least sample a *tostada con jamón* with tomato and olive oil. One of the best places for hamming up is **La Taberna de Rokelin** (*Calle de Tozal 33*), a narrow bar with a beautiful rack of smoked pig hocks.

Getting There & Away
The **bus station** (*Ronda de Ambeles*), just north of the old town, has daily buses heading to Barcelona (6½ hours), Cuenca (2¾ hours), Valencia (two hours) and Madrid (€15, 4½ hours).

By rail, Teruel is about midway between Valencia and Zaragoza, with three trains a day to both places. The **RENFE station** (*Calle de la Estación*) is on the southeastern corner of the old city.

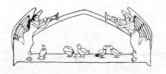

Switzerland

Chocolate, cheese and clocks; strait-laced bankers and big business – the cliches paint only a limited picture of Switzerland. Broader brushstrokes might add elegant cities buzzing with nightlife, a taste for eclectic culture, and some of the most exquisite natural beauty on the continent. The poet and novelist Goethe's description of the country as a combination of 'the colossal and the well-ordered' still fits, typified by awe-inspiring Alps set against tidy, efficient, watch-precise towns and cities.

Switzerland has one of the highest standards of living in the world, so even generous budgets will take a beating here, but the payoff is a super-slick infrastructure giving quick and easy access to everything the country has to offer. Switzerland blends the flavours of Germany, France and Italy to create a three-cultures-in-one experience.

Its distinct regional personalities are all the while united by a sophisticated sensibility and financial savvy.

Add an unassailable independent streak born of an obsession with getting along with the neighbours and it's plain why Switzerland remains an oasis of stability hardly touched by the political storms around it. The cynics who say that Switzerland is wasted on the Swiss are just jealous.

Facts about Switzerland

HISTORY

The first inhabitants of the region were a Celtic tribe, the Helvetii. The Romans arrived in 107 BC via the Great St Bernard Pass, but were gradually driven back by the Germanic Alemanni tribe, which settled in the region in the 5th century. Burgundians and Franks also came to the area, and Christianity was gradually introduced.

The territory was united under the Holy Roman Empire in 1032, but central control was never tight, and neighbouring nobles fought each other for local influence. The Germanic Habsburg expansion was spearheaded by Rudolph I, who gradually brought the squabbling nobles to heel.

The Swiss Confederation

Upon Rudolph's death in 1291, local leaders saw a chance to gain independence. The forest communities of Uri, Schwyz and Nidwalden formed an alliance on 1 August 1291, which is seen as the origin of the Swiss Confederation (their struggles against the Habsburgs are idealised in the legend of William Tell). This union's success prompted

SWITZERLAND

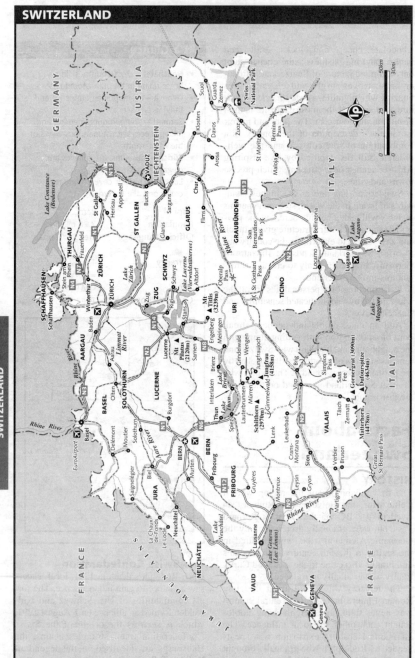

other communities to join: Lucerne (1332) was followed by Zürich (1351), Glarus and Zug (1352), and Bern (1353).

Encouraged by successes against the Habsburgs, the Swiss acquired a taste for territorial expansion. More land was seized. Fribourg, Solothurn, Basel, Schaffhausen and Appenzell joined the confederation, and the Swiss gained independence from the Holy Roman Emperor Maximilian I after their victory at Dornach in 1499.

Finally the Swiss over-reached themselves. They took on a superior force of French and Venetians at Marignano in 1515 and lost. Realising they could no longer compete against larger powers with better equipment, they declared their neutrality. Even so, Swiss mercenaries continued to serve in other armies for centuries, and earned an unrivalled reputation for skill and courage.

The Reformation during the 16th century caused upheaval throughout Europe. The Protestant teachings of Luther, Zwingli and Calvin spread quickly, although the inaugural cantons remained Catholic. This caused internal unrest that dragged on for centuries.

The French Republic invaded Switzerland in 1798 and established the Helvetic Republic. The Swiss vehemently resisted such centralised control, causing Napoleon to restore the former confederation of cantons in 1803. Yet France still retained overall jurisdiction. Following Napoleon's defeat by the British and Prussians at Waterloo, Switzerland finally gained independence.

The Modern State

Throughout the gradual move towards one nation, each canton remained fiercely independent, to the extent of controlling coinage and postal services. The cantons lost these powers in 1848, when a new federal constitution was agreed upon, with Bern as the capital. The Federal Assembly was set up to take care of national issues, but the cantons retained legislative (Grand Council) and executive (States Council) powers to deal with local matters.

Having achieved political stability, Switzerland could concentrate on economic and social matters. Poor in mineral resources, it developed industries dependent on highly skilled labour. A network of railways and roads was built, opening up previously inaccessible regions of the Alps and helping the development of tourism.

The Swiss carefully guarded their neutrality in the 20th century. Their only involvement in WWI was organising units of the Red Cross (founded in Geneva in 1863 by Henri Dunant). Switzerland joined the League of Nations after peace was won, however, only if its involvement was financial and economic rather than military. Apart from some accidental bombing, WWII left Switzerland largely unscathed.

While the rest of Europe underwent the painful process of rebuilding from the ravages of war, Switzerland expanded its already powerful commercial, financial and industrial base. Zürich developed as an international banking and insurance centre. Many international bodies, such as the World Health Organisation, based their headquarters in Geneva. Workers and employers struck agreements under which industrial weapons such as strikes and lockouts were renounced. Social reforms, such as old-age pensions (1948), were also introduced.

Afraid that its neutrality would be compromised, Switzerland managed to avoid joining the United Nations (UN) for over 50 years, restricting itself to observer status. However, in a March 2002 referendum, after much lobbying by government, economists and the media, the Swiss people finally voted in favour of membership. The government proudly announced that Switzerland's days of sitting on the sidelines were over.

The Swiss aren't quite as keen on joining the EU, however. Switzerland's 1992 application remains frozen, after voters twice failed to endorse the federal government's strategy. Nevertheless, the 1999 bilateral agreements promised market access, and free movement of people and transport between Switzerland and the EU.

In the 1990s the country's WWII record came under critical scrutiny. Swiss banks were accused of holding huge sums deposited by Jews who later became victims of the Holocaust. In 1998, facing a class action lawsuit in the US by Holocaust survivors, the banks agreed to pay US$1.25 billion to settle all outstanding claims. In 2002 an independent commission of historians set up by the Swiss government confirmed that tens of thousands of Jewish refugees were turned back from Switzerland's border, and left to face their fate in Nazi Germany. Swiss banks were also accused of banking Nazi plunder during WWII. A sum of at least US$400 million (US$3.8 billion today) was deposited.

Despite its long-standing military neutrality, Switzerland maintains a 400,000-strong civilian army. Every able-bodied male undergoes national service at 20 and stays in the reserves for 22 years, all the while keeping his rifle and full kit at home. Some complain of the high cost of keeping the civilian army going, and a 2001 referendum was held to decide whether the army should be scrapped. However, the people gave the army a reprieve...for now.

GEOGRAPHY

Mountains make up 70% of Switzerland's 41,290 sq km. Not a square inch of land is wasted in this compact country, with 30% meadow and pasture, 32% forest, 10% arable and 28% put to other use. Farming of cultivated land is intensive and cows graze on the upper slopes in summer as soon as the retreating snow line permits.

The Alps occupy the central and the southern regions of the country. The Dufourspitze (4634m), a peak on the Monte Rosa massif, is the highest point, although the Matterhorn (4478m) is more famous.

Glaciers account for an area of 2000 sq km, most notably the Aletsch Glacier, which at 169 sq km is the largest valley glacier in Europe.

The St Gotthard Massif, in the centre of Switzerland, is the source of many lakes and rivers, such as the Rhine and the Rhône. The Jura Mountains straddle the border with France, and peak at around 1700m. Between the two mountain systems is the Mittelland, also known as the Swiss Plateau, a region of hills crisscrossed by rivers, ravines and winding valleys.

CLIMATE

Ticino in the south has a hot, Mediterranean climate, and Valais in the southwest is noted for being dry.

Elsewhere the temperature is typically from 20° to 25°C in summer and 2° to 6°C in winter, with spring and autumn temperatures hovering around the 7° to 14°C mark. Summer tends to bring a lot of sunshine, however, it also brings the most rain. You will need to be prepared for a range of temperatures depending on your altitude.

Look out for the *Föhn*, a hot, dry wind that sweeps into the valleys, can be oppressively uncomfortable and can strike at any time of year.

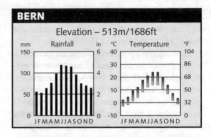

ECOLOGY & ENVIRONMENT

Switzerland has long been an environmentally aware nation. Its citizens diligently recycle household waste and cities encourage the use of public transport. The policy in the mountains is to contain rather than expand existing resorts.

GOVERNMENT & POLITICS

The modern Swiss Confederation is made up of 23 cantons; three are subdivided, bringing the total to 26. Each has its own constitution and legislative body for dealing with local issues.

National legislative power is in the hands of the Federal Assembly, which has two chambers. The lower chamber, the National Council, has 200 members elected by proportional representation. The upper chamber, the States Council, has 46 members, two per full canton. The Federal Assembly elects seven members to form the Federal Council, which holds executive power. All elections are for a four-year term except the posts of president and vice-president of the confederation, which are rotated annually. The vice-president always succeeds the president.

Under the 1874 constitution, Swiss citizens enjoy direct democracy: 50,000 signatories are needed to force a full referendum on proposed laws, and 100,000 to initiate legislation. Citizens regularly vote in referendums on national, local and communal issues. Yet surprisingly, women only won the right to vote in federal elections in 1971. It was 1991 before women gained a cantonal vote in Appenzell, the last remaining canton that still conducts votes by a show of hands in an Landsgemeinde (open-air parliament).

ECONOMY

Though poor in natural resources, Switzerland has a strong and stable market economy thanks to international trade and banking.

High prices in Switzerland are matched by high wages, and a good proportion of the wealth generated is channelled back into the community via social-welfare programmes. The Swiss generally enjoy moderate tax rates, low inflation (0.6% in 2002) and negligible unemployment rates (2.2% in 2002).

Due to the absence of other raw materials, hydroelectric power is the main source of energy. Chemicals, machine tools, and watches and clocks are the most important exports, and Swiss banks are a magnet for foreign funds attracted to political and monetary stability. Tourism is the country's third-biggest industry and an excellent infrastructure makes life easy for visitors. Swiss breakthroughs in science and industry include vitamins, DDT, gas turbines and milk chocolate.

POPULATION & PEOPLE

With a population of 7.28 million, Switzerland averages 174 people per square kilometre. Alpine districts are sparsely populated, while the Mittelland is very densely settled, especially around the shores of the larger lakes. Zürich is the largest city (339,300) followed by Geneva (176,000), Basel (163,800) and Bern (122,000). Most of the people are of Germanic origin, as reflected in the breakdown of the four national languages (see Language later in this section). Around 20% of the people living in the country are residents but not Swiss citizens; the foreign influx started after WWII, particularly from southern Europe.

ARTS

Switzerland does not have a very strong tradition in the arts, though there are several noteworthy exceptions. Paul Klee (1879–1940), the best-known native painter, created bold, hardlined abstract works. The writings of philosopher Jean-Jacques Rousseau (1712–78) in Geneva played an important part in the development of democracy. Critically acclaimed postwar dramatists and novelists, Max Frisch (1911–91) and Friedrich Dürrenmatt (1921–90), entertained readers with their dark tragicomedies, satire and morality plays. On the musical front, Arthur Honegger (1892–1955) is Switzerland's most recognised composer. The tranquillity of the mountains and lakes also seduced many foreign writers and artists (such as Voltaire, Byron and Shelley), who made their homes in Switzerland.

Gothic and Renaissance architecture are prevalent in urban areas, especially Bern. Rural Swiss houses vary according to region, but are generally characterised by ridged roofs with wide, overhanging eaves, and balconies and verandas enlivened by colourful floral displays, especially geraniums.

SOCIETY & CONDUCT

The Swiss are polite, law-abiding people who usually see no good reason to break the rules. You'll see few local litterbugs or jaywalkers here. Living quietly with your neighbours is a national obsession, with strict rules about noise levels (no baths or flushing toilets after 10pm – tourist accommodation excepted). Lunch is another designated quiet time, when many businesses shut up shop, and most workers and schoolchildren head home to eat with the family.

Good manners infuse the national psyche, and politeness is the cornerstone of all social intercourse. Always shake hands when being introduced to a Swiss, and kiss on both cheeks to greet and farewell friends. Don't forget to greet shopkeepers when entering shops. Remember to say *Grüezi* (hello) before launching into your question or request.

When drinking with Swiss, always wait until everyone has their drink and toast each of your companions, looking them in the eye and clinking glasses. Drinking before the toast is unforgivable, and will lead to seven years of bad sex...or so the superstition goes. Don't say you weren't warned.

Switzerland is a dog-friendly country, and some travellers may be surprised to find them everywhere – on trains, in restaurants and cafés, even hanging out with their owners in late-night bars. For a nation of such fit and active people, the Swiss are no more enlightened than the rest of Europe when it comes to smoking. A pungent blue haze hovers in most bars, restaurants and cafés.

In a few mountain regions such as Valais, people still wear traditional rural costumes, but dressing up is usually reserved for festivals. Yodelling, playing the alp horn and Swiss wrestling are also part of the Alpine tradition.

RELIGION

Protestantism and Roman Catholicism are equally widespread, though their concentration varies between cantons. Strong Protestant areas are Bern, Vaud and Zürich, whereas

Valais, Ticino and Uri are mostly Catholic. Most Swiss make a financial contribution by way of a *Kirchensteuer* (church tax), a percentage of their income tax that the government distributes to the churches through state subsidies.

LANGUAGE

Located in the corner of Europe where Germany, France and Italy meet, Switzerland is a linguistic melting pot with three official federal languages: German (spoken by 64% of the population), French (19%) and Italian (8%). A fourth language, Rhaeto-Romanic, or Romansch, is spoken by less than 1% of the population, mainly in the canton of Graubünden. Derived from Latin, it's a linguistic relic that has survived in the isolation of mountain valleys. Romansch was recognised as a national language by referendum in 1938 and given federal protection in 1996.

Though German-speaking Swiss have no trouble with standard High German, they use *Schwyzertütsch* (Swiss German) in most nonofficial situations. Swiss German covers a wide variety of melodic dialects that differs markedly from High German. Visitors will probably note the frequent use of the suffix *-li* to indicate the diminutive, or as a term of endearment.

English-speakers will have few problems being understood in the German-speaking parts. However, it is simple courtesy to greet people with the Swiss-German *Grüezi* and to inquire *Sprechen Sie Englisch?* (Do you speak English?) before launching into English.

In French Switzerland you shouldn't have too many problems either, though the locals' grasp of English probably will not be as good as the German-speakers'. Italian Switzerland is where you will have the greatest difficulty.

Most locals speak some French and/or German in addition to Italian. English has a lower priority, but you'll still find that the majority of hotels and restaurants have at least one English-speaking staff member.

See the Language chapter at the back of the book for German, French and Italian pronunciation guidelines and useful words and phrases.

Facts for the Visitor

HIGHLIGHTS

For mountain vistas you'll never forget the Jungfrau region, with the Schilthorn (2970m) and its neighbour, the Jungfrau (4158m). Challenging hikes and dazzling views can be enjoyed from the peaks overlooking Lake Lucerne and at Zermatt, in the shadow of the Matterhorn. Catch a lake steamer to Château de Chillon, on Lake Geneva, justifiably the most famous castle in Switzerland. For buzzing nightlife and medieval town centres creaking with history, head to Bern and Zürich. Culture buffs will find plenty of interest in Basel and Geneva, with many fine museums and galleries. But whatever you do, wherever you go, remember to stop and taste the chocolate!

SUGGESTED ITINERARIES

Depending on the length of your stay, you might want to see and do the following:

Two days
   Visit Interlaken and the Jungfrau, with an excursion to the mountains.
One week
   Spend two days in the Jungfrau, two days in Lucerne taking a lake steamer and going on mountain hikes, and a few days on Lake Geneva, visiting Château de Chillon.
Two weeks
   As above, but spend longer in the mountains, and visit Bern, Basel and Zürich.
One month
   As above, but make time for Geneva, Zermatt and the Matterhorn, and the Italian towns in Ticino.
Two months
   As above, but take your time. Include visits to Neuchâtel and the Jura Mountains, St Moritz and Graubünden, and the northeast towns of Schaffhausen, Appenzell and St Gallen.

LANGUAGE AREAS

- Romansch
- German
- French
- Italian

Basel • Zürich •
• Bern • Lucerne
Lausanne •   • Chur
                      St Moritz •
• Bellinzona
Geneva

PLANNING
When to Go
Visit Switzerland from December to April
for winter sports, and May to October for
general sightseeing and hiking. Alpine resorts all but close down in late April, May
and November.

Maps
Michelin covers the whole country with four
maps. The *Landeskarte der Schweiz* (Topographical Survey of Switzerland) series is
larger in scale and especially useful for hiking. Kümmerly + Frey maps are also good
for hikers. All these maps are sold throughout Switzerland. Swiss banks, especially the
UBS branches, are a good source of free
maps.

What to Bring
Take a sturdy pair of boots if you intend to
walk in the mountains, and warm clothing for
those cold nights at high altitude. Hostel
membership is invaluable and it's cheaper to
join before you get to Switzerland.

TOURIST OFFICES
Local Tourist Offices
Verkehrsbüro or *Tourismus* (tourist offices)
are extremely helpful. They have reams of literature to give out, including maps (nearly always free), and staff invariably speak English.
Offices can be found everywhere tourists are
likely to go and will often book hotel rooms
and organise excursions. If you are staying in
resorts, ask the local tourist office whether
there's a Visitor's Card, which is excellent for
discounts.

Switzerland Tourism also sells the **Swiss
Museum Passport** *(w www.museums.ch;
adult/student Sfr30/25)*, which will save big
bucks if you plan to visit more than a handful
of museums.

Tourist Offices Abroad
Switzerland Tourism has a free-phone number
for **Europe** *(☎ 00800 100 200 30)* and the
USA/Canada *(☎ 011800 100 200 30)*. Offices can be found in:

UK (☎ 020-7734 1921, fax 7437 4577; e info
.uk@switzerland.com) 10th Floor, Swiss Centre,
10 Wardour St, London W1D 6QF
USA (☎ 1-877-794-8037; e info.usa@switzer
landtourism.ch) 608 Fifth Ave, New York, NY
10020

Canadian queries are now handled through the
US office.

VISAS & DOCUMENTS
Visas are not required for passport holders of
the UK, USA, Canada, Australia, New Zealand
or South Africa. A maximum three-month stay
applies although passports are rarely stamped.

EMBASSIES & CONSULATES
Swiss Embassies & Consulates
Swiss embassies can be found in:

Australia (☎ 02-6273 3977, fax 6273 3428;
e vertretung@can.rep.admin.ch) 7 Melbourne
Ave, Forrest, Canberra, ACT 2603
Canada (☎ 613-235 1837, fax 563 1394;
e vertretung@ott.rep.admin.ch) 5 Marlborough Ave, Ottawa, Ontario K1N 8E6
New Zealand (☎ 04-472 1593, fax 499 6302;
e vertretung@wel.rep.admin.ch) 22 Panama
St, Wellington
UK (☎ 020-7616 6000, fax 7724 7001; e swiss
embassy@lon.rep.admin.ch) 16-18 Montague
Place, London W1H 2BQ
USA (☎ 202-745 7900, fax 387 2564;
e vertretung@was.rep.admin.ch) 2900 Cathedral Ave NW, Washington, DC 20008-3499

Embassies & Consulates in Switzerland
All embassies are in Bern (the Bern tourist office lists them in the free *Bern Aktuell*). They
include:

Canada (☎ 031 357 32 00) Kirchenfeldstrasse 88
France (☎ 031 359 21 11) Schosshaldenstrasse 46
Germany (☎ 031 359 41 11) Willadingweg 83
Ireland (☎ 031 352 14 42) Kirchenfeldstrasse 68
Italy (☎ 031 350 07 77) Elfenstrasse 14
UK (☎ 031 359 77 00) Thunstrasse 50
USA (☎ 031 357 70 11) Jubiläumsstrasse 93

Foreign consulates include:

Australia (☎ 022 799 91 00) Chemin des Fins 2,
Geneva
Canada (☎ 022 919 92 00) Ave de l'Ariana 5,
Geneva
France (☎ 022 319 00 00) Rue Imbert Galloix 11,
Geneva
Germany (☎ 022 730 11 11) Chemin du Petit-
Saconnex 28C, Geneva
New Zealand (☎ 022 734 95 30) Chemin du
Petit-Saconnex 28A, Geneva
UK (☎ 022 918 24 00) Rue de Vermont 37-39,
Geneva
USA (☎ 022 840 51 60) Rue Versonnex 7, Geneva;
(☎ 01 422 25 66) Dufourstrasse 101, Zürich

SWITZERLAND

CUSTOMS

Visitors from Europe may import 200 cigarettes, 50 cigars or 250g of pipe tobacco (twice as much for visitors from non-European countries). The allowance for alcoholic beverages is the same for everyone: 1L of alcohol above 15% and 2L below 15%. Tobacco and alcohol may only be brought in by people aged 17 or older.

MONEY
Currency

Swiss francs (Sfr, written CHF locally) are divided into 100 centimes (called *rappen* in German-speaking Switzerland). There are notes for 10, 20, 50, 100, 500 and 1000 francs, and coins for five, 10, 20 and 50 centimes, and one, two and five francs.

All major travellers cheques and credit cards are accepted. Virtually all train stations have money-exchange facilities open daily. Commission is not usually charged for changing cash or cheques but it's gradually creeping in. Shop around for the best exchange rates. Hotels usually have the worst rates.

Having money sent to Switzerland should be straightforward. No charge is made at Swiss American Express (AmEx) offices for receiving Moneygram transfers. Likewise for money sent to Western Union offices, of which there are many, particularly at larger train stations. Automatic teller machines (ATMs), known as Bancomats in banks and Postomats in post offices, are everywhere, and many give credit-card advances.

There are no restrictions on the amount of currency that can be brought in or taken out of Switzerland.

Exchange Rates

country	unit		Swiss franc
Australia	A$1	=	Sfr0.89
Canada	C$1	=	Sfr1.03
euro zone	€1	=	Sfr1.47
Japan	¥100	=	Sfr1.26
New Zealand	NZ$1	=	Sfr0.75
UK	UK£1	=	Sfr2.29
USA	US$1	=	Sfr1.57

Costs

Affluent Switzerland has one of the highest standards of living in Europe, and prices are inevitably high. Some travellers can scrimp by on about Sfr60 a day after buying a rail pass. This is survival level – camping or hostelling, self-catering when possible and allowing nothing for nonessentials. If you want to stay in pensions, see some sights and have a beer, count on spending twice as much. Minimum prices per person are around Sfr25/50 in a hostel/hotel and Sfr10/15 for lunch/dinner (excluding drinks).

Tipping & Bargaining

Tipping is not strictly necessary as hotels, restaurants and bars are required by law to include a 15% service charge on bills. Nevertheless, locals often 'round up' and a few extra francs for good service is appreciated. Prices are fixed, but travellers have successfully haggled for lower hotel rates in the low season.

Taxes & Refunds

VAT (MWST or TVA) on goods and services is levied at a rate of 7.5% (3.5% for hotel bills). Nonresidents can claim back the tax on purchases over Sfr500 (not hotel/restaurant bills). This can be done by presenting the goods and an export declaration to customs officials at airports and major border crossings when leaving the country. Ask for the documentation when making the purchase.

Switzerland has a motorway tax (see Car & Motorcycle in the Getting There & Away section later in this chapter).

POST & COMMUNICATIONS
Post

Postcards and letters to Europe cost Sfr1.30/1.20 priority/economy; to elsewhere they cost Sfr1.80/1.40. The term poste restante is used nationwide or you could use the German term, *Postlagernde Briefe*. Mail can be sent to any town with a post office and is held for 30 days; show your passport to collect mail. AmEx also holds mail for one month for people who use its cheques or cards.

Post office opening times vary but typically are 7.30am to noon and 2pm to 6.30pm Monday to Friday and until 11am Saturday. The largest post offices offer services outside normal hours (to late evening daily), but some transactions are subject to a Sfr1 to Sfr2 surcharge.

Telephone & Fax

The privatised Swisscom is the main telecommunications provider. The minimum charge in Swisscom payphones is Sfr0.60, though per-minute rates are low. Swisscom charges the same rate for national or local calls. During the day it's Sfr0.08 per minute, and during evenings and weekends it drops to Sfr0.04. Most phone boxes also allow you to send short emails worldwide for Sfr1.50 each.

The country code for Switzerland is ☎ 41. In March 2002 regional codes were incorporated into the subscriber number to create 10-digit numbers (with the exception of Zürich, which has nine-digit numbers). Drop the initial zero on the subscriber number when dialling from overseas.

International call prices have dropped substantially in recent years. A standard-rate call to the USA/Australia/UK costs Sfr0.12/0.25/0.12 per minute. Standard rates apply on weekdays (day or night), and there are reduced rates on weekends and public holidays. Many telephone boxes no longer take coins; the prepaid *taxcard* comes in values of Sfr5, Sfr10 and Sfr20, and is sold in post offices, kiosks and train stations.

Hotels can charge as much as they like for telephone calls, and they usually charge a lot, even for direct-dial calls.

To send a one-page fax at post offices costs Sfr7/8/9 for Switzerland/Europe/elsewhere, plus Sfr1/4/5 for each following page.

Email & Internet Access

Most large towns have an Internet café, and most cities have several. Rates range from reasonable (Sfr8 per hour) to ridiculous (Sfr24 per hour!!). Youth hostel Internet corners are often the best places to do a quick email check. Keep an eye out for cyber happy hours elsewhere.

DIGITAL RESOURCES

Switzerland has a strong presence on the Internet, with most tourist-related businesses having their own website; a good place to start is **Switzerland Tourism (W** *www.myswitzerland .com)*, with many useful links. For current news, try the **W** www.sri.ch website, and for in-depth coverage of major cities, check out **W** www.swisstownguide.ch.

BOOKS

See Lonely Planet's *Switzerland* and *Walking in Switzerland* guides for more detailed information on Switzerland and its walks. *Living and Working in Switzerland* by David Hampshire is an excellent practical guide. *Why Switzerland?* by Jonathan Steinberg explores the country's history and culture, and enthusiastically argues that Switzerland is *not* a boring country. Paul Bilton's slim volume *The Xenophobe's Guide to the Swiss* is informative and amusing. *The Swiss, the Gold and the Dead* by Jean Ziegler details shady banking deals during WWII. Fiction about Switzerland is surprisingly scarce, but Anita Brookner won the Booker Prize in 1984 for *Hotel du Lac*, a novel set around Lake Geneva.

English-language books are widely available in Switzerland, though for foreign titles you always pay more than the cover price. Check second-hand bookshops in cities.

NEWSPAPERS & MAGAZINES

Various English-language newspapers and magazines *(The Times, International Herald Tribune, Newsweek, Time)* are widely available and cost around Sfr3 to Sfr6.

RADIO & TV

Swiss Radio International broadcasts in English. Pick it up on 3985kHz, 6165kHz and 9535kHz. The English-language World Radio Geneva is on the FM band at 88.4mHz. Multichannel, multilingual cable TV is widespread; nearly all hotels have it.

TIME

Swiss time is GMT/UTC plus one hour. Daylight savings comes into effect at midnight on the last Saturday in March, when the clocks are moved forward one hour; they go back again on the last Saturday in October.

LAUNDRY

It usually costs about Sfr10 to wash and dry a 5kg load in a coin-operated or service laundrette. Many hostels also have washing machines (around Sfr8).

TOILETS

Public toilets are invariably spick-and-span, with a vast array of whizz-bang, self-cleaning models. Urinals are usually free but there's often a pay slot for cubicles. Note that the McClean chain of toilets in train stations charges as much as Sfr2 for a pee.

WOMEN TRAVELLERS

Women travellers should experience few problems with sexual harassment in Switzerland. However, some Ticino males suffer from machismo leanings, so you may experience

SWITZERLAND

unwanted attention in the form of whistles and catcalls. It's best to ignore the perpetrators.

GAY & LESBIAN TRAVELLERS

Attitudes to homosexuality are reasonably tolerant and the age of consent is 16. Zürich has a lively gay scene and hosts the Christopher Street Day march in late June. It's also home to *Cruiser* magazine (☎ 01 388 41 54; e info@cruiser.ch; w www.cruiser.ch), which lists significant gay and lesbian organisations, and has extensive listings of bars and events in Switzerland (Sfr4.50). For more insights into gay life in Switzerland, check out **Pink Cross** (w www.pinkcross.ch).

DISABLED TRAVELLERS

Many hotels have disabled access and most train stations have a mobile lift for boarding trains. For useful travel information, you can contact Switzerland Tourism or the **Swiss Invalid Association** (*Schweizerischer Invalidenverband;* ☎ 062 206 88 88, fax 062 206 88 89; w www.siv.ch; *Froburgstrasse 4, Olten CH-4601*).

DANGERS & ANNOYANCES

Crime rates are low, but that's no reason to forget your street smarts. Remember to be security-conscious and keep your valuables safely tucked away. Take special care in the mountains as **helicopter rescue** (☎ 1414) is expensive (make sure your travel insurance covers alpine sports).

BUSINESS HOURS

Most shops are open 8am to 6.30pm Monday to Friday, with a 90-minute or two-hour break for lunch at noon. In towns there's often a late shopping day till 9pm, typically on Thursday or Friday. Closing times on Saturday are usually 4pm or 5pm. At some places, such as large train stations, you may find shops are open daily. Banks are open 8.30am to 4.30pm weekdays, with some local variations.

Emergency Services

Emergency telephone numbers are: police ☎ 117, fire brigade ☎ 118, and ambulance (most areas) ☎ 144. The national 24-hour number for roadside assistance in the event of breakdown is ☎ 140.

PUBLIC HOLIDAYS & SPECIAL EVENTS

National holidays are 1 January, Good Friday, Easter Monday, Ascension Day, Whit Monday, 1 August (National Day), and 25 and 26 December. Some cantons observe 2 January, 1 May (Labour Day), Corpus Christi and 1 November (All Saints' Day). Many events take place at a local level throughout the year (check with the local tourist offices). Dates often vary from year to year. This is just a brief selection:

Costumed Sleigh Rides Experience archetypal Swiss kitsch in the Engadine in January.

Fasnacht In February, a lively spring carnival of wild parties and parades is celebrated countrywide, but with particular enthusiasm in Basel and Lucerne.

Combats de Reines From March to October, the lower Valais stages traditional cow fights.

Landsgemeinde On the last Sunday in April, Appenzellers gather in the main square to take part in a unique open-air parliament.

Montreux Jazz Festival Big-name rock/jazz acts hit town in July for this famous festival.

National Day On 1 August, celebrations and fireworks mark the country's National Day.

Street Parade In early August, Zürich lets its hair down with an enormous techno parade with 30 lovemobiles and more than half a million ravers.

Vintage Festivals You can down a couple in wine-growing regions such as Neuchâtel and Lugano in October.

Onion Market In late November, Bern takes on a carnival atmosphere for a unique market day.

Escalade Festival This historical festival held in Geneva celebrates deliverance from would-be conquerors.

ACTIVITIES

There are dozens of ski resorts throughout the Alps, the pre-Alps and the Jura, with some 200 ski schools. Resorts favoured by the package-holiday companies don't necessarily have better skiing facilities, but they do tend to have more off-slope activity when it comes to après-ski. Equipment hire is available at resorts and ski passes allow unlimited use of mountain transport.

There's no better way to enjoy Switzerland's spectacular scenery than to walk through it. There are 50,000km of designated paths, often with a convenient inn or café en route. Yellow signs marking the trail make it difficult to get lost, and each gives an average walking time to the next destination. Slightly more strenuous mountain paths have white-red-white markers. The **Schweizer Alpen-Club** (SAC; ☎ 031 370 1818, fax 031 370 18 00; W *www.sac-cas.ch*; *Monbijoustrasse 61, Bern*) maintains huts for overnight stays at altitude and can help with extra information. Lonely Planet's *Walking in Switzerland* contains track notes for walking in the Swiss countryside.

You can water-ski, sail and windsurf on most lakes. Courses are usually available, especially in Central Switzerland. There are over 350 lake beaches. Anglers should contact the local tourist office for a fishing permit valid for lakes and rivers. The Rotsee near Lucerne is a favourite place for rowing regattas. Rafting is possible on many Alpine rivers, including the Rhine and the Rhône.

Bungy-jumping, paragliding, canyoning and other high-adrenalin sports are widely available throughout Switzerland, especially in the Interlaken area.

WORK

Switzerland's bilateral agreement with the EU on the free movement of persons has eased regulations for EU citizens. Non-EU citizens officially need special skills to work legally but people still manage to find casual work in ski resorts – anything from snow clearing to washing dishes. Hotel work has the advantage of including meals and accommodation.

In theory, jobs and work permits should be sorted out before arrival, but if you find a job once you're in the country the employer may well have unallocated work permits. The seasonal 'A' permit is valid for up to nine months, and the elusive and much sought-after 'B' permit is renewable and valid for a year. Many resort jobs are advertised in the Swiss weekly newspaper *hotel + tourismus revue*. Casual wages are higher than in most other European countries.

ACCOMMODATION
Camping

There are about 450 camping grounds, classified from one to five stars depending upon amenities and the convenience of location. Nightly charges are around Sfr7 per person plus Sfr5 to Sfr10 for a tent, and around Sfr5 for a car. Many sites offer a slight discount if you have a Camping Carnet (earned by membership of a camping club). Free camping is discouraged and you should be discreet. Contact the **Schweizerischer Camping und**

Caravanning-Verband (*Swiss Camping & Caravanning Federation*; ☎ 041 210 48 22; *Habsburgerstrasse 35, Lucerne CH-6004*) for more information.

Hostels

There are 63 official Swiss Youth Hostels (*Jugendherberge, auberge de jeunesse, alloggio per giovani*) that are automatically affiliated to the international network. Nearly all youth hostels include breakfast and sheets in the price. Average high-season prices are Sfr30/50/80 for dorm beds/singles/doubles. Most hostels charge a few francs less during the low season (this chapter quotes high-season prices). Many places have double or family rooms available (with single or bunk beds), and around half of the Swiss hostels have kitchen facilities. Reception desks are often closed during the day, with check-in usually available from mid-late afternoon. It's wise to ring ahead to check on suitable check-in times.

Membership cards must be shown at hostels. Nonmembers pay a Sfr6 'guest fee' to stay in Swiss hostels; six of these add up to a full international membership card. Buying an international membership before you leave home is usually cheaper.

Hostels do get full, so it's wise to book ahead. Bookings can made by phone, email or via the website W www.youthhostel.ch (you'll need a credit card to book online). You can also ask your Swiss hostel to reserve ahead for your next one (Sfr1 plus a Sfr9 refundable deposit). A map, giving full details of all hostels, is available free from hostels and some tourist offices. For more information contact the **Schweizer Jugendherbergen** (*Swiss Youth Hostel Association or SYHA*; ☎ 01 360 14 14; e *marketing@youthhostel.ch; Schaffhauserstrasse 14, Zürich CH-8042*).

Some of the best budget accommodation you'll find is in independent 'backpacker hostels' – they're listed in *Swiss Backpacker News*, free from hostels and some tourist offices, and on the website W www.backpacker.ch. Prices are similar to SYHA hostels and membership is not required. The independents often have a more laid-back atmosphere and allow you to escape the bane of hostel living – noisy school groups. Many offer double rooms and kitchens and some have their own bars and clubs.

In ski resorts, some hotels have an annexe with a dormitory (*Touristenlager* or *Massenlager* in German, *dortoir* in French).

SWITZERLAND

Schweizer Alpen-Club maintains around 150 dormitory-style mountain huts at higher altitudes.

Hotels

Swiss accommodation is geared towards value for money rather than low costs, so even budget rooms are fairly comfortable (and pricey). The high-season prices quoted in this chapter could be reduced by 10% (towns) to 40% (alpine resorts) during the low season. Hotels are star rated. Prices start at around Sfr50/90 for a basic single/double. Count on at least Sfr10 more for a room with a private shower. Rates generally include breakfast, which tends to be a buffet in mid-range and top-end hotels. Half-board (ie, including dinner) is common in ski resorts. 'Hotel Garni' means a B&B establishment without a restaurant. Note that some train stations have hotel information boards with a free telephone. For more information contact the **Schweizer Hotelier-Verein** (*Swiss Hotel Association;* ☎ *031 370 41 11;* w *www .swisshotels.ch; Monbijoustrasse 130, Bern CH-3001*).

Other Accommodation

Private houses in rural areas sometimes offer inexpensive rooms; look out for signs saying *Zimmer frei* (rooms vacant). Some farms also take paying guests. Self-catering accommodation is available in holiday chalets, apartments or bungalows. Local tourist offices have lists of everything on offer in the area.

FOOD

Lactose intolerants will struggle in this dairy-obsessed country, where cheese is a way of life. The best-known Swiss dish is fondue, in which melted Emmental and Gruyére are combined with white wine, served in a large pot and eaten with bread cubes. Another popular artery-hardener is *Raclette*, melted cheese, served with potatoes. *Rösti* (fried, buttery, shredded potatoes) is German Switzerland's national dish, and is served with everything.

Many dishes are meaty, and veal is highly rated throughout the country; in Zürich it is thinly sliced and served in a cream sauce (*Geschnetzeltes Kalbsfleisch*). *Bündnerfleisch* is dried beef, smoked and thinly sliced. Like their northern neighbours, the Swiss also munch on a wide variety of *Wurst* (sausage).

Vegetarians won't have any trouble in the cities and larger towns, where there are often several dedicated vegetarian restaurants. Most eateries will also offer a small selection of nonmeat options, including large salad plates and the less appealing 'Toast Hawaii'. Soups are popular and are often a meal in themselves.

International fast-food chains proliferate, but better quality budget meals can often be found in markets and street stalls. In German-speaking Switzerland, pretzel shops and bratwurst stands abound, but thanks to an influx of Middle Eastern and North African communities, more exotic fare is easy to come by.

Buffet-style restaurant chains, such as Manora, have a huge selection of freshly cooked food at low prices. Their salad and dessert buffet bars are particularly tempting. Many budget travellers rely on picnic provisions from the supermarkets. Migros and Coop are the main supermarket chains (closed Sunday, except at some train stations). Larger branches have good quality self-service restaurants, which are typically open until around 6.30pm on weekdays and to 4pm or 5pm on Saturday.

Eating out in restaurants can be pricey. Look out for the fixed-menu dish of the day (*Tagesteller plat du jour*, or *piatto del giorno*), which often has several courses and is much cheaper than à la carte choices. Main meals are eaten at noon, and restaurants tend to have a closing day, often Monday.

Finally, Switzerland makes some of the most delectable chocolate in the world – don't miss it!

DRINKS

Rivella is a refreshing soft-drink alternative, made from the milk by-product whey (it's much nicer than it sounds). For simpler tastes, mineral water is readily available and tap water is drinkable everywhere.

Buying drinks in restaurants is inevitably expensive. Head to the local supermarkets if you're on a tight budget. Lager comes in 0.5L or 0.3L bottles, or on draught (*vom Fass* or *à la pression*) with measures ranging from 0.2L to 0.5L. Cardinal is a popular local brand, though small breweries all over the country serve up their own brews.

Wine is considered an essential accompaniment to lunch and dinner. Local vintages are generally good quality, but you might never have heard of them, as they are rarely exported. The main growing regions are the Italian- and French-speaking areas, particularly in Valais and by lakes Neuchâtel and Geneva. Both red and white wines are produced, and each region has its speciality (eg, Merlot in Ticino). There is also a choice of locally produced fruit brandies, often served with or in coffee.

ENTERTAINMENT

In the cities, nightlife centres on a thriving café culture and an ever-changing wave of hip bars and clubs. Check free newspapers or city listing guides for the latest hotspots. Many places open early for breakfast and stay open all day, transforming from cafés/restaurants into bars/clubs at night. There's a robust alternative scene, with old factories and warehouses being converted into clubs, restaurants, art spaces and live-music venues. Ski resorts have a distinctive atmosphere, with the après-ski scene keeping things buzzing until late. Cinemas usually show films in their original language. Check posters for the upper-case letter: for instance, E/d/f indicates English with both German and French subtitles. In French Switzerland you might see 'VO' instead, which signifies 'original version'.

SPECTATOR SPORTS

Switzerland might not breed bands of obsessive sports fanatics, but football (soccer) still has a strong following, with most towns having their own professional teams. Ice hockey is also popular and tennis has won its fair share of fans, particularly since naturalised Swiss Martina Hingis started hitting winners on the world circuit. Not surprisingly, winter sports are where the Swiss really come into their own, with most ski resorts hosting popular annual events, including long-distance cross-country contests and dramatic downhill races.

SHOPPING

Switzerland is known for producing high-quality luxury items such as watches, jewellery and exquisite chocolates. Swiss army knives are popular, whether it's a simple blade (Sfr10) or a mini-toolbox (Sfr100 or more); the larger youth hostels sell them at below-list price. Textiles and embroidery are best bought in St Gallen or Appenzell, and for woodcarvings head to Brienz. For a country that prides itself on quality and style, a surprising amount of tacky tourist gear fills the souvenir shops. Lovers of kitsch will be in their element, with a vast array of cuckoo clocks and cowbells to choose from.

Getting There & Away

AIR

The busiest international airports are Zürich and Geneva, each with several nonstop flights a day to major transport hubs such as London, Paris and Frankfurt. Budget airline **easyJet** (**w** www.easyjet.com) offers regular services from London to/from Zürich and Geneva. EuroAirport, near Mulhouse in France, serves Basel, while both Bern and Lugano have small airports.

After a 2001 crisis in the airline industry, Swissair's subsidiary Crossair was rebadged Swiss International Air Lines (known simply as 'Swiss'), becoming the new national airline. Swiss luggage check-in facilities are at major train stations around the country. For reservations throughout Switzerland, call ☎ 0848-85 2000 (local rate).

Airport departure taxes range from Sfr15 for Lugano up to Sfr24.50 for Zürich, and are always included in the ticket price.

LAND

Bus

With such cheap flights available, few people travel to Switzerland by bus these days. The trip from London to Geneva (UK£145 return, three to seven per week) or Zürich (UK£100 return, one to two per week, via Basel) is an exhausting 18- to 20-hour journey. For those with Busabout passes, there are stops in Geneva, Interlaken, Lucerne and Lauterbrunnen. For more information, see the website (**w** www.busabout.com). Geneva also has bus connections to Barcelona, and Zürich has various services to Eastern Europe. See the Geneva and Zürich entries later in this chapter for details.

Train

Located in the heart of Europe, Switzerland is a hub of train connections to the rest of the continent. Zürich is the busiest international terminus. It has two direct day trains and one night train to Vienna (nine hours). There are several trains daily to both Geneva and Lausanne from Paris (three to four hours by superfast TGV). Travelling from Paris to Bern takes 4½ hours by TGV. Most connections from Germany pass though Zürich or Basel. Nearly all connections from Italy pass through Milan before branching off to Zürich, Lucerne, Bern or Lausanne. Reservations on international trains are subject to a surcharge of Sfr5 to Sfr30, which depends upon the date and the service.

Car & Motorcycle

Roads into Switzerland are good despite the difficulty of the terrain, but special care is needed to negotiate mountain passes. Some, such as the N5 route from Morez (France) to Geneva, are not recommended if you have not had previous mountain-driving experience. Upon entering Switzerland you will need to decide whether you wish to use the motorways (there is a one-off charge of Sfr40). Arrange to have some Swiss francs ready, as you might not always be able to change money at the border. Better still, pay for the tax in advance from Switzerland Tourism or a motoring organisation. The sticker (called a *vignette*) you receive is valid for a year and must be displayed on the windscreen. A separate fee must be paid for trailers and caravans (motorcyclists must pay too). Some Alpine tunnels incur additional tolls.

BOAT

Switzerland can be reached by lake steamers: from Germany via Lake Constance (Bodensee); from Italy via Lake Maggiore; and from France via Lake Geneva (Lac Léman).

Getting Around

PASSES & DISCOUNTS

Swiss public transport is an efficient, fully integrated and comprehensive system which incorporates trains, buses, boats and funiculars. Convenient discount passes make the system even more appealing.

The Swiss Pass is the best deal for people planning to travel extensively, offering unlimited travel on Swiss Federal Railways, boats, most Alpine postbuses, and trams and buses in 35 towns. Reductions of 25% apply to funiculars and mountain railways. These passes are available for four days (Sfr240), eight days (Sfr340), 15 days (Sfr410), 22 days (Sfr475) and one month (Sfr525); prices are for 2nd-class tickets. The Swiss Flexi Pass allows free, unlimited trips for three to eight days within a month and costs Sfr230 to Sfr420 (2nd class).

With either pass, two people travelling together get 15% off.

The Swiss Card allows a free return journey from your arrival point to any destination in Switzerland, 50% off rail, boat and bus excursions, and reductions on mountain railways. It costs Sfr165 (2nd class) or Sfr240 (1st class) and it is valid for a month. The Half-Fare Card is a similar deal minus the free return trip. It costs Sfr99 for one month.

Except for the Half-Fare Card, these passes are best purchased before arrival in Switzerland from Switzerland Tourism or a travel agent. The Family Card gives free travel for children aged under 16 if they're accompanied by a parent and is available free to pass purchasers.

Regional passes, valid for a specific tourist region, provide free travel on certain days and half-price travel on other days within a seven or 15-day period.

All the larger lakes are serviced by steamers, for which rail passes are usually valid (Eurail is valid; Inter-Rail often gets 50% off).

AIR

Internal flights are not of great interest to most visitors, owing to the short distances and excellent ground transport. **Swiss International Air Lines** (W www.swiss.com) is the local carrier, linking major towns and cities several times daily, including Zürich, Geneva, Basel, Bern and Lugano.

BUS

Yellow postbuses are a supplement to the rail network, following postal routes and linking towns to the more inaccessible regions in the mountains. In all, routes cover some 8000km of terrain. Services are regular, and departures tie in with train arrivals. Postbus stations are next to train stations, and offer destination and timetable information.

TRAIN

The Swiss rail network covers 5000km and is a combination of state-run and private lines. Trains are clean, reliable, frequent and as fast as the terrain will allow. Prices are high, though the travel passes mentioned earlier will cut costs. All fares quoted in this chapter are for 2nd class; 1st-class fares are about 65% higher. In general, Eurail passes are not valid for private lines and Inter-Rail pass holders get a 50% discount. All major stations are connected by hourly departures, but services stop from around midnight to 6am.

Train stations offer luggage storage, either at a counter (usually Sfr5 per piece) or in 24-hour lockers (Sfr2 to Sfr7). They also have excellent information counters that give out free timetable booklets and advice on connections. Train schedules are revised yearly, so double-check details before travelling. For train information, consult the excellent website for the **Schweizerische Bundesbahnen** *(SBB;* w *www.sbb.ch)* or phone ☎ 0900-300 300 (Sfr1.19 per minute).

CAR & MOTORCYCLE
Be prepared for winding roads, high passes and long tunnels. Normal speed limits are 50km/h in towns, 120km/h on motorways, 100km/h on semi-motorways (designated by roadside rectangular pictograms showing a white car on a green background) and 80km/h on other roads. Don't forget you need a vignette to use motorways and semi-motorways (see the Getting There & Away section earlier in this chapter). Mountain roads are good but stay in low gear whenever possible and remember that ascending traffic has right of way over descending traffic, and postbuses always have right of way. Snow chains are recommended in winter. Use dipped lights in *all* road tunnels. Some minor Alpine passes are closed from November to May – check with tourist offices or motoring organisations such as the **Swiss Touring Club** *(TCS;* ☎ 022-417 2727; w *www.tcs.ch).*

Switzerland is tough on drink-driving; if your blood alcohol level is over 0.05% you face a large fine or imprisonment.

Rental
For the best deals, you have to prebook – see the Getting Around chapter. One-way drop-offs are usually free of charge within Switzerland, though collision-damage waiver costs extra. Multinationals provide similar rates – around Sfr100 to Sfr130 for one day's rental (unlimited kilometres and the lowest-category car), with reductions beyond three days. Look out for special weekend deals. Local operators may have lower prices (the local tourist office will have details), though you won't get a 'one-way drop-off' option.

BICYCLE
Despite the hilly countryside, many Swiss choose to get around on two wheels. You can hire bikes from most train stations (adult/child Sfr30/25 per day) and return to any station with a rental office, though this incurs a Sfr6 surcharge. Bikes can be transported on most trains; SBB rentals travel free (maximum five bikes per train). If you have your own wheels you'll need a bike pass (one day Sfr15, with Swiss travel pass Sfr10). Look for the *Cycling in Switzerland* booklet (Sfr37.80) in bookshops, which covers nine routes and 3300km of bike paths. Local tourist offices often have good cycling information. Bern, Basel, Geneva and Zürich offer free bike loans – see the city sections.

HITCHING
Lonely Planet does not recommend hitchhiking. Indigenous Swiss are not very forthcoming with lifts and most hitchers will be picked up by foreigners. Although illegal on motorways, hitching is allowed on other roads. A sign is helpful. Make sure you stand in a place where vehicles can stop. To try to get a ride on a truck, ask around the customs post at border towns.

LOCAL TRANSPORT
City Transport
All local city transport is linked together on the same ticketing system and you need to buy tickets before boarding. One-day passes are usually available and are much better value than paying per trip. There are regular checks for fare dodgers; those caught without a ticket pay an on-the-spot fine of Sfr40 to Sfr60.

Taxis are always metered and tend to wait around train stations, but beware – they are expensive!

Mountain Transport
Vertigo sufferers will be challenged by the five main modes of transport used in steep Alpine regions. A funicular *(Standseilbahn, funiculaire)* is a pair of counterbalancing cars on rails, drawn by cables. A cable car *(Luftseilbahn, téléphérique)* is dramatically suspended from a cable high over a valley. A gondola *(Gondelbahn, télécabine)* is a smaller version of a cable car except that the gondola is hitched onto a continuously running cable as soon as the passengers are inside. A cable chair *(Sesselbahn, télésiège)* is likewise hitched on to a cable but is not enclosed. A ski lift *(Schlepplift, téléski)* is a T-bar hanging from a cable, which the skiers hold on to while their feet slide along the

snow (these are gradually being phased out because of safety concerns).

ORGANISED TOURS

Tours are booked through local tourist offices. The country is so compact that excursions to the major national attractions are offered from most towns. A trip up to Jungfraujoch, for example, is available from Zürich, Geneva, Bern, Lucerne and Interlaken.

Bern

pop 122,000

Bern, the nation's capital, is the fourth-largest city and retains a relaxed, small-town charm. Surrounded on three sides by the deep-green Aare River, its medieval old town features 6km of covered arcades and countless historic fountains and monuments. Founded in 1191 by Berchtold V, Bern was named for the unfortunate bear (*Bärn* in local dialect) who was Berchtold's first hunting victim. Today, the bear remains the heraldic mascot of the city.

Orientation

The compact centre of the old town is contained within a sharp U-bend of the Aare River. On the western edge of the old town, the main train station is within easy reach of all the main sights, and offers bike rental and airline check-in.

Information

Tourist Offices Located in the train station, **Bern Tourismus** (☎ *031 328 12 28;* **e** *info -res@bernetourism.ch; open 9am-8.30pm daily June-Sept, 9am-6.30pm Mon-Sat & 10am-5pm Sun Oct-May)* offers a two-hour city tour by coach (Sfr25; daily April to October, weekly November to March) and an on-foot version (Sfr14; daily June to September) in summer. Its free booklet, *Bern aktuell*, has plenty of useful information, and the online **Bern Youth Guide** (**w** *www.youthguide.ch)* has some excellent tips and links. There's another tourist office by the bear pits.

Money The **SBB exchange office** (*open 6.30am-9pm daily)* is in the lower level of the train station.

Post & Communications The **main post office** (*Schanzenstrasse; open 7.30am-6.30pm*

Mon-Fri, 8am-noon Sat) has convenient automatic stamp machines if you get there after hours.

ispace (☎ *031 327 76 77;* **e** *info@compe rio.ch; Zeughausgasse 14; free/Sfr4/6 for 10/ 30/45min; open 9am-5.30pm Mon-Fri)*, in the basement of the Medienhaus, is a good place to do a quick email check for free. **Loeb department store** (*Spitalgasse 47-51; Sfr5/10 for 30/60min)* has an Internet café in the basement. There are two free terminals, but you'll have to wait during busy times.

Bycom Internet Pub (☎ *031 313 81 91; Aarbergergasse 46; Sfr5 per hour; open 6am-11.30pm Mon-Thur & Sun, 6am-3am Fri, 9am-3am Sat)* is a two-level lounge bar-cum-Internet café with 50 coin-operated computer terminals, a fully stocked bar and a groovy atmosphere.

Travel Agencies The budget and student travel agency **STA Travel** (☎ *031 302 03; 12 Falkenplatz 9 ● 031 312 07 24; Zeughausgasse 18; both open 9.30am-6pm Mon-Fri, 10am-1pm Sat)* can help with travel advice.

Bookshops English-language books fill an entire floor at **Stauffacher** (☎ *031 311 24 11; Neuengasse 25)*. You can also browse the second-hand bookshops of Rathausgasse or Kramgasse.

Medical Services There is a **university hospital** (☎ *031 632 21 11; Freiburgstrasse)*. For help in locating a doctor or dentist call ☎ 0900 57 67 47.

Things to See & Do

The city map available from the tourist office (Sfr1) sends you on a sightseeing stroll through the old town. The core of the walk is Marktgasse and Kramgasse, with their covered arcades, colourful fountains, and cellars with hidden shops, bars and theatres.

Check out the **ogre fountain** in Kornhausplatz, depicting a giant enjoying a meal of wriggling children.

Dividing Marktgasse and Kramgasse is the **Zytglogge**, a colourful clock tower with revolving figures that herald the chiming hour. People gather a few minutes before the hour on the eastern side to watch them twirl. Nearby is **Einstein House** (☎ *031 312 00 91; Kramgasse 49; adult/student/child Sfr3/2/2; open 10am-5pm Tues-Fri, 10am-4pm Sat*

BERN

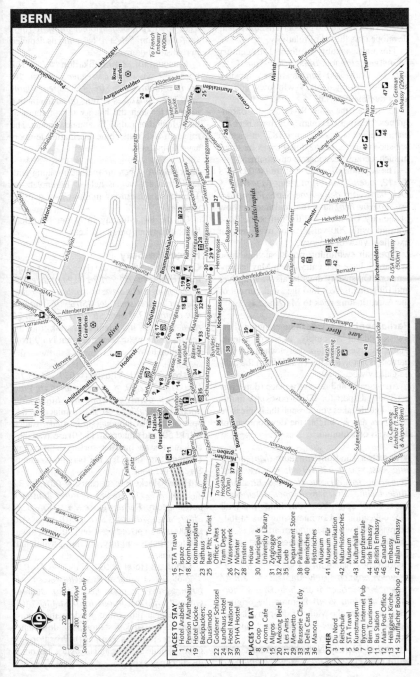

Some Streets Pedestrian Only

0   200   400m
0   200   400yd

PLACES TO STAY
1   Hotel Arabelle
2   Pension Marthahaus
19 Hotel Glocke
    Backpackers;
    Quasimodo
22 Goldener Schlüssel
24 Landhaus Hotel
37 Hotel National
39 SYHA Hostel

PLACES TO EAT
8   Coop
9   Aroma Cafe
15 Migros
20 Mekong Beizli
21 Les Amis
29 Menuetto
33 Brasserie Chez Edy
34 Della Casa
36 Manora

OTHER
3   Du Nord
4   Reitschule
5   STA Travel
6   Kunstmuseum
7   Bycom Internet Pub
10 Bern Tourismus
11 Bus Station
12 Main Post Office
13 Heiliggeist Kirche
14 Stauffacher Bookshop

16 STA Travel
17 ispace
18 Kornhauskeller;
    Kornhausplatz
23 Rathaus
25 Bear Pits; Tourist
    Office; Altes
    Tram Depot
26 Wasserwerk
27 Münster
28 Einstein

30 Municipal &
    University Library
31 Zytglogge
32 Adriano's
35 Loeb
    Department Store
38 Parlament
40 Bernisches
    Historisches
    Museum
41 Museum für
    Kommunikation
42 Naturhistorisches
    Museum
43 Kulturhallen
    Dampfzentrale
44 Irish Embassy
45 British Embassy
46 Canadian
    Embassy
47 Italian Embassy

Mar-Oct, 1pm-5pm Tues-Fri, 12pm-4pm Sat Feb & Nov), where the physicist lived when he developed his theory of relativity.

The unmistakably Gothic, 15th-century **Münster** *(cathedral; open 10am-5pm Tues-Sat, 11.30am-5pm Sun)* features imposing, 12m-high, stained-glass windows and an elaborate main portal.

Just across the Aare River are the **Bären-graben** (bear pits). Though bears have been the entertainment at this site since 1857, it's sad to see such majestic beasts doing tricks for treats in such a cramped, concrete environment.

The adjoining **Tourist Centre** *(☎ 031 328 12 12; open 10am-4pm daily Mar-May & Oct, 9am-6pm daily June-Sept, 11am-4pm Fri-Sun Nov-Feb)* has a free multimedia show of the city's history. Up the hill is the **Rose Garden**, with 200 varieties of roses and an excellent view of the city.

Open-air swimming pools, such as those at Marzili, have free entry (open May to September). On steamy days locals walk upriver and fling themselves into the swift current of the Aare, floating back to Marzili.

Parliament The **Bundeshäuser**, home of the Swiss Federal Assembly, is worth a look. There are free tours (six daily) when the parliament is not in session (watch from the public gallery when it is).

Arrive early and reserve a place (don't forget your passport for ID purposes). A multilingual guide takes you through the impressive chambers and highlights the development of the Swiss constitution.

Museums The **Kunstmuseum** *(Museum of Fine Arts; ☎ 031 328 09 44; w www.kunst -museumbern.ch; Hodlerstrasse 8-12; adult/ student/child Sfr7/5/free; open 10am-9pm Tues, 10am-5pm Wed-Sun)* holds the Paul Klee collection and an interesting mix of Italian masters, Swiss and modern art.

Many museums are clustered on the southern side of the Kirchenfeldbrücke. **Bernisches Historisches Museum** *(☎ 031 350 77 11; w www.bhm.ch; Helvetiaplatz 5; adult/ student Sfr5/3; open 10am-5pm Tues & Thur-Sun, 10am-8pm Wed)* features the original sculptures from the Münster doorway depicting the *Last Judgment* and Niklaus Manuel's macabre *Dance of Death* panels.

The kid-friendly **Naturhistorisches Museum** *(☎ 031 350 71 11; w www.nmbe.ch;*

Bernastrasse 15; adult/student/child Sfr5/3/ free; open 2pm-5pm Mon, 9am-5pm Tues-Fri, 10am-5pm Sat-Sun) has animals depicted in realistic dioramas.

Museum für Kommunikation *(☎ 031 357 55 55; w www.mfk.ch; Helvetiastrasse 16; adult/student/child Sfr6/4/2; open 10am-5pm Tues-Sun)* takes visitors on an interactive journey through the history of communications, including radio, TV and new media. The museum also runs some fascinating temporary exhibitions.

Markets An open-air market groaning with fresh fruit and veg is held at Bärenplatz on Tuesday and Saturday mornings, or daily in summer.

On the last Monday in November, Bern hosts its famous onion market.

Places to Stay

Camping Nestled by the river Aare is **Camping Eichholz** *(☎ 031 961 26 02; Strandweg 49; e camping.eichholz@swissonline.ch; camp site per person/small tent Sfr6.90/5, bungalow rooms 2/3/4 beds Sfr15/17/22; open 20 April-30 Sept)*. It's a half-hour walk from the centre, or the weary can ride tram No 9 from the station to Wabern.

Hostels The **SYHA hostel** *(☎ 031 311 63 16, fax 031 312 52 40; w www.jugibern.ch; Weihergasse 4; dorm beds from Sfr29.80, singles/ doubles Sfr42.80/75.60)* is in a quiet riverside spot below Parliament (signposted). Lunch (Sfr12.50) and dinner (Sfr11.50) are available, and there's an Internet surfing happy hour (midnight to 7am) for the bargain-basement Sfr2.50 per hour.

Hotel Glocke Backpackers *(☎ 031 311 37 71, fax 031 311 10 08; e info@chilisback packers.com; Rathausgasse 75; dorm beds Sfr27, singles/doubles Sfr75/110)*, renovated in 2000, has a prized position in the old town, spotless rooms and tiny, sparkling-white hall bathrooms.

Landhaus Hotel *(☎ 031 331 41 66, fax 031 332 69 04; e landhaus@spectraweb.ch; Altenbergstrasse 4; dorm beds Sfr30, doubles without/with bathroom from Sfr110/140)*, near the bear pits, offers modern minimalist rooms and a slick restaurant/bar downstairs (live jazz Thursday evenings). Private room prices include bedding and breakfast, but dorm dwellers pay extra.

Hotels Near the train station there's the **National** (☎ *031 381 19 88, fax 031 381 68 78;* e *info@nationalbern.ch; Hirschengraben 24; singles/doubles from Sfr60/95, with bathroom from Sfr85/130)*, a grand, old-world, family-run hotel, kept in the style of 100 years ago.

Pension Marthahaus (☎ *031 332 41 35, fax 031 333 33 86;* e *info@marthahaus.ch; Wyttenbachstrasse 22a; bus No 20 to Gewerbeschule; singles/doubles/triples Sfr60/95/ 120, with bathroom Sfr90/120/150)*, 1km out of town in a quiet residential area, is warm and welcoming, with comfy rooms, Internet access and a share kitchen.

Goldener Schlüssel (☎ *031 311 02 16, fax 031 311 56 88;* e *info@goldenerschluessel .ch; Rathausgasse 72; singles/doubles Sfr82/ 115, with bathroom Sfr108/145, half-/full board Sfr24/40)*, once a horse market, is now faded but functional. Its bustling ground-floor restaurant serves fondue and other favourites.

Hotel Arabelle (☎ *031 301 03 05, fax 031 302 42 62;* e *info@arabelle.ch; Mittelstrasse 6; bus No 12 to Mittelstrasse; singles/doubles Sfr105/155)*, near the university, has modern, bright and breezy rooms.

Places to Eat

Wall-to-wall cafés and restaurants line the popular meeting places of Bärenplatz and Theaterplatz, as well as the more upmarket Gerechtigskeitsgasse.

For both convenience and delicious fresh food, try the **Manora** (*Bubenbergplatz 5a; salads Sfr4.40-9.40, pizzas Sfr6.90-8.90; open 6.30am-10.45pm Mon-Sat, 8.30am-10.45pm Sun)*, a busy, two-level, buffet-style restaurant.

Aroma (*Genfergasse 8; snacks Sfr4.90-13.50; open 7am-9pm Mon-Fri, 7am-7pm Sat, 11am-8pm Sun)* is a popular coffee stop. Its carefully crafted mugs of coffee sport love-hearts in the froth.

Brasserie Chez Edy (☎ *031 311 38 93; Bärenplatz; mains Sfr24-34; open 11am-11pm)* is the best of the Bärenplatz bunch. Try the speciality mussels (served 10 different ways), or the Bernese Platter, with more sauerkraut and sausages than you can finish.

Don't be fazed by the dingy entrance to **Della Casa** (☎ *031 311 21 42; Schauplatzgasse 16; lunch menu from Sfr18.50, mains Sfr22.50-42; open 8am-11.30pm Mon-Fri, 9am-3pm Sat)*. Inside you'll find an old but cosy eatery with floral curtains, leadlight lamps and traditional Swiss specialities.

Menuetto (☎ *031 311 14 48; Herrengasse 22; meals Sfr13.80-23.50; open 11.15am-2.15pm & 5.30pm-10pm Mon-Sat)* is a mecca for vegetarians, serving up seriously wholesome dishes to a seriously wholesome crowd.

Hidden below a popular grungy bar, **Les Amis** (☎ *031 311 51 87; Rathausgasse 63; mains Sfr30-37.50; open 6.30pm-12.30am Tues-Sat)* specialises in French and Italian dishes.

MeKong Beizli (☎ *031 311 26 00; Chindlifrässer-Passage, Kornhausplatz 7; starters Sfr10.50, mains Sfr21-29; open 10am-11pm daily)*, at the entrance to an arcade, is perfect for a chilli fix, with spicy Thai soups and Chinese stir-fries.

Self-caterers can buy up big at **Coop** (*Neuengasse*) and **Migros** (*Marktgasse 46*), which also have cheap self-service restaurants.

Entertainment

Bern has a thriving nightlife, with countless bars and clubs to choose from. See the website w www.bernbynight.ch for an extensive list.

Du Nord (☎ *031 332 23 38; Lorrainestrasse 2; open 8am-12.30pm Mon-Fri, 9am-12.30pm Sat, 4pm-12.30pm Sun)* is a spacious, semi-grungy, bar-restaurant with a laid-back atmosphere and a social conscience.

Altes Tramdepot (☎ *031 368 14 15; Am Bärengraben; open 11am-12.30am daily)*, beside the bear pits, brews its own beer on the premises (sample three types for Sfr9.50). This cavernous converted tram depot has snacks and monster meals, and sweeping views across the river.

Adriano's (☎ *031 318 88 31; Theaterplatz 2; open 7am-12.30pm Mon-Sat, 10am-11.30pm Sun)* transforms from hip bar with black-clad regulars at night to mellow prework breakfast niche the next morning.

Kornhauskeller (☎ *031 327 72 72; Kornhausplatz 18; open 6pm-1am Mon-Wed, 6pm-2am Thur-Sat, 6pm-12.30am Sun)* is a magnificent, underground gallery bar and restaurant with vaulted ceilings, frescoes and comfy sofas overlooking diners below. Drinks are dear, but it's worth sipping slowly on a fruit juice (Sfr5) to soak up the atmosphere.

Wasserwerk (☎ *031 312 12 31;* w *www .wasserwerk.ch; Wasserwerkgasse 5; gigs free-Sfr30; open 9pm-1.30am Sun-Thur, 9pm-2.30am Fri-Sat)*, in a converted riverside warehouse, is a favourite hang-out for local pool-players and clubbers, with international DJs and regular special events. See the website for the latest programme.

Quasimodo (☎ 031 311 13 81; *Rathaus-gasse 75; admission free; open 4pm-1.30am Mon-Wed, 4pm-3.30am Thur-Sat*), underneath Hotel Glocke, is a dimly lit techno bar/ club pumping out a hard electronic pulse.

There's almost always something interesting on at **Kulturhallen Dampfzentrale** (☎ 031 311 63 37; **w** *www.dampfzentrale.ch; Marzili-strasse 47; bus No 30 to Marzili*), with an eclectic mix of acts from jazz and flamenco to classical and club DJs. The late-night Moonlinerbus shuttles from Dampfzentrale to the station on weekends.

The **Reitschule** (☎ 031 306 69 69; **w** *www .reitschule.ch; Schützenmattstrasse*), a graffiti-covered alternative arts centre in a grotty area, attracts a left-leaning crowd looking for dance, theatre, cinema and live music. There's also a bar, restaurant and women's centre. It's rather run-down. There are plans for renovation.

Getting There & Away

There are daily flights to/from Lugano, London, Paris, Amsterdam and other European destinations from Bern-Belp airport. Postbuses depart from the western side of the train station. There are at least hourly train connections to most Swiss towns, including Geneva (Sfr50, 1¾ hours), Basel (Sfr37, 70 minutes), Interlaken (Sfr25, 50 minutes) and Zürich (Sfr48, 70 minutes).

There are three motorways that intersect at the northern end of the city. The N1 runs from Neuchâtel in the west and Basel and Zürich in the northeast. The N6 connects Bern with Thun and the Interlaken region in the southeast. The N12 is the route from Geneva and Lausanne in the southwest.

Getting Around

Belp airport is some 9km southeast of the city centre. A bus links the airport to the train station (Sfr14). It takes 30 minutes and is coordinated with flight arrivals and departures.

Bus and tram tickets cost Sfr1.60 (maximum six stops) or Sfr2.50. A day pass for the city and regional network is Sfr8. A 24/48/72-hour pass for the city costs Sfr6.50/10.50/14.50. Buy single-journey tickets at stops and passes from the tourist office or the **BernMobil office** (*Bubenbergplatz 5*).

Many taxis wait by the train station. They charge Sfr6.80 plus Sfr3.10 per kilometre (Sfr3.40 after 8pm daily and on Sunday).

From May to October there are *free* daily loans of city bikes outside the train station. ID and Sfr20 deposit are required.

AROUND BERN

There are some excellent excursions close to Bern. About 30km west of Bern is **Murten**, a historic walled town overlooking a lake. There are hourly trains from Bern (Sfr11.80).

Fribourg, to the southwest, has an enticing old town-centre and an **Art & History Museum** which is well stocked with late-Gothic sculpture and painting. It's easily accessible by train (Sfr11.80, 30 minutes).

Further south is **Gruyéres**, about an hour away from either Fribourg or Montreux, with a 13th-century **castle** on the hill. Fromage fanciers flock to **La Maison du Gruyére** (☎ 026 921 84 00; **w** *www.lamaisondu gruyere.ch; tours Sfr5; open 9am-7pm daily June-Sept, 9am-6pm daily Oct-May*), which offers daily cheese-making tours. Fans of the *Alien* movie can pay homage to its designer at the **Musée HR Giger** (☎ 026 921 22 00; *adult/child Sfr10/5; open 10am-6pm daily summer, 10am-5pm Tues-Sun daily winter*).

Neuchâtel & the Jura

The northwest corner of the country hugs the border with France, sharing its language, food and sensibility. Neuchâtel is a wine-making region featuring rolling hills and a postcard-perfect lake as well as a proud watch-making heritage. The Jura region is often overlooked by foreign visitors but attracts its fair share of Swiss holidaymakers. Dominated by the Jura mountain range, its landscape of forests, pastures and gentle slopes makes it ideal territory for a range of sports and outdoor activities.

NEUCHÂTEL
pop 32,000

Neuchâtel is the canton's capital, on the northwest shore of the large lake that shares its name. This laid-back French-style resort, surrounded by vineyards, has a cruisey café culture and an inviting medieval old town.

The train station (Gare CFF) has daily money exchange and bike rental. The central pedestrian zone and Place Pury (the hub of local buses) are about 1km away down the hill along Ave de la Gare.

The **tourist office** (☎ 032 889 68 90; e *tourisme.neuchatelois@ne.ch; Place du Port; open 9am-7pm daily mid-May–mid-Oct, 9am-noon & 1.30pm-5.30pm Mon-Fri, 9am-noon Sat mid-Oct–mid-May)* is in the main post office by the lake.

Things to See & Do
The centrepiece of the old town is the 12th-century **Chateau de Neuchâtel** *(tours daily Apr-Sept)*, now housing cantonal offices, and the adjoining **Collegiate Church**. The church features a striking cenotaph of 15 statues dating from 1372. Nearby, the **Prison Tower** *(admission Sfr1; open Apr-Aug)* offers broad views of the town and lake.

Visit the **Musée d'Art et d'Histoire** *(Museum of Art & History;* ☎ 032 717 79 20; *Esplanade Léopold-Robert 1; adult/student Sfr7/4, free Wed; open 10am-6pm Tues-Sun)*, on the waterfront, to see the museum's beloved 18th-century clockwork figures.

Tropical Gardens Papiliorama/Nocturama (☎ 038 33 43 44; *adult/student/child Sfr11/9/5; open 9am-6pm daily summer, 10am-5pm daily winter)* has a complex of lush vegetation with colourful butterflies and tropical birds, as well as a faux moonlit world for Latin American night creatures. It's 6km east of Neuchâtel at Marin (take bus No 1 from Place Pury).

The tourist office has information on nearby walking trails and boat trips on the lake.

Places to Stay
Oasis Neuchâtel (☎ 032 731 31 90, fax 032 730 37 09; e *auberge.oasis@bluewin.ch; Rue du Suchiez 35; dorm beds Sfr25-32, twins Sfr64; open Apr-Oct)* is 2km from the centre; take bus No 1 (Cormondréche) to Vauseyon, then follow the signs towards Centre Sportive. This friendly, independent hostel is a bit of a hike, but rewards you with glorious views. At the time of writing there was talk of renovation or closure, so ring ahead before traipsing uphill.

Hôtel Marché (☎ 032 723 23 30, fax 032 723 23 33; e *info@hoteldumarche.ch; Place des Halles 4; singles/doubles/triples Sfr70/100/125)* offers basic rooms right in the thick

of it, overlooking the cafés of bustling Place des Halle.

Hotel des Arts (☎ 032 727 61 61, fax 032 727 61 62; e *info@hotel-des-arts.ch; Rue Pourtales 3; singles/doubles/suites from Sfr108/150/200)*, a couple of blocks from the main drag, was spruced up in early 2002, and has bright, cheerful rooms.

The **Hôtel Alpes et Lac** (☎ 032 723 19 19, fax 032 723 19 20; e *hotel@alpesetlac.ch; station-side singles/doubles from Sfr120/180, lakeside from Sfr145/207)*, opposite the train station, is an elegant option with renovated rooms and a generous breakfast buffet. It's worth paying an extra Sfr20 for panoramic views over Neuchâtel's rooftops.

Places to Eat
Bach et Buck Creperie (☎ 032 725 63 53; *Ave du 1er-Mars 22; crepes Sfr6-10.50; open 11.30am-1.45pm & 5.30pm-9.45pm Mon-Thur, 11.30am-1.45pm & 5.30pm-11.30pm Fri-Sat, 5pm-9.45pm Sun)* has a menu of 130 crepes and good vegie options in a café dominated by refreshing green-themed decor.

Cafe des Halles (☎ 032 724 31 41; *Rue du Trésor 4; mains Sfr14-23; open 8am-midnight Mon-Sat, 10am-midnight Sun)*, in an impressive high-ceilinged historic house on the main square, has scrumptious pizzas, pastas and a large shaded terrace.

Night owls should keep an eye out for Neuchâtel's **restaurants de nuit** *(all-night eateries; open 9pm-6am)*, which are strung all over town.

Self-caterers can stock up on local wines and cheeses at **Coop** *(Rue de la Treille 4)* and **Aux Gourmets** *(cnr Rue de Seyon & Rue de L'Ancien Hotel-de-Ville)*, both near Place Pury.

Entertainment
Chauffage Compris (☎ 032 721 43 96; *Rue des Moulins 37; open 7am-1am Mon-Thur, 7am-2am Fri, 8am-2am Sat, 3pm-midnight Sun)* is a funky café/bar with quality coffee, a range of spirits and beers and a daily lunch menu. Grab a board game from the bar and settle in for a few hours.

Café du Cerf (☎ 724 27 44; *Rue de L'Ancien Hotel-de-Ville 4; open 8am-midnight Mon-Fri, 8am-1am Sat & Sun)* is a friendly, popular beer-lover's paradise (150 choices) with Cambodian specialities from the linked restaurant Le Lotus upstairs.

Also worth a look are **Bar de L'Univers** (☎ 032 721 43 40; Rue du Coq d'Inde 22), a cool, smoky, studied-grunge bar for all ages, tucked into the corner of a quiet square; and **Brasserie Cafe du Theatre** (☎ 032 725 29 77; Faubourg du Lac 1), a glass-fronted place attracting all types for a chat and a late supper.

Getting There & Around

There are hourly fast trains to Geneva (Sfr42, 70 minutes) and Bern (Sfr17.20, 35 minutes). Postbuses heading to the Jura leave from the station.

Local buses cost Sfr1.60 to Sfr2.60 per trip, or Sfr7 for a 24-hour pass.

AROUND NEUCHÂTEL
La Chaux-de-Fonds

Watch- and clock-making have a long history here, and the town even boasts its own **Musée International D'Horlogerie** (Horology Museum; ☎ 032 967 68 61; Rue des Musées 29; adult/student Sfr8/4; open 10am-6pm Tues-Sun Jun-Sept, 10am-noon & 2pm-5pm Oct-May), with over 4500 timekeeping exhibits being displayed. Just 20km northwest of Neuchâtel and accessible by train in 30 minutes (Sfr10.40), it's an ideal day trip.

JURA CANTON

The youngest canton in Switzerland is the Jura, which only broke away from the Bern canton in 1974. Though the capital is Delémont, outdoor enthusiasts head to Franches-Montagnes (Free Mountain), a magnet for mountain-bikers, hikers and cross-country skiers. Some 1500km of hiking trails and 200km of prepared cross-country ski trails lead through scenic pastures and woodlands.

It's also horse country, with over 30 towns and villages boasting equestrian centres that offer all-inclusive weeks, weekends or simply hourly rides.

The main town in Franches-Montagnes is Saignelégier, where you will find **Jura Tourisme** (☎ 032 952 19 53, fax 032 952 19 50; www.juratourisme.ch; Place du 23-Juin 6, Saignelégier). Staff can help with accommodation and outdoor activities.

Saignelégier can be reached by train from La Chaux-de-Fonds (Sfr12.60, 40 minutes) and Basel (Sfr27, 95 minutes with change at Glovelier).

Geneva

pop 176,000

Geneva (Genève, Genf, Ginevra), Switzerland's third-largest city, sits comfortably on the shore of Lake Geneva (Lac Léman). The canton is surrounded by France on three sides and the Gallic influence is everywhere. Birthplace of the Red Cross, once League of Nations headquarters and now European home of the UN, Geneva has been an important centre of both diplomacy and business for decades. The city belongs not so much to Switzerland as to the whole world. More than 40% of residents are non-Swiss and this city of bankers, diplomats and transients has a truly international flavour. Despite the obvious affluence of the city and its impressive lakeside position, take a step into the backblocks and you'll find a scruffier, seedier side.

Orientation

The Rhône River runs through the city, dividing it into *rive droite* (right bank, ie, north of the Rhône) and *rive gauche* (left bank). On the northern side is the main train station, Gare de Cornavin; south of the river lies the old town. In summer, Geneva's most visible landmark is the **Jet d'Eau**, a giant fountain on the southern shore.

In France, **Mont Salève** yields an excellent view of the city and Lake Geneva. Take bus No 8 to Veyrier and walk across the border. The cable car costs Sfr19 return and runs daily in summer, but infrequently in winter.

Information

Tourist Offices For advice on accommodation or attractions, go to **Genéve Tourisme** (☎ 022 909 70 00; e info@geneve-tourism .ch; Rue du Mont-Blanc 18; open 9am-6pm Mon-Sat, plus 9am-6pm Sun summer). Grab a copy of the excellent (and free) *Vélo-Cité* map or the budget-conscious brochure *Genéve info-jeunes*. There's also the **city information office** (☎ 022 311 98 27; Pont de la Machine; open noon-6pm Mon, 9am-6pm Tues-Fri, 10am-5pm Sat) and **Centre d'Accueil et de Renseignements** (CAR; ☎ 022 731 46 47; open 9am-11pm daily mid-June–mid-Sept), with youth-oriented information dispensed from a bus parked at the station end of Rue du Mont-Blanc.

Watchful Castelo de São Jorge, Lisbon, Portugal

Palácio da Pena, Sintra, Portugal

Flamenco in a Barcelona club

One of Alicante's many vibrant nightclubs, Spain

Galathea's tower, part of Teatre-Museu Dalí, Figueres, Spain

The Hemisfèric, Valencia, Spain

BILL WASSMAN

The fairy-tale *alcázar* (fortress), Segovia, Spain

SIMON BRACKEN

Gaudí's La Sagrada Família, Barcelona, Spain

DONALD C & PRISCILLA ALEXANDER EASTMAN

Dazzling Plaza de España, Seville, Spain

CLEM LINDENMAYER

Mirror image of the Matterhorn, Valais, Switzerland

MARTIN MOOS

Boating is popular on Lake Maggiore, Switzerland

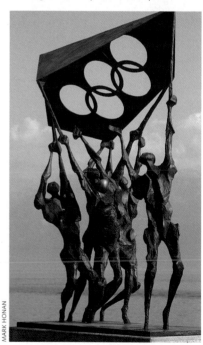
MARK HONAN

Musée Olympique statue, Lausanne, Switzerland

Money There is an **exchange office** *(open 6.45am-9.30pm daily summer, 6.50am-7.40pm Mon-Sat, 6.50am-6.40pm Sun rest of year)* in Gare de Cornavin.

Post & Communications Not far from the station is the **main post office** *(Rue du Mont-Blanc 18; open 7.30am-6pm Mon-Fri, 8.30am-noon Sat)*.

Near the tourist office you'll find excellent Internet rates (Sfr1/3/4 for 10/30/60 minutes) at **Video Club** *(☎ 022 731 47 48; Rue des Alpes 19; open 11am-midnight Mon-Thur, 11am-2am Fri-Sat, noon-midnight Sun)*. In the train station, **Internet Cafe de la Gare** offers bargain nightly rates between 9pm and 11pm (Sfr3 per hour), but prices rise at other times.

Travel Agencies Among a string of travel agents and airline offices is **American Express** *(☎ 022 731 76 00; Rue du Mont-Blanc 7; open 8.30am-5.45pm Mon-Fri year-round, 9am-noon Sat-Sun in summer)*. On the other side of town, there's a branch of **STA Travel** *(☎ 022 329 97 33; Rue Vignier 3; open 9.15am-6pm Mon-Fri, 9am-noon Sat)*.

Medical Services Ring ☎ 111 for medical information. For medical services there's the **Cantonal Hospital** *(☎ 022 372 33 11; Rue Micheli-du-Crest 24)* or a private 24-hour clinic, **Permanence Médico Chirurgicale** *(☎ 022 731 21 20; Rue de Chantepoulet 1-3)*. The **Servette Clinique** *(☎ 022 733 98 00; Ave Wendt 60)* offers emergency dental treatment.

Things to See & Do

The city centre is so compact that it's easy to see many of the main sights on foot. Start a scenic walk through the old town at the **Île Rousseau**, home to a statue in honour of the celebrated free thinker. Head west along the southern side of the Rhône until you reach the 13th-century **Tour de L'Île**, once part of the medieval city fortifications. Walk south down the narrow, cobbled Rue de la Cité until it becomes Grand-Rue. **Rousseau's birthplace** is at No 40.

A short detour off Grand-Rue there's the part-Romanesque, part-Gothic **Cathédrale St Pierre**, where John Calvin preached from 1536 to 1564. There are good views from the **tower** *(admission Sfr3; open 9am-5pm daily June-Sept, 10am-noon & 2pm-5pm Mon-Sat, 11am-12.30pm & 1.30pm-5pm Sun*

Oct-May). The cathedral location has been a place of worship since the 4th century, and you can witness evidence of this in the **archaeological site** *(adult/student Sfr5/3; open Tues-Sun)*.

Grand-Rue terminates at **Place du Bourg-de-Four**, which is the site of a medieval marketplace that features both a fountain and street cafés.

Take Rue de la Fontaine to reach the lakeside. Anticlockwise round the shore is the **Jet d'Eau**. Calling this a fountain is an understatement. The water shoots up with incredible force (200km/h, 1360HP), to create a 140m-high plume. At any one time there are seven tonnes of water is in the air, and much of it falls on spectators who venture out on the pier. It's not activated in winter or in high winds.

United Nations The European arm of the UN and the home of 3000 international civil servants is the Art-Deco **Palais des Nations** *(☎ 022 907 48 96; Ave de la Paix 9-14; tour adult/student Sfr8.50/6.50; open 10am-5pm daily July-Aug, 10am-noon & 2pm-4pm daily Apr-June & Sept-Oct, 10am-noon & 2pm-4pm Mon-Fri Nov-Mar)*. You can see where decisions about world affairs are made on the hour-long tour (bring your passport to get in). Take Bus No 5 or 8 from the station.

Museums There are plenty of museums (many free) to keep you busy on a rainy day. **Musée d'Art et d'Histoire** *(Museum of Art and History; ☎ 022 418 26 00; Rue Charles-Galland 2)* has a vast collection of paintings, sculpture, weapons and archaeological displays. **Musée d'Histoire Naturelle** *(Museum of Natural History; ☎ 022 418 63 00; Route de Malagnou 1)* delights the kiddies with dioramas and anthropological displays. **Maison Tavel** *(☎ 022 418 37 00; 6 Rue du Puits Saint Pierre)* gives visitors an insight into the everyday, with a focus on the history of urban life in Geneva. These museums are free and are open 9.30am or 10am to 5pm Tuesday to Sunday.

The **International Red Cross & Red Crescent Museum** *(☎ 022 748 95 25; Av de la Paix 17; Bus No 5 or 8; adult/student Sfr10/5; open 10am-5pm Wed-Mon)*, next to the UN, proudly tells the story of the world's first humanitarian organisation, and keeps you up to date with current work in the field.

SWITZERLAND

GENEVA (GENÈVE)

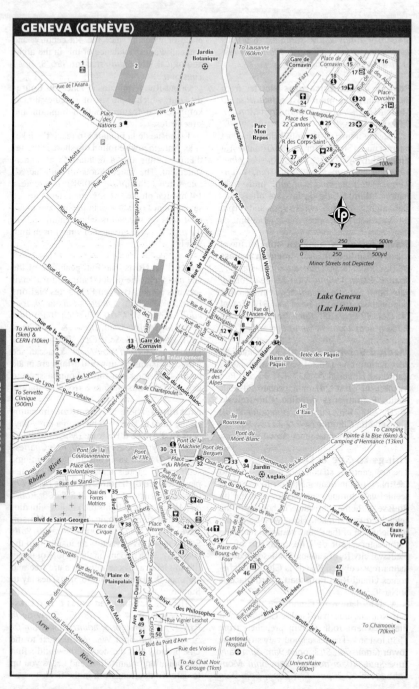

To Lausanne (60km)

Jardin Botanique

Gare de Cornavin

Place de Cornavin

Place Dorcière

James-Fazy

Rue de Berne

Rue des Alpes

Rue du Mont-Blanc

Rue de Chantepoulet

Place des 22 Cantons

Rue Rousseau

R des Corps-Saint

R Grenus

R des Étuves

0   100m

Ave de l'Ariana

Route de Ferney

Place des Nations

Ave de la Paix

Rue de Lausanne

Parc Mon Repos

Ave Giuseppe-Motta

Rue de Vermont

Ave de la France

Rue du Vidollet

Rue de Montbrillant

Rue du Grand Pré

Rue de la Servette

To Airport (5km) & CERN (10km)

Rue des Gares

Rue du Valais

Rue Ferrier

Rue de Lausanne

Rue Rothschild

Quai Wilson

Lake Geneva (Lac Léman)

Rue de la Prairie

Rue de Lyon

Rue de Lyon

To Servette Clinique (500m)

Rue Voltaire

James-Fazy

Rue du Môle

Rue de la Navigation

Rue de Berne

Rue de Zürich

Rue de Monthoux

Rue de l'Ancien-Port

Rue Philippe-Plantamour

Quai du Mont-Blanc

Bains des Pâquis

Jetée des Pâquis

Gare de Cornavin

Rue du Mont-Blanc

Rue de Chantepoulet

Rue Rousseau

Place des Alpes

Île Rousseau

Jet d'Eau

To Camping Pointe à la Bise (6km) & Camping d'Hermance (13km)

Pont de la Machine

Pont des Bergues

Pont du Mont-Blanc

Quai du Seujet

Pont de la Coulouvrenière

Pont de l'Île

Place du Rhône

Quai du Général-Guisan

Promenade du Lac

Jardin Anglais

Quai Gustave-Ador

Rhône River

Quai des Volontaires

Place des Volontaires

Rue du Stand

Quai des Forces Motrices

Rue de la Confédération

Rue du Rhône

Rue de Rive

Rue Pierre-Fatio

Quai Versonnex

Ave Pictet de Rochemont

Gare des Eaux-Vives

Blvd de Saint-Georges

Rue Bovy Lysberg

Rue du Général Dufour

Place Neuve

Rue de la Corraterie

Rue de la Croix-Rouge

Grand-Rue

Rue de la Fontaine

Rue du Marché

Rue Ferdinand-Hodler

Place du Cirque

Rue Georges-Favon

Rue du Conseil-Général

Promenade des Bastions

Place du Bourg-de-Four

Rue Charles-Galland

Ave de Sainte-Clotilde

Rue Gourgas

Rue des Vieux Grenadiers

Plaine de Plainpalais

Ave Henri-Dunant

Rue du Carouge

Cours des Bastions

Blvd Jaques Dalcroze

Blvd Helvétique

Rue François D'Ivernois

Rue Lefort

Blvd des Tranchées

Route de Malagnou

Rue des Bains

Quai Ernest-Ansermet

Ave du Mail

Rue Vignier Leschot

Blvd des Philosophes

Route de Florissant

To Chamonix (70km)

Arve River

Rue des Voisins

Blvd du Pont d'Arve

Cantonal Hospital

To Au Chat Noir & Carouge (1km)

To Cité Universitaire (400m)

0   250   500m
0   250   500yd
Minor Streets not Depicted

See Enlargement

SWITZERLAND

GENEVA

PLACES TO STAY		35	La Mamounia		23	Permanence Médico
3	Centre Masaryk	37	Le The			Chirurgicale
4	SYHA Hostel	38	Victoria		24	Notre-Dame
5	City Hostel	45	Chez Ma Cousine		28	Mulligans
10	Hôtel de la Cloche	51	Café Universal		30	Tour de l'Île
15	Hôtel Bernina				31	City Information Office
25	Hôtel Excelsior	**OTHER**			32	Free Bicycle Rental
27	Hotel Saint-Gervais	1	International Red Cross &		33	MGN boat departure
50	Hôtel le Prince		Red Crescent Museum		34	CGN Ticket Booth
52	Hôtel Carmen	2	Palais des Nations (UN)		36	L'Usine
		9	Free Bicycle Rental		39	Flanagan's Irish Bar
PLACES TO EAT		11	Sixt		40	Alhambar
6	Migros	13	Genev' Roule		41	Maison Tavel
7	L'amalgam	17	Video Club		42	Rousseau's Birthplace
8	Edelweiss	18	CAR Information Centre		43	Reformation Monument
12	Espresso Club	19	Post Café		44	Cathédrale St Pierre
14	Kong Restaurant	20	Genéve Tourism;		46	Musée d'Art et d'Histoire
16	Al-Amir		Main Post Office		47	Musée d'Histoire Naturelle
26	Manora	21	International Bus Terminal		48	Fruit market
29	Sugar Hut	22	American Express		49	STA Travel

Parks & Gardens Geneva has more parkland than any other Swiss city, much of it along the lakefront.

There's the **Jardin Anglais**, near the jet, featuring a large flower clock; and, in the north of the city, the impressive **Jardin Botanique** (admission free; open 9.30am-5pm daily winter, 8am-7.30pm daily rest of year), with exotic plants and an aviary.

South of Grand-Rue is **Promenade des Bastions**, containing a massive monument to the Reformation: the giant figures of Bèze, Calvin, Farel and Knox are flanked by smaller statues of other important figures, and depictions of events instrumental in the spread of the movement.

CERN Some 10km northwest of the centre is the European Centre for Nuclear Research (CERN; ☎ 022 767 84 84; e visits.service@ cern.ch; Route de Meyrin; bus No 9 from train station; admission free; open 9am-5pm Mon-Sat). Its educational Microcosm exhibition covers particle accelerators and the Big Bang; real enthusiasts can get up close to the large hadron collider on one of the guided tours that run at 9am and 2pm (take your passport and book well in advance).

Special Events

The Geneva Festival, a 10-day event in early August, features parades, fireworks and live music, most of it along the lake. In early December, L'Escalade celebrates the foiling of an invasion by the Duke of Savoy in 1602 with a costumed parade and day of races around the old town.

Places to Stay

Camping Some 7km northeast of the centre, on the southern lakeshore, is **Camping Pointe á la Bise** (☎ 022 752 12 96; Chemin de la Bise 19; camp site per adult/child/tent Sfr6.70/ 3.10/6; open Apr-Oct) in Vesenaz. Take bus E from Rive. Further away, but a cheaper option, is **Camping d'Hermance** (☎ 022 751 14 83; Rue de Nord 44; open Apr-Oct) at the terminus of bus E, 14km from the centre.

Hostels Above an International School for tots near the UN, **Centre Masaryk** (☎ 022 733 07 72; Ave de la Paix 11; Bus No 5 or 8; dorm beds Sfr30, singles/doubles/triples Sfr40/76/ 99) has large rooms with lots of character, creaky floorboards and wonderful views over parkland. Get a key for late access and beware of stray building blocks.

Closer to the centre is the **SYHA hostel** (☎ 022 732 62 60, fax 022 738 39 87; w www .yh-geneva.ch; Rue Rothschild 28-30; dorm beds from Sfr25, doubles without/with bath Sfr70/80), a big, busy, concrete box of a building with helpful staff. Breakfast is included and dinners cost Sfr12.50.

The independent **City Hostel** (☎ 022 901 15 00; e info@cityhostel.ch; Rue Ferrier 2; dorm beds in 4-/3-/2-bed rooms Sfr25/28/31, singles/doubles Sfr55/80) is in a charmless

'70s-style building. It offers adequate rooms, kitchen and Internet access (Sfr4 for 30 minutes).

Cité Universitaire (☎ 022 839 22 22, fax 022 839 22 23; Ave de Miremont 46; dorm beds Sfr20, singles for students/nonstudents Sfr42/49, studios Sfr75), south of the Rhône, is an enormous jumble of student accommodation with Internet, reading room and restaurant (open 7am to 10pm; breakfast Sfr7). Basic dorms are only available from mid-June to September, but ask for affordable singles at other times. Take bus No 3 from Gare de Cornavin to the terminus at Champel.

Hotels Geneva has a huge number of five- and four-star hotels that fill quickly with business clientele.

See the tourist office, or **W** www.geneva-tourism.ch, for some upmarket choices. For the budget-conscious, there are a few good-value options in town.

Hôtel de la Cloche (☎ 022 732 94 81, fax 022 738 16 12; **e** hotelcloche@span.ch; Rue de la Cloche 6; singles/doubles Sfr60/85, doubles with shower & toilet Sfr120) is a small, old-fashioned hotel with expansive rooms, ageing furniture, dramatic chandeliers and towering ceilings. It's liable to be full so call ahead.

Hotel Saint-Gervais (☎/fax 022 732 45 72; Rue des Corps-Saints 20; singles/doubles from Sfr62/78) is a tiny place with tiny rooms, but its convenient location and unorthodox design (one room has tartan-covered ceiling, door and floor) have won fans.

Near the university, **Hôtel Carmen** (☎ 022 329 11 11, fax 022 781 59 33; Rue Dancet 5; singles/doubles Sfr55-100, doubles Sfr75-126) is a friendly, family-run place with some of the best-value rooms in town. Studio apartments are available for longer stays. If Carmen is booked out, try the nearby **Hôtel le Prince** (☎ 022 807 05 00, fax 022 807 05 29; **W** www.hotel-le-prince.ch; 16 Rue des Voisins; singles/doubles from Sfr85/110), with modest but comfortable rooms.

If you're looking for convenience, there are several tourist-class hotels clustered near the train station. Reliable options include **Hôtel Bernina** (☎ 022 908 49 50, fax 022 908 49 51; **e** info@bernina-geneve.ch; Place de Cornavin 22; singles/doubles from Sfr130/160), offering renovated rooms directly across the road; and **Hôtel Excelsior**

(☎ 022 732 09 45, fax 022 738 43 69; Rue Rousseau 34; singles/doubles from Sfr120/180), around the corner.

Places to Eat

Geneva is the cuisine capital of Switzerland, with a wide range of choices, from Chinese to Lebanese to North African. You'll find cheapish Asian and Middle Eastern eateries in the seedy streets north of Rue des Alpes, or on Boulevard de Saint-Georges south of the river. Don't miss the best kebab in town from the hole-in-the-wall Lebanese takeaway **Al-Amir** (Rue de Berne 22; kebabs Sfr8; open 11am-2am daily).

For tasty dishes and extensive salad and dessert bars, head to **Manora** (Rue de Cornavin 4; small/large meals Sfr6.90/8.90; open 7.30am-9.30pm Mon-Sat, 9am-9.30pm Sun).

Restaurants Tuck into the plentiful plat du jour (Sfr16) at **La Mamounia** (☎ 022 329 55 61; Blvd Georges-Favon 10; dishes Sfr23-29; open noon-2pm & 7pm-midnight daily) and you won't need dinner. The Moroccan eatery has generous melt-in-your-mouth couscous dishes with an array of condiments; weekend diners often score a belly-dancer bonus.

West of the station, **Kong Restaurant** (Rue de la Servette 31; mains Sfr10-26; open noon-2pm & 6.45pm-10pm Mon-Sat, 6.45pm-10pm Sun) satisfies the biggest appetites with its all-you-can-eat buffet (Sfr17.50; available Tuesday to Friday).

At the other end of the scale, there's **Le The** (☎ 079 436 77 18; Rue des Bains 65; tea Sfr4, dishes Sfr4-8), a tiny boutique teahouse with exquisite Chinese infusions (61 varieties) and bite-size delicacies.

For flavoursome Thai food, there's the busy, intimate **Sugar Hut** (☎ 022 731 4613; Rue des Etuves 16; mains Sfr22-28; open noon-2pm & 7pm-2am Mon-Fri, 7pm-2am Sat-Sun), with a good seafood selection.

Road-testing Swiss specialities in Geneva is not out of the question either. **Victoria** (☎ 022 807 11 99; Rue Bovy-Lisberg 2; dishes Sfr21-49; open 10.30am-3pm & 5.30pm-midnight Mon-Sat) is a stylish brasserie run by gourmet chefs specialising in Genevese food. Or go the whole hog at kitschy **Edelweiss** (☎ 022 731 49 40; Place de la Navigation 2), with pots of steaming fondue (from Sfr23) in a Swiss-chalet setting and a folklore show (from 7pm nightly).

Cafés In the old town, terrace cafés and restaurants crowd along the medieval Place du Bourg-de-Four. **Chez Ma Cousine** (☎ 022 310 96 96; Place du Bourg-de-Four 6; meals Sfr13.90; open 7am-midnight Mon-Fri, 11am-midnight Sat, 11am-11pm Sun) entices local lunchers with its country-cottage decor and plates piled high with its signature dish (half-chicken, potatoes and salad).

The walk-in-wardrobe-sized **Espresso Club** (☎ 022 738 84 88; Rue des Paquis 25; meals Sfr13-22; open 6am-2am Mon-Fri, 7am-2am Sat, 8am-7pm Sun) is a popular cruisey café serving up pizza, pasta, salads and industrial-strength coffee.

Around the corner is **L'amalgam** (Rue de l'Ancien-Port 13; meals Sfr16-18) which is all African art, palms and ochre tones, with simple fusion food and a mellow mood.

Café Universal (☎ 022 781 18 81; Blvd du Pont d'Arve 26; mains Sfr24-32, plat du jour Sfr17-18) is French, smoky and cool, and features monster mirrors, 1920s posters, glittering chandeliers and an arty crowd.

Self-Catering Stock up at **Migros** (Rue des Pâquis; open 8am-7pm Mon-Fri, 8am-6pm Sat), which also sells baguettes (Sfr2) and sandwiches (Sfr3.60) from its self-service restaurant. **Aperto** (open 6am-10pm daily), in the train station, has fresh produce and a mini bakery. You can pick up seasonal goodies at the fruit and vegie markets scattered around (the one at Plainpalais operates five days a week).

Entertainment

The latest nightclubs, live music venues and theatre events are well covered in the weekly Genéve Agenda, free from the tourist office.

Alhambar (☎ 022 312 13 13; 1st floor, Rue de la Rôtisserie 10; open noon-2pm Mon, noon-2pm & 6pm-2am Tues-Fri, 5pm-2am Sat, 11am-midnight Sun) is an oasis of theatricality in an otherwise staid shopping district, with a buzzing atmosphere, an eclectic music programme and the best Sunday brunch in town.

An odd blend of Brit fixtures and loud blues music attracts a mixed crowd at the **Post Café** (Rue de Berne 7), near the tourist office. Other pubs popular with the city's English-speakers are **Mulligans** (14 Rue Grenus) and **Flanagan's Irish Bar** (Rue du Cheval-Blanc). Both open daily at 5pm and

keep the Guinness flowing well into the wee hours.

L'Usine (☎ 022 328 08 18; Place des Volontaires 4), a converted factory, contains an art-house cinema, experimental theatre and a venue for local and visiting bands.

Described by tourist boffins as the 'Greenwich Village' of Geneva, Carouge (south of town) is full of groovy shops, bars and clubs. One of the most popular is **Au Chat Noir** (☎ 022 343 49 98; Rue Vautier 13, Carouge; entry free-Sfr15; open 6pm-4am Mon-Thur, 6pm-5am Fri, 9pm-5am Sat-Sun), serving up funk, African beats, jazz and DJs.

Getting There & Away

Air Geneva airport is an important transport hub and has frequent connections to every major European city.

Bus International buses depart from **Place Dorcière** (☎ 022 732 02 30), off Rue des Alpes.

There are several buses a week to London (Sfr145, 17 hours) and Barcelona (Sfr100, 10 hours).

Train There are more or less hourly connections to most Swiss towns; the Zürich trip takes three hours (Sfr76), as does Interlaken (Sfr63), both via Bern.

There are regular international trains going to Paris (Sfr95 by TGV, 3½ hours; reservations essential), Hamburg (Sfr280, 10 hours), Milan (Sfr81, four hours) and Barcelona (Sfr100, nine hours). **Gare des Eaux-Vives** is the best station for Annecy and Chamonix. To get there from the Gare de Cornavin, take tram No 16.

Car & Motorcycle An autoroute bypass skirts Geneva, with major routes intersecting southwest of the city: the N1 from Lausanne joins with the E62 to Lyon (130km) and the E25 heading southeast towards Chamonix. Toll-free main roads follow the course of these motorways.

Sixt (☎ 022 732 90 90; Place de la Navigation 1) has the best daily car rental rates (from Sfr89 per day, unlimited kilometres). Its 72-hour weekend deal is Sfr159.

Boat Next to Jardin Anglais is a ticket booth for **Compagnie Générale de Navigation** (CGN; ☎ 022 312 52 23; Ⓦ www.cgn.ch),

SWITZERLAND

which operates a steamer service to all towns and major villages bordering Lake Geneva, including those in France.

Boats operate throughout the year, but the busy summer timetable runs from May to September. Destinations include Lausanne (Sfr34.80, 3½ hours) and Montreux (Sfr40.80, 4½ hours).

Eurail and Swiss passes are valid on CGN boats or there are CGN boat day passes for Sfr55 and circular excursions.

Getting Around

To/From the Airport Getting from the airport is easy with regular trains into Gare de Cornavin (Sfr5.20, six minutes). Bus No 10 (Sfr2.20) does the same 5km trip. A taxi would cost Sfr25 to Sfr35.

Public Transport The city is efficiently serviced by buses, trams, trains and boats, and ticket dispensers are found at all stops. Tickets cost Sfr1.80 (within one zone, 30 minutes) and Sfr2.20 (two zones, 60 minutes). A day pass costs Sfr6 for the city or Sfr12 for the whole canton. Tickets and passes are also valid for MGN boats that travel along the city shoreline.

Taxi Taxis are Sfr6.30 flag fall and Sfr2.90 per kilometre (Sfr3.50 per kilometre from 8.30pm to 6.30am).

Bicycle You can rent bikes from **Genev' Roule** (☎/fax 022 740 13 43; Place de Montbrillant 17; Sfr10/42 per day/week; open 8am-6pm Mon-Sat, 10am-6pm Sun), right next to the station.

If you're willing to ride a bike covered in advertising, it will only cost you Sfr7. From May to October, Genev' Roule even has bikes free of charge, available here and at Bains des Pâquis, Place du Rhône and Plaine de Plainpalais. Some ID and Sfr50 deposit is required.

Boat In addition to CGN (see under Getting There & Away earlier in this section), smaller companies operate excursions on the lake between April and October (no passes valid). Ticket offices and departures are along the Quai du Mont-Blanc and next to the Jardin Anglais. Trips range from 45 minutes (Sfr8) to two hours (Sfr20), with commentary in English.

Lake Geneva Region

LAUSANNE
pop 115,500

Capital of the Vaud canton, Lausanne is a beautiful hillside city overlooking Lake Geneva, with several distinct personalities. There's the former fishing village, Ouchy, with its summer beach-resort feel; Place St-Francois, with stylish, cobblestoned shopping streets; and Flon, a warehouse district of bars, galleries and boutiques.

On the lake south of the train station is Ouchy, while to the north is Place St François (the main hub for local transport). The **main tourist office** (☎ 021 613 73 21; e informa tion@lausanne-tourisme.ch; open 9am-6pm daily Oct-Mar, 9am-8pm Apr-Sept) is in the Ouchy metro station. The train station also has a **tourist office** (open 9am-7pm daily), as well as bicycle rental and money exchange.

The **main post office** (open 7.30am-6.30pm Mon-Fri, 8am-noon Sat) is by the train station. Across the road is **Quanta** (open 9am-midnight daily), a video-games centre offering Internet access for Sfr4/8 for 30/60 minutes.

Things to See & Do

Worth the hill climb is the glorious Gothic **Cathedrale de Lausanne** (open 7am-7pm Mon-Fri, 8am-7pm Sat-Sun Apr-Sept; closes 5.30pm Oct-Mar), built in the 12th and 13th centuries. Highlights include the stunningly detailed carved portal, vaulted ceilings and archways, and carefully restored stained-glass windows.

Musée de l'Art Brut (☎ 021 647 54 35; w www.artbrut.ch; Ave de Bergiéres 11; adult/student Sfr6/4; open 11am-1pm & 2pm-6pm Tues-Fri, 11am-6pm Sat-Sun) is a fascinating amalgam of 15,000 works of art created by untrained artists – psychiatric patients, eccentrics and incarcerated criminals. Biographies and explanations are in English.

The Olympic movement is alive and well in Lausanne, home of the IOC headquarters. Sports aficionados can immerse themselves in archive footage, interactive computers and memorabilia at information-packed **Musée Olympique** (☎ 021 621 65 11; w www.olym pic.org; Quai d'Ouchy 1; adult/student/child Sfr14/9/7; open 9am-6pm Mon-Wed & Fri-Sun, 9am-8pm Thur May-Sept; closed Mon Oct-Apr).

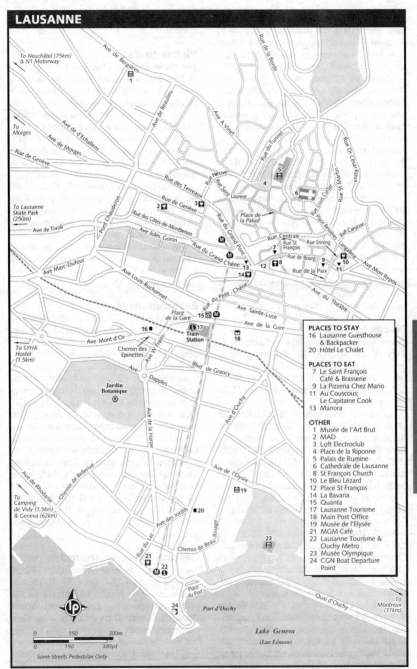

LAUSANNE

To Neuchâtel (75km)
& N1 Motorway

Ave de Bergières

To Morges

Ave de d'Echallens

Ave de Morges

Rue de Genève

To Lausanne Skate Park (250m)

Ave de Tivoli

Ave Jules Gonin

Rue des Côtes-de-Montbenon

Ave Marc-Dufour

Ave Louis-Ruchonnet

To SYHA Hostel (1.5km)

Ave Mont d'Or

Chemin des Epinettes

Blvd de Grancy

Ave du Dapples

Jardin Botanique

To Camping de Vidy (1.5km) & Geneva (62km)

Ave de Rhodanie

Chemin de Bellerive

Ave de la Harpe

Ave d'Ouchy

Ave de l'Elysée

Ave des Jordils

Rue du Lac

Chemin de Beau-Rivage

Place du Port

Port d'Ouchy

Lake Geneva
(Lac Léman)

To Montreux (31km)

Quai d'Ouchy

Rue de la Borde

Ave de Beaulieu

Ave A Vinet

Rue du Tunnel

Rue Dr César Roux

Rue des Terreaux

Rue Neuve

Rue Saint Laurent

Rue St François

Rue Louis Curtat

Place Bessières

Rue Caroline

Rue de Genève

Rue du Grand Pont

Place de la Palud

Rue Centrale

Rue St François

Rue Enning

Rue de Bourg

Rue de la Paix

Ave Mon Repos

Rue du Grand Chêne

Rue du Petit Chêne

Ave du Théâtre

Place de la Gare

Ave Sainte-Luce

Ave de la Gare

Ave W Frass

PLACES TO STAY
16 Lausanne Guesthouse
   & Backpacker
20 Hôtel Le Chalet

PLACES TO EAT
7 Le Saint François
   Café & Brasserie
9 La Pizzeria Chez Mario
11 Au Couscous;
   Le Capitaine Cook
13 Manora

OTHER
1 Musée de l'Art Brut
2 MAD
3 Loft Electroclub
4 Place de la Riponne
5 Palais de Rumine
6 Cathédrale de Lausanne
8 St François Church
10 Le Bleu Lézard
12 Place St François
14 La Bavaria
15 Quanta
17 Lausanne Tourisme
18 Main Post Office
19 Musée de l'Elysée
21 MGM Café
22 Lausanne Tourisme &
   Ouchy Metro
23 Musée Olympique
24 CGN Boat Departure
   Point

Train Station

0   150   300m
0   150   300yd

Some Streets Pedestrian Only

SWITZERLAND

For a range of museum subjects under one roof, the **Palais de Rumine** (Place de la Riponne 6; most museums open 11am-5pm Tues-Sun) is a one-stop shop covering fine arts, natural history, geology and zoology.

Musée de l'Elysée (☎ 021 316 99 11; W www.elysee.ch; Ave de L'Elysée 18; adult/student/child Sfr8/4/free; open 11am-6pm daily) is a photography museum exhibiting thought-provoking classical and contemporary works.

Windsurfing and waterskiing are popular on the lake, particularly in summer. Would-be yachties can try the **Ouchy Sailing School** (☎ 021 635 58 87; W www.ecole-de-voile.ch).

It's no surprise that inline skating has taken off in steep-streeted Lausanne. Enthusiasts should check out the **Lausanne Skate Park** (☎ 021 626 37 93; W www.fievre.ch; Sévelin 36), with large indoor and outdoor courses.

If a tipple (not a topple) is more your style, consider walking the **vineyard trails** in Lavaux, between Ouchy and Montreux. The tourist office can help with lists of vineyards, and walking and cycling maps.

Places to Stay

Lakeside camping is available at **Camping de Vidy** (☎ 021 622 50 00; e info@camping lausannevidy.ch; Chemin du Camping 3; bus No 1; adult/child/tent/car park Sfr7.70/5/8/3, bungalows 2/4 persons Sfr55.30/87.30; open year-round).

Lausanne Guesthouse & Backpacker (☎ 021 601 80 00, fax 021 601 80 01; e info@lausanne-guesthouse.ch; Chemin des Epinettes 4; dorm beds Sfr29-34, singles Sfr80-88, doubles Sfr86-98), in an elegant, tastefully renovated 1894 townhouse, is high on the hill near the train station. It offers stunning views of the lake and Alps, sparkling white bathrooms and a nonsmoking, allergen-free environment.

The **SYHA hostel** (☎ 021 626 02 22, fax 021 626 02 26; e lausanne@youthhostel.ch; Chemin du Bois-de-Vaux 36; bus No 2; dorm beds from Sfr28, singles/doubles from Sfr53/80, with bathroom Sfr78/94) provides no-frills accommodation by the lake.

Hôtel Le Chalet (☎ 021 616 52 06; Ave d'Ouchy 49; metro to Jordils stop; singles/doubles with hall showers from Sfr50/90), with a charming garden, is a welcoming old-world family hotel whose owner has an infectious joie de vivre. Swedish playwright Johan

August Strindberg lived here in the late 19th century.

Places to Eat

The **Manora** (Place St François 17; meals from Sfr10.40) is the best place in town to fill up with delicious fresh food, with particularly tempting salad and dessert buffets.

Dig into North African sausages, spiced rice and couscous at **Au Couscous** (☎ 021 22 20 17; 1st floor, Rue Enning 2; meals Sfr19-34; open 11.30am-2.30pm & 6.30pm-midnight Mon-Sun), a Tunisian and macrobiotic specialist.

La Pizzeria Chez Mario (☎ 021 323 74 01; 1st floor, Rue de Bourg 28; dishes Sfr13-21; open 11.30am-12.30am daily) serves up pasta and delicious pizzas in a graffiti-plastered den. Follow the scrawl to find the entrance.

Sweet-toothed aesthetes won't be able to resist the delights of **Le Saint François Café & Brasserie**, on Place St-François, where each cake is a work of art.

Entertainment

Le Bleu Lézard (☎ 021 321 38 35; Rue Enning 10; La Cave open 8pm-1am Tues-Thur & Sun, 8pm-3am Fri-Sat) offers snacks by day and a cave-like basement bar for concerts, jam sessions and DJs by night.

La Bavaria (☎ 021 323 39 13; Rue du Petit-Chêne 10; open 8am-1am Mon-Sat) serves up big beers in dark-wood Bavarian surrounds. Other popular watering holes are the shoulder-to-shoulder **Le Capitaine Cook** (Rue Enning 2), under Au Couscous; or the mellow **MGM Café** (Rue du Lac 14) on the waterfront.

With its large student population, Lausanne has a thriving club scene, particularly in the Flon district. Check out **MAD** (☎ 021 312 11 22; Rue de Genéve) or **Loft Electroclub** (☎ 021 311 64 00; Place Bel Air 1). Both clubs get going from 11pm and are closed Monday and Tuesday.

Getting There & Around

There are trains to/from Geneva (Sfr18.80, 50 minutes, three hourly), Bern (Sfr30, 70 minutes, one or two hourly) and Interlaken Ost (Sfr52, two hours, two hourly). For boat services, see Getting There & Away in the Geneva section earlier.

Climbing Lausanne's steep streets can be a slog, but you can save your legs by catching the metro. Many locals buzz around on mopeds.

MONTREUX

pop 22,300

Centrepiece of the 'Swiss Riviera', Montreux is an affluent lakeside town with stunning views of the French Alps, excellent lakeside walks and the ever-popular Château de Chillon.

The **train station** and **main post office** are on Ave des Alpes, with the town centre to the left (south). The **tourist office** (☎ 021 962 84 36; e tourism@montreuxtourism.ch; open 9am-12.30pm & 1.30pm-6pm Mon-Fri, 10am-2pm Sat-Sun) is in the pavilion on the lakeshore (descend the stairs or lift opposite the post office).

Things to See & Do

The **Château de Chillon** (☎ 021 966 89 10; w www.chillon.ch; adult/student/child Sfr8.50/6.50/4; open 9am-7pm daily Apr-Sept, 9.30am-5pm Mar & Oct, 10am-4pm Jan-Feb & Nov-Dec) deservedly receives more visitors than any other historical building in Switzerland. The fortress was originally constructed on the shores of Lake Geneva in the 11th century, and caught the public imagination when Lord Byron wrote *The Prisoner of Chillon* about Bonivard, a prior chained in the dungeons for almost four years in the 16th century.

You can easily spend a couple of hours touring the tower, courtyards, dungeons and staterooms containing weapons, frescoes and furniture.

The castle is a pleasant 45-minute walk along the lakefront from Montreux. It's accessible by local train (Sfr2.60; Veytaux-Chillon stop) or bus No 1 (Sfr2.60; Veytaux stop).

Montreux's idyllic location has attracted writers, musicians and artists for hundreds of years. To learn more about such icons as Noel Coward, Vladimir Nabokov and Charlie Chaplin and their local connections, ask for the **Hemingway Trail** walking tour map from the tourist office. Or take the **Poet's Ramble** along the shoreline from Vevey to Montreux, featuring a series of 'speaking benches' which quote famous texts in several languages.

Montreux also has many famous music links. You may already know it as the subject of Deep Purple's famous *Smoke on the Water*. Queen's Freddy Mercury was a regular visitor, recording most of his music here (see the statue on the waterfront). And then there's the annual **Jazz Festival** (☎ 021 963 82 82; w www.montreuxjazz.com), which transforms the town every July. Visit the website for a full programme.

Places to Stay

The modern **SYHA hostel** (☎ 021 963 49 34, fax 021 963 27 29; Passage de l'Auberge 8, Territet; bus No 1; dorm beds Sfr30, doubles without/with bathroom Sfr76/84; open mid-Feb–mid-Nov), a 30-minute walk from the centre, is on the waterfront just 15 minutes from Château de Chillon.

Hotel Wilhelm (☎ 021 963 14 31, fax 021 963 32 85; e hotel.wilhelm@span.ch; Rue de Marché 13-15; singles/doubles Sfr60/100, with bathroom Sfr70/120) is a traditional family-run hotel a few paces from the train station.

Hostellerie du Lac (☎ 021 963 32 71, fax 021 963 18 35; Rue du Quai 12; singles Sfr50-140, doubles Sfr150; open Mar-Nov) has a faded grandeur and a prime lakeside position. Rooms vary dramatically in price, style and facilities – some even have lakeside balconies.

If you can't secure a lakeside spot, try **Hotel Elite** (☎ 021 966 03 03; Ave du Casino 25; singles/doubles with breakfast from Sfr70/130), a small, quiet alternative with friendly staff and spacious renovated rooms.

Places to Eat

Paradise (☎ 021 963 19 35; Grand-Rue 58; meals from Sfr8; open 7am-1am Tues-Thur, 7am-2am Fri-Sat) has a sprawling salad buffet with 40 dishes (Sfr2.80 per 100g) and flavoursome kebabs and souvlakis.

Delicious buttery perch fillets are a highlight at the **Hostellerie du Lac restaurant** (mains Sfr31; open 11.30am-9.30pm Wed-Mon). Its large, open terrace which overlooks the lakeside promenade is just perfect for people-watching.

For pizza and pasta, try the wood-panelled **Brasserie des Alpes** (☎ 021 963 21 20; Ave des Alpes 23; pizzas Sfr14-22). Coffee lovers can get a caffeine fix at **Mokaccino**, a busy café in the Forum shopping centre on Ave du Casino. In the same centre is **piMi**, the fast-food section of Migros supermarket, with good-value croissants and baguettes.

Getting There & Away

There are trains to/from Geneva (Sfr26, 70 minutes, hourly) and Lausanne (Sfr9.80, 25

SWITZERLAND

minutes, three hourly). Make the scenic journey to Interlaken via the **GoldenPass Panoramic**, with changeovers at Zweisimmen and Spiez (Sfr54, rail passes valid, three hours).

The track winds its way up the hill for excellent views over Lake Geneva. For boat services, see the Geneva Getting There & Away section earlier.

VEVEY
pop 15,400
Another popular pitstop on the Swiss Riviera is Vevey, a few kilometres west of Montreux. Its sprawling square on the waterfront becomes a bustling **marketplace** on summer Saturdays, with traditionally dressed merchants selling local handicrafts and wines.

For overnight stays, try the independent hostel **Yoba Riviera Lodge** (☎ 021 923 80 40, fax 021 923 80 41; e info@rivieralodge .ch; Place du Marché; dorm beds Sfr24-29, doubles Sfr80), in a 19th-century townhouse near the waterfront.

Some of the best budget eating in town is at the **Manora**, opposite the train station, or the **Migros restaurant** on Rue de Lausanne.

Sip on a coffee or beer at **Charly's Bar** (☎ 021 921 50 06; Rue du Lac 45; open 8am-1.30am Mon-Thur, 8am-2.30am Fri-Sat, 10am-midnight Sun), which is a busy glass-fronted place with fantastic views.

VAUD ALPS
To get off the beaten track and enjoy the Alpine experience, consider staying in quiet, untouristed **Gryon** (1130m), southeast of Montreux. It's close to the ski fields of Villars and 30 minutes by train from Bex (on the Lausanne–Sion rail route).

The popular **Swiss Alp Retreat** (☎ 024 498 33 21, fax 024 498 35 31; e info@gryon.com; dorm beds/doubles from Sfr18/50) is a homely wooden chalet with kitchen, sundeck and log fire. Phone ahead for check-in.

Another tranquil Alpine spot, **Leysin** attracts skiers, snowboarders, hikers and meditators. It is accessible from Aigle on the Lausanne-Sion route.

For an overnight stay, head to the **Hiking Sheep** (☎/fax 024 494 35 35; e hiking sheep@leysin.net; dorm beds/doubles from Sfr23/60). This 19th-century guesthouse provides breathtaking views, combined with a pine-forested back yard and a friendly laid-back atmosphere.

Valais

The dramatic Alpine scenery of Valais (Wallis in German) once made it one of the most inaccessible regions of Switzerland. Today, the mountains and valleys have been opened up for keen skiers and hikers by an efficient network of roads, railways and cable cars. It's an area of extraordinary natural beauty and, naturally enough, each impressive panorama has spawned its own resort.

Valais villages are also well known for the bizarre cow fights waged to determine the best beast to lead the herd to summer pastures. Far from a blood sport, the bovine battles merely leave the beasts exhausted. The unfortunate winner is rewarded with an enormous bell to lug around. Fights are held on selected Sundays from late March to October; for an up-to-date programme, see the Valais Tourism website (w www.matterhornstate.com).

SION
pop 27,500
With two ancient fortifications that dominate the town, the capital of the Lower Valais is worth a stop en route from Montreux to Zermatt. **Château de Tourbillon** and the 11th-century church **Basilique de Valère** sit atop twin hills and offer excellent views of the Rhône Valley below. Several Valais regional museums are also based in the town. Overnighters will find basic four-bed dorms at the modern **SYHA hostel** (☎ 027 323 74 70, fax 027 323 74 38; Rue de l'Industrie 2; dorm beds from Sfr28), behind the station.

ZERMATT
pop 5340
This skiing, mountaineering and hiking mecca bathes in the reflected glory of the most famous peak in the Alps, the Matterhorn (4478m). The town is small and easy to navigate, and it's car-free except for tiny electric taxis and vans that whisk guests around the streets. The main street is Bahnhofstrasse, but street names are rarely used.

Zermatt Tourismus (☎/fax 027 966 81 00; e zermatt@wallis.ch; open 8.30am-noon & 1.30pm-6pm Mon-Fri, 8.30am-noon Sat) is beside the train station. During high season it's also open Saturday afternoon and Sunday. Next door is **Zermatt Tour**, a travel agency that also changes money.

Alpin Center (☎ 027 966 24 60; open 8am-11.30am & 4pm-6.30pm daily), on Bahnhofstrasse near the post office, is a one-stop shop for all adventure needs, whether it be ski passes, heli-skiing, mountain guiding or snowboard lessons.

Activities

Zermatt is arguably the country's best ski resort, with many demanding slopes to test the experienced skier and panoramic views at every turn (beginners have fewer possibilities). February to April is peak time, but high-altitude ski fields make **skiing** possible right through summer. Stunning vistas of Monte Rosa and the Matterhorn can be seen from the network of cable cars and gondolas.

The cog-wheel railway to **Gornergrat** (3090m; Sfr63 return; departures every 20 minutes) is a particular highlight. Topped by the highest cable station in Europe (3820m), the Klein Matterhorn provides access to summer skiing slopes, as well as the ski route down to Cervinia in Italy (don't forget your passport). A day pass for all ski lifts, excluding Cervinia, costs Sfr64. Ski shops open daily for rental – for one day, hire prices are Sfr28 for skis and stocks and Sfr15 for boots.

Of course, in summer, Zermatt becomes a hub for **hikers**, attracted by 400km of trails through high-Alpine scenery with views of Europe's highest mountains.

A walk in the **cemetery** is a sobering experience for any would-be mountaineers, with many monuments and gravestones commemorating deaths on Monte Rosa and the Matterhorn. The **Hinter Dorf**, just north of the church, is another interesting part of town. Here, the touristy chalets make way for traditional Valais wooden huts.

Places to Stay & Eat

Tourism is big business in Zermatt, and holiday chalets and apartments dominate the town. The tourist office can help with a full list. Be warned that many hotels and restaurants close between seasons.

The **SYHA hostel** (☎ 027 967 23 20, fax 027 967 53 06; e zermatt@youthhostel.ch; dorm beds with half-board from Sfr48; closed mid-Apr–June), a 20-minute walk from the station, is a five-storey chalet high on the hill with excellent views of the Matterhorn.

Matterhorn Hostel (☎ 027 968 19 19, fax 027 968 1915; w www.matterhornhostel .com; Schluhmattstrasse 32; dorm beds Sfr29, doubles Sfr78; open year-round), a short walk from the station, is the independent option, with Internet access (Sfr2 for 10 minutes), its own restaurant and après-ski bar.

Directly opposite the station is **Hotel Bahnhof** (☎ 027 967 24 06, fax 027 967 72 16; e welcome@hotelbahnhof.com; dorm beds Sfr30, singles/doubles Sfr56/86, with shower Sfr68/96), with an impressive industrial-size kitchen, ski storage room in the basement, large dorms, and twins with balconies facing the Matterhorn.

Squeezed between old mountain huts on cobblestoned streets, **Hotel Gabelhorn** (☎ 027 967 22 35; singles/doubles from Sfr40/80; closed May, Jun & Oct), in the Hinter Dorf area, is a traditional family-run pension. It's full of character but a little cramped.

A favourite hang-out for resort workers is the **Brown Cow** (Hotel de la Poste; ☎ 027 967 19 32; snacks Sfr6-14; open 9am-1.30am daily), with great music, hearty food and cowhide decor. Don't miss the monster vegie burger with chunky chips for Sfr10.50. Within the same complex underneath the Hotel de la Poste is the **Old Spaghetti Factory** (open 7pm-11pm daily) and **Broken's Pizza Factory** (open 7pm-1.30am).

For Valais specialities, there's **Walliserkanne** (☎ 027 966 46 10; Bahnhofstrasse; meals from Sfr15), by the post office. Or fill up with raclette and rosti at **Restaurant Weisshorn** (meals Sfr12.50-30) and **Café du Pont** (meals Sfr11-22), which sit side by side beyond the church on Bahnhofstrasse.

Head to the **North Wall Bar** (☎ 027 967 28 63; open 6.30pm-12.30am daily) for cheap beer, inspirational ski videos and 'the best pizza in town' (from Sfr12). Or catch the latest Hollywood blockbuster at **Vernissage Cultural Centre** (☎ 027 967 66 36; Hofmattstrasse 4; open 5pm-2am), with a cinema, bar and nightclub just off the main drag.

Getting There & Away

Hourly trains depart from Brig, calling at Visp en route, a steep, scenic journey (Sfr35/69 one way/return, 80 minutes). Swiss Passes are valid and Inter-Rail passes give 50% off for those under 26. The only way out is to backtrack, but if you're going to Saas Fee you can divert there from Stalden-Saas. The popular scenic *Glacier Express* travels to/from St Moritz from Zermatt (see the St

Moritz Getting There & Away section later in this chapter for details).

As Zermatt is car-free, you need to park cars at Täsch (Sfr4.50 to Sfr12 per day) and take the train from there (Sfr7.40). Parking is free near Visp station if you take the Zermatt train.

OTHER RESORTS

Saas Fee, the self-styled 'Pearl of the Alps', is in the valley adjoining its more famous neighbour, Zermatt, ringed by 4000m peaks. It has summer skiing and the highest metro in the world to **Mittelallalin** (3500m), where there's an *ice pavilion* (admission Sfr7) and fabulous views. Summer hikers have access to 280km of marked **trails**. The **tourist office** (☎ 027 958 18 68; e to@saas-fee.ch), opposite the bus station, can help with hiking maps and accommodation options. Car-free Saas Fee cannot be reached by train. Buses depart from Brig via Visp (Sfr17.20, one hour, hourly). Travelling to/from Zermatt, you must transfer at Stalden-Saas. There are car parks at the village entrance.

Other popular ski resorts include **Verbier**, in west Valais, with 400km of ski runs (ski passes Sfr51 per day); and the lesser-known **Leukerbad**, west of Brig (Sfr43 per day), which also boasts Europe's largest alpine **thermal baths**.

Ticino

South of the Alps, Ticino (Tessin in German) enjoys a Mediterranean climate and an unmistakable Italian flavour. Indeed, it belonged to Italy until the Swiss Confederation seized it in 1512.

Cuisine, architecture and plantlife mirrors that of its southern neighbour, and Italian is the official language of the canton. Many people also speak French and German, but English is less widely spoken.

The region also boasts spectacular Swiss scenery, with dramatic gorges in the north and languid, lakeside towns in the south. Free open-air music festivals include Bellinzona's Piazza Blues (late June), and Lugano's Estival Jazz (early July) and Blues to Bop Festival (late August).

BELLINZONA
pop 16,700

Ticino's capital is a city of castles situated in a valley at the southern side of the San Bernardino and St Gotthard Alpine Passes. World Heritage-listed in 2000, Bellinzona's imposing battlements and towers at one time played a significant role in fortifiying the region and still dominate the town today. You can roam the ramparts of the two larger castles, **Castelgrande** or **Castello di Montebello**, and visit the **museums** (admission Sfr4 each; open Tues-Sun), however, there's limited English translation. The smallest castle, set high on the hill, is **Castello di Sasso Corbaro**.

The **tourist office** (☎ 091 825 21 31, fax 825 38 17; e bellinzona.turismo@bluewin.ch; Viale Stazione 18; open 9am-6.30pm Mon-Fri, 9am-noon Sat), in the post office, can provide information on Bellinzona and the whole canton.

Places to Stay & Eat

The **SYHA hostel** (☎ 091 825 15 22; e bellinzona@youthhostel.ch; Via Nocca 4; dorm beds from Sfr35, singles/doubles Sfr50/90) shares the grand old Villa Montebello with a private school and a catering company (which supplies the inclusive buffet breakfast). At the foot of the Montebello Castle, it's a 10-minute walk from the station.

For budget rooms closer to the station, there's **Garni Moderno** (☎/fax 091 825 13 76; Viale Stazione 17b; singles/doubles Sfr55/90, doubles with bath Sfr120), part of Caffé della Posta (closed Sunday).

Ristorante Corona (☎ 091 825 28 44; Via Camminata 5; pizzas Sfr11-17; open 7am-midnight Mon, 7am-1am Tues-Sat) serves enormous thin-crust pizzas in the friendly front pub area. For fancier fare, there's a formal restaurant behind.

As usual, the best budget eats can be found in **Manora** (Manor department store, Viale Stazione); there's also a good self-service restaurant at the **Coop** (Via H Guisan).

Getting There & Away

Bellinzona is on the train route connecting Locarno (Sfr7.20, 25 minutes) and Lugano (Sfr11.40, 30 minutes).

It's also on the Zürich-Milan route. Postbuses head northeast to Chur; please note that you will need to reserve your postbus seat the day before on ☎ 091 825 77 55, or at the train station.

There is a scenic cycling track along the Ticino River to Lake Maggiore and Locarno.

LOCARNO
pop 14,600

Locarno, at the northern end of Lake Maggiore, has a quaint old town with Italianate townhouses, piazzas and arcades, and a laid-back summer-resort atmosphere.

Piazza Grande is the centre of town and the location of the **main post office**. In the nearby casino complex is the **tourist office** (☎ 091 751 03 33, fax 091 751 90 70; e locarno@ticino.com; open 9am-6pm Mon-Fri, 10am-5pm Sat, 10am-noon & 1pm-3pm Sun). It stocks brochures on many parts of Switzerland.

A five-minute walk east is the train station, where there's an **Aperto supermarket**, **money exchange** and **bike rental**. You can gulp down shots and smoke Cuban cigars while checking your email at the Latino-style **Pardo Bar** (☎ 091 752 21 23; Via della Motta 3; Sfr4 for 20min; open 11am-1am Mon-Sat, 4pm-1am Sun). On Piazza Imbarcadero, near the waterfront, the **Visitors Center** offers Internet access at the **Cyberbox** and charges Sfr2/5 for 10/30 minutes.

Things to See & Do

Don't miss the formidable **Madonna del Sasso**, up on the hill with panoramic views of the lake and town. The sanctuary was built after the Virgin Mary appeared in a vision in 1480. It features a church with 15th-century paintings, a small museum and several distinctive statues. There is a funicular from the town centre, but the 20-minute climb is not demanding (take Via al Sasso off Via Cappuccini) and you pass some shrines on the way.

In the old town, there are a couple of churches worth visiting, including the 17th-century **Chiesa Nuova** (Via Cittadella), with an ornate ceiling and frolicking angels.

Locarno has more hours of sunshine than anywhere else in Switzerland, perfect for strolls and bike rides around the lake. **Giardini Jean Arp** is a small lakeside park off Lungolago Motta, where sculptures by the surrealist artist are scattered among palm trees and springtime tulips.

In August, over 150,000 film buffs hit town for the **Locarno International Film Festival**, with a huge open-air screen in Piazza Grande. For more information see w www.pardo.ch.

Places to Stay

Delta Camping (☎ 091 751 60 81; camp sites low/high season Sfr21/47, plus Sfr11/18 per person; open Mar-Oct) is family friendly but pricey. There are plenty of cheaper options on Lake Maggiore outside Locarno; ask the tourist office for the Camping Ticino brochure.

The **SYHA hostel** (☎ 091 756 15 00, fax 091 756 15 01; e locarno@youthhostel.ch; Via Varenna 18; dorm beds/doubles from Sfr32/72), 500m west of Piazza Grande, is in the charmless Palagiovani (Palace of Youth), which also houses a radio station, music school and youth bureau.

The staff are all smiles at **Pensione Cittá Vecchia** (☎/fax 091 751 45 54; e cittavecchia@datacomm.ch; Via Toretta 13; dorm beds Sfr28-35, singles/doubles Sfr37/74; open Mar-Nov), a nonsmoking hostel with basic dorms (breakfast included). It's uphill from Piazza Grande via a lane next to the Manor department store.

Convenient to the station and lake is clean, clinical **Garni Montaldi** (☎ 091 743 02 22, fax 091 743 54 06; Piazza Stazione; singles/doubles Sfr58/110, with shower from Sfr60/120). Rates include continental breakfast; ask for deals out of season. The reception is also here for **Stazione** (singles/doubles from Sfr44/88; open Apr-Oct), an older building to the rear with spacious, rudimentary rooms.

Places to Eat

Manora (Via Stazione 1; meals from Sfr6.90; open 7.30am-9pm Mon-Sat, 8am-9pm Sun), by the train station, has excellent self-service hot meals and salad plates.

Lungolago (Lungolago Motta; pizza from Sfr12.50; open 7am-1am daily), a popular haunt for snackers and beer-guzzlers, is perfect for steamy summer evenings. The more sophisticated **Hotel Ristorante Zurigo** (☎ 091 743 16 17; Via Verbano 9; mains Sfr16-37; open 7am-11pm daily) has moreish Mediterranean meals and a lakeside outlook.

In the backblocks, **Ristorante Cittadella** (☎ 091 751 58 85; Via Cittadella 18; dishes Sfr35-50; open 8am-2pm & 5.30pm-midnight daily) has a ground-floor trattoria with pizzas and pastas, and an elegant upstairs eatery serving seafood.

On Piazza Grande there's a **Coop supermarket** and a **Migros De Gustibus** snack bar opposite.

Getting There & Away

The St Gotthard Pass provides the road link (N2) to central Switzerland. There are trains

SWITZERLAND

every one to two hours from Brig, passing through Italy en route (Sfr50, 2½ hours). You change trains at Domodóssola across the border, so take your passport.

One-day travel passes for boats on Lake Maggiore cost Sfr12 to Sfr21, depending on the coverage. For more information, contact **Navigazione Lago Maggiore** (*NLM;* ☎ *091 751 18 65)*. There is a regular boat and hydrofoil service from Italy (except in winter).

LUGANO
pop 25,900

Switzerland's southernmost tourist town is a sophisticated slice of Italian life, with colourful markets, upmarket shops, pedestrian-only piazzas and lakeside parks. Resting on the shore of Lake Lugano with Montes San Salvatore and Bré rising on either side, it's also a great base for lake trips, water sports and hillside hikes.

The train station has **money exchange, bike rental** and an **Aperto supermarket**, all open daily. The old town is a 10-minute walk down the hill to the east. On the lake side of the Municipio building is the **tourist office** (☎ *091 913 32 32, fax 091 922 76 53;* **e** *info@lugano -tourism.ch; Riva Albertolli; open 9am-6.30pm Mon-Fri, 9am-12.30pm & 1.30pm-5pm Sat, 10am-3pm Sun; closed weekends in winter)*. The **main post office** *(Via della Posta 7)* is in the centre of the old town. There are four stand-up Internet terminals (Sfr5 for 30 minutes) on the 3rd floor of the **Manor** department store *(Piazza Dante)*.

Things to See & Do

Stroll through the winding alleyways of Lugano's old town and go window-shopping along the stylish arcade-lined **Via Nassa** (street of fishing nets).

At the end, pop into the **Santa Maria degli Angioli Church** *(Piazza Luini)*, featuring a vivid 1529 fresco of the *Crucifixion* by Bernardino Luini.

There are many worthwhile museums in the waterfront town and the surrounding region. Art lovers can get their fix of 19th- and 20th-century works at the **Museo Cantonale d'Arte** (☎ *091 910 47 80;* **w** *www.museo-can tonale-arte.ch; Via Canova 10; adult/student Sfr7/5; open 2pm-5pm Tues, 10am-5pm Wed-Sun)*, with examples by Renoir, Hodler and Klee. The café set can pay homage at the **Coffee Museum** in Balerna or the **Alpenrose**

Chocolate Museum in Caslano. Ask the tourist office for a full museum list.

Waterbabies will love the **Lido** *(adult/child Sfr6/4; open 9am-7pm May-Sept)*, east of the Cassarate River, with a swimming pool and sandy beaches.

Take a **boat trip** to one of the many photogenic villages hugging the shoreline of Lake Lugano. One of the most popular is car-free **Gandria**, a tiny hillside village with historic homes and shops and narrow winding alleyways right down to the water. If you hit town at mealtimes you can tuck into a traditional Ticinese dish in one of the many **grotti**. You can also see how the smugglers plied their trade at the **Swiss Customs Museum** (☎ *091 910 48 11; admission free; open 1.30pm-5.30pm daily Apr–mid-Oct)*, across the water.

Swissminiatur *(adult/child Sfr12/7, including boat trip Sfr27.80/14.40; open 9am-6pm daily mid-Mar–Oct)*, in Melide, is a kitschy display of 1:25 scale models of national attractions. You can get there by bus, train or boat.

There are excellent hikes and views from **Monte San Salvatore** and **Monte Bré**. The **funicular** *(one-way/return ticket Sfr12/18)* from Paradiso up Monte San Salvatore operates from mid-March to mid-November. To ascend Monte Bré, take the year-round **funicular** *(one-way/return Sfr13/19)* from Cassarate. The tourist office can help with hiking information.

If you've got some spare francs, you can pick up bargain Prada and Versace at **Foxtown** *(Via A Maspoli;* **w** *www.foxtown.ch; open 11am-7pm daily)*, an enormous, discount, factory-outlet complex 15km south of Lugano.

Places to Stay

An excellent budget option close to the station is **Hotel Montarina** (☎ *091 966 72 72, fax 091 966 00 17;* **e** *info@montarina.ch; Via Montarina 1; dorm beds Sfr25, sheets Sfr4 for whole stay, singles/doubles Sfr70/100, with bathroom Sfr80/120; open mid-Mar–Oct)*. This lovingly renovated 19th-century villa is heaven in summer, with a swimming pool, large dorms and a garden with palm trees.

The **SYHA hostel** (☎ *091 966 27 28, fax 091 968 23 63; Via Cantonale 13; dorm beds/doubles Sfr31/72; open mid-Mar–Nov)* is a hard 20-minute walk uphill from the train station (signposted), or take bus No 5 to Crocifisso. Breakfast is included and you can cool off in the swimming pool.

Closer to the old town is **Albergo Ristorante Pestalozzi** (☎ 091 921 46 46, fax 091 922 20 45; e pestalo@bluewin.ch; Piazza Indipendenza 9; singles/doubles Sfr60/100, with bathroom from Sfr92/144), an inviting Art Nouveau hotel with a variety of renovated rooms.

In Paradiso, near the foot of Monte San Salvatore, there's the homely **Hotel Dischma** (☎ 091 994 21 31, fax 091 994 15 03; e dischma@swissonline.ch; Vicolo Geretta 6; bus No 1; singles/doubles from Sfr60/106).

Places to Eat
Head to the pedestrian-only **piazzas** to tempt the tastebuds, with panini (Sfr5) and gelati (Sfr3) from street stalls, or larger meals in the pizzerias and cafés spilling on to the streets.

You can produce your own pizzettes at the sprawling **Manora** (meals from Sfr8.90; open 7.30am-10pm Mon-Sat & 10am-10pm Sun), with a wide range of self-service food. It's up the stairs on the northern side of Piazza Cioccaro.

On the southern side is **Sayonara** (☎ 091 922 01 70; Via Soave 10; pasta from Sfr10, pizza Sfr15.50-20.50; open 6.30am-midnight daily), with delicious Italian cuisine and a good wine list (try the Ticinese white Merlot).

Panino Gusto (☎ 091 922 51 51; Via Motta 7a; panini Sfr9-19; open 11am-7pm Mon-Wed, 11am-midnight Thur-Sat) offers panini with smoked meats, salmon and cheeses.

Ristorante Pestalozzi (see Places to Stay earlier in the Lugano section; meals from Sfr11; open 11am-9.30pm daily) has a changing daily menu with plenty of vegie options in a large alcohol-free dining room.

The critically acclaimed **La Tinéra** (Via dei Gorini; dishes Sfr11-27; open 8.30am-3pm & 5.30pm-11pm Mon-Sat), off Piazza della Riforma, is a tiny cellar restaurant serving local specialities to a jam-packed crowd.

For drinks, pitta bread and tapas amid tropical decor, try **Ethnic** (Quartiere Maghetti; tapas Sfr4-8, meals Sfr8-18; open 6pm-midnight Mon-Sat). Self-caterers can stock up at the large **Migros** (Via Pretorio) opposite Via Emilio Bossi.

Getting There & Away
Lugano is on the same road and rail route as Bellinzona. Two postbuses run to St Moritz daily in summer, cut back to one during winter (and only on Friday, Saturday and Sunday

during some weeks). It costs Sfr50 (plus Sfr12 reservation fee) and takes 4½ hours. Reserve your seat the day before at the **bus station** or the **train information office**, or by phoning ☎ 091 807 85 20. Buses leave from the bus station on Via Serafino Balestra, though the St Moritz bus also calls at the train station. A three-/seven-day regional holiday pass costs Sfr72/92 and is valid for all regional public transport, including funiculars and boats on Lake Lugano.

Graubünden

Graubünden (Grisons, Grigioni, Grishun) is the largest Swiss canton and it has some of the most developed winter sports centres in the world, including Arosa, Davos, Klosters, Flims and, of course, famous St Moritz. Away from the international resorts, Graubünden is a relatively unspoiled region of rural villages, alpine lakes and hill-top castles. Dazzling scenery and outdoor pursuits are the region's main attractions, and tourism is one of its biggest money-spinners. In the north, the locals speak German, in the south Italian, and in between mostly Romansch.

CHUR
pop 31,800
Chur, the canton's capital and largest town, is also one of the oldest settlements in Switzerland, tracing its history back some 3000 years. Today it serves as a gateway for the region. For a town map and accommodation options see the **tourist office** (☎ 081 252 18 18; Grabenstrasse 5; open 1.30pm-6pm Mon, 8.30am-noon & 1.30pm-6pm Tues-Fri, 9am-noon Sat). For information on the canton, try the **regional tourist office** (☎ 081 254 24 24; e contact@graubuenden.ch; Alexanderstrasse 24; open 8am-6pm Mon-Fri).

The old town features 16th-century buildings, fountains and alleyways. Worth a visit are the 1491 **Church of St Martin**, with stained-glass windows created by Augusto Giacometti, and the imposing **cathedral**, dating from 1150. The **Kunstmuseum** (Postplatz; adult/student Sfr10/7; open 10am-noon & 2pm-5pm Tues-Wed & Fri-Sun, 10am-noon & 2pm-8pm Thur) has a collection of artwork by the three Giacomettis (Alberto, Augusto and Giovanni), and exhibits by local sci-fi artist HR Giger (of Alien fame).

Chur is only 90 minutes by fast train from Zürich (Sfr35) and two hours from St Moritz (Sfr38). It's on the *Glacier Express* route (see the St Moritz Getting There & Away section later), and there are also rail connections to Davos, Klosters, Arosa, and Sargans (Sfr9.80, 25 minutes), the station for Liechtenstein.

ST MORITZ
pop 5600
St Moritz has built its reputation as the playground of the international jet set for more than a century, but the curative properties of its waters have been known for 3000 years. The plush main town, St Moritz Dorf, lounges on the slopes overlooking Lake St Moritz. In winter, superb skifields are the main drawcard; in summer, visitors come for the hiking, windsurfing, 'kitesurfing' and inline skating.

Orientation & Information
Hilly St Moritz Dorf is above the train station, with luxury hotels, restaurants and shops. To the southwest, 2km around the lake, lies the more downmarket St Moritz Bad; buses run between the two. St Moritz is seasonal and becomes a ghost town during November and late April to early June.

The **train station** near the lake rents out bikes in summer and changes money from 6.50am to 8.10pm daily. Up the hill on Via Serlas is the **post office** and five minutes further on is the **tourist office** (☎ 081 837 33 33, fax 081 837 33 77; e information@stmoritz.ch; Via Maistra 12; open 9am-6pm Mon-Sat, 4pm-6pm Sun high season; 9am-noon & 2pm-6pm Mon-Fri, 9am-noon Sat low season), with friendly, helpful staff.

You can check your favourite websites at **Bobby's Pub** (☎ 081 834 42 83; Via dal Bagn 50a; open 9am-1.30am Mon-Sat, 2pm-1.30am Sun) which charges Sfr2 for 10 minutes of Net access.

Activities
There are 350km of **downhill runs** around St Moritz, although the choice for beginners is limited. A one-day ski pass costs Sfr63, and ski and boot rental is about Sfr43 per day. There are also 160km of **cross-country trails** (equipment rental Sfr20) and 120km of marked **hiking paths**.

Sporting activities abound both in winter and summer. You can try golf (including on the frozen lake in winter), tennis, inline skating,

fishing, horse riding, sailing, windsurfing and river rafting, to mention a few. The tourist office has a list of prices and contacts. People-watching in St Moritz is another great sport and it's fun and free. If a touch of rest and recovery is on the agenda, try a health treatment in the **spa** (w www.stmoritz-spa.ch).

Places to Stay & Eat
The **Olympiaschanze camping ground** (☎ 081 833 40 90; camp site per adult/tent Sfr8/6.30; open late May-late Sept) is 1km southwest of St Moritz Bad.

Naturally, cheaper digs are found in the 'Bad' part of town. Backing on to forest and the cross-country ski course is the **SYHA hostel** (☎ 081 833 39 69, fax 081 833 80 46; Via Surpunt 60; w www.youthhostel.ch/st.moritz; dorm beds with half-board Sfr45.50, doubles without/with bathroom Sfr117/140), a large, modern, ochre-coloured centre with excellent facilities. There's mountain bike rental, compulsory half-board, a ski room and Internet access (Sfr4 for 15 minutes).

If the hostel is full, head next door to the **Hotel Stille** (☎ 081 833 69 48, fax 081 833 07 08; e hotel.stille@bluewin.ch; singles/twins Sfr57/114 in summer, Sfr72/144 in winter), which attracts a young, sporty crowd. Breakfast is included and dinner is available in winter for Sfr19.

You'll get basic budget rooms in a convenient lakeside location at **Bellaval** (☎ 081 833 32 45, fax 081 833 04 06; e hotel-bellaval@ bluewin.ch; Via Grevas 55; singles/doubles from Sfr55/110, with bathroom from Sfr80/ 140). Prices include breakfast.

The pretty, peach-coloured **Hotel Languard Garni** (☎ 081 833 31 37, fax 081 833 45 46; e languard@bluewin.ch; Via Veglia 14; singles/doubles from Sfr105/190) is a three-star, family hotel in St Moritz Dorf overlooking the lake. It's worth paying Sfr20 extra for a room with a view.

Heading into St Moritz Bad, there's a clutch of good-value pizzerias and Italian restaurants, including **La Fontana** (☎ 081 833 12 66; Via dal Bagn 16; mains Sfr12-28; open 9am-10.30pm Mon-Sat), a cosy rustic restaurant with candles; and **Pizzeria La Botte** (☎ 081 833 39 88; Via dal Bagn 15; mains Sfr16-24; open 11am-2pm & 4pm-1am daily), with rich, buttery Italian dishes. Next to La Fontana, there also is a **Coop supermarket** for self-caterers.

Getting There & Away

The *Glacier Express* plies one of Switzerland's most famous scenic train routes, connecting St Moritz to Zermatt via the 2033m Oberalp Pass. It takes 7½ hours to cover 290km and cross 291 bridges (Sfr138, plus a Sfr9 to Sfr12 supplement depending on the season). Novelty drink glasses in the dining car have sloping bases to compensate for the hills – but remember to keep turning them around!

Two postbuses run to/from Lugano daily in summer – in winter, there's a daily bus on Friday, Saturday and Sunday. You must reserve a seat the day before on ☎ 081 837 67 64.

Nine daily trains travel south to Tirano in Italy with connections to Milan.

AROUND ST MORITZ

The Engadine Valley, running northeast and southwest of St Moritz, has an interesting combination of plush resorts and unspoilt villages. In **Guarda** and **Zuoz** you can see homes displaying traditional **sgraffito** designs (patterns scratched on wall plaster) that are characteristic of the Engadine.

In the **Davos/Klosters** region there are 320km of ski runs, mostly medium to difficult, including one of the hardest runs in the world, the **Gotschnawang**. **Arosa** is another top-notch resort, easily reached by train from Chur. Most other ski resorts in Graubünden have easy to medium runs. Ski passes for the top resorts average Sfr50 for one day (cheaper by the week); passes for smaller places cost less.

The annual Engadine Cross-country Ski Marathon between Maloja and Zuoz is on the second Sunday in March. The route crosses ice-covered lakes and passes by St Moritz Lake. Trains and buses run regularly along the valley.

Flora and fauna abound in the 169 sq km **Swiss National Park** (☎ 081-856 13 78; w www.nationalpark.ch; open June-Oct). The park information centre near Zernez has details of hiking routes and the best places to see particular animals. Call or check the website.

Zürich

pop 339,300

Switzerland's most populous city offers an ambience of affluence, style and culture. Banks and art galleries greet you at every turn in a marriage of finance and aesthetics, and at night, the pinstripe brigade yields the streets to bar-hoppers and clubbers.

Zürich started life as a Roman customs post and graduated to the status of free city under the Holy Roman Empire in 1218. The city's reputation as a cultural and intellectual centre began after it joined the Swiss Confederation in 1351, and Huldrych Zwingli brought the Reformation doctrines to the city in the early 16th century. Zürich's status as a business centre was boosted by the energetic administrator and railway magnate Alfred Escher in the 19th century. WWI saw Switzerland become temporary home to luminaries such as Lenin, Trotsky and James Joyce; and Tristan Tzara and Hans Arp, key figures in the founding of Dadaism in 1916 at Cabaret Voltaire.

Orientation

Zürich is at the northern end of Lake Zürich (Zürichsee), with the city centre split by the Limmat River. Like many Swiss cities, it is compact and easy to navigate. The main train station (Hauptbahnhof) is on the western bank of the river, close to the old centre.

Information

Tourist Offices The **Zürich Tourist Service** (☎ 01 215 40 00, fax 01 215 40 44; e *infor mation@zurichtourism.ch; open 8.30am-8.30pm Mon-Fri, 8.30am-6.30pm Sat & Sun Nov-Mar, 8.30am-7pm Mon-Fri, 9am-6.30pm Sat & Sun Apr-Oct)* is in the train station's main hall. There's a free city map, but Sfr3 gets you a more detailed map with a street index.

Money There's no shortage of choice when exchanging money in this banking city. Banks are open 8.15am to 4.30pm Monday to Friday (until 6pm Thursday). There is an **exchange office** *(open 6.30am-10pm daily)* in the main train station.

Post & Communications The main post office is **Sihlpost** (☎ 01 296 21 11; *Kasernenstrasse 95-97; open 7.30am-8pm Mon-Fri, 8am-4pm Sat)*, but there's a more convenient post office at the main train station.

Several tables of terminals vie for space with video games in **Quanta Virtual Fun Space** *(cnr Niederdorfstrasse & Mühlegasse)* where Net access costs Sfr10 an hour.

Stars Bistro *(open 11am-11pm Mon-Sat, 10am-11pm Sun)*, in the main hall of the train

ZÜRICH

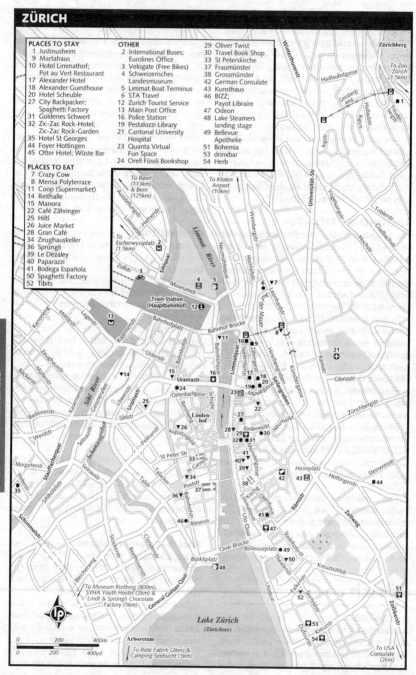

PLACES TO STAY
1 Justinusheim
9 Martahaus
10 Hotel Limmathof;
   Pot au Vert Restaurant
17 Alexander Hotel
18 Alexander Guesthouse
20 Hotel Scheuble
27 City Backpacker;
   Spaghetti Factory
31 Goldenes Schwert
32 Zic-Zac Rock-Hotel;
   Zic-Zac Rock-Garden
35 Hotel St Georges
44 Foyer Hottingen
45 Otter Hotel; Wüste Bar

PLACES TO EAT
7 Crazy Cow
8 Mensa Polyterrace
11 Coop (Supermarket)
14 Reithalle
15 Manora
22 Café Zähringer
25 Hiltl
26 Juice Market
28 Gran Café
34 Zeughauskeller
36 Sprüngli
39 Le Dézaley
40 Paparazzi
41 Bodega Española
50 Spaghetti Factory
52 Tibits

OTHER
2 International Buses;
   Eurolines Office
3 Velogate (Free Bikes)
4 Schweizerisches
   Landesmuseum
5 Limmat Boat Terminus
6 STA Travel
12 Zurich Tourist Service
16 Main Post Office
16 Police Station
19 Pestalozzi Library
21 Cantonal University
   Hospital
23 Quanta Virtual
   Fun Space
24 Orell Füssli Bookshop

29 Oliver Twist
30 Travel Book Shop
33 St Peterskirche
37 Fraumünster
38 Grossmünster
42 German Consulate
43 Kunsthaus
46 BIZZ;
   Payot Libraire
47 Odeon
48 Lake Steamers
   landing stage
49 Bellevue
   Apotheke
51 Bohemia
53 drinxbar
54 Herb

SWITZERLAND

station, is a sprawling smoky café with Internet access (Sfr5 for 20 minutes).

Travel Agencies For help with travel suggestions and budget fares there's **STA Travel** (☎ 01 261 97 57; Leonhardstrasse 10; open 10am-6pm Mon-Wed & Fri, 10am-8pm Thur, 10am-1pm Sat).

Bookshops & Libraries A great source of fiction, nonfiction and travel books in English is **Orell Füssli Bookshop** (☎ 01 211 04 44; Bahnhofstrasse 70). **Payot Libraire** (☎ 01 211 54 52; Bahnhofstrasse 9) specialises in both English- and French-language titles.

The **Travel Book Shop** (☎ 01 252 38 83; Rindermarkt 20) sells English-language travel books and maps. You can also read English-language newspapers in the **Pestalozzi Library** (☎ 01 261 78 11; Zähringerstrasse 17; open 10am-7pm Mon-Fri, 10am-4pm Sat).

Medical & Emergency Services For medical and dental help, ring ☎ 01 269 69 69. The **Cantonal University Hospital** (☎ 01 255 11 11; Rämistrasse 100) has a casualty department, and there's a 24-hour chemist at **Bellevue Apotheke** (☎ 01 252 56 00; Theaterstrasse 14). **Police HQ** (☎ 01 216 71 11; Bahnhofquai 3) is in an impressive building overlooking the river.

Things to See & Do

The cobblestoned pedestrian streets of the old town on each side of the Limmat River are worth a wander. Explore intimate alleyways with surprises at every turn – 16th- and 17th-century houses and guildhalls, tiny boutiques and cafés, courtyards and fountains.

For a brief history lesson, the tourist office runs two-hour **walking tours** (adult/student/child Sfr20/15/10; daily May-Oct).

Elegant **Bahnhofstrasse** is simply perfect for window-shopping and affluent Zürcher-watching. The bank vaults beneath the street are said to be crammed with gold and silver. Above ground, you'll find luxury shops selling the best Switzerland can offer, from watches and clocks to chocolates, furs, porcelain and fashion labels galore.

Walks around Lake Zürich are a pleasant diversion from city crowds. Wander down the west bank and concrete walkways give way to parkland in the **Arboretum**. On the eastern bank, the **Zürichhorn** park has sculptures and a

Chinese Garden. In summer, the lakeside park buzzes with food stalls and entertainment. Take the S10 train to **Uetliberg** (813m) for hikes and sweeping views.

Places of Worship The 13th-century tower of **St Peterskirche** (St Peter's Church) is hard to miss, with the largest clock face in Europe (8.7m in diameter). Also west of the Limmat River, the part Romanesque, part Gothic **Fraumünster** features *The Heavenly Paradise* window by Augusto Giacometti and magnificent stained-glass works created by surrealist Marc Chagall when in his 80s. Across the river, the dual-towered **Grossmünster** looms. Highlights are the choir windows designed by Augusto Giacometti (1933) and an imposing statue of Charlemagne (1107) with giant crown and sword in the crypt. Zwingli preached here in the 16th century.

Museums With one of the best collections in the country, **Kunsthaus** (Museum of Fine Arts; ☎ 01 253 84 84; w www.kunsthaus.ch; Heimplatz 1; adult/student/child Sfr10/6/free, free Wed; open 10am-9pm Tues-Thur, 10am-5pm Fri-Sun) has works by Dali, Man Ray, Hockney, Renoir, Monet and Marc Chagall. Temporary exhibitions incur an extra charge.

Schweizerisches Landesmuseum (Swiss National Museum; ☎ 01 218 65 11; w www.musee-suisse.ch; Museumstrasse 2; adult/student/child Sfr5/3/free; open 10am-5pm Tues-Sun) delves into cultural history, with sections on church art, weapons, coins and room interiors, all housed in a mock castle built in 1898.

Museum Rietberg (☎ 01 202 45 28; w www.rietberg.ch; Gablerstrasse 15; tram No 7; adult/student from Sfr12/6; open 10am-5pm Tues & Thur-Sun, 10am-8pm Wed) has wonderful collections of art and artefacts from Africa and Asia. Also keep an eye out for numerous private galleries around the city.

Other Attractions The **Lindt & Sprüngli chocolate factory** (☎ 01 716 22 33; Seestrasse 204; bus No 165 from Bürkliplatz to Schooren; admission free; open 10am-noon & 1pm-4pm Wed-Fri) has a small exhibit and corny documentary; free chocolate samples abound. For choc fanatics only.

Zoo Zürich (☎ 01 254 25 00; Zürichbergstrasse 221; tram No 6; adult/student

SWITZERLAND

Sfr14/7; open 8am-6pm daily Mar-Oct, 8am-5pm daily Nov-Feb) exhibits 1800 animals nestled within Zürichberg, a beautiful wood ideal for walks away from the city.

Special Events

On the third Monday in April, Zürich celebrates the arrival of warmer weather with Sechseläuten. The guild members parade the streets in historical costume and tour the guildhalls, playing music. A fireworks-filled 'snowman' (the Böögg) is ignited at 6pm.

Zürich lets its hair down in August, with the techno Street Parade (second only to Berlin's Love Parade), attracting well over half a million ravers who flock to the city to party. A three-hour parade is followed by all-night parties around the city.

In February, just after Ash Wednesday, the city celebrates Fasnacht, with parades and festive costumes. Zürcher Festspiele, from mid-June to mid-July, offers a programme of music, dance and theatre.

Places to Stay

Accommodation can be hard to find, particularly from August to October. Cheaper hotels fill early. Book ahead or use the information board and free phone in the train station. The tourist office can sometimes get lower rates (no booking fee).

Camping On the west shore of the lake 4km from the centre (signposted), **Camping Seebucht** (☎ 01 482 16 12; Seestrasse 559; bus No 161 or 165 from Bürkliplatz; camp sites per adult/tent/car park/camper van Sfr8.50/12/3/16; open May-Sept) has good facilities including a shop and café.

Hostels The SYHA hostel (☎ 01 482 35 44, fax 01 480 17 27; e zurich@youthhostel.ch; Mutschellenstrasse 114, Wollishofen; dorm beds from Sfr32, singles/doubles from Sfr69/90) is large and modern with two- to six-bed dorms, 24-hour service and excellent facilities. Take tram No 6 or 7 to Morgental, or S-Bahn 8 to Wollishofen.

Bar-hoppers will feel reallt at home at the **City Backpacker** (☎ 01 251 90 15, fax 01 251 90 24; e backpacker@access.ch; Niederdorfstrasse 5; dorm beds without/with sheets Sfr29/32, singles/doubles/triples/quads Sfr66/92/126/164), in the heart of the busy Niederdorfstrasse. Take a wander up the narrow steps to the 2nd floor to find reception. Facilities include Internet access (Sfr5 for 25 minutes) and a rooftop area.

Removed from the busy city streets is the tranquil student home **Justinusheim** (☎ 01 361 38 06, fax 01 362 29 82; Freudenbergstrasse 146; singles/doubles/triples Sfr50/80/120, with shower Sfr60/100/140). Overlooking carefully tended gardens, spartan but spacious rooms are available during student holidays (particularly mid-July to mid-October), though there are vacancies during term too. A few paces from the Zürichberg woods, it has views of the city and lake far below. Take tram No 10 from the train station to Rigiblik, then the frequent Seilbahn (every six minutes) to the top station, opposite the hostel.

Foyer Hottingen (☎ 01 256 19 19, fax 01 256 19 00; e info@foyer-hottingen.ch; Hottingerstrasse 31; dorm beds Sfr35, singles/doubles/triples Sfr70/110/140, with bathroom Sfr105/150/190) has sparkling, white, minimalist rooms and a peaceful pace, away from the hubbub. Dorm beds are available for women only.

Hotels On the west bank of the Sihl River, **Hotel St Georges** (☎ 01 241 11 44, fax 01 241 11 42; e st-georges@bluewin.ch; Weberstrasse 11; singles/doubles Sfr78/102, with bathroom Sfr104/136) is a bit of a hike, but it's quiet, comfortable and includes continental breakfast.

A more convenient option is the recently renovated **Martahaus** (☎ 01 251 45 50, fax 01 251 45 40; e info@martahaus.ch; Zähringerstrasse 36; dorm beds Sfr37, singles/doubles/triples from Sfr75/98/129), just a five-minute walk from the station. Privacy even prevails in the six-bed dorms with individual cubicles fashioned from partitions and curtains. Book ahead as it's often full.

Hotel Limmathof (☎ 01 261 42 20, fax 01 262 02 17; Limmatquai 142; singles/doubles/triples with bathroom Sfr110/168/198) is an easy stumble from Niederdorfstrasse's nightlife, but is inevitably noisy. The **pot au vert** vegetarian restaurant is on the 1st floor.

Zic-Zac Rock-Hotel (☎ 01 261 21 81, fax 01 261 21 75; e rockhotel.ch@bluewin.ch; Marktgasse 17; singles from Sfr75, doubles without/with bathroom Sfr120/160), features a bold paint job, rock-star room names and gold discs, and is a bit of a novelty, but it is cramped.

Alexander Hotel (☎ 01 251 82 03, fax 01 252 74 25; e info@hotel-alexander.ch; Niederdorfstrasse 40; singles/doubles Sfr160/220, guesthouse Sfr95/140) offers three-star accommodation with mod cons and breakfast, but ask about its linked two-star **guesthouse** in Zähringerstrasse, with much simpler, better-value rooms.

Goldenes Schwert (☎ 01 266 18 18, fax 01 266 18 88; e hotel@rainbow.ch; Marktgasse 14; singles/doubles from Sfr130/155) is a gay-friendly hotel with murals and mirror balls in some rooms and a disco downstairs.

Otter Hotel (☎ 01 251 22 07, fax 01 251 22 75; Oberdorfstrasse 7; singles/doubles from Sfr100/130), on fashionable Oberdorfstrasse, is flamboyantly quirky, with 17 room choices including hot pink, desert-island and Arabian-nights themes – a basic breakfast is included.

Simple and elegant, **Hotel Scheuble** (☎ 01 251 87 95, fax 01 251 76 78; e info@ scheuble.ch; Mühlegasse 17; singles Sfr140-210, doubles 190-400) offers newly renovated rooms and sleek modern furniture.

Places to Eat

Zürich has a thriving café culture and hundreds of restaurants serving all types of local and international cuisine. A good place to start exploring is Niederdorfstrasse and the backstreets nearby, with wall-to-wall cafés, restaurants and bars of every description.

Restaurants With a fun, buzzing atmosphere, **Spaghetti Factory** (☎ 01 251 94 00; Niederdorfstrasse 5; pasta Sfr13.50-22; open 11am-2am daily) serves big, steaming bowls of its namesake dish (22 choices). Night owls with the munchies can fill up at a second **branch** (Theaterstrasse 10; open all night Fri-Sat).

For melt-in-your-mouth garlic mushrooms and other delicious tapas, head to the ground-level café section of **Bodega Española** (☎ 01 251 23 10; Münstergasse 15; tapas Sfr4.80; open 11.45am-2pm & 6pm-11pm).

Hiltl (☎ 01 227 70 00; Sihlstrasse 28; mains Sfr20-25; open 7am-11pm Mon-Sat, 11am-11pm Sun) is an institution, serving tasty vegie meals to Zürchers since 1898 (when vegetarians were commonly thought of as crackpots). Try the Indian buffet (Sfr4.60 per 100g, Sfr42 all-you-can-eat; from 5pm nightly).

Another local eatery with a long history is the touristy **Zeughauskeller** (☎ 01 211 26 90; Bahnhofstrasse 28a; mains Sfr15-30; open 11.30am-11pm daily), a meat-lovers' heaven (with Swiss specialities and 'sausage of the month') which is housed in a 500-year-old former armoury.

In the shadow of Grossmünster is stylish **Le Dézaley** (☎ 01 251 61 29; Römergasse 7; dishes from Sfr22; open 11am-2pm & 5pm-11pm Mon-Sat), the locals' choice for fondue and Vaudois specialities.

Dining becomes entertainment at the big, bright, irreverent **Crazy Cow** (☎ 01 261 40 55; Leonhardstrasse 1; dishes from Sfr17; open 6.30am-midnight daily). There's a giant Toblerone pillar and an unreadable 'Swiss-German' menu as well as delicious chicken wings served in toy supermarket trolleys.

Reithalle (☎ 01 212 07 66; Theaterhaus Gessnerallee; Gessnerallee 8; mains Sfr20-25; open 11am-midnight Mon-Fri, 6pm-4am Sat, 5pm-11pm Sun), in a large converted horse stable, has a mixed menu (pastas and curries) and is often packed with theatre-goers. The Saturday-night diners get in free to the disco.

Cafés Next to the Polybahn (funicular) top station, **Mensa Polyterrace** (Leonhardstrasse 34; dishes Sfr10.50; open 7am-7pm Mon-Fri during term) is an enormous, bustling university cafeteria.

Pile your plate high with tasty fresh food at the buffet-style **Manora** (5th floor, Manor department store, Bahnhofstrasse; mains from Sfr8.90; open 9am-8pm Mon-Fri, 9am-5pm Sat).

Creative vegetarian options are a highlight at **Tibits** (☎ 01 260 32 22; Seefeldstrasse 2; open 6.30am-midnight Mon-Fri, 8am-midnight Sat, 9am-midnight Sunday), a sprawling modern vegie restaurant with purple walls and comfy lounges. The salad bar has 30 different choices for Sfr3.50 per 100g.

If you need to detox after a night on the fondue, **Juice Market** (☎ 01 211 69 33; Augustinergasse 42; juices Sfr6.50-9; open 8am-7pm Mon-Fri, 8am-5pm Sat) makes fresh protein shakes and smoothies, and a range of healthy snack alternatives.

Run by a collective, **Café Zähringer** (☎ 01 252 05 00; Zähringerplatz 11; snacks Sfr5.50-7.50, meals Sfr10.50-22; open 6pm-midnight Mon, 8am-midnight Tues-Thur, 8am-12.30am Fri-Sat, 8am-midnight Sun) provides mellow music, a relaxed atmosphere and scrumptious low-fat soups and snacks.

Paparazzi (☎ 01 250 55 88; Nägelihof 1, Limmatquai; snacks Sfr5-14; open 8.30am-10pm Mon-Thur, 8.30am-midnight Fri-Sat) is a fun place to hang out among old movie posters, cameras and early paparazzi snaps.

Old photos of famous folk also adorn the **Gran Café** (☎ 01 252 31 19; Limmatquai 66; open 6am-11.30pm Mon-Fri, 7am-midnight Sat, 7.30am-11.30pm Sun), by the river, with a bargain all-you-can-eat spaghetti for Sfr10.90 (from 6pm).

Sprüngli (☎ 01 244 47 11; Bahnhofstrasse 21; open 7am-6.30pm Mon-Fri, 7.30am-5.30pm Sat, 10am-5pm Sun) is a must for chocoholics. Choose from a huge range of truffles and cakes from display cases downstairs, or mingle with the well-heeled crowd in the elegant 1st-floor tearooms for a rather special experience.

Self-Catering Cheap eats abound around the train station, especially in the underground Shopville, which has a **Migros** (open 7am-8pm Mon-Fri, 8am-8pm Sat-Sun). Above ground by the station, there is a large **Coop supermarket**. Niederdorfstrasse has a string of **snack bars** offering pretzels, bratwurst, kebabs and Oriental food.

Entertainment

Like most big cities, Zürich has a fickle, ever-changing entertainment scene. Pick up the free events magazine Züritipp from the tourist office or check daily listings at **w** www.zueritipp.ch. Tickets for many events are available from **Billettzentrale** (BIZZ; ☎ 01 221 22 83; Bahnhofstrasse 9; open 10am-6.30pm Mon-Fri, 10am-2pm Sat).

Late-night pubs, clubs and discos clutter Niederdorfstrasse and its adjoining streets. English speakers gravitate towards the Irish pub **Oliver Twist** (Rindermarkt 6) and the constantly crowded, American-style **Zic-Zac Rock-Garden** (Marktgasse 17).

Lenin and James Joyce once downed drinks at the **Odeon** (☎ 01 251 16 50; Am Bellevue; open 7am-2am Mon-Thur & Sun, 7am-4am Fri-Sat), a swish, smoky bar packed with an arty crowd. More laid-back is **Bohemia** (☎ 01 383 70 60; am Kreuzplatz; open 7am-1am Mon-Fri, 9am-2am Sat, 10am-1am Sun), a spacious, Cuban-themed café/bar. **Wüste Bar** (☎ 01 251 22 07; Oberdorfstrasse 7; open

10am-midnight Mon-Thur, 10am-2am Fri-Sat), underneath the Otter Hotel, is small and groovy with plush red seats and a cowhide bar.

You'll pay around Sfr15 admission for most clubs, however a couple of small, central establishments have no cover charge. Try **Herb** (Kreuzstrasse 24; open 9pm-2am Mon-Wed, 9pm-3am Thur-Sat) and **drinxbar** (Dufourstrasse 24; 5pm-midnight Mon-Wed, 5pm-2am Thur-Sat, 5pm-midnight Sun).

Factories in the industrial quarter, west of the train station, are gradually being taken over by a wave of hip bars, clubs and restaurants. Head to Escherwyssplatz (tram No 4 or 13) and follow your ears. The **Peugeot Bar** (☎ 01 273 11 25; Pfingstweidstrasse 6) draws big crowds with its unpretentious atmosphere and produce-market setting. Nearby, **Moods Jazz Club** (☎ 01 276 80 00; Schiffbaustrasse 6), in a former ship-building factory, shares its cavernous postmodern space with a theatre, bar and stylish restaurant.

Rote Fabrik (☎ 01 481 9143; Seestrasse 395; bus No 161 or 165 from Bürkliplatz), once a cutting-edge centre for alternative arts, is more mainstream these days. It offers a range of music, original-language films, theatre, dance and a bar/restaurant.

Cinema prices are around Sfr15, reduced to Sfr11 on Monday. There's also an **open-air cinema** in Zürichhorn park from mid-July to mid-August. The **Comedy Club** performs plays in English – check venues in events magazines or free newspapers by tram stops.

Getting There & Away

Air Kloten airport is 10km north of the city centre and has several daily flights to/from all major destinations. **Swiss** (☎ 0848 85 2000; open 8.30am-6.30pm Mon-Fri, 9.30am-2.30pm Sat) has an office in the main train station.

Bus Various buses head east to Budapest, Belgrade, Dubrovnik and other destinations. The **Eurolines office** (☎ 01 272 40 42) is behind the train station, and is open daily, but intermittently.

Train There are direct trains to Stuttgart (Sfr62, three hours), to Munich (Sfr89, 4½ hours), to Innsbruck (Sfr69, four hours) and to Milan (Sfr75, four hours), as well as many other international destinations. There are also at least hourly departures to most of the Swiss towns including Lucerne (Sfr22, 50 minutes), Bern (Sfr48, 70 minutes) and Basel (Sfr32, 65 minutes).

Car & Motorcycle The N3 approaches Zürich from the south along the shore of Lake Zürich. The N1 is the fastest route from Bern and Basel and the main entry point from the west. The N1 also services routes to the north and east of Zürich.

Getting Around

To/From the Airport Regular trains make the 10-minute trip from the airport to the main train station (Sfr5.40). Taxis cost around Sfr50.

Public Transport There's a comprehensive, unified bus, tram and S-Bahn service in the city that includes boats plying the Limmat River. All tickets must be bought in advance from dispensers at stops. Short trips under five stops are Sfr2.30. A one-hour/24-hour pass for the city costs Sfr3.60/7.20, while a 24-hour pass including travel to/from the airport is Sfr10.80. For unlimited travel within the canton, including extended tours of the lake, a day pass costs Sfr28.40, or Sfr20 after 9am (9-Uhr-Pass).

Lake steamers depart from Bürkliplatz from early April to late October (Swiss Pass and Eurail valid, Inter-Rail 50% discount). A popular option is the two-hour journey to Rapperswill (round trip Sfr20). For more information, contact **Zürichsee-Schifffahrtsgesellschaft** (ZSG; ☎ 01 487 13 33; **w** www.zsg.ch).

Taxi & Bicycle Taxis in Zürich are expensive, even by Swiss standards, at Sfr6 plus Sfr3.50 per kilometre. Use of city bikes is free of charge from **Velogate** (platform 18, main train station; open 7.30am-9.30pm year-round). Bring photo ID and Sfr20 deposit.

Central Switzerland

This is the region that many visitors consider the 'true' Switzerland. Rich in typical Swiss features – mountains, lakes, tinkling cowbells and alpine villages – it's also where Switzerland began as a nation 700 years ago. The original pact of 1291, which was signed by the communities of Uri, Schwyz and Nidwalden, can be viewed in the **Bundesbriefarchiv hall** in Schwyz town centre.

LUCERNE
pop 57,100

Ideally situated in the historic and scenic heart of Switzerland, Lucerne (Luzern in German) is an excellent base for mountain excursions, with easy access to the towering peaks of Mt Pilatus and Mt Rigi. It also has a great deal of character in its own right, particularly the medieval town centre.

The mostly pedestrian-only old town is on the northern bank of the Reuss River. The train station is centrally located on the southern bank. Beside platform three is **Luzern Tourismus** (☎ 041 227 17 17; **e** luzern@luzern.org; Zentralstrasse 5; open 8.30am-7.30pm Mon-Fri, 9am-7.30pm Sat & Sun Apr-Oct; closes 6pm Nov-Mar). In front of the train station is the **boat landing stage** and across the road is the **main post office** (open 7.30am-6.30pm Mon-Fri, 8am-noon Sat).

Internet access can be pricey in Lucerne. For the best deal (Sfr2 for 30 minutes) head to the **Stadtbibliothek** (Library; Löwenplatz 10; open 1.30pm-6.30pm Mon, 10am-6.30pm Tues-Wed & Fri, 10am-9pm Thur, 10am-4pm Sat).

American Express (☎ 041 410 00 77; Schweizerhofquai 4; open 8.30am-5pm Mon-Fri, plus 8.30am-noon Sat in summer) has an ATM and money exchange.

Ask for the visitor's booklet (available from your accommodation) for various discounts on excursions.

Things to See

Your first port of call should be the medieval **old town**, with ancient rampart walls and towers, 15th-century buildings with painted facades and the two much-photographed covered bridges. **Kapellbrücke** (Chapel Bridge), dating from 1333, is Lucerne's best-known landmark, famous for its distinctive water tower and the spectacular 1993 fire that nearly destroyed it. Though it has been rebuilt, fire damage is still obvious on the 17th-century pictorial panels under the roof. In better condition, but rather dark and dour, are the Dance of Death panels under the roofline of **Spreuerbrücke** (Spreuer Bridge).

There's a fine view of the town and lake from the Gütsch Hotel; climb uphill for 20 minutes or treat your feet by taking the clunky **Gütschbahn** (Sfr3).

Make sure that you set aside a few hours for the fascinating **Gletschergarten** (Glacier Garden; ☎ 041 410 43 40; Denkmalstrasse 4;

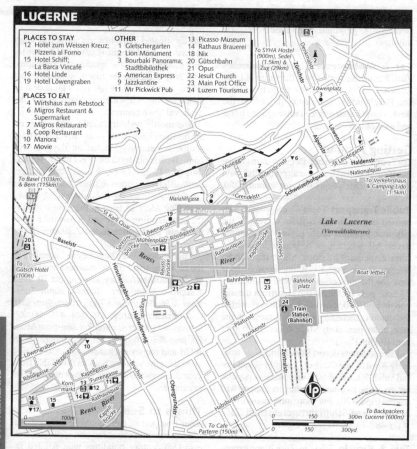

LUCERNE

PLACES TO STAY
12 Hotel zum Weissen Kreuz;
   Pizzeria al Forno
15 Hotel Schiff;
   La Barca Vincafé
16 Hotel Linde
19 Hotel Löwengraben

PLACES TO EAT
4 Wirtshaus zum Rebstock
6 Migros Restaurant &
   Supermarket
7 Migros Restaurant
8 Coop Restaurant
10 Manora
17 Movie

OTHER
1 Gletschergarten
2 Lion Monument
3 Bourbaki Panorama;
   Stadtbibliothek
5 American Express
9 Jazzkantine
11 Mr Pickwick Pub

13 Picasso Museum
14 Rathaus Brauerei
18 Nix
20 Gütschbahn
21 Opus
22 Jesuit Church
23 Main Post Office
24 Luzern Tourismus

www.gletschergarten.ch; adult/student/child Sfr9/7/5.50; open 9am-6pm daily Apr-Oct, 10am-5pm daily Nov-Mar). Most visitors come here to peer into the giant glacial potholes that prove Lucerne's prehistory as a subtropical palm beach, but don't miss Amrein's House, with collections of antique maps and paintings, and the entertaining, century-old Alhambra Hall of Mirrors.

Nearby is the poignant **Lion Monument**, carved in natural rock in 1820 and dedicated to the Swiss soldiers who died in the French Revolution. Another moving historical exhibit is the **Bourbaki Panorama** (☎ 041 412 30 30; Löwenplatz 11; *www.panorama-luzern.ch; adult/student/child Sfr7/6/5; open 9am-6pm daily),* an 1100 sq metre circular painting with commentary depicting the

first Red Cross efforts during the Franco-Prussian War.

The **Picasso Museum** (☎ 041 410 35 33; Furrengasse 21; adult/student/child Sfr6/3/3; open 10am-6pm daily Apr-Oct, 11am-1pm & 2pm-4pm daily Nov-Mar) has a small artwork exhibit, but the main attraction is its collection of intimate black-and-white photos of the artist, his muse Jacqueline and his children.

Verkehrshaus (Transport Museum; ☎ 041 370 44 44; Lidostrasse 5; bus No 6, 8 or 24 from Bahnhofplatz; adult/student/child Sfr21/19/12; open 10am-6pm daily Apr-Oct, 10am-5pm daily Nov-Mar), east of the city centre, is a huge complex devoted to Switzerland's proud transport history. There are trains, planes and automobiles, a communications display, simulators, planetarium and IMAX theatre (costs extra). For unrivalled views of the town and lake, take off in the Hiflyer, a captive balloon you can ride for an extra Sfr20 (15 minutes' duration).

Culture buffs should consider buying the Lucerne museums pass (Sfr29, valid for one month).

From mid-August through mid-September, Lucerne hosts the annual **Internationale Musikfestwochen** (International Festival of Music; ☎ 041 226 44 00; w www.lucerne -music.ch).

Activities
If you want an adrenalin rush, contact **Outventure** (☎ 041 611 14 41; w www.outventure.ch), which has a wide range of adventure sports (eg, bungy-jumping, paragliding and canyoning in the Lucerne/Engelberg region).

Organised Tours
There are many options for scenic cruises on the lake, including on old-fashioned paddle-steamers. Swiss and Eurail passes are valid on all boat trips and Inter-Rail pass holders travel half-price. A 2nd-class day pass for unlimited boat travel is Sfr44. Also popular are trips to the nearby mountains (ask tourist office staff about special deals in winter).

A popular option is the **Golden Roundtrip** (Sfr78.20), which includes a lake steamer to Alpnachstad, a steep cog railway (open May to November) up craggy Mt Pilatus (2120m), a cable car down to Kriens and bus back to Lucerne.

To visit Mt Titlis (3020m), Central Switzerland's highest lookout, there's the tourist office's all-inclusive **guided tour** (Sfr95), including coach trip, Titlis rotating cable car and guide. If you prefer to go it alone, you'll pay Sfr88 for the return journey to Titlis, including cable cars and a train to Engelberg.

Nearby Mt Rigi offers 100km of excellent hiking trails. A combination lake steamer, cog railway and cable-car excursion up Mt Rigi (1797m) costs Sfr87. Rail pass holders should ask about reductions on tour prices.

Places to Stay
Camping Lido (☎ 041 370 21 46; Lidostrasse 8; bus No 6, 8 or 24; camp site per adult/tent/car Sfr8.70/5/5, bunk in cabin Sfr15; open mid-Mar–Oct) entices happy campers with its tranquil spot near the Lido and transport museum.

Backpackers Lucerne (☎ 041 360 04 20, fax 041 360 04 42; Alpenquai 42; dorm beds in 4-/2-bed rooms Sfr24/30), a 12-minute walk southeast of the station, is a cheerful independent with sprawling parkland frontage and a scrap of lakefront beach nearby.

The **SYHA hostel** (☎ 041 420 88 00, fax 041 420 56 16; e luzern@youthhostel.ch; Sedelstrasse 12; bus No 18 from Bahnhofplatz; dorm beds from Sfr31.50, singles/doubles Sfr64/78, with bathroom Sfr70/90), around 1km north of the city walls, is a large, modern, reliable option.

Good for novelty value is **Hotel Löwengraben** (☎ 041 417 12 12, fax 041 417 12 11; e hotel@loewengraben.ch; Löwengraben 18; dorm beds from Sfr30, singles/twins/doubles with breakfast Sfr120/165/190, suites Sfr250-300), a converted prison with basic, white-washed, 'cell-like' rooms and some fancier suites (albeit with bars on the windows). Its transformation comes complete with a stylish restaurant (see Places to Eat later), trendy bar and nightclub, and Internet access.

Simple but central is **Hotel Linde** (☎ 041 410 31 93; Metzgerrainle 3; singles/doubles Sfr44/88; open Apr-Oct), off Weinmarkt in the old town, offering six cheap and cheerful rooms with crisp white linen. Check-in is through the ground-floor Italian restaurant.

At the three-star **Hotel zum Weissen Kreuz** (☎ 041 418 82 20, fax 041 418 82 30; e wkreuz@tic.ch; singles/doubles with breakfast from Sfr100/180), nestled in a cobble-stoned alleyway, there are casual, comfortable rooms a few paces from the water.

Hotel Schiff (☎ 041 418 52 52, fax 041 418 52 55; e contact@hotel-schiff-luzern.ch; Unter der Egg 8; singles/doubles with breakfast from Sfr80/120, with bathroom from Sfr150/190), overlooking the Reuss River, has mostly spacious, renovated rooms, though they vary in style and price.

Places to Eat
Good eating is easy to find in Lucerne, particularly along the Reuss River, around Kornmarkt or in the winding maze of streets in the old town.

A fairly reliable cheapie is the buffet-style **Manora** (5th floor, Weggisgasse 5; salads Sfr4.40-9.40; open 9am-6.30pm Mon-Wed, 9am-9pm Thur-Fri & 8am-4pm Sat), with a small rooftop terrace with mountain vistas.

For speedy service, try **Pizzeria al Forno** *(1st floor, Hotel zum Weissen Kreuz; pizza/pasta from Sfr14/13; open 11am-11.30pm Tues-Sat, 11am-10pm Sun-Mon)*, with 34 varieties of mouthwatering wood-fired pizza. At the converted prison, **Hotel Löwengraben** *(mains Sfr24-28; open 11am-2pm Mon-Fri, 6pm-12.30am Tues-Sat)*, bread and water has been replaced by tasty Asian dishes. Try the daily menu (Sfr17 to Sfr18).

Movie *(☎ 041 410 36 31; Metzgerrainle 9; mains Sfr18.50-36; open 11.30am-2.30pm & 5.30pm-1.30am Mon-Fri, 11.30am-1.30am Sat, 10am-11pm Sun)* is a popular light-hearted theme restaurant with an elaborate film-studio decor, a movie-reel menu and American-style food. Be prepared for intermittent trailers of mainstream flicks on the diner's big screen.

Wirtshaus zum Rebstock *(☎ 041 410 35 81; St Leodegarstrasse 3; dishes Sfr16-42)*, in an ivy-covered historic building, has an eclectic blend of cuisine, from the Rebstock Teller, a meat-fest of fillets (Sfr42.80), to creative vegie dishes such as ravioli curry with shitake mushroom sauce (Sfr17.50).

Wander in and smell the coffee at **La Barca Vincafé**, hidden away under the Hotel Schiff, an antipasto bar serving up super-strong Italian blends.

Self-caterers should head to Hertensteinstrasse, where cheap eats are plentiful. There are numerous **hole-in-the-wall shops** selling pretzels (from Sfr2) and baguettes (from Sfr5). There's also a **Coop restaurant**, two **Migros restaurants** and a **supermarket**.

Entertainment

Jazzkantine *(☎ 041 410 73 73; Grabengasse 8; open 7am-12.30am Mon-Sat, 4pm-12.30am Sun)* is a groovy hang-out frequented by the young, creative types from the adjoining jazz school. There's cool music, counter meals and Saturday-night gigs and weeknight jazz workshops.

More laid-back is **Cafe Parterre** *(☎ 041 210 40 93; Mythenstrasse 7; open 7am-12.30am Mon-Fri, 9am-12.30am Sat & Sun)*, south of the train station, with industrial decor, beer garden and pool tables in the back bar. Breakfast is served into the afternoon for late risers.

Bar-hoppers can choose from the **Rathaus Brauerei** *(Unter der Egg 2)*, serving big home brews on the waterfront; **Nix** *(Mühlenplatz 4)*, a low-key wine bar with abstract artwork and

tasty bar snacks; **Mr Pickwick Pub** *(Rathausquai 6)* for Brit beer, food and footy; or the upmarket **Opus** *(Bahnhofstrasse 16)*, with a choice of 600 wines (25 by the glass).

Behind Lake Rotsee near the youth hostel there is **Sedel** *(☎ 041 420 63 10)*, a former women's prison with rock concerts and DJs at the weekend.

Getting There & Around

Hourly trains connect Lucerne to Zürich (Sfr11, 50 minutes), Interlaken (Sfr29, two hours), Bern (Sfr32, 1½ hours), Lugano (Sfr58, 2½ hours) and Geneva (Sfr70, 3¼ hours). The N2/E9 motorway which connects Basel and Lugano passes by Lucerne, and the N14 provides the road link to Zürich.

INTERLAKEN
pop 15,000

Interlaken, flanked by the stunning Lakes Thun and Brienz and within yodelling distance of the mighty peaks of the Jungfrau, Mönch and Eiger, is a popular base for exploring the delights of the Jungfrau region. Lovers of kitsch will have a field day in the town itself, with horse-drawn carriages and the souvenir shops overflowing with tacky tourist mementoes. Interlaken is also a mecca for thrillseekers. It has a flourishing adventure-sports industry offering a range of white-knuckle, high-adrenalin sports.

Orientation & Information

Most of Interlaken lies between its two train stations, Interlaken Ost and West, which both offer bike rental and daily money-exchange facilities. Behind each station is a landing for lake boat services. The main shopping street, Höheweg, runs between the stations, and you can walk from one to the other in 20 minutes.

Near Interlaken West is the **main post office** *(cnr Marktgasse & Höheweg)* and **Interlaken Tourismus** *(☎ 033 826 53 00; e mail@interlakentourism.ch; Höheweg 37; 8am-6.30pm Mon-Fri, 8am-5pm Sat, 10am-noon & 4pm-6pm Sun July-Aug; shorter hours & closed Sun between seasons)*. There's a hotel board and free phones outside the tourist office and at both train stations. You can check your email at **Buddy's Pub** *(Höheweg 33)*, where the costs is Sfr5/9/16 for 15/30/60 minutes of Net access, but the hostels (particularly Backpackers Villa; see Places to Stay later in this section) often have cheaper access.

Things to See & Do

Interlaken is an active town, bursting with options for hiking, rafting, bungy-jumping, heli-skiing, skydiving and paragliding. The adventure-sports industry continues to thrive, despite the tragic canyoning disaster in 1999 in which 21 people lost their lives. Local operators include **Alpin Raft** (☎ 033 823 41 00; w www.alpinraft.ch) and the **Alpin Center** (☎ 033 823 55 23; w www.alpincenter.ch). One of the more bizarre summer activities is **zorbing** (offered by Alpin Center for Sfr95), where you are enclosed in an enormous transparent ball and sent plummeting down a snow-covered hill.

Hiking trails dot the area surrounding Interlaken, all with signposts giving average walking times. For an excellent panorama and more signposted hiking trails, catch the funicular up to **Harder Kulm** (Sfr21 return; open May to October).

Find time to get out on a lake if possible. Ferries chug along to several towns and villages (Swisspass and Eurail valid, Inter-Rail 50% off). **Lake Thun** has the greater number of resorts and villages, including Spiez (Sfr13/8.60 by steamer/train) and Thun (Sfr19.20/13.60). Medieval castles dominate both towns. Another fine castle is the 13th-century **Schloss Oberhofen** – boats stop right outside.

St Beatus Höhlen (Caves; ☎ 033 841 16 43; adult/student/child Sfr16/14/8; w www .beatushoehlen.ch; open 10.30am-5pm daily Apr-Oct) has some impressive stalagmite formations, a small museum, and a rather feeble reconstruction of a prehistoric settlement. The caves are a 90-minute walk, or save your legs by catching the boat (Sfr5.80).

Lake Brienz has a more rugged shoreline and fewer resorts than its neighbour. The enormous **Freilichtmuseum Ballenberg** (Ballenburg Open-Air Museum; w www.ballen berg.ch; adult/child Sfr16/8; open 10am-5pm daily mid-Apr–Oct) gives visitors a taste of Swiss rural life, with farm animals, craftsmen at work and 100 century-old houses. A shuttle bus operates from the train station at Brienz (Sfr12.40/6 by steamer/train).

Places to Stay

The Guest Card (available from accommodation places) provides useful discounts.

There are a dozen camping grounds in and around Interlaken. Most convenient is **Sackgut** (☎ 033 822 44 34; e sackgut@swisscamps.ch; Brienzstrasse; adult/child/tent from Sfr8.20/5.20/6.50; open Apr-Oct), behind Interlaken Ost station. For alternatives, visit the website at w www.campinginterlaken.ch.

The **SYHA hostel** (☎ 033 822 43 53, fax 033 823 20 58; e boenigen@youthhostel.ch; Aareweg 21, am See, Bönigen; bus No 1; dorm beds from Sfr27.70, singles/doubles Sfr40.70/81.40; closed early Nov–mid-Dec), a 20-minute walk around Lake Brienz from Interlaken Ost, has large dorms and breakfast buffet. What this hostel lacks in elegance it makes up for with its fantastic view over the marine-green Lake Brienz.

For 50 years now, young Americans have flocked to **Balmer's Herberge** (☎ 033 822 19 61, fax 033 823 32 61; e balmers@tcnet.ch; Hauptstrasse 23-25; dorm beds Sfr24-26, singles/doubles/triples/quads Sfr40/68/90/120). It has excellent facilities (games rooms, kitchen, bar and restaurant) and a raucous summer-camp feel, but it's definitely not for everyone. It's a 15-minute walk (signposted) from either station.

For a similarly raucous but Australasian flavour, head to the **Funny Farm** (☎ 079-652 61 27; e james@funny-farm.ch; dorm beds from Sfr25), a converted farmhouse behind the Mattenhof Hotel. The perfect antidote to Swiss-style regimentation, this free-and-easy place has basic, colourful rooms, didgeridoo workshops, swimming pool, bar and party atmosphere. Rooms with better facilities are available in the linked **Mattenhof** (dorm beds Sfr35).

If you need some shut-eye, try the **Backpackers Villa** (☎ 033 826 71 71, fax 033 826 71 72; e backpackers@villa.ch; Alpenstrasse 16; dorm beds Sfr32, doubles Sfr88), an ordered Christian hostel with spacious, renovated rooms. It's well worth the extra Sfr5 surcharge for a 'Jungfrau room' with balcony and mountain view.

The aptly named **Happy Inn Lodge** (☎ 033 822 32 25, fax 033 822 32 68; e info@happy-inn.com; Rosenstrasse 17; dorms Sfr19-30, singles/doubles from Sfr30/60 per person) has basic rooms and a merry bartender/owner serving drinks in the pub below.

Choose between the old and new at **Hotel Alphorn** (☎ 033 822 30 51, fax 033 823 30 69; e accommodation@hotel-alphorn.ch; Rugenaustrasse 8; singles/doubles Sfr90/150), where rooms are either minimalist and modern or filled with florals and antiques. It's in a quiet residential street near the West train station, and some spacious three-star options are available in the linked **Hotel Eiger** *(singles/doubles Sfr110/180).*

Each room is different in the **Hotel Splendid** *(☎ 033 822 76 12, fax 033 822 76 79;* e *info@splendid.ch; Höheweg 33; singles/ doubles Sfr135/210),* above Buddy's Pub, which offers three-star comfort in the heart of town.

Places to Eat
Brasserie 17 *(open 8.30am-12.30am Mon-Sat, 5pm-12.30am Sun),* underneath Happy Inn Lodge, is a fun local hang-out serving up chicken wings, spareribs and live music on Thursday night.

For simple Italian home cooking, try **Ristorante Arobaleno** *(☎ 033 823 12 43; Hotel Post Hardimannli, Haupstrasse 18; mains Sfr20.50-35.50; open 9am-12.30am daily),* with an excellent two-course daily menu.

The ravenous can fill up with tasty thin-crust pizzas and plentiful pasta plates at **Pizzeria Mercato** *(☎ 033 827 87 71; Postgasse 1; pizzas from Sfr14; open 10am-midnight daily mid-Apr–Sept, 10am-2.30pm & 5-11.30pm daily Oct–mid-Apr).*

Gasthof Hirschen *(☎ 822 15 45; Haupstrasse 11; mains Sfr16.50-34; open Mon & Thur-Fri from 2pm, Sat-Sun from 11am)* is a wisteria-strewn rustic chalet with fondue, rosti and a meaty menu. More central is **Hotel Splendid** *(open 6pm-late daily summer, 6pm-late Fri-Sat in winter; closed April & Nov),* with a popular 1st-floor restaurant serving steaming fondue (from Sfr19.50) and other local specialities.

More exotic options include **Spice of India** *(Postgasse 6),* serving delicious dishes with a kick; or **El Azteca** *(Jungfraustrasse 30),* with friendly waitresses and passable Mexican food.

Self-caterers can pick up all their supplies at **Migros** *(cnr Rugenparkstrasse & General Guisan-Strasse)* and **Coop**, with branches on Bahnhofstrasse and opposite Interlaken Ost.

Entertainment
If too much kitsch is not enough, catch the Swiss Folklore Show at the **Kursaal** *(Casino; ☎ 033 827 61 00; show Sfr20, with dinner Sfr39-59.50; 7.30pm daily May-Sept).* Sip on a cocktail and enjoy the sweeping mountain views from **Top o'Met** *(18th floor, Höheweg 37).* Other popular watering holes include the tiny, English-style **Buddy's Pub** *(Höheweg 33; 10am-1am Sun-Thur, 10am-1.30am Fri-Sat);* the larger, rowdier **Café-Bar Hüsi** *(Postgasse 3; open 4pm-12.30am Tues-Sun);* and the grungy **Postiv Einfach** *(Centralstrasse; open 5pm-12.30am Mon-Thur & Sun, 5pm-1.30am Fri-Sat),* with DJs, live music and black-clad crowd. Most of the hostels also have their own bars and bistros. For house music, check out the Hotel Mattenhof's **Club Caverne** in summer.

Getting There & Away
Trains to Lucerne (Sfr30, two hours) depart hourly from Interlaken Ost. Trains to Brig and Montreux (via Bern or Zweisimmen) depart from Interlaken West or Ost. Main roads head east to Lucerne and west to Bern, and the only way south for vehicles, without a major detour around the mountains, is the car-carrying train from Kandersteg, south of Spiez.

JUNGFRAU REGION
The views get better the further south you go from Interlaken. Outdoor enthusiasts will find it hard to tear themselves away. The region's most popular peaks are the Jungfrau and the Schilthorn, but you can also enjoy marvellous vistas and hikes from Schynige Platte, Männlichen and Kleine Scheidegg. In winter, the Jungfrau is a magnet for skiers and snowboarders, with 200km of pistes, ranging from amateur slopes to intermediate to demanding runs down the Schilthorn. Ski passes cost Sfr52/95 for one/two days (discounts for seniors and teens).

Grindelwald
Once a simple farming village, Grindelwald is now the largest ski resort in the Jungfrau, nestled in a valley under the north face of the Eiger. In the First region there are 90km of **hiking trails** above 1200m, with 48km open year-round. The First is the main **skiing** area in winter, with runs stretching from **Oberjoch** at 2486m to the village at 1050m. You can catch the longest **cable car** in Europe from Grindelwald-Grund to Männlichen, where there are more extraordinary views and hikes (one-way/return Sfr29/46).

Grindelwald Tourism *(☎ 033 854 12 12;* e *touristcenter@grindelwald.ch; open 8am-7pm Mon-Fri, 8am-6pm Sat, 9am-noon & 2pm-5pm Sun July-Sept; shorter hours & closed Sun between seasons)* is in the centre at the Sportzentrum, 200m from the train station.

Places to Stay & Eat Grindelwald has several **camping grounds** and countless **holiday apartments** and **chalets** from which to choose. Ask the tourist office for a complete list.

The **SYHA hostel** (☎ *033 853 10 09, fax 033 853 50 29;* e *grindelwald@youthhostel .ch; Terrassenweg; dorm beds from Sfr29.50),* a hillside wooden chalet above the town, has magnificent views. The bad news is it's a tough 20-minute climb from the station. Avoid the slog by taking the Terrassenweg-bound bus to the Gaggi Säge stop.

If the hostel's full, try the nearby **Naturfreundehaus** (☎ *033 853 13 33, fax 033 853 43 33;* e *nfhostel@grindelwald.ch; Terrassenweg; dorm beds from Sfr27, with breakfast/ half-board Sfr33/50).* Both hostels are closed between seasons.

Near the Mälichen cable-car station, the modern **Mountain Hostel** (☎ *033 853 39 00;* e *mhostel@grindelwald.ch; dorm beds/ doubles with breakfast from Sfr34/88)* is a good base for sports junkies eager to get to the slopes. Big, bright and blue, it's impossible to miss.

Lehmann's Herberge (☎*/fax 033 853 31 41; singles/doubles from Sfr40/80),* in the village centre, provides spartan rooms and a buffet breakfast. It's situated just off the main street (signposted).

The **Hirschen Hotel** (☎ *033 854 84 84;* e *hirschen.grindelwald@bluewin.ch; singles/ doubles Sfr105/180),* on the main street, is a friendly and family-run three-star hotel with cheerful, wood-panelled rooms.

Most hotels in town have their own restaurants and some also have bars and clubs. For tasty traditional food and staggering views of the Eiger, try **Rendez-vous Restaurant** (☎ *033 853 11 81; mains Sfr13.50-27; closed Tues)* on the main street. Fondue is Sfr21.50, or launch yourself into a platter of Grindelwald cheese or cold meats.

Onkel Tom's Hütte (☎ *033 853 52 39; pizza from Sfr10; open 6pm-10.30pm Tues, noon-11.30pm Wed-Sat, noon-9pm Sun),* on the way out of town, is a cosy California-style barn with cheap tucker and an excellent wine list.

Self-caterers can stock up at **Coop supermarket** opposite the tourist office.

Getting There & Away Grindelwald is only 40 minutes by train from Interlaken Ost (Sfr9.40 each way), and is easily reached by road.

Lauterbrunnen Valley

The Lauterbrunnen Valley branches out from Interlaken with sheer rockfaces and towering mountains on either side, attracting an army of hikers and mountain bikers. Cow bells echo in the valley and every house and hostel has a postcard-worthy view. The first village reached by car or rail is **Lauterbrunnen,** known mainly for the trickling **Staubbach Falls** and the much more impressive **Trümmelbach Falls** (*admission Sfr10; open Apr-Oct),* 4km out of town. Find out more from the **tourist office** (☎ *033 855 19 55;* e *info@lauterbrunnen.tourismus .ch),* on the main street.

Above the village (via the funicular) there's Grütschalp, where you switch to the train to **Mürren** (Sfr9.40 total), a skiing and hiking resort. The ride yields tremendous unfolding views across the valley to the Jungfrau, Mönch and Eiger peaks. Mürren's efficient **tourist office** (☎ *033 856 86 86;* e *info@muerren.ch)* is in the sports centre. A pleasant 40-minute walk downhill from Mürren is tiny **Gimmelwald,** a minute rural village with a pungent barnyard aroma.

Gimmelwald and Mürren can also be reached from the valley floor by the **Stechelberg cable car,** which runs up to **Schilthorn** (2971m). From the top there's a fantastic panorama, and film shows will remind you that James Bond performed his stunts here in *On Her Majesty's Secret Service.* The standard return fare for Schilthorn is Sfr89, but ask about low-season or first/last ascent of the day discounts.

Places to Stay & Eat Gimmelwald and Lauterbrunnen have some of the cheapest accommodation in the region. Another base with plenty of appeal is Wengen, a hiking and skiing centre clinging to the eastern side of the valley. It has several hotels and the reader-recommended backpacker hostel **Hot Chili Peppers** (☎ *033 855 50 20;* e *chilis@wengen .com; dorm beds/doubles Sfr26/99),* with chatty staff and a popular ground-floor bar.

Lauterbrunnen With views of the falls, **Camping Schützenbach** (☎ *033 855 12 68; adult/child/tent Sfr8.40/3.90/14, dorm beds*

SWITZERLAND

Sfr18.50) and **Camping Jungfrau** *(☎ 033 856 20 10; adult/child/tent Sfr10.60/5/15, dorm beds Sfr22)* offer excellent facilities and a range of accommodation.

You won't get much cheaper than **Matratzenlager Stocki** *(☎ 033 855 17 54; dorm beds Sfr13; closed Nov & Dec)*, a cosy, mountain cabin with a homely feel and extremely close quarters.

Another excellent option is the newish **Valley Hostel** *(☎/fax 033 855 20 08;* **e** *valley hostel@bluewin.ch; dorm beds/doubles from Sfr22/52)*, which offers comfy rooms (many with balconies) and a mellow, nonsmoking environment.

Chalet im Rohr *(☎ 033 855 21 82; singles/doubles Sfr26/52)*, across from the church, is a large, creaky wooden chalet with balconies and overflowing flowerboxes.

Cheap eats are harder to track down. Stock up in the **Coop** near the tourist office, or try one of the **hotel restaurants**. For a snack, beer, email check or serious game of darts, head to the **Horner Pub/Hotel** *(☎ 033 855 16 73; open 9am-1.30am daily)*.

Gimmelwald Close to the cable-car station, **Mountain Hostel** *(☎ 033 855 17 04, fax 033 855 26 88;* **e** *mountainhostel@tcnet.ch; dorm beds Sfr18)* has jaw-dropping views, snacks and beer for hungry guests, Internet access and a pool table. If you don't mind the occasional roll in the hay, **Esther's Guesthouse** *(☎ 033 855 54 88;* **e** *evallmen@bluewin.ch)* offers beds of straw in a big, old barn (Sfr20, including a generous breakfast of organic food). Health nuts can pick up biodynamic farm produce from Esther's 'Little Farmer Shop'.

Restaurant-Pension Gimmelwald *(☎/fax 033 855 17 30;* **e** *pensiongimmelwald@ tcnet.ch; dishes from Sfr14)* has hearty home cooking, including fondue and farmers' barley soup. Five minutes up the hill there's the **Mittaghorn** *(Walter's;* ☎ *033 855 16 58; dorm beds/doubles Sfr25/70)*, with basic accommodation and a small café.

Mürren By the train station is **Eiger Guesthouse** *(☎ 033 855 35 35, fax 033 855 35 31;* **e** *eigerguesthouse@muerren.ch; dorm beds Sfr45, singles Sfr65-90, doubles Sfr110-150)*, with a bar, restaurant and games room. **Hotel Edelweiss** *(☎ 033 855 13 12, fax 033 855 42 02;* **e** *edelweiss@muerren.ch; singles Sfr90-120, doubles Sfr190-240)* offers comfortable

three-star rooms with views of the Eiger and Jungfrau (ask for a balcony). Don't leave town without trying the hearty home cooking at **Staegerstübli**, with generous helpings of delicious traditional food. Self-caterers can stock up at the **Coop supermarket** next door.

Jungfraujoch

The trip to Jungfraujoch by train (the highest in Europe) is excellent – if it's a clear day. Unfortunately, the price is as steep as the track and you're at the mercy of the weather gods (call ☎ 033 855 10 22 for taped forecasts or check cable TV). From Interlaken Ost, trains go via Grindelwald or Lauterbrunnen to Kleine Scheidegg. From here, the line is less than 10km long but took 16 years to build. Opened in 1912, the track powers through both the Eiger and the Mönch, pausing briefly for travellers to take happy snaps of views from two windows blasted in the mountainside, before terminating at Jungfraujoch (3454m).

On the summit, there is free entry to the **ice palace** (exhibition rooms cut within the glacier) and free use of plastic disks for sliding down glacial slopes. From the terrace of the **Sphinx Research Institute** (a weather station) the panorama of peaks and valleys is unforgettable, including the **Aletsch Glacier** to the south, and mountains as distant as the Jura and the Black Forest. Take warm clothing and sunglasses (for glacier walking).

From Interlaken Ost, the journey is 2½ hours each way (Sfr162 return). Allow at least three hours at the site. There's a cheaper 'good morning ticket' of Sfr125 if you can drag yourself out of bed for the early train (6.35am from Interlaken) and leave the summit by noon. From 1 November to 30 April the reduction is valid for the 6.35am and 7.35am trains, and the noon restriction does not apply. Eurail passholders get 25% off, and Swisspass holders slightly more.

Northern Switzerland

This region is important for industry and commerce, yet by no means lacks tourist attractions. Take time to explore the tiny rural towns set among green rolling hills, and Lake Constance (Bodensee) and the Rhine on the German border.

BASEL

pop 163,800

Basel (Bâle in French) is an affluent city squeezed into the top left corner of the country, bordering France and Germany. Although a major hub of commerce and industry, it has an idyllic old town and many enticing museums. The famous Renaissance humanist, Erasmus of Rotterdam, was associated with the city and his tomb rests in the cathedral.

Orientation & Information

Basel's strategic position on the Rhine, beside France and Germany, has been instrumental in its development. On the northern bank of the river is Kleinbasel (Little Basel), surrounded by German territory. The pedestrian-only old town and most popular sights are on the south bank in Grossbasel (Greater Basel).

The **Basel Tourismus** (☎ 061 268 68 68; e office@baseltourismus.ch; Schifflände 5; open 8.30am-6pm Mon-Fri & 10am-4pm Sat) is by the Mittlere Brücke. There's a hole-in-the-wall **tourist office** in the main **SBB train station**, which also has **bike rental** and **money exchange** (open 6am-9pm daily) and a **Migros supermarket** (open 6am-10pm Mon-Fri, 7.30am-10pm Sat-Sun & holidays).

The **main post office** (Freie Strasse; open 7.30am-6.30pm Mon-Wed & Fri, 7.30am-10pm Thur, 8am-noon Sat) is situated in the city centre and there's another **branch** by the train station.

You can check your emails in quiet, modern comfort at the **Tiscali Internet Center** (☎ 0844 89 19 91; e info@tiscalinet.ch; Steinentorstrasse 11; open 9am-10pm Mon-Thur, 9am-8pm Fri, 9am-5pm Sat) where Net access costs Sfr5/8 for 30/60 minutes. With better hours, but sharing space with noisy computer games, there's **Domino** (☎ 061 271 13 50; e ngc@net-generation.ch; Steinenvorstadt 54; open 9.30am-midnight Mon-Thur, 9.30am-1am Fri-Sat, 1pm-midnight Sun) where Net access costs Sfr10/60 for an hour/day.

Things to See & Do

Take a self-guided walk through the **old town**, with its cobbled streets, colourful fountains, and Middle-Age churches and stately buildings. The tourist office distributes leaflets with suggested routes, and it can also arrange two-hour **guided walks** (adult/child Sfr15/7.50; 2.30pm daily May–mid-Oct, 2.30pm Sat mid-Oct–Apr).

In Marktplatz is the impressive rust-coloured **Rathaus** (town hall), with frescoed courtyard. The 12th-century **Münster** (cathedral) is another highlight, with Gothic spires and Romanesque St Gallus doorway. Don't miss the stunning view of the Rhine behind the Münster, where office workers lunch and visitors gaze across the river to Kleinbasel.

Theaterplatz is a crowd-pleaser, with a curious **fountain**, designed by Swiss sculptor Jean Tinguely. His madcap scrap-metal machines perform a peculiar water dance, delighting children and weary travellers alike. Also check out the 700-year-old **Spalentor** gate tower, a remnant of the town's old city walls, with a massive portal and grotesque gargoyles.

Basel has over 30 museums from which to choose – the BaselCard costs Sfr25/33/45 for one/two/three days and gives free entry to them all.

The **Kunstmuseum** (Art Museum; ☎ 061 206 62 62; w www.kunstmuseumbasel.ch; St Albangraben 16; adult/student/child Sfr10/8/free, free 1st Sun of month; open 10am-5pm Tues-Sun) features religious and local art, a cubism collection including a palette of Picassos, and a copper-etchings gallery. Admission also grants entry to the **Museum für Gegenwartskunst** (☎ 061 272 81 83; St Alban-Rheinweg 60; same hours), in a converted factory, exhibiting contemporary art pieces including works by Andy Warhol and Joseph Beuys.

Contemporary-art devotees should also make sure to visit the **Museum Jean Tinguely Basel** (☎ 061 681 93 20; w www.tinguely.ch; Grenzacherstrasse/Solitude-Park; adult/child Sfr7/5; open 11am-7pm Wed-Sun), east of the city centre, a shrine to the mechanical work of the local artist.

For a change of pace, the BaselCard provides free entry to Basel's **zoo** (☎ 061 295 35 35; Binningerstrasse; w www.zoobasel.ch; adult/child/family Sfr14/5/30; open 8am-6pm daily), known locally as the 'Zolli'.

Of interest, but possibly more for novelty value than anything else, is Drei Länder Eck (Three Countries Corner), where the Swiss, German and French borders meet. Take tram No 8 to the last stop, from where it's a 10-minute walk.

If you're lucky enough to be in town on the Monday after Ash Wednesday you'll be treated to Fasnacht, a three-day spectacle of parades, masks, music and costumes, all starting at 4am.

SWITZERLAND

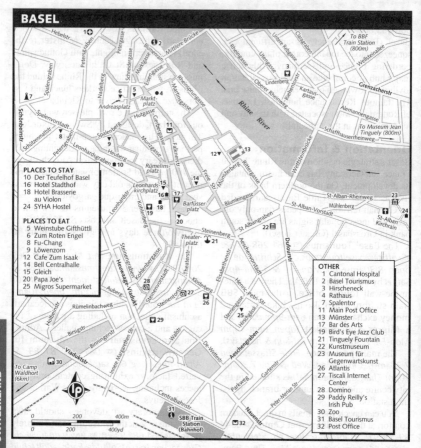

BASEL

PLACES TO STAY
10 Der Teufelhof Basel
16 Hotel Stadthof
18 Hotel Brasserie
   au Violon
24 SYHA Hostel

PLACES TO EAT
5 Weinstube Gifthüttli
6 Zum Roten Engel
8 Fu-Chang
9 Löwenzorn
12 Cafe Zum Isaak
14 Bell Centralhalle
15 Gleich
20 Papa Joe's
25 Migros Supermarket

OTHER
1 Cantonal Hospital
2 Basel Tourismus
3 Hirscheneck
4 Rathaus
7 Spalentor
11 Main Post Office
13 Münster
17 Bar des Arts
19 Bird's Eye Jazz Club
21 Tinguely Fountain
22 Kunstmuseum
23 Museum für
   Gegenwartskunst
26 Atlantis
27 Tiscali Internet
   Center
28 Domino
29 Paddy Reilly's
   Irish Pub
30 Zoo
31 Basel Tourismus
32 Post Office

Places to Stay

Hotels are often full during Basel's numerous
trade fairs and conventions, so book ahead.
The tourist offices offer a reservation service
for a fee (Sfr10/15 for Basel/out-of-town) and
can help with cheaper, out-of-town accommodation. Don't forget to ask your accommodation for the Mobility Card, which entitles you
to free local transport.

Camp Waldhort (☎ 061 711 64 29;
e camp.waldhort@gmx.ch; Heideweg 16,
Reinach; adult/child/tent/camper van Sfr7/
4.50/11/17; open Mar-Oct) is in a small village, 6km south of the train station.

The **SYHA hostel** (☎ 061 272 05 72, fax
061 272 08 33; St Alban Kirchrain 10; dorm
beds Sfr30-32, singles/doubles Sfr80/100),
10 minutes from the centre, is in a converted

textiles factory in St Alban, a quiet, leafy, old-
money part of town. It has small spick-and-
span rooms and Internet access (Sfr5 for 20
minutes).

Hotel Stadthof (☎ 061 261 87 11, fax 061
261 25 84; e info@stadthof.ch; Gerbergasse
84; singles/doubles from Sfr70/120) offers
rudimentary rooms with shared hall shower.
Tucked in the corner of buzzing Barfüsser-
platz, its bar and **restaurant** do a roaring trade.

Climb the ancient stone stairs to **Hotel
Brasserie au Violon** (☎ 061 269 87 11, fax
061 269 87 12; e auviolon@iprolink.ch; Im
Lohnhof 4; singles/doubles from Sfr90/140),
a majestic former monastery and prison with
tastefully decorated rooms. There's an elegant
restaurant downstairs for breakfast (Sfr14)
and other meals.

Der Teufelhof Basel (☎ 061 261 10 10, fax 061 261 10 04; e info@teufelhof.com; Leonhardsgraben 47; singles/doubles from Sfr250/277, in Galeriehotel annexe from Sfr180/255) is a unique option for more creative souls. Each of the nine rooms features theme-based 'environmental art' created by a different artist. The Galeriehotel annexe has cheaper rooms, and there's a small theatre, stylish **restaurant** and wine shop.

Places to Eat
For a quick, cheap bite on the run, the daily **market** on Marktplatz has tasty bratwurst (Sfr5) and delicious breads (Sfr3 to Sfr7). Alternatively, there's pedestrian-only **Steinenvorstadt**, with its countless fast-food outlets, cafés and restaurants.

Cafe Zum Roten Engel (☎ 061 261 20 08; Andreasplatz 15; meals Sfr9-14; open 9am-midnight Mon-Sat, 10am-10pm Sun), hidden away in a quiet, leafy courtyard, is a busy student hang-out serving delicious vegie snacks and gigantic mugs of coffee.

Gleich (☎ 061 261 48 83; Leonhardsberg 1; mains Sfr16-26; open 10.30am-9.30pm Mon-Fri), in a laneway off Gerbergasse, is another favourite haunt for nonmeat-eaters.

Zum Isaak (☎ 061 25 77 11; Kaffihaus am Munsterplatz 16; open 9am-10.30pm Tues-Sat, 9am-6pm Sun; tea/coffee Sfr4.30, meals Sfr8-18) blends quirky artwork with a laid-back atmosphere and a range of 20-plus teas.

For Basel specialities and a traditional atmosphere, try **Weinstube Gifthüttli** (☎ 061 261 16 56; Schneidergasse 11; mains Sfr25-38; open 9am-11.30pm Mon-Sat) or **Löwenzorn** (☎ 061 261 42 13; Gemsberg 2; mains Sfr27.50-44; open 9am-11.45pm Mon-Sat). Both restaurants offer a meaty daily lunch menu for Sfr17 to Sfr20.

Papa Joe's (☎ 061 274 04 04; am Barfi; meals Sfr22.50-48.50; open 11.30am-2pm & 5pm-late Mon-Fri, 5pm-late Sat & Sun) is a Tex-Mex-style restaurant serving burgers, ribs and nachos to appreciative locals. Its adjoining bar, with terracotta tiles, plastic toucans and American paraphernalia, attracts a cocktail-quaffing crowd.

Fu-Chang (☎ 061 261 98 71; Schützenmattstrasse 1; lunches Sfr12.50-15; open 11.30am-3pm & 5.30pm-10pm Mon-Fri, 11am-3pm Sat), a stone's throw from the towering Spalentor, serves generous helpings of tasty Asian dishes.

For self-caterers, there's the local **Migros** (Sternengasse 17; open 7.30am-6.30pm Mon-Wed & Fri, 7.30am-10pm Thur, 7.30am-5pm Sat). Or for a huge selection of organic local produce (including 200 different cheeses), try the **Bell Centralhalle** (cnr Streitgasse & Weisse Gasse; open 8am-6pm Mon-Fri, 8am-10pm Thur, 8am-5pm Sat).

Entertainment
In Steinenvorstadt, there's a string of **cinemas** with latest-release movies. There's also a bar/café/restaurant to suit every taste. **Paddy Reilly's Irish Pub** (☎ 061 281 33 36; Steinentorstrasse 45; bar meals Sfr5-12.50; open 11.30am-1am Sun-Wed, 11.30am-2am Thur-Sat) entices expats with Brit beers and big-screen TV. The spacious, stylish **Bar des Arts** (☎ 061 273 57 37; Am Barfüsserplatz 6; open 11am-1am Mon-Wed, 11am-2am Thur, 11am-3am Fri-Sat, 3pm-midnight Sun) has a piano player tickling the ivories and an extensive drinks menu (happy hour 5pm to 7pm).

For everything from house to pop, soul and R&B, there's **Atlantis** (☎ 061 228 96 96; Klosterberg 13). Wrapped in garish gold, it's impossible to miss. In Kleinbasel, there's the grungier **Hirscheneck** (☎ 061 692 73 33; Lindenberg 23; entry Sfr8-15) which is a melting pot of nonconservatives, with DJs and thrashy live music on weekends and the occasional weekday.

For smoother grooves, try the **Bird's Eye Jazz Club** (☎ 061 263 33 41; Kohlenberg 20; entry from Sfr10; open 8pm-1am Tues-Wed & Sun, 8pm-2am Thur-Sat).

Getting There & Away
Basel is a major European rail hub. On most international trains you pass through the border controls in the station, so allow extra time. Trains to France leave from the **SNCF section** of SBB station; there are seven daily to Paris (Sfr69, five hours). Germany-bound trains stop at **Badischer Bahnhof** (BBF) on the northern bank; local trains to the Black Forest stop only at BBF, though fast EC services stop at SBB, too.

Main destinations along this route are Amsterdam (Sfr180, eight hours), Frankfurt (Sfr80, three hours) and Hamburg (Sfr198, 6½ hours). Services within Switzerland leave from SBB: there are two fast trains hourly to both Geneva (Sfr71, three hours; via Bern or Biel/Bienne) and Zürich (Sfr30, 70 minutes).

By motorway, the E25/E60 heads from Strasbourg and passes by the EuroAirport, and the E35/A5 hugs the German side of the Rhine.

Getting Around

For the EuroAirport, catch bus No 50 from in front of the SBB Station (Sfr6.60). City buses and trams run every six to 10 minutes (Sfr1.80 for four or fewer stops, Sfr2.80 for central zone, Sfr8 for day pass). By the SBB station is a **hut** offering *free* bike loans in summer.

SCHAFFHAUSEN
pop 32,900

Schaffhausen is a quaint medieval town on the northern bank of the Rhine, surrounded by German territory. Beautiful oriel windows, painted facades and ornamental fountains crowd the streets of the **old town**. See the finest examples of these in Vordergasse and Vorstadt, which intersect at Fronwagplatz. **Schaffhausen Tourism** (☎ 052 625 51 41; e tourist@swissworld.com) can help with a map and sightseeing options.

For the best views around, climb up to the 16th-century hill-top **Munot fortress** (admission free; open 8am-10pm daily May-Sept, 9am-5pm daily Oct-Apr). By the cathedral is the **Allerheiligen Museum** (☎ 052 633 07 77; Klosterstrasse; admission free; open noon-5pm Tues-Wed & Fri-Sun, noon-8pm Thur), with art and archaeological exhibits.

Rhine Falls (Rheinfall) is a 40-minute stroll westward along the river, or take bus No 1 to Neuhausen. Though the drop is only 23m, the waterfall is considered the largest in Europe, with an extraordinary amount of water thundering over it. The 45km of the Rhine from Schaffhausen to Constance is one of the river's most stunning stretches, passing by meadows, castles and ancient villages, including **Stein am Rhein**, 20km to the east, where you could easily wear out your camera in Rathausplatz.

Places to Stay & Eat

Schaffhausen is an easy day trip from Zürich, but overnighters won't regret a stay at the **SYHA hostel** (☎ 052 625 88 00; fax 052 624 59 54; Randenstrasse 65; dorm beds from Sfr24; open Mar-Nov), in an impressive 16th-century former manor house.

If you've got the munchies, look for pretzel and bratwurst **stalls** on Vordergasse. There are also cheap eats at **Migros** (Vorstadt 39), **China**

Town Take Away (Vorstadt 36) or **Manora** (Manor department store, Vordergasse).

Getting There & Away

Hourly trains run to Zürich (Sfr17.20, 50 minutes). Constance and Basel can be reached by either Swiss or (cheaper) German trains. **Untersee Und Rhein** (☎ 052 634 08 88; e info@urh.ch) operates steamers to/from Constance (Sfr38, four hours, four daily May to October). Schaffhausen has good roads in all directions.

ST GALLEN
pop 70,300

In AD 612, an itinerant Irish monk called Gallus fell into a briar. An irritating mishap, most people would think, but Gallus interpreted it as a sign from God and decided to stay put and build a hermitage. From this inauspicious beginning the town of St Gallen evolved and developed into an important medieval cultural centre.

The **main post office** is opposite the train station. Two minutes away there's **St Gallen-Bodensee Tourismus** (☎ 071 227 37 37; e info@stgallen-bodensee.ch; Bahnhofplatz 1a; open 9am-noon & 1pm-6pm Mon-Fri, 9am-noon Sat).

St Gallen has an interesting pedestrian-only **old town**. Many buildings have distinctive oriel windows, with the best on Gallusplatz, Spisergasse and Kugelgasse. Don't miss the twin-tower **Kathedrale**, with an ostentatious interior which includes dark ceiling frescoes by Josef Wannenmacher and the marine-green stucco-work by the Gigel brothers. Also note the pulpit, arches and woodcarvings around the confessionals.

Bookworms will treasure a sticky-beak through the nearby **Stiftsbibliothek** (Abbey Library; ☎ 071 227 34 16; adult/student Sfr7/5; closed three weeks in Nov), one of the oldest libraries of the Western world. It contains some manuscripts from the Middle Ages and an opulent rococo interior.

Places to Stay & Eat

The modern **SYHA hostel** (☎ 071 245 47 77; fax 071 245 49 83; Jüchstrasse 25; dorm beds Sfr26, singles/doubles Sfr46.50/72; open Mar–mid-Dec) is a signposted 15-minute walk east of the old town; take the Trogenerbahn from the station to 'Schülerhaus' (Sfr2.40).

Closer to town is the **Hotel Vadian Garni** (☎ 071 228 18 78, fax 071 228 18 79;

Gallusstrasse 36; singles/doubles from Sfr70/
100, with bathroom Sfr92/140), a friendly
and alcohol-free, family-run hotel close to
the cathedral. The recently renovated **Weisses
Kreuz** (☎/fax 071 223 28 43; Engelgasse 9;
singles/doubles from Sfr61/108) is central
and good value, with reception in the mellow
bistro-bar downstairs.

Fast-food stalls proliferate around the
old town, selling St Gallen sausage and bread
for around Sfr6. There's also a buffet-style
Manora (4th floor, Manor department store,
Marktgasse), with a wide selection of freshly
cooked meals.

Restaurant Marktplatz (☎ 071 222 36 41;
Neugasse 2; mains Sfr14.50-19.80; open
8.30am-midnight Mon-Sat, 10am-midnight
Sun) is a rowdy beer-hall-style restaurant serving beer, pizza and local meaty dishes.

For a calmer atmosphere and traditional
Swiss food, try **Wirtschaft Zur Alten Post**
(☎ 071 222 66 01; Gallusstrasse 4; mains
Sfr20-42; open 11am-2pm & 5.30pm-11pm
Tues-Sat), near the cathedral. Small and cosy,
it fills quickly so reserve ahead.

Getting There & Away
St Gallen is a short train ride from Lake Con-
stance (Bodensee), upon which boats sail to
Bregenz in Austria, and to Constance and

Lindau in Germany (but not in winter). There
are also regular trains to Bregenz (Sfr16, 40
minutes), Constance (Sfr16.60, one hour) and
Zürich (Sfr26, 70 minutes).

APPENZELL
Parochial Appenzellers, inherently resistant to
change, are often the butt of Swiss jokes. Appenzell village, nestled in the middle of lush
farmland, reflects this conservatism, with an
old-fashioned ambience that's popular with
tourists. Cobblestoned streets are lined with
traditional old houses with painted facades,
and souvenir shops selling everything from
cowbells and chocolate to embroidered linen.

The streets are bedecked with flags and
flowers on the last Sunday in April, when the
locals vote on cantonal issues by a show of
hands in the open-air parliament (Landsgemeinde). Many men carry swords or bayonets
(often heirlooms) as proof of citizenship, but
the women produce a simple licence to vote
(they only won the right to vote in cantonal affairs in 1991).

There are hourly connections from St
Gallen by narrow-gauge train, which meanders along, mostly following the course of the
road (45 minutes). There are also trains to/
from Zürich (Sfr32, two hours), changing at
Gossau or St Gallen.

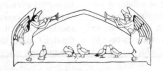

Appendix – Telephones

Dial Direct

You can dial directly from public telephone boxes from almost anywhere in Europe to almost anywhere in the world. This is usually cheaper than going through the operator. In much of Europe, public telephones accepting phonecards are becoming the norm and in some countries coin-operated phones are difficult to find.

To call abroad simply dial the international access code (IAC) for the country you are calling from (most commonly ☎ 00 in Europe but see the following table), the country code (CC) for the country you are calling, the local area code (usually dropping the leading zero if there is one) and then the number. If, for example, you are in Italy (international access code ☎ 00) and want to make a call to the USA (country code ☎ 1), San Francisco (area code ☎ 415), number ☎ 123 4567, then you dial ☎ 00-1-415-123 4567. To call from the UK (☎ 00) to Australia (☎ 61), Sydney (☎ 02), number ☎ 1234 5678, you dial the following: ☎ 00-61-2-1234 5678.

Home Direct

If you would rather have somebody else pay for the call, you can, from many countries, dial directly to your home country operator and then reverse charges; you can also charge the call to a phone company credit card. To do this, simply dial the relevant 'home direct' or 'country direct' number to be connected to your own operator. For the USA there's a choice of AT&T, MCI or Sprint Global One home direct services. Home direct numbers vary from country to country – check with your telephone company before you leave, or with the international operator in the country you're ringing from. From phone boxes in some countries you may need a coin or local phonecard to be connected with the relevant home direct operator.

In some places (particularly airports), you may find dedicated home direct phones where you simply press the button labelled USA, Australia, Hong Kong or whatever for direct connection to the operator. Note that the home direct service does not operate to and from all countries, and that the call could be charged at operator rates, which makes it expensive for the person paying. Placing a call on your phone credit card is more expensive than paying the local tariff.

Dialling Tones

In some countries, after you have dialled the international access code, you have to wait for a second dial tone before dialling the code for your target country and the number. Often the same applies when you ring from one city to another within these countries: wait for a dialling tone after you've dialled the area code for your target city. If you're not sure what to do, simply wait three or four seconds after dialling a code – if nothing happens, you can probably keep dialling.

Phonecards

In major locations phones may accept credit cards: simply swipe your card through the slot and the call is charged to the card, though rates can be very high. Phone-company credit cards can be used to charge calls via your home country operator.

Stored-value phonecards are now almost standard all over Europe. You usually buy a card from a post office, telephone centre, newsstand or retail outlet and simply insert the card into the phone each time you make a call. The card solves the problem of finding the correct coins for calls (or lots of correct coins for international calls) and generally gives you a small discount.

Call Costs

The cost of international calls varies widely from one country to another: a US$1.20 call from Britain could cost you US$6 from Turkey. The countries shown in the 'Telephone Codes & Costs' table that follows are rated from * (cheap) to *** (expensive), but rates can vary depending on which country you are calling to (for example, from Italy it's relatively cheap to call North America, but more expensive to call Australia). Reduced rates are available at certain times, usually from mid-evening to early morning, though it varies from country to country – check the local phone book or ask the operator for more details. Calling from hotel rooms can be very expensive.

Telephone Codes & Costs

	CC	cost (see text)	IAC	IO
Albania	355	***	00	12
Andorra	376	**	00	821111
Austria	43	*	00	09
Belarus	375	***	8(w)10	(017) 233 2971
Belgium	32	**	00	1224 (private phone)
				1223 (public phone)
Bosnia-Hercegovina	387	**	00	900/901/902
Bulgaria	359	**	00	0123 (calls)
				0124 (inquiries)
Croatia	385	**	00	901
Cyprus	357	***	00	
Cyprus (Turkish)	90+392		00	
Czech Republic	420	*	00	1181/0149
Denmark	45	**	00	141
Estonia	372	***	000	165
Finland	358	**	00, 990, 994, 999	020222
France	33	*	00(w)	12
Germany	49	*	00	11834
Gibraltar	350	***	00	100
Greece	30	*	00	161
Hungary	36	*	00(w)	199
Iceland	354	***	00	5335010
Ireland	353	*	00	114
Northern Ireland	44+28	*	00	155
Italy	39	**	00	15
Latvia	371	***	00	115
Liechtenstein	423	***	00	114
Lithuania	370	***	00	194/195
Luxembourg	352	**	00	0010
Macedonia	389	***	99	901
Malta	356	**	00	194
Moldova	373	***	8(w)10	973
Morocco	212	***	00(w)	12
Netherlands	31	**	00	0800-0410
Norway	47	**	00	181
Poland	48	**	00	901
Portugal	351	*	00	099
Romania	40	***	00	971
Russia	7	**	8(w)10	
Slovakia	421	**	00	0149
Slovenia	386	**	00	115
Spain	34	**	00(w)	025
Sweden	46	**	00	0018
Switzerland	41	**	00	114
Tunisia	216	**	00	
Turkey	90	***	00	115
UK	44	*	00	155
Ukraine	380	**	810	079/073
Yugoslavia	381	***	99	901

CC – Country Code (to call into that country)
IAC – International Access Code (to call abroad from that country)
IO – International Operator (to make inquiries)
(w) – wait for dialling tone

Other country codes include: Australia ☎ 61, Canada ☎ 1, Hong Kong ☎ 852, India ☎ 91, Indonesia ☎ 62, Israel ☎ 972, Japan ☎ 81, Macau ☎ 853, Malaysia ☎ 60, New Zealand ☎ 64, Singapore ☎ 65, South Africa ☎ 27, Thailand ☎ 66, USA ☎ 1

Language

This language guide contains pronunciation guidelines and basic vocabulary to help you get around Western Europe. For background information on each language, see the individual country chapters. For more extensive coverage of the languages included in this guide, get yourself a copy of Lonely Planet's *Europe phrasebook*.

Dutch

Pronunciation
Vowels

a	short, as the 'u' in 'cut'
a, aa	long, as the 'a' in 'father'
au, ou	pronounced somewhere between the 'ow' in 'how' and the 'ow' in 'glow'
e	short, as in 'bet', or as the 'er' in 'fern' (without pronouncing the 'r')
e, ee	long, as the 'ay' in 'day'
ei	as the 'ay' in 'day'
eu	a tricky one; similar to the 'eu' in French *couleur* – try saying 'eh' with rounded lips and the tongue forward, then slide the tongue back and down to make an 'oo' sound;
i	short, as in 'it'
i, ie	long, as the 'ee' in 'meet'
ij	as the 'ey' in 'they'
o	short, as in 'pot'
o, oo	long, as in 'note'
oe	as the 'oo' in 'zoo'
u	short, similar to the 'u' in 'urn'
u, uu	long, as the 'u' in 'flute'
ui	a very tricky one, similar to the 'eui' in French *fauteuil*, without the slide to the 'i'; pronounced somewhere between au/ou and eu

Consonants

ch, g	in the north, a hard 'kh' sound as in the Scottish *loch*; in the south, a softer, lisping sound
j	as the 'y' in 'yes'; also as the 'j' in 'jam' or the 's' in 'pleasure'
r	in the south, a trilled sound; in the north it varies, often guttural
s	as in 'so'; or as the 'z' in 'zoo'
w	similar to English 'w'

Basics

Hello.	*Dag/Hallo.*
Goodbye.	*Dag.*
Yes.	*Ja.*
No.	*Nee.*
Please.	*Alstublieft/Alsjeblieft.*
Thank you.	*Dank U/je (wel).*
You're welcome.	*Geen dank.*
Excuse me.	*Pardon.*
Sorry.	*Sorry.*
Do you speak English?	*Spreekt U/spreek je Engels?*
How much is it?	*Hoeveel kost het?*
What's your name?	*Hoe heet U/je?*
My name is ...	*Ik heet ...*

Getting Around

What time does the ... leave/arrive?	*Hoe laat vertrekt/ arriveert de ...?*
(next)	*(volgende)*
boat	*boot*
bus	*bus*
tram	*tram*
train	*trein*
I'd like to hire a car/bicycle.	*Ik wil graag een auto/fiets huren.*
I'd like a one-way/ return ticket.	*Ik wil graag een enkele reis/een retour.*
1st class	*eerste klas*
2nd class	*tweede klas*
left luggage locker	*bagagekluis*
bus stop	*bushalte*
tram stop	*tramhalte*
train station	*treinstation*
ferry terminal	*veerhaven*
Where is the ...?	*Waar is de ...?*
Go straight ahead.	*Ga rechtdoor.*

Signs – Dutch

Ingang	**Entrance**
Uitgang	**Exit**
Informatie/ Inlichtingen	**Information**
Open	**Open**
Gesloten	**Closed**
Kamers Vrij	**Rooms Available**
Vol	**Full/No Vacancies**
Politiebureau	**Police Station**
Verboden	**Prohibited**
WC/Toiletten	**Toilets**
Heren	**Men**
Dames	**Women**

Turn left.	*Ga linksaf.*
Turn right.	*Ga rechtsaf.*
near	*dichtbij*
far	*ver*

Around Town

a bank	*een bank*
the ... embassy	*de ... ambassade*
my hotel	*mijn hotel*
the post office	*het postkantoor*
the market	*de markt*
the pharmacy	*de drogist*
the newsagency	*de krantenwinkel*
the stationers	*de kantoorboekhandel*
the telephone centre	*de telefooncentrale*
the tourist office	*de VVV/het toeristenbureau*
What time does it open/close?	*Hoe laat opent/ sluit het?*

Accommodation

hotel	*hotel*
guesthouse	*pension*
youth hostel	*jeugdherberg*
camping ground	*camping*
Do you have any rooms available?	*Heeft U kamers vrij?*
single room	*eenpersoons kamer*
double room	*tweepersoons kamer*
one night	*één nacht*
two nights	*twee nachten*
How much is it per night/ per person?	*Hoeveel is het per nacht/ per persoon?*
Does it include breakfast?	*Zit er ontbijt bij inbegrepen?*

Time, Days & Numbers

What time is it?	*Hoe laat is het?*
today	*vandaag*
tomorrow	*morgen*
yesterday	*gisteren*
in the morning	*'s morgens*
in the afternoon	*'s middags*
Monday	*maandag*
Tuesday	*dinsdag*
Wednesday	*woensdag*
Thursday	*donderdag*
Friday	*vrijdag*
Saturday	*zaterdag*
Sunday	*zondag*

Emergencies – Dutch

Help!	*Help!*
Call a doctor!	*Haal een dokter!*
Call the police!	*Haal de politie!*
Go away!	*Ga weg!*
I'm lost.	*Ik ben de weg kwijt.*

0	*nul*
1	*één*
2	*twee*
3	*drie*
4	*vier*
5	*vijf*
6	*zes*
7	*zeven*
8	*acht*
9	*negen*
10	*tien*
11	*elf*
100	*honderd*
1000	*duizend*
one million	*één miljoen*

French

Pronunciation

French has a number of sounds which are difficult for Anglophones to produce. These include:

- The distinction between the 'u' sound (as in *tu*) and 'oo' sound (as in *tout*). For both sounds, the lips are rounded and projected forward, but for the 'u' the tongue is towards the front of the mouth, its tip against the lower front teeth, whereas for the 'oo' the tongue is towards the back of the mouth, its tip behind the gums of the lower front teeth.

- The nasal vowels. During the production of nasal vowels the breath escapes partly through the nose and partly through the mouth. There are no nasal vowels in English; in French there are three, as in *bon vin blanc* (good white wine). These sounds occur where a syllable ends in a single 'n' or 'm'; the 'n' or 'm' is silent but indicates the nasalisation of the preceding vowel.

- The 'r'. The standard 'r' of Parisian French is produced by moving the bulk of the tongue backwards to constrict the air flow in the pharynx while the tip of the tongue rests behind the lower front teeth. It's similar to the noise made by some people before spitting, but with much less friction.

Basics

Hello.	*Bonjour.*
Goodbye.	*Au revoir.*
Yes.	*Oui.*
No.	*Non.*
Please.	*S'il vous plaît.*
Thank you.	*Merci.*
That's fine, you're welcome.	*Je vous en prie.*
Excuse me. (attention)	*Excusez-moi*
Sorry. (apology)	*Pardon*
Do you speak English?	*Parlez-vous anglais?*
How much is it?	*C'est combien?*
What's your name?	*Comment vous appelez-vous?*
My name is ...	*Je m'appelle ...*

Getting Around

When does the next ... leave/arrive?	*À quelle heure part/ arrive le prochain ...?*
boat	*bateau*
bus (city)	*bus*
bus (intercity)	*car*
tram	*tramway*
train	*train*
left luggage (office)	*consigne*
timetable	*horaire*
bus stop	*arrêt d'autobus*
tram stop	*arrêt de tramway*
train station	*gare*
ferry terminal	*gare maritime*
I'd like a ... ticket.	*Je voudrais un billet ...*
one-way	*aller simple*
return	*aller retour*
1st-class	*première classe*
2nd-class	*deuxième classe*
I'd like to hire a car/bicycle.	*Je voudrais louer une voiture/un vélo.*
Where is ...?	*Où est ...?*
Go straight ahead.	*Continuez tout droit.*
Turn left.	*Tournez à gauche.*
Turn right.	*Tournez à droite.*
near	*proche*
far	*loin*

Around Town

a bank	*une banque*
the ... embassy	*l'ambassade de ...*
my hotel	*mon hôtel*
post office	*le bureau de poste*
market	*le marché*
chemist/pharmacy	*la pharmacie*
newsagency	*l'agence de presse*
stationers	*la papeterie*
a public telephone	*une cabine téléphonique*
the tourist office	*l'office de tourisme/ le syndicat d'initiative*
What time does it open/close?	*Quelle est l' heure de ouverture/fermeture?*

Accommodation

the hotel	*l'hôtel*
the guesthouse	*la pension (de famille)*
the youth hostel	*l'auberge de jeunesse*
the camping ground	*le camping*
Do you have any rooms available?	*Est-ce que vous avez des chambres libres?*
for one person	*pour une personne*
for two people	*deux personnes*
for one night	*une nuit*
for two nights	*deux nuits*
How much is it per night/ per person?	*Quel est le prix par nuit/ par personne?*
Is breakfast included?	*Est-ce que le petit dé- jeuner est compris?*

Time, Days & Numbers

What time is it?	*Quelle heure est-il?*
today	*aujourd'hui*
tomorrow	*demain*

yesterday	hier
morning	matin
afternoon	après-midi

Monday	lundi
Tuesday	mardi
Wednesday	mercredi
Thursday	jeudi
Friday	vendredi
Saturday	samedi
Sunday	dimanche

1	un
2	deux
3	trois
4	quatre
5	cinq
6	six
7	sept
8	huit
9	neuf
10	dix
100	cent
1000	mille

| one million | un million |

German

Pronunciation

Unlike English or French, German has no real silent letters: you pronounce the **k** at the start of the word *Knie*, 'knee', the **p** at the start of *Psychologie*, 'psychology', and the **e** at the end of *ich habe*, 'I have'.

Vowels

As in English, vowels can be pronounced long, as the 'o' in 'pope', or short, as in 'pop'. As a rule, German vowels are long before one consonant and short before two consonants, eg, the **o** is long in the word *Dom*, 'cathedral', but short in the word *doch*, 'after all'.

a	short, as the 'u' in 'cut' or long, as in 'father'
au	as the 'ow' in 'vow'
ä	short, as in 'cat' or long, as in 'care'
äu	as the 'oy' in 'boy'
e	short, as in 'bet' or long, as in 'obey'
ei	as the 'ai' in 'aisle'
eu	as the 'oy' in 'boy'
i	short, as in 'it' or long, as in 'marine'
ie	as the 'brief'
o	short, as in 'not' or long, as in 'note'
ö	as the 'er' in 'fern'
u	as in 'pull'
ü	similar to the 'u' in 'pull' but with lips stretched back

Consonants

Most German consonants sound similar to their English counterparts. One important difference is that **b**, **d** and **g** sound like 'p', 't' and 'k', respectively when word-final.

b	as in 'be'; as 'p' when word-final
ch	as in Scottish *loch*
d	as in 'do'; as 't' when word-final
g	as in 'go'; as 'k' when word-final (except after i, when it's as 'ch' in Scottish *loch*)
j	as the 'y' in 'yet'
qu	as 'k' plus 'v'
r	can be trilled or guttural, depending on the region
s	as in 'sun'; as the 'z' in 'zoo' when followed by a vowel
sch	as the 'sh' in 'shjp'
sp, st	as 'shp' and 'sht' when word-initial
tion	the 't' is pronounced as the 'ts' in 'its'
v	as the 'f' in 'fan'
w	as the 'v' in 'van'
z	as the 'ts' in 'its'

Basics

Good day.	Guten Tag.
Hello. (in Bavaria and Austria)	Grüss Gott.
Goodbye.	Auf Wiedersehen.
Bye. (informal)	Tschüss.
Yes.	Ja.
No.	Nein.
Please.	Bitte.
Thank you.	Danke.
You're welcome.	Bitte sehr.
Sorry. (excuse me, forgive me)	Entschuldigung.
Do you speak English?	Sprechen Sie Englisch?
How much is it?	Wieviel kostet es?

What's your name?	*Wie heissen Sie?*
My name is ...	*Ich heisse ...*

Getting Around

What time does ... leave/arrive?	*Wann (fährt ... ab/ kommt ... an)?*
the boat	*das Boot*
the bus (city)	*der Bus*
the bus (intercity)	*der (überland) Bus*
the tram	*die Strassenbahn*
the train	*der Zug*

What time is the next boat?	*Wann fährt das nächste Boot?*
I'd like to hire a car/bicycle.	*Ich möchte ein Auto/ Fahrrad mieten.*
I'd like a one-way/ return ticket.	*Ich möchte eine Einzel- karte/Rückfahrkarte.*

1st class	*erste Klasse*
2nd class	*zweite Klasse*
left luggage lockers	*Schliessfächer*
timetable	*Fahrplan*
bus stop	*Bushaltestelle*
tram stop	*Strassenbahnhaltestelle*
train station	*Bahnhof (Bf)*
ferry terminal	*Fährhafen*

Where is the ...?	*Wo ist die ...?*
Go straight ahead.	*Gehen Sie geradeaus.*
Turn left.	*Biegen Sie links ab.*
Turn right.	*Biegen Sie rechts ab.*
near	*nahe*
far	*weit*

Around Town

a bank	*eine Bank*
the chemist/ pharmacy	*die Apotheke*
the ... embassy	*die ... Botschaft*
my hotel	*mein Hotel*
the market	*der Markt*
the post office	*das Postamt*
the newsagency	*der Zeitungshändler*
the stationers	*der Schreibwaren- geschäft*
the telephone centre	*die Telefonzentrale*
the tourist office	*das Verkehrsamt*

What time does it open/close?	*Um wieviel Uhr macht es auf/zu?*

Accommodation

hotel	*Hotel*
guesthouse	*Pension, Gästehaus*
youth hostel	*Jugendherberge*
camping ground	*Campingplatz*

Signs – German

Eingang	**Entrance**
Ausgang	**Exit**
Auskunft	**Information**
Offen	**Open**
Geschlossen	**Closed**
Zimmer Frei	**Rooms Available**
Voll/Besetzt	**Full/No Vacancies**
Verboten	**Prohibited**
Polizeiwache	**Police Station**
Toiletten (WC)	**Toilets**
Herren	**Men**
Damen	**Women**

Do you have any rooms available?	*Haben Sie noch freie Zimmer?*

a single room	*ein Einzelzimmer*
a double room	*ein Doppelzimmer*
one night	*eine Nacht*
two nights	*zwei Nächte*

How much is it per night/person?	*Wieviel kostet es pro Nacht/Person?*
Is breakfast included?	*Ist Frühstück in- begriffen?*

Time, Days & Numbers

What time is it?	*Wie spät ist es?*
today	*heute*
tomorrow	*morgen*
yesterday	*gestern*
in the morning	*morgens*
in the afternoon	*nachmittags*

Monday	*Montag*
Tuesday	*Dienstag*
Wednesday	*Mittwoch*
Thursday	*Donnerstag*
Friday	*Freitag*
Saturday	*Samstag, Sonnabend*
Sunday	*Sonntag*

0	*null*
1	*eins*
2	*zwei/zwo*
3	*drei*
4	*vier*
5	*fünf*
6	*sechs*
7	*sieben*
8	*acht*
9	*neun*
10	*zehn*

Emergencies – German

Help!	*Hilfe!*
Call a doctor!	*Holen Sie einen Arzt!*
Call the police!	*Rufen Sie die Polizei!*
Go away!	*Gehen Sie weg!*
I'm lost.	*Ich habe mich verirrt.*

11	*elf*
12	*zwölf*
13	*dreizehn*
100	*hundert*
1000	*tausend*

one million   *eine Million*

Greek

Alphabet & Pronunciation

Pronunciation of Greek letters is shown in the table below using the closest-sounding letter in English.

Greek Alphabet

Greek	English	Pronunciation
Α α	a	as in 'father'
Β β	v	as the 'v' in 'vine'
Γ γ	gh, y	like a rough 'g', or as the 'y' in 'yes'
Δ δ	dh	as the 'th' in 'then'
Ε ε	e	as in 'egg'
Ζ ζ	z	as in 'zoo'
Η η	i	as the 'ee' in 'feet'
Θ θ	th	as the 'th' in 'throw'
Ι ι	i	as the 'ee' in 'feet'
Κ κ	k	as in 'kite'
Λ λ	l	as in 'leg'
Μ μ	m	as in 'man'
Ν ν	n	as in 'net'
Ξ ξ	x	as the 'ks' in 'looks'
Ο ο	o	as in 'hot'
Π π	p	as in 'pup'
Ρ ρ	r	slightly trilled 'r'
Σ σ	s	as in 'sand' ('ς' at the end of a word)
Τ τ	t	as in 'to'
Υ υ	i	as the 'ee' in 'feet'
Φ φ	f	as in 'fee'
Χ χ	kh, h	as the 'ch' in Scottish *loch*, or as a rough 'h'
Ψ ψ	ps	as the 'ps' in 'lapse'
Ω ω	o	as in 'lot'

Letter Combinations

Some pairs of vowels are pronounced separately if the first has an acute accent (eg, **ά**), or the second has a dieresis (eg, **ï**). All Greek words of two or more syllables have an acute accent which indicates where the stress falls.

ει, οι	i	as the 'ee' in 'feet'
αι	e	as in 'bet'
ου	u	as the 'oo' in 'mood'
μπ	b	as in 'be'
	mb	as in 'amber' (or as the 'mp' in 'ample')
ντ	d	as in 'do'
	nd	as in 'bend' (or as the 'nt' in 'sent')
γκ	g	as in 'go'
γγ	ng	as the 'ng' in 'angle'
γξ	ks	as in 'yaks'
τζ	dz	as the 'ds' in 'suds'

The suffix of some Greek words depends on the gender of the speaker, eg, *asthmatikos* (masculine) and *asthmatikya* (feminine), or *epileptikos* (m) and *epileptikya* (f).

Basics

Hello.	*yasu* (informal)
	yasas (polite/plural)
Goodbye.	*andio*
Yes.	*ne*
No.	*okhi*
Please.	*sas parakalo*
Thank you.	*sas efharisto*
That's fine/ You're welcome.	*ine endaksi/parakalo*
Excuse me. (forgive me)	*signomi*
Do you speak English?	*milate anglika?*
How much is it?	*poso kani?*
What's your name?	*pos sas lene/ pos legeste?*
My name is ...	*me lene ...*

Getting Around

What time does the ... leave/arrive?	*ti ora fevyi/ftani ...?*
boat	*to plio*
bus (city)	*to leoforio (ya tin poli)*
bus (intercity)	*to leoforio (ya ta proastia)*
tram	*to tram*
train	*to treno*

I'd like a ... ticket.	tha ithela isitirio ...
one-way	horis epistrofi
return	me epistrofi
1st-class	proti thesi
2nd-class	dhefteri thesi

left luggage	horos aposkevon
timetable	dhromologhio
bus stop	i stasi tu leoforiu

Go straight ahead.	pighenete efthia
Turn left.	stripste aristera
Turn right.	stripste dheksya
near/far	konda/makria

Around Town

Where is a /the ...?	pu ine ...?
bank	mia trapeza
... embassy	i ... presvia
hotel	to ksenodhokhio
market	i aghora
newsagency	to efimeridhon
pharmacy	to farmakio
post office	to takhidhromio
telephone centre	to tilefoniko kentro
tourist office	to ghrafio turistikon pliroforion

What time does it open/close?	ti ora aniyi/klini?

Accommodation

a hotel	ena xenothohio
a youth hostel	enas xenonas neoitos
a camp site	ena kamping

I'd like a ... room.	thelo ena dhomatio ...
single	ya ena atomo
double	ya dhio atoma

How much is it per person/night?	poso kostizi ya ena atomo/vradhi?

for one night	ya mia nichta
for two nights	ya dhio nichtes

Is breakfast included?	simberilamvanete to proiono?

Time, Days & Numbers

What time is it?	ti ora ine?
today	simera
tomorrow	avrio
yesterday	hthes
in the morning	to proi
in the afternoon	to apoyevma

Monday	dheftera
Tuesday	triti
Wednesday	tetarti
Thursday	pempti
Friday	paraskevi
Saturday	savato
Sunday	kiryaki

1	ena
2	dhio
3	tria
4	tesera
5	pende
6	eksi
7	epta
8	okhto
9	enea
10	dheka
100	ekato
1000	khilya

one million	ena ekatomirio

Italian

Pronunciation
Vowels

a	as the second 'a' in 'camera'
e	as the 'ay' in 'day', but without the 'i' sound
i	as the 'ee' in 'see'
o	as in 'dot'
u	as the 'oo' in 'too'

Consonants

c	as 'k' before **a**, **o** and **u**; as the 'ch' in 'choose' before **e** and **i**
ch	a hard 'k' sound
g	as in 'get' before **a** and **o**
gh	as in 'get'
gli	as the 'lli' in 'million'
gn	as the 'ny' in 'canyon'
h	always silent
r	a rolled 'rrr' sound
sc	as the 'sh' in 'sheep' before **e** and **i**; a hard sound as in 'school' before **h**, **a**, **o** and **u**
z	as the 'ts' in 'lights' or as the 'ds' in 'beds'

Note that the **i** in **ci**, **gi** and **sci** isn't pronounced when followed by **a**, **o** or **u**, unless it's accented. Thus the name 'Giovanni' is pronounced 'joh-**vahn**-nee' – the 'i' sound after the 'G' is not pronounced.

Stress

Double consonants are pronounced as a longer, often more forceful sound than a single consonant.

Stress often falls on the next to last syllable, as in 'spaghetti'. When a word has an accent, the stress is on that syllable, as in *città* (city).

Basics

Hello.	*Buongiorno.* (polite)
	Ciao. (informal)
Goodbye.	*Arrivederci.* (polite)
	Ciao. (informal)
Yes.	*Sì.*
No.	*No.*
Please.	*Per favore/Per piacere.*
Thank you.	*Grazie.*
That's fine/	*Prego.*
You're welcome.	

Signs – Italian

Ingresso/Entrata	**Entrance**
Uscita	**Exit**
Informazione	**Information**
Aperto	**Open**
Chiuso	**Closed**
Camere Libere	**Rooms Available**
Completo	**Full/No Vacancies**
Polizia/Carabinieri	**Police**
Questura	**Police Station**
Proibito/Vietato	**Prohibited**
Gabinetti/Bagni	**Toilets**
Uomini	**Men**
Donne	**Women**

Excuse me.	*Mi scusi.*
Sorry. (excuse me/ forgive me)	*Mi scusi/Mi perdoni.*
Do you speak English?	*Parla inglese?*
How much is it?	*Quanto costa?*
What's your name?	*Come si chiama?*
My name is ...	*Mi chiamo ...*

Getting Around

When does the ... leave/arrive?	*A che ora parte/ arriva ...?*
boat	*la barca*
ferry	*il traghetto*
bus	*l'autobus*
tram	*il tram*
train	*il treno*
bus stop	*fermata dell'autobus*
train station	*stazione*
ferry terminal	*stazione marittima*
1st class	*prima classe*
2nd class	*seconda classe*
left luggage	*deposito bagagli*
timetable	*orario*
I'd like a one-way/ return ticket.	*Vorrei un biglietto di solo andata/ di andata e ritorno.*
I'd like to hire a car/bicycle.	*Vorrei noleggiare una macchina/bicicletta.*
Where is ...?	*Dov'è ...?*
Go straight ahead.	*Si va sempre diritto.*
Turn left.	*Giri a sinistra.*
Turn right.	*Giri a destra.*
near	*vicino*
far	*lontano*

Around Town

a bank	*una banca*
the ... embassy	*l'ambasciata di ...*
my hotel	*il mio albergo*
post office	*la posta*
market	*il mercato*
chemist/pharmacy	*la farmacia*
newsagency	*l'edicola*
stationers	*il cartolaio*
telephone centre	*il centro telefonico*
the tourist office	*l'ufficio di turismo*
What time does it open/close?	*A che ora (si) apre/chiude?*

Accommodation

hotel	*albergo*
guesthouse	*pensione*
youth hostel	*ostello per la gioventù*
camping ground	*campeggio*

Emergencies – Italian

Help!	*Aiuto!*
Call a doctor!	*Chiama un dottore/ un medico!*
Call the police!	*Chiama la polizia!*
Go away!	*Vai via!*
I'm lost.	*Mi sono perso* (m)/ *persa.* (f)

Do you have any rooms available?	*Ha delle camere libere/ C'è una camera libera?*
How much is it per night/per person?	*Quanto costa per la notte/ciascuno?*
Is breakfast included?	*È compresa la colazione?*
a single room	*una camera singola*
a twin room	*una camera doppia*
a double room	*una camera matri- moniale*
for one night	*per una notte*
for two nights	*per due notti*

Time, Days & Numbers

What time is it?	*Che ora è?/ Che ore sono?*
today	*oggi*
tomorrow	*domani*
yesterday	*ieri*
morning	*mattina*
afternoon	*pomeriggio*
Monday	*lunedì*
Tuesday	*martedì*
Wednesday	*mercoledì*
Thursday	*giovedì*
Friday	*venerdì*
Saturday	*sabato*
Sunday	*domenica*

1	*uno*
2	*due*
3	*tre*
4	*quattro*
5	*cinque*
6	*sei*
7	*sette*
8	*otto*
9	*nove*
10	*dieci*
100	*cento*
1000	*mille*
one million	*un milione*

Portuguese

Portuguese pronunciation can be tricky for the uninitiated; like English, vowels and consonants have more than one possible sound depending on position and stress. Moreover, there are nasal vowels and diphthongs in Portuguese with no English equivalents.

Vowels

a   short, as the 'u' in 'cut' or long, as the 'ur' in 'hurt'
e   short, as in 'bet' or longer, as in 'heir'; silent at the end of a word and in unstressed syllables
é   short, as in 'bet'
ê   long, as the 'a' in 'gate'
i   short, as in 'ring' or long, as the 'ee' in 'see'
o   short, as in 'pot'; long as in 'note'; as the 'oo' in 'good'
ô   long, as in 'note'
u   as the 'oo' in 'good'

Nasal Vowels

Nasalisation is represented by an 'n' or an 'm' after the vowel, or by a tilde over it, eg, ã. The nasal 'i' exists in English as the 'ing' in 'sing'. For other vowels, try to pronounce a long 'a', 'ah', or 'e', 'eh', holding your nose, as if you have a cold.

Diphthongs

Vowel combinations are relatively straightforward:

au   as the 'ow' in 'now'
ai   as the 'ie' in 'pie'
ei   as the 'ay' in 'day'
eu   as 'e' followed by 'w'
oi   similar to the 'oy' in 'boy'

Nasal Diphthongs

Try the same technique as for nasal vowels. To say *não*, pronounce 'now' through your nose.

ão   nasal 'ow' (owng)
ãe   nasal 'ay' (eing)
õe   nasal 'oy' (oing)
ui   similar to the 'uing' in 'ensuing'

Consonants

c   as in 'cat' before **a**, **o** or **u**; as the 's' in 'sin' before **e** or **i**

ç	as the 'c' in 'celery'
g	as in 'go' before **a**, **o** or **u**; as the 's' in 'treasure' before **e** or **i**
gu	as in 'guest' before **e** or **i**
h	never pronounced when word-initial
nh	as the 'ni' in 'onion'
lh	as the 'lli' in 'million'
j	as the 's' in 'treasure'
m	not pronounced when word-final – it simply nasalises the previous vowel, eg, *um* (oong), *bom* (bõ)
qu	as the 'k' in 'key' before **e** or **i**; elsewhere as in 'queen'
r	when word-initial, or when doubled (**rr**) within a word it's a harsh, guttural sound similar to the 'ch' in Scottish loch; in the middle or at the end of a word it's a rolled 'r' sound. In some areas of Portugal it's always strongly rolled.
s	as in 'so' when word-initial and when doubled (**ss**) within a word; as the 'z' in 'zeal' when between vowels; as 'sh' when it precedes a consonant, or at the end of a word
x	as the 'sh' in 'ship', as the 'z' in 'zeal', or as the 'x' in 'taxi'
z	as the 's' in 'treasure' before a consonant or at the end of a word

Word Stress

Word stress is important in Portuguese, as it can affect meaning. In words with a written accent, the stress always falls on the accented syllable.

Note that Portuguese uses masculine and feminine word endings, usually '-o' and '-a' respectively – to say 'thank you', a man will therefore use *obrigado*, a woman, *obrigada*.

Basics

Hello.	*Bom dia.*
Goodbye.	*Adeus.*
Yes.	*Sim.*
No.	*Não.*
Please.	*Se faz favor.*
Thank you.	*Obrigado/a.* (m/f)
You're welcome.	*De nada.*
Excuse me.	*Com licença.*
Sorry. (forgive me)	*Desculpe.*
Do you speak English?	*Fala Inglês?*
How much is it?	*Quanto custa?*
What's your name?	*Como se chama?*
My name is ...	*Chamo-me ...*

Getting Around

What time does the ... leave/arrive?	*A que horas parte/ chega ...?*
boat	*o barco*
bus (city)	*o autocarro*
bus (intercity)	*a camioneta*
tram	*o eléctrico*
train	*o combóio*
bus stop	*paragem de autocarro*
train station	*estação ferroviária*
timetable	*horário*
I'd like a ... ticket.	*Queria um bilhete ...*
one-way	*simples/de ida*
return	*de ida e volta*
1st-class	*de primeira classe*
2nd-class	*de segunda classe*
I'd like to hire ...	*Queria alugar ...*
a car	*um carro*
a bicycle	*uma bicicleta*
Where is ...?	*Onde é ...?*
Go straight ahead.	*Siga sempre a direito/ Siga sempre em frente.*
Turn left.	*Vire à esquerda.*
Turn right.	*Vire à direita.*
near	*perto*
far	*longe*

Around Town

a bank	*um banco*
the chemist/ pharmacy	*a farmácia*
the ... embassy	*a embaixada de ...*
my hotel	*o meu hotel*
the market	*o mercado*
the newsagency	*a papelaria*
the post office	*os correios*
the stationers	*a tabacaria*
the telephone centre	*a central de telefones*
the tourist office	*o (posto de) turismo*

Signs – Portuguese

Entrada	**Entrance**
Saída	**Exit**
Informações	**Information**
Aberto	**Open**
Fechado	**Closed**
Quartos Livres	**Rooms Available**
Posto Da Polícia	**Police Station**
Proíbido	**Prohibited**
Empurre/Puxe	**Push/Pull**
Lavabos/WC	**Toilets**
Homens (h)	**Men**
Senhoras (s)	**Women**

Emergencies – Portuguese

Help!	*Socorro!*
Call a doctor!	*Chame um médico!*
Call the police!	*Chame a polícia!*
Go away!	*Deixe-me em paz!/*
	Vai-te embora! (inf)
I'm lost.	*Estou perdido.* (m)
	Estou perdida. (f)

What time does it open/close?	*A que horas abre/ fecha?*

Accommodation

hotel	*hotel*
guesthouse	*pensão*
youth hostel	*pousada da juventude*
camping ground	*parque de campismo*
Do you have any rooms available?	*Tem quartos livres?*
How much is it per night/per person?	*Quanto é por noite/ por pessoa?*
Is breakfast included?	*O pequeno almoço está incluído?*
a single room	*um quarto individual*
a twin room	*um quarto duplo*
a double bed room	*um quarto de casal*
for one night	*para uma noite*
for two nights	*para duas noites*

Time, Days & Numbers

What time is it?	*Que horas são?*
today	*hoje*
tomorrow	*amanhã*
yesterday	*ontem*
morning	*manhã*
afternoon	*tarde*
Monday	*segunda-feira*
Tuesday	*terça-feira*
Wednesday	*quarta-feira*
Thursday	*quinta-feira*
Friday	*sexta-feira*
Saturday	*sábado*
Sunday	*domingo*

1	*um/uma*
2	*dois/duas*
3	*três*
4	*quatro*
5	*cinco*
6	*seis*
7	*sete*
8	*oito*
9	*nove*
10	*dez*
11	*onze*
100	*cem*
1000	*mil*
one million	*um milhão*

Spanish

Pronunciation
Vowels

Unlike English, each of the vowels in Spanish has a uniform pronunciation which doesn't vary. For example, the Spanish **a** has one pronunciation rather than the numerous pronunciations we find in English, such as 'cat', 'cake', 'cart', 'care', 'call'. An acute accent (as in *días*) generally indicates a stressed syllable and doesn't change the sound of the vowel. Vowels are pronounced clearly even if they are in unstressed positions or at the end of a word.

a	as the 'u' in 'nut', or a shorter sound than the 'a' in 'art'
e	as in 'met'
i	somewhere between the 'i' in 'marine' and the 'i' in 'flip'
o	similar to the 'o' in 'hot'
u	as the 'oo' in 'hoof'

Consonants

Some Spanish consonants are pronounced as per their English counterparts. The pronunciation of others is dependent on following vowels and also on which part of Spain you happen to be in. The Spanish alphabet also contains three consonants that aren't found in the English alphabet: **ch**, **ll** and **ñ**.

b	as in 'but' when word-initial or preceded by a nasal; elsewhere it's almost a cross between English 'b' and 'v'
c	a hard 'c' as in 'cat' when followed by **a**, **o**, **u** or a consonant; as the 'th' in 'thin' before **e** and **i**
ch	as in 'church'
d	as in 'do' when word-initial; elsewhere as the 'th' in 'then'
g	as in 'get' when word-initial and before **a**, **o** and **u**; elsewhere much softer. Before **e** or **i** it's a harsh, breathy sound, similar to the 'h' in 'hit'
h	silent

j	a harsh, guttural sound similar to the 'ch' in Scottish loch
ll	as the 'lli' in 'million'; some pronounce it rather like the 'y' in 'yellow'
ñ	a nasal sound, as the 'ni' in 'onion'
q	as the 'k' in 'kick'; q is always followed by a silent u and is combined only with the vowels e (as in *que*) and i (as in *qui*)
r	a rolled 'r' sound; longer and stronger when initial or doubled
s	as in 'see'
v	the same sound as b
x	as the 'ks' sound in 'taxi' when between vowels; as the 's' in 'see' when it precedes a consonant
z	as the 'th' in 'thin'

Semiconsonant

Spanish also has the semiconsonant **y**. When at the end of a word or when standing alone as a conjunction it's pronounced like the Spanish **i**. As a consonant, it's somewhere between the 'y' in 'yonder' and the 'g' in 'beige', depending on the region.

Basics

Hello.	*¡Hola!*
Goodbye.	*¡Adiós!*
Yes.	*Sí.*
No.	*No.*
Please.	*Por favor.*
Thank you.	*Gracias.*
You're welcome.	*De nada.*
I'm sorry. (forgive me)	*Lo siento/Discúlpeme.*
Excuse me.	*Perdón/Perdoneme.*
Do you speak English?	*¿Habla inglés?*
How much is it?	*¿Cuánto cuesta?/ ¿Cuánto vale?*

Signs – Spanish

Entrada	**Entrance**
Salida	**Exit**
Información	**Information**
Abierto	**Open**
Cerrado	**Closed**
Habtaciones Libres	**Rooms Available**
Completo	**Full/No Vacancies**
Comisaría	**Police Station**
Prohibido	**Prohibited**
Servicios/Aseos	**Toilets**
Hombres	**Men**
Mujeres	**Women**

What's your name?	*¿Cómo se llama?*
My name is ...	*Me llamo ...*

Getting Around

What time does the next ... leave/arrive?	*¿A qué hora sale/ llega el próximo ...?*
boat	*barco*
bus (city)	*autobús, bus*
bus (intercity)	*autocar*
train	*tranvía*

I'd like a ... ticket.	*Quisiera un billete ...*
one-way	*sencillo/de sólo ida*
return	*de ida y vuelta*
1st-class	*primera clase*
2nd-class	*segunda clase*

left luggage	*consigna*
timetable	*horario*
bus stop	*parada de autobus*
train station	*estación de ferrocarril*

I'd like to hire ...	*Quisiera alquilar ...*
a car	*un coche*
a bicycle	*una bicicleta*

Where is ...?	*¿Dónde está ...?*
Go straight ahead.	*Siga/Vaya todo derecho.*
Turn left.	*Gire a la izquierda.*
Turn right.	*Gire a la derecha/recto.*
near	*cerca*
far	*lejos*

Around Town

a bank	*un banco*
chemist/pharmacy	*la farmacia*
the ... embassy	*la embajada ...*
my hotel	*mi hotel*
the market	*el mercado*
newsagency	*el quiosco*
stationers	*la papelería*
the post office	*los correos*
the telephone centre	*el locutorio*
the tourist office	*la oficina de turismo*

What time does it open/close?	*¿A qué hora abren/ cierran?*

Accommodation

hotel	*hotel*
guesthouse	*pensión/casa de huéspedes*
youth hostel	*albergue juvenil*
camping ground	*camping*

Do you have any rooms available?	*¿Tiene habitaciones libres?*

LANGUAGE

Emergencies – Spanish

Help!	*¡Socorro!/¡Auxilio!*
Call a doctor!	*¡Llame a un doctor!*
Call the police!	*¡Llame a la policía!*
Go away!	*¡Váyase!*
I'm lost.	*Estoy perdido.* (m)
	Estoy perdida. (f)

a single room	*una habitación individual*
a double room	*una habitación doble*
a room with a double bed	*una habitación con cama de matrimonio*
for one night	*para una noche*
for two nights	*para dos noches*
How much is it per night/per person?	*¿Cuánto cuesta por noche/por persona?*
Is breakfast included?	*¿Incluye el desayuno?*

Time, Days & Numbers

What time is it?	*¿Qué hora es?*
today	*hoy*
tomorrow	*mañana*
yesterday	*ayer*
morning	*mañana*
afternoon	*tarde*

Monday	*lunes*
Tuesday	*martes*
Wednesday	*miércoles*
Thursday	*jueves*
Friday	*viernes*
Saturday	*sábado*
Sunday	*domingo*

1	*uno, una*
2	*dos*
3	*tres*
4	*cuatro*
5	*cinco*
6	*seis*
7	*siete*
8	*ocho*
9	*nueve*
10	*diez*
11	*once*
12	*doce*
13	*trece*
14	*catorce*
15	*quince*
16	*dieciéis*
100	*cien/ciento*
1000	*mil*
one million	*un millón*

Thanks

FROM THE AUTHORS

Susie Ashworth First and foremost I would like to thank Gordon for his unwavering support and encouragement every step of the way. Thanks to Markus Hoffmann and Julie for their hospitality and guided tour of Basel; Russell and Marg Huntington in Zürich for their time and energy; Markus Leuthard and Doris Stüker for fantastic local tips and advice; and Terry Carter and Lara Dunstan for spot-on foodie suggestions. Back in Oz, Gabrielle, Ronnie and Yvonne offered some excellent pretrip insights, while Kieran Grogan and Craig MacKenzie at LP were particularly helpful and patient. Finally, thanks to my parents, John and Lil, for taking charge in our absence.

David Atkinson Thanks to Ann Noon at the Maison de la France in London, Charles Page at Rail Europe, Nicole Mitchell at Eurostar, Sarah Barnes on behalf on Buzz, Daniel Spendrup in Chamonix, Sylvie Bonnafond in Lyon, and LP readers Paul Pederson, Anne Underwood and Katherine B for their useful input.

Chris Baty Thanks to Heike Neumann in Volksdorf for her unfailing kindness, and bottomless pots of strong coffee. A *danke* to old friends Anke and Philipp Bergman in Düsseldorf who were there to help me over the wall, and to Katja Bode, Queen of Göttingen. Much gratitude to Frau Schick in the Frankfurt tourist office, and Frau Mertens in the Kiel tourist office. And a final thanks to purveyors of milk chocolate and *Apfeltaschen* throughout Germany; your selfless dedication to the confectionary arts is an inspiration.

Andrew Bender Thanks first to German tourism representatives in Los Angeles, Helmut Helas and Kristina von Sachs of the GNTO, and Kirsten Schmidt of Berlin Tourismus Marketing, for the warm welcome even before my departure. That spirit continued courtesy of Natascha Kompatzki and Britta Grigull in Berlin, Brigit Wachs and staff in Stralsund, Sabine Weigand in Rostock, Christine Lambrecht in Dessau, Stephan Schellhass in Lutherstadt Wittenberg, Annett Morche in Leipzig and Christoph Münch and Christine Ross in Dresden. Chris Baty and Matt Lane were a pleasure to work with, Andrea Schulte-Peevers came through in a pinch, and thanks finally to Chris Wyness for the opportunity.

Duncan Garwood Thanks, in no particular order, to Viviana, Daniele, Anna, Marco, Elisa and Marco in Bologna; Sabrina and Alessandro for their cheerful company in Milan and Maria Ferrara for her tips on that city's nightlife; Antonello and Dora in Genoa; Richard McKenna and everybody at the British School in Cinecittà, Rome, for giving me the time off and covering my courses; Sally O'Brien for her support and help; my mum for push-starting me into having a go; and Lidia for putting up with my absences and, probably worse for her, my presence.

Susie Grimshaw Thanks to Teresa Ventura at the Portuguese tourist office in London, Fernanda Reis at Porto Turismo, Vanda Brito at Ask Me Lisboa (I did), and Carla Rodrigues at Arco de Cego for endless patience and good humour. Thanks also to Luis Kuski, Elsa Denninhoff Stelling, Celina Piedade and Carla Cavaço for insider tips, and to Jorge and Ole for help researching entertainment sections. Also to Julia and John for moral (and practical) support, and Paul Piaia for mapping expertise. Finally, a big thank you to Mark for putting up with my lengthy absence and remembering to feed the cat.

Kathryn Hanks A huge thanks to all at LP, but particularly Kieran Grogan for having the patience of a saint, and David Else and Tom Downs for consistently fighting in the authors' corner and making a difference. Thanks also to the many helpful tourist offices up and down the UK – I owe you all a fortune in leaflets; George Taylor for his boundless knowledge of Newcastle; Ryan and all the crew in York; the 'Whitby Walkers'; May Stiggins; Hel Robinson; and of course Ma, Pa, and Tom Parkinson for endless cups of tea and just the right amount of 'helpful' advice.

Sarah Johnstone Thanks to friends and family who helped in various ways, especially Helle, Richard, Alex, Lindsay, Marusa and Luka, Annette, Lisa, Ros, Beth and Brian. Thanks, too, to Andrea and Rhys for the Heuriger experience. (We made it in the end!) I owe a huge debt to various bods in Austrian tourist offices, including Helga Percht in Salzburg, Friedrich Kraft in Innsbruck, Heinrich Wagner and Rebecca in St Anton am Arlberg, and Barbara Gigler, at the Austrian National Tourist Office in London.

Alex Landragin I owe a huge debt of gratitude to Dani Valent, Annabel Hart and especially the infinitely kind and diligent Miles Roddis. My thanks also to the editors at LP for their patience and for giving me the job in the first place, to my father for navigating and for showing me a side of France I never knew, to various relatives for putting me up (read: putting up with me), and to the hundreds of thousands of protesters I bumped into in France's streets – *no pasaran!*

Matt Lane My first big thanks goes to Paul, my best man, and he knows why. On the road, I had invaluable help from many tourist offices, most notably Vera and the crew in Munich, Karin in Stuttgart, Renate in Erfurt, Kerstin in Weimar, the girls in Regensburg and Andrea in Heidelberg. Thanks to numerous travellers who helped along the way, and all the hostel and hotel staff who made the job easier. Special thanks to my drinking partners in Heidelberg and Munich for keeping me sane. Lastly, thanks to my wife, Simone, who patiently waited for me despite being a newlywed.

Cathy Lanigan In the Netherlands, thanks to Hans, Marie-Louise, Michelle and Femke de Groot for friendship and hospitality, Gitta de Groot for assistance checking out bars, Nick and Corrie Plomb, and Tos and Ko van der Knijff for the Den Bosch adventure, Marleen Blijleven for Rotterdam insider info, Hans van Amsterdam for providing a necessary link, Justine DallaRiva and Eveline for laughs, staff at VVV offices and all those people who gave us tips and helped with the stroller! In England, thanks to Julie Powell and Roy Willis, Sarah Crute and Yousef Goosani for warmth and friendship. Special thanks to John and Zoe van der Knijff for being there every step of the way.

Leanne Logan & Geert Cole Special thanks to the ever helpful staff at many tourist offices in all three countries. In particular we appreciate the warm-hearted support of Jean-Claude Conter from the Luxembourg National Tourist Office, Els Maes at Toerisme Vlaanderen and Sabine Rosen at the Office de Promotion du Tourisme in Brussels. Also invaluable were the comments of those readers who wrote in. To Roos and Bert in Antwerp, *bedankt* for keeping your social and very vocal granddaughter entertained. Thanks to Alan Trubody for the warm hospitality and entertaining storytelling; to Marianne for coming to the computer rescue; and to our neglected buddies, Sixy and Bluey – next time we promise there'll be more beers.

Craig MacKenzie I'm particularly grateful to Emma Sangster who provided invaluable assistance during a difficult period for her. Thanks also to Chris Adlam (Automobile Association), David Burnett, Yvonne Byron, Emma Cafferty (YHA England & Wales), Brigitte Ellemor, Paul Guy (HI Northern Ireland), Bibiana Jaramillo, Hilary Rogers, and Joyce Turton (HI Canada).

Lisa Mitchell To Matt Waite, my partner, for his patience, invaluable editorial support and encouragement. Enduring thanks to big sis Kerry Jones, for her editorial backup. Warm thanks to Yiannis and Katerina in Athens for their hospitality and contacts, and Spiros Gianotis from *Hellenic Travelling* magazine and Theo Spordilis on Chios for their research assistance. To Mike Emm Akalestos on Paros – could there be a more generous host? To Nikos and Angela Perlakis on Naxos, thank you for showing me the local delights. Thank you to the kind souls who offered refreshments, and the busy travel agents and tourist information staff who answered my flurry of questions.

Sally O'Brien Thanks to Tony Davidson for the work; Duncan Garwood for his help and his great work; Craig MacKenzie for editing and Adrian Persoglia for designing the chapter; Maria Grazia Montenucci at APT Roma for her assistance; Marie-Claire Muir for the bar/restaurant research laughs in Rome and Naples; Jenny Hoskins, Sam Adams and Glenn for their kindness and humour in Naples; Fabian Muir for rekindling my interest in running madly across Rome; and the many tourist office staff, locals and travellers who offered opinions. Once again, a big salute to Lara and Jody for looking after my stuff and my parents, Barbara and Peter.

Josephine Quintero Thanks to Hannah Reineck, Jonathan Symon, David Forrest, Naomi and Glen Mitchell, Craig Jenkins, Suman Bolar, Rose Brannon, Vijay Panjeti and Neil Allies.

Kalya Ryan Laura Pusey deserves a big hug for keeping me sane while on the road. A huge thank you to Kenny, fireman 541 and Donald at the Bettyhill Hotel for proving to me that Scots have the world's best sense of humour. Special thanks to Ingrid and Barney for the use of a comfy couch. Cheers to my lovely flatmates, Lachlan and Will, for keeping my room free for my return (and to Bill for putting all my furniture back into exactly the right place). Thanks to Kieran Grogan and Craig

MacKenzie at LP and to Leanne Logan and Geert Cole. Most importantly, thanks to my Hugh, for generally being great and for his patience throughout a long, cold, lonely Melbourne winter.

Andrew Stone I'm so grateful to Johnny and Jane Walsh and to the Herron and McGale families for all their kindness and hospitality. Particular thanks to Helen, Julian, Brian and Nigel McGale, and Paul for showing me such a great time in Belfast. Thanks to Katherine McCluskey, Lisa McMurray, John Lahiff and Katrina Doherty and their respective tourism offices for efficient, friendly help. To Celia Fleur, thanks for a memorable afternoon skimming stones, drinking Guinness and exploring hidden Castletownbere. Thanks to all at the Kinsale Castlepark Marina Hostel and to Darragh for being my guide on Sherkin. To Pete Groom, thanks so much for the loan of the flat – I owe you several Stellas.

Rachel Suddart Thanks to Paul Gowen from the RAC for 'behind-the-wheel' knowledge, Mark Waters from the CTC for all things bicycle-related, LP's UK IT team for all their patience and expertise, and Tom Hall for never getting sick of hearing 'Can I just run something past you...' A hearty cheers to one and all.

Dani Valent Thanks to Karl Quinn, Liam Alexander-Quinn, Stephanie Bremner, Sally Ross, Miranda Epstein, Jeanne Oliver, Steve Fallon (who should never grow up) and the Corsican pigs that died to create all those brilliant sausages.

Vivek Wagle *Muchísimas gracias* to my fellow authors and to the production staff in Melbourne for making Spain such a smooth ride. Special thanks to Tony Davidson and Mary Neighbour for overseeing the project and to Ryan Ver Berkmoes for presenting me with the opportunity. *Un montón de agradecimiento* to travelling companion Cara Forster, whose support and assistance were invaluable. Love, as always, to Mom, Dad, Nani and Ayesha. And *mucho cariño* to all my US LP and ex-LP friends. It's been a great ride.

David Willett I'd like to thank all the friends who have contributed so much to my understanding of Greece over the years, especially Maria Economou from the Greek National Tourism Office, the Kanakis family, Ana Kamais, Matt Barrett, Tolis Houtzoumis, Petros and Dimitris in Nafplio, Yiannis in Sparti, the irrepressible Voula in Gythio, the Dimitreas family from Kardamyli, and Andreas the magician from Patras. Special thanks to my partner, Rowan, and our son Tom, who formed my support team around the Peloponnese and northern Greece.

OTHER THANKS

Many thanks to the travellers who used the last edition and wrote to us with helpful hints, useful advice and interesting anecdotes:

Alwyn Adams, Nick Adlam, Anthony Andrews, Cynthia Ang, Mike Appleyard, Mary Ara, Gary Artim, John Arwe, Andrei Avram, Jerry Azevedo, Allison Azzopardi, Theo Baak, Renee Banky, John Barbano, Christine Barbour, Leah Barnett, Amy Bartlett, Montse Baste-Kraan, Ken Baxter, Paul Beach, Gregory Becker, John Bedford, CB Belcher, Tony Bellette, Barb Bellinger, Tony Benfield, Mark Bersten, Heather Beswick, Rebecca Bevers, Bill Birch, Lars Björk, Misty Bliss, Jessica and Furseth Bodil, Sarah Boniface, Melissa Bowtell, Clare Bradley, Domi Branger, George Aaron Broadwell, Carol Brown, Hanna Bruin, Craig Bryant, Ian Buchanan, Jan Bullerdieck, Nick Burchell, Cameron Bush, Anna Caffyn, Doris Calhoun, Andrew and L Campbell, Kent Carter, Scott Casban, Melissa Casley, Terry Casstevens, Carolyn Castiglia, Sandy Ceniseros, Dr CW Chen, Annette and Bill Chessum, Melody Chong, KM Chow, Alfred Choy, Leigh Churchill, Daniele Clavenzani, Mark Clewlow, Diana Clough, Stephen Coast, Peter Collins, Helen Conway, Paul Conway, David Cope, Rose Corney, Michael Counsell, Alma Cristina, Martin Croker, Jody Culham, Desmond Cumiskey, P Cuypers, Harry Davidson, Shane de Malmanche, Johan De Roeck, Johan de Vetti, Michael R Decker, Marius den Hartog, Vinay Deolalikar, Philippe Desplenter, David Deutscher, Stelios N Deverakis, Nathan Dhillon, Kostis Diamantopoulos, Marianna Dioxini, Mathew Dolenac, Steffi Domagk, Sue Donovan, Coen Dortmond, Majorie Douglass, Amy Duckworth, Annie Dude, John Dynan, Jutta Eberlin, Ben Edmunds, Bronwyn Edwards, Katie Elder, Ruth Emblin, Martin Fagerer, Trasy Fahle, Michael Falk, Teresa Fanning, Gillian Farley, Cameron Fincher, Wendy Finch-Turner, Derek M Fisher, Tyler Flood, Dell Forrester, Brad Fortner, Liz Foulis, Rob Fowler, Viola Franke, Peter Franzese, Paul Fraser, Gemma French, Christian Friederich, Marvin Ross Friedman, Jan and Yeni Fritzen, Gaelen Gates, Bart Giepmans, Ewan Girvan, Jemma Golding, Antonio Gonzalez-Avila, Athina Gorezis, Paul

Graalman, Nicholas Graham, Gordon Grant, Nancy Grant, Phyllis Grant, Dan Greenberg, Frederik Grufman, Karen Grunow, Janine Hagens, James Hall, Warren Halliday, Simone Hanks, Donald Hatch, David Haugh, Thomas Haunstein, Esther Hecht, Masami Heiser, Wesley Heiser, KG Hellyen, Dale Henderson, Alyson and David Hilbourne, Carolyn Hill, Gerald Holt, Karen Howat, Michael Huber, Thng Hui Hong, Joanne Hutchinson, Samantha Ipsa, Marcia Jackson-Smith, Diana James, Rok Jarc, Graham S Jarvis, Marie Javins, Hayley Jenkins, David John, George John, Sally Jo Johnson, Stephanie Johnson, Jenny Jones, Marius Jones, Benno Kaestli, Martjin Katan, Bryan and Louise Kelly, Christoph Kessel, Seamus King, Wim Klumpenhouwer, Andrew Knox, Csaba Kobol, Diana Lachiondo, Stephen Lamb, Francesca Lanaro, Dr Hazem Lashin, Antonio Lee, Denise Lee, Sabine Legrand, Dr PA Lekhi, Desmond Leow, Juha Levo, George Liangas, Tan Shuh Lin, Jeroen Lintjens, Simon Looi, Juliet and Heini Lux, Alex MacKenzie, Emily MacWilliams, Kevin Madden, Diana Maestre, Rebecca Manvell, Tracey Marek, John Marquis, Margaret Marszal, Steve Martin, Olivier Mauron, Glenn McAllister, Kathryn McDonnell, Brenda McDowell, Andrea McEneaney, David McGowan, Duane K Meek, Lucas Meijknecht, Lori Mendel, Gunnar Merbach, Lin Merry, Julian Mettler, Alister Miller, Sarah Milligan, Eric Milsom, Nicki Miquel, Basit Mirza, Martin Mischkulnig, Arkajyoti Misra, Charlene Mogdan, Rebecca Morarhy, Jason Mote, Molly Murphy, Sean Murphy, Roberta Murray, Gabe Murtagh, Jonas Nahm, Margaret and Pat Nankivell, MaryAnne Nelson, Vicky Nicholas, Jen Noble, Judith O'Brien, Con O'Conaill, Elka Olsen, Jacquie Olsen, Andre Oord, Gustavo Orlando-Zon, Michaela Osborne, Aoife O'Shea, Megan Packer, Thea Parkin, RF Parsons, James Payne, Roger Peake, Jill Pearson,

Valentina M Pennazio, Jan M Pennington, Steve Penny, Maxime Philibert, Marion Phillips, Eric Philpott, Chris Phoenix, John Pilgrim, Niki Pilidou, David John Pitts, Scott Plimpton, Adrian Pritchard, Marc Purnal, Roy Pyne, Maria Ralph, Francesco Randisi, Bernt Rane, Vince and Julieta Raschilla, Kurt Rebry, Dean A Redmann, Hanneke Renes, Helen Richards, Tony Richmond, Dan Robinson, Jason Rodrigues, Kang Rong, Brenda Roscoe, Matthew Rothschild, John Rowe, Nagiller Rudolf, Melissa Russel, Patti Ryan, Sharon Sadler, Caroline Sargent, Karl Scharbert, Jeremias Schmidt, Sabine Schmitz, Eric Schwenter, Paola Sconzo, Amber Senneck, Sean Seurin, Rick Seymour, Brett Shackelford, U Shalit, Mary Sheargold, Eric Sheppard, Jessica Sherwood, Bogdan Siewierski, Arnis Siksna, Juanita Simmonds, Carol and Ron Simmons, Vern and Cindy Simpson, Anneke Sips, Alec Sirken, Kara Slaughter, Ann Snyder, David Spiers, Kevin Stanes, Julie Stenberg, Timothy Sullivan, Ann Sy, Amanda Fay Szumutku, Andrew Tan, Sue Taylor, Anke Temmink, Vera ten Hacken, Katrin Thomas, Anouchka-Virginie Thouvenot, Robert Tissing, Phil Torcasio, Michael Travis, Dana and Nick Tsamaidis, Loredana Tsamaidis, Metaxia Tsoukatos, Ronaldo Uliana de Oliveria, Dave Upton, Erwin van Engelen, Brigette van Haasteren, Jacqueline van Klaveren, Theodora Van Leeuwen Boomkamp, Janet Van Meter, Matthew Van Meter, Dirk van Rooy, Nathalie van Spaendonck, Mike Viechweg, Matthew Vincent, George S Vrontos, Fons Vrouenraths, Pauline Waddell, Jost Wagner, Janine Waliszewski, Heather Wallace, Karen Walsh, Jo Watkins-Wade, A Watson, Jeremy Watts, Renee Webster, Jennifer Wells, Tony Weston, Valda White, Rod Whyte, Hanna Wilhelm, Veryan Wilkie-Jones, Scott Williamson, Fiona Wilson, Jon Wilton, Roxanne Winkler, Joanne Woo, Peta Woodland, Norman Yap, Kathryn Young, D Yudhope, RA Zambardino, Holger Zimmermann

Index

Abbreviations

AND – Andorra
A – Austria
B – Belgium
CH – Switzerland
D – Germany

E – Spain
F – France
FL – Liechtenstein
GB – Britain
GR – Greece

I – Italy
IRL – Ireland
L – Luxembourg
NL – Netherlands
P – Portugal

Text

Bold indicates maps.

Bold indicates maps.

Bold indicates maps.

Bold indicates maps.

MAP LEGEND

CITY ROUTES

Freeway	Freeway
Highway	Primary Road
Road	Secondary Road
Street	Street
Lane	Lane
On/Off Ramp	

Unsealed Road	
One Way Street	
Pedestrian Street	
Stepped Street	
Tunnel	
Footbridge	

REGIONAL ROUTES

Tollway, Freeway	
Primary Road	
Secondary Road	
Minor Road	

BOUNDARIES

International	
State	
Disputed	
Fortified Wall	

HYDROGRAPHY

River, Creek	
Canal	
Lake	

Dry Lake; Salt Lake	
Spring; Rapids	
Waterfalls	

TRANSPORT ROUTES & STATIONS

Train	
Underground Train	
Metro	
Tramway	
Funicular Railway	

Ferry	
Walking Trail	
Walking Tour	
Path	
Pier or Jetty	

AREA FEATURES

Building	
Park, Gardens	

Market	
Sports Ground	

Beach	
Cemetery	

Forest	
Plaza	

POPULATION SYMBOLS

✪ CAPITAL .... National Capital	● CITY .... City	○ Village	.... Village
◉ CAPITAL .... State Capital	● Town .... Town		.... Urban Area

MAP SYMBOLS

■ ....Place to Stay	▼ ....Place to Eat	● .... Point of Interest

✈	Airport	▣	Cinema	★	Police Station	▦	Swimming Pool
⊗	Bank	▢	Embassy, Consulate	▣	Post Office	▣	Synagogue
⦿	Border Crossing	♆	Fountain	▣	Pub or Bar	▣	Taxi Rank
▣	Bus Station	✛	Hospital	▣	Pub or Bar (Ire)	▣	Telephone
▣	Cable Car, Funicular	▣	Internet Cafe	▣	Ruins	▣	Theatre
▣	Castle, Chateau	▲	Mounment	▣	Shopping Centre	❶	Tourist Information
▣ ▣	Cathedral, Church	▥	Museum	⚲	Ski Field	▣	Zoo

Note: not all symbols displayed above appear in this book

LONELY PLANET OFFICES

Australia
Locked Bag 1, Footscray, Victoria 3011
☎ 03 8379 8000 fax 03 8379 8111
email: talk2us@lonelyplanet.com.au

USA
150 Linden St, Oakland, CA 94607
☎ 510 893 8555 TOLL FREE: 800 275 8555
fax 510 893 8572
email: info@lonelyplanet.com

UK
10a Spring Place, London NW5 3BH
☎ 020 7428 4800 fax 020 7428 4828
email: go@lonelyplanet.co.uk

France
1 rue du Dahomey, 75011 Paris
☎ 01 55 25 33 00 fax 01 55 25 33 01
email: bip@lonelyplanet.fr
www.lonelyplanet.fr

World Wide Web: www.lonelyplanet.com *or* AOL keyword: lp
Lonely Planet Images: lpi@lonelyplanet.com.au